So you turn to the major section of your thesaurus, looking for **273. Ship**. You get there quickly by scanning the numbers in red that appear at the top of each page. You find the beginning of **273. Ship** on page 84. The synonyms you see read in part as follows:

---

272. Vehicle

barb, roan, jade, hack, bidet, pad, cob, tit [*dial.*], punch [*dial.*], roadster, goer; race–, droshki *or* drosky.
dogcart, trap [*colloq.*], whitechapel, buggy, char-à-bancs (*pl. chars-à-bancs*) [*F.*], shandry-dan *or* shandradan [*Scot., Ir., & dial. Eng.*].
team, pair, span, tandem, random; spike team *or* spike, unicorn; four-in-hand.
litter, palanquin *or* palankeen, sedan *or* sedan chair; palki, jampan, dandy *or* dandi, dooly

or doolie, munchil [*all India*]; cacolet [*F.*]; tonjon [*Ceylon*], brancard, horse litter; stretcher,

adj. **vehicular**, curricular [*rare*], vehiculatory [*rare*]; ambulatory etc. (*traveling*) 266.

273. Ship

n. **ship**, vessel, sail; craft, bottom.
navy, marine, fleet, flotilla.
shipping, man-of-war etc. (*combatant*) 726; transport, tender, storeship; merchant ship,

84

---

274. Velocity

merchantman; packet, liner; whaler, slaver, collier, coaster, freight-steamer, freighter, lighter; fishing–, pilot- boat; trawler, hulk; yacht; baggala; floating -hotel, –palace; ocean greyhound [*colloq.*].
ship, bark *or* barque; shipentine, four-masted bark *or* barque; brig, snow, hermaphrodite brig; brigantine, barkentine *or* barquentine, schooner; topsail–, fore-and-aft- schooner; fore-and-after [*colloq.*]; three–, four–, five–, six- masted schooner; chasse-marée [*F.*], sloop, cutter, corvet *or* corvette, clipper, foist [*obs.*], yawl, dandy, ketch, smack, lugger, barge, hoy, cat, catboat, buss; sailer, sailing vessel; windjammer; steamer, steamboat, steamship; mail–, paddle–, turbine–, screw- steamer; tug; line of steamers etc.

adv. **afloat**, aboard; on board, on ship board; hard-a-lee, –port, –starboard, –weather.

274. Velocity

n. **velocity**, speed, celerity; swiftness etc. *adj.;* rapidity, eagle speed, lightning speed; expedition etc. (*activity*) 682; pernicity [*obs.*], acceleration; haste etc. 684.
spurt, sprint, rush, dash, race, steeple chase; automobile race; Marathon race *or* Marathon; smart–, lively–, swift etc. *adj.* –, rattling [*colloq.*] –, spanking [*slang*] –, strapping [*colloq.*]- –rate, –pace; round pace; flying, flight.
pace, gallop, canter, trot, round trot, run, scamper; hand–, full- gallop; swoop.
[comparisons] lightning, light, electricity, wind; cannon ball, rocket, arrow, dart, hydrargyrum,

---

As you can see, the words are grouped according to meaning, and the first word in each paragraph tells you the kinds of words you will find in a given paragraph.

You then search for the precise word you have in mind. Is the word you want *clipper*, *steamer*, *steamship*, *windjammer*, or another of the many types of ships listed? Now, for example, you can write:

The *windjammer* sailed at dawn.

Caution: When you locate a word in a thesaurus and you are not certain of its meaning, be sure to look up the word in a dictionary. You want to make sure that the word you choose means what you think it means.

Family Handbook

with

Roget's University Thesaurus

Family Handbook

with

Roget's University Thesaurus

THE SOUTHWESTERN COMPANY
Nashville, Tennessee

Roget's University Thesaurus
was originally published under the title
Roget's International Thesaurus of English Words and Phrases.

ROGET'S UNIVERSITY THESAURUS.
Copyright 1911, 1922, 1930, 1932, 1936, 1938, 1939, copyright © 1958, 1959, 1960, 1963, 1985
by Harper & Row, Publishers, Inc.
All rights reserved.

Copyright under the Universal Copyright Convention;
the International Copyright Union; Pan-American Conventions
of Montevideo, Mexico, Rio de Janeiro, Buenos Aires, and Havana

Family Handbook copyright © 1988, 1987, 1985
The Southwestern Company

All rights reserved

Printed in the United States of America

Preface

The *Family Handbook with Roget's University Thesaurus* is the most practical reference book ever designed for use by the American family. All members of the family—students looking ahead to advanced schooling or that important first job, those out of school and wanting to advance their careers, parents concerned with the organization and management of their lives, senior citizens wishing to remain active—will discover essential information about increasing their enjoyment from life by becoming healthier, wealthier, and wiser. The *Family Handbook* covers in a single volume subjects that ordinarily require an entire shelf of books. Thus, it is an indispensable home reference book to be kept next to the other, more specialized books you may already have: cookbooks, telephone books, the Bible, etc.

Though the *Family Handbook* is completely independent and can be consulted separately, it is expressly designed to be the third volume in the well-known and popular *Student Handbook* set. The *Student Handbooks* are intended to help students improve at school. They assemble in an easy-to-learn way the many subjects taught in elementary, junior high, and high schools.

The *Family Handbook,* on the other hand, offers help to the whole family in its everyday activities. It is especially useful for those who are looking for a job or who want to move ahead in their careers, and for those who are retired and want new ways to make life more interesting and productive. Thus, the *Family Handbook* is a lifelong resource. It will be as useful to you decades from now as it will be the first time you consult it.

The *Family Handbook* is in two major parts: PART ONE covers all practical aspects of home management, such as finances, health, and the law; and all aspects of career advancement, such as computers, letter writing, memory improvement, speaking, and writing. If published separately, each of these topics would be a book in itself.

PART TWO is a world-famous thesaurus, a treasury of words that will help you find exactly the right one to express your every thought.

The 15 sections of PART ONE are:
 1. *Understanding Computers*—You too can be knowledgeable about computers.
 2. *Advancing Your Career*—How to get a job, get along in your job, change careers, or start your own business.
 3. *Health and Fitness*—How to eat well and stay healthy, with good advice for every family member, even senior citizens.
 4. *You and Modern Medicine*—What to do when you are sick; how to choose a doctor; generic drugs; your hospital stay; medical payments.
 5. *Managing the Family's Money*—Credit, banking, investment, shopping, vacationing, retirement, money-saving ideas.
 6. *You and the Law*—Wills and estates, consumers' rights, criminal law, finding a lawyer.
 7. *Improving Your Memory*—A tested and successful way to learn how to remember anything: names, numbers, essential facts, school subjects, on-the-job information.
 8. *Building Your Vocabulary*—How to learn new words and their meanings; 15 days to a more forceful vocabulary; vocabulary tests; words you should know.
 9. *Improving Your Speech*—How to say what you want clearly and effectively; public speaking made easy; Robert's Rules of Order.
 10. *Writing Effective Letters*—Social letters, business letters, hard-to-write letters, postal information, scores of examples for every need.
 11. *Improving Your Reading*—How to read better and faster; learning to read special kinds of texts; reading lists.

12. *Taking Aptitude Tests*—How to prepare for tests; sample questions from those all-important General Educational Development Tests (GED's), Scholastic Aptitude Tests (SAT's), American College Testing (ACT's), and Graduate Record Examinations (GRE's).
13. *Review of French Grammar*—Parts of speech, rules governing their use, verb tables, sample sentences, important expressions, plus a concise French-English dictionary and English-French dictionary.
14. *Review of German Grammar*—Parts of speech, rules governing their use, verb tables, sample sentences, important expressions, plus a concise German-English dictionary and English-German dictionary.
15. *Review of Spanish Grammar*—All parts of speech, rules governing their use, verb tables, sample sentences, important expressions, plus a concise Spanish-English dictionary and English-Spanish dictionary.

PART TWO is the complete, newly revised publication of the famous *Roget's University Thesaurus,* printed here for the first time in two colors to make it easier and quicker to use. This thesaurus, though it has been modernized, is based on the family word book devised over a hundred years ago by Peter Mark Roget. It has proven so useful that it has been in print continuously ever since. Your family will find it helpful in writing letters, student papers, and reports.

We invite you to turn the pages of the practical and beautifully designed *Family Handbook.* Note that each section begins with its own table of contents, including page numbers, so that you can turn immediately to the particular subject that interests you most. Each section offers charts, checklists, and boxes of special information that you will use again and again. The *Family Handbook* presents a wealth of practical information. Learn how the famous *Roget's University Thesaurus* will help you find the word you need and assist you in building your vocabulary, simply and quickly. Are you intimidated by the world of computers? Have a look at the very first section for an introduction to these marvelous machines that every member of your family can use with ease. Are you interested in brushing up on your French, German, or Spanish? In the *Family Handbook* the essentials are laid out in a new, easy-to-learn way. Note, finally, that there is a general index that gives you quick access to every topic in the book.

We are certain you will find the *Family Handbook* of lasting value for the whole family.

—*Gorton Carruth, Editor-in-Chief*

Table of Contents

Part 1
Family Handbook

Understanding Computers 2
- What is a computer? 3
- The microcomputer 5
- Computers and education 12
- Financial and business programs 14
- Word processing 16
- Staying healthy with computers 17
- Glossary 18

Advancing Your Career 22
- Preparing for the job search 24
- Going after the job 32
- Getting the job 40
- Moving up the ladder 41
- Changing careers 44
- Getting back into the work force 47
- Starting your own business 49
- Matching yourself to the world of work 52

Health and Fitness 58
- Fatigue 59
- Stress 60
- Eye care 62
- Ear care 63
- Foot care 63
- Health nutrients 64
- Good nutrition 69
- Watch your weight 72
- Get back into shape 74
- Home medical testing 75
- Glossary 76

You and Modern Medicine 78
- You and the doctor 78
- You and the hospital 82
- You and emergency rooms 85
- You and drugs 87
- Your mental health 92
- Medical payments 95
- Glossary 96

Managing the Family's Money 110

- Planning and record-keeping 111
- Using credit wisely 114
- Dealing with your bank 115
- Saving and investing 118
- Looking ahead to tax time 120
- Buying insurance 122
- Putting your affairs in order 126
- Planning for retirement 127
- Managing your shopping 130
- Your shelter dollar 132
- Managing your car 134
- An economical vacation 135
- Glossary 136
- Booklets on request 139

You and the Law 140

- Your family and the law 141
- Your home and the law 147
- Wills and estates 154
- Consumers' rights 156
- Personal property 159
- Injuries and damages 162
- Earning a living 164
- Criminal law and procedure 167
- How to find a lawyer 169
- Glossary 171

Improving Your Memory 180
- Observation 182
- Paying attention 183
- Getting organized 186
- Image formation 187
- Peg words 188
- Link method 190
- Everyday applications 192
- Names and faces 194
- Suggestions for students 196
- Appendix 198

Building Your Vocabulary 206
- Your Word Power file 207
- A permanent memory system 209
- How words are used 210
- Natural settings for words 215
- 15 days to a forceful vocabulary 224
- Preparing for vocabulary tests 232
- American English 234
- Puzzles and word games 236
- Words you should know 238

Improving Your Speech 244
- The five keys 245
- Correct speech 252
- Body language 254
- Prepare to speak 257
- Everyday uses of speech 261
- Robert's Rules of order 264

Writing Effective Letters 266
- Social letters 266
- Business letters 276
- Clubs and organizations 290
- Tips for retired people 292
- Postal information 298
- Forms of address 300

Improving Your Reading 302
- Enjoy the benefits of reading 302
- What is good reading? 306
- Efficient reading 310
- Special types of reading 318
- Continuing to improve 322
- Reading lists 324

Taking Major Tests 328
- Improve your test taking 329
- The GED 332
- The SAT 336
- The ACT 343
- The GRE 349

Review of French Grammar 352
- Articles 352
- Pronouns and adjectives 354
- Verbs 360
- Numbers, dates, time 368
- French-English dictionary 370
- English-French dictionary 375

Review of German Grammar 382
- Articles 382
- Nouns 383
- Pronouns 384
- Prepositions 386
- Adjectives and adverbs 387
- Verbs 388
- Conjunctions 391
- Numbers, dates, time 392
- German-English dictionary 396
- English-German dictionary 402

Review of Spanish Grammar 408
- Articles 409
- Nouns 410
- Adjectives and adverbs 410
- Pronouns 412
- Prepositions 415
- Verbs 416
- Numbers, dates, time 424
- Spanish-English dictionary 426
- English-Spanish dictionary 432

Index 438–444

Part 2
Roget's University Thesaurus

ILLUSTRATION CREDITS: *page 5* Sperry Corporation, *(inset)* Texas Instruments; *6* Ric DelRossi/Mulvey Associates; *7 (left)* Mike Heck; *8* Spiegel/Black Star; *9* Peter Loewer/Graphos Studios; *12 (left)* Mike Heck, *(right)* Ogden/Art Resource; *14* Mike Heck; *15 (both)* Mike Heck; *17* UPI; *18* Mike Heck; *19* Ric DelRossi/Mulvey Associates; *29* Peter Loewer/Graphos Studios; *37* Ric DelRossi/Mulvey Associates; *39 (left)* Mahon/Monkmeyer, *(right)* Hankin/Stock, Boston; *41, 43, 46* Ric DelRossi/Mulvey Associates; *47 (art)* Ric DelRossi/Mulvey Associates, *(photo)* Wendy's International; *48* Ric DelRossi/Mulvey Associates; *51 (left)* Hankin/Stock, Boston, *(right)* Shelton/Monkmeyer; *58* Forsyth/Monkmeyer; *59* Ric DelRossi/Mulvey Associates; *61* Wolinsky/Stock, Boston; *64, 68, 69, 70, 73, 75, 76 (bottom)* Ric DelRossi/Mulvey Associates; *76 (top)* Peter Loewer/Graphos Studios; *78* Rotker/Taurus Photos; *80* Lambert/Frederic Lewis; *83* Ric DelRossi/Mulvey Associates; *84* Hewlett Packard; *88 (both), 89 (bottom)* Ric DelRossi/Mulvey Associates; *89 (top)* Rotker/Taurus Photos; *92* Strickler/Monkmeyer; *93* Gatewood/Stock, Boston; *94 (left)* Rotker/Taurus Photos, *(right)* Delevingne/Stock, Boston; *95* Forsyth/Monkmeyer; *96 (top, middle)* Ric DelRossi/Mulvey Associates, *(bottom)* Wilks/Stock, Boston; *110* Schlossberg/Monkmeyer, H. Armstrong Roberts, Sacks Art Resource; *111* Ric DelRossi/Mulvey Associates; *112* Rachelle Friedle; *115* Ric DelRossi/Mulvey Associates; *116* Rachelle Friedle; *117* Ric DelRossi/Mulvey Associates; *119* Greenberg/Monkmeyer; *120, 123, 125, 127, 129* Ric DelRossi/Mulvey Associates; *130* Peter Loewer/Graphos Studios; *135 (top)* Ric DelRossi/Mulvey Associates, *(bottom)* National Park Service; *136 (top)* Rotker/Taurus Photos, *(bottom)* SUVA/DPI; *140* AP/Wide World; *141* Ric DelRossi/Mulvey Associates; *143, 144* Bill Colrus/Mulvey Associates; *146, 147, 148, 152* Ric DelRossi/Mulvey Associates; *155* National Kidney Foundation of New York/New Jersey; *157, 159* Ric DelRossi/Mulvey Associates; *160* Coleman/Frederic Lewis; *162* Bill Colrus/Mulvey Associates; *163* UPI/Bettmann; *166* Ric DelRossi/Mulvey Associates; *170* Levick/Black Star; *172, 173, 180, 181* Ric DelRossi/Mulvey Associates; *182, 183* Bill Colrus/Mulvey Associates; *184* Ric DelRossi/Mulvey Associates; *185 (first row, left to right)* Forsyth/Monkmeyer, Sidney/Monkmeyer, Forsyth/Monkmeyer, *(second row)* Forsyth/Monkmeyer, Prelutsky/Stock, Boston, Franken/Stock, Boston, *(third row)* Morrow/Stock, Boston, Forsyth/Monkmeyer, Forsyth/Monkmeyer, *(fourth row)* Conklin/Monkmeyer, Forsyth/Monkmeyer, Albertson/Stock, Boston; *187 (both)* Bill Colrus/Mulvey Associates; *188 (all)* Ric DelRossi/Mulvey Associates; *189, 190, 191, 192* Bill Colrus/Mulvey Associates; *194* Ric DelRossi/Mulvey Associates; *195 (top row, all)* Forsyth/Monkmeyer, *(second row, left to right)* Albertson/Stock, Boston, Franken/Stock, Boston, Forsyth/Monkmeyer, *(third row)* Conklin/Monkmeyer, Forsyth/Monkmeyer, Morrow/Stock, Boston, *(fourth row)* Sidney/Monkmeyer, Prelutsky/Stock, Boston, Forsyth/Monkmeyer; *197, 198 (all), 199 (all)* Ric DelRossi/Mulvey Associates; *206* Ray Hand; *207* Ric DelRossi/Mulvey Associates; *211* Bill Colrus/Mulvey Associates; *212, 215, 216 (top)* Ray Hand; *216 (bottom), 217, 218 (bottom)* Ric DelRossi/Mulvey Associates; *218 (top), 219, 220 (top)* Ray Hand; *220 (bottom), 221 (both)* Ric DelRossi/Mulvey Associates; *222* Bill Colrus/Mulvey Associates; *225* Bettmann; *226* Ray Hand; *227* Ric DelRossi/Mulvey Associates; *228* Ray Hand; *229, 230* Ric DelRossi/Mulvey Associates; *235* Frederic Lewis; *236, 238 (top)* Ric DelRossi/Mulvey Associates; *238 (bottom)* Ray Hand; *244, 246* Forsyth/Monkmeyer; *247* Krathwohl/Stock, Boston; *248 (top)* Southwick/Stock, Boston; *248 (bottom), 249 (bottom)* Forsyth/Monkmeyer; *249 (top)* Franken/Stock, Boston; *251* Ric DelRossi/Mulvey Associates; *253* Falk/Monkmeyer; *255 (top row, left to right)* Leinwand/Monkmeyer, Wolinsky/Stock, Boston, Herwig/Stock, Boston, *(second row)* Sidney/Monkmeyer, Dunn/Stock, Boston, Balzer/Stock, Boston, *(third row)* Cox/Stock, Boston, Smolan/Stock, Boston; *256 (left)* Siteman/Stock, Boston, *(right)* Southwick/Stock, Boston; *257, 261 (left)* Ric DelRossi/Mulvey Associates; *261* Buck/Stock, Boston; *262* AP/Wide World; *263* Smolan/Leo de Wys, Inc.; *271* Ric DelRossi/Mulvey Associates; *282* Bill Colrus/Mulvey Associates; *302* Sidney/Monkmeyer; *303* Rogers/Monkmeyer; *304* Rutledge/Taurus Photos; *307* Ric DelRossi/Mulvey Associates; *308* Leinwand/Monkmeyer; *317, 319* Ric DelRossi/Mulvey Associates; *323* Mahon/Monkmeyer; *328* Ric DelRossi/Mulvey Associates; *331* Rachelle Friedle; *334* Minassian/Woodfin Camp & Assoc.; *339, 343 (top)* Ric DelRossi/Mulvey Associates; *343 (bottom)* Collidge/Taurus Photos; *345, 346* Ric DelRossi/Mulvey Associates; *349* Paireault/Magnum; *351, 352 (both)* Ric DelRossi/Mulvey Associates; *364* Greene/Frederic Lewis; *367, 369, 372, 374* Ric DelRossi/Mulvey Associates; *376* Reichman/Monkmeyer; *377* Peter Arnold; *378 (both)* Ric DelRossi/Mulvey Associates; *390* McKoy/Taurus Photos; *393, 394, 395* Ric DelRossi/Mulvey Associates; *397* UPI/Bettmann; *400* Ric DelRossi/Mulvey Associates; *406* Bill Colrus/Mulvey Associates; *407, 408 (both)* Ric DelRossi/Mulvey Associates.

SAT and GRE questions and explanations on pages 336–342 and 349–351 are excerpted and reprinted by permission of Educational Testing Service, from: *Taking the SAT* and *10 SATs*. College Entrance Examination Board, 1986 and *GRE Information Bulletin, 1984–1986*. Permission to reprint the above material does not constitute review or endorsement by Educational Testing Service, the College Board, or the GRE Board of this publication or any testing information it may contain. The ACT questions on pages 343–348 © 1984 by The American College Testing Program. All rights reserved. Reprinted with permission. The GED questions on pages 332–335 are reprinted from *Official GED Practice Test, Form A* with the permission of GED Testing Service, © 1985.

Editorial development of the *Family Handbook* was directed by
The Hudson Group, Inc., Pleasantville, N.Y. 10570.

Administrative editor:	Eugene Ehrlich
Editor-in-chief:	Gorton Carruth
Managing editor:	Hayden Carruth
Copy-editing:	Felice Levy/AEIOU, Inc.
Contributors:	Renni Browne/The Editorial Department
	Frances E. Barth, Else Behrendt, Marietta Burrowes, Delia Bye, Gisele Carruth, Karl Friese, John Harrington, Sylvia Helm, Lawrence Heyl, Jr., Helene Isaac, Naomi Katz, Seymour Levine, John Maloney, Elizabeth Rich
Special advisor:	"Improving Your Memory," Harry Lorayne
Design and production:	Pam Forde Graphics
Production:	Rachelle Friedle, Kathleen Marks
Illustrations:	Ric Del Rossi, Bill Colrus/Mulvey Associates, H. Peter Loewer/Graphos Studio, Ray Hand, Rachelle Friedle, Tara Forde
Photo researcher:	Lenore Weber

Part 1

Family Handbook

Understanding Computers

- What is a computer? 3
- The microcomputer 5
- Computers and education 12
- Financial and business programs 14
- Word processing 16
- Staying healthy with computers 17
- Glossary 18

Today, computers are everywhere you look, even in places where you might be surprised to find them. Nearly all of us use computers every day, whether we realize it or not.

Computers process your checks at the bank by reading the computer-scannable numbers on the bottom left-hand corner of your check. Computers in automated cash or teller machines let you withdraw and deposit money regardless of banking hours. Airline ticketing and reservation agents book you on a flight by using a computerized system that keeps track of routes, fares, and seats.

Computers scan the Universal Product Code on your groceries, tally your bill, and adjust the store's inventory. Computers tune the radio, pump gas, set thermostats, and control or monitor engine emissions and fuel economy.

Computers are on your wrist (digital watches) and in your pocket (calculators). If you have a microwave oven, you have a computer. When you press the "redial" button on a telephone receiver, a computer remembers and dials the number you last called.

Computers are creating an enormous job market, and almost every job soon may require some level of computer use. Computer-related occupations will grow 47 percent in the next ten years, according to the U.S. Bureau of Labor Statistics. That is three times the rate of all other occupations. By 1990, we will need 1.5 million computer programmers in a variety of businesses.

The computer age is *your* age. You have the right to live in it comfortably, without feeling threatened by this pervasive new technology. A computer is just another tool for you to use.

Numerous tasks at home can be performed by a computer. You can bank at home, shop at home, and read newspapers on the computer; you can even use your computer as a library. You can also monitor your health and advance your education by means of a computer.

The computer will make it possible for you to bring work home. Some insurance and financial companies already allow employees to work on company-owned terminals placed in employees' homes.

In our schools, the push is on to make children "computer literate." This means learning more about computers themselves, and being able to use a computer to learn about other subjects. Many parents and teachers fear that those students who are not familiar with computers will be left behind. They know that long after youngsters leave school, computers will remain a powerful tool in their lives.

This chapter will explain what a computer is, and what it can and cannot do. It will tell you how you can use one in your home to improve your job skills, earn extra income, and enjoy more leisure time.

What is a computer?

Historically, a computer, broadly defined, was a device that helped in computation—counting, calculating, adding, subtracting, multiplying, dividing, etc.—as you might guess from the root of the word *computer*. Today the word computer is used to describe an electronic device that stores, manipulates, and analyzes information. Computers no longer simply perform mathematical calculations: they can perform a much wider range of tasks, as described in the second half of this chapter.

The first computers. Stonehenge, the prehistoric circular stone monuments in Great Britain, and the abacus are two examples of early computers.

Stonehenge is a manmade device used to *calculate* the movement of the stars and planets in order to *measure* the seasons and *predict* seasonal change.

The abacus, although it is associated almost exclusively with the Chinese, was also used in some version by early Romans, Greeks, and Egyptians to *count* and *calculate*. The abacus was the first genuine calculating machine.

Gottfried Leibniz (b. 1646) and Blaise Pascal (b. 1623) each invented calculating machines in the 17th century. Leibniz also developed the system of using the base-two (binary) number system that computers use today. Consult the glossary under *binary* for a fuller explanation.

How computers work. Five steps are always required to make a computer work:
1. **Input:** the parts of the problem must be entered into the computer;
2. **Storage:** the computer must hold ("remember") the problem;
3. **Sequencing:** the computer must decide on the steps required to tackle the problem ("control");
4. **Calculation:** the computer must solve the problem; and
5. **Output:** the computer must deliver the answer.

The shrinking computer. Although Pascal's simple calculator (which could add and subtract) came before that of Charles Babbage, Babbage is considered the father of the modern computer. An early 19th-century Englishman, Babbage developed the principles on which modern computers are based.

The Difference Engine. Babbage started by inventing a small machine, the Difference Engine, in 1822. The machine computed algebraic expressions with many terms (polynomials), but it did only that. Babbage decided to build a machine that could solve virtually any mathematical problem and perform any kind of mathematical calculation.

The Analytical Engine. Babbage's design—a general-purpose computing machine—encompassed the main elements of a modern computer: it had input, storage, control, and output mechanisms. It was controlled by punched cards and was digital. (Think of a digital computer as a machine that counts on its fingers, or digits.)

Babbage planned for his Analytical Engine to be capable of storing thousands of figures, but as with many modern computer designs, his plans and his machine were never fully realized.

Hollerith's tabulating machine. Across the Atlantic Ocean, about 50 years after Babbage's work, the U.S. Census Bureau was having trouble tabulating the 1880 census, even though the next one was fast approaching. Herman Hollerith, a census agent, was asked to invent a mechanized tabulating system for the 1890 census.

Hollerith's system used paper tape initially, but punched cards worked better. Census takers punched holes in census cards to record data. The cards were fed into Hollerith's device, which had pins that stuck through the punched holes to form a closed electrical circuit, causing the information in each census category to be recorded.

The machine was a success. Hollerith went on to form his own concern, the Tabulating Machine Company, which became the International Business Machines Corporation (IBM) in 1914.

Understanding Computers

Mark I. Thirty years later, World War II gave the development of the computer its next big push. In 1944, the Mark I was built at Harvard University for IBM. Instead of punched cards, it used electric relay switches, and punched paper tape for input. The Mark I, which was used to set up tables of artillery gradations for the Army, produced figures accurate to 23 digits in .3 seconds.

ENIAC. The world's first *electronic* digital computer was ENIAC—the *E*lectronic *N*umerical *I*ntegrator *a*nd *C*alculator. Until ENIAC was developed, computers were mechanical.

ENIAC was room-sized, taking up 15,000 square feet. It was built of 18,000 vacuum tubes, and it weighed 30 tons. ENIAC, developed by a U.S. government team in 1946 to test weapons development and ballistics strength, was 17 times faster than Mark I, performing 5000 additions per second.

UNIVAC. Business first computerized with UNIVAC, the *Uni*versal *A*utomatic *C*omputer, which was smaller than its predecessors in size. UNIVAC, introduced in 1951, correctly tabulated the results of the 1952 presidential election.

Beginning with UNIVAC, people began to see computers as powerful, fast, accurate—and threatening. In the movie *2001: A Space Odyssey,* a computer named Hal does exactly what people are afraid computers will do some day: take over.

Transistors. The invention of the transistor at Bell Laboratories in 1947 quickly made possible a miniature world of transistor radios, hearing aids, and electronic equipment of all kinds. The transistor was smaller than a thimble. While the computer memory storage in use in the late 1950's was only 1.2 million figures, transistorized computers introduced by IBM in 1964 had a storage capacity of 8 million figures.

As memory went up, prices went down. Transistors made computers cheaper. In 1965, Digital Equipment Corporation of Maynard, Massachusetts, introduced the PCP-8, a *minicomputer.* It cost $20,000, while other, physically larger, computers of that time cost $1 million.

Computers that once took up an entire floor of a building could now be fit into the corner of an office. The next invention, the *microchip,* would make possible a computer small enough to fit on your lap.

Common questions about computers

Q: Do I need to know a lot about computers in order to use one?

A: No. Here is what you *do not need* to know. You do not need to know how to program a computer. You do not need to know programming languages. You do not have to possess scientific or mathematical aptitude. In fact, you do not have to know any math at all. You do not even have to know how the computer works. Most users do not.

Q: What should I know about my computer's disk operating system (DOS)?

A: All you have to know about a computer's DOS is which kind it is: common types are CP/M and MS-DOS. No advantages separate them. Your choice determines the range of software you can use. All the software you buy has to run on your operating system, or you cannot use it. Think of your DOS as speaking, say, French—unable to "read" German or Russian programs.

Q: Do I have to be computer-literate in order to use a computer?

A: You may be intimidated by what is called computer literacy. There is no need to be. Other than the experience of using a computer and a software program or two, nothing is required to qualify anyone for the ranks of the computer qualified.

Why do you want a computer?

How do you translate the things a computer does well into the kinds of things *you* might want a computer to do?

Some common reasons for wanting a computer are listed here to get you started. Look at this list and check off the things you want your computer to do.

_____Balance the checkbook
_____Chat with other computer users
_____Do calculations in class, at meetings, on trips
_____Do taxes
_____Draw pictures/graphs/charts
_____Improve job skills
_____Keep addresses
_____Keep Christmas mailing list
_____Keep personal records
_____Keep recipes
_____Keep the family budget
_____Learn more about computers
_____Organize records and tapes
_____Play games
_____Start or run a small business
_____Teach programming languages
_____Teach spelling, math, or other subjects
_____Tie into computer data banks
_____Track the stock market
_____Write music
_____Write term papers or reports

---

4   **Understanding Computers**

The microcomputer

A *microcomputer,* also called a micro, is simply a computer that is very much smaller in size than previously built computers. Microcomputers are also called *personal computers* because they can be owned and used by individuals, and because only one person at a time can use them. A *home computer* is a simple, inexpensive personal computer, such as the type people use to play games.

The microchip.
The core of the microcomputer is the *microprocessor,* a computer on a microchip. The microchip is integrated electronic circuitry on a silicon base. It made its debut in 1959.

The electronic components and circuitry on a microchip, also called a chip, serve the same function as did the relay switches and vacuum tubes of the older, larger computers. A chip can hold 1 million electronic components (electric transistors, wiring, and circuitry) on the space of a baby's thumbnail. The chip offers ten times the capacity of ENIAC at 1/30,000th of the cost. It performs a million calculations a second—200 times the number that ENIAC could perform.

You would have to use a microscope to examine the circuitry on a chip. It carries hundreds of thousands of transistors connected by microscopic "wires" on a sliver of silicon. Ten million transistors on a chip are expected in a few years. To "remember" 16K (store in memory 16 kilobytes, or about 16,000 pieces of data or numbers), a computer memory bank of the 1950's had to be taller and larger than an average adult standing up. That same amount of memory can now be stored on a tiny 16-K memory chip.

The same technology that put these myriad transistors on one chip has also reduced drastically the price of the computer. Today, personal computers that rival those once available only to government and big business can be purchased by small businesses, private individuals, and families.

Development of the microchip made possible ever smaller computers, from the room-size ENIAC to the desk-size personal computer.

Understanding Computers

The parts of a computer

CPU, keyboard, monitor, and disk drives in one unit.

The main part of the computer, the *c*entral *p*rocessing *u*nit (CPU), may be the only part of the computer that an advertisement or a salesperson refers to when offering a computer at what sounds like a price too good to be true.

Though the CPU is the "brains" of the computer, you will not be able to do anything with a CPU by itself. You need some way to communicate with it.

The computer's ears. The computer has to "hear" what you say. That is accomplished with *input devices*, such as game controls or a keyboard.

You use *game controls* to communicate with your computer. These controls, sometimes called joy sticks, come with or without a number pad. The stick moves up, down, right, and left in a two-dimensional axis and controls the movements of the game (your space ship, your hero, etc.) on the screen. Or the stick is a trigger that fires a weapon or, perhaps, a Ping-Pong ball at your command.

A more advanced way of communicating with your computer is to use a typewriterlike *keyboard*. The keys may include a number pad similar to that on a calculator.

The computer's mouth. The computer has to communicate back to you what it has done. It "talks" to you through *output devices*.

A *screen*, such as that on a television set, is an output device for game playing as well as for other more advanced or professional applications, such as word processing. It is often called a CRT (cathode ray tube) or a monitor.

A *printer* is an output device that records what the computer has done on paper. It is essential if you use your computer for writing or business.

If you want to store what you did on the computer, you need a *storage device*, such as a cassette (tape) recorder or a disk drive. Printers and storage devices are discussed in more detail later in the chapter.

Understanding Computers

Some low-priced computers turn out to be, upon closer investigation, next to useless without add-ons like monitors, disk drives, and printers, which can end up being more expensive than the computer itself.

Bit/Byte

How does a bit differ from a byte?

Bit is a contraction of "*b*inary dig*it*" and refers to the smallest unit of information a computer can process. Everything a computer does is done with electric circuitry, and electric current has two states: on and off. These two states are represented by the base two, or binary, number system, which has two symbols (0 and 1) to represent all numbers.

A byte is a group of bits, usually eight, forming a character, letter, number, punctuation mark, etc.

Here are some examples:

letter   byte:
The letter A is 01000001
The letter B is 01000010
The letter C is 01000011

It is never too late to learn!

In an adult education class at your local school you can learn how to use a personal computer. For those out of work or seeking a new job, experience in using a computer will provide new opportunities. Even if you have been out of school for a long time, it is not too late to learn how the computer can help you at home or on the job. In addition, many computer programs are designed to be easily learned: they lead you step by step throught their use, eliminating the need to memorize dozens of commands.

Understanding Computers

Computer programs. The computer that you use to play video games on your television set is dedicated to one task: playing games. You tell your computer what to do (play a game) by inserting a game cartridge. More expensive, sophisticated computers also need instructions to tell them what to do. These instructions are called programs, or *software*.

You can write a program yourself, but you certainly do not have to. Many computer owners hire someone to write a program for them. Businesses and some professionals (doctors, accountants, etc.) tailor programming to the exact requirements of their offices. Although you, too, could hire someone to write a program for your computer, the cost would probably exceed the price of the computer itself.

Far more likely, you will buy canned programs sold off the shelf, without any modification for personal quirks. You buy these programs exactly the way you buy a phonograph record or tape cassette, in a store or by mail. You then put the disk or tape in your computer and run it. A set of instructions, usually called documentation, comes with software programs.

There are two broad categories of software: *system* and *applications*.

System software. This category includes operating systems, utilities (software programs of a specific type), and languages.

A *disk operating system* (DOS) is what the computer uses to run itself. It directs the transfer of information from one part of the computer to another, and controls its storage in memory and on disk. It consists of a supervisory core and a collection of utility programs.

Utilities help tell the operating system how to work. They fill in the gaps where the operating system creates them. Gaps exist because a computer's operating system cannot—and does not have to—be all things for all uses. Two of the most common utilities include one that copies files from one disk drive to another and one that lets you specify exactly how you want something to be printed. Some of the more exotic utilities can examine and change specific bytes or groups of bytes in memory.

Good applications software is made easy for a beginner to use. Here is a response that makes you feel good and tells you what to do next.

Levels of computer literacy

How computer-literate are you? Perhaps more than you think. Instead of being intimidated by computers, check yourself against these criteria to find out where you fit on a computer literacy scale.

Level 1: You have used a computer. You have run a very simple computer program, such as a game cartridge.

Level 2: You have bought a software program that fits your personal needs, such as a word processing or spreadsheet program, and have used it.

Level 3: You are familiar with a computer language, such as BASIC. You have copied a program from a book or magazine, perhaps modified it, and run it on a computer.

Languages let you talk to the computer. Computers are machines that work with electrical impulses; computer languages let you "talk" to the computer without knowing anything about the machine's internal processes. Consider the language to be your interpreter.

Applications software. This term describes the task-oriented software programs that your computer uses to run your business, play games, type term papers, teach you or your family how to program, etc.

The difference between system software and applications software has been compared to the difference between knowing how to build a house and living in one: you do not need the former to do the latter. Unless you want to design or modify a software program, you will not need to use or understand system software.

The applications software (other than games) that you are most likely to use are programs in the fields of
- business/financial
- education
- health
- word-processing

Later in this chapter you will learn more about software categories and how to use them.

Compatibility. The computer's disk operating system (DOS) determines the kinds of software that will or will not work on your computer. Applications software is run (made to work) by the computer's operating system. For example, Apple computers can

8 **Understanding Computers**

Home computer limitations

Entertainment or home computers play arcade games and cost anywhere from $100 to $700. However, such computers have limitations. If you want a computer for extensive typing or for business use (accounting, inventory, mailing lists, etc.), you may not be able to expand a home computer's capability to meet your needs. Some home computers, for example, will not accept a disk drive. And you cannot necessarily expand the internal memory of the system (the RAM—*r*andom *a*ccess *m*emory) to the requirements of professional software. You are likely to be limited in your choice of software in any case: entertainment computers primarily come with game software.

---

only run Apple-DOS software. IBM PC computers can only use PC-DOS software.

Some operating systems work on several types of computers, called *compatible* computers. Most computers, however, are not compatible with each other, and most software will run on only one type of computer. This is similar to the situation with automobile parts: you cannot put a Cadillac El Dorado carburetor on a Volkswagen Rabbit.

Software, sometimes called parts, is built up around computer brands. There is no standardization in the computer market. You cannot use IBM PC software on an Apple computer. That is why you are advised to pick out software first—to know in advance what you want your computer to do for you—before you buy hardware (the computer itself, the printer, etc.).

Buying software.
Take your list to a computer store—or to any large retail store that sells computers—and ask to see a demonstration of software that will perform the tasks you want. In addition, look through computer magazines for the names of software programs that do the tasks you have selected. Then ask to see these programs demonstrated as well.

While you are trying out software, you will also get a chance to see different types of computers. The best way to begin selecting a computer is to actually try it out, watching it do what you want it to.

Although the conventional approach is to buy software first, this has become less important recently because of the many different versions of the same software programs for different machines. There are many software programs continually being developed to perform everyday tasks on home computers.

Shop around for the best price for both software and hardware.

Selecting hardware.
To select the right computer for you—the hardware—go back to the list of things you want your computer to do.

Do you want to buy a computer to become computer-literate or to play games? Then consider a basic, inexpensive computer.

Many of these units use the family television set as a screen. A beginner, spending less than $100, can learn how to use a computer with these low-cost models.

Game computers can introduce the family to computers without requiring any other investment in hardware. You can hook a game computer up to your existing television set with a converter (usually included). The converter translates computer signals into video signals for television display. It will come with a set of game paddles. You buy game cartridges for the games you want to play. Cartridges are the easiest software to use and are ideal for very young children.

Education computers will give you games plus education. You will spend about $100 to $500 for a computer with a keyboard as well as game paddles. You can still use the television set for the visual display. This simple setup will introduce you to how computers work. If you wish, you can even learn programming.

Personal computers. To run business programs and to do business typing, a computer with disk drives, costing $1000 or more, a typewriter keyboard with a numerical keypad and function keys, a high-resolution display screen, and a printer are required. This kind of computer can play games, too, but it would be a waste of money to buy it solely for entertainment.

Storing your data.
One fact of computer life that people often forget (with sometimes tragic results), is that when you turn off the computer, or the power fails, you lose any information that was stored only in the internal electronic memory of the computer. If you want to keep records, balance the checkbook, plan the budget, keep recipe files, or organize your record collection, then you want your computer to remember what you did the last time you used it. This requires a *storage device.* With inexpensive learning or entertainment computers, the storage device is a cassette recorder. The computer remembers your information by recording it on cassette tapes.

Cassette tapes are the least expensive of the storage devices. Running them is like running a tape recorder: you put the tape in the recorder and push the "play" button. Tapes are slow to use and are not available with

Understanding Computers　　　　9

a full range of software programs. The advantage is that they are inexpensive and easy to use.

Disks and disk drives. The next step up in computer storage is the *floppy disk*, which runs on a *disk drive*. You can upgrade some, but not all, home entertainment computers with a disk drive that will expand the amount of material you can manipulate and store. For a computer with disk drive, you should anticipate spending at least $1000, and should intend using your computer for serious applications, such as running a business from your home. Disk drives are used by more expensive personal, desk-top, or business computers to store data on disks, either floppy or hard. Disk drives are similar in purpose to a tape recorder that records data on cassette tapes, but the drives are much faster. Unlike a tape recorder, disk drives can "read" data anywhere on a disk without playing through all the recorded material sequentially.

Both floppy disk drives and hard disk drives are usually a physical part of the main computer housing. The essential difference between them is that a floppy disk can be removed from its drive, while a hard disk is permanently fixed in its drive.

Floppy disks may be single- or double-sided, and single- or double-density. Just as a double-sided disk will hold twice as much information as a single-sided disk, a double-density disk holds twice as much information as a single-density disk. A double-sided, double-density disk will hold from 320K to 400K depending on the operating system. Hard disks generally are available in the 5-, 10- or 20-megabyte (millions of bytes) capacity ranges.

The storage capacity that you need will be determined for the most part by the applications you intend using the computer for. Some applications programs are very large and can only be stored on one of the higher capacity disks. If you intend to use your computer to create a very large database, you may need a hard disk. This is something you should discuss with your computer salesman.

What about those expensive add-ons?

The following are extra features that can be bought as add-on, peripheral (side) devices or can be built into the computer. They are nonessential, and in some cases quite expensive.

Touch screens	Some computers allow you to tell them what to do by touching the video display screen instead of the keyboard.
Voice	Some computers recognize voice commands. Speech recognition is rudimentary right now, but it is an important feature for those who cannot use a keyboard.
Mice	Using a mouse is another way of telling the computer what to do. Instead of using a typewriterlike keyboard, you use a hand-held controller, or mouse, which you move over a rectangular pad. The upper left-hand corner of the pad corresponds to what you see on the upper left-hand corner of the video display screen.
Hard disks	These are storage devices for sophisticated business-type uses of personal computers. They have a storage capacity in the 10-megabyte (millions of bytes) range, as compared with the 180- or 360- kilo byte (thousands of bits) range of floppy disks commonly found on home computers. The disks are sealed inside a disk drive. They can come as part of the computer or they can be bought as extras.
Modems	These devices let a computer talk over telephone lines to other computers. Sometimes a modem is built-in, most common in portable or transportable computers. More often, however, you have to buy the modem. You need a modem to tap into the information services that carry stock quotes, airline guides, and user bulletin boards. If you do not want your computer to communicate with other computers, you do not need a modem.
Sound synthesizers	These plug into the computer and create sounds, including spoken words and music. You can compose and play music on your computer with special extras you plug in or add on to it, although some computers do come with this ability built-in.

Printers

Certain uses you may have for your computer—writing letters or research papers, keeping your budget, running a business from your home—will require putting the output of your computer on paper. This is called hard copy and it requires a printer.

There are several kinds of printers. Two popular choices are the daisywheel and dot matrix printers. Both names describe the kind of printing element that produces their distinctive type of character. Each has advantages (+) and disadvantages (−).

Daisywheels. These printers have a printing element that resembles a flat circular hub with spokes radiating outward, something like a daisy. Daisywheel printers

− Are relatively expensive ($600 up).
+ Produce high-quality print, good for professional-looking (letter quality) correspondence, manuscripts, etc.
− Are slow, printing only 12 to 50 characters per second. At that rate, an average letter on 8½″ × 11″ stationery, 65 characters across, would take about half a minute to print.
− Cannot produce graphs (bar graphs, charts, drawings, tables, etc.). Because daisywheel printers have actual letters, numbers, and punctuation on the "petals" of the print element, they are not useful for graphics, which are formed with dots instead of letters.

Dot matrix. These printers have a printing element that produces everything on a keyboard, such as letters, numbers, and punctuation, plus graphs and pictures, by "drawing" them with a series of tiny dots at a speed of 80 to 350 characters per second. The "matrix" may consist of a grid of five rows of seven dots (5 × 7), nine rows of nine dots (9 × 9), and so on. The greater the number of dots, the higher the quality of character produced. Dot matrix printers

+ Can produce graphics.
+ Are very fast.
+ Are relatively inexpensive ($100 to $600 or more).
− Are noisier than daisywheel printers.
− Do not produce print that looks like that of a typewriter.

Which printer is for you? Quality is in the eye of the beholder. You have to look at the print and decide if it is what you want.

A 9 × 9 matrix on a dot matrix printer is considered to rival daisywheel print quality. Each character is produced from a total of 82 dots, and it is clear and well delineated. A 5 × 7 matrix, on the other hand, may not print the tails of descenders (*j, q, p, y,* and *g*) deeply enough.

While you are looking at the print, listen to the printer. Any impact printer (including both daisywheel and dot matrix) is noisy. Thermal printers, a type of nonimpact printer that burns the print into specially treated paper, are quiet. The disadvantage lies in the treated paper you must use with a thermal printer. Ink-jet printers are also nonimpact and quiet—and expensive. They sell for about $5000.

Pin-feed advance mechanisms use "pins" on the platen to advance the paper through the printer. Page after page, the alignment of your line of copy stays perfect because of the way the paper is locked on the pins on the right and left sides. However, those pins require that all your paper be specially made with holes along both margins.

Friction-feed advance mechanisms grip paper between the platen and roller, like a typewriter, but the paper may slip after continued use. Some printers have both methods of advancing paper, a definite plus.

Understanding Computers

Computers and education

Educational software for children that is also fun to use can be an important learning aid. However, not all educational software is for children. There are many programs for older students and adults.

Why are computers good for learning new things? Computers can entertain as they educate, with engaging graphics, colors, sounds, movement, and simulations. Computer learning can be fun.

Computers can force one-to-one attention (one person, teacher, or computer to one student), which is known to speed learning.

Unlike a textbook, computers can encourage you when you have grasped the material. By making a sound or by flashing a message on the screen ("GREAT WORK!"), they can congratulate you on a job well done.

Computers are endlessly patient when you are wrong, going over and over the material until you get it right. No harsh words, no lost tempers.

Young children are especially good candidates for computer education because they are fascinated with how a computer works. Early education software takes advantage of a child's natural delight with games, and combines games with learning to produce a painless teaching environment.

Educational software.
A wide variety of educational software is now available for use on home computers. For the most part, they come packaged in one of two ways.

Plug-in cartridges for use on even low-cost computers allow the youngest of users to count, spell, read, etc., on a home computer. If you have very young children, consider buying an inexpensive home computer that uses software cartridges that the child can plug in without help.

Floppy disks containing many educational programs are now available. They can teach typing, logical analysis, programming, science subjects, and more.

Evaluating the software.
Some educational software consists of nothing more than expensive flash cards, such as those you used in school to learn multiplication and addition. Such software does not take advantage of the full potential of your computer.

How can you tell a good educational software program from a bad one? How do you go about finding a good one?

1. **For children, start in the school.** If your child's school has computers, ask the teacher what kind of software they use. You may wish to duplicate or complement the software your child is already using. Or you may want to use the next, more advanced program in a series.

   If the school does not have computers, your child's teacher may still have some recommendations. Be prepared, however; the teacher may know no more than you do.

2. **Next, go to a computer store and try out some programs.** If you are buying the software for children, take them into the store to try it out with you. The software should be labeled with suggested age levels, but a test run will ensure that the software is appropriate for your children. Let them use it.

3. **Read the manual** (the documentation, or instructions that go with the program). Are the instructions easy to read? Some are written very poorly, and some are useless. It is not your fault if you cannot understand the instructions. If they are incomprehensible, look for another program; if the program has no documentation, do not buy it.

4. **When you test-run the program,** look for these features:

Two educational software examples

Speed reading. Speed-reading courses outside the home are often quite expensive, and they require you to spend hours in a classroom that may be far from home. With a computer, you can learn to increase your reading speed, at home, much more economically. You can buy a speed-reading software program for about $70. More than one member of your family can take the same "course," which brings the cost down even further.

The computer is an especially effective tool for learning speed reading. It can train your eye movements to extend your peripheral (side) vision, so that you read larger groups of words at a time instead of one or two at a time. It can flash individual words on the screen at faster and faster rates, enabling you to build up your comprehension. It can also roll text across the screen at increasingly faster rates to train you to read actual running text more and more quickly.

Some of these techniques are the same ones used in speed-reading courses given outside the home. But when you are working on your own computer, you can insert your own reading material so that the selections you use for practice are the kinds of material you enjoy reading.

History. How does history take shape? Instead of memorizing names and dates of famous people and wars, you can use the computer to study factors that influence the way history unfolds. Some history programs trace the interplay of economic, political, religious, and other influences. The programs use the software to present a "model" that allows for the random selection of events within the established limits (historical period, countries, etc.).

Instead of reading the names of kings and generals and the locations of the major wars, for example, you could put yourself in tenth-century Spain or the American Civil War. Then, you could manipulate the historical, economic, and human factors as variables on the computer. The result is a model of theoretical history.

The program is unique each time it runs, although it preserves the broad historical overview. Color displays are used to show maps and graphic detail for the time period, as well as political or religious areas of influence.

The models offer information you might also get from books or a course, but learning through models allows you to make choices and participate in the process.

- *Friendliness.* Is the structure of the program nonthreatening and easy to use? It should be. This does not mean that the course content of the program should be something your child can breeze through, thereby learning nothing. It means that the program itself should be something you and your child can use on the computer without major problems.

  In addition, the content of the program, the actual material to be learned, should be neither above nor below your child's ability. Just because the package says "Ages 5–8" does not mean that your seven-year-old will find the program useful. Your child may not be ready, or may be too advanced, for that particular program.

- *Usefulness.* What does this program purport to do? Read the claims on the package or brochure. It should clearly state what the program will teach your child. Is this what your child wants or needs? Do not waste money on programs that your child cannot, or will not, benefit from.

- *Encouragement.* The software should assess your child's progress. If an answer is incorrect, does the program just move on, or does it offer help, and review the material when an answer is incorrect? Better yet, does it rephrase the original explanation, presenting the material in a new way for those who did not understand it the first time? A program that simply indicates wrong answers is not as good as one that offers feedback and encouragement.

- *Flexibility.* A good program has the flexibility to adjust to progress. If the child grasps the material with no difficulty (three answers right in a row, for example), the program should adjust accordingly: it should become progressively more challenging. Some programs are flexible enough to let you add new material—for example, extra passages for reading comprehension, additional vocabulary, or a whole new text with questions. When the original content has been mastered, such programs remain useful so long as you continue making additions to them.

- *Entertainment.* Finally, the software should take full advantage of the computer's ability to enhance the learning experience with movement, color, interesting displays, simulations, etc. If the program simply presents screen after screen of straight text, followed by multiple choice questions, it offers no advantages over a textbook. Do not buy it. You do not need a computer to read a book, unless you are learning how to speed read.

Financial and business programs

- Are you thinking of starting an income-producing business at home?
- Do you run a small business?
- Do you take work home from the office frequently?
- Do you want tighter control over the family budget?

Using a personal computer for financial or business applications will probably justify the cost. For simply balancing your checkbook, a pocket calculator is more cost-effective than a computer, and it is more time-efficient. But if you also want to set up a small business in your home, then a computer is a wise purchase.

The computer offers invaluable assistance for business-oriented tasks, such as:
- maintaining inventory records
- keeping a customer file for billings or advertising
- accounting

Applications

Word processing. Writing on a computer—word processing—is discussed on page 16. If you prepare long or repetitious documents on a typewriter, a computer with word processing software can make you more productive.

Number crunching. Simple addition, subtraction, multiplication, and division—the kind you do to balance the checkbook—do not require a computer. Figuring out how much a mortgage would cost at five different interest rates, for five different down payments, over a $20,000 range in housing prices, is, however, the kind of complicated calculation made easier and quicker by a computer. Computers perform these kinds of math gymnastics, called "crunching," with electronic spreadsheet software.

Database management. Also called information management, this software allows multiple arrangements of files of data. For a business, a database management program could sort your customer list by zip code for cheaper mailing rates, or target the big spenders for advertising promotions, or select them by any other category you enter into the computer.

Computer-drawn illustrations can be instantly revised. Changing the percentages will automatically cause the pie to be redrawn.

Graphics. Do you make sales presentations? You can turn numbers into charts, graphs, and other visual displays with a computer and a graphics printer.

Buy or lease?

If you are buying a computer for business reasons, the 10 percent investment tax credit on the purchase price is a definite advantage of outright purchase.

But leasing, too, has its advantages:
- You avoid being stuck with out-of-date technology. At the end of a short-term lease, you turn the computer in and get the latest model.
- If anything goes wrong, you do not have to pay for repairs.
- If you are leasing for business, you can deduct all the leasing expenses.
- Leases can cost less than purchases, especially if you have the lessor pass the tax credits through to you.

Leasing also has its disadvantages:
- You lose depreciation and other deductions that you would have gotten had you bought the equipment. Those benefits include a one-time $7500 ($10,000 in 1986) writeoff, investment tax credit, accelerated depreciation, loan interest deductions (if you borrow money to buy the computer), and business expense deductions. You may be entitled to partial tax advantages if you buy the computer for both home and business use. (For strictly personal home use, you cannot claim business tax deductions.)
- You will have to pay a security deposit.
- If you do not read the fine print carefully, you may find yourself paying additional charges (service and maintenance) or getting locked into an extension of the lease.

Sample business software titles

pfs: File	*Lotus 1-2-3*
pfs: Report	*Symphony*
BPS Graphics	*Wordstar*
Market Analyzer	*dBase III*
Financier II	*Framework*

---

14   **Understanding Computers**

The electronic spreadsheet

The software most used in business is the spreadsheet program. In fact, it is the electronic spreadsheet that made microcomputers popular. It was invented by a student at the Harvard Business School in 1978. He knew there had to be an easier way to do the recalculations required every time one element changed in accounting or recordkeeping. His invention made it possible for the recalculations to be done on a microcomputer.

What is a spreadsheet? Think of an electronic spreadsheet as a computer program that duplicates the rows and columns printed on accounting graph paper, and does all the arithmetic you would have to do to fill in all those rows and columns (254 horizontal rows and 63 vertical columns on most spreadsheets).

To do an accounting or recordkeeping spreadsheet by hand often means doing not one spreadsheet but many, each one different, each involving a multitude of complicated, repetitive calculations. Changing one figure requires changing related figures. A mistake in one figure produces a chain of mistakes in related figures.

Unlike people, the computer thrives on doing things over and over again, and it does not make mathematical errors. It does all its calculations in seconds. You simply enter the figures, or in a few places change them, and the entire spreadsheet is recalculated in an instant with no mistakes.

What can you use a spreadsheet to do? You can analyze a business or personal budget using a spreadsheet program. You can see the effect of changes in income or of different deductions on your taxes; you can keep track of your investments; you can control your cash flow; or you can project your profits.

You can, to use a more specific example, make use of "what if" scenarios. Suppose you want to buy a new house. Into a spreadsheet you could enter figures for varying

- down payments: $5000 $7500 $10,000 $15,000 $20,000
- purchase prices: $30,000 $50,000 $80,000 $100,000
- interest rates: 9%   10%   12%   14%

Now you can find out how much house you can afford if interest rates go up, or if you put down a larger or smaller down payment, or if you buy a more or less expensive house.

In business the electronic spreadsheet can help answer questions like these:

- Should you build or buy? What would the difference in cost be?
- How much should you charge for a new product in order to recoup your cost?
- How much should you charge to make a profit?
- What would your financial situation be if you gave every employee a raise?
- What would the impact on your business be if sales fell by 10 percent next quarter?
- How much new business will you have to generate to recoup the cost of advertising?

The problem-solving capabilities of the spreadsheet are nearly limitless.

By using a spreadsheet program you can automatically revise a whole table to reflect a change in only one number. In this example the sales figure in October for the Marina was corrected, resulting in instant recalculation of the totals in three places.

Understanding Computers

Word processing

If you want to use your computer for running a home-based business, improving your job skills, or writing long research papers, word processing is the application software for you. In fact, word processing has become the most important use for most people who have computers in the home.

There are also word processors (that is, computers) that have advanced word-processing programs built into their systems. They are intended for heavy duty, professional use.

Word processing: how it works.

Word processing is typing by computer, with a big plus. Word processing software can turn your computer into a typewriter, a typesetter, a printer, a dictionary, a thesaurus, an editor, and a secretary.

Instead of using paper to try out your ideas, you use the computer's memory. Instead of typing and retyping on paper, you type a first draft of a document into the computer. The computer lets you correct or revise it without retyping the whole document.

What can word processing do?

Whether you use a word processor or—as is more likely and much less expensive—a computer, running a word processing program, such as MultiMate™ or WordStar®, allows anyone who can type to do word processing. What can word processing do that a typewriter cannot?

Related software

A spelling checker. A spelling checker automatically looks through your typed document for spelling errors. Any word that is misspelled will be highlighted for you to correct.

An electronic thesaurus. Do you keep using the same words over and over? With this software, you can be creative instead of repetitive in your word choice. At the stroke of a key, synonyms for the word you want to replace appear on the computer screen.

Mailing lists. You can coordinate word processing software with programs that can handle any mailing list—your Christmas cards, your business clients. Each letter will carry an individual salutation with its own address.

---

1. **It can justify margins** automatically. That means that everything on the right and left side of the page or column will be lined up evenly.
2. **It can rearrange the order** of anything you have typed. You can move sentences, words, and paragraphs up or down on the page without retyping them.
3. **You can copy automatically** any part of the document, or even another document, and deposit it at another location using one key.
4. **You can change the format** of material. You can make the margins much wider, or you can make them much narrower if you prefer. Without any retyping.
   You can center material
   with one keystroke.
You can underline, highlight, number and renumber the pages, insert footnotes automatically, type ^{above} or below the line, **use bold type for emphasis.**
5. **You save time** because you do not have to retype. Also, because you do not have to retype the whole document, you reduce the possibility of introducing new errors while correcting old ones. If you are sending one letter, manuscript, or document to several people, the computer saves you even more time.

What equipment do you need?

A keyboard. If you intend to do a lot of typing (whether of words or numbers), you should have a computer with a typewriterlike keyboard. Instead of such a keyboard, some computers have a membrane with the letters and symbols painted on; some have thin little keys somewhat like those on pocket calculators. Neither is adequate for heavy word processing.

A printer. You will need some kind of printer for the output of your typing.

A word processing program. You need not buy a word processor to do word processing. A word processor is expensive, and word processing is the only thing it can do. Fortunately, you can buy word-processing software for inexpensive home computers. For business or demanding professional use, you will need a more elaborate program, one costing several hundred dollars, and a more professional computer, costing at least $1000.

A video display. You can use your television set for viewing copy, but for long stints of typing, the resolution (sharpness) on a television screen is not clear enough, and your eyes will tire. For this reason, you may want to buy a computer video display.

Staying healthy with computers

From improving the hearing to monitoring heart disease, computer-based health aids are helping people live longer and better. A computer can affect your health and well-being in two major ways.

Staying healthy.
If you are already in good health, or simply need a little push to get there, there are computer programs that monitor your lifestyle to make sure you stay healthy.

Programs you may want include the following:

Computerized medical records keep track of doctor visits, immunizations, and health problems. They schedule checkups and record the health history for every member of your family.

Exercise programs monitor the quality of your exercise. Some exercise devices have their own built-in computer.

Diet software translates your meals into the nutrients and calories you get from them. The programs typically use the U.S. Department of Agriculture's nutritional data values, focusing on 24 nutrients in 1000 foods. Some programs combine diet and exercise, analyzing your exercise and your food intake to see if you have met a weight-loss or weight-maintaining goal.

Computerized meal-planning programs range from gourmet cookbooks to simple menu planners that analyze and plan meals so that all nutritional needs are covered. Such programs can recalculate calories and nutrients for reduced servings or substitutions ("What if I use cottage cheese instead of sour cream?").

Handling a health impairment.
Microcomputers are also used in a variety of devices designed to help people with various disabilities. They improve the quality of life. They can make the difference between idleness and productivity, or between dependence and independence. Here are some of the many devices and inventions that are already helping disabled people:

- *Bio-ears,* implanted behind the ear, offer hearing for the severely impaired.
- *Prostheses* (artificial limbs) can be electronically activated by computer circuitry.
- *Electronic reading aids* for the visually impaired include devices that translate a printed word into a vibrating tactile form.
- *Game paddles* help physically impaired computer users.
- *Expanded computer keyboards* accommodate people with motor disabilities.
- *Microprocessors for Braille* combine computers and Braille communication.
- *Microcomputer-based devices* allow the hearing-impaired to send and receive messages over the telephone.
- *Sonar-guided wheelchairs* and *voice-operated robot arms* are two sophisticated computer aids. The wheelchair uses a microcomputer for steering and speed control.
- *Blood pressure monitors* that you can wear during your normal day-to-day activities have an electronic memory and use a computer display. They are more likely to reflect a normal blood pressure reading than the inflated reading a visit to the doctor's office sometimes produces.

Also in development is a computer aid to help the blind to see: a small television camera attached to an even smaller computer.

For more information about disabilities and personal computers, see the list of books on page 21.

A microcomputer, which is carried over the shoulder, can be tuned to adjust a prosthetic knee joint for different gaits: normal walking, running, or climbing stairs.

Understanding Computers

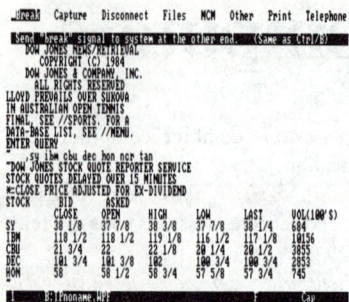

Dow Jones averages from online database

Glossary of computer terms

Some standard keyboard characters with their ASCII equivalents

033	!	063	?	093	]		
034	"	064	@	094	^		
035	#	065	A	095	_		
036	$	066	B	096	'		
037	%	067	C	097	a		
038	&	068	D	098	b		
039	'	069	E	099	c		
040	(	070	F	100	d		
041	)	071	G	101	e		
042	*	072	H	102	f		
043	+	073	I	103	g		
044	,	074	J	104	h		
045	-	075	K	105	i		
046	.	076	L	106	j		
047	/	077	M	107	k		
048	0	078	N	108	l		
049	1	079	O	109	m		
050	2	080	P	110	n		
051	3	081	Q	111	o		
052	4	082	R	112	p		
053	5	083	S	113	q		
054	6	084	T	114	r		
055	7	085	U	115	s		
056	8	086	V	116	t		
057	9	087	W	117	u		
058	:	088	X	118	v		
059	;	089	Y	119	w		
060	<	090	Z	120	x		
061	=	091	[	121	y		
062	>	092	\	122	z		

acoustic coupler. A type of modem with two "ear muffs" into which you place your telephone handset (see illustration) to let your computer "talk" over phone lines to other computers. See also *modem*.

ADP. Automatic data processing.

AI (artificial intelligence). The field or study of computer use to reproduce human intelligence. Also describes the ability of computers to simulate human intelligence and reasoning, as well as attempts to make computers "think."

algorithm. The mathematical or logical steps needed to solve a problem.

ASCII (the *A*merican *S*tandard *C*ode for *I*nformation *I*nterchange). An internationally used coding scheme for representing information digitally. With ASCII, any two computers—regardless of operating system or brand—can communicate. ASCII uses 128 seven- or eight-digit codes to represent the letters of the alphabet, the numbers 0 through 9, and punctuation marks. The codes are based on the binary system (for example, the lower-case letter "a" is represented by 0110001).

BASIC (*B*eginner's *A*ll-purpose *S*ymbolic *I*nstruction *C*ode). The most widely used programming language on home computers. Also considered one of the easiest to use. See also *language*.

baud. Measuring unit of the speed of computer information transfer. Usually calculated in bits per second (bps). Three hundred or 1200 are two common speeds for modems used with home computers. This means that if you were sending information through a modem at 300 baud, your computer would be transmitting the information at a rate of about 300 words per minute. As a rule of thumb, the baud rate is approximately equal to the number of English words per minute at a given baud rate. You can read 300 baud material moving across your screen. You cannot read 1200 baud, which moves too fast. Twelve hundred baud is used for transferring long files or programs from computer to computer.

binary, binary system. The base-two number system used by computers (see chart). The two digits used in base two, and in the binary system, are 0 and 1. Each space to the left of the decimal is a progressive power of two. Base two is used in computers because it represents the basis of computer operations: on-off or high-low electric current.

bit, binary digit. The basic unit of encoded computer data. A bit is one unit of storage space in a computer. Each electric pulse is one bit. Generally, eight bits form one byte.

boot. To start up a program (pull it up by its bootstraps). Bootstrapping, or booting, is the process used to start up the computer with its first instructions.

Bps. Bits per second. A way of measuring the speed at which a computer sends information. See also *baud*.

bug. An error in the computer or its programming software. Legend has it that an early large mainframe computer malfunctioned because of an insect trapped somewhere in the computer's tubes. The insect was discovered and removed. Since then, the word "bug" has come to describe general computer problems. Getting rid of the problems is called debugging the computer.

18

Understanding Computers

byte. Eight bits, the number required to encode one letter or number or symbol.

chip. A tiny piece of silicon (the size of a baby's fingernail) that contains thousands of transitors joined by very fine metal circuitry. A modern computer will have one or more chips, also called microchips.

command. Any instruction given to a computer. Commands are frequently preset by the software program you use.

CP/M (R). Control program for microcomputers. An operating system used by a number of microcomputers.

CPU (central processing unit). The computer's "brains," actually a chip. See also *microprocessor.*

CRT (cathode ray tube). The video display (looks like a television screen) where computer output is displayed.

database. Computer-organized and computer-maintained filing. In databasing, you type into your computer addresses, recipes, etc.—whatever information you want it to keep track of. **Online database,** also called **information utility,** offers information services (about 1500 of them) that you can tap into with your computer, some communications software, a modem, and your phone line. Online database/information services give you access to business information, stock quotes, legal research and case law, games, restaurant and movie reviews, classified ads, advice and so on.

disk/diskette. The magnetic-coated flexible disk (looks something like a 45 rpm phonograph record though you can bend it) on which software programs are stored, and on which you can store your own data (documents, files, etc.).

Computer communicating

Your computer can communicate. You can use it like a telephone, to call and chat, using the keyboard and monitor, with other computer users. You can program it to send calls to other computer owners late at night, when rates are cheap.

You can also use your computer to gain access to libraries of books, newspapers, and magazines through computer information services and bibliographic databases.

How it works. Your computer can talk to another computer any distance away over telephone lines. To use normal phone lines, you have to convert the binary or digital signals your computer makes into the voice-frequency signals telephone lines carry.

Modems do that, among other things. They translate digital signals produced by your computer into oscillating signals, and vice versa (when in the receiving mode). That process is one of *mo*dulation and *dem*odulation, hence the name modem.

Equipment. There are two popular types of modems that are used with microcomputers.

Acoustic coupler modems consist of a cradle, or earmuffs, into which you place the handset of your telephone. Acoustic couplers have one drawback: they allow noise onto the line, which can interfere with data transmission.

Direct connect modems, as the name suggests, connect the computer to a phone jack directly.

What must you buy? Some computers are sold with built-in telecommunications ability. But many microcomputers do not have this capability, which means you will need additional hardware and peripheral equipment:
- an asynchronous board with RS232-C port and cable,
- the modem itself,
- and a telephone line to connect the modem into a wall jack.

You also will need *communications software:* programming on a disk telling your computer how to interact with other computers. You may find modem hardware and communications software sold together.

You can buy good programs for under $200—sometimes well under. *PC-talk* is a public domain program (free, uncopyrighted software), highly regarded, with good features and documentation. You can find public domain software in magazines, through computer clubs, etc.

Understanding Computers

documentation. The instructions for using a computer or software.

expansion slot, port. Space in the main body of the computer for board with additional memory or capability.

floppy disk. See *disk*.

hard or fixed disk. A disk sealed in a hard disk drive with a storage capacity in the millions of bytes.

hardware. The computer and related machine equipment, such as the printer.

home computer. A basic, inexpensive personal computer.

input/output (I/O). What goes in and what comes out of the computer.

K (kilobyte). One thousand and twenty-four bytes. K is an abbreviation for the Greek word *kilo*, or thousand. However, in the binary system, which is based on two, the closest corresponding power of two is 1024.

language. The means by which you talk to your computer. Has special vocabulary you can use to write programs or command instructions for the computer.

load. To enter data or programming into the computer.

logo. An easy-to-learn and easy-to-use computer language for programming and for learning programming. Frequently used in schools, especially for young children. Created at Massachusetts Institute of Technology.

list-merge. Combines a list of names and addresses with correspondence or any other file or data. Used for mailings, it is frequently combined with word-processing software.

mainframe. Large business and academic computers. They can be used by many people at one time. They can also be hooked up to and used by other, smaller computers.

```
list                              run
10 PRINT "What is your name":     What is your name? David
20 INPUT X$                       Hello David!
30 PRINT "Hello ";X$;"!"
40 END
```

Programing languages like BASIC, in which this simple program is written, allow you to make a computer do exactly what you want it to do.

Mb (megabytes). Million(s) of bytes. See also *byte*.

memory. The storage capability (circuitry and devices) of the computer.

menu. Selections, choices, and options presented on the video screen for a program, or for an information or electronic database. See also *database*.

microcomputer, micro. A computer that uses the microprocessor as its "brain." A personal computer.

microprocessor. The primary chip in a typical microcomputer. Like other chips, it is silicon-based circuitry wrapped in plastic or ceramic; but this particular chip contains the "brains" of the computer.

modem. A machine that translates computer signals into signals that can be carried over telephone wires.

mouse. A hand-held pointer used with a computer for word processing, graphics, etc. Bypasses the keyboard as a means of telling the computer what you want it to do.

Pascal. A programming language named after the French philosopher, mathematician, and inventor Blaise Pascal.

peripheral. A side item used with a computer. Peripherals include modems, joy sticks, and printers. Usually either an input or output device.

personal computer. A microcomputer, designed for personal use by an individual at home or in a business.

pin-feed. One way of pulling paper through a printer. Also called *tractor* or *sprocket feed* because the paper-advance mechanism consists of raised sprockets on the printer's platen that fit into holes on the right and left margins of the paper to pull it through the printer.

pixel. The unit of picture elements on a computer's video (visual) display. The equivalent of a dot. Used to measure the quality of the picture (resolution).

platen. The cylinder in a printer that corresponds to the platen in a typewriter. This cylinder rolls paper through the printer and serves as the backing against which the print element strikes.

program. Any instructions telling the computer what to do. See also *software*.

RAM (*r*andom *a*ccess *m*emory). The computer memory available for your use. It "forgets" whatever is in it when the computer is turned off.

RF (radio frequency) modulator. Adapts computer signals for use with a television type display.

ROM (*r*ead *o*nly *m*emory). The computer memory that is permanent. It is programmed when the computer is manufactured, and is not part of the memory available for you to use.

RS-232, 232C. A standard connector for computers and

Understanding Computers

peripheral devices, such as a modem.

save. To store a program or data on a storage device, either cassette or disk.

scroll. To move text on a screen vertically or horizontally.

semiconductor. Used for computer circuitry switches. Any material that transmits electricity better than a resistor or insulator, but not as well as a true metal conductor, is a semiconductor. The level of a semiconductor's ability to conduct electricity can be changed by temperature variation or by introducing impurities into it.

software. The instructions telling a computer what to do. Also called programs. There are two main types of software: systems and applications. Systems software gives the computer general instructions telling it how to do what it does. Applications software tells the computer how to perform a specific task.

unix. An operating system.

user friendly. A term that indicates that a computer or piece of software is easy to use.

user groups. Clubs of computer owners, usually organized around one particular type of computer or software. Some user groups have software libraries—programs members can try out, copy, and use. This is public domain (free, uncopyrighted) programming, often written by group members.

vacuum tubes. Glass tubes that control and amplify electric current. Used in early computers.

Winchester. When the Winchester hard disk was developed at IBM, its project number was 3030, and it was nicknamed Winchester after the Winchester 30-30 rifle.

For further reference

General
Bates, William
The Computer Cookbook
Doubleday

Bradbeer, Robin, De Bono, Peter, and Laurie, Peter
The Beginner's Guide to Computers
Addison-Wesley

Edelhart, Mike, and Garr, Doug
The Complete Computer Compendium
Addison-Wesley

Laurie, Peter
The Joy of Computers
Little, Brown

Leventhal, Lance, and Stafford, Irvin
Why Do You Need a Personal Computer?
John Wiley & Sons

Makower, Ernest
Personal Computers A–Z
Doubleday

Spencer, Donald
What Computers Can Do
Scribner's

How to buy a computer
Bates, Timothy, and Wright, Judith
Choosing the Right Small Business Computer
Hayden

Birnbaum, Mark, and Sickman, John
How to Choose Your Small Business Computer
Addison-Wesley

Hillman, Howard
Complete Computer Buyer's Checklist
Macmillan

How to Buy a Home Computer
Electronic Industries Association (free booklet)

Children and computers
Gerber, Carole
Turn Your Kid into a Computer Genius
Dutton

Hammond, Ray
Computers and Your Child
Ticknor & Fields

Walsh Burke, Anna Mae
Microcomputers Can be Kidstuff
Hayden

Computer games
Ahl, David
Basic Computer Games
Workman Publishing

Mau, Ernest
Create Word Puzzles with Your Microcomputer
Hayden

Computer history
Kidder, Tracy
The Soul of a New Machine
Little, Brown

Levy, Steven
Hackers: The Wizards of the Computer Revolution
Doubleday

The Microchip
National Geographic
Vol. 162, No. 4, October, 1982

Parker, Donna
Crime by Computer
Scribner's

Special applications
Brand, Stewart
The Whole Earth Software Catalogue
Doubleday

Edelhart, Mike, and Davies, Owen
Omni Online Database Directory
Macmillan

McWilliams, Peter
Computers and the Disabled
Doubleday

McWilliams, Peter
Questions and Answers on Word Processing
Prelude

Mau, Ernest
Secrets of Better Basic
Hayden

Ross, Peter
Introducing Logo
Addison-Wesley

Understanding Computers

Advancing Your Career

- Preparing for the job search 24
- Going after the job 32
- Getting the job 40
- Moving up the ladder 41
- Changing careers 44
- Getting back into the work force 47
- Starting your own business 49
- Matching yourself to the world of work 52

Whether you are interested in part-time work or a lifetime career commitment, careful reading of this chapter will inform you of the many possibilities before you. If you have already chosen your career, the information will help prepare you for promotion. It will also help those who simply want to ensure that they keep their jobs. Starting a new career in mid-life or after retirement calls for special advice and encouragement.

Here are some of the forecasts worth considering before making any new career decisions:
- About 131 million men and women are expected to comprise the 1995 labor force—3.8 million more than the figure named in earlier projections.
- Nearly two-thirds of the increase will be among women. Already, two-income families are the norm rather than the exception in today's economy.
- Job growth in the service industries (such as transportation, communications, public utilities, trade, finance, insurance, real estate, fast food, and government) is expected to account for nearly 75 percent of all new jobs between 1985 and 1995.
- By 1990, over 4.3 million senior citizens will have retired. Many of them will be taking advantage of the new Social Security laws (1984) that allow them to earn additional income (from $5160 to $6960, depending on age and yearly cost-index adjustments).
- High-school graduates are quickly entering the job market, often foregoing college in favor of computer schools and vocational training institutions.
- A shortage of college graduates is starting to show up in such fields as computer engineering and telecommunications.
- The demand for typists will decrease as the use of word processors creates openings for computer operators and programmers.
- Two of the fastest growing occupations will be repairmen for the computers and electrical equipment being produced, and health technicians to operate the new medical equipment being developed.
- Employment of teachers for preschool children is expected to surge in the next ten years, increasing by more than 40 percent. This demand will be created in part by the children of those born during the baby boom.

Specific, practical advice follows in each of the following sections.

Job opportunities in rapidly growing fields

Fastest growing industry	*Fastest growing occupation*	*Jobs with most openings*	*Annual openings*
Medical and dental instruments and other medical services	occupational therapists physical therapists physical therapy assistants medical insurance clerks	nurses' aides, orderlies, and attendants registered nurses licensed practical nurses	94,000 85,000 60,000
Business services	legal assistants office machine repairers banking and insurance credit clerks employment interviewers	secretaries and stenographers cashiers bookkeepers accountants typists real estate agents and brokers bank clerks receptionists	305,000 119,000 96,000 61,000 59,000 50,000 45,000 41,000
Computers and peripheral equipment and scientific and controlling equipment	computer systems analysts computer programmers computer operators peripheral EDP equipment operators	fast growing but small industry engineers	
Radio and television broadcasting	electrical engineers electrical and electronic technicians	engineers	total in engineering occupations: 46,500
Electronic components	electronic engineers electrical and electronic technicians	engineers	
New construction	surveyors' helpers mechanical engineers mechanical engineering technicians	blue-collar workers and supervisors local truck drivers carpenters construction laborers	69,000 64,000 58,000 49,500
Plastics products	compression and injection mold plastics machine operators	industrial assemblers machinery repairers	77,000 58,000

Advancing Your Career

Preparing for the job search

Assessing your abilities. When preparing for a job search, take the time to sit quietly and assess what you have done with your life. In addition to any work experience, what abilities do you have that qualify you for the job market? If you look closely at your past experiences, you may be surprised at the possibilities they point to for your future.

Take a pencil and paper and list all the skills and talents you have taken for granted all your life. What abilities do you use in your nonpaid activities? Can you cook, drive a car, write letters, sing in the church choir? See how you might apply the skills that you enjoy using most to a job situation.

How to start. To draw up your success chart, start as far back in your life as you wish. For instance, you may have had to recite a soliloquy from Shakespeare in tenth grade, or a poem in Sunday school when you were even younger. Whatever your age at the time, recitation in front of a group indicates poise, some public speaking ability, commitment—and courage.

Divide your life into five-year intervals. List each success or accomplishment in the first column, the skills or experience gained in a second column. It is also a good idea to consider negative experiences. Perhaps you hated selling Girl Scout cookies. You should ask yourself if this typifies your attitude toward selling

Matching yourself with the World of Work

	1. Leadership/Persuasion	2. Helping/Instructing others	3. Problem-solving/Creativity	4. Initiative	5. Work as part of team	6. Frequent public contacts	7. Manual dexterity	8. Physical stamina	9. Hazardous	10. Outdoors	11. Confined
Automobile mechanics			•		•	•	•	•		•	
Bank clerks				•							•
Bank tellers				•	•						
Blue-collar supervisors		•	•	•			•	•			
Dental hygienists		•			•	•	•				
Dieticians	•	•	•	•	•	•					
Drafters			•		•	•					•
Employment counselors	•	•	•	•							•
Firefighters		•	•		•	•	•	•	•		
Landscape architects			•	•		•	•				
Librarians	•	•	•	•	•	•					
Mail carriers						•	•	•		•	
Market research analysts	•		•		•	•					
Police officers	•	•	•	•	•	•		•	•		
Photographic process workers						•					•
Secondary school teachers	•	•	•		•	•					
Secretaries					•	•	•				
Waiters, waitresses			•		•	•	•				

Advancing Your Career

and, if so, remind yourself to stay out of that field.

Stick to your positive experiences when making an entry on the success chart. Consider what satisfactions and rewards came out of each experience. List these in a third column.

Matching your skills with work. Your success chart will give you the information about your marketable skills that you will need to apply to the Department of Labor *World of Work* chart. A sample from this chart is shown on page 24; you will find the entire chart on page 52.

The average person's length of time at the same job is 4.8 years. Although your career decisions are important, they are not necessarily meant to last forever. Once you have developed some experience at self-assessment, you will be able to go through the process more efficiently five years hence if need be. It would be wise to keep all you paperwork filed away for future reference.

The two examples shown on this page and on page 26 show the success charts of Julie Parsons, a homemaker who wants to reenter the work force, and Edward Stubbs, a hospital administrator who wants to start his own business (with his wife, Alice) after he retires. The amount of your work experience will determine where you start your success chart.

Julie Parsons started her chart back in childhood, which increased her confidence for job-hunting because she saw the range of her own experience. Edward and Alice Stubbs started with adult work experience. Though the Stubbses had tested most of their abilities, they wanted to develop a full profile of themselves because going into business on their own was a big and somewhat risky step for them.

Broad experience is useful in business

Edward and Alice Stubbs's catering business is a perfect example of a business formed from skills that are most enjoyed. Their access to advertising in their community theater program enabled them to reach exactly the right market at a low cost. Their big old house was well suited to their business needs and activities.

Past social and volunteer participation gave them the opportunity to show off their talents to the community and to gain experience and a good reputation.

CATERING SERVICE	Finance budgeting	Public Relations	Organizational ability	Communication	Working with people	Leadership	Cooperation	Dexterity cooking	Creativity	Risk	
Edward Stubbs age 65	•	•	•	•	•	•	•	•	•	•	Alice Stubbs age 63
Hospital Administrator 35 yrs.	•	•	•	•	•	•	•				
Gourmet cook 40 yrs.								•	•		Gourmet club Secretary 10 yrs.
Budget chairman 15 yrs. Finance committee	•	•	•								
Board of Directors 7 yrs. Community theater	•	•	•	•	•	•		•	•		Board of Directors Community theater 15 yrs.
Co-chairman social committee 8 yrs.			•	•		•	•	•			Co-chairman social committee 14 yrs.
Member of Chamber of commerce 30 yrs.		•			•						
Church Deacon 30 yrs.		•	•	•	•						Deaconess of Church 30 yrs.
		•	•	•	•	•	•				Publicity Chairman community theater 14 yrs.
			•	•	•	•					Subscription Drive 8 yrs.
		•	•	•	•						Secretary of Church choir 13 yrs.
			•	•	•	•	•				Volunteer at hospital cafeteria 25 yrs.

Advancing Your Career

JULIE PARSONS' SUCCESS CHART

Age	Successes	Skills used/acquired	Enjoyment/rewards
5-10	Recited poem at school assembly	Courage, poise, following directions, public speaking	Public acclaim, applause, approval
	Learned to swim	Physical fitness, athletic dexterity	Feeling of fitness, prize for diving
	Won spelling contest	Competition, self-motivation	Prize, public acclaim
11-15	Sold most Scout cookies	Salesmanship, competition, teamwork, self-motivation	Prize, personal satisfaction, helped troop
	Babysitting	Dependability, trust, child care	Approval, earning money
16-19	Editor of yearbook	Typing, design, layout, organization, photography, public relations, dependability, leadership	Concrete proof of accomplishment: book, name in print; problem-solving
	Lead in school musical	Teamwork, poise, following directions, dependability	Public acclaim, approval, using talent
	Class treasurer for 3 years	Mathematical ability, leadership, dependability	Problem-solving, public approval, trust, popularity
	Graduation	Intelligence, public relations, leadership	Diploma, feeling of accomplishment
20-25	Job as library assistant	Public relations, mathematical ability	Feeling of independence, earning money
	Church choir	Musical talent, teamwork, dependability	Public approval, using talent
	Marriage	Economics, math, sewing, teamwork, budget management, public relations	Personal acceptance, independence, trust, love
	Mother	Nursing, laundress, instructor, chef, counselor, public relations, arbitrator, flexibility	Trust, approval, love, problem-solving
26-30	Cub Scout leader and Sunday school teacher	Organization, leadership, fund-raising, trust, commitment	Public approval, teamwork, problem-solving
	Treasurer of church fair and fund-raising drive	Mathematical ability, trust, popularity	Teamwork, public approval, leadership
	Treasurer of reading club, member of library board of directors	Mathematical ability, trust, leadership, knowledge of books	Working with books and math again

Advancing Your Career

Career goals

Ultimate goals. Carefully consider your success chart and see what patterns show up. On Julie Parsons' chart, two interests keep reappearing: math/accounting and books/publishing. These patterns caused Julie to list "comptroller of her local newspaper" as her ultimate goal.

Edward Stubbs found the confidence to begin his own catering business after reviewing his success chart. He saw that throughout their 40 years of marriage, he and his wife had gained great satisfaction and given great pleasure to others through cooking, a joint hobby.

Now is the time to let yourself think about your ideal job. Refer to your success chart and ask yourself what you would most like to do with the remainder of your working years. Consider what contribution your work could make to society and make sure that your goal fits your values. A sample goal statement is shown at the top of this page.

Intermediate goals. With your goal statement in front of you, consider what intermediate goals you can set for yourself that will logically lead to your ideal job. If you want to be a teacher, education courses would be one of your intermediate goals. An even shorter range intermediate goal would be finding out about available courses. The point is to break your tasks down into manageable steps so that you can embark enthusiastically on taking the first one.

GOAL STATEMENT	PAUL CARTER
1. Career goal:	Chief computer programmer in medical diagnostics
2. Preparation:	B.S. electrical engineering and computer programming
3. Company:	High-tech industries
4. Social value:	Contributing to medical research

If you find yourself procrastinating, you may have made your intermediate goals too general. Rework them until you have made them so specific that at least one of them can be accomplished immediately. Making a list is an important visual aid, and you have the added pleasure of checking off each step that you complete. Below you will find an intermediate goal scoreboard used by a young man preparing for a job interview.

Paul Carter's scoreboard illustrates one way of setting down intermediate steps. Set up your own scoreboard any way that works for you, as long as it is

Paul Carter's monthly plan

SUN	MON	TUES	WED	THUR	FRI	SAT
	1 SEND FOR HI-TECH ANNUAL REPORT	2 CHECK LIBRARY FOR RECENT ARTICLES ABOUT HI-TECH; LOOK FOR NAMES	3 Call Friends who might know someone in HI-TECH field	4	5	6
7	8 See College Placement officer Ask for References	9	10 FIND NAME TO WRITE TO IN ANNUAL REPORT	11 Talk with Professors in Related courses; Ask for References	12 CHECK COLLEGE DIRECTORY FOR ALUMNAE IN HI-TECH JOBS; TELL THEM OF PLANNED VISIT	13 CHECK ALL MATERIAL FOR JOB DESCRIPTIONS
14	15 Begin work on resumé	16	17	18 FINISH RESUMÉ	19 HAVE RESUMÉ PRINTED PROFESSIONALLY	20
21	22 VISIT HI-TECH FIRMS; SPEAK WITH CONTACTS; TAKE NOTES FOR INTERVIEW	23 PICK UP RESUMÉ	24 WRITE FOR INTERVIEW; SEND RESUMÉ AND COVER LETTER OF INTRODUCTION	25 SEND THANK YOU NOTES TO ALL CONTACTS	26 Plan questions for interview	27
28	29	30 Follow up Letter with call for appointment GET APPOINTMENT!!	31			

Advancing Your Career

specific. Some useful questions to ask yourself are:
- Keeping in mind your ultimate goal, what skills must you develop? How?
- What are the available jobs in your area and how do your qualifications fit their needs? How do *your* needs fit their requirements?
- What are the priorities among the steps you must take to qualify for your ideal job?
- What resources are necessary—money, education, equipment, uniforms, etc.?
- What reasonable time limits can you set for accomplishing each intermediate goal?

If the intermediate goal is a course, when can the course be completed? If it is an interview, when will you set that up? Be realistic, write everything down, and then do your best to stick to your timetable.

If unexpected delays occur, rewrite your scoreboard so that it is once more realistic and manageable. If you face long-term career preparation, such as completing a course, serving an apprenticeship, or getting an advanced degree, divide your goals into yearly steps until they can be broken down into monthly or weekly tasks, as Paul Carter has done.

What schooling do you need?

To school or not to school? If you have been out of the job market for a while, you may immediately think of additional schooling as a solution to your dilemma. Often it is the appropriate first step to embarking on a new or different career. Nevertheless, make sure you do not rush to the registrar's office before taking an inventory of your skills. Lack of confidence rather than lack of education may be your problem.

The essential diploma. There is only one diploma that should not be questioned—your high school diploma. If your high school career was interrupted, there is a basic exam you may take to earn your General Equivalency Diploma (GED). This certificate will make you eligible for jobs requiring the completion of high school.

Your local high school guidance office will refer you to the nearest adult learning center where you can find out what steps are necessary to obtain your GED. Often you can study independently at home and pass your exam without having to go back into the classroom. You may take the exam as many times as necessary to earn your GED.

Going back to school?

Pros and cons. If you are undecided about the necessity of additional schooling, consider these arguments for and against. Applying such arguments to your own situation can help you make the right decision.

PROS
- An additional degree may advance your career in a specific way.
- A particular course of study may guarantee you a job.
- A master's degree may guarantee you a higher salary in your field.
- You may need more education to break into the field of your choice.
- All education is useful and may be applied in unexpected ways in the future.

CONS
- A liberal arts degree does not guarantee a job.
- Most people do not end up working in their field of study.
- Approximately 80 percent of the new jobs (see chart on next page) do not require a degree, though they may require vocational training.
- Many companies prefer to do their own training.
- You may price yourself out of the job market with more degrees, especially in the field of education.

Checklist: Getting the most out of additional training

Recall your previous educational experience. Consider each of the following and check one.

1. You prefer:
   ( ) Studying by yourself
   ( ) Studying with others

2. What suits you best is:
   ( ) Learning at your own speed
   ( ) Learning at the speed of a group

3. You learn best:
   ( ) In a lecture course taking notes
   ( ) In a course where you learn by doing

4. You prefer having material presented:
   ( ) By using words and ideas
   ( ) By sounds, pictures, and objects

Try to tailor any courses you take to fit the choices checked above. You will learn more easily in a situation that suits your educational preferences.

More school = more pay

Earnings: L = $145 − 225, M = $225 − 360, H = $360 −

Degree jobs

Administration
- Buyers — H
- City managers — H
- FBI agents — H
- Secondary school administrators — H

Clergy
- Ministers — M
- Priests — M
- Rabbis — H

Education
- Counselors — M

Engineering and science
- Oceanographers — H
- Physicists — H

Professional, technical
- Chemists — H
- Computer systems analysts — H
- Dentists — H
- Laboratory technicians — H
- Lawyers — H
- Librarians — M
- Registered nurses — M

Social scientists
- Psychologists — H
- Social workers — L

Teachers
- College and university — H
- Elementary — M

Technicians
- Airplane pilots — H
- Radio and TV announcers — L

Writers, artists, entertainers
- Painters — M
- Publicity writers — H
- Reporters — H

Nondegree jobs

Clerical-type workers
- Bank tellers — L
- Bookkeepers — M
- Counter clerks — L
- Insurance adjusters — H
- Mail carriers — H
- Payroll clerks — M
- Receptionists — L
- Secretaries, medical — M
- Teachers' aides — L
- Telephone operators — H

Craft-type workers
- Bakers — M
- Carpenters — M
- Electricians — H
- Heavy equipment mechanics — H
- Painters, maintenance workers — M
- Radio/TV repairpersons — M
- Tool and die makers — H

Food service
- Bartenders — L
- Waiters, waitresses — L

Health and personal service workers
- Child care workers — L
- Hairdressers — M

Operatives
- Bottlers and canners — L
- Earth drillers — H

Selling
- Insurance agents, brokers — H
- Real estate agents — H
- Sales clerks — M

Transportation
- Taxi drivers — M
- Truck drivers — M

Lifetime earnings estimates by education and age

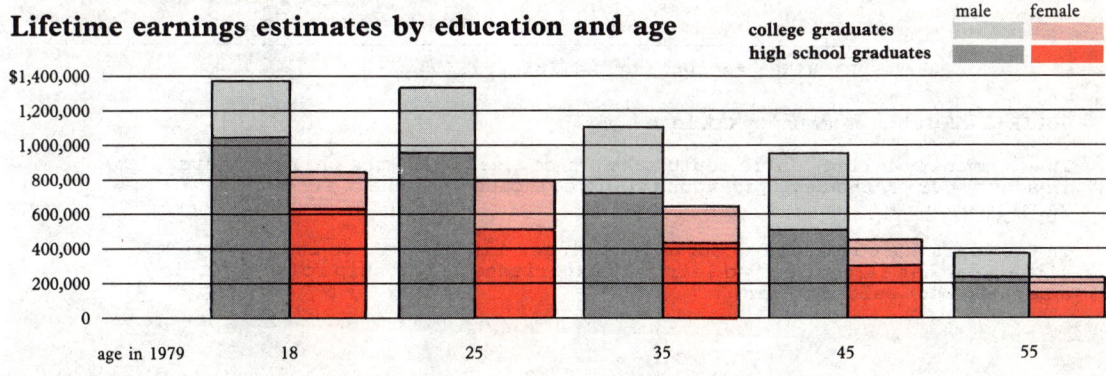

college graduates / high school graduates — male / female

age in 1979: 18, 25, 35, 45, 55

Advancing Your Career

29

Weighing the alternatives.

Julie Parsons, the homemaker who filled out one of the success charts shown earlier, wants to reenter the job market now that her children are in high school. As is the case with many families, the Parsons will find an additional salary more than welcome when the time comes to put two children through college.

How should Julie Parsons go about qualifying for a job in the field of her choice? Although she has had very little paid job experience, the skills she discovered from her success chart affirm her enjoyment of and talent for math and her interest in the field of publishing. Matching her skills to the Department of Labor occupational charts, Julie has decided on a career in public accounting and publishing. Her ultimate goal—her ideal job—is to be the comptroller of her town newspaper. Does Julie need to go back to school?

Julie Parsons has many responsibilities to juggle while preparing herself for a career. She cannot abandon her role of homemaker to become a full-time student. She still wants to participate in activities with her children, and knows she must find a way to advance her knowledge and expertise in the field of public accounting. Can she do all of these?

Educational alternatives.

Getting a Bachelor of Arts or Bachelor of Science (B.A. or B.S.) degree usually involves a four-year commitment, a luxury many people cannot afford. Fortunately, there are other options that still will allow you to advance your career. Listed on the next page are a series of alternatives to a four-year degree. Evaluate each one in the light of your particular career situation and needs.

Going for the college degree

Deciding on the institution. Colleges and universities will send catalogs on request, but your local library may have copies of the ones you are interested in.

SHOULD JULIE PARSONS GO TO COLLEGE?

ULTIMATE GOAL: Treasurer of town paper

JOB DESCRIPTION: Position requires excellent bookkeeping and accounting skills, ability to deal directly with the public, and the leadership qualities necessary to supervise a business office.

QUALIFICATIONS	JULIE'S EXPERIENCE

Knowledge of newspaper business	Editor of yearbook
	  organizational skills
	  leadership
	  initiative

Experience
  bookkeeping
  budgeting
  accounting
	Treasurer—various organizations
	  problem-solving
	  bookkeeping
	  budgeting

Skills
  problem-solving
  leadership
  initiative
  administrative
	History of public relations
	  dependability

LACKING: accounting; administrative

JULIE'S CHOICE: Community College

In a community college Julie could take her courses while the children were in school during the day. Vacations would coincide with their school vacations.

In two years she completed a course in business administration in a classroom situation that allowed her to learn and experience leadership roles again in a setting best suited to her.

Make an appointment with your local high school guidance counselor, who has all the information you need—and, probably, some helpful advice. These guidance services are available to any taxpayer, no matter how long ago or where you received your high school diploma. The counselor will help you choose a college and make out the application.

How do you pay for college? When Paul Carter, the graduating high school student interested in a job in computer programming, decided to go to the state university, his family could not afford to support him throughout his college career. Paul was an exceptionally bright student and he earned a scholarship. This helped but did not entirely solve his financial problems. His guidance counselor referred him to *Financial Aid Guide for College*, a book by Elizabeth W. Suchar (Monarch Press, Simon & Schuster, NY). If your local guidance counselor does not have a copy, try your library. Suchar's book contains excellent information.

How to get credit for what you know
(alternative routes to educational credit)

Contact: Women's Bureau
Department of Labor
200 Constitution Avenue
Washington, DC 20210

(Note: This pamphlet is intended for both men and women.)

For veterans:
Read *The Guide to the Evaluation of Educational Experiences in the Armed Services*, published by the American Council on Education, which is available in most libraries and at many Veterans Administration offices.

Alternatives to a four-year degree

Community colleges: Most of these colleges vary their courses to fit the needs of the community where they are located. Usually, courses in both vocational training and management are offered. Specific training courses (hotel and restaurant management, accounting, nursing, hairstyling, dental hygiene, etc.) generally take two years to complete. Associate degrees in applied arts and sciences are often awarded for the completion of a two-year course of study. The academic courses are similar to those given at four-year colleges, and credits are transferable for those who wish to continue their education.

Vocational training schools: Courses are offered full- or part-time to prepare you for a particular occupation. The placement rate for these schools is high, and the costs are reasonable.

Correspondence and evening courses: These courses may take longer to complete than those in which attendance is required, but they make the exploration of new fields available to everyone, no matter where they live. People who cannot attend classes regularly may continue their education or job advancement at their own pace without putting a strain on their financial resources.

Apprenticeship programs: These are offered by many companies or, in some instances, by master craftsmen. Usually the company or craftsman will pay the apprentice and guarantee a job if the program is successfully completed.

Employee training programs: Many companies prefer to train their own personnel (airlines, for example). The training may be considered part of the job in that it requires a full-time commitment and is paid at the same rate as the base salary of the job itself. Often it is regarded as on-the-job training.

Armed services: The U.S. government offers training in marketable skills applicable to civilian life in return for an armed-service career commitment of two to four years.

Temporary services: There are many temporary services throughout the country that offer part-time work, mainly in clerical jobs. Working for one or more of them can be a productive way for a person who has been out of the job market a long time to become familiar with office procedures, earn a salary, and get an idea of what work is available. Getting some experience in a field unfamiliar to you may reveal talents you did not know you had. In addition, working for a company as a temporary employee may lead to a permanent job offer.

Going after the job

Résumés. Résumés are a useful if overrated tool in a job search. Sending out résumés is not an effective way of seeking job interviews. In fact, statistics show that you will receive a response on the average of one out of every 40 to 50 résumés; depending on the competition in the field you want to enter, the response could be as low as one out of every thousand. You could end up very discouraged if you depend on your résumé to launch you. You will, however, need a résumé at some point before being employed.

An important function of your résumé is to serve as a reminder to a prospective employer of your suitability for the job available. A résumé can also serve to notify the company that you have skills or abilities they may wish to call upon in the future. The wisest course is to carry your résumé with you to interviews rather than send it on ahead to be thrown away, or to be filed away, with dozens of other résumés.

Some experts advise writing the résumé *after* the interview, tailoring it to the job. You would then send the résumé along with a thank-you letter. Some people use a heavy beige or cream-colored paper for their résumé so that it will stand out from all the rest. Those sending out a great many résumés should use a professional copying machine or service.

The short form. Anyone faced with writing a résumé knows the frustration of trying to stretch the relevant information to a full page—or to cut it down to fit just one page. The most important thing to remember is that the résumé must point out a special talent or interest you have that matches the job desired. Although the rule is to make your résumé precise and concise, keeping it to one page if possible, you should never crowd the information so that it is hard to read. Special circumstances may necessitate a two- or even three-page résumé. Just make sure that it is neatly typed, correctly spelled, and attractively arranged on the paper. If your typing is inadequate or nonexistent, professional résumé services are available at a small cost. Since a messy, badly typed résumé will represent you very poorly indeed, this expenditure is well worth the investment.

Job search detective work. Once you have prepared yourself for a career in the field of your choice, you need to become a detective dedicated to finding the best job for you. Unless you are lucky enough to have the right job offered to you early in your job search, finding it in the shortest possible time is—and should be—a full-time occupation in itself.

```
JEROME DAY
56 Cash Street
Catersville, Kansas 09376
(814) 773-5791

JOB OBJECTIVE
Electrician

WORK EXPERIENCE   Tom's Small Engines
1976-Present      Catersville, Kansas
                  Repaired electrical equipment
                  and parts of engines,
                  hand-crafted parts for
                  obsolete machines.

1961-1975         Jansen Tool and Electrical Parts
                  56 Center Street
                  Evansville, Kansas
                  Apprenticed and worked up
                  to position of foreman of ten men
                  doing industrial wiring.

EDUCATION
1961-1964         Electrician's Apprenticeship
                  Completed all courses
                  including blueprint reading.

1959              General Equivalency Diploma

ARMED SERVICES    U.S. Army. Private to Sergeant.
1959-1961         Served in California and Japan.
                  Inventoried electrical parts.

PERSONAL          Excellent health. Free to travel.

REFERENCES        Furnished upon request.
```

```
JULIE PARSONS
Halfbend Road
Turnston, Indiana 32557
(702) 560-1422

JOB OBJECTIVE
Accountant, Administrative Assistant

WORK EXPERIENCE   Turnston Standard Journal
1980-Present      45 Main Street
                  Turnston, Indiana
                  Sold classified advertising.
1965-1980         Retired to raise family.
1964-1966         Assistant in Turnston Library.
EDUCATION
1980-1985         Part-time courses in Accounting
                  and Business Administration
                  Turnston Community College
                  Certificate of Completion
                  with distinction.

VOLUNTEER WORK    Served as treasurer of community
Accounting        organizations for 15 years
and               (Parent-Teachers Assn., Reading Club,
Budgeting         church fund-raising campaign and fairs).
Public Relations  Appeared on local radio and TV
and               during fund-raising campaigns,
Communications    promoting church fair and shows.
Publishing        Editor of high school yearbook;
                  in charge of layout, editing,
                  financing, printing, and bookkeeping.

PERSONAL          Mature, in good health,
                  own and drive a car.
REFERENCES        Furnished upon request.
```

Your future is worth your concentrated attention to the details that could make the difference between earning your salary in a boring, dead-end job or advancing over the years in a satisfying and rewarding career.

Looking for valuable clues. You have chosen your field and identified geographically where you are likely to be most successful in your job search. The next step is to target the companies or institutions that could actually offer you the job you want. Your local library and magazine stand are logical places to begin your research.

Magazines covering business generally or concentrating on the particular field you hope to enter will give you an idea about the successful companies, the future trends, and even the openings in new areas. A search through the periodical (newspaper and magazine) catalogs in your library can provide valuable information about any company you are interested in working for.

When you have narrowed down your choice of places to apply, your detective work should focus on learning everything you can about those companies. Ask people in the field for information about the company's future, its problems, its new products, its expansion plans, and, of course, any expected layoffs. Sending for the company's newsletter and promotional material will add bits and pieces to the overall picture of your potential employer. No clue you find to a possible job should be overlooked.

Organizing the job search

Networking. Much has been written on the "old boy network"—a seemingly closed club of powerful men making executive decisions among themselves. Though most of us do not qualify for chairperson of the board, we can thank the "old boys" for a good idea. Realize the power of networking, and create your own network. Enlist the help of people you know or meet in your job search. Tell them what your goals are and ask them to help you in any way they can.

You will be surprised at the way useful bits of information turn up if you keep asking friends and acquaintances what they know about your field or company of choice.

Your butcher, your minister, your car mechanic—do not hesitate to let everyone with whom you are on friendly terms know that you are job hunting. Your mechanic may service a manager in the company where you want to work and may have overheard him mention a problem or an opening. You never know.

Another way to create your own network is to go to conventions or civic interest groups frequented by the personnel of a company you have targeted as a prospect. Make yourself known to these people and listen to any advice they have. There is, of course, a fine line between showing enthusiasm for your job search and making a nuisance of yourself. Watch people's faces, listen to their tone of voice, and politely withdraw if you feel a chill.

Checklist for writing your résumé

1. **Your name, address, and phone number** should be typed at the top of the page.

2. **Your job objective** comes next. Be as specific as you can. Your research should have informed you of the job that the company has available or the area that you want to pursue for your career.

3. **List your work experience and education,** along with any special experience (volunteer work, avocations) that enhances your qualifications for the job. There is no need to list jobs or bosses that were a career mistake for you.

4. **Add personal information** if you wish. Personal information should never be negative (such as "Divorced"). In fact, all the information on your résumé should be positive. Do not lie, but do omit any negative information, such as being fired, or negative preferences, such as "Hate to type."

5. **References** need only be furnished on request; however, you should have your references readily available should they be called upon. Everyone (friends and past employers alike) appreciates advance notice that a stranger may be calling to ask questions about you. This consideration will keep your source from being embarrassed and caught off-guard, and will probably result in a better recommendation for you.

Suggested reading

Résumés that get jobs
Résumé Service
Jane Reed, Editor
Arco Publishing Co., N.Y.

What Color Is Your Parachute: A Practical Manual for Job and Career Changers
Richard Nelson Bolles
Ten Speed Press

Introduction to the Job Hunt Success Kit
Center for Career Development
Phyllis Martin
11385 Landon Lane
Cincinnati, Ohio 45246

Advancing Your Career

Resources for researching careers

For information about particular fields:
A Guide to Special Book Collections in Libraries
Lee Ash and Denis Lorenz, editors
New York: Bowker

For information about organizations:
Annual reports, house organs, stock reports, public relations offices, newspapers, historical societies

For information about occupations:
Directory of Professional and Trade Organizations
(check local societies)

For information about people:
Who's Who in America;
Who's Who in the East;
Who's Who in the West
Professional directories

Let Uncle Sam help you in your search

The federal government has agencies engaged in continuous research on careers. This work is funded by your tax dollars. Let them work for you. Here are a few places to write for assistance:

Director, Office of Plans, Policies, and Design
Employment Service
Employment and Training Administration
Department of Labor
601 D Street NW
Washington, DC 20213

Job seekers and employers will be sent a list of placement related services funded by the government.

Division of Applicant Services
Office of Program Services
Employment Service
Employment and Training Administration
Department of Labor
601 D Street NW
Washington, DC 20213

This job information service is located within local employment centers. The office provides a *Job Bank Book* that enables the applicant to conduct his own search.

Department of Labor
601 D Street NW
Washington, DC 20213

For any questions regarding the job possibilities in your area or forecasts with respect to employment, an inquiry to this agency will prove useful.
Your letter will be directed to the proper office, which will send you the information you have requested.

Computerized Placement System
Automated Matching System Division
Office of Program Services
Employment Service
Employment and Training Administration
601 D Street NW
Washington, DC 20213

This office provides a daily printout of all jobs listed with the employment service in your area and distributes it to local employment service offices. Automated Matching System uses computers to identify registered jobs for which a particular applicant is qualified.

Where to look for job openings

- Local Chamber of Commerce
- Local Better Business Bureau
- *Commerce and Industry Directory*
  (Contacts Influential
  Market Research and Development Services
  321 Bush Street
  San Francisco CA 94014
  Check your library first.)
- *Career Guide to Professional Associations*
  Garrett Park Press
  Garrett Park, MD 20766
- *National Trade and Professional Associations of the United States and Canada and Labor Unions*
  Garrett Park Press
  Garrett Park, MD 20766

- *How to Reach Anyone Who's Anyone*
  by Michel Levine
  Price/Stern/Sloan Publications, Inc.
  410 North La Cienega Blvd.
  Los Angeles, CA 90048
- *What Color Is Your Parachute?: A Practical Manual for Job-Hunters & Career-Changers*
  by Richard Nelson Bolles
  Ten Speed Press
  P.O. Box 7123
  Berkeley, CA 94707
  Published annually, this book is an invaluable source for job-hunters.

Reading want ads

Quite a bit of time may be required to go through want ad columns. You must read enough of each ad to discover whether it interest you, whether you are qualified for the job offered, and—most important—whether you should apply. This is time well spent. With experience, you will be able to read the ads faster because the wording used will become familiar. You will learn, for example, that EOE means equal opportunity employer, a term indicating that the firm offering the job does not discriminate against women or minority groups. FEE PAID or F/PD means that the firm offering the job will pay the employment agency's fee. EXPD F/T means experienced, full-time.

Most important, however, is the caution you develop in deciding whether a job offered in an ad is realistic. Can one really believe a claim that an untrained person can make $35,000 a year at a job? Incidentally, ads that make such claims often do not mention what the job is. Other ads offer work at home for unrealistically high rates of pay. It is wise to be careful.

Know your salary range

Before you go to an interview, you should know the salary range for the job you want. Money is always an intimidating subject, so prepare yourself with as much knowledge as possible. Here are some sources to consult for information.

- **Visit your library.** You will find a number of books listed in the card catalogs under "salaries" and under the occupations you are interested in.
- **Write to the Department of Labor,** Bureau of Labor Statistics, Washington, DC 20212. Ask for Area Wage Surveys and the Bureau of Labor Statistics News Releases.
- **Consult the professional organization that serves your chosen field.** The Encyclopedia of Associations (at your local library) will tell you where to write.
- **Call the personnel office of the company you want to interview.** Tell them you are doing research on various careers and ask about their salary range for the job or jobs you are interested in. Such a call should, of course, be made well before any interview letter is sent or appointment made.
- **Inquire at your college placement office.** Here you can find up-to-date material on professional and higher level careers.
- **Check the want ads.** These newspaper advertisements are good for learning about salaries offered for entry-level jobs.

Know the value of fringe benefits

Find out whether the salary includes such fringe benefits as insurance, health plans, vacation, education, and retirement programs. *These benefits can add as much as 25 percent to the value of a salary.* A salary of $1000 a month with maximum benefits is really $1250.

Advancing Your Career

The job interview

Writing for an interview. Consult the letter-writing section of this volume for samples of interview letters. What you want to say about yourself in the letter will be more important than the form. You should know specifically to whom you are writing and be clear about what you have to offer in the job you want. You should conclude the letter by informing the employer that you will phone the following week for an appointment.

If you have briefly referred to experience, education, or training that qualify you for a job, you need not include a résumé with your request for an interview. Even if you have no friend or acquaintance to recommend you, it helps to refer to some reputable person of whom the interviewer may have heard: "Professor Johnson of State University Biology Department suggested that I write to you" is a reasonable approach.

Your letter must make the interviewer want to see you. Think of ways you can contribute to the company even though there may not be a job opening at the time. Your letter may even suggest ways to increase sales or solve a problem or meet a challenge that your research has uncovered. If you are inventive, enthusiastic, and organized in your presentation, you may convince the interviewer to create a job for you. This happens more often than you might imagine, but it takes research, confidence, and imagination to prepare yourself with a solid proposal. On the other hand, you have nothing to lose if the company you want to work for has no openings. Making a good impression on interviewers may serve you well at some future time, when jobs you are suited for do fall open.

How to avoid preinterview jitters. The day of the interview, make sure you allow enough time to make your appearance impeccable. Get up an hour earlier or cancel other appointments. Make sure your appearance matches the appropriate points on the checklist and the drawings on the next page. For instance, if you have a heavy beard growth and your interview is scheduled for late afternoon, allow time for a fresh shave. Confronting your five o'clock shadow in the revolving door as you go into a building for an interview can throw you off balance and ruin your composure. These checkpoints are only guidelines, of course. Showing a clean appearance is obvious to most of us. Yet every one of us has forgotten the obvious under stress, and job interviews may certainly qualify as stressful situations. You should check every detail before you leave for your appointment.

Conservative dress is the recommendation of all experts in the employment field. Loud colors and flamboyant styles are not appropriate when interviewing for most jobs. Nevertheless, the ultimate judge of appropriate dress is you. If you are interviewing for a job as a construction worker, you may decide that clean work clothes would be most appropriate. Surveys have shown, however, that even in occupations where a certain type of clothing is necessary on the job, taking the care to dress up instead of down for the interview impresses the employer and may even lead to an offer of a job at a higher level than the one you seek.

It never hurts to present yourself properly dressed. It is the first signal to the interviewer that you are concerned with detail. He will certainly see it as a sign of respect for him and your serious intent about the job.

Finally, write down and memorize the name of the person who will be interviewing you. If possible, find out and write down the names of any company personnel you will be dealing with before or after the interview.

Preinterview checklist

Once your research and detective work are completed, check off these next steps:

1. Make sure you have used *all* your contacts and resources to inform yourself thoroughly about the company. Have you been able to identify the person who is in a position to hire you?

2. Ask yourself if you have done everything you can to have an interview arranged by someone in your network. All it takes is one sentence—"A good friend of mine asked me to recommend that you see a young journalism graduate"—and there you have an interview, thanks to the intervention of a stranger. But *you* have to set the process in motion and follow up.

3. Deal with personnel departments when you must. They are useful for entry-level jobs and are sometimes a necessary channel in setting up interviews with the department head you want to see. You may walk into most personnel departments without telephoning in advance. Have with you (in your head or on paper) a list of questions you wish to have answered, and leave with copies of any informational material (annual reports, benefit plan pamphlets, etc.) that may be useful to you.

4. Make use of employment agencies. They can sometimes be the fastest route to a job for which you are qualified. Use them if you feel you are bogging down in your own efforts. Every interview is a learning experience, and your ideal job can turn up through any channel.

5. If none of these approaches is successful, write a letter asking for an interview.

Checklist for night before interview

1. **Hair** trimmed. Check supplies of shampoo, deodorant, toothpaste, etc., for morning shower.

2. **Fingernails** filed conservatively and cleaned. For women, polish should be neutral or coordinated to blend with your clothes and makeup.

3. **Clothes** freshly cleaned and pressed.

4. **Two pairs of hose** ready (one pair for your handbag) is a good idea for women. A sudden unsightly run need not be the cause for panic.

5. **A clean handkerchief** or a packet of tissues. Nervousness often makes the nose run; snuffling your way through an interview is likely to make both you and the interviewer uncomfortable.

6. **A small notebook and pen** for taking notes, such as names of secretaries, assistants, and receptionists. Make sure the notebook already contains the list of questions you want to ask, and the names of the people you will be seeing.

Looking good

Checklist for arrival at interview

1. **Arrive early enough** to visit the rest room and check your appearance.

2. **Consult your notebook** to refresh your memory on the questions and names you have written down.

3. **Focus your attention** on what is happening around you. Be alert to people's expressions, the atmosphere of the office, and any clues as to how smoothly things are functioning. If what you notice is positive, say so in the interview: "The atmosphere here is electric. It must be an exciting place to work. . . . I find I do my best work in a calm environment like this one. . . . I like the way everything is neat and organized. . . . Your employees seem so cheerful and friendly. . . . I work best in a busy, fast-paced office like this one."

4. **Comment only on what is true and positive.** Negative thoughts should be kept to yourself and noted for your private consideration in accepting or rejecting the job. If noisy, chaotic work areas disturb you, do not think you are going to change the atmosphere. A better decision would be to turn down the job if it is offered.

Advancing Your Career

Tips for the interview

1. **Always knock** on doors before entering.

2. **Use the interviewer's name** when acknowledging the introduction *and* when saying goodby. Introduce yourself by name if there is no one to perform the introduction. Be prepared to shake hands but do not initiate the gesture.

3. **Speak clearly and slowly.**

4. **Do not smoke or chew gum.**

5. **Listen well:**
   - Face the person squarely.
   - Establish eye contact.
   - Sit upright with straight but relaxed posture.
   - Keep hands away from face, preferably resting in your lap.
   - Lean forward to show interest.

6. **Do not use slang** or questionable language.

7. **Be prepared for leading questions:** "Tell me about yourself." Have clear, brief answers rehearsed. "What do you think you could do for this job?" "Why are you interested in us?"

8. **Ask open questions** as much as possible:
   "I would like to know more about the qualifications for the job."
   "What do you think Hi Tech's future [production, sales] will hold in the next few years?"
   This sort of question leads to more information and a chance for you to participate by pointing out ways in which your qualifications fit the job description or the company's goals.

9. **When appropriate, ask questions or make comments that reveal your knowledge of the company:** "Hi Tech chose one of my favorite architects to design their executive offices.... I am very impressed with SeaLinks' support of the Olympics (or involvement in the community)."

10. **Do not interrupt;** always let the interviewer be the guide. Eye contact will enable you to tell if the interviewer expects you to fill in a silence. If he looks down at something on his desk, he may be thinking a point over. Wait until he looks up again before continuing the conversation.

11. **Do not get flustered** when asked a question you have no answer for. This is an opportunity to show your presence of mind and composure. Simply say, "I don't have the answer right now, but I will get back to you tomorrow." Make an entry on your note pad and follow through.

12. **Do not volunteer negative information.** If you left a previous job because you hated it, a positive but truthful comment might be that you wanted to move on to something more challenging. If you were fired, do not lie about it if asked, but do not volunteer the information. "My previous job was terminated," is just as truthful and less negative-sounding than "I was fired."

13. **Describe yourself by your skills** ("I have good secretarial skills") instead of letting your skills describe you ("I am a secretary"). The message thus conveyed is that you are not limited to a certain job category but can apply your skills to different jobs.

14. **Be alert to signs that the interview is over.** If the interviewer does not seem to know how to conclude, you might say, "I know your time is valuable. Thank you for seeing me. Is there anything more you would like to know about me?"

15. **Say goodby and thank you** (when appropriate) **to assistants, secretaries, and receptionists.** Use their names whenever possible.

16. **Always write a thank-you note.** Include any new information you think relevant, or any responses to unanswered questions. Attach your résumé (tailored to fit the job and preferably on beige or cream-colored paper).

A job search may begin (left) *at a state employment office. A warm handshake* (right) *may signal successful conclusion of a search and the start of a promising career.*

Interviewers are people too. Most people who conduct interviews do not think they are very good at it. It is unlikely to be their main occupation. In fact, they may dread the interviewing process more than you do.

Interviewers fear they will fail to screen out applicants who are:

1. Chronic abusers of sick time.
2. Too passive to take any initiative or too headstrong to take instruction.
3. Abrasive or disruptive around coworkers.
4. Dishonest, incompetent, or irresponsible.

Any of these defects showing up in an employee would reflect badly on the interviewer's judgment and represent an expensive mistake for the company. In other words, hiring you could end up costing the interviewer his or her job.

It is up to you to address these silent questions and real fears by conveying the message that you will not turn out to be a problem. Here are some possible ways to do this:

Character: The interviewer is looking for signs that you are honest, trustworthy, and responsible. A mention of charitable activities, volunteer work, personal recommendations, or awards you have received may be appropriate.

Competence: How to handle this subject depends on your previous experience and the type of work you are seeking. The hardest situation is when you want to convey your ability to perform effectively in a job where you have no experience. Your enthusiasm and confidence will have to convince the interviewer. "I'm a quick learner and know I have abilities in this area from [mention avocational experience]. . . . I particularly enjoy mastering new skills. . . . I have always taken pride in my work. . . . I have always had a knack for detail work. . . . I'm good at working with people."

Health: "I never used up my sick time in my previous job," or simply, "I keep myself fit by regular exercise." Or, "My feeling is that if I'm home sick, I'm not doing the job I'm being paid to do."

Your interview rights

Federal law prohibits a hiring decision based on race, color, national origin, religion, sex, pregnancy, marital status, parenthood, age, height, weight, or criminal record.

There are rare exceptions in which an employer is entitled to demand a certain race or sex as a bona fide occupational qualification, as in a job for an actress.

Finally, the law prohibits asking personal questions or questions irrelevant to the position for which you are applying.

How to handle illegal questions

1. Answer politely with a question: "Is this relevant to the requirements of the job?"
2. Answer the question and ignore the fact that it is illegal if the job is important enough to you, or if you think the question is actually innocent of discriminatory intent.
3. Contact the nearest Equal Employment Opportunity Commission Office and file a complaint if you believe you have been discriminated against.

Advancing Your Career

Getting the job

The job offer. Finally your search comes to a successful conclusion. You are offered a job, or perhaps several jobs. At this point, take time to consider before accepting a job.

Show your appreciation for the job offer and ask when your decision is expected. If the employer says immediately, then you must give an answer unless you can use your negotiating skills to convince him or her that you need some time to reflect. You certainly can indicate that you are very interested while postponing your decision for a few days to allow consideration.

Evaluating the job offer. Often a series of interviews is necessary before a job is offered. This gives your prospective employers the opportunity to find out more about you and to observe you at different times; it also gives you the same opportunity. Take the time to consider these questions:

Challenge: Will the work keep you motivated and enthusiastic?

Personalities: Do you like what you have seen of your coworkers? Do you think you can work well with them?

Environment: Is the work space acceptable to you; for example, if you are allergic to smoke, will you be surrounded by chain smokers? Have you observed any safety violation?

Job security: Have you investigated the future of this company? What is the long-range economic outlook for the industry?

Reputation: Do the values of this company come up to your standards? Will you be asked to do anything that would compromise your integrity? (One job applicant thought she had found a job selling by phone until the employer informed her she must lie and say that her husband is a paraplegic.) Save yourself embarrassment by finding these things out ahead of time.

Never sell yourself short. Your research will have given you an idea of the salary range for the job offered. Where you fall in that range will depend on your negotiating ability. There can be as much as a $2000 to $3000 difference in your salary. Your employer wants to save the company that dollar difference as much as you want to earn it.

One negotiating expert has suggested the following tactic for securing the highest salary. Suppose the salary range is $12,000 to $15,000. When the employer asks you what salary you are thinking about, say that you are thinking about $16,000 as fairly representing your abilities, but that you cannot consider an offer under $13,500. Your lowest salary consideration falls

---

What is your bottom line?

To arrive at a salary figure you can live with, list all your necessary **monthly** expenses:

    rent   _____
    food   _____
    gas/electricity   _____
    transportation   _____
    clothes   _____
    miscellaneous   _____
        subtotal   _____
    __% of city, state, and federal taxes*   _____
    add another 15% for emergencies and   _____
      inflation
    monthly salary   _____
    multiply subtotal by 12 for yearly salary   _____
    divide by 52 for weekly   _____

This is your bottom line—weekly, monthly, and yearly. You cannot accept a job paying less without changing your lifestyle.

*Find the approximate percentage of taxes on the income you have arrived at by calling your local tax office.

Can you afford *this* job?

1. **Are there hidden expenses,** such as transportation, day care/babysitting, or nursing for elderly members of your family? Are you required to buy equipment or uniforms?

2. **What is the travel time** to and from the work place? Is employee parking provided?

3. **How much overtime is expected?** Is it reimbursed? At what rate? If you are required to work late hours, will you be safe returning home?

4. **Do you need flexible hours** occasionally if children or elderly relations living at home become sick? Will your employer agree to them?

5. **Is it possible to do some of your work at home?**

6. **Are the fringe benefits** (medical, insurance, retirement, vacation, sick days) acceptable to you? If not provided, how much additional salary will you need in order to assume the cost of these benefits?

within their range but is well above the bottom. And if you have impressed them with your abilities enough to make them stretch their salary offer above their range limit, you are on your way to a resounding success.

This is also the time to clarify the company's policy on raises, fringe benefits, and vacations. Often these items are negotiable. It is up to you to put the highest value on yourself. If you know what is possible, your employer can only respect you for wanting to secure the best offer possible. He may even envision your using your negotiating skill on behalf of the company.

Once terms are agreed upon, you should get them in writing. A good way to protect yourself is to write a letter to your boss immediately after these face-to-face negotiations, formally accepting the job. Include a rundown of your verbal agreements and ask him to inform you if you have misunderstood any point. Keep a copy of the letter and of any response to it in case a misunderstanding develops in the future.

Job descriptions

Unless your duties are self-evident or absolutely cut and dried, you should ask for a written copy of your job description when you accept the position. It will save both you and your boss a lot of time in the long run, and it serves as a protection for both of you.

Remember, your job description is a guideline, not a law written in stone. When you see things that need to be done that do not come under your job description, you have a choice. If you choose to take on additional work, your job description will verify your initiative. If you refuse (because of overwork or distaste for the extra work), the job description is your proof that these tasks were not to be expected of you.

Moving up the ladder

Work rules. Every organization has work rules. It is a great mistake to assume that they do not apply to you. Find out from the start what the basic rules are and show your cooperation. Remember, there is usually a good reason for every rule. Employers expect that their employees will live up to work rules.

Common rules of employment

Attendance: You are expected to work a certain number of days or hours for your salary. Most businesses allow you sick leave; some give you days for personal leave, such as funerals; nearly all grant vacation time. Find out *exactly* what is allowed and stick to the rules.

Punctuality: You will be told what time you are expected to be at work each day. Plan accordingly, taking traffic and weather into account. There is seldom a good excuse for being late. Coffee breaks and lunches have set time frames: observe them.

Dress: If you have any questions about what the dress codes are for your job, do not hesitate to ask. Some jobs require dress rules to meet safety standards, such as hard hats, safety glasses, long-sleeved shirts, etc. Do not wear strong perfume or after-shave lotion. Your chewing gum should be left at home.

Safety: Many companies have weekly safety meetings. For instance, public service companies have standards dealing with the parking of their trucks, wearing apparel, the handling of equipment in private homes, the backing out of driveways, etc. Safety rules will be prominently posted. It is your responsibility to observe them for the protection of everyone.

Protocol: Leave your personal business at home. Make personal phone calls *only* in emergencies. Give the respect due a superior. Bypassing the next in line or going over someone's head could cost you your job. Take the time to find out who is in charge and take the care to go through proper channels. These practices are good job insurance.

Communicating on the job.

As a new employee, you will be busy mastering your job. Establishing good relations with your coworkers can provide you with much-needed advice and support.

Avoid the pitfalls of participating in office gossip and taking sides in disputes. Your early communications should be especially friendly and courteous. Your curiosity should be focused on ways to perform your job as efficiently and thoroughly as possible.

Be helpful to your fellow workers but not at the expense of your own job performance. If you have any complaints, direct them to the proper person to solve the problem. Be observant of what is going on around you, but avoid jumping to conclusions. If you are patient and stay uninvolved in any potentially explosive situation, your options will eventually become clear to you. Your long-range assessment of the situation will probably be quite different from your immediate reactions during the first few weeks on the job.

Making suggestions

Suggestion box. As a relatively new employee, you may bring a fresh approach to solving company problems. Many companies have a suggestion box. Unless you have been hired specifically as a troubleshooter, the suggestion box is the best place to direct your ideas. Such initiative often pays off in the form of a bonus or even a promotion.

Direct suggestions. You may soon develop a close enough relationship with your superior to make a written memo to him an appropriate way to make a suggestion. If you can relate the inspiration of the suggestion to your superior ("something you mentioned made me think of the possibility of . . ." or "in keeping with your work philosophy, I would like to suggest . . ."), you have expressed support for your superior and created a positive atmosphere for your suggestion.

Suggesting changes can be risky without the support and enthusiasm of the decision-makers. Sharing the credit by allowing them to feel that they were in part the source of the idea allows them to join you in carrying out a constructive suggestion. Learning to communicate diplomatically is a major key to success.

How to be supportive to your employer

1. **Have a positive attitude:** Take note of your superior's contributions, acknowledge the good ones, and keep quiet about the bad ones.
2. **Know your boss:** Learn his or her working methods and adjust your own to harmonize with them. Be clear on your boss's priorities.
3. **Be informed:** Do your homework by keeping up to date in your field. Read carefully all memos and annual reports.
4. **Become a team worker:** Cooperate with coworkers; contribute whatever you can to a pleasant working environment.
5. **Be honest:** The best way to be supportive to your boss is to be honest, responsible, and trustworthy.

The art of listening.

One of the more satisfying rewards of teaching is the profound silence of someone listening. If you can give this attention to your boss, he will not fail to notice.

Most new employees want to impress everyone with how much they know, their speed in catching on, and their enthusiasm. They are much more concerned with feedback ("How am I doing?") than with giving appreciation to their boss or mentor.

Remember, it may be lonely at the top. Your boss needs appreciation for his contributions as much as you do. In fact, directing your attention to listening and acknowledging him can open blocked channels of communication for everyone.

Yearly job assessments. Many companies now make it a practice to require their employees to turn in statements of their yearly goals and assessments of their past job performances. This exercise can be very helpful. Even though your company may not require it, you

---

Tips for getting along on the job	Checklist for making suggestions
1. Make your job performance your top priority. 2. Become a team worker. 3. Be willing to accept more responsibility. 4. Be loyal to your boss or keep quiet if you are not. 5. Treat everyone with courtesy. 6. Avoid office gossip. 7. Avoid making personal phone calls.	1. Examine your suggestion carefully before you submit it. 2. Make sure you do not imply criticism of a superior or jeopardize anyone's job. 3. Phrase you suggestion positively. 4. Check it from all angles for clarity and detail. 5. Leave no chance for misinterpretation.

could celebrate your yearly anniversary by reflecting on your progress. Experience can change your direction. Yearly assessments will clarify your focus on future progress and serve as a useful guide for making changes if you are dissatisfied. And reviewing your progress can be an enormous help when you are asking for a raise.

Shifts in responsibility

Asking for a lighter load. Sometimes your success on the job can create a situation in which it is wise to request a decrease in responsibility. For example, maybe your workload has increased to the point where you cannot possibly keep up with your work or perform it to your (or anyone else's) satisfaction. Or perhaps a classroom teacher has been promoted to assistant principal, a logical next step up the ladder of success. But that promotion may have robbed her of her greatest pleasure, teaching her students, and may have put her in an administrative position where she has no particular skills.

Awareness of your strengths, preferences, and limitations when a well-intentioned promotion is offered is important. If you are competent and enthusiastic in a job, think twice before accepting a promotion that does not feel right to you. More money and prestige are seldom worth the giving up of duties you love for those you dislike or cannot perform well.

If union membership is mandatory

1. Become familiar with union rules on payment of dues, work, and behavior.
2. Use your union's services responsibly. It exists to improve your working conditions and salary, and to protect you.
3. Do not discuss union business with nonunion employees or with members of other unions.
4. Work for changes if you are dissatisfied with your union leadership. Complaining without constructive suggestions is counterproductive. On the other hand, constructive suggestions may be welcomed and result in improved organizational procedures.
5. Look for a job in another field if you cannot support your union and are unwilling to change it.

Increasing responsibilities. As you become more experienced in your job, responsibilities may be assigned to you that are not in your job description. If you are ambitious and like the challenge, you may

Asking for a promotion

1. Do you have the necessary qualifications, including experience, to do your present job well?
2. Have you been on your present job long enough to warrant a promotion?
3. Where do you stand in line for a promotion?
4. Do you have a clear understanding of the new position and all it involves?
5. Are you willing to make the necessary commitment to the new job?
6. Does your employer know what your expectations are?
7. Are you on good terms with fellow workers?

Steps in asking for a raise

1. **Check company policy:** Some companies have automatic raises that go into effect at scheduled intervals; some use a merit system. Others will grant increases for merit in addition to regularly scheduled increases.
2. **Use good judgment:** Check salaries for jobs in companies similar to yours. Make sure your own company is in a financial position to grant an increase at this time.
3. **Review your record:** Read over your yearly assessments if you have made them. Have firmly in mind your contributions as an employee—from good attendance and/or productivity to increasing the efficiency of your department.
4. **Be assertive:** Tie your request for a raise to the specific factors most appropriate in your case: your time on the job, comparable salaries in the field, your career goals, your contributions to the company, etc. Asking for a raise is difficult for all of us; taking the first three steps will make this one easier for you—and make you more likely to succeed.

Advancing Your Career

welcome the extra work. After proving yourself sufficiently, you should take the opportunity to review your job description with your superior.

It is a good idea to bring two copies of your old job description with you, plus a new description of your present job as you see it. If you have been assigned more work than you can handle efficiently, make constructive suggestions for dealing with the problem. If you think additional training is necessary, present your request for it along with a specific plan. If you need to hire an assistant, back up your request with facts about productivity and costs.

This is a good time to ask for a raise. It is certainly reasonable to ask for confirmation of your new job description and to inquire what increase in salary accompanies the increase in your responsibilities.

Changing careers

Case history. Paul Carter's mother, Carol, has taught English at the local high school for 15 years. Although she enjoys her work, she has always dreamed of becoming a travel agent: she loves travel, and has a real aptitude for learning foreign languages. For the past four years, while Paul has been at college, Carol has been researching her dream job. She has worked part-time in a friend's travel agency every summer, and is now ready to resign from teaching and take a full-time job with the agency.

One of the reasons Carol Carter can afford to give up the superior fringe benefits and security of teaching is that her husband, Jeffrey, has been promoted from his job as sports equipment buyer for a local department store.

It was Jeffrey Carter who came up with the idea of expanding the sports department into a separate facility to include a health club and restaurant. He presented his expansion plan so convincingly that he was made a vice president of the store and put in charge of the entire new operation.

When to make a change. Unlike Carol Carter, who considered her career change for a number of years before she came to a decision, some people wake up one morning and experience a moment

---

Carol Carter consulted this list from the *Department of Labor Occupational Outlook Quarterly* and was pleased to find her background in English related to skills needed in her new career choice.

Occupations related to English

High school graduate
Actor or actress
Claims adjuster
Court clerk
Court reporter
Flight attendant

Insurance agent
Printer
Proofreader
Receptionist
Reservation/ticket passenger agent
Salesperson

Secretary
Service representative
Telephone operator
Travel guide or agent
Typesetter
Typist

Two years of college
Computer operator
Film editor
Legal secretary

Library technician and assistant
Licensed practical nurse
Maitre d'hotel

Medical secretary
Paralegal
Police officer

College graduate +
Administrator
Advertising executive
Advertising writer
Announcer–radio, TV
Archivist
Buyer
Criminologist
Drama coach
Editor
Editorial assistant
Education and public affairs director
Educator

Employment counselor
Executive
Job analyst
Journalist
Librarian
Market research analyst
Missionary/minister/rabbi/priest
Personnel and labor relations worker
Physician
Political scientist
Producer–TV, films, plays
Program director–radio/TV

Psychologist
Public relations worker
Publisher
Registrar–college and university
School counselor
Script writer–radio, TV, movies
Social worker
Speech pathologist/clinician
Teacher
Translator
Tutor
Writer

of truth: their job is no longer challenging or satisfying, and no money or benefits are worth so much dissatisfaction.

If this happens to you, do not quit your present job or even start discreetly exploring other possibilities immediately. First, make yourself a plan.

Jeffrey Carter was bored with his job when he got an inspiration from observing the health-club boom spreading across the country. Having always been a fitness addict, Jeffrey now dreamed of opening a health club. He had to restrain himself from putting in his resignation so that he could work full-time on financing his dream.

Instead, he used his spare time to work out a plan, researching it thoroughly and devising a presentation that was practical and specific. Jeffrey was prepared to resign and launch the venture on his own if his proposal met with a negative response. As it was, he got his health club, a big raise and promotion.

Every employee experiences some job dissatisfaction some of the time. If yours is serious and pervasive, however, a change may be indicated. Before you do anything, look at your situation from every possible angle. Sometimes a well-thought-out plan or even a single good idea can make it possible for you to change jobs within your organization.

Changing jobs: what to consider

1. Can you make a job change within your present company?
2. Would you increase your chances of getting a job you like better by staying where you are?
3. Have you done everything you can to increase the rewards in your present job?
4. Are you using the abilities you enjoy most? Are you learning skills important to your career advancement?
5. Are you fulfilling a need for yourself or the community in your present job?
6. Are you willing to risk the loss of security and/or your present benefits if you make a change?
7. Is your family supportive of your desire to change?
8. Can you financially afford to make a change?
9. Would a change involve a geographic move?
10. Is it possible to work part-time in another job to see how well it suits you before leaving your present job?

If you decide to quit

If you are certain that there will be no openings for advancement at your present job, give the boss the proper notice when you decide to leave. He or she should honor your good record with a letter of recommendation. The usual required notice is two weeks, but check your work rules.

Where the jobs are

American workers have always shown an enthusiasm for going after the job if the job will not come to them. If your occupation is threatened with extinction, or if jobs are scarce in your area, you may choose to make a geographic as well as a career move. Consult these charts before you decide.

10 best states

Number employed in thousands

	1973	1983	Percent change
Alaska	110	213	+94
Nevada	245	405	+65
Wyoming	126	203	+61
Texas	4,142	6,174	+49
Arizona	715	1,064	+49
Colorado	936	1,322	+41
Florida	2,779	3,893	+40
N. Mexico	346	478	+38
Oklahoma	852	1,170	+37
Washington	1,152	1,579	+37

10 worst states

Number employed in thousands

	1973	1983	Percent change
Michigan	3,284	3,186	−3
Indiana	2,028	2,007	−1
Ohio	4,113	4,084	−1
Pennsylvania	4,507	4,519	0
Illinois	4,470	4,501	+1
New York	7,132	7,285	+2
W. Virginia	562	581	+3
Iowa	961	1,018	+6
Rhode Island	366	393	+7
Missouri	1,771	1,917	+8

Advancing Your Career

If you lose your job. If you have been fired, ask questions if you do not know why. The truth may be difficult to face; but only if you know the truth, can you make constructive use of your experience. If you were fired for unreliability, you can try to avoid making the same mistakes next time. If you were dismissed because your company or field is in trouble, you can try to avoid putting yourself in a similar situation next time. Ask for a letter of recommendation.

There is no need to panic, or to rush into a new job you do not want. If you were fired or laid off, you automatically qualify for unemployment insurance to assist you in your search for another job (your local unemployment office will give you all the information you need).

Your time between jobs offers an opportunity to consider carefully where you were, what you have learned, where you are now, and where you want to go.

Warning signs!

1. The company is suffering unusual losses.
2. People are getting laid off.
3. You are not invited to the usual meetings.
4. You feel uninformed.
5. People seem to be avoiding you.
6. You were passed over for a promotion.
7. Your boss shows continued dissatisfaction and impatience with your performance.
8. Your boss leaves.
9. The new boss starts bringing in his own people.
10. Little by little, your responsibilities are being assigned to other people.

You are fired. Why?

1. Were you qualified for the job? Did you honestly represent your skills before you were hired?
2. Were you truly suited for the job?
3. Should you have taken additional courses to keep you up to date?
4. Did you make costly mistakes?
5. Did you get along with your fellow workers?
6. Did you participate in office gossip and politics?
7. Were you given warnings before being fired? Did you make constructive use of criticism from superiors?
8. Did you often find yourself making excuses for work not finished, getting to work late, leaving early, taking excessive sick leave?
9. Have you been fired before? If so, why?
10. Do you see a pattern forming? For example, do you always become bored in your jobs?

Taking an unflinching look at what went wrong can be invaluable for finding the right job in the future and for recognizing how you can perform that job more effectively.

Applying for unemployment insurance

Go *immediately* to your nearest office of unemployment with two forms of identification (driver's license, birth certificate, passport, etc.) and your Social Security number (your Social Security card does not qualify as identification). Pride is *not* a factor: get in line and sign up.

How to survive until the first unemployment check comes

1. Call or visit your local office of Human Services for information about:
   a. food stamps   b. rent allowances   c. fuel assistance

2. An employee laid off or fired will normally receive at least two weeks' severance pay.

3. Look in the first few pages of your telephone book for a special section commonly called Community Service Numbers. There you will find the local telephone number for job services, unemployment, food stamps, and other social services that can help you.

46 Advancing Your Career

Getting back into the work force

Opportunities for retirees. Many companies have a mandatory retirement age, as do certain occupations (pilots must retire at age 60, for example). Some retirees are surprised to find that they do not adjust well to so much leisure time and are not happy unless they are in a work-related environment. For others, continuing to work for pay is not a matter of choice but of simple economics: Social Security and pension checks are often inadequate to provide a comfortable or even a reasonable standard of living.

There are many opportunities for older people to get back into the work force or work-related activities. For those who are not concerned with more income, programs such as ACTION, Retired Senior Volunteer Program (RSVP), VISTA, Peace Corps, Foster Grandparents, and Senior Companion urgently need older Americans who are willing to share their concern and expertise. See pages 296-297 for more information.

If you discover that your retirement income will be inadequate before you have actually retired, you may be able to arrange with your employer for part-time work as a consultant or during vacation or peak periods. You may even find that full- or part-time work in an entirely different capacity from your present job can be arranged. The fact that you still work for the company gives you more leverage than you would have as a former employee in the months after retirement.

Retirement often allows people the security to take the risk of trying to make money out of a new activity or one formerly considered recreational. America is the home of success stories like those of Ray Kroc and Colonel Saunders, who came out of retirement to start McDonald's and Kentucky Fried Chicken. It is also the home of thousands of cottage industries started all over the country by retirees who turned their hobbies into profit-making ventures.

If you cannot find any work in your field, the JTPS (Job Training Partnership Act) is a state-funded program that assists low-income people over 55 who need job training and placement.

Other areas to investigate are local churches, YMCA and YWCA occupational services, professional or trade associations, labor union employment services, and Forty-Plus Clubs. Ample help and counseling are available if you know where to look.

Another avenue to explore is the office of your state representative or senator. Their local offices have workers who collect information in all problem areas, especially unemployment. Upon request they will provide this information and assist you in any other way they can.

Odd jobs can solve problems

For retirees, there are many ways to make money without actually working at a regular job. Clara Peller became famous for her "Where's the Beef?" commercial. Here are some ideas to start you thinking:

1. Retired teachers or anyone with expertise in a particular area (in a foreign language, for example) can tutor at home. An ad in your local paper, a call or visit to a school or college in your area, even a notice on a supermarket or shopping-mall bulletin board can help attract this kind of business.

2. In most communities, those qualified to supply music, art, or drama coaching can attract willing students.

3. Anyone who can sew or tailor is likely to find a ready supply of customers.

4. Those who have no specific area of expertise can make money running errands, chauffering, house-sitting, babysitting, or assisting the elderly and infirm.

5. Gardening can be profitable to those who sell their own vegetables, flowers, or fruits. Tending other people's gardens while they are traveling can be enjoyable and profitable. Landscaping can supplement your income even more.

6. There is a market in most communities for hand-crafted items, from dolls and pillows to furniture. Homemade baked goods are easy to sell, and can be the start of a home catering business.

7. For more ideas write for an eight-page fact sheet compiled by the government telling where to look for both paid and unpaid jobs:
   Consumer Information Center
   Pueblo, Colorado 81009

Advancing Your Career

Women who work. Approximately 131.4 million people will make up the 1995 labor force—3.8 million more than originally projected. Nearly two-thirds of that growth will be among women. For example, according to the Department of Labor, the employment of preschool teachers (nearly all of them women) is expected to increase 40 percent from now to 1995.

The majority of people reentering the work force are also women. In 1960, slightly more than 23 million women held paying jobs. Today, the number is more than twice that, and rising every year. Women comprise over 53 percent of the work force in America today. Many of these women are supplementing the family income or working their way up in a chosen career. The majority of them are in the work force because of economic necessity. Over 50 percent of women reentering the work force are single parents.

Far-reaching social changes have contributed to the surge of women workers. More and more women choose to defer marriage and/or motherhood. Equal pay and antidiscrimination laws, along with new tax allowances for child-care expenses, have opened up the job choices available to women. It is still true that many more women are employed in service rather than goods-producing industries; but it is also true that the service industries are expanding while manufacturing is on the decrease. Service industries (public relations, transportation, communications, finance, insurance, real estate, etc.) are projected to account for nearly 75 percent of all new jobs between now and 1995.

Over half of women with children under six are now in the work force. Lack of adequate child care remains the most significant problem for working mothers, although the picture is considerably brighter than it was a few years ago. Federally funded day-care centers, where tuition is scaled to income, are still on the increase. Many corporations, and some local schools, are now providing day-care centers.

About three out of four employed adult American women work full time. Forty-five percent of American mothers with infants are employed outside the home. Sixty percent of American mothers with children between ages three and five are employed outside the home.

Alternative work patterns

For information on part-time work, flexible work schedules, and shared jobs, write to:

New Ways to Work Newsletter
  New Ways to Work
  149 Ninth Street
  San Francisco, CA 944103

Alternative Work Patterns: Changing Approaches to Work Scheduling, by David Robinson
  Work in America Institute, Inc.
  700 White Plains Road
  Scarsdale, NY 10583

First National Directory on Part-Time and Flexitime Programs
  National Council for Alternative Work Programs
  1925 K Street NW, Suite 308A
  Washington, DC 20036

Many companies now offer flexible hours in certain jobs. This trend is a great boon to working mothers, who can arrange their assigned number of hours per week to accommodate their children's schedules. For example, a parent need not miss a child's graduation or school play: the hours can be made up before or after the normal working day, or on the weekend.

Job-sharing is another trend in meeting the special needs of working women. Two people can share the same job, working out their hours and finances between them along whatever lines seem fair to both parties. So long as they get the job done satisfactorily, it does not matter to the employer which worker does what. This arrangement can allow each employee to hold a more challenging or better paying job than part-time work could offer either of them.

Help is as near as your mailbox

The U.S. government spends millions of dollars each year printing information invaluable to women in—or entering—the work force. Write to:
  Information Office
  Women's Bureau
  Department of Labor
  200 Constitution Ave. NW
  Washington, DC 20210

Ask for a list of their publications. There is likely to be one pertaining to any problem you may have or supplying any information you seek.

Advancing Your Career

Starting your own business

Starting your own *successful* business can be best described as turning your passion into your profession. The secret ingredient in the formula for a successful small business is likely to be an obsessed owner—one willing to put in the time needed to get the job done (often well over eight hours a day) and full of unflagging enthusiasm.

It is likely that running your own business will be harder than working at a regular job. Studies have demonstrated that most entrepreneurs are not motivated primarily by the desire to make money. The satisfactions lie more in the areas of independence, power over the future, and the pleasure of doing a good job.

Whether a business succeeds or fails most often depends on a simple thing called "cash flow." If there is not enough cash coming in or reserved to pay the expenses of running the business, the business will soon fail. It does not matter how much money is owed to you (debtors may also be suffering a cash flow problem); what counts is *cash in hand*.

Smart entrepreneurs reserve every bit of cash they can for unexpected expenses or dry periods. Giving in to the temptation to expand too quickly or display the fruits of sudden profits can turn an apparent success into a sudden failure.

Here are some questions to ask yourself before you embark on any business venture of your own. Answering them thoughtfully will help you decide whether starting your own business is right for you.

Starting your own business

1. Do you have a clear idea of the business you would like to start in terms of the product or service?
2. Do you have (or can you acquire) the necessary knowhow to run that type of business?
3. Have you gained experience in that field or in a related field?
4. Do you have any necessary equipment, or the money to acquire it?
5. Do you have the kind of contacts you will need to launch your business—bankers, accountants, potential customers, promoters, etc.?
6. Do you have the time and energy necessary to commit to a new business? (Remember, this may mean 18-hour work days and seven-day work weeks.)
7. Does your family support your endeavor?
8. Do you have the temperament for taking risks?
9. Are you practical enough to implement your ideas?
10. Are you capable of picking the right people to help you?
11. Do you have a good supply of self-confidence?
12. Are you willing to admit your mistakes and learn from them?
13. Can you tolerate the uncertainty that characterizes any new business?
14. Do you have a plan to provide for you and your family if the business fails?
15. Do you have plans to expand where necessary if the business succeeds?

Advantages and disadvantages of starting your own business

ADVANTAGES
- You are totally responsible for any success.
- You can work at your own speed.
- Your schedule will be flexible.
- You will reap the profits of your hard work and have many tax advantages.
- Your business may provide security and even jobs for your family.
- You will not face forced retirement.

DISADVANTAGES
- You are totally responsible for any failure.
- You may work during all your waking hours.
- You will have no paid vacation; you may have no vacation at all.
- You will have no weekly paycheck or fringe benefits.
- You may go deeply into debt; you may have almost no time to spend with your family.
- If the business fails, your savings and property can be eaten up by debts, leaving nothing for your retirement.

Advancing Your Career

The birth of a small business.

Edward and Alice Stubbs, whose success chart appears on page 25, want to start a catering business now that Edward is retired. They have had many years of volunteer catering experience at their church and community theater. More important, they both love to cook and have ample kitchen facilities in a large house with plenty of storage space.

If you want to start your own business, make an analysis similar to the Stubbs's. Think of every contingency for success and failure. Write everything down. Consult anyone who might have valuable advice or experience, including people operating a similar business far enough out of your area to be noncompetitive. Visit or write to the Small Business Administration, whose retired business people are available for free consultation. Inform yourself about your proposed business from all sources mentioned in this section. It is particularly important to get help in arriving at the right profit margin for your product or services (many businesses fail because they are priced too low). If you are thinking about opening a retail shop, for example, you will probably find that doubling the cost to you of items for sale will not be adequate. Finally, make sure you have enough cash to carry you until the business can carry itself.

Stubbs's catering service: An analysis

Market: Their initial market already existed, since their reputation as splendid cooks was well established in the community.

Pricing: After doing research at the library and drawing from their own knowledge about the actual cost of preparing dishes, they marked up the price of their ingredients three times in order to ensure a profit. Dishes or meals especially time-consuming to prepare were marked up five times.

Competition: The only catering service in their community was a firm that catered for guest lists of 50 or more. The Stubbses were interested in providing a small, personal service.

Goods and overhead: Because they operated out of their own large kitchen, relatively little initial investment was required. They needed trays and some large pots and platters, but their expenditures were minimal. They used their own station wagon for deliveries, making it a company car and a tax deduction.

Regulations: The Stubbses worked out of their home, so there was no need for health department inspections (although theoretically there could have been).

Risk: Relatively little risk was involved. The Stubbs's policy was to ask for one-third to one-half of their fee in advance, which covered their costs. They either sent a bill for the remainder or collected upon delivery, depending on the customer. After consulting a lawyer, they had a legal form drawn up that each customer signed upon ordering. They consulted their insurance agent and took out a liability policy that covered them in the event of a lawsuit from a customer. These precautions protected the Stubbses from unanticipated threats to their business and personal investment and property, and, more important to their everyday business, ensured their cash flow.

Time commitment: At first, the Stubbses were capable of handling all of the business themselves. They worked long hours to keep overhead to a minimum, not minding because theirs was a labor of love. Eventually, the volume of business became too much for them and they hired an assistant.

Start-up expenses checklist

1. Do you need printed business cards, stationery, invoices, wrapping paper, shopping bags, etc.?
2. Do you need to buy a mailing list or lists?
3. Do you need to rent work space, furniture, typewriters, cash registers, etc.?
4. Do you need a separate phone line for the business?
5. What are the advertising rates in the local newspapers? Can you arrange to have a promotional article written about your new business?
6. Will you need a telephone answering service or machine?
7. Do you need to file the name of your business in your state? Do you need to incorporate?

Think of every hidden expense and write it down. Talk with people in similar businesses and ask them what expenses, including unexpected ones, are likely to come up. Then draw up a budget and compare it with your cash on hand to estimate how much money you will have to raise.

How your government can help

Some of the best information is supported by your tax dollars. It is yours for the asking. Write to:

Office of Small Business Development Centers
Management Assistance
Small Business Administration
1441 L Street NW
Washington, DC 20416

Ask for their complete kit of information. Write to the Office of Management Counseling Services, Management Assistance, at the Small Business Administration for free personal counseling.

Special help for women. Helping women become successful entrepreneurs is a special goal of the Small Business Administration. Write to:

Office of Women's Business Enterprise Division
Small Business Administration
1441 L Street NW
Washington, DC 20416

If you want to start a business out of your home, write to: National Alliance of Homebased Businesswomen
P.O. Box 95
Norwood, New Jersey 07648

Starting out

Starting Out Series publications are available free from the Small Business Administration Washington District Office, 1111 18th Street NW, 6th Floor, Washington, DC 20417. Tel. (202) 634-6156.

101 Building Service Contracting	118 The Nursery Business	135 Printing
102 Service Stations	119 The Wholesale Nursery Business	136 Fabricare
103 Catering	120 The Garden Center Business	137 The Bookstore
104 Radio-Television Repair Shop	121 The Landscaping Business	138 Home Furnishings
105 Retail Florist	122 Apparel Store	139 Handbags
106 Franchise Businesses	123 Pharmacies	140 Bake Shops
107 Hardware Store or Home Center	124 Retail Photography Store	141 Portable Sanitation
108 Home Building, Small Volume	125 Office Products	142 Ice Cream
109 Travel Agency	126 Automotive Parts & Accessories	143 Recreational Vehicles
110 Restaurants	127 Motels	144 Real Estate
111 Sporting Goods Stores	128 Paint & Decorating Store	145 Sewing Centers
112 Dry Cleaning	129 Interior Design Services	146 Exhibit Design and Production
113 Car Wash	130 Fish Farming	147 Electric Vehicles
114 Beauty Salon	131 Day-Care Centers–Preschoolers	148 Personnel Referral Service
115 Pest Control	132 Men's Outerwear	149 Selling by Mail Order
116 Marine Retailers	133 Bicycles	150 Solar Energy
117 Retail Grocery Stores	134 Roofing Contractors	201 Breakeven Point for Independent Truckers

A hobby developed into a marketable skill and eventually became a promising small business (left) for an ambitious couple. Another innovative entrepreneur (right) saw a big future in a commodity that always is in demand.

Advancing Your Career

Matching yourself to the World of Work

L = lowest level
M = middle level
H = highest level

[1] Estimates not available.
[2] Vary, depending on job.

Job requirements:
1. Leadership/persuasion
2. Helping/instructing others
3. Problem-solving/creativity
4. Initiative
5. Work as part of a team
6. Frequent public contacts
7. Manual dexterity
8. Physical stamina
9. Hazardous
10. Outdoors
11. Confined

Work environs:
12. Jobs concentrated geographically
13. Part-time

Occupational characteristics:
14. Earnings
15. Employment growth
16. Entry requirements

Occupation	1	2	3	4	5	6	7	8	9	10	11	12	13	14	15	16
Administrative and Managerial Occupations																
Accountants and auditors		•	•	•	•							•		M	M	H
Bank officers and managers	•	•	•	•	•	•						•		H	M	H
Buyers	•		•	•	•									M	M	H
College student personnel workers	•	•	•	•	•	•								1	1	H
Construction inspectors (government)		•	•	•	•		•			•				M	H	M
Credit managers	•	•	•	•	•							•		M	L	H
Health services administrators	•		•	•	•									H	H	H
Hotel managers and assistants	•	•	•	•	•									1	H	M
Medical record administrators	•		•	•	•									H	H	H
Occupational safety and health workers		•	•	•	•			•		•				H	1	H
Personnel and labor relations specialists	•	•	•	•	•									M	L	H
Purchasing agents	•		•		•									1	L	H
School administrators	•	•	•	•	•	•								H	L	H
Engineers, Surveyors, and Architects																
Architects			•	•		•	•							H	H	H
Landscape architects			•	•		•	•							1	H	H
Surveyors and surveying technicians				•		•	•			•				L	M	M
Engineers																
Agricultural engineers			•	•	•									H	H	H
Chemical engineers			•	•	•									H	M	H
Civil engineers and electrical engineers			•	•	•									H	H	H
Electrical engineers			•	•	•									H	H	H
Industrial and mechanical engineers			•	•	•									H	H	H
Metallurgical and mining engineers			•	•	•									H	H	H
Natural Scientists and Mathematicians																
Mathematical scientists and systems analysts																
Mathematicians			•	•										H	L	H
Statisticians			•	•										M	M	H
Systems analysts		•	•	•	•							•		H	H	H
Physical scientists																
Astronomers			•	•										H	L	H
Chemists			•	•										H	M	H
Geographers			•	•	•									H	M	H
Geologists and geophysicists			•	•	•				•					H	H	H
Meteorologists			•	•	•									H	L	H
Oceanographers			•	•	•				•		•			H	M	H
Physicists			•	•										H	L	H

52   **Advancing Your Career**

Job requirements / Work environs / Occupational characteristics

Columns:
1. Leadership/persuasion
2. Helping/instructing others
3. Problem-solving/creativity
4. Initiative
5. Work as part of a team
6. Frequent public contacts
7. Manual dexterity
8. Physical stamina
9. Hazardous
10. Outdoors
11. Confined
12. Jobs concentrated geographically
13. Part-time
14. Earnings
15. Employment growth
16. Entry requirements

Occupation	1	2	3	4	5	6	7	8	9	10	11	12	13	14	15	16
Life scientists																
Agricultural and biological scientists			•	•										1	M	H
Biochemists			•	•										H	M	H
Food technologists			•	•										H	L	H
Foresters			•	•	•			•	•	•				M	L	H
Soil conservationists		•	•	•						•				H	L	H
Social Scientists, Social Workers, Religious Workers, and Lawyers																
Lawyers	•	•	•	•	•	•								H	M	H
Social scientists																
Anthropologists			•	•	•									H	M	H
Economists			•	•										H	H	H
Historians			•	•										H	L	H
Political scientists			•	•	•	•								H	L	H
Psychologists		•	•	•		•								H	M	H
Sociologists			•	•	•									H	L	H
Social and recreation workers																
Recreation workers	•	•	•	•	•	•		•		•			•	L	M	M
Social workers	•	•	•	•	•	•								L	M	H
Religious workers																
Ministers and priests	•	•	•	•	•	•								L	1	H
Rabbis	•	•	•	•	•	•								H	1	H
Teachers, Librarians, and Counselors																
College career counselors	•	•	•	•	•	•								M	1	H
College and university faculty	•	•	•	•	•	•							•	H	L	H
Employment counselors	•	•	•	•	•	•						•		1	1	H
Kindergarten, school teachers	•	•	•	•	•	•	•	•					•	M	M	H
Librarians	•	•	•	•	•	•							•	M	L	H
Rehabilitation counselors	•	•	•	•	•	•								1	1	H
School counselors	•	•	•	•	•	•								M	L	H
Secondary school teachers	•	•	•	•	•	•								M	L	H
Health Diagnosing and Treating Practitioners																
Chiropractors	•	•	•	•	•	•	•	•					•	H	M	H
Dentists	•	•	•	•	•	•	•	•						H	M	H
Optometrists	•	•	•	•	•	•	•	•						H	M	H
Physicians	•	•	•	•	•	•	•	•	•					H	H	H
Veterinarians	•	•	•	•	•	•	•	•						H	H	H
Registered Nurses, Pharmacists, Dietitians, etc.																
Dietitians	•	•	•	•	•	•							•	L	H	H
Occupational therapists	•	•	•	•	•	•	•	•						1	H	H
Pharmacists	•	•	•	•	•	•						•	•	H	L	H
Physical therapists	•	•	•	•	•	•	•	•						M	H	H
Physician assistants	•	•	•	•	•	•	•	•						M	1	H
Registered nurses	•	•	•	•	•	•	•	•					•	M	H	M

Advancing Your Career

Job requirements / Work environs / Occupational characteristics

Columns:
1. Leadership/persuasion
2. Helping/instructing others
3. Problem-solving/creativity
4. Initiative
5. Work as part of a team
6. Frequent public contacts
7. Manual dexterity
8. Physical stamina
9. Hazardous
10. Outdoors
11. Confined
12. Jobs concentrated geographically
13. Part-time
14. Earnings
15. Employment growth
16. Entry requirements

Occupation	1	2	3	4	5	6	7	8	9	10	11	12	13	14	15	16
Health Technologists and Technicians																
Dental hygienists		•		•	•	•	•				•		•	L	H	M
Electrocardiograph technicians		•		•	•	•					•			1	H	M
Emergency medical technicians		•	•	•	•	•	•	•						L	M	M
Licensed practical nurses		•		•	•	•	•						•	L	H	M
Medical laboratory workers				•		•	•		•					L	H	2
Radiologic (x-ray) technicians		•		•	•		•		•				•	L	H	M
Surgical technicians		•			•		•	•						L	H	M
Writers, Artists, and Entertainers																
Communications occupations																
Public relations workers	•		•	•	•	•								M	M	H
Radio and television announcers and newscasters	•	•		•	•	•						•		L	H	H
Reporters and correspondents	•		•	•	•	•								1	M	H
Writers and editors	•		•	•	•							•		1	M	H
Design occupations																
Commercial, graphic designers			•	•			•						•	1	L	M
Display workers	•		•	•		•	•	•						L	M	L
Floral designers			•			•	•					•		1	L	L
Industrial designers			•	•	•		•							1	L	H
Interior designers			•	•	•	•	•							1	M	M
Photographers			•	•			•	•					•	L	L	M
Performing artists																
Actors and actresses			•	•	•	•		•				•	•	L	M	M
Dancers and musicians			•	•	•	•		•				•	•	L	M	M
Singers			•	•	•	•		•				•	•	1	L	M
Technologists and Technicians, Except Health																
Air-traffic controllers		•	•	•	•							•		H	L	H
Broadcast technicians			•		•							•		L	L	M
Drafters				•			•							M	H	M
Forestry technicians					•		•	•	•					1	H	M
Engineering, science technicians		•		•		•		2	2	2				M	M	M
Legal assistants			2	•	2									M	H	L
Programmers		•		•								•		M	H	H
Technical writers			•	•	•							•		1	H	M
Marketing and Sales Occupations																
Advertising workers	•		•	•										1	1	H
Automobile parts counter workers		•			•		•							L	M	M
Automobile salesworkers	•		•		•									M	H	L
Cashiers					•	•						•	•	L	H	L
Insurance agents and brokers	•	•	•	•		•							•	M	M	M
Models					•	•		•				•	•	1	1	L
Real estate agents and brokers	•	•	•	•		•				•			•	M	H	M
Retail trade salesworkers	•			•		•	•						•	L	M	L
Travel agents	•	•	•	•		•								1	H	M

54

Advancing Your Career

Job requirements / Work environs / Occupational characteristics

Columns:
1. Leadership/persuasion
2. Helping/instructing others
3. Problem-solving/creativity
4. Initiative
5. Work as part of a team
6. Frequent public contacts
7. Manual dexterity
8. Physical stamina
9. Hazardous
10. Outdoors
11. Confined
12. Jobs concentrated geographically
13. Part-time
14. Earnings
15. Employment growth
16. Entry requirements

Administrative Support Occupations, Including Clerical

Occupation	1	2	3	4	5	6	7	8	9	10	11	12	13	14	15	16
Airline reservation, ticket agents		•	•		•	•						•		M	L	L
Bank clerks				•								•	•	L	H	L
Bank tellers				•	•							•	•	L	M	L
Bookkeepers and accounting clerks				•								•	•	L	L	L
Collection workers	•		•	•	•							•		L	M	L
Computer operating personnel		•		•			•					•		L	M	M
Mail carriers				•	•	•		•						M	L	L
Postal clerks				•	•	•	•				•	•		M	L	L
Receptionists		•		•	•								•	L	M	L
Secretaries and stenographers			•	•	•	•								L	H	L
Teacher aides	•	•		•	•	•							•	L	M	L
Telephone operators		•			•							•		L	L	L
Typists				•			•						•	L	M	L

Service Occupations

Protective service occupations

Occupation	1	2	3	4	5	6	7	8	9	10	11	12	13	14	15	16
Correction officers	•	•		•				•	•		•			1	H	L
Firefighters		•	•		•		•	•	•				•	M	M	L
Guards				•	•			•		•				L	M	L
Police officers	•	•	•	•	•	•		•	•	•				M	M	L

Food and beverage preparation and service occupations

Occupation	1	2	3	4	5	6	7	8	9	10	11	12	13	14	15	16
Bartenders				•		•	•	•					•	L	M	M
Cooks and chefs				•			•	•					•	L	M	M
Food and counterworkers				•		•	•	•					•	L	H	L
Waiters and waitresses				•		•	•	•					•	L	M	L
Kitchen helpers				•			•	•					•	L	H	L

Health service occupations

Occupation	1	2	3	4	5	6	7	8	9	10	11	12	13	14	15	16
Dental assistants				•	•	•	•						•	L	H	L
Medical assistants				•	•	•								L	H	L
Occupational and physical therapy assistants		•		•	•	•							•	1	H	M

Cleaning and building service occupations

Occupation	1	2	3	4	5	6	7	8	9	10	11	12	13	14	15	16
Hotel housekeepers and assistants						•	•	•						L	M	L

Personal service occupations

Occupation	1	2	3	4	5	6	7	8	9	10	11	12	13	14	15	16
Barbers					•	•	•					•		L	L	M
Bellhops and bell captains				•	•	•						•		L	L	L
Cosmetologists				•	•	•	•				•			L	L	M
Flight attendants		•			•	•	•							M	L	L

Mechanics and Repairers

Vehicle and mobile equipment mechanics and repairers

Occupation	1	2	3	4	5	6	7	8	9	10	11	12	13	14	15	16
Aircraft mechanics			•		•		•	•	•					H	L	M
Automobile body repairers			•				•	•	•					M	M	M
Automobile mechanics			•		•		•	•	•					L	M	M
Farm equipment mechanics			•				•	•	•	•				L	M	M
Truck and bus mechanics			•				•	•	•					M	M	M

Advancing Your Career

	Job requirements	Work environs	Occupational characteristics
	1. Leadership/persuasion / 2. Helping/instructing others / 3. Problem-solving/creativity / 4. Initiative / 5. Work as part of a team / 6. Frequent public contacts / 7. Manual dexterity / 8. Physical stamina / 9. Hazardous / 10. Outdoors / 11. Confined	12. Jobs concentrated geographically / 13. Part-time	14. Earnings / 15. Employment growth / 16. Entry requirements

	1	2	3	4	5	6	7	8	9	10	11	12	13	14	15	16
Electrical and electronic equipment repairers																
Appliance repairers		•	•		•	•								L	M	M
Central office craft occupations		•		•			•	•	•					1	L	L
Computer service technicians		•	•		•		•							M	H	M
Line installers and cable splicers		•		•			•	•	•	•				M	L	L
Maintenance electricians		•	•		•		•	•	•					M	M	M
Telephone installers, repairers		•		•	•	•	•	•	•					M	L	L
Television, radio technicians		•	•		•		•					•		M	H	M
Other mechanics and repairers																
Air-conditioning, refrigeration, and heating mechanics			•				•		•					M	M	M
Business machine repairers		•	•	•			•							M	H	M
Industrial machinery repairers			•				•	•	•					M	M	M
Piano and organ tuners and repairers							•							L	L	M
Watch repairers		•	•	•		•					•		•	L	L	M
Construction and Extractive Occupations																
Construction occupations																
Bricklayers and stonemasons		•					•	•	•	•				M	H	M
Carpenters		•					•	•	•	•				M	M	M
Electricians (construction)		•					•	•	•	•				H	M	M
Floorcovering installers					•		•	•						L	M	M
Glaziers		•		•			•	•	•	•				L	M	M
Insulation workers							•	•	•					M	H	M
Ironworkers				•			•	•	•	•				H	M	M
Painters and paperhangers		•			•		•	•	•	•				L	L	M
Plasterers							•	•						M	L	M
Plumbers and pipefitters		•			•		•	•	•	•				H	M	M
Roofers				•			•	•	•	•				L	L	M
Sheet-metal workers		•					•	•						M	M	M
Extractive occupations																
Coal mining operatives							•		•	•	•	•		M	H	L
Production Occupations																
Blue-collar worker supervisors	•	•	•	•		•		•						M	L	M
Precision production occupations																
Bookbinders and bindery workers		2			•	•					•	2		L	L	M
Dental and laboratory technicians					•									L	H	M
Furniture upholsterers					•		•					•	•	L	L	M
Instrument makers (mechanical)		•	•	•	•		•							M	M	M
Jewelers		•	•	•	•		•					•	•	L	M	M
Lithographers					•		•							H	H	M
Machinists			•		•		•	•	•					M	M	M
Molders (foundry)					•		•	•	•					M	L	M
Patternmakers (foundry)					•	•		•						H	L	M
Photoengravers					•			•						1	L	M
Tool-and-die makers			•		•	•	•	•						H	L	M

56   Advancing Your Career

Job requirements / Work environs / Occupational characteristics

Columns:
1. Leadership/persuasion
2. Helping/instructing others
3. Problem-solving/creativity
4. Initiative
5. Work as part of a team
6. Frequent public contacts
7. Manual dexterity
8. Physical stamina
9. Hazardous
10. Outdoors
11. Confined
12. Jobs concentrated geographically
13. Part-time
14. Earnings
15. Employment growth
16. Entry requirements

Occupation	1	2	3	4	5	6	7	8	9	10	11	12	13	14	15	16
Plant and system operators																
Stationary engineers			•				•	•	•					M	L	M
Water treatment operators			•	•			•		•	•				L	L	M
Machine operators, tenders, and setup workers																
Boiler tenders							•	•	•					M	L	M
Forge shop occupations							•	•	•		•			M	L	M
Machine tool operators			•				•	•			•			M	M	M
Machine tool setup workers			•				•	•						M	M	M
Printing press operators							•	•			•			M	L	M
Fabricators, assemblers, and hand-working occupations																
Assemblers				•			•				•			L	M	L
Automotive painters							•	•	•					H	H	M
Welders and flamecutters							•	•	•					M	M	M
Transportation and Material Moving Occupations																
Motor vehicle operators																
Bus drivers				•		•	•				•		•	H	L	M
Truck drivers					•			•						M	M	L
Other transportation and material moving occupations																
Airplane pilots		•	•	•	•				•					H	L	M
Merchant marine sailors			•		•	•	•	•	•					M	L	M
Operating engineers							•	•	•	•				M	L	M

For further reference

Barth, George Francis
Your Aptitudes
Lothrop, Lee & Shepard

Bolles, Richard Nelson
What Color Is Your Parachute: A Practical Manual for Job and Career Changers
Ten Speed Press

Brown, Denver
The Entrepreneur's Guide
Ballantine

Figler, Howard
The Complete Job-Search Handbook
Holt, Rinehart & Winston

Guide to Federal Career Literature
Superintendent of Documents
U.S. Government Printing Office
Washington, DC 20402

Jablonski, Donna M.
How to Find Information About Companies
Washington Research
918 16th Street NW
Washington, DC 20006

Jawin, Ann J.
A Woman's Guide to Career Preparation: Scholarships, Grants, and Loans
Doubleday/Anchor Press

Lieberoff, Allen
Climb Your Own Ladder
Simon & Schuster

Martin, Phyllis
Introduction to the Job Hunt Success Kit
Center for Career Development
11385 Landon Lane
Cincinnati, Ohio 45246

Reed, Jane
Résumés That Get Jobs
Arco

Advancing Your Career

Health and Fitness

- Fatigue 59
- Stress 60
- Eye care 62
- Ear care 63
- Foot care 63
- Healthy nutrients 64
- Good nutrition 69
- Watch your weight 72
- Get back into shape 74
- Home medical testing 75
- Glossary 76

During the past few decades, a great change has taken place in the attitude of the general public and professionals toward the maintenance of good health. A growing number of individuals are concerned about their own health care and that of members of their family. Doctors, as well as other medical and health professionals, are placing greater emphasis on *preventive medicine:* the use of appropriate measures to help prevent illness.

A century ago, human effort accounted for one-third of all the energy needed to run the factories, farms, businesses, and homes in the United States. However, in the late 20th century, human effort provides only one-half of one percent of the energy needed. We lead softer lives physically, but the pace of life has been stepped up to the point where unbridled stress has become a common problem. The harmful effects of stress contribute to our foremost health concerns: heart disease, stroke, cancer, and high blood pressure.

These degenerative diseases can be controlled and to some extent prevented by your habits and lifestyle. If these diseases were wiped out, the average current life expectancy of 74.5 years would be raised to 90.5 years. This statistical projection, made by the U.S. Public Health Service, is not unrealistic. It can be attained with changes in lifestyle, nutrition and diet, the handling of stress, weight control, and physical activity. Preventive medicine can not only add years to your life, it can put more life into those years.

In this chapter, you will find useful information on nutrition, stress, exercise, and other essentials that can provide preventive health care for your entire family. The highlighted *Health Care Alert* boxes, listing signals of major diseases, are intended to help you in recognizing early symptoms of disease and in reporting them in detail to your doctor. Because there are still so many myths and misconceptions about various health issues, we have included another feature, *Fact or Fiction,* which separates false notions from factual information.

Many such notions are obtained from articles appearing in popular magazines and from product advertising that is misleading in the presentation, or lacks factual information. The Food and Drug Administration advises everyone to review carefully all advertisements, especially those making claims for medical remedies. Bogus medical products include certain weight reduction pills or diets, arthritis and cancer cures, and panaceas for whatever ails you.

Answers to specific medical questions, or medical treatment, should be sought from a reputable doctor. While a majority of medical professionals are trustworthy, there are still many quack doctors who make promises of quick cures to unsuspecting victims of such serious diseases as cancer and arthritis. Choose your doctor carefully and know the drugs you use. For helpful suggestions, see "You and Modern Medicine" on page 78.

Fatigue

Fatigue is a common complaint, one for which you yourself can often pinpoint the reason quite readily: a sleepless night, on-the-job frustration, frazzled nerves from trying to run a busy household.

There are many other less obvious, but equally plausible, explanations for a feeling of tiredness. All too often, people fail to see the connection between poor nutrition and fatigue. A lack of B vitamins or an inadequate intake of carbohydrates may interfere with the production of body energy. Too little activity may result in too little oxygen reaching the tissues.

Unless your tired feeling is related to a specific disease or medical problem, you can fight it with some simple changes in your daily routine. However, before you decide how to deal with fatigue, it is important for you to know what is causing it. Under any circumstances, if tiredness continues for more than a few weeks, you should check with a doctor. Such fatigue may be due to an illness that needs medical treatment.

Basically, fatigue may be placed into three major categories: physical (of the body), pathological (from a disease), psychological (of the mind).

Physical.
This fatigue may be brought on by strenuous activity such as jogging or heavy housework. It may also be caused by such factors as poor muscle tone or bad posture.

Pathological.
A tired feeling is often one symptom present in such conditions as iron-deficiency anemia, heart disease, cancer, arthritis, and diabetes; however, other and even more specific symptoms are also usually in evidence.

Certain prescription drugs (for example, tranquilizers and allergy remedies) may induce fatigue. If medication you are taking seems to rob you of vital energy, ask your doctor to prescribe an alternate drug. Excessive use of alcohol or caffeine, cigarette smoking, and poor eating habits are other factors that may result in fatigue.

Psychological.
Severe emotional stress, tension, anxiety, and other psychogenic factors are predominant in causing a feeling of constant tiredness. The person who feels trapped in a job situation or a marriage, for example, is bound to suffer from a persistent fatigue and lack of energy.

There are any number of ways in which you can fight that tired feeling. Take stock of your lifestyle, and see what you can do to take out the monotony, the frustration, or the stress in your day-to-day routines.

A working couple may need to share household responsibilities more equally; a "workaholic" may need to fit in some time for relaxation; and a weary housewife may need to hire a babysitter and join an exercise or art group. Make certain, too, that you include the essential nutrients in your daily diet; they are all needed for top performance by your body. Get enough exercise and rest, and try not to undertake too many demanding activities at one time.

Fact or fiction?

Exercise will make you feel more tired.
Fiction. Exercise releases tensions, improves sleep patterns, and promotes fitness. Those who exercise regularly get more done with less effort.

A sweet snack will *not* give you energy.
Fact. You will probably feel even more tired an hour or so after a sweet snack between meals. Have some fresh fruit instead.

Coffee or colas will give you energy.
Fiction. Caffeinated drinks may keep you awake, but too much can interfere with sleep and simply add to that tired feeling.

A light supper helps you sleep.
Fact. A high protein meal induces wakefulness; supper should be a low-protein, high-carbohydrate meal.

Health and Fitness

Energy-boosters to fight fatigue

- **Eat three well-balanced meals a day.** Include the four basic food groups (milk, meat, vegetables and fruits, breads and cereals).
- **Choose a conditioning exercise that you enjoy.** Aerobic exercises (increasing the heart rate and flow of oxygen to the blood) are especially beneficial. Jogging, bicycling, aerobic dancing, and brisk walking fall into this category.
- **Be certain to get as many hours of sleep as *you* need.** Different people require different amounts of sleep.
- **Plan activities according to your natural body rhythms.** If you have more energy in the morning, do your most demanding work at that time, and keep lesser tasks for another time of day.
- **Pace yourself, balancing out your work demands and social activities.** Take revitalizing breaks throughout the day.
- **Cut down, or avoid, the use of caffeine, alcoholic substances, and tobacco.**
- **Do not use over-the-counter drugs to pep you up;** do not become dependent upon sleeping pills (they have a bad effect upon the quality of sleep).

Stress

Stress is an essential part of our lives, and we would not want to be without it. Many types of stress provide the impetus that makes us excel at a chosen task, or at reaching a desired personal goal. Other kinds of stress, however, particularly that arising from the complexities of modern life, can have a disturbing effect upon those who do not know how to handle it.

Simply defined, stress is the total response of your body (physical, mental, and chemical) to events that irritate, frighten, endanger, confuse, or excite you. Some stress is of your own making, as when you enter college, embark on a new career, or get married. Other pressures are forced upon you, such as nerve-wracking job or home situations, or sudden injury or illness. Whatever the nature of the stress, the important thing is how you come to grips with it.

There is no one foolproof way of dealing with stress, but learning to identify the "stressor," or stressful event, can be the first step in turning your stress into positive energy. Stressful situations can help you to be receptive to changes and challenges, and to think and act clearly. On the other hand, if not handled right, stress can thwart clear thinking and decisive action and become a threat to good health. It can add to the likelihood of developing such high stress conditions as anxiety, chronic headaches, ulcers, arthritis, high blood pressure, asthma, and heart disorders.

Remember: Experiencing stress is normal. But sometimes stress can be a real problem. The trick is to turn it from a destructive to a positive force.

Body protection against stress.

The father of modern research on stress, Hans Selye, described stress in terms of a syndrome—the adaptive energy syndrome. Dr. Selye believed that each one of us is born with an individualized amount of adaptive energy and that we use up some of this supply every time we draw upon it.

There are three stages to the adaptive energy syndrome: 1) the alarm reaction, 2) the resistance stage, and 3) the exhaustion stage.

In the alarm reaction, the body is subjected to stress and it responds with a significant drop in its level of resistance. Adrenalin (the stress hormone) is pumped into the bloodstream, the pulse races, and breathing speeds up. The blood supply is promptly redirected from the internal organs to other parts of the body, particularly the muscles, where it is needed to respond during the emergency.

The resistance stage represents the continuing attempt of the body to develop defenses in combatting the stressor. During this period, the body works hard to raise its level of resistance well above normal. Gradually, the distinctive indicators of the alarm reaction disappear and the body seemingly returns to normal. However, if the body remains mobilized for an overlong period of time, the above normal level of resistance will not continue and will drop below normal. At this point, the exhaustion stage sets in, making the body increasingly vulnerable to disease related to stress, organic dysfunction, and even death.

Executives should have hobbies sufficiently different from their office routines to help relieve the stresses of the work day. Gourmet cooking is relaxing and fun.

HEALTH CARE ALERT

STRESS

Signals of badly channeled stress

Many commonly experienced stress reactions signal potential stress damage to the body. These reactions may include heart palpitations or a pounding pulse, nagging headaches, irritability, and a feeling of tightness in the chest, neck, or shoulders. Other symptoms may be difficulty in falling asleep, back pain, upset stomach, loss of appetite, lack of concentration, and fatigue.

With increased stress, the stress reactions intensify and signal possible greater damage to the body. A person may find it impossible to unwind or enjoy physical relaxation, become impatient or depressed, do more drinking or smoking than usual, spend sleepless nights, or have frequent headaches and stomach disturbances.

Eventually, if negatively channeled stress continues for a long time, the accumulated effects can contribute to such serious ailments as asthma, heart disease, migraine headaches, high blood pressure, stomach ulcers, alcoholism, and drug addiction.

Some common stressors

Stressors mean different things to different people. What is high stress to one person may cause no reaction in another.

Day-to-day living: being stuck in traffic; standing on long supermarket or bank lines; a rough day at home or at work; marital discord.

Emotional: negative feelings such as anger, fear, or worry; positive feelings such as profound joy, love, or excitement.

Environmental: intense noise or air pollution; bright blinking lights; exposure to extremes of heat or cold.

Health: allergies or chemotherapy; serious illness; accidents or physical injury; excesses of drugs, alcohol, caffeine, or nicotine.

Life cycle: adolescent's struggle for independence and identity; pregnancy and motherhood; oldsters adjusting to physical limitations of aging.

Life milestones: start of formal education; graduating from school; getting married; embarking on a new career.

Social: overcrowding or unpleasant surroundings; unsuccessful interpersonal relationships at work or at home.

Some ways to beat stress

Basically, a good stress skill is anything that can help *you* deal with the stress you feel. There is little help to be found in the use of alcohol or drugs, or "stress-formula" products bought at the drugstore. If a situation becomes too difficult for you to handle, see a doctor or therapist.

- **Change your attitude.** Either decide to work out or get out of a stressful situation.
- **Give yourself a break.** Get away from yourself and your problems. Take 10-minute breaks during the day; get away for a day, a week, or longer if possible.
- **Eat sensibly.** Eat plenty of high-energy foods each day. Avoid, or greatly limit, the use of sugar, salt, coffee, and alcohol.
- **Exercise regularly.** Keep physically active: walk, run, swim, bicycle to keep trim and strong, and to relieve pent-up feelings.
- **Get moral support.** At times, talking over a problem with family or friends can be of help in deciding how best to deal with it.
- **Learn to relax.** Take up a hobby: art or music, vegetable gardening or flower arranging, handicrafts or photography.

Health and Fitness

Eye care

It has been estimated that no less than 50,000 Americans become blind each year. *This number could be reduced by one-half if people took proper measures to guard against accident and disease.* By taking simple commonsense precautions, you can help to preserve your sight.

Proper lighting

Reading or close work. A room should have at least 200 watts of general lighting or 100 watts of general lighting and 75 to 100 watts of direct lighting.

Glare. Arrange lighting so that it is not reflected by a book or other reading material. Make certain, too, that no shadows fall upon the reading material.

Television. To avoid eyestrain, a child should sit at least 6 feet from the TV set and at about the same level as the screen. Some other light in the room is necessary, but the TV set should be located where it cannot reflect light from a lamp. Video games are especially tiring for the eyes as children tend to stay closer to the screen and watch it more steadily than when watching TV. Home computers may cause similar problems.

Eye changes in children. Vision problems occur in 5 percent of all preschool children and 25 percent of all school-age youngsters. Ophthalmologists advise a first test when the child is six months, and again at three or four years of age.

Parents can help their children maintain healthy eyes by being alert to various changes in the eye, and by having their children's eyes examined periodically.

Appearance: an eye that turns in, out, up, or down. Red-rimmed, encrusted, or swollen lids. Inflamed or watery eyes, recurring sties, an enlarged eye, an eye that appears cloudy, or a white spot in the pupil.

Behavior: excessive rubbing of the eyes, shutting or covering of one eye. Tilting or thrusting the head forward. Difficulty in reading or doing close work. Blinking more than usual or irritability when doing close work. Inability to see distant objects clearly, squinting, or frowning.

Complaints: itching, burning, or scratchy feeling. Inability to see well, dizziness, headaches, or nausea following close work. Blurred or double vision.

Health hints on eye care

Rubbing and poking	Children especially need to be reminded not to put their fingers into their eyes, particularly if their hands are soiled or if they have touched an open infectious cold sore or wound. Spread of a virus infection to the eye can ulcerate and scar the cornea, a primary cause of blindness.
Safety goggles	These should be worn to protect the eyes from accident or injury. For example, wear goggles when using electric tools such as saws and drills, lawn mowers, and hedge clippers; chemicals such as pesticidal or herbicidal sprays and household cleaning products; and in sports, particularly squash and racketball. An optician can help you choose proper goggles.
Sunglasses	Use sunglasses in reflected sunlight (on the water or the beach). Do not wear sunglasses indoors or for night driving. When selecting sunglasses, check the label to see that they filter out ultraviolet rays. Ask an optician for help, if necessary.
Drugs	At times, prescription drugs may cause complications. If you are taking a medication to control a condition such as high blood pressure, ask your doctor if the drug you are taking can affect the eye in any way.
Visits to the eye doctor	See your eye doctor (ophthalmologist) about any injury to the eye so that he or she can make sure that there is no damage. Check out any eye symptoms such as sudden pain or extreme sensitivity to light. After age 40, eyes should be checked for glaucoma (increased pressure in the eye) every two or three years. Begin checking after age 30 if there is a family history of glaucoma.

Ear care

Together with your eyes, your ears are the most vital sense organs. They are the lines of communication with the world around you.

Wax in the ear. Sometimes wax accumulates in the outer auditory canal; this can impede hearing. Do not remove the wax by using a hairpin, matchstick, or other sharp object. You may cause damage by scratching or perforating the eardrum. If you have a wax plug, an insect, or any foreign body in your ear, keep in mind the advice not to put anything in your ear smaller than your elbow. See your doctor for proper treatment.

Hearing problems. Some people are born deaf. Many others suffer hearing loss as a result of an accident or an infection. When the delicate inner ear structure has been damaged by meningitis or scarlet fever, "nerve deafness" occurs, and very little, if anything, can be done to relieve the condition.

Children who seem to be inattentive at school and who have learning disabilities are often afflicted with hearing problems. To avoid such difficulties, a child's hearing should be checked regularly. The value of good hearing can hardly be overestimated, and any change in hearing ability calls for prompt examination by an ear doctor.

Foot care

Foot problems afflict at least 75 percent of the American adult population. The most common problems are corns and bunions. Proper care of the feet will help keep feet strong and healthy. The most important protective measure is to keep your feet clean and dry. Take soothing foot baths as needed to relieve soreness. Allow toenails to grow to the tip of the toe; then cut straight across, not on a curve. Exercise your feet to keep them flexible and to strengthen the arches.

A large number of foot problems (flat feet, corns, bunions, calluses, and ingrown toenails) are caused by poorly fitted shoes. Select shoes with sensible heels and plenty of toe room. Always try on *both* shoes of a pair for size (one foot is usually larger than the other). Make certain that the back of the shoe fits snugly, and that the shoe has an inner or outer cushioning sole.

Simple care for minor foot problems

Bunions (hallux valgus)	Some people, such as diabetics, need special foot care. Any foot problems that are troublesome should be checked with your doctor or podiatrist (foot specialist). To avoid bunion pain, pressure on the prominent joint must be eliminated. Chiefly, this is a matter of wearing sensible shoes with plenty of toe room.
Calluses and corns (clavus)	After your bath or shower, gently rub your feet with a piece of pumice smeared with soap to remove excess calluses. Use of an emery board a few times a week will help reduce a hard corn. Medicated corn drops must be used very carefully so that there is no damage to good skin. The use of doughnut-shaped corn pads may also afford some relief.
Ingrown toenail (onyxia)	Try to wedge a small piece of cotton (soaked in castor oil) under the edge of the embedded nail. Apply a clean gauze pad to protect the nail from pressure. Soak the foot in water daily.
Athlete's foot (tinea pedis)	To help avoid this infection, keep feet clean and thoroughly dry, especially between the toes. Dusting with a medicated or other foot powder can help keep feet free of moisture.

Health and Fitness

Healthy nutrients

There are about 50 different nutrients that your body needs to stay healthy, including vitamins, minerals, carbohydrates, proteins, and fats. In this section, you will find out more about fiber, trace minerals, vitamins, and water.

On the whole, the American diet is thought to be relatively low in fiber. Most experts agree that the average person could probably double the amount of dietary fiber consumed, increasing intake to about 30 to 40 grams a day.

Mainly, there are two forms of minerals: macrominerals (needed in comparatively large amounts by the body) and microminerals (needed by the body in only very small amounts). There are some additional minerals, such as cobalt and nickel, which will take on greater nutritional importance as research determines the full extent of their usefulness in the human body.

Vitamins, organic substances derived from plants and animals, are required in the diet in very small amounts for normal health and growth. Although vitamins do not supply energy, they do help to trigger biochemical reactions that convert food into usable substances by the body.

In a listing of important nutrients, water is not always mentioned, yet the entire body mechanism needs water to function properly. Active people often fail to drink enough fluids; this may result in muscle fatigue, even upon moderate exertion. During strenuous exertion, as when running a marathon, an inadequate amount of water may be scarcely tolerable and even life-threatening.

Eat more high in fiber foods. To get enough fiber in your diet, eat whole-grain breads and cereals, nuts, fruits, and vegetables. Some good

You should eat some foods high in fiber each day, but beware of high-fiber diets. Eating too much fiber may interfere with the body's absorption of essential nutrients. Regular servings of whole wheat bread, vegetables, and fruit should provide enough fiber for most people.

sources are found in dried figs and apricots, avocados, and apples with their skins, green beans and peas, broccoli, Brussels sprouts, turnips, lentils, black beans, whole-wheat breads, and crackers. Adding fiber to foods that contain fiber is of no value.

All fibers are not the same, which is why you must include some of the various available types in your daily diet. Most fibers prove beneficial in weight control, and whole grains may help tighten a flabby stomach. But pectins and gums are needed for the proper body use of fats, cholesterol, and carbohydrates. A *high-fiber* diet, compared with one that is *adequate* in fiber, can interfere with intestinal absorption, which may result in the loss of essential nutrients. You will probably get enough fiber in your diet by eating two servings of vegetables and two servings of whole grains (whole-wheat bread, for instance) each day.

How to add fiber to your diet

DO'S

- **Make certain** to eat a wide variety of foods in reasonable amounts.
- **Be sure** to drink adequate liquids when you eat fiber to avoid constipation.
- **Look for** the words "whole grain," "whole wheat," or "whole oats" on breads and cereals. Generally, coarse fiber is more effective than the same fiber ground fine.
- **Include** fresh fruits and raw vegetables in your diet. Their fiber content is more useful than peeled, cooked, or puréed fruits and vegetables.

DON'TS

- **Do not** depend upon fiber pills or tablets. You would have to take a whole bottle to get any benefit.
- **Do not** use fiber as a food additive. Change the kinds of foods you eat *gradually* to avoid a bloated feeling, diarrhea, or gas.
- **Do not** cut out all refined carbohydrates at one time. Replace them slowly with natural, whole-grain foods.
- **Do not** concentrate on one or another type of fiber; consider them all.

Trace minerals. Mineral elements account for only about four percent of total body weight. However, the body holds enough iron to make a good size nail, and enough sodium to fill a small salt shaker. More needs to be learned about the exact daily requirements of trace minerals, but a diet with a sufficient amount of natural foods should be adequate to maintain good health.

Food sources and body functions

Trace mineral	Chief food sources	Chief body functions
Chromium	Liver, beef, dried beans, cheese, whole-grain breads and cereals, peanuts, brewer's yeast, molasses, and beets.	Aids the body, together with insulin, in deriving energy from glucose (blood sugar). Plays an important role in the synthesis of fatty acids and cholesterol in the liver.
Copper	Oysters, fish, nuts, dried peas, beans, beef and pork liver, organ meats, eggs, spinach, asparagus, and corn-oil margarine.	Aids in the manufacture of red blood cells, and helps the body store iron. A component of several respiratory enzymes, copper is also part of the enzyme that helps make melanin (the pigment in the skin).
Fluorine (Fluoride)	Fish, tea, most animal foods, fluoridated water, and foods grown with or cooked in fluoridated water.	Helps form strong teeth and resistance to decay. Aids in maintenance of bone strength.
Iodine	Seafood, saltwater fish, seaweed, sea salt, and iodized salt.	A component of thyroid hormones that control the body's metabolism. Aids in the development and functioning of the thyroid gland, and in the prevention of goiter.
Iron	Liver (especially pork, followed by calf, beef, and chicken), kidneys, red meat, egg yolks, green leafy vegetables, dried raisins, apricots, prunes, dried beans, peas, potatoes, blackstrap molasses; enriched, whole-grain cereals.	Helps form red blood cells and myoglobin in muscles that supply oxygen in cells. Found in enzyme systems, including one that works to produce energy in the body.
Manganese	Nuts, whole grains, fruits, vegetables, tea, instant coffee, and cocoa powder.	Aids in proper function of the nervous system, normal bone structure, and reproduction. Extremely important in many vital enzyme systems in the body. Needed for utilization of iron.
Molybdenum	Legumes, cereal grains, liver, kidney, some dark green vegetables.	Required by three important enzymes. May aid in prevention of tooth decay. Associated with carbohydrate metabolism.
Selenium	Seafood, whole-grain cereals, meat, egg yolks, chicken, and milk.	Antioxidant, preventing breakdown of fats and other body chemicals. Interacts with Vitamin E in protecting cell membranes.
Zinc	Beef, liver, eggs, poultry, seafood, especially oysters, peas, carrots, whole grains, and pure maple syrup.	A component of as many as 100 enzymes in the body. Involved in normal wound healing. Needed for growth and development.

Know your vitamins. There are 13 compounds considered to be vitamins. Four—A, D, E, and K—are soluble in fat. The eight B vitamins and C are soluble in water. The fat-soluble vitamins, stored in body fat, are not readily excreted and therefore do not need to be replaced as often as the water-soluble

How vitamins can keep you healthy

Vitamin	*Food sources*	*How they help you*
Vitamin A Retinol (discovered 1913)	Yellow, orange, and dark green vegetables, liver, cheese, milk, eggs, and butter.	Known as the growth vitamin, Vitamin A is essential in maintaining healthy skin, hair, mucous membranes, and bone. It provides visual pigments that allow you to see.
Vitamin B_1 Thiamin (discovered 1936)	Whole-wheat grains, wheat germ, liver and kidney, pork, peas, beans, peanuts, oranges, and many other fruits and vegetables.	All B vitamins play a similar role in the body: they help enzymes to do their job. B_1 acts as a cofactor for 24 enzymes, aiding cells to utilize carbohydrates. It assists in the proper functioning of the nervous system and digestive tract.
Vitamin B_2 Riboflavin (discovered 1935)	Liver, kidney, lamb, beef, veal, eggs, whole-wheat products, yeast, asparagus, beets, peas, and dark green vegetables.	A cofactor in enzymes helping cells to use carbohydrates, proteins, and fats, and producing energy. Promotes growth, healthy skin, and mucous membranes.
Vitamin B_3 Niacin Nicotinamide Nicotinic acid (discovered 1867)	Lean meat, fish, liver, yeast, eggs, whole-grain breads and cereals, peas, beans, and nuts.	An essential component of enzymes that contribute to the production of energy in cells. Also assists in the breakdown of fats.
Vitamin B_6 Pyridoxine Pyridoxal (discovered 1934)	Poultry, fish, liver, whole grains, cereals, breads, tomatoes, yellow corn, spinach, green beans, bananas, and yogurt.	An essential activator of many enzymes, pyridoxine aids in breaking down protein, carbohydrates, and fat, and in forming hormones such as adrenalin and insulin. It also helps to regenerate red blood cells and produce antibodies.
Folic acid Folicin (discovered 1946)	Liver, kidneys, green leafy vegetables, and dried legumes.	Necessary for formation of red and white cells. Aids in protein metabolism and in creating some components of the DNA molecule.
Vitamin C Ascorbic acid (discovered 1919)	Abundant in most fruits and vegetables, especially citrus fruits, tomatoes, potatoes, green peppers, and dark green vegetables.	Enhances the activity of certain enzymes. Aids body use of iron and blood clotting as needed. Helps formation of teeth, gums, and bones; aids in healing of bone fractures and wounds.
Vitamin D Calciferol (discovered 1925)	Egg yolks, butter, fortified milk, liver, fish liver oils, tuna, salmon, herring, sardines, and oysters.	Known as the "sunshine vitamin." Aids in the normal growth and development of bones and teeth. Important in the intestinal absorption of calcium and phosphorus. Affords antirachitic activity.
Vitamin E Alpha tocopherol (discovered 1936)	Lettuce and other leafy green vegetables, seed oils, whole grains, dried beans, and liver.	Helps in the production of red blood cells and in the strengthening of muscles and other tissues. An antioxidant, it protects Vitamin A and fats from reacting with oxygen.

Health and Fitness

vitamins. These must be included in your daily diet in adequate amounts. On the whole, vitamins can be used and reused by the body, which explains why you need only small amounts to replace those lost in the urine or feces. Studying this table will help you choose the right foods for a balanced diet.

Research indications

In animal tests, some researchers found that a lack of Vitamin A can increase the toxicity of aflatoxin (a natural poison produced by a fungus living in peanuts and grains), and with it the chance of getting cancer of the colon. It is also becoming more evident that Vitamin A may play an important part in preventing epithelial cancers, such as are produced by smoking cigarettes.

Vitamin B_1 deficiency is implicated in all stages of alcoholism; a diet rich in B_1 will help prevent polyneuritis in alcoholics. There has been some success in treating children suffering repeated episodes of fever and gland swellings (unresponsive to conventional therapy) with B_1 supplementation.

Vitamin B_2 helps the body obtain energy from food. One study has shown that women who exercise vigorously and regularly may need almost twice as much riboflavin as those who are less active. This may be owed to the part Vitamin B_2 has in producing energy.

Niacin has been used effectively to lower high cholesterol levels associated with familial hypercholesterolemia, which cannot be controlled by diet alone and which quintuples the risk of heart disease.

In test animals, a diet lacking pyridoxine and other B vitamins, and with exposure to aflatoxin, increased the likelihood of cancer of the liver. Pyridoxine has been used medically to treat the toxic effects of carbon disulfide. A diet rich in pyridoxine may help prevent cirrhosis in alcoholics.

Preliminary British studies with pregnant women indicate that a large dose (4 mg daily) of this vitamin may help prevent such congenital defects as spina bifida (a defect in the wall of the spinal canal) and encephalocele (a defect involving the brain). An American study indicates that a megadose (10 mg daily) may lower the risk of cervical cancer in women on the pill who show cervical cell abnormalities.

In animal studies, Vitamin C has shown a possible activity against gum disease. Research shows that large doses of Vitamin C may be able to help the body detoxify such poisonous substances as malathion, lead, and cancer-causing nitrosamines.

Rickets and osteomalacia due to a lack of Vitamin D can be effectively treated with a form of Vitamin D known as 25-hydroxy-cholecalciferol. It has been found that Vitamin D breaks down in the body into compounds that may act as hormones. A synthetic compound, 1-25 Vitamin D, has been approved for use as an agent to promote bone growth.

Animal tests have shown that Vitamin E can lessen the damage that two air pollutants, ozone and nitrogen dioxide, can have on the lungs. Vitamin E, together with Vitamin C and zinc, may reduce toxicity to cadmium. Reportedly, Vitamin E may relieve chronic cystic mastitis in many cases; also, nighttime leg cramps.

Fact or fiction?

Vitamin C is a cure for the common cold.
Fiction. To date, there is no accepted medical evidence to support such a claim. Excessive doses, many times higher than the recommended 30 to 60 milligrams a day, may cause health problems in some people, such as the formation of kidney or bladder stones.

Vitamin D should be used carefully.
Fact. Too high doses of Vitamin D can result in nausea, loss of appetite, excessive thirst, and excessive urination. The heart, lungs, kidneys, and joints may develop calcium deposits, while the bones may become fragile.

Laxatives can cause vitamin deficiencies.
Fact. For example, the frequent use of mineral oil can rob your body of vitamins A, D, and K. Vitamin deficiencies due to overuse of laxatives make the user more susceptible to many toxic substances and to carcinogens.

There is no danger in taking large amounts of Vitamin A.
Fiction. A form of Vitamin A, retinol, taken in very high doses, can be quite toxic. If too much is taken, retinol can cause various conditions, including headaches, fatigue, blurred vision, intestinal disturbances, liver and kidney damage, hair loss, and brain damage.

HEALTH CARE ALERT

OSTEOPOROSIS

Signs of brittle bones

In the United States, women over 45 suffer a million fractures each year. Most are associated with a condition in which there is a degenerative thinning of the bones.

Detection in the early stages is difficult. X-rays, for example, will not show bone loss until there is a loss of 30 to 50 percent. There are a few simple signs that may alert a person to the presence of osteoporosis.

Decrease in height may give the earliest detectable sign, and it is one that often goes unnoticed. It is suggested that people at high risk of osteoporosis (such as menopausal women, alcoholics, and the elderly) keep a record of their height and check it every six to twelve months. Any height loss should be reported to a doctor.

Another sign is tooth loss brought on by periodontal (gum) disease. Gum inflammation, attributed to the formation of plaque on teeth, can also be due to bone degeneration. Regular visits to the dentist will prevent the development of gum disease.

To help avoid brittle bones, women over 35 should get an adequate amount of calcium, magnesium, and vitamins C and D in their diet. Regular exercise, such as walking and stretching, is most important, as it improves calcium absorption and stimulates bone formation. Excessive intake of coffee and alcohol, and smoking, add to bone loss and should be avoided.

Water is a vital nutrient. Your body is about two-thirds water, and contains about 40 to 50 quarts of water. In women, water content averages 55 to 65 percent, while it is around 65 to 75 percent in men.

Every living body cell needs water to perform its vital function. Water aids in the digestion and absorption of nutrients, such as vitamins. It transports oxygen to the cells and removes both liquid and solid wastes. It helps the body maintain a normal temperature, and lubricates the joints. It provides a protective cushion for the tissues, and keeps skin from drying out.

How much water should you drink? Most people drink far less water than the six to eight 8-ounce glasses considered nutritionally adequate even though the fluid requirement includes fruit juices, soft drinks, milk, coffee, and tea as well as plain water. Even greater amounts of liquid are needed during periods of increased water loss in hot weather, strenuous exercise, and illness accompanied by fever. Infants and child-bearing women also require extra fluids.

Water forms the larger part of most solid foods. Fruits and vegetables are about 80 percent water, green beans 89 percent, and lettuce 95 percent. Even milk is 87 percent water, and fish foods around 75 percent. Meat is half water, while bread is about one-third water by weight.

The body excretes about 2 quarts of water a day, most of it as urine. Water may also be lost in sizeable amounts through the skin by sweating, through the lungs in the process of breathing, and upon extreme exertion in strenuous exercise.

Good nutrition

Eating less meat and other high cholesterol foods will reduce deaths caused by heart disease, from which 555,000 die each year.

Most Americans eat too much. There is too much fat, refined sugar, and salt in our diets. On the whole, our diets consist of about 50 percent nonessential foods. You can, however, easily improve your eating habits for the better. Start by cutting down on fats and using polyunsaturated for saturated fats. Eat more lean meats and poultry, and fewer dairy products. Instead of overloading your diet with foods high in sugar, substitute fresh fruits and vegetables. Use low-calorie for high-calorie foods whenever possible. Limit your salt intake, using herbs to flavor food.

Heart attacks. The average American, eating a diet high in saturated fats and cholesterol, is at greater risk of having a heart attack than other populations consuming diets low in fat and cholesterol. In the opinion of the American Heart Association, reduction of fat intake is one of the most important steps a person can take to lower the risk of heart disease. Most people obtain their total daily calories from fat. It is recommended that fat intake be cut to 30 percent, and that fats in the diet be equally divided among saturated, polyunsaturated, and monounsaturated fats.

Types of fats

Saturated *Avoid use of* (tend to raise blood cholesterol)	butter cheese coconut, coconut oil egg yolks lard	meat milk chocolate palm oil vegetable shortening whole milk
Monounsaturated *Use occasionally* (have no effect on blood cholesterol)	avocados cashews olives, olive oil	peanuts peanut butter peanut oil
Polyunsaturated *Good to use* (tend to lower blood cholesterol)	almonds corn oil cottonseed oil filberts fish margarine	pecans safflower oil salad dressing soybean oil sunflower oil walnuts

---

HEALTH CARE ALERT

HEART ATTACK

A key signal: chest pain

In a heart attack, pain may range from a feeling of slight pressure in the chest to a crushing sensation.
- Generally, pain lasts for hours.
- Pain does not respond to rest, or the use of nitroglycerin.
- The face turns ashen gray, and a cold sweat appears.
- Retching, belching, or vomiting may occur, which can easily be confused with an attack of indigestion.
- Pain responds only to use of a narcotic drug.
- *Act promptly:* call for medical help at once, or take victim to the nearest hospital emergency room.

Chest pain may be due to a number of different causes, some of a minor nature, such as gum chewing, drinking too much carbonated water, and excessive smoking. Chest pain may also be caused by such conditions as bruised or fractured ribs or angina pectoris. Angina is similar to a heart attack in that it usually comes on with exertion (for example, running to catch a bus or train), but the type, extent, and duration of pain are quite dissimilar.

Health and Fitness

Cancer. *Faulty diets, according to a report from the National Academy of Sciences, account for 30 to 40 percent of all cancers in men and as high as 60 percent in women.* The cancers most exclusively linked to diet are cancers of the stomach, colon, breast, and, to a lesser extent, the lung and prostate.

Eat more fruits, vegetables, fiber. Fresh dark green, orange, and yellow vegetables (broccoli, carrots, and others) are rich in a substance called beta-carotene, which the body converts into Vitamin A. Cabbage-family vegetables (Brussels sprouts, cabbages, and others) contain several chemicals that have been found to inhibit cancer in animals. Their plentiful use is associated with a reduced risk of certain cancers, especially of the colon.

Get plenty of foods rich in Vitamin C, especially citrus and red fruits and dark green vegetables. Laboratory studies have shown that Vitamin C stops the formation of certain chemicals causing cancer. In studies of persons at high risk of cancer, Vitamin C reduced the incidence of stomach or esophageal cancer.

When dietary fiber (whole grains, fresh fruits, and vegetables) intake amounts to 20 to 40 grams a day, there is possible protection against colon and rectal cancer.

Eat less fats, smoked foods. Avoid or limit intake of dietary fats. Both saturated (for example, animal fats, butter fat, palm oil, coconut oil) and unsaturated fats (mostly vegetable oils) have been linked with increased cancer, in particular, of the breast and colon. A 25 percent reduction in *all* dietary fats is recommended.

Fact or fiction?

Cow's milk is a perfect food.
Fiction. Cow's milk may be a relatively good food for young children, but most infants fare better on mother's milk. Milk is a good food but does not contain enough of some important nutrients, especially iron, copper, and Vitamin C.

Enriched breads are nutritious.
Fact. Important vitamins and minerals (thiamin, riboflavin, niacin, and iron) are partially removed in the milling of flour. By enrichment, these substances are replaced to a level equivalent to those in whole-wheat flour or bread.

Vegetarians often develop severe nutritional deficiencies.
Fact. Strict vegetarians do not get enough Vitamin D or Vitamin B_{12} (the only B vitamin not found in any vegetable). For good sources of these vitamins, as well as calcium and protein, we must depend upon foods of animal origin.

Eating out . . . healthily and enjoyably

Be in control of your diet, no matter where you eat or what the occasion.

- **Ask that dishes be prepared as you wish:** with reduced salt or no salt at all; with margarine instead of butter; with entrees broiled, roasted, or baked.
- **Avoid rich sauces,** or ask that sauces be served on the side. Spoon off as much sauce as you can when you are served a precooked dish with a rich sauce. Also, pass up such salads as shrimp and tuna.
- **Trim off all fat and skin** from served meats.
- **If high sodium seasonings,** such as soy sauce, monosodium glutamate (MSG), and salt are used, ask that they be used sparingly, or not at all.
- **Snack on nonfattening foods** at a buffet party and leave the patés, dips, smoked fish, and the like.

Smoked, salt-cured, or pickled foods should be used sparingly. In smoking and curing, foods are exposed to certain compounds, such as the nitrosamines. These compounds cause cancer in animals and are suspect in humans.

The consumption of alcohol should be limited to one or two drinks a day, or eliminated. More than a few drinks a day has been linked to cancer of the mouth, larynx, esophagus, and respiratory tract, and beer drinking has been linked to cancer of the colon and rectum. The risk is increased with cigarette smoking.

HEALTH CARE ALERT

CANCER

Seven signals

1. Change in bowel or bladder habits.
2. A sore that does not heal.
3. Unusual bleeding or discharge.
4. Thickening or lump in the breast or any other part of the body.
5. Indigestion or difficulty in swallowing.
6. Obvious change in wart or mole.
7. Nagging cough or hoarseness.

If you have any of these signals, it does not necessarily mean that you have cancer. It does mean that something is wrong in your body, and you need to check with your doctor.

Cigarette smoking is a major cause of lung cancer. For more than a decade, the number of women smokers has been increasing steadily. Today, lung cancer will kill more women than breast cancer.

Fast foods. Probably nothing has changed the eating habits of millions of Americans more than the fast-food eateries found nearly everywhere and the introduction of convenience foods, which are steadily increasing in number and variety.

Many of these foods are labeled junk foods. They provide few or no nutrients other than sugar calories. These are rightly called empty calories because they are mostly carbohydrate and contain no proteins, minerals, or vitamins. Most popular soft drinks, pastries, candies, and ice creams contain as much as 100 percent of sugar calories.

While fast foods do not fall into the junk food category, they supply either too little or too much of one or more essential nutrients. Even pizza, which contains more protein and less fat than most other fast foods, has a rather high calorie and salt content. *The average American consumes nearly 10 grams of salt a day, which is more than three times the recommended daily allowance.* This excessive use of salt has led health authorities to suggest that salt intake be restricted to 5 grams a day.

It pays to read food labels. You can readily check packaged foods for their sugar, sodium, or fat content by reading the labels. In general, the ingredient with the highest amount of a given substance is listed first, followed by others in descending order of content.

Familiarize yourself with other names for sugar, sodium, or fat content in packaged foods. Sugar may be listed as sucrose, glucose, zylose, fructose, mannose, and disaccharides or monosaccharides. Sodium is the main ingredient in monosodium glutamate (MSG), phosphates, nitrites, and baking soda as well as in table salt. Some manufacturers give the milligram content of sodium per serving. A product is considered high in sodium if it contains more than 350 to 500 milligrams per serving.

In general, the term "shortening," either animal or vegetable, implies that the fat is saturated, and the term "liquid vegetable oil" suggests a polyunsaturated fat. If the label lists "vegetable oil" as a main ingredient but does not specify the kind, or if it lists coconut or palm oil (high in saturated fat), it is best to avoid use of the product.

Food values of fast foods

Fast food	Calories	Protein (grams)	Carbohydrates (grams)	Fats (grams)	Sodium (mg)
Burger Chef Hamburger	258	26	39	31	962
Burger King French Fries	214	3	28	10	5
Burger King Vanilla Shake	332	11	50	11	159
Burger King Whaler	486	18	64	46	735
Burger King Whopper	606	29	51	32	909
Dairy Queen Banana Split	540	10	91	15	N.A.*
Dairy Queen Cheese Dog	330	15	24	19	N.A.*
Dairy Queen Onion Rings	300	6	33	17	N.A.*
Kentucky Fried Chicken Extra Crispy Dinner (3 pieces chicken)	950	52	63	54	1,915
Kentucky Fried Chicken Original Recipe Dinner	830	52	56	46	2,285
Long John Silver's Fish (2 pieces)	318	19	19	19	N.A.*
McDonald's Apple Pie	300	2	31	19	414
McDonald's Big Mac	541	26	39	31	962
McDonald's Chocolate Shake	364	11	60	9	329
McDonald's Egg McMuffin	352	18	26	20	914
McDonald's Filet-o-Fish	402	15	34	23	709
Pizza Hut Thick 'n Chewy Pepperoni Pizza (½ of 10-inch pie)	560	31	68	18	N.A.*
Pizza Hut Thin 'n Crispy Cheese Pizza (½ of 10-inch pie)	450	25	54	15	N.A.*
Taco Bell Taco	186	15	14	8	79
Arthur Treacher's Coleslaw	123	1	11	8	266
Arthur Treacher's Fish Sandwich	440	16	39	24	836

Source: Data supplied by the companies to the Senate Select Committee on Nutrition and Human Needs.
*N.A.—not available.

Health and Fitness

Watch your weight

As a nation we are becoming more obese, with the typical American adult male averaging 20 to 30 pounds of excess weight, and the typical female carrying 15 to 30 extra pounds. Overweight people are more likely to run the risk of high blood pressure, diabetes, high blood cholesterol, and heart disease.

To maintain ideal weight, it is necessary to keep your body energy needs in balance. Take in *more* energy than is needed and your body will store it as excess fat and you will gain weight. Take in *less* energy than is used up, and your body will withdraw some from the stored fat and you will lose weight. For the average person, it takes about 3500 extra calories to produce a pound of fat and, conversely, about 3500 fewer calories to use up a pound of stored fat. The easiest way to keep your weight constant is to lose any weight gain promptly, even if it is only 1 pound.

Ideal body weight may be determined by checking a table of suggested body weights. Such tables give no absolute answers on what constitutes ideal weight, but they can be helpful in determining your weight range.

Cut calories, not nutrients. There are almost as many diet plans as there are dieters. They embrace a variety of weight-loss theories: crash diets, liquid protein diets, cleansing and no-food diets, fruit juice, vegetable, or meat diets, high-fat and low-carbohydrate diets, low-fat and high-carbohydrate diets, to mention a few. To this list must be added the numerous reducing drugs that can be bought at the drugstore.

Many diet plans are nutritionally unbalanced. Most are disappointing as they seldom result in permanent weight loss. The repeated gaining, losing, and regaining of weight is considered by some health professionals to have a more damaging effect upon health than being consistently and moderately overweight. In sensible weight loss, you reduce your calorie intake without depriving your body of the nutrients needed for good health.

In the long run, the only diet that can do you real good is one that changes your bad eating habits for the better. The need is not for a 7-, or 10- or 21-day reducing plan, but a lifetime diet that includes all the

Metropolitan Life height and weight tables

Compared with figures as revised in 1959, this latest update on height and weight tables issued by the Metropolitan Life Insurance Company shows that adults can now weigh more than previously. There is an average increase in weight of 13 pounds for short men and 10 pounds for short women; 7 pounds for men of medium height, and 3 pounds for women of medium height; and 2 pounds for tall men, and 3 pounds for tall women. These tables apply to people from ages 25 to 59. The weight is stated in pounds, according to body frame size and the wearing of indoor clothing (5 pounds for men and 3 pounds for women in shoes with 1-inch heels).

Men Height	Small frame	Medium frame	Large frame	Women Height	Small frame	Medium frame	Large frame
5' 2"	128–134	131–141	138–150	4' 10"	102–111	109–121	118–131
5' 3"	130–136	133–143	140–153	4' 11"	103–113	111–123	120–134
5' 4"	132–138	135–145	142–156	5' 0"	104–115	113–126	122–137
5' 5"	134–140	137–148	144–160	5' 1"	106–118	115–129	125–140
5' 6"	136–142	139–151	146–164	5' 2"	108–121	118–132	128–143
5' 7"	138–145	142–154	149–168	5' 3"	111–124	121–135	131–147
5' 8"	140–148	145–157	152–172	5' 4"	114–127	124–138	134–151
5' 9"	142–151	148–160	155–176	5' 5"	117–130	127–141	137–155
5' 10"	144–154	151–163	158–180	5' 6"	120–133	130–144	140–159
5' 11"	146–157	154–166	161–184	5' 7"	123–136	133–147	143–163
6' 0"	149–160	157–170	164–188	5' 8"	126–139	136–150	146–167
6' 1"	152–164	160–174	168–192	5' 9"	129–142	139–153	149–170
6' 2"	155–168	164–178	172–197	5' 10"	132–145	142–156	152–173
6' 3"	158–172	167–182	176–202	5' 11"	135–148	145–159	155–176
6' 4"	162–176	171–187	181–207	6' 0"	138–151	148–162	158–179

© 1983 Metropolitan Life Insurance Company/Source of basic data 1979 Build Study, Society of Actuaries and Association of Life Insurance Medical Directors of America, 1980.

essential nutrients obtained from a variety of foods. It is never too late to correct faulty eating habits, and by doing so you can help children learn good eating habits as they grow up.

To gain weight, add calories.

To those who are forever fighting the battle of the midriff bulge, putting on extra pounds may seem to be an easy task. Such, however, is not always the case. Some people are naturally thin because of their inherited body build; others cannot put on weight no matter how much food rich in calories they consume. In some cases, medical problems such as hyperthyroidism or diabetes must be corrected before considering a program to gain weight.

If you are underweight, it may be due to faulty eating habits, or just eating too little food. You may not have a good appetite, which in itself may signal an underlying illness, and you may also suffer from poor digestion and absorption of food. A physical checkup may be needed to determine the cause of being underweight, or having continued weight loss, before deciding on the measures necessary to assure weight gain.

In general, a person who desires to gain weight needs to eat more nutritious food and to increase the total number of calories in the daily diet. Proper living habits are important, too: eat regular meals, take mild exercise, get sufficient sleep, and avoid tension.

Fact or fiction?

You can shed pounds by skipping breakfast.
Fiction. Breakfast should be your first meal of the day, providing essential nutrients to assure body function at a high level of energy. Without breakfast, you may be tempted to snack between meals, or eat too much at the next meal.

The more exercise, the bigger the appetite.
Fiction. You will not only use up calories with regular moderate exercise, but you will keep physically fit. In many cases, inactivity is a main reason for obesity in children as well as adults.

You can lose ten pounds in ten days.
Fact. This is possible, but it will probably be mostly a water loss, which will be quickly replaced once you go off the crash diet. A sound weight loss program recommends a slow, sure loss of 1 or 2 pounds a week.

With determination, everyone can reduce.
Fact. People who claim they cannot lose weight are usually themselves at fault. Many persons do not eat to appease hunger, but to satisfy a craving. Hunger signals the body's need for food; appetite, based on remembered eating pleasures, is a desire for certain types of food.

Food for thought

If you eat . . .	you add on . . .	to lose, you must walk
2 strips of bacon	100 calories	20 minutes
10 potato chips	100 calories	20 minutes
1 doughnut	150 calories	29 minutes
1 piece cake	358 calories	68 minutes
1 slice apple pie	375 calories	73 minutes
1 malted milk shake	500 calories	97 minutes

Substitute . . . burn off more calories. By substituting one ingredient for another in the preparation of food, and eating one type of food for another, you can reduce your total calorie intake. An ounce of pure protein or carbohydrate will produce 110 calories; an ounce of fat will supply 250 calories. These figures may help you calculate your own calorie intake from a meal or dietary plan.

Food preparation Instead of . . .	Substitute	Food consumption Instead of . . .	Substitute . . .	Saved calories
whole milk	skim milk	2 tbsp. regular mayonnaise	2 tbsp. diet mayonnaise	about 150
cream	evaporated milk	1 cup ice cream	1 cup ice milk	about 90
sour cream	yogurt	1 regular hamburger	1 lean hamburger	about 76
cream cheese	low-fat cottage cheese	1 serving French fries	1 baked potato	about 200
whole milk cheese	skim-milk or low-fat cheese	1 can (6½ oz.) tuna, oil-packed, drained	1 can (6½ oz.) tuna water-packed, drained	about 100

Health and Fitness

Get back into shape

Moderate and regular exercise, which is good for you at any time of life, is doubly important when losing weight. It can help your body burn up unwanted fat faster while firming up muscles and flattening out bulges. Physical activity can also keep your body flexible, and help maintain muscle tone, stimulate body functions, especially the circulatory and respiratory systems, and help relieve tension.

To keep physically fit, you need not take up strenuous exercise or a demanding sport. If you make a conscious effort, you can even find plenty of opportunity to stretch and bend while you are doing some everyday task—dusting, sweeping, making the beds, weeding the garden, doing small repair jobs around the house.

Choose an exercise that you enjoy, and one suited to your physical condition, body build, age, and lifestyle. While you will benefit little from doing exercise in a lax manner, you should not overexercise to the point of physical pain or injury.

Exercise works. Walking is an excellent form of exercise, considered by health authorities to be the best overall nonstrenuous activity for the heart and legs. All you need is a comfortable pair of walking shoes. *A brisk 20- to 30-minute walk each day can help you take weight off and keep it off.*

Swimming, jogging, or bicycling are exercises that develop a strong heart, while calisthenics and gymnastics improve strength, agility, and muscle tone. Whatever your choice of activity, it is important to remember that it will only be beneficial and improve your state of health if you stick with it.

Energy expenditures

This table gives approximate energy expenditures by a 150-pound person in various activities.

Activity	*Calories per hour*
Bicycling, 5½ mph	210
Bicycling, 13 mph	660
Bowling	270
Domestic work	180
Driving an automobile	120
Gardening	220
Golf	250
Lawn mowing (power mower)	250
Lying down or sleeping	80
Roller skating	350
Running, 10 mph	900
Sitting	100
Skiing, 10 mph	600
Square dancing	350
Squash and handball	600
Standing	140
Swimming, ¼ mph	300
Tennis	420
Volleyball	350
Walking, 2½ mph	210
Walking, 3¾ mph	300
Wood chopping or sawing	400

Source: Based on material prepared by Robert E. Johnson, M.D., Ph.D., and colleagues, University of Illinois.

HEALTH CARE ALERT
ARTHRITIS

There are many forms of arthritis but, in general, sufferers are afflicted with either osteoarthritis or rheumatoid arthritis. Osteoarthritis takes a decade or longer to develop, so most sufferers are at least middle-aged. In this condition, the protective cartilage normally cushioning a joint begins to break down, causing pain and stiffness, and inflammation in some cases.

Rheumatoid arthritis (RA), unlike osteoarthritis, strikes children and young adults as well as older adults. In this arthritic disorder, the body's immune system (defense network) goes haywire and turns on the body itself. There is pain and recurrent inflammation. RA can be severely crippling.

Do not ignore these signals.
Medical care in the early stages of arthritis can often lessen the permanent damage to diseased joints. If you experience any of the symptoms listed below for more than two weeks, check with your physician.
- Swelling in one or more joints.
- Recurring pain or tenderness in any body joint.
- Inability to move a joint properly, or to perform normal activities.
- Obvious redness and warmth in one of the joints.
- Persistent early morning pain and stiffness in joints. Unexplained weight loss, fever, weakness, or fatigue combined with joint pain.

Health and Fitness

Home medical testing

Medical tests help to determine the cause of pain or disease, and in themselves become meaningful only after your physician has studied them in the light of your complete medical history. There are any number of medical tests that can be performed at home. Some require nothing more than close observation, while others, such as various urine tests, require certain medical supplies (which can be purchased at a local pharmacy), and a knowledge of how the tests should be performed. Still others, such as taking your blood pressure, call for the purchase of special equipment and must be carefully performed to be useful. Before buying medical supplies or equipment, it is advisable to check with your doctor to see if there is any drawback to home testing and to obtain detailed instructions on performing a test correctly.

Home medical testing should not be regarded as a means of making a self-diagnosis, or instituting self-treatment. Any body signals, such as persistent pain, unexplained bleeding, skin or other growths, difficulties in breathing, seeing, or hearing, or uncoordinated movements, should be promptly brought to the attention of your physician.

The tests included in this discussion do not call for the purchase of special supplies or equipment. They are intended to help you learn more about your own or your family's health, and to communicate more effectively with your doctor if a medical problem arises.

Two important tests

Taking your pulse. Pulse measurements generally consist of rate, rhythm, and character. The most frequently used location is the wrist. With the palm up, place two or three fingers of the examining hand on the thumb side of the wrist being examined. Do *not* use the thumb, and be careful not to apply too much pressure.

Rest for ten minutes before taking your pulse, and then take it in a sitting position. To begin with, you may want to count the pulse beats for a full minute, timing them by the second hand of a watch. As you become more experienced, you can shorten the time to half a minute, and then 15 seconds, multiplying the result by four. Normal pulse rates may range from 60 to 70 beats per minute for men and from 70 to 80 beats per minute for women. Wide variations in pulse rate, or a weak or irregular pulse, should be checked out with your doctor. Pulse rhythm may be observed at the

same time that the pulse rate is being counted. It should be regular without pauses; that is, there should be no skipped beats or extra beats between normal beats. Pulse character is determined by the smoothness of the beat: no beat should be any stronger or weaker than any of the others.

Testing your sense of smell. This type of test is more useful than it may seem at first. There are many people who live in danger of serious harm because they are unable to detect the odor that accompanies spoiled or contaminated foods, smoke from fire, escaping gas from a heating apparatus, and lethal chemical fumes.

Gather together at least three items with familiar odors, such as an onion or garlic, milk chocolate, turpentine, fresh flowers with a distinctive scent (roses, lilacs), and a burning paper match, or burning paper in an ashtray. With the exception of the burning match and paper, the items are best tested by being enclosed in a tightly closed container, and then opened for a few seconds when the test is being made.

Before starting, make certain that your nasal passages are clear. Then, begin the test by closing one nostril (apply pressure to it with a finger). Close your eyes, and smell the odor being tested through the open nostril; repeat with the other nostril. Both sides of the nose should be able to smell the tested odors with equal efficiency.

Health and Fitness

Glossary

fructose sources

Blood pressure readings

Pressure is written as a fraction: $^{120}/_{80}$ mm Hg, or 120 over 80 millimeters of mercury, which is generally regarded as an average normal pressure in an adult. The higher figure is the systolic pressure, when the heart contracts. The lower figure is the diastolic pressure, when the heart relaxes between beats. Blood pressure that consistently remains at $^{140}/_{90}$ or higher is considered to be high blood pressure, requiring medical attention.

High blood pressure is often called the silent disease, because it produces no specific symptoms and many people are unaware that they have it. You should have your blood pressure checked regularly.

For definitions of additional medical terms, see Glossary on page 96.

angina pectoris. Painful oppression about the heart which is usually severe and radiates from the heart to the shoulder and down the left arm.

antioxidant. An agent inhibiting oxidation and thereby preventing oils or fats from becoming rancid through the process of oxidation.

aromatic. The series of carbon compounds in which the carbon atoms form closed rings, such as benzene.

arthritis. An inflammatory condition of the joints in which there is usually pain and changes in structure.

asthma. A term generally used to mean bronchial asthma, which is a condition of the lungs having widespread narrowing of the airways.

calorie. The energy value of foods, calculated by the amount of heat needed to raise one kilogram of water through 1° C, a kilocalorie.

carbohydrates. Sugar; saccharides. A class of organic compounds in which hydrogen and oxygen are in the same ratio as they are in water.

cells. Minute structures that are the physical basis of all plant and animal life processes.

cellulose. A plant fiber, or fibrous form of carbohydrate, which aids peristaltic stimulation and intestinal elimination.

cholesterol. A sterol (fatlike substance) widely distributed in animal tissues, and occurring in egg yolk, various oils, fats, and nerve tissue (brain and spinal cord).

cornea. A transparent membrane that is part of the outer coat of the eyeball.

degenerative. The state in which a body part or organ becomes impaired or deteriorates.

disaccharides. One of a group of carbohydrates, dissacharose is a complex sugar that may be split into two molecules of monosaccharides.

DNA (deoxyribonucleic acid). A nucleic acid that is found in chromosomes of the nuclei of cells. It is considered to be the carrier of genetic information and the chemical basis of heredity.

enzymes. Complex proteins that are capable of inducing chemical changes in other substances without themselves becoming altered in the process.

fructose. Levulose; a fruit sugar found in corn syrup, honey, and fruit juices. Produces glycogen and maintains normal glucose content in the blood.

glaucoma. Eye disease marked by increased pressure in the eye that results in atrophy of the optic nerve and blindness.

glucose. A sugar that is formed during digestion. It is the most important carbohydrate in body metabolism.

glycogen. A polysaccharide, it is the main carbohydrate reserve in the body that is readily converted into sugar.

goiter. An enlargement of the thyroid gland.

hydrocarbon. A compound made up only of hydrogen and carbon.

hydrogenation. Adding hydrogen to a compound, especially to an unsaturated fat. In this way, soft fats or oils are solidified or "hardened."

hypertension. Condition in which a person has higher blood pressure than is considered to be normal.

mannose. An aldohexose (sugar) obtained from various plant sources: mannons (various legumes).

76   Health and Fitness

monosaccharide. A simple sugar (fructose, galactose, glucose) that is absorbed directly. It maintains the glucose content of the blood and aids in the production of glycogen.

monosodium glutamate. Sodium salt of glutamic acid; a white crystalline substance with a meatlike taste. It is used to flavor foods.

myoglobin. Muscle protein that transports oxygen, similar in function to blood hemoglobin.

nitrosamines. A combination of nitrites with a type of organic chemical in food known as amines. Nitrosamines are potent cancer-causing substances.

nutrient. A food supplying the body with essential elements. Carbohydrates, proteins, and alcohol provide energy. Water, electrolytes (acids, bases, salts), minerals, and vitamins are needed for metabolism.

nutrition. The taking in and utilization of food substances for body growth, repair, and maintenance. Successive stages are known as digestion, absorption, metabolism (assimilation), and excretion.

osteomalacia. A disease that is marked by increased softening of the bone. This makes bone flexible and brittle, resulting in deformities.

pectin. Plant carbohydrate that forms a gelatinous mass in the cooking of fruits and vegetables, causing them to jell.

polysaccharide. One of a group of carbohydrates that, upon hydrolysis, yields more than two molecules of simple sugars.

polyunsaturated. Refers to long-chain carbon compounds, especially fats that have many carbon atoms joined by double or triple bonds.

saccharides. A group of carbohydrates (including sugars) that is divided into these classifications: monosaccharides, disaccharides, trisaccharides, and polysaccharides.

saturated. Carbon compounds in which all the atoms are linked by single bonds.

sodium. Sodium salts are found in body fluids, serum, blood, lymph, and tissues. These salts are needed to maintain a balance between calcium and potassium for normal heart function, and for equilibrium of the body.

synthesis. In general, this is the process involved in the formation of a complex substance from simpler elements or compounds; for example, the synthesis of proteins from amino acids.

HEALTH CARE ALERT

DIABETES

In this disorder, the body does not make proper use of sugar. Sugar, derived from the food we eat, is an important fuel needed by the body to supply energy. Normally, insulin (a substance made in the pancreas) allows sugar to reach the muscles, fat, and other tissues and be burned to produce energy. In diabetes, there is not enough insulin; consequently, the sugar cannot enter the tissues.

Diabetes is found most often in persons who have a relative with diabetes, are overweight, or elderly. In some cases, adults become diabetic without developing any symptoms.

Signals of diabetes

Check with your doctor if you notice any of the following symptoms:
1. Excessive thirst
2. Increased appetite
3. Frequent urination
4. Itching of the skin, especially the genital area
5. Weakness and tiredness
6. Weight loss
7. Pain, numbness, or tingling in the hands and feet
8. Disturbances of vision
9. Irritability, nervousness, or nausea

For further reference

Bright, Deborah
  Creative Relaxation: Turning Your Stress Into Positive Energy
  Harcourt Brace Jovanovich
Brody, Jane
  Nutrition Book: A Lifetime Guide
  W. W. Norton & Company
Calabrese, E. J. and Dorsey, Michael W.
  Healthy Living in an Unhealthy World
  Simon & Schuster
Davis, Adelle
  Let's Stay Healthy: A Guide to Lifelong Nutrition
  Harcourt Brace Jovanovich

Schroeder, Henry A.
  The Trace Minerals and Man: Some Positive and Negative Aspects
  The Devin-Adair Company
Tubesing, D.A.
  Kicking Your Stress Habits: A Do-It-Yourself Guide for Coping With Stress
  Whole Person Associates
Wenck, D. A.
  A Supermarket Nutrition
  Reston Publishing Company
Wentzler, R.
  The Vitamin Book: A Complete Guide to Vitamins, Minerals and Essential Nutrients
  Gramercy Publishing Company

Health and Fitness

You and Modern Medicine

- You and the doctor 78
- You and the hospital 82
- You and emergency rooms 85
- You and drugs 87
- Your mental health 92
- Medical payments 95
- Glossary 96

There are doctors practicing today who have never seen a case of polio, smallpox, typhoid, childbed fever, or any number of other diseases that devastated human society in the past. As a generation, our life expectancy is longer than that of any other generation in history. Organ transplants and miraculous surgical techniques seem to promise an even brighter future.

We also live in a time when technology has outrun man's ability to absorb its implications or to use it safely and wisely. Life-saving devices are frequently perverted into death-prolonging machinery. Drugs proliferate at a rate beyond the ordinary doctor's capability to use them. Medical costs have skyrocketed, giving us the most expensive system in the world, with many of us living in dread of a catastrophic illness that could bankrupt us.

The average American is caught in the middle. This chapter is a guide for those consumers of medical services who wish to take better control of their lives and to use the medical system to their advantage.

You and the doctor

A doctor is an ordinary human being, highly and expensively trained to treat disease. He sees himself as a saver of lives. All of his training has led him to expect unquestioning obedience from his own staff, hospital personnel, and his patients.

In the past, most patients agreed that "doctor knows best," but as specialization and technology have eroded the patient-doctor relationship, many have begun to ask questions.

Recent court decisions have affirmed patients' right to know and right to informed consent. Informed consent means that the doctor must not only tell his patient what he proposes as treatment, but must make sure that the patient truly understands. A consent form, read and signed, is not enough.

Not all doctors are comfortable with this arrangement, and not all patients are ready to give up a dependent relationship.

When to look for a doctor. The key to good medical care is having a competent, knowledgeable, well-trained primary care physician. Many people postpone finding such a doctor for years. They use an orthopedist if they break a bone, or consult a dermatologist for skin problems. It is only when they become seriously ill that they begin the search. This is the very worst time to look.

A primary care physician has the opportunity to know his patients, their families, and their lifestyles. He is the logical keeper of medical records, an invaluable go-between in the mystifying world of specialists, an important member of the hospital treatment team, and more likely to treat the whole person than just the disease.

The hole left by the disappearing general practitioner is being filled by a growing number of young doctors who choose "family practice" as their specialty. The general internist also serves as a primary care physician. Pediatricians are primary care doctors for children.

How to find a doctor.

Talking to as many people as possible is a good beginning in finding the right doctor. Since other doctors and medical associations are rarely frank about their fellow professionals, the most reliable source of information about doctors are friends, neighbors, storekeepers, pharmacists, and nurses.

Once a tentative list of names is compiled, *The American Medical Directory* (available in libraries) and your local medical association can be consulted about medical schools, medical degrees, board certification, and hospital affiliations.

Particular attention should be paid to the hospital affiliations of doctors under consideration. You should be sure that the doctor you choose is entitled to admit patients to the hospital you determine to be the best in your community.

When the list of doctors has been narrowed to one or two, it is time to make an appointment with the doctor who sounds most promising.

A good strategy is to make a list of things you wish to observe and learn. Time and extent of office hours, who takes over when the doctor is not available, and how he can be reached in an emergency should be among the items on the list. You will want to inquire about fees, and how and when they are payable. Women will ask whether the doctor handles routine gynecological matters, and people with children will ask at what age their children will be accepted as patients.

How a doctor's office is run can affect the quality of medical care. A crowded waiting room may mean poor scheduling. The amount of time you are kept waiting on your first visit probably will not change. Only you can decide what your limits are.

A concerned, courteous, and helpful office staff is an important link between patient and doctor. An arrogant, disinterested, or rude staff can put a real stumbling block in the way of your getting the most for your medical dollar.

Getting the most from a doctor.

A successful patient is one who has reasonable expectations from his doctor; who learns as much as he can

Do not lie to the doctor

Many people have things in their lives that they do not want anyone to know about. These things should not be kept from the doctor. Drinking more than just occasionally is a habit he needs to know about—not only because of its possible effect on physical health, but because it can influence the kinds of medications he may safely prescribe. A three-pack-a-day smoker should own up, as should users of drugs, even recreationally. Venereal diseases are treatable but not if you are too embarrassed to describe your symptoms. If you are not comfortable discussing such things with your doctor, you should not hesitate to change to someone you are comfortable with.

It is not uncommon for a patient to accept a prescription and then, for some reason, not use it. The doctor should know about this, too. Consulting another doctor when not satisfied is a mistake only when you fail to tell your own doctor in advance.

You and Modern Medicine

You and your doctor are partners in the enterprise of recovering your health. Like all successful partnerships, it requires mutual trust.

about his own illness and treatment; and who follows instructions or informs his doctor when he is not doing so and why. He gets to know the office nurse and talks frankly and openly to her about why he is calling and what he expects from the phone call. He learns to be explicit and insistent with the answering service, and he also learns the value of an early call when he is feeling ill (perhaps making it easier for him to place a call in the middle of the night). A combination of assertiveness and consideration is as effective in dealing with a doctor as it is in dealing with the rest of the world.

When to change doctors.

A continuing feeling of dissatisfaction is a valid reason for changing doctors. The frequent changing of doctors is deplored by the medical profession, and may be an indication that the patient has unrealistic expectations;

When to call the doctor

People are often reluctant to call the doctor for fear of being either a nuisance or an alarmist. There are symptoms that call for an immediate call to the doctor and an immediate response from him.

Symptoms to take seriously
- Chest pain; sudden rapid or irregular pulse
- Difficulty in breathing
- Sudden coughing up of blood
- Severe nosebleed
- Inability to urinate or defecate
- Sudden and profuse vaginal bleeding
- Severe abdominal pain
- Blood in the stool
- Uncontrollable vomiting or diarrhea
- Inability to swallow
- Sudden loss of vision
- Eye pain or double vision
- Loss of balance, hearing, or sudden weakness
- Mental confusion, fainting, or vertigo
- Headache accompanied by stiff neck
- Very high or very low temperature

GET A SECOND OPINION!

Surgery is not always the only effective treatment. Check with another qualified surgeon before agreeing to even minor surgery.

however, when needs are not being met, it is time for a change.

In the case of doctor error, each case should be decided on its own merits. A mistake that is freely acknowledged and does not represent a pattern of carelessness is not necessarily a reason for change. An error that is life-threatening may permanently shake our confidence, however, and make a change advisable.

Do you need a specialist?

The decision to consult a specialist should always be made after consultation with your primary care doctor. A referral from him will insure that you are seeing someone whose competence he trusts, and that your care will continue in the hands of someone *you* trust.

A consultation with a specialist does not mean that you will continue to see him on an extended basis. Although your internist may wish you to see a cardiologist for diagnosis of a heart problem, he is quite capable of monitoring and managing heart conditions himself. Not only will this make you more comfortable; it will save you money as well because internists' fees are usually lower than those of specialists.

What about surgery?

Surgeons not only save lives but improve the quality of life for many people. They also are rather single-minded in that they are inclined to think only in terms of surgical procedures, frequently rejecting alternative methods of treatment. Since even minor surgery can be hazardous, the patient and his primary care doctor must be on guard against unnecessary surgery.

Many insurance companies now require and pay for a second opinion when surgery is recommended. There are certain operations that are widely considered to be overperformed. If any of the operations listed below are advised, it is wise to ask for a second opinion.

Overused surgical procedures. These operations, which used to be considered more or less routine, are often thought to be unnecessary today. As with any operation, be sure you get the very best advice before proceeding with:

Hysterectomy	Gallbladder removal
Oophorectomy	Radical mastectomy
(removal of ovaries)	Dilation and curettage
Tonsillectomy	Caesarean section

Doctors: Who they are and what they do

Primary care
Family Practitioner. Receives additional training in family medicine. Replaces old general practitioner. Provides care from birth to death.
Internist. Not to be confused with intern, a recent medical school graduate. Practices "internal medicine." Training qualifies him to care for adult patients in all matters that do not require surgery.
Pediatrician. Trained to deliver primary care to children from infancy to adolescence.

Specialists
Allergist. Treats such diseases as asthma, hay fever, or skin allergy.
Anesthesiologist. Administers anesthetics, or pain killers, during an operation.
Cardiologist. Highly trained to treat complicated diseases of the heart and blood vessels.
Dermatologist. Specializes in diseases of the skin.
Endocrinologist. Deals with disorders of the glandular system.
Gastroenterologist. Treats diseases of the digestive organs—esophagus, stomach, bowels, liver, and pancreas.
Gerontologist. Deals with aging and the problems of old people.
Hematologist. Expert in diseases of the blood.
Infectious Disease Specialist. Helps treat patients with serious or baffling diseases.
Nephrologist. Specializes in diseases of the kidney.
Neurologist. Qualified to treat illnesses of the nervous system.
Obstetrician/Gynecologist. Manages pregnancies, delivers babies, and handles problems concerning the reproductive organs of women.
Oculist. Deals with diseases of the eye.
Oncologist. Treats malignancies; decides on appropriate treatment and administers it.
Pulmonary Specialist. Treats diseases of the lungs; performs pulmonary function tests and bronchoscopy.
Radiologist. Gives and interprets x-ray photographs.
Rheumatologist. Cares for patients with diseases of the joints, and treats diseases such as rheumatoid arthritis, systemic lupus erythematosus, and scleroderma.

Nonmedical Specialists
Osteopath. Licensed to practice medicine and perform surgery, specializes in musculoskeletal manipulation.
Chiropractor. Licensed in most states to practice a system of manipulation of the spine.
Optometrist. Tests the eye for defective vision in order to prescribe corrective lenses.
Podiatrist. Trained in a four-year program as a specialist in disorders of the feet. Admitted to practice in many hospitals, but usually treat and operate on an outpatient basis.

Surgeons
General. Trained to perform abdominal, gynecological, and vascular surgery. In most urban areas, removes gallbladders, appendixes, moles, and cysts. Performs hysterectomies and repairs hernias.
Cardiac. Performs heart surgery such as coronary bypass and grafts. Removes aortic aneurysms.
Neurosurgeon. Operates on brain and spinal tumors, performs back surgery, repairs carotid arteries.
Obstetric/Gynecologic. Performs surgery related to the female reproductive system.
Ophthalmologic. Eye surgeons. Will also treat diseases of the eye.
Orthopedic. Sets bones, replaces joints, pins hips, and cares for traumatic injuries.
Otolaryngologic. Ear, nose, and throat.
Plastic. Performs both cosmetic and reconstructive surgery.
Urologic. Operates on the prostate, scrotum, bladder, and kidneys.

You and Modern Medicine

You and the hospital

The modern hospital is a remarkable place. It is a scene of human drama, where lives are saved, pain is eased, babies are born, and people die. The hospital is also a place where serious errors in treatment may be made, where unnecessary surgery may be performed, where technology may prolong life when there is no hope for survival, and where even strong-minded individuals are reduced to childlike dependency.

Increasingly, doctors and insurance companies recognize the advantages of limiting hospital stays, not only to save money for the patient and his insurer, but to assure the ultimate well-being of the individual.

Before you go. When the doctor recommends putting you in the hospital, it is time to ask serious questions and to make sure they are answered satisfactorily. Are there alternatives? What are the benefits? What are the risks? Is it an emergency? Can it be postponed? Is a second opinion advisable? How long will I be there?

Frequently, hospitalization is suggested by a specialist, and it may be wise to postpone decisions until you have discussed the situation with your primary care doctor.

Which hospital to choose. Factors such as what is available in the community, where your doctor has admission privileges, or where an ambulance takes you after an accident often limit your choices. Large and famous is not always better. Open heart surgery is probably best performed in a large medical center where there is a concentration of specific skills and experience; the gallbladder patient, however, may actually receive better care in a small community hospital.

Although differences may be blurred in specific cases, the kinds of hospitals can be categorized:

Teaching hospitals are connected with medical schools, are usually large, and are staffed by students, residents, and doctors who both teach and attend patients.

Public hospitals are the large institutions funded by local, county, state, or federal governments. They also have interns, residents, and a permanent medical staff.

Private and community hospitals are usually operated on a not-for-profit basis. They may or may not have a house staff, and they are operated for the convenience of the doctors who admit patients.

Nursing and convalescent homes are designed for patients who no longer need full medical facilities and who cannot be cared for at home.

There are no simple guidelines, but a little research into available facilities, before they are needed, will help a great deal. Nursing homes, particularly, should be investigated in advance. When you visit, talk with patients and their families. Ask your own doctor if a particular home is a place he recommends.

Your decision is made. Before packing a bag and finding your health insurance card, choose a member of your family or a close friend to act as your personal advocate during your stay in the hospital. When the person in the admitting office asks for "next of kin," give the name of the person you wish to serve as advocate. If the hospital requires further authorization, you will be informed at that time. Your advocate will be able to keep track of your treatment, ask questions on your behalf, register legitimate complaints, and stand between you and hospital bureaucracy.

Defend against hospital error. Most people emerge from the hospital in better health than when they went in. Usually, their most serious complaints deal with the food or difficulty in sleeping.

Can you stay out of the hospital?	How to help yourself in the hospital
1. Not all surgery requires hospitalization. 2. Many tests and procedures can be performed on an outpatient basis. 3. Many kinds of medical care can be delivered at home through the use of community services. 4. Families of the terminally ill have more options as a result of the hospice movement and changing attitudes toward care of the dying.	*Ask questions!* *Do not remain ignorant of what is being done for you.* 1. Make sure you get the right medication. 2. Make sure you get your medication on time. 3. Make sure you get the right tests—not someone else's tests. 4. Make sure you get the food your doctor ordered for you.

However, wrong medications, wrong tests, and needless exposure to invasive procedures are all hazards.

Patients are not helpless. The person who constantly asks questions or has his personal advocate ask them in his behalf is putting up a good defense against error. No procedure, test, or medication should come as a surprise—it could be meant for someone else. Make a point of knowing your medication schedule; if medication does not come on time, ask for it. If it is new or unfamiliar, make sure that it is intended for you.

If you have been told to take nothing by mouth prior to surgery or a diagnostic test, do not assume that the arrival of your breakfast tray means that someone has changed his mind.

What to pack for your stay.
As an antidote to the loss of identity that usually occurs when you walk through hospital doors, take part of your home with you: snapshots, a favorite bathrobe, even if it is old, your own cosmetics, deodorant, shaving cream, and toothpaste. Leave valuables at home, but you may want to take a small battery-run radio with earphones. Arrange to have your favorite newspaper delivered. Maintaining a sense of your own personality will help you to stand up for yourself and to make the best use of the facilities that exist to restore you to health.

Be sure to take some of your personal belongings to the hospital. Do not forget your eye glasses so that you can read or watch television.

When you get there.
Checking into a hospital used to be an interminable ordeal. Today, many hospitals arrange for blood tests, x-rays, urine analyses, and many diagnostic tests to be done well in advance of admission. The vast amount of preadmission paperwork is handled by the admitting office before you arrive. This has worked to shorten hospital stays and has nearly eliminated those weekend admissions that once resulted in a patient's being tucked into a very expensive hospital bed days in advance of his need for it.

The Patient's Bill of Rights

The patient has a right to:

- **Complete, current information** concerning his diagnosis, treatment, and prognosis in terms he can understand.

- **Information necessary to give informed consent** prior to any medical procedures, except in emergencies, including knowledge of significant risks, duration of incapacitation, alternatives for care or treatment, and the names of persons who will perform the procedures.

- **Refuse treatment** to the extent permitted by law, and to be informed of the medical consequences of refusal.

- **Privacy** concerning medical care, diagnosis, and records.

- **Reasonable response** to requests for services.

- **Not be transferred** to another facility without his permission.

- **Be advised** if treatment involves human experimentation.

- **Refuse** such experimentation.

- **Continuity** of care following discharge.

- **Examine** and receive an explanation of charges regardless of source of payment.

—excerpted from a document prepared by the American Hospital Association

You and Modern Medicine

What about all those tests?

As diagnostic techniques have improved and expanded, and words like "CAT scan" and "sonogram" have entered ordinary language, doctors have an increasingly difficult time knowing when to stop testing. Hospitals have enormous sums of money invested in machinery; the way to pay for them is to charge for their use.

Another factor in overtesting is the doctor's real fear of malpractice suits. This seems to be a byproduct of overspecialization on the part of the medical profession. A patient who has developed a comfortable and trusting relationship with his doctor rarely sues, even when things go wrong.

You and your primary doctor can work together to ensure that you get only those tests that are absolutely necessary. High-risk, invasive procedures, such as arteriograms or surgical biopsies, require especially careful consideration. They will not be performed without your consent, but before giving that consent be sure to ask about benefits, risks, and alternatives.

New computer-aided testing equipment has made the diagnosis of illness more reliable. This is an ultrasound image of the heart at work.

What they mean when they say . . .

CAT scan	(Computerized tomography) An x-ray technique that photographs cross-sections of the body. Normal x-rays produce pictures that are flat, like a photograph; the CAT scan sends rays through the body that are picked up by a scanner, fed into a computer, and visualized on a screen. This procedure has eliminated many complicated and high-risk tests.
Sonogram	(Ultrasound examination) High-frequency sound waves are directed at the body; the echoes are received on a TV screen and recorded photographically. This procedure is often performed in the last trimester of pregnancy to determine the position and health of the fetus.
EEG	(Electroencephalogram) Electrodes are glued to the scalp, and the electrical activity of the brain is painlessly recorded.
EKG	(Electrocardiogram) A machine records the electrical activity of the heart. It gives information about heartbeat, the strength of the heart, and the location of any injury. A stress test is an EKG given while the patient is exercising.
Spinal tap	(Lumbar puncture) A small amount of fluid is drawn from the spinal column to test the internal pressure or to provide a sample for laboratory testing.
Biopsy	A surgical procedure, often performed under a local anesthetic, in which a small amount of tissue is obtained for laboratory study.
GI series	(Upper and lower) X-ray pictures are taken of the digestive tract after the introduction of barium, by mouth or by enema, to make the tract visible.
Amniocentesis	Fluid is drawn from the amniotic sac surrounding the fetus during the end of the first trimester of pregnancy. Cells grown in the laboratory provide information about such genetic defects as Down's syndrome.

You and emergency rooms

Some emergency rooms are little more than first-aid stations with a nurse on duty and a doctor on call; others are full-scale trauma centers attached to major medical centers. The average emergency room falls somewhere in between. Locating and evaluating emergency rooms in your immediate area could save a life. The closest place to go is not always the best place to go in a true emergency.

What to look for. A well-run emergency room is staffed around the clock by doctors trained in emergency medicine. If there is not a permanent house staff, specialists are on call. Emergency rooms attached to good hospitals have access to cardiac and intensive care units; these can assume great importance for patients needing such care.

A talk with your doctor about nearby facilities should prove helpful; your choice will be governed by his hospital affiliations whenever possible.

Before you go. No matter how serious the emergency, a cool head is essential. A call to your own doctor for his help in evaluating the seriousness of the emergency is wise. His call to the emergency room—warning them that you are on the way and ordering whatever tests or treatments he thinks necessary—will cut a lot of red tape and assure fast attention. If you cannot reach your doctor before leaving, have the hospital call him on arrival.

In the face of an emergency, calling an ambulance is almost a reflex action. When there is a suspected heart attack, poisoning, severe pain, impaired breathing, or any condition in which rapid medical help is essential, it is best to use whatever transportation is available—personal car, taxi, or police car. Many police departments have trained their officers in basic first aid and equipped their cars with life-saving apparatuses.

If there is time, locate insurance cards, regular medication, and, in the case of poisoning or drug overdose, the original container the substance came in. If there is not enough time, a neighbor or a friend can follow soon after with the appropriate information.

DO NOT BE TIMID!

Remember to leave tact and good manners at home. An emergency room is no place to assume automatically that somebody else knows best or to let consideration of other people sway your judgment. If you know that the condition is serious, do whatever is necessary to make sure that the doctor and nurses know it too.

When you get there. At a glance, the average emergency room looks like a scene of total chaos. Despite appearances, there *is* a system functioning called "triage." This means that a nurse, a doctor, or other emergency room personnel will determine who will have first call on limited facilities and personnel. Top priority is assigned to patients with suspected heart attacks, seriously injured accident victims, cases of poisoning or drug overdose, or those in need of immediate attention.

Although many people tell horror stories about interminable hours spent waiting for attention, as a rule those who need help the most get it the quickest. To the parent of an hysterical child who has suffered a non-life-threatening injury, the system may seem unfair and insensitive. But remember, the person in charge must balance urgent need against discomfort and inconvenience.

Children and emergencies. Mothers of large families may, when the children are grown up, swear that they spent most of their children's younger years in one emergency room or another. The most common reasons for these trips are accidents, poisoning, and difficulties in breathing.

Often there seems to be a conflict of interest between medical personnel and parents. No child should be left unattended by a familiar adult or made to go through

---

True emergencies

- Severe and uncontrolled bleeding
- Serious difficulty in breathing
- Choking
- Poisoning
- Severe chest pain
- Convulsions
- Heat stroke
- Unconsciousness
- Severe injuries
- Stabbing or bullet wounds, severe burns
- Diabetic acidosis or shock from hypoglycemia
- Hypothermia

You and Modern Medicine

any procedure alone. Parents are often asked to leave the room in the interest of the child's welfare. The answer to that request is an emphatic "No!" Keep quiet and calm, but stay. Your leaving may be better for the doctors and nurses, but it is not better for the child.

The elderly and emergencies.
Fractures are the most common reason for trips by the elderly to emergency rooms. Pseudo-dementia is a close second. If an elderly person becomes suddenly disoriented, hallucinates, or shows signs of paranoia, he may be suffering from a drug reaction. If the attending doctor has a list of all the prescription and nonprescription drugs that the patient is taking, it may save time, money, and discomfort. The tests to determine organic causes, such as those in Alzheimer's disease, stroke, etc., are complicated, upsetting, and expensive.

The emergency room doctor.
If the emergency room does not have a permanent medical staff, it does have a list of doctors who are on call. Make clear to the admitting desk, and to the doctor you see, that you do have your own doctor and that you do wish to have him informed as soon as possible. Although you may receive excellent care from the available doctor, if hospital admission is indicated, you may not welcome the discovery that you have inadvertently changed doctors. It is better to be clear in the beginning than to try to sort things out later.

Misusing the emergency room.
The hospital emergency room has become a substitute for a personal doctor in many people's lives. Families often postpone finding a doctor when they move to a new community and fall into the habit of going to the nearest emergency room whenever anyone in the family needs medical care. Tetanus shots, medication for sore throats, or examination of a sick child are very expensive when delivered by an emergency room.

Other people have a very low tolerance for suffering, their own as well as that of other people. A bump on the head when there is no loss of consciousness, a minor cut that bleeds profusely, mild muscle sprains or strains, and vomiting when there is no indication of poisoning are not reasons for taking up valuable time and space in a busy emergency room. A course in first aid at the local Red Cross—and a greater use of your doctor's telephone number—will save money.

Should you be admitted?
Admission to the hospital is not necessarily the outcome of a visit to an emergency room. If your own doctor is on hand or on the other end of a telephone, this decision should be made under his guidance.

If your own doctor is not available, the discussion will need to be carried on with the attending physician. No one would think of taking a suspected heart attack victim home until his condition has been verified, but a bump on the head may be a different matter. Careful questioning, followed by the use of your own common sense, should resolve the matter.

Unless you are far from home or have been taken by an ambulance to a hospital where your doctor does not have admitting privileges, try to make sure that the hospital has the name of your primary care doctor. If your doctor is not available, you are entitled to be admitted by a private doctor of your choice.

If you are not admitted to the hospital, you should inquire about follow-up care. For example, who will remove the stitches?

Post a note by the telephone

Display prominently the telephone number of your local police and your own street address. Emergency police cars can arrive at your house in minutes. Also, households with young children or elderly parents should place a notice near the telephone for use by babysitters or caretakers.

> **POLICE • FIRE AMBULANCE**
> **555-7000**
> Compliments of
> Your Volunteer Fire Department

- If you have found a primary care doctor, investigated local hospitals and emergency rooms, and located a pharmacist you can rely on, this information should be readily available when you are out of the house.

- Current medications, how they are taken, and for what conditions should be noted.

- If children are likely to have croup or experience allergic reactions, the measures to take in case of an attack should be described.

- Working mothers with regular, reliable babysitters or housekeepers should make certain that the doctor knows their names and whether or not they are empowered to act in your behalf.

You and drugs

Most drugs simply alleviate symptoms, modify the course of an illness, or assist the body to achieve normal functioning. Our own bodies fight most illnesses better than most drugs. Given time, many conditions improve without any treatment. For example, early diabetes can often be controlled by diet alone. And drugs used to control high blood pressure need assistance from a modified diet and appropriate exercise.

Otherwise sensible people cling to the notion that all they need to recover from any illness, from a cold to cancer, are the right words written on a prescription blank, or the right bottle of nonprescription medicine brought home from the drugstore.

Any drug powerful enough to have a significant effect on a disease also has the potential to cause harm. The risks range from slight to major, and it is the job of the patient and his doctor to weigh risks against benefits. Powerful drugs are to be reserved for serious illnesses.

No one should refuse medication that is thoughtfully and knowledgeably prescribed, but the wise person guards against misuse and overuse of medication by assuming personal responsibility for knowing as much as possible and for following directions.

Warning signs when taking medication

- Rash, nausea, swelling, muscle cramps
- Trouble with urination, heart, breathing, circulation, headaches, vision
- Yellowing of skin or eyes
- Depression or exhilaration
- Weight gain or loss
- Stomach upset, constipation, or diarrhea
- Feeling worse or showing no sign of improvement

Doctors are human.

Most of us have nagged our doctors for a prescription that we think we need to make us feel better, and most doctors have written unnecessary prescriptions for the same reason. In the past, doctors had a very limited number of effective drugs they could use, so they sometimes offered their patients "sugar pills" to make them feel better.

Today, however, modern pharmacology has made a bewildering number of drugs available to doctors, making it difficult for them to keep up with their names, much less their efficacy and side effects. When today's physician reaches for his copy of the *Physician's Desk Reference* to look up a drug he is about to prescribe, he is demonstrating sound medical sense and taking care to prescribe the right drug for the right condition.

The smart patient should not hesitate to use the same reference book, which is available in libraries and pharmacies, before starting a new medicine. Although the information may seem too extensive and too technical, it will provide a basis for asking further questions of your doctor. Understanding all you can about your medication should make it easier to follow instructions and to make the most effective use of it.

Doctors complain that their patients accept prescriptions that they never fill, fill prescriptions that they never take, and take medication only until they feel better. If the goal is to form a full partnership with a doctor, thus ensuring better care, such quirks on the part of a patient get in the way. A doctor needs to know about the course of a disease—what worked and what did not, why a patient seemed to recover and then had a relapse, etc. Good information is one way to ensure good care.

How to use your pharmacist.

Pharmacists are highly trained professionals who are well informed on the use, composition, and effects of drugs. They are qualified not only to advise the consumer, but the doctor as well. They are not allowed to prescribe medications, make a diagnosis, or refuse to fill a prescription. They can offer advice about nonprescription medicines and are usually willing to take the time to answer questions about prescription drugs.

Many good pharmacists keep a complete drug record on each customer; as more and more stores are computerized, this information is stored for instant retrieval.

In an effort to save money, many people use the discount drug stores and chain stores. The pharmacists in these large operations are inaccessible to customers and do not keep personal drug profiles. It is advisable to balance the advantages and disadvantages in making a choice between a well-stocked neighborhood pharmacy and a large commercial operation.

Over-the-counter drugs.

After this category of drugs was studied by the Food and Drug Administration (FDA), many over-the-counter drugs were taken off the market because they were judged to be ineffective.

Some drugs do not mix safely

(see drug chart on pages 90-91)

Do not take even an aspirin without consulting your doctor or pharmacist if you are taking prescription medication. Aspirin, for example, taken with anticoagulants, increases the anticoagulant effect of the aspirin and internal bleeding can result.

Alcohol, even in small quantities, can have fatal effects when combined with barbituates.

It is reasonably safe to use nonprescription drugs for such conditions as a bad cold, headache, mild allergic reaction, constipation, mild diarrhea, or any condition that is self-limiting—so long as you receive some guidance from a doctor or pharmacist.

Elderly people, young children, pregnant women, or people who are taking prescription medication should exercise particular care.

Make sure to read the label, avoiding medications that contain more than two active ingredients. Make sure *not* to use these preparations to put off a visit to the doctor for a condition that might be serious.

Brand name vs. generic.
Achromycin is a brand name antibiotic that costs just under $10. Tetracycline is its generic equivalent; it costs about half that amount. The drugs are equally effective and pharmacists in all states are permitted to fill a prescription with either drug, providing the doctor has not specifically forbidden it.

Unfortunately for the consumer, not all brand-name drugs have a generic equivalent available. Some are still protected by patent. Until recently, the Food and Drug Administration (FDA) made approval of generic copies so complicated and expensive that there was no real incentive for other drug companies to manufacture copies, even when the patent expired.

But now, under a recent FDA ruling, drug companies will be able to issue generic copies so long as they demonstrate that the generic drugs are chemically the same and that they perform in the same way as the brand-name drugs. Any FDA-approved generic drug is as safe and effective as any brand-name drug. The saving to the consumer should be enormous.

Medicine and high-risk groups.
These three groups are at particular risk, and extra precautions must be taken to ensure that medications are effective and do no harm.

Children. Children not only require smaller doses of drugs than adults, but they frequently react in opposite ways. Sedatives may stimulate, and stimulants may sedate. Children should be given only those medicines prescribed for them by their own doctor.

Adults should make their own medicine-taking a very private affair. Many doctors and psychologists feel that children who observe their parents taking drugs for any discomfort are getting a message that could pave the way for drug abuse at a later age.

Pregnant women. Extraordinary care must be exercised when taking medication during pregnancy. Nursing mothers should practice the same restraint. The fetus was once considered totally secure while in the womb. The tragic thalidomide babies were a testament to the fallacy of that perception.

Not all pregnant women can forego all medication, but they must cooperate closely with an obstetrician who is sensitive to the possible dangers.

The elderly. This group can present their doctors, their caretakers, and even themselves with troublesome medication problems. They complain of lack of sleep, lose their appetites, develop aches and pains, break bones, lose their sharpness of sight and hearing, and find that their vital organs have slowed in their

Darvon is one of a half-dozen brands, all relatively expensive, for the common generic analgesic Propoxyphene Hydrochloride, which costs much less.

functioning. As a result, many of them become doctor shoppers and enthusiastic consumers of vast quantities of prescription and over-the-counter drugs. To add to their problems, many old people swap drugs with each other. The result may be a drug-induced nightmare for those who love the elderly and care for them.

A single primary care physician—a gerontologist or an internist—can act as a deterrent to freewheeling drug use. Not only will one doctor have a record of all the drugs taken, but the patient can be encouraged to substitute exercise, relaxation, and good nutrition for some of the medication. An introduction to commonly prescribed drugs, their generic names, and a guide to possible problems appears on the next page.

The home medicine cabinet

The bathroom medicine cabinet is often a disorderly jumble of deodorants, toothpaste, expired prescriptions, cosmetics, dried-up cough syrups, and empty Band-Aid boxes. This may lead to a small child's being rushed to the emergency room after eating a bottle of aspirin.

The smart thing to do is to clean up and lock up. Medications belong in a locked cabinet, preferably located in a cool, dry place. All out-of-date medications should be discarded. The pharmacist will usually be willing to make recommendations about what to keep and what to flush down the toilet.

Home remedies should be confined to a few reliable kinds, and first-aid supplies should be kept organized and ready to use.

A well-ordered medicine cabinet will reduce the temptation to self-medicate with leftover prescription drugs.

Suggestions for the home pharmacy

Keep	*For*
Aspirin or nonaspirin pain reliever	Pain or fever
Antacid	Upset stomach
Adhesive tape and bandages	Covering minor wounds
Hydrogen peroxide	Antiseptic
Sodium bicarbonate	For soaking
Syrup of ipecac	To induce vomiting
Milk of magnesia	Constipation
Kaopectate	Diarrhea
Eyedrops	Simple irritation
Hydrocortisone ointment	Poison ivy, other rashes

Home remedies and first-aid supplies should be kept in one place. Teach children not to open the cabinet doors, which should be kept locked. Do not give old medicines to friends. Destroy them by flushing them down the toilet.

You and Modern Medicine

A sample listing of frequently prescribed drugs

Brand name	Generic	Possible problems
Pain killers		
Darvon	Propoxyphene hydrochloride	Habit forming; avoid alcohol, muscle relaxants, tranquilizers, nervous system depressants
Percodan	Oxycodone, aspirin, phenacetin, caffeine	Avoid alcohol, sedatives, antihistamines, oral diabetes drugs, muscle relaxants
Antibiotics		
Achromycin V, SK-Tetracycline, Sumycin	Tetracycline	Avoid milk, dairy products, exposure to sun; oral anticoagulants may have increased effects
Amcill, Omnipen, SK-Ampicillin	Ampicillin	Avoid other antibiotics and antacids
E. E. S., E-Mycin, Erypar, Erythrocin, Ethril	Erythromycin	Avoid other antibiotics and alcohol
Penicillin, SK-Penicillin VK, Pen-Vee K	Penicillin	Avoid if you have a past history of allergy to any penicillin; to be taken for full treatment on empty stomach; do not take with fruit juice; avoid antacids
Anticoagulants		
Coumadin, Panwarfin	Warfarin	Avoid if pregnant or a nursing mother
Antihypertensives		
Aldactatone	Spirionolactone plus hydrochlorothiazide	This group of drugs, used to control high blood pressure, must be taken under regular supervision of the doctor with attention to high or low potassium levels; before any surgical procedure, the surgeon and anesthetist must know about the medication (this includes dental surgery); Regroton can cause sensitivity to sunlight
Apresoline	Hydralazine plus hydrochloride	
Inderal	Propranolol plus hydrochloride	
Lopressor	Metoprolol plus tartrate	
Regroton	Resperine plus chlorthalidone	
Oral antidiabetics		
Diabinese	Chlorpropamide	Avoid taking anticoagulants, aspirin, diuretics, or any other medication without consulting a doctor
Ulcer medication		
Cogentin	Benztropine mesylate	Can cause sensitivity to sunlight; do not take within an hour of antacid or diarrhea medication
Tagamet	Cimetidine	Avoid anticoagulants, some penicillins, Valium, Librium, etc., and alcohol and caffeine

Psychiatric medications

Brand name	Generic	Possible problems
Major tranquilizers		
Thorazine	Chlorpromazine	These are important drugs used in controlling serious mental illness; they have many side effects when taken over an extended period of time; many patients discontinue medication when they feel better or because of side effects; taking these drugs can mean the difference between being hospitalized or being able to live in the community; cooperation on the part of the patient and careful management on the part of the doctor are essential
Prolixin	Fluphenazine	
Mellaril	Thioridazine hydrochloride	
Stelazine	Trifluoperazine	
Haldol	Haloperidol	
Navane	Thiothixene	
Minor tranquilizers		
Librium	Chlordiazepoxide	No other medication should be taken without consulting a doctor; alcohol can be highly dangerous
Valium	Diazepam	
Equanil	Meprobamate	
Serax	Oxazepam	
Tranxene	Clorazepate	
Xanax	Alprazolam	
MAO inhibitor antidepressants		
Marplan	Isocarboxazid	Aged cheese, aged meat, pods of broad beans, beer, wine, pickled herring, yogurt, liver, yeast extract, heavy amounts of caffeine, bananas, soy sauce, anchovies, avocados, and sour cream (all with high tramine content) must be avoided; can cause dangerous rise in blood pressure
Nardil	Phenelezine	
Parnate	Transylcypromine sulfate	
Tricyclic antidepressants		
Tofranil	Imipramine	Take two to six weeks to become effective; do not combine with other medication except on doctor's specific instruction; avoid alcohol; may have side effects like dry mouth or constipation; people over 60 years of age should have heart and blood pressure checked before beginning medication and regularly thereafter
Norpramin	Desipramine	
Elavil	Amitriptyline	
Sleeping pills		
Seconal	Secobarbital	Tolerance develops very quickly and physical addiction can occur from extended use; withdrawal can be dangerous if not undergone slowly; absolutely avoid combining with alcohol
Nembutal	Phenobarbital	
Sodium Amytal	Amobarbital	

You and Modern Medicine

You and mental health

Many people are uncomfortable with discussions of mental illness. A persistent stomach ache sends us to the doctor at once, yet the pain from a deep depression may be endured for months or years out of fear or shame. We talk freely of triple bypass heart surgery or kidney dialysis, but speak of schizophrenia in whispers. Alcoholism or drug addiction may be fervently denied in the face of incontrovertible evidence.

What is mental illness? Mental illnesses fall roughly into two categories: neuroses and psychoses. Neurotic symptoms may become disabling, but they respond well to psychotherapy. Psychosis is a term for serious organic mental illness often thought to be caused by a disruption in the brain's chemistry. These illnesses, such as schizophrenia and manic-depression, are treated by a combination of hospitalization, medication, and supportive therapy for both the patient and his family.

When to go for help. Few people escape periodic feelings of depression. Death, job loss, broken marriages or relationships, and major illness all make normal people feel sad, angry, or unhappy. But when those feelings persist over an extended period of time, even when the situation changes, or when there seems to be no rational explanation for the feelings, it is time to look for outside help. Researchers have found that therapy helps most people to some extent, no matter who delivers it.

Depression is the most common reason for people to seek help. Anxiety attacks, eating disorders, marital conflict, phobias, and some psychosomatic illnesses are all responsive to psychotherapy.

Depression checklist

- Sad moods and crying spells
- Feelings of despair
- Recurring guilt feelings
- Loss of pleasure
- Forgetfulness and lack of concentration
- Insomnia or abnormal amounts of sleep
- Loss of appetite or abnormal hunger
- Loss of interest in sex
- Suicidal thoughts
- Vague or actual physical complaints
- Irritability

Other mental illnesses, such as psychoses, alcoholism, and drug addition, are rarely helped by psychotherapy alone.

How to get help. The phone book is a good place to begin for mental health centers, Alcoholics Anonymous, and drug and alcohol treatment centers, but it is probably the very worst way to locate a psychotherapist.

Although proper credentials are important, they are not as vital as a sense of caring and warmth. A recommendation from a primary care doctor is useful, but word of mouth is also valuable. Talking to people who have been in therapy and who have been helped can put you on the right track.

Many clergymen are trained as counselors. For some people, this help is the most accessible and the least expensive.

Who are the mentally ill?

One out of ten American families has a member who is seriously mentally ill. If you do not have a victim in your own family, the family down the block probably does. It is particularly important not to dismiss a "blue Monday" teenager as just going through an adolescent stage. Seek professional advice if your daughter or son seems persistently depressed.

You and Modern Medicine

Understanding alcoholism.

Alcoholism is defined by the American Medical Association as a disease that, if not checked, leads to death. Yet the image of the alcoholic as the town drunk sleeping it off on a park bench fades slowly. Since most people in our society drink safely, it is easy to view alcoholism as the result of moral weakness and poor self-control.

Alcoholism is a leading cause of death and is implicated in 90 percent of physical assaults, 50 percent of murders, and 25 percent of suicides. Drunken drivers account for 25,000 deaths on the highway each year.

The causes of alcoholism are still obscure, although recent research points toward a genetic predisposition in many cases. Young people who combine alcohol with drugs account for a new phenomenon—17- and 18-year-olds who are as physically and mentally ill as older alcoholics who have been drinking for 30 or 40 years.

Who are the alcoholics? Despite the popular stereotype, alcoholics are found in corporate board rooms, on the police force, in the classroom, in the medical profession, among priests, ministers, and rabbis, and in suburban homes. Alcoholism permeates our entire society.

Because the progress of the disease is often slow, many people cross the line into alcoholism without being aware of it. Any wife who has tried to convince her husband that he is drinking too much knows how difficult it is for someone else to make an alcoholic recognize his own problem.

Can an alcoholic be helped? Very real help is available to the alcoholic who is able to recognize his need for it. Lifelong abstinence sounds like a grim sentence in a society that celebrates all occasions with alcohol. However, many people considered "hopeless" by their families, employers, and doctors have recovered through participation in Alcoholics Anonymous (A.A.), the self-help group with the best track record. Many people combine A.A. with alcohol counseling.

Many large corporations now have outreach programs for their employees, often financing extended treatment. Local governments are establishing alcohol treatment centers, and in many states, insurance companies are required by state law to provide coverage for both in-hospital and outpatient treatment.

Are you in trouble with alcohol?

- Do you need a drink to make you feel relaxed? Self-confident? To have a good time?
- Do you drink every day?
- Do you look forward all day to your first drink?
- Are you drinking more than you used to? More than you want to?
- Do you have a drink before going to a party?
- Have you changed your favorite drink lately to help you cut down?
- Have friends, family, or your employer mentioned your drinking?
- Do you frequently plan to stop drinking?
- Do you ever hide bottles or lie about the amount you drink?
- Do you drink in the morning, alone, or at work?
- Do you ever carry liquor in your breast pocket or pocketbook?
- Do you have blackouts, severe hangovers, or guilt feelings?
- Are you proud of being able to hold your liquor?
- Are most of your friends heavy drinkers?

There is no passing grade for this quiz. If you answer "yes" to more than one question, it is probably time to take a hard look at your "social" drinking.

You and Modern Medicine

Understanding drug addiction.

The drug addict is as poorly understood as the alcoholic. Although alcohol is available at the corner liquor store, drugs are available only from illegal sources—which puts the drug user at odds with the law.

Some drugs, such as heroin and morphine, are truly addictive. Others are considered to be "habituating." The effect is frequently the same. It is not uncommon for someone to try "recreational" drugs as an experiment at a party, to like the effect, and in time to become as addicted as the heroin user.

Prescription drug abusers are a hidden element in the drug addiction picture. Many people start taking tranquilizers or sleeping pills as recommended by their doctor and find themselves not only addicted but forced to seek illegal sources if they do not have a compliant doctor.

Can the drug addict be helped? The same conditions prevail for the drug addict as for the alcoholic. He must want to stop and be willing to turn to appropriate channels for assistance. Detoxification is almost always essential in the case of such drugs as heroin, amphetamines, barbiturates, and some tranquilizers. "Cold turkey" withdrawal from heroin is merely painful, but with some other drugs, it can cause convulsions and even death.

Chapters of Narcotics Anonymous are appearing all over the country, as are fine drug rehabilitation centers. Although addiction is seemingly intractable, many people do recover from its effects and go on to lead normal, drug-free, productive lives.

What about mental patients?

The discovery of major tranquilizers promised a new era in the treatment of the mentally ill. The hospitals were emptied of long-term patients, and promises were made to support their existence in the community. Those promises were not kept, and many communities find heavily medicated former patients wandering the streets, frequently with no place to live. Some are leading sad and dreary lives, with no supervision, as residents of shamefully inadequate rooming houses.

If serious mental illness strikes someone in your family, becoming informed about treatment, medication, and management is vital for your family's survival and for the well-being of your sick family member. Joining advocacy groups, support groups, and becoming active in your community mental health center will provide a focus.

Schizophrenics who learn to manage their illness, who are properly medicated, and who receive family and community support are often able to lead nearly normal lives, spending most of their time outside a hospital setting.

What are psychiatric medications? Psychotropic (psychiatric) medicines are tools used by psychiatrists in treating many kinds of mental illnesses. These medicines do not cure; they ease symptoms or, in the case of psychotic illnesses, control the disease.

As with any other medication, these drugs carry risks that have to be balanced against benefits. The major tranquilizers, for example, carry the potential for serious, permanent side effects; yet they can make the difference between long-term hospitalization and the possibility of living independently.

Managing medication—whether it involves an antidepressant or a major tranquilizer—should be a joint effort on the part of the therapist, the patient, and the patient's family. See page 91 for a chart of psychiatric drugs, their uses and side effects.

Methadone stations like this one exist all over the United States. Methadone helps the addict to overcome his or her dependence on heroin.

Former mental patients often live in group homes where they gain support from each other and live constructive lives.

Who are the therapists?

Psychiatrist (M.D.)
A medical doctor who is trained in diagnosis and therapy. He is the only choice when medication is necessary as an adjunct to therapy.

Psychologist (Ph.D.)
A nonmedical doctor trained in therapeutic techniques, skilled at helping people who do not suffer from psychosis. Cannot prescribe medication. Fees are generally lower than those of a psychiatrist.

Psychiatric Social Worker (M.S.W.)
Trained in counseling and particularly effective in family therapy.

Medical payments

Health insurance is a major element in a family's economic security. Many people are insured through their employers and have only a vague idea of their coverage until a sudden, major illness strikes. Sometimes the extent of that coverage comes as a painful and expensive surprise. It is also not uncommon to forget that health coverage stops unless converted to a personal policy when an employee is dismissed.

Get to know your health policy.
If the language of your policy is difficult to understand, consult the person in your company who handles the coverage.

There are a number of important things to know: Is there coverage for office visits? What about prescription drugs? Out-of-hospital tests? Pregnancy? Newborns? Premature births? What are the dollar limits and when does the insurance company begin to pay? Do you pay in advance and get reimbursed later? Are doctors and surgeons fees paid in full or according to an established fee schedule? When does your coverage run out?

Major medical insurance.
Many people who are self-employed or who have minimal coverage turn to major medical insurance. Basically, this insurance either picks up when primary insurance stops or provides full coverage when medical expenses pass a predetermined amount, the deductible.

Major medical insurance can be very expensive, but it can frequently be tailored to an individual family's needs.

How does your doctor get paid?
The day of doctors' bills being sent to the home seems to be passing. It is quite common, today, to be expected to pay as you go. If this is not possible, discuss it with the doctor himself, since his office staff is merely following his instructions. Price is often negotiable, particularly if you are a long-time patient or if your means are limited.

Specialists' fees. Specialists and surgeons set their own fees, sometimes at a scale that has made many patients gasp upon hearing them. This is a very sound reason for using specialists only when your primary care doctor thinks it absolutely necessary. If a surgeon's fee is beyond your ability to pay immediately, make arrangements in advance to pay it over an extended period of time.

Medicaid and Medicare. The simplest thing to remember about these two government-subsidized health benefits is this: Medicaid is linked to income and/or disability; Medicare is linked to age and/or permanent disability.

A doctor must accept the standard of fees set by Medicaid. He is not bound to a fee schedule for Medicare, under which patients pay part of their medical bills.

Many retired persons choose to supplement their Medicare coverage with additional private coverage.

Further information is contained in the chapter *Managing the Family's Money* on page 110, or in the government pamphlet on the subject listed at the end of this chapter.

You and Modern Medicine

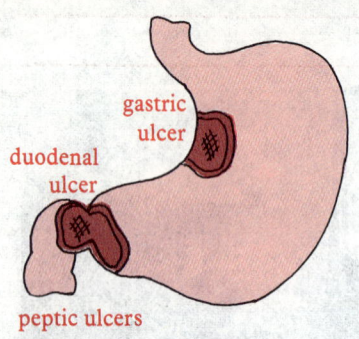
peptic ulcers — gastric ulcer, duodenal ulcer

Glossary

hiatus hernia, gallbladder, appendix, inguinal hernia, femoral hernia

pacemaker

abdominal distention. Condition that may be due to overeating or to gross enlargement of any abdominal organ. Other causes include fluid in the abdomen and gas in the bowels.

abscess. A localized collection of pus (dead cell debris) that can develop in any part of the body. Commonly, abscesses are caused by bacteria, but fungi, yeasts, and amoebae may also be involved.

acromegaly. Slowly progressive disease that produces a characteristic appearance: enlarged bones, a protruding jaw, and a coarsening and thickening of all features.

addiction. Medically, the habitual use of alcohol or drugs.

Addison's disease. Condition caused by inadequate secretion of the adrenal glands. Early symptoms include weakness, loss of energy, and muscular aches.

aerophagia. The habitual swallowing of air as while eating fast, drinking large amounts of carbonated beverages, or chewing gum. In severe cases, there may be abdominal distention, difficult breathing, and palpitations.

alcoholism. The compulsive abuse of alcohol, with resultant extreme nervousness, loss of appetite, vitamin deficiencies, nausea, and vomiting. When chronic, there is liver and kidney dysfunction, and DTs (delirium tremens).

allergy. An unusual reaction in an individual to a substance that usually does not affect other people. Most often, dust, feathers, animal hair, cosmetics, some foods and drugs, and fabrics are involved.

Alzheimer's disease. Generally noted between the ages of 40 and 60. It is associated with gradual memory loss, disorientation, and apathy, and is caused by a disorder of the cells of the brain.

amenorrhea. The absence of menstrual flow. Occurs most commonly during pregnancy and the menopause. Menstruation not started by age 18 is termed primary amenorrhea, while cessation of periods after they have begun is called secondary amenorrhea.

amniocentesis. Diagnostic procedure used to assess various genetic defects and some hereditary disorders of the fetus.

anaphylaxis. A potentially life-threatening type of allergic reaction that can result from the injection of some drugs or diagnostic agents. It may also be caused by wasp stings or such foods as shellfish and strawberries.

anemia. A variety of conditions marked by excessive loss, destruction, or faulty production of red blood cells. Iron-deficiency anemia, the most common form, is often due to a lack of dietary iron.

aneurysm. A swelling or localized bulging of a weakened arterial wall, particularly dangerous when it involves the aorta or arteries in the brain. If ruptured, it can lead to massive internal bleeding that may prove fatal.

angina pectoris. A condition marked by sudden pain in the chest. Generally occurs during strenuous exertion, such as shoveling snow or climbing stairs, which makes the heart work harder.

angiography. X-ray technique in which blood vessels are made visible by injection of a radiopaque substance. The test is useful in detecting the presence of tumors, atherosclerosis, and aneurysms.

96   You and Modern Medicine

anorexia nervosa. A condition that mainly affects adolescent girls and younger women who eat less and less food. As food intake and weight continue to drop, severe nutritional deficiencies and even death by starvation may occur.

antibiotics. Various natural and synthetic substances widely used to treat infectious diseases. If bactericidal, an antibiotic kills organisms; if bacteriostatic, it prevents their growth.

anticoagulant. Term used to describe the prevention of blood coagulation, or an agent that prevents coagulation.

appendicitis. An inflammation of the worm-shaped (vermiform) appendix, which is located at the tip of the cecum (part of the large bowel). A perforated appendix is a serious complication with the potential of peritonitis.

arrhythmia. An alteration in the regular rhythm of the heart, either in the formation or conduction of heart impulses. Such disturbances may be functional or due to disease.

arteriogram. An x-ray picture of an artery after it has been injected with a contrast medium.

arteriosclerosis. Commonly referred to as hardening of the arteries. Involves thickening, hardening, and loss of elasticity of the artery walls.

arthritis. An inflammation of the joints. Rheumatoid arthritis is a chronic and generally progressive inflammatory disease marked by pain and swelling of the joints. Osteoarthritis is a chronic degenerative disease mainly of weight-bearing joints. See also *Still's disease.*

asthma. A condition marked by difficult breathing and wheezing, chronic or episodic. Three major contributory factors are allergy, respiratory infection, and emotional stress.

atherosclerosis. A form of arteriosclerosis in which fatty substances are deposited in the arteries and their inner layers become tough and sinewy.

athlete's foot (tinea pedis). An infection caused by a fungus that thrives on dead skin cells between the toes. It is commonly found in locker rooms, public showers, and swimming pool walkways.

beta blockers. Drugs that reduce the workload of the heart and thereby lower the demand of the coronary arteries for blood. Beta-blocking agents are prescribed for the treatment of angina pectoris, hypertension, and cardiac arrhythmias.

biopsy. The excision and microscopic examination of tissue samples and cells to determine abnormalities. Indicated when cancer, or certain liver or kidney diseases, are suspected.

bone marrow. The soft red (in spongy bones) or yellow (in long bones) tissue filling the interior cavities of bones. Red marrow is the site of production of the red and white blood cells and the platelets.

brain death. Condition in which there is irreversible coma and evidence of irreparable brain damage. There is lack of electrical activity for a prolonged period, no response to external stimuli, fixed pupils, and absence of spontaneous breathing.

brain scan. Diagnostic technique in which a radioactive isotope or tracer is injected into a vein, usually the arm. A scintillation scanner is used to detect the tiny radioactive emissions as the tracer flows through the blood vessels in the brain.

bronchitis. An acute inflammatory condition usually due to exposure to cold and dampness. When chronic and uncontrolled, bronchitis can create serious lung problems.

bronchoscopy. A diagnostic procedure that permits inspection of the interior of the tracheobronchial tree through a bronchoscope. The technique is helpful in obtaining biopsy specimens and removing obstructions.

bursitis. A painful inflammation of the bursa, which are small fluid-filled sacs that facilitate movement of body joints. Most commonly, the shoulder, elbow, hip, and knee are involved.

Caesarean section. A technique in which the fetus is removed by means of an incision into the uterus, usually via the abdominal wall. Generally, it is employed when there is an overly large fetus or an abnormally small pelvis.

cancer. Many diseases, all characterized by an irregular and uncontrolled growth of body cells. These malignant cells may remain in the area where they formed or may spread via the blood and lymph to other parts of the body.

candidiasis. A yeastlike fungus. *Candida albicans* is responsible for this infection, called thrush when it is localized in the mouth or throat, vaginitis when it affects the vaginal walls.

cardiac arrest. A sudden cessation of heartbeat and breathing. This is a medical emergency calling for immediate attention. Cardiopulmonary resuscitation (CPR) is potentially life-saving, but can only be performed by a person trained in the technique.

CAT scan. See *computerized axial tomography.*

chemotherapy. The use of drugs or chemical agents that have a specific and toxic effect upon disease-causing microorganisms. The term is often applied to potent drugs that destroy cancer cells.

chicken pox (varicella). A highly contagious infectious disease that occurs mostly in children. Symptoms include fever, headache, malaise, and at times a sore throat. A red rash that crusts develops.

childbed fever (puerpural fever). Occurs after a prolonged or difficult childbirth and is marked by septicemia. There is absorption of septic products into blood and tissues, or disease-causing organisms that may multiply in these areas.

cholecystitis. Inflammation of the gallbladder, either acute or chronic, often due to obstruction of the bile duct by gallstones. Symptoms include pain, nausea, vomiting, and fever.

cholecystography. The examination of the gallbladder by x-ray study. Useful in detecting gallstones or gallbladder dysfunction.

cholesterol. A sterol, this fatlike substance is found in animal fats and oils, nerve tissue, bile, blood, and egg yolk. A normal constituent of bile, cholesterol can also be manufactured in the liver.

chromosome. A microscopic J- or V-shaped body present in all living cells. Chromosomes contain genes, the particles responsible for determining hereditary characteristics. The normal number of chromosomes in each human cell is 46, arranged in 23 pairs.

cirrhosis. Chronic condition in which there are degenerative changes in the liver cells and thickening of surrounding tissue; interferes with normal liver function. Often associated with advanced alcoholism.

collagen. An insoluble protein that represents about 30 percent of total body protein. Found in the white fibers of connective tissue, cartilage, and bone.

collagen diseases. Various conditions causing cellular changes affecting the body's connective tissue. Diseases include lupus erythematosus, rheumatoid arthritis, and scleroderma.

colonoscopy. Permits examination of the upper portion of the rectum with an elongated speculum. May also be useful in removing polyps and obtaining tissue samples for biopsy.

colostomy. Temporary or permanent surgical opening made from the colon through the abdominal wall. Creates an artificial passage for the elimination of solid wastes to the outside of the body.

computerized axial tomography (CAT scan). A computer-aided x-ray system that can be used with safety and effectiveness, exposing a person to about the same amount of radiation as obtained from a chest x-ray. Provides highly detailed imaging of internal structures of the brain, lungs, pancreas, and kidneys.

concussion. Commonly the result of a severe blow to the head. Brain concussion may be accompanied by temporary or prolonged unconsciousness. Recovery may be gradual, depending upon age, damage, and care given.

congestive heart failure. Impaired circulation when the heart cannot pump sufficient blood to supply the body's needs. Congestion, or fluid accumulation, may develop in the lungs, legs, or abdomen.

conjunctivitis. Refers to inflammation of the conjunctiva, the mucous membrane lining the eyelids and white of the eye. Causative factors include allergy, bacterial and viral infections, smoke, dust, or wind.

convulsions. Condition marked by involuntary jerking movements, often with momentary unconsciousness. Some possible causes may be epilepsy, stroke, meningitis, hypoglycemia, skull fracture, brain tumor, and drug reactions.

coronary bypass. A major operative procedure in which a blocked coronary artery is bypassed with a section of vein taken from the leg and grafted into position. Double, triple, and quadruple bypass can be performed.

coronary occlusion. Blockage of vessels supplying blood to the myocardium (heart muscle). May be produced by growth of plaque (fatty materials), or by growth of a thrombus (blood clot) plugging the artery.

corpus luteum. Ovarian follicle after it has released its ovum. Produces the hormone progesterone, which prepares the uterine lining for possible implantation of the ovum.

crib death. See *sudden infant death*.

cross-eye. See *strabismus*.

croup. An acute viral infection that occurs most often in infants and young children. Marked by difficult breathing and a hoarse cough.

cryosurgery. Surgical procedure in which cells are destroyed by the application of extreme cold (the tissue is usually cooled to below 0° F (−20° C). Used in the treatment of malignant tumors and certain precancerous conditions.

culdoscopy. Examination of the female internal organs and pelvic cavity with an endoscope. Used in cases of suspected abnormal uterine tissue growth, infertility, and pelvic disorders.

curettage. Scraping of a cavity with a curette. In uterine curettage, scraping is done to remove contents of the uterus, obtain diagnostic specimens, or remove growths.

cyst. An abnormal sac or swelling filled with fluid or a semisolid material; may occur anywhere in the body. Sebaceous cysts, often forming on the scalp, consist of a small sac containing a yellowish-white caseous matter.

cystocele. A hernia sometimes associated with childbirth, where part of the bladder protrudes into the vagina. The condition may be accompanied by bladder incontinence or infection.

cystoscopy. An examination of the inside of the bladder and urethra with a cystoscope. Indicated when there is a suspicion of bladder or urinary tract cancer or polyps.

D&C (dilation and curettage). Procedure in which the cervix is enlarged (dilated) to facilitate scraping of the uterine walls. Undertaken to remove unwanted tissue from the uterus, remove growths, or obtain tissue for examination.

decubitus ulcers. Bedsores caused by poor circulation in the area under pressure. Common in bedridden patients who must lie in one position. Buttocks, shoulders, elbows, and heels are often involved.

dermatitis. An inflammation of the skin which, in extremely sensitive persons, may be due to contact with such skin irritants as acids and alkalis, cosmetics, fabrics, and animal hair. Marked by itching, redness, and skin lesions.

diabetes insipidus. Form of diabetes in which there is a chronic excretion of very large amounts of urine, accompanied by extreme thirst. Ordinarily results from an insufficient production of the antidiuretic hormone by the pituitary gland.

diabetes mellitus. A metabolic disorder in which the body is unable to utilize carbohydrates, primarily due to the inadequate production of insulin by the pancreas. It is detected by the presence of sugar in the blood and urine.

diagnosis. The use of various methods to determine the cause and nature of a disease. Among the methods are study of the signs and symptoms of a disease, laboratory data, and special tests.

dialysis. A process employed to separate or extract certain substances in solution by diffusion through a porous membrane. Used to purify the blood (hemodialysis) in persons with one or both kidneys defective or absent.

diarrhea. A condition that is marked by the frequent passage of loose, watery stools. May be caused by infection, food poisoning, overeating, or certain drugs.

diverticular disease. Condition marked by diarrhea, colic, and abdominal pain. Diverticula are pouches or pockets that form on the large bowel. In diverticulosis, the colon contains dozens of these pouches.

DNA (deoxyribonucleic acid). A nucleic acid present in chromosomes of the nuclei of cells. Considered the chemical basis of heredity, and the carrier of genetic information.

Down's syndrome. Congenital abnormality, also known as mongolism, marked by moderate to severe mental retardation. Children born with Down's have a sloping forehead, low-set ears, slanted eyes, and a generally dwarfed physique.

dysmenorrhea. Painful or difficult menstruation. Discomfort is usually felt in the lower abdomen and sometimes the lower back. Often the condition improves with age and may disappear after childbirth.

dysplasia. Abnormal tissue development that can occur in the cervix, lungs, and other parts of the body. Women with cervical dysplasia must be examined regularly as it may become cancerous.

electrocardiogram (ECG or EKG). A graphic record of the electrical activity of the heart. Can indicate whether electrical conduction is normal and whether there is dead tissue due to a previous heart attack.

electroencephalogram (EEG). Graphic recording of the electric activity of the brain. May be used for a number of different purposes, such as diagnosing epilepsy and for research into sleep and dream patterns.

embolism. An obstruction of a blood vessel by a transported solid (an embolus): a blood clot, bacterial mass, or other foreign material. The severity of the condition is in direct relationship to the size and location of the blocked vessel.

emphysema. A chronic lung disease. The alveoli (air sacs) become greatly distended, bronchioles become thinned, and, eventually, the architecture of the lungs is destroyed. Chronic bronchitis or bronchial asthma, smoking, and air pollution may be implicated.

endocardiography. Method used to record the size, motion, and composition of various cardiac structures. Indicated in

heart valve problems that are difficult to diagnose.

endocarditis. An inflammation of the heart lining (endocardium). Persons with damaged heart valves are most vulnerable. The condition is often observed in young adults and the middle-aged.

endometriosis. A nonmalignant condition in which tissue normally located in the lining of the uterus (endometrium) begins to grow elsewhere. Often seen in the ovaries, the Fallopian tubes, the bladder, or between the rectum and vagina.

enzyme. One of various complex proteins produced by living cells. Enzymes alter the chemical reactions in other substances while remaining unchanged in the process, and help break down food particles into simple, more readily absorbed compounds.

epilepsy. Includes a group of nervous disorders characterized by either convulsive or nonconvulsive seizures and, generally, a temporary loss of consciousness. Seizures are associated with a sudden unruly pattern of brain waves.

epistaxis (nosebleed). Included among the causes are high blood pressure, injury, infection, foreign bodies, and a direct blow to the nose. If severe or uncontrolled, nosebleed requires medical attention.

erythrocyte sedimentation rate. A laboratory test that determines how fast red blood cells (erythrocytes) in a blood specimen settle to the bottom of a long narrow tube. The speed of settling is increased in various infections, pregnancy, and cancer.

fever (pyrexia). A body temperature above the normal, which, taken orally, is 98.6° F (37° C). Generally, a fever of 101° F (39° C) calls for medical attention.

fibroma. A benign tumor derived from fibrous tissue. May vary in size from a millet seed to large enough to fill the entire abdominal cavity. May be single or multiple in number.

fistula. An abnormal tubelike passage that leads from a normal cavity or tube to the free surface, or to another cavity. Fistulae may be congenital or result from abscesses, injuries, or inflammatory processes.

flatulence. An excessive amount of gas in the stomach and intestine. May be due to habitual air swallowing or indigestion. If it is worse after eating fatty foods, there may be gallstones.

flu. See *influenza*.

fluoroscopy. A technique that permits examination of inner parts of the body by means of the fluoroscope. In the upper body, there is x-ray visualization of the esophagus, stomach, and duodenum; in the lower body, the large intestine is visualized.

gallstones. Concretions or stonelike masses that form in the gallbladder or bile ducts. May not cause much distress or may be associated with painful attacks.

gamma globulin. Various proteins found in the lymphatic system, bone marrow, and spleen, associated with the production of antibodies. They circulate in the blood and help the body to resist infection.

gastritis. Inflammation of the mucous membrane of the stomach. May be due to viral infection, hot spicy food, food poisoning, or overindulgence in alcoholic beverages.

gastroscopy. Inspection of the inner surface of the stomach by the use of an endoscope. Useful in confirming stomach ulcers, unexplained bleeding, or other abnormalities.

genetics. The branch of science that is concerned with heredity.

German measles (rubella). An acute contagious disease similar to measles and scarlet fever. Women who have not had rubella in childhood should be protected against this disease before considering pregnancy.

glandular. Relates to the nature of a gland, a secreting organ or structure. There are many types of glands, and they serve different purposes throughout the body.

glaucoma. A disease of the eye marked by an unaccountable rise in fluid pressure within the eyeball. If unrelieved, it can cause permanent damage to the eye and result in partial or total blindness.

glossitis. Inflammation of the tongue, which may be associated with stomatitis (inflammation of the mouth). The tongue becomes tender and painful; thick saliva makes swallowing difficult.

goiter. An enlarged thyroid. Due to overactivity of the gland in secreting an excessive amount of hormones. In severe cases, the thyroid gland may swell to several times its normal size and be observable as a large growth on the front of the throat.

gonorrhea. A sexually transmitted disease that, if untreated, can lead to serious damage. In the male, it can cause epididymitis; in women, it may result in painful infection of the Fallopian tubes, often causing sterility.

graft. Insertion of skin or other living substance into similar substance for the purpose of overcoming a defect. In skin graft, a piece of skin is removed from one part of the body to another to cover a large superficial burn.

gynecology. A branch of medicine that deals with diseases of women, in particular, the genital tract and the female endocrine and reproductive systems.

habituation. The act of becoming accustomed to something by frequent use. In general, it refers to the psychological dependence that develops with the continued use of a drug, eventually resulting in drug addiction.

Hashimoto's disease. A chronic form of thyroiditis (inflammation of the thyroid gland) manifested by a particular type of goiter.

headache (cephalalgia). A symptom that is associated with a great many diseases and emotional states. Infection and tension are among the causes.

heart attack. See *myocardial infarction*.

heartburn. An abnormal return of acid liquid from the stomach into the esophagus. Produces a burning sensation deep in the chest together with an oppressive tightening sensation.

hematoma. A localized mass of blood that has escaped from a vessel into the tissues, occurring at the site of an injury where the blood vessels have broken.

hemodialysis. A procedure that is used to purify the blood in persons with kidney failure; usually requires 20 hours a week; 10 hours twice a week; or 6½ hours three times a week.

hemophilia. An hereditary blood disease in which the blood fails to clot and there is an abnormal tendency to bleed from a cut or other injury. Transmitted from mother to son as a sex-linked recessive condition.

hemorrhoids (piles). Varicose (enlarged or swollen) veins of the anal and rectal area. External hemorrhoids occur on the outside of the anal sphincter; internal hemorrhoids develop within the anal canal.

hepatitis (infectious). Acute disease of the liver. Viral hepatitis type A is transmitted by the oral-fecal route. It is spread from person to person by infected food handlers or contaminated food, water, feces, or bedpans.

hepatitis (serum). Viral hepatitis type B. Transmitted by injection of infected blood or by the use of contaminated needles or instruments. Similar to type A, it is caused by a virus found in blood and tissues rather than in the feces.

hepatitis (toxic). An inflammation of the liver caused by exposure to certain chemicals (carbon tetrachloride, insecticides, solvents). In those overly sensitive to such drugs as ioniazid and bromates, liver damage may result.

hernia. A weak point in the abdominal wall through which a part of the intestine can protrude. Commonly seen types are inguinal (groin), umbilical (navel), and femoral (thigh).

hernia (hiatus). Protrusion of the upper part of the stomach into the chest cavity. This condition is associated with weakness in the area where the esophagus opens up into the diaphragm. This impairment permits leakage of acid stomach contents into the esophagus.

herpes simplex. A virus infection that causes painful fluid-filled blisters, called cold sores or fever blisters. Other forms of herpes simplex are denoted according to site; for example, herpes genitalis.

herpes zoster (shingles). A completely different disease from herpes simplex, this painful vesicular eruption occurs along the course of a nerve. It is due to the same virus, herpes varicella, as that causing chicken pox.

Hodgkin's disease. A malignant disease that mostly afflicts men. It is marked by painless and progressive swelling of the lymph glands with enlargement of the spleen. Some symptoms are anemia, fever, and fatigue.

hydrocephalus. An increased accumulation of cerebrospinal fluid within the hollow spaces (ventricles) of the brain. It may result from a malformation, infection, injury, or a brain tumor.

hypertension. High blood pressure denoting arterial pressure that is consistently elevated. Added pressure on the blood vessel walls makes the heart work harder; untreated, it can cause organ damage.

hyperthyroidism (Graves' disease). The result of an overproduction of hormones by the thyroid gland. Besides exophthalmos goiter, symptoms include increased nervousness and heart rate, weight loss, and heat intolerance.

hypoglycemia. An abnormally low concentration of sugar in circulating blood. May be due to an insulin overdose or a missed meal by a diabetic. In nondiabetics, poor diet may be a cause.

hypothermia. A technique used to lower body temperature and so reduce the need for oxygen during surgery. It is especially useful when the heart and the nerves are involved.

hypothyroidism (myxedema). Condition in which the thyroid gland is underactive, failing to secrete an adequate amount of hormones. As the condition progresses, there is slowed pulse rate, sluggish movement, facial puffiness, and muscle weakness.

hysterectomy. An operative procedure that involves removal of the uterus. It is usually indicated when tumors are present, whether benign or malignant.

immunosuppressive agent. Belonging to a group of drugs that interfere with the body's natural immune system. Used before surgical transplant of a foreign organ, such as a kidney, to avert body rejection.

indigestion. Often caused by eating too much too fast, not chewing food well, eating when emotionally upset, or swallowing large amounts of air. Symptoms may be heartburn, gas, and belching.

infarction (infarct). Condition in which there is death of tissue and consequent scarring in an organ deprived of an adequate supply of blood. Myocardial infarction describes such an occurrence in the heart.

influenza (flu). A respiratory infection caused by one of several related, yet distinct, viruses. It strikes suddenly with chills, fever, headache, muscle aches, and a dry cough, most of which subside after a few days.

insomnia. Inability to sleep. In itself, not a disease, but it may be a symptom of disease, either of a slight or serious nature. Most often due to pain or anxiety.

insulin shock. A low blood sugar reaction that can be caused by an insulin overdose. Often the result of lowered blood sugar brought on by a break in normal routine or emotional upset.

irritable bowel syndrome. A common gastric disorder marked by abdominal pain, diarrhea, and/or constipation. In general, the problem is not organic but stems from the nature of a person's personality, particularly an inability to deal with stress.

jaundice. An excessive amount of bile pigment in the blood and a yellowish discoloration of the skin. Associated with diseases of the liver, gallbladder, bile ducts, and certain blood diseases.

laryngitis. An inflammation of the larynx. May be due to improper use or overuse of the voice. May also be caused by upper respiratory infections, the inhalation of irritating vapors or dust, or tobacco smoke.

lead poisoning. Results from the ingestion of lead, as during prolonged exposure to lead dust in the workplace, when using lead vessels for eating or drinking, or when chewing on lead toys.

legionnaires' disease. Applies to a severe pneumonialike disease that felled 249 American Legion conventioneers in Philadelphia (July, 1976). Marked by fever, cough, and bloody sputum. Additional symptoms may not be distinguishable from other types of pneumonia.

leukemia. A form of cancer in which there is a rapid increase of white blood cells in the bloodstream. The cells infiltrate body tissues and, in particular, bone marrow. This condition leads to anemia, hemorrhaging, and infection.

lumpectomy. Surgical procedure in which only a primary tumor and a varying amount of surrounding breast tissue is removed. Radiation therapy is used postoperatively.

lupus erythematoses. Systemic, and possibly chronic, disease in which a skin rash spreads across the bridge of the nose and face in a butterfly pattern. The disease affects the blood vessels.

lymphatic vessels. Vessels that transport lymph (the clear fluid bathing all body tissues), lymphocytes (a type of white blood cell), and other substances needed for the body's immune system. These vessels are part of the lymph system along with the lacteals, lymph capillaries, ducts, and nodes.

malignancy. Term that describes a condition occurring in severe form, growing worse, and resisting treatment. In cancer, it denotes uncontrollable growth and dissemination, or recurrence after removal of a tumor, or both.

mammography. Specialized x-ray technique for detecting breast abnormalities, especially early cancers. Recent improvements assure more accurate information and smaller amounts of radiation.

manic-depressive psychoses. A major mental disorder in which a person displays severe changes of mood: overelation and excessive activity during the manic state; depression and anxiety while in the depressed state.

mastectomy. A surgical procedure that involves removal of the breast. If simple, only breast tissue is excised; if major, the underlying chest muscles and the lymph nodes in the armpit are also removed.

mastoiditis. Infection that spreads through the ear to the mastoid process (part of the temporal bone). When acute, symptoms include chills, fever, malaise, and headache. When chronic, mastoid tissue is destroyed and there is loss of hearing.

measles. A highly communicable viral disease that usually occurs in early childhood. Marked by nasal discharge, fever, cough, and reddening of the eyes; also, a blotchy rash and fine white spots inside the mouth.

medication. A medicinal substance that is a medicine or remedy. Also refers to treatment with a remedy. (See pages 90-91 for a list of prescription drugs.)

Ménierè's disease. An impairment of the balancing mechanism of the inner ear. Attacks often come on with alarming suddenness. Symptoms include vertigo, ringing or other disturbing noises in the ear, and progressive loss of hearing.

meningitis. An inflammation of the meninges, the delicate membranes covering the layers of the brain. A local infection of the ears, sinuses, or tonsils may spread the infection to the meninges, or be carried into the bloodstream.

menopause. The cessation of menstruation that brings to a close the reproductive life of a woman. Natural menopause may occur as early as age 35, and as late as 58. Usually, it takes place between the ages of 47 and 52.

metabolism. The sum of chemical changes affecting the function of nutrition. Two fundamental processes are involved: anabolism—converting small molecules into large; and catabolism—converting large molecules into small.

microorganisms. Living organisms too small to be seen with the naked eye. Only a relatively small number are pathogenic (capable of causing disease). Protozoa, bacteria, fungi, rickettsiae, and viruses are all microorganisms.

migraine. A severe, periodic, vascular type of headache, usually one-sided. It may be preceded or accompanied by various symptoms: visual disturbances, extreme sensitivity to light, and nausea.

mole. A congenital discolored spot raised above the skin surface. Generally, moles are harmless unless there is irritation in the area.

mongolism. See *Down's syndrome*.

mononucleosis (infectious). An acute infection, also called glandular fever, believed to be due to a virus. It is manifested by a sore throat, fever, swollen lymph nodes, headache, and a faintly red eruption.

multiple sclerosis (MS). A chronic disease of the central nervous system in which there is degeneration of the myelin (a fatlike substance) sheath in the brain and spinal cord. Symptoms may come and go for years, but incapacitation worsens with progress of the disease.

mumps (epidemic parotitis). An acute febrile disease marked by inflammation of the parotid salivary glands (just below the ears). Although not as communicable as chicken pox or measles, mumps are quite contagious.

muscular dystrophy (Duchenne's disease). A hereditary disorder that primarily affects boys. There is progressive weakness and wasting of muscles, first affecting the abdomen and buttocks, then the chest and other body parts.

musculoskeletal. Relates to the muscles and the skeleton.

myasthenia gravis. A chronic neuromuscular disorder caused by a defective transmission of nerve impulse to the muscles. Marked by extreme muscular weakness, but no wasting of muscles.

myelitis. An inflammation of the spinal cord or of bone marrow. A potentially serious condition that calls for prompt diagnosis and treatment. If the spinal nerves are involved, there may be partial or total paralysis.

myocardial infarction (heart attack). Condition in which part of the heart muscle is deprived of blood and dies, being gradually replaced by a fibrous scar (infarct).

nephritis. Inflammation of the kidneys. Denotes a group of noninfectious diseases involving widespread kidney damage. The glomeruli (filtering units of the kidney) or the tubules may be affected.

nephrolithiasis. Condition in which calculi, or stones, are formed in the kidney and urinary bladder. Many kidney stones eventually pass out; others must be removed surgically.

neuritis. May be inflammation of a nerve (mononeuritis) or nerves (polyneuritis), usually characterized by pain. May be caused by injury, infection, metallic poisoning, or a metabolic disturbance.

neurosis. A psychological or behavioral disorder with the chief underlying factor being anxiety. In contrast with psychosis, persons with neurosis maintain contact with reality and undergo no major personality changes.

nonspecific urethritis. Condition in which the specific organism causing inflammation of the urethra is unknown. May be due to Chlamydia trachomatis, the same microbe that causes the eye disease trachoma.

nosebleed. See *epistaxis*.

oophorectomy. Surgical procedure in which an ovary or a portion of it is removed; also called ovariectomy.

osteoarthritis. Form of arthritis in which there is chronic degeneration of the joints, especially the weight-bearing (spinal column, hip, and knee) joints. Swelling may appear at the sides of each finger joint (Heberden's nodes).

osteomalacia. Disease in which bones gradually become soft due to bonelike tissue that fails to calcify. Bones become flexible and brittle, resulting in pain and deformation.

osteomyelitis. An inflammation of bone marrow and adjacent bone involving sudden pain, fever, and bone tenderness. Movement is painful and restricted, with subsequent swelling over the bone and often the nearby joint.

osteoporosis. A disorder characterized by the loss of bone mass. Increases the potential for fractures, particularly of the weight-bearing vertebrae. With compression of vertebrae, there is loss of height and, at times, kyphosis (humpback).

otitis. Inflammation of the ear differentiated by the part of the ear affected: otitis externa, the outer ear; otitis media, the middle ear; and otitis interna, the inner ear.

otosclerosis. Formation of spongy bone around the stapes (a small bone in the middle ear) that results in progressively worsening deafness. This hearing loss can be corrected surgically or with a hearing aid.

ovarian cyst. An abnormal fluid-filled sac that develops within an ovary. It afflicts many women between the ages of 30 and 60. Enlarged, painful cysts are removed surgically.

pacemaker. Defines any rhythmic center that controls heart rhythm; normally, the sinus node. An artificial pacemaker is a device that substitutes for the normal pacemaker and controls heart rhythm.

Paget's disease (osteitis deformans). Generalized skeletal disease seen mainly in older persons. It is marked by an increased breakdown and reforming of bone that leads to abnormal thickening and softening of the bones.

pancreatitis. Condition in which there is inflammation of the pancreas. In the acute form, may lead to areas of tissue destruction and scattered hemorrhages. Complaints include abdominal pain, nausea, vomiting, and fever.

paralysis. A temporary or permanent loss of voluntary muscular movement in a part of the body. There are many different causes, including injury, infection, and stroke.

paraplegia. Paralysis caused by injury to the spinal cord. Paraplegics suffer paralysis in both legs and, usually, the lower trunk. Quadriplegics have paralysis in all four limbs.

paratyphoid fever. Similar to but less severe than typhoid fever. Caused by an infection of Salmonella bacteria. The infection is transmitted by contaminated food, milk, or water.

Parkinson's disease (paralysis agitans). A chronic, progressive disease involving the brain. Symptoms include a masklike face, muscular tremor of the head and extremities, and muscular stiffness with slowed voluntary movement.

pediculosis. An infestation of the body with lice. The infection is spread by direct contact with an infected person, or by the use of infected clothing or objects. There are three kinds of lice: head, body, and pubic.

pellagra. Chiefly a B vitamin deficiency (nicotinic acid). May also be caused by intestinal diseases or alcoholism. In severe cases, there is inflamed mouth and tongue, skin rash, diarrhea, and anemia.

peptic ulcer. May be a stomach ulcer (gastric) or of the duodenum (duodenal). It is associated with a decreased ability of the organ to withstand bathing by the acid gastric juices (pepsin and hydrochloric acid).

pericarditis. Condition in which there is inflammation of the pericardium, the membranous sac enveloping the heart. It is often accompanied by shortness of breath and chest pains that may be aggravated on coughing or deep breathing.

peritonitis. Inflammation of the peritoneum, the membrane lining the abdominal cavity. Acute peritonitis is caused by infection, such as that caused by a ruptured appendix, which requires immediate hospitalization and treatment.

pheochromocytoma. A disorder caused by a tumor of the adrenal gland. Usually manifested by sustained high blood pressure. Symptoms, varying widely from person to person, include nausea, headache, palpitations, and weakness.

phlebitis. Inflammation of a vein, most often noted in a leg. May involve injury to the vein, obesity, infection, or a problem related to blood circulation.

pleurisy (pleuritis). Inflammation of the membrane covering the lungs. Usually due to a bacterial or viral infection. In acute cases, there is stabbing pain in the affected side, high fever, and a dry cough.

pneumonia. An inflammatory condition of the lungs, marked by cough, chest pains, and fever. Causative agents are bacteria or viruses, but mostly the pneumococcus—*Diplococcus pneumoniae*—is involved.

pneumothorax. A condition in which air or gas escapes into the pleural cavity. It usually results from a penetrating chest wound, or may be due to various lung diseases. In either case, the lung or parts of the lung collapse.

poliomyelitis (infantile paralysis). A viral infection that attacks the gray matter of the spinal cord. This can lead to muscular paralysis, especially of the limbs and of the muscles involved with breathing.

polyarteritis. Condition marked by widespread inflammation of the smaller arteries. Often leads to complications, such as kidney disease and high blood pressure.

polyp. An abnormal, often benign, stalklike growth. Usually occurs in vascular organs, such as the nose, uterus, and rectum. If there is any sign of malignancy, polyps should be removed surgically.

Pontiac fever. A pneumonialike disease first noted in Pontiac, Michigan (1968). The bacteria are believed to be slightly different strains of the same bacteria as those causing legionnaires' disease.

positron emission tomography (PET). A scanner that makes images of the body from radioactive isotopes; the images are deciphered by computers. It is an invasive means of visualizing brain sites to detect neuropsychiatric disorders.

Pott's disease. Spinal tuberculosis. The condition may also affect the hips and knees. It occurs mainly in children and adults up to 40 years of age.

preeclampsia and eclampsia. Conditions commonly referred to as toxemias of pregnancy. Preeclampsia is often marked by fluid retention and high blood pressure. In eclampsia, convulsions occur and pregnancy must be terminated.

pregnancy tests.
Slide test. Simple test that involves mixing urine with a solution on a slide and examining results. It is most accurate when done at least seven weeks after the last menstrual period.
Tube (hemagglutination inhibition) test. Typical of home pregnancy tests, urine is mixed with a testing solution in a tube. It is slightly more accurate and can be done about a week earlier than the slide test.
Radioreceptor assay (RRA) blood test; beta-HCG (human chorionic gonadotropin) test; monoclonal antibodies test. The newest of available tests with which accurate positive results can be obtained as early as the time of the first missed period.

prognosis. Foretelling of the probable course and outcome of a disease.

prolapse. Downward or forward displacement of a part of the body. Most often used in denoting a displaced or "fallen" uterus.

prostaglandins. A group of fatty acid derivatives present in many body tissues. They can lower blood pressure, stimulate uterine contractions, and regulate body temperatures.

prostatitis. Inflammation of the prostate. In the acute bacterial form, marked by fever, chills, and back pain. There is usually accompanying difficulty in urination, as well as pain in muscles and joints.

prothrombin time (PT). Test that measures the time needed for a fibrin (a protein formed by the action of thrombin on fibrinogen) clot to form in a treated blood sample.

pseudodementia. Condition in which a person experiences an exaggerated indifference to his surroundings. However, there is no actual impairment of mental capacity.

psittacosis. A viral disease that may be transmitted to humans by infected birds, especially parrots, parakeets, love birds, and canaries. It is generally acquired by breathing in the dust from the cage contents or feathers of the infected birds.

psoriasis. A skin condition marked by formation of unsightly reddish, silvery-scaled patches. In general, the elbows, knees, legs, lower back, chest, and scalp are affected.

psychiatry. A medical specialty that deals with the diagnosis and treatment of mental illness. Psychotherapy employs mental rather than physical means.

psychosis. Mental disorders in which there is disturbed thought, disintegration of personality, and lack of touch with reality. Schizophrenia is the most common psychosis.

psychosomatic. The influence of the mind (emotions, fears, desires) upon the body functions, especially as it pertains to disease.

psychotropic. All that affects the mind and its processes. Also refers to psychotropic drugs, which have an effect on psychic function, behavior, and experience.

pulmonary embolism. A clot in an artery of the lungs, often due to a detached clot from a leg vein. Those most vulnerable are the bedridden or those with heart or lung disease, cancer, or hip fractures.

purpura. A group of bleeding disorders due to various causes. Characterized by bleeding into the skin and other tissues, mucous membranes, and internal organs.

pyelography. X-ray examination of the renal pelvis and ureter.

It is indicated in cases of recurrent kidney or bladder infection, or severe symptoms of prostate enlargement.

pyelonephritis. Inflammation of the kidney as well as the renal pelvis, commonly caused by an ascending bacterial infection. When chronic, the kidney suffers irreversible changes.

Q fever (query fever, Balkan grippe). An acute infective disease. When first noted, its cause was unknown and the Q stood for "query." The organism is carried by livestock and transmitted to humans by inhalation of infected dusts, or by drinking of contaminated milk of infected animals.

radiation sickness. An illness resulting from chronic exposure to or excessive amounts of high-energy radiation. Symptoms may be mild or may result in serious disturbances in blood cell formation, leukemia, and other changes.

radioisotope scanning. The study of the function and condition of internal organs, vessels, or body fluids with radioactive forms of chemicals, such as iodine.

radiotherapy (radiation, roentgenography). Treatment of disease by the use of roentgen rays (x-rays), radium, ultraviolet, and other radiations. It may be used alone or in combination with surgery or drugs.

Raynaud's disease. Condition in which there is spasm in the blood vessels of the extremities, especially in response to cold temperatures that would not normally affect a person. Most often, the fingers are affected.

reticular activating system (RAS). A complex system of nerve cells and fibers in the brain stem, hypothalamus, and adjacent areas. It plays an important part in maintaining alertness or wakefulness.

retinitis pigmentosa. Chronic and progressive disease that usually starts in childhood. It is marked by retinal degeneration, widespread changes in retinal pigmentation, wasting of the optic nerve, and defective night vision.

Reye's syndrome. Potentially fatal disorder that usually afflicts children under 18 following a viral infection such as chicken pox. It is marked by increased pressure on the brain and fatty degeneration of the liver.

Rh blood factor (Rhesus factor). A factor discovered in red blood cells of the rhesus monkey. It is present in about 85 percent of the human population who are said to be Rh positive (Rh+). Those not having this substance in the blood are Rh negative (Rh−).

rheumatic fever. A disease of childhood and adolescence that often follows symptoms of throat infection. If untreated, it can lead to heart damage.

rheumatoid arthritis. A chronic and usually progressive inflammatory disease of the joints that affects women more than men. Pain and swelling of the joints result in restricted movement.

rickets. A childhood disease primarily due to a lack of dietary Vitamin D, or inadequate exposure to sunlight, or both. Rickets interferes with the normal deposition of calcium.

RNA (ribonucleic acid). The "message" molecule that carries information from the nucleus (the vital body in cell protoplasm) to cytoplasma (cell protoplasm outside the nucleus) sites.

Rocky Mountain spotted fever. An infectious disease caused by a species of rickettsia. Usually acquired in man from the bite of infected ticks. Marked by high fever, muscle and bone pain, and rash.

Salmonellosis. The most common form of food poisoning, caused by ingestion of food contaminated with bacteria of the genus Salmonella. There is severe inflammation of the stomach lining and intestines.

salpingitis. Inflammatory condition of a Fallopian tube usually caused by a bacterial infection spreading upward from the uterus, cervix, or vagina.

sarcoma. A general term for cancer. Composed of cells from connective tissues of the body, such as bone or muscle. The bladder, kidneys, lungs, liver, spleen, and nearby tissues may be involved.

scabies. Highly infectious skin disease caused by the itch mite, *Sarcoptes scabiei*, and spread by close contact with infected persons. Most often, the hands, wrists, armpits, breasts, and thighs are affected.

scarlet fever. Acute contagious disease caused by a bacterial infection. Marked by sore throat, fever, and a scarlet rash. The infection is spread by the breath or cough of an infected person, or by handling contaminated objects.

schistosomiasis (snail fever). Parasitic infestation due to blood flukes (a type of worm) belonging to a species of Schistosoma. Man becomes infected by bathing in water containing parasitic worms issued from snails.

schizophrenia. A group of mental disorders in which there are disturbances in thinking, mood, and behavior. In some cases, there is an altered sense

sciatica. A severe pain involving the sciatic nerve, which extends from the back of the thigh down through the inside of the leg. The pain is sharp, usually more intense when standing, and often accompanied by tingling, numbness, and tenderness.

scleroderma. Progressive skin disease involving collagen tissue. There is widespread hardening of the skin due to swelling and thickening of fibrous tissue. This may be followed by skin atrophy and pigmentation.

scoliosis. An abnormal sideways curvature of the spine. There may be just one curve or a compensatory curve in the opposite direction. It may be due to a congenital defect, injury, disease, or poor posture.

senile dementia (senility, senile psychosis). A wide variety of mental and emotional changes affecting the elderly. Symptoms of this condition include loss of recent memory, short attention span, and irritability.

shingles. See *herpes zoster*.

shock. A state of deep mental and physical depression after receiving severe physical injury or undergoing emotional stress. Some causes are heart failure, hemorrhage, drug reaction, or poisoning.

sickle-cell anemia. An inherited blood disorder marked by a genetic abnormality of the red blood cells in which the cells become crescent or sickle-shaped.

sigmoidoscopy. A technique that permits inspection, through a tubular speculum called a sigmoidscope, of the interior of the sigmoid colon. It is indicated for detection of polyps, cancer, and bowel abnormalities.

sinusitis. Inflammation of the lining membrane of any sinus, but especially the nasal sinus. Most often, the condition occurs as an extension of nasal infections.

sleeping sickness. See *trypanosomiasis*.

slipped disk (prolapsed disk). Herniation or rupture of part of the intervertebral disk, which is normally held in place by fibrous tissues. When fibers weaken, protrusion from between the vertebrae occurs.

smallpox (variola). An acute, contagious, febrile disease that begins with chills, high fever, backache, and headache. Symptoms subside within five days and a skin eruption appears, ending up in dry scabs that fall off and mark the skin.

snail fever. See *schistosomiasis*.

specialist. A physician who, on completion of specialized postgraduate training, is able to practice a particular branch of medicine, such as surgery or obstetrics. (See page 81 for a description of various specialists.)

spinal tap. Involves lumbar puncture, which is used in cases of suspected meningitis and in certain types of spinal cord or brain damage.

Still's disease (juvenile rheumatoid arthritis). Similar to rheumatoid arthritis found in adults; however, children are affected much more severely during the development of the disease and less so in the later stages.

Stokes-Adams syndrome. Characterized by light-headedness or sudden loss of consciousness. Condition is associated with various disorders of the heart that disrupt its normal pumping action and consequent output of blood.

strabismus (cross-eye, squint). Condition in which the eyes fail to point in the same direction. Involves one or more muscles controlling eyeball movement.

stroke (apoplexy). Sudden loss of consciousness and paralysis on one side due to blockage of a cerebral artery by an embolus or thrombus or rupture of a blood vessel in the brain.

sudden infant death (SIDS; crib death). Unexplained death of an apparently well infant occurring most often between the second week and the first year of life. About 10 percent of cases are associated with cardiovascular or central nervous systems.

symptom. Any noticeable change in the body or its functions that indicates the presence of an illness or disease. May be of a general nature or pertain to the part of the body affected.

syphilis. A venereal disease caused by bacterial infection of the species *Treponema pallidum*. Spread almost exclusively by sexual intercourse with an infected partner.

tachycardia. Condition in which there is an abnormally fast heartbeat, especially over 100 beats per minute. May result from an overactive thyroid gland or some form of heart disease.

tapes dorsalis (locomotor ataxia). A late manifestation of syphilis involving the spinal cord. Occurs in persons having had inadequate or no treatment during early stages of syphilis.

Tay-Sachs disease. An hereditary disease caused by transmission of an abnormal gene. It results in a specific enzyme deficiency and is marked by progressive mental and physical retardation, paralysis, spasticity, and blindness.

telangiectasia. Dilation of capillaries, or a group of small blood vessels, which causes a small dark red elevation on the skin. May appear as a birthmark or become noticeable in young children.

temporal arteritis. Inflammation of the arteries that supply the sides of the scalp. Of unknown origin, it is becoming increasingly recognized in the elderly.

tetanus. An acute infection caused by the bacteria *Clostridium tetani*. These bacteria enter the body through a scratch or wound, where they release their poison (toxin) by growth and multiplication.

tetany. Nervous disorder in which there are intermittent tonic spasms involving the extremities. It can occur after a critical drop in the amount of calcium circulating in the blood.

thalassemia. An hereditary form of anemia characterized by the development of abnormally thin and fragile red blood cells. There are several variants of the disease, but no specific treatment is obtainable.

thalidomide. A hypnotic drug widely used in European countries as a sleeping pill in the early 1960's. Use of the drug was discontinued when it was found to cause severe limb deformities in developing fetuses.

therapeutic. The treatment of disease, or the results obtained from treatment. It may also pertain to a healing agent, or having healing properties.

thermography. A technique used to detect, record by a sensitive scanner, and interpret the significance of radiant heat thrown off by tissues affected by disease. It is used to study blood flow in limbs and to detect cancer.

thrombocytopenia. An abnormal decrease in the number of platelets (thrombocytes) in the circulating blood. It results in an inability of the blood to clot efficiently.

tinnitus. Condition in which a person experiences in one or both ears the sensation of noises that are not caused by external sound vibrations. It may be nothing more serious than impacted wax, or it may be an early sign of inner ear disease.

tonsillitis. An inflammation of tonsillar tissue. Tonsils appear enlarged and red, and are painful on swallowing. There may also be high fever, chills, and headache. It is more frequent in children than in adults.

toxic. A poisonous substance, a condition caused by a poison, or pertaining to a toxin. A toxin is a poisonous substance of animal or plant origin.

toxic shock syndrome. A fast-spreading, often deadly form of toxic reaction that sometimes kills or permanently disables a person within hours. About 80 percent of the cases occur in menstruating women using tampons.

toxoplasmosis. An infection caused by a parasite. Usually transmitted to humans through cat litter or from raw or uncooked meat. In pregnant women, the infectious organism can be transmitted to the fetus and cause jaundice, anemia, or nerve damage.

tranquilizer. Drug that acts to reduce mental tension and anxiety without causing depression in the user. Such drugs have facilitated treatment of certain severely disturbed psychiatric patients.

trichinosis. A parasitic disease caused by eating raw or inadequately cooked or processed pork or pork products infected with *Trichinella spiralis*. Symptoms may be absent or there may be pain, nausea, and diarrhea.

trichomoniasis vaginitis. One of the most common vaginal diseases, it is caused by a single-celled organism. Sometimes, it produces no symptoms, but often there is discharge and itching. Untreated, it can cause urinary problems.

trypanosomiasis (sleeping sickness). May be one of several diseases occurring in man and domestic animals caused by a trypanosome. The infection is marked by drowsiness, lethargy, muscular weakness, and cerebral symptoms.

tuberculosis. Three types of tubercle bacillus cause this infection: human, bovine, and avian. The human type is most responsible for the infection in man. Generally, contact is with an infected person or with contaminated milk from an infected cow.

typhoid fever. A bacterial infection caused by ingesting contaminated food, milk, or water. The bacteria responsible, *Salmonella typhosa*, are excreted in the feces and sometimes the urine of infected persons or carriers of the disease.

ulcerative colitis. Inflammation combined with ulceration of the mucous membrane lining the large intestine. Marked by acute abdominal pain, tenderness, and watery stools.

ultrasonography. The use of sound waves to produce an image or photograph of an organ or tissue. It is indicated where there is a suspicion of thyroid or gallbladder dysfunction, in certain heart problems, and in the last trimester of

pregnancy to determine size and position of fetus.
ultrasound (sonogram). Procedure that produces velocities in tissues that differ in density and elasticity from others. Outlines the shape of various body tissues and organs.
uremia. A toxic condition in which the kidneys fail to filter out various nitrogen-containing waste products in the blood, especially urea.
urticaria. An allergic skin reaction, more commonly called hives or nettle rash. Produces an eruption of wheals (red or white raised patches on the skin) that is accompanied by intense itching.
vaginitis. An inflammation of the vagina that may be caused by a bacterial, fungal, or protozoan infection. May also be due to irritation from chemical douches or foreign bodies, or poor hygiene of the vulval area.
varicose veins. Enlarged, twisted veins, usually in the leg, caused by damage to their one-way valves (which normally prevent a backward flow of blood); stretching of their relatively thin walls results.
vascular. The blood vessels. Collectively, the blood vessels together with the heart and lymph vessels constitute the vascular system.
vertigo. A sensation of whirling about, either of oneself or external objects, associated with difficulty in keeping one's balance. May be due to drug reactions, middle ear disease, or infection.
volvulus. A twisting upon itself of a section of intestine, causing a serious obstruction. Signs and symptoms include severe, sudden abdominal pain followed by vomiting and distention.

wart (verruca). A small skin tumor caused by papilloma viruses. They are usually benign, and may disappear spontaneously. Warts may form on fingers, elbows, face, soles of feet, or genitalia.
whooping cough (pertussis). An acute infectious disease caused by *Bordetella pertussis* and spread in the air by the cough of an infected person. Highly contagious, it is a serious childhood disease.
xanthema. Condition in which a yellow pigment, carotene, is present in the blood. Marked by yellowing of the skin and a pseudo, rather than a true, jaundice, as there is no yellow discoloration of eye whites.
x-rays. Electromagnetic radiation of a wavelength shorter than visible light or ultraviolet radiation. X-rays have the ability to penetrate the body and most other solids, and to act on photographic film, making them valuable in diagnosing diseases.
yeast infection. A popular term for several fungal infections: candidiasis, thrush, and some forms of vaginitis. Yeasts, which reproduce by budding, are unicellar fungi of the genus *Saccharomyces*.
Zollinger-Ellison syndrome. A condition characterized by tumors of the pancreas, about 60 percent of which are malignant. With the secretion of too much hydrochloric acid and pepsin, there is eventual ulceration of the intestinal lining and the stomach.

For further reference

The American Medical Directory
 American Medical Association
Angel, Jack E.
 Physicians Desk Reference
 Medical Economics Company
Belsky, Marvin S., M.D.
 How to Choose Your Doctor
 Arbor House
Berkow, Robert, M.D.
 The Merck Manual (Diagnosis and Therapy)
 Merck & Company
Directory of Medical Specialists
 A.N. Marquis Company
It's Good to Know About Mental Health
 U.S. Government Printing Office
 1724-0037
Medicaid-Medicare, Which Is Which?
 U.S. Government Printing Office
 MSA-901-70

Mindell, Earl
 Earl Mindell's Pill Bible
 Bantam Books
Sehnert, Keith W., M.D.
 How to Be Your Own Doctor
 Grosset & Dunlap
Someone Close to You Drinks Too Much
 U.S. Government Printing Office
 HE 20.8302:D 83 (SB) $2
Vickery, Donald, M.D. and Fries, James F., M.D.
 Take Care of Yourself: A Consumer's Guide to Medical Care
 Addison-Wesley Publishing Company
Wolfe, Sidney and Coley, Christopher
 Pills That Don't Work
 Farrar Strauss & Giroux

Information resources:
American Hospital Association
 840 North Lake Shore Drive
 Chicago, IL 60611
Joint Commission on Accreditation of Hospitals
 875 N. Michigan Avenue
 Chicago, IL 60611

The National Cancer Institute
 Building 31, Room 10 A
 Bethesda, MD 20205
The American Heart Association
 44 East 23rd Street
 New York, NY 10010
The U.S. Government Printing Office
 Washington, DC 20402

You and Modern Medicine

Managing the Family's Money

- Planning and record-keeping 111
- Using credit wisely 114
- Dealing with your bank 115
- Saving and investing 118
- Looking ahead to tax time 120
- Buying insurance 122
- Putting your affairs in order 126
- Planning for retirement 127
- Managing your shopping 130
- Your shelter dollar 132
- Managing your car 134
- An economical vacation 135
- Glossary 136
- Booklets on request 139

When we do think about money, it is either about how it comes in or how it goes out. This section will not tell you how to make more money come in—except through prudent investing. It will tell you some of the ways you can control the way money goes out. Managing the family's money means keeping track of it and making sure you put it to the best use in the ways you spend and save it.

In this age of inflation, high interest rates, and wide-ranging opportunities for saving and investing, money management has captured the interest of people everywhere. People who never spent much time thinking about the subject before are now paying for the advice of professional financial planners.

There are many paths on the financial landscape, and not all of them lead where we might hope. But there are some basic facts that can help us make sensible choices. This section sets many of them forth.

The information here is generally correct for the entire United States, but state laws do vary in some cases. If you think your state requirements might differ, ask your elected representative to check them for you.

The seven ages of your economic life

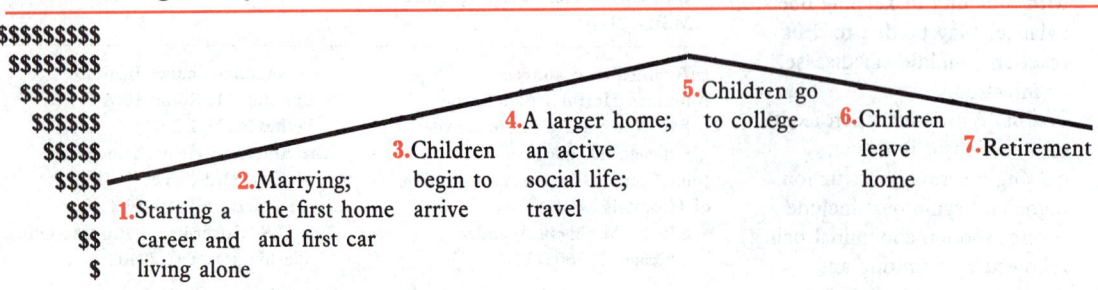

Planning and record-keeping

Dwight D. Eisenhower is said to have remarked when he was a general, "It's not the plan that counts, it's the planning." What he meant, of course, was that the very act of planning—setting goals, gathering facts, deciding what is important, figuring out how to get where you want to go—is worthwhile in itself. It helps you to understand what you are doing and why you are doing it. The particular plan you come up with may have to be changed or discarded in favor of a better one, but the discipline and knowledge that come from working up a plan will always be to your advantage.

Managing the family's money begins with planning. You set your goals for the kind of life you want to lead and the things you want your family to have. You get all the facts you can about how much you will need to save, to spend, and to invest. You also need to know how to make the best use of credit, the services that are available, and the potential pitfalls.

Good record-keeping is essential. You must keep receipts for important items and make note of important cash outlays. To do this, you must find a way to keep records that suits you. For one person, it might be a ledger book with neatly written entries. For another, a shoebox would be just right for keeping records on separate pieces of paper. There is nothing wrong with a shoebox provided you use it consistently and start a new one at regular intervals—every six months or a year—putting each important sales slip or receipt into it and making sure that each item is identified on the slip. Include gifts to charity, interest expense items, sales tax, and all other items you would not find recorded in your checkbook.

Planning also means keeping permanent records of basic information (such as that suggested on the next page). This information can be useful to you and your family at various times throughout the year and is absolutely essential when a family member dies. The mere act of filling out the form may suggest ideas to you. Perhaps you have partly overlapping insurance policies, or not enough coverage. As you review the record at least once a year, changing conditions will suggest other revisions.

Your financial plan should start with your estimate of how much you are worth. Use the chart on page 112 as your guide.

Your net worth at any one time does not mean very much by itself. But if you go through the exercise of figuring out your net worth every year and you find that it is going down, this is a clear signal that something is wrong.

Next it is time to work up a budget, based on how much you earn and how much you should reasonably

Paying for college

Saving enough to send a child to college is unrealistic for most families.

Some schools offer tuition budget plans. You make monthly payments while your son or daughter is in college.

The federal government's Guaranteed Student Loan (GSL) program enables freshmen and sophomores to borrow up to $2625 a year and juniors and seniors up to $4000 a year at low interest rates. Repayment begins six months after studies are completed. The student has to show need to be eligible for a GSL. Loans for Parents are available up to $4000 a year with higher interest rates and repayment beginning in 60 days.

Students who can show need are eligible for Supplemental Educational Opportunity Grants (SEOG) of $100 to $2000.

Unusually needy students borrowing for the first time can get loans at 5 percent from the Carl D. Perkins National Direct Student Loan program. The Pell Grant program provides grants based on need up to $2300 a year.

Managing the Family's Money

spend. Before you draw up a budget, have your family keep an informal record of expenses for a month. Then estimate how much you spend on once-a-year events like a vacation and Christmas, dividing such expenses by twelve. Make sure you take into account all other outlays that come up during the year, such as quarterly tax payments. Then summarize all your income during the year, including interest payments from the bank and dividends on life insurance. With this information on inflow and outgo, you have the basis for your budget.

If the figures show that there is not much left over for savings, review your expense items with your family and decide on what can be cut back or eliminated. Be sure to make some provision for unexpected expenses. A budget will soon fail if it is too tightly drawn up.

$1 × 10 years = 50¢

The problem of our time

Underlying all your planning, there should be an awareness of the unavoidable problem of our time—inflation. Remember this rule of thumb: a 7 percent increase each year means a doubling in ten years, which means that you would need $2 ten years from now to buy what $1 buys today.

When you see an advertisement for an Investors Retirement Account (IRA) that states $2000 a year may grow to a million dollars at your time of retirement, remember that a million dollars in the 2020's will be worth $125,000 in today's dollars, assuming 6 percent inflation.

How much are you worth?

Like a business, a family that manages its money effectively starts with a balance sheet. The difference between the assets and the liabilities is what cost accountants call *net worth*.

Assets
Cash and marketable securities
    Cash in checking and
        savings accounts   _____
    Certificates of deposit   _____
    Mutual fund shares   _____
    U.S. Savings Bonds   _____
    Life insurance cash value
        (obtainable from your
        insurance agent)   _____

Other assets
    Real estate (including
        your home)   _____
    Pension value   _____
    IRA and Keogh accounts   _____
* Automobiles   _____
* Furniture and appliances   _____
* Personal possessions   _____
          Total assets   _____

Liabilities
Current liabilities
    Bills payable   _____
    Installment loans   _____

Long-term liabilities
    Mortgage   _____
    Bank loans   _____
          Total liabilities   _____
*Depreciated   **Net worth**   _____

The family budget

No budget format would be right for all families, but here are typical items that should be included in an annual budget.

Income
Salaries   _____
Interest   _____
Dividends   _____
Sale of securities or property
    (these should be recognized
    as unusual items unless you
    sell securities every year)   _____
Bonuses
    (also to be treated as
    unusual items)   _____
          Total income   _____

Outgo
Food   _____
Clothing   _____
Automobile operating costs   _____
Shelter costs, including
    mortgage payments   _____
Miscellaneous purchases   _____
Health care   _____
Entertainment   _____
Vacation   _____
Education   _____
Interest expense   _____
Insurance premiums   _____
Charitable contributions   _____
Taxes   _____
          Total outgo   _____
      **Balance available for
      saving and investing**   _____

The family record

Information related to money management that should be available to everyone in your family.

Your name:	Date and place of birth:
Your Social Security number:	
Your spouse's name:	Date and place of birth:
Spouse's Social Security number:	
First child's name:	Date and place of birth:
Social Security number:	
Same information for each additional child:	
Your employer's name and address:	
Name and telephone number of your supervisor:	
Spouse's employer's name and address:	
Name and telephone number of supervisor:	
Your attorney's name and telephone number:	
Your accountant's, or tax advisor's, name and telephone number:	
Your insurance agent's name and telephone number:	
Your bank or savings institution officer:	
Date and location of your will:	
Your executor:	
Numbers of bank checking and savings accounts and certificates of deposit:	
Interest income:	
Location of check recordbooks, passbooks, and certificates:	
Your safe deposit box location and number:	
Location of keys:	
Description of valuable possessions and serial numbers (of such items as cameras):	
Description of real estate you own:	
Date and cost of purchase:	
Name and address of mortgage holder:	
Descriptions of investments, such as mutual fund shares:	
Income from investments:	Dates investments were made:
Name of investment company, bank or broker, and numbers of the accounts:	
Name of life insurance company:	
Numbers and face values of the policies on your life:	Loans against the policies:
Same information for policies on your spouse's life:	Premium due dates:
Name of automobile insurance company:	
Number and amount of the policy:	Premium due date:
Name of health and disability insurance company:	
Number and amount of the policy:	Premium due date:
Name of home-owner's insurance company:	
Number and amount of the policy:	
Loans outstanding:	Interest payment dates:
Repayment dates:	
Mortgage balance and monthly payment:	
Installment loans:	Payments due:
Credit card account numbers:	
Address of issuer to be notified:	
Your Social Security benefit (if applicable):	

Managing the Family's Money

Using credit wisely

Like fire and water, credit is a good servant but a poor master. The nation's economy runs on credit, and most of us have come to depend on it every day of our lives.

For most people, credit is not difficult to obtain, whether in the form of a charge account or installment credit at a store, a credit card from a bank, or a loan from a credit union.

Applying for credit. When you apply for credit, you will be asked questions about your stability in society and your ability to pay off loans. How long have you been with your present employer? Do you own your own home? If not, how long have you rented the space where you now live? Do you have checking and savings accounts? Do you have a history of paying your bills on time?

There is no fixed credit rating that follows you wherever you go. Lenders judge you by their own standards.

Credit at a store. When you open a charge account at a department store, you may be offered a revolving account. This has a set limit on how much you can owe the store at one time, with interest to be paid every month on the unpaid balance.

If you want to buy something on the installment plan, ask yourself these two questions first: Would I pay cash for this if I had the cash available? Is what I am buying going to last longer than it will take me to pay off this loan?

Before you sign the installment contract, ask the seller for the annual percentage rate (APR). The APR, which is the total finance charge expressed as a percentage of the amount you are borrowing, is the true interest cost, and it may be higher than you realize. For example, if you paid off a loan of $100 with twelve equal monthly installments totaling $110, your true interest was not 10 percent; it was 18 percent. The amount you owed kept declining while you continued to pay interest on the total loan.

Also ask the seller for the total cost of the loan, including payments and principal, the cost of late charges, and the penalties, if any, for paying off early.

Credit unions. If you live in an area where there are few banks or savings institutions competing with each other, an economical source of credit is a local credit union. Members purchase shares in the association, and loan applications are reviewed by a committee of members. Since members do much of the administrative work with the help of a small paid staff, a credit union can give its members better value.

Credit card tips

- Be sure to sign your credit card promptly.
- Do not carry more cards than you absolutely need.
- Do not give your card to a salesperson without making sure that you get your own card back.
- When your card expires and a new one is issued, cut the old card in half before you discard it.
- When you get your credit card receipt, ask for and then destroy both of the little pieces of carbon paper. Wastebaskets are searched by credit card defrauders, who can copy your number and signature from the carbon paper, or even manufacture a fake card with your name and number.
- Do not give your credit card number to strangers who telephone you.
- Keep the numbers and issue dates of your cards with your personal records.
- Report the loss of your card immediately, even if someone telephones you to say he has found it and will return it. He may be stalling for time in which to run up charges in your name. You are not liable for any charges if you report the loss promptly.

"Plastic" from the bank. Credit cards issued by banks, such as Visa and MasterCharge, are by far the most widely used form of credit. If you have "plastic," the best rule is to think of it not as a *credit* card but as a *charge* card—a convenience that you have with you to avoid the trouble and risk of carrying cash. A card also saves you money by enabling you to take advantage of unexpected sales and bargains. In addition, it offers the great convenience of shopping by telephone.

With many bank cards, it has been possible to obtain free credit by paying the bill in full before the monthly due date. Increasingly, however, banks are charging interest from the day they receive each charge slip from the participating establishment.

If you let your balance accumulate, you are paying interest at the rate of 18 to nearly 20 percent a year, although some banks introduce credit cards with rates as low as approximately 12 percent. Your bank will not object if you take your time paying off the balance, provided you pay the relatively small monthly minimum—a sure sign that this arrangement is to the bank's advantage, not yours. By paying off more than the minimum, you significantly reduce your interest costs.

Dealing with your bank

A bank borrows at wholesale and lends at retail. Besides paying you interest on money you deposit and charging you higher interest on money you borrow, a commercial—or full-service—bank offers a wide range of services.

In addition to checking and savings accounts, banks offer money market accounts, Individual Retirement Accounts (IRA's), Keogh accounts, certificates of deposit (CD's), home improvement loans, home mortgages, automobile loans, personal loans, and credit cards. They also provide such services as automatic teller machines (ATM's), safe deposit boxes, purchasing government bonds on your behalf, paying utility bills out of your account, and automatically depositing your paychecks or Social Security checks. Savings institutions offer some of these services, including negotiable orders of withdrawal (NOW) accounts, which are interest-bearing checking accounts.

Choosing your bank.
In selecting your bank or savings institution, remember that no service is truly free. Compare the rates and service charges with those of their competitor institutions and look at the details of the various savings plans, including certificates of deposit and money market accounts.

Ask about savings plans. Among the questions you should ask about savings plans are these: How frequently is interest compounded? What is the effective annual yield, not just the interest rate? Is interest compounded from day of deposit to day of withdrawal? Is there an interest penalty for early or frequent withdrawal? Are deposits insured? How quickly do funds become available?

Banks and savings institutions now pay the same interest on passbook savings accounts, but the relatively low rate makes such an account unattractive for depositing more than a few hundred dollars.

The checking account.
The greatest convenience a bank or savings institution offers is the checking account. A check is essentially theftproof and, once it has been paid and returned to you, indisputable proof that payment was made. Your check recordbook gives you a dependable and up-to-the-minute record of your cash inflow and outgo.

Many banks offer as many as five different kinds of checking accounts. Find out if the checking services in the bank you are considering are competitive on interest paid (if any), number of checks allowed, service charges, and minimum balance required.

Do not choose a bank on the basis of its giveaways. Instead read the bank's fine print about its interest rates and service charges.

Special checking usually involves a fee but no minimum balance; it is best suited to someone who writes less than half a dozen checks a month. *Regular checking*, for people who write more checks, is likely to require a minimum balance or service charge. A *NOW account*, at either a bank or savings institution, pays interest close to savings account rates. A *Super NOW account* pays higher rates, like those of the bank's money market deposit account, but it may require a minimum balance, and it imposes relatively high service charges. The Super NOW is of greatest use to people who need quick access to a lot of cash and who write many checks. As we shall see later, banks also offer overdraft accounts, for convenient borrowing at high interest rates.

A *joint checking account* is a convenience for a couple, provided they both enter all their transactions in the same recordbook, which the bank provides along with the blank checks. A couple should be aware that any money in a joint account belongs legally to either person and can be completely withdrawn without the other's knowledge. Since some states freeze a joint account when one of the co-owners dies, it is essential for the survivor to have access to other funds at such a time.

Do not make out a check to "cash" unless you immediately give it to the recipient, because you have thereby turned your check into cash. If your checkbook is stolen, notify the bank immediately so that your account can be frozen. The bank will honor only those checks that you have written.

If you write a check and then decide you do not want it honored, call the bank's stop-payment department. It will stop payment for a fee, provided there would have been enough in your account to pay the check anyway. Notify the person to whom you issued the check.

When you make a deposit into your checking account, allow several working days for your account to be credited. Always deposit a check as soon as you receive it.

Managing the Family's Money

Balancing your checkbook.

After you receive your checking account statement from the bank, balance your check recordbook against the statement within a few days. If you wait longer and find an error in the bank's statement, it may be too late for them to locate their error speedily.

Although it should be a simple matter to balance your check recordbook, some people find it confusing because not all of the checks that have been written clear the bank by the time a statement is completed.

The figure on the last line of your table should equal the balance on the bank statement. If it is off by a significant amount, check your arithmetic, making sure you did not add when you should have subtracted, or vice versa. If your balance is off by an insignificant amount, assume the bank statement to be correct and make a compensating entry on the first open line of your check recordbook.

How to balance your checkbook

1. Arrange the canceled checks in numerical order.
2. Check them off in pencil against the debit column of the bank's statement.
3. Go through the canceled checks again, this time checking them off in pencil against the entries in your check recordbook. The lowest-numbered checks will probably include a few that did not clear before the previous statement.
4. When you come to a check in your recordbook that has not yet cleared the bank, draw a circle in red around the number of that check in the recordbook.
5. Go through the same two procedures with your deposit slips. If you have entered a deposit in your check recordbook that does not show up on the bank statement, draw a red circle around it in the recordbook.
6. Draw a red line underneath the last check in your recordbook that is also shown on the bank statement. This is the cutoff point.
7. Enter in your recordbook the bank's debit for charges and credit for interest (if any), so that these amounts will be reflected in your own balance before the next statement comes from the bank.
8. Draw up a simple table on a piece of paper like this:

Your recordbook balance
  (the last balance above the red line you drew)   _____

Plus Total of outstanding checks
  (those you circled in red)   + _____

Plus Any interest credited to your statement (if it is an interest-bearing account)   + _____
                                                    Total   _____

Minus Recent deposits entered by you but not yet credited by the bank (circled in red)   − _____
                                              Difference   _____

Minus Service charges shown on the bank statement   − _____
                              Difference: Your balance   _____

Do's and don'ts of writing a check

Face of check
1. Name and address printed on check make it easier to cash.
2. Number your checks if they are not already numbered.
3. Date properly; never postdate. It *is* legal to date a check on a Sunday or holiday.
4. Do not use Mr., Mrs., Ms., or Miss.
5. Do not leave a space between $ and the first digit.
6. Start writing at the end of the line. The written figure with the fraction is the amount the bank pays.
7. Draw a line between the fraction and "dollars."
8. The memo entry is for your convenience only.
9. Sign the same way every time. Do not write in pencil, even though it is legal. If you make a mistake, tear up the check and cross out the check number in your check recordbook.

Back of check
10. Endorse on back of left end.
11. Endorse exactly as your name appears on the face of the check as payee. Write your regular name underneath in parentheses.
12. Writing "for deposit only" will prevent the check from being cashed by someone else.

116

Managing the Family's Money

Other kinds of checks. For an unusual transaction, you may be asked to pay with a certified check. In this case, you write your own check for a specific amount to a specific payee and take it to your bank, where it will be signed and stamped by a bank officer. At the same time, the officer will reserve that amount from your account so that there will be enough to pay the check when it comes in, regardless of what other checks you write. At this point, your certified check is as good as cash and should be given directly to the payee.

A cashier's check has similar uses. It is made out and signed by an officer of the bank in return for a payment by you to the bank. It is best to have it made out to your name so that there is a record that the payment is going through your hands. You can then endorse it to the payee when you hand it over, and be sure to get a receipt.

Most banks provide traveler's checks, which are issued by a few large banks or other financial institutions known around the world. Traveler's checks are useful when you are traveling or moving because they are usually accepted everywhere while personal checks are not. If lost, traveler's checks can be replaced and the money returned. But they should not be held for a long time. When you buy one, you are in effect lending the bank your money at no interest, and at a small charge to you.

A place for your savings.
Banks compete vigorously for your savings. In addition to the traditional passbook savings account, many banks and savings institutions now offer time deposit accounts with fixed interest at much higher rates. Usually referred to as CD's, these insured accounts have minimum periods of deposit ranging from three months to as long as ten years, with penalties for early withdrawal. The minimum deposit in many banks is $1000 for certificates of deposit of less than a year and $500 for longer terms.

Banks also offer money market deposit accounts, which pay interest that is adjusted periodically in line with interest rates in the money market. This is the market where short-term debt securities are traded. Some banks require a minimum deposit in a money market account.

A place to borrow.
On the other side of the banking business, there is at least as much competition to lend you money.

One of the simplest and most economical ways to borrow at a bank or savings institution is to borrow against your own passbook. The interest rate is lower than on a regular loan, and you continue to earn interest on your entire deposit.

Do not carry your ATM number

- Be sure *not* to write your ATM identification number on anything you carry or keep at your place of work. Keep the only record of the number in a safe place at home.
- Always check your receipt before leaving.
- Make sure the machine is back to its original setting.
- As soon as you get home, enter your ATM transaction in your recordbook.
- If you lose your ATM access card, call the bank immediately. If the card is used by someone who has found out your ATM identification number, you will have to file a report with the police.

Many banks also offer overdraft checking accounts under various names. You activate your account simply by writing one of the special checks for that account given to you by the bank. Each month you receive a statement specifying the part of the loan to be paid back that month and the high interest rate charges you have to pay.

You can obtain loans at banks for a variety of specific needs. In applying for such a loan, be sure to ask the annual percentage rate. This is the total finance charge—more than simple interest—expressed as a percentage of the amount borrowed.

Some banks also offer debt consolidation loans, for people who are unable to keep up with their bills. The idea sounds appealing because your monthly payment for the loan can be less than the monthly total for all your bills. The bank achieves this sleight-of-hand by stretching out the payments over a long period of time; thus, the total interest you pay is very high.

Other bank services.
Automatic teller machines (ATM's) enable you to make deposits or withdrawals at any hour of the day, including weekends and holidays. This means you can make a deposit without carrying cash or checks around, and you can begin earning interest immediately. It also means you can obtain cash whenever you need it.

Safe deposit boxes are useful for storing items difficult to replace. These include securities; the deed to your house; the title to your automobile; birth and marriage certificates; your home-owner's insurance policy; an inventory of possessions in your house; and a copy—not the original—of your will. Since some states seal safe deposit boxes on the death of the owner, do not store any items that would be needed right after your death. Keep a list at home of the contents of your box.

Managing the Family's Money

Saving and investing

Everyone knows it is wise to put something aside regularly. Everyone also knows of good uses for the money saved—an untroubled retirement, a vacation home, a weekend cottage.

Clearly, some ways of saving are easier than others, and some investments are safer than others. U.S. Savings Bonds purchased through the payroll savings plan and mutual fund shares acquired with regular monthly payments offer good investment and good savings.

Savings bonds. U.S. Savings Bonds, Series EE, once considered an unappealing investment choice in a time of rising interest rates, are now more attractive. The most secure of all savings or investments, because they are backed by the U.S. government, they now offer—when held for five years or more—an annual interest rate that equals 85 percent of the average yield on U.S. Treasury five-year notes over the period, with a guaranteed minimum of 6.0 percent. They can be bought in multiples of $25 and can be redeemed at any time between the fifth and tenth years. After ten years, an EE bond purchased for $25 is worth $50 or more, depending on how much interest has been accumulated; it will continue to earn interest for another 40 years if it is not redeemed. Federal income taxes do not have to be paid on any of the interest until the bonds are redeemed, an attractive feature for people approaching retirement who expect to be in a lower income tax bracket when they cash in the bonds. Like other U.S. government securities, EE bonds are never subject to state and local income tax.

Great American tax shelters. In recent years, two forms of investment have been introduced through changes in the tax laws. They have made it highly attractive for employed and self-employed people to save for their retirement.

Investment Retirement Accounts (IRA's). An IRA offers any man or woman earning at least $2000 a year who is not covered by an employer pension plan (or, if covered, with an adjusted gross income of less than $25,000) an opportunity to take a tax deduction for $2000, if the same amount is deposited in an IRA account. You can take this deduction even if you do not itemize deductions on your tax return. More important in the long run, any income earned in the IRA account is sheltered from income tax until you withdraw it after the age of 59½. This has a powerful multiplier effect, since tax-sheltered income on your original investment can be reinvested to produce further income that is also tax-sheltered.

Compounding makes the difference

Always ask for the effective annual yield when you are planning to deposit money in a bank or savings institution.

Here is why. Simple interest—that is, without compounding—on $10,000 at 7.15 percent would be $715 for a year.

With daily compounding, the interest would be $26 more.

SAVINGS BANK RATES
(not typical of all savings banks)
Compounded Daily

Account	Annual rate %	Annual yield %
1 year	6.20	6.40
2 years	6.65	6.88
4 years	7.15	7.41

No tax is due until you begin withdrawals, which can be as early as age 59½. At age 70½, withdrawals must begin according to a schedule based on your life expectancy.

If you need to, you may borrow the funds needed to deposit in your IRA; it would likely be to your advantage to borrow for this purpose in view of the tax benefits. Your deposit can be made as late as April 15 in the year following the year for which you want to take the deduction on your income tax. The sooner you make the deposit, however, the sooner it will begin earning tax-sheltered income for you.

IRA accounts at banks, savings institutions, and credit unions are all insured up to $100,000. If your account is with a mutual fund company, it will have more potential for gain at possibly greater risk than in a bank or savings institution, and it will not be federally insured. Insurance companies also offer IRA's, but they tend to charge higher fees for opening accounts.

If only one member of your family is earning income, a joint IRA account can be opened with an annual deposit and tax deduction of $2250. For a working couple not covered by employer pension plans (or with an adjusted gross income of less than $40,000 if filing jointly and if either is covered by an employer pension plan), the amount would be $4000.

Keogh accounts. Self-employed people can invest not only in IRA's but also in Keogh accounts, which work in a similar way.

Managing the Family's Money

If you are self-employed, you can invest in a Keogh plan and claim a deduction each year for as much as 25 percent of your earned income, or a maximum of $30,000, whichever is less. This would be in addition to the $2000 that you invest in an IRA. As in an IRA, the deposit can be made as late as April 15 of the year following the year of the tax deduction, you can begin withdrawals as early as age 59½ without a tax penalty, and you must begin withdrawing by age 70½.

There is, however, one other requirement of a Keogh plan. If you have any employees who have worked for you for at least three years, you must contribute to your Keogh plan on your employees' behalf a percentage of their income equal to the percentage of your own income that you are contributing. Any contributions that you make for your employees are deductible as business expenses.

Your investment choices.
Many people look for opportunities for investment, but few have the expert knowledge to select from the many choices offered by the financial markets. Except for the wealthy person who can pay for expert advice, it is nearly impossible for an investor to obtain professional, unbiased recommendations on which stocks or bonds to buy and, sometimes more important, when to sell.

Mutual funds. Many investors meet the problem of obtaining expert advice by purchasing shares in mutual funds. Owning large, diversified portfolios of stocks or bonds selected and continuously reviewed by professional managers, mutual funds spread the risk, and they can be bought and sold easily.

Many mutual funds have a sales charge as high as 8.5 percent of the investment. These are called "load" funds. "No-load" funds, so called because they have no sales commission and charge only a management fee of typically no more than 1 percent a year, perform in many cases as well as the load funds or better.

In either case, you can select a fund according to its investment objective—income (from high-dividend stocks and corporate or government bonds); growth (with investments in stocks that involve more than average risk); or balance (offering both income and growth). Funds are rated according to their performance every year in magazines that you will find at your library, including *Forbes* and *Money*.

Mutual funds can be purchased under various plans. If you do not have a large sum to invest at once, you might consider the contractual plan, under which you pay a fixed amount each month.

Dividends are paid every quarter from the income on the fund's portfolio of investments. Once a year, the fund makes a capital gain distribution based on any increase in the value of the shares of the stocks it owns.

Money market funds. Many investment companies that manage mutual funds also offer money market funds. These funds are directly competitive with banks' money market accounts, and tend to have somewhat higher returns on investment. Unlike the banks' accounts, money market funds are not insured by the government; but you can, if you wish, select a fund that invests only in U.S. Treasury securities, which is as good as insurance. Some money market funds require an initial investment of $1000. You can write checks on your account, usually with a minimum of $500.

A family of funds. If you have not invested in mutual funds before, you could pick an investment company with a family of funds and start in their money market fund until you build up a substantial amount of cash. Then you could switch all or part of that money to one or more of the other funds in the same group.

Real estate.
A completely different kind of investment—and, in the view of many, a hedge against inflation—is real estate. Before the Tax Reform Act of 1986 took effect, real estate investments offered significant tax advantages to people in higher income brackets. But tax considerations aside, there are some disadvantages to real estate for investors to keep in mind.

If the neighborhood deteriorates, you may have to sell at a sacrifice. In a time of depression, any real estate value is likely to suffer. If your property stays undeveloped, it produces no income but still gets taxed. Values are no longer rising as they did in the early 1980's, and in some areas they are falling.

If you are, nevertheless, persuaded by the argument that the supply of land is fixed while the number of people keeps growing, limit your real estate investing to opportunities in your own area. Then you can see for yourself what is happening to values. Experts say the best residential real estate investment, whether you live in it or not, is a medium-priced house in a neighborhood that is desirable or improving.

For those in high-tax brackets, municipal bonds are often a good investment because they are tax-free for people living in the issuer's jurisdiction.

Managing the Family's Money

Looking ahead to tax time

Income tax instructions have been simplified in recent years, and several inexpensive books are available to help you prepare your return. Whether you do your own return or have it done for you, it is essential to keep good records throughout the year. These include
- property tax receipts;
- canceled checks for gifts to charity, tax payments, and other deductible items;
- receipted bills for moving expenses;
- medical bills;
- bills for expenses in connection with your job, such as safety equipment, for which you have not been reimbursed.

The Internal Revenue Service (IRS) urges you to continue keeping such records three years after a return is filed, after which the statute of limitations runs out for that return.

The IRS also suggests that you read the tax form when you receive it at the beginning of the year and make sure that you understand it; collect all your records early; begin to work on the sample sheets; and call the nearest IRS office if you have any questions. The earlier in the year you do this, the easier it will be to get their attention.

After you have filled out your return, wait until just before April 15 to mail it. The funds that you have to provide with the return can be earning money for you at the bank until the filing date. More important, you are likely to pick up an error you may have made if you give yourself plenty of time to review the figures. The IRS says that people who prepare their returns just before the deadline make the most errors.

Income you do not have to report

- Accident and health insurance benefits
- Benefits from disability insurance you purchased yourself
- Federal income tax refunds
- Gifts to you
- Life insurance dividends (unless they include interest on reinvested dividends)
- Life insurance proceeds
- Sick pay (if permanently and totally disabled)
- Social Security benefits (unless your adjusted gross income—including half of Social Security retirement benefits—is more than $25,000 for you alone or $32,000 for you and your spouse filing jointly)
- Veterans' benefits
- Welfare payments
- Workmen's compensation

Start work on completing your tax return early, but wait until the last minute before returning it with your check.

Confusing income tax terms

exemption: reduces each taxpayer's income by $1900 in 1987 and more in later years; if your income was $1900 or less, you are exempt from paying taxes.

deduction: an amount that you are allowed to subtract from your income *before* computing your tax.

credit: an amount that you subtract from your tax *after* computing it; thus, it is worth more, dollar for dollar, than a deduction.

deferral: a tax obligation that you do not have to pay as long as the income is sheltered.

Do you like to get a big refund?

If you like to get a big refund on your income tax, you are not managing your money the best way.

Getting a refund means you have given the government the use of your money for nothing, because a refund comes to you with absolutely no interest.

If you got a big refund last year, try doing an estimate of what your tax is going to be for the current year. If you find that too much of your income is being withheld, ask your employer for a W-4 form. Using the formula on the form, figure out how many allowances to request in order to bring your total withholding for the year close to your estimated tax.

You will not have a nice refund to look forward to, but you will have the use of funds to invest yourself.

Tax facts

Loss on sale. You cannot deduct a loss on a sale of property or goods to close relatives—grandparents, parents, children, brothers, sisters, spouse. In-laws are no problem.

Working at home. If you are unable to set aside a whole room as an office for a business that you carry on at home, you can meet the IRS test for a home office by setting up a partition to separate the office area from the rest of the room.

Selling your house. If you sell your house when you are 55 or older, you can avoid tax on up to $125,000 of the profit on the sale. But you can do this only once, and, if the profit is less than $125,000, you cannot save the balance for another tax-exempt sale. The $125,000 allowance must also include any deferred profits on sales of houses you made before you were 55. (If you sold a house at a profit before 55, the capital gain was deferred for tax purposes if you bought another house costing at least as much.)

Job deductions. You can deduct the cost of looking for a new job *in the same line of work* as you are currently in, along with the cost of courses to maintain or improve your job skills.

Marriage penalty. A working married couple is penalized in comparison with two single people with the same incomes. For 1986, a working couple could take a deduction up to $3000 to reduce the penalty, but this deduction was repealed effective in the tax year 1987, making the penalty more severe.

Itemizing deductions. Nearly all home owners save taxes by itemizing deductions instead of taking the standard deduction, chiefly because of interest costs on the mortgage.

State tax deduction. Your deduction for state income taxes should be the actual cash outlay for the tax year, not the amount shown on your latest state tax return.

Moving costs. Moving costs and unreimbursed employee business expenses can be subtracted from your income even if you are not itemizing deductions. The moving deduction is allowed only if a change in your work place has added at least 35 miles to the distance from your previous home to the new work place.

Travel expenses. Although daily travel expenses from home to work are definitely not deductible, you can deduct travel expenses from one regular job to another.

Child care credit. If both parents are working full-time, or if you are a single working parent, you are entitled to a credit against your tax of 20 percent of the total costs of care of a child or a dependent relative living with you and incapable of self-care. But this credit cannot exceed your income from employment.

Baby exemption. A baby born on December 31 counts as an exemption for the whole year.

Deceased spouse. If your spouse dies during the year, you may file a joint return for that year and continue to do so for two more years, provided you have at least one dependent child and do not remarry during that time.

Filing for the deceased. If you are an executor, administrator, or legal representative of someone who died during the year and had taxable income, you must file a return for that person for that year. Taxes are paid out of the estate.

Quarterly intervals. If you file a quarterly return, remember that the amount is not due at regular three-month intervals. Starting with the April 15 filing, succeeding intervals are two months, three months, four months, and three months.

Managing the Family's Money

Buying insurance

When you take out an insurance policy, you are betting that something unfortunate will happen to you at some time. The insurance company is betting it will not happen, at least for quite a while. If nothing happens to you for many years, you and the insurance company both win—in different ways. If something does happen to you, nobody wins, but the insurance coverage helps protect you or your family from financial disaster.

The rates you pay for insurance reflect to some degree the odds of something happening to you. But there is clearly more to buying insurance than knowing the odds. In each field—life, health, home owners, and automobile—you have to make your choice from many types of policies offered by many companies at different prices. Some kinds of coverage are far more economical and effective than others.

Life insurance.
The first rule about life insurance is not to buy it until someone is dependent on the earning power of the insured person. That is why it makes no sense to buy it when you are just out of college, or to insure the life of a child, as some people do.

A rule of thumb many people follow is to buy enough life insurance to make up for five years of the breadwinner's take-home pay. You should also find out how much your family would receive in Social Security survivors' benefits if the breadwinner died now. Your local Social Security office will figure this out for you if you make it clear that you are not asking them to estimate how much you will get in retirement benefits at a future date.

After you have decided how much coverage you need, it is time to select an insurance company. Do not wait for an agent to call on you; he or she will come primed with all the reasons why you should buy from a particular company. If you have a good library nearby, ask to see a copy of *Best's Insurance Reports*, which rates the quality of companies from A+ to C. Then, no matter where you live, make sure that the company you are considering is licensed to write insurance in New York State, which has the strictest standards in the country.

There are two basic kinds of life insurance policy—whole life (also called straight, ordinary, or permanent) and term insurance.

Whole life. This is a combination of insurance and savings, since it eventually builds up a cash value that you can borrow against or cash in. Insurance companies will not tell you how much of your whole life premium is going for savings, but you would probably

---

Insurance-buying strategy

Whether you are buying major medical, homeowner's, or automobile liability insurance, a simple strategy can give you the most effective coverage and help protect you from being financially wiped out.

The strategy is to *accept the highest deductible you think you can handle.* Then, using the money you save, buy the highest coverage you can afford. In exchange for the temporary hardship that a high deductible may cause, you will be buying protection against a financial disaster that could impoverish you and your family for life.

For example, if you increased the deductible on your automobile insurance from $200 to $500, you would save about $80 a year. It would cost you only $30 additional to increase your automobile liability insurance from maximum coverage of $300,000 for all the people in one accident to $1,000,000 coverage.

---

do almost as well to save money in a passbook loan account. From a savings point of view, the return on your investment in a whole life policy is negative for about the first ten years.

When you take out a whole life policy, the premiums are fixed for life. Since the cost of one company's coverage is hard to compare with that of another, ask your agent to show you the interest adjusted cost index for the policy. This takes into account dividends, cash value, and interest you would have earned if you had invested elsewhere. The lower the index figure, the more favorable the comparison.

Some companies also offer whole life without dividends, which means lower premiums. Ask whether the policy has a waiver of premium in the event of your total and permanent disability, and double indemnity in the event of your accidental death. Also ask about discounts for nonsmokers and people who exercise regularly.

The head of a family needs the most insurance when he or she is young and with dependents. Thus, there may come a time when it no longer seems necessary to continue paying premiums on whole life insurance. At that time, take the cash value, which is roughly two-thirds of the face value after 25 to 30 years, or accept reduced coverage without further premiums. Or convert to term insurance, with the same coverage for a limited time.

When you have built up cash value in a whole life policy, it is the most accessible source of funds for borrowing, short of a passbook loan. Insurance companies typically charge no more than 8 percent annual interest for loans against whole life policies. The interest is tax deductible, unless you choose not to pay it, in which case the insurance company simply adds the unpaid interest to your outstanding loan. Because there is no time limit on a policy loan—it is really your own money you are borrowing—there is a great temptation not to pay it back. Some investors deliberately do not pay it back because they do so much better by putting the funds elsewhere. If you do this, of course, there would be less coverage for your heirs, or less value for you if you decided to cash in the policy.

Term insurance. This is life insurance pure and simple, without any savings feature. It starts off in the early years with premiums as low as one-fifth of whole life. That is why insurance agents make lower commissions selling term and thus have far less enthusiasm for it than they do for whole life. Like whole life, term insurance can be bought without dividends, which makes the premiums even lower.

The early years of marriage, when you have children and your spouse may be dependent on you, are not only the years when you need a lot of coverage, they are also the years during which you are less able to pay high premiums; hence, the great appeal of term insurance. The most popular way to buy term is called "annual, renewable, and convertible." This means that the rates go up every year on a fixed schedule; you have the right to renew at the end of each term (generally five years) until you are in your sixties or older; you can convert without a physical examination to whole life whenever you choose. Future premiums are stated in the contract and cannot be changed. But term insurance has no cash value and coverage lasts only as long as you pay premiums.

Since term premiums rise sharply as you get older, you may wish to convert to whole life, with its fixed rates. The time to do this is before the age of 45 for men and 48 for women, after which rates go up significantly.

Universal life. A third basic type of life insurance, universal life, combines term insurance with savings that earn bond-market rates. You are told, moreover, how much of your premiums are going into savings, which is not the case with whole life. Because of administrative fees, universal life is not economical in policies of less than about $50,000.

Mail order life insurance. Some life insurance is sold by mail to members of associations or such groups as users of an oil company credit card. This is generally an economical way to buy insurance, provided the company is well rated by Best's and licensed in New York State, and you cannot be turned down when you apply. Bear in mind, however, that premium rates are not guaranteed and you lose the coverage if you happen to leave the group.

Health insurance.
Every one needs three kinds of health insurance, and a wage-earner needs a fourth as well.

The three kinds are for hospitalization; other basic medical expenses, including surgery and doctors' fees; and major medical fees, in the event of a lengthy or catastrophic illness. The fourth kind, which most wage-earners tend to skimp on, is for disability coverage, to make up for loss of income if a breadwinner is disabled for a long time.

Some private companies offer comprehensive insurance, which combines the first three types. Such a policy is not necessarily the most economical. The National Insurance Consumer Organization, an independent group, estimates that the typical private company pays out about 60 cents of every dollar it takes in, while Blue Cross and Blue Shield, which are not-for-profit organizations with great economies of scale, pay out in the range of 85 to 90 cents on each dollar they take in.

The "Blues." Blue Cross, available through group plans at places of employment or on an individual basis, covers hospitalization. Blue Shield covers the other basic medical expenses. The "Blues" provide major medical coverage, however, only to groups, with minor exceptions.

Life insurance over 55?

Advertisements on TV may sound appealing: life insurance for people over 55 with no medical examination and a monthly premium of a few dollars. But "over 55" does not necessarily include applicants 65 and over. The premium is likely to be for $1000 of coverage. Multiply that by twelve months and the number of thousands you want, and the annual premium may not sound like much of a bargain. Finally, it makes no sense to buy life insurance unless someone is dependent on your earning power.

Managing the Family's Money

Have you thought of joining an HMO?

If your company has 25 or more employees and offers health benefits, you have the choice of joining a Health Maintenance Organization (HMO). You also can join on your own if you are not an employee.

Bringing the physician, the laboratory, and the clinic together, an HMO provides—for a flat fee paid in advance—virtually all the medical services you might need, except dental and long-term psychiatric care.

Compared with private health insurance and your out-of-pocket medical expenses, an HMO would be low in cost. Compared with Blue Cross/Blue Shield, it would cost more but provide more comprehensive service.

The Blues have different plans for different areas of the country, with rates based on where you live and how many people are covered, rather than on age, sex, or health. The family rate covers a family of any size, a particular attraction for large families. The hospital and the other providers of service are paid directly, saving you the need to have cash available. The policies are guaranteed renewable, and any one may sign up during the annual open enrollment period. The Blues may, however, exclude coverage for a preexisting condition for a certain period. As economical and dependable as Blue Cross/Blue Shield coverage is, you may want to consider purchasing additional major medical coverage from a private company to supplement your coverage from the Blues.

When you purchase major medical coverage, accept a high deductible and buy maximum coverage. Ask whether the maximum applies to each illness or injury, or whether it is merely a lifetime total. The latter is clearly less desirable. Also find out whether the "internal limits" of coverage are adequate—the hospital day rate, for example.

When you purchase disability insurance, the amount of income it would pay should be enough to make up for your loss of wages until you are, say, 65. Make sure the policy is not cancelable and that there is no question about the company's definition of disability: you are unable to work at the occupation for which you have been trained. Premiums will be cheaper if you buy coverage that does not begin until a certain period, such as 90 days after you are disabled. Many wage-earners who buy life insurance have never seriously considered disability insurance, not realizing how much of a burden to a family a disabled person would be.

Home-owner's insurance. This is the insurance that covers damage to your home and belongings, and provides liability coverage for injury to others on your property. It also covers damage to other people's property *accidentally* caused by you or your family, or by accidents originating on your property, such as falling trees.

Two particular points to remember about this insurance are that it does not include damage from floods or earthquakes and that the coverage you buy should be at least 80 percent of the replacement cost—not the market value—of your house. Again, accept a high deductible and use the savings to buy liability coverage that will keep you from being wiped out. Awards by juries of a million dollars are not uncommon. "Umbrella liability" insurance to cover you up to that amount can be purchased as a wrap-around for adequate home-owner's and automobile policies for not much more than $100.

Home-owner's insurance comes in various packages. The most popular, called Home-Owner's 3 (HO-3), includes all-risk coverage on your dwelling—for everything except floods, earthquakes, wars, nuclear accidents, and anything else specified—plus "Broad Form" coverage on your personal belongings. Broad Form is not as complete as the most expensive form of coverage. It covers damage from broken pipes but not the pipes themselves, for example.

When you insure your house for 80 percent or more of its replacement cost, damage to any part of the house, such as a bathroom, will be covered at full replacement cost. If the entire house is destroyed, you will receive only 80 percent of the total replacement cost. If you can afford it, you should consider 100 percent coverage on the house.

Your belongings in the house are covered for 50 percent of the insured value of the house, which you may want to increase if you have unusually valuable possessions. Your home-owner's policy will also pay your additional temporary living expenses if your house is too damaged to live in, and it will cover losses away from home of belongings up to 10 percent of their value. The standard personal liability coverage is only $25,000, making it essential to purchase additional coverage.

Because replacement costs increase every year although the market value of a house may not, it is essential to keep your coverage in step with inflation. You can have an "inflation-guard" provision added to a new or existing policy. This will provide for automatic increases in coverage and save you from having to review your policy each year.

Flood and earthquake coverage

Flood and earthquake coverage, not included in home-owner's policies, can be obtained under separate policies.

For information about flood coverage, which is written by local insurance agents and guaranteed by the federal government, call the National Flood Insurance Program, 800-638-6620.

Automobile insurance. As with health and home-owner's insurance, accept a high deductible and buy extra liability coverage. A rule of thumb for a deductible on automobile insurance is slightly more than a week's take-home pay.

Automobile insurance includes five different kinds of coverage.

Liability. Typical coverage is called 50/100/10: $50,000 for injury to one person, $100,000 maximum for all the people in one accident, $10,000 for property damage. Even if you have umbrella coverage, you should consider increasing your liability coverage to 100/300/10 or even 300/500/10. The additional coverage costs only a little more.

Insurance planning worksheet: a checklist

To find out if you have enough insurance—or more than you need—it pays to look through your policies.

Life insurance
What is the total coverage you have (including group coverage by your employer)?
What is the value of each policy and what is the annual premium and dividend?
Do the policies have double indemnity (double payment in case of death by accident)?
What do you estimate to be the cash value? (Your agent can help you.)
What loans have you made against any of the policies?
What assets would your heirs receive in addition to Social Security survivors' benefits?
How long would you expect your survivors to need to adjust to the loss of your income?

Health and disability insurance
How much coverage do your various policies provide?
What is the cost to you?
How much could you afford to pay yourself in case of an extended illness?
How much disability insurance coverage do you have from your employer?

Home-owner's insurance
What do you estimate is the replacement cost of your home?
How much of that cost could you assume in the event the house was totally destroyed?
What is the value of your personal possessions?
If a valuable possession were lost, how much of the replacement cost would you be able to assume?

Automobile insurance
How much coverage does your policy provide for injury to one person?
What is the maximum for all the people in one accident?
How much coverage do you have for collision insurance? Could you afford a larger deductible?
When will your car be five years old and thus no longer worth covering with collision insurance?
Would your uninsured driver coverage be adequate if the breadwinner in your family were seriously injured?

Umbrella insurance
Do you have umbrella insurance to increase your protection against damage awards not adequately covered by home-owner's or automobile insurance? Is your umbrella coverage adequate in light of the million-dollar-or-more awards frequently granted?

Managing the Family's Money

Collision. The most expensive automobile insurance, this covers damage you yourself cause to your car. It should be dropped when a car is four to five years old.
Comprehensive. Also expensive, this covers damage other than that caused by collisions.
Uninsured driver. Cheap and highly desirable, this insurance covers injuries caused by an uninsured or insufficiently insured driver, or a hit-and-run driver.

Medical. This automobile insurance covers treatment for you and your passengers. It is included in your basic coverage except in certain states that have no-fault insurance.

It is worth shopping around for automobile insurance, since rates and quality of service vary widely. Some companies have lower rates for people over 65 no longer driving to work.

Putting your affairs in order

Your estate is what you leave when you die. It consists of all your property, including real estate, investments, bank accounts, life insurance proceeds, personal possessions, and any interests you might have in business ventures. From the total value of your estate are deducted funeral expenses, fees for executors and lawyers, state inheritance taxes, and any outstanding debts.

What is left is subject to federal *estate* taxes—not income taxes. As a result of changes in the tax laws in recent years, few estates are subject to federal taxes. For 1986, no return need be filed for a gross estate (before deductions) of less than $500,000. For 1987, the minimum rises to $600,000, where it will remain in subsequent years. It is estimated that 95 percent of estates will be exempt from federal tax in 1987. Moreover, you can leave any amount in any year to your spouse without incurring a federal estate tax.

After a person dies, his or her will is probated. Probate is the process of filing a will with the appropriate court and having it declared valid; this process can take several months. Certain property, however, passes directly to the beneficiaries without their having to wait for probate. This includes life insurance proceeds (which are paid directly by the insurance company when notified by your agent); pension benefits to a beneficiary named by the pensioner (although not all pension arrangements call for the survivor to receive benefits); U.S. Savings Bonds (if jointly held or if solely held with a designated beneficiary named on the face of the bond); property held in joint tenancy (that is, with the survivor having the right to receive the property); and joint bank accounts.

Your heirs do not have to pay any *income* taxes on life insurance proceeds or anything else they receive from your estate, whether written into the will or not.

In some states, joint bank accounts may be frozen and safe deposit vaults sealed until the state is satisfied that state taxes have been paid for the year in which the person died. That is why it is important for your survivors to have access to funds outside of joint bank accounts—and why your vault should not contain any document, such as a life insurance policy, that would be needed right after your death.

Funeral arrangements should be made clear in the instructions left for survivors. A recent federal law requires funeral directors to break down the costs of the various services they provide when quoting a price for a funeral.

There are certain facts a funeral director might not mention unless asked. No state requires embalming unless a body is to be shipped, but funeral directors do it routinely. Burial vaults required for caskets by certain cemeteries can be simpler and far less costly than the ones recommended by many funeral directors. Caskets usually are not required for cremation. Cremation costs far less than burial.

> **What to do when the head of the family dies**
>
> - Notify employer.
> - Notify lawyer who drew up the will.
> - Notify life insurance agent.
> - Cancel all credit cards, or convert them to the name of the surviving spouse.
> - Notify the local Social Security office, which will arrange for a funeral benefit of $255.
> - Notify the nearest Veterans Administration (VA) office if the deceased was in the armed services. The VA will provide for a wartime veteran or any veteran who suffered a disability a $250 funeral allowance, a $150 allowance if the burial is not in a national cemetery, and a flag for the casket. (Burial in a national cemetery—Arlington is virtually out of the question—is free for any veteran, his spouse, and children in the same grave.)

126

Managing the Family's Money

Planning for retirement

The time to start planning for retirement is when you still have many paychecks ahead of you.

Social Security and, for those who have them, pensions are only a base on which to build a satisfactory retirement income. To achieve an income at the desirable level of two-thirds of your preretirement income, you clearly need your own savings and investments. The sooner you start setting aside a certain amount for retirement out of every paycheck, the smaller the monthly amount will have to be.

In planning your retirement income, consider a variety of investments because your Social Security and pension benefits may not be adequate.

Your retirement needs.

Allowing for continued inflation, you can project how much income you are likely to need after you retire. Some of your needs, such as transportation, may end. Taxes will be lower. Some of your costs, such as your mortgage, will remain fixed and thus insulated from inflation. Your savings are likely to earn higher interest as inflation continues, and your Social Security benefits will be indexed for inflation.

On this page is a table that suggests how you can go about estimating your retirement living costs. If you are still many years away from retirement, it is too early to work out a close estimate of your income from Social Security; in addition, your local Social Security office will be reluctant to help you until you get much closer to retirement. Your pension would also be difficult to estimate many years ahead. But it is still worth trying to get some idea of your retirement needs so that you can plan your savings and investment program wisely.

How much retirement income will you need?

Item	What each item costs you now per month*	What it would cost you in retirement today (current dollars)	What it would cost you in future retirement (inflated dollars)
Food	_____	_____	_____
Shelter (including mortgage, maintenance, fuel, and utilities)	_____	_____	_____
Transportation	_____	_____	_____
Clothing	_____	_____	_____
Medical	_____	_____	_____
Insurance	_____	_____	_____
Vacation	_____	_____	_____
Entertainment	_____	_____	_____
Savings and investments	_____	_____	_____
Total	_____	_____	_____

To calculate for inflation, use a compound interest table from your local library to see how much one dollar of expense would increase over the number of years until you retire. For example, at 5 percent annual inflation for ten years, it would increase to $1.63. Multiply the current figure by that amount to get an inflation-adjusted total.

*For items that do not come up every month, such as a vacation, divide the total yearly cost by 12.

Managing the Family's Money

Social Security. Your Social Security benefits are based on the number of years you have been paying Social Security taxes and your earnings over certain of those years. No one has to work more than ten years, or 40 quarters, to qualify for retirement benefits, but the amount of your monthly check will depend on how much you earned over the years. Do not assume that you will get the highest benefits shown on various tables you may see because you always earned the maximum amount covered by Social Security taxes.

Every few years, you should make sure your Social Security account is being properly credited with your taxes. One way to do this is to copy the form shown on this page and mail it to: Social Security Administration, P.O. Box 57, Baltimore, MD 21203. Another way is to request a postcard from your local Social Security office and send it in.

Inequities in the system. Families with similar incomes often receive different benefits. For example, a family in which only the husband was a wage-earner will receive higher benefits than a family in which both husband and wife worked with a combined income equal to the husband's income in the first family.

This is one of various inequities embedded in a system that originated half a century ago, when attitudes and social conditions were different. With all the problems Social Security now faces, such inequities are unlikely to be removed. Contrary to what many people believe, Social Security is not a fund into which people make "contributions" that they withdraw after retirement. It is a pay-as-you-go system under which working people and their employers are taxed in order to provide benefits for retired people, survivors, and the disabled.

Figuring out approximately how much you will receive in retirement benefits under Social Security is not hard if your retirement is just a few years away. Visit or call your local Social Security office and ask for the leaflet, "Estimating Your Social Security Check."

Although you are eligible for full retirement benefits when you reach 65, you can, if you choose, begin receiving benefits as early as 62. Monthly benefits in that case will be 80 percent of regular benefits (or a prorated percentage for any age between 62 and 65) and will be fixed at that percentage for the rest of your life.

If you delay starting benefits until age 65 to 72, your monthly benefits will be higher than the basic full rate by 3 percent for each year you delay. This is hardly worth doing unless your self-employment income is so high that you receive almost no Social Security benefits.

When a married man is receiving Social Security benefits, his wife can begin receiving *her* benefits at 50 percent of his rate when she reaches 65. She never receives more than 50 percent of his benefits while he is alive. If she chooses to begin receiving benefits at any age between 62 and 65, she will get between 37½ per-

---

REQUEST FOR STATEMENT OF EARNINGS

ACCOUNT NUMBER: ___ ___ ___ / ___ ___ / ___ ___ ___ ___
DATE OF BIRTH: _____ / _____ / 19_____
                          Month   Day   Year

Please send me a Statement of Earnings recorded in my Social Security account.

PLEASE PRINT NAME & ADDRESS IN INK OR USE TYPEWRITER:

NAME: Mr/Mrs/Ms _____
STREET AND NUMBER _____
CITY, P.O. _____
STATE AND ZIP _____
SIGN YOUR NAME AS YOU
USUALLY WRITE IT: _____

Sign your own name only. Under the law, information in your Social Security record is confidential, and anyone who signs someone else's name can be prosecuted.

If your name has been changed from that shown on your Social Security account number card, please copy your name exactly as it appears on that card below:

_____

Managing the Family's Money

cent and 50 percent of her husband's retirement check. This lower rate will continue until her husband dies, after which she would receive a survivor's benefit, explained below.

If the wife has been working and paying Social Security taxes herself, she can receive either a spouse's benefit or a benefit based on her own Social Security taxes, but she cannot receive both. In many cases, a working wife will receive no more from Social Security than if she had been a housewife all her life.

If the husband dies first, the wife can receive 100 percent of his benefit beginning at age 65, or 71.5 percent beginning at age 60 (with percentages in between for starting at any age from 60 to 65).

If the husband dies before the wife reaches 60, and after the youngest child reaches 16, the wife receives no benefits as a survivor until age 60. The child receives benefits until age 18.

All of these examples assume that the husband is the principal wage-earner.

Applying for benefits. To apply for benefits, you must visit your Social Security office three months before the date that you will become eligible, or the date when you choose to begin receiving your retirement checks, if that is later.

When the husband applies, it is not necessary for the wife to be there, unless she is also applying for her benefits. Take the following documents with you: Social Security card and proof of age (birth certificate or baptismal papers); marriage certificate (if applying as a spouse); copy of W-2 form showing the latest year's earnings, or a copy of the latest income tax return.

Medicare coverage. Apply for Medicare at the same time that you apply for retirement benefits. If you have already begun receiving Social Security payments before 65, you will automatically get your Medicare card in the mail by your 65th birthday, which is when Medicare coverage begins.

If you plan to delay the start of retirement checks past age 65, you and your spouse must each remember to apply for Medicare three months before each of you is 65.

Medicare consists of two parts—A and B. Part A, which costs you nothing, pays for your hospital bills. Part B, medical insurance, pays doctors' bills and a number of other items not covered by Part A. For Part B, you pay a monthly premium that covers your spouse and eligible dependents. This premium, which is deducted from your retirement check, is the same for everybody and increases every year on July 1.

Part B is optional. If you do not enroll for Part B within three years after your 65th birthday, you are no longer eligible for that coverage.

Part A helps pay for up to 90 days in each benefit period at any participating hospital. A benefit period runs from the first day of hospital treatment to the 60th

Questions about your pension

If your company has a pension plan, your employer is obligated to give you a description of it once a year. You should know the answers to these questions:

- Is your particular job covered by the plan?
- How long do you have to work before you are vested (before the pension is guaranteed)?
- How old do you have to be for regular or early retirement benefits?
- Is the pension federally insured?
- Is there a benefit for your spouse?

day after release from a hospital or nursing home. Part B generally pays 80 percent of approved medical charges after an annual deductible that you pay.

If you decide to buy supplementary health insurance, which is widely advertised, make sure that the policy does not duplicate any part of Medicare, or that different policies you buy do not duplicate each other.

Your pension.
For many employed people, a pension offers additional retirement income. Most pensions are based, to some extent, on Social Security benefits. The employer usually takes your Social Security benefits into account in deciding how much of a pension to provide for you.

If you die before early retirement age, benefits for your spouse are not likely unless you have contributed to the pension plan yourself.

When you retire, you can choose to have your pension cover your spouse in the event that you die first. In that case, your own monthly payments are reduced while you are living. Depending on your spouse's age, benefits after your death could be as little as 50 percent of your own benefits.

Some pension plans give you a choice of receiving your benefits in monthly payments or in a lump sum. Monthly payments are guaranteed for life but are not adjusted for inflation, unless your employer volunteers to do so. A lump sum can be invested by you, most likely in a rollover Individual Retirement Account, into which you can deposit the entire sum without paying taxes at the time. Unlike a conventional IRA, there is no tax deduction for making the investment, but there are very large tax savings because the income from the investment is sheltered from tax until you make withdrawals, which must begin at age 70½. Assuming that you or your spouse do not draw out all the funds in the account, there would still be money left for your heirs, in contrast to a pension.

Managing the Family's Money

How post-retirement earnings affect Social Security benefits

Social Security benefits ▬
(approximately $7000 maximum in this example)
Earned income ▬

Thousands of dollars a year

1. $8160 is the most a person age 65 to 69 can earn in 1987 without losing some part of Social Security benefits.
2. A person earning approximately this amount or more loses all Social Security benefits until age 70.

Working for yourself. In these inflationary times, many people augment their retirement income by continuing to work.

If you are self-employed and use part of your home as a business, you are allowed significant deductions on your income tax. Check with your local Internal Revenue Service office.

But you will be required to pay self-employment tax as long as you work to help support the Social Security system, even though you may already be drawing Social Security benefits. This tax, which has been slowly increasing year by year, leveled off at 12 percent of net self-employment income from 1986 to 1989. In 1990, a new formula will bring it into line with Social Security taxes paid by employees.

When self-employed people receive Social Security payments, any amount they earn over a certain level reduces their Social Security benefits by one dollar for every two earned. The deduction is made from Social Security benefits at the beginning of the calendar year. In 1986, a retired person age 65 to 69 could earn up to $7800 a year without losing any Social Security retirement benefits. This limit has been increasing every year. From age 70 on, under present regulations, you can earn as much as you want without losing any Social Security benefits.

Managing your shopping

Shopping is where management of the family's money begins. Planning what you are going to buy and following simple rules when you shop can mean the difference between just making ends meet and having money to save.

Going to the supermarket. At least once a week or so, someone in the family has to shop for food and other household needs. Here are some guidelines that can bring considerable savings.

- Do not shop more than once a week. Read the newspaper ads on Wednesdays and Thursdays and plan where you will shop and what you will buy each week. Jot down several menus featuring the specials advertised and note the staples on sale—unperishable items you can stock up on for weeks ahead. Clip coupons, but only for items you really need. Make a shopping list to take with you.
- Go to the supermarket shortly after you have eaten so that you will not have an appetite for expensive treats. Try to shop early in the morning, when stocks of produce and fresh meats and fish offer the greatest choice. Just before a long weekend, you might try shopping late in the day to take advantage of last-minute markdowns. Schedule your shopping trip without your children and, if you are a woman, without your husband. Their impulses can wipe out your economies.
- Do not overstock on produce, the most profitable line for most supermarkets. Do not buy the first of a new crop of fruit or vegetables; prices should come down later. Remember that frozen food prices also go up and down with the season, so try stocking up on a frozen vegetable when the same vegetable is as good a buy as fresh produce. Buy canned fruits and vegetables at the end of summer, when many prices are reduced before the fresh packs come in.
- Keep portions in mind when you are buying meat. Steaks and chops will serve for only one meal; a roast can last for several days.
- Read labels and note how much you are paying per ounce. The large size is not always the economy size.

- Try buying day-old bakery products. After you freeze and thaw them, most people cannot tell them from fresh.
- Remember that junk food is costly, apart from its lack of nourishment. A six-pack of supermarket-brand raisins costs no more than many snack items and less than some.
- Think hard about convenience foods. Instant coffee can be more economical than regular, but does it make sense to pay someone to make your iced tea for you?
- Soft drinks in cans and bottles are an expensive way to buy water—with tiny percentages of artificial flavor. For about the same cost as two 12-ounce cans of soft drink, you can make a sparkling genuine fruit drink by adding store-brand carbonated water to a 6-ounce can of frozen concentrated fruit juice.

Shopping in other stores. In your other shopping, it is important to time certain purchases according to the seasons and to take advantage of sales. Not all sales, however, are what they appear to be. Some, such as department store white sales, feature items that may have been especially manufactured for the sale. Certain goods ordered by mail are not manufactured until after your order has been received. When a sale is announced, look for words that mean the goods have been marked down from a quoted figure. If the ad uses terms like "special purchase" or "comparable value," the prices may not be genuine reductions.

When you purchase a big-ticket item such as a refrigerator or a television set, you will probably be urged to buy a service contract, which provides that repairs will be made at no additional cost for the life of the contract. What some stores do not tell you is that the service contract may partly duplicate the coverage already offered in the warranty, such as parts and repairs at no cost for a full year. Service contracts, moreover, are usually sold for the early years of the life of your purchase, when a problem is less likely to develop. A study at Cornell University concluded that most service contracts are not good buys.

Those glossy catalogs. Unsolicited catalogs that come in the mail have become a popular way to shop for clothes, gifts, and a broad range of unusual items. Catalogs offer convenience and, for people away from large cities, a wide choice of high-priced items.

Some catalogs do offer sales from time to time, but most catalog prices are not competitive, not even with other catalogs. If an item in a catalog catches your eye, watch for it in other catalogs and in your local stores, since prices vary widely. If you do order an item, be prepared to wait a few weeks. According to federal regulations, you have the right to receive any mail-order item within 30 days unless the seller has specified a longer delivery time. If the deadline is not met, you have the right to cancel and get all your money back.

Returns may be a problem unless your catalog is from a nearby department store.

Do you shop at the co-op?

If there is a co-op in your area, you might try it for dairy products, produce, meat, and various staples, on which big savings are possible.

Run by volunteer members, co-ops buy in large quantities, either from commercial wholesalers or wholesalers that are themselves cooperatives. Working members take orders from fellow members, compile the orders and telephone them in to the wholesaler, pick up the orders and break them down for the members, and calculate how much each member owes. Savings can be significant and quality is likely to be higher than in stores. People who have a choice of working for pay or contributing time to the cooperative, however, may find that they just about break even on the co-op.

If there is no co-op in your area and you would like to start one, write for information to:

National Cooperative Business Center
1401 New York Avenue, NW
Washington, DC 20005

A shopper's calendar

The best times to buy what you need

January–February	Dress fabrics (except cotton)
February	Bedding Curtains
After Easter	Storewide clearance sales
June	Men's summer wear Cotton dress fabrics
After July 4	Storewide clearance sales
August	Children's clothing Camping equipment
October–November	Women's coats
November	Women's woolens
November–December	Men's suits and coats
After Christmas	Women's dressy clothes Lingerie Storewide clearance sales

Managing the Family's Money

Your shelter dollar

The American ideal of owning a one-family home has become difficult for many to achieve. Young families seeking a home for the first time find that they have to settle for far less space than they wanted at a cost that takes a disproportionate share of their income.

The principal question to be answered is how much home can you afford. The table that appears directly below shows how much income you should expect to have and how much your monthly mortgage payments would be for a typical single-family house of about 1500 square feet in two different cities. Real estate costs vary widely from region to region.

The figures that are shown here do not include closing costs, which are identified in the adjoining table. Closing costs for the examples below were estimated to be just over $4000 in Philadelphia but a little under $3000 in Los Angeles.

Total interest payments alone are 2.3 times the cost of the house itself in the Los Angeles example and 2.6 times in the Philadelphia example. If the 9.75 percent mortgage were for 15 years instead of 30, the total principal and interest payments would be only two-thirds as much.

Partly offsetting the high cost of interest payments is the tax advantage of owning your home, since interest as well as property taxes are deductible from federal income tax. On a 30-year $100,000 mortgage at 14 percent interest, over 95 percent of your payment in the first year is deductible interest. By the 15th year, interest on this mortgage would still be well over 80 percent of the monthly payments.

Lenders' smorgasbord. Lending institutions have come up with a smorgasbord of alternatives to the traditional fixed mortgage. When you select a lender—a bank, savings institution, mortgage banker, or credit union—find out first if mortgages are fairly easy to obtain at that institution. Do they charge a fee for originating the mortgage? (This consists of a one-time charge called "points," explained in the glossary.) Do they offer a choice of mortgage plans? Is there a prepayment penalty?

Traditional fixed rate. This type of mortgage, on which the figures in the table are based, appears at first glance to be the most expensive. That is because the interest rate is higher than starting rates for other kinds of mortgage now being offered. But this appearance is deceptive. The fixed rate mortgage is not only the most certain, it is likely to be the most economical in a time of rising interest rates.

Adjustable rate. The most common of the other types of mortgage available is the adjustable rate mortgage (ARM). Starting at a lower rate than the fixed rate mortgage, the ARM can be adjusted at any time, with 30 days' notice, to reflect changes in interest rates. The change could affect your monthly payment, or the outstanding principal, or the length of the mortgage. There is, however, no penalty for prepayment.

Mortgage costs

Real estate industry figures show wide ranges from city to city in typical prices of houses and, correspondingly, in the annual income required to purchase one. Here are typical 1986 figures, with payments for fixed mortgages at an interest rate of 9.75 percent for two cities. Philadelphia had the lowest cost among large cities and Los Angeles the second highest (after New York).

	Philadelphia	Los Angeles
Typical house price	$72,000	$150,000
Annual income required	30,000	49,000
Down payment	7,200	30,000
Monthly mortgage payment	700	1,225

Ask your bank or savings institution for figures based on local costs and mortgage rates.

Checklist of closing costs

When you buy the house, you will encounter a whole battery of additional costs, called closing costs. Buyers can expect to pay most or all of these charges, in addition to the purchase price of the house. Actual costs vary from locality to locality; get an estimate from your lawyer or a local real estate man.

- Title search fees
- Judgment search fees
- Title insurance policy fee
- Survey costs
- Attorney's fee
- Loan origination fee for mortgage
- Credit report fee
- Fee for bank's lawyer
- Insurance premium
- Taxes, recording fees
- Adjustment for costs paid by seller (fuel, water, etc.)

Managing the Family's Money

Borrowing on your house

To home owners who have paid a large part or all of their mortgages, lending institutions are actively offering equity conversion. This is a loan with your equity in your house as collateral. Another form is a line of credit, on which you can draw by writing checks.

Unlike other kinds of interest payments, mortgage interest is deductible under the 1986 Tax Reform Act if the loans do not exceed the original cost of the house plus the cost of improvements.

But equity conversion advertising does not always make it clear that your monthly payments may be for interest only, with the original amount of the loan to be paid off in a "balloon" at the end of the term. Nor do the ads always tell you that you have to pay closing costs as well as interest.

> **INTRODUCING EQUITYLINK.™ THE HOME EQUITY CREDIT LINE OF UP TO $200,000 THAT MAKES GETTING A LOAN AS EASY AS WRITING A CHECK.**
>
> Getting a loan from a bank can be enough to get you down.
>
> Especially when you realize you've got to go through the whole thing all over again next time you need money.
>
> But now there's a better way. Equitylink from The Bank of New York.
>
> Equitylink lets you turn the equity in your home into a

If the terms of an ARM include a cap on the monthly amount you pay, a rise in interest rates could result in negative amortization. If your payments are not sufficient to cover interest charges at current rates, the lender can make up the difference by increasing the principal—the amount of your loan. This is the opposite of building up equity under a conventional mortgage. To avoid negative amortization, the term of an ARM could be extended, but to no more than 40 years.

Graduated payment. In the Graduated Payment Mortgage (GPM), the rates begin low and build up on a fixed schedule, ending at a higher level than rates on a conventional fixed mortgage.

Buy-down. Still another choice is the buy-down, offered as an incentive to the buyer by house builders. The builder turns over to the lending institution part of the money he receives for the house. This money is used to reduce your interest payments for a limited number of years.

If you choose one of the new types of mortgage, do not expect the lending institution to judge your ability to meet higher payments in future years. Borrowers today are being accepted if it appears they can manage the low introductory rate, regardless of how much rates may go up later.

For any kind of mortgage, the lender is likely to urge you to take out mortgage insurance. Like other life insurance on credit purchases, this is more for the convenience and protection of the lender than for yours, since you could probably purchase term insurance more economically on your own. If you do find it convenient to take out mortgage insurance, make sure the policy is *not* made out to the lender; your family might prefer to keep the mortgage and invest the insurance proceeds.

Ways to save energy in your home

Everyone knows that you can save energy by insulating a home and turning off the lights, but here are some points you may not have thought about:

- In cold weather, use the sun's heat by opening blinds or curtains; in summer keep them closed as much as possible.
- When the outside temperature is 78° or cooler, turn off the air conditioner and open the windows.
- Run the dishwasher and clothes washer only with full loads. In the clothes washer, use warm or cold water cycles when you can.
- A shower uses about half as much hot water as a tub bath.
- Clean the condenser coils on the back or bottom of your refrigerator with a vacuum or brush at least once a year.
- Check the gasket on the refrigerator door by seeing if it will resist letting you pull out a slip of paper. Replace it if necessary.
- Do not open the refrigerator or oven doors more than necessary. Opening the oven door lowers the temperature about 25°.
- Check the refrigerator temperature to make sure the settings are correct. The refrigerator compartment should be about 40° and the freezer should be 0°.
- The refrigerator should have enough space around food to let air circulate, but the freezer should be solidly packed, even if it means filling a milk carton with water and freezing it to take up space.
- One 100-watt incandescent bulb gives more light with less energy than two 60-watt bulbs.

Managing the Family's Money

Managing your car

> ### How long a car loan?
>
> If you take out a loan for a period of more than three years, there could be a span of well over a year when the car is worth less than the loan still to be paid off. If you trade in the car during that period, or if it is stolen or wrecked, you will not receive enough to pay off the loan.

> ### Best time to buy
>
> If you decide to buy a new car, and you are thinking of a domestic make, plan to buy it just before the new models come out. The next best time is mid-December to late February—especially Christmas week—when salesmen spend a lot of time looking out of the showroom window.

The most economical way to own a car, according to a study made by the U.S. Department of Transportation, is to keep driving it until it cannot go anymore.

Most drivers would prefer not to put that proposition to the test, but there is no question that it is less expensive to keep running an old car that is in tolerably good condition than to buy a new one.

Nearly half the depreciation of a new car occurs in the first two years of ownership. In fact, a new car depreciates by as much as a third as soon as you drive it out of the showroom. Repairs and maintenance tend to be at their highest level in the fourth to seventh years, when the original parts begin to fail. That is why many people who could afford new cars used to trade them in after three years. More recently, as car prices have soared, drivers keep their new cars longer, which means fewer choices for used-car buyers.

Buying a new car.
Before you go to the showroom, you can find out what the dealer paid for the car you have your eye on. The figure is shown as the base price in one of the guidebooks to new automobile prices available in paperback or at your public library. The sticker on a showroom model will tell you the charges for optional equipment, freight, and dealer preparation. Add those to the base price in the book and you will know how much leeway you have for bargaining on the dealer's price to you.

You should also know the value of the old car you are trading in. Ask your bank lending officer, to whom you will be returning after you buy the car, to let you see his Red Book of Official Used Car Market Values. Knowing the old-car value will alert you to a fairly common practice among dealers—"highballing," or offering a high trade-in to attract the customer while making the price of the new car correspondingly higher.

When the dealer offers you a package of options, remember that his profit margin on them is higher than on the car itself. The most expensive option is factory-installed air conditioning.

Your dealer will be more than happy to arrange financing for your car, because that is likely to be another source of profit for him. In many cases, you can probably get a better deal by financing through your bank.

Buying a used car.
A used car is estimated, on an average, to be about 40 percent less expensive than a comparable new one. In selecting a dealer, it is usually wise to go to a well-regarded new car dealer; he has a reputation to protect and hopes to sell you a new car some day. Insist on being allowed to give the car a road test—more than just around the block. You might take it to an automobile diagnostic service listed in the yellow pages under that heading.

Tips for economical driving

- Do not leave the motor idling if you are stopping for more than a minute. It is more economical to turn off the engine and restart it later than to let it run.
- Speed kills economy. Remember that wind resistance cuts mileage above 50 mph, and the most economical speed is about 45 to 50. Tire treads wear twice as fast at 70 as they do at 45.
- Switch wheels every 5000 miles so that tires wear evenly.
- Maintain tire pressure, and check it only when the tires are cool.
- Check wheel alignment regularly.
- Avoid sudden stops as well as sudden starts. If you have to brake hard at a traffic light or a toll booth, you were using too much gasoline to get to that point.
- Do not try to maintain speed going up a long grade.

Managing the Family's Money

An economical vacation

Camping. Certainly the most economical way to vacation and, in many ways, the most rewarding, is to take the family camping.

If camping is your choice and you are looking for out-of-the-way places, write to the Wilderness Society, Western Regional Office, 4260 Evans Avenue, Denver, CO 80222. They can provide information on wilderness area locations for hiking, backpacking, canoeing, and horseback riding. You can also write to the Superintendent of Documents, Washington, DC 20402 for the publication "Camping in the National Park System," available at a small charge. For information about recreation areas run by a particular state, write to the Office of the Governor at the state capital.

If you plan to visit several places maintained by the federal government in one calendar year, send $10 for a Golden Eagle Passport to the National Park Service Headquarters, Room 1013, U.S. Department of the Interior, Washington, DC 20240. This will entitle you and your family to visit, in your private vehicle, any federal outdoor recreation area that charges an entrance fee, as well as historical houses and museums in federal areas. It does not cover fees such as those charged for camping, and it is good only for the calendar year when issued.

Managing money properly should always include planning for your vacation, but it is not necessary to spend more than you can comfortably afford.

Sleeping indoors. If you prefer to sleep indoors on your vacation, there are still ways to hold down costs.

Two people traveling a considerable distance may find that a fly-and-drive trip can be more economical than driving the whole way. To take advantage of airfare bargains, however, you may not be able to leave and return at the time when you would most like to. Moreover, the economical car rental services are not as conveniently located at airports as the well-known ones. But the savings on gasoline and en route motel costs could make this kind of trip worthwhile.

Finally, plan your route carefully. Do not try to cover too many miles in one day; this would necessitate wasteful and tiring high-speed driving. Try also to avoid urban and resort areas, where prices are likely to be higher.

For senior citizens

People 62 and older may obtain free of charge from the National Park Service a lifetime permit that admits them, and anyone accompanying them in a private vehicle, to federal recreation areas that charge fees. It also provides a 50 percent discount on use fees in park areas, but not on prices charged by concessionaires.

The Golden Age Passport must be obtained in person with suitable identification (not a Medicare card) and is available at most federally operated recreation areas.

Trimming vacation expenses

- Schedule your trip just before or just after the busy season, generally from Memorial Day to Labor Day, when rates are likely to be lower in vacation-area motels.
- If you are in a hot climate, start driving quite early in the morning and stop around mid-afternoon. This will save on use of the air conditioner and give you a better choice of economical accommodations. (It also makes the driving more agreeable if you are heading west with the sun in your eyes.)
- Do not carry a container on the roof, where it will increase wind resistance.
- Take along a small heating coil so that you can make your own coffee or tea. With fruit juice and pastry picked up the day before, you can have breakfast in your room.
- Save on lunch as well by taking along a simple picnic kit. Buy fruit, cold cuts, and other easy-to-eat items in very small quantities along the way.
- Eating only one meal a day in a restaurant means considerable savings.

Managing the Family's Money

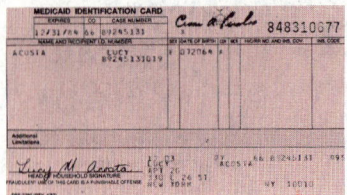

Medicaid identification card

Glossary

one share of common stock

Invest like a pro

- Get all the information you can—from books in your library, trade publications, newspapers, and TV programs on business-related topics.
- Talk to people who have done a lot of investing about what they have done right and what they have done wrong.
- Draw up a list of your investment objectives, and decide how much risk you can accept at your age.
- Do not get into collectibles unless you know a great deal about them.
- Do not agree to buy anything from a stranger who telephones you.

amortize. To reduce the principal of a loan by regular payments.

annual percentage rate (APR). The true interest cost of an installment payment, as distinct from simple interest; true interest takes into account the fact that the debt is being paid off during the time the interest is paid.

balance. The difference in an account between debits and credits.

balloon payment. The unpaid part of a mortgage that is due at one time (not typical of most mortgage arrangements).

bankruptcy. The condition of being insolvent and thus unable to meet one's obligations.

binder. A temporary contract issued by an insurance agent that covers the insured until the policy is prepared and executed; it is customary for fire insurance and other insurance protecting property.

blue chip stocks. Stocks issued by leading companies known for a continuing record of good earnings and dividend payments.

bond. An IOU or promissory note of a corporation or government, with a promise to pay a specified amount of interest for a specified length of time, and to repay the face value of the bond when it matures.

bottom line. The net income, which is the last line on an income statement.

bracket creep. A slang term referring to the way inflation pushes salaries and wages into higher tax brackets.

buy-down. Money offered by a builder as an inducement, which reduces monthly mortgage payments.

cash surrender value. Amount for which you can cash in your whole life insurance policy.

certificate of deposit (CD). A savings certificate with a fixed interest rate and a fixed maturity from 90 days to 10 years.

closing. The conclusion of a real estate transaction when all documents are signed and the deed is transferred to the new owner.

co-insurance. Condition, usually in major medical, in which you and the insurance company share costs; typically, the insurer pays 80 percent and you pay the rest.

collateral. Anything you own of value against which you can borrow money.

common stock. Securities that represent an ownership interest in a corporation.

compound interest. Interest that is computed on both the principal and the previously earned interest; in a savings account, interest left on deposit will itself earn interest.

condominium. Individually owned real estate consisting of a dwelling unit and an undivided interest in joint facilities and areas that serve the multi-unit complex.

consumer price index. A measure of the relative change in prices paid for a "market basket" of consumer goods by a typical wage-earner.

contractual plan. In mutual funds, a plan under which the total amount you intend to invest is stated, with a commitment to invest regular amounts monthly.

convertibles. Securities, such as bonds, that can be converted into other securities, such as stocks, at a certain price.

co-operative. Real estate ownership in which each person owns stock in a corporation, which owns and administers the residential units.

debenture. A debt certificate issued by a company that is not

136

Managing the Family's Money

secured by a specific asset but by the company's credit in general.

deductible. In insurance, the sum you must pay before insurance coverage begins.

defined benefit pension. A type of pension in which a worker is guaranteed a certain amount of retirement income.

demand deposit. A bank deposit, such as in a passbook or checking account, that is payable to the depositor on demand (unlike a certificate of deposit).

discretionary income. The part of an individual's income that is left after paying taxes and buying necessities.

disposable income. The part of an individual's income that is left after paying taxes.

dividend. A payment made from earnings to the stockholders of a corporation; a payment made by an insurance company to holders of ordinary life or term insurance (if they choose a dividend-paying policy).

double indemnity. A policy rider that provides for double the face amount of the policy in the event of death by accident.

earnings per share. The after-tax earnings of a company divided by the number of shares outstanding.

effective annual interest rate. The total amount, expressed as a percentage, that one dollar will earn in one year; it is higher than the nominal rate when interest is compounded during the year.

equity. The residual value of a business or property beyond any remaining debt.

equity conversion. A loan for which your equity in your house serves as collateral.

escrow. Deposit of money with a neutral third party, as during the sale of a home.

estate tax. A tax imposed by the federal government and some state governments on the value of property transferred at death.

extended coverage. In insurance, extension of a policy to provide coverage against hazards not covered by the basic policy.

face value. In investing, the principal of a debt instrument, such as a bond or certificate of deposit, on which interest is computed and which is payable at maturity; in life insurance, the amount of the death benefit (as opposed to the cash value, which is less).

fee simple. Comprehensive ownership of real estate, with the right to pass it on to one's heirs.

float. In banking, the value of checks that have been written by you but not yet paid by the bank; in credit cards, the value of charges made to the account but not yet paid by the cardholder; in travelers' checks, the value of checks purchased but not yet cashed (in the second case, the cardholder benefits; in the third case, the bank benefits).

government bonds. Obligations of the U.S. government, considered the highest-grade bonds anywhere.

guaranty. A promise that merchandise will perform as claimed; differs from a warranty in that the latter is absolute assurance and failure to perform may void the basic contract; a guaranty merely provides that the guarantor will be liable (the two terms are often used interchangeably).

head of family. A person who maintains a family unit (not necessarily a father or husband).

Individual Retirement Account (IRA). A retirement program for anyone with earned income under which people can benefit from tax deductions and tax deferrals while investing funds for retirement.

insufficient funds. A statement stamped on a check by a bank when the account does not have enough funds to cover that check.

interest. Money paid for the use of borrowed money.

investment company. A company that invests in stocks or bonds of other companies and sells shares to the public.

joint tenancy. The holding of property by two or more persons in such a manner that, upon the death of one, the survivor or survivors take the entire property.

Keogh plan. A retirement program for self-employed people under which they can benefit from tax deductions and tax deferrals while investing funds for retirement.

lien. A claim against a person's property.

liquid assets. Cash, or assets that can readily be converted into cash without serious loss.

major medical. Protection against the expenses of a catastrophic or very lengthy illness.

market value. The value in a free market transaction agreed to by a willing seller and a willing buyer.

Medicaid. Combined federal-state program that pays for many medical expenses of the poor.

Medicare. The comprehensive federal health and medical insurance program that covers almost all people over 65.

money market account. An account offered by a bank with funds invested in short-term securities in the money market; the deposit is federally insured.

money market funds. Mutual funds that trade in short-term securities in the money market.

money markets. Financial markets where short-term debt securities are traded.

mutual fund. An investment managed by a company that pools the money of individual investors and buys a diversity of securities, such as stocks and bonds, to reduce risk.

net income. Also called net earnings or net profit, it is the difference between a company's sales and its expenses, before payment of dividends.

over the counter. Trading in securities that are not listed on major exchanges such as the New York Stock Exchange or the American Exchange.

payroll tax. The tax that an employee and employer each pay to support the Social Security program.

points. A one-time charge by a lending institution for originating a mortgage; one point equals 1 percent of the value of the loan.

price-earnings ratio. The market price of a company's common stock divided by its earnings per share.

prime rate. The interest rate that commercial banks charge their most creditworthy customers (lower than rates charged for loans to most individuals).

promissory note. A written promise to pay a debt.

rate of return. The annual percentage of an investment that is returned to the investor.

recipient. A person who receives public assistance or welfare payments, as distinguished from a "beneficiary," who works in covered employment and pays Social Security taxes.

rollover IRA. A special kind of Individual Retirement Account in which an employee deposits a lump-sum pension, paying no taxes on the lump sum or on the income it earns until starting to withdraw the money after age 59½.

simple interest. The interest earned by the principal only, and thus not compounded.

term life insurance. Insurance without any cash value that provides coverage for a limited term; it can be renewed at specified increasing rates; it is considerably cheaper than ordinary life in the early years but more expensive in later years.

treasury bill. A short-term obligation of the U.S. Treasury that is issued at a discount without interest.

treasury bond. A U.S. Treasury obligation that pays interest and matures in more than seven years.

treasury note. A U.S. Treasury obligation that pays interest, with a maturity of from one to seven years.

vesting. The acquisition by an employee of an interest in the contributions made by the employer to the pension fund, or to other employee-benefit funds.

warranty. A statement that merchandise is as represented; a false warranty is cause for legal action.

yield. Dividends on a stock or interest on a bond expressed as a percentage of current price.

For further reference

Annual Buying Guide Issue
  Consumer Reports magazine
Boyer, Richard, and Savageau, David
  Places Rated Retirement Guide
  Rand McNally
The Consumers Union Report on Life Insurance
  Holt, Rinehart & Winston
Donoghue, William E.
  No-Load Mutual Fund Guide
  Bantam
Downs, Hugh, and Roll, Richard
  The Best Years Guide: How to Plan for Fulfillment, Security and Happiness in the Retirement Years
  Delacorte
Hallman, G. Victor, and Rosenbloom, Jerry
  Personal Financial Planning
  McGraw-Hill
The Handbook for No-Load Fund Investors
  McGraw-Hill
How to Live on Your Income
  The Reader's Digest Association
J. K. Lasser Tax Institute
  J. K. Lasser's Your Income Tax
  Simon & Schuster
Jehle, Faustin F.
  The Complete & Easy Guide to Social Security & Medicare
  Dell
Loeb, Marshall
  Marshall Loeb's Money Guide
  Little, Brown
Mobil Travel Guide (seven area editions)
  Rand McNally
Porter, Sylvia
  Sylvia Porter's New Money Book for the 80's
  Doubleday
Quinn, Jane Bryant
  Everyone's Money Book
  Delacorte
Rugg, Donald D., and Hale, Norman B.
  The Dow Jones-Irwin Guide to Mutual Funds
  Dow Jones-Irwin
Sloan, Leonard
  The New York Times Book of Personal Finance
  Times Books
Unthank, L.L., and Behrendt, Harry M.
  What You Should Know About Individual Retirement Accounts
  Dow Jones-Irwin
Weinstein, Grace W.
  The Lifetime Book of Money Management
  New American Library

Booklets on request (free unless otherwise noted)

College
"Federal Student Aid Programs"
Department DEA—88
Pueblo, CO 81009

Investing
A directory of no-load mutual funds with information on their investment goals.

Investors Directory
P.O. Box 2004
New York, NY 10116

(send $2 check payable to No-Load Mutual Fund Association

Income tax
"Your Federal Income Tax"
Write the I.R.S. Forms Distribution Center for your area (address is on the next-to-last page of Federal Income Tax Forms and Instructions).

Tax information publications and forms are available for reference and photocopying at your public library.

"Tax Benefits for Older Americans"
I.R.S. Publication 554
U.S. Government Printing Office
Washington, DC 20402

Insurance
"Buyers' Guide to Insurance"
National Insurance Consumer Organization
121 North Payne Street
Alexandria, VA 22314

(send self-addressed envelope with $1)

Vacation
"Travel Tips for Senior Citizens"
Superintendent of Documents
U.S. Government Printing Office
Department 33
Washington, DC 20402

(send $1)

Retirement
"Your Social Security"
"Thinking About Retiring"
"How You Earn Social Security Credits"
"Estimating Your Social Security Retirement Check"
"How Work Affects Your Social Security Checks"
"Part of Your Benefits May be Taxable"
"A Brief Explanation of Medicare"

From your Social Security office.

Catalog of Publications and Materials (C-48)
American Association of Retired Persons
1909 K Street NW
Washington, DC 20049

Shopping
List of available publications of
U.S. Department of Agriculture
Office of Communication, Room 507A
U.S. Department of Agriculture
Washington, DC 20250

(includes titles of guides to buying and use of food)

"Consumer Information Catalog"
Consumer Information Center—Z
P.O. Box 100
Pueblo, CO 81002

Managing the Family's Money

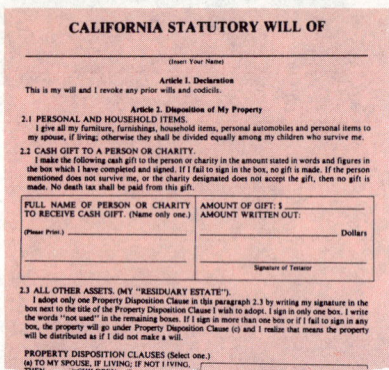

You and the Law

- Your family and the law 141
- Your home and the law 147
- Wills and estates 154
- Consumers' rights 156
- Personal property 159
- Injuries and damages 162
- Earning a living 164
- Criminal law and procedure 167
- How to find a lawyer 169
- Glossary 171

What is the law? Basically, the law is the set of rules that enables the members of a society to live and work together in reasonable harmony and to settle their disputes without violence. Some laws are in the form of written constitutions or statutes; others are legal principles that have arisen over the years from custom, experience, and common acceptance. Law is not confined to courts and legislatures. It pervades our day-to-day relationships with our families, our neighbors, the people we deal with on our jobs, and the members of our community.

When you pick up the phone and order something from a store, you make a contract governed by the law of sales. When you drive your car, you are subject to traffic laws and the laws of negligence and liability. Your wages and working conditions depend on your contract with your employer, perhaps a union contract, and federal and state labor laws. When a couple marries or a child is born, the law establishes the rights and duties of family members. When a person dies, the law determines who gets his or her property and who will care for the children. Even as you sleep at night, you are protected by laws against burglary and trespass—and perhaps by zoning laws that prevent a boiler factory from being built next door.

Most of the time we attend to our everyday affairs without running into any legal problems. Inevitably, though, conflicts arise. The goods we order fail to arrive, or they are unsatisfactory. Accidents happen and people are injured. Disputes arise between employers and employees, or between landlords and tenants. Families break up, or fight among themselves about inheritance or other rights. The person with no knowledge of the law may find that he has put himself in a weak legal position or incurred legal obligations that he never intended. Unscrupulous persons may take advantage of him, or he may simply not know what his rights are or what to do about them.

The purpose of this chapter is to help you deal with legal situations and, if possible, prepare for them. Reading the chapter will not make you a legal expert, but it may help you to recognize the problems most likely to arise in everyday situations, the pitfalls to look out for and errors to avoid, and the means by which you can protect and enforce your legal rights.

This chapter deals with general legal principles; but each state has its own special rules, which may differ from other states. Always check your own state and local law before making any important decisions.

The *Glossary* at the end of this chapter defines some technical terms you may come across in the newspaper or in other reading. *For further reference* lists a number of nontechnical books on law. Many more can be found at your local library, always a good source of information. For more technical information, try the courthouse library. If you are not familiar with using a law library, do not be afraid to ask the librarian for help.

Your family and the law

Marriage. Marriage is a contract, but not an ordinary one. Because of the importance of the family, society sets rules and imposes duties and obligations that usually do not apply to purely private agreements.

A marriage is valid everywhere if valid in the state where it takes place. *Each state sets its own rules,* which usually include a license, a blood test, a waiting period, and a ceremony performed by a clergyman or judge. Some marriages are prohibited because of blood relationship, age, prior marriage, or physical or mental incapacity.

Annulments. Marriages that do not conform to the rules are not automatically void. Unless incestuous or bigamous, a marriage will be valid unless one or both parties takes legal action and has it annulled within a reasonable time. (If an underage person marries, the child's parents can have the marriage annulled.) Annulments may also be obtained on grounds of fraud if, for example, one party expressed a desire for children knowing that he or she could not or would not have any.

Each state sets its own rules.

Common law marriage. Newspapers often use the term "common law marriage" to refer to the state of any couple living together; such use of the phrase is not accurate. A common law marriage is an agreement to marry and live together as man and wife without going through a ceremony. In states where they are permitted, common law marriages are exactly the same, legally, as any other marriage. The difficulty lies in proving the agreement and the intention of the parties, especially if one or both is dead and there is a dispute over inheritance.

Most states no longer recognize common law marriages. However, they will recognize a common law marriage that was valid at the time it was entered into, or one made in a state that does recognize them.

Changing your name

A married woman often wants to continue using her maiden name; she may, for example, have established a useful professional reputation under that name. Using a maiden name is perfectly legal. In fact, anyone can use any name he or she wants, so long as there is no intent to defraud. (You could not, for example, use the name of a well-known person in order to borrow money.) Getting a court order to change your name makes it official; but it is not necessary.

State laws. Some states do require women to use their married names on drivers' licenses or other documents. The state can do this, as it is responsible for public records. In these states, a woman must either comply or go to court and have her name officially changed.

Updating records. Most women do take their husbands' names. Those women should immediately notify the Social Security Administration to avoid any possible confusion in the records, as well as employers, insurance companies, department stores where they have charge accounts, and anyone else whose records should be changed.

Children. A child born to a married woman is presumed to be legitimate, even if the marriage turns out to be invalid. Illegitimate children become legitimate if their parents later marry each other.

Scientific developments, such as artificial insemination and "test-tube babies," pose new legal problems. Many states have passed laws requiring the consent of both husband and wife to these methods of conception or birth. If the law is complied with, the children are legitimate.

Illegitimate children. With respect to their mother, illegitimate children have full legal rights. They also have the right to support from their father; it may, however, take a lawsuit and a court order to establish paternity. Inheritance rights of illegitimate children from their fathers vary from state to state. Many states allow illegitimate children to inherit if the father has acknowledged the child in writing.

Abortion. The U.S. Supreme Court has ruled it unconstitutional to forbid abortion during the first three months of pregnancy. In other situations, each state can set its own abortion laws, and they vary widely.

Adopted children. Adopted children have the same legal relationship to their parents as natural children. In some states, an adopted child may also inherit from his or her natural parents, but in no state can natural parents inherit from the child. The right of adopted children to inherit from the adopting parents' relatives (where there is no will) varies widely from state to state. The trend is toward allowing inheritance rights.

How to adopt a child

Learn your state's law and follow it to the letter. Consent must be obtained from the natural parents unless they have been legally deprived of custody. Consent may also be required from the child, if above a certain age.

The rules vary. Some states allow adoptions by single persons, but singles usually find it hard to get approval. Religious requirements are not absolute but the state may give preference to adoptive parents of the same religion as the child's natural parents.

The essential point. You must satisfy a court, at a hearing, that you are of good moral character, able to provide a good home, and financially responsible. The court usually accepts the recommendation of the social agency in charge, but if it is unfavorable, you can introduce evidence to overturn it. A deaf couple, for instance, overcame an unfavorable report by showing that they had successfully raised their own children, who had normal hearing.

Adults may be adopted. The practice is uncommon, but it has sometimes been done to establish inheritance rights.

Legal status of minors

Contracts	Minors cannot be held to a contract or agreement while underage. Moreover, they can repudiate and cancel a contract at any time. (*Exception:* Real estate contracts cannot be repudiated while the minor is underage.) If the minor does not repudiate and cancel the contract before coming of age or within a reasonable time afterward, the contract will be valid. A minor can cancel a sale and get his money back. This rule does not apply to food, clothing, medical care, or other necessities. However, a minor who bought a car was able to get his money back, even though he had cracked it up. As a general rule, anyone who deals with a minor acts at his own risk, even if he does not know that the person is underage.
Liability for damages	Minors are responsible for injuries they cause to other people or to their property. They can be sued for damages; the damages can be paid from property owned or later acquired by the minor. Parents are usually not liable for the acts of their children, but some states have changed this rule.
Crimes	Under traditional law, a minor over seven could be tried as an adult. Today, children under 16 are charged with juvenile delinquency, not crime, to keep them from being encumbered by a criminal record. (The age may vary in some states.) Minors charged with juvenile delinquency have the right to a trial, a lawyer, and all constitutional safeguards.

Since an underage teenager can not be held to a contract, his father must cosign a car loan and become legally responsible for making the payments. But the son can be held responsible for the damage he does with his car.

Legal capacity

Children. Children do not have full legal rights and duties until they reach the *age of majority*. Traditionally, this age was 21, but many states have lowered it to 18, along with the voting age. Most states also have age limits for specific privileges, such as buying alcoholic beverages or obtaining a driver's license.

Incompetent adults. Adults are presumed to have full legal rights and capacities unless declared incompetent by a court after a full hearing. This procedure has severe drawbacks:

- It stigmatizes the person as mentally unsound.
- It is not appropriate for physical disabilities or mental difficulties, such as forgetfulness, that fall far short of mental unsoundness.
- The incompetent loses most of his or her legal rights, including the right to vote, make contracts, buy or sell, lend or borrow money, make gifts, marry, travel, or choose a place of residence. The incompetent may even be committed to a mental hospital.

Property	Minors can own property of all types, but it must be managed by a parent or guardian. A child's earnings legally belong to his father (or mother), unless the child is "emancipated"—no longer dependent upon his parents for support. Examples of emancipated minors are those in the armed forces, those who have married, and those whose parents will not support them.
Right to sue	Lawsuits may be brought on a child's behalf by a parent, guardian, or person appointed by a court. Children can sue parents for intentional injuries, but not for negligence (auto accidents, for example). Some states allow negligence suits against a parent who does not have custody.
School rights	Children have a right to an education, but parents cannot be compelled to send them to public schools. Many states recognize the right of handicapped or retarded children to special education; parents can participate in the decision to send or not send their children to special classes. Schools have the right to maintain reasonable discipline, but a child cannot be expelled or suspended without a hearing, except in emergencies. Parents have a right to see their children's records and correct any misinformation. The records cannot be shown to others without the parents' consent (except to school officials or to protect a child's health or safety).

You and the Law

A gift belongs legally to the person who receives it. But household furnishings usually belong to the husband, except in those states that have community property laws. A paycheck belongs to the person who earned it.

In some states it is possible to appoint a conservator to manage a person's property simply by showing that he is unable to handle it himself due to mental or physical disability. The usual proof is a doctor's statement. The person has the right to contest the proceeding, but is less likely to do so because he is not declared incompetent and does not lose his other legal rights.

Aliens. Resident aliens have the same rights as citizens, except that they cannot vote or hold elective office. They must register and must get a permit to work in the United States. In some states, they are ineligible for public employment. Illegal aliens may be deported.

Legal rights and duties. At one time, married women could not manage their own property; in fact, their legal status was almost that of children. These laws are a thing of the past. Husbands and wives have equal legal rights and powers.

Property. Except in community property states, wages and salaries belong to the person who earns them. Income from property belongs to the person who owns it. Property belongs to the person who bought it or in whose name it is placed. Household furnishings belong to the husband unless proven otherwise.

Gifts, including gifts between husband and wife, belong to the person who receives them. However, a man

Planning for old age, illness, or incapacity

Old age is not necessarily incapacity. Elderly people lose none of their legal rights, but the infirmities of age may make it difficult for some to handle their legal affairs. There are ways to plan against possible incapacity without the need for court proceedings; the same methods can be used by persons who simply want to be relieved of business responsibilities, and by people who wish to have someone else take care of their affairs.

Power of attorney	A power of attorney, which must be in writing, gives someone else the power to act on your behalf. It can be a *general* power to handle your affairs, or a *special* power, limited as you see fit. It can be revoked at any time and ends at your death. In some states, you may provide that the power of attorney is to take effect only if your physician certifies you are no longer able to handle your own affairs.
Trusts	You can put your money or property in a trust (see *Glossary*), and appoint a trustee to manage it for your benefit. The trust can be set up to take effect only on your doctor's certification that you are incapacitated; another way is to appoint yourself as trustee and name a co-trustee to take over automatically if you are incapacitated. You can put whatever you want into the trust, impose any limitations you want on the trustee, and reserve the right to cancel the trust at any time and take back the property.
Married couples	Do not keep everything in one spouse's name. If that spouse becomes incapacitated, the other will be in a financial bind. Legal proceedings to straighten things out may be time consuming. Each spouse should have at least enough money or separate property to provide for emergency situations.

You and the Law

who "gave" his wife money to save for his old age was able to get it back by proving no gift was intended. Contrary to popular belief, wedding gifts do not belong to the bride; they belong to both partners, unless clearly intended for just one (a necklace, for example).

Joint bank accounts and other joint property are owned equally by husband and wife; if one dies, the other gets the property. Some states recognize a special form of real estate ownership called "tenancy by the entireties." It is similar to joint ownership, but neither party can sell or mortgage his or her share without consent of the other. Also, creditors cannot get at the property except for debts owed jointly by husband and wife. This form of ownership ends if the parties are divorced; they become ordinary co-owners. See also "Community property laws," page 146.

Antenuptial agreements. Husband and wife can make a property agreement before marriage; each can give up any right to inherit from the other. Agreements are common among people with children from prior marriages; they assure that the children get their property free of any claims from a second spouse. These agreements are enforced by the courts unless grossly unfair. One was set aside because the husband, who had only a moderate income when he married, later became rich.

Husband and wife. Despite the trend toward equality, the husband is still "head of the family" in most states. He can decide where the family is to live. If his wife refuses to accompany him, she cannot charge him with desertion or abandonment. The husband also has the right to direct the children's education and religious upbringing.

Duty to support. A husband has a duty to support his wife and children, even if they have money of their own. If the husband is unable to support the family, the duty passes to the wife.

Support means the provision of "necessaries," but this includes more than the bare necessities of life. It means providing a standard of living in keeping with the father's financial condition. Some courts have held that a father must give his children a college education if he is financially able.

Purchases. A wife can buy necessities for the family and charge them to her husband; she is acting as his agent. A merchant can assume she is acting for the family unless the husband has notified him not to extend credit. A newspaper announcement, such as "I will not be responsible for debts incurred by my wife," is sufficient, but *only if the merchant knows of it.*

There are limits to the rule. It applies to purchases that are reasonable—not to sable coats or Rolls-Royces. If, however, the couple has a joint charge account or credit card, either is entitled to make purchases on it.

Indigent parents. Some states require adult children to support their parents if the parents cannot support themselves and would otherwise have to apply for public assistance.

Divorce and separation.

Traditionally, a divorce could be granted only for an offense committed by one spouse against the other. The "guilty party" was often barred from remarrying and from receiving alimony, which is why most divorce actions were brought by the wife.

Grounds for divorce include adultery, desertion, cruelty, conviction of crime, and habitual drunkenness or drug addiction. Defenses to a lawsuit for divorce include "condonation" (forgiveness of the offense), collusion, and justification (for instance, abandonment by the wife might be justified by the cruelty of the husband).

No-fault divorce. Most states now permit divorces for incompatibility, irreconcilable differences, or separation for a long period of time. No one need be at fault.

"Quickie" divorces. Most divorces, even those granted from foreign countries, will be recognized if both parties have appeared in court, either personally or through an attorney. But "mail-order" divorces and divorces where the defendant was not notified will be set aside if challenged.

Separation. A separated couple can make an agreement between themselves or go to court for a legal separation. The rules are similar to the rules in divorce cases, but a separation does not dissolve the marriage or change the parties' legal status as married persons.

A newspaper ad may not always protect a person from a spouse's debts. Consult a lawyer before placing an ad.

I, CHRISTOPHER SMARTS, also known professionally and publicly as CHRIS MILLS, do hereby declare that I am not responsible for any debts incurred by MISS BETTY WHITE or BETTY SMARTS as of June 15, 1985. I am in the process of challenging the legality of this marriage in Nevada and at no time did Miss White or myself establish residence in Boston or any other city in the United States.

You and the Law

Alimony and property settlements. Courts today base their decisions on equity and fairness, not on set rules or formulas. For instance, wives have been awarded alimony for a period of time while attending college or taking training courses to enable them to support themselves. In a few cases, alimony has been awarded to the husband. If the parties can agree to a settlement between themselves, the court will usually accept it and make it a part of the court order.

Property settlements are permanent, but alimony or child support orders can be modified. Alimony normally ends if the wife remarries, but a father's duty to support his children is not ended by the remarriage. A support order may continue even after the child comes of age. For example, the court may find that the father is financially able to help the child through college or to help support a child who is incompetent. The amount, however, can always be modified to reflect changes in the parents' financial status.

Enforcement. A husband who fails to pay is guilty of contempt of court and can be punished by being sent to jail. This is done rarely, but the threat is always there.

Child custody. The welfare of the child is the primary consideration; but, in practice, the mother is almost always awarded custody (unless clearly unfit), with visitation rights for the husband. Recently, there has been a trend toward shared custody.

Custody fights are the bitterest of all lawsuits. One study showed that, even in uncontested divorces, over half the couples with children wound up in court later in custody battles. Couples would be well advised to settle their differences, perhaps with the help of a clergyman or social worker, before engaging in never-ending court battles. Such custody suits can do great harm to children.

Divorce and taxes

While uncontested divorces can be handled by a legal clinic at low fees—or even with a do-it-yourself divorce kit—you should be sure to talk with your tax adviser. There are some tricky income tax points that may depend on the wording of the divorce decree.

Alimony is deductible. Alimony payments are deductible from the husband's income; they are taxable income to the wife. Child support payments are not deductible, and are not income to the wife. Payments are considered alimony if they meet the following rules:

- They are made under a written agreement or court order.
- They are scheduled to continue for at least six years.
- They are to terminate at the death of the wife.
- They are not specifically designated as something other than alimony (such as child support).
- They do not depend on the status of a child (for example, if payments are scheduled to end when a child reaches 18, they are considered child support, not alimony).

Other payments. Property settlements are not taxable to either spouse, but later sales may be taxable. Payments under oral agreements are considered gifts and are not tax deductible.

Fees. Legal fees for getting a divorce are not deductible. Fees for tax advice are. Get separate bills.

Community property laws

Eight states—Arizona, California, Idaho, Louisiana, Nevada, New Mexico, Texas, and Washington—have community property laws for married couples. The laws vary, but the basic features of community property are these:

Anything owned before marriage remains the property of the person who owns it.

Gifts and inheritances, before or after marriage, are the property of the person who receives them.

All other property acquired after marriage (including wages, salaries, and other earnings) is community property shared equally by husband and wife, no matter how the property was acquired or whose name it is in.

If the couple is divorced, the property is split between them. If one dies, community property does *not* automatically go to the survivor. It goes to the person named in the deceased spouse's will, or to the next of kin if there is no will.

If you are moving into or out of a community property state, it may be a good idea to check on any problems that might arise. Talk to a lawyer in the community property state; lawyers in other states often know little about community property law.

Your home and the law

Buying a home. This may be the biggest financial deal of your life, and the one most important to the happiness of your family. Do not let yourself be rushed or pressured. You should probably consult a lawyer as early as possible, before you commit yourself to anything.

Land and buildings are called *real property*. All contracts for the sale of real property *must* be in writing, and cannot be changed except in writing. Never sign anything on the assurance that "It doesn't really mean anything" or "We'll change that later if you don't like it." You are legally bound by anything you sign, and an oral agreement to change it is worthless.

You are bound by anything you sign.

If you buy through a real estate broker, he or she may ask you to leave a deposit and sign a binder agreement to hold the property until you can get together with the seller. Do not sign unless you have spoken to a lawyer. And get a receipt for any deposit.

Down payments. When you sign the sales contract, or before, you will have to put down a deposit. Make sure

Questions to ask *before* signing a contract

About the property	Exactly what is included in the sale? Stoves, refrigerators, ovens? Carpets, shelves, Venetian blinds, storm windows, screens? Awnings? TV antennas? Is a survey needed? Who pays for it? Are there any old mortgages on the house, judgments against the seller, or payments due to contractors or repairmen?
About the sale	When will the sale be completed? When can I take possession? Are any delays likely? Are there penalties for delays? Who is to pay escrow fees, taxes, insurance, etc.? Are there any hidden fees?
About the mortgage	Can I cancel the contract if I cannot get the kind of mortgage I want? Under what conditions? How much time do I have?
About inspection	Do I have the right to inspect? What if the inspection shows damage from termites or other causes? Suppose the house needs repair? Who pays for it? Can I cancel the contract if the inspection shows the house is unsatisfactory?
About restrictions	Are there any restrictions on building or on the use of the property? What are the zoning regulations? Does the town have a building code? Can I build a tennis court? Put in a swimming pool? Keep a horse? Other pets? Store my old car in the backyard? Practice with my band? Can I run a business out of my home? What kind?
About the neighborhood	What kind of neighborhood is the house in? Who are my neighbors? What school will my children go to? Where can I do my shopping? Is the neighborhood entirely residential, or are there some businesses? What kind? Are there any plans to build a factory in the neighborhood, or run a highway through it?

You and the Law

the contract states when you are entitled to get it back. For example, the contract may take effect only if you can get a "satisfactory" mortgage. The bank offers a mortgage, but the interest rate is too high. The seller might argue that the mortgage was "satisfactory," in which case you would have to go to court to get your money back. You might not succeed. The contract should have defined exactly what, in this particular case, is meant by "satisfactory."

The sales contract. To be valid, the contract must contain all essential terms of the agreement, including enough information to identify the property, the buyer, the seller, the date of sale, the price, and how the money is to be paid.

Some tips to the buyer

- **Make sure of the identity of the seller.** Swindlers usually pass themselves off as someone else.
- **Insist that the seller's spouse sign,** in case he or she has any claim on the property.
- **Beware of printed forms.** They favor the seller.
- **Do not sign without having the house and property inspected,** unless the contract gives you the right to cancel if an inspection shows the place to be unsatisfactory.

Contract clauses of importance to buyers. Make sure your lawyer covers them.

Type of deed	A *quitclaim* deed simply releases all right, title, and interest that the seller has in the property. A *warranty* deed also guarantees that he actually does have the right, title, and interest that he claims to have. Buyers should insist on a warranty deed. If the contract does not specify, the seller only has to give a quitclaim deed.
Date of sale	If it is absolutely imperative that you have the house by a certain date (for example, you have to move from your old house), you can request a clause saying "time is of the essence." This makes the seller responsible for any financial loss you suffer from delay. If such a clause is too strict to be accepted, the seller may at least agree to a clause imposing monetary penalties for each day's delay.
Encumbrances	Property may be "encumbered" by unpaid taxes, old mortgages, court judgments against the seller, claims of third parties, etc. Such encumbrances are what the title insurance company looks for when searching the records. Until the search is made, do not sign any agreement to buy "subject to all encumbrances" unless they are listed specifically. (Title insurance protects you against any unknown or undiscovered encumbrances that turn up in the future.)
Fixtures	Items permanently affixed to the property, such as furnaces or plumbing, are part of the real property. Movables, such as tables or chairs, are not. Many other items, such as storm windows, are borderline. The contract should state exactly what goes with the house and what does not.
Risk of loss	Be sure to include a clause canceling the sale if the house is lost by fire or other disaster before the sale is completed.

148

You and the Law

How the contract is enforced. What if the seller refuses to go through with the deal? The buyer can sue for any damages and can also sue for "specific performance," which is a court order directing the seller to complete the sale. The seller has the same remedies if the buyer backs out. Most likely, though, he will just keep the down payment and sell the house to someone else.

Title closing. The sale is completed and the deed transferred at the closing. Usually, the buyer, the seller, their lawyers, a representative of the bank or other mortgage lender, and a lawyer from the title insurance company are present. Costs and fees are settled, including the buyer's share of costs already paid by the seller, such as taxes, insurance, fuel, etc.

Escrow. If there are encumbrances on the land, such as judgments or unpaid taxes, part of the purchase price may be put in escrow. This means that a neutral third party will hold the money until the seller removes the encumbrances.

When the sale is complete. Finally, the seller gets his money and the buyer gets his home. Besides the deed, the buyer should receive all insurance policies, tax receipts, and a bill of sale for any personal property, such as furniture, that has been purchased along with the house. The buyer will also receive a title insurance policy and a mortgage statement from the bank.

It is important to have the deed recorded immediately to protect your title. Dishonest persons sometimes sell property to more than one buyer. If the first buyer has not recorded his deed, a person who buys later but is first to record his deed may have a valid claim to the property.

Get it in writing.

Building a home. Contracts to build should be in writing, though it is not legally required. The best way to avoid legal disputes with contractors is to make the contract and specifications as exact and detailed as possible, including types and quality of materials and equipment, colors, and brand names. Any changes should require your written approval.

Method of payment. Partial payments are usually made at various stages of construction, with final payment due when the house is completed. If an architect drew the plans, you might hire him to supervise construction and make payment to the contractor subject to his approval. At the very least, you should have periodic inspections by someone who knows the construction business.

The contract may provide for penalties if the contractor does not finish on time, except in the case of causes beyond his control.

Liens. Serious problems can arise if the contractor does not pay his workmen, suppliers, or subcontractors. Even though you did not deal with them directly, they can file liens, or claims, against the property for the amount owed them. The legal status of these liens depends on your state's law, but they are encumbrances on the property and have roughly the same effect as unpaid mortgages. The contractor is liable for

The home owner should always exercise caution when coming to terms with a contractor. The slip shown below is an estimate, not a contract. It does not bind the contractor to do the work for the stated price.

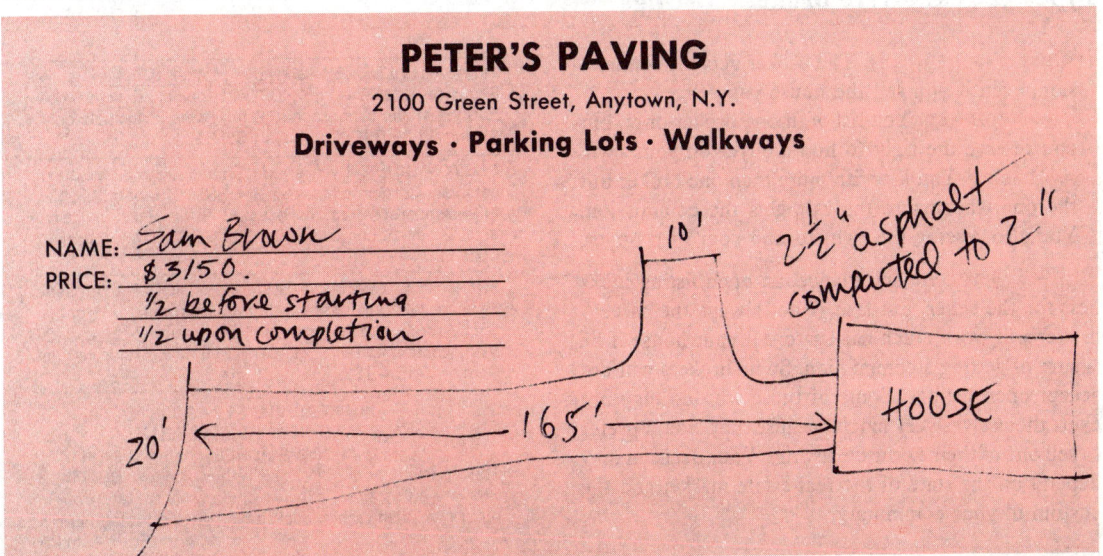

You and the Law

satisfying these claims, but that will not help if he becomes bankrupt or cannot pay.

If you get notice of a lien, do not make any further payments to the contractor until he removes the lien by paying the claim.

One way to protect yourself. You might require the contractor to post a bond to guarantee payment of any claims. Bonds can be obtained from insurance companies; they are common in big commercial projects. There are drawbacks. The premium charged by the insurance company will probably add to the cost of the house, and the insurance company will have a voice in any changes you want to make in the plans or specifications.

Selling your home.
Sellers have the same legal problems as buyers—but in reverse. If a sales contract is conditional on the buyer's obtaining a mortgage or having an inspection made, be sure to set a time limit, or the sale may be held up indefinitely. Also, stipulate that the buyer relies *solely* on the inspection, not on any promises or statements made by you.

If the buyer cannot get a mortgage, you may be willing to finance all or part of the price by a *purchase money mortgage*. This means you agree to be paid in installments and you retain a mortgage on the property, just like a bank, in case the buyer does not pay.

Real estate brokers. If you sell through a real estate broker, the broker is entitled to his commission if he produces a buyer who is "ready, willing, and able" to buy at your price. Even if the buyer backs out or cannot get a mortgage, the broker may be entitled to his commission unless you protect yourself by a clause in the contract with the broker.

How to save on taxes when you sell

If you sell your house, you normally have to pay capital gains tax on the profit. But you can postpone the tax by purchasing or building a new house within two years before or after you sell the old one. The postponed tax will become due if you sell the second house, but you can postpone again by buying still another house. There is no limit on the number of postponements. The tax may never become due.

Tax break for the elderly. If you have reached age 55, you can sell your home and pay no tax on up to $125,000 of profit. If spouses own the home jointly, the rule applies if either has reached age 55. This tax option is permitted only once in your lifetime.

Figuring your tax correctly. If you do not qualify for these tax breaks, you can keep taxes to a minimum by remembering to deduct the following costs from your profit:
- Costs of buying and selling, such as legal fees, brokers' commissions, and recording fees.
- Costs of any capital improvements, such as additional rooms, air-conditioning systems, swimming pools, and landscaping (but not ordinary repairs).
- "Fixing-up costs" to put the house in shape to sell.

Keep records. Be sure to keep all bills, records, and documents *permanently*. You can never tell when you might need them.

Types of real estate brokers' listings

Exclusive right to sell. The broker gets his commission, even if you sell the house yourself.

Exclusive listing. You list with one broker only, but you reserve the right to find a buyer on your own.

Open listing. You list with more than one broker but the one who makes the sale gets the commission. You also reserve the right to find your own buyer.

Which is best? At first glance, an open listing looks best for the seller, but that is not always the case. A broker will work much harder to sell your house if he is sure of getting a commission. Some brokers will not accept open listings. Some of those who do may not exert themselves very much because they would prefer to sell one of their exclusive listings. Your decision may depend on the state of the real estate market and the custom in your community.

PLEASANTVILLE, BY OWNER; Mother/daughter split. Separate entrances. EIK, DR/with deck, LR with wood burning stove. 5 bedrooms, 2 full baths. Principals only. Asking $179,900. Call days 555-2111.

★CUSTOM BUILT: 3 years young, immaculate 2,900 sq.ft. colonial. All room oversized. 3-4 BR's, 2½ bath, LR, DR, EIK w/separate breakfast area. FF w/fireplace, exclusive area. Excellent commute IBM. $176,900. Owner, broker, 555-1234.

SUNNYSIDE COMMUTE-DIST III SCHOOLS: Fantastic value, new 2-story contemporary. 3 Bedrooms, 2½ baths, family room with fireplace, full basement, 2-car garage. Many custom extras $169,900. Call now. Exclusive King George. 555-4321

PUTNAM HILL $124,900
BRAND NEW 50' BI-LEVEL
ON 6 ACRES
This spacious home offers LR w/bow window, DR, EIK, 3 BRs & 2 baths. Many extras include W/W carpet throughout, range, dishwasher, deck, paved driveway, aluminum &

You and the Law

Brokers' contracts. Contracts are normally in writing, and should have a time limit, such as six months. When the contract expires, get a list of persons to whom the broker has shown the property. Otherwise, one of those persons may come back later and buy the property. You would then owe the broker a commission because he first produced the buyer.

Look out for the fine print. As always, beware of printed contracts. They favor the broker.

Owners' rights and duties.

Your use of your property may be subject to restrictions for the benefit of other persons or the public in general. Here are some of the most common restrictions.

Covenants and conditions. Deeds often contain restrictions on property, such as a ban on commercial use or rules on the type and size of buildings. Developers often put these rules in deeds to maintain the character of the development. The restrictions are binding on future buyers. If the property has passed through several hands, a thorough search of the records may be needed to discover the restrictions.

If a restriction is made a *condition* of ownership, a violation could cost the owner the title to the property. Most restrictions, however, are *covenants* (promises); if they are violated, nothing happens automatically, but persons who are affected, such as neighbors, can get a court order (injunction) requiring the owner to comply with the covenant. Courts may refuse to enforce covenants if they make no sense because the neighborhood has changed. If in doubt, a landowner can ask for a court ruling in advance. Some covenants are illegal, such as restrictions based on race or religion.

An "Application for Zoning & Building Permit" must be filed with the building department of your local government. The application usually requires specifications about the proposed renovation or new building and may require a survey or architectural drawings.

Public laws. Most communities have zoning laws restricting land use, but they normally do not apply to land or buildings already constructed or in use when the law is passed. Most towns also have building codes and require a permit before building. If you want an *exception* or *variance* from the zoning laws, you have to apply to the zoning board and show good cause. It is very important to show that your neighbors have no objection to the proposed use or construction.

Co-ownership of property

Ownership of property of any kind may be shared by two or more persons. Co-owners are either *tenants in common* or *joint tenants.* (Married couples may also be "tenants by the entirety" or share "community property"—see pages 144–145.

Do not be confused by the word "tenants." It usually refers to renters of property, but here it means owners.

Tenants in common. Each owns a *fractional* share in the entire property; no one owns any specific part. Each may sell or mortgage his share; creditors may reach it for payment of debt. When a tenant in common dies, his share does not go to the co-owners, but to the person named in his will, or to his next of kin.

Joint tenants. Each owns an *equal* share in the property. Each can sell or mortgage his share, and creditors can reach it. When a joint tenant dies, his share goes to the survivor or survivors. If a joint tenant sells his share, the survivorship feature ends, and the new owner is a tenant in common.

Is co-ownership desirable? Except possibly for married couples or business partners, co-ownership is usually not a good idea. The owners may disagree on what to do with the property. A sale may be missed if one co-owner holds out, as the buyer may be unwilling to take less than full ownership. Even if owners agree on managing the property, one may die or sell out, in which case there would be a new owner to deal with. If the new owner is a minor, the property can be tied up for years.

If the owners are deadlocked, the only solution may be a court order of "partition," which will physically divide the property among the owners.

Neighbors have duties to each other. One cannot create a nuisance to the other, such as by polluting a stream or continuously making a loud noise. Local laws vary, so be careful about taking action on your own. Consult a lawyer.

Easements. Other persons may have the right to use your property or pass through it. Such easements and rights of way may be purchased, or they may arise from continuous use over a long period of time. If one neighbor has an easement or right of way in the property of another, it will continue even if either or both properties are sold.

Condemnation. The government has the power (eminent domain) to take all or part of your property for public purposes, such as for highways or schools. The power may also be exercised on behalf of public utilities; for example, an electric company may need to run power lines over the land. Landowners are entitled to reasonable compensation, which is decided at a condemnation proceeding, where there is presented evidence from appraisers and experts. You may also be entitled to compensation if the use of your land is interfered with, even if it is not actually taken; for example, low-flying planes from a nearby airport may lessen the value of the property.

Mortgages. If you fail to make mortgage payments, the bank cannot just take your home; it must go to court in a *foreclosure* proceeding. In every state, you are given a period of time (usually a year or more) to make the payments and *redeem* your house—or else work out a new arrangement with the bank, such as smaller payments over a longer period of time.

If you are unable to pay and the mortgage is foreclosed, the property will be sold at auction. If the price does not cover the mortgage, you still owe the balance. If the price is higher than the mortgage, you are entitled to the difference.

Air, water, and mineral rights. You own the air over your land (subject to reasonable use by airplanes) and the minerals beneath it. Air and mineral rights can be sold separately from the land itself, and can be extremely valuable; if you get an offer, see a lawyer.

You own any body of water entirely on your property, such as a pond. But rivers and streams flowing through your land or next to it are subject to the rights of downstream owners. You may not pollute the river, dam it up, or divert it from its course. (Navigable bodies of water are under the jurisdiction of the federal government.)

Neighbors' rights. Neighbors owe each other a duty of *lateral support;* this means they cannot make excavations that would weaken the other's land. If their buildings share a *party wall,* neither can weaken the wall.

Neighbors may not use their land in such a way as to create a *nuisance,* such as loud noise or foul odors. The remedy is to get an injunction banning the nuisance. Overhanging branches from a neighbor's tree may constitute a nuisance, and a landowner has the right to cut them down, but check local laws first.

Insurance. If you have a mortgage, the bank will insist you have fire insurance, but the bank only requires enough insurance to cover the mortgage. You may want to buy more. The cost of replacing a home is likely to be more than the original price because of inflation.

Homeowners should also have liability insurance, in case anyone is injured on the premises. Property owners' liability for injuries is a complicated subject. If you buy insurance, the insurance company will take care of all claims. Some companies sell *comprehensive* policies, which cover most or all kinds of insurance a homeowner wants.

Renting a home.

A contract to rent is a *lease.* Most leases are in a writing, but an oral lease is valid. If no period of time is specified, either the landlord or the tenant can cancel at any time, usually by one giving a month's notice to the other.

Most written leases specify how long they are to last, usually a year or more. A tenant who stays on after the lease has run out is called a holdover tenant. The landlord has the choice of evicting him, or of regarding the lease as renewed for another term.

Unless the lease states otherwise, the tenant can sublet or assign (transfer) the lease. Most leases, however, ban or restrict the right to assign or sublet, except with the owner's consent.

Landlord's duties. The landlord is responsible for keeping the building structurally sound. The old rule held the tenant responsible for ordinary repairs, but in many states, the landlord is now considered responsible for repairs in residential property, unless otherwise provided in the lease. (In commercial property, the tenant usually makes repairs.) In apartment buildings, the landlord is responsible for maintaining hallways, staircases, driveways, laundry rooms, and other areas used by all the tenants.

A *constructive eviction* occurs if the landlord lets the building run down to the point where it is not fit for use. The tenant can move out, does not have to pay any more rent, and can sue the landlord.

Tenant's duties. The tenant's main obligation is to pay rent. If he moves before the lease expires, he must continue to pay rent until the end of the lease or until the landlord rents the property to someone else. Under traditional law, the tenant had to pay the rent even if the landlord violated his part of the agreement—or even if the house burned down. This rule has been modified in many states.

Some states recognize an "implied warranty of habitability," which means the landlord is regarded as promising that the property is fit for the tenant to live in, even if the lease contains no actual promise or guarantee. Tenants can sue for violation of the implied promise or withhold payment of the rent. How serious does a violation have to be to justify not paying the rent? That depends on the rules of the state. Check with a lawyer or with a tenants' group before trying it.

Tenants are liable for any damage they do to the property. Landlords usually require a security deposit when the lease is signed. The tenant gets the deposit back when he leaves, if he has not damaged the property and does not owe any rent. Sometimes the deposit serves in place of the final month's rent. Some states require the landlord to pay interest on the security deposit.

Government regulations. Many state and local governments have passed laws that extensively regulate the relationship between landlords and tenants, especially in communities with housing shortages; some have rent control. Landlords' associations and tenants' groups will provide members with information and, sometimes, legal counsel.

Co-operatives and condominiums

"Co-ops" and "condos" are the fastest growing type of housing in the United States.

Co-ops. A co-operative apartment house is owned by a corporation. The residents are the stockholders; they own shares in proportion to the value of their apartments. Each has the exclusive use of his own apartment and the right to use common areas: stairways, halls, basement, grounds, driveways. The mortgage covers the entire building; stockholders are not personally liable for payment, but must make up the difference if any stockholder defaults, or risk foreclosure of the mortgage. Anyone who wants to sell must get approval from the other stockholders, who rule on the desirability of the proposed new resident.

Condos. Each condominium resident actually *owns* his apartment and shares ownership of the common areas. Each separate apartment can be mortgaged. This sometimes makes condos easier to buy and sell than co-ops, as banks are more willing to lend money if they can get a mortgage on the owner's apartment. (Co-op owners have only their shares of stock to pledge as security for a loan; the primary mortgage is on the whole building.) Condos are also easier to sell because approval of the other owners is not required (though owners may reserve the right to buy the condo themselves if they do not like a proposed owner).

Both co-ops and condos are run by a committee of residents; often, they hire a professional manager. Residents pay a monthly fee, which often includes maintenance, taxes, mortgage payments, etc. The ground floor is sometimes rented to commercial tenants, but there are legal limitations on how much of the building can be rented.

Advantages of co-ops and condos over renting:
- The residents actually own property. They can sell it or raise money on it. Tenants own nothing.
- Owners usually take better care of property than tenants do.
- Property owners get valuable tax breaks that renters do not, including tax deductions for mortgage interest and real estate taxes.

Wills and estates

What is a will? A will is a way for a person (the testator) to direct who will get his property (estate) after his death. The will has no effect before death and can be changed or revoked at any time. A will is valid even if it does not dispose of *all* the testator's property; anything not mentioned in the will goes to the next of kin under state law. Normally, a will contains a "residuary clause" naming a person or persons to get everything not specifically left to someone else.

Why do you need a will? If you have no will, your property will be distributed according to state law, regardless of your wishes or your family's needs. The court will appoint an administrator (and a guardian if you leave children). They will have to post bond, which will be payable from your estate, along with their fees. If any money or property goes to minors, it will be tied up until they come of age. The guardian will not be able to touch it, even for education or medical costs, without getting a special court order.

If you have a will, you can be sure your property will go to the persons of your choice. You can appoint an executor to handle the estate, and guardians or trustees for the property of children. You can give the persons you appoint any powers that you see fit, or impose any limitations. You can direct what is to happen if you and your spouse (or other heirs) should die at the same time —in an auto accident, for example.

You can also appoint a personal guardian for your minor children; the appointment is not binding, but the court will usually follow your wishes.

How to make a will. The testator must be at least 18 years old and of sound mind. The will must be in writing and signed in the presence of two witnesses (three, in some states); the witnesses should also sign. Witnesses cannot inherit under a will, so do not pick as a witness anyone you are leaving anything to.

If you die without a will . . .

- **If you leave a spouse and children,** they get your estate. In some states, it is divided half and half; in others the children take two-thirds and the spouse one-third. If you leave no spouse, the children get it all. If any of your children die before you, their children take what would have been their share. If you leave no children, the spouse either gets everything or, in some states, divides the estate with your parents, brothers, and sisters.

- **If you leave no wife or descendants,** your parents take the estate; if they are not alive, your brothers and sisters (or their children, if they are deceased) divide the estate.

- **If you leave no close relatives,** you can figure out who is your next of kin by counting generations to and from a common ancestor. For example, you and your first cousins have a common grandparent; so you count back two generations to the grandparent, and two generations down to your cousins. They are of the fourth degree of relationship. Their children would be of the fifth degree. Your estate will be split equally among all those of the nearest degree of relationship. Some states do not allow relatives beyond a specified degree to inherit.

- **If you leave no next of kin,** everything goes to the state.

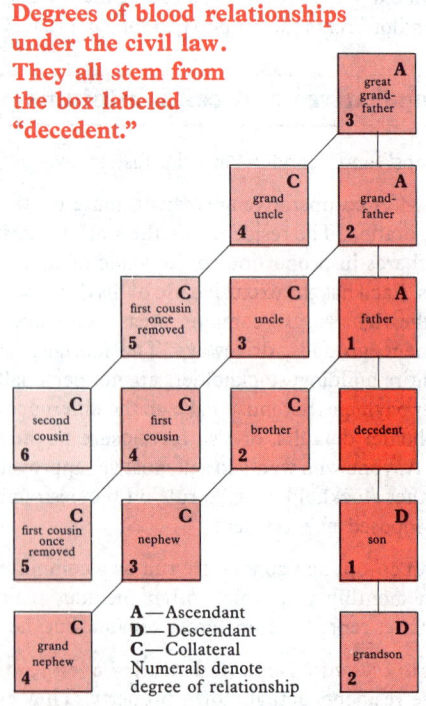

Degrees of blood relationships under the civil law. They all stem from the box labeled "decedent."

A—Ascendant
D—Descendant
C—Collateral
Numerals denote degree of relationship

There are exceptions. Some states require no witnesses to a *holographic* will, one entirely in the testator's handwriting. Some states allow *oral* wills in special circumstances, such as on a deathbed or when a serviceman is going overseas. Holographic or oral wills should be used only in emergencies, and replaced by a regular will as soon as possible.

Changes to a will (codicils) must also be in writing, signed, and witnessed.

A will may be declared invalid if the testator was of such unsound mind that he did not understand what he was doing, or if the will was made because of force, duress, fraud, mistake, or undue influence.

Revoking a will. A will can be revoked by another will or written document, signed and witnessed. It can also be revoked by physical destruction, such as tearing it up or burning it; but this is *not* a good idea. If you die and your will is not found, no one will know whether it was destroyed or just lost. A lost will, however, can be given effect if there is a copy, or some other proof of what was in it.

A will may be revoked by a later marriage or the birth or adoption of a child. In some states, the revocation is only partial. The wife or child gets what he or she would have inherited if there were no will; the balance, if any, is distributed according to the will.

Your rights to your body

You do not have an absolute right to decide where you will be buried or what service will be performed. The right belongs to the next of kin. Normally, however, your wishes will be respected.

You do have the right to leave your body to a hospital, college, or medical school for scientific purposes, or to donate any parts of your body for organ transplants. You can do this in your will or by using a special form; one common form is called a "Universal Donor Card." (Using a will may be too slow, especially in the case of transplants.)

Make your decision known. If you are donating your body, be sure to notify your family, your doctor, and any hospital you are in. You should also keep a copy of the donor card with you, in your wallet or purse, in case you die in an accident or away from home.

Sample will clauses

Specific bequests	I bequeath to my niece Jane Roberts, now residing at 4 Main Street, Centerville, IL, the sum of three thousand dollars ($3,000.00).
	I bequeath to my son John Jones, now residing at 2 Main Street, Centerville, IL, all my jewelry and any other personal effects and mementos which he may desire.
Residuary clause	I give, devise, and bequeath all of the rest, residue, and remainder of my estate to my wife Mary Jones if she survives me. If she fails to survive me, then I give the remainder of my estate to my friend William Brown, now residing at 10 Elm Street, Centerville, IL.
Common disaster clause	In the event that my wife Mary Jones and I die under circumstances where it cannot be established who died first, it shall be presumed that I survived my wife and this will and all dispositions contained herein shall be interpreted on the basis of that presumption.
Appointment of executor	I nominate my son John Jones as executor of my estate, to serve without bond. If my son predeceases me or is for any reason unable or unwilling to serve, then I appoint the First National Bank of Centerville, IL, as executor.
Appointment of guardian	Should my son John Jones be under the age of 18 years when I die, then I nominate my brother Thomas Jones and his wife Ann Jones, now residing at 12 Elm Street, Centerville, IL, to be guardians of his person. I appoint the First National Bank of Centerville to be guardian of all my son's property, subject to the following rules (enumerate powers and limitations on guardian).

Limitations on wills. You can disinherit any relative, including children, but you cannot totally disinherit a spouse. All states require that a certain minimum be left to the spouse. If it is not, the spouse can elect to get the share he or she would have received had the testator died without a will.

Some states limit the amount you can leave to charity if you are survived by a spouse, children, or other close relatives.

Mutual wills. Contracts to make wills or leave property to specific persons are enforceable. Sometimes, husbands and wives make mutual wills. Each leaves his or her property to the other, with the entire property to go to named beneficiaries (such as children) upon the death of the survivor. If the wills are made by agreement, the surviving spouse cannot change his or her will. But the agreement should be stated clearly in the will or in a separate written document. The mere fact that the two wills are the same does not prove that they were made by contractual agreement.

Probate and how to avoid it.
Court proceedings to establish your will and settle the estate (probate) are usually necessary, even if you die without a will. The court will appoint an administrator, usually your next of kin. Some property, however, need not go through court. Joint property goes directly to the joint owner. Insurance proceeds are paid directly to the beneficiary.

Some people want to avoid court proceedings to save costs and delay, and to maintain privacy (court records are open to the public). The best way is to put all your property in a trust (see *Glossary*), naming yourself as beneficiary for life and designating the persons you want to receive the property at your death, just as in a will. You should still have a will, however, as you may own property at your death without realizing it. For example, if you die in an accident, your estate may have a claim against the person responsible. Or you may have inherited property that has not yet been distributed.

Consumers' rights

You may have heard of the old legal rule Caveat emptor, Latin for "Let the buyer beware." If a buyer purchased shoddy goods, paid exorbitant prices, or failed to read the fine print in a contract, any problem was considered to be his own fault. This is still the law in the case of some business deals, but state and federal laws protect consumers in most transactions.

A consumer loan or transaction is for the purchase of goods or services for personal, family, or household purposes, and sometimes for agricultural purposes.

Getting out of bad deals.
Federal and state laws ban false, fraudulent, and deceptive advertising. Not only outright falsehoods are banned, but also deceptive practices such as "bait and switch" advertising, in which a merchant advertises a bargain to get you into his store (the bait), then tells you the bargain item is sold out and talks you into buying something more expensive (the switch).

You may be able to cancel a sale or a contract on grounds of fraudulent advertising, but it is hard to prove. Mere sales talk or exaggeration about a product is not enough; and if a salesman does tell an outright lie, he will probably deny it. The best course is not to be taken in by tricky advertising in the first place. Many agencies have published pamphlets and booklets telling consumers what to look out for. Write your state consumer agency, or the Consumer Information Center, Pueblo, CO 81009.

Mail-order sales. If you buy something by mail, you can cancel the order and get your money back if the goods are not shipped within 30 days.

You absolutely do not have to pay for unsolicited goods sent through the mail. You do not have to send them back either. Just treat them as a gift.

Door-to-door sales. If you sign a contract with a door-to-door salesman, you have three business days to think it over. Within this period, you can cancel the sale and get back any payments just by giving written notice to the seller. However, if you request immediate delivery, you lose this right.

Warranties.
A warranty is a guarantee or promise about the quality or condition of goods and products; sometimes it includes a promise to repair. An express warranty is one actually made by the manufacturer or seller. Whether or not he makes an express warranty, the law regards him as making an implied warranty that the goods are fit for the purpose they are

---

"Caveat emptor."
Let the buyer beware.

LIMITED ONE-YEAR WARRANTY
Name _____
Address _____
City _____ State _____ Zip code _____
Date purchased _____ Store name _____
Product name _____ Model number _____

A warranty gives you specific legal rights, but you may also have other rights that vary from state to state. Consult your lawyer.

being purchased for. The seller can avoid this, however, by specifically stating that he makes no warranties whatsoever; this statement is called a disclaimer.

If the goods do not live up to the warranty, the buyer can sue for damages or get his money back.

Federal law. A seller who makes a written warranty must designate the warranty as *full* or *limited*. Under a full warranty, if repeated attempts to repair a product fail, the consumer must be given the choice of a replacement or his money back.

Defective products. What redress is available if someone is injured by an exploding bottle, contaminated food, or an appliance that catches fire? The buyer can sue under the product warranty. But suppose someone else is hurt, or the seller has specifically disclaimed any warranties?

In the past, it was necessary to prove the injury was caused by negligent or improper manufacture or handling of the product. Sometimes negligence is obvious (a dead mouse is found in a bottle of soda). But in many cases it may be difficult to prove negligence in manufacture, or to determine just who was at fault.

The modern trend. Today, many states impose *strict liability* on anyone who sells a consumer product, from the manufacturer to the retailer. The injured person need only prove that the product was defective and caused the injury. The rule of strict liability is applied in most cases involving food, drugs and medicines, clothing, cosmetics, and other products intended for bodily use, and products inherently dangerous, such as automobiles. In other cases, it may still be necessary to prove negligence in manufacturing. It depends on state law.

Credit.
Anyone who makes a loan or extends credit for consumer purposes must disclose all terms and conditions in clear, understandable language, including the annual interest rate, any other charges, and what happens if there is a dispute or if the consumer fails to pay. Credit may not be denied because of race, religion, national origin, age, sex, marital status, or receipt of public assistance. If you are denied credit (a loan, a charge account, a credit card) you must be told why—in writing.

Protecting your credit rating. If you are turned down because of an unfavorable report from a credit rating bureau or agency, you must be told which agency. Upon request, the agency must tell you the nature and source of the unfavorable information (but it does not have to show you its file). It must also disclose the names and addresses of all persons who have been given the information within the past six months (two years if the information was given for employment purposes).

If you disagree, you may insist that the agency reinvestigate. If you still disagree, you may put a brief statement of your own in the file (up to 100 words) telling your side of the story.

Small claims court

All states have small claims courts to handle cases involving less than a maximum amount set by state law. The federal Tax Court has a Small Case Division to handle tax disputes up to $10,000. Small claims courts provide a speedy, inexpensive way for people to assert their legal rights without the time, trouble, and cost of a major lawsuit.

Bringing a lawsuit. The court clerk will help you fill out the forms to start the case. There is a small fee, which the other side will pay if you win. The other party will be notified. Often, this will be enough to get him to settle. If not, you will be notified of the time and place of trial.

Caution: If the other party pays up, you can just drop the case. But if he only *promises* to pay, be sure to show up on the trial date and tell the judge. The case will then be held open, to make sure that you get paid.

Trials are informal. You can have a lawyer, but you do not need one. Here are some tips on how to behave:
- Dress well, but do not dress up.
- Stand when you talk to the judge. Call him or her "Your Honor."
- Describe your case in a general way before going into detail. Be sure to bring with you all documentary evidence, such as bills, canceled checks, letters, forms, etc.
- Testify yourself and call any witnesses.
- Do not fight or argue with the other party. Do not act like a lawyer. Do not ever argue with the judge.
- Do what the judge says. If he or she asks you a question, answer it. If he or she tells you not to say anything, be silent.

Credit cards. If your card is lost or stolen, you should notify the credit card company at once. But even if someone has used the card before you notify the company, you can be held liable for no more than $50.

If you find an error on your monthly statement, you must notify the company within 60 days, in writing, stating your name, address, card number, and the nature and amount of the mistake. *A phone call is not sufficient, nor is a note written on the monthly bill.* Write a separate letter. The company must investigate and give you a written answer within two billing periods, but not longer than 90 days.

Until then, the company may not try to collect the disputed amount; it may not revoke your card; and it may not report you as a delinquent payer to anyone, such as a credit rating bureau.

If the company, after investigation, still insists that you owe the money, it must furnish you with documentary evidence upon your request. If you still disagree, you should protect your credit rating by writing to the company again. If the company then reports you to anyone as delinquent, it must also report that the matter is in dispute and must notify you of the report.

Defective goods. If you buy merchandise that turns out to be defective or worthless, you do not have to pay the credit card company, provided:
- The transaction was for more than $50.
- It was made in your home state or within 100 miles of your home.
- You made an honest attempt to settle the dispute with the merchant.

The rule applies only to the unpaid balance. You cannot get back payments already made. Of course, you can try to get your money back from the merchant.

Bill collectors. Bill collection agencies operate under federal restrictions. The law does not apply, however, to persons or companies trying to collect their own debts. The following practices by collection agencies are forbidden:
- Telling anyone, including your employer, that you owe a debt (but they may ask for your address).
- Contacting you at unreasonable times or places (no middle-of-the-night phone calls).
- Using forms or envelopes that look official.
- Sending collection notices on postcards that other people might read.
- Using any abusive, deceptive, or unfair methods.

Moreover, the agency must stop *all* bill collection efforts if you notify them in writing to stop, or tell them you dispute the debt, or hire a lawyer.

If the agency violates the law, you can sue for actual damages, plus up to $1000 additional damages (if the court so decides), plus costs and attorneys' fees.

Are your debts too big?

Although you should always exercise care not to accumulate too many debts, it may happen that you become overwhelmed by the amount of money you owe. Declaring bankruptcy is the solution of last resort. Prudent management of your money will not only help you avoid bankruptcy, it can often get you out of your overwhelming debt. Read carefully "Managing the Family's Money," pages 110-139, for good advice on how not to overextend yourself. Sometimes it makes sense to consolidate your debts in order to avoid high monthly payments (see page 117 for more information). In order to get a fresh start, however, you may have to file for personal bankruptcy in a federal court.

How it works. You give the court a list of everything you own, the debts you owe, and any debts owed to you. The court appoints a trustee to collect your assets and distribute them to creditors. Mortgaged property or property pledged as security (collateral) goes to the particular creditor involved; the rest is distributed proportionately to all. If you have not misrepresented or concealed anything, your debts will be canceled (discharged) except for taxes, alimony, and child support.

Caution: Judges have the power to deny discharges if they find that the debtor *can* pay his debts and is improperly trying to take advantage of the bankruptcy law.

What you keep. Not everything you own can be taken. You can keep personal belongings, most household goods, your car (up to $1200 in value), the tools of your trade, and a certain amount of cash. But if you own a home, you could be in danger of losing it. There is a "homestead exemption" of $7500, but if your house is worth more, it will be sold, and you will receive only the $7500.

Wage earner plans. The bankruptcy law provides another alternative, under which you submit to the court a plan to pay a specified amount each month, depending on your income, how much you owe, and the needs of your family. If the court approves the plan and you make the monthly payments, your creditors are not allowed to demand more. Eventually, you will be free of debt.

Personal property

Your neighbor is responsible for your lawnmower if he borrows it for his own use, but you are not responsible for his car if you let him park in your garage.

Land and buildings are *real* property. All other property is *personal* property, including cash, movable goods, stocks, bonds, and intangible legal rights.

Abandoned property belongs to the finder. *Lost* property belongs to the finder only if the real owner cannot be found. Many states require that anything over a certain value be turned over to the police; the finder gets it if the owner fails to turn up within a specified period. *Stolen* property continues to belong to the owner; he can get it back, even from people who bought it without knowing that it was stolen. The exception is *cash*. If cash is stolen, you can recover it only if it is still in the possession of the thief.

Owners and possessors

Bailments. Temporary transfers of possession, but not ownership, of property are called bailments. If someone borrows property for his own use (your neighbor borrows your lawnmower), he is normally required to return it or pay for any loss or damage. If the bailment is for the benefit of the owner (you let someone keep his car in your garage), you, the possessor, are responsible only for intentional damage or gross negligence.

Most bailments are business transactions for mutual benefit (you take your TV set to the repair shop, or leave your jewelry as security for a loan). The possessor must use reasonable care, and is responsible for loss or damage that results from his negligence.

Some special cases. Hotels and motels are usually protected by state laws limiting liability to a small amount—and then only if the property is put in the hotel safe. Common carriers, such as railroads or trucking companies, are held to a high standard of care. They are generally liable for all loss or damage, unless caused by improper packing or an act of God, such as lightning, a flood, or a hurricane.

Liens. Repairmen, hotelkeepers, and others have a lien on goods in their possession; they can keep them until their bill is paid. If you want your property back, you have no choice but to pay—or go to court. (If you are overcharged, consider suing in small claims court—see page 157.)

Ideas as property. You cannot "own" an idea. If you have a business idea you think is worth money, do not divulge it to anyone unless you get an agreement to pay for its use, or to keep it confidential.

Copyrights protect writing, music, works of art, and computer programs. What is protected is not the idea, but the form in which it is expressed. The copyright belongs to the producer of the work (or to his employer, if the work was done for hire). Copyrights can be registered, but need not be.

Patents are issued by the U.S. Patent Office to protect inventors. No one else may copy or manufacture the invention for a period of years. There is an exception, however. The inventor's employer may own the invention or have rights in it if it was invented during the course of employment.

Trademarks are names, designs, or slogans associated with a company or product; they may not be copied by competing companies. Trademarks may be registered or may simply arise from long use and association.

Installment sales. Sales of autos, furniture, and the like are often *conditional sales*. The buyer takes possession, but the seller remains legal owner until the goods are paid for. He can repossess the goods (if this can be accomplished without violence) or get them back from third parties if the buyer has sold or transferred them.

Watch out for this trap. An installment buyer usually signs a *promissory note* for the amount due. If a merchant sells the note to a finance company, the buyer will find himself in debt to the finance company even if the goods are defective or worthless. The finance company is a "holder in due course," not responsible for the condition of the goods. Many states have modified this rule. If you find yourself in this spot, talk to a lawyer or consumers' rights agency.

You and the Law

Your car. Legally, buying a car is no different from buying any other consumer product, but mistakes can be more costly. (For the law of conditional sales, see page 159; for the law of warranty, see page 156.) Be sure to read the warranty you get with your car. It tells you what rights you have if anything goes wrong.
"Lemon" laws. Many states have laws, stronger than the federal law, protecting consumers who buy cars that turn sour. The laws vary, but most work like this: If, within a year (or the warranty period, if less than a year), the dealer or manufacturer has been unable to repair a defect after four tries, or if the car has been out of commission for 30 days or more, the buyer is entitled to a new car or his money back.
Used cars. If you buy from a used car dealer, you are probably buying at your own risk, except for whatever warranty the dealer may give you. This holds even more so when you buy from a private party, unless you can show that you were defrauded.
Registration. A dealer will probably handle the registration of the car. If you buy privately, you may have to handle it yourself, and you may have to pay a sales tax to get the car registered. Contact your local motor vehicle bureau.
Insurance. Most states require car owners to carry liability insurance to cover any claims arising from auto accidents. Other types of insurance, such as fire, theft, or collision, are not required. You can buy them or not, as you choose.

If your new car does not work properly, you may be able, under the laws of your state, to get another car or your money back.

Accidents.
More lawsuits arise from auto accidents than from any other single cause. If you are involved in one, notify your insurance company immediately. The company will handle any claim against you, provide a lawyer if you are sued, and pay any judgment. If the judgment is for more than your insurance coverage, you are liable for the balance. You are required to cooperate with the insurance company in the defense of the case.
If you are injured. You may wish to make a claim for personal injuries or property damage. Write to the owner or driver of the other car, stating that you are making a claim, and asking him to turn it over to his insurance company, which will probably contact you. *Do not give the opposing insurance company any written statement about the accident;* it can be used against you. If you do not have a lawyer, you will have to communicate the nature of your claim and provide evidence, such as doctors' reports and repair bills. Do not give more evidence than is necessary, and never make any admissions. (If you have a lawyer, he will handle all this; it would be improper for the other side to contact you personally.)
Should you get a lawyer? A lawyer can probably get more than you can from the insurance company, but he will take part of it for his fee. Most accident cases are on a *contingent fee* basis. The lawyer gets nothing if you lose; but if you win he gets a percentage, which may run from a third to a half. It may even be more for small claims, as the lawyer may have to do as much paperwork in a small case as a large one. If the percentage seems too high, you might try to settle the claim yourself. You can call in a lawyer later, if necessary.
Evaluating a claim. You are entitled to be paid for actual losses, such as lost wages, repair bills, and medical costs (even if paid by insurance). These are called special damages. You are also entitled to damages for pain and suffering. As a general rule, a settlement should run from two to four times the amount of special damages. If there is doubt as to who was at fault in the accident, the settlement may be less. If there are permanent injuries, it will be much more, since future losses, expenses, and pain and suffering must be taken into account.

The law of negligence.
Except in states with no-fault insurance, you can recover damages only from a person who has caused an accident through negligence (carelessness). Negligence means the failure to use the ordinary care that could be expected of a reasonable person. Violation of the traffic laws is evidence of negligence, but a driver may be negligent without violating any law.
Who may recover? In some states, the injured person may not recover damages if he has also been guilty of

negligence, even in the slightest degree. This is called contributory negligence. Other states follow a rule of comparative negligence. The injured party can recover, but the amount he gets will be reduced in proportion to the extent he was at fault for the accident. A jury, for example, might find that the injured party was 20 percent responsible, and reduce his damages by that percentage.

Owner's liability. The driver is liable for his negligence. Under traditional law, the owner of the vehicle was liable only if the driver was his employee or was acting on the owner's behalf. In some states, it was presumed that any member of the owner's family was acting on his behalf (family purpose rule).

Many states now hold the owner responsible whenever the car is being driven with his consent.

Uninsured motorist laws. Many states have passed laws and established funds to pay persons injured by stolen cars, cars that do not carry insurance, and hit-and-run drivers who cannot be identified.

Who can sue? One spouse cannot sue the other for negligence. A minor child is usually not allowed to sue a parent for negligence. Some states allow a child to sue if the parent does not have custody.

Some states have "guest statutes" that ban a guest in an automobile from suing the owner. The guest can, of course, sue the driver of the other car.

No-fault insurance

A growing number of states are adopting no-fault insurance laws, under which persons injured in auto accidents are paid for their economic losses no matter who was at fault, including lost wages and out-of-pocket medical expenses (not covered by medical insurance). Under this system, you apply to your own insurance company for payment instead of suing the other driver. Passengers in your car also apply to your company. Injured pedestrians apply to the company carrying insurance on the car that hit them.

Lawsuits are still possible. In serious cases, you can also sue the other driver for damages, including pain and suffering. A serious case is one involving death or permanent injury, or medical expenses above a threshold amount, which is set by state law.

A good idea? Advocates of no-fault insurance claim that it speeds payments, avoids lawsuits, and cuts the cost of insurance. Some claimants receive smaller amounts than under the old system, but they save the cost of a lawyer.

What to do if you are involved in an accident

1. Get help	First of all, get medical help for anyone who is injured. If the accident is at all serious, call the police.
2. Exchange information	Exchange information with the other driver. Get his name, address, phone number, license number, and the make and license number of his car. If the driver does not own the car, get the owner's name, address, and phone number.
	Do not admit you were at fault. Do not get into any argument about who was at fault. Stay calm and simply exchange information.
3. Get evidence	Get names, addresses, and phone numbers of passengers and witnesses. If the police come to the scene, get the officers' names and badge numbers, and the address and phone number of their station.
	If you have a camera with you, take pictures of the scene. Otherwise, get photographs as soon after the accident as possible. Write down the details of the accident as soon as you get the chance, while you still remember them clearly. Include all details, such as the weather, time of day, and visibility.
4. Give notice	All states require a report to the police if anyone was injured. It is also required for property damage beyond a certain amount, set by state law. If in doubt, play it safe and file a report.
	Notify your insurance company as soon as you possibly can. Failure to report, or unnecessary delay, could jeopardize your insurance coverage.

You and the Law

Injuries and damages

Property owners must exercise reasonable care that customers or guests are not injured on their property.

A wrongful act that injures another person or his property is called a tort. Torts are classified as intentional or negligent. Auto accidents are the most common examples of negligent tort; another is malpractice by doctors, lawyers, or other professionals.

Property owners' liability. Many lawsuits arise over injuries on someone else's property; for example, someone trips and falls. Whether the property owner is liable may depend on who is injured. Here are the rules:

- **Invitees** are invited on the premises for business purposes; an example is customers in a store. The owner owes them a duty of reasonable care and is liable for any negligence.
- **Licensees** are persons allowed on the premises who are not business invitees. Social guests generally fall into this category. Licensees are on the premises at their own risk, but owners are under a duty to warn of hidden dangers, such as a loose floorboard.
- **Trespassers** have no right on the premises, and owners owe them no duty except to refrain from intentional harm. However, if the trespassers are children, and the owner knows that some building, structure, condition, or object on the property is likely to attract children, he may be held liable for any failure to exercise reasonable care.

Intentional torts. The word "intentional" does not necessarily imply an intention to hurt anyone. For example, if you slap someone on the back, thinking he is an old friend, and he turns out to be a stranger with a heart condition, you are liable for any damage.

Intention to harm (malice) is necessary to recover *punitive damages*. Punitive damages, over and above any actual damages, may be awarded to punish the wrongdoer and deter him (and others) from repeating the wrongful act.

Assault and battery. Assault is a threat of violence that puts someone in fear of bodily harm. Battery is the actual physical contact. Either (or both) is grounds for a lawsuit.

Self-defense is the only legal excuse. Insults or provocative language do not excuse assault and battery; but the jury may consider them in awarding damages.

Illegal confinement. This term includes any interference with personal liberty, including false arrest, false imprisonment, or any detention by physical barriers, force, or the threat of force. Normally, no one may be detained against his will. But most states permit shopkeepers and others to detain persons suspected of theft, provided they have reasonable grounds for suspicion and do not use excessive force or make unnecessary false public accusations.

Private citizens who make citizen's arrests do so at their own risk. If the arrested person is released or acquitted, he may sue. (For police arrests, see pages 167-168.)

Defamation of character. Defamation is the communication of false statements that injure the reputation of a living person. False statements about the dead, or about groups in general, are not defamation, no matter how offensive.

Libel is written defamation; slander is spoken defamation. Traditionally, libel was more serious, as the written word can be more widely circulated. Radio and TV have made the distinction less important. Pictures or other communications may be defamatory, as well as words.

A statement is automatically defamatory if it accuses a person of crime, immoral or unethical conduct, loathsome disease, unfitness for one's trade or profession, or unchastity (if female). Even if there is no financial damage, a person may sue to vindicate his reputation. For other statements, a person must show in what way they were defamatory and what damages were suffered.

Publication. To be defamatory, a statement must be communicated to a third person; private insults do not count. But communication to even one other person is enough to constitute publication. Anyone who repeats or republishes a defamation also commits defamation.

Defenses. If you are sued for defamation, there are several ways to defend yourself.
- By showing the statement was *true*.
- By proving the person gave *consent* to the statement.
- By showing the statement was *fair comment* on a matter of public interest. (A fair comment is one based on fact, or an honest expression of belief or opinion, and not made from malice or dishonorable motives.)
- By showing you had a *privilege* to make the statement. Any statement is absolutely privileged if made between husband and wife, or if made in court, legislative, or other government proceedings.

There is also a *qualified privilege* for statements by an employer who is asked about an employee, and for statements by newspapers or other media about public figures. But the privilege is lost if the statement was made with malice and with either a knowledge of its falsity or a reckless disregard for the truth.

Invasion of privacy. No one may use your name or picture for commercial or advertising purposes without your consent. You can sue for damages and can also get a court order stopping such use.

There has been much discussion of the right of privacy and the danger of computerized data banks that hold information about private lives and personal affairs. So far, however, there are few laws on the subject, except for laws prohibiting government employees from disclosing confidential information.

Trespass. Anybody who goes on someone else's land (or enters their buildings) without permission, or places or throws anything on the property, is a trespasser and can be sued for any damage to the property. Even if no damage is done, the owner may want to sue, to establish his right to keep the person off the property.

Conversion. Trespass applies to real property; the term conversion applies to personal property. Anyone who takes another's personal property or uses it without permission, or obtains it by fraud or trickery, or destroys or damages it, or disposes of it without permission by sale, gift, lease, or other means, has committed a conversion (meaning he "converted" the property to his own purposes). Even if someone has legal possession of another's property, he commits conversion if he damages it, loses it, gives it to someone else, or refuses to return it to its owner. The owner can sue for any damage to the property, or the full value, if it is lost or destroyed.

A lawsuit for conversion is a lawsuit for money. If

Jacqueline Onassis charged that her civil rights were violated when this photo, used in an ad, showed her look-alike in the background.

the owner wants the actual property back, he may file a lawsuit known as replevin. This is appropriate for property that is unique in some way—such as a work of art or a family heirloom.

Emotional damages

Courts are reluctant to award damages when the only injury is emotional. There is too much chance of fraud or of exaggerated claims for hurt feelings. But where there has been actual physical injury, the court or jury may award additional damages for emotional harm. The physical injury proves the claim is not a fraud and that it involves more than hurt feelings.

Recent trends. Recently, there has been a trend toward allowing damages solely for emotional harm where it is obvious that the harm is real. For instance, a mother who watched her child run down by a car recovered emotional damages from the driver. Damages will also be awarded if they result from some illegal act.

There has also been a trend toward allowing damages for *intentional* infliction of emotional harm. Examples would include vicious harassment by bill collectors, and obscene phone calls.

A special case. Common carriers, such as railroads and bus lines, are obligated to provide passengers with courteous service. Therefore, they can be sued for insulting behavior on the part of their employees.

You and the Law

Earning a living

Your job. At one time, employers could hire, fire, and set the terms and conditions of work almost at will. About all an employee could do was quit or accept the conditions. Today, employees' rights are protected by federal and state laws, enforced by government agencies. Some laws give employees the right to sue on their own, but it is usually better to go to an agency and take advantage of its services. Some important laws and agencies are in the chart below.

Who are employees? If your boss has the right to control the manner and means by which you do your job, you are an employee. If not, you are an independent contractor. A good example of an independent contractor is your doctor; you hire him to cure your illness, but you do not tell him how to examine you or

> PLACEMENT SUPERVISOR: (Work-site) to provide vocational training to handicapped adults for job placement in area business & industry. Community work-site position working with handicapped people. Related Bachelor's Degree required. Prior experience in rehabilitation desirable. Reply Box 204, EOE, M/F.

An Equal Opportunity Employer will not discriminate when hiring on the grounds of race, age, sex, religion, or national origin.

what medicine to prescribe. Some occupations are borderline cases; some commission salesmen are employees, some are not.

Persons working at home may be employees: an example would be women hired by clothing manufacturers to do sewing. Some office workers now work at home, with a computer tie-in to the office.

Officers of a corporation are employees, but partners are not employees of the partnership.

Laws protecting employees rights and the agencies that enforce them

Union activity	Protected and regulated for nonsupervisory employees by National Labor Relations Act. *Contact:* National Labor Relations Board.
Racial, ethnic, or religious discrimination	Banned by Civil Rights Act of 1964. *Contact:* Equal Employment Opportunity Commission (EEOC).
Sex discrimination	Banned by Civil Rights Act of 1964. *Contact:* EEOC. Wage discrimination banned by Equal Pay Act. *Contact:* U.S. Labor Department, Wage and Hour Division.
Age discrimination	Banned, for persons aged 40 to 69, by the Age Discrimination in Employment Act. *Contact:* U.S. Labor Department, Wage and Hour Division.
Safety and health	Occupational Safety and Health Administration sets workplace and industry standards and conducts inspections. Special laws apply for coal miners and other hazardous occupations.
Wages and salaries	Fair Labor Standards Act guarantees a minimum wage and time and a half for hours worked over 40 a week to most nonsupervisory employees. *Contact:* U.S. Labor Department, Wage and Hour Division. Consumer Credit Protection Act limits the amount of wages and salaries a creditor can seize for payment of a debt.
Veterans	Right to reemployment at previous job. *Contact:* Veterans Administration.
Child labor	Limited and restricted by Fair Labor Standards Act. *Contact:* U.S. Department of Labor, Wage and Hour Division.
Miscellaneous	Some states provide stronger protection than federal laws. State laws also ban any discrimination against employees serving on jury duty. Many states ban or restrict the use of lie detector tests by employers. *Contact:* State Labor Department or Commission on Human Rights.

Employment is a contract. Except in union plants, the contract is usually oral, and either employer or employee can end it at will, with or without notice. But as long as the contract lasts, both parties must comply with its terms. Your employer, for example, cannot cut your salary for work already done.

Some courts have ruled that company manuals, employee handbooks, and the like are to be considered part of the contract; employees are entitled to all benefits described in them. Many companies, however, now put a specific statement in company publications reserving the right to make changes at any time.

Unlawful discharge. Traditionally, employers had an absolute right to fire at will, subject only to antidiscrimination laws and union contracts. Recent court decisions cast doubt on the old rule. Courts have awarded damages to employees dismissed for refusing to give false testimony at a hearing, and to employees dismissed for filing workers' compensation claims. Employees have sued when fired for opposing company practices or products they considered unethical or against public policy—such as products harmful to the environment. Some won, some lost. The law is changing in the direction of greater employee rights; but no one knows how far the change will go.

Union contracts. Employers must deal with unions representing a majority of workers in a bargaining unit, which may be the whole company, a division, or some group of employees. The National Labor Relations Board (or a state board) decides the proper bargaining unit and holds elections, if necessary. In a union shop, you must join the union or, at least, pay dues (except in a minority of states, which have right-to-work laws).

Wages and conditions of employment are set by a written collective bargaining agreement between company and union. Most contain grievance or arbitration procedures for resolving disputes. If you have a grievance or dispute with your employer, you must go through the union; if it decides not to press your claim, you have no remedy. There is an exception. The union owes a "duty of fair representation" to its members and cannot discriminate against any of them. If the union violates this duty, a member may be able to sue.

Union members have the right to run for union office, vote in union elections, and express their opinions on union matters—subject to reasonable regulations.

Employee benefits.
Some benefits are required by law:
Social Security pays benefits to retired or disabled workers and their families, and families of deceased workers. It includes Medicare. (For details, see pages 95 and 128-130.)
Unemployment insurance pays benefits to workers laid off or unemployed through no fault of their own. They must be ready, willing, and able to work.
Disability insurance is required by a few states (including California, New York, and New Jersey). It is similar to unemployment insurance, but applies to those unable to work because of illness, not unemployment. Some companies carry disability insurance even when not required.
Workers' compensation pays medical bills and sick benefits to workers injured on the job.
Pensions are *not* required by law. But if an employer does have a pension system, it must comply with federal pension law, which sets minimum standards for eligibility, length of service, etc. It also requires that participants be given a summary of the plan, written in language the average man can understand, explaining all the rules and provisions of the plan. It is important to read the summary; if you have any questions, ask the company personnel people for an explanation.
Other benefits. Many companies and union contracts provide other fringe benefits, including highly important ones, such as life insurance and medical insurance. Be sure to learn your rights to these benefits, and find out what will happen if you leave the company or are laid off. How long will the insurance continue? Can you renew it on your own? How much will it cost?

Starting your own business.
If you have the money to set up or buy a full-scale business, you undoubtedly have a lawyer. Many people, though, start out on a small scale, often working from their homes, sometimes as a sideline to their regular jobs. Many housewives do typing at home or run small telephone answering services. Here are some legal problems that may arise with a new business.

How to save on taxes. If you operate from your home, reserve part of the home *exclusively* for business. You can take a percentage of household costs as a home office business deduction, including heat, repairs, maintenance, utilities, depreciation, and rent.

Hobbies, such as photography or woodworking, can often be turned into profitable businesses. But the Internal Revenue Service will be suspicious, especially if you show a loss (as many new business do, at first). If you are just pursuing a hobby, you cannot deduct any losses or home office expenses. To prove you are really in business, you should operate in a businesslike fashion. Keep records of income and expenses. Get business cards. Put out a sign, or advertise. Comply with any licensing or registration laws. You do not have to be making a profit, but you must show that you are trying to. (*Note:* If you make a profit in two years out of five, the law presumes you are in business for profit.)

There may be tax advantages in hiring your spouse and children. Check with your accountant.

Hiring employees. You must comply with all labor laws. You must also withhold taxes and send them in to the government, including Social Security and unemployment. You must buy workers' compensation insurance.

If you need only part-time or occasional help, you can avoid these problems by using free-lance workers or independent contractors, such as public stenographers who do clerical work. Another way is to get your help from a temporary agency. The agency is the legal employer of the employees. You pay a fee to the agency, and the agency pays the employees.

Government regulations. You need a license for some occupations, especially those affecting public health or safety. If your business has anything to do with food or drink, you will certainly be subject to regulation and inspection. If you use a business name (Acme Plumbing Co.), you may have to register it somewhere. For information, contact local authorities or any business group.

Partnerships. Each partner acts as agent for the others. Each is personally liable for all debts of the business; this means that creditors can get at a partner's home, bank account, or other property—not just the property of the partnership. Partners share profits (or losses) in any way they agree on. It is best to have a written agreement, specifying what each partner is entitled to, how much money he is to invest, how much time he is to put in, and any other agreements between the partners.

Every partnership must have at least one *general* partner. It may also have *limited* partners, who put money in the partnership and are entitled to share in the profits, but who have no say in running the business. Limited partners are personally liable for partnership debts only to the extent of their investment.

Buying a franchise. A franchise is the right to use a name or trademark, or to manufacture or sell a product. Fast food chains like McDonald's are well-known examples. Local people own and operate the restau-

Should you form a corporation?

A corporation is a legal "person," separate and distinct from the stockholders who own it. Its great advantage is *limited liability*. Stockholders are not personally liable for corporate debts; they may lose their investment, but no more. (Small businesses, however, may find it difficult to get bank loans or credit unless officers or stockholders agree to be personally liable.)
Other advantages:
- Corporations can raise money by issuing stock; it is a lot easier to sell shares of stock than a percentage interest in a business.
- Corporations go on, even if individual stockholders die.
- Family corporations can be used to split income among family members to save on taxes.

A disadvantage is double taxation. Corporations pay income tax; then stockholders pay personal income tax when profits are distributed to them. On the other hand, if the corporation grows in value, so does the stock. And if a stockholder sells, he is taxed on only 40 percent of the profit.

Small corporations can avoid double taxation by electing to be taxed as if they were partnerships.

Forming a corporation is simple, legally. What you need more than a lawyer is a good accountant or businessman to advise you.

Doing business with relatives

Your brother has a great idea for a new business, so you stake him to the money to get started. A few months later, he dies in an auto accident. What happens now?
- *If the money was a loan,* you can get it back.
- *If the money was a gift,* you cannot get it back; you may even owe a gift tax.
- *If the money was an investment,* you might be considered your brother's partner, entitled to a share of any business profit. On the other hand, you might be liable for business debts.

You probably have nothing in writing, and you cannot remember exactly what was said. In fact, neither you nor your brother may even have thought about the possibilities. As a result, you may be faced with the trouble of a lawsuit, with no assurance of getting your money.

The moral is, when making a loan to a friend or relative, setting up a partnership, or doing anything with legal consequences, *put it in writing,* just as you would with a stranger. Aside from the possibility of a death, you never know when there may be a falling out in the family. Any lawyer can tell you that family disputes are more bitter than any other.

In addition, the Internal Revenue Service is always suspicious of family deals. If your taxes are ever audited, you may need proof of exactly what transpired.

rants, using the companies' names. Other common franchises are gas stations and automobile dealerships. The owner gets the benefit of the name, the advertising, and a lot of management and financial help. There is a drawback. The franchising company will retain a great deal of control.

Before signing any agreement, have it read by your lawyer. These are important questions to ask: How long will the franchise last? Is it permanent? Can I sell it? Can I lose it? If so, under what circumstances? Do I have to buy only from certain suppliers? What are the restrictions on my right to run the business?

Getting help. The U.S. Small Business Administration gives information, counseling, financial aid, and help in getting bank loans and government contracts. A special division aids minority businesses.

Criminal law and procedure

What is a crime?
A *felony* is a serious crime, such as murder, manslaughter, rape, robbery, arson, burglary, or assault with a weapon. Lesser crimes are *misdemeanors*. Traffic violations or violations of local ordinances are not crimes. An attempt to commit a crime is itself a crime. An *accessory* (one who aids in a crime though not present when it is committed) is guilty of a crime.

No law may make an act a crime, if the act was not a crime when it was performed. Nor may penalties be increased retroactively.

Who can commit a crime?
An insane person cannot commit a crime. Insane means "unable to understand the nature of his act, or unable to know right from wrong." Drunkenness or voluntary use of drugs is not insanity and is not a defense to crime; but a person whose mind is affected by drugs prescribed as medicine may be excused. Children under a specified age set by state law (usually 15 or 16) cannot commit a crime (juvenile delinquency is not a crime). Young people over that age may be treated as "youthful offenders," and their crime later expunged from the record if not repeated.

Defenses. Ignorance of the law is not a defense, but ignorance of the fact may be. For example, a person may take another's property believing it to be his own.

If a person reasonably believes himself to be in danger of death or bodily harm, he may use force and even kill another person in self-defense.

Arrests. A policeman may arrest a person who commits *any* crime in his presence. He may arrest on reasonable suspicion in cases of *felony*. Otherwise, he needs a warrant.

Searches. An officer may make a search in the course of a lawful arrest. He may search a person for weapons if he thinks it is necessary to ensure his own safety. He may search a vehicle if he has reasonable grounds to believe that it contains evidence of a crime and that it may be driven away before he can get a search warrant.

If your child is arrested

If you are ever unlucky enough to get a phone call informing you that your son or daughter has been arrested, *what you do next can affect your child's whole future.* So do not panic, however you may feel. Here is what to do:

- **Get all the information you can,** including the address of the police station, the names and badge numbers of the arresting officers and the desk sergeant, the district attorney's man in charge of the case, and when and where your child will be taken for arraignment (a court hearing to advise the defendant of the charges and set bail).

- **Ask to talk to the desk sergeant and tell him you do not want your child questioned until you or your lawyer get there.** Ask him to write this request down. If your child has medical or emotional problems requiring any special treatment, tell the desk sergeant. (As soon as you can, have the child's doctor call the police.)

- **When you talk to the child, try to calm him down.** If possible, one parent should keep the child on the phone while the other goes to the station. Tell the child to be courteous and polite to the police and not to antagonize them, but not to answer any questions.

- **Do not argue or fight with the child at the station,** no matter how you feel. It is important to show the police a good family relationship. Get the child out on bail; if there is any delay, try to have him held at the station house, not the county jail. Jails are not safe, and can be a harrowing experience for young people.

- **Get a lawyer who is experienced at criminal law,** and do what he says.

You and the Law

**Answer no questions.
Get a lawyer.**

In other cases, he must get a warrant. If a search is unlawful, nothing that is discovered can be admitted as evidence against the person searched.

Rights of accused persons.
Anyone charged with a crime has the right to remain silent. He has the right to a lawyer and a speedy trial before a jury. He has the right to confront and cross-examine his accusers, and he is entitled to be considered innocent until proven guilty "beyond a reasonable doubt." Even if convicted, he may not be subjected to "cruel or unusual punishment."

When a person is arrested, he must be informed of his rights, including the right to a lawyer and the right to remain silent. Otherwise, any admission or confession may not be used as evidence against him. This rule applies only to arrests.

When the police are questioning witnesses or persons at the scene of a crime, they are not required to give any warning, and anything a person says at that time may be used against him.

What to do if you are arrested. There are two basic rules: (1) Do not answer questions, and (2) Get a lawyer. The more serious the charge, the more important these rules are. Most non-criminals have a strong urge to explain themselves. Resist the urge. You can always make a statement later after you have talked to your lawyer.

If you do say anything, tell the truth. Any lies will probably be found out, and no one will believe anything you say after that.

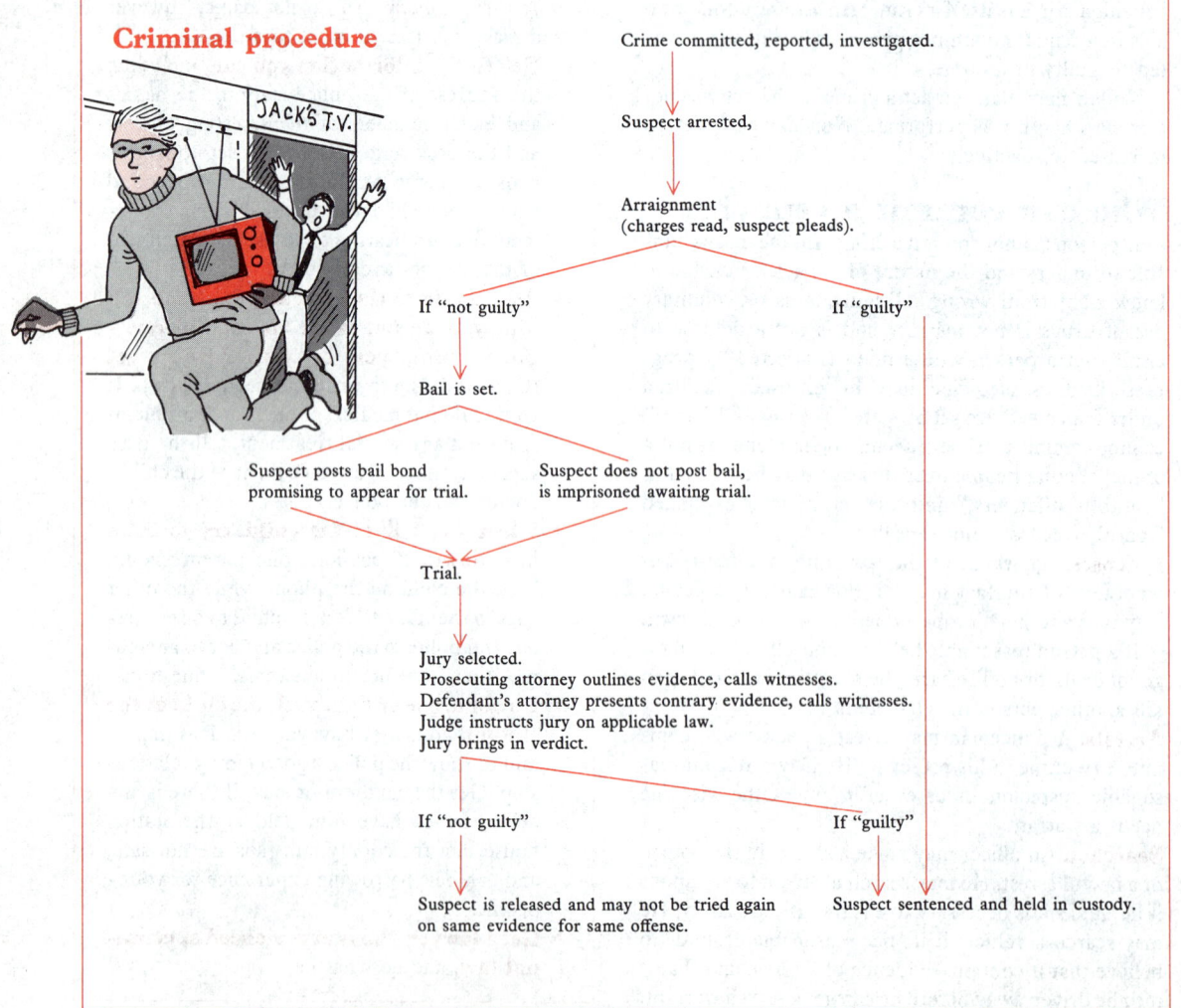

Criminal procedure

Crime committed, reported, investigated.
↓
Suspect arrested.
↓
Arraignment
(charges read, suspect pleads).

If "not guilty" / If "guilty"

Bail is set.

Suspect posts bail bond promising to appear for trial. / Suspect does not post bail, is imprisoned awaiting trial.

Trial.

Jury selected.
Prosecuting attorney outlines evidence, calls witnesses.
Defendant's attorney presents contrary evidence, calls witnesses.
Judge instructs jury on applicable law.
Jury brings in verdict.

If "not guilty" / If "guilty"

Suspect is released and may not be tried again on same evidence for same offense. / Suspect sentenced and held in custody.

How to find a lawyer

Do you need one? Many simple legal matters can be handled without a lawyer. Simple wills, uncontested divorces with no property or custody complications, personal bankruptcies, even settling simple estates often involve nothing more than filling out standard forms available at legal supply stores or from the courts. But be careful not to take legal advice from anyone who is not a lawyer.

Many books contain sample clauses for wills, contracts, leases, etc. You can find them at your library or the law library at the courthouse. Ask the librarian for help.

Here are other inexpensive ways to handle legal matters:

- **Legal clinics** handle routine matters for a small fee. Often the work is done by *paralegals*—nonlawyers trained in specific areas—under a lawyer's supervision.
- **Prepaid legal services,** a form of insurance like medical insurance, are provided by many employers and union contracts. If you need legal help, use a participating lawyer and the insurance pays the fee.
- **Arbitration** is used extensively in labor and commercial disputes, and now in consumer and housing disputes. Arbitration is like an informal court hearing, and the arbitrator's decision is binding. Usually, both sides must agree, in advance, to arbitrate the dispute.

Civil procedure

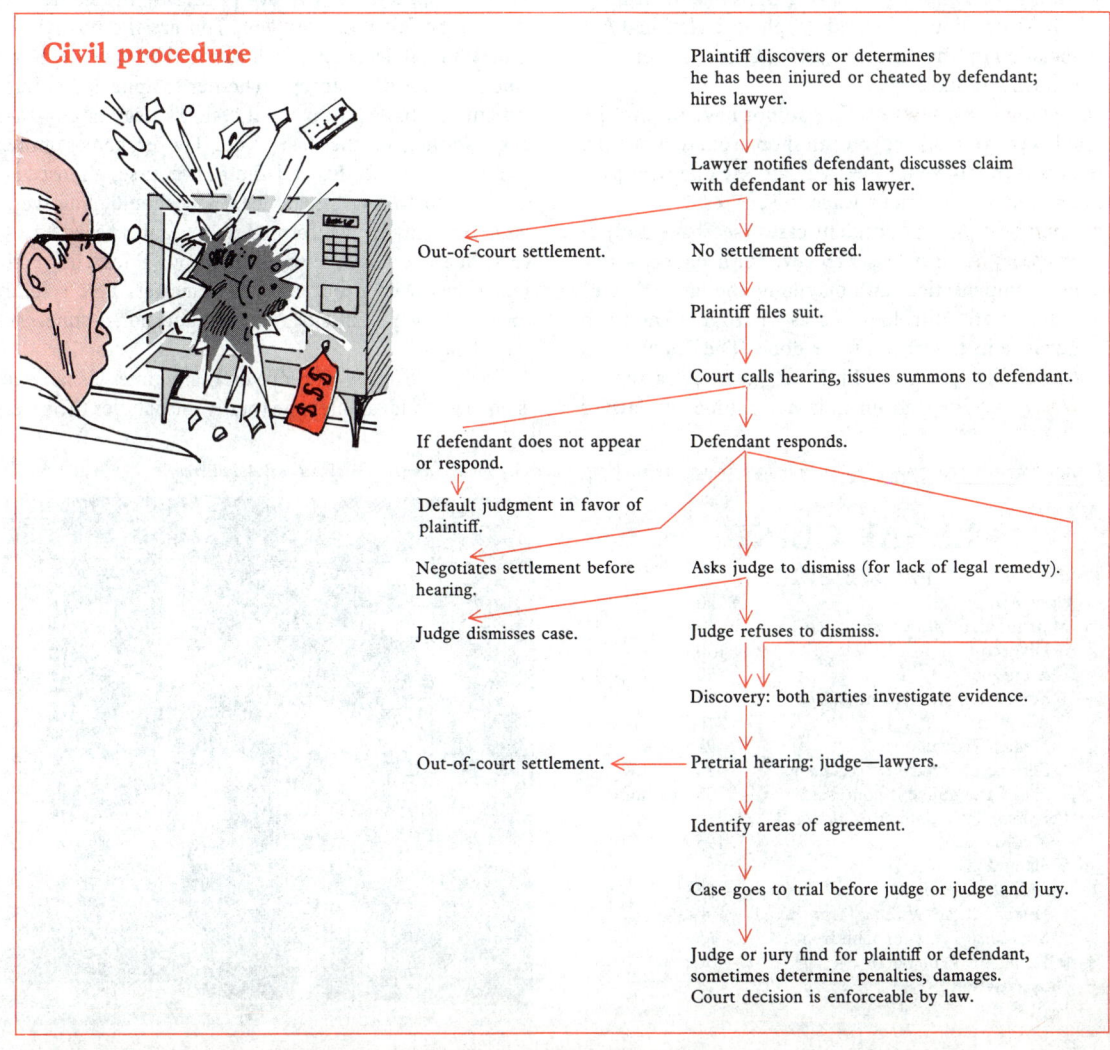

Plaintiff discovers or determines he has been injured or cheated by defendant; hires lawyer.

Lawyer notifies defendant, discusses claim with defendant or his lawyer.

Out-of-court settlement. ← No settlement offered.

Plaintiff files suit.

Court calls hearing, issues summons to defendant.

If defendant does not appear or respond.
Default judgment in favor of plaintiff.

Defendant responds.

Negotiates settlement before hearing.
Judge dismisses case.

Asks judge to dismiss (for lack of legal remedy).

Judge refuses to dismiss.

Discovery: both parties investigate evidence.

Out-of-court settlement. ← Pretrial hearing: judge—lawyers.

Identify areas of agreement.

Case goes to trial before judge or judge and jury.

Judge or jury find for plaintiff or defendant, sometimes determine penalties, damages. Court decision is enforceable by law.

You and the Law

If you do need a lawyer, look for someone with experience in your type of case. Many lawyers specialize, particularly in the fields of criminal law, accident and negligence law, domestic relations law, real estate law, tax law, and various kinds of business law. If you do not know any lawyers, here are some people to ask:

- *Friends* who have had a similar legal problem.
- *Your boss,* on business matters.
- *Your union,* on employment matters or questions of your entitlement to benefits.
- *Your clergyman,* or a social worker, on family matters, divorce, child custody, and so on.
- *Your accountant or banker* on financial, tax, or inheritance matters.
- *Your doctor* on injury cases. He has probably been called to testify, and may know a good lawyer.
- *People who work at the courthouse.* They see the lawyers in action.
- *Civic or community groups,* or groups like the American Association of Retired People, the National Association for the Advancement of Colored People, or women's groups.

Interviewing a lawyer. You do not have to hire the first lawyer you talk to; you can shop around. Never be reluctant to talk about fees; you are the one who pays them. There are various ways to set fees:

- *Contingent fees,* in accident cases (see page 160).
- *Statutory fees* may be set by law. For instance, workers' compensation laws may limit the lawyer's fee.
- *Flat fees* are suitable for cases where it is known in advance just what has to be done. The drawback is that the lawyer is not likely to put in extra time.
- *Hourly fees* depend on how much time the lawyer puts in. That sounds fair, but there is a danger: the longer the case drags on, the higher the fee, so your lawyer may be in no hurry to get anything done. Put a limit, in advance, on how much you can afford to pay.

Other factors affecting fees are the difficulty of the case, the amount of money involved, the skill and experience of the lawyer, and the customary fee charged in your community. (Local bar associations used to set minimum fee schedules. No lawyer who was a member could charge less. The practice has been banned by the U.S. Supreme Court as illegal price-fixing. Unfortunately, it still goes on, though not openly.)

What is a retainer? When you hire a lawyer, you make a down payment on the fee, called a retainer, which binds the lawyer to act in your interests and to accept no business that conflicts with your interests. You should have a written payment schedule, and insist that all bills show just what services were performed, especially if you are paying by the hour.

Working with your lawyer. You are the boss. You make all final decisions, such as whether to settle, how much to offer or to accept, whether to appeal, etc. But it would be foolish to try to dictate strategy or day-to-day handling of the case. Your lawyer knows more about it than you do, and the best course, almost always, is to follow his advice. You should, however, insist on being kept informed on a regular basis. Lawyers, like everybody else, tend to put things off, and sometimes need prodding. Legal matters take a long time anyway; you do not want any additional unnecessary delays.

You can dismiss your lawyer at any time. Usually, it is not a good idea unless he totally mishandles the case.

Usually lawyers charge what is customary in their communities. But if you cannot afford a lawyer, consult a Legal Aid attorney.

LEGAL CLINIC
FEE SCHEDULE

Consultation	$ 20
Matrimonial *(uncontested)*	
Divorce	150
Annulment	250
Separation Agreement *(simple)*	95
Adoption	210
Name Change	95
Service of Papers *(if necessary)*	25
All of the above if contested	35 per hour
Personal Bankruptcy *(uncontested,*	
limited assets)	195
Wills and Estates	
Individual *(simple)*	60
Husband and Wife *(separate wills)*	90
Standard Trust for Children	65
Filing for Probate	150
Incorporation	175
Real Estate	

You and the Law

You have to pay him for work already done, and you will have to pay a new lawyer as well. If a case is already on trial, changing lawyers can make a bad impression on a judge or jury.

Cooperate with your lawyer. Do not lie or conceal anything from him. The more damaging the information, the more the lawyer needs to know it. Anything you tell your lawyer is *absolutely confidential.* He is not allowed to tell anyone else, even if he wants to; the same rule applies to his employees.

Do not try to decide what is important and what is not. That is what you hire a lawyer for. There is no way that he can win a case if the other side comes up with evidence he knows nothing about. This advice is not limited to lawsuits. A lawyer who is drawing a will or a contract has to understand the entire situation. Most lawsuits about the meaning of legal documents arise because something has been left out, or some aspect of the situation has not been covered.

How to complain.
You can file a complaint with the bar committee, which can take disciplinary action or even recommend disbarment. If your lawyer has actually stolen or misappropriated your money, you can file a criminal complaint. (Lawyers are supposed to keep clients' money separate from their own; it is entirely improper to mingle the funds.)

You can also sue for malpractice, which means failure to exercise the reasonable care expected of a professional. Making an error of judgment would not be malpractice; but failure to know the elementary principles of law would. So would a failure to file a lawsuit on time, thereby costing the client the right to sue.

Where to go if you cannot afford a lawyer

The Legal Aid Society gives free legal help to those who cannot afford to pay. It does not handle divorces or criminal cases.

Lawyers referral services of local bar associations do not offer free aid, but they may refer you to a lawyer who bases his charges on what the client can afford.

The Legal Services Corporation, federally funded, provides legal help to poor people. Neighborhood Justice Centers try to settle disputes without lawyers.

Government agencies, such as consumer agencies, human rights commissions, and labor departments, will bring legal actions on behalf of people who file complaints.

Law schools sometimes run legal clinics staffed by law students. If not, the school can give you information.

Civil rights groups, such as the NAACP Legal Defense Fund and the American Civil Liberties Union, may handle a case or refer you to someone who can help.

Private organizations, such as landlords' and tenants' groups, trade associations, business groups, and labor unions, may provide legal services for their members.

Questions to ask before hiring a lawyer

Do you handle cases like mine? Ask the lawyer about some of them. How did they come out? How long did they take? What were the costs? Were there any special problems?

Will you actually do the work? If the lawyer's secretary or staff does the work, will the bill be reduced? You do not want to pay high professional rates for a clerk filling out a standard form.

What are your fee arrangements and billing practices? Some lawyers, for instance, bill by the quarter-hour. If they make a two-minute phone call, they bill for the full quarter hour. A few phone calls and your bill starts to mount. You should also check on other costs that may be incurred: Xeroxing of documents, filing fees and other court costs, and the cost of taking depositions from witnesses.

About how long will the whole thing take? You want to know, first, what the total period of time will be, and second, how much time the lawyer will actually put in.

How closely do you work with clients? You want to be kept informed and have some say in what is being done.

What happens if something goes wrong or we disagree? Suppose you have a dispute over fees? If your lawyer mismanages, will he still expect to be paid? Will he agree to submit disputes to an impartial arbitrator other than the bar association? (Bar associations are notorious for favoring lawyers over clients.)

You and the Law

circumstantial evidence

Glossary

encroachment

libel

felony

ab initio. From the beginning.
abatement. Reduction or decrease.
accord and satisfaction. An agreement between two persons that settles a claim or lawsuit.
administrative law. The law regulating the procedure to be followed by government agencies.
adverse possession. Acquisition of ownership of land by continuous use for a long period of time, usually 20 years.
affidavit. A written statement made under oath.
agent. One who has authority to act for another (the principal). Acts or promises of the agent are binding on the principal.
alibi. Latin for "elsewhere." Alibi does not mean excuse. It means a person was somewhere else when a crime was committed.
alienate. To transfer ownership of property.
amicus curiae. Friend of the court. A person not a party in a case, but allowed to participate because of some indirect interest.
amortization. Payment of a debt over a period of time, usually a mortgage or bond.
appellant. A person who requests a higher court to review the decision of a lower court. The other party is called the *appellee* or *respondent*.
arraignment. Bringing a person charged with crime before a court to be advised of the charges against him.
assign. Transfer one's right or interest in something to another.
attachment. Seizure of property for payment of debt.
attestation. Witnessing the signature of a will or document.
attorney. One who has power to act for another.
bail. Money or property deposited in court to guarantee the appearance of a criminal defendant at his trial.
bailee. One in legal possession of another's property (has nothing to do with criminal bail; see page 159).
bench warrant. A court order for someone's arrest.
bequest. A gift of personal property in a will.
bill of exchange. A written order directing one person to pay a sum of money to another. The most common bill of exchange is a check, which directs a bank to pay a sum of money to the person named on the check.
bill of lading. A written contract for delivery of goods by freight.
bill of particulars. A written statement of the details of a claim in a lawsuit.
bill of sale. Written transfer of rights for personal property.
bona fide. In good faith; genuine.
breach of the peace. Disturbance of public order, usually by fighting.
brief. Written statement by a lawyer in support of his legal position in a case.
burden of proof. The obligation to produce evidence in support of allegations in a lawsuit. Whoever alleges a fact has the burden of proving it if it is disputed.
burglary. The crime of breaking into and entering property with intention to commit a felony.
capital. The money invested in a business, adjusted each year for the business's profits or losses.
capital crime. A crime punishable by death.
capital stock. The stock issued by a corporation.
causa mortis. "In contemplation of approaching death." Gifts made causa mortis are subject to special legal rules.

172

You and the Law

cause of action. The legal basis of a lawsuit, such as negligence, debt, breach of contract, or libel.

certiorari. A legal procedure by which a higher court reviews the decision of a lower one.

challenge. An objection to a juror. A juror may be challenged "for cause," if, for example, he is biased in favor of one side. In addition, each side has a certain number of peremptory challenges, for which no reason need be given.

chattel. An item or article of personal property.

chattel mortgage. A loan on which personal property is put up as security; for example, an auto loan or a loan on jewelry.

circumstantial evidence. Evidence from which a fact can be inferred; for example, a person's fingerprint is evidence of his presence at the place the fingerprint was found.

C.O.D. Cash on delivery. A type of sale in which the buyer pays when the goods are delivered to him.

codicil. An amendment to a will (see page 155).

collateral. Property pledged as security for a debt.

collateral relatives. Relatives other than direct ancestors or descendants.

common carrier. A transportation facility, such as a railroad or trucking company, in the business of transporting passengers or goods for a price.

common law. The body of law that has grown up over the centuries from custom and from the decisions of the courts—as opposed to statutory law, which is law passed by legislatures.

common law marriage. Marriage without a formal ceremony (see page 141).

commutation. Reduction in punishment, ordered by the governor or another authority.

complaint. A document in a lawsuit setting forth the claim that is being made.

condemnation. Taking of property by the government (see page 152).

condition. A provision in a contract which *must* be performed, or the contract loses its validity.

condonation. Forgiveness (see page 145).

consanguinity. Blood relationship.

consideration. See *contract.*

consortium. A person's right to the sex, services, and society of his or her spouse. Traditionally, a husband could sue for loss of consortium if his wife were injured. In many states today, a wife can sue for loss of consortium if her husband is injured.

conversion. Misappropriation or misuse of personal property.

convey. To transfer property in writing.

corpus delicti. Latin for "body of the crime." Proof that a crime was committed; it does *not* mean the body of the victim.

co-signer or co-maker. One who signs a note or other

Contract

contract. An agreement by which one person promises to do something in return for the act or promise of another. Contracts usually arise from an *offer* by one person and *acceptance* by the other. An *executory* contract is one consisting of promises that have not yet been *executed.*

Consideration is the legal term for the act or promise of one side that induces the act or promise of the other. For example, I agree to sell you my watch for $100. My promise to sell the watch is the consideration for your promise to pay the $100, and vice versa.

A mere promise, without consideration, is not a contract and cannot be enforced. But a promise given for consideration is binding, even if the consideration is of no benefit to the promisor. *Example:* You promise to give your nephew $1000 if he does not smoke or drink until he is 21. If he performs his side of the bargain, you must give him the $1000 even though his act (not smoking or drinking) is of no material benefit to you.

Contracts may be written or oral, and may be *implied* from conduct or even silence. For example, if you go into a restaurant and eat a meal, you have to pay for it. If you let someone perform services for you knowing that he expects to be paid, you have to pay him. Implied contracts are sometimes called quasicontracts (*quasi* is Latin for "as if"). You accepted the benefit of another's action, so you must pay for it *as if* you had made a contract.

Some contracts, because of their importance, are required to be in writing or they will not be enforced by the courts. The most common are:

- Contracts for the sale of real property.
- Contracts which, by their terms, cannot be performed within one year.
- Contracts holding one responsible for the debt of another.
- Contracts to sell goods for more than a specified amount of money (the amount varies from state to state).

You and the Law 173

document and makes himself liable to pay if the original signer does not.

counterclaim. A claim made by the defendant in a lawsuit against the plaintiff.

covenant. A promise in a deed (see page 151).

curtesy. A widower's legal right to a share of the lands owned by his wife.

damages. Money awarded to compensate for injury to person or property.

decedent. A person who has died and whose estate is being settled.

decree. Written judgment of a court.

deed. A document transferring ownership of land.

defamation. A false statement that injures a person's reputation (see page 162).

default. Failure to appear for trial. The defaulting party loses unless he can show good reason for not appearing. Also refers to failure to perform a contract or failure to make payments when due—for example, defaulting on a mortgage.

defendant. The person who is being sued. In criminal cases, the person being tried for a crime.

demurrer. A denial by the defendant that there are any legal grounds for the lawsuit.

deposition. A written statement made under oath, generally for use in a lawsuit.

descent and distribution. The law governing the disposition of property of someone who dies without a will.

devise. To transfer real property by will.

dictum. A statement of law made by a judge, but not necessary to decide the case, and therefore not binding.

discovery. See *pretrial procedure*.

dishonor. To refuse to accept an obligation; for example, a bank dishonors a check, if it refuses to pay it.

dispossess. To evict a tenant from the premises he rents.

dividend. Money paid to stockholders of a corporation from the profits of the corporation.

domicile. A person's permanent place of residence.

donee. A person to whom a gift is made.

donor. A person who makes a gift.

double indemnity. A provision in an insurance policy under which the company must pay double the face amount if a person dies by accidental means.

double jeopardy. Trying a person more than once for the same crime; prohibited by the U.S. Constitution.

dower. The right of a widow to a share of her husband's lands.

draft. A written order directing one person to pay a sum of money to another. For example, a person may direct his bank to pay a sum of money to someone.

due process. The constitutional right not to be deprived of life, liberty, or property, except after fair legal proceedings.

duress. Force or threat of force to compel someone to do something against his will.

earnest money. A down payment to make a contract binding.

easement. A right to use the land of another (see page 152).

ejectment. A legal action to remove a person who is wrongfully occupying land.

embezzlement. The crime of misappropriating money by a person to whom it has been entrusted.

eminent domain. The right of the government to take private property for public purposes (see page 152).

encroachment. Something that extends on the land of another, such as part of a building or fence.

encumbrance. Any claim against property that diminishes its value, such as an unpaid mortgage or a lien.

endorsement. Writing one's name on the back of a check or promissory note to cash or transfer it. An endorser normally guarantees the check or note, and is liable if the original signer cannot pay.

enjoin. To direct someone to do something or refrain from doing something.

equity. Court action in a case where money damages are not enough. Examples of equity include a court order directing a person to stop the commission of a nuisance; and an order of specific performance directing a seller to go through with a contract to sell land.

equity of redemption. The right of a landowner to redeem his land by paying the mortgage at any time before it is foreclosed.

escheat. Return of property to the state when there is no one to inherit it.

escrow. Delivery of money or property to a neutral party, to be held until certain conditions are fulfilled.

estate. The property left by a person who has died. (The term may also refer to property in general or any interest in property.)

estoppel. Refusal to allow a person to change his statement or legal position if he has induced people to act on the basis of his previous statement or position.

ex parte. A legal action taken by one side without notice to the other.

ex post facto law. A law making an act a crime, although it was not a crime when it was done;

prohibited by the U.S. Constitution.

executor. The person named in a will to handle and distribute an estate.

exemplary damages. Punitive damages.

extortion. The crime of obtaining money by threats.

extradition. Return of a fugitive from justice to the state in which he is wanted.

false arrest. Unlawful arrest (see page 162).

false imprisonment. Unlawful restraint (see page 162).

fee simple. Absolute ownership.

felony. A serious crime, usually one punishable by imprisonment in the state penitentiary.

fiduciary. One who holds or manages property for another and is held to a high standard of conduct because of his position of trust.

fixture. An item of personal property that becomes real property by being "affixed" to the realty, for example, a furnace.

F.O.B. Free on board. A type of sale in which the seller agrees to deliver the goods to a carrier, such as a railroad, for shipment to the buyer.

foreclosure. Court proceedings to take over property for failure to pay a mortgage.

forgery. The crime of fraudulently making or changing writing or a signature, with intent to deceive.

franchise. The right to vote. A form of business arrangement (see pages 166-167).

fraud. False statement or misrepresentation made to deceive someone into taking an action he would not have taken had he known the truth.

garnishment. Taking all or part of a person's salary in payment of a debt. The amount that can be taken is limited by law.

guaranty. A promise to perform some act or pay some debt on behalf of another if the other fails to perform or pay.

guardian. One legally entrusted with the duty of caring for the person or property of a minor or incompetent adult.

habeas corpus. Latin for "you have the body." A legal proceeding (called a "writ") commanding that a prisoner be brought before a court to decide whether he is legally being held.

hearsay evidence. Evidence of what someone else said, rather than what the witness knows.

heir. One who inherits the property of a person who dies.

holder in due course. A purchaser of a negotiable instrument in good faith without knowledge of any defect (see page 159).

holdover tenant. One who remains on the property after the lease has expired (see page 153).

holographic will. A will entirely in a person's own handwriting (see page 155).

homicide. The killing of one human being by another. "Justifiable" homicide is in self-defense.

impeach. Challenge the truthfulness of a witness. Bring charges against a public official to remove him from office.

implied. Understood from the circumstances, although not directly stated, as an implied promise or an implied contract.

indemnity. An insurance or other agreement guaranteeing payment if a person suffers a loss.

indenture. A formal written contract.

indictment. An accusation of crime made by a grand jury.

infant. A minor. In law, the term refers to any minor, not just a small child.

information. A written accusation of crime by a district attorney or prosecuting officer without a grand jury.

injunction. A court order directing a person to do something or to refrain from doing something.

inquest. Any inquiry by a court to determine a disputed fact. Most commonly, it refers to a coroner's inquest to discover the cause of death.

insolvency. Inability to meet one's debts as they come due.

interest. Any legal right or claim. The amount charged for the use of money.

interlocutory decree. A preliminary decree that does not become final until some further action is taken.

interrogatories. A set of written questions to be proposed to a witness in a pending lawsuit, or to the opposing party.

intestate. Without a will.

joint tenancy. A form of co-ownership (see page 151).

judgment. The decision of a court.

judicial notice. Recognition of certain facts by a court without the need for proof, such as historical events, scientific laws, or geographic facts.

jurisdiction. The authority of a court to decide a case. The jurisdiction of a court is generally set out in the law establishing the court.

jurisprudence. The study of law in general.

kidnapping. The crime of stealing and carrying away a human being.

laches. Excessive delay in asserting a legal right.

larceny. The crime of taking another's property.

leading question. A question that suggests the answer, such as, "Were you walking past Mr. Johnson's house at noon on January 12th?" The proper question would be, "Where

You and the Law

were you at noon on January 12th?"

lease. A contract to rent.

legacy. A gift made in a will.

lessee. The tenant under a lease.

lessor. The owner or landlord under a lease.

letters of administration. A court document appointing someone to handle the estate of a person who died without a will.

letters testamentary. A court document authorizing the executor named in a will to take charge of the estate.

levy. A tax. A seizure of property by order of court to pay a judgment.

libel. Written defamation (see page 162).

lien. A claim or charge against property, such as an unpaid mortgage or other debt.

life estate. An interest in property during a person's lifetime ending upon the person's death. For example, a husband's will leaves his house to his wife for her lifetime, and then to his children.

life tenant. A person who owns a life estate in property.

liquidated damages. A specified sum of money agreed on beforehand as damages in case one party to a contract fails to perform.

lis pendens. A notice filed in a county office stating that a lawsuit is pending over a designated piece of real property. Anyone who purchases the property is bound by the result of the lawsuit.

living will. A document by which a person directs whether or not he is to be kept alive by artificial devices if he should fall into an irreversible coma. Living wills are not legally binding in most states, but people often prepare them to inform the family of their wishes.

majority. The age at which a person is considered an adult, with full legal rights and capacities.

malfeasance. Performing an act that is wrong; see also *misfeasance*.

malice. Intention to harm.

malicious mischief. Intentional destruction of property.

malicious prosecution. Knowingly bringing criminal charges that are false.

mandamus. A court order directing a public official to perform his official duty.

manslaughter. The crime of killing a human being without premeditation or malice aforethought.

mayhem. The crime of violently depriving a person of the use of a member, such as an arm, leg, or eye.

mechanic's lien. A claim against property by someone who has done work on it, as a repairman or a workman on a house.

misdemeanor. A crime less serious than a felony.

misfeasance. An act that is not wrong but is improperly performed; see also *malfeasance*.

mistrial. A trial that ends because of some procedural error, or because the jury cannot agree on a verdict.

moot question. A question that is undecided and subject to argument, but is not directly related to a case.

motion. An application to a court for a ruling, decision, or order, usually in connection with some pending case.

murder. The crime of killing a human being, with premeditation or malice aforethought.

naturalization. The process of becoming a citizen. Normally, an alien must reside in the United States for at least five years before he can apply for citizenship; but the period is shortened for aliens married to or adopted by American citizens. The alien must show that he is mentally and morally fit to become a citizen. Minor children of naturalized citizens also become citizens.

negligence. Failure to use reasonable care, thereby causing an injury to person or property (see pages 160-161).

negotiable instrument. A document, such as a check or promissory note, that can be endorsed and transferred from person to person, almost like cash. Whether an instrument is negotiable depends entirely on how it is worded.

nisi. Latin for "unless." A decree nisi is a court order to take effect on a specified date unless some action is taken in the meantime.

nolle pros. Short for *nolle prosequi*, a decision not to proceed with a prosecution or lawsuit.

nolo contendere. Latin for "I will not contest it." In criminal cases, a plea with the same effect as a plea of guilty, but without actually admitting guilt.

non compos mentis. Latin for "not of sound mind."

nonage. Underage; the period during which a person is a minor.

nonfeasance. Failure to perform an act required by law; for example, nonperformance of duties by a public official.

notary public. An official authorized to administer oaths, witness signatures, and certify to affidavits or other documents.

note. A written promise to pay.

novation. The making of a new contract or agreement to replace one that now exists.

nuncupative will. An oral will (see page 155).

oath. A promise to tell the truth, sworn on one's belief in a

Supreme Being. An *affirmation* is a similar promise by those who have religious or other scruples against taking oaths.

obligee. A person to whom some contractual obligation is owed.

obligor. The person who owes an obligation.

option. The right to buy or sell property at a specified time for a specified price.

palimony. A term applied to lawsuits for payments similar to alimony, brought when an unmarried couple separates after living together. Courts have not recognized any right to such payments, but they have sometimes recognized a contractual right to payment for services rendered, as when a woman gives up her career and provides companionship, assistance, and business help to her male partner. (Note, however, that a contract to pay for sexual relations is against public policy and will not be enforced by a court.)

parol evidence. Oral evidence. The parol evidence rule is that a written document may not be changed or amended by oral testimony.

partition. A court order physically dividing property owned by co-owners who cannot agree on the use to be made of the property. Sometimes the property is sold and the proceeds divided among the owners.

party wall. A common wall shared by two adjoining buildings, providing support to both.

patent. The exclusive right to manufacture and sell an invention.

per capita. In the law of wills, equal division of property among all persons with the same relationship to the deceased. For example, if a will leaves property to grand- children per capita, each grandchild gets an equal share.

per curiam. An opinion by the entire court, rather than an opinion written by one judge.

per stirpes. In the law of wills, division of property by groups rather than individuals. For example, if the deceased had a son who had two children, and a daughter who had three, the two children of the son would get half the property, and the three children of the daughter would get the other half.

perjury. The crime of making false statements under oath.

personal property. Any movable property; anything but land and buildings (see page 159).

petit jury. A jury that decides cases. A *grand jury* decides whether a person should be charged with a crime.

plaintiff. The person who brings a lawsuit.

plea bargaining. An agreement between a prosecutor and a criminal defendant by which the charge is reduced, or a lesser sentence agreed on, in return for the defendant's plea of guilty. Most plea bargaining is unavoidable, as it would be impossible to hold all the trials that would be necessary if most defendants did not plead guilty.

pleadings. The written documents in a lawsuit that state the position of the parties. The usual pleadings are a complaint by the plaintiff and an answer by the defendant. In some cases, further pleadings may be submitted by both sides.

pledge. Delivery of property to a creditor, as security for a debt.

polling the jury. Asking each juror individually for his verdict.

postmortem. Latin for "after death." Usually applied to the medical examination of a dead body to determine the cause of death.

power of attorney. A written authorization giving one person the power to act for another.

precedent. A previous court decision on a case similar to the one being tried.

prescription. A way of acquiring an interest in property by long and continuous use.

presumption. A rule requiring a judge or jury to draw certain conclusions from certain facts. For example, from the fact that a child is born to a married woman, the conclusion must be drawn that the child is legitimate. A *conclusive* presumption is one that cannot be disproven. Other presumptions can be overcome by evidence to the contrary.

pretrial procedure. The process, before a lawsuit comes to trial, of taking depositions, producing documents, conferring with the judge, etc. It is intended to help settle cases or, at least, to make sure that each party is aware of the issues.

prima facie case. Sufficient evidence to win a lawsuit, provided the other side cannot contradict or explain it.

privileged communication. A statement, made in private, which the other party is not allowed to divulge in court, and which cannot be used in evidence. The most common examples are communications between husband and wife, attorney and client, doctor and patient, priest and penitent.

probate. Proving a will. In a wider sense, all the proceedings relating to an estate (see page 156).

probation. In criminal law, a suspended sentence on condition of continued good behavior.

promissory note. A negotiable instrument consisting of a written, unconditional promise to pay a sum of money.

proof. Evidence that is believed by the judge or jury.

protest. A formal notice that a negotiable instrument, such as a check or promissory note, was presented for payment, and that payment was refused.

proximate cause. In the law of torts, an act that directly leads to and results in an injury.

proxy. One entitled to vote on behalf of another; usually applied to meetings of stockholders of a corporation. Proxy marriages were once recognized, but no longer.

public defender. A lawyer hired by the state to defend persons accused of crime who cannot afford their own lawyers.

publication. Making a statement public. In the law of defamation, telling one person constitutes publication.

punitive damages. Damages over and above actual damages, awarded to punish a wrongdoer and deter him from repeating the wrong (see page 162).

quantum meruit. Latin for "amount deserved." A sum of money awarded for services rendered when no specific sum is provided by contract.

quash. To annul or set aside.

quitclaim. A type of deed (see page 148).

quorum. The number of people who must be present at a meeting of a group in order to legally transact business.

rape. The crime of having sexual intercourse with a woman against her will. Statutory rape is the crime of having sexual intercourse with a minor below the age of consent.

ratification. Approval or confirmation of an act already done.

real property. Land and buildings.

rebuttal. Introduction of evidence to contradict a claim made in a lawsuit.

receiver. A person appointed by a court, in a lawsuit about property, to hold and manage the property at the court's direction.

recidivist. A repeater; an habitual criminal.

referee. A person appointed by a court to hear testimony, receive evidence, and report back to the court on his findings.

release. A document giving up a legal claim or right, usually when a case is settled. When an insurance company pays a claim, for example, it will require the claimant to sign a release.

remand. Send back a case from a higher court to a lower one for additional or corrective action.

replevin. A legal action for the return of property (see page 163).

reply. In a lawsuit, the plaintiff's written answer to a counterclaim by the defendant.

res ipsa loquitur. Latin for "the thing speaks for itself." A presumption of negligence, applied when there is no direct proof, but no other explanation makes sense. For example, if something falls from a window sill and injures a passerby, negligence will be presumed, even if it is impossible to prove what caused the accident.

res judicata. A legal or factual dispute that has already been decided by the judgment of a court, and that cannot be disputed any further.

respondent. See *appellant*.

restrictive endorsement. An endorsement when a check or other negotiable instrument is transferred for a specific purpose; for example, "for collection only," or "for deposit only."

retainer. A down payment to a lawyer to retain his services (see page 170).

retroactive. Relating backward in time, as a retroactive pay increase.

reversion. The return of property to its original owner after a trust or a gift for a period of years.

robbery. The crime of taking property by force or threat of force.

royalties. Payments (often a share of profits) to inventors, authors, songwriters, etc., or to owners of mineral or oil rights.

satisfaction piece. A document stating that a recorded mortgage has been paid.

seisin or seizin. The right to possession of real property.

service. Delivery of a summons to a defendant, informing him of a lawsuit against him.

setoff. A claim by the defendant against the plaintiff that reduces or eliminates the plaintiff's claim.

slander. Spoken defamation (see page 162).

specific performance. A court order to perform a contract for the sale of land (see page 149).

statute. A law passed by a legislative body, such as Congress.

statute of limitations. The time limit for bringing a lawsuit (or criminal prosecution). Different types of lawsuits have different limitation periods, but once the particular time limit has passed, no legal action may be taken.

stipulation. An agreement between parties to a lawsuit.

subornation of perjury. Persuading or bribing another to give false testimony.

subpoena. A document commanding a person to appear in court, either as a witness or as a party to a lawsuit.

subpoena duces tecum. A subpoena directing someone to produce documents or records in court.

substantive law. That part of the law that deals with legal rights rather than legal procedures; see also *adjective law*.

summary judgment. A court decision, made without a trial, when there are no facts in dispute.

summons. The first document in a lawsuit, advising the defendant that the lawsuit is being filed.

surety. One who promises to pay a debt if the original debtor fails to pay.

surrogate's court. A court that handles wills and estates.

tenancy by the entireties. A form of ownership by husband and wife (see pages 145, 151).

tenancy in common. A form of co-ownership (see page 151).

testament. A will.

testator. A person who has made a will or testament.

title. Evidence of one's right to property.

title search. A search of public records to trace the history of ownership of land.

tort. A wrongful act that injures another person (see page 162).

treason. The crime of waging war against the United States or aiding its enemies (treason is the only crime defined in the U.S. Constitution).

trespass. Any wrongful act affecting real property.

true bill. An indictment by a grand jury charging someone with a crime.

usury. Charging more than the legal rate of interest on a loan.

vendee. A purchaser.

vendor. A seller.

venue. The place where a trial is to be held.

verdict. The decision of a jury.

verification. An affidavit swearing that a writing or document is true.

voidable. Anything that can be made void; for example, a contract made by a minor is voidable at the option of the minor.

warrant. A legal document, signed by a judge, authorizing an arrest or a search.

Trust

trust. Money or property legally owned by one person (the trustee) for the benefit of another. The person who establishes the trust, and sets out its terms, conditions, and purposes, is called the *grantor* or *settlor*. The person entitled to the income is the *income beneficiary*. The person who gets the property when the trust comes to an end is the *remainderman*, except when the property is to be returned to the grantor.

A trust may be set up during the grantor's life (living trust) or by his will (testamentary trust). It may be *revocable* or *irrevocable*; in a revocable trust, the grantor reserves the right to cancel the trust and take back the property. In an irrevocable trust, the grantor may not cancel the trust.

The trustee must manage the trust for the sole benefit of the beneficiaries. He may not make any profit for himself, directly or indirectly. He may, however, charge a fee for his services. Many financial institutions, such as banks, have special departments set up for the management of trusts.

Trusts may be set up for many purposes; here are some of the most common:

- To provide an income for children who are minors until they come of age.
- To provide for people who are not good at handling business or financial affairs.
- To provide a lifetime income for someone (such as yourself or your spouse) with the property eventually to revert to someone else (such as your children).
- To provide income to someone for a temporary period.
- To make gifts for charitable purposes.

For further reference

Ashley, Paul P.
You and Your Will
McGraw-Hill

Brown, Robert N.
The Rights of Older Persons
Avon Books

Coughlin, George Gordon
Your Introduction to Law
Barnes & Noble Books

Kling, Samuel G.
The Complete Guide to Everyday Law
Jove Publications, Inc.

Lasson, Kenneth
Representing Yourself
Farrar Straus Giroux

Ross, Martin J. and Steven, Jeffrey
Handbook of Everyday Law
Ballantine Books

Schimmerl, David and Fischer, Louis
Rights of Parents in the Education of Their Children
The National Committee for Citizens in Education

Schwartz, Robert
The Home Owner's Legal Guide
Collier Macmillan

Smith, Robert Ellis
Workrights
E.P. Dutton, Inc.

Improving Your Memory

- Observation   182
- Paying attention   183
- Getting organized   186
- Image formation   187
- Peg words   188
- Link method   190
- Everyday applications   192
- Names and faces   194
- Suggestions for students   196
- Appendix   198

When you learn something, you practice three skills: *finding* what you need to know, *remembering* what you find, and *applying* that information usefully and effectively. Everyone who attends school, from first grade through college, is drilled over and over in the skills of finding and applying useful information. But without the middle skill—remembering—the other two are short-lived at best. However, most schools do not teach memory skills; they teach you to learn by rote memory—by routine drill—without your necessarily understanding or thinking about the text material. And so, very soon, you tend to forget.

Good memory is not a trick, nor does it require great intellectual resources. It does require systematic mental organization, that is, concentration on what you need to remember. The rest is practice, and the rewards—remembering people, places, and things that you always used to forget—are self-sustaining.

Through the centuries, some of the world's greatest thinkers and philosophers have tried to promote systems of memory improvement. No one system ever caught on; each one turned out to be too personal for general application. In this century mnemonists—memory experts—have shied away from complicated personal systems in favor of simpler methods with everyday applications. You will learn such step-by-step methods in this chapter. "There is memory without learning," writes memory expert Harry Lorayne, "but there is no learning without memory."

Think about that for a moment. How can one say that he has learned something effectively if he cannot recall it when it is needed. This is true whether we are talking about a particular skill or a bit of knowledge or an entire procedure or a religion or a philosophy. True learning puts information, ideas, or systems of thought at one's fingertips, ready for immediate use when needed, ready for direct application, ready for explanation to others, in short, for whatever application is generally called for.

As a result, the process of learning can only be considered complete when you have stored in your memory the subject to be learned. It is for this reason that so much emphasis must be placed on training the memory, especially for those who customarily find difficulty in recalling things they think they have learned, in recalling tasks they must perform, in bringing to mind thoughts they seek to explain to others. The objective of memory training is to make complete the process of learning: *finding, remembering,* and *applying* knowledge.

Self-training. No one is born with a poor memory. As you grow up, you develop highly personal habits of awareness and observation. You choose to see and hear, touch and taste certain things, and you choose to ignore most others. Quite likely, you began as a child to organize your daily life around those things you needed most, or were pleased by, or had an interest in. Those meaningful things constitute your earliest memories. Happy childhoods tend to be remembered longer and more fully.

Normally, you pay attention to those things around you that are important, potentially rewarding, and potentially pleasurable, and you teach yourself to remember them. As a child, for instance, your mother may have given you a dime and made you memorize your own phone number ("Always call home if you get lost somewhere"). Now, as an adult, you probably have immediate recall of at least one phone number—your own—even though you may seldom use it. But the memory seed was planted long ago, and you trained yourself to always know your own phone number. It was a start.

Think of how effective your memory is. Besides recalling your telephone number whenever you wish—even though you may hardly ever use it—you also have stored within your memory an enormous number of other bits of information. But you cannot always remember everything you are sure you know. This chapter will help you overcome that problem and greatly improve your recall.

Because your memory is yours alone, you can profitably train yourself to improve what needs improvement. Check your memory out with this list of facts and numbers:

Wait a minute . . . it's on the tip of my tongue

(No peeking, please.
Answer everything from memory.)

1. What is your home phone number?
2. Your license plate number?
3. Your Social Security number?
4. Whose face is on the $20 bill?
5. What is your mother's birthday?
6. How many days are there in June?
7. How many pints are in a gallon?
8. Name the Great Lakes.
9. Name your U.S. congressman.
10. What is your father's birthday?
11. Name your first-grade teacher.
12. Diamond-shaped road signs always indicate what?
13. Top to bottom, name the three colors on a stop light.

A high-school diploma or a college degree cannot help you answer any of these questions. But the succeeding pages will help you remember all of them.

Improving Your Memory 181

Observation

Memory—even short-term memory—can be affected by heightened emotions. A studio audience observing a staged struggle cannot be relied on to report just what happened.

How observant are you? How observant do you think you are? Most people assume they are competent eyewitnesses. The fact is, nearly everyone sees the same sequence of events differently.

Testing observation. TV talk show hosts once were fond of a stunt that included the studio audience in addition to the viewers at home. While the host chatted with his guest onstage, a scuffle would break out in the audience. Angry voices would be raised, stopping the onstage conversation. Members of the audience would look on. Suddenly, one of the combatants would whip out a handgun and shoot one or both of the other participants. Then all the troublemakers would scurry for the exits. Total elapsed time: about one minute.

Of course, the whole drama was staged, and there were no bullets. But the studio audience was taken by surprise. At this point, the TV host would choose four members of the audience and bring them onstage to describe what happened, who was involved, and what the perpetrators looked like. These eyewitness accounts turned out to be at odds. The audience members rarely agreed about anything—who started it, who shot whom, what they wore, what they said, even their sexes. Finally, the perpetrators—two or three actors—would reappear onstage and reenact the "crime," and the studio audience would see it all clearly for the first time.

The point of this exercise is that eyewitness testimony is too often distorted by shock and surprise. Every viewer at home, untouched by the heat of the moment, was a better witness to the crime than the studio audience that was part of it.

How well do we observe? For the most part, you see what you are accustomed to seeing. You glimpse something, and you have immediate recall of whatever you have trained yourself to expect to see. Your powers of observation, over the years, are restricted to self-imposed limits, to a field of vision that is relevant to your personal or professional life. The television audience was prepared to be entertained. When the unexpected happened, it was a blur.

Whenever there is a dramatic story on the TV news —a violent crime, a fire, or a natural disaster—you are likely to see an interview with a witness or a victim. "How do you feel?" the reporter asks. "Can you tell us what happened?"

The answer rarely makes any sense. The distraught victim may be in shock and is usually too confused to say anything coherent.

Then the same reporter interviews a fireman or a policeman who, with sirens wailing in the background, supplies a precise reconstruction of the tragedy without tears or emotion. The uniformed man is not hardhearted or all-knowing. He is trained to make sense out of what seem to be chaotic events. You, too, can train yourself to observe with detachment what others might recoil from in horror or disgust. Better yet, you can learn to remember anything.

For a moment, think of something completely familiar—your wristwatch. Try to remember: Does it have a six on it? A Roman numeral VI? A dot? An empty space? If yours is a digital watch, how many lines are there in the number eight? Even if you answered correctly, chances are you had to double-check to make sure.

The tests and drills in these pages are designed to get you in the habit of memorizing by stages: observing, paying attention, organizing, forming images, and applying the methods of memory training. All these steps are part of the memory habit and, like most habits, this one can be maintained only through exercise.

Untrained memory is haphazard and unreliable. Trained memory brings all recollections to the surface. **Try this.** The following three exercises are designed to test your native, untrained memory. You may not do well at all, but take heart: in the pages that follow you will learn the techniques for memorizing lists, names, and numbers. And you can gauge your training progress. The tests will be repeated on pages 198-199.

Quick-recall tests

1. Study this 15-digit number for two minutes. Then try to duplicate it exactly on a piece of paper—without looking at the number here

238158649376914

2. Here are seven phone numbers, each corresponding to a local tradesman or professional. Study the list for six minutes, then copy the seven titles in any order. Finally, without looking, match the memorized numbers to the titles.

Doctor 762-5881
Grocer 616-2053
Plumber 358-0854
Florist 784-3579
Lawyer 681-9558
Dentist 386-9156
Electrician 872-9647

3. This is an apparently random list of twelve objects found in the home. Study it for just two minutes, then reconstruct the list from memory, in order.

couch, refrigerator, newspaper, clock, television, mirror, toaster, lamp, toilet, stove, carpet, window

Paying attention

There is nothing wrong with this story, but read it carefully:

You are driving a bus that contains 50 passengers. At 57th Street, ten people get off and three get on. At 55th, seven get off and two get on. At 53rd and at 51st, four passengers get off each time; three get on at 53rd, no one at 51st. The bus breaks down at 51st, and eight passengers get crosstown transfers and leave. The bus starts up again and proceeds to 49th, where it breaks down once again. The remaining passengers ask for transfers and leave the bus.

Most of us, by paying strict attention, can probably answer several anticipated questions about this bus story (answers below). How many passengers finally got off? How many got transfers? How many stops did the bus make?

But hardly anyone can answer the most obvious question of all: *What is the bus driver's name?*

(Answers in order: 26, 34, 5)

Improving Your Memory

Remember the very first word in the story? *You.* You drove the bus; your own name is the answer. Of course, this was a trick. By misdirection you were led to overlook that critical first word, and to pay close attention to everything else. More important, you tried hard to figure out that story; you were interested in all those bus riders, and you probably had a moving picture in your mind of that bus on its route. The building blocks of memory were all there: concentration plus attention plus image formation—minus misdirection.

Memory needs no notes.
One early step in memory improvement is difficult: *no more note-taking.* If your interest is genuine, part of the drill is to throw away your pencil and paper. As you come to know new memory techniques, you must trust your ability to employ them. Constant list-making, note-taking, and memo-writing betray a lack of self-confidence in your memory and a lack of commitment to memory training. But once you start to remember names and numbers that you never remembered before, you will no longer need to stuff your wallet or pocketbook with little scraps of paper—half of whose messages and numbers make no sense to you when you finally read them.

Memory and high intelligence are not necessarily related. The absent-minded professor knows all there is to know about his academic specialty, but cannot remember to wear two socks of the same color. The professor focuses so hard on one thing that he forgets nearly everything else. At the other end of the spectrum, medical literature contains intriguing case histories of idiots savants—mentally defective people who can play classical piano instinctively, or immediately name the day of the week for any date in history. Like the professor, the idiot savant has a one-track mind: his concentration is perfectly focused and his interest is single-minded. And his memory is pure.

Most of us, in fact, possess a store of useless information that has come to be known as trivia. Boys often have a knack for memorizing the batting averages of hundreds of baseball players. Many women have an astonishing recall of what other women wore, or looked like, when last met. Gamblers stake huge sums on their memory of a single deck of cards. Whatever you are most interested in, you tend to remember best. Memory building, in large part, is a matter of broadening your interests.

Names and faces.
What do you *want* to remember better? Names and faces top the list for most people. Study the faces on the next page for a few minutes, then match them to the names. Cover up the names and see if you can put the right name to the right face. This is rote memorization; even if you can do the match-ups successfully, chances are that the achievement will be short-lived. As you learn better name/face memorization techniques, you may want to refer back to these names and faces and match the memorized names to the anonymous faces on page 195.

In a later section you will learn precise methods for memorizing names and faces. For now, as you study the page, try to isolate a single outstanding feature from each face. These are strangers, after all; trying to memorize an entire new countenance—plus eleven others—is too great a task. Focusing your attention on just one feature (nose, mouth, eyebrows, etc.) will serve your purpose best.

Some of the names may defy rote memorization. They may sound like nothing else you have ever heard, nor look like any word in English. But everyone's name —if you study it hard enough—can be manipulated in sound into *something* else that sticks in your mind. And the mental effort of that transformation has value in itself. When you take the time and trouble to turn O'Bradovich into Over the Bridge, you are not likely to forget that name soon.

For the time being, first names are less important than last names. Concentrate on a distinguishing facial feature, plus a last-name word association, and try to knit them together in your mind. (You can use the same technique later to remember first names, which usually are easier.) This exercise is really just a warm-up to test your capacity to memorize by rote. When you next come across these same names and faces on page 195, you will be much better equipped to remember them. No matter how good your rote memory powers may be, the gains from using them are fleeting. *Trained memory* lasts and lasts.

Paper slips—and our recollection of what they mean—are rapidly lost.

Improving Your Memory

Vinnie Dodson
 Russell Meredith
 Eileen Murray

 Samantha Kearns
 Vicky Seaton
 Clinton Montgomery

 Sue Young
 Neil Keenan
 Angelo Rivera

 Juan Sanchez
 Judy Sommers
 Olaf Christenson

Improving Your Memory

Getting organized

Everyone has immediate memory, and almost anyone can get by with a functional short-term memory. But a good long-term memory requires conscious and systematic organizational skills. Foremost among these skills is a technique called *chunking*. Several items (or numbers) worth remembering are grouped together—chunked—for longer and easier recall. A list of nine seems unmanageable unless written down. But three chunks of three, properly organized, can be retained in your head.

Take a grocery shopping list, for instance. Say you need milk, cereal, coffee, lettuce, cheese, sugar, tomatoes, eggs, and celery. Now try to organize your list: three of the items are dairy products (milk, eggs, and cheese); three are dry foods (cereal, coffee, and sugar); and three are vegetables (lettuce, celery, and tomatoes).

Once in the supermarket, you really need only remember dairy (3), dry goods (3), and vegetables (3). Those cues will likely call to mind your specific items. (Similarly, the quantities you need do not have to clutter your mental list.) Of course, if you are thoroughly familiar with the store, you can chunk your purchases according to sections or aisles.

Chunking. Try the chunking principle on your next shopping expedition. Plan ahead in your mind. Group your purchases into categories, colors, things beginning with the same letter, or goods located in the same part of the store. Put them in chunks of three or four and they become infinitely more memorable—and manageable—than they were in one huge lump. Your list is organized, and so is your brain.

Chunking is made to order for numbers. Many numbers are too big to remember, and no wonder. Memory specialists say that the upper limit for long-term number retention is seven digits—and it is no coincidence that phone numbers are just that long. Nor is it coincidence that, when area codes came into everyday use, the extra three digits were traditionally separated from the original seven by parentheses. Three digits in parentheses happens to be a perfect example of a chunk, set neatly apart from the already memorized number.

Graphically, the memory advantage of chunking is quickly apparent. Consider a twelve-digit number:

> 4 9 2 3 5 7 1 6 8 2 4 7

Even in mathematical order—492 billion, and so on—it is too big to grasp, much less hold on to. But now try chunking it:

> (492) (357) (168) (247).

> **Using acronyms**
>
> Suppose you are going to the store to buy *peas, mustard, soda, artichokes,* and *tea.* Reorder to *s* oda, *t* ea, *a* rtichokes, *m* ustard, and *p* eas:
>
> **STAMP**
>
> You have created a mnemonic.

Suddenly it becomes comprehensible: you may think of it as four area codes. If you need to know an absurdly long number—a charge account or bank account code, for instance—try using the chunking method. If the number does not break down into neat multiples of three, tack on a one- or two-digit prefix. With practice, and habit, chunking works.

Some useful facts have been imprinted on your memory bank in a peculiarly childish way, through rhymes and ditties that you learned in school or at home. They may be childish, but they save everyone a lot of time and trouble. You probably know these:

(calendar)	Thirty days hath September, April, June, and November ...
(time change)	Spring forward, fall back
(spelling)	*I* before *E*, except after *C*, Or when sounded like *A* ...
(treble clef)	*E*very *G*ood *B*oy *D*eserves *F*udge

Mnemonics. Each of these is an example of a *mnemonic* (nee-MON-ik): a learning aid, often a rhyme, that cues your conscious mind to recall some fact in your long-term memory bank. Some mnemonics are best left to serious memory experts, but many others (supplied in succeeding pages) are accessible to all learners. Each new technique represents a mnemonic progression from some previous level of memory training, and none involves parlor tricks or special intellectual gifts.

Every level of memory building will involve a sustained effort on your part: close *observation,* concentrated *attention,* and mental *organization.* Your progress may be shaky at first, slower than you like, but there will be nothing painful about it, and no one will grade your performance. Best of all, the reward will be considerable: never forgetting names and faces again, no more list-making and note-taking, and the sure self-knowledge that you are more fully aware of everything happening around you.

Image formation

Ridiculous associations can be an aid to memory. For example, you may visualize a dog-food sandwich to help remember dog food and bread.

Image formation, or imaging, is a cornerstone of memory building. You probably do it already, nearly every night, when you dream. Every time you dream, you indulge your natural capacity for forming images. In memory training you teach yourself to dream consciously, on purpose, with your eyes open, in order to make forgettable things memorable.

Any common object can be made memorable by mentally assigning three qualities to it: *detail, color,* and *movement.* Consider something you may frequently misplace. A key is a good example. It is small, dull and much like any other key. Now make your key special in your mind: gleaming, flashing gold in the light, with sharp teeth that might cut you if you are not careful. Next, imagine that this thing is alive and has a mind of its own—if you do not keep track of it, it is likely to jump up and lock you up. You might even give it a name. Once you see this key as somehow distinctive or dangerous, you will be unlikely to lose it again.

Paired images. Remembering two different things is much easier if you pair them in your mind, however improbably. Unpaired, they are readily forgotten. "Oh, and on the way back would you please pick up some dog food and some bread?" On your way home you may vaguely recall something—two things—you were supposed to get at the store, but you are unlikely to recall what they were. But if you had drawn this picture in your mind, you would not soon forget it: a dog-food sandwich, two slices of white bread enclosing three inches of golden brown canine chunks.

In making paired images, it is important to remember that logic, reality, even propriety must be discarded. The idea is to imprint on your mind a truly outrageous and colorful picture, one that takes imagination to come up with. At first this process, like learning to paint, will require time and thought, but soon enough the process will seem easy. In fact, most people find it fun. Image formation is a conscious investment in remembering. Having made that investment, you will be unlikely to give it up easily.

Most lists of things to remember contain more than two or three items. However, your mind picture can accommodate an extensive list, this one, for example:

1. culottes
2. tennis racket
3. rain hat
4. fur-topped boots
5. knee pads
6. bib overalls
7. swim goggles
8. windbreaker
9. ski gloves
10. duck-hunting whistle

Imagine yourself wearing or using all this gear at once, from top to bottom, from the inside out. Silly? Certainly, but not nearly as silly as it could have been—if half your list had been grocery items, for instance.

The primary trick in image formation is to *gather everything together in one room,* or *hang everything on one person.* Construct a situation in which each item belongs with another one, in which unrelated objects become related through the medium of your imagination. By seeing yourself equipped with all ten items in the list, you will be able to remember all ten. Imaging is a useful memory tool.

When trying to remember a long list of items, you might relate each to yourself. Find a way to wear or hold each item on your list.

Improving Your Memory

Peg words

To prepare for the use of peg words in building memory, try to imagine that every number, 0 through 9, *looks like* a certain letter of the alphabet. Here is the version that memory experts use and memory students find most useful. It is sometimes called the number/consonant system or the letter-number alphabet:

Number	Letter/sound	Reason
0	z (*or* s)	zero begins with *z*
1	t (*or* d)	vertical stroke of a *t* looks like number *1*
2	n	printed *n* has *2* downstrokes
3	m	printed *m* has *3* downstrokes
4	r	written-out *4* ends in *r*
5	l	your *5*-fingered left hand, thumb out, forms an *L*
6	ch (j *or* g *or* sh)	turned-around *j* looks like a *6*
7	k (*or* c)	European *7* looks like a *k*
8	f (*or* v)	written *f* looks like a skinny *8*
9	p (*or* b)	mirror-image of *p* is a *9*

Remember one phrase—TeN MoRe LoGiC FiBS—minus the vowels—and you will know 1 through 10. Now you are ready to work with peg words.

The letter-number alphabet, with its single-letter equivalent numbers, is not suitable for all numerical combinations, especially the long ones. The true *memory pegs* for all numbers are pictorial equivalents: 1 = t = a picture (in your mind) of a tie. Tie, of course, begins with t and can be tacked on to almost any word picture you can think up. Each effective pictorial equivalent, or peg, must be short, must begin with the correct letter, and must be readily transferable into picture form. You might think of 1 to 10 this way:

Tie (1) should be a loud necktie or bow tie.
Noah (2) is usually thought of as an old man in robes, with a flowing white beard.
Ma (3) can be your mind's-eye view of your own mother, or any other motherly person.
Rye (4) works well as a loaf of bread.
Law (5) is John Law, a policeman or sheriff.
Shoe (6) stands for a single shoe, preferably a large one.
Cow (7) is the dairy animal. (The hard *c* in cow is the same as phonetic *k*.)
Ivy (8) is the climbing vine, capable of growing on anything. (This is the only exception to the rule that peg words should begin with the correct letter, but ivy is easy to see in your mind and so is remembered easily.)
Bee (9) is the noisy insect.
Toes (10) combine 1 and 0—the *t* sound plus the *z* sound. They stand for your toes.

Peg words for 1–10: TeN MoRe LoGiC FiBS

1 = Tie	2 = Noah	3 = Ma	4 = Rye	5 = Law
6 = Shoe	7 = Cow	8 = Ivy	9 = Bee	10 = Toes

It takes some doing to construct a picture such as this for a telephone number. But once it's done, you'll never forget the number.

The numbers 1 to 10 are enough to learn for now; they include all the basic peg sounds, peg words, and peg pictures. With them alone you can memorize any phone number and itemize any short list in your head. But first you need practice. At every reasonable opportunity, practice using these pegs with phone numbers and street addresses until every number you hear immediately sparks a picture in your mind. Then you can start stringing numbers together in multiples. Your word pictures will become murals. With them, you can start trying to memorize almost any complicated combination. But start modestly.

Peg words are *substitutes* for numbers. Because they are based on the letter-number alphabet, and because they are backed by pictorial equivalents, they are clearly superior to plain numbers as memory builders. (There are peg words for 11 to 100 also, listed in the Appendix, pages 198-199.) By using letter *and* picture substitutes for numbers, every new number takes on two- or three-dimensional significance in your mind's eye.

When you attempt to memorize a phone number, for example, 246-3579, using one-dimensional rote memory, you will usually forget it by the next day. This is because there is nothing memorable about that number. Its letter-number equivalent is a different story. The number 246-3579 becomes *NoRwiCH MiLKuP*, a country scene one can easily remember. Now consider one more version—the pictorial equivalent—of the same phone number:

(246) Picture old Noah (2), arms outstretched, with a ham on Rye (4) sandwich in one hand and a huge Shoe (6) in the other.

(3579) There goes your Ma (3) riding double with an Officer of the Law (5) on a Cow (7), galloping away from a swarm of Bees (9) in hot pursuit.

That is a picture. More importantly, it is a phone number you will not soon forget. Take your own phone number, fill in the right peg sounds and peg pictures, and see what you come up with. You will soon become good at using letter-number equivalents and peg words.

Improving Your Memory

Link method

The hardest things to remember are those that lack logical association between the items. By contrast, for example, it is easy to remember the multiplication tables—the logic of 1 times 2, 1 times 3, etc. is apparent to all of us. When it comes to remembering to buy shoes, shirts, and soap, the association is missing.

Links are the mortar that holds individual memories together. Links make mental connections between unrelated objects, numbers, or items. Names of objects can be linked in two ways: by placing them one after another in a narrative, or by constructing new words from the first letters of those objects (using the initial method plus connecting vowels, as in NoRwiCH MiLKuP).

Initial method. For example, suppose you want to remember the sites of the last six Olympic Games. Beginning in 1964, they are Tokyo, Mexico City, Munich, Montreal, Moscow, and Los Angeles. You could invent a narrative—a travelogue—that took you to all those cities in order, but you need not do so. It would be better, because there are only six of them, to try the first-initial method. Here is how it might work:

Too	MuCh	M&MMs	LAnguage
(Tokyo)	(Mexico City)	(Munich, Montreal, Moscow)	(Los Angeles)

Many of us enjoy M & M candy, so now we can link together Too MuCh M&MMs LAnguage, not the greatest of thoughts but surely a fine story of someone enjoying candy. When you invent your own link phrase, you become the author of your own memory aid. The phrases are yours alone, and you will remember them.

Narrative method. The other kind of link association, the narrative method, requires all the imagination you can come up with. Nothing is too outrageous, *if it helps you remember*. As an example, take the nine-item grocery list used earlier (page 186):

> milk, cheese, eggs, cereal, coffee,
> sugar, lettuce, tomatoes, celery

For the sake of demonstration, this is a short and easy list. With practice, the link narrative method will work equally well even for a much longer and more varied shopping list. First, put yourself in the center of the picture: everything that happens will be made to happen by you.

A trip to the supermarket

You are going—in your mind, of course—to the supermarket. You are on a mission of mercy. Some people, you have decided, need groceries more than you do. You commandeer nine shopping carts, tucked into one another, and make your way down the first aisle: Dairy. A young mother is trying to corral her two small youngsters who are sampling everything on the shelves.

"Need some *milk*?" you ask her. She nods. You hand each child a gallon jug of milk—nearly as big as they are—and lift the boys and the milk into the first of your shopping carts. The mother smiles and heads for the check-out counter.

Just then a burly young man comes by with about 15 packages of hamburger buns under each arm.

"*Cheese*burgers?" you ask. He nods, and you heap the second of your carts with dozens of prewrapped packages of assorted cheeses; the young man dumps his hamburger meat on top of it and is on his way, with thanks.

Across the aisle an old lady is painstakingly opening every cardboard *egg* carton in the display to check for breakage. "It would be easier to do that at home," you say pleasantly, and soon the old lady is pushing your third cart filled with 45 dozen eggs. You have made her day.

You come across a little girl in tears, vainly trying to rip open the bottom of a box of *cereal* to get at the prize. No problem: the young lady is packed off in your fourth cart with 24 boxes of cereal, calling out to her mother, "Mommy, I won!"

190 Improving Your Memory

Hidden in a corner is an enormous aluminum *coffee* urn, steaming from the top, with no sign attached. "The coffee must be free," you conclude. You unplug the coffee-maker and wrestle it into your fifth shopping cart—a perfect fit, with just enough room for three dozen styrofoam cups.

"Take a break, shoppers!" you announce. "Hot coffee. On me." You lead a growing procession to the middle aisle of the store and start dispensing coffee from your cart. More than one shopper remarks that the brew is too bitter.

Not for long: you empty two 5-pound bags of *sugar* into the urn and load your sixth cart with five more bags. Your fellow shoppers are enjoying themselves. But not the store manager, who has been watching you from the moment the coffee urn disappeared. (The coffee was free, but it tasted so bad that the store wanted it hidden.) He is right behind you as you approach your last stop: Produce.

"Pardon me," the manager says, "could I have a word with you in my office?"

"Just a minute," you say. "I'm mixing a salad." You have three shopping carts left. You fill the first with heads of *lettuce,* the second with dozens of *tomatoes,* and the third with every bunch of *celery* in the bin. The shoppers raid each cart and buy out the entire supply, which brings a smile to the store manager's face at last.

"Now, my good man, I believe I owe you for two bags of sugar," you say on your way out, peeling off a five-dollar bill. "Charge the coffee to good customer relations."

Now that is a shopping excursion you will remember —which means, of course, that will also remember your nine-item shopping list. Most shopping lists, however, leave little to the imagination. They are colorless and lifeless. The storytelling method, on the other hand, contains everything a list does not: detail, color, and movement. In addition, of course, you are the star performer in your own story. Like an actor, you have only to remember to follow through the sequence of events. Imagination and the patience to concoct a scenario are the only requirements. After you practice a few times, it will take far less effort to make up a story than it does to write down a list.

Always try to paint your mind pictures in the broadest possible strokes, freely using disproportion, movement, exaggeration, and even substitution. Substitution means using one object in place of another—a potato, say, in place of a prizefighter's broad lumpy nose—because the resemblance is clearly there or because the image is so memorable. Using linked mind pictures, you can learn to memorize lists of 20 or more items that have no apparent relation to one another.

Improving Your Memory

Everyday applications

Even as a beginner in the use of memory systems, you can go a long way with the link method and your ten peg words. Links are used to memorize anything in sequence; pegs help you remember any kind of number, in or out of sequence. Pegs and links can be combined to memorize schedules and appointments.

Using links.
Suppose one morning you have eight things to do: (1) phone the vet about your cat; (2) get the car washed; (3) make a deposit at the bank; (4) mail a package at the post office; (5) buy four items at the hardware store (light bulbs, extension cord, duplicate key, and catnip); (6) buy a watchband at the jeweler's; (7) pick up three food items at the convenience store; and (8) stop by a friend's house, where you left your umbrella.

Now for your links. Your movie for the day begins at breakfast, where you imagine yourself milking cows—one cow is sick, call the vet (1). As you get in your car, imagine that it is dripping wet and clean (2). See yourself driving up to the bank teller's drive-in window (3). Your bank deposit slip could be considered postage for your package, which it is time to mail (4). While you are at the post office, study the "Wanted" posters and imagine that you are pictured there as a burglar. You will need tools from the hardware store (5): light bulbs for bright ideas, an extension cord for second-story work, a skeleton key, and catnip. Right down the street from the hardware store is the jeweler's where you treat yourself to a new watchband (6). The rest is easy. You always pass the convenience store on your way home and you nearly always stop for something. Milk, bread, and eggs (7) are needed this time. So is your umbrella. It always rains when you do not have it. It is raining now—in your mental movie—so you stop at your friend's house to retrieve it (8). Eight errands and eight links, combining to fashion a chain of actions.

Using pegs.
The other way to memorize this schedule/list is to peg each stop to its pictorial symbol. You might wear a Tie (1) to talk to the vet. Imagine your car being washed by Noah himself (2). Your Ma (3), wearing an eyeshade, might be the bank teller. Your parcel for mailing might be a loaf of Rye (4) bread. Your imaginary burglar's foray at the hardware store would be thwarted by the Law (5). Your Shoe (6) might be held together by a watchband. Your milk is custom-dispensed by a Cow (7). Finally, your umbrella is found to be upholstered with Ivy (8).

For a short list, the peg method permits a briefer scenario and seems to make more sense. But good sense and good memorability are not always the same. For most students of memory, the link method seems to yield more satisfaction.

Links and pegs

Two surefire ways to memorize the otherwise forgettable:

Link

Peg

192　　Improving Your Memory

Links and pegs in action

Phone numbers   Your task is, of course, very much simplified if you only want to memorize local numbers. You already know the prefix; just deal with the last four numbers. For simplicity, try to make a peg word from those final four numbers; 3819, for example, might become MuFf-Top, which prompts a picture of a fur-topped boot. Link the peg word to the face (or figure) of the person you want to call.

Historical dates   First get rid of the extraneous factors. Replace the names of months with their sequential numbers, 1 to 12. As for years, eliminate the first two century numbers; you already know what century you are dealing with. Thus Lincoln's Gettysburg Address, November 19, 1863, becomes 11 19 63, whose first (peg) initials form TaTTeD SHaM. Picture Mr. Lincoln tatting a sham—that is, stitching a pillowcase—while he tries to memorize the Gettysburg Address.

Playing cards   Think up your own peg words to represent all the cards in the deck, with 13 *s* words in the spade suit, 13 *h* words in hearts, 13 *d* words in diamonds, and 13 *c* words in clubs. Your own one-syllable pegs will be better than a ready-made set, because you will have to memorize them perfectly and practice thoroughly before applying your knowledge of unplayed cards in a game of chance.

Foreign words   This advice is limited to individual words, short expressions, and proper names. Memorization is no substitute for learning a foreign language, but it is a great help in learning useful words. Whatever word gives you trouble can be manipulated, somehow, to approximate an English substitute—a word or name that sounds like the foreign one. Whenever you see or hear the foreign version, a mind picture of your version will give you an instant translation. Pronunciation is not important in this aspect of the work involved in learning a foreign language.

Birthdays   Use the same method as for historical dates, but make a special birthday link between the peg date and the person. If one of your nephews was born on August 2, 1965, for instance, streamline the date—8 2 65—and make a first-letter peg substitution: INSoLe, your nephew's bare foot. The same principle applies to anniversaries, except that you have two people to keep in your mind picture.

Aging and absent-mindedness

Resistance to change is most noticeable when a grandparent or great-grandparent simply stops paying attention; the suspicion sets in that our beloved seniors are finally just too old to function, that senility is taking its toll.

Senility can easily be a misdiagnosis. Old-age mental infirmity, usually called senility, may be the natural product of two maladies of old age: inattention and inactivity. Usually, both are easily reversible, and neither is indicative of true memory loss, which is a clinical condition accompanying physical deterioration. Memory loss rarely shows itself as an isolated symptom.

A leading authority on adult education, Edward L. Thorndike, once stated that "age is no handicap to learning a new trade, profession, or anything you want to do at any time of life." Remember: *anything you want to do*. Your brain can always use exercise. A sedentary brain means a sedentary memory. Absent-mindedness may simply mean not caring.

By practicing the memory-building exercises in this chapter, older people are likely to tap reserves of vitality they thought they had outlived. Memory experts agree: the best memory students are often the oldest. The alertness and involvement you use in practicing a memory system not only sharpen memory but sharpen all your mental faculties as well. Every flex of a memory muscle strengthens it.

Improving Your Memory

Names and faces

If you are like most people, you wish you could remember names and faces better. After all, any man or woman who remembers *your* name is likely to win your respect and attention; it is almost disrespectful if you fail to reply in kind. And when someone knows your name, and assumes you remember his, there is rarely a graceful way out if you do not. First a word of reassurance: do not assume that you are cursed with the inability to remember names. You simply have never gone about it in a systematic way.

Getting a name right.
To begin with, you may have never listened to an introduction properly. On meeting someone—a perfect stranger—at some social function, attend to these ground rules:
- Hear his or her whole name clearly.
- If unclear, ask for the spelling.
- If odd, comment on it.
- Repeat the name during conversation.
- Say the name once more on parting.

Surnames fall into three categories for the purpose of memorization. The first two are easy:

1. Self-descriptive names (Baker, Cook, White, Day, Knight, Brown, Foote, Post, and so on) that in themselves have meaning or spark images.
2. Same-as or sound-like names that duplicate or approximate those of famous people, historical figures, or well-known brand names.

You should have no trouble associating these names with a pictorial equivalent, whether it be a celebrity, an occupation, or a color.

But the third category—meaning 90 percent of all surnames—will require some work. Except to linguists, most names mean nothing by themselves; they defy visualization or definition, perhaps even pronunciation, and they are meaningless as words. The solution: a substitute word or words to stand for the difficult name and to make a picture for deposit in your memory bank. Each syllable in a name will likely add a picture, and then the pictures must be linked. Below are some names, along with suggested pictorial equivalents, to get you started.

After you have practiced this substitution technique, no one's name should be meaningless anymore. But that is only half the battle. It is essential, of course, to memorize someone's name, but it is equally important to match that name to its owner's face. So there is one last association technique to learn. Match your outlandish mind picture (from the name) to *one* outstanding feature of that person's face.

Just as you take pains to get his or her name right, so you must look the other person straight in the face to get it right, too. Almost certainly something will strike you as distinctive—a scar, a hairline (or lack of it), a wide (or pursed) mouth, high cheekbones, a disproportionate nose, a drooping eyelid, a five o'clock shadow, a long chin, squinty eyes or prominent eyeglasses, a long (or dimpled) chin. Then take that one facial feature and combine (link) it with your mind picture of the person's last name. Never mind the ridiculousness of your finished portrait; its lack of logic is what makes it memorable.

Knowing what you have just read, try once more to truly memorize the names and faces on page 185. Then turn back to this page and note your improvement.

Making pictures of names

Name	Phrase	Picture
Cohen	ice cream *cone*	
Olzcewski	old + chef + ski-ing	
Gordon	vegetable *garden*	
Kassebaum	castle + bomb	
Pottinger	pot + injure	
Pfeiffer	*fife* player	

Improving Your Memory

Suggestions for students

Too many people go through high school and college and adult education courses stuffing themselves with information one day only to disgorge it all the next. They cram for an exam, take it, and emerge with little or no permanent knowledge. Why is all that information forgotten so quickly?

The scholastic method of memory building is rote repetition without regard for meaning. Thus, such students will read something over and over again until it sinks in—for a little while. To memorize something by rote is not really to learn it, and certainly not to understand it. Learning is not a one-shot recital of facts or ideas; it is the informed application of information and ideas. When you build true memory, you absorb facts and ideas in such a way that you store them away, ready to be employed profitably for the rest of your life.

So far you have learned the fundamentals of the peg and link methods of memory, both unsurpassed for the recollection of tangible objects and numbers, and both suitable for translation into mind pictures.

Pegs and links will not work, however, in certain fields of academic study. There is no practical way to conjure up a picture of a French verb, a mathematical equation, or a scientific term. Something else is needed to aid the memory.

Memory techniques for students

English vocabulary Some words do not look at all like what they mean. In such cases, break the word into separate syllables and give each part a new meaning in a new linkage.
Execrate—to hate, detest. Imagine having to put *eggs* in a *crate* all the time. You would *detest* such a chore.
Hirsute—hairy. Look at that woman in the woolen suit—*her suit* is all covered with *hair*.
Litany—a kind of prayer. Think of yourself *praying* on one knee—praying for mercy because you just *lit* your other *knee* with the votive candle.

English spelling There is no magical way to become a better speller. The most practical solution is to seize on a habitually misspelled word like "calendar" and write it down five times wrong—c-a-l-e-n-d-e-r—and then cross out the second *e*. Then write it five times correctly and circle the second *a*. Or you might make associations between words you know already and troublesome words you want to know. See *all* lines as par*all*el, *iron* as part of the env*iron*ment, a *guar*d as *guar*anteeing safety, and *loss* as being co*loss*al.

Mathematics Your knowledge of peg sounds 1 to 10 (and 1 to 100, on pages 198-199) can be put to good use for learning fractions, formulas, equations, measurements, ratios, and theorems. Use the first-initial link method for individual numbers, then tie them together in a mind picture. The pictures thus formed may be ridiculous in the extreme, but they are intended only to make you familiar with a mathematical concept. When you truly learn it, you will have memorized the concept, not the funny picture.

Biology Unlike most sciences, biology is well adapted to memory building because most of its terms have direct application to something you can visualize—a human body, an animal, a neural network. Take what you need to know, shorten it to pegs and links, and picture it right on or in the body part to which it belongs.

Chemistry The language of chemistry is made up of symbols, and symbols are made to order for changing into pegs and links. You can, for instance, treat a subscript—the 2 in H_2O, for example—as its peg sound equivalent. The task is to make something from a chemical formula that illustrates the substance.
H_2SO_4 is sulfuric acid. Using pegs, H_2SO_4 might become HeN SORe. Why is the hen sore? Because it was doused in sulfuric acid.

Substitution. The something else is the *substitution* method. If you are faced with an intangible or abstract nugget of information, find a sound-alike English substitute for it, something you can *picture* in your mind. Here is how substitution works with two French words:

Pont means bridge. In pronunciation it is similar to the English word *pawn*. You might remember both the word and its pronunciation if you make a mind picture of yourself dragging a bridge—the Brooklyn Bridge or the Golden Gate—to a pawnshop.

Pamplemousse means grapefruit. Imagine a big *moose* head on the wall with an enormous *dimple* on its cheek. The dimple is so large that you are able to balance a grapefruit in it.

To help remember that the French word pont *means bridge, picture yourself dragging a bridge into a pawnshop.*

Lectures	Your goal is to *stop taking lecture notes* altogether. In lectures you are supposed to be listening and understanding. Remember the memory virtues: close *observation,* strict *attention,* and systematic *organization.* Practice doing these in your head, not your notebook. Lecturers are as eager to make sense to you as you are to make sense of them, so pay attention. In their opening remarks, lecturers will tell you what they will talk about. The lecturers then will talk about their subjects at length. Finally they will usually summarize what they have just said. The middle part—the mental note-taking part—is the most difficult part of a lecture for the audience. The opening remarks and the conclusion, which may last a combined total of five minutes, contain most of what must be retained. Most people, however, are not listening at those times. They are still settling in with note-taking paraphernalia at the start, and they are packing up to leave at the conclusion. A practiced listener should know in advance what the lecture subject is, and write that down. At first, you may need to take minimal notes on paper, as if they were chapter headings. Eventually, with practice, you will be able to take mental notes only.
Reading	As you become more fluent in the construction and use of word pictures, using substitute word pegs, you are likely to find yourself visualizing peculiar mind's-eye views of things you read. Do not be alarmed. This is a sign that pegs, links, and substitutes are becoming part of your conscious memorization process. Without those mind pictures, the reading material might never be recalled at all. The substitution method is most useful for memorizing quotations and lines of poetry. If the line or passage is a philosophical thought, or simply beautiful language, then make sound-alike substitutions to fix it in your mind. Never forget that it is difficult to memorize anything unless you invest it with *detail, color,* and *movement.* Your aim should be to simplify whatever you read to its memorable essence, and then, through substitutions, to fix it in your mind.
Maps	First consult a map of the United States. From the western border, draw approximately vertical lines southward from the borders of the northernmost states. The West Coast grid, or zone, will take in Washington, Oregon, and California plus Alaska and Hawaii. The East Coast grid, by far the largest, may encompass as many as 17 states under Maine. Try to place all the states within six or eight zones. Then figure out your own substitute word for each state, form a link word picture for each zone, and you will have a six- or eight-chapter mind picture of the map of America.

Improving Your Memory

Appendix

Quick-recall tests

For those readers who had little or no success the first time (page 183), try this test again.

1. Study this 15-digit number for two minutes. Then try to duplicate it exactly on a piece of paper.

   238158649376914

Peg words 1–100

198

Improving Your Memory

2. Here are seven phone numbers, each corresponding to a local tradesman or professional. Study the list for six minutes, then copy the seven titles in any order. Finally, without looking, match the memorized numbers to the titles.

Doctor	762-5881	Lawyer	681-9558
Grocer	616-2053	Dentist	386-3579
Plumber	358-0864	Florist	784-3579
Electrician	872-9647		

3. This is a list of twelve objects found in the home. Study it for just two minutes, then reconstruct the list from memory, in order.

couch, refrigerator, newspaper, clock, mirror, toaster, lamp, toilet, stove, television, carpet, window

Improving Your Memory   199

Names and their pictorial equivalents

Feminine

Abby: abbey, a bee
Abigail: a big ale
Ada: aid her
Addy: add E
Adelaide: a dell aid, addle aid
Adele: a dell
Adeline: add a line
Agatha: agate tore
Agnes: egg nest
Alberta: Al bought her
Alexandra: lick sand raw
Alexis: all ex's, all legs
Alice: blue gown
Alicia: a leash
Aline: lean
Alvira: I'll wire her
Amanda: a man there, amend, a mender
Amelia: a meal yeah
Amy: aim me, hey me
Andrea: hand dryer, angrier
Angela: angel, and Jell-o
Angelina: angel leaner
Anita: anteater, an eater
Annabel: a new bell
Annette: a net
Antoinette: ant turn net
Arlene: I lean
Audrey: all dry, aw dry
Augusta: gust her
Avis: a whiz
Babette: bad bet
Babs: bobs, blabs
Barbara: barber
Becky: bad key, peck E
Bernadette: burn a debt
Bernice: burn niece, burnoose
Bess: best, bass
Beth: bet bath
Beverly: beef early
Bobbie: pin, bob E
Bonnie: bony, bone knee, bonnet
Brenda: bran there
Candace: canned ace, candy
Candy: candy
Carla: car law
Carmen: car men
Caroline: carry line
Carrie: carry
Cecile: says seal
Cecilia: steal ya
Celeste: see less, see last
Celia: seal ya
Charlene: char lean
Cheryl: chair ill
Chrissie: cross E
Christine: pristine, grist in
Cicely: Sicily, sees a lea

Cindy: cinder, sin D
Clara: clearer, clarify
Clarissa: clear as air
Claudia: claw D, clawed ya
Clementine: clam on time
Colleen: call in, coal lean
Conchita: conch eater
Constance: con stands, cons dance
Consuelo: con swallow
Cora: core, corer
Cordelia: core deal ya
Corinne: chlorine, core in
Cornelia: corn kneel
Crystal: crystal, cross tall
Cynthia: send to ya, sin tear
Daphne: deaf knee
Darleen: darling, door lean
Deborah: the borer
Deirdre: deer draw
Delia: deal ya
Denise: the niece, dentist
Diana: piano, die on her, dye Anna
Dinah: diner
Dixie: south, dig sea
Dolly: doll
Dolores: the law is
Dora: door, adore her
Doreen: tureen, door in
Dorothy: adore a tea, door tea
Dot: dot
Eden: eatin', E den
Edith: edict
Edwina: head winner
Eileen: I lean, eye lean
Eleanor: a lean oar
Elena: a loner, a leaner
Elise: a lease, release
Eliza: L icer, he lies t'her
Elizabeth: he lifts a bed
Ellie: alley, a lea
Eloise: hello ease, yellow E's
Elsa: L saw, else
Elsie: L sea, el see
Elva: elf, L where?
Elvira: elf higher, L wirer
Emily: a mill E, M in lea
Emma: hey Ma, hemmer
Enid: he knit, in it
Erica: error car
Ernestine: earnest in, a nest in
Essie: ess sea, S see, I see, icy
Estelle: S tell
Esther: yester(day), yes dear, ess tear
Etta: eater, editor
Eugenia: ewe genius, ewe jeans

Evangeline: evangelist
Eve: eve, heave
Evelyn: evil in, a violin
Faith: faith
Fay: fade, fail
Felicia: full leash
Flo: flow
Flora: flower, floor
Florence: floor ants
Flossie: floor see
Frances: France is
Francesca: France's car
Francine: France seen, ran scene
Freda: freed her
Fritzie: ritzy, frisky
Gabrielle: horn, gabby L
Gail: gale
Genevieve: gem verve
Georgia: gorga ya, gorgeous, gorge
Geraldine: chair old dine
Germaine: German, germane
Gertrude: protrude, go through
Gilda: gill there, gild, guild
Gina: china, gee no
Ginny: gin knee
Gisele: gazelle
Glenda: lender, glen deer
Grace: grace, race
Greta: get her, (re)gretter
Gretchen: retchin', great chin
Griselda: grows older
Gussie: gassy, gust sea
Gwen: when, goin'
Gwendolyn: mandolin, wend all in
Hannah: hand her
Harriet: hurry it, harried
Hattie: had tea, hat tea
Hazel: nut, haze, hassle
Heather: heather, feather
Hedda: header, head her
Hedy: heady
Heidi: hide E, hide
Helen: hellin', hailin'
Helena: hill leaner
Helga: held car
Henrietta: hen reader
Hermione: her my own knee
Hester: S tore, has tear
Hettie: heady
Hilary: hilarious, hill airy
Hilda: builder, hill there
Hildegarde: hill the guard
Holly: holly, holy
Honey: honey
Hope: hope
Hortense: horse sense
Ida: cider

Ilka: ilk, elk, ill car
Ilse: ills, else
Imogene: emergin', in motion
Ina: iron, eye no, I know
Inez: iron S, inn Ess
Ingrid: in grid, ink rid
Irene: eye ran, iron in
Irma: I'm a, her Ma
Isabel: is a bell
Isadora: is a door, adorer
Jackie: jack key
Jacqueline: jackal in, jack line
Jane: jay hen, chain
Janet: chain it, chain net
Janice: chain ice, chain ease
Jean: jeans
Jeannette: gem net, shine it
Jeannie: jean knee, chain knee
Jennifer: chain off her, gem fur
Jenny: jay knee, chain knee
Jessica: sick car, chase a car
Jessie: chase E
Jewel: jewel, chew L
Jill: chill, jail
Jo: show, (G.I.) Joe
Joan: showin', own
Joanna: show Anna, showin' her
Jocelyn: jostlin'
Jody: show D, show tea
Josephine: show sip fine
Joyce: juice, (re)joice, choice
Juanita: one eater, war neater
Judith: showed it, chewed it
Judy: chew D
Julia: jewel, jewel yeah
Juliana: shoe lea Anna
Julie: jewel E
Juliet: balcony, jewel ye
June: chewin'
Justine(ina): just in, just tea
Karen: carryin', carin'
Kate: gate
Katherine: cat run, cat tore in
Kathleen: cat lean
Kathy: cat see
Katie: katydid, K tea
Katrina: cat runner
Kay: K, cake, key
Kim: come, grim
Kirsten: curse tin
Kit: kit, cat
Kitty: kitty, kit E
Laura: lurer
Lauren: lurin', lowerin'
Laurette: lower it, lorgnette
Laurie: lower E, lorry

Laverne: love urn
Lavinia: love in here
Leah: lea ah, leader
Lee: lea, lee (shelter)
Lena: leaner
Leonora: lea and aura, lee and oar
Leslie: less lea
Letitia: the teacher
Letty: let E
Lila: lie low
Lillian: lily in
Linda: lender, lint
Lisa: leaser, lease her
Liza: lies here
Lois: loose
Lola: loller, low lair
Lolita: low lighter, low leader
Loretta: lure a tire, lower it
Lorna: law no, (for)lorn, lawn
Lorraine: low rain
Lottie: lottery, lot tea
Louisa: low icer
Louise: low ice, low ease
Lucia: lose ya'
Lucille: loose sail, low sill
Lucinda: lose cinder, loose in there
Lucy: loose E, low sea
Lulu: tutu, (that's a) lulu, lullaby
Lydia: lid here, lady, lid ya'
Lynne: lin(iment), lean
Mabel: may bell, may bull
Madeleine: mad lean
Madge: mad G, badge
Mae: may(pole)
Magda: make door, nagged her
Magdalena: make door leaner
Maggie: magpie, my key
Maisie: maize, maze E, may see
Malvina: mail wiener
Mamie: maim me
Mandy: mandolin, man D, man handy
Marcella: Ma cellar
Marcy: Ma see
Margie: march E
Margot: Ma go
Marguerite(ta): Ma car eat
Maria: mare here
Marian: marryin'
Marie: marry, mare E
Marietta: marry Etta
Marilyn: merrily, marry lin(iment)
Marion: marryin', carry on
Marjorie: Ma jury

Marsha: marsh, marcher
Mary: marry
Mathilda: mat ill there
Mattie: mat E
Maureen: more in, tureen
Mavis: may whiz
Maxine: Macks(trucks) in
Mehitabel: me hit a bell
Melanie: melody, melon knee
Melissa: me listen, mail a saw
Mercedes: Benz, me say D's, mercy
Meredith: married it, merry dish
Mildred: mill dread
Millicent: mill sent, mini cent
Millie: mill, mill E
Mimi: me me, mime me
Minerva: my nerve
Minnie: my knee
Miranda: veranda, mirror and door
Miriam: mirror him, merry ham
Mitzi: mitt sea
Molly: tropical fish, Ma lea
Mona: moaner
Monica: money car, Monaco
Morna: more no, mourner
Muriel: mural
Myra: my rah, mirer
Myrtle: me tell, more till
Nadine: neigh dine
Nan: nun
Nancy: nun see
Nanette: nun net, no net
Naomi: neigh owe me
Natalie: not tell E, gnat toll E, naturally
Nell: knell, kneel
Nellie: knell E
Nettie: net E, net eel
Nicole: nickel, nick hole
Nicolette: nickel let
Nina: knee no
Nita: neater
Noel: Christmas, no el
Nona: no no
Nora: gnaw her
Noreen: gnaw in, no rain
Norma: no Ma, normal
Octavia: hocked a view
Odette: owed debt
Olga: old car, ogre
Olive: olive
Olivia: oh liver
Opal: opal, old pal
Pam: bam, P ham
Pamela: pummel her
Pandora: box, pan door, panda

Pansy: pansy, pan sea
Pat: pat
Patricia: pat richer
Patty: (meat)patty, pat E
Paula: pull her
Pauline: pull in, poor line
Pearl: pearl
Peg: peg
Peggy: peg E, piggy
Penelope: pen elope
Penny: penny
Philippa: full lip
Philomena: fill meaner
Phoebe: fee bee
Phyllis: fill us
Polly: parrot, pulley
Priscilla: press cellar
Prudence: prude ants
Prue: true, rue, rude
Rachel: ray chill
Ramona: ray moaner, ram owner
Rebecca: ray
Regina: reach in, reachin' her
Rena: rain her
Renee: run hay, grenade
Renni: wren E, runny
Rhoda: road
Rita: reader
Roberta: robe hurt her
Robin: robbin', robin (red breast)
Rochelle: row shell
Rosa: rose
Rosalie: rose lea
Rosaline: rose land
Rosalyn: rose lin(iment)
Rosamund: rose mount
Rose: rose
Rosemarie: rose marry
Rosita: rose eater
Rowena: row wiener
Roxanne: rocks in
Ruby: ruby, rude bee
Ruth: Babe(Ruth), ruth(less)
Sabina: soapin' her, sap eye now
Sadie: say D, lady
Sally: sail E, sally
Salome: veil, salami
Samantha: saw man there
Sandra: sander, sand draw
Sandy: sandy
Sarah: say rah, sharer
Sasha: sash
Saundra: sauna, sundry
Selma: sell Ma
Shari: share E, chair ease
Sharon: chair on
Shawn: shorn
Sheila: shield
Sherry: sherry, cherry

Sheryl: chair ill, share ill
Shirley: surely, surly
Sibyl: see bill
Sidney: sit knee
Sigrid: sea grid, secret
Simone: sea moan
Sonia: sewin' ya', sun ya', sun
Sophia: sew fire, sew fee
Sophie: sew fee
Stacy: stay see
Stella: stellar, cella
Stephanie: staff a knee
Sue: sue
Sue Ann: sue ant
Susan: sues Ann, snoozin', (lazy) Susan
Susannah: sues Anna
Susie: sue sea
Sylvia: silver
Tammy: tan me
Terry: terry(cloth) towel
Tess: toss, test
Tessie: toss E, dressy
Thelma: tell Ma
Theodora: see a door
Theresa: tear easy, terrace
Tilda: tell door
Tillie: till E, dilly
Tina: teeny
Toby: toe bee
Toni: toe knee
Tracey: trace E
Tricia: tree share
Trixie: trick see
Trudy: true D, threw D
Una: owner
Ursula: ice cellar
Valerie: valet read
Vanessa: van a saw
Velma: well Ma
Vera: veer, fear
Verna: firmer
Vicky: icky, V key
Victoria: victory
Vida: feed her
Viola: viola
Violet: violet, file it, violent
Vivian: we win, vivid inn
Wanda: wander
Wendy: wend windy
Wilhelmina: will helm inn
Wilma: will Ma
Winifred: when if red, win if red
Winnie: whinny, win knee
Yetta: yeah tar
Yolanda: you launder
Yvette: he wet, E vet
Yvonne: he won, heave on
Zelda: sell there, seldom
Zoe: sew E

Improving Your Memory

Names and their pictorial equivalents

Masculine

Aaron: air run
Abe: hey bee, ape
Abel: able, a bell
Abner: abnor(mal), nab knee
Abraham: ape ram, a bear ham
Abram: ape ram, a broom, bram(ble)
Adam: atom, at 'em
Adolph: a dolph(in)
Adrian: aid dream, a dream
Alan: a lens, a land
Albert: Prince (Albert)
Alden: all den
Alec: a lick
Alex: all eggs, legs
Alexander: leg sander
Alfred: half red
Algernon: all jaw nun
Alonzo: alone sew
Aloysius: all wishes
Alvin: all win
Ambrose: ham browse
Amos: hey miss
André: hand ray
Andrew: hand drew
Andy: handy
Angelo: angel low
Archibald: arch bald
Archie: archer
Armand: almond
Arnold: arm old
Arthur: author
Ashley: ash lea
Aubrey: orb ray
August: gust
Augustine: gustin'
Augustus: gust us
Austin: awes tin, oars tin
Avery: aviary
Axel: axle
Baldwin: bald one
Barnaby: barn a bee
Barney: bar knee, barn E
Barry: bury
Bart: bought, bart(er)
Bartholomew: bottle anew
Basil: bay sill
Bayard: bay yard
Benedict: benedict(ion)
Benjamin: bend a man
Bennett: bend net
Benny: bend E
Bentley: bent lea
Bernard: burn hard
Bernie: burn knee
Bert: bird
Bertram: bought ram
Bertrand: bird ran
Bobby: bob E
Boris: bore us

Boyd: bird
Bradford: bread ford
Bradley: bread lea
Brandon: brandin'
Brian: brine, buyin'
Bruce: bruise
Bruno: burn O
Burton: buy ton
Byron: buy run
Calvin: cave in
Cameron: camera on
Carlos: car loose
Carter: carter, car tear, cart her
Cary: carry
Casper: cast pear
Cecil: cease ill, see sill
Chad: charred, chat
Charles: quarrels, chars
Charlie: char lea
Charlton: quarrel ton, char ton
Chester: chest, jester
Chet: jet
Chris: cross, kiss, grist
Christian: cross tin
Christopher: grist fur, kissed a fur
Clarence: clearance
Clark: clock
Claude: clawed
Clayton: clay ton
Clement: cement, (in)clement
Clifford: cliff oared, cliff awed
Clifton: cliff ton
Clint: lint
Clinton: clean ton
Clive: alive
Clyde: slide, lied, clod
Cole: coal
Colin: coal in, callin'
Connie: con D, con knee
Conrad: con rat, comrade
Corey: core E
Craig: crack
Curtis: caught us, curt
Cyril: see reel, cereal
Cyrus: sires
Damon: demon
Dana: deign, day, dinner
Daniel: den yell
Danny: den knee
Darren: darin'
Darryl: barrel, dare ill
Dave: dive, gave
David: gave it, save it, slingshot
Davy: day V
Dennis: tennis
Derek: derrick
De Witt: the wit, do it

Dexter: deck stir
Dick: tick, detective
Dirk: dark, dirk, Turk
Dominick: down my neck
Donald: duck, darn old
Douglas: dug glass
Duane: D wane
Dudley: dud lea, deadly
Duke: duke, duck
Duncan: dunkin'
Dustin: dustin'
Dwight: white, D white
Earl: oil
Eddie: eddy, a D, heady
Edgar: headgear
Edmund: head mount
Edward: head ward
Edwin: head win, head wind
Egbert: egg butt
Elbert: el butt
Eldred: el dread
Eli: eel eye
Elias: eel highest
Eliot: L E yacht, eel yacht
Ellery: celery
Elmer: el Ma, el more
Emanuel: manual, he man
Emil: a mill, hem ill
Emmett: hem met, aim it
Enoch: he knock
Ephraim: half ram, F rim
Erasmus: erase most
Erastus: erased us, he razzed us
Eric: a rick(shaw), air egg
Ernest: earnest, her nest, honest
Ernie: earn knee
Errol: error
Ervin: I win, urban
Erwin: her win
Eugene: you jean, ewe jean, huge E
Eustace: used us
Evan: a van, heaven
Everett: ever et (ate), over it
Ezekiel: a Z kill L, seek L
Ezra: S roar, ess raw
Felix: feel eggs
Ferdinand: bull, fur in hand
Fletcher: lecher, fetcher
Floyd: flood
Foster: forced her
Francis: fan sis
Frank: frank(furter)
Franklin: Benjamin (Franklin)
Fred: red, fret
Freddy: ready
Frederick: red rick(shaw)
Fritz: freeze
Gabriel: horn, gave reel
Garrett: garret, carry it

Gary: carry, gory
Gaston: gas ton
Gavin: gave in
Gaylord: gay lord
Gene: jean
George: gorge, judge
Gerald: chair old
Gerard: chair hard
Gideon: Bible, giddy on
Gifford: give Ford
Gil: gill, kill
Gilbert: gill butt
Giles: guiles
Gino: gee no
Godfrey: got free
Godwin: God win, good win
Gordie: gaudy
Graham: cracker, gray ham
Grant: grant, granite
Greg: grog, crack, dreg
Gregory: grog airy, crack gory
Griff: gruff, grip
Griffin: grippin', grip fin
Grover: grove
Gunther: gun tore
Gus: gas, gust
Gustave: gas stove
Hadley: head lea, heady
Hal: hall, hail
Hank: hanky, yank
Hans: hands, hens
Harold: hair old
Harry: hairy
Harvey: hard V
Hector: hick tore
Henry: hen, hen ray
Herb: herb
Herbert: her boot
Herman: her man, ermine
Hilary: hilarious, hill airy
Hiram: hire 'im, eye ram
Homer: homer
Horace: her ace
Horatio: ratio, her ratio
Howard: how ward, coward
Hoyt: hurt
Hubert: you bet, ewe bet
Hugh: you, ewe, hue
Hugo: ewe go, you go
Humphrey: home free
Hy: high
Hyman: high man
Ian: eon, ion
Ignace: egg nice, egg nuts
Ignatius: egg nauseous
Ingram: ink ram
Ira: eye rah, irate
Irving: nerve ink, serving
Irwin: I win
Isaac: eye sack, I sick
Isadore: is a door
Israel: his rail, is real**

202   **Improving Your Memory**

Ivan: eye van
Ivor: I wore, ivy ore
Jacob: Jacob('s ladder), shake up
Jake: shake
James: aims
Jamie: aim me
Jarvis: jar whiz
Jason: jay son
Jasper: just pair, gasp pear
Jay: jay(bird), jail
Jed: shed
Jeff: shave, shove, chaff, chef
Jeffrey: shove free, chef free
Jeremiah: chair mire
Jeremy: chair on me
Jerome: d'ya' roam?, chair room
Jerry: cherry
Jess: jazz
Jesse: James, d'ya see?, let's see
Jim: gym
Jimmy: jimmy (a door), gimme
Joel: jewel, jowl
Joey: showy, chewy
Johnny: on knee, john
Jonah: whale, show new
Jonas: showin' us
Jonathan: john thin
Jordan: Jordan (River), jaw down
José: oh say, hose
Joseph: shows off
Joshua: josh shoe, josh shower
Juan: one, won, wan
Jud: jut
Jude: chewed
Judson: jut son
Jules: jewels
Julian: jewel in
Julie: jewel, July
Justin: just in, justice
Keith: keys
Kenneth: can it
Kent: can't, canned
Kevin: cave in
Kimball: come bull
Kirk: kick
Lance: lance, lands
Lancelot: lance a lot
Larry: lair E, leery
Lawrence: lower ants
Lemuel: lamb mule
Lenny: lend knee
Leo: lion, lea O
Leon: lean on, lea on
Leonard: lean hard
Leopold: leap old, leap pole
Leroy: lea roil
Leslie: less lea

Lester: less tear
Lionel: lion el, lion L
Lloyd: lewd
Lonny: low knee
Louis: loose
Lowell: low el, lower, loll
Lucas: luke kiss
Ludwig: load wig
Luther: looser
Malcolm: mail come
Manny: many, man E, manly
Marcus: mark us
Mario: marry O
Marmaduke: Mom a duke
Marshall: marshal, marsh ill
Marty: Ma tea
Marvin: Ma win, move in
Mason: mason, my son
Matthew: mat ewe
Maurice: more rice
Maury: more E
Maximilian: makes a million
Maxwell: mix well
Maynard: main yard
Melvin: melt win, delve in
Meredith: married it
Mervin: movin'
Meyer: mire
Michael: my call, mike ill
Mickey: my key
Milton: melt on
Mitchell: mitt shell
Monroe: man row
Montague: mount glue
Montgomery: mount gum airy
Monty: mount tea, mountie
Morgan: more can
Mortimer: morti(fy) Ma, more tea Ma
Morton: more ton
Morty: more tea
Moses: Moseys, Ma says
Murray: more ray
Myron: my run, mire on
Nathan: nay sun
Nathaniel: neigh tan yell
Neil: kneel
Nelson: half nelson
Nero: fiddler, knee row
Neville: never, never ill
Nicholas: nick alas
Niles: miles, Niles (rivers)
Noah: ark, no air
Noel: Christmas, no el
Norbert: no berth
Norman: no man, Norseman
Norton: no ton
Ogden: egg den
Olaf: oh laugh, O laugh
Oliver: olive
Orson: oar sun

Oscar: Academy Award
Otis: elevator
Owen: owin'
Ozzie: ah see, I see
Patrick: pat rick(shaw)
Pattie: (meat) patty
Pedro: pet row
Percy: per se, purse see
Perry: bury, pear E, pair eel
Peter: eater, pea eater
Philip: full lip, fill up
Pierce: pierce
Pierre: pea air
Prescott: press cot
Preston: press ton
Quentin: went in
Quincy: win sea
Ralph: rough
Randall: ran doll
Randolph: ran dolph(in)
Randy: ran D
Raoul: rah oil, roll
Raphael: rah fail
Raymond: ray mount
Reggie: red G
Reginald: red G old
Reuben: ruby in
Rex: king (Latin), wrecks
Reynold: ran old
Richard: rich hard
Richie: rich E
Robbie: rob bee
Robert: robber
Robin: robin (red breast), robbin'
Roddy: ruddy, ready
Roderick: ruddy rick(shaw)
Rodney: rod knee
Roland: row land, rollin'
Rolph: roll off
Ronald: run old
Ronnie: run knee, runny
Rory: roar E
Roscoe: rescue
Ross: roars
Rudolph: rude dolph(in), rude doll off
Rufus: roof us
Rupert: rude pat
Russell: rustle
Sammy: ham me, hammy
Samson: biblical strong man
Samuel: some mule
Sandy: sandy
Schuyler: scholar
Scott: Scott(ish kilt)
Sean: shorn, sh yawn
Sebastian: sea bashed in
Seymour: see more
Shelley: shell E, shell ease
Sherman: sure man, German
Sidney: sit knee

Silas: silence, silo
Silvester: silver vest, investor
Simeon: see me on
Simon: says, sigh man
Sinclair: sin clear, sink lair
Solomon: wise man, solo man
Spence: dispense, pens
Spencer: spend sore
Stanley: stand lea
Stephen: steep hen
Stewart: steward
Teddy: ready, dead E
Terence: tear ants
Terry: terry(-cloth towel)
Theo: see O
Theodore: see a door
Thomas: tom-tom, the miss
Timmy: tinny, dim E
Timothy: dim tea
Titus: tied us
Tobias: toe buy us, bias
Toby: toe bee
Tod: toddy, toward
Tommy: tummy
Tonio: tone E O
Tony: toe knee
Tracy: trace E
Tristan: twistin'
Tyrone: throne, tie rowin'
Upton: uptown
Uriah: you're higher
Valentine: heart, valley dine
Vance: vans
Vergil: verge L
Verne: V earn, fern
Vernon: fur nun
Victor: victor
Vince: wince
Vincent: win cent
Vinnie: fini, V knee
Wade: wade
Waldo: wall dough
Wallace: wall lace, walrus
Wally: wall E
Walter: wall tear
Wayne: wane
Wendell: wend L
Wesley: west lea
Whitney: white knee
Wilbur: will burr, will bear
Wilfred: wolf red
Willard: will lard
William: will yam
Willis: will lace
Willy: willy(-nilly), will E
Winston: wins ton
Winthrop: win troop
Wyatt: Y hat, white
Zachary: sack airy, sack hairy
Zeke: seek

Improving Your Memory

Names and their pictorial equivalents

Surnames

Abbott: abbott, I bought
Abelson: a bell son
Abrams: rams, ape rams
Acheson: hatch a son
Ackerman: hacker man
Addison: add a son
Adler: add law, paddler
Alcott: old cot
Alexander: lick sand, lick sander
Altman: old man
Ambrose: ham browse
Anderson: hand and son
Andrews: Ann draws
Arnold: arm old, darn old
Ashburn: ash burn
Atkins: hat kin
Atkinson: hat kin son
Atwater: at water
Austin: awes tin
Bailey: bale E, bay leaf
Baldwin: bald one, bald win
Ballinger: ball injure
Bankhead: bank head
Barnett: bar net, barn hat
Bartlett: bottle it
Baxter: back stir, backs tear
Begley: beg lea
Benham: bend ham
Benson: bend son
Bentley: band lay, English car
Bergman: (ice)berg man
Bernstein: burn stein
Blum: plum
Borden: milk, boarding
Braddock: bad dock
Bradley: brad lay
Bradshaw: bad shore
Brandt: brand
Brennan: burnin', bran nun
Brent: rent, bent
Brewster: brew stir, rooster
Brock: rock, broke
Brody: broad E
Brophy: trophy
Bryant: buy ant, buoyant
Buchanan: blue cannon
Buckley: buckle
Burgess: purchase
Burke: (ice)berg, perk
Byron: buy run
Cabot: cab butt
Cahill: gay hill
Caldwell: cold well, called well
Callahan: call a hand
Cameron: camera on
Campbell: soup, camp bell
Carlson: call son
Carmichael: car mike call

Carson: car son
Carter: car tear, cart her
Cassidy: cast tea
Cates: gates
Cavanaugh: cave in oar
Chamberlain: chamber lain
Chandler: chandelier
Channing: chaining
Chester: chest tear, jester
Chilton: chill ton
Christenson: Christian son
Clark: clock, clerk
Clinton: clean ton
Colby: cold bee
Coleman: cold man, coal man
Collins: collie, (Tom) Collins
Compton: camped on
Cooper: (chicken) coop, coo pair, barrel maker
Cosgrove: cost grove
Costello: cost hello
Coughlin: coughin'
Cowen: cow in
Crandall: ran doll
Crawford: crawl Ford
Crosby: Bing Crosby
Cunningham: cunning ham
Curtis: curt, caught us
Cushing: cushion
Custer: custard
Dalton: dull ton
Davenport: havin' port
Davis: Davis Cup
Dawson: door son
Delaney: delay knee
Denham: den ham
Denton: dent ton
Devlin: devil in
Diaz: dais
Dillon: tillin', dill on
Dixon: ticks on
Dodson: dud son
Donahue: don a hue (color)
Donaldson: darn old son
Donovan: don a van
Dooley: duel lea
Dougherty: dough in tea
Douglas: dug glass, dug less
Dowling: dowel ink, toweling
Driscoll: drizzle
Drummond: drummin'
Duffy: the fee, toughy
Dugan: do again, due again
Duncan: dunkin'
Dunlap: down lap, down lip
Durant: the rent, tour ant
Durham: door ham
Dutton: button, the ton
Dwyer: wire, dryer
Easley: easy, ease lea, easily

Eastman: yeast man
Eberhardt: ever hard
Eldridge: held ridge
Elliott: yacht, lot, L E hot
Ellsworth: el's worth
Endicott: end a cot
Ericson: a rig son
Ettinger: head injure
Everett: ever et (ate), over it
Farley: far lea
Farrell: far rail, barrel
Faulkner: fork near
Ferguson: fur go son
Findlay: find lea, finned lee
Finney: fishy, fini
Fitzgerald: fits chair old
Fitzpatrick: fits pat rick(shaw)
Flanagan: fan again
Fletcher: fetch her, lecher
Foley: fall E, foal
Forrester: forest, forest tear
Foster: forced her
Fowler: foul law, fouler
Frazer: freezer, raise her
Frederick: red rick(shaw)
Freund: friend, frond
Fuller: full, brush
Fulton: full ton
Galbraith: gal breath
Gaynor: gain her
Geller: gala, gal law, kill her
Gibbons: ribbons
Gilbert: kill bed, gill butt
Gillespie: kills pea
Giordano: jawed an O
Gladstone: glad stone
Gleason: glee son, grease on
Gonzales: guns are less
Gordon: garden
Gorman: gore man
Gould: gold, cooled
Graham: cracker, gray ham
Granger: ranger
Gregory: grog airy
Gulliver: giant, gull over
Gunther: gun tore
Haber: hay bear
Haggerty: haggard tea
Halpern: help urn
Hamilton: hammer ton
Hammond: ham mount
Hanrahan: hen ran
Hansen: hansom (cab), handsome
Harrington: herring ton
Harrison: hairy son
Hartley: heart lea, hardly
Hastings: haste inks
Hathaway: hat away
Hawkins: hawk inns
Hayden: hay den
Haynes: hay nose

Hecht: hacked
Hellman: held man
Henderson: hen son
Hendricks: hen tricks
Herbert: her boot
Hernandez: hurryin' ant is
Higgins: he gains
Hobart: whole bar, hope bard
Hobbs: hops
Hodges: hedges
Hoffman: huff man, half man
Hogan: hoe can, whole can
Holden: hold in, hold den
Hooper: hoop
Hopkins: hop kin
Horton: her ton, hurtin'
Houlihan: hold a hand
Houston: house ton, use ton
Howard: how hard, coward
Hubbard: cupboard
Humphrey: home free
Hutchinson: hutch in son
Hyatt: high hat
Hyman: high man
Ingersoll: anger soul
Ingram: ink ram
Irving: serving
Isaacs: eye sacks, ice axe
Jackson: jack son
Jacobs: cobs, Jacob's (ladder)
Jacobson: shake off son
Jacoby: jack cold bee
Jamison: aim at son
Jarrett: jar it
Jeffers: chef airs
Jeffries: chef freeze
Jenkins: chain cans
Johanson: show hand son
Jonas: showin' us
Jordan: jaw down
Joseph: shows off
Josephson: hose off son
Joyce: juice, choice, joyous
Kaiser: geyser, guy sore
Kaufman: cough man
Kearns: coins
Keenan: keen nun
Keith: keys
Kelleher: killer her
Kelly: call E, kill E
Kemp: camp
Kenny: can knee, penny
Keogh: keyhole
Kessler: cast law, wrestler
Kimball: gamble, come ball
Kingsley: kings lea
Knapp: nap, knap(sack)
Knowles: Noels, knolls
Koenig: king, coin nick
Krakauer: crack hour
Kramer: creamer, gray Ma

Kroger: crow gore
Kruger: crew gore, cruder
Lafferty: laugh tea
Lambert: lamb butt
Landau: land dough
Langer: longer, linger
Larson: larceny, arson
Lawrence: law ants, lower ants
Lawson: law son
Lazarus: lather us
Lederman: leader man, letter man
Lehman: layman
Leonard: lean hard
Leopold: leap old, leap pole
Lester: less tear, jester
Leventhal: lovin' tall
Levinson: level son
Levitt: love it, leave it
Lewis: lose, loose, who is
Lieberman: labor man
Lindsey: lint sea, lindy (hop)
Lindstrom: lint strum
Livingston: living stone
Logan: low again
Loring: low ring, lowering
Loughran: lock ran
Lovell: love el
Lovett: love it
Lowell: low el
Lowenthal: low and tall
Lubin: low bin
McCarthy: Mack cart tea
McCormick: Mack core mike
McDonald: Mack darn old
McGraw: Mack raw
MacGregor: Mack rigor
McKay: Mack hay, my key
McMann: Mack man
Mahoney: Ma hold knee
Maloney: alone knee, baloney
Manning: man ink, manning
Marcus: mark us
Marshall: marshal, Ma shall
Martin: Ma tin, mar tin
Martinez: martinets
Martinson: Ma tin son
Matheson: matter son
Matthew(s): mat ewe(s)
Maxwell: makes well, mix well
Maynard: mane hard
Mercer: mercy
Meredith: married it
Metcalf: met calf
Michaelson: mike call son
Middleton: middle ton
Mitchell: shell, mitt shell
Montgomery: mount gum airy

Morales: morals, more or less
Morgan: more can
Morrison: marry son
Morse: moss
Morton: mutton, more ton
Moynihan: mind a hand
Murray: more ray
Nash: gnash
Nathanson: no tan son
Nichols: nickels
Nicholson: nickel son
Noonan: new nun
Norman: no man, Norseman
Norris: no risk
Norton: no ton, gnaw ton
Nugent: new gent
O'Brien: oh burn, brine
O'Connor: O con her
O'Donnell: ode down hill
Ogden: egg den, egged on
O'Malley: home alley
Oppenheim: open home
O'Reilly: oar oily
O'Rourke: O roar
Ortiz: oared ease
Osborne: is born
Osgood: is good
Otis: elevator
Owen: owin'
Padgett: patch it, page it
Palmer: palm, palm Ma
Papadopoulos: Papa topple us
Patterson: pat a son
Pawley: pulley
Pearce: pierce
Pearson: pierce son
Pendleton: peddle ton
Perlman: pearl man
Peterson: eater son
Phelps: helps
Phillips: full lips
Platt: plate
Poindexter: point egg stir
Pollock: pole lock
Prentiss: parent is, parenthesis

Proctor: doctor
Quentin: went in
Quinn: win
Raleigh: roll lea, raw lea, roll E
Ramirez: ram ear ess (curve)
Randall: ran doll
Randolph: ran dolph(in)
Raymond: ray mount
Reeves: reefs
Reinhard: rain hard
Reynolds: ran old
Richardson: rich son, rich yard son
Rigney: rig knee
Riley: rye lea, rile E
Riordan: rear down, reared on
Rivera: river
Robeson: robe son
Robinson: robbin' son
Romero: roam arrow
Rooney: ruin knee
Rossiter: rose sitter
Rudolph: rude dolph(in)
Rutherford: rode a Ford
Ryan: cryin', rind, Rhine (River)
Samuelson: some mules on
Sanchez: send chest
Sanders: sand, senders
Saunders: sanders, sun doors
Saxon: sacks on
Schultz: shields, shoots
Seaton: see ton, sit on
Sedgwick: search wick
Seiden: side in, sigh den
Seward: steward, seaward
Seymour: see more
Schaeffer: shave four
Shannon: shine on, chainin'
Sheehan: sheen
Shelton: shell ton, shelter
Sheridan: share a den
Sherman: show man, sure man

Simpson: simple son, simper son
Sinclair: sin clear
Slater: slayed her
Sommers: summers
Spaulding: sprawled ink
Spenser: expense her
Stafford: staff ford
Stoddard: stood hard
Sutherland: other land
Sweeney: sweet knee, sweety
Tate: tight, tea ate
Thatcher: that chair, thatcher
Thompson: tom-tom son
Thorpe: tore up
Tompkins: thump kin
Travers: traverse
Tucker: tuck'er
Ullmann: old man
Unger: hunger, hung her
Vance: vans
Vaughn: warn
Vincent: win cent
Wallace: wall lace, wall is, wall ace
Walsh: waltz
Warner: warn her
Warrington: warring ton
Watson: what son
Waverly: wave early, waver lea
Welch: grape juice, welsh
Wesley: west lea
Whalen: whalin', whale, wailing
Whitney: white knee
Whittaker: wit taker, with a car
Wilkinson: milkin' son
Williamson: will yam son
Winston: Churchill
Winthrop: win troop
Woolsey: wool see
Wrightson: write son
York: cork
Young: baby
Zachary: sack airy

For further reference

Cermak, Laird S.
Improving Your Memory
McGraw-Hill

Gallant, Roy A.
Memory: How It Works and How to Improve It
Four Winds Press

Lorayne, Harry
How to Develop a Super-Power Memory
Frederick Fell

Lorayne, Harry
Remembering People
Stein and Day

Lorayne, Harry, and Lucas, Jerry
The Memory Book
Stein and Day

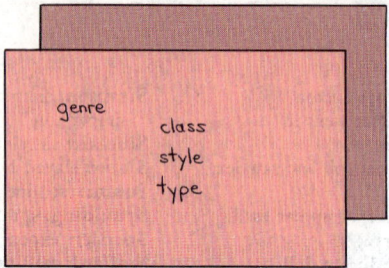

Building Your Vocabulary

- Your word power file 207
- A permanent memory system 209
- How words are used 210
- Natural settings for words 215
- 15 days to a forceful vocabulary 224
- Preparing for vocabulary tests 232
- American English 234
- Puzzles and word games 236
- Words you should know 238

"There is a weird power in a spoken word . . . And a word carries far—very far—deals destruction through time as the bullets go flying through space."
Joseph Conrad, 1857–1924

The world recognizes Joseph Conrad as one of the great English novelists. Yet he knew little of the language before he was twenty. A Polish orphan, the teenage Conrad sailed on British ships, where he learned English from his fellow seamen. Conrad was awed by the power of words, and set about becoming a writer. The quotation above is from his masterpiece, *Lord Jim*.

"A powerful agent is the right word. Whenever we come upon one of those intensely right words in a book or a newspaper the resulting effect is physical as well as spiritual, and electrically prompt."
Mark Twain, 1835–1910

Starting his career as a twelve-year-old apprentice newspaper printer, Mark Twain never lost his ambition to be a Mississippi riverboat pilot. Twain, whose real name was Samuel Clemens, used life along the river as background for *The Adventures of Tom Sawyer* and *Adventures of Huckleberry Finn*. Like Joseph Conrad, he was self-taught. Both writers respected the power of words and used them with extreme precision.

A key to success. Those women and men who possess a large vocabulary usually advance more rapidly in their careers and ultimately attain more responsible positions than those whose vocabularies are limited. The Human Engineering Laboratory has studied thousands of successful executives pursuing a wide variety of careers. It found that the only trait the executives held in common was their command of large vocabularies.

What does "to command a large vocabulary" mean? Knowing the meanings of words is part of it; but another part is knowing how to use those words effectively. Other sections in this volume help you learn how to write and speak well. See "Writing Effective Letters," pages 266–301, "Improving Your Reading," pages 302–327, and "Improving Your Speech," pages 244–265. You will also want to consult volume 1, pages 30–62, and volume 2, pages 254–283.

Do not assume that because you know the jargon of your own field, as in accounting, say, or nursing, law, or medicine, that you can communicate successfully. Just think of your own doctor, whom you, as a lay person, may not understand because he uses only incomprehensible medical words. For most people, a vocabulary rich in depth and wide in scope is more useful than one limited to the confines of a particular field. A famous professor at Columbia University once said that graduates from the English department generally ended their careers earning more money and having more responsible positions than graduates from any other field.

So you will gain considerably from the mastery of a large vocabulary. When you are interviewed for a job, or are talking to a manager at your current place of employment, the words you use are an important part of the impression you make.

Even before you are interviewed for a job or a promotion, you may be asked to take a vocabulary test. A passing grade is a necessity. To gain that passing grade, you will want to know the meanings of hundreds of new words. You will learn, and remember, 300 to 400 interesting new words as you read the next three dozen pages. But more than that, you will find three full pages of hints and techniques for passing verbal/vocabulary tests, together with questions similar to the ones you can expect to find in examination booklets.

Memorizing lists of new words and their definitions is not a recommended method for improving your vocabulary. There are several more effective ways to acquire a larger stock of words and the ability to use them correctly.

Those paths to a more powerful vocabulary are explored on the pages of this section. Whichever method you choose to follow, it will work best when you have begun building your own *Word Power* file.

Your Word Power file. Keep a file card or small notebook in your pocket or handbag. During the day, jot down unknown or puzzling words that you read in newspapers, magazines, or on signs, or hear in conversations or on radio broadcasts. You might even overhear an unknown term as two strangers are talking together near you on a crowded bus.

Wherever you come across it, write the word on your card. If possible, try to include a portion of the way it was used in conversation or a portion of the sentence in which you read it. A typical day's entries might look like the cards at the right.

Using one of the new techniques you have mastered, there is a good chance you will have an approximate idea of the meanings of these new words. But your aim is to use more words with greater accuracy, so approximate meanings are not good enough.

The solution: At the end of each day, write each word on a separate 3×5 card. Put into your own words a dictionary's definition of the word, and enter that on the card. Also add a synonym or two if the dictionary lists them. (A **synonym** is a word that has the *same meaning* as the original word. *Grand* and *magnificent* are synonyms, as are *punish* and *discipline*.)

Keep the cards in alphabetical order. When you add new entries in your *Word Power* file, select a handful of the existing cards at random. Glance at the words but not their meanings. Test yourself. Reinforce the power of your burgeoning vocabulary. (There's a good one to start with: **burgeoning**.)

Keep a notebook in your pocket or purse so you can jot down immediately those new, unknown words you meet in your daily activities.

Building Your Vocabulary

How do you rate?

How much larger will your vocabulary be when you have mastered most of the techniques in this section? That depends on the effort you expend, beginning today. The percentage of your gain can be measured by taking this simple test, recording your score, and a month from now comparing it with your score on the test that appears on page 237.

For each of the questions, select the one term that *most nearly defines* the meaning of the word in dark print. Other readers will be using this book, so please do not write in it; mark your selections on a separate sheet of paper.

1. **acrimony** a) agility; b) court-ordered payments; c) bitterness; d) dryness
2. **adulation** a) growing up; b) adding water; c) hero worship; d) mixture
3. **appellation** a) name; b) maintain; c) small bullet; d) country
4. **capillary** a) form of butterfly; b) slender tube; c) large quantity; d) head, or top
5. **cobalt** a) metallic element; b) African antelope; c) partner; d) garden tool
6. **covert** a) secret; b) ditch, or gutter; c) lid; d) quarrelsome
7. **destitute** a) illegal; b) wicked; c) poverty-stricken; d) enhanced
8. **diffident** a) unlike; b) shy; c) argumentative; d) shining
9. **diurnal** a) under water; b) easily fooled; c) selfish; d) daily
10. **effigy** a) easy task; b) image; c) degree; d) ratio of output to input
11. **exude** a) put away; b) clear out; c) investigate; d) ooze
12. **famished** a) done, completed; b) starved; c) mixed up; d) related, as a cousin or aunt
13. **florid** a) warm; b) ornate; c) damp; d) southern
14. **glean** a) gather bit by bit; b) tilt dangerously; c) flash of light; d) smooth
15. **grotesque** a) bizarre; b) cavelike; c) comical; d) hyacinth
16. **martial** a) art; b) judo; c) general; d) warlike
17. **mendicant** a) remedy; b) ointment; c) beggar; d) prescription
18. **migrant** a) traveler; b) move to another country; c) severe headache; d) worker
19. **natal** a) Asian; b) living under water; c) birth; d) federal
20. **phobia** a) small bird; b) fear; c) drowning; d) falling
21. **pinnacle** a) peak; b) card game; c) evergreen tree; d) sail
22. **sallow** a) empty; b) yellow; c) not deep; d) filled with salt water
23. **tactile** a) crawling; b) touchable; c) pointy; d) cottonlike material
24. **troll** a) streetcar; b) mischievous dwarf; c) drumbeat; d) three of a kind
25. **usury** a) putting on makeup; b) illegal interest rate; c) impersonation; d) counterfeiting

Answers. Score one point for each correct answer. 1, c; 2, c; 3, a; 4, b; 5, a; 6, a; 7, c; 8, b; 9, d; 10, b; 11, d; 12, b; 13, b; 14, a; 15, a; 16, d; 17, c; 18, a; 19, c; 20, b; 21, a; 22, b; 23, b; 24, b; 25, b.

Analyze your score. A score of 25 is perfect (and quite rare), 22 to 24 very good, 18 to 21 above average, and 15 to 18 the score that most adults achieve. With *Word Power* you will gain during the next few weeks. It should be interesting to see how much better you do when you test yourself again.

A permanent memory system

Suppose you are reading a news magazine and come across this sentence: "She attributed the superiority of her tomatoes to the **humus** in which she grew them." You think humus has something to do with the amount of moisture in the gardener's backyard, but you are not sure. You look up the word in your dictionary and learn that it means "organic matter; decayed plants that provide nutriments to soil."

If you merely read a definition in a dictionary, make a mental note of it, and go on with your reading, your chances of retaining the meaning are slim. If you write the new word down, however, you greatly increase the probability that you will remember the meaning of **humus**. Experts in educational psychology say that the act of writing increases a person's ability to remember by as much as 100 percent.

But you are not an ordinary reader who wants to learn the meaning of an occasional new word. You are actively engaged in a campaign to radically increase your *Word Power*. To reinforce your learning process, you require additional techniques to make the new words you encounter every day a part of your working vocabulary.

Review the four-step system that follows.

Four steps to a larger vocabulary

1. **Understand what the word means, in your own terms.** If the dictionary tells you that **perfidy** means "a calculated breach of faith," do not try to add the word and that meaning to your active vocabulary in that form. Instead, read the entire dictionary entry and rephrase it, perhaps as "acts of a traitor; deliberate breaking of trust; spies engage in *perfidious* activities."

2. **Write the meaning on a card.** It requires some discipline to make a habit of the daily transference of words from your pocket notes to a permanent file card. You may be tempted to let it go for the weekend, but weekends often are more crammed with activities than we thought they would be, and file-building may be postponed yet again. The way to guarantee success is to establish a routine: fill out your file cards before you settle down for an evening's television watching or magazine reading. And keep your pocket card with you during those two activities so that any new words you hear or read will be included in the next day's entries.

    If a newspaper or magazine is the source of a word, you may want to clip the sentence from the page; then you can tape the printed sentence right on your *Word Power* card.

3. **Add the new card to your file.** An empty box, any shoebox-sized container, makes a fine storage space for your *Word Power* cards. If you have a special interest or two, you may want to color-code the cards that pertain to it for extra review. Words from the world of law and order, for example, could have green dots in the cards' upper right corners.

    Do you own a home computer? If you do, it will be easy to program a cumulative list of words, definitions, and examples of their use. Prepared software packages for vocabulary building are available, but you will find them less effective than the *Word Power* file you build for yourself.

4. **Systematically use your file.** During your first week of file-building, you may accumulate 20 or more *Word Power* cards. Once you have that many, you are ready to establish a routine that will reinforce your familiarity with the words' meanings.

    All that is required is to take out a handful of cards. Do not shuffle them, or they will have to be repositioned in alphabetical order later. Just lift one card from the pack, glance at the main word, and define it without looking at the printed definition. Then read the definition to see if you remember it correctly. If you do, replace the card and select another word. If you get it wrong, jot down the word on a list you keep for this purpose. A day or two later, look at the list and try to recall the word's meaning. If you remember a new word correctly for several days, in all probability you will remember it for many years.

    By reaching into the box and randomly choosing eight or ten words to test yourself on each day, you are certain to repeat many of the cards. Do not abandon the system. Repetitive practice, as with an athlete's training, brings superior performance.

Building Your Vocabulary

How words are used

Words, like bricks or shingles, do not have much value when standing alone—a single brick on a patch of bare ground, or a solitary word on a page, is not of much use. But when a number are arranged in a purposeful pattern, both words and bricks are extremely useful.

When you read a newspaper and notice an unfamiliar word, you are seeing it in **context**. That is, you are seeing it in use, among other words. Context can give you clues to an unknown word's meaning. Often, the clues are so strong that you will be able to define the word without **recourse** to a dictionary.

The sense of a sentence. The way in which *recourse* was used in the previous sentence gives you a strong clue as to its meaning. "Without recourse to a dictionary" might mean without returning to a dictionary, or perhaps, without the heaviness of a dictionary. But neither of those possibilities makes much sense. What does make sense is being able to understand the word's meaning without turning to or consulting a dictionary. And that is exactly what *recourse* means in the context of that sentence.

Echo words. At times, the context of an unfamiliar word includes another word that closely duplicates its meaning. "She had never before seen on a tray so many beautiful glasses as she saw on Mrs. March's large **salver**." In this sentence, it is easily understood that the glasses are, at the same time, on a tray and on a *salver*. The two words have the same meaning; they are *synonyms*.

Easy opposites. Just as echo words, or *synonyms*, are strong context clues, so are opposites, or *antonyms*. "Carl's blueprint specified rigid sheets of plastic, but the ones he brought were **malleable**." The key clues here are "rigid" and "but." In the context, **malleable** refers to a kind of plastic that is the opposite of rigid. It is correct to assume that the target word means pliable or easily bent.

Read on a bit further. The last of the more common contextual techniques takes you beyond the sentence in which the unknown word appears. If there is no clue to the word's meaning in that sentence—read on. The definition may become clear a sentence or two later. Here is an example: "We recognized those sagging **jowls**. No one else ever had such baggy *jaws*." There you have a clear definition of the wanted word, right in the next sentence.

On this page and the following pages are paragraphs, each containing several unfamiliar words. Examine those words in the context of their sentences and paragraphs. Then check your conclusions against the explanations printed right below the paragraphs. Of course, you will want to add to your *Word Power* file all words that are new or that you never have used in conversation.

The six-story **edifice** symbolized the values of **bourgeois, bustling** prewar Chicago. The building's solid **facade**, though granite and limestone, had a certain warmth. Built as the **abode** of bankers, it still was **accessible** by trolley car and other public transportation.

In the first two sentences, we learn that the paragraph describes a six-story building. *Edifice*, therefore, means building. *Bourgeois* and *bustling* are harder; you might guess the pair of words refers to busy or businesslike values of prewar Chicago. The precise definition of *bourgeois* is respectable, middle-class, property-owning. *Bustling* means busy, hurrying, or active.

Facade, a form of the word "face," refers to the front of a building. "The *abode* of bankers" can be understood to mean, loosely, their home. And if the building is *accessible* by public transportation, those trolleys have access to it; they can reach it easily.

Though the reason can't be pinned down, Mackey strikes some viewers as a **vaguely** unprofessional anchorman. It might be his slight speech **impediment** (trouble with "r's") or his **wry**, dry sense of humor. Yet, among each night's **welter** of disturbing facts and new worries, Mackey brings comfort to a large audience.

Vaguely tells us something about how or why some viewers think Mackey is unprofessional. Studying the sentence, we see that *vaguely* echoes the "can't be pinned down" quality of their feelings. *Vaguely* means indistinct, or no definite reason. If Mackey has trouble pronouncing "r's," something is standing in the way of clear speech; that is exactly what *impediment* means: an obstacle.

Wry and *dry*, when applied to sense of humor, are synonyms. The two words have the same meaning. *Welter* is not surrounded by enough clues to provide an accurate definition, but it clearly refers to a number of "facts and worries." Later, when you look it up, you will find it means a miscellaneous, hodge-podge grouping; a jumble.

Building Your Vocabulary

Try to visualize the situation, or context, in which new words appear and you may be able to guess their meanings and remember them better.

Her friends at work **twitted** Elaine about her **obsession** with her new grandchild. She was a **caricature** of an adoring grandma, **incessantly recounting** examples of the baby's brilliance. And, of course, she carried **myriad** photographs of the infant.

Her friends probably would not be mean or cruel to Elaine, but they would tease her and make fun of her constant bragging about her granddaughter. *Twitted* means teased. Elaine's mind is occupied with thoughts of the infant: she is *obsessed* with those thoughts. Drawings or actors' portrayals of easily recognizable characters, done in an exaggerated manner, are *caricatures*.

To *recount* a story is to tell it over again, and to do it continually, or without ceasing, is to do it *incessantly*. (Sometimes a story or anecdote is called an "account." Telling it again is to *recount* it.) If you did not know the meaning of *myriad*, you might guess that Elaine would carry very many photographs of the baby. *Myriad* does mean a very large number.

I wondered about Joanne's interest in **exotic** Peruvian shawls. The ancient woolens were harsh and too rough for comfort. The designs were childlike and **rudimentary**, almost primitive. Later, when her husband **confided** that Joanne was a **curator** at the Field Museum, I understood.

It would be difficult, from the context in which it is used, to know exactly what is meant by *exotic*. But the flavor, the general sense, of "exotic Peruvian shawls" indicates that the shawls are strange or foreign in appearance. And that is very close to the exact meaning of *exotic*: unusual, from another part of the world.

Rudimentary designs are described as "childlike" and "primitive." It is clear that the word means basic, elementary, or an early form. You may recognize *confided* as a form of the word *confidential* (secret). When "Joanne's husband *confided*," he made a private, almost secret, statement.

We can associate Joanne's interest in Peruvian weavings, and also the word *curator*, with her work at the museum. Actually, a *curator* is a person who is in charge of a department in a museum, library, or art gallery.

A soccer superstar for a dozen years, Ivor remained an **enigma** to his fans. They could not understand his childlike, stubborn **petulance** and his sudden temper **tantrums**. At the same time, they puzzled over his equally sudden bursts of **altruism**. Within moments, Ivor could be as generous as he had been **irascible** and mean.

If Ivor's fans could not understand his behavior, even after twelve years, *enigma* must refer to his puzzling habits. An *enigma* is a puzzle. Clues to the meaning of *petulance* are the echo words "childlike, stubborn." Ivor is grumpy, with flashes of quick, unreasonable anger. You can assume that his *tantrums* are fits of bad temper. He might kick the ball up into the stands, or shout rude remarks to the fans.

If Ivor has all those unpleasant traits, and *altruism* is strangely different, it might be related to "generous," mentioned in the last sentence. That is exactly right; *altruism* means unselfish help to others. Now, with all we know about Ivor, *irascible* becomes quite clear. It is a form of *irate*, and it means easily angered.

Building Your Vocabulary

Now that you have seen how the *context method* works when **assessing** the meanings of words, you may be ready to use it with some harder examples. (Did *assessing* stump you? Or did you recognize that it means estimating; forming an opinion of something?) The sample sentences on this page use less of the echo words technique, described on page 210, than the sentences you have worked on so far. But the other techniques for using context clues still **obtain.** (Note the unusual use of *obtain*. Very likely you are familiar only with the meaning to get, or gain possession of. In this instance, *obtain* completes the thought that other techniques exist or are accepted.)

> meticulous
> Very careful about small details.
> Almost too concerned. "Precise."
>   experience entering her kitchen. The spices
>   were lined up meticulously on a shelf
>   carefully lined with heavy white paper.
>   Every pot, every pan, was
> Syn: fussy; super-careful

Make sure your Word Power *file grows every day. In a short time you will learn many new words. Use them in your conversation and writing.*

Anyone who owns a cat knows that domestic **felines** have certain behavior patterns. They are **unremitting** in their care of their fur. All cats' tails **undulate** gently when cats hunt. And they are **discriminating** eaters, refusing new or suspicious kinds of food.

This short article is about *felines*, the family of animals that includes lions, tigers, and "domestic *felines*"—the ones that live with people. Cats. *Unremitting* has few context clues. You may have guessed, though, that it means unstopping or ceaseless.

If you have ever seen a cat creeping toward an unsuspecting bird, you know its tail waves gently. It *undulates*. *Discrimination,* as we most commonly use it, means to select or choose certain people, for unfair reasons. But *discriminating* can refer to the careful selection of certain objects. Cats are quite particular—or *discriminating*—about the food they will accept.

The Milwaukee-based sporting goods company is known for its **innovation.** It was the first to develop a safe, **incombustible** tent, and it pioneered an unsinkable, one-hulled **catamaran.** The company's sales are the **cynosure** of the industry.

If the company is first to develop one product and "pioneered" another, it is known for its new ideas. That is what *innovative* means: creative. A safe tent might be one of several kinds, including one that will not blow over. But an *incombustible* tent is one that cannot burn. *Catamarans* almost always are boats with two bottoms, or hulls, so a reference to an *innovative*, unsinkable item of sporting goods with one hull provides a strong context clue to *catamaran's* meaning. *Cynosure* refers to sales that are the envy of the industry; other companies admire and look up to that company's record.

Denizens of towns and cities never **encounter** deer in their natural **habitats.** The **visualize** Bambi or Rudolph, lovable big-eyed creatures. Farmers and **exurbanites,** often **plagued** by deer, see them as **voracious** animals that devour crops and shrubbery. Moreover, the **marauders** never travel alone, but in herds.

Reading all four sentences of the paragraph and then coming back to the target words will make the words' meanings clearer. *Denizens* must be people who are in towns and cities; actually, it means residents or inhabitants—people who live there. *Encounter,* in this context, obviously means to meet or see deer. The exact meaning is to meet unexpectedly. What could be a deer's natural *habitat*? Not towns or cities, but the woods and fields where deer live. (Their *habitation* is their home, or where they are most likely to be found.) You know that *audiovisual* is something you hear and see, and that *invisible* means cannot be seen. *Visualize* is related to those words; it means to see in your mind, or to imagine. City people imagine that deer are big-eyed, lovable creatures.

Urbanites are people who live in cities. *Exurbanites,* together with farmers, live far out from cities. You know that a *plague* is a disaster, generally an epidemic of serious sickness or disease. The word has come to mean any severe annoyance or nuisance. "Animals that devour crops and shrubbery" is a strong clue to the meaning of *voracious*—a huge appetite; greedy; eats great amounts of food.

Marauders is more difficult; you may have seen an athletic team with that name, and recall them using a pirate as their symbol. Like pirates, *marauders* roam around, raiding and stealing others' property. They never travel alone, but in bands.

Test questions. There are two kinds of test questions that often appear in civil service, employment, and college entrance examinations. Both kinds ask you to define words in the context of a sentence.

Supply a synonym.
Their lawyer, unfortunately, avoided the **salient** issues.
scrupulous   prominent   foreign   childish

You are asked to select the word among the four choices that most closely duplicates the meaning of *salient*.

Starting with *scrupulous*, which means conscientious, or very careful, we see it makes no sense in that sentence. *Prominent*, if we recognize it as meaning standing out or important, does make sense. *Foreign?* Not likely that it would be unfortunate if the lawyer avoided the *foreign* issues. And the last choice, *childish*, makes no sense in the context of the sentence.

In most questions of this kind, the possibilities narrow down to two choices, as the other two words are unlikely or obviously unsuitable. When all four, or three of the four, choices are difficult new words, selecting the right answer becomes considerably harder. You will find some of those difficult questions in the samples on this page. All the words you do not know should be added to your *Word Power* file.

Learning synonyms

1. The Red Cross set up emergency tents in the **devastated** areas of the valley.
   remote   wasted   elevated   largest

1. *Devastated* means *wasted*. Think about the Red Cross's mission. Few people live in *remote*, or far away, sections of the valley. There is no obvious reason to set up tents in *elevated*, high regions, nor in the *largest* areas of the valley.

2. After failing two inspections, the diner's license was **revoked.**
   revised   released   reissued   recalled

2. *Revoked* means *recalled*. It is clear that the diner lost its license, so *revised* is inappropriate; it means fixed, or made over. *Released*, a commonly used word, does not fit either. And the license would not be *reissued*, or given out again, if the diner failed to pass inspections.

3. Sharks were seen in the **vicinity**, but all three divers continued their work.
   nearby area   deeper water   emptiness   undersea wreck

3. *Vicinity* means *nearby area*. *Deeper water* and *undersea wreck* might make sense, but *vicinity* is used in everyday language, and should be recognized. *Emptiness* is totally out of place in the context of the sentence.

4. Outraged parents and dog lovers sent **irate** letters to the school board.
   legal   lengthy   angry   questioning

4. *Irate* means *angry*. "Outraged" is the clue to the tone of the parents' letters. The letters might have been *legal, lengthy*, or *questioning*, but *angry* is the word called for by the context of the sentence.

5. Is the association a **vestige** of times past, when streets were dusty and unpaved?
   trace   memory   religion   raiment

5. *Vestige* means *trace*, or remnant, of something that has disappeared over the years. *Religion* and *raiment* (clothing) do not make sense. *Memory* comes close, but it would be awkward referring to an association as a *memory* of times past.

6. $700,000 was granted to a **consortium** of four states, to form a defense against tax evaders.
   legislatures   association   treasury   police

6. A *consortium* is an *association* or grouping together of people or organizations, for a specific purpose. Several churches might form a *consortium* calling for stricter laws against drunk drivers. *Legislatures*, a plural word, should not follow the singular article 'a.' One *treasury* cannot belong to four states. It would be unusual for *police* to deal with tax evaders.

Building Your Vocabulary

Fill in the blank. The second type of context-based examination question is like the first kind in that you are offered a choice of four words. But it has a slightly different format. Instead of supplying a synonym for the target word as it is used in a sentence, you are asked to fill in the word—from among the four choices—that best completes the sentence.

Your procedure will be much like the one you followed in answering type 1 questions. Try each of the four words. Think how it relates to the central thought of the sentence. Eliminate the one or two impossible selections. Does either of the remaining words conflict with any of the **adjectives** (describing words)? Even if you are unfamiliar with a new word's meaning, does it give you a feeling of belonging—of not destroying the sentence's logic?

Choose the right word

1. It was the same _____ whose advice Julius Caesar had ignored.
   criminal   gesture   soothsayer   cravat

1. A *soothsayer* reads such signs as cloud formation or tea leaves, and gives advice. He is a fortune teller. (An old term for truth was *sooth;* a soothsayer 'says the truth.') Julius Caesar ignored a fortune teller's advice, not a *criminal* or a *gesture*. A *cravat* is a kind of necktie or scarf.

2. We hear about adolescent _____, yet most teenagers in this town are pleasant and likable.
   translucence   alienation   allegory   viability

2. *Alienation* is the right word. *Aliens* are foreign; they do not belong to the society in which they find themselves. Adolescents sometimes feel out of place, or isolated: *alienated*. The clue here is knowing that this town's adolescents behave in a manner opposite to *alienation;* they are pleasant and likable.

3. Imagine Joan's _____ after she prepared that marvelous barbecue and only three guests showed up.
   frustration   cuisine   perception   hallucination

3. *Frustration* is what Joan felt. It means discouragement; a sense of being unable to accomplish one's goal. *Cuisine* is the French word for kitchen; it is an awkward, improper fit. *Perception* means vision or seeing. *Hallucinations* are imaginary sights, nightmares, or the visions of unstable persons.

4. Maria's family was _____, in their sorrow, by a visit from the bishop.
   rewarded   cosseted   controlled   consoled

4. Maria's family was comforted in their sorrow; they were *consoled* by the bishop's visit. He brought them *consolation,* or sympathy, as well as comfort. There is no reason he would try to *reward* or *control* the family. The fourth choice, *cosseted,* means pampered, petted, or made a great fuss of.

5. When a modern shopping mall opened, the downtown merchants were forced to use strong _____ against it.
   textiles   tactics   statutes   covenants

5. The merchants used strong *tactics* against their competitor, the shopping mall. Those were maneuvers or actions. Two others of the four choices, *statutes* and *covenants,* are on the right track. They refer to laws. *Textiles* is entirely wrong; it means fabrics or materials, like woven cotton in a dress.

6. Secrecy surrounded the ambassador's plans, and his _____ chef was transferred to another post.
   rustic   perceptive   garrulous   esteemed

6. The ambassador's chef was *garrulous,* or talkative. *Rustic* refers to country life; rough and simple furniture is called *rustic* furniture. One who sees meanings is called *perceptive*. And though the chef might have been *esteemed*—thought well of, or honored—that would have been no reason for the ambassador to transfer him to another post.

Natural settings for words

A powerful aid to remembering the meanings of new words is to discover them in settings that hold interest for you: in the pages of a magazine or book, or on a television or radio broadcast. Here, where your aim is to come into contact with as many new words as possible, the grouping of target words serves as an effective substitute for those "natural" settings.

On the next few pages you will find such headings as *Health and medicine, Films and theater,* and *Sports*. For each category, there will be a list of six words, followed by six sentences, each containing one blank space. Select the one word from the list that best completes the thought expressed in each sentence. Below the sentences you will find the correct solutions; often, there also will be a brief explanation for the choice.

Note that you will not be able to use the context method for defining all the words in this section, but it can be applied to many of them. Every word here, though, is a perfect one to add to your growing *Word Power* file. Make out a card for each and you will add more than six dozen new words to your vocabulary.

Try creating natural settings of your own and provide new words to fit them. Be sure to make your *Word Power* file grow every day.

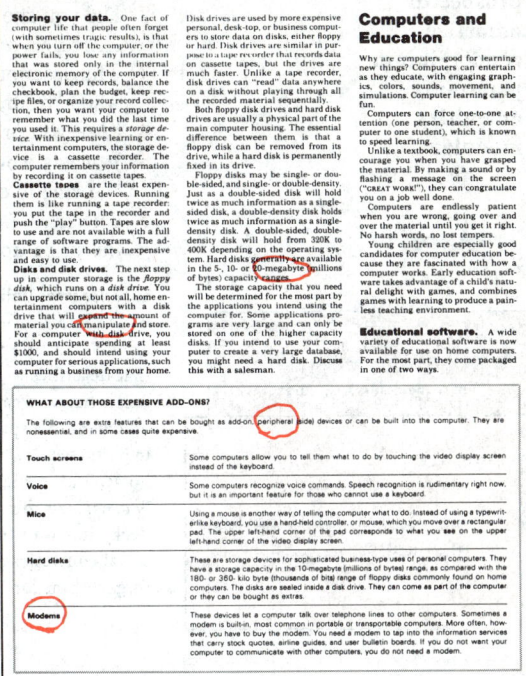

New words in natural settings

Health and medicine

insomnia
intermittently
epidemiology
anatomical
chronic
sedentary

1. _____ liver disease is diagnosed without much difficulty using techniques easily available to most doctors.
2. A _____ person has much lower resistance to muscular strains than one who is active.
3. The symptoms were not present constantly, but appeared _____.
4. Determining rates of disease in population groups, and studying the causes, is what _____ is all about.
5. The amount of sleep necessary for good health varies from person to person, and _____ can cause serious discomfort.
6. Through endless study of the body, Galen, who died in 203 A.D., became known as the father of _____ research.

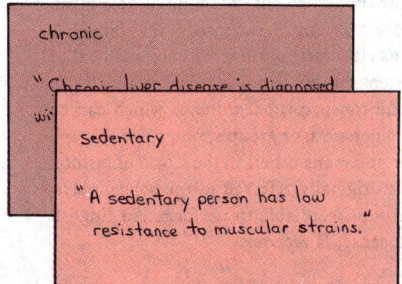

1. *chronic:* lasting for a long time; continual. It refers to time, as in *chronometer,* a precise clock or watch. **2.** *sedentary:* too much sitting; too little exercise. An active person is exactly the opposite of one who is *sedentary.* **3.** *intermittently:* stopped and started. The symptoms appeared and disappeared, or were *intermittent,* which is why they were not present constantly. **4.** *epidemiology:* the sentence itself is a definition of the word. It is related to *epidemic,* a widespread incidence of disease in a community or territory. **5.** *insomnia:* inability to sleep; unhealthy wakefulness. A *somnolent* person is a sleepy one; *insomnia* is the opposite condition. **6.** *anatomical:* the structure of the body, or any of its parts. *Anatomy* sometimes is used in its wider sense, meaning a general structure: She understood the *anatomy* of company management, and was well paid for her knowledge.

Building Your Vocabulary 215

New words in natural settings

Buying a home

prospectus
amortize
condominium
panorama
amenities
modular

1. We decided to buy the house when we stood on the front steps and saw the _____ of autumn leaves.
2. Did you know that your neighbors were musicians before you bought the _____?
3. The description in the _____ was far different from the building we saw when we drove out to the lake.
4. "Are you prepared to _____ this debt in 20 years?" asked the banker.
5. It was a wonderful day for the Kroeger family, for their _____ home was finally delivered from the factory.
6. The _____, including the carpeting, were attractive, but they brought the price up beyond our reach.

1. *panorama:* unlimited view over a wide area. 2. *condominium:* apartment or portion of a building owned by its occupants, while the rest of the building, and the grounds around it, are owned in common with other owners. 3. *prospectus:* a brochure (booklet) that describes a property offered for sale. A *prospect* is an expectation; a *prospectus* tells what you can expect from your purchase of this property. 4. *amortize:* to pay off a debt in a specified amount of time—in this instance, 20 years. 5. *modular:* made in parts that are later assembled. A child's building blocks are *modular* toys. A *modular* home, like a block construction, is composed of separate parts that fit together. 6. *amenities:* things that increase an object's value or comfort. A swimming pool, sun deck, and wall-to-wall carpeting are *amenities*. Another use of the word refers to social courtesies or pleasantries: Charlie overlooked the *amenities,* and Martha never forgave him for his rudeness.

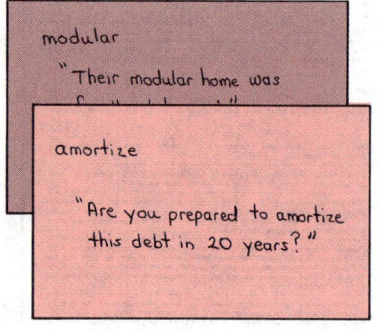

modular
"Their modular home was ..."

amortize
"Are you prepared to amortize this debt in 20 years?"

Design and fashion

nonchalant
pretentious
beguiling
intricately
repertoire
hybrid

1. The furniture seemed a _____ of two styles, French provincial and early American.
2. We admired Robert's _____ appearance as he strolled along the boulevard with his fiancée.
3. Doris selected a _____ version of a modern classic, the coatdress.
4. Above the mantel was a mirror with an _____ carved wooden frame.
5. Kate decided not to buy the bracelet, calling it "_____ and showy."
6. After she had attended four sessions of the sewing class, Beverly's _____ of techniques had tripled.

1. *hybrid:* mixture. The word's origin is in the natural sciences, where selected strains of plants and animals are bred to produce *hybrids* with mixed characteristics. 2. *nonchalant:* a word borrowed from the French, meaning casual, cool, unworried. Robert's carefree appearance could also be described as *debonair.* 3. *beguiling:* demanding attention, or distracting. At the same time, it means charming or delightful. *Bewitching* is sometimes used as a synonym for *beguiling.* 4. *intricately:* the frame has many carefully carved details; *intricate* means elaborate, or done with a great deal of skill and effort. 5. *pretentious:* demanding attention that is not justified. *Showy* is an echo word with almost the same meaning and tone; so is *ostentatious,* which can be added to your *Word Power* file. 6. *repertoire:* a person's, or group's, range of skills and accomplishments. This word, like *nonchalant* and many others in the world of fashion and design, is borrowed from the French. It originally referred to the songs, plays, or compositions that dramatic or musical groups were able to perform. An English version of the word, used in that theatrical sense, is *repertory.*

hybrid

216   **Building Your Vocabulary**

Sports

foiled
caliber
interim
regimen
grimaced
spate

1. When Dr. Newbold retired, Chris Stanley was named as _____ head coach of the Blue Devils.
2. Josephine had unusual natural ability, but was unwilling to stick to the training _____ demanded of professional athletes.
3. He fell on the field and _____ in intense pain after colliding with Parrish.
4. A _____ of matches against weak opponents gave Miss Yerby a strong boost in the tournament standings.
5. An eighth-inning triple by Hunt _____ pitcher Ken Leslie's attempt at a no-hitter.
6. Reporters agreed Miss Bryant was a superior player, but not quite Olympic _____.

regimen

1. *interim:* temporary, or the time between. Chris Stanley's appointment is not permanent. He will act as head coach only between the time that Dr. Newbold resigned and a new coach is appointed. 2. *regimen:* a system or process; routine procedures. Governments, or *regimes*, control the way many things are done, and *regimen* is formed from that word. 3. *grimaced:* made a distorted or "scrunched-up" facial expression. A *grimace* usually indicates pain, though sometimes it expresses anger or displeasure. 4. *spate:* a sudden rush. Miss Yerby had a flood of tennis matches, all during a short time. *Spate's* original meaning was a sudden downpour of heavy rain. 5. *foiled:* upset, or prevented from being successful. A synonym is *thwarted*. 6. *caliber:* a measure of worth or quality. The inside of a gun barrel is measured as .22, .38, or some other specific *caliber*. From that single meaning, the measure of a bullet's size, the word has come to mean a measure of any kind.

More sports

climactic
peripheral
disparity
conceded
soared
snared

1. "Most of my shots from mid-court are lucky to hit the rim," Anna _____.
2. Jerry Lloyd caught a seemingly impossible pass and trotted away with the _____ six points.
3. The crowd rose to its feet when Thompson _____ a line drive in the third inning.
4. A split second after the ball met her bat, it _____ into the left-field stands.
5. Crowley was paid a star's salary, but was kept in a _____ position all season.
6. Marge acknowledged the _____ in their national rankings, but insisted on first-class travel accommodations.

peripheral

1. *conceded:* gave, admitted, yielded; acknowledged as true. Anna admitted that most of her shots from mid-court fell short. 2. *climactic:* refers to a *climax*, the final and most important part of an action. 3. *snared:* trapped, or caught. A *snare* is a trap for catching animals or birds, but the word has come to have a broader meaning. 4. *soared:* flew through the air. Hawks *soar* above valleys, and baseballs *soar* when a batter hits a high fly. 5. *peripheral:* off to one side; not in the center of things. 6. *disparity:* inequality. Marge may have ranked 34th, but she insisted on the same accommodations (airplane seats and hotel rooms) as the top-ranking players.

Building Your Vocabulary

New words in natural settings

Films and theater

antagonist
documentary
choreographer
improvise
interlude
genre

1. The city council budgeted $500,000 to make a _____ film about its new mental health center.
2. After a brief musical _____, the curtain rose on the second act of Shakespeare's comedy.
3. "I'm particularly proud to be awarded this Oscar," she said, "because romances are my favorite _____ of film."
4. In those early James Cagney movies, it was usually a G-man or detective who was Jimmy's _____.
5. The brilliant young team of comics rarely work from a script; they _____ nearly every sketch they perform.
6. By the time she had grown too old for an active career as a dancer, she had begun to win notice as a _____.

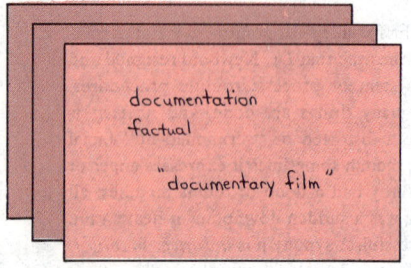

1. *documentary:* factual. Most *documentary* films explain a social, historical, or natural event as accurately as possible, using a narrator's (announcer's) voice rather than actors' speeches. 2. *interlude:* something that comes between the acts of a theatrical entertainment. The word's meaning extends beyond the theater to indicate any in-between period or activity, such as an *interlude* between wars. 3. *genre:* type, class, or style. The actress may have felt comfortable acting in comedies and mysteries, too, but romances were her favorite type of movie. 4. *antagonist:* a person who is opposed to another one; an *adversary.* The opposite of *antagonist* is *protagonist,* a person who is friendly—a hero. 5. *improvise:* invent, or make up as one goes along. 6. *choreographer:* a person who creates dances or ballets.

Food

piquant
cholesterol
mandatory
ramekin
complement
entails

1. Excess amounts of _____, a substance present in dairy products and animal fats, should be avoided.
2. More and more consumers are taking time to read the _____ information printed on food package labels.
3. Following her aunt's recipes, Molly made some of the most _____ sauces we ever had tasted.
4. Ron has become a popular host ever since he has learned that barbecuing _____ constant, extremely high heat.
5. They ended the meal with a _____ of custard for each guest.
6. In some Near Eastern recipes, raisins are used as a tasty _____ to rice.

mandatory

1. *cholesterol* is defined in the sentence. A doctor or nurse can advise you about diets that contain normal and excessive amounts of *cholesterol.* 2. *mandatory:* required by regulations. Laws require food manufacturers to list the ingredients of their products on the packages. *Mandates* are regulations that must be obeyed. 3. *piquant:* spicy; pleasantly sharp taste. The word is an uncommon one, but would make a fine addition to anyone's vocabulary. 4. *entails:* is a necessary part of an action or thing. Cooking over extremely high heat is a necessary part of barbecuing. In legal matters, to *entail* has a totally different meaning—to prevent the transfer of property or real estate: The building's title was *entailed,* so the owner was not allowed to sell it. 5. *ramekin:* a small dish, used for both baking and serving individual portions. 6. *complement:* something that *completes* a whole, or goes with another thing. To avoid confusing this word with *compliment* (making pleasant or flattering comments), remember that *complement* and *complete* both begin with *comple.*

Building Your Vocabulary

Law and courtroom procedure

ordinance
warrant
jeopardy
precedent
jurisdiction
arraignment

1. The court issued a search _____, and Sgt. Mellon made the arrest.
2. Within a week, he appeared at his _____ and entered a plea of "not guilty."
3. Mary had never heard of the antinoise _____, but still was ordered to pay the fine.
4. "This court has no _____ over matters in Jefferson County," the judge explained.
5. The Constitution prohibits trials that would put a defendant in double _____.
6. "This may set a _____ for families with similar problems," she told the judge.

1. *warrant:* a certificate authorizing an officer to make an arrest or search or seize property. 2. *arraignment:* a time at which an accused person is called before a court. *Arraignments* take place before trials are scheduled. 3. *ordinance:* a law or regulation. A similar word, lacking an "i," is *ordnance*; it has an entirely different meaning—military weapons and ammunition. 4. *jurisdiction:* the right and power to apply the law; or the territory in which a law is applied. Words that begin with *jur* refer to law—among them are *juror, jury,* and *jurisprudence* (formal study of the law). 5. *jeopardy:* risk or danger. In courtrooms, *jeopardy* refers to the danger of being found guilty and convicted. The Constitution states that a person can be tried only once for any crime; he cannot be put at risk twice for the same crime. 6. *precedent:* an action or legal decision that sets an example for similar cases that follow.

jurisdiction

"This court has no jurisdiction over matters in Jefferson County."

Books and reading

creed
squibs
narrative
paraphrase
appendix
prose

1. "To _____ Gertrude Stein," he wrote, "a dog is a dog is a dog."
2. Berryman had gained his reputation as a poet, but _____ seemed beyond his reach.
3. We looked carefully through the _____, but could not find the source of the statistics in chapter 4.
4. The author said that this is her _____: "Never take your writing too seriously—or too lightly."
5. It was a lively _____, but far too long to finish reading in one evening.
6. Young E. B. White got his start writing _____ that were published in newspapers of the day.

1. *paraphrase:* put someone else's writings or thoughts in your own language, or change them somewhat. Gertrude Stein, a noted author of the 1920's, had written "... a rose is a rose is a rose." 2. *prose:* ordinary speech or writing, not poetry. Novels and newspapers are written in *prose*. 3. *appendix:* additional material that "hangs" at the end of a book. 4. *creed:* a statement of belief or opinion. 5. *narrative:* story. A reporter might *narrate* a true story, while a comedian might *narrate* a series of jokes that he made up on his way to the studio. 6. *squibs:* short, usually humorous, items in a newspaper or magazine. *Squibs* are used by editors to fill the space at the bottom of a column of print.

creed

> "I believe in the supreme worth of the individual and in his right to life, liberty and the pursuit of happiness."
> —JOHN D. ROCKEFELLER, JR.

Building Your Vocabulary

New words in natural settings

Music

libretto
uninhibited
syncopated
searing
idiom
ovation

1. Until we got to New Orleans, we had never heard the wonderful tones of rhythmic, _____ riverboat music.
2. Her _____ high notes won Miss Larcher a Golden Recording award.
3. The audience rose to its feet in a wild, frenzied _____.
4. Ray Charles's vocal style was strongly influenced by a modern gospel _____.
5. Once he had the idea for an opera's music, Mozart searched for a poet who could write a suitable _____.
6. Her boisterous, _____ approach to country music made her a great favorite on the West Coast.

1. *syncopated:* music played with a strong beat where it might normally be expected to have a weaker beat. Dixieland music has a toe-tapping, *syncopated* quality. **2.** *searing:* literally means scorching or burning. In music, *searing* refers to extremely high notes, sung or played on an instrument. **3.** *ovation:* continued, enthusiastic applause. We often hear the phrase standing *ovation* to describe a wildly cheering audience that has risen to its feet in tribute to a performer. (Are you sure about the meaning of "frenzied" in sentence 3? Check it in the dictionary if you have any doubt.) **4.** *idiom:* a special style of artistic expression. Singers might be influenced by a gospel *idiom,* an operatic *idiom,* or any of many other schools of singing. The word more often refers to spoken or written language that is not easily understood by anyone who is a foreigner to that language. "Up to snuff" is an *idiomatic* expression. **5.** *libretto:* the words that are sung in an opera. **6.** *uninhibited:* unrestrained; not held back. A singer who lets herself go is *uninhibited.*

idiom
Special style of artistic expression.

libretto
words sung in an opera

Personalities

contagious
tenacity
affability
skylarking
boisterous
sarcastic

1. Marc's reputation for _____ helped when the vice president was deciding whom to make sales manager.
2. Not everyone appreciated Linda's _____ laughter, but her husband never failed to enjoy it.
3. When Linda laughed, Harry found it _____; it broke him up and left him gasping.
4. "I've had enough of his _____ comments," Hope complained. "He can't say a word without cutting my friends to ribbons."
5. His supervisor made Jess understand that a supermarket was no place for _____ and clowning around.
6. "With all the long faces you see around here," Mr. Watkins said, "Helen's _____ makes her a standout—she's a delight."

1. *tenacity:* holding fast to one's views; persistent. Probably, the aspect of Marc's *tenacity* that appealed most to his boss was Marc's habit of not giving up, even when the competition seemed likely to win. **2.** *boisterous:* loud, noisy, uncontrolled. **3.** *contagious:* spreading from one person to another; catching. Measles is a *contagious* disease; to Linda's husband, her laughter was a *contagious* emotion. **4.** *sarcastic:* remarks intended to be biting, cutting, belittling. *Sarcasm* is usually expressed as humor—but humor that is intended to ridicule someone or something. **5.** *skylarking:* frolicking and fooling around. **6.** *affability:* friendliness, gentleness.

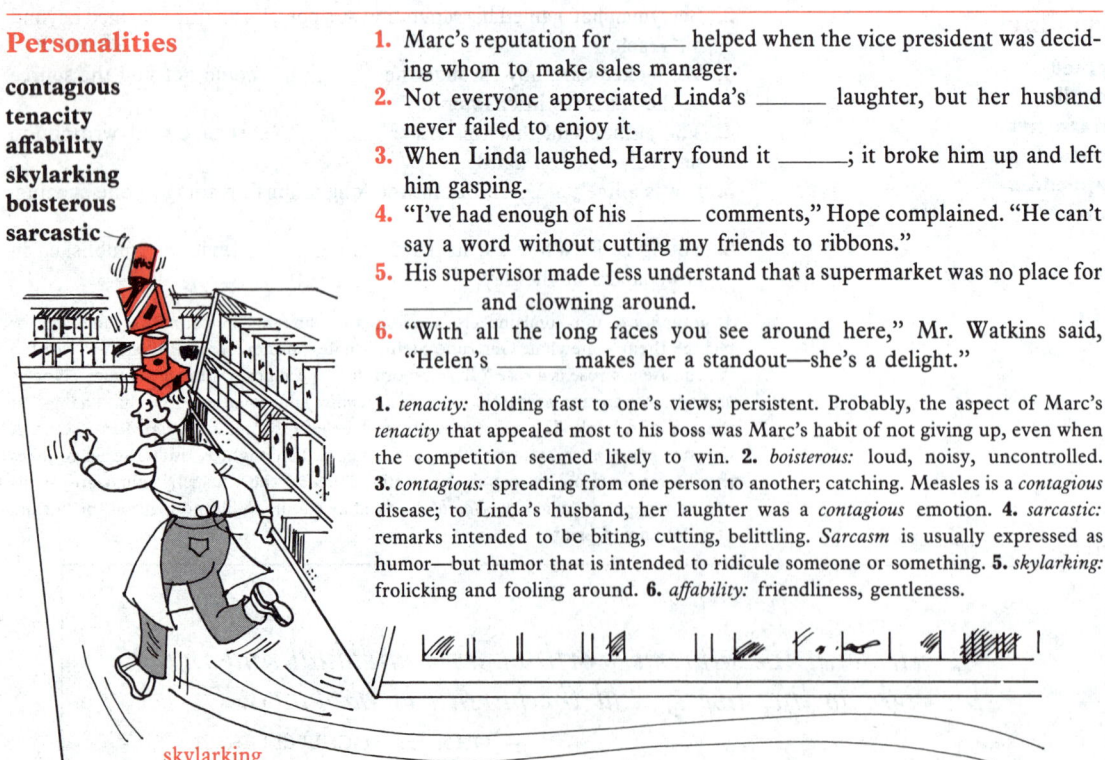

skylarking

Building Your Vocabulary

Gardening

herbicide
lobes
defoliate
prostrate
dormant
variegated

1. It was an uncommon type of ivy, with a streaked, _____ leaf.
2. Don paid no attention to the warning on the _____ label, so he killed all the grass in his front yard.
3. "Don't worry," she told me, "these bushes aren't dead. They are _____ in the winter."
4. The rounded _____ of the leaf were the size of half dollars.
5. It resembled a moss, lying low along the soil, but we learned it was a healthy _____ shrub.
6. It took the beetles only four days to completely _____ our entire crop of peas.

1. *variegated:* patches of different color. *Streaked* is an echo word that gives a strong clue to the meaning of *variegated.* **2.** *herbicide:* a substance that kills plants. Words ending in *icide* refer to *death—suicide,* killing oneself; *matricide,* killing one's mother; *fungicide,* killing fungi (mushroomlike plants). **3.** *dormant:* inactive, resting, seemingly asleep. *Dormant* plants grow leaves and become active in the spring. A related word, *dormitory,* means place where people sleep. **4.** *lobes:* rounded parts. You will recall that the rounded, lower part of your ear is called an *earlobe.* **5.** *prostrate:* in plants, growing flat along the ground. People who *prostrate* themselves bow or kneel down before a superior person; sometimes they throw themselves flat on the ground. **6.** *defoliate:* to remove all the leaves from a plant or tree. Leaves are referred to as *foliage;* to remove them is to *defoliate* them, as to remove frost from frozen food is to *defrost* it.

defoliate

Television

indispensable
vernacular
ennui
eclipsed
absorbed
chide

1. In surveys among American families, television has _____ radio in listener-hours per household.
2. It is the one medium _____ by all ages: small children, adolescents, young adults, and the elderly.
3. Politicians find television _____ for getting their messages into voters' households.
4. On newscasts, political candidates gain the opportunity to _____ their opponents and be seen by huge audiences.
5. "We ran my comedy series for five years, and then dropped it before _____ set in," she explained.
6. The newscaster's popularity was due, in part, to his use of the _____.

1. *eclipsed:* we know that as television has become more important over the years, radio has become less so. *Eclipse* originally referred to one star or planet being hidden behind another. It now means any person's or thing's giving way to a more popular one. **2.** *absorbed:* taken up. All ages are totally interested in watching television. A synonym is *engrossed.* **3.** *indispensable:* cannot do without; necessary. **4.** *chide:* scold, reprimand, or express disapproval. **5.** *ennui:* boredom, general dissatisfaction. (A French word, pronounced *ahn-we'.*) **6.** *vernacular:* commonly used language, as opposed to the more formal, literary language used in some books and newspapers.

vernacular

Building Your Vocabulary

Pairs, pears

Our language is laced with sets of words that sound alike—or enough alike to confuse many people—yet have entirely different meanings. On these pages we offer some of the most confusing of those pairs of words and their definitions. Be on the lookout, as you read and listen during the coming months, for additional pairs of "confusers." Adding these pairs to your *Word Power* file is a **diverting** way to build your vocabulary.

A military colonel *and a seed or grain called a* kernel *are pronounced the same but spelled very differently.*

annal, annual. An *annal* is a written chronicle or record of events. *The annals of baseball. Annual* means yearly. *We payed our annual taxes.*

arc, ark. An *arc* is a curved or arched shape resembling a rainbow. An *ark* is a boat. In the Old Testament, the *ark* was Noah's boat during the Flood.

ardorous, arduous. A person who is *ardorous* has strong emotions, enthusiasms, or love. An *arduous* task is a difficult one, filled with hardship.

bazaar, bizarre. *Bazaar* refers to one shop, or a street of shops, selling various items. *Bizarre* means odd or extraordinary. *A bizarre costume.*

carat, carrot. A *carat* (also spelled *karat*) is a unit of weight for gems and jewels. *A half-carat diamond. Carrots* are common, orange-colored vegetables.

cite, site. To *cite* is to mention or quote as proof. *Their record was cited in the* World Almanac. A *site* is a place, or the location of a building or group of buildings. *The mayor conducted an on-site inspection.*

colonel, kernel. A military *colonel* (ker'-nell) is an officer ranking above a lieutenant colonel and below a brigadier general. A *kernel* is a grain or seed, usually one that can be eaten.

deceased, diseased. A *deceased* person is a dead person. One who is *diseased* is sick, infected, cannot function normally.

decent, descent. A *decent* appearance or person is modest, not shocking, meeting accepted standards. *A decent rate of pay. Descent* is the act of moving downward. Sometimes it means following from. *She traced the descent of jazz from early 20th-century New Orleans to today.*

demean, demeanor. To *demean* oneself is to act in a way that causes a loss of dignity and respect. *Demeanor* is the manner in which a person conducts himself; a synonym is *deportment*.

flounder, founder. A *flounder* is a flat saltwater fish. To *flounder* means to flop around clumsily, like a fish out of water; to be off balance. To *founder* is to sink. *John quit the foundering company* means that John quit because the company was going under.

flout, flaunt. To *flout* means to disobey openly and scornfully. *He flouted the law.* To *flaunt,* on the other hand, means to display proudly or in a showy way. *She flaunted her new red dress. A man who flaunts his disrespect for women flouts the common courtesies of civilization.*

gauge, gouge. A *gauge* (gayj) is a meter or dial for measuring an activity or amount. It is also the act of measuring or estimating. A *gouge* (gowj) is a chisel-like tool, or the scooping-out action of such a tool.

hawk, hock. A *hawk* is a falcon, or eaglelike, bird. To *hawk* is slang for to sell by calling out. *He hawked programs in the theater lobby.* To *hock* is slang for to pawn—to pledge personal property in return for a cash loan.

impromptu, improper. An *impromptu* speech is one given without preparation or rehearsal. An *improper* action is one that is irregular, not suitable, offensive.

language, languish. *Language* is the spoken words and written symbols that humans use to communicate thoughts. To *languish* is to lose strength, to become feeble and weak; to lie around doing nothing; to be neglected.

lop, lope. To cut off, or trim, part of a bush or tree is to *lop* it off. To *lope* is to run, or to ride a horse, at a steady, even rate.

lucid, ludicrous. *Lucid* writing is easily understood; its meaning is clear. A person who is *lucid* is sane and can make himself understood. *Ludicrous* statements or actions are laughable, ridiculous, or absurd.

lumbar, lumber. *Lumbar* refers to the lower back. *She had a pinched nerve in her lumbar vertebrae. Lumber* is wood in the form of boards or planks.

miller, milliner. A *miller* mills, or grinds, grain into flour or meal. A *milliner* makes or sells women's hats.

morning, mourning. *Morning* is the early part of the day, from sunrise to noon. *Mourning* is grieving for the dead. *Bereavement* is a synonym for *mourning*.

noisome, noisy. A *noisome* odor is one that is foul or disgusting, or giving off dangerous fumes. *Noisy* means making sounds, usually loud and unwanted.

occult, oculist. *Occult* happenings are supernatural, unexplained, ghostly. An *oculist* is an eye doctor—sometimes called an *optometrist*.

pampas, pamper. The *pampas* is a huge grassy area of South America, principally in Argentina, much like our Western prairies. To *pamper* is to pay too much attention to one's own, or another's, desires. *Indulge* and *spoil* are synonyms for *pamper*.

pitfall, pitiful. *Pitfalls* are traps made by digging deep holes, then covering them over lightly. *Pitfall* also means a danger that is not easily seen. *Pitiful* means pathetic; arousing sorrow. Less charitably, it can mean inferior.

quarry. *Quarry* has two entirely different meanings: 1) an open mine or pit, as a gravel *quarry;* 2) a hunted animal, or a person who is pursued.

quota, quote. A *quota* is a number of persons or things. The number is calculated to make the *quota* become a certain share of the whole. To *quote* is to repeat or copy another's words. It also means to state a price.

rouse, ruse. To *rouse* (rhymes with *how's*) someone is to wake him from sleep, or excite him into activity. A *ruse* is a trick, or ploy, meant to mislead someone.

scarce, scares. A *scarce* item is one that is seldom seen or found; it is rare. A dog that *scares* the neighbors is one that frightens them.

several, severance. *Several* means more than two or three, but not many. *She drew several flowers in a bowl. Severance* is the act of cutting off or separating. *The company gave Ruth a large amount of severance pay.*

sheik, chic. A *sheik* is the leader of an Arab family or tribe. *Chic* (sheek) is a French word meaning stylish; sophisticated and classy.

slew. *Slew* has two entirely different meanings: 1) killed (the past form of *slay*); 2) a large amount of things or people. *We watched a whole slew of actors perform.*

stake, steak. A wooden or metal *stake* is sharp at one end, which is hammered into the ground. A *steak* is the familiar cut of beef or other meat.

tracked, tract. *Tracked* is the past form of to *track*, to follow footprints or other traces or also to observe. *The police tracked her on their radar. Tract* has two meanings: 1) a piece of property or land; 2) a booklet or paper stating a special point of view, such as a political *tract*.

vanish, varnish. To *vanish* is to disappear; to be no longer able to be seen. *Varnish* is a paintlike coating for surfaces, usually wooden. It leaves a hard, smooth finish.

Groups of word parts

In classrooms and textbooks, it has long been the custom to teach vocabulary lessons through *word parts*. This method is also called *derivations*, because many of our English words are *derived* from (*came* from, or *arrived* from) Latin and Greek terms.

In all likelihood, you are not a student of Latin or Greek, so you will **benefit** from the more practical nonderivative techniques for building *Word Power* in this section of your handbook. Yet, you should still know just a few word-source facts.

ben, the first part of *benefit*, is called a *prefix*. *Ben* means good, and the whole word means good deed or advantage. Other words starting with *ben* are *benediction*, good speech or blessing; and *benevolent*, kindly, or one who is charitable.

Here are four of the hundreds of word parts that form our modern English language.

aud—hear
    audience—people gathered to hear an event
    audition—hear actors or musicians demonstrate their skills
    audiophile—person extremely interested in hearing sounds, particularly electronic reproduction

locut, loqu—to talk, speak
    loquacious—talkative; garrulous
    colloquy—conversation; talking together
    ventriloquist—person who makes his voice "come from his stomach"
    interlocutor—person who speaks between, or interrupts.
    soliloquy—one person's thoughts; a speech by one person in a play

nav—ship
    naval—pertaining to ships or a navy
    navigable—water deep enough to sail on
    navigate—to control the course of a ship or an airplane

pend—to hang, or be inclined toward
    pendulum—hangs from a clock's works
    depend—to hang on, or need, someone or something
    impending—hanging on, or waiting, for an event to take place
    appendage—a connected part, perhaps hanging from the main part

Building Your Vocabulary

15 days to a forceful vocabulary

Studies have shown that the average American uses relatively few words—about 2000—for normal conversation. That same person may recognize another 12,000 to 13,000 words when he hears or sees them. But he hesitates to try them; he feels uncomfortable because he is not certain of the meanings of the words.

If you have been adding 40 or more words a week to your working vocabulary, you are moving far ahead of the average. Here is a way to boost your rate even higher. In just 15 days, you can add approximately 125 new terms to your working stock. Spend only 15 minutes a day beyond your regular *Word Power* activities and you will have accomplished that gain in less than three weeks!

Each day's activity is designed to be stimulating and enjoyable. Yet, before you start, keep in mind that there is nothing magical about the number "15." If an unexpected drain on your time prevents you from working the plan suggested for day six on the day following day five, do not be concerned. As long as you eventually get back to the routine, and maintain your *Word Power* file at the same time, the plan will work.

DAY 1: A few cents' worth

A daily newspaper is the easiest and least expensive source of new words. For variety and added challenge, get a copy of an out-of-town paper: one from the largest city in your state or a neighboring state. Or get a Washington, D.C., Houston, or New York daily, or *The Wall Street Journal*.

Make a list of eight or ten words that you are not sure about, and the sentences in which you find them. Using your dictionary, add them to your *Word Power* file.

Here are eight sentences, slightly paraphrased, from papers published on the same day in Illinois, Florida, and California.

1. Hungary was the first Soviet **bloc** nation to question the agricultural policy.
2. As he has during much of his **tenure,** Mr. Richards took issue with the district attorney.
3. "We cannot continue to operate on this level, at only half of our full sales **potential**."
4. All except one commander agreed to a **phased** withdrawal of the land forces.
5. Eight more terrorists were seen on the **outskirts** of the city.
6. His manager demanded an aplogy, saying, "They cannot call Sam a **demagogue** and get away with it."
7. The state of Colorado argued that it had not **delegated** that authority to Boulder.
8. "They never actually said we lied, but I do believe the word **prevaricate** was heard."

1. *bloc:* a group of organizations, nations, or persons united for a common purpose. **2.** *tenure:* the time during which a person holds an office or a job. **3.** *potential:* capability for growth that has not yet been realized. **4.** *phased:* done in stages. In *phase* one they pulled out the tanks, in *phase* two the artillery. **5.** *outskirts:* parts away from the central area; the *periphery.* **6.** *demagogue:* an unprincipled political leader who appeals to the emotions of citizens. **7.** *delegated:* a person or organization authorized to act for, or represent, another. **8.** *prevaricate:* to avoid the truth, or twist it to one's purposes.

224

Building Your Vocabulary

DAY 2: Upping the price slightly

Move upward, in price and degree of specialization, from newspapers to magazines. The periodicals that are most widely read—*People, Time, Cosmopolitan,* and *Reader's Digest,* among others—are good sources of vocabulary-stretching words.

Any single issue is almost sure to provide several useful additions to your *Word Power* file. The sentences to the right were gathered from just three magazines.

1. Reservation services often are **biased** in an airline's favor.
2. Pain caused by bursitis can become **excruciating** with the slightest movement.
3. A mix of traditional English and American styles produced the rich **patina** of years.
4. It was a **premise** stated with authority, but one we had great difficulty accepting.
5. I had become **adept** at using the smaller keyboard.
6. Pat's high school ring had something resembling an **amethyst** at the center.
7. **Trend**-conscious designers abandoned the "layered look."

1. *biased:* prefers one person or thing; prejudiced. **2.** *excruciating:* intensely, agonizingly painful. **3.** *patina:* appearance of aging. Originally, a thin coating of brown or green on bronze or other metals. **4.** *premise:* an underlying or basic statement that can be assumed to be true. **5.** *adept:* skillful. **6.** *amethyst:* a purple semiprecious stone. **7.** *trend:* movement toward a new fashion or style.

DAY 3: Name-words

Late in the 19th century, all across the United States people watched for news of the completion of the Brooklyn Bridge. Knowing it was the focus of so much attention, a publicity-seeking young man called the newspapers, climbed one of the towers, and dived into the East River. He survived the dive, and his name survives in the language as a synonym for "high dive" or "publicity stunt." He was Steve Brody, the originator of "taking a Brody."

Once you know the stories behind some of the names that have become often-used words in our language, it becomes easier to remember their meanings and how they are used. Here is a group of such words—some of them derived from names, others from places.

Annie Oakley: a free pass to a show or concert is called an *Annie Oakley*. Annie was a star of Buffalo Bill Cody's Wild West Show in the 1890's; she shot holes in playing cards and other small targets. A free ticket, punched full of holes, reminded people of her act.

bowdlerize: to take out from, or change, portions of a book that are thought to be offensive. In 1818 an Englishman, Thomas Bowdler, published an edition of Shakespeare's plays "suitable for reading aloud to a family." Bowdlerized versions of stories or plays often are weaker and less effective than the originals.

boycott: to refuse to have anything to do with a person or thing. Captain Boycott was a land agent in Ireland who was shunned by everyone because he bought up the property of evicted farmers.

billingsgate: rude, abusive, often foul language. A fishmarket has been located for centuries near the ancient London tower of Billingsgate. The language used there by fish merchants gave rise to the word.

donnybrook: a brawl or free-for-all commotion. Yearly, in Donnybrook, Ireland, a fair was held. Every year there were said to be blackened eyes, bloodied noses, and many arrests.

Draconian: extremely harsh. Draco was a Greek lawmaker who ruled that death must be the punishment for all crimes, even small ones. A *Draconian* measure is a severe ruling.

gerrymander: to divide a voting district into parts that give an unfair advantage to one party. Elbridge Gerry, 1744–1814, was a governor of Massachusetts who created an odd-shaped election district that looked like a salamander.

malapropism: a comical confusion of words, especially those that sound alike ("a shrewed (for rude) awakening"). The word comes from Mrs. Malaprop in a famous comedy, *The Rivals,* by Richard Sheridan.

gerrymander

Building Your Vocabulary

DAY 4: Time-words

Hundreds of words in our language have *prefixes*, or parts placed in front of a main stem, that give a special meaning to the word. Some of the most commonly used prefixes indicate *time;* that is, one action's occurrence in relation to another's. Looking at a few examples of the way these prefixes work is the easiest way to understand prefixes that indicate time.

rebound
bounce back

ante (Latin): before
 antebellum before the Civil War (*bellum* = war).
 antedate at a time before the time mentioned.
archa (Greek): old
 archaeology the study of old (ancient) life and culture.
 archaic belonging to a much earlier time.
neo (Greek): new
 neoclassicism revival of classical form in arts.
 neologism a recently invented word or phrase.
 neonate a newborn infant.
post (Latin): after
 postdate to use a date, as on a check, later than the actual date.
 postmeridian afternoon (*meridian* is the highest part of the sun's course across the sky).
pre (Latin): before
 preadolescence a child's age, ten to twelve, before adolescence.
 predict to say, or make known, before an act happens.
 premature growing or existing before the customary time.
re (Latin): again
 rebound bounce back again.
 recognize know something or someone again.
 rehearse practice in preparation for a performance (originally, hear again).

DAY 5: Your lucky number

As a change from yesterday's word-gathering based on formations and derivations from classical languages, try this relaxer. Write down any seven numbers from one to one thousand—roughly, the number of pages in your dictionary. Then turn to each of those numbered pages. Select any unknown words on those pages that come to your notice. Make a *Word Power* card for them, and put the cards in your file.

Here are ten "lucky number words" chosen by one word-collector on a recent evening.

deride (p. 204 in his dictionary): to speak with scorn, laughter, or contempt; to ridicule.
astral (p. 45): of or about the stars; star-shaped.
nectar (p. 501): the drink of the mythic gods; any sweet or delicious drink.
polyp (p. 579): a growth in the lining of the stomach, nose, or other body part.
extort (p. 267): to gain something by forcing it from another person, often by threats or intimidation.
compunction (p. 155): a sense of guilt; uneasiness.
legume (p. 428): a plant, eaten as a vegetable, that bears seeds in a pod (as peas or beans).
sobriquet (p. 709): a nickname; an alias or assumed name.
triturate (p. 800): to grind or crush into a very fine powder; to chew thoroughly.
quadruped (p. 609): any animal with four feet.

---

legroom   428   **leprechaun**

of mutton: said of a sleeve that puffs out toward the shoulder, etc.
leg·room (leg′room′) *n.* adequate space for the legs while seated, as in a car
leg·ume (leg′yoom, li gyoom′) *n.* [< Fr. < L. *legumen* < *legere*, to gather] **1.** any of a large family of plants, including the peas, beans, clovers, etc., with fruit that is a pod splitting along two sutures: many legumes are nitrogen-fixing **2.** the pod or seed of some members of this family, used for food
le·gu·mi·nous (li gyoo′min əs) *adj.* **1.** of, having the nature of, or bearing legumes **2.** of the family of plants to

length·en (-'n) *vt., vi.* to make or become longer —**length′-en·er** *n.*
length·wise (-wiz′) *adv., adj.* in the direction of the length: also **length′ways′** (-wāz′)
length·y (-ē) *adj.* **length′i·er, length′i·est** long; esp. too long —**length′i·ly** *adv.* —**length′i·ness** *n.*
le·ni·ent (lē′ni ənt, lēn′yənt) *adj.* [< L. prp. of *lenire*, to soften < *lenis*, soft] not harsh or severe in disciplining, judging, etc.; mild; merciful —**le′ni·en·cy,** *pl.* **-cies, le′ni·ence** *n.* —**le′ni·ent·ly** *adv.*
Len·in (len′in; *Russ.* lye′nyin), **V(ladimir) I(lyich)** (orig. surname *Ulyanov*: also called **Nikolai Lenin**) 1870-1924; *Russ.* Communist revolutionary leader; premier of the

DAY 6: The study of studies

Any word that ends in *ology* refers to the study of, or the science of, the subject named in the first part of the word. Since that hard-to-know first part is sometimes a Greek or Latin word, your job is not easy. **Dermatology,** for example, is the study of the skin—and a **dermatologist** is a doctor who specializes in that study.

As your working vocabulary widens, you will find many basic word parts appearing again and again. You will recognize *derm* as part of *hypodermic*—under the skin—and the meaning of *dermatologist* will be reinforced.

For now, here are 14 *study of* words. They will form the **nucleus** (core; center) of this part of your vocabulary.

anthropology: the study of the biologic history and habits of mankind.
archaeology: the study of ancient civilizations through buildings, pottery, and other traces that remain.
biology: the study of life processes and living organisms.
chronology: time-connected studies. The word has come to mean a sequence of events, as they took place in time.
entomology: the study of insects.
etymology: the study of words—how they originated and how they took their present form. (Do not confuse this word with the previous one. There is an "n" in *insect*—and none in *etymology*.)
geology: the study of the structure and development of Earth's crust and its strata.
ichthyology: the study of fish.
meteorology: the study of the atmosphere.
oenology: the study of wine making.
ornithology: the study of birds.
philology: the study of languages and their development.
psychology: the study of the mind, mental processes, and the way humans respond to events around them.
theology: the study of religion.

DAY 7: Words that are *before*

We have already seen two word parts that mean *before* in the sense of time, or when an event happened. One is *ante;* the other is *pre*. Both come to us from Latin and are in common use. Another Latin word part that we use frequently also means before, but in the sense of in front of, concerned with space rather than time. It is *pro,* the first syllable of the following nine words.

proboscis: a long, flexible nose, as of an elephant. Also, an insect's noselike feeding tube. A human nose, if large, is sometimes called a *proboscis*.
proceed: to go before.
prodigal: wasteful, reckless, extravagant. The word's origin is not easily recognized in English, but in Latin it means driving recklessly ahead.
produce: to bring forth, make, or give rise to. Its roots are in *to lead forward*.
profile: the outline of a human head or other object. Also, an essay, graph, or table summarizing an idea or thing; it goes before a full, extended description.
program: a listing of events. It is writing that comes before the event.
progress: movement forward, or toward a goal.
prologue: a short speech or dramatic action presented before a play begins.
promontory: a high ridge of land extending out into the sea.

proboscis

Building Your Vocabulary

DAY 8: Words that are *against,* and some that are *with*

It is possible that this sudden **immersion** (dunking; a teabag is *immersed* in hot water) into the ancient roots of words has proved confusing. So day eight will be used to clarify a few of the ideas that may have bewildered you.

Take **ante,** for example. We saw that it is Latin and that it means before, or earlier, as in *antedate.* But how about **antifreeze?** The answer lies in the spelling. *Ante* with an "e" means before—*anti* with an "i" means against, or opposing. Some of the *opposing* words are **antibacterial, antibody, anticlimax, anticlockwise, antidepressant, antimagnetic, antipoverty,** and **antitrust.**

You may have wondered where, among all those **pro** words, was **con**—as in "they argued *pro and con* the new rent laws." *Con* is short for the Latin *contra,* meaning against. The full *contra* is used in such English words as *contrary, contraband,* and *contravene.*

When you do see *con* at the beginning an English word, it nearly always means together, or with. These are some typical uses of *con* as the first syllable of a word:

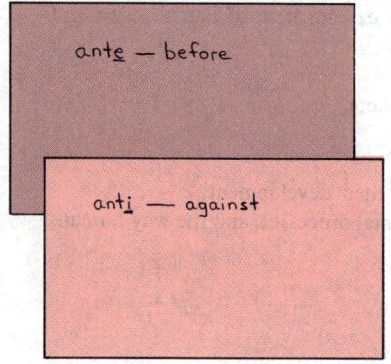

concentrate: to direct or bring together toward a common center.
concert: to work (or produce music) together.
conclave: a secret meeting.
concrete: real, existing things. *A table is a concrete object.* Also, a construction material of mortar or cement mixed together with pebbles or stones.
confabulate: to talk informally, or chat, together.
confederate: an ally, accomplice, or fellow member in a *conspiracy.*
congest: to overfill; bring together too many.
connect: to unite, join, or fasten together.

DAY 9: Culling the classroom

Does a neighbor, or a friend, have a son who is in junior high school? Or does your cousin's daughter go to high school or college not far from where you live? If you know someone who regularly attends school, enlist his or her help in your *Word Power* campaign.

Just ask your helping student to be on the lookout, in the books he reads and the assignments he does, for words he does not recognize. Instead of passing them by, ask him to note them on a piece of paper.

You will notice that the heading for day nine reads "**Culling** the classroom." Is *culling* an unfamiliar term? To *cull* is to select, or gather, from a place; here, to collect new words from the classroom. Here is a typical day's catch.

savant: one who knows many answers; a wise person. (A French word that means knowing.)
perfunctory: done in a routine, uninspired manner; careless; merely getting the job done.
levity: a joking, light manner; frivolity.
matrix: the surrounding environment in which an object is found. *Her ambition must be viewed within the matrix of her family's poverty.*
exacting: making severe demands. *Joan objected to her employer's exacting requirements.*
corpulent: fat; obese.
grapple: to hold or seize something or someone; to struggle, wrestle. A *grappling iron* is a large hook, dragged along a river bottom to seize submerged objects or drowned persons.
jetty: a large pier or wharf that protects a harbor or coastline from damage by the tide.
correlate: to compare or connect in a systematic way.
riposte: a quick retort or counterattack.
fatuous: foolish, silly.
propitious: favorable.
marauding: going in search of plunder or prey.
perverse: obstinately doing something different from what is reasonable or expected.
recondite: refers to an obscure subject, or to writing about an obscure subject.

DAY 10: Largeness

Think about those times when you have tried to describe to someone something you have seen earlier in the day. It was a big accident, or a big crowd, or something else much larger than ordinary. You probably had to hesitate to find exactly the right word—and settled for "huge" or "very big."

That need not happen again. There are dozens of easily used words for expressing *bigness*, and each of them has a distinct, separate meaning. Learn most of them on this list, and you will have made an **imposing** gain in your *Word Power*.

vast: very great area, space, or number of things. *A vast acreage of forest.*
immense: extremely large; so vast it cannot be measured.
substantial: a large number or size; large enough to be worthy of notice.
expansive: open and wide; capable of growing larger or stretching. *We saw an expansive stretch of beach.*
mammoth: huge. *Mammoths* were prehistoric forms of elephants; the word often describes giant animals or people.
monster: actually means "a frightening creature." Has come to mean an abnormally large person or object.
massive: bulky; a very large organism or undertaking. *The Girl Scouts undertook a massive charity drive.*
monumental: outstanding; enduring; remembered; amazing. *She displayed monumental ability to overcome disease.*
towering: higher than all surrounding objects; outstanding in its group or class.
tremendous: extremely large; enormous. Actually means "so large it makes one tremble."
enormous: immense; tremendous. Actually means "so large it is abnormal."

mammoth
petite

DAY 11: Smallness

When it is not the idea of largeness that makes us pause and search for just the right word, it is often the very opposite **concept** (idea)—smallness.

It is not hard to come up with, say, *tiny* when we want to express extreme smallness: The doll's house contained the *tiniest* table and chair I've ever seen.

Sometimes, though, *tiny* and *very small* do not seem exactly right. For those times, here is a collection of words expressing smallness. Some may be ones you know, others may be unfamiliar. All will add strength to your *Word Power* abilities.

diminutive: of very small size. Also, a name that indicates smallness, as *booklet* for "a small book."
minute (min-oot'): exceptionally small; too small for ordinary notice. The Latin *min* in a word almost always indicates smallness, as in *miniature* and *diminish*.
pygmy: an individual or object of unusually small stature (height). Called after a race of African or Asian people who are about 4 feet tall.
infinitesimal: an amount or thing so small it cannot be measured.
insignificant: an amount or thing too small to matter; easily ignored or overlooked.
trace: a barely visible amount.
speck: a very small bit, or spot, or mark.
petite (peh-teet'): dainty, fragile. From the French word for *little*.
bantam: diminuitive, miniature. From a small, domestic fowl.
microscopic: too small to be seen.
midget: extremely small. From midge, a very small, gnatlike insect.
grain: a small particle, such as a *grain of sand*.
mite: a very small quantity, such as *a mite of sympathy*.

Building Your Vocabulary

DAY 12: Words about words

As you learn more words, you will find it interesting to learn more *about* words. There is, in fact, a whole body of terms that describes specific aspects of word study. Some of those terms you already have added to your *Word Power* file: *etymology* and *neologism* are two. You will rediscover two more in this list.

The word acronym is a good one to learn. Here MADD stands for "Mothers Against Drunken Driving."

lexicography: the work of putting together a dictionary. A person who does this work is a **lexicographer,** and the dictionary itself is a **lexicon.** *Lexicon* also refers to the special terms used in a trade or profession. *The word "quit" was not in the ballplayers' lexicon.*

linguistic: relating to language, or a person who speaks several languages.

locution: a style of speaking; words and phrases used in a style of speaking.

acronym: a word formed by the initial letters of an organization or name, as EPA for Environmental Protection Agency.

provincial: an unsophisticated, heavily rustic word or term, as *taters* instead of *potatoes*.

homonym: a word that sounds like another word: *pail* and *pale*, or *shear* and *sheer*. (You already know the other two terms of the *nym* trio—*antonym* and *synonym*.)

interjection: a word that stands alone and expresses sudden thoughts or emotions. *Darn!* and *Oops!* are interjections. They often come between *(inter)* other thoughts.

usage: the way that a word expresses a thought in a language. See volume 1, pages 272-283 for explanations of correct modern English *usage*.

DAY 13: Free—on the shelves

The fullest, most "official" dictionary—the *Oxford English Dictionary* (O.E.D.)—gives the meanings of more than 500,000 words. Several million words are devoted to those definitions; the complete, multivolume O.E.D. is too heavy for an average man or woman to lift.

Yet right on the nearest shelf of your local library is nearly as good a source of *Word Power*—and easily lifted, too. It is any book that you pick out, skim through—or read fully, if the subject interests you—and from which you select unknown words. Why nearly as good as the OED? Because you see the words in context, actually being used by a writer.

Here, from a book about a scandal in New York City's Department of Water Supply, Gas and Electricity (*A Percentage of the Take*, by Walter Goodman) are a handful of words as they appear, together with their meanings. (The sentences have been shortened for inclusion here.)

That story was **diligently** *reported in the city's newspapers.* Carefully; conscientiously; done with unsparing effort.

What is striking is the **passivity** *of the press.* Accepting without argument, inquiry, or objection.

Marcus's comments about toughness **comprised** *a great deal of the conversation.* Filled.

He was a man whose profession required that a grudge not be lightly **relinquished.** Given up; abandoned; put aside.

This version contains an **inherent implausibility.** *Inherent:* an essential part; without it, the whole could not exist. *Implausibility:* difficulty in believing. (An important part of this version is difficult to believe, so it is difficult to believe the entire story.)

The newspaper commented on Albano's **"adroit** *footwork."* Nimble, agile.

The lawyer had appeals of his own for the **neophyte** *politician, whose hold was* **faltering.** *Neophyte:* beginner or novice. *Faltering:* slipping, missing one's step; beginning to make mistakes.

His stock began a **precipitous** *drop.* Steep; dropping sharply, as when falling off a *precipice* (cliff).

Observers regarded the electric company as highly **paternal** *to its employees.* Like a father. (Providing many of the needs of the employees beyond their salaries.)

230   Building Your Vocabulary

DAY 14: Sending out scouts

Your campaign to improve your vocabulary need not be a **solitary** one (done by one person only—you). It will make your project considerably more interesting if you let others participate in it.

If you have a neighbor who works in an auto showroom, for example, have him or her bring you ten words that are used in the trade. Or your cousin may work for the phone company. What are some new words that he has heard? Here is a sampling of what you might expect from two kinds of "word scouts."

Sheriff's assistant

deterrent: something that prevents or discourages an action. *Increasing the police force would be a deterrent to crime.*
larceny: theft or robbery.
recidivism: slipping back into criminal behavior after being released from prison.
subpoena (suh-peen´-a): an order requiring the receiver to appear in court.

Carpenter/housing contractor

ferrule: a metal ring near the end of a wooden pole or tool handle, to prevent splitting.
shim: a thin wedge of wood or metal, used to level parts or fill spaces.
miter: cutting each of two surfaces at a 45° angle, to form a right angle when they are joined.
rabbet: a groove cut into a piece of wood, in which another piece of wood will be glued or screwed.

DAY 15: Tripling your list

During the past 14 days you have added more than 125 new words to your working vocabulary. No need for you to be modest about it—that is an extraordinary leap beyond the average person's rate of word **accretion** (gradual growth by adding or including new material) and you deserve congratulations.

Better yet, you can triple—or at least double—your number of new words by going back over the 14 formulas and reworking them. Use them to produce two or three sets of all-new words.

Be flexible. If you are not too sure about day six techniques, or if you feel uncomfortable with day eight, skip them. Try to concentrate on those days' plans that interest you the most.

You probably will find a thesaurus extremely helpful, if not essential. Turn now to the *Roget's University Thesaurus* at the back of this book. Study it carefully. Look up some general subjects and add the words you do not know to your *Word Power* file.

Or working at a library—at least in the planning stage of your tripling-up project—may give you just the help you need. You will find the librarian, who works with words all day, a knowledgeable, helpful collaborator.

Building Your Vocabulary

Preparing for vocabulary tests

Any time you are applying for some step upward—admission to college, or a new job, or a promotion—there seems to be a vocabulary test involved.

That is because a broad vocabulary is recognized as a reliable indicator of intelligence (and, often, education). Also, vocabulary tests are easy to administer and to score: they are right or wrong, pass or fail, with no maybes or gray areas.

Now that you have a significantly improved vocabulary, be sure you know the ins and outs of testing.

Confidence. For most of us, an attitude of *I'm going to win* goes a long way toward making us actually win. Salesmen who know they are going to make that sale, even before they walk in the door, are much more likely to get the order.

This will hold true for you when you are faced with a vocabulary test. You have worked on the plans and strategies and projects in these pages. You have built an impressive *Word Power* file. So be confident.

Samples. Know beforehand, as exactly as possible, the kinds of questions you will be asked to answer. There are four commonly used forms of vocabulary questions. They are explained on these pages, and samples are provided for extra practice; see also pages

Four forms of questions

1. Select the appropriate word or term that is most nearly the same in meaning as the capitalized word.

   Sample: **ignite**   a) look away   b) put out   c) set fire   d) sleep

   There are no context clues, so it is necessary to know or recognize the words themselves in this type of test. Be aware that one or two wrong answers are designed to mislead you. *Look away* might make you think of *ignore,* which could be confused with *ignite;* and *sleep* might relate to the *nite* (night) sound in *ignite.* The right answer is c) *set fire.* Here are some practice questions.

joggle	a) shake slightly	b) run slowly	c) ankle	d) turn a corner
seance	a) after	b) rabbit	c) sofa	d) meeting
buzzard	a) saw	b) fox	c) intestines	d) vulture
evict	a) send to jail	b) put out	c) raise up	d) saying
align	a) line up	b) marker	c) insult	d) press down

   answers: joggle, a; seance, d; buzzard, d; evict, b; align, a.

2. For each statement, select the choice that best completes it or answers the question.

   Sample: To be **profuse** with compliments means to
   a) be obscene   b) give them freely   c) withhold them   d) be vague

   Your only clue is the prefix *pro,* which we have seen means *forward* or *in front of.* Among the four choices, all have a negative or backward implication, except b). To be *profuse* means to give freely, even extravagantly. There is no easy way to answer type 2 questions; the more words you know, the better you will do. Practice with these typical questions.

   Farmland that is **parched** is
   a) elevated   b) dry   c) flooded   d) posted

   A **turquoise** would most likely be found in a
   a) zoo   b) tunnel   c) bracelet   d) restaurant

   A **seamy** neighborhood is
   a) sordid   b) morbid   c) elegant   d) hot

   The **barrage** consisted of
   a) wooden sheds   b) gunfire   c) tiles   d) clear plastic

   Who gave the **compress** to Jason?
   a) a barber   b) a carpenter   c) a nurse   d) a teacher

   answers: parched, b; turquoise, c; seamy, a; barrage, b; compress, c.

Building Your Vocabulary

328-333 for more help on taking tests.

Usually, you can obtain copies of last year's test, or special review copies of tests similar to the one you will be taking. They are in review books and easily obtainable from a guidance counselor, library, or the testing organization itself.

Learn the rules. Should you guess at answers you are not quite sure of? Or are points taken off your score for wrong answers? And what about time? How many minutes will you be allowed?

When you practice for a particular vocabulary test, you will want to do it under conditions that are much like those under which the real test is administered. You should become accustomed to working within a time frame similar to the actual one. If there is no penalty for wrong answers, and there usually is not, you should practice guessing at every question.

The school, government office, or employer that will be testing you will answer your questions well in advance of test day. Phone or drop by in person. Make sure you are talking to someone who really knows the procedures, not a clerk who is only guessing.

Relax. Do not put unnecessary pressure on yourself as you prepare for the test. Cramming until late the night before the test guarantees that you will be groggy on the big day. There is no need for last-minute panic if you have been building *Word Power* day by day, week by week.

Know exactly how you will get to the test place, and plan to arrive ten or fifteen minutes early, with a pocket full of extra pens and pencils. Then relax and let your *Word Power* take over.

---

3. Each question consists of four pairs of words. In one pair among the four, both words have the same meaning: they are synonyms. Select that pair.

Sample: a) magnify-diminish   b) section-partition   c) capitulate-defy   d) encrust-salvage

By looking closely at all four pairs, you may recall that *diminish* means "to make smaller," and is the opposite of *magnify*. *Capitulate* and *defy* are opposites, too; and though you may not be sure about d), you probably will recognize that in b) a *section* and a *part* are the same thing. Your answer is b). See how well you do with these practice questions.

1. a) simile-quote   b) monastery-monograph   c) bisect-divide   d) create-basket
2. a) deprecate-belittle b) crass-cliff   c) ominous-many   d) biology-oculist
3. a) captain-demagogue b) curator-bishop   c) fiasco-failure   d) flagrant-tramp
4. a) familiar-intimate b) recognize-venal   c) proximity-distance   d) thermal-sunshine
5. a) tripod-oyster   b) confide-trust   c) reveal-conceal   d) unite-sever

answers: 1 c; 2 a; 3 c; 4 a; 5 b.

---

4. For each of the following statements, select T if the statement is *true*, F if is *false*.

Sample: A **parable** is a type of umbrella.   T F
The question was designed to mislead you slightly. A sunshade, very much like an umbrella, is called a *parasol*. But a *parable* is a story illustrating a religious or moral lesson, so the correct answer is F. Decide if each of these examples is true or false.

1. A **saga** is a long story or report.   T F
2. A **terminal** is the last car of a railroad train.   T F
3. To **mediate** is to apply bandages to a wound or a rash.   T F
4. **Archives** are written records.   T F
5. **Largesse** is a large, generous gift.   T F

answers: 1. T; 2. F (a *caboose* is the last car; a *terminal* is a station at the end of the line, or the final portion of a thing); 3. F (to *mediate* is to come between two opposing parties, to resolve their differences); 4. T; 5. T.

Building Your Vocabulary

American English

American English is made up, to a large extent, of borrowings from the many immigrants who arrived on U.S. shores, each speaking his native tongue. Even the American Indians were immigrants, arriving across a land bridge to Alaska from Asia that no longer exists. And they brought their language with them, too.

American Indian. Among the words that Indians have given to modern American English are **tomahawk; moccasin; wigwam; tepee;** and **cayuse** (horse). Probably, the Indians' most lasting contribution is place names. Consider the following states:

Arkansas: land of south wind people.
Idaho: light on the mountains.
Illinois: warriors (**Chicago,** for some reason, meant place that smells bad).
Iowa: the sleepy people, referring to a local tribe of the Dakota nation.
Kentucky: meadowland.
Minnesota: sky-blue water.
Mississippi: big river.

Spanish. The Indians of the Southwest mingled closely with the Spanish settlers of that territory. The area attracted pioneers from the settled eastern colonies, and the mingled westerners put their own stamp on the language. These cowboy terms are Spanish in origin: **buffalo** (explorer DeSoto's word for our native bison); **chaps** (short for *chaparejos,* a cowboy's leather leg protectors); **cinch; corral; buckaroo** (derived from Spanish *vaquero*); **lariat; lasso; pinto** (spotted horse); **rodeo; pronto; canyon; loco; cabana; fiesta; hombre; siesta; tequila; tortilla; vamoose.** We call a low island a **key** and a common insect pest a **cockroach;** both terms are based on similar Spanish words. If we want someone to leave in a hurry, we tell him to **vamoose**—one more Spanish borrowing.

African. When slaves were shipped to America in chains, they brought with them African words that were converted to the nation's growing language. Among them are **banana; banjo; goober** (peanut); **juke** (to misbehave, much later adapted to mean a tavern music player, or *jukebox*); **tote** (carry).

The various waves of settlers brought with them customs and words they used in their new homes. Dutch, French, English, German, Scandinavian, Italian, and many, many other ethnic groups contributed to the growing language. Here are a few borrowings.

Dutch

bedspread	**cookie**	**sauerkraut**
boss	**hex**	**sleigh**
bush	**landscape**	**waffle**
cole slaw	**Santa Claus**	**Yankee**

French

barrage	**depot**	**music**
castle	(railroad station)	**pantry**
chowder	**détente**	**parlor**
crime	(easing of tensions)	**prairie**
dance	**manor**	**procession**

Among French place names are **Baton Rouge** (LA), red stick; **Des Moines** (IA), the monks; **Terre Haute** (IN), high ground; **Vermont,** green mountain; and **Louisiana,** for King Louis XIV.

German

and how	**dumb**	**klutz**
bub	**ecology**	(clumsy person)
bum	**frankfurter,**	**phooey**
(loafer, tramp)	**hamburger**	**pumpernickel**
check	(styles of meat	**vampire**
(restaurant bill)	served in	("to vamp,"
dachshund	Frankfurt and	bewitch)
delicatessen	Hamburg)	

Italian. A nation of brilliant cooks and dedicated eaters, Italians changed forever the composition of American menus. Among the additions:

espresso	**macaroni**	**spaghetti**
lasagna	**ravioli**	**tortoni**

And, of course, **pizza.** Contrary to legend, the word does not mean pie. It refers to pinching or plucking the dough, as in the musical term *pizzicato*—to pluck a violin string.

Yiddish. The first large waves of Jewish immigrants from Central and Eastern Europe arrived in the late 1800's. By 1910, 3 million had settled in the United States, mostly in the North Atlantic states. Jews had been colonists in New York, Rhode Island, and Massachusetts since 1654, but their contributions to American English became most significant in the period before and after World War I.

Most American Jews do not speak Hebrew. Their original tongue was Yiddish, a German-based language used by Jews in Central and Eastern Europe. These Yiddish words are common in our language.

bagel: doughnut-shaped hard roll.
chutzpah: audacity; nerve; impudence.
ghetto: living area in which a minority is confined by the majority.
kibitz: give unwanted advice (kibitz at a card game).
kosher: proper, legitimate (derived from special dietary laws observed by Orthodox Jews).
lox: smoked salmon.
mavin: an expert, an authority.
schlemiel: a foolish, clumsy person.
schlep: to drag or carry.

Our evolving language. Words you might overhear spoken in Springfield, Massachusetts, or any other American town or city, would be widely different from those you might hear in Peterborough or any other English city or town. We lift the *hood* on our car; they lift the *bonnet*. We might see a *cop* on his *vacation;* an Englishman would see a *bobby* on *holiday*.

Our two languages, of course, started as one. Over a 300-year span, the division has encompassed more than variations in common terms and their usages. Americans have coined their own words and phrases. These are some from various periods in American history:

The Revolutionary War
militia: a reserve force; a citizen army.
redcoats: British soldiers.
rifle: a musket with a spiraled inner barrel.
stockade: a fort protected by a wall of pointed stakes.

The Civil War
carpetbagger: an unscrupulous northerner who went south in 1868 for cheap land; an opportunist.
scalawag: southerner who accepted Reconstruction.

World War I
doughboy: infantry soldier; also used, to a lesser extent, in the Civil War.
goldbrick: to loaf or avoid work (Army term).
rookie: new recruit.

Prohibition
flapper: a "modern," unconventional young woman.
gang wars: battles for supremacy among rival groups of gangsters.
public enemy: notorious criminal, high on the FBI's most-wanted list.
scram: get out of here; leave.
speakeasy: illegal tavern or barroom.
teetotaler: one pledged to total abstinence from intoxicating beverages.

World War II
black market: trafficking in rationed, scarce goods.
Dear John: a letter to a soldier from his sweetheart, calling off their relationship.
GI: an ordinary soldier; based on the term *government issue*, applied to all military materials.
wild blue yonder: the sky, as it applied to the site of aerial battles.

The '50's, '60's, and '70's
dove: one who advocates peaceful overtures, particularly to the Soviets.
game plan: strategy; used in business and politics.
hawk: one who advocates a hard line, particularly against the Soviets; the term was first used, in another context, in Jefferson's era.
leak: disclosure of government papers and plans.
stonewall: resist investigation, as during the Watergate episode of the Nixon Presidency

The '80's
burnout: exhaustion caused by intensive work over an extended period.
computerese: terms used by computer operators; examples are **byte** (unit of information stored in the computer's memory); **glitch** (error); **user-friendly** (program that is easy to operate).

Stud, draw, or deuces wild

Poker is the most American of card games. (Only basketball and baseball have stronger claims to being "the Great American game"—they were invented by Yankees. Poker is an old European card game, and its name is derived from the French *poque.*)

In all parts of the nation, daily, people who do not know a pair of eights from a royal flush use poker terms. A few that have become ingrained in our national speech follow.

poker face: a wooden, nonrevealing expression.
on the come, on the blind: hoping or acting as if an event will happen, without really knowing if it will.
go the limit: extend oneself as far as possible.
penny ante: insignificant, petty action or game.
bluff: overblown actions calculated to make an opponent think you are stronger than you are.
wild card: an unexpected factor; may change the outcome.
dead man's hand: two aces and two eights, said to be the hand Billy the Kid was holding when he was murdered.
stand pat: stay with what you have; do not budge.
playing with a short deck: not too bright; dim-witted.
four flusher: cheater; needs five, has only four.

Building Your Vocabulary

Puzzles and word games

What is good for us is often bad tasting—but there are exceptions. You can enjoy yourself as you progress on several of the paths to a more powerful vocabulary. Word games and puzzles, whether played alone or in competition, are effective learning devices. They really do reinforce your knowledge of new words' meanings, and build considerably your ability to recall those words.

Crossword puzzles.
Americans seem to be a nation of crossword puzzlers. Newspapers print daily puzzles; paperback and hardcover books of puzzle collections fill several shelves in most bookstores; crossword puzzle dictionaries and other specialized aids are widely available.

If you are new to the world of crosswords, consider these tips:

1. Search around, while you are still getting the hang of it, for a source of *easy* puzzles. Ones that are difficult are likely to discourage you.
2. Use pencil, write lightly, and do not hesitate to erase guesses that might be wrong.
3. For your first move, skim through the puzzle and insert words you are sure about: names of people or movies; places; facts about games, crafts, or instruments. Then you will have enough letters in place to give you hints for words you are less sure about.

Packaged word games

Any bookstore or toy store should be a good source for a half-dozen or more different word games, packaged and ready for spreading out on your table.

Examine the game; read the rules before purchasing it. You may decide it is too specialized or requires too extensive a vocabulary for the people who will be playing it.

Anagrams: the granddaddy of all "take-a-card" or "take-a-tile" word games. Players form their own words, capture opponents' words, and the whole family joins in.

Scrabble:® each player forms a word with any number of his seven randomly selected tiles. He lays the letters on the board's marked spaces. Some letters and spaces are good for bonus points. Players add on to, or branch out from, previously laid-down words.

Boggle:® 25 letters appear in a square. Players compose hidden lists of all possible words, using only letters that are touching one another. After three minutes, lists are compared and a winner declared.

Ghosts

This age-old game requires two or more players. Each player in turn calls out a letter. If, from the fourth letter on, a player completes a word, he loses that round, and must "carry" letter G.

A new round is begun. If there is a new loser, he too carries letter G. Losers of subsequent rounds must carry G, then H, then O, S, T, and S. When one player has all six letters, he loses. The others play on until one winner remains.

If it is Mary's turn and the letters VAL, for example, have been named, she might call letter I. If she had called E, the word VALE would have been spelled, and she would have lost that round. If the next player cannot think of a word starting VALI, he can challenge Mary, who will say VALISE or VALID. Mary proves she has a word in mind, so the challenger loses that round.

Hangman

This word game requires at least two players. One of the players, the leader, has a word in mind. He tells the other players the number of letters in the word. The other players try to guess the word by calling out letters. When a letter is guessed correctly, the leader tells the others at what position or positions in the word the letter falls.

However, for every letter that is called out that is not in the word, the leader draws a portion of a stick figure. Usually, the figure is made up of a head, eyes, nose, mouth, torso, arms, hands, legs, and feet. If the figure is completed before the word is guessed, then the figure is considered hanged, and the leader has won the game. If someone guesses the word, then that person becomes the next leader.

Building Your Vocabulary

Rate yourself again

Some time ago, when you were setting out to build your *Word Power*, you tested yourself. ("How do you rate?" on page 208.) Now that you nearly have completed the program, it will be interesting to measure your gain over your earlier effort.

To make the comparison valid, you should test your facility with difficult words—ones that you have examined and added to your vocabulary. All of the target words in this self-exam appear and are defined in the preceding pages.

For each of the questions, select the one term that *most nearly defines* the meaning of the word in dark print. Score one point for each correct answer.

If you are determined to improve your vocabulary, but score 17 or under, start over. Work on your *Word Power* file daily. Be certain that you understand the meaning of each word before progressing to the next one. Go back over your new vocabulary. A daily review can go a long way toward cementing new words in your memory.

1. **dubious** a) twin; b) prejudiced; c) doubtful; d) double
2. **humus** a) amateur comedian; b) good feelings; c) bad reputation; d) decayed plants
3. **perfidy** a) smells good; b) large taxes; c) traitor's actions; d) risk
4. **meticulous** a) precise; b) fingernails; c) angry; d) foolish
5. **impediment** a) fooling; b) showing; c) statue; d) blocking
6. **facade** a) front; b) mimic; c) framework; d) mobility
7. **accessible** a) can be captured; b) must leave; c) can be reached; d) too much
8. **curator** a) doctor's assistant; b) museum director; c) bullfighter's sword; d) church official
9. **enigma** a) puzzle; b) birthmark; c) pride; d) energetic
10. **petulance** a) birdlike; b) grumpiness; c) shyness; d) holiday
11. **altruism** a) honesty; b) generosity; c) completion; d) conservatism
12. **irascible** a) held up; b) easily angered; c) ready for action; d) green
13. **felines** a) fish; b) snakes; c) criminals; d) cats
14. **undulate** a) wave; b) chew; c) blink; d) shout
15. **cynosure** a) show; b) deterrent; c) detergent; d) swan
16. **habitat** a) farmyard; b) home; c) unpleasant; d) nun
17. **voracious** a) gets in front; b) eats huge amounts; c) frightening; d) never wins
18. **incombustible** a) untidy; b) unburnable; c) unbreakable; d) can't be equaled
19. **marauders** a) raiders; b) jumpers; c) winners; d) swimmers
20. **gregarious** a) religious; b) young; c) frightened; d) sociable
21. **devastated** a) exasperated; b) humbled; c) wasted; d) enlarged
22. **vestige** a) clothing; b) appropriate; c) persuasion; d) remnant
23. **consoled** a) comforted; b) entertained; c) controlled; d) welcomed
24. **garrulous** a) talkative; b) plump; c) foolish; d) proud
25. **antagonist** a) sufferer; b) opponent; c) follower; d) merchant

Answers. 1, c; 2, d; 3, c; 4, a; 5, d; 6, a; 7, c; 8, b; 9, a; 10, b; 11, b; 12, b; 13, d; 14, a; 15, a; 16, b; 17, b; 18, b; 19, a; 20, d; 21, c; 22, d; 23, a; 24, a; 25, b. A score of 25 is perfect, 22–24 very good, 18–21 above average.

Building Your Vocabulary

askance

Words you should know

gist — the main point of a topic.

empirical — believing things that one has observed for oneself.

insouciant — carefree, nonchalant, untroubled

Word Power cards

absolve. To clear or pardon; to pronounce that no blame exists.
abstract. 1. Not concrete or definite (an *abstract* thought). 2. A portion reprinted from a larger book or article.
acerate. Sharpened; pointed at one end.
acquiesce. To agree; consent; to go along with a suggestion.
acrylic. A resin-based synthetic fiber.
acute. 1. Sharp, pointed. 2. Important. 3. Sensitive (an *acute* sense of hearing).
agitate. 1. To move suddenly or violently; to shake up. 2. To disturb. 3. To interest in a cause (*agitated* for higher pay).
albatross. 1. Large sea bird. 2. A burden, handicap, or curse (this meaning is derived from a poem, *The Rime of the Ancient Mariner,* by Coleridge).
alewife. Small, herringlike fish.
anemic. A disease in which too few red blood cells results in weakness and fatigue.
aorta. The largest of the arteries carrying blood from the heart.
apothecary. Druggist; pharmacist.
appalling. Frightening; upsetting (the filth was *appalling*).
askance (a-skans'). Disapproval or distrust; a sidewise glance indicating doubt.
aspect. 1. Appearance. 2. The direction something faces.
assert. To state positively or forcefully.
assuage (a-swaje'). To remedy; make easier, less painful.
badinage (bad-n-ahj'). Playful, joking talk; chitchat.
baste. 1. To sew loosely, temporarily. 2. To keep moist (as with sauce or melted butter) while cooking.
bastion. Fort or strongly held position (the league was a *bastion* of patriotism).
behoove. Necessary or proper (*behooves* us to pay attention).

bellow. To roar or shout; the roar of a large animal, as a buffalo.
benign. Harmless, kindly, mild.
bequeath. To pass on, or leave, as in a will.
bequest. That which has been *bequeathed* (Mary's aunt left her a *bequest* of $50,000).
bigamy. Being married to two persons at one time, a criminal offense.
blackguard (blag'-erd). An unprincipled rascal; a scoundrel.
blanch. To bleach or whiten; to remove the color from an object.
blather. Nonsensical or foolish talk.
blemish. A flaw or spot that spoils the appearance of an object or a person.
blunder. A mistake caused by stupidity or confusion.
bob. To move up and down (Jim *bobbed* alongside the boat).
bolster. 1. A pillow or cushion. 2. To support or prop up (contributions *bolstered* her campaign funds).
bountiful. Plentiful; generous.
Brahmin. Descendant of old, exclusive family (a New England *Brahmin*); derived from Hindu term for *highest rank.*
bravado. A show of false, swaggering bravery.
calligraphy. Handwriting; penmanship.
camber. 1. An arched surface. 2. The way in which automobile wheels are set slanting inward toward their tops.
caster. A small, swiveled wheel under furniture or another heavy object.
cherish. To treat with love and tenderness; to hold dear.
circa. Approximately, about (first used *circa* 1900).
cistern. A tank for holding rainwater.
constrict. To squeeze, compress, make smaller.

238 **Building Your Vocabulary**

consummate. 1. To conclude or bring to perfection. 2. Perfect; highly skilled (a *consummate* baker of pastries).
cougar. A mountain lion.
covenant. An agreement or contract that binds two or more persons.
cringe. To move back in fear (synonym: *cower*).
croissant (kwoss-sahn′). A crescent-shaped roll of light, sweet dough.
damsel. A girl or maiden (used in ancient times, but rarely heard today).
decimate. To kill or destroy a large part of something; to kill one-tenth.
desecrate. To disturb something sacred; to profane.
detonate. To explode.
dire. Dreadful, terrible, extreme; having horrible consequences (a *dire* threat).
discord. Tension, strife, lack of agreement.
divan. A backless couch.
dominant. The highest; the one in control, with the most authority.
dominate. To rule or control; to be higher than others.
dub. To apply a nickname (they *dubbed* him "Mr. Careful").
dynasty. A group or family that keeps power for several generations.
edgy. Tense; nervous; anxious.
eject. To throw out; to evict (the noisy couple was *ejected* from the theater).
ember. A dying coal in a fire that is partially out.
embroil. To involve in an argument or contest; to entangle.
empirical. Believing ideas, actions, or things that one has observed for oneself (*empirical* evidence).
epicure. One who has uncommon, highly refined preferences in food and wine.
evince. To demonstrate clearly.

expire. 1. To end; to die; a last breath. 2. To breathe out.
expostulate. To present one's reasons; to argue intelligently.
extol. To praise highly.
extricate. To free or release from an entanglement.
farce. Far-fetched, humorous show; broad, exaggerated comedy.
fastidious. 1. Careful, exacting attention to detail. 2. Overly attentive to good manners.
fervent. Showing great emotional depth; highly enthusiastic.
fetish. 1. Something that is said to have mystic powers. 2. An excessively strong habit or attitude (Tim made a *fetish* of washing his hands).
fickle. Unpredictably changeable in regard to attitudes and affections.
figment. Something made up or invented (the whole story was a *figment* of his imagination).
forage. 1. To look for food. 2. Hay, grain, or other food for domestic animals.
forfeit (for′-fit). Something given up, in punishment for a crime or offense; that which is forfeited.
forlorn. Extreme sadness or loneliness; the appearance of a sad, lonely person.
furl. To roll up a flag.
gabardine. Cotton twill fabric.
gaggle. 1. A flock of geese. 2. A group of silly or cackling people.
gape. To stare, with mouth opened wide in wonderment.
garret. An attic.
genial. Friendly; pleasant; a kindly manner.
gird. 1. To prepare for action. 2. To put on a belt or band.
gist. The main point of a topic; the core, or essence, of a subject.
gnash (nash). To grind one's teeth together.
graphic. Relating to writing, drawing, painting, typesetting, and other representations on paper or a similarly flat surface (*graphic* arts).
grave. 1. Serious, important, dangerous (declaring war was a *grave* decision). 2. A burial place.
guffaw. Coarse, noisy laughter.
gustatory. Relating to the sense of taste (eating at Joe's was a *gustatory* experience).
gyrate. To circle or revolve around a point or axis.
hack. To chop, cut, or break up.
hagiology. Study of the lives of saints.
hale. To drag or pull; to compel someone to go somewhere (*haled* into court). 2. Healthy; not sickly.
hark. To listen carefully.
harridan. Unpleasant, complaining woman.
hearth. The floor of a fireplace, and that part of it extending into a room.
hepatitis (hep′-a-tie-tiss). A serious disease of the liver.
heretic. A person who disagrees with generally accepted opinions, or dissents from religious views.
hexagonal. Six-sided.
hindsight. Noticing the importance and cause of an event after it has happened.
hormone. A chemical substance formed in the body and carried in the bloodstream.
horticulture. The growing of fruits, vegetables, or plants; gardening.
hospice. 1. A place or program that cares for patients who are incurably ill. 2. A shelter for needy travelers.
huckster. 1. A peddler; one who sells merchandise in the street. 2. A writer of advertisements.
hydraulic. Related to water pressure (*hydraulic* pump; *hydraulic* engineer).
iconoclast. One who attacks and destroys popularly held, or traditional, values. (Ancient

Greeks called religious statues *icons*. *Iconoclasts* were "breakers of statues," or breakers of ideas.)
ignominious. Disgraceful; shameful.
immune. Not affected; excepted from a general condition.
immutable. Unchangeable.
imperial. 1. Relating to an empire or emperor. 2. A nation that maintains control over colonies.
imperturbable. Calm; cannot be shaken or disturbed.
implicit (im-plis'-it). Understood, though stated only indirectly (an *implicit* understanding).
impunity. Will not be punished or harmed (state your opinions with *impunity*).
inception. The beginning; start.
incumbent. Currently holding an office or position (the *incumbent* governor).
inept. Clumsy; foolish; incompetent; not suitable.
influx. Flowing in (an *influx* of immigrants).
inordinate. More than could be expected; an unreasonable amount.
insouciant (in-soo'-see-ont). Carefree, nonchalant, untroubled.
interrogate. Ask questions.
iota. An extremely small amount (we did not care one *iota* what their opinion might be).
itinerant. One who travels from place to place, as part of his work; traveling in such a way.
jamb (jam). The vertical framework of a door or window.
jibe. To agree (your information *jibes* with ours).
jubilant. Joyful; happy enough to sing or laugh aloud.
juxtapose. To put one thing or idea next to another in order to compare them.
kamikaze (ka-me-kah'-zee). A suicidal crash attack (a tactic used by Japanese pilots in World War II).
keynote. Main theme (President Kennedy gave the *keynote* speech at the convention).
koala. An Australian animal, the model for teddy bears.
labyrinth (lab'-a-rinth). Mazelike series of connecting passages and tunnels.
lacerate. To tear, wound, rip, or cut.
laconic (la-kon'-ick). Using few words; short-spoken (Coolidge, who was *laconic,* was called "Silent Cal").
lacuna (la-koo'-nah). An empty space; missing part; gap.
laggard. Straggler; one who falls behind the others.
laity (lay'-ih-tee). People who are not members of a given profession; in churches, those who are not members of the clergy.
lament. To mourn or grieve; to express sorrow; a spoken or written expression of grief.
lapse. 1. To slip or drift backward; to neglect or overlook. 2. A missed opportunity or privilege; the amount of time during which the privilege expired.
late. In addition to the common meaning of coming after the expected time, late also means dead, or recently died (the *late* Mrs. Patterson).
lax. Not strict. Unfirm.
LED. The display of letters or numerals, as on a calculator, furnished by a semiconductor; *LED* is an acronym for Light Emitting Diode.
lenient (lee'-ne-yent). Not inclined to punish; forgiving.
levitate. To rise into the air with no apparent support; a mystical act or illusion that defies gravity.
libation. An alcoholic drink; a drink offered to a god.
limber. Moving easily; supple; working without effort (he sent a more *limber* player into the game).
linear. (linn'-ee-er). Relating to a straight line (a *linear* descendant of the Adams family).
locus. A place or location.
lozenge. A medicated tablet for relief from coughs and colds.
macadam. A type of road made of stone and asphalt or tar.
machination (mack'-in-ayshun). 1. The act of plotting or scheming, usually for an evil purpose; the plot itself.
maculate. Spotted or soiled; to spot or stain (*immaculate* means "without spots," or pure, clean, unstained).
magnate. Powerful person, usually a businessman or industrialist (a lumber *magnate*).
malcontent. Unhappy or discontented; also, a person in that condition *(mal* means bad, or generally negative, as in *malformed* and *malodorous*).
manacle. Handcuff.
mangle. 1. To ruin through clumsiness (Howard *mangled* his speech). 2. To cut, hack, or otherwise physically ruin.
mare's nest. 1. A tangled, complicated situation. 2. A fraud.
marginal. 1. Near the edge or border. 2. Of barely passable quality.
maroon. 1. A color, ranging from reddish brown to reddish purple. 2. To abandon a person; to put him off a boat with little hope of rescue.
martinet. A rigid military leader or taskmaster; one who demands total obedience.
mediate. To settle disputes by acting as a neutral party.
melange (may-lahnj'). A mixture.
menial (mean'-ee-al). 1. A servant. 2. Relating to a job or task that a servant might do.
metamorphosis. A change in shape, appearance, or function (a tadpole's *metamorphosis* into a frog).

metropolis. A large city.
microcomputer. A very small computer (*micro* means small or greatly reduced in size).
mien (mean). Facial expression or the way one carries oneself; appearance.
mildew. A fungus, similar to a mold, that grows on leather, plants, cloth, or paper under damp conditions.
minatory. Threatening; fearsome.
minutia (mi-noo'-sha). A very small, unimportant item (we cannot bother with the *minutia* of their complaints).
mode. A way of doing something; a style of action (an unusual *mode* of dress, or of speech).
molest. To harass, bother, or physically disturb.
monarch. A king, emperor, or ruler.
monogram. The initials of a person's name formed into a design.
moot. A matter that can be argued in any of several ways; not easily decided.
mucilage (myoo'-si-laj). Glue.
murky. Dark, gloomy; heavy mist or fog; thick, unclear waters (a *murky* atmosphere).
nape. The back of the neck.
nether. Lower or below (the *nether* regions).
niggling. Fussy; petty; too concerned with unimportant detail.
novel. 1. New, different (Bill's wagon had a *novel* design). 2. A book of fiction; prose narrative.
obfuscate. To hide slightly, or make obscure (he deliberately *obfuscated* the facts about the accident).
Occident. Europe and the western hemisphere (Asia and the Pacific islands are the *Orient*).
offing. Soon, or the near future (a large gift is in the *offing*).
oratory. The skill of public speaking; rhetorical style.

ossify. 1. To become bony. 2. To become set in an unchanging pattern.
ostracize. To shut out or exclude from a group; to banish.
palate. The roof of the mouth.
palette. 1. A hand-held board on which an artist mixes colors. 2. The range of colors used by an artist.
panacea (pan-a-see-a). A cure for all diseases or difficulties, the value of which is doubtful.
paradox. A statement, difficult to believe, that is true (*paradoxically*, the two opponents were brothers).
paragon. A model of excellence.
peccadillo. A small fault; a prank.
pewter. Silver-gray metal used for kitchen and cooking utensils.
pillage. To rob or plunder, as by invading armies in wartime.
poise. 1. To balance, or the state of being balanced. 2. Bearing oneself with dignity and composure (she exhibited *poise* and maturity).
ponder. To think carefully; to consider.
predator. One who preys on others for his own profit, as an animal preys on (kills and eats) weaker animals.
propinquity (pro-pin'-kwi-tee). Nearness (*propinquity* is at the root of most friendships).
quagmire. 1. Swampy, boggy land into which a walker might sink. 2. A predicament or difficult situation that might entrap a person.
quail. 1. To move backward in fear. 2. A small, chickenlike bird; a bobwhite.
quash. To put down; suppress; set aside (the judge *quashed* the motion for appeal).
quiver. 1. To tremble or shake. 2. A case in which an archer's arrows are carried.
radiate. 1. To spread out from a central point (spokes of a wheel *radiate* from the hub). 2. To issue energy—heat, light, or sound.
radical. Carried to an extreme; not moderate.
rail. To speak strongly against; to verbally abuse (Ken *railed* against the new tax collector).
rampart. A fort or defensive position higher than the surrounding ground.
rant. To shout in a violent manner; to rave.
rapport (ra-pour'). A good relationship, marked by mutual trust and admiration.
rationale (rash-a-nal'). A reason (sometimes used as an excuse) for doing something.
redundant. Unnecessarily repeated; not needed.
refute. To disprove; to argue against.
regress. To move backward, usually to a worsened condition (the opposite of *progress*).
reiterate. To say again; repeat.
relent. To soften an attitude; to give up a previously held, harder position.
remonstrate. To protest; object; argue.
repartee (re-par-tay'). Witty, clever conversation, particularly a witty reply.
replete. Plenty, or an oversupply. (a party *replete* with butlers and waitresses).
rife. Appears frequently; often occurs (his work was *rife* with errors).
rook. 1. A crow. 2. To cheat or swindle.
ruminate. 1. To think about something for a long time; to reflect on it. 2. For cattle, to chew and rechew.
Rx. A prescription for medicine or pharmaceutical drugs.
saccharine (sack'-a-rin). Too sweet (*saccharin* is the white, powdery substitute for sugar).
salutation. A greeting, especially at the start of a letter ("Dear Mr. Brenner," for example).

sanctum. A holy place; sacred part of a church or temple.
sarcophagus (sar-kof'-a-gus). A stone coffin.
savvy. *(Slang)* To understand; knowhow (he is *savvy* enough to make a good deal).
scale. Thin, flaky substance on the skins of animals, fishes, or plants. 2. Rate of pay, determined by union schedules, for musicians and other skilled technicians. 3. A device for weighing; a measure.
scant. Meager; a small degree less than a specified amount (a *scant* four miles).
scenario. 1. An outline of a play or book. 2. The probable way in which events will take place, if certain unpredictable circumstances govern the action (here is the *scenario* for our rescue operation, if all the bridges flood out).
scow. A large flat-bottomed boat.
scrawny. Skinny; bony.
scuffle. To grapple or fight with someone in an indeterminate, confused manner.
sealing wax. A soft substance when heated, it hardens to seal bottles and packages.
secondary school. High school.
seethe. 1. To be extremely excited; agitated. 2. To have a motion like that of boiling water.
semantics. The study of the meaning of language.
seminary. 1. A school for the training of religious persons—ministers, priests, rabbis. 2. A school of higher education for young women.
sensor. A machine that receives or sends impulses, like light or heat, not otherwise detected by humans.
sentient. Conscious; able to experience thought and feelings.
sequester. To move away; set apart; place in seclusion (they chose to *sequester* themselves in a far valley).

serrated. Having an edge that is notched or saw-toothed.
servile. Subordinate or submissive in attitude, like a servant.
sham. False, fraudulent; a trick intended to pass off someone or something as other than as it really is.
shear. To remove hair or fleece from an animal (the farmer *sheared* his sheep; the barber *sheared* Don's hair too short).
shoal. Shallow water, sometimes unexpectedly so and a threat to navigators.
shoddy. Inferior; made of poor quality materials.
shortfall. A shortage; an amount below the expected, usually referring to money.
showboating. Showing off; attempting to attract attention.
showdown. An act that forces the outcome of an issue or event (the feud had gone on long enough, so the families arranged a *showdown*).
shrew. 1. A woman who nags and scolds; an unpleasant, constantly criticizing woman. 2. A small, mouselike animal with poor vision.
shrewd. Clever, sharp, cunning; quick-witted.
shrivel. To shrink and dry up, remaining in a wrinkled condition.
shun. To deliberately avoid (Carol walked across the street, *shunning* her nephew).
sickle. A tool with a long, curved blade used for cutting grain, grass, or other tall plants (the Communist flag is known as the hammer and sickle because those two tools are depicted on it).
sidereal. About, or relating to, the stars; stellar.
sidle. To step or move sideways; usually done when trying to avoid another person, or to remain unnoticed.
significant. Having a valuable or important meaning.

silent treatment. To totally ignore an unliked person, as a means of expressing contempt (everyone in the class gave Kim the *silent treatment*).
simper. A silly, childish smile.
simulate. 1. To imitate, or take on the manner and appearance of another person or thing. 2. To pretend (Carl *simulated* interest in Rose's career).
sketchy. Slight; incomplete; leaving out many of the details and finer points.
skimpy. Not enough; too small an amount for the purpose, often due to insufficient money having been spent.
slake. To satisfy; to lessen a condition that had existed (the announcement *slaked* Dan's rage; the water *slaked* Ann's thirst).
snide. Sarcastic; offensive in a rude, superior manner.
solar. Having to do with the sun. (*solar* heat; *solar* rays; *solar* blindness).
sonar. A technique of using sound waves, reflected off objects under water.
sordid. 1. Extremely dirty; filthy; vile. 2. Motivated solely by greed.
souvenir (soo'-va-neer). A memento; something that helps one remember a place or an event (we were given key rings as *souvenirs* of the party).
spectrum. A range of ideas, thoughts, or activities (the whole *spectrum* of medical science).
stalwart. Strong, determined.
stance. One's attitude or position; the way one stands; also, one's thoughts on a controversial issue.
stifle. 1. To smother; suffocate. 2. To cut off opposition.
stunt. To slow or stop the growth of a person or thing.
taboo. A strict rule or custom against an action, imposed by social or religious beliefs.

tactful. Sensitive, considerate; taking care not to offend.
taint. To infect; to stain someone's reputation (the *taint* of his dishonorable discharge).
tension. 1. The act of stretching or being stretched. 2. A condition of nervous strain.
thwart. To frustrate; to prevent an action or event desired by another person from taking place.
tirade. A long, angry speech, aimed at an enemy or an enemy's position.
topsy-turvy. Totally confused; upside-down.
torrid. 1. Very hot and dry, parched. 2. Passionate, intense.
touchy. 1. Quick to take offense; too sensitive. 2. A situation that requires delicate handling.
tranquil. Calm and undisturbed.
transitory. Existing only for a brief time; short-lived; an in-between period.
traverse. To move across or through; to travel up or down, or backward and forward, through a place or region.
trounce. To beat, as in a fight.
tumult. Noise and commotion caused by an unruly crowd.
tyrant. A harsh, cruel ruler.
unvailing. Useless.
uncouth. Clumsy, crude, impolite.
unflappable. Calm and unexcited.
ungainly. Awkward; lacking grace; moving clumsily.
unpalatable. Not easily swallowed or accepted; unpleasing; unpleasant.
valor. Bravery; courage (a *valiant* person is one who exhibits *valor*).
vandalism. Meaningless, criminal destruction of property.
veer. To turn in another direction; to move off one's course.
venerable. Honored and respected because of age, position, or reputation.

vicissitudes (vi-siss′-i-toods). Unexpected shifts and changes in one's life; commonly used to mean hardships (the *vicissitudes* of widowhood).
vivid. Bright; strongly experienced; distinct; described in a lifelike manner.
wane. To decline, come to an end, decrease.

wary. Watchful; cautious; on one's guard.
wistful. Vaguely, or sadly, wishful.
word processing. Producing reports, books, and other documents via the use of computers.
wrest. To forcefully pull or grab an object from another person.

For further reference

American language
Boatner, Maxine T. and Gates, J. E.
  A Dictionary of American Idioms
  Barron's. Four thousand commonly used expressions, including slang, proverbs, and clichés. For each entry, definitions and examples of use in sentences.
Mathews, Mitford M.
  Americanisms
  Phoenix. A dictionary of words that first came into use in the United States. Includes the earliest recorded use of each word.
Mencken, H. L.
  The American Language (one-volume abridged edition)
  Knopf. The enduring classic study of our language: how it evolved and how it is used today. Still as fascinating as when written more than 60 years ago.

Vocabulary building
Davidson, Jessica
  How to Improve Your Spelling and Vocabulary
  Franklin Watts. Rules, tips, procedures, exercises, and games for students and young adults.
Evans, Bergen
  Comfortable Words
  Random House. Witty, brief analyses of the origins and accurate meanings of commonly used words and phrases.

Specialized interests
Barnhart, Clarence L., Steinmetz, Sol, and Barnhart, R.
  The Second Barnhart Dictionary of New English
  Harper & Row. Definitions of new words that appeared in print during the years 1973 to 1979.

Bernstein, Theodore M.
  Reverse Dictionary
  Quadrangle. Meanings are arranged alphabetically; the word that is defined follows its meaning (for example: "Rope or cable for mooring or towing: HAWSER").
Partridge, Eric
  Origins
  Macmillan. An etymological dictionary, providing information about the evolution of 12,000 commonly used words.
Pei, Mario
  Language of the Specialists
  Funk & Wagnalls. Specialists in 20 categories—astronomy, literature, and medicine are typical—each select and define a hundred or more terms.
Webster's New Dictionary of Synonyms
  G. & C. Merriam Company. Helpful for finding the right word with precisely the meaning you require.

Games and puzzles
Brandreth, Gyles
  The World's Best Indoor Games
  Pantheon. Complete rules and explanations for dozens of word games from "Ghosts" to "Guggenheim."
Hill, Norman
  How to Solve Crossword Puzzles
  Funk & Wagnalls.
Kurzban, Stan and Rosen, Mel
  The Compleat Cruciverbalist
  Van Nostrand Reinhold. Subtitled "How to solve and compose crossword puzzles for fun and profit." (*Cruciverbalist* is a made-up word meaning "crossword.")

Building Your Vocabulary

Improving Your Speech

- The five keys   245
- Correct speech   252
- Body language   254
- Preparing to speak   257
- Everyday uses of speech   261
- Robert's Rules of order   264

It is said that man is instinctively afraid of only two things: falling and speaking in public. Just a clever remark, you may think, and not one that applies to you. But think a moment longer. Do any of the following cause you anxiety?
- Making an important phone call.
- Being introduced to an important person.
- Trying to convince someone.

Many people are uneasy in such everyday situations, and they betray their anxiety by the way they speak. On the phone, an anxious person may stumble or mumble, and the other party may quickly stop listening. Meeting an influential stranger, an anxious person may launch into a self-promoting one-way conversation—and forget to introduce himself. During a good-natured exchange involving a difference of opinion, an anxious person may undermine his argument by unintentionally bullying or ridiculing his opponent.

What do these situations have to do with public speaking? Most phone calls, many two-way discussions, and all introductions take place between you and a stranger, between you and your "public." Whatever you say is going to leave an indelible first impression; how you speak to a stranger is as memorable to him as your face. For this reason, your private conversation may need improvement before you are ready to go public.

Broadly interpreted, public speaking is the art of communicating effectively. It is a learned skill, always starting at the level of one-to-one communication. By understanding the way people exchange information verbally and symbolically, you can learn to improve the way you speak—to friends, co-workers, and even strangers.

Formal speechmaking is, of course, the highest form of public speaking. But there are virtually no natural public speakers, born to the podium. The great spellbinders in history—politicians, preachers, and actors—were polished and well-rehearsed performers who knew precisely what they were doing. All of them practiced hundreds of times before hundreds of audiences. In fact, every great speaker is likely to remember at least one time when he was terrified: his first time.

Until the basics of speaking are mastered, the best-written speech on Earth will not be truly heard. On the next pages you will find the five keys to effective speech:

1. Pronunciation; 2. Pace; 3. Attention; 4. Eye contact; and 5. Pauses.

Take each key in order, then apply it to your own mannerisms. (Here as elsewhere in this chapter, access to a tape recorder will be highly useful.) The five keys might be called the tools of your private communications trade; all of them together, in order and ready to use, make up your public speaking tool kit. Each of the five is essential if you expect to be a fully effective speaker.

The five keys

Pronunciation. Beginning now, imagine that everything you say is for someone else's consumption. First, ask yourself if you are usually understood when you talk to anyone outside of your immediate family (families sometimes speak in code). Do you make an effort to enunciate each word? Or do you run the words together as if in a hurry to get the sentence over with? Among friends, face to face, you may get by with careless pronunciation. But do you notice any problem in being understood by people who do not know you? By older people? By people with different regional accents?

Your own regional accent or dialect need not concern you; it is part of your personality and may well be part of your charm. Three of the last six U.S. Presidents had pronounced regional accents, and they made no attempt to change them.

Many English words sound similar, but the slightest adjustment between tongue and lips can make the difference between one sound (or word) and another—between *far* and *fire*, for example. One self-test for pronunciation addresses itself to words beginning with *d, t,* and *th.* Try saying *din, tin, thin,* and *then.* Can you hear the difference clearly? If you cannot, perhaps a friend can. Ask other friends if they have any trouble understanding the way you pronounce words. When you read or hear a difficult word or name, write it down and practice saying it. Soon you will develop a highly desirable pronunciation habit: *wanting* to say things right.

Reading from a prepared text, you will have the time to look up the pronunciation of any word about which you feel uncertain—and the time will be well spent. Proper names, too, can be found phonetically notated in large dictionaries. A correctly pronounced proper name or place is always well received by an audience. A mispronounced name is, at best, unnecessary; at worst, it is insulting. Most common mispronunciations arise through constant misuse.

For best results with the following list, cover up the *wrong* and *right* columns and read the words aloud, using a tape recorder if possible. Some of the words on the list are routinely mispronounced by some of the most prominent people in the United States. But no matter who says *new*-cue-ler at a press conference, it is wrong.

Test your pronunciation

	Wrong	*Right*
accidentally	ak-si-*dent*-ly	ak-si-*den*-tal-ly
across	a-*krost*	a-*kross*
anyway	*en*-ee-wayz	*en*-ee-way
anywhere	*en*-ee-wayrze	*en*-ee-ware
asked	axed	asked
burst	bust	burst
drowned	drown-did	drownd
escape	ek-*scape*	es-*cape*
film	*fill*-um	film
government	*guv*-mint	*guh*-vern-ment
heartrending	*hart*-ren-der-ing	*hart*-ren-ding
height	*hite*-th	hite
hold	a-*hold*	hold
hundred	*hun*-nert	*hun*-drid
incidentally	in-si-*dent*-ly	in-si-*den*-tal-ly
interesting	*in*-nur-es-ting	*in*-tur-es-ting
judgment	*judg*-uh-ment	*judg*-ment
nowhere	*no*-wayrze	*no*-ware
nuclear	*new*-cue-ler	*new*-clee-ur
often	*off*-ten	*off*-en
police	*poh*-leece	poh-*leece*
recur	re-o-*cur*	re-*cur*
regardless	ir-ri-*gard*-liss	ri-*gard*-liss
scared	uh-*scared*	scared
toward	tuh-*ward*	tawrd
unaware	un-uh-*wayrze*	un-uh-*ware*
undoubtedly	un-*dow*-tuh-blee	un-*dow*-tid-lee

Improving Your Speech

Pace. The initial requirement for effective speech is intelligibility. If you are not understood, your thoughts are not conveyed, and if you are to be understood, then you must speak at a pace that enables your listeners to get your message. Rapid-fire speech may be acceptable for comic effect, but it is unacceptable for the purpose of communication.

Most Americans harbor the prejudice that people who speak a foreign language talk too fast. Whatever is unfamiliar, in your own language or another, nearly always seems to be spoken too fast.

Perhaps you have been told that you speak too fast, or too slowly; or perhaps you suspect that your conversational speed is not quite right for public speaking. To test your speaking rate, choose a page from a favorite book and read it aloud, at your normal speed, for three minutes. Then count the number of words you have just read. Fewer than 400 is considered too slow; 450 is the comfortable spoken average; and 500 words or more is too fast.

Most people find after taking this test that they read faster than they thought. Reading aloud takes longer, of course, than normal conversation; your own words are spoken more easily than someone else's. As a starting point, assume that you should try to speak slower in public than in private.

An aid to slower speaking is louder speaking. Trying to talk louder will cause you to slow your pace. Think for a moment about how people respond to fast, soft speech. In a classroom, for example, a student who rattles off an answer in a whispery voice will neither be heard nor understood—even if his answer is correct. The student who speaks deliberately and clearly makes a better impression—even if his facts are not quite right. In terms of public speaking, slower and louder are usually better.

To be sure, you cannot learn effective speaking pace from a book. There are far too many variables in a speech: points of emphasis, pauses for effect, audience responses and interruptions, and catches of breath. Some novices are fearful that they will not have enough to say, or that what they *do* have to say will take up no more than five minutes. (They are often surprised to discover, once they have finished, that they have held forth for ten, even fifteen minutes.) Others are fearful that they will not cover all their points in the time allotted, and speak at a disconcertingly fast pace.

You will find that just a few prepared remarks, or notes for reference, can go a long way in your actual presentation. It is better to have a few well-chosen things to say, and to say them slowly and with conviction, than to overstay your welcome. Remember, once you get started, time goes by much faster for the speaker than for the audience.

This speaker has captured the attention of her audience, but will her message be understood?

For the present, try to get to know the sound of your own voice. Use a tape recorder if possible. Listen to your normal talking speed. Ask yourself if the pace seems unhurried, or slightly frantic. Practice will enable you to speak at a rate that is comfortable for you.

Attention. When speaking to others, your task is to get them to pay attention to *you*. Presumably, standing in front of an audience will give you their attention to begin with. Now you must keep it.

First you must cope with the fear of speaking in public. The best defense against stage fright is an offense. In public speaking, offense usually means loudness. Assuming that you will not use a microphone, you will need to speak louder in performance than you ever did in practice. Most speakers find the process helpful; by concentrating on talking louder than usual, you become less preoccupied with your fear of talking in the first place. Loudness, in its best sense, becomes outspokenness; outspokenness quickly breeds confidence.

Overcoming problems. The most common failing of inexperienced speakers is mumbling—talking too low, not saying things clearly, and sounding apologetic. Consider the way mumblers look when they talk: slouched shoulders, shuffling feet, downward head, eyes darting in every direction except that of the audience. This type of body language will undermine the effectiveness of any spoken language that accompanies it. Clearly the mumbler has no confidence in what he is saying; that message is plain to anyone who sees or hears him. The speaker who mumbles gets sympathy, not attention.

Attention is gotten by a speaker who talks loudly, who stands up straight and leans slightly forward, and who looks as though he believes what he is saying. A loud and forceful delivery also requires more time and energy, thus slowing you down. The extra effort makes

A cigar clenched between one's teeth while talking is a surefire way to obscure one's words.

you pay more attention to each word, improving your enunciation. If you are too loud, your audience will signal you quickly by the expressions on their faces. It is far easier to tone down your voice than to raise it.

Before you speak in front of an audience, consider how effective you are—or are not—at holding attention when you speak. Among friends, for instance, do you find it difficult to make yourself heard? Are you accused of making short stories long? Do you have trouble remembering the punch line of a joke or the windup of a story? These are common shortcomings of inexperienced speakers; all are overcome through practice and preparation. When you are thoroughly familiar with what you want to say and how you are going to say it, you will stop worrying about making mistakes. You will speak up. An audience will feel your confidence. You will get—and hold—their attention.

Speech improvement tools. A tape recorder is an invaluable tool for getting to know your best voice level. Most people are surprised and dismayed when they hear themselves for the first time on tape. Both the tone and the volume of your voice sound like someone else's. "I hate the way I sound" is a common reaction. But take heart: the very playback that has dismayed you can help you make truly dramatic improvements. Listen to yourself again and again. Then rerecord your voice, making any adjustments in loudness that seem indicated. You may, for example, find that too many words are being emphasized with volume, creating a strident effect, such as the effect a writer creates who constantly uses italics. Whatever the problem, with loudness or any other aspect of your delivery, a few sessions with a tape recorder can be very revealing.

Another useful aid to self-improvement is the radio. Nearly all radio announcers are chosen for their quality of voice: tone, precise enunciation, and smoothness of delivery. It took years of practice for them to achieve a level of consistency and professionalism that sounds effortless and natural to the listener. Parrot the words of a newscaster as he reads his copy, using his pauses to supply your own version a split second after his. Compare your sound with the newscaster's. Make adjustments and repeat the process. If you do this exercise often enough, improvement will take place on a subconscious as well as a conscious level.

Going a step further, try this experiment. Turn on a baseball game, a football game, or a tennis match, and turn off the sound on the TV. "Broadcast" the whole game, using a tape recorder. Most top sportscasters have used just such radio/TV exercises to learn their trade. They also started out just like you: unsure of themselves (and their voices) and quite anxious about speaking in public. They conquered their uncertainty and anxiety, and so can you.

How your voice comes across

Many people make value judgments based on the way your voice comes across to them. Using a tape of your normal, conversational speaking voice, monitor yourself for the following:

- **Crispness.** If you slur your words, even unintentionally, your listener is likely to think you are in no condition to talk.

- **Rapidity.** Talking too fast in a conversation gives the listener—particularly a stranger—the idea that he or she will be given no chance to speak at all.

- **Harshness.** A listener or an audience will be put off by harsh, strident tones, which are the verbal equivalent of shaking someone by the arm.

- **Rising inflection.** The habit of ending phrases and sentences on an upward note makes declarations sound like questions. Listeners will question your self-assurance.

- **Falling inflection.** Phrases or sentences that trail off make you sound as if you changed your mind (or lost your conviction) in mid-sentence.

- **Shrillness.** Speaking at too high and sharp a pitch will alienate most listeners. It comes across as overemotionalism, immaturity, or poor argument.

- **Tenseness.** A slight amount of tension showing up in the voice of a public speaker is quite common and need not concern you. The best cure for a noticeably tense voice, which makes a speaker sound nervous, is practice.

- **Whispering.** Low, "sexy," or whispery tones should be avoided. A whispery voice is hard to hear, and will keep listeners from taking you seriously.

Improving Your Speech

How to get attention and control of an audience

We all admire speakers who can hold an audience from the time they begin to speak until the moment they finish. No one is born with this talent; experience and the following good practices can build it.

1. Find out how many people will be in your audience. (You can speak less formally in front of a small group.)
2. Determine how many are friends and how many are strangers. (Strangers warrant a different approach than friends.)
3. Decide on what sort of message the audience is likely to appreciate. (Never offend the audience's self-interest.)
4. Keep your ideas and remarks to the intellectual level of the audience.
5. Learn the age level of the audience. (Young people may be unfamiliar with historical references.)
6. Learn how many men and how many women will be in attendance. (Avoid language and examples that are sex-biased.)
7. Find out, approximately, the racial and ethnic composition of the audience. (Giving offense to part of an audience usually affects the whole audience.)
8. Determine beforehand the probable reaction of your audience to your subject. (If you invite controversy, be ready to defend your position.)
9. Eliminate *all* irrelevant material. (A knowledgeable audience will be uninterested in hearing what it knows already, and not at all impressed that you know it, too.)
10. Find out beforehand how well the audience knows *you*. If not at all, take some time at the beginning to introduce yourself, personally and professionally.

Tips for using a microphone

A microphone can frighten even an experienced speaker who has never used one. These tips will help:

- Remember that the microphone will make it possible for for your normal speaking voice to be heard easily by everyone in the room—even a large room. Think of it as a friend.

- If possible, arrive early when you know you will be using a microphone. This will give you time to make sure it is in working order and to test your voice level without an audience.

- Check the height of a stationary microphone before you say anything. If it is uncomfortably high or low, you can adjust the height.

- When you reach the podium, stand at a comfortable speaking distance from the microphone and ask, "Can you hear me?" If your voice is underamplified, the audience will let you know. If it is overamplified, *you* will know. Someone in charge will adjust the mike, or you can take care of the problem yourself by taking a step or two backward or forward.

- Do not lean forward over the microphone. It will be able to pick up your voice from a close but comfortable distance without your bending over.

- Do not touch a stationary microphone, or the head of a hand-held microphone. Your lightest touch can produce a resounding thump or a high, piercing whine.

- If you are given a hand-held microphone, hold it about 6 inches from your mouth and ask, "Can you hear me?" Make any adjustments necessary, moving the mike farther away from or closer to your mouth.

- Stay put behind a podium with a microphone. If you move, you will be moving away from the mike, and you will no longer be heard at the same voice level.

Eye contact.

If you use your voice to get attention, you use your eyes to hold attention. People tend to believe you, trust you, and listen to what you say if you are looking at them. "Shifty-eyed" and "cross-eyed" are not negative adjectives by chance. Direct eye contact is not just preferable; it is essential to effective private conversations and public addresses.

As a tool for public speaking, your eyes are second only to your voice. While you are speaking, you judge your audience to determine how they are reacting to your words. Their eyes, mirrored by the expressions on their faces, tell the story. Even at a distance you can gauge whether your listeners are attentive.

Why look away from someone you are greeting? Lack of eye contact (top) *says, "I do not mean what I'm saying." Good eye contact* (above) *with your audience says, "I mean every word I'm saying."*

Never forget for a moment that your listeners watch your eyes just as intently. How you look at them will determine to a great extent how faithfully they will listen to you. If your eyes never stray from your prepared text, never acknowledge the presence of your live audience, then you might as well hand out copies of your speech instead of delivering it. Without eye contact, you seem to dismiss your audience. Why should they listen if you do not seem to care whether or not you are heard? But when you take pains to establish eye contact with your listeners, they know you mean what you say.

There are three basic ways to use eye contact to your advantage:

Look your listener straight in the eye. Looking someone in the eye while you speak has a similar effect to that of shining your car headlights on a deer: he is transfixed, your captive audience so long as you maintain the beam. The eyes are the meaningful target—

Improving Your Speech

foreheads, lips, and chins are not good enough—and the other person's eyes can tell the difference. Direct eye contact assures your listener that you are sincere, that you care about what you are saying. Direct eye contact enables direct communication to take place.

For contrast, imagine the consequences of these examples of indirect eye contact:

- At a party, you follow the progress of other guests with your eyes while you chat with a friend.
- Standing with a shorter friend, you direct your remarks to the top of his head.
- Making a deal with a business acquaintance, you shake on it—while staring at his shoes.

Look the whole audience straight in the eye. Maintaining eye contact is a simple enough matter when you are face to face with one other person. But what if you are addressing two people? Ten people? Scores of people in a large room?

The answer lies in the target method. For each sentence you speak, zero in on the eyes of a different (target) member of the audience. Use an orderly right-left-center pattern, fixing your gaze on one particular man or woman for each phrase or sentence. The method may sound simplistic, but professional speakers adhere to it with excellent results. The whole audience feels included, cared for, spoken to. Targeting takes some effort to master, but it is worth the effort.

Let your eyes talk for you. Your eyes are the best indicator of your emotions. If you talk about courage and perseverance while your eyes show fear and indecision, your listeners will probably stop listening, and will certainly stop believing you.

Pauses.

Everyone pauses from time to time in the course of giving a talk. There are good pauses, for an intended effect, and there are bad ones. The bad ones leave you sounding unprepared. There are constructive ways to fill speaking space. First, however, learn to avoid the destructive ways.

An almost universal space filler is hemming and hawing: the all-purpose *uh* and its cousin *um*. These syllables find their way into nearly every phone conversation, where they are simply an irritant if noticed at all by either party. But they can destroy the effectiveness of anyone speaking in public.

Listen again to yourself speaking (not reading) on tape. Just as you may not have realized that you talk too fast, you may be surprised at how many ums and uhs show up in your speech. You do not hear yourself using them, and it is unlikely that anyone else will point them out. Fortunately, the habit is easily broken.

The best cure for such space fillers is the simplest: breathing space. If you find yourself bogging down in mid-sentence, just stop. Pause for a few seconds and collect your thoughts. Once you resume your sentence, it is likely to end up better than it started out. It will certainly *sound* better, uncluttered by uhs or ums—which tend to make your audience forget what preceded them. Best of all, mid-sentence pauses lend any speaker an aura of thoughtfulness, gravity, and maturity that a space-filling hem or haw cannot match. So take your time. You, the speaker, have the floor.

A particularly irksome space filler is "y'know?" It is not even logical. If your audience already knows, there is no point in telling them. If *you* already know, then "y'know?" cues the audience that you lack the verbal equipment to say what you know. In either case, "y'know?" has no place in good speaking. It may not bother you, and it may not bother your friends, but the average audience reacts to this space filler very poorly indeed. Avoid it.

Grammar counts too. Proper grammar is an essential part of correct speech, particularly since an audience is likely to judge you as much on how you say things as on what you say. The following list consists of common errors in American diction. Do any of them apply to you?

25 words and phrases to watch for

Incorrect	*Correct*
a criteria	a criterion
a phenomena	a phenomenon
Can I go now?	May I go now? (if asking permission)
finalize	complete; finish up
for free	free; for nothing
hardly nothing	hardly anything; almost nothing
hisself	himself
I ain't; it ain't	I am not; it is not
I been	I have been
I can't help but feel	I can't help feeling
I can't hardly	I cannot; I can hardly
I done	I did; I have done
it don't	it does not
off of	off
out loud	aloud
over with	over; finished; done with
quote (as noun)	quotation
reason is because	reason is
snuck	sneaked
supposing I am	suppose I am
theirselves	themselves
the media	the press; a medium
this here	this
this point in time	now; then
thusly	thus

250   **Improving Your Speech**

Help yourself

Pronunciation, pace, attention, eye contact, pauses; each of the five keys is an integral part of successful speechmaking; none can be overlooked. To check your progress, try these three self-help exercises:

- Talk to yourself in front of a mirror, with strict emphasis on making eye contact.

- Tape-record yourself—reading from a text and talking extemporaneously—to check your pronunciation, pace, and voice level.

- Listen carefully to the tape playbacks to see how poised you are during pauses.

Tape recorder checklist

You are your own worst judge of your own voice. You simply do not hear yourself accurately. Your ears are misplaced for the purpose, and you need an outside, objective opinion. A tape recorder is the obvious solution, and it makes no judgments at all.

With a tape recorder, you have plenty of time to make adjustments and refinements. Start simply. Talk conversationally into the machine, merely recounting what is on your mind or what you might like to say to somebody else if he were present. Sessions like these teach you what your "normal" voice level is.

As you get more comfortable with self-recording, you can record emotional flare-ups, perhaps, or tiny tantrums. With diligence and patience, you can learn from your tapes just how you sound to everyone else at your best and your worst. Then you can begin to change what you do not like. Remember, this vocal self-improvement is a strictly private matter, between you and your machine.

Here are some tape-playback questions to ask yourself:

1. Do you pronounce each word clearly?
2. Does any of the pronunciation sound uncertain?
3. Do you sometimes run two or more words together?
4. Do you talk too fast to be understood easily?
5. Do you sound tired or bored?
6. Do you speak loudly enough for each word to be heard clearly?
7. Does your speech sound too soft to reach a large audience?
8. Do you sound timid or uncertain?
9. Do you sound angry or belligerent?
10. Is your tone monotonous?
11. Within sentences, do you emphasize certain words?
12. Do you put emphasis on the wrong words?
13. Do you start sentences with the word "well"?
14. Does "y'know?" creep into your speech?
15. Do you handle pauses silently, without hemming or hawing?
16. Are there any grammatical mistakes? Incorrect words?
17. Is your speech marred by slang or profanity?
18. If you were in the audience, would you trust this speaker?
19. Do you sound as if you mean what you are saying?
20. Could you say what you have said on tape to an audience?
21. Do you sound better now than you did when you began taping?

Usually, it is best to listen for one or two speech habits at a time. If you prefer, listen to the tape several times in a row, making notes about whatever you observe. Make adjustments and rerecord. In a surprisingly short time, your answer to Number 21 will be "yes."

Improving Your Speech

Correct speech

Speaking correctly means using the English language correctly. That, necessarily, means paying attention to grammar and word usage. You may have a great deal to say, but if you do not say it right—according to the rules—your listeners will not take you seriously. Sloppy grammar and mispronunciation often go together; the speaker who uses words incorrectly will often mispronounce them as well.

Your basic diction—the way you use and apply words—is probably well grounded as the result of reading, writing, and hearing others talk. But you may be unaware of some common misuses and misapplications of everyday speech. Check your own diction against the following examples. Some of these words are used mistakenly all the time in informal speech.

You may wonder why you should be so careful about your diction. Your friends understand you anyway, and you want to sound like your normal self when you speak in public. But your friends have learned to read between the lines of what you say; you do the same thing when you listen to them. Sometimes, among friends and spouses, almost no words are needed.

This is not so in public speaking. In public, among strangers, the rules of grammar and correct speech are universal. A public speaker wants and needs to be understood the first time—which may be his only time. By learning and using proper diction, you increase your chances of expressing yourself clearly, whoever your audience. However unsophisticated an audience may be, it will understand and respect good diction.

Words commonly confused

affect, effect. *Affect* is a verb meaning to influence. *Effect*, though it can be a verb, usually is a noun meaning result.

compare, contrast. Use *compare* for pointing out similarities *and* differences between things. Use *contrast* only to show differences.

compare to, compare with. Use *compare to* when drawing a comparison between two things that are not really similar: "*Compared to* a glacier, you move quickly." Use *compare with* when drawing a comparison between two things that are similar: "*Compared with* her, you are a fast runner."

each. In formal prose and speech, treat each as meaning *each one* (singular): "*Each* of the soldiers did *his* duty."

either. Always a singular pronoun, meaning *either one*: "*Either* of the teams *is* capable of winning."

exhausting, exhaustive. Use *exhausting* to mean using up completely, especially using up energy, that is, becoming fatigued: "*Exhausting* exercise is not recommended for me." Use *exhaustive* to mean thorough: "My physician gave me an *exhaustive* examination and declared me fit as a fiddle."

farther, further. *Farther* means measurable distance; *further* means intangible distance: "There is no point in talking any *further* if you keep moving *farther* away."

flaunt, flout. Use *flaunt* to mean display conspicuously: "She *flaunted* her new car before all of us." Use *flout* to mean treat with contempt. "Some people *flout* traffic laws."

imply, infer. *Imply* is what the speaker does; *infer* is what the listener does: "The professor *implied* that he was not through yet. I *inferred* that he had yet to conclude his lecture."

it is I, it is me. In strictly formal speech, "It is *I*" is preferred.

kind of, sort of. Use *kind of* and *kinds of* to refer to definite things and commodities. *Sort of* and *sorts of* should be saved for indefinite, imprecise types and categories: "The *kind of* speaker who says he's *kind of* sorry will not be taken seriously." (Note: never use *kind of a* or *sort of a* in formal discourse.)

lay, lie. These are among the most misused verbs in the language. *Lay (laid, lain)* is a transitive verb; it takes an object. *Lie (lay, lain)* is an intransitive verb; it does not take an object: "Are you tired? Why not *lay* down your suitcase." "Thanks, but I need to *lie* down for a while."

learn, teach. *Learn* is intransitive, *teach* is transitive: "I *learned* so much French in a year abroad that I ended up *teaching* it to my classmates this year."

less, few. *Less* refers to amounts measured, and *few* refers to things counted: "We have *less* gas than I thought we had, but just a *few* more miles to go."

like, as. *Like* is a preposition, used for comparisons, and *as* is a conjunction, used to link phrases: "We picked up the suspect just *as* he left the premises. We're sticking to him *like* glue."

slow, slowly. *Slow* is an adjective, *slowly* an adverb: "Can you believe it? Danny ran *slowly* again. I'm afraid he's just a *slow* runner."

**ALWAYS be yourself.
NEVER address your audience
as less intelligent
than yourself.**

Word choice.
The best advice to inexperienced speakers is also the oldest: be yourself. Only a trained actor should stand in front of people he does not know and pretend to be Mark Twain, or Emily Dickinson, or Clarence Darrow. Most likely you will be speaking words that you wrote, so you had better use ones that you are comfortable with. Think about the way you would normally use persuasion on another person, or marshal your forces for an argument with that person. Those words are precisely the kind you should choose for a talk before a group. Only this time, your argument will be unopposed. Public speakers have that luxury.

A great deal of specialized jargon has crept into American speech, thanks to television, the press, and rock music. Public speakers who use this jargon—often in an attempt to sound "in"—usually end up sounding phony, presumptuous, or condescending.

Anyone can aspire to be a plain speaker. The chief requirements are telling the truth as you see and know it, telling it simply, and treating your audience as intellectual equals. All of these are healthy underpinnings for any public speaking appearance.

Choosing the right words is often complicated by changing times and fashions. Yesterday's "in" word or phrase is today's cliche. At the right is a list of overworked words. Many of them may remind you of others that you may have fallen into the habit of using. Get rid of them, too.

Choosing the right word

Fad words and phrases. Coming from politics, business, and the social sciences, these words sound pretentious in conversational speech. Some examples are:
bottom line, in context, time frame, viable

Pet words. Most of these words are legacies from adolescence. They say (vaguely) what you feel, but never what you think. They make *you* sound dated. A small sampling:
fabulous, cute, far out, right on, awesome

Extra words. More eloquent than *um* or *uh* (but no more meaningful), these extra words are creatures of habit. A thoughtful pause would be more eloquent than:
you know, frankly, so to speak, well

Slang words. Formal language is always acceptable, colloquial language is generally permissible, but slang usage is risky. When in doubt, use your dictionary. Misused slang sounds vulgar or tasteless.

Exaggeration. Most superlatives should be avoided; they are so overused that they have lost their meaning. Personalize your feelings and value judgments with, I think . . . , In my opinion . . . , etc. Meaningless superlatives include:
great, fantastic, terrific, incredible, the most

Pejorative words. Racial slurs and epithets—you know them all. Avoid them.

Adding -wise. Adding *-wise* to nouns is as unnecessary as it is ill-advised. Try the constructions *as to* or *speaking of*.

Profanity. Despite what you see in current movies, read in novels, and hear from comedians, profanity still has no place at all in formal speech or polite society. Swearing is generally offensive to people who know better ways to express themselves.

Overworked words to avoid

alienated	operative
articulate *(as a verb)*	oppressed
awesome	overreact
concept	paranoid
credibility	posture *(for attitude)*
depersonalization	prioritize
dynamic	rhetoric
elegant	ripoff
enrichment	scenario
holistic	structure *(as a verb)*
involved	substantive
manic	superlative
obscene	veritable

Improving Your Speech   253

Clichés to avoid

When you say...	Do you mean?	When you say...	Do you mean?
advance planning	planning	game plan	strategy
as far as	as for; as to	guesstimate	rough guess
as you know	as you may know; let me remind you	head tripping	thinking
		impact *(as a verb)*	affect
at this/that point in time	now *or* then	in my opinion	I think
beautiful	good, kind, cooperative	in point of fact	in fact
be that as it may	nonetheless; but	insightful	perceptive
bleep out	censor	learning experience	experience
by the same token	also	love	like; approve; admire
charisma	appeal	meaningful dialogue	discussion
confrontation	meeting	meaningful experience	experience
consciousness-raising	educational	more unique	singular
consensus of opinion	consensus; agreement	my personal opinion	my opinion
curiously enough	curiously	needless to say	obviously
dialogue	conversation; meeting	out of sight	impressive
disadvantaged	poor	out of this world	impressive
due to the fact	because	personal friend	friend
encounter	meet	presently	now
escalate	rise; raise	prior to	before
expertise	knowledge; skill	relationship	friendship; acquaintance
fabulous/ fantastic/ far out	good; excellent; acceptable	underprivileged	poor
		valid	true; genuine
for free	free	validate	confirm
frame of reference	background	with reference to	as to; about

Body language

Your eyes are the most obvious indicator of your attitudes and emotions, but your facial expressions, posture, and gestures—singly or together—can just as surely cue an attentive observer to your state of mind. Your most eloquent words cannot dispel the mistrust that is invited by negative body language.

Just as you can train your eyes to make contact with a single listener as well as an entire audience, you can learn to control the attentiveness of the rest of your body—if you become aware of your body language.

Facial expression. Variety is important. If you smile all the time, you may be considered insincere, perhaps even frivolous. By contrast, an unvarying solemn expression may be interpreted as insensitive, even dangerous. Look at photographs of yourself. Are you characteristically gloomy, grinning, frowning, close-mouthed? Are you noticeably out of step with the occasion? An appropriate variety of facial expressions will encourage an audience to trust you.

Posture. Sitting or standing, you want to look poised. Whether you are sitting behind a table or not, sit up straight. If you are on your feet, do not stand at military attention; it is clearly uncomfortable for most speakers. At the same time, slouching is uncomfortable for most audiences—it signals the speaker's lack of interest or his disrespect. Try to find an intermediate posture, with both feet balanced on the floor, in which you lean slightly *toward* your audience. That alone will focus the audience's attention on your eyes and mouth, which is where you want it.

Gestures. The best advice for novice speakers is to do nothing with your hands—rest them on the podium or clasp them behind your back. Do not fold your arms across your chest; that means, in body language, that you are challenging the audience. Hand gestures to emphasize your words can be highly effective, but they must be learned, usually in performance and often in response to the mood of the moment. Furthermore, hand language must be nearly perfectly synchronized to your spoken words or it will look foolish. Practice before a mirror may be helpful here, but audience feedback—time and time again—is the only sure test.

Body language checklist

Here are some suggestions about silent communication for public and nonpublic speaking occasions:

Fussing with your hair tells your audience your mind is elsewhere.

A sidewise glance says you surely distrust the speaker.

Your eyes and posture can say I do not take you seriously.

Your hands can say I worry about what you are telling me.

Self-assurance can easily become oppressive self-importance.

When neither person looks the other in the eye, who trusts whom?

Close attention is apparent in eyes that stay on the speaker.

Eye contact plus legs crossed toward one another equal rapt attention.

Improving Your Speech

Members of a mature audience are more likely to listen receptively to a speaker whose dress and grooming resemble their own. A younger audience might prefer a speaker less carefully groomed.

Personal appearance. A speaker needs more than voice plus message to make a good impression. There are silent factors, too, that contribute to your listeners' acceptance or rejection of what you have to say. Your good looks or lack of them are *not* a factor, but your clothes and grooming definitely are. Before you speak a word, they show your opinion of yourself and affect other people's opinion of you—for good or ill.

Department store salespeople know this well. They do significantly more business when they dress up fully for work, even if the weather is hot and the air conditioning inadequate. Customers, they find, are reluctant to buy from salesmen in shirtsleeves or saleswomen in pants. Experienced job seekers know this, too. Applicants who show up for an interview in business clothes increase their chances of being hired, even for blue collar jobs.

For public speaking or for important personal engagements, the rules are the same: dress to show yourself to best advantage. For men, this usually means a pressed suit, shined shoes, a tasteful tie, and a freshly pressed shirt with an unfrayed collar. Good grooming is important, too. The absence of a shave will reflect poorly on any speaker, as will unruly hair or a long-overdue haircut.

Women speakers should take care to avoid being too elaborately dressed, coiffed, or made up. A simple, becoming dress or suit, neatly styled hair, and carefully applied tasteful makeup will increase the speaker's confidence and prevent her audience from being distracted by her appearance. As for accessories, leave attention-drawing jewelry, scarves, etc., at home, and make sure that the shoes you choose are shined or cleaned and not run down at the heels.

If you know the audience you will be addressing, then you can predict with reasonable accuracy how they will be dressed and then dress yourself accordingly. You probably own at least one outfit in which you know you look well. Wear it. You will feel most comfortable in the clothes you like best—which, with very few exceptions, are your best choice for a speaking engagement.

You want to look like your best self, not like someone else. After all, *you* are the one who has been invited to speak. If you pay careful attention to clothes and grooming, you will increase the audience's confidence in you right along with your confidence in yourself.

Preparing to speak

What is needed for a successful outline? A central idea. A clear understanding of the audience that will be addressed. A beginning, middle, and end—all connected and all headed in the same direction.

Why do people make speeches? There are three reasons for speechmaking that will probably never change: the speaker has something special to say; he believes he has an audience receptive to his ideas; and he is confident he can make his case in the allotted time and place. With those reasons in mind, here is a speaker's three-part blueprint for a talk:

1. A receptive audience.
2. A central idea.
3. A beginning, middle, and end.

Unless all three of these fundamentals are present, a speaker probably cannot deliver a successful speech. Why?

—Without a receptive audience, one's points cannot be made.

—Without a central idea, a speech is pointless.

—Without a beginning-to-end structure, very few in the audience will get the point.

These basics of public speaking have not been improved upon in the 2400 years since Aristotle explained them in his great book, *Rhetoric*. Every successful speech, from a three-minute talk to a thirty-minute oration, will adhere to the time-tested formula that states, before you say anything, know your audience and organize your thoughts.

A receptive audience.
Who will be in the audience? In most cases, you will know your listeners or at least be known to them (fellow students, townspeople, club or union members, kindred political spirits, etc.). If this is not the case, find out who will be there, or check with someone likely to know. If you find that your listeners will be older or younger than you expected, better educated or less well informed, all male or all female, then tailor your remarks accordingly. A clear idea of who your audience will be gives you the best possible chance of getting through to them in your speech.

A central idea.
Ask yourself why you are motivated to speak in the first place. What is your point? A central idea is easier to arrive at than you might think. The problem is to distill it, to break it down to *one or two sentences* at the most. That brevity is what will make your central idea memorable. Whenever you can make your point memorably, you know you have succeeded.

A beginning, middle, and end.
Briefly, the *beginning* of your talk should do two things: get your listeners' attention and introduce your central idea. The *middle* portion (the longest by far) will support your central idea and expand on it, with examples or evidence, in some depth. The *end* will restate the central idea, summing up with supporting evidence. Ideally, you will come up with a quotable line, perhaps the central idea itself, that members of the audience can take home with them.

When composing your talk, *begin in the middle*. The bulk of your research and the meat of your argument will be found in the middle portion. No doubt your best ideas will stem from there, too. Try to hold off on composing the beginning of your speech—setting forth your central idea—until you have explored the fertile territory in the middle ground.

Because so many professional speakers do it, you may be tempted to begin or end your talk with a humorous anecdote, a topical or local joke. Resist the temptation. The pros know how to get laughs because they do it all the time. A novice speaker should not risk

Improving Your Speech

> **FORGET the jokes.**
> **FORGET the big fancy words.**

not getting a laugh, which can undermine the effectiveness of a speech at the very beginning.

If you stick to the three basics and honor the beginning–middle–end framework, you will not embarrass yourself—even if you are a first-time speaker. The rest of your preparation will consist of researching your subject matter, writing out your speech (one draft is not enough), and reading it aloud.

The best written speech does not always translate from the page to the podium, just as certain great novels do not read well aloud. Plan to read your text aloud before giving it the final touches. You are likely to make minor alterations that will significantly improve the way your speech "plays."

As in most things, skill is achieved through experience. The first time is the worst by far. Because novice speakers are so apprehensive, they tend to remember, vividly, all their mistakes. Knowing those mistakes, they usually do not repeat them. Members of such organizations as Toastmasters, or Dale Carnegie, or the self-help anonymous groups usually find, after they speak the first time, that they enjoy talking in public. It was only that first time that frightened them, like a plunge into cold water.

You will soon be ready to take that plunge.

Writing a speech.
Speechwriting differs from ordinary prose writing in one crucial respect: speeches are read aloud. Prose is meant to be read silently; it is designed solely for transfer from the printed page directly into the reader's mind. Speechwriting is consciously designed to be transferred by a speaker to a listener; the effect of the spoken word must be emotional as well as intellectual.

Even though you take great pains to write it, a good speech should sound as much like normal conversation as possible, using unadorned language that people can understand. A speech that you write should also conform to the way you normally talk—your tone of voice, choice of words, and cadence. Here is how to begin:

1. Using just one page of a yellow legal pad, outline your talk vertically under the three-part basic framework:
   appeal to audience
   central idea
   beginning–middle–end
   (Allow 80 percent of the page for the last grouping, and most of that for the middle.)

2. Make short notes to "set" each of the three themes above: your informed appeal to a particular audience; a short statement of your central idea; and your beginning–middle–end structure (starting with the middle).

So far your written preparations for speaking will not have taken up more than a page. But you may already have saved hours in wasted time. You now have a clear idea of whom to convince, your intention, and how to hold your argument together.

A first draft of a speech should be written in longhand or typed quickly. Many writers need to use a typewriter or word processor because they need execution that keeps up with their thoughts. It is helpful to get your spontaneous thoughts down, before you start writing like a writer rather than a talker. Here are some time-tested ingredients of an effective speech that should be of help whatever your subject matter:

- **Beginning.** Start by thanking your host or your sponsoring organization. Then introduce your central idea.
- **Middle.** Drawing on your knowledge of the audience, compliment your listeners. If appropriate, suggest ways in which your central idea coincides with certain goals they have or values they believe in.
- **End.** Work toward what salesmen call the *close*, in which the audience becomes persuaded that your central idea, once a hypothesis, is now a given.

When you write your final draft, remember that a typewritten page takes considerably longer to read aloud than you may think. A ten-minute talk translates to five typewritten pages or less. Try to retain most of the unrehearsed scribbled or hastily typed language of your first draft: that is how you really talk. *Given a choice between a big fancy word and a short plain one, take the little one.* Keep your sentences short, too. Long sentences may be artful on paper, but they are deadly when read aloud. Last of all, *never fail to thank the audience* for their attention.

To illustrate a well-written speech, it might be useful to study one of the very best: Lincoln's Gettysburg Address.

For all its deserved fame, for all its renowned eloquence, Lincoln's address was only 280 words long and required only three minutes to deliver. As an accomplished speaker he knew intuitively the appropriate message to deliver at Gettysburg. How would Lincoln have sketched out the Gettysburg Address?

Abraham Lincoln, when he wrote out the Gettysburg Address (supposedly on the back of an envelope), came up with some phrases that will live forever in American prose. He may have memorized the whole speech; he may have read it. But what if he had restricted himself to one small index card for prompting purposes? The card on the next page shows what it might have looked like.

Lincoln's Gettysburg Address

Fourscore and seven years ago our fathers brought forth on this continent a new nation, conceived in liberty, and dedicated to the proposition that all men are created equal. Now we are engaged in a great civil war, testing whether that nation, or any nation so conceived and so dedicated, can long endure. We are met on a great battlefield of that war. We have come to dedicate a portion of that field, as a final resting place for those who here gave their lives that that nation might live. It is altogether fitting and proper that we should do this. But, in a larger sense, we cannot dedicate—we cannot consecrate—we cannot hallow—this ground. The brave men, living and dead, who struggled here, have consecrated it, far above our poor power to add or detract. The world will little note, nor long remember, what we say here, but it can never forget what they did here. It is for us the living, rather, to be dedicated here to the unfinished work which they who fought here have thus far so nobly advanced. It is rather for us to be here dedicated to the great task remaining before us—that from these honored dead we take increased devotion to that cause for which they gave the last full measure of devotion—that we here highly resolve that these dead shall not have died in vain—that this nation, under God, shall have a new birth of freedom—and that government of the people, by the people, for the people, shall not perish from the earth.

How the speech was planned

1. **Audience** —survivors and mourners of the casualties of Gettysburg. (The occasion is the consecration of the battlefield.)
2. **Central idea** —Civil war is a dreadful, wasteful undertaking, but in the course of history a noble ideal—an indissoluble union—must on occasion be tested by fire.
3. **Rhetorical structure**
   a. *Beginning*— the framers of the Constitution foresaw a nation conceived in liberty, in which all men are created equal.
   b. *Middle*— thousands of Americans, from North and South, died at Gettysburg to test the proposition that the nation can endure, at whatever price.
   c. *End*— everyone here today must now profit from the awful witness of Gettysburg: none of these soldiers shall have died in vain; a new nation shall rise from these ashes; the spirit of the Founding Fathers shall somehow transcend the tragic waste and sacrifice of this battlefield.

A card Lincoln might have used

```
(beginning)   Fourscore and seven years ago...
              nation conceived in liberty...
              all men equal

(middle)      world will forget us...
              but not men who died here

(end)         new birth of freedom...
              government of, by, and for people last forever
```

Improving Your Speech

Reading a speech. Mark Twain once said, "It usually takes me more than three weeks to prepare a good impromptu speech." He meant it, too. The best speakers, like the best actors, have to practice hard in order to appear natural.

There are three methods for speaking in public: (1) from a written text; (2) extemporaneously (from minimal notes); and (3) impromptu (from no notes at all). At first the alternatives may seem progressively less difficult. But in fact, number three is always the riskiest and often the hardest. A novice speaker should never consider "winging it" in front of a group until he is thoroughly familiar with his own voice, his own style, and his own words—written out. In order, here is how each method works:

Delivery from a written text. Written, as used here, refers to remarks or to a speech that you have written yourself. The first rule is not to read your speech at all—that is, never appear to be reading it word for word. This would necessitate your staring at your text, as if it were an unfamiliar book, and rarely coming up for air. Your audience might conclude that their presence does not matter at all. It would also appear that you have no familiarity with your own words. The only situation in which it is not a mistake to read aloud to a live audience is when broadcasting on the radio. And people who read scripts on the radio are usually professional actors or newscasters. In person you must do more than read; you must communicate.

Never forget that your listeners crave eye contact. You cannot begin to establish whole-room eye contact if your head is buried in your text most of the time. The remedy is twofold. First, practice reading your speech over and over again until the beginning of each section or paragraph is a memory cue to the rest. When you know your material well enough, type your final draft in capital letters, with extra space between words so that you can make it out easily from a distance. Next, underline the crucial first words and phrases of paragraphs and sections—or highlight them in yellow, or type them in red—so that you can be a glancer, not a reader. Glancing is a natural thing to do while speaking; reading is patronizing.

Extemporaneous delivery. When you become sufficiently adept at cuing yourself from first words and phrases, you are but a short step away from making seemingly offhand talks—with careful preparation, but no written-out text. For this method it is best to compose a single-page *master note* (see the Lincoln sample on the previous page). This will include, in digest form, the same information as an outline for a written address: appeal to audience, central idea, and beginning–middle–end linkage.

Impromptu delivery. This method is appropriate for speakers who address audiences frequently and are

---

NEVER read your entire speech.

---

very sure of themselves and their subject matter. Impromptu speaking, in fact, requires more expertise and self-confidence than many experienced speakers are likely to possess. Nonprofessionals are well advised to opt for delivery from a written text, or for extemporaneous delivery.

If proper preparation for speaking involves so much rehearsal and homework, why not simply memorize your remarks? Unless you are a trained actor, this method almost never works. At some time you may have been compelled to memorize stanzas of poetry, or lines from plays, or famous historical orations. Were you pleased with the way you sounded in recitation? Most likely, your version of those great words sounded monotonous, or painfully self-conscious, or both. An entire speech, minus an actor's intonation and dramatic embroidery, would probably sound more awkward still. The moment you memorize something, your delivery stops being spontaneous and genuine. Without spontaneity and sincerity, you cannot persuade anyone of anything.

Practicing a speech. Most of your speech preparation can be done all by yourself. One crucial part, however, will require the cooperation of another person and the use of a tape recorder, as discussed earlier.

Record a normal conversation with your cooperating friend. When you play the conversation back, note how he or she reacts to whatever you say. Pay even closer attention to your own "performance." Can you be clearly understood? Is your speaking tone monotonous, tired-sounding, markedly accented, or too excitable? Imagine yourself listening to this voice on the tape for the first time. Does the tone make you feel anxious? Bored? Angry?

Practicing for a specific talk, try to simulate difficult conditions for yourself. Turn on a portable fan or a noisy air conditioner; play a radio in the background; train a lamp or two on your face—whatever might disturb your concentration, because something probably will when you actually speak in front of an audience. As you start the tape recorder, make note of the time; however quickly you get through your trial run, your actual speech will almost surely run longer. Do not talk too loudly—only loud enough to overcome your distractions. Wherever you think an audience reaction (laughter, murmurs, applause) is likely or appropriate, pause until the floor is yours again.

Practice under noisy conditions can help you deal with distractions that occur when giving a talk.

Practicing an illustrated talk before giving it can iron out difficulties with visual aids.

If you have a full-length mirror, use it to practice eye contact. Practice your most comfortable speaking stance as well—standing still or shifting slightly, weight on the balls of your feet or on one foot at a time. (Behind a solid lectern, of course, your feet will not be a problem.) If you feel you must use hand gestures, try to limit them to the few that come most naturally to you.

The whole idea here is to get thoroughly comfortable with your text, voice, pace, stance, etc. If you take the care to go through with this rehearsal as many times as seems necessary, there can be few things that will surprise or unnerve you when you are in front of an audience.

Visual aids help. Some rehearsal is essential in situations where visual aids—slides, blackboards, flip charts, etc.—are to be used. Unfamiliarity with blackboard techniques can produce the high, screeching noise that causes most people to shudder. (You might bring your own soft chalk with you.) Botched slide presentations can turn a lecture into an unintended comedy routine. (Insert the slides yourself and run through each of them beforehand.) And someone else's flip chart can too often fall over. Any of these mishaps can become the most memorable aspect of your well-intentioned presentation. But routine rehearsal and practice should forestall all of them.

Most public speakers find that they can quickly remedy their shortcomings. That worst shortcoming of all —dread of the first time out—is largely self-imposed, and all of these tips are designed to do away with it entirely. A well-organized and well-researched speech, thoroughly rehearsed, can actually inspire anticipation rather than dread. All that preparation means that you are ready, that you have every reason to be confident. Look yourself in the mirror one more time, then go out and let the audience know *you* know what you are talking about.

Everyday uses of speech

Telephone speaking. Have you ever tried to determine how much time you spend on the phone each day? The average time is one hour. You may spend more, or less, but telephone conversation is likely to be a significant part of your daily routine. It makes little sense to undermine your phone communications with discourtesy, incoherence, or impatience.

Most people jump to answer the phone when it rings. Perhaps nothing else in your daily or business life commands such instant obedience. Following such a response, it is curious that so many people answer their phone with an ill-tempered snarl. Whoever is calling will not be likely to call again soon. It is, however, remarkably simple to change your telephone etiquette, starting with the way you answer the phone. The best way is the simplest: "Hello? This is [your name]."

Common courtesy and a positive attitude, practiced and maintained, will serve you well in any conceivable at-home telephone conversation. Business calls, however, frequently require another ingredient: patience. When you place a business call, be organized. Know precisely whom you want to reach (or his or her department or assistant), and state that intention.

Improving Your Speech   261

Telephone pointers

- **Voice.** Unless someone happens to tell you, you may have no idea of how you sound on the phone—too loud perhaps, or too soft, or too fast. Find out. Ask a friend about it or record yourself on tape.
- **Attitude.** When a nervous, inexperienced salesman or fund-raiser calls you, you can tell almost instantly what the call is about. To counteract a bad first impression, try to start every phone conversation as if you really care, as if this call is just the one you were expecting. If it is not, it will not take long to end the conversation.
- **Courtesy.** Before you dial, ask yourself a few questions. Is this an inconvenient time? Is the other person likely to be too busy to talk? Should you call back later? Most of these questions can be answered early in your conversation, before inconsideration sets in. If you reach an answering machine, either hang up or leave a short, straightforward message.

Emotions show through even when you are using a telephone. Bear this in mind when you talk.

If your quarry is "in conference," it means he or she cannot or will not talk to you now. No matter. Leave your number and call back an hour later if your call is not returned. Call back a second time, even a third, if necessary. Your man or woman's secretary will have dropped the conference excuse by this time, and your courteous persistence cannot fail to make an impression. Your name will go to the top of the call-back list. Courtesy, persistence, and patience all have an important place in telephone business transactions.

Every time you talk to a stranger on the phone you are practicing the same arts of persuasion that you use when speaking in public. On-the-phone training is a daily refresher course. Make the most of it, and try your best to be pleasant.

Salesmanship.
The art of salesmanship is primarily a one-to-one test of wits between you, the seller, and your listener, the buyer. (See the *Careers* chapter for a discussion of speaking in a job interview.) Before the buyer orders anything, he must be convinced that the salesman means what he says, that his word is his bond regardless of his product. Effective public speaking operates on the same principle. The listener must be persuaded that you, the speaker, are worthy of belief and trust. Persuasiveness, in both selling and speaking, rests on four fundamental precepts:

1. **Knowledge.** Speakers, like salesmen, must know their subjects—particularly their central ideas or selling points—better than their listeners. You may need to anticipate tricky (even mean-spirited) questions and have a ready answer for anything, which is where research and practice come in. The best salesmen always have tailor-made reasons why *anybody* can use their product. The best speakers, especially debaters, always seem capable of summoning a convincing argument on the spot.

2. **Empathy.** Not to be confused with sympathy (feeling *for* the other person), empathy is the ability to step into the other person's shoes, to feel *with* him or her. In terms of public speaking, empathy is the learned talent for saying the right thing in the right words to markedly different listeners. A skilled speaker delivers the same basic message time and time again, simply altering his tone and his style so as not to offend his present audience, and even to flatter them a bit. Top salesmen must do this constantly, of course, trying to convince a housewife, a teenager, and a grandfather that the same car is the right choice for each of them.

3. **Sincerity.** Presumably, you would not choose to talk, publicly, about something you did not believe in. But the moment you decide to stand up and sound off about a subject, your own faith and belief in it is not enough. You must demonstrate, through your delivery technique, that you truly mean what you say. If anything undermines that sincerity—a monotonous tone of voice, shifty eyes, sloppy posture—your credibility will be damaged and may even disappear.

4. **Enthusiasm.** You may not be able to define enthusiasm, but you know it when you see it: excitement, energy, contagious self-confidence. Those who know how to transfer that feeling to others are usually outstanding in their field: successful coaches, teachers, businesspeople, politicians, and religious leaders. Such a talent is too easily passed off as speaking ability. What it really is, when practiced and sustained, is inspirational leadership.

Knowledge, empathy, sincerity, and enthusiasm. All are essential to both selling and speaking in public. Knowledge and enthusiasm are largely a matter of thorough preparation and vigorous delivery; empathy and sincerity are largely determined by your listener's perception of your intentions. Salesmen have a harder time with listeners' misconceptions than speakers do—but not much harder.

Another technique shared by salesmen and speakers is the use of the "grabber" in the first paragraph. In sales, the grabber is the unique selling point; in speaking it is the central idea. Whichever form it takes, it should be mentioned early and often. As a public speaker you must never forget that you are selling *yourself* to whomever you address, just as a politician sells himself in painstakingly crafted 30-second spots on television. You, however, will be "live," not taped. Your only product is yourself. It is important to mean what you say about that product—with your words, your eyes, your body language, and your attitude.

Parliamentary procedure.

There are thousands of community organizations and service groups in the United States. Very few of them would accomplish much of anything unless they depended on *Robert's Rules* for order, decorum, and proper parliamentary procedure. Although every conceivable point of order is covered in *Robert's*, the group chairman is responsible for invoking, enforcing, and interpreting each parliamentary dispute. (A condensed table of *Robert's Rules* may be found on pages 264-265.)

Even in an informal meeting, a chairman has the responsibility of conducting proceedings fairly.

If you know your rules of procedure, local meetings can provide excellent on-the-floor training for self-assertiveness and for making your points aloud and under pressure. If you become disruptive or obstructionist, the chairperson of the meeting will let you know soon enough. When you learn such a lesson in a crowd, you tend to remember it. Here are some examples of ways—within *Robert's Rules*—to influence the course of a public meeting:

Important procedural rules

Adjournment	The chairperson can hold off a hurry-up vote on adjournment until proper consideration is given to the entire scheduled agenda.
Obstructionism	A chairperson is empowered to tell a troublemaker that he will not be recognized to speak—that he is out of order—until he agrees to behave in accordance with the rules.
Recess	As in a courtroom, the chairperson may declare a short recess at a time when feelings are running too high—or when it looks as if an ill-advised vote is in the offing.
Brokering	The chairperson is entitled to interrupt debate and propose a vote whenever he pleases, or to advise postponement of a vote if he does not like the probable outcome.
Quorum	Organizations establish the requirements for a quorum, the minimum number of people that must be present at a meeting before its proceedings can be regarded as valid. If the quorum criterion is not met, the meeting is invalid.

Improving Your Speech

Robert's Rules of order

Table of precedence of parliamentary motions, points of order, and procedural questions

Type of motion		May be debated	May be amended
Privileged category	Fix time of next meeting	yes[1]	yes
	Adjourn	no	no
	Take a recess	yes[1]	no[2]
	Point of privilege (e.g., group comfort)	no	no
	Point of order (refer, agenda)	no	no
Incidental category	Point of order (refer, ruling)	no	no
	Appeal ruling of the chair	yes[4]	no
	Parliamentary inquiry	no	no
	Withdraw motion[6]	no	no
	Suspend the rules (temporary)	no	no
	Object to consideration	no	no
Subsidiary category	Lay on the table (postpone)	no	no
	Close debate (vote previous question)	no	no
	Limit debate	no	yes
	Postpone (to specific time)	yes	yes
	Refer to committee	yes	yes
	Make amendment	no[8]	yes
	Postpone indefinitely	yes	no
Main or unclassified category	Primary motion	yes	yes
	Take up from the table	no	no
	Reconsider[9]	no[8]	no
	Rescind	yes	yes

264   Improving Your Speech

Type of vote	Needs second	May interrupt speaker
majority	yes	no
majority	yes	no
majority	yes	no
majority[3]	no	yes
no vote	no	yes
majority[3]	no	yes
majority[5]	yes	yes
no vote	no	yes
no vote[7]	no	no
2/3	yes	no
2/3	no	yes
majority	yes	no
2/3	yes	no
2/3	yes	no
majority	yes	no
majority	yes	no
majority	yes	no
majority	yes	no
majority	yes	no
majority	yes	no
majority	yes	yes
2/3[10]	yes	no

Explanatory footnotes

[1] May be debated *except* when another motion is already on the table.
[2] Only the length of the recess may be amended.
[3] The chair decides—but a majority may overrule.
[4] May be debated *except* when it pertains to a rules violation or to indecorum.
[5] A tie vote upholds the chair's ruling.
[6] Only the person who made the motion may withdraw it.
[7] No objection, no vote. If there is an objection, a majority vote is required.
[8] May be debated *only* if the original motion was ruled debatable.
[9] This is complicated. Only a person who voted on the prevailing side may move to reconsider—and that only on the same day that the original vote was taken (or the next day of the same session). The following motions may *not* be reconsidered: adjourn, point of order (agenda), lay on the table (postpone), point of order (ruling), point of privilege, recess, refer to committee, suspend the rules, and take up from the table.
[10] If notice was given at a previous meeting that a vote to rescind would take place, then a majority vote would suffice. Without such notice, a two-thirds vote is required.

For further reference

Braden, Waldo Warder
  Public Speaking: The Essentials
  Harper & Row
Ehrlich, Eugene and Hawes, Gene R.
  Speak for Success
  Bantam Books
Newman, Edwin
  Strictly Speaking
  Bobbs Merrill
Prochnow, Herbert V. and Herbert V., Jr.
  The Toastmaster's Treasure Chest
  Harper & Row

Rogers, Natalie
  Talk-Power
  Dodd, Mead
Stedman, Raymond William
  A Guide to Public Speaking
  Prentice-Hall
Strunk, William, Jr., and White, E.B.
  The Elements of Style
  Macmillan

Improving Your Speech

Writing Effective Letters

- Social letters 266
- Business letters 276
- Clubs and organizations 290
- Tips for retired people 292
- Postal information 298
- Forms of address 300

Letters are an important part of life. They can bring you closer to friends and family. They can bring comfort and cheer and inspire affection and love. The right letter can get you a job, sell your products or services, influence others, initiate action, and build goodwill. Knowing how to write the right letter for the right occasion can be a powerful asset in your social and business life, and it is a skill that anyone can learn.

The secret of writing a successful letter is knowing what you want to say and how to say it. Although neither is necessarily difficult, when confronted by a blank piece of paper, *you* may go blank—because, you think, you do not know what to say. In fact, this is rarely the case. You always have at least one reason for writing a letter and need only ask yourself what it is.

More often, the problem is that you do not know *how* to express yourself. The solution to this problem lies in knowing the kind of letter that you wish to write, whether it is a social or a business letter, and, if it is social, whether it is formal or informal and personal. There are specific techniques for each type of letter. Formal letters, such as announcements, invitations, and responses, have a standard form and wording that are simple to follow. Informal or personal letters to friends and relations are like a "visit" on paper; the trick in writing them is to write as you ordinarily talk. Business letters are written with a specific goal in mind, and usually require some advance preparation. You must decide on your goal and organize your supporting material, facts, arguments, requests, or questions *before* you start writing. In this chapter you will find the ways and means of doing this—techniques for organizing your thoughts, correct forms, and samples that you can use as models for the many occasions in your social and business life when you want to say the right thing in the right way.

Social letters

Your personal letters to friends and family can be relaxed and original in form and content. This is not the case, however, for the "letters of etiquette," the communications of social life that have a specific purpose (invitations, announcements, acceptances and regrets, thank yous, notes of congratulation or condolence). For these, it is important to be correct, to follow the standard social conventions in appearance and content. This section gives valuable help on writing both informal and formal social letters.

Parts of a letter. This five-part form is standard for all informal letters:

Heading. This is simply your address and the date or, if you have a printed letterhead, just the date. It goes at least an inch from the top, with at least a ¾-inch margin (larger, if you have a short letter) on the right. Cities and street names should be spelled out, but you can abbreviate the states. *You will notice that the date and return address have been omitted from most of the sample letters in this chapter. This was done to save space, but you should always include them in your letters.*

Salutation. This is the greeting. It goes on the left, at least half an inch below the heading, with the left margin equal to the right margin. The standard form is "Dear Sally" or "Dear Mrs. Thomson," depending on how well you know the person you are writing to. In the United States, "My Dear Mr. Jones" is considered more formal, but in England it is less formal. Salutations such as "Dear Friend," "Dear Sir," or "Dear Madam" are impolite for social letters.

Body. This is the message and there is no special form.

Complimentary closing. How you say "goodby" depends on how well you know the person you are writing to. In the past, closings were elaborate, but today's style is short and simple, such as "Yours sincerely" "Sincerely yours." Closing with just "Yours" sounds abrupt; but "Cordially" and "Sincerely" do not. "Respectfully" is usually reserved for writing to employers or customers.

Signature. This goes below the closing, a little to the right, in ink. The social convention is that you never use a title, such as Dr., Mr., Miss, or Mrs. when signing. A married woman would sign Betty Jordan, but she could, and *would* for business correspondence, add Mrs. Donald Jordan underneath her signature in parentheses. A divorced woman, but not a widow, would add Mrs. Betty Jordan.

Addressing the envelope. Use either the block form or indented form. The return address goes in the upper left. The convention is that women use Miss, Mrs., or Ms., but men do not use Mr. A boy under twelve is addressed as Master (that is, Master John Smith). Boys are not addressed as Mister until they are 18 or girls as Miss until they are 16. Use just the boy's full name when he is between the ages of 13 and 17, and the girl's full name when she is under 16. When addressing a husband and wife, the man's name comes first. You may write Mr. and Mrs. John Smith or John and Mary Smith. The address should be complete. Do not abbreviate people's names (unless *they* always do) or words like Street, Road, or Parkway, and do not forget the zip code. This can go on the same line as the town or city and state or on a separate line after the state.

You may add in the lower left corner:

PERSONAL—when you are sending a purely social and confidential letter to someone's office.

PLEASE FORWARD—when you know only the former address.

OPENED BY MISTAKE—when you mistakenly receive and open another person's mail. If you reseal the envelope, write "Opened by Mistake," sign your name, and mail it for the post office to redeliver, you will not be legally liable if the letter is lost.

Heading
63 Glover Street
Pleasantville, CT zip code
March 29, 1985

Salutation
Dear Sally,   *Body*

  Thank you so much for the lovely weekend. It was wonderful to see you and Jerry again and such a treat for Tom and me to get out of the city. We loved meeting Betty and Jim Henderson. It is always a pleasure to meet fellow sailors. I think it would be wonderful for us all to go sailing together this summer, but I hope you and Jerry will come for a visit way before then. You are such marvelous hosts and I only hope we can show you as good a time.

Closing Affectionately,
Signature Betty
           Betty

Writing Effective Letters   267

Stationery. Choose the best quality paper you can afford. Paper comes in different weights: the heavier the weight, the better the quality. A good choice is a 20-pound rag bond.

For formal correspondence (see page 270) that is not printed, the rule is to use plain white paper, a double sheet that folds once into its matching envelope.

For general informal correspondence (everything but personal letters), you have a wide choice, but you will always be in good taste if you stay with subdued shades. The rule used to be, a large sheet of paper, 8 × 10 or 7½ × 10, with matching envelopes in white, cream, or gray for men; and a folded sheet of blue, 5½ × 6½ or 6 × 8, that folds once again into a matching envelope, for women. Today, the larger sizes and a variety of colors are considered suitable for both men and women. For personal letters bright colors are popular and correct now for men and women.

Monograms and letterheads. Stationery printed with your monogram or letterhead costs more but it makes an excellent impression. A monogram is fine for personal letters, but a letterhead (including your telephone number, if you wish) is better for general-purpose letters.

Women have traditionally used the "informal," a folded card of white or off-white with the name engraved in black on the front (Mrs. John Jones, or Harriet Jones if unmarried) for social notes. While this is still correct, today informals can have both the husband's and wife's names, include the address, and be in any color, with printing or engraving in a contrasting color.

Typing vs. writing.
It was once considered bad taste to type personal letters, but this is no longer true. Go ahead and type them, especially if your handwriting is hard to read, but remember to always sign your letters by hand, in ink. Formal invitations and replies, however, are never typed. Although there is no firm rule, it is usually considered more polite, more personal, and more sincere to write short thank-you notes or notes of congratulation or sympathy by hand. (When you type, use larger sheets and do not type on the back of the page.)

Page sequence and folding.
For folded sheets, social notes should be short enough to go on the first page. Longer personal notes are written on pages one and three. A long letter simply follows the natural sequence.

The main point in having matching envelopes is to have as few folds as possible. A double sheet is folded once and put in the envelope fold first, as is a small single sheet. A larger single sheet is folded in three equal sections and inserted with the closed end first in such a way that the letter will be opened right side up.

How to be yourself

- **Visualize the person you are writing to.** Imagine you are face to face. What would you say? What questions would you ask? What questions would the person ask you?
- **Ask, "What would I say to *this* person?"** You would not talk the same way to your dearest friend as you would to a casual acquaintance, your child's school principal, or your boss.
- **Write the way you speak.** Keep thinking about *what* you want to say and do not edit. Your first thought is usually your best. Use the words you normally would in speaking. Most people use contractions (I can't, rather than I cannot) and short, simple words (I *went* to a movie, not I *attended* a movie). Try not to make a special effort to be correct; the result may sound forced and insincere.
- **Use conversational techniques.** You emphasize certain words in conversation by changing your inflection or tone; you can do the same in writing by underlining (Your dinner was *terrific!*), but do not overdo it. You can also occasionally mention the name of the person you are writing to (I wish I could see you, Betty).

Personal letters.
These letters to friends and family can be the most fun to write because they are like a friendly visit. Their purpose is to share experiences and feelings and to give pleasure. Of all the different kinds of letters you write, personal letters give you the best chance to be yourself—which is also the key to writing them well.

Lord Chesterfield, the 18th-century English essayist and social critic, put it very well in this advice to his son: "Write as you speak! Write as though you were seated in a room with me, talking in plain, simple language about the things you have seen and done and thought and experienced since you wrote to me last."

Being yourself or finding your own "voice" is something all good writers must learn. You can tell when you have found your voice because your writing will sound relaxed and easy. Your thoughts and words flow, though this is not always easy to achieve. "Writer's block" can be experienced by letter writers, too. You become tongue-tied, freeze, and feel as though you have nothing to say. That blank piece of paper is intimidating you. The trick to overcoming this, as Lord Chesterfield knew, is to relax and imagine that you are having a conversation with the person you are writing to. Some hints to help you do that are above.

Letters to friends and relatives

Get well

```
Dear Uncle Bob,
    I spoke to Margaret last night
and she told me about your kidney
stone and that you were much better
and would be home from the hospital
today. Hurrah! I'm sure you'll be
just fine again in no time. In the
meantime, here's a new book by our
favorite, Guy Murtchie, that I
hope you'll like. Get well soon!
                        Cordially,
                        Hank
```

Travel

Dearest Sandy,

I'm in Fez at the famous Hotel Jamai, where I stayed 40 years ago when it was about one-sixth the size. In a week I'll be home and eager to see you. I know you'd love Morocco. I'm traveling with Gloria French. Gloria knows a lot about rugs, and we intend to visit all the museums.

There are really impressive Roman ruins of temples, much destroyed, but many stones are standing, one 10 feet high.

As for painting, I've been working—produced three pictures and I've done a lot of work on the book. I'm really on the last lap now. I think of you all the time, for your dear friendship and all of your help on my book.

Much love,
Anne

Christmas letter to a sister

Dearest Sis,

It's so good to be back in Jerome and to have all the children with us after the past few years of being all over the map. It has made it a wonderful Christmas, though we miss you and Jim and wish you could be here with us. Maybe next year!

Of course, there's lots of news. Wes has been working on the pipeline, as you know, and Mike has joined him. Mike is in love with a lovely girl. Her name is Tessie and it looks as though they will get married this summer and settle down in Alaska. Caroline took a job with an engineering firm in Nome—so except for Hank, we're all together again. Hank came up from San Diego in the most incredible van (about a block long). He's joined forces with a friend who manufactures water skis and they're going to promote them on a grand tour of European spas—thus, the van. But you'll see for yourself, as he's coming east in March to ship the van to France and, of course, he'll come and see you.

You can imagine what fun it's been in Jerome. We're staying in the hotel (our house is rented for another year yet). We've been spending lots of time downstairs in the Spirit Room, where Wes threw a gigantic party for our anniversary. Lots of people remember you and Jim from your visit three years ago. Tom and Shirley, Dr. Joe and Margaret, and Burt send their best regards, as do Wes and the kids. Let me hear form you! My love to you and Jim.

With love,
Sarah

When you do not know what to say

If, in spite of everything, you still draw a blank, you can simply say, "I don't know what to say," but say *why*. That's what Michael Faraday, the English physicist famous for his work on electricity, did in this letter written to Sarah Bernard in 1820. Sarah Bernard and Michael Faraday were married soon after this letter was written and had a long and happy life together, a tribute in part, perhaps, to the power of the written word.

My Dear Sarah,

It is astonishing how much the state of the body influences the powers of the mind. I have been thinking all the morning of the very delightful and interesting letter I would send you this evening, and now I am so tired, and yet have so much to do, that my thoughts are quite giddy, and run round your image without any power of themselves to stop and admire it. I want to say a thousand kind and, believe me, heartfelt things to you, but am not master of words fit for the purpose; and still, as I ponder and think on you, chlorides, trials, oil, steel, miscellanea, mercury, and fifty other professional fancies swim before and drive me further and further into the quandry of stupidness.

From your affectionate
Michael

Writing Effective Letters

Invitations

Formal vs. informal. A formal event, such as a large church wedding or dinner-dance, requires a formal invitation. An informal invitation can be used for an informal event such as a small at-home wedding or country weekend. Informal invitations are simply handwritten notes in the first person. Formal invitations can be engraved or handwritten, but they have a specific form. They are written in the third person and are centered on the first page of folded white paper.

Acceptances and regrets. Any invitation should be answered right away. Formal invitations require a handwritten reply that follows the exact form of the invitation.

R.S.V.P. This means "Repondez si'il vous plait," French for "answer please." It can also be written R.s.v.p. and goes in the lower left with an address beneath on formal invitations, or with a phone number, if you wish, on informal ones. For informal events such as cocktail parties, where you need to know how many people are coming and also want to speed replies, you can write "Regrets only" and your phone number.

Please come to a party to celebrate the publication of Sam Jones's new mystery, A Death in the Afternoon, *at the Little Tor Bookshop, 100 River Road, Grandview, NY.*

Regrets only
555-1212

Formal dinner

> John Gordon and Mary Gordon Green
> the children of
> Henry and Elizabeth Gordon
> request the pleasure of your company
> at a dinner in honor of their parents'
> Golden Wedding Anniversary
> on Saturday, the sixteenth of June
> at eight o'clock
> Tumblebrook Country Club
>
> R.S.V.P.
> Mrs. Robert Green
> 140 Old Mountain Road
> West Hartford, CT zip code

Informal dinner

> Dear Edith,
>
> My brother John and I are giving a small dinner in honor of our parents' Golden Wedding Anniversary on Saturday, June 16th at eight o'clock at the Tumblebrook Country Club. The celebration wouldn't be complete without you and Harry. I do hope you can come.
>
> Cordially,
> Mary Green

Formal acceptance

> Mr. and Mrs. Harold Smith
> accept with pleasure
> the kind invitation of
> John Gordon and Mary Gordon Green
> to a dinner in honor of
> the Golden Wedding Anniversary
> of their parents
> Henry and Elizabeth Gordon
> on Saturday, the sixteenth of June
> at eight o'clock
> at the Tumblebrook Country Club

Informal acceptance

> Dear Mary,
>
> Harry and I will be delighted to come on Saturday at eight to celebrate your parents' Golden Wedding Anniversary. What a wonderful occasion! Thank you so much for asking us.
>
> Yours sincerely,
> Edith Smith

Formal regret

> Mr. and Mrs. Harold Smith
> regret that they are unable to accept
> the kind invitation of
> John Gordon and Mary Gordon Green
> to a dinner in the honor of
> the Golden Wedding Anniversary
> of their parents
> Henry and Elizabeth Gordon
> on Saturday, the sixteenth of June
> at eight o'clock
> at the Tumblebrook Country Club

Informal regret

> Dear Mary,
>
> I'm so sorry, but we can't come to what I know will be a wonderful party. We will be away that whole week in Montreal to meet Joe's fiancée and her family, but thank you so much for asking us. Harry and I both wish we could be there.
>
> Yours sincerely,
> Edith Smith

Formal wedding. An invitation to a formal church wedding may include another invitation to the reception afterward. If the reception is held before one o'clock, it is called a breakfast; after one, a reception. If space is limited in the church, guests are also sent an admission card or a card for reserved seating "within the ribbon." Invitations are enclosed in *two* envelopes. The inside envelope is not sealed. It holds the invitation and enclosures and is addressed with only the names of the guests.

Formal reply. Formal wedding invitations do not require a reply, but an invitation to the reception does. You can use the shorter form shown at right, or you can repeat the exact wording of the invitation.

Formal wedding invitation

Mr. and Mrs. Richard Cameron
request the honor of your presence
at the marriage of their daughter
Nancy Susan
to
Mr. Henry McQuiston
on Saturday morning, the second of June
at ten o'clock
Grace Unitarian Church
Pleasantville, NY

Mr. and Mrs. Richard Cameron
request the pleasure of your company
at breakfast
Saturday, the second of June
at twelve o'clock
Forty-five Riversville Road
Pleasantville, NY

The favor of a reply
is requested

Please present this card
at Grace Unitarian Church
Saturday, June second

Mr. and Mrs. Thomas Putnam
accept with pleasure
Mr. and Mrs. Richard Cameron's
kind invitation for
Saturday, the second of June
at twelve o'clock

If a husband and wife receive an invitation and only one can attend, the acceptance is stated first, then the regret.

Mrs. Thomas Putnam
accepts with pleasure etc.
Mr. Thomas Putnam
regrets exceedingly etc.

Informal wedding invitation

Dear Sally,
Marlene is being married here at home to Ted Smith on Friday, May 25, at four o'clock. We do hope that you and Jack can come and that you will be able to stay for tea after the ceremony.
Love,
Helen

Informal reply

Dear Helen,
We are so happy about Marlene's forthcoming marriage and are delighted to be included. We look forward to seeing you on May 25, at four.
Love,
Sally

Formal acceptance

Mr. and Mrs. Thomas Putnam
accept with pleasure
Mr. and Mrs. Richard Cameron's
kind invitation to be present
at the marriage of their daughter
Nancy Susan
to
Mr. Henry McQuiston
on Saturday, the second of June
at twelve o'clock
and afterward at the wedding breakfast

Recalling invitations. When a wedding must be postponed or canceled, guests can be notified by telephone, telegram, or, if there is time, by printed cards. The wording is formal, but the style does not have to be indented. Reasons are given for a postponement, but not for a cancellation.

Mr. and Mrs. Raymond Brown regret that owing to their daughter's illness they are obliged to recall the invitations to her wedding on Sunday, the third of June.

Mr. and Mrs. Raymond Brown
announce that the marriage of their daughter
Suzanne to Mr. Henry Harrison
will not take place

Mary Ann Shaw
January 1, 1985

Mr. and Mrs. Robin Shaw

17 Cherry Lane · Springfield, Ohio

Announcements

Wedding. A wedding is usually announced by calling the society editor of your local paper, but when a wedding is small and private (or when the couple has eloped), formal announcements can be sent out as soon as possible after the event.

Mr. and Mrs. Anthony Jerome
announce the marriage of their daughter
Charlotte
to
Mr. Peter Gates
Captain United States Army
on Friday, the fifteenth of June
Saratoga, New York

NOTE: When the bride or groom is an officer, it is customary to give the military title, but the title can be omitted for a noncommissioned officer or an enlisted person.

Birth. A traditional and formal way to announce a baby's birth is shown above. The baby's card is attached to the parents' joint card with a pink, blue, or white ribbon, or, an engraved card can be sent.

Mr. and Mrs. Robin Shaw
announce with joy
the birth of their daughter
Mary Ann
on the first of January, 1985

Requests and responses

Excuse for absence from school

Dear Mrs. Shepard,

Please excuse Peter's absence from school this past Monday, Tuesday, and Wednesday. He had a bad cold and I thought it would be best (and best for the other children) to keep him home. Could you please tell Peter, or send me a note, if there is any work to be made up?

Thank you.

Yours sincerely,
Ruth Jones

Excuse for lateness

Dear Mrs. Shepard,

Please excuse Peter's lateness this morning. During the storm last night, our electricity must have been off for an hour, as all our clocks and alarms were an hour off, and he missed the school bus. I'm driving him in myself and hope you will forgive his unavoidable lateness.

Sincerely,
Ruth Jones

Excuse for future absence

Dear Miss Costanza,

Sally will be absent from school next Thursday and Friday, October 4th and 5th, as this is an important religious holiday (Yom Kippur) and she will be attending services.

If it's possible to give Sally assignments to make up the class work she will miss, she'll do that over the weekend. Thank you.

Very truly yours,
Mary Green

Apologetic answer to a complaint about a child

Dear Mr. Johnson,

I can certainly understand your being upset about Tommy's hitting a baseball through your windshield. We've told the boys not to play baseball in the street and now they know why.

K & R Auto says the replacement cost would be $40. I've enclosed a check for that amount, which Tommy will make up out of his paper-route money. He is very sorry about what happened and will be over soon to tell you so himself. I am so sorry about the trouble this has caused you.

Yours sincerely,
Sally Smith

Nonapologetic answer to a complaint about a child

Dear Mrs. Henderson,

Billy has told us how upset you were about the noise the children made playing in the vacant lot next to your house over the weekend. I'm sorry that you were disturbed and Billy is, too.

As he explained it, he and his friends have been playing softball in that lot for several years now. The people who used to live in your house, the Jenkins, never objected and it didn't occur to any of the children that you would mind.

He's told me that he and his friends have talked it over and will play future games on the baseball diamond over at the grammar school.

Yours very truly,
Hattie Brown

Thank you notes.

You are expected to send thank-you notes for wedding and shower gifts and for being entertained for the weekend, but there are many other times when they are appropriate—such as for birthday or Christmas presents or when someone has done you a favor or shown you or your family some particular kindness. Thank-you notes can be quite short, but they should be specific and personal. It is easier, and more polite, to write them right away, while the pleasure of receiving a present, or of having a lovely time, is still fresh in your mind.

For a retirement party and gift

Dear John,

This is just to tell you how much I have enjoyed working with you over the years, and also to thank you for your part in that fine farewell gift. I have always wanted a matched set of golf clubs and these are superb. Thanks again for making my last day at Acme so memorable.

Sincerely,
Henry Maxwell

For the weekend.

When a couple is entertained for the weekend, the "bread and butter" letter is usually written by the wife to the hostess.

Dear Mary Ann,

Thank you so much for an absolutely wonderful weekend. It was such a treat to spend time with you and Jim. Tom hasn't stopped talking about your chocolate soufflé and what a fantastic cook you are. We were especially thrilled with the whale-watching boat trip. How thoughtful of you to know that would be just what we'd love and to arrange it! Thank you again for everything.

Love,
Sarah

For a Christmas gift

Dear Larry,

Thank you so much for the beautiful lamp. It is truly just what I needed. I've clipped it to my drawing board and it not only looks terrific (I love the red color), but it also eliminates the shadows, which is a big help in my work. I feel lucky to have such a wonderful, thoughtful cousin.

Much love,
Sally,

For a wedding gift

Dear Aunt Sarah,

Tom and I are thrilled with your wonderful wedding present. We have always admired Grace Steven's work, and to have an entire dinner set of her beautiful pottery is just fantastic!

I know it will look spendid on our table and I want you and uncle Joe to come for dinner and see for yourselves as soon as we get back from Bermuda. I will call you then to set a date.

Love,
Polly

For a baby gift

Dear Sally,

Angelo doesn't have any words yet, but if he did I know he would thank you for your beautiful present. The baby sack is just what he needed—just the right weight—and the rose and blue stripes make him look so handsome! Thank you so much.

Cordially,
Bianca

Thank you notes from children

For a gift

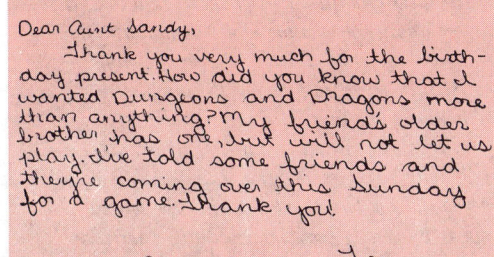

For the weekend

Dear Margie,

Thank you very much for a wonderful time. Your birthday party was great. I loved the treasure hunt (and winning the prize) and I loved staying with you. It was just like old times.

Please thank your Mom for me and ask her to send my Mom her recipe for spaghetti. It's the best I ever tasted. Thanks for everything.

Love,
Tina

Writing Effective Letters

Sympathy and condolence.

Writing to someone on the death of a spouse, relative, or friend is difficult for most people and yet there is probably no time when a letter can mean so much and be so deeply appreciated. Your natural feeling of sympathy for someone's loss is what matters here. Your letter can be short, but it should be tactful—not dwelling on the circumstances of the death—and it should be sincere and simple.

To a neighbor

Dear Rose,

I cannot tell you how shocked and sorry I am to learn of Bob's sudden death. He was such a wonderful man and I have such warm memories of his many kindnesses. I know that I will miss him very much and can only imagine what a terrible loss this is to you. Please accept my deepest sympathy.

Most sincerely,
Harriet Jones

To a friend

Dear Margaret,

I have just heard the very sad news that you lost your father and I want you to know how sorry I am. I know how much you loved him and how painful this loss must be for you and your mother.

I wish that words could help, but I know that only time does that. Please know that my loving thoughts and deepest sympathy are with you both.

Love,
Sarah

To an employee

Dear Harry,

I was sorry to hear of your wife's death and can only imagine how terrible this loss must be for you. Although words can do so little, I want you to know that you have my deepest sympathy.

If there is anything that I can do to help in any way, please do not hesitate to call on me.

Yours sincerely,
Franklin Rogers

Acknowledgments.

It is considered correct to send a short thank-you note to everyone who sends a condolence letter. This does not have to be written as promptly as an ordinary thank-you letter, but it should, if possible, be sent within six weeks.

Dear Carol,

I cannot tell you how much your thoughtfulness when my father died meant to me. You are a true and dear friend and I thank you for all your kindness.

Love,
Nancy

Dear Mr. Brown,

Thank you for your very kind and thoughtful letter. It is wonderful to know how well thought of John was among the people he worked with, and I very much appreciate your telling me.

Yours sincerely,
Jane Smith

Lincoln's letter to Mrs. Bixby

One of the most famous letters in American history is Abraham Lincoln's to Mrs. Lydia Bixby after being told by the governor of Massachusetts that she had lost her five sons in the Civil War. That the information turned out to be wrong—that one son survived as a prisoner of war, one went to sea, and one deserted to the Confederate Army—changed the facts upon which the letter was based, but not its substance or its eloquence.

Executive Mansion
Washington, Nov. 21, 1864

To Mrs. Bixby, Boston, Mass.

Dear Madam,

I have been shown in the files of the War Department a statement of the Adjutant General of Massachusetts that you are the mother of five sons who have died gloriously on the field of battle. I feel how weak and fruitless must be any word of mine which should attempt to beguile you from the grief of a loss so overwhelming. But I cannot refrain from tending you the consolation that may be found in the thanks of the republic they died to save. I pray that our Heavenly Father may assuage the anguish of your bereavement, and leave you only the cherished memory of the loved and lost, and the solemn price that must be yours to have laid so costly a sacrifice upon the altar of freedom.

Yours very sincerely and respectfully,
A. Lincoln

Announcing a death. Often a member of the family of someone who has died will have to tell other family members or friends the sad news that someone close to them has died. This should be done as gently as possible, with an attempt to lessen the shock. It is hard to find a better example of this kind of letter than the one that Charles Dickens wrote to his wife, who was ill and away from home, to prepare her for finding out that their infant daughter had died. (See below.)

To a relative

Dear Uncle Ben,

I'm so sorry to be writing with some very sad news that I know will be a great shock to you: Uncle Harry passed away last night after having had a stroke two days ago. The funeral will be held at St. Agnes Church on Elm Street in New London, Thursday at two o'clock, and afterward family and friends will go to Aunt Mary's.

Affectionately,
Betty

To a friend of the deceased

Dear Mr. Jones,

I am writing to let you know that my father, Timothy Johnson, died in his sleep last night after a short illness. Father spoke of you so often as a friend that I felt you would want to know.

Yours sincerely,
Fred Johnson

Death and funeral notices

These are prepared by the person in charge of the funeral and are then phoned into the newspaper, either as news or as a paid advertisement. The paper will need the following information:

1. Name of deceased (and maiden name of a married woman)
2. Address
3. Date of death
4. Age
5. Names and relationships of survivors
6. Time and place of funeral and burial
7. Whether services are private or open to the public
8. Whether the family wishes no flowers to be sent or the organization and its address to which a memorial contribution can be sent.

Death notice

HENDERSON, MARY (née Bronson), of 27 Pine Street, Harrison, New York, died suddenly on May 12, in her 55th year, beloved wife of John Henderson. She is also survived by their son Howard Henderson, daughters Alice (Mrs. John Lagrange) and Mary (Mrs. Robert Johnson), and grandchildren Ramond and Susan Lagrange. Funeral services at Community Church, corner of Central and Lafayette Avenues, Harrison, NY, 11 AM Monday, May 14. Interment is private. In lieu of flowers, contributions may be made to the Community Care Society, Box 4000, Harrison, NY zip code.

Dickens' letter to his wife

Often family members or friends will have to be told that someone close to them has died. This should be done as gently as possible. It is hard to find a better example than this letter Charles Dickens wrote to his wife to prepare her for the news that their daughter had died.

Devonshire-terrace
Tuesday morning, 15th April, 1851

My dearest Kate,

Now observe you must read this letter very slowly and carefully. If you have hurried on thus without quite understanding (apprehending some bad news) I rely on your turning back and reading again.

Little Dora, without being in the least pain, is suddenly stricken ill. There is nothing in her appearance but perfect rest—you would suppose her quietly asleep, but I am sure she is very ill, and I cannot encourage myself with much hope of her recovery. I do not (and why should I say I do to you, my dear?) I do not think her recovery at all likely.

I do not like to leave home, I can do no good here, but I think it right to stay. You will not like to be away, I know, and I cannot reconcile it to myself to keep you away. Foster, with his usual affection for us, comes down to bring you this letter and to bring you home, but I cannot close it without putting the strongest entreaty and injunction upon you to come with perfect composure—To remember what I have often told you, that we never can expect to be exempt, as to our many children, from the afflictions of other parents, and that if—if when you come I should even have to say to you, "Our little baby is dead," you are to do your duty to the rest, and to show yourself worthy of the great trust you hold in them.

If you will only read this steadily I have a perfect confidence in your doing what is right.

Ever affectionately,
Charles Dickens

Writing Effective Letters

Business letters

A successful business letter is not only grammatically correct and neat, it is also friendly and courteous. It is simple, brief, easy to read, and gets right to the point. Such a letter creates a good impression. It makes your reader feel that you are the kind of person or firm that it is good to do business with. In short, a successful business letter looks good and sounds good. Here are some helpful hints.

Looking good.
Business letters are almost always typed on a standard 8½" × 11" good quality paper. Most businesses use a letterhead with their name, address, and phone number. The standard formats are shown below. Although some businesses prefer the block form because it saves time for the typist, most use either the modified block or modified semiblock forms.

Basic rules for spacing.
Follow these rules no matter which format you use.

1. Place the address two lines below the date, which is two lines below the heading.
2. Place the salutation two lines below the address.
3. Begin the opening sentence or paragraph two lines below the salutation.
4. Single space for the heading, address, and within paragraphs.
5. Double space between paragraphs.
6. Place the complimentary closing two lines below the last paragraph.
7. Place the typed signature four lines below the complimentary closing.
8. Put any additional data (such as enclosures or initials of the writer and typist) two lines below the typed signature, beginning at the left margin.

Styles

Block

```
ABC Company
100 Main Street
Anytown, Florida zip code
January 1, 1985

Mr. John Smith
12 Broadway
Apple City, New York zip code

Dear Mr. Smith:

This is an example of the block form
of business letter. You will notice that
the heading, inside address, closing, and
signature all line up at the left and the
paragraphs are not indented.

This style saves the typist time and that
is why some businesses prefer it.

Yours sincerely,
Thomas Rider
Thomas Rider
```

Modified semiblock

```
                ABC Company
                100 Main Street
                Anytown, Florida zip code
                January 1, 1985

Mr. John Smith
12 Broadway
Apple City, New York zip code

Dear Mr. Smith:

    Here is an example of the modified
semiblock form. You will notice that the
heading, closing, and signature are aligned
vertically near the center of the page
and that the paragraphs are indented.
This last point is the only difference
between this and the modified block form
shown at the right.

                Yours sincerely,
                Thomas Rider
                Thomas Rider
```

Parts of a business letter

Modified block format

Heading — Warner Widget Company
100 Marvin Gardins
Centerville, New Jersey zip code
March 10, 19—

Inside address — Mr. Mark Harris
M & H Manufacturing Company
Paradise, Rhode Island zip code

Salutation — Dear Mr. Harris:

Body — Thank you for your letter of February 24 and for your interest in our products. I am sending you our latest brochure describing our entire selection of widgets and particularly refer you to pages 8 and 9, where you will find some widgets well-suited to your needs.

Jack Armstrong, our New England sales representative, will be calling on you soon and will be happy to answer any further questions you may have. I hope that we may soon count you among our many satisfied customers.

Closing — Yours sincerely,

Signature — Frank Jones
Frank Jones, Manager
Product Information

Additional data — FJ/ms
Enclosure

Sounding good. You will be able to write successful business letters by following five basic rules:
1. **Be friendly.** Your letter will build goodwill and be more likely to accomplish its purpose if you maintain a friendly tone. Even if you are angry, avoid sarcasm or insults.
2. **Be specific.** Tell the reader exactly what he or she needs to know. If you have a complaint, say precisely what is wrong and what you want done about it. If you need information, note clearly what you need to know.
3. **Be positive.** Even a letter that must say no can do it in a positive way. Compare, for example, "We regret to inform you that the postal strike makes it impossible to ship your order until . . ." with "Thank you for your order. The merchandise will be shipped to you immediately after the postal strike is settled."
4. **Keep your reader's point of view in mind.** Try to see things from his or her vantage point, not yours. One way to tell whether you have done this is to count the "I's" and the "you's." You want lots of you's and few I's. You can usually get the right effect by rephrasing. Compare these examples:
   I: *I* want to express *my* sincere thanks for the kind words *I* received today from . . .
   You: Thank *you* for *your* very kind words.
   Or:
   I: *We* make four styles in all sizes.
   You: *You* may have *your* choice of four styles in all sizes.
5. **Remember the golden rule.** Write the kind of letter you would like to get if you were in the reader's position.

Anatomy of a letter. You will find it easier to write a clear, well-organized letter if you think of it as having a basic structure—a beginning, a middle, and an end.

The beginning. The purpose of the first sentence is to get the reader's attention and interest. This can often be done by asking a question. An insurance sales letter might ask: "Do you want to save 40 percent on your auto insurance?" Keep the first sentence short. The rest of the opening paragraph explains it.

The emphasis should be on what the *reader* needs, not what *you* need. This holds true even for a letter of complaint. You might, for example, begin such a letter with, "I know you want to maintain good relationships with your customers, but . . ."

The middle. This is where you state and explain *your* purpose. It is important to present your supporting facts or arguments in order of their importance.

It helps to make notes or an outline (see volume 2, page 262) before you start to write.

Often, you are trying to motivate your reader to take some action, or you may be explaining why you will or will not take some action. Give the facts first and then the conclusion. A tenant might say to an uncooperative landlord, "I have talked to my lawyer about your failure to have my water pipes repaired after my repeated requests and was told that under this jurisdiction I may withhold my rent until repairs are made. I plan to do so unless repairs are made this month."

The end. If the purpose of your letter is to get the reader to take some action, sum up at the end with a direct and positive statement. Sounding tentative or doubtful invites rejection. It is better to say, "Your cooperation in sending a check by return mail will be greatly appreciated," than to say, "We hope you will pay as soon as possible." "Our representative will call for an appointment next week" is better than, "May we send our representative to see you soon?" You should be clear (if you want some action taken), courteous (avoid a cold, curt ending), and complete (the reader should feel you have said everything you have to say).

What's wrong with this letter?

The letter below is a good example of what *not to do* in business writing.

> Dear Sir:
>
> We have the latest edition of your Readers' Complete Bookshelf. After reviewing it very thoroughly with my wife and children, the very best we can find to say about it is that we are completely disgusted with it. We have, however, found that it is very useful in teaching our children how the art of misinformation is being used to deceive Americans. We have found many examples in your book.
>
> Please do not send Volume Three.
>
> Howard Case
> Howard Case

The tone of this letter could be improved, but the real problem is that the letter is vague. The writer does not give any concrete examples. A better letter would read,

> *I have gone over the latest volume of your Readers' Complete Bookshelf and am deeply disappointed with it—particularly in the chapter on the War Between the States. I felt you were unjustly critical of the South and not critical enough of what the North did during Reconstruction. There were also several historical inaccuracies. You have the wrong Confederate commander for the Battle . . .*

Writing Effective Letters

Job applications. A letter written to apply for a job is really a sales letter. You are selling your own qualifications as a prospective employee. As in any sales letter, you want to get your reader's interest, stress what you can do for the reader, and persuade him or her to take an action—in this case, give you an interview. You would also include a résumé that lists your educational and work experience, but the letter of application has the advantage of being written for *this particular job,* as most résumés do not, and allows you to select and emphasize the experience and abilities that qualify you for that job. (For information on choosing a career and finding the job you want, see Advancing Your Career, page 22.)

A famous letter, written to the Duke of Milan in 1482, is hard to beat as an example of super-salesmanship, but then it was written by an extraordinary man who could do everything he said he could do and more. His name was Leonardo Da Vinci. Below are some excerpts from that letter. Leonardo got the job and he kept it for 16 years, until the French Army marched into Milan and took the Duke prisoner.

"Having, most illustrious lord, seen and considered the experiments of all those who pose as masters in the art of inventing instruments of war, and finding that their inventions differ in no way from those in common use, I am emboldened, without prejudice to anyone, to solicit an appointment of acquainting your Excellency with certain of my secrets.

1. I can construct bridges which are very light and strong and very portable, with which to pursue and defeat the enemy; and others more solid, which resist fire and assault, yet are easily removed and placed in position; and I can also burn and destroy those of the enemy.

2. In case of siege I can cut off water from the trenches and make pontoons and scaling ladders and other similar contrivances. . . .

4. I can also make a kind of cannon which is light and easy of transport, with which to hurl small stones like hail, and of which the smoke causes great terror to the enemy, so that they suffer heavy loss and confusion. . . .

10. In time of peace, I believe that I can give you as complete satisfaction as anyone else in the construction of buildings both public and private, and in conducting water from one place to another.

I can further execute sculpture in marble, bronze or clay, also in painting I can do as much as anyone else, whoever he may be.

And if any of the aforesaid things should seem to anyone impossible or impracticable, I offer myself as ready to make trial of them in your park or in whatever place shall please your Excellency. . . .

If you are looking for your first full-time job, you probably do not have much work experience, but you do have some "life experience." Your letter should emphasize your personal qualities and any relevant work, school, or extracurricular activities:

Letter from a college graduate

354 Hardscrabble Road
Anytown, N.Y. zip code
June 1, 1985

Dear Mr. Johnson:

With my college degree in Business and my strong interest in sales, I believe I could do an excellent job as a management trainee with your company. I have achieved high grades in marketing courses and am sure I could learn to market a product successfully.

I know how valuable successful communication is in business, and feel that being editor of our college newspaper has helped me develop communication skills. You will find a complete résumé of my educational experience and extracurricular activities enclosed. I will call on Monday, June 4th, to arrange an interview so that we may discuss my qualifications for your management-trainee program.

Yours sincerely,
Nancy Graham
Nancy Graham

From prospective high-school graduate

Mr. Harold Long
Personnel Director
Carter Paper Company
52 Broadway
Apple City, New York zip code

Dear Mr. Long:

I will graduate from Centerville High School this June and my guidance counselor, Mr. Herbert Jones, suggested that I write to you about a sales position with your company.

I have worked part-time as an ad salesman for the Centerville Bulletin for the past two years. As advertising manager of our high-school yearbook, I produced a $1500 profit - a first for Centerville High. I've also been manager of the track team for the past two years and organized the successful fund-raising campaign that sent the team to the national meet in Washington this year.

I like sales, think I am good at it and want to make it my career - if possible, with the Carter Paper Company. I will call next Monday for an appointment.

Yours sincerely,
Jack Hudson

Writing Effective Letters

Putting it the right way. Helpful sentences:

Salary   I would be happy to discuss salary with you when we meet. My range is —, — to —, —.

I will be glad to discuss the matter of salary with you at a personal interview.

Salary considerations are not as important as the career opportunity this position offers. I am sure we can arrive at a satisfactory arrangement.

References   The following people can tell you about my work from several different points of view:

I refer you specifically to the following people with whom I have worked over the past few years.

My former employers and clients will vouch for my integrity and good reputation in the trade. I refer you to the following:

Selling yourself   I would be happy to show you my proposal for increasing your next year's sales by at least 25 percent.

I would like to show you how I can save you money on your company's liability insurance and will call on Monday for an appointment.

I shall phone your secretary next week to arrange for a meeting at your convenience.

I would very much like to discuss my qualifications for your buyer–training program and will call on Monday to set up an appointment.

Experienced worker answering an advertisement

```
Box 000, Times
Centerville, NY zip code

Dear Sir:
    In response to your advertisement in
this morning's Times for an experienced
secretary, I would like to apply for that
position. I have been a secretary for the
past ten years for three prominent executives
who will vouch for my efficiency and
dependability. They are:

    Mr. Harry Ricer, ABC Company,
    Centerville, NY (Hospital Supplies)
    19-- to 19--

    Mr. John Kramer, Consolidated Products,
    Newton, NY (Building Materials)
    19-- to 19--

    Mr. Peter Kent, Hawkins, Smith &
    Barnes, Inc., Centerville, NY
    (Management Consultants) 19-- to 19--

    I have worked for Mr. Kent for the past
five years. He is being transferred to
Minneapolis, and so I am looking for another
position.
    I would like to come in and talk to
you personally, and have enclosed a self-
addressed card for you to let me know the
most convenient time for you. You can also
call me at work. The number is Hudson 5-1212,
extension 400.

                     Sincerely yours,
                     Susan Graham
                     Susan Graham
```

Follow-up letter. It is a very good idea to write again *after* an interview to thank the interviewer and remind him or her of your interest and abilities.

Dear Mr. Smith:

I very much enjoyed talking with you and meeting the members of your staff yesterday afternoon.

I am glad you mentioned the importance of budget constraints and feel that my record of cost-effectiveness as a project manager under government contracts would be a definite asset to your organization. I would be happy to discuss this further and will call again in a few days.

Yours sincerely,

Gerald Simms

Thank-you letter. After you get the job, it is a good idea to write thank-you notes to the people who helped you.

Dear Mr. Jones:

I am very happy to be able to tell you that I am now a project manager at Consolidated Technologies. Mr. Smith told me about the fine letter of recommendation you sent and I am sure that that had a lot to do with my getting the job. Thank you very much for your encouragement and help.

Yours sincerely,

Gerald Simms

Getting help.

Asking for information or services, particularly from the government or corporate bureaucracy, can be frustrating and time-consuming. Yet you can do it easily by writing the right kind of letter. Here are some hints.

State your reason for writing in the first sentence. This saves your reader time and energy.

Include all reference numbers and dates. If you are writing about a bill, an order, or a missing shipment, you will need to include such things as the invoice number or date of purchase. If a company gives you a reference number to use in writing to them, be sure to use it.

Confine your inquiry or request to one point. Do not confuse your reader by covering several subjects. Write a different letter for each. Be short and specific.

Gentlemen:

Could you give me an explanation of line 30 of Commerce Department Form 638: Employer Liability. Specifically, does line 30 refer only to office workers or does it cover field representatives?

When you want action, request it clearly. Do this at the end of your letter. Some examples are:

Please send me a refund.
Please send me a corrected bill.

Be brief. Keep your letter to one page if possible. Write a draft first, put it aside for a while, then see what you can eliminate.

Write to an individual whenever possible. This will speed a reply. Although you can use just the person's title, a name—which you can usually find out by calling the company—is better. When in doubt, write to the president or department head, who will see that the right person gets it. (For help in finding the right person, see box at top right.)

To a drug company

Mr. Frank Jones, President
ABC Vitamin Company
Deercrossing, Colorado zip code

Dear Mr. Jones:

I am writing to ask about the safety of your special Vitamin x compound, Wondervite. I have been taking this vitamin for some time and have just read in the Health and Science section of the Portland Times *that it does not lower cholesterol and that it can cause serious side effects.*

I would appreciate your sending me a summary of your laboratory reports on the action and side effects of this vitamin as soon as possible.

Yours sincerely,

Angela Black

Finding the person to write to

Consumer affairs. A pamphlet listing state, city, and county consumer protection offices, Better Business Bureaus, and names and addresses of corporate consumer contacts is available without charge by writing to:

Consumer Resource Handbook
Consumer Information Center
Pueblo, Colorado 81009

U.S. government officials. *The United States Government Manual* is updated regularly to tell you who's who in Congress and all government agencies. You can buy it from the Superintendent of Documents, U.S. Government Printing Office, Washington, D.C. 20402, *but* you must write first for the price (which changes) and the correct order form. You may find it at the public library. *Congressional Staff Directory* is published by Congressional Staff Director, Ltd., Mt. Vernon, Va. 22121. It, too, may be found at the library.

To a company

John Smith, Sales Manager
Acme Office Supplies
Newton, Illinois zip code

Dear Mr. Smith:

Please send me samples and a price quotation for 100 metal paper clips, Product Number 2000 on page 36 of your catalog. I would also like to know the price for an order of 1 million clips.

I would appreciate your sending this information by the end of the week.

Yours sincerely,

Frank Davis

To the Food and Drug Administration

Gentlemen:

I need to know whether it is safe to use the anti-inflammatory drug, Cureall. The drug is produced by Universal Drug Company, Weaver, Illinois. The code number on the label is Y-8000.

I bought the drug about six months ago from my local druggist, Robert Morley, 200 Main Street, Centerville, New York. I have since heard that the drug has been declared unsafe. Could you let me know the current status of this product?

Yours sincerely,

Helen Smith

A request for aid

```
The Reverend Frank E. Roberts
Christ Church
Centerville, New York zip code

Dear Dr. Roberts:

Some of the employees at Consolidated
Industries are repairing broken toys to
be given as Christmas presents to
children in the county. We hoped you
might help us with this project by
setting up a collection depot at the
church and asking parishioners to
contribute broken toys.

I have asked Sandra Smith, an employee
who is one of your parishioners, to speak
to you further about this. Let me just
say that your help would be much
appreciated.
                        Yours sincerely,
                        Thomas Brown
                        Thomas Brown
```

To a dress company

Manager, Customer Services
Jennie de Woolfe, Inc.
New York, NY zip code

Dear Sir or Madam:

I saw an advertisement for your silk shirtwaist dress on page 35 of the April Vogue magazine and would very much like to buy it.

Could you please tell me if any stores in Marblehead carry the dress or, if not, where I could buy it in Boston?

Yours sincerely,

Barbara Ann Blake

To the Veterans Administration

Dear Mr. (look up proper person):

Please tell me if you offer educational benefits to children of soldiers killed in action. My husband, Henry Greene, Serial number 000-000, died in Vietnam in 1970. He was a sergeant in the Marine Corps. My son Henry will be ready for college next year and I need to know whether he is eligible for benefits.

Please let me know as soon as possible.

Yours sincerely,

Ruth Greene

Letter of inquiry.
The following letter follows the formula for a letter of inquiry: it gets the reader's attention; states what is wanted, who wants it, and why; motivates action; and expresses appreciation.

Dear Alumna or Alumnus,

Exciting news! The first Address Register of the Alumnae and Alumni of Evergreen College in ten years will be published in 1985. This new volume will contain an alphabetical listing of alumnae/i names and addresses, cross-referenced with name in college, plus class and geographical listings.

We need your help in completing the register. Please check your listing for accuracy, and return the questionnaire in the enclosed envelop by June 1. Please note that the register will be available only to alumnae/i, faculty, and officers of Evergreen College. Your address will not be given out for noncollege use.

An order blank for your copy of the 1985 AAEC Register is attached to the questionnaire. The register is available at the prepublication price of $10. (It will be $15 after June, 1985.)

We hope you will take the time to fill out all of the enclosed questionnaire. If you are one of the 8000 alumnae/i who have joined AAEC's ranks since 1975, do not miss your first chance to tell us about your activities since graduation. If you are one of the 31,000 who were listed in the 1975 directory, this is your chance to bring your record up to date. Information about your current interests and accomplishments helps us in developing our many programs—including our guided travel tours and summer seminars.

Many thanks for your cooperation in filling out this questionnaire. We hope to be flooded by completed answers from all of you!

Yours sincerely,

Annabel Kemp Smith
President, AAEC

Enclosures

Notification of address change

Dear Sir:

Please send all future compensation checks to my new address:
    1400 Wharton Avenue
    Centerville, New York zip code.
My former address was:
    10 Henry Street
    Hartsdale, New Jersey zip code.

Yours truly,

Frank Dean

Writing Effective Letters

Complaints that get action. People often have a hard time writing an effective letter of complaint because they are angry and they let their anger take over. The anger becomes the important thing. However, what really matters is getting some action that will remedy the situation. This is much more likely if your tone is reasonable and calm. In some situations, it helps to use humor; in others, just to present the facts clearly and briefly. Sometimes it helps to go ahead and write your enraged letter *and put it away*. Then, with you mind clear, you can write the letter you will actually mail. Here are some hints to help you:

Write to the right person. Think carefully about who will be most likely to take action or get action on your complaint. If you are having a problem with the credit department of a store, for example, you will be more likely to get action if you write directly to the store's president, *not* to the credit department. In general, it is always best to write to the boss—you would be surprised how few people do this.

Keep copies of your letters. Knowing when you said what to whom and when may be important to solving the problem.

Do not lose your temper if you want to write a letter of complaint that gets results.

Do not get personal. Do not be sarcastic or insulting to your reader. You may be angry about the situation, but remember that the person and the situation are different. Try to put yourself in the other person's place and enlist his or her cooperation.

Organize your ideas. It is important to be clear about what you want, why you want it, and how you think you can get it *before* you start to write. A good way to do this is to make a list of your major points. A general list, with examples for a specific case, is given below.

Sending enclosures. You may want to support your complaint or argument by enclosing such items as bills, receipts, canceled checks, previous correspondence, invoices, and newspaper or magazine articles. If you do, be sure to keep the originals for your records and send a copy to the person you are writing to.

How to get organized

Here is how the master list of major points is applied to the specific case of writing a letter of complaint to a state senator about his position on the death penalty. The final letter appears at the right.

Major points	Examples
1. What you want the reader to do in order to remedy what you are complaining about.	1. I want Senator Green to change his mind regarding the death penalty.
2. Your reasons for wanting a remedy—that is, why it is important to *you*.	2. I believe it is morally wrong to take a life and that the government has no right to do this.
3. What information your reader needs in order to act.	3. There is a lot of evidence that the death penalty is not a deterrent to violent crime. Various presidential commissions on crime and violence have found that the real deterrents are social (doing something about such factors as poverty, unemployment, and family disorganization) and legal (having the court system react quickly so that criminals are tried, convicted, and sent to jail in a relatively short time).
4. What is likely to motivate your reader to take action. This includes appealing to your reader's self-interest and any pressure you can bring to bear.	4. I will not vote for Senator Green again unless he changes his position. I will support any opponent of his who is against the death penalty.

Complaint about fraud. The following letter could be sent to the Better Business Bureau and/or the Federal Trade Commission (note that the writer encloses a copy of his receipt, not the original).

Gentlemen:

I am making a complaint about fraudulent pricing. On December 10, I went to Snazzy Sam's Audio Outlet at 81 Spruce Street in Centerville, New York, to buy a CB radio. The salesman claimed that the Star Monitor CB, which he showed me and which I subsequently purchased, was being offered at a special discount price of $50—half the normal retail price. I have enclosed a copy of my receipt. A few days later, at Janes' Department Store in Centerville, I saw the same radio being sold for $35 and was told that this was its normal retail price.

I can only conclude that the salesman at Snazzy Sam's deliberately misrepresented the price of the radio. I am sure you will agree that this store should be investigated and am turning the matter over to you as it involves interstate commerce. Please let me know what action you plan to take.

Yours sincerely,

Arnold Smart

Letter to state senator

63 Sunnyside Avenue
Anytown, N.Y. zip code
May 15, 1985

Dear Senator Green:

I strongly oppose your position on the death penalty. I do not believe, as you do, that the death penalty is a deterrent to violent crime. I appreciate and support your strong stand against crime, but I think your remedy is wrong.

There is a great deal of evidence that the deterrents to violent crime are social and legal, that violent crime decreases where there are adequate opportunities for work, health care, and education, and a court system that functions efficiently and quickly so that criminals are invariably sentenced and sent to jail. I refer you to the various presidential commissions on crime and violence over the years—beginning with President Johnson's—all of which have come to the same conclusions.

I think your emphasis on the death penalty as a deterrent is not only useless, it also diverts attention from the real remedies. I urge you to change your position. If you do not, I will not be able to support your bid for reelection to the State Senate.

Yours very truly,

Lucy Fuller

Lucy Fuller
(Mrs. David Fuller)

Complaint about billing error

Gentlemen:

I have just received my July bill from Universal Utilities and feel that you must have made a mistake. The bill was not only much higher than usual for that month (I have enclosed copies of this and last year's July and August bills), but also our family was away for the entire month.

I always pay my bills promptly and shall continue to do so—as soon as I receive a corrected statement or an explanation of this discrepancy.

Yours sincerely,

Alice Jones
(Mrs. Sidney Jones)

Complaint about a warranty (note that the writer refers to a previous letter and gives the company's file number).

File #6000-B

Dear Mr. Brandt:

I believe you are wrong about the term of my warranty on the Gallactic Food Processor that I bought from your company in June of 1982. Your letter of March 1 says that my warranty expired last year. In fact, it is a five-year warranty and will not expire until 1987. I am therefore sending the Gallactic Food Processor back to you C.O.D., and trust that you will have it repaired and returned postage-paid as your warranty promises.

Yours sincerely,

Ruth Green

Letters to the editor. If you confine your letter to one issue, it will be more forceful.

To the Editor of the Centerville Times:

I strongly disagree with your March 1st editorial recommending that the north end of Wadsworth Park along Central Avenue be used as the site for the new middle school.

Your editorial quotes Mayor Barnes as saying that this use of the land will save the taxpayers' hard-earned money, which it will. But you do not say what this loss of parkland will mean to the citizens of Centerville.

The 40 acres of Wadsworth Park is the last remaining open, green space in Centerville, providing a retreat from our ever-encroaching urban area, a place for relaxation and quiet walks, and a sanctuary for birds and many small wild animals.

Removing even 10 acres of the park would represent a major loss to the city and would set a dangerous precedent. In the long run, it would be uneconomical to lose even a small part of our precious, irreplaceable parkland.

Yours sincerely,

Tom Jones

Writing Effective Letters

Answering inquiries. Whether you are answering a personal inquiry or are answering on behalf of your company, your letter should include the following:

- An acknowledgment of the inquiry, mentioning the date and general subject of the letter to you.
- A detailed response to the questions, or an explanation of why you have to refuse.
- Additional information that may be helpful.
- An offer of further help where appropriate.

To an insurance company

Dear Mr. Smith:

Your letter of March 1 asks me to itemize our losses in the flood last month.

As the damage to furniture, carpets, and appliances was extensive, I have prepared the enclosed list with the approximate cost or value of each item. I hope this will be sufficient for your purposes. Please let me know if you need any further information.

Sincerely yours,
Jim Kiley

enc.

To a prospective customer

Dear Mrs. Blake:

In response to your inquiry about the Jennie deWoolfe dress shown in the advertisement in the April Vogue, you can buy it in Marblehead at Design Research or, in Boston, at Kemp & Co., Market Fair, or Woman's Haberdasher. All these stories regularly carry our line.

Many thanks for your interest.

Yours sincerely,
Harry Ross
Customer Service

To a mail order company

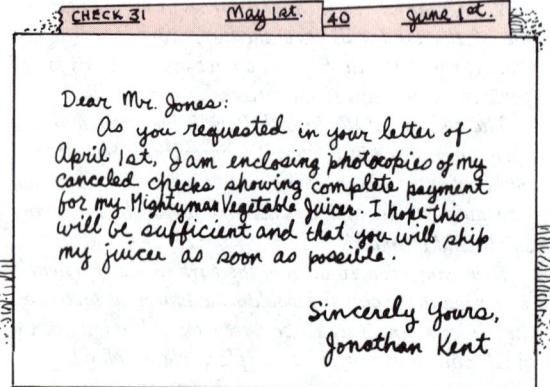

Turning inquiries into sales.

Answering an inquiry provides a golden opportunity for a company to create goodwill and promote sales. A courteous and helpful reply can be and will be very good for business. See how this works in the following letter to a potential customer:

Dear Mr. Smith:

Many thanks for your inquiry, just received, about our Miracle Re-Circulating Wood Stoves.

As a builder, you know the importance of first-rate equipment. As heating suppliers, we welcome the chance to tell you more about our fine product.

First, it uses a revolutionary design. The curved ducts and chimney fan capture the heat ordinarily lost up the chimney and blow warm air out at floor level, which improves air circulation.

Second, it is efficient. It burns less wood because its airtight construction causes wood to burn slowly.

Third, it is practical. Its small size allows it to fit easily in most existing fireplaces. For new-home construction, it is unobtrusive and easily installed.

Finally, and perhaps most important, it is safe. Our Teflon-coated stovepipe reduces dangerous creosote build-up and does not need to be cleaned as frequently as ordinary stovepipes.

I have enclosed a brochure showing our complete line of stoves and direct your attention particularly to pages 6 and 7, showing models suitable for small summer homes. I would be happy to answer any further questions and arrange for a demonstration. Just call our toll-free number as soon as you are ready.

Yours sincerely,
Ted Jones

enc.

Answering complaints.

What if you need to *respond* to a complaint. How you respond depends on the particular situation and on whether or not you feel that you (or your company) is at fault. Whatever the case, it is best to be reasonable and courteous. It will help if you do the following things *before you begin to write:*

Organize your response

- Determine the real nature of the complaint. It is important to know exactly what the complainant thinks is wrong.
- Determine your position. Decide on what you want to accomplish with your letter—that is, if you want to apologize, defend your actions without an apology, or something in between.

How to get organized

Major points

As in writing most other kinds of letters, setting down the points you want to make in a clear and logical sequence is important in answering complaints effectively.

1. Summarize the complaint in your first sentence or your first paragraph.
2. Make your position clear in your next paragraph. Say whether you are sorry or think the person complaining has made a mistake.
3. Explain your position. Give the information that justifies or at least explains your actions.
4. State what action you plan to take or want your reader to take in your last paragraph.

Example

The following response includes the major points and has a cooperative tone that should gain time until the facts have been determined.

Dear Mr. Jones:

1. *You believe that we have put our driveway across your property line.*
2. *We are having our lawyer check the deed, since we thought we put in the driveway entirely within our own property.*
3. *We realize that many of the old markers are unclear, so we would like to do more research before we come to any conclusions.*
4. *We know you are concerned about this and will be in touch with you as soon as we hear from our lawyer.*

Yours truly,

Harry Green

Responding to customer complaints. In answering complaints, particularly when you have to refuse a request for an adjustment, a company or an individual businessperson wants to keep the goodwill of the customer without acting against the best interests of his or her business. The best way to do this is to avoid an accusatory tone and to present your facts courteously, simply, and clearly so that the customer will find it hard to argue with your conclusion. This is the case in the following letter, in which the service manager refuses to honor his company's warantee because the damage to the company's product was caused by the owner's misuse.

Dear Mr. Jones:

 We do agree with you that your new Easywriter should not have broken down after three months and we were concerned to find out why it did.

 That is why we sent it to our laboratory for a thorough examination as soon as we received it. It appears that the machine had been dropped several times and that it must have been left uncovered—a great deal of dust was found inside the motor. Unfortunately, no typewriter can withstand such treatment. If you think it over, we are sure you will agree and will understand why we cannot repair or replace it under the terms of our warranty.

 If you have any questions please do not hesitate to call me.

Yours truly,

Howard Smith
Service Manager

When to apologize. This depends on whether you think the complaint has merit. Here are two different responses to slightly different situations:

Apologetic

Dear Mrs. Ashley:

 I am very sorry to learn that you are unhappy about the work I did on your house. I want you to be completely satisfied with the job.

 I would be glad to come back and touch up the woodwork and window frames as soon as I am available—which should be in about a week. I will call you then to arrange for my completing the work.

Yours truly,

Bob Adams

Nonapologetic

Dear Mrs. Ashley:

 I am very sorry that you are unhappy about the completed paint job on your house, particularly the color of the living room and hall.

 I would be happy to make any changes you would like, but will have to charge you for the additional time and paint to redo the living room and hall. Under our original agreement, my payment constituted your acceptance of the job.

 If you would call me, I would be glad to give you an estimate and arrange for doing the additional work.

Yours truly,

Bob Adams

Writing Effective Letters

Collection letters.
Letters asking for money owed are sent after the first bill has not been paid. They include the following points:
- How much is owed (a bill may be enclosed).
- Arguments for payment, including any action you plan (where appropriate).
- Request for payment by a certain date.

A delicate situation. Requests for overdue payments may put you in a somewhat delicate position. You want to get the money owed without antagonizing and losing your customer. You want to convey understanding and tact while remaining firm. Here are some techniques to help you do that.

1. **Put yourself in the other person's place.** Try to see that in most cases the person who owes you money would like to be able to pay on time and is sensitive about being unable. You can make this sensitivity work for you by appealing to his or her self-interest and sense of pride.

2. **Avoid unwarranted threats.** Be careful, you can be held legally liable for threats or insults. Do not accuse your debtor of dishonest behavior or intentions and do not threaten legal action without consulting a lawyer.

3. **Fit the letter to the situation.** Try to think why the payment may be late and use an appropriate approach. It is possible, for example, that the bill was lost or mislaid, that your customer did not understand the terms of sale or credit, or that he or she normally lets small bills accumulate. In such cases, all that is usually needed is a gentle reminder. Here are some examples:

When you opened this letter, I am sure it reminded you of something you meant to do, but forgot—to send us your check. Why not do it now? The amount due is $22.30. Please accept our apologies and thanks if you have already paid.

Perhaps we did not make it clear that our policy is to extend credit for a two-week period only, following the date of purchase.

Your payment of $135.62 was due last week on May 7. We would very much appreciate your sending us your check by return mail.

You may not have noticed that your past-due account with us now totals $236.14. We are trying to clear our books before December 31 and would appreciate your settling your account within the next few days.

Letters in a series. Often collection letters are written in a series, each successive letter getting stronger in tone. It is wise to make sure that your last collection letter reaches the person who owes you money. Send it certified mail, return receipt.

1.
Dear Mrs. Kent:
  We find in checking our accounts that you have an unpaid balance for September of $62.42.
  I thought that you would want us to bring it to your attention. If your check is already in the mail, just disregard this letter.
            Yours truly,

2.
Dear Mrs. Kent:
  As you usually pay your bills on time, we wonder why you have overlooked your September bill. The amount, $62.42, is now more than three months overdue. If there is some reason why you are not paying it, I trust you will let us know.
  If I do not hear from you, I will look forward to getting your check within a few days.
            Yours truly,

3.
Dear Mrs. Kent:
  As you know, we do not usually extend credit for more than a month unless some agreement for partial payment has been made. Your bill for $62.42 is now four months overdue.
  I urge you, therefore, to send us your check right away. If you cannot pay right now or can make only a partial payment, I am sure we could come to some arrangement. Do let me hear from you about this right away.
            Yours truly,

4.
Dear Mrs. Kent:
  I am extremely sorry that you have not responded to any of my letters about your overdue bill of $62.42.
  I am afraid that unless I get your check in a few days, I will have to turn the matter over to our lawyers, Smith, French and Block, for legal action.
            Yours truly,

Family business.

Opening charge accounts, ordering merchandise, paying bills, planning vacations, contracting for work done to the house or yard—there are many occasions in a family's day-to-day life that require the writing of business letters. It is better to write than to telephone because you will not only have a record of your request, but the recipient will have a constant reminder before him. Here are a few examples:

Request for a delay in paying bills

Gentlemen:

Thank you for your recent letter reminding me that my account is long past due and inquiring as to when you can expect to receive payment.

I am enclosing a check for $50 toward the sum of $250, which is currently owed on my account.

Please accept my apologies for being in arrears. Recent medical expenses have placed a severe financial burden on me that I did not expect when I made the purchases at your store last spring.

I can manage to pay you $50 a month and if I do not hear otherwise from you, I will assume that this schedule is satisfactory. Thank you for your patience about this.

Yours truly,

Mary Snow
(Mrs. Richard Snow)

enc.

To report a lost credit card

```
                          10 Overlook Drive
                          Essex, CT, zip code

                          May 5, 19--

Galaxy Gas, USA
Credit Card Center
P O Box 1000
Houston, TX, zip code

Gentlemen:
     I wish to make a formal report of the
loss of my Galaxy Credit Card, Number
600-200-000-4 on May 4 in New York City.
I called your 800 number immediately to
report its loss and understand that I am
not liable for any amount over $50 charged
to my card.
     Please send me a new card with a new
charge number. Thank you.

                          Yours truly,

                          Robert Brown
                          Robert Brown
```

Opening a charge account

Gentlemen:

I would like to open a charge account at your store. I currently have charge accounts at Lord & Taylor, B. Altman, and Saks Fifth Avenue.

If you require further information or references, please let me know.

Yours truly,

Alice McCoy
(Mrs. Robert McCoy)

Making a hotel reservation

Gentlemen:

Please reserve a double room with bath for my husband and myself for the week of July 9th through July 15th. We would prefer a room overlooking the lake and, if possible, twin beds.

We will be arriving by train about noon on the 9th and will take a taxi directly to the hotel. Since we will rent a car during our stay, please send us a list of rental fees.

Please confirm and send your rate schedule.

Yours sincerely,

Harriet Brownly
(Mrs. John Brownly)

Contract in a letter

```
Dr. Raymond Brown
1 Rolls Plaza
Centerville, New York zip code

Dear Dr. Brown:
    This is to confirm our financial arrangement for
Nancy's orthodontic treatment as explained by you
in your office last week.
    The cost of the treatment is $2080. I agree to
make an initial payment of $400 at the beginning
of the treatment and to pay the balance of $1680
in 24 monthly payments of $70 each. I understand
that there is no finance charge or interest on the
balance due.
    I also understand that the treatment does not
include x-rays, but does include any necessary
fillings or extractions.
    If these arrangements are agreeable to you,
please sign the enclosed copies of this letter and
return one to me.
    I am very pleased that you are going to treat
Nancy and am sure the treatment will be
successful.
                              Yours truly,
                              Henry Graham
                              Henry Graham

enc.
```

Writing Effective Letters

Letters that sell

The basic formula. The formula for a successful sales letter, according to an expert on direct mail, is:

INTEREST—DESIRE—CONVICTION—ACTION.

If you can stimulate each of these in your reader, you have made your sale.

An important point that all good salesmen know is this: people are more interested in the "secondary gains" of *what the product or service will do for them* than they are in the product or service itself. As one advertising professional puts it, "You don't sell the steak, you sell the sizzle."

What people want. Experts have compiled lists of the basic reasons why people buy anything from a magazine subscription to a car. The main ones are:

1. Better Health
2. To make money
3. To save money
4. Popularity
5. To look better
6. Security in old age
7. Praise from others
8. Sexual attractiveness
9. Comfort
10. Increased enjoyment
11. Leisure
12. Business advancement
13. Social advancement
14. Cleanliness
15. To escape physical pain
16. To save time

These basic human desires are the "sizzle."

Seven steps that sell the sizzle

1. Capture attention. Pique your reader's interest and get his or her attention with your first sentence. This is the first thing a good business letter does—often by asking a question, such as, "Do you want to improve your memory 100 percent?"

2. Make an offer. Promise something important that your product can do for the reader and make him or her want to find out more about it.

3. Appeal to some human need (see checklist).

4. Find at least one way that your product is different from similar ones and show how this difference is important.

5. Back up claims with facts. Prove the value of what you are selling. Make your reader agree.

6. Persuade your reader to take advantage of the opportunity you are offering.

7. Close with a request for action. Give your reader something specific to do right away, such as telephoning or filling out an enclosed order form.

Sample sales letter using the 7 steps

Dear Mr. Jones:

1. How would you like to improve your reading speed by 400 percent and remember everything you have read? How would you like to give your children the chance to improve their reading skills and comprehension in the vital early years?

2. We have developed a foolproof programmed course of instruction that will enable the entire Jones family to develop and perfect these essential skills in only four short months.

3. There is no better investment you could make in your own career or your wife's, or in your children's future.

4. Easyreader is different from any other speed-reading program you may have read or heard about because we give you two complete programs—*one for adults and one for children. The children's program goes from grades 1 through 12. The adults' begins with short stories and ends with market analyses and international relations.*

5. The Howard Smith family of Brocton, Illinois, wrote us that the Easyreader Program was responsible for their son Tom's getting all A's in his last year of high school. Tom Green from Hanover, New Hampshire, said, "My performance on the job was so improved that I got two raises in one year."

6. Do not deprive yourself or your family of this wonderful opportunity to increase your learning and earning power and to enrich your lives. The cost is only $15 a month.

7. So act now. Phone us toll-free (800-100-1000) or fill out the enclosed form. It will be one of the best and most rewarding decisions you ever made!

Yours truly,

Fred Little

enc.

Magazine subscription renewal. Humor can be an important ingredient in a sales letter. It is a good way to get attention and build goodwill, especially when it is likely that a routine letter would be ignored. This is a common problem for the people who write letters soliciting magazine subscriptions and renewals. The following letter uses humor for a "soft sell" approach.

Dear Reader:

This is to tell you that your future issues of Motor Boat Monthly *are being held captive in the guts of a computer.*

You will never know about the incredible new designs for speed and power, or get a chance to win a family vacation on the Inland Waterway, or read about the amazing race down the Mississippi— unless *you send us your check or money order at our special $10 renewal rate, now!*

This is no time to hesitate. Act now or you will never see your beloved Motor Boat Monthly *again.*

Yours anonymously,

MBM Subscription Gang

Letter to boss. Here the writer has a new idea that he thinks would be good for business and he wants to "sell" his boss on it. He uses a slightly different approach and does not specifically include steps 3, 4, or 6. But step 5 is particularly important: he backs up his proposal with facts based on a recognized authority.

Milkman's letter for holiday products

Dear Customer:

The holiday season is coming and I'm sure you won't want to run out of all the things you'll need for entertaining friends and family.

Neilson's Dairy is offering two new holiday products this season, which I'm sure you'll enjoy—frozen strawberry cream and frozen lemon soufflé.

Why not use the enclosed form and order everything you'll need in advance?

With best wishes for the holiday season,

George Wilson

Letter promoting winterizing service

Dear Prospective Winter Driver:

Winter is coming. There's a chill in the air that could spell future trouble for your car. Don't wait for signs of trouble. Come in and give your car the attention and cold-weather servicing it needs—right now!

We have the expert mechanics and up-to-date equipment to give your car a thorough inspection and locate any possible difficulties, and repair them. And we are having early-bird specials on replacing coolant, changing oil and oil filters, and putting on snow tires.

Don't put winterizing off and be sorry later. Come in now. You and your car will be glad you did!

Yours truly,

enc.

Tom Benton

MEMO

TO: Mr. Thomas Grant
FROM: Tony Newman
DATE: August 1, 19—
SUBJECT: Establishing Hang-gliding Training Programs

   I believe Grant's Glorious Gliders could take advantage of the current surge of interest in hang-gliding to promote our product and build goodwill among a growing group of prospective buyers.

   I propose that we initiate a series of hang-gliding training programs and charge an appropriate fee to those who enroll. This would teach many of the inexperienced people who are buying hang-gliders how to use them safely and responsibly, and would enhance our reputation as a company that cares about its products and its customers.

   Our expenses in setting up the course would, I believe, represent a sound financial investment in view of the rate at which the sport is growing. Our own sales, as you know, are up 25 percent over the last three months. According to this month's Hang-gliding News, not only is the sport growing nationwide, but enthusiasts are spending up to $2000 on the average for first-time purchases and from $300 to $1000 per year on maintenance and replacement parts. The article goes go on to say that enthusiasts are becoming more aware and concerned about good proceedure and safety.

   If you approve of this proposal, I would like to discuss with you my ideas for putting it into practice. I can meet with you whenever it is convenient.

T.N.

Tony Newman

Clubs and organizations

Letters from clubs and organizations can include anything from announcing a meeting to thanking a speaker.

Announcement of meetings.
Include the names, time, date, and place. For a regular meeting, a simple postcard will be quicker and less expensive than a letter.

> Monthly Meeting
> South Hampton Garden Club
> Saturday, May 26
> 10:00 A.M.
> at the home of Mrs. John Jones
> 32 Job Lane, South Hampton
>
> Judy Greer, Sec.
> Tel. 555-1212

A special business meeting would require a letter:

> Notice of the 25th Annual Meeting
> of the John and Marian Macy Charity Fund
>
> The annual meeting of the trustees of the John and Marian Macy Charity Fund will be held in the Palisades Community Center on March 1, 1985, at 2:00 P.M. for the purpose of considering and acting on the following:
> 1. Report of the Secretary
> 2. Report of the Treasurer
> 3. Report of the Committee on Disbursements
> 4. Distribution of Income
> 5. Election of Trustees
>
> Harriet Drew
> Secretary
>
> January 15, 1985

Saving money on postage

Your club or organization may be able to save money by applying to the post office for a third-class mailing permit. If yours is a nonprofit organization, the savings compared with first-class postage can be 75 percent. Even a commercial third-class bulk rate saves about 50 percent. Though there are fees for a permit, the savings can be large on frequent mailings.

Announcement of a special event

Dear Parents:

"Bloomsday" is coming and it's only six weeks away! That is the all-new magic show and musical review being presented by the Bloomfield High School Dramatic Club and Marching Band.

Some of the treats in store for you are:
- A mini-musical comedy with songs, dancing, and lots of laughs in one splendid act.
- Astounding feats of magic by that master magician, School Superintendent Jim Rawson.

It should be a marvelous evening, but that's not all. Proceeds will go to the Bloomfield High School College Scholarship Fund, so the cost of your tickets is tax deductible.

This extraordinary event will take place Friday, June 8, at 8:00 P.M. in the Bloomfield High School Auditorium on North Main Street.

Tickets are $4 each. Just fill out the coupon below and send it to us along with your check and we'll send you your tickets right away—or, for $4.50 each, you may buy them at the door. Come and bring your friends and family. You'll be glad you did.

Yours very truly,
Gertrude Troy
Gertrude Troy
Chairman, Scholarship Fund

Yes, I want to have a wonderful time! Send my tickets at once! Here is my check for $_____
Name _____
Address _____
Phone _____

Note the selling techniques of this letter. Its purpose is to convince the reader to buy a product, which is the ticket, and further, to spend money for the good cause of the scholarship fund. The letter accomplishes its purpose by using the following specific techniques:
- It gets attention and creates interest by giving the event an intriguing name.
- It describes a part of the event to develop the interest further.
- It gives two reasons for buying tickets: the event itself and the scholarship fund, and says that the ticket money is *tax deductible*.
- It does not give the date, time, and place until near the end, *after* the event has been described in an exciting way.
- It suggests an action the reader can take (buying tickets). It provides an easy way to do it (the coupon

at the bottom) and an incentive for doing it (lower price).
- It ends with a final encouragement to come.

Fund raising.
In today's tight economy, many clubs and organizations have to raise funds, either for their own needs or for civic purposes. The following letters might be part of an annual drive.

Fund drive letter to the editor

To the Editor:

Centerville Memorial Hospital needs your help. Some 25,000 new people have come to our town in the past ten years and our hospital has to grow to keep up. We urgently need a new wing with at least 50 beds, additional operating rooms, and diagnostic equipment. This will cost some $3 million and the Centerville Chamber of Commerce is sponsoring a drive for funds.

Very soon you will be receiving letters asking for pledges and contributions. You will see announcements of special sporting events, concerts, and dinners—all to help us reach our $3 million goal. But you can help us get off to a flying start right now by sending your check made out to "Centerville Memorial Hospital Fund." Send it to me today, at the Centerville Chamber of Commerce, 100 Main Street, Centerville, Ohio, zip code. No contribution is too small. All contributions are tax deductible.

Yours sincerely,

Frank Ross, President
Centerville Chamber
of Commerce

To the general public

Dear _____ (to be filled in):

Did you know that the population of Centerville has grown by some 25,000 over the past ten years? The people at Centerville Memorial Hospital know this only too well, because the hospital must grow to keep up. An additional 50 beds are badly needed, as are more operating rooms and diagnostic facilities.

This is why the Chamber of Commerce is sponsoring a campaign to raise $3 million for a new wing. Only your dollars will make this possible. Your contribution of $100 or more can buy bricks or a bed or a new piece of equipment. It can be dedicated to whomever you wish, and a memorial plaque will be placed in the lobby upon your request. So please send your check or pledge today in the enclosed return envelope. No amount is too small (or too large) and all contributions are tax deductible.

Yours sincerely,

Frank Ross, President
Centerville Chamber
of Commerce

Thanks to a company for their contribution

Dear Mr. Smith:

Your company's generous contribution to the Centerville Memorial Hospital Fund has enabled the hospital to purchase a CAT scanner, which will give it the most modern diagnostic facilities of any hospital in the area. We are deeply grateful.

Yours sincerely,

Frank Ross, President
Centerville Chamber

Invitation to speak

Dear Mr. Hunt:

The American Association of Railroads is going to hold its annual convention this year at the Palmer House in Minneapolis from Monday, May 8 through Friday, May 11. We would very much like to have you speak at the May 10 session.

This session is devoted to safety problems in freight handling, an area in which your own contributions are well known throughout the industry. I have enclosed our tentative schedule of speakers and a short list of suggested topics.

The association will, of course, pay your travel expenses to Minneapolis and hotel expenses for two nights. We are happy we can also offer you an honorarium.

I hope you will be able to accept, as your views on solving current safety problems would be of great interest to our membership.

Very truly yours,

George Brant, Chairman
Organizing Committee

Acceptance

Dear Mr. Brant:

I would be happy to speak at the May 10 session of the American Association of Railroads' annual convention. Your list of speakers is impressive and I am honored to be included. The suggested topic—the application of systems engineering—is fine. I will send you an outline next week.

Yours sincerely,

Robert Hunt

Thanking a speaker

Dear Mr. Hunt:

This year's convention was a big success, due in no small part to your contribution. Many of the people who attended your session told me what a fine and interesting presentation you made. Thank you very much.

Yours sincerely,

George Brant

Writing Effective Letters

Tips for retired people

Power in numbers. Today more than 26 million Americans are over 65 years old. This group has grown by some 31 percent since the 1970 census and is expected to reach 29 million by the year 2000.

This means that older Americans are an important interest group as consumers and as voters, and a group whose importance can only increase as their numbers grow. So if you have an opinion or complaint, if you need information or assistance—it matters. There are people out there ready to hear from you and ready to help: write to them.

Government agencies. Almost every department of the federal government has policies that affect older people. Special programs on state and local levels were set up by the Older Americans Act and the Older Americans Comprehensive Services Amendments, in such areas as employment, nutrition, recreation, health care, and care of the frail elderly (75 and over).

Finding one's way through the bureaucratic welter can be difficult, but there is a central clearinghouse for information—The Office for the Aging—which also acts as an advocate and mediator between the elderly and various government agencies. There is at least one office in every state. These offices are an invaluable source of information.

Organizations. The number of voluntary organizations of older people who address themselves to a variety of issues on both national and local levels is also growing rapidly. A list of national organizations appears at the end of this section.

You are entitled. If you need help or information in such areas as housing, finance, health, education, travel, recreation, or employment—you are entitled to it. Do not hesitate to ask for it. You can use the telephone, but it is usually better to write a letter. In this section we give you some hints and sample letters to help you do that.

Housing

To a state office for the aging about tax relief

Dear Sir or Madam:

My wife and I are both over 65 and own our own home. I would like to know whether we are eligible for tax abatements, and if so, how we apply.

Yours truly,

John Harris

About eligibility for rent subsidy

```
New York State Office for the Aging
Empire State Plaza
Albany, NY 12230

Gentlemen:
    I would like to know whether I am
eligible for a rent subsidy under any
federal, state, or local program.
    My wife and I are both over 65 and have
been renting the same apartment for 25 years.
We are now living on my pension as a retired
postman and on my wife's Social Security
benefits.  It is sometimes very hard to make
ends meet.  Accordingly, I am eager to know
whether any financial aid is available to
us.  I would appreciate your answer as
soon as possible.
                           Yours truly,
                           Frank Smith
                           Frank Smith
```

About moving to another state

South Carolina Commission on Aging
915 Main Street
Columbia, SC 29201

Dear Sir or Madam:

I plan to retire next year and am very interested in South Carolina as a possible place to live. I need some general information to help me focus on specific towns. I would like to know about the locations of available housing, cost of living and taxes, health care, and special facilities for seniors, including tax exemptions.

My wife and I anticipate a joint income from pensions and Social Security of about $15,000 per year. We plan to sell our house and purchase a small, easily maintained house or apartment for retirement.

I would appreciate any information you can send me on the suitability of South Carolina for retirement, including a list of local Chambers of Commerce to which I can write for more detailed information. Thank you very much.

Yours sincerely,

Henry Crawford

Finances. Finances are of concern to everyone, but never more than to people who are living, or who are about to begin living, on the reduced income that is a fact of life for so many retirees. If you are planning to retire, finding out before you retire about what is likely to be your future financial situation is an excellent idea. The best way to get started is by writing letters.

Some people will be enrolled in private or company pension plans. Some will be entitled to veterans' benefits or survivor benefits. Some will be eligible for food stamps; most for Social Security benefits. Find out about these as soon as possible. There are several ways to go about it:

Send for the Social Security Handbook. You get it without charge by writing to:

Social Security Handbook
U.S. Government Printing Office
Washington, DC 20402

Visit or write to your local Social Security office. Make an appointment to come in and discuss your situation and options.

Get an accounting. There is a credit system for Social Security benefits measured in quarter years, which do not have to be consecutive. What you get depends on your average wages, when you start to collect, and how much you are earning when you put in a claim. If you want to find out where you stand, you can get an accounting of your Social Security earnings at any age, at any time, by writing to:

The Social Security Administration
P.O. Box 57
Baltimore, MD 21203

To make an appointment

Social Security Administration
410 Nanuet Mall
Anytown, N Y zip code

Dear Sir or Madam:

I am 64 years old and plan to retire next year. I want to plan for my retirement and need to know what my benefits will be. May I come in and discuss this with you? I can take time off from work any morning, provided I give advance notice. Please let me know when I can come in. I'd appreciate your answer as soon as possible.

Yours truly,

Margaret Green

To request an accounting. Requests should be made on either of two forms which you can get from the Social Security Administration. They are (1) Social Security Request for Detailed Earnings Information, which will provide a year-by-year breakdown, and (2) Request for Statement of Earnings, which will cover a group of years. You should sign your form exactly as you signed your original card. See page 128 for more information.

> The Social Security Administration
> P.O. Box 57
> Baltimore, Md. 21203
>
> Dear Sir or Madam:
>   Would you please send me your form, Social Security Request for Detailed Earnings Information, as soon as possible? Thank you.
>
>   Yours truly,
>   Robert Stone

To a local utility

Town Gas and Electric Co.
Town, State zip code

Dear Sir or Madam:

I am writing to inquire about your special rates for senior citizens, and want to know what your eligibility requirements are. I am also interested in any help you could give me on energy conservation and weatherization. I am 70 years old, a widow, and live on a small pension.

Yours truly,

Harriet James

To inquire about food stamps

> Department of Social Services
> County, State zip code
>
> Dear Sir or Madam:
>
>   I would like to find out if my husband and I are eligible for food stamps. I am 65 and my husband is 72. As it is very hard for us to get to your offices, I wonder if it is possible to conduct an interview in our home or over the telephone. Also, please tell me what material you will need from us to decide whether we are eligible.
>
>   Sincerely yours,
>   Jane Duffy
>   Jane Duffy
>   (Mrs. Thomas Duffy)

Health

Health insurance. Information on *Medicare*, the health insurance program that covers everyone over 65, and on *Medicaid*, the financial assistance program for needy people of all ages who meet their state's requirements, is available from any Social Security office.

Assistance. Your state or county Office for the Aging can also tell you how to arrange for home care, day care, home meals, and medical transportation.

To request information

Office for the Aging
Rockland County Health Center
Pomona, NY zip code

Dear Sir or Madam:

I need transportation from my home to my doctor's office in Pearl River every other month. I am 75 years old and am confined to a wheelchair. Can you provide this service for me on a regular basis?

Yours truly,

Ruth Daley

To apply for Medicaid. You must apply in person, or send a representative if you are unable to come yourself. When you make an appointment, be sure to ask for an application form with its checklist of required information and documents.

Department of Social Services
Medicaid Unit
Sanatorium Road
Pomona, NY zip code

Dear Sir or Madam:

 I wish an interview in order to apply for Medicaid. Please send me an application form and a list of what I will need to prove eligibility. I can come in any morning.

Yours truly,

Ruth Daley
Ruth Daley

Education.

One of the wonderful things you can do with more time is go back to school. You can finish or further your education and explore new interests, taking courses for credit toward a degree.

Write for information about the many programs available for adult and continuing education from your local school district or community college and from state and private colleges. For summer studies in the United States, Canada, and abroad, investigate ELDERHOSTEL. This program also offers limited fall/winter and winter/spring courses. Write for a catalog (see address on sample letter below).

To a community college

The Institution for Senior Education
Rockland County Community College
Suffern, NY zip code

Dear Sir or Madam:

I have recently retired and would now very much like to finish my college education. Please send me information about your program and about how to apply. I would like to enroll this fall as a sophomore, if that is possible. Please let me hear from you as soon as possible.

Sincerely,

Jane Baker

To inquire about a summer program. There are many special programs open only to retired or elderly people. Here is an example of one:

ELDERHOSTEL
100 Boyston Street
Boston, MA 02116

Dear Sir or Madam:

 I am very interested in finding out about the ELDERHOSTEL program. Please send me your summer catalog and any other information you have about the program.

 I do have some special questions:
1) Are there are facilities for the hearing-impaired?
2) Can you provide any financial assistance? If so, can you send me the necessary application forms?
3) Must students make their own travel arrangements?

 I look forward to hearing from you in regard to these questions and to receiving your catalog.

Yours truly,

Harry Smith
Harry Smith

Travel and transportation

Special services. Many municipalities offer transportation to senior centers, doctors and dentists, and grocery stores, but appointments must usually be made well in advance. For information, contact your state or county Office for the Aging.

To request transportation

County Office for the Aging
County Road
City, State zip code

Dear Sir or Madam:

Can you provide transportation from my home to my local senior center and back on Mondays, Thursdays, and Fridays for the next three months? A recent hip operation has confined me to a wheelchair for that period. Thank you.

Yours truly,

John Rudd

To obtain a senior I.D. pass

Rockland County Office for the Aging
Rockland County Health Center
Sanatorium Road
Pomona, NY zip code

Dear Sir or Madam:

I obtained my senior I.D. pass from your office last year and have found it very helpful for my half-fare bus service, and many other discounts. However, I have lost it. Can you send me another or is it necessary for me to come in to your office? Please let me know about this as soon as possible.

Yours truly,

Alice Jones

To a travel agency

Dear Sir or Madam:

I am interested in finding out about group tours on behalf of my Senior Citizens Club. We are interested in spending a week in the White Mountains in New Hampshire. We would need a congenial place that is wheel-chair accessible, with interesting walks (we have quite a few bird watchers), swimming, and golf. There are ten women and eight men in our group.

Could you recommend some hotels that would be appropriate for our needs and send me brochures and rate schedules? We would like to go by chartered bus and would need information on this, as well. I look forward to hearing from you. Thank you.

Yours truly,

Albert Mills

A Directory of Senior Centers in the U.S. is available for $2 from
    The Government Printing Office
    Superintendent of Documents
    Washington, DC 20402

Recreation. One of the pleasures retired people have is more leisure time. They also have the pleasure of figuring out what to do with it. Local senior centers, which you can find out about from the State or County Office for the Aging, are a valuable source of information.

Inquiry about a senior center

New York State Office for the Aging
Empire State Plaza
Albany, NY 12230

Dear Sir or Madam:

I would like to know which senior center is nearest to my home. Also, please tell me whether noon meals are available at this center, what special programs they offer, and whether transportation is available.

Yours truly,

Frank Parker

To get a recreational pass

National Park Service
Room 1013
U.S. Department of the Interior
18th & C Streets, NW
Washington, DC 20240

Dear Sir or Madam:

Please send me your list of the federal recreational areas where I can obtain a Golden Age Pass. I understand this will provide me with free entrance and a 50 percent discount on fees for all park facilities. Thank you.

Yours truly,

Roger Williams

Requesting a catalog

Sam's Art Supplies
10 Main Street
Centerville, New York zip code

Dear Sir or Madam:

I see from your advertisement that you offer a 10 percent senior citizens discount. Could you please send me your catalog of art supplies? It would be a great convenience to me to be able to order through the mail.

Yours truly,

Harriet Jackson

Employment

Finding work again. The Age Discrimination in Employment Act of 1969 prohibits discrimination against people between the ages of 40 and 65. Nonetheless, finding employment can be difficult for older people.

Remember that you have a lot to offer a prospective employer—the invaluable experience and skills learned over the years, plus the generally excellent record in terms of productivity and dependability that older people have on the job. You need to tell people what you can do, and a very good way to do this is through letters. It usually takes a lot of letters to get a response, but do not get discouraged. You have nothing to lose by trying.

Start a letter campaign. Select a number of companies in the field where you have experience and write directly to them. Explain the type of job you want and that you are not interested in joining a pension plan.

People starting service businesses, such as landscaping and lawn care, catering or real estate, can also use a letter campaign to good advantage. In addition, you can investigate the various government-funded employment programs by writing to the appropriate agency (see table below).

Write to friends and former business associates. Many jobs are found through personal contacts and here, as someone who has been in the business world for many years, you have a definite advantage. Use it.

To a former business associate

> 15 India Street
> Scotch Plains, NJ zip code
> September 3, 1985
>
> Mr. James Morris
> Morris and Burgess, Inc.
> 120 Main Street
> Pleasant Valley, NJ zip code
>
> Dear Jim:
>
> As you know, I retired from McKinsey and Otis last spring when Janet and I moved to Scotch Plains. I find now that I really miss my work as an architectural draftsman (Janet and I miss the income, too) and would very much like to go back to work again.
>
> I wondered, specifically, whether you need additional drafting services in your new office—either full-time or on a free-lance basis. If you don't need anyone right now, do you know of any openings with other architectural firms in our area?
>
> I know you were always pleased with the work I did for you at McKinsey and Otis and I would very much appreciate any help or suggestions you can give me about job possibilities. Again, I would like to work full-time, but would be happy to take on free-lance assignments until I can find something permanent.
>
> I hope to hear from you soon.
>
> Yours truly,
> Henry Scott
> Henry Scott

Write to people that you think might know, or know someone who knows, about job possibilities.

Government employment programs

Action programs. For information about the following programs, write to ACTION, 806 Connecticut Avenue, NW, Washington, DC 20525.

Peace Corps. This international program has no upper age limit. You can also write directly to Senior Citizens Liaison Office of the Peace Corps, Specialized Recruiting, Washington, DC 20525

VISTA (Volunteers in Service to America). This is a domestic Peace Corps which also provides a stipend and living allowance for workers in poor urban and rural areas.

Foster Grandparents. This program pays an hourly wage to low-income people over 60 who care for hospitalized or institutionalized children. Training is provided.

Senior Companion Program. This program is similar to Foster Grandparents, but serves adults with special needs. You visit people who are unable to leave their homes or who are in nursing homes or hospitals.

Department of Labor Programs. This is only a partial listing. Check with the State or County Office for the Aging for other local federally funded programs.

Operation Mainstream. For low-income, unemployed people in about 20 states. Write to U.S.D.A. Forest Service, Manpower Program, P.O. Box 2417, Washington, DC 20013.

Green Thumb. For low-income men over 55. Outdoor work improving public areas. Write to Green Thumb, Inc., National Farmers Union, 1012 14th Street, NW, Washington, DC 20005.

Senior Community Service Aide. Part-time work in Social Security and state employment offices and a variety of service programs. Write to the National Council on Aging, 600 Maryland Avenue, SW, West Wing 100, Washington, DC 20024.

Senior Aides. Part-time work performing a variety of local services such as child care and home health. Write to your State or County Office on the Aging for information.

National organizations

Senior citizens

American Association of Retired Persons (AARP)
1909 K Street, NW
Washington, DC 20006

Open to anyone over 55, AARP offers world tours, bimonthly news bulletins, a hospitality house, out-of-hospital major medical insurance (for members 65 and over), life insurance, reduced prices on prescription and nonprescription drugs, a nursing home in California, and Institutes of Lifetime Learning in Long Beach, California, and Washington, D.C. There are almost 500 local chapters.

National Association of Retired Civil Employees (NARCE)
1909 Que Street, NW
Washington, DC 20009

Organized in 1921, NARCE has more than a thousand chapters in the 50 states. NARCE is active in promoting needed legislation and also has separately administered subsidiaries that provide favorable rates in life, casualty, hospital, fire, and automobile insurance. The annual dues include the monthly magazine *Retirement Life*.

National Council of Senior Citizens (NCSC)
1627 K Street, NW
Washington, DC 20006

Established in 1961, NCSC reports a membership of more than 2 million with more than 2000 affiliated clubs in all the states. NCSC is primarily concerned with promoting the general welfare of older people through public understanding and legislation. It also provides low-cost travel, medical, and other services for its members. Its monthly publication is *Senior Citizen News*.

National Council of the Aging (NCOA)
600 Maryland Avenue, SW
West Wing 100
Washington, DC 20024

NCOA is a central, national resource. General services include professional consultation, gathering and dissemination of information, a special lending library (largest of its kind), conferences, institutes and seminars, special studies and projects, general liaison with government, and the development and design of funded demonstrations.

National Retired Teachers Association (NRTA)

NRTA was founded in 1947 as a separate organization, but now functions as part of AARP, sharing headquarters, staff, and executive director. It has over 800 local associations in all the states. Annual membership dues include the bimonthly *NRTA Journal* and *News Bulletin*.

Retired Offices Association (ROA)
1625 Eye Street, NW
Washington, DC 20006

ROA was established in 1929 and reports a membership of more than 92,000 officers from all the services. It encourages legislation that benefits retired military personnel, and provides employment, travel, insurance, and other services for its members. Annual dues include the magazine *The Retired Officer*.

Senior Citizens of America (SCA)
4109 17th Street, NW
Washington, DC 20011

This is an educational organization, founded in 1954, to help older persons become more effective in community service and personal growth and to bring about a better understanding of aspects of the aging process. SCA serves as a clearinghouse and offers general information services, publications, correspondence, and special counseling service to firms and agencies to prepare employees for retirement.

Gray Panthers
3700 Chestnut Street
Philadelphia, PA 19104

This group was originally called the Coalition of Older and Younger Adults—which is what it is, a loosely knit network of social activists working for change in all areas affecting older people.

Minority groups

National Association for the Spanish Speaking Elderly
3875 Wilshire Boulevard, Suite 401
Los Angeles, CA 90010

National Caucus and Center on Black Age, Inc.
1424 K Street, NW
Washington, DC 20005

You and your post office

The U.S. Postal Service has a lot more to offer than stamps, including many special products and services they would like you to know about. Ask for information at your local post office, or write to:

Consumer Advocate
U.S. Postal Service
Washington, DC 20260-3620

Here is a brief overview:

Classes of mail

Designation	Type of mail	Restrictions	Delivery	Rates
1st class	Letters, documents, postcards	At least 3" × 5" and at least .007" thick. Must not weigh more than 12 oz.	Usually 2 days, but depends on destination. All 1st-class mail going over 500 miles is delivered by air	22 cents for 1st oz., 17 cents each additional oz.
Priority mail (1st-class mail over 12 oz.)	Letters, documents, etc.	Same as above, weighing over 12 oz.	Same as above	Rates for priority mail are determined by zone. Check with your post office.
2nd class	Newspapers, periodicals		Varies	Ask post office for single and bulk rates
3rd class	Commercial (advertising); parcels	Must weigh under 16 oz.	Varies	Single and bulk rates for advertising mail. Rates for parcels are the same as for 1st class up to 4 oz. Over 4 oz., check with post office
4th class	Parcels, printed matter	Weighing over 1 lb.	8–10 days	Rates for most 4th-class mail are determined by zone (ask at your post office). "Book rate" is a special rate available for 24 or more bound pages of material: 69 cents for 1st lb., 25 cents up to 7 lbs., 15 cents thereafter

Mailing valuables

Registered mail	Anything of value to you (jewelry, documents, etc.)	Valued over $400	Delivery is according to class of mail. May be insured for up to $10,000 for domestic. Optional insurance up to $25,000 against loss or damage. Return receipt	$3.55 without postal insurance; $3.60 with postal insurance (up to $100) included
Insured mail	Same as above	Under $500	Reimbursement up to $400	Varies for different classes of mail
Money orders	Alternative to sending cash	Up to $700	1st class	75 cents up to $25; $1 up to $700
Express mail	See "Fast delivery" section for insurance coverage			

Writing Effective Letters

For fast delivery

Designation	Type of mail	Restrictions	Delivery	Rates
Express mail	Letters, parcels	Check with post office for areas serviced and for daily deadline	Overnight to areas serviced (most zip codes and some foreign countries). Guaranteed (money back) and insured (up to $500 reimbursement for merchandise and up to $50,000 for loss or damages). Includes weekends and holidays	$10.75 up to 2 lbs.; over 2 lbs. depends on zone
Airmail	Letters, packages	Up to 70 lbs. Maximum size: 100 sq. in. Mark "Airmail"	Depends on destination; check with post office	Domestic: 1st-class rates if going over 500 miles. International: 44 cents per half oz. up to 2 oz. for foreign countries other than Colombia, Venezuela, and Caribbean countries, which are 39 cents per half oz. up to 2 oz.
Aerogram	Lightweight self-mailer	Must have an overseas destination. Self-mailer is single sheet	Depends on destination; check with post office	36 cents to all destinations
Special delivery	Letters, parcels	No bulk 3rd class	Includes evenings, Sundays, and holidays	$2.95 plus postage for 1st class, $3.10 for all others
Mailgrams (night letters)	Letters	None	Overnight via Western Union or Office Telex or TWX	$7.50 for 1st 50 words, $2.25 thereafter for each additional group of 50 words
INTEL POST service	Documents	Service only between U.S. and designated foreign countries	Documents are scanned by a facsimile reader and transmitted via satellite, printed in destination country, and delivered by regular mail (1st class)	$5 per page

Proof of mailing

Designation	Type of mail	Restrictions	Delivery	Rates
Certificate of mailing	Letters, parcels	Items of no intrinsic value	According to class of mail. Sender gets a mailing receipt, but post office keeps no record	40-cent fee plus postage according to weight and class of mail
Certified mail	Letters, parcels	1st-class mail only, for items of no intrinsic value	Sender gets a mailing receipt, and post office keeps a record	75-cent fee plus postage
Return receipt	Letters, parcels	Given for Certified, Registered, C.O.D., and Express mail, and for any mail insured over $20	According to class/designation of mail. Receipt, returned to sender, constitutes proof of delivery	70 cents plus postage

Writing Effective Letters

Correct forms of address

Government officials

Person	Address	Salutation
The President	The President The White House Washington, DC 20510	Dear Mr. President or Madam President
The Vice President	The Vice President United States Senate Washington, DC 20510	Dear Mr. Vice President or Madam Vice President
Cabinet Officers	The Honorable John Smith Secretary of the Interior Washington, DC zip code	Dear Mr. Secretary or Madam Secretary
The Attorney General	The Honorable John Smith Attorney General Washington, DC zip code	Dear Mr. Attorney General or Madam Attorney General
Chief Justice of the United States (same applies for a State Supreme Court)	The Chief Justice of the United States The Supreme Court Washington, DC 20543	Dear Mr. Chief Justice or Madam Chief Justice
Associate Justice	Mr. Justice Smith The Supreme Court Washington, DC 20543	Dear Mr. Justice or Madam Justice
U.S. Senator	The Honorable John Smith United States Senate Washington, DC 20510	Dear Senator Smith
U.S. Representative	The Honorable John Smith The United States House of Representatives Washington, DC zip code	Dear Mr. Smith
Governor	The Honorable John Smith Governor of (State) State Capital	Dear Governor Smith
Lieutenant Governor	The Honorable John Smith Lt. Governor of (State) State Capital	Dear Mr. Smith
State Senator	The Honorable John Smith The State Senate State Capital	Dear Senator Smith
State Assemblyman or Representative	The Honorable John Smith State House of Representatives (or Assembly) State Capital	Dear Mr. Smith
Mayors	The Honorable Jane Smith Mayor of (City or Town) Address	Dear Mayor Smith or Dear Madam Mayor
Lawyers	John Smith, Esq. Address	Dear Mr. Smith
Federal Judge	The Honorable John Smith United States District Judge	Dear Judge Smith

For further reference

Adler, Joan
   The Retirement Book
   William Morrow
Amy Vanderbilt's Etiquette
   Doubleday and Company
Blumenthal, Lassor A.
   The Art of Letter Writing
   Grosset & Dunlap
Buckley, Earle C.
   How to Write Better Business Letters
   McGraw-Hill
Mager, N.H. and S.K.
   The Complete Letter Writer
   Pocket Books
Paxson, William C.
   The Business Writing Handbook
   Bantam Books
Schuster, M. Lincoln (ed.)
   A Treasury of the World's Great Letters
   Simon & Schuster
Silverstone, Barbara and Hyman, Helen Kandel
   You and Your Aging Parent
   Pantheon Books
Watson, Lilian Eichler
   The Bantam Book of Correct Letter Writing
   Bantam Books

Members of the clergy

Person	Address	Salutation
Catholic clergy		
The Pope	His Holiness, the Pope Vatican City Rome, Italy	Your Holiness
Cardinals	His Eminence, John Cardinal Smith	Dear Cardinal Smith
Archbishops and Bishops	The Most Reverend John Smith	Dear Archbishop (Bishop)
Abbot	The Right Reverend John Smith Abbot of (abbey)	Dear Father Abbot
Canon	The Very Reverend Canon John Smith	Dear Canon Smith
Monsignors	The Right (Very or Most)* Reverend Msgr. John Smith	Dear Monsignor Smith
Priest	The Reverend John Smith	Dear Father Smith
Brothers	Brother John Smith Name of Community	Dear Brother John
Sisters	Sister (full religious name) Name of Convent	Dear Sister

*The form of address depends on rank. When in doubt, consult the Official Catholic Directory.

Protestant clergy		
Presiding Bishop of the Episcopal Church, U.S.A.	The Most Reverend John Smith, D.D.	Dear Bishop Smith
Episcopal Bishops	The Right Reverend John Smith, D.D. Bishop of (area)	Dear Bishop Smith
Dean	The Very Reverend John Smith Dean of (cathedral or seminary)	Dear Dean Smith
Minister or Priest	The Reverend John Smith	Dear Mr. Smith (or, if the person has a doctorate, Dear Dr. Smith)
Jewish clergy		
Rabbi	Rabbi John Smith	Dear Rabbi Smith (or, as above, Dear Dr. Smith)
Cantor	Cantor John Smith	Dear Cantor Smith

Members of the armed forces

The convention for addressing Army, Navy, Air Force, Coast Guard, and Marine officers and enlisted personnel is: full rank followed by the full name, a comma, and the abbreviation for the branch of service.

The abbreviations for the branches of service are: Army—U.S.A.; Army Reserve—U.S.A.R.; Air Force—U.S.A.F.; Air Force Reserve—U.S.A.F.R.; Navy—U.S.N.; Navy Reserve—U.S.N.R.; Coast Guard—U.S.C.G.; Coast Guard Reserve—U.S.C.G.R.; Marine Corps—U.S.M.C.; Marine Corps Reserve—U.S.M.C.R.

Retired generals and admirals keep their military titles in civilian life. The abbreviation (Ret.) is added after the service initials. Inactive reserve officers or retired officers of lower rank do not keep their titles. A retired brigadier general in the Army Reserve would be addressed as Brigadier General John Smith, U.S.A.R. (Ret.). The salutation would be Dear General Smith. Ensigns, petty officers, and warrant officers would be addressed according to the formula, but the salutation would be written Dear Mr. Smith.

Writing Effective Letters

Improving Your Reading

- Enjoy the benefits of reading 302
- What is good reading? 306
- Efficient reading 310
- Special types of reading 318
- Continuing to improve 322
- Reading lists 324

In the world we live in, our everyday actions depend to a great extent on our ability to read. We are always reading, often without even being aware of it: we read traffic signs, recipes, words on a television screen, and billboard advertisements. Surrounded by the printed word, many of us often take reading for granted. We come to think of our reading habits and skills as fixed, unchangeable parts of ourselves.

But good readers have one thing in common—they have *made* themselves good readers, often at a late age. One of the most famous books on reading is Mortimer Adler's *How to Read a Book;* in it he wrote: "I did not discover I could not read until after I had left college." Of course he could read newspapers, magazines, and books. But he discovered that he was not a good reader because he was not getting everything possible out of the things he read, nor was he reading with speed, pleasure, and satisfaction.

This chapter will help any reader become a better one, and it will help make reading more enjoyable. Most people want to improve their reading ability but do not know how. Here you will discover exactly how to improve your reading skills through an effective reading improvement program that will meet your own needs. You will also learn of the many benefits of good reading skills.

Enjoying the benefits of reading

The best reason for improving your reading is one of the most neglected. Reading gives pleasure. Good reading skills make reading even more pleasurable. Most of the books offered by a library or bookstore are for leisure reading, because reading is one of the most stimulating ways people can spend free time. Yet many people avoid reading because they think of it as a kind of chore or a kind of homework that they outgrew when they left school. But think of this: as a reader you have a world of entertainment at your fingertips. You can enjoy reading wherever you find yourself and whenever you wish, without depending on others or on the schedules that control movies and television.

The pleasures of reading are not limited to novels or stories. Good readers enjoy the personal satisfaction of learning more about their fields of interest, such as history or biography or sports, and also the satisfaction of developing new interests. People who enjoy reading usually become engrossed in current events. This gives them the satisfaction of understanding in depth the news of the day that is only skimmed by radio or television. Reading does not prevent activity. It makes people more active. Good readers of all ages use "how to" books on home improvement or hobbies for ideas on improving and broadening their leisure activities. Readers do not dislike parties or sports. In fact, they have more enthusiasm for these activities because they are stimulated by reading to seek more exciting ways to live.

In addition to these personal benefits, good reading skills help promote career advancement. Reading lists of required and recommended books are the heart of any formal education, and the ability to master these books fully and quickly is essential for the success of those planning for college, now in college, or returning to college. Independent reading can also open the doors to occupational advancement or to career changes. Because good readers enjoy reading and do more of it, they are more likely to find the books that will help them to obtain promotions or inspire new job ideas. Reading skills are also closely related to important occupational skills, such as writing and public speaking.

Finally, the benefits of good reading habits are felt by the entire family. Children are more likely to read well if they come from homes where books are valued. Reading is not necessarily a solitary activity. It lends itself to group activities, such as reading aloud or discussing the contents of mutually shared books. Children brought up by people who care about reading benefit from the ideas and discussions stimulated by books. Adults, in turn, can better understand their own reading habits by observing their children and by becoming involved with required school reading. Good reading habits can be learned and relearned by all members of the family together.

Evaluating your reading.
To improve your reading, you should first find out where you now stand as a reader. This self-evaluation will enable you to concentrate on areas that need attention. It will also make it possible for you to judge your overall improvement as you work on your reading.

Thus, to benefit from the program in reading improvement described in this chapter, your first task is

> "He that loves reading, has everything within his reach. He has but to desire, and he may possess himself of every species of wisdom to judge and power to perform."
>
> —*William Godwin*

to examine your reading performance for symptoms of a possible problem. Then you will examine individual habits to isolate the ones that can hold you back. Even if your reading performance is acceptable, you can set new, higher goals and achieve them by continuing to work on fundamental habits with the techniques described here.

The most obvious symptom of a reading problem is boredom. No author tries to bore a reader. Rather, most authors spend considerable effort trying to interest their readers. Without knowing it, people who find

The enjoyment of reading is limitless. Reading is not restricted to a particular time or place.

Improving Your Reading

Executives and professionals read for many hours each day to keep up with new developments and advance in their careers.

to keep up with reading as a purposeful activity. They need to renew their sense of reading for specific information, whether to pass a school course, secure a job promotion, or obtain a personal benefit.

Finally, the family benefits of reading are lost by people who make no attempt to master what they read. People who find it difficult to retain what they read can regain this ability by discussing their reading with friends, family members, people who are familiar with the same book, or people who may be interested in hearing about a book.

Boredom, failure to comprehend material, and failure to retain information are only the most general symptoms of reading problems. But these symptoms can help you identify specific reading habits that should be corrected or improved in order to better your overall reading performance. The checklist provided here will help you analyze specific reading habits. These habits are discussed later in this chapter.

themselves bored with books and magazines are working against the benefits of reading. In adults, this is usually because their reading habits have deteriorated since their school years.

The personal benefits of reading for pleasure and information are easily undone by neglecting to keep up with reading as a regular activity. People who pick up a book only when they are bored can hardly hope to be anything but bored while reading it. Good readers plan to read regularly, and they keep material at hand that they look forward to reading.

Similarly, the professional and educational benefits of reading are undone by reading without a purpose. People who have trouble getting started in reading, and who find themselves with only a vague understanding of isolated facts when they have finished, have failed

Essential steps to good reading.

If you are dissatisfied with your present reading ability, if you are unsure of how to improve your reading skills, or if you wish to enjoy reading more, this chapter will give you the practical advice you need. You, in turn, must have the willingness to follow a program of regular practice in special reading skills. You may be asked to break habits caused by years of little or no contact with books. You may also find yourself asked to develop new habits, many of which may seem difficult to adopt. But if you accept the fact that reading is an acquired skill rather than a natural talent, and if you agree that all skills can be sharpened by practice, then you are in an excellent position to begin your own program for reading improvement.

Checklist of reading habits

Answer all questions in this checklist for an inventory of your reading habits.

1. Do you suffer from eyestrain or headaches as you read?
2. Do you find yourself distracted as you read?
3. Do you point at words as you read?
4. Do you audibly or silently say words as you read?
5. Do you frequently reread words or phrases?
6. Do you read everything at a single speed?
7. Do you skip over new words without understanding them?
8. Do you quickly forget what you have read?
9. Do you lack a sense of purpose before you begin reading?
10. Do you find certain kinds of reading especially difficult?
11. Do you go many days without reading at all?
12. Do you read only a single kind of book?
13. Do you lack ideas on what new things you might read?

The questions that you answer "yes" identify your reading habits that need improvement. This chapter provides advice on each of them. Questions 1 through 4 are discussed in the section "What is good reading?"; questions 5 through 8 in the sections on "Reading for speed" and "Reading for comprehension"; 9 and 10 in "Special types of reading"; and 11 through 13 in "Continuing to improve."

Setting realistic goals. We all know of highly advertised schemes for miraculous accomplishments in reading improvement. Most of them concentrate only on reading speed. They advertise success as the ability to skim a novel such as Leo Tolstoy's massive *War and Peace* in a few hours. Such schemes may indeed be able to teach people to turn all 1200 pages of that novel in a short amount of time. But the schemes are flawed on two counts: first, no one can understand that novel in a few hours; second, no one can enjoy that novel in a few hours. A further problem with such promises is the proven fact that superspeed reading ability does not last.

The primary goals of this program are to help you enjoy reading more; to allow you to learn the satisfactions of reading well; and to encourage you to want to read more often for pleasure and self-improvement. You will certainly enjoy reading more if you read faster; this program will help you to double your normal reading speed and beyond. But to increase your enjoyment of books, you must also read better; this program will help you to improve your comprehension so you can enjoy stimulating and challenging books. Both of these goals can be achieved by most people in about eight weeks of daily reading practice for about one hour at a time. This is not an overnight key to superspeed reading. It is a responsible program for achieving long-lasting benefits in reading with only 50 to 60 hours of practice.

To begin, *read every day* for about one hour. If possible, this reading session should be scheduled at the same time each day, but make certain that you avoid a time when you are too tired or too distracted to concentrate. For the first two weeks, read any easy material you find enjoyable. Read at your present natural reading speed. As the days go by, work to improve that reading speed by following the advice on "Reading for speed" given in this chapter. Your goal is to double your natural reading speed within two weeks. Then you will be prepared to develop a repertoire of reading speeds for material of different levels of difficulty. This skill is described in the section of this chapter called "Developing three speeds." From week three to week eight, vary the difficulty of your reading material each day. In this stage you will be taking advantage of the advice in the section on "Reading for comprehension." You will also concentrate on special reading skills, and on reading for special purposes. In this way, you will be developing your ability to read different sorts of books and articles with proficiency. At the end of eight weeks of these daily one-hour reading sessions, compare your initial speed and comprehension with your final speeds and comprehension.

Charting your progress. You will need a record of your daily reading to chart your progress through the eight weeks. The best record is a diary of brief entries recorded after each day's reading. You can keep such a diary in any pad or notebook. The box on this page shows the items of information to record as you complete the program. In the first two weeks, you will be concerned only with the first five items. In later weeks, as you work on special skills, you will want to keep track of all ten questions for a thorough evaluation of your improving skills.

Your reading program

This outline of a good program for reading improvement requires only a single hour each day for a period of eight weeks.

Weeks 1–2: Measure beginning reading speed.
Read one hour a day.
Read easy material.
Check reading speed daily.
Work to double beginning reading speed.

Weeks 3–8: Measure three reading speeds:
rapid, *normal*, and *study*.
Read one hour a day.
Alternate readings of easy, average, and difficult levels of complexity.
Check one reading speed daily.
Review what has been read.
Keep notes on aspects of reading that need work.

A reader's diary

To keep track of your reading, make brief, daily notes in a diary or notebook. The diary sample shown here supplies all the important questions affecting reading plus answers given by one reader.

When you start your diary, only the first questions will be answered in the first weeks. In later weeks, you will answer all these questions.

> Date: 4-6-85
> Words read: 5500
> Reading speed: 360 wpm
> Level of difficulty: average
> Level of speed: normal
> Summary completed: clear presentation of personnel evaluation process
> Special difficulties: none

What is good reading?

Being a competent reader means having a sufficient knowledge of the fundamental habits necessary for success. Poor readers never examine their habits, so they never discover the wasted movements or persistent distractions that prevent them from increasing their speed and comprehension. Good readers scrutinize their basic habits to find ways to improve. Thus, moving toward competent reading begins with self-examination.

Before you read. The eyes are the most important physical tools for reading. Schools regularly check the vision of children, so many minor eye problems are identified early in life. The most common of these are *nearsightedness*, which is clear focus only on close objects, and *farsightedness*, which is clear focus only on more distant ones. Another common problem is *astigmatism*, a blurred perception in one eye that causes eyestrain. All these problems are easily corrected by prescription eyeglasses.

After youth, however, the eyes continue to change, and so adults have as much need as children for regular eye examinations. Because of natural changes in the way the eyes focus, adults may require prescription lenses for the first time or new prescriptions to replace old ones. Adults must also be concerned with diseases of the eyes associated with aging. These include *cataracts*, which cause a clouding of the lens of the eye, and *glaucoma*, which is an increase in the pressure within the eye.

Any weakness in eyesight can lead to eyestrain, headaches, fatigue, and restlessness. But correctly prescribed lenses can correct vision, insuring that reading is both more effective and more pleasant. It is a good habit to have your eyes examined at least once every two years.

Congenial surroundings are another fundamental consideration. Good readers make a habit of reading in an environment conducive to concentration. Poor readers often complain of boredom with books when improper surroundings have made concentration impossible.

First, reading requires proper light. Poor lighting can strain the best of eyes. Reading lamps should throw sufficient light on the printed page without causing glare. Ideally, the light should come from behind the reader—usually over the left shoulder—and be shaded from the reader's eyes. Single bright lights in otherwise dark rooms also cause eyestrain, so make certain that your reading room is also lit by a background lamp.

Second, reading requires the quiet essential for concentration. Many people find some background noise, such as a radio, more conducive to concentration than complete silence. That is because the noise remains in the background, is unobtrusive, and has a soothing effect. Other kinds of noise, however, are specifically designed to attract attention. Television commercials, for example, are designed to draw attention from whatever anyone is doing, including reading. It is important, therefore, to test your tolerance for noise while reading. No one needs a private study or library in order to read well, but readers must control their surroundings in order to eliminate distractions that make concentration difficult.

Finally, reading requires an appropriate seating arrangement. This, too, is largely a matter of personal preference. It may seem too obvious a point to bear repeating, but reading in bed is more conducive to sleeping than to reading effectiveness. Everyone enjoys reading as relaxation, but good readers are aware of their physical posture and choose the one best for a particular reading purpose. A comfortable armchair is best for becoming absorbed in a favorite novel or magazine, but a chair and desk or table are necessary for study. While seated before a desk or table, good readers are able to take notes or reach for a handy dictionary or other reference work without the distraction of moving elsewhere to find the necessary book. Your daily reading for this program should be done at a well lighted desk or table in a quiet room. This promotes alertness and concentration on the reading material itself and the particular reading skill you may be practicing that day.

The act of reading. Reading is primarily a mental activity, requiring only turning pages and moving the eyes. Any other actions are distractions and impediments to understanding. By indulging in bad habits, poor readers often make reading hard for themselves, but good readers free their minds for speedy absorption of written material. To improve your reading, it is important to identify and eliminate physical habits that slow you down while reading.

Eye movements. In reading, the eyes make small, split-second movements across the lines of the page. Only when the eyes stop is vision possible. Thus, only when the eyes stop can reading taking place.

The first person to connect this physical fact with the reading process was the French ophthalmologist Emile Javal. In 1878 he gave the name *saccades* to the jerky jumps of the eye moving across the printed page

> ### Observing eye movements
>
> Most people are unaware of the physical eye movements of reading. Observe the eye movements of another person while reading in order to better understand your own.
>
> 1. Have a friend sit in a straight-backed chair.
> 2. Have the friend hold a book at eye level about 12 inches from the face.
> 3. As the friend reads, look just over the top of the book at the eyes in motion.
> 4. Note the movements and pauses of the eyes while reading. Look for regressions and for return eye sweeps from the end of one line to the beginning of the next.

from left to right. He called the pauses between the jumps *fixations*. We are not aware of it as we read, but each line of print is crossed by the eye in a series of these jumps and pauses. For obvious reasons, we cannot observe our own eye movements. But we can observe the eye movements of other people who are reading, and this is a helpful exercise because it demonstrates how our own eyes behave as we read.

During reading, most people fixate on the beginning of a word because their eyes are drawn by the spaces between words. Everyone's reading is a sequence of these fixations. Good readers are able to keep the time of fixation to a minimum, thus speeding the eye along the printed line and on to the next. This increases their interest in the material and their mastery of ideas. Good readers are also able to eliminate *regressions,* the name given to backtracking to words already read. This ensures that they encounter the author's ideas as written and not as a confusing jumble of rearranged and reread words and phrases. As you observe the eye movements of other readers, you can expect to see different numbers of fixations and regressions.

It is important to observe and understand reading eye movement because you can control it. Among the most common bad habits of poor readers are slow or sloppy eye movements and frequent regressions. Both make it harder, not easier, to understand an author's ideas. Both are unnecessary, and both are easy to correct. Prove this to yourself by reading a single page at a slightly faster than normal rate and without any regressions at all. Move your eyes rapidly along the line and do not regress. It takes time to make this a habit, but you will soon notice that the effort increases reading speed and efficiency without any loss in comprehension. (More information on eye movements is provided in the section on "Reading for speed.")

Hand movements. Many young children are instructed to point at words while they are learning to read. Usually these words are in a list, and the exercise is designed to increase vocabulary. Unfortunately, many adult readers are held back because they fail to shed this habit. They read by pointing at words with a finger or a pencil, or even at a whole line of words with a ruler.

The problem with using hand movements is that they not only limit but actually distort reading. Fingers, pencils, and rulers introduce an unnecessary physical act into the reading process—complicating it, slowing it down, and distracting the eye. Habitual hand motions are usually performed at a single speed, making it difficult to achieve the flexibility of speed necessary for efficient reading. Finally, pointers distort reading comprehension because they locate *places on a page* rather than *ideas in a sentence*.

Good readers concentrate on ideas by eliminating the physical distraction of pointing.

Hand movements are a bad reading habit that is easy to correct. Simply refuse to let yourself touch the page when you read. Unless you are taking notes or underlining, place your book on a reading stand or hold it with both hands. A single hour of reading like this will demonstrate that pointing is simply unnecessary. Because a physical hindrance to understanding has been removed, later practice sessions will show improved comprehension.

Lip movements. Although reading is a mental process, many poor readers limit themselves by pronouncing the words they read. This habit is known to specialists as *vocalization,* and it can take several forms. Some people may actually read aloud. Others murmur to themselves. Most vocalizers silently mouth words as they read. These physical actions are the simplest

Improving Your Reading 307

One can tell that this reader is reading efficiently. She does not distract herself by pointing at the words as she reads, nor does she move her lips. The silent reading she practices is truly silent. Her attention is on the ideas and information she seeks, not on individual words.

forms of vocalization. More often, people have the habit of *subvocalization,* or mentally reproducing the sound of written words without any apparent physical action. These readers are listening to an interior voice rather than seeing words on a page.

Vocalization and subvocalization are not found among good readers because these habits interfere with both comprehension and speed. As in the case of hand movements, these physical or mental actions are a distraction from the ideas of a written work. These habits also substitute sound for meaning, causing a delay or even a loss in understanding. Since good readers focus on ideas, they are not hindered by vocal distractions.

It is easy to prove to yourself how seriously vocalization and subvocalization can slow your reading. Most speakers are able to read a passage aloud at about 125 words per minute. Mentally listening to the sound of printed words produces a reading rate only insignificantly faster. But even slow readers free from vocalizing habits proceed at close to twice this speed. Open any book or magazine you have handy and select two pages with approximately the same number of words. Time yourself while reading the first page aloud. Then time yourself while reading the second page as quickly as you can without any vocalization at all. Do not be surprised if you find you have read the second page a hundred words a minute faster than the first.

Many good readers have cured themselves of the habit of vocalizing. Some have done this merely by resisting the temptation to speak or hear the words they read; they insist, "I will *not* vocalize," and overcome the habit by willpower. But there is another method. You used it already if you did the exercise just described. *Simply force yourself to read faster.* If you work at reading fast, your vocal or subvocal voice will not be able to keep up with your eyes. Continued practice at reading faster with your eyes alone will break the vocalization habit and also improve your ability to read for speed.

How we read.

One of the most frequent complaints of poor readers is that they get lost when they begin to read. They get a few pages or paragraphs into a book or article and then find themselves confused. The author seems to be saying something they cannot understand, or the author does not seem to be saying anything at all. The result? Boredom and frustration.

These readers have the bad habit of beginning with the first word of a book or article and treating all the words as if they were of equal importance. These readers have failed to use the signposts provided by writers to help guide readers to the points being made. Good readers make a habit of using these pointers to focus on key ideas.

Prereading. You can preview anything you wish to read, thus locating these pointers before you begin to work your way carefully through the text. This is often called *skimming* or *scanning* the written work. It is a good habit because it helps you to read faster and with better understanding. But it is no substitute for careful reading, and so it is useful to think of this process as *prereading.* You will not want to preread casual leisure reading; few readers of mystery novels, for example, enjoy knowing the outcome of the story in advance. But for all difficult or scholarly reading, you will want to preread the text as a technique that will help you understand the text more completely and more quickly.

Published books and articles include many signposts to help the reader. Some of these signposts are part of the format of the work, for example, chapter titles and subheadings within chapters. Others are part of the organization of the work, such as introductory and summary paragraphs. All are intended to help you get a sense of an author's ideas before you begin to read. Good readers take advantage of these signposts and are not likely to get lost while reading. They already know where they are going.

The first step in prereading is to study titles. Books and magazine articles usually have main titles and subtitles. These indicate both the general subject and the author's special approach to it. When you are reading a book, study the chapter titles in the table of contents. Chapter titles can give you an idea of what to expect in the book. If you are reading a magazine, look for subheadings within articles. These break up the text just as chapter titles in longer works do. Subheadings provide clues to the ideas in sections of the article and an outline of the contents of each article.

Depending on the kind of material you are reading, you may be given other signposts. Textbooks often include study questions. They should be consulted *before* you read so you know in advance what to look for and concentrate on. Many books also include important illustrations, diagrams, charts, or graphs. These are visual aids to be consulted in prereading for a quick hint about important concepts. Finally, many books and magazines use boxes to set off important quotations, definitions, and key ideas.

In the second stage of prereading, skim the text itself to understand its organization. This can be done with an entire magazine article, but in books you will want to skim each chapter as you come to it. First, examine the opening and closing paragraphs. Opening paragraphs often introduce you to the material, arouse interest, or identify important ideas. Closing paragraphs often restate conclusions or recapitulate the information presented. Then briefly check the interior paragraphs. This can be done by reading only the opening sentences of the paragraphs. These are called topic sentences when they announce the point of the paragraph.

What to preread

Reading material is full of signposts to check *before* you read. These are the kinds of places you can find pointers to the main ideas in any work.

Full titles	Main titles on opening page
Chapter titles	Found in table of contents
Subheadings	Breaks in text
Study questions	At the ends of some chapters
Illustrations	Visual examples with captions
Boxed text	Words in enlarged type
Opening paragraphs	Introduction for all readers
Closing paragraphs	Conclusion in its plainest form
Topic sentences	Informative openings of paragraphs

Prereading, of course, will not answer all of your questions about a work. That can be done only by careful reading according to the principles described later in this chapter. But prereading is a good reading habit because it shows you what writers call the *shape* of the material. This will help you decide what to read, how fast to read it, and what to look for in it.

Prereading

Prereading alerts you to signposts directing attention to important points. Among these signposts are the topic sentences of paragraphs. Scan the passage below by reading only topic sentences, which are printed in boldface. Then read the passage from beginning to end. You will see that your first prereading scan gives you an excellent preliminary idea of the content of the entire passage.

THE SAN FRANCISCO EARTHQUAKE
by Jack London

Within an hour after the earthquake shock, the smoke of San Francisco's burning was a lurid tower visible a hundred miles away. And for three days and nights this lurid tower swayed in the sky, reddening the sun, darkening the day, and filling the land with smoke.

On Wednesday morning at quarter past five came the earthquake. A minute later the flames were leaping upward. In a dozen different quarters south of Market Street, in the working class ghetto and in the factories, fires started. There was no opposing the flames. There was no organization, no communication. All the cunning adjustments of a twentieth-century city had been smashed by the earthquake. The streets were humped into ridges and depressions, and piled with the debris of fallen walls. The steel rails were twisted into perpendicular and horizontal angles. The telephone and telegraph systems were disrupted. And the great water mains had burst. All the shrewd contrivances and safeguards of man had been thrown out of gear by thirty seconds' twitching of the earth-crust.

By Wednesday afternoon, inside of twelve hours, half the heart of the city was gone. At that time I watched the vast conflagration from out on the bay. It was dead calm. Not a flicker of wind stirred. Yet from every side wind was pouring in upon the city. East, west, north, and south, strong winds were blowing upon the doomed city. The heated air rising made an enormous suck. Thus did the fire of itself build its own colossal chimney through the atmosphere. Day and night this dead calm continued, and yet, near to the flames, the wind was often half a gale, so mighty was the suck.

Wednesday night saw the destruction of the very heart of the city. Dynamite was lavishly used, and many of San Francisco's proudest structures were crumbled by man himself into ruins, but there was no withstanding the onrush of the flames.

Improving Your Reading

Efficient reading

Efficiency in any operation is getting the best results with minimum effort. An efficient machine produces quality work quickly. Should it be too slow, goods cannot be produced economically. But should it be too fast, the loss of quality offsets any gain by speed.

The same can be said of reading, an operation that should produce maximum understanding with minimum time and effort. Read too fast, and you will not understand what you read. Read too slowly, and you risk losing interest.

Good readers are efficient because they balance these dual concerns of speed and comprehension. In this section you will be given instructions on how to read for speed and how to read for comprehension. First you will concentrate on speed, learning how you can double your reading speed with only a few days of practice. Then you will work on comprehension, learning special skills to help you master even difficult study material.

Reading for speed. Most poor readers proceed at about 150 to 200 words a minute. Average readers read about 250 to 300 words a minute. Good readers read from 400 to 500 and even more words a minute. But the most important skill of good readers is that they read at more than a single speed. They have a *repertoire of speeds*, an assortment of speeds for easy, average, and difficult material. Like the physical mannerisms discussed earlier, reading speeds are habits that can be corrected and improved. With a little practice, you can increase your average reading speed and develop a repertoire for special occasions

Measure your reading speed. The first step in your program for improvement is to measure your present reading speed. This establishes your beginning point; later, you can check your improvement against this original speed.

For this self-assessment you will need a quiet place, a book you consider easy to read, a watch or clock with a second hand, and paper and pencil. Make sure you will be free from interruptions or distractions. Also make sure you choose reading material you like, so you get an accurate measurement of your speed. Time yourself with the watch, and keep a permanent record of the results on paper.

Reading speed is always measured in words per minute. So the first step is to calculate the words on an average page of the book you will use for the test. The simplest way to do this is to count the words on single lines of text. Count the words in each of five full lines of text. Add the total number of words and divide by five. Now you know the average number of words in each line. You can now count the number of lines on a page. All full pages of text in your book will have

---

How to measure your reading speed

To find your average reading speed, first calculate the words on a page of the book you are going to use. When doing this, count both parts of hyphenated words as separate words. Then calculate your reading speed in words per minute (WPM) on a test. To arrive at an accurate figure, you should complete at least five brief tests and combine the results of each to reach your personal average reading speed.

Calculating words per page

Words in first line	=____
Words in second line	=____
Words in third line	=____
Words in fourth line	=____
+ Words in fifth line	=____
Total	=____
Divided by	5
Average words per line	=____
Multiplied by lines per page	×____
Average words per page	=____

Calculating words per minute (WPM)

$$\frac{\text{Total words read}}{\text{Time in seconds}} \times 60 = \underline{\qquad} \text{WPM}$$

Calculating average reading speed

First test WPM	=____
Second test WPM	=____
Third test WPM	=____
Fourth test WPM	=____
Fifth test WPM	=____
Total	=____
Divided by	5
Average WPM	=____

about the same number of lines. You can now multiply the average number of words in a line by the number of lines on a page, thereby obtaining a quick estimate of words per page. Make notes on these counts for later reference. What is the average number of words in a line? What is the average number of lines on a page? What is the average number of words on a page?

Using the same book, test your reading speed. After noting the time, read five pages. Read at your normal speed, making sure you understand the material. Do not rush; you are testing yourself. After five pages, stop and note the elapsed time. You can now calculate your reading speed in words per minute by following the directions in the box on this page.

In this test it is important that you understand what you have read. Rushing to beat the clock is pointless: it makes reading unpleasant and comprehension impossible, and it produces a false estimate of your normal reading speed. After you have finished reading, take a moment to review the main ideas or facts in the pages you have read. If your recall seems poor, you may have read too fast. Another good test is to try to describe what you have read to a family member or friend. If he or she cannot understand the passage from your description of it, then you may not have understood it either. If you do not understand the material, slow down in the next tests and read more carefully.

You will need to conduct five tests in all, for each reading five pages, in order to have an accurate measurement of your average reading speed. After each test, carefully record your speed in words per minute. Relax for a few minutes between tests. It is not necessary to complete all five tests in a single sitting.

After five tests on passages you have understood, average your reading rates for a reliable estimate of your normal reading speed. This is the beginning point for your program to improve your reading speed.

Increasing your reading speed. Your beginning reading speed reflects habits you have developed over a period of years. This means that you cannot expect to increase it dramatically overnight. But it also means that reading speed can be improved by developing new habits.

First, you must focus on the problem of regressions, the backtracking habit you observed while watching the eye movements of another reader. *Regression* is going back to reread a word or, more often, a group of words. For example, suppose a 200-word-per-minute reader regressed five times in a minute to reread five groups of ten words each. In a minute this reader reread 50 words. This reader is actually reading at least 250 words per minute, but all the eye motion is not forward. Eliminating regressions would immediately improve this reader's speed at least 25 percent.

Of course, not all regressions can or even should be eliminated instantly. There are two types of regressions, and it is helpful to distinguish between them. *Voluntary regressions* are necessary searches for key ideas. To read with good comprehension, you must be prepared to reverse occasionally to review information, even at a loss of speed. Remember that speed itself is worthless if it means rushing blindly forward without full understanding. Good readers read for ideas, even if it means some backtracking. If you concentrate and control possible distractions, these voluntary regressions should be infrequent. *Involuntary regressions* are unnecessary. Many poor readers have the bad habit of regressing many times on a page without even being aware that they are doing so.

To correct habitual, unnecessary regressions, do your best to read with concentration and *read forward*. If you feel you are about to go back, ask yourself if it is absolutely necessary. If you have been concentrating, the answer most often will be "no," and you can proceed forward without loss of comprehension. After a few sessions of this exercise, you will find yourself regressing much less often, and so increasing your reading speed.

Another consideration is the *eye return*, the movement of the eye from the end of one line to the beginning of the next. Any typist knows that carriage returns, or the return of the paper for a new line, occupy a surprisingly large portion of typing time. Similarly, eye returns can occupy a large portion of reading time. Lazy eye returns are a bad reading habit, because they also invite distraction and loss of concentration.

To increase your reading speed, you should concentrate on eye returns. Force yourself to move quickly from one line to the next in a swift sweep from right to left without any opportunity for distracting thoughts or daydreams. This is an easily learned good reading habit, one that simultaneously improves both speed and comprehension. Work on eye returns by sweeping from the ends to the beginnings of lines on a page without reading the page at all. Make sure you always sweep to the next line. Readers who do not concentrate may often sweep to the wrong line. Practice demonstrates how fast the return can be if you are conscious of it and its importance.

The key to improved reading speed is practice. Set aside one hour each day. Practice on reading material that is easy and pleasant. Be sure to practice at a well-lit desk in a room free of distractions. As you read, concentrate on eliminating regressions and on speedy return sweeps. This is the way to increase reading speed permanently: practice and force yourself to go faster. Set your goals at a level higher than your present reading speed, and work at achieving them. Push yourself to read faster, eliminate regressions, and concentrate on speedy eye returns. As you achieve one

Regressions

Regressions make reading slower and harder to understand. The two passages printed here are identical except that one shows what a reader sees in making five regressions. You can see that these regressions make the passage longer and far more confusing.

If put to guess his calling and livelihood, I should have taken him for a country schoolmaster as soon as taken him for a country schoolmaster as soon as anything else. He was dressed in a rusty black frock coat and pantaloons, unbrushed, and worn so faithfully that the suit had faithfully that the suit had adapted itself to the curves and angularities of his figure and angularities of his figure, and had grown to be an outer skin of the man. His hair was black, still unmixed with gray, stiff, somewhat bushy, and had apparently been acquainted had apparently been acquainted with neither brush nor comb that morning, after neither brush nor comb that morning, after the disarrangement of the pillow; and as to a nightcap, Uncle Abe probably knows nothing of such effeminacies.
—*Nathaniel Hawthorne, "Abraham Lincoln"*

If put to guess his calling and livelihood, I should have taken him for a country schoolmaster as soon as anything else. He was dressed in a rusty black frock coat and pantaloons, unbrushed, and worn so faithfully that the suit had adapted itself to the curves and angularities of his figure, and had grown to be an outer skin of the man. His hair was black, still unmixed with gray, stiff, somewhat bushy, and had apparently been acquainted with neither brush nor comb that morning, after the disarrangement of the pillow; and as to a nightcap, Uncle Abe probably knows nothing of such effeminacies.
—*Nathaniel Hawthorne, "Abraham Lincoln"*

If put to guess his calling and livelihood, I should have taken him for a country schoolmaster as soon as anything else. He was dressed in a rusty black frock coat and pantaloons, unbrushed, and worn so faithfully that the suit had adapted itself to the curves and angularities of his figure, and had grown to be an outer skin of the man. His hair was black, still unmixed with gray, stiff, somewhat bushy, and had apparently been acquainted with neither brush nor comb that morning, after the disarrangement of the pillow; and as to a nightcap, Uncle Abe probably knows nothing of such effeminacies.

WPM (words per minute) goal, it becomes your natural speed. Then you may work on achieving still greater speed.

No matter what your beginning reading speed, you can double it, at least, in only a few days. Continue this daily practice for two weeks. Record your reading speed for each day in your reading diary. Small dips in your reading speed are inevitable because of outside forces such as interruptions or fatigue. With regular practice over two weeks, however, you will soon be reading at your new, faster speed without any special effort or need to slow down.

Developing three reading speeds. As you have already learned, one characteristic of good readers is that they have more than one reading speed. They can shift reading speeds much as a car shifts gears. A car needs different gears for going uphill, downhill, or cruising. Good readers use different speeds for similar reasons. You can prove this to yourself by reading a few pages in a favorite novel and then trying to read a legal document, for example, a mortgage or a lease. One is much less difficult and complex than the other, and so it is neither possible nor desirable to read both at the same speed.

For efficient reading, you should have three speeds. Such a repertoire enables you to get the most out of any material you read and to do so with minimum time and effort. No matter what you read, shifting gears will keep you from reading so slowly that you become bored or reading so quickly that you lose comprehension. The three speeds are *study reading, normal reading,* and *rapid reading.*

Study reading is the slowest speed. It is used, for example, for textbooks and work manuals, which require you to retain facts and master concepts. Naturally, this takes care and concentration, and it would be foolish to rush headlong through such material. In studying, therefore, you should slow down so that you absorb the material in a single reading. For that reason, good readers study at a rate of about 200 words per minute, or even less.

Normal reading is the middle speed for works of average complexity. It is used for books and magazine articles that require close attention, but not intense study. This speed is suitable for books and articles that present facts without demanding an analysis of concepts, and for novels and general nonfiction read for relaxation. Normal reading speed can also be useful for reviewing difficult material that has already been studied once. Most good readers have a normal reading speed close to twice as fast as their study speed. A good normal reading speed would be anywhere from 300 to 400 words per minute.

Rapid reading is used for easy reading material or for sampling material to find out whether you want to read it completely. Rapid reading is used for magazines, newspapers, and other quick reading for general information. The rapid reading speed is the one you will find it easiest to improve quickly. Good rapid reading proceeds at speeds up to 500 words per minute and sometimes even beyond. The maximum reading speed attainable in easy reading without skipping is about 800 words per minute.

Two considerations will help you choose the speed for any reading material. First ask yourself, what is the level of difficulty? Using your prereading skills, check the material for vocabulary, subject matter, amount of important facts, and complexity of important concepts. Grade the work on a scale from difficult to easy and choose the appropriate reading speed. Then ask yourself, why are you reading it? Decide if your purpose is to study, to be generally informed, or to relax. The answers to these questions usually point to a choice of study, normal, or rapid reading.

After working on your average reading speed for at least two weeks, begin to practice the three reading speeds by varying the kind of material you read. Your first practice was on easy material, at a speed closest to your rapid rate. But in your third week of daily reading, begin to practice with difficult and average as well as easy reading matter. You will quickly find your own beginning speed for each; then work to improve it.

You can now begin to add the level of difficulty to your reading diary and to keep track of three reading speeds. Once you have calculated your beginning speed at all three paces, set personal goals for all three speeds. As always, push yourself to go faster, to eliminate regressions, and to make speedy eye returns. After reading, record your speed and review the passage in your mind to check for comprehension. If you have not understood what you have read, you will have to slow down. But if you continue to practice and to vary your reading material, you will find your words per minute scores at all three speeds beginning to improve.

Reading speeds

Good readers have three reading speeds. They are efficient readers because they can choose the proper speed for any kind of reading material. Here is the basic repertoire of a good reader, illustrating the uses of each speed and the rates attainable with practice. The youth shown here is reading a manual on entomology. Because his purpose is careful analysis, he reads at a slow rate.

Speed	*Materials*	*Purposes*	*Complexity*	*WPM*
Study	Textbooks Work manuals	Careful analysis Memorization Test preparation	Difficult	200 or less
Normal	Novels Nonfiction	Leisure reading General information	Average	300–400
Rapid	Newspapers Magazines	Locating facts Prereading Sampling	Easy	500 or more

Improving Your Reading

Test your speed and comprehension

Time yourself on this passage. Read at your normal speed. When finished, calculate your reading speed using the information provided at the end of the passage. Then test your comprehension with the questions provided. If you cannot answer most of the questions, you need to slow down and work on comprehension. If you can answer most of them, you are ready to practice reading faster.

Most of us have grown up with unfair stereotypes of those Puritan forefathers we heard so much about in high school. We imagine very joyless people, dressed in black, with little taste for experimentation in life.

In fact, the Puritans were among the most innovative people of all times, and certainly among the most adventurous and daring of any people who came to America in the early days of its colonial history. The very name "Puritan" was once synonymous with experimentation, and those who came to Massachusetts in the 17th century were as contentious a bunch as ever sat in the bistros popularized by the poets of Paris. The origins of the movement can be located in the Protestant Reformation launched in England by Henry VIII, who differed from the Pope on matters of divorce law. Henry founded the Church of England, but some thought that his own church needed to be purified even further of some old traditions, and that is why they became known as Puritans.

The first group to land in the new world were bound, aboard the *Mayflower*, for a place around New York bay. But blown off course, they landed in Massachusetts on December 21, 1620, according to tradition, at Plymouth Rock, near Boston. A group of 103 had left on the voyage that took 64 days; by the time they landed at Plymouth in a snowstorm, two had died and one had been born. Unsure of how to govern themselves, they invented a method: it was called the Mayflower Compact, and it is considered one of the forerunners of the United States Constitution.

Landing in winter was a dreadful mistake. By April of 1621 only 50 of the landing 102 had survived "the great sickness," a combination of scurvy contracted aboard ship and starvation through the winter. As their leader, William Bradford, described it, they arrived in a "howling wilderness" of previously unimaginable proportions. Actually, one key problem on Bradford's mind was the extent of the jungle before him. He imagined a "hideous and desolate wilderness" extending forever, or perhaps to some theoretical "South Sea," or Pacific Ocean, limit, populated only by "savage barbarians ready to fill our sides full of arrows." The Puritans knew this as they huddled in their tents—not log cabins—through that first winter. But when the *Mayflower*, with its shipload of skeptical sailors, left North America for home on April 5, 1621, not one of the surviving Puritans chose to return with the ship.

The Puritans, whom we still think of as rigid and impersonal, made the best of their situation. Three thousand miles by sailing ship from any civilized place, they made what friends they could. They met with Indians—the very people the popular stereotype suggests would most horrify the straight-laced Puritans. Miles Standish, Priscilla Mullins, and the rest of these true pioneers readily sat down and ate with visitors whose names have been recorded, no doubt inaccurately, as Samoset and Squanto. Their Thanksgiving probably never happened on November 24, but the Puritans were open-minded and adventurous enough to celebrate, in the fall of 1621, their own survival with a people completely opposite in culture and personal habit. It was this flexibility, this ability to deal honestly with people whose beliefs were light-years away from their own, that enabled the Puritans, in Bradford's words: "To fit up their houses and dwellings against winter, being all well recovered in health and strength and with all things."

$$\frac{\text{Total words} = 580}{\text{Reading time in seconds} =} \times 60 = \underline{\qquad} \text{ WPM}$$

1. The author's major point is:
   a. The Puritans have little to do with modern life.
   b. The Puritans are poorly understood by us.
   c. The Puritans should have emigrated to Virginia.

2. The author appreciates the Puritans for their:
   a. Ability to relate to strangers.
   b. Religious piety.
   c. Political activism.

3. Puritans got their name because they:
   a. Hoped to purify the Church of England.
   b. Hoped to purify the Roman Catholic Church.
   c. Hoped to purify the Presbyterian Church.

4. The Puritans came to Massachusetts in the:
   a. 16th century.
   b. 17th century.
   c. 18th century.

5. This passage to tells us:
   a. Whom the Puritan fought against.
   b. The importance of enduring hardship.
   c. Why the Puritans deserve attention.

Answers: 1 (b); 2 (a); 3 (a); 4 (b); 5 (c).
Being able to answer *most* of these questions means correct responses to 3 or more. If you answered 2 or less correctly, you may have read too fast.

Reading for comprehension.

Reading faster is a physical skill. For the most efficient reading, this physical skill must be matched by an intellectual one. Thus, speed must be based on the ability to comprehend written material quickly. Complete comprehension is easier to manage at slow reading speeds, but efficient readers are able to absorb ideas even when pushing to move through a book at rapid reading speed.

Four basic habits are essential to good comprehension: locating key ideas, marking a book while reading, using reference books, and reviewing what has been read.

Locating key ideas. As you have already learned, prereading is possible because all words on a page are not of equal importance. Prereading establishes this fact. The process of prereading is one of locating key ideas embodied in important words and phrases. Even in difficult material, many words may be read quickly —think of "as," "an," and "the," for example. The important words, however, are crucial terms. They carry specific definitions in any written work, such as the term "prereading" in this chapter. Important words also include words or phrases of transition. They signal the direction of ideas. The word "however" is a good example. Efficient readers are able to comprehend material as they read quickly because they are alert to such important words as they push ahead.

Crucial terms are the heart of any written work, because they contain in single words the focused ideas of the author. For example, government spokesmen in both the Soviet Union and the United States are likely to use the word "propaganda" as a crucial term in their statements. One accepted meaning of propaganda is "promotion of ideas," and the spokesmen of both countries mean this when they use the word in reference to political policies. But by this term the spokesman of one country may mean "important and necessary ideas," while the spokesman from the other may mean "false and misleading ideas." For this reason, recognizing uses of this crucial term is essential to comprehending fully the statements made by spokesmen from competing nations.

Good readers spot a crucial term when they read at any speed, and if necessary they pause to consider the term, to locate its definition in the work, or to check its accepted definition in a dictionary. A crucial term can be located by its frequent recurrence in a work. The appearance of a crucial term may be signaled to the reader through the use of italics or the use of the word in chapter titles or subheadings. Any book on American history, for example, can be expected to use the word "Reconstruction" to refer to the post-Civil War era. Good readers recognize this as a crucial term that the author must define. Having met it for the first time in a chapter title or important topic sentence to a paragraph, they then look for the definition the author will attach to it—what years are included in "Reconstruction" and what gives the era its significance. This may take a moment, but the pause helps both comprehension and speed because the term can be read confidently and quickly when met again.

Transition words and phrases are another class of important words that indicate key ideas. Transition words and phrases indicate directions and relationships. We are all familiar with the basics of this concept. We all know that the word "and" signals a second action, idea, or fact similar in kind to a first one: "Ulysses S. Grant was a Civil War general *and* a United States President." We know that the word "but" signals a second action or idea different from a first one: "Ulysses S. Grant was an effective Civil War general *but* an ineffective United States President." We also know that the word "then" signals a sequence of ideas or actions: "Ulysses S. Grant was a Civil War general and *then* a United States President." We all know these word indicators of direction, but good readers use this knowledge to their advantage as they read for speed. Good readers look for transition words and phrases that show relationships of ideas.

The transition words and phrases you can look for in your reading all fall into three groups. Some, such as "and," signal *similarity*. Others, such as "but," signal *difference*. The last group, such as "then," signals *sequence*. The table of transition terms shown here provides further examples of the words and phrases that fall into each of these three groups. By looking for

---

Transition words and phrases

Good readers identify relationships between ideas by spotting transition words and phrases. Pivotal terms, such as those listed here, indicate similarity, difference, or sequence. Paying attention to them helps comprehension at any reading speed.

Similarity	*Difference*	*Sequence*
and	but	then
as well as	although	first, second
also	however	earlier
furthermore	nevertheless	later
likewise	despite	before
similarly	yet	after
in addition	on the other hand	last
another	on the contrary	finally
moreover	instead	as a result
so	though	next

Improving Your Reading

transition terms, you can more easily and completely comprehend the relationships between key ideas in your reading.

Marking books. By consciously searching for crucial terms and for transition words or phrases, good readers keep themselves alert and so improve both their speed and comprehension. Another habit they use to make reading an active, conscious process is annotating, or *marking*, their books. Obviously, you cannot mark up a book that does not belong to you, whether it comes from a library or from a friend. Nor will you want to bother with careful annotations on easy material intended to be read at your rapid speed. But for all difficult material that is read at your study speed, and some average material that is read at your normal speed, you will find your comprehension improved if you pause to mark the key ideas in the book. Some people are reluctant to mark up a book because they mistakenly believe that this destroys it. But most books, usually relatively inexpensive, easily replaceable, and salable after use even if marked, are not often heirloom possessions to be preserved in mint condition. Rather, they are objects to be used to acquire knowledge, and good use implies some wear and tear. By marking a book, you make it your own.

Marking books is a good reading habit because it increases concentration and alertness. It also improves your reading ability by reminding you that you are searching for the key ideas that deserve annotation. Marking books also improves your ability to retain what you have read because the physical act of underlining or circling words or phrases on a page impresses them on your memory. Finally, having the marks on the page makes it easier to review books later on for study purposes or for personal interest.

Many adults still own books they marked up in school. A quick examination of one of them will prove how useful annotations are when studying or reviewing reading material. Many people who mark up their books limit themselves to underlining or coloring over lines of text with a soft-tipped marker. Because good reading distinguishes between ideas, and because you are free to mark books in any way you wish, do not limit yourself to a single kind of marking. Good readers develop a variety of markings to use for different purposes when studying difficult material. While working to improve your reading, develop your own markings, remembering that it is essential to have various marks for a variety of purposes. A typical system might mix circles for crucial terms with underlining for their definitions. It could also use marginal numbers for ideas in a sequence, and stars for important facts.

Using reference books. Good readers often are ambitious. They read for pleasure and relaxation, but they also read to broaden their understanding of various fields of knowledge. In books they discover new interests, and they pursue these new interests in other books. Like any rewarding enterprise, this sort of ambitious reading is a challenge. In pursuing interests through books, you will inevitably encounter works that present challenges in ideas and vocabulary.

No one should make reading an unpleasant chore. If

How to mark a book

Marking your books can help you to understand and review what you are reading. It is helpful, therefore, to develop a system of marking you find useful. The passage below shows how one reader marked it, using circles for crucial terms, underlining for definitions, using numbers for ideas in a sequence and stars for important facts.

(Historians) undertake to arrange sequences—called stories, or histories—assuming in silence a relation of cause and effect. These assumptions, hidden in the depths of dusty libraries, have been astounding, but commonly unconscious and childlike; so much so, that if any captious critic were to drag them to light, historians would probably reply, with one voice, that they had never supposed themselves required to know what they were talking about. Adams, for one, had toiled in vain to find out what he meant. He had even ★ published a dozen volumes of American history for no other purpose than to satisfy himself whether, by the severest process of stating, with the least possible comment, such facts as seemed sure, in such order as seemed rigorously consequent, he could fix for a familiar moment a necessary sequence of human move- ★ ment. The result had satisfied him as little as at Harvard College. Where he saw sequence, other men saw something quite different, and no one saw the same unit of measure. He cared little about his experiments and less about his statesmen, who seemed to him quite as ignorant as himself and, as a rule, no more honest; but he insisted on a relation of sequence, and if he could not reach it by one method, he would try as many methods as science knew. Satisfied that the se- ① quence of men led to nothing and that the sequence ② of their society could lead no further, while the mere ③ sequence of time was artificial, and the sequence of ④ thought was chaos, he turned at last to the sequence ⑤ of force; and thus it happened that, after ten years' pursuit, he found himself lying in the Gallery of Machines at the Great Exposition of 1900, with his historical neck broken by the sudden eruption of forces totally new.

Improving Your Reading

a book seems impenetrable, feel free to abandon it. Choose another on the same subject, or switch to another of your interests. However, many good readers get special satisfaction from mastering difficult works. This is because they have the good reading habit of using *reference books,* most often dictionaries and encyclopedias. Many of the advertised methods to quadruple your reading speed overnight actually advise against using reference books. They do this because they are interested only in how *fast* something is read, not in how *well* it is read. Speed is part of good reading, as this section on efficient reading has stressed, but to read something well at any speed, to gain the satisfaction of mastering demanding works, you will surely have to pause occasionally to consult dictionaries and encyclopedias.

Reference works are used because different authors envision different audiences for their books. For example, authors of high-school textbooks on economics write for an audience that is different from that intended by authors of advanced books on United States economy. The difference is that authors of the advanced books assume that the reader will be familiar with certain words and concepts, so there are fewer explanations in advanced books than in textbooks. The authors of textbooks will, for example, provide a complete definition of "capitalism," while authors of advanced works will assume that their readers already understand the definition.

The meanings of words are the domain of the dictionary. Many people mistakenly think that using a dictionary is childish. In fact, most scholars work with a dictionary close at hand. They do this because the dictionary provides precise definitions of its terms. In addition, dictionaries provide information on the pronunciation, derivation, and multiple meanings of a word. With this knowledge, the precise meaning of a word as it is used in context becomes clear.

Facts and ideas are the domain of the encyclopedia. Most encyclopedia entries open with a brief, precise identification of a person, place, or idea, and then move into more detailed explanation. Thus, a quick look at the opening of an encyclopedia entry may be all you need to return to your book confident that you understand a general concept. Also, many encyclopedia entries are pleasurable and informative reading. If you understand a concept mentioned in your reading but want to go deeper into it, you might make a note to consult an encyclopedia when you have finished reading or before you resume again. A final great advantage of consulting an encyclopedia is that it can lead you to other books of interest on the same subject. Many attach bibliographies to their substantial entries.

There are two sorts of reference works. The most common are general encyclopedias and dictionaries.

Keep a dictionary close at hand.

These are all-purpose reference works that cover all fields of knowledge. Southwestern's *Volume Library* and the dictionaries in its *Student Handbooks* are general reference works. The second type of reference works comprises specialized dictionaries and encyclopedias. These cover single fields of knowledge, such as medicine, art, literature, or history. All homes should have general reference works available for use by readers of all ages. Specialized reference works, which are consulted less often, can be used in any local library.

Reviewing what you read. A final consideration in reading for comprehension is the ability to retain information obtained from books. Reading and understanding are not the same thing as memorization. No one is expected to retain everything read in a book. In fact, because reading is a process of understanding and assimilating information, no one should even desire complete recall. Good readers concentrate on ideas, intending to retain the main concepts and facts from whatever they are reading. They help themselves retain this information by developing the habit of reviewing what they have read before going on to another activity. In reviewing material that is difficult, average, or easy, repeat the key ideas to yourself and create a double impression of them in your memory, once in reading and once in reviewing. You should be able to review mentally all reading you do, even leisure reading of easy material. However, reviewing is most important for material that is complex enough to require your normal or study speeds. Reviewing is an important part of any overall program to improve your reading speed and comprehension. If your review suggests lack of comprehension, you will have to slow down and read more carefully.

Good readers review material immediately on finishing their reading. In this way they create that double impression on their memory before the information can slip away.

Improving Your Reading

Questions and sample answers for reviewing what you read

Many readers have only a vague recollection of books they have read. Your comprehension and retention of books and articles can be improved by briefly reviewing what you read soon after finishing it. With a series of general questions, you can focus your reactions. This process will improve both your understanding of books and your ability to remember their content. These five general questions can be asked of any reading material:

The general questions for review can help you to form a memorable impression of the ideas in your reading. Here is the way a reader might answer those questions, mentally or on paper, for the reading about the Puritans given as a speed test on page 314.

1. What was the author's general point?

1. The author's general point was to make us interested in what we have to learn from the Puritans.

2. What individual ideas did the author use to support his point?

2. The individual idea used to suggest this was the way the Puritans made friends with the Indians.

3. What were the crucial terms discussed by the author?

3. The name "Puritan" reflects the fact that Puritans hoped to purify their church even more than the English Protestants had already done.

4. What important facts were cited by the author?

4. The Puritans came to America in 1620. They landed in Massachusetts even though they intended to go to New York.

5. What did you like or dislike in this work?

5. The Puritans may be more interesting than I had thought. I think I will read more about them.

The first step in reviewing is to ask yourself fundamental questions about what you have read. What were the important ideas? What were the important facts? If you have concentrated on locating key ideas by spotting crucial terms and transitions, you should be able to remember these in their proper sequence. If you have taken the time to mark your book, you can use this brief review period to leaf back over the pages you have read, glancing at the key ideas identified by your markings.

The second step in the review process is to summarize the key ideas in your own words. For easy reading material, this can be done mentally. But for difficult material, especially if you have read for study purposes, take the time to summarize on paper what you have read. This can be done in the form of brief notes.

You will find such notes handy for later reference.

Now begin to add this consideration to your reading diary. As described early in this chapter, the diary has space for these new notes on review. First, note whether you have summarized your reading in your mind or on paper. Summarizing readings is always a good habit, but you need not always do so, especially on days when you practice easy reading. Then honestly describe your own sense of your level of comprehension simply by describing your effort at summary as *excellent, mediocre,* or *poor.* As your reading diary grows, you will be able to correlate this information on comprehension against your entries on reading speed. Then you can determine whether you are achieving a balance between speed and comprehension; that is, whether you are progressing toward efficient reading.

Special types of reading

To become a proficient reader, you must learn to vary your reading speed to suit different sorts of reading material. But complete proficiency requires the additional skill of learning how to suit reading methods to reading purposes. If an adult seeking relaxation picks up a classic modern novel, for example, that reader has a reading purpose different from that of a college student reading the same novel for a course in literature.

You should formulate your purposes and expectations before beginning to read. The checklist on this page provides some key questions that can help you do so.

Reading for self-improvement.

Reading for self-improvement requires interest in accumulating general knowledge about a subject. Once you have begun to pursue this interest, your reading purpose should be to add to your fund of knowledge by testing the persuasiveness of different opinions on the subject. An interest in British history, for example, logically begins with some general surveys of events in that long history. But from that point on, you will encounter contradictory accounts and interpretations of the significant movements and periods in British history. Thus, in reading for self-improvement, you should eventually begin to read against your fund of background knowledge, to consider new ideas in the light of older ones.

Reading for this purpose requires regular contact with your chosen subject and careful reading at normal reading speed. Reading for self-improvement also demands the frequent consultation of reference works, which can be counted on to provide relatively objective overviews and impartial summaries of long-standing disputes and differences of opinion. Because this sort of reading constitutes an informal course of study, you probably will not feel it necessary to keep notes on what you read. Another aid to interest and understanding in reading for self-improvement comes from sharing and debating books. That can be done in a reading discussion group, described in the "Continuing to improve" part of this chapter.

Reading for advancement.

No kind of reading provokes a clearer sense of interest and purpose than reading that is intended to develop occupational skills needed for career promotion or change. Here you have a personal interest more intensely felt than that generally found in purely intellectual or leisure pursuits.

Your interest in reading for professional advancement is especially well focused—you want to know what special skill any book or article can teach you. Your purpose in reading is twofold: to determine the relevance of the advice to your position and to master it completely for application to your job or career plans. These two purposes imply two reading strategies. The first demands especially careful prereading so you do not waste your time with irrelevant advice. Most occupational guides are designed to facilitate prereading. Pay close attention to the chapter titles, subtitles, summaries, and questions for review (these are standard features of this sort of reading material). Your second purpose demands that you closely read material of proven relevance at your study speed.

Occupational guides attach special importance to a vocabulary of crucial terms, and mastery of these terms is important in achieving a better job. For that reason, careful note-taking is essential to reading for professional advancement. Be sure to mark your books for later review, and be sure to keep written summaries of especially valuable information. For any occupation, there are likely to be a number of useful guides to advancement. Note-taking can be especially helpful because it makes it possible for you to gather notes on practical advice from many sources.

Reading for pleasure.

Reading for pleasure is the least formal sort of reading endeavor. Your interest in the material might derive from any of the full range of literary pleasures: enjoyment of stories, identification with dynamic characters, or delight in a particular narrative style. Your purpose in reading is a desire for the stimulating and unpredictable entertainment that only books can offer.

But even in reading for pleasure, your repertoire of reading skills is essential for preserving and continually satisfying your desire to read. Reading for enjoyment is best pursued with attention to consciously formulating your interest in the material. Your interest may stem from a particular author's style, the presence of the same interesting character in several novels, or the suspense of a particular kind of plot. Whatever the reason for your interest, you will be led logically to other, similar works that can provide the same enjoyment.

The method of reading for pleasure is as unstructured as the purpose. You should feel free to shift from normal to rapid reading speeds and back again as your interest dictates. Slowing down unnecessarily, however, invites the risk of flagging interest. Brisk reading of works chosen for no interest other than enjoyment can, in fact, intensify delight in them by more quickly and more frequently bringing to the reader the individual features cherished most. No note-taking should intrude on pleasure reading, but you will find it useful to keep some sort of record of your favorite works, either on a shelf that holds your personal library or in a diary of authors and titles.

Study or pleasure? Tailor your approach to your purpose.

Special kinds of reading. Different purposes can change your reading strategy, but differences in reading materials may require special strategies. Technical journals, for example, may rely on complicated charts, graphs, and diagrams to explain ideas discussed in the text or to introduce supplementary ideas. Literary magazines, on the other hand, are rarely broken by any such illustrative material. In the first case, your beginning strategy should be to master the charts, graphs, and diagrams. In the second case, you might begin by prereading titles, subtitles, and topic sentences.

Visual contrasts among kinds of reading materials represent differences of format, both in page arrangements and layouts. But format is indicative of fundamental differences in organization as well. Because a technical journal uses charts, graphs, and diagrams, it may adopt a particular kind of organization.

Kinds of reading

Newspapers. It has been said that no one *reads* newspapers, people just peruse them. There is some truth to this exaggeration. The sheer bulk of your daily newspaper may prohibit careful reading.

Most people read newspapers for quick information on recent events. Newspaper editors know this, and so their news stories feature essential information in the opening paragraphs. There is a journalism school maxim for how to open a news story: Who? What? Where? When? Why? and How? You can see how these important facts find their way into the opening of the sample newspaper story shown on this page. By concentrating only on the opening paragraphs of the news story, you can easily and quickly determine if your are interested enough to read further.

This is true only of news stories. Other parts of the newspaper, such as features and editorials, are organized more along the lines of a magazine article.

Where?
When?
Who?
What?

Why?

How?

MORRISON ELECTION VICTOR

New York City, March 18—Jennifer Morrison was elected president of the new American Federation of Teachers today in a stunning upset over the incumbent, Michael A. Conroy. The vote ended the union's national congress at the convention center here and convincingly demonstrated Ms. Morrison's ability to control the votes of union members disenchanted with the union's pension policies.

The new president made her acceptance speech after midnight from a dais strewn with confetti and streamers. Mr. Conroy, despite losing by a clear margin of 2 to 1, had issued no concession speech.

Magazines. Magazine articles, newspaper editorials, and newspaper features may differ from news stories in at least one important respect: they may be based on opinion rather than fact. For this reason, they are always signed by authors, or, in the case of editorials, they appear on the newspaper's editorial page. Because such articles are not primarily concerned with facts, they open with no recitation of who, what, where, when, why, and how.

Magazines, in particular, tend to pile up as they arrive in the mail. To keep abreast of your magazine reading, you can take advantage of this knowledge of their organization. Preread the table of contents to get an overview of the magazine's contents. Check the full titles and subheadings of individual articles for indications of their special focus. Then go through the opening paragraphs to reach the announcement of the article's purpose and content. If you are interested enough to want to read the entire article, go on. Few good readers ever bother to read all of a magazine.

Mid-Life Career Change: One Man's Story

by Robert Miller

His job had been "obsoleted," as the supervisor said, by new automation that churned out the product faster, better, and cheaper. His daughters, already enrolled in college by then, had been forced to withdraw in mid-semester. His home, carefully reworked for his family's needs over twenty years of amateur handyman projects, had been repossessed by the bank and shown to strangers. Then, hitting rock bottom, William Jameson found himself on an endless line in an overcrowded office filing for welfare benefits.

Last week Congress opened debate on the nation's chronic unemployment problem. The discussion in Washington has to do with hundreds of thousands of workers, but unemployment is also a personal catastrophe. . . .

Recognizing a format and understanding the organization it implies is a matter of knowing facts about the organization of different sorts of publications and of practicing the reading strategy best suited to each. The following pages give you practical facts about several kinds of reading material.

The reading diary you prepared included a final notation for "special difficulties." At this point in your program for reading improvement, you are ready to begin using that notation. Keep track of the single kinds of written material that seem most confusing. Because you are also already varying daily the difficulty of your reading, you should begin to see a pattern emerging. You will be able to recognize potential stumbling blocks in news articles, magazine stories, reference book entries, or visual aids. Then you can consult or review the relevant information given on these pages.

Reference books. Reference books are concise compilations of essential knowledge on a wide variety of subjects. They make this knowledge available in individual entries, organized topically or alphabetically. Each entry begins with a broad statement of the subject's significance. Only then does it proceed to a discussion of individual aspects of the subject.

In the sample biographical entry shown, you can see how a reference book gives easy access to essential information, such as dates and nationality.

In reference books you will also find keys to related articles, such as the cross-reference here to a separate entry on "stream of consciousness." If you were only interested in finding out who James Joyce was, you could have stopped reading this entry after the second paragraph. But if your interest went further, you would have continued to the end, where you would likely have found a bibliography.

> **JOYCE, JAMES A.** (1882–1941). Irish novelist. Although he wrote some poetry (*Chamber Music*, 1907) and one play (*Exiles*, 1918), James Joyce's most important contributions to modern literature were the stories collected in *Dubliners* (1907) and the novels *Portrait of the Artist as a Young Man* (1916), *Ulysses* (1922), and *Finnegans Wake* (1939).
>
> By almost any evaluation, James Joyce ranks as one of the most difficult and most important novelists of the twentieth century. His works have had enormous influence on all subsequent writers because they developed a technique of STREAM OF CONSCIOUSNESS for presentation of the disorganized flow of frequently commonplace thoughts through the minds of their characters.
>
> James Joyce was born in Dublin on. . . .

Tables and graphs. Tables require close study. You should first note the title and the column and row identifications. In this table, for example, it is important to note that the figures are for five-year periods. Notes and explanations attached to tables are crucial. (Here the notes tell you that all figures except the first row are in billions of dollars; they also tell that the statistics have been obtained from the federal government). After acquainting yourself with a table, analyze the figures for trends.

A line graph like the one shown here is read like a grid. To interpret any point on the lines you must move from it to the vertical or horizontal reference points that explain its value. This graph clearly indicates the overall trend of increase in both liabilities and assets of savings and loan associations. It also shows how closely liabilities follow assets, a fact not as obvious in the table on the same subject. Graphs are limited, however, because they can provide only approximate values.

**Balance sheet of savings and loan associations
1960–1980**
All figures in billions of dollars except number of associations

	1960	1965	1970	1975	1980
Number of associations	6,320	6,185	5,669	4,931	4,613
Total assets	$71.5	$129.6	$176.2	$338.2	$630.0
Cash	7.9	12.1	16.5	30.9	57.6
Mortgages	60.1	110.3	150.3	278.6	502.8
Other	3.5	7.2	9.3	28.7	69.4
Liabilities	66.5	120.9	163.8	318.5	596.5
Net worth	$5.0	$8.7	$12.4	$19.7	$33.5

Source: U.S. Federal Home Loan Bank Board

Assets and liabilities of savings and loan associations 1960–1980

Improving Your Reading   321

Continuing to improve

At the end of eight weeks of daily practice of the principles of good reading, as described in this chapter, you will see a marked improvement in your reading speed and comprehension. Even more important, you will have acquired a new set of reading habits that will make you a better reader and make your reading more enjoyable. You can verify your improvements in speed and comprehension over the eight weeks by comparing the first and the last entries in your reading diary. You can also verify your improvements in reading habits over the same period by answering once again the questions on the "Checklist of reading habits" on page 304.

These improvements will have made you a competent, efficient, and proficient reader by giving you a mastery of important particular skills. But once acquired, the skills must be maintained. People improve their golf or swimming abilities, for example, through a series of lessons. When the lessons are complete, they must practice continually to protect their new abilities at these sports. In the same way, you must practice to protect your new reading skills. This is easier and more enjoyable than learning new habits, because your improved ability will make the practice itself more satisfying and pleasurable.

The checklist for continued improvement shown on this page itemizes the key considerations for maintaining an ongoing reading program of your own. You should periodically review the entire list to protect your new reading skills.

Practice reading. Daily practice is essential for preserving reading speed and comprehension. You can help yourself with short readings for speed during work breaks. You can mentally summarize your recent reading at virtually any time. Ideally, though, you will continue to set aside a regular reading time each day. Most people find that in addition to keeping their reading skills sharp, regular reading periods become a positive influence on their daily lives, particularly when they choose books of inspirational value or intellectual interest.

Your interest in daily reading can be maintained by varying what you read. There is no need to alternate easy, average, and difficult reading material as rigorously as you did over the eight-week program, but switching from novels to occupational journals or from history books to popular magazines introduces a pleasant variety into your reading and also helps reinforce your repertoire of speeds and your comprehension skills. Even though you may stop thinking about study,

My checklist for continuing to improve

1. I read daily.
2. I vary the kinds of things I read.
3. I vary my reading speeds.
4. I test my speed and comprehension regularly.
5. I follow the principles of good reading.
6. I am always conscious of my purpose in reading.
7. I keep interesting things to read at home.
8. I pursue my reading interests.
9. I visit bookstores and libraries.
10. I share my reading with friends and family.

normal, and rapid reading speeds, you will find yourself shifting automatically into these speeds if you vary the kinds of things you read.

As a final check on maintaining your new reading speeds and strategies, test yourself periodically. A quick calculation of your reading speed on different sorts of materials every few weeks will remind you of the need to continue to work on your new speeds. Periodic tests will also indicate particular aspects of your reading ability that may still require special attention, such as your high speed reading. A brief review of the advice in this chapter, on any aspect of your reading, along with a few refresher practice sessions, will ensure that you preserve your complete repertoire of reading skills.

Group reading. One of the best ways to continue your reading improvement is to read as a social activity. Sharing reading with friends has two good effects. It increases your interest in reading, because comments from others force you to think about what you have read and give you ideas for what you might read in the future. Sharing reading with others also helps keep you on a continuing program for improvement by encouraging you to finish books so that you can discuss them intelligently with others.

Reading as a family activity. Many people have fond memories of being read to in their childhood. But family reading is not just a memory from the past. Many families continue to read aloud regularly, and reading is often their only group recreational activity. Reading aloud to others is not just for parents with young children. Sharing readings with one's entire family is a gratifying experience; once introduced, such reading quickly proves its value. Family reading offers a refreshing alternative to television, so anyone seri-

Reading is a family activity with lifelong benefits for all members, from the youngest to the most senior. Ideas for books on a wide variety of subjects can often be obtained from book reviews that appear in your local newspaper and in magazines you read.

The Oxford Illustrated Literary Guide to the United States by Eugene Ehrlich and Gorton Carruth (Oxford, 464 pages; $29.95). Hawaii? Rupert Brooke went to Oahu in 1913 and wrote the sonnet "Waikiki," which is reprinted in the guide. Whittier, Calif.? Maxwell Anderson became head of the Whittier College English department in 1917. And Samuel Clemens was everywhere. Richly illustrated with photographs and carefully organized by regions, this guide reveals, among other curiosities, the peculiar restlessness of American writers.

ously interested in reading should begin to share this activity with the family.

Reading as a social activity. Reading discussion groups are a contagious kind of social activity that can become a regular part of one's life. These discussion groups offer an alternative means of getting together with friends for an evening. Many reading groups thrive for years. Often there is a revolving membership of people of many backgrounds who find that they have much to offer as well as much to learn.

To start a reading group, all you need are a few friends interested in reading the same book. Arrange a time to meet together after everyone has had a chance to finish the book. Most discussions of the book will begin by chatting casually about what the book says and what members of the group have found good or bad about it. Reactions will differ, of course, but different opinions of a book, an author, or a character's worth will enhance the discussion. There is no need to focus on purely intellectual problems, although these may finally become the focus of the discussion.

Reading groups generally vote on the next book to be read. They may also invite additional friends to join the next discussion. Whether the meetings are weekly or monthly, a large membership is useful because it ensures stimulating discussion despite the occasional absence of some regular members.

Keeping in touch with books.

Your reading will be helped by making certain you have an ample supply of books you want to read. More than 40,000 new titles are published in the United States every year. Despite this abundance, many people do not value books highly. While the skill of reading can be acquired through conscious effort, the love of books develops through contact with them.

Bookstores stimulate reading through attractive displays of current books and standard titles that continue to attract readers. Bookstore managers know the books people enjoy reading at any time as well as other works that might match your current reading interests. In comparison with other ages, books in our time are relatively inexpensive. New, hardbound best-sellers may seem difficult to afford, but their worth should be considered in terms of the hours of pleasure or the practical benefits they offer. Almost any reading interest can also be served well by reliance on paperbacks.

Booksellers—often students working their way through college—who come to your door may also offer books of lasting value. Many families fill their bookshelves in this way, establishing reading resources that serve more than a single generation.

Local libraries acquire books they think may be of interest to the taxpayers who support them. A single visit to a library can produce a reading list that will serve for months, and the books may be borrowed at no cost. Libraries, even more than bookstores, keep on hand a variety of books for readers of all ages. Often their books are shelved by age group, so the reading interests of children, young adults, or adults can be fueled simply by browsing along the shelves. All libraries also stock extensive collections of books printed in oversized, especially legible typefaces. These are intended for readers who suffer from poor eyesight. In this way, books become accessible to those who might otherwise be denied.

With bookstores, booksellers, and libraries, you can always keep your home well stocked with books enjoyable to you and all members of your family. Well chosen books, plus attention to the principles of reading discussed in this chapter, can help anyone become and remain a better reader.

Reading lists

Making reading a lifelong activity. Books lead to books. This means that one book is likely to lead you to another on the same subject or by the same author. The connections are made in the books themselves, in the topical groupings of library shelves, or in shared displays in bookstores.

What follows is a list of worthwhile books in general fields of interest. Any one of these books can serve as the beginning point in a reading hobby that may travel far from these selections or subject areas, but part of the charm of regular reading is that it takes off in unpredictable directions.

Take full advantage of all available sources of interesting titles: friends who read, your local library, bookstores and booksellers, and the book review columns of magazines and newspapers.

Science and nature

Attenborough, David. *Life on Earth* (1981). Attractively illustrated introduction to natural history.

Bell, Eric. *The Magic of Numbers* (1946). Fascinating demonstrations of the power and allure of mathematics.

Bronowski, Jacob. *The Ascent of Man* (1974). The history of scientific advancement since primitive times.

Carson, Rachel. *Silent Spring* (1962). A classic and harrowing account of the dangers of pollution.

Commoner, Barry. *Science and Survival* (1966). The mixed virtues of science, plainly stated.

Crick, Francis. *Of Molecules and Men* (1966). Narrative account of the Nobelist's achievements in biology.

Eisley, Loren. *The Immense Journey* (1957). Philosophical thoughts on the history of human development.

Freud, Sigmund. *General Introduction to Psychoanalysis* (1920). A general overview of the subject.

Geertz, Clifford. *The Interpretation of Cultures* (1973). Academic introduction to social anthropology.

Jastrow, Robert. *Red Giants and White Dwarfs* (1979). A popular guide to new knowledge of astronomy.

Kidder, Tracy. *The Soul of a New Machine* (1981). Exciting story of the construction of a computer.

McPhee, John. *Basin and Range* (1981). An account of learning geology in the field.

Milgram, Stanley. *Obedience to Authority* (1974). Controversial experiment on our will to obey overwhelming our moral precepts.

Sagan, Carl. *Broca's Brain* (1979). A patient and persuasive refutation of pseudo-scientific superstitions.

Sears, Paul B. *The Living Landscape* (1967). Elegantly written summation of ecological issues.

Thomas, Lewis. *Lives of a Cell* (1974). Enjoyable essays on the lessons drawn from biology.

Turnbull, Colin. *The Mountain People* (1972). A description of a field anthropologist's work.

Ulam, Stanislaw. *Adventures of a Mathematician* (1976). A scientist's story of his work on the atom bomb.

Watson, James D. *The Double Helix* (1967). Exciting narrative of the discovery of DNA.

Wiener, Norbert. *Cybernetics* (1961). A demanding, groundbreaking discussion of the computer age.

Wilson, Edmund O. *Sociobiology* (1975). Challenging behavioral theory of the dominance of genes over will.

History

Allen, Frederick L. *Only Yesterday* (1931). Engaging, novelistic portrait of the years after World War I.

Boorstin, Daniel. *The Americans* (1958–73). Three-volume popular epic by the librarian of Congress.

Braudel, Fernand. *The Mediterranean* (1972). One of the great modern social histories: life in the 16th century.

Carlyle, Thomas. *The French Revolution* (1832). Dramatic saga of heroes and villains of the uprising.

Catton, Bruce. *The Centennial History of the Civil War* (1961–63). Three eminently readable volumes.

Durant, Will and Ariel. *The Story of Civilization* (1935–75). Eleven volumes of enthusiastic history of ideas.

Fitzgerald, Frances. *Fire on the Lake* (1972). Early prize-winning account of the Vietnam War.

Fussell, Paul. *The Great War and Modern Memory* (1975). Literate and surprising discussion of the special significance of World War I.

Gibbon, Edward. *The Decline and Fall of the Roman Empire* (1776–78). The work that created our image of Rome.

Halberstam, David. *The Best and the Brightest* (1972). How the Kennedy administration slipped toward war in Southeast Asia.

Hamilton, Edith. *The Greek Way* (1930). A persuasive and lucid paean to the merits of ancient Greece.

Hersey, John. *Hiroshima* (1946). The effects of the atomic bomb, focused on the stories of six survivors.

Morison, Samuel Eliot. *The Great Explorers* (1978). A sailor's history of early global navigation.

Plumb, J. H. *The Italian Renaissance* (1965). A beautifully written history of the great flowering.

Shirer, William. *The Rise and Fall of the Third Reich* (1960). A journalist's account of the Hitler years.

Stratton, Joanna L. *Pioneer Women* (1981). Edited diaries of frontier women on the American prairies.

Thomas, Hugh. *A History of the World* (1978). A contemporary overview for background.

Toynbee, Arnold. *A Study of History* (1934–61). A twelve-volume analysis for knowledgeable readers.

Trevor-Roper, H. R. *The Rise of Christian Europe* (1965). A masterly and witty survey for general readers.

Tuchman, Barbara. *A Distant Mirror* (1978). The story of the Middle Ages told through the life of one man.

Wills, Garry. *Inventing America* (1978). A journalist's investigation of the Declaration of Independence.

Wood, Gordon S. *The Creation of the American Republic* (1965). A sophisticated political analysis.

Woodham-Smith, Cecil. *The Great Hunger* (1962). Graphic description of the Irish potato famine in 1848.

Young, George W. *Victorian England* (1964). An academic survey of the pivotal 19th century in Britain.

Places

Abbey, Edward. *Cactus County* (1973). A naturalist's appreciation of the Sonora Desert, with photographs.

Barzini, Luigi. *The Italians* (1964). Native's discursive reflections on the distinctive features of his culture.

Belloc, Hillaire. *The Path to Rome* (1902). A literary critic travels on foot to the Italian capital.

Bellow, Saul. *To Jerusalem and Back* (1976). An American novelist's portrait of Israel.

Benedict, Ruth. *The Chrysanthemum and the Sword* (1946). Noted anthropologist's visit to Japan.

Dos Passos, John. *Brazil on the Move* (1963). Novelist's journalistic account of the South American nation.

Douglas, William O. *My Wilderness* (1960). A distinguished jurist's salute to the Pacific Northwest.

Fisher, M. F. K. *Map of Another Town* (1964). A noted writer on food describes southern France.

Frady, Marshall. *Southerners* (1980). Magazine writer's irreverent look at his native region.

Gornick, Vivian. *In Search of Ali Mahmoud* (1973). Jewish-American feminist meets modern Egypt.

Hoagland, Edward. *Notes of a Century Before* (1969). Compelling journal of frontier British Columbia.

Krutch, Joseph Wood. *The Forgotten Peninsula* (1961). A scholar and naturalist on the Mexican Baja.

Lavender, David. *The Rocky Mountains* (1980). History and lore tied to the modern state of the region.

McGinniss, Joe. *Going to Extremes* (1980). Desperate lives in the magnificent environment of Alaska.

Mehta, Ved. *Portrait of India* (1970). By an Indian blind since childhood.

Naipaul, V. S. *Among the Believers* (1981). Prominent novelist's exploration of Islamic nations.

Orwell, George. *Burmese Days* (1934). Author recalls his youth in what was a British colony.

Pritchett, V. S. *The Spanish Temper* (1955). An affectionate analysis by a noted English writer and critic.
Smith, Hedrick. *The Russians* (1976). A *New York Times* reporter reflects on his years in Moscow.
Snow, Edgar. *Red Star over China* (1968). One of the first American accounts of life in Communist China.
Steinbeck, John. *Travels with Charley* (1962). The novelist's celebrated cross-country drive, with dog.
Thoreau, Henry David. *The Maine Woods* (1865). Early explorations by the author of *Walden Pond*.
Warner, William W. *Beautiful Swimmers* (1976). Natural history of the Chesapeake.
West, Rebecca. *Black Lamb and Grey Falcon* (1941). A tour of the Balkans in the company of H. G. Wells.

People

Adams, Henry. *The Education of Henry Adams* (1906). Autobiography of a troubled member of a famous family.
Boswell, James. *The Life of Samuel Johnson* (1791). One of the first and finest detailed records of a life.
Coe, Urling C. *Frontier Doctor* (1939). A popular self-portrait of a general practitioner.
Curie, Eve. *Madame Curie* (1937). The life of the famous scientist, as told by her daughter.
Ellmann, Richard. *James Joyce* (1982). Revised edition of a great modern biography.
Erikson, Erik H. *Gandhi's Truth* (1969). Theory of identity crisis; portrait of a remarkable man.
Flexner, James Thomas. *Washington: The Indispensable Man* (1979). The author's own condensation of a longer work.
Franklin, Benjamin. *The Autobiography of Benjamin Franklin* (1791). Commonsense and humor, for his son.
Fraser, Antonia. *Cromwell: The Lord Protector* (1973). Best of the author's works on British leaders.
Jones, Ernest. *The Life and Work of Sigmund Freud* (1961). Abridgment of a remarkable life, told by a disciple.
Josephson, Matthew. *Edison* (1963). The inventor's deeds made all the more fascinating by demystification.
Kaplan, Justin. *Walt Whitman: A Life* (1980). The poet in the context of 19th-century American society.
Mabee, Carlton T. *The American Leonardo* (1943). The life of Samuel Morse, painter and inventor.
Malcolm X. *The Autobiography of Malcolm X* (1964). Searing story of ghetto and political life.
Manchester, William. *American Caesar: Douglas MacArthur* (1978). Sumptuous life of the general.
Mizener, Arthur. *The Far Side of Paradise* (1951). The tragic career of F. Scott Fitzgerald.
Muir, John. *Story of My Boyhood* (1913). The naturalist's youth in Scotland and in America.
Murray, K. M. Elizabeth. *Caught in the Web of Words* (1977). Life of the editor of the *Oxford English Dictionary*.
Pais, Abraham. *Subtle Is the Lord* (1982). Portrait of Albert Einstein, physicist and humanist.
Royko, Mike. *Boss: Richard J. Daley of Chicago* (1971). The life of the mayor and his political machine.
Sandburg, Carl. *Abraham Lincoln* (1926). A stately study of the man and President.
Schoenbaum, Samuel. *Shakespeare's Lives* (1970). The facts and the fiction about the life of the bard.
Strachey, Lytton. *Queen Victoria* (1921). Portrait of the matriarch, by a noted biographer.
Sullivan, J. W. N. *Beethoven* (1927). Convincing links between the man's emotions and the composer's music.
Thurber, James. *The Years with Ross* (1959). Endearing, hilarious life of the first editor of *The New Yorker*.

Literature

Amis, Kingsley. *Lucky Jim* (1954). The most famous of comic novels about professors.
Anderson, Sherwood. *Winesburg, Ohio* (1919). Famous stories of small-town life in the Midwest.
Auchincloss, Louis. *The Rector of Justin* (1964). Mixed devotion and hatred of prep school headmaster.
Austen, Jane. *Pride and Prejudice* (1813). Among the wittiest of novels about marriageable ladies.
Baldwin, James. *Go Tell It on the Mountain* (1953). Tense story of black adolescent.
Bronte, Emily. *Wuthering Heights* (1847). The tempestuous romance of Cathy and Heathcliff.
Burgess, Anthony. *A Clockwork Orange* (1962). Horrific vision of violence in the future.
Caldwell, Erskine. *God's Little Acre* (1933). Folksy story of Georgia mountain families.
Camus, Albert. *The Stranger* (1946). Plainly written novel of modern man's disorientation and loss of self.
Chandler, Raymond. *The Big Sleep* (1939). Philip Marlowe, the archetype of hardboiled detectives.
Cheever, John. *The Stories of John Cheever* (1979). Suburban settings, unpredictable doings, comic tone.

Conrad, Joseph. *Heart of Darkness* (1902). Intricate, enigmatic tale of horrors of African colonization.

Crane, Stephen. *The Red Badge of Courage* (1895). The first, perhaps the best novel of inglorious war.

Dickens, Charles. *David Copperfield* (1850). Poverty and the journey to adulthood in Victorian England.

Donleavy, J. P. *The Ginger Man* (1955). Scandalous novel of literary bohemians in Dublin.

Dostoevski, Feodor. *The Brothers Karamazov* (1880). Murder, false accusations, moral implications.

Elkin, Stanley. *The Dick Gibson Show* (1971). Almost surreal tale of late-night radio host.

Ellison, Ralph. *Invisible Man* (1952). To many, the best novel ever of black American experience.

Farrell, James T. *Studs Lonigan* (1935). Best of a trilogy of novels about the Irish in Chicago.

Fitzgerald, F. Scott. *The Great Gatsby* (1925). Tragic undoing of a gloriously romantic hero.

Flaubert, Gustave. *Madame Bovary* (1857). Important modern novel of restless wife's petty ambitions.

Greene, Graham. *Brighton Rock* (1938). Suspenseful story of gang wars at a British resort.

Hammett, Dashiell. *The Thin Man* (1934). Classic American detective fiction.

Hardy, Thomas. *The Mayor of Casterbridge* (1886). A modern man doomed by fate and accident.

Heller, Joseph. *Catch-22* (1961). Bleakly humorous novel of combat and red tape in World War II.

Hemingway, Ernest. *A Farewell to Arms* (1929). Terse, understated story of World War I desertion.

Huxley, Aldous. *Brave New World* (1932). Science fiction vision of an impersonal future.

James, Henry. *The Ambassadors* (1902). Complexly told story of American experience in Europe.

Jones, James. *From Here to Eternity* (1951). Military life in Hawaii at the time of Pearl Harbor.

Joyce, James. *Dubliners* (1914). Subtle, deceptive short stories, useful as introduction to his novels.

Kafka, Franz. *The Castle* (1926). Nightmarish vision of personal alienation and social bureaucracy.

Kennedy, William. *Billy Phelan's Greatest Game* (1978). Powerful tale of gambling in the 1930's.

Lawrence, D. H. *Sons and Lovers* (1913). Coming of age in the milieu of the English coal mines.

London, Jack. *The Call of the Wild* (1903). The classic animal story, good reading for all ages.

Melville, Herman. *Moby Dick* (1851). The epic sea story, with modernistic digressions on good and evil.

O'Connor, Flannery. *A Good Man Is Hard to Find* (1955). Short stories about the South.

O'Flaherty, Liam. *The Informer* (1926). Study of accidental betrayal during the Irish uprising.

Pasternak, Boris. *Dr. Zhivago* (1958). A man's struggle to preserve personal goals in the midst of the Russian revolution.

Percy, Walker. *The Moviegoer* (1961). Complicated story of film overwhelming reality in the South.

Poe, Edgar Allan. *Tales of the Grotesque* (1840). Unsurpassed stories of Gothic horrors.

Shelley, Mary. *Frankenstein* (1818). The original tale, more chilling than the movies or imitations.

Tolstoy, Leo. *War and Peace* (1866). Expansive panorama of Russian lives disrupted by Napoleonic invasions.

Twain, Mark. *The Adventures of Huckleberry Finn* (1885). Social satire from a boy's perspective.

Updike, John. *Rabbit Run* (1960). Gritty view of small-town life in Pennsylvania.

Wolfe, Thomas. *Look Homeward, Angel* (1929). An American epic of families and coming of age.

Woolf, Virginia. *To the Lighthouse* (1927). Modern novel told in stream-of-consciousness technique.

For further reference

Adams, W. Royce
Increasing Reading Speed
Macmillan

Agardy, Franklin J.
How to Read Faster and Better
Simon & Schuster

Berger, Gilda
Learning Disabilities and Handicaps
Watts

Cohn, Marvin
Helping Your Teen-age Student: What Parents Can Do to Improve Reading and Study Skills
Dutton & Co.

Ervin, Jane
Your Child Can Read and You Can Help
Doubleday

Lewis, Norman
How to Read Better and Faster
Harper & Row

Miller, William M.
Reading Faster and Understanding More
Little, Brown

Osman, Betty B.
Learning Disabilities: A Family Affair
Random House

Improving Your Reading

Taking Major Tests

- Improve your test taking 329
- How to take a test 330
- The GED 332
- The SAT 336
- The ACT 343
- The GRE 349

Nearly all people who want to advance their educations or careers must at some time take at least one of the major tests. These tests are designed to evaluate general knowledge, aptitude for college, or qualifications for graduate school. All of these tests are developed by nonprofit organizations, and their scores are generally accepted by employers and educators across the United States.

The achievement test called General Educational Development, or GED, is designed to assess whether a person knows as much as a typical high-school graduate. It is administered to people who dropped out of high school or who never entered high school. A passing grade on the GED is accepted by most employers and colleges as the equivalent of a high-school diploma.

Most colleges, however, want students who are better than the typical high-school graduate. They also want to be able to evaluate the best student in a poor high school against an ordinary student in a good high school. While the best students in poor high schools may be at least as good as ordinary students in good schools, they may actually be much better or much worse. By giving the same aptitude test to everyone who applies for admission, college administrators hope to obtain an objective evaluation. Of course, colleges do not rely on tests alone, but the scores provided by standardized tests may indicate whether a student with poor grades in school may have unrealized potential.

Colleges use one of two aptitude tests to acquire the information they need. (Some colleges will accept scores from either.) The test used most in the eastern United States is the Scholastic Aptitude Test, or SAT, prepared by the College Entrance Examination Board. The SAT is the grandfather of all the major aptitude tests and many tests have imitated it. Elsewhere in the United States, the American College Testing Program, or ACT, is used more than the SAT. It is important to remember, though, that around the country individual colleges have different requirements. The admissions offices of the colleges to which you are applying should be consulted as to whether you need to take an aptitude test and, if so, which test.

These tests are called *aptitude tests* because they are intended to measure ability, not knowledge. Some colleges also require *achievement tests*, which measure knowledge of specific subjects, such as French or calculus, rather than ability.

Just as college admissions offices want to have standards to judge applicants from different high schools, administrators of graduate schools want to have similar objective standards for college graduates. The Graduate Record Examination, or GRE, is designed to test the kinds of skills needed in graduate school. Not every graduate school requires the GRE, especially where there are programs that lead directly from a college into a specific course of graduate study. Nevertheless, the GRE is frequently required, and failure to pass it can keep a person out of a graduate program.

Improve your test-taking

Though everyone wants to do as well as possible on tests, some students know more than they are ever able to show because they are test-shy. These students often perform more poorly than students who know less than they do. Thus, good test-takers have an advantage over classmates who do not test well. For this reason, you should learn about various tests and try to become "test-wise," that is, comfortable when taking tests and capable of figuring out correct answers even when you do not have firm knowledge to guide you.

Most good test-takers follow a few simple rules that help them get better scores. Some of these rules apply to all tests. Others are specific for multiple-choice tests, or even more specific for a single test, such as the SAT. The first and most important rule, however, is that the better prepared you are, the easier you will find the test and the better your score will be.

Attitude. Perhaps the most important rule to help you improve your test-taking is to adopt the right attitude. You cannot do well on a test if your mind is blocked by worry. Remember, tests are designed to measure your mastery of a skill or your knowledge of a subject. They are not designed to embarrass you, fool you, or terrify you. In a sense, taking a test should be no harder for you than taking your temperature.

Forget about the students around you—what they do is of no concern. Forget about the teacher, about the plans you have for after the test, and about anything else that may be on your mind. Until the test is over, the only two things that matter are you and the test. With this single-minded attitude, you are ready to concentrate and do your very best. You may feel keyed up, like an athlete before a game. Being keyed up can make you more alert and ready, but you should not feel agitated or worried.

Preparation. Not less important than attitude is preparation for a test. There are two kinds of preparation for any test, whether it is an end-of-course achievement test or a general aptitude test. The first is study of the subject matter. Even in taking an aptitude test, knowing the subject matter will help you get a high score. If you do not know the subject matter, only your test-wiseness can help you.

Some students study hard but do not master the material. They may read a chapter over and over, desperately trying to memorize hundreds of facts, or they may run in circles, trying over and over again to master a new problem without first understanding it.

If the test is on subject matter from a book, try this approach. Instead of reading the material over and over, read it once. Then spend some time organizing it on paper. What are the major facts or themes of the material? What are the important names or dates or other facts—those necessary to understand the whole? Many of the names and dates may be less important—in fact, some of them can safely be forgotten.

If you are learning a skill, go back to an example, either in the book or in your notes, and follow it step by step, making sure that you see how the right answer was reached. Then take a new problem and follow exactly the same steps. If you still do not understand, ask for help from a classmate or teacher.

There are many aids available to you in preparing for these major tests. The sample items with explanations that are on pages 332–351 are a good place to begin. The box on page 330 lists some other options.

If you are having trouble, it is important that you begin preparing for the test early. Otherwise, there will not be time to ask for help. An early start is a good idea in any case, especially when learning the vocabulary of a foreign language or such basic facts as the multiplication table. The mind needs lots of time and much repetition to fix the information firmly. No amount of cramming on the night before the test is likely to make up for work not done ahead of time. Even if you do manage to remember part of the material for the test, you probably will forget it soon afterward; in that case, you will have to do extra studying for the next test.

Ten ways to improve your test scores

Though there are many kinds of tests, with some requiring different techniques from others, here are a few tips that apply to all major tests:

1. **Take a course** that will prepare you if you are unsure about your ability to deal with a test. Such courses are offered in most major cities. Some are available by mail or on computer programs. Such courses are particularly useful for achievement tests. Although some test-makers believe that such courses cannot improve aptitude test scores, other experts think these courses help. Books available in most bookstores contain more sample questions than those offered here. The testing organizations themselves publish free or inexpensive booklets that contain helpful information and sample questions.

2. **Take at least one sample test.** This book supplies a few sample questions, but you can obtain a complete sample test, often from your school library or local bookstore. Try to take the test in the same time limit set for the actual test. The experience should not only prepare you but relax you for the actual test. It also might show up weak areas that require more study.

3. **Be prepared.** Make sure you have whatever is required to take the test when you arrive at the testing place. Some tests require an admission ticket, personal identification (such as a driver's license or birth certificate), and Number 2 pencils. Be sure you know what is needed for your test so you do not forfeit your place.

4. **Relax.** More tests are fouled up because test-takers are too tense than because they are too calm. The time to stay up nights studying for a test is in the weeks preceding it, when you can use that excess energy for studying. You should be well-rested by the time the actual test starts. A good night's sleep is better than staying up late and cramming.

5. **Take a moment to look through the whole test** before you begin to answer any questions. Read the instructions or directions especially carefully. If you do not know exactly what is wanted, it is easy to make mistakes that reduce your score.

6. **Try to estimate how much time you have** for answering each question. Count quickly how many questions there are altogether, and estimate the time needed for each. If the test has several parts, jot down a rough timetable for handling each part.

7. **Read each question carefully.** If you misunderstand the question, you will probably answer it wrong, no matter how much you know about the subject. Some tests have questions with tricky wording just to test your understanding. Especially when a question is complicated, read it a second time to be sure you have it right.

8. **Answer all the easy questions first** and skip questions you are not sure about. Use the remaining time to consider carefully the hard-to-answer questions. Answering easy questions will warm you up and help keep you from getting a mental block, a temporary inability to remember something that you really know. Answering easy questions first also will ensure that you have answered everything you know best before time runs out.

9. **Answer first questions from parts of the test that carry higher values** than others do. Obviously, if you know which parts count most and the correct answers, it is better to answer those parts right away to be sure of getting the highest possible score.

10. **If you have time left,** do not turn in your test or stop working on it. Use the remaining minutes to read through all the questions and answers. You may find, for example, that you have failed to answer some items whose answers you know. In multiple choice tests with separate answer sheets, take the time to make sure that you have put your answers in the right spaces or columns. Take a moment to determine that each answer seems reasonable, especially in a mathematics test; if an answer is wrong, do not be too lazy to do your calculations again.

The second kind of preparation for any test has nothing at all to do with subject matter. It consists of making sure that you are physically and mentally ready to do well. One important factor is a good night's sleep. The day before a test, remember to take a few minutes now and then to relax. Finish your studying early so that you can get to bed and be ready for sleep at your regular bedtime. In the morning, eat a good breakfast. At the same time, train yourself to put aside any worries or excitement for a few hours, until the test is over. You need all your powers of concentration for the test.

During the test.
Arrive early and have with you the pencils or any other tools you will need. At this point you should be well enough prepared not to think about the test for a moment or two. Do something else if you can, such as chat with a friend.

When the test is handed out, read it through quickly before you answer any of the questions. Be sure you understand *how* you are to provide the answers. Do not, for example, write on the test booklet if a separate answer sheet is required. In fact, it is a good idea to read all the instructions twice—just to make sure. Getting a poor grade because you did not follow the rules is worse than getting a poor grade because you did not know the material. Once you have read through the whole test, do the easy items first. In that way, even if you are short of time, you will make sure you get credit for what you know. After the easy items are done, tackle the items you are not sure of.

Obviously, if you do not know the correct answer to a test item, you will have a more difficult time than if you do know the answer. But you still have many ways to improve your score. For one thing, your unconscious mind usually knows more than your conscious mind does. Although you skip over an item because you do not remember the answer, the answer may pop into your mind later. In addition, if you weed out answers that you know are wrong, you have a good chance of coming up with the correct answer. For example, if you eliminate two of four answers in a multiple choice item, you have a fifty-fifty chance of getting the right answer from the remaining two.

If you are really in trouble, there are other rules you

Get a good night's sleep and eat a proper breakfast.

can use for guessing. Be warned, however, that the people who write the tests know these rules also. For example, correct answers often have to be qualified extensively, which means that the right answer will normally be the longest one. Test-makers know this, of course, so they deliberately try to think of wrong answers that will be longer than the right ones. As a result, the second-longest answer is sometimes the right one. Similarly, absolute qualifiers, such as *always, never,* or *none,* generally apply to incorrect answers, since few things in this world are ever absolute. Test-makers know this also, and sometimes they add absolute qualifiers to incorrect answers in order to trap the unwary. Finally, the test-makers want there to be about equal numbers of answers labeled A, B, C, D, and E. Each letter should, in this case, get about 20 percent of the answers. While test-makers know that students might exploit this to improve their test scores, most are reluctant to let one answer predominate over the others. Thus, in a multiple choice test, you can use the number of answers for each letter among the items you are sure of as a rough guide to guessing the items of which you are not sure.

Scoring multiple-choice tests.
Multiple-choice tests are used most often to test mastery of facts. Be sure to read each question and its possible answers carefully. Sometimes, more than one answer may seem correct; in that case, choose the one that you think is most accurate.

Short multiple-choice tests usually are graded on the number of right answers. This means that if you do not know the answer to a question, you can guess at answers without being penalized.

On long multiple-choice tests, such as standardized reading and mathematics tests, you are penalized for guessing. For this kind of test you should not guess at an answer if you have no idea what the answer is. You should guess if you can eliminate one or more of the possible answers as surely wrong.

Sample test questions

Sample questions from the four major tests follow. You will notice that the same kinds of questions often appear on more than one test. Each question is accompanied by a short explanation of why one of the answers is correct. Study these explanations carefully; they will reveal techniques of thinking you can use over and over. Note that in multiple-choice questions, the part that sets up the choices is sometimes called the *stem.*

GED

The General Educational Development examination has been developed by the American Council on Education to qualify students who have not finished high school or the equivalent of a secondary school diploma. It is rare for high-school dropouts to make a success of their lives without passing the GED. The GED consists of five parts: writing skills, social studies, science, reading, and mathematics. It generally takes about three and a half hours to complete. The writing skills section is a test of written English, including spelling, capitalization, punctuation, usage, sentence structure, and organization. There is no penalty for guessing, so you should complete all items even if you do not have the slightest idea of what the correct choices are.

Writing skills

Directions: The following sentences contain problems in capitalization and punctuation. If there is an error, select the one underlined part that must be changed to make the sentence correct. No sentence contains more than one error. If there is no error, mark answer space 5.

Until recently, almost all history book's ignored the
                                    1   2

contributions and achievements of the various minor-
       3

ity cultures within the country. No error
                   4   5

Part 2 contains the error, since *book's* has an apostrophe, indicating that it is in the possessive case. All that is needed here is a simple plural. The sentence refers to more than one book, not to a book that owns something. The correct form is *books*.

Directions: Beneath each sentence you will find five ways of writing the underlined part. Choose the answer that makes the best sentence and mark the number of that answer on your answer sheet. Answer (1) is always the same as the underlined part and is sometimes the right answer.

Representative Jones was first sent to Washington by a huge majority vote, who reelected her for three more terms.

(1) a huge majority vote
(2) a great majority of the voters
(3) a vote of large majority
(4) the larger part of voters
(5) more votes on her side

The key here is the word *who*, following the underlined part. *Who* must refer to a person or persons. Only choices (2) and (4) allow *who* to refer to the voters instead of the vote. Choice (2) has exactly the same meaning as the underlined part, so it is correct. "The larger part" in choice (4) does not carry the same meaning as "a huge majority" in the underlined part.

Directions: In each sentence find what is wrong, if anything. If there is an error, decide which underlined part must be changed to make the sentence correct; then blacken the space having the same number as the answer you have chosen. If there is no error, mark answer space 5. No sentence contains more than one error.

It is fortunate that waterpower has been so abundant
                                    1

in Quebec and Ontario, two areas that have hardly
          2   3

no coal at all. No error
  4   5

The word *hardly* has the meaning of *only just*. It cannot precede *no coal* because no one would say, "The areas have only just no coal." The error, then, is in choice 4. The correct form would be *hardly any coal*.

Directions: Read the following passage before you answer the questions based on it. For each question, select the one best answer. Then blacken the corresponding space on your answer sheet.

[1]Skylab was a huge space station that was put into orbit around Earth in 1973. [2]It was to be used for scientific experiments by three teams of scientist–cosmonauts. [3]While Skylab was being launched unmanned, a protective shield was torn off. [4]Without the shield, the sun's rays heated the inside of Skylab to a temperature you couldn't stand.

In sentence 4, a temperature you couldn't stand should be

(1) left as it is
(2) changed to a really hot temperature
(3) changed to hotter than you would think
(4) changed to hot temperatures
(5) changed to unbearable temperatures

The underlined part needs to be changed, since *you* could not refer to the scientists–cosmonauts in Skylab. A temperature that the scientist–cosmonauts "couldn't stand" would be unbearable. Therefore, choice (5) is correct.

Taking Major Tests

Social studies

Directions: Choose the one best answer to each question.

In the United States, a governor of a state has the power to do all of the following EXCEPT

(1) prepare a budget for the next year
(2) veto a law passed by the state legislature
(3) send an ambassador to a foreign country
(4) campaign for the members of his or her political party
(5) suggest laws he or she would like to see passed

Choices (1), (2), and (5) describe activities that might be performed by the governor of a state. Choice (4) describes an activity common to most elected officials. The correct answer is choice (3). Only the federal government of the United States—the President with the advice and consent of the Senate—can send ambassadors to other countries.

According to the graph above, the year the population was evenly distributed between urban and rural areas was approximately

(1) 1880   (2) 1900   (3) 1920   (4) 1940   (5) 1960

First, it is important to understand that "evenly distributed between urban and rural areas" means that the two populations are equal. In a line graph such as the one given here, two quantities are equal when the lines for both quantities cross; that is, because the height of the line above the base represents the quantity, the lines will cross when the heights are the same. The lines for the urban and rural areas cross just once, above the time 1900. Therefore, the correct choice is (2).

Answer every question on the GED. There is no penalty for guessing.

The next two questions refer to the following map.

Which area is associated with the Gold Rush of 1849?

(1) 1   (2) 2   (3) 3   (4) 4   (5) 5

Many GED items rely on knowledge that the person taking the test is supposed to have. This is one of them, but you can also eliminate some choices even if you do not remember that the Gold Rush of 1849 brought many people to California. For example, the region east of the Mississippi was filled with people in the 1800's, so choice (5) (region 5) can be ruled out. With only four choices left, you have a better chance of guessing the correct choice, which is (1).

In the middle of the 19th century, American industry was most heavily concentrated in which area?

(1) 1   (2) 3   (3) 4   (4) 6   (5) 7

Make sure that you remember that the 19th century is the same as the 1800's, so this question centers about the years around 1850. As in the previous item, you can eliminate choices (1), (2), and (3) (regions 1, 3, and 4) because these regions did not have enough people to support heavy industry at that time. If you do not remember that heavy industry was concentrated mostly in New England at that time, which is choice (5) (region 7), you still have a fifty-fifty chance of guessing the correct choice.

All of the following are undesirable results of man's efforts to improve his standard of living EXCEPT

(1) erosion of soils
(2) desalination of seawater
(3) destruction of wildlife habitats
(4) exhaustion of mines
(5) pollution of air and water

In this kind of a question, there is a "hidden double negative" that can confuse the person taking the test. The "EXCEPT" in the stem means that you want to find a choice that is not undesirable. "Not undesirable" is not necessarily the same as desirable. It means that you need to reject four choices that *are* undesirable. Choices (1), (3), (4), and (5) all describe results that are undesirable. Choice 2 describes something that can be desirable, so it is correct.

Taking Major Tests

Reading

<u>Directions:</u> Choose the <u>best</u> answer to each question.

What Is Poetry?

What is poetry? Who knows?
Not the rose, but the scent of the rose;
Not the sky, but the light of the sky;
Not the fly, but the gleam of the fly;
Not the sea, but the sound of the sea;

Not myself, but what makes me
See, hear, feel something that prose
Cannot, and what it is, who knows?

Reprinted by permission of Harold Ober Associates Inc. © 1938 by Eleanor Farjeon, renewed.
Copyright 1938, Eleanor Farjeon. Reprinted by permission of J.B. Lippincott Company.

According to the poem, poetry, unlike prose, does which of the following?

(1) relates to feelings rather than to objects
(2) explains things fully and logically
(3) deals with everyday life
(4) concerns itself with things, not people
(5) describes things in simple words

Choice (2) is not generally thought of as relating to poetry, so it can be rejected. The poem does not refer to everyday life (3) or simple words (5), so they can be eliminated. Choice (1) fits better than choice (2) because *scent, light, gleam,* and *sound* involve human *feelings* about the objects that are mentioned.

In a recent survey, three out of four people interviewed said that they liked Soothies better than the other leading pain reliever. Here's what some of those people had to say:

Ms. R. Jones: "Soothies really make me feel better fast. I've told my friends about them."
Mr. L. Smith: "Soothies taste better than the other leading pain reliever. My children chew Soothies like candy. And for the same price, you get more Soothies than pills of the other leading brand."
Dr. Q. Brown: "I recommend Soothies for fast relief. They work best for me."

Soothies cost less than the other leading pain reliever. So get the best for less! Try Soothies.

Dr. Brown recommends Soothies because they

(1) taste good to him   (2) help most people
(3) are inexpensive   (4) bring him relief
(5) are the leading brand

When asked for a specific detail in a reading passage, focus only on the part that contains the information asked for. In this case, you can go directly to what Dr. Brown has said. Choice (4) is the only one with this idea, so it is correct.

Science

<u>Directions:</u> Each of the questions or incomplete statements below is followed by five suggested answers or completions. Select the one that is best in each case and then blacken the corresponding space on the answer sheet.

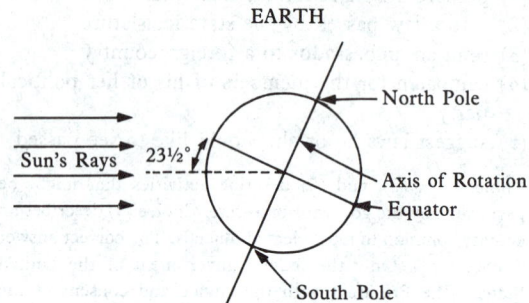

In the diagram above, the sun's rays and the axis of rotation of Earth are both in the plane of the page. The diagram best represents the position of Earth nearest to

(1) March 21
(2) June 21
(3) July 1
(4) September 23
(5) December 21

This is the kind of question that asks you to see something in your mind's eye. As you look at the diagram, picture the time of the year when the northern hemisphere is tilted away from the warming rays of the sun: wintertime. This corresponds to choice (5), which is correct.

Evidence indicates that cigarette smoking results in

(1) cardiovascular stress
(2) hepatitis
(3) whooping cough
(4) pneumonia
(5) pleurisy

Most people think of lung cancer when they think of the effects of cigarette smoking, but lung cancer is not among the choices. Emphysema, another common disease associated with smoking, also is not present. You might think that choices (3), (4), or (5)—all associated with the lungs—might be correct, but this is one of those cases in which the testmaker has been deliberately misleading. If you recognize that choices (2), (3), (4), and (5) all are infectious diseases, then none of them can be caused by cigarette smoking. Therefore, the correct choice must be (1), cardiovascular stress. It is also helpful to know that *cardiovascular* relates to the heart and blood vessels, and smoking is often thought of as being damaging to the heart.

Mathematics

Directions: For all problems choose the one best answer.

During the month of July the Herbert family spent $32.28, $27.39, $37.54, $54.80, and $52.20 for food. How much did they spend on food for the month?

(1) $184.21   (2) $193.11   (3) $193.21
(4) $203.19   (5) $204.21

Speed helps in getting through a test. While this item can be answered by actually adding the amounts, you should notice at once that three of the choices end in 21 cents. Add just the cents: 0.28 + 0.39 + 0.54 + 0.80 + 0.20 = 2.21, so (as could be suspected) the correct choice has to be (1), (3), or (5). Now look at the dollars. Both (2) and (3) have $193. Since (3) is on the possibly correct list and (2) is not, the correct answer is most likely (3). Check by estimating the sum (round off the numbers to whole dollars): $32 + $27 + $38 + $55 + $52 = 204. The correct choice must be (5), not (3). The test-maker was trying to mislead you.

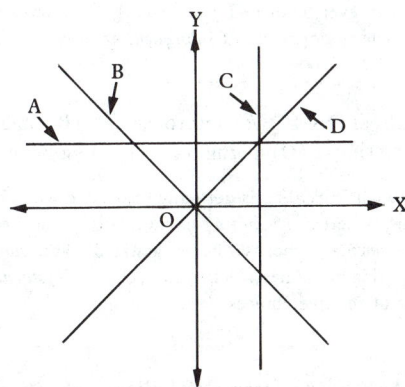

Which of the lines shown in the figure above has zero slope?

(1) A   (2) B   (3) C   (4) D
(5) None of the above

If you have studied slope, it is essential to remember the difference between a slope of zero and no slope. Line A has a slope of zero, while line C has no slope (its slope is undefined). If you have not studied slope, you can still guess that slope refers to the degree of slantedness or steepness of a line. The line that is not slanted, or has zero steepness, is line A. The correct choice is (1).

For further information on the GED, contact your provincial or state department of education, or:
American Council on Education
One Dupont Circle
Washington, DC 20036

One statute mile is equal to 5280 feet. If one nautical mile is approximately 1.15 statute miles, then one nautical mile is equal to approximately how many feet?

(1) 4590   (2) 5165   (3) 5395
(4) 5545   (5) 6070

With a question such as this one, you may find it easy to perform the indicated multiplication: $1.15 \times 5280 = 6072$. If multiplication is not easy for you, you may find it easier to approach the problem the following way.

The statement that a nautical mile is 1.15 statute miles means that a nautical mile is 15 percent larger than a statute mile. Since a nautical mile is larger than a statute mile, you can eliminate choices (1) and (2) automatically. You also can note that 15 percent is halfway between 10 and 20 percent. It is easy to calculate that 10 percent of 5280 is 528 and that twice 528 is 1056, 20 percent of 5280. Therefore, a nautical mile must be about 700 or 800 feet larger than a statute mile. Only choice (5) is anywhere near correct. The method of estimation is especially good, since the actual product of 1.15 and 5280 is 6072.40, not 6070.

On the number line above, which lettered point could represent the number $-\frac{9}{8}$?

(1) A   (2) B   (3) C   (4) D   (5) E

From the labels below the number line, it is clear that all the negative numbers are to the left, so you can eliminate points D and E easily. It may help then to think of $-\frac{9}{8}$ as $-1\frac{1}{8}$. Just as $+1\frac{1}{8}$ is a number between $+1$ and $+2$, $-1\frac{1}{8}$ is between -1 and -2, so only A or B could be correct choices. Since $-1\frac{1}{8}$ must be closer to -1 than it is to -2, the correct choice is (2) (point B).

If $x + y = 36$ and $x = 2y$, then $x =$

(1) 9   (2) 12   (3) 18   (4) 24   (5) 27

This problem can be solved by a formal method, but it is probably easier, faster, and just as accurate to treat this as a problem in reasoning, not a problem in algebra. Since $x = 2y$, the value of x must be twice the value of y, or y must be one half of x. This rules out odd numbers for x, since the sum of x and y would then contain a fraction. Of the remaining choices (2), (3), and (4), choices (2) and (3) are easily seen to be too small, so the correct choice must be (4). Always check problems if you can. If $x = 24$, then $y = 12$, and $24 + 12 = 36$. (Another approach is to use substitution. Since $x = 2y$, substitute 2y for x in $x + y = 36$. This produces $2y + y = 36$, or $3y = 36$. Therefore, $y = \frac{36}{3}$, or 12. Now go back to $x = 2y$ to see that x is twice 12, or 24.)

Taking Major Tests   335

SAT

The SAT requires about three hours to complete and consists of two sections, verbal and mathematics. Each section is made up of several subtests. The verbal and mathematics sections are scored individually on a scale of 200 to 800. Guessing is penalized on the SAT. The penalty is so slight, however, that you should guess if you can eliminate even one of the choices.

Verbal

The verbal sections of the SAT contain four types of questions:
- 25 antonyms,
- 20 analogies,
- 15 sentence completions, and
- 25 questions based on reading passages.

The antonyms usually take the least time per question, followed by analogies, sentence completion questions, and, finally, reading comprehension questions. Individual students spend varying amounts of time working on the different types of questions. Some students can answer two or three antonyms a minute, but the same students may take more than seven minutes to read a 400-word passage and answer five questions on it.

Antonyms (opposites). Antonym questions primarily test the extent of your vocabulary. The vocabulary used in the antonym questions includes words that you are likely to come across in your general reading, although some words may not be the kinds you use in everyday speech.

Among the five choices offered, you are looking for the word that means the *opposite* of the given word. Words that have exactly the same meaning as the given word are not included among the five choices.

You are looking for the *best* answer. Read all of the choices before deciding which one is best, even if you feel sure you know the answer.

Few words have exact opposites, that is, words that are opposite in all of their meanings. You should find the word that is *most nearly* opposite.

You need to be flexible. A word can have several meanings.

You will often recognize a word you have encountered in your reading but have never looked up in the dictionary. If you do not know the dictionary meaning of a word but have a feeling for how the word should be used, try to make up a short phrase or sentence using the word. This may give you a clue as to which choice is an opposite, even though you may not be able to define the word precisely.

Directions: Each question below consists of a word in capital letters, followed by five lettered words or phrases. Choose the word or phrase that is most nearly opposite in meaning to the word in capital letters. Since some of the questions require you to distinguish fine shades of meaning, consider all the choices before deciding which is best.

SUBSEQUENT: (A) primary (B) recent (C) contemporary (D) prior (E) simultaneous

Subsequent means "following in time or order; succeeding." Someone working quickly might choose (B) *recent* because it refers to a past action and *subsequent* refers to an action in the future. However, choice (D) *prior* is the best answer. It is more nearly the opposite of *subsequent* than is *recent*.

FERMENTING: (A) improvising (B) stagnating (C) wavering (D) plunging (E) dissolving

Even though *fermenting* is normally associated with chemical reactions, whereas *stagnating* is normally associated with water, *fermenting* means "being agitated" and *stagnating* means "being motionless." Therefore, choice (B) *stagnating* is the best of the five choices.

DEPRESS: (A) force (B) allow (C) clarify (D) elate (E) loosen

The word *depress* can mean "to push down." However, no word meaning "to lift up" is included among the choices. Therefore, you must consider another meaning of *depress*, to sadden or discourage. Option (D) *elate* means to fill with joy or pride. The best answer is (D) *elate*.

INCUMBENT: (A) conscious (B) effortless (C) optional (D) improper (E) irrelevant

You may remember *incumbent* used in a sentence such as "It is incumbent upon me to finish this." If you can think of such a phrase, you may be able to recognize that *incumbent* means "imposed as a duty" or "obligatory." Of the five choices, (A), (B), and (D) are in no way opposites of *incumbent* and you can easily eliminate them. Choice (E) means "not pertinent" and choice (C) means "not compulsory." Although choice (E) may look attractive, choice (C) *optional* is more nearly an exact opposite to *incumbent*. Choice (C), therefore, is the answer.

336 Taking Major Tests

Analogies. Analogy questions test your ability to see a relationship in a pair of words, to understand the ideas expressed in the relationship, and to recognize a similar or parallel relationship.

For the analogy below, just state the relationship between the original pair of words and then decide which pair of words from choices (A)–(E) has the same relationship.

Remember that a pair of words can have more than one relationship.

Directions: Each question below consists of a related pair of words or phrases, followed by five lettered pairs of words or phrases. Select the lettered pair that best expresses a relationship similar to that expressed in the original pair.

SUBMISSIVE : LED ::   (A) wealthy : employed
(B) intolerant : indulged   (C) humble : humiliated
(D) incorrigible : taught
(E) inconspicuous : overlooked

The relationship between *submissive* and *led* can be expressed as "to be submissive is to be easily led." Only choice (E) has the same relationship: to be inconspicuous is to be easily overlooked.

To be *intolerant* is not to be easily *indulged,* to be *humble* is not to be easily *humiliated,* and to be *incorrigible* (or incapable of being reformed) is not to be easily *taught.* With regard to choice (A), although the wealthy may find it easier to get employment than do the poor, the statement "to be wealthy is to be easily employed" is an expression of opinion and not an expression of the relationship between the words according to their dictionary meanings.

SONG : REPERTOIRE ::   (A) score : melody
(B) instrument : artist   (C) solo : chorus
(D) benediction : church   (E) suit : wardrobe

The best answer is choice (E). The relationship between the words can be expressed as "several (first word) make up a (second word)." Several (songs) make up a (repertoire) as several (suits) make up a (wardrobe).

REQUEST : ENTREAT ::   (A) control : explode
(B) admire : idolize   (C) borrow : steal
(D) repeat : plead   (E) cancel : invalidate

The best answer is choice (B). Although both of the capitalized words have similar meanings, they express different degrees of feeling; to (entreat) is to (request) with strong feeling as to (idolize) is to (admire) with strong feeling.

To answer analogy questions, you must think carefully about the precise meanings of words. For instance, if you thought the word *entreat* meant only to ask instead of to ask urgently, you would have trouble establishing the correct relationship between *request* and *entreat.*

AMPLIFIER : HEAR ::   (A) turntable : listen
(B) typewriter : spell   (C) platter : eat
(D) camera : feel   (E) microscope : see

The best answer is choice (E). An (amplifier) magnifies in order to help a person (hear) in the same way that a (microscope) magnifies in order to help a person (see). Note that, in (A), while a *turntable* is part of a larger mechanism that allows a person to *listen,* the choice is not as good an answer as (E) because a *turntable* does not magnify anything. Choice (D) is also wrong for a similar reason: a *camera* produces pictures that may make a person *feel* something, but a *camera* does not magnify in order to help a person to *feel.*

PRIDE : LION ::   (A) snake : python
(B) pack : wolf   (C) rat : mouse
(D) bird : starling   (E) dog : canine

A possible relationship between *pride* and *lion* might be that the first word describes a characteristic of the second (especially in mythology). Using this reasoning, you might look for an answer such as *wisdom : owl,* but none of the given choices has that kind of relationship. Another relationship between *pride* and *lion* is "a group of lions is called a pride"; therefore, the answer is (B) *pack : wolf,* since a group of wolves is called a pack.

KNIFE : INCISION ::   (A) bulldozer : excavation
(B) tool : operation   (C) pencil : calculation
(D) hose : irrigation   (E) plow : agriculture

On the most general level, the relationship between *knife* and *incision* is that the object indicated by the first word is used to perform the action indicated by the second word. Since a (knife) is used to make an (incision), a (bulldozer) is used to make an (excavation), and a (hose) is used for (irrigation), there appear to be two correct answers. You need to go back and state the relationship more precisely. Some aspect of the relationship between the original pair exists in only one of the choices. A more precise relationship between *knife* and *incision* could be expressed as: "a knife cuts into something to make an incision" and "a bulldozer cuts into something to make an excavation." This relationship eliminates *hose : irrigation* as a possible answer. The best answer is choice (A).

Publications containing current information about the SAT may be obtained from your high school guidance office, or from:
College Board ATP
CN 6200
Princeton, NJ 08541-6200

Taking Major Tests

Sentence completion. Sentence completion questions test your ability to recognize relationships among parts of a sentence. Each question has a sentence with one or two words missing. You must choose the word or set of words that best fits with the other parts of the sentence. You will find that even if you are not familiar with the topic of a sentence, there is enough information in the sentence for you to find the correct answer from the context of the sentence itself.

For a better understanding of sentence completion questions, read the following sample questions and explanations.

Directions: Each sentence below has one or two blanks, each blank indicating that something has been omitted. Beneath the sentence are five lettered words or sets of words. Choose the word or set of words that best fits the meaning of the sentence as a whole.

Although its publicity has been ----, the film itself is intelligent, well-acted, handsomely produced, and altogether ----.

(A) tasteless . . respectable
(B) extensive . . moderate
(C) sophisticated . . amateur
(D) risqué . . crude
(E) perfect . . spectacular   ● Ⓑ Ⓒ Ⓓ Ⓔ

The word *although* suggests that the publicity gave the wrong impression of the movie, so look for two words that are more or less opposite in meaning. Also, the second word has to fit in with "intelligent, well-acted, handsomely produced." Choices (D) and (E) are not opposites. The words in choice (B) are somewhat opposite in meaning, but do not logically fulfill the expectation set up by the word *although*. Choice (C) can't be the correct answer, even though *sophisticated* and *amateur* are nearly opposites, because an "intelligent, well-acted, handsomely produced" film isn't amateurish. Only choice (A), when inserted in the sentence, makes a logical statement.

She is a skeptic, ---- to believe that the accepted opinion of the majority is generally ----.

(A) prone . . infallible   (B) afraid . . misleading
(C) inclined . . justifiable   (D) quick . . significant
(E) disposed . . erroneous

The words to be inserted in the blank spaces in the question above must result in a statement that is consistent with the definition of a skeptic. Since a skeptic would hardly consider the accepted opinion of the majority as *infallible, justifiable,* or *significant,* you can eliminate choices (A), (C), and (D). A skeptic would not be afraid that the accepted opinion of the majority is misleading; a skeptic would believe that it was. Therefore, choice (B) is not correct. Only choice (E) *disposed . . erroneous* makes a logical sentence.

Nearly all the cultivated plants utilized by the Chinese have been of ---- origin; even rice, though known in China since Neolithic times, came from India.

(A) foreign   (B) ancient   (C) wild   (D) obscure
(E) common

To answer this question, you need to consider the entire sentence—the part that comes after the semicolon as well as the part that comes before it. If you only consider the first part of the question, all five choices seem plausible. The second part of the sentence adds a specific example—that rice came to China from India. This idea of origin supports and clarifies the "origin" mentioned in the first part of the sentence and eliminates (C), (D), and (E) as possible answers. The mention of Neolithic times makes (B) harder to eliminate, but the sentence is not logical when (B) is used to fill in the blank because the emphasis in the second part of the sentence— country of origin—is inconsistent with that in the first—age. Only choice (A) produces a sentence that is logical and consistent.

The excitement does not ---- but ---- his senses, giving him a keener perception of a thousand details.

(A) slow . . diverts
(B) blur . . sharpens
(C) overrule . . constricts
(D) heighten . . aggravates
(E) forewarn . . quickens

Since the sentence has two blanks to be filled, you must make sure that both words make sense in the sentence. If you look for grammatical clues within the sentence, you will see that the word *but* implies that the answer will involve two words that are more or less opposite in meaning. If you keep this in mind, you can eliminate all of the choices except for (B) *blur . . sharpens*. Only the words in choice (B) imply opposition. Also, "sharpens his senses" is consistent with the notion that he has a "keener perception of a thousand details."

They argue that the author was determined to ---- his own conclusion, so he ---- any information that did not support it.

(A) uphold . . ignored
(B) revise . . destroyed
(C) advance . . devised
(D) disprove . . distorted
(E) reverse . . confiscated

The logic of the sentence makes it fairly easy to eliminate choices (B), (D), and (E). The first word in choice (A), *uphold,* and the first word in (C), *advance,* seem all right. However, the second word in choice (C), *devised,* does not make sense in the sentence. Why would an author who wished to advance his theory devise information that did not support it? Only choice (A) makes a logically consistent sentence.

338   Taking Major Tests

Reading comprehension. The reading comprehension questions on the SAT test your ability to read and understand a passage. Each passage contains the information you need for the questions that follow it.

Several types of questions are asked about the passage. Some ask about the main idea of a passage. Some questions ask about those ideas that are stated directly in the passage. Some ask you to recognize applications of the author's principles or opinions. In some questions you must make an inference from what you have read. In others you must evaluate the way the author develops and presents the passage.

Following are a sample passage, sample questions, and explanations of each of the questions.

Directions: The passage below is followed by questions based on its content. Answer all questions following the passage on the basis of what is <u>stated</u> or <u>implied</u> in that passage.

Between guilds and modern business firms there is a profound gulf. Unlike modern firms, the purpose of guilds was not first and foremost to make money. Rather, it was to preserve a certain orderly way of life —a way that envisaged a decent income for the master craftsmen but that was certainly not intended to allow any of them to become "big" businessmen. On the contrary, guilds were specifically designed to ward off any such outcome of an uninhibited struggle among their members. The terms of service and wages were fixed by custom. So, too, were the terms of sale: a guild member who cornered the supply of an item or bought wholesale to sell at retail was severely punished. Competition was strictly limited and profits were held to prescribed levels. Advertising was forbidden, and even technical progress in advance of one's fellow guildsmen was considered disloyal.

Surely the guilds represent a more "modern" aspect of feudal life than the manor, but the whole temper of guild life was still far removed from the goals and ideals of modern business enterprise. There was no free competition and no restless probing for advantage. Existing on the margin of a relatively moneyless society, the guilds were organizations that sought to take the risks out of their slender enterprises. As such, they were as drenched in the medieval atmosphere as the manors.

According to the passage, modern business enterprises, compared to the medieval guilds, are

(A) more concerned with increasing profits
(B) influenced more by craftsmen than by tradesmen
(C) more subordinate to the demands of consumers
(D) less progressive in financial dealings
(E) less interested in quantity than quality

SAT reading passages contain all the information you'll need to answer the questions.

Relax.

To answer this question, locate the parts of the passage that compare guilds and modern business—the beginnings of the first and second paragraphs. Lines 2–3 suggest that the foremost purpose of modern firms is to make money. Lines 21–22 indicate that "free competition" and "restless probing for advantage" are central to modern business enterprise. Choice (A) is the most appropriate answer among the choices given. There is no justification in the passage for any of the other choices. Some people might argue from their own experience or opinion that (C) is a possible answer. However, since the question says, "According to the passage . . . ," the answer must be based on what is stated in the passage.

It can be inferred that the guilds were organized as they were because

(A) life on the manors was boring and drab
(B) technical improvements were still improbable
(C) they stressed preservation and stability, not progress
(D) people in medieval times were interested in advancing individual liberty
(E) social status was determined by income

This question is not answered simply and directly in the passage itself, but the passage gives you information to draw on. In the first paragraph, the author notes that the purpose of guilds "was to preserve a certain orderly way of life" and that guilds were specifically designed "to ward off . . . uninhibited struggle among their members." In the second paragraph, the author states that the guilds "were organizations that sought to take the risks out of their slender enterprises." From these statements and the comparisons between guilds and modern business firms that the author makes elsewhere in the passage, choice (C) is the most reasonable conclusion to draw. Choice (A) is not related to the purpose of the organization of the guilds. The statement about technical progress made in lines 16–17 weakens the plausibility of the inference in (B). The passage does not provide enough information to justify the inferences made in (D) and (E). This is a fairly easy and straightforward inference question. You may be asked others that will require somewhat more sophisticated reasoning processes.

There is a slight penalty for guessing on the SAT. If you can eliminate a choice, you should guess.

Taking Major Tests

Mathematics

Two types of multiple-choice questions are used in the mathematical sections of the SAT:
1. Standard multiple-choice questions (approximately two-thirds of the math questions)
2. Quantitative comparison questions (approximately one-third of the math questions)

Standard multiple-choice

Directions: In this section solve each problem, using any available space on the page for scratch work. Then decide which is the best of the choices given and blacken the corresponding space on the answer sheet.

If $2a + b = 5$, then $4a + 2b =$

(A) $\frac{5}{4}$ (B) $\frac{5}{2}$ (C) 10 (D) 20 (E) 25

This is an example of a problem that requires realizing that $4a + 2b = 2(2a + b)$. Therefore, $4a + 2b = 2(2a + b) = 2(5) = 10$. The correct answer is (C).

If $16 \cdot 16 \cdot 16 = 8 \cdot 8 \cdot P$, then $P =$

(A) 4 (B) 8 (C) 32 (D) 48 (E) 64

This question can be solved by several methods. A time-consuming method would be to multiply the three 16s and then divide the result by the product of 8 and 8. A quicker approach would be to find what additional factors are needed on the right side of the equation to match those on the left side. These additional factors are two 2's and a 16, the product of which is 64. The correct answer is (E).

If a car travels X kilometers of a trip in H hours, in how many hours can it travel the next Y kilometers at this rate?

(A) $\frac{XY}{H}$ (B) $\frac{HY}{X}$ (C) $\frac{HX}{Y}$ (D) $\frac{H+Y}{X}$

(E) $\frac{X+Y}{H}$

You can solve this problem by using ratios or by using the distance formula.

Using the ratio method, X kilometers is to H hours as Y kilometers is to $\square$ hours, where $\square$ represents the amount of time required to travel Y kilometers:

$$\frac{X}{H} = \frac{Y}{\square}$$

$X \square = HY$

$\square = \frac{HY}{X}$

The correct answer is (B).

Do your scratch work right on the test paper.

The town of Mason is located on Eagle Lake. The town of Canton is west of Mason. Sinclair is east of Canton, but west of Mason. Dexter is east of Richmond, but west of Sinclair and Canton. Assuming all these towns are in the United States, which town is farthest west?

(A) Mason (B) Dexter (C) Canton
(D) Sinclair (E) Richmond

For this kind of problem, drawing a diagram may help. In this case, a line can be effectively used to locate the relative position of each town. Start with the statement "The town of Canton is west of Mason" and, using abbreviations, draw the following:

W———————C————————M———E

From the remaining information, place the other towns in their correct order:

W———R-D-C————————S————M———E

The final sketch shows that the town farthest west is Richmond (R) and the correct answer is (E).

If the symbol $\triangledown$ between two expressions indicates that the expression on the right exceeds the expression on the left by 1, which of the following is (are) true for all real numbers x?

I. $x(x + 2) \triangledown (x + 1)^2$

II. $x^2 \triangledown (x + 1)^2$

III. $\frac{x}{y} \triangledown \frac{x+1}{y+1}$

(A) None (B) I only (C) II only
(D) III only (E) I and III

This kind of problem involves working with a newly defined symbol. One approach is to check the statements one at a time. Statement I reduces to $x^2 + 2x \triangledown x^2 + 2x + 1$, so the expression on the right does exceed the expression on the left by 1. Therefore, statement I is true. Statement II reduces to $x^2 \triangledown x^2 + 2x + 1$, so the right expression exceeds the left expression by $2x + 1$, which is not equal to 1 except when $x = 0$. This makes statement II false. Statement III is more difficult to check, but you can verify by subtraction, or by substituting numbers (for example, $x = 3, y = 5$), that the expression on the right does not exceed the expression on the left by 1. Therefore, statement III is false. The only true statement is I, so the correct answer is (B).

In a problem of this kind, if you are able to decide about only one or two statements, you can still eliminate some choices and guess among those remaining. For example, if you can conclude that I is true, then the correct answer is either (B) or (E) because these choices contain statement I.

Taking Major Tests

A number is divisible by 9 if the sum of its digits is divisible by 9. Which of the following numbers is divisible by 45?

(A) 63,345 (B) 72,365
(C) 99,999 (D) 72,144
(E) 98,145

It would be very time-consuming to divide each choice by 45. In order for a number to be divisible by 45 it must be divisible by both 9 and 5. Choices (A), (B), and (E) are divisible by 5, but choices (C) and (D) are not, so you can eliminate choices (C) and (D) immediately. You are given that a number is divisible by 9 if the sum of its digits is divisible by 9. The sums of the digits in choices (A), (B), and (E) are 21, 23, and 27, respectively.

Of these choices only 27 is divisible by 9. The correct answer is (E). Your scratch work for this problem might appear as follows:

(A) 63,345   ~~21~~
(B) 72,365   ~~23~~
(C) ~~99,999~~
(D) ~~72,144~~
(E) 98,145   ㉗

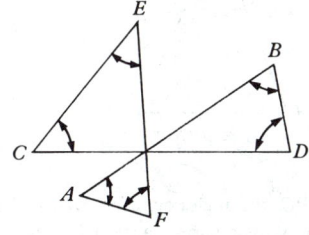

In the triangles above, if AB, CD, and EF are line segments, what is the sum of the measures of the six marked angles?

(A) 180° (B) 360° (C) 540° (D) 720°
(E) It cannot be determined from the information given.

This problem requires a creative problem-solving approach. One solution involves recognizing that the sum of the three unmarked angles in the triangles is 180°.

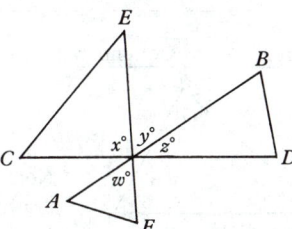

Because CD is a line segment, the sum of angles x, y, and z is 180°. Also, $y = w$ because they are vertical angles. Therefore, $x + w + z = 180$. Since the sum of the measures of all angles in the three triangles is 540° (3 · 180°) and the sum of the unmarked angles of the triangles in the original figure equals 180°, it follows that the sum of the marked angles is 540° − 180° = 360°. The correct answer is (B).

If the average of seven x's is 7, what is the average of fourteen x's?

(A) $\frac{1}{7}$ (B) $\frac{1}{2}$ (C) 1 (D) 7 (E) 14

Do not get caught up in the wording of this problem, which might lead you to choose (E) 14. The average of any number of equal numbers such as x is always x. Since you are given that the average of seven x's is 7, it follows that $x = 7$ and that the average of 14 x's is also 7. The correct answer is (D).

If 90 percent of P is 30 percent of Q, then Q is what percent of P?

(A) 3% (B) 27% (C) 30% (D) 270%
(E) 300%

Writing an algebraic equation for this percent problem not only simplifies the work, it also helps you organize your thoughts. "90 percent of P is 30 percent of Q" can be written as $0.90P = 0.30Q$ (or $\frac{9}{10}P = \frac{3}{10}Q$). "$Q$ is what percent of P" tells you to find $\frac{Q}{P}$ and express it as a percent. $\frac{Q}{P} = 3$; therefore, Q is 300 percent of P and the correct answer is (E).

The figure above shows a piece of paper in the shape of a parallelogram with measurements as indicated. If the paper is tacked at its center to a flat surface and then rotated about its center, the points covered by the paper will be a circular region of diameter

(A) $\sqrt{3}$ (B) 2 (C) 5 (D) $\sqrt{28}$ (E) $\sqrt{39}$

The first step in solving the problem is to realize that the center of the parallelogram is the point of intersection of the two diagonals; thus, the diameter you are looking for is the length of the longer diagonal AC. One way to find AC is to think of the additional lines drawn as shown below.

The triangles at each end are congruent (equal in size and shape), so the lengths of DE and CE are 1 and $\sqrt{3}$, respectively. AEC is a right triangle; therefore, the Pythagorean theorem can be used in solving the problem:

$AC^2 = CE^2 + AE^2$

$AC^2 = (\sqrt{3})^2 + (6)^2 = 3 + 36 = 39$

The diameter AC is $\sqrt{39}$ and the correct answer is (E).

Taking Major Tests

Quantitative comparison. Quantitative comparison questions emphasize the concepts of equalities, inequalities, and estimation. They generally involve less reading, take less time to answer, and require less computation than regular multiple-choice questions. Quantitative comparison questions may not be as familiar to you as other types of questions. Therefore, give special attention to the directions ahead of time. Be careful not to mark answer option E when responding to the four-choice quantitative comparison questions.

To solve a quantitative comparison problem, compare the quantities in the two columns and decide whether one quantity is greater than the other, whether the two quantities are equal, or whether the relationship cannot be determined from the information given.

Problems are clearly separated and the *quantities to be compared are always on the same line as the number of the problem.* Figures and additional information provided for some problems appear *above* the quantities to be compared. The following are some practice problems with explanations to help you understand this type of question.

Directions: Each of the following questions consists of two quantities, one in Column A and one in Column B. You are to compare the two quantities and on the answer sheet blacken space

A if the quantity in Column A is greater;
B if the quantity in Column B is greater;
C if the two quantities are equal;
D if the relationship cannot be determined from the information given.

Notes: 1. In certain questions, information concerning one or both of the quantities to be compared is centered above the two columns.
2. In a given question, a symbol that appears in both columns represents the same thing in Column A as it does in Column B.
3. Letters such as x, n, and k stand for real numbers.

Column A	Column B
1. $(37)(\frac{1}{43})(58)$	$(59)(\frac{1}{43})(37)$

Because the numbers in this problem are fairly large, it may save time to study the multipliers first before attempting the calculations. Note that (37) and $(\frac{1}{43})$ appear in both quantities; thus, the only numbers left for you to compare are 58 and 59. Since $59 > 58$, the quantity on the right is greater and the correct answer is (B).

Answer the easy questions first.

Column A	Column B	
2. The perimeter of the square	The perimeter of the rectangle	← Quantities to be compared

It can be assumed that the units used to indicate measures in a given problem are the same in all figures in that problem unless otherwise stated. The correct answer is (C) because the perimeter of the square is $4 \cdot 7 = 28$ units and the perimeter of the rectangle is $(2 \cdot 5) + (2 \cdot 9) = 28$ units.

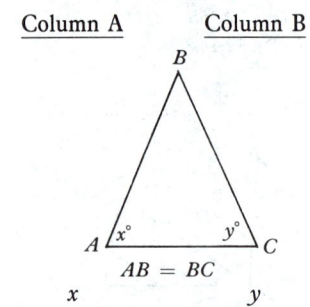

Column A	Column B
3. x	y

Since $AB = BC$, the angles opposite AB and BC are equal; therefore, $x = y$. The correct answer is (C).

Column A	Column B
4. $\sqrt{2} - 1$	$\sqrt{3} - 1$

For any positive number x, the symbol $\sqrt{x}$ denotes the positive square root of x. The fact that $\sqrt{3} > \sqrt{2}$ leads to the conclusion that $\sqrt{3} - 1 > \sqrt{2} - 1$. The correct answer is (B). Note that $x^2 = 9$ has two solutions, $x = 3$ or $x = -3$. However, $\sqrt{9} = 3$, not ± 3.

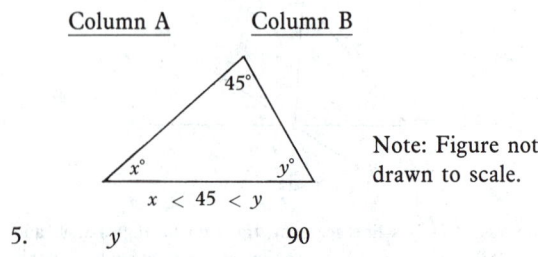

Note: Figure not drawn to scale.

Column A	Column B
5. y	90

Because the sum of the angles of a triangle is 180, $x + y + 45 = 180$ or $x + y = 135$. Since $x < 45$, it follows that $y > 90$. The answer is (A). In this problem, do not try to determine the answer from the appearance of the figure because the note indicates that the figure is not drawn to scale.

ACT

The ACT takes about three hours to complete. It consists of four sections: mathematics usage (commonly called mathematics reasoning), English usage, social studies reading, and natural sciences reading. The two reading tests involve items based on passages either in the social studies (largely history) or science sections. Specific content knowledge is not necessary for these items; however, other items do test content knowledge in social studies and science. Note that nothing is taken off for wrong answers, so guessing can help when you do not know an answer. Every item should be completed, even if you have no idea of what the right answer is. As the following explanations show, it is often possible to find a helpful clue to the correct answer.

English usage

Directions: In the passages that follow, certain words and phrases are underlined and numbered. In the right-hand column, you will find alternatives for each underlined part. You are to choose the one that best expresses the idea, makes the statement appropriate for standard written English, or is worded most consistently with the style and tone of the passage as a whole. If you think the original version is best, choose "NO CHANGE." Read each passage through once before you begin to answer the questions that accompany it. You cannot determine most answers without reading several sentences beyond the phrase in question. Be sure that you have read far enough ahead each time you choose an alternative.

As late as 1945, no baseball team in either the American nor National
                    1
League had accepted a black player. Some blacks were playing professional baseball, as a result. A Negro league had
              2
managed to survive many and countless
                         3
difficulties. In this league, were many
                         4
fine players, including one named Jackie Robinson.

During Robinson's high school days in California, an outstanding athlete was developed,
                 5
excelling in several sports. After two years at UCLA and a stint in the army, he began playing baseball in the Negro league. Where
                                                      6
Branch Rickey, president of the Brooklyn

(continued)

1. A. NO CHANGE
   B. either the American or
   C. either the American and
   D. neither the American and

   Choice B is correct, since *either* must be paired with *or*, not *nor* or *and* (C). *Neither* cannot be paired with *and* (D).

2. F. NO CHANGE
   G. therefore.
   H. however.
   J. consequently.

   Choice H is correct, since *however* describes a logical relationship between the first and second sentences. The other choices do not.

3. A. NO CHANGE
   B. many countless
   C. many numerous
   D. countless

   Choice D is correct. *Many and countless* (A), *many countless* (B), and *many numerous* (C) are redundant.

4. F. NO CHANGE
   G. league are
   H. league were
   J. league,

   Choice H is correct, since a comma incorrectly separates the verb *were* from the rest of the predicate, *in this league*. Choice G, *league are*, is present tense and therefore wrong.

5. A. NO CHANGE
   B. he expanded into an outstanding athlete,
   C. he developed into an outstanding athlete,
   D. he was developed by becoming an outstanding athlete,

   Choice C is correct, since it supplies a subject, *he*, for the verb *developed*. *Expanded* (B) would be a poor choice of verb, and *was developed by becoming* is redundant (D).

6. F. NO CHANGE
   G. When
   H. There
   J. While

   Choice H is correct, since it explains that Rickey discovered him *there*, meaning in the Negro league. G and J refer to time, not place. F would be correct if the two sentences were joined.

Taking Major Tests   343

Dodgers, now known as the Los Angeles Dodgers—discovered him. When Rickey announced plans to sign Robinson, a star player threatened to resign, but he proceeded. Thus, in 1947, Jackie Robinson broke the color barrier in major league baseball.

    Robinson's debut was unimpressive, however. He was undoubtedly apprehensive as he faced the packed stadium. In his three times at bat, he grounded out initially, struck out the second time, and his final out was a pop fly. His performance did not improve over the next several games.

Although taunted by spectators until he seriously considered quitting. He persevered and after the season was acclaimed Rookie of the Year.

    By the time Jackie Robinson left baseball, he had become a legend. Six years after retirement, he was inducted, into baseball's Hall of Fame. In his induction speech, he spoke for himself and other black players when he praised Rickey for helping he and they overcome the racial injustice that had so long plagued major sports in America.

---

7. A. NO CHANGE
   B. Dodgers (now being the Los Angeles Dodgers)
   C. Dodgers—which is now the Los Angeles Dodgers
   D. Dodgers,

Choice D is correct. The phrase *now known as the Los Angeles Dodgers* must be enclosed in commas.

8. F. NO CHANGE
   G. he proceeded on his plans.
   H. Rickey proceeded on his plans.
   J. Rickey proceeded with his plans.

Choice J is correct. *Rickey* is needed in place of *he*, and the correct idiom is *proceeded with*, not *on* (H).

9. A. NO CHANGE
   B. apprehensive as the stadium was packed.
   C. apprehensive and facing the packed stadium.
   D. apprehensive, the stadium was packed.

Choice A is correct. The other choices make no sense whatever.

10. F. NO CHANGE
   G. hit a pop fly for his final out.
   H. hitting a pop fly for his final out.
   J. he hit a pop fly for his final out.

Choice G is correct, since there are three elements in parallel. J is also parallel with the first two elements, but mistakenly repeats the subject *he*, which is lacking in the second element.

11. A. NO CHANGE
   B. Although, taunted by spectators until he seriously considered quitting,
   C. Although taunted by spectators until he seriously considered quitting, he
   D. Although taunted by spectators, until he seriously considered quitting. He

Choice C is correct. The original (A) is a sentence fragment, as is D, so both are wrong. Choice B is wrong because *Although* followed by a comma would be incorrect.

12. F. NO CHANGE
   G. (Begin new paragraph) Now that
   H. (Begin new paragraph) In the time that
   J. (Do NOT begin new paragraph) Now that

Choice F is correct. G and J confuse a past action with the present, and H makes no sense.

13. A. NO CHANGE
   B. inducted into baseball's
   C. inducted, into baseballs'
   D. inducted into baseballs'

Choice B is correct. A comma after *inducted* interrupts the predicate, so A and C are wrong. D is wrong because the apostrophe is in the wrong place.

14. F. NO CHANGE
   G. he and them
   H. him and they
   J. him and them

Choice J is correct. The objects of *helping* must be in the objective case, so F, G, and H are incorrect.

Mathematics usage

<u>Directions</u>: Solve each problem, choose the correct answer, and then blacken the corresponding space on your answer sheet.

Do not linger over problems that take too much time. Solve as many as you can; then return to the others in the time you have left.

<u>Note</u>: Illustrative figures are not necessarily drawn to scale and are assumed to lie in a plane unless otherwise stated.

A company employs a total of 750 people in 3 departments. Department A employs 100 more people than department B and twice as many people as department C. How many people are employed in department A?

A. 340
B. 260
C. 250
D. 240
E. 170

Think of the other departments in terms of department A. Department B, then, is A − 100, and department C is 0.5 × A. You were told that A + B + C = 750. Substitute for B and C in the equation. A + (A − 100) + (0.5 × A) = 750. Add the terms with A in them. This gives 2.5 × A − 100 = 750, so 2.5 × A = 850. Divide 850 by 2.5 to get the correct answer, 340. Notice that it is easier to work this problem with decimals than with fractions.

The product of 2 numbers is 1 less than the sum of the numbers. If one of the numbers is 5 and the other is x, which of the following equations could be used to find x?

F. $5x = (x + 5) - 1$
G. $5x = (x + 5) + 1$
H. $5x = (x - 5) - 1$
J. $5x = (x - 5) + 1$
K. $5x = (5 - x) - 1$

Substitute 5 and x for *2 numbers* in the first sentence of the problem. The sentence becomes *The product of 5 and x is 1 less than the sum of 5 and x*. Now you can see that answer F is correct. People sometimes have trouble interpreting the meaning of *1 less than*. It means *subtract 1 from whatever follows*. If you read carefully, you will have no trouble solving problems like this one.

Answer every question on the ACT. There is no penalty for wrong answers.

In the figure below, the lengths of $\overline{AB}$ and $\overline{BC}$ are equal, $\overline{AD}$ is a straight line, and the measure of exterior ∠DBC is 100°. What is the measure of ∠CAB?

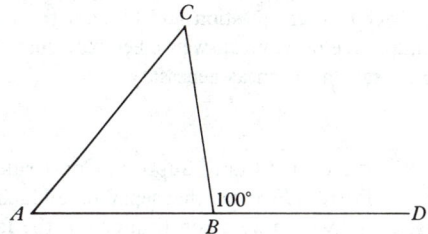

A. 25°
B. 40°
C. 50°
D. 80°
E. 100°

Since AD is a straight line, ∠CBA is the supplement of 100°. Thus, ∠CBA is 180° − 100°, or 80°. Since AB and BC are equal in length, the triangle is isosceles and the base angles (at A and C) are equal. Finally, since the sum of the angles in a triangle is 180°, the sum of the angles at A and C is 180° − 80°, or 100°. Since these angles are equal, each is 50°, answer C. (Remembering that the sum of the remote interior angles in a triangle is equal to the exterior angle would have saved a step.)

Last month an organization spent 30% of its income on postage and 10% of its income on the telephone bill. The postage costs were $240 more than the telephone bill. What was the organization's income last month?

F. $2,400
G. $1,200
H. $ 800
J. $ 600
K. $ 300

Let x = monthly income. Then .30x = the amount of the postage and .10x = the amount of the telephone bill. Since the postage is $240 more than the telephone bill, .30x = .10x + 240. Thus, .20x = 240, and solving the equation gives x = $1,200 (choice G).

For additional information about the ACT, inquire at your high school guidance office, or write:
American College Testing Program
P.O. Box 168
Iowa City, Iowa 52243

Taking Major Tests

Social studies reading

Directions: Each passage in this test is followed by several questions. After reading a passage, choose the best answer to each question and blacken the corresponding space on your answer sheet. You may refer to the passage as often as necessary.

In 1896 the United States Supreme Court ruled in the case of *Plessy* v. *Ferguson* that separate rail facilities for blacks and whites were constitutional if the facilities were equal. The decision was used for years, especially in the South, to justify segregation in public accommodations such as restaurants, hotels, and theaters.

The *Plessy* ruling was also employed to justify the creation and perpetuation of segregation in the public schools of several states. Dual school systems were expanded confidently, also supported by the contention that public education is a state rather than federal responsibility under the constitutional theory of "separation of powers."

Despite the Court's mandating of equality, states made little effort to give black children the same opportunity as white children. After 1896 various state cases questioned whether segregation caused inequality, but not until 1954 did the Supreme Court fundamentally alter *Plessy*. In that year the Court ruled on a case involving Linda Brown, an eight-year-old student in the Topeka, Kansas, school system.

The *Brown* case, like *Plessy*, rested on an interpretation of the Fourteenth Amendment. Chief Justice Earl Warren spoke for a unanimous Court when he wrote: "To separate Negro children from others of similar age and qualification solely because of their race generates a feeling of inferiority as to their status in the community that may affect their hearts and minds in a way unlikely ever to be undone."

The Court held that segregation by race in public schools was unconstitutional. The separate-but-equal doctrine was finally repudiated. With the *Brown* decision providing a touchstone, civil rights activism and litigation began to reverse the pattern of segregation established by the *Plessy* case as they forced the legal integration of public accommodations.

Although in 1955 the Court ordered that public schools be integrated "with all deliberate speed," the process of integration has been slow. Objections over methods like busing and the problem of de facto segregation in housing patterns have delayed the full-scale implementation of the Court order. A quarter century after the *Brown* decision, racial segregation had not disappeared.

Which of the following statements is NOT constitutionally acceptable today?

F. There is a basic principle of separation of powers in our government.
G. Separation with equality in education may be established in state law.
H. A Supreme Court decision is the law of the land.
J. Public education is a state responsibility.

Choice G is correct, based on the first sentence of the fifth paragraph. *Separation* is another way of saying *segregation* when discussing the topic of segregation of students in public schools.

The Supreme Court's order to desegregate public schools was based upon its judicial power to:

A. enforce states' rights.
B. interpret the Constitution.
C. control public education.
D. review actions of the executive branch.

Choice B is correct, since the first sentence of the fourth paragraph states that the *Brown* case, like the *Plessy* case, rested on interpretation of the Fourteenth Amendment to the U.S. Constitution. Interpretation of any part of the Constitution is interpretation of the Constitution.

In the *Brown* decision, the Supreme Court ruled that states could NOT:

F. decide on educational issues.
G. use federal money to integrate schools.
H. require segregated schools.
J. bus students to distant school districts.

Choice H is correct, since the first sentence of the fifth paragraph states that the Court held segregation by race in public schools unconstitutional. In other words, the Supreme Court ruled that states could not require segregated schools.

The author implies that incidents like the Montgomery, Alabama, bus boycott of 1956 would illustrate the:

A. failure of the civil rights movement.
B. impact of the *Brown* decision.
C. weakness of the NAACP.
D. determination of the federal government to implement integration.

Choice B is correct. This question deals with an implication, so the answer is not given directly. Surely, however, there is no implication of failure (A), weakness (C), or federal determination (D).

In the North, school segregation mainly stems from:

F. community housing patterns.
G. local school boards' refusal to obey the Supreme Court.
H. old state laws still in effect.
J. a continued belief in separate but equal facilities.

Choice F is correct, since the second sentence of the final paragraph cites *de facto segregation in housing patterns* as one reason for delay in full implementation of the Court order in the *Brown* case. It also mentions the problem of busing methods, but this topic does not appear in the questions.

Social studies

The following questions are not based on a reading passage. You are to answer these questions on the basis of your previous school work in the social studies.

Cases that are ruled upon by the Supreme Court often begin with:

A. bills that the President has vetoed.
B. bills that are reported favorably out of Senate committees.
C. cases decided in previous sessions of the Court in which the vote of the justices had been very close.
D. appeals of decisions rendered by lower state and federal courts.

Choice D is correct, since the Supreme Court has ultimate responsibility for deciding appeals of decisions made by lower state and federal courts. The Court plays no role in regard to bills vetoed by the President (A) or bills reported out of Senate committees (B). As for C, decisions by the Court, no matter how close, are not reviewed by it unless a new suit is first brought.

The Sioux taught the Cheyenne how to dress buffalo hides. This illustrates cultural:

F. invention.
G. diffusion.
H. generation.
J. parallelism.

Choice G is correct, since the question deals with how cultural achievements spread from one group to another. It does not deal with *invention* (F); *generation,* which refers to creation of a culture (H); or *parallelism,* which refers to similarities between cultures (J).

A family that consists of only the parents and their children is termed:

A. a nuclear family.
B. a patrilocal family.
C. a polygamous family.
D. an authoritarian family.

Choice A is correct, since *nuclear family* is defined as one consisting of a father, mother, and children. A *patrilocal family* (B) is one located with or near the husband's kinsmen. A *polygamous family* (C) is one that has additional husbands or wives, but usually additional wives. An *authoritarian family* (D) describes a family in which the father or mother exercises complete or almost complete control over the other members.

Read the directions twice.

Natural sciences

The following questions are not based on a reading passage. You are to answer these questions on the basis of your previous school work in the natural sciences.

Which factor determines whether moisture condensing out of the atmosphere will produce dew rather than frost?

A. Atmospheric pressure
B. Temperature
C. Relative humidity
D. Availability of condensation surfaces

The main difference between dew and frost is that dew remains liquid while frost freezes solid. Therefore, the correct response is B, temperature. Although relative humidity and the availability of condensation surfaces affect the formation of both dew and frost, the test item states that moisture is *condensing out of the atmosphere.* Therefore, humidity (C) and condensation surfaces (D) cannot be considered determining factors. Atmospheric pressure (A) has no effect on condensation.

Plants that have thick, waxy cuticles most likely also have:

F. desert environments.
G. long lifespans.
H. aerial roots.
J. no leaves.

A cuticle is a covering, the outer skin of something. A thick, waxy cuticle would help prevent passage of water through it. In a desert environment, this feature would help retain water within the plants that otherwise would be lost through evaporation. Therefore, the correct response is F, desert environments. Waxy cuticles are not necessarily associated with long lifespans (G), aerial roots (H), or absence of leaves (J).

Which of the time periods listed below is closest to the shortest time period in which one could observe every constellation that possibly could be observed directly overhead at midnight from a location on the equator of Earth?

A. 1 month
B. 1 year
C. 10 years
D. 100 years

As Earth travels in its orbit around the sun, the point directly opposite the sun changes each night. That point is always between the tropics of Cancer and Capricorn. Thus, in one year the entire circle of the night sky can be viewed by the observer, and the correct answer is B.

Taking Major Tests

Natural sciences reading

Directions: Each passage in this test is followed by several questions. After reading a passage, choose the best answer to each question and blacken the corresponding space on your answer sheet. You may refer to the passage as often as necessary.

Earth's atmosphere was not always the same as the air we breathe today. Geologic evidence indicates that Earth's atmosphere at one time consisted mainly of water vapor, nitrogen, hydrogen, oxides of carbon and sulfur, and probably methane and ammonia.

Soon after the formation of the atmosphere, certain changes occurred. Some gases were added to it, certain gases were removed, and some gases were changed into others. Through *outgassing*—the release of gases locked up in rocks inside Earth's mantle and crust—volcanic activity added gases to the atmosphere. Eruptions today emit carbon dioxide, sulfur oxides, nitrogen, and chlorine. Prehistoric volcanoes probably also emitted these gases.

While volcanic activity was adding gases to the atmosphere, certain gases were also being removed. Small amounts of hydrogen escaped into space, and water-soluble gases, such as ammonia, were dissolved by rain water and removed from the atmosphere. These solutions eventually reacted with substances on land or went into solution in seawater.

As gases were added to and removed from the atmosphere, certain gaseous compounds were changed into others. Some gases reacted with each other to form new ones. Hydrogen and fluorine, for example, reacted to form hydrogen fluoride. Other gases were transformed by *photodissociation*—the splitting of molecules into their parts by radiant energy. The sun's ultraviolet rays broke apart small numbers of water molecules into hydrogen and oxygen. The oxygen released by photodissociation amounted to less than 0.1 percent of all atmospheric gases.

Although these inorganic processes had been working for a long time, the appearance of life had a much greater impact upon the nature of the atmosphere. Before life was formed, the atmosphere contained little carbon dioxide or free oxygen. Early life forms released carbon dioxide into the atmosphere. Somewhat later, photosynthetic organisms developed and began to process water and carbon dioxide, releasing oxygen as a metabolic byproduct. The buildup of oxygen was slow, and by half-a-billion years ago the activity of photosynthetic marine plants had raised the level of oxygen to about 1 percent of the atmosphere. Since then it has risen to its present level of 21 percent of all atmospheric gases. Oxygen and nitrogen are the two major constituents of the present-day atmosphere.

The most direct way to maintain the present level of atmospheric oxygen would be to:

F. screen out all ultraviolet rays from the sun.
G. evaporate large quantities of water.
H. increase volcanic activity.
J. ensure the survival of photosynthetic plants.

The level of oxygen in the atmosphere is quite high. Before photosynthetic plants developed, this level was low. Paragraphs 2 and 4 show that volcanoes did not emit oxygen and ultraviolet radiation acting on water produced little oxygen, so J is correct.

Some scientists believe our present atmosphere contains very little ammonia compared to the earliest atmosphere because ammonia:

A. is used by plants in large amounts.
B. is not emitted by volcanoes.
C. contains a form of nitrogen that decays radioactively.
D. readily goes into solution in water.

The only mention of ammonia removal is in paragraph 3, which states that ammonia is dissolved by rain water and removed from the atmosphere. *Dissolved by rain water* is equivalent to *readily goes into solution in water*, making D correct.

Which statement best describes the relationship between the atmosphere and seawater?

F. The ocean is the major source of atmospheric gases.
G. The ocean contains dissolved atmospheric gases.
H. The volume of the ocean is reduced by reactions with atmospheric gases.
J. Reactions triggered by atmospheric gases produce seawater.

Paragraph 3 says some gases *went into solution in seawater*, that is, dissolved in the ocean, so G is correct.

The earliest life forms on Earth must have been able to survive without taking in:

I. water.
II. free oxygen.
III. carbon dioxide.

A. III only
B. I and II only
C. II and III only
D. I, II, and III

Paragraph 5 states that the early atmosphere contained little carbon dioxide or free oxygen. Organisms that needed these gases could not have survived. On the other hand, the presence of water in the atmosphere is mentioned several times. Therefore, choice C is the correct answer.

If outgassing had been the only process in the formation of the atmosphere, the atmosphere would NOT contain:

A. chlorine.
B. nitrogen.
C. free oxygen.
D. carbon dioxide.

Paragraph 2 says outgassing produces chlorine, nitrogen, and carbon dioxide, so C, free oxygen, is correct. Free oxygen in the atmosphere is produced by photosynthesis.

GRE

The GRE takes three and a half hours of actual test time. It consists of seven general sections. In addition to the general sections, test-takers can elect to take one of the 17 special sections. We cover the general sections only. The seven general sections test verbal ability, quantitative ability, and analytical ability. The general sections do not penalize for guessing. Complete every item whether you are sure of an answer or not.

Antonyms

Although antonym questions test knowledge of vocabulary more directly than do any of the other verbal question types, the purpose of the antonym questions is to measure not merely the strength of one's vocabulary but also the ability to reason from a given concept to its opposite.

<u>Directions:</u> The question below consists of a word printed in capital letters followed by five lettered words or phrases. Choose the lettered word or phrase that is most nearly <u>opposite</u> in meaning to the word in capital letters. Since some of the questions require you to distinguish fine shades of meaning, be sure to consider all the choices before deciding which one is best.

PARSIMONIOUS :   (A) initial   (B) vegetative   (C) prodigal   (D) affluent   (E) impromptu

The answer to this question is (C); *parsimonious* means "frugal to the point of stinginess," and *prodigal*, which means "extravagant to the point of wastefulness," is the only answer choice opposite in meaning. At first, answer choice (D), *affluent*, may seem plausible in that it may be thought that wealth is an opposite concept to frugality—but it is well known that not all wealthy persons are generous.

Analogies

Analogy questions test the ability to recognize relationships among words and the concepts they represent and to recognize when these relationships are parallel.

<u>Directions:</u> In each of the following questions, a related pair of words or phrases is followed by five lettered pairs of words or phrases. Select the lettered pair that best expresses a relationship similar to that expressed in the original pair.

COLOR : SPECTRUM ::   (A) tone : scale   (B) sound : waves   (C) verse : poem   (D) dimension : space   (E) cell : organism

The relationship between *color* and *spectrum* is not merely that of part to whole, in which case (E) or even (C) might be defended as correct. A *spectrum* is made up of a progressive, graduated series of colors, as a *scale* is of a progressive, graduated sequence of tones. Thus, (A) is correct. Here, the best answer must be selected from a group of fairly close choices.

Sentence completions

The sentence completion questions measure the ability to recognize words or phrases that both logically and stylistically complete the meaning of a sentence.

<u>Directions:</u> The sentences below have two blanks, each blank indicating that something has been omitted. Beneath the sentence are five lettered words or sets of words. Choose the word or set of words for each blank that <u>best</u> fits the meaning of the sentence as a whole.

Early ------- of hearing loss is ------- by the fact that the other senses are able to compensate for moderate amounts of loss, so that people frequently do not know that their hearing is imperfect.

(A) discovery . . indicated
(B) development . . prevented
(C) detection . . complicated
(D) treatment . . facilitated
(E) incidence . . corrected

The statement that other senses compensate for partial loss of hearing indicates that hearing loss is not *prevented* or *corrected*, eliminating choices (B) and (E). The ability to compensate for hearing loss does not facilitate early *treatment* (D) or early *discovery* (A) of hearing loss. It is reasonable, however, that early *detection* of hearing loss is *complicated* by the ability to compensate for it. The correct answer is (C).

The ------- science of seismology has grown just enough so that the first overly bold theories have been -------.

(A) magnetic . . accepted
(B) fledgling . . refuted
(C) revolutionary . . analyzed
(D) predictive . . protected
(E) exploratory . . recalled

At first reading, there may appear to be several answer choices that make sense when substituted in the blanks of the sentence. (A) and (D) can be dismissed fairly readily when it is seen that *accepted* and *protected* are not compatible with *overly bold* in the sentence. The sentence yielded by (C) is logically more acceptable but not as strong as the sentences yielded by (B) and (E). Of these two latter choices, (B) is superior on stylistic grounds: theories are not *recalled* (E), and *fledgling* (B) reflects the idea of growth present in the sentence.

Taking Major Tests   349

Quantitative comparison

The quantitative comparison questions test the ability to reason quickly and accurately about the relative sizes of two quantities or to perceive that not enough information is provided to make such a decision.

Directions: The following question consists of two quantities, one in Column A and one in Column B. You are to compare the two quantities and choose

A if the quantity in Column A is greater;
B if the quantity in Column B is greater;
C if the two quantities are equal;
D if the relationship cannot be determined from the information given.

Note: Since there are only four choices, NEVER MARK (E).

Common
Information: In a question, information concerning one or both of the quantities to be compared is centered under the two columns. A symbol that appears in both columns represents the same thing in Column A as it does in Column B.

	Column A	Column B
	$(273 \times 87) + q = 29{,}235$	
	$(273 \times 87) + p = 30{,}063$	
1.	p	q

It is unnecessary to do much computation to solve this problem. The sum of a number and q is less than the sum of the same number and p. Therefore $q < p$, and the answer is A.

	Column A	Column B
	$x^2 = y^2 + 1$	
2.	x	y

From the given equation, it can be determined that $x^2 > y^2$; however, the relative sizes of x and y cannot be determined. For example, if $y = 0$, x could be 1 or -1 and, since there is no way to tell which number x is, the answer is D.

	Column A	Column B
3.	$(-6)^4$	$(-6)^5$

Since $(-6)^4$ is the product of four negative factors and the product of an even number of negative numbers is positive, $(-6)^4$ is positive. Since the product of an odd number of negative numbers is negative, $(-6)^5$ is negative. Therefore $(-6)^4$ is greater than $(-6)^5$ since any positive number is greater than any negative number. The correct answer is A. Do not waste time determining that $(-6)^4 = 1{,}296$ and that $(-6)^5 = -7{,}776$. This information is not needed to make the comparison.

Discrete quantitative

Each question contains all information needed for answering it except for the basic mathematical knowledge assumed common to the backgrounds of examinees.

Directions: Each of the following questions has five answer choices. For each of these questions, select the best of the answer choices given.

The average of x and y is 20. If $z = 5$, what is the average of x, y, and z?

(A) $8\frac{1}{3}$ (B) 10 (C) $12\frac{1}{2}$ (D) 15 (E) $17\frac{1}{2}$

Since the average of x and y is 20, $\frac{x+y}{2} = 20$ or $x + y = 40$. Thus $x + y + z = x + y + 5 = 40 + 5 = 45$ and therefore $\frac{x+y+z}{3} = \frac{45}{3} = 15$. The correct answer is (D).

Several years ago, Minnesota produced $\frac{2}{3}$ and Michigan $\frac{1}{6}$ of all the iron ore produced in the United States. If all the other states combined produced 18 million tons in a year, how many million tons did Minnesota produce that year?

(A) 27 (B) 36 (C) 54 (D) 72 (E) 162

Since Minnesota produced $\frac{2}{3}$ and Michigan $\frac{1}{6}$ of all the iron ore produced in the United States, the two states together produced $\frac{5}{6}$ of the iron ore. Therefore, the 18 million tons produced by the rest of the United States was $\frac{1}{6}$ of the total production. Thus, total United States production was $6 \cdot 18 = 108$ million tons, and Minnesota produced $\frac{2}{3}(108) = 72$ million tons. The correct answer is (D).

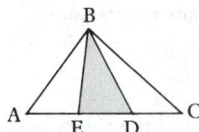

In the figure above, if $AE = ED = DC$ and the area of the shaded region is 5, what is the area of $\triangle ABC$?

(A) 10 (B) 12.5 (C) 15 (D) 20 (E) 25

In this problem, the shaded triangular region has a base that is $\frac{1}{3}$ that of $\triangle ABC$ and has the same height as $\triangle ABC$. Therefore, the area of the shaded region is $\frac{1}{3}$ the area of $\triangle ABC$, and the area of $\triangle ABC = 3(5) = 15$. The answer is (C).

Publications containing current information about the GRE may be obtained from your school guidance office, or from:
  Graduate Record Examinations
  CN 6000
  Princeton, NJ 08541-6000

Taking Major Tests

Analytical reasoning

Analytical reasoning questions test the ability to understand a given structure of arbitrary relationships among fictitious persons, places, things, or events; to deduce new information from the relationships given; and to assess the conditions used to establish the structure of relationships.

To apply to college a student must see the school counselor, obtain a transcript at the transcript office, and obtain a recommendation from Teacher A or Teacher B.

A student must see the counselor before obtaining a transcript.

The counselor is available only Friday mornings and Tuesday, Wednesday, and Thursday afternoons.

The transcript office is open only Tuesday and Wednesday mornings, Thursday afternoons, and Friday mornings.

Teacher A is available only Monday and Wednesday mornings.

Teacher B is available only Monday afternoons and Friday mornings.

A student has already seen the counselor and does not care from which teacher she obtains her recommendation. Which of the following is a complete and accurate list of those days when she could possibly complete the application process in one day?

(A) Friday (B) Monday, Wednesday
(C) Monday, Friday (D) Wednesday, Friday
(E) Monday, Wednesday, Friday

To complete the application process in one day, the student has to obtain a transcript and a recommendation on the same day. This will be possible on Wednesdays, when both the transcript office and Teacher A are accessible, and on Fridays, when both the transcript office and Teacher B are accessible, and at no other time. The only other day a teacher recommendation can be obtained is Monday, but on Mondays no transcripts can be obtained. Thus, the correct answer is (D).

A student completed his application procedure in one day. Which of the following statements must be true?

I. He obtained his recommendation from Teacher A.
II. He obtained his recommendation from Teacher B.
III. He completed the procedure in the morning.

(A) I only (B) II only (C) III only
(D) I and III only (E) II and III only

If a student completed the entire application procedure in a single day, that day must have been a Friday. It could not have been a Monday, since on Mondays neither counselor nor transcript office is accessible. It could not have been either a Tuesday or a Thursday, because on neither of these days would a teacher have been available for a recommendation. And it could not have been a Wednesday because on Wednesdays one cannot see the counselor before obtaining a transcript. Now, given that the student in question must have done everything on a Friday, I must be false since Teacher A is not available on Fridays, II must be true since Teacher B is both available on Fridays and the only teacher to be so available, and III must also be true since on Fridays all of the relevant business can be conducted only in the morning. Therefore, the correct answer is (E).

Logical reasoning

Logical reasoning questions test the ability to understand, analyze, and evaluate arguments. Some of the abilities tested by specific questions include recognizing the point of an argument, recognizing assumptions on which an argument is based, drawing conclusions from given premises, inferring material missing from given passages, applying principles governing one argument to another, identifying methods of argument, evaluating arguments and counterarguments, and analyzing evidence.

There is no reason to rule out the possibility of life on Uranus. We must, then, undertake the exploration of that planet.

The argument above assumes that

(A) life exists on Uranus
(B) Uranus is the only other planet in the solar system capable of supporting life
(C) Uranian life would be readily recognizable as life
(D) the search for life is a sufficient motive for space exploration
(E) no one has previously proposed the exploration of Uranus

The argument is based on the weak claim that there is a possibility that life may exist on Uranus and not on the stronger claim that life on Uranus actually exists; since logically weak claims do not presuppose logically stronger claims, (A) is not an assumption. (B) is likewise readily eliminated since the author's argument is presented as independent of any comparison of Uranus with other planets. (E) is also clearly not the correct answer: There is no hint in the argument that its author takes it to be a novel one or takes its conclusion to be a novel one. (C) comes closer to being an assumption of the argument: If the mere possibility of the existence of life on Uranus is taken as an impetus for exploration, we can safely conclude that a major aim of any such exploration would be to ascertain whether or not there actually was life on Uranus. But this search for life does not presuppose that the techniques scientists on Earth have for detecting life will be adequate for recognizing possibly alien life forms in every case. Even less is it presupposed that this task will be relatively easy. So (C) cannot be an assumption of the argument. The correct answer is (D), for, if (D) is true, the mere possibility of there being life on Uranus is indeed a compelling reason for the exploration of the planet.

Taking Major Tests

Review of French Grammar

- Articles 352
- Pronouns and adjectives 354
- Verbs 360
- Numbers, dates, time 368
- French-English dictionary 370
- English-French dictionary 375

French grammar shares certain characteristics with English grammar, as you may recall from the time when you first studied these languages. For the most part, the names of the parts of speech and the terms used to show how words function in a sentence are the same. If you have any difficulty in recalling the meanings of any words used in this chapter, consult the dictionary in volume 2 of the Student Handbook. No matter how long you have been away from the formal study of French, you will quickly find yourself recalling what you once knew.

Articles

Definite articles

Nouns normally are preceded by a definite or indefinite article or by another introductory word. The uses of the definite article *(le, la, les, l')* are shown in the following examples.

Before a noun used in a general or abstract sense.
  L'argent ne fait pas le bonheur.
  Money does not make for happiness.

Articles

	Singular Masc.	Fem.	Plural Both genders
Definite	le, l'	la, l'	les
Indefinite	un, de	une, de	des

With a title of office or profession followed by a name, except in direct address.
  Le président Mitterrand. President Mitterrand.
With proper nouns that are modified.
  La pauvre Louise. Poor Louise.
With the name of a language, except immediately after *parler* and after *en.*
  Il apprend l'italien. He is learning Italian.
  Il parle italien. He speaks Italian.
  en italien in Italian
In the singular, with days of the week, to show regularly repeated action.
  Il vient ici le mardi et le jeudi.
  He comes here on Tuesdays and Thursdays.
With names of seasons and colors.
  L'été est la plus chaude des saisons.
  Summer is the hottest of the seasons.

Le rose ne vous va pas bien.
Pink does not suit you.

To express "in" with a part of the day.
Le matin je me lève de bonne heure.
In the morning I get up early.

With nouns of weight and measure to express "a," "an," or "per."
trente-cinq francs le kilo
thirty-five francs a kilo

quinze francs la bouteille
fifteen francs a bottle

Cette soie coûte cent francs le mètre.
This silk costs one hundred francs a meter.

To express frequency of occurrence, *par* is used.
deux fois par an twice a year

With place names, except names of cities.
le Japon, l'Amérique, l'Asie Japan, America, Asia

To express "in," "to," and "from" with names of countries and continents.

For all European countries (except Belgium, Luxembourg, and the Netherlands) and all countries and continents whose names are feminine singular.

For "to" and "in," use *en* and omit the article.
For "from," use *de* and omit the article.
J'ai voyagé en Espagne. I have traveled in Spain.
Je reviens d'Espagne. I am returning from Spain.

With countries whose names are plural and all countries outside of Europe whose names are masculine singular.

For "to" and "in," use *à* and the article (*à le = au*).
For "from," use *de* and the article (*de le = du*).
Nous allons au Canada, au Mexique, au Japon.
We are going to Canada, Mexico, and Japan.

Nous revenons du Canada, du Mexique, du Japon.
We are coming back from Canada, Mexico, and Japan.

With names of parts of the body, and often with articles of clothing, when the possessor is clear.
Elle m'a donné la main.
She gave me her hand.

Il avait le chapeau sur la tête.
He had his hat on his head.

Indefinite articles

The indefinite article (*un, une, de, des*) is omitted before an unmodified noun denoting nationality, profession, religion, etc.

Nationality.
Est-il américain? Is he an American?
Profession.
Il est étudiant et il voudrait devenir acteur.
He is a student and would like to become an actor.
Religion.
Êtes-vous protestant? Are you a Protestant?
Before nouns in apposition.
M. Durand, professeur de français
Mr. Durand, a French teacher
Before the numbers *cent* and *mille*.
cent fois a hundred times
mille baisers a thousand kisses
After an exclamatory adjective (*quel, quelle,* etc.).
Quelle fraise délicieuse!
What a delicious strawberry!
In numerical titles of monarchs.
Henri Quatre Henry the Fourth
If a noun is modified, the article must be used.
C'est un acteur célèbre.
He is a famous actor.

Partitives

A partitive (*de, de la, de l', du, des*) corresponds to "some" or "any," whether expressed or not. *Des* may express either the partitive plural or indefinite plural.

Singular.
Il a un crayon. He has a pencil.
La carotte est un légume. The carrot is a vegetable.
Plural.
Il a des crayons.
He has pencils.

On cultive des légumes de toutes sortes en France.
They grow vegetables of all kinds in France.
Partitive.
Donnez-lui du pain. Give him some bread.
Avez-vous du sucre? Do you have any sugar?
Il a acheté des légumes. He bought vegetables.

Review of French Grammar

Uses of *de*
Without the article after a negative expression.
Elle ne fait pas de fautes.
She does not make mistakes.
When an adjective precedes the noun.
J'ai vu de beaux papillons.
I saw some beautiful butterflies.
After expressions of quantity.
Il a beaucoup de cousins. He has many cousins.

With adverbs of quantity
The following adverbs of quantity, with certain exceptions, take only *de*.

assez	enough
autant	as much, as many
beaucoup	much, many, a lot
combien	how much, how many
moins	less
peu	little, few
plus	more
tant	so much, so many
trop	too much, too many

The partitive is omitted after *sans* and *ni . . . ni*.
Il n'y a pas de rose sans épines.
There are no roses without thorns.
Il n'a ni frères ni soeurs.
He has neither brothers nor sisters.

The partitive is omitted after expressions that normally take *de*: *avoir besoin de* "to need," *se passer de* "to get along without," *se servir de* "to use," *se souvenir de* "to remember," *s'approcher de* "to approach," *remplir de* "to fill with," *couvrir de* "to cover with."
Elle ne peut pas se passer de sucre.
She cannot get along without sugar.
Elle a besoin de secours.
She needs help.

If the noun is omitted, the idea of "some" or "any" is expressed by the pronoun *en*.
Avez-vous des amis? Oui, j'en ai.
Have you any friends? Yes, I have some.
Avez-vous besoin de votre voiture? Oui, j'en ai besoin.
Do you need your car? Yes, I need it.

Pronouns and adjectives

Personal pronouns

Pronoun-verb order
Personal object pronouns directly precede the verb, except in affirmative commands. In the *affirmative imperative*, object pronouns are placed directly after the verb and are linked to it by hyphens. The pronouns *me* and *te* become *moi* and *toi* after the verb, but when followed by *en*, they become *m'* and *t'*.
Me réveillez-vous? Are you waking me up?
Ne les a-t-il pas réveillés? Didn't he wake them up?
Ne les réveillez pas. Do not wake them up.
Réveillons-la. Let's wake her up.
Réveillez-moi. Wake me up.

Double object pronouns, like single object pronouns, as well as *y* and *en*, directly precede the verb, except in the case of the affirmative imperative where they follow the verb.
Je compte la lui raconter. I propose to tell it to him.
Tu me la prêtes. You lend it to me.
Il les y a trouvés. He found them there.

Forms of personal pronouns

Conjunctive				Disjunctive
Subject	Direct object	Indirect object	Reflexive	
je (j')	me (m')	me (m')	me (m')	moi
tu	te (t')	te (t')	te (t')	toi
il	le (l')	lui	se (s')	lui
elle	la (l')	lui	se (s')	elle
nous	nous	nous	nous	nous
vous	vous	vous	vous	vous
ils	les	leur	se (s')	eux
elles	les	leur	se (s')	elles

Order of personal pronouns

me	before	le	before	lui	before	y	before	en
te		la		leur			before verb	
se		les						
nous								
vous								

Tu me la prêtes

Il n'en a pas besoin. He does not need any.
Il nous les a donnés. He gave them to us.
Donnez-le-moi. Give it to me.
Donnez-m'en. Give me some.

Uses of disjunctive pronouns

After a preposition.
   avant toi before you
   sans lui without him
   derrière eux behind them
   pour elle for her
When there is no verb.
   pas moi not I

   Qui l'a dérangé? Elle.
   Who disturbed him? She.

   Il a plus d'argent qu'eux.
   He has more money than they.
As a complement after *être*.
   C'est lui. It is he.   *C'est moi.* It is I.
   C'est elle. It is she.   *Ce sont eux.* It is they.
For emphasis.
   Lui, il l'a fait. He did it.
   Elles ne l'aiment pas, lui. They don't like him.
When a subject or object is separated from its verb.
   Lui seul peut le dire. He alone can say it.
   Il n'a vu ni lui ni elle. He saw neither him nor her.
With two subjects, objects, or indirect objects.
   Lui et moi nous sommes partis hier.
   He and I left yesterday.

   Je vous ai vus, vous et elle.
   I saw you and her.
With *même* or *mêmes* for emphasis.
   Je l'ai fait moi-même.
   I did it myself.

   Ils y sont allés eux-mêmes.
   They went there themselves.

Forms of relative pronouns

qui	as subject of the verb: who or which
que	as direct object of the verb: whom, which, or that
lequel, laquelle lesquels, lesquelles	as object of a preposition: whom or which
qui quoi dont	whose, of whom, of which

Relative pronouns

Qui is used as subject of the verb of a relative clause.
   C'est l'enfant qui a fait cela.
   It is the child that did that.

   C'est le livre qui est sur la table.
   It is the book that is on the table.
Que is used as direct object of the verb of a relative clause.
   C'est la femme que vous connaissez.
   It is the woman you know.

   Ce sont les livres que vous m'avez donnés.
   These are the books you gave me.
Lequel, laquelle, lesquels, and *lesquelles* agree in gender and number with their antecedents. *Lequel, lesquels,* and *lesquelles* contract with the preposition *à* into *auquel, auxquels,* and *auxquelles;* with the preposition *de* into *duquel, desquels,* and *desquelles. Laquelle* does not combine.
For persons, *qui* is generally preferred to *lequel, laquelle,* etc.
   Où sont les messieurs avec qui vous parliez?
   Where are the gentlemen with whom you were talking?
For things, a form of *lequel* has to be used.
   La voiture auprès de laquelle il était lui appartient.
   The car he was near belongs to him.
The invariable *dont* combines the sense of *de* plus a relative pronoun (*qui, lequel, quoi*).
   le garçon dont le père est médecin
   the boy whose father is a doctor

   le crayon dont je me sers
   the pencil I am using
The order of words in a relative clause is *dont* (or *duquel, de laquelle,* etc.) + subject + verb + object. To avoid mistakes in translation of sentences with the relative "whose," replace "whose" with "of whom," "of which," "from which," "in which."
   un livre dont j'ai oublié le titre
   a book whose title I have forgotten
Où may serve as an adverb replacing *à, en, dans, sur,* plus *lequel,* when the antecedent is a noun of place.
   la maison où j'habite
   the house in which I live

   le trottoir où la neige tombait
   the sidewalk on which the snow was falling

   le village d'où je viens
   the village from which I come
The words "which," "what," and "that" (= a thing *which,* the thing *which,* that *which*) may be translated as follows:
ce qui, subject of a verb
   Ce qui est sur la table est à moi.
   What is on the table belongs to me.

Review of French Grammar

ce que, direct object of a verb
  Ce que tu m'as dit est un secret.
  What you told me is a secret.
ce dont, used with expressions taking *de*
  Comprends-tu ce dont il parle?
  Do you understand what he is talking about?
ce à quoi, used with expressions taking *à*
  Personne ne pouvait deviner ce à quoi je pensais.
  No one could guess what I was thinking of.

Interrogatives

Qui a cassé la tasse?
Qui est-ce qui a cassé la tasse?
Who broke the cup?

Qui regardez-vous?
Qui est-ce que vous regardez?
Whom are you looking at?

Avec qui parle-t-il?
Avec qui est-ce qu'il parle?
With whom is he talking?

De quoi est-ce qu'il parle?
A quoi pensez-vous?
What is he talking about?
What are you thinking of?

When *à* and *de* are used with forms of *lequel,* the usual contractions take place.
  Laquelle de ces filles est la vôtre?
  Which of these girls is yours?

  Auquel de ces garçons avez-vous parlé?
  To which one of these boys did you speak?

Quel (quelle, quels, quelles) is the interrogative adjective "which" or "what."
  Quelle robe as-tu choisie?
  Which dress did you choose?

  Quel livre lisez-vous?
  What book are you reading?

Possessives

Adjectives and pronouns agree in gender and number with the object possessed.
  Il a pris mon livre et le sien.
  He took his book and mine.

  Il emmène sa fille et la mienne.
  He is taking his daughter and mine.

  Son père est plus sévère que le nôtre.
  Her father is stricter than ours.

With parts of the body, the possessive adjective is often replaced by the definite article if the identity of the possessor is clear.
  Elle s'est coupé le doigt.
  She cut her finger.

  Elles se sont lavé les mains.
  They washed their hands.

The definite article preceding the possessive pronoun contracts after *à* and *de.*
  Cette valise est-elle aux (not *à les*) *enfants?*
  Is this suitcase the children's?

  Non, elle est aux filles.
  No, it's the girls'.

Idiomatic expressions with possessives.
  un de mes voisins
  a neighbor of mine

  bonjour ma tante
  good morning, aunt

  une de ses soeurs
  one of his sisters

  Dites-leur bonjour de ma part.
  Say hello to them for me.

  Serez-vous des nôtres?
  Will you join us?

The word "own" is expressed by *propre.*
  Il l'a écrit de sa propre main.
  He wrote it with his own hand.

Forms of interrogative pronouns

	Subject	Direct object	Object of preposition
persons	*qui* who *qui est-ce qui* who	*qui* whom *qui est-ce que* whom	*qui* whom
things	*qu'est-ce qui* what	*que* what *qu'est-ce que* what	*quoi* what
persons and things	*lequel,* etc. which *and* which one	*lequel,* etc. which *and* which one	*lequel,* etc. which *and* which one
after prepositions	*qui*	*quoi*	

Demonstratives

The following examples illustrate the uses of demonstrative adjectives.

cet avion this or that	airplane
ce livre	book
cette robe	dress
ces avions these or those	airplanes
ces livres	books
ces robes	dresses

Uses of -ci, -là, etc.

In principle *-ci* refers to the nearest object, *-là* to the farthest, but this distinction is not strictly observed unless objects are contrasted.

Comment trouvez-vous ces maisons?
How do you like these (those) houses?

Je préfère cette maison-ci, celle-là est trop grande.
I like this house better; that one is too big.

With demonstrative pronouns, *-ci* or *-là* must be added when the pronoun is not followed by a relative clause or by a prepositional complement. *Celui, celle, ceux,* and *celles* cannot be used alone.

Quelle route faut-il prendre?
What road must we take?

Celle-ci ou celle-là?
This one or that one?

Prenons celle de droite.
Let's take the one on the right.

Ceci, cela, ça, and *ce* are invariable demonstrative pronouns.

ceci this, it	*ça* this, that, it
cela that, it	*ce* it

Ne prenez pas ceci, prenez cela.
Do not take this; take that.

Ça ne fait rien.
It does not matter.

Ceci or *cela* must be used instead of *ce* when emphasis is desired and when "this" and "that" are contrasted

Forms of demonstratives

	Adjectives		Pronouns	
	Singular	*Plural*	*Singular*	*Plural*
Masc.	ce (before a consonant) cet (before a vowel)	ces	celui	ceux
Fem.	cette	ces	celle	celles

and the pronoun is separated from the verb by any word other than *ne*.

Ceci est correct, cela ne l'est pas.
This is correct; that is not.

Cela n'est pas vrai.
That is not true.

The neuter demonstrative *ce* is used as the subject of *être* (or *devoir* or *pouvoir être*) only in four instances.

1. When *être* is followed by an adjective, *ce* designates something not previously named, or refers to a thought expressed or understood, or refers to a statement.

   Paris est une grande ville; c'est la plus belle du monde.
   Paris is a beautiful city; it is the most beautiful in the world.

   Ce devait être interressant.
   It must have been interesting.

2. When a noun or pronoun follows *être*.
   Ce doit être celle de mon frère.
   It must be my brother's.

3. When an antecedent is *ceci* or *cela*.
   Goûtez ceci. C'est très bon.
   Taste this. It is very good.

4. When *être* is followed by an adverb or complement.
   Ce n'est pas assez. It is not enough.

Forms of possessive adjectives

	Singular		Plural
	Masc.	*Fem.*	
my	mon	ma	mes
your	ton	ta	tes
his, her, its	son	sa	ses
our	notre	notre	nos
your	votre	votre	vos
their	leur	leur	leurs

Note: Use *mon, ton, son* instead of *ma, ta, sa* before a word beginning with a vowel or a silent *h*.

Forms of possessive pronouns

	Singular		Plural	
	Masc.	*Fem.*	*Masc.*	*Fem.*
mine	le mien	la mienne	les miens	les miennes
yours	le tien	la tienne	les tiens	les miennes
his, hers, its	le sien	la sienne	les siens	les siennes
ours	le nôtre	la nôtre	les nôtres	les nôtres
yours	le vôtre	la vôtre	les vôtres	les vôtres
theirs	le leur	la leur	les leurs	les leurs

Review of French Grammar

Indefinites

Uses of *on*
To translate the indefinite "one," "we," "you," "they," or "people" when there is no definite antecedent.

On n'est pas toujours heureux.
One is not always happy.

On ne sait jamais.
You never know.

On ne fait pas cela ici.
People don't do that here.

Il faut qu'on se dépêche.
We must hurry.

On ne doit pas toujours parler de soi.
One must not speak always about himself.

On répare notre voiture.
Our car is being repaired.

Ici on ne sera pas dérangés.
Here we will not be disturbed.

Uses of *quelque*
Quelque and *quelques* are adjectives. In using these words there is no agreement in gender or elision of the final *-e* in the singular. *Quelque* and *quelques* are slightly more specific than the partitive.

On va acheter quelques pommes.
We are going to buy some apples.

Quelqu'un, quelqu'une, quelques uns, and *quelques unes* are the corresponding pronouns.

Quelqu'un l'a cassé.
Someone broke it.

Donnez-moi quelques unes de vos fleurs.
Give me some of your flowers.

Quelque chose, a pronoun meaning "something" or "anything," is followed by *de* before an adjective. It does not require agreement in gender.

Y a-t-il quelque chose qui manque?
Is anything missing?

Oui, il y a quelque chose qui manque.
Yes, something is missing.

Similarly with *pas grand'chose* "little," *autre chose* "something else," and *peu de chose* "little," or "not much."

Common indefinite adjectives and pronouns
Plusieurs, plural adjective and pronoun meaning "several." It shows no agreement for gender.

Nous y sommes allés plusieurs fois.
We went there several times.

J'en ai vu plusieurs.
I saw several of them.

Chaque, singular pronoun meaning "each" or "every." It shows no agreement for gender, no elision.

Chaque artiste est orgueilleux de son oeuvre.
Every artist is proud of his work.

Chacun and *chacune*, singular pronouns meaning "each" or "each one."

Chacun a ses propres traditions.
Each one has its own traditions.

Tout, toute, tous, and *toutes*, pronouns and adjectives meaning "all," "entire," and "every." In the singular (*tout, toute*) without an article, these words mean "every"; with the article, "the whole." In the plural (*tous, toutes*), these words are always accompanied by an article or similar word. As adjectives they precede the noun and the article. These words are never followed by *de*.

Tout chemin mène à Rome.
Every road leads to Rome.

Toutes les bêtes s'étaient sauvées.
All the animals had escaped.

Tous les hommes avaient embarqué.
All the men had embarked.

Tous avaient embarqué.
All had embarked.

Tel, telle, tels, telles, adjectives and pronouns meaning "such," "similar," and "the like." *Tel* as an adjective agrees in gender and number with the noun it modifies. It is preceded by an indefinite article or partitive (*un, une, de*) when *tel* does not introduce a comparison.

Il ne s'attendait pas à une telle chance.
He did not expect such luck.

Tel père tel fils.
Like father like son.

Un and *une* are pronouns only in two constructions:
1. When followed by *de* as one of the objects or persons indicated.
   Une de ces tasses est cassée.
   One of these cups is broken.
2. In contrast with *autre: l'un, l'autre; les uns, les autres.*
   Nous avons besoin l'un de l'autre.
   We need each other.

Même and *mêmes* are used as adjectives meaning "same" before a noun, or "very" or "itself" after a noun; as an adverb meaning "even."

à l'heure même il arrivait à Paris
at the very hour he was arriving in Paris

Ce n'est pas la même chose.
It is not the same thing.

Ce n'est même pas vrai.
It is not even true.

Quiconque, a pronoun meaning "anyone who" or "whoever."

Quiconque le fera sera récompensé.
Whoever does it will be rewarded.

Quelconque, an adjective meaning "any," "of whatever sort," and "no matter what," as an attributive or predicate adjective, meaning "ordinary."

Cette femme est quelconque.
This woman is common.

Donnez-moi un crayon quelconque.
Give me any pencil at all.

Qui que, quoi que, quel que, relative pronouns and adjectives combined with *que* and followed by the subjunctive have an all inclusive sense, and are translated as follows: *qui que ce soit* "whoever it may be," *quoi que ce soit* "whatever it may be," *quel que soit* "whatever," as in *quel que soit l'heure,* "whatever the time." These expressions are the most emphatic forms of *quelque chose* and *quelqu'un.*

Si vous dîtes quoi que ce soit à qui que ce soit, vous le regretterez.
If you say anything at all (whatever it may be) to anyone (without exception, whoever it may be), you will regret it.

Negation

Negation is expressed by *ne* before the verb plus the second part of a negative expression after it. The principal negative expressions are shown here in two groups.

Group A
ne . . . que	only, none but
ne . . . ni . . . ni	neither . . . nor
ne . . . personne	nobody
ne . . . aucun	no, none, not any

Group B
ne . . . pas	not
ne . . . point	not (less common than ne . . . pas)
ne . . . guère	hardly, scarcely
ne . . . plus	no more, no longer
ne . . . jamais	never
ne . . . rien	nothing

Placement of the negative expression

In a declarative sentence with a verb in a simple tense, the two parts of the negative are placed before and after the verb.

Elle ne mange pas. She does not eat.
Il n'est pas ici. He is not here.

With compound tenses, the two parts of the negative of Group A expressions are placed before and after the auxiliary verb *(avoir* or *être).*

Je n'ai jamais fait cela. I have never done that.
Il n'a guère mangé. He scarcely ate.

With compound tenses, the two parts of the negative of Group B expressions are placed before and after the complete verb.

Il n'a lu aucun de ces livres.
He read none of these books.

Il n'a vu personne.
He saw no one.

Additional rules of negation

Only conjunctive and reflexive object pronouns *(me, te, le, lui, nous, vous, les, leur, se, y, en)* can come between *ne* and the verb.

Il ne lui parle pas. He does not speak to him.
Elle ne les a pas vus. She did not see them.

Ne . . . aucun!
Ne . . . jamais!

When the negative is used with an infinitive, both parts come before the infinitive and its pronoun objects, if any.

Il a promis de ne plus la voir.
He promised not to see her again.

The *que* of *ne . . . que* immediately precedes the word it modifies.

Je n'ai acheté que deux livres.
I bought only two books.

Je n'ai parlé qu'à lui seul.
I spoke only to him.

Personne, rien, and *aucun* may be used as subjects and as objects of verbs as well as objects of prepositions. *Ne* must not be omitted.

Personne ne peut faire cela. No one can do that.
Aucun n'est venu. No one came.
Je n'ai rien entendu. I heard nothing.

Ne may sometimes be used without *pas* with the verbs *cesser, oser, savoir,* and *pouvoir,* especially when followed by an infinitive and in some expressions that imply hesitancy rather than definite negation.

Je n'ose le dire. I hardly dare say it.
Je ne saurais vous le dire. I couldn't tell you.
Elle ne cesse de parler. She does not stop talking.

Si must be used instead of *oui* in answering a negative question affirmatively.

Ne l'avez-vous pas vu? Haven't you seen it?
Si, je l'ai vu. Yes, I have.

Jamais used without *ne* means "ever."

A-t-on jamais vu pareille chose?
Has anyone ever seen such a thing?

Rien used without *ne* means "anything."

Y a-t-il rien de plus beau?
Is there anything lovelier?

Review of French Grammar

Verbs

Regular verbs
The infinitives of regular verbs end in *-er, -ir,* or *-re.* The examples shown here are *donner, finir,* and *rompre.*

Formation of tenses
The simple tenses of all regular verbs and most irregular verbs derive from four forms of the verb.

Conjugation of regular verbs

Formation of tenses

Use the *infinitive* to form:

Future
Infinitive plus -ai, -as, -a, -ons, -ez, -ont.
Example: *donner*ai

Conditional
Infinitive plus -ais, -ais, -ait, -ions, -iez, -aient.
Example: *donner*ais
In the third conjugation the final *e* is dropped.
Example: *rompr*ai

Use the *present participle* to form:

Imperfect indicative
Change *-ant* to -ais, -ais, ait, -ions, -iez, -aient.
Example: *donn*ais

Present subjunctive
Change *-ant* to -e, -es, -e, -ions, -iez, -ent.
Example: *donn*e

Moods

Indicative

Present
I give, finish, break
I do give, finish, break

				Imperfect I was giving, finishing, breaking		
je	donne	finis	romps	donnais	finissais	rompais
tu	donnes	finis	romps	donnais	finissais	rompais
il	donne	finit	romp	donnait	finissait	rompait
nous	donnons	finissons	rompons	donnions	finissions	rompions
vous	donnez	finissez	rompez	donniez	finissiez	rompiez
ils	donnent	finissent	rompent	donnaient	finissaient	rompaient

Conditional

Present
I should give, finish, break

je	donnerais	finirais	romprais
tu	donnerais	finirais	romprais
il	donnerait	finirait	romprait
nous	donnerions	finirions	romprions
vous	donneriez	finiriez	rompriez
ils	donneraient	finiraient	rompraient

Subjunctive

Present
that I give, finish, break

que je	donne	finisse	rompe
que tu	donnes	finisses	rompes
qu'il	donne	finisse	rompe
que nous	donnions	finissions	rompions
que vous	donniez	finissiez	rompiez
qu'ils	donnent	finissent	rompent

Don't forget to write

le 5 septembre, 1985.

Mon cher Georges,
    J'avais promis de vous mettre au courant de tout ce qui m'arriverait pendant mon séjour à New York. Je ne sais que trop bien que j'ai manqué de parole, car je serai de retour à Paris bientôt. Cependant, je vous prie de ne pas me tenir rigueur de ma négligence. J'ai été tellement occupé que c'est à peine si j'ai eu le temps d'écrire à mes parents.
    À bientôt.

Ton ami,
Robert

Infinitive	*-er*	*-ir*	*-re*
	donner	finir	rompre
	to give	to finish	to break

Participles			
Present	giving	finishing	breaking
	donnant	finissant	rompant
Past	given	finished	broken
	donné	fini	rompu

Imperative			
Singular	give	finish	break
	donne	finis	romps
Plural	let's give	let's finish	let's break
	donnons	finissons	rompons
	give	finish	break
	donnez	finissez	rompez

Use the *present indicative* to form:
Imperative
The pronoun subject is dropped from the second person singular and from the first and second person plural. The *-s* of the first conjugation is dropped except before *y* and *en*.
Example: *donne, donnons, donnez*

Use the *past definite* to form:
Imperfect subjunctive
Change the final *-i* or *-s* of the first person singular form to *-sse, -sses, -t, -ssions, -ssiez, -ssent*. A circumflex accent is placed over the last vowel of the third person singular.
Example: *donnât*

Past definite
I gave, finished, broke

donnai	finis	rompis
donnas	finis	rompis
donna	finit	rompit
donnâmes	finîmes	rompîmes
donnâtes	finîtes	rompîtes
donnèrent	finirent	rompirent

Future
I shall give, finish, break

donnerai	finirai	romprai
donneras	finiras	rompras
donnera	finira	rompra
donnerons	finirons	romprons
donnerez	finirez	romprez
donneront	finiront	rompront

September 5, 1985

Dear George,
   I had promised to tell you all the things that happened to me during my visit to New York. I know too well that I have broken my promise, but I shall be back in Paris soon. However, I hope you will not hold this against me. I have been so busy that I have not had time even to write to my parents.
   See you soon.

                    Your friend,
                    Robert

Review of French Grammar

Verbal spelling irregularities

Spelling changes often occur in regular verbs. These changes appear to be needed to retain the original sounds within the infinitive forms. As you will shortly see, for example, by adding a cedilla to *c*, the soft *c* of verbs ending in *cer* is retained before vowels that normally would make the *c* hard.

Spelling irregularities of regular verbs

Verb ending	*Change*	*Example Present participle*	*Present indicative*	*Imperfect indicative*	*Past definite*	*Imperfect subjunctive*
-cer *avancer* to advance	requires the soft *c* sound throughout the conjugation.	avançant	avance avançons	avançais avancions	avançai avançâmes	avançasse avançassions
-ger *manger* to eat	requires the soft *g*, so *g* followed by *a* or *o* becomes *ge*.	mangeant	mange mangeons	mangeais mangions	mangeai mangeâmes	mangeasse mangeassions

		Present indicative	*Future*	*Conditional*	*Present subjunctive*
-oyer **-uyer** *netoyer* to clean	*y* changes to *i* before *e* in conjugation, but not elsewhere.	nettoie, etc.	nettoierai	nettoierais	nettoie, etc.
-ayer **-eyer** *payer* to clean	may either retain *y* throughout, or change to *i* before *e*.	paye paie	payerai paierai	payerais paierais	paye paie
-er when unaccented and followed by a single consonant *mener* to lead	*e* changes to *è* when the ending begins with an unstressed *e*	mène mènes mène menons menez mènent	mènerai mèneras mènera mènerons mènerez mèneront	mènerais mènerais mènerait mènerions mèneriez mèneraient	mène mènes mène menions meniez mènent
-eter **-eler** (most verbs) *appeler* to call	the *l* or *t* is doubled to cause the first *e* to be stressed.	appelle appelles appelle appelons appelez appellent	appellerai appelleras appellera appellerons appellerez appelleront	appellerais appellerais appellerait appellerions appelleriez appelleraient	appelle appelles appelle appelions appeliez appellent
jeter to throw		jette	jetterai	jetterais	jette
-eter **-eler** (some verbs) *acheter* to buy	follows the rule for unaccented *e*, as in *mener* above.	achète	achèterai	achèterais	achète

362 **Review of French Grammar**

The auxiliary verbs

Avoir combines with the past participle to form the compound tenses of all transitive verbs and most intransitive verbs. Both *avoir* and *être* themselves are conjugated with *avoir*.

Il a eu besoin d'argent. He needed money.
Il a été malade. He was sick.
Il a acheté des fleurs. He bought some flowers.

Etre is used as the auxiliary to form
1. The compound tenses of all reflexive verbs.
    Elle s'est levée. She got up.
    Elles se sont assises. They sat down.
2. The passive voice.
    Elle est admirée de tous. She is admired by all.
3. The compound tenses of intransitive verbs and their derivatives that indicate motion or change of state:

aller	to go	venir	to come
arriver	to arrive	partir	to leave
entrer	to go in	sortir	to go out
monter	to go up	descendre	to go down
naître	to be born	mourir	to die
rester	to remain	retourner	to go back
tomber	to fall	devenir	to become

Certain normally instransitive verbs may also be used transitively, with a corresponding change in meaning. They are conjugated with *avoir* when used transitively.

J'ai descendu ma valise. I took down my suitcase.
Il a sorti les chaises. He took out the chairs.
Il a rentré les chaises. He took in the chairs.

When a verb that is not reflexive is conjugated with *être*, the participle agrees in gender and number with the subject.

Elle est partie ce soir. She left tonight.

When a verb is conjugated with *avoir*, the past participle agrees in gender and number with the direct object, if the direct object precedes the verb.

Il a acheté des fleurs et il les a données à sa mère.
He bought some flowers and gave them to his mother.

Les fleurs qu'il a achetées sont belles.
The flowers he bought are beautiful.

All reflexive verbs are conjugated with *être*. It sometimes is hard to determine whether the reflexive pronoun is the direct object or the indirect object of the verb. In the sentence, *Elle s'est coupée* (she cut herself) the reflexive pronoun, *se*, representing "herself" is the direct object. For this reason there is agreement of the past participle with the direct object. But if the sentence reads *Elle s'est coupé le doigt* (she cut her finger) the direct object is *doigt*. The reflexive pronoun is indirect, merely indicating the possessor. The verb may have but one direct object, so the past participle will not agree with *se*.

As another example, consider the following:

Les chemises qu'il s'est achetées sont belles.
The shirts he bought for himself are pretty.

In this case the preceding direct object is *que* (referring to *chemises*, feminine plural) and *se* is an indirect object. The agreement is with *que: achetées*.

Reflexive verbs may express reciprocal action, that is action which the individuals that are the subject of the verb perform upon each other.

Ils se sont parlé. They spoke to each other.

Auxiliary verbs

Infinitives		avoir to have	être to be
Participles	Present	ayant having	étant being
	Past	eu had	été been
Indicative	Present	j'ai	je suis
		tu as	tu es
		il a	il est
		nous avons	nous sommes
		vous avez	vous êtes
		ils ont	ils sont
	Imperfect	j'avais	j'étais
		tu avais	tu étais
		il avait	il était
		nous avions	nous étions
		vous aviez	vous étiez
		ils avaient	ils étaient
	Past definite	j'eus	je fus
		tu eus	tu fus
		il eut	il fut
		nous eûmes	nous fûmes
		vous eûtes	vous fûtes
		ils eurent	ils furent
	Future	j'aurai	je serai
		tu auras	tu seras
		il aura	il sera
		nous aurons	nous serons
		vous aurez	vous serez
		ils auront	ils seront

Review of French Grammar

Uses of verb tenses

Use the past indefinite when expressing simple past tense and when the verb expresses successive actions.

J'ai frappé à la porte et il me l'a ouverte.

I knocked at the door and he opened it for me.

Use the imperfect for past time only when the verb expresses:

1. A mental state.
   Je savais bien que tu connaissais la vie.
   I knew well that you understood life.
2. A condition, continuing action, or an action occurring while another action occurred.
   Je déjeunais quand il est entré.
   I was having lunch when he came in.
3. A repeated or habitual action.
   Je faisais les courses tous les matins.
   I used to do errands every morning.
4. A permanent characteristic.
   Le jardin était plein de fleurs.
   The garden was full of flowers.

The imperfect is used with *depuis* when the verb conveys an action begun in the past and continuing into a later time.

J'étais là depuis trois jours quand il est arrivé.

I had been there for three days when he arrived.

When an action begun in the past is described as continuing up to the present, the present is used with *depuis*.

Elle est ici depuis deux jours.

She has been here for two days.

Conditional sentences

A conditional sentence consists of two parts: a clause expressing a condition, and a clause expressing a result. When the result clause is in the future, the condition clause is in the present.

Si j'étudie, je réussirai à mon examen.

If I study, I will pass my exam.

When the result clause is in the conditional, the condition clause is in the imperfect.

Important irregular verbs

aller   *Present:* vais, vas, va, allons, allez, vont
Imperfect: allais, allais, allait, allions, alliez, allaient
Present participle: allant
Past participle: allé

Infinitive	Present indicative	Future	Present participle	Past participle
asseoir	assieds	assiérai	asseyant	assis
battre	bats	battrai	battant	battu
conduire	conduis	conduirai	conduisant	conduit
courir	cours	courrai	courant	couru
couvrir	couvre	couvrirai	couvrant	couvert
craindre	crains	craindrai	craignant	craignis
devoir	dois	devrai	devant	dû
dormir	dors	dormirai	dormant	dormi
écrire	écris	écrirai	écrivant	écrit
mentir	mens	mentirai	mentant	menti
mettre	mets	mettrai	mettant	mis
mourir	meurs	mourrai	mourant	mort
offrir	offre	offrirai	offrant	offert
partir	pars	partirai	partant	parti
recevoir	reçois	recevrai	recevant	reçu
sentir	sens	sentirai	sentant	senti
sortir	sors	sortirai	sortant	sorti
souffrir	souffre	souffrirai	souffrant	souffert
venir	viens	viendrai	venant	venu
vêtir	vêts	vêtirai	vêtant	vêtu

Si j'étais riche, je voyagerais beaucoup.
If I were rich, I would travel a lot.

The same rule applies to the auxiliaries of compound tenses.

*Si je n'étais pas sorti,
je n'aurais pas manqué mes amis.*
If I had not gone out,
I would not have missed my friends.

Clauses with *quand* etc.

The future is used after *quand, lorsque, dès que, aussitôt que,* and *tant que* if the action takes place at a future time.

Dès que j'aurai écrit cette lettre, je l'enverrai.
As soon as I have written this letter, I will send it.

Quand je parlerai français, j'irai en France.
When I speak French, I will go to France.

Uses of the infinitive

The infinitive may be used as the subject of a verb.

Réussir est très important.
To succeed is very important.

The infinitive may be used as a complement.

Tu n'arriveras pas à faire ce problème.
You will not succeed in working this problem.

The infinitive may be used after many prepositions to express the English present participle.

Il a passé deux jours sans dormir.
He spent two days without sleeping.

The preposition *après* is followed by a past infinitive. The past infinitive has two parts: an auxiliary *(avoir or être)* and the past participle of the verb.

Après avoir dîné, je suis allé au cinéma.
After eating, I went to the movies.

Most adjectives and nouns are followed by *de* before an infinitive, but a few common adjectives are followed by *à* before the infinitive: *habile, lent, prêt, premier, dernier,* and *seul.*

Il est prêt à partir.
He is ready to leave.

Elle est toujours la première à finir.
She is always the first one to finish.

When an infinitive is passive in meaning, it is preceded by *à.*

Elle avait encore tout son travail à faire.
She still had all her work to do.

Some verbs are followed directly by the infinitive without a preposition.

aimer mieux	to prefer	*oser*	to dare
aller	to go	*paraître*	to appear
compter	to intend	*pouvoir*	to be able to
croire	to believe	*préférer*	to prefer
désirer	to wish, want	*regarder*	to watch
devoir	to have to	*savoir*	to know
entendre	to hear	*sembler*	to seem
espérer	to hope	*souhaiter*	to wish
faire	to do	*venir*	to come
laisser	to allow, let	*voir*	to see

Some verbs require *à* before the infinitive, as in *apprendre à conduire,* learn to drive.

aider	to help	*renoncer*	to give up
apprendre	to learn	*réussir*	to succeed
arriver	to succeed	*s'amuser*	to enjoy
avoir	to have	*s'attendre*	to expect
chercher	to seek	*se décider*	to decide
commencer	to begin	*se mettre*	to start
enseigner	to teach	*tarder*	to delay
hésiter	to hesitate	*tenir*	to insist on
inviter	to invite	*venir*	to happen

The infinitive preceded by *à* is used with certain nouns to express function or purpose.

une salle à manger a dining room
une machine à laver a washing machine

Subjunctive

The subjunctive mood is used after certain verbs or expressions that indicate desire, doubt, emotion, necessity, or uncertainty. Verbs in the subjunctive are almost always used in dependent clauses. Such clauses are introduced usually by *que* but sometimes by a relative pronoun.

The present subjunctive is formed by dropping the *-ent* of the third person present indicative form and adding *-e, -es, -e, -ions, -iez, -ent.* These endings are the same for all verbs except *avoir* and *être.*

*avoir j'aie, tu aies, il ait,
        nous ayons, vous ayez, ils aient*

*être   je sois, tu sois, il soit,
        nous soyons, vous soyez, ils soient*

A few irregular verbs use only one irregular stem for all forms.

faire: je fasse . . .   pouvoir: je puisse . . .
falloir: il faille . . . savoir: je sache . . .

Nous cherchons quelqu'un qui puisse faire le travail.
We are looking for someone who can do the work.

Some irregular verbs form the present subjunctive by using one stem for the *nous* and *vous* forms (from the imperfect indicative) and one for the other forms. The most common verbs of this type are as follows.

aller	*que j'aille, tu ailles, il aille, nous allions, vous alliez, ils aillent*
boire	*que je boive, tu boives, il boive, nous buvions, vous buviez, ils boivent*
croire	*que je croie, tu croies, il croie, nous croyions, vous croyiez, ils croient*
devoir	*que je doive, tu doives, il doive, nous devions, vous deviez, ils doivent*
prendre	*que je prenne, tu prennes, il prenne, nous prenions, vous preniez, ils prennent*

Review of French Grammar

venir que je vienne, tu viennes, il vienne,
  nous venions, vous veniez, ils viennent

vouloir que je veuille, tu veuilles, il veuille,
  nous voulions, vous vouliez, ils veuillent

The subjunctive is used in a dependent clause when the subject of the dependent clause is different from the subject of the main clause.

Je veux qu'elle fasse sa chambre.
I want her to clean her room.

Je veux faire ma chambre.
I want to clean my room.

The subjunctive is used after certain expressions.
Emotion.

avoir peur	to be afraid
craindre	to fear
être content	to be happy
être désolé	to be sorry
être enchanté	to be delighted
être fâché	to be angry
être heureux	to be happy
être surpris	to be surprised
regretter	to be sorry
s'étonner	to be surprised

Il est fâché qu'elle ne soit pas rentrée.
He is angry that she has not returned.

Verbs of wishing, asking, commanding, permitting, or prohibiting.

aimer mieux	to prefer	permettre	to permit
défendre	to forbid	préférer	to prefer
demander	to ask	souhaiter	to wish
exiger	to demand	vouloir	to want
ordonner	to demand		

J'aime mieux qu'il fasse ses devoirs maintenant.
I prefer that he do his homework now.

Je ne crois pas qu'il puisse partir.
I do not think he can leave.

The subjunctive is used when the antecedent is modified by a superlative or by *premier, dernier,* or *seul.*

C'est le premier livre que nous ayons lu.
It is the first book we have read.

The subjunctive is used after certain conjunctions.

afin que	in order that
à moins que	unless
avant que	before
bien que	although
jusqu'à ce que	until
pour que	in order that
pourvu que	provided that
quoique	although

The subjunctive is also used with all conjunctions of condition except *si.*

Pourvu qu'il soit là à temps, c'est tout ce que je veux.
All I want is for him to be on time.
(As long as he is on time, that is all I want.)

Interrogation

There are several ways of changing a declarative sentence to an interrogative sentence.

By prefixing *est-ce que.* No change in word order is needed.

Ce livre est intéressant.
This book is interesting.

Est-ce que ce livre est intéressant?
Is this book interesting?

By inversion of subject and verb.

When the subject is a personal pronoun or *ce* or *on,* it follows the verb and is joined to it by a hyphen.

Est-il chez lui?
Is he at home?

Est-ce vrai?
Is it true?

Parle-t-on toujours d'elle?
Do people still speak of her?

When the subject is a noun, demonstrative pronoun, possessive pronoun, or indefinite pronoun, the subject precedes the verb and is repeated after it in the form of a pronoun.

Votre ami est-il parti? Has your friend left?
Les vôtres sont-ils ici? Are yours here?
Cela est-il vrai? Is that true?
Quel livre choisit-il? What book does he choose?

The noun subject need not be repeated in pronoun form when three conditions are met: (1) the sentence must be introduced by an interrogative adverb *(combien, comment, où, quand)*; (2) the verb must be in a simple tense: present, imperfect, future, conditional, or past definite; and (3) the verb must have neither an object nor a modifying phrase.

Combien coûte ce livre?
How much does this book cost?

Comment va votre soeur?
How is your sister?

When the verb is not a simple tense or has an object or adverbial phrase, subject and verb are inverted or *est-ce que* is used.

Pourquoi votre mère a-t-elle acheté ces fruits?
Why did your mother buy that fruit?

A quelle heure votre ami arrivera-t-il à la gare?
When will your friend arrive at the station?

For the traveler

Stores

la bijouterie	jewelry shop
la boucherie	butcher shop
la boulangerie	bakery
le bureau de tabac	tobacco shop
la charcuterie	delicatessen
le coiffeur pour dames	beauty parlor
le grand magasin	department store
la librairie	bookstore
la pâtisserie	pastry shop
la pharmacie	drugstore

English	French
Pardon me, sir, where is the tourist office?	*Pardon, Monsieur, où est le bureau de tourisme?*
It is there, to the right, next to door number 9.	*Il est là-bas, à droite à côté de la porte numéro 9.*
Thank you, sir. Goodbye.	*Merci, Monsieur. Au revoir.*
Good morning, miss. Could you please tell me if there is a good hotel, not very expensive, near here?	*Bonjour Mademoiselle, pourriez-vous m'indiquer un bon hôtel, pas très chère, et près d'ici s'il vous plaît?*
Do you speak English? I do not speak French.	*Parlez-vous anglais? Je ne parle pas français.*
I do not understand.	*Je ne comprends pas.*
Speak more slowly, please.	*Parlez plus lentement s'il vous plaît.*
What does that mean?	*Qu'est-ce que ça veut dire?*
A room for two, with bath.	*Une chambre pour deux personnes, avec salle de bain.*
It is expensive.	*C'est très cher.*
Is there a phone?	*Y a-t-il un téléphone?*
What time is breakfast?	*A quelle heure est le petit déjeuner?*
I would like to buy a summer dress.	*Je voudrais acheter une robe d'été.*
How much does it cost?	*Elle coûte combien?*
It is not expensive.	*Elle n'est pas chère.*
Taxi. Are you free? I want to go to the station.	*Taxi. Vous êtes libre? Je veux aller à la gare.*
Can you tell me where there is a good, inexpensive restaurant?	*Pouvez-vous me dire où il y a un bon restaurant pas trop cher?*
A table for two near the window please?	*Une table pour deux, près de la fenêtre, s'il vous plaît.*
Waiter. The menu, please.	*Garçon. La carte, s'il vous plaît.*
I will have antipasto, chicken, and French fries.	*Je prendrais des hors-d'oeuvre variés et ensuite du poulet et des pommes frites.*
The bill, please.	*L'addition, s'il vous plaît.*

Review of French Grammar

Numerals, time, and dates

Cardinal numbers

The word *et* is used in numbers only in 21, 31, 41, 51, 61, and 71. In all other compound numbers through 99, the hyphen is used.

Vingt and *cent* are made plural when multiplied and modifying a noun, but drop the *s* before another number.

> *quatre-vingts garçons*
> eighty boys

> *quatre-vingt-deux garçons*
> eighty-two boys

> *quatre cents mots*
> four hundred words

> *quatre cent cinquante mots*
> four hundred fifty words

Cent and *mille* are not preceded by the indefinite article. Numbers, except *un* and *une,* do not show gender.

> *cent bateaux* a hundred boats
> *six cents bateaux* six hundred boats

Mille does not change in the plural.

> *mille fois* a thousand times
> *six mille plantes* six thousand plants

Periods, not commas, are used with numbers.

> 2.000.000 2,000,000

Ordinal numbers

Ordinals are formed from cardinals by adding *-ième*. Silent *e* is dropped before *-ième*.

> *deuxième* second
> *quatrième* fourth

Exceptions to this rule:

> *premier, première* first
> *second, seconde* second
> *cinquième* (*u* inserted) fifth
> *neuvième* (*f* changes to *v*) ninth
> *quatre-vingtième* (*s* omitted) eightieth

Fractions are formed by combining cardinal and ordinal numbers. *Quart, moitié,* and *tiers* are irregular. *Moitié* is a noun and must have an article. *Demi,* generally used as an adjective, is connected by a hyphen when it precedes the noun and is invariable. When *demi* follows a noun it modifies, it agrees with it in gender.

> *la moitié de la bouteille* half the bottle
> *une demi-heure* half an hour
> *une heure et demie* an hour and a half

cardinal numbers

0	*zero*	45	*quarante-cinq*
1	*un, une*	50	*cinquante*
2	*deux*	51	*cinquante et un*
3	*trois*	53	*cinquante-trois*
4	*quatre*	60	*soixante*
5	*cinq*	61	*soixante et un*
6	*six*	64	*soixante-quatre*
7	*sept*	70	*soixante-dix*
8	*huit*	71	*soixante et onze*
9	*neuf*	75	*soixante-quinze*
10	*dix*	78	*soixante-dix-huit*
11	*onze*	80	*quatre-vingts*
12	*douze*	81	*quatre-vingt-un*
13	*treize*	87	*quatre-vingt-sept*
14	*quatorze*	90	*quatre-vingt-dix*
15	*quinze*	91	*quatre-vingt-onze*
16	*seize*	100	*cent*
17	*dix-sept*	101	*cent un*
18	*dix-huit*	122	*cent vingt-deux*
19	*dix-neuf*	200	*deux cents*
20	*vingt*	206	*deux cent-six*
21	*vingt et un*	1000	*mille*
22	*vingt-deux*	1001	*mille un*
30	*trente*	1100	*mille cent*
33	*trente-trois*	3000	*trois mille*
40	*quarante*	1,000,000	*un million*

Time

To express time, *heure* (hour) is used for "o'clock." To express time after the hour, the number of minutes is added. The word *et* is used only with *quart* and *demie. Moins* is used to express time before the hour.

In public announcements, such as timetables, the 24-hour system is used. Starting at midnight: *neuf heures* = 9 A.M. 14 *heures* = 2 P.M.

Quelle heure est-il?	What time is it?
Il est une heure.	It is one o'clock.
Il est deux heures.	It is two o'clock.
Il est dix heures dix.	It is ten past ten.
Il est huit heures et quart.	It is a quarter past eight.
Il est neuf heures et demie.	It is half-past nine.
Il est dix heures moins le quart.	It is quarter of ten.
Il est onze heures moins dix.	It is ten minutes of eleven.
Il est midi.	It is noon.
Il est minuit.	It is midnight.

Dates

The cardinal numbers are used to express dates, except for the first day of a month, week, etc. The masculine definite article always precedes the date.

le premier avril April first
le vingt-cinq décembre December 25th
dix-neuf cent vingt-huit 1928
en dix-sept cent quatre-vingt-neuf in 1789

Months, days, seasons

janvier	January	*lundi*	Monday
février	February	*mardi*	Tuesday
mars	March	*mercredi*	Wednesday
avril	April	*jeudi*	Thursday
mai	May	*vendredi*	Friday
juin	June	*samedi*	Saturday
juillet	July	*dimanche*	Sunday
août	August		
septembre	September	*le printemps*	spring
octobre	October	*l'été*	summer
novembre	November	*l'automne*	autumn
décembre	December	*l'hiver*	winter

Countries

l'Allemagne	Germany
l'Angleterre	England
l'Autriche	Austria
la Belgique	Belgium
l'Espagne	Spain
la Hongrie	Hungary
l'Irlande	Ireland
l'Italie	Italy
les Pays Bas	Netherlands
la Pologne	Poland
le Portugal	Portugal
la Suisse	Switzerland

les États-Unis d'Amérique
United States of America

Le menu

Alose à la provençale
shad baked with garlic, onions, tomatoes, black olives, spinach, and parsley

Blanquette de veau
a stew made of veal and a white sauce, and garnished with onions, mushrooms, and parsley

Boeuf bourguignon
a beef dish made with red wine plus braised onions and mushrooms

Bouillabaisse
a fish stew made with fish available in season, and flavored with thyme, rosemary, fennel seeds, saffron, onions, fresh tomatoes, orange rind, and olive oil.

Choucroute garnie
a combination of two or more types of sausages plus shredded white cabbage fermented in salt and flavored with caraway and juniper berries, all cooked with smoked pork, lean bacon, goose fat, white wine, and boiled potatoes.

Moules marinières
mussels cooked in a large kettle, with a sauce made of butter, shallots, pepper, parsley, and white wine.

Talking with a waiter

Une table pour quatre, s'il vous plaît.	A table for four, please.
La carte, s'il vous plaît.	The menu, please.
Une tasse de café avec du pain et du beurre, s'il vous plaît.	A cup of coffee and bread and butter, please.
Je prendrais du boeuf bourguignon.	I will have *boeuf bourguignon*.
Une bouteille de vin du pays, s'il vous plaît.	A bottle of the local wine, please.
Donnez-moi du beurre, s'il vous plaît.	Please give me some butter.
Avez-vous de la crème?	Have you any cream?
L'addition, s'il vous plaît.	The check, please.

Review of French Grammar

La figure The face

Dictionary

Le corps humain The human body

Dictionary abbreviations. Nouns are identified as masculine *(m)* or feminine *(f)*. Adjectives are identified as *adj*, adverbs as *adv*, conjunctions as *conj*, interjections as *interj*, prepositions as *prep*, pronouns as *pron*, and verbs as *v*. Plurals are identified as *pl*.

French-English

A

à *prep* at, in, to
absence *f* absence
accepter *v* accept
accident *m* accident
accourir *v* run up
accueillir *v* welcome
acheter *v* buy
acquérir *v* acquire, get
activité *f* activity
affaire *f* matter, business
afin de *prep* in order to
afin que *conj* in order that
agent *m* agent
agréable *adj* pleasing
aider *v* help
aimable *adj* friendly, pleasant
aimer *v* love, like
aimer mieux *v* prefer
aller *v* go
amener *v* bring
Américain *adj and noun m* American
Amérique *f* America
ami *m* friend
amie *f* friend
amuser *v* entertain
an *m* year
ancien *adj* old, ancient, former
année *f* year
appartenir *v* belong, pertain
appeler *v* call
apporter *v* bring
apprendre *v* learn, teach
approcher *v* bring near
approuver *v* approve
après *adv* afterward
après *prep* after
après que *conj* after
arbre *m* tree
argent *m* money, silver
arrêter *v* stop
arriver *v* arrive, happen
asseoir *v* seat, **s'asseoir** sit down
assez *adv* enough, **assez de** enough of
attendre *v* wait for, expect
aucun *adj and pron* none, no one, not one, not any
auprès de *prep* near, beside
aussi *adv* also, as, and so
aussitôt *adv* immediately
aussitôt que *conj* as soon as
autant *adv* as much
autant que *conj* as much as
autre *adj* other
autrefois *adv* formerly
avancer *v* move, go forward
avant *adv and prep* before
avertir *v* warn, give notice
avertissement *m* warning
avion *m* plane
avis *m* notice, opinion
avocat *m* lawyer
avoir *v* have

B

bain *m* bath
baiser *m* kiss
bataille *f* battle
bateau *m* boat
battre *v* beat, **se battre** fight
beau, bel *adj m*, **belle** *f* beautiful, handsome, fine, fair
beaucoup *adv* much, many
bénéfice *m* profit
besoin *m* need, **avoir besoin** *v* need
bête *f* animal, beast, brute, fool
beurre *m* butter
bien *adv* well
bien que *conj* although
bière *f* beer
billet *m* ticket
blesser *v* wound, hurt
boire *v* drink
bois *m* wood, forest
boisson *f* drink, beverage
bon *adj m*, **bonne** *f* good
bonheur *m* happiness
bouteille *f* bottle
bruit *m* noise, rumor

370   **Review of French Grammar**

brun *adj* brown, brunette
bureau *m* desk, office
but *m* purpose, aim, goal

C

cadeau *m* gift, present
café *m* coffee
carte *f* card, map, chart
casser *v* break
causer *v* chat, cause
céder *v* yield, give in
célèbre *adj* famous
cesser *v* stop, cease
chaise *f* chair
chance *f* luck
chanson *f* song
chanter *v* sing
chapeau *m* hat
chaque *adj* each
charpentier *m* carpenter
chaud *adj* hot
chemin *m* road, path
chemise *f* shirt
chercher *v* seek, look for
chez *prep* at (the home, shop, etc. of . . .)
choisir *v* choose
chose *f* thing, object
clef, clé *f* key
client *m* customer
colère *f* anger, **en colère** angry
colis *m* package
combien *adv* how much, how many
comme *adv* as, how, *conj* as, like
commencer *v* begin, start
comment *adv* how
comprendre *v* understand
compter *v* count, **compter sur** count on
conduire *v* lead, take, drive
conférence *f* lecture, conference
connaissance *f* acquaintance, knowledge
connaître *v* be acquainted with, know
consentir *v* consent
construire *v* build
contenir *v* contain, restrain
content *adj* content, glad
corriger *v* correct
costume *m* suit, costume
coucher *v* put to bed, **se coucher** lie down
coupable *adj* guilty
couper *v* cut
courage *m* courage
courir *v* run
course *f* race, errand
couteau *m* knife
coûter *v* cost
couvrir *v* cover
craindre *v* fear
crainte *f* fear
crayon *m* pencil
croire *v* believe
cueillir *v* gather
cuire *v* cook
cultiver *v* cultivate

D

dame *f* lady
décider *v* decide
déclarer *v* declare, affirm
découvrir *v* discover
décrire *v* describe
défendre *v* defend, forbid
déjeuner *m* lunch, **petit déjeuner** breakfast
délicieux *adj m*, **délicieuse** *f* delicious
demain *adv* tomorrow
demander *v* ask for
demeurer *v* dwell
demi *adj and noun m* half
départ *m* departure
dépit *m* spite, **en dépit de** in spite of
depuis *adv and prep* since
déranger *v* disturb
dernier *adj m* last
dès *prep* since, **dès que** *conj* as soon as
descendre *v* go down, come down
désirer *v* desire, wish
désoler *v* grieve
dessous *m* underside, **au-dessous de**, beneath
dessus *adv* above
devenir *v* become
deviner *v* guess
devoir *m* duty, homework
devoir *v* owe, have to, ought
difficile *adj* difficult, hard
dire *v* say, tell
doigt *m* finger
domestique *m and f* servant
dommage *m* damage, **c'est dommage** that's too bad
donner *v* give
dormir *v* sleep
douter *v* doubt
droit *m* right, law
droit *adj and adv* right, fair
droite *f* right, **à droite** to the right

E

eau *f* water
éblouir *v* dazzle
écarter *v* put aside
échouer *v* fail
écouter *v* listen
écrire *v* write
église *f* church
élève *m or f* pupil
embarquer *v* embark
emmener *v* take away, lead away
empêcher *v* prevent, hinder
encore *adv* again, still, yet
encre *f* ink
endroit *m* place
enfant *m or f* child
enfin *adv* at last, finally
enseigner *v* teach
entendre *v* hear
entrer *v* enter, come in
envie *f* envy, desire, **avoir envie de** feel like
envoyer *v* send, **envoyer chercher** send for
épine *f* thorn, spine
éprouver *v* experience, feel
erreur *f* error, mistake
escalier *m* stairway
espérer *v* hope, await
essuyer *v* wipe
et *conj* and
été *m* summer
éteindre *v* extinguish
étendre *v* extend, stretch out
étonner *v* surprise
étrange *adj* strange, curious
étudiant *m* student
étudier *v* study
évident *adj* evident, obvious
éviter *v* avoid, spare
examen *m* examination, test
exiger *v* require, demand
exprimer *v* express

F

fable *f* fable, story
fabriquer *v* manufacture
fâcher *v* anger, **se fâcher** become angry
facile *adj* easy
faim *f* hunger
faire *v* do, make
falloir *v* be necessary
famille *f* family
fatigué *adj* tired
faute *f* fault, mistake
femme *f* woman, wife
fermer *v* close
fête *f* celebration, holiday, party
feuille *f* leaf, sheet
fier *adj* proud
figure *f* face
fille *f* daughter, girl
fils *m* son
fin *f* end
finir *v* finish
fleur *f* flower
fois *f* instance, time
forcer *v* compel, force
fraise *f* strawberry
franc *m* franc, **franc** *adj m* frank, open
franche *adj f* frank, open
frapper *v* knock, strike
frère *m* brother
froid *m and adj* cold
fuir *v* flee, shun

G

gagner *v* acquire, gain, win
gant *m* glove
garçon *m* boy, waiter
garder *v* keep, guard
gare *f* station
gêner *v* hinder, bother
goûter *v* taste
grand *adj* large, tall, great
grange *f* barn
guère *adv* hardly
guerre *f* war

H

habile *adj* able, clever
habiller *v* dress, **s'habiller** put on one's clothing
habit *m* clothes, coat
habiter *v* inhabit, dwell in
habituer *v* accustom, familiarize
haut *adj* high, **à haute voix** aloud, **en haut** upstairs
hésiter *v* hesitate
heure *f* hour, time, **de bonne heure** early
heureux *adj m*, **heureuse** *f* happy, lucky
hier *adv* yesterday
histoire *f* history, story
homme *m* man
honnête *adj* honest, upright
horloge *f* clock
hôte *m* host, guest

I

ici *adv* here
informer *v* inform, **s'informer** make inquiries
ingénieur *m* engineer
intelligent *adj* bright, clever
intéresser *v* interest, concern
interrompre *v* interrupt
inutile *adj* useless, unnecessary
inviter *v* invite

J

jamais *adv* ever, never, **à jamais** forever
jardin *m* garden
jaune *adj* yellow
jeter *v* throw, cast
jeune *adj* young
joli *adj* pretty
jouet *m* toy
jour *m* day
jus *m* juice
jusqu'à *prep* up to, as far as, until
juste *adj* just, right, exact
juste *adv* just, exactly

K

kilo *m* kilogram

L

lac *m* lake
lacet *m* shoelace
laisser *v* allow
lancer *v* throw
langage *m* language
langue *f* tongue, language
larme *f* tear
laver *v* wash, **se laver** wash oneself
leçon *f* lesson
légume *m* vegetable
lent *adj* slow
lettre *f* letter
lever *v* raise
ligne *f* line
lire *v* read
lit *m* bed
livre *m* book, **livre** *f* pound
longtemps *adv* longtime
lorsque *conj* when
louer *v* rent
loyer *m* rent
luire *v* gleam

M

magasin *m* store
main *f* hand
maintenant *adv* now
mais *conj* but
maison *f* house
malade *adj* ill
malle *f* trunk
manger *v* eat
manière *f* manner
manquer *v* miss, fail, lack
marchand *m* merchant
marier *v* marry
matin *m* morning
mauvais *adj* bad
médecin *m* physician, doctor
méfier *v* **se méfier** mistrust
meilleur *adj* better, **le meilleur** the best
même *adj* same
mener *v* lead
mentir *v* lie
mère *f* mother
métier *m* trade, craft, loom
mètre *m* meter
mettre *v* put, set
meuble *m* furniture
midi *m* noon, midday
mieux *adv* better, best
mille *m* mile, *adj and noun m* thousand
minuit *m* midnight
moins *adv* less, least
mois *m* month

moitié *f* half
monde *m* world, society
monter *v* go up, take up
moquer *v* **se moquer de** make fun of, mock
mourir *v* die

N

nager *v* swim, float
naissance *f* birth
naître *v* be born
négliger *v* neglect
neige *f* snow
nettoyer *v* clean
neuf *adj and noun m* nine
neuf *adj m,* **neuve** *f* new
ni *conj* nor, **ni . . . ni** neither . . . nor
nier *v* deny
nom *m* name, noun
note *f* grade, note
nouvelle *f* news
nuire *v* harm
nuit *f* night

O

obéir *v* obey
observer *v* observe, notice
oeil *m* eye, *pl* **yeux**
oeuvre *f* work, labor
offrir *v* offer, present
or *m* gold
orage *m* storm
ordonner *v* order, command
ordre *m* order
orgueilleux *adj m,* **orgueilleuse** *f* proud, haughty
oser *v* dare
ou *conj* or
où *adv* where, at, on
oublier *v* forget
oui *adv* yes
ouvrir *v* open

P

page *m* pageboy
page *f* page
pain *m* bread
paix *f* peace
pâlir *v* become pale, fade
panne *f* accident, lard
papier *m* paper
papillon *m* butterfly
paraître *v* appear, seem
pardessus *m* overcoat
pardonner *v* pardon
pareil *adj* like
parier *v* bet
parler *v* speak, talk
parmi *prep* among
partager *v* divide, share
partie *f* part, party
partir *v* leave, go away
passer *v* pass, go by
patiner *v* skate
pauvre *adj* poor
pavé *m* pavement
payer *v* pay
pays *m* country
peine *f* pain, penalty
pendant *prep* during
pendant que *conj* while
penser *v* think, **penser à** think of
perdre *v* lose
père *m* father
péril *m* danger
périr *v* perish
permettre *v* allow, permit
personne *f* person
personne *pron* no one, nobody
petit *adj* small, little, petty
peu *m* little, few
peur *f* fear
pièce *f* piece, coin, play
pied *m* foot
pierre *f* stone
plaindre *v* pity
plaire *v* please
plante *f* plant
plein *adj* full
pleurer *v* weep, cry, mourn
pleuvoir *v* rain
plier *v* fold
pluie *f* rain
plume *f* pen, feather
plupart *f* majority, most
plus *adv* more, most
plusieurs *adj and pron* several
poche *f* pocket
pomme *f* apple, **pomme de terre** potato
porte *f* door
porter *v* carry, bear
pourquoi *adv* why
pourvu que *conj* provided that
pouvoir *v* be able, can
préférer *v* prefer
premier *adj* first
prendre *v* take
près *adv* near, **près de** *prep* near
présenter *v* introduce, present
prêt *adj* ready
prêter *v* lend
projet *m* project, plan
promener *v* take out walking
promettre *v* promise
propos *m* talk, subject, **à propos de** with regard to
propre *adj* own, very, same, clean
propriétaire *m* proprietor
protester *v* protest
provoquer *v* provoke
puis *adv* then

Q

qualifier *v* qualify
qualité *f* quality, nature
quand *conj* when
quart *m* quarter, fourth
quelque *adj* some, any, **quelque chose** something
quelquefois *adv* sometimes
quelqu'un *pron* someone, anyone
quitter *v* leave
quoique *conj* although
quotidien *adj* daily

R

raconter *v* tell, narrate
rafraîchir *v* cool, refresh
raison *f* reason, **avoir raison** be right
ralentir *v* slow down, slacken
ramasser *v* pick up
ramener *v* bring back, take back
rapide *adj* swift
rappeler *v* remember
ravi *adj* delighted
recevoir *v* receive
récompense *f* reward
reconnaissance *f* gratitude, recognition
reconnaître *v* recognize
reculer *v* fall back, go back
réfléchir *v* reflect, think
regarder *v* look
règle *f* rule
regretter *v* regret, be sorry for

rejoindre *v* join
relier *v* bind, connect
remarquer *v* notice
remplir *v* fill
remuer *v* move, stir
rencontrer *v* meet
rendre *v* give back
renoncer *v* renounce, give up
rentrer *v* go home, go back
repas *m* meal
répondre *v* reply, answer
reposer *v* rest
résoudre *v* resolve
rester *v* remain, stay
retard *m* delay, **en retard** late
retourner *v* return, turn around
retrouver *v* find again
réussir *v* succeed
rêve *m* dream
réveiller *v* waken
révéler *v* reveal
revenir *v* come back, return
riche *adj* rich
rien *pron* nothing
rire *v* laugh
robe *f* dress
roman *m* novel
rompre *v* break
rond *adj* round
route *f* road, **en route** under way
rue *f* street

S

sable *m* sand
sage *adj* wise
saisir *v* seize
saison *f* season
sale *adj* dirty
salon *m* parlor
sans *prep* without
sauf *prep* except
sauter *v* leap, jump
sauver *v* save, **se sauver** run away
savoir *v* know, know how
savon *m* soap
secours *m* help
selon *prep* according to
semaine *f* week
sembler *v* seem
sentir *v* feel, smell
serviette *f* napkin, towel
servir *v* serve, **se servir de** use

seul *adj* alone, only, single
sévère *adj* strict, severe
si *conj* if, whether
si *adv* so, yes
soeur *f* sister
soie *f* silk
soif *f* thirst
soigner *v* care for
soir *m* evening
soleil *m* sun
sommeil *m* sleep
sonner *v* sound, ring, strike
sorte *f* kind
sortir *v* go out, get out
souffrir *v* suffer, bear
souhaiter *v* wish
soulager *v* relieve
soulever *v* raise, lift up, arouse
sourire *v* and *n m* smile
souvenir *m* remembrance, **se souvenir de** remember
souvent *adv* often
sucre *m* sugar
suffire *v* suffice
suivre *v* follow
sur *prep* on, upon, over, about
sûr *adj* sure
surtout *adv* above all, especially

T

table *f* table
tableau *m* picture, blackboard
taire *v* keep quiet, **se taire** be silent
tandis que *conj* while, whereas
tant *adv* so many, so much, **tant que** as long as
tante *f* aunt
tard *adv* late
tarder *v* delay, put off
tasse *f* cup
tel *adj* such
temps *m* time, weather
tenir *v* hold, possess
tenter *v* attempt
terre *f* earth, ground, land
tête *f* head
timbre *m* stamp
tirer *v* draw, pull
tomber *v* fall
tort *m* wrong, **avoir tort** be wrong
tôt *adv* soon, early
toucher *v* touch

toujours *adv* always, yet
tourner *v* turn
tout *adj* all, each, every
tout *pron* everything
tranquille *adj* quiet
travailler *v* work
traverser *v* cross
très *adv* very
tromper *v* deceive, **se tromper** make a mistake, be wrong
trop *adv* too much, too
trottoir *m* sidewalk
trouver *v* find

U

usage *m* use
utile *adj* useful
utiliser *v* use

V

vacances *f pl* vacation
vague *f* wave
vaincre *v* conquer
vaisselle *f* dishes
valise *f* suitcase
valoir *v* be worth
vendre *v* sell
verre *m* glass
vêtir *v* dress
viande *f* meat
vide *adj* empty
vie *f* life
vieillard *m* old man
vieille *adj f* old, *noun f* old woman
vieux *adj m* old
village *m* village
ville *f* city, town
vin *m* wine
vite *adv* quick
vivre *v* live
voici *v* here is, here are
voilà *v* there is, there are
voir *v* see
voisin *m* neighbor
voiture *f* car, automobile
voix *f* voice
vouloir *v* wish, want
voyager *v* travel
vrai *adj* true, real

Y

y *adv* there, in it, to it

Dictionary abbreviations. Nouns are identified as masculine *(nm)* or feminine *(nf)*. Adjectives are identified as *adj*, adverbs as *adv*, conjunctions as *conj*, interjections as *interj*, prepositions as *prep*, pronouns as *pron*, and verbs as *v*. Plurals are identified as *pl*.

English-French

A

able *adj* capable, **be able** *v* pouvoir
about *prep* environ, à peu près
above *adv* dessus, au dessus, par dessus
absence *n* absence *f*
accept *v* accepter
accident *n* accident *m*
according to *prep* selon, d'après
accustom *v* habituer
acquaintance *n* connaissance *f*
acquire *v* acquérir
act *v* agir
activity *n* activité *f*
add *v* ajouter, additionner
advise *v* conseiller
afraid *adj* éffrayé
after *adv* après
after *conj* après que
afternoon *n* après-midi *m or f*
afterward *adv* après, ensuite, plus tard
again *adv* encore
agent *n* agent, représentant *m*
ago *adv* il y a, **two days ago** il y a deux jours
agreement *n* accord *m*
aim *n* but *m*
airplane *n* avion *m*
all *adj* tout, tous, toute, toutes
allow *v* laisser, permettre
alone *adj* seul
aloud *adv* à haute voix
already *adv* déjà
also *adv* aussi
although *conj* bien que, quoique
always *adv* toujours
among *prep* parmi, entre
amuse *v* amuser
ancient *adj* ancien, antique
and *conj* et
anger *n* colère *f*
anger *v* fâcher, mettre en colère
animal *n* bête *f*
answer *v* répondre
any *pron* en
anything *pron* quelque chose, **not anything** ne . . . rien, **anything at all** n'importe quoi
anyone *pron* quelqu'un, **not . . . personne**
anywhere *adv* quelque part, **not . . . nulle part**
appear *v* paraître, sembler
apple *n* pomme *f*
approach *v* s'approcher
approve *v* approuver
arrest *v* arrêter
arrive *v* arriver
as *adv* comme, aussi, que
as *conj* comme, en tant que, tel que, **as . . . as** aussi . . . que
ask *v* demander, **ask a question** poser une question
at *prep* à
attain *v* atteindre
aunt *n* tante *f*
automobile *n* automobile *f*, voiture *f*
avoid *v* éviter
await *v* attendre, espérer
away *adv* absent, loin, au loin

B

bachelor *n* célibataire *m*
back *n* dos *m*, dossier *m*, derrière *m*
back up *v* reculer
bad *adj* mauvais
badly *adv* mal
barely *adv* guère, à peine
barn *n* grange *f*
bath *v* bain *m*
battle *n* bataille *f*
be *v* être
bear *v* porter
beast *n* bête *f*
beat *v* battre, vaincre, frapper
beautiful *adj* beau *and* bel *m*, belle *f*
because *conj* parce que

become *v* devenir
bed *n* lit *m*
beer *n* bière *f*
before *adv* avant, devant
begin *v* commencer, se mettre à
behind *adv* derrière
believe *v* croire
belong *v* appartenir
below *prep* sous, dessous, en bas
bend *v* plier
beside *prep* à côté de, auprès de
besides *adv* d'ailleurs
best *adv* mieux, *adj* le meilleur
bet *v* parier, *n* pari *m*
better *adj* meilleur, *adv* mieux
between *prep* entre
big *adj* grand, gros
bird *n* oiseau *m*
birth *n* naissance *f*
bite *v* mordre
blanket *n* couverture *f*
body *n* corps *m*
book *n* livre *m*
born (be) *v* naître
borrow *v* emprunter
both *adj and pron* les deux
bother *v* déranger, gêner
bottle *n* bouteille *f*
box *n* boîte *f*
bread *n* pain *m*
break *v* casser, rompre, briser
breakfast *n* petit déjeuner *m*
bright *adj* brillant, clair, intelligent
bring *v* amener, apporter
bring back *v* ramener
broad *adj* large
brother *n* frère *m*
build *v* construire
business *n* affaires *f pl*
busy *adj* occupé
but *conj* mais
butter *n* beurre *m*
butterfly *n* papillon *m*
buy *v* acheter
by *prep* par, de, à, près de

C

café *n* café *m*
call *v* appeler
can *v* pouvoir
car *n* voiture *f*

Review of French Grammar 375

carpenter *n* charpentier *m*
carry *v* porter
cast *v* jeter
cat *n* chat *m*
cause *n* cause *f*
cease *v* cesser, discontinuer
celebration *n* fête *f*
certain *adj* certain
chair *n* chaise *f*
chance *n* chance *f*, hasard *m*
chart *n* carte marine *f*
chat *n* causerie *f*, entretien *m*
cheap *adj* bon marché
child *n* enfant *m* or *f*
choose *v* choisir
church *n* église *f*
city *n* ville *f*
class *n* classe *f*
clean *adj* propre, *v* nettoyer
clear *adj* clair
clever *adj* habile
climb *v* grimper, monter
clock *n* horloge *f*, pendule *f*
close *v* fermer
clothe *v* habiller, vêtir
clothes *n* habits *m pl*, vêtements *m pl*
cloud *n* nuage *m*
coat *n* habit *m*, manteau *m*
coffee *n* café *m*
cold *adj* froid
come *v* venir
command *v* commander, ordonner
company *n* compagnie *f*
compare *v* comparer
compel *v* forcer
complain *v* se plaindre
complaint *n* plainte *f*
concern *v* interesser
conquer *v* vaincre
consent *v* consentir
consider *v* considérer
consist *v* consister
construct *v* construire, fabriquer
contain *v* contenir
contents *n* contenu *m*
continue *v* continuer
convince *v* convaincre
cook *v* cuire
cool *adj* frais *m*, fraîche *f*
cool *v* rafraîchir
correct *v* corriger
cost *v* coûter
costs *n* frais *m pl*

count *v* compter
country *n* pays (nation) *m*, patrie (native country) *f*, campagne (rural area) *f*
courage *n* courage *m*
course *n* cours *m*
cover *v* couvrir
cross *n* croix *f*
cry *v* pleurer
cultivate *v* cultiver
cup *n* tasse *f*
customer *n* client *m*
cut *v* couper

D

daily *adj* quotidien, tous les jours
damage *n* dommage *m*, *v* endommager
dance *n* danse *f*
dance *v* danser
danger *n* danger *m*, péril *m*
dangerous *adj* dangereux
dare *v* oser
date *n* date *f*
daughter *n* fille *f*
day *n* jour *m*, journée *f*
dazzle *v* éblouir
dealer *n* marchant *m*
deceive *v* tromper
decide *v* décider
declare *v* déclarer
defeat *v* vaincre
delay *v* tarder
delicious *adj* délicieux
delight *n* joie *f*, plaisir *m*
delight *v* ravir
delighted *adj* joyeux, ravi
deny *v* nier
depart *v* s'en aller, partir
descend *v* descendre
describe *v* décrire
deserve *v* mériter
desire *v* désirer, vouloir
desk *n* bureau *m*
despair *v* désespérer
destroy *v* détruire
die *v* mourir
difficult *adj* difficile
dine *v* dîner
dining room *n* salle à manger *f*
direct *v* diriger
dirty *adj* sale
dishes *n* vaisselle *f*
displease *v* déplaire

disturb *v* déranger, troubler
dive *v* plonger
divide *v* diviser, partager
do *v* faire
dog *n* chien *m*
door *n* porte *f*
doubt *n* doute *m*
doubt *v* douter
draw *v* tirer (pull), dessiner (sketch)
drawer *n* tiroir *m*
drawing room *n* salon *m*
dress *n* robe *f*
dress *v* vêtir, habiller
drink *n* boisson *f*
drink *v* boire
drive *v* conduire
during *prep* pendant
dust *n* poussière *f*
duty *n* devoir *m*
dwell *v* demeurer, habiter

E

each *adj* chaque, tout
each one *pron* chacun
ear *n* oreille *f*
early *adv* de bonne heure, tôt
earn *v* gagner, mériter
earth *n* terre *f*
easy *adj* facile
eat *v* manger
effort *n* effort *m*
egg *n* oeuf *m*
either *adv* ou
else *adv* autrement, ou bien
elsewhere *adv* ailleurs, autre part
embark *v* embarquer
employ *v* employer
empty *adj* vide
encourage *v* encourager
end *n* fin *f*
end *v* finir, terminer
engineer *n* ingénieur *m*
enjoy *v* jouir
enough *adv* assez
enter *v* entrer
entire *adj* entier, complet
evening *n* soir *m*
equal *adj* égal
error *n* erreur *f*, faute *f*
especially *adv* surtout
even *adv* même

event *n* événement *m*
ever *adv* jamais
every *adj* tout, chaque
everybody *pron* tout le monde
everything *pron* tout
everywhere *adv* partout
evident *adj* évident, clair
exactly *adv* exactement
examination *n* examen *m*
example *n* exemple *m*
except *prep* excepté, sauf
expect *v* attendre, espérer
expensive *adj* cher, coûteux
experience *v* éprouver
explain *v* expliquer
express *v* exprimer, **express** *adj* exprès
extend *v* étendre
extinguish *v* éteindre
eye *n* oeil *m*, yeux *m pl*

F

fable *n* fable *f*
face *n* figure *f*, face *f*
face *v* faire face à, affronter, donner sur
fail *v* échouer, manquer
fair *adj* juste
fairly *adv* assez, pas mal, honnêtement
faithful *adj* fidèle
fall *v* tomber
false *adj* faux *m*, fausse *f*
familiar *adj* familier
family *n* famille *f*
far *adv* loin
fast *adv* vite
father *n* père *m*
fault *n* faute *f*
fear *n* crainte *f*, peur *f*
fear *v* craindre, avoir peur
feed *v* nourrir
feel *v* sentir, tâter (touch)
feel like *v* avoir envie de
few *adj* peu de, quelques, *pron* peu, quelques-uns
fill *v* remplir
fight *v* se battre
finally *adv* enfin, à la fin
find *v* trouver
find out *v* découvrir
finger *n* doigt *m*
finish *v* finir
fire *n* feu *m*

first *adj* premier, *adv* d'abord
fish *n* poisson *m*
fish *v* pêcher
fit *v* aller à, *adj* convenable, capable
flee *v* se sauver, s'enfuir
flower *n* fleur *f*
fly *v* voler
fold *v* plier
follow *v* suivre
food *n* nourriture *f*
foot *n* pied *m*
for *prep* pour, *conj* car
forbid *v* défendre
force *n* force *f*, puissance *f*
force *v* force, obliger
forget *v* oublier
former *adj* ancien
free *adj* libre
freeze *v* geler
friend *n* ami *m*, amie *f*
from *prep* de, depuis (since)
full *adj* plein
fun *n* amusement, plaisanterie, **make fun** se moquer
furniture *n* meubles *m pl*
future *n* avenir *m*

G

gain *n* profit *m*, gain *m*, avantage *m*
gain *v* gagner
game *n* jeu *m*, gibier (hunting) *m*
garden *n* jardin *m*
gate *n* porte *f*, portail *m*, barrière *f*
gather *v* cueillir, ramasser, se réunir
get *v* prendre, avoir, obtenir, gagner, **go and get** aller chercher
gift *n* cadeau *m*, présent *m*
girl *n* fille *f*
give *v* donner
give up *v* renoncer à
glad *adj* content
glass *n* verre *m*
glove *n* gant *m*
go *v* aller, se rendre, **go out** sortir, **go down** descendre
goal *n* but *m*
gold *n* or *m*

good *adj* bon *m*, bonne *f*, **for good** pour de bon
great *adj* grand, gros, **a great deal** beaucoup
greet *v* saluer
ground *n* terre *f*, **on the ground** par terre
grow *v* grandir, pousser
guard *v* garder
guess *v* deviner
guilty *adj* coupable

H

habit *n* habitude *f*
hair *n* cheveux *m pl*
half *adj* demi, *n* moitié *f*
hall *n* vestibule (entrance) *m*, salle (large room) *f*
hand *n* main *m*
happen *v* arriver, se passer
happy *adj* heureux, content
hard *adj* dur
hardly *adv* à peine, ne . . . guère
harm *v* nuire
hat *n* chapeau *m*
hate *v* détester, haïr
haughty *adj* orgueilleux
have *v* avoir
hear *v* entendre
help *n* aide *f*, secours *m*, *interj* au secours!
help *v* aider
here *adv* ici
hesitate *v* hésiter
high *adj* haut
hinder *v* gêner, empêcher
history *n* histoire
hit *v* frapper, battre
hold *v* tenir
holiday *n* fête
home *n* foyer *m*, maison *f*, chez soi, à la maison
homework *n* devoir *m*
honest *adj* honnête
hope *v* espérer
hot *adj* chaud
hour *n* heure *f*
house *n* maison *f*
how *adv* comment, comme (in exclamation), **how much** combien
however *adv* cependant
hunger *n* faim *f*
hurt *v* blesser, faire mal
husband *n* mari *m*, époux *m*

Review of French Grammar 377

I

ice *n* glace *f*
idea *n* idée *f*
ill *adv* mal, *adj* malade
in *prep* dans, à, en
incite *v* encourager, provoquer
inform *v* informer, renseigner
inhabitant *n* habitant *m*
ink *n* encre *f*
insist *v* insister, tenir à
instance *n* fois *f*
instead of *prep* au lieu de
intend *v* avoir l'intention de
interest *v* intéresser
interrupt *v* interrompre
introduce *v* introduire, présenter
invite *v* inviter

J

join *v* relier, joindre
joke *v* plaisanter
journey *n* voyage *m*
jump *v* sauter
just *adj* juste, précis
just *adv* justement, donc, **to have just** venir de

K

keep *v* garder, tenir, **keep from** empêcher
key *n* clef *f*
kill *v* tuer
kilogram *n* kilo *m*
kind *adj* aimable, *n* genre *m*, sorte *f*
knife *n* couteau *m*, **pocketknife** canif *m*
knock *v* frapper
know *v* savoir, connaître
knowledge *n* science *f*, connaissances *f pl*

L

lace *n* dentelle *f*, **shoelace** *n* lacet *m*
land *n* terre *f*
land *v* débarquer (ship), atterrir (airplane)
language *n* langage *m*, langue *f*
large *adj* grand, gros
last *adj* dernier, **last night** hier soir
last *v* durer
late *adj* tard, en retard
later *adj* plus tard
laugh *v* rire, **laugh at** se moquer
law *n* droit *m*
lawyer *n* avocat *m*, avoué *m*
lead *n* plomb *m*
lead *v* mener, conduire
leaf *n* feuille *f*
leap *v* sauter
learn *v* apprendre
least *adv, adj, n m* moins
leave *v* quitter, partir, laisser
lecture *n* conférence *f*
leg *n* jambe *f*
lend *v* prêter
less *adv* moins, *adj* moindre, moins de
lesson *n* leçon *f*
let *v* laisser, permettre
letter *n* lettre *f*
lie *v* se coucher
lie *n* mensonge *f*, *v* mentir
life *n* vie *f*, existence *f*
light *n* lumière *f*
light *adj* léger
like *v* aimer
like *adj* comme, pareil, semblable
line *n* ligne *f*
listen *v* écouter
little *adj* petit, *adv* peu
live *v* demeurer, vivre, habiter
living room *n* salon *m*
long *adj* long *m*, longue *f*, *adv* longtemps
look *n* regard *n*
look *v* regarder
look for *v* chercher
look like *v* avoir l'air de
lose *v* perdre
loud *adv* fort, haut
love *v* aimer
luck *n* chance *f*, fortune *f*
lunch *v* déjeuner, *n* déjeuner *m*

M

machine *n* machine *f*
maid *n* bonne à tout faire *f*
main *adj* principal
majority *n* la plupart *f*
make *v* faire, fabriquer
man *n* homme *m*
manner *n* manière *f*
many *adv* beaucoup de
map *n* carte *f*
market *n* marché *m*
marry *v* se marier, épouser
matter *n* matière *f*, sujet *m*
meal *n* repas *m*
mean *v* vouloir dire, signifier
mean *adj* méchant
meat *n* viande *f*
meet *v* rencontrer, rejoindre
midday *n* midi *m*
midnight *n* minuit *m*
mind *n* esprit *m*, intelligence *f*
mirror *n* miroir *m*
miss *v* manquer
mistake *n* erreur *f*, faute *f*
mistrust *v* se méfier
money *n* argent *m*
month *n* mois *m*
more *pron* en ... davantage, *adj and adv* plus, encore
morning *n* matin *m*
most *adv* très, bien, *adj* la plupart, *n* le plus *m*
mother *n* mère *f*
mountain *n* montagne *f*
move *v* remuer, avancer
much *adv* beaucoup, **as much** autant
must *v* falloir, devoir

N

name *n* nom *m*
name *v* appeler
napkin *n* serviette *f*
narrate *v* raconter
narrow *adj* étroit
near *adj* proche, *adv* près, *prep* près de
necessary *adj* nécessaire
need *n* besoin *m*
need *v* avoir besoin
neglect *v* négliger
neighbor *n* voisin *m*
never *adv* jamais
new *adj* neuf *m*, nouveau *m*, neuve *f*, nouvelle *f*
news *n* nouvelles *f pl*
newspaper *n* journal *m*
next *adj* prochain
noise *n* bruit *m*
noon *n* midi *m*
note *v* noter, remarquer
nothing *pron* rien

notice *n* avis *m*
notice *v* remarquer
novel *n* roman *m*
novel *adj* nouveau *m*, nouvelle *f*
now *adv* maintenant, à present

O

obey *v* obéir
observe *v* observer
obvious *adj* évident, clair
offend *v* offenser
offer *v* offrir
office *n* bureau *m*
often *adv* souvent
old *adj* vieux *m*, vieil *m*, vieille *f*
once *adv* une fois, autrefois
only *adj* seulement, seul
open *v* ouvrir
opinion *n* avis *m*
or *conj* ou
order *v* commander, ordonner
order *n* ordre *m*
other *adj* autre
out *adv* dehors
outside *adv* au dehors
overcoat *n* pardessus *m*
owe *v* devoir
own *v* posséder

P

package *n* colis *m*
pageboy *n* page *m*
pail *n* seau *m*
pain *n* peine *f*
paper *n* papier *m*
pardon *v* pardonner, faire grâce
part *n* partie *f*
part *v* se séparer
pass *v* passer, réussir
past *adj* passé
path *n* chemin *m*
pay *v* payer
peace *n* paix *f*
pen *n* plume *f*, stylo *m*
pencil *n* crayon *m*
people *n* gens *m*, monde *m*
perish *v* périr
permit *v* permettre
person *n* personne *f*
physician *n* médecin *m*, docteur *m*
pick *v* ceuillir
pick out *v* choisir

picture *n* tableau *m*
pity *v* plaindre
place endroit *m*, lieu *m*
place *v* placer, mettre
plane *n* avion *m*
play *n* pièce *f*, comédie *f*
play *v* jouer
pleasant *adj* agréable
please *v* plaire
pleasure *n* plaisir *m*
pocket *n* poche *f*
pocketknife *n* canif *m*
pond *n* étang *m*
poor *adj* pauvre, mauvais
possess *v* posséder
potato *n* pomme de terre *f*
pound *n* livre *f*
predict *v* deviner
prefer *v* préférer, aimer mieux
prepare *v* préparer
pretty *adj* joli
prevent *v* empêcher
professor *n* professeur *m*
profit *n* bénéfice *m*, profit *m*
project *n* projet *m*
promise *v* promettre
proud *adj* fier
provided that *conj* pourvu que
pull *v* tirer
punish *v* punir
pupil *n* élève *m and f*
put *v* mettre, poser, **put out** éteindre

Q

qualify *v* qualifier
quality *n* qualité *f*
quantity *n* quantité *f*
quarter *n* quart *m*
question *v* questionner, interroger
quick *adj* rapide, vite
quiet *adj* tranquille, calme
quit *v* quitter
quite *adv* tout à fait, complètement
quiz *n* petit examen *m*

R

race *n* course *f*
rain *v* pleuvoir
rain *n* pluie *f*, **rain** *v* pleuvoir
raise *v* lever, soulever

reach *v* atteindre
read *v* lire
ready *adj* prêt
real *adj* vrai
realize *v* se rendre compte
really *adv* réellement
reason *n* raison *f*
receive *v* recevoir
recognize *v* reconnaître
reflect *v* réfléchir
refresh *v* rafraîchir
regard *v* considérer
regret *v* regretter
relative *n* parent *m*, *adj* relatif
remain *v* rester
remark *n* remarque *f*, propos *m*
remember *v* se rappeler, se souvenir
renounce *v* renoncer
rent *n* loyer *m*
rent *v* louer
repair *v* réparer
reply *v* répondre, répliquer
require *v* exiger, demander
resolve *v* résoudre
rest *n* repos *m*
rest *v* se reposer
retain *v* garder, retenir
return *v* revenir
reward *n* récompense *f*
rich *adj* riche
right *adj* juste, correct, **be right** avoir raison
ring *v* sonner
road *n* route *f*
room *n* place *f*, chambre *f*, salle *f*
round *adj* rond
rule *n* règlement *m*, règle *f*
rumor *n* bruit *m*
run *v* courir

S

sadden *v* désoler, attrister
safe *adj* sûr, en sûreté
salary *n* salaire *m*
same *adj* même, pareil
sand *n* sable *m*
satisfied *adj* satisfait, content
save *v* sauver (rescue), épargner (economize)
say *v* dire
scarcely *adv* à peine, guère

Review of French Grammar 379

school *n* école *f*
season *n* saison *f*
seat *v* asseoir
see *v* voir
seek *v* chercher
seem *v* paraître, sembler
sell *v* vendre
send *v* envoyer, **send for** envoyer chercher
sentence *n* phrase *f*
servant *n* servante *f*, valet *m*, domestique *m* and *f*, bonne *f*
serve *v* servir
set *n* serie *f*
set *v* mettre, **set up** monter, dresser
several *adj* plusieurs
share *v* partager
shine *v* briller, luire
shirt *n* chemise *f*
show *n* spectacle *m*
show *v* montrer, faire voir
sidewalk *n* trottoir *m*
sign *v* signer
silk *n* soie *f*
silver *n* argent *m*
similar *adj* pareil, semblable
since *conj* depuis que, puisque, **since** *adv and prep* depuis
sing *v* chanter
sister *n* soeur *f*
sit *v* s'asseoir, **be seated** être assis
skate *v* patiner
slacken *v* ralentir
sleep *n* sommeil *m*
sleep *v* dormir
slow *adj* lent, tardif, en retard
slow down *v* ralentir
small *adj* petit
smell *v* sentir
smile *n* sourire *m*, *v* sourire
smoke *v* fumer
so *adv* si, de telle manière, ainsi
some *adj* quelque, quelques-uns
someone *pron* quelqu'un
something *n* quelque chose *m*
sometimes *adv* quelque fois, parfois
somewhere *adv* quelque part
son *n* fils *m*
song *n* chanson *f*
soon *adv* bientôt
sorrow *n* peine *f*
sorry *adj* fâché, **be sorry** être fâché, regretter
sound *v* sonner
spare *v* épargner, ménager, céder, éviter
speak *v* parler
speech *n* discours *m*
speed *n* vitesse *f*, rapidité *f*
spend *v* dépenser (money), passer (time)
stairs *n* escalier *m*
stamp *n* timbre *m*
start *v* partir, se mettre en route, commencer
station *n* gare *f*, station *f*
stay *n* séjour *m*
stay *v* demeurer, rester
still *adv* encore, toujours, *adj* tranquille, *conj* cependant
stir *v* remuer
stone *n* pierre *f*
stop *v* arrêter, cesser
store *n* magasin *m*, boutique *f*
storm *n* orage *m*
story *n* histoire *f*, récit *m*, conte *m*, étage (floor) *m*
straight *adj* droit
strange *adj* étrange
strawberry *n* fraise *f*
street *n* rue *f*
stretch *v* tendre, étendre
strict *adj* sévère, étroit, strict
strike *v* frapper, sonner
study *n* étude *f*
study *v* étudier
succeed *v* réussir
such *adj* tel pareil, semblable
suffer *v* souffrir, subir, endurer
suffice *v* suffire, satisfaire
sugar *n* sucre *m*
suit *n* complet *m*, procès (law) *m*
suitcase *n* valise *f*
summer *n* été *m*
sun *n* soleil *m*
sure *adj* sûr
surprise *v* surprendre, étonner
swift *adj* rapide
swim *v* nager

T

table *n* table *f*
take *v* prendre, porter, emporter, conduire

tale *n* conte *m*
talk *v* parler, causer
tall *adj* grand, haut
task *n* tâche *f*, besogne *f*
taste *n* goût *m*
tea *n* thé *m*
teach *v* enseigner, apprendre
teacher *n* professeur *m*, maître *m*, instituteur *m*
tear *n* larme *f*
tear *v* déchirer
tell *v* raconter, dire, annoncer
test *n* épreuve *f*, examen *m*
thank *v* remercier
then *adv* alors, ensuite, puis
there *adv* là, **there is** il y a, voilà
thing *n* chose *f*, affaire *f*
think *v* penser, croire
thirst *n* soif *f*
thorn *n* épine *f*
throw *v* jeter
ticket *n* billet *m*
tie *v* lier, attacher
till *v* cultiver
time *n* temps *m*, fois *f*, époque *f*
tired *adj* fatigué
today *adv* aujourd'hui
together *adv* ensemble
tomorrow *adv* demain
tongue *n* langue *f*
touch *v* toucher
toward *prep* vers, envers
towel *n* serviette *f*
town *n* ville *f*
trade *n* marché *m*, commerce *m*
travel *v* voyager
tree *n* arbre *m*
trouble *v* déranger, gêner
true *adj* vrai
trunk *n* malle *f*
trust *v* avoir confiance, se fier à
truth *n* vérité *f*
try *v* tâcher, essayer
turn *n* tour *m*
turn *v* tourner
twice *adv* deux fois

U

under *prep* sous, *adv* au-dessous
underneath *adv* en dessous
understand *v* comprendre
unless *conj* à moins que
unnecessary *adj* inutile

unpleasant *adj* désagréable
until *prep* jusqu'à, *conj* jusqu'à ce que
up *adj* en haut, **go up** *v* monter
up to *prep* jusqu'à
use *n* emploi *m*
use *v* se servir de, employer
useful *adj* utile
useless *adj* inutile
usually *adv* ordinairement
utensil *n* ustensile *m*
utilize *v* utiliser

V

vacation *n* vacances *f pl*
vaccinate *v* vacciner
vaccine *n* vaccin *m*
valiant *adj* vaillant
valley *n* vallée *f*
vanilla *n* vanille *f*
vanish *v* s'évanouir
variety *n* variété *f*
various *adj* divers
vary *v* varier
vault *n* voûte *f*
vegetable *n* légume *m*
vehicle *n* véhicule *m*
veil *n* voile *m*
vein *n* veine *f*
very *adv* très, bien, fort, beaucoup
village *n* village *m*
visit *n* visite *f*
visit *v* faire visite à
voice *n* voix *f*

W

wager *v* parier
wait *v* attendre
waiter *n* garçon *m*
walk *n* promenade *f*, **walk** *v* marcher, se promener
wall *n* mur *m*
want *v* vouloir, avoir envie de
war *n* guerre *f*
warm *adj* chaud
warm *v* chauffer
warn *v* avertir
wash *v* laver
watch *n* montre *f*
watch *v* regarder, surveiller
water *n* eau *f*
way *n* route *f*, voie *f*, chemin *m*, moyen (means) *m*

wear *v* porter
weather *n* temps *m*
week *n* semaine *f*
weep *v* pleurer
welcome *v* accueillir
well *adv* bien, **as well as** aussi bien que
when *conj* quand
where *adv* où
whether *conj* si
while *conj* pendant que, tandis que
whole *adj* tout, entier
wide *adj* large
will *v* vouloir
win *v* gagner
wine *n* vin *m*
wipe *v* essuyer
wise *adj* sage
wish *v* vouloir, désirer, souhaiter
with *prep* avec
withdraw *v* se retirer
within *prep* dedans
without *prep* sans

woman *n* femme *f*
wonder *v* se demander
wood *n* bois *m*
word *n* mot *m*, parole *f*
work *n* travail *m*, besogne *f*, ouvrage *m*, tâche *f* oeuvre
work *v* travailler, marcher
world *n* monde *m*
worry *n* ennui *m*, souci *m*, *v* préoccuper
worst *adj* pire, *adv* pis
worth *n* valeur *m*, prix *m*
write *v* écrire
wrong *adj* faux, **be wrong** *v* avoir tort

Y

year *n* an *m*, année *f*
yellow *adj* jaune
yesterday *adv* hier
yet *conj* pourtant, cependant, *adv* encore, déjà
yield *v* céder
young *adj* jeune

For further reference

Grammars

Barson, John
   La Grammaire à l'oeuvre
   Holt, Rinehart and Winston
Comeau, Raymond F., Bustin Normand, Francine L., and Lamoureux, L.
   Ensemble: Grammaire
   Holt, Rinehart and Winston
Daudon, René
   French in Review
   Harcourt Brace Jovanovich
Dubois, J., Jouannon, G., and Lagane, R.
   La Grammaire Française
   Librairie Larousse

Fraser, Ian Forbes
   French Reviewed
   Holt, Rinehart and Winston
Grevisse, Maurice
   Grammaire Française
   Librairie A. Hatier
Grevisse, Maurice
   Précis de Grammaire Française
   Editions J. Duculot
Jenkins, E. S.
   French Grammar
   David McKay Company

Dictionaries

Deak, Etienne
   Dictionnaire d'américanismes
   Edition du Dauphin
Hanse, Joseph
   Dictionnaire des difficultés grammaticales et lexicologiques
   Les Editions Scientifiques et Littéraires
Levieux, Michel and Eleanor
   Beyond the Dictionary in French
   Cassell

Mansion, J.E.
   Harrap's New Standard French and English Dictionary
   Charles Scribner's Sons
Micro Robert
   Le Robert
Thomas, Adolphe V. and Toro, Michel de
   Dictionnaire de Poche des difficultés
   Librairie Larousse

Review of German Grammar

- Articles 382
- Nouns 383
- Pronouns 384
- Prepositions 386
- Adjectives and adverbs 387
- Verbs 388
- Conjunctions 391
- Numbers, dates, time 392
- German-English dictionary 396
- English-German dictionary 402

The grammar of German is closely related to the grammar of English. This is because English, to a large extent, is Germanic in origin, as is obvious from the large number of English words that derive from Germanic sources. Consider *Vater* and father, *Mutter* and mother, *Sohn* and son, to name just a few examples of the many cognates the two languages exhibit.

As you can expect, therefore, German phrases, clauses, and sentences are constructed in somewhat the same way in both languages. The greatest exceptions appear in the relative absence of gender in English nouns, compared with the German noun genders. Another aspect of gender that is missing in English, in contrast with German, is the agreement of adjectives with the gender of the nouns they modify.

To cite an additional difference, German nouns (as well as the adjectives used to modify them) are declined to show their functions in sentences. This means that a noun will change in form to show that it is being used, for example, as the subject of a verb, the object of a verb, or the indirect object of a verb. Yet another form of this linguistic process of declension is the genitive, which we know as the possessive. In English, nouns rarely decline to show function. Instead we show subject, object, and indirect object by placement of the noun within the phrase, clause, or sentence. We do, however, use an apostrophe and the letter *s* to show possession with certain nouns.

Articles

Definite articles

Definite articles agree in gender and number with the nouns they modify: *der* for the masculine singular, *die* for the feminine singular, and *das* for the neuter singular. All three genders have *die* in the plural.

der Mann the man
die Frau the woman
das Kind the child
die Männer the men
die Frauen the women
die Kinder the children

The case of the noun determines the case of the article:
Das Kind sieht den Mann. The child sees the man.
die Frau des Mannes the man's wife
Der Mann gibt dem Kind. The man gives the child.
The dative and the accusative singular of the definite article are often contracted with a preposition. For example, *am* is used instead of *an dem,* at the. Other

Declension of articles: Definite | Indefinite

Case	Singular Masc.	Singular Fem.	Singular Neuter	Plural	Singular Masc.	Singular Fem.	Singular Neuter	Plural
Nominative	der	die	das	die	ein	eine	ein	einige
Genitive	des	der	des	der	eines	einer	eines	einiger
Dative	dem	der	dem	den	einem	einer	einem	einigen
Accusative	den	die	das	die	einen	eine	ein	einige

contractions for prepositions with articles are:
 ans = an das beside the
 beim = bei dem at the
 im = in dem in the
 ins = in das into the
 zum = zu dem to the

The definite article is used before abstract nouns.
 Es lebe die Demokratie! Long live democracy!

Diminutives formed with the endings *chen* and *lein* are always neuter:
 das Mädchen the girl
 das Fräulein the miss
 das Kindchen the little child

Indefinite articles

Indefinite articles agree in gender with the nouns they modify: *ein* for the masculine singular, *eine* for the feminine singular, and *ein* for the neuter singular. There is no plural for the indefinite article. The word *einige*, some, is used for more than one person or thing.
 ein Vater a father   *einige Väter* some fathers
 eine Mutter a mother   *einige Mütter* some mothers
 ein Kind a child   *einige Kinder* some children

The case of the noun determines the case of the indefinite article:
 ein Kind eines Vaters
 a child of a father

 einer Mutter Kinder
 children of a mother

 Eine Mutter hat einige Kinder.
 A mother has some children.

 die Kinder eines Mannes
 a man's children

Nouns

Declining singular nouns

Nouns are either masculine, feminine, or neuter. Nouns are declined. In the genitive singular form, for example, most masculine and neuter nouns add *s* to the nominative singular form.
 Nominative *der Bruder* the brother
 Genitive   *des Bruders* of the brother

 Nominative *das Wetter* the weather
 Genitive   *des Wetters* of the weather

If a noun is monosyllabic, *es* is added in the genitive singular.
 Nominative *der Sohn*   the son
 Genitive   *des Sohnes* of the son

 Nominative *das Haus*   the house
 Genitive   *des Hauses* of the house

Some nouns ending in *e* add *n* in the genitive singular.
 Nominative *der Verwandte*   the relative
 Genitive   *des Verwandten* of the relative

Review of German Grammar

Der Sohn des Bruders ist der Neffe.
The brother's son is the nephew.

Der Vater des Kindes ist alt.
The child's father is old.

The dative and accusative forms of a masculine or neuter singular noun are usually the same as those of the nominative. If the nominative ends in *e*, however, *n* is added.

Dative   *dem Bruder* to the brother
Accusative *den Bruder* the brother

Dative   *dem Haus*   to the house
Accusative *das Haus*   the house

Feminine singular nouns remain unchanged in all cases.

Die Tochter der Mutter ist schön.
The mother's daughter is beautiful.

Die Frau gibt der Tochter die Birne.
The woman gives the daughter the pear.

Declining plural nouns

The plural of all genders is formed in four ways. Adding an umlaut to the singular form.

der Bruder the brother *die Brüder* the brothers

Adding *er* plus an umlaut to the singular form.

der Mann the man *die Männer* the men

Adding *e* plus an umlaut to the singular form.

die Nacht the night *die Nächte* the nights

Adding *en* to the singular form.

die Frau the woman *die Frauen* the women

The nominative, genitive, and accusative of plural nouns are all spelled identically. The dative adds *n* to all plural forms, with the exception of plurals formed by adding *en* to the singular.

	men	brothers	women
Nominative	die Männer	die Brüder	die Frauen
Genitive	der Männer	der Brüder	der Frauen
Dative	den Männern	den Brüdern	den Frauen
Accusative	die Männer	die Brüder	die Frauen

All nouns are capitalized.

Forms of the noun

Certain nouns have two forms, one for masculine gender, the other for feminine gender. For such nouns, the feminine form adds *in* to the masculine form.

Masc.	*Fem.*	
der Anwalt	die Anwältin	the lawyer
der Arzt	die Ärztin	the physician
der Künstler	die Künstlerin	the artist
der Lehrer	die Lehrerin	the teacher
der Wirt	die Wirtin	the host, the hostess

Compound nouns take the gender and declension of the last noun.

das Haus + *die Tür* = *die Haustür*
the house + the door = the door to the house

der Schlaf + *das Zimmer* = *das Schlafzimmer*
the sleep + the room = the bedroom

die Tasche + *das Tuch* = *das Taschentuch*
the pocket + the cloth = the handkerchief

Pronouns

Personal pronouns

Personal pronouns agree in number and gender with their antecedents.

	Nominative singular	*Nominative plural*
1st person	ich I	wir we
2nd person	du you (informal)	ihr you (informal)
3rd person	er, sie, es he, she, it	sie they
		Sie you (formal)

The pronoun *ich* is capitalized only when it is the first word of a sentence. The formal pronoun *Sie* is always capitalized.

Ich sehe dich.
I see you.

Der Tisch ist gross; er ist braun.
The table is big; it is brown.

Die Kinder spielen in dem Haus; sie singen in ihm.
The children play in the house; they sing in it.

Er gibt uns das Brot; er gibt es uns.
He gives us the bread; he gives it to us.

Reflexive pronouns

A reflexive pronoun functions as a direct or indirect object referring to the subject of a verb. It agrees in number and gender with the subject of the verb.

Dieter zieht sich an. Dieter dresses himself.
Wir waschen uns. We wash ourselves.

Ich wasche mir die Hände. I myself wash my hands.

Ihr ärgert euch. You are angry.

Some verbs that are reflexive in German are not reflexive in English.

sich anziehen to dress
sich erinnern to remember
sich freuen to be glad
sich fürchten to be afraid
sich hüten to be careful
sich trennen to separate
sich verbergen to hide
sich verlassen to rely
sich vorsehen to be careful

Declension of pronouns

Personal pronouns

	Singular			Plural		
	First person	*Second person*	*Third person*	*First person*	*Second person*	*Third person*
Nominative	ich I	du you	er he, sie she, es it	wir we	ihr you	sie they
Genitive	meiner of me	deiner of you	seiner his, ihrer her, seiner its	unser of us	euer of you	ihrer of them
Dative	mir to me	dir to you	ihm to him, ihr to her, ihm to it	uns to us	euch to you	ihnen to them
Accusative	mich me	dich you	ihn him, sie her, es it	uns us	euch you	sie them, Sie you (formal)

Reflexive pronouns

Subject	*Direct object*	*Indirect object*
ich I	mich myself	mir (to) myself
du you	dich yourself	dir (to) yourself
er, sie, es he, she, it	sich himself, herself, itself	sich (to) himself etc.
wir we	uns ourselves	uns (to) ourselves
ihr you	euch yourselves	euch (to) yourselves
sie they	sich themselves	sich (to) themselves
Sie you (formal)	sich yourselves	sich (to) yourselves

Relative pronouns
der who, which, that

	Singular			Plural
	Masc.	*Fem.*	*Neuter*	*All genders*
Nominative	der	die	das	die
Genitive	dessen	deren	dessen	deren
Dative	dem	der	dem	denen
Accusative	den	die	das	die

welcher who, which, that

Nominative	welcher	welche	welches	welche
Genitive	dessen	deren	dessen	deren
Dative	welchem	welcher	welchem	welchem
Accusative	welchen	welche	welches	welche

Demonstrative pronouns
dieser this

	Singular			Plural
	Masc.	*Fem.*	*Neuter*	*All genders*
Nominative	dieser	diese	dieses	diese
Genitive	dieses	dieser	dieses	dieser
Dative	diesem	dieser	diesem	diesen
Accusative	diesen	diese	dieses	diese

jener that

Nominative	jener	jene	jenes	jene
Genitive	jenes	jener	jenes	jener
Dative	jenem	jener	jenem	jenen
Accusative	jenen	jene	jedes	jede

Interrogative pronouns
wer who **was** what

Nominative	wer	was
Genitive	wessen	(no form)
Dative	wem	(no form)
Accusative	wen	was

Review of German Grammar

Demonstrative pronouns
Demonstrative pronouns agree in number and gender with their antecedents. The demonstrative pronouns are *dieser* this, and *jener* that.
> *Dieses Buch ist besser als jenes.*
> This book is better than that.

Relative pronouns
Relative pronouns agree with their antecedents in number and gender. The masculine is *der*, who, that, or which; the feminine is *die*, who, that, or which; and the neuter is *das*, who, that, or which.
> *Der Eimer, der in der Küche ist, ist voll.*
> The pail that is in the kitchen is full.

> *Die Tante, die im Garten arbeitet, ist hübsch.*
> The aunt who is working in the garden is pretty.

Welcher, welche, welches are relative pronouns, with the same meanings as *der, die,* and *das*. They are usually found in the written language.
> *Dem Schüler, welchem ich das Buch gab, traue ich.*
> I trust the student to whom I gave the book.

Interrogative pronouns
The interrogative pronouns are *wer* for persons; *was* for things. *Welcher, welche,* and *welches* are used for "which one." There is no plural for *wer* or *was*.
> *Wer ist das?* Who is this?
> *Was gebt ihr?* What are you giving?

English questions introduced by "with what," "from what," etc. are expressed in German by *wo* "where," plus a preposition.
> *Wovon spricht er?* What is he talking about?
> *Womit schreibt ihr?* What do you write with?
> *Wofür gibt er Geld?* What is he giving money for?

Wo becomes *wor* before a vowel.
> *Woran denkst du?*
> What do you think about?

> *Worin liegt die Tugend?*
> Where is the virtue?

> *Worüber liegen die Bücher?*
> What are the books above?

Possessive pronouns
Possessive pronouns are formed in the following ways. By adding *er, e,* or *es* to the possessive adjective. For example, *meiner, meine, meines.*
> *Wessen Tasse ist das? Es ist meine.*
> Whose cup is this? It is mine.

By adding *e* to the possessive adjective and employing the definite article. For example, *der deine, die deine, das deine.*
> *Wessen Glas ist das? Es ist das deine.*
> Whose glass is this? It is yours.

By adding *ige* to the possessive adjective and employing the definite article. For example, *der seinige, die seinige, das seinige.*
> *Ist das dein Papier? Nein, es ist das seinige.*
> Is this your paper? No, it is his.

Prepositions

Prepositions are followed by words in the genitive, dative, or accusative case.

Prepositions taking the genitive
anstatt instead of *trotz* in spite of
ausserhalb outside of *während* during
innerhalb inside of *wegen* on account of
oberhalb above

> *wegen des Wetters* because of the weather
> *trotz der Musik* in spite of the music

Prepositions taking the dative
aus out of *nach* after
ausser besides *seit* since
bei at *von* from, of
gegenüber opposite of *zu* at, to
mit with

> *Bei mir spricht man deutsch.*
> At my house everyone speaks German.

> *Nach der Schule gehe ich nach Hause.*
> After school I go home.

Prepositions taking the accusative
durch through *ohne* without
für for *um* around, about
gegen against, toward

> *Ich stimme für den Kandidaten.*
> I vote for the candidate.

Prepositions taking the dative or the accusative
The following prepositions take the dative case when they answer the question Where? They take the accusative when they answer the question Where to?

an on *über* over, above
auf on, upon *unter* under, among
hinter behind *vor* before
in in, into *zwischen* between
neben near, beside

> *Ich stehe vor der Tür.*
> I am standing in front of the door.

> *Ich lege das Buch auf den Tisch.*
> I put the book on the table.

Adjectives and adverbs

Forms of adjectives

Predicative adjectives never change form.
   Der Tiger ist zahm. The tiger is tame.
   Das Kind ist frech. The child is impudent.
Attributive adjectives add *e* when they modify a noun preceded by a definite article. They add *er* for the masculine, *e* for the feminine, and *es* for the neuter when they modify a noun preceded by an indefinite article.
   der grosse Baum the big tree
   das kleine Brot the small bread
   ein kleiner Baum a small tree
   ein kleines Brot a small bread
The plural adds *en* in all genders and cases.
   die schweren Bücher the heavy books
There is no plural form for adjectives used with indefinite articles.

Possessive adjectives

Possessive adjectives agree in number and gender with the nouns they modify and are declined like them.
   meine Katze my cat
   seines Hundes of his dog
The plural here refers to the number of the noun modified.
   deine Bücher your books
   ihre Brüder her brothers

Declension of adjectives

with definite article

	Masc.	Singular Fem.	Neuter
Nominative	grosse the big	grosse	grosse
Genitive	grossen of the big	grossen	grossen
Dative	grossen to the big	grossen	grossen
Accusative	grossen the big	grosse	grosse

with indefinite article

Nominative	grosser a big	grosse	grosses
Genitive	grossen of a big	grossen	grossen
Dative	grossen to a big	grossen	grossen
Accusative	grossen a big	grosse	grosses

Forms of possessive adjectives

	Masc.	Singular Fem.	Neuter	Plural All genders
my	mein	meine	mein	meine
your	dein	deine	dein	deine
his	sein	seine	sein	seine
her	ihr	ihre	ihr	ihre
its	sein	seine	sein	seine
our	unser	unsere	unser	unsere
your	euer	eure	euer	eure
their	ihr	ihre	ihr	ihre

Declension of possessive adjectives

Nominative	mein	meine	mein	meine
Genitive	meines	meiner	meines	meiner
Dative	meinem	meiner	meinem	meinen
Accusative	meinen	meine	mein	meine
Nominative	dein	deine	dein	deine
Genitive	deines	deiner	deines	deiner
Dative	deinem	deiner	deinem	deinen
Accusative	deinen	deine	dein	deine
Nominative	sein	seine	sein	seine
Genitive	seines	seiner	seines	seiner
Dative	seinem	seiner	seinem	seinen
Accusative	seinen	seine	sein	seine
Nominative	ihr	ihre	ihr	ihre
Genitive	ihres	ihrer	ihres	ihrer
Dative	ihrem	ihrer	ihrem	ihren
Accusative	ihren	ihre	ihr	ihre
Nominative	sein	seine	sein	seine
Genitive	seines	seiner	seines	seiner
Dative	seinem	seiner	seinem	seinen
Accusative	seinen	seine	sein	seine
Nominative	unser	unsere	unser	unsere
Genitive	unseres	unserer	unseres	unserer
Dative	unserem	unserer	unserem	unseren
Accusative	unseren	unsere	unser	unsere
Nominative	euer	eure	euer	eure
Genitive	eures	eurer	eures	eurer
Dative	eurem	eurer	eurem	euren
Accusative	euren	eure	euer	eure
Nominative	ihr	ihre	ihr	ihre
Genitive	ihres	ihrer	ihres	ihrer
Dative	ihrem	ihrer	ihrem	ihren
Accusative	ihren	ihre	ihr	ihre

Review of German Grammar

Adverbs

Adverbs are identical with adjectives but are not declined.

Er geht langsam. He goes slowly.

Comparative forms

The comparative form usually adds *er* to the adjective.

schnell fast *schneller* faster

Sometimes an umlaut is added before the *er.*

arm poor *ärmer* poorer

The comparatives of certain adjectives and adverbs are not formed in the conventional way.

gut good *besser* better
viel much *mehr* more
gern gladly *lieber* rather

Ich lese viel aber er liest mehr.
I read much but he reads more.

Superlatives

The superlative is formed by adding *ste* or *este* to the adjective. An umlaut is sometimes added to the vowel preceding the *ste* or *este.*

der ärmste the poorest
die kleinste the smallest
das dümmste the least intelligent
der älteste the oldest

Adjectives with irregular comparative forms also have irregular superlatives.

viel, mehr, am meisten much, more, most
gut, besser, am besten, good, better, best

Verbs

Conjugation of auxiliary verbs

The verbs *sein* to be, *haben* to have, and *werden* to become, are used in the compound tenses of other verbs.

Rules for using verbs

There is only one present tense, but it translates in three ways into English.

Ich gehe zur Schule.
I go to school. I am going to school.
I do go to school.

To form a question, subject and verb are reversed.

Du spielst. You are playing.
Spielst du? Are you playing?

In a negative sentence *nicht* is placed after the verb:

Wir lesen nicht. We do not read.

Conjugation of auxiliary verbs

Infinitive		sein to be	haben to have	werden to become			
Indicative	*Present*				*Imperfect*		
	ich	bin	habe	werde	war	hatte	wurde
	du	bist	hast	wirst	warst	hattest	wurdest
	er, sie, es	ist	hat	wird	war	hatte	wurde
	wir	sind	haben	werden	waren	hatten	wurden
	ihr	seid	habt	werdet	wart	hattet	wurdet
	sie	sind	haben	werden	waren	hatten	wurden
(formal)	Sie	sind	haben	werden	waren	hatten	wurden
	Perfect				*Future*		
	ich	bin gewesen	habe gehabt	bin geworden	werde sein	werde haben	werde werden
	du	bist gewesen	hast gehabt	bist geworden	wirst sein	wirst haben	wirst werden
	er, sie, es	ist gewesen	hat gehabt	ist geworden	wird sein	wird haben	wird werden
	wir	sind gewesen	haben gehabt	sind geworden	werden sein	werden haben	werden werden
	ihr	seid gewesen	habt gehabt	seid geworden	werdet sein	werdet haben	werdet werden
	sie	sind gewesen	haben gehabt	sind geworden	werden sein	werden haben	werden werden
(formal)	Sie	sind gewesen	haben gehabt	sind geworden	werden sein	werden haben	werden werden

Formation of tenses

To form the perfect tense of any verb, the present tense of *haben* or *sein* is used together with the past participle of the verb.

Er hat gehabt. He has had.
Sie sind gewesen. They have been.

To form the future tense of any verb, the present tense of *werden* is used with the infinitive of the verb.

Du wirst essen. You will eat.
Wir werden tanzen. We shall dance.

Weak and strong verbs

Weak verbs are known in English as regular verbs. The infinitive, past tense, and past participle are shown here for the weak verb *zahlen*.

zahlen, zahlte, gezahlt (to) pay, paid, paid

Strong verbs are known in English as irregular verbs. The infinitive, past tense, and past participle are shown here for the strong verb *singen*.

singen, sang, gesungen (to) sing, sang, sung

Whether weak or strong, all infinitives end in *en*.

machen (to) make   *gehen* (to) go

Dropping the *en* yields the stem of the verb, for example, *mach* for *machen*, *geh* for *gehen*. The endings for the various tenses can then be added to the stem.

Present tense

To form the present tense, the same endings are used for weak verbs and strong verbs: *e, st, t, en, t, en, en*.

Imperfect tense of weak verbs

The imperfect tense of weak verbs is formed by adding the endings *te, test, te, ten, tet, ten* to the stem of the verb.

If the infinitive stem of a verb ends in *d* or *t*, an *e* precedes the endings. In the verb *warten*, for example, the stem is *wart*. The imperfect of *warten*, therefore, is as follows:

ich wartete	I waited	*wir warteten*	we waited
du wartetest	you waited	*ihr wartetet*	you waited
er wartete	he waited	*sie warteten*	they waited

Past participle of weak verbs

The past participle of weak verbs is formed by putting *ge* before the third person singular of the present tense of the verb.

(er) spielt he plays, *gespielt* played
(er) dankt he thanks, *gedankt* thanked

Conjugation of weak and strong verbs

		weak	strong				
Infinitive		*machen*	*gehen*				
		to make	to go				

Indicative	*Present*			*Imperfect*		**Imperative**	
	I make	I go		I made	I went	(fam. sing.)	*mache*
	I do make	I do go		I did make	I did go	(fam. pl.)	*macht*
	I am making	I am going		I was making	I was going	(formal)	*machen Sie*
ich	*mache*	*gehe*		*machte*	*ging*		
du	*machst*	*gehst*		*machtest*	*gingst*	(fam. sing.)	*gehe*
er, sie, es	*macht*	*geht*		*machte*	*ging*	(fam. pl.)	*geht*
wir	*machen*	*gehen*		*machten*	*gingen*	(formal)	*gehen Sie*
ihr	*macht*	*geht*		*machtet*	*gingt*		
sie	*machen*	*gehen*		*machten*	*gingen*		
(formal) *Sie*	*machen*	*gehen*		*machten*	*gingen*		

	Perfect			*Future*		**Participles**	
	I have made	I have gone		I shall make	I shall go	*Past*	*gemacht*
ich	*habe gemacht*	*bin gegangen*		*werde machen*	*werde gehen*	*Present*	*machend*
du	*hast gemacht*	*bist gegangen*		*wirst machen*	*wirst gehen*		
er, sie, es	*hat gemacht*	*ist gegangen*		*wird machen*	*wird gehen*	*Past*	*ist gegangen*
wir	*haben gemacht*	*sind gegangen*		*werden machen*	*werden gehen*	*Present*	*gehend*
ihr	*habt gemacht*	*seid gegangen*		*werdet machen*	*werdet gehen*		
sie	*haben gemacht*	*sind gegangen*		*werden machen*	*werden gehen*		
(formal) *Sie*	*haben gemacht*	*sind gegangen*		*werden machen*	*werden gehen*		

Review of German Grammar

Perfect tense of weak verbs
The perfect tense of weak verbs is formed by conjugating *sein* to be, or *haben* to have, plus the past participle. Among the verbs forming the perfect with *sein* are verbs of motion.
Ich bin gegangen. I have gone.
Er ist ihm gefolgt. He has followed him.
All reflexive verbs form the perfect with *haben* and the past participle. This is true both for weak and strong verbs.
Sie hat sich gewaschen. She has washed herself.
Wir haben uns gestritten. We have quarreled.
Er hat sich gefreut. He was glad.
Note that past participles are placed at the end of the sentence or independent clause.
Du hast das Buch gelesen. You have read the book.

Imperfect and past participle of strong verbs
Strong verbs form their own imperfect and past participle. Some examples of strong verbs are shown here.

Infinitive	Imperfect	Past participle
fliegen (to) fly	*flog*	*geflogen*
kommen (to) come	*kam*	*gekommen*
lassen (to) let	*liess*	*gelassen*
leiden (to) suffer	*litt*	*gelitten*
rufen (to) call	*rief*	*gerufen*
schlafen (to) sleep	*schlief*	*geschlafen*

Future tense
The future tense of all verbs, whether weak or strong, is formed by conjugating *werden* in the present tense plus the infinitive of the verb.
ich werde halten I shall hold
du wirst halten you will hold
er wird halten he will hold
wir werden halten we will hold
ihr werdet halten you will hold
sie werden halten they will hold

Imperative mood
The imperative with the polite *Sie* is formed by using the infinitive of a verb, followed by *Sie*. To be very polite, the word *bitte* (please) may be added:
Schreiben Sie bitte. Please write.
Gehen Sie bitte. Please go.
The imperative with the *du* form is expressed by deleting the *en* of the infinitive.

Infinitive		Imperative	
spielen (to) play		*spiel* play	
singen (to) sing		*sing* sing	

The imperative for the *ihr,* you plural, form uses the present tense *ihr* form of the verb without the pronoun *ihr.*
ihr geht you go   *geht* go
ihr nehmt you take   *nehmt* take
The imperative of the first person plural is expressed by the infinitive followed by *wir* we.
helfen wir let us help   *geben wir* let us give

Forming the passive voice
To form the passive, the auxiliary verb *werden* (to become) is conjugated and followed by the past participle of the main verb:
Sie wird getragen.
She is being carried.

Er wurde gehört.
He was heard.

Wir werden gelobt werden.
We are going to be praised.

Impersonal verbs
Many verbs are used only in the third person singular with the pronoun *es* it. They are used in all tenses. Some examples follow.
es regnet it is raining
es schneit it is snowing
es klopft there is a knock
es gelingt mir I succeed
es gibt there is, there are
wie geht es dir? how are you?
es geht mir gut I am fine
es tut mir leid I am sorry

Verbal prefixes
There are two types of verbal prefixes: inseparable and separable. Although these prefixes may change the meaning of a verb, they do not affect conjugation. Some examples of inseparable verbal prefixes follow.
be as in *besuchen* (to) visit
ent as in *entspannen* (to) relax
er as in *erlangen* (to) get
ge as in *gelingen* (to) succeed
miss as in *misstrauen* (to) mistrust
ver as in *vertrauen* (to) trust
zer as in *zerbrechen* (to) break

Separable verbal prefixes are prefixes that also function as prepositions. Some examples follow.
anhören (to) listen   *an* at, on, to
aufstehen (to) get up   *auf* on, onto
untergehen (to) perish   *unter* under, among
vorstellen (to) introduce *vor* before

In the simple tenses, the verbal prefix separates from the verb and is placed at the end of the sentence. Consider this example, which uses the verb *untergehen.*
Die Sonne geht unter. The sun sets.
In compound tenses, the verbal prefix does not separate. The *ge* of the past participle appears between the prefix and the verb.
Er hat zugehört. He has listened.
Wir wurden angestellt. We were hired.

Modal auxiliary verbs

Six verbs expressing certain modes of action have a conjugation of their own.

dürfen (to) be allowed to, expressing permission
können (to) be able to, expressing ability
mögen (to) like to, expressing desire
müssen (to) have to, expressing obligation
sollen (to) be obliged to *or* to be said to, expressing obligation
wollen (to) want, expressing intent

The principal forms of the modal auxiliaries follow.

Infinitive	Imperfect	Past participle
dürfen	durfte	gedurft
können	konnte	gekonnt
mögen	mochte	gemocht
müssen	musste	gemusst
sollen	sollte	gesollt
wollen	wollte	gewollt

The following sentences show typical uses of the modal auxiliary verbs. (Modal auxiliaries are used frequently, since they express thoughts commonly needed in situations that arise in the everyday lives of people of all types.)

Willst du nach Hause gehen?
Do you want to go home?

Er darf nicht spielen.
He is not allowed to play.

Wir konnten rennen.
We were able to run.

Sie mag keine Milch.
She does not like milk.

Er hat sprechen gekonnt.
He was able to speak.

Sie muss üben.
She must exercise.

Present tense of modal auxiliary verbs

	dürfen I may	können I can	mögen I may, I like	müssen I must	sollen I should	wollen I want
ich	darf	kann	mag	muss	soll	will
du	darfst	kannst	magst	musst	sollst	willst
er, sie, es	darf	kann	mag	muss	soll	will
wir	dürfen	können	mögen	müssen	sollen	wollen
ihr	dürft	könnt	mögt	müsst	sollt	wollt
sie	dürfen	können	mögen	müssen	sollen	wollen

Conjunctions

There are two types of conjunctions: coordinating conjunctions and subordinating conjunctions.

Coordinating conjunctions

Coordinating conjunctions connect principal clauses and do not affect word order.

Ich trinke Wein, aber Dieter trinkt Bier.
I drink wine but Dieter drinks beer.

Er liest nicht, sondern schläft.
He does not read but sleeps.

Common coordinating conjunctions follow.

aber but
denn for
entweder . . . oder either . . . or
oder or
sondern but (on the contrary)
und and

Subordinating conjunctions

Subordinating conjunctions introduce a dependent clause. Subordinating conjunctions affect the word order.

Er geht langsam, weil er müde ist.
He goes slowly because he is tired.

Sie spielte, obgleich sie müde war.
She was playing although she was tired.

In sentences containing an independent clause and a dependent clause, the auxiliary verb comes last and is preceded by the past participle or an infinitive.

Ich schrieb, nachdem ich angekommen war.
I wrote after I had arrived.

Er trank, weil er durstig gewesen ist.
He drank because he was thirsty.

Common subordinating conjunctions follow.

als when, then
als ob as if
bevor before
bis until
da since, when
damit in order that
dass so that
obgleich although
seit, seitdem since
sobald as soon as
weil because

Review of German Grammar

Numbers, time, dates

Cardinal numbers

Cardinal numbers are not declined.
Zehn is added to the numbers three to nine to form thirteen to nineteen. Note the difference in spelling:
  sechs 6, *sechzehn* 16; *sieben* 7, *siebzehn* 17.
Zig is added to the numbers three to nine to form thirty, etc. Note the differences in spelling:
  zwei 2, *zwanzig* 20;
  drei 3, *dreissig* 30;
  sechs 6, *sechzig* 60
  sieben 7, *siebzig* 70.
The numbers from twenty to thirty and so on up to 99 are formed by using the single numbers first and adding *und* and.

Ordinal numbers

Ordinal numbers are declined as adjectives. They are usually formed by adding *te* to the cardinal numbers. With ordinal numbers beginning with *zwanzig* 20, add *ste* to form the cardinal number.

Time of day

The time of day is expressed in two ways.
  Es ist drei Uhr. It is three o'clock.
  um drei Uhr at three o'clock
The progression of time is expressed in two ways. For example, ten-fifteen can be expressed as follows.
  ein Viertel nach zehn a quarter after ten
  ein Viertel elf a quarter past ten
Ten-thirty is *halb elf.* Ten-forty-five is *drei Viertel elf.* The progression of time can also be expressed by employing minutes.
  zehn Minuten vor sieben ten minutes before seven
  zehn Minuten nach sieben ten minutes after seven
In timetables time is expressed on a twenty-four hour basis. From 12 noon to midnight, the hours are 13 to 24 o'clock.
  acht Uhr fünfundzwanzig 8:25 A.M.
  zwanzig Uhr zehn 8:10 P.M.

	Cardinal numbers	*Ordinal numbers*	
1	*eins*	*(der, die, das) erste*	first
2	*zwei*	*zweite*	second
3	*drei*	*dritte*	third
4	*vier*	*vierte*	fourth
5	*fünf*	*fünfte*	fifth
6	*sechs*	*sechste*	sixth
7	*sieben*	*siebente*	seventh
8	*acht*	*achte*	eighth
9	*neun*	*neunte*	ninth
10	*zehn*	*zehnte*	tenth
11	*elf*	*hundertste*	hundredth
12	*zwölf*	*tausendste*	thousandth
13	*dreizehn*	*millionste*	millionth
14	*vierzehn*		
15	*fünfzehn*		
16	*sechzehn*		
17	*siebzehn*		
18	*achtzehn*		
19	*neunzehn*		
20	*zwanzig*		
21	*einundzwanzig*		
22	*zweiundzwanzig*		
30	*dreissig*		
40	*vierzig*		
50	*fünfzig*		
60	*sechzig*		
70	*siebzig*		
80	*achtzig*		
90	*neunzig*		
100	*hundert*		
101	*hunderteins*		
200	*zweihundert*		
1000	*tausend*		
2000	*zweitausend*		
2300	*zweitausenddreihundert*		
4002	*viertausendzwei*		
10900	*zehntausendneunhundert*		
1000000	*eine Million*		

Review of German Grammar

Dates

When numbers are used in expressing dates, they generally are not written out. Instead, a numeral is used and followed by a period.

am 18. Dezember 1983 December 18, 1983
der 19. Mai May 19th

Days

Montag	Monday
Dienstag	Tuesday
Mittwoch	Wednesday
Donnerstag	Thursday
Freitag	Friday
Sonnabend	Saturday
Sonntag	Sunday

Seasons

Frühling	spring
Sommer	summer
Herbst	autumn
Winter	winter

Months

Januar	January	*Juli*	July
Februar	February	*August*	August
März	March	*September*	September
April	April	*Oktober*	October
Mai	May	*November*	November
Juni	June	*Dezember*	December

Arithmetical expressions

Vier und vier ist acht. Four and four are eight.
Instead of *und*, *plus* can be used.
Acht weniger sechs ist zwei. Eight minus six is two.
Instead of *weniger*, *minus* can be used.
Drei mal sieben ist einundzwanzig.
Three times seven is twenty-one.

Zehn geteilt durch zwei ist fünf.
Ten divided by two is five.

To indicate a fraction, *tel* is added to the cardinal number.

viertel ¼   *fünftel* ⅕   *sechstel* ⅙

An exception is *ein halb* ½, which is an adjective and is declined.

Er isst einen halben Kuchen. He eats a half a cake.
Another exception is *ein drittel*, which derives from *drei* three.

Indefinite numbers and amounts are not declined.

ein bisschen	a little	*etwas*	some
ein paar	a few	*genug*	enough
ein wenig	a little	*mehr*	more

Note that *ein Paar* means a pair.

Countries

With few exceptions, the names of countries are not preceded by an article. The exceptions follow.

die Niederlande the Netherlands
die Schweiz Switzerland
die Türkei Turkey

Adjectives describing a country or its people are not capitalized.

der deutsche Wein
German wine

die amerikanische Bevölkerung
the American population

die Vereinigten Staaten von Amerika
United States of America

Country	*People*	*Language*
Belgien Belgium	*Belgier* Belgian	*Französisch* French
Dänemark Denmark	*Däne* Dane	*Dänisch* Danish
Deutschland Germany	*Deutsche* German	*Deutsch* German
England England	*Engländer* Englishman	*Englisch* English
Frankreich France	*Franzose* Frenchman	*Französisch* French
Polen Poland	*Pole* Pole	*Polnisch* Polish
Russland Russia	*Russe* Russian	*Russisch* Russian
Schweden Sweden	*Schwede* Swede	*Schwedisch* Swedish
Spanien Spain	*Spanier* Spaniard	*Spanisch* Spanish

Review of German Grammar

Word order

Normal word order
As a rule the word order within a sentence is subject, verb, object.
Der Bruder liest das Buch.
The brother reads the book.

If a sentence contains a direct and an indirect object, the indirect object precedes the direct object.
Der Bruder gibt dem Vater das Buch.
The brother gives the father the book.

If the direct object is a pronoun, the direct object precedes the indirect object.
Der Bruder gibt es ihm.
The brother gives it to him.

Der Bruder gibt's dem Vater.
The brother gives it to the father.

Inverted word order
Inverted word order is used in forming questions.
Kann er lesen? Does he know how to read?
Inverted word order is used in expressing commands.
Kommen Sie her! Come here!
Inverted word order is used in sentences beginning with expressions of time or place.
Heute schlafe ich nicht.
Today I do not sleep.

In der Stadt gibt es viele Theater.
There are many theaters in the city.

In the future tense and with a modal auxiliary verb, an infinitive is placed at the end of the sentence.
Sie werden heute spielen. They will play today.
Sie können heute spielen. They can play today.
A past participle is placed at the end of a sentence.
Sie sind angekommen. They have arrived.

This highway sign illustrates typical German word order: STOPPT (stop) includes the subject "you" understood; the object AUSPUFF-PEST (exhaust pest) follows. Above this message appear the words Unsere Luft *(our air).*

Participles
A separable prefix becomes inseparable in the past participle.

A past participle precedes the auxiliary verb in sentences containing an independent clause and a dependent clause.
Wir wissen, dass er gehört hat.
We know that he has heard.

Writing letters

Date
14. August 1984 August 14, 1984

Inside address
The destination is supplied after the name of the addressee. The house number follows the street.
Herrn Max Schulz Mr. Max Schulz
Düsseldorf   8 Hauptstrasse
Hauptstrasse 8   Düsseldorf

Salutation
(informal)
  Lieber Herr Schulz Dear Mr. Schulz
(formal)
  Sehr geehrter Herr Schulz Dear Mr. Schulz

Complimentary close
(informal)
  Mit freundlichen Grüssen
  With kindest regards
(formal)
  Hochachtungsvoll Very truly yours
A letter to friends or family may close in three ways.
  Mit vielen Grüssen
  With many regards

  Mit den besten Grüssen
  With best regards

  Viele Grüsse und Küsse
  With many regards and kisses

For the traveler

Basic expressions and idioms

auf alle Fälle	at any rate
danke	
danke sehr	
danke vielmals	thank you
besten Dank	
vielen Dank	
es tut mir leid	I am sorry
gestern abend	last night
Glück haben	to be lucky
glückliche Reise	have a good trip
herzlichen Glückwunsch	congratulations
heute in acht Tagen	a week from now
Hunger (Durst) haben	to be hungry (thirsty)
ich heisse	my name is
nehmen Sie Platz	please sit down
schönen Gruss an	remember me to
was ist los?	What is going on?
zu Fuss gehen	to walk
zu Hause	at home

A street in West Berlin with many attractions for German shoppers as well as tourists from abroad.

Reading a menu in a German restaurant

Breakfast *Frühstück*

rolls	*Brötchen*	pancakes	*Pfannkuchen*	coffee	*Kaffee*
crescent rolls	*Hörnchen*	scrambled eggs	*Rühreier*	cocoa	*Kakao*
dry toast	*Zwieback*	fried eggs	*Spiegeleier*	tea	*Tee*
		soft-boiled eggs	*weichgekochte Eier*		

Lunch and dinner *Mittagessen und Abendessen*

cold cuts	*Aufschnitt*	roast beef	*Rinderbraten*	potato dumplings	*Kartoffelklösse*
sandwich	*belegtes Brot*	roast chicken	*Brathuhn*	mashed potatoes	*Kartoffelpüree*
cheese	*Käse*	roast goose	*Gänsebraten*	boiled potatoes	*Salzkartoffeln*
sausage	*Wurst*	roast veal	*Kalbsbraten*		
frankfurters	*Würstchen*	roast pork	*Schweinebraten*	dessert	*Nachtisch*
		meatballs	*Klopse*	ice cream	*Eis*
consommé	*Brühe*			stewed fruit	*Kompott*
noodle soup	*Brühe mit Nudeln*	fish	*Fisch*	tarts	*Törtchen*
soup	*Suppe*	codfish	*Cabeljau*	fruit	*Obst*
		flounder	*Flunder*		
salad	*Salat*	halibut	*Heilbut*		
cucumber salad	*Gurkensalat*				
tomato salad	*Tomatensalat*	vegetables	*Gemüse*		
mixed salad	*Gemischter Salat*	mushrooms	*Champignons*		
		peas	*Erbsen*		
		vegetable plate	*Gemüseplatte*		
		green beans	*grüne Bohnen*		
		cabbage	*Kohl*		
		carrots	*Mohrrüben*		

Review of German Grammar

das Gesicht The face

Dictionary

der Körper The human body

Dictionary abbreviations. Nouns are identified as masculine *(m)*, feminine *(f)*, or neuter *(nt)*. Adjectives are identified as *adj*, adverbs as *adv*, conjunctions as *conj*, interjections as *interj*, prepositions as *prep*, pronouns as *pron*, and verbs as *v*. Plurals are identified as *pl*.

German-English

A

Abend *m* evening
Abenteur *nt* adventure
aber *conj* but
ablehnen *v* decline
ähnlich *adj* similar
also *conj* therefore, so
alt *adj* old
alt werden *v* age
Angina *f* sore throat
Angst *f* fear
Anleihe *f* loan
Ansprache *f* speech
anständig *adj* decent
Antwort *f* reply, answer
antworten *v* answer
Anzug *m* suit
Arbeit *f* work
arbeiten *v* work
Arm *m* arm
arm *adj* poor
Armbanduhr *f* wristwatch
Arzt *m* medical doctor
atmen *v* breathe
auch *conj* also
Aufgabe *f* task
aufpassen *v* watch
aufstehen *v* get up, rise
aufwachen *v* wake up
auf Wiedersehen *interj* goodbye
aufziehen *v* (watch) wind
Auge *nt* eye
Ausflug *m* excursion, outing
Ausgang *m* exit
ausrotten *v* eradicate
ausser *prep* except
Autobahn *f* highway
Autofahrer *m* driver

B

backen *v* bake
Bahnhof *m* station
bald *adv* soon
Ball *m* ball
Bank *f* bench

Bart *m* beard
bauen *v* build, construct
Baum *m* tree
bedeuten *v* mean
beeindrucken *v* impress
behalten *v* keep
Bein *nt* leg
beinahe *adv* almost
bekannt werden *v* become acquainted
Belagerung *f* siege
belasten *v* burden
bellen *v* bark
Belohnung *f* reward
benutzen *v* use
beobachten *v* observe
bequem *adj* comfortable
bereit *adj* ready, prepared
berühmt *adj* famous
bescheiden *adj* modest
Bescheidenheit *f* modesty
beschreiben *v* describe
Beschwerde *f* complaint, burden
Besen *m* broom
besonders *adv* particularly
bestechen *v* bribe
Bestechung *f* bribery, graft
bestimmen *v* determine
bestrafen *v* punish
Besuch *m* visit
besuchen *v* visit
beten *v* pray
Bett *nt* bed
Bevölkerung *f* population
bezahlen *v* pay
billig *adj* cheap
bitte *adv* please
blass *adj* pale
blau *adj* blue
bleiben *v* stay
Bleistift *m* pencil
blind *adj* blind
Blinddarm *m* appendix
Blitz *m* lightning
Blume *f* flower
borgen *v* borrow
Brandstiftung *f* arson

396 Review of German Grammar

brauchen *v* need
braun *adj* brown
Braut *f* bride
Bräutigam *m* bridegroom
Bremse *f* brake
Brief *m* letter
Briefmarke *f* stamp
Briefumschlag *m* envelope
Brot *nt* bread
Brücke *f* bridge
Bruder *m* brother
Buch *nt* book
Bürger *m* citizen

C

Charakter *m* character
Chef *m* boss
Chemie *f* chemistry
Chirurg *m* surgeon
christlich *adj* Christian

D

Dame *f* lady
Dampf *m* steam
Dank *m* gratitude, thanks
danken *v* thank
Daumen *m* thumb
denken *v* think
deswegen *conj* therefore
dichten *v* write poetry
Dichter *m* poet
dick *adj* thick
Dieb *m* thief
Ding *nt* thing
diskutieren *v* discuss
Donner *m* thunder
Draht *m* wire
draussen *adv* outside
dringend *adj* urgent
Druck *m* pressure
dumm *adj* stupid
dunkel *adj* dark
Durst *m* thirst
durstig *adj* thirsty

E

Ecke *f* corner
Efeu *m* ivy
Egoismus *m* egotism
Ehefrau *f* wife
Ehemann *m* husband
Ei *nt* egg

Eid *m* oath
Eigentum *nt* property
einbrechen *v* burglarize
Einbrecher *m* burglar
Eindruck *m* impression
Einfuhr *f* import
einführen *v* introduce
Eingang *m* entrance
Einkommen *nt* income
einladen *v* invite
Einladung *f* invitation
Einschnitt *m* incision
Einwanderer *m* immigrant
Ellbogen *m* elbow
Eltern *pl* parents
Ende *nt* end
endlich *adv* finally
Engel *m* angel
Enkel *m* grandchild
entlassen *v* dismiss
Entlassung *f* dismissal
entwickeln *v* develop
erbärmlich *adj* miserable
erforderlich *adj* necessary
Ergebnis *nt* result
erhalten *v* receive
erinnern *v* remind
erklären *v* explain
erleichtern *v* facilitate, lighten
ernst *adj* earnest
erschöpfen *v* exhaust
ertragen *v* tolerate
essen *v* eat
Europa *nt* Europe
exponieren *v* expose

F

fähig *adj* capable, able
fahren *v* drive, ride
Fahrer *m* driver
Fahrplan *m* timetable
falsch *adj* wrong, false
Familie *f* family
Farbaufnahme *f* color photo
Farbe *f* color
fegen *v* sweep
Fehler *m* mistake
feiern *v* celebrate
Feiertag *m* holiday
Feind *m* enemy
Ferien *pl* vacation
Ferne *f* distance
feucht *adj* damp
Feuchtigkeit *f* dampness

Feuer *nt* fire
finden *v* find
Finger *m* finger
Flasche *f* bottle, flask
fleissig *adj* diligent
Flugzeug *nt* airplane
fordern *v* request
Forderung *f* request
fortfahren *v* continue
Frage *f* question
Frankreich *nt* France
französisch *adj* French
Frau *f* woman, wife
Fräulein *nt* miss
Freiheit *f* liberty
Freund *m* friend
freundlich *adj* kind, friendly
frieren *v* freeze
fröhlich *adj* merry, cheerful
Frucht *f* fruit
früh *adv* early
Frühling *m* spring
Frühstück *nt* breakfast
Fuchs *m* fox
Führerschein *m* driver's license
Funke *m* spark
funkeln *v* spark
funktionieren *v* function, work
für *prep* for
fürchten *v* fear
Fuss *m* foot
Fussboden *m* floor

G

Gabel *f* fork
Gans *f* goose
garantieren *v* vouch for
garnieren *v* adorn
Gast *m* guest
Gastarbeiter *m* foreign worker
Gastgeber *m* host
geben *v* give
Gebirge *nt* mountain range
Gebühr *f* fee
Geburt *f* birth
Geburtstag *m* birthday
Gedächtnis *nt* memory
Gedanke *m* thought, idea
Gedicht *nt* poem
Geduld *f* patience
geduldig *adj* patient
Gefahr *f* danger
gefährlich *adj* dangerous
gegen *prep* against, toward

Gegend *f* area
Gegenwart *f* presence
Gegner *m* adversary
geheim *adj* secret
Geheimnis *nt* secret
gehen *v* go, walk
gehören *v* belong
gehorsam *adj* obedient
Gehorsamkeit *f* obedience
gelb *adj* yellow
Geld *nt* money
Gelegenheit *f* occasion
genau *adv* precisely
genug *adj* enough
geräumig *adj* spacious
Geräusch *nt* noise
Gerüst *nt* scaffolding
Geschenk *nt* present
Gesetz *nt* law
Gesicht *nt* face
Gespenst *nt* ghost
Geständnis *nt* confession
gestehen *v* confess
gestern *adv* yesterday
gesund *adj* healthy
gewaltsam *adj* violent
Gewalttätigkeit *f* violence
gewiss *adv* certainly
Gewissen *nt* conscience
Gewissensbisse *m* remorse
gewissenhaft *adj* conscientious
gewissermassen *adv* so to speak
Gewitter *nt* thunderstorm
Glas *nt* glass
glatt *adj* slippery
Glatze *f* baldness
gleichzeitig *adv* simultaneously
Glocke *f* bell
Glück *nt* luck
Gott *m* god
göttlich *adj* divine
gottlos *adj* godless
Grab *nt* tomb
Graben *m* ditch
graben *v* dig
gratulieren *v* congratulate
Grippe *f* flu
gross *adj* big, tall
grün *adj* green
Grundlage *f* basis
gründlich *adj* profound
Gruppe *f* group
grüssen *v* greet
gültig *adj* valid
gut *adj* good

H

Haar *nt* hair
Hafen *m* harbor
Hagel *m* hail
Hals *m* neck
Hand *f* hand
Handlung *f* action
Handschuh *m* glove
Handtuch *nt* towel
hauptsächlich *adv* chiefly, *adj* principal
Hauptstadt *f* capital
Hauptstrasse *f* main street
Haus *nt* house
Hauswirt *m* landlord
Haut *f* skin
Heide *f* heath
heilen *v* cure, heal
Heiligabend *m* Christmas eve
heiraten *v* marry
helfen *v* help, assist
Hemd *nt* shirt
Herausgeber *m* publisher
Herbst *m* fall, autumn
herrlich *adj* splendid
Herz *nt* heart
herzlich *adj* affectionate
heute *adv* today
heute abend *adv* tonight
hier *adv* here
Hilfe *f* help
hilflos *adj* helpless
Himmel *m* sky, heaven
hinter *prep* behind, beyond
Hintergrund *m* background
hinzufügen *v* add
hoch *adj* high, tall
Hochzeit *f* wedding
hoffen *v* hope
hoffentlich *adv* I hope
Hoffnung *f* hope
höflich *adj* polite
Hölle *f* hell
Holz *nt* wood
hören *v* hear
Hose *f* pants
hübsch *adj* pretty, handsome
Hunger *m* hunger
hungern *v* starve
hungrig *adj* hungry
Husten *m* cough
husten *v* cough
Hut *m* hat
Hütte *f* cabin

I

immer *adv* always
impfen *v* inoculate
Ingenieur *m* engineer
Inhaltsverzeichnis *nt* table of contents
interessant *adj* interesting
Irrtum *m* error

J

Jagd *f* chase
jagen *v* chase
jedoch *conj* nevertheless
jemand *pron* somebody
jenseits *adv* beyond
jetzt *adv* now
Jugend *f* youth
jugendlich *adj* youthful
jung *adj* young

K

kahl *adj* bold
kalt *adj* cold
Kammermusik *f* chamber music
Kampf *m* fight
kämpfen *v* fight
Kapitel *nt* chapter
Karfreitag *m* Good Friday
Kartoffel *f* potato
Käse *m* cheese
Kassier *m* bank teller
kauen *v* chew
kaufen *v* buy
kaum *adv* hardly
Kehle *f* throat
Keim *m* germ
kennenlernen *v* get acquainted, meet
Kern *m* pit
Kind *nt* child
Kirche *f* church
Kissen *nt* pillow
Klasse *f* class
Klatsch *m* gossip
Klavier *nt* piano
Kleid *nt* dress
klein *adj* little, small
klingeln *v* ring
klug *adj* clever
Knie *nt* knee
kochen *v* cook, boil
Koffer *m* suitcase

kommen *v* come
Konditorei *f* coffee shop
Konkurs *m* bankruptcy
Konzept *nt* plan, draft
Kopf *m* head
Kopfschmerz *m* headache
krank *adj* sick, ill
Krankenhaus *n* hospital
Krebs *m* cancer
Krieg *m* war
krumm *adj* crooked
Krüppel *m* cripple
Küche *f* kitchen
Kuchen *m* cake
Kunde *m* customer
Kunst *f* art
Künstler *m* artist
künstlich *adj* artificial
kürzlich *adv* recently
Kusine *f* female cousin
Kuss *m* kiss

L

lächeln *v* smile
lachen *v* laugh
Lachs *m* salmon
Laken *nt* sheet
langsam *adj* slow
Last *f* burden
lästig *adj* burdensome
Leben *nt* life
leben *v* live
ledig *adj* unmarried
leer *adj* empty
Lehrer *m* teacher
Lehrling *m* apprentice
leicht *adj* easy
leider *adv* unfortunately
leihen *v* lend
leise *adv* softly, *adj* soft
lernen *v* learn
lesen *v* read
Leute *pl* people
Licht *nt* light
Liebe *f* love
lieben *v* love
lieber *adv* rather
lieber haben *v* prefer
Literatur *f* literature
Locke *f* curl
Löffel *m* spoon
Luft *f* air
lügen *v* lie
Lust haben *v* like to

M

machen *v* make
Mädchen *nt* girl
Mahlzeit *f* meal
manchmal *adv* sometimes
Mann *m* man, husband
Mantel *m* overcoat
Märchen *nt* fairy tale
Markt *m* market
Maschine *f* machine
Maus *f* mouse
Mehl *nt* flour
mehrere *adj* several
Mensch *m* human being
merken *v* notice
Merkmal *nt* identification mark
messen *v* measure
Messer *nt* knife
Milch *f* milk
mit *prep* with
Mitglied *nt* member
Mittag *m* noon
Mitte *f* middle
Mitternacht *f* midnight
möglich *adj* possible
Monat *m* month
Mord *m* murder
Mörder *m* murderer
morgen *adv* tomorrow
Morgen *m* morning
Motor *m* engine, motor
Muschel *f* shell
Musik *f* music
Mutter *f* mother

N

Nachfolge *f* succession
Nachname *m* last name
Nachricht *f* news
Nacht *f* night
Nachteil *m* disadvantage
Nachtisch *m* dessert
Nadel *f* needle
nahe *adj* near, close
nähren *v* nurse
Nahrung *f* food
Name *m* name
Nase *f* nose
nass *adj* wet
Nässe *f* wetness
Natur *f* nature
natürlich *adj* natural, *adv* of course

neben *prep* next to, beside
Neffe *m* nephew
nehmen *v* take
Neid *m* envy
neiden *v* envy
Nichte *f* niece
nichts *pron* nothing
nieder *prep* down
Niedergang *m* decline
niedrig *adj* low
niemand *pron* nobody
Nummer *f* number

O

ob *prep* whether
Ober *m* waiter
obgleich *conj* although
oder *conj* or
Ofen *m* stove
öffnen *v* open
oft *adv* often
ohne *prep* without
ohnegleichen *adv* unequaled
ohnehin *adv* in any case
Ohr *nt* ear
Ohrfeige *f* slap in the face
Onkel *m* uncle
Oper *f* opera
Opfer *nt* sacrifice, victim
Ort *m* spot

P

packen *v* pack
Paket *nt* package
Panne *f* breakdown
Papagei *m* parrot
Papier *nt* paper
Papierkorb *m* wastepaper basket
Park *m* park
Pass *m* passport
Passagier *m* passenger
passieren *v* happen
Person *f* person
Pfeife *f* pipe
Pferd *nt* horse
Platz *m* place
Polizei *f* police
Polizeiwache *f* police station
Priester *m* priest
Programm *nt* program
prüfen *v* examine
Prüfung *f* examination
pünktlich *adj* punctual

Review of German Grammar

Q

Qual *f* torture
quälen *v* torture
Qualität *f* quality

R

Rabe *m* raven
Rad *nt* wheel
Rauch *m* smoke
rauchen *v* smoke
rechnen *v* calculate, count
Recht *nt* right
recht *adj* right
recht haben *v* be right
rechtzeitig *adv* on time
Regen *m* rain
Regenmantel *m* raincoat
Regenschirm *m* umbrella
Regierung *f* government
regnen *v* rain
Reifen *m* tire
reinigen *v* clean
reisen *v* travel
reissen *v* tear
rennen *v* run
Reservereifen *m* spare tire
Rock *m* skirt
Roman *m* novel
rot *adj* red
Rücken *m* back
Rucksack *m* knapsack
Ruderboot *nt* rowboat
rufen *v* call
ruhig *adj* quiet, calm

S

sammeln *v* collect
Sammlung *f* collection
Sand *m* sand
Satz *m* sentence
schaffen *v* create
Schaffner *m* conductor
Schaffung *f* creation
scharf *adj* sharp
Scheibenwischer *m* windshield wiper
Schere *f* scissors
Schiff *nt* ship
Schinken *m* ham
schlafen *v* sleep
Schlagsahne *f* whipped cream
schlecht *adj* bad
schliessen *v* close
Schlips *m* necktie
Schloss *nt* castle
schmeicheln *v* flatter
schmutzig *adj* dirty
Schnee *m* snow
schneiden *v* cut
schnell *adj* fast, quick
Schokolade *f* chocolate
schön *adj* beautiful
Schornstein *m* chimney
schreiben *v* write
Schuh *m* shoe
Schule *f* school
Schurke *m* villain
schwach *adj* feeble, weak
schwarz *adj* black
Schwein *nt* pig
schwer *adj* heavy
Schwester *f* sister
Schwiegermutter *f* mother-in-law
Schwiegervater *m* father-in-law
sehen *v* to see
sehr *adv* much
seit *prep* since
Seite *f* page
seltsam *adj* strange
senden *v* send
Serviette *f* napkin
sich sorgen *v* worry
sich setzen *v* sit down
singen *v* sing
sitzen *v* sit
sogar *adv* even
Sohn *m* son
Sommer *m* summer
Sonne *f* sun
Sorge *f* worry
sparen *v* save
Speisekarte *f* menu
Spiegel *m* mirror
Spinne *f* spider
spinnen *v* spin
Sprache *f* language
sprechen *v* speak
Sprecher *m* speaker
Stadt *f* city, town
stark *adj* strong
Staub *m* dust
Stein *m* stone
sterben *v* die
steuern *v* conduct, steer
Steuerrad *nt* steering wheel
Stimme *f* voice, vote
Strand *m* beach
Strasse *f* street
streiten *v* quarrel, fight
studieren *v* study
Studium *nt* study
Stuhl *m* chair
Stunde *f* hour
suchen *v* seek, look for
Suppe *f* soup
surren *v* buzz
suspendieren *v* suspend
Szene *f* scene

T

Tag *m* day
Tankstelle *f* gas station
Tante *f* aunt
Tanz *m* dance
tanzen *v* dance
Tasse *f* cup
taub *adj* deaf
Tee *m* tea
teilnehmen *v* take part, participate
Telefon *nt* telephone
telefonieren *v* telephone
telegraphieren *v* telegraph
Teller *m* plate
teuer *adj* expensive
Theater *nt* theater
tief *adj* deep, low
Tier *nt* animal
Tierarzt *m* veterinarian
Tinte *f* ink
Tisch *m* table
Tochter *f* daughter
Topf *m* pot
Torte *f* fancy cake
tot *adj* dead, *n* **Tot** *m*
totmüde *adj* dead tired
tragen *v* carry
trauern *v* mourn
Traum *m* dream
träumen *v* dream
traurig *adj* sad
Treppe *f* staircase
treu *adj* faithful
trinken *v* drink
Trinkgeld *nt* tip
trocken *adj* dry
Trost *m* consolation
trösten *v* comfort
Tür *f* door
Turm *m* tower

U

über *prep* above, over
überraschen *v* surprise
Überraschung *f* surprise
übertreiben *v* exaggerate
Übertreibung *f* exaggeration
Übung *f* exercise
Uhr *f* clock, watch
ungeduldig *adj* impatient
ungefähr *adv* approximately
ungesund *adj* unhealthy
ungewöhnlich *adj* uncommon
unglücklich *adj* unhappy
Universität *f* university
unter *prep* underneath
unterbrechen *v* interrupt
Unterbrechung *f* interruption
Unterhaltung *f* conversation
Unterricht *m* instruction
unterschreiben *v* sign
unverschämt *adj* impudent
unvollendet *adj* unfinished
unzufrieden *adj* dissatisfied
Ursache *f* cause
ursprünglich *adv* originally

V

Vater *m* father
verbessern *v* improve
verbrennen *v* burn
vereinen *v* unite
vergessen *v* forget
verkaufen *v* sell
Verkehr *m* traffic
Verkehrsampel *f* traffic light
verlangen *v* demand
verlieren *v* lose
vermehren *v* increase
veröffentlichen *v* publish
verrückt *adj* crazy
verschwinden *v* disappear
versenden *v* ship
Versicherung *f* insurance
Verspätung *f* delay
verstehen *v* understand
Versuch *m* attempt
verteidigen *v* defend
vertraut *adj* familiar
verwunden *v* wound
verzeihen *v* pardon, forgive
Vetter *m* cousin
viel *adv* much
Vogel *m* bird

Volkslied *nt* folk song
Volksstamm *m* tribe
voll *adj* full
Vorbereitung *f* preparation
vorgestern *adv* day before yesterday
vorhaben *v* plan
vorher *adv* before
Vorhersage *f* prediction
vorhersagen *v* predict
vorhersehen *v* anticipate
Vorname *m* first name
Vorschlag *m* proposal
vorschlagen *v* propose
vorsichtig *adj* careful
Vorstadt *f* suburb
Vorstellung *f* performance
Vorteil *m* advantage

W

Waage *f* scale
wachsen *v* grow
wagen *v* risk
Wahl *f* election
wählen *v* choose
während *prep* during
Wahrheit *f* truth
wandern *v* wander
warm *adj* warm
warnen *v* warn
Warnung *f* warning
warten *v* wait
warum *adv and conj* why
Wasser *nt* water
wechseln *v* change
Weg *m* path
weich *adj* soft
weil *conj* because
weinen *v* cry
weiss *adj* white
weit *adj* far
weitergehen *v* go on
Welt *f* world
wenig *adj* little
wetten *v* bet
Wetter *nt* weather
wichtig *adj* important
wieder *adv* again
wiederholen *v* repeat
wiegen *v* weigh
wild *adj* wild
Windel *f* diaper
windig *adj* windy
Windschutzscheibe *f* windshield

Winter *m* winter
Winterfrische *f* winter resort
Wintergarten *m* conservatory
winterlich *adj* wintry
winzig *adj* tiny
wir *pron* we
wirbeln *v* whirl
wirken *v* work
wirklich *adj* actual, real
Wirtshaus *nt* inn
wissen *v* know
Wissenschaft *f* science, learning
Woche *f* week
wöchentlich *adv* weekly
Wolkenkratzer *m* skyscraper
Wörterbuch *n* dictionary
Wunder *nt* miracle
wunderbar *adj* wonderful
Wunderkind *n* prodigy
Wunsch *m* desire, wish
wünschen *v* want

Z

zahlen *v* pay
Zahn *m* tooth
Zahnarzt *m* dentist
Zahnbürste *f* toothbrush
zährtlich *adj* tender
Zehe *f* toe
zeigen *v* show
Zeitalter *nt* age
Zeitung *f* newspaper
Zentrum *nt* center
zerbrechen *v* break
ziehen *v* pull
Ziel *nt* aim
ziemlich *adv* rather
Zimmer *nt* room
zittern *v* tremble
zögernd *adv* reluctantly
Zorn *m* anger
Zucker *m* sugar
Zufall *m* accident
Zug *m* train
zuhören *v* listen
zumachen *v* close
Zündung *f* ignition
Zunge *f* tongue
zurück *adv* back, behind
zurückkommen *v* return
zusammen *adj* together
zwingen *v* force
Zwinger *m* kennel
zwischen *prep* between

Review of German Grammar

Dictionary abbreviations. Nouns are identified as masculine *(nm)*, feminine *(nf)*, or neuter *(nt)*. Adjectives are identified as *adj*, adverbs as *adv*, conjunctions as *conj*, interjections as *interj*, prepositions as *prep*, pronouns as *pron*, and verbs as *v*. Plurals are identified as *pl*.

English-German

A

above *prep* über
action *n* Handlung *f*
add *v* hinzufügen
adorn *v* garnieren
advantage *n* Vorteil *m*
adventure *n* Abenteuer *nt*
adversary *n* Gegner *m*
again *adv* wieder
against *prep* gegen
age *n* Zeitalter *nt*
age *v* altern
air *n* Luft *f*
airplane *n* Flugzeug *nt*
alleviate *v* erleichtern
almost *adv* fast
already *adv* schon
although *conj* obgleich
always *adv* immer
angel *n* Engel *m*
animal *n* Tier *nt*
answer *n* Antwort *f*, *v* antworten
anticipate *v* vorhersehen
appendix *n* (medical) Blinddarm *m*
apprentice *n* Lehrling *m*
approximately *adv* ungefähr
arm *n* Arm *m*
arrive *v* ankommen
arson *n* Brandstiftung *f*
art *n* Kunst *f*
artist *n* Künstler *m*
attempt *n* Versuch *m*
attempt *v* versuchen
aunt *n* Tante *f*
autumn *n* Herbst *m*
award *n* Belohnung *f*

B

back *adv* zurück
background *n* Hintergrund *m*
bad *adj* schlecht
bake *v* backen
ball *n* Ball *m*
ban *v* verbannen
bark *v* bellen
beach *n* Strand *m*
beard *n* Bart *m*
beautiful *adj* schön
because *adv* weil
bed *n* Bett *nt*
before *adv* vorher
behind *prep* hinter
bell *n* Glocke *f*
belong *v* gehören
beside *prep* neben
bet *v* wetten
between *prep* zwischen
beyond *adv* jenseits
big *adj* gross
birth *n* Geburt *f*
birthday *n* Geburtstag *m*
bite *v* beissen
black *adj* schwarz
blind *adj* blind
bloom *v* blühen
blue *adj* blau
book *n* Buch *nt*
borrow *v* borgen
boss *n* Chef *m*
bottle *n* Flasche *f*
brake *n* Bremse *f*
bread *n* Brot *nt*
breakdown *n* Panne *f*
breakfast *n* Frühstück *nt*
breath *n* Atem *m*
breathe *v* atmen
bribe *n* Bestechung *f*
bribe *v* bestechen
bride *n* Braut *f*
bridegroom *n* Bräutigam *m*
bridge *n* Brücke *f*
broom *n* Besen *m*
brother *n* Bruder *m*
brown *adj* braun
build *v* bauen
burden *n* Last *f*
burden *v* belasten
burglar *n* Einbrecher *m*
burn *v* brennen
but *conj* aber
buy *v* kaufen

C

cabin *n* Hütte *f*
cake *n* Kuchen *m*
cancer *n* Krebs *m*
capable *adj* fähig
capital *n* Hauptstadt *f*
careful *adj* vorsichtig
carry *v* tragen
castle *n* Schloss *nt*
cause *n* Ursache *f*
cautious *adj* vorsichtig
certainly *adv* gewiss
chair *n* Stuhl *m*
chamber music *n* Kammermusik *f*
change *v* wechseln, *n* Kleingeld *nt*
character *n* Charakter *m*
chase *v* jagen
cheese *n* Käse *m*
chemistry *n* Chemie *f*
chew *v* kauen
chiefly *adv* hauptsächlich
child *n* Kind *nt*
chimney *n* Schornstein *m*
chocolate *n* Schokolade *f*
choose *v* wählen
Christian *adj* christlich
Christmas eve *n* Heiligabend *m*
church *n* Kirche *f*
citizen *n* Bürger *m*
city *n* Stadt *f*
class *n* Klasse *f*
clean *v* reinigen
clever *adj* klug
close *v* schliessen
coat *n* Mantel *m*
coffee shop *n* Konditorei *f*
cold *adj* kalt
collect *v* sammeln
collection *n* Sammlung *f*
color *n* Farbe *f*
color picture *n* Farbaufnahme *f*
come *v* kommen
comfortable *adj* bequem
compassion *n* Mitleid *nt*
compassionate *adj* mitleidig
complain *v* sich beschweren
complaint *n* Beschwerde *f*
conductor *n* (train) Schaffner *m*
confess *v* gestehen
confession *n* Geständnis *nt*
congratulate *v* gratulieren
conscience *n* Gewissen *m*

consolation *n* Trost *m*
contents *n* Inhalt *m*
continuation *n* Fortsetzung *f*
continue *v* fortfahren
cook *n* Koch *m*, *v* kochen
corner *n* Ecke *f*
cough *v* husten
courage *n* Mut *m*
cousin *n* Vetter *m*, Kusine *f*
create *v* schaffen
creation *n* Schaffung *f*
cup *n* Tasse *f*
customer *n* Kunde *m*
cut *v* schneiden

D

daily *adj.* täglich
damp *adj* feucht
danger *n* Gefahr *f*
dangerous *adj* gefährlich
dark *adj* dunkel
daughter *n* Tochter *f*
day *n* Tag *m*
dead *adj* tot
dead tired *adj* todmüde
deaf *adj* taub
death *n* Tod *m*
decent *adj* anständig
decline *n* Niedergang *m*
decline *v* ablehnen
deep *adj* tief
defend *v* verteidigen
defense *n* Verteidigung *f*
delay *n* Verzögerung *f*
describe *v* beschreiben
description *n* Beschreibung *f*
desire *n* Wunsch *m*
determine *v* bestimmen
develop *v* entwickeln
dictionary *n* Wörterbuch *nt*
die *v* sterben
difficult *adj* schwierig
dig *v* graben
diligent *adj* fleissig
disadvantage *n* Nachteil *m*
dismiss *v* entlassen
dismissal *n* Entlassung
dissatisfied *adj* unzufrieden
distinguish *v* unterscheiden
ditch *n* Graben *m*
divine *adj* göttlich
doctor *n* Arzt *m*
dog *n* Hund *m*
donkey *n* Esel *m*

door *n* Tür *f*
dream *n* Traum *m*
dress *n* Kleid *n*
drink *v* trinken
driver *n* Fahrer *m*
driver's license *n* Führerschein *m*
drugstore *n* Drogerie *f*
dry *adj* trocken
during *prep* während
dust *n* Staub *m*

E

eagle *n* Adler *m*
ear *n* Ohr *nt*
early *adv* früh
easy *adj* leicht
eat *v* essen
egg *n* Ei *nt*
egotism *n* Egoismus *m*
elbow *n* Ellbogen *m*
elect *v* auserwählen
election *n* Wahl *f*
emigrant *n* Auswanderer *m*
empty *adj* leer
end *n* Ende *nt*
enemy *n* Feind *m*
engine *n* Motor *m*
enough *adv* genug
enrich *v* bereichern
entrance *n* Eingang *m*
envelope *n* Umschlag *m*
envoy *n* Gesandte *m*
envy *n* Neid *m*
envy *v* neiden
eradicate *v* ausrotten
error *n* Fehler *m*
Europe *n* Europa *nt*
even *adv* sogar
evening *n* Abend *m*
exaggerate *v* übertreiben
exaggeration *n* Übertreibung *f*
except *prep* ausser
excess *n* Übermass *nt*
excursion *n* Ausflug *m*
exhaust *n* Auspuff *m*
exhaust *v* erschöpfen
exhausted *adj* erschöpft
exhibit *n* Austellung *m*
exhibit *v* ausstellen
exit *n* Ausgang *m*
expensive *adj* teuer
explain *v* erklären
eye *n* Auge *nt*

F

face *n* Gesicht *nt*
facilitate *v* erleichtern
fairy tale *n* Märchen *nt*
faithful *adj* treu
false *adj* falsch
familiar *adj* vertraut
family *n* Familie *f*
famous *adj* berühmt
far *adj* weit
fast *adj* schnell
father *n* Vater *m*
father-in-law *n* Schwiegervater *m*
fear *n* Furcht *f*, *v* fürchten
fee *n* Gebühr *f*
fight *n* Kampf *m*, *v* kämpfen
finally *adv* endlich
find *v* finden
finger *n* Finger *m*
fire *n* Feuer *nt*
first name *n* Vorname *m*
fish *n* Fisch *m*
fish *v* fischen
flatter *v* schmeicheln
flour *n* Mehl *nt*
flower *n* Blume *f*
flue *n* Grippe *f*
food *n* Nahrung *f*
foot *n* Fuss *m*
for *prep* für
force *v* zwingen
foreign worker *n* Gastarbeiter *m*
forget *v* vergessen
forgive *v* vergeben
fox *n* Fuchs *m*
France *n* Frankreich *nt*
freeze *v* frieren
French *adj* französisch
friend *n* Freund *m*, Freundin *f*
friendly *adj* freundlich
fright *n* Furcht *f*
frog *n* Frosch *m*

G

gas station *n* Tankstelle *f*
get up *v* aufstehen
girl *n* Mädchen *nt*
give *v* geben
glass *n* Glas *nt*
glove *n* Handschuh *m*
go *v* gehen
God *n* Gott *m*

Review of German Grammar

good *adj* gut
goodby *interj* auf Wiedersehen
gossip *n* Klatsch *m*
government *n* Regierung *f*
grandchild *n* Enkel *m*, Enkelin *f*
gratitude *n* Dankbarkeit *f*
green *adj* grün
greet *v* grüssen
greeting *n* Gruss *m*
group *n* Gruppe *f*
grow *v* wachsen
guest *n* Gast *m*

H

hail *n* Hagel *m*, *v* hageln
hair *n* Haar *nt*
ham *n* Schinken *m*
hand *n* Hand *f*
happen *v* passieren
harbor *n* Hafen *m*
hardly *adv* kaum
hat *n* Hut *m*
hay *n* Heu *nt*
head *n* Kopf *m*
headache *n* Kopfschmerz *m*
heal *v* heilen
healthy *adj* gesund
hear *v* hören
heart *n* Herz *nt*
heartily *adv* herzlich
heath *n* Heide *f*
heavy *adj* schwer
hell *n* Hölle *f*
help *n* Hilfe *f*, *v* helfen
helpless *adj* hilflos
here *adv* hier
high *adj* hoch
highlight *n* Höhepunkt *m*
highly *adv* höchst
hilarious *adj* ausgelassen
holiday *n* Feiertag *m*
hope *n* Hoffnung *f*
hope *v* hoffen
horse *n* Pferd *nt*
hospital *n* Krankenhaus *nt*
host *n* Gastgeber *m*
hour *n* Stunde *f*
house *n* Haus *nt*
human being *n* Mensch *m*
hunger *n* Hunger *m*
hungry *adj* hungrig
hunt *n* Jagd *f*
hunt *v* jagen
husband *n* Mann *m*

I

idea *n* Gedanke *m*
ignition *n* Zündung *f*
ill *adj* krank
immigrant *n* Einwanderer *m*
impatient *adj* ungeduldig
import *n* Einfuhr *f*
import *v* einführen
important *adj* wichtig
impress *v* beeindrucken
impression *n* Eindruck *m*
improve *v* verbessern
impudent *adj* unverschämt
incision *n* Einschnitt *m*
income *n* Einkommen *nt*
increase *v* vermehren
inexpensive *adj* billig
ink *n* Tinte *f*
inn *n* Wirtshaus *nt*, Gasthaus *nt*
instead of *conj* anstatt
instruction *n* Unterricht *m*
insurance *n* Versicherung *f*
interesting *adj* interessant
interrupt *v* unterbrechen
interruption *n* Unterbrechung *f*
introduce *v* bekannt machen, einführen
invent *v* erfinden
invention *n* Erfindung *f*
invite *v* einladen
ivy *n* Efeu *m*

K

kennel *n* Zwinger *m*
kind *adj* freundlich, *n* Art *f*
kiss *n* Kuss *m*
kitchen *n* Küche *nt*
knee *n* Knie *nt*
knife *n* Messer *nt*
know *v* wissen

L

lady *n* Dame *f*
landlord *n* Hauswirt *m*
last name *n* Nachname *m*
laugh *n* Lachen *nt*, *v* lachen
law *n* Gesetz *nt*
lazy *adj* faul
learn *v* lernen
leg *n* Bein *nt*
lend *v* leihen
letter *n* Brief *m*

liberty *n* Freiheit *f*
lie *v* (recline) liegen, (tell untruth) lügen, *n* (untruth) Lüge *f*
light *adj* (color) hell, (weight) leicht
lightning *n* Blitz *m*
like to *v* gern
listen *v* zuhören
literature *n* Literatur *f*
little *adj* klein
live *v* leben
living room *n* Wohnzimmer *nt*
loan *n* Anleihe *f*
lock *v* zuschliessen
lose *v* verlieren
loud *adj* laut
love *n* Liebe *f*, *v* lieben
low *adj* niedrig
luck *n* Glück

M

machine *n* Maschine *f*
Main Street *n* Hauptstrasse *f*
majority *n* Mehrheit *f*
make *v* machen
man *n* Mann *m*
many *adj* viel
market *n* Markt *m*
meal *n* Mahlzeit *f*
mean *v* meinen
measure *n* Mass *nt*
measure *v* messen
meet *v* treffen
member *n* Mitglied *nt*
memory *n* Gedächtnis *nt*
menu *n* Speisekarte *f*
merry *adj* fröhlich
middle *n* Mitte *f*
midnight *n* Mitternacht *f*
milk *n* Milch *f*
minority *n* Minderhait *f*
miracle *n* Wunder *n*
mirror *n* Spiegel *m*
miserable *adj* erbärmlich
mistake *n* Fehler *m*
modest *adj* bescheiden
modesty *n* Bescheidenheit *f*
money *n* Geld *nt*
month *n* Monat *m*
mother *n* Mutter *f*
mother-in-law *n* Schwiegermutter *f*
mountain *n* Berg *m*

mourning *n* Trauer *f*
mouse *n* Maus *f*
murder *n* Mord *m*
murderer *n* Mörder *m*
muscle *n* Muskel *m*
music *n* Musik *f*

N

name *n* Name *m*
name *v* ernennen
napkin *n* Serviette *f*
naturally *adv* natürlich
near *adv* nahe
necessary *adj* nötig
neck *n* Nacken *m*
necktie *n* Krawatte *f*, Schlips *m*
needle *n* Nadel *f*
nephew *n* Neffe *m*
never *adv* nie
news *n* Nachricht *f*
next to *prep* neben
niece *n* Nichte *f*
night *n* Nacht *f*
noise *n* Lärm *m*
noon *n* Mittag *m*
no one *pron* niemand
nose *n* Nase *f*
notebook *n* Heft *nt*
nothing *pron* nichts
notice *v* merken
nurse *n* Krankenschwester *f*
nurse *v* nähren

O

oath *n* Eid *m*
obedience *n* Gehorsam *m*
obedient *adj* gehorsam
observation *n* Beobachtung *f*
observe *v* beobachten
occasion *n* Gelegenheit *f*
often *adv* oft
old *adj* alt
on time *adv* rechtzeitig
open *v* öffnen, *adj* offen
opera *n* Oper *f*
or *conj* oder
originally *adv* ursprünglich
otherwise *adv* sonst
outside *adv* draussen

P

pack *v* packen
package *n* Paket *nt*

page *n* Seite *f*
pale *adj* blass
paper *n* Papier *nt*
parents *n* Eltern *pl*
park *n* Park *m*
parrot *n* Papagei *m*
passenger *n* Passagier *m*
passport *n* Pass *m*
patience *n* Geduld *f*
patiently *adv* geduldig
pay *v* zahlen
peculiar *adj* besonders
pea *n* Erbse *f*
peace *n* Friede *m*
pencil *n* Bleistift *m*
people *n* Leute *pl*
person *n* Person *f*
piano *n* Klavier *nt*
pig *n* Schwein *nt*
pillow *n* Kissen *nt*
pipe *n* Pfeife *f*
place *n* Platz *m*
plate *n* Teller *m*
please *interj* bitte, *v* gefallen
poem *n* Gedicht *m*
poet *n* Dichter *m*
police *n* Polizei *f*
police station *n* Polizeiwache *f*
polite *adj* höflich
poor *adj* arm
population *n* Bevölkerung *f*
possible *adj* möglich
pot *n* Topf *m*
potato *n* Kartoffel *f*
pray *v* beten
precisely *adv* genau
predict *v* vorhersagen
prediction *n* Vorhersage *f*
prefer *v* vorziehen
presence *n* Gegenwart *f*
present *n* (gift) Geschenk *nt*
pressure *n* Druck *m*
pretty *adj* hübsch
priest *n* Priester *m*
prison *n* Gefängnis *nt*
profound *adv* gründlich
program *n* Programm *nt*
property *n* Eigentum *nt*
proposal *n* Vorschlag *m*
propose *v* vorschlagen
publish *v* veröffentlichen
publisher *n* Herausgeber *m*
punctual *adj* pünktlich
punish *v* bestrafen
purchase *v* kaufen

Q

quarrel *v* streiten
question *n* Frage *f*
quick *adj* schnell
quiet *adj* ruhig

R

rain *n* Regen *m*, *v* regnen
raincoat *n* Regenmantel *m*
read *v* lesen
ready *adj* bereit
receive *v* erhalten
recently *adv* kürzlich
red *adj* rot
relative *n* Verwandte *m*
reluctant *adj* zögernd
remember *v* sich erinnern an
remorse *n* Gewissensbisse *pl*
request *n* Forderung *f*
request *v* fordern
responsible *adj* verantwortlich
result *n* Ergebnis *nt*
retain *v* zurückbehalten
ride *v* fahren
ring *v* klingeln
rob *v* rauben
robbery *n* Raub *m*
room *n* Zimmer *nt*
runner *n* Läufer *m*

S

sad *adj* traurig
sand *n* Sand *m*
save *v* sparen
scarce *adj* selten
scarcely *adv* kaum
school *n* Schule *f*
science *n* Wissenschaft *f*
scientist *n* Wissenschaftler *m*
scissors *n* Schere *f*
secret *n* Geheimnis *m*
secret *adj* geheim
see *v* sehen
seek *v* suchen
sell *v* verkaufen
send *v* schicken
sentence *n* (grammar) Satz *m*, (judgment) Urteil *nt*
serious *adj* ernst
several *adj* mehrere
share *n* Anteil *m*
share *v* teilen

Review of German Grammar

sharp *adj* scharf
sheet *n* Laken *nt*
shell *n* Muschel *f*
ship *n* Schiff *nt*
ship *v* versenden
shirt *n* Hemd *nt*
shoe *n* Schuh *m*
show *v* zeigen
shut *v* schliessen
sick *adj* krank
siege *n* Belagerung *f*
sign *n* Zeichen *nt*,
   v unterschreiben
similar *adj* ähnlich
simultaneously *adv* gleichzeitig
since *prep* seit
sing *v* singen
sit down *v* sich setzen
skin *n* Haut *f*
skirt *n* Rock *m*
sky *n* Himmel *m*
skyscraper *n* Wolkenkratzer *m*
slaughter *v* schlachten
sleep *v* schlafen
slippery *adj* glatt
slow *adj* langsam
smile *n* Lächeln *nt*, *v* lächeln
smoke *n* Rauch *m*, *v* rauchen
snow *n* Schnee *m*
soft *adj* weich
softly *adv* leise
soiled *adj* schmutzig
somebody *pron* jemand
sometimes *adv* manchmal
son *n* Sohn *m*
soon *adv* bald
soup *n* Suppe *f*
spacious *adj* geräumig
spare tire *n* Ersatzreifen *m*
spark *n* Funke *m*
spark *v* funkeln
speak *v* sprechen
speaker *n* Sprecher *m*
spider *n* Spinne *f*
splendid *adj* herrlich
spoon *n* Löffel *m*
spring *n* Frühling *m*
stamp *n* Briefmarke *f*
staircase *n* Treppe *f*
starve *v* hungern
station *n* (train) Bahnhof *m*
steam *n* Dampf *m*
steer *v* steuern
steering wheel *n* Steuerrad *nt*
stone *n* Stein *m*

stove *n* Ofen *m*
strange *adj* seltsam
street *n* Strasse *f*
strong *adj* stark
study *n* Studium *nt*, *v* studieren
succession *n* Nachfolge *f*
suddenly *adv* plötzlich
sugar *n* Zucker *m*
suit *n* Anzug *m*
suitcase *n* Koffer *m*
summer *n* Sommer *m*
sun *n* Sonne *f*
surgeon *n* Chirurg *m*
swallow *n* Schwalbe *f*
swallow *v* schlucken
sweep *v* fegen

T

table *n* Tisch *m*
table of contents *n*
   Inhaltsverzeichnis *nt*
take *v* nehmen
take part *v* teilnehmen
tale *n* Erzählung *f*
tall *adj* gross
task *n* Aufgabe *f*
tea *n* Tee *m*
teacher *n* Lehrer *m*, Lehrerin *f*
telephone *n* Telefon *nt*
telephone *v* telefonieren
tell *v* erzählen
teller *n* (bank) Kassier *m*
temporary *adj* vorübergehend
thank *v* danken
theater *n* Theater *nt*
therefore *adv* also
thick *adj* dick
thief *n* Dieb *m*
thing *n* Ding *nt*
think *v* denken
thirst *n* Durst *m*
thought *n* Gedanke *m*
thumb *n* Daumen *m*
thunder *n* Donner *m*
thunderstorm *n* Gewitter *nt*
time *n* Zeit *f*
timetable *n* Fahrplan *m*
tip *n* Trinkgeld *nt*
tire *n* Reifen *m*
today *adv* heute
together *adv* zusammen
tolerate *v* ertragen
tomorrow *adv* morgen
tongue *n* Zunge *f*

torture *n* Qual *f*
torture *v* quälen
towel *n* Handtuch *nt*
town *n* Stadt *f*
trade *n* Handel *m*
traffic *n* Verkehr *m*
traffic light *n* Verkehrsampel *f*
train *n* Zug *m*
transmission *n* Übertragung *f*
transmit *v* übertragen
travel *v* reisen
tree *n* Baum *m*
tribe *n* Volksstamm *m*
true *adj* wahr
truth *n* Wahrheit *f*

U

umbrella *n* Regenschirm *m*
uncle *n* Onkel *m*
uncommon *adj* ungewöhnlich
under *prep* unter
understand *v* verstehen
unfinished *adj* unvollendet
unfortunately *adv* leider
unhappy *adj* unglücklich
unhealthy *adj* ungesund
university *n* Universität *f*
unmarried *adj* ledig
unusual *adj* ungewöhnlich
urgent *adj* dringend
use *v* benutzen

V

vacation *n* Ferien pl
valid *adj* gültig
very *adv* sehr
veterinarian *n* Tierarzt *m*
victim *n* Opfer *nt*
villain *n* Schurke *m*
violence *n* Gewalttätigkeit *f*
violent *adj* heftig
visit *n* Besuch *m*, *v* besuchen
voice *n* Stimme *f*
vote *v* wählen
voter *n* Wähler *m*
vouch for *v* garantieren

W

wait *v* warten
waiter *n* Ober *m*
war *n* Krieg *m*
wash *v* waschen

waste basket n Papierkorb m
watch v aufpassen
water n Wasser nt
waterfall n Wasserfall m
waterproof adj wasserdicht
wave n Welle f
waver v schwanken
wavy adj wellig
wax n Wachs nt
way n Weg m
we pron wir
weak adj schwach
weaken v schwächen, **feel weak** v schwach werden
weakness n Schwäche f
wealth n Reichtum m
wealthy adj reich
weapon n Waffe f
wear v tragen
wear out v abtragen
weary adj müde
weather n Wetter nt
wedding n Hochzeit f
week n Woche f
weekly adv and adj wöchentlich
weep v weinen
weigh v wiegen
weight n Gewicht nt
weird adj unheimlich
welcome n Willkommen nt
welcome v bewillkommnen
welfare n Wohlergehen nt
well adv gut, (health) gesund
well n Brunnen m
well-known adj bekannt
west n Westen m
western adj westlich
wet adj nass
wetness n Nässe f
wheel n Rad nt
when conj als, adv wann
whether conj ob
which adj and pron welcher
whichever adj and pron welcher
while conj während
while n Weile f
whim n Laune f
whip n Peitsche f
whip v schlagen
whipped cream n Schlagsahne f
whirl v wirbeln
whirlpool n Strudel m
whirlwind n Wirbelwind m
whisker n Barthaar nt
whiskey n Whisky m

whisper v flüstern
whistle n Flöte f
whistle v flöten
white adj weiss
wife n Frau f
wig n Perücke f
wild adj wild
wilderness n Wildnis f
will n Wille m
will v (future) werden, (bequeath) vermachen, (want to) wollen
willful adj eigensinnig
willow n Weide f
wilt v welken
wilted adj welk
win v gewinnen
wind n Wind m
wind v aufziehen
windshield n Windschutzscheibe f
windshield wiper n Scheibenwischer m
windy adj windig
winter n Winter m
wire n Draht m
wire v drahten
wish n Wunsch m, v wünschen
with prep mit
within prep innerhalb
without prep ohne
witness n Zeuge m
witty adj witzig
woe n Leid nt
wolf n Wolf m
woman n Frau f
wood n Holz nt
woods n Wald m

word n Wort nt
work n Arbeit f, v arbeiten
world n Welt f
worldly adj weltlich
worm n Wurm m
worn-out adj abgenutzt
worry n Sorge f
worry v sich sorgen
worse adj schlechter
worship n Verehrung f
worship v verehren
worst adj schlechtest
worth n Wert m
worthless adj wertlos
worthy adj würdig
wound n Wunde f
wound v verwunden
wrap n Umhang m
wrap v wickeln
wrath n Zorn m
wreath n Kranz m
wreck n Wrack nt
wreck v demolieren
wrist n Handgelenk nt
wristwatch n Armbanduhr f
write v schreiben
write poetry v dichten

Y

year n Jahr nt
yell v schreien
yellow adj gelb
yesterday adv gestern
young adj jung
youth n Jugend f
youthful adj jugendlich

For further reference

Texts

Huebener, Theodore, and Newmark, Maxim
A First Course in German
D.C. Heath and Company

Lange, Eva C.
German in 20 Lessons
R.D. Cortina

Steinhauer, Harry
Read, Write, Speak German
Bantam Books

Steinhauer, Harry, and Sundermeyer, William
Introduction to German
Macmillan

Dictionaries

Cassell
German/English; English/German
Macmillan

Wehrle, Hugo
Deutscher Wortschatz
Ernst Klett Verlag

Review of Spanish Grammar

- Articles 409
- Nouns 410
- Adjectives and adverbs 410
- Pronouns 412
- Prepositions 415
- Verbs 416
- Numbers, dates, time 424
- Spanish–English dictionary 426
- English–Spanish dictionary 432

Spanish grammar shares certain characteristics with English grammar, as you may recall from the time when you first studied these languages. For the most part, the names of the parts of speech and the terms used to show how words function in a sentence are the same. If you have any difficulty in recalling the meanings of any words used in this chapter, consult the dictionary in volume 2 of the *Student Handbooks*. No matter how long you have been away from the formal study of Spanish, you will quickly find yourself recalling what you once learned.

Spanish in Spain and Spanish America

Pronunciation. The *z*, *ce*, and *ci* are pronounced alike. In southern Spain and Spanish America, they are pronounced like the *s* in *sin*. In central and northern Spain, they are pronounced like the *th* in *thin* and *fifth*.

azúcar sugar
ah-soo-kahr (Spanish America, southern Spain)
ah-thoo-kahr (central and northern Spain)

quince fifteen
keen-say (Spanish America, southern Spain)
keen-thay (central and northern Spain)

hacienda farm
ah-see-en-dah (Spanish America, southern Spain)
ah-thee-en-dah (central and northern Spain)

The *ll* in southern Spain and Spanish America is pronounced like the *y* in *yes*. In central and northern Spain, the *ll* is pronounced like the *ly* sound in the second syllable of *million*.

gallo rooster
gah-yoh (Spanish America, southern Spain)
gah-lyoh (central and northern Spain)

Vocabulary. Certain words and expressions differ in Spain and Spanish America, but the differences are minor. A native of one Spanish-speaking country is easily understood by natives of other Spanish-speaking countries.

to drive	*conducir*	(Spain)
	manejar	(Spanish America)
bus	*autobús*	(Spain)
	camión	(Mexico)
peas	*guisantes*	(Spain)
	chícharos	(Spanish America)

The *tortilla* in Spain is an omelet; in Mexico and Guatemala it is a flat corn cake.

Articles

Definite and indefinite articles

	Singular		Plural	
	Masc.	*Fem.*	*Masc.*	*Fem.*
Definite: the	el	la	los	las
Indefinite: a, an	un	una		
some, a few			unos	unas

The neuter article *lo* is used with adjectives and past participles when they are used as nouns.
   lo bueno y lo malo the good and the bad

Agreement
Articles agree in number and gender with the nouns they modify.
   el niño the boy   *una niña* a girl

El is used instead of *la* before a feminine singular noun that begins with a stressed *a* or *ha*.
   el hacha the ax

Contractions of *el*
The prepositions *de* and *a* combine with the masculine article *el* to form *del* and *al*.
   Voy al cine. I am going to the movies.

Uses of the definite article
Before each noun in a series.
   El padre y el hijo van al centro.
   The father and son are going downtown.

Before the names of languages except directly after *hablar, en,* or *de*.
   El español es importante hoy.
   Spanish is important today.
   Mi padre habla alemán.
   My father speaks German.

Before titles such as *señor, doctor,* and *profesor,* except in direct address.
   El señor López llegó ayer.
   Mr. Lopez arrived yesterday.
   ¿Cómo está usted, señora Gómez?
   How are you, Mrs. Gomez?

Instead of the possessive with clothing and parts of the body.
   Me lavo las manos. I wash my hands.

To express "o'clock."
   Son las ocho. It is eight o'clock.

Before nouns used in a general or abstract sense.
   La medicina es una profesión noble.
   Medicine is a noble profession.

Before an infinitive used as a noun.
   El comer es necesario. Eating is necessary.

With the names of seasons.
   La primavera empieza en marzo.
   Spring begins in March.

With days of the week, except after *ser.*
   Voy de compras el sábado.
   I'm going shopping on Saturday.
   Hoy es jueves.
   Today is Thursday.

Before certain geographic names such as:
   la Argentina Argentina
   el Brasil Brazil
   los Estados Unidos United States

To express *a* or *an* with weights or measures.
   dos pesos el metro two pesos a meter

Omission of the definite article
Before nouns in apposition.
   Antonio, criado de los García, llegó tarde.
   Anthony, the Garcias' servant, arrived late.

Before numerals expressing numerical order of rulers.
   Carlos Quinto Charles the Fifth

Omission of the indefinite article
Before unmodified predicate nouns indicating occupation, profession, or nationality.
   Su hermano es médico. His brother is a physician.

Before *cien, cierto, mil, otro,* and *tal.*
   cien dólares a hundred dollars
   cierto libro a certain book
   mil estudiantes a thousand students
   otro amigo another friend
   tal padre such a father

After the exclamatory *¡qué!*
   ¡Qué mujer! What a woman!

Nouns

Gender
Nouns referring to males and nouns ending in *o* are generally masculine.
   el cuaderno the notebook
   el abuelo the grandfather
Nouns referring to females and nouns ending in *-a, -ión, -dad, -tad, -tud,* or *-umbre* are generally feminine.
   la nación the nation   *la madre* the mother

Exceptions
Feminine nouns ending in *o.*
   la mano the hand   *la radio* the radio
Masculine nouns ending in *a.*
   el drama the drama
   el clima the climate
   el poeta the poet
   el problema the problem
   el tranvía the streetcar
   el idioma the language
   el mapa the map

Plurals
For nouns ending in a vowel, add *s;* for nouns ending in a consonant, add *es.*
   el libro, los libros the book, the books
   la pared, las paredes the wall, the walls
For nouns ending in *z,* change *z* to *c* before adding *es.*
   la luz, las luces the light, the lights
Nouns ending in an unaccented syllable with final *s* remain unchanged in the plural.
   el cumpleaños, los cumpleaños
   the birthday, the birthdays
For nouns ending in an accented syllable with final *n* or *s,* drop the written accent in the plural.
   el jardín, los jardines the garden, the gardens
Nouns indicating rank or relationship may be used in the masculine plural to designate individuals of either sex.
   los reyes the kings, or the king and queen

Adjectives and adverbs

Adjectives
Adjectives whose masculine singular forms end in *o* and adjectives of nationality have two singular, two plural forms. All others have one singular, one plural.

Agreement
An adjective agrees in gender and number with the noun modified. An adjective modifying nouns of different genders is generally masculine plural.
   Los lápices y las plumas son caros.
   The pencils and pens are expensive.

Position
A descriptive adjective usually follows the noun it modifies.
   el papel blanco the white paper

A limiting adjective such as a possessive, a demonstrative, or a number, and an adjective of quantity usually precede the noun.
   ese vaso that glass
The following adjectives drop the final *o* before a masculine singular noun: *bueno, malo, uno, primero, tercero, alguno, ninguno.*
   el primer día the first day
Grande becomes *gran* before a singular noun of either gender.
   un gran pintor a great painter
Ciento becomes *cien* immediately before a noun of either gender.
   cien vacas one hundred cows

Forms of adjectives

	Singular Masc.	Fem.	Plural Masc.	Fem.
tall	*alto*	*alta*	*altos*	*altas*
English	*inglés*	*inglesa*	*ingleses*	*inglesas*
poor	*pobre*	*pobre*	*pobres*	*pobres*
easy	*fácil*	*fácil*	*fáciles*	*fáciles*

Common adjectives that change meaning with a change in position

	AFTER the noun	BEFORE the noun
antiguo	old (ancient)	old (former), old-time
cierto	sure, reliable	a certain
grande	large, big	great, famous
nuevo	new	another, different
pobre	poor	unfortunate
simple	silly, simple-minded	simple, mere

Demonstrative adjectives

	Masc.	Fem.
this	este	esta
these	estos	estas
that	ese	esa
those	esos	esas
that	aquel	aquella
those	aquellos	aquellas

Demonstrative adjectives

Demonstrative adjectives precede the nouns they modify and agree with them in number and gender.

esas manzanas those apples

Este refers to what is near the speaker. *Ese* refers to what is near the person addressed.

Aquel refers to what is remote from both the speaker and the person addressed.

Juan, déme Vd. aquellos libros que están en la sala.
John, give me those books that are in the living room.

Adverbs

Many adverbs are formed by adding the suffix *-mente* to the feminine singular form of the adjective.

un hombre ricamente vestido
a richly dressed man

La tortuga anda lentamente.
The turtle walks slowly.

¡Habla claramente!
Speak clearly!

Maneja cuidadosamente.
He drives carefully.

In a series of two or more adverbs normally formed with *-mente*, the suffix is used only with the last adverb.

Arturo escribió clara y facilmente.
Arthur wrote clearly, and easily.

Comparison

Comparison with adjectives

Superiority *Juan es más rico que María.*
John is richer than Mary.

Equality *Juan es tan rico como María.*
John is as rich as Mary.

Inferiority *Juan es menos rico que María.*
John is not as rich as Mary.

The superlative of an adjective is formed by placing the definite article or possessive adjective before the comparative form.

Miguel es el estudiante más inteligente de la clase.
Michael is the most intelligent student in the class.

Comparison with adverbs

Adverbs are compared as shown in this example.

rápidamente quickly
más (menos) rápidamente more (less) quickly
lo más (menos) rápidamente the most (least) quickly

The article *lo* is used with the superlative form.
The superlative form of the adverb is followed by *de*.
The English word "than" is usually translated as *que*.

Tiene más dinero que Ana.
He has more money than Anna.

Before a number, "than" is translated as *de* if the sentence is affirmative and by *que* if negative.

Recibió más de cien dólares.
He received more than one hundred dollars.

Comparisons of equality are expressed by *tan* plus an adjective or adverb plus *como*.

Manuel es tan alto como Andrés.
Manuel is as tall as Andrew.

Tanto (-a, -os, -as) plus a noun plus *como* is used to express as much (as many) as.

Tengo tantas llaves como tú.
I have as many keys as you.

Tanto (-a, -os, -as) plus *como* is used to express as much (as many) as.

Antonio trabaja tanto como su hermano.
Anthony works as much as his brother.

Comparative forms of adjectives

Positive	Comparative	Superlative
bueno good	mejor better	el mejor the best
malo bad	peor worse	el peor the worst
grande great, big	mayor greater, older más grande larger menos grande not as large	el mayor the greatest, the oldest el más grande the largest el menos grande the least large
pequeño small	menor minor, lesser, younger más pequeño smaller menos pequeño less, small	el menor the least, the youngest el más pequeño the smallest el menos pequeño the least small

Review of Spanish Grammar

Possession

Possession is expressed by *de* + the possessor.
   la cama de mi hermano my brother's bed

Possessive adjectives

The short form always precedes the noun; the long form always follows the noun. Both forms agree in gender and number with the person or thing possessed.
   nuestros amigos our friends
   las maletas tuyas your suitcases

Possessive pronouns

A possessive pronoun is formed by the definite article plus the long form of the possessive adjective.
   el tuyo yours

A possessive pronoun agrees in number and gender with the noun it replaces.
   mi pelota y la tuya my ball and yours

Possessive adjectives

	Short form Singular	Plural	Long form Singular Masc.	Fem.	Plural Masc.	Fem.
my	mi	mis	mío	mía	míos	mías
your (familiar singular)	tu	tus	tuyo	tuya	tuyos	tuyas
your, his, her, its, their	su	sus	suyo	suya	suyos	suyas
our			nuestro	nuestra	nuestros	nuestras
your (familiar plural)			vuestro	vuestra	vuestros	vuestras

Possessive pronouns

	Singular Masc.	Fem.	Plural Masc.	Fem.
mine	el mío	la mía	los míos	las mías
yours (familiar singular)	el tuyo	la tuya	los tuyos	las tuyas
your, his, hers, its, theirs	el suyo	la suya	los suyos	las suyas
ours	el nuestro	la nuestra	los nuestros	las nuestras
yours (familiar plural)	el vuestro	la vuestra	los vuestros	las vuestras

Pronouns

Subject pronouns

Subject pronouns are used for clarity, emphasis, or politeness. The English word "it" is not expressed as a subject.
   Es difícil hacer. It is difficult to do.

The plural form *vosotros* is used in Spain. In Spanish America, *ustedes* is preferred.

Object pronouns

A pronoun used as the object of a preposition always follows the preposition.

The pronouns *mí, ti* and *sí* combine with the preposition *con* as follows:
   conmigo with me
   contigo with you (familiar)
   consigo with yourself, himself, herself, themselves

These pronoun forms do not change in gender or number.

An object pronoun, whether direct or indirect, is usually placed immediately before the verb. In an affirmative command, infinitive, or present participle, the object pronoun follows and is joined to the verb. In a negative command, the object pronoun precedes the verb. When the object pronoun is joined to an affirmative command or present participle, an accent mark is needed over the vowel of the accented syllable.

Double object pronouns

When a verb has two object pronouns, the indirect object pronoun precedes the direct object pronoun.
   Me los entregan. They deliver them to me.

When both object pronouns are in the third person, the indirect object is written as *se*.
   Se lo digo. I tell it to her.

The various meanings of *se* may be clarified by adding *a Vd., a Vds., a él, a ella, a ellos, a ellas*.
   No se la enseñamos a ellos.
   We don't show it to them.

Forms of pronouns (see also Possession on page 412)

Subject pronouns

Singular	Plural
yo I	nosotros, -as we
tú you (familiar)	vosotros, -as you (familiar)
usted (Vd. or Ud.) you	ustedes (Vds. or Uds.) you
él he	ellos they
ella she	ellas they

Pronouns used as objects of prepositions

Singular	Plural
mí me	nosotros, -as us
ti you (familiar)	vosotros, -as you (familiar)
usted (Vd. or Ud.) you	ustedes (Vds. or Uds.) you
él him, it	ellos them (masc.)
ella her, it	ellas them (fem.)
sí yourself, himself, herself, itself	sí yourselves, themselves

Object pronouns

Indirect	Direct	Reflexive
Singular	*Singular*	*Singular*
me to me	me me	me myself
te to you (familiar)	te you (familiar)	te yourself (familiar)
le to you, to him, to her, to it	le you (masc.), him; lo him, it (masc.); la you (fem.), her, it (fem.)	se yourself, himself, herself, itself
Plural	*Plural*	*Plural*
nos to us	nos us	nos ourselves
os to you (familiar)	os you (familiar)	os yourselves (familiar)
les to you, to them	los you, them (masc.); las you, them (fem.)	se yourselves, themselves

Position of object pronouns

Finite verb	Les doy el regalo.	I give them the gift.
Infinitive	Quieren verlo.	They want to see it.
	Lo quieren ver.	
Present participle	Estoy esperándolo.	I am waiting for it.
	Lo estoy esperando.	
Affirmative command	Envíelo Vd.	Send it.
Negative command	No lo envíe Vd.	Don't send it.

Relative pronouns and adjectives

que that, which, who
quien (-es) who
el (la, los, las) cual (-es) which, who
lo cual which
el (la) que (the one) which, (the one) who, he (she) who
los (las) que (the ones) which, (the ones) who, those who
lo que what, which
cuyo (-a, -os, -as) whose (as relative adjective)

Demonstrative pronouns

	Masc.	Fem.	Neut.
this (one)	éste	ésta	esto
these	éstos	éstas	
that (one)	ése	ésa	eso
those	ésos	ésas	
that (one)	aquél	aquélla	aquello
those	aquéllos	aquéllas	

Review of Spanish Grammar

The placement of double object pronouns is the same as that given above for single object pronouns. Double object pronouns are always kept together.
When both object pronouns are attached to the verb, a written accent mark is used to keep the original stress.

Va a servírselo. He is going to serve it to him.

Demonstrative pronouns
Demonstrative pronouns agree in number and gender with the nouns they represent.

Me gustan estas faldas y aquéllas.
I like these skirts and those (distant).

Neuter forms of demonstrative pronouns indicate things indefinitely referred to, or general ideas and situations.

No haré esto. I shall not do this.

Relative pronouns and adjectives
Relative pronouns and adjectives are never omitted in Spanish.

La revista que compraste es interesante.
The magazine you bought is interesting.

Que refers to both persons and things. After a preposition, however, *que* refers only to things; *quien (-es)* refers to persons.

el chico que jugó   *el chico con quien jugué*
the boy who played   the boy with whom I played

Negation, interrogatives, and exclamations

Negative words and their opposites

Negative	*Affirmative*
no no, not	*sí* yes
nadie no one, nobody, not anyone	*alguien* someone, somebody
nada nothing, not anything	*algo* something
nunca, jamás never, not ever	*siempre* always
tampoco neither, not either	*también* also
ninguno (-a) no, none, not any	*alguno (-a)* some, any
ni . . . ni neither . . . nor, not . . . nor	*o . . . o* either . . . or
sin without	*con* with

The negative word *no* precedes the verb.

¿No encontró usted el reloj?
Didn't you find the watch?

If an object pronoun precedes the verb, the negative word precedes the object pronoun.

No lo recibió. He didn't receive it.

All negative sentences must have a negative word preceding the verb. If the negative word follows the verb, then *no* must precede the verb.

Nunca lo haré. I shall never do it.
No lo haré nunca. I shall never do it.

When *nadie* is the object of the verb, it is preceded by the personal *a*.

No veo a nadie. I don't see anyone.

But is expressed as *sino* when the first element is negative and the second is in direct contrast.

No llevaba abrigo negro, sino azul.
He wasn't wearing a black coat, but a blue one.

Interrogative expressions
¿qué? what?
¿quién (-es)? who?
¿cuál (-es)? which, which one(s)?
¿dónde? where?
¿adónde? where? to where? (with verbs of motion)
¿cuándo? when?
¿cuánto (-a)? how much?
¿cuántos (-as)? how many?
¿cómo? how?
¿por qué? why?

Note that all interrogative expressions carry an accent mark.

Exclamations
All exclamatory words carry written accent marks. The most common are:

¡Qué . . . ! What . . . ! What a . . . ! How . . . !
¡Cuánto (a) . . . ! How much . . . !
¡Cuántos (as) . . . ! How many . . . !

Exclamatory sentences have an inverted exclamation point (¡) at the beginning and a regular exclamation point at the end.

¡Qué día! What a day!

Review of Spanish Grammar

Prepositions

Prepositions with infinitives

The infinitive is the only verb form that may follow a preposition.

Después de vestirse, salió.
After getting dressed, he went out.

The infinitive is used after many verbs. In many cases it follows the verb directly.

Quiere salir temprano. He wants to leave early.

In other cases the infinitive is preceded by a preposition. The following common verbs do not require a preposition before an infinitive.

creer	to believe	*necesitar*	to need
deber	ought to, should	*poder*	to be able, can
desear	to wish, desire	*querer*	to wish, want
esperar	to hope	*saber*	to know how to

Verbs expressing beginning, motion, teaching, or learning and several other verbs require the preposition *a* before a following infinitive.

beginning	*comenzar*	motion	*correr* to run
	empezar		*ir* to go
	ponerse		*llegar* to arrive
	principiar		*salir* to go out to
teaching	*enseñar*	other	*invitar* to invite
learning	*aprender*	verbs	*ayudar* to help
			llamar to call

Los niños empezaron a llorar.
The children began to cry.

The following verbs require the preposition *de* before an infinitive.

acabar	to have just	*dejar*	to cease, stop, fail
acordarse	to remember	*olvidarse*	to forget
alegrarse	to be glad to	*tratar*	to try
cesar	to cease, stop		

Trató de esconderse. He tried to hide.

Uses of the personal *a*

The personal *a* is used before direct objects that denote persons or personified things. The personal *a* is not translated.

Visitan a su abuelo They visit their grandfather.

The personal *a* is used before pronouns referring to persons, even when used in a negative sense.

No veo a nadie. I see no one.

The personal *a* is omitted after the verb *tener* with the meaning "to have."

Tiene muchos amigos. He has many friends.

The personal *a* is used with *querer* when it means "to love" and omitted when it means "to want."

El niño quiere su madre.
The child wants his mother.

El niño quiere a su madre.
The child loves his mother.

A striker in Chicago, Illinois, carrying a sign that translates as "On strike for our contract."

Uses of *para*

Purpose:
Como para vivir. I eat in order to live.
Destination:
Saldrá para España. He will leave for Spain.
Use:
Es una caja para dulces. It is a candy box.
Future time:
Estará listo para el sábado.
It will be ready by Saturday.
"Considering the fact that":
Para estudiante, toca muy bien.
For a student, he plays very well.
"Be about to" after *estar*:
Estoy para salir. I am about to leave.

Uses of *por*

"For the sake of":
Lo hizo por su hermano. He did it for his brother.
Price or exchange:
Compró la revista por un peso.
He bought the magazine for a peso.
Length of time:
Quedó en Perú por dos semanas.
He stayed in Peru for two weeks.
"In the morning, afternoon, or night":
Trabajo por la tarde. I work in the afternoon.
"By, through, along":
Dan un paseo por el parque.
They take a walk through the park.
"For" after the verbs *ir, enviar, luchar, llamar,* or *preguntar*:
Fue por el médico. He went for the doctor.

The following verbs are not followed by *para* or *por,* since "for" is part of the meaning of the verb:
buscar to look for,
esperar to wait for,
pedir to ask for.

Buscaron una mesa. They looked for a table.

Review of Spanish Grammar

Verbs

Conjugation of regular verbs

The three conjugations are distinguished by the infinitive endings: *-ar, -er,* and *-ir.*

Conjugation of regular verbs

Simple tenses
Indicative

	Present			*Imperfect*		
	I take, eat, live			I was taking, eating, living		
	I do take, eat, live			I used to take, eat, live		
yo	tomo	como	vivo	tomaba	comía	vivía
tú	tomas	comes	vives	tomabas	comías	vivías
Vd., él, ella	toma	come	vive	tomaba	comía	vivía
nosotros, nosotras	tomamos	comemos	vivimos	tomábamos	comíamos	vivíamos
vosotros, vosotras	tomáis	coméis	vivís	tomabais	comíais	vivíais
Vds., ellos, ellas	toman	comen	viven	tomaban	comían	vivían

Subjunctive

	Present			*Imperfect*		
	that I may take, eat, live			that I might take, eat, live		
				that I should take, eat, live		
yo	tome	coma	viva	tomara	comiera	viviera
				or		
				tomase	comiese	viviese
tú	tomes	comas	vivas	tomaras	comieras	vivieras
				or		
				tomases	comieses	vivieses
Vd., él, ella	tome	coma	viva	tomara	comiera	viviera
				or		
				tomase	comiese	viviese
nosotros, nosotras	tomemos	comamos	vivamos	tomáramos	comiéramos	viviéramos
				or		
				tomásemos	comiésemos	viviésemos
vosotros, vosotras	toméis	comáis	viváis	tomarais	comierais	vivierais
				or		
				tomaseis	comieseis	vivieseis
Vds., ellos, ellas	tomen	coman	vivan	tomaran	comieran	vivieran
				or		
				tomasen	comiesen	viviesen

Compound tenses
Indicative

Present perfect
Present of *haber* plus past participle
I have taken   I have eaten   I have lived
he tomado   he comido   he vivido

Pluperfect
Imperfect of *haber* plus past participle
I had taken   I had eaten   I had lived
había tomado   había comido   había vivido

Subjunctive

Present perfect
Present subjunctive of *haber* plus the past participle
that I may have taken   that I may have eaten   that I may have lived
haya tomado   haya comido   haya vivido

Progressive

The present participle is used with *estar* to denote continuing action.
I am taking   I am eating   I am living
estoy tomando   estoy comiendo   estoy viviendo

Review of Spanish Grammar

In all but the future and conditional tenses, the inflexional endings are added to the stem of the verb, for example: *tom*, *com*, and *viv* for *tomar*, *comer*, and *vivir*. Future and conditional endings are added to the infinitive. These endings are the same for all verbs.

Preterite
I took, ate, lived
I did take, eat, live

tomé	comí	viví
tomaste	comiste	viviste
tomó	comió	vivió
tomamos	comimos	vivimos
tomasteis	comisteis	vivisteis
tomaron	comieron	vivieron

Future
I shall take, eat, live
I will take, eat, live

tomaré	comeré	viviré
tomarás	comerás	vivirás
tomará	comerá	vivirá
tomaremos	comeremos	viviremos
tomaréis	comeréis	viviréis
tomarán	comerán	vivirán

Conditional
I should take, eat, live
I would take, eat, live

tomaría	comería	viviría
tomarías	comerías	vivirías
tomaría	comería	viviría
tomaríamos	comeríamos	viviríamos
tomaríais	comeríais	viviríais
tomarían	comerían	vivirían

Infinitives

	-ar verb	-er verb	-ir verb
	tomar	comer	vivir
	to take	to eat	to live

Participles

Present	taking	eating	living
	tomando	comiendo	viviendo
Past	taken	eaten	lived
	tomado	comido	vivido

Imperative

	take	eat	live
Familiar s.	toma	come	vive
Familiar pl.	tomad	comed	vivid
Polite s.	tome Vd.	coma Vd.	viva Vd.
Polite pl.	tomen Vds.	coman Vds.	vivan Vds.

Preterite perfect
Preterite of *haber* plus past participle
I had taken   I had eaten   I had lived
hube tomado   hube comido   hube vivido

Future perfect
Future of *haber* plus past participle
I shall have taken   I shall have eaten   I shall have lived
habré tomado   habré comido   habré vivido

Pluperfect
Either form of the imperfect subjunctive of *haber* plus past participle
that I might have taken   that I might have eaten   that I might have lived
hubiera (hubiese) tomado   hubiera (hubiese) comido   hubiera (hubiese) vivido

Conditional *perfect*
Conditional of *haber* plus past participle
I should have taken   I should have eaten   I should have lived
habría tomado   habría comido   habría vivido

Review of Spanish Grammar

Stem changing verbs

In conjugating Spanish verbs, we are accustomed to changes in the verb endings, but certain verbs also change the spelling of their stems.

Stem changes are not uncommon in English. Consider the way the verb "eat" changes in English: I eat, I ate. Consider the verb "go": I go, I went. Finally, consider the verb "be": I am, I was.

Conjugation of stem-changing verbs

First class

Certain verbs of the first and second conjugations with stem vowels *e* or *o* change *e* to *ie*, *o* to *ue* when stressed. Note that *jugar*, to play, is conjugated as if it were a first class stem-changing verb with stem vowel *o*.

Examples:

pensar — to think
volver — to return

Review: First class verbs e→ie & o→ue when stressed.

Present participle
pensando   volviendo

Present indicative		Present subjunctive		Imperative	
pienso	vuelvo	piense	vuelva		
piensas	vuelves	pienses	vuelvas	piensa	vuelve
piensa	vuelve	piense	vuelva	piense	vuelva
pensamos	volvemos	pensemos	volvamos	pensemos	volvamos
pensáis	volvéis	penséis	volváis	pensad	volved
piensan	vuelven	piensen	vuelvan	piensen	vuelvan

Second class

Certain verbs of the third conjugation with stem vowels of *e* or *o* change *e* to *ie*, *o* to *ue* when stressed. Changes are the same as those listed above with the addition of *e* changing to *i*, and *o* to *u*, when the following syllable contains a stressed *a*, *ie*, or *io*.

Examples:

(ie) sentir — to feel
(ue) dormir — to sleep

Present participle
sintiendo   durmiendo

Present indicative		Present subjunctive		Preterite		Imperfect subjunctive		Imperative	
siento	duermo	sienta	duerma	sentí	dormí	sintiera	durmiera		
sientes	duermes	sientas	duermas	sentiste	dormiste	sintieras	durmieras	siente	duerme
siente	duerme	sienta	duerma	sintió	durmió	sintiera	durmiera	sienta	duerma
sentimos	dormimos	sintamos	durmamos	sentimos	dormimos	sintiéramos	durmiéramos	sintamos	durmamos
sentís	dormís	sintáis	durmáis	sentisteis	dormisteis	sintierais	durmierais	sentid	dormid
sienten	duermen	sientan	duerman	sintieron	durmieron	sintieran	durmieran	sientan	duerman

Third class

Certain verbs of the third conjugation with stem vowel *e* change *e* to *i* in all forms affected in the first and second classes of stem-changing verbs.

Example:

(i) pedir — to ask for

Present participle
pidiendo

Present indicative	Present subjunctive	Preterite	Imperfect subjunctive	Imperative
pido	pida	pedí	pidiera	
pides	pidas	pediste	pidieras	pide
pide	pida	pidió	pidiera	pida
pedimos	pidamos	pedimos	pidiéramos	pidamos
pedís	pidáis	pedisteis	pidierais	pedid
piden	pidan	pidieron	pidieran	pidan

Review of Spanish Grammar

Spelling change verbs

This class of verbs undergoes changes in spelling during conjugation, with the effect of preserving the sound of the consonant found in the infinitive.

The chart below supplies examples of changes in the verbs *buscar* search, *jugar* play, *averiguar* investigate, *vencer* conquer, *conocer* know, *escoger* choose, *leer* read, and *seguir* follow.

Spelling change verbs

Verb ending	*Spelling change*	*Examples*
in verbs ending in *car*	*c* changes to *qu* before an *e*	*buscar* → *busqué*
in verbs ending in *gar*	insert *u* before an *e*	*jugar* → *jugué*
in verbs ending in *guar*	put dieresis over *u* before an *e*	*averiguar* → *averigüé*
in verbs ending in *cer* or *cir* preceded by a consonant	replace the *c* by *z* before an *a* or *o*	*vencer* → *venzo*
in verbs ending in *cer* or *cir* preceded by a vowel	insert *z* before *c* when followed by an *a* or *o*	*conocer* → *conozco*
in verbs ending in *ger* or *gir*	replace the *g* with *j* before an *a* or *o*	*escoger* → *escojo*
in verbs ending in *er* or *ir*	change the *i* of the endings *ie* and *io* to *y*	*leer* → *leyó*
in verbs ending in *guir* when the *u* is silent	drop the *u* before an *a* or *o*	*seguir* → *sigo*

Correspondencia Correspondence

La carta comercial A business letter

ciudad, fecha city, date	*Miami, 8 de mayo de 19*___	Miami, May 8, 19___
destinatario, dirreccion inside address	*Sr. Juan Encina* *Avenida de las Américas 20* *Lima, Perú*	
el saludo salutation	*Estimado (a) señor (a):*	Dear Sir (Madam):
despedida closing	*Atentamente,* Attentively, *Sinceramente,* Sincerely,	
firma signature	José Antonio Rivera	

Carta personal A friendly letter

ciudad, fecha city, date	*Nueva York, 20 de julio de 19*___	New York, July 20, 19___
saludo salutation	*Querido (a) amigo (a),*	Dear friend,
despedida closing	*Cariñosamente,* Lovingly, *Recuerdos,* Regards,	
firma signature	José	

Review of Spanish Grammar

Irregular verbs

Irregular verbs are the most difficult verbs to learn. Yet, perhaps unfortunately, they describe actions and states of being that are most frequently needed in speaking and writing Spanish. The verb forms given in the chart below and continuing for two more pages take nineteen irregular verbs through nine tenses. As you will see, the verb endings for certain tenses are the same as those you will encounter in conjugating regular verbs.

Conjugation of irregular verbs

Infinitive	Indicative				Conditional	Subjunctive			Imperative
	Present	Imperfect	Preterite	Future	Present	Present	Imperfect (1st form)	(2nd form)	
andar to go, walk	ando andas anda andamos andáis andan	andaba andabas andaba andábamos andabais andaban	anduve anduviste anduvo anduvimos anduvisteis anduvieron	andaré andarás andará andaremos andaréis andarán	andaría andarías andaría andaríamos andaríais andarían	ande andes ande andemos andéis anden	anduviera anduvieras anduviera anduviéramos anduvierais anduvieran	anduviese anduvieses anduviese anduviésemos anduvieseis anduviesen	anda ande andemos andad anden
dar to give	doy das da damos dais dan	daba dabas daba dábamos dabais daban	di diste dio dimos disteis dieron	daré darás dará daremos daréis darán	daría darías daría daríamos daríais darían	dé des dé demos deis den	diera dieras diera diéramos dierais dieran	diese dieses diese diésemos dieseis diesen	da dé demos dad den
decir to say, tell	digo dices dice decimos decís dicen	decía decías decía decíamos decíais decían	dije dijiste dijo dijimos dijisteis dijeron	diré dirás dirá diremos diréis dirán	diría dirías diría diríamos diríais dirían	diga digas diga digamos digáis digan	dijera dijeras dijera dijéramos dijerais dijeran	dijese dijeses dijese dijésemos dijeseis dijesen	di diga digamos decid digan
estar to be	estoy estás está estamos estáis están	estaba estabas estaba estábamos estabais estaban	estuve estuviste estuvo estuvimos estuvisteis estuvieron	estaré estarás estará estaremos estaréis estarán	estaría estarías estaría estaríamos estaríais estarían	esté estés esté estemos estéis estén	estuviera estuvieras estuviera estuviéramos estuvierais estuvieran	estuviese estuvieses estuviese estuviésemos estuvieseis estuviesen	está esté estemos estad estén
haber to have	he has ha hemos habéis han	había habías había habíamos habíais habían	hube hubiste hubo hubimos hubisteis hubieron	habré habrás habrá habremos habréis habrán	habría habrías habría habríamos habríais habrían	haya hayas haya hayamos hayáis hayan	hubiera hubieras hubiera hubiéramos hubierais hubieran	hubiese hubieses hubiese hubiésemos hubieseis hubiesen	he haya hayamos habed hayan
hacer to make, do	hago haces hace hacemos hacéis hacen	hacía hacías hacía hacíamos hacíais hacían	hice hiciste hizo hicimos hicisteis hicieron	haré harás hará haremos haréis harán	haría harías haría haríamos haríais harían	haga hagas haga hagamos hagáis hagan	hiciera hicieras hiciera hiciéramos hicierais hicieran	hiciese hicieses hiciese hiciésemos hicieseis hiciesen	haz haga hagamos haced hagan

> **El Directorio Páginas Amarillas**
> **Es El Camino Más Corto Para Hacer Sus Compras**
>
> *Let your fingers do the walking: "The yellow pages directory is the shortest route for making your purchases."*

Conjugation of irregular verbs (continued)

Infinitive	Indicative				Conditional	Subjunctive			Imperative
	Present	*Imperfect*	*Preterite*	*Future*	*Present*	*Present*	*Imperfect (1st form)*	*(2nd form)*	
ir to go	voy	iba	fui	iré	iría	vaya	fuera	fuese	
	vas	ibas	fuiste	irás	irías	vayas	fueras	fueses	ve
	va	iba	fue	irá	iría	vaya	fuera	fuese	vaya
	vamos	íbamos	fuimos	iremos	iríamos	vayamos	fuéramos	fuésemos	vamos
	vais	ibais	fuisteis	iréis	iríais	vayáis	fuerais	fueseis	id
	van	iban	fueron	irán	irían	vayan	fueran	fuesen	vayan
oir to hear	oigo	oía	oí	oiré	oiría	oiga	oyera	oyese	
	oyes	oías	oíste	oirás	oirías	oigas	oyeras	oyeses	oye
	oye	oía	oyó	oirá	oiría	oiga	oyera	oyese	oiga
	oímos	oíamos	oímos	oiremos	oiríamos	oigamos	oyéramos	oyésemos	oigamos
	oís	oíais	oísteis	oiréis	oiríais	oigáis	oyerais	oyeseis	oíd
	oyen	oían	oyeron	oirán	oirían	oigan	oyeran	oyesen	oigan
poder to be able	puedo	podía	pude	podré	podría	pueda	pudiera	pudiese	
	puedes	podías	pudiste	podrás	podrías	puedas	pudieras	pudieses	puede
	puede	podía	pudo	podrá	podría	pueda	pudiera	pudiese	pueda
	podemos	podíamos	pudimos	podremos	podríamos	podamos	pudiéramos	pudiésemos	podamos
	podéis	podíais	pudisteis	podréis	podríais	podáis	pudierais	pudieseis	poded
	pueden	podían	pudieron	podrán	podrían	puedan	pudieran	pudiesen	puedan
poner to put	pongo	ponía	puse	pondré	pondría	ponga	pusiera	pusiese	
	pones	ponías	pusiste	pondrás	pondrías	pongas	pusieras	pusieses	pon
	pone	ponía	puso	pondrá	pondría	ponga	pusiera	pusiese	ponga
	ponemos	poníamos	pusimos	pondremos	pondríamos	pongamos	pusiéramos	pusiésemos	pongamos
	ponéis	poníais	pusisteis	pondréis	pondríais	pongáis	pusierais	pusieseis	poned
	ponen	ponían	pusieron	pondrán	pondrían	pongan	pusieran	pusiesen	pongan
querer to want, love	quiero	quería	quise	querré	querría	quiera	quisiera	quisiese	
	quieres	querías	quisiste	querrás	querrías	quieras	quisieras	quisieses	quiere
	quiere	quería	quiso	querrá	querría	quiera	quisiera	quisiese	quiera
	queremos	queríamos	quisimos	querremos	querríamos	queramos	quisiéramos	quisiésemos	queramos
	queréis	queríais	quisisteis	querréis	querríais	queráis	quisierais	quisieseis	quered
	quieren	querían	quisieron	querrán	querrían	quieran	quisieran	quisiesen	quieran
saber to know	sé	sabía	supe	sabré	sabría	sepa	supiera	supiese	
	sabes	sabías	supiste	sabrás	sabrías	sepas	supieras	supieses	sabe
	sabe	sabía	supo	sabrá	sabría	sepa	supiera	supiese	sepa
	sabemos	sabíamos	supimos	sabremos	sabríamos	sepamos	supiéramos	supiésemos	sepamos
	sabéis	sabíais	supisteis	sabréis	sabríais	sepáis	supierais	supieseis	sabed
	saben	sabían	supieron	sabrán	sabrían	sepan	supieran	supiesen	sepan

Review of Spanish Grammar

Conjugation of irregular verbs (continued)

Infinitive	Indicative				Conditional	Subjunctive			Imperative
	Present	*Imperfect*	*Preterite*	*Future*	*Present*	*Present*	*Imperfect (1st form)*	*(2nd form)*	
salir to go out	salgo sales sale salimos salís salen	salía salías salía salíamos salíais salían	salí saliste salió salimos salisteis salieron	saldré saldrás saldrá saldremos saldréis saldrán	saldría saldrías saldría saldríamos saldríais saldrían	salga salgas salga salgamos salgáis salgan	saliera salieras saliera saliéramos salierais salieran	saliese salieses saliese saliésemos salieseis saliesen	sal salga salgamos salid salgan
ser to be	soy eres es somos sois son	era eras era éramos erais eran	fui fuiste fue fuimos fuisteis fueron	seré serás será seremos seréis serán	sería serías sería seríamos seríais serían	sea seas sea seamos seáis sean	fuera fueras fuera fuéramos fuerais fueran	fuese fueses fuese fuésemos fueseis fuesen	sé sea seamos sed sean
tener to have	tengo tienes tiene tenemos tenéis tienen	tenía tenías tenía teníamos teníais tenían	tuve tuviste tuvo tuvimos tuvisteis tuvieron	tendré tendrás tendrá tendremos tendréis tendrán	tendría tendrías tendría tendríamos tendríais tendrían	tenga tengas tenga tengamos tengáis tengan	tuviera tuvieras tuviera tuviéramos tuvierais tuvieran	tuviese tuvieses tuviese tuviésemos tuvieseis tuviesen	ten tenga tengamos tened tengan
traer to bring	traigo traes trae traemos traéis traen	traía traías traía traíamos traíais traían	traje trajiste trajo trajimos trajisteis trajeron	traeré traerás traerá traeremos traeréis traerán	traería traerías traería traeríamos traeríais traerían	traiga traigas traiga traigamos traigáis traigan	trajera trajeras trajera trajéramos trajerais trajeran	trajese trajeses trajese trajésemos trajeseis trajesen	trae traiga traigamos traed traigan
valer to be worth	valgo vales vale valemos valéis valen	valía valías valía valíamos valíais valían	valí valiste valió valimos valisteis valieron	valdré valdrás valdrá valdremos valdréis valdrán	valdría valdrías valdría valdríamos valdríais valdrían	valga valgas valga valgamos valgáis valgan	valiera valieras valiera valiéramos valierais valieran	valiese valieses valiese valiésemos valieseis valiesen	val valga valgamos valed valgan
venir to come	vengo vienes viene venimos venís vienen	venía venías venía veníamos veníais venían	vine viniste vino vinimos vinisteis vinieron	vendré vendrás vendrá vendremos vendréis vendrán	vendría vendrías vendría vendríamos vendríais vendrían	venga vengas venga vengamos vengáis vengan	viniera vinieras viniera viniéramos vinierais vinieran	viniese vinieses viniese viniésemos vinieseis viniesen	ven venga vengamos venid vengan
ver to see	veo ves ve vemos veis ven	veía veías veía veíamos veíais veían	vi viste vio vimos visteis vieron	veré verás verá veremos veréis verán	vería verías vería veríamos veríais verían	vea veas vea veamos veáis vean	viera vieras viera viéramos vierais vieran	viese vieses viese viésemos vieseis viesen	ve vea veamos ved vean

Uses of *ser* and *estar*

Both *ser* and *estar* mean *to be*. They are used in the following ways:

ser

With adjectives to express an inherent or permanent quality, such as age, characteristic, color, possession, shape, size, and wealth.

La casa es blanca. The house is white.

With the preposition *de* to express ownership, material, or origin.

La pulsera es de oro. The bracelet is gold.

With a predicate noun or pronoun.

Él es médico. He is a doctor.

With the past participle in a passive construction.

El libro fue escrito por él.
The book was written by him.

In impersonal expressions

Es mejor hacerlo ahora. It is better to do it now.

estar

With adjectives to express an accidental or temporary condition.

La chica está ausente. The girl is absent.

In expressions of location

Barcelona está en España. Barcelona is in Spain.

In expressions of health.

Estaban enfermos. They were sick.

With the past participle used as an adjective to express a condition.

Las ventanas están cerradas.
The windows are closed.

With the present participle to form the present progressive tense.

Estaba durmiendo. He was sleeping.

Gustar

Gustar, which literally means to be pleasing, is used to translate the verb "to like." For example, in the sentence *Me gustan las revistas,* I like the magazines, the subject becomes the indirect object, *me,* and the direct object *revistas,* becomes the subject of the verb *gustar.*

Reflexive verbs

Reflexive verbs are designated by *se* attached to the infinitive so *lavarse* means to wash oneself. Reflexive pronouns are used with reflexive verbs in any tense, so *se lavaron* means they washed themselves.

Uses of the subjunctive mood

The subjunctive is used mainly in certain types of subordinate clauses introduced by *que*. In general, a verb in the subjunctive expresses a feeling or thought in the mind of the speaker rather than an established fact.

After verbs of volition (with a subject change).

Quiero que lo hagas. I want you to do it.

After verbs of emotion (with a subject change).

Se alegra de que venga.
He is happy that I am coming.

After impersonal expressions followd by a definite subject in the subordinate clause.

Es probable que me escriba.
It is likely that he will write to me.

After verbs of doubt and denial in the affirmative.

Dudo que lo sepa. I doubt that he knows it.

After verbs of thinking and believing used in the interrogative or negative.

No creo que tenga razón. I don't think he is right.

In a relative clause modifying a negative or an indefinite antecedent.

No conozco a nadie que hable alemán.
I don't know anyone who speaks German.

After conjunctions of time, purpose, restriction, or result.

Iré con tal que volvamos temprano.
I shall go provided that we return early.

After certain indefinite expressions, such as *dondequiera que* and *cualquier cosa que*.

Dondequiera que viva será feliz.
Wherever she lives, she will be happy.

Idioms

a tiempo on time
  Vuelve a tiempo si quieres ver la película.
  Return on time if you want to see the movie.

darse prisa to hurry
  Date prisa! Ya son las seis.
  Hurry up! It's six o'clock.

de repente suddenly
  De repente abrió la puerta.
  Suddenly he opened the door.

en seguida immediately
  Pagó la cuenta y salió en seguida.
  He paid the check and left immediately.

estar de vuelta to be back (in a place)
  Mi hijo está de vuelta en Nueva York.
  My son is back in New York.

hacer frío (calor) of weather: to be cold (warm)
  Hace frío hoy.
  It is cold today.

hacer un viaje to take a trip
  Hice un viaje a España.
  I took a trip to Spain.

tener hambre (sed) to be hungry (thirsty)
  Tengo mucha hambre.
  I am very hungry.

tratar de to try to
  Trata de terminar el trabajo.
  He tries to finish the work.

Hace frio!   **Date prisa!**

Review of Spanish Grammar

Numerals, time, and dates

Cardinal numbers
The numbers 16 to 19 and 21 to 29 may be written as single words. Note that as single words, 16, 22, 23, and 26 carry accent marks on the final syllable.

   16 *dieciséis*, 22 *veintidós*

The only numbers that change with gender are *uno* and the compounds of *ciento* from 200 through 900.

   quinientas dos escuelas
   five hundred and two schools

Ciento becomes *cien* before nouns and before the numbers *mil* and *millones*. In all other numbers, the full form *ciento* is used.

   cien soldados one hundred soldiers

Millón requires the preposition *de* before the noun it multiplies.

   tres millones de pesos three million pesos

Un is not used before *ciento* or *mil*. It is used before *millón*.

   ciento doce sillas one hundred and twelve chairs
   un millón de pesos a million pesos

Ordinal numbers

1st *primero*	4th *cuarto*	8th *octavo*
2nd *segundo*	5th *quinto*	9th *noveno*
3rd *tercero*	6th *sexto*	10th *décimo*
	7th *séptimo*	

Ordinal numbers are generally used only through *tenth;* beyond that, the cardinal numbers are used. An ordinal number agrees in number and gender with the noun it modifies.

   la Quinta Avenida Fifth Avenue

The ordinal numbers *primero* and *tercero* drop the final *o* before a masculine singular noun.

   el tercer edificio the third building

Cardinal numbers

0	*cero*	30	*treinta*
1	*uno, una*	31	*treinta y uno*
		32	*treinta y dos*
2	*dos*	40	*cuarenta*
3	*tres*	41	*cuarenta y uno*
4	*cuatro*	50	*cincuenta*
5	*cinco*	51	*cincuenta y uno*
6	*seis*	60	*sesenta*
7	*siete*	61	*sesenta y uno*
8	*ocho*	70	*setenta*
9	*nueve*	71	*setenta y uno*
10	*diez*	80	*ochenta*
11	*once*	81	*ochenta y uno*
12	*doce*	90	*noventa*
13	*trece*	91	*noventa y uno*
14	*catorce*	100	*ciento (cien)*
15	*quince*	101	*ciento uno*
16	*diez y seis (dieciséis)*	102	*ciento dos*
		200	*doscientos (-as)*
17	*diez y siete (diecisiete)*	201	*doscientos uno*
		300	*trescientos (-as)*
18	*diez y ocho (dieciocho)*	400	*cuatrocientos (-as)*
		500	*quinientos (-as)*
19	*diez y nueve (diecinueve)*	600	*seiscientos (-as)*
		700	*setecientos (-as)*
20	*veinte*	800	*ochocientos (-as)*
21	*veinte y uno (veintiuno)*	900	*novecientos (-as)*
		1,000	*mil*
22	*veinte y dos (veintidós)*	2,000	*dos mil*
		100,000	*cien mil*
23	*veinte y tres (veintitrés)*	500,000	*quinientos mil*
		1,000,000	*un millón*

Time
The article *la* is always used when expressing *one o'clock, las* when expressing the other hours.

After or *past* is expressed by *y; to* or *of,* by *menos*. After half past the hour, time is expressed by the following hour minus *(menos)* the minutes.

¿Qué hora es?	What time is it?
Es la una.	It is one o'clock.
Son las dos.	It is two o'clock.
Son las tres y media.	It is three-thirty.
Son las cuatro y cuarto (quince).	It is a quarter past four.
Son las cinco menos cuarto.	It is a quarter to five.
Son las once y diez.	It is ten minutes past eleven.
Son las ocho menos cinco.	It is five minutes to eight.
Son las siete en punto.	It is exactly seven o'clock.
Es mediodía (medianoche).	It is noon (midnight).
¿A qué hora?	At what time?
Las nueve de la mañana.	Nine in the morning.

Review of Spanish Grammar

Dates

¿Cuál es la fecha de hoy?	What is today's date?
¿A cuántos estamos hoy?	
Es el primero de marzo.	It is March 1.
Llegó el dos de junio de mil novecientos cincuenta.	He arrived June 2, 1950.
Salió el cuatro de mayo.	He left on May 4.

Cardinal numbers are used for all dates except *primero* (first).

Months, days, seasons

The names of the months, days of the week, and seasons are written with small letters.

enero	January	*el lunes*	Monday
febrero	February	*el martes*	Tuesday
marzo	March	*el miércoles*	Wednesday
abril	April	*el jueves*	Thursday
mayo	May	*el viernes*	Friday
junio	June	*el sábado*	Saturday
julio	July	*el domingo*	Sunday
agosto	August		
septiembre	September	*la primavera*	spring
octubre	October	*el verano*	summer
noviembre	November	*el otoño*	autumn
diciembre	December	*el invierno*	winter

The English word "on" before a day of the week or a date is expressed by the definite article.

Los sábados voy de compras.
On Saturdays I go shopping.

The years are expressed in thousands and hundreds.

Nació en mil novecientos setenta.
He was born in nineteen seventy.

Age

Age is expressed with the verb *tener*.

¿Cuántos años tienes tú? How old are you?
Tengo once años. I am eleven.

Arithmetic

Sumar Add
 Dos y tres son cinco.
 Two and three are five.
Restar Subtract
 Quince menos ocho son siete.
 Fifteen minus eight are seven.
Multiplicar Multiply
 Nueve por cuatro son treinta y seis.
 Nine times four are thirty six.
Dividir Divide
 Sesenta dividido por diez son seis.
 Sixty divided by ten are six.

Names of countries

Alemania	Germany	*Inglaterra*	England
Austria	Austria	*Italia*	Italy
Bélgica	Belgium	*Perú*	Peru
Canadá	Canada	*Rusia*	Russia
Dinamarca	Denmark	*Suecia*	Sweden
España	Spain	*Suiza*	Switzerland

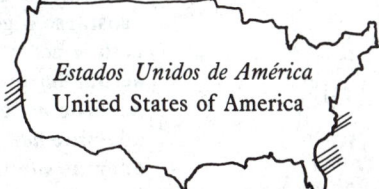

Estados Unidos de América
United States of America

El menú

arroz con pollo
saffron-flavored rice and chicken
bistec a la parrilla
grilled steak
churrasco
barbecued steak (South America)
churro
a twist of batter deep fried, often eaten as a snack with hot chocolate in Spain

enchilada
(Mexico and Guatemala)
a corn cake stuffed with meat or chicken, rolled and baked with tomato sauce flavored with chili
flan
custard
horchata
a cold drink made of almonds
paella
saffron-flavored rice, chicken, seafood, and peas
tortilla
omelet; in Mexico and Guatemala, corn meal cake

Review of Spanish Grammar

La cara The face

Dictionary

El cuerpo humano The human body

Dictionary abbreviations. Nouns are identified as masculine *(m)* or feminine *(f)*. Adjectives are identified as *adj*, adverbs as *adv*, conjunctions as *conj*, interjections as *interj*, prepositions as *prep*, pronouns as *pron*, and verbs as *v*. Plurals are identified as *pl*.

Spanish-English

A

a *prep* at, to
abajo *adv* below, down
abeja *f* bee
abierto *adj* open
abogado *m* lawyer
abrigo *m* overcoat
abrir *v* open
acá *adv* here
acabar *v* finish, **acabar de** to have just . . .
aceite *m* oil
acento *m* accent
aceptar *v* accept
acera *f* sidewalk
acerca de *prep* about, concerning
acercarse *v* approach
acero *m* steel
acompañar *v* accompany
aconsejar *v* advise
acordarse *v* remember
acostarse *v* go to bed
acto *m* act
actual *adj* present
acuerdo *m* agreement
adelante *adv* forward
además *adv* besides
adentro *adv* inside
adiós *interj and m* goodbye
admirar *v* admire
adónde *adv* where
aduana *f* custom house
aeropuerto *m* airport
afecto *m* affection
afilado *adj* sharp
afuera *adv* out, outside
agradable *adj* pleasant, agreeable
agradecer *v* be grateful for
agua *f* water
aguardar *v* wait for
agudo *adj* sharp
águila *f* eagle
aguja *f* needle
ahí *adv* there
ahora *adv* now
aire *m* air

al *prep* to the, at the
albóndiga *f* meatball
alcalde *m* mayor
alcanzar *v* reach, catch
alcoba *f* bedroom
aldea *f* village
alegrarse *v* be glad
alegre *adj* happy
alegría *f* joy
alfiler *m* pin
alfombra *f* carpet, rug
algo *pron* something
algodón *m* cotton
alguien *pron* someone
alguno *adj* some
alimento *m* food
allá *adv* there
allí *adv* there
alma *f* soul
almacén *m* department store
almohada *f* pillow
almorzar *v* lunch
almuerzo *m* lunch
alrededor *adv* around
alto *adj* tall, high
altura *f* height
alumbrar *v* illuminate, light
alumno, -a *n* pupil, student
alzar *v* raise, lift
amable *adj* amiable, kind, pleasant
amar *v* love
amargo *adj* bitter
amarillo *adj* yellow
ambos *adj and pron* both
americano *adj and n* American
amigo, -a, *n* friend
amistad *f* friendship
amor *m* love
ancho *adj* wide
anciano *adj* old
andar *v* walk
ángel *m* angel
anillo *m* ring
anoche *adv* last night
antes *adv* before, formerly
antiguo *adj* former

426   **Review of Spanish Grammar**

añadir *v* add
año *m* year
apagar *v* extinguish
aparecer *v* appear, show up
apenas *adv* hardly
aplicado *adj* diligent
aprender *v* learn
aquí *adv* here
árbol *m* tree
arena *f* sand, arena
armario *m* closet
arreglar *v* arrange, fix, repair
arriba *adv* above, up
asar *v* roast
así *adv* so, thus
asiento *m* seat
asistir *v* attend
asustar *v* frighten
atar *v* tie
atrás *adv* behind
avenida *f* avenue
averiguar *v* find out
avisar *v* inform, notify
ayer *adv* yesterday
ayudar *v* help
azul *adj* blue

B

bailar *v* dance
bajar *v* descend, lower
banco *m* bank, bench
bandera *f* flag
baño *m* bath, bathroom
barato *adj* cheap
barba *f* beard, chin
barbero *m* barber
barco *m* ship
barrio *m* district
bastante *adv and adj* enough
beber *v* drink
bello *adj* beautiful
beso *m* kiss
biblioteca *f* library
bien *adv* well
billete *m* ticket
bizcocho *m* cake, biscuit
blanco *adj* white
bolígrafo *m* ballpoint pen
bolsa *f* purse
bolsillo *m* pocket
bonito *adj* pretty
bosque *m* forest
botella *f* bottle
bueno *adj* good

burro *m* donkey
buscar *v* look for
butaca *f* armchair

C

caballero *m* gentleman
caballo *m* horse
cabello *m* hair
cabeza *f* head
cada *adj* each, every
cadena *f* chain
caer *v* fall
café *m* coffee, café
caja *f* box
calentar *v* heat, warm
caliente *adj* hot
calle *f* street
calor *m* heat
cama *f* bed
cambio *m* change, exchange
caminar *v* walk
camino *m* road
campo *m* country
canción *f* song
cansado *adj* tired
cantar *v* sing
cara *f* face
cariño *m* affection
caro *adj* expensive
carro *m* car
carta *f* letter
casa *f* house
casarse *v* get married
casi *adv* almost
cena *f* supper
cepillo *m* brush
cerca *adv* near
cerdo *m* pig, hog
cerrar *v* close
cerveza *f* beer
cielo *m* sky, heaven
cita *f* appointment
ciudad *f* city
clavel *m* carnation
coche *m* car
cocina *f* kitchen
cocinar *v* cook
colina *f* hill
comedia *f* comedy, play
comedor *m* dining room
comenzar *v* begin
comer *v* eat
comercio *m* commerce
comida *f* food, meal, dinner

como *adv and conj* as, like
cómo *interj* how
cómoda *f* dresser
comprar *v* buy
comprender *v* understand
con *prep* with
conocer *v* know
conseguir *v* obtain
contar *v* count, tell
contento *adj* happy
contestar *v* answer
continuar *v* continue
contra *prep* against
copa *f* goblet
correo *m* mail, post office
correr *v* run
corrida *f* race, **corrida de toros** bullfight
cortina *f* curtain
corto *adj* short
cosa *f* thing
costar *v* cost
creer *v* believe
criada *f* maid
cristiano *m and adj* Christian
cuadro *m* picture
¿cuál? *interj* which
¿cuándo? *interj* when
¿cuánto? *interj* how much?
¿cuántos? *interj* how many?
cuarto *m* room, quarter
cuchara *f* spoon
cuchillo *m* knife
cuenta *f* bill
cuero *m* leather
cuidado *m* care, caution
cumpleaños *m* birthday

CH

charla *f* chat
cheque *m* check
chico, -a *n* boy, girl
chiste *m* joke
choque *m* collision

D

dama *f* lady
daño *m* damage
dar *v* give
de *prep* of, from
debajo *adv* beneath
deber *v* ought, should, owe
débil *adj* weak

Review of Spanish Grammar

decir *v* say, tell
dejar *v* leave
delante de *prep* in front of
delgado *adj* thin
demasiado *adv and adj* too much, too many, too
dentista *m* dentist
dentro *adv* within
derecho *adj and adv* straight
desastre *m* disaster
desayunarse *v* breakfast
desayuno *m* breakfast
descansar *v* rest
descubrir *v* discover
desear *v* wish, desire
despacio *adv* slowly
despertar *v* wake
después de *prep* after
detrás de *prep* in back of
devolver *v* return
día *m* day
difícil *adj* difficult
dinero *m* money
Dios *m* God
dolor *m* pain
don, doña *n* titles given to gentlemen and ladies. Used with first names.
dónde *conj and adv* where
dormir *v* sleep
dormitorio *m* bedroom, dormitory
duda *f* doubt
dueño *m* master, owner
dulce *adj* sweet
duro *adj* hard

E

e *conj* and
echar *v* throw
edad *f* age
edificio *m* building
ejemplo *m* example
ejército *m* army
empleado *m* employee
empresa *f* enterprise
empujar *v* push
en *prep* in, on, at
encantador *adj* charming
encontrar *v* find, meet
enfermo *adj* sick
enfrente de *prep* facing
enojado *adj* angry
enseñar *v* teach

entender *v* understand
entero *adj* entire, whole
entonces *adv* then
entrada *f* entrance
entre *prep* between, among
enviar *v* send, ship
equivocado *adj* mistaken
escalera *f* staircase
escoba *f* broom
escoger *v* choose
escribir *v* write
escuchar *v* listen to
escuela *f* school
español *m and adj* Spanish
espejo *m* mirror
esperar *v* hope, wait
esposa *f* wife
esposo *m* husband
esquina *f* corner
estación *f* station, season
estado *m* state, condition
estar *v* be
este *m* east
estrecho *adj* narrow
estrella *f* star
estudiar *v* study
evitar *v* avoid
éxito *m* success
extranjero *m* foreigner

F

fábrica *f* factory
fácil *adj* easy
factura *f* invoice, bill
falda *f* skirt
falta *f* lack, mistake, fault
familia *f* family
fecha *f* date
feliz *adj* happy
feo *adj* ugly
ferrocarril *m* railroad
fiebre *f* fever
fiesta *f* holiday, festival
figurarse *v* imagine
fin *m* end, purpose
fino *adj* fine
firmar *v* sign
flan *m* custard
flor *f* flower
fonda *f* inn
fondo *m* bottom
francés *m and adj* Frenchman, French
frase *f* sentence

frazada *f* blanket
fresco *adj* cool, fresh
frío *m* cold, **tener frío** *v* feel cold
fuego *m* fire
fuente *f* fountain
fuera *adv* outside
fuerte *adj* strong, loud
fumar *v* smoke

G

gallina *f* hen
gallo *m* rooster
ganar *v* earn, win
ganga *f* bargain
gastar *v* spend
gato *m* cat
gemelos *m pl* cufflinks
gente *f* people
golpe *m* blow
gordo *adj* fat
gozar *v* enjoy
gracia *f* grace, wit
gracias *f pl* thanks, thank you
grande *adj* large, great
gritar *v* shout
guapo *adj* handsome
guardar *v* keep, guard
guerra *f* war
gustar *v* please
gusto *m* pleasure, taste

H

haber *v* have
habitación *f* room
hablar *v* speak
hacer *v* do, make
hacia *prep* toward
hallar *v* find
hambre *f* hunger, **tener hambre** be hungry
hasta *prep* until, **hasta luego** until later
hay *v* there is, there are
hecho *m* fact
hermoso *adj* beautiful
hielo *m* ice
hierba *f* grass
hija *f* daughter
hijo *m* son
hilo *m* thread
hoja *f* leaf
hombre *m* man

hora *f* hour, time
hoy *adv* today
hueso *m* bone
huevo *m* egg

I

idioma *m* language
iglesia *f* church
igualmente *adv* equally
inglés *m and adj* Englishman, English
inquieto *adj* anxious, worried
ir *v* go
isla *f* island
izquierdo *adj* left

J

jabón *m* soap
jamás *adv* never
jardín *m* garden
jefe *m* chief, boss
joven *adj* young
joya *f* jewel, gem
judío *m and adj* Jew, Jewish
juego *m* game
jugar *v* play
jugo *m* juice
junto *adj* together

L

labio *m* lip
lado *m* side
ladrón *m* thief
lago *m* lake
lágrima *f* tear
lana *f* wool
lápiz *m* pencil
largo *adj* long
lástima *f* pity
lata *f* tin, tin can
lavandería *f* laundry
lavar *v* wash
lectura *f* reading
leer *v* to read
legumbres *f pl* vegetables
lejos *adv* far
lento *adj* slow
levantar *v* raise, lift, **levantarse** *v* get up, rise
ley *f* law
libra *f* pound
libre *adj* free

libro *m* book
ligero *adj* light
limpiar *v* clean, wash
lindo *adj* pretty
listo *adj* clever, ready
lobo *m* wolf
loco *adj* crazy
lograr *v* achieve
lucha *f* fight
luego *adv* then
lugar *m* place
luna *f* moon
luz *f* light

LL

llamar *v* call
llamarse *v* be named
llave *f* key
llegar *v* arrive
lleno *adj* full
llevar *v* carry, wear
llorar *v* cry
llover *v* rain
lluvia *f* rain

M

madera *f* wood
madre *f* mother
maestro *m* teacher
maíz *m* corn
mal *adv* badly
maleta *f* suitcase
malo *adj* bad, sick
mandar *v* send
manga *f* sleeve
mano *f* hand
manta *f* blanket
mantel *m* tablecloth
mar *m and f* sea
marido *m* husband
martillo *m* hammer
más *adj and adv* more
matador *m* bullfighter
matar *v* to kill
mayor *adj* greater, older
medianoche *f* midnight
médico *m* doctor
medio *m* half
mejor *adj* better
menor *adj* smaller, younger
mentira *f* lie
mercado *m* market
mes *m* month

mesa *f* table
metro *m* meter, subway
miedo *m* fear
mientras *conj* while
milla *f* mile
mirar *v* look at
mismo *adj* same
modo *m* manner
molestar *v* trouble, disturb
moneda *f* coin
mono *m* monkey
montar *v* mount, climb
moreno *adj* dark, brunette
morir *v* die
mozo *m* waiter, porter, lad
muchacho, -a *n* boy, girl
mucho *adj* much
mueble *m* furniture
muerte *f* death
mujer *f* woman, wife
mundo *m* world
museo *m* museum
muy *adv* very

N

nacer *v* be born
nada *pron* nothing
nadar *v* swim
nadie *pron* nobody
nariz *f* nose
Navidad *f* Christmas
necesitar *v* need
negar *v* deny
negocio *m* business
negro *adj* black
nevar *v* snow
nieta *f* granddaughter
nieto *m* grandson
nieve *f* snow
niña *f* girl
niño *m* boy
no *interj and adv* no, not
noche *f* night
nombre *m* name, noun
norte *m* north
noticia *f* news
novia *f* sweetheart
novio *m* sweetheart
nube *f* cloud
nubile *adj* marriageable
nublado *adj* cloudy
nuevo *adj* new
número *m* number
nunca *adv* never

Review of Spanish Grammar

O

o *conj* or
obra *f* work
océano *m* ocean
ocupado *adj* busy, occupied
oeste *m* west
oído *m* ear (inner)
oír *v* hear
olor *m* odor
olvidar *v* forget
orar *v* pray
orgulloso *adj* proud
orilla *f* shore
oro *m* gold
oso *m* bear
otro *adj* another, other, **otra vez** *adv* again
oveja *f* sheep

P

pagar *v* pay
país *m* country
pájaro *m* bird
palabra *f* word
paloma *f* dove
pañuelo *m* handkerchief
papel *m* paper
paquete *m* package
par *m* pair, equal
para *prep* for
paraguas *m* umbrella
pardo *adj* brown
parecer *v* seem
pariente *m* relative
parque *m* park
partida *f* departure
pasajero *m* passenger
paseo *m* walk
paso *m* step
paz *f* peace
pedir *v* ask (for)
peinarse *v* comb one's hair
pelota *f* ball
peluquero *m* hairdresser
pena *f* pain, grief, trouble
pensar *v* think
peor *adj* worse
pequeño *adj* small
perder *v* lose
perezoso *adj* lazy
periódico *m* newspaper
pero *conj* but
perro *m* dog
pesado *adj* heavy
piedra *f* stone
pintor *m* painter
pintura *f* painting
piso *m* floor
plata *f* silver
plátano *m* banana
playa *f* beach
pluma *f* pen
pobre *adj* poor
poco *adj and adv* little
poder *v* be able
poner *v* put
por *prep* for, by, through
por favor *adv* please
porque *conj* because
por qué *pron* why
precio *m* price
pregunta *f* question
preguntar *v* ask
prestar *v* lend
primero *adj and adv* first
prisa *f* hurry
probar *v* prove
pronto *adv* soon
propina *f* tip
propio *adj* own, proper
pueblo *m* town, people
puerta *f* door
pulsera *f* bracelet

Q

que *pron* that, than
qué *pron* what
quedar *v* remain
queja *f* complaint
quemar *v* burn
querer *v* want, love
querido *adj* dear, beloved
quien *pron* who
quién *pron* who
quitar *v* remove
quizá *adv* perhaps

R

raíz *f* root
rana *f* frog
rápido *adj* fast
rato *m* while
raya *f* dash, stripe
razón *f* reason
realizar *v* accomplish
recibir *v* receive
recibo *m* receipt
recoger *v* gather
recordar *v* remember
recuerdo *m* remembrance, memory
redondo *adj* round
regalo *m* gift
regla *f* rule
regresar *v* return
reina *f* queen
reír *v* laugh
reloj *m* watch, clock
repetir *v* repeat
resfriado *m* cold (illness)
respirar *v* breathe
responder *v* answer
respuesta *f* answer
resto *m* remainder
resultado *m* result
retrete *m* toilet
reunión *f* meeting
revista *f* magazine
rey *m* king
rezar *v* pray
rico *adj* rich
rincón *m* corner
río *m* river
robar *v* steal
rogar *v* beg
rojo *adj* red
romper *v* break
rubio *adj* blond
rueda *f* wheel
ruido *m* noise

S

sábana *f* sheet
saber *v* know
sabio *adj* wise
sabor *m* flavor
sacar *v* take out
sacerdote *m* priest
sal *f* salt
sala *f* livingroom
salida *f* exit, departure
salir *v* leave
saltar *v* jump
salud *f* health
saludar *v* greet
sandía *f* watermelon
sangre *f* blood
sano *adj* healthy, sane
sastre *m* tailor
satisfecho *adj* satisfied

seco *adj* dry
sed *f* thirst
seda *f* silk
seguida *f* succession, **en seguida** immediately
seguir *v* follow
seguro *adj* sure
sello *m* stamp
semana *f* week
semejante *adj* similar
señal *f* signal
señor *m* sir, Mr., gentleman
señora *f* madam, Mrs., lady
señorita *f* young lady, Miss
sentarse *v* sit down
sentido *m* meaning, sense
sentir *v* regret, feel, sense
ser *v* be
servicio *m* service
servilleta *f* napkin
servir *v* serve
si *conj* if
sí *interj* yes
siempre *adv* always
sierra *f* mountain range
siglo *m* century
significar *v* mean, signify
siguiente *adj* following
silla *f* chair
simpático *adj* congenial, nice
sin *prep* without
sobre *m* envelope
sobre *prep* on
socio *m* associate, partner
sol *m* sun
solamente *adv* only
solo *adj* alone
sombra *f* shadow
sonar *v* sound
sordo *adj* deaf
sorpresa *f* surprise
subir *v* ascend
suceder *v* happen
sucio *adj* dirty
suelo *m* floor, ground
sueño *m* dream
suerte *f* luck
sur *m* south
susto *m* fright

T

tal *adj* such
tamaño *m* size
también *adv* also

tampoco *adv* neither, either
tan *adv* so
tanto *adj* so much
tarde *f* afternoon
tarjeta *f* card
taza *f* cup
teatro *m* theater
techo *m* ceiling, roof
teléfono *m* telephone
temprano *adv and adj* early
tenedor *m* fork
tener *v* have
terminar *v* end, terminate
tesoro *m* treasure
tiempo *m* time, weather
tienda *f* store
tierra *f* earth, land
tirar *v* throw
tiza *f* chalk
tocar *v* touch, play (instrument)
todo *adj* all
tomar *v* take, drink
tonto *m and adj* fool, foolish
torero *m* bullfighter
toro *m* bull
trabajar *v* work
traducir *v* translate
traer *v* bring
tranvía *m* streetcar
trapo *m* floor, ground
tratar de *v* try to
tren *m* train
trigo *m* wheat
triste *adj* sad
tronco *m* trunk

U

u *conj* or (before *o* or *ho*)
último *adj* last
único *adj* only
unir *v* unite
usar *v* wear, use
útil *adj* useful
uva *f* grape

V

vaca *f* cow
vacaciones *f pl* vacation
vacío *adj* empty
valer *v* be worth
valle *m* valley
vapor *m* steam
varios *adj* several

vaso *m* glass
vecino *m* neighbor
vender *v* sell
venir *v* come
venta *f* sale
ventana *f* window
ver *v* see
veras, de *adv* really
veraz *adj* truthful
verbo *m* verb
verboso *adj* talkative
verdad *f* truth
verde *adj* green
verede *f* path
veredicto *m* verdict
vergonzoso *adj* shameful, shy
vergüenza *f* shame
verificar *v* verify
verja *f* grating
verosímil *adj* likely
vestir *v* dress
vez *f* time, turn
viajar *v* travel
viaje *m* trip
vida *f* life
viejo *adj* old
viento *m* wind
vino *m* wine
visita *f* visit
visitar *v* visit
vista *f* view
viudo, -a *n* widower, widow
vivir *v* live
vivo *adj* living, alive
volar *v* fly
voz *f* voice
vuelta *f* return, turn

Y

y *conj* and
ya *adv* already
yacer *v* lie
yema *f* egg yolk
yerba *f* grass
yerro *m* error

Z

zapatería *f* shoe store
zapato *m* shoe
zarzuela *f* musical comedy
zona *f* zone
zorra *f* vixen
zorro *m* fox

Review of Spanish Grammar

Dictionary abbreviations. Nouns are identified as masculine *(n m)* or feminine *(n f)*. Adjectives are identified as *adj*, adverbs as *adv*, conjunctions as *conj*, interjections as *interj*, prepositions as *prep*, pronouns as *pron*, and verbs as *v*. Plurals are identified as *pl*.

English-Spanish

A

a, an *adj* un, una
able *adj* capaz, **be able** *v* poder
abode *n* residencia *f*
about *prep* acerca de
above *adv* arriba
absent *adj* ausente
accent *n* acento *m*
accept *v* aceptar
accompany *v* acompañar
accomplish *v* realizar
ache *n* dolor *m*
achieve *v* lograr
act *n* acto *m*
add *v* añadir
admire *v* admirar
advantage *n* ventaja *f*
advise *v* consejar
affection *n* afecto *m*, cariño *m*
after *prep* después de
afternoon *n* tarde *f*
again *adv* otra vez
age *n* edad *f*
agreement *n* acuerdo *m*
air *n* aire *m*
airport *n* aeropuerto *m*
all *adj* todo
almost *adv* casi
alone *adv* solo
already *adv* ya
also *adv* también
always *adv* siempre
American *adj and nm* americano
among *prep* entre
and *conj* y, e
angel *n* ángel *m*
angry *adj* enojado
answer *v* responder, contestar
anxious *adj* inquieto
appear *v* aparecer
appointment *n* cita *f*, nombramiento *m*
approach *v* acercarse a
apron *n* delantal *m*
armchair *n* butaca *f*
army *n* ejército *m*
around *adv* alrededor
arrange *v* arreglar
arrive *v* llegar
as *adv and conj* como
ascend *v* subir
ask *v* preguntar
ask for *v* pedir
associate *n* socio *m*
at *prep* a, **at the** al
attend *v* asistir a
aunt *n* tía *f*
author *n* autor *m*
avenue *n* avenida *f*
avoid *v* evitar
awful *adj* horrible, terrible

B

back *adv* atrás, **in back of** detrás de
backward *adj* atrasado
bad *adj* malo
badly *adv* mal
ball *n* pelota *f*
ballpoint pen *n* bolígrafo *m*
banana *n* plátano *m*
bank *n* banco *m*
barber *n* barbero *m*
bargain *n* ganga *f*
bath *n* baño *m*
bathroom *n* cuarto de baño *m*
be *v* ser, estar
beach *n* playa *f*
bear *n* oso *m*
beard *n* barba *f*
beautiful *adj* bello, hermoso
because *conj* porque
bed *n* cama *f*, **go to bed** acostarse
bedroom *n* alcoba *f*, dormitorio *m*
bee *n* abeja *f*
beer *n* cerveza *f*
before *adv* antes
beg *v* rogar
begin *v* comenzar, empezar
behind *adv* detrás, *prep* detrás de
believe *v* creer
bell *n* campana *f*
below *adv* abajo
bench *n* banco *m*
beneath *adv* debajo
besides *adv* además
better *adj and adv* mejor
between *prep* entre
bill *n* cuenta *f*, factura *f*
bird *n* pájaro *f*
birthday *n* cumpleaños *m*
bitter *adj* amargo
black *adj* negro
blanket *n* manta *f*, frazada *f*
blind *adj* ciego
blond *adj* rubio
blood *n* sangre *f*
blow *n* golpe *m*
blue *adj* azul
boat *n* barco *m*
bone *n* hueso *m*
book *n* libro *m*
born, be *v* nacer
both *adj and pron* ambos
bottle *n* botella *f*
bottom *n* fondo *m*
box *n* caja *f*
boy *n* niño *m*, chico *m*, muchacho *m*
bracelet *n* pulsera *f*
break *v* romper
breakfast *n* desayuno *m*, *v* desayunar
breathe *v* respirar
bring *v* traer
broom *n* escoba *f*
brother *n* hermano *m*
brown *adj* pardo
brunette *adj and nm* moreno
brush *n* cepillo *m*
building *n* edificio *m*
bull *n* toro *m*
bullfight *n* corrida de toros *f*
bullfighter *n* torero *m*, matador *m*
burn *v* quemar
bus *n* autobús *m*
business *n* negocios *m pl*, comercio *m*
busy *adj* ocupado
butter *n* mantequilla *f*
buy *v* comprar

C

cabin *n* cabaña *f*
cage *n* jaula *f*
cake *n* bizcocho *m*
call *v* llamar
car *n* carro *m*, coche *m*
care *n* cuidado *m*
carnation *n* clavel *m*
carpet *n* alfombra *f*
carry *v* llevar
castle *n* castillo *m*
cat *n* gato *m*
ceiling *n* techo *m*
century *n* siglo *m*
chain *n* cadena *f*
chair *n* silla *f*
chalk *n* tiza *f*
change *n* cambio *m*
charming *adj* encantador
chat *n* charla *f*
cheap *adj* barato
check *n* (banking) cheque *m*
chief *n* jefe *m*
chin *n* barba *f*
choose *v* escoger
Christmas *n* Navidad *f*
church *n* iglesia *f*
city *n* ciudad *f*
clean *v* limpiar
clever *adj* listo
clock *n* reloj *m*
close *v* cerrar
closet *n* armario *m*
cloud *n* nube *f*
coffee *n* café *m*
coin *n* moneda *f*
cold *n* frío *m*, (illness) resfriado *m*
collar *n* cuello *m*
collision *n* choque *m*
comb (one's hair) *v* peinarse
come *v* venir
comedy *n* comedia *f*
commerce *n* comercio *m*
concerning *prep* acerca de
congenial *adj* simpático
continue *v* continuar
cool *adj* fresco
corn *n* maíz *m*
corner *n* esquina *f*, rincón *m*
cost *v* costar
cotton *n* algodón *m*
count *v* contar
country *n* campo *m*, país *m*

cow *n* vaca *f*
crash *n* choque *m*
crazy *adj* loco
cry *v* llorar
cufflinks *n* gemelos *m pl*
cup *n* taza *f*
custard *n* flan *m*
custom *n* costumbre *f*
customhouse *n* aduana *f*
cut *v* cortar

D

daily *adj* diario
damage *n* daño *m*
dance *v* bailar
dark *adj* moreno
dash *n* raya *f*
date *n* fecha *f*
daughter *n* hija *f*
day *n* día *m*
dead *adj* muerto
deaf *adj* sordo
dear *adj* querido
death *n* muerte *f*
decide *v* decidir
deep *adj* hondo
dentist *n* dentista *m, f*
deny *v* negar
department store *n* almacén *m*
departure *n* partida *f*, salida *f*
descend *v* bajar
dew *n* rocío *m*
difficult *adj* difícil
diligent *adj* aplicado
dining room *n* comedor *m*
dinner *n* comida *f*
dirty *adj* sucio
disaster *n* desastre *m*
discover *v* descubrir
dish *n* plato *m*
district *n* barrio *m*
disturb *v* molestar
do *v* hacer
doctor *n* médico *m*
dog *n* perro *m*
donkey *n* burro *m*
door *n* puerta *f*
doubt *n* duda *f*
dove *n* paloma *f*
down *adv* abajo
dozen *n* docena *f*
dream *n* sueño *m*, *v* soñar
dress *n* vestido *m*, *v* vestir
dresser *n* cómoda *f*

drink *v* beber
dry *adj* seco
during *prep* durante

E

each cada *adj*
eagle *n* águila *f*
ear *n* (inner) oído *m*, (outer) oreja *f*
early *adv and adj* temprano
earn *v* ganar
east *n* este *m*
Easter *n* Pascua Florida *f*
easy *adj* fácil
eat *v* comer
egg *n* huevo *m*
employee *n* empleado *m*
empty *adj* vacío
end *n* fin *m*, *v* terminar
enjoy *v* gozar
enough *adj and adv* bastante
enterprise *n* empresa *f*
entire *adj* entero
entrance *n* entrada *f*
envelope *n* sobre *m*
equally *adv* igualmente
even *adj* igual, *adv* hasta
example *n* ejemplo *m*
exchange *n* cambio *m*
exit *n* salida *f*
expensive *adj* caro
extinguish *v* apagar

F

face *n* cara *f*
facing *prep* enfrente de
fact *n* hecho *m*
factory *n* fábrica *f*
fall *v* caer
false *adj* falso
family *n* familia *f*
far *adv* lejos
farm *n* granja, hacienda *f*
fat *adj* gordo
fear *n* miedo *m*, *v* temer
feel *v* sentir
festival *n* fiesta *f*
fever *n* fiebre *f*
fight *n* lucha *f*
find *v* encontrar, hallar
find out *v* averiguar
fine *adj* fino, *adv* muy bien
finish *v* acabar

Review of Spanish Grammar

fire *n* fuego *m*
first *adj and adv* primero
flavor *n* sabor *m*
floor *n* piso *m*, suelo *m*
flower *n* flor *f*
fly *v* volar, *n* mosca *f*
follow *v* seguir
following *adj* siguiente
food *n* comida *f*
fool *n* tonto *m*
for *prep* por, para
foreigner *n* extranjero *m*
forest *n* bosque *m*
forget *v* olvidar *v*
fork *n* tenedor *m*
former antiguo *adj*
forward adelante *adv*
fountain *n* fuente *f*
frankly *adv* francamente
free libre *adj*
French *adj and nm* francés
fresh fresco *adj*
friend *n* amigo *m*
friendship *n* amistad *f*
fright *n* susto *m*
frighten asustar *v*
frog *n* rana *f*
from *prep* de
front *n* frente *m*, **in front of** delante de
full *adj* lleno
furniture *n* mueble *m*

G

gaiety *n* alegría *f*
game *n* juego *m*
garbage *n* basura *f*
garden *n* jardín *m*
garlic *n* ajo *m*
gasoline *n* gasolina *f*
gather *v* recoger
gem *n* joya *f*
gentleman *n* caballero *m*, señor *m*
gift *n* regalo *m*
girl *n* chica *f*, muchacha *f*, niña *f*
give *v* dar
glad *adj* contento, **be glad** *v* alegrarse
glass *n* vaso *m*
glove *n* guante *m*
go *v* ir
go out *v* salir
goblet *n* copa *f*

God *n* Dios *m*
gold *n* oro *m*
goodbye *interj* adiós
grace *n* gracia *f*
granddaughter *n* nieta *f*
grandson *n* nieto *m*
grape *n* uva *f*
grass *n* hierba *f*
grateful *adj* agradecido, **be grateful for** *v* agradecer
great *adj* gran, grande
greater *adj* mayor
green *adj* verde
greet *v* saludar
grief *n* pena *f*
ground *n* suelo *m*
guess *v* advinar

H

hair *n* cabello *m*, pelo *m*
hairdresser *n* peluquero *m*
hammer *n* martillo *m*
hand *n* mano *f*
handkerchief *n* pañuelo *m*
handsome *adj* guapo
happen *v* suceder
happy *adj* alegre, feliz, contento
hard *adj* duro
hardly *adv* apenas
have *v* tener, haber
head *n* cabeza *f*
health *n* salud *f*
healthy *adj* sano
hear *v* oír
heat *n* calor *m*, *v* calentar
heavy *adj* pesado
height *n* altura *f*
help *v* ayudar
hen *n* gallina *f*
here *adv* aquí, acá
hill *n* colina *f*
holiday *n* fiesta *f*
honest *adj* honesto
hope *v* esperar
horse *n* caballo *m*
hot *adj* caliente
hour *n* hora *f*
house *n* casa *f*
how *interj* como
how much, how many *interj* cuánto, cuántos
hunger *n* hambre *f*
hurry *n* prisa *f*
husband *n* esposo, marido *m*

I

ice *n* hielo *m*
if *conj* si
illuminate *v* alumbrar
imagine *v* figurarse
immediately *adv* en seguida
in *prep* en
inform *v* avisar
inn *n* fonda *f*
inside *adv* adentro, *adj and nm* interior
invoice *n* factura *f*
island *n* isla *f*

J

Jew *n* judío *m*, **Jewish** *adj* judío
jewel *n* joya *f*
joke *n* chiste *m*, *v* bromear
joy *n* alegría *f*
juice *n* jugo *m*
jump *v* saltar

K

keep *v* guardar
key *n* llave *f*
kill *v* matar
kind *adj* amable
king *n* rey *m*
kitchen *n* cocina *f*
knife *n* cuchillo *m*
know *v* saber, conocer

L

lack *n* falta *f*, *v* faltar
lady *n* dama *f*, señora *f*, **young lady** señorita *f*
lake *n* lago *m*
land *n* tierra *f*
language *n* idioma *m*
large *adj* grande
last *adj* último
last night *adv* anoche
later, see you hasta luego
laugh *v* reír
laundry *n* lavandería *f*
law *n* ley *f*
lawyer *n* abogado *m*
lazy *adj* perezoso
leaf *n* hoja *f*
learn *v* aprender
leather *n* cuero *m*

leave *v* dejar, salir
left *adj* izquierdo
lend *v* prestar
let *v* dejar
letter *n* carta *f*
library *n* biblioteca *f*
lie *n* mentira *f*, *v* mentir
life *n* vida *f*
light *adj* ligero, *nf* luz
lip *n* labio *m*
listen (to) *v* escuchar
little *adj* poco
live *v* vivir
living *adj* vivo
livingroom *n* sala *f*
look *n* mirada *f*, **look at** *v* mirar, **look for** buscar
lose *v* perder
love *n* amor *m*, *v* amar, querer
luck *n* suerte *f*
lunch *n* almuerzo *m*, *v* almorzar

M

madam *n* señora *f*
magazine *n* revista *f*
maid *n* criada *f*
mail *n* correo *m*
make *v* hacer
man *n* hombre *m*
manner *n* modo *m*
market *n* mercado *m*
marry *v* casarse con
master *n* dueño *m*
mayor *n* alcalde *m*
meal *n* comida *f*
mean *v* significar
meaning *n* sentido *m*
meatball *n* albóndiga *f*
meet *v* encontrar
meeting *n* reunión *f*
meter *n* metro *m*
midnight *n* medianoche *f*
mile *n* milla *f*
mirror *n* espejo *m*
miss *n* señorita *f*
mistake *n* falta *f*
mistaken *adj* equivocado
money *n* dinero *m*
month *n* mes *m*
moon *n* luna *f*
mother *n* madre *f*
mount *v* montar
mountain range *n* sierra *f*
Mr. *n* señor *m*

Mrs. *n* señora *f*
much *adj* mucho, **so much** tanto, **too much** demasiado
museum *n* museo *m*

N

name *n* nombre *m*
napkin *n* servilleta *f*
narrow *adj* estrecho
near *adv* cerca
need *v* necesitar
needle *n* aguja *f*
neighbor *n* vecino *m*
neither *adv* tampoco
never *adv* jamás, nunca
new *adj* nuevo
news *n* noticias *f pl*
newspaper *n* periódico *m*
night *n* noche *f*
no *adv* no
nobody *pron* nadie
noise *n* ruido *m*
north *n* norte *m*
nose *n* nariz *f*
not *adv* no
nothing nada *pron*
now *adv* ahora
number *n* número *m*

O

obtain *v* conseguir
ocean *n* océano *m*
odor *n* olor *m*
of *prep* de
oil *n* aceite *m*
old *adj* anciano, viejo
older *adj* mayor
on *prep* en, sobre
only *adv* solamente
open *adj* abierto, *v* abrir
or *conj* o, u
other *adj* otro
ought *v* deber
out *adv* afuera
outside *adv* fuera
overcoat *n* abrigo *m*
own *adj* propio
owner *n* dueño *m*

P

package *n* paquete *m*
pain *n* dolor *m*, pena *f*

painter *n* pintor *m*
painting *n* pintura *f*, cuadro *m*
pair *n* par *m*
paper *n* papel *m*
park *n* parque *m*, *v* estacionar
partner *n* socio *m*
passenger *n* pasajero *m*
pay *v* pagar, *n* pago, salario *m*
pen *n* pluma *f*
pencil *n* lápiz *m*
people *n* gente *f*, pueblo *m*
perhaps *adv* quizá
picture *n* cuadro *m*
pig *n* cerdo *m*
pillow *n* almohada *f*
pin *n* alfiler *m*
place *n* lugar *m*
play *n* comedia *f*, *v* jugar
pleasant *adj* agradable
please *v* gustar, *adv* por favor
pleasure *n* gusto *m*
pocket *n* bosillo *m*
poor *adj* pobre
porter *n* mozo *m*
post office *n* correo *m*
pound *n* libra *f*
pray *v* rezar, orar
present *adj* actual, presente, *n* regalo *m*
pretty *adj* bonito, lindo
price *n* precio *m*
priest *n* sacerdote *m*
proud *adj* orgulloso
prove *v* probar
pupil *n* alumno, -a
purse *n* bolsa *f*
push *v* empujar
put *v* poner

Q

quarter *n* cuarto *m*
queen *n* reina *f*
question *n* pregunta *f*

R

rag *n* trapo *m*
railroad *n* ferrocarril *m*
rain *v* llover, *n* lluvia *f*
raise *v* alzar
reach *v* alcanzar
read *v* leer
reading *n* lectura *f*
ready *adj* listo

Review of Spanish Grammar 435

reason *n* razón *f*
receipt *n* recibo *m*
receive *v* recibir
red *adj* rojo
regret *v* sentir, *n* pena *f*
relative *n* pariente *m*
remain *v* quedar
remainder *n* resto *m*
remember *v* acordarse, recordar
remembrance *n* recuerdo *m*
remove *v* quitar
repeat *v* repetir
rest *v* descansar, *n* descanso *m*
result *n* resultado *m*
return *v* volver, devolver, regresar, *n* vuelta *f*
rich *adj* rico
right *adj and n* derecho *m*
ring *n* anillo *m*
rise *v* levantarse
river *n* río *m*
road *n* camino *m*
roast *v* asar
roof *n* techo *m*
room *n* cuarto *m*, habitación *f*
rooster *n* gallo *m*
root *n* raíz *f*
round *adj* redondo
rule *n* regla *f*
run *v* correr

S

sad *adj* triste
sale *n* venta *f*
salt *n* sal *f*, *v* salar
same *adj and pron* mismo
sand *n* arena *f*
satisfied *adj* satisfecho
say *v* decir
school *n* escuela *f*
sea *n* mar *m and f*
season *n* estación *f*
seat *n* asiento *m*
see *v* ver
seem *v* parecer
sell *v* vender
send *v* enviar, mandar
sentence *n* frase *f*
serve *v* servir
service *n* servicio *m*
shadow *n* sombra *f*
shame *n* vergüenza *f*
sharp *adj* afilado, agudo
sheep *n* oveja *f*

sheet *n* sábana *f*
ship *n* barco *m*
shoe *n* zapato *m*
shoe store *n* zapatería *f*
shore *n* orilla *f*
short *adj* corto
should *v* deber
shout *v* gritar
sick *adj* enfermo, malo
side *n* lado *m*
sidewalk *n* acera *f*
sign *v* firmar
signal *n* señal *f*
silk *n* seda *f*
silver *n* plata *f*
similar *adj* semejante, parecido
sing *v* cantar
sir *title* señor
sit down *v* sentarse
size *n* tamaño *m*
skirt *n* falda *f*
sky *n* cielo *m*
sleep *v* dormir
sleeve *n* manga *f*
slow *adj* lento
slowly *adv* despacio
small *adj* pequeño
smaller *adj* menor
smile *v* sonreír, *n* sonrisa *f*
smoke *v* fumar
snow *v* nevar, *n* nieve *f*
so *adv* tan, así
so much *adj* tanto
soap *n* jabón *m*
some *adj and pron* alguno
someone *pron* alguien
something *pron* algo
song *n* canción *f*
soon *adv* pronto
soul *n* alma *f*
sound *v* sonar, *n* sonido *m*
south *n* sur *m*
Spanish *adj and n m* español
speak *v* hablar
spend *v* gastar
spoon *n* cuchara *f*
staircase *n* escalera *f*
stamp *n* sello *m*
star *n* estrella *f*
state *n* estado *m*
station *n* estación *f*
steal *v* robar
steam *n* vapor *m*
steel *n* acero *m*
step *n* paso *m*

stone *n* piedra *f*
store *n* tienda *f*
straight *adj* derecho
street *n* calle *f*
streetcar *n* tranvía *m*
stripe *n* raya *f*
strong *adj* fuerte
study *v* estudiar
subway *n* metro *m*
success *n* éxito *m*
such *adj* tal
suitcase *n* maleta *f*
sun *n* sol *m*
supper *n* cena *f*
sure *adj* seguro
surprise *n* sorpresa *f*
sweet *adj* dulce
sweetheart *n* novio, -a
swim *v* nadar

T

table *n* mesa *f*
tablecloth *n* mantel *m*
tailor *n* sastre *m*
take *v* tomar
take out *v* sacar
tall *adj* alto
teach *v* enseñar
teacher *n* maestro, -a
tear *n* lágrima *f*
telephone *n* teléfono *m*
tell *v* decir
than *conj* que
that *pron* que
then *adv* entonces, luego
there *adv* ahí, allá, allí
there are hay
there is hay
thief *n* ladrón *m*
thin *adj* delgado
thing *n* cosa *f*
think *v* pensar
thirst *n* sed *f*
thread *n* hilo *m*
throw *v* tirar, echar
thus *adv* así
ticket *n* billete *m*
tie *v* atar
time *n* hora *f*, tiempo *m*, vez *f*
tin *n* lata *f*
tin can *n* lata *f*
tip *n* propina *f*
tired *adj* cansado
to *prep* a

436   **Review of Spanish Grammar**

today *adv* hoy
together *adj* junto
toilet *n* retrete *m*
too *adv* demasiado, también
touch *v* tocar
toward *prep* hacia
town *n* pueblo *m*
train *n* tren *m*
translate *v* traducir
travel *v* viajar
treasure *n* tesoro *m*
tree *n* árbol *m*
trip *n* viaje *m*
trouble *v* molestar, *n* apuro *m*, pena *f*
trunk *n* tronco *m*
truth *n* verdad *f*
try to *v* tratar de

U

ugly *adj* feo
umbrella *n* paraguas *m*
understand *v* comprender, entender
unite *v* unir
use *v* usar
useful *adj* útil

V

vacation *n* vacaciones *f pl*
valley *n* valle *m*
view *n* vista *f*
village *n* aldea *f*
visit *n* visita *f*, *v* visitar
voice *n* voz *f*

W

wait for *v* aguadar, esperar
waiter *n* mozo *m*, camarero *m*
wake *v* despertar
walk *v* andar, caminar
want *v* querer
war *n* guerra *f*
wash *v* lavar
watch *n* reloj *m*
water *n* agua *f*
watermelon *n* sandía *f*
weak *adj* débil
weather *n* tiempo *m*
week *n* semana *f*
well *adv* bien, *adj* bueno
west *n* oeste *m*

what *interj pron* qué
wheat *n* trigo *m*
wheel *n* rueda *f*
when *adv* cuándo, *conj* cuando
where *adv* adónde, dónde, *conj* donde
which *pron* cuál
while *conj* mientras, *n* rato *m*
white *adj* blanco
who *pron* quién, quien
whole *adj* entero
why *adv* por qué
wide *adj* ancho
widow *n* viuda *f*
widower *n* viudo *m*
wife *n* esposa *f*
wild *adj* bárbaro
wilderness *n* desierto *m*
wilt *v* marchitar
win *v* ganar
wind *n* viento *m*
window *n* ventana *f*
wine *n* vino *m*
wing *n* ala *f*
winner *n* ganador *m*
winter *n* invierno *m*
wipe *v* limpiar
wise *adj* sabio
wish *v* desear, *n* deseo *m*
wit *n* gracia *f*
with *prep* con
within *adv* dentro
without *prep* sin
wolf *n* lobo *m*
woman *n* mujer *f*
wood *n* madera *f*
wool *n* lana *f*
word *n* palabra *f*
work *n* obra *f*, *v* trabajar
world *n* mundo *m*
worried *adj* inquieto
worse *adv* peor
worth *n* valor *m*, **be worth** *v* valer
write *v* escribir

Y

year *n* año *m*
yellow *adj* amarillo
yes *adv* sí
yesterday *adv* ayer
young *adj* joven
younger *adj* menor

For further reference

Grammars

Greenfield, Eric V.
 Spanish Grammar
 Barnes and Noble
Jarvis, Ana C., Lebredo, Raquel, and Mena, Francisco
 Basic Spanish Grammar
 D. C. Heath and Company

Kendris, Christopher
 301 Spanish Verbs
 Barron's

Dictionaries

Castillo, Carlos and Bond, Otto
 The University of Chicago Spanish-English, English-Spanish Dictionary
 Pocket Books
Cuyás, Arturo
 Appleton's New Cuyás English-Spanish, Spanish-English Dictionary
 Prentice-Hall
Dutton, Brian, Harvey, L.P., and Walker, Roger M.
 Cassell's Compact Spanish-English, English-Spanish Dictionary
 Dell Publishing

Velázquez de la Cadena, Mariano, Gray, Edward, and Iribas, Juan R.
 New Revised Velázquez Spanish-English, Diccionario Inglés-Español
 New Century Publishers
Williams, Edwin B.
 The Bantam New College Spanish and English Dictionary
 Bantam Books

Review of Spanish Grammar

Index

How to use the index. The INDEX to the *Family Handbook* is arranged alphabetically according to a letter-by-letter system. All entries, regardless of punctuation or spaces between words, are in precise alphabetical order; there are no exceptions:

    Cataract
    Catering
    Catholic Church
    CAT scan

Each entry ends with a period. Following the period is the number of the page or pages on which the term will be found:

    Lincoln, Abraham. 258–259, 274, 312

Handy cross-references are provided when a listing may be ambiguous or confusing. Few abbreviations are used in the index, and those that are used are so standard as to eliminate the need for an abbreviations list.

Books, plays, and other titles are not indexed, but authors, artists, composers, etc., are. Monarchs are listed in numerical order:

    Charles I (King of England)
    Charles II (King of England)
    Charles V (Holy Roman Emp.)
    Charles VII (King of France)

A

Abacus. 3
Abdomen. 96
Abortion. 142
Abscess. 96
Accidents. *See* Safety
Accounting. 23, 52, 55
Achievement tests. 328
Acromegaly. 96
ACTION. 47, 296
Addiction (drug). *See* Narcotics
Addison's disease. 96
Adjectives. 214
Adler, Mortimer. 302
Adoption. 142
Adrenal gland. 104
Adrenalin. 60, 66
Advertising. 44, 54, 58, 156
Aerophagia. 96
Aflatoxin. 67
African languages. 234
Age Discrimination in Employment Act (1969). 296
Airplane. 29, 54, 55, 57
Air rights. 152
Alaska. 45
Alcohol. 59, 60, 61, 67, 70, 79, 88, 90, 91, 92, 93, 96, 98
Alcoholics Anonymous (A.A.). 93
Algebra. 3
Aliens. *See* Citizenship
Alimony. 146, 177

Allergy. 81, 88, 96, 98
Alzheimer's disease. 86, 96
Amenorrhea. 96
American Association of Retired Persons (AARP). 297
American College Testing program (ACT). 328, 343–348
American Revolution. 235
Amniocentesis. 84, 96
Amphetamines. 94
Anaphylaxis. 96
Anemia. 59, 96, 107, 108
Anesthesia. 81
Aneurysm. 96
Angina pectoris. 76, 96
Angiography. 96
Annual percentage rate (APR). 114, 136
Annulment (marriage). 141
Anorexia nervosa. 97
Anthropology. 227
Antibiotics. 90, 97
Anticoagulants. 88, 90, 97
Antonyms. *See* Synonyms and antonyms
Anxiety. 59, 60
Appendix (body). 97
Aptitude tests. 328
Archaeology. 227
Architecture. 52
Aristotle. 257
Arizona. 45, 146
Arkansas. 234

Armed forces (U.S.). 31, 301
Arrythmia. 97
Art. *See* Graphic arts; Painting
Arteriogram. 97
Arteriosclerosis. 97
Artery (human). 97, 105, 108
Arthritis. 58, 59, 60, 74, 76, 81, 97, 98, 103–104, 106, 107
Ascorbic acid. *See* Vitamin C
Aspirin. 88, 89
Assault and battery. 162
Asthma. 60, 61, 76, 97, 99
Astigmatism. 306
Atherosclerosis. 97
Athlete's foot. 63, 97
Attorneys. *See* Legal profession
Audio-visual materials. 261
Automobiles. 24, 54, 55, 125–126, 134, 160–161

B

Babbage, Charles. 3
Baked goods. 29, 47, 131
Bank finance and banking. 23, 24, 29, 52, 55, 114–115, 117, 137, 145. *See also* Checking accounts
Bankruptcy. 136, 158
Barbiturates. 88, 94
Baton Rouge (La.). 234
Bedsores. 99
Bell Laboratories. 4
Beta blockers. 97

Beverages. 131
Bill collection. *See* Collection (bill)
Billingsgate Tower (London). 225
Billy the Kid. 235
Biology. 196, 227
Biopsy. 84, 97
Birds. 105, 227
Bixby, Lydia. 274
Blacks. 297
Bladder. 99, 100, 103, 106
Blindness. 17, 62
Blood. 81, 101, 105, 106, 108
Blood cells. 65, 66, 100
Blood pressure. 17, 60, 75, 76, 87, 90, 101
Blue Cross and Blue Shield. 123–124
Body (human). 155. *See also* specific body parts and diseases
Body language. 246, 254–256
Bond (financial). 118, 119, 126, 136, 137, 138
Bone. 65, 66, 68, 77, 97, 103, 104
Bookkeeping. 29, 55
Books. *See* authors' names; Libraries; Literature; Reading; Reference books; Textbooks
Bowdler, Thomas. 225
Bowel. 102
Boycott. 225
Braille. 17
Brain. 96, 97, 98, 101, 105, 106
Bread. 64, 70
Breast. 102
Bronchitis. 97, 99
Brooklyn Bridge. 225
Budgeting. 111–112
Buffalo Bill (Cody). 225
Building. *See* Construction
Bunions. 63
Burglary. *See* Theft
Bursitis. 97
Business. 14, 23, 25, 49–51, 130, 165–167, 276–277

C

Cadmium. 67
Caffeine. 59, 60, 61

Calciferol. *See* Vitamin D
Calculator. 3
California. 146
Calluses (foot). 63
Calorie. 72–74, 76
Camping. 135
Cancer. 58, 59, 67, 70, 81, 97, 98, 99, 102, 106
Candidiasis. 97
Carbohydrates. 59, 64, 66, 76
Careers. 22–57, 278–279, 296, 303, 319. *See also* specific fields, jobs, and professions
Carotene. 109
Carpentry. 23, 29, 56
Cars. *See* Automobiles
Catalogs. 131
Cataract. 306
Catering. 50
Catholic Church. *See* Roman Catholic Church
CAT scan. 84, 98
Cellulose. 76
Census Bureau (U.S.). 3
Certificates of deposit (CD's). 115, 117, 136
Cervix. 99
Charge account. *See* Credit
Charity. 121
Charts. *See* Graph; Tables
Checking accounts. 115–117
Chemistry and chemicals. 29, 52, 196
Chemotherapy. 97
Chesterfield (Lord). 268
Chicago (Ill.). 234
Chicken pox. 98
Childbed fever. 98
Children. 12–13, 29, 48, 62, 81, 85–86, 88, 121, 142–143, 146, 164, 167. 272–273. *See also* Abortion; Adoption; Reading
Chiropracty. 81
Cholesterol. 64, 65, 67, 69, 76, 98
Christmas. 273
Chromium. 65
Chromosome. 98
Cigarettes. *See* Tobacco
Cirrhosis. 98

Cities. 29
Citizenship. 144
Civil Rights Act (1964). 164
Civil War (U.S.). 235
Clemens, Samuel Langhorne. 206, 260
Clergy. *See* Religion
Clerks. *See* Office work
Clothing. 36–37, 41, 131, 216, 256
Clubs and organizations. 290–291, 292, 297
Coffee. 59
Cola. 59
Cold, common. 68, 88
Collagen. 98
Collection (bill). 158, 286, 287
Colleges and universities. 22, 28–31, 44, 53, 111, 139, 145, 294, 303
Colon (body part). 70, 98, 99, 107
Colorado. 45
Common law marriage. 141, 173
Computers. *See* Data processing
Condominium. 136, 153
Congress (U.S.). 300
Conjunctivitis. 98
Conrad, Joseph. 206
Construction. 23, 56, 149
Consumer price index. 136
Consumer protection. 156–158
Contracts. 142, 143, 147–149, 151, 156, 165, 173, 287. *See also* Lease
Convulsions. 98
Co-ops (food). 131
Co-ops (housing). 153
Copper. 65, 70
Copyright. 159
Cornea. 76
Cornell University. 131
Corns (foot). 63
Corporation. 166
Courts. 157, 172–179, 219, 300
Credit. 114–115, 117, 134, 157–158, 159, 287. *See also* Mortgages
Crib death. 107
Crime. 142, 167–168, 172–179
Cross-eye. 107
Croup. 98
Cryosurgery. 98

Index 439

Culdoscopy. 98–99
Curettage. 99
Cyst. 99
Cystocele. 99

D

Damages (legal). 162–163, 174, 178
Data processing. 2–21, 22, 23, 29, 44, 54, 55, 56
Da Vinci, Leonardo. *See* Leonardo da Vinci
De Soto, Hernando. 234
Death. 121, 126, 275. *See also* Estate
Defamation of character. 162–163, 178
Dentistry. *See* Teeth
Depression (mental). 91, 92
Des Moines (Iowa). 234
Diabetes. 59, 77, 87, 99, 101
Diarrhea. 89, 99
Dickens, Charles John Huffam. 275
Diction. 250, 252
Dictionary. 230, 317
Diets. *See* Weight
Digestive system. 66, 81, 84, 102
Digital Equipment Corp. 4
Disability insurance. 165
Disaccharide. 71, 76
Discrimination. 39, 151, 164. *See also* Minorities; specific groups
Disease. *See* Medicine and health; specific diseases
Diverticula. 99
Divorce. 145–146
DNA (deoxyribonucleic acid). 66, 76, 99
Doctors. *See* Medicine and health
Donnybrook (Ireland). 225
Down's syndrome. 84, 99
Draco. 225
Drama. *See* Theater
Drugs. 58, 59, 60, 61, 62, 79, 87–91. *See also* Narcotics; specific drugs
Dutch language. 234
Dysmenorrhea. 99
Dysplasia. 99

E

Ear. 63, 102, 103, 104, 108. *See also* Hearing
Earthquake. 125, 309
Economics. 110–139
Education. 9, 12–13, 22, 24, 28–31, 44, 47, 53, 143, 294, 297
EEG (electroencephalogram). 84, 99
Eisenhower, Dwight David. 111

EKG (electrocardiogram). 84, 99
Elderly. *See* Old age
Electricity. 22, 23, 29, 56
Electronics. 23, 56. *See also* Data processing
Embezzlement. 174
Embolism. 99, 105
Eminent domain. 152, 174
Emphysema. 99
Employment. 46, 164–165
Encyclopedia. 317
Energy (power). 121, 133
Engineering. 22, 23, 29, 52, 54
English-French dictionary. 375–381
English-German dictionary. 402–407
English language. 44, 196, 234–235. *See also* Reading; Vocabulary; parts of speech
English-Spanish dictionary. 432–437
ENIAC (computer). 4, 5
Entertainment. 44, 54
Enzymes. 65, 66, 76, 100
Epilepsy. 100
Erythrocytes. 100
Escrow. 149, 174
Estate. 121, 126, 137, 154–156, 174, 175, 176, 177
Etiquette. 266
Executor. *See* Estate
Exercise. 17, 59, 60, 61, 67, 68, 73, 74
Extortion. 175
Eye. 62, 81, 98, 100, 106, 249–250, 306–307, 311. *See also* Blindness

F

Fair Labor Standards Act. 164
Fallopian tube. 106
Family. 141–146, 322–323
Farsightedness. 306
Fashion. *See* Clothing
Fatigue. 59–60
Fats. 64, 65, 66, 69, 70, 71, 76, 77
FBI (Federal Bureau of Investigation). 29
Feet. 63, 81
Fever. 100
Fiber. 64, 70
Fibroma. 100
Films. *See* Motion pictures
Finances. 14, 110–139, 293
Fire. 24, 55
Fish and fishing. 227
Fistula. 100
Fitness. *See* Medicine and health
Flatulence. 100
Flood. 125
Florida. 45
Flu. *See* Influenza

Fluorine. 65
Fluoroscopy. 100
Folic acid. 66–67
Food. 53, 55, 59–60, 61, 70–71, 130–131, 218, 293. *See also* Catering; Nutrition; Weight
Food and Drug Administration (FDA). 58, 87, 88
Forgery. 175
Foster Grandparents. 47, 296
Franchise. 166–167
Frankfurt (Ger.). 234
Fraud. 175, 283
French adjectives. 357–358
French articles. 352–354
French-English dictionary. 370–374
French language. 234, 352–381
French pronouns. 354–359
French verbs. 354, 360–366
Fructose. 71, 76
Fruit. 64, 68, 70, 130
Funerals. *See* Death

G

Gallbladder. 98, 100
Games. 8, 9, 17, 236
Gamma globulin. 100
Gardening. 47, 221
Gastritis. 100
General Educational Development (GED) test. 328, 332–335
Genetics. 99, 100
Geology. 227
German adjectives and adverbs. 387
German articles. 382–383
German conjunctions. 391
German-English dictionary. 396–401
German language. 234, 382–407
German measles (rubella). 100
German nouns. 383–384
German prepositions. 386
German pronouns. 384–386
German verbs. 388–391
Gerry, Elbridge. 225
Gerrymander. 225
Gettysburg Address. 258–259
Gifts. 144–145, 146, 172
Glands. 81, 100
Glaucoma. 62, 76, 100, 306
Glossitis. 100
Glucose. 65, 71, 76
Glycogen. 76
Godwin, William. 303
Goiter. 65, 76, 100
Gonorrhea. 100
Government. 292, 300
Government bond. *See* Bond (financial)

Graduate Record Examination (GRE). 328, 349–351
Grammar. 250, 252
Graph. 321
Graphic arts. 14
Graves' disease. 101
Gray Panthers. 297
Greek language. 223, 226, 227
Green Thumb. 296
Grooming. 36–37, 256
Guaranteed Student Loan program. 111
Guaranties and warranties. 137, 138, 156–157, 160, 175, 283, 285
Gum. 64
Gynecology. 81, 101

H

Hair. 29, 37, 55
Hamburg (Ger.). 234
Hand. 307
Handicapped. 17, 143
Handicrafts. 47
Harvard University. 4, 15
Hashimoto's disease. 101
Hawthorne, Nathaniel. 312
Headache. 60, 61, 88, 101, 103
Health. See Medicine and health
Health insurance. 123–124, 125, 126, 136, 137. See also Medicaid; Medicare
Hearing. 4, 17, 63
Heart. 59, 60, 61, 67, 69, 76, 81, 97, 98, 99–100, 102, 103, 104, 107
Heartburn. 101
Hematoma. 101
Hemophilia. 101
Hemorrhoids. 101
Hepatitis. 101
Hernia. 99, 101
Heroin. See Narcotics
Herpes. 101
Hispanic-Americans. 297
History. 13
HMO (Health Maintenance Organization). 124
Hodgkin's disease. 101
Hollerith, Herman. 3
Homes. See Home-owner's insurance; Housing; Mortgages
Homonyms. 222–223
Home-owner's insurance. 124, 125
Hospitals. 82–86
Hotels. See Motels and hotels
Housing. 121, 147–153, 216, 292. See also Condominium; Energy; Home-owner's insurance; Mortgages; Real estate
Human Engineering Laboratory. 206

Hydrocarbon. 76
Hydrocephalus. 101
Hydrogenation. 76
Hypertension. See Blood pressure
Hypoglycemia. 101
Hypothermia. 101
Hysterectomy. 102

I

IBM (International Business Machines). 3, 4, 21
Idaho. 146, 234
Illegitimacy. 142
Illinois. 45, 234
Illness. See Medicine and health; specific diseases
Immune system. 102
Income. 137, 138, 144
Income tax. See Tax
Indiana. 45
Indians (N. Am.). 234
Indigestion. See Digestive system
Inflation. 110, 112, 119, 127
Influenza. 102
Inheritance. 142, 146. See also Estate
Insect. 227
Insomnia. See Sleep
Installment payments. See Credit
Insulin. 101, 102
Insurance. 29, 44, 54, 122–126, 137, 139, 150, 152, 160–161. See also specific types, e.g., Life insurance
Interest (financial). 110, 111, 114, 115, 118, 136, 137, 138, 157, 175. See also Mortgages
Internal Revenue Service (IRS). 120, 165
Interviews (job). 36–39
Intestines. 109
Investment (financial). 119, 137
Iodine. 65
Iowa. 45, 234
IRA (Individual Retirement Account). 112, 115, 118, 129, 137, 138
Iron (element). 65, 70, 96
Italian language. 234

J

Jaundice. 102
Javal, Emil. 306
Jews. 234, 301
Jobs. See Careers; Labor
Joyce, James. 321

K

Kentucky. 234
Keogh accounts. 115, 118–119, 137

Kidney. 81, 99, 101, 103, 106, 109
Kroc, Ray. 47

L

Labeling. 71, 130
Labor. 43, 121, 164–167. See also Careers; Employment; specific fields
Labor, Department of (U.S.). 296
Lamp. See Light
Landscape architecture. 24, 52
Language. 227. See also Speech and speaking; Vocabulary; specific languages
Larynx. 102
Latin language. 223, 226, 227, 228
Law. 140–179, 219
Lawyers. See Legal profession
Laxatives. 68
Lead (metal). 102
Lease. 152–153, 176
Lectures. 197
Legal profession. 23, 29, 44, 53, 54, 160, 169–171, 172
Legionnaires' disease. 102
Leibniz, Gottfried. 3
Leonardo da Vinci. 278
Letter writing. 36, 266–301
Leukemia. 102
Libel. 162–163
Libraries. 24, 29, 44, 53, 323
Lice. 104
Lien. 149–150, 159, 176
Life insurance. 122–123, 125, 138
Light. 62, 306
Lincoln, Abraham. 258–259, 274, 312
Lip. 307
Listening. 38, 42
Literature. 219
Liver. 65, 67, 98, 101
London, Jack. 309
Lorayne, Harry. 180
Louis XIV (King of France). 234
Louisiana. 146, 234
Lungs. 70, 81, 99, 104–105
Lupus erythematoses. 81, 98, 102
Lymph system. 102

M

Ménierè's disease. 103
Machines. 57
Magazines. 225, 289, 308–309, 313, 320
Mail. See Postal service
Mail order. 123, 156
Manganese. 65
Manic depression. 102
Mannose. 71, 76
Maps. 197
Mark I (computer). 4

Index 441

Marketing. *See* Selling
Market research. 24, 44
Marriage. 121, 141, 144–145, 271–273. *See also* Divorce
Mastoid. 102
Mathematics. 3, 14, 18, 52, 196
Measles. 102–103
Meat. 130
Medicaid. 95, 137, 294
Medicare. 95, 129, 137, 294
Medicine and health. 17, 22, 23, 44, 53–54, 55, 58–77, 78–109, 144, 215, 294. *See also* Hospitals; Mental illness; specific body parts and diseases
Melanin. 65
Memory. 180–205, 209
Meningitis. 103
Menopause. 103
Menstruation. 96, 99, 103
Mental illness. 91, 92–95, 103, 105, 143
Metabolism. 103
Meteorology. 227
Michigan. 45
Microchip. 4, 5, 20
Microcomputer. 5, 9, 17, 20
Microorganisms. 103
Microphone. 249
Milan, Duke of. 278
Milk. 70
Minerals. 64–65, 152
Minicomputer. 4
Minnesota. 234
Minorities. 297. *See also* specific minority groups
Mississippi. 234
Missouri. 45
Mole (skin). 103
Molybdenum. 65
Money. 110–139
Money market accounts and funds. 117, 119, 137–138
Mongolism. *See* Down's syndrome
Mononucleosis. 103
Monosaccharide. 71, 77
Morphine. 94
Mortgages. 115, 121, 127, 132–133, 136, 145, 147, 150, 152, 173
Motels and hotels. 159, 287
Motion pictures. 218
Movies. *See* Motion pictures
Moving. 121
MSG (monosodium glutamate). 70, 71, 77
Multiple sclerosis. 103
Mumps. 103
Murder. 175, 176
Muscle. 103
Muscular dystrophy. 103
Music. 47, 220
Mutual funds. 119, 138, 139
Myasthenia gravis. 103

Myelitis. 103
Myocardial infarction. *See* Heart
Myoglobin. 77

N

Names (personal). 141, 184, 194, 200–205
Narcotics. 92, 94, 96, 101
National Association of Retired Civil Employees (NARCE). 297
National Council of Senior Citizens (NCSC). 297
National Council of the Aging (NCOA). 297
National Direct Student Loan program. 111
National Retired Teachers Association (NRTA). 297
Nearsightedness. 306
Negligence (legal). 160–161, 176
Negroes. *See* Blacks
Nervous system. 65, 66, 81, 103
Nevada. 45, 146
New Mexico. 45, 146
Newspapers. 224, 313, 320
New York State. 45, 122, 123
Niacin. *See* Vitamin B₃
Nicotine. 61
Nitrogen dioxide. 67
Nitrosamines. 77
No-fault insurance. 161
Noise. 306
Nose. 100
NOW accounts. 115
Nursing. 23, 29, 44, 53–54
Nursing homes. 82
Nutrition. 17, 24, 64–71, 77

O

Oakley, Annie. 225
Obesity. *See* Weight
Ocean. 29, 52
Office work. 23, 29, 52, 55. *See also* Secretaries
Ohio. 45
Oil (animal and plant). 71
Oklahoma. 45
Old age. 22, 47, 81, 86, 88–89, 107, 127–130, 135, 139, 144, 150, 164, 193, 292–297
Older Americans Act. 292
Operation Mainstream. 296
Organizations. *See* Clubs and organizations; specific organizations
Osteomalacia. 77
Osteoporosis. 68
Ovary. 98, 100, 103, 104
Oxford English Dictionary. 230
Oxygen. 59
Ozone. 67

P

Paget's disease. 104
Pain. 90
Painting. 29, 47
Pancreas. 104, 109
Paralysis. 104
Paratyphoid fever. 104
Parkinson's disease. 104
Parliamentary procedure. 263–265
Partnership (business). 166
Pascal, Blaise. 3, 20
Patent. 159, 177
Peace Corps. 47, 296
Pectin. 64, 77
Pell Grants. 111
Pellagra. 104
Peller, Clara. 47
Penicillin. 90
Pennsylvania. 45
Pensions. 129, 137, 165. *See also* Social insurance
Peritonitis. 104
Perjury. 177, 178
Personal appearance. *See* Grooming
Personal computer. *See* Microcomputer
Personnel. 24, 44
Pharmaceuticals. *See* Drugs
Phlebitis. 104
Photography. 24, 54
Physicians. *See* Medicine and health
Physics. 29, 52
Pizza. 71
Plastics. 23
Plastic surgery. 81
Pleurisy. 104
Pneumonia. 104
Poisoning. 106, 108
Poker (card game). 235
Police. 24, 44, 55
Polio. 105
Polyps. 105
Polysaccharide. 77
Pontiac fever. 105
Postal service. 24, 29, 55, 290, 298–299
Pott's disease. 105
Prefixes. 226
Pregnancy. 81, 84, 88, 97, 105, 108
President (U.S.). 300
Printing. 6, 11, 16, 21
Privacy. 163
Probate. *See* Estate
Profanity. 253
Programming (computer). *See* Data processing
Property. 143–146, 159, 162–163, 173, 178. *See also* Estate; Real estate

Prostaglandins. 105
Prostate. 105
Protestantism. 301
Prothrombin time (PT). 105
Pseudodementia. 105
Psittacosis. 105
Psoriasis. 105
Psychiatry. 95, 105
Psychology. 29, 44, 53, 227
Publishing. 44
Pulse (human). 75
Puritans. 314, 318
Purpura. 105
Puzzles. *See* Games
Pyelography. 105
Pyridoxine. *See* Vitamin B$_6$

Q

Q fever. 106

R

Radiation. 106
Radio. 4, 23, 29, 44, 54, 56, 247
Rape. 178
Raynaud's disease. 106
Reading. 13, 17, 197, 219, 302–327
Real estate. 23, 29, 54, 119, 136, 145, 150–151. *See also* Housing; Mortgages
Record-keeping. 111–113, 116
Recreation. 295
Red blood cells. *See* Blood cells
Reference books. 316–317, 321
Refrigerator. 133
Religion. 29, 44, 53, 227, 301
Renting. 152–153
Repairs. 23, 29, 55, 56, 134, 153, 159
Restaurants. 24, 29, 44, 55
Résumés. 32–33
Retina. 106
Retinol. *See* Vitamin A
Retired Officers Association (ROA). 297
Retired Senior Volunteer Program (RSVP). 47
Retirement. *See* Old age
Reye's syndrome. 106
Rheumatic fever. 106
Rh factor. 106
Rhode Island. 45
Riboflavin. *See* Vitamin B$_2$
Rickets. 106
RNA (ribonucleic acid). 106
Robbery. *See* Theft
Robert's Rules. 263–265
Rocky Mountain spotted fever. 106
Roman Catholic Church. 301

S

Saccharides. 77
Safety. 41, 160–163, 164
Salary. *See* Wages
Sales. *See* Selling
Salmonellosis. 106
Salt. 70, 71
San Francisco (Calif.). 309
SAT's. *See* Scholastic Aptitude Tests
Saunders, Colonel. 47
Savings accounts. 115, 117
Scabies. 106
Scalp. 108
Scarlet fever. 106
Schizophrenia. 92, 94, 106–107
Scholastic Aptitude Tests (SAT's). 328, 329, 336–342
Schools. *See* Education
Sciatic nerve. 107
Science. 52–53. *See also* specific fields
Scleroderma. 81, 98, 107
Scoliosis. 107
Search and seizure. 167–168, 179
Secretaries. 23, 24, 29, 44, 55
Selenium. 65
Selling. 24, 29, 44, 54, 156, 262–263, 284, 288, 290
Selye, Hans. 60
Semiconductor. 21
Senility. 107
Senior citizens. *See* Old age
Senior Citizens of America (SCA). 297
Senior Companion Program. 296
Separation (marital). 145–146
Services. 22, 29, 44, 47, 48, 52–57. *See also* specific fields and industries
Sewing. 47
Sheridan, Richard Brinsley. 225
Shingles. *See* Herpes
Shock (physiological). 107
Shoes. 63
Shopping. 130–131, 139
Sickle-cell anemia. 107
Silicon. 5
Sinus. 107
Skin. 81, 99, 100, 105, 106, 109
Slander. 162–163
Slang. 38, 253
Sleep. 59, 60, 61, 91, 102
Sleeping sickness. 108
Slipped disk. 107
Smallpox. 107
Smell. 75
Smoking. *See* Tobacco
Snail fever. 106
Social insurance. 22, 47, 115, 120, 122, 127–130, 138, 141, 165–166, 293

Social welfare. 29, 44, 53
Sodium. 70, 71, 77
Software (computer). 8–9, 12, 14, 15, 21
Solar energy. 121
Sonogram. 84, 109
Sound. 108. *See also* Sonogram
Sound recording. 246, 247, 251
Spanish adjectives and adverbs. 410–414
Spanish articles. 409
Spanish-English dictionary. 426–431
Spanish language. 234, 408–437
Spanish nouns. 410
Spanish prepositions. 415
Spanish pronouns. 412–414
Spanish verbs. 416–423
Speech and speaking. 44, 244–265
Spelling. 16, 196
Spine. 81, 84, 103, 104, 105, 107
Sports. 217
Spreadsheet (electronic). 15
Stationery. 268
Still's disease. 107
Stock (financial). 136, 137, 138, 172
Stokes-Adams syndrome. 107
Stomach. 100, 101
Stonehenge (Eng.). 3
Stress. 59, 60–61
Stroke (apoplexy). 107
Suchar, Elizabeth W. 31
Sugar. 71, 101, 102
Supermarket. 130
Supreme Court (U.S.). 300
Surgery. 80–81, 82, 95, 98, 101
Synonyms and antonyms. 16, 210, 213
Syphilis. 107

T

Tables (charts). 321
Tape recorder. *See* Sound recording
Tax. 118, 120–121, 126, 137, 138, 139, 146, 150, 165–166, 292
Taxis. 29
Tay-Sachs disease. 107
Teaching. *See* Education
Teeth. 23, 24, 29, 53–54, 55, 65, 66, 68
Telangiectasia. 108
Telecommunications. 22
Telephone. 29, 44, 56, 261–262
Television. 23, 29, 44, 56, 62, 221
Terre Haute (Ind.). 234
Testing. 213–214, 232–233, 328–351
Testing (medical). 75, 82–84, 86, 96–109
Tetanus. 108

Index   443

Tetany. 108
Texas. 45, 146
Textbooks. 309, 313, 317
Thalassemia. 108
Thalidomide. 108
Theater. 44, 47, 218
Theft. 159, 167, 172
Thermography. 108
Thiamin. *See* Vitamin B₁
Thorndike, Edward. 193
Thyroid. 65, 100, 101
Time. 226
Tissue (physiol.). 59
Title (property). 149, 179
Tobacco. 59, 60, 61, 67, 70, 79
Toe. 63
Tongue. 100
Tonsils. 108
Tort. 162, 179
Toxic shock syndrome. 108
Toxoplasmosis. 108
Trademark. 159
Tranquilizers. 91, 94, 108
Transistor. 4, 5
Transportation. 295
Travel. 121, 295
Traveler's checks. 117
Trespass. 162, 163, 179
Trichinosis. 108
Trichomoniasis. 108
Trucks. 23, 29, 55, 57
Trust (financial). 144
Tuberculosis. 105, 108
Twain, Mark. *See* Clemens, Samuel Langhorne
Typewriter. 22, 23, 44, 55, 268
Typhoid fever. 108

U

Ulcerative colitis. 108
Ulcers. 60, 61, 90, 99, 104
Ultrasound. *See* Sonogram

Unemployment. *See* Employment
Unions. *See* Labor
UNIVAC (computer). 4
Uremia. 109
Urethra. 103
Urticaria. 109
Uterus. 99, 100, 102, 105

V

Vacations. 135
Vacuum tube. 21
Vagina. 99, 100, 108, 109
Varicose veins. 109
Vascular system. 109
Vegetables. 64, 68, 70, 130
Vegetarianism. 70
Venereal disease. 79. *See also* specific diseases
Vermont. 234
Vertigo. 109
Veterans. 164
Vision. *See* Eye
VISTA. *See* Volunteers in Service to America
Vitamin A. 66–68, 70
Vitamin B. 59, 104
Vitamin B₁. 66–67
Vitamin B₂. 66–67
Vitamin B₃. 66–67
Vitamin B₆. 66–67
Vitamin B₁₂. 70
Vitamin C. 66–68, 70
Vitamin D. 66–68, 70
Vitamin E. 65, 66–67
Vitamins. 64, 66–67
Vocabulary. 196, 206–243, 253–254
Vocalization. 307–308
Vocational training. 22, 31
Voice. 247
Volunteers in Service to America (VISTA). 47, 296

W

Wages. 35, 40–41, 43, 164–165
Waiters and waitresses. *See* Restaurants
Wart. 109
Washington (state). 45, 146
Water. 64, 68, 152
Wax (ear). 63
Weight. 17, 58, 64, 72–73, 97
Welfare. *See* Social welfare
West Virginia. 45
Whooping cough. 109
Will. *See* Estate
Wine. 227
Women. 22, 48, 51, 68, 141, 144–145, 164
Word processing. 14, 16, 22
Words. *See* Vocabulary
Workers' compensation. 165, 166
World War I. 235
World War II. 235
Writing. 29, 44, 54. *See also* Letter writing
Wyoming. 45

X

Xanthema. 109
X-rays. 81, 83, 96, 97, 98, 102, 105, 109

Y

Yeast. 109
Yiddish language. 234
Youth. *See* Children

Z

Zinc. 65
Zollinger-Ellison syndrome. 109
Zoning. 151

Part 2

Roget's University Thesaurus

Roget's University Thesaurus

Edited by
Eugene Ehrlich

This work was originally published under the title
Roget's International Thesaurus of English Words and Phrases.

ROGET'S UNIVERSITY THESAURUS.
Copyright 1911, 1922, 1930, 1932, 1936, 1938, 1939, copyright © 1958, 1959, 1960, 1963, 1985
by Harper & Row, Publishers, Inc.
All rights reserved.

Preface

This edition of *Roget's University Thesaurus* remains true to the original formulation of Peter Mark Roget, followed by all his distinguished successors, including the late C. O. Sylvester Mawson, who edited the first *University Thesaurus*. The distinguishing feature of the present edition is that it responds to the particular needs of all family members, young and old, who are students. The day does not go by when writing or when preparing a speech that an appropriate word or phrase is difficult to recall. It is at those times that the *University Thesaurus* proves invaluable.

The *University Thesaurus* offers its users

1. a large list of synonyms and antonyms;
2. a special grouping of comparisons and related terms;
3. systematic treatment of specialized terminology;
4. a grouping of synonyms in individual paragraphs supplying words more or less related and interchangeable;
5. characterization of all obsolete, obsolescent, rare, archaic, colloquial, dialectal, and slang words, as well as British, foreign, and special terms;
6. plural forms in all cases of unusual difficulty;
7. numerous phrases and idioms;
8. citations from modern authors.

The words new in the *University Thesaurus* run well into the thousands and embrace all aspects of knowledge, particularly in the sciences and social sciences. The aim has been to suggest ideas and turns of thought. The arrangement of synonyms and antonyms peculiar to the Roget scheme adds to the usefulness of the work: Roget gives *goodness* and *badness*, for example, in sequential entries. There is no need to refer to another part of the book.

Another distinguishing feature of Roget is the inclusion of phrases. Not only does the use of phrases enlarge the group of synonyms for any particular word, but in many instances the phrase furnishes the only possible synonym. Improvement of this feature in the *University Thesaurus* has received painstaking attention.

Our language marches with no frontiers; English is a world possession. Every race and country is reflected in its vocabulary. The *University Thesaurus* is alive to this universality, and, in order to assist writers and speakers in giving local color, the birthplace of every imported word is duly recorded.

Attention must be drawn to the need for using any thesaurus in tandem with a dictionary. Synonyms are often only related words. The dictionary provides precise definitions of individual words, so it must be consulted before using a word or phrase new to the reader.

Eugene Ehrlich

Table of Contents

Roget's University Thesaurus

- Preface   iii
- Abbreviations   vi
- How to Use the Thesaurus   viii
- Tabular Synopsis of Categories   x
- **Roget's University Thesaurus**   3
- Index Guide   366

Abbreviations

abbr. abbreviated, abbreviation
adj. adjective, adjectival expression
adv. adverb, adverbial expression
Afr. Africa
Am. *or* **Amer.** America, American
Am. hist. American history
anat. anatomy
anc. ancient
Anglo-Ind. Anglo-Indian
anon. anonymous
antiq. antiquities
Ar. Arabic
arch. architecture
archaeol. archaeology
arith. arithmetic
A.-S. Anglo-Saxon
astrol. astrology
astron. astronomy
Austral. Australian
Bib. Biblical
biol. biology
bot. botany
Brit. British
Can. Canada, Canadian
Can. F. Canadian French
Celt. Celtic
chem. chemistry
Chin. Chinese
Ch. of Eng. Church of England
class. classical
colloq. colloquial
com. commerce, commercial
conj. conjunction

Du. Dutch
Dan. Danish
derog. derogatory
dial. dialect, dialectal
dim. diminutive
E. East
eccl. ecclesiastical
econ. economics
elec. electricity
Eng. English, England
erron. erroneous, erroneously
esp. especially
exc. except
F. French
fem. feminine
fig. figurative, figuratively
G. *or* **Ger.** German
Gr. Greek
gram. grammar
Gr. Brit. Great Britain
Heb. Hebrew
her. heraldry
Hind. Hindustani
hist. history, historical
Icel. Icelandic
Ind. Indian
Ir. Irish, Ireland
int. interjection
It. Italian
Jap. Japanese
Jew. Jewish
joc. jocular
L. Latin

l.c. lower case
masc. masculine
math. mathematics
Meth. Methodist
Mex. Mexico, Mexican
mil. military
Moham. Mohammedan
myth. mythology
N. North
n. noun
N. Am. North American
naut. nautical
N. E. *or* **New Eng.** New England
neut. neuter
Nfld. Newfoundland
NL. New Latin
Norw. Norwegian
N. W. Northwest, Northwestern
N. Z. New Zealand
obs. obsolete
obsoles. obsolescent
OE. Old English
opp. opposed
orig. original, originally
parl. parliamentary
path. pathology
Per. Persian
Pg. Portuguese
pharm. pharmacy
philos. philosophy
physiol. physiology
P. I. Philippine Islands
pl. plural

pol. *or* **polit.** political	**S. Am.** South American	**theat.** theatrical
pop. popular, popularly	**Scand.** Scandinavian	**theol.** theology
prep. preposition	**Scot.** Scottish, Scotland	**theos.** theosophy
Prot. Epis. Protestant Episcopal	**sing.** singular	**Turk.** Turkish
prov. proverb, provincial	**Skr.** Sanskrit	**typog.** typography
psychol. psychology	**Sp.** Spanish	**Univ.** University
R. C. Ch. Roman Catholic Church	**Sp. Amer.** Spanish American	**U. S.** United States
relig. religion	**surg.** surgery	**v.** verb
rhet. rhetoric, rhetorical	**Sw.** Swedish	**W.** West
Russ. Russian	**S. W.** Southwest, Southwestern	**W. Ind.** West Indies
S. *or* **So.** South	**S. W. U. S.** Southwest United States	**zool.** zoology
S. Afr. South African	**tech.** technical	

Dashes and hyphens are used to avoid the repetition of a term common to each word or phrase in the same group. For example:

"over-, above- the mark;"	=	"over the mark," "above the mark"
"on the -verge, -brink, -skirts of;"	=	"on the verge of," "on the brink of," "on the skirts of"
"brush-, whisk-, turn-, send- -off, -away;"	=	"brush off," "brush away," "whisk off," "whisk away," "turn off," "turn away," "send off," "send away"
"quick-, keen-, clear-, sharp- -eyed, -sighted, -witted;"	=	"quick-eyed," "quick-sighted," "quick-witted," "keen-eyed," "keen-sighted," "keen-witted," "clear-eyed," "clear-sighted," "clear-witted," "sharp-eyed," "sharp-sighted," "sharp-witted"
"away from-, foreign to-, beside- the -purpose, -question, -transaction, -point;"	=	"away from the purpose," "away from the question," "away from the transaction," "away from the point," "foreign to the purpose," etc., "beside the purpose," etc.
"fall, -to the ground;"	=	"fall," "fall to the ground"
"shortness etc. *adj.;*" "shortly etc. *adj.;*" "shortening etc. *v.;*"	=	in a similar manner form other words from the groups of *adjectives* or *verbs* in the same category

How to Use the Thesaurus

1. To find a synonym or antonym for any given WORD:

Turn to the Index Guide and find the particular word or any term of kindred meaning; then refer to the category indicated. Under the part of speech sought for [*n., v., adj., adv.*] will be found a wide choice of synonymous and related terms, with their antonyms in the following category or in the preceding category. For example, suppose a synonym is wanted for the word "rare" in the sense of "choice." Turn to the Index Guide, where the following references will be found:

> **rare** *unique* 20
> *exceptional* 83
> *few* 103
> *infrequent* 137
> *underdone* 298
> *tenuous* 322
> *neologic* 563
> *choice* 648

The italicized words denote the general sense of the related terms in the respective categories. Turning to No. 648 (the sense required), we select the most appropriate expression from the comprehensive list presented. To widen the selection, suggested references are given to allied lists; while in No. 649 are grouped the corresponding antonyms. The groups are arranged, not merely to supply synonyms for some special word, but to suggest new lines of thought and to stimulate the imagination.

The writer at a loss for some archaism, colloquialism, or even slang, will find the *University Thesaurus* a veritable mine, such terms being clearly indicated in the text.

2. To find suitable words to express a given IDEA:

Find in the Index Guide some word relating to the idea, and the categories referred to will supply the need. Thus, suppose a writer wishes to use some less hackneyed phrase than "shuffle off this mortal coil," let him look up "die" or even the phrase itself, and reference to No. 360 will immediately furnish a generous list of synonymous phrases.

3. To find appropriate words or new ideas on any given SUBJECT:

Turn to the subject or any branch of it. The Index Guide itself will frequently suggest various lines of thought, while reference to the indicated groups will provide many words and phrases that should prove helpful.

Thus, suppose "philosophy" is the theme, No. 451 will be found most suggestive. Or again, the subject may be "the drama" (599), "music" (415), "zoology" (368), "psychical research" (992a), or "mythology" (979). Writers may perhaps be hazy about the titles of the ruling chiefs of India. The Thesaurus (875) will prevent applying a Hindu title to a Mohammedan prince. The subject may be such an everyday one as "food" (298), "automobiles" (272), "aviation" (267 and 269a), or various kinds of "amusements" (840); whatever it is, the Thesaurus will prove profitable as regards ideas. Writers and speakers who have acquired the Roget habit do not need to be reminded of this valuable aid.

N.B. To grasp the underlying principle of the classification, study the *Tabular Synopsis of Categories*, which begins on the next page. Reference may be made direct from this Synopsis to the body of the work; but it is usually found more convenient to consult the Index Guide first.

The Guide numbers always refer to the *section numbers* in the text and *not* to pages.

Tabular Synopsis of Categories

Class 1. Abstract Relations
Section 1. Existence
1. ABSTRACT
   - 1. Existence
   - 2. Nonexistence
2. CONCRETE
   - 3. Substantiality
   - 4. Unsubstantiality
3. FORMAL
   - *Internal*
   - 5. Intrinsicality
   - *External*
   - 6. Extrinsicality
4. MODAL
   - *Absolute*
   - 7. State
   - *Relative*
   - 8. Circumstance

Section 2. Relation
1. ABSOLUTE
   - 9. Relation
   - 10. Irrelation
   - 11. Consanguinity
   - 12. Correlation
   - 13. Identity
   - 14. Contrariety
   - 15. Difference
2. CONTINUOUS
   - 16. Uniformity
   - 16a. Nonuniformity
3. PARTIAL
   - 17. Similarity
   - 18. Dissimilarity
   - 19. Imitation
   - 20. Nonimitation
   - 20a. Variation
   - 21. Copy
   - 22. Prototype
4. GENERAL
   - 23. Agreement
   - 24. Disagreement

Section 3. Quantity
1. SIMPLE
   - *Absolute*
   - 25. Quantity
   - *Relative*
   - 26. Degree
2. COMPARATIVE
   - 27. Equality
   - 28. Inequality
   - 29. Mean
   - 30. Compensation
   - *By Comparison with a Standard*
   - 31. Greatness
   - 32. Smallness
   - *By Comparison with a Similar Object*
   - 33. Superiority
   - 34. Inferiority
   - *Changes in Quantity*
   - 35. Increase
   - 36. Decrease
3. CONJUNCTIVE
   - 37. Addition
   - 38. Nonaddition
      Deduction
   - 39. Adjunct
   - 40. Remainder
   - 40a. Decrement
   - 41. Mixture
   - 42. Simpleness
   - 43. Junction
   - 44. Disjunction
   - 45. Vinculum
   - 46. Coherence
   - 47. Incoherence
   - 48. Combination
   - 49. Decomposition
4. CONCRETE
   - 50. Whole
   - 51. Part
   - 52. Completeness
   - 53. Incompleteness
   - 54. Composition
   - 55. Exclusion
   - 56. Component
   - 57. Extraneous

Section 4. Order
1. GENERAL
   - 58. Order
   - 59. Disorder
   - 60. Arrangement
   - 61. Derangement

x

2. CONSECUTIVE		62. Precedence	63. Sequence
		64. Precursor	65. Sequel
		66. Beginning	67. End
			68. Middle
		69. Continuity	70. Discontinuity
		71. Term	
3. COLLECTIVE		72. Assemblage	73. Nonassemblage Dispersion
		74. Focus	
4. DISTRIBUTIVE		75. Class	
		76. Inclusion	77. Exclusion
		78. Generality	79. Speciality
5. CATEGORICAL		80. Rule	81. Multiformity
		82. Conformity	83. Unconformity

Section 5. Number

1. ABSTRACT		84. Number	
		85. Numeration	
		86. List	
2. DETERMINATE		87. Unity	88. Accompaniment
		89. Duality	
		90. Duplication	91. Bisection
		92. Triality	
		93. Triplication	94. Trisection
		95. Quaternity	
		96. Quadruplication	97. Quadrisection
		98. Five, etc.	99. Quinquesection, etc.
3. INDETERMINATE		100. Plurality	100a. Fraction
			101. Zero
		102. Multitude	103. Fewness
		104. Repetition	
		105. Infinity	

Section 6. Time

1. ABSOLUTE		106. Time	107. Neverness
		Definite	*Indefinite*
		108. Period	109. Course
		108a. Contingent Duration	
		110. Diuturnity	111. Transience
		112. Perpetuity	113. Instantaneity
		114. Chronometry	115. Anachronism
2. RELATIVE	*1. To Succession*	116. Priority	117. Posteriority
		118. Present time	119. Different time
		120. Synchronism	
		121. Futurity	122. Preterition
	2. To a Period	123. Newness	124. Oldness
		125. Morning	126. Evening
		127. Youth	128. Age
		129. Infant	130. Veteran
			131. Adolescence

xi

3. To an Effect or Purpose	132. Earliness	133. Lateness
	134. Occasion	135. Intempestivity
3. RECURRENT	136. Frequency	137. Infrequency
	138. Periodicity	139. Irregularity

Section 7. Change
1. SIMPLE	140. Change	141. Permanence
	142. Cessation	143. Continuance
	144. Conversion	
		145. Reversion
	146. Revolution	
	147. Substitution	148. Interchange
2. COMPLEX	149. Changeableness	150. Stability
	Present	*Future*
	151. Eventuality	152. Destiny

Section 8. Causation
1. CONSTANCY OF SEQUENCE	*Constant Antecedent*	*Constant Sequence*
	153. Cause	154. Effect
	Assignment of Cause	*Absence of Assignment*
	155. Attribution	156. Chance
2. CONNECTION BETWEEN CAUSE AND EFFECT	157. Power	158. Impotence
	Degrees of Power	
	159. Strength	160. Weakness
3. POWER IN OPERATION	161. Production	162. Destruction
	163. Reproduction	
	164. Producer	165. Destroyer
	166. Paternity	167. Posterity
	168. Productiveness	169. Unproductiveness
	170. Agency	
	171. Energy	172. Inertness
	173. Violence	174. Moderation
4. INDIRECT POWER	175. Influence	175a. Absence of Influence
	176. Tendency	
	177. Liability	
5. COMBINATION OF CAUSES	178. Concurrence	179. Counteraction

Class 2. Space

Section 1. Space in General
1. ABSTRACT SPACE	*Indefinite*	180a. Inextension
	180. Space	*Definite*
		181. Region
		Limited
		182. Place
2. RELATIVE SPACE	183. Situation	
	184. Location	185. Displacement
3. EXISTENCE IN SPACE	186. Presence	187. Absence
	188. Inhabitant	189. Abode
	190. Contents	191. Receptacle

Section 2. Dimensions
1. GENERAL	192. Size	193. Littleness
	194. Expansion	195. Contraction
	196. Distance	197. Nearness
	198. Interval	199. Contiguity
2. LINEAR	200. Length	201. Shortness
	202. Breadth	203. Narrowness
	Thickness	Thinness
	204. Layer	205. Filament
	206. Height	207. Lowness
	208. Depth	209. Shallowness
	210. Summit	211. Base
	212. Verticality	213. Horizontality
	214. Pendency	215. Support
	216. Parallelism	217. Obliquity
	218. Inversion	
	219. Crossing	
	220. Exteriority	221. Interiority
	222. Centrality	
	223. Covering	224. Lining
	225. Investment	226. Divestment
	227. Circumjacence	228. Interjacence

3. Centrical	*1. General*	229. Circumscription	
		230. Outline	
		231. Edge	
		232. Inclosure	
		233. Limit	
	2. Special	234. Front	235. Rear
		236. Laterality	237. Contraposition
		238. Dextrality	239. Sinistrality

Section 3. Form
1. General	240. Form	241. Amorphism
	242. Symmetry	243. Distortion
2. Special	244. Angularity	
	245. Curvature	246. Straightness
	247. Circularity	248. Convolution
	249. Rotundity	
3. Superficial	250. Convexity	252. Concavity
	251. Flatness	
	253. Sharpness	254. Bluntness
	255. Smoothness	256. Roughness
	257. Notch	
	258. Fold	
	259. Furrow	
	260. Opening	261. Closure
	262. Perforator	263. Stopper

Section 4. Motion
1. Motion in General	264. Motion	265. Quiescence
	266. Journey	267. Navigation
	268. Traveler	269. Mariner
		269a. Aeronaut
	270. Transference	
	271. Carrier	
	272. Vehicle	273. Ship
2. Degrees of Motion	274. Velocity	275. Slowness
3. Conjoined with Force	276. Impulse	277. Recoil
4. With reference to Direction	278. Direction	279. Deviation
	280. Precession	281. Sequence
	282. Progression	283. Regression
	284. Propulsion	285. Traction
	286. Approach	287. Recession
	288. Attraction	289. Repulsion
	290. Convergence	291. Divergence
	292. Arrival	293. Departure
	294. Ingress	295. Egress
	296. Reception	297. Ejection
	298. Food	299. Excretion
	300. Insertion	301. Extraction
	302. Passage	
	303. Overrun	304. Shortcoming
	305. Ascent	306. Descent
	307. Elevation	308. Depression
	309. Leap	310. Plunge
	311. Circuition	
	312. Rotation	313. Evolution
	314. Oscillation	
	315. Agitation	

Class 3. Matter
Section 1. Matter in General
316. Materiality	317. Immateriality
318. World	
319. Gravity	320. Levity

Section 2. Inorganic Matter
1. Solids	321. Density	322. Rarity
	323. Hardness	324. Softness
	325. Elasticity	326. Inelasticity
	327. Tenacity	328. Brittleness
	329. Texture	
	330. Pulverulence	
	331. Friction	332. Lubrication
2. Fluids	*1. In General*	333. Fluidity	334. Gaseity
		335. Liquefaction	336. Vaporization

	2. *Specific*		337. Water	338. Air
			339. Moisture	340. Dryness
			341. Ocean	342. Land
			343. Gulf Lake	344. Plain
			345. Marsh	346. Island
	3. *In Motion*		347. Stream	
			348. River	349. Wind
			350. Conduit	351. Air Pipe
	3. IMPERFECT FLUIDS		352. Semiliquidity	353. Bubble Cloud
			354. Pulpiness	355. Unctuousness
				356. Oil
				356a. Resin

Section 3. Organic Matter

1. VITALITY	1. *In General*		357. Organization	358. Inorganization
			359. Life	360. Death
				361. Killing
				362. Corpse
				363. Interment
	2. *Special*		364. Animality	365. Vegetation
			366. Animal	367. Vegetable
			368. Zoology	369. Botany
			370. Cicuration	371. Agriculture
			372. Mankind	
			372a. Anthropology	
			373. Man	374. Woman
2. SENSATION	1. *General*		375. Sensibility	376. Insensibility
			377. Pleasure	378. Pain
	2. *Special*	(1) *Touch*	379. Touch	
			380. Sensations of Touch	381. Numbness
		(2) *Heat*	382. Heat	383. Cold
			384. Calefaction	385. Refrigeration
			386. Furnace	387. Refrigeratory
			388. Fuel	
			389. Thermometer	
		(3) *Taste*	390. Taste	391. Insipidity
			392. Pungency	
			393. Condiment	
			394. Savoriness	395. Unsavoriness
			396. Sweetness	397. Sourness
		(4) *Odor*	398. Odor	399. Inodorousness
			400. Fragrance	401. Fetor
		(5) *Sound*	(i) *Sound in General*	
			402. Sound	403. Silence
			404. Loudness	405. Faintness
			(ii) *Specific Sounds*	
			406. Snap	407. Roll
			408. Resonance	408a. Nonresonance
				409. Sibilation
			410. Stridor	
			411. Cry	412. Ululation
			(iii) *Musical Sounds*	
			413. Melody Concord	414. Discord
			415. Music	
			416. Musician	
			417. Musical Instruments	
			(iv) *Perception of Sound*	
			418. Hearing	419. Deafness
		(6) *Light*	(i) *Light in General*	
			420. Light	421. Darkness
				422. Dimness
			423. Luminary	424. Shade
			425. Transparency	426. Opacity
				427. Semitransparency
			(ii) *Specific Light*	
			428. Color	429. Achromatism
			430. Whiteness	431. Blackness
			432. Gray	433. Brown
			434. Redness	435. Greenness

436.	Yellowness	437.	Purple
438.	Blueness	439.	Orange
440.	Variegation		

(iii) *Perceptions of Light*

441.	Vision	442.	Blindness
		443.	Dim-sightedness
444.	Spectator		
445.	Optical Instruments		
446.	Visibility	447.	Invisibility
448.	Appearance	449.	Disappearance

Class 4. Intellect
Division 1. Formation of Ideas

Section 1. Operations of Intellect in General

450.	Intellect	450a.	Absence of Intellect
451.	Thought	452.	Incogitance
453.	Idea	454.	Topic

Section 2. Precursory Conditions and Operations

455.	Curiosity	456.	Incuriosity
457.	Attention	458.	Inattention
459.	Care	460.	Neglect
461.	Inquiry	462.	Answer
463.	Experiment		
464.	Comparison		
465.	Discrimination	465a.	Indiscrimination
466.	Measurement		

Section 3. Materials for Reasoning

467.	Evidence	468.	Counterevidence
		469.	Qualification

Degrees of Evidence

470.	Possibility	471.	Impossibility
472.	Probability	473.	Improbability
474.	Certainty	475.	Uncertainty

Section 4. Reasoning Processes

476.	Reasoning	477.	Intuition
			Sophistry
478.	Demonstration	479.	Confutation

Section 5. Results of Reasoning

480.	Judgment	481.	Misjudgment
480a.	Discovery		
482.	Overestimation	483.	Underestimation
484.	Belief	485.	Unbelief
			Doubt
486.	Credulity	487.	Incredulity
488.	Assent	489.	Dissent
490.	Knowledge	491.	Ignorance
490a.	Science		
492.	Scholar	493.	Ignoramus
494.	Truth	495.	Error
496.	Maxim	497.	Absurdity

Faculties

498.	Intelligence	499.	Imbecility
	Wisdom		Folly
500.	Sage	501.	Fool
502.	Sanity	503.	Insanity
		504.	Madman

Section 6. Extension of Thought

1. To the Past

505.	Memory	506.	Oblivion

2. To the Future

507.	Expectation	508.	Inexpectation
		509.	Disappointment
510.	Foresight		
511.	Prediction		
512.	Omen		
513.	Oracle		

Section 7. Creative Thought

514.	Supposition	
515.	Imagination	

Division 2. Communication of Ideas

Section 1. Nature of Ideas Communicated

516.	Meaning	517.	Unmeaningness
518.	Intelligibility	519.	Unintelligibility
		520.	Equivocalness
521.	Metaphor		
522.	Interpretation	523.	Misinterpretation
524.	Interpreter		

Section 2. Modes of Communication

525.	Manifestation	526.	Latency
527.	Information	528.	Concealment

xv

			529. Disclosure	530. Ambush
			531. Publication	
			532. News	533. Secret
			534. Messenger	
			535. Affirmation	536. Negation
			537. Teaching	538. Misteaching
				539. Learning
			540. Teacher	541. Learner
				542. School
			543. Veracity	544. Falsehood
				545. Deception
				546. Untruth
			547. Dupe	548. Deceiver
				549. Exaggeration

Section 3. Means of Communication
    1. *Natural Means*

			550. Indication	
			551. Record	552. Obliteration
			553. Recorder	
			554. Representation	555. Misrepresentation
			556. Painting	
			Black and white	
			557. Sculpture	
			558. Engraving	
			559. Artist	
	2. *Conventional Means*	1. *Language Generally*	560. Language	
			561. Letter	
			562. Word	563. Neology
			564. Nomenclature	565. Misnomer
			566. Phrase	
			567. Grammar	568. Solecism
			569. Style	
			Qualities of Style	
			570. Perspicuity	571. Obscurity
			572. Conciseness	573. Diffuseness
			574. Vigor	575. Feebleness
			576. Plainness	577. Ornament
			578. Elegance	579. Inelegance
		2. *Spoken Language*	580. Voice	581. Aphonia
			582. Speech	583. Stammering
			584. Loquacity	585. Taciturnity
			586. Allocution	587. Response
			588. Interlocution	589. Soliloquy
		3. *Written Language*	590. Writing	591. Printing
			592. Correspondence	593. Book
			594. Description	
			595. Dissertation	
			596. Compendium	
			597. Poetry	598. Prose
			599. The Drama	

Class 5. Volition
Division 1. Individual Volition
Section 1. Volition in General
    1. *Acts*

			600. Will	601. Necessity
			602. Willingness	603. Unwillingness
			604. Resolution	605. Irresolution
			604a. Perseverance	
			606. Obstinacy	607. Tergiversation
				608. Caprice
			609. Choice	609a. Absence of Choice
				610. Rejection
			611. Predetermination	612. Impulse
			613. Habit	614. Desuetude
	2. *Causes*		615. Motive	615a. Absence of Motive
			617. Plea	616. Dissuasion
	3. *Objects*		618. Good	619. Evil

Section 2. Prospective Volition
    1. *Conceptional*

			620. Intention	621. Chance
			622. Pursuit	623. Avoidance
				624. Relinquishment
			625. Business	

		626. Plan	
		627. Method	
		628. Mid-course	629. Circuit
		630. Requirement	
	2. *Subservience to Ends*	1. *Actual Subservience*	
		631. Instrumentality	
		632. Means	
		633. Instrument	
		634. Substitute	
		635. Materials	
		636. Store	
		637. Provision	638. Waste
		639. Sufficiency	640. Insufficiency
		641. Redundance	
		2. *Degree of Subservience*	
		642. Importance	643. Unimportance
		644. Utility	645. Inutility
		646. Expedience	647. Inexpedience
		648. Goodness	649. Badness
		650. Perfection	651. Imperfection
		652. Cleanness	653. Uncleanness
		654. Health	655. Disease
		656. Salubrity	657. Insalubrity
		658. Improvement	659. Deterioration
		660. Restoration	661. Relapse
		662. Remedy	663. Bane
		3. *Contingent Subservience*	
		664. Safety	665. Danger
		666. Refuge	667. Pitfall
		668. Warning	
		669. Alarm	
		670. Preservation	
		671. Escape	
		672. Deliverance	
	3. *Precursory Measures*	673. Preparation	674. Nonpreparation
		675. Essay	
		676. Undertaking	
		677. Use	678. Disuse
			679. Misuse
Section 3. Action			
	1. *Simple*	680. Action	681. Inaction
		682. Activity	683. Inactivity
		684. Haste	685. Leisure
		686. Exertion	687. Repose
		688. Fatigue	689. Refreshment
		690. Agent	
		691. Workshop	
	2. *Complex*	692. Conduct	
		693. Direction	
		694. Director	
		695. Advice	
		696. Council	
		697. Precept	
		698. Skill	699. Unskillfulness
		700. Proficient	701. Bungler
		702. Cunning	703. Artlessness
Section 4. Antagonism			
	1. *Conditional*	704. Difficulty	705. Facility
	2. *Active*	706. Hindrance	707. Aid
		708. Opposition	709. Cooperation
		710. Opponent	711. Auxiliary
		712. Party	
		713. Discord	714. Concord
		715. Defiance	
		716. Attack	717. Defense
		718. Retaliation	719. Resistance
		720. Contention	721. Peace
		722. Warfare	723. Pacification
		724. Mediation	
		725. Submission	
		726. Combatant	
		727. Arms	
		728. Arena	

Section 5. Results of Action

	729. Completion	730. Noncompletion
	731. Success	732. Failure
	733. Trophy	
	734. Prosperity	735. Adversity
		736. Mediocrity

Division 2. Intersocial Volition
Section 1. General

737. Authority	738. Laxity
739. Severity	740. Lenity
741. Command	
742. Disobedience	743. Obedience
744. Compulsion	
745. Master	746. Servant
747. Scepter	
748. Freedom	749. Subjection
750. Liberation	751. Restraint
	752. Prison
753. Keeper	754. Prisoner
755. Commission	756. Abrogation
	757. Resignation
758. Consignee	
759. Deputy	

Section 2. Special

760. Permission	761. Prohibition
762. Consent	
763. Offer	764. Refusal
765. Request	766. Deprecation
767. Petitioner	

Section 3. Conditional

768. Promise	768a. Release
769. Compact	
770. Conditions	
771. Security	
772. Observance	773. Nonobservance
	774. Compromise

Section 4. Possessive Relations

1. Property in General

775. Acquisition	776. Loss
777. Possession	777a. Exemption
778. Participation	
779. Possessor	
780. Property	
781. Retention	782. Relinquishment

2. Transfer of Property

783. Transfer	
784. Giving	785. Receiving
786. Apportionment	
787. Lending	788. Borrowing
789. Taking	790. Restitution
791. Stealing	
792. Thief	
793. Booty	

3. Interchange of Property

794. Barter	
795. Purchase	796. Sale
797. Merchant	
798. Merchandise	
799. Mart	

4. Monetary Relations

800. Money	
801. Treasurer	
802. Treasury	
803. Wealth	804. Poverty
805. Credit	806. Debt
807. Payment	808. Nonpayment
809. Expenditure	810. Receipt
811. Accounts	
812. Price	813. Discount
814. Dearness	815. Cheapness
816. Liberality	817. Economy
818. Prodigality	819. Parsimony

Class 6. Affections
Section 1. Affections in General

820. Affections	
821. Feeling	
822. Sensibility	823. Insensibility
824. Excitation	
825. Excitability	826. Inexcitability

Section 2. Personal

1. Passive

	827. Pleasure	828. Pain
	829. Pleasurableness	830. Painfulness
	831. Content	832. Discontent
		833. Regret
	834. Relief	835. Aggravation
	836. Cheerfulness	837. Dejection
	838. Rejoicing	839. Lamentation
	840. Amusement	841. Weariness
	842. Wit	843. Dullness
	844. Humorist	

2. Discriminative

	845. Beauty	846. Ugliness
	847. Ornament	848. Blemish
		849. Simplicity
	850. Taste	851. Vulgarity
	852. Fashion	
		853. Ridiculousness
		854. Fop
		855. Affectation
		856. Ridicule
		857. Laughingstock

3. Prospective

	858. Hope	859. Hopelessness
		860. Fear
	861. Courage	862. Cowardice
	863. Rashness	864. Caution
	865. Desire	867. Dislike
	866. Indifference	
		868. Fastidiousness
		869. Satiety

4. Contemplative

	870. Wonder	871. Expectance
	872. Prodigy	

5. Extrinsic

	873. Repute	874. Disrepute
	875. Nobility	876. Commonalty
	877. Title	
	878. Pride	879. Humility
	880. Vanity	881. Modesty
	882. Ostentation	
	883. Celebration	
	884. Boasting	
	885. Insolence	886. Servility
	887. Blusterer	

Section 3. Sympathetic

1. Social

	888. Friendship	889. Enmity
	890. Friend	891. Enemy
	892. Sociality	893. Seclusion
	894. Courtesy	895. Discourtesy
	896. Congratulation	
	897. Love	898. Hate
	899. Favorite	
		900. Resentment
		901. Irascibility
		901a. Sullenness
	902. Endearment	
	903. Marriage	904. Celibacy
		905. Divorce Widowhood

2. Diffusive

	906. Benevolence	907. Malevolence
		908. Malediction
		909. Threat
	910. Philanthropy	911. Misanthropy
	912. Benefactor	913. Evildoer

3. Special

	914. Pity	914a. Pitilessness
	915. Condolence	

4. Retrospective

	916. Gratitude	917. Ingratitude
	918. Forgiveness	919. Revenge
		920. Jealousy
		921. Envy

Section 4. Moral

1. Obligations

	922. Right	923. Wrong
	924. Dueness	925. Undueness
	926. Duty	927. Dereliction
		927a. Exemption

	2. Sentiments	928.	Respect	929.	Disrespect
				930.	Contempt
		931.	Approbation	932.	Disapprobation
		933.	Flattery	934.	Detraction
		935.	Flatterer	936.	Detractor
		937.	Vindication	938.	Accusation
	3. Conditions	939.	Probity	940.	Improbity
				941.	Knave
		942.	Disinterestedness	943.	Selfishness
		944.	Virtue	945.	Vice
		946.	Innocence	947.	Guilt
		948.	Good Man	949.	Bad Man
		950.	Penitence	951.	Impenitence
		952.	Atonement		
	4. Practice	953.	Temperance	954.	Intemperance
				954a.	Sensualist
		955.	Asceticism		
		956.	Fasting	957.	Gluttony
		958.	Sobriety	959.	Drunkenness
		960.	Purity	961.	Impurity
				962.	Libertine
	5. Institutions	963.	Legality	964.	Illegality
		965.	Jurisprudence		
		966.	Tribunal		
		967.	Judge		
		968.	Lawyer		
		969.	Lawsuit		
		970.	Acquittal	971.	Condemnation
				972.	Punishment
		973.	Reward	974.	Penalty
				975.	Scourge

Section 5. Religious

	1. Superhuman Beings and Regions	976.	Deity		
		977.	Angel	978.	Satan
		979.	Mythic and Pagan Deities	980.	Evil Spirits
		981.	Heaven	982.	Hell
	2. Doctrines	983.	Theology		
		983a.	Orthodoxy	984.	Heterodoxy
		985.	Revelation (Biblical)	986.	Sacred Writings (non-Biblical)
	3. Sentiments	987.	Piety	988.	Impiety
				989.	Irreligion
	4. Acts	990.	Worship	991.	Idolatry
				992.	Sorcery
				992a.	Psychical Research
				993.	Spell
				994.	Sorcerer
	5. Institutions	995.	Churchdom		
		996.	Clergy	997.	Laity
		998.	Rite		
		999.	Canonicals		
		1000.	Temple		

Roget's University Thesaurus

Class 1. Abstract Relations

Section 1. Existence

1. Existence

n. **existence**, being, entity, *ens* [*L.*], *esse* [*L.*], subsistence; quid, hypaxis [*rare*], automaton.
  reality, actuality; positiveness etc. *adj.;* fact, matter of fact, sober reality; truth etc. 494; actual existence.
  presence etc. (*existence in space*) 186; coexistence etc. 120.
  stubborn fact; not a dream etc. 515; no joke.
  essence, inmost nature, center of life, inner reality, vital principle.
  [science of existence] ontology.

v. **exist**, be; having being etc. *n.;* subsist, live, breathe, stand, obtain, be the case; occur etc. (*event*) 151; have place, rank, prevail; find oneself, pass the time, vegetate.
  come into existence etc. *n.;* arise etc. (*begin*) 66; come forth etc. (*appear*) 446.
  become etc. (*be converted*) 144; bring into existence etc. 161; coexist, postexist [*rare*], preëxist [*rare*].
  consist in, lie in; be comprised in, be contained in, be constituted by.
  abide, continue, endure, last, remain.

adj. **existing** etc. *v.;* existent, subsistent, under the sun; in existence etc. *n.;* extant; afloat, on foot, current, prevalent; undestroyed.
  real, actual, positive, absolute; factual, veritable, true etc. 494; substantial, substantive; self-existing, self-existent; essential.
  well-founded, well-grounded; unideal, unimagined; not potential etc. 2; authentic.

adv. **actually** etc. *adj.;* in fact, in point of fact, in reality; indeed; *de facto* [*L.*], *ipso facto* [*L.*].

2. Nonexistence

n. **nonexistence**, nonsubsistence; inexistence; nonentity, *nil* [*L.*]; negativeness etc. *adj.;* nullity; nihility; nihilism; *tabula rasa* [*L.*], blank; abeyance; absence etc. 187; no such thing etc. 4; nonbeing, nothingness, oblivion, *non esse* [*L.*].
  annihilation; extinction etc. (*destruction*) 162; extinguishment, extirpation, Nirvana, obliteration.

v. **not exist** etc. 1; have no existence etc. 1; be null and void; cease to exist etc. 1; pass away, perish; be *or* become extinct etc. *adj.;* die out; disappear etc. 449; melt away, dissolve, leave not a rack behind; go, be no more; die etc. 360.
  annihilate, render null, nullify; abrogate etc. 756; destroy etc. 162; take away; remove etc. (*displace*) 185; obliterate, extirpate, deracinate [*rare*].

adj. **inexistent**, nonexistent etc. 1; negative, blank; null, minus, missing, omitted; absent etc. 187; insubstantial, shadowy, spectral, visionary.
  unreal, potential, virtual; baseless, *in nubibus* [*L.*]; unsubstantial etc. 4; vain.
  unborn, uncreated, unbegotten, unconceived, unproduced, unmade.
  perished, annihilated etc. *v.;* extinct, exhausted, gone, lost, departed; defunct etc. (*dead*) 360.
  fabulous, ideal etc. (*imaginary*) 515; supposititious etc. 514.

adv. negatively, virtually etc. *adj.*

3. Substantiality

n. **substantiality**, hypostasis; person, thing, object, article; something, a being, an existence; creature, body, substance, flesh and blood, stuff, substratum; matter etc. 316; corporeity, element, essential nature, groundwork, materiality, substantialness, vital part.
  [totality of existences] world etc. 318; *plenum* [*L.*].

adj. **substantive**, substantial; hypostatic *or* hypostatical; personal, bodily, practical, effective; tangible etc. (*material*) 316; corporeal; right, sober.

adv. **substantially** etc. *adj.;* bodily, essentially.

4. Unsubstantiality

n. **unsubstantiality**, insubstantiality; nothingness, nihility; no degree, no part, no quantity, no thing.
  nothing, naught, *nil* [*L.*], nullity, zero, cipher, no one, nobody; never a one, ne'er a one; no such thing, none in the world; nothing whatever, nothing at all, nothing on earth; not a particle etc. (*smallness*) 32; all talk, all moonshine, all stuff and nonsense; matter of no importance, matter of no consequence.
  thing of naught, man of straw, John Doe and Richard Roe, fagot (*or* faggot) voter [*polit. cant, Eng.*]; *nominis umbra* [*L.*], nonentity, cipher, nought, nothing, obscurity, lay figure; flash in the pan, *vox et praeterea nihil* [*L.*].
  phantom etc. (*fallacy of vision*) 443; shadow; dream etc. (*imagination*) 515; *ignis fatuus*

5. Intrinsicality

[*L.*] etc. (*luminary*) 423; "such stuff as dreams are made on" [*Tempest*]; air, thin air; bubble etc. 353; mockery.

blank; void etc. (*absence*) 187; hollowness.

inanity, fatuity, fool's paradise.

v. **vanish**, evaporate, fade, fleet, sink, fly, dissolve, melt away; die, die away, die out; disappear etc. 449.

adj. **unsubstantial**; baseless, groundless; ungrounded; without foundation, having no foundation.

visionary etc. (*imaginary*) 515; immaterial etc. 317; spectral etc. 980; dreamy; shadowy; ethereal, airy, gaseous, imponderable, tenuous, vague, vaporous, dreamlike, mushroom; cloud-built, cloud-formed; gossamery, illusory, insubstantial, unreal, unsolid [*rare*], slight, bodiless.

vacant, vacuous; empty etc. 187; eviscerated; blank, hollow; nominal; null; inane [*rare*].

5. Intrinsicality

n. **intrinsicality**, intrinsicalness, inbeing, inherence, inhesion, immanence, indwelling; subjectiveness; ego; egohood; essence, quintessence, elixir; essentialness etc. *adj.;* essential part, incarnation, quiddity, gist, pith, core, kernel, marrow, sap, lifeblood, backbone, heart, soul, life, substance, flower; important part etc. (*importance*) 642.

principle, nature, constitution, character, type, quality, crasis, diathesis.

temper, temperament; spirit, humor, grain, nature, vein, mood, frame, cue; disposition; habit.

capacity, endowment; capability etc. (*power*) 157.

aspects, moods, declensions, features; peculiarities etc. (*specialty*) 79; idiosyncrasy; idiocrasy etc. (*tendency*) 176; diagnostics.

v. be in the blood, run in the blood; be born so; be intrinsic etc. *adj.*

adj. **intrinsic**, intrinsical; derived from within, subjective; idiocratic *or* idiocratical, idiosyncratic *or* idiosyncratical; fundamental, normal; implanted, inherent, essential, natural; innate, inborn, inbred, ingrained, indwelling, inwrought; coeval with birth, genetic, genetous, haematobious, syngenic; radical, incarnate, thoroughbred, hereditary, inherited, immanent; congenital, congenite [*obs.*]; connate, running in the blood; ingenerate, ingenit *or* ingenite [*obs.*], ingenita [*obs.*], indigenous; in the grain etc. *n.;* bred in the bone, instinctive; inward, internal etc. 221; to the manner born; virtual.

characteristic etc. (*special*) 79, (*indicative*) 550; invariable, incurable, ineradicable, fixed.

adv. **intrinsically** etc. *adj.;* at bottom, in the main, in effect, practically, virtually, substantially, *au fond* [*F.*]; fairly.

6. Extrinsicality

n. **extrinsicality**, objectiveness, *non ego* [*L.*]; extraneousness etc. 57; accident.

adj. **extrinsic**, extrinsical; derived from without; objective; extraneous etc. (*foreign*) 57; modal, adventitious; ascititious, adscititious; incidental, accidental, nonessential, unessential, accessory; contingent, fortuitous, casual, subsidiary.

implanted, ingrafted; inculcated, infused.

outward etc. (*external*) 220.

adv. **extrinsically** etc. *adj.*

7. State

n. **state**, condition, category, estate, lot, case, trim, mood, temper; aspect etc. (*appearance*) 448.

dilemma, pass, predicament, quandary, corner, hole, *impasse* [*F.*], fix, pickle, plight.

frame, fabric etc. 329; stamp, set, fit, mold *or* mould; constitution, habitude, diathesis.

form, fettle, shape, kilter *or* kelter; tone, tenor, turn; trim, guise, fashion, light, complexion, style, character; build etc. 240; mode, modality, schesis [*obs.*]

v. be in–, possess–, enjoy- a state etc. *n.;* be on a footing, do, fare; come to pass.

adj. **conditional**, modal, formal; structural, organic.

adv. **conditionally** etc. *adj.;* as the matter stands, as things are; such being the case etc. 8; *quae cum ita sint* [*L.*].

8. Circumstance

n. **circumstance**, situation, phase, position, posture, attitude, place, point; terms; *régime* [*F.*]; footing, standing, status.

occasion, juncture, conjuncture; contingency etc. (*event*) 151.

predicament; emergency; exigency, crisis, pinch, pass, plight, push; occurrence; turning point.

bearings, how the land lies.

adj. **circumstantial**; given, conditional, provisional; critical; modal; contingent, incidental; adventitious etc. (*extrinsic*) 6; limitative.

detailed, minute, full, fussy.

adv. **thus**, in such wise; in *or* under the circumstances etc. *n.;* in *or* under the conditions etc. 7.

accordingly; that being the case; such being the case; that being so; since, seeing that.

as matters stand; as things go, as times go.

conditionally, provided, if, in case; if so, if so be, if it be so; if it so happen, if it so turn out; in the event of; in such a contingency, in such a case, in such an event; provisionally, unless, without.

according to circumstances, according to the occasion; as it may happen, as it may turn out, as it may be; as the case may be, as the wind blows.

Section 2. Relation

9. Relation

n. **relation**, bearing, reference, connection, concern, cognation, applicability, apposition, appositeness; correlation etc. 12; analogy; similarity etc. 17; affinity, homology, alliance, nearness, rapport, homogeneity, association; approximation etc. (*nearness*) 197; filiation etc. (*consanguinity*) 11; interest; relevancy etc. 23; dependency, relationship, relative position; correlation, interrelation, interconnection.

ratio, proportion; comparison etc. 464.

link, tie, bond of union, privity [*law*].

v. **be related** etc. *adj.;* have a relation etc. *n.;* relate to, refer to; bear upon, regard, concern, touch, affect, have to do with; pertain to, belong to, appertain to; answer to; interest.

associate, connect; bring into relation with, bring to bear upon; draw a parallel; link etc. 43.

adj. **relative**; correlative etc. 12; relating to etc. *v.;* relative to, in relation with, referrable *or* referable *or* referrible to; belonging to etc. *v.;* appurtenant to, in common with.

related, connected; implicated, associated, affiliated; allied, allied to; collateral, connate [*rare*], cognate, congenerous, connatural, affinitive, paronymous; *en rapport* [*F.*], in touch with.

approximative, approximating; proportional, proportionate, proportionable; allusive, comparable, equiparable [*obs. or rare*].

relevant etc. (*apt*) 23; applicable, equiparant; in the same category etc. 75; like etc. 17.

adv. **relatively** etc. *adj.;* pertinently etc. 23.

thereof; as to, as for, as respects, as regards; about; concerning etc. *v.;* anent; relating to, as relates to; with relation to, with reference to, with respect to, with regard to; in respect of; speaking of, *à propos* [*F.*] of; in connection with; by the way, by the by; whereas; for as much as, in as much as; in point of, as far as;

on the part of, on the score of; under the head of etc. (*class*) 75; in the matter of, *in re* [*L.*].

10. Irrelation
[want or absence of relation]

n. **irrelation**, dissociation; misrelation; inapplicability; inconnection; multifariousness; disconnection etc. (*disjunction*) 44; inconsequence, independence; incommensurability; irreconcilableness etc. (*disagreement*) 24; heterogeneity; unconformity etc. 83; irrelevancy, impertinence, *nihil ad rem* [*L.*]; intrusion etc. 24; non-pertinence.

v. **not concern** etc. 9; have no relation to etc. 9; have no bearing upon, have no concern with etc. 9; have no business with; have nothing to do with, have no business there; intrude etc. 24.
bring–, drag–, lug- in by the head and shoulders.

adj. **irrelative**, irrespective, unrelated, disrelated, irrelate [*rare*]; arbitrary; independent, unallied; disconnected, unconnected, adrift, isolated, insular; extraneous, strange, alien, foreign, outlandish, exotic.

not comparable, incommensurable, heterogeneous; unconformable etc. 83.

irrelevant, inapplicable; not pertinent, not to the purpose; impertinent [*legal*], unessential, inessential, accidental, inapposite, beside the mark; aside from–, away from–, foreign to–, beside- the -purpose, –question, –transaction, –point; misplaced etc. (*intrusive*) 24; traveling out of the record.

remote, far-fetched, out-of-the-way, forced, neither here nor there, quite another thing; detached, apart, segregated, segregate; disquiparant.

multifarious; discordant etc. 24.

incidental, parenthetical, *obiter dictum* [*L.*], episodic.

adv. **parenthetically** etc. *adj.;* by the way, by the by; *en passant* [*F.*], incidentally, *obiter* [*L.*]; irrespectively etc. *adj.;* without reference to, without regard to; in the abstract etc. 87; *a se* [*L.*].

11. Consanguinity
[relations of kindred]

n. **consanguinity**, relationship, kindred, blood; parentage etc. (*paternity*) 166; filiation, affiliation; lineage, agnation, connation [*obs.*], cognation, connection, alliance; people [as, my *people*], family, family connection, family tie; ties of blood, blood relation; nepotism.

12. Correlation

kinsman, kinsfolk; kith and kin; relation, relative; connection; sib [*rare*]; next of kin; uncle, aunt, nephew, niece; cousin, cousin-german; first cousin, second cousin; cousin once removed, cousin twice removed etc.; near relation, distant relation; brother, sister, one's own flesh and blood.
family, fraternity; brotherhood, sisterhood, cousinhood.
race, stock, generation; sept etc. 166; stirps, side; strain; breed, clan, tribe.

v. **be related to** etc. *adj.;* claim relationship with etc. *n.*

adj. **related**, akin, sib [*Scot. or archaic*], consanguineous, of the blood, family, allied, collateral; cognate, agnate, connate [*rare*]; kindred; affiliated; fraternal.
intimately related, nearly related, closely related, remotely related, distantly related; intimately allied, nearly allied, closely allied, remotely allied, distantly allied; affinal, german.

12. Correlation
[double or reciprocal relation]

n. **reciprocalness** etc. *adj.;* reciprocity, reciprocality, reciprocation; mutuality, correspondence, correlation, interrelation, interconnection, interdependence; interchange etc. 148; exchange, barter, *quid pro quo* [*L.*].
alternation, seesaw, shuttle [*rare*], to-and-fro. reciprocitist.

v. **reciprocate**, alternate, interact; interchange etc. 148; exchange; counterchange.

adj. **reciprocal**, mutual, commutual [*rare*], correlative; correspondent, corresponding; alternate; interchangeable; international; complemental, complementary; equivalent.

adv. *mutatis mutandis* [*L.*]; *vice versa* [*L.*]; each other; by turns etc. 148; reciprocally etc. *adj.*

13. Identity

n. **identity**, sameness, identicalness, unity, selfsameness, coincidence, coalescence; convertibility; equality etc. 27; selfness, self, oneself; identification.
connaturality, connature, connaturalness, homogeneity.
monotony; tautology etc. (*repetition*) 104.
facsimile etc. (*copy*) 21; homoousia; *alter ego* [*L.*] etc. (*similar*) 17; *ipsissima verba* [*L.*] etc. (*exactness*) 494; same; self-same, very same, one and the same; counterpart; very thing, actual thing; no other.

v. **be identical** etc. *adj.;* coincide, coalesce.

treat as the same, render the same; treat as identical; render identical; identify; recognize the identity of.

adj. **identical**; self, ilk [*archaic*]; the identical same etc. *n.;* selfsame, homoousian, one and the same; ditto.
coincident, coinciding, coalescing, coalescent, indistinguishable; one; equivalent etc. (*equal*) 27; much the same, much of a muchness; unaltered.

adv. **identically** etc. *adj.;* on all fours with; *ibidem* [*L.*], *ibid.*

14. Contrariety
[noncoincidence]

n. **contrariety**, contrast, foil, antithesis, antipode, counterpole, counterpoint; counterpart; complement; *vis-à-vis* [*F.*], oppositeness; contradiction; antagonism etc. (*opposition*) 708; clashing, repugnance, antipathy.
inversion etc. 218; the opposite, the reverse, the inverse, the converse, the antipodes, the other extreme.

v. **be contrary** etc. *adj.;* contrast with, oppose, antithesize [*rare*]; differ *toto coelo* [*L.*].
invert, reverse, turn the tables; turn topsy-turvy, turn end for end, turn upside down; retrograde, transpose, invaginate, intussuscept.
contradict, contravene; antagonize etc. 708.

adj. **contrary**, contrarious [*archaic*], contrariant [*rare*], opposite, counter, dead against; adverse, averse, converse, reverse; opposed, antithetical, contrasted, antipodean, antagonistic, opposing; conflicting, inconsistent, contradictory, at cross purposes; negative; hostile, inimical etc. 703.
differing *toto coelo* [*L.*]; diametrically opposite; as opposite as black and white, as opposite as light and darkness, as opposite as fire and water, as opposite as the poles; "Hyperion to a satyr" [*Hamlet*]; quite the contrary, quite the reverse; no such thing, just the other way, *tout au contraire* [*F.*].

adv. **contrarily** etc. *adj.;* contra, contrariwise, *per contra* [*L.*], on the contrary, nay rather; *vice versa* [*L.*]; on the other hand etc. (*in compensation*) 30.

15. Difference

n. **difference**; variance, variation, variety; diversity, divergence, heterogeneity, disconguity, contrast, inconformity, incompatibility, antithesis, antitheticalness, discrepation [*rare*], dissimilarity etc. 18; disagreement etc. 24; disparity etc. (*inequality*) 28; distinction,

17. Similarity

dissimilitude [*rare*], distinctness, contradiction, contradictoriness, contrariety, contradistinction; alteration.

nice distinction, fine distinction, delicate distinction, subtle distinction; shade of difference, nuance; discrimination etc. 465; differentia.

different thing, something else, apple off another tree, another pair of shoes; this, that, or the other.

modification, commutation [*rare*], moods and tenses.

v. **be different** etc. *adj.;* differ, vary, ablude [*obs.*], mismatch, contrast; diverge from, depart from, deviate from, disaccord with, discrepate [*rare*]; divaricate; differ *toto coelo* [*L.*], differ *longo intervallo* [*L.*].

vary, modify etc. (*change*) 140.

discriminate etc. 465.

adj. **differing** etc. *v.;* different, diverse, heterogeneous; distinguishable; varied, variant, divergent, contrastive, incongruous, discrepant, dissonant, inharmonious, disparate, inconformable, differential, modified; diversified, various, divers [*archaic*], all manner of; variform etc. 81.

other, another, not the same; unequal etc. 28; unmatched; widely apart.

distinctive, characteristic; discriminative, differentiative, distinguishing; diacritic, diacritical; diagnostic.

adv. **differently** etc. *adj.*

16. Uniformity

n. **uniformity**; homogeneity, homogeneousness; stability, continuity, permanence, consistency; connature [*rare*], connaturality [*rare*], connaturalness; homology; accordance; conformity etc. 82; agreement etc. 23; consonance, uniformness.

regularity, constancy, evenness, sameness, unity, even tenor, routine; monotony.

v. **be uniform** etc. *adj.;* accord with etc. 23; run through.

become uniform etc. *adj.;* conform to etc. 82.

render uniform etc. *adj.;* assimilate, level, smooth, dress.

adj. **uniform**; homogeneous, homologous; of a piece, consistent, connatural; singsong, drear [*rare*], drearisome, dreary, monotonous, even, equable, constant, level; invariable; regular, unchanged, undeviating, unvaried, undiversified, unvarying; jog-trot.

adv. **uniformly** etc. *adj.;* uniformly with etc. (*conformably*) 82; in harmony with etc. (*agreeing*) 23; in a rut.

always, ever, evermore, perpetually, forever, everlastingly, invariably, without exception, never otherwise; by clockwork.

16a. Nonuniformity
[absence or want of uniformity]

n. **diversity**, irregularity, unevenness; multiformity etc. 81; unconformity etc. 83; roughness etc. 256; dissimilarity, dissimilitude, divarication, divergence, heteromorphism, heterogeneity.

adj. **diversified**, varied, irregular, checkered, daedal, uneven, rough etc. 256; multifarious; multiform etc. 81; of various kinds; all manner of, all sorts of, all kinds of.

adv. in all manner of ways; here, there, and everywhere.

17. Similarity

n. **similarity**, resemblance, likeness, similitude [*rare*], semblance, consimilarity [*rare*]; affinity, approximation, parallelism; agreement etc. 23; analogy, analogicalness; correspondence, homoiousia, parity.

connaturalness, connature [*rare*], connaturality [*rare*]; brotherhood, family likeness.

alliteration, rime *or* rhyme, pun.

repetition etc. 104; sameness etc. (*identity*) 13; uniformity etc. 16; isogamy.

analogue; the like; match, pendant, fellow, companion, pair, mate, twin, double, congener, counterpart, brother, sister; one's second self, *alter ego* [*L.*], chip of the old block, *par nobile fratrum* [*L.*], *Arcades ambo* [*L.*], birds of a feather, *et hoc genus omne* [*L.*]; *gens de même famille* [*F.*].

simile; parallel; type etc. (*metaphor*) 521; image etc. (*representation*) 554; photograph; close–, striking–, speaking–, faithful etc. *adj.* —likeness, –resemblance.

v. **be similar** etc. *adj.;* look like, resemble, favor [*colloq.*], follow, echo, reproduce, bear resemblance; savor of, smack of; approximate; parallel, match, rime *or* rhyme with; take after; imitate etc. 19; span; hunt in couples, run in couples.

render similar etc. *adj.;* assimilate, approximate, bring near; connaturalize, make alike; rime *or* rhyme, pun.

adj. **similar**; resembling etc. *v.;* like, alike; twin.

analogous, analogical; parallel, of a piece; such as, so; homoiousian.

connatural, correlative, corresponding, cognate, congeneric, congenerous, allied to; akin to etc. (*consanguineous*) 11.

7

18. Dissimilarity

approximate, much the same, near, close, something like, near- [as *near*-silk, *colloq.*], such like; a show of; mock, pseudo, simulating, representing.

exact etc. (*true*) 494; lifelike, faithful; true to nature, true to life; the very image of, the very picture of; for all the world like, *comme deux gouttes d'eau* [*F.*], as like as two peas, as like as it can stare; *instar omnium* [*L.*], cast in the same mold, ridiculously like.

adv. **as if**, so to speak; as it were, as if it were; *quasi* [*L.*], just as.

18. Dissimilarity

n. **dissimilarity**, dissimilitude; unlikeness, diversity, disparity, dissemblance; divergence, variation; difference etc. 15; novelty, originality; creativeness; oögamy.

v. **be unlike** etc. *adj.;* vary etc. (*differ*) 15; bear no resemblance to, differ *toto coelo* [*L.*].
render unlike etc. *adj.;* vary etc. (*diversify*) 140.

adj. **dissimilar**, unlike, disparate; divergent, nonidentical, unidentical; of a different kind etc. (*class*) 75; unmatched, unique; new, novel; unprecedented etc. 83; original.

nothing of the kind; no such thing, quite another thing; far from it, other than, cast in a different mold, *tertium quid* [*L.*], as like a dock as a daisy, "very like a whale" [*Hamlet*]; as different as chalk from cheese, as different as Macedon and Monmouth; *lucus a non lucendo* [*L.*].

diversified etc. 16*a*.

adv. **otherwise**, elsewise; alias.

19. Imitation

n. **imitation**; copying etc. *v.;* transcription; repetition, duplication, reduplication; quotation; reproduction; mimeography.
mockery, apery, mimicking, mimicry.
simulation, personation; parrotism, parrotry; representation etc. 554; semblance, pretense; copy etc. 21; assimilation.
paraphrase, parody etc. 21.
plagiarism; forgery etc. (*falsehood*) 544.
imitator, echo, cuckoo, parrot, ape, monkey, mocking bird, mimic; copyist.

v. **imitate**, copy, mirror, reflect, reproduce, repeat; do like, echo, reëcho, catch; transcribe; match, parallel.
mock, take off, borrow, mimic, ape, simulate, personate; act etc. (*drama*) 599; represent etc. 554; counterfeit, forge, parody, travesty, caricature, burlesque.

follow in the steps of, follow in the footsteps of; follow in the wake of; tread in the steps of, tread in the footsteps of; take pattern by; follow suit [*colloq.*], follow the example of; walk in the shoes of, take a leaf out of another's book, strike in with; take after, model after; emulate.

adj. **imitated** etc. *v.;* mock, mimic; modeled after, molded on.
paraphrastic; literal; imitative; secondhand; imitable; aping, apish, mimicking, borrowed, counterfeit, imitation, false, pseudo, near- [as, *near*-silk, *colloq.*].

adv. **literally**, to the letter, verbatim, *literatim* [*L.*], *sic* [*L.*], *totidem verbis* [*L.*], word for word, *mot à mot* [*F.*], *verbatim et literatim* [*L.*]; exactly, precisely.

20. Nonimitation

n. **nonimitation**, no imitation; originality; creativeness.

adj. **unimitated**, uncopied; unmatched, unparalleled; inimitable etc. 33; unique, original, archetypal, prototypal, prototypical, primordial, creative, untranslated; exceptional, rare, *sui generis* [*L.*], uncommon, unexampled, out-of-the-way, insuitate [*rare*], unwonted, *recherché* [*F.*], unordinary [*rare*], supernormal.

20a. Variation

n. **variation**; alteration etc. (*change*) 140.
modification, moods and tenses; discrepance, discrepancy.
divergency etc. 291; deviation etc. 279; aberration; innovation.

v. **vary** etc. (*change*) 140; deviate etc. 279; diverge etc. 291; alternate, swerve.

adj. **varied** etc. *v.;* modified; diversified etc. 16*a;* dissimilar etc. 18.

21. Copy
[result of imitation]

n. **copy**, facsimile, counterpart, *effigies* [*L.*], effigy, form, likeness, similitude, semblance, cast, tracing, ectype, electrotype; imitation etc. 19; model, representation, adumbration, study; "counterfeit presentment" [*Hamlet*]; portrait etc. (*representment*) 554; resemblance.

duplicate; transcript, transcription; counterscript; reflex, reflexion; shadow, echo; chip off the old block; reprint, replica, offprint, transfer, reproduction; second edition etc. (*repetition*) 104; *réchauffé* [*F.*]; apograph, fair copy, revise, rewriting.

matter; manuscript, typescript, flimsy [*cant*].

parody, caricature, burlesque, travesty, *travestie* [*F.*], paraphrase; cartoon.

servile copy, servile imitation; counterfeit etc. (*deception*) 545; *pasticcio* [*It.*].

adj. **faithful**; lifelike etc. (*similar*) 17; close, exact, strict, conscientious.

22. Prototype
[thing copied]

n. **prototype**, original, model, pattern, precedent, standard, scantling [*rare*], type; archetype, antitype; protoplast, protoplasm, plasm [*obs.*], proplasm [*rare*], module, exemplar, example, ensample [*archaic*], paradigm; lay-figure; fugleman, guide.

copy, text, design; keynote.

die, mold; matrix, last, mint, seal, punch, intaglio, negative; stamp.

v. be an example, set an example; set a copy.

23. Agreement

n. **agreement**, accord, accordance; unison, harmony; concord etc. 714; concordance, concert; understanding, mutual understanding; gentleman's agreement, *entente cordiale* [*F.*], consortium; unanimity, consension [*rare*], consentaneity.

conformity etc. 82; conformance; uniformity etc. 16; assonance, consonance, consentaneousness, consistency; congruity, congruence *or* congruency; keeping; congeniality; correspondence, concinnity, parallelism, apposition, union.

fitness, aptness etc. *adj.*; relevancy; pertinence *or* pertinency; sortance [*obs.*]; case in point; aptitude, coaptation, propriety, applicability, admissibility, commensurability, compatibility; cognation etc. (*relation*) 9.

adaptation, adaption, adjustment, graduation, accommodation; reconciliation, reconcilement; assimilation.

consent etc. (*assent*) 488; concurrence etc. 178; consensus, *rapport* [*F.*], meeting of minds, coöperation etc. 709.

right man in the right place, very thing; quite the thing, just the thing.

v. **be accordant** etc. *adj.*; agree, accord, harmonize; correspond, tally, respond; meet, suit, fit, befit, do, adapt itself to; fall in with, chime in with, square with, quadrate with, consort with, comport with; dovetail, assimilate; fit like a glove; fit to a tittle, fit to a T; match etc. 17; become one; homologate.

consent etc. (*assent*) 488.

render accordant etc. *adj.*; fit, suit, adapt, accommodate; graduate; adjust etc. (*render equal*) 27; dress, regulate, readjust; accord, harmonize, reconcile; fadge, dovetail, square.

adj. **agreeing**, suiting etc. *v.*; in accord, accordant, concordant, consonant, congruous, consentaneous [*archaic*], answerable, correspondent, congenial; coherent; becoming; harmonious, reconcilable, conformable; in accordance with, in harmony with, in keeping with, in unison with etc. *n.*; at one with, of one mind, of a piece; consistent, compatible, proportionate; commensurate; on all fours with.

apt, apposite, pertinent, pat; to the point, to the purpose; happy, felicitous, germane, *ad rem* [*L.*], in point, bearing upon, applicable, relevant, admissible.

fit, adapted, *in loco* [*L.*], *à propos* [*F.*], appropriate, seasonable, sortable, suitable, idoneous [*rare*], deft; meet etc. (*expedient*) 646.

at home, in one's proper element.

adv. *à propos* of; pertinently etc. *adj.*

24. Disagreement

n. **disagreement**; discord, discordance, discordancy; dissonance, dissidence, disunity, disunion, discrepancy; unconformity etc. 83; incongruity, incongruence; discongruity, *mésalliance* [*F.*]; jarring etc. *v.*; dissension etc. 713; conflict etc. (*opposition*) 708; bickering, clashing, misunderstanding, wrangle.

disparity, mismatch, disproportion, dissimilitude, inequality; disproportionateness etc. *adj.*; variance, divergence, repugnance.

unfitness etc. *adj.*; inaptitude, impropriety; inapplicability etc. *adj.*; inconsistency, inconcinnity; irrelevancy etc. (*irrelation*) 10.

misjoining, misjoinder; syncretism, intrusion, interference.

fish out of water.

v. **disagree**; clash, conflict, dispute, quarrel, jar etc. (*discord*) 713; interfere, intrude, come amiss; not concern etc. 10; mismatch; *humano capiti cervicem jungere equinam* [*L.*].

adj. **disagreeing** etc. *v.*; discordant, discrepant; at variance, at war; hostile, antagonistic, repugnant, inaccordant, clashing, jarring, factious, dissentient, dissentious, dissident, inacquiescent, incompatible, irreconcilable, inconsistent with; unconformable, exceptional etc. 83; intrusive, incongruent, incongruous; disproportionate, disproportioned; unharmonious; unconsonant; divergent, repugnant to.

25. Quantity

inapt, unapt, inappropriate, malappropriate [*rare*], improper; unsuited, unsuitable; inapplicable; unfit, unfitting, unbefitting; unbecoming; ill-timed, ill-adapted, dissuitable [*rare*], infelicitous, unseasonable, *mal à propos* [*F.*], inadmissible; inapposite etc. (*irrelevant*) 10.

uncongenial; ill-assorted, ill-sorted; mismatched, misjoined, misplaced; unaccommodating, irreducible, uncommensurable; unsympathetic.

out of character, out of keeping, out of proportion, out of joint, out of tune, out of place, out of season, out of its element; at odds, at variance with.

adv. in defiance of, in contempt of, in spite of; discordantly etc. *adj.; à tort et à travers* [*F.*].

Section 3. Quantity

25. Quantity
[absolute quantity]

n. **quantity**, magnitude; size etc. (*dimensions*) 192; amplitude, mass, amount, quantum, measure, measurement, substance, strength.

[science of quantity] mathematics, mathesis [*rare*].

[logic] category, general conception, universal predicament.

[definite or finite quantity] armful, handful, mouthful, spoonful, capful; stock, batch, lot, dose; quota, quotiety [*rare*], quotum, pittance, driblet, grist.

v. **quantify**, rate.

adj. **quantitative**, some, any, more or less.

adv. to the tune of.

26. Degree
[relative quantity]

n. **degree**, grade, step, extent, measure, amount, ratio, stint *or* stent, standard, height, pitch; reach, amplitude, range, scope, caliber; gradation, shade; tenor, compass; sphere, station, rank, standing; rate, way, sort.

point, mark, stage etc. (*term*) 71; interval, line [*music*], space [*music*]; intensity, strength etc. (*greatness*) 31.

v. **graduate**, calibrate, measure; rectify.

adj. **comparative**; gradual, gradational, gradatory [*rare*], shading off; within the bounds etc. (*limit*) 233.

adv. **by degrees**, gradually, inasmuch, *pro tanto* [*L.*]; however, howsoever; step by step, bit by bit, little by little, inch by inch, drop by drop; by inches, by slow degrees, by little and little; in some degree, in some measure; to some extent; *di grado in grado* [*It.*].

27. Equality
[sameness of quantity or degree]

n. **equality**, parity, coextension, symmetry, balance, poise; evenness, monotony, level.

equivalence; equipollence, equipoise, equilibrium, equiponderance; par, quits; not a pin to choose; distinction without a difference, six of one and half a dozen of the other; identity etc. 13; similarity. etc. 17; coequality, coevality [*rare*], isonomy, isopolity, isotropy, parallelism.

equalization, equation; equilibration, coördination, adjustment, readjustment.

tie, dead heat; drawn game, drawn battle; neck-and-neck race.

match, peer, compeer, equal, mate, fellow, brother; equivalent.

v. **be equal** etc. *adj.;* equal, match, reach, keep pace with, run abreast; come to, amount to, come up to; be on a level with, lie on a level with; balance; cope with; come to the same thing, even off.

render equal etc. *adj.;* equalize, level, dress, balance, equate, handicap, give points, trim, adjust, poise; fit, accommodate; adapt etc. (*render accordant*) 23; strike a balance; establish equality, restore equality, establish equilibrium, restore equilibrium; readjust; stretch on the bed of Procrustes.

adj. **equal**, even, level, monotonous, coequal, symmetrical, coördinate; on a par with, on a level with, on a footing with; up to the mark; equiparant, equiparate [*rare*].

equivalent, tantamount; quits; homologous; synonymous etc. 522; resolvable into, convertible, much at one, as broad as long, neither more nor less; much the same as, the same thing as, as good as; all one, all the same; equipollent, equiponderant, equiponderous, equibalanced; equalized etc. *v.;* drawn; half and half; isochronal, isochronous; isoperimetric *or* isoperimetrical; isobath, isobathic.

adv. **equally** etc. *adj.; pari passu* [*L.*], *ad eundem* [*L.*], *caeteris paribus* [*L.*], *in equilibrio* [*L.*]; to all intents and purposes.

28. Inequality
[difference of quantity or degree]

n. **inequality**, inequalness [*rare*]; disparity, imparity [*rare*]; odds; difference etc. 15; unevenness; inclination of the balance, partiality;

shortcoming; casting weight, makeweight; superiority etc. 33; inferiority etc. 34; inequation, inadequation [*archaic*], inadequacy.

v. **be unequal** etc. *adj.;* countervail; have the advantage, give the advantage; turn the scale; kick the beam; topple, topple over; overmatch etc. 33; not come up to etc. 34.

adj. **unequal**, inequal [*rare*], uneven, disparate, partial, inadequate; overbalanced, unbalanced; top-heavy, lopsided; disquiparant; unequaled, unparalleled, fellowless [*rare*], unmatched [*rare*], unrivaled, unique, unapproached, matchless, inimitable, transcendent, peerless, nonpareil, unexampled, unpatterned [*rare*], unpeered [*rare*].

adv. **unequally** etc. *adj.*

29. Mean

n. **mean**, medium, intermedium [*obsoles.*], average, balance, normal, rule, run; mediocrity, generality; golden mean etc. (*mid-course*) 628; middle etc. 68; compromise etc. 774; middle course, middle state; neutrality.

v. **average**, split the difference; take the average etc. *n.;* reduce to a mean etc. *n.;* strike a balance, pair off.

adj. **mean**, intermediate; medial, middle etc. 68; average, normal, standard; neutral.

mediocre, middle-class, *bourgeois* [*F.*], commonplace etc. (*unimportant*) 643.

adv. **on an average**, in the long run; taking one with another, taking all things together, taking it for all in all; *communibus annis* [*L.*], in round numbers.

in the middle, *in medias res* [*L.*].

30. Compensation

n. **compensation**, equation; commutation; indemnification; compromise etc. 774; neutralization, nullification; counteraction etc. 179; reaction; measure for measure; retaliation etc. 718; equalization etc. 27; redemption, recoupment.

set-off, offset; makeweight, casting weight; counterpoise, ballast; indemnity, equivalent, *quid pro quo* [*L.*]; bribe, hush money; gift, donation etc. 784; amends etc. (*atonement*) 952; counterbalance, counterclaim, countervailing; cross debt, cross demand.

pay, payment, reward etc. 973.

v. **compensate**, compense [*obs.*], make compensation, indemnify; counteract, countervail, counterpoise; balance; counterbalance, offset, outbalance, overbalance, set off; hedge, square, give and take; make up for, make leeway; cover, fill up, neutralize, nullify; equalize etc. 27; make good; recoup, redeem etc. (*atone*) 952; pay, reward etc. 973.

adj. **compensating**, compensatory, compensative, amendatory, indemnificatory, reparative; countervailing etc. *v.;* in the opposite scale; equivalent etc. (*equal*) 27.

adv. **for a consideration**, in return, in consideration.

notwithstanding, but, however, yet, still, nevertheless; although, though; howbeit, albeit; at all events, in spite of, in despite of, despite, at any rate; be that as it may, for all that, even so, on the other hand, at the same time, *quand même* [*F.*], however that may be; after all, after all is said and done; taking one thing with another etc. (*average*) 29.

31. Greatness

n. **greatness** etc. *adj.;* magnitude; size etc. (*dimensions*) 192; multitude etc. (*number*) 102; immensity, enormity, muchness; infinity etc. 105; might, strength, intensity, fullness.

great quantity, quantity, deal [*colloq.*], power [*colloq.*], sight [*colloq.*], pot [*colloq.*], volume, world; mass, heap etc. (*assemblage*) 72; stock etc. (*store*) 636; peck, bushel, load, cargo; cartload, wagonload, shipload; flood, spring tide; abundance etc. (*sufficiency*) 639.

principal part, chief part, main part, greater part, better part, major part, best part, essential part; bulk, mass etc. (*whole*) 50.

fame, distinction, grandeur, dignity; importance etc. 642; generosity.

v. **be great** etc. *adj.;* run high, soar, tower, loom, tower above, rise above, transcend; rise to a great height, carry to a great height; bulk, bulk large; know no bounds; ascend, mount.

enlarge etc. (*increase*) 35, (*expand*) 194.

adj. **great**; greater etc. 33; large, considerable, fair, above par; big, bulky, huge etc. (*large in size*) 192; titanic, Atlantean, Herculean, cyclopean, voluminous; ample; abundant etc. (*enough*) 639; wholesale; many etc. 102; full, intense, strong, sound, passing [*archaic*], heavy, plenary, deep, high; signal, at its height, in the zenith.

worldwide, widespread, far-famed, extensive.

goodly, noble, precious, mighty; sad, grave, serious; far gone, arrant, downright; uttermost; crass, gross, tall, mickle [*archaic*], arch, profound, intense, consummate; rank, unmitigated, red-hot desperate; glaring, flagrant, stark staring; thorough-paced, thorough-going; roaring, whacking [*colloq.*], magnitudinous [*rare*],

32. Smallness

thumping; extraordinary; important etc. 642; unsurpassed etc. (*supreme*) 33; complete etc. 52.

august, grand dignified, sublime, majestic etc. (*repute*) 873.

vast, immense, enormous, extreme; inordinate, excessive, extravagant, exorbitant, outrageous, preposterous, unconscionable, swinging, monstrous, overgrown; towering, stupendous, prodigious, astonishing, incredible, pronounced, fearful [*colloq.*], thundering [*slang*], terrible [*colloq.*], dreadful [*colloq.*], terrific [*colloq.*]; marvelous etc. (*wonder*) 870.

unlimited etc. (*infinite*) 105; unapproachable, unutterable, indescribable, ineffable, unspeakable, inexpressible, beyond expression, fabulous.

undiminished, unabated, unreduced, unrestricted.

absolute, positive, stark, decided, unequivocal, essential, perfect, finished.

remarkable, of mark, marked, pointed, veriest; notable, noticeable, noteworthy; renowned.

adv. [**in a positive degree**] truly etc. (*truth*) 494; decidedly, unequivocally, purely, absolutely, seriously, essentially, fundamentally, radically, downright, in all conscience; for the most part, in the main.

[in a complete degree] entirely etc. (*completely*) 52; abundantly etc. (*sufficiently*) 639; widely, far and wide.

[in a great or high degree] greatly etc. *adj.;* much, muckle [*archaic*], well, indeed, very, very much, a deal, no end of, most, not a little; pretty, pretty well; enough, in a great measure, no end, passing, richly; to a large extent, to a great extent, to a gigantic extent; on a large scale; so; never so, ever so; ever so much; by wholesale, mighty [*colloq.*], mightily, powerfully; ultra, in the extreme, extremely, exceedingly, intensely, exquisitely, acutely, indefinitely, immeasurably; beyond compare, beyond comparison, beyond measure, beyond all bounds; out of sight [*colloq.*]; incalculably, infinitely.

[in a supreme degree] preëminently, superlatively etc. (*superiority*) 33.

[in a too great degree] immoderately, monstrously, preposterously, inordinately, exorbitantly, excessively, enormously, out of all proportion, with a vengeance.

[in a marked degree] particularly, remarkably, singularly, curiously, uncommonly, unusually, peculiarly, notably, signally, strikingly, pointedly, mainly, chiefly; famously, egregiously, prominently, glaringly, emphatically, strangely, wonderfully, amazingly, surprisingly, astonishingly, incredibly, marvelously, awfully, stupendously.

[in an exceptional degree] peculiarly etc. (*unconformity*) 83.

[in a violent degree] furiously etc. (*violence*) 173; severely, desperately, tremendously, extravagantly, confoundedly, deucedly [*slang*], devilishly [*colloq.*], with a vengeance, *à outrance* [*F.*], *à toute outrance* [*F.*].

[in a painful degree] painfully, sadly, grossly, sorely, bitterly, piteously, grievously, miserably, cruelly, woefully, lamentably, shockingly, frightfully, dreadfully, fearfully, terribly, horribly, distressingly, balefully, dolorously.

32. Smallness

n. **smallness** etc. *adj.;* littleness etc. (*small size*) 193; tenuity; paucity; fewness etc. (*small number*) 103; meanness, insignificance etc. (*unimportance*) 643; mediocrity, moderation.

small quantity, modicum, minimum; vanishing point; material point, atom, particle, electron, molecule, muon, photon, quark, corpuscle, point, speck, dot, mote, jot, iota, ace; minutiae, details; look, thought, idea, *soupçon* [*F.*], dab, dight [*dial.*], whit, tittle, shade, shadow; spark, scintilla, gleam; touch, cast; grain, scruple, granule, globule, minim, sup, sip, sop, spice, drop, droplet, sprinkling, dash, *morceau* [*F.*], screed [*Scot.*], smack, tinge, tincture; inch, patch, scantling, tatter, cantle, cantlet, flitter, gobbet, dole, mite, bit, morsel, crumb; scrap, shred, tag, splinter, rag; seed, fritter, shive; snip, snippet; snick, snack [*dial.*], snatch, slip, chip, chipping; shiver, sliver, driblet, clipping, paring, shaving, hair.

nutshell; thimbleful, spoonful, handful, capful, mouthful; fragment; fraction etc. (*part*) 51; drop in the ocean.

animalcule etc. 193.

trifle etc. (*unimportant thing*) 643; mere nothing, next to nothing; hardly anything; just enough to swear by; the shadow of a shade.

finiteness, finite quantity.

v. **be small** etc. *adj.;* lie in a nutshell.

diminish etc. (*decrease*) 36, (*contract*) 195.

adj. **small**, little; diminutive etc. (*small in size*) 193; minute, miniature, minikin; fine; inconsiderable, dribbling, paltry etc. (*unimportant*) 643; faint etc. (*weak*) 160; slender, light, slight, scanty, scant, limited; meager etc. (*insufficient*) 640; sparing; few etc. 103; low; soso *or* so-so *or* so so [*colloq.*], middling, tolerable, no great shakes [*slang*]; below par, under par, below the mark, under the mark; at a low ebb; halfway; moderate, modest; tender, subtle.

inappreciable, evanescent, infinitesimal, homeopathic, very small; atomic, corpuscular, microscopic, molecular; skin-deep.

mere, simple, sheer, stark, bare; near run.

dull, petty, shallow, stolid, phlegmatic, unintelligent; Boeotian, ungifted etc. 499.

adv. [in a small degree] to a small extent, on a small scale; a little, a wee bit; slightly etc. *adj.;* imperceptibly; miserably, wretchedly; insufficiently etc. 640; imperfectly; faintly etc. 160; passably, pretty well, well enough.

[in a certain or limited degree] partially, in part; in a certain degree, to a certain degree; to a certain extent; comparatively; some, rather, middling [*colloq.*]; in some degree, in some measure; something, somewhat; simply, only, purely, merely; at least, at the least, at most, at the most; ever so little, as little as may be, *tant soit peu* [*F.*], in ever so small a degree; thus far, *pro tanto* [*L.*], within bounds, in a manner, after a fashion.

almost, nearly, well-nigh, short of, not quite, all but; near upon, close upon; *peu s'en faut* [*F.*], near the mark; within an ace of, within an inch of; on the brink of; scarcely, hardly, barely, only just, no more than.

[in an uncertain degree] about, thereabouts, somewhere about, nearly, say; be the same more or less, be the same little more or less.

[in no degree] noway *or* noways, nowise, not at all, not in the least, not a bit, not a bit of it, not a whit, not a jot, not a shadow; in no wise, in no respect; by no means, by no manner of means; on no account, at no hand.

33. Superiority
[supremacy]

n. **superiority**, majority, plurality; greatness etc. 31; advantage; pull [*slang*]; preponderance, preponderation; vantage ground, prevalence, partiality; personal superiority; scepter, sovereignty, sovranty [*poetic*]; nobility etc. (*rank*) 875; Triton among the minnows, *primus inter pares* [*L.*], *nulli secundus* [*L.*]; superman, overman; captain; crackerjack [*slang*].

supremacy, supremeness, supremity [*rare*], primacy, paramountcy, preëminence; lead; maximum, record; crest, climax; culmination etc. (*summit*) 210; transcendence; *ne plus ultra* [*L.*]; lion's share, Benjamin's mess; excess, surplus etc. (*remainder*) 40; redundance etc. 641.

v. **be superior** etc. *adj.;* exceed, excel, transcend; outdo, outbalance, outweigh, outrank, outrival, out-Herod Herod; pass, surpass, get ahead of; overtop, override, overpass, overbalance, overweigh, overmatch; top, o'ertop, cap, beat, cut out [*colloq.*]; beat hollow [*colloq.*]; outstrip etc. 303; eclipse, throw into the shade, take the shine out of [*colloq.*], put one's nose out of joint [*colloq.*]; have the upper hand, have the whip hand of, have the advantage; turn the scale; play first fiddle etc. (*importance*) 642; preponderate, predominate, prevail; precede, take precedence, come first; come to a head, culminate; beat etc. all others, bear the palm; break the record; take the cake [*slang*].

become *or* render larger etc. (*increase*) 35, (*expand*) 194.

adj. **superior**, greater, major, higher; exceeding etc. *v.;* great etc. 31; distinguished, ultra; vaulting; more than a match for.

supreme, greatest, maximal, maximum, utmost, paramount, preëminent, foremost, crowning, hegemonic [*rare*]; first-rate etc. (*important*) 642, (*excellent*) 648; unrivaled; peerless, matchless; second to none, *sans pareil* [*F.*]; unparagoned, unparalleled, unequaled, unapproached, unsurpassed; superlative, inimitable, *facile princeps* [*L.*], incomparable, sovereign, without parallel, *nulli secundus* [*L.*], *ne plus ultra* [*L.*]; beyond compare, beyond comparison; culminating etc (*topmost*) 210; transcendent, transcendental; *plus royaliste que le Roi* [*F.*].

increased etc. (*added to*) 35; enlarged etc. (*expanded*) 194.

adv. **beyond**, more, over; over the mark, above the mark; above par; upwards of, in advance of; over and above; at the top of the scale, at its height.

[in a superior or supreme degree] eminently, egregiously, preëminently, surpassing, prominently, superlatively, supremely, above all, of all things, the most, to crown all, *par excellence* [*F.*], principally, especially, particularly, peculiarly, *a fortiori* [*L.*], even, yea, still more.

34. Inferiority

n. **inferiority**, minority, subordinacy [*obs.*], subordinance [*obs.*]; shortcoming, deficiency; minimum; smallness etc. 32; imperfection; subjacency [*rare*]; lower quality, lower worth; meanness, poorness, baseness, shabbiness.

[personal inferiority] commonalty etc. 876; juniority, subordinacy; subaltern, sub [*colloq.*].

35. Increase

- *v.* **be inferior** etc. *adj.;* fall short of, come short of; not pass, not come up to; want.
  become smaller, render smaller etc. (*decrease*), 36, (*contract*) 195; hide its diminished head, retire into the shade, yield the palm, play second fiddle, take a back seat [*colloq.*], kick the beam.
- *adj.* **inferior,** deterior [*rare*], smaller; small etc. 32; minor, less, lesser, deficient, minus, lower, subordinate, secondary, junior, humble; second-rate etc. (*imperfect*) 651; sub-, subaltern.
  least, smallest etc. (*see* little, small etc. 193); lowest.
  diminished etc. (*decreased*) 36; reduced etc. (*contracted*) 195; unimportant etc. 643.
- *adv.* **less;** under the mark, below the mark, under par, below par; at the bottom of the scale, at a low ebb, at a disadvantage; short of, under.

35. Increase

- *n.* **increase,** augmentation, increasement [*rare*], addition, enlargement, extension; dilatation etc. (*expansion*) 194; increment, accretion; accession etc. 37; development, growth; aggrandizement, accumulation, reënforcement, redoubling, intensification, inflation, enhancement, aggravation; rise; ascent etc. 305; exaggeration, exacerbation; spread etc. (*dispersion*) 73; flood tide, spring tide.
  gain, produce, product, profit, gettings [*archaic*], advantage, booty, plunder, superlucration [*rare*], clean-up.
- *v.* **increase,** augment, add to, enlarge; dilate etc. (*expand*) 194; grow, wax, get ahead, gain strength; advance; run up, shoot up; rise; swell, mount, ascend etc. 305; sprout etc. 194.
  aggrandize; raise, exalt; deepen, heighten, lengthen, greaten [*archaic*], thicken; eke [*archaic*], inflate; strengthen, intensify, enhance, magnify, redouble, double, triple, etc.; aggravate, exaggerate; exasperate, exacerbate; add fuel to the flame, *oleum addere camino* [*L.*]; superadd etc. (*add*) 37; spread etc. (*disperse*) 73.
- *adj.* **increased** etc. *v.;* on the increase, undiminished; additional etc. (*added*) 37.
  increasing, growing, crescent, crescive [*rare*], lengthening, multiplying, intensifying, intensive, intensitive [*rare*], incretionary [*rare*]; crescendo.
- *adv.* crescendo, increasingly.

36. Nonincrease, Decrease

- *n.* **decrease,** diminution, decrescence, decrement, diminishment, lessening etc. *v.;* subtraction etc. 38, reduction, rebatement [*rare*], abatement, declension; shrinkage etc. (*contraction*) 195; coarctation [*obs.*]; curtailment, abridgment etc. (*shortening*) 201; extenuation.
  subsidence, wane, ebb, decline; ebb tide, neap tide, ebbing; descent etc. 306; reflux, depreciation, wear and tear, erosion, consumption; deterioration etc. 659; anticlimax; mitigation etc. (*moderation*) 174; catabasis [*med.*].
- *v.* **decrease,** diminish, lessen; abridge etc. (*shorten*) 201; shrink etc. (*contract*) 195; drop off, fall off, tail off; fall away, waste, wear; wane, ebb, decline, descend etc. 306; subside; melt away, die away; retire into the shade, hide its diminished head, fall to a low ebb, run low, languish, decay, crumble, erode, consume away.
  bate, abate [*archaic*], dequantitate [*obs.*]; discount, belittle, minify [*rare*], minimize, minish [*rare*], depreciate; extenuate, lower, weaken, attenuate, fritter away; mitigate etc. (*moderate*) 174; dwarf, throw into the shade; reduce etc. 195; shorten etc. 201; subtract etc. 38; deliquesce, ease, remit [*rare*].
- *adj.* **unincreased** etc. (*see* increase etc. 35); decreased, decreasing etc. *v.;* decrescent, reductive; deliquescent, contractive; descrescendo; on the wane etc. *n.*
- *adv.* decrescendo, decreasingly.

37. Addition

- *n.* **addition,** annexation, adjection [*rare*], junction etc. 43; superposition, superaddition, superjunction, superfetation; accession, reënforcement; increase etc. 35; increment.
  affix, codicil, subscript, tag, rider, appendage, continuation, equation, postscript, adjunct, etc. 39; supplement; accompaniment etc. 88; interlineation, interposition etc. 228; insertion etc. 300.
  computation, footing, totaling, casting, summation.
- *v.* **add,** annex, affix, superadd, subjoin, superpose; clap on, saddle on; tack to, append, tag, adject [*rare*], attach, postfix, adjoin [*rare*], ingraft; saddle with; sprinkle; introduce etc. (*interpose*) 228; insert etc. 300.
  compute, foot up, total, cast, sum, count up.
  become added, accrue; supervene, advene.
  reënforce or reinforce, restrengthen; strengthen, swell the ranks of; augment etc. 35.
- *adj.* **added** etc. *v.;* additional; supplement, supplemental, supplementary; suppletive [*rare*], supervenient [*rare*], suppletory, subjunctive;

adjectitious, adscititious, ascititious; additive, extra, further, fresh, more, new, ulterior, other, remanent [*rare*]; auxiliary, contributory, accessory; spare.

adv. au reste [*F.*]; in addition, more, plus, extra; and, also, likewise, too, furthermore, further, item; and also, and eke [*archaic*]; else, besides, to boot; et cetera, etc.; and so on, and so forth; into the bargain, *cum multis aliis* [*L.*], over and above, moreover.

with, withal; including, inclusive, as well as, not to mention, let alone; together with, along with, coupled with, in conjunction with; conjointly; jointly etc. 43.

38. Nonaddition, Deduction

n. **deduction**, subtraction, subduction; retrenchment; removal; sublation [*rare*], ablation; abstraction etc. (*taking*) 789; garbling etc. *v.;* mutilation, detruncation; amputation; recision, abscision, excision; abrasion; curtailment etc. 201.

rebate etc. (*decrement*) 40a; minuend, subtrahend; decrease etc. 36.

v. **subduct**, subtract, deduct, deduce; bate, retrench; remove, withdraw; take from, take away; detract; garble.

mutilate, amputate, detruncate; cut off, cut away, cut out; abscind, excise.

pare, thin, prune, decimate, eliminate, rebate; bant [*colloq.*], reduce; abrade, scrape, file.

geld, castrate, envirate [*rare*], cut, spay (*female*), capon *or* caponize (*a cock*), eunuchize [*rare*], unman, emasculate.

diminish etc. 36; curtail etc. (*shorten*) 201; deprive of etc. (*take*) 789; weaken.

adj. **subtracted** etc. *v.;* subtractive.

tailless, acaudal, acaudate.

adv. **in deduction** etc. *n.;* less; short of; minus, without, except, excepting, with the exception of, barring, bar, save, exclusive of, save and except, with a reservation, ablatitious [*rare*].

39. Adjunct
[thing added]

n. **adjunct**; addition, additament; *additum* [*L.*], affix, appendage, annex; augment, augmentation; increment, reënforcement, supernumerary, accessory, item; garnish, sauce; accompaniment etc. 88; adjective, addendum (*pl.* addenda); complement, supplement; continuation.

rider, offshoot, episode, side issue, corollary, codicil etc. (*addition*) 37.

flap, lug, lapel, apron, tab, fly, tuck, lap, piece, lappet, skirt, embroidery, trappings, cortege *or cortège* [*F.*]; tail, suffix etc. (*sequel*) 65; wing.

v. **add**, annex etc. 37.

adj. **additional** etc. 37.

winged, alate *or* alated.

adv. in addition etc. 37.

40. Remainder
[thing remaining]

n. **remainder**, residue; remains, remanet [*rare*], relict [*rare*], remanence [*rare*], remnant, rest, relic; leavings, heeltap, odds and ends, cheeseparings, candle ends, orts; residuum; dregs etc. (*dirt*) 653; refuse etc. (*useless*) 645; stubble, result, educt; fag-end; ruins, wreck, skeleton, stump, rump; alluvium.

surplus, overplus, excess; balance [*commercial slang*], complement; surplusage; superfluity etc. (*redundance*) 641; survival, survivance [*rare*]; fossil, shadow, *caput mortuum* [*L.*].

v. **remain**; be left etc. *adj.;* exceed, survive; leave.

adj. **remaining**, left; left behind, left over; residual, residuary; over, odd; unconsumed, sedimentary; surviving; net; exceeding, over and above; outlying, outstanding; cast off etc. 782; superfluous etc. (*redundant*) 641.

40a. Decrement
[thing deducted]

n. **decrement**, discount, rebate, rebatement, tare, offtake, drawback, draft, reprise; defect, loss, deduction; afterglow; eduction; waste.

41. Mixture
[forming a whole without coherence]

n. **mixture**, admixture, mixtion [*obs.*], admixtion, commixture, commixtion *or* commixion [*obs.*], intermixture, immixture, minglement, eucrasy [*med.*], interfusion, intertanglement, interlacement, interlacery, intertexture, levigation, alloyage; matrimony; junction etc. 43; combination etc. 48; miscegenation.

impregnation; infusion, diffusion, suffusion, transfusion; infiltration; seasoning, sprinkling, interlarding; interpolation etc. 228; adulteration, sophistication.

[thing mixed] tinge, tincture, touch, dash, smack, sprinkling, spice, seasoning, infusion, *soupçon* [*F.*].

[compound resulting from mixture] alloy, amalgam; brass, chowchow, pewter; magma, half-and-half, *mélange* [*F.*], *tertium quid* [*L.*], miscellany, medley, mess, hash, hodgepodge,

42. Simpleness

hotchpotch, hotchpot, *pasticcio* [*It.*], patchwork, odds and ends, all sorts; jumble etc. (*disorder*) 59; salad, sauce, mash, omnium-gatherum [*colloq.*], gallimaufry, olla-podrida, olio, salmagundi, potpourri, Noah's ark; texture; mingled yarn; mosaic etc. (*variegation*) 440.

half-blood, half-breed, half-caste; mulatto; quarteron *or* quarteroon [*rare*], quintroon *or* quinteron, quadroon, octoroon, sambo *or* zambo; cafuzo; Eurasian; fustee *or* fustie [*W. Ind.*], mestee [*W. Ind.*], mestizo (*fem.* mestiza), griffe, ladino, marabou, sacatra; zebrule; catalo; mule; cross, hybrid, mongrel; cross-breed etc. (*unconformity*) 83.

v. **mix**; join etc. 43; combine etc. 48; commix, immix, intermix; levigate, mix up with, mingle; commingle, intermingle, bemingle; shuffle etc. (*derange*) 61; pound together; hash up, stir up; knead, brew; impregnate with; interlard etc. (*interpolate*) 228; intertwine, interweave etc. 219; associate with; miscegenate.

be mixed etc.; get among, be entangled with.

imbue; infuse, suffuse, transfuse, instill *or* instil, infiltrate, dash, tinge, tincture, season, sprinkle, besprinkle, attemper, medicate, blend, cross; alloy, amalgamate, compound, adulterate, sophisticate, infect.

adj. **mixed** etc. *v.;* implex [*rare*], composite, half-and-half, linsey-woolsey, medley, chowchow, hybrid, mongrel, heterogeneous; motley etc. (*variegated*) 440; miscellaneous, promiscuous, indiscriminate; miscible.

adv. **among**, amongst, amid, amidst; with; in the midst of, in the crowd.

42. Simpleness
[freedom from mixture]

n. **simpleness** etc. *adj.;* purity, homogeneity.

elimination; sifting etc. *v.;* purification etc. (*cleanness*) 652.

v. **render simple** etc. *adj.;* simplify.

sift, winnow, bolt, eliminate; exclude, get rid of; clear; purify etc. (*clean*) 652; disentangle etc. (*disjoin*, 44).

adj. **simple**, uniform, of a piece, homogeneous, Attic, homespun, single, pure, clear, sheer, neat.

unmixed, unmingled, unblended, uncombined, uncompounded; elemental, elementary, undecomposed; unadulterated, unsophisticated, unalloyed, untinged, unfortified; *pur et simple* [*F.*]; incomplex, incomposite [*rare*].

free from, exempt from; exclusive.

adv. **simply** etc. *adj.;* only.

43. Junction

n. **junction**; joining etc. *v.;* joinder, union; connection, conjunction, conjugation; annexion, annexation, annexment [*rare*]; astriction, attachment, compagination [*rare*], subjunction, vincture [*obs.*], ligation, alligation; accouplement; marriage etc. (*wedlock*) 903; infibulation, inosculation, symphysis, anastomosis, confluence, communication, concatenation; meeting, reunion; assemblage etc. 72.

coition, copulation; sexual congress, sexual conjunction, sexual intercourse.

joint, joining, juncture, chiasm, osculature, pivot, hinge, articulation, commissure, seam, gore, gusset, suture, stitch; link etc. 45; miter, mortise.

contingency, emergency, predicament, crisis, concurrence.

closeness, tightness etc. *adj.;* coherence etc. 46; combination etc. 48.

annexationist.

v. **join**, unite; conjoin, connect; associate; put together, lay together, clap together, hang together, lump together, hold together, piece together, tack together, fix together, bind up together; embody, reëmbody; roll into one.

attach, fix, affix, immobilize, saddle on, fasten, bind, secure, clinch, twist, make fast etc. *adj.;* tie, pinion, string, strap, sew, lace, stitch, tack, knit, button, buckle, hitch, lash, truss, bandage, braid, splice, swathe, gird, tether, moor, picket, harness, chain; fetter etc. (*restrain*) 751; lock, latch, belay, brace, hook, grapple, leash, couple, accouple, link, yoke, bracket; marry etc. (*wed*) 903; bridge over, span.

pin, nail, bolt, hasp, clasp, clamp, screw, rivet; impact, solder, braze; cement, set; weld together, fuse together; tighten, trice up, screw up; wedge, rabbet, mortise, miter, jam, dovetail, enchase; graft, ingraft, inosculate.

entwine *or* intwine; interlink, interlace, intertwine, intertwist, interweave; entangle; twine round, belay.

be joined etc.; hang together, hold together; cohere etc. 46.

adj. **joined** etc. *v.;* joint; conjoint, conjunct; corporate, compact; hand in hand.

firm, fast, close, tight, taut *or* taught, secure, set, intervolved [*obs.*]; inseparable, indissoluble, insecable [*obs.*], inseverable.

adv. **jointly** etc. *adj.;* in conjunction with etc. (*in addition to*) 37; fast, firmly, etc. *adj.;* intimately.

44. Disjunction

- *n.* **disjunction**, disconnection, disunity, disunion, disassociation, disengagement, dissociation, disjointure; discontinuity etc. 70; abjunction [*obs.*]; cataclasm; inconnection [*obs.*]; abstraction, abstractedness; isolation; insularity, insulation; oasis; island; separateness etc. *adj.*; severalty; *disjecta membra* [*L.*]; dispersion etc. 73; apportionment etc. 786.

  separation; parting etc. *v.;* circumcision, detachment, segregation; divorce, sejunction [*obs.*], seposition [*obs.*], diduction [*rare*], diremption [*rare*], discerption; elision; caesura, division, subdivision, break, fracture, rupture; compartition [*obs.*]; dismemberment, disintegration, dislocation; luxation; severance, disseverance; scission; rescission, abscission; laceration, dilaceration; disruption, abruption; avulsion, divulsion; section, resection, cleavage; fission; partibility, separability, separatism.

  fissure, breach, rent, split, rift, crack, slit, incision.

  dissection, anatomy; decomposition etc. 49; cutting instrument etc. (*sharpness*) 253; buzz saw, circular saw.

  separatist.

- *v.* **be disjoined** etc.; come off, come to pieces, fall off, fall to pieces; peel off; get loose.

  disjoin, disconnect, disengage, disunite, dissociate, dispair [*obs.*]; divorce, part, dispart, detach, separate, cut off, rescind, segregate; set apart, keep apart; insulate, isolate; throw out of gear; cut adrift; loose; unloose, undo, unbind, unchain, unlock etc. (*fix*) 43, unpack, unravel; disentangle; set free etc. (*liberate*) 750.

  sunder, divide, subdivide, sever, section, sectionize [*rare*], segment, dissever, abscind; circumcise; cut; incide [*obs.*], incise; saw, snip, nib [*obs.*], nip, cleave, rive, rend, slit, split, splinter, chip, crack, snap, break, tear, burst; rend etc., asunder, rend in twain; wrench, rupture, shatter, shiver, crunch, craunch *or* cranch, chop; cut up, rip up; hack, hew, slash; whittle; haggle, hackle, discind [*obs.*], lacerate, scamble [*obs.*], mangle, gash, hash, slice; cut up, carve, quarter, dissect, anatomize; dislimb; take to pieces, pull to pieces, pick to pieces, tear to pieces; tear to tatters, tear piecemeal; divellicate; skin etc. 226.

  disintegrate, dismember, disbranch, disband; disperse etc. 73; dislocate, disjoint; break up; mince; comminute etc. (*pulverize*) 330; apportion etc. 786.

  partition, parcel, demarcate [*rare*], graduate, district, chapter, canton.

  part, part company; separate, leave; alienate, estrange.

- *adj.* **disjoined** etc. *v.;* discontinuous etc. 70; bipartite, biparted [*rare*], multipartite, abstract; disjunctive; secant; isolated etc. *v.;* insular, separate, disparate, discrete, apart, asunder, far between, loose, free; lobate, lobulate, lobulated, lobulose, digitate; unattached, unannexed, unassociated, unconnected; distinct; adrift; straggling; rift, reft, cleft.

  [capable of being cut] scissile, divisible, discerptible [*rare*], partible, separable, severable, dividuous [*rare*].

- *adv.* **separately** etc. *adj.;* one by one, severally, apart; adrift, asunder, in twain; in the abstract, abstractedly.

45. Vinculum
[connecting medium]

- *n.* **vinculum**, link; connective, connection; junction etc. 43; bond of union, copula, intermedium, hyphen; bracket; bridge, stepping-stone, isthmus.

  bond, tendon, tendril; fiber; cord, cordage; ribband, ribbon, rope, guy, cable, line, halser [*obs.*], hawser, painter, moorings, wire, chain; string etc. (*filament*) 205.

  fastening, tie; ligament, ligature; strap; tackle, rigging; standing rigging; running rigging; traces, harness; yoke; band, bandage; brace, roller, fillet; inkle; with, withe, withy; thong, braid; girder, tiebeam; girth, girdle, cestus, garter, halter, noose, lasso, surcingle, knot, running knot; *cabestro* [*Sp. Amer.*], cinch, lariat, *legadero* [*Sp. Amer.*], oxreim [*S. Africa*]; suspenders.

  pin, corking pin, nail, brad, tack, skewer, staple, clamp; cramp, cramp iron, detent, *larigo* [*Sp. Amer.*], pawl, terret, screw, button, buckle, clasp, hasp, bar, hinge, hank, catch, latch, bolt, latchet, tag; tooth; hook, hook and eye; lock, holdfast, padlock, rivet, couple, coupler, ring; anchor, grappling iron, treenail *or* trennel, stake, post; prop etc. (*support*) 215.

  cement, glue, gum, paste, size, wafer, solder, lute, putty, birdlime, mortar, stucco, plaster, grout; viscum.

  shackle, rein etc. (*means of restraint*) 752.

- *v.* **bridge over**, span; connect etc. 43; hang etc. 214.

46. Coherence

- *n.* **coherence**, cohesion, cohesiveness, adherence, adhesion, adhesiveness; concretion, accretion;

47. Incoherence

conglutination, conglomeration, agglutination, agglomeration; aggregation; consolidation, set, cementation; sticking, soldering etc. *v.;* connection; dependence.

tenacity, toughness; stickiness etc. 352; inseparability, inseparableness; bur *or* burr, remora.

conglomerate, concrete etc. (*density*) 321.

v. **cohere**, adhere, coagulate, stick, cling, cleave, hold, take hold of, hold fast, close with, clasp, hug; grow together, hang together; twine round etc. (*join*) 43.

stick like a leech, stick like wax, stick like the paper on the wall; stick closer than a brother; stick close; cling like ivy, cling like a bur; adhere like a remora, adhere like Dejanira's shirt.

glue; agglutinate, conglutinate; cement, lute, belute [*rare*], paste, gum; solder, weld; ferruminate [*archaic*]; cake, consolidate etc. (*solidify*) 321; agglomerate.

adj. **adhesive**, cohesive, adhering, cohering etc. *v.;* tenacious, tough; sticky etc. 352.

united, unseparated, sessile, inseparable, inextricable, infrangible; compact etc. (*dense*) 321.

47. Incoherence
[nonadhesion, immiscibility]

n. **incoherence**, nonadhesion; immiscibility; looseness etc. *adj.;* laxity; relaxation; loosening etc. *v.;* freedom; disjunction etc. 44; rope of sand.

v. **make loose** etc. *adj.;* loosen, slacken, relax; unglue etc. 46; detach etc. (*disjoin*) 44.

adj. **nonadhesive**, immiscible; incoherent, detached, loose, baggy, slack, lax, relaxed, flapping, streaming; disheveled; segregated, like grains of sand; unconsolidated etc. 231; uncombined etc. 48; noncohesive.

48. Combination

n. **combination**; mixture etc. 41; junction etc. 43; union, unification, synthesis, synizesis, syneresis, incorporation, amalgamation, embodiment, coalescence, crasis, fusion, coalescing, blend, blendure [*rare*], blending, absorption, centralization.

alloy, compound, amalgam, composition, *tertium quid* [*L.*]; resultant, impregnation.

v. **combine**, unite, incorporate, inosculate, consubstantiate, alloy, intermix, interfuse, interlard, syncretize, interlace, agglutinate, amalgamate, embody, absorb, reëmbody, blend, merge, fuse, melt into one, consolidate, coalesce, solidify, commix [*archaic*], contemper, centralize, impregnate; put together, lump together.

league, interleague [*rare*], federate, confederate, fraternize, club, associate, amalgamate, cement a union, marry, couple, pair, ally.

adj. **combined** etc. *v.;* wedded; indiscrete, conjunctive, conjugate, conjoint; impregnated with, ingrained; imbued, inoculated.

allied, amalgamated, federate, confederate, corporate, leagued.

49. Decomposition

n. **decomposition**, analysis, dieresis, dissection, resolution, catalysis, dissolution, break-up; dispersion etc. 73; disjunction etc. 44; disintegration.

decay, rot, putrefaction, putrescence, putridity, caries; corruption etc. (*uncleanness*) 653.

electrolysis, electrolyzation, hydrolysis, proteolysis, thermolysis, catalysis.

v. **decompose**, decompound [*rare*]; analyze, disembody, dissolve; resolve into its elements, separate into its elements; dissect, decentralize, break up; disintegrate, disperse etc. 73; unravel etc. (*unroll*) 313; crumble into dust.

corrupt [*archaic*], rot, decay, consume; putrefy, putresce.

electrolyze, hydrolyze, thermolyze, catalyze.

adj. **decomposed** etc. *v.;* catalytic, analytical; resolvent, separative, solvent.

50. Whole
[principal part]

n. **whole**, totality, integrity; totalness etc. *adj.;* entirety, entire [*rare*], *ensemble* [*F.*], collectiveness; unity etc. 87; completeness etc. 52; indivisibility, indiscerptibility; integration, embodiment; integer, integral.

all, general [*archaic*], the whole, total, aggregate, one and all, gross amount, sum, sum total, the altogether [*humorous*], *tout ensemble* [*F.*], length and breadth of, Alpha and Omega, "be all and end all"; complex, *complexus* [*L.*]; lock, stock, and barrel.

bulk, mass, lump, tissue, staple, body, compages; trunk, torso, bole, hull, hulk, skeleton; greater part, major part, best part, principal part, main part; essential part etc. (*importance*) 642; lion's share, Benjamin's mess; the long and the short; nearly all, almost all.

v. **form a whole**, constitute a whole; integrate, embody, amass; aggregate etc. (*assemble*) 72; amount to, come to.

adj. **whole**, total, integral [*rare*], integrate [*rare*], entire; complete etc. 52; one, individual.

unbroken, uncut, undivided, unsevered, unclipped, uncropped, unshorn; seamless; undiminished; undemolished, undissolved, undestroyed, unbruised.
indivisible, indissoluble, indissolvable, indiscerptible.
wholesale, sweeping; comprehensive.
adv. **wholly**, altogether; as a whole, one and indivisible; totally etc. (*completely*) 52; entirely, all, all in all, wholesale, in a body, collectively, all put together; in the aggregate, in the lump, in the mass, in the gross, in the main, in the long run; *en masse* [*F.*], on the whole, bodily, *en bloc* [*F.*], *in extenso* [*L.*], throughout, every inch; substantially.

51. Part

n. **part**, portion; dose; item, particular; aught, any; division; ward, parcel [*law or archaic*], count; sector, segment; fraction, fragment; cantle, cantlet; frustum [*rare*]; detachment, subdivision.
section, chapter, verse; article, clause, phrase, paragraph, passage, number, book, fascicle, fascicule *or* fasciculus, *livraison* [*F.*].
piece, lump, bit, snatch; cut, cutting; chip, chunk, collop, slice, scrap, crumb, scale; lamina etc. 204; small part, morsel, moiety, particle etc. (*smallness*) 32; installment, dividend; share etc. (*allotment*) 786.
oddments, *débris* [*F.*], odds and ends, detritus; *excerpta* [*L.*], excerpt.
member, limb, lobe, lobule, arm, wing, scion, branch, bough, joint, link, offshoot, ramification, twig, bush, spray, sprig; runner, tendril; leaf, leaflet; stump; component part etc. 56; sarmentum.
cue, role, cast; lines, pageant [*archaic*].
compartment; department etc. (*class*) 75; county etc. (*region*) 181.
v. **part**, divide, break etc. (*disjoin*) 44; partition etc. (*apportion*) 786.
adj. **fractional**, fragmentary, portional [*rare*]; sectional, aliquot; divided etc. *v.;* in compartments, multifid; disconnected, incomplete, partial.
divided, broken, cut, severed, clipped, cropped, shorn; seamed.
divisible, dissoluble, dissolvable, discerptible.
adv. **partly**, in part, partially; piecemeal, part by part; by installments, by snatches, by inches, by driblets; bit by bit, inch by inch, foot by foot, drop by drop; in detail, in lots.

52. Completeness

n. **completeness** etc. *adj.;* completion etc. 729; integration; allness [*rare*], totality, integralness, totalness, integrality [*rare*], integrity.
entirety; perfection etc. 650; solidity, solidarity; unity; all; *ne plus ultra* [*L.*], ideal, limit; undividedness, intactness, universality.
complement, supplement, make-weight; filling up etc. *v.*
fill; impletion; saturation, saturity [*obs.*]; high water; high tide, flood tide, springtide; load, bumper, bellyful; brimmer; sufficiency etc. 639.
v. **be complete** etc. *adj.;* come to a head.
render complete etc. *adj.;* complete etc. (*accomplish*) 729; fill, charge, load, stevedore, replenish; make up, make good; piece out, eke out; supply deficiencies; fill up, fill in, fill to the brim, fill the measure of; satiate; saturate.
go the whole hog [*colloq.*], go the whole length; go all lengths; go the limit [*colloq.*].
adj. **complete**, entire; whole etc. 50; perfect etc. 650; full, good, absolute, thorough, plenary; solid, undivided; with all its parts; all-sided.
exhaustive, radical, sweeping, thorough-going; dead.
regular, consummate, unmitigated, sheer, unqualified, unconditional, free; abundant etc. (*sufficient*) 639.
brimming; brimful, topful; chock-full, chokefull; saturated, crammed; replete etc. (*redundant*) 641; fraught, laden; full-laden, full-fraught, full-charged; heavy laden.
completing etc. *v.;* supplemental, supplementary; ascititious.
adv. **completely** etc. *adj.;* altogether, outright, wholly, totally, *in toto* [*L.*], quite; all out; over head and ears; effectually, for good and all, nicely, fully, through thick and thin, head and shoulders, out of sight [*slang*]; neck and heel, neck and crop; in all respects, in every respect; at all points, out and out, to all intents and purposes; *toto coelo* [*L.*]; utterly; clean, clean as a whistle; to the full, to the utmost, to the limit, to the backbone; hollow, stark; heart and soul, root and branch, down to the ground.
to the top of one's bent, as far as possible, *à outrance* [*F.*].
throughout; from first to last, from beginning to end, from end to end, from one end to the other, from Dan to Beersheba, from head to foot, from top to toe, from top to bottom; *de fond en comble* [*F.*]; *à fond* [*F.*]; *a capite ad*

53. Incompleteness

calcem [*L.*]; *ab ovo usque ad mala* [*L.*]; fore and aft; every whit, every inch; *cap-à-pie* [*F.*], to the end of the chapter; up to the brim, up to the ears, up to the eyes; as . . . as can be.

on all accounts; *sous tous les rapports* [*F.*]; with a vengeance.

53. Incompleteness

n. **incompleteness** etc. *adj.;* deficience [*rare*], deficiency, short weight, short measure; shortcoming etc. 304; want, lack, insufficiency etc. 640; imperfection etc. 651; immaturity etc. (*nonpreparation*) 674; half measures.

[part wanting] defect, deficit, defalcation, omission; caret; wantage [*rare*], ullage, shortage; interval etc. 198; break etc. (*discontinuity*) 70; noncompletion etc. 730; missing link.

v. **be incomplete** etc. *adj.;* fall short of etc. 304; lack etc. (*be insufficient*) 640; neglect etc. 460.

adj. **incomplete**; imperfect etc. 651; unfinished; uncompleted etc. (*see* complete etc. 729); defective, deficient, wanting, failing; bobtailed; in default, in arrear; short, short of; hollow, meager, jejune, poor, scarce, lame, half-and-half, perfunctory, sketchy; crude etc. (*unprepared*) 674.

mutilated, garbled, hashed, mangled, butchered, docked, lopped, truncated.

in progress, in hand; going on, proceeding.

adv. **incompletely** etc. *adj.;* by halves.

54. Composition

n. **composition**, constitution; crasis, synizesis, syneresis; confection [*rare*], synthesis, compaction [*rare*], make, make-up; combination etc. 48; inclusion, admission, comprehension, reception; embodiment; formation.

authorship, compilation, composition, *recueil* [*F.*], production, inditing *or* inditement, conflation, invention; writing etc. 590.

hymnody, hymnology, instrumentation; opus, aria etc. (*music*) 415.

painting, scenography, etching, design etc. (*painting*) 556; relief, relievo etc. (*sculpture*) 557.

typesetting, typography etc. (*printing*) 591.

v. **be composed of**, be made of, be formed of, be made up of; consist of, be resolved into.

include etc. (*in a class*) 76; contain, hold, comprehend take in, admit, embrace, embody; involve, implicate; drag into; synthesize.

compose, constitute, form, make; make up, fill up, build up; fabricate, weave, construct; compile, redact, collate, dash off, address, indite, score, scribble, draw, write; set (*in printing*); enter into the composition of etc. (*be a component*) 56.

adj. containing, constituting etc. *v.*

55. Exclusion

n. **exclusion**, nonadmission, omission, exception, rejection, repudiation; exile etc. (*seclusion*) 893; noninclusion, preclusion, debarrance [*rare*], debarment, lock-out, disfellowship [*rare*], ostracism, prohibition.

separation, segregation, seposition [*obs.*], elimination, expulsion; cofferdam.

v. be excluded from etc.

exclude, bar; leave out, shut out, bar out; reject, repudiate, blackball, ostracize; lay apart, lay aside, put apart, put aside, set apart, set aside; relegate, segregate; throw overboard; strike off, strike out; neglect etc. 460; banish etc. (*seclude*) 893; separate etc. (*disjoin*) 44.

pass over, omit; garble; eliminate, weed, winnow.

adj. **excluding** etc. *v.;* exclusive, exclusory; excluded etc. *v.;* unrecounted, not included in; inadmissible, preclusive, preventive, prohibitive.

adv. exclusive of, barring; except; with the exception of; save; bating.

56. Component

n. **component**, integrant; component part, integral part, integrant part; element, constituent, ingredient, leaven; part and parcel; contents; appurtenance; feature; member etc. (*part*) 51; personnel.

v. **enter into**, enter into the composition of; be a component etc. *n.;* be *or* form part of etc. 51; merge in, be merged in; be implicated in; share in etc. (*participate*) 778; belong to, appertain to; combine, inhere in, unite.

form, make, constitute, compose, precompose, recompose; sonnetize [*rare*]; fabricate etc. 54.

adj. **forming** etc. *v.;* inherent, intrinsic, essential.

inclusive, all-embracing, compendious, comprehensive, inclusory.

57. Extraneousness

n. **extraneousness** etc. *adj.;* extrinsicality etc. 6; exteriority etc. 220; alienage, alienism.

foreign body, foreign substance, foreign element.

alien, stranger, intruder, interloper, foreigner, *novus homo* [*L.*], newcomer, jackaroo [*Australia*], griffin [*Anglo-Ind.*]; recruit, immigrant, emigrant; creole, Africander; outsider, outlander [*archaic*], barbarian, extern [*rare*], tramontane [*rare*], ultramontane; tenderfoot.

adj. **extraneous**, foreign, alien, ulterior, exterior, external, outlandish, outside, outland [*archaic*]; barbaric, barbarian, metic, oversea, tramontane [*rare*], ultramontane.

excluded etc. 55; inadmissible; exceptional.

adv. **abroad**, in foreign parts, in foreign lands; beyond seas; oversea, overseas; on one's travels.

Section 4. Order

58. Order

n. **order**, regularity, uniformity, symmetry, *lucidus ordo* [*L.*]; harmony, music of the spheres.

gradation, progression; series etc. (*continuity*) 69.

course, even tenor, routine; method, disposition, arrangement, array, system, economy, discipline; orderliness etc. *adj.;* subordination.

rank, place etc. (*term*) 71.

v. **form**; be *or* become in order etc. *adj.;* fall in, draw up; arrange itself, range itself, place itself; fall into one's place, fall into rank, take one's place, take rank; rally round.

adjust, methodize, regulate, systematize, standardize, normalize; time, police.

adj. **orderly**, regular; in order, in trim, in apple-pie order, in its proper place; neat, tidy, *en règle* [*F.*], well regulated, correct, methodical, uniform, symmetrical, shipshape, businesslike, systematic, systematical, normal, habitual; unconfused etc. (*see* confuse etc. 61); arranged etc. 60.

adv. **in order**; methodically etc. *adj.;* in turn, in its turn; step by step; by regular steps, by regular gradations, by regular stages, by regular intervals; *seriatim* [*NL.*], systematically, by clockwork, gradatim; at stated periods etc. (*periodically*) 138.

59. Disorder

[absence or want of order, etc.]

n. **disorder**; derangement etc. 61; irregularity; deray [*archaic*], deordination [*rare*]; anomaly etc. (*unconformity*) 83; anarchy, anarchism; want of method; untidiness etc. *adj.;* disunion; discord etc. 24.

confusion; confusedness etc. *adj.;* mishmash, mix; disarray, jumble, topsy-turvy, botch, huddle, litter, lumber; *cahotage* [*F.*]; farrago; mess, mash, muddle, muss, hash, hodgepodge, hotchpotch, hotchpot; what the cat brought in [*colloq.*]; imbroglio, chaos, omnium-gatherum [*colloq.*], medley; mere mixture etc. 41; fortuitous concourse of atoms, *disjecta membra* [*L.*].

complexity; complexness etc. *adj.;* complexus, complication, implication; intricacy, intrication [*rare*]; perplexity; network, maze, labyrinth; wilderness, jungle; involution, raveling, entanglement, dishevelment; coil etc. (*convolution*) 248; sleave, tangled skein, knot, Gordian knot, wheels within wheels; kink, gnarl *or* knarl [*obs.*]; webwork.

turmoil; ferment etc. (*agitation*) 315; to-do [*colloq.*], trouble, pudder [*obs. or dial.*], pother, row [*colloq.*], disturbance, convulsion, tumult, uproar, riot, rumpus [*colloq.*], stour [*archaic*], scramble, fracas, embroilment, *mêlée* [*F.*], spill and pelt, rough and tumble; whirlwind etc. 349; bear garden, pandemonium, Babel, Saturnalia, Donnybrook, confusion worse confounded, most admired disorder, *concordia discors* [*L.*]; Bedlam broke loose, hell broke loose; bull in a china shop; all the fat in the fire, *diable à quatre* [*F.*], Devil to pay; pretty kettle of fish; pretty piece of work.

slattern, slut, drab, dowdy, trollop, sloven, draggle-tail [*colloq.*].

v. **be disorderly** etc. *adj.;* ferment, play at cross-purposes.

put out of order; botch, derange etc. 61; drag from under the bed [*colloq.*]; ravel etc. 219; ruffle, rumple.

adj. **disorderly**, orderless; out of order, out of place, out of gear, out of kilter [*colloq.*]; irregular, desultory; anomalous etc. (*unconformable*) 83; acephalous; aimless; disorganized; straggling; unmethodical, immethodical; unsymmetric, unsystematic; untidy, slovenly, messy [*colloq.*], hugger-mugger, dislocated; out of sorts; promiscuous, indiscriminate; chaotic, anarchic, anarchical; unarranged etc. (*see* arrange etc. 60); confused; deranged etc. 61; topsy-turvy etc. (*inverted*) 218; shapeless etc. 241; disjointed, out of joint; gnarled *or* knarled [*obs.*].

complex, complexed; intricate, complicated, perplexed, involved, raveled, entangled, knotted, tangled, inextricable; irreducible.

troublous, tumultuous, turbulent; riotous etc. (*violent*) 173.

adv. **irregularly** etc. *adj.;* by fits, by fits and snatches, by fits and starts; pellmell; higgledy-piggledy; helter-skelter [*colloq.*], harum-scarum [*colloq.*]; in a ferment; at sixes and sevens, at cross-purposes; upside down etc. 218.

60. Arrangement
[reduction to order]

n. **arrangement**; plan etc. 626; preparation etc. 673; disposal, disposition, disposure; collocation, allocation; distribution; sorting etc. *v.;* assortment, allotment, apportionment, taxis, taxonomy, syntaxis, graduation, organization, ordination, grouping, groupage.
  analysis, classification, division, systematization, categorization, codification, digestion.
  [result of arrangement] orderliness, form, lay, array, digest; synopsis etc. (*compendium*) 596, syntagma, table, atlas; register etc. (*record*) 551; cosmos, schematism, organism, architecture; instrumentation, orchestration, score etc. (*music*) 415; stipulation, settlement, *bandobast* or *bundobust* [*Anglo-Ind.*].
  [instrument for sorting] sieve, riddle, screen, bolter, colander, grate, grating.
  file, card index.

v. **reduce to order**, bring into order; introduce order into; rally.
  arrange, dispose, place, form; put in order, set in order, place in order; set out, collocate, allocate, compose, space, range, pack, marshal, array, size, rank, group, parcel out, allot, distribute, deal; cast the parts, assign the parts; dispose of, assign places to; assort, sort; sift, riddle; put to rights, put into shape, put in trim, put in array, set to rights, set into shape, set in trim, set in array; tidy; apportion.
  class, classify; divide; file, list, string together, thread; register etc. (*record*) 551; catalogue, tabulate, index, alphabetize, graduate, digest, grade, codify; orchestrate, score, harmonize.
  methodize, regulate, systematize, coördinate, organize, brigade, echelon, seriate [*rare*], settle, fix.
  unravel, disentangle, unweave, ravel, card; disembroil; feaze.

adj. **arrange** etc. *v.;* embattled, in battle array; cut and dried; methodical, orderly, regular, systematic, on file; tabular, tabulate.

61. Derangement
[subversion of order; bringing into disorder]

n. **derangement** etc. *v.;* muss, mess, disorder etc. 59; evection, discomposure, disturbance; disorganization, deorganization; dislocation; perturbation, interruption; shuffling etc. *v.;* inversion etc. 218; corrugation etc. (*fold*) 258; involvement; insanity etc. 503.

v. **derange**; misarrange, disarrange, displace, misplace; mislay, discompose, disorder; disorganize; embroil, unsettle, disturb, confuse, trouble, perturb, jumble, tumble; huddle, shuffle, muddle, toss, hustle, fumble, riot; bring into disorder, put into disorder, throw into disorder etc. 59; muss, mess; break the ranks, disconcert, convulse; break in upon.
  unhinge, dislocate, put out of joint, throw out of gear.
  turn topsy-turvy etc. (*invert*) 218; bedevil; complicate, involve, perplex, confound; embrangle or imbrangle, tangle, entangle, ravel, tousle, dishevel, ruffle; rumple etc. (*fold*) 258; dement, become insane etc. 503.
  litter, scatter; mix etc. 41.

adj. **deranged** etc. *v.;* syncretic, syncretistic; mussy.

62. Precedence

n. **precedence**; predecession [*rare*]; coming before etc. *v.;* the lead, *le pas* [*F.*]; superiority etc. 33; importance etc. 642; premise *or* premiss; antecedence *or* antecedency; anteriority etc. (*front*) 234; precursor etc. 64; priority etc. 116; precession [*rare*] etc. 280; anteposition; epacme; preference.
  prefix, prefixture [*rare*], prelude, affix, preamble, overture, ritornel, *ritornello* [*It.*], voluntary.

v. **precede**, forerun, forego [*archaic*], prevene [*rare*]; come before, come first; head, lead, take the lead; lead the way, lead the dance; introduce, prologize [*rare*], usher in; have the *pas* [*F.*]; set the fashion etc. (*influence*) 175; open the ball, lead the cotillion, lead the german; rank, outrank; take precedence, have precedence; have the start etc. (*get before*) 280.
  place before; prefix; premise, prelude, preface; affix.

adj. **preceding** etc. *v.;* precedent, antecedent; anterior; prior etc. 116; before; former, foregoing; before mentioned, above mentioned, aforementioned; aforesaid, said; precursory, precursive; prevenient, preliminary, prefatory, introductory; prelusive, prelusory; proemial, preparatory.

adv. **before**; in advance etc. (*precession*) 280.

63. Sequence

n. **sequence**, train, coming after; pursuance, going after etc. (*following*) 281; consecution, succession; posteriority etc. 117.
  continuation, prolongation; mantle of Elijah; order of succession; successiveness; paracme.

secondariness; subordinancy [*obs.*], subordinacy etc. (*inferiority*) 34.

afterbirth, afterburden, afterclap, aftercrop, afterglow, aftergrass, aftermath, afterpain, afterpiece, aftertaste; placenta, secundines; sequelae.

v. **succeed**; come after, come on, come next; follow, ensue, step into the shoes of; alternate.

follow, tag [*colloq.*], heel, dog, dodge, shadow, hound, bedog, hunt; trace, retrace.

place after, suffix, append, subjoin.

adj. **succeeding** etc. *v.;* sequent; subsequent, consequent; sequacious, proximate, next; consecutive etc. (*con*tinuity) 69; alternate, amoebean.

latter; posterior etc. 117.

adv. **after**, subsequently; behind etc. (*rear*) 235.

64. Precursor

n. **precursor**, antecedent, precedent, predecessor; forerunner, apparitor, vancourier [*obs.*]; pioneer, prodrome [*obs.*], prodromos [*Gr.*], prodromus [*rare*], outrider; leader, bellwether; herald, harbinger; dawn; bellmare, *avant-coureur* [*F.*], avant-courier, *avant-courrier* [*F.*], forelooper *or* foreloper *or* forelouper [*S. Afr.*], voorlooper [*Dutch*], voortrekker [*Dutch*].

prelude, preamble, preface, prologue, foreword, *avant-propos* [*F.*], protasis, proemium, prolusion [*rare*], proem, prolepsis, prolegomena, prefix, exordium, introduction; heading, frontispiece, groundwork; preparation etc. 673; overture, voluntary, ritornel, *ritornello* [*It.*], descant, symphony; premises.

prefigurement etc. 511; omen etc. 512.

adj. **precursory**; prelusive, prelusory, preludious; proemial [*rare*], introductory, preludial, prefatory, prodromous [*rare*], inaugural, preliminary; precedent etc. (*prior*) 116.

65. Sequel

n. **sequel**, suffix, successor; tail, queue, train, wake, trail, rear; retinue, suite; appendix, postscript, subscript, postlude, conclusion, epilogue; peroration; codicil; continuation, sequela [*pl.* sequelae]; appendage, tailpiece, heelpiece; tag, more last words; colophon.

follower, successor, sectary, heeler [*slang*], pursuer, adherent, partisan, disciple, client; sycophant, parasite.

aftercome [*Scot.*], aftergrowth, afterpart, afterpiece, after course, aftergame, afterthought; *arrière pensée* [*F.*], second thoughts; outgrowth.

66. Beginning

n. **beginning**, incunabula [*pl.*], commencement, opening, outset, incipience, incipiency, inception, inchoation, inchoacy [*rare*]; introduction etc. (*precursor*) 64; alpha, initial; inauguration, ingress, *début* [*F.*], *le premier pas* [*F.*], embarkation, rising of the curtain; curtain-raiser, maiden speech; exordium; outbreak, onset, brunt; initiative, move, first move; prelude, prime, proem, gambit; narrow *or* thin end of the wedge, fresh start, new departure.

first stage, first blush, first glance, first impression, first sight.

origin etc. (*cause*) 153; source, rise; bud, germ etc. 153; egg, embryo, rudiment; genesis, birth, nativity, cradle, infancy; forefront, outstart, start, starting point etc. 293; dawn etc. (*morning*) 125.

head, heading; title-page; van etc. (*front*) 234; caption, *fatihah* [*Ar.*].

entrance, entry; inlet, orifice, mouth, chops, lips, porch, portal, portico, propylon, door; gate, gateway; postern, wicket, threshold, vestibule; propylaeum; skirts, border etc. (*edge*) 231; tee.

rudiments, elements, principia, outlines, grammar, protasis, alphabet, ABC.

v. **begin**, commence, inchoate, rise, arise, originate, conceive, initiate, open, start, gin [*archaic*], dawn, set in, take its rise, enter upon, enter; set out etc. (*depart*) 293; embark in; incept [*rare*], institute.

usher in; lead off, lead the way, take the lead, take the initiative; inaugurate, auspicate, head; stand at the head, stand first, stand for; lay the foundations etc. (*prepare*) 673; found etc. (*cause*) 153; set up, set on foot, set agoing, set abroach, set the ball in motion; apply the match to a train; launch, broach; open up, open the door to; set about, set to work; make a beginning, make a start; handsel; take the first step, lay the first stone, cut the first turf; break ground, break the ice, break cover; pass the Rubicon, cross the Rubicon; open fire, open the ball; ventilate, air; undertake etc. 676.

come into existence, come into the world; make one's *début* [*F.*], take birth; burst forth, break out; spring up, crop up.

recommence; begin at the beginning, begin *ab ovo* [*L.*], begin again, begin *de novo* [*L.*]; start afresh, make a fresh start, shuffle the cards, resume.

adj. **beginning** etc. *v.;* initial, initiatory, initiative; inceptive, introductory, incipient; proemial

67. End

[*rare*], inaugural, inauguratory; inchoate, inchoative [*rare*]; embryonic, rudimentary, rudimental; primal, primary, prime, premier [*rare*], primigenial, primigenious *or* primigenous, primogenial; primeval etc. (*old*) 124; aboriginal; natal, nascent.

first, foremost, front, head, leading; maiden.

begun etc. *v.;* just begun etc. *v.*

adv. at *or* in the beginning etc. *n.;* first, in the first place, *imprimis* [*L.*], first and foremost; *in limine* [*L.*]; in the bud, in embryo, in its infancy; from the beginning, from its birth; *ab initio* [*L.*], *ab ovo* [*L.*], *ab incunabilis* [*L.*], *ab origine* [*L.*]; formerly, erst [*archaic*].

67. End

n. **end**, close, termination; desinence [*rare*], conclusion, finis, finale, period, term, terminus, last, omega; extreme, extremity; gable end, butt end, fag-end; tip, nib, point; tail etc. (*rear*) 235; verge etc. (*edge*) 231; tag, peroration, appendix, epilogue; bottom dollar [*colloq.*], bitter end, tail end [*colloq.*], terminal, apodosis.

consummation, *dénouement* [*F.*]; finish etc. (*completion*) 729; fate; doom, doomsday; crack of doom, day of Judgment, fall of the curtain; goal, destination; limit, stoppage, end-all, wind-up [*colloq.*]; determination; expiration, expiry; dissolution, death etc. 360; end of all things; finality; eschatology.

break up, *commencement de la fin* [*F.*], last stage, evening (*of life*); turning point; *coup de grâce* [*F.*], deathblow; knock-out, knock-out blow; sockdolager [*slang*], K. O. [*slang*].

v. **end**, close, finish, terminate, conclude, be all over; expire; die etc. 360; come to a close, draw to a close etc. *n.;* perorate; have run its course; run out, pass away.

bring to an end etc. *n.;* put an end to, make an end of; determine; get through; achieve etc. (*complete*) 729; stop etc. (*make to cease*) 142; shut up shop; hang up the fiddle [*colloq.*], hang up the gloves [*colloq.*].

adj. **ending** etc. *v.;* final, terminal, terminative [*rare*], conclusive, conclusory, determinative, definitive; crowning etc. (*completing*) 729; last, ultimate; hindermost, rear etc. 235; caudal; vergent [*rare*].

conterminate [*obs.*], conterminous, conterminable [*rare*].

ended etc. *v.;* at an end; settled, decided, over, played out, set at rest; conclusive.

penultimate; last but one, last but two, etc.

adv. **finally** etc. *adj.;* in fine; at the last; once for all.

68. Middle

n. **middle**, midst, mid [*rare*], thick, midmost, middlemost [*rare*], mediety [*obs.*]; mean etc. 29; medium, middle term; center etc. 222, midcourse etc. 628; *mezzo termine* [*It.*], *mezzo cammin* [*It.*]; *juste milieu* [*F.*] etc. 628; halfway house, nave, navel, omphalos; nucleus, nucleolus.

equidistance, bisection, half distance; equator, diaphragm, midriff; interjacence etc. 228.

adj. **middle**, medial, mesial, mesian, mean, mid, middlemost, midmost, midway [*rare*], midship, mediate [*rare*]; intermediate etc. (*interjacent*) 228; equidistant; central etc. 222; mediterranean, equatorial; homocentric.

adv. **midway**, halfway; in the middle; midships, amidships, *in medias res* [*L.*] meden agan [*Gr.*].

69. Continuity
[uninterrupted sequence]

n. **continuity**, continuousness, unbrokenness; consecution, consecutiveness etc. *adj.;* succession, round, suite, progression, series, train, catena, chain; catenation, concatenation; scale; gradation, course; ceaselessness, constant flow, unbroken extent; perpetuity.

procession, column; retinue, *cortège* [*F.*], cavalcade, parade; funeral, ovation, triumph; rank and file, line of battle, array.

pedigree, genealogy, lineage, history, tree, race; ancestry, descent, family, house; line, line of ancestors; strain.

rank, file, line, row, range, tier, string, thread, team; suit; colonnade.

v. **form a series** etc. *n.;* fall in; follow in a series etc. *n.*

arrange in a series etc. *n.;* string together, file, list, thread, graduate, tabulate.

adj. **continuous**, continued; consecutive; progressive, gradual; serial, successive; immediate, unbroken, entire; linear; in a line, in a row etc. *n.;* uninterrupted, unintermitting; unremitting; perennial, evergreen; constant.

adv. **continuously** etc. *adj.; seriatim* [*NL.*]; in a line etc. *n.;* in succession, in turn; running, gradually, step by step, gradatim, at a stretch; in file, in column, in single file, in Indian file.

70. Discontinuity
[interrupted sequence]

n. **discontinuity**, discontinuousness, discreteness, disconnectedness; disjunction [*rare*] etc. 44; anacoluthon; interruption, break, fracture, flaw, fault, crack, cut; gap etc. (*interval*) 198;

solution of continuity, caesura; broken thread; parenthesis, episode, rhapsody, crazy quilt [*colloq.*], patchwork; intermission; alternation etc. (*periodicity*) 138; dropping fire.

v. **be discontinuous** etc. *adj.;* alternate, intermit.
discontinue, pause, interrupt; intervene; break, break in upon, break off; interpose etc. 228; break the thread, snap the thread; disconnect etc. (*disjoin*) 44; dissever.

adj. **discontinuous**, unsuccessive, disconnected, broken, interrupted, *décousu* [*F.*]; disconnected, unconnected; discrete, disjunct [*rare*], disjunctive; fitful etc. (*irregular*) 139; spasmodic, desultory; intermitting etc. *v.*, intermittent; alternate; recurrent etc. (*periodic*) 138.

adv. **at intervals**; by snatches, by jerks, by skips, by catches, by fits and starts; skippingly, *per saltum* [*L.*]; *longo intervallo* [*L.*].

71. Term

n. **term**, rank, station, stage, step; degree etc. 26; scale, remove, grade, link, peg, round of the ladder, status, state, position, place, point, mark, *pas* [*F.*], period, pitch; stand, standing; footing, range.

v. hold a place, occupy a place, find a place, fall into a place etc. *n.;* rank.

72. Assemblage

n. **assemblage**; collection, collocation, colligation; compilation, levy, gathering, ingathering, mobilization, meet, forgathering, muster, *attroupement* [*F.*]; team; concourse, conflux, congregation, contesseration [*obs.*], convergence etc. 290.
meeting, levee, reunion, drawing room, at home; *conversazione* [*It.*] etc. (*social gathering*) 892; assembly, congress, house, senate, legislature, convocation; caucus, séance, eisteddfod, gemot *or* gemote; convention, conventicle; conclave etc. (*council*) 696; Noah's ark.
company, platoon, faction, caravan, claque, posse, *posse comitatus* [*L.*]; watch, squad, corps, troop, troupe; army, regiment etc. (*combatants*) 726; host etc. (*multitude*) 102; populousness.
miscellany, *collectanea* [*L.*]; museum, menagerie etc. (*store*) 636; museology.
crowd, throng; flood, rush, deluge; rabble, mob, rout, press, crush, *cohue* [*F.*], horde, body, tribe; crew, gang, knot, squad, band, party; swarm, shoal, school, covey, flock, herd, drove; kennel; *atajo* [*Sp. Amer.*]; bunch, drive, force, *mulada; remuda* [*Sp.*]; round-up; array, bevy, galaxy.
clan, brotherhood, association etc. (*party*) 712.
group, cluster, Pleiades, clump, pencil; set, batch, lot, pack; budget, assortment, bunch; parcel; packet, package; bundle, fascine, bale, *seron* [*Sp.*], fagot, wisp, truss, tuft; grove, thicket, plump [*archaic*]; shock, rick, fardel, stack, sheaf, haycock, swath; fascicle, fascicule, fasciculus, gavel, hattock [*dial. Eng.*], stook [*dial.*].
volley, shower, storm, cloud.
accumulation etc. (*store*) 636; congeries, heap, lump, pile, rouleau, tissue, mass, pyramid; bing [*obs.*]; drift; snowball, snowdrift; acervation [*rare*], cumulation, amassment; glomeration, agglomeration; conglobation; conglomeration, conglomerate; coacervation [*rare*], coagmentation [*obs.*], aggregation, concentration, congestion, omnium-gatherum [*colloq.*], *spicilegium* [*L.*], Black Hole of Calcutta; quantity etc. (*greatness*) 31.
collector, gatherer; whip, whipper-in.

v. [be or come together] assemble, collect, muster; meet, unite, join, rejoin; cluster, flock, swarm, surge, stream, herd, crowd, throng, associate; congregate, conglomerate, concentrate; center round, rendezvous, resort; come together, flock together, get together, pig together; forgather *or* foregather; huddle; reassemble.
[get or bring together] assemble, muster; bring together, get together, put together, draw together, scrape together, lump together; collect, collocate, colligate; get in, whip in; gather; hold a meeting; convene, convoke, convocate; rake up, dredge, heap, mass, pile; pack, put up, truss, cram; acervate [*rare*]; agglomerate, aggregate; compile; group, aggroup, concentrate, unite; collect into a focus, bring into a focus; amass, accumulate etc. (*store*) 636; collect in a dragnet; heap Ossa upon Pelion.

adj. **assembled** etc. *v.*, closely packed, dense, serried, crowded to suffocation, teeming, swarming, populous; as thick as hops; swarming like maggots; all of a heap, fasciculated; cumulative.

73. Nonassemblage. Dispersion

n. **dispersion**; disjunction etc. 44; divergence etc. 291; aspersion; scattering etc. *v.;* dissemination, diffusion, dissipation, distribution; apportionment etc. 786; spread, respersion [*obs.*], circumfusion, interspersion, spargefaction [*obs.*], affusion.
waifs and estrays, flotsam and jetsam, *disjecta membra;* waveson.

v. **disperse**, scatter, sow, disseminate, diffuse, radiate, shed, spread, bestrew, overspread, dis-

74. Focus

pense, disband, disembody, dismember, distribute; apportion etc. 786; blow off, let out, dispel, cast forth, draft (*or* draught) off; strew, straw [*obs.*], strow [*archaic*]; ted; spurtle *or* spirtle [*obs.*], cast, sprinkle; issue, deal out, retail, utter; intersperse, resperse [*obs.*]; set abroach, circumfuse.

spread like wildfire, disperse themselves.

turn adrift, cast adrift; scatter to the winds; sow broadcast.

adj. **unassembled** etc. (*see* assemble etc. 72); diffuse, disseminated scattered, strown, strewn, dispersed etc. *v.,* dispersive, dissipative, diffusive, dispellent [*rare*]; sparse, dispread, broadcast, sporadic, widespread; epidemic etc. (*general*) 78; adrift, stray; disheveled, streaming resolvent, discutient [*med.*].

adv. **sparsim** [*L.*], here and there, *passim* [*L.*].

74. Focus
[place of meeting]

n. **focus**; point of convergence etc. 290; corradiation [*rare*]; center etc. 222; gathering place, resort; haunt; retreat; venue; rendezvous; rallying point, headquarters, home, club; depot etc. (*store*) 636; tryst, trysting place; place of meeting, place of resort, place of assignation; *point de réunion* [*F.*] issue

v. bring to a point, bring to a focus, bring to an issue, focus, corradiate [*rare*].

75. Class

n. **class**, division, subdivision, category, head, order, section; department, province, domain, sphere.

kind, sort, estate, genus, species, variety, family, race, tribe, caste, sept, phylum, clan, breed; clique, coterie; type, kit, sect, set; assortment; feather [*rare*], kidney; suit; range; gender, sex, kin.

manner, description, denomination, persuasion, connection, designation, character, stamp; predicament; indication, particularization, selection, specification.

similarity etc. 17.

76. Inclusion
[comprehension under, or reference to, a class]

n. **inclusion**, admission, incorporation, comprisal, comprehension, reception.

composition etc. (*inclusion in a compound*) 54.

v. **be included** in etc.; come under, fall under, range under; belong to, pertain to; range with; merge in.

include, comprise, comprehend, contain, admit, embrace, subsume, receive, inclose etc. (*circumscribe*) 229; incorporate, cover, embody, encircle.

reckon among, enumerate among, number among; refer to; place under, place with, arrange under, arrange with; take into account.

adj. **inclusive**, inclusory; included, including etc. *v.;* congener [*rare*], congenerous; of the same class etc. 75; comprehensive, sweeping, all-embracing, liberal, unexclusive [*rare*].

77. Exclusion[1]

n. **exclusion** etc. 55.

[1]The same set of words is used to express *Exclusion from a class* and *Exclusion from a compound*. Reference is therefore made to the former at 55. This identity does not occur with regard to *Inclusion,* which therefore constitutes a separate category.

78. Generality

n. **generality**, generalization; universality; catholicity, catholicism; miscellany, miscellaneousness; dragnet; common run; worldwideness.

Pan-Americanism, Pan-Anglicanism, Pan-Hellenism, Pan-Germanism, Pan-slavism *or* Pansclavism.

everyone, everybody, *tout le monde* [*F.*]; all hands [*colloq.*], all the world and his wife [*humorous*]; anybody, N or M, all sorts.

prevalence, rifeness, run.

v. **be general** etc. *adj.;* prevail, be going about, stalk abroad.

render general etc. *adj.;* spread, broaden, universalize, generalize.

adj. **general**, generic, collective; current, wide, broad, comprehensive, sweeping; encyclopedic *or* encyclopedical, panoramic; widespread etc. (*dispersed*) 73.

universal; catholic, catholical; common, worldwide, nationwide, statewide, heavenwide, ecumenical; prevalent, prevailing, rife, epidemic, besetting; all over [*colloq.*], covered with.

Pan-American, Pan-Anglican, Pan-Hellenic, Pan-Germanic, Panslavic *or* Pansclavic, Panslavonic, Panslavonian; panharmonic.

every, all; unspecified, impersonal, indefinite.

customary etc. (*habitual*) 613.

adv. whatever, whatsoever; to a man, one and all.

generally etc. *adj.;* always, for better for worse; in general, generally speaking; speaking generally; for the most part; in the long run etc. (*on an average*) 29; by and large, roughly speaking.

79. Specialty

n. **specialty**, *spécialité* [*F.*]; individuality, individuity [*obs.*]; particularity, peculiarity; *je ne sais quoi* [*F.*], *nescio quid* [*L.*]; idiocrasy etc. (*tendency*) 176; personality, characteristic, mannerism, idiosyncrasy, physiognomic [*rare*], diagnostic; specificness etc. *adj.;* singularity etc. (*unconformity*) 83; reading, version, lection; state; trait; distinctive feature; technicality; differentia.

particulars, details, items, counts; minutiae.

I, self, I myself; myself, himself, herself, itself.

v. **specify**, particularize, individualize, realize, specialize, designate, determine; denote, indicate, point out, select, differentiate, come to the point.

itemize, detail, descend to particulars, enter into detail.

adj. **special**, particular, individual, specific, proper, personal, original, private, respective, definite, determinate, minute, especial, certain, esoteric, endemic, partial, party, peculiar, marked, intimate, appropriate, several, characteristic, diagnostic, exclusive, restricted; singular etc. (*exceptional*) 83; idiomatic; typical, representative.

this, that; yon, yonder.

adv. **specially** etc. *adj.;* in particular, *in propria persona* [*L.*]; *ad hominem* [*L.*]; for my part.

each, apiece, one by one; severally, respectively, each to each; *seriatim* [*NL.*], in detail, bit by bit; *pro hac vice* [*L.*], *pro re nata* [*L.*].

namely, that is to say, *videlicet* [*L.*], viz.; to wit.

80. Rule

n. **regularity**, uniformity, constancy, clockwork precision; punctuality etc. (*exactness*) 494; even tenor, rut; system; routine etc. (*custom*) 613; formula; canon, convention, maxim, rule etc. (*form, regulation*) 697; keynote, standard, model; precedent etc. (*prototype*) 22; conformity etc. 82.

law, capitular *or* capitulary, gnomology [*rare*], *règlement* [*F.*], order of things; normality, normalcy; normal state, normal condition, natural state, natural condition, ordinary state, ordinary condition, model state, model condition; standing dish, standing order; Procrustean law; law of the Medes and Persians; hard and fast rule; nature, principle.

adj. **regular**, uniform, symmetrical, constant, steady; according to rule etc. (*conformable*) 82; normal, habitual, customary etc. 613; methodical, orderly, systematic, systematical.

81. Multiformity

n. **multiformity**, omniformity; variety, diversity; multifariousness etc. *adj.;* varied assortment.

adj. **multiform**, multifold, multifarious, multigenerous, multiplex; variform [*rare*], diversiform, amoebiform, manifold, many-sided; omniform, omnigenous, omnifarious; polymorphic, polymorphous, multiphase, metamorphotic, protean, proteiform, heterogeneous, motley, mosaic; epicene.

indiscriminate, desultory, irregular, diversified, different, divers; all manner of; of every description, of all sorts and kinds; *et hoc genus omne* [*L.*]; and what not?

82. Conformity

n. **conformity**, conformance; observance; habituation; naturalization; conventionality etc. (*custom*) 613; agreement etc. 23.

example, instance, specimen, sample, quotation; exemplification, illustration, case in point; object lesson; elucidation.

pattern etc. (*prototype*) 22.

conventionalist, formalist, bromide [*slang*], Philistine.

v. **conform to**, conform to rule; accommodate oneself to, adapt oneself to; rub off corners.

be regular etc. *adj.;* move in a groove, move in a rut, travel in a rut; follow-, observe-, go by-, bend to-, obey- -rules, -precedents; agree with, comply with, tally with, chime in with, fall in with; be guided by, be regulated by; fall into a custom, fall into a usage; follow the fashion, follow the multitude; assimilate to, shape, harmonize, conventionalize, pass muster, do as others do, *hurler avec les loups* [*F.*]; do in Rome as the Romans do; go with the -stream, -current, -tide; swim with the -stream, -current, -tide; pass current; tread the beaten track etc. (*habit*) 613; keep one in countenance.

exemplify, illustrate, example, sample, type [*rare*], cite, quote, put a case; produce an instance etc. *n.;* elucidate, explain.

adj. **conformable to rule**; adaptable, consistent, agreeable, compliant; regular etc. 80; according to regulation, according to rule, according to Cocker, according to Gunter, according to Hoyle [*all colloq.*]; *en règle* [*F.*], *selon les règles* [*F.*], well regulated, orderly; symmetric etc. 242.

conventional etc. (*customary*) 613; of daily occurrence, of everyday occurrence; in the natural order of things; ordinary, common, habitual,

83. Unconformity

usual, commonplace, prosaic, bromidic, Philistine.
in the order of the day; naturalized.
typical, normal, formal; canonical, orthodox, sound, strict, rigid, positive, uncompromising, Procrustean.
secundum artem [*L.*], shipshape, point-device [*archaic*], technical.
exemplary, illustrative, in point.

adv. **conformably** etc. *adj.;* by rule; agreeably to; in conformity with, in accordance with, in keeping with; according to; consistently with; as usual, *ad instar* [*L.*], *instar omnium* [*L.*]; *more solito* [*L.*], *more majorum* [*L.*].
for the sake of conformity; of course, as a matter of course; *pro forma* [*L.*], for form's sake, by the card.
invariably etc. (*uniformly*) 16.
for example, for instance; *exempli gratia* [*L.*]; *e. g.; inter alia* [*L.*].

83. Unconformity

n. **nonconformity** etc. 82; unconformity, disconformity; unconventionality, informality, abnormity, anomaly; anomalousness etc. *adj.;* exception, peculiarity; infraction–, breach–, violation–, infringement- of -law, –custom, –usage; teratism, eccentricity, *bizarrerie* [*F.*], oddity, *je ne sais quoi* [*F.*], monstrosity, rarity; freak of nature.
individuality, idiosyncrasy, singularity, selfness [*rare*], originality, mannerism.
aberration; irregularity; variety; singularity; exemption; salvo [*rare*] etc. (*qualification*) 469.
nonconformist, bohemian, nondescript, character [*colloq.*], original, nonesuch [*rare*], freak, crank [*colloq.*], prodigy, wonder, miracle, curiosity, missing link, flying fish, black swan, monster, white blackbird, basilisk, salamander, *lusus naturae* [*L.*], *rara avis* [*L.*], queer fish [*slang*].
mongrel; half-caste, half-blood, half-breed etc. 41; metis, crossbreed, hybrid, mule, mulatto; *tertium quid* [*L.*], hermaphrodite.
monster, phoenix, chimera, hydra, sphinx, minotaur; griffin *or* griffon; centaur, xiphopagus; hippogriff, hippocentaur; sagittary; kraken, cockatrice, wivern *or* wyvern [*obs.*], roc, dragon, sea serpent; mermaid; unicorn; Cyclops, "men whose heads do grow beneath their shoulders" [*Othello*]; teratology.
fish out of water; neither one thing nor another; neither fish, flesh, fowl, nor good red herring; one in a way, one in a thousand.

outcast, outlaw, Ishmael, pariah.

v. **be uncomformable** etc. *adj.;* abnormalize; leave the beaten track, leave the beaten path; infringe–, break–, violate - a -law, –habit, –usage, –custom; stretch a point; have no business there; baffle all description, beggar all description.

adj. **uncomformable**, exceptional; abnormal, abnormous; anomalous, anomalistic; out of order, out of place, out of keeping, out of tune, out of one's element; irregular, arbitrary; teratogenic, teratogenetic; lawless, informal, aberrant, stray, wandering, wanton; peculiar, exclusive, unnatural, eccentric, egregious; out of the beaten track, out of the common, out of the common run, out of the pale of; misplaced; funny [*colloq.*].
unusual, unaccustomed, uncustomary, unordinary, unwonted, uncommon; rare, singular, unique, curious, odd, extraordinary, strange, monstrous; wonderful etc. 870; unexpected, unaccountable; *outré* [*F.*], out of the way, remarkable, noteworthy, *recherché* [*F.*], queer, quaint, nondescript, *sui generis* [*L.*]; original, unconventional, supernormal [*rare*], bohemian, sulphitic [*slang*], unfashionable; undescribed, unprecedented, unparalleled, unexampled, unheard of, unfamiliar; fantastic, newfangled, grotesque, bizarre; outlandish, exotic, *tombé des nues* [*F.*], preternatural; denaturalized.
heterogeneous, heteroclite, amorphous, mongrel, amphibious, epicene, half blood, hybrid; androgynous, androgynal; unsymmetric etc. 243; adelomorphic *or* adelomorphous, gynandrous, bisexual, hermaphrodite, androgynic, androgynous, monoclinous.

adv. **unconformably** etc. *adj.;* except, unless, save, barring, beside, without, save and except, let alone.
however, yet, but.

int. what on earth! what in the world!

Section 5. Number

84. Number

n. **number**, symbol, numeral, figure, cipher, digit, integer; counter; round number; formula; function; series.
sum, difference, complement, subtrahend; product, total, aggregate; multiplicand, multiplier, multiplicator; coefficient, multiple; dividend, divisor, factor, quotient, submultiple, fraction; mixed number; numerator, denominator; deci-

mal, circulating decimal, repetend; common measure, aliquot part; reciprocal; prime number; totient; quota, quotum [*rare*].

figurate numbers, pyramidal numbers, polygonal numbers.

permutation, combination, variation; election.

ratio, proportion; progression; arithmetical progression, geometrical progression, harmonical progression; percentage.

power, root, radix, exponent, index, logarithm, antilogarithm; modulus. differential, integral, fluxion, fluent.

adj. **numeral**, complementary, divisible, aliquot, reciprocal, prime, fractional, decimal, figurate, incommensurable.

proportional, exponential, logarithmic, logometric, differential, fluxional, integral, totitive.

positive, negative; rational, irrational; surd, radical, real, imaginary, impossible.

85. Numeration

n. **numeration**; numbering etc. *v.;* pagination; tale, tally, telling [*archaic*], recension, enumeration, summation, reckoning, computation, supputation [*obs.*]; calculation, calculus; algorithm, rhabdology, dactylonomy; measurement etc. 466; statistics, logistics.

arithmetic, analysis, algebra, fluxions; differential calculus, integral calculus, infinitesimal calculus; calculus of differences.

[statistics] dead reckoning, muster, poll, census, capitation, roll call, recapitulation; account etc. (*list*) 86.

[operations] notation, addition, subtraction, multiplication, division, proportion, rule of three, practice, equations, extraction of roots, reduction, involution, evolution, approximation, interpolation, differentiation, integration, indigitation [*rare*].

[instruments] abacus, calculator, computer, suan pan, logometer, slide rule, tallies, Napier's bones, calculating machine, difference engine; adding machine; cash register.

arithmetician, calculator, geodesist, abacist; algebraist, geometrician, trigonometrician, mathematician, actuary, statistician.

v. **number**, count, tell; call over, run over; take an account of, enumerate, call the roll, muster, poll, recite, recapitulate; sum; sum up, cast up; tell off, score, cipher, reckon, reckon up, tally estimate, make an estimate, furnish an estimate, make up accounts, compute, calculate, suppute [*obs.*], add, subtract, multiply, divide, extract roots, algebraize.

check, prove, demonstrate, balance, audit, overhaul, take stock.

page, affix numbers to, foliate, paginate.

amount to, come to, total.

adj. **numeral**, numerical; arithmetical, analytic, algebraic, statistical, countable, reckonable, numberable, computable, calculable, rhabdological; commensurable, commensurate; incommensurable, incommensurate.

86. List

n. **list**, catalogue *or* catalog, inventory, schedule, calends [*rare*]; register etc. (*record*) 551; account; bill, bill of costs; syllabus; terrier, tally, file; calendar, index, table, atlas, contents; book, ledger; synopsis, *catalogue raisonné* [*F.*]; scroll, brief [*obs.*], screed, manifest, invoice, bill of lading; prospectus, program; bill of fare, menu, carte; score, bulletin, *tableau* [*F.*], census, statistics, returns; Red Book, Blue Book, Domesday Book; directory, gazetteer.

almanac; army list, clergy list, civil service list, navy list; Statesman's Yearbook, Whitaker's Almanack, *Almanach de Gotha*, cadastre *or* cadaster, *cadre* [*F.*], card index; Lloyd's Register, Nautical Almanac, Who's Who.

dictionary, lexicon, glossary, word-book, thesaurus, gloss [*rare*], gradus.

roll; check roll, checker roll, bead roll; muster roll, muster book; roll of honor; roster, slate, rota, poll, panel; chartulary *or* cartulary, diptych.

v. **list**, enroll, schedule, inventorize [*rare*], inventory, register, catalogue *or* catalog, invoice, bill, book, indent, slate, post, manifest, docket; matriculate, empanel, calendar, tally, file, index, tabulate, enter, score, keep score; census.

adj. inventorial, cadastral; listed etc. *v.*

87. Unity

n. **unity**; oneness etc. *adj.;* individuality; solitude etc. (*seclusion*) 893; isolation etc. (*disjunction*) 44; unification etc. 48; completeness etc. 52.

one, unit, ace, monad; individual; none else, no other, nought beside.

integer, item, point, module.

v. **be one**, be alone etc. *adj.*

isolate etc. (*disjoin*) 44.

render one; unite etc. (*join*) 43, (*combine*) 48.

adj. **one**, sole, only-begotten, single, solitary, companionless; individual, apart, alone; kithless.

unaccompanied, unattended; *solus* (*fem., sola*) [*L.*], single-handed; singular, odd, unique,

88. Accompaniment

unrepeated, azygous, first and last; isolated etc. (*disjoined*); insular.

monadic, monadical; unific, uniflorous, unilobed, uniglobular, unifoliolate, unigenital, uniliteral, unilocular, unimodular, unitary; monospermous.

inseverable, indiscerptible; compact, irresolvable.

lone, lonely, lonesome; desolate, dreary.

adv. **singly** etc. *adj.;* alone, by itself, *per se* [*L.*], only [*rare*], apart, in the singular number, in the abstract; one by one, one at a time; simply; one and a half, *sesqui-*.

88. Accompaniment

n. **accompaniment**; adjunct etc. 39; context; appendage, appurtenance.

company, association, companionship; coexistence, concomitance; partnership, copartnership; coefficiency.

concomitant, accessory, coefficient; companion, attendant, fellow, associate, *fidus Achates* [*L.*], consort, spouse, colleague; partner, copartner; satellite, hanger-on, shadow; escort, *cortège* [*F.*], suite, train, convoy, follower etc. 65; attribute.

v. **accompany**, coexist, attend, company [*archaic*], convoy, chaperon; hang on, wait on; go hand in hand with; synchronize etc. 120; bear company, keep company; row in the same boat; bring in its train; associate with, couple with.

adj. **accompanying** etc. *v.;* concomitant, fellow, twin, joint; associated with, coupled with; accessory, attendant, comitant [*rare*], obbligato.

adv. **with**, withal; together with, along with, in company with; hand in hand, side by side; cheek by jowl; arm in arm; therewith, herewith; and etc. (*addition*) 37.

together, in a body, collectively, in conjunction.

89. Duality

n. **duality**, dualism; duplicity; biplicity [*rare*], biformity; polarity.

two, deuce, couple, couplet, both, twain, brace, pair, cheeks, twins, Castor and Pollux, gemini, Siamese twins; fellows; yoke, conjugation; dispermy, doublets, dyad, duad, twosome [*rare*], distich, span.

v. [unite in pairs] pair, couple, bracket, yoke; conduplicate; mate, span [*U.S.*].

adj. **two**, twain; dual, dualistic; binary, binomial; twin, biparous; dyadic; conduplicate; duplex etc. 90; biduous, binate, binary, binal [*rare*], diphyletic, dispermic, paired, unijugate; *tête-à-tête* [*F.*].

coupled etc. *v.;* conjugate.

both, both the one and the other.

90. Duplication

n. **duplication**; doubling etc. *v.;* gemination, ingemination; reduplication; iteration etc. (*repetition*) 104; renewal.

duplicate, facsimile, copy, replica, counterpart etc. (*copy*) 21.

v. **double**; redouble, reduplicate; geminate [*rare*]; repeat etc. 104; renew etc. 660.

adj. **double**; doubled etc. *v.;* bicipital, bicephalous, bidental, bilabiate, bivalve, bivalvular, bifold, biform, bilateral, bifarious, bifacial; twofold, twosided; disomatous; duple [*rare*], duplex; double-faced, double-headed; twin, duplicate, geminous [*rare*], geminate, ingeminate; second: dual etc. 89.

adv. **twice**, once more; over again etc. (*repeatedly*) 104; as much again, twofold.

secondly, in the second place, again.

91. Bisection

[division into two parts]

n. **bisection**, bipartition; dichotomy, subdichotomy [*rare*]; halving etc. *v.;* dimidiation.

bifurcation, furcation, forking, branching, ramification, divarication; fork, crotch, furculum, prong; fold.

half, moiety.

v. **bisect**, halve, hemisect [*rare*], divide, split, cut in two, cleave, dimidiate, dichotomize.

go halves, divide with.

separate, fork, bifurcate, furcate, divaricate; branch off *or* out; ramify.

adj. **bisected** etc. *v.;* cloven, cleft; bipartite, dimidiate, divaricate, biconjugate, bicuspid, bifid; bifurcous [*rare*], bifurcate, bifurcated; bigeminate, distichous, distichal, dichotomous, furcular, furcate, lituate [*rare*]; semi-, demi-, hemi-.

92. Triality

n. **triality** [*rare*], trinity, triunity, Trimurti [*Hindu*], triplicity, trialism [*rare*].

three, triad, triplet, ternion, ternary, trine [*rare*], trey, trio, leash; shamrock, tierce, delta, trefoil; triangle, trident, triennium, trigon [*rare*], trinomial, trionym, triplopia *or* triplopy, tripod, trireme, triseme, triskelion *or* triskele, trisul *or* trisula, triumvirate.

third power, cube.

adj. **three**; triform, trinal, trinomial; tertiary; triune; triarch, triadic.

93. Triplication

- *n.* **triplication**, triplicity; trebleness, terza, trine; trilogy.
- *v.* **treble**, triple, triplicate, cube.
- *adj.* **treble**, triple; tern, ternary, ternate, tertiary; triplicate, threefold, trilogistic; triplasic; third; trinal, trine [*rare*].
- *adv.* **three times**, thrice, in the third place, thirdly, threefold, triply, trebly etc. *adj.*

94. Trisection
[division into three parts]

- *n.* **trisection**, tripartition, trichotomy; third, third part.
- *v.* **trisect**, divide into three parts, third.
- *adj.* **trifid**; trisected etc. *v.;* tripartite, trichotomous, trisulcate; ternal, trident, tridental.
  triadelphous, triangular, trichotomic, tricuspid, tricapsular, tridental, tridentate *or* tridentated, tridentiferous, trifoliolate, trifurcate *or* trifurcated, trigonoid, trigonous, trigonal, trigrammic *or* trigrammatic, tripedal, trilateral, tripetalous, tripodal, tripodic, triquetral, triquetrous.

95. Quaternity

- *n.* **quaternity** [*rare*], four, tetrad, quartet *or* quartette, quatre [*rare*], quadruplet, quaternion, square, quadrilateral, quadrinomial, biquadrate, quarter, quarto, tetract, tetragon.
  quadrangle, quadrature, quadruplet; quatrefoil; tetragram, tetragrammaton; tetrahedron, tetrapody, tetrology, quatrefoil *or* quadrefoil.
- *v.* **square**, biquadrate, reduce to a square.
- *adj.* **four**; quaternary, quaternal; quadratic; quartile, quartic, quadrifid, quadriform, quadric, biquadratic; tetract, tetractine, tetractinal [*zool.*], four-rayed; tetrad, quadrivalent; quadrangular, tetragonal, quadrilateral, tetrahedral.

96. Quadruplication

- *n.* **quadruplication**.
- *v.* **quadruplicate**, biquadrate, multiply by four.
- *adj.* **fourfold**; quadrable, quadruple, quadruplex, quadruplicate, quadrible; fourth.
- *adv.* **four times**; in the fourth place, fourthly.

97. Quadrisection
[division into four parts]

- *n.* **quadrisection**, quadripartition; quartering etc. *v.;* fourth; quart, quarter, quartern; farthing.
- *v.* **quarter**, divide into four parts, quadrisect.
- *adj.* **quartered** etc. *v.;* quadrifid, quadripartite [*rare*]; quadrifoliate, quadrigeminal, quadrigeminous, quadrigeminate, quadripennate, quadriplanar, quadriserial, quadrivial, quadrifurcate, quadrumanal, quadrumane, quadrumous.

98. Five, etc.

- *n.* **five**, cinque, quint, quincunx, quintet *or* quintette, quintuple, quintuplet, quinary [*rare*], pentad; pentagon, pentagram, pentameter, pentapody, pentarchy, pentastich, Pentateuch.
  six, sise *or* size [*rare*], hexad, sextuplet, hexagon, hexahedron, hexagram, hexameter, hexapod, hexapody, hexastich, Hexateuch, sextet, half-a-dozen.
  seven, heptad, septenary [*rare*], heptagon, heptahedron, heptameter, heptarchy, Heptateuch.
  eight, octave, octonary, octad, ogdoad, octagon, octahedron, octameter, octastyle, octavo, octet.
  nine, novenary [*rare*], ennead, nonary [*rare*]; nonagon, three times three; *novena* [*R. C. Ch.*].
  ten, decad [*rare*], decade, dicker; decagon, decagram, decahedron, decapod, decare, decastere, decastyle, decasyllable, decemvir, decemvirate, decennium.
  eleven; **twelve**, dozen; **thirteen**; long dozen, baker's dozen; **twenty**, score; twenty-four, four and twenty, two dozen; twenty-five, five and twenty, quarter of a hundred; forty, twoscore; fifty, half a hundred; sixty, sexagenary, threescore; seventy, threescore and ten; eighty, fourscore; ninety, fourscore and ten.
  hundred, centenary, hecatomb, century, bicentenary, tercentenary; hundredweight, cwt.; one hundred and forty-four, gross.
  thousand, chiliad, milliad [*rare*], millenary [*rare*], millennium; myriad, ten thousand; one hundred thousand, lac *or* lakh [*India*], plum [*obs.*], million; ten million, crore [*India*]; thousand million, billion, milliard.
  billion, trillion etc.
- *v.* quintuplicate, sextuple, centuplicate, centuriate [*obs.*].
- *adj.* **five**, fifth, quinary, quintuple; quintuplicate, pentangular, pentagonal, pentastyle.
  sixth, senary [*rare*], sextuple, hexagonal, hexangular, hexastyle, hexahedral, sextan.
  seventh, septuple, septenary, septimal [*rare*]; heptagonal, heptahedral, heptamerous, heptangular.
  eighth, octuple, octonary; octagonal, octahedral, octan, octangular, octastyle.
  ninth, ninefold, novenary [*rare*], nonary [*rare*], enneahedral, enneastyle.

99. Quinquesection, etc.

tenth, tenfold, decimal, denary, decuple, decagonal, decahedral, decasyllabic.
eleventh, undecennial, undecennary.
twelfth, duodenary, duodenal.
in one's teens, thirteenth, etc.
twentieth, vicenary, vicennial, vigesimal, vicesimal.
sixtieth, sexagesimal, sexagenary.
seventieth, septuagesimal, septuagenary.
centuple, centuplicate, centennial, centenary, centurial; secular, hundredth; thousandth, millenary, millennial etc.

99. Quinquesection, etc.

n. **quinquesection** etc.; division by five etc. 98; decimation; fifth etc.
v. **decimate**; quinquesect; decimalize.
adj. **quinquefid**, quinqueliteral, quinquepartite.
sexpartite; octofid; decimal, tenth, tithe; duodecimal, twelfth; sexagesimal, sexagenary; hundredth, centesimal; millesimal etc.

100. Plurality
[more than one]

n. **plurality**; a number, a certain number; one or two, two or three etc.; a few, several; multitude etc. 102; majority.
adj. **plural**, more than one, upwards of, some, certain; not, not alone etc. 87.
adv. et cetera, etc.

100a. Fraction
[less than one]

n. **fraction**, fractional part; part etc. 51.
adj. **fractional**, fragmentary, inconsiderable, partial, portional.

101. Zero

n. **zero**, nothing; naught, nought; cipher, none, nobody; *nichts* [*Ger.*], goose egg, nix [*slang*]; not a soul; absence etc. 187; unsubstantiality etc. 4.
adj. **no**, not one, not any.

102. Multitude

n. **multitude**; multitudinousness, numerousness etc. *adj.;* numerosity, numerality [*obs.*]; multiplicity; profusion etc. (*plenty*) 639; legion, host; great number, large number, round number, enormous number; a quantity, numbers, array, sight, army, sea, galaxy; scores, peck, bushel, shoal, oodles [*colloq.*], pile [*colloq.*], heap [*colloq.*], power [*colloq.*], sight [*colloq.*], lot [*colloq.*], lots [*colloq.*], swarm, bevy, cloud, flock, herd, drove, flight, covey, hive, brood, litter, farrow, fry, nest; mob, crowd etc. (*assemblage*) 72; all the world and his wife [*humorous*].
[increase of number] greater number, majority; multiplication, multiple.
v. **be numerous** etc. *adj.;* swarm with, teem with, be alive with, creep with; crowd, swarm, come thick upon; outnumber, multiply; people; swarm like locusts, swarm like bees.
adj. **many**, several, sundry, divers, various, not a few; Briarean; a hundred, a thousand, a myriad, a million, a billion, a quadrillion, a nonillion, a thousand and one; some ten or a dozen, some forty or fifty etc.; half a dozen, half a hundred etc.; alive with; very many, full many, ever so many; numerous; profuse, in profusion; manifold, multifold, multiplied, multitudinous, multiple, multinomial, teeming, populous, peopled, outnumbering, crowded, thick, studded; galore [*colloq.*].
thick coming, many more, more than one can tell, a world of; no end of, no end to; *cum multis aliis* [*L.*], thick as hops, thick as hail; plenty as blackberries; numerous as the stars in the firmament, numerous as the sands on the seashore, numerous as the hairs on the head; and what not, and heaven knows what; endless etc. (*infinite*) 105.

103. Fewness

n. **fewness** etc. *adj.;* paucity, scarcity, sparseness, sparsity, small number; only a few; small quantity etc. 32; rarity; infrequency etc. 137; handful; minority; exiguity.
[diminution of number] reduction; weeding etc. *v.;* elimination, sarculation [*obs.*], decimation; eradication.
v. **be few** etc. *adj.*
render few etc. *adj.;* reduce, diminish, diminish the number, weed, eliminate, thin, decimate.
adj. **few**; scant, scanty; thin, rare, scarce, sparse, thinly scattered, few and far between; exiguous; infrequent etc. 137; *rari nantes* [*L.*]; hardly any, scarcely any; to be counted on one's fingers, to be counted on the fingers of one hand; reduced etc. *v.;* unrepeated.
adv. here and there.

104. Repetition

n. **repetition**, iteration, reiteration, iterance [*rare*], reiterance [*rare*], alliteration, duplication, reduplication, monotone, harping, recurrence, succession, run; battology, tautology; monotony, tautophony; rhythm etc. 138; diffuseness, pleonasm, redundancy.

chimes, repetend, echo, reëcho, encore, dilogy [*rare*], *ritornello* [*It.*], burden of a song, refrain, undersong; rehearsal; *réchauffé* [*F.*], *rifacimento* [*It.*], recapitulation.

cuckoo etc. (*imitation*) 19; reverberation etc. 408; drumming etc. (*roll*) 407; renewal etc. (*restoration*) 660.

twice-told tale, chestnut [*slang*], old stuff [*slang*], old story, old song; second edition, new edition; reappearance, reproduction; periodicity etc. 138.

v. **repeat**, iterate, reiterate, reproduce, echo, reëcho, drum, harp upon, battologize, tautologize, hammer, redouble.

recur, revert, return, reappear; renew etc. (*restore*) 660.

rehearse; do over again, say over again; ring the changes on; harp on the same string; din in the ear, drum in the ear; conjugate in all its moods, tenses and inflexions; begin again, go over the same ground, go the same round, duplicate, reduplicate, never hear the last of; resume, return to, recapitulate, reword.

adj. **repeated** etc. *v.;* warmed up, warmed over, repetitional, repetitionary, repetitive, repetitious, reduplicatory [*rare*], reduplicative, recurrent, recurring; ever recurring, thick coming; frequent, incessant; redundant, pleonastic, tautological, tautologous, tautophonical, inexhaustible, unplumbed.

monotonous, harping, iterative, unvaried; mocking, chiming; retold; habitual etc. 613; another.

aforesaid, aforenamed; above-mentioned, said.

adv. **repeatedly**, often, again, anew, over again, afresh, once more; ditto, encore, *de novo* [*L.*], bis, *da capo* [*It.*].

again and again; over and over, over and over again; many times over; time and again, time after time; times without number; year after year; day by day etc.; many times, several times, a number of times; many a time, full many a time; frequently etc. 136; inexhaustibly, depth beyond depth.

105. Infinity

n. **infinity**, infinitude, infiniteness etc. *adj.;* perpetuity etc. 112; inexhaustibility, immensity, boundlessness.

v. **be infinite** etc. *adj.;* know no limits, know no bounds, have no limits, have no bounds; go on forever.

adj. **infinite**; immense; numberless, countless, sumless, measureless, innumerable, immeasurable, incalculable, illimitable, interminable, unfathomable, unapproachable; exhaustless, indefinite; without number, without measure, without limit, without end; incomprehensible; limitless, endless, boundless, termless; untold, unnumbered, unmeasured, unbounded, unlimited, illimited; perpetual etc. 112.

adv. **infinitely** etc. *adj.; ad infinitum* [*L.*].

Section 6. Time

---

106. Time

n. **time**, duration; period, term, stage, space, tide [*archaic*], span, spell, season; the whole time, the whole period; course etc. 109; snap.

intermediate time, while, bit, breathing, interim, interval, pendency; intervention, intermission, intermittence, interregnum, interlude; respite.

era, epoch, Kalpa, eon, cycle; time of life, age, year, date; decade etc. (*period*) 108; point, bell, moment etc. (*instant*) 113; reign etc. 737.

glass of time, ravages of time, whirligig of time, noiseless foot of Time; scythe of Time.

v. **continue**, last, endure, stay, go on, remain, persist, subsist, abide, run, stand, dure [*archaic*], perdure [*rare*], perennate [*rare*], stick [*colloq.*]; intervene; elapse etc. 109; hold out.

take time, take up time, fill time, occupy time.

pass time; pass away time, spend time, while away time, consume time, talk against time; tide over; use time, employ time; seize an opportunity etc. 134; linger on, drag on, drag along, tarry etc. 110; waste time etc. (*be inactive*) 683; procrastinate etc. 133.

adj. **continuing** etc. *v.;* on foot; permanent etc. (*durable*) 110; timely etc. (*opportune*) 134.

adv. **while**, whilst, during, pending; during the time, during the interval; in the course of; for the time being, day by day; in the time of, when; meantime, meanwhile; in the meantime, in the interim; *ad interim* [*L.*], *pendente lite* [*L.*]; *de die in diem* [*L.*]; from day to day, from hour to hour etc.; hourly, always; for a time, for a season; till, until, up to, yet; the whole time, all the time; all along; throughout etc. (*completely*) 52; for good etc. (*diuturnity*) 110.

then, hereupon, thereupon, whereupon; *anno Domini* [*L.*], A.D.; *ante Christum* [*L.*], A.C.; before Christ, B.C.; *anno urbis conditae* [*L.*], A.U.C.; *anno regni* [*L.*], A.R.; once upon a time, one fine morning.

107. Neverness

n. "neverness"; absence of time, no time; *dies non* [*L.*]; St. Tib's eve; Greek Calends (*or* Kalends).

adv. never, ne'er; at no time, at no period; on *or* at the Greek Calends (*or* Kalends); on no occasion, never in all one's born days [*colloq.*], *jamais de ma vie* [*F.*], nevermore, *sine die* [*L.*], in no degree.

108. Period
[definite duration, or portion of time]

n. period; second, minute, hour, day, week, month, octave, *novena* [*L.*], semester, quarter, year, decade, decennium, luster *or* lustrum, indication; cycle–, era– of indiction (*or* indictions); quinquennium, lifetime, generation; epoch, era, epact, ghurry *or* ghari [*India*], lunation, moon. century, age, millennium; *annus magnus* [*L.*], *annus mirabilis* [*L.*].

adj. horary; hourly, annual, epochal etc. (*periodical*) 13; *ante bellum* [*L.*].

108a. Contingent Duration

adv. during pleasure, during good behavior; *quandiu se bene gesserit* [*L.*].

109. Course
[indefinite duration]

n. corridors of time, sweep of time, vista of time, halls of time, course of time, progress of time, process of time, succession of time, lapse of time, flow of time, flux of time, stream of time, tract of time, current of time, tide of time, march of time, step of time, flight of time; duration etc. 106.

[indefinite time] aeon *or* eon, age, Kalpa; aorist.

v. elapse, lapse, flow, run, proceed, advance, pass; roll on, wear on, press on; flit, fly, slip, slide, glide; crawl, drag; run its course, run out; expire; go by, pass by; be past etc. 122.

adj. elapsing etc. *v.;* aoristic; transient etc. 111; progressive.

adv. in time; in due time, in due season, in due course; in course of time, in process of time, in the fullness of time.

110. Diuturnity
[long duration]

n. diuturnity [*rare*]; a long time, length of time; an age, aeon *or* eon, a century, an eternity; slowness etc. 275; coeternity, sempiternity, perpetuity etc. 112; blue moon [*colloq.*], coon's age [*colloq.*], dog's age [*colloq.*].

durableness, durability; persistence, eternalness, lastingness etc. *adj.;* continuance, standing; permanence etc. (*stability*) 150; survival, survivance; longevity etc. (*age*) 128; distance of time.

protraction of time, prolongation of time, extension of time; delay etc. (*lateness*) 133.

v. last, endure, stand, remain, abide, continue etc. 106; brave a thousand years.

tarry etc. (*be late*) 133; drag on, drag its slow length along, drag a lengthening chain; protract, prolong; spin out, eke out, draw out, lengthen out; temporize; gain time, make time, talk against time.

outlast, outlive; survive; live to fight again.

adj. durable, endurable [*rare*]; lasting etc. *v.;* of long duration, of long standing; permanent, chronic, longstanding; diuturnal [*rare*]; intransient, intransitive; intransmutable, persistent; lifelong, livelong; longeval [*rare*], longevous, endless, fixed, immortal, perdurant [*rare*], perdurable, long-lived, macrobiotic, evergreen, perennial; sempervirent [*rare*], sempervirid; unintermitting, unremitting; perpetual etc. 112.

lingering, protracted, prolonged, spun out etc. *v.;* long-pending, long-winded; slow etc. 275.

adv. long; for a long time, for an age, for ages, for ever so long, for many a long day; long ago etc. (*in a past time*) 122; *longo intervallo* [*L.*].

all the day long, all the year round; the livelong day, as the day is long, morning, noon and night; hour after hour, day after day etc.; for good, for good and all; permanently etc. *adj.;* *semper et ubique* [*L.*].

111. Transience
[short duration]

n. transience, transiency, ephemerality, transientness [*rare*] etc. *adj.;* evanescence, impermanence *or* impermanency, preterience [*rare*], volatility, fugacity, caducity [*rare*], mortality, span; nine days' wonder, bubble, Mayfly; spurt; temporary arrangement, interregnum, interim.

velocity etc. 274; suddenness etc. 113; changeableness etc. 149.

ephemeron; transient, transient boarder, transient guest, transient rates.

v. be transient etc. *adj.;* flit, pass away, fly, gallop, vanish, fleet, sink, melt, fade, evaporate; pass away like a –cloud, –summer cloud, –shadow, –dream.

adj. transient, transitory, transitive; passing, evanescent, fleeting; flying etc. *v.;* fugacious, fugitive; transeunt, interim, shifting, slippery; spasmodic.

115. Anachronism

temporal, temporary; provisional, provisory; cursory, short-lived, ephemeral, ephemerous [*rare*], preterient [*rare*], caducous [*rare*], deciduous; perishable, mortal, precarious; impermanent.

brief, quick, brisk, fleet, cometary, meteoric, volatile, extemporaneous, summary; pressed for time etc. (*haste*) 684; sudden, momentary etc. (*instantaneous*) 113.

adv. **temporarily** etc. *adj.; pro tempore* [*L.*]; for the moment, for a time; awhile, *en passant* [*F.*], *in transitu* [*L.*]; in a short time; soon etc. (*early*) 132; briefly etc. *adj.;* at short notice; on the point of, on the eve of; *in articulo mortis* [*L.*]; between cup and lip.

112. Perpetuity
[endless duration]

n. **perpetuity**, eternity, everness,[1] aye, sempiternity, perenniality [*rare*], coeternity, immortality, athanasy, athanasia; everlastingness etc. *adj.;* perpetuation; continued existence, uninterrupted existence; perennity [*obs.*].

v. **have no end**; last forever, endure forever, go on forever.

eternize, immortalize, eternalize, monumentalize, perpetuate.

adj. **perpetual**, eternal; everduring, everlasting, everliving, everflowing; continual, sempiternal, sempiternous [*rare*], eviternal [*rare*]; coeternal; endless, unending; ceaseless, incessant, uninterrupted, indesinent [*obs.*], unceasing; interminable, eterne [*poetic*], having no end; unfading, evergreen, amaranthine; never-ending, never-dying, never-fading; deathless, immortal, undying, imperishable.

adv. **perpetually** etc. *adj.;* always, ever, evermore [*archaic*], aye; forever, for aye, forevermore, forever and a day, forever and ever; forever and aye, in all ages, from age to age; without end; world without end, time without end; *in secula seculorum* [*L.*]; to the end of time, to the crack of doom, to the "last syllable of recorded time" [*Macbeth*]; till doomsday; constantly etc. (*very frequently*) 136.

113. Instantaneity
[point of time]

n. **instantaneity**, instantaneousness; suddenness, abruptness.

moment, instant, second, minute; twinkling, flash, breath, crack, jiffy [*colloq.*], *coup* [*F.*], burst, flash of lightning, stroke of time.

time; epoch, time of day, time of night; hour, minute; very minute etc., very time, very hour; present time, right time, true time, exact time, correct time.

v. **be instantaneous** etc. *adj.;* twinkle, flash.

adj. **instantaneous**, momentary, extempore, sudden, instant, abrupt; subitaneous [*obs.*], hasty; quick as thought, quick as lightning; rapid as electricity.

adv. **instantaneously** etc. *adj.;* in no time, in less than no time; presto, *subito* [*It. and L.*], instanter, forthright [*archaic*], eftsoon *or* eftsoons [*archaic*], in a trice, in a jiffy [*colloq.*], suddenly, at a stroke, like a shot; in a moment etc. *n.;* in the twinkling of an eye; in one's tracts; right away; *toute à l'heure* [*F.*]; at one jump, in the same breath, *per saltum* [*L.*], *uno saltu* [*L.*]; at once, all at once; plump, slap [*colloq.*]; "at one fell swoop" [*Macbeth*]; at the same instant etc. *n.;* immediately etc. (*early*) 132; extempore, on the moment, on the spot, on the dot [*colloq.*], on the spur of the moment; just then; slapdash etc. (*haste*) 684.

114. Chronometry
[estimation, measurement, and record of time]

n. **chronometry**, horometry, chronology, horology; date, epoch; style, era, age.

almanac, calendar, ephemeris; standard time, daylight-saving time; register, registry; chronicle, annals, journal, diary, chronogram, isochronon.

[instruments for the measurement of time] clock, watch; chronometer, chronoscope, chronograph; repeater; timekeeper, timepiece; dial, sundial, gnomon, horologe, horologium [*rare*], hydroscope, *pendule* [*F.*], hourglass, clepsydra; ghurry *or* ghari [*Hind.*].

chronographer, chronologer, chronologist, horologer; annalist.

v. **fix the time**, mark the time; date, register, chronicle, chronologize; measure time, beat time, mark time; bear date.

adj. **chronologic** *or* chronological, chronometric *or* chronometrical, chronogrammatical; data [*rare*], temporal, isochronous, isochronal, cinquecento, quattrocento, trecento.

adv. o'clock.

115. Anachronism
[false estimate of time]

n. **anachronism**, metachronism, parachronism, prochronism; prolepsis; misdate; anticipation, antichronism [*rare*].

35

116. Priority

disregard of time, neglect of time, oblivion of time.
intempestivity [*rare*] etc. 135.
- *v.* **misdate**, antedate, postdate, overdate; anticipate; take no note of time; anachronize [*rare*].
- *adj.* **misdated** etc. *v.;* undated; overdue; out of date, anachronous, anachronistic, intempestive, behind time.

116. Priority

- *n.* **priority**, antecedence, anteriority, precedence, preëxistence; precession etc. 280; precursor etc. 64; the past etc. 122; premises.
- *v.* **precede**, come before; forerun; prevent [*rare*], antecede; go before etc. (*lead*) 280; preëxist; dawn; presage etc. 511; herald, usher in, announce.
  be beforehand etc. (*be early*) 132; steal a march upon, anticipate, forestall; have the start, gain the start.
- *adj.* **prior**, previous; preceding, precedent [*rare*]; anterior, antecedent; preëxistent; former, aforegoing, aforesighted, aforementioned, aforethought, fore [*obs.*], foregoing; beforementioned, above-mentioned; aforesaid, said; introductory etc. (*precursory*) 64; prodromal.
- *adv.* **before**, prior to; earlier; previously etc. *adj.;* afore [*obs.*], aforehand [*archaic*], ere, theretofore, erewhile; ere then, ere now, before then, before now; already, yet, beforehand; or ever, aforetime; on the eve of.

117. Posteriority

- *n.* **posteriority**; succession, sequence; following etc. 281; subsequence, subsequency, supervention; continuance, prolongation; futurity etc. 121; successor; sequel etc. 65; remainder, reversion.
- *v.* **follow after** etc. 281, come after, go after; succeed, supervene; ensue, attend, emanate [*rare*], occur, result; step into the shoes of.
- *adj.* **subsequent**, posterior, following, after, later, succeeding, sequacious [*rare*], successive, sequential [*rare*], ensuing, consecutive, attendant, sequent, postliminary [*rare*], postnate [*obs.*]; postdiluvial, postdiluvian; posthumous; future etc. 121; after-dinner, postprandial.
- *adv.* **subsequently**, after, afterwards, since, later; at a subsequent period, at a later period; next, in the sequel, close upon, thereafter, thereupon, upon which; eftsoon *or* eftsoons [*archaic*]; from that time, from that moment; after a while, after a time; in process of time.

118. Present Time

- *n.* **the present time**, the present day, the present moment, the present juncture, the present occasion; the times, existing time, time being; twentieth century; crisis, epoch, day, hour.
  age, time of life.
- *adj.* **present**, actual, instant, current, nonce, latest, existing, that is.
- *adv.* **at this time**, at this moment etc. 113; at the present time etc. *n.;* now, at present; at hand.
  at this time of day, to-day, now-a-days; already; even now, but now, just now; on the present occasion; for the time being, for the nonce; on the nail, on the spot; on the spur of the moment, on the spur of the occasion.
  until now; to this day, to the present day.

119. Different Time
[time different from the present]

- *n.* different time, other time.
  [indefinite time] aorist.
- *adj.* aoristic; indefinite.
- *adv.* **then**, at that time, at that moment, at that instant; at which time, at which moment, at which instant; on that occasion, upon.
  when; whenever, whensoever; whereupon, upon which, on which occasion; at another time, at a different time, at some other time, at any time; at various times; some of these days, one of these days, some fine morning, one fine morning; some fine day, on divers occasions, sooner or later; some time or other.
  once, formerly, once upon a time.

120. Synchronism

- *n.* **synchronism**; coexistence, coincidence; simultaneousness etc. *adj.;* concurrence, concomitance, unity of time, interim.
  [having equal times] isochronism.
  contemporary, coeval, coetanian [*obs.*].
- *v.* **coexist**, concur, accompany, go hand in hand, keep pace with; synchronize, isochronize.
- *adj.* **synchronous**, synchronal, synchronic *or* synchronical, synchronistic *or* synchronistical, simultaneous, coexisting, coincident, concomitant, concurrent; coeval, coevous [*obs.*]; contemporary, contemporaneous; coetaneous [*rare*], coinstantaneous, coterminous, collateral, coeternal; isochronous.
- *adv.* **at the same time**; simultaneously etc. *adj.;* together, in concert, during the same time; in the same breath; *pari passu* [*L.*]; in the interim.
  at the very moment etc. 113; just as, as soon as; meanwhile etc. (*while*) 106.

121. Futurity
[prospective time]

n. **futurity**, futurition [*rare*]; future, hereafter, time to come; approaching—, coming—, subsequent—, after- -time, —age, —days, —hours, —years, —ages, —life; morrow, tomorrow, by and by, the yet [*rare*]; millennium, chiliad [*rare*], millenary, doomsday, day of judgment, crack of doom, remote future.
approach of time, advent, time drawing on, womb of time; destiny etc. 152; eventuality.
heritage, heirs, posterity, descendants.
prospect, anticipation etc. (*expectation*) 507; foresight etc. 510.

v. **look forward**; anticipate etc. (*expect*) 507, (*foresee*) 510; forestall etc. (*be early*) 132.
approach, await, threaten; impend etc. (*be destined*) 152; come on, draw on; draw near.

adj. **future**, to come; coming etc. (*impending*) 152; next, near; near at hand, close at hand; eventual, ulterior; anticipant, expectant, prospective, in prospect etc. (*expectation*) 507; millenary, millennial.

adv. **prospectively**, hereafter, in future; on the knees of the gods; *kal* [*Hind.*], to-morrow, the day after tomorrow; in course of time, in process of time, in the fullness of time; eventually, ultimately, sooner or later; proximo; *paulo post futurum* [*L.*]; in after time; one of these days; after a time, after a while.
from this time; henceforth, henceforwards; thence; thenceforth, thenceforward; whereupon, upon which.
soon etc. (*early*) 132; on the eve of, on the point of, on the brink of; about to; close upon.

122. Preterition
[retrospective time]

n. **preterition**; priority etc. 116; the past, past time; heretofore [*rare*]; days of yore, days of old, days past, days gone by; times of yore, times of old, times past, times gone by; bygone days; old **times**, ancient times, former times; foretime [*rare*]; yesterday, the olden time, good old time; langsyne; eld [*obs.* or *poetic*].
antiquity, antiqueness, ancientness, *status quo* [*L.*]; time immemorial, distance of time; history, remote age, remote time; remote past; rust of antiquity.
paleontology, paleography, paleology; palaetiology, archaeology; archaism, antiquarianism, medievalism, Pre-Raphaelitism.
retrospection, looking back; memory etc. 505.
antiquary, antiquarian; paleologist, archaeologist etc.; Oldbuck, Dryasdust; *laudator temporis acti* [*L.*]; medievalist, Pre-Raphaelite.
ancestry etc. (*paternity*) 166.

v. **be past** etc. *adj.*; have expired etc. *adj.*, have run its course, have had its day; pass; pass by, pass away, pass off; go by, go away, go off; lapse, blow over.
look back, trace back, cast the eyes back; exhume.

adj. **past**, gone, gone by, over, passed away, bygone, foregone [*archaic*]; elapsed, lapsed, preter-lapsed [*rare*], expired, no more, run out, blown over, that has been, bypast, agone [*archaic*], whilom [*archaic*], extinct, never to return, exploded, forgotten, irrecoverable; obsolete etc. (*old*) 124.
former, pristine, quondam, *ci-devant* [*F.*], late; ancestral.
foregoing; last, latter; recent, overnight, preterit *or* preterite, past, plu-perfect, past perfect.
looking back etc. *v.*; retrospective, retroactive; archaeological etc. *n.*

adv. **formerly**; of old, of yore; erst [*archaic* or *poetic*], erstwhile [*archaic*], whilom [*archaic*], erewhile [*archaic*], time was, ago, over; in the olden time etc. *n.*; anciently, long ago, long since; a long while ago, a long time ago; years ago, ages ago; some time ago, some time since, some time back.
yesterday, the day before yesterday; last year, last season, last month etc.; *ultimo* [*L.*]; lately etc. (*newly*) 123.
retrospectively; ere now, before now, till now; hitherto, heretofore; no longer; once, once upon a time; from time immemorial; in the memory of man; time out of mind; already, yet, up to this time; *ex post facto* [*L.*].

123. Newness

n. **newness** etc. *adj.*; novelty, recency; neology, neologism; immaturity; youth etc. 127; gloss of novelty.
innovation; renovation etc. (*restoration*) 660.
modernist, neoteric; neologist.
upstart, *narikin* [*Jap.*], start-up [*rare*], *nouveau riche* [*F.*], parvenu.
modernism, modernness, modernity; modernization; *dernier cri* [*F.*]; latest fashion; mushroom.

v. **renew** etc. (*restore*) 660; modernize.

adj. **new**, novel, recent, fresh, green; young etc. 127; evergreen; raw, immature; virgin; untried, un-

124. Oldness

handseled, unheard-of, untrodden, unbeaten; fire-new, span-new.

modern, late, neoteric, neoterical; new-born, new-fashioned, newfangled, newfledged; of yesterday; just out [*colloq.*], brand-new, up-to-date [*colloq.*]; *fin-de-siècle* [*F.*], vernal, renovated; sempervirent [*rare*], sempervirid [*rare*]. fresh as a rose, fresh as a daisy, fresh as paint [*colloq.*]; spick-and-span, spick-and-span-new, unhandled.

adv. **newly** etc. *adj.;* afresh, anew, lately, just now, only yesterday, the other day; latterly, of late. not long ago, a short time ago.

124. Oldness

n. **oldness** etc. *adj.;* age, antiquity, eld [*obs. or poetic*]; cobwebs of antiquity.
maturity, matureness, ripeness.
decline, decay; senility etc. 128.
seniority, eldership, primogeniture.
archaism etc. (*the past*) 122; thing of the past, relic of the past; megatherium; Babylonian, Assyrian, Sanskrit.
tradition, prescription, custom, immemorial usage, common law; folklore.

v. **be old** etc. *adj.;* have had its day, have seen its day.
become old etc. *adj.;* age, fade.

adj. **old**, ancient, olden [*archaic*], eldern [*archaic*], antique; of long standing, time-honored, venerable, hoary, vetust [*obs.*]; elder, eldest; firstborn.
primitive, prime, primeval, primigenous, primigenial, primigenious; paleoanthropic; primordial, primordiate [*rare*]; aboriginal etc. (*beginning*) 66; diluvian, antediluvian, protohistoric, prehistoric, dateless, patriarchal, preadamite; palaeocrystic; fossil, paleozoic, preglacial, antemundane; archaic, Vedic, classic, medieval, Pre-Raphaelite, ancestral; black-letter.
immemorial, traditional, traditive, traditionary [*rare*], prescriptive, customary, unwritten, whereof the memory of man runneth not to the contrary; inveterate, rooted.
antiquated, of other times, old as the hills, of the old school, after-age, obsolete; out-of-date, out-of-fashion; stale, old-fashioned, old-fangled [*rare*], fusty, outworn, moth-eaten [*humorous*], behind the age; old-world; exploded; gone out, gone by, *passé* [*F.*], extinct, dead, disused, past, run out; senile etc. 128; timeworn; crumbling etc. (*deteriorated*) 659; secondhand.

old as the hills, old as Methuselah, old as Adam, old as history.

adv. since the world was made, since the year one, since the days of Methuselah.

125. Morning
[noon]

n. **morning**, morn, matins [*eccl.*], morningtide [*rare or poetic*], forenoon, *a.m.,* prime, dawn, daybreak; dayspring, foreday [*chiefly Scot.*], sun-up, peep of day, break of day; aurora; first blush of the morning, first flush of the morning, prime of the morning; twilight, crepuscle *or* crepuscule, sunrise; daylight, daypeep, cockcrow, cockcrowing; the small hours, the wee sma' hours [*Scot.*].
noon, midday, noonday, noontide, meridian, prime; nooning, noontime.
spring, springtide, springtime, seedtime; vernal equinox.
summer, summertide, summertime, midsummer.

adj. **matin**, matutinal, matinal, matutinary [*rare*]; crepuscular.
noon, noonday, midday, meridional [*rare in this sense*].
spring, vernal, vernant [*obs.*].
summer, aestival *or* estival.

adv. **at sunrise** etc. *n.;* with the lark, when the morning dawns.

126. Evening
[midnight]

n. **evening**, eve; decline of day, fall of day, close of day; candlelight, candlelighting; eventide, evensong [*eccl. or archaic*], vespers [*eccl.*], nighttide [*archaic*], nightfall, curfew, dusk, twilight, eleventh hour; sunset, sundown; going down of the sun, cockshut [*obs.*], dewy eve, gloaming, bedtime.
afternoon, *post meridiem* [*L.*], *p.m.*
midnight; dead of night, witching hour of night, witching time of night, killing-time.
autumn; fall, fall of the leaf; harvest, autumnal equinox; Indian summer, St. Luke's summer, St. Martin's summer.
winter, *hiems* [*L.*].

adj. **vesper**, vespertine, nocturnal; autumnal.
wintry, winterly, brumous, brumal.

127. Youth

n. **youth**; juvenility, juvenescence [*rare*]; juniority; infancy; babyhood, childhood, boyhood, girlhood, youthhood [*archaic*]; incunabula; minority, boyage [*rare*], immaturity, nonage, teens, tender age, bloom.

cradle, nursery, leading strings, puberty, pucelage.
flower of life, springtide of life, seedtime of life, prime of life, golden season of life; heyday of youth, school days; rising generation.

adj. young, youthful, juvenile, juvenescent, green, callow, budding, sappy, puisne [*law*], beardless, under age, in one's teens, *in statu pupillari* [*L.*]; younger, junior; hebetic, unfledged, unripe.

128. Age

n. age; oldness etc. *adj.* old age, advanced age; senility, senescence; years, anility, gray hairs, climacteric, grand climacteric, declining years, decrepitude, hoary age, caducity [*rare*], eld [*archaic*], superannuation; second childhood, childishness; dotage; vale of years, decline of life, senectitude [*rare*], "sear and yellow leaf" [*Macbeth*]; threescore years and ten; green old age, ripe age; longevity; time of life.
seniority, eldership; elders etc. (*veteran*) 130; firstling; *doyen* [*F.*], dean, father; primogeniture.
[science of old age] nostology; geriatrics *and* gerontology *and* gerocomy [*med.*].

v. be aged etc. *adj.*; grow old, get old etc. *adj.*; age; decline, wane, senesce [*rare*].

adj. aged; old etc. 124; elderly, eldern [*archaic*], senile; matronly, anile; in years; ripe, mellow, run to seed, declining, waning, past one's prime; gray, grayheaded; hoar, hoary; venerable, time-worn, antiquated, *passé* [*F.*], effete, decrepit, superannuated; advanced in life, advanced in years; stricken in years; wrinkled, marked with the crow's foot; having one foot in the grave; doting etc. (*imbecile*) 499; like the last of pea time.
years old; of a certain age, no chicken [*colloq.*], old as Methuselah; ancestral; patriarchal etc. (*ancient*) 124; gerontic.
older, elder, oldest, eldest; senior; firstborn.

129. Infant

n. infant, babe, baby; nursling, suckling, yearling, weanling; papoose, *bambino* [*It.*]; vagitus.
child, bairn [*Scot.*], tot, mite, scrap, chick, kid [*slang*], *butcha or bacha* [*Hind.*]; little one, brat, chit, pickaninny, urchin; bantling, bratling elf.
youth, boy, lad, laddie, slip, sprig, stripling, youngster, younker [*colloq.*], whipster [*rare*], youngling [*rare*], damoiseau [*archaic*], cub, callant [*Scot.*], whippersnapper [*colloq.*], schoolboy, hobbledehoy, hopeful, cadet, minor, master.
scion, sapling, seedling; tendril, olivebranch, nestling, chicken, duckling, larva, chrysalis, tadpole, whelp, cub, pullet, fry, callow [*obs.*], codling *or* codlin; fetus, calf, colt, pup, puppy, foal, kitten; lamb, lambkin; aurelia, caterpillar, cocoon, nymph, nympha, pupa, staddle.
girl, lass, lassie; wench [*dial.*], miss, damsel; damoiselle, damosel *or* damozel [*archaic*]; demoiselle; maid, maiden; virgin; nymph, colleen, girleen, flapper [*slang*], girly [*colloq.*], minx, missy, baggage, hussy; schoolgirl; hoyden, tomboy, romp.

adj. infantine, infantile; puerile; boyish, girlish, childish, babyish, kittenish; childly [*rare*], boylike, girllike, kiddish [*colloq.*], dollish [*colloq.*]; youngling, infant, baby; newborn, unfledged, newfledged, callow.
in the cradle, in swaddling clothes, in long clothes, in arms, in leading strings; at the breast; in one's teens; young etc. 127.

130. Veteran

n. veteran, old man, reverend sir, seer, patriarch, graybeard; grandfather, grandsire [*archaic*], grisard [*rare*], oldster [*colloq.*], pantaloon [*obs.*]; gaffer, sexagenarian, octogenarian, nonagenarian, centenarian; *doyen* [*F.*], old stager; dotard etc. 501.
granny, grandam *or* grandame [*archaic*], gammer [*dial. Eng.*], crone, hag, oldwife, beldam *or* beldame.
preadamite, Methuselah, Nestor, old Parr; elders; forefathers etc. (*paternity*) 166; Darby and Joan, Philemon and Baucis, "John Anderson, my jo" [Burns].

adj. veteran; aged etc. 128.

131. Adolescence

n. adolescence, pubescence, majority; adultism; adulthood, adultness etc. *adj.*; manhood, virility; flower of age; full bloom; spring of life.
man etc. 373; woman etc. 374; adult, pubescent, no chicken [*colloq.*].
middle age, *mezzo cammin* [*It.*], maturity, full age, ripe age, prime of life, meridian of life.

v. come of age, come to man's estate, come to years of discretion; attain majority, put on long trousers, assume the *toga virilis* [*L.*]; have cut one's eyeteeth [*colloq.*], settle down, have sown one's wild oats.

adj. adolescent, pubescent, of age; of full age, of ripe age; out of one's teens, grown up, full-blown, in

132. Earliness

full bloom, full-grown, manly, manlike, virile, adult; womanly, matronly; marriageable, marriable, nubile.

middle-aged, mature, in one's prime; matronly.

132. Earliness

n. **earliness** etc. *adj.;* morning etc. 125.

punctuality; promptitude etc. (*activity*) 682; haste etc. (*velocity*) 274; suddenness etc. (*instantaneity*) 113.

prematurity, precocity, precipitation, anticipation, prevenience; a stitch in time.

v. **be early** etc. *adj.;* be beforehand etc. *adv.;* keep time, take time by the forelock, anticipate, forestall; have the start, gain the start; steal a march upon; gain time, draw on futurity; bespeak, secure, engage, preëngage.

accelerate; expedite etc. (*quicken*) 274; make haste etc. (*hurry*) 684.

adj. **early**, prime, timely, seasonable, in time, punctual, forward; prompt etc. (*active*) 682; summary.

premature, precipitate, precocious; prevenient, anticipatory; rath *or* rathe [*obs. or poetic*].

sudden etc. (*instantaneous*) 113; unexpected etc. 508; imminent, impending, near, near at hand; immediate.

adv. **early**, soon, anon, betimes, rath *or* rathe [*poetic*]; eftsoon *or* eftsoons [*archaic*]; ere long, before long; punctually etc. *adj.;* to the minute; in time; in good time, in military time, in pudding time [*obs.*], in due time; time enough, on time, on the dot [*slang*].

beforehand; prematurely etc. *adj.;* precipitately etc. (*hastily*) 684; too soon; before its time, before one's time; in anticipation; unexpectedly etc. 508.

suddenly etc. (*instantaneously*) 113; before one can say "Jack Robinson," at short notice, extempore; on the spur of the moment, on the spur of the occasion [Bacon]; at once; on the spot, on the instant; at sight; off hand, out of hand; *à vue d'oeil* [*F.*]; straight, straightway, straightforth; forthwith, incontinently, summarily, instanter, forthright [*archaic*], immediately, briefly, shortly, erewhile [*archaic*], quickly, speedily, apace, before the ink is dry, almost immediately, presently, at the first opportunity, in no long time, by and by, in a while, directly.

133. Lateness

n. **lateness** etc. *adj.;* tardiness etc. (*slowness*) 275.

delay, cunctation [*rare*] tarriance, moration [*rare*], delation [*archaic*], procrastination; deferring etc. *v.;* postponement, adjournment, prorogation, retardation, respite; protraction, prolongation; after-time; circumlocution office [*ridicule*], "circumlocution court" [Dickens], chancery suit, Fabian policy, *médecine expectante* [*F.*], moratorium; leeway; high time; truce, reprieve, demurrage; stop, stay, suspension, remand.

v. **be late** etc. *adj.;* tarry, wait, stay, bide, take time; dawdle etc. (*be inactive*) 683; linger, loiter; bide one's time, take one's time; gain time; hang fire; stand over, lie over; hang, hang around *or* about [*colloq.*], hang back [*colloq.*], hang in the balance, hang in the hedge, hang up [*colloq.*], sit up for, stay up for.

put off, defer, delay, lay over, suspend; shift off, stave off; waive, retard, remand, postpone, adjourn; procrastinate; dally; prolong, protract; spin out, draw out, lengthen out; prorogue; keep back; tide over; push to the last, drive to the last; let the matter stand over; table, lay on the table, shelve; respite [*rare*], perendinate [*rare*]; reserve etc. (*store*) 636; temporize, filibuster, stall [*slang*]; consult one's pillow, sleep upon it.

be kept waiting, dance attendance; kick one's heels [*colloq.*], cool one's heels [*colloq.*]; *faire antichambre* [*F.*]; wait impatiently; await etc. (*expect*) 507; sit up, sit up at night; lose an opportunity etc. 135.

adj. **late**, tardy, slow, cunctatious *or* cunctative [*rare*], behindhand, serotine [*rare*], belated, postliminary [*rare*], posthumous, backward, unpunctual, impunctual [*rare*], overdue, moratory; dilatory etc. (*slow*) 275; delayed etc. *v.;* in abeyance.

adv. **late**; backward, lateward [*obs.*], late in the day; at sunset, at the eleventh hour, at length, at last; ultimately; after time, behind time; too late; too late for etc. 135.

slowly, leisurely, deliberately, at one's leisure; *ex post facto* [*L.*]; *sine die* [*L.*].

134. Occasion

n. **occasion**, opportunity, opening, room, scope, space, place, liberty, show [*colloq., U. S.*]; suitable time, suitable season, proper time, proper season; high time; opportuneness etc. *adj.;* tempestivity [*obs.*].

nick of time; golden opportunity, well-timed opportunity, fine opportunity, favorable opportunity; clear stage, fair field; *mollia tempora* [*L.*]; spare time etc. (*leisure*) 685.

crisis, turn, emergency, juncture, conjuncture; turning point, given time.

v. **improve the occasion**; seize etc. (789) an opportunity *or* an occasion; use etc. (677) an opportunity *or* an occasion; give etc. (784) an opportunity *or* an occasion.

suit the occasion etc. (*be expedient*) 646.

strike the iron while it is hot, *battre le fer sur l'enclume* [*F.*], make hay while the sun shines, seize the present hour, take time by the forelock, *prendre la balle au bond* [*F.*].

adj. **opportune**, timely, well-timed, timeful [*obs.*], seasonable, tempestive [*archaic*], timeous [*rare*].

lucky, providential, fortunate, happy, favorable, propitious, auspicious, critical; suitable etc. 23; *obiter dicta* [*L.*].

occasional, accidental, extemporaneous, extempory; contingent etc. (*uncertain*) 475.

adv. **opportunely** etc. *adj.;* in proper time, in proper course, in proper season; in due time, in due course, in due season; for the nonce; in the nick of time, in the fullness of time; all in good time; just in time, at the eleventh hour, now or never.

by the way, by the by; *en passant* [*F.*], *à propos* [*F.*]; *pro hac vice* [*L.*]; *par parenthèse* [*F.*], parenthetically, by way of parenthesis; while on this subject, speaking of; *par exemple* [*F.*]; extempore; on the spur of the moment, on the spur of the occasion; on the spot etc. (*early*) 132.

135. Intempestivity

n. **intempestivity** [*rare*]; unsuitable time, improper time; unreasonableness etc. *adj.;* evil hour; *contretemps* [*F.*], misventure [*archaic*], misadventure; intrusion; anachronism etc. 115.

v. **be ill-timed** etc. *adj.;* mistime, intrude, come amiss, break in upon; have other fish to fry; be busy, be occupied, be engaged.

lose an opportunity; throw away an opportunity, waste an opportunity, neglect etc. (460) an opportunity; allow *or* suffer the opportunity *or* occasion to -pass, -slip, -go by, -escape, -lapse; waste time etc. (*be inactive*) 683; let slip through the fingers, lock the stable door when the steed is stolen.

adj. **ill-timed**, mistimed; ill-fated, ill-omened, ill-starred; untimely, intrusive, unseasonable; out of date, out of season; inopportune, timeless [*archaic*], inconvenient, intempestive [*rare*], untoward, *mal à propos* [*F.*], unlucky, inauspicious, unpropitious, unfortunate, unfavorable; unsuited etc. 24; inexpedient etc. 647.

unpunctual etc. (*late*) 133; too late for; premature etc. (*early*) 132; too soon for; wise after the event.

adv. **inopportunely** etc. *adj.;* as ill luck would have it, in an evil hour, the time having gone by, a day after the fair.

136. Frequency

n. **frequency**, frequence, oftness [*rare*], oftenness [*rare*], quotiety [*rare*]; repetition etc. 104.

v. **keep**, keep on; recur etc. 104; do nothing but.

adj. **frequent**, often [*archaic*], many, many times, not rare, thickcoming, incessant, perpetual, continual, constant, repeated etc. 104; habitual etc. 613; hourly etc. 138.

adv. **often**, oft, ofttime [*archaic*], ofttimes, oftentimes; oftentime [*rare*], oftentide [*obs.*], not seldom, frequently; repeatedly etc. 104; unseldom, not unfrequently; in quick succession, in rapid succession; many a time and oft; oftly [*rare*], daily, hourly etc.; every day, every hour, every moment etc.

perpetually, continually, constantly, incessantly, unchangingly, steadfastly, without ceasing, at all times, daily and hourly, night and day, day and night, day after day, morning noon and night, ever and anon.

commonly etc. (*habitually*) 613; most often.

sometimes, occasionally, at times, now and then, from time to time, there being times when, *toties quoties* [*L.*], often enough, again and again.

137. Infrequency

n. **infrequency**, infrequence, unfrequency [*rare*], rareness, rarity; sparseness, fewness etc. 103; seldomness; uncommonness.

v. **be rare** etc. *adj.*

adj. **infrequent**, unfrequent [*rare*], seldseen [*archaic*], uncommon, sporadic; rare, rare as a blue diamond; few etc. 103; scarce; almost unheard of, scarce as hen's teeth [*colloq.*], unprecedented, which has not occurred within the memory of the oldest inhabitant, not within one's previous experience.

adv. **seldom**, rarely, scarcely, hardly; not often, unfrequently, infrequently, uncommonly, sparsely, unoften; scarcely ever, hardly ever; once in a blue moon [*colloq.*].

once; once for all, once in a way; *pro hac vice* [*L.*].

138. Regularity of recurrence. Periodicity

n. **periodicity**, intermittence; beat; oscillation etc. 314; pulse, pulsation; systole and diastole; rhythm; alternation, alternateness, alternacy [*rare*], alternativeness, alternity [*rare*].

139. Irregularity of recurrence

round, revolution, rotation, bout, turn, say.
anniversary, biennial, triennial, quadrennial, quinquennial, sextennial, septennial, octennial, decennial; tricennial, jubilee, centennial, centenary, bicentennial, bicentenary, tercentenary; birthday, birthright, natal day, fête day, saint's day.
catamenia, courses, menses, menstrual flux.
[regularity of return] rota, cycle, period, stated time, routine; days of the week; Sunday, Monday etc.; months of the year; January etc.; feast, festival, fast etc.; Christmas, Yuletide, New Year's day, Ash Wednesday, Maundy Thursday, Good Friday, Easter; Allhallows, Allhallowmas, All Saints' Day; All Souls' Day; Candlemas, Dewali [*Hindu*], Holi *or* Hoolee [*Hindu*], Memorial *or* Decoration Day, Independence Day, Labor Day, Thanksgiving, ground-hog day, woodchuck day [*U. S.*], Halloween, Hallowmas, Lady Day; leap year, bissextile; Bairam, Ramadan, Muharram [*Mohammedan*]; St. Swithin's Day; Midsummer Day; May Day etc. (*holiday*) 840; yearbook.
punctuality, regularity, steadiness.

v. **return**, revolve; recur in regular -order, -succession; come again, come in its turn; come round, -again; beat, pulsate; alternate; intermit.

adj. **periodic**, periodical; serial, recurrent, cyclic, cyclical, rhythmic *or* rhythmical; recurring etc.*v.*; intermittent, remittent; alternate, every other; every.
hourly; diurnal, daily, quotidian [*rare*]; tertian, weekly; hebdomadal, hebdomadary; biweekly, fortnightly; bimonthly; monthly, catamenial, menstrual; yearly, annual; biennial, triennial etc.; centennial, secular; paschal, lenten etc.
regular, steady, constant, methodical, punctual, regular as clockwork.

adv. **periodically** etc. *adj.;* at regular intervals, at stated times; at fixed periods, at established periods; punctually etc. *adj.; de die in diem* [*L.*]; from day to day, day by day.
by turns; in turn, in rotation; alternately, every other day, off and on, ride and tie, round and round.

139. Irregularity of recurrence

n. **irregularity**, uncertainty, unpunctuality; fitfulness etc. *adj.;* capriciousness, ecrhythmus; acatastasia [*med*].

adj. **irregular**, uncertain, unpunctual, capricious, erratic, heteroclite, ecrhythmic, ecrhythmous, desultory, fitful, flickering; rambling, rhapsodical; spasmodic; immethodical, unsystematic, unequal, uneven, variable.

adv. **irregularly** etc. *adj.;* by fits and starts etc. (*discontinuously*) 70.

Section 7. Change

140. Change
[difference at different times]

n. **change**, alteration, mutation, permutation, variation, novation [*rare*], modification, modulation, inflection *or* inflexion, mood, qualification, innovation, eversion, deviation, shift, turn; diversion; break.
transformation, transfiguration, transfigurement; metamorphosis; metabola *or* metabole [*med.*], transmorphism [*rare*], transmutation; deoxidization, deoxidation; transubstantiation; metagenesis, transanimation, transmigration, metempsychosis, version [*rare*]; metasomatism *or* metasomatosis, metathesis; metabolism, metastasis; transmogrification [*colloq.*]; avatar; alterative.
resolution, conversion etc. (*gradual change*) 144; revolution etc. (*sudden or radical change*) 146; inversion etc. (*reversal*) 218; displacement etc. 185; transference etc. 270.
changeableness etc. 149; tergiversation etc. (*change of mind*) 607.

v. **change**, alter, vary, wax and wane; modulate, diversify, qualify, tamper with; turn, shift, veer, gybe *or* jibe, jib, tack, chop, shuffle, swerve, warp, deviate, dodge, tergiversate, turn aside, evert, intervert [*obs.*]; pass to, take a turn, turn the corner, resume.
work a change, modify, vamp, patch, piece, vamp up, superinduce; transform, transfigure, transmute, transmogrify [*colloq.*], transume [*rare*], transverse [*rare*], transshape [*rare*], metabolize, convert, transubstantiate, resolve, revolutionize; chop and change; metamorphose, ring the changes.
innovate, introduce new blood, shuffle the cards; give a turn to, give a color to; influence, turn the scale; shift the scene, turn over a new leaf.
recast etc. 146; reverse etc. 218; disturb etc. 61; convert into etc. 144.

adj. **changed** etc. *v.;* newfangled; eversible; changeable etc. 149; transitional; modifiable; metagenetic; alterative.

adv. mutatis mutandis [*L.*].

int. quantum mutatus! [*L.*].

141. Permanence
[absence of change]

n. **permanence**, permanency, fixity, persistence, endurance; durableness, durability, lastingness; standing, *status quo* [*L.*]; maintenance, preservation, conservation; conservatism; *laisser faire* [*F.*], *laisser aller* [*F.*]; law of the Medes and Persians; standing dish.

stability etc. 150; quiescence etc. 265; obstinacy etc. 606.

v. **let alone**, let be; persist, remain, stay, tarry, rest; hold, hold on; last, endure, bide, abide, aby *or* abye [*archaic*], dwell, maintain, keep; stand, –still, –fast, –pat [*colloq.*]; subsist, live, outlive, survive; hold–, keep- one's -ground, –footing; hold good.

adj. **permanent**; stable etc. 150; persisting etc. *v.;* established; fixed, irremovable, durable; pucka *or* pukka *or* pakka [*Hind.*]; unchanged etc. (change etc. 140); renewed; intact, inviolate; persistent; monotonous, uncheckered; unfailing, unfading.

undestroyed, unrepealed, unsuppressed; conservative, *qualis ab incepto* [*L.*]; prescriptive etc. (*old*) 124; stationary etc. 265.

adv. **finally**; *in statu quo* [*L.*]; for good, at a stand, at a standstill, *uti possidetis* [*L.*]; without a shadow of turning; as you were!

142. Cessation
[change from action to rest]

n. **cessation**, discontinuance, desistance, desinence. intermission, remission; suspense, suspension; interruption; stop; hitch [*colloq.*]; stopping etc. *v.;* stoppage, halt; arrival etc. 292.

pause, rest, lull, respite, truce, truce of God, armistice, stay, drop; interregnum, abeyance.

[in debate] closure, cloture, *clôture* [*F.*].

deadlock, checkmate, backwater, dead water, dead stand, dead stop; end etc. 67; death etc. 360.

punctuation, comma, semicolon, colon, period, full stop, caesura.

v. **cease**, discontinue, desist, stay; break off, leave off; hold, stop, pull up, stop short; check, check in full career, deadlock; stick, hang fire; halt; pause, rest.

come to a -stand, –standstill, –deadlock, –full stop; arrive etc. 292; go out, die away; wear away, wear off; pass away etc. (*be past*) 122; be at an end.

have done with, give over, surcease, shut up shop; give up etc. (*relinquish*) 624.

hold–, stay- one's hand; rest on one's oars, repose on one's laurels.

interrupt, suspend, interpel [*obs.*]; intermit, remit; put an end to, put a stop to, put a period to; derail; bring to a -stand, –standstill; stop, stall, cut short, arrest, stem the -tide, –torrent; pull the check-string.

int. **stop**! hold! enough! avast! [*naut.*], have done! a truce to! soft! leave off! *tenez!* [*F.*], fade away! [*slang*], let up! [*slang*], cut it out! [*slang*].

143. Continuance in action

n. **continuance**, continuation; run, pursuance, maintenance, extension, perpetuation, prolongation; persistence etc. (*perseverance*) 604a; repetition etc. 104.

v. **continue**, persist; go on, jog on, keep on, run on, hold on; abide, keep, pursue, stick to; take–, maintain- its course; carry on, keep up, drag on, stick [*colloq.*], persevere, endure, carry on.

sustain, uphold, hold up, keep on foot; follow up, perpetuate, prolong, maintain; preserve etc. 604a; harp upon etc. (*repeat*) 104.

keep going, keep alive, keep the pot boiling [*colloq.*], keep up the ball [*colloq.*]; die in harness; plug at it *or* along [*slang*]; keep the field, keep the ball rolling, keep at it, keep up; hold on–, pursue -the even tenor of one's way.

let be; *stare super antiquas vias* [*L.*]; *quieta non movere* [*L.*]; let things take their course.

adj. **continuing** etc. *v.;* uninterrupted, unintermitting, unvarying, persistent, unceasing, unremitting, unshifting; unreversed, unstopped, unrevoked, unvaried; sustained; chronic; undying etc. (*perpetual*) 112; inconvertible.

int. carry on! stand fast!

144. Conversion
[gradual change to something different]

n. **conversion**, reduction, transmutation, resolution, assimilation; chemistry, alchemy; lapse, assumption, growth, progress; naturalization; transportation.

proselytization, regeneration, Catholicization, Protestantization.

passage, transit, transition, transmigration; shifting etc. *v.;* flux; phase; conjugation; convertibility.

laboratory etc. 691; crucible, alembic, caldron, retort, mortar; potter's wheel, anvil, lathe, blowpipe.

convert, neophyte, catechumen, proselyte; pervert, renegade, apostate, turncoat.

145. Reversion

v. **be converted into**; become, get, wax; come-, turn- -to, -into; turn out, lapse, shift; run-, fall-, pass-, slide-, glide-, grow-, ripen-, open-, resolve itself-, settle-, merge- into; melt, grow, come round to, mature, mellow; assume the - form, -shape, -state, -nature, character- of; illapse [*rare*]; assume a new phase, undergo a change.

convert into, resolve into; make, render; mold, form etc. 240; remodel, new-model, refound, reform, reorganize; assimilate to, bring to, reduce to.

adj. **converted into** etc. *v.;* convertible, resolvable into; conversible [*rare*], chemical, transitional; naturalized.

adv. gradually etc. (*slowly*) 275; *in transitu* [*L.*] etc. (*transference*) 270.

145. Reversion

n. **reversion**, return; revulsion.
turning point, turn of the tide; *status quo ante bellum* [*L.*]; calm before a storm.
alternation etc. (*periodicity*) 138; inversion etc. 219; recoil etc. 277; retrocession, retrospection, regression etc. 283; restoration etc. 660; relapse etc. 661; atavism, throwback; vicinism; escheat.

v. **revert**, reverse, return, turn back; relapse etc. 661; invert etc. 219; recoil etc. 277; retreat etc. 283; restore etc. 660; undo, unmake; turn the tide, turn the scale; escheat.

adj. **reverting** etc. *v.;* revulsive, reactionary; retrorse.

adv. **revulsively**, retrorsely, on the rebound, *à rebours* [*F.*].

146. Revolution
[sudden or violent change]

n. **revolution**, revolt, *bouleversement* [*F.*], subversion, breakup; destruction etc. 162; sudden-, radical-, sweeping-, organic- change; clean sweep, debacle, *débâcle* [*F.*], overturn, overthrow, *coup d'état* [*F.*], rebellion, rising, uprising, mutiny, sansculottism, bolshevism, counter-revolution.
spasm, convulsion, throe, revulsion; storm, earthquake, eruption, upheaval, cataclysm, transilience *or* transiliency [*rare*], jump, leap, plunge, jerk, start, dash; explosion.
legerdemain etc. (*trick*) 545.

v. **revolutionize**, revolt, rebel, insurrect, rise; new-model, remodel, recast; strike out something new, break with the past; change the face of, unsex.

adj. **unrecognizable**; transilient.
revolutionary, catastrophic, cataclysmic, cataclysmal, convulsionary, insurgent, Red, insurrectional, insurrectionary, mutinous, rebellious, sansculottic, bolshevist *or* bolshevik.

147. Substitution
[change of one thing for another]

n. **substitution**, commutation, subrogation [*law*], surrogation [*rare*]; supplanting etc. *v.,* supersession, supersedence, supersedure; metonymy etc. (*figure of speech*) 521.
[thing substituted] substitute, succedaneum, makeshift, temporary expedient; shift, apology, *pis aller* [*F.*], stopgap, jury mast, *locum tenens* [*L.*], alternate, warming pan [*colloq.*], dummy, scapegoat; double; changeling; *quid pro quo* [*L.*], alternative; representative etc. (*deputy*) 759; palimpsest.
price, purchase money, consideration, equivalent.

v. **substitute**, put in the place of, change for; make way for, give place to; supply-, take- the place of; surrogate [*rare*], subrogate [*law*], supplant, supersede, replace, cut out [*colloq.*], serve as a substitute; step into the shoes of, stand in the shoes of; make a shift with, put up with; borrow of Peter to pay Paul; commute, redeem, compound for.

adj. **substituted** etc. *v.;* vicarious, vicarial, substitutional, subdititious [*rare*].

adv. **instead**; by proxy; in place of, in lieu of, in the stead of, in the room of; *faute de mieux* [*F.*].

148. Interchange
[double or mutual change]

n. **interchange**, exchange; commutation, permutation, intermutation; reciprocation, transposition, transposal, shuffle, shuffling; alternation, reciprocity; castling [at chess]; hocus-pocus; swap [*colloq.*].
barter etc. 794; a Roland for his Oliver; tit for tat etc. (*retaliation*) 718; cross fire, battledore and shuttlecock; *quid pro quo* [*L.*].
interchangeableness, interchangeability.

v. **interchange**, exchange, counterchange; bandy, barter, transpose, shuffle, change hands, swap [*colloq.*], permute, reciprocate, commute; interwork, give and take, return the compliment; play at -puss in the corner, -battledore and shuttlecock; take in one another's washing; retaliate etc. 718; requite.

adj. **reciprocal**, interactive, mutual, commutative, interchangeable; interchanged etc. *v.;* intercurrent [*rare*].
international, interstate, interurban, intercollegiate, intertribal, interdenominational, interscholastic.

adv. **in exchange**, *vice versa* [*L.*], conversely, *mutatis mutandis* [*L.*], backwards and forwards, forward and back, to and fro, back and forth, by turns, turn about, contrariwise, commutatively, turn and turn about; each in his turn, every one in his turn.

149. Changeableness

n. **changeableness** etc. *adj.;* mutability, inconstancy; versatility, mobility; instability, unstable equilibrium; vacillation etc. (*irresolution*) 605; fluctuation, vicissitude; dysphoria; alternation etc. (*oscillation*) 314; transientness etc. 111.

[comparisons] moon, Proteus, kaleidoscope, chameleon, quicksilver, shifting sands, weathercock, vane, weathervane, harlequin, turncoat, Vicar of Bray, Cynthia of the minute, April showers; wheel of Fortune.

restlessness etc. *adj.;* fidgets, disquiet; disquietude, inquietude; unrest; agitation etc. 315.

v. **fluctuate**, vary, waver, flounder, flicker, flitter [*archaic*], flit, flutter, shift, shuffle, shake, totter, tremble, vacillate, wamble [*dial.*], turn and turn about, ring the changes; sway–, shift- to and fro; change and change about; oscillate etc. 314; vibrate–, oscillate- between two extremes; alternate; have as many phases as the moon.

adj. **changeable**, changeful; changing etc. 140; mutable, variable, checkered, ever changing, kaleidoscopic; protean, proteiform; versatile.

inconstant, unstaid, unsteady, unstable, unfixed, unsettled; fluctuating etc. *v.;* restless, uneasy; agitated etc. 315; erratic, fickle; mercurial, irresolute etc. 605; capricious etc. 608; touch and go; inconsonant, fitful, spasmodic; vibratory; vagrant, feathery [*rare*], lightheaded, wayward; desultory; afloat; alternating; alterable, plastic, mobile; transient etc. 111; wavering.

adv. **seesaw** etc. (*oscillation*) 314; off and on.

150. Stability

n. **stability**; immutability etc. *adj.;* unchangeableness etc. *adj.;* constancy; stable equilibrium, immobility, soundness, vitality, stabiliment [*rare*], stabilization; stiffness, ankylosis, solidity, *aplomb* [*F.*]; coherence.

permanence etc. 141; obstinancy etc. 606.

fixture, establishment; rock, pillar, tower, foundation, leopard's spots, Ethiopian's skin; law of the Medes and Persians.

standpatter [*politics*].

v. **be firm** etc. *adj.;* stick fast; stand firm, keep firm, remain firm; stand pat; weather the storm.

establish, settle, stablish [*archaic*], ascertain, fix, set, stabilitate [*obs.*], stabilize; stet [*printing*],

retain, keep hold; make good, make sure; fasten etc. (*join*) 43; set on its legs [*colloq.*], set on its feet; float; perpetuate.

settle down; strike root, take root; take up one's abode etc. 184; build one's house on a rock.

adj. **unchangeable**, immutable; unaltered, unalterable; not to be changed, constant; permanent etc. 141; invariable, unyielding, undeviating; stable, durable; perennial etc. (*diuturnal*) 110.

fixed, steadfast, firm, firm as Gibraltar, firm as a rock, on a rock; tethered, anchored, moored, at anchor, firmly-seated, –established etc. *v.;* deeprooted, ineradicable; fast, steady, balanced; confirmed, inveterate, valid; fiducial; immovable, irremovable, reveted, rooted; stated, settled, stereotyped, established etc. *v.;* obstinate etc. 606; vested; incontrovertible, indeclinable.

stuck fast, transfixed, aground, high and dry, stranded.

incommutable, indefeasible, irretrievable, intransmutable, irresoluble, irrevocable, irreversible, reverseless, inextinguishable, irreducible; indissoluble, indissolvable; indestructible, undying, imperishable, indelible, indeciduous; insusceptible, –of change.

int. stet [*L., printing*].

151. Eventuality

n. **eventuality**, eventuation, event, occurrence, supervention, incident, affair, transaction, proceeding, fact; matter of fact, naked fact; phenomenon: advent.

circumstance, particular, casualty, accident, happening, adventure, passage, crisis, pass, emergency, contingency; concern, business.

consequence, issue, result, termination, conclusion.

affairs, matters; the world, life, things, doings; things–, affairs- in general; the times, state of affairs, order of the day; course–, tide–, stream–, current–, run–, march-of-things, –events; ups and downs of life; chapter of accidents etc. (*chance*) 156; situation etc. (*circumstances*) 8; memorabilia.

v. **happen**, occur; take place, take effect; come, become of; come -off, –about, –round, –into existence, –forth, –to pass, –on; pass, present itself; fall; fall out, turn out; run, be on foot, fall in; befall, betide, bechance; prove, eventuate, draw on; turn up, crop up, spring up, cast up; supervene, survene, [*obs.*] issue, arrive, ensue, result, eventuate, arise, start, hold, take its course; pass off etc. (*be past*) 122.

experience; meet with; fall to the lot of; be one's -chance, –fortune, –lot; find; encounter, un-

152. Destiny

- dergo; pass through, go through; endure etc. (*feel*) 821.
- *adj.* **happening** etc. *v.;* going on, doing, current; in the wind, afloat; on foot, on the carpet, on the tapis; at issue, in question; incidental.
  - **eventful**, stirring, bustling, full of incident; memorable, momentous, signal.
- *adv.* **eventually**, ultimately, finally; in the event of, in case; in the course of things; in the natural *or* ordinary course of things; as things go, as times go; as the world -goes, -wags; as the tree falls, as the cat jumps [*colloq.*]; as it may -turn out, -happen.

152. Destiny

- *n.* **destiny** etc. (*necessity*) 601; future existence, postexistence; hereafter; foredoom, future state, next world, world to come, after life; futurity etc. 121; everlasting life, everlasting death; life beyond the grave, life to come, world beyond the grave; prospect etc. (*expectation*) 507.
- *v.* **impend**; hang over, lie over; threaten, loom, await, hover, come on, approach, stare one in the face; foreordain, preordain; predestine, doom, foredoom, have in store for.
- *adj.* **impending** etc. *v.;* destined; about to be, about to happen; coming, in store, to come, going to happen, instant, at hand, near; near at hand, close at hand; overhanging, hanging over one's head, imminent; brewing, preparing, forthcoming; in the wind, in the cards [*colloq.*], in reserve; that will be, that is to be; in prospect etc. (*expected*) 507; looming in the -distance, -horizon, -future; postexistent, unborn, in embryo; in the womb of -time, futurity; on the knees of the gods, in the future; pregnant etc. (*producing*) 161.
- *adv.* **in time**, in the long run; all in good time; eventually etc. 151; whatever may happen etc. (*certainly*) 474; as chance etc. (156) would have it.

Section 8. Causation

153. Cause

[constant antecedent]

- *n.* **cause**, origin, source, principle, element; prime mover, *primum mobile* [*L.*], primordium [*rare*]; *vera causa* [*L.*], ultimate cause, Great First Cause; author etc. (*producer*) 164; mainspring, agent; leaven; groundwork, foundation etc. (*support*) 215.
  - **spring**, fountain, well, font; fountainhead, springhead, reservoir, headspring, wellspring, wellhead; *fons et origo* [*L.*], genesis; descent etc. (*paternity*) 166; remote cause; influence.
  - **pivot**, hinge, turning point, lever; key; heart, nucleus, hub, focus; proximate cause, *causa causans* [*L.*]; the straw that breaks the camel's back.
  - **reason**, reason why; ground; why and wherefore [*colloq.*], rationale, occasion, derivation; final cause etc. (*intention*) 620; *les dessous des cartes* [*F.*]; undercurrents.
  - **rudiment**, egg, germ, embryo, fetus, bud, root, radix, radical, radication [*rare*], etymon, nucleus, seed, stem, stock, stirps, trunk, taproot, gemma, gemmule, radicle, semen, sperm.
  - **nest**, cradle, nursery, womb, nidus, birthplace, breeding-place, hotbed.
  - **causality**, causation; origination; causative; production etc. 161.
- *v.* **be the cause of** etc. *n.;* originate; give origin to, give rise to, give occasion to; cause, occasion, sow the seeds of, kindle, suscitate [*obs.*]; bring on, bring to pass, bring about; produce; create etc. 161; set up, set afloat, set on foot; found, broach, institute, lay the foundation of; lie at the root of.
  - **procure**, induce, draw down, open the door to, superinduce, evoke, entail, operate; elicit, provoke.
  - **contribute**; conduce to etc. (*tend to*) 176; have a hand in; have a finger in the pie [*colloq.*]; determine, decide, turn the scale, have the deciding vote, have the final word; have a common origin; derive its origin etc. (*effect*) 154.
- *adj.* **caused** etc. *v.;* causal, aetiological *or* etiological, original; primary; primitive, primordial; aboriginal; originative, generative, inceptive, productive, creative, constitutive, procreative, formative, demiurgic, protogenic, protogenal; radical; in embryo, embryonic, embryotic; *in ovo* [*L.*]; seminal, germinal; at the bottom of; connate, having a common origin.
- *adv.* **from the beginning**, in the first place, before everything; because etc. 155; behind the scenes.

154. Effect

[constant sequent]

- *n.* **effect**, consequence; aftercome [*Scot.*], aftergrowth, afterclap, aftermath, aftercrop, derivative, derivation; result; resultant; upshot, issue, outcome, resultance [*rare*], *dénouement* [*F.*], conclusion; falling action, catastrophe, end etc. 67; impress, impression; development, outgrowth; blossom, bud, ear, fruit, crop, harvest, product.

production, produce, work, handiwork, fabric, performance; creature, creation; offspring, offshoot; first fruits, firstlings; heredity, telegony; premices [*obs.*], primices [*obs.*].

v. **be the effect of** etc. *n.;* be due to, be owing to; originate in *or* from; rise from, arise from, take its rise from, spring from, proceed from, emanate from, come from, grow from, bud from, sprout from, germinate from, issue from, flow from, result from, follow from, derive its origin from, accrue from; come to, come of, come out of; depend upon, hang upon, hinge upon, turn upon.

take the consequences, reap where one has sown, make one's bed and lie on it, sow the wind and reap the whirlwind.

adj. **owing to**; resulting from etc. *v.;* resultant, firstling; derivable from; due to; caused by etc. 153; dependent upon; derived from, evolved from; derivative; hereditary; telegonous.

adv. **consequently**, of course, it follows that, naturally; as a consequence, in consequence; through, necessarily, eventually.

155. Attribution
[assignment of cause]

n. **attribution**, theory, ascription, assignment, reference to, rationale; accounting for etc. *v.;* etiology, imputation, derivation from.

filiation, affiliation; filiality; pedigree etc. (*paternity*) 166.

explanation etc. (*interpretation*) 522; reason why etc. (*cause*) 153.

v. **attribute to**, ascribe to, impute to, refer to, lay to, point to, trace to, bring home to; put down to, set down to; blame; blame upon [*colloq.*]; charge on, ground on; invest with, assign as cause, lay at the door of, father upon, saddle, filiate, affiliate; account for, derive from, point out the reason etc. 153; theorize; tell how it comes; put the saddle on the right horse; find the real culprit.

adj. **attributed** etc. *v.;* attributable etc. *v.;* referable *or* referrible; due to, derivable from; affiliate, derivate [*rare*]; owing to etc. (*effect*) 154; putative; ecbatic.

adv. **hence**, thence, therefore, for, since, on account of, because, owing to; on that account; from this cause, from that cause; thanks to, forasmuch as; whence, *propter hoc* [*L.*].

why? wherefore? whence? how comes it? how is it? how happens it? how come? [*colloq.*] how does it happen? how so?

in some way, in some such way; somehow, somehow or other.

156. Chance[1]
[absence of assignable cause]

n. **chance**, indetermination, accident, fortune, hazard, hap [*rare*], haphazard, chance-medley, random, luck, *raccroc* [*F.*], fluke [*cant*], casualty, fortuity, contingence, adventure, hit; fate etc. (*necessity*) 601; equal chance; lottery; tombola; lotto; toss-up [*colloq.*] etc. 621; turn of the -table, –cards; hazard of the die, chapter of accidents; cast–, throw- of the dice; heads or tails, wheel of Fortune; *sortes* [*L.*], *sortes Virgilianœ* [*L.*].

probability, possibility, contingency, odds, long odds, run of luck; accidentalness, accidentalism, accidentality; main chance.

theory of -probabilities, –chances; bookmaking; assurance; gamble, speculation, gaming etc. 621.

v. **chance**, hap, turn up; fall to one's lot; be one's fate etc. 601; stumble on, light upon; blunder upon, hit, hit upon; take one's chance etc. 621.

adj. **casual**, fortuitous, accidental, chance, chanceable [*archaic*], chanceful [*archaic*], haphazard, random, casual, adventive, adventitious, causeless, incidental, contingent, uncaused, undetermined, indeterminate; possible etc. 470; unintentional etc. 621.

adv. **by chance**, by accident; at random, casually; perchance etc. (*possibly*), 470; for aught one knows; as -good, –bad, –ill-luck etc. *n.*- would have it; as it may -be, –chance, –turn up, –happen; as the case may be.

[1]The word *Chance* has two distinct meanings: the first, the absence of assignable *cause*, as above; and the second, the absence of *design*—for the latter see 621.

157. Power

n. **power**; potency, potentiality; jiva [*theos.*]; puissance, might, force; energy etc. 171; dint; right hand, right arm; ascendancy, sway, control; prepotency, prepollence *or* prepollency [*rare*]; almightiness, omnipotence; *carte blanche* [*F.*], authority etc. 737; strength etc. 159; predominance.

ability; ableness etc. *adj.;* competency; efficiency, efficacy, validity, cogency; enablement; vantage ground; influence etc. 175.

pressure, electromotive force, high pressure; conductivity; elasticity; gravity, electricity, magnetism, magneto-electricity, galvanism, voltaic electricity, voltaism, electromagnetism,

158. Impotence

electrostatics, electrokinetics, electrodynamics; electromotion, electrification; magnetization, galvanization; attraction, pull; *vis inertiae* [*L.*], *vis mortua* [*L.*], *vis viva* [*L.*]; potential–, dynamic- energy; friction, suction; live-circuit, –rail, –wire; volt, voltage.

[instruments] galvanometer, rheometer; variometer, magnetometer, magnetoscope, electrometer, electroscope, galvanoscope, electrophorus, electrodynamometer, voltameter, ammeter, voltammeter, voltmeter, wattmeter.

capability, capacity; *quid valeant humeri quid ferre recusent* [*L.*]; faculty, quality, attribute, endowment, virtue, gift, property, qualification, susceptibility.

v. **be powerful** etc. *adj.;* gain power etc. *n.*

belong to, pertain to; lie–, be- in one's power; can.

empower; give–, confer–, exercise-power etc. *n.;* enable, invest; indue, endue, endow, arm; strengthen etc. 159; compel etc. 744.

electrify, magnetize, energize, galvanize, attract.

adj. **powerful**, puissant; potent, potential [*rare*]; capable, able; equal to, up to; cogent, valid; effective, effectual; efficient, efficacious, adequate, competent; multipotent [*rare*], plenipotent [*rare*], prepollent [*rare*], predominant; mighty, ascendent, prepotent, omnipotent, armipotent, mightful [*archaic*]; almighty.

forcible etc. *adj.* (*energetic*) 171; influential etc. 175; productive etc. 168.

electric, electrodynamic, electrokinetic, electromagnetic, electrometric, electrometrical, electromotive, electronegative, electropositive, electroscopic; magnetic, magneto-electric *or* magneto-electrical, magnetomotive; voltametric, voltaic; galvanic, galvanometric, galvanoscopic, dynamo-electric *or* dynamo-electrical; dynamic, static, potential.

adv. **powerfully** etc. *adj.;* by virtue of, by dint of.

158. Impotence

n. **impotence**; inability, disability; disablement, impuissance [*rare*], caducity, imbecility; incapacity, incapability, inaptitude, ineptitude; indocility; invalidity, inefficiency, incompetence, disqualification.

telum imbelle [*L.*], *brutum fulmen* [*L.*], blank cartridge, flash in the pan, *vox et praeterea nihil* [*L.*], dead letter, bit of waste paper, dummy; Quaker gun; cripple.

inefficacy etc. (*inutility*) 645; failure etc. 732.

helplessness etc. *adj.;* prostration, paralysis, palsy, apoplexy, syncope, sideration [*obs.*], vincibility, vincibleness, deliquium, collapse, exhaustion, softening of the brain, senility, superannuation, atony, decrepitude, imbecility, neurasthenia, invertebracy, inanition; emasculation, orchotomy; eunuch.

mollycoddle, old woman, muff [*colloq.*], tenderling [*rare*], milksop, molly [*colloq.*], sissy [*colloq.*], mother's darling.

v. **be impotent** etc. *adj.;* not have a leg to stand on. *vouloir rompre l'anguille au genou* [*F.*], *vouloir prendre la lune avec les dents* [*F.*].

collapse, faint, swoon, fall into a swoon, drop; go by the board; end in smoke etc. (*fail*) 732.

render powerless etc. *adj.;* depotentiate [*rare*], deprive of power; disable, disenable; disarm, incapacitate, disqualify, unfit, invalidate, disinvigorate [*rare*], undermine, deaden, cramp, tie the hands; double up, prostrate, paralyze, muzzle, cripple, becripple, maim, lame, hamstring, unsinew [*rare*], draw the teeth of; throttle, strangle, garrote *or* garrotte, ratten [*trade-union cant*], silence, sprain, clip the wings of, put *hors de combat* [*F.*], spike the guns; take the wind out of one's sails, scotch the snake, put a spoke in one's wheel; break the -neck, –back; unhinge, unfit; put out of gear.

unman, unnerve, devitalize, effeminize, attenuate, enervate; emasculate, evirate [*rare*], spay, eunuchize [*rare*], caponize, castrate, geld, alter.

shatter, exhaust; weaken etc. 160.

adj. **powerless**, impotent, unable, incapable, incompetent; inefficient, ineffective; inept; unfit, unfitted; unqualified, disqualified; unendowed; doddering [*colloq.*], wambly [*Scot. and dial. Eng.*], inapt, unapt; crippled, disabled etc. *v.;* armless; senile, decrepit, superannuated.

harmless, unarmed, weaponless, defenseless, *sine ictu* [*L.*], unfortified, mightless [*archaic*], indefensible, vincible, pregnable, untenable.

paralytic, paralyzed; palsied, imbecile; nerveless, sinewless, marrowless, pithless, lustless; emasculate, disjointed; out of joint, out of gear; unnerved, unhinged; waterlogged, on one's beam ends, rudderless; laid on one's back; done up [*colloq.*], done for [*colloq.*], done brown [*colloq.*], done [*colloq.*], dead-beat [*colloq.*], exhausted, shattered, atonic, demoralized; graveled [*colloq.*] etc. (*in difficulty*) 704; helpless, unfriended, fatherless; without a leg to stand on, *hors de combat* [*F.*], laid on the shelf.

nugatory, null and void, inoperative, good for nothing, invertebrate, ineffectual etc. (*failing*) 732; inadequate etc. 640; inefficacious etc. (*useless*) 645.

159. Strength
[degree of power]

- *n.* **strength**; power etc. 159; energy etc. 171; vigor, force; main–, physical–, brute- force; spring, elasticity, tone, tension, tonicity.
  [comparisons] adamant, steel, iron, oak, heart of oak; iron grip; bone.
  virility, vitality; stoutness etc. *adj.;* lustihood, stamina, nerve, muscle, sinew *or* sinews, thews and sinews, physique; grit, pith, pithiness.
  athletics, athleticism; gymnastics, acrobatism, agonistics, feats of strength.
  athlete, gymnast, pancratiast, acrobat; Atlas, Hercules, Antaeus, Samson, Cyclops, Briareus, Colossus, Polyphemus, Titan, Brobdingnagian, Goliath; tower of strength; giant refreshed
  strengthening etc. *v.;* invigoration, refreshment, refocillation [*obs.*].
  [science of forces] dynamics, statics.
- *v.* **be strong** etc. *adj.,* be stronger; overmatch.
  render strong etc. *adj.;* give strength etc. *n.;* strengthen, invigorate, potentiate [*rare*], brace, nerve, fortify, buttress, sustain, harden, case-harden, steel, gird; screw up, wind up, set up; gird–, brace-up one's loins; recruit, set on one's legs [*colloq.*]; vivify; refresh etc. 689; refect [*archaic*], reinforce *or* reënforce etc. (*restore*) 660.
- *adj.* **strong**, mighty, vigorous, forcible, hard, adamantine, stout, robust, sturdy, husky, doughty, hardy, powerful, potent, puissant, valid.
  resistless, irresistible, invincible, proof against, impregnable, unconquerable, indomitable, inextinguishable, unquenchable; incontestable; more than a match for; overpowering, overwhelming; all-powerful, all-sufficient, sovereign.
  able-bodied; athletic, gymnastic, carobatic, agonistic, palaestral [*rare*]; Herculean, Briarean, Brobdingnagian, Titanic, Cyclopean, Atlantean; muscular, brawny, wiry, well-knit, broad-shouldered, sinewy, sinewous [*rare*], strapping, stalwart, gigantic.
  manly, manlike, manful; masculine, male, virile, in the prime of manhood.
  unweakened, unallayed, unwithered, unshaken, unworn, unexhausted; in full force, in full swing; in the plentitude of power.
  sound; stubborn, thick-ribbed, made of iron, deep-rooted; strong as -a lion, –an ox, –a horse -brandy; sound as a roach; in fine feather, in high feather [*both colloq.*]; like a giant refreshed.
- *adv.* **strongly** etc. *adj.;* by force etc. *n.;* by main force etc. (*by compulsion*) 744.

160. Weakness

- *n.* **weakness** etc. *adj.;* debility, atony, relaxation, languor, enervation; impotence etc. 158; infirmity, effeminacy, feminality; fragility, flaccidity; inactivity etc. 683.
  [comparisons] reed, thread, rope of sand, house of cards, house built on sand.
  anemia, bloodlessness, deficiency of blood, poverty of blood.
  invalidation; declension–, loss–, failure- of strength; delicacy, decrepitude, asthenia, adynamy [*rare*], cachexia *or* cachexy, sprain, strain.
  weakling; softling [*obs.*]; infant etc. 129; youth etc. 127.
- *v.* **be weak** etc. *adj.;* drop, crumble, give way, totter, dodder, tremble, shake, halt, limp, fade, languish, decline, flag, fail, have one foot in the grave.
  render weak etc. *adj.;* weaken, enfeeble, debilitate, invalidate, shake, deprive of strength, relax, enervate; unbrace, unnerve; cripple, unman etc. (*render powerless*) 158; cramp, reduce, sprain, strain, blunt the edge of; dilute, impoverish; decimate; extenuate; reduce in strength, reduce the strength of; *mettre de l'eau dans son vin* [*F.*].
- *adj.* **weak**, feeble, debile [*obs.*]; impotent etc. 158; relaxed, unnerved etc. *v.;* sapless, strengthless, powerless; weakly, unstrung, flaccid, adynamic, asthenic; nervous.
  soft, effeminate, feminate [*obs.*], womanish.
  frail, fragile, shattery; flimsy, sleazy, gossamery, papery, unsubstantial, gimcrack, gingerbread; rickety, jerry-built, *kucha or kachcha* [*Hind.*], cranky; craichy [*dial. Eng.*], drooping, tottering, doddering [*colloq.*] etc. *v.;* broken, lame, withered, shattered, shaken, crazy, shaky, tumbledown; palsied etc. 158; decrepit.
  unsound, poor, infirm; faint, faintish; sickly etc. (*disease*) 655; dull, slack, evanid [*obs.*], languid; spent, short-winded, effete; weather-beaten; decayed, rotten, forworn [*archaic*], worn, seedy, languishing, wasted, washy, wishy-washy [*colloq.*], laid low, pulled down, the worse for wear.
  unstrengthened etc. 159, unsupported, unaided, unassisted; aidless, defenseless etc. 158.
  on its last legs; weak as a -child, –baby, –chicken, –cat, –rat, –rag; weak as -water, –water gruel, –gingerbread, –milk and water; colorless etc. 429.

161. Production

n. **production**, creation, construction, formation, fabrication, manufacture; building, architecture, erection, edification; coinage; disaster; organization; *nisus formativus* [*L.*]; putting together etc. *v.;* establishment; workmanship, performance; achievement etc. (*completion*) 729.

flowering, fructification, fruition; inflorescence.

bringing forth etc. *v.;* parturition, birth, birth throe, childbirth, delivery, confinement, *accouchement* [*F.*], travail, labor, midwifery, obstetrics; geniture [*obs.*]; gestation etc. (*maturation*) 673; assimilation; evolution, development, growth; entelechy; fertilization, gemination, germination, heterogamy, genesis, generation, histogenesis, breeding, begetting, isogamy, epigenesis, procreation, progeneration, propagation; fecundation, impregnation; albumen etc. 357.

spontaneous generation; archigenesis, archebiosis, abiogenesis, biogenesis, biogeny, dysmerogenesis, eumerogenesis, heterogenesis, oögenesis, merogenesis, metogenesis, monogenesis, parthenogenesis, homogenesis, xenogenesis.

dissogeny, digenesis, physiogeny, phylogeny, ontogeny, ontogenesis, mitosis, xenogeny; theogony, tocogony, tocology, vacuolation, vacuolization.

publication; works, *oeuvres* [*F.*], opus (*pl.* opera) [*L.*]; authorship

structure, building, edifice, fabric, erection, pile, tower; flower, fruit, blossom.

v. **produce**, perform, operate, do, make, gar [*obs.*], form, construct, fabricate, frame, contrive, manufacture; weave, forge, coin, carve, chisel; build, raise, edify, rear, erect, put together; set up, run up; establish, constitute, compose, organize, institute; achieve, accomplish etc. (*complete*) 729.

flower, burgeon, blossom, bear fruit, fructify, teem, ean [*obs.*], yean, farrow, drop, pup, whelp, kitten, kindle [*obs.*], spawn, spat; bear, lay, bring forth, give birth to, lie in, be brought to bed of, evolve, pullulate, usher into the world.

make productive etc. 168; create; beget, get, generate, fecundate, impregnate; procreate, progenerate, propagate; engender; bring–, call- into -being, –existence; breed, hatch, develop, bring up.

induce, superinduce; suscitate [*obs.*]; cause etc. 153; acquire etc. 775.

adj. **produced, producing** etc. *v.*, productive of; prolific etc. 168; creative; formative; procreant, generative, genitive, genetic, genial [*rare*], genital; pregnant; *enceinte* [*F.*], big with, fraught with; in the family way [*colloq.*], teeming, parturient, in the straw [*colloq.*], brought to bed of; lying-in; puerperal, puerperous [*rare*].

digenetic, heterogenetic, oögenetic, xenogenetic; ectogenous, gamic, hematobious, sporogenous, sporophorous.

architectonic *or* architectonical, constructive.

162. Destruction
[nonproduction]

n. **destruction**; waste, dissolution, breaking up; disruption; diruption [*obs.*], consumption; disorganization.

fall, downfall, ruin, perdition, debacle, *débâcle* [*F.*], crash, *éboulement* [*F.*], smash [*colloq.*], havoc, *délabrement* [*F.*], breakdown, break-up; prostration, cave-in [*colloq.*]; desolation, *bouleversement* [*F.*], wreck, wrack [*archaic*], shipwreck, cataclysm; washout.

extinction, annihilation; destruction of life etc. 361; knock-out, K. O. [*slang*], knock-out blow, knock-down blow; doom, crack of doom.

destroying etc. *v.;* demolition, demolishment [*rare*], overthrow, subversion, suppression; abolition etc. (*abrogation*) 756; biblioclasm; sacrifice; ravage, devastation, razzia; incendiarism; revolution etc. 146; extirpation etc. (*extraction*) 301; *commencement de la fin* [*F.*], road to ruin; dilapidation etc. (*deterioration*) 659; *sabotage* [*F.*].

v. **be destroyed** etc.; perish; fall, fall to the ground; tumble, topple; go–, fall- to pieces; break up; crumble, -to dust; go to -the dogs, –the wall, –smash, –shivers, –wreck, –pot [*colloq.*], –wrack and ruin; go by the board, go down the drain [*colloq.*]; be all over with, be all up with [*colloq.*], go to glory [*colloq.*], go to pieces, go under, go up the spout [*colloq.*], totter to its fall.

destroy; do–, make- away with nullify; annul etc. 756; sacrifice, demolish; tear up; overturn, overthrow, overwhelm; upset, subvert, put an end to seal the doom of, do for [*colloq.*], dish [*slang*], undo; break up, cut up; break down, cut down, pull down, mow down, blow down, beat down; suppress, quash, put down; cut short, take off, blot out; efface, obliterate, cancel, erase, strike out, expunge, delete, dele; dispel, dissipate, dissolve; consume.

smash, crash, quell, squash [*colloq.*], squelch [*colloq.*], crumple up, shatter, shiver; batter;

tear–, crush–, cut–, shake–, pull–, pick -to pieces; laniate [*rare*]; nip; tear to -rags, –tatters; crush–, knock- to atoms; ruin; strike out; throw down, throw over, knock down, knock over, lay out [*slang*], lay by the heels, fell, sink, swamp, scuttle, wreck, shipwreck, engulf *or* ingulf, submerge; lay in ashes, lay in ruins; sweep away, raze; level, –with the -ground, -dust.

deal destruction, lay waste, ravage, gut; disorganize; dismantle etc. (*render useless*) 645; devour, swallow up, desolate, devastate, sap, mine, blast, confound; exterminate, extinguish, quench, annihilate; snuff out, put out, stamp out, trample out; lay–, trample- in the dust; prostrate; tread–, crush–, trample- under foot; lay the ax to the root of; make short work of, make a clean sweep of, make mincemeat of; cut up root and branch; fling–, scatter- to the winds; throw overboard; strike at the root of, sap the foundations of, spring a mine, blow up; ravage with fire and sword; cast to the dogs; eradicate etc. 301.

adj. **destroyed** etc. *v.;* perishing etc. *v.;* trembling–, nodding–, tottering- to its fall; in course of destruction etc. *n.;* extinct; all-destroying, all-devouring, all-engulfing.

destructive, subversive, ruinous, incendiary, deletory [*obs.*]; destroying etc. *n.;* suicidal; deadly etc. (*killing*) 361.

adv. with crushing effect, with a sledge hammer.

163. Reproduction

n. **reproduction**, renovation; restoration etc. 660; renewal; new edition, reprint etc. (*copy*) 21; revival, regeneration, palingenesis, revivification; apotheosis; resuscitation, reanimation, resurrection, resurgence, reappearance; regrowth; Phoenix.

generation etc. (*production*) 161; multiplication.

v. **reproduce**; restore etc. 660; revive, renovate, renew, regenerate, revivify, resuscitate, reanimate, refashion, stir the embers, put into the crucible; multiply, repeat; resurge.

crop up, crop out, spring up like mushrooms.

adj. **reproduced** etc. *v.;* renascent, resurgent, reappearing; reproductive, proligerous [*rare*], progenitive, proliferous, gametal; hydra-headed; suigenetic.

164. Producer

n. **producer**, originator, inventor, author, founder, generator, mover, architect, grower, raiser, introducer, deviser, constructor, begetter, creator; maker etc. (*agent*) 690; prime mover.

165. Destroyer

n. **destroyer** etc. (*destroy* etc. 162); cankerworm etc. (*bane*) 663; assassin etc. (*killer*) 361; executioner etc. (*punish*) 975; biblioclast; eidoloclast, iconoclast, idoloclast; vandal, destructor [*rare*], Hun, nihilist.

166. Paternity

n. **paternity**; parentage; consanguinity etc. 11.

parent, father, sire, dad, papa, governor [*Engl. slang*], pater [*Engl. colloq.*], daddy [*colloq.*], paterfamilias, abba; genitor [*rare*], progenitor, procreator, begetter; ancestor; grandsire, grandfather; great-grandfather; fathership, fatherhood; *mabap* [*Hind.*].

motherhood, maternity, motherhead [*rare*], mothership; mother, dam, mamma *or* mama, mammy, mam [*colloq.*], motherkin, matriarch, materfamilias; grandmother.

stem, trunk, tree, stock, stirps, pedigree, house, lineage, line, family, tribe, sept, race, clan; genealogy, family tree, descent, extraction, birth, ancestry; forefathers, forbears, patriarchs.

adj. **parental**; paternal; maternal; family, ancestral, linear, patriarchal; racial, phyletic.

167. Posterity

n. **posterity**, progeny, breed, issue, offspring, brood, litter, seed, farrow, spawn, spat; family, children, grandchildren, heirs; great-grandchildren.

child, son, daughter, bairn, baby, kid [*colloq.*], papoose [*Am. Ind.*], imp, brat, moppet [*archaic*], lambkin, cub, cherub, nestling, tot, innocent, urchin, chit [*colloq.*]; infant etc. 129; *butcha* or *bacha* [*Hind.*]; bantling, scion; acrospire, plumule, shoot, sprout, olive-branch, sprit, branch; offshoot, offset; ramification; descendant; heir, heiress; heir-apparent, heir-presumptive; chip of the old block; heredity; rising generation.

lineage, straight descent, sonship, line, filiation, primogeniture.

adj. **filial**; diphyletic.

168. Productiveness

n. **productiveness** etc. *adj.;* fecundity, fertilization, fertility, luxuriance, uberty [*obs.*].

[comparisons] milch cow, rabbit, hydra, warren, seed plot, land flowing with milk and honey.

aftermath, second crop, aftercrop, aftergrowth, arrish [*dial. Eng.*], eddish [*dial. Eng.*], rowen.

multiplication, multiparity, propagation, procreation; superfetation, pregnancy, pullulation [*rare*], fructification.

169. Unproductiveness

- *v.* **make productive** etc. *adj.;* fructify; procreate, pullulate, generate, fertilize, spermatize, impregnate; fecundate, fecundify; teem, spawn, multiply; produce etc. 161; conceive.
- *adj.* **productive**, prolific, copious; teeming, teemful [*dial.*]; fertile, fruitful, frugiferous [*obs.*], fructuous [*rare*], plenteous, proliferous, fructiferous, fruitbearing; fecund, luxuriant; pregnant, uberous.

  procreant, procreative; generative, life-giving, spermatic, inceptive, originative; multiparous; omnific; propagable.

  parturient etc. (*producing*) 161; profitable etc. (*useful*) 644.

169. Unproductiveness

- *n.* **unproductiveness** etc. *adj.;* infertility, sterility, infecundity; impotence etc. 158; unprofitableness etc. (*inutility*) 645.

  waste, desert, Sahara, wild, karoo, wilderness, howling wilderness.
- *v.* **be unproductive** etc. *adj.;* hang fire, flash in the pan, come to nothing.
- *adj.* **unproductive**, acarpous, inoperative, barren, addle, unfertile, unprolific, arid, sterile, unfruitful, infecund, [*rare*], jejune, infertile; useless, otiose; *sine prole* [*L.*]; fallow; teemless, issueless, fruitless, infructuose [*rare*]; unprofitable etc. (*useless*) 645; null and void, of no effect.

170. Agency

- *n.* **agency**, operation, force, working, strain, function, office, maintenance, exercise, work, swing, play; interworking, interaction; procuration procurement.

  causation etc. 153; mediation, intermediation, instrumentality etc. 631; conation, influence etc. 175; action etc. (*voluntary*) 680; *modus operandi* [*L.*] etc. 627.

  quickening–, maintaining–, sustaining- power; home stroke.
- *v.* **be in action** etc. *adj.;* operate, work; act, act upon; perform, play, support, sustain, strain, maintain, take effect, quicken, strike.

  come–, bring- into -operation, –play; have play, have free play; bring to bear upon.
- *adj.* **operative**, operant [*rare*], efficient, efficacious, practical, exertive, conative, effectual.

  at work, on foot; acting etc. (*doing*) 680; in operation, in force, in action, in play, in exercise; acted upon, wrought upon.
- *adv.* **by the agency of** etc. *n.;* through etc. (*instrumentality*) 631; by means of etc. 632.

171. Energy

- *n.* **energy**, physical energy, force; keenness etc. *adj.;* intensity, vigor, backbone [*colloq.*], vim [*colloq.*], mettle, *vis viva* [*L.*], *vis vitae* [*L.*], pep [*slang*], ginger [*slang*], go [*colloq.*]; strength, elasticity; high pressure; fire; rush; human dynamo.

  activity, agitation, effervescence; ferment, fermentation; ebullition, splutter, perturbation, stir, bustle; voluntary energy etc. 682; quicksilver.

  exertion etc. (*effort*) 686; excitation etc. (*mental*) 824; resolution etc. (*mental energy*) 604.

  acrimony, acridity, acritude [*obs.*]; causticity, virulence, poignancy; harshness etc. *adj.;* severity, edge, point; pungency etc. 392.

  excitant, stimulant; Spanish fly, cantharides; seasoning etc. (*condiment*) 393.
- *v.* **give energy** etc. *n.;* energize, stimulate, kindle, excite, exert; activate, potentialize [*rare*], dynamize, doubleshot; sharpen, intensify; inflame etc. (*render violent*) 173; wind up etc. (*strengthen*) 159.

  strike, –into, –hard, –home; make an impression.
- *adj.* **energetic**, strong, forcible, active, strenuous, forceful, mettlesome, enterprising; go-ahead [*colloq.*]; intense, deep-dyed, severe, keen, vivid, sharp, acute, incisive, trenchant, brisk.

  rousing, irritating; poignant; virulent, caustic, corrosive, mordant, harsh, stringent; double-edged, double-shotted, double-distilled; drastic, escharotic; racy etc. (*pungent*) 392; excitant, excitative, excitatory.

  potent etc. (*powerful*) 157; radioactive.
- *adv.* **strongly** etc. *adj.; fortiter in re* [*L.*]; with telling effect.

172. Inertness

- *n.* **inertness**, physical inertness, inertia, *vis inertiae* [*L.*], inertion, inactivity, torpor, languor; dormancy, *fainéance* [*F.*], quiescence etc. 265; latency, inaction; passivity; stagnation; dullness etc. *adj.*

  mental inertness; sloth etc. (*inactivity*) 683; inexcitability etc. 826; irresolution etc. 605; obstinacy etc. 606; permanence etc. 141.
- *v.* **be inert** etc. *adj.;* hang fire, smolder *or* smoulder.
- *adj.* **inert**, inactive, passive; torpid etc. 683; sluggish, stagnant, *fainéant* [*F.*], dull, heavy, flat, slack, tame, slow, blunt; lifeless, dead, uninfluential.

  latent, dormant, smoldering *or* smouldering, unexerted.
- *adv.* **inactively** etc. *adj.;* in suspense, in abeyance.

173. Violence

n. **violence**, inclemency, vehemence, might, impetuosity, furiosity [*rare*]; boisterousness etc. *adj.;* effervescence, ebullition; turbulence, bluster; uproar, callithump, riot, row [*colloq.*], rumpus, le diable à quatre [*F.*], devil to pay [*colloq.*], the fat in the fire [*colloq.*].

ferocity, rage, fury; exacerbation, exasperation, malignity; severity etc. 739.

force, brute force; outrage; coup de main [*F.*]; strain, shock, shog [*rare*].

fit, paroxysm, spasm, convulsion, throe; hysterics, passion etc. (*state of excitability*) 825; orgasm, aphrodisia.

outbreak, outburst; debacle; burst, bounce, dissilience [*rare*], discharge, volley, explosion, blow-up, blast, detonation, rush, eruption, displosion [*obs.*], torrent.

turmoil etc. (*disorder*) 59; ferment etc. (*agitation*) 315; storm, tempest, rough weather; squall etc. (*wind*) 349; earthquake, volcano, thunderstorm.

fury, berserk, dragon, demon, tiger, beldam *or* beldame, madcap, wild beast; fire eater [*colloq.*] etc. (*blusterer*) 887; Erinys (*pl.* Erinyes), Eumenides, Tisiphone, Megaera, Alecto.

v. **be violent** etc. *adj.;* run high; ferment, effervesce; romp, rampage; run wild, run riot; break the peace; rush, tear; rush headlong, rush headforemost; run amuck, raise a storm, make a riot; make–, kick up– a row [*colloq.*]; rough-house [*slang*]; bluster, rage, roar, riot, storm; boil, boil over; fume, foam, come in like a lion, wreak, bear down, ride roughshod, out-Herod Herod; spread like wildfire.

explode, go off, displode [*obs.*], detonate, detonize, fulminate, let off, let fly, discharge, thunder, blow up, flash, flare, burst; shock, strain.

break open, force open, prize open, pry open; break out, fly out, burst out.

render violent etc. *adj.;* sharpen, stir up, quicken, excite, incite, urge, lash, stimulate; irritate, inflame, kindle, suscitate [*obs.*], foment; accelerate, aggravate, exasperate, exacerbate, convulse, infuriate, madden, lash into fury; fan the flame, add fuel to the flame; oleum addere camino [*L.*].

adj. **violent**, vehement; warm; acute, sharp; rough, tough [*colloq.*], vicious [*colloq.*], rude, ungentle, bluff, boisterous, wild; brusque, abrupt, waspish; impetuous; rampant.

turbulent; disorderly; blustering, towering, raging etc. *v.;* troublous, riotous; tumultuary, tumultuous; obstreperous, uproarious; extravagant; unmitigated, immitigable; ravening, tameless; frenzied etc. (*insane*) 503; desperate etc. (*rash*) 863; infuriate, furious, outrageous, frantic, hysteric, in hysterics.

fiery, flaming, scorching, hot, red-hot, ebullient.

savage, fierce, ferocious, fierce as a tiger.

excited etc. *v.;* unquelled, unquenched, unextinguished, unrepressed, unbridled, unruly; headstrong; ungovernable, unappeasable, unmitigable; uncontrollable, incontrollable; insuppressible, irrepressible; orgastic.

spasmodic, convulsive, explosive; detonating etc. *v.;* volcanic, meteoric, stormy etc. (*wind*) 349.

adv. **violently** etc. *adj.;* amain; by storm, by force, by main force; with might and main; tooth and nail, vi et armis [*L.*], at the point of the –sword, –bayonet; at one fell swoop; with a high hand, through thick and thin; in desperation, with a vengeance; à outrance [*F.*], à toute outrance [*F.*]; headlong, headfirst, headforemost.

aphrodisiac, aphrodisiacal, aphroditous.

174. Moderation

n. **moderation**; lenity etc. 740; temperateness, temperance, passability, passableness, gentleness etc. *adj.;* sobriety; quiet; mental calmness etc. (*inexcitability*) 826.

moderating etc. *v.;* anaphrodisia; relaxation, remission, mitigation, tranquilization, assuagement, alleviation, contemperation [*obs.*], pacification.

mean, measure, juste milieu [*F.*], golden mean, meden agan [*Gr.*], ariston metron [*Gr.*].

moderator; lullaby, sedative, calmative, lenitive, palliative, demulcent, antispasmodic, carminative; laudanum; rose water, balm, poppy, chloroform, opium: soothing sirup, opiate, anodyne, milk.

v. **be moderate** etc. *adj.;* keep within –bounds, –compass; sober down, settle down; keep the peace, remit, relent; take in sail.

moderate, soften, mitigate, temper, accoy [*obs.*]; attemper, contemper [*obs.*], mollify, lenify [*rare*], dulcify, dull, take off the edge, blunt, obtund, sheathe, subdue, chasten; sober down, tone down, smooth down, slow down; weaken etc. 160; lessen etc. (*decrease*) 36; check; palliate.

tranquilize, assuage, appease, suage *or* swage [*dial.*], lull, soothe, compose, still, calm, cool, quiet, hush, quell, sober, pacify, tame, damp, lay, allay, rebate [*archaic*], slacken, smooth, al-

175. Influence

leviate, rock to sleep, deaden, smother; throw cold water on, throw a wet blanket over; slake; curb etc. (*restrain*) 751; tame etc. (*subjugate*) 749; smooth over; pour oil on the -waves, −troubled waters; pour balm into; mettre de l'eau dans son vin [*F.*].

go out like a lamb, "roar you as gently as any sucking dove" [*Midsummer Night's Dream*].

adj. **moderate**; lenient etc. 740; gentle, mild; cool, sober, temperate, reasonable, measured; tempered etc. *v.;* calm, laid back [*slang*], unruffled, quiet, tranquil, still; slow, smooth, untroubled; tame; peaceful, peaceable; pacific, halcyon.

unexciting, unirritating; soft, bland, oily, demulcent, lenitive, anodyne; hypnotic etc. 683; sedative, calmative, assuaging, assuasive, calmant; antiorgastic, anaphrodisiac.

mild as mother's milk, mild as milk, milk and water, gentle as a lamb.

adv. **moderately** etc. *adj.;* gingerly; piano; under easy sail, at half speed, in moderation; within bounds, within compass; in reason.

175. Influence

n. **influence**; importance etc. 642; weight, pressure, preponderance, prevalence, sway; predominance, predominancy; ascendancy; dominance, reign; control, domination, pull [*colloq.*]; authority etc. 737; power, potency, capability etc. (*power*) 157; interest; spell, magic, magnetism.

footing; purchase etc. (*support*) 215; play, leverage, vantage ground, advantage.

tower of strength, host in himself; protection, patronage, auspices; patron etc. (*auxiliary*) 711.

v. **have influence** etc. *n.;* be influential etc. *adj.;* carry weight, sway, bias, actuate, weigh, tell; have a hold upon, magnetize, bear upon, gain a footing, work upon; take root, take hold; strike root in.

pervade, run through; spread like wildfire, be rife etc. *adj.;* rage, gain head.

dominate, subject, predominate; outweigh, overweigh; override, overbear; have-, get-, gain- -the upper hand, −full play; prevail.

be recognized, be listened to; make one's voice heard, gain a hearing; play a -part, −leading part- in; lead, control, rule, manage, master, get the mastery of, get control of, make one's influence felt; take the lead, pull strings; wind round one's finger; turn-, throw one's weight into- the scale; set the fashion, lead the dance.

adj. **influential**, effective, effectual [*rare*], potent; important etc. 642; weighty; prevailing etc. *v.;* prevalent, rife, rampant, dominant, regnant, predominant, in the ascendant, hegemonical; authoritative, recognized, telling.

adv. with telling effect, with authority.

175a. Absence of Influence

n. **impotence** etc. 158; powerlessness; inertness etc. 172; irrelevancy etc. 10.

v. have no influence etc. 175.

adj. **uninfluential**; unconducing [*rare*], nonconductive, unconductive; forceless, powerless etc. 158; irrelevant etc. 10.

176. Tendency

n. **tendency**; aptness, aptitude; proneness, proclivity, bent, turn, tone, bias, set, warp, leaning (*with* to *or* towards), predisposition, inclination, tendence [*rare*], propensity, susceptibility; conatus, conation [*obs.*], nisus; liability etc. 177; quality, nature, temperament; idiocrasy, idiosyncrasy; cast, vein, grain; humor, mood; trend; drift etc. (*direction*) 278; conduciveness, conducement; applicability etc. (*utility*) 644; subservience etc. (*instrumentality*) 631.

v. **tend**, contribute, conduce, lead, influence, dispose, incline, verge, bend to, warp, turn, work towards, trend, affect, carry, redound to, bid fair to, gravitate towards; promote etc. (*aid*) 707.

adj. **tending** etc. *v.;* conative, conducent [*obs.*], conducive, working towards, in a fair way to, likely to, calculated to; liable etc. 177; subservient etc. (*instrumental*) 631; useful etc. 644; subsidiary etc. (*helping*) 707; idiocratic, indiosyncratic, idiosyncratical.

adv. for, whither; for the purpose of.

177. Liability

n. **liability**, liableness; possibility, contingency; susceptivity, susceptiveness, susceptibility.

v. **be liable** etc. *adj.;* incur, lay oneself open to, be subjected to, run the chance, stand a chance; lie under, expose oneself to, open a door to.

adj. **liable**, subject, susceptive; in danger etc. 665; open to, exposed to, obnoxious to; answerable, responsible, accountable, amenable; unexempt from; apt to; dependent on; incident to.

contingent, incidental, possible, on the cards, within range of, at the mercy of.

178. Concurrence

n. **concurrence**, coöperation, coagency; union; coadunation, coaction [*rare*], coworking [*rare*], synergy, collaboration, conformity, conformableness, agreement etc. 23; consilience;

consent etc. (*assent*) 488; alliance; concert etc. 709; partnership etc. 712.

v. **concur**, conduce, conspire, contribute; agree, unite, harmonize, jibe [*colloq.*], coadunate, combine; hang–, pull- together etc. (*coöperate*) 709; help to etc. (*aid*) 707.

keep pace with, run parallel; go with, go along with, go hand in hand with.

adj. **concurring** etc. *v.;* concurrent, conformable, corresponsive [*rare*], joint, coöperative, concomitant, coincident, concordant, harmonious, consentaneous [*archaic*]; coadunate, coadunative, consilient, in alliance with, banded together, of one mind, at one with.

adv. with one consent.

179. Counteraction

n. **counteraction**, opposition; contrariety etc. 14; antagonism, polarity; clashing etc. *v.;* collision, interference, resistance, renitency, friction; reaction; retroaction etc. (*recoil*) 277; counterblast; neutralization etc. (*compensation*) 30; vis inertiae [*L.*]; check etc. (*hindrance*) 706.

voluntary opposition etc. 708; voluntary resistance etc. 719; repression etc. (*restraint*) 751.

v. **counteract**; run counter, clash, cross; interfere with, conflict with; contravene; jostle; go–, run–, beat–, militate- against; stultify; antagonize, frustrate, oppose etc. 708; traverse; overcome, overpower, withstand etc. (*resist*) 719; impede, hinder etc. 706; repress etc. (*restrain*) 751; react etc. (*recoil*) 277.

undo, neutralize, offset, cancel; counterpoise etc. (*compensate*) 30; overpoise.

adj. **counteracting** etc. *v.;* antagonistic, conflicting, retroactive, renitent, reactionary; contrary etc. 14.

adv. **although** etc. 30; against; mauger, malgre [*obs.*], malgrado [*obs.*], notwithstanding; in spite of etc. 708.

Class 2. Space

Section 1. Space in General

180. Space
[indefinite space]

n. **space**, extension, extent, superficial extent, expanse, stretch; room, accommodation, capacity, scope, range, latitude, field, way, expansion, compass, sweep, play, swing, spread.

spare room, elbowroom, houseroom; leeway, seaway, headway, stowage, roomage [*obs.*], tankage, margin; opening, sphere, arena.

open space, free space; void etc. (*absence*) 187; waste, desert, wild; wildness [*obs.*], wilderness; moor, down, downs, upland, moorland; prairie, steppe, llano [*Sp. Amer.*], campagna.

unlimited space; heavens, ether, plenum, infinity etc. 105; world, wide world; ubiquity etc. (*presence*) 186; length and breadth of the land; abyss etc. (*interval*) 198.

proportions, acreage; acres, –roods and perches; square -inches, –yards etc.; ares, arpents.

adj. **spacious**, roomy, extensive, expansive, capacious, ample; widespread, vast, world-wide, wide, far-flung, vasty [*rare*], uncircumscribed; boundless etc. (*infinite*) 105; shoreless, trackless, pathless; extended; beyond the verge, far as the eye can see.

adv. **extensively** etc. *adj.;* wherever; everywhere; far and -near, –wide; right and left, all over, all the world over; throughout the world, –length and breadth of the land; under the sun, in every quarter; in all -quarters, –lands; here, there, and everywhere; from pole to pole, from China to Peru [*Johnson*], from Indus to the pole [*Pope*], from Dan to Beersheba, from end to end; on the face of the earth, in the wide world, on the face of the waters, "from the four corners of the earth" [*Merchant of Venice*], from all points of the compass; to the four winds, to the uttermost parts of the earth.

180a. Inextension

n. **inextension**, nonextension, point, dot, speck, spot, pinprick, tittle; atom etc. (*small, ness*) 32.

181. Region
[definite space]

n. **region**, sphere, ground, soil, area, realm, hemisphere, quarter, orb, circuit, circle; pale etc. (*limit*) 233; compartment, department; clearing; domain, tract, terrain, dominion, colony,

182. Place

commonwealth, territory, country, fatherland, motherland.

canton, county, shire, province, *arrondissement* [*F.*], mofussil [*India*], parish, diocese, township, commune, ward, wapentake [*hist.*], hundred, riding, soke [*hist.*], tithing, bailiwick; principality, duchy, palatinate, archduchy, dukedom, kingdom, empire.

precinct, arena, *enceinte* [*F.*], walk, march, district, beat; patch, plot, inclosure, close, enclave, field, garth, court; street etc. (*abode*) 189; paddock etc. (*inclosure*) 232.

clime, climate, zone, meridian, latitude.

adj. **territorial**, local, parochial, provincial, regional, insular.

ins and outs; every hole and corner.

adv. **somewhere**, in some place, wherever it may be, here and there, in various places, *passim* [*L.*].

182. Place
[limited space]

n. **place**, lieu, spot, whereabouts, point, dot; niche, nook etc. (*corner*) 244; hole; pigeonhole etc. (*receptacle*) 191; compartment; confine, premises, precinct, station; area, courtyard, square, *place* [*F.*], *piazza* [*It.*], *plaza* [*Sp.*], forum [*L.*], *agora* [*Gr.*], hamlet, village etc. (*abode*) 189; pen etc. (*inclosure*) 232; countryside, location, site, locality etc. (*situation*) 183.

183. Situation

n. **situation**, position, locality, locale (*properly,* local), status, latitude and longitude; footing, standing, standpoint, post; stage; aspect, attitude, posture, set [*colloq.*], pose.

place, site, situs, station, seat, venue, whereabouts, environment, ground; bearings etc. (*direction*) 278; spot etc. (*limited space*) 182.

topography, geography, chorography; map etc. 554.

v. **be situated**, be situate, be located; lie; have its seat in.

adj. **situate**, situated; local, topical, topographical etc. *n.*

adv. **in situ** [*L.*], *in loco* [*L.*]; here and there, *passim* [*L.*]; hereabouts, thereabouts, whereabouts; in place, here, there.

in-, amidst- such and such -surroundings, -environs, -*entourage* [*F.*].

184. Location

n. **location**, localization; lodgment; deposition, reposition; stowage; collocation; packing, lading; establishment, settlement, installation; fixation; insertion etc. 300.

anchorage, roadstead, mooring, encampment.

settlement, plantation, colony, cantonment; situation; quarters, barracks; habitation etc. (*abode*) 189; "a local habitation and a name" [*Midsummer Night's Dream*].

domestication, cohabitation, colonization; endenization [*obs.*], naturalization.

v. **place**, situate, locate, localize, make a place for, put, lay, set, seat, station, lodge, quarter, post, install; house, stow; establish, fix, pin, root; graft; plant etc. (*insert*) 300; shelve, pitch, camp, lay down, deposit, reposit, store, store away, cradle; moor, tether, picket; pack, tuck in; embed, imbed; vest, invest in.

billet on, quarter upon, saddle with.

load, lade, stevedore, freight; pocket, put up, bag.

inhabit etc. (*be present*) 186; domesticate, colonize, found, people; take root, strike root; anchor; cast–, come to an- anchor; sit down, settle down; settle; take up one's -abode, –quarters; plant–, establish–, locate- oneself; have one's legal residence at; hang out one's shingle [*colloq.*]; squat, perch, hive, *se nicher* [*F.*], bivouac, burrow, get a footing; encamp, pitch one's tent; put up -at, –one's horses at; keep house.

naturalize, endenizen [*rare*], adopt.

put back, replace etc. (*restore*) 660.

adj. **placed** etc. *v.;* situate, posited, ensconced, imbedded, embosomed, rooted; domesticated; vested in, unremoved.

moored etc. *v.;* at anchor.

185. Displacement

n. **displacement**, elocation [*obs.*], heterotopy, transposition.

ejectment etc. 297; exile etc. (*banishment*) 893.

removal etc. (*transference*) 270; unshipment, transshipment *or* transshipment, unplacement [*rare*], moving, shift.

misplacement, dislocation etc. 61; fish out of water.

v. **displace**, displant, dislodge, disestablish; misplace, unplace [*rare*], translocate [*rare*], unseat, disturb, disniche; exile etc. (*seclude*) 893; ablegate [*obs.*], set aside, remove; take away, cart away; take off, draft off; lade etc. 184.

unload, empty etc. (*eject*) 297; transfer etc. 270; dispel.

vacate; depart etc. 293.

adj. **displaced** etc. *v.;* unplaced, unhoused, unharbored, unestablished, unsettled; houseless, homeless, harborless [*archaic*]; out of place, out of a situation.

misplaced, out of its element.

186. Presence

n. **presence**, presentness, occupancy, occupation; attendance.

permeation, pervasion; diffusion etc. (*dispersion*) 73.

whereness, ubiety, ubiquity, ubiquitariness; omnipresence.

bystander etc. (*spectator*) 444.

v. **be present** etc. *adj.;* assister [*F.*]; make one -of, –at; look on, attend, remain; find–, present- oneself; show one's face; fall in the way of, occur in a place; exist in space, lie, stand; occupy.

inhabit, dwell, reside, stay, sojourn, live, abide, lodge, bunk, room, nestle, roost [*colloq.*], perch; take up one's abode etc. (*be located*) 184; tenant; people.

frequent, resort to, haunt; revisit.

pervade, permeate; be diffused through, be disseminated through; overspread, overrun; fill, run through; meet one at every turn.

adj. **present**; occupying, inhabiting etc. *v.;* moored etc. 184; resiant [*obs.*], resident, residential, residentiary; domiciled.

ubiquitous, ubiquitary; omnipresent; universally present.

peopled, populous, full of people, inhabited.

adv. here, there, where, everywhere, aboard, on board, at home, afield; on the spot; here there and everywhere etc. (*space*) 180; in presence of, before; under the eyes of, under the nose of; in the face of; *in propria persona* [*L.*].

187. Absence

[nullibicity]

n. **nullibicity**, nullibiety [*rare*], absence; awayness [*rare*], cut [*colloq.*]; inexistence etc. 2; nonresidence, absenteeism; nonattendance, alibi.

emptiness etc. *adj.;* void, vacuum; vacuity [*rare*], vacancy, voidness [*rare*], *tabula rasa* [*L.*]; exemption; hiatus etc. (*interval*) 198; lipotype.

truant, absentee.

nobody; nobody -present, –on earth; not a soul; no man, nix [*slang*].

v. **be absent** etc. *adj.;* keep away, keep out of the way; play truant, absent oneself, stay away; slip off, slip out, slip away; keep–, hold- aloof.

withdraw, make oneself scarce [*colloq.*], retreat, retire, vacate; go away etc. 293.

adj. **absent**, not present, away, nonresident, gone, from home; missing; lost; wanting; omitted; nowhere to be found; inexistent etc. 2.

empty, void; vacant, vacuous; blank, null; untenanted, unoccupied, uninhabited; tenantless; desert, deserted; devoid; unhabitable, uninhabitable.

exempt from, not having.

adv. **without**, minus, nowhere; elsewhere; neither here nor there; in default of; sans; behind one's back.

188. Inhabitant

n. **inhabitant**; resident, residentiary; dweller, indweller, habitant [*rare*]; addressee; occupier, occupant; householder, lodger, roomer, inmate, tenant, incumbent, sojourner, *locum tenens* [*L.*], commorant; settler, squatter, backwoodsman, colonist; islander; denizen, citizen; burgher, oppidan, cockney, cit [*colloq.*], townsman, burgess; villager; cottager, cottier, cotter; compatriot; backsettler, boarder; hotel keeper, innkeeper; habitant; paying guest; planter.

native, indigene [*rare*], aborigines, autochthon (*pl.* autochthones), aboriginal; newcomer etc. (*stranger*) 57.

American; Briton, Englishman, Britisher, John Bull; Canadian, Canuck [*slang*]; downeaster; Scot, Scotchman, Scotsman, Caledonian; Hibernian, Irishman, Paddywhack, Paddy, Mick, Teague, Greek *or* Grecian [*slang*]; Welshman, Cambrian, Taffy; Frenchman, Parleyvoo, Frog *or* Froggy [*slang*]; Chinaman, Celestial; Uncle Sam, Yankee, Brother Jonathan.

people etc. (*mankind*) 372; colony, settlement; household; mir [*Russia*]; garrison, crew; population.

v. **inhabit** etc. (*be present*) 186; endenizen [*rare*] etc. (*locate oneself*) 184.

adj. **indigenous**; native, natal; autochthonal, autochthonous; British, English; American; Canadian; Irish, Hibernian; Scotch, Scottish; Welsh, Cambrian; French, Gallic; Chinese, Celestial, Sinaean, Sinaic *or* Sinic [*rare*]; domestic; domiciliated, domiciled; naturalized, vernacular, domesticated; domiciliary; colonial.

occupied by, in the occupation of; garrisoned by.

189. Abode

[place of habitation, or resort]

n. **abode**, dwelling, lodging, domicile, residence, address, habitation, where one's lot is cast, local habitation, berth, diggings [*colloq.*], seat, lap, sojourn, housing, pad [*slang*], quarters, head-

190. Contents

quarters, resiance [*obs.*], tabernacle, throne, ark.

home, fatherland, motherland, country; homestead, home stall [*Eng.*], fireside; hearth, hearthstone; chimney corner, ingleside; harem, seraglio, zenana; household gods, *lares et penates* [*L.*], roof, household, housing, *dulce domum* [*L.*], paternal domicile; native soil, native land, "God's country," down home [*colloq.*]

quarter, parish etc. (*region*) 181.

retreat, haunt, resort; nest, nidus, snuggery [*colloq.*], arbor, bower etc. 191; lair, den, cave, hole, hiding place, cell, sanctum sanctorum, aerie, eyrie *or* eyry, rookery, hive; habitat, covert, perch, roost; nidification; *kala jagah* [*Hind.*].

camp, bivouac, encampment, cantonment; castrametation; barrack, casemate, casern *or* caserne; tent etc. 223.

tenement, messuage, farm, farmhouse, grange, hacienda [*Sp. Amer.*], toft [*Scot., and dial. Eng.*].

cot, cabin, hut, chalet *or* châlet [*F.*], croft, shed, booth, stall, hovel, bothy *or* boothy, shanty, dugout [*U.S.*], wigwam; pen etc. (*inclosure*) 232; barn, bawn [*obs.*], kennel, sty, doghole, cote, coop, hutch; byre, cowhouse, cowshed, cowbyre; stable, dovecote, columbary, columbarium; shippen [*dial.*]; igloo *or* iglu [*Eskimo*], jacal; lacustrine–, lake–, pile– dwelling; log cabin, log house; shack [*colloq.*], shebang [*slang*], tepee, topek.

house, mansion, place, villa, cottage, box, lodge, hermitage, *rus in urbe* [*L.*], folly, rotunda, tower, *château* [*F.*], castle, pavilion, hotel, court, manor-house, messuage, hall, palace; kiosk, brownstone, bungalow, chummery [*esp. Anglo-Indian*], casa [*Sp., Pg. and It.*], country seat; apartment–, frame–, ranch–, shingle- house; duplex, flat, high-rise, tenement; building etc. (*construction*) 161; room, chamber etc. (*receptacle*) 191; buildings, mews.

hamlet, village, bustee *or* basti [*Hind.*], thorp *or* thrope, dorp, kraal [*S. Africa*], rancho [*Sp. Amer.*].

town, borough, burgh, ham [*now used only in compounds*], city, capital, metropolis; suburb; provincial town, county town, county seat; courthouse; ghetto.

street, place, terrace, parade, esplanade, *alameda* [*Sp.*], board walk, embankment, road, row, lane, alley, court, quadrangle, quad [*colloq.*], wynd [*dial.*], close, yard, passage.

square, polygon, circus, crescent, mall, piazza, arcade, colonnade, peristyle, cloister; gardens, grove, residences; block of buildings, market place, *place* [*F.*], plaza.

anchorage, roadstead, roads; dock, basin, wharf, quay, port, harbor.

assembly room, auditorium, concert hall, armory, gymnasium; cathedral, church, chapel, meetinghouse etc. (*temple*) 1000; parliament etc. (*council*) 696.

inn, hostel [*archaic*], hostelry [*archaic*], hotel, tavern, caravansary *or* caravanserai, xenodochium, dak bungalow [*India*], khan, hospice; public house, alehouse, pothouse, mughouse; gin palace; bar, barroom cocktail lounge; cabaret, chophouse; club, clubhouse; cookshop, dive; grill room, saloon, shebeen [*Irish and Scot.*]; coffee-house, eating-house; canteen, restaurant, buffet, café, *estaminet* [*F.*], *posada* [*Sp.*]

almshouse, flophouse, poorhouse, townhouse.

garden, park, pleasure ground, pleasance *or* plaisance [*archaic*], demesne.

sanatorium, health resort, Hill station *or* the Hills [*India*], health retreat, sanitarium, spa, watering-place, pump room.

v. **inhabit** etc. (*be present*) 186; take up one's abode etc. (*locate oneself*) 184.

adj. **urban**, oppidan [*rare*], metropolitan; suburban; provincial, rural, rustic, agrestic, country, countrified, regional; domestic; cosmopolitan; palatial.

190. Contents
[things contained]

n. **contents**; cargo, lading, freight, shipment, load, bale, burden, jag [*Engl. colloq.*]; cartload, shipload; cup of, basket of etc. (*receptacle*) 191; inside etc. 221; stuffing.

v. **load**, lade, ship, charge, weight, pile, fill, stuff.

191. Receptacle

n. **receptacle**, container; inclosure etc. 232; recipient, receiver, reservatory [*obs.*].

compartment; cell, cellule; follicle; hole, corner, niche, recess, nook; crypt, stall, pigeonhole, cove, oriel; cave etc. (*concavity*) 252; mouth.

capsule, vesicle, cyst, pod, calyx, cancelli, utricle, bladder; pericarp, udder.

stomach, paunch, belly, venter, ventricle, ingluvies, crop, craw, maw, gizzard, breadbasket [*slang*], Little Mary [*slang*]; omasum, manyplies, abomasum, rumen, reticulum.

bag, sac, sack, saccule, wallet, pocket, pouch, fob, sheath, scabbard, socket, cardcase, scrip [*archaic*], poke [*chiefly dial.*], knapsack, haversack, satchel, reticule, budget [*dial.*], net; dittybag, –box; housewife *or* hussif; saddlebags; portfolio; quiver etc. (*magazine*) 636.

case, chest, box, coffer, caddy, casket; pyx *or* pix, monstrance [*R. C. Ch.*]; caisson; desk, bureau, reliquary, shrine; trunk, portmanteau, bandbox, valise, grip *or* gripsack [*colloq.*], suitcase, handbag, Boston bag, school bag, brief case, travelingbag, Gladstone *or* Gladstone bag; skippet, vasculum; boot, imperial [*now rare*]; *vache* [*F.*]; cage, manger, rack.

vessel, vase, bushel, barrel; canister, jar; pottle, basket, pannier; buck basket, clothes basket, hopper, maund [*obs.*], creel, cran *or* crane [*Scot.*], crate, cradle, bassinet, whisket *or* wisket [*dial. Eng.*]; *jardinière* [*F.*], *corbeille* [*F.*], hamper, dosser *or* dorser, tray, hod, scuttle, utensil; brazier; cuspidor, spittoon.

[for liquids] cistern etc. (*store*) 636; vat, caldron *or* cauldron, barrel, cask, puncheon, keg, rundlet, tun, butt, firkin, kilderkin, carboy, amphora, bottle, jar, decanter, ewer, cruse, carafe, crock, kit [*dial. Eng.*], canteen, flagon; demijohn; flask, flasket; stoup *or* stoop, noggin, vial, phial, cruet, caster; urn, epergne, salver, patella, *tazza* [*It.*], patera; piggin; biggin, percolator, coffeepot, coffee urn, teapot, tea urn, samovar; tig *or* tyg [*dial. Eng.*], nipperkin [*now rare*], pocket pistol [*slang*], tub, bucket, pail, skeel [*dial.*], pot, tankard, jug, pitcher, mug, pipkin; gallipot; matrass *or* mattrass, receiver, retort, alembic, bolthead, capsule, can, kettle; bowl, basin, jorum [*colloq.*], punch bowl, cup, goblet, chalice, tumbler, glass, rummer, horn, saucepan, skillet, posnet [*obs.*], tureen, stein.

bail, beaker, billy [*Australia*], cannikin *or* canakin; catch basin, catch drain; chatti *or* chatty [*India*], lota *or* lotah [*India*], mussuk *or* mussuck [*India*]; schooner, spider, terrine, toby, *urceus* [*L.*].

plate, platter, dish, trencher, calabash, porringer, potager [*obs.*], saucer, pan, crucible; glassware, tableware; vitrics.

ladle, dipper, tablespoon, spoon; shovel, trowel, spatula.

cupboard, closet, commode, cellaret, chiffonier *or* chiffonnier, *chiffonnière* [*F.*], locker, bin, bunker, buffet, press, clothespress, safe, sideboard, drawer, chest of drawers, till, escritoire, scrutoire [*obs.*], secretary, *secrétaire* [*F.*], davenport, bookcase, cabinet, canterbury; *étagère* [*F.*], vargueno, vitrine.

chamber, apartment, room, cabin; office, court, hall, atrium; suite of rooms, apartment, flat, story; saloon, *salon* [*F.*], parlor; by-room, cubicle; presence chamber; living–, sitting–, drawing–, reception–, state-room; best room [*colloq.*], keeping room [*dial. Eng.*]; gallery, cabinet, closet, pew, box; boudoir; adytum, sanctum; bedroom, dormitory; refectory, dining room, *salle-à-manger* [*F.*]; nursery, schoolroom; library, study; studio; billiard room, bathroom, lavatory, toilet, powder room, smoking room; den; state room, tablinum, tenement.

attic, loft, garret, cockloft, clerestory; cellar, vault, hold, cockpit; cubbyhole; cook house; *entre-sol* [*F.*]; mezzanine *or* mezzanine floor; ground floor, *rez-de-chaussée* [*F.*], basement, kitchen, pantry, *bawarchi-khana* [*Hind.*], scullery, offices; storeroom etc. (*depository*) 636; lumber room; dairy, laundry, coach house; garage; hangar; outhouse, penthouse; lean-to.

portico, porch, stoop [*U.S.*], veranda, lobby, court, hall, vestibule, corridor, passage; anteroom, antechamber; lounge; piazza [= veranda, *U.S.*].

bower, arbor, summerhouse, alcove, grotto, hermitage; conservatory, greenhouse.

lodging etc. (*abode*) 189; bed etc. (*support*) 215.

carriage etc. (*vehicle*) 272.

adj. capsular; saccular, sacculated; recipient; ventricular, cystic, vascular, vesicular, cellular, camerated, locular, multilocular, polygastric; gastric, stomachic, gasteral [*rare*]; marsupial; siliquose, siliquous.

Section 2. Dimensions

192. Size

n. **size**, magnitude, dimension, bulk, volume; largeness etc. *adj.*; greatness etc. (*of quantity*) 31; expanse etc. (*space*) 180; amplitude, mass; proportions.

capacity; tonnage *or* tunnage; cordage; caliber *or* calibre; scantling [*obs.*].

corpulence, obesity; plumpness etc. *adj.*; *embonpoint* [*F.*], corporation [*colloq.*], flesh and blood, lustihood; turgidity etc. (*expansion*) 194.

hugeness etc. *adj.*; enormity, immensity; monstrosity.

giant, Brobdingnagian, Antaeus, Goliath, Polyphemus, Colossus, Titan, Titaness, Briareus,

193. Littleness

Norn, Hercules, Cyclops, Gog and Magog, Gargantua, King Kong; monster, mammoth, cachalot, whale, porpoise, behemoth, leviathan, elephant, jumbo, hippopotamus; colossus.

lump, bulk, block, loaf, mass, swad [*slang*], clod, nugget, tun, cord, bushel; thumper [*slang*], whopper *or* whapper [*colloq.*], spanker [*slang*], strapper [*slang*]; "Triton among the minnows" [*Coriolanus*].

mountain, mound; heap etc. (*assemblage*) 72.

full-size, life-size; largest portion etc. 50.

v. **be large** etc. *adj.;* become large etc. (*expand*) 194.

adj. **large**, big; great etc. (*in quantity*) 31; considerable, bulky, voluminous, ample, massive, massy; capacious, comprehensive, spacious etc. 180; mighty, towering, fine, magnificent.

stout, corpulent, fat, plump, squab, full, lusty, strapping [*colloq.*], bouncing; portly, burly, well-fed, full-grown; corn-fed, gram-fed [*Anglo-Ind.*]; stalwart, brawny, fleshy, goodly; in good -case, -condition; in condition, in shape; chopping, jolly; club-faced [*obs.*], chubby-faced.

large as life; plump as a -dumpling, -partridge; fat as -a pig, -a quail, -butter, -brawn, -bacon [*all colloq.*].

hulky, hulking, unwieldy, lumpish, lubberly, gaunt, spanking [*slang.*], whacking [*colloq.*], whopping [*colloq.*], thumping [*colloq.*], thundering [*colloq.*], overgrown; puffy etc. (*swollen*) 194.

huge, immense, enormous, titanic, mighty; vast, vasty [*archaic*]; stupendous; monster, monstrous; gigantic; elephantine; giant, giantlike; colossal, Cyclopean, Brobdingnagian, Gargantuan; infinite etc. 105.

193. Littleness

n. **littleness** etc. *adj.;* smallness etc. (*of quantity*) 32; exiguity, inextension; parvitude [*rare*], parvity [*obs.*]; duodecimo; epitome; microcosm; rudiment; vanishing point; thinness etc. 203.

dwarf, pygmy *or* pigmy, Liliputian, Negrito, Negrillo; chit, fingerling [*rare*], Pigwiggen, pigwidgeon [*rare*], urchin, elf; atomy, dandiprat [*archaic*], doll, puppet; Tom Thumb, hop-o'-my-thumb; manikin *or* mannikin; micromorph [*rare*], homunculus, dapperling.

mite, insect, arthropod, ephemerid, ephemera, bug [*pop.*], larva, emmet, fly, midge, gnat, shrimp, minnow, worm, maggot, grub; tit, tomtit, runt, mouse, small fry; millet seed, mustard seed; barleycorn; pebble, grain of sand; molehill, button, bubble.

atom, monad, animalcule, animalculum (*pl.* animalcula), diatom, dyad, triad, tetrad, pentad, hexad, heptad, octad, molecule, microbe, germ, microörganism, bacterium (*pl.* bacteria), microphyte, microzyme, amoeba, microzoa, entozoön (*pl.* entozoa), phytozoaria, infusoria.

particle etc. (*small quantity*) 32; point, micron; scintilla; fragment etc. (*small part*) 51; powder etc. 330; point of a pin, mathematical point; minutiae etc. (*unimportance*) 643.

micrography; micrometer, microscope, interferometer, vernier; scale.

v. **be little** etc. *adj.;* lie in a nutshell; become small etc. (*decrease*) 36, (*contract*) 195.

adj. **little**; small etc. (*in quantity*) 32; minute, diminutive, microscopic; inconsiderable etc. (*unimportant*) 643; exiguous, puny, runty, tiny, wee [*colloq.*], petty, minikin [*obs.*], miniature, pygmy *or* pigmy, elfin; undersized; dwarf, dwarfed, dwarfish; spare, stunted, limited; cramp, cramped; pollard, Liliputian, Negritic, dapper, pocket; portative, portable; duodecimo; dumpy, squat; short etc. 201.

impalpable, intangible, evanescent, imperceptible, invisible, inappreciable, infinitesimal, homeopathic; rudimentary, rudimental; embryonic, vestigial.

animalcular, amoebic, amoeboid, diatomaceous, diatomic, microzoal, microbial, microbic, molecular, atomic, corpuscular.

scant, weazen [*obs.*], scraggy, scrubby; thin etc. (*narrow*) 203; granular etc. (*powdery*) 330; shrunk etc. 195; brevipennate.

adv. in a small compass, in a nutshell; on a small scale.

194. Expansion

n. **expansion**, dilation, expansibleness; increase etc. 35 -of size; enlargement, extension, augmentation; amplification, ampliation; aggrandizement, spread, increment, growth, development, pullulation [*rare*], swell, dilatation, rarefaction; turgescence *or* turgescency, turgidness, turgidity; dispansion [*obs.*]; obesity etc. (*size*) 192; hydrocephalus, hydrophthalmus; dropsy, tumefaction, intumescence, swelling, tumor, diastole, distension; puffing, puffiness; inflation; pandiculation.

dilatability, expansibility.

growth, upgrowth; accretion etc. 35; germination, budding, gemmation.

bulb etc. (*convexity*) 250; plumper; superiority of size.

overgrowth, overdistension; hypertrophy, tympany.

v. **become larger** etc. (large etc. 192); expand, widen, enlarge, extend, grow, increase, incrassate, swell, gather; fill out; deploy, take open order, dilate, stretch, spread; mantle, wax; grow up, spring up; bud, burgeon *or* bourgeon, shoot, sprout, germinate, put forth, vegetate, pullulate, open, burst forth; gain flesh, gather flesh; outgrow; spread like wildfire, overrun.

be larger than; surpass etc. (*be superior*) 33.

render larger etc. (large etc. 192); expand, spread, extend, aggrandize, distend, develop, amplify, spread out, widen, magnify, rarefy, inflate, puff, blow up, stuff, pad, cram, bloat; exaggerate; fatten.

adj. **expanded** etc. *v.;* larger etc. (large etc. 192); swollen; expansive; wide open, widespread; fan-shaped, flabelliform; overgrown, exaggerated, bloated, fat, turgid, tumid, hypertrophied, dropsical; pot-bellied, swagbellied [*obs.*]; edematous, corpulent, obese, puffy, pursy, blowzy, distended; patulous; bulbous etc. (*convex*) 250; full-blown, full-grown, full-formed; big etc. 192; abdominous, enchymatous, rhipidate; tumefacient, tumefying.

195. Contraction

n. **contraction**, reduction, diminution; decrease etc. 36 -of size; defalcation, decrement; lessening, shrinking etc. *v.;* compaction [*rare*], tabes, collapse, emaciation, attenuation, tabefaction [*rare*], consumption, marasmus, atrophy; systole, syncopation, syncope; neck, hourglass.

compression, condensation, constraint, astriction [*rare*], compactness; compendium etc. 596; squeezing etc. *v.;* strangulation; corrugation; constringency, astringency; astringents, sclerotics; contractibility, contractibleness, contractility, compressibility, compressibleness, coarctation.

inferiority in size.

v. **become small**, become smaller; lessen, decrease etc. 36; grow less, dwindle, shrink, contract, narrow, shrivel, syncopate, collapse, wither, lose flesh, wizen [*dial.*], fall away, waste, wane, ebb; decay etc. (*deteriorate*) 659.

be smaller than, fall short of; not come up to etc. (*be inferior*) 34.

render smaller, lessen, diminish, contract, draw in, narrow, pucker, cockle, coarct *or* coarctate [*rare*]; boil down; deflate, exhaust, empty; constrict, constringe; condense, compress, squeeze, corrugate, crush, crumple up, warp, purse, purse up, pack, stow; pinch, tighten, strangle; cramp; dwarf, bedwarf; shorten etc. 201; circumscribe etc. 229; restrain etc. 751.

pare, reduce, attenuate, rub down, scrape, file, grind, chip, shave, shear.

adj. **contracting** etc. *v.;* astringent, constringent, shrunk, shrunken, tabescent, tabetic, contractible, contracted etc. *v.;* strangulated, tabid, wizened, weazen, weazeny [*colloq.*], corky, stunted; waning etc. *v.;* neap, compact, compacted.

unexpanded etc. (expand etc. 194); contractile; compressible; smaller etc. (small etc. 193).

196. Distance

n. **distance**; space etc. 180; remoteness, farness; far cry to; longinquity [*rare*], elongation; easting, westing, drift, offing, background; remote region; removedness; parallax; reach, span, stride.

outpost, outskirt; horizon, sky line; aphelion; foreign parts, *ultima Thule* [*L.*], *ne plus ultra* [*L.*], antipodes; jumping-off place [*colloq.*], long range, giant's stride.

dispersion etc. 73.

v. **be distant** etc. *adj.;* extend to, stretch to, reach to, spread to, go to, get to, stretch away to; range, outreach, outlie [*rare*].

remain at a distance; keep-, stand--away, -off, -aloof, -clear of.

adj. **distant**; far off, far away; remote, telescopic, distal, wide of; stretching to etc. *v.;* yon, yonder; ulterior; transmarine, transpontine, transatlantic, transpacific, transoceanic, transalpine; tramontane; ultramontane, ultramundane; hyperborean, antipodean; inaccessible, out-of-the-way, God-forsaken [*colloq.*]; unapproached, unapproachable; incontiguous [*obs.*].

adv. **far off**, far away; afar, -off; off; away; a -long, -great, -good- way off; wide away, beyond range, aloof; wide of, clear of; out of -the way, -reach; abroad, yonder, farther, further, beyond; *outre mer* [*F.*], over the border, far and wide, "over the hills and far away" [Gay]; from pole to pole etc. (*over great space*) 180; to the -uttermost parts, -ends- of the earth; out of range, out of hearing, nobody knows where, *à perte de vue* [*F.*], out of the sphere of, wide of the mark; a far cry to.

apart, asunder; wide apart, wide asunder; *longo intervallo* [*L.*]; at arm's length.

197. Nearness

n. **nearness** etc. *adj.;* proximity, propinquity; vicinity, vicinage; neighborhood, adjacency, nigh-

198. Interval

ness [*archaic*], appropinquity [*rare*]; contiguity etc. 199.

short -distance, -step, -cut; earshot, close quarters, range, stone's throw; bowshot, gunshot, pistol shot; hair's breadth, span.

purlieus, neighborhood, vicinage, environs, *alentours* [*F.*], suburbs, *faubourg* [*F.*], confines, *banlieue* [*F.*], borderland; whereabouts.

bystander, spectator; neighbor *or* neighbour, borderer.

approach etc. 286; convergence etc. 290; perihelion.

v. **be near** etc. *adj.;* adjoin, abut, neighbor, hang about, trench on; border upon, verge upon; stand by, approximate, tread on the heels of, cling to, clasp, hug; huddle; hang upon the skirts of, hover over; burn [*colloq.*].

bring *or* draw near etc. 286; converge etc. 290; crowd etc. 72; place side by side etc. *adv.*

adj. **near**, nigh; close-, near- at hand; close, neighboring, vicinal, propinquent [*rare*]; bordering upon, contiguous, adjacent, adjoining; proximate, proximal; at hand, warm [*colloq.*], handy; near the mark, near run; home, intimate.

adv. **near**, nigh; hard by, fast by; close to, close upon; hard upon; at the point of; next door to; within -reach, - call, -hearing, -earshot, -range; within an ace of; but a step, not far from, at no great distance; on the -verge, -brink, -skirts- of; in the environs etc. *n.;* at one's -door, -feet, -elbow, -finger's end, -side; on the tip of one's tongue; under one's nose; within a stone's throw etc. *n.;* in sight of, in presence of; at close quarters; cheek by jowl, cheek to cheek, shoulder to shoulder; beside, alongside, side by side, *tête-à-tête* [*F.*]; in juxtaposition etc. (*touching*) 199; yardarm to yardarm; at the heels of; on the confines of, at the threshold, bordering upon, verging to; in the way.

about; hereabout *or* hereabouts, thereabout *or* thereabouts; roughly, in round numbers; approximately, approximatively; as good as, wellnigh.

198. Interval

n. **interval**, interspace; separation etc. 44; hiatus, caesura; interruption, interregnum; interstice, intersection, lacuna.

parenthesis etc. (*interjacence*) 228; void etc. (*absence*) 187; incompleteness etc. 53.

cleft, break, gap, opening; hole etc. 260; chasm, mesh, crevice, chink, rime [*rare*], creek, cranny, crack, chap, slit, fissure, scissure, rift, fault, flaw, breach, fracture, rent, gash, cut, leak, dike, ha-ha.

gorge, defile, ravine, cañon, crevasse, abyss, abysm; gulf; inlet, frith, strait, gully, nullah [*India*]; pass; furrow etc. 259; *abra* [*Sp. Amer.*], barranco [*Sp.*]; clove, gulch, notch, yawning gulf; *hiatus maxime deflendus* [*L.*], *hiatus valde deflendus* [*L.*].

v. **gape** etc. (*open*) 260; separate etc. 44.

adj. with an interval, far between; breachy; rimose, rimous, rimulose.

adv. **at intervals** etc. (*discontinuously*) 70; *longo intervallo* [*L.*].

199. Contiguity

n. **contiguity**, contiguousness, contact, proximity, apposition, abuttal, juxtaposition, touching etc. *v.;* abutment, osculation; meeting, appulse, appulsion, *rencontre* [*F.*], rencounter, syzygy, conjunction, conjugation, coincidence, coexistence; adhesion etc. 46.

borderland; frontier etc. (*limit*) 233; tangent; abutter.

v. **be contiguous** etc. *adj.;* join, adjoin, abut on, neighbor, border, march with; graze, touch, meet, osculate, come in contact, coincide; coexist; adhere etc. 46.

adj. **contiguous**; touching etc. *v.;* in contact etc. *n.;* conterminous, end to end, osculatory; pertingent [*obs.*]; tangential.

hand to hand; close to etc. (*near*) 197; with no interval etc. 198.

200. Length

n. **length**, longitude, longness [*rare*], extent, span; mileage.

line, bar, rule, stripe, streak, spoke, radius.

lengthening etc. *v.;* prolongation, production, protraction; tension, tensure [*obs.*]; extension.

[measures of length] line, nail, inch, hand, palm, foot, cubit, yard, ell, fathom, rood, pole, furlong, mile, knot, league; chain; arpent, handbreadth, *jornada* [*Sp. Amer.*], kos [*Hind.*], vara [*Sp. & Pg.*]; meter, kilometer, centimeter etc.

pedometer, odometer, odograph, viameter, viatometer, log [*naut.*], speedometer, telemeter, perambulator; scale etc. (*measurement*) 466.

v. **be long** etc. *adj.;* stretch out, sprawl; extend to, reach to, stretch to; make a long arm, "drag its slow length along" [*Pope*].

render long etc. *adj.;* lengthen, extend, elongate; stretch; prolong, produce [*rare*], protract; let out, draw out, spin out; drawl.

  enfilade, look along, view in perspective.
adj. **long**, longsome [*archaic*]; elongate *or* elongated, longish, lengthy, wiredrawn, outstretched, extended; lengthened etc. *v.;* sesquipedalian etc. (*words*) 577; interminable, no end of [*colloq.*].
  linear, lineal; longitudinal, oblong.
  lanky, lank, slabsided [*slang*], rangy; tall etc. 206; macrocolous, long-limbed.
  as long as -my arm, –to-day and to-morrow; unshortened etc. (shorten etc. 201).
adv. **lengthwise**, at length, longitudinally, endlong [*archaic*], endways, endwise, along; tandem; in a line etc. (*continuously*) 69; in perspective.
  from end to end, from stem to stern, from head to foot, from the crown of the head to the sole of the foot, from tip to toe, from top to toe; fore and aft; over all.

201. Shortness

n. **shortness** etc. *adj.;* brevity littleness etc. 193; a span.
  shortening etc. *v.;* abbreviation, abbreviature [*obs.*], abridgment, concision, retrenchment, curtailment, decurtation [*obs.*], epitomization, obtruncation [*rare*], condensation; reduction etc. (*contraction*) 195; epitome etc. (*compendium*) 596.
  elision, ellipsis; conciseness etc. (*in style*) 572.
  abridger, epitomist, epitomizer, obtruncator [*rare*].
v. **be short** etc. *adj.;* **render short** etc. *adj.;* shorten, curtail, abridge, abbreviate, take in, reduce; compress etc. (*contract*) 195; epitomize etc. 596.
  cut short, retrench, obtruncate [*rare*], scrimp, cut, chop up, hack, hew; cut down, pare down; clip, dock, lop, prune, shear, shave, mow, reap, crop; snub; truncate, pollard, stunt, nip, check the growth of; foreshorten [*drawing*].
adj. **short**, brief, curt; compendious, compact; stubby, pudgy, tubby [*colloq.*], squatty, squidgy [*rare*]; scrimp; shorn, stubbed; stumpy [*colloq.*], thickset, pug; chunky, curtate, curtal [*archaic*], decurtate; *retroussé* [*F.*], turned up; scrub, stocky; squab, squabby; squat, squattish, dumpy; little etc. 193; curtailed of its fair proportions; short by; oblate; abbreviatory; concise etc. 572; summary.
adv. **shortly** etc. *adj.;* in short etc. (*concisely*) 572.

202. Breadth, Thickness

n. **breadth**, width, latitude, amplitude; diameter, bore, caliber, radius; superficial extent etc. (*space*) 180.
  thickness, crassitude [*obs.*]; corpulence etc. (*size*) 192; dilatation etc. (*expansion*) 194.
v. **be broad** etc. *adj.;* become *or* render broad etc. *adj.;* expand etc. 194; thicken, widen, calibrate.
adj. **broad**, wide, ample, extended; discous, discoid; fanlike; outspread, outstretched; "wide as a church-door" [*Romeo and Juliet*]; latifoliate [*rare*], latifolious [*rare*].
  thick, dumpy, squab, squat, thickset, stubby etc. 201; thick as a rope.

203. Narrowness, Thinness

n. **narrowness** etc. *adj.;* closeness, exility [*rare*]; exiguity etc. (*little*) 193.
  line; hair's-, finger's- breadth; strip, streak, vein.
  thinness etc. *adj.;* tenuity; emaciation, marcor [*obs.*], macilence *or* macilency [*rare*].
  shaving, slip etc. (*filament*) 205; thread paper, skeleton, shadow, scrag, atomy [*obs. or joc.*], anatomy, [*archaic*], study in anatomy [*humorous*], spindle-shanks [*humorous or contemptuous*], bare-bone, lantern jaws, mere skin and bone.
  middle constriction, stricture, coarctation [*med.*]; neck, waist, isthmus, wasp, hourglass; ridge, ghat *or* ghaut [*India*], pass; ravine etc. 198.
  narrowing, angustation, tapering; contraction etc. 195.
v. be narrow etc. *adj.;* narrow, taper, contract, etc. 195; render narrow etc. *adj.*
adj. **narrow**, close; slender, gracile, thin, fine; threadlike etc. (*filament*) 205; finespun, taper, slim, slight-made; scant, scanty; spare, delicate, incapacious; contracted etc. 195; unexpanded etc. (*expand* etc. 194); slender as a thread.
  lean, emaciated, meager *or* meagre, gaunt, macilent; lank, lanky; weedy [*colloq.*], skinny; scrawny, slinky [*dial.*]; starved, starveling; attenuated, shriveled, pinched, poor, peaked [*colloq.*], lathy [*colloq.*], skeletal, flatsided [*colloq.*], slabsided [*slang*]; spindle-legged, spindle-shanked, spindling; coarctate, angustate, tabic, tabelic, tabid, extenuated, marcid [*obs.*], rawboned; herring-gutted [*colloq.*]; worn to a shadow, "lean as a rake" [*Chaucer*]; thin as a -lath, –whipping post, –wafer; hatchet-faced; lantern-jawed.

204. Layer

n. **layer**, stratum, course, bed, couch, coping, zone, substratum, floor, flag, stage, story, tier, slab, escarpment; table, tablet; dess [*Scot. & dial. Eng.*]; flagstone; board, plank; trencher, platter.

205. Filament

    leaf, lamina, lamella, sheet, flake, foil, wafer, scale, coat, peel, pellicle, membrane, film, lap, ply, slice, shive, cut, rasher, shaving, plate; overlay, integument etc. (*covering*) 223; eschar.

    stratification, lamination, delamination, foliation; scaliness, nest of boxes, coats of an onion.

v.   **slice**, shave, pare, peel, skive; delaminate; plate, coat, veneer; cover etc. 223.

adj.   **lamellar**, lamelliferous, lamellate *or* lamellated, lamelliform; laminate *or* laminated, laminiferous; micaceous; schistose, schistous; scaly, filmy, membranous, membranaceous, flaky, squamous; foliated, foliaceous; stratified, stratiform; tabular, discoid; spathic, spathose.

205. Filament

n.   **filament**, line; fiber, fibril; funicle, vein, hair, cobweb, capillary, ciliolum, capillament [*rare*], cilium, cirrus, barbel, strand, tendril, gossamer; hair stroke; veinlet, venula, venule. beard etc. (*roughness*) 256; ramification.

    thread, threadlet, harl, yarn, pack-thread, cotton, sewing silk.

    string, twine, twist, whipcord, cord, rope, hemp, oakum, jute; tape, ribbon, wire.

    strip, shred, slip, spill, list, taenia *or* tenia, band, fillet, fascia; ribbon, ribband *or* riband [*archaic*], roll, lath, splinter, shiver, shaving; ligule *or* ligula.

adj.   **filamentous**, filamentiferous, filaceous [*rare*]; filiform; fibrous, fibrillous, fibrilliform, fibrilliferous; thread-like, wiry, stringy, ropy; capillary, capilliform; funicular, wire-drawn; anguilliform; flagelliform; barbate, hairy etc. (*rough*) 256; taeniate, taeniform, taenioid; venose, venous; ligulate *or* ligulated.

206. Height

n.   **height**, altitude, elevation; eminence, pitch; loftiness etc. *adj.*; sublimity, celsitude [*rare*].

    tallness etc. *adj.*; stature, procerity [*rare*]; prominence etc. 250; apex, zenith, culmination.

    colossus etc. (*size*) 192; giant, grenadier; giraffe, camelopard.

    height, mount, mountain; hill, *alto* [*Sp.*], butte, monticule, monticle [*obs.*], fell [*obs. exc. in proper names*], knap; cape; headland, foreland; promontory; ridge, hogback *or* hog's-back, dune, rising–, vantage- ground; down; moor, moorland; Alp; uplands, highlands, heights etc. (*summit*), 210; knob, *loma, pena, picacho* [*Sp.*], tump [*dial.*]; knoll, hummock, hillock, barrow, mound; steeps, bluff, cliff, craig [*Scot.*], tor, peak, pike [*dial.*], clough [*obs.*]; escarpment, edge, ledge, brae [*Scot. & dial. Eng.*]; dizzy height.

    tower, pillar, column, obelisk, monument, belfry, steeple, spire, minaret, campanile, turret, dome, cupola; pylon, *tourelle* [*F.*], barbican, martello tower; pyramid, pagoda, mole [*Rom. antiq.*],

    ceiling etc. (*covering*) 223; upstairs.

    pole, pikestaff, maypole, flagstaff; mast, mainmast, topmast, topgallant mast.

    high water; high–, flood–, spring-tide.

    hypsography, hypsometry, hypsometer, altimeter, altimetry etc. (*angle*) 244; hypsophobia.

v.   **be high** etc. *adj.*; tower, soar, command; hover; cap, culminate; overhang, hang over, impend, beetle; bestride, ride, mount; perch, surmount; cover etc. 223; rise above, overtop etc. (*be superior*) 33; stand on tiptoe.

    become high etc. *adj.*; grow, grow higher, grow taller; upgrow; rise etc. (*ascend*) 305.

    render high etc. *adj.*; heighten etc. (*elevate*) 307.

adj.   **high**, elevated, eminent, exalted, lofty; tall; gigantic etc. (*big*) 192; Patagonian; towering, beetling, soaring, mountained, hanging [gardens]; elevated etc. 307; higher, superior, upper, supernal; highest etc. (*topmost*) 210; high-reaching, insessorial, perching; hill-dwelling, monticoline, monticolous.

    tall as a -maypole, –popular, –steeple; lanky etc. (*thin*) 203.

    upland, moorland; hilly, knobby; mountainous, alpine, subalpine, heaven-kissing; cloud-topt, cloud-capt, cloud-touching; aërial.

    overhanging etc. *v.*; incumbent; overlying; superincumbent, supernatant, superimposed; prominent etc. 250.

    hypsographic, hypsographical, hypsometric, hypsometrical.

adv.   **on high**, high up, aloft, up, above, aloof, overhead; airward; upstairs, above stairs; in the clouds; on tiptoe, on stilts, on the shoulders of; over head and ears; breast high.

    over, upwards; from top to bottom etc. (*completely*) 52.

207. Lowness

n.   **lowness** etc. *adj.*; debasement; prostration etc. (*horizontal*) 213; depression etc. (*concave*) 252; subjacency; lowlands.

    ground floor; *rez de chaussée* [*F.*]; street floor.

    basement, basement floor, cellar; hold; base etc. 211.

    [comparison] feet, heels; molehill.

low water; low–, ebb–, neap- tide.
- v. **be low** etc. *adj.;* lie low, lie flat; underlie; crouch, slouch, wallow, grovel; lower etc. (*depress*) 308.
- adj. **low**, neap, debased; lower, inferior, under, nether; lowest, nether-most, lowermost; flat, level with the ground; lying low etc. *v.;* crouched, subjacent, squat, prostrate etc. (*horizontal*) 213; depressed.
- adv. **under**; beneath, underneath; below; down, downwards; adown, at the foot of; underfoot, underground; downstairs, belowstairs; at a low ebb; below par.

208. Depth

- n. **depth**; deepness etc. *adj.;* profundity, depression etc. (*concavity*) 252.
  pit, shaft, hollow, well, crater; gulf etc. 198; deep, abyss, bowels of the earth, bottomless pit, hell.
  soundings, depth of water, water, draft *or* draught, submersion; plummet, sound, probe; sounding-rod, –line; lead; bathometer, bathymeter, bathymetry; benthos; submarine, sub [*colloq.*], U-boat; depth bomb.
- v. **be deep** etc. *adj.;* render deep etc. *adj.;* deepen.
  sound, heave the lead, take soundings; dig etc. (*excavate*) 252; plunge etc. 310.
- adj. **deep**, deep-seated, deep-bosomed; profound, sunk, buried; submerged etc. 310; subaqueous, submarine, subterranean, subterrene [*obs.*], subterraneous; underground.
  knee-deep, ankle-deep.
  bottomless, soundless, fathomless; unfathomed, unfathomable; abysmal; deep as a well; bathycolpian *or* bathukolpic *or* bathukolpian; deep-sea, benthal, benthopelagic; bathymetric, bathymetrical; bathypelagic, bathysmal; down-reaching, yawning.
- adv. **out of one's depth**; beyond one's depth; over head and ears.

209. Shallowness

- n. **shallowness** etc. *adj.;* shoals; mere scratch.
- adj. **shallow**, slight, superficial; skin–, ankle–, knee-deep; depthless, just enough to wet one's feet; shoal, shoaly.

210. Summit

- n. **summit**, top, vertex, apex, summit [*obs.*], zenith, pinnacle, acme, culmination, meridian, utmost height, *ne plus ultra* [*L.*], height, pitch, maximum, climax; culminating–, crowning–, turning- point; turn of the tide, fountainhead; watershed, water parting; sky, pole.

tip, tiptoe; crest, crow's nest, cap, truck, peak, nib; end etc. 67; crown, brow; head, nob [*slang*], noddle [*colloq.*], pate [*humorous*]; capsheaf.
high places, heights.
topgallant mast, skyscraper; quarter deck, hurricane deck.
architrave, frieze, cornice, corona, coping, coping stone, zoöphorus, capital, headpiece, capstone, fastigium, larmier, epistyle, sconce, pediment, entablature; tympanum; ceiling etc. (*covering*) 223.
attic, loft, garret, housetop, upper story, roof.
- v. **crown**, top, cap, crest, surmount; overtop etc. (*be superior to*) 33; culminate.
- adj. **highest** etc. (high etc. 206); top; topmost, overmost, uppermost; tiptop; culminating etc. *v.;* meridian, meridional; capital, head, polar, supreme, supernal, apical, culminate [*rare*], culminal [*rare*], topgallant, skyward.
- adv. **atop**, at the top of the tree; *en flûte* [*F.*]; *à fleur d'eau* [*F.*].

211. Base

- n. **base**, basement; plinth, dado, wainscot; baseboard, mopboard; bedrock, hardpan; foundation etc. (*support*) 215; substructure, substratum, ground, earth, pavement, floor, paving, flag, carpet, ground floor, deck; footing, ground work, basis; hold, bilge, sump; cullet.
  bed, basin, channel, coulee [*Western N. Amer.*], cañon etc. (*interval*) 198.
  bottom, nadir, foot, sole, toe, hoof, keel, root; centerboard.
- adj. **bottom**, undermost, nethermost; fundamental; founded on, based on, grounded on, built on.

212. Verticality

- n. **verticality**; erectness etc. *adj.;* perpendicularity, aplomb; right angle, normal; azimuth circle.
  cliff, steep, crag, bluff, palisades; wall, precipice.
  elevation, erection; square, plumb line, plummet.
- v. **be vertical** etc. *adj.;* stand -up, –on end, –erect, –upright; stick up, cock up.
  render vertical etc. *adj.;* set up, stick up, raise up, cock up; erect, rear, raise, pitch, raise on its legs.
- adj. **vertical**, upright, erect, perpendicular, unrecumbent [*rare*], plumb, normal, straight, bolt upright; rampant; straight up; standing up etc. *v.;* rectangular orthogonal.
- adv. **vertically** etc. *adj.;* up, on end; up–, right- on end; *à plomb* [*F.*], endwise; on one's legs; at right angles.

213. Horizontality

n. **horizontality**; flatness; level, plane; stratum etc. 204; dead level, dead flat; level plane.
recumbency; lying down etc. *v.;* reclination, decumbence *or* decumbency, discumbency [*obs.*]; proneness etc. *adj.;* accubation, supination, resupination, prostration; azimuth.
[level surfaces] plain, floor, platform, bowling green; cricket ground; croquet -ground, -lawn; billiard table, pool table; terrace, estrade [*rare*], esplanade, parterre, table-land, plateau, ledge.

v. **be horizontal** etc. *adj.;* lie, recline, couch; lie -down, -flat, -prostrate; sprawl, loll; sit down.
render horizontal etc. *adj.;* lay, lay down, lay out; level, flatten, even, raze, equalize, smooth, align.
prostrate, knock down, floor, fell, ground, drop, grass [*slang*]; cut-, hew-, mow- down.

adj. **horizontal**, level, even, plane, flush; flat etc. 251; flat as a -billiard table, -bowling green, -pool table, -pancake; alluvial; calm, -as a mill pond; smooth, -as glass.
recumbent, procumbent, accumbent, decumbent [*bot.*]; lying etc. *v.;* prone, supine, couchant, jacent [*rare*], prostrate, recubant [*rare*], resupinate.

adv. **horizontally** etc. *adj.;* on one's back, on all fours, on its beam ends.

214. Pendency

n. **pendency**, dependency; suspension, hanging etc. *v.*
pendant, drop, eardrop, tassel, tippet, lobe, tail, train, flap, skirt, queue, pigtail, pendulum; hangnail.
peg, knob, button, hook, nail, stud, ring, staple, tenterhook; fastening etc. 45; spar, horse.
chandelier, gaselier, electrolier.

v. **be pendent** etc. *adj.;* hang, depend, swing, dangle, lower, droop: swag [*dial.*]; daggle, flap, trail, flow; beetle, jut, overhang.
suspend, hang, sling, hook up, hitch, fasten to, append.

adj. **pendent**, pendulous, pendulant [*rare*], decumbent, penduline [*rare*], pensile; hanging etc. *v.;* beetle; beetling, jutting over, overhanging, projecting; dependent; lowering; suspended etc. *v.;* loose, flowing.
having a pendant etc. *n.;* tailed, caudate.

215. Support

n. **support**, ground, foundation, base, basis; *terra firma* [*L.*], bearing, fulcrum, bait, caudex, crib; *point d'appui* [*F.*], *pou sto* [*Gr.*], purchase, footing, hold, *locus standi* [*L.*]; landing, -stage, -place; stage, platform; block; rest, resting place; groundwork, substratum, riprap, sustentation [*now rare*], sustention [*rare*], subvention; floor etc. (*basement*) 211.
supporter; aid etc. 707; prop, stand, anvil, fulciment [*obs.*]; cue rest, jigger [*slang*], monkey [*builders' slang*], hod; stay, shore, skid, rib, truss, bandage; sleeper; stirrup, stilts, shoe, sole, heel, splint, lap; bar, rod, boom, spirit, outrigger; ratline *or* ratlin *or* ratling.
pedicle, pedicel *or* pedicellus *or* pediculus, peduncle [*all bot.*], stalk.
board, ledge, shelf, hob, bracket, trivet, arbor, rack; mantel, mantelpiece, mantelshelf; slab, console; counter, dresser; flange, corbel; table, trestle; shoulder; perch; horse; easel, desk; clotheshorse, hatrack; retable, predella, teapoy.
staff, stick, crutch, alpenstock, baton, crosier, cross, crook, lituus [*Rom. antiq.*], caduceus, thyrsus, staddle; bourdon, cowlstaff [*archaic*], *lathi* [*Hind.*], maulstick *or* mahlstick.
post, pillar, shaft, thill, column, pilaster; pediment, pedestal; plinth, shank, leg, socle *or* zocle; buttress, jamb, mullion, stile, abutment; baluster, banister, stanchion; balustrade; headstone.
frame, framework; scaffold, skeleton, beam, rafter, girder, lintel, joist, travis *or* traviss [*dial. Eng.*], trave, corner stone, summer, breastsummer *or* bressomer, summertree, transom; rung, round, step, sill; angle-rafter, hip-rafter; cantilever, modillion; crown-post, king-post; vertebra, modiolus.
columella, backbone; keystone; axle, axletree; axis; arch, mainstay.
trunnion, pivot, rowlock; peg etc. (*pendency*) 214; tiebeam etc. (*fastening*) 45; thole pin.
seat, throne, dais; divan, musnud *or* masnad [*Ar.*], guddee *or* gaddi [*Hind.*]; chair, bench, form, sofa, davenport, couch, day-bed, settee, stall; wingchair, armchair, easychair, elbow-chair, rocking-chair; *fauteuil* [*F.*], woolsack, ottoman, settle, squab, bench; long chair, long-sleeve chair [*Anglo-Ind.*], *chaise longue* [*F.*], morris chair; *lamba chauki* or *lamba kursi* [*Hind.*]; saddle, aparejo, panel *or* pannel, pillion; sidesaddle, packsaddle; pommel, horn.
stool, foldstool, *prie-dieu* [*F.*], hassock, footstool; tabouret; tripod.
bed, berth, pallet, tester-bed, crib, cot, hammock, shakedown, truckle-bed, trundle-bed, cradle, litter, stretcher, bedstead; four-poster, French

bed; bunk, kip [*dial.*], *palang* [*Hind.*]; roost [*slang*]; bedding, *bichhana* [*Hind.*], mattress, paillasse; pillow, bolster; mat, rug, cushion.

Atlas, Herakles *or* Hercules; tortoise that supports the earth.

[in architecture] atlas (*pl.* atlantes), telamon (*pl.* telamones), caryatid (*pl.* caryatids *or* caryatides).

v. **be supported** etc.; lie–, sit–, recline–, lean–, loll–, rest–, stand–, step–, repose–, abut–, bear–, be based etc.-on; have at one's back; bestride, bestraddle.

support, bear, carry, hold, sustain, shoulder; hold up, back up, bolster up, shore up; uphold, upbear; brace, truss, cradle, pillow, prop; underprop, underpin, underset; riprap; bandage etc. 43.

give–, furnish–, afford–, supply–, lend- -support, -foundations; bottom, found, base, ground, embed, imbed.

maintain, keep on foot; aid etc. 707.

adj. **supporting**, supported, etc. *v.;* Atlantean, columellar, columelliform; sustentative, sustentational; fundamental; dorsigerous.

having a pedicle etc. *n.;* pedunculate, pedicellate.

adv. **straddle**, astride on.

216. Parallelism

n. **parallelism**, coextension, equidistance, concentricity; collimation.

v. **be parallel** etc. *adj.;* parallel, equal; collimate.

adj. **parallel**, coextensive, equidistant, collateral, concentric, concurrent; abreast, aligned, equal, even, alongside.

adv. **alongside** etc. (*laterally*) 236.

217. Obliquity

n. **obliquity**, inclination, incline, slope, slant, skew, thrawnness [*Scott. & dial. Eng.*]; crookedness etc. *adj.;* slopeness; leaning etc. *v.;* bevel, ramp, pitch, bezel, tilt; bias, list, twist, swag [*prov. Eng.*], sag, cant, lurch; distortion etc. 243; bend etc. (*curve*) 245; tower of Pisa.

acclivity, rise, ascent, gradient [*chiefly Brit.*], grade [*U. S.*], *khudd* [*Hind.*], glacis, rising ground, hill, bank, declivity, downhill, dip, fall, devexity [*obs.*]; gentle–, rapid- slope; easy -ascent, –descent; shelving beach; talus; *montagne Russe* [*F.*]; *facilis descensus Averni* [*L.*].

steepness etc. *adj.;* cliff, precipice etc. (*vertical*) 212; escarpment, scarp; chevron.

[measure of inclination] clinometer; sine, cosine, cotangent, angle, hypothenuse.

diagonal; zigzag.

v. **be oblique** etc. *adj.;* slope, slant, skew, lean, incline, shelve, stoop, decline, descend, bend, keel, careen, sag, swag [*dial.*], seel [*obs.*], slouch, cant, sidle.

render oblique etc. *adj.;* sway, bias; slope, slant; incline, bend, crook; cant, tilt; distort etc. 243.

adj. **oblique**, inclined; sloping etc. *v.;* tilted etc. *v.;* recubant [*rare*], recumbent, clinical, skew, askew, slant, bias, aslant, plagihedral, indirect, wry, awry; agee *or* ajee, thrawn [*both Scot. & dial. Eng.*], crooked; sinuous, zigzag, zigzaggy, chevrony; knock-kneed etc. (*distorted*) 243; bevel, out of the perpendicular; aslope; asquint, backhand *or* backhanded.

uphill, rising, ascending, acclivous.

downhill, falling, descending; hanging (as, *hanging* gardens), declining, declivitous, proclivous [*rare*], declivous, devex [*obs.*], synclinal, anticlinal.

steep, abrupt, precipitous, breakneck.

diagonal; transverse, transversal; athwart, antiparallel; curved etc. 245; loxic, loxotic, loxodromic.

adv. **obliquely** etc. *adj.;* on one side, all on one side; askew, askance *or* askant, awry, skew, skewed, edgewise, at an angle; sidelong, sideways; slopewise, slantwise; by a side wind.

218. Inversion

n. **inversion**, eversion, subversion, reversion, retroversion, introversion; retroflexion; contraposition etc. 237; contrariety etc. 14; reversal; turn of the tide etc. (*reversion*) 145.

overturn; somersault *or* summersault, somerset *or* summerset; *culbute* [*F.*] eversion [*archaic*]; revulsion; pirouette.

transposition, transposal, anastrophy, metastasis, hyperbaton, anastrophe; hysterology, hysteron proteron; hypallage, synchysis, tmesis, parenthesis; metathesis; palindrome; ectropion [*path.*]; invagination, intussusception.

pronation and supination.

v. **be inverted** etc.; turn–, go–, wheel- -round, –about, –to the right-about [*colloq.*]; turn–, go–, tilt–, topple- over; capsize, turn turtle.

invert, subvert, retrovert, introvert; reverse; turn the cat in the pan [*obs*]; upturn, overturn, upset, overset, *bouleverser* [*F.*], evert [*archaic*]; turn topsy-turvy etc. *adj.; culbuter* [*F.*]; transpose, put the cart before the horse, turn the tables; invaginate, intussuscept.

219. Crossing

adj. **inverted** etc. *v.;* wrong side -out, –up; inside out, upside down; bottom–, keel- upwards; supine, on one's head, topsy-turvy, *sens dessus dessous* [*F.*]; ectropic.
inverse; reverse etc. (*contrary*) 14; opposite etc. 237; palindromic *or* palindromical.
topheavy, unstable.
adv. **inversely** etc. *adj.;* heels over head, head over heels.

219. Crossing

n. **crossing** etc. *v.;* intersection, interdigitation; decussation, transversion; chiasm *or* chiasma; convolution etc. 248; level crossing [*Eng.*], grade crossing.
network, reticulation, cancellation; inosculation, anastomosis, intertexture, mortise.
net, plexus, plexure, web, mesh, twill, skein, Hippocrates' sleeve, sleave [*archaic*]; sieve, sifter, riddle rocker, screen, cradle; felt, lace; wicker; mat, matting; plait, trellis, wattle, lattice, grating, grille, gridiron, tracery, fretwork, filigree, reticle [*obs.*]; tissue, netting, moke [*dial. Eng.*]; rivulation.
cross, chain, wreath, braid, cat's cradle, knot; entanglement etc. (*disorder*) 59.
crucifix, cross, rood, crisscross, christcross, tau; crux.
[woven fabrics] cloth, linen, muslin, cambric, *toile* [*F.*], drill, homespun, silk, satin, broadcloth, tweed etc.
v. **cross**, decussate; intersect, interlace, intertwine, intertwist, interweave, interdigitate, interlink, intercross [*rare*], crisscross, crossbar.
twine, entwine, weave, inweave, twist, wreathe; anastomose, inosculate, dovetail, splice, link.
mat, plait, pleat, plat, braid, felt, twill; tangle, entangle, ravel; net, knot; dishevel, raddle.
adj. **crossing** etc. *v.;* crossed, matted etc. *v.;* transverse; intersected, decussate *or* decussated; chiasmal.
cross, cross-shaped cruciform, crucial; netlike, retiform, reticular, reticulate, areolar, cancellate *or* cancellated, cancellous, latticed, grated, barred, streaked; textile; crossbarred, cruciate, secant; cruciferous; plexal, plexiform; anastomotic; web-footed, palmiped.
adv. **cross**, thwart, athwart, transversely; at grade; crosswise, thwartwise [*rare*].

220. Exteriority

n. **exteriority**; outside, exterior; surface, superficies; skin etc. (*covering*) 223; superstratum; disk *or* disc; face, facet; extrados.
eccentricity; circumjacence etc. 227.
v. **be exterior** etc. *adj.;* lie around etc. 227.
place exteriorly, place outwardly, place outside; put out, turn out.
externalize, objectize [*rare*], objectify, visualize, envisage, actualize.
adj. **exterior**, external, extraneous; outer, outermost; outward, outlying, outside, outdoor, *alfresco* [*It.*]; round about etc. 227; extramural; extralimitary, extramundane, extraterrene, extraterrestrial, extraterritorial, exterritorial; extern [*rare*].
extraregarding; eccentric *or* eccentrical; outstanding; extrinsic etc. 6; ecdemic, exomorphic.
superficial, skin-deep; frontal, discoid.
adv. **externally** etc. *adj.;* out, without, over, outwards, *ab extra* [*L.*], out of doors; *extra muros* [*L.*].
in the open air; *sub Jove* [*L.*], *sub dio* [*L.*]; *à la belle étoile* [*F.*], *alfresco* [*It.*].

221. Interiority

n. **interiority**; inside, interior; interspace, subsoil, substratum; intrados.
contents etc. 190; substance, pith, marrow; backbone etc. (*center*) 222; heart, bosom, breast; abdomen.
vitals, viscera, entrails, bowels, belly, intestines, guts [*vulgar or tech.*], chitterlings, chitlings *or* chitlins, womb, lap [*obs.*], rectum, cecum *or* caecum, ileum, duodenum, jejunum.
gland, glandule [*rare*], gland cell; thyroid, parotid, prostate; liver, kidney.
penetralia, recesses, innermost recesses; cave etc. (*concavity*) 252.
enterology, enterotomy, enteropathy, enteritis, splanchnology; peristalsis, vermiculation.
inmate, intern, inhabitant etc. 188.
v. **be inside** etc. *adj.;* be within etc. *adv.*
inclose etc. (*circumscribe*) 229; intern embed *or* imbed etc. (*insert*) 300; place within, keep within.
adj. **interior**, internal; inner, intern [*archaic*], intraneous [*rare*], intimate, inside, inward, intraregarding; inmost, innermost; deep-seated; intestine, intestinal, visceral, rectal, duodenal, splanchnic; subcutaneous; abdominal, celiac *or* coeliac, endomorphic.
intracanal, intracellular, intralobular, intramarginal, intramolecular, intramundane, intraocular, intraseptal, intratelluric, intrauterine, intravascular, intravenous, intraventricular.
interstitial etc. (*interjacent*) 228; inwrought etc. (*intrinsic*) 5; inclosed etc. *v.*

    home, inland, domestic, family, indoor, intramural, vernacular; endemic.
adv. **internally** etc. *adj.;* inwards, within, in, inly; herein, therein, wherein, *ab intra* [*L.*]; indoors, within doors; at home, in the bosom of one's family.

222. Centrality

n. **centrality**, centricalness, centricality, center *or* centre; middle etc. 68; focus etc. 74.
    center of -gravity, –pressure, –percussion, –oscillation, –buoyancy etc.; metacenter.
    core, kernel; nucleus, nucleolus; heart, pole, axis, bull's-eye, nave, hub, navel, umbilicus; marrow, pith; backbone; vertebra, vertebral column; hotbed.
    concentration etc. (*convergence*) 290; centralization; symmetry; metropolis.
v. **be central** etc. *adj.;* converge etc. 290.
    render central, centralize, concentrate; bring to a focus.
adj. **central**, centrical; middle etc. 68; axial, pivotal, nuclear, nucleate, centric, focal, umbilical, concentric; middlemost; rachial, rachidial *or* rachidian; spinal, vertebral; metropolitan.
adv. **middle**; midst; centrally etc. *adj.*

223. Covering

n. **covering**, cover, baldachin *or* baldaquin; canopy, *shamianah* [*Hind.*], tilt, awning, tent, marquee, marquise, wigwam, tepee, *tente d'abri* [*F.*], umbrella, parasol, sunshade; veil (*shade*) 424; shield etc. (*defense*) 717.
    roof, ceiling, thatch, tile, pantile, tiling, slates, slating, leads, shingles; dome, cupola, mansard, hip roof; barrack, *plafond* [*F.*], planchment, tiling, shed etc. (*abode*) 189.
    top, lid, covercle [*obs.*], door, operculum; bulkhead.
    wrapping, bandage, dressing, plaster, lint, dossil, pledget, finger stall.
    coverlet, counterpane, sheet, quilt, blanket, rug, drugget; housing; tidy, antimacassar, eiderdown quilt *or* eiderdown; comforter *or* comfortable *or* comfort, numdah [*Hind.*], pillowcase, pillowslip, linoleum, oilcloth; tarpaulin; saddle blanket, saddlecloth; tilpah, apishamore, poncho.
    tegmen (*pl.* tegmina), integument, tegument; skin, pellicle, fleece, fell, fur, leather, lambskin, sable, miniver, beaver, ermine, shagreen, hide, coat, buff, pelt, peltry [*collective noun*]; cordwain [*archaic*]; robe, buffalo robe.

    cuticle, cutis, dermis, corium, scarfskin, epidermis, derm [*rare*], derma; ectoderm, epithelium, ecderon, ecteron, enderon.
    exuviae, desquamation, slough, cast, cast-off skin.
    clothing etc. 225; mask etc. (*concealment*) 530.
    peel, crust, bark, rind. cortex, husk, shell, epicarp, testa; eggshell, glume.
    capsule; sheath, sheathing; pod, cod [*dial.*], casing, case, theca; elytron, elytrum; involucrum; wrapping, wrapper; envelope, vesicle; cornhusk, cornshuck.
    dermatography, dermatology, dermatogen, dermoplasty, dermatopathy, dermatophyte; conchology; testaceology.
    veneer, facing; pavement; imbrication, scale etc. (*layer*) 204; anointing etc. *v.;* ointment etc. (*grease*) 356; inunction; incrustation, superposition, obduction [*obs.*]; coating, paint, stain, engobe; varnish etc. (*resin*) 356a; ground, enamel, whitewash, plaster, stucco, roughcast, plasterwork, scagliola, compo; cerement; cerecloth, shroud.
v. **cover**; superpose, superimpose; overlay, overspread; wrap etc. 225; incase, encase, enchase; face, case, veneer, pave, paper; tip, cap, bind; bulkhead, bulkhead in; clapboard, shingle; imbricate.
    overlie, overarch; endome [*rare*]; conceal etc. 528.
    coat, paint, stain, varnish, flat, incrust, encrust, crust, cement, roughcast, stucco, dab, plaster, tar; wash; besmear; bedaub; anoint, do over; gild, plate, japan, lacquer, lacker, enamel, whitewash; parget; lay it on thick.
adj. **covering** etc. *v.;* cutaneous, dermal, cortical, cuticular, tegumentary, tegumental, tegmental, integumentary, integumental, epidermal *or* epidermic, endermic, epicarpal, testaceous, dermatopathic, dermatological, dermoplastic, dermatophytic, subcutaneous, hypodermic.
    scaly, squamate, squamiferous, squamous; covered etc. *v.;* imbricate, imbricated, loricate, loricated, armored, encuirassed, armor-plated, ironclad, under cover.
    hooded, cowled, cucullate *or* cucullated, tectiform, rooflike; vaginate.
    skinlike, dermic, dermoid, dermatoid, epidermoid, skinny.

224. Lining

n. **lining**, inner coating; coating etc. (*covering*) 223; stalactite, stalagmite.
    filling, stuffing, wadding, padding, facing; bushing.

225. Investment

wainscot, parietes, wall, brattice, sheathing.
v. line, stuff, incrust, wad, pad, fill, face, ceil, bush, wainscot, sheathe.
adj. lined etc. *v.*

225. Investment

n. investment; covering etc. 223; dress, clothing, raiment, drapery, costume, attire, guise, toilet, toilette, trim; habiliment; vesture, vestment; garment, garb, palliament [*obs.*], apparel, wardrobe, wearing apparel, clothes, things.
array; tailoring, millinery; best bib and tucker [*colloq.*]; finery etc. (*ornament*) 847; full dress etc. (*show*) 882; garniture; theatrical properties.
outfit, equipment, trousseau; uniform, khaki, olive-drab, regimentals; continentals [*Am. hist.*]; canonicals etc. 999; livery, gear, harness, turnout, accouterment, caparison, suit, rigging, trappings, traps [*colloq.*], slops, togs [*colloq.*], toggery [*colloq.*]; masquerade.
dishabille or deshabille, morning dress, tea gown, wrapper, negligee or *négligé* [*F.*], dressing gown, undress; kimono; shooting coat; smoking jacket; mufti [*chiefly Eng.*]; rags, tatters, old clothes; mourning, weeds; duds [*colloq.*]; slippers.
robe, tunic, paletot, habit, gown, coat, frock, blouse, middy blouse or middy, jumper, shirt waist, suit; one-piece -, two-piece- suit; toga, smock, frock; Prince Albert coat [*colloq.*]; frock–, sack–, tail- coat.
dress suit, dress clothes, evening dress, swallow-tailed coat [*colloq.*], claw-hammer coat [*colloq.*]; dinner -coat, -jacket; tuxedo, soup-and-fish [*colloq.*]; glad rags [*slang*].
cloak, pall [*archaic*], mantle, mantua, mantelet or mantlet, sagum, shawl, pelisse, wrapper; veil; cape, kirtle [*archaic*], plaid [*Scot.*], tippet, muffler, comforter, balaklava helmet, haik, huke [*obs.*], chlamys, mantilla, tabard, housing, horse cloth, burnoose or burnous, roquelaure; houpland [*hist.*]; surcoat, overcoat, greatcoat; surtout, spencer; oilskins, slicker, mackintosh, waterproof, ulster, dreadnaught or dreadnought, wraprascal, poncho; pea-coat, pea-jacket; cardinal, pelerine; chuddar or chadar [*Hind.*], jubbah [*Hind.*], pullover, pyjamas or pajamas, pilot jacket, sweater, blazer, coatee, cardigan or cardigan jacket; Mackinaw coat or Mackinaw; talma.
jacket, vest, jerkin [*hist. or dial.*], chaqueta [*Sp.*], sontag, waistcoat, doublet, gaberdine; stays, corsage, corset, bra, *brassière* [*F.*], camisole, corselet, bodice; stomacher.

skirt, petticoat, farthingale, kilt, filibeg or philibeg, jupe, crinoline, bustle, panier, apron, pinafore; bloomer, bloomers; *tablier* [*F.*].
loin cloth, dhoti [*Hindu*], lungi [*Burmese*]; G string.
trousers, breeches, pantaloons, inexpressibles [*humorous*], trews [*Scot.*], innominables [*humorous*], unmentionables [*humorous*], continuations [*slang*], kicks [*slang*]; overalls, smalls [*colloq. or archaic*], smallclothes [*archaic*]; pants [*colloq.*]; shintiyan; shorts; tights, drawers; knickerbockers, knickers [*Engl. colloq.*].
headdress, headgear, coiffure [*F.*], head, headcloths, chignon [*F.*]; chapeau [*F.*], crush hat, opera hat; kaffiyeh [*Ar.*]; taj, tam-o'-shanter, topee or topi [*India*], sola topi [*India*], puggree or pagri [*Hind.*]; sombrero, sundown, cap, hat, beaver, castor, bonnet, tile [*slang*], wide-awake, panama, leghorn; derby, bowler [*Eng.*], billycock [*Eng.*]; wimple; nightcap, skullcap; mobcap, boudoir cap, Dutch cap; Salvation-Army bonnet; hood, coif, capote, calash, kerchief, snood; crown etc. (*circle*) 247; pelt, wig, front, peruke, periwig, caftan, turban, fez, tarboosh, shako, busby; kepi, forage cap, campaign hat, overseas cap, bearskin; helmet etc. 717; mask, domino.
body clothes; linen; hickory shirt [*U. S.*]; shirt, O.-D. (olive-drab) shirt; sark [*archaic or dial.*], smock, shift, chemise; nightgown, nightshirt; bed-gown, *sac de nuit* [*F.*]; jersey; underclothing, underwaistcoat, undershirt, undervest, chemisette, guimpe.
tie, neckerchief, neckcloth; ruff, collar, cravat, stock, handkerchief, scarf; bib, tucker; boa; girdle etc. (*circle*) 247; cummerbund [*India*], rumal [*Hind.*], rabat [*F.*], rabato.
shoe, pump, sneakers, boot, slipper, sandal, galosh or galoshe, patten, clog; high-low; Blucher–, Wellington–, Hessian–, jack–, top- boot; Oxford -shoe, -tie; Balmoral; arctics, bootee, bootikin, brogan, brogue, *chaparajos* [*Mex. Sp.*], chaps [*colloq.*], *chivarras or chivarros* [*Sp. Amer.*]; gums [*U. S.*], larrigan [*N. Amer.*], rubbers; snowshoe, ski; stogy, veldtschoen [*Dutch*], legging, puttee or putty, buskin, greave, galligaskin [*dial.*], moccasin, gambado, gaiter, spatterdashes, spats, gamashes [*archaic or dial. Eng.*], *gamache* [*F.*]; antigropelos.
stocking, hose, gaskins [*obs.*], trunk hose, sock; hosiery.
glove, gauntlet, mitten, mitt.
cuff, wristband; sleeve.
baby linen, swaddling clothes, diaper, layette.

[suppliers] clothier, tailor, snip [*slang*], tailoress, milliner, costumer, costumier, seamstress *or* sempstress, dressmaker, *modiste* [*F.*], habit-maker; breeches-maker; shoemaker, Crispin cordwainer, cobbler; hosier, hatter, glover, draper, linen draper, haberdasher, mercer; hairdresser, *friseur* [*F.*].

v. **invest**; cover etc. 223; envelop, lap, involve; inwrap *or* enwrap; wrap; fold up, wrap up, lap up, muffle up; overlap; sheathe, swathe, swaddle, roll up in, shroud, circumvest [*obs.*].

clothe, vest [*rare*], array, dress, dight [*archaic*], bedight [*archaic*], drape, robe, enrobe, attire, apparel, tire [*archaic*], habilitate [*rare*], garb, enclothe, breech, coat, jacket, gown, accouter, rig, fit out; dizen, bedizen, deck etc. (*ornament*) 847; perk, equip, harness, caparison.

wear; don; put on, huddle on, slip on; mantle.

adj. **invested** etc. *v.;* habited; dight, dighted; barbed, barded; clad, *costumé* [*F.*], shod, *chaussé* [*F.*]; *en grande tenue* [*F.*] etc. (*show*) 882; *décolletée* [*F.*].

sartorial, sartorian [*rare*].

226. Divestment

n. **divestment**; taking off etc. *v.*

nudity; bareness etc. *adj.;* undress; dishabille etc. 225; altogether; *tout ensemble* [*F.*]; nudation [*rare*], denudation; decortication, depilation, excoriation, desquamation, slough etc. 223; molting *or* moulting, exuviation; exfoliation; trichosis.

baldness, hairlessness, alopecia.

v. **divest**; uncover etc. (cover etc. 223); denude, bare, strip; disfurnish; undress, disrobe etc. (dress, enrobe etc. 225); uncoif; dismantle; put off, take off, cast off; doff.

peel, pare, decorticate, desquamate, slough, excoriate, skin, scalp, flay, bark, husk, rind; expose, lay open; exfoliate, molt *or* moult, exuviate, mew [*archaic*]; cast the skin.

adj. **divested** etc. *v.;* bare, naked, nude; undressed, undraped, unclad, ungarmented, unclothed, unappareled, unarrayed; exposed; in dishabille.

in a state of nature, in nature's garb, in the buff, in native buff, in birthday suit; *in puris naturalibus* [*L.*]; with nothing on, stark-naked; bare as the back of one's hand.

out at elbows; threadbare, ragged, callow, roofless; barefoot; bareback, barebacked; leafless, napless, hairless.

bald, hairless, depilous [*rare*], glabrous, glabrate, tonsured, beardless, bald as a coot.

exuvial, sloughy, desquamative, desquamatory.

227. Circumjacence

n. **circumjacence** *or* circumjacency, circumfluence [*rare*], circumambience environment, encompassment; atmosphere, medium; surroundings, *entourage* [*F.*].

outpost; border etc. (*edge*) 231; girdle etc. (*circumference*) 230; outskirts, boulevards, suburbs, purlieus, precincts, *faubourgs* [*F.*], environs, environment, entourage, *banlieue* [*F.*], neighborhood, vicinage, vicinity.

v. **lie around** etc. *adv.;* surround, beset, compass, encompass, environ, inclose *or* enclose, encircle, encincture [*rare*], circle, girdle, ensphere, hedge, embrace, circumvent, lap, gird, belt; begird, engird; skirt, twine round; hem in etc. (*circumscribe*) 229; beleaguer, invest, besiege, beset, blockade.

adj. **circumjacent**, circumambient, circumfluent; ambient; surrounding etc. *v.;* circumferential, suburban.

adv. **around**, about; without; on every side, on all sides; right and left, all round, roundabout.

228. Interjacence

n. **interjacence** *or* interjacency, intercurrence, intervenience *or* interveniency [*rare*], interlocation, interdigitation, interpenetration; permeation.

interjection, interpolation, interlineation, interspersion, intercalation; embolism.

intervention, interference, interposition, intromission, intrusion, obtrusion; insinuation; insertion etc. 300; dovetailing; infiltration.

intermedium, intermediary; go-between, interagent, middleman, intervener, mean, medium, bodkin [*colloq.*], intruder, interloper; parenthesis, episode, flyleaf.

partition, septum, interseptum, phragma, septulum, mediastinum, diaphragm, midriff; dissepiment; party wall, panel, bulkhead, brattice, *cloison* [*F.*], perpend, halfway house.

v. **lie between**, come between, get between; intervene, slide in, interpenetrate, permeate.

put between, introduce, import; throw in, wedge in, edge in, jam in, worm in, foist in, run in, plow in, work in; interpose, interject, intercalate, interpolate, interline, interleave, intersperse, interweave, interlard, interdigitate; let in, dovetail, splice, mortise; insinuate, smuggle; infiltrate, ingrain.

interfere, put in an oar, stick one's nose in; intrude, obtrude; have a finger in the pie; introduce the thin end of the wedge; thrust in etc. (*insert*) 300.

229. Circumscription

adj. **interjacent**, intervenient [*rare*], intervening etc. *v.;* intercalary, intercolumnar, intercostal, intercurrent, interfacial, intergrowth, interlineal, interlobular, interlocular, intermedial, intermediary, intermediate, intermaxillary, intermolecular, intermundane, internasal, interneural, internodal, interoceanic, interosseal, interosseous, interplanetary, interpolar, interradial, interrenal, interscapular, interseptal, interstellar, interstitial, intervalvular, intervascular, interventricular, intervertebral; septal, embolismal.

parenthetical, episodic; mediterranean; intrusive; embosomed; merged.

mean, medium, mesne, middle, median.

adv. **between**, betwist; 'twixt; among *or* amongst; amid, amidst; 'mid, 'midst; in the thick of; betwixt and between [*colloq.*]; sandwich-wise; parenthetically, *obiter dictum* [*L.*].

229. Circumscription

n. **circumscription**, limitation, inclosure; confinement etc. (*restraint*) 751; circumvallation; encincture; envelope etc. 232.

v. **circumscribe**, limit, bound, confine, inclose *or* enclose; surround etc. 227; compass about; imprison etc. (*restrain*) 751; hedge in, wall in, rail in; fence round, hedge round; picket; corral.

enfold, bury, incase, pack up, enshrine, inclasp *or* enclasp; wrap up etc. (*invest*) 225; embay, embosom.

adj. **circumscribed** etc. *v.;* begirt, circumambient, girt, cinct [*rare*], circumcinct [*rare*], lapt; buried in, immersed in; embosomed, in the bosom of, imbedded, encysted, mewed up; imprisoned etc. 751; landlocked, in a ring fence.

230. Outline

n. **outline**, circumference; perimeter, periphery; ambit, circuit, lines, *tournure* [*F.*], contour, profile, silhouette, relief, lineaments; bounds; coast line.

zone, belt, girth, band, baldric, zodiac, girdle, tire, cingle [*rare*], clasp, girt, girth; cordon etc. (*inclosure*) 232; circlet etc. 247.

v. **outline**, contour, delineate, silhouette, block, sketch, profile; circumscribe etc. 229.

adj. **outlined** etc. *v.;* circumferential, perimetric, perimetrical, peripheral.

231. Edge

n. **edge**, verge, brink, brow, brim, margin, border, confine, skirt, rim, flange, side, mouth; jaws, chops, chaps, fauces; lip, muzzle.

shore, coast, strand, bank; bunder, bund [*both Oriental*], quay, wharf, dock, mole, landing.

fringe, flounce, frill, list, trimming, edging, skirting, hem, selvage *or* selvedge, welt; furbelow, valance; frame; exergue.

threshold, door, porch; portal etc. (*opening*) 260.

v. **edge**, border, skirt, fringe, marginate.

adj. **border**, marginal, skirting; labial, labiated, marginated.

232. Inclosure

n. **inclosure** *or* enclosure, envelope; case etc. (*receptacle*) 191; wrapper; girdle etc. 230.

pen, fold; sty, penfold, sheepfold; paddock, croft, pasture, wood lot; pound; corral; yard, compound; net, seine net.

fence etc. (*defense*) 717; pale, paling, balustrade, rail, railing, quickset hedge, park paling, circumvallation, *enceinte* [*F.*]; ring fence; wall; hedge, hedgerow; espalier.

barrier, barricade; gate, gateway; weir; bent, dingle; door, hatch, cordon; prison etc. 752.

dike, ditch, fosse, trench, drain, dugout, *tranchée* [*F.*], *coupure* [*F.*], moat.

v. **inclose** *or* enclose; circumscribe etc. 229.

233. Limit

n. **limit**, boundary, bounds, confine, enclave, term, bourn *or* bourne, verge, curbstone, but [*Scot.*], pale; termination, terminus, terminal; stint, stent; frontier, precinct, marches; backwoods.

boundary line, landmark; line of -demarcation, –circumvallation; pillars of Hercules; Rubicon, turning point; *ne plus ultra* [*L.*]; sluice, floodgate.

v. **limit**, bound, compass, confine, define, circumscribe, demarcate, delimit.

adj. **definite**; conterminate [*obs.*], conterminable; terminable, limitable; terminal, frontier, bordering, border, limitary, boundary, limital [*rare*].

adv. **thus far**, –and no further.

234. Front

n. **front**; fore, fore part *or* forepart; foreground, forefront; face, disk *or* disc, frontage, façade, proscenium, facia, frontispiece; priority, anteriority; obverse (*of a medal*).

van, vanguard; advanced guard; forerank, front rank; outpost; first line; scout.

brow, forehead, visage, physiognomy, phiz [*colloq.*], features, countenance, mug [*slang*]; metoposcopy; chin, mentum; rostrum, beak, bow, stem, prow, prore, jib, bowsprit.

pioneer etc. (*precursor*) 64; metoposcopist, physiognomist
- *v.* **front**, face, confront, breast, buck [*slang*], brave, dare, defy oppose, outbrazen; bend forwards; come to the front, come to the fore; be *or* stand in front etc. *adj.*
- *adj.* **fore**, forward, anterior, front, frontal; metopic
- *adv.* **before** in front, in the van, in advance; ahead right ahead; foremost, headmost in the foreground, in the lee of; before one's -face, −eyes: face to face, *vis-à-vis* [*F.*]; *front à front* [*F.*].

235. Rear

- *n.* **rear**, back, posteriority; rear rank, rear guard, rearward [*archaic*]; background, hinterland. occiput, nape; heels.
  spine, backbone, rachis, spinal column, chine.
  tail, scut, brush, appendage [*humorous*].
  rump, croup, buttock, posteriors, fundament, bottom [*colloq.*], stern [*colloq.*], seat, backside [*vulgar*], breech, dorsum, tergum, loin; dorsal–, lumbar-region; hind quarters; aitchbone.
  stern, poop, counter, mizzenmast, postern door, tailpiece, after-part, heel-piece, crupper.
  wake; train etc. (*sequence*) 281.
  reverse; other side of the shield.
- *v.* **be behind** etc. *adv.;* fall astern; bend backwards; bring up the rear; heel, tag, shadow, follow etc. (*pursue*) 622.
- *adj.* **back**, rear; hind, hinder, hindmost, hindermost; sternmost; postern, posterior, dorsal, after; caudal, tergal, neural, spinal, vertebral, lumbar; mizzen.
- *adv.* **behind**; in the -rear, −background; behind one's back; at the -heels, −tail, −back- of; back to back.
  after, aft, abaft, baft, astern, aback, rearward, hindward, backward.

236. Laterality

- *n.* **laterality** [*rare*]; side, flank, quarter, lee; hand; cheek, jowl *or* jole, wing; profile; temple, paries (*pl.* parietes), loin, haunch, hip; beam.
  gable, gable-end; broadside; lee side.
  points of the compass; East, sunrise, Orient, Levant; West, Occident, sunset; orientation.
- *v.* **flank**, outflank; sidle; skirt, border, wing; orientate; be on one side etc. *adv.*
- *adj.* **lateral**, sidelong; collateral; parietal, flanking, skirting; flanked; sideling.
  many-sided; multilateral, bilateral, trilateral, quadrilateral.
  eastern, eastward, east, orient, oriental, auroral *or* aurorean; Levantine.
  western, west, westerly, westward, occidental, Hesperian.
- *adv.* **sideways** *or* sideway, sidewise, sideling, sidelong; broadside on; on one side, abreast, alongside, beside, aside; by, by the side of; side by side; cheek by jowl etc. (*near*) 197; to windward, to leeward; laterally etc. *adj.;* right and left; on her beam ends.

237. Contraposition

- *n.* **contraposition**, opposition; polarity; inversion etc. 218; opposite side; reverse, inverse; counterpart; antithesis.
  antipodes, opposite poles, North and South.
- *v.* **be opposite** etc. *adj.;* subtend.
- *adj.* **opposite**; reverse, inverse, converse; antipodal, diametrical, antithetic, counter, subcontrary; fronting, facing, diametrically opposite.
  northern, north, northerly, northward, hyperborean, septentrional, boreal, polar, arctic.
  southern, south, southerly, meridional, southward, Austral, antarctic.
- *adv.* **over**, over the way, over against; against; face to face, *vis-à-vis* [*F.*]; as poles asunder.

238. Dextrality

- *n.* **dextrality**; right, right hand; dexter, offside, starboard.
- *adj.* **dextral**, dexterous *or* dextrous, right-handed; dexter, dextrorsal, dextrorse.
  ambidexter, ambidextrous, ambidextral.
- *adv.* **dextrad**, dextrally; ambidextrously.

239. Sinistrality

- *n.* **sinistrality**, sinistration; left, left hand, southpaw; *sinistra* or *sinistra mano* [*music, It.*]; nearside, larboard, port.
- *adj.* **left-handed**, sinister-handed [*obs.*], sinister, sinistral, sinistrorsal, sinistrorse, sinistrous, ambilevous [*rare*]; sinistrogyrate, sinistrogyric.
- *adv.* **sinistrad**, sinistrally, sinistrously.

Section 3. Form

240. Form

- *n.* **form**, figure, shape; conformation, configuration; make, formation, frame, construction, cut, set, build, *tournure* [*F.*], outline, get-up [*colloq.*], trim, cut of one's jib [*colloq.*]; stamp, type, cast, mold *or* mould; fashion; contour etc. (*outline*) 230; structure etc. 329; plasmature [*obs.*].

241. Amorphism

    feature, lineament, turn; phase etc. (*aspect*) 448; posture, attitude, pose.
    [science of form] morphology.
    [similarity of form] isomorphism; isomorph.
    formation, figuration, efformation [*rare*]; forming etc. *v.;* sculpture; plasmation [*rare*].

v. **form**, shape, figure, fashion, efform [*rare*], carve, cut, chisel, hew, cast; roughhew, roughcast; sketch; block out, hammer out; trim; lick–, put- into shape; model, knead, work up into, set, mold, sculpture; cast, stamp; build etc. (*construct*) 161.

adj. **formed** etc. *v.;* structural, morphologic *or* morphological.
    shapely, well-proportioned, symmetrical, well-made, well-formed, comely, trim, neat.
    [receiving form] plastic, fictile; formative, impressible, creative.
    [giving form] plasmatic, plasmic; protoplasmic.
    [similar in form] isomorphic, isomorphous.

241. Amorphism
[absence of form]

n. **amorphism**, misproportion, informity [*rare*]; uncouthness; rough diamond; unlicked cub; *rudis indigestaque moles* [*L.*]; disorder etc. 59; deformity etc. 243.
    disfigurement, defacement; mutilation; deforming.

v. [destroy form] deface, disfigure, deform, mutilate, truncate; derange etc. 61; blemish, mar.

adj. **shapeless**, amorphous, formless; unshapely, misshapen, unsymmetrical, malformed, unformed, unhewn, unfashioned, unshapen; anomalous.
    rough, rude, Gothic, barbarous, rugged, scraggy, vandalic; in the rough.

242. Symmetry
[regularity of form]

n. **symmetry**, shapeliness, finish; beauty etc. 845; proportion, eurythmy *or* eurhythmy, eurythmics *or* eurhythmics, uniformity, parallelism; bilateral–, trilateral–, multilateral-symmetry; centrality etc. 222; radiation, regularity, evenness.
    arborescence, branching, ramification; arbor vitae; peloria.

adj. **symmetrical**, shapely, well set, finished; beautiful etc. 845; classic, chaste, severe.
    regular, uniform, radiate, radiated, balanced; equal etc. 27; parallel, coextensive.

    arborescent, arboriform; dendriform, dendroid *or* dendroidal; branching; ramous, ramose; fern-shaped, filiciform, filicoid; subarborescent; papilionaceous.

243. Distortion
[irregularity of form]

n. **distortion**, detortion [*rare*], contortion, contortuosity, knot, warp, buckle, screw, twist; crookedness etc. (*obliquity*) 217; grimace; deformity; malformation, malconformation; harelip; monstrosity, misproportion, want of symmetry, anamorphosy, anamorphosis; ugliness etc. 846; talipes, club-foot; teratology.

v. **distort**, contort, twist, warp, buckle, screw, wrench, writhe, gnarl, wrest, writhe, make faces, deform, misshape.

adj. **distorted** etc. *v.;* out of shape, irregular, unsymmetric, anamorphous, awry, wry, askew, crooked; not true, not straight; on one side, crump [*obs.*], deformed; harelipped; misshapen, misbegotten; misproportioned, ill-proportioned; ill-made; grotesque, crooked as a ram's horn; camelbacked, humpbacked, hunchbacked, bunchbacked, crook-backed; bandy; bandylegged, bowlegged; bowkneed, knock-kneed; splayfooted, taliped *or* talipedic, club-footed; round-shouldered; snub-nosed; curtailed of one's fair proportions; stumpy etc. (*short*) 201; gaunt (*thin*) etc. 203; bloated etc. 194; scalene; simous.

adv. all manner of ways.

244. Angularity

n. **angularity**, angularness; aduncity; angle, cusp, bend; fold etc. 258; notch etc. 257; fork, furculum, bifurcation.
    elbow, knee, knuckle, ankle, groin, crotch, crutch; crane, fluke, scythe, sickle; zigzag.
    corner, nook, recess, niche, oriel, coign (*as in* "coign of vantage").
    right angle etc. (*perpendicular*) 212; obliquity etc. 217; angle of 45 degrees, miter; acute–, obtuse–, salient–, reëntering -, spherical- angle.
    angular -measurement, –elevation, –distance, –velocity; trigonometry, goniometry; altimeter, pantometer, altimetry; clinometer, graphometer, goniometer; theodolite; transit *or* transit theodolite, sextant, quadrant; dichotomy.
    triangle, trigon, wedge; rectangle, square, lozenge, diamond; rhomb, rhombus, rhomboid, rhom-

bohedron, quadrangle, quadrilateral; parallelogram; quadrature; polygon, pentagon, hexagon, heptagon, octagon, oxygon, decagon.

Platonic bodies; cube, rhomboid; tetrahedron, pentahedron, hexahedron, octahedron, dodecahedron, icosahedron; prism, pyramid; parallelepiped *or* parallelepipedon; curb–, gambrel–, French–, mansard– roof.

v. **fork**, furcate, divaricate, branch, ramify, bifurcate, bend, crinkle.

adj. **angular**, bent, crooked, aduncous, adunc *or* aduncal, aduncate *or* aduncated, uncinated, aquiline, jagged, serrated; falciform, falcated; furcal, furcate, furcated, forked, bifurcate, crotched, zigzag, furcular, hooked; dove-tailed; knockkneed, crinkled, akimbo, kimbo [*obs.*], geniculated; oblique etc. 217.

wedge-shaped, cuneiform; cuneate, multangular, oxygonal; triangular, trigonal, trilateral; quadrangular, quadrilateral, foursquare, rectangular, square; multilateral; polygonal etc. *n.*; cubical, rhombic *or* rhombical, rhomboidal, pyramidal.

245. Curvature

n. **curvature**, curvity [*rare*], curvation; incurvature, incurvity [*obs.*], incurvation; bend; flexure, flexion; conflexure [*obs.*]; crook, hook, bought [*obs.*], bending; deflexion, inflexion; concameration; arcuation, devexity [*obs.*], turn; deviation, detour *or* détour [*F.*], sweep; curl, curling; bough; recurvity [*rare*], recurvation [*rare*]; sinuosity etc. 248; aduncity.

curve, arc, arch, arcade, vault, bow, crescent, meniscus, half-moon, lunule, horseshoe, loop, crane neck; parabola, hyperbola; catacaustic, diacaustic; geanticline, geosyncline; catenarian, catenary, festoon; conchoid, cardioid; caustic; tracery; arched– ceiling, –roof; bay window, bow window.

v. **be curved** etc. *adj.*; sweep, swag [*obs. or dial.*], sag; deviate etc. 279; turn; reënter.

render curved etc. *adj.*; bend, curve, incurvate; deflect, inflect; crook; turn, round, arch, arcuate, arch over, embow, recurvate [*rare*], concamerate [*rare*]; bow, coil, curl, recurve, frizzle, friz *or* frizz.

adj. **curved** etc. *v.*; curvate *or* curvated, lobiform; curviform, curvilineal *or* curvilinear; devex [*obs.*], devious; recurved, recurvous; crump [*obs.*]; bowed etc. *v.*; vaulted; geanticlinal, geosynclinal; bow-legged etc. (*distorted*) 243; oblique etc. 217; circular etc. 247.

beak-shaped, beaked, rostrate, rostriform, rostroid, rhamphoid.
bell-shaped, campaniform, campanular, campanulous, campanulate.
boat-shaped, navicular, cymbiform, naviform, scaphoid.
bow-shaped, arcuate *or* arcuated, arcual; arciform, arclike, embowed.
crescent-shaped, crescent, crescentiform, crescentic, convexo-concave, sigmoid, semilunar, horned, meniscal, bicorn, bicornute *or* bicornuate, bicornuous [*rare*], bicorned *or* bicornous, semicircular.
heart-shaped, cordiform, cardioid, cordate.
helmet-shaped, galeiform, galeate, galeated, cassidiform.
hook-shaped, hooked, hooklike, unciform, uncate, uncinal, uncinate, hamulate, hamate, hamiform, hamose *or* hamous [*both rare*]; unguiform, unguiculate *or* unguiculated; curvated, aduncate, aduncous, adunc.
kidney-shaped, reinform.
lens-shaped, lenticular, lentoid, lentiform, meniscal, meniscoid.
moon-shaped, lunar, lunate *or* lunated, luniform, lunular, lunulate *or* lunulated, crescent-shaped (*q. v.*); Cynthian.
oar-shaped, remiform [*rare*].
pear-shaped, pyriform; obconic.
shell-shaped, conchate, conchiform, conchylaceous [*rare*], conchoidal [*min.*].
shield-shaped, scutate, scutiform, peltate, clypeate *or* clypeated, clypeiform.
sickle-shaped, falcate, falciform, falculate [*rare*].
tongue-shaped, linguiform, lingulate, ligulate.
turnip-shaped, napiform.

246. Straightness

n. **straightness**, rectilinearity, rectilinearness; directness; inflexibility etc. (*stiffness*) 323; straight–, bee–, right–, direct– line; short cut.

v. **be straight** etc. *adj.*; have no turning; not -incline, –bend, –turn, –deviate- to either side; go straight; steer for etc. (*direction*) 278.

render straight, straighten, rectify; set–, put- straight; unbend, unfold, uncurl etc. 248; unravel etc. 219, unwrap.

adj. **straight**; rectilinear, rectilineal; direct, even, right, true, in a line; virgate, unbent etc. *v.*; undeviating, unturned, undistorted, unswerving; straight-lined, straight as an arrow etc. (*direct*) 278; inflexible etc. 323.

perpendicular, plumb, vertical, upright, erect.

247. Circularity
[simple circularity]

n. **circularity**, roundness; rotundity etc. 249.
circle, circlet, ring, areola, hoop, roundlet, annulus, annulet, bracelet, armlet; ringlet; eye, loop, wheel; cycle, orb, orbit, rundle, zone, belt, cordon, band; contrate–, crown– wheel; hub, nave; sash, girdle, cestus, cest *or* ceste, cincture, baldric, fillet, fascia, wreath, garland; crown, corona, coronet, chaplet, snood, necklace, collar; noose, lasso.
ellipse, oval, ovule; ellipsoid, cycloid, epicycloid, epicycle.
semicircle; quadrant, sextant, sector.

v. **make round** etc. *adj.;* round.
go round; encircle etc. 227; describe a circle etc. 311.

adj. **round**, rounded, circular, annular, orbicular, orbiculate *or* orbiculated; oval, ovate, obovate, ovoid, ovoidal [*rare*], elliptic, elliptical, egg-shaped; pear-shaped etc. 245; cycloidal etc. *n.;* spherical etc. 249; fasciate *or* fasciated.

248. Convolution
[complex circularity]

n. **convolution**, involution, circumvolution; winding etc. *v.;* wave, undulation, tortuosity, anfractuosity; sinuosity, sinuation, sinuousness, flexuosity, tortility; meandering, circuit, circumbendibus [*humorous*], twist, twirl, windings and turnings, ambagiousness, ambages; torsion; inosculation; reticulation etc. (*crossing*) 219; rivulation.
coil, roll, curl, buckle, spiral, helix, corkscrew, worm, volute, whorl, rundle; tendril; scollop, scallop, escalop *or* escallop; kink; ammonite, snakestone.
serpent, snake, eel; maze, labyrinth.

v. **be convoluted** etc. *adj.;* wind, twine, turn and twist, twirl; wave, undulate, meander; inosculate; entwine *or* intwine; twist, coil, roll; wrinkle, curl, crisp, twill; frizz, frizzle; crimp, crape, indent, scollop, scallop; wring, intort; contort; wreathe etc. (*cross*) 219.

adj. **convoluted**; winding, twisted etc. *v.;* tortile, tortive [*obs.*]; wavy; undate *or* undated [*rare*], undulatory; circling, snaky, snakelike, serpentine, serpentiform, anguilliform, anguiform, anguilloid, anguillous, vermiform, vermicular; mazy, tortuous, sinuose, sinuous, sinuate, flexuous; undulating, undulated, wavy; anfractuous, reclivate [*rare*], rivulose, scolecoid; sigmoid, sigmoidal; spiriferous, spiroid.

wreathy, frizzly, *crêpé* [*F.*], buckled; raveled etc. (*in disorder*) 59.
involved, intricate, complicated, perplexed; labyrinthic, labyrinthian, labyrinthine; circuitous, ambagious; peristaltic; Daedalian; kinky, curly.
spiral, coiled, helical; cochlear, cochleate, cochleous [*rare*]; screw-shaped; turbinated, turbiniform, turbinoid, turbinal.

adv. in and out, round and round.

249. Rotundity

n. **rotundity**; roundness etc. *adj.;* cylindricity; sphericality, sphericity, spheroidicity *or* spheroidity, globoseness, globosity, globularity, annularity, orotundity, orbiculation.
cylinder, cylindroid; barrel, drum; roll, roller; rouleau, column, rolling-pin, rundle.
cone, conoid; pear-shape, egg-shape, bell-shape.
sphere, globe, ball, bowlder *or* boulder; spheroid, geoid, globoid, ellipsoid; oblong–, oblate-spheroid; drop, spherule, globule, vesicle, bulb, bullet, pellet, clew, pill, marble, pea, knob, pommel, horn, knot; oval etc. 247.

v. **render spherical** etc. *adj.;* form into a sphere, sphere, roll into a ball; give rotundity etc. *n.;* round.

adj. **rotund**; round etc. (*circular*) 247; cylindric *or* cylindrical, cylindroid *or* cylindroidal, columnar, vermiform, lumbriciform; conic, conical; spherical, spheroidal; globular, globous, globose; gibbous; fungiform; bulbous; *teres atque rotundus* [*L.*]; round as –an orange, –an apple, –a ball, –a billiard ball, –a cannon ball.
bead-shaped, beadlike, moniliform, monilated.
bell-shaped, campaniform, campanulate, campanulous, campanular.
egg-shaped, ovoid, oviform, ovoidal, ovate, globoid, globate *or* globated; obovate, obovoid [*both bot.*].
pear-shaped, pyriform.
rice-shaped, riziform.

250. Convexity

n. **convexity**, prominence, projection, swelling, gibbosity, bilge, bulge, protuberance, protrusion, excrescency; camber, swell.
intumescence, tumidity; tumor *or* tumour; tubercle, tuberousness, tuberosity, carunculation, bubo.
excrescence, hump, hunch, bunch; knob, knur, knurl, gnarl, knot; bow, boss, embossment, bump, mamelon, clump; bulb, node, nodule, nodosity.

253. Sharpness

tooth, molar; lip, flange; tongue; withers, shoulder, back, dorsum; elbow.

process, apophysis, condyle.

wheel, hub, hubble.

peg; button, stud; ridge, rib, trunnion, snag; sugar loaf etc. (*sharpness*) 253.

pimple, wen, whelk, papula, papule, pustule, pock, proud flesh, growth, sarcoma, caruncle, corn, wart, verruca, furuncle, polypus, fungus, fungosity, exostosis, bleb, blister, bulla, blain; boil etc. (*disease*) 655; air bubble, blob.

papilla, nipple, teat, pap, breast, dug, mammilla.

proboscis, nose, olfactory organ, neb, beak, snout, nozzle.

belly, corporation [*colloq.*], paunch, epigastrium, abdomen.

arch, cupola, dome, vault, beehive; balcony; eaves.

relief, relievo, cameo; low relief, bas-relief, basso-relievo *or* basso-rilievo [*It.*]; half relief, mezzo-relievo *or* mezzo-rilievo [*It.*]; high relief, alto-relievo *or* alto-rilievo [*It.*]; pilaster.

point of land, hill etc. (*height*) 206; cape, promontory, mull; foreland, headland; hummock, ledge, spur; naze, ness; mole, jetty, jutty.

v. **be prominent** etc. *adj.;* project, bulge, protrude, bag, belly, carunculate, pout, bouge [*obs.*], bunch; jut out, stand out, stick out, poke out; stick up, bristle up, start up, cock up, shoot up; swell over, hang over, bend over; beetle.

render prominent etc. *adj.;* raise 307; emboss, chase.

adj. **prominent**, protuberant, protrusile, protrusive; undershot, underhung; projecting etc. *v.;* bossed, bossy, nodular, convex, bunchy; clavate, clavated, claviform; hummocky, *moutonné* [*F.*]; caruncular *or* carunculous, carunculate *or* carunculated; furuncular, furunculous, furunculoid; mammiform; papulous, papulose; hemispheric, bulbous; bowed, arched; bold; bellied; tuberous, tuberculous; tumorous; cornute, odontoid; lentiform, lenticular; gibbous; club-shaped, hubby, hubbly, knobby, papillose; saddle-shaped, selliform; subclavate, torose, ventricose, verrucose; excrescential.

salient, in relief, raised, *repoussé* [*F.*]; bloated etc. (*expanded*) 194.

251. Flatness

n. **flatness** etc. *adj.;* smoothness etc. 255.

plane; level etc. 213; plate, platter, table, tablet, slab.

v. **flatten**; render flat; squelch, squash, fell; level etc. 213.

adj. **flat**, plane, even, flush, scutiform, discoid; complanate, flattish, homaloid; level etc. (*horizontal*) 213; flat as -a pancake, -a fluke, -a flounder, -a board, -my hand; smooth.

adv. **flat**, flatly [*rare*], flatways, flatwise, lengthwise, horizontally.

252. Concavity

n. **concavity**, depression, dip; hollow, hollowness; indentation, intaglio, cavity, vug *or* vugg *or* vugh, dent, dint, dimple, follicle, pit, sinus, antrum, alveolus, lacuna; honeycomb.

excavation, pit, sap, mine, shaft, colliery; caisson, *fougasse* [*F.*], countermine; trough etc. (*furrow*) 259; bay etc. (*of the sea*) 343.

cup, basin, crater, punch bowl; cell etc. (*receptacle*) 191; socket.

valley, vale, dale, dell, dingle, coomb *or* combe, bottom, slade [*obs.*], strath [*Scot.*], gill *or* ghyll [*Scot. & dial. Eng.*], glade, grove, glen, donga [*S. Africa*], nullah [*India*], park.

cave, subterrane, cavern, cove; grot, grotto; alcove, blind alley, *cul-de-sac* [*F.*], hole, burrow, kennel, tunnel; gully etc. 198; arch etc. (*curve*) 245.

excavator, sapper, miner.

v. **be concave** etc. *adj.;* retire, cave in.

render concave etc. *adj.;* depress, dish, hollow; scoop, scoop out; gouge, dig, delve, excavate, dent, dint, mine, sap, undermine, burrow, tunnel, stave in.

adj. **depressed** etc. *v.;* alveolate, alveolar, calathiform, cup-shaped, dishing; favaginous, faveolate, favose; scyphiform, scyphose; concave, hollow, vuggy, stove in; retiring; retreating; cavernous; porous etc. (*with holes*) 260; cellular, spongy, spongious; honey-combed; infundibular, infundibuliform, funnel-shaped, bell-shaped, campani-form, capsular; vaulted, arched.

253. Sharpness

n. **sharpness** etc. *adj.;* acuity, acumination, mucronation; spinosity.

point, spike, spine, spiculum; needle, pin; prick, prickle; spur, rowel, barb; spit, cusp; horn, antler; snag; tag; thorn, bristle; Adam's needle, bear grass, tine, yucca.

nib, tooth, tusk; spoke, cog, ratchet.

beard, cheval-de-frise (*pl.* chevaux-de-frise), porcupine, hedgehog, brier, bramble, thistle; comb; awn, beggar's lice, bur *or* burr, catchweed, cleavers *or* clivers, goose grass, hairif

254. Bluntness

or hariff [*dial. Eng.*], flax comb, hatchel *or* hackle *or* heckle.

peak, crag, crest, arête [*F.*], cone, sugar loaf, pike, aiguille; spire, pyramid, steeple.

cutting-edge, knife-edge, blade, edge tool, cutlery, knife, penknife, whittle, razor; scalpel, bistoury, lancet; plowshare, colter; hatchet, ax *or* axe, pickax, mattock, pick, adz *or* adze, bill; billhook, cleaver, cutter; scythe, sickle, scissors, shears; sword etc. (*arms*) 727; wedge; bodkin etc. (*perforator*) 262; beduque [*F.*], bowie knife, paring knife; bushwhacker; drawing knife *or* drawknife, drawshave.

sharpener, hone, strop; grindstone, whetstone; novaculite; steel, emery.

v. **be sharp** etc. *adj.;* taper to a point; bristle with, acuminate.

render sharp etc. *adj.;* sharpen, point, aculeate, acuminate, whet, barb, spiculate, set, strop, grind.

cut etc. (*sunder*) 44.

adj. **sharp**, keen; acute; acicular; aciform; aculeate *or* aculeated, acuminate *or* acuminated, pointed; tapering; mucronate *or* mucronated, mucronulate; spiked, spiky, peaked, salient; cusped, cuspidate *or* cuspidated; prickly, echinate *or* echinated, acanaceous, acanthophorous, spiny, spinous, spinulose, spinulescent, spinuliferous; apiculate *or* apiculated; thorny, bristling, muricate *or* muricated, corniculate, pectinate *or* pectinated, studded, thistly, briery; craggy etc. (*rough*) 256; snaggy, digitate *or* digitated, two-edged.

arrow-shaped, arrowheaded, arrowy, sagittal, sagittate, sagittated, sagittiform.

barbed, glochidiate, spurred, aristate, awned, awny, bearded, barbate, crestate, setarious, subulate, tetrahedral.

cone-shaped, conic, conical, coniform [*rare*], pyramidal.

horn-shaped, corniform, cornute *or* cornuted; crescent-shaped; horned, corniculate.

lance-shaped, lanceolate, lanciform.

reed-shaped, calamiform [*rare*], arundinaceous, reedy.

scimitar-shaped, acinaciform.

spear-shaped, hastate, hastiform [*rare*], lance-shaped (*q.v.*).

spindle-shaped, fusiform.

star-shaped, stellate *or* stellated, stelliform, stellular, starlike, starry.

sword-shaped, gladiate, ensate, ensiform, xiphoid.

tooth-shaped, dentiform, toothlike, odontoid, dentoid.

keen-edged, cutting; sharp-edged, knife-edged; sharp–, keen– as a razor; sharp as a needle; sharpened etc. *v.;* set.

254. Bluntness

n. **bluntness** etc. *adj.*

v. **be** *or* **render blunt** etc. *adj.;* obtund, dull; take off the -point, -edge; unedge [*rare*], turn.

adj. **blunt**, obtuse, dull, dullish, pointless, unpointed; unsharpened, bluff; edentate, toothless.

255. Smoothness

n. **smoothness** etc. *adj.;* polish, gloss; lubricity, lubrication.

[smooth surfaces] bowling green etc. (*level*) 213; glass, ice, slide; asphalt, granolithic pavement, wood pavement, flags; down, velvet, silk, taffeta, satin, velveteen, velumen.

smoother; roller, steam roller; sandpaper, emery paper; flatiron, sadiron; burnisher, chamois *or* shammy, turpentine and beeswax.

v. **smooth**, smoothen [*rare*]; plane; file; mow, shave; level, roll; macadamize; polish, burnish, sleek, planish, levigate, calendar, glaze; iron, hot-press, mangle; lubricate etc. (*oil*) 332.

adj. **smooth**; polished etc. *v.;* leiodermatous, slick [*colloq.*], velutinous, even; level etc. 213; plane etc. (*flat*) 251; sleek, glossy; silken, silky; lanate, downy, velvety; glabrous, slippery, glassy, lubricious *or* lubricous, oily, soft; unwrinkled; smooth as -glass, –ice, –monumental alabaster, –ivory, –satin, –velvet, –oil; slippery as an eel; woolly etc. (*feathery*) 256.

256. Roughness

n. **roughness** etc. *adj.;* tooth, grain, texture, ripple; asperity, rugosity, salebrosity [*obs.*], corrugation, nodosity, nodulation; arborescence etc. 242; pilosity.

hair, brush, beard, shag, mane, whiskers, moustache, imperial, trees, lock, curl, ringlet, fimbria, eyelashes, lashes, cilia, villi; lovelock; beaucatcher; curl paper; goatee; papillote, scalp lock, scolding locks [*colloq.*], elf locks, mop, mat, thatch; fringe, toupee; hair shirt.

plumage, plumosity; plume, panache, crest; feather, tuft.

nap, pile, floss, velvet, plush, fur, down, wool, fluff; byssus, moss, bur *or* burr.

v. **be rough** etc. *adj.;* go against the grain.

render rough etc. *adj.;* roughen, knurl, crinkle, ruffle, crisp, crumple, corrugate, engrail;

roughcast; set on edge, stroke the wrong way, rub the fur the wrong way, rumple.
- *adj.* **rough**, uneven; scabrous, knotted; rugged, rugose, rugous, rugulose; nodose, nodular, nodulated; knurled, cross-grained, knurly; asperous [*obs.*], crisp, salebrous [*obs.*], gnarled, gnarly, scraggly, scragged, scraggy; jagged; unkempt, unpolished, unsmooth, rough-hewn; craggy, cragged; crankling [*obs.*]; prickly etc. (*sharp*) 253; arborescent etc. 242; leafy, well-wooded.
  feathery, plumose, plumigerous.
  hairy, bristly, hirsute, hispid, pappous *or* pappose, pileous, pilose, pilous; trichogenous, trichoid; tufted, ciliated, filamentous; crinose, crinite; bushy; villous, nappy; bearded, shaggy, shagged; setous [*obs.*], setose, setaceous, setiferous, setigerous, setiform; "like quills upon the fretful porcupine" [*Hamlet*]; rough as a -nutmeg grater, −bear.
  downy, velvety, flocculent, woolly, lanate, lanated, lanuginous, lanuginose; tomentose; fluffy.
  fringed, befringed, fimbriate, fimbriated, fimbricate, laciniate *or* laciniated, laciniform, laciniose.
- *adv.* **against the grain**; the wrong way of the goods; in the rough; on edge.

257. Notch

- *n.* **notch**, dent, nick, cut; dimple; scotch, indent, indentation, denticulation, serration, serrature.
  saw, tooth, crenel *or* crenelle, scallop *or* scollop; rickrack, picot edge, vandyke; depression, jag.
  embrasure, battlement, machicolation.
- *v.* **notch**, nick, pink, mill, score, cut, dent, indent, jag, scarify, scotch, crimp, scallop *or* scollop, crenulate, crenelate *or* crenellate, vandyke.
- *adj.* **notched** etc. *v.;* crenate *or* crenated; dentate *or* dentated, denticulate *or* denticulated, crenelated *or* crenellated, toothed, palmate *or* palmated, serriform, serrate *or* serrated, serrulate.

258. Fold

- *n.* **fold**, plicature, plication, pleat, plait, ply, crease; knife-pleat, knife-plait, box-pleat, box-plait; accordion pleat, accordion plait; tuck, gather; flexion, flexure, joint, elbow, double, doubling, duplicature, gather, wrinkle, rimple, crinkle, crankle, crumple, rumple, rivel [*archaic*], ruck, ruffle, dog's-ear, corrugation, frounce [*obs.*], flounce, lapel; pucker, crow's-feet.
- *v.* **fold**, double, plicate, pleat, plait, crease, wrinkle, crinkle, crankle, curl, smock, shrivel, cockle up, cocker [*dial.*], rimple, rumple, frizzle, frounce [*archaic*], rivel [*archaic*], twill, corrugate, ruffle, crimple [*obs.*], crumple, pucker; turn−, double- -down, −under; dog's-ear, tuck, ruck, hem, gather.
- *adj.* **folded** etc. *v.*

259. Furrow

- *n.* **furrow**, groove, rut, sulcus, scratch, streak, striae, crack, score, incision, slit; chamfer, fluting; corduroy road, cradle hole [*sleighing*].
  trench, ditch, dike *or* dyke, moat, fosse, trough, channel, gutter, ravine etc. (*interval*) 198; depression, tajo.
- *v.* **furrow** etc. *n.;* flute, groove, chamfer, carve, corrugate, cut, chisel, plow; incise, engrave, etch, enchase, mezzotint, crosshatch, hatch, grave, bite in.
- *adj.* **furrowed** etc. *v.;* ribbed, striated, sulcated, fluted, canaliculate *or* canaliculated; bisulcous *or* bisulcate *or* bisulcated; canaliferous; unisulcate; trisulcate; corduroy; costate, rimiform [*rare*].

260. Opening

- *n.* **opening**, aperture, apertness [*archaic*]; hiation [*rare*], yawning, oscitance *or* oscitancy, dehiscence, patefaction [*obs.*], pandiculation; chasm etc. (*interval*) 198.
  outlet, inlet; vent, venthole, blow-hole, airhole, spiracle; vomitory [*Rom. arch.*]; embouchure; orifice, mouth, sucker, muzzle, throat, gullet, weasand, wizen [*dial.*], nozzle; placket.
  window, casement; embrasure, *abatjour* [*F.*]; light; skylight, fanlight; lattice; bay window, bow window, oriel, dormer; lantern.
  portal, porch, gate, ostiary [*obs.*], postern, wicket, trapdoor, hatch, door; arcade; cellarway, driveway, gateway, doorway, hatchway, gangway; lich gate *or* lych gate [*archaic*].
  way, path etc. 627; thoroughfare; channel, gully; passage, passageway.
  tube, pipe, main; water pipe etc. 350; air pipe etc. 351; vessel, tubule, canal, gut, fistula; ajutage *or* adjutage; ostium; smokestack; chimney, flue, tap, funnel.
  tunnel, mine, pit, adit, drift, shaft; gallery.
  alley, lane, mall, aisle, glade, vista.
  bore, caliber *or* calibre; pore; blind orifice; fulgurite, thunder tube.

261. Closure

hole, foramen; puncture, perforation; fontane *or* fontanelle; transforation; pinhole, keyhole, loophole, porthole, peephole, mousehole, pigeonhole; eye, eye of a needle; eyelet; slot.
porousness, porosity; sieve, strainer, colander *or* cullender; cribble, riddle, screen; honeycomb.
perforation, apertion [*archaic*]; piercing etc. *v.*; terebration, empalement, pertusion [*obs.*], puncture, acupuncture, penetration.
opener, key, master key, *passepartout* [*F.*], clavis, open-sesame.

v. **open**, ope [*poetic*], gape, yawn, hiate [*rare*], dehisce, bilge; fly open.
perforate, pierce, empierce [*obs.*], tap, bore, drill; mine etc. (*scoop out*) 252; tunnel; transpierce, transfix; enfilade, impale, spike, spear, gore, spit, stab, pink, puncture, lance; trepan, trephine; stick, prick, riddle, punch; stave in.
cut a passage through; make way for, make room for.
uncover, unclose, unrip, rip; lay–, cut–, rip–, throw- open.

adj. **open**; perforated etc. *v.*; perforate; wide open, patulous, agape, dehiscent, ringent, ajar, unclosed, unstopped; oscitant, gaping, yawning; patent.
tubular, cannular, fistulous; pervious, permeable; foraminous; vesicular, vascular; porous, follicular, cribriform, honeycombed, infundibular *or* infundibulate, riddled; tubulose *or* tubulous, tubulate *or* tubulated; piped, tubate, tubiform.
opening etc. *v.*; aperient.

int. open sesame! gangway! passageway!

261. Closure

n. **closure**, occlusion, blockade; shutting up etc. *v.*; obstruction etc. (*hindrance*) 706; embolism, embolus; contraction etc. 195; infarct, infarction; constipation, obstipation; blind -alley, –corner; keddah [*India*], *cul-de-sac* [*F.*]; cecum *or* caecum; imperforation, imperviousness etc. *adj.*; impermeability; stopper etc. 263; operculum.

v. **close**, occlude, plug; block up, stop up, fill up, bung up, cork up, button up, stuff up, shut up, dam up; blockade; obstruct etc. (*hinder*) 706; bar, bolt, stop, seal, plumb; choke, throttle; ram down, dam, cram; trap, clinch; put to–, shut- the door; slam, clap, snap.

adj. **closed** etc. *v.*; shut, operculated; unopened, blank.

unpierced, imporous, caecal; embolic; infarcted, imperforate, impervious, impermeable; impenetrable; impassable, unpassable, invious [*obs.*]; pathless, wayless; untrodden.
tight, unventilated, air-tight, water-tight, hermetically sealed; snug.

262. Perforator

n. **performator**, piercer, borer, auger, chisel, gimlet, drill, wimble, awl, bradawl, scoop, terrier [*obs.*], corkscrew, dibble, trocar, trepan, trephine, probe, bodkin, needle, stylet, stiletto, broach, reamer, rimer, lancet; punch, puncheon; spikebit, gouge; spear etc. (*weapon*) 727; puncher; punching machine, punching press; punch pliers.

263. Stopper

n. **stopper**, stopple; plug, cork, bung, spike, spill, spile, stopcock, tap, faucet; rammer; ram, ramrod; piston; stop-gap; wadding, stuffing, padding, stopping, dossil, pledget, sponge [*surg.*], tampion *or* tompion, tourniquet.
valve, vent peg, spigot, slide valve, cover etc. 223.
doorkeeper, gatekeeper, janitor, janitress [*fem.*], janitrix [*fem.*], *concierge* [*F.*], porter, portress [*fem.*], warder, beadle, tiler *or* tyler [*Freemasonry*], durwaun [*Hind.*], usher, guard, sentinel; beefeater, yeoman of the guard [*Eng.*]; Cerberus, watch dog, ostiary.

Section 4. Motion

264. Motion

[successive change of place]

n. **motion**, movement, motility, motivity; move; going etc. *v.*; mobility; movableness, motive power, motorium; laws of motion; mobilization. stream, flow, flux, run, course, stir; conduction; evolution; kinematics; telekinesis.
rate, pace, tread, step, stride, gait, port, footfall, cadence, carriage, velocity, angular velocity; clip [*colloq.*], progress, locomotion; journey etc. 266; voyage etc. 267; transit etc. 270.
restlessness etc. (*changeableness*) 149; unrest.

v. **be in motion** etc. *adj.*; move, go, hie, gang [*Scot. & dial. Eng.*], budge, stir, pass, slit; hover -round, –about; shift, slide, glide; roll, roll on; flow, stream, run, drift, sweep along; wander etc. (*deviate*) 279; walk etc. 266; change–, shift- one's -place, –quarters; dodge; keep going, keep moving.

266. Journey

    put in motion, set in motion; move; impel etc. 276; propel etc. 284; render movable, mobilize.

adj. **moving** etc. *v.;* in motion; traveling, transitional, metabatic; motory [*rare*], motive; shifting, movable, mobile, motiferous, motile, motific [*rare*], motor, motorial, quicksilver, mercurial, unquiet; restless etc. (*changeable*) 149; nomadic etc. 266; erratic etc. 279.

    telekinetic, kinematic *or* kinematical, evolutionary.

adv. **under way**; on the -move, –wing, –fly, –tramp, –march.

265. Quiescence

n. **rest**; stillness etc. *adj.;* quiescence; stagnation, stagnancy; fixity, immobility, catalepsy; indisturbance [*rare*]; quietism.

    quiet, tranquillity, calm; repose etc. 687; peace; dead calm, anticyclone; statue-like repose; silence etc. 403; not a breath of air, not a mouse stirring; not a leaf stirring; sleep etc. (*inactivity*) 683.

    pause, lull etc. (*cessation*) 142; stand, standstill; standing still etc. *v.;* lock; deadlock, dead stop, dead stand; full stop; fix; embargo.

    resting place; *gîte* [*F.*]; bivouac; home etc. (*abode*) 189; pillow etc. (*support*) 215; haven etc. (*refuge*) 666; goal etc. (*arrival*) 292.

v. **be quiescent** etc. *adj.;* stand still, stand fast, stand firm, lie still; keep quiet, repose, rest one's bonnet on a chair [*dial.*], rest one's face and hands [*dial.*], hold the breath.

    remain, stay; stand, lie to, ride at anchor, remain *in situ*, tarry, mark time; bring to, heave to, lay to; pull up, draw up; hold, halt; stop, stop short; rest, pause, anchor; cast anchor, come to anchor; rest on one's oars; repose–, rest- on one's laurels; lie back on one's record; take breath; stop etc. (*discontinue*) 142.

    vegetate, stagnate; *quieta non movere* [*L.*]; let alone, let well enough alone; abide, rest and be thankful; keep within doors, stay at home, go to bed, live the life of a claim.

    dwell etc. (*be present*) 186; settle etc. (*be located*) 184; alight etc. (*arrive*) 292; stick, stick fast; stand, stand like a post; not stir a -peg, –step; stand like a stuck pig [*colloq.*]; be at a stand etc. *n.*

    quell, becalm, hush, calm, still, stay, lull to sleep, lay an embargo on, put the brakes on.

adj. **quiescent**, still; motionless, moveless; fixed; stationary; immotile; at rest, at a stand, at a standstill, at anchor; stock-still; standing still etc. *v.;* sedentary, untraveled, stay-at-home; becalmed, stagnant, quiet; unmoved, undisturbed, unruffled; calm, restful; cataleptic; immovable etc. (*stable*) 150; sleeping etc. (*inactive*) 683; silent etc. 403; still as - a statue, –a post, –a stone, –a mouse, –death.

adv. **at a stand** etc. *adj.; tout court* [*F.*]; at the halt.

int. **stop!** stay! avast! [*naut.*], halt! hold hard! whoa! hold! *sabr karo!* [*Hind.*], *arrêtez!* [*F.*], *halte!* [*F.*].

266. Journey
[locomotion by land]

n. **travel**; traveling etc. *v.;* wayfaring, campaigning, nomadization.

    excursion, journey, expedition, tour, trip, grand tour, *Wanderjahr* [*Ger.*], circuit, peregrination, discursion [*obs.*], ramble, pilgrimage, hadj *or* hajj [*Ar.*], trek [*S. Africa*], course, ambulation, march, walk, promenade, constitutional [*colloq.*], stroll, saunter, hike [*colloq.*], tramp, jog trot, turn, stalk, perambulation; outing, ride, drive, airing, jaunt.

    nightwalking, noctambulation, noctambulism; somnambulism, sleep walking, somnambulation.

    riding, equitation, horsemanship, manège, manage [*archaic*], ride and tie.

    roving, vagrancy, pereration [*obs.*]; marching and countermarching; nomadism; vagabondism, vagabondage; hoboism; gadding; flit, flitting; migration; emigration, immigration, demigration [*obs.*], intermigration; *Wanderlust* [*Ger.*].

    itinerary, plan, guide; handbook, travel guide, roadbook; Baedeker, Bradshaw, Michelin, Murray.

    procession, parade, cavalcade, caravan, file, *cortège* [*F.*], column.

    organs and instruments of locomotion] cycle, automobile, motor car etc. (*vehicle*) 272; trolley, locomotive; palanquin *or* palankeen, litter, dandy *or* dandi [*India*], jinrikisha *or* jinricksha; roller skates, skates, skis, snowshoes; legs, shanks, feet; pegs, pins, trotters [*colloq.*].

    traveler etc. 268.

    station, stop, stopping place, terminal, terminus, depot, railway station, *gare* [*F.*].

v. **travel**, journey, course; take–, go- a journey; railroad [*U. S.*]; flit, take wing; migrate, emigrate, immigrate; trek [*S. Africa*]; scour–, traverse- the country; peragrate [*obs.*]; perambulate, circumambulate; tour, peregrinate, itinerate [*rare*], nomadize.

267. Navigation

motor, motorcycle, bicycle, cycle, spin, speed, burn up the road; trolley; go by -car, -trolley, -automobile, -rail, -train etc.
motorize, electrify.
wander, roam, range, prowl, rove, jaunt, ramble, stroll, saunter, hover, go one's rounds, straggle; gad, gad about; expatiate [*rare*]; patrol, pace up and down, traverse; take a walk etc. *n.;* go out for a walk etc. *n.;* have a run, take the air; noctambulate; somnambulate.
take horse, ride, drive, trot, amble, canter, prance, fisk [*obs.*], frisk, *caracoler* [*F.*], caracole; gallop etc. (*move quickly*) 274.
walk, march, step, tread, pace, plod, wend [*archaic*]; promenade; trudge, track, hoof it [*slang*], hike [*colloq.*], tramp; stalk, stride, straddle, strut, foot it, stump, bundle, bowl along, toddle; paddle; tread-, follow-, pursue- a path.
peg on, jog on, wag on, shuffle on; stir one's stumps [*colloq.*]; bend one's -steps, -course; make-, find-, wend-, pick-, thread-, plow- one's way.
glide, slide, coast, skim, skate.
file off, march in procession, defile.
go to, repair to, resort to, hie to, betake oneself to.
adj. **traveling** etc. *v.;* ambulatory, itinerant, peripatetic, perambulatory, mundivagant [*rare*], roving, rambling, gadding, discursive, vagrant, migratory, nomadic; circumforanean [*obs.*], circumforaneous.
night-wandering, noctivagant [*rare*], noctambulistic, noctivagous, somnambulistic *or* somnambular, somnambulant.
self-moving, automobile, automotive, locomotive, locomobile, automatic.
wayfaring, wayworn; travel-stained.
adv. on foot, on horseback, on shanks' mare; by the Marrowbone stage; *in transitu* etc. 270; en route etc. 282.
Int. come along! step on it!

267. Navigation
[locomotion by water or air]

n. **navigation**; volatility; aquatics; boating, yachting, cruising; ship etc. 273.
oar, scull, sweep, pole; paddle, screw, turbine; sail, canvas.
natation, swimming; fin, flipper, fish's tail.
aeronautics, aerostatics, aerostation, aerodonetics, aerial navigation, aeronautism; aeromechanics, aerodynamics, balloonery; balloon etc. 273; ballooning; aviation, airmanship; flying, flight, volitation; volplaning, planing [*colloq.*], hydroplaning, volplane, glide, dive, nose-dive, spin, looping the loop; wing' pinion, aileron.
voyage, sail, cruise, passage, circumnavigation, periplus; headway, sternway, leeway; fairway.
mariner etc. 269; **aeronaut** etc. 269a.
v. **sail**; put to sea etc. (*depart*) 293; take ship, weigh anchor, get under way; spread -sail, -canvas; gather way, have way on; make-, carry- sail; plow the -waves, -deep, -main, -ocean; ride the waves, ride the storm, buffet the waves, walk the waters.
navigate, warp, luff, scud, boom, kedge; drift, course, cruise, steam, coast; hug the -shore, -land; circumnavigate.
row, paddle, ply the oar, pull, scull, punt.
float, swim, skim, *effleurer* [*F.*], dive, wade.
[in aeronautics] fly, soar, drift, hover, be wafted, aviate, volplane, plane [*colloq.*], glide, dive, fly over, nose-dive, spin, loop the loop, land; take wing, take a flight; wing one's flight, wing one's way.
adj. **sailing** etc. *v.;* seafaring, nautical, maritime, naval; seagoing, coasting; afloat; navigable; grallatorial *or* grallatory.
aeronautic, aeronautical, aerostatic, *or* aerostatical, aeromechanic *or* aeromechanical, aerodynamic, aerial, volant, volitant, volatile, volitational.
aquatic, natatory, natatorial, natational.
adv. **under -way**, -sail, -canvas, -steam; on the wing.

268. Traveler

n. **traveler**, wayfarer, voyager, itinerant, passenger, transient, commuter, straphanger [*colloq.*].
tourist, excursionist, explorer, adventurer, mountaineer, Alpine Club; peregrinator, wanderer, rover, straggler, rambler; landsman, landlubber, horse marine; bird of passage; gadabout [*colloq.*], gadling [*obs.*]; vagrant, scattering [*obs.*], landlouper *or* landloper, waifs and estrays, wastrel, stray; loafer, swagman *or* swagsman [*Australia*], tramp, vagabond, nomad, Bohemian, gypsy, Arab, Wandering Jew, hadji *or* hajji [*Ar.*], pilgrim, palmer; peripatetic; comers and goers, immigrant; *émigré* [*F.*], emigrant; runagate, runaway, renegade, fugitive, refugee; beachcomber; booly [*Irish hist.*]; globe-girdler, globetrotter [*colloq.*]; hobo [*U. S.*], runabout, trekker [*S. Africa*], camper, *zingaro* (*pl.* zingari) [*It.*].
sleepwalker, somnambulist, somnambulator [*rare*], nightwalker, noctambulist.

courier, messenger, express, *estafette* [*F.*], runner; Mercury, Iris, Ariel; comet.

pedestrian, walker, foot passenger, hiker [*colloq.*], perigrinator [*rare*], tramper.

rider, horseman, horsewoman [*fem.*], equestrian, equestrienne [*fem.*], cavalier, jockey, rough-rider, trainer, breaker, huntsman, whip, postilion *or* postillion, postboy.

driver, coachman, Jehu [*humorous*], charioteer, carter, wagoner, drayman; cabman, cabdriver; *voiturier* [*F.*], *vetturino* [*It.*], *condottiere* [*It.*], gharry-wallah *or* gari-wala [*Hind.*], hackman, syce [*India*], truckman.

[railroad] engine driver [*Brit.*], engineer, fireman, stoker, conductor, guard [*Brit.*], motorman.

[automobile] driver, chauffeur, chauffeuse [*fem.*], automobilist, motorist, truck driver, mechanician; scorcher [*slang*], speed maniac, road hog [*slang*].

269. Mariner

n. **mariner**, sailor, navigator; seaman, seafarer, seafaring man, sea dog [*colloq.*], hand, water dog [*colloq.*], shellback [*slang*]; Ancient Mariner, Flying Dutchman; dock walloper [*slang*]; Jack, Jack Tar *or* jack-tar, tar, jacky (*pl.* jackies) [*landsman's term*], shipman [*obs. or poet.*], gob [*slang*]; salt, able seaman, A. B.; man-of-war's man, bluejacket, galiongee *or* galionji, marine, devil-dog [*slang*], jolly [*slang*]; midshipman, middy [*colloq.*]; lascar, *mangee* or *manjhi* [*Hind.*], *matelot* [*F.*], captain, commander, master mariner, skipper; mate; boatman, ferryman, waterman, lighterman, bargeman, longshoreman; bargee, gondolier; oar, oarsman; rower; boatswain.

steersman, coxswain *or* cockswain, cox [*colloq.*], helmsman, wheelman, pilot, *patron* [*F.*]; crew.

269a. Aeronaut

n. **aeronaut**, aviator, aeroplanist, airman, airwoman, flyer, birdman [*colloq.*], birdwoman [*colloq.*], aviatress *or* aviatrix, navigator, manbird [*colloq.*], wizard of the air, monoplanist; pilot, observer, spotter, scout, bombardier *or* bomber, ace; balloonist, Icarus.

270. Transference

n. **transfer**, transference; translocation, elocation [*obs.*]; displacement; metastasis, metathesis; removal; remotion; amotion; relegation; deportation, asportation, extradition, conveyance, draft; carrying, carriage; convection, conduction, contagion, infection; transfusion; transfer etc. (*of property*) 783.

transit, transition; passage, ferry, gestation; portage, porterage, freightage, carting, cartage; shoveling etc. *v.;* vection [*obs.*], vecture [*obs.*], vectitation [*obs.*]; shipment, freight, waftage; transmission, transport, transporation, transumption [*rare*], transplantation, translation; shifting, dodging; dispersion etc. 73; transposition etc. (*interchange*) 148; traction etc. 285; *portamento* [*music, It.*].

[thing transferred] drift, alluvion, alluvium, detritus, deposit, moraine; deed, gift, bequest, legacy, lease; quitclaim; freight, cargo, mail, baggage, luggage, goods.

transferee, grantee, assignee; donee, legatee, consignee, indorsee, devisee.

v. **transfer**, transmit, transport, transplace, transplant, transfuse; convey, carry, bear, fetch and carry; carry over, ferry over; hand, pass, forward; shift; conduct, convoy, bring, fetch, reach; tote.

send, delegate, consign, relegate, turn over to, deliver; ship, freight, embark; waft; shunt; transpose etc. (*interchange*) 148; displace etc. 185; throw etc. 284; drag etc. 285; mail, post.

ladle, bail *or* bale, bucket, lade, dip, drip; shovel, decant, draft off.

adj. **transferred** etc. *v.;* drifted, movable; portable, portative; conductive, contagious, infectious; metastatic, metathetic *or* metathetical; transumptive [*rare*].

transferable, assignable, conveyable, devisable, bequeathable, negotiable, transmittible, transmissible; mailable.

adv. from hand to hand, from pillar to post; by freight, by rail, by steamer, by aeroplane, by trolley, by motor truck, by express, by mail, by special delivery.

on the way, by the way; on the road, on the wing; as one goes; *in transitu* [*L.*], *en route* [*F.*], *chemin faisant* [*F.*], *en passant* [*F.*], in mid-progress.

271. Carrier

n. **carrier**, porter, red cap, bearer, tranter [*obs.*], conveyer; *cargador* [*P.I.*], freighter, express, expressman; stevedore; coolie; conductor, chauffeur, truck driver; letter carrier, postman, man of letters [*humorous*], aerial mail-carrier.

beast of burden, beast, cattle, horse, steed, nag, palfrey, Arab, blood horse, thoroughbred, galloway, charger, courser, racer, hunter, jument [*obs.*], pony; Shetland, –pony; filly, colt, foal,

272. Vehicle

barb, roan, jade, hack, bidet, pad, cob, tit [*dial.*], punch [*dial.*], roadster, goer; race–, pack–, draft–, cart–, dray–, post- horse; shelty *or* sheltie; garran *or* garron [*Brit.*], jennet *or* genet, bayard, mare, stallion, gelding; broncho *or* bronco, cayuse; creature, critter; cow pony, mustang, Narragansett, waler; stud.

ass, donkey, jackass, burro, cuddy [*Scot. & dial. Eng.*], moke [*slang*]; wild ass, onager.

mule, hinny; sumpter -horse, –mule; ladino.

reindeer; camel, dromedary, llama, elephant; carrier pigeon.

Pegasus, Bucephalus, Rosinante *or* Rocinante, Alborak, Bayard, Incitatus, Kantaha, Veillantif, Vindictive, Black Bess, Kelpie *or* Kelpy.

[means of transport] locomotive, motor, trolley, carriage etc. (*vehicle*) 272; ship etc. 273.

adj. equine, asinine; electric, motor, express.

272. Vehicle

n. **Vehicle**, conveyance, carriage, caravan, car, van; wagon *or* waggon, wain [*archaic*], dray, cart, lorry.

cariole *or* carriole; truck, tram; limber, tumbrel *or* tumbril, pontoon; barrow; wheelbarrow, handbarrow; perambulator; Bath–, wheelchair; chaise; police van, patrol wagon, black Maria [*colloq.*]; conestoga wagon *or* wain; jinrikisha *or* jinricksha, ricksha [*colloq.*], dearborn, dump cart, hack, jigger, horse car; kittereen, mail stage, manumotor, rig, rockaway, prairie schooner, shay [*colloq.*], sloven [*Can.*], team, tonga [*India*], Cape cart [*S. Africa*], hackery [*India*], ekka [*India*]; gharri *or* gharry *or* gari [*India*]; gocart.

equipage, turnout [*colloq.*]; coach, chariot, phaeton, mail phaeton, wagonette, break *or* brake, drag, curricle, tilbury, whiskey [*obs.*], landau, barouche, victoria, brougham, clarence, calash, *calèche* [*F.*], britzka, araba [*Oriental*], kibitka; berlin; sulky, *désobligeant* [*F.*], sociable, *vis-à-vis* [*F.*], *dormeuse* [*F.*], jaunting–, outside- car; runabout; *vettura* [*It.*].

post chaise; diligence [*F.*], stage, stagecoach; mail–, hackney–, glasscoach; stage wagon; car, omnibus, bus [*colloq.*]; fly [*Eng.*], cabriolet, cab, hansom, four-wheeler, growler [*slang, Eng.*], droshki *or* drosky.

dogcart, trap [*colloq.*], whitechapel, buggy, char-à-bancs (*pl.* chars-à-bancs) [*F.*], shandrydan *or* shandradan [*Scot., Ir., & dial. Eng.*].

team, pair, span, tandem, random; spike team *or* spike, unicorn; four-in-hand.

litter, palanquin *or* palankeen, sedan *or* sedan chair; palki, jampan, dandy *or* dandi, dooly *or* doolie, munchil [*all India*]; *cacolet* [*F.*]; tonjon [*Ceylon*], brancard, horse litter; stretcher, hurdle; ambulance.

sled, bob, bobsled *or* bobsleigh; cutter; doubleripper, doublerunner; jumper [*U. S. & Can.*], sledge, sleigh, toboggan, cariole *or* carriole [*Can.*], pung; ski (*pl.* ski *or* skis), snowshoes, skates, roller skates.

cycle, monocycle, bicycle, bicycle built for two, tricycle, quadricycle, hydrocycle, tandem; machine [*colloq.*], wheel [*colloq.*], bike [*slang*], safety bicycle *or* safety [*colloq.*], motor cycle *or* motorcycle; velocipede, hobbyhorse, draisine *or* draisene.

automobile, motor car *or* motorcar, limousine, sedan, touring car, roadster, coupé, motor, machine, car, auto, locomobile, autocar, steamer, electric, runabout, couplet, racer, torpedo; truck, tractor; taxicab, taxi, taxicoach, bus, motor bus *or* motorbus; flivver [*slang*], jitney [*colloq.*], tacot [*F. mil. slang*].

[allied automobile terms] tonneau, trunk, chassis, hood, top, ignition, spark plug, trunk, generator, distributor, magneto, self-starter, gear, gear box, differential, cylinder, manifold, intake, exhaust, carburetor; four–, six–, eight–, twelve- cylinder; twin six, ammeter, speedometer, oil gauge, primer, clutch, universal joint, crank shaft, transmission, tire, rim; gasoline, petrol [*Brit.*]; trailer; garage; chauffeur etc. 268.

train; express, mail; accommodation–, passenger–, express–, special–, limited–, mail–, corridor–, parliamentary–, luggage [*Brit.*] -, freight–, train; 1st-, 2d-, 3d-class- -train, –carriage, –compartment; rolling stock; cattle truck; car, coach, carriage [*Brit.*]; baggage–, freight–, chair–, drawing- room–, parlor–, Pullman–, sleeping-car; surface–, tram- car; trolley *or* trolley car [*U. S. & Can.*], electric car, electric [*colloq.*]; trollbus, trackless trolley; box car, box wagon; horse box [*Brit.*], horse car; lightning express; mail car, mail van [*Brit.*]; baggage car, luggage van [*Brit.*].

hand car, trolley *or* trolley.

[utensils & implements] spoon, spatula, ladle, hod, hoe; spade, shovel, spaddle [*obs.*], boy [*Ir.*]; spud; pitchfork.

adj. **vehicular**, curricular [*rare*], vehiculatory [*rare*]; ambulatory etc. (*traveling*) 266.

273. Ship

n. **ship**, vessel, sail; craft, bottom.

navy, marine, fleet, flotilla.

shipping, man-of-war etc. (*combatant*) 726; transport, tender, storeship; merchant ship, merchantman; packet, liner; whaler, slaver, collier, coaster, freight-steamer, freighter, lighter; fishing–, pilot- boat; trawler, hulk; yacht; baggala; floating -hotel, –palace; ocean greyhound [*colloq.*].

ship, bark *or* barque; shipentine, four-masted bark *or* barque; brig, snow, hermaphrodite brig; brigantine, barkentine *or* barquentine, schooner; topsail–, fore-and-aft- schooner; fore-and-after [*colloq.*]; three–, four–, five–, six- masted schooner; chasse-marée [*F.*], sloop, cutter, corvet *or* corvette, clipper, foist [*obs.*], yawl, dandy, ketch, smack, lugger, barge, hoy, cat, catboat, buss; sailer, sailing vessel; windjammer; steamer, steamboat, steamship; mail–, paddle–, turbine–, screw- steamer; tug; line of steamers etc.

boat, pinnace, launch; lifeboat, long-boat, jollyboat, bumboat, flyboat, cockboat, ferry-boat, canal boat; ark, bully [*N fld.*], bateau [*Can.*], broadhorn, dory, drogher, dugout, Durham boat, galiot *or* galliot, flatboat, shallop, gig, funny [*Eng.*], skiff, dinghy *or* dingey *or* dingy, scow, cockleshell, wherry, coble, punt, cog, lerret [*dial. Eng.*]; eight–, four–, pair- oar; randan; outrigger; float, raft, pontoon; ice-boat, ice-canoe, ice-yacht.

catamaran, coracle, gondola, caravel *or* carvel, felucca, caique, canoe; galley, bilander, dogger, hooker *or* howker [*obs.*]; argosy, carack *or* carrack [*hist.*], galleass *or* galliass, galleon; polacre *or* polacca, corsair, piragua, bunderboat [*India*], tartane, junk, lorcha, praam, proa *or* prahu, saic, sampan, xebec, dhow; dahabeah; nuggar; kayak, keel boat, canoe, pirogue; quadrireme, trireme; stern-wheeler; wanigan *or* wangan, wharf boat; derelict.

[aeronautics] balloon; airship, aeroplane, airplane, monoplane, biplane, triplane; avion [*F.*], aeronat, dirigible, zeppelin, zepp [*colloq.*]; air cruiser, battle–, bombing–, combatplane; two-seater, biplace [*F.*]; single-seater, monoplace [*F.*], aeroboat, aerobus, aero-hydroplane, aeroyacht, flying boat; aircraft; hydroplane, aerodrome [*obsoles.*], air–, pilot–, captive–, fire-balloon; aerostat, Montgolfier; kite, parachute.

[allied aeronautical terms] fuselage, gondola, wings, ailes [*F.*], controls, aileron, lifting power, camouflage, rudder; tail, empennage [*F.*]; cabane, hangar; aeronaut etc. 269a.

adj. **marine**, maritime, naval, nautical, seafaring, ocean-going; A1, A1 at Lloyd's; seaworthy.

aeronautic *or* aeronautical, aerial; airworthy; volant etc. 267.

adv. **afloat**, aboard; on board, on ship board; hard-a -lee, –port, –starboard, –weather.

274. Velocity

n. **velocity**, speed, celerity; swiftness etc. *adj.;* rapidity, eagle speed, lightning speed; expedition etc. (*activity*) 682; pernicity [*obs.*], acceleration; haste etc. 684.

spurt, sprint, rush, dash, race, steeple chase; automobile race; Marathon race *or* Marathon; smart–, lively–, swift etc. *adj.* –, rattling [*colloq.*] –, spanking [*slang*] –, strapping [*colloq.*]- -rate, –pace; round pace; flying, flight.

pace, gallop, canter, trot, round trot, run, scamper; hand–, full- gallop; swoop.

[comparisons] lightning, light, electricity, wind; cannon ball, rocket, arrow, dart, hydrargyrum, quicksilver, Mercury; wireless, telegraph, express train; swallow flight; torrent.

eagle, antelope, courser, race horse, barb, gazelle, greyhound, hare, doe, squirrel, camel bird, swallow, chickaree, chipmunk, hackee, ostrich.

scorcher [*slang*], joy rider, speedster, speed maniac.

Mercury, Ariel, Puck, Camilla, Harlequin.

[measurement of velocity] velocimeter, speedometer, patent log, log, log line.

v. **move quickly**, trip, fisk [*obs.*]; speed, hie, hasten, spurt, sprint, post, spank, scuttle; scud, scuddle [*obs. or Scot.*], scurry, whiz; thunder -by, –on; scour, scour the plain; scamper; run, run like mad [*colloq.*], fly, race, run a race, cut away, shoot, tear, whisk, sweep, skim, brush; skedaddle [*colloq.*], cut and run [*colloq.*], cut along [*colloq.*], bowl along; scorch [*colloq.*]; rush etc. (*be violent*) 173; dash on, dash off, dash forward; bolt; trot, gallop, bound, flit, spring, dart, boom; march in -quick, –double- time; ride hard, get over the ground; give her the gas, step on her tail, run wide open.

hurry etc. (*hasten*) 684; bundle, bundle along; bundle on; accelerate, put on; quicken; quicken–, mend -one's pace; clap spurs to one's horse; make haste, make rapid strides, make forced marches, wing one's way, set off at a score; carry sail, crowd sail; go off like a shot, go ahead, gain ground; outstrip the wind, fly on the wings of the wind.

keep up with, keep pace with.

outstrip etc. 303; outmarch.

adj. **fast**, speedy, swift, rapid, quick, fleet; nimble, agile, expeditious; express; active etc. 682; flying, galloping etc. *v.;* light-footed, nimble-footed; winged, eagle-winged, mercurial, electric, telegraphic; light-legged, light of heel;

275. Slowness

swift as an arrow etc. *n.;* quick as lightning etc. *n.;* quick as thought.

adv. **swiftly** etc. *adj.;* with speed etc.*n.;* apace; at a great rate, at full speed, at railway speed; full drive, full gallop; posthaste, in full sail, tantivy; like a shot [*colloq.*], like greased lightning [*colloq.*]; trippingly; instantaneously etc. 113.

under press of -sail, –canvas, –sail and steam; *velis et remis* [*L.*], on eagle's wing, in double-quick time; with rapid strides, with giant strides, *à pas de géant* [*F.*], in seven-league boots; whip and spur; *ventre à terre* [*F.*]; as fast as one's -legs, –heels- will carry one; as fast as one can lay feet to the ground, at the top of one's speed; by leaps and bounds; with haste etc. 684; in high (gear *or* speed).

275. Slowness

n. **slowness** etc. *adj.;* languor etc. (*inactivity*) 683; drawl; creeping etc. *v.,* lentor [*rare*].

jog-trot, dog-trot; amble, rack, pace, single-foot, walk; mincing steps; dead march, slow march, slow time.

retardation; slackening etc. *v.;* delay etc. (*lateness*) 133; claudication [*obs.*].

slow goer, slow coach [*colloq.*]; lingerer, loiterer, sluggard, tortoise, snail; slow poke [*slang*]; dawdle etc. (*inactive*) 683.

v. **move slowly** etc. *adv.;* creep, crawl, lag, slug [*dial.*], walk, drawl, linger, loiter, saunter; plod, trudge, stump along, lumber; trail, drag; dawdle etc. (*be inactive*) 683; grovel, worm one's way, inch, inch along, steal along; jog on, rub on, toddle, waddle, wabble *or* wobble, wamble, traipse [*dial. or colloq.*], slouch, shuffle, halt, hobble, limp, claudicate [*obs.*], shamble: flag, falter, totter, stagger; mince, step short; march in slow time, march in funeral procession; take one's time; hang fire etc. (*be late*) 133.

retard, relax, slacken, check, moderate, rein in, curb; reef; strike–, shorten–, take in- sail; put on the drag, brake, apply the brake; clip the wings; reduce the speed; slacken speed, slacken one's pace, backwater, back pedal, throttle down, lose ground.

adj. **slow**, slack; tardy; dilatory etc. (*inactive*) 683; gentle, easy; leisurely; deliberate, gradual; insensible, imperceptible; languid, sluggish, apathetic, phlegmatic, lymphatic; moderate, slowpaced, tardigrade [*rare*], snail-like; creeping etc. *v.;* reptatorial *or* reptatory.

dull, slow [*colloq.*], prosaic, unentertaining, boresome, wearisome, uninteresting etc. (*dull*) 843.

adv. **slowly** etc. *adj.;* leisurely; *piano* [*It.*], *adagio* [*It.*], *largo* [*It.*], *larghetto* [*It.*], at half speed, under easy sail; at a -foot's, –snail's, –funeral-pace; dead slow [*colloq.*]; slower than- death, –cold molasses [*colloq.*], –a funeral; in slow time; with mincing steps, with clipped wings; in low (gear *or* speed).

gradually etc. *adj.;* gradatim; by degrees, by slow degrees, by inches, by little and little; step by step; inch by inch, bit by bit, little by little, *seriatim* [*L.*], consecutively.

276. Impulse

n. **impulse**, impulsion, impetus; momentum; push, pulsion, thrust, shove, jog, jolt, brunt, boom, booming, boost, throw; explosion etc. (*violence*) 173; propulsion etc. 284.

clash, collision, occursion [*obs.*], encounter, appulsion, appulse, shock, crash, bump; impact; *élan* [*F.*]; charge etc. (*attack*) 716; percussion, concussion; beating etc. (*punishment*) 972.

blow, dint, stroke, knock, tap, rap, slap, smack, pat, dab; fillip; slam, bang, hit, whack, thwack; cuff etc. 972; squash, douse *or* dowse, whap [*dial.*], swap [*obs.*], punch, thump, pelt, kick, punce [*obs.*], calcitration; *ruade* [*F.*]; arietation [*obs.*]; cut, thrust, lunge, yerk [*obs.*]; carom *or* carrom, clip [*slang*], jab, plug [*slang*], sidewinder [*slang*], sidewipe [*slang*].

hammer, sledge hammer, mall, maul, mallet, flail; ram, rammer; ramrod; battering-ram, monkey, tamper, tamping iron, pile driver, pile-driving engine, punch, bat; cant hook; cudgel etc. (*weapon*) 727; ax etc. (*sharp*) 253.

[science of mechanical forces] mechanics, dynamics; kinematics, kinetics; dynamograph, dynamometer; seismometer.

v. **impel**, give an impetus etc. *n.;* push; start, give a start to, set going; drive, urge, boom; thrust, prod, foin [*archaic*]; cant; elbow, shoulder, jostle *or* justle, hustle, hurtle, shove, jog, jolt, encounter; run–, bump–, butt- against; knock–, run- one's head against; impinge; boost, bunt, carom *or* carrom, clip [*slang*]; fan, –out; jab, plug [*slang*].

strike, knock, hit, tap, rap, slap, flap, dab, pat, thump, beat, bang, slam, dash; punch, thwack, whack; hit–, strike- hard; swap [*obs.*], batter, douse *or* dowse [*obs.*], tamp, baste, paste [*slang*], pelt, patter, buffet, belabor; fetch one a blow; poke at, pink, lunge, yerk [*obs.*]; kick, calcitrate; butt, strike at etc. (*attack*) 716; whip etc. (*punish*) 972.

collide; come–, enter- into collision; foul; fall–, run- foul of; telescope, throw etc. (*propel*) 284.

adj. **impulsive**, impellent, propulsive, pulsive [*rare*], booming; dynamic, dynamical; kinetic, kinematic *or* kinematical; impelled etc. *v.;* impelling etc. *v.*

277. Recoil

n. **recoil**; reaction, retroaction; revulsion; rebound, ricochet, backlash, repercussion, recalcitration: kick, *contrecoup* [*F.*]; springing back etc. *v.;* elasticity etc. 325; reflexion, reflex, reflux; reverberation etc. (*resonance*) 408; rebuff, repulse; return.

ducks and drakes; boomerang; spring.

reactionary, reactionist, recalcitrant.

v. **recoil**, react; balk, jib; spring–, fly–, bound-back; rebound, reverberate, repercuss, recalcitrate; echo, ricochet.

adj. **recoiling** etc. *v.;* refluent, repercussive, recalcitrant, reactionary, revulsive, retroactive.

adv. on the recoil etc. *n.*

278. Direction

n. **direction**, bearing, course, set, trend, run, drift, tenor; tendency etc. 176; incidence; bending, trending etc. *v.;* dip, tack, aim, collimation; steering, steerage.

points of the compass, cardinal points; north, east, south, west; NNE, NE, ENE, E, etc.

rhumb, azimuth, line of collimation.

line, path, road, range, quarter, line of march; alignment; air line, bee line; straight shot.

v. **tend toward**, bend toward, point toward; conduct to, go to; point -to, -at; bend, trend, verge, incline, dip, determine.

steer for, steer towards, make for, make toward; aim at, level at; take aim; keep–, hold- a course; be bound for; bend one's steps toward; direct–, steer–, bend–, shape- one's course; align one's march; go straight, -to the point; make a bee line; march -on, -on a point.

ascertain one's direction etc. *n.; s'orienter* [*F.*], see which way the wind blows; box the compass; take the air line.

adj. **directed** etc. *v.,* - toward; pointing toward etc. *v.;* bound for; aligned with; direct, straight; undeviating, unswerving; straightforward; north, northern, northerly, etc. *n.*

directable, steerable, leadable, dirigible, guidable, aimable, determinable.

adv. **towards**; on the -road, -high road- to; *en avant* [*F.*]; *versus* [*L.*], to; hither, thither, whither; directly; straight, -forwards, -as an arrow; point-blank; in a -bee, -direct, -straight- line -to, -for, -with; in a line with; full tilt at, as the crow flies.

before–, near–, close to–, against-the wind; windward, in the wind's eye.

through, *via* [*L.*], by way of; in all -directions, -manner of ways; *quaqua-versum* [*L.*], from the four winds.

279. Deviation

n. **deviation**; swerving etc. *v.;* obliquation [*obs.*], warp, refraction; flection *or* flexion; sweep; deflection, deflexure; declination.

diversion, digression, departure from, aberration, drift, sheer, divergence etc. 291; zigzag; detour etc. (*circuit*) 629; divagation, disorientation, exorbitation [*rare*].

[desultory motion] wandering etc. *v.;* vagrancy, evagation [*obs.*]; bypaths and crooked ways; byroad.

[motion sideways, oblique motion] sidling etc. *v.;* jibe, tack, yaw [*all naut.*]; passage, right passage, left passage [*manège*]; echelon [*mil.*]; knight's move at chess.

v. **deviate**, alter one's course, depart from, turn, trend; bend, curve etc. 245; swerve, heel, bear off; jibe, break, yaw, wear, sheer, tack [*all naut.*].

deflect; intervert [*obs.*]; divert, divert from its course; put on a new scent; shift, shunt, switch, draw aside, crook, warp.

stray, straggle; sidle, edge; diverge etc. 291; tralineate [*obs.*], digress, wander; wind, twist, meander; veer, divagate; go astray, go adrift; lose one's way; ramble, rove, drift.

sidetrack; turn aside, turn a corner, turn away from; wheel, steer clear of; dodge; step aside, ease off, make way for, shy, jib.

glance off, fly off at a tangent; wheel about, face about; turn–, face-to the right-about; echelon [*mil.*]; waddle etc. (*oscillate*) 314; go out of one's way etc. (*perform a circuit*) 629.

adj. **deviating** etc. *v.;* aberrant, errant; excursive, discursive; devious, desultory, loose; rambling; stray, erratic, vagrant, undirected; circuitous, round-about, crooked, sidelong, indirect, zigzag; crab-like.

adv. **astray from**, round about, wide of the mark; to the right about; all manner of ways; circuitously etc. 629.

obliquely, sideling, sidelong, like the knight's move [*chess*].

280. Precession
[going before]

n. **precession**, leading, heading; precedence etc. 62; priority etc. 116; the lead, *le pas* [*F.*]; van etc. (*front*) 234; precursor etc. 64.

v. **precede**, go before, go ahead, go in the van, go in advance; forerun, forego [*archaic*]; usher in,

281. Sequence

introduce, herald, head, take the lead; lead, lead the way, lead the dance; get-, have- a start; steal a march; get before, get ahead, get in front of; outstrip etc. 303; take precedence etc. (*first in order*) 62.

adj. **leading**, precedent etc. *v.;* first, foremost.

adv. **in advance**, before, ahead, in the van; foremost, headmost; in front.

281. Sequence
[going after]

n. **sequence**; sequel; coming after etc. (*order*) 63, (*time*) 117; following; pursuit etc. 622; run [*cards*].

follower, attendant, satellite, pursuer, shadow, dangler, train.

v. **follow**; pursue etc. 622; go after, fly after.

attend, beset, dance attendance on, dog; tread in the steps of, tread close upon; be-, go-, follow- in the -wake, -trail, -rear- of; follow as a shadow, hang on the skirts of; tread-, follow- on the heels of; camp on the trail.

lag, loiter, linger, get behind.

adj. **following** etc. *v.*

adv. **behind**; in the rear etc. 235, in the train of, in the wake of; after etc. (*order*) 63, (*time*) 117.

282. Progression
[motion forward; progressive motion]

n. **progression**, progress, progressiveness; advancing etc. *v.;* advance, advancement; ongoing; flood tide, headway; march etc. 266; rise; improvement etc. 658.

v. **advance**; proceed, progress; get on, get along, get over the ground; gain ground; forge ahead; jog on, rub on, wag on [*obs.*], go with the stream; keep-, hold on- one's course; go-, move-, come-, get-, pass-, push-, press- -on, -forward, -forwards, -ahead; press onward *or* onwards, step forward; make-, work-, carve-, push-, force-, edge-, elbow- one's way; make -progress, -head, -way, -headway, -advances, -strides, -rapid strides etc. (*velocity*) 274; go ahead, shoot ahead; drive -on, -ahead; go full steam ahead; distance; make up leeway.

adj. **advancing** etc. *v.;* ongoing; progressive, profluent; advanced.

adv. **forward**, onward; forth, on, ahead, under way, *en route* for, on -one's way, -the way, -the road, -the high road- to; in progress, in mid-progress; *in transitu* [*L.*] etc. 270.

283. Regression
[motion backward]

n. **regression**, regress, retrocession, retrogression, retrogradation, retroaction; *reculade* [*F.*], retreat, withdrawal, retirement, remigration; recession etc. (*motion from*) 287; recess [*obs.*]; crab-like motion.

reflux, refluence, backwater, regurgitation, ebb, return; resilience, resiliency; reflexion (*recoil*) 277; *volte-face* [*F.*].

countermotion, countermovement, countermarch; veering, tergiversation, recidivation [*obs. exc. in criminology*], backsliding, fall; deterioration etc. 659; recidivism *or* recidivity, relapse.

turning point etc. (*reversion*) 145; climax.

v. **recede**, regrade, return, revert, retreat, remigrate, retire; retrograde, retrocede; back, back out [*colloq.*], back down [*colloq.*], balk; crawfish [*slang*], crawl [*slang*]; withdraw; rebound etc. 277; go-, come-, turn-, hark-, draw-, fall-, break-, get-, put-, run- back; lose ground; fall astern, drop astern; backwater, put about [*naut.*], take the back track; veer, veer round; double, wheel, countermarch; ebb, regurgitate; jib, shrink, shy.

turn tail, turn round, turn upon one's heel, turn one's back upon; retrace one's steps, dance the back step; sound-, beat- a retreat; go home.

adj. **receding** etc. *v.;* retrograde, retrogressive; regressive, refluent, reflex, recidivous, resilient; crab-like; contraclockwise, counterclockwise; balky; reactionary etc. 277.

adv. **back**, backward; reflexively, to the right-about; *à reculons* [*F.*], *à rebours* [*F.*].

284. Propulsion
[motion given to an object situated in front]

n. **propulsion**, projection; propelment; *vis a tergo* [*L.*], push etc. (*impulse*) 276; jaculation, ejaculation; ejection etc. 297; throw, fling, toss, shot, discharge, shy.

[science of propulsion] gunnery, ballistics, archery.

propeller, screw, twin-screws, turbine.

missile, projectile, ball, shot; spear, arrow; gun etc. (*arms*) 727; discus, quoit; brickbat.

shooter, shot; archer, toxophilite; bowman, rifleman, marksman, gun [*cant*], gunner, good shot, dead shot, crack shot; sharpshooter etc. (*combatant*) 726.

v. **propel**, project, throw, fling, cast, pitch, chuck, toss, jerk, heave, shy, hurl; flirt, fillip.
dart, lance, tilt; ejaculate, jaculate [*rare*], fulminate, bolt, drive, sling, pitchfork.
send; send off, let off, fire off; discharge, shoot; launch, send forth, let fly; dash.
start; put–, set- in motion; set agoing, give a start to, give an impulse to; bundle, bundle off; impel etc. 276; trundle etc. (*set in rotation*) 312; expel etc. 297.
carry one off one's legs; put to flight.
adj. propelled etc. *v.*; propelling etc. *v.*; propulsive, projectile, ballistic.

285. Traction
[motion given to an object situated behind]

n. **traction**; drawing etc. *v.*; draft *or* draught, pull, haul; rake; "a long pull, a strong pull, and a pull all together"; towage, haulage.
v. **draw**, pull, haul, lug, rake, snake [*slang*], trawl, draggle, drag, tug, tow, trail, train; take in tow.
wrench, jerk, twitch; yank [*U.S.*].
adj. **drawing** etc. *v.*; tractile, tractive, tractional, ductile.

286. Approach
[motion toward]

n. **approach**, approximation, approximateness, appropinquation; access; appulse, appulsion; afflux, affluxion; advent etc. (*approach of time*) 121; pursuit etc. 622.
v. **approach**, approximate [*archaic*], appropinquate [*rare*]; near; get–, go–, draw- near; come, –near, –to close quarters; move towards, set in towards; drift; make up to [*dial. or slang*]; gain upon; pursue etc. 622; tread on the heels of; bear up; make land; hug the shore, hug the land.
adj. **approaching** etc. *v.*; approximate, approximative; affluent; converging, connivent, convergent; impending, imminent etc. (*destined*) 152.
adv. on the road.
int. **approach**! come hither! here! come! come near! forward!

287. Recession
[motion from]

n. **recession**, retirement, withdrawal; retreat; regression, regress, retrogradation, retrocession etc. 283; departure, etc. 293; recoil etc. 277; flight etc. (*avoidance*) 623.

switch, by-pass, shunt.
v. **recede**, go, move back, move from, retire, withdraw, retrograde, retrogress, regress, ebb; shrink; come–, move–, go–, get–, drift- away; depart etc. 293; retreat etc. 283; move off, stand off, sheer off, swerve from; fall back, stand aside; run away etc. (*avoid*) 623.
switch, shunt, sidetrack, turn, remove.
adj. **receding** etc. *v.*; recessive, retrogressive, regressive.

288. Attraction
[motion toward, actively]

n. **attraction**, attractiveness; attractivity; pull, drawing to, pulling towards, attrahent, adduction, magnetism, gravity, attraction of gravitation.
loadstone *or* lodestone, lodestar *or* loadstar, polestar, lode [*archaic*]; magnet, magnetite, siderite.
lure, bait, charm, decoy.
v. **attract**, adduct; draw–, pull–, drag- towards; pull, draw, magnetize, bait, trap, decoy, charm; adduce.
adj. **attracting** etc. *v.*; attrahent, attractive, adducent, adductive.

289. Repulsion
[motion from, actively]

n. **repulsion**; driving from etc. *v.*; repulse, abduction, retrusion [*rare*].
v. **repel**; push from, drive from etc. 276; chase, dispel; retrude [*rare*]; abduce [*obs.*], abduct; send away; repulse; repercuss.
keep at arm's length, turn one's back upon, give the cold shoulder; send -off, –away- with a flea in one's ear [*colloq.*]; send about one's business; send packing.
adj. **repellent**, repulsive; repelling etc. *v.*; abducent, abductive, repercussive.

290. Convergence
[motion nearer to]

n. **convergence** *or* convergency, confluence, concourse, conflux, congress, concurrence, concentration; appulse, meeting; corradiation [*rare*].
assemblage etc. 72; resort etc. (*focus*) 74; asymptote.
v. **converge**, concur; come together, unite, meet, fall in with; close with, close in upon; center *or* centre, center round, center in; enter in; pour in.

291. Divergence

        concentrate, bring into a focus; gather together, unite.

adj. **converging** etc. *v.;* convergent, confluent, concurrent; centripetal; asymptotic *or* asymptotical; confluxible [*rare*].

291. Divergence
[motion further off]

n. **divergence** *or* divergency, divarication, ramification, forking; radiation; separation etc. (*disjunction*) 44; dispersion etc. 73; deviation etc. 279; aberration, declination.

v. **diverge**, divaricate, radiate; ramify; branch off, glance off, file off; fly off, fly off at a tangent; spread, scatter, disperse etc. 73; deviate etc. 279; part etc. (*separate*) 44.

adj. **diverging** etc. *v.;* divergent, divaricate, radiant, radial, centrifugal; aberrant; broadcast.

adv. broadcast; *passim* [*L.*].

292. Arrival
[terminal motion at]

n. **arrival**, advent; landing; debarkation, disembarkation.

        reception, welcome; *vin d'honneur* [*F.*].

        destination, bourn *or* bourne, goal; landing -place, -stage; bunder *or* bandar [*Pers. & India*]; resting place; harbor, haven, port; terminus, terminal; halting -place, -ground; home, journey's end; anchorage etc. (*refuge*) 666; completion etc. 729.

        return, recursion [*obs.*], remigration, reëntry.

        meeting, joining, recounter, encounter, rejoining.

v. **arrive**; get to, come to; come; reach, attain; come up, -with, -to; overtake; make; fetch; come from, hail from; complete etc. 729; join, rejoin.

        visit, pitch one's tent; sit down etc. (*be located*) 184; get to one's journey's end; be in at the death; come-, get- -back, -home; return; come in etc. (*ingress*) 294; make one's appearance etc. (*appear*) 446; drop in; detrain; out-span, offsaddle [*both S. Africa*].

        light, alight, dismount.

        land, make land, cast anchor, put in, put into; go ashore, debark, disbark [*rare*], disembark

        meet; encounter, rencounter [*rare*], come in contact; come to hand; come at, come across; hit; come-, light-, pop [*colloq.*] -, bounce [*colloq.*] -, plump [*colloq.*]-, burst-, pitch- upon.

adj. **arriving** etc. *v.;* homeward bound, terminal.

adv. **here**, hither.

int. **welcome**! hail! all hail! good-day! good-morrow! come in and rest your bonnet on a chair! [*Southern U. S.*], bienvenu! [*F.*].

293. Departure
[initial motion from]

n. **departure**, decession [*rare*], decampment; embarkation; outset, start, headway, inspan [*S. Africa*], debouchment, debouch *or* débouché [*F.*]; removal; exit etc. (*egress*) 295; congé [*F.*], exodus, hegira, flight.

        leave-taking, valediction, adieu, farewell, good-by *or* good-bye, Godspeed, stirrup cup; valedictorian.

        starting point, starting post; point-, place- of -departure, -embarkation; port of embarkation.

v. **depart**; go, go away, part [*archaic*], take one's departure, set out; set-, march-, put-, start-, be-, move-, get-, whip-, pack-, go-, take oneself-off; start, boun [*archaic*], issue, march out, debouch; go forth, sally forth; sally, set forward; be gone.

        leave a place, quit, vacate, evacuate, abandon; go off the stage, make one's exit; retire, withdraw, remove; "use your legs" [*Merchant of Venice*]; vamose *or* vamoose [*slang, U. S.*], mizzle [*slang*], skip [*slang*], cut [*colloq. or slang*], go one's way, go along, go from home; take flight, take wing; spring, fly, flit, wing one's flight; fly away, whip away; strike tents, decamp; break camp, break away, break ground, walk one's chalks [*slang*], cut one's stick *or* cut stick [*slang*], cut and run [*colloq.*]; take leave; say-, bid- good-by etc. *n.;* disappear etc. 449; abscond etc. (*avoid*) 623; entrain; saddle, bridle, harness up, hitch up [*colloq.*], inspan [*S. Africa*]; "speed the parting guest" [*Pope*].

        embark; go on board, go aboard; set sail; put to sea, go to sea; sail, take ship; hoist the blue Peter; get under way, weigh anchor.

adj. **departing** etc. *v.;* valedictory; outward bound.

adv. **hence**, whence, thence; with a foot in the stirrup; on the wing, on the move.

int. **begone**! etc. (*ejection*) 297; cut! cut away! cut off! [*all colloq.*], away! to horse! boot! saddle! all aboard! busk and boun ye! [*archaic*].

        farewell! adieu! good-by *or* goodbye! good-day! *au revoir!* [*F.*], *vale!* [*L.*], fare you well! God bless you! Godspeed! *auf Wiedersehen!* [*G.*], *au plaisir de vous revoir!* [*F.*], *bon voyage!* [*F.*], *glückliche Reise!* [*G.*], *vive valeque!* [*L.*], bye-bye! [*colloq.*], be good! [*slang*], so long! [*slang*], come again!

294. Ingress
[motion into]

n. **ingress**; entrance, entry; introgression, ingressiveness, influx, intrusion, inroad, incursion, invasion, irruption; ingression; penetration, interpenetration; illapse [*rare*], infiltration; insinuation etc. (*interjacence*) 228; insertion etc. 300.

immigration, incoming, foreign influx; admission etc. (*reception*) 296.

import, importation; imports.

immigrant, visitor, incomer, newcomer, comeling [*archaic*], colonist, Buttinsky [*humorous*].

inlet; way in; mouth, door, etc. (*opening*) 260; barway; path etc. (*way*) 627; conduit etc. 350.

v. **enter**; go–, come–, pour–, flow–, creep–, slip–, pop–, break–, burst- -into, -in; have the entrée; set foot on; ingress [*obs.*]; burst–, break-in upon; invade, insinuate itself; interpenetrate, penetrate; infiltrate; find one's way–, wriggle–, worm oneself- into; intrude, butt in [*slang*] horn in [*slang, U. S.*].

give entrance to etc. (*receive*) 296, insert etc. 300

adj. **incoming**, inbound, ingressive, inward, entrant [*rare*]; entering etc. *v.*

295. Egress
[motion out of]

n. **egress**, exit, issue; emersion, emergence; outbreak, outburst, proruption [*rare*], eruption; emanation; egression; evacuation, disemboguement, exudation, transudation; extravasation, perspiration, sweating, leakage, percolation, lixiviation, leaching, distillation, seep, oozing; gush etc. (*water in motion*) 348; outpour, outpouring; effluence, effusion; efflux, effluxion; drain; dribbling etc. *v.;* defluxion; drainage; outcome, output; outflow, discharge etc. (*excretion*) 299.

export, exportation; exports, shipments.

emigration, exodus etc. (*departure*) 293; expatriation, remigration.

emigrant, migrant, redemptioner, colonist, émigré [*F.*].

outlet, vent, spout, tap, sluice, flood-gate; vomitory, outgate, sallyport; debouch [*mil.*], débouché [*F.*]; way out; mouth, door etc. (*opening*) 260; path etc. (*way*) 627; conduit etc. 350; airpipe etc. 351; pore, emunctory.

v. **emerge**, emanate, issue; egress; go–, come–, move–, pass–, pour–, flow- out of; pass off, evacuate.

exude, transude; leak; run, –out, –through; lixiviate, leach, percolate, transcolate [*obs.*]; egurgitate [*rare*]; strain, distill; perspire, sweat, drain, seep, ooze; filter, infiltrate, filtrate; dribble, gush, spout, flow out; well, –out; pour, trickle, etc. (*water in motion*) 348; effuse, extravasate, disembogue, discharge itself, debouch; come–, break forth; burst -out, –through; find vent; escape etc. 671.

adj. **emergent**, emerging, erumpent, eruptive, emanant, emanational, emanative, exudative, porous, pervious, leaky, sweaty, transudatory; effused etc. *v.;* outgoing, outbound, outwardbound.

percolative, oozing, gushing, transuding etc. *v.;* effluent, emunctory, effusive, excretory.

296. Reception
[motion into, actively]

n. **reception**; admission, admittance, entrée, importation; initiation, introduction, intromission; immission, ingestion, imbibition, introception, absorption, resorbence, engorgement, ingurgitation, inhalation; suction, sucking; eating, drinking etc. (*food*) 298; insertion etc. 300; interjection etc. 228; introit.

v. **give entrance to**, give admittance to, give the entrée; introduce, usher, admit, initiate, intromit [*rare*], receive, import, bring in, immit [*rare*], open the door to, throw open, ingest, absorb, imbibe, instill, implant, infiltrate, induct, inhale; let in, take in, suck in; readmit, resorb, reabsorb; snuff up.

swallow, ingurgitate; engulf, engorge; gulp; eat, drink etc. (*food*) 298.

adj. **introductory**, introductive, initiatory, initiary [*rare*], preliminary, ingestive; imbibitory, introceptive, intromittent, intromissive; admissible; absorbent, resorbent; admitting etc. *v.*, admitted etc. *v.*

297. Ejection
[motion out of, actively]

n. **ejection**, emission, effusion, rejection, expulsion, eviction, extrusion, detrusion, trajection; discharge.

egestion, evacuation, vomition; emesis, eruption, eruptiveness, eruptivity, voidance, disgorgement; ructation, eructation; bloodletting, venesection, phlebotomy, extravasation, paracentesis; expuition [*rare*], exspuition [*rare*]; tapping, drainage; emetic; vomiting; excretion etc. 299; clearance, clearage.

dislodgment; deportation; banishment etc. (*punishment*) 972; rogue's march; relegation; extradition.

298. Food

ejector, bouncer [*slang, U. S.*], chucker-out [*slang*].

v. **eject**, reject; expel, discard; cut [*colloq.*], ostracize, send to Coventry, boycott; *chasser* [*F.*]; banish etc. (*punish*) 972; bounce [*slang*]; fire [*slang*]; throw etc. (284) -out, -up, -off, -away, -aside; push etc. (276) -out, -off, -away, -aside; shovel-, sweep- -out, -away; brush-, whisk-, turn-, send- -off, -away; discharge; send-, turn-, cast- adrift; turn out, bundle out; throw overboard; give the sack to [*slang*]; send packing, send about one's business, send to the right-about; strike off the roll etc. (*abrogate*) 756; turn out -neck and heels [*colloq.*], -head and shoulders, -neck and crop [*colloq.*]; pack off; send away with a flea in the ear [*colloq.*]; send to Jericho [*colloq.*]; bow out, show the door to.

evict, oust, dislodge; turn out of -doors, -house and home; unhouse, unkennel; unpeople, dispeople; depopulate; relegate, deport.

let out, give out, pour out, send out; dispatch *or* despatch, exhale, excern [*obs.*], excrete; embogue [*obs.*], disembogue; extravasate, shed, void, egest, evacuate; emit; open the -sluices, -floodgates; turn on the tap; give exit to, give vent to; extrude, detrude; effuse, spend, expend; pour forth; squirt, spurt *or* spirt, spill, slop; perspire etc. (*exude*) 295; breathe, blow etc. (*wind*) 349.

tap, draw off; bale out, lade out; let blood, broach.

empty; drain, -to the dregs; sweep off; clear, -off, -out, -away; suck, draw off; clean out, make a clean sweep of, clear decks, purge.

disembowel, embowel [*rare*], disbowel [*rare*], eviscerate, gut.

root out, root up, unearth; eradicate, averruncate [*obs.*]; weed out, get out; eliminate, get rid of, do away with, shake off; exenterate [*rare*].

vomit, spew, puke]*vulgar*], keck, retch, upchuck [*colloq.*]; cast up, bring up; disgorge.

salivate, ptyalize, expectorate, clear the throat, hawk, spit, sputter, splutter, slobber, drivel, slaver, slabber, drool.

belch, eruct, eructate.

unpack, unlade, unload, unship; break bulk; dump.

emerge, ooze etc. 295; be let out.

adj. **ejective**, emissive, extrusive; egestive; salivant; vomitive, vomitory; emitting, emitted etc. *v.*

int. **begone**! get you gone! get-, go- -away, -along, -along with you! go your way! away, -with! off with you! go! go about your business! be off! avaunt! aroint *or* aroynt! [*archaic*], allez-vous-en! [*F.*], jao! [*Hind.*], va-t'en! [*F.*], scoot! [*colloq.*], shoo! "get thee behind me, Satan!" [*Bible*].

298. Food
[eating]

n. **eating** etc. *v.;* deglutition, gulp, epulation [*rare*], mastication, manducation [*rare*], rumination; gastronomy, gastrology, pantophagy, hippophagy, carnivorism, carnivorousness, herbivority [*rare*], vegetarianism, ichthyophagy; gluttony etc. 957.

carnivore; herbivore, vegetarian.

mouth, jaws, gob [*slang*], mandible, mazard, chaps, chops.

drinking etc. *v.;* potation, draft *or* draught, libation; compotation, symposium; carousal etc. (*amusement*) 840; drunkenness etc. 959.

food, pabulum; aliment, nourishment, nutriment; sustenance, sustentation; nurture, subsistence, provender, corn, feed, fodder, provision, ration, keep, commons, board; commissariat etc. (*provisions*) 637; prey, forage, pasture, pasturage; fare, cheer; diet, dietary; regimen; belly timber [*facetious, dial.*], staff of life; bread, -and cheese; liquid diet, spoon victuals.

eatables, comestibles, victuals, edibles, ingesta; grub [*slang*], prog [*slang*], meat; bread, breadstuffs; cereals, viands, cates [*obs.*], delicacy, dainty, creature comforts, creature, contents of the larder, fleshpots; festal board; ambrosia; good cheer, good living.

[breadstuffs and desserts] biscuit, cracker, bun, cooky *or* cookie, doughnut, cruller, hard-tack, pilot bread, sea biscuit, pilot biscuit, ship biscuit, hoecake, ashcake, corncake, corndodgers, corndabs, shortbread, scone, rusk, matzo [*Jewish*], chupatty [*India*], damper [*Australia*], flapjack, waffle, pancake, griddlecake, pastry, *pâtisserie* [*F.*], pie, *pâté* [*F.*], pasty, patty, turnover, *vol-au-vent* [*F.*], apple dumpling, apple slump, apple dowdy, pandowdy, mince pie, pudding, supawn, apple pie, blueberry pie, custard pie, lemon pie, pumpkin pie, squash pie, charlotte russe, plum pudding, tart, compote, apple fritters, *beignets de pommes* [*F.*], banana fritters, macaroon, meringue, marchpane *or* marzipan, *massepain* [*F.*], whipped cream, *crème fouettée* [*F.*], cake, *gâteau* [*F.*], stewed prunes, *pruneaux* [*F.*], stewed apples, *compote de pommes* [*F.*], blancmange, cornstarch, jam, *confiture* [*F.*], Bar-le-Duc, red currant jelly, *gelée de groseilles* [*F.*], ice cream,

298. Food

crème glacée [*F.*], ice, sundae; vanilla–, strawberry–, chocolate–, coffee–, Neapolitan–, country club-ice cream; banana royal, water ice, sherbet; sweets etc. 396; see **fruit**.

[cereals] hominy, oatmeal, mush, hasty pudding, porridge, gruel, crowdie *or* crowdy [*Scot. & dial. Eng.*], *atole* [*Mex. Sp.*], samp, hulled corn, frumenty.

[soups] *potage* [*F.*], pottage, broth, *bouillon* [*F.*], gravy soup, *consommé* [*F.*], thick soup, *purée* [*F.*], bisque, mulligatawny, turtle soup, mock-turtle soup, oyster stew, oyster chowder, clam chowder, fish chowder, *julienne* [*F.*], *potage à la julienne* [*F.*], vermicelli soup, *potage au vermicelle* [*F.*], chowder, spoon-meat, trepang, ox-tail soup, gumbo, okra soup, stock, *bouillabaisse* [*F.*].

[fish] *poisson* [*F.*], salmon, *saumon* [*F.*], sole, fried sole, *sole frite* [*F.*], shad, plaice, bluefish, whiting, *merlan* [*F.*], trout, *truite* [*F.*], mackerel, *maquereau* [*F.*], herring, *hareng* [*F.*], bloater, kipper, kippered herring, cod, *morue* [*F.*], sturgeon ("Albany beef"), sardines, haddock, *aiglefin* [*F.*], finnan haddie *or* haddock, scrod, sturgeon roe, caviar *or* caviare, shad roe, tarpon, tuna, lobster, *homard* [*F.*], lobster à la King, lobster Newburg, periwinkles, prawns, shrimps, *crevettes* [*F.*], oysters, *huitres* [*F.*], oyster stew, blue points, sea slug, *bêche de mer* [*F.*], clams, eel, *anguille* [*F.*], crab, crab meat, soft-shell crab, crawfish *or* crayfish, *écrevisse* [*F.*].

[meats] *rôti* [*F.*], joint, *pièce de résistance* [*F.*], *relevé* [*F.*], hash, *réchauffé* [*F.*], stew, ragout, fricassee, mince, chow mein, chop suey, salmis, fatling, barbecue, kickshaws, mincemeat, forcemeat, meat balls, croquettes, goulash *or* Hungarian goulash; condiment etc. 393; haggis [*Scot.*], bubble and squeak, pilau *or* pilaw [*India*], curry, aspic jelly; turtle, terrapin, diamond-back terrapin.

beef, *boeuf* [*F.*], porterhouse steak, boiled beef, bouilli, beef à la mode, beefsteak, roast beef, *rosbif* [*F.*], *bifteck* [*F.*], sirloin, rump, chuck.

veal, *veau* [*F.*], fricandeau, calf's head, *tête de veau* [*F.*], tongue, *langue* [*F.*], fried brains, *cervelle frite* [*F.*], sweetbread, *ris de veau* [*F.*], calf's liver, *foie de veau* [*F.*].

mutton, *mouton* [*F.*], mutton chop, *côtelette de mouton* [*F.*], plain chop, *côtelette au naturel* [*F.*], *côtelette à la maître d'hôtel* [*F.*], *côtellette à la jardinière* [*F.*], broiled kidneys, *rognons à la brochette* [*F.*], lamb, *agneau* [*F.*], saddle, *selle* [*F.*]

pork, *porc* [*F.*], pork chop, *côtelette de porc frais* [*F.*], sausage, *saucisson* [*F.*], frankfurter, hot dog [*slang, U. S.*], bacon, ham, *jambon* [*F.*], sucking pig, *cochon de lait* [*F.*], pig's knuckles, pig's feet, trotters, *pieds de cochon* [*F.*], crackling.

poultry, *volaille* [*F.*], capon, *chapon* [*F.*], *poularde* [*F.*], pigeon, fowl, broiler, chicken, *poulet* [*F.*], duck, *canard* [*F.*], muscovy duck, roast duck, *canard rôti* [*F.*], goose, *oie* [*F.*], turkey, *dinde (masc. dindon)* [*F.*], wing, *aile* [*F.*], leg, *cuisse* [*F.*], breast, *filet (of a goose)* [*F.*], *blanc (of a fowl)* [*F.*], drumstick.

game, venison, *chevreuil* [*F.*], hare, *lièvre* [*F.*], jugged hare, *civet* [*F.*], rabbit, *lapin* [*F.*], pheasant, *faisan* [*F.*], partridge, *perdrix* [*F.*], snipe, *bécasse* [*F.*], quail, *caille* [*F.*], wild duck, *canard sauvage* [*F.*], canvasback, teal, *sarcelle* [*F.*], grouse, ricebird [*Southern U. S.*], pigeon, squab.

[eggs] *oeufs* [*F.*], boiled eggs, *oeufs à la coque* [*F.*], fried eggs, *oeufs sur le plat* [*F.*], poached eggs, *oeufs pochés* [*F.*], scrambled eggs, *oeufs brouillés* [*F.*], new-laid eggs, *oeufs frais* [*F.*], buttered eggs, dropped eggs, shirred eggs, stuffed eggs, omelet, *omelette* [*F.*], soufflé *or* soufflée [*F.*].

[cheese dishes] cheese, *fromage* [*F.*], cheesecake, *talmouse* [*F.*], cheese-mold, *moule à fromage* [*F.*], Welsh rabbit *or* Welsh rarebit [*an erroneous form*], *rôtie au fromage* [*F.*], golden buck, cheese straws, cheese fondue; cream–, cottage–, Neuchatel–, Swiss (*Schweizerkäse or Schweitzerkäse or Schweitzer*) –, Gruyère –, Emmenthaler–, Dutch–, Edam–, Roquefort–, Brie–, Limburg *or* Limburger–, Wensleydale-cheese.

[vegetables] *légumes* [*F.*], greens, asparagus, *asperge* [*F.*], green peas, *petits pois* [*F.*], artichoke, *artichaut* [*F.*], cabbage, *chou* [*F.*], coleslaw, Brussels sprouts, *choux de Bruxelles* [*F.*], cauliflower, *chou-fleur (pl. choux-fleurs)* [*F.*], lettuce, *laitue* [*F.*], romaine, cos lettuce, *laitue romaine* [*F.*], lima beans, string beans, French beans, *haricots verts* [*F.*], kidney beans, *haricots blancs* [*F.*], baked beans, potatoes, *pommes de terre* [*F.*], yams, sweet potatoes, *patates* [*F.*], spinach, *épinards* [*F.*], endive, *chicorée* [*F.*], pumpkin, squash, sauerkraut, *choucroute* [*F.*], eggplant, oyster plant, salsify, *salsifis* [*F.*], tomato, *tomate* [*F.*], celery, *céleri* [*F.*], cress, *cresson* [*F.*], watercress, *cresson de fontaine* [*F.*], beets, beetroot [*Brit.*], *betterave* [*F.*], parsnips, *panais* [*F.*], turnip, *navet*

299. Excretion

[F.], radish, *radis* or *rave* [F.], horse radish, *raifort* [F.], onion, *oignon* [F.], scallion, shalot, *échalote* [F.], cucumber, *concombre* [F.], mushrooms, *champignons* [F.], rhubarb, truffles, succotash.

[fruit] figs, *figues* [F.], raisins, nuts, *noisettes* [F.], almonds: *les quatres mendiants* [F.]; apple, *pomme* [F.], pear, *poire* [F.], alligator pear, avocado, apricot, *abricot* [F.], peach, *pêche* [F.], plantain, banana, breadfruit, grapefruit, mango, mangosteen, grapes, pineapple, *ananas* [F.], walnuts, *noix* [F.], orange, lemon, lime, cherries, *cerises* [F.], watermelon, currants, cranberry, loganberry, blueberry, blackberry, gooseberry, whortleberry, huckleberry, raspberry, strawberry.

table, *cuisine*, bill of fare, menu, *table d'hôte* [F.], ordinary, *à la carte* [F.], cover, *couvert* [F.]; American plan, European plan.

meal, repast, feed [*archaic or colloq.*], spread [*colloq.*]; mess; dish, plate, course; side dish, *hors-d'oeuvre* [F.], entrée, *entremets* [F.], remove, dessert [*in U. S., often includes pastry or pudding*]; regale; regalement, refreshment, entertainment; refection, collation, picnic, feast, banquet, junket; breakfast, lunch, luncheon; *déjeuner* [F.], *déjeuner à la fourchette* [F.]; bever [*dial.*], tiffin, dinner, supper, snack [*colloq.*], whet, bait [*dial.*]; potluck; hearty–, square–, substantial–, full– meal; blowout [*slang*]; light refreshment; *chota hazri, bara hazri, bara khana* [*all Hind.*].

mouthful, bolus, gobbet [*archaic*], tidbit, kickshaw, morsel, sop, sippet.

drink, beverage, liquor, broth, soup; potion, dram, draft *or* draught, drench, swill [*slang*]; nip, sip, sup, gulp.

[beverages] wine, spirits, liqueur, beer, ale, malt liquor, (Sir) John Barleycorn, stingo [*old slang*]; heavy wet [*slang, Eng.*]; grog, toddy, flip, purl, punch, negus, cup, bishop, wassail; hooch [*slang*], whisky *or* whiskey, the creature [*humorous*]; gin etc. (*intoxicating liquor*) 959; coffee, chocolate, cocoa, tea, "the cup that cheers but not inebriates"; bock–, lager–, Pilsener–, schenk–, near– beer; Brazil tea, cider, claret, ice water, maté, mint julep.

restaurant, eating house etc. 189.

v. **eat**, feed, fare, devour, swallow, take; gulp, bolt, snap; fall to; dispatch *or* despatch, discuss [*colloq.*]; take–, get–, gulp– down; lay in, lick, pick, peck; tuck in [*slang*], gormandize etc. 957; bite, champ, munch, craunch *or* cranch, crunch, chew, masticate, nibble, gnaw, mumble.

live on; feed–, batten–, fatten–, feast– upon; browse, graze, crop, regale; carouse etc. (*make merry*) 840; lick one's chops [*colloq.*], make one's mouth water; eat heartily, do justice to, play a good knife and fork [*dial. Eng.*], banquet.

break bread, break one's fast; breakfast, lunch, dine, take tea, sup.

drink, –in, –up, –one's fill; quaff, sip, sup; suck, –up; lap; swig [*dial. or colloq.*], swill [*slang*], tipple etc. (*be drunken*) 959; empty one's glass, drain the cup; toss off, toss one's glass; wash down, crack a bottle [colloq.], wet one's whistle [*colloq.*].

cater, purvey etc. 637.

adj. **eatable**, edible, esculent, comestible, gustable, alimentary; cereal, cibarious [*rare*]; dietetic; culinary; nutritive, nutritious; gastric; succulent.

underdone, rare, *saignant* [F.]; well-done, *bien cuit* [F.]; overdone; with gravy, *au jus* [F.]; high [*of game*]; ripe [*of cheese*].

drinkable, potable, potulent [*obs.*]; bibulous.

omnivorous, carnivorous, herbivorous, granivorous, graminivorous, phytivorous, phytophagous, ichthyophagous; omophagic, omophagous; pantophagous, xylophagous.

299. Excretion

n. **excretion**, discharge, emanation, ejection; exhalation, exudation, extrusion, secretion, effusion, extravasation, ecchymosis, evacuation, dejection, feces, defecation, cacation, excrement; bloody flux; celiac *or* coeliac, flux; dysentery; perspiration, sweat; subation [*obs.*], exudation; diaphoresis; sewage; eccrinology.

hemorrhage, bleeding; outpouring etc. (*egress*) 295; menses, menstrual discharge, menstrual flow, catamenial discharge; leucorrhea *or* leucorrhoea, the whites.

ejecta (*pl.*), saliva, spittle, sputum (*pl.* sputa); spit, rheum; ptyalism, salivation, catarrh; diarrhea *or* diarrhoea, egesta (*pl.*), excreta; lava; exuviae etc. (*uncleanness*) 653.

v. **excrete** etc. (*eject*) 297; secrete, secern; emanate etc. (*come out*) 295.

adj. **excretory**, fecal, feculent, secretory.

ejective, eliminative, eliminant.

300. Insertion

[forcible ingress]

n. **insertion**, infixion, implantation, introduction; embolism, interpolation, intercalation, interlineation, insinuation etc. (*intervention*) 228; planting etc. *v.*; injection, inoculation, importation, infusion; forcible ingress etc. 294; immersion; submersion, submergence, dip, plunge; bath etc. (*water*) 337; interment etc. 363.

enema, clyster, glyster, lavage, lavement.

v. **insert**, introduce, intromit, put into, run into; import; inject; imbed, inlay, inweave; interject etc. 228; infuse, instill *or* instil, inoculate, impregnate, imbue, imbrue.

insert etc. itself; plunge *in medias res* [*L.*].

graft, ingraft, engraft, bud, plant, implant; dovetail.

obtrude; thrust in, stick in, ram in, stuff in, tuck in, press in, drive in, pop in, whip in, drop in, put in: impact; pierce etc. (*make a hole*) 260.

immerse, immerge, merge; bathe, soak etc. (*water*) 337; dip, plunge etc. 310.

bury etc. (*inter*) 363.

adj. **inserted** etc. *v.*

301. Extraction
[forcible egress]

n. **extraction**; extracting etc. *v.;* removal, elimination, extrication, eradication, evulsion, extirpation, extermination; ejection etc. 297; export etc. (*egress*) 295; avulsion, wrench, forcible separation.

expression, squeezing; distillation.

extractor, corkscrew, forceps, pliers.

v. **extract**, draw; take out, draw out, pull out, tear out, pluck out, pick out, get out; wring from, wrench; extort; root–, weed–, grub–, rake–up, –out; eradicate; pull–, pluck– up by the roots; averruncate [*obs.*]; unroot; uproot, pull up, extirpate, dredge.

educe, elicit, evolve, bring forth, draw forth; extricate.

eliminate etc. (*eject*) 297; eviscerate etc. 297; remove.

express, squeeze out, press out, distill *or* distil.

adj. **extracted** etc. *v.*

302. Passage
[motion through]

n. **passage**, transmission; permeation; penetration, interpenetration; transudation, infiltration; exosmosis *or* exosmose; osmosis *or* osmose, endosmosis, endosmose; intercurrence; ingress etc. 294; egress etc. 295; path etc. 627; conduit etc. 350; opening etc. 260; journey etc. 266; voyage etc. 267.

v. **pass**, pass through; perforate etc. (*hole*) 260; penetrate, permeate, thread, thrid [*archaic or dial.*], enfilade; go through, go across, go over, pass over; cut across; ford, cross; pass and repass, work; make–, thread–, worm–, force– one's way; make–, force– a passage; cut one's way through; find its -way, –vent; transmit, make way, clear the course; traverse, go over the ground.

adj. **passing** etc. *v.;* intercurrent; endosmosmic, endosmotic, exosmotic *or* exosmic, osmotic.

adv. **en passant** [*F.*] etc. (*transit*) 270.

303. Overrun
[motion beyond]

n. **overrun**, transcursion [*obs.*], transilience *or* transiliency [*rare*], transgression; trespass; inroad, advancement, intrusion, infraction, encroachment, infringement; extravagation [*obs.*], transcendence; redundancy etc. 641.

v. **surpass**, transgress, pass; go beyond, go by; show in front, come to the front; shoot ahead of; steal a march upon, gain upon.

overstep, overpass, overreach, overgo, override, overleap, overjump, overskip, overlap, overshoot the mark; outstrip, outleap, outjump, outgo, outstep, outrun, outride, outrival, outdo; beat, beat hollow [*colloq.*]; distance; leave in the -lurch, –rear; throw into the shade; exceed, transcend, surmount; soar etc. (*rise*) 305.

encroach, trespass, infringe, intrude, invade, accroach [*rare*], advance upon, trench upon, intrench on; strain; stretch–, strain– a point; pass the Rubicon.

adj. **surpassing** etc. *v.*

adv. **ahead**, beyond the mark.

304. Shortcoming
[motion short of]

n. **shortcoming**, failure; falling short etc. *v.;* default, defalcation, delinquency; leeway; labor in vain, no go [*colloq.*]; fizzle [*colloq.*], dud [*slang*], slump [*colloq.*]; flash in the pan.

incompleteness etc. 53; imperfection etc. 651; insufficiency etc. 640; noncompletion etc. 730; failure etc. 732.

v. **fall short**, –of; come short, –of; stop short, –of; not reach; want; keep within -bounds, –the mark, –compass.

collapse, fail, break down, stick in the mud, flat out, come to nothing; fall down, slump, fizzle out [*all colloq.*]; fall through, fall to the ground; cave in [*colloq.*], end in smoke, miss the mark; lose ground; miss stays [*naut.*]; miss one's moorings.

adj. **unreached**; deficient; short, short of; minus; out of depth; perfunctory etc. (*neglect*) 460.

adv. **within the mark**, within compass, within bounds; behindhand; *re infecta* [*L.*]; to no purpose; far from it.

305. Ascent
[motion upwards]

n. **ascent**, ascension; rising etc. *v.;* rise, upgrowth, upward flight, upgrade; leap etc. 309; grade, gradient [*Eng.*], ramp, acclivity, hill etc. 217.

stairway, staircase, stair [*esp. in Scot.*], stairs; flight of -steps, -stairs; ladder, scaling ladder; Jacob's ladder, companionway, companion, companion ladder [*all naut.*]; escalator, elevator etc. 307.

[comparisons] rocket, skyrocket, lark, skylark; Alpine Club.

v. **ascend**, rise, mount, arise, uprise; go up, get up, work one's way up, start up, spring up, shoot up; aspire, aim high.

plane, swim, float.

climb, shin [*colloq.*], swarm [*colloq.*], clamber, ramp [*rare*], scramble, escalade, surmount; wind upward; scale, -the heights.

tower, soar, hover, spire, go-, fly- aloft; surge; leap etc. 309.

adj. **rising** etc. *v.;* upcast; scandent, buoyant; supernatant, superfluitant; excelsior.

adv. **up**, upward *or* upwards, skyward. heavenward, toward the empyrean; upturned; uphill.

306. Descent
[motion downwards]

n. **descent**, descension [*rare*], inclination, declension, declination; decurrence [*rare*], downcome, comedown, downcast, setback, fall; falling etc. *v.;* slump [*colloq.*], drop, cadence; subsidence, lapse; downfall, tumble, slip, tilt, trip, lurch; culbute [*F.*], titubation, stumble; fate of -Icarus, -Phaëthon, -Lucifer.

avalanche, debacle, *débâcle* [*F.*], landslip [*Eng.*], landslide, slide, snowslip, snowslide, glissade.

declivity, dip, decline, pitch, drop, down-grade.

elevator etc. 307.

stairway etc. 305.

v. **descend**; go-, drop-, come- down; fall, gravitate. drop, slip, slide, settle; decline, set, sink, droop, come down a peg [*colloq.*], slump [*colloq.*].

get down, dismount, alight, light; swoop, souse; stoop etc. 308; fall prostrate, precipitate oneself; let fall etc. 308.

tumble, trip, stumble, titubate [*rare*], lurch, pitch, swag, topple; topple-, tumble- -down, -over; tilt, sprawl, plump, plump down; come-, fall-, get- a cropper [*colloq. or slang*].

adj. **steep**, sloping, declivitous, declivous; beetling etc. (*high*) 206; bottomless etc. (*deep*) 208.

descending etc. *v.;* down, downcast; descendent; decurrent, decursive; labent [*rare*], deciduous; nodding to its fall.

adv. **downward** *or* downwards, downhill.

307. Elevation

n. **elevation**; raising etc. *v.;* erection, lift; sublevation, upheaval; sublimation, exaltation; prominence etc. (*convexity*) 250.

lever etc. 633; crane, derrick, windlass, capstan, winch; dredge, dredger, dredging machine.

elevator, *ascenseur* [*F.*], lift [*chiefly Eng.*], dumb-waiter, escalator.

v. **elevate**, raise, heighten, lift, erect; set up, stick up, perch up, perk up, tilt up; rear, hoist, heave; uplift, upraise, uprear, upbear, upcast, uphoist, upheave; buoy, weigh, mount, give a lift; exalt; sublimate; place-, set- on a pedestal.

take up, drag up, fish up; dredge.

stand up, rise up, get up, jump up; spring to one's feet; hold oneself up, hold one's head up; draw oneself up to his full height.

adj. **elevated** etc. *v.;* upturned, *retroussé* [*F.*]; stilted, attollent, rampant.

adv. on stilts, on the shoulders of, on one's legs, on one's hind legs [*colloq.*].

308. Depression

n. **depression**; lowering etc. *v.;* dip etc. (*concavity*) 252; abasement; detrusion; reduction.

overthrow, overset, overturn; upset, prostration, subversion, precipitation.

bow; curtsy *or* curtsey, dip [*colloq.*], bob, obedience [*archaic*], duck, genuflexion, kotow *or* kowtow [*Chinese*]. obeisance, salaam *or* salam.

v. **depress**, lower; let-, take- -down, -down a peg [*colloq.*]; cast; let drop, let fall; sink, debase, bring low, abase, reduce, detrude, pitch, precipitate.

overthrow, overturn, overset; upset, subvert, prostrate, level, fell; down [*archaic or colloq.*], cast down, take down, throw down, fling down, dash down, pull down, cut down, knock down, hew down; raze, raze to the ground; trample in the dust, pull about one's ears; come off-, pull off- one's high horse [*slang*]; come off-, get off- one's perch [*slang*].

sit, sit down, couch, squat; recline etc. 213.

crouch, stoop, bend, cower.

bow; curtsy *or* curtsey, genuflect, kotow [*Chinese*], duck, bob, dip, kneel; bend-, bow- the

-head, -knee; incline, make obeisance, salaam *or* salam, prostrate oneself, bow down.

adj. **depressed** etc. *v.;* at a low ebb; prostrate etc. (*horizontal*) 213; detrusive.

309. Leap

n. **leap**, jump, hop, spring, bound, vault, pole vault, leaping, saltation [*rare*].

caper; dance, curvet, caracole *or* caracol; gambade, gambado, gambol, frisk, prance, dido, capriole, demivolt; buck, -jump; hop skip and jump; falcade.

[comparisons] kangaroo, jerboa, chamois, goat, frog, grasshopper, flea; buckjumper; wallaby.

v. **leap**; jump -up, -over the moon; hop, spring, bound, vault, negotiate [*cant*], clear, ramp, trip, skip.

prance, dance, caper; buck, buck-jump; curvet, caracole *or* caracol; foot it, bob, bounce, flounce, start; frisk etc. (*amusement*) 840; jump about etc. (*agitation*) 315; cut capers [*colloq.*], cut a dido [*colloq.*]; trip it on the light fantastic toe, dance oneself off one's legs, dance the soles off one's feet.

adj. **leaping** etc. *v.;* saltatorial, saltatoric *or* saltatory; frisky, lively.

adv. on the light fantastic toe.

310. Plunge

n. **plunge**, dip, dive, nose dive [*aviation*], header [*colloq.*]; ducking etc. *v.*

submergence, submersion, immersion, engulfment [*rare*].

diver; diving bird, loon, auk, penguin, grebe, sea duck etc.

v. **plunge**, dip, souse, duck; dive, plump; take a -plunge, -header [*colloq.*]; make a plunge; bathe etc. (*water*) 337; pitch.

submerge, submerse; immerse; douse *or* dowse, sink, engulf, send to the bottom; send to -Davy Jones's locker, -feed the fishes.

founder, welter, wallow; get out of one's depth; go to the bottom, go down like a stone.

adj. **plunging** etc. *v.;* submergible, submersible; soundable.

311. Circuition

[curvilinear motion]

n. **circuition** [*archaic*], circulation, volutation; turn, curvet; excursion; circumvention, circumnavigation, circumambulation, circumambience *or* circumambiency, circumflexion, circumfluence [*rare*], circummigration, circumvolation [*rare*]; Northwest Passage; wheel, gyre, ambit, compass, lap, circuit etc. 629.

turning etc. *v.;* wrench; evolution; coil, spiral, corkscrew.

v. **turn**, bend, wheel; go about, put about [*both naut.*]; heel; go-, turn- -round, -to the right- about; turn on one's heel.

circle, encircle, circumscribe; circuit; make-, describe- a -circle, -complete circle; go-, pass- through -180°, - 360°; circumnavigate, circumambulate, circumvent; "put a girdle round about the earth" [*Midsummer Night's Dream*]; go the round, make the round of, circumvolate [*rare*], circumflex.

round; turn-, round- a corner; double a point [*naut.*]; make a detour etc. (*circuit*) 629.

wind, circulate, meander; whisk; twirl; twist etc. (*convolution*) 248.

wallow, welter, roll, volutate.

adj. **circuitous**; turning etc. *v.;* circumforaneous, circumfluent, roundabout; devious, deviatory; circumambient, circumflex, circumfluent, circumfluous, circumvolant, circumnavigable.

adv. round about.

312. Rotation

[motion in a continued circle]

n. **rotation**, revolution, gyration, circulation, roll; circumrotation, circumvolution [*rare*], circumgyration; circumfusion, circination [*obs.*], turbination, pirouette, convolution.

eddy, vortex, whirlpool, swirl, gurge [*rare*]; verticity [*obs.*]; vertiginousness; whir, whirl; countercurrent; cyclone, tornado; surge; vertigo, dizzy round; maelstrom, Charybdis.

Ixion; Wheel of Fortune.

[comparisons] wheel, screw, propeller, turbine, whirligig, rolling stone, windmill; treadmill; top, teetotum; roller; cogwheel, gear, gearwheel, flywheel, jack, smokejack, turnspit; gyroplane, gyroscope, gyrostat, gyrocar; caster.

axis, axle, spindle, pivot, pin, hinge, pole, swivel, gimbals, arbor, bobbin, spool, reel, mandrel.

[science of rotatory motion] trochilics, gyrostatics.

v. **rotate**; roll, roll along; revolve, spin; turn, turn round; circumvolve [*rare*], circumgyrate [*rare*], circumvolute, circumfuse, turbinate [*rare*], encircle; circulate, gurge [*rare*], swirl, gyre, gyrate, wheel, whirl, twirl, trundle, troll, bowl, roll up, furl.

box the compass; spin like a -top, -teetotum.

adj. **rotating** etc. *v.;* rotatory, rotary; circumrotatory, trochilic, vertiginous, gyral, circumgyratory, circumvolutory, gyratory, gulfy; vorticular, vortical, vorticose; gyrostatic, gyroscopic.

313. Evolution

adv. **round and round**, head over heels, like a horse in a mill, in circles, clockwise.

313. Evolution
[motion in a reverse circle]

n. **evolution**, unfolding, development; evolvement; unfoldment; eversion etc. (*inversion*) 218.

v. **evolve**; unfold, unroll, unwind, uncoil, untwist, unfurl, untwine, unravel; disentangle; develop.

adj. **evolutional**, evolutionary; evolving etc. *v.;* evolved etc. *v.*

314. Oscillation
[reciprocating motion, motion to and fro]

n. **oscillation**; vibration, vibratility, libration; motion of a pendulum; nutation, circumnutation; undulation; pulsation; pulse, beat, throb; seismicity, seismism, seismology.

alternation; coming and going etc. *v.;* ebb and flow, flux and reflux, systole and diastole; libration -of the moon, -in latitude; ups and downs; crossruff [*in cards*].

fluctuation; vacillation etc. (*irresolution*) 605.

swing, wave, vibratiuncle [*rare*], beat, shake, wag, seesaw, teeter; dance, lurch, dodge.

rocking stone, logan (*or* loggan) stone.

[instruments] vibroscope, vibrograph; seismograph, seismoscope.

v. **oscillate**; nutate, vibrate, librate; undulate, wave; rock, sway, swing; pulsate, beat; wag, waggle; nod, bob, curtsy *or* curtsey, tick; play; wamble, wabble; dangle, swag [*obs. or dial.*].

fluctuate, dance, curvet, reel, quake; quiver, quaver; shake, flicker; wriggle; roll, toss, pitch; flounder, stagger, totter; move-, bob- up and down etc. *adv.*

alternate, pass and repass, shuttle, ebb and flow, come and go; vacillate etc. 605.

brandish, shake, flourish; agitate etc. 315.

adj. **oscillating** etc. *v.;* oscillatory, undulatory, pulsatory, libratory; vibratory, vibrative, vibratile; seismic *or* seismical, seismal, seismographic, seismological; pendulous; shuttlewise.

adv. **to and fro**, up and down, backwards and forwards, back and forth, in and out, seesaw, zigzag, wibble-wabble [*colloq.*], in and out, from side to side, like buckets in a well.

315. Agitation
[irregular motion]

n. **agitation**, stir, tremor, shake, ripple, jog, jolt, jar, jerk, shock, succussion, trepidation, quiver, quaver, dance, tarantella, tarantism; vellication, jactation, jactitation, quassation [*rare*]; shuffling etc. *v.;* twitter, flicker, flutter.

disquiet, perturbation, commotion, turmoil, turbulence; tumult, tumultuation [*obs.*]; hubbub, rout, bustle, fuss, racket.

twitching, subsultus, floccillation, carphology *or* carphologia; staggers, megrims, epilepsy, fits; chorea, the jerks [*colloq.*], St. Vitus's dance, tilmus.

spasm, throe, throb, palpitation, pitapatation [*humorous*], convulsion, paroxysm, seizure, grip, cramp.

disturbance etc. (*disorder*) 59; restlessness etc. (*changeableness*) 149.

ferment, fermentation; ebullition, effervescence, hurly-burly, *cahotage* or *cahotement* [*F.*], cahot [*Can.*]; tempest, storm, ground swell, heavy sea, whirlpool, vortex etc. 312; whirlwind etc. (*wind*) 349.

v. **be agitated** etc.; shake; tremble, -like an aspen leaf; shake like a jelly, quiver, quaver, quake, shiver, twitter, twire [*obs.*], writhe, toss, jactitate [*rare*], shuffle, tumble, stagger, bob, reel, sway; wag, waggle, wriggle, -like an eel; dance, stumble, shamble, flounder, totter, flounce, flop, curvet, prance, cavort; squirm; bustle.

toss about, jump about; jump like a parched pea; shake like an aspen leaf; shake to its -center, -foundations; be the sport of the winds and waves; reel to and fro like a drunken man; move-, drive- from post to pillar and from pillar to post; keep between hawk and buzzard.

throb, pulsate, beat, palpitate, go pitapat.

flutter, flitter [*archaic*], flicker, bicker; twitch, vellicate.

ferment, effervesce, foam; boil, boil over; bubble, bubble up; simmer.

agitate, shake, convulse, toss, tumble, bandy, wield, brandish, flap, flourish, whisk, jerk, hitch, jolt; jog, joggle; jostle, buffet, hustle, disturb, stir, shake up, churn, jounce, wallop [*dial.*], whip.

adj. **agitated**, tremulous; subsultory [*obs.*], desultory, successive, saltatorial, saltant, saltatoric *or* saltatory; quassative [*rare*]; shambling; giddy-paced, convulsive, jerky; effervescent, effervescive, vellicative, unquiet, restless, all of a twitter [*colloq.*], all of a flutter; shaking etc. *v.*

adv. **by fits and starts**; subsultorily [*obs.*] etc. *adj.; per saltum* [*L.*]; hop, skip, and jump; in convulsions, in fits, in a flutter.

Class 3. Matter

Section 1. Matter in General

316. Materiality

n. **materiality**, materialness; corporeity, corporality; substantiality, substantialness, materialization, material existence, incarnation, flesh and blood, plenum; physical condition.
    matter, body, substance, brute matter, protoplasm, plasma, stuff, element, principle, parenchyma, material, substratum, hyle, *corpus* [*L.*], pabulum; frame.
    object, article, thing, something; still life; stocks and stones; *matériel* [*F.*]; materials etc. 635.
    [science of matter] physics; somatology, somatics; natural–, experimental- philosophy; physicism; physical science, *philosophie positive* [*F.*], materialism, hylism, hylicism, hylotheism, somatism, substantialism.
    materialist; physicist; somatologist, somatist, corporealist [*rare*], hylicist, hylotheist, substantialist.
v. **materialize**, incorporate, substantiate, substantialize, insubstantiate [*rare*], incorporate, embody, incarnate, corporify [*obs.*].
adj. **material**, bodily; corporeal, corporal; physical; somatic, somatoscopic; mundane etc. (*terrestrial*) 318; sensible, tangible, ponderable, palpable, substantial, somatologic *or* somatological; embodied, fleshy.
    neuter, unspiritual, materialistic *or* materialistical, hylic, hylotheistic *or* hylotheistical, parenchymatous.
    objective, impersonal, nonsubjective.

317. Immateriality

n. **immateriality**, immaterialness; incorporeity, dematerialization, insubstantiality, incorporality, decarnation [*obs.*], unsubstantiation, unsubstantiality, spirituality; inextension; astral plane.
    personality; I, myself, me.
    ego, spirit etc. (*soul*) 450; astral body, etheric double, subliminal self, subconscious self, higher self.
    immaterialism; spiritualism, spiritism, animism, Platonism; Platonic -Idea, -Ideal.
    immaterialist, spiritualist, spiritist, animist, Platonist.
v. **immaterialize**, dematerialize, unsubstantialize [*rare*]; disembody, spiritualize.

adj. **immaterial**, immateriate, incorporeal, incorporal, incorporate, unsubstantial, insubstantial, immateriate [*obs.*], spiritistic, animistic; unfleshly; supersensible; asomatous, unextended; unembodied, discarnate, bodiless, decarnate *or* decarnated, disembodied; extramundane, unearthly; pneumatoscopic; spiritual etc. (*psychical*) 450; Platonistic.
    subjective, personal, nonobjective.

318. World

n. **world**, creation, nature, universe; earth, globe, wide world; cosmos; Midgard; terraqueous globe, sphere; macrocosm, megacosm; music of the spheres.
    heavens, sky, welkin [*archaic*], empyrean; starry -cope, –heaven, –host; firmament, *caelum* [*L.*], hyaline, supersensible regions; *varuna* [*Skr.*]; vault–, canopy- of heaven; celestial spaces.
    heavenly bodies, luminaries, stars, asteroids; nebulae; galaxy, Milky Way, galactic circle, *via lactea* [*L.*].
    sun, orb of day, day-star [*poetic*], Helios, Apollo, Phoebus etc. (*sun god*) 423; photosphere, chromosphere; solar system; planet, planetoid; Venus, Aphrodite Urania, Hyades; comet; satellite; moon, orb of night, Diana, Luna, Phoebe, Cynthia, Selene, "glimpses of the moon" [*Hamlet*], silver-footed queen; aerolite, meteor; falling–, shooting-star; meteorite, uranolite.
    constellation, zodiac, signs of the zodiac; Charles's Wain, The Dipper; Great Bear, Ursa Major; Little Bear, Ursa Minor; Southern Cross, Orion's Belt, Cassiopeia's Chair, Pleiades.
    colures, equator, ecliptic, orbit.
    [science of heavenly bodies] astronomy; uranography, uranology; uranometry, cosmology, cosmography, cosmogony; eidouranion, orrery; geodesy etc. (*measurement*) 466; star-gazing; observatory; planetarium.
    cosmologist, cosmographer, cosmogonist, geodesist, geographer; astronomer, star-gazer.
adj. **cosmic** *or* cosmical, mundane; terrestrial, terrestrious [*obs.*], terraqueous, terrene, terrenous, [*obs.*]; fluvioterrestrial, geodesic *or* geodesical, geodetic *or* geodetical, cosmogonal, cosmogonic, cosmographic *or* cosmographical; telluric, earthly, under the sun; sublunary, subastral.

319. Gravity

solar, heliacal; lunar; empyreal, celestial, heavenly, sphery; starry, stellar, stellary, bespangled, sidereal; sideral, astral; nebular; uranic.

adv. in all creation, on the face of the globe, here below, under the sun.

319. Gravity

n. **gravity,** gravitation; weight; heft, heaviness etc. *adj.;* specific gravity; ponderation [*rare*], ponderousness, ponderance [*rare*], ponderosity, pressure, load; burden *or* burthen; ballast, counterpoise; mass; lump–, mass–, weight-of.
[comparisons] lead, millstone, mountain; Ossa on Pelion.

weighing, ponderation, trutination [*obs.*]; weights; avoirdupois–, troy–, apothecaries' weight; grain, scruple, drachma, dram *or* drachm, ounce, pound, lb., arroba, load, stone, hundred-weight, cwt., ton, quintal, carat, penny-weight, tod; gram *or* gramme, decagram, hectogram, kilogram *or* kilo, myriagram, decigram, centigram, milligram.
[weighing instrument] balance, scales steelyard, beam, weighbridge, spring balance.
[science of gravity] statics.

v. **be heavy** etc. *adj.;* gravitate, weigh, press, cumber, load.
[measure the weight of] weigh, counterweigh, scale [*rare*], poise.

adj. **weighty**; weighing etc. *v.;* heavy, –as lead; ponderous, ponderable; lumpish, lumpy, cumbersome, burdensome; cumbrous, unwieldy, massive; static *or* statical.
incumbent, superincumbent.

320. Levity

n. **levity**; lightness etc. *adj.;* imponderability, buoyancy, volatility; imponderables [*tech.*].
[comparisons] feather, dust, mote, down, thistledown, flue, fluff, cobweb, gossamer, straw, cork, bubble; float, buoy; ether, air.
ferment, leaven, barm, yeast, zyme, enzyme, pepsin, diastase.

v. **be light** etc. *adj.;* float, swim, be buoyed up.
render light etc. *adj.;* lighten.
ferment, work, raise, leaven.

adj. **light,** subtile, subtle, airy; imponderous, imponderable; astatic, weightless, ethereal, sublimated; gossamery; suberose *or* suberous, subereous; uncompressed, volatile; buoyant, floating etc. *v.;* foamy, frothy; portable.
light as -a feather, –thistledown, –air.
fermenting, fermentative, zymogenic, zymologic *or* zymological, diastatic, yeasty.

Section 2. Inorganic Matter

321. Density

n. **density,** solidity; solidness etc. *adj.;* impenetrability, impermeability; incompressibility; imporosity; cohesion etc. 46; costiveness, constipation, consistence, spissitude.
specific gravity; hydrometer, areometer.
condensation; caseation; solidation [*obs.*], solidification, consolidation, concretion, coagulation; petrification etc. (*hardening*) 323; crystallinity, crystallizability, crystallization, precipitation; deposit, precipitate; inspissation; incrassation, crassitude; thickening etc. *v.*
indivisibility, indiscerptibility, indissolvableness [*rare*], infrangibility, infrangibleness, indissolubility, indissolubleness.
solid body, mass, block, knot, lump; concretion, concrete, conglomerate; cake, stone, bone, gristle, cartilage.
clot, coagulum, casein, crassament [*obs.*], crassamentum, legumin, curd; clabber, bonnyclabber, clotted cream, Devonshire cream, grume.
sediment, lees, dregs, settlings.

v. **be dense** etc. *adj.;* become *or* render solid etc. *adj.;* solidify, solidate; concrete, set, take a set, consolidate, congeal, coagulate; curd, curdle, cruddle [*dial.*], lopper; fix, clot, cake, candy, precipitate, deposit, cohere, crystallize; petrify etc. (*harden*) 323.
condense, thicken, inspissate, incrassate.
compress, squeeze, ram down, constipate [*rare*].

adj. **dense,** solid; solidified etc. *v.;* caseate, caseous; pucka *or* pakka [*Hind.*], coherent, cohesive etc. 46; compact, close, serried, thickset; substantial, massive, lumpish; impenetrable, impermeable, imporous; incompressible; constipated, costive; crass, spiss [*obs.*], clabber, kern [*chiefly dial.*]; concrete etc. (*hard*) 323; knotted, knotty; gnarled; crystallitic, crystalline, crystallizable; thick, grumose, grumous, stuffy.
undissolved, unmelted, unliquefied, unthawed.
indivisible, indiscerptible, infrangible, indissolvable [*rare*], indissoluble, insoluble, infusible.

322. Rarity

n. **rarity**; tenuity; absence of solidity etc. 321; subtility; subtility; sponginess, compressibility.
rarefaction, rarefication [*rare*], expansion, dilatation, inflation, subtilization.
ether etc. (*gas*) 334.

v. **rarefy,** expand, dilate, subtilize [*rare*], attenuate, thin.

100

adj. **rare**, subtile [*now rare*], subtle, thin, fine, tenuous, compressible, flimsy, slight; light etc. 320; cavernous, porous, spongy etc. (*hollow*) 252.
    rarefied etc. *v.*; unsubstantial; uncompact, uncompressed; rarefiable, rarefactive, rarefactional.

323. Hardness

n. **hardness** etc. *adj.;* rigidity; renitency *or* renitence; inflexibility, temper, callosity, durity [*obs.*].
    induration, petrifactioon; lapidification, lapidescence [*rare*]; cornification, chondrification, vitrification, vitrescence, ossification; crystallization.
    [comparisons] stone, pebble, flint, marble, rock, fossil, crag, crystal, quartz, granite, adamant; bone, cartilage; calculus; hardware; heart of oak, block, board, deal board; iron, steel; cast-, decarbonized-, wrought- iron; nail; brick, concrete; cement; osmiridium, iridosmine *or* iridosmium.

v. **harden**; render hard etc. *adj.;* stiffen, indurate, petrify, temper, ossify, vitrify, lithify, lapidify, cement.

adj. **hard**, rigid, stubborn, stiff, firm; starch, starched; stark, unbending, unlimber, renitent, unyielding; inflexible, tense; indurate, indurated; gritty, proof.
    adamantine, adamantean; concrete, stony, rocky, granitic, calculous, lithic, vitrescent, vitrifiable, vitrescible, vitreous; horny, cornified, callous, corneous; bony, ossipid, osseous, ossific; cartilaginous; lapideous, lapidific *or* lapidifical [*rare*]; crystallized, crystalloid; hard as a -stone etc. *n.;* stiff as -buckram, -a poker.

324. Softness

n. **softness**, pliableness etc. *adj.;* flexibility; pliancy, pliability; sequacity [*obs. in this sense*], malleability, ductility, ductibility, tractability, tractility, extensibility, extendibility; plasticity; inelasticity, flaccidity, laxity, flabbiness, flocculence; mollescence, mollification; softening etc. *v.*
    [comparisons] clay, alumina, argil; wax, putty, butter, dough, pudding; cushion, pillow, feather bed, down, eider down, padding, wadding.

v. **soften**; render soft etc. *adj.;* mollify, mellow, milden, tender [*rare*], gentle [*rare*], dulcify; relax, temper; mash, knead, massage, squash [*colloq.*].
    bend, yield, relent, relax, give.

adj. **soft**, tender, supple; pliant, pliable; flexible, flexile; lithe, lithesome; lissom, limber, plastic; ductile, ductible [*rare*], tractile, tractable; malleable, extensile, extensible, lax, sequacious [*obs. in this sense*], inelastic; aluminous; remollient [*obs.*], mollient, mollescent, mollitious, mollified.
    yielding etc. *v.;* flabby, limp, flimsy.
    flaccid, flocculent, downy; spongy, oedematous *or* edematous, medullary, doughy, clayey, argillaceous, mellow.
    soft as -butter, -down, -silk, -putty, -a feather bed; yielding as wax; tender as a chicken.

325. Elasticity

n. **elasticity**, springiness, spring, resilience *or* resiliency, renitency, buoyancy, tensibility, tensibleness, tensility, extensibility; recoil, rebound, reflex.
    [comparisons] India rubber *or* india-rubber, caoutchouc, gum elastic, whalebone, baleen; turf, moss; balloon, battledore.

v. **be elastic** etc. *adj.;* spring back etc. (*recoil*) 277.

adj. **elastic**, tensile, tensible, springy, resilient, renitent, ductile, extensible, buoyant.

326. Inelasticity

n. **inelasticity** etc. (*softness*) 324; want of-, absence of- elasticity etc. 325; irresilience.

adj. **inelastic** etc. (*soft*) 324; irresilient.

327. Tenacity

n. **tenacity**, toughness, strength; cohesiveness, cohesion etc. 46; sequacity, sequaciousness [*both obs. in this sense*]; stubbornness etc. (*obstinacy*) 606; gumminess, glutinousness, viscidity etc. 352.
    [comparisons] leather; white leather *or* whitleather, tawed leather; gristle, cartilage.
    claw, talon, pincers, nippers, vise; bulldog.

v. **be tenacious** etc. *adj.;* resist fracture.

adj. **tenacious**, cohesive, tough, strong, resisting, adhesive, stringy, viscid, gummy, glutinous, gristly, cartilaginous, leathery, coriaceous, tough as whitleather; stubborn etc. (*obstinate*) 606.

328. Brittleness

n. **brittleness** etc. *adj.;* fragility, friability, frangibility, fissility [*rare*], frailty, cold-shortness; house of -cards, -glass.

v. **be brittle** etc. *adj.;* live in a glass house.
    break, crack, snap, split, shiver, splinter, crumble, crash, crush, break short, burst, fly, give way; fall to pieces; fall to dust; crumble -to, -into- dust.

329. Texture

adj. **brittle**, brash, frangible, breakable, friable, delicate, shattery [*rare*], fragile, frail, gimcrack, shivery, fissile; splitting etc. *v.;* lacerable, splintery, crisp, crimp, short, brittle as glass, cold-short; crisp as celery.

329. Texture
[structure]

n. **structure**, organization, anatomy, frame, mold *or* mould, fabric, construction; framework, carcass, architecture; stratification, cleavage.
substance, stuff, compages, parenchyma; constitution, staple, organism.
[science of structures] organology, osteology, myology, splanchnology, neurology, angiology, adenology; angiography, adenography, organography.
texture, intertexture, contexture; tissue, grain, web, surface; warp and -woof, –weft; gossamer, homespun, linsey-woolsey, frieze, fustian, satin, velvet; tooth, nap etc. (*roughness*) 256; fineness–, coarseness- of grain; dry goods.
[science of textures] histology.

adj. **structural**, organic; anatomic *or* anatomical; splanchnic, splanchnological, visceral, adenological.
textural, textile; fine-grained, coarse-grained, ingrained, ingrain; fine, delicate, subtle, subtle, gossamer, gossamery, filmy; coarse; homespun, linsey-woolsey.

330. Pulverulence

n. [state of powder] **pulverulence**; sandiness etc. *adj.;* efflorescence; friability, friableness, arenosity, sabulosity.
particle etc. (*smallness*) 32; powder, dust, sand, shingle; sawdust; grit; meal, bran, flour, farina, rice, paddy, spore, sporule; crumb, seed, grain; limature [*obs.*], filings, *débris* [*F.*], detritus, scobs, magistery, fine powder; flocculi.
smoke; cloud of -dust, –sand, –smoke; puff–, volume- of smoke; sand storm, dust storm.
[reduction to powder] pulverization, comminution, attenuation, granulation, disintegration, subaction, contusion, trituration, levigation, abrasion, detrition, multure limitation; tripsis; filing etc. *v.*
[instruments for pulverization] mill, arrastra, gristmill, grater, rasp, file, pestle and mortar, nutmeg grater, teeth, grinder, grindstone, kern [*dial.*], quern, quernstone, millstone.
[science] koniology.

v. **come to dust**; be disintegrated, be reduced to powder etc.

pulverize, comminute, granulate, triturate, levigate; reduce *or* grind to powder; scrape, file, abrade, rub down, grind, grate, rasp, pound, bray, bruise, contuse, contund [*rare*]; beat, crush, craunch *or* cranch, crunch, scranch [*colloq.*], crumble, disintegrate; attenuate etc. 195.

adj. **powdery**, pulverulent, granular, mealy, floury, farinaceous, branny, furfuraceous, flocculent, dusty, sandy, sabulous, psammous; detrital, arenaceous, arenose, arenarious, gritty; efflorescent, impalpable; lentiginous, lepidote, sabuline; sporaceous, sporous.
pulverable *or* pulverizable; friable, crumbly, shivery; pulverized etc. *v.;* attrite; in pieces.

331. Friction

n. **friction**, attrition; rubbing etc. *v.;* attriteness, attritus, erasure; confrication [*obs.*], contrition [*obs.*]; affriction [*obs.*], abrasion, arrosion [*obs.*], limature [*obs.*], anatripsis, anatripsology, frication, rub; elbow grease [*colloq.*]; rosin; massage.
masseur (*fem. masseuse*) [*F.*], massagist, rubber.

v. **rub**, abrade, scratch, scrape, scrub, fray, rasp, graze, curry, scour, polish, rub out, raze, erase, gnaw; file, grind etc. (*reduce to powder*) 330; rosin; massage.
set one's teeth on edge.

adj. **abrasive**, anatriptic; attrite [*rare*], attritive [*obs.*].

332. Lubrication
[absence of friction. prevention of friction]

n. **lubrication**, lubrification [*rare*], lubricity; anointment; oiling etc. *v.*
smoothness etc. 255; unctuousness etc. 355.
lubricant, lubricator, synovia; glycerin, oil etc. 356; saliva; lather; ointment, salve, balm, unguent, unguentum [*pharm.*], lenitive, unction.

v. **lubricate**, lubricitate [*obs.*]; oil, grease, lather, soap; wax; anoint; salivate.

adj. **lubricated** etc. *v.;* lubricous, lubricant, lubric [*rare*]; lenitive, synovial.

333. Fluidity

n. **fluidity**, liquidity, liquefaction; liquidness etc. *adj.;* gaseity etc. 334; solution, chylifaction, serosity.
fluid, inelastic fluid; liquid, liquor, lymph, humor, juice, sap, serum, blood, gravy, rheum, ichor, sanies; chyle.
solubility, solubleness.

[science of liquids at rest] hydrology, hydrostatics, hydrodynamics, hydrometry, hydrokinetics.
hydrometer, hydrophone, hydrostat, meter.
- *v.* **be fluid** etc. *adj.;* flow etc. (*water in motion*) 348; liquefy etc. 335.
- *adj.* **liquid**, fluid, serous, juicy, succulent, sappy; ichorous; rheumy, chylous, sanious, lymphatic; fluent etc. (*flowing*) 348.
  liquefied etc. 335; uncongealed; soluble.
  hydrological, hydrostatic *or* hydrostatical, hydrodynamic *or* hydrodynamical, hydrometric *or* hydrometrical.

334. Gaseity

- *n.* **gaseity**, gaseousness, vaporousness etc. *adj.;* flatulence *or* flatulency; volatility; aeration, aerification; gasification.
  elastic fluid, gas, air, vapor *or* vapour, ether, steam, fume, reek, effluvium, flatus; cloud etc. 353; ammonia, ammoniacal gas; volatile alkali.
  [science of elastic fluids] pneumatics, pneumatology, pneumatonomy, pneumatostatics; aerostatics, aerodynamics, aeroscopy, aerography, aerology, aeromechanics.
  pneumatoscope, pneumatometer, gasometer, gas meter; air−, swimming-bladder, sound (*of a fish*).
- *v.* **gasify**, aërify, aërate; emit vapor etc. 336.
- *adj.* **gaseous**, gasiform, aeriferous, aëriform, ethereal, aery, aerial, airy, vaporous, volatile, evaporable, flatulent.
  pneumatolytic, aerostatic *or* aerostatical, aerodynamic, aeromechanic.

335. Liquefaction

- *n.* **liquefaction**; liquescence, liquescency; deliquescence; melting etc. (*heat*) 384; colliquation [*obs.*], colliquefaction [*obs.*]; thaw; solubleness, deliquation [*obs.*], liquation; lixiviation, dissolution.
  solution, decoction, apozem [*rare*], infusion, flux; alloy; lixivium.
  solvent, diluent, resolvent, dissolvent, menstruum, alkahest.
- *v.* **render liquid** etc. 333; liquefy, run; deliquesce; melt etc. (*heat*) 384; solve; dissolve, resolve; liquate; hold in solution.
  leach, lixiviate, percolate.
- *adj.* **liquefied** etc. *v.,* liquescent, liquefiable; deliquescent, soluble, dissoluble, dissolvable, colliquative; leachy, porous.
  solvent, diluent, resolutive, resolvent, dissolvent.

336. Vaporization

- *n.* **vaporization**, volatilization; gasification; evaporation, vaporation [*rare*], vaporishness, vaporosity, atomization, distillation, cupellation, cohobation, sublimation, exhalation; volatility.
  fumigation, steaming.
  vaporizer, atomizer, spray, evaporator, cohobator, finestill, still, retort.
  bay salt, chloride of sodium.
- *v.* **render gaseous** etc. 334; vaporize, volatilize, atomize. spray; distill, sublime, sublimate, evaporate, exhale, smoke, transpire, emit vapor, fume, reek, steam, fumigate; cohobate; finestill.
- *adj.* **volatile**, evaporable, vaporizable, vaporific, vapory, vaporous, gaseous; volatilized etc. *v.;* reeking etc. *v.*

337. Water

- *n.* **water**, lymph; aqua [*L.*], eau [*F.*], flood, crystal [*poetic*], Adam's ale [*humorous*], agua [*Sp.*], pani [*Hind.*]; diluent, serum etc. 333.
  washing etc. *v.;* immersion, mersion [*obs.*]; dilution, maceration, lotion; humectation, infiltration, spargefaction [*obs.*], affusion, irrigation, seepage, balneation, bath.
  deluge etc. (*water in motion*) 348; high water, flood tide, springtide.
  sprinkler, sparger, aspergillum *or* aspergill, shower *or* shower bath, douche, enema; nozzle; atomizer etc. 336.
- *v.* **be watery** etc. *adj.;* reek.
  water, wet; moisten etc. 339; dilute, add water, dip, immerse, merge; soak, drouk [*Scot.*]; affuse [*rare*], immerge, douse *or* dowse, submerge; plunge, souse, duck, drown; steep, macerate, wash, sprinkle, sparge, humect *or* humectate [*rare*], lave, bathe, splash, swash, drench; dabble, slop, slobber, irrigate, inundate, deluge; infiltrate, percolate, seep; slosh; marinate *or* marinade, pickle.
  inject, gargle; syringe, douche.
- *adj.* watery, aqueous, aquatic, hydrous, lymphatic; balneal; diluent, solvent, hydrotic *or* hydrotical; infiltrative, seepy; drenching etc. *v.;* diluted etc. *v.;* weak; wet etc. (*moist*) 339.

338. Air

- *n.* **air** etc. (*gas*) 334; common−, atmospheric− air; atmosphere; aerosphere [*rare*].
  the open, −air; sky, lift [*archaic*], welkin [*archaic*], the blue, blue serene, blue sky; cloud etc. 353.

339. Moisture

    weather, climate; rise and fall of the -barometer, –mercury.
    isopiestic line, isobar.
    exposure to the -air, –weather; ventilation.
    [science of air] aerology, aerometry, aeroscopy, aerography; meteorology, climatology; pneumatics; aeronautics; eudiometry; eudiometer, barometer, vacuometer, climatometer, aerometer, aeroscope; aneroid, baroscope, weatherglass, weathergauge, barograph.
    aerostation etc. (*aeronautics*) 267; aeronaut etc. 269a.
    weathervane, weathercock, vane, cock.
v. **air,** ventilate, perflate [*rare*]; fan etc. (*wind*) 349.
    fly, soar, drift, hover; aviate etc. (*aeronautics*) 267.
adj. **containing air,** flatulent, effervescent; windy etc. 349.
    atmospheric, airy; aerial, aeriform; aery, pneumatic.
    meteorologic *or* meteorological, aerological, aerometric, eudiometric *or* eudiometrical, barometric *or* barometrical, barographic, baroscopic *or* baroscopical; isobaric, isopiestic; aerographic *or* aerographical; weatherwise.
adv. **in the open air,** *à la belle étoile* [*F.*], in the open, out of the blue, under the stars, out of doors, outdoors; *al fresco* [*It.*]; *sub Jove* [*L.*], *sub dio* [*L.*].

339. Moisture

n. **moisture;** moistness etc. *adj.;* humidity, humectation; madefaction [*obs.*], dew; *serein* [*F.*]; marsh etc. 345.
    hygrometry, hygrometer.
v. **moisten,** wet; humect *or* humectate [*rare*]; sponge, damp, bedew; imbue, imbrue, infiltrate, saturate; soak, sodden, seethe, sop, dampen; drench etc. (*water*) 337.
    be moist etc. *adj.;* not have a dry thread; perspire etc. (*exude*) 295.
adj. **moist,** damp; watery etc. 337; madid [*now rare*], undried, humid, wet, dank, muggy, dewy; roric; roriferous, rorifluent [*both rare*], roral [*obs.*], rorid [*obs.*]; roscid [*rare*]; juicy.
    saturated etc. *v.;* wringing wet; wet through, wet to the skin.
    sodden, swashy [*dial.*], soppy, soggy, dabbled; reeking, dripping, soaking, droukit [*Scot.*], soft, sloppy, muddy; swampy etc. (*marshy*) 345; irriguous.

340. Dryness

n. **dryness** etc. *adj.;* siccity [*rare*], siccation, aridness, aridity, drought *or* drouth.
    ebb tide, low water.
    desiccation, exsiccation [*rare*], dehydration, insolation, anhydration, anhydromyelia [*med.*], evaporation, arefaction [*rare*], dephlegmation, drainage.
    drier, desiccative, desiccator.
v. **be** *or* **render dry** etc. *adj.;* dry; dry up, soak up; sponge, swab, wipe. drain, parch, sear.
    be fine, hold up; be bright and fair.
    desiccate, exsiccate, dehydrate, anhydrate, evaporate, insolate, infumate, torrefy, siccate [*rare*], arefy.
adj. **dry,** arid; droughty, waterless, siccaneous [*rare*], siccate [*obs.*], aneroid, sear *or* sere, siccant [*rare*], siccific, desiccatory; adjust, arescent; dried etc. *v.;* undamped; dephlegmatory; juiceless, sapless; corky; husky; rainless, without rain, fine; dry as -a bone, –dust, –a stick, –a mummy, –a biscuit; waterproof, watertight.
    anhydrous, desiccated, desiccate, anhydric, dehydrated, insolated.

341. Ocean

n. **ocean,** sea, main, deep, blue, brine, salt water, waters, waves, billows, high seas, offing, great waters, watery waste, "vasty deep" "briny deep," "swan-bath" [*A.-S.*], "swan-road" [*A.-S.*], "whale-path" [*A.-S.*], mere [*archaic*], herring pond *or* pond [*humorous for Atlantic*], hyaline, the Seven Seas, *kala pani* [*Hind.*]; wave, tide etc. (*water in motion*) 348; ocean basin; ocean lane, steamer track.
    Neptune, Poseidon, Oceanus, Thetis, Triton, Naiad, Nereid; sea nymph, Siren, mermaid, merman; trident, dolphin.
    oceanography, hydrography; oceanographer, hydrographer.
adj. **oceanic,** marine, maritime; pelagic; seaworthy, seagoing; hydrographic *or* hydrographical, oceanographic *or* oceanographical; bathybic, cotidal.
adv. at sea, on sea; afloat; oversea *or* overseas, oceanward *or* oceanwards.

342. Land

n. **land,** earth, ground, soil, dry land, *terra firma* [*L.*].
    continent, mainland, main, peninsula, chersonese, delta; tongue–, neck- of land; isthmus, oasis; promontory etc. (*projection*) 250; highland etc. (*height*) 206.
    realty, real estate etc. (*property*) 780; acres.
    coast, shore, scar *or* scaur, strand, beach; *playa* [*Sp.*]; bank, lea; seaboard, seaside, sea

bank, seacoast, seabeach; seashore, rock-bound coast, iron-bound coast; loom of the land; derelict; innings; reclamation, made land, alluvium, alluvion; ancon [*S. W. U. S.*].

region etc. 181; home, fatherland etc. (*abode*) 189.

soil, glebe, clay, loam, marl, cledge [*dial. Eng.*], chalk, gravel, mold *or* mould, subsoil, clod, clot [*dial.*].

rock, crag, cliff.

geography, geodesy, geology, geognosy, geogony, agriculture, agronomics, agronomy, geoponics, georgics.

geographer, geodesist, geologist, geognost.

landsman, landlubber, tiller of the soil; agriculturist etc. 371.

v. **land**, disembark, debark, come to land; set foot on -the soil, -dry land; come-, go- ashore.

adj. **earthy**; continental, midland; terrene etc. (*world*) 318.

littoral, riparian, riparial, riparious, ripicolous, ripuarian; alluvial.

landed, predial, territorial; geophilous.

geographic *or* geographical, geodesic *or* geodesical, geodetic *or* geodetical, geognostic *or* geognostical, geologic *or* geological, geoponic; agricultural etc. 371.

adv. **ashore**; on shore, on land, on dry land, on *terra firma* [*L.*].

343. Gulf. Lake

n. **gulf**, gulph, bay, inlet, bight, estuary, arm of the sea, bayou, fiord, armlet; frith *or* firth, ostiary [*obs.*], mouth; lagoon *or* lagune; indraft *or* indraught [*obs.*], cove, creek; natural harbor; roads; strait; narrows; euripus; sound, belt, gut, kyle [*Scot.*].

lake, loch [*Scot.*], lough, [*Ir.*], mere, tarn, plash, broad [*Eng.*], pond, pool, sump [*Scot. or dial. Eng.*], slab [*dial.*], linn *or* lin [*Scot.*], tank, puddle, well, artesian well; standing-, dead-, sheet of- water; fish-, mill- pond; ditch, dike *or* dyke, dam, race, mill race; reservoir etc. (*store*) 636; alberca [*Sp. Amer.*], hog wallow, buffalo wallow.

adj. **lacustrine**, lacustral.

344. Plain

n. **plain**, tableland, face of the country; open-, champaign-country; basin, downs, waste, weary waste, desert, wild, steppe, tundra, peneplain, pampas, savanna, prairie etc. (*grassland*) 367; heath, common, wold, veldt *or* veld, moor, moorland; bush, plateau etc. (*level*) 213; campagna [*obs. as Eng.*], champaign, uplands, fell [*Brit.*]; reach, stretch, expanse; alkali flat, llano; mesa, mesilla, *playa* [*Sp.*]; shaking-, trembling- prairie; vega [*Sp. Amer.*].

meadow, mead, haugh [*Scot. & dial. Eng.*], pasture, lea, ley *or* lay [*dial.*], pasturage, field.

lawn, green, plat, plot, grassplat.

greensward, sward, turf, sod, grass; heather.

grounds; maidan [*India*], park, common, campus, *agostadero* [*Sp.*].

adj. **champaign**, campestral, campestrial [*obs.*], campestrian, campestrine.

alluvial, fluvio-marine.

adv. in the bush.

345. Marsh

n. **marsh**, swamp, morass, marish [*archaic*], peat bog, moss, fen, bog, quagmire, slough, sump [*Scot. or dial. Eng.*], bottoms, holm [*Eng.*], wash; mud, squash, slush; baygall, ciénaga [*Sp.*], jhil [*India*], vlei [*S. Africa*].

adj. **marsh**, marshy, swampy, boggy, plashy, poachy, quaggy, soft; muddy, sloppy, squashy, spongy; paludal; moorish, moory; fenny, marish [*archaic*].

346. Island

n. **island**, isle, islet, ait *or* eyot, holm, reef, atoll; archipelago; islander.

v. **insulate**, island, enisle [*rare*], isle [*rare*].

adj. **insular**, insulary [*rare*], seagirt, archipelagic.

347. Stream

[fluid in motion]

n. **stream** etc. (*of water*) 348, (*of air*) 349.

v. **flow** etc. 348; **blow** etc. 349.

348. River

[water in motion]

n. running water.

jet, swash, spurt *or* spirt, squirt, spout, splash, rush, gush, *jet d'eau* [*F.*]; sluice.

waterspout, waterfall; fall, cascade, force *or* foss [*dial. Eng.*], linn *or* lin [*Scot.*], gill *or* ghyll; Niagara; cataract, catadupe [*obs.*], cataclysm; debacle, inundation, deluge; chute, washout.

rain, rainfall; *serein* [*F.*]; plash, shower, scud [*dial.*]; downpour; downflow, pour, cloudburst, drencher; driving-, drenching- rain; predominance of Aquarius, reign of St. Swithin; drisk, brash [*dial.*], mizzle [*dial.*], drizzle, stillicidium, dropping etc. *v.;* rains, rainy season, monsoon, *bursat or barsat* [*Hind.*]; falling weather [*colloq.*].

hyetology, hyetography; hyetograph, rain chart.

349. Wind

stream, course, flux, flow, profluence; effluence etc. (*egress*) 295; defluxion; flowing etc. *v.*; current, tide, race, mill race, tide race.

spring; fount, fountain; rill, rivulet, rillet; streamlet, brooklet; branch; runnel, runlet; sike, burn [*both dial. Eng. & Scot.*], beck [*Eng.*], brook, river; reach; tributary.

body of water, torrent, rapids, flush, flood, swash; spring-, high-, flood-, full- tide; bore, eagre *or* hygre; fresh, freshet; indraft *or* indraught; ebb, refluence, reflux, undercurrent, undertow, eddy, vortex, gurge [*rare*], whirlpool, Charybdis, Maelstrom (*also* maelstrom), regurgitation, overflow, alluvion; confluence, corrivation [*obs.*].

wave, billow, surge, swell, ripple, *anerithmon gelasma* [*Gr.*]; beachcomber, riffle, tidal wave, comber, chop, choppiness, roll, rollers, ground swell, surf, breakers, white horses; rough-, heavy-, cross-, long-, short-, choppy-, chopping- sea.

[science of fluids in motion] hydrodynamics; hydraulics, hydrostatics, hydrokinetics, hydromechanics, pegology, pluviometry.

[measures] hyetometer, hyetometrograph, hydrodynamometer, nilometer, fluviometer, fluviograph, marigraph, hydrometer, hydrometrograph, udometer, ombrometer, rain gauge *or* gage, pluviometer, pluviograph.

irrigation etc. (*water*) 337; pump; watering- pot, -cart; hydrant, standpipe, syringe, siphon, *mussuk* [*Hind.*].

water carrier, bheesty *or* bheestie [*India*], Water Bearer, Aquarius.

v. **flow**, run; meander; gush, pour, spout, roll, jet, well, issue; drop, drip, dribble, plash, spirtle, trill, trickle, distill, percolate; stream, gurge [*rare*], surge, swirl, overflow, inundate, deluge, flow over, splash, swash; guggle, murmur, babble, bubble, purl, gurgle, sputter, spurt, regurgitate; ooze, flow out etc. (*egress*) 295.

flow into, fall into, open into, drain into; discharge itself, disembogue.

[cause a flow] pour; pour out etc. (*discharge*) 297; shower down; irrigate, drench etc. (*wet*) 337; spill, splash.

[stop a flow] stanch *or* staunch; dam, dam up etc. (*close*) 261; obstruct etc. 706.

rain, -hard, -in torrents, -cats and dogs, -pitchforks [*both colloq.*]; pour, shower, sprinkle, pour with rain, drizzle, spit [*colloq.*], set in; mizzle.

adj. **fluent**, deliquescent, defluent, profluent [*rare*], diffluent; affluent; tidal; flowing etc. *v.*; meandering, meandrous, meandry [*obs.*], flexuous, fluvial, fluviatile, streamy, streamful; choppy, rolling; stillicidious [*obs.*], stillatitious [*rare*]; hydragogue [*med.*].

rainy, showery, pluvial [*rare*], pluvious, pluviose [*rare*], drizzly, drizzling, mizzly, wet; pluviometric *or* pluviometrical.

349. Wind
[air in motion]

n. **wind**, draught, flatus, afflatus, sufflation [*rare*], insufflation, perflation, inflation, afflation, indraft *or* indraught, efflation; air; breath, -of air; puff, whiff, whiffet, zephyr, blow, drift; aura; stream, current; undercurrent.

Aeolus *or* Eolus, Boreas, Euroclydon, Eurus, Notus [*rare*], Zephyr *or* Zephyrus, Favonius; cave of Aeolus *or* Eolus; Wabun (east wind), Kabibonokka (north wind), Shawondasee (south wind), Mudjekeewis (west wind) [*all four from Hiawatha*].

gust, blast, breeze, capful of wind, fresh breeze, stiff breeze, keen blast, squall, half a gale, gale.

trade wind, trades, monsoon.

storm, tempest, hurricane, whirlwind, tornado, samiel, cyclone, typhoon, simoom *or* simoon, harmattan, sirocco, mistral, *bise* [*F.*], *tramontana* [*It.*], tramontane, levant, levanter; blizzard, barber [*Can.*], *candelia* [*Sp. Am.*], chinook, foehn, khamsin, norther, northeaster, northeast gale, *vendaval* [*Sp.*], wuther [*dial.*], willy-willy [*Austral.*].

windiness etc. *adj.*; ventosity [*obs.*]; rough-, dirty-, ugly-, wicked-, foul-, stress of- weather; dirty sky, mare's-tail, mackerel sky; cloud etc. 353; thick-, black-, white- squall.

anemography, anemology, anemometry, aerology, aerography, aerodynamics.

wind-gauge, anemometer, anemoscope, anemograph, anemometrograph; weathercock, weathervane, vane.

breathing, respiration, inspiration, inhalation, expiration, exhalation; blowing, fanning, etc. *v.*; ventilation; sneezing etc. *v.*; errhine; sternutation; hiccup *or* hiccough, eructation, catching of the breath; inspirator, respirator, ejector.

air pump, lungs, bellows, pulmotor, blowpipe; branchiae, gills.

fan, punkah *or* punka [*India*], flabellum, thermantidote, electric fan; *ventilabrum* [*L.*].

ventilator, louver, aerator [*rare*], transom; air-pipe etc. 351; hygrometer, psychrometer.

353. Bubble. Cloud

v. **blow**, waft; blow -hard, –great guns, –a hurricane etc. *n.;* storm; wuther [*dial.*], stream, issue.
respire, breathe, inhale, exhale; inspire, expire; puff; whiff, whiffle; gasp, wheeze; snuff, snuffle; sniff, sniffle; sneeze, cough, hiccup *or* hiccough; belch, eruct [*rare*].
fan, ventilate; inflate, pump, perflate [*obs.*]; blow up.
whistle, scream, roar, howl, sing, sing in the shrouds, growl.

adj. **windy**, airy, aeolian *or* eolian, borean, favonian; ventilative; blowing etc. *v.;* breezy, gusty, squally.
stormy, tempestuous, blustering, cyclonic, typhonic; boisterous etc. (*violent*) 173.
anemographic, anemological, anemometric *or* anemometrical, aerologic *or* aerological, aerographic *or* aerographical, aerodynamic.
pulmonic, pulmonary, pulmonate.
nasal, errhine; sternutative, sternutatory.
flatulent, gassy, windy, ventose.

350. Conduit
[channel for the passage of water]

n. **conduit**, channel, duct, watercourse, cañon *or* canyon, coulee *or* coulée [*geol.*], water gap, gorge, ravine, chasm; race; head–, tail– race; abito [*F. Amer.*], aboideau *or* aboiteau [*local Can.*], bito [*dial., U. S.*]; acequia [*Sp. Amer.*], acequiador [*Sp. Amer.*], arroyo; adit, aqueduct, canal, trough, gutter, pantile; flume, dike, main; gully, gullet [*rare*], gulch, moat, ditch, drain, sewer, culvert, cloaca, sough [*dial. Eng.*], kennel, siphon; piscine, piscina; pipe etc. (*tube*) 260; funnel; tunnel etc. (*passage*) 627; water–, waste- pipe; emunctory, gully hole, spout, scupper; ajutage; hose; gargoyle *or* gurgoyle; penstock, pentrough, weir, lock weir, floodgate, water gate, sluice, lock, valve; rose, rosehead; waterworks.
[for metal] ingate, runner, tedge.
[anatomy] artery, vein, *vena* [*L.*], blood vessel, lymphatic, pore; aorta; intestines, bowels; small intestine, duodenum, jejunum, ileum; large intestine, cecum *or* caecum, colon, rectum; esophagus, gullet; throat.

adj. **vascular** etc. (*with holes*) 260.
excretory, eliminative.

351. Air Pipe
[channel for the passage of air]

n. **air pipe**, air tube, air hole, blowhole, breathing hole, spiracle, touchhole, vent hole, spile hole, bung, bunghole; shaft, airway, air shaft, smoke-shaft, flue, chimney, funnel, vent, ventage; ventiduct, ventilator; pipe etc. (*tube*) 260; blowpipe etc. (*wind*) 349.
nostril, nozzle, throat, weasand, bronchus (*pl.* bronchi), larynx, tonsils, windpipe, trachea.
louver, Venetian blind, Venetian shutter, *jalousie* [*F.*], *jhilmil* [*India*].

352. Semiliquidity

n. **semiliquidity**; stickiness etc. *adj.;* viscidity, viscosity, mucidness, gummosis, emulsification, jellification; gummosity [*rare*], glutinosity [*rare*], mucosity; crassitude, spissitude; lentor [*now rare*]; pastiness; adhesiveness etc. (*cohesion*) 46; succulence *or* succulency; lactescence.
inspissation, incrassation, crassamentum, coagulum; thickening.
[comparisons] jelly, gelatin, carlock, ichthyocol, ichthyocolla, isinglass; mucus, pus, phlegm, pituite; lava; paste; library–, flour- paste; glair, starch, gluten, albumen, milk, cream, protein; treacle, rob, syrup, molasses; gum, size, glue, varnish, mastic, mucilage, fish glue; wax, beeswax; emulsion; gruel, porridge; *purée* [*F.*], soup.
squash, mud, slush, slime, ooze; moisture etc. 339; marsh etc. 345.

v. **inspissate**, incrassate; coagulate, gelatinate, gelatinize; jellify, jelly, jell; emulsify, thicken; mash, squash, churn, beat up.

adj. **semifluid**, semiliquid; half-melted, half-frozen; milky, muddy etc. *n.;* lacteal, lactean [*rare*], lacteous, lactescent, lactiferous; emulsive, curdled, thick, succulent, uliginose *or* uliginous.
gelatinous, albuminous, mucilaginous, glutinous; gummous, spissated [*rare*], crass, tremelloid, tremellose, amylaceous, ropy, clammy, clotted; viscid, viscous, sticky, tacky; slab [*dial.*], slabby; lentous [*obs.*], pituitous, mucid, muculent, mucous.

353. Bubble. Cloud
[mixture of air and water]

n. **bubble**; foam, froth, head, spume, scum, fume, lather, suds, spray, surf, yeast, barm, spoondrift *or* spindrift.
effervescence, fermentation; bubbling etc. *v.;* evaporation, exhalation, emanation.
cloudiness etc. (*opacity*) 426; nebulosity etc. (*dimness*) 422.
cloud, vapor, fog, mist, haze, steam; scud, rack, nimbus; cumulus, nebula, meteor, woolpack, cirrus, curl cloud, thunderhead, stratus; cirro-

354. Pulpiness

stratus, cumulo-stratus; cirro-cumulus; mackerel sky, mare's-tail, colt's-tail, cat's-tail, cocktail, dirty sky; frost smoke.

[science of clouds] nephology, nephelognosy, meteorology; nephoscope, nephelometer, nephograph.

v. **bubble**, boil, foam, spume, froth, mantle, sparkle, guggle, gurgle; effervesce, pop, ferment, fizzle; aerate.

cloud, overcast, overcloud, befog, becloud, adumbrate [*rare*], mist, fog, overshadow, shadow.

adj. **bubbling** etc. *v.;* frothy, nappy [*obs.*], effervescent, sparkling, *mousseux* [*F.*], fizzy, heady, with a head on, with a collar on [*slang*], up [*colloq.*].

cloudy etc. *n.;* cirrous, cirrose; nubiferous, cumulous, thunderheaded; vaporous, nebulous, overcast.

nephological, nepheloscopic, nephelometric, meteorologic *or* meteorological.

354. Pulpiness

n. **pulpiness** etc. *adj.;* pulp, paste, dough, sponge, batter, clotted cream, curd, pap, jam, pudding, poultice, grume.

v. **pulp**, pulpify [*rare*], mash, squash [*colloq.*], masticate, macerate; coagulate etc. 352.

adj. **pulpy** etc. *n.;* pultaceous, grumous; baccate; [*of fruit*] fleshy, succulent.

355. Unctuousness

n. **unctuousness** etc. *adj.;* unctiousness [*rare*], unguent, unctuosity, lubricity; salve, cerate; ointment etc. (*oil*) 356; anointment; lubrication etc. 332.

v. **oil**, anoint, lubricate etc. 332; smear, salve, grease, lard, pinguefy.

adj. **unctuous**, unctious [*rare*], unguentary, unguentous, oily, oleaginous, adipose, sebaceous, unguinous, fat, fatty, greasy; waxy, butyraceous, soapy, saponaceous, pinguid, lardaceous; slippery.

356. Oil

n. **oil**, fat, butter, cream, grease, tallow, suet, lard, dripping, exunge [*obs.*], blubber; glycerin *or* glycerine, stearin, elain *or* elaine, olein, oleagine; coconut butter; soap; soft soap, wax, cerement; paraffin, benzine, gasoline, petrol, spermaceti, adipocere; petroleum, mineral–, rock–, crystal- oil; vegetable–, colza–, olive–, salad–, linseed–, cottonseed–, coconut–, palm–, nut- oil; animal–, neat's-foot–, train- oil; ointment, pomade, pomatum, unguent, liniment; amole, Barbados tar; fusel–, grain–, rape–, seneca-oil; hydrate of amyl, ghee *or* ghi [*India*], kerosene, naphtha.

356a. Resin

n. **resin**, rosin, colophony, gum; lac, shellac, sealing wax; amber, ambergris; bitumen, pitch, tar; asphalt *or* asphaltum; camphor; varnish, copal, mastic, megilp *or* magilp, lacquer, japan, Brunswick black.

v. **varnish** etc. (*overlay*) 223; rosin, resin.

adj. **resinous**, resiny, rosinous [*rare*], lacquered, japanned, camphorated, tarred, tarry, pitched, pitchy, gummed, gummy, gummous, waxed; bituminous, asphaltic, asphaltite.

Section 3. Organic Matter

357. Organization

n. **organization**, organized world, organized nature, living nature, animated nature; living beings; organic remains; organism, bion [*physiological individual*]; morphon [*morphological individual*]; biota, animal and plant life, fauna and flora.

fossils, fossilization, lapidification, petrification, petrifaction, paleontology *or* palaeontology, paleozoölogy *or* paleozoölogy; paleontologist.

[science of living beings] biology, natural history; zoölogy etc. 368; botany etc. 369; physiology, anatomy, cytology, embryology, organic chemistry, morphology; promorphology, tectology; cell theory *or* cellular theory, evolution, metabolism; abiogenesis, spontaneous generation; archigenesis etc. (*production*) 161; biotaxy, ecology, ontogeny, phylogeny, polymorphism, oxidation, invagination, vertebration.

Darwinism, Lamarckism, neo-Lamarckism, Weismannism.

naturalist, biologist, zoölogist, botanist, bacteriologist, embryologist, Darwinian.

protoplasm, plasma *or* plasm, cytoplasm, metaplasm, karyoplasm, bioplasm, trophoplasm, idioplasm; cell, proteid, protein, albumen, albumin, albuminoid; structure etc. 329; chromatin; centrosome, nucleolus, karyosome, vacuole, chromosome; protoplast, protozoan, amoeba; karyaster, erythroblast, dysmeromorph, antherozoid.

ovum, oösperm, zygote, oösphere, oöcyte, ooecium, ovicell, oögonium; oöphyte, oöspore, oögamy, heterogamy, isogamy, oögenesis; gamete, gametophore, gametophyte, sporophyte, sporocyte, sporocyst, sporocarp, cystocarp, sporogonium, sporozoite, gametangium, antheridium *or* antherid; macrospore, megasporangium; microspore, microsporangium; biophore; spermatozoid, zoöspore, macrogamete, microgamete, spermatozoön, spermatium, spermatia, spermatocyte, spermatogenesis, spermatophore, spermatozoid, spermatozooid; spermogonium, spermary, sperm gland, testis, testicle, ovary; germ cell, blastoderm, mesoblast *or* mesoplast, meroblast (*opp. to* holoblast); germinal matter, biogenesis *or* biogeny, germ plasm, zooid.

v. **organize**, systematize, form, arrange, construct.
fossilize, petrify, lapidify, mummify.

adj. **organic**, organized; biotic, zooid, zooidal.
fossilized, petrified, petrifactive, lapidined; paleontologic, paleontological *or* palaeontological, paleozoölogical *or* palaeozoölogical.
protoplasmic, plasmatic *or* plasmic, cytoplasmic, metaplasmic, karyoplasmic, bioplasmic, trophoplasmic, idioplasmic; cellular, cellulous; proteid, proteinaceous, albuminous *or* albuminose, albuminoidal, structural; nuclear, nucleate, nucleolar, nucleolate *or* nucleolated; vacuolar, protoplastic, protozoan, amoebic, amoeboid.
ovarian, oviferous, oviparous (*opp. to* viviparous), ovicular; oöphytic, oösporic, oösporous, oögamous, heterogamous (*opp. to* autogamous *or* isogamous); gamic, sporogenous; spermatic, spermatogenetic, spermatoid, spermatophoral, spermatozoal; blastodermic, mesoblastic (*opp. to* holoblastic), biogenetic, germinal; zoögleic, zoögleoid; unsegmentic, dioecious *or* diecious (*opp. to* monoecious *or* monecious).

358. Inorganization

n. **mineral kingdom**, mineral world; unorganized-, inorganic-, brute-, inanimate- matter.
[science of the mineral kingdom] mineralogy, geology, geognosy, geoscopy, metallurgy, metallography, lithology, petrology, oryctology [*obs.*], oryctography [*obs.*].

v. **mineralize**; pulverize, turn to dust.

adj. **inorganic**, inanimate, unorganized *or* inorganized, lithoid, *or* lithoidal; azoic; mineral.

359. Life

n. **life**; vitality, viableness, viability; animation.
vital spark, vital flame, Promethean spark, lifeblood; respiration, wind; breath of life, breath of one's nostrils; Archeus *or* Archaeus; *anima* [*L.*], *anima bruta* [*L.*], *anima divina* [*L.*], *anima mundi* [*L.*]; world -soul, -spirit, -principle; existence etc. 1.
vivification; oxygen; vital -air, -force; life force; vitalization; revival; revivification etc. 163; Prometheus; Deucalion and Pyrrha; life to come etc. (*destiny*) 152.
"a short summer" [Johnson]; "a bubble" [Browne]; "a battle" [Aurelius]; "one dem'd horrid grind" [Dickens].
[science of life] physiology, biology, etiology, embryology; animal economy.
nourishment, staff of life etc. (*food*) 298.

v. **live**; be alive etc. *adj.;* breathe, respire, suspire; subsist etc. (*exist*) 1; walk the earth; (a poor player that) "struts and frets his hour upon the stage" [*Macbeth*]; be spared.
be born, see the light, come into the world; fetch-, draw- -breath, -the breath of life; breathe the vital air; quicken; revive; come to, -life.
give birth to etc. (*produce*) 161; bring to life, put into life, vitalize; vivify, vivificate [*rare*]; reanimate etc. (*restore*) 660.
keep alive, keep body and soul together, keep the wolf from the door; support life.
have nine lives like a cat.

adj. **living**, alive; in life, in the flesh, in the land of the living; on this side of the grave, above ground, breathing, quick, animated; animative; lively etc. (*active*) 682; alive and kicking [*colloq.*]; tenacious of life.
vital, vitalic; vivifying, vivified etc. *v.;* viable, zoëtic; Promethean.

adv. *vivendi causa* [*L.*].

360. Death

n. **death**; decease, demise; mortality; dying; passing -away, -of the soul; dissolution, departure, obit, release, rest, eternal rest, quietus, fall; loss, bereavement.
end etc. 67-, cessation etc. 142-, loss-, extinction-, ebb- of life etc. 359.
death-warrant, deathwatch, death rattle, deathbed; stroke-, agonies-, shades-, valley of the shadow-, summons-, jaws-, hand-, bridge-, river- of death; Jordan, Jordan's bank, "one more river to cross"; last -breath, -gasp, -agonies; dying -day, -breath. -agonies; swan song, *chant du cygne* [*F.*]; *rigor mortis* [*L.*]; Stygian shore; "crossing the bar" [Tennyson]; the great adventure.
euthanasia, euthanasy [*rare*]; happy release, *bona mors* [*L.*]; break-up of the system; natural -death, -decay; sudden-, violent- death; un-

361. Killing

bed; at the point of death, at death's door, at the last gasp; near one's end, given up, given over, booked [*slang*]; with one foot in –, tottering on the brink of- the grave.

timely end, taking off [*colloq.*], watery grave; debt of nature; mortification, heart failure, suffocation, asphyxia; fatal disease etc. (*disease*) 655; deathblow etc. (*killing*) 361.

angel of death, death's bright angel, Azrael; King -of terrors, –Death; Death, doom etc. (*necessity*) 601; "Hell's grim Tyrant" [Pope].

necrology, bills of mortality, obituary.

death song etc. (*lamentation*) 839.

v. **die**, expire, perish; meet one's -death, –end; pass away, pass over, be taken; yield–, resign- one's breath; resign one's -being, –life; end one's -days, –life, –earthly career; breathe one's last; cease to -live, –breathe; depart this life; be no more etc. *adj.;* go off [*colloq.*], drop off [*colloq.*], pop off [*slang*]; lose–, lay down–, relinquish–, surrender- one's life; drop–, sink- into the grave; close one's eyes; fall–, drop- -dead, –down dead; break one's neck; give–, yield- up the ghost; be all over with one.

pay the debt to nature, shuffle off this mortal coil, take one's last sleep; go the way of all flesh; hand–, pass- in one's checks, –in one's chips [*all slang*]; go over to the–, join the- -greater number, –majority, –great majority; join the choir invisible; awake to life immortal; come–, turn- to dust; give an obolus to Charon; cross the Stygian ferry; go to one's long account, go to one's last home, go to Davy Jones's locker, go to glory [*colloq.*]; receive one's death warrant, make one's will, step out [*colloq.*], die a natural death, go out like the snuff of a candle; come to an untimely end; catch one's death; go off the hooks, kick the bucket, hop the twig, turn up one's toes [*all slang*]; die a violent death etc. (*be killed*) 361.

die for one's country, make the supreme sacrifice, go West [*World War I euphemism*].

adj. **dead**, lifeless; deceased, demised, departed, defunct; late, gone, no more; exanimate [*rare*], inanimate; out of the world, taken off, released; bereft of life; stone dead; departed this life etc. *v.;* dead and gone; dead as -a doornail, –a doorpost, –mutton, –a herring, –nits [*all slang or colloq.*]; launched into eternity, gathered to one's fathers, numbered with the dead; born into a better world, born into the next world; gone to a better land; dying–, dead- in the Lord; asleep in Jesus; with the saints.

stillborn; mortuary; deadly etc. (*killing*) 361.

dying etc. *v.;* moribund, morient [*obs.*]; Hippocratic; *in articulo* [*L.*], *in extremis* [*L.*]; in the -jaws, –agony- of death; going, –off; *aux abois* [*F.*]; on one's -last legs [*colloq.*], –death-

adv. post obit [*L.*], post mortem [*L.*].

361. Killing
[destruction of life; violent death]

n. **killing** etc. *v.;* homicide, manslaughter, murder, assassination, trucidation [*obs.*], occision [*obs.*]; effusion of blood; blood, bloodshed; gore, slaughter, carnage, butchery; *battue* [*F.*]; bomb explosion, electrocution, shipwreck; gladiatorial combat; lapidation.

massacre; fusillade, *noyade* [*F.*]; thuggism, thuggee, thuggery; saturnalia of blood, sacrifice to Moloch; organized massacre, *pogrom* [*Russia*].

war, warfare, "organized murder," *horrida bella* [*L.*], crusade, jihad *or* jehad [*Moham.*]; battle; war to the death etc. (*warfare*) 722; Armageddon; gigantomachy; deadly weapon etc. (*arms*) 727.

deathblow, finishing stroke, *coup de grâce* [*F.*], quietus; execution etc. (*capital punishment*) 972; judicial murder; martyrdom.

suffocation, strangulation, garrote *or* garrotte; hanging etc. *v.*

slayer, butcher, murderer, Cain, assassin, cutthroat, garroter *or* garrotter, bravo, Thug *or* thug, Moloch, matador, *sabreur* [*F.*]; *guet-apens* [*F.*]; gallows, executioner etc. (*punishment*) 975; man-eater, Apache, hatchet man, highbinder, gunman, bandit, lapidator [*rare*].

regicide, parricide, fratricide, infanticide; feticide, aborticide; uxoricide, vaticide [*these words ending in -cide refer to both doer and deed*].

suicide, self-murder, self-destruction, *felo-de-se* (*pl. felos-de-se*), seppuku [*Jap.*], hara-kiri [*Jap.*], suttee, sutteeism, car of Jagannath *or* Juggernaut [*an erroneous assumption*]; immolation, holocaust.

fatal accident, violent death, casualty, disaster, calamity.

Aceldama (*often l.c.*), potter's field, field of blood.

[destruction of animals] slaughtering; phthiozoics; sport, sporting; the chase, venery; hunting, coursing, shooting, fishing; pig-sticking.

sportsman, huntsman, fisherman; hunter, Nimrod.

shambles, slaughterhouse, *abattoir* [*F.*].

v. **kill**, put to death, slay, shed blood; murder, assassinate, butcher, slaughter, victimize, immolate; massacre; take away–, deprive of- life; make away with, put an end to; dispatch *or* despatch; burke, settle [*colloq.*], do to death, do for [*colloq.*]; hunt.

shoot, –dead; blow one's brains out; brain, knock on the head, blackjack; drop in one's tracks; stone, lapidate; give–, deal- a deathblow; give the -quietus, *–coup de grâce* [*F.*].

strangle, garrote *or* garrotte, hang, throttle, choke, stifle, suffocate, stop the breath, smother, asphyxiate, drown.

saber *or* sabre; cut -down, –to pieces, –the throat; jugulate; stab, run through the body, bayonet; put to the -sword, –edge of the sword.

execute, behead, guillotine, hang, electrocute; bowstring etc. (*execute*) 972.

cut off, nip in the bud, launch into eternity, send to one's last account, sign one's death warrant, strike the death knell of.

give no quarter, pour out blood like water; decimate; run amuck *or* amok; wade knee-deep in blood; dye–, imbrue- one's hands in blood.

die a violent death, welter in one's blood; dash–, blow- out one's brains; commit suicide; kill–, make away with–, put an end to- oneself; suicide [*colloq.*]; disembowel, commit hara-kiri.

adj. **murderous**, slaughterous, sanguinary, sanguinolent, blood-stained, blood-thirsty; killing etc. *v.;* homicidal, red-handed; bloody, bloody-minded; ensanguined, gory, sanguineous.

mortal, fatal, lethal; deadly, deathly; mortiferous [*obs.*], lethiferous; unhealthy etc. 657; mutually destructive, internecine; suicidal.

sporting; piscatorial, piscatory.

int. thumbs down! *habet! hoc habet!* [*L.*], let him have it!

362. Corpse

n. **corpse**, corse [*archaic*], carcass, cadaver, bones, skeleton, dry bones; defunct, relics, reliquiae, remains, mortal remains, dust, ashes, earth, clay; mummy; carrion; food for -worms, –fishes; tenement of clay, "this mortal coil" [*Hamlet*]; "this too, too solid flesh" [*Hamlet*].

ghost, shade, manes, phantom, specter *or* spectre, apparition, spirit, revenant, sprite [*archaic*], spook [*colloq.*].

organic remains, fossils.

adj. **cadaverous**, cadaveric, corpse-like; unburied etc. 363.

363. Interment

n. **interment**, burial, sepulture, entombment *or* intombment, inhumation, humation [*obs.*]; obsequies, exequies; funeral, wake.

cremation, burning; pyre, funeral pile.

funeral rite, funeral solemnity; knell, passing bell, death bell, funeral ring, tolling; dirge etc. (*lamentation*) 839; cypress, obit, dead march, muffled drum; elegy; funeral -oration, –sermon.

undertaker, mortician, funeral director.

mourner, mute, keener [*Ireland*], lamenter; pall-bearer, bearer.

graveclothes, shroud, winding sheet, cerecloth; cerements.

coffin, casket, shell, sarcophagus.

urn, cinerary urn; pall, bier, litter, hearse, catafalque.

burial place, grave, pit, sepulcher *or* sepulchre, tomb, vault, crypt, catacomb, mausoleum, cenotaph, golgotha, house of death, narrow house, low green tent, low house, long home, last home; cemetery, necropolis; burial ground; graveyard, churchyard; God's acre; potter's field; cromlech, barrow, tumulus, cairn; ossuary; bonehouse, charnel-house, deadhouse; morgue, mortuary; lich gate; burning ghât *or* ghaut [*India*]; crematorium, crematory; mastaba *or* mastabah [*Egypt*], tope *or* stupa [*Buddhist*]; dokhma, Tower of Silence [*Parsee*].

gravedigger, sexton, *fossoyeur* [*F.*].

monument, cenotaph, shrine; gravestone, headstone, tombstone; *memento mori* [*L.*]; hatchment, stone, marker, cross; epitaph, inscription.

necropsy, necroscopy, autopsy, *post mortem* examination *or post mortem* [*L.*].

exhumation, disinterment.

v. **inter**, bury; lay in–, consign to- the -grave, –tomb; entomb *or* intomb; inhume; hold–, conduct- a funeral; put to bed with a shovel [*colloq.*]; inurn; cremate.

lay out; embalm, mummify; toll the knell.

exhume, disinter, unearth.

adj. **funereal**, funebrial [*now rare*], funeral, funerary, mortuary, sepulchral, cinerary; buried etc. *v.;* burial; elegiac; necroscopic *or* necroscopical.

adv. *hic jacet* [*L.*], *ci-gît* [*F.*], R. I. P.; in memoriam [*L.*]; *post obit* [*L.*], *post mortem* [*L.*]; beneath the sod, under the sod, underground; at rest.

364. Animality

n. **animality**, animalism, animal life; animation, animalization, animalness.

corporeal nature, human system; breath; flesh, flesh and blood; physique; strength etc. 159.

365. Vegetation

- *v.* **animalize**; incarnate, incarn [*rare*], incorporate.
- *adj.* **fleshly**, carnal, human, corporeal.

365. Vegetation

- *n.* **vegetation**, vegetable life, vegetability [*obs.*], vegetativeness, vegetism, vegetality [*rare*]; herbage, flowerage.
- *v.* **vegetate**, germinate, sprout, grow, shoot up, luxuriate, fungate; grow -rank, -lush, -like a weed; flourish etc. 367; cultivate.
- *adj.* **vegetative**, vegetal, vegetable; leguminous etc. 367.

   luxuriant, rank, dense, lush, wild, jungly.

366. Animal

- *n.* **animal kingdom**, fauna, brute creation.

   animal, creature, created being; creeping thing, living thing; dumb animal, dumb friend, dumb creature; brute, beast.

   mammal, quadruped, bird, reptile, fish, crustacean, shellfish, mollusk, worm, insect, zoöphyte; plankton, nekton, benthos; animalcule etc. 193.

   beasts of the field, fowls of the air, denizens of the day; flocks and herds, live stock, domestic animals; wild animals, *ferae naturae* [*L.*], game.

   [domestic animals] horse etc. (*beast of burden*) 271; cattle, kine, ox; bull, bullock; cow, milch cow, Alderney, Guernsey, Holstein, Jersey, calf, heifer, shorthorn, yearling, steer, stot [*prov. Eng.*]; sheep; lamb, lambkin, ewe lamb, pet lamb; ewe, ram, tup, wether, tag [*prov. Eng.*], teg [*prov. Eng.*]; pig, swine, boar, hog, sow; yak, zebu, Indian buffalo.

   dog, hound, canine; pup, puppy; whelp, cur [*contemptuous*].

   house-, watch-, sheep-, shepherd's-, sporting-, hunting-, fancy-, lap-, toy- dog; collie; mastiff; bulldog, English bulldog, Boston bull, bull terrier, French bull; police dog, bloodhound, greyhound, staghound, deerhound, foxhound, coach dog, bandog, lurcher, Russian *or* Siberian wolfhound, boarhound, St. Bernard, husky *or* Eskimo dog; otter-hound; harrier, beagle, spaniel, pointer, setter, retriever, Newfoundland; water -dog, -spaniel; pug, poodle; turnspit; terrier; fox-, Airedale-, Yorkshire-, Irish-, Skye-, toy-terrier; Dandie Dinmont; dachshund, badger dog; brindle; Pomeranian, cocker spaniel, King Charles spaniel, toy spaniel, spitz dog; chow *or* chow-dog, Japanese poodle.

   pariah dog, pye-dog *or* pie-dog [*India*]; mongrel, mutt [*slang*].

   female, bitch, slut, brach, brachet, lady [*euphemistic*].

   cat, feline, puss, pussy, grimalkin, tomcat *or* tom, gib [*rare*], Angora, Persian, Maltese, tortoiseshell, mouser; tabby; kitten, kit, catling, kitling [*dial.*].

   [wild animals] **deer**, buck, doe, fawn, stag, hart, hind, roe, roebuck, caribou, elk, moose, reindeer, sambar, wapiti *or* American elk, mule deer, black-tailed deer *or* Virginia deer, fallow deer, red deer.

   antelope, gazelle, nilghau, eland, gnu, hartebeest, springbok *or* springbuck, oryx, steinbok, ibex; American antelope *or* pronghorn, chamois, koodoo *or* kudu.

   armadillo, peba, poyou, tatouay; wild ass, kiang, dziggetai, onager; bear, polar bear, grizzly bear, brown bear; beaver; bison, buffalo; musk ox, giraffe, okapi, tapir; wild boar, babiroussa *or* babirussa; ape, monkey, gorilla, marmoset, chimpanzee, lemur, baboon, orang-utan *or* orang-outang; kangaroo, opossum; wild horse, zebra; elephant, *hathi* [*Hind.*]; fox, reynard, Reynard, vixen [*fem.*], varmin *or* varmint [*dial.*], prairie fox, gray fox, red fox, arctic fox; dingo, coyote; wildcat, lynx, bobcat; skunk; hippopotamus, rhinoceros, lion, tiger etc. (*wild beast*) 913; squirrel, chipmunk, gopher, prairie dog, ferret, stoat, weasel, mongoose, raccoon *or* coon, bandicoot, rat, mouse; bat, flying mouse, flying phalanger, flying squirrel; flying fox, flying lemur, colugo.

   lizard, saurian, iguana, eft, newt, chameleon, gecko, Gila monster, dragon, horned toad, horned lizard.

   crocodilian, crocodile, mugger *or* magar [*India*], gavial [*India*], alligator, cayman, American crocodile.

   whale, sperm whale, baleen whale; shark, porpoise, walrus, seal, octopus, devilfish; swordfish; pike; salmon etc. (*food*) 298.

   [birds] feathered tribes, feathered songster, singing bird, warbler, dickybird [*colloq.*].

   canary, vireo, linnet, finch, goldfinch, brown thrasher, siskin, crossbill, aberdevine, chewink, peewee, lapwing [*Scot.*], titmouse *or* chickadee, nightingale, lark; magpie, cuckoo, mocking bird, catbird, laughing jackass, starling, myna *or* mina; bobolink, reedbird, ricebird, cardinal, cowbird, crow, rook, jackdaw, raven; pigeon, dove, cushat, ringdove, wood pigeon; swan, cygnet, goose, gander, duck, drake, wild duck, mallard; flamingo, heron, crane, stork, eagle, kingfisher, sandpiper, lyre bird, robin, thrush, hermit thrush, veery, mavis, missel thrush, ouzel *or* ousel, blackbird, red-winged blackbird; kingbird, fly-catcher; woodpecker, flicker; sparrow, song sparrow, chipping sparrow, vesper sparrow; swallow, swift, martin, sand martin, oriole, bluebird, meadow lark; bird of paradise, parrot, parrakeet *or* parakeet; penguin, pelican; gull, sea gull, albatross, petrel, stormy petrel *or* Mother Carey's chicken, fulmar *or* Mother Carey's goose; ostrich, emu; owl, bird of night; hawk, vulture, buzzard, turkey buzzard; eagle, bird of freedom, bird of Jove.

game, black game, black grouse, ruffed grouse, grouse, blackcock, duck, plover, rail, snipe; pheasant etc. 298.

poultry, fowl, cock, rooster, chanticleer, dunghill fowl, barndoor fowl, barnyard fowl, hen, Partlet, chicken, chick, chickabiddy; guinea fowl, guinea hen; peafowl, peacock, bird of Minerva, peahen.

[insects] ant, bee, honeybee, queen bee, drone; ant, white ant, termite; wasp, sawfly, locust, grasshopper, cicada, cicala, cricket; dragon fly, June fly, caddis fly; beetle; butterfly, moth; fly, May fly, thrips, aphid, bug; ant lion, hellgramite *or* hellgamite, earwig; springtail, podura, lepisma; buffalo bug, buffalo carpet beetle etc. (*injurious insects*) 913.

vermin, lice, cooties [*slang*], flies, fleas, cockroaches *or* roaches, water bugs *or* Croton bugs, bugs, bedbugs, Norfolk Howards [*slang*], mosquitoes; rats, mice, weasels.

snake, serpent, viper; asp, adder, copperhead, coral snake *or* harlequin snake, sidewinder, krait [*India*], viper, cobra, cobra de capello, king cobra, rattlesnake *or* rattler, copperhead, constrictor, boa constrictor, boa, python, Kaa [*Kipling*], ophidian.

[mythological] dipsas (*pl.* dipsades), basilisk, cockatrice, amphiobaena, Python, Hydra.

salamander; griffin *or* griffon *or* gryfon; chimaera; Cerberus.

adj. **animal**, zoic, zooid *or* zooidal, zoölogical.

equine; bovine, vaccine; canine; feline; fishy, piscatory, piscatorial; molluscous, vermicular; gallinaceous, rasorial, solidungulate, soliped; planktonic, nekteric, benthonic.

ophidian, ophiologic, ophiomorphous, reptilian, anguine, ophic [*rare*], snakelike, serpentiform [*rare*], viperine, colubrine.

367. Vegetable

n. **vegetable**, vegetable kingdom; flora.

organism, plant, tree, shrub, bush, creeper, vine; herb, seedling, plantlet, exotic, annual, perennial, biennial, triennial; legume, pulse, vetch, greens; asparagus etc. (*vegetables*) 298.

foliage, leafage, verdure, foliation, frondescence [*rare*]; prefoliation, vernation; branch, bough, ramage, stem, tigella *or* tigelle *or* tigellum *or* tigellus; leaf, spray, leaflet, frond, foliole, bract, bractlet, bracteole, cotyledon, pad, flag, petal, needle, sepal; spray etc. 51; petiole, petiolule, bine; shoot, tendril.

flower, blossom, bud, burgeon, blow, blowth [*rare*]; floweret, floret, floscule, flowering plant; inflorescence, flowerage.

tree, sapling, seedling, stand, pollard, dryad [*fig.*]; oak, elm, beech, birch, timber tree, pine, palm, spruce, fir, hemlock, yew, larch, cedar, savin *or* savine, juniper, chestnut, maple, alder, ash, myrtle, magnolia, walnut, olive, poplar, willow, linden, lime; apple etc. (*fruit trees*) 298; arboretum etc. 371.

banyan, teak, acacia, deodar, pipal *or* pipal tree; fig tree, eucalyptus, gum tree.

woodlands, virgin forest, forest primeval, forest, wood, timberland, timber, wood lot; hurst, frith, holt [*poetic or dial.*], weald, wold [*obs.*], park, chase [*Eng.*], greenwood, grove, copse, coppice, bocage [*F.*], tope [*India*], clump of trees, thicket, spinet [*obs.*], spinney [*Eng.*], bosk, chaparral, ceja [*Texas*], motte [*local, U. S.*]; jungle, bush.

undergrowth, underwood, brushwood, brake, "the mid-forest brake" [Keats], boscage, scrub, palmetto barrens, bosch [*Dutch*]; heath, heather, fern, bracken, furze, gorse, whin, broom, genista, sedge, rush, bulrush, bamboo; weed, moss, foggage [*Scot.*], lichen, Iceland moss, mushroom, toadstool, fungus; turf, turbary, mold *or* mould.

grass, fog, second growth, second crop; herbage.

alfalfa, lucern *or* lucerne, alfilaria, clover, bent *or* bent grass, timothy, redtop *or* English grass, switch grass *or* black bent, blue grass, Kentucky blue grass, ribbon grass, meadow grass, spear grass, wire grass, blue joint, crab grass, bunch grass, meadow fescue, meadow foxtail, grama *or* mesquite grass, gama *or* sesame grass, sheep's fescue; cereal, wheat, barley, buckwheat, maize *or* Indian corn, oats, rice, rye.

368. Zoology

grassland, greensward, green, lawn, sward, common, maidan [*India*], mead, meadow, pasture, pasturage, prairie, pampas, steppe, llano, savanna, campo, plain, field, campus.

seaweed, alga (*pl.* algae), fucus, fucoid, conferva (*pl.* confervae), confervoid, wrack, dulse, kelp, rockweed, sea lettuce, gulfweed, sargasso, sargassum; plankton, benthos; Sargasso Sea.

v. **vegetate**, grow, flourish, bloom, flower, blossom; bud etc. (*expand*) 194; timber, retimber, coppice, copse; bush, plant, trim, cut.

adj. **vegetable**, vegetal, vegetive [*obs.*], vegetative, vegetarian; leguminous, herbaceous, herbal, botanic *or* botanical; arborary, arboreous, arborescent, arborical [*obs.*], arboreal, arboral; silvan *or* sylvan; treelike, dendriform, dendritic *or* dendritical, dendroid; grassy, verdant, verdurous; floral, floreal [*rare*], lignose *or* lignous [*rare*], ligneous, lignescent, wooden, woody; bosky, cespitose, copsy; mossy, turfy, turf-like, fungous, fungiform, fungoid; tigellate, radiculose, radicular, radiciform, radiciflorous, rhizanthous, radicated; endogenous, exogenous; deciduous, evergreen.

native, domestic, indigenous, native-grown, home-grown.

algal, fucoid, confervoid; planktonic, benthonic.

368. Zoology
[science of animals]

n. **zoology**, zoonomy, zoography, zootomy; morphology, anatomy, histology, embryology; comparative anatomy, animal physiology, comparative physiology; mammalogy.

anthropology, anthropotomy, ornithology, ornithotomy, ichthyology, ichthyotomy, herpetology, herpetotomy, ophiology, malaeology, helminthology, entomology, entomotomy; oryctology [*obs.*], paleontology *or* palaeontology; mastology, vermeology; taxidermy.

zoologist, zoographer, zoographist, zootomist, anatomist, anthropotomist, morphologist, promorphologist, anthropologist, ornithologist, ornithotomist, ichthyologist, ichthyotomist, herpetologist, herpetotomist, ophiliologist, malacologist, helminthologist, entomologist, entomotomist; oryctologist [*obs.*], paleontologist *or* palaeontologist; vermeologist, taxidermist.

[principal groups] **protozoa** (the simplest animals): Rhizopoda, rhizopod; Foraminifera, foraminifer; Radiolaria, radiolarian; Flagellata; Infusoria, infusorian; Gregarinae, gregarine.

coelentera *or* **coelenterata** (sponges, corals, jellyfishes): Porifera, poriferan; Cnidaria, cnida; Spongiae *or* Spongiaria *or* Spongiozoa, sponge, calcareous sponges, siliceous sponges; Anthozoa, anthozoan, coral polyps; Hydrozoa, hydrozoön, hydroid, medusa.

echinodermata (crinoids, starfishes, and sea urchins): Pelmatozoa, Asterozoa, Echinozoa; Cystidea *or* Cystoidea, cystid, cystidean; Crinoidea, stone lilies, crinoidean; Blastoidea, blastoid; Ophiuroidea *or* Ophiurioidea, brittle stars, ophiuroid *or* ophiurid; Asterioidea *or* Asteridea, starfishes, asteridian; Echinoidea, sea urchins, echinoid; Holothurioidea, sea cucumbers, holothurian, holothure.

vermes (worms): Platyhelminthes *or* Plathelminthes, flatworms, platyhelminth; Rotifera, rotifer; Nemathelminthes *or* Nematelminthes, roundworms; Gephyrea, marine annelids, gephyrean, gephyreoid; Annelida, annelid, annelidan, annelloid.

molluscoidea (mollusk-like animals): Bryozoa *or* Polyzoa, sea mosses, bryozoan; Brachiopoda, lamp shells, brachiopod.

mollusca (mollusks): Pelecypoda *or* Lamellibranchia, bivalves, lamellibranch; Scaphopoda, tooth-shells *or* tusk-shells, scaphopod; Amphineura, chitons; Gastropoda, univalves, snails, gastropod; Cephalopoda, nautilus, cuttlefish, squid, octopus, cephalopod *or* cephalopode.

arthropoda (articulates): Branchiata, Tracheata; Crustacea, crustacean; Trilobita, trilobite; Limuloidea *or* Xiphosura, horseshoe crab, limulus; Entomostraca, ostracoids, barnacles, entomostracan; Malacostraca, lobsters, crabs, malacostracan; Myriapoda, centipedes, galleyworms, millipeds, myriapod; Arachnida *or* Arachnoidea, spiders, scorpions, mites, ticks, arachnid, arachnidan; Insecta, insects.

vertebrata (vertebrate animals): Cyclostomata *or* Cyclostoma, lampreys; Pisces, fishes; Selachii, sharks, rays, selachian; Holocephali *or* Holocephala, chimaeras, spooks; Dipnoi, lungfishes; Teleostomi, ordinary fishes, ganoids, teleost, teleostean; Amphibia, amphibians, batrachians; Reptilia, reptiles; Aves, birds; Mammalia, mammals; Monotremata *or* Prototheria, monotremes; Marsupialia, marsupials, marsupialian *or* marsupian; Placentalia, placentals.

adj. **zoological**, zoologic; zoonomic; zoographical etc.
n.

protozoan, rhizopodous; foraminiferous, foraminous, foraminated; radiolarian; flagellate; infusorial, infusory; gregarine.

coelenterate, poriferan, spongiose *or* spongious, spongoid, spongiform; anthozoan, anthozoic, corallaceous, coralliferous, coralliform, coralligenous, coralligerous, coralloid, coralloidal; polyparous, polypean; hydrozoal, hydroid; medusiform, medusoid.

echinodermatous, echinodermal; pelmatozoan; crinoidal, crinoid; ophiuran, ophiuroid; asteridian; echinoid, holothurian.

vermicious, vermicular, vermiculate, vermiculose *or* vermiculous, vermiform; gephyrean, gephyreoid; annelid *or* annelidan, annelidous.

molluscoid, molluscoidal; bryozoan; brachiopod.

molluscan, molluscoid, molluscous; lamellibranch, lamellibranchiate, bivalvular, bivalvous, bivalved; gastropodous, univalve *or* univalved, univalvular; cephalopodic, cephalopodous, nautiloid.

arthropodal, articulate; branchial, branchiate; branchiferous; tracheate; crustacean, crustaceous; arachnoid, arachnoidal, arachnidan, arachnidial; insectile, insected.

vertebrate, vertebrated, vertebral; cyclostome, cyclostomous; piscatorial *or* piscatory, pisciform, piscine; amphibian, amphibial [*rare*], amphibious; batrachian, batrachoid; reptilian; avicular; mammalian, mammiferous.

369. Botany
[science of plants]

n. **botany**; physiological–, structural–, systematic- botany; phytography, phytology, phytotomy, phytobiology, phytogenesis *or* phytogeny, phytonomy, phytopathology; phytochemistry, phytochimy [*obsoles.*], vegetable chemistry; pomology; vegetable physiology, herborization, dendrology, mycology, fungology, algology; flora, Flora, Pomona; botanic garden etc. (garden) 371; *hortus siccus* [*L.*]; herbarium, herbal [*obs.*].

phyton, phytomer *or* phytomeron.

[principal groups] **thallogens** *or* **thallophytes** (thallus plants): algae and algoid forms: Cyanophyceae, blue-green algae; Chlorophyceae, green algae; Phaeophyceae, brown algae; Rhodophyceae, red algae.

fungi and fungoid forms: Schizomycetes, fission fungi, bacteria; Myxomycetes, slime molds; Phycomycetes, algae fungi, water molds; Ascomycetes, sac fungi, lichen fungi; Basidiomycetes, basidium fungi, rusts, mushrooms.

bryophytes (moss plants): Hepaticae, liverworts; Musci, mosses.

pteridophytes (fern plants): Lycopodiales: Sigillaria, Stigmaria, Lepidodendra, fossil trees, lepidodendrid, lepidodendroid; Lycopodiaceae; club mosses: Equisetales, calamites, Equisetacae, horsetails, equisetum; Filicales: Cycadofilices, cycad ferns; Filices, ferns, filicoid.

spermatophytes (seed plants): Gymnospermae (naked-seeded plants): gymnosperm. Cycadales, cycads; Gnetales, gnetums; Ginkgoales, ginkgo (*pl.* ginkgoes); Coniferae, conebearing evergreens, conifer.

Angiospermae (covered-seeded plants): angiosperm; Monocotyledones, monocotyledon, cereals, palms, lilies, orchids, banana, pineapple etc., endogens; Dicotyledones: oak, apple, sunflower, pea, dicotyledon.

botanist, phytologist, phytotomist, phytobiologist, dendrologist; mycologist, fungologist; phytopathologist, horticulturist etc. 371; herbalist, herbist, herbarist [*obs.*], herborist, herbarian; pomologist.

v. **botanize**, herborize.

adj. **botanic** *or* botanical, phytoid, dendroid *or* dendroidal, herbose *or* herbous, dendriform, dendritic *or* dendritical, dendrologous, herby, herbal; fungoid, fungous, mycologic *or* mycological, mycetoid, phytobiological, phytochemical, phytogenetic *or* phytogenous, pomological, horticultural.

thalloid, thalline; hepatic, musciform, muscoid, lycopodiaceous, lepidodendroid, equisetaceous, equisetiform, filicoid, filiciform, gymnospermous, cycadaceous, coniferous, angiospermous, angiospermatous, monocotyledonous, endogenous, dicotyledonous.

370. Cicuration
[economy or management of animals]

n. **cicuration** [*obs.*], taming etc. *v.*; zoohygiantics; domestication, domesticity; manège *or* manege, veterinary art; farriery; breeding; pisciculture; apiculture.

menagerie, vivarium, zoological garden, zoo [*colloq.*]; bear pit; aviary, apiary, alvearium, alveary, beehive, hive; aquarium, fishery, fish hatchery, fish pond; swan pond, duck pond; incubator.

371. Agriculture

[destruction of animals] phthisozoics etc. (*killing*) 361.

[keeper] herder, oxherd, neatherd (*obs.*), cowherd, grazier, drover, cowkeeper; shepherd, shepherdess; keeper, gamekeeper; trainer, breeder; bull whacker, cowboy, cow puncher, *vaquero* [*Sp. Amer.*]; horse trainer, bronchobuster [*slang*]; apiarian [*rare*], apiarist, apiculturist.

veterinarian, veterinary surgeon, vet [*colloq.*], horse doctor, horse leech [*rare*]; farrier [*obsoles. as veterinarian*], horseshoer.

inclosure, stable, barn, byre; cage etc. (*prison*) 752; hencoop, bird cage, coif, cauf; sheepfold etc. 232.

v. **tame**, domesticate, domesticize, acclimatize, breed, tend, corral, round up, break in, gentle, cicurate [*obs.*], break, bust [*slang*], break to harness, train; ride, drive etc. (*take horse*) 266; cage, bridle, etc. (*restrain*) 751; guide, spur, prick, lash, goad, whip; trot, gallop etc. (*move quickly*) 274; bolt; yoke, harness, harness up [*colloq.*], hitch, hitch up [*colloq.*], cinch.

groom, rub down, brush, currycomb; water, feed, fodder; bed, bed down, litter; drench, embrocate.

tend stock, milk, shear; water etc. (*groom*) *v.*; herd; raise, bring up, bring up by hand.

hatch, incubate, sit, brood, cover.

swarm, hive.

adj. **pastoral**, bucolic, rural; agricultural etc. 371.

tame, domestic, domesticated, broken, gentle, docile.

371. Agriculture
[economy or management of plants]

n. **agriculture**, cultivation, husbandry, farming; georgics, geoponics; agronomy, agronomics, tillage, tilth, gardening, spade husbandry, vintage; horticulture, arboriculture, silviculture, forestry; floriculture; landscape gardening; viticulture.

husbandman, horticulturist, gardener, florist; agricultor [*rare*], agriculturist, agronomist, yeoman, farmer, cultivator, tiller of the soil, plowman *or* ploughman, reaper, sower; logger, lumberman, lumberjack, forester, woodcutter, pioneer, backwoodsman; granger, habitant, *vigneron* [*F.*], viniculturist, vine-grower, vintager, viticulturist; Triptolemus.

garden; botanic–, winter–, ornamental–, flower–, kitchen–, market–, truck–, hop- garden; nursery; greenhouse, hothouse, conservatory, forcing house, cold-frame; bed, border, seed plot; grassplot *or* grassplat, lawn; parterre; shrubbery, plantation, avenue, arboretum, pinery, pinetum, orchard; vineyard, vinery, orangery.

field, meadow, mead, green, common, maidan [*India*]; park etc. (*pleasure ground*) 840; farm etc. (*abode*) 189.

v. **cultivate**, till, till the soil, farm, garden, sow, plant; reap, mow, cut; manure, dress the ground, dig, spade, delve, dibble, hoe, plow *or* plough, harrow, rake, weed, lop and top; backset; force, seed, turf, transplant, thin out, bed, prune, graft.

adj. **agricultural**, agronomic, geoponic, georgic, agrestical [*obs.*], agrestian, praedial *or* predial; horticultural, viticultural.

arable, plowable *or* ploughable, tillable.

rural, rustic, country, agrarian, pastoral, bucolic, Arcadian.

372. Mankind

n. **mankind**, man; human -race, –species, –kind, –nature; humanity, mortality, flesh, generation.

[science of man] anthropology, anthropogeny, anthropography, anthroposophy; ethnology, ethnography; anthropotomy, androtomy; humanitarianism.

human being; person, personage; individual, creature, fellow creature, mortal, body, somebody, one; such a one, some one; soul, living soul; earthling; party, head, hand; member, members of the cast, *dramatis personae* [*L.*]; *quidam* [*L.*].

people, persons, folk, public, society, world; community, –at large; general public; nation, nationality; state, realm; commonweal, commonwealth; republic, body politic; million etc. (*commonalty*) 876; population etc. (*inhabitant*) 188.

cosmopolite; lords of creation; ourselves.

adj. **human**, mortal, personal, individual, national, civic, public, social; cosmopolitan; anthropoid.

372a. Anthropology

n. **anthropology**; physical anthropology, anthropometry, human evolution, human paleontology; cultural anthropology *or* social anthropology, ethnology, ethnography, archaeology, linguistics.

[eras of recent life] Cenezoic era; Tertiary period *or* Age of Mammals (Paleocene epoch, Eocene epoch, Oligocene epoch, Miocene epoch, Pliocene epoch), Quaternary period *or* Age of Man (Pleistocene epoch, Holocene epoch).

372a. Anthropology

[fossil primates] Parapithecus; Propliopithecus; Dryopithecus, Dryopithecus fontani, Dryopithecus rhenanus, Dryopithecus darwini; Proconsul africanus; Pliopithecus; Australopithecus africanus, Paranthropus robustus, Plesianthropus transvaalensis.

[fossil races of man] Gigantanthropus or Gigantopithecus blacki, Meganthropus paleojavanicus; Pithecanthropus robustus, Pithecanthropus erectus, Pithecanthropus modjokertensis; Sinanthropus pekinensis or Peking man; Homo soloensis or Solo man; Homo Africanthropus; Homo heidelbergensis or Heidelberg man; Homo neanderthalensis or Neanderthal man, Rhodesian group, Mousterian group, Ehringsdorf group (Ehringsdorf forms, Tabun Mt. Carmel forms, Steinheim forms), Skhul Mt. Carmel forms, Galilee forms; Homo Sapiens, Galley Hill man, London man, Swanscombe man, Fontechevade man; Cro-Magnon man, Grimaldi man, Predmost man, Brünn man, Chancelade man, Ofnet man; Wadjak man, Keilor man, Talgai man; Oldoway man, Boskop man, Springbok man, Fish Hoek man; Eoanthropus dawsoni or Piltdown "man."

[prehistoric cultural eras] Eolithic or Dawn Stone Age; Paleolithic or Old Stone Age, Lower Paleolithic Age (pre-Chellean stage, Chellean stage, Acheulean stage), Middle Paleolithic Age or Mousterian stage, Upper Paleolithic Age (Aurignacian stage, Solutrean stage, Magdalenian stage); Epipaleolithic or Mesolithic Age or Azilian-Tardenoisian stage; Neolithic or New Stone Age; Metal Age; Bronze Age, Early Bronze Age, Middle Bronze Age, Late Bronze Age; Iron Age.

[races] Caucasoid (Ainu, Australoid, Dravidian, Vedda; Alpine, Armenoid, Mediterranean, Nordic; Dinaric, East Baltic, Polynesian); Mongoloid (Asiatic, Indonesian-Malay, American Indian); Negroid (Forest Negro, Negrito; Hottentot-Bushman, Nilote or Nilotic Negro, Oceanic Negro).

index; acrocranic index, acromiocristal index, bodily fullness index, brachial index, cephalic index (dolichocephalic index, mesocephalic index, brachycephalic index), cranial index, cranial breadth-height index, cranial length-height index, crural index, facial index (euryprosopic index, mesoprosopic index, leptoprosopic index), femorohumeral index, forearm-hand index, gnathic index, hand index, intermembral index, ischium-pubis index, length-breadth sacral index, lower leg-foot index, maxillo-alveolar index, morphological or Naccarati's index, nasal index (platyrrhine index, mesorrhine index, leptorrhine index), orbital index, palatal index, pelvic breadth-height index, pelvic inlet index, pilastric index, platycnemic index, platymeric index, sicklemia index, stem-leg length or Manouvrier's skelic index, thoracic index, tibio-femoral index, tibio-radial index, total facial index, transverse fronto-parietal index, trunk index, upper facial index, vertical lumbar index; Frankfort line or Frankfort plane; Mongoloid eye; epicanthic or Mongoloid fold, external epicanthic fold, internal epicanthic fold; Negroid lip; prognathism; peppercorn hair; steatopygy or steatopygia; genotype, phenotype; blood type or group; constitutional type, pyknic type, leptosome type, athletic type; ectomorphy, mesomorphy, endomorphy.

culture; culture pattern, ideal pattern, behavioral pattern; integration of culture; function, theme, configuration, drive, postulate, affirmation; Apollonian configuration, Dionysian configuration; culture trait or element; trait complex or culture complex; age area, culture area, culture center or nucleus, marginal area; cultural evolution, savagery, barbarism, civilization; invention, discovery; convergence, parallelism; cultural transmission or borrowing; diffusion, stimulus diffusion; assimilation; acculturation, antagonistic acculturation, marginal acculturation, planitational acculturation; evolutionism, diffusionism (heliolithic diffusionism, culture-historical diffusionism), Kulturkreis, functionalism.

folkway; custom; mos; moral; law, collective responsibility; tort or private wrong crime or public wrong; sanction, legal or organized sanction; oath, compurgation; ordeal.

kinship; kin group; consanguine kinship, affinal kinship; unilateral kinship or descent, bilateral kinship or descent, mixed kinship or descent; patrilineal or agnatic kinship, matrilineal or uterine kinship; sibling; cross-cousin, parallel cousin or ortho-cousin; family; nuclear family, stem family, elementary family, composite family, extended family, joint family (patrilocal joint family, matrilocal joint family); conjugal or biological or small family, consanguineal family; patriarchal family; paternal family, maternal family; sib; clan; complex or genealogical clan, equalitarian clan; patrilineal clan, matrilineal clan; gens; lineage, unilocal lineage,

373. Man

multilocal lineage; phratry; moiety, simple moiety, compound moiety; tribe; familiarity *or* privileged familiarity, kin familiarity (avunculate, amitate), joking relationship; kin avoidance.

373. Man

n. **man**, male, he; manhood etc. (*adolescence*) 131; gentleman, sir, master, dan [*archaic*], don, huzur [*India*], sahib [*India*]; yeoman, chap [*colloq.*], wight [*now chiefly jocose*], swain, fellow, blade, beau, gaffer [*dial. Eng.*], goodman [*archaic*]; husband etc. (*married man*) 903; boy etc. (*youth*) 129.

mister, Mr., *monsieur* (*abbr.* M., *pl.* MM. *or* Messrs.) [*F.*], *Herr* [*Ger.*], *signor* [*It., used before name*], *signore* [*It.*], *signorino* [*It., dim. of signore*], signior [*Eng. form*], seignior, *señor* [*Sp.*], *senhor* [*Pg.*].

[male animal] cock, drake, gander, dog, boar, stag, hart, buck, horse, entire horse, stallion; gib [*rare*], tom, tomcat; he-goat, billy-goat [*colloq.*]; ram, tup; bull, bullock; capon; ox, gelding; steer, stot [*prov. Eng.*].

adj. **male**, he, masculine; manly, virile; unwomanly, unfeminine.

374. Woman

n. **woman**, she, female, petticoat; skirt, jane [*both slang*].

feminality, femininity, femineity, feminacy, feminity, muliebrity; gynics.

womankind; womanhood etc. (*adolescence*) 131; the sex, the fair; fair sex, softer sex; weaker vessel.

dame [*archaic except as an elderly woman*], madam, mastress [Chaucer, *obs.*], lady, Donna, belle, matron, dowager, goody, grammer [*dial. Eng.*], memsahib [*Anglo-Ind.*], sahiba [*Hind.*], bibi [*Hind.*], frow, vrouw [*Du.*], good woman, good wife [*archaic*]; squaw; wife etc. (*marriage*) 903; matronage, matronhood.

bachelor girl, new woman, feminist, suffragist, suffragette; spinster, old maid.

nymph, houri, wench, grisette; girl etc. (*youth*) 129.

mistress, Mrs., *madame* (*pl. mesdames*) [*F.*], *Frau* [*Ger.*], *signora* [*It.*], *señora* [*Sp.*], *senhora* [*Pg.*]; Ms.; miss, *mademoiselle* (*pl. mesdemoiselles*) [*F.*], *Fräulein* [*Ger.*], *signorina* [*It.*], *señorita* [*Sp.*], *senhorita* [*Pg.*].

[effeminacy] betty, cot betty, cotquean, henhussy, molly, mollycoddle, muff, old woman, tame cat [*all contemptuous*].

[female animal] hen; bitch, slut, brach, brachet; sow, doe, roe, mare; she-goat, nanny-goat [*colloq.*], nanny [*colloq.*]; ewe, cow; lioness, tigress; vixen.

harem, gynaeceum *or* gynaecium, seraglio, zenana [*India*], purdah [*India*].

adj. **female**, she; feminine, womanly, ladylike, matronly, girlish, maidenly; womanish, effeminate, unmanly; gynecic *or* gynaecic.

375. Physical Sensibility

n. **sensibility**; sensitiveness etc. *adj.;* physical sensibility, feeling, impressibility, perceptivity, susceptibility, aesthetics *or* esthetics; moral sensibility etc. 822.

sensation, impression; consciousness etc. (*knowledge*) 490.

external senses.

v. **be sensible of** etc. *adj.;* feel, perceive; feel keenly, –exquisitely.

render sensible etc. *adj.;* sharpen, refine, excite, stir, cultivate, tutor.

impress, cause sensation; excite–, produce– an impression.

adj. **sensible**, sensitive, sensuous; aesthetic *or* esthetic, perceptive, sentient; conscious etc. (*aware*) 490; alive, alive to impressions, answering quickly to, impressionable, responsive, easily affected, quick in response.

acute, sharp, keen, vivid, lively, impressive, thin-skinned.

adv. **to the quick**; on the raw [*slang*].

376. Physical Insensibility

n. **insensibility**, physical insensibility; obtuseness etc. *adj.;* palsy, paralysis, anaesthesia *or* anesthesia, narcosis, narcotization, hypnosis, stupor, coma; twilight sleep, *Dämmerschlaf* [*Ger.*]; sleep etc. (*inactivity*) 683; moral insensibility etc. 823; hemiplegia, motor paralysis.

anaesthetic *or* anesthetic, anaesthetic agent; local–, general– anaesthetic; opium, ether, chloroform, chloral; nitrous oxide, laughing gas; exhilarating gas, protoxide of nitrogen; cocaine, novocain; refrigeration.

v. **be insensible** etc. *adj.;* have a –thick skin, –rhinoceros hide.

render insensible etc. *adj.;* blunt, cloy, satiate, pall, obtund, benumb, numb, deaden, freeze, paralyze; anaesthetize *or* anesthetize, put under the influence of chloroform etc. *n.;* put to sleep, hypnotize, stupefy, stun.

adj. **insensible**, unfeeling, senseless, impercipient, callous, thick-skinned, pachydermatous; hard, hardened; case-hardened; proof; obtuse, dull; anaesthetic *or* anesthetic; paralytic, palsied, numb, dead.

377. Physical Pleasure

n. **pleasure**; physical–, sensual–, sensuous - pleasure; bodily enjoyment, animal gratification, delight, sensual delight, hedonism, sensuality; luxuriousness etc. *adj.;* dissipation, round of pleasure; titillation, gusto, creature comforts, comfort, ease; pillow etc. (*support*) 215; luxury, lap of luxury; purple and fine linen; bed of -down. –roses; velvet, clover; cup of Circe etc. (*intemperance*) 954.

treat; diversion, entertainment, banquet, regalement, refreshment, regale; feast; delice [*obs.*]; dainty etc. 394; *bonne bouche* [*F.*].

source of pleasure etc. 829; happiness, felicity, bliss, beatitude etc. (*mental enjoyment*) 827.

v. **enjoy**, pleasure [*rare*]; feel–, experience–, receive- pleasure; relish; luxuriate–, revel–, riot–, bask–, swim–, wallow- in; feast on; gloat -over, –on; smack the lips; roll under the tongue.

live on the fat of the land, live in comfort etc. *adv.;* bask in the sunshine, *faire ses choux gras* [*F.*].

give pleasure etc. 829; charm, delight, enchant.

adj. **enjoying** etc. *v.;* luxurious, voluptuous, sensual, comfortable, cosy, snug, in comfort, at ease, in clover [*colloq.*].

agreeable etc. 829; grateful, refreshing, comforting, cordial, genial; gratifying, titillative, sensous; apolaustic, hedonic, hedonistic, palatable etc. 394; sweet etc. (*sugar*) 396; fragrant etc. 400; melodious etc. 413; lovely etc. (*beautiful*) 845.

adv. **in comfort** etc. *n.;* on a bed of roses etc. *n.;* at one's ease; on flowery beds of ease.

378. Physical Pain

n. **pain**; suffering, sufferance [*rare*]; bodily–, physical- -pain, –suffering; mental suffering etc. 828; dolor *or* dolour, ache; aching etc. *v.;* smart; shoot, shooting; twinge, twitch, gripe, hurt, cut; sore, soreness; discomfort; headache, *malaise* [*F.*], megrim, migraine, cephalalgy, cephalalgia; otalgia, earache, ischiagra, lumbago, arthritis, neuritis, gout, podagra, rheumatism, sciatica, ischialgia, neuralgia, tic douloureux, toothache, odontalgia; stiffneck, torticollis.

spasm, cramp; nightmare, ephialtes; kink, crick, stitch; convulsion, throe; throb etc. (*agitation*) 315; pang; colic; tormina, gripes.

sharp–, piercing–, throbbing–, grinding–, stabbing–, shooting–, gnawing–, burning- pain.

torment, torture, agony, anguish, laneination, rack, cruciation, crucifixion, martyrdom; vivisection.

martyr, sufferer; toad under a harrow.

v. **suffer**; feel–, experience–, suffer–, undergo- pain etc. *n.;* ache, smart, bleed; tingle, shoot; twinge, twitch, lancinate; writhe, wince, make a wry face; sit on -thorns, –pins and needles.

pain, give pain, inflict pain; lacerate; hurt, chafe, sting, bite, gnaw, stab, grind, gripe, pinch, tweak; grate, gall, fret, prick, pierce, wring, convulse; torment, torture; rack, agonize; crucify; cruciate [*obs.*], excruciate, break on the wheel, put to the rack; flog etc. (*punish*) 972; grate on the ear etc. (*harsh sound*) 410.

adj. **in pain** etc. *n.,* in a state of pain; under the harrow; pained etc. *v.;* gouty, podagric, torminous, torminal.

painful; aching etc. *v.;* poignant, pungent, torturous, baleful [*rare*], biting; with exposed nerves, sore, raw.

379. Touch
[sensation of pressure]

n. **touch**; tact, taction, tactility; contact, tangency, tangence [*rare*], impact, attain [*archaic*]; feeling, kiss, osculation, graze, glance, brush; lick, licking, lambency, palpation, palpability; contrectation [*rare*]; manipulation, palmation [*obs.*], contaction [*obs.*]; stereognosis; rubbing, kneading, massage.

[organ of touch] hand, palm, finger, forefinger, thumb, paw, feeler, antenna; tongue, palpus.

v. **touch**, feel, handle, finger, thumb, paw, fumble, grope, grabble; twiddle, tweedle [*obs. or dial.*]; pass–, run- the fingers over; stroke, palpate, palm, massage, rub, knead, manipulate, wield; throw out a feeler.

adj. **tactual**, tactile; tangible, palpable, tangent, contactual [*rare*], lambent; touching etc. *v.;* stereognostic.

380. Sensations of Touch

n. **itching** etc. *v.;* formication; aura [*med.*].
tickling, titillation.
itch, scabies, psora, pruritus, prurigo [*all med.*]; mange.

v. **itch**, tingle, creep, thrill, sting; prick, prickle.
tickle, titillate.

adj. **itching**, tingling etc. *v.*
ticklish, titillative.

119

381. Numbness

itchy, psoric, scabious, mangy; creepy, crawly; prurient.

381. Numbness
[insensibility to touch]

n. **numbness** etc. (*physical insensibility*) 376; anaesthesia *or* anesthesia, narcosis, narcotization; pins and needles [*colloq.*].

v. **benumb** etc. 376; stupefy, narcotize, drug, deaden, paralyze.

adj. **numb**; benumbed etc. *v.;* insensible, unfeeling, anaesthetic *or* anesthetic, deadened; intangible, impalpable; dazed, dazy [*rare*], comatose, torporific, narcotic, carotic.

382. Heat

n. **heat**, caloric; temperature, warmth, fervor, calidity [*obs.*], torridity; incalescence *or* incalescency [*rare*], incandescence; recalescence, decalescence; adiathermancy, athermancy, diathermacy, diathermance *or* diathermancy *or* diathermaneity; phlogiston [*old chem.*], phlogisis; thermogenesis; liquation.

summer, dog days, canicule, canicular days; baking etc. 384-, white-, tropical-, Afric-, Indian-, Bengal-, summer-, blood- heat; sirocco, simoom *or* simoon, hot wave, sun at noon, "the bloody Sun, at noon" [Coleridge], vertical rays, broiling sun; insolation; warming etc. 384.

flush, glow, blush, bloom, redness; rubicundity; fever, hectic; febricity, pyrexia.

fire, spark, scintillation, flash, flame, blaze; bonfire; firework, pyrotechny; wildfire; sheet of fire, lambent flame; devouring element; pyrotechnics.

sun etc. (*luminary*) 423.

hot springs, geysers; thermae, hot baths; sauna, hot tub; Turkish-, electric-, Russian-bath; steam.

fire worship, pyrolatry, sun worship, heliolatry, Sabaeanism *or* Sabeanism *or* Sabeism, Parsiism *or* Parseeism, Zoroastrianism; pyrolator, heliolator, Sabaean *or* Sabean, Parsi *or* Parsee, Zoroastrian.

[science of heat] pyrology; thermology, thermotics; thermometer etc. 389.

v. **be hot** etc. *adj.;* glow, flush, sweat, swelter, bask, smoke, reek, stew, simmer, seethe, boil, burn, singe, scorch, scald, grill, broil, blaze, flame; smolder *or* smoulder; parch, fume, pant.

heat etc. (*make hot*) 384; insolate, incandesce, recalesce.

thaw, fuse, melt, liquate, liquefy; give.

adj. **warm**, mild, genial, tepid, lukewarm, unfrozen; calid; warm as -toast, -wool.

hot, heated, fervid, fervent; roasting, sweltry; reeking etc. *v.;* ardent, aglow; baking etc. 384; sunny, sunshiny, aestival *or* estival, canicular, torrid, tropical; thermal, thermic; calorific.

red-, white-, smoking-, burning etc. *v.* -, piping- hot; like -a furnace, -an oven; hot as -fire, -pepper; hot enough to roast an ox.

close, sultry, stifling, stuffy, suffocating, oppressive.

fiery; incandescent, incalescent [*rare*]; candent, ebullient, glowing, smoking, live; on fire; blazing etc. *v.;* in flames, in a blaze; alight, afire, ablaze; unquenched; unextinguished; smoldering *or* smouldering; in a -heat, -glow, -perspiration, -sweat; sudorific; sweltering, sweltered; blood-hot, blood-warm; recalescent, decalescent, thermogenic, thermogenous, thermogenetic, thermotic *or* thermotical; pyrotechnic *or* pyrotechnical; phlogotic *or* phlogistic; pyrological.

[transmitting radiant heat] diathermic, diathermal, diathermanous.

[not transmitting radiant heat] athermanous, adiathermal, adiathermanous, adiathermic.

volcanic, plutonic, igneous.

isothermal, isothermic, isothermical.

feverish, febrile, febricose [*rare*], febrific, febrifacient, pyretic, pyrexic [*rare*], inflamed, burning; in a fever.

383. Cold

n. **cold**, coldness etc. *adj.;* frigidity, gelidity, algidity, glaciation, gelidness [*rare*], frore [*poetic*], inclemency, fresco [*obs.*]; "a hard, dull bitterness of cold" [Whittier].

winter; depth of-, hard- winter; Siberia, Nova Zembla; Arctic, North Pole; Antarctic, South Pole.

ice; sleet; hail, hailstone; frost, rime, hoarfrost; rime-, white-, hard-, black-, sharp-frost; barf [*Hind.*], glaze, lolly [*N. Amer.*]; icicle, thick-ribbed ice; iceberg, floe, berg, ice field, ice float *or* ice floe, ice pack, glacier; nevé [*F.*], sérac [*F.*]; pruina [*L. & It.*]; icequake.

snow, snowflake, snowdrift, fall of snow, snowstorm, heavy fall; snowball, snowslide, snow-slip, snow avalanche.

[sensation of cold] chilliness etc. *adj.;* chill; shivering etc. *v.;* goose flesh, goose skin, rigor, horripilation, aching, ache, chilblains, frostbite, chattering of teeth.

385. Refrigeration

v. **be cold** etc. *adj.;* shiver, starve [*rare in U. S.*], quake, shake, tremble, shudder, didder, quiver; perish with cold; chill etc. (*render cold*) 385; horripilate, glaciate [*obs.*].

adj. **cold,** cool; chill, chilly; gelid, frigid, frore [*poet.*], algid; fresh, keen, bleak, raw, inclement, bitter, biting, cutting, nipping, piercing, pinching; clay-cold; starved etc. (*made cold*) 385; shivering etc. *v.;* aguish, *transi de froid* [*F.*], frostbitten, frost-bound, frost-nipped.

cold as - a stone, −marble, −lead, −iron, −a frog, −charity, −Christmas; cool as -a cucumber, −custard.

icy, glacial, ice-built, frosty, freezing, wintry, brumal, hibernal, boreal, arctic, Siberian, hiemal *or* hyemal; hyperborean, hyperboreal [*rare*]; snow-bound, ice-bound; frozen out.

unwarmed, unheated; unthawed.

lukewarm, tepid; warm etc. *adj.* 382.

isocheimal, isocheimenal, isocheimic.

adv. **coldly,** bitterly etc. *adj.;* à pierre fendre [*F.*]; with chattering teeth.

384. Calefaction

n. **calefaction,** tepefaction, torrefaction; increase of temperature; heating etc. *v.;* melting, fusion; liquefaction etc. 335; burning etc. *v.;* combustion; incension [*obs.*], accension [*archaic*]; concremation, cremation; scorification; cautery, cauterization; ustulation [*rare*], calcination; incineration; carbonization; cupellation.

ignition, kindling, inflammation, adustion [*rare*], flagration [*obs.*], deflagration, conflagration; empyrosis, incendiarism; arson; *auto-da-fé* [*Pg.*], *auto-de-fe* [*Sp.*], the stake, burning at the stake; suttee.

incendiary, arsonist, arsonite, *pétroleur* (*fem. pétroleuse*) [*F.*], pyromaniac, fire bug, macher [*slang*].

boiling etc. *v.;* coction, ebullition, ebullience *or* ebulliency, aestuation *or* estuation, elixation [*obs.*], decoction; ebullioscope, ebulliometer; hot spring, geyser.

crematory, crematorium, burning ghat [*India*], incinerator, calcinatory; cupel; furnace etc. 386.

wrap, blanket, flannel, wool, fur; muff, mittens, wristers; muffler, fascinator, comforter, comfortable; ear-muffs, ear-flaps; shawl; wadding etc. (*lining*) 224; clothing etc. 225.

cauterant, scorifier; match etc. (*fuel*) 388; caustic, lunar caustic, apozem, moxa; aqua fortis, aqua regia; catheretic, nitric acid, nitrochlorhydric acid, nitromuriatic acid, radium.

sunstroke, *coup de soleil* [*F.*]; insolation [*rare*], siriasis, [*med.*]; sunburn, burn, tan, suntan, ambustion [*rare*].

pottery, ceramics, crockery, porcelain, china; earthenware, stoneware; pot, mug, terra cotta, brick.

[products of combustion] cinder, ash, scoriae; embers, slag, cinders, clinker, coke, carbon, charcoal.

inflammability, combustibility, accendibility.

[transmission of heat] diathermance *or* diathermancy etc. 382; transcalency.

v. **heat,** warm, chafe, foment; make hot etc. 382; sun oneself, bask in the sun.

fire, set fire to, set on fire; kindle, enkindle, light, ignite, strike a light; apply the -match, −torch- to; rekindle, relume; fan-, add fuel to- the flame; poke−, stir−, blow- the fire; make a bonfire of; build a campfire.

melt, thaw, fuse; liquefy etc. 335.

burn, inflame, roast, toast, fry, grill, incinerate, singe, parch, bake, torch [*slang*], torrefy, scorch; brand, cauterize, sear, burn in; corrode, char, carbonize, calcine, incinerate, calefy, calcinate [*rare*], tepefy, cupel, cupellate [*rare*], deflagrate [*chem.*]; smelt, scorify; reduce to ashes; burn to a cinder; commit−, consign- to the flames.

take−, catch- fire; blaze etc. (*flame*) 382.

boil, digest, stew, cook, seethe, ebullate [*rare*], scald, parboil, simmer; do to rags [*colloq.*].

adj. **heated** etc. *v.;* molten, sodden; *réchauffé* [*F.*]; heating etc. *v.;* adjust; ambustial [*rare*], calefactive, deflagrable [*chem.*], ustulate; calcinatory, cauterant; aestuous [*rare*]; apozemial, scoriaceous; transcalent; burnt etc. *v.;* volcanic.

inflammable, burnable, inflammatory, accendible, combustible.

diathermic, diathermal, diathermanous.

radioactive; salamandrine.

385. Refrigeration

n. **refrigeration,** infrigidation, reduction of temperature; cooling etc. *v.;* congelation, conglaciation [*obs.*], glaciation, regelation; ice etc. 383; solidification etc. (*density*), 321; ice box, cooler, ice chest; refrigerator, freezer, etc. 387.

fire-extinguisher, *extincteur* [*F.*]; fire annihilator; amianthus, amianth, earth flax, mountain flax; asbestos, flexible asbestos; fireman, fire brigade, fire department, fire engine.

incombustibility, incombustibleness etc. *adj.*

v. **cool,** fan, refrigerate, infrigidate, refresh, ice; congeal, freeze, glaciate; benumb, starve

386. Furnace

[*rare in U. S.*], pinch, chill, petrify, chill to the marrow, regelate, nip, cut, pierce, bite, make one's teeth chatter.

damp, slack; quench; put out, stamp out; extinguish.

go out, burn out, die.

adj. **cooled** etc. *v.;* frozen out; cooling etc. *v.;* frigorific, infrigidative [*rare*], refrigerative [*rare*].

incombustible, asbestic, nonflammable, unflammable, uninflammable; fireproof; amianthine, amianthoid *or* amianthoidal.

386. Furnace

n. **furnace**, stove; air-tight-, Franklin-, Dutch-, gas-, oil-, electric- stove; cookstove, cooker, oven, brick oven, tin oven, Dutch oven, range, kitchener [*Eng.*]; fireless- heater, -cooker; forge, fiery furnace; kiln, brickkiln, limekiln; tuyère, brasier, salamander, heater, warming pan, foot-stove, foot-warmer; radiator, register, coil; boiler, caldron *or* cauldron, seething caldron, pot; urn, kettle, frying pan, stew pan, spider, broiler, skillet, tripod, chafing dish; retort, crucible, alembic, still; waffle irons; flatiron, sadiron; curling tongs; toasting fork, toaster.

galley, caboose *or* camboose; hothouse, conservatory, bakehouse, washhouse, laundry; athanor, hypocaust, reverberatory; volcano.

fireplace, hearth, grate, firebox, andiron, firedog, fire-irons; poker, tongs, shovel, hob, trivet; damper, crane, pothooks, chains, turnspit, spit, gridiron.

hot bath; thermae, calidarium, tepidarium, vaporarium, sudatorium [*all L.*]; sudatory; Turkish-, Russian -vapor-, electric-, sitz-, hip-, shower-, warm - bath; tub, hot tub, sauna; lavatory.

387. Refrigeratory

n. **refrigeratory**, refrigerator; frigidarium; cold storage; ice-, freezing-, refrigerating-machine; refrigerating plant; icehouse, ice pail, ice bag, ice box, ice chest, ice pack, cold pack; cooler, wine cooler.

refrigerant, freezing mixture, ice, ammonia.

388. Fuel

n. **fuel**, firing, combustible, coal, wallsend [*Eng.*], anthracite, blind coal, glance coal; bituminous-, egg-, stove-, nut-, pea- coal; culm, coke, carbon, briquette, slack, cannel coal *or* cannel, lignite, charcoal; turf, peat; oil, gas, natural gas, electricity; ember, cinder etc. (*products of combustion*) 384; ingle; port-fire; fire-barrel, fireball, firebrand.

log, backlog, yule log *or* yule clog, firewood, fagot *or* faggot, kindling wood, kindlings, brushwood, bavin [*dial. Eng.*].

tinder, touchwood; punk, German tinder, amadou; smudge [*U. S. & Can.*], pyrotechnic sponge.

fumigator, incense, joss-stick; sulphur, brimstone, disinfectant.

[illuminants] candle etc. (*luminary*) 423; oil etc. (*grease*) 356.

brand, torch, fuse *or* fuze, wick; spill, match, safety match, lights [*chiefly Eng.*], light, lucifer, congreve, vesuvian, vesta, fusee *or* fuzee, locofoco [*obs.*], linstock [*obs. or hist.*].

v. coal, stoke; feed, fire etc. 384.

adj. carbonaceous; combustible, inflammable; slow-burning, free-burning.

389. Thermometer

n. **thermometer**, thermocouple, thermometrograph, thermopile, thermostat, thermoscope; differential thermometer, telethermometer, pyrometer, calorimeter, radiomicrometer.

390. Taste

n. **taste**, flavor, gust [*archaic*], gusto, savor; goût [*F.*], relish; sapor [*obs.*], sapidity; twang [*dial. Eng.*], smack, smatch [*dial. Eng.*]; aftertaste, tang.

tasting; degustation, gustation.

palate; tongue; tooth; stomach.

v. **taste**, savor, smatch [*dial. Eng.*], smack, flavor; tickle the palate etc. (*savory*) 394; smack the lips.

adj. **sapid**, saporific, gustable, gustatory, gustative, tastable, savory, gustful, tasty; strong; flavored, spiced, tanged [*obs.*]; palatable etc. 394.

391. Insipidity

n. **insipidity**; tastelessness etc. *adj.;* jejuneness.

v. **be tasteless** etc. *adj.*

adj. **insipid**; void of taste etc. 390; tasteless, gustless [*obs.*], unsavory, unflavored, jejune, savorless; ingustible [*obs.*], mawkish, milk and water, weak, stale, flat, vapid, fade [*F.*], wishy-washy [*colloq.*], mild; untasted.

392. Pungency

n. **pungency**, piquancy, poignancy, haut-goût [*F.*], acrity [*obs.*], strong taste, twang [*dial. Eng.*], race, tang, nip, kick [*slang*].

sharpness etc. *adj.;* acrimony, acridity; roughness etc. (*sour*) 392; unsavoriness etc. 395.

[pungent articles] niter, saltpeter; mustard, cayenne, caviare; seasoning etc. (*condiment*) 393; brine; carbonate of ammonia; sal-ammoniac, sal-volatile; smelling salts; hartshorn.

dram, cordial, nip, toothful [*colloq.*], tickler [*colloq.*], bracer [*colloq.*], pick-me-up [*colloq.*], potion, liqueur, *pousse-café* [*F.*].

tobacco, Lady Nicotine, Nicotiana, nicotian [*rare*], nicotine; snuff, quid; cigar *or* segar, cigarette, fag [*slang*], cheroot, Trichinopoli cheroot, Trichi [*colloq.*], Havana *or* Habana [*Sp.*], Cuban tobacco; weed [*colloq.*]; fragrant–, Indianweed; Cavendish, fid [*dial.*], rappee, stogy, old soldier [*slang*].

v. **be pungent** etc. *adj.*; bite the tongue.

render pungent etc. *adj.*; season, spice, bespice, salt, pepper, pickle, brine, devil, curry.

use tobacco, smoke, chew, inhale, take snuff.

adj. **pungent**, strong; high-flavored, full-flavored; high-tasted, high-seasoned; gamy, high; sharp, stinging, rough, piquant, racy; biting, mordant; spicy; seasoned etc. *v.*; hot, –as pepper; peppery, vellicative, vellicating, escharotic, meracious [*obs.*]; acrid, acrimonious, bitter; rough etc. (*sour*) 397; unsavory etc. 395.

salt, saline, brackish, briny; salt as -brine, –a herring, –Lot's wife.

393. Condiment

n. **condiment**, flavoring, salt, ketchup *or* catsup, mustard, pepper, cayenne, cinnamon, nutmeg, curry, seasoning, sauce, spice, relish, *sauce piquante* [*F.*], *sauce tartare* [*F.*], caviare, pot herbs, onion, sauce-alone, hedge garlic, garlic, pickle; achar [*Hind.*], allspice, appetizer; bell–, Jamaica–, red- pepper; horseradish, capsicum, chutney, tabasco; cubeb, pimento.

v. **season** etc. (*render pungent*) 392.

394. Savoriness

n. **savoriness** etc. *adj.*; nectareousness; relish, zest.

appetizer, *apéritif* [*F.*], *hors d'oeuvre* [*F.*]

delicacy, titbit, dainty, ambrosia, nectar, delice [*obs.*], *bonne-bouche* [*F.*]; game, turtle, venison; delicatessen.

v. **be savory** etc. *adj.*; tickle the -palate, –appetite; tempt the appetite, taste good, taste of something; flatter the palate.

render palatable etc. *adj.*

relish, like, smack the lips.

adj. **savory**, to one's taste, tasty, good, palatable, good-tasting, pleasing, nice, dainty, delectable; toothful [*obs.*], toothsome; gustful, appetizing, lickerish *or* liquorish [*rare*], delicate, delicious, exquisite, rich, luscious, ambrosial, ambrosian, nectareous, distinctive.

adv. per amusare la bocca [*It.*].

395. Unsavoriness

n. **unsavoriness** etc. *adj.*; amaritude [*rare*], acrimony, acritude [*obs.*], acridity, acridness, roughness etc. (*sour*) 397; acerbity, austerity. gall and wormwood, rue, quassia, aloes, asafetida *or* asafoetida; hemlock; sickener; Marah.

v. **be unpalatable** etc. *adj.*; sicken, disgust, nauseate, pall, turn the stomach.

adj. **unsavory**, unpalatable, unsweet; ill-flavored; bitter, bitter as gall; amarulent [*obs.*], acrid, acrimonious; rough.

offensive, repulsive, nasty; sickening etc. *v.*; nauseous; loathsome, fulsome; unpleasant etc. 830.

396. Sweetness

n. **sweetness**, dulcitude, saccharinity.

sugar, saccharin *or* saccharine, saccharose, crystallose; cane–, beet–, loaf–, lump–, granulated- sugar.

preserve, conserve, confiture [*obs.*], jam, julep; sugar candy, sugarplum; marmalade.

sweets, confectionery, caramel, lolly [*colloq.*], lollipop, bonbon, licorice, jujube, comfit, sweetmeat, confection, confectionery; honey, manna; apple butter, glucose, sucrose, dulcin [*chem.*], dulcite [*chem.*]; sirup *or* syrup, treacle, molasses, maple sirup *or* syrup, maple sugar; *mithai* [*India*], sorghum, taffy, butterscotch.

[sweet beverages] nectar; hydromel, mead, metheglin, liqueur, sweet wine, *eau sucrée* [*F.*].

pastry, cake, pie, tart, puff, pudding.

dulcification, dulcoration [*obs.*], saccharification, saccharization, edulcoration.

v. **be sweet** etc. *adj.*

render sweet etc. *adj.*; sweeten, sugar, saccharize, saccharify, sugar off [*local, U. S. & Can.*]; edulcorate; dulcorate [*obs.*], dulcify [*obs.*]; candy; mull.

adj. **sweet**, sugary, saccharine, sacchariferous, saccharoid *or* saccharoidal; dulcet, candied, honied, luscious, cloying, honey-sweet, nectarious [*rare*], nectareous, nectareal, nectarous, nectarean, nectarian; melliferous; sweetened etc. *v.*

sweet as -sugar, –honey.

397. Sourness

n. **sourness** etc., *adj.*; acid, acetosity, acerbity, acidity. subacidity; acescence *or* acescency; acetous fermentation.

[sour articles] vinegar, acetum, tartar, verjuice, crab, alum; acetic acid; lime, lemon, crab apple, chokeberry, chokecherry; unripe-, green fruit.
- v. **be sour**, turn sour etc. *adj.;* set the teeth on edge.
render sour etc. *adj.;* acidify, acidulate, acetify, acetize [*are*], tartarize, ferment.
- *adj.* **sour**; acid, acidulous, acidulated; tart, crab, crabbed; acetous, acetose, acerb, acetic; sour as vinegar, sourish; acescent, subacid; hard, rough, unripe, green; astringent, styptic.

398. Odor

- *n.* **odor** *or* odour, smell, odorament [*obs.*], scent, effluvium; emanation, exhalation; fume, essence, trail, nidor [*obs.*], redolence.
scent; sense of smell; act of smelling etc. *v.;* olfaction, olfactories.
- *v.* **have an odor** etc. *n.;* smell, -of, -strong of; exhale, effluviate [*rare*]; give out a smell etc. *n.;* scent.
smell, scent; snuff, -up; sniff, nose, inhale.
- *adj.* **odorous**, odorant [*rare*], odoriferous; smelling, strong-scented, effluvious, redolent, nidorous, pungent.
[relating to the sense of smell] olfactory, olfactive, olfactible *or* olfactable; quick-scented.

399. Inodorousness

- *n.* **inodorousness**; absence-, want- of smell. deodorization; deodorizer, deodorant.
- *v.* **be inodorous** etc. *adj.;* not smell. deodorize.
- *adj.* **inodorous**, inodorate [*obs.*], scentless; without-, wanting- smell etc. 398. deodorized, deodorizing.

400. Fragrance

- *n.* **fragrance**, aroma, redolence, incensation, thurification [*rare*], perfume, bouquet; sweet smell, sweet odor *or* odour, aromatic perfume, scent.
[comparisons] agalloch *or* agallochum, agalwood, eaglewood, aloes wood, sandalwood, cedar, champak, calambac *or* calambour, lignaloes, linaloa; bayberry, bay leaf, balsam, fir balsam; wild clove, wild cinnamon, Jamaica bayberry, oil of myrcia, bay rum; horehound, Marrubium, mint, musk root, muskrat, napha water, olibanum.
perfumery; incense, frankincense; musk, pastil *or* pastille; myrrh, perfumes of Arabia; attar *or* ottar *or* otto; bergamot, balm, civet, potpourri, pulvil [*obs.*]; tuberose, hyacinth, heliotrope, rose, jasmine, lily, lily of the valley, violet, arbutus, carnation, sweet pea, sweet grass, new-mown hay, lilac; pomade, pomatum, pomander, toilet water; *eau de cologne* [*F.*], cologne, cologne water.
bouquet, nosegay, posy [*archaic or colloq.*], boughpot *or* bowpot; *boutonnière* [*F.*], buttonhole [*colloq.*].
spray; wreath, garland, chaplet.
[scent containers] smelling bottle, scent bottle, vinaigrette; scent bag, sachet; thurible, censer, incense burner, incensorium, incensory; atomizer, spray.
perfumer, *parfumeur* [*F.*]; thurifer.
- *v.* **be fragrant** etc. *adj.;* have a perfume etc. *n.;* smell sweet, scent, perfume; embalm.
incense, cense, thurificate, thurify [*rare*]; aromatize.
- *adj.* **fragrant**, aromatic, redolent, spicy, balmy, scented; sweet-smelling, sweet-scented; perfumed, perfumatory [*rare*], perfumy, incense-breathing, thuriferous; fragrant-, sweet- as a rose, muscadine, ambrosial.

401. Fetor

- *n.* **fetor** *or* foetor; bad etc. *adj.* -smell, -odor *or* odour; stench, stink; foul odor, malodor *or* malodour, fetidness, mephitis, empyreuma; fustiness, mustiness etc. *adj.;* rancidity, reastiness *or* reasiness [*dial. Eng.*]; foulness etc. (*uncleanness*) 653.
[comparisons] stoat, polecat, skunk, zoril; foumart *or* foulmart, fitchew, fitchet, peccary; asafetida *or* assafoetida; fungus, garlic, onion, leek, skunk cabbage; stinkpot, stinkball, stinker, stinkhorn, stinkbush, stinkstone, stinkweed, stinkwood.
- *v.* **have a bad smell** etc. *n.;* smell, empyreumatize; stink, -in the nostrils, -like a polecat; smell strong etc. *adj.*, smell to heaven, stench [*obs.*], smell offensively.
- *adj.* **fetid**; strong-smelling; high, bad, strong, fulsome, offensive, graveolent, noisome, rank, rancid, reasty *or* reasy [*dial. Eng.*], moldy *or* mouldy, tainted, musty, frowsty [*dial. Eng.*], fusty, frowsy *or* frouzy; olid, olidous [*obs.*]; nidorous [*rare*], smelling, stinking; putrid etc. 653; suffocating, mephitic; empyreumatic *or* empyreumatical.

402. Sound

- *n.* **sound**, noise; sonority, sonorosity [*obs.*], sonification, strain; accent, twang, intonation, tune, cadence; sonorescence, sonorousness etc. *adj.;* audibility; resonance etc. 408; voice etc. 580; phonation; aspirate; phonogram, ideophone; rough breathing.

[science of sound] acoustics, acoumetry, diacoustics, catacoustics, diaphonics, cataphonics, polycoustics, phonics, phonetics, phonology, phonography; telephony, radiophony, photophony; polyphony, homophony; phonetism; acoustician.

- v. **produce sound**; sound, make a noise; give out sound, emit sound; phonate, consonate [*rare*], resound etc. 408.
phoneticize, phonetize [*rare*].
- adj. **sounding**; soniferous; sonorous, sonorescent; sonorific [*rare*]; sonorant, sonoric; resonant, audible, distinct; auditory, acoustic, acoustical, diacoustic, polycoustic; stertorous, ear-splitting.
phonic, phonetic; homophonic *or* homophonous (*opp. to* polyphonic), monodic, monophonic; sonant; ideophonous; phonocamptic [*rare*].

403. Silence

- n. **silence**; stillness etc. (*quiet*) 265; peace, hush, lull; rest [*music*]; muteness etc. 581; solemn–, awful–, dead–, deathlike– silence; silence of the -tomb, –grave.
- v. **be silent** etc. *adj.*; hold one's tongue etc. (*not speak*) 585; whist [*dial. Eng.*].
render silent etc. *adj.*; silence, still, hush; stifle, muffle, gag, stop; muzzle, put to silence etc. (*render mute*) 581.
- adj. **silent**; still, stilly; noiseless, quiet, calm, hush [*archaic*], echoless, speechless, soundless; hushed etc. *v.*; aphonic, surd, mute etc. 581.
solemn, soft, awful, deathlike; silent as the -tomb, –grave; inaudible etc. (*faint*) 405.
- adv. **silently** etc. *adj.*; *sub silentio* [*L.*]; in–, in dead–, in perfect- silence.
- int. **hush**! silence! soft! whist! mum! sh! chut! tut! pax! [*L.*], *tais-toi!* [*F.*], hold your tongue! shut up! [*colloq.*], be quiet! be silent! be still! *chup!* [*Hind.*], *chup rao!* [*Hind.*], *tace!* [*L.*].

404. Loudness

- n. **loudness**, power; vociferation, uproariousness.
din, loud noise, clang, clangor, clatter, noise, bombilation, roar, uproar, racket, clutter, hullabaloo, pandemonium, hell let loose; outcry etc. 411; hubbub; explosion, detonation; bobbery, fracas, charivari.
blare, trumpet blast, flourish of trumpets, fanfare, tintamarre [*archaic*]; blast; peal, swell, larum [*archaic*], alarum, boom; resonance etc. 408.
lungs; stentor; megaphone; calliope, steam siren, steam whistle; watchman's rattle.

[comparisons] artillery, cannon, guns, bombs, shells, barrage; thunder.
- v. **be loud** etc. *adj.*; peal, swell, clang, boom, thunder, fulminate, bombilate [*rare*], roar; resound etc. 408; speak up, shout etc. (*vociferate*) 411; bellow etc. (*cry as an animal*) 412.
clatter, clutter, racket, uproar [*rare*].
rend the air, rend the skies; fill the air; din–, ring–, thunder- in the ear; pierce–, split–, rend-the-ears, –head; deafen, stun; *faire le diable à quatre* [*F.*]; make one's windows shake; awake the echoes, startle the echoes; give tongue.
- adj. **loud**, sonorous; high-sounding, big-sounding; deep, full, powerful, noisy, blatant, clangorous, multisonous; thundering, deafening etc. *v.*; trumpet-tongued; ear-splitting, ear-rending, ear-deafening, piercing; shrill etc. 410; obstreperous, rackety, uproarious; enough to wake the -dead, –seven sleepers; clamorous etc. (*vociferous*) 411; stentorian, stentorophonic [*obs.*].
- adv. **loudly** etc. *adj.*; aloud; with one wild yell; at the top of one's -lungs, –voice; lustily, in full cry.

405. Faintness

- n. **faintness** etc. *adj.*; faint sound, whisper, breath; undertone, underbreath; murmur, hum, buzz, purr, lap [*of waves*], plash; sough, moan, rustle, susurration [*rare*], tinkle; "still small voice."
hoarseness etc. *adj.*
silencer, muffler; soft pedal, damper, mute, *sordino* [*It.*], sordine [*all music*].
- v. **whisper**, breathe; mutter etc. (*speak imperfectly*) 583; susurrate [*rare*].
murmur, purl, hum, gurgle, ripple, babble, flow; rustle, tinkle.
steal on the ear, melt in the air, float on the air.
muffle, deaden, mute, subdue.
- adj. **faint**, scarcely–, barely–, just-audible; low, dull; stifled, muffled; inaudible; hoarse, husky; gentle, soft; floating, purling, flowing etc. *v.*; muttered; whispered etc. *v.*; liquid; soothing; dulcet etc. (*melodious*) 413; susurrant [*rare*], susurrous [*rare*].
- adv. **in a whisper**, with bated breath, *sotto voce* [*It.*], between the teeth, aside; piano, pianissimo [*both music*], *sordamente* [*It.*], *sordo* [*It.*], *à la sourdine* [*F.*]; out of earshot; inaudibly etc. *adj.*

406. Snap
[sudden and violent sounds]

- n. **snap** etc. *v.*; toot, shout, yell, yap [*dial.*], yelp, bark; rapping etc. *v.*

125

407. Roll

report, decrepitation, crepitation; thump, knock, clap, thud; burst, thunderclap, thunderburst, eruption, blowout [*tire*], explosion, discharge, detonation, firing, salvo, volley.

detonator, bomb, gun, rifle; torpedo, squib, cracker, firecracker, popgun, rattle.

v. snap, rap, tap, knock; click; clash; crack, crackle; crash; pop; slam, bang, clap; thump, toot, yap [*dial.*], yelp, bark, fire, explode, rattle, burst on the ear; crepitate, flump.

adj. rapping etc. *v.;* crepitant.

adv. slap-bang or slam-bang [*colloq.*], bang [*colloq.*].

int. bang! crash!

407. Roll
[repeated and protracted sounds]

n. roll etc. *v.;* drumming etc. *v.; berloque* [*F.*], ululation, howl, bombilation, bombination, rumbling; dingdong; tantara, rataplan, ratatat, rubadub, tattoo; pitapat; quaver, clutter, brustle [*dial.*], charivari, racket; cuckoo; repetition etc. 104; peal of bells, devil's tattoo; drum fire, barrage; whirr, rattle, drone; reverberation etc. 408.

v. roll, drum, rataplan, boom; whirr, rustle, tootle, clutter, roar, drone, rumble, rattle, clatter, patter, clack; bombinate, bombilate [*rare*].

hum, trill, shake; chime, peal, toll; tick, beat.

drum in the ear, din in the ear.

adj. rolling, etc. *v.;* monotonous etc. (*repeated*) 104; like a bee in a bottle.

408. Resonance

n. resonance; ring etc. *v.;* ringing etc. *v.;* reflection *or* reflexion; clangor, bell-note, tintinnabulation, vibration, reverberation.

low-, base-, bass-, flat-, grave-, deep- note; bass; *basso* [*It.*], *basso profondo* [*It.*]; barytone *or* baritone, contralto; pedal point, organ point.

v. resound, reverberate, reëcho; ring, sound, jingle *or* gingle, chink, clink, tink, tinkle; chime; gurgle etc. 405; plash, guggle, echo, ring in the ear.

adj. resonant, reverberant, resounding etc. *v.;* tinnient [*obs.*], tintinnabula *or* tintinnabulary; deep-toned, -sounding, -mouthed; hollow, sepulchral; gruff etc. (*harsh*) 410.

408a. Nonresonance

n. nonresonance; mutescence; thud, thump, dead sound; muffled drums, cracked bell; damper, *sordino* [*It.*], sordine, mute, muffler, silencer.

v. muffle, deaden, mute; sound dead; stop-, damp-, deaden-, the -sound, -reverberations; use *or* employ the *sordino* [*It.*] etc. *n.*

adj. nonresonant, dead, mute; muffled etc. *v.*

409. Sibilation
[hissing sounds]

n. sibilation; zip; hiss etc. *v.;* sternutation; high note etc. 410.

goose, serpent, snake.

v. hiss, buzz, whiz, rustle; fizz, fizzle; wheeze, whistle, snuffle; squash; sneeze; sizz [*colloq.*], sizzle, swish.

adj. sibilant; hissing etc. *v.;* wheezy; sternutative.

410. Stridor
[harsh or high sounds]

n. stridor, harshness, roughness, sharpness etc. *adj.;* raucousness, raucity; creak etc. *v.;* creaking etc. *v.;* discord, etc. 414; cacophony; cacoëpy.

high note, acute note; soprano, treble, tenor, alto, falsetto; *voce di testa* [*It.*], head voice, head tone; shriek, yell; cry etc. 411.

penny trumpet, piccolo, fife, whistle; penny-, willow- whistle; Panpipes, syrinx; pipes, bagpipes, doodlesack [*Scot.*].

v. grate, creak, saw, snore, jar, burr, pipe, twang, jangle, clank, clink; scream etc. (*cry*) 411; yelp etc. (*animal sound*) 412; buzz etc. (*hiss*) 409.

set the teeth on edge, *écorcher les oreilles* [*F.*]; pierce-, split- the -ears, -head; offend-, grate upon-, jar upon- the ear.

adj. grating, creaking etc. *v.;* stridulous, strident, harsh, coarse, hoarse, horrisonant [*obs.*], raucous, metallic, horrisonous [*obs.*], rough, rude, jangly [*rare*], gruff, grum, sepulchral, hollow.

high, sharp, acute, shrill; trumpet-toned; piercing, ear-piercing, high-pitched, high-toned; cracked; discordant etc. 414; cacophonous.

411. Cry

n. cry etc. *v.;* voice etc. (*human*) 580; view halloo, yoicks [*both hunting*]; hubbub; bark etc. (*animal*) 412.

outcry, vociferation, hullabaloo, chorus, clamor *or* clamour, hue and cry, plaint; lungs; Stentor, stentor.

v. cry, roar, shout, bawl, brawl, halloo, halloa, yo-ho, yoick, whoop *or* hoop [*rare*], yell, bellow, howl, scream, screech, screak, shriek, shrill, squeak, squeal, squall, whine, pule, pipe, yap, yaup *or* yawp.

cheer, huzza, hurrah; hoot.

moan, grumble, groan.

snort, snore; grunt etc. (*animal sounds*) 412.

vociferate; raise-, lift up- the voice; yell out, call out, sing out, cry out; exclaim; rend the air;

make the welkin ring; split the -throat, –lungs; thunder–, shout- at the -top of one's voice, –pitch of one's breath; *s'égosiller* [*F.*]; strain the -throat, –voice, –lungs; give cry; give a cry etc.; clamor *or* clamour.

adj. **clamant,** clamorous; crying etc. *v.;* vociferous; stentorian etc. (*loud*) 404; open-mouthed; full-mouthed.

412. Ululation
[animal sounds]

n. **ululation,** howling, mugiency [*obs.*], reboation [*rare*]; cry etc. *v.;* crying etc. *v.;* call, note, howl, bark, yelp, bow-wow, latration, belling; woodnote; insect cry, twittering, fritiniancy [*obs.*], drone; cuckoo.

v. **ululate,** howl, cry, roar, bellow, blare, rebellow, latrate, bark, yelp, bay, bay the moon; yap, growl, yarr [*obs.*], yawl [*dial.*], yaup *or* yawp, snarl, howl; grunt, gruntle; snort, squeak; neigh, bray; mew, mewl, purr, caterwaul, miaow; bleat, low, moo; troat [*rare*], croak, crow, screech, caw, coo, gobble, quack, cackle, gaggle, guggle; chuck, chuckle; cluck, clack; chirp, cheep, chirrup, chirk [*obs.*], peep, sing, pule, twitter, chatter, hoot, wail, cuckoo; hum, buzz; hiss, blatter, blat [*colloq.*].

adj. **ululant,** crying etc. *v.;* blatant, latrant, remugient [*obs.*], mugient; deep-mouthed, full-mouthed; rebellowing, reboant [*rare*].

adv. in full cry.

413. Melody. Concord

n. **melody,** rhythm, measure; rime *or* rhyme etc. (*poetry*) 597.

[musical terms] pitch, timbre, intonation, tone, overtone.

orchestration, harmonization, modulation, phrasing, temperament, syncope, syncopation, preparation, suspension, solution, resolution.

staff *or* stave, line, space, brace; bar, rest; *appoggiato* [*It.*], *appoggiatura* [*It.*]; *acciaccatura* [*It.*], trill *or* shake, turn, *arpeggio* [*It.*].

note, musical note, notes of a scale; sharp, flat, natural; high note etc. (*shrillness*) 410; low note etc. 408; interval; semitone; second, third, fourth etc.; diatessaron [*ancient music*].

breve, semibreve *or* whole note, minim *or* half note, crotchet *or* quarter note, quaver *or* eighth note, semiquaver *or* sixteenth note, demisemiquaver *or* thirty-second note, hemidemisemiquaver *or* sixty-fourth note; sustained note, drone, bourdon, burden.

scale, gamut; diapason; diatonic–, chromatic–, enharmonic- scale; key, clef, chords.

tonic; key–, leading–, fundamental- note; supertonic, mediant, dominant; pedal point, organ point; submediant, subdominant; octave, tetrachord; Dorian *or* Doric - mode, –tetrachord; major–, minor- -mode, –scale, –key; passage, phrase.

harmony, concord, emmeleia; euphony, euphonism; tonality; consonance; concent [*archaic*], concentus; part.

unison, unisonance; chime, homophony.

[science of harmony] harmony, harmonics; thorough bass, fundamental bass; counterpoint; faburden [*medieval music*].

opus (*pl.* opera) [*L.*], piece of music etc. 415.

composer, harmonist, contrapuntist.

v. **harmonize,** chime, symphonize, transpose, orchestrate; blend, put in tune, tune, accord, string; be harmonious etc. *adj.*

adj. **harmonious,** harmonic, harmonical; in concord etc. *n.,* in tune, in concert, in unison; unisonant, concentual *or* concentuous [*rare*], symphonizing, isotonic, homophonous, assonant; ariose, consonant.

measured, rhythmic *or* rhythmical, diatonic, chromatic, enharmonic.

melodious, musical; melic; tuneful, tunable; sweet, dulcet, canorous; mellow, mellifluous; soft; clear, –as a bell; silvery; euphonious, euphonic *or* euphonical, symphonious; enchanting etc. (*pleasure-giving*) 829; fine-toned, silver-toned, full-toned, deep-toned.

adv. **harmoniously** etc. *adj.*

414. Discord

n. **discord,** discordance; dissonance, cacophony, want of harmony, caterwauling; harshness etc. 410; charivari, shivaree [*dial., U. S.*], racket; consecutive fifths.

[confused sounds] Babel, pandemonium; Dutch concert, cat's concert, marrowbones and cleavers [*all colloq.*].

v. **be discordant** etc. *adj.;* jar etc. (*sound harshly*) 410; shivaree [*dial., U. S.*].

adj. **discordant,** dissonant, absonant; out of tune, tuneless; unmusical, untunable; immelodious, unmelodious, unharmonious, inharmonious, unsweet [*rare*], singsong; cacophonous; harsh etc. 410; jarring.

415. Music

n. **music;** strain, tune, air; melody etc. 413; piece of music, *morceau* [*F.*], rondo, rondeau, pas-

416. Musician

torale [*It.*], pastoral, cavatina, fantasia, *toccata* [*It.*], *toccatella* [*It.*], *toccatina* [*It.*], *capriccio* [*It.*], fugue, canon; potpourri, medley, incidental music; variations, roulade, cadenza, cadence, trill; serenade, *notturno* [*It.*], nocturne; *passamezzo* [*It.*]; staff *or* stave etc. 413.

instrumental music; orchestral score, full score; minstrelsy, tweedledum and tweedledee [*applied by John Byrom to the feuds between Handel and Bononcini*]; band, orchestra etc. 416; composition, *opus* (*pl. opera*) [*L.*], movement, concert piece, concerted piece, symphony, *concerto* [*It.*], sonata, symphonic poem, tone poem; chamber music; overture, prelude, voluntary, *Vorspiel* [*Ger.*]; string quartet *or* quartette.

lively music, polka, reel etc. (*dance*) 848; ragtime, disco, reggae, rock, hard rock, acid rock, punk rock, jazz; syncopation; *allegro* etc. *adv.*

slow music, slow movement, Lydian measures; *adagio* etc. *adv.*; minuet; siren strains, soft music; lullaby, cradle song, *berceuse* [*F.*]; dump [*obs.*]; dirge etc. (*lament*) 839; pibroch, coronach [*Scot. & Ir.*], dead march, martial music, march; waltz etc. (*dance*) 840.

vocal music, vocalism; chaunt [*archaic*], chant; psalm, psalmody, hymnology; hymn; song etc. (*poem*) 597; oratorio, opera, operetta; canticle, cantata, lay, ballad, ditty, carol, pastoral, recitative *or* recitativo, *aria parlante* [*It.*], aria, arietta *or* ariette, canzonet; bravura, coloratura [*It.*], coloratura; virtuoso music, cantabile.

solo, duet, *duo* [*It.*], trio, terzetto, quartet *or* quartette, quintet *or* quintette, sestet *or* sextet, septet, double quartet, chorus; part song, descant, glee, madrigal, catch, round, chorale; antiphon, antiphony; accompaniment; inside part, second, alto, tenor, bass; score, piano score, vocal score; burden, bourdon, drone.

concert, musicale, musical [*colloq.*], recital, chamber concert, popular concert *or* pop [*colloq.*], open-air concert, rock concert, serenade, *aubade* [*F.*]; community singing, singsong [*colloq.*].

method, *solfeggio* [*It.*], tonic sol-fa, solmization; sight -singing, -reading; reading at sight.

composer etc. 413; **musician** etc. 416.

v. **compose**, write, set to music, arrange etc. 416; attune.

perform, execute, play etc. 416.

adj. **musical**; instrumental, vocal, choral, lyric, melodic, pure, operatic; classic, modern, orchestral, symphonic, contrapuntal, program;

imitative, falsetto; harmonious etc. 413; Wagnerian.

adv. adagio; largo, larghetto, andante, andantino; alla cappella; maestoso, moderato; allegro, allegretto; spiritoso, vivace, veloce; presto, prestissimo; con brio; capriccioso; scherzo, scherzando; legato, staccato, crescendo, diminuendo, rallentando, affettuoso; arioso, parlante, cantabile; obbligato; pizzicato; desto [*all It.*].

416. Musician
[performance of music]

n. **musician**, *artiste* [*F.*], virtuoso, performer, player, minstrel; bard etc. (*poet*) 597; accompanist, instrumentalist, organist, pianist, violinist, tweedledee [*Scot.*], fiddler, catgut scraper [*slang*]; flutist *or* flautist; harpist *or* harper, fifer, trumpeter, cornetist, piper, drummer; accordionist.

orchestra; string -orchestra, -quartet; strings, woodwind, brass; band, brass band, military band, German band, jazz band; street musicians, waits.

vocalist, melodist, singer, warbler; songster, chanter *or* chaunter [*archaic*]; *cantatore* [*It.*], *cantatrice* [*F.*], improvisator, *improvvisatore* or *improvisatore* [*It.*]; *improvvisatrice* or *improvisatrice* [*It.*], songstress, chantress *or* chauntress [*archaic*]; chorister; chorus singer.

choir *or* quire [*archaic*]; chorus; *Liedertafel* [*Ger.*], *Liederkranz* [*Ger.*]; choral -club, -society; singing -club, -society; festival chorus, eisteddfod [*Welsh*].

song bird, nightingale, philomel, lark, ringdove, bulbul, cuckoo, thrush, mavis.

[*patrons*] Orpheus, Apollo, Apollo Musagetes, the Muses, Polyhymnia, Erato, Euterpe, Terpsichore; Pierides, sacred nine, tuneful nine, tuneful quire [*archaic*]; Siren.

composer etc. 413.

conductor, choirmaster, bandmaster, concert master *or* *Konzertmeister* [*Ger.*], drum major, song leader, precentor.

performance, execution, touch, expression.

v. **play**, tune, tune up, pipe, pipe up, strike up, sweep the chords, fiddle, scrape [*derog.*], strike the lyre, beat the drum; blow-, sound-, wind- the horn; doodle [*Scot. or colloq.*]; toot, tootle, grind the organ; touch the guitar etc. (*instruments*) 417; twang, pluck, pick, paw the ivories [*slang*]; pound, thump; drum, thrum, strum, beat time.

execute, perform; accompany; sing-, play- a second.

compose, set to music, arrange, harmonize, orchestrate.

sing, chant *or* chaunt [*archaic*], intone, hum, warble, carol, yodel, chirp, chirrup, lilt, purl, quaver, trill, shake, twitter, whistle; sol-fa; do-re-mi.

have an ear for music, have a musical ear, have a correct ear, have absolute pitch.

adj. **musical**; lyric, dramatic; *coloratura* [*It.*], bravura, florid, brilliant; playing etc. *v.*

adv. adagio [*It.*], andante [*It.*] etc. (*music*) 415.

417. Musical Instruments

n. **musical instruments**; orchestra, band; string band, military band, brass band; orchestrion, orchestrina.

[stringed instruments] polychord, harp, lyre, lute, archlute, theorbo, cithara, cither, cittern *or* cithern, gittern, zither, psaltery, guitar, banjo, banjo-zither; rebec *or* rebeck, mandola, mandolin *or* mandoline, ukulele [*Hawaii*]; *bandurria* [*It.*], samisen [*Jap.*]; bina, vina [*India*].

violin, Cremona, Stradivarius; fiddle, kit; viol, vielle; viola, –d'amore, –di gamba; tenor, violoncello, bass viol *or* base viol; double bass, *contrabasso* [*It.*], *violone* [*It.*]; bow, fiddlestick, strings, catgut.

piano *or* pianoforte; grand–, concert-grand–, baby-grand–, square–, upright - piano; harpsichord, monochord [*hist.*], clavichord, clarichord, manichord *or* manichordon, clavier, spinet, virginals, dulcimer; hurdy-gurdy, street piano, piano organ; pianette, pianino, piano player, player piano, player; Aeolian (*or* Eolian) harp.

[wind instruments] organ; church–, pipe–, reed-organ; seraphine *or* seraphina, harmonium, cabinet organ, American organ; harmoniphon [*obs.*], barrel organ, hand organ, melodeon, accordion, concertina; humming top.

flute, fife, piccolo, flageolet, clarinet *or* clarionet, bass clarinet, basset horn, *corno di bassetto* [*It.*], musette, oboe *or* hautboy, *cor anglais* [*F.*], English horn, *corno inglese* [*It.*], bassoon, double bassoon, *contrafagotto* [*It.*], serpent, bag-pipes, union pipes, doodlesack [*Scot.*]; ocarina, Panpipes *or* Pandean pipes; reed instrument; pipe, pitch-pipe; whistle; willow–, penny- whistle; calliope, siren *or* sirene; catcall.

horn, bugle, cornet, cornet-à-pistons, cornopean [*obs.*], clarion [*now chiefly poetic*], trumpet, trombone, tuba, bombardon, bass tuba, ophicleide; French horn, bugle horn, post horn, saxhorn, *Flügelhorn* [*Ger.*], alt horn *or* althorn, tenor horn, sackbut, euphonium.

[vibrating surfaces] cymbals, bell, gong; drum, tambour, snare drum, side drum, tabor *or* tabour, taboret *or* tabouret, kettle drum, timpano (*pl.* timpani), timbal *or* tymbal, tom-tom *or* tam-tam, timbrel, tambourine, castanet, bones; musical glasses, musical stones; mouth organ, harmonica; sounding-board, *abatvoix* [*F.*]; rattle, watchman's rattle; phonograph, graphophone, gramophone, stereo, victrola [*trade-mark name*]; zambomba [*Sp.*].

[vibrating bars] reed, tuning fork, triangle, jew's-harp, music box *or* musical box, harmonicon, xylophone.

mute, sourdine, *sordino* [*It.*], sordine, sordet, sourdet.

418. Hearing
[sense of sound]

n. **hearing** etc. *v.;* audition, auscultation; audibility; acoustics etc. 402; eavesdropping.

acute–, nice–, delicate–, quick–, sharp–, correct–, musical- ear; ear for music.

ear, auricle, pinna, concha, labyrinth, lug [*Scot.*], lobule *or* lobe, acoustic organs, auditory apparatus, eardrum, tympanum; malleus, incus, stapes, vestibule, cochlea, auditory nerve, Eustachian tube.

ear trumpet, speaking trumpet; telephone, phonograph, microphone; gramophone, phonograph, victrola [*trademark name*], megaphone, phonorganon; dictagraph *or* dictograph [*trade-mark name*], dictophone [*trade-mark name*], audiphone, dentiphone; stethoscope; telephone etc. 527.

hearer, auditor, auditory, audience, listener, eavesdropper.

otology, otoscopy, auriscopy; otoscope, auriscope; otopathy, otography, otoplasty; otorrhea, tympanitis; otologist, aurist.

v. **hear**, overhear; hark, hearken *or* harken; list, listen; give–, lend–, bend- an ear; strain one's ears, attend to, give attention, catch a sound, prick up one's ears; give ear, give a hearing to, give audience to.

hang upon the lips of, be all ear, listen with both ears.

become audible; meet–, fall upon–, catch–, reach- the ear; be heard; ring in the ear etc. (*resound*) 408.

adj. **hearing** etc. *v.;* auditory, otic, aural, acoustic, acoustical, phonic; auriculate, auricular; auricled, eared; auditive.

adv. arrectis auribus [*L.*]; all ears.

419. Deafness

int. **hark**! hark ye! hear! list! listen! oyez *or* oyes! attend! attention! lend me your ears!

419. Deafness

n. **deafness**, hardness of hearing, surdity [*obs.*], deaf ears; inaudibility, inaudibleness.
adder, beetle, slowworm, blindworm; deaf-mute.
dactylology, deaf-and-dumb alphabet.

v. **be deaf** etc. *adj.;* have no ear; shut–, stop–, close- one's ears; turn a deaf ear to.
render deaf, stun, deafen; split the -ears, -eardrum.

adj. **deaf**, earless, surd; hard–, dull- of hearing; deaf-mute; stunned, deafened; stone deaf; deaf as -a post, –an adder, –a beetle, –a trunkmaker; inattentive etc. 458.
inaudible, out of -earshot, –hearing.

420. Light

n. **light**, ray, beam, stream, gleam, streak, pencil; sunbeam, moonbeam; aurora, dawn.
day; sunshine; light of -day, –heaven; sun etc. (*luminary*) 423, daylight, broad daylight, noontide light; noontide, noonday.
glow etc. *v.;* afterglow, sunset glow; glimmering etc. *v.;* glint; glare; play–, glare–, flood- of light; phosphorescence, lambent flame.
halo, glory, nimbus, aureola, aureole, gloriole [*rare*], aura.
spark, scintilla; facula; sparkling etc. *v.;* emication [*obs.*], scintillation, flash, blaze, coruscation, fulguration [*now rare*]; flame etc. (*fire*) 382; lightning, levin; *ignis fatuus* [*L.*] etc. (*luminary*) 423.
luster *or* lustre, sheen, shimmer, reflection *or* reflexion; gloss, tinsel, spangle, brightness, brilliancy, splendor *or* splendour, effulgence, refulgence; fulgor, fulgidity [*rare*]; dazzlement, resplendence *or* resplendency, transplendency [*rare*], luminousness etc. *adj.;* luminosity; lucidity; nitency [*rare*]; radiance, radiation; irradiation, illumination.
[science of light] optics; photology, photics; actinology, actinometry, radiology, heliology, radiometry, radioscopy, photometry, dioptrics, catoptrics; photography, photolithography, photomicography, phototelegraphy, radiotelegraphy; phototherapy, heliotherapy, radiotherapy; heliometry, heliography.
actinic rays, actinism; radioactivity, radium emanation, exradio; Röntgen *or* Roentgen rays, X-rays, ultra-violet rays; photometer etc. 445; heliometer, refractometer.
[distribution of light] *chiaroscuro* or *chiaroscuro* [*It.*], clair-obscure, *clair-obscure* [*F.*], mezzotint, mezzotinto, half tone *or* half-tone, demitint, half tint; breadth, light and shade, black and white, tonality.
reflection, refraction, dispersion; refractivity.
illuminant, artificial light; gas etc. 423.

v. **shine**, glow, beam, glitter; glister, glisten; twinkle, gleam; flare, flare up; glare, shimmer, glimmer, flicker, sparkle, scintillate, coruscate, flash, blaze; be bright etc. *adj.;* reflect light, daze, dazzle, bedazzle, radiate, shoot out beams; fulgurate, phosphoresce.
clear up, brighten.
lighten, enlighten; levin; light, light up; irradiate, shine upon; give–, hang out a - light; cast–, throw–, shed-luster, -light- upon; illume, illumine, illuminate; relume, strike a light; kindle etc. (*set fire to*) 384.

adj. **luminous**, luminiferous; shining etc. *v.;* lucid, lucent, luculent, luciferous [*rare*], lucific [*rare*]; illuminate [*archaic*], illuminant, light, lightsome; bright, vivid, splendent, nitid, lustrous, shiny, beamy, scintillant, fulgurant, radiant, lambent; sheen, sheeny; glossy, burnished, glassy, sunny, orient, meridian; noonday, noontide; cloudless, clear; unclouded, unobscured.
garish; resplendent, transplendent [*rare*]; refulgent, effulgent, fulgid, fulgent, relucent, splendorous *or* splendrous, splendid, blazing, in a blaze, ablaze, rutilant, meteoric, phosphorescent; aglow.
bright as silver; light–, bright- as -day, –noonday, –the sun at noonday.
[scientific] actinic, radioactive; optic, optical, photologic *or* photological, heliological; photogenic, photographic; heliographic; heliophagous.

421. Darkness

n. **darkness** etc. *adj.;* tenebrosity, umbrageousness, dunness [*rare*], caliginousness, lightlessness, sootiness; blackness etc. (*dark color*) 431; obscurity, gloom, murk *or* mirk, murkiness *or* mirkiness, darksomeness; dusk etc. (*dimness*) 422.
Cimmerian–, Stygian–, Egyptian-darkness; night; midnight; dead of–, witching hour of–, witching time of- night; darkness visible; "darkness which may be felt" [*Bible*]; "the palpable obscure" [*Milton*]; "embalméd darkness" [*Keats*]; Erebus; "the jaws of darkness" [*Midsummer Night's Dream*]; "sable-vested Night" [*Milton*].

shadow, shade, umbra, penumbra; skiagraphy *or* sciagraphy; skiagram *or* sciagram, skiagraph *or* sciagraph; radiograph.

obscuration; obumbration [*rare*]; obtenebration [*rare*], offuscation [*obs.*], caligation [*obs.*], adumbration; extinction; eclipse, total eclipse; gathering of the clouds.

shading; distribution of shade; *chiaroscuro* [*It.*] etc. (*light*) 420.

v. be dark etc. *adj.;* be in darkness etc. *n.*

darken, obscure, shade; dim; tone down, lower; overcast, overshadow; cloud, cloud over, darken over, murk *or* mirk; eclipse; offuscate [*obs.*], obumbrate, obtenebrate [*rare*], obfuscate; adumbrate; cast into the shade; becloud, bedim, bedarken; cast–, throw–, spread- a -shade, –shadow, –gloom; "walk in darkness and in the shadow of death" [*Book of Common Prayer*].

extinguish, put out, blow out, snuff out, dout [*obs. or dial. Eng.*].

adj. dark, darksome, darkling; obscure, tenebrious, tenebrous, sombrous, pitch dark, pitchy; caliginous [*archaic*]; black etc. (*in color*) 431.

dark as -pitch, –the pit, –Erebus.

sunless, lightless etc. (*see* sun, light, etc. 423); somber, dusky; unilluminated etc. (*see* illuminate etc. 420); nocturnal; dingy, lurid, gloomy; murky *or* mirky, murksome *or* mirksome, sooty, shady, umbrageous; overcast etc. (*dim*) 422; cloudy etc. (*opaque*) 426; darkened etc. *v.*

benighted; noctivagant, noctivagous.

adv. in the -dark, –shade; at night, by night, through the night; darkling, darklings [*rare*].

422. Dimness

n. dimness etc. *adj.;* darkness etc. 421; paleness etc. (*light color*) 429.

half light, *demi-jour* [*F.*]; partial shadow, partial eclipse; "shadow of a shade" [*Aeschylus*]; "shadows numberless" [*Keats*]; glimmer, glimmering; nebulosity, nebulousness, obnubilation [*rare*]; cloud etc. 353; eclipse.

twilight, aurora, dusk, nightfall, gloaming, gloam [*rare*], blind man's holiday, *entre chien et loup* [*F.*], *inter canem et lupem* [*L.*], shades of evening, crepuscule, cockshut time [*obs.*]; break of day, daybreak, dawn.

moonlight, moonbeam, moonglade, moonshine; owl's-light, starlight, candlelight, rushlight, firelight; farthing candle.

v. be *or* grow dim etc. *adj.;* gloom; cloud over; flicker, twinkle, glimmer, loom, lower; fade; pale, "pale his uneffectual fire" [*Hamlet*].

render dim etc. *adj.;* dim, bedim, obscure, shade, shadow; encompass with -gloom, –shadow; darken, dark [*archaic*], cloud, becloud, darkle.

adj. dim, dull, lackluster, dingy, darkish, dusky, shorn of its beams; dark etc. 421.

faint, shadowed forth; glassy; cloudy; misty etc. (*opaque*) 426; blear; fuliginous; nebulous, nebular, obnubilated [*rare*], obnubilous [*obs.*].

lurid, leaden, dun, dirty; overcast, muddy; looming etc. *v.*

twilight, crepuscular, crepusculous [*rare*], crepusculine [*rare*].

pale etc. (*colorless*) 429; confused etc. (*invisible*) 447.

423. Luminary
[source of light]

n. luminary; light etc. 420; flame etc. (*fire*) 382.

spark, scintilla; phosphorescence.

[heavenly bodies] sun, orb of day, day-star [*poetic*], Aurora; star, orb, meteor; falling star, shooting star; blazing star, dog star, canicula, Sirius, Aldebaran; constellation, galaxy, Milky Way; pole star, Polaris; Cynosure; anthelion; morning star, Lucifer, Phosphor, Phosphorus; Venus, Hesperus, evening star; mock sun, parhelion, sun dog *or* sundog, moon etc. 318.

sun god, Helios, Titan, Phaëthon, Phoebus, Apollo, Hyperion, Ra *or* Re [*Egypt*], Shamash [*Babylon & Assyria*].

lightning, levin; chain–, fork–, sheet–, summer- lightning.

phosphorus; *ignis fatuus* [*L.*]; Jack o'–, Friar's- lantern; will-o'-the-wisp, firedrake, Fata Morgana, St. Elmo's fire, Castor and Pollux [*naut.*], corposant.

glowworm, firefly.

polar lights, northern lights, *aurora borealis* [*L.*], *aurora australis* [*L.*]; aurora; zodiacal light.

[artificial light] gas, gaslight, electric light; headlight, searchlight, spotlight, flashlight, limelight, calcium light, lamplight, lamp; lantern, lanthorn [*archaic*]; electric torch, dark lantern, bull's-eye; candle; wax–, tallow–, bayberry- candle; farthing dip, tallow dip [*colloq.*]; bougie, taper, rushlight; oil etc. (*grease*) 356; wick, burner; Argand, moderator, duplex; torch, flambeau, link, brand; gaselier, chandelier, electrolier; candelabrum, girandole, sconce, luster *or* lustre, candlestick.

firework, Catherine wheel, Roman candle, fizgig; pyrotechnics.

424. Shade

signal light, rocket, balefire, beacon fire; lighthouse etc. (*signal*) 550.
pyre, funeral pyre; death fire; corpse candle.
v. **illuminate** etc. (*light*) 420.
adj. **self-luminous**; phosphoric, phosphorescent; radiant etc. (*light*) 420.

424. Shade

n. **shade**; awning etc. (*cover*) 223; parasol, sunshade, umbrella.
screen, curtain, chick [*India*], purdah [*India*], portière [*F.*]; shutter, blind, Venetian blind, jalousie [*F.*].
gauze, veil, mantle, mask, yashmak [*Turk.*].
cloud, mist; gathering of clouds; smoke screen [*mil.*].
umbrage [*archaic*], glade; shadow etc. 421; ambush, covert.
blinkers, blinders; smoked glasses, colored spectacles.
v. **veil** etc. *v.;* draw a curtain; put up–, close- a shutter; cast a shadow etc. (*darken*) 421.
adj. **shady**, umbrageous, shadowy, bowery.

425. Transparency

n. **transparency**, transparence, translucence, translucency, diaphaneity, diaphanousness; lucidity, pellucidity, limpidity; fluorescence; transillumination, translumination.
transparent medium, glass, crystal, lymph, water, hyalite, hyaline.
v. **be transparent** etc. *adj.;* transmit light.
adj. **transparent**, pellucid, lucid, diaphanous; translucent, tralucent [*obs.*], limpid, clear, serene, crystalline, clear as crystal, pervious [*rare*], vitreous, transpicuous [*rare*], glassy, hyaline, hyaloid [*rare*], vitreform.

426. Opacity

n. **opacity**; opaqueness etc. *adj.;* obfuscation, fuliginosity, nubilation.
film; cloud etc. 353.
v. **be opaque** etc. *adj.;* obstruct the passage of light; obfuscate, offuscate [*obs.*].
adj. **opaque**, impervious to light; adiaphanous; dim etc. 422; turbid, thick, muddy, opacous [*obs.*], obfuscated, fuliginous, cloudy, nubilous, nubilose [*obs.*], foggy, vaporous, nubiferous.
smoky, fumid [*obs.*], murky *or* mirky, smeared, dirty.

427. Semitransparency

n. **semitransparency**, opalescence, milkiness, pearliness.
[*comparisons*] gauze, muslin, cypress *or* cyprus [*hist.*], bombyx, thin silk; film; mica, mother-of-pearl, nacre, opal glass, opaline, frosted glass; mist etc. (*cloud*) 353.
adj. **semitransparent**, semipellucid, semidiaphanous, semiopacous [*obs.*], semiopaque; opalescent, opaline; pearly, milky, frosted, nacreous; hazy, misty.
v. **cloud**, frost, cloud over, frost over; become –pearly, –milky, –misty.
be opalescent etc. *adj.;* opalesce.

428. Color

n. **color** *or* colour, hue, tint, tinct [*archaic*], tinction, tinge, dye, complexion, shade, tincture, cast, livery, coloration, chromatism *or* chromism, glow, flush; tone, key.
pure–, positive–, primary–, primitive–, complementary- color; three primaries; spectrum, chromatic dispersion; broken–, secondary–, tertiary- color.
local color, coloring, keeping, tone, value, aerial perspective.
[science of color] chromatics, spectrum analysis; chromatography, chromatology, chromatoscopy; chromatograph, chromatometer, chromatoscope, chromoscope, chromatrope, chromometer, colorimeter; prism, spectroscope, kaleidoscope.
pigment, coloring matter, paint, dye, wash, distemper, stain, chromogen; medium; mordant; oil paint etc. (*painting*) 556.
v. **color** *or* colour, dye, tinge, stain, tint, tinct [*archaic*], hue, tone, complexion [*rare*]; paint, wash, distemper, ingrain, grain, illuminate, emblazon, imbue; paint etc. (*fine art*) 556.
adj. **colored** etc. *v.;* colorific, tingent [*rare*], tinctorial; chromatic, prismatic; full–, high–, rich–, deep- colored; double-dyed; polychromatic; chromatogenous; chromatophoric, chromatophorous; tingible.
bright, vivid, intense, deep; fresh, unfaded; rich, gorgeous; bright-colored, gay.
gaudy, florid; garish; showy, flaunting; flashy; many-colored, party-colored *or* parti-colored, variegated; raw, crude; glaring, flaring; discordant, inharmonious.
mellow, harmonious, pearly, sweet, delicate, subtle, tender.
dull, sad, somber *or* sombre, sad-colored, grave, gray, dark.

429. Achromatism
[absence of color]

n. **achromatism**, achromatization; decoloration, decolorization, discoloration; pallor, pallidity; paleness etc. *adj.;* etiolation.

neutral tint, monochrome, black and white.
- *v.* **lose color** etc. 428; fade, fly, go, become colorless etc. *adj.;* turn pale; pale, fade out, bleach out; wan; fly, go.
  deprive of color, decolor *or* decolour, decolorize *or* decolourize, whiten, bleach, tarnish, achromatize, blanch, etiolate, wash out, tone down.
- *adj.* **colorless**; achromatic; uncolored etc. (*see* color etc. 428); etiolated; hueless, pale, pallid; pale-faced, anemic, tallow-faced; faint, dull, cold, muddy, leaden, dun, wan, sallow, dead, dingy, ashy, ashen, ghastly, cadaverous, glassy, lackluster; discolored etc. *v.*
  pale as -death, -ashes, -a witch, -a ghost, -a corpse.
  light-colored, fair, blond, ash-blond; white etc. 430; tow-headed, tow-haired.

430. Whiteness

- *n.* **whiteness** etc. *adj.;* whitishness, canescence; argent, argentine.
  albification, albication, albinism, albinoism; leucopathy, leucoderma *or* leucodermia [*med.*], dealbation, albescence, etiolation; lactescence.
  [comparisons] snow, paper, chalk, milk, lily, ivory, silver, alabaster; albata, eburin *or* eburine *or* eburite, German silver, white metal, barium sulphate, *blanc fixe* [*F.*], pearl white; white lead, ceruse, carbonate of lead, Paris white, zinc white, flake white, Chinese white.
  whitewash, whiting, whitening, calcimine.
- *v.* **be white** etc. *adj.*
  render white etc. *adj.;* whiten, bleach, blanch, etiolate, silver, besnow, dealbate [*obs.*], albify [*rare*], frost.
  whitewash, calcimine, white.
- *adj.* **white**; snow-white; snowy, niveous; candent, candid [*archaic*], frosted, hoar, hoary; silvery, silver, argent, argentine; canescent, chalky, cretaceous; lactescent, milk-white, milky, marmoreal *or* marmorean; albificative, albicant, albescent; albinistic.
  white as -a sheet, -driven snow, -a lily, -silver; like ivory etc. *n.*
  whitish, creamy, pearly, ivory, fair, blond, ash-blond; blanched etc. *v.;* high in tone, light.

431. Blackness

- *n.* **blackness** etc. *adj.;* darkness etc. (*want of light*) 421; swarthiness, swartness; lividity; dark -color, -tone; *chiaroscuro* [*It.*] etc. 420.
  nigrification [*rare*], nigrefaction [*obs.*], nigrescence, denigration, infuscation [*rare*].
  [comparisons] jet, ink, ebony, ebon [*now poetic*], coal, pitch, soot, charcoal, sloe; smut, smutch, smudge, smirch; raven, crow.
  negro, negress, blackamoor, man of color, colored man, colored woman, black, Black, Ethiop, Ethiopian, buck [*colloq.*], kala admi [*Hind.*], Melanesian, Hottentot, Pygmy, Bushman, Negrillo [*African Pygmy*], Negrito [*Asiatic Pygmy*], African, Mandingo, Senegambian, Sudanese, Papuan, blackfellow, Australian aborigine.
  [pigments] lamp–, ivory–, blue-black; writing–, printing–, printer's–, Indian- ink.
- *v.* **be black** etc. *adj.*
  render black etc. *adj.;* black, blacken, infuscate [*rare*], denigrate, nigrify; blot, blotch, smut, smudge, smutch, smirch; darken etc. 421.
- *adj.* **black,** sable, somber *or* sombre, livid, dark, inky, ebon, atramentous, jetty; coal-black, jet-black; fuliginous, pitchy, sooty; *dhu* [*Ir. & Gaelic*], swart, swarthy, dusky, dingy, murky *or* mirky; blotchy, smudgy, smutty; nigrine [*rare*], nigricant, nigrescent, Ethiopian, Ethiopic; low-toned, low in tone; of the deepest dye.
  black as -jet etc. *n.,* - my hat, -a shoe, -a tinker's pot, -November, -the ace of spades, -thunder, -midnight; nocturnal etc. (*dark*) 421; gray etc. 432; obscure etc. 421.
- *adv.* in mourning.

432. Gray

- *n.* **gray** *or* grey etc. *adj.;* neutral tint, silver, dove-color, pepper and salt, *chiaroscuro* [*It.*], grisaille.
  grayness *or* greyness etc. *adj.*
  [pigments] Payne's gray; black etc. 431.
- *v.* **render gray** etc. *adj.;* gray *or* grey.
- *adj.* **gray** *or* grey; iron-gray, dun, drab, dingy, leaden, livid, somber, sad, pearly, calcareous, limy, silver, silvery, silvered; French–, steel–, Quaker–, dapple- gray; dappled; dove-colored, *gorge-de-pigeon* [*F.*]; ashen, ashy, favillous; cinereous, cineritious; grizzly, grizzled; slate-colored, stone-colored, mouse-colored, ash-colored; cool.

433. Brown

- *n.* **brown** etc. *adj.;* brownness.
  [pigments] bister *or* bistre, brown ocher *or* ochre, mummy, sepia, Vandyke brown.
- *v.* **render brown** etc. *adj.;* brown, tan, embrown, imbrown, bronze.
- *adj.* **brown,** adust [*rare*], castaneous, toast-brown, nut-brown, seal-brown, cinnamon, hazel, fawn,

434. Redness

puce, musteline, musteloid, écru, *feuille-morte* [*F.*], tawny, fuscous, chocolate, maroon, tan, brunette, whity-brown; fawn-colored, snuff-colored, liver-colored; brown as -a berry, –mahogany, –oak leaves; khaki.

reddish-brown, terra cotta, rufous, russet, russety, russetish, ferruginous, rust, foxy, bronze, coppery, copperish, copper-colored; bay, bayard, roan, sorrel, henna, auburn, chestnut, mahogany; rubiginous, rubiginose, rust-colored; lurid.

sun-burnt; tanned etc. v.

434. Redness

n. **red**, scarlet, cardinal, cardinal red, vermilion, carmine, crimson, pink, rose, cerise, cherry, rouge, coquelicot, salmon, lake, maroon, carnation, *couleur de rose* [*F.*], *rose du Barry* [*F.*]; magenta, solferino, damask, flesh -color, -tint; color; fresh–, high-color; warmth; gules [*her.*].

redness etc. *adj.;* rubescence, rubicundity, ruddiness, rubefaction, rubrication, rubification; erubescence, blush.

[comparisons] ruby, *grenat* [*F.*], garnet, carbuncle; rust, iron mold *or* mould; rose, cardinal flower, lobelia; cardinal-bird, –grosbeak; redstart.

[dyes and pigments] cinnabar, cochineal, red ocher *or* ochre, stammel, fuchsine *or* fuchsin, vermilion; ruddle, madder; Indian red, palladium red, light red, Venetian red; red ink, annatto *or* annotto, realgar, minium, red lead.

v. **be** *or* **become red** etc. *adj.;* blush, flush, color, color up, mantle, redden.

render red etc. *adj.;* redden, rouge, crimson, encrimson [*rare*], empurple; rubify [*rare*], rubricate; incarnadine; ruddle, rust.

adj. **red** etc. *n.,* reddish; incarnadine, sanguine, sanguineous, bloody, gory; coral, coralline, rosy, roseate; stammel, blood-red, laky, wine-red, wine-colored, vinaceous; incarmined [*rare*], rubiform [*rare*], rufous, rufulous, murrey, bricky, lateritious [*rare*]; rubineous, rubious, rubricate, rubricose; Pompeiian red; reddish-brown etc. 433.

rose–, ruby–, cherry–, claret–, flame–, flesh–, peach–, salmon–, brick–, rust-colored.

red as -fire, –blood, –scarlet, -a turkey cock, –a lobster; warm, hot.

red-complexioned, red-faced, florid, burnt, rubicund, ruddy, red, blowzed, blowzy, glowing, sanguine, blooming, rosy, hectic, flushed, inflamed; blushing etc. *v.;* erubescent, rubescent; reddened etc. *v.*

[of hair] sandy, carroty, brick-red, Titian red, auburn, chestnut.

435. Greenness

n. **green** etc. *adj.;* blue and yellow; vert [*her.*].
greenness, verdancy, verdure, viridescence, viridity.
[comparisons] emerald, malachite, chrysoprase, jasper, chrysolite *or* olivine, beryl; verd antique, verdigris, aquamarine; reseda, mignonette, absinthe, *crême de menthe* [*F.*].
[pigments] *terre verte* [*F.*], viridian, bice, verditer, verdine, celadon.

v. **render green** etc. *adj.;* green.

adj. **green**, verdant; glaucous, olive; green as grass; verdurous, citrine *or* citrinous, porraceous, olivaceous, smaragdine [*rare*].
emerald–, pea–, grass–, apple–, sea–, olive–, cucumber–, leaf–, Irish–, Nile–, Kelly–, bottle- green.
greenish, virent [*rare*], virescent, viridescent [*rare*], chlorine; aquamarine, blue-green.

436. Yellowness

n. **yellow** etc. *adj.;* or [*her.*]; yellowness etc. *adj.;* xanthocyanopia *or* xanthocyanopsia, xanthochroia.
[comparisons] crocus, jonquil, saffron, topaz; xanthite; gold, gilding, gilt; yolk; jaundice, icterus; London fog.
[pigments] gamboge, fustic, massicot; cadmium–, chrome–, Indian–, king's–, lemon-yellow; orpiment, yellow ocher, Claude tint, aureolin; xanthein, xanthin; xanthophyll.

v. **render yellow** etc. *adj.;* yellow, gild; jaundice.

adj. **yellow**, aureate, golden, gold, gilt, gilded, flavous [*obs.*], citrine, citreous, lemon, fallow; fulvous, fulvescent, fulvid [*rare*]; sallow, lutescent, luteolous, luteous, tawny, cream, creamy, sandy; xanthic, xanthous; jaundiced; auricomous, ocherous *or* ochreous, ochery *or* ochry, flaxen, yellowish, buff, écru; icterine, icteritious *or* icteritous, icteroid; xanthochroid, yellow complexioned.
gold–, saffron–, citron–, lemon–, sulphur–, amber–, straw–, primrose–, cream-colored; xanthocarpous, xanthopous [*bot., rare*].
yellow as a -quincy, –crow's foot; yellow as saffron.

437. Purple

n. **purple** etc. *adj.;* blue and red, bishop's purple; gridelin, amethyst; damson, heliotrope; purpure [*her.*].

        lividness, lividity.
v. **render purple** etc. *adj.;* purple, empurple.
adj. **purple**, violet, plum-colored, lavender, lilac, puce, mauve, purplish, purpurate [*archaic*], violaceous, hyacinthine, amethystine, magenta, solferino, heliotrope; livid.

438. Blueness
n. **blue** etc. *adj.;* garter-blue; watchet [*obs.*]; blueness, bluishness; bloom.
    [comparisons] *lapis lazuli* [*L.*], sapphire, turquoise; indicolite.
    [pigments] ultramarine, smalt, cobalt, cyanogen; Prussian–, syenite- blue; bice, indigo; zaffer.
v. **render blue** etc. *adj.;* blue.
adj. **blue**, azure, cerulean, cyanic; sky-blue, sky-colored, sky-dyed; navy blue, midnight blue, cadet blue, robin's-egg blue, baby blue, ultramarine, aquamarine, electric blue *or* electric, steel blue *or* steel; cerulescent; bluish; atmospheric, retiring; cold.

439. Orange
n. **orange**, red and yellow; old gold; gold color etc. *adj.*
    [pigments] ocher *or* ochre, Mars orange, cadmium.
v. **gild**, engild, deaurate [*rare*], warm.
adj. **orange**; ocherous *or* ochreous, ochery *or* ochry; henna, burnt orange; orange–, gold–, brass–, apricot- colored; warm, hot, glowing, flame-colored.

440. Variegation
n. **variegation**; dichroism, trichroism; iridescence, irisation, play of colors, polychrome, maculation, spottiness, striae.
    [comparisons] spectrum, rainbow, iris, tulip, peacock, chameleon, butterfly, zebra, leopard, jaguar, panther, cheetah, ocelot, ophite, nacre, mother-of-pearl, tortoise shell; opal, cymophane, marble; mackerel, mackerel sky; harlequin; Joseph's coat; tricolor.
    check, plaid, tartan, patchwork; marquetry, parquet, parquetry, mosaic, tesserae, tessellation, checkerwork; chessboard, checkers *or* chequers.
v. **variegate**, stripe, streak, checker *or* chequer, fleck, bespeckle, speckle, besprinkle, sprinkle; stipple, maculate, dot, bespot; tattoo, inlay, tessellate. damascene; embroider, braid, quilt.
    be variegated etc. *adj.*
adj. **variegated** etc. *v.;* many-colored, many-hued; divers-colored, party-colored *or* parti-colored, dichromatic, polychromatic; bicolor, tricolor, versi-color; of all the colors of the rainbow, of all manner of colors; kaleidoscopic, naevose *or* nevose, daedal.
    iridescent, opaline, opalescent, prismatic, nacreous, pearly, shot, *gorge-de-pigeon* [*F.*], chatoyant; irised, irisated, pavonine; tortoise-shell.
    mottled, pied, piebald, skewbald; motley, marbled, pepper-and-salt, paned, dappled, clouded, cymophanous.
    checkered *or* chequered, mosaic, tessellated, plaid.
    spotted, spotty; punctate *or* punctuated [*rare*], powdered; speckled etc. *v.;* freckled, flea-bitten, studded; flecked, fleckered.
    striated, barred, veined; brinded, brindled, tabby; watered; strigose, strigillose, strigate, striolate; listed; embroidered etc. *v.*

441. Vision
n. **vision**, sight, optics, eyesight.
    view, look, espial, glance, ken, *coup d'oeil* [*F.*]; glimpse, glint, peep, peek; gaze, stare, leer; perlustration [*rare*], contemplation; conspection [*obs.*], conspectuity [*obs.*]; regard, survey; inspection, introspection; reconnoissance, reconnaissance, speculation, watch, espionage, *espionnage* [*F.*]; autopsy; ocular -inspection, –demonstration; sight-seeing, globe-trotting.
    viewpoint, standpoint, point of view; gazebo, loophole, belvedere, watchtower.
    field of view; theater *or* theatre, amphitheater *or* amphitheatre, arena, vista, horizon; commanding view, bird's-eye view, panoramic view.
    visual organ, organ of vision; eye; naked eye, unassisted eye; retina, pupil, iris, cornea, white; optics, orbs; saucer–, goggle–, gooseberry- eyes.
    short sight etc. 443; clear–, sharp–, quick–, eagle–, piercing–, penetrating-sight, –glance, –eye; perspicacity, discernment; catopsis.
    [comparison] eagle, hawk; cat, lynx, weasel; Argus.
    evil eye, blighting glance; basilisk, cockatrice.
    [optical devices] spectacles, eyeglass, lorgnette, monocle, reading glass, field glass, opera glass; telescope etc. 445; microscope, periscope.
v. **see**, behold, discern, perceive, have in sight, descry, sight, make out, discover, distinguish, recognize, spy, espy, ken [*archaic*]; get–, have–, catch- a -sight, –glimpse -of; command a view of; witness, contemplate, speculate; cast–, set- the eyes on; be a spectator of etc. 444; look on

442. Blindness

etc. (*be present*) 186; see sights etc. 455; see at a glance etc. 498.

look, view, eye; lift up the eyes, open one's eye; look -at, –on, –upon, –over, –about one, –round; survey, scan, inspect; run the eye -over, –through; reconnoiter *or* reconnoitre, glance- round, –on, –over; turn–, bend- one's looks upon; direct the eyes to, turn the eyes on, cast a glance.

observe etc. (*attend to*) 457; watch etc. (*care*) 459; see with one's own eyes; watch for etc. (*expect*) 507; peep, peek, peer, pry, take a peep; play at bopeep.

look full in the face, look hard at, look intently; strain one's eyes; fix–, rivet- the eyes upon; stare, gaze; pore over, gloat on, gloat over; leer, ogle, glare; goggle; cock the eye, squint, gloat, look askance *or* askant.

adj. **ocular**; seeing etc. *v.*; visual, optic *or* optical; ophthalmic.

clear-sighted etc. *n.*; clear-eyed, far-sighted; eagle–, hawk–, lynx–, keen–, Argus-eyed.

visible etc. 446.

adv. **visibly** etc. 446; in sight of, with one's eyes open.

at sight, at first sight, at a glance, at the first blush; *prima facie* [*L.*].

int. **look**! etc. (*attention*) 457.

442. Blindness

n. **blindness**, sightlessness, benightedness, anopsia *or* anopsy, cecity, excecation [*obs.*], cataract, ablepsia *or* ablepsy [*rare*], prestriction [*obs.*]; dim-sightedness etc. 443; amaurosis, *gutta serena* ["drop serene" *of* Milton], teichopsia.

[type for the blind] Braille *or* Braille type, New York point, Gall's serrated type, Howe's American type *or* Boston type, Moon's type; Alston's Glasgow type, Lucas's type, Frere's type; string alphabet, writing stamps, noctograph.

v. **be blind** etc. *adj.*; not see; lose sight of; have the eyes bandaged; grope in the dark.

not look; close–, shut–, turn away–, avert- the eyes; look another way; wink etc. (*limited vision*) 443; shut the eyes to, be blind to; wink at, blink at.

render blind etc. *adj.*; excecate [*obs.*], blind, blindfold; hoodwink, dazzle; put one's eyes out; throw dust into one's eyes; *jeter de la poudre aux yeux* [*F.*]; screen from sight etc. (*hide*) 528.

adj. **blind**; eyeless, sightless, visionless, dark; stoneblind, stark-blind, sand-blind [*archaic*]; undiscerning; dimsighted etc. 443.

blind as -a bat, –a buzzard, –a beetle, –a mole, –an owl; wall-eyed.

blinded etc. *v.*

adv. **blindly**, blindfold; darkly.

443. Dim-sightedness
[imperfect vision]

n. dim–, dull–, half–, short–, near–, long–, double–, astigmatic–, failing- sight; dim etc. -sightedness; purblindness, monocularity, blearedness, lippitude; myopia, presbyopia; confusion of vision; astigmatism; color blindness, chromato-pseudoblepsis, Daltonism; day blindness, hemeralopia; snow blindness; xanthocyanopia *or* xanthocyanopsia; ophthalmia; cataract; nyctalopia, moon blindness.

squint, cross-eye, strabismus, strabism, nystagmus; cast in the eye, swivel eye, cockeye, goggle-eyes; obliquity of vision.

winking etc. *v.*; nictitation, nictation; blinkard, albino.

dizziness, swimming, scotomy *or* scotoma [*med.*].

[limitation of vision] blinker, blinder; screen etc. (*hider*) 530.

[fallacies of vision] *deceptio visus* [*L.*]; refraction, distortion, illusion, false light, anamorphosis, virtual image, spectrum, mirage, looming, phasma [*obs.*]; phantasm, phantasma, phantom; vision; specter *or* spectre, apparition, ghost; *ignis fatuus* [*L.*] etc. (*luminary*) 423; specter of the Brocken; magic mirror; magic lantern etc. (*show*) 448; mirror, lens etc. (*instrument*) 445.

v. **be dim-sighted** etc. *n.*; see double; "see men as trees walking" [*Bible*]; have a mote in the eye, have a mist before the eyes, have a film over the eyes; see through a -prism, –glass darkly; wink, blink, nictitate, nictate; squint; look askance *or* askant, screw up the eyes, glare, glower.

dazzle, glare, swim, blur, loom.

adj. **dim-sighted** etc., myopic, nearsighted, shortsighted; presbyopic; astigmatic; moon–, blear–, goggle–, gooseberry–, one- eyed; blind of one eye, monoculous *or* monocular *or* monoculate; half-blind, purblind; cockeyed [*colloq.*], dim-eyed, mole-eyed, mope-eyed [*obs.*]; dichroic.

blind as a bat etc. (*blind*) 442; winking etc. *v.*

444. Spectator

n. **spectator**, beholder, observer, looker-on, onlooker, *assistant* [*F.*], viewer, gazer, witness, eye-witness, bystander, passer-by; sightseer; rubberneck.

136

spy, scout; sentinel etc. (*warning*) 668.
grandstand [*fig.*], bleachers, gallery, the gods [*slang*].

v. **witness**, behold etc. (*see*) 441; look on etc. (*be present*) 186; rubber *or* rubberneck.

445. Optical Instruments

n. **optical instruments**; lens, meniscus, magnifier; microscope, simple microscope *or* single microscope, compound microscope, projecting microscope, ultramicroscope; spectacles, glasses, barnacles [*colloq., Eng.*], gig lamps [*slang*], goggles, eyeglass, *pince-nez* [*F.*]; periscopic lens; telescope, glass, teinoscope, prism telescope; lorgnette, binocular; spyglass, opera glass, field glass; burning glass, convex lens.

prism; camera, hand camera, kodak [*trade name*], moving-picture machine; camera-lucida, camera-obscura; magic lantern etc. (*show*) 448; megascope; stereopticon; chromatrope, thaumatrope; stereoscope, pseudoscope, polyscope, kaleidoscope, kaleidophon *or* kaleidophone.

photometer, optometer, eriometer, actinometer, lucimeter, radiometer; abdominoscope, gastroscope, helioscope, polariscope, polemoscope, spectroscope, spectrometer.

mirror, reflector, speculum; looking-glass, pier-glass, cheval-glass; hand mirror.

optics, optician; photography, photographer; optometry, optometrist; abdominoscopy; gastroscopy; microscopy, microscopist.

446. Visibility

n. **visibility**, perceptibility, perceivability; conspicuousness, distinctness etc. *adj.;* conspicuity [*rare*]; appearance etc. 448; basset [*geol.*]; exposure; manifestation etc. 525; ocular-proof, –evidence, –demonstration; field of view etc. (*vision*) 441; periscopism.

v. **be** *or* **become visible** etc. *adj.;* appear, open to the view; meet–, catch-the eye; basset [*geol.*], crop out; present–, show–, manifest–, produce–, discover–, reveal–, expose–, betray-itself; stand forth, stand out; materialize; show; arise; peep out, peer out; start up, spring up, show up [*colloq.*], turn up, crop up; glimmer, gleam, glitter, glow, loom; glare; burst forth; burst upon the -view, –sight; heave in sight [*naut. or colloq.*]; come in sight, come into view, come out, come forth, come forward; see the light of day; break through the clouds; make its appearance, show its face, appear to one's eyes, come upon the stage, float before the eyes, speak for itself etc. (*manifest*) 525; attract the attention etc. 457; reappear; live in a glass house.

expose to view etc. 525.

adj. **visible**, perceptible, perceivable, discernible, apparent; in view, in full view, in sight; exposed to view, *en évidence* [*F.*]; unclouded.

distinct, plain, clear, definite; obvious etc. (*manifest*) 525; well-defined, well-marked; in focus; recognizable, palpable, autoptic *or* autoptical; glaring, staring, conspicuous; stereoscopic *or* stereoscopical; in bold relief, in strong relief, in high relief.

periscopic *or* periscopical, panoramic.

adv. **before one**; under one's -nose, –very eyes; before–, under- one's eyes; *à vue d'oeil* [*F.*], in one's eye, *oculis subjecta fidelibus* [*L.*]; visibly etc. *adj.;* in sight of; *veluti in speculum* [*L.*].

447. Invisibility

n. **invisibility**, invisibleness, nonappearance, imperceptibility; indistinctness etc. *adj.;* mystery, delitescence *or* delitescency.

concealment etc. 528; latency etc. 526.

v. **be invisible** etc. *adj.;* be hidden etc. (*hide*) 528; lurk etc. (*lie hidden*) 526; escape notice.

render invisible etc. *adj.;* conceal etc. 528; put out of sight.

not see etc. (*be blind*) 442; lose sight of.

adj. **invisible**, imperceptible; undiscernible, indiscernible; unapparent, nonapparent; out of sight, not in sight; *à perte de vue* [*F.*], behind the -scenes, –curtain; viewless, sightless; unconspicuous, inconspicuous; unseen etc. (*see* see etc. 441); covert etc. (*latent*) 526; eclipsed, under an eclipse.

indistinct; dim etc. (*faint*) 422; mysterious, dark, obscure, confused; indistinguishable, undiscernible *or* undiscernable, shadowy, indefinite, undefined; ill-defined, ill-marked; blurred, blurry, fuzzy, out of focus; misty etc. (*opaque*) 426; veiled etc. (*concealed*) 528; delitescent.

448. Appearance

n. **appearance**, phenomenon, sight, spectacle, show, premonstration [*obs.*], scene, species, view, *coup d'oeil* [*F.*]; lookout, outlook, prospect, vista, perspective, bird's-eye view, scenery, landscape, seascape, picture, tableau; display, exposure, *mise en scène* [*F.*], rising of the curtain.

449. Disappearance

phantasm, phantom etc. (*fallacy of vision*) 443.
spectacle, pageant; peep show, raree-show, galanty (*or* gallanty) show; ombres chinoises [*F.*]; magic lantern, phantasmagoria, dissolving views; biograph, cinematograph, cinema, moving pictures, movies, photoplay, photodrama; panorama, diorama, cosmorama, georama; coup de théâtre [*F.*], jeu de théâtre [*F.*]; pageantry etc. (*ostentation*) 882; insignia etc. (*indication*) 550.
aspect, angle, phase, phasis, seeming; shape etc. (*form*) 240; guise, look, complexion, color, image, mien, air, cast, carriage, port, demeanor; presence, expression, first blush, face of the thing; point of view, light.
lineament, feature, trait, lines; outline, outside; contour, silhouette, face, countenance, visage, phiz [*colloq.*], cast of countenance, profile, tournure [*F.*], cut of one's jib [*colloq.*], outside etc. 220.
physiognomy, metoposcopy, phrenology; physiognomist, metoposcopist, phrenologist.

v. **appear**; be *or* become visible etc., 446; seem, look, show; present-, wear-, carry-, have-, bear-, exhibit-, take-, take on-, assume- the -appearance, -semblance- of; look like; cut a figure, figure; present to the view; show etc. (*make manifest*) 525.

adj. **apparent**, seeming, ostensible; on view.
adv. **apparently**; to all seeming, to all appearance; ostensibly, seemingly, as it seems, on the face of it, prima facie [*L.*]; at the first blush, at first sight; in the eyes of; to the eye.

449. Disappearance

n. **disappearance**, evanescence, eclipse, occultation; insubstantiality.
  departure etc. 293; exit; vanishing, vanishment, vanishing point; dissolving views.
v. **disappear**, vanish, dissolve, fade, melt away, pass, go, avaunt [*obs.*]; be gone etc. *adj.*; leave no trace, "leave not a rack behind" [*Tempest*]; go off the stage etc. (*depart*) 293; suffer-, undergo-an eclipse; retire from sight; be lost to view, be lost to sight, see no longer, fade away [*slang*], pass out of sight.
  lose sight of.
  efface etc. 552.
adj. **disappearing** etc. *v.;* evanescent; missing, lost; lost to sight, lost to view; gone.
int. **vanish**! disappear! fade! [*slang*], beat it! [*slang*], avaunt! etc. (*ejection*) 297.

Class 4. Intellect

Division 1. Formation of Ideas

Section 1. Operations of Intellect in General

450. Intellect

n. **intellect**, mind, understanding, reason, thinking principle; rationality; cogitative-, cognitive-, discursive-, reasoning-, intellectual-faculties; faculties, senses, consciousness, observation, percipience *or* percipiency, apperception, mentality, intelligence, intellection [*obs.*], intuition, association of ideas, instinct, conception, judgment, wits, parts, capacity, intellectuality, genius; brains, cognitive-, intellectual-powers; wit etc. 498; ability etc. (*skill*) 698; wisdom etc. 498; Vernunft [*Ger.*], Verstand [*Ger.*].
ego, soul, spirit, ghost [*archaic*], inner man, heart, breast, bosom, penetralia mentis [*L.*], divina particula aurae [*L.*], anima divina [*L.*], heart's core; psyche, pneuma, subconscious self, subliminal consciousness, supreme principle, the Absolute.
seat of thought, organ of thought, sensorium, sensory, brain; head, headpiece; pate [*colloq.*], noodle [*colloq.*], noddle [*slang*], skull, pericranium, cerebrum, cranium, brain pan, brain box, brain case, sconce [*colloq.*], upper story [*colloq.*].
[science of mind] metaphysics; philosophy etc. 451; psychics; pneumatology, psychology, psychogenesis; noölogy, noöscopics, ideology; mental-, moral-philosophy; philosophy of the mind.
phrenology; craniology, cranioscopy; psychometry, psychophysics, psycho-analysis.
ideality, idealism; transcendentalism, immateriality etc. 317; universal -concept, -conception; mahat [*theos.*].

psychical research; telepathy, thought transference, thought reading; clairaudience; clairvoyance, mediumship; spiritualism etc. 992a.

metaphysician, philosopher, psychiatrist, psychologist, psychometer, psychopath, psychophysicist psychotherapist; psychic, medium, spiritist; adept, mahatma, yogi [*Hinduism*].

v. **reason**, understand, think, reflect, cogitate, excogitate, conceive. judge, contemplate, meditate; ruminate etc. (*think*) 451.

note, notice, mark; take -notice, –cognizance- of; be aware of, be conscious of; realize; appreciate; fancy etc. (*imagine*) 515.

adj. [**relating to intellect**] intellectual, mental, rational, endowed with reason; subjective, noöscopic, psychological; cerebral; percipient, appercipient, animastic; brainy [*colloq.*].

hyperphysical, superphysical; subconscious, subliminal; telepathic, clairaudient, clairvoyant; psychic *or* psychical, spiritual, ghostly; metaphysical, transcendental.

immaterial etc. 317.

450a. Absence or want of Intellect

n. **absence of intellect**, want of intellect etc. 450; apartments to let [*slang*], nobody home [*slang*], nobody home upstairs [*slang*], *non compos mentis* [*L.*], unintellectuality; imbecility etc. 499; brutality, brute instinct, brute force.

adj. unendowed with–, void of- reason; unintelligent etc. (*imbecile*) 499.

451. Thought

n. **thought**; exercitation–, exercise- of the intellect; intellection; reflection, cogitation, consideration, meditation, study, lucubration, speculation, deliberation, pondering; head work, brainwork; cerebration; mentation, deep reflection; close study, application etc. (*attention*) 457.

association–, succession–, flow–, train–, current- of -thought, –ideas.

mature thought; afterthought, reconsideration, second thoughts; retrospection etc. (*memory*) 505; excogitation; examination etc. (*inquiry*) 461; invention etc. (*imagination*) 515.

thoughtfulness etc. *adj.*

abstraction, abstract thought, contemplation, musing; brown study etc. (*inattention*) 458; reverie *or* revery, depth of thought, workings of the mind, thoughts, inmost thoughts; self-counsel, self-communing, self-consultation.

451. Thought

[philosophy] philosophical -opinions, –systems, –schools; the handmaid of theology, *ancilla theologioe* [*L.*].

oriental philosophy: Vedânta *or* Uttara-Mîmâmsâ ["later investigation"]; Pûrva-Mîmâmsâ ["prior investigation"]; Sâmkhyas–, Yoga–, Nyâya–, Vaisheshika- philosophy.

greek and greco-roman philosophy: Ionian–, Pythagorean–, Eleatic- school; Atomism; Sophism *or* Sophistic philosophy.

Socratic–, Megarian *or* Eristic–, Elean- school; Cynic philosophy; Cyrenaic *or* Hedonistic school, Hedonism; Platonism; philosophy of the -Absolute, –Academy; Aristotelianism, philosophy of the Lyceum; Peripatetic school [historical formula: *concept, Idea, essence*].

Stoic philosophy, Stoicism, philosophy of the Porch; Epicureanism, philosophy of the Garden; Scepticism; Eclecticism.

Neo-Phythagoreanism; Neo-Platonism.

patristic philosophy: Gnosticism, Manicheism; Alexandrian school; philosophy of the Ante-Nicene Fathers, philosophy of the Post-Nicene Fathers.

scholastic philosophy: Scholasticism; Eclecticism; Mysticism, Mystic philosophy; Pantheistic school, pantheism; Thomism, Scotism, voluntarism; Averroism.

modern philosophy: Post-Reformation philosophy; Humanism, rationalism, political philosophy; Cartesianism; Spinozism; empiricism, moralism; idealistic philosophy, idealism; Leibnitzianism *or* Leibnizianism, Berkeleian philosophy, Berkeleyism; pan-phenomenalism.

modern German philosophy: Kantianism, Fichteanism, Schelling's philosophy, Hegelianism, Herbartianism, Schopenhauer's philosophy; neocriticism; Freudianism, Freudian theory; Einstein theory, relativism.

modern French philosophy: traditionalism; psychologico-spiritualistic school; Positivism; sociological school; Bergsonism.

modern English philosophy: associational psychology, utilitarianism, Darwinism, evolutionistic ethics; Spencerian philosophy; agnosticism, idealism, Neo-Hegelianism.

modern Italian philosophy: Vicoism, sensism, empiricism, criticism, idealism, ontologism, Neo-Scholasticism.

American philosophy: Transcendentalism, pragmatism, neo-voluntarism, new ethical movement; Neo-Hegelianism, Neo-Hegelian movement.

452. Incogitance

v. **think**, reflect, cogitate, excogitate, consider, reason, deliberate; bestow -thought, –consideration -upon; speculate, contemplate, meditate, ponder, muse, dream, ruminate; brood over, con over, study; mouse over, mull over, sweat over [*colloq.*]; bend–, apply- the mind etc. (*attend*) 457; digest, discuss, hammer at, hammer out, weigh, perpend [*archaic*]; realize, appreciate; fancy etc. (*imagine*) 515; trow [*archaic*].

rack–, ransack–, crack–, beat–, cudgel- one's brains; set one's -brain, –wits- to work; cerebrate, mentalize [*rare*].

harbor–, entertain–, cherish–, nurture- an idea etc. 453, take into one's head; bear in mind; reconsider.

take into consideration; take counsel etc. (*be advised*) 695; commune with oneself, bethink oneself; collect one's thoughts; revolve–, turn over–, run over-in the mind; chew the cud upon [*colloq.*], sleep upon; take counsel of–, advise with- one's pillow.

suggest itself, present itself, occur; come–, get- into one's head; strike one, flit across the view, come uppermost, run in one's head; enter–, pass in–, cross, –, flash on–, flash across–, float in–, fasten itself on–, be uppermost in–, occupy- the mind; have in one's mind.

make an impression; sink–, penetrate- into the mind; engross the thoughts.

adj. **thoughtful**, pensive, meditative, reflective, cogitative, excogitative, museful, wistful, contemplative, speculative, deliberative, studious, sedate, introspective, Platonic, philosophical; thinking etc. *v.*

under consideration, in contemplation, under advisement.

absorbed, rapt; lost in thought etc. (*inattentive*) 458; engrossed in etc. (*intent*) 457.

adv. all things considered, taking everything into -account, –consideration.

452. Incogitance
[absence or want of thought]

n. **incogitance** *or* incogitancy, vacancy, inunderstanding, vacancy of mind, poverty of intellect etc. 499; thoughtlessness etc. (*inattention*) 458; inanity, fatuity, vacuity.

v. **not think** etc. 451; not think of; dismiss from the -mind, –thoughts etc. 451.

indulge in reverie etc. (*be inattentive*) 458.

put away thought; unbend–, relax–, divert- the mind; make the mind a blank, let the mind lie fallow.

adj. **vacant**, inane, unintellectual, nonunderstanding, unideal, unoccupied, unthinking, incogitant, incogitative, unreasoning, inconsiderate, thoughtless; absent etc. (*inattentive*) 458; diverted; irrational etc. 499; narrow-minded etc. 481.

unthought of, undreamt of, unconsidered; off one's mind; incogitable, inconceivable, not to be thought of.

453. Idea
[object of thought]

n. **idea**, notion, conception, thought, apprehension, impression, perception, image, eidolon, sentiment, reflection, observation, consideration; abstract idea; archetype, formative notion; guiding–, organizing- conception; image in the mind, regulative principle.

view etc. (*opinion*) 484; theory etc. 514; conceit, fancy; phantasy etc. (*imagination*) 515.

viewpoint, point of view; aspect etc. 448; field of view.

454. Topic
[subject of thought]

n. **subject of thought**, material for thought; food for the mind, mental pabulum.

subject, subject matter; matter, *motif* [*F.*], theme, *noemata* [*Gr.*], topic, what it is about, thesis, text, business, affair, matter in hand, argument; motion, resolution; head, chapter; case, point; proposition, theorem; field of inquiry; moot point, debatable point, point at issue, point in question; problem etc. (*question*) 461.

v. float–, pass- in the mind etc. 451.

adj. **thought of**; uppermost in the mind; *in petto* [*It.*].

adv. **under consideration**, under advisement; in question, in the mind; at issue, up for discussion, before the house, on foot, on the docket, on the carpet, on the tapis, *sur le tapis* [*F.*]; relative to etc. 9.

Section 2. Precursory Conditions and Operations

455. Curiosity
[desire of knowledge]

n. **curiosity**, curiousness; interest, thirst for knowledge, mental acquisitiveness; newsmongery, inquiring mind; inquisitiveness.

questioner, *enfant terrible* [*F.*], walking question mark [*humorous*], quidnunc.

458. Inattention

busybody, newsmonger; Peeping Tom, Paul Pry, eavesdropper; gossip etc. (*news*) 532.

sight-seer, rubberneck.

v. **be curious** etc. *adj.;* take an interest in, stare, gape; prick up the ears, see sights, lionize; rubber *or* rubberneck.

pry, nose, search, ferret out, poke one's nose into.

adj. **curious**, inquisitive, burning with curiosity, overcurious, nosey [*colloq.*]; inquiring etc. 461; prying; inquisitorial; agape etc. (*expectant*) 507.

456. Incuriosity
[absence of curiosity]

n. **incuriosity**; incuriousness etc. *adj.;* apathy, insouciance etc. 866; indifference.

v. **be incurious** etc. *adj.;* have no curiosity etc. 455; be bored by, take no interest in etc. 823; mind one's own business, pursue the even tenor of one's way, glance neither to the right hand nor to the left.

adj. **incurious**, uninquisitive, indifferent; impassive etc. 823; uninterested, bored.

457. Attention

n. **attention**; mindfulness etc. *adj.;* intentness, intentiveness [*rare*]; alertness; thought etc. 451; advertence *or* advertency; observance, observation; consideration, reflection, perpension [*obs.*]; heed; heedfulness; particularity; notice, regard etc. *v.;* circumspection etc. (*care*) 459; study, scrutiny; inspection, introspection; revision, revisal.

active–, diligent–, exclusive–, minute–, close–, intense–, deep–, profound–, abstract–, labored–, deliberate- -thought, –attention, –application, –study.

absorption of mind etc. (*abstraction*) 458.

minuteness, meticulosity, meticulousness, finicality, finicalness; circumstantiality, attention to detail.

indication, calling attention to etc. *v.*

v. **be attentive** etc. *adj.;* attend, advert to, observe, look, see, view, remark, notice, regard, take notice, mark; give–, pay- -attention, –heed- to; know what time it is [*colloq.*], know the time of day [*colloq.*]; incline–, lend- an ear to; trouble one's head about; give a thought to, animadvert; occupy oneself with; contemplate etc. (*think of*) 451; look -at, –to, –after, –into, –over; see to; turn–, bend–, apply–, direct–, give- the -mind, –eye, –attention -to; have an eye to, have in one's eye; bear in mind; take into -account, –consideration; keep in -sight, –view; have regard to, heed, mind, take cognizance of, entertain, recognize; make–, take- note of; note.

examine, –closely, –intently; scan, scrutinize, consider; give–, bend- one's mind to; overhaul, revise, pore over; inspect, review, pass under review; take stock of; get the gist of; fix–, rivet–, devote- the -eye, –mind, –thoughts, –attention- on *or* to; hear out, think out; mind one's business, attend to one's business.

examine cursorily; glance -at, –upon, –over; cast–, pass- the eyes over; run over, turn over the leaves, dip into, perstringe [*obs.*]; skim etc. (*neglect*) 460; take a cursory view of.

revert to, hark back to; watch etc. (*expect*) 507, (*take care of*) 459; hearken *or* harken to, listen to; prick up the ears; have–, keep- the eyes open; come to the point.

meet with attention; fall under one's -notice, –observation; be under consideration etc. (*topic*) 454.

catch–, strike- the eye; attract notice; catch–, awaken–, wake–, invite–, solicit–, attract–, claim–, excite–, engage–, occupy–, strike–, arrest–, fix–, engross–, absorb–, rivet- the -attention, –mind, –thoughts; be present to the mind, be uppermost in the mind.

call attention to, bring under one's notice; point -out, –to, –at, –the finger at; lay the finger on, indigitate [*obs.*], indicate; direct attention to; show; put a mark upon etc. (*sign*) 550; call soldiers to "attention"; bring forward etc. (*make manifest*) 525.

adj. **attentive**, mindful, heedful, intentive [*rare*], advertent, all eyes and ears, observant, regardful; alive to, awake to; on the job [*colloq.*]; there with the goods [*colloq.*], with it [*slang*]; observing etc. *v.;* alert; taken up with, occupied with; engaged in, engrossed in, wrapped in; absorbed, rapt; breathless; preoccupied etc. (*inattentive*) 458; watchful etc. (*careful*) 459; intent on, all eyes [*colloq.*], open-eyed; breathless, undistracted, upon the stretch; on the watch etc. (*expectant*) 507.

steadfast etc. (*persevering*) 604a.

int. **see**! look! look you! look to it! mark! lo! behold! soho! hark! hark ye! mind! look out! look alive! [*colloq.*]; look here! [*colloq.*]; halloo! observe! lo and behold! attention! *nota bene* [*L.*]; **n.b.**; *, †; I'd have you know! notice! O yes! Oyez! dekko! [*Hind.*], ecco! [*It.*], yo-ho! ho!

458. Inattention

n. **inattention**, inconsideration, want of consideration; inconsiderateness etc. *adj.;* oversight; in-

459. Care

advertence *or* inadvertency, nonobservance, disregard.

supineness etc. (*inactivity*) 683; étourderie [*F.*]; want of thought; heedlessness etc. (*neglect*) 460; insouciance etc. (*indifference*) 866.

abstraction; absence of mind, absorption of mind; preoccupation, distraction, reverie *or* revery, brown study [*colloq.*], woolgathering, moonraking [*dial. Eng.*], pipe dream [*colloq.*], castle in the air, château en Espagne [*F.*], fancy, deep musing, fit of abstraction.

v. **be inattentive** etc. *adj.*; overlook, disregard; pass by etc. (*neglect*) 460; not observe etc. 457; think little of.

close-, shut- one's eyes to; pay no attention to; dismiss-, discard-, discharge- from one's -thoughts, -mind; drop the subject, think no more of; set-, turn-, put- aside; turn away from, turn one's attention from, turn a deaf ear to, turn one's back upon.

abstract oneself, dream, be somewhere else, be absent, be woolgathering, indulge in reverie *or* revery.

escape notice, escape attention; come in at one ear and go out at the other; forget etc. (*have no remembrance*) 506.

call off-, draw off-, call away-, divert-, distract- the -attention, -thoughts, -mind; put out of one's head.

confuse, disconcert, discompose, put out, perplex, bewilder, moider [*dial. Eng.*], fluster, flurry, rattle [*colloq.*], muddle, dazzle.

adj. **inattentive**; unobservant, unmindful, unheeding, undiscerning; inadvertent; mindless, regardless, respectless; listless etc. (*indifferent*) 866; blind, deaf; hen-headed [*colloq.*], flighty, giddy-pated, giddy-headed, bird-witted; hand over head [*rare*]; cursory, percursory [*rare*], volatile, scatter-brained, hare-brained; unreflecting, écervelé [*F.*], inconsiderate, offhand, thoughtless, dizzy, muzzy [*colloq.*], brainsick; giddy, -as a goose; wild, harum-scarum [*colloq.*], rantipole, heedless, careless etc. (*neglectful*) 460.

abstracted, absent, distrait [*F.*], woolgathering, moonraking [*dial. Eng.*], dazed, absent-minded, lost; lost-, wrapped- in thought; rapt, in the clouds, bemused, day-dreaming; dreaming of-, musing on- other things; preoccupied, engrossed etc. (*attentive*) 457; in a reverie etc. *n.*; off one's guard etc. (*inexpectant*) 508; napping; dreamy; caught napping.

disconcerted, put out etc. *v.*; rattled [*colloq.*].

adv. **inattentively**, inadvertently etc. *adj.*; per incuriam [*L.*], sub silentio [*L.*].

459. Care
[vigilance]

n. **care**, solicitude, heed, concern, reck [*poetic*], heedfulness etc. *adj.*; scruple etc. (*conscientiousness*) 939.

vigilance; watchfulness etc. *adj.*; surveillance, eyes of a lynx, eyes of Argus, watch, vigil, lookout, watch and ward, l'oeil du maître [*F.*].

espionage etc. (*reconnoitering*) 461; invigilation, watching.

alertness etc. (*activity*) 682; attention etc. 457; prudence etc., circumspection etc. (*caution*) 864; anxiety; forethought etc. 510; precaution etc. (*preparation*) 673; tidiness etc. (*order*) 58, (*cleanliness*) 652; accuracy etc. (*exactness*) 494; minuteness, meticulousness, meticulosity, circumstantiality, attention to detail.

watcher, watchdog etc. 664.

v. **be careful** etc. *adj.*; reck [*archaic*]; take care etc. (*be cautious*) 864; pay attention to etc. 457; take care of; look-, see- -to, -after; keep an eye upon, keep a sharp eye upon; chaperon, matronize, play gooseberry; keep watch, keep watch and ward; mount guard, set watch, watch; keep in -sight, -view; mind, mind one's business.

look sharp, look about one; look with one's own eyes; keep a -good, -sharp-lookout; have all one's -wits, -eyes-about one; watch for etc. (*expect*) 507; keep one's eyes open, have the eyes open, sleep with one eye open; catch a weasel asleep.

do one's best etc. 682; mind one's Ps and Qs [*colloq.*], speak by the card, pick one's steps.

take precautions etc. 673; protect etc. (*render safe*) 664.

adj. **careful**, regardful, heedful; taking care etc. *v.*; particular; prudent etc. (*cautious*) 864; considerate; thoughtful etc. (*deliberative*) 451; provident etc. (*prepared*) 673; alert etc. (*active*) 682; sure-footed.

guarded, on one's guard; on the -qui vive [*F.*], -alert, -watch, -lookout; awake, broad awake, vigilant; watchful, wakeful, Argus-eyed, lynx-eyed; wide awake etc. (*intelligent*) 498; on the watch for etc. (*expectant*) 507.

scrupulous etc. (*conscientious*) 939; tidy etc. (*orderly*) 58, (*clean*) 652; accurate etc. (*exact*) 494; cavendo tutus [*L.*] etc. (*safe*) 664.

adv. **carefully** etc. *adj.*; with care, gingerly.

142

460. Neglect

n. **neglect**; carelessness etc. *adj.;* trifling etc. *v.;* negligence; omission, laches [*obs.*], deferment, cunctation, procrastination, default; supineness etc. (*inactivity*) 683; conspiracy of silence; inattention etc. 458; nonchalance etc. (*insensibility*) 823; imprudence, recklessness etc. 863; slovenliness etc. (*disorder*) 59, (*dirt*) 653; improvidence etc. 674; noncompletion etc. 730; inexactness etc. (*error*) 495.

paraleipsis or paralipsis or paralepsis [*rhet.*].

trifler, waiter on Providence; Micawber; waster [*colloq.*], wastrel [*dial. Eng.*], drifter [*colloq.*], bum [*slang*], hobo, tramp, Knight of the Road [*humorous*], down-and-outer [*colloq.*], deadbeat, dead one [*slang*], stiff [*slang*], roustabout, sundowner [*Australia*]; slacker.

v. **be negligent** etc. *adj.;* take no care of etc. (take care of etc. 459); neglect; let slip, let go; lay –, set –, cast –, put– aside; keep –, leave– out of sight; lose sight of.

delay, defer, procrastinate, postpone, adjourn, pigeonhole, tie up with red tape, shelve, stay, suspend, table, lay on the table.

overlook, disregard; pass over, pass by; let pass; blink; wink at, connive at; gloss over; take no -note, -notice, -thought, -account- of; pay no regard to; *laisser aller* [*F.*].

scamp; trifle, fribble; do by halves; slight etc. (*despise*) 930; play with, trifle with; slur; skimp [*dial. & colloq.*]; skim, -the surface; *effleurer* [*F.*]; take a cursory view of etc. 457; slur –, slip –, skip –, jump– over; pretermit, miss, skip, jump, cut [*colloq.*], omit, push aside, throw into the background, sink.

ignore, refuse to notice, shut one's eyes to, refuse to hear, turn a deaf ear to, leave out of one's calculation; not attend to etc. 457, not mind; not trouble -oneself, -one's head- -with, -about: forget etc. 506.

be caught napping etc. (*not expect*) 508; leave a loose thread; let the grass grow under one's feet.

render neglectful etc. *adj.;* put *or* throw off one's guard.

adj. **neglecting** etc. *v.;* unmindful, negligent, neglectful; heedless, careless, thoughtless, inconsiderate; perfunctory, remiss.

unwary, unwatchful, unguarded, incircumspect [*rare*], uncircumspect, off one's guard, offhand.

supine etc. (*inactive*) 683; inattentive etc. 458; insouciant etc. (*indifferent*) 823; imprudent, reckless etc. 863; slovenly etc. (*disorderly*) 59, (*dirty*) 653; inexact etc. (*erroneous*) 495; improvident etc. 674.

neglected etc. *v.;* unheeded, uncared for, unperceived, unseen, unobserved, unnoticed, unnoted, unmarked, unattended to, unthought of, unregarded, unremarked, unmissed; shunted, shelved.

unexamined, unstudied, unsearched, unscanned, unweighed, unsifted, unexplored.

abandoned; buried in a napkin; hid under a bushel.

adv. **negligently** etc. *adj.;* hand over head [*obs.*], in any old way [*colloq.*], anyhow; in an unguarded moment etc. (*unexpectedly*) 508; *per incuriam* [*L.*]; when the cat is away.

int. **never mind**, no matter, let it pass; it will be all the same a hundred from now; *mañana* [*Sp.*].

461. Inquiry
[subject of inquiry. question]

n. **inquiry**; request etc. 765; search, research, quest; pursuit etc. 622.

examination, review, scrutiny, investigation, indagation [*obs.*]; perquisition, perscrutation [*rare*], pervestigation [*obs.*]; inquest, inquisition; exploration; exploitation, ventilation.

sifting; calculation, analysis, dissection, resolution, induction; Baconian method.

**strict –, close –, searching –, exhaustive– inquiry; narrow –, strict-search; study etc. (*consideration*) 451.

scire facias [*L.*], *ad referendum* [*L.*]; trial.

questioning etc. *v.;* interrogation, interrogatory; interpellation; challenge, examination, third degree [*colloq.*], cross-examination, catechism, catechesis; feeler, Socratic method, zetetic philosophy; leading question; discussion etc. (*reasoning*) 476.

reconnoitering, reconnaissance *or* reconnoissance, prying etc. *v.;* espionage, *espionage* [*F.*]; domiciliary visit, peep behind the curtain; lantern of Diogenes.

question, query, problem, poser, desideratum, point to be solved, porism; subject –, field– of -inquiry, -controversy; point –, matter– in dispute; moot point; issue, question at issue; bone of contention etc. (*discord*) 713; plain –, fair –, open– question; enigma etc. (*secret*) 533; knotty point etc. (*difficulty*) 704; *quodlibet* [*L.*]; threshold of an inquiry.

inquirer, investigator, inquisitor, inspector, querist, examiner, probator, catechist; scruta-

462. Answer

tor, scrutineer, scrutinizer; analyst; quidnunc etc. (*curiosity*) 455.

v. **inquire**, seek, search; make inquiry etc. *n.;* look -for, -about for, -out for; scan, reconnoiter *or* reconnoitre, explore, sound, rummage, ransack, pry, peer, look round; look-, go- -over, -through; give the once-over [*slang*]; spy, overhaul.

scratch the head, slap the forehead.

look-, peer-, pry- into every hole and corner; visit-, look- behind the scenes; nose, nose out, trace up; hunt out, fish out, ferret out; unearth; leave no stone unturned.

track, seek a clew *or* clue; hunt, trail, shadow, mouse, dodge, trace; follow the -trail, -scent; pursue etc. 662; beat up one's quarters; fish for; feel for etc. (*experiment*) 463.

investigate; take up-, institute-, pursue-, follow up-, conduct-, carry on-, prosecute- an inquiry etc. *n.;* look at, look into; pre-examine; discuss, canvass, agitate.

examine, mouse over, study, consider, calculate; dip-, dive-, delve-, go deep- into; make sure of, probe, sound, fathom; probe to the -bottom, -quick; scrutinize, analyze, anatomize, dissect, parse, resolve, sift, winnow; view-, try- in all its phases; thresh out.

bring in question, subject to examination, pose; put to the proof etc. (*experiment*) 463; audit, tax, pass in review; take into consideration etc. (*think over*) 451; take counsel etc. 695.

question, ask, demand; put-, propose-, propound-, moot-, start-, raise-, stir-, suggest-, put forth-, ventilate-, grapple with-, go into- a question.

interrogate, put to the question, catechize, pump; cross-question, cross-examine; roast [*colloq.*], grill [*colloq.*], put through the third degree [*colloq.*]; dodge; require an answer; pick-, suck- the brains of; feel the pulse.

be in question etc. *adj.;* undergo examination.

adj. **inquiring** etc. *v.;* inquisitive etc. (*curious*) 455; requisitive [*obs.*], requisitory; catechetical, inquisitorial, analytic; in search of, in quest of; on the lookout for, interrogative, zetetic; all-searching.

undetermined, untried, undecided, tentative; in question, in dispute, in issue, in course of inquiry; under -discussion, -consideration, -investigation etc. *n.;* *sub judice* [*L.*], moot, proposed; doubtful etc. (*uncertain*) 475.

adv. **what**? why? wherefore? *pourquoi?* [*F.*], *warum?* [*Ger.*], whence? whither? where? *quoere?* [*L.*]; how comes it? how does it happen? how is it? what is the reason? what's the matter? what's in the wind? what's afoot? what's up? what's in the air? what is it all about? what on earth? when? who? *nicht wahr?* [*Ger.*].

462. Answer

n. **answer**, response, reply, replication, riposte *or* ripost, subjoinder, rejoinder, retort, repartee; rescript, rescription [*archaic*]; antiphon, antiphony; acknowledgment; password; echo; counterstatement, counterblast, countercharge, contradiction.

[*law*] defense, plea, surrebutter, surrejoinder, reply, rejoinder, rebutter.

solution etc. (*explanation*) 522; discovery etc. 480*a;* rationale etc. (*cause*) 153; clew *or* clue etc. (*indication*) 550.

Oedipus; oracle etc. 513; return etc. (*record*) 551.

v. **answer**, respond, reply, rebut, riposte *or* ripost, retort, rejoin; give answer, return for answer; acknowledge, echo.

[*law*] defend, plead, surrebut, surrejoin, rebut, reply.

explain etc. (*interpret*) 522; solve etc. (*unriddle*) 522; discover etc. 480*a;* fathom, hunt out etc. (*inquire*) 461; satisfy, set at rest, determine.

adj. **answering** etc. *v.;* responsive, respondent; antiphonal; Oedipean, oracular; conclusive.

adv. **for this reason**; because etc. (*cause*) 153; on the scent, on the right scent.

int. **eureka**.

463. Experiment

n. **experiment**; essay etc. (*attempt*) 675; analysis etc. (*investigation*) 461; docimasy, trial, tentative method, *tâtonnement* [*F.*].

verification, probation, *experimentum crucis* [*L.*], proof, criterion, diagnostic, test, crucial test; assay, ordeal.

reagent, crucible, check, touchstone, pyx *or* pix [*Brit. mint*], curcuma paper, turmeric paper.

empiricism, rule of thumb.

feeler; pilot-, messenger- balloon; pilot engine; scout; straw to show the wind.

speculation, random shot, leap in the dark.

experimenter, experimentist, experimentalist, assayer, analyst, analyzer; prospector *or* prospecter, Forty-Niner, adventurer; speculator, gambler, stock gambler, plunger [*slang*].

v. **experiment**; essay etc. (*endeavor*) 675; try, assay; make an experiment, make trial of; give a trial to; put upon-, subject to- trial; experiment upon; rehearse; put-, bring-, submit- to the

-test, –proof; prove, verify, test, touch, practice upon, try one's strength.

grope; feel–, grope- -for, –one's way; fumble, *tâtonner* [*F.*], *aller à tâtons* [*F.*]; put–, throw- out a feeler; send up a pilot balloon; see how the -land lies, –wind blows; consult the barometer; feel the pulse; fish for, bob for; cast–, beat- about for; angle, trawl, cast one's net, beat the bushes.

venture; try one's fortune etc. (*adventure*) 675; explore etc. (*inquire*) 461.

adj. **experimental**, probative, probatory, probationary; analytic, docimastic *or* docimastical, speculative, tentative; empirical.

tried, tested, proved.

on trial, on examination, on *or* under probation, "on suspicion," under suspicion; on one's trial.

464. Comparison

n. **comparison**, collation, contrast, parallelism, balance; identification; comparative–, relative- estimate.

simile, similitude, parallelization [*rare*]; allegory etc. (*metaphor*) 521.

v. **compare**, –to, –with; collate, confront; place side by side etc. (*near*) 197; set–, pit– against one another; contrast, balance.

compare notes; institute a comparison; *parva componere magnis* [*L.*].

parallel, parallelize; draw a parallel.

adj. **comparative**, relative, contrastive; metaphorical etc. 521.

compared with etc. *v.;* comparable; judged by comparison.

adv. **relatively** etc. (*relation*) 9; as compared with etc. *v.*

465. Discrimination

n. **discrimination**, distinction, differentiation, diagnosis, diorism; nice perception; perception–, appreciation- of difference; estimation etc. 466; nicety, refinement; taste etc. 850; critique, judgment; tact; discernment etc. (*intelligence*) 498; acuteness, penetration; *nuances* [*F.*].

tip, pointer, dope [*slang*]; past performances, record.

v. **discriminate**, distinguish, severalize [*obs.*]; separate; draw the line, sift; separate–, winnow- the chaff from the wheat; separate the wheat from the tares; separate the sheep from the goats; split hairs.

estimate etc. (*measure*) 466; tip, tip off, sum up, criticize; know which is which, know what's what [*colloq.*], know one's way about, know a thing or two, know what o'clock it is, know the time of day, have cut one's eyeteeth, know the ways of the world [*all colloq.*]; "know a hawk from a handsaw" [*Hamlet*].

take into -account, –consideration; give–, allow- due weight to; weigh carefully.

adj. **discriminating** etc. *v.;* dioristic *or* dioristical [*obs.*], critical, diagnostic, perceptive, discriminative, distinctive; nice, acute.

465a. Indiscrimination

n. **indiscrimination**; indistinctness, indistinction; want of distinction, want of discernment, inability to discriminate; uncertainty etc. (*doubt*) 475.

v. **not discriminate** etc. 465; overlook etc. (*neglect*) 460- a distinction; confound, confuse, jumble, jumble together, heap indiscriminately; swallow whole, judge in a lump, use loosely.

adj. **indiscriminate**, indistinguishable, lacking distinction, undistinguished, undistinguishable; unmeasured; promiscuous, undiscriminating.

466. Measurement

n. **measurement**, admeasurement, mensuration, metage, survey, valuation, appraisement, assessment, assize; estimate, estimation; dead reckoning [*naut.*]; reckoning etc. (*numeration*) 85; gauging etc. *v.;* horse power, candle power, candle foot, foot candle, volt ampere, kilowatt; foot pound, foot poundal, foot ton.

metrology, weights and measures, compound arithmetic.

measure, yard measure, standard, rule, foot rule, spirit level, plumb line; square, T-square, steel square, compass, dividers, calipers; gauge *or* gage, standard gauge, broad *or* wide gauge, narrow gauge; log, log-line, patent log [*naut.*]; meter, line, rod, check.

flood mark, high-water mark, load-line mark, Plimsoll mark; index etc. 550.

scale; graduation, graduated scale; nonius; vernier etc. (*minuteness*) 193; quadrant, theodolite, transit *or* transit theodolite, viagraph; scale, beam, steelyard, weighing machine, balance etc. (*weight*) 319; anemometer etc. (*wind*) 349; barometer etc. (*air*) 338; bathometer etc. (*depth*) 208; dynamometer etc. (*force*) 276; galvanometer etc. (*power*) 157; goniometer etc. (*angle*) 244; hyetometer etc. (*fluids in motion*) 348; landmark etc. (*limit*) 233; pedometer etc. (*length*) 200; photometer etc. (*optical instruments*) 445; radiometer etc. (*light*) 420; stethoscope etc. (*medical*) 662; thermometer etc. 389.

467. Evidence

coordinates, ordinate and abscissa, polar coordinates, latitude and longitude, declination and right ascension, altitude and azimuth.

geometry, stereometry, planimetry, hypsometry, altimetry, hypsography, chorometry, chorography, topography, cartography; surveying, land surveying, geodesy, geodetics, geodaesia *or* geodesia, orthometry; cadastre *or* cadaster; cadastral survey, cadastration.

astrolabe, armillary sphere.

surveyor, land surveyor; geometer, chorographer, topographer, cartographer.

v. **measure**, meter, mete; value, assess, rate, appraise, estimate, form an estimate, set a value on; appreciate; standardize.

span, pace, step, inch, dial; caliper, divide, apply the compass etc. *n.;* gauge *or* gage; balance, poise, hold the scales, place in the beam, kick the beam; plumb, probe, sound, fathom; heave the -log, -lead; survey, plot, block in, block out, rule, draw to scale.

take an average etc. 29; graduate, calibrate.

adj. **measuring** etc. *v.;* metric, metrical; measurable; geodetical, cadastral, hypsographic *or* hypsographical, hypsometric *or* hypsometrical, chorographic *or* chorographical, topographic *or* topographical, cartographic *or* cartographical.

Section 3. Materials for Reasoning

467. Evidence
[on one side]

n. **evidence**; facts, premises, data, praecognitum (*pl.* praecognita), grounds; indication etc. 550; criterion etc. (*test*) 463.

testimony, testification; attestation; affirmation, declaration; deposition etc. 535; examination.

authority, warrant, credential, diploma, voucher, certificate, docket; *testamur* [*L.*]; record etc. 551; muniments; document; *pièce justificative* [*F.*]; deed, warranty etc. (*security*) 771; autograph, handwriting, signature, seal etc. (*identification*) 550; exhibit; citation, reference, quotation; admission etc. (*assent*) 488.

witness, indicator, eyewitness, earwitness, deponent; sponsor; cojuror, oath-helper [*hist.*]; compurgator [*hist.*].

evidence in chief; oral-, documentary-, hearsay-, external-, extrinsic-, internal-, intrinsic-, circumstantial-, cumulative-, *ex parte* [*L.*]-, presumptive-, collateral-, constructive- evidence; proof etc. (*demonstration*) 478; finger print, thumb print.

secondary evidence; confirmation, corroboration, support; ratification etc. (*assent*) 488; authentication; compurgation [*hist.*], wager of law [*hist.*], comprobation [*obs.*].

writ, summons etc. (*lawsuit*) 696.

v. **be evidence** etc. *n.;* evince, show, betoken, tell of; indicate etc. (*denote*) 550; imply, involve, argue, bespeak, breathe.

have weight, carry weight; tell, speak volumes; speak for itself etc. (*manifest*) 525.

rest upon, depend upon; repose on.

bear witness etc. *n.;* give evidence etc. *n.;* testify, depose, witness, vouch for; sign, seal, undersign, set one's hand and seal, sign and seal, deliver as one's act and deed, certify, attest; acknowledge etc. (*assent*) 488.

confirm, make absolute, ratify, corroborate, indorse *or* endorse, countersign, support, bear out, vindicate, uphold, warrant.

adduce, attest, evidence, cite, quote; refer to, appeal to; call, call to witness; bring forward, bring on, bring into court; allege; plead; produce-, confront- witnesses; collect-, bring together-, rake up- evidence.

establish; have-, make out- a case; authenticate, circumstantiate, substantiate, verify, make good, quote chapter and verse; bring home to, bring to book, bring off.

adj. **evidential**; showing etc. *v.;* indicative, indicatory; deducible etc. 478; grounded on, founded on, based on; first-hand, authentic, verificative, verifiable, veridical, cumulative, corroborative, confirmatory; significant, weighty, overwhelming, damning, conclusive.

oral, documentary, hearsay etc. (*evidence in chief*) *n.*

adv. **by inference**; according to, witness, *a fortiori* [*L.*]; still more, still less; *raison de plus* [*F.*]; in corroboration of etc. *n.;* *valeat quantum* [*L.*]; under seal, under one's hand and seal; at first hand, at second hand.

468. Counterevidence
[evidence on the other side]

n. **counterevidence**; evidence on the other -side, -hand; disproof; refutation etc. 479; negation etc. 536; conflicting evidence.

plea etc. 617; vindication etc. 937; counter-protest; *tu quoque* [*L.*] argument; other side-, re-

verse- of the shield; *reductio ad absurdum* [*L.*].
- *v.* **countervail**, oppose; rebut etc. (*refute*) 479; subvert etc. (*destroy*) 162; check, weaken; contravene; run counter; contradict etc. (*deny*) 536; tell another story, turn the scale, alter the case; turn the tables; cut both ways; prove a negative. *audire alteram partem* [*L.*].
- *adj.* **countervailing** etc. *v.;* contradictory, in rebuttal.
  unattested, unauthenticated, unsupported by evidence; supposititious, trumped up.
- *adv.* **conversely**, on the other hand, on the other side, in opposition; *per contra* [*L.*].

469. Qualification

- *n.* **qualification**, limitation, modification, coloring.
  allowance, grains of allowance, consideration, extenuating circumstances; mitigation.
  condition, proviso, exception; exemption; salvo [*rare*], saving clause; discount etc. 813; restriction.
- *v.* **qualify**, limit, modify, affect, leaven, take color from, give a color to, introduce new conditions, narrow, temper.
  allow for, make allowance for; admit exceptions, take into account; modulate.
  take exception, file exceptions, object, raise objections, rise to a point of order.
- *adj.* **qualifying** etc. *v.;* modificatory, extenuatory, mitigatory, lenitive, palliative; conditional; exceptional etc. (*unconformable*) 83.
  hypothetical etc. (*supposed*) 514; contingent etc. (*uncertain*) 475.
- *adv.* **provided**, –always; if, unless, but, yet; according as; conditionally, admitting, supposing; on the supposition of etc. (*theoretically*) 514; with the understanding, even, although, though, for all that, after all, at all events.
  if possible etc. 470; with grains of allowance, *cum grano salis* [*L.*]; *exceptis excipiendis* [*L.*], wind and weather permitting.
  subject to; with this proviso etc. *n.*

470. Possibility

- *n.* **possibility**, potentiality, potency; what may be, what is possible etc. *adj.;* compatibility etc. (*agreement*) 23.
  practicability, feasibility, workability, workableness; practicableness etc. *adj.*
  contingency, chance etc. 156.
- *v.* **be possible** etc. *adj.;* stand a chance; have a leg to stand on; admit of, bear.

  render possible etc. *adj.;* put in the way of, bring to bear, bring together.
- *adj.* **possible**; on the -cards, -dice; *in posse* [*L.*], within the bounds of possibility, conceivable, imaginable, credible; compatible etc. 23; likely.
  practicable, feasible, workable, performable, achievable; within -reach, –measurable distance; accessible, superable, surmountable; attainable, obtainable; contingent etc. (*doubtful*) 475.
- *adv.* **possibly**, by any possibility; perhaps, perchance, peradventure; may be, it may be, haply, mayhap.
  if possible, wind and weather permitting, God willing, *Deo volente* [*L.*], D. V.; as luck may have it.

471. Impossibility

- *n.* **impossibility** etc. *adj.;* what cannot be, what can never be; sour grapes; hopelessness etc. 859; infeasibility, infeasibleness, impracticality; discrepancy etc. (*disagreement*) 241.
  [comparisons] Canute (commanding the tide), Mrs. Partington (and her mop).
- *v.* **be impossible** etc. *adj.;* have no chance whatever.
  attempt impossibilities; square the circle, find the elixir of life, discover the philosopher's stone, discover the grand panacea, find the fountain of youth, discover the secret of perpetual motion; wash a blackamoor white; skin a flint; make a silk purse out of a sow's ear, make bricks without straw; have nothing to go upon; weave a rope of sand, build castles in the air, *prendre la lune avec les dents* [*F.*], extract sunbeams from cucumbers, milk a he-goat into a sieve, catch a weasel asleep, *rompre l'anguille au genou* [*F.*], be in two places at once; gather grapes from thorns, fetch water in a sieve, catch wind in cabbage nets, fling eels by the tail, make cheese of chalk.
- *adj.* **impossible**; not possible etc. 470; absurd, contrary to reason; at variance with the facts; unlikely; unreasonable etc. 477; incredible etc. 485; beyond the bounds of -reason, –possibility; from which reason recoils; visionary; inconceivable etc. (*improbable*) 473; prodigious etc. (*wonderful*) 870; unimaginable, inimaginable [*obs.*], not to be thought of, unthinkable.
  impracticable, unachievable; unfeasible, infeasible; insuperable; insurmountable *or* unsurmountable, unattainable, unobtainable; out of reach, out of the question; not to be had; be-

472. Probability

yond control; desperate etc. (*hopeless*) 859; incompatible etc. 24; inaccessible, uncomeatable [*colloq.*], impassable, impervious, innavigable, inextricable; self-contradictory.

out of-, beyond- one's -power, -depth, -reach, -grasp; too much for; *ultra crepidam* [*L.*].

472. Probability

n. **probability**, likelihood; credibleness; likeliness etc. *adj.;* *vraisemblance* [*F.*], verisimilitude, plausibility; color, semblance, show of; presumption; presumptive-, circumstantial- evidence; credibility.

reasonable-, fair-, good-, favorable- -chance, -prospect; prospect, well-grounded hope; chance etc. 156.

v. **be probable** etc. *adj.;* give-, lend- color to; point to; imply etc. (*evidence*) 467; bid fair etc. (*promise*) 511; stand fair for; stand a chance; stand-, run- a good chance; stand-, run- an even chance.

presume, infer, venture, suppose, take for granted, think likely, dare say, flatter oneself; expect etc. 507; count upon etc. (*believe*) 484.

adj. **probable**, likely, hopeful, to be expected, in a fair way.

plausible, specious, ostensible, colorable, *ben trovato* [*It.*], well-founded, reasonable, credible, easy of belief, presumable, presumptive, apparent.

adv. **probably** etc. *adj.;* belike [*archaic*]; in all probability, in all likelihood; very-, most- likely; like enough; very like; ten etc. to one; apparently, seemingly, to all seeming, as like as not [*colloq.*], according to every reasonable expectation; *prima facie* [*L.*]; to all appearance etc. (*to the eye*) 448.

473. Improbability

n. **improbability**, unlikelihood; unfavorable-, bad-, ghost of a-, little-, small-, poor-, scarcely any-, no- chance; bare possibility; long odds; incredibility etc. 485.

v. **be improbable** etc. *adj.;* violate-, stretch- the probabilities; go beyond reason, strain one's credulity; run counter to the laws of nature; have a small chance etc. *n.;* stand a poor show [*colloq.*].

adj. **improbable**, unlikely, contrary to all reasonable expectation; contrary to -fact, -experience; implausible, rare etc. (*infrequent*) 137; unheard of, inconceivable; unimaginable, inimaginable [*obs.*]; incredible etc. 485; more than doubtful.

int. **not likely**! no fear! [*chiefly Eng.*]; I ask you! [*slang*]; catch me! [*slang*].

474. Certainty

n. **certainty**; necessity etc. 601; certitude, sureness, surety, assurance; dead-, moral- certainty; infallibleness etc. *adj.;* infallibility, reliability, reliableness; indubitableness, inevitableness, unquestionableness.

gospel, scripture, church, pope, court of final appeal; *res adjudicata,* [*L.*], *res judicata* [*L.*]; ultimatum.

fact; positive fact, matter of fact; *fait accompli* [*F.*].

bigotry, positiveness, dogmatism, dogmatization; fanaticism.

dogmatist, dogmatizer, doctrinaire, bigot, opinionist, Sir Oracle; dogmatic theorist; zealot, fanatic; *ipse dixit* [*L.*].

v. **be certain** etc. *adj.;* stand to reason.

render certain etc. *adj.;* insure *or* ensure, assure; clinch, make sure; determine, find out once for all, decide, set at rest, "make assurance double sure" [*Macbeth*]; know etc. (*believe*) 484; dismiss all doubt, admit of no doubt.

dogmatize, lay down the law.

adj. **certain**, sure; assured etc. *v.;* solid, well-founded.

unqualified, absolute, positive, determinate, definite, clear, unequivocal, categorical, unmistakable, decisive, decided, ascertained.

inevitable, unavoidable, avoidless; ineluctable.

conclusive, unimpeachable, undeniable, unquestionable; indefeasible, indisputable, incontestable, incontrovertible, indubitable; irrefutable etc. (*proven*) 478; without power of appeal, inappealable, final.

indubious; without-, beyond a-, without a shade or shadow of- -doubt, -question; past dispute; clear as day; beyond all -question, -dispute; undoubted, uncontested, unquestioned, undisputed; questionless, doubtless.

authoritative, authentic, official, governmental, curule.

sure as -fate, -death and taxes, -a gun [*colloq.*].

evident, self-evident, axiomatic; clear, -as day, -as the sun at noonday; apparent etc. (*manifest*) 525.

infallible, unerring; unchangeable etc. 150; to be depended on, trustworthy, reliable, bound.

dogmatic, opinionative, opinionated, dictatorial, doctrinaire; fanatical, bigoted.

adv. **certainly** etc. *adj.;* for certain, certes [*archaic*], sure, no doubt, doubtless, and no mistake [*colloq.*], *flagrante delicto* [*L.*]; sure enough, to be sure, of course, as a matter of course, *a coup sûr* [*F.*], *sans doute* [*F.*], questionless [*rare*], for a certainty, of a certainty, to a certainty; in truth etc. (*truly*) 494; at any rate, at all events; without fail; *coûte que coûte* [*F.*], *coûte qu'il coûte* [*F.*]; whatever may happen, if the worse come to the worst; come what may, come what will, happen what may, happen what will; sink or swim; rain or shine, live or die.

475. Uncertainty

n. **uncertainty**, incertitude, doubt; doubtfulness etc. *adj.;* dubiety, dubitation, dubitancy [*obs.*], dubiosity, dubiousness.

hesitation, suspense, state of suspense; perplexity, embarrassment, dilemma, Morton's fork [*hist.*], bewilderment; botheration [*colloq.*]; puzzle, quandary; timidity etc. (*fear*) 860; vacillation etc. 605; aporia, diaporesis, indetermination; sealed orders.

vagueness etc. *adj.;* haze, fog; obscurity etc. (*darkness*) 421; ambiguity etc. (*double meaning*) 520; contingency, double contingency, possibility upon a possibility; open question etc. (*question*) 461; *onus probandi* [*L.*], blind bargain, pig in a poke, leap in the dark, something or other; needle in a haystack; roving commission.

fallibility; unreliability, unreliableness, untrustworthiness; precariousness etc. *adj.*

v. **be uncertain** etc. *adj.;* wonder whether.
lose the -clew *or* clue, -scent; miss one's way, wander aimlessly, beat about, hang around.
not know -what to make of etc. (*unintelligibility*) 519, -which way to turn, -whether one stands on one's head or one's heels; float in a sea of doubt, hesitate, flounder; lose oneself, lose one's head; muddle one's brains.

render uncertain etc. *adj.;* put out, pose, puzzle, perplex, embarrass; muddle, confuse, confound, fluster; bewilder, bother, moider [*dial.*], rattle [*colloq.*], nonplus, addle the wits, throw off the scent, keep in suspense, keep one guessing.

doubt, etc. (*disbelieve*) 485; hang in the balance, tremble in the balance; depend.

adj. **uncertain**, unsure; casual; random etc. (*aimless*) 621; changeable, changeful etc. 149.

doubtful, dubious; dazed; insecure, unstable, indecisive; unsettled, undecided, undetermined; in suspense, open to discussion; controvertible; in question etc. (*inquiry*) 461.

vague; indeterminate, indefinite; ambiguous, equivocal; undefined, undefinable, confused etc. (*indistinct*) 447; mysterious, cryptic, veiled, obscure, oracular.

perplexing etc. *v.;* enigmatic, paradoxical, apocryphal, problematical, hypothetical; experimental etc. 463.

fallible, questionable, precarious, slippery, ticklish, debatable, disputable; unreliable, untrustworthy.

unauthentic, unauthenticated, unauthoritative; unascertained, unconfirmed; undemonstrated; untold, uncounted.

contingent, contingent on, dependent on; subject to; dependent on circumstances; occasional; provisional.

in a state of uncertainty, on the horns of a dilemma, in a cloud, in a maze; bushed, off the track; derailed; ignorant etc. 491; afraid to say; out of one's reckoning, out of one's bearings, astray, adrift; at sea, at fault, at a loss, at one's wit's end, at a non-plus; puzzled etc. *v.;* lost, abroad, *désorienté* [*F.*]; distrait, distracted, distraught.

adv. **uncertainly** etc. *adj.;* at random, until things straighten out, while things are so uncertain, in this state of suspense; *pendente lite* [*L.*]; sub spe rati [*L.*].

Section 4. Reasoning Processes

476. Reasoning

n. **reasoning**; ratiocination, rationalism; dialectics, dialecticism, induction, generalization.

discussion, comment; ventilation; inquiry etc. 461.

argumentation, controversy, debate; polemics, wrangling; contention etc. 720; logomachy, disputation, disceptation [*archaic*]; paper war.

logic, art of reasoning.

process-, train-, chain- of reasoning; deduction, induction; synthesis, analysis.

argument; case, plea, *plaidoyer* [*F.*], opening; premise *or* premiss; lemma, proposition, terms, premises; postulate, data, starting point, principle; inference etc. (*judgment*) 480.

prosyllogism, syllogism; enthymeme, sorites, dilemma, *a fortiori* reasoning, *a priori* reasoning, *reductio ad absurdum* [*L.*], horns of a dilemma, *argumentum ad hominem* [*L.*], comprehensive argument; empirema, epagoge.

477. Intuition

logical sequence; good case; correct-, just-, sound-, valid-, cogent-, irrefutable-, logical-, forcible-, persuasive-, persuasory [*rare*]-, consectary [*obs.*]-, conclusive etc. 478-, subtle- reasoning; force of argument; strong -point, -argument.

arguments, reasons, pros and cons.

reasoner, logician, dialectician; disputant; controversialist, controvertist; wrangler, arguer, debater, devil's disciple, polemic, casuist, rationalist; scientist; eristic.

v. **reason**, argue, discuss, debate, dispute, wrangle; argufy *or* argify [*dial.*], bandy -words, -arguments; chop logic; hold-, carry on- an argument; controvert etc. (*deny*) 536; canvass; comment-, moralize- upon; consider etc. (*examine*) 461.

try conclusions; open a -discussion, -case; join-, be at- issue; moot; come to the point; stir-, agitate-, ventilate-, torture- a question; take up a -side, -case.

contend, take one's stand upon, insist, lay stress on; infer etc. 480.

follow from etc. (*demonstration*) 478.

adj. **reasoning** etc. *v.*; rational, ratiocinative, rationalistic; argumentative, controversial, dialectic, polemical; discursory, discursive; disputatious; logomachic *or* logomachical; Aristotelian, eristic *or* eristical.

debatable, controvertible.

logical; syllogistic, soritical, epagogic, inductive, deductive, synthetic *or* synthetical, analytic *or* analytical; relevant etc. 23.

adv. **for**, because, hence, whence, seeing that, since, sith [*archaic*], then, thence, so; for -that, -this, -which- reason; for as much as *or* forasmuch as, in as much as *or* inasmuch as; whereas, *ex concesso* [*L.*], considering, in consideration of; therefore, argal [*archaic*], wherefore; consequently, *ergo* [*L.*], thus, accordingly; *a priori* [*L.*]; *a fortiori* [*L.*].

finally, in conclusion, in fine; after all, *au bout du compte* [*F.*], on the whole, taking one thing with another; pro and con; rationally etc. *adj.*

477. Intuition
[absence of reasoning]

Sophistry
[specious reasoning]

n. **intuition**, instinct, association; presentiment; rule of thumb.

sophistry, paralogy, perversion, casuistry, jesuitry, equivocation, evasion, mental reservation; chicane, chicanery; quiddit [*obs.*], quiddity; mystification; special pleading; speciousness etc. *adj.*; nonsense etc. 497; word fence, tongue fence; overrefinement, hairsplitting, quibbling etc. *v.*

false-, fallacious-, specious-, vicious- reasoning; begging of the question, *petitio principii* [*L.*], *ignoratio elenchi* [*L.*]; *post hoc ergo propter hoc* [*L.*]; *non sequitur* [*L.*], *ignotum per ignotius* [*L.*].

misjudgment etc. 481; false teaching etc. 538.

sophism, solecism, paralogism; quibble, quirk, elench, elenchus, fallacy, *quodlibet* [*L.*], subterfuge, shift, subtlety, quillet [*archaic*]; inconsistency, antilogy; claptrap, mere words; "lame and impotent conclusion" [*Othello*].

meshes-, cobwebs- of sophistry; flaw in an argument; weak point, bad case.

sophist, casuist, paralogist.

v. **judge intuitively**, judge by intuition; hazard a proposition, talk at random.

pervert, quibble; equivocate, mystify, evade, elude; gloss over, varnish; misteach etc. 538; mislead etc. (*error*) 495; cavil, refine, subtilize, split hairs; misrepresent etc. (*lie*) 544.

reason ill, reason falsely etc. *adj.*; misjudge etc. 481; paralogize.

beg the question, reason in a circle, cut blocks with a razor, beat about the bush, play fast and loose, blow hot and cold, prove that black is white and white black, travel out of the record, *parler à tort et à travers* [*F.*], put oneself out of court, not have a leg to stand on.

adj. **intuitive**, instinctive, impulsive; independent of-, anterior to- reason; gratuitous, hazarded; unconnected.

illogical, unreasonable, false, unsound, invalid; unwarranted, not following, incongruous, inconsequent, inconsequential; inconsistent; absonous [*obs.*], absonant, unscientific; untenable, inconclusive, incorrect; fallacious, fallible; groundless, unproved.

specious, sophistic *or* sophistical, jesuitic *or* jesuitical, casuistic *or* casuistical, paralogistic, paralogical; deceptive, illusive, illusory; hollow, plausible, *ad captandum* [*L.*], evasive; irrelevant etc. 10.

weak, feeble, poor, flimsy, loose, vague, irrational; nonsensical etc. (*absurd*) 497; foolish etc. (*imbecile*) 499; frivolous, pettifogging, quibbling; finespun, overrefined.

at the end of one's tether, *au bout de son latin* [*F.*].

adv. **intuitively** etc. *adj.*; by intuition.

illogically etc. *adj.*

478. Demonstration

n. **demonstration**, proof, irrefragability; conclusiveness etc. *adj.;* apodeixis *or* apodixis, probation, comprobation [*obs.*].
logic of facts etc. (*evidence*) 467; *experimentum crucis* [*L.*] etc. (*test*) 463; argument etc. 476; rigorous–, absolute- establishment.

v. **demonstrate**, prove, establish, make good; show, evince etc. (*be evidence of*) 467; verify etc. 467; settle the question, reduce to demonstration, set the question at rest.
make out, –a case; prove one's point, have the best of the argument; draw a conclusion etc. (*judge*) 480.
follow, –of course; stand to reason; hold good, hold water [*colloq.*].

adj. **demonstrating** etc. *v.;* demonstrative, demonstrable; probative, unanswerable, conclusive, convincing; apodeictic *or* apodictic, apodeictical *or* apodictical; irresistible, irrefutable, irrefragable, undeniable.
categorical, decisive, crucial.
demonstrated etc. *v.;* proven; unconfuted, unanswered, unrefuted; evident etc. 474.
deducible, consequential, consectary [*obs.*], inferential, following.

adv. **of course**, in consequence, consequently, as a matter of course.

479. Confutation

n. **confutation**, refutation; answer, complete answer; disproof, conviction, redargution, invalidation; exposure, exposition, *exposé* [*F.*], clincher [*colloq.*], retort, *reductio ad absurdum* [*L.*]; knock-down-; *tu quoque*- argument; sockdolager [*slang*].

v. **confute**, refute; parry, negative, disprove, redargue, expose, show up, show the fallacy of, rebut, defeat; demolish etc. (*destroy*) 162; overthrow, overturn; scatter to the winds, explode, invalidate; silence; put–, reduce- to silence; clinch -an argument, –a question; stop the mouth, shut up; have, have on the hip, have the better of; confound, convince.
not leave a leg to stand on, cut the ground from under one's feet; smash all opposition; knock the bottom out of an argument [*colloq.*].
be confuted etc.; fail; expose–, show- one's weak point.

adj. **confutable**, confutative, refutable; confuting, confuted, etc. *v.;* capable of refutation.
condemned -on one's own showing, –out of one's own mouth; "hoist with his own petar" [*Hamlet*].

Section 5. Results of Reasoning

480. Judgment
[conclusion]

n. **judgment**, decision, determination, finding, verdict, sentence, decree; *res adjudicata* [*L.*], *res judicata* [*L.*]; opinion etc. (*belief*) 484; good judgment etc. (*wisdom*) 498.
result, conclusion, upshot; deduction, inference, ergotism [*obs.*], illation; corollary, porism; moral.
estimation, valuation, appreciation, judication; dijudication, adjudication; arbitrament, arbitrement, arbitration; assessment, ponderation [*rare*]; valorization.
estimate, award; review, criticism, critique, notice, report.
plebiscite, plebiscitum, voice, casting vote; vote etc. (*choice*) 609.
arbiter, arbitrator; judge, umpire; assessor, referee; inspector, inspecting officer; censor.
reviewer, critic; connoisseur; commentator etc. 524.

v. **judge**, conclude, opine; come to–, draw–, arrive at- a conclusion; ascertain, determine, make up one's mind.
deduce, derive, gather, collect, infer, draw an inference, make a deduction, weet [*obs.*], ween [*archaic*].
estimate, form an estimate, appreciate, value, count, assess, rate, rank, account; regard, consider, think of; look upon etc. (*believe*) 484; review; size up [*colloq.*].
decide, settle; pass–, give- an opinion; try, pronounce, rule; pass -judgment, –sentence; sentence, doom, decree; find; give–, deliver- judgment; adjudge, adjudicate, judicate [*rare*]; arbitrate, award, report; bring in a verdict; make absolute, set a question at rest; confirm etc. (*assent*) 488.
hold the scales, sit in judgment; try a cause, hear a cause.
review, comment, criticize; pass under review etc. (*examine*) 457; investigate etc. (*inquire*) 461.

adj. **judging** etc. *v.;* judicious etc. (*wise*) 498; determinate, conclusive, confirmatory.
critical, hypercritical, hairsplitting, censorious.

adv. **on the whole**, all things considered, taking all this into consideration, this being so, *quae cum ita sint* [*L.*], therefore, wherefore.

480a. Discovery
[result of search or inquiry]

n. **discovery**, detection, disenchantment; ascertainment, disclosure, find, revelation.
trover etc. 775.

v. **discover**, find, determine, evolve; fix upon; find–, trace–, make–, hunt–, fish–, worm–, ferret–, dig–, root- out; fathom; bring out, draw out; educe, elicit, bring to light; dig up, grub up, fish up; unearth, disinter.

solve, resolve; unriddle, unravel, ravel, ravel out, unlock; pick–, open- the lock; find a clew *or* clue to; interpret etc. 522; disclose etc. 529.

trace, get at; hit it, have it; lay one's -finger, –hands- upon; spot [*colloq.*], see through a millstone [*colloq.*]; get–, arrive- at the -truth etc. 494; put the saddle on the right horse, hit the right nail on the head.

scent, be near the truth, be warm [*colloq.*], burn [*colloq.*]; smoke, sniff, smell out, smell a rat [*colloq.*].

see through, see daylight, see in its true colors, see the cloven foot; open the eyes to; detect; catch, catch tripping.

meet with; pitch–, fall–, light–, hit–, stumble–, pop- upon; come across; fall in with.

recognize, realize, verify, make certain of, identify.

int. eureka! I have it! at last!

481. Misjudgment

n. **misjudgment**, obliquity of judgment, warped judgment; miscalculation, miscomputation, misconception etc. (*error*) 495, hasty conclusion.

preconception, prejudgment, prejudication [*rare*], prejudice; foregone conclusion; prenotion, prevention [*Gallicism*], predilection, prepossession, preapprehension, presumption, presentiment, foreboding; fixed idea; *idée fixe* [*F.*], obsession, preconceived idea, *mentis gratissimus error* [*L.*]; fool's paradise.

partisanship, *esprit de corps* [*F.*], party spirit, mob spirit, class prejudice, class consciousness, race prejudice, provincialism, clannishness, prestige.

quirk, shift, quibble, equivocation, evasion, subterfuge.

bias, warp, twist; hobby, whim, craze, fad, crotchet, partiality, infatuation, blind side, blind spot, mote in the eye.

one-sided–, partial–, narrow–, confined–, superficial- -views, –ideas, –conceptions, –notions; purblindness, *entêtement* [*F.*]; narrow mind; bigotry etc. (*obstinacy*) 606; *odium theologicum* [*L.*]; pedantry; hypercriticism.

doctrinaire etc. (*positive*) 474.

v. **misjudge**, misestimate, misesteem, misthink, misconjecture, misconceive etc. (*error*) 495; fly in the face of facts; miscalculate, misreckon, miscompute.

overestimate etc. 482; underestimate etc. 483.

prejudge, forejudge; presuppose, presume, prejudicate [*rare*], dogmatize; have a bias etc. *n.;* have only one idea; *jurare in verba magistri* [*L.*], run away with the notion; jump–, rush- to a conclusion; go off half-cocked [*colloq.*]; look only at one side of the shield; view with jaundiced eye, view through distorting spectacles; not see beyond one's nose; *dare pondus fumo* [*L.*]; get the wrong sow by the ear etc. (*blunder*) 699.

bias, warp, twist; give a -bias, –twist; prejudice, prepossess.

adj. **misjudging** etc. *v.;* ill-judging, wrong-headed; prejudiced, prepossessed; jaundiced; short-sighted, purblind; partial, one-sided, superficial.

narrow, narrow-minded, narrow-souled; provincial, parochial, insular; mean-spirited; confined, illiberal, intolerant, besotted, infatuated, fanatical, *entêté* [*F.*], positive, dogmatic, dictatorial; pragmatic *or* pragmatical, egotistical, conceited; opinioned, opinionated, opinionate [*rare*], opinionative [*rare*], opinative [*obs.*], opiniative [*obs.*]; self-opinionated; self-opinioned, wedded to an opinion, *opiniâtre* [*F.*]; bigoted etc. (*obstinate*) 606; crotchety, fussy, impracticable; unreasonable, stupid etc. 499; credulous etc. 486; warped.

misjudged etc. *v.*

adv. *ex parte* [*L.*].

482. Overestimation

n. **overestimation** etc. *v.;* exaggeration etc. 549; vanity etc. 880; optimism, pessimism.

much cry and little wool, much ado about nothing; storm in a teacup; fine talking; fine writing, rodomontade, gush [*colloq.*], hot air [*slang*].

egoism, egotism, bombast, conceit, swelled head [*slang*], megalomania.

egoist, egotist, megalomaniac; optimist, booster, pessimist; Rodomont, Braggadochio, braggart, boaster, braggadocio, swaggerer; hot-air artist [*slang*], gas-bag [*slang*], wind-bag [*slang*].

v. **overestimate**, overrate, overvalue, overprize, overweigh, overreckon, overstrain, overpraise;

estimate too highly, attach too much importance to, make mountains of molehills, catch at straws; strain, magnify; exaggerate etc. 549; set too high a value upon; think-, make- -much, -too much- of; out-reckon.

have too high an opinion of oneself etc. (*vanity*) 880.

eulogize, panegyrize, optimize, gush [*colloq.*], gush over [*colloq.*], boost; puff *or* puff up [*colloq.*]; extol, -to the skies; make the -most, -best, -worst- of; make two bites of a cherry.

adj. overestimated etc. *v.;* oversensitive etc. (*sensibility*) 822.

inflated, puffed up; grandiose, stilted, pompous, pretentious, megalomaniacal, braggart, bombastic.

483. Underestimation

n. **underestimation;** depreciation etc. (*detraction*) 934; pessimism; self-detraction, self-depreciation; undervaluation, miosis, litotes [*rhet.*]; undervaluing etc. *v.;* modesty etc. 881.

pessimist, depreciator, knocker [*slang*], crape-hanger [*slang*].

v. **underrate,** underestimate, undervalue, under-reckon; depreciate; disparage etc. (*detract*) 934; not do justice to; misprize, disprize; ridicule etc. 856; pessimize; slight etc. (*despise*) 930; neglect etc. 460; slur over.

make -light, -little, -nothing, -no account- of; belittle, knock [*slang*], slam [*slang*], run down [*colloq.*], minimize, think nothing of; set no store by, set at naught; shake off like water from a duck's back, shake off as dewdrops from the lion's mane.

adj. **depreciating** etc. *v.;* depreciative, depreciatory.

depreciated etc. *v.;* unappreciated, unvalued, unprized.

484. Belief

n. **belief;** credence; credit; assurance; faith, trust, troth, confidence, presumption, sanguine expectation etc. (*hope*) 858; dependence on, reliance on.

conviction, persuasion, convincement, plerophory [*rare*], self-conviction; certainty etc. 474; opinion, mind, view; conception, thinking; impression etc. (*idea*) 453; surmise etc. 514; conclusion etc. (*judgment*) 480.

tenet, dogma, principle, persuasion, views, way of thinking; popular belief etc. (*assent*) 488.

firm-, implicit-, settled-, fixed-, rooted-, deep-rooted-, staunch-, unshaken-, steadfast-, inveterate-, calm-, sober-, dispassionate-, impartial-, well-founded- -belief, -opinion etc.; *uberrima fides* [*L.*].

doctrine, system of opinions, school, articles, canons; article-, declaration-, profession- of faith; tenets, credenda, creed, credo, thirty-nine articles etc. (*orthodoxy*) 983a; gospel, gospel truth; catechism; assent etc. 488; propaganda etc. (*teaching*) 537.

credibility etc. (*probability*) 472.

v. **believe,** credit; give -faith, -credit, -credence- to; see, realize; assume, receive; set down for, take for; have it, take it; consider, esteem, presume.

count-, depend-, calculate-, pin one's faith-, reckon-, lean-, build-, rely-, rest- upon; cast one's bread upon the waters; lay one's account for; make sure of.

make oneself easy -about, -on that score; take on -trust, -credit; take for -granted, -gospel; allow-, attach- some weight to.

know, -for certain; be in the know [*slang*]; have-, make- no doubt; doubt not; be-, rest- -assured etc. *adj.;* persuade-, assure-, satisfy- oneself; make up one's mind.

confide in, believe in, put one's trust in; give one credit for; place-, repose- implicit confidence in; take one's word for, take at one's word; place reliance on, rely upon, swear by, regard to.

think, hold; take, take it; opine, be of opinion, conceive, trow [*archaic*], ween [*archaic*], fancy, apprehend; have-, hold-, possess-, entertain-, adopt-, imbibe-, embrace-, get hold of-, hazard-, foster-, nurture-, cherish- -a belief, -an opinion etc. *n.*

view as, consider as, take as, hold as, conceive as, regard as, esteem as, deem as, look upon as, account as, set down as; surmise etc. 514.

get-, take- it into one's head; come round to an opinion; swallow etc. (*credulity*) 486.

persuade; cause to be believed etc. *v.;* satisfy, bring to reason, have the ear of, gain the confidence of, assure; convince, convict, convert; wean, bring round; bring-, win- over; indoctrinate etc. (*teach*) 537; cram down the throat; produce-, carry- conviction; bring-, drive- home to.

find credence, go down, pass current; be received etc. *v.,* be current etc. *adj.;* possess-, take hold of-, take possession of- the mind.

adj. **believing** etc. *v.;* certain, sure, assured, positive, cocksure [*colloq.*], satisfied, confident, unhesitating, convinced, secure.

485. Unbelief. Doubt

under the impression; impressed–, imbued–, penetrated- with.

confiding, trustful, suspectless [*obs.*], unsuspecting, unsuspicious, void of suspicion; credulous etc. 486; wedded to.

believed etc. *v.;* accredited, putative; unsuspected, trusted, undoubted.

worthy of–, deserving of–, commanding- -belief, –confidence; credible, reliable, trustworthy, to be depended on; satisfactory; probable etc. 472; fiducial, fiduciary; persuasive, impressive.

doctrinal, relating to belief.

adv. **in the opinion of**, in the eyes of; *me judice* [*L.*]; meseems [*archaic*], methinks [*archaic*]; to the best of one's belief; in my opinion, in my judgment, according to my belief; I dare say, I doubt not, I have no doubt, I am sure; cocksure, sure enough etc. (*certainty*) 474; depend–, rely- upon it; be–, rest-assured; I'll warrant you etc. (*affirmation*) 535.

485. Unbelief. Doubt

n. **unbelief**, disbelief, misbelief; discredit, miscreance *or* miscreancy [*archaic*]; infidelity etc. (*irreligion*) 989; wrangling, ergotism [*rare*]; dissent etc. 489; change of opinion etc. 484; retractation etc. 607.

doubt etc. (*uncertainty*) 475; skepticism *or* scepticism, misgiving, demur; distrust, mistrust; misdoubt, suspicion, jealousy, scruple, qualm; *onus probandi* [*L.*].

incredibility, incredibleness, incredulity, unbelievability.

agnostic, skeptic *or* sceptic; unbeliever etc. 487.

v. **disbelieve**, discredit; not believe etc. 484; misbelieve; refuse to admit etc. (*dissent*) 489; refuse to believe etc. (*incredulity*) 487.

doubt; be doubtful etc. (*uncertain*) 475; doubt the truth of; be skeptical as to etc. *adj.;* diffide [*obs.*], distrust, mistrust; suspect, smoke, scent, smell, smell a rat [*colloq.*], have–, harbor–, entertain- -doubts, -suspicions; have one's doubts.

throw doubt upon, raise a question; bring–, call- in question; question, challenge; dispute; deny etc. 536; cause–, raise–, start–, suggest–, awake- a -doubt, -suspicion; cavil, wrangle, ergotize [*rare*].

demur, stick at, pause, hesitate, shy at, scruple; stop to consider, waver.

hang in suspense, hang in doubt.

stagger, startle; shake–, stagger- one's -faith, -belief.

adj. **unbelieving**; skeptical *or* sceptical, incredulous–, skeptical- as to; distrustful of, shy of, suspicious of; doubting etc. *v.*

doubtful etc. (*uncertain*) 475; disputable; unworthy–, undeserving- of -belief etc. 484; questionable; suspect [*archaic*], suspicious; open to -suspicion -doubt; staggering, hard to believe, incredible, unbelievable, not to be believed, inconceivable.

fallible etc. (*uncertain*) 475; undemonstrable; controvertible etc. (*untrue*) 495.

adv. **with caution**, *cum grano salis* [*L.*]; with grains of allowance.

486. Credulity

n. **credulity**, credulousness etc. *adj.*; gullibility, cullibility [*obs.*]; gross credulity, infatuation; self-delusion, self-deception; superstition; one's blind side; bigotry etc. (*obstinacy*) 606; hyperorthodoxy etc. 984; misjudgment etc. 481.

credulous person etc. (*dupe*) 547.

v. **be credulous** etc. *adj.; jurare in verba magistri* [*L.*]; follow implicitly; swallow, swallow whole, gulp down; take on trust; take for -granted, –gospel; take on faith; run away with -a notion, –an idea; jump–, rush- to a conclusion; think the moon is made of green cheese; take–, grasp- the shadow for the substance; catch at straws.

impose upon etc. (*deceive*) 545.

adj. **credulous**, gullible; easily deceived etc. 545; simple, green, soft, childish, silly, stupid; easily convinced; overcredulous, overconfident, overtrustful; infatuated, superstitious; confiding etc. (*believing*) 484.

487. Incredulity

n. **incredulity**. incredulousness; skepticism, free thought, Pyrrhonism; want of faith etc. (*irreligion*) 989; minimifidianism; unbelief etc. 485.

suspiciousness etc. *adj.;* scrupulosity; suspicion etc. (*unbelief*) 485; inconvincibility.

unbeliever, skeptic *or* sceptic, miscreant [*archaic*], doubting Thomas, disbeliever, agnostic, infidel, misbeliever, nullifidian, minimifidian, zendik [*Oriental*], freethinker, Pyrrhonist etc. (*irreligion*) 989; heretic etc. (*heterodox*) 984.

v. **be incredulous** etc. *adj.;* distrust etc. (*disbelieve*) 485; refuse to believe; shut one's eyes to, shut one's ears to; turn a deaf ear to; hold aloof; ignore, *nullius jurare in verba magistri* [*L.*].

adj. **incredulous**, skeptical *or* sceptical, dissenting, unbelieving, inconvincible; hard of belief, shy of belief; suspicious, scrupulous, distrustful, disposed to doubt, indisposed to believe; heterodox.

488. Assent

n. **assent**, assentment [*archaic*]; acquiescence, admission; nod; accord, concord, concordance; agreement etc. 23; affirmance, affirmation; recognition, acknowledgment, avowal, recognizance [*rare*], confession, confession of faith.

unanimity, common consent, consensus, acclamation, chorus, *vox populi* [*L.*]; popular-, current- -belief, -opinion; public opinion; concurrence etc. (*of causes*) 178; cooperation etc. (*voluntary*) 709.

ratification, confirmation, corroboration, approval, acceptance, visa, *visé* [*F.*]; indorsement etc. (*record*) 551.

consent etc. (*compliance*) 762.

affirmant, assentant [*obs.*], professor [*esp. in relig.*], confirmist, consenter, covenantor, subscriber, indorser *or* endorser; upholder etc. (*auxiliary*) 711.

v. **assent**; give-, yield-, nod- assent; acquiesce; agree etc. 23; receive, accept, accede, accord, concur, lend oneself to, consent, coincide, reciprocate, go with; be at one with etc. *adj.;* go along with, chime in with, strike in with, close with; echo, enter into one's views, agree in opinion; vote for, give one's voice for; recognize; subscribe-, conform-, defer- to; say -yes, -ditto, -amen, -aye- to.

go-, float-, swim- with the stream; float with the current; get on the band wagon [*slang*]; be in the fashion, join in the chorus; be in every mouth.

arrive at-, come to- -an understanding, -terms, -an agreement.

acknowledge, own, admit, allow, avow, confess; concede etc. (*yield*) 762; come round to; abide by; permit etc. 760.

confirm, affirm; ratify, approve, indorse, visa, *visé* [*F.*], countersign; corroborate etc. 467.

adj. **assenting** etc. *v.;* of one -accord, -mind; of the same mind, affirmant, assentaneous [*rare*], assentant [*obs.*], at one with, agreed, acquiescent, content; willing etc. 602.

uncontradicted, unchallenged, unquestioned, uncontroverted.

carried-, agreed- -*nem. con.* [*L.*] etc. *adv.;* unanimous; agreed on all hands, carried by acclamation.

affirmative etc. 535.

adv. **yes**, yea, aye *or* ay, true; good; well; how true, very -well, -true; well and good; granted; even so, just so; to be sure, as you say, sure, surely, assuredly, "thou hast said"; truly, exactly, precisely, that's just it, indeed, certainly, certes [*archaic*], *ex concesso* [*L.*], of course, unquestionably, no doubt, doubtless.

be it so; so be it, so let it be; so mote it be, with all one's heart; amen; willingingly etc. 602.

affirmatively, in the affirmative.

unanimously, *unâ voce* [*L.*], by common consent, in chorus, to a man; with one -consent, -voice, -accord; *nem. con.* [*L.*]; *nemine contradicente* [*L.*], *nemine dissentiente* [*L.*], without a dissentient voice; as one man, one and all, on all hands.

489. Dissent

n. **dissent**, nonconsent, discordance etc. (*disagreement*) 24; difference-, diversity- of opinion.

nonconformity etc. (*heterodoxy*) 984; protestantism, recusancy, schism; disaffection; secession etc. 624; recantation etc. 607.

dissension etc. (*discord*) 713; discontent etc. 832; caviling, wrangling, ergotism [*rare*].

protest; contradiction etc. (*denial*) 536; noncompliance etc. (*rejection*) 764.

dissentient, dissenter, nonconformist; sectary, separatist, recusant, schismatic, protestant; heretic etc. (*heterodoxy*) 984.

v. **dissent**, nonconsent, demur; call in question etc. (*doubt*) 485; differ in opinion, disagree, agree to differ; say no etc. 536; refuse -assent, -to admit; cavil, wrangle, ergotize [*rare*], protest, raise one's voice against, repudiate; contradict etc. (*deny*) 536.

have no notion of, differ *toto coelo* [*L.*], revolt at, revolt from the idea.

shake the head, shrug the shoulders; look askance *or* askant.

secede; recant etc. 607.

adj. **dissenting** etc. *v.;* negative etc. 536; dissident, dissentient; unconsenting etc. (*refusing*) 764; noncontent, nonjuring; protestant, recusant; unconvinced, unconverted.

unavowed, unacknowledged; out of the question.

unwilling etc. 603; extorted; discontented etc. 832.

sectarian, sectary [*rare*], denominational, schismatic; heterodox; intolerant.

adv. **no** etc. 536; at variance with, at issue with; under protest.

490. Knowledge

int. **God forbid**! not for the world! I'll be hanged if! [*colloq.*]; not another word! no, sirree!; not if I know it! I beg to differ; never tell me! pardon me.

490. Knowledge

n. **knowledge**; cognizance, cognition, cognoscence [*obs.*]; acquaintance, experience, ken, privity, insight, familiarity; comprehension, apprehension; recognition; appreciation etc. (*judgment*) 480; intuition; conscience, consciousness; perception, apperception, precognition; acroamatics.

system-, body- of knowledge; science, philosophy, pansophism, pansophy; acroama; theory, aetiology *or* etiology; circle of the sciences; pandect, doctrine, body of doctrine; cyclopedia *or* cyclopaedia, encyclopedia *or* encyclopaedia, circle of knowledge; school etc. (*system of opinions*) 484.

tree of knowledge; republic of letters etc. (*language*) 560.

enlightenment, light; glimpse, inkling, glimmer, glimmering, dawn; scent, suspicion; impression etc. (*idea*) 453; discovery etc. 480*a*.

learning, erudition, lore, scholarship, reading, letters; literature; book madness; book learning, bookishness; bibliomania, bibliolatry; information, general information; store of knowledge etc.; education etc. (*teaching*) 537; culture, *Kultur* [*Ger.*], cultivation, menticulture, attainments; acquirements, mental acquisitions; accomplishments; proficiency; practical knowledge etc. (*skill*) 698; liberal education, higher education; dilettantism; rudiments etc. (*beginning*) 66.

deep-, profound-, solid-, accurate-, acroatic-, acroamatic-, vast-, extensive-, encyclopedic- -knowledge, -learning; omniscience, pantology.

march of intellect; progress-, advance- of -science, -learning; schoolmaster abroad.

v. **know**, ken [*dial.*], scan, wot [*archaic*]; wot of [*archaic*], be aware of etc. *adj.;* ween [*archaic*], weet [*obs.*], trow [*archaic*]; have, possess.

conceive; apprehend, comprehend; take, realize, understand, savvy [*slang*], be wise to [*slang*], appreciate; fathom, make out; recognize, discern, perceive, see, get a sight of, experience.

know full well; have-, possess- some knowledge of; be *au courant* [*F.*] etc. *adj.;* have in one's head, have at one's fingers' ends; know by -heart, -rote; be master of; *connaître le dessous des cartes* [*F.*], know what's what [*colloq.*] etc. 698.

discover etc. 480*a;* see one's way.

learn, come to one's knowledge etc. (*information*) 527.

adj. **knowing** etc. *v.;* cognitive; acroamatic *or* acroamatical, apperceptive, appercipient.

aware of, cognizant of, conscious of; acquainted with, made acquainted with; privy to, no stranger to; *au fait* [*F.*], *au courant* [*F.*]; in the secret; up to [*colloq.*], alive to; behind the -scenes, –curtain; let into; apprised of, informed of; undeceived.

proficient in, versed in, read in, forward in, strong in, at home in; conversant with, familiar with.

educated, erudite, instructed, learned, lettered; well-informed, well-versed, well-read, well-grounded, well-educated; enlightened, shrewd, *savant* [*F.*], bluestocking, high-brow [*slang*], bookish, scholastic, solid, profound, deep-read, book-learned, aetiological *or* etiological, pansophic *or* pansophical; accomplished etc. (*skillful*) 698; omniscient; self-taught, self-educated, autodidactic; self-made.

known etc. *v.;* ascertained, well-known, recognized, received, notorious, noted; proverbial; familiar, –as household words, –to every schoolboy; hackneyed, trite, commonplace.

knowable, cognizable, cognoscible.

adv. to–, to the best of- one's knowledge; as every schoolboy knows.

490a. Astronomy

n. **astronomy**, cosmogony, interpretational astronomy, observational astronomy, descriptive astronomy, astrometry, geometrical astronomy, celestial mechanics; astrophysics, astrionics, radio astronomy, solar radio astronomy; astrobiology; planetology, heliography, actinometry, areography, cometography, astrography; celestial navigation, astrogation, nautical astronomy.

Ptolemaic system; Copernican system; evolutionary theory of the universe, expanding universe hypothesis, nebular hypothesis, collision hypothesis; planetismal hypothesis, protoplanet hypothesis; Lorentz-Fitzgerald contraction theory; infinity of the universe; Newton's universal laws of motion; Bode's law; Kepler's laws; Fechner's law; fission theory.

universe, cosmos, metagalaxy; firmament, space, deep space, interplanetary space, intergalactic space, interstellar space; lunar space, solar space.

490a. Astronomy

solar system; planet; inner planets, outer planets; minor planets, major planets; inferior planets, superior planets; Mercury, Venus, Earth, Mars, Jupiter, Saturn, Uranus, Neptune, Pluto; evening star, morning star; satellite; asteroid, planetoid; comet (nucleus, coma, tail), periodic comets (Encke, Giacobini-Zinner, Pons-Winnecke, Biela, Faye, Arend, Westphal, Olbers, Halley, Herschel-Rigollet), comet group, comet family.

meteor, fire ball, bolide; meteor shower, Aquarids, Arietids, Draconids, Geminids, Leonids, Perseids; micrometeorite; meteorite, aerolite, achrondite, siderite, ataxite, siderolite.

sun; photosphere, sunspots, granules, faculae, plages, maculae; M regions; reversing layer; chromosphere, flocculi, spicules; corona, K corona, F corona; prominences, jets; limb; aureole; halo; Zeeman effect.

moon, new moon, first quarter, crescent moon, half-moon, last quarter gibbous moon, full moon; harvest moon, hunter's moon; lunar plains *or* maria *or* seas (Mare Foecunditatis, Mare Nectaris, Mare Crisium, Mare Tranquillitatis, Mare Serenitatis, Mare Imbrium, Oceanus Procellarum, Mare Nubium, Mare Humorum), lunar mountain ranges, lunar rays, lunar rills, lunar craters (Alphonsus, Archimedes, Aristarchus, Aristoteles, Arzachel, Bullialdus, Catharina, Clavius, Copernicus, Cyrillus, Eratosthenes, Furnerius, Gassendi, Grimaldi, Kepler, Langrenus, Maginus, Maurolycus, Petavius, Plato, Proclus, Ptolemaeus, Schickard, Theophilus, Tycho).

star, circumpolar star, double star, binary star, lucid star, lucida, faint companion star, astrometric companion, multiple star, nova, supernova, Kepler's star; Population I stars, Population II stars; main sequence stars; dwarf, subdwarf, white dwarf, subgiant, giant, red giant, blue giant, supergiant; variable star, Cepheid variables, RR Lyrae variables, irregular variables, eclipsing variables, Mira-type stars; high velocity stars; star cluster, galactic cluster, globular cluster, moving cluster; Hertzsprung-Russell diagram, color-magnitude diagram, color index; magnitude, apparent magnitude, absolute magnitude, bolometric magnitude; absolute luminosity, period-luminosity relation; Messier number.

[stars] Achernar, Acrux, Adhara, Albireo, Alcor, Aldebaran, Algol, Alioth, Alkaid, Alphard, Alphecca, Alpheratz, Altair, Antares, Arcturus, Bellatrix, Benetnasch, Betelgeuse, Canopus, Capella, Caph, Castor, Cor Caroli, Deneb, Deneb Kaitos, Denebola, Dubhe, Fomalhaut, Hamal, Kaus Australis, Kochab, Marfak, Markab, Megrez, Merak, Mira, Mizar, Phad, Polaris, Pollux, Procyon, Rasalhague, Regulus, Rigel, Rigil Kentaurus, Saiph, Shaula, Sirius, Spica, Thuban, Vega; (constellations) Andromeda, Aquarius, Aquila, Ara, Aries, Auriga, Boötes, Canes Venatici, Canis Major, Canis Minor, Capricornus, Carina, Cassiopeia, Centaurus, Cepheus, Cetus, Columba, Corona Borealis, Corvus, Crux, Cygnus, Delphinus, Draco, Eridanus, Gemini, Grus, Hercules, Hydra, Hydrus, Leo, Lepus, Libra, Lupus, Lyra, Musca, Ophiuchus, Orion, Pavo, Pegasus, Perseus, Phoenix, Puppis, Sagitta, Sagittarius, Scorpius, Serpens, Taurus, Triangulum, Triangulum Australe, Tucana, Ursa Major, Ursa Minor, Vela, Virgo.

nebulae, galactic nebulae, bright nebulae, dark nebulae, planetary nebulae, diffuse nebulae; Orion Nebula, Coal Sack Nebula, Loop Nebula; extragalactic nebulae, external galaxy, galaxy, spiral galaxy, barred spiral galaxy, elliptical galaxy, irregular galaxy; galactic cluster; galactic window; Milky Way; Magellanic Clouds, Andromeda Nebula.

celestial sphere; celestial equator, celestial poles, celestial meridian, antimeridian, zenith, nadir, vertical circle, diurnal circle, horizon, azimuth; hour angle, hour circle; amplitude; altitude, altitude circle, altitude difference; declination; apex, antapex; culmination; astronomical latitude, celestial latitude, astronomical longitude, celestial longitude; ecliptic; right ascension; equinox, autumnal equinox, vernal equinox; solstice, summer solstice, winter solstice.

celestial motion; proper motion; rotation; revolution; orbit, perihelion, aphelion, apogee, perigee; inclination, perturbation; libration; precession, nutation; acceleration, deceleration; antecedence; arc of progression, arc of retrogression; anomaly; inequality; daily aberration, annual aberration.

transit; occultation; immersion; eclipse, annular eclipse, partial eclipse, total eclipse, umbra, penumbra; conjunction, inferior conjunction, synodic period, sidereal period.

gravity; acceleration of gravity, g; antigravity; barycenter; galactic center; atmospheric tides.

[instruments] accelerometer; astrolabe; astronomical triangle; barograph, barometer; chronometer, chronograph, astronomical clock; helioscope, spectrohelioscope, spectroheliograph, coronagraph, heliometer, magnetograph; illuminometer; sextant; thermocouple;

490b. Chemistry

spectroscope, spectrograph, spectrobolometer, micrometer; telescope, astronomical telescope, meridian circle telescope, equatorial telescope; reflecting telescope, Newtonian telescope, coelostat; refracting telescope; radio telescope; astronomical observatory; planetarium.

490b. Chemistry

n. **chemistry**, general chemistry, inorganic chemistry, organic chemistry, analytical chemistry (qualitative analysis, quantitative analysis), biological chemistry *or* biochemistry, radiochemistry *or* nuclear chemistry, theoretical chemistry *or* physical chemistry.

matter, organic matter, inorganic matter; homogeneous matter, substance, stable substance, unstable substance, volatile substance, amorphous substance, crystalline substance; element, active element, inactive element, nonmetal, metal, alkali metal, alkaline earth metal, amphoteric element; free state, combined state; allotropic forms, allotropy.

[chemical notation] symbol, coefficient, subscript, radical; formula, equation, word equation, skeleton equation, balanced equation, ionic equation; molecular weight, formula weight; valence, negative valence, positive valence, zero valence.

mixture; compound, binary compound, ternary compound, electrovalent compound, ionic compound, chain compound, covalent compound; covalent linkage; law of definite proportions; heat of formation, heat of neutralization.

chemical change, chemical reaction, chemical combination, decomposition, displacement, double decomposition; irreversible reaction, completion, reversible reaction, complete reaction, incomplete reaction; endothermic reaction, exothermic reaction, photochemical reaction; dynamic equilibrium, equilibrium constant, ionization constant, solubility product constant; common ion effect; catalyst *or* catalytic agent; law of conservation of matter, law of mass action.

ionization *or* dissociation, nonionization, electrolytic dissociation; electrolyte, nonelectrolyte; electrolysis; ion, positive ion *or* cation, negative ion *or* anion; positive electrode *or* anode, negative electrode *or* cathode; Ionization Theory *or* Theory of Electrolytic Dissociation; activity coefficient.

acid, binary acid, ternary acid, monobasic acid, dibasic acid, tribasic acid; weak acid (*or* base), strong acid (*or* base); base, alkali, monoacid base, diacid base, triacid base; salt, binary salt, ternary salt, acid salt, basic salt, normal salt, double salt, complex salt; neutralization, hydrolysis, titration; indicators, litmus, phenolphthalein, methyl orange, methyl violet, alizarin yellow; hydrogen ion concentration *or* pH.

ascorbic acid, benzoic acid, boric acid, butyric acid, carbolic acid, citric acid, formic acid, gallic acid, hydrochloric acid, hydrofluoric acid, lactic acid, malic acid, nitric acid, oleic acid, oxalic acid, phosphoric acid, picric acid, prussic acid, salicylic acid, stearic acid, sulfuric acid, tannic acid, tartaric acid; (bases) ammonium hydroxide, calcium hydroxide, magnesium hydroxide, potassium hydroxide, sodium hydroxide; (salts) ammonium chloride, bismuth subnitrate, calcium carbonate, potassium chloride, potassium nitrate, sodium acetate, sodium acid phosphate, sodium bicarbonate, sodium bisulfite, sodium chloride.

solution, gaseous solution, liquid solution, solid solution, dilute solution, concentrated solution, unsaturated solution, supersaturated solution; molar solution, molal solution, normal solution, standard solution; solute, solvent; seeding, precipitate, filtration; suspension.

crystal, ionic crystal, atom crystal, molecule crystal; crystal symmetry, isometric crystal (cube), hexagonal crystal, tetragonal crystal, orthorhombic crystal, monoclinic crystal, triclinic crystal; water of crystallization *or* water of hydration; hydrate, anhydrous compound; decrepitation, sublimation; deliquescent substance, hygroscopic substance, efflorescent substance.

oxide, metallic oxide *or* basic anhydride, nonmetallic oxide *or* acid anhydride, amphoteric oxide, neutral oxide, suboxide, saline oxide, peroxide; oxidation, rapid oxidation, combustion, spontaneous combustion, slow oxidation, organic oxidation, inorganic oxidation; oxidizing agent; reduction, reducing agent; kindling temperature, temperature of combustion, heat of combustion.

hydrocarbons; aliphatic hydrocarbons, saturated *or* methane series (methane, ethane, propane), unsaturated series, ethylene series (ethylene, propylene, butylene), acetylene series (acetylene, allylene); aromatic hydrocarbons, benezene series (benzene, toluene, xylene), naphthalene series (naphthalene), anthracene series (anthracene).

[hydrocarbon derivatives] halogen substitution products (chloroform *or* trichloromethane); alcohols, monohydroxy alcohols, dihydroxy alcohols (methyl alcohol, ethyl alcohol); aldehydes (formaldehyde, acetaldehyde); ketones (acetone, butanone); organic acids; ethers (diethyl ether); esters (methyl acetate); carbohydrates (sugars, starches, cellulose); proteins (albumin, globulin, glutelin).

colloid, natural colloid, lyophobic colloid, hydrophobic colloidal system, lyophilic colloid, hydrophilic colloidal system; sol, gel; dispersed medium, dispersing medium; condensation *or* coagulation method, dispersion method (mechanical disintegration, peptization, emulsification); emulsion, temporary emulsion, permanent emulsion; emulsifying agent *or* protective colloid; miscible liquids, nonmiscible liquids; dialysis, adsorption, flotation process, Cottrell process, cataphoresis, electroendosmosis.

[apparatus] aspirator, blowpipe, Büchner funnel, Bunsen burner, burette *or* buret, crucible, disiccator, distiller, etna, Kipp apparatus, matrass, mortar, pestle, reagent bottle, receiver, retort, ring, ring stand, still, test tube.

490c. Geology

n. **geology**, mineralogy, petrology, stratigraphy, paleontology, structural geology, glacial geology, geomorphology, oceanography, meteorology, geophysics, terrestrial magnetism, seismology, geodesy, geochemistry, petroleum geology, economic geology, engineering geology, hydrology.

crystal, crystallization; euhedral crystal, subhedral crystal, anhedral crystal; crystal symmetry, isometric system, hexagonal system, tetragonal system, orthorhombic system, monoclinic system, triclinic system.

minerals, amphibole group, feldspar group, mica group, pyroxene group; hornblende, apatite, azurite, bauxite, bornite, calcite, carnotite, cassiterite, chalcopyrite, chert, chlorite, chromite, copper, corundum, diamond, dolomite, epidote, microcline, orthoclase, albite, labradorite, anorthite, fluorite, galena, garnet, gold, graphite, gypsum, halite, hematite, kyanite, limonite, magnetite, malachite, biotite, lepidolite, muscovite, olivine, pyrite, augite, pyrrhotite, quartz, serpentine, sillimanite, sphalerite, staurolite, sulfur, talc, tourmaline.

[properties of minerals], specific gravity, cleavage, hardness, fracture, luster (adamantine luster, vitreous luster, resinous luster, greasy luster, pearly luster, silky luster), color, streak, taste, radio-activity, magnetism, opalescence, fluorescence; twinning.

[gross features of earth's crust] continent, continental shield, young folded mountain belt; zone of transition, continental margin, continental shelf, continental slope, continental rise; island arcs; ocean basin, deep oceanic crust, mid-ocean ridges; ocean currents; drift, tide, tidal current, wave, breaker, surf, sea, ground swell.

earthquake, shallow earthquake, intermediate earthquake, deep earthquake, volcanic earthquake; seismism; elastic rebound, foreshock, aftershock; shock wave, P wave *or* dilational wave *or* compressional wave *or* longitudinal wave, S wave *or* shear wave *or* transverse wave; Rayleigh wave; seismograph, seismometer, seismogram, accelerograph.

[deformation of earth's crust] isostasy; epeirogeny, uplifting, downwarping; orogeny, mountain building; diastrophism, confining pressure, stress, strain; fold, anticline, sycline, dome, basin, monocline; fault, fault plane, slickensides, hanging-wall side, foot-wall side, strike-slip movement, dip-slip movement, oblique-slip movement, normal fault, reverse fault, scissors fault, transverse fault, thrust fault, fault scarp, graben, horst, klippe, nappe *or* decke; fracture, tension fracture, shear fracture, rock cleavage; unconformity.

metamorphism, rock flowage; granulation, recrystallization, recombination; contact metamorphism, dynamic metamorphism; foliated metamorphic rock, nonfoliated metamorphic rock; slates, schists, gneisses, phyllites, marble, quartzite, hornfels, amphiboles.

volcano, cinder cone, lava cone, composite cone; shield volcano, flood basalt; vent, fumarole, solfatara, spatter cone, caldera; volcanism, eruption, explosion, expulsion, lava flow; (pyroclastic materials) blocks, bombs, lapilli, ash, volcanic dust; gases; lava, basalt lavas, rhyolite lavas, andesite lavas.

igneous rock, magmas, basaltic magma, granitic magma; (discordant igneous intrusions) batholith, stock, dike; (concordant igneous intrusions) sill, laccolith, lopolith; aphanitic rock, phaneritic rock, porphyritic rock, glassy rock; granite, graphic granite, granite pegmatite, orbicular granite, syenite, diorite, gabbro, peridotite, dunite, pyroxene, hornblendite, felsite, basalt, dolerite, obsidian, pitchstone, pumice, scoria; pyroclastic debris, tuff, agglomerate, volcanic breccia.

490d. Physics

sedimentary rock; marine environment, transitional environment, continental environment; residual deposits, transported deposits; mechanical deposition, chemical deposition, organic deposition; rudaceous rocks, arenaceous rocks, silty rocks, argillaceous rocks, chemically deposited siliceous rocks, carbonate rocks, chemically deposited ferruginous rocks, salt rocks, organically deposited siliceous rocks, calcareous rocks, phosphatic rocks, organically deposited ferruginous rocks, carbonaceous rocks; conglomerate, breccia; sandstone, arkose, graywacke; siltstone, loess; mudstone, shale; sinter, chert-flint; tufa, travertine, oölitic limestone, dolostone, lithographic limestone; ironstone, caliche, gypsum, anhydrite, halite; radiolarian ooze, diatom ooze; fossiliferous limestone, chalk, marl; rock phosphates, guano; bog iron ore; coal.

erosion, weathering; mechanical weathering, thermal contraction *and* expansion, unloading, crystal growth, freezing; chemical weathering, oxidation, hydration, carbonation; (specialized erosion) deflation, corrasion, abrasion, impact, corrosion, hydraulicking, quarrying, plucking, solution, slump, rolling, sliding, dislodgement, falling; transportation; deposition.

[wind erosion] undercut hill, cave rock, table, mushroom rock, ventifact, desert pavement, lag gravel; (running water erosion) river valley, pediment, peneplain, river terrace, wadi, pothole; (glacial erosion) striation, groove, drumlin, crescentic mark, u-shaped valley, truncated spur, hanging valley, cirque, fiord, col, arête, horn; (ground water erosion) cave, sinkhole, karst topography; (mass movement erosion) slide scar, surface subsidence; (ocean erosion) cliff, terrace, guyot, stack, arch, sea cave, notch.

geologic time, era, period, epoch, age; rock system, rock series, rock stage; Precambrian Era; Paleozoic Era, Cambrian Period, Ordovician Period, Silurian Period, Devonian Period, Mississippian Period, Pennsylvanian Period, Permian Period; Mesozoic Era, Triassic Period, Jurassic Period, Cretaceous Period; Cenozoic Era, Paleogene Period, Paleocene Epoch, Eocene Epoch, Oligocene Epoch, Neogene Period, Miocene Epoch, Pliocene Epoch, Pleistocene Epoch.

490d. Physics

n. **physics**, classical physics, modern physics; mechanics (kinematics, dynamics, statics, hydrostatics, hydrodynamics, hydraulics), heat (thermometry, calorimetry, thermodynamics), sound, acoustics, light, optics, spectroscopy, electricity (electrostatics, electronics), magnetism; high-energy physics *or* elementary-particle physics, nuclear physics, atomic physics, molecular physics, solid-state physics, physics of liquids, physics of gases, plasma physics, biophysics, low-temperature physics, mathematical physics, theoretical physics, space physics.

atom, neutral atom, ion, nucleus, atomic number, atomic weight, mass number, isobar, isotope; elementary particles *or* subatomic particles; hyperons, nucleons, mesons, leptons, photons; proton, neutron, electron, positron; element; molecule; chemical change, nuclear change, physical change.

matter; solid, liquid, gas, extension *or* volume, mass, weight, density, fluid; specific gravity, impenetrability; elasticity, stress, strain, elastic limit; malleability, ductility; adhesion, cohesion, surface tension, capillarity, diffusion, osmosis, Brownian movement, buoyancy, viscosity; pressure, atmospheric pressure, air pressure; Hooke's law, kinetic theory of matter *or* molecular theory of matter, Pascal's law, Archimedes' principle, Bernoulli's principle; pycnometer, hydrometer, barometer, aneroid barometer, barograph, altimeter, manometer.

fusion, heat of fusion, melting, melting point; freezing, freezing point; regelation; vaporization, heat of vaporization; boiling, boiling point; evaporation, dew point, humidity, absolute humidity, relative humidity; sublimation, volatile liquid *or* solid; condensation *or* liquefaction, critical temperature, critical pressure, vapor; distillation, fractional distillation, distillate.

motion, rectilinear motion, curvilinear motion, circular motion, projectile motion, rotation *or* rotary motion, precession, revolution; velocity, terminal velocity, acceleration, speed, momentum, impulse, inertia; Newton's laws of motion; projectile, trajectory; pendulum, simple pendulum, compound pendulum, compensation pendulum, seconds pendulum; center of percussion; oscillation *or* vibration, amplitude, period, frequency.

force, centrifugal force, centripetal force, parallel forces, couple, component forces, effective component, ineffective component, resultant force; friction, coefficient of friction; equilibrant, equilibrium; resolution of forces, composition of forces, moment of force *or* torque; vector, vector quantity, scalar quantity; dyne, poundal, slug, newton; gravitation, gravity; free fall; Newton's law of universal gravitation.

work; foot-pound, foot-poundal; gram-centimeter, kilogram-meter; erg, joule; power, horsepower; energy, potential energy, kinetic energy; law of conservation of energy.

machines, simple machine, compound machine; inclined plane, screw, wedge, lever and fulcrum, wheel and axle, pulley; mechanical advantage, ideal mechanical advantage, actual mechanical advantage; efficiency, input, output.

[heat] conduction, conductor, conductometer; insulator, convection; radiation; law of heat exchange, Newton's law of cooling; expansion, linear expansion, coefficient of linear expansion, differential expansion; bimetallic bar, compound bar, thermostat; pressure coefficient of gases, general gas law, Boyle's law, Charles's law, Gay-Lussac's law; standard conditions, standard pressure, standard temperature; absolute zero; heat engine, internal-combustion engine, external-combustion engine, turbine; Joule's equivalent; temperature, degree; thermometer, absolute scale, Kelvin scale, Fahrenheit scale, centigrade scale; foot-pound-second system, centimeter-gram-second system; British thermal unit, btu; calorie, kilogram-calorie; specific heat.

[sound] wave, wavelength, sound wave, longitudinal wave (condensation, rarefaction); transverse wave (crest, trough); pitch, intensity, loudness; bel, decibel; beat, echo, reverberation; interference, resonance; frequency, audio frequency, ultrasonic frequency, infrasonic frequency.

[musical sound] tone, fundamental tone, overtone, quality, major chord, musical interval; consonance, dissonance; noise; musical scale, chromatic scale *or* tempered scale, diatonic scale; standing wave, node, antinode, loop, segment.

[light] luminosity, incandescence, fluorescence, illuminated body; opaque body, translucent body, transparent body; shadow, umbra, penumbra; photometry, photometer; luminous intensity, candle power, candle, foot-candle, lumen, illumination; quantum, quantum theory; Einstein's special theory of relativity, Einstein's general theory of relativity; Doppler effect.

reflection, diffusion, angle of reflection, angle of incidence; image, real image, virtual image; magnification; mirror, concave mirror, convex mirror; center of curvature, radius of curvature, principal axis; focus, virtual focus, focal length, principal focus, focal plane; spherical aberration.

refraction, angle of refraction, index of refraction, critical angle; diffraction; convex lens *or* positive lens, concave lens *or* negative lens; optical center, optical density; achromatic lens, chromatic aberration; diopter.

color, primary colors, complementary colors; pigments, primary pigments; complementary pigments; monochromatic light, polychromatic light, polarized light, polarization; polarizer, analyzer.

spectrum; dispersion; electromagnetic spectrum, electromagnetic radiations (infrared rays, ultraviolet rays, X-rays, gamma rays); angstrom; continuous spectrum, absorption spectrum (Fraunhofer lines); bright-line spectrum, dark-line spectrum; spectroscope.

[magnetism], induced magnetism, residual magnetism; magnet, saturated magnet, temporary magnet, permanent magnet; lodestone, magnetic compass, dipping needle; magnetic retentivity; magnetic poles, south-seeking pole, north-seeking pole; magnetic line of force, magnetic field, magnetic flux, magnetic permeability, magnetic transparency; magnetic delination, isogonic line, agonic line; magnetic inclination, isoclinic line, magnetic equator, aclinic line.

[electricity], static electricity; electric current, direct current, D.C., alternating current, A.C.; induced current; eddy current; electromagnetism; electric field; circuit, parallel circuit, series circuit; electromotive force *or* e.m.f.; resistance, specific resistance *or* resistivity; reactance, inductive reactance, capacitive reactance; impedance; conduction, conductance, conductor; induction, electromagnetic induction, inductance; self-inductance; capacitance; electrolysis; dissociation; electroplating; electrolyte, nonelectrolyte, Ohm's law, Coulomb's law, inverse-square law, Lenz's law.

generator, motor; armature *or* keeper, commutator, brush, slip rings; electrophorus; capacitor *or* condenser; insulator *or* dielectric; transformer; primary coil, secondary coil; rectifier; rheostat, galvanoscope; oscillator, relay; shunt; electrode, anode *or* plate, cathode; electrolytic cell; Leyden jar, voltaic cell, storage cell.

coulomb, ohm, ampere, volt, henry, farad, watt; watt-hour, kilowatt-hour; electroscope, ammeter, galvanometer, voltmeter.

491. Ignorance

diode, triode, vacuum tube; cathode-ray tube, cathode rays; photoelectric cell, photoelectric effect; transistor.

[radioactivity], alpha particle, beta particle, gamma rays, cosmic rays; isotope, radioactive isotope; transmutation of elements; particle accelerator *or* atom smasher, betatron, cyclotron, synchrotron; nuclear reactor, uranium-graphite pile; atomic energy, nuclear energy; fission, chain reaction, critical mass; fusion, thermonuclear reaction.

491. Ignorance

n. **ignorance**, nescience, *tabula rasa* [*L.*], illiteracy, unlearnedness, crass ignorance, *ignorance crasse* [*F.*]; unacquaintance; unconsciousness etc. *adj.;* darkness, blindness; incomprehension, inexperience, simplicity.

sealed book, *terra incognita* [*L.*], virgin soil, unexplored ground; dark ages.

unknown quantities; *x, y, z.*

[imperfect knowledge] smattering, superficiality, half-learning, shallowness, sciolism, glimmering; bewilderment etc. (*uncertainty*) 475; incapacity.

[affectation of knowledge] pedantry, charlatanry, charlatanism; Philistine, *Philister* [*Ger.*].

v. **be ignorant** etc. *adj.;* not know etc. 490; know -not, -not what, -nothing of; have no -idea, -notion, -conception; not have the remotest idea.

ignore, be blind to; keep in ignorance etc. (*conceal*) 528.

see through a glass darkly; have a film over the eyes, have a glimmering etc. *n.;* wonder whether; not know what to make of etc. (*unintelligibility*) 519; not pretend to say, not take upon oneself to say.

adj. **ignorant**; nescient; unknowing, unaware, unacquainted, unapprised, unwitting, unweeting [*obs.*], unconscious; witless, weetless [*obs.*]; a stranger to; unconversant.

uninformed, uncultivated, unversed, uninstructed, untaught, uninitiated, untutored, unschooled, unscholarly, unguided, unenlightened; Philistine; behind the age.

shallow, superficial, green, rude, empty, half-learned, half-baked [*colloq.*], low-brow [*slang*]; illiterate; unread, uninformed, uneducated, unlearned, unlettered, unbookish; empty-headed; pedantic.

in the dark; benighted, belated; blinded, blindfold; hoodwinked; misinformed; *au bout de son latin* [*F.*], at the end of his tether, at fault; at sea etc. (*uncertain*) 475; caught tripping, caught napping.

unknown, unapprehended, unexplained, unascertained, uninvestigated, unexplored, unheard of, unperceived; concealed etc. 528; novel.

adv. **ignorantly** etc. *adj.;* unawares; for anything one knows, for aught one knows; not that one knows.

int. God-, Heaven-, the Lord-, nobody- knows!

492. Scholar

n. **scholar**, *savant* [*F.*], pundit *or* pandit [*India*], schoolman, professor, graduate, wrangler [*Cambridge Univ., Eng.*], academician, academist [*obs.*], doctor, fellow, don [*Eng. Univ. cant*], graduate, postgraduate, clerk [*archaic*]; *Artium Magister* [*L.*], A.M. *or* M.A., master of arts; *Artium Baccalaureus*, A.B. *or* B.A., bachelor of arts; bookman [*rare*], classicist, licentiate, gownsman; philosopher, philomath; scientist, connoisseur, sophist, sophister; linguist; etymologist, philologist; philologer [*now rare*]; lexicographer, glossographer, glossologist, lexicologist, scholiast, commentator, annotator; grammarian; *littérateur* [*F.*], literati [*L.*], dilettanti [*It.*], illuminati; mayven [*Jew.*], munshi *or* moonshee [*India*], mullah [*Moslem*], moolvi [*India*], guru [*India*]; Hebraist, Hellenist, Graecist, Sanskritist; sinologist, sinologue.

bookworm, *helluo librorum* [*L.*], bibliophile, bibliophilist, bibliomaniac, blue-stocking [*colloq.*], *bas-bleu* [*F.*], high-brow [*slang*].

Admirable Crichton, Mezzofanti, "learned Theban" [*King Lear*], Dominie Sampson [*Guy Mannering*], Socrates.

learned man, literary man; *homo multarum literarum* [*L.*]; man of -learning, -letters, -education, -genius; giant of learning, colossus of knowledge, prodigy.

antiquarian, antiquary, archaeologist, Assyriologist, Egyptologist, sage etc. (*wise man*) 500.

pedant, doctrinaire; pedagogue, Dr. Pangloss; pantologist; instructor etc. (*teacher*) 540.

student, learner, classman, senior, junior, sophomore, freshman, pupil, schoolboy etc. (*learner*) 541.

adj. **learned** etc. 490; brought up at the feet of Gamaliel.

493. Ignoramus

n. **ignoramus**, illiterate, dunce, duffer, woodenhead [*colloq.*], bonehead [*slang*], solid ivory [*slang*], numskull [*colloq.*], wooden spoon [*Cambridge Univ., Eng., cant*]; no scholar.

sciolist, smatterer, dabbler, half scholar; charlatan; wiseacre.

novice, tenderfoot; greenhorn etc. (*dupe*) 547; plebe *or* pleb [*cant, U. S.*]; tyro etc. (*learner*) 541; lubber etc. (*bungler*) 701; fool etc. 501.

adj. **bookless**, shallow, simple, lumpish, dull, dumb [*colloq.*], dense, crass, imbecile; wise in his own conceit; ignorant etc. 491.

494. Truth
[object of knowledge]

n. **truth**, verity; fact, reality etc. (*existence*) 1; plain matter of fact; nature etc. (*principle*) 5; gospel; orthodoxy etc. 983a; authenticity; veracity etc. 543.

plain-, honest-, sober-, naked-, unalloyed-, unvarnished-, unqualified-, stern-, exact-, intrinsic- truth; *nuda veritas* [*L.*]; the very thing; not an illusion etc. 495; real Simon Pure; unvarnished tale; the truth, the whole truth and nothing but the truth; just the thing.

accuracy, exactitude; exactness, preciseness etc. *adj.*; precision, delicacy; rigor, mathematical precision, fidelity; clockwork precision etc. (*regularity*) 80; conformity to rule; nicety.

orthology; *ipsissima verba* [*L.*], the very words; realism.

v. **be true** etc. *adj.*, be the case; stand the test; have the true ring; hold good, hold true, hold water.

render true, prove true etc. *adj.*; substantiate etc. (*evidence*) 467.

get at the truth etc. (*discover*) 480a.

adj. **true**, real, actual etc. (*existing*) 1; veritable; certain etc.; 474; substantially-, categorically- true etc.; true -to the letter, -as gospel, -as steel, -to life, -to the facts; unimpeachable; veracious etc. 543; unrefuted, unconfuted; unideal, unimagined; realistic.

exact, accurate, definite, precise, well-defined, just, right, correct, strict, severe; close etc. (*similar*) 17; orthological, literal; rigid, rigorous; scrupulous etc. (*conscientious*) 939; religiously exact, punctual, punctilious, mathematical, scientific; faithful, constant, unerring; curious, particular, nice, meticulous, delicate, fine; clean-cut, clear-cut.

authentic, genuine, legitimate; orthodox etc. 983a; official, *ex officio* [*L.*].

pure, natural, sound, sterling, true-blue; unsophisticated, unadulterated, Simon-Pure [*colloq.*], unvarnished, uncolored; in its true colors.

valid, well-grounded, well-founded; solid, substantial, pukka *or* pucka *or* pakka [*Hind.*], tangible; undistorted, undisguised; unaffected, unexaggerated, unromantic, unflattering.

adv. **truly** etc. *adj.*; verily, indeed, in reality; in very truth, in fact, as a matter of fact, to state the facts; beyond -doubt, -question; with truth etc. (*veracity*) 543; certainly etc. (*certain*) 474; actually etc. (*existence*) 1; in effect etc. (*intrinsically*) 5.

exactly etc. *adj.*; *ad amussim* or *adamussim* [*L.*], verbatim, *verbatim et literatim* [*L.*]; word for word, literally, *literatim* [*L.*], *totidem verbis* [*L.*], *sic* [*L.*], to the letter, chapter and verse, *ipsissimis verbis* [*L.*]; *ad unguem* [*L.*]; to an inch; to a -nicety, -hair, -tittle, -turn, -T; *au pied de la lettre* [*F.*]; neither more nor less; in every respect, in all respects; *sous tous les rapports* [*F.*]; at any rate, at all events; strictly speaking.

495. Error

n. **error**, fallacy; misconception, misapprehension, misunderstanding; aberration, aberrance *or* aberrancy; inexactness etc. *adj.*; laxity; misconstruction etc. (*misinterpretation*) 523; anachronism; miscomputation etc. (*misjudgment*) 481; *non sequitur* [*L.*] etc. 477; misstatement, misreport; mumpsimus.

mistake; miss, fault, blunder, cross-purposes, oversight, misprint, erratum, corrigendum, slip, blot, flaw, loose thread; trip, stumble etc. (*failure*) 732; botchery etc. (*want of skill*) 699; slip of the tongue, *lapsus linguae* [*L.*]; slip of the pen, *lapsus calami* [*L.*], clerical error; bull etc. (*absurdity*) 497; Spoonerism, Malapropism, Leiterism [*U. S.*], Mrs. Partington; haplography.

delusion, illusion; false-, warped-, distorted- -impression, -idea; bubble; self-deceit, self-deception; mists of error; exploded -notion, -idea, -superstition.

heresy etc. (*heterodoxy*) 984; hallucination etc. (*insanity*) 503; false light etc. (*fallacy of vision*) 443; dream etc. (*fancy*) 515; fable etc. (*untruth*) 546; bias etc. (*misjudgment*) 481; misleading etc. *v.*

v. **be erroneous** etc. *adj.*

mislead, misguide; lead astray, lead into error; cause error; beguile, misinform etc. (*misteach*) 538; delude; give a false -impression, -idea; falsify, misstate; deceive etc. 545; lie etc. 544.

err; be in error etc. *adj.*, be mistaken etc. *v.*; be deceived etc. (*duped*) 547; mistake, receive a false impression, deceive oneself; fall into-, lie

496. Maxim

under–, labor under– an error etc. *n.;* be in the wrong, blunder; misapprehend, misconceive, misunderstand, misreckon, miscount, miscalculate etc. (*misjudge*) 481.

play–, be– at cross purposes etc. (*misinterpret*) 523.

trip, stumble; lose oneself etc. (*uncertainty*) 475; go astray; fail etc. 732; be in the wrong box; take the wrong sow by the ear etc. (*mismanage*) 699; put the saddle on the wrong horse; reckon without one's host; take the shadow for the substance etc. (*credulity*) 486; dream etc. (*imagine*) 515.

adj. **erroneous**, untrue, false, devoid of truth, faulty, erring, fallacious, apocryphal, unreal, ungrounded, groundless; unsubstantial etc. 4; heretical etc. (*heterodox*) 984; unsound; illogical etc. 477.

inexact, unexact, inaccurate, incorrect; indefinite etc. (*uncertain*) 475.

illusive, illusory, delusive; mock, ideal etc. (*imaginary*) 515; spurious etc. 545; deceitful etc. 544; perverted.

controvertible, unsustainable, unsustained, unauthentic, unauthenticated, untrustworthy.

exploded, refuted, discarded.

mistaken etc. *v.;* in error, under an error etc. *n.;* tripping etc. *v.;* out, out in one's reckoning; aberrant; beside–, wide of– –the mark, –the truth; astray etc. (*at fault*) 475; on –a false, –the wrong– –scent, –trail; in the wrong box; at cross-purposes, all in the wrong; at sea, bewildered.

adv. more or less.

496. Maxim

n. **maxim**, aphorism; apothegm *or* apophthegm; dictum, saying, adage, saw, proverb, epigram, gnomic saying, gnome, sentence, mot [*Gallicism*], motto, word, byword, bromide, bromidium [*slang*], commonplace, moral, phylactery, protasis [*rare*].

wise–, sage–, received–, admitted–, recognized– maxim etc.; true–, common–, hackneyed–, trite–, commonplace– saying etc.

axiom, theorem, scholium, truism, postulate.

principle, principia; profession of faith etc. (*belief*) 484; settled principle, formula; reflection etc. (*idea*) 453; conclusion etc. (*judgment*) 480; golden rule etc. (*precept*) 697.

adj. **aphoristic**, aphorismic, aphorismatic, proverbial, phylacteric; axiomatic *or* axiomatical, gnomic *or* gnomical.

adv. as the saying is, as they say, as it was said by them of old.

497. Absurdity

n. **absurdity**, absurdness etc. *adj.;* imbecility etc. 499; alogy [*obs.*], comicality, nonsense, paradox, inconsistency; stultiloquy [*rare*], stultiloquence [*rare*], stultification, futility, nugacity.

blunder, muddle, bull; Irishism, Hibernicism; anticlimax, bathos; sophism etc. 477.

farce, galimatias, burlesque, parody, fiddle-faddle [*colloq.*], amphigory *or* amphigouri, rhapsody; farrago etc. (*disorder*) 59; bêtise [*F.*]; extravagance, romance; sciamachy.

pun, sell [*colloq.*], catch [*colloq.*], verbal quibble, macaronic composition, limerick, joke.

jargon, slipslop [*colloq.*], gibberish, balderdash, bombast, claptrap, fustian, twaddle etc. (*no meaning*) 517; exaggeration etc. 549; moonshine, stuff; mare's-nest, quibble, self-delusion.

tomfoolery, vagary, mummery, monkeyshine, monkey trick, boutade [*F.*], frisk, practical joke, escapade.

v. **play the fool** etc. 499; stultify, blunder, muddle; employ absurdity etc. *n.;* rhapsodize; romance, sell [*slang*], fiddle-faddle [*colloq.*]; talk nonsense, parler à tort et à travers [*F.*]; battre la campagne [*F.*]; anemolia bazein [*Gr.*]; be absurd etc. *adj.;* frisk, caper, joke, play practical jokes.

be the fool, be the goat [*colloq.*], bite [*colloq.*].

adj. **absurd**, nonsensical, farcical, preposterous, egregious, senseless, inconsistent, stultiloquent [*rare*], stulty [*obs.*], ridiculous, extravagant, quibbling; self-annulling, self-contradictory; paradoxical, macaronic *or* maccaronic, punning.

burlesque, foolish etc. 499; sophistical etc. 477; unmeaning etc. 517; amphigoric; without rhyme or reason; fantastic *or* fantastical, rhapsodic *or* rhapsodical, bombastic, high-flown.

int. fiddledeedee! pish! pooh! pooh-pooh! bah! stuff and nonsense! fiddle-faddle! bosh! come off! [*slang*].

498. Intelligence. Wisdom

n. **intelligence**, capacity, comprehension, understanding; cuteness [*colloq.*], sabe [*slang*], savvy [*slang*]; intellect etc. 450; nous [*colloq.*], docity [*dial.*], parts, sagacity, mother wit, wit, esprit [*F.*], gumption [*colloq.*], quick parts, grasp of intellect; acuteness etc. *adj.;* acumen, longheadedness, arguteness, subtility, subtlety, penetration, perspicacy [*obs.*], perspicacity, discernment, due sense of, good judgment; discrimination etc. 465; cunning etc. 702; refinement etc. (*taste*) 850.

head, brains, gray matter [*colloq.*], brain-stuff [*colloq.*], headpiece, upper story [*colloq.*], long head.

eagle -eye, –glance; eye of a lynx, eye of a hawk.

wisdom, sapience, sense; good–, common–, horse - [*colloq.*], plainsense; clear thinking, rationality, reason; reasonableness etc. *adj.;* judgment, solidity, depth, profundity, caliber *or* calibre; enlarged views; reach–, compass- of thought; enlargement of mind.

genius, lambent flame of intellect, inspiration, *Geist* [*Ger.*], fire of genius, heaven-born genius, soul; talent etc. (*aptitude*) 698.

[wisdom in action] prudence etc. 864; vigilance etc. 459; tact etc. 698; foresight etc. 510; sobriety, self-possession, *aplomb* [*F.*], ballast, mental poise, balance.

a bright thought, an inspiration, not a bad idea.

v. **be intelligent** etc. *adj.;* have all one's wits about one; be brilliant, be witty, scintillate, coruscate; understand etc. (*intelligible*) 518; catch–, take in- an idea; take a -joke, –hint.

penetrate; see through, see at a glance, see with half an eye, see far into, see through a millstone [*colloq.*]; discern etc. (*descry*) 441; foresee etc. 510.

discriminate etc. 465; know what's what [*colloq.*] etc. 698; listen to reason.

adj. **[applied to persons] intelligent**, quick of apprehension, keen, acute, alive, brainy [*colloq.*], awake, bright, quick, sharp; quick–, keen–, clear–, sharp- -eyed, –sighted, –witted; wide-awake; canny, sly, pawky [*dial.*], shrewd, astute; clear-headed; farsighted etc. 510; discerning, perspicacious, penetrating, piercing; argute; nimble-witted, needle-witted; sharp as a tack; alive to etc. (*cognizant*) 490; clever etc. (*apt*) 698; arch etc. (*cunning*) 702; *pas is bête* [*F.*]; acute etc. 682.

wise, sage, sapient [*often in irony*], sagacious, reasonable, rational, sound, in one's right mind, sensible, *abnormis sapiens* [*L.*], judicious, strong-minded.

impartial, unprejudiced, unbiased, unbigoted, unprepossessed; undazzled, unperplexed; of unwarped judgment, equitable, fair.

cool; cool–, long–, hard–, strong-headed; long-sighted, calculating, thoughtful, reflecting; solid, deep, profound.

prudent etc. (*cautious*) 864; sober, staid, solid; considerate, politic, wise in one's generation; watchful etc. 459; provident etc. (*prepared*) 673; in advance of one's age; wise as -a serpent, –Solomon, –Solon, –Nestor, –Mentor.

oracular; heaven-directed, heaven-born.

[applied to actions] **wise**, sensible, reasonable, judicious; well-judged, well-advised; prudent, politic; expedient etc. 646.

499. Imbecility. Folly

n. **imbecility**; want of intelligence etc. 498, want of intellect etc. 450; shallowness, unwisdom, silliness, foolishness etc. *adj.;* morosis, incapacity, vacancy of mind, poverty of intellect, clouded perception, poor head; apartments–, rooms–, space- to let [*all slang*]; nobody home [*slang*]; stupidity, insulsity [*rare*], stolidity; hebetude, dull understanding, meanest capacity, short-sightedness; incompetence etc. (*unskillfulness*) 699.

bias etc. 481; infatuation etc. (*insanity*) 503; one's weak side.

simplicity, puerility, babyhood; senility, dotage, anility, second childishness, fatuousness, fatuity; idiocy, idiotism, jobbernowlism [*colloq., Eng.*], driveling, driveling idiocy; senile dementia.

folly, frivolity, irrationality, trifling, ineptitude, nugacity, futility, inconsistency, lip wisdom, conceit; sophistry etc. 477; giddiness etc. (*inattention*) 458; eccentricity etc. 503; extravagance etc. (*absurdity*) 497; rashness etc. 863.

act of folly etc. 699.

v. **be imbecile** etc. *adj.;* have no -brains, –sense etc. 498; have a screw loose [*colloq.*].

trifle, drivel, *radoter* [*F.*], dote, ramble etc. (*madness*) 503; play the -fool, –monkey; take leave of one's senses; not see an inch beyond one's nose; stultify oneself etc. 699; talk nonsense etc. 497.

adj. **[applied to persons] unintelligent**, unintellectual, unreasoning; mindless, witless, reasonless, brainless; half-baked [*colloq.*], having no head etc. 498; not bright etc. 498; inapprehensive, thick [*colloq.*].

blockish, unteachable; Boeotian, Boeotic; bovine; ungifted, undiscerning, unenlightened, unwise, unphilosophical; apish, simious, simian.

weak–, addle–, puzzle–, blunder–, muddle- [*colloq.*], jolter–, jolt–, chowder–, pig–, beetle–, buffle- [*obs.*], chuckle–, mutton–, gross-headed; maggot-pated [*obs.*], beef-headed, beef-witted, fat-headed, fat-witted.

weak-minded, feeble-minded; dull–, shallow–, lack- brained; rattle- brained, –headed; saphead [*colloq.*], muddy-brained, addle-brained; half–, lean–, short–, shallow–, dull–, blunt-witted; shallow–, clod–, addle- pated; dim–, short- sighted; thick-skulled; thick-headed;

500. Sage

weak in the upper story [*colloq.*], inapprehensible, nutty [*slang*], batty [*slang*], loony [*slang*].

shallow, *borné* [*F.*], weak, wanting, soft [*colloq.*], sappy, spoony *or* spooney [*slang*]; dull, —as a beetle.

stupid, heavy, insulse [*rare*], obtuse, blunt, stolid, doltish; asinine; inapt etc. 699; prosaic etc. 843; hebetudinous, hebetate, hebete [*rare*].

childish, childlike; infantine, infantile, babyish, babish; puerile, senile, anile; simple etc. (*credulous*) 486; old-womanish.

imbecile, fatuous, idiotic, driveling; blatant, babbling; vacant; sottish; bewildered etc. 475.

foolish, silly, senseless, irrational, insensate, nonsensical, inept; maudlin.

narrow-minded etc. 481; bigoted etc. (*obstinate*) 606; giddy etc. (*thoughtless*) 458; rash etc. 863; eccentric etc. (*crazed*) 503.

[applied to actions] **foolish**, unwise, injudicious, improper, unreasonable, without reason, ridiculous, silly, stupid, asinine; ill-imagined, ill-advised, ill-judged, ill-devised; *mal entendu* [*F.*]; inconsistent, irrational, unphilosophical; extravagant etc. (*nonsensical*) 497; sleeveless [*obs.*], idle; useless etc. 645; inexpedient etc. 647; frivolous etc. (*trivial*) 643.

500. Sage

n. **sage**, wise man; master mind, master spirit of the age; longhead, thinker, philosopher.

authority, oracle, mentor, luminary, shining light, *esprit fort* [*F.*], *magnus Apollo* [*L.*], Solon, Solomon, Buddha, Confucius, Mentor, Nestor, the Magi; Seven Wise Men of Greece, Seven Sages, Philosophical Pleiad; "second Daniel."

savant [*F.*], pundit etc. (*scholar*) 492; wiseacre [*archaic or ironical*]; expert etc. 700; wizard etc. 994.

adj. **venerable**, venerated, reverenced, revered, honored, looked up to; authoritative, wise, oracular; erudite etc. (*knowledge*) 490; *emeritus* [*L.*].

501. Fool

n. **fool**, idiot, tomfool, wiseacre, simpleton, Simple Simon, moron, gaby [*colloq.*], witling, dizzard [*obs.*], donkey, ass; ninny, ninny hammer, chowderhead [*dial.*], jolterhead *or* jolthead, chucklehead [*colloq.*], dolt, booby, tomnoddy, loony [*slang*], looby, hoddy-doddy [*obs.*], noddy, nonny [*dial.*], noodle, nizy [*obs.*], owl, goose, imbecile; *radoteur* [*F.*], nincompoop [*colloq.*], *badaud* [*F.*], zany; trifler, babbler; pretty fellow; natural, *niais* [*F.*].

child, baby, infant, innocent, milksop, sop.

oaf, lout, loon *or* lown [*dial.*]; bullhead, blunderhead, addle-pate, addlebrain, addlehead [*all colloq.*]; blockhead, dullhead, bonehead [*slang*], rattlepate, dullard, doodle [*obs.*], calf [*colloq.*], colt, buzzard [*obs.*], block, put, stick [*colloq.*], stock, numps [*obs.*], tony [*obs.*]; loggerhead, beetlehead, grosshead [*obs.*], muttonhead [*colloq.*], noodlehead, giddyhead [*colloq.*], numskull [*colloq.*], thickhead [*colloq.*], thick skull; lackbrain, shallowbrain; half-wit, lackwit; dunderpate; lunkhead.

sawney [*dial. Eng.*], clod, clodhopper; clodpoll, clodpate, clotpole *or* clotpoll [*obs.*], clotpate [*obs.*], soft *or* softy [*colloq. or slang*], saphead [*slang*], bull calf [*colloq.*], spoony *or* spooney [*slang*], gawk, gawky, gowk, Gothamite, lummox [*dial.*], rube; men of Boeotia, wise men of Gotham.

un sot à triple étage [*F.*], sot [*Scot.*], jobbernowl [*colloq., Eng.*], changeling [*archaic*], mooncalf, *gobe-mouches* [*F.*].

greenhorn etc. (*dupe*) 547; dunce etc. (*ignoramus*) 493; lubber etc. (*bungler*) 701; madman etc. 504; solid ivory.

one who -will not set the Thames on fire, –did not invent gunpowder, –does not exactly scintillate; *qui n'a pas inventé la poudre* [*F.*]; no conjurer; no Solomon.

dotard, driveler; old fogy *or* fogey [*colloq.*], old woman; crone, grandmother; cotquean [*archaic*], henhussy, betty [*contempt*].

502. Sanity

n. **sanity**; soundness etc. *adj.*; rationality, normalcy, normality, sobriety, lucidity, lucid interval; senses, sober senses, common sense, horse sense [*colloq.*], sound mind, *mens sana* [*L.*].

v. **be sane** etc. *adj.;* retain one's senses, –reason.
become sane etc. *adj.;* come to one's senses, sober down, cool down, get things into proportion, see things in proper perspective.
render sane etc. *adj.;* bring to one's senses, sober, bring to reason.

adj. **sane**, rational, normal, wholesome, right-minded, reasonable, *compos mentis* [*L.*], of sound mind; sound, sound-minded; lucid.
self-possessed; sober, sober-minded.
in one's -sober senses, –right mind; in possession of one's faculties.

adv. **sanely** etc. *adj.;* in reason, within reason, within bounds; according to the dictates of -reason, –common sense; in the name of common sense.

503. Insanity

- *n.* **insanity**, lunacy; madness etc. *adj.*, mania, rabies, furor, mental alienation, aberration, amentia, paranoia; dementation, dementia, demency [*rare*], morosis, idiocy; *dementia a potu* [*L.*], delirium tremens, d.t.'s, the horrors [*colloq.*]; phrenitis, frenzy, raving, incoherence, wandering, delirium, calenture of the brain, delusion, hallucination; lycanthropy.
  derangement; disordered -reason, -intellect; diseased-, unsound-, abnormal- mind; unsoundness.
  vertigo, dizziness, swimming, sunstroke, *coup de soleil* [*F.*], siriasis.
  oddity, eccentricity, twist, monomania; fanaticism, infatuation, craze; kleptomania, dipsomania; hypochondriasis etc. (*low spirits*) 837; melancholia, hysteria.
  screw-, tile-, slate-loose; bee in one's bonnet, rats in the upper story, bats in the belfry, bee in the head [*all colloq.*].
  dotage etc. (*imbecility*) 499.
- *v.* **be** or **become insane** etc. *adj.;* lose one's senses, -reason, -faculties, -wits; go mad, run mad; rave, dote, ramble, wander; drivel etc. (*be imbecile*) 499; have a screw loose etc. *n.*, have a devil; *avoir le diable au corps* [*F.*]; lose one's head etc. (*be uncertain*) 475.
  derange; render or drive mad etc. *adj.;* madden, dementate [*rare*], addle the wits, derange the head, infatuate, befool; turn the brain, turn one's head.
- *adj.* **insane**, mad, lunatic; crazy, crazed, *aliéné* [*F.*], *non compos mentis* [*L.*], not right, dement [*rare*], dementate, cracked [*colloq.*], touched; bereft of reason; all-possessed, unhinged, unsettled in one's mind; insensate, reasonless, beside oneself, demented, maniacal, daft; frenzied, frenetic or frenetical; possessed, -with a devil; deranged, far gone, maddened, moonstruck; shatterpated, shatterbrained, madbrained, scatterbrained, crack-brained; off one's head.
  Corybantic, dithyrambic; rabid, giddy, vertiginous, wild; haggard, mazed; flighty; distracted, distraught; bewildered etc. (*uncertain*) 475.
  mad as a -March hare, -hatter; of unsound mind etc. *n.;* touched-, wrong-, not right- in one's -head, -mind, -wits, -upper story [*colloq.*]; out of one's -mind, -senses, -wits; not in one's right mind; nutty [*slang*].
  odd, fanatical, infatuated, eccentric; hypochondriac, hyppish [*rare*], hipped or hypped [*colloq.*], hippish [*colloq.*].

  delirious, light-headed, incoherent, rambling, doting, wandering; frantic, raving, stark mad, stark staring mad.
  imbecile, silly, etc. 499.
- *adv.* like one possessed.

504. Madman

- *n.* **madman**, lunatic, maniac, bedlamite, candidate for Bedlam, raver, phrenetic, madcap; energumen [*eccl. antiq.*]; automaniac, monomaniac, dipsomaniac, kleptomaniac, paranoiac; hypochondriac etc. (*low spirits*) 837; crank, Tom o' Bedlam; nut [*slang*].
  dreamer etc. 515; rhapsodist, seer, highflyer or highflier [*obs.*], enthusiast, fanatic, *fanatico* [*It.*], *exalté* [*F.*], Don Quixote, Ophelia, Madge Wildfire.
  idiot etc. 501.

Section 6. Extension of Thought

505. Memory

- *n.* **memory**, remembrance; retentivity, retention, retentiveness; tenacity; tablets of the memory; readiness.
  retentive-, tenacious-, trustworthy-, capacious-, faithful-, correct-, exact-, ready-, prompt- memory; Memory's halls, Memory's pictures.
  recollection, reminiscence, recognition, recurrence, rememoration [*rare*], rememorance [*rare*]; retrospect, retrospection; "that inward eye" [Wordsworth]; afterthought.
  reminder; suggestion etc. (*information*) 527; prompting etc. *v.;* hint, token of remembrance, memento, souvenir, keepsake, relic, memorandum (*pl.* memoranda); remembrancer, flapper; memorial etc. (*record*) 551; commemoration etc. (*celebration*) 883.
  things to be remembered, memorabilia.
  mnemonics; art of-, artificial- memory; *memoria technica* [*L.*]; mnemotechnics, mnemotechny; Mnemosyne.
  aids to memory, jogger [*colloq.*], memorandum book, notebook, promptbook, engagement book.
  fame, celebrity, renown, reputation etc. (*repute*) 873.
- *v.* **remember**, mind [*obsoles.*], rememorate [*rare*]; retain the -memory, -remembrance- of; keep in view.
  have-, hold-, bear-, carry-, keep-, retain- in or in the -thoughts, -mind, -memory,

506. Oblivion

-remembrance; be in–, live in–, remain in–, dwell in–, haunt–, impress- one's -memory, -thoughts, -mind.

sink in the mind; run in the head; not be able to get it out of one's head; be deeply impressed with; rankle etc. (*revenge*) 919.

recognize, bethink oneself, recall, call up, conjure up, retrace; look–, trace- -back, –backwards; think upon, look back upon; review; call–, recall–, bring- to -mind, –remembrance; carry one's thoughts back; rake up the past.

redeem from oblivion; keep the -memory alive, –wound green; *tangere ulcus* [*L.*]; keep the memory green, keep up the memory of; commemorate etc. (*celebrate*) 883.

recollect, recur to the mind; flash on the mind, flash across the memory.

remind; suggest etc. (*inform*) 527; prompt; put–, keep- in mind; fan the embers; call up, summon up; renew; *infandum renovare dolorem* [*L.*]; task–, tax–, jog–, flap–, refresh–, rub up–, awaken- the memory; pull by the sleeve; bring back to the memory, put in remembrance, memorialize.

memorize, commit to memory; con, –over; fix–, rivet–, imprint–, impress–, stamp–, grave–, engrave–, store–, treasure up–, bottle up–, embalm–, bury–, enshrine- in the memory; load–, store–, stuff–, burden- the memory with; get–, have–, learn–, know–, say–, repeat- by -heart, –rote; get–, drive- into one's head; bury in the mind; say one's lesson; repeat, –like a parrot; have at one's fingers' ends.

make a note of etc. (*record*) 551.

adj. **remembering**, remembered etc. *v.;* mindful, reminiscential; alive in memory; retained in the memory etc. *v.;* pent up in one's memory; fresh; green, –in remembrance; still vivid, rememorant [*rare*]; not–, never -to be erased, –to be forgotten; unforgettable *or* unforgetable; enduring, –in memory; unforgotten, present to the mind; within one's memory etc. *n.;* indelible; uppermost in one's thoughts; memorable etc. (*important*) 642; suggestive.

adv. **by heart**, *par coeur* [*F.*], by rote; without book, *memoriter* [*L.*].

in memory of; *in memoriam* [*L.*]; *memoria in aeterna* [*L.*].

506. Oblivion

n. **oblivion**; forgetfulness etc. *adj.;* obliteration etc. (552) of–, insensibility etc. (823) to- the past. short–, treacherous–, loose–, slippery–, failing- memory; decay–, failure–, lapse- of memory; mind–, memory- like a sieve; untrustworthy memory; waters of -Lethe, –oblivion; amnesia.

amnesty, general pardon.

v. **forget**; be forgetful etc. *adj.;* fall–, sink- into oblivion; have a short memory etc. *n.,* have no head.

forget one's own name, have on the tip of one's tongue, come in one ear and go out the other.

slip–, escape–, fade from–, die away from- the memory; lose, lose sight of.

efface etc. (552)–, discharge- from the memory; unlearn; consign to -oblivion, –the tomb of the Capulets; think no more of etc. (*turn the attention from*) 458; cast behind one's back, wean one's thoughts from; let bygones be bygones etc. (*forgive*) 918.

adj. **forgotten** etc. *v.;* unremembered, past recollection, bygone, out of mind; buried–, sunk- in oblivion; clean forgotten; gone out of one's -head, –recollection.

forgetful, oblivious, mindless, Lethean; insensible etc. (823) to the past; heedless.

507. Expectation

n. **expectation**, expectance, expectancy; anticipation, contingency, contingent, reckoning, calculation; foresight etc. 510; contemplation, prospection.

prospect, lookout [*chiefly Eng.*], perspective, horizon, vista; destiny etc. 152; futures [*stock exchange*].

suspense, waiting, abeyance; curiosity etc. 455; anxious–, ardent–, eager–, breathless–, sanguine- expectation; torment of Tantalus.

assurance, confidence, presumption, reliance; hope etc. 858; trust etc. (*belief*) 484; prognosis [*med.*], prognostic, prognostication; auspices etc. (*prediction*) 511.

v. **expect**; look -for, –out for, –forward to; hope for, anticipate; have in -prospect, –contemplation; keep in view; contemplate, promise oneself; not wonder at *or* if etc. 870.

wait for, tarry for, lie in wait for, watch for, bargain for; keep a -good, –sharp -lookout for; await; stand at "attention," abide, mark time, bide one's time, watch.

prick up one's ears, hold one's breath.

foresee etc. 510; prepare for etc. 673; forestall etc. (*be early*) 132; count upon etc. (*believe in*) 484; think likely etc. (*probability*) 472; bargain for; make one's mouth water.

predict, prognosticate, forecast; lead one to expect etc. (*predict*) 511; have in store for etc. (*destiny*) 152.

adj. **expectant**; expecting etc. *v.;* in expectation etc. *n.;* on the watch etc. (*vigilant*) 459; open-eyed, open-mouthed; agape, gaping, all agog; on tenterhooks, on tiptoe, on the tiptoe of expectation; *aux aguets* [*F.*]; ready, prepared, provided for, provisional, provident; curious etc. 455; looking forward to; on the rack.

expected etc. *v.;* long expected, foreseen; in prospect etc. *n.;* prospective, future, coming; in one's eye, in view, on the horizon; impending etc. (*destiny*) 152.

adv. **expectantly**; on the watch etc. *adj.;* in the event of; as a possible contingency; with muscles tense, on edge [*colloq.*]; with eyes–, with ears -strained; with ears pricked forward; *arrectis auribus* [*L.*]; with breathless expectation etc. *n.,* with bated breath.

soon, shortly, forthwith, anon [*archaic*], presently; prospectively etc. 121.

508. Inexpectation

n. **inexpectation** [*rare*], nonexpectation; unforeseen contingency, the unforeseen; false expectation etc. (*disappointment*) 509; miscalculation etc. 481.

surprise, sudden burst, thunderclap, blow, shock; bolt out of the blue; astoundment [*rare*], astonishment, mazement [*rare*], amazement; wonder etc. 870; eye opener.

v. **not expect** etc. 507; be taken by surprise; start; miscalculate etc. 481; not bargain for; come–, fall- upon.

be unexpected etc. *adj.;* come unawares etc. *adv.;* turn up, pop [*colloq.*], drop from the clouds; come–, burst–, flash–, bounce–, steal–, creep- upon one; come–, burst- like a -thunderclap, -thunderbolt; take–, catch- -by surprise, –unawares; catch napping, catch off one's guard; yach [*S. Africa*].

surprise, startle, take aback [*colloq.*], electrify, stun, stagger, take away one's breath, throw off one's guard; pounce upon, spring, spring upon, spring a mine upon; stound [*archaic*], astound; astonish etc. (*strike with wonder*) 870.

adj. **nonexpectant**, inexpectant; surprised etc. *v.;* unwarned, unaware; off one's guard; inattentive etc. 458.

unexpected, unanticipated, unlooked for, unforeseen, unhoped for; dropped from the clouds; beyond–, contrary to–, against- expectation; out of one's reckoning; unheard of etc. (*exceptional*) 83, startling; sudden etc. (*instantaneous*) 113.

adv. **unexpectedly**, abruptly, plump, pop, *à l'improviste* [*F.*], unawares; without -notice, –warning, –saying "by your leave"; like a thief in the night, like a thunderbolt; like a lightning flash; in an unguarded moment; suddenly etc. (*instantaneously*) 113.

int. heydey! etc. (*wonder*) 870; do tell!

509. Disappointment
[failure of expectation]

n. **disappointment**; blighted hope, disillusion, balk; blow; slip 'twixt cup and lip; non-fulfillment of one's hopes; sad–, bitter- disappointment; trick of fortune; afterclap; false–, vain- expectation; miscalculation etc. 481; fool's paradise; much cry and little wool.

v. **be disappointed**; look blank, look blue [*colloq.*]; look *or* stand aghast etc. (*wonder*) 870; find to one's cost; laugh on the wrong side of one's mouth [*colloq.*], laugh out of the other corner of the mouth [*colloq.*]; find one a false prophet.

disappoint; crush–, dash–, balk–, disappoint–, blight–, falsify–, defeat–, not realize- one's -hope, –expectation; balk, jilt, bilk; play one -false, –a trick; dash the cup from the lips; tantalize; dumfounder *or* dumbfounder, dumfound *or* dumbfound, disillusion, disillusionize; come short of; dissatisfy, make dissatisfied, disgruntle.

adj. **disappointed** etc. *v.;* disconcerted, aghast; disgruntled; out of one's reckoning; short of expectations.

510. Foresight

n. **foresight**, prospicience, prevision, long-sightedness, farsightedness; anticipation; providence etc. (*preparation*) 673.

forethought, forecast; predeliberation, presurmise; foregone conclusion etc. (*prejudgment*) 481; prudence etc. (*caution*) 864.

foreknowledge, precognition, prescience, prenotion, presentiment; second sight; sagacity etc. (*intelligence*) 498; antepast, prelibation; prophasis [*med.*], prognosis [*med.*].

prospect etc. (*expectation*) 507; foretaste; prospectus etc. (*plan*) 626.

v. **foresee**; look -forward to, –ahead, –beyond; scent from afar; feel it in one's bones [*colloq.*]; look–, pry–, peep- into the future.

see one's way; see how the -land lies, –wind blows, –cat jumps [*colloq.*].

511. Prediction

anticipate; expect etc. 507; be beforehand etc. (*early*) 132; predict etc. 511; foreknow, forejudge, forecast; surmise; have an eye to the -future, -main chance; *respicere finem* [*L.*]; keep a sharp lookout etc. (*vigilance*) 459; forewarn etc. 668.

adj. **foreseeing** etc. *v.;* prescient, anticipatory; farseeing, farsighted, long-sighted; sagacious etc. (*intelligent*) 498; weatherwise; provident etc. (*prepared*) 673; on the lookout, -for; prospective etc. 507.

adv. against the time when; for a rainy day.

511. Prediction

n. **prediction**, announcement; program *or* programme etc. (*plan*) 626; premonition etc. (*warning*) 668; prognosis, prognostic, presage, presagement, precurse [*obs.*], prophecy, vaticination, mantology [*rare*], prognostication, premonstration [*obs.*]; augury, auguration [*obs.*], ariolation [*obs.*], hariolation [*obs.*], foreboding, aboding [*obs.*], abode [*obs.*], bode [*obs.*], bodement, abodement; omniation [*obs.*], auspice (*pl.* auspices), forecast, omen etc. 512; horoscope, nativity; sooth [*obs.*], soothsaying, fortune-telling; divination.

adytum, oak of Dodona; cave of the Cumaean Sibyl, Sibylline leaves, Sibylline books; tripod of the Pythia.

prefiguration, prefigurement; prototype, type.

[divination by the stars] astrology, astromancy, horoscopy, genethlialogy, judicial *or* mundane astrology.

oracle, prophet, seer etc. 513.

[means of divination] crystal, ink, tea leaves, cards; Hallowe'en -nuts, mirror; divining-rod, witch-hazel; hand of glory; wax image; teraphim; shadows etc. [*see footnote*]; spell, charm etc. 993.

sorcery, magic, necromancy etc. 992; heteroscopic divination.[1]

v. **predict**, prognosticate, prophesy, vaticinate, divine, foretell, soothsay, augurate, tell fortunes; cast a horoscope, cast a nativity; advise; forewarn, prewarn etc. 668.

presage, augur, bode, abode [*obs.*], forebode; foretoken, betoken; prefigure, prefigurate, augurate [*rare*], ariolate [*rare*], figure [*obs.*], forecast, precurse, portend; preshow, foreshow, foreshadow; shadow forth, typify, pretypify, ominate [*obs.*], signify, point to.

hold out-, raise-, excite- -expectation, -hope; bid fair, promise, lead one to expect; be the precursor etc. 64.

herald, usher in, premise, announce; lower.

adj. **predicting** etc. *v.;* predictive, prophetic, fatidic *or* fatidical, precursal, precurrent, presageful, vaticinal, oracular, fatiloquent [*rare*], haruspical; Sibylline; weatherwise.

ominous, portentous; augurous, augurial, augural, precursive, precursory, auspicial, auspicious; prescious [*rare*], prescient, monitory, extispicious [*obs.*], premonitory, significant of, pregnant with, big with the fate of.

[1]The following terms, expressive of different forms of divination, have been collected from various sources, and are here given as a curious illustration of bygone superstitions:

Divination *by oracles,* theomancy; *by the Bible,* Bibliomancy; *by ghosts,* psychomancy; *by crystal gazing,* crystallomancy; *by shadows or manes,* sciomancy; *by appearances in the air,* aeromancy, chaomancy; *by the stars at birth,* genethliacs; *by meteors,* meteoromancy; *by winds,* austromancy; *by sacrificial appearances,* aruspicy (*or* haruspicy), hieromancy, hieroscopy; *by the entrails of animals sacrificed,* extispicy, hieromancy; *by the entrails of a human sacrifice,* anthropomancy; *by the entrails of fishes,* ichthyomancy; *by sacrificial fire,* pyromancy; *by redhot iron,* sideromancy; *by the smoke from the altar,* capnomancy; *by mice,* myomancy; *by birds,* orniscopy, ornithomancy; *by a cock picking up grains,* alectryomancy (*or* alectoromancy); *by snakes,* ophiomancy; *by herbs,* botanomancy; *by water,* hydromancy; *by fountains,* pegomancy; *by a wand,* rhabdomancy; *by dough of cakes,* crithomancy; *by meal,* aleuromancy, alphitomancy; *by salt,* halomancy; *by lead,* molybdomancy; *by dice,* cleromancy; *by arrows,* belomancy; *by a balanced hatchet,* axinomancy; *by a balanced sieve,* coscinomancy; *by a suspended ring,* dactyliomancy; *by dots made at random on paper,* geomancy; *by precious stones,* lithomancy; *by pebbles,* pessomancy; *by pebbles drawn from a heap,* psephomancy; *by mirrors,* catoptromancy; *by writings in ashes,* tephramancy; *by dreams,* oneiromancy; *by the hand,* palmistry, chiromancy; *by nails reflecting the sun's rays,* onychomancy; *by finger rings,* dactylomancy; *by numbers,* arithmancy; *by drawing lots,* sortilege; *by passages in books,* stichomancy; *by the letters forming the name of the person,* onomancy, nomancy; *by the features,* anthroposcopy; *by the mode of laughing,* geloscopy; *by ventriloquism,* gastromancy; *by walking in a circle,* gyromancy; *by dropping melted wax into water,* ceromancy; *by currents,* bletonism; *by the color and peculiarities of wine,* oenomancy; *by the shoulder blade,* scapulimancy *or* scapulomancy, omoplatoscopy.

512. Omen

n. **omen**, portent, presage, prognostic, augury, auspice; sign etc. (*indication*) 550; harbinger etc. (*precursor*) 64; yule candle, yule log *or* clog.

bird of ill omen; halcyon birds; signs of the times; gathering clouds, thunder, lightning, rainbow, comet, shooting star; rain of blood, warning etc. 668.

prefigurement etc. 511; adytum etc. 511.

adj. **ill-boding**, ill-omened, inauspicious.

513. Oracle

n. **oracle**; prophet, seer, soothsayer, augur, medium, clairvoyant, palmist, fortune teller, prophetess, sibyl, witch, geomancer, haruspice *or* aruspice, haruspex *or* aruspex; Sibyl; python, pythoness, Pythia; Pythian oracle, Delphian (*or* Delphic) oracle; Monitor, Sphinx, Tiresias, Cassandra, Sibylline leaves; oak–, oracle- of Dodona; sorcerer etc. 994; interpreter etc. 524.

weather prophet, weather sharp [*slang*], weather bureau, Old Probabilities *or* Old Prob. [*humorous nickname for U. S. weather bureau*]; Old Moore, Zadkiel.

Section 7. Creative Thought

514. Supposition

n. **supposition**, assumption, supposal, supposableness [*rare*], suppositality [*obs.*], postulation [*rare*], condition, presupposition, hypothesis, postulate, postulatum, theory, data; proposition, position; thesis, theorem; proposal etc. (*plan*) 626; assumed position.

bare–, vague–, loose- -supposition, –suggestion; conceit; conjecture; guess, guesswork; rough guess, shot [*colloq.*]; conjecturality [*rare*], suggestiveness, presurmise, surmise, suspicion, inkling, suggestion, association of ideas, hint; presumption etc. (*belief*) 484; divination, speculation, shot in the dark.

theorist, theorizer, speculatist [*rare*], speculator, notionalist, hypothesist, hypothetist [*rare*], doctrinaire, doctrinarian.

v. **suppose**, conjecture, surmise, suspect, guess, divine; theorize; presume, presuppose; assume, fancy, wis [*archaic*], take it; give a guess, speculate, believe, dare say, take it into one's head, take for granted.

propound, propose, put forth; start, put a case, submit, move, make a motion; hazard–, venture–, throw out–, put forward- a -suggestion, –conjecture, –supposition; hypothesize.

suggest, allude to, hint, put it into one's head. suggest itself etc. (*thought*) 451; run in the head etc. (*memory*) 505; marvel - wonder- -if, –whether.

adj. **supposing** etc. v.; given, mooted, postulatory [*now rare*]; assumed etc. v.; suppositive, supposititious; gratuitous, speculative, conjectural, conjecturable, hypothetical, theoretical, academic, supposable, presumptive, putative; suppositional, suppositionary.

suggestive, allusive, stimulating.

adv. **if**, if so be; an [*archaic*]; on the supposition etc. n.; ex hypothesi [*L.*], in case, in the event of; if that [*archaic*], so that, whether; quasi, as if, provided; perhaps etc. (*by possibility*) 470; for aught one knows.

515. Imagination

n. **imagination**, originality, invention; fancy; inspiration; verve.

warm–, heated–, excited–, sanguine–, ardent–, fiery–, boiling–, wild–, bold–, daring–, playful–, lively–, fertile- -imagination, –fancy.

"mind's eye" [*Hamlet*]; "the mind's internal heaven" [Wordsworth]; "such stuff as dreams are made on" [*Tempest*].

ideality, idealism; romanticism, utopianism, castle-building; dreaming; frenzy, ecstasy; calenture etc. (*delirium*) 503; reverie *or* revery, brown study, pipe dream, daydream, trance; somnambulism.

conception, *Vorstellung* [*Ger.*], excogitation, "a fine frenzy" [*Midsummer Night's Dream*]; cloudland, dreamland; flight–, fumes- of fancy; "thick-coming fancies" [*Macbeth*]; creation–, coinage- of the brain; imagery; word painting.

fantasy, conceit, figment, myth, dream, vision, shadow, chimera; phantasm, phantasy, fancy; maggot, whim, whimwham, whimsey *or* whimsy, vagary, rhapsody, romance, gest *or* geste, extravaganza; "air-drawn dagger" [*Macbeth*], bugbear, nightmare; flying Dutchman, great sea serpent, man in the moon, castle in the air, castle in Spain, *château en Espagne* [*F.*], pleasure dome of Kubla Khan, Utopia; Heavenly City, New Jerusalem; Atlantis, Happy Valley [Johnson], millennium, fairyland; land of Prester John, kingdom of Micomicon; Estotiland *or* Estotilandia [Milton]; Laputa; Cockagne, Lubberland; Arabian nights; *le pot au lait* [*F.*]; pot of gold at the end of the rainbow; dream of Alnaschar etc. (*hope*) 858; golden dream.

[creative works] work of fiction etc. (*novel*) 594; poetry etc. 597; play, tragedy, comedy etc. (*drama*) 599; sonata etc. (*music*) 415.

illusion etc. (*error*) 495; phantom etc. (*fallacy of vision*) 443; *Fata Morgana* [*L.*] etc. (*ignis*

516. Meaning

fatuus) 423; vapor etc. (*cloud*) 353; stretch of the imagination etc. (*exaggeration*) 549; mythogenesis.

idealist, romanticist, visionary; mopus [*slang*], romancer, daydreamer, dreamer; somnambulist; rhapsodist etc. (*fanatic*) 504; castle-builder, fanciful projector; "sweetest Shakespeare, Fancy's child" [Milton].

v. **imagine**, fancy, conceive; idealize, realize; dream, –of; "gives to airy nothing a local habitation and a name" [*Midsummer Night's Dream*].

set one's wits to work; strain–, crack- one's invention; rack–, ransack–, cudgel- one's brains; excogitate.

give -play, –the reins, –a loose [*obs.*]- to the- -imagination, –fancy; tilt at windmills; indulge in reverie.

conjure up a vision; fancy–, represent–, picture–, figure- to oneself; *vorstellen* [*Ger.*]; "see visions and dream dreams" [*Bible*].

float in the mind; suggest itself etc. (*thought*) 451.

create, originate, devise, invent, make up, coin, fabricate; improvise, strike out something new.

adj. **imagined** etc. *v.; ben trovato* [*It.*]; air-drawn, air-built.

imaginative; imagining etc. *v.;* original, inventive, creative, fertile, productive, ingenious.

extravagant, romantic, high-flown, flighty, preposterous; rhapsodic *or* rhapsodical; fanatic, enthusiastic, Utopian, Quixotic.

ideal, unreal; in the clouds, *in nubibus* [*L.*]; unsubstantial etc. 4; illusory etc. (*fallacious*) 495; fictitious, theoretical, hypothetical.

fanciful; fabulous, legendary, mythic *or* mythical, mythological, chimerical; imaginary, visionary; dream-beset, dream-ridden, dreamy, entranced, notional, fancy, fantastical, high-fantastical, fantasied, maggoty, made of empty air, vaporous, whimsical; fairy, fairylike.

Division 2. Communication of Ideas

Section 1. Nature of Ideas Communicated

516. Meaning
[idea to be conveyed]
[thing signified]

n. **meaning**; signification, significance; sense, expression; import, purport; implication, connotation, essence, force; drift, tenor, spirit, bearing, coloring; scope.

allusion etc. (*latency*) 526; suggestion etc. (*information*) 527; interpretation, acceptation etc. 522; acceptance [*rare*].

general–, broad–, substantial–, colloquial–, literal–, primary–, accepted–, essential–, plain–, simple–, natural–, unstrained–, true etc. (*exact*) 494–, honest etc. 543–, *prima facie* [*L.*] etc. (*manifest*) 525- meaning.

literality; literal–, obvious–, real- -meaning, –sense, –interpretation.

equivalent meaning; interchangeable word, figure of speech etc. 521; equivalent, synonym etc. 522.

thing signified, matter, subject, subject matter, substance, sum and substance; gist etc. 5; argument, text.

v. **mean**, signify, connote, denote, express; import, purport; convey, imply, breathe, indicate, bespeak, bear a meaning, bear a sense; tell of, speak of; touch on; point to, allude to; drive at; involve etc. (*latency*) 526; declare etc. (*affirm*) 535.

understand by etc. (*interpret*) 522.

synonymize, express by a synonym; paraphrase, state differently.

adj. **meaning** etc. *v.;* expressive, suggestive, allusive; significant, significative, significatory; pithy; meaningful; full of–, pregnant with- meaning; explicit etc. 525.

declaratory etc. 535; intelligible etc. 518.

literal, metaphrastic *or* metaphrastical, word-for-word, verbatim; exact, real.

synonymous; tantamount etc. (*equivalent*) 27.

implied etc. (*latent*) 526; understood, tacit.

adv. **to that effect**; that is to say etc. (*being interpreted*) 522.

verbatim, literally; evidently, apparently, from the context.

517. Unmeaningness
[absence of meaning]

n. **unmeaningness** etc. *adj.;* scrabble, scribble, scrawl, pothooks.

empty sound, dead letter, *vox et praeterea nihil* [*L.*]; "a tale told by an idiot, full of sound and fury, signifying nothing" [*Macbeth*]; "weasel words" [Roosevelt]; "sounding brass or a tinkling cymbal" [*Bible*].

nonsense, jargon, gibberish, jabber, mere words, hocus-pocus, fustian, rant, bombast, balderdash, palaver, patter, flummery, verbiage, babble, *bavardage* [*F.*], *baragouin* [*F.*], platitude, *niaiserie* [*F.*]; inanity; flapdoodle [*colloq.*]; rigmarole, rodomontade; truism; twaddle, twattle, fudge, trash; poppy-cock; stuff, –and nonsense; bosh [*colloq.*], rubbish, moonshine, wish-wash [*slang*], fiddle-faddle [*colloq.*]; absurdity etc. 497; imbecility, folly etc. 499; unintelligibleness, ambiguity, vagueness etc. (*unintelligibility*) 519.

v. **mean nothing**; be unmeaning etc. *adj.;* twaddle, quibble, jabber, rant, rodomontade, palaver, babble, fiddle-faddle [*colloq.*].

scribble, scrawl, scrabble, scratch.

adj. **unmeaning**; meaningless, senseless; nonsensical etc. 497; void of sense etc. 516.

inexpressive, unexpressive; vacant; not significant etc. 516; insignificant.

trashy, washy, wishy-washy [*colloq.*], inane, wash [*obs.*], rubbishy, vague, trumpery, trivial, fiddle-faddle [*colloq.*], twaddling, quibbling.

unmeant, not expressed; tacit etc. (*latent*) 526.

inexpressible, undefinable, ineffable, unutterable, incommunicable.

int. **fudge**! stuff! stuff and nonsense! bosh! fiddle-faddle! [*colloq.*]; poppycock! *oh! la-la!* [*F.*]; rubbish! fiddledee-dee! etc. 497.

518. Intelligibility

n. **intelligibility**; clearness, clarity, explicitness etc. *adj.;* lucidity, comprehensibility, perspicuity; legibility, plain speaking etc. (*manifestation*) 525; precision etc. 494; *phonanta sunetoisi* [*Gr.*], a word to the wise.

v. **be intelligible** etc. *adj.;* speak for itself, speak volumes; tell its own tale, lie on the surface.

render intelligible etc. *adj.;* popularize, simplify, clear up; elucidate etc. (*explain*) 522.

understand, comprehend; take, –in; catch, grasp, follow, collect, master, make out; see with half an eye, see daylight, see one's way [*all colloq.*]; enter into the ideas of; come to an understanding.

adj. **intelligible**; clear, clear as -day, -noonday, –crystal; lucid; perspicuous, transpicuous; luminous, transparent.

easily understood, easy to understand, for the million, intelligible to the meanest capacity, popularized.

plain, distinct, clear-cut, hard-hitting, to the point, explicit; positive; definite etc. (*precise*) 494.

unambiguous, unequivocal, unmistakable etc. (*manifest*) 525, unconfused; legible, recognizable; obvious etc. 525.

graphic, telling, vivid; expressive etc. (*meaning*) 516; illustrative etc. (*explanatory*) 522.

adv. in plain -terms, –words, –English; hitting the nail on the head.

519. Unintelligibility

n. **unintelligibility**, incomprehensibility, imperspicuity [*rare*]; inconceivableness, unknowability, unknowableness, vagueness etc. *adj.;* obscurity; ambiguity etc. 520; doubtful meaning; uncertainty etc. 475; perplexity etc. (*confusion*) 59; spinosity; *obscurum per obscurious* [*L.*]; mystification etc. (*concealment*) 528; latency etc. 526; transcendentalism.

pons asinorum [*L.*], asses' bridge; double Dutch, high Dutch [*slang*], Greek, Hebrew, Choctaw; jargon etc. (*unmeaning*) 517.

enigma, riddle etc. (*secret*) 533; paradox; *dignus vindice nodus* [*L.*]; sealed book; steganography, cryptography, freemasonry.

v. **be unintelligible** etc. *adj.;* require explanation etc. 522; have a doubtful meaning, pass comprehension.

render unintelligible etc. *adj.;* conceal etc. 528; darken etc. 421; confuse etc. (*derange*) 61; mystify, perplex etc. (*bewilder*) 475.

not understand etc. 518; lose, –the clew; miss; not know what to make of, be able to make nothing of, give it up; not be able to -account for, –make head or tail of; be at sea etc. (*uncertain*) 475; wonder etc. 870; see through a glass darkly etc. (*ignorance*) 491.

not understand one another; play at cross-purposes etc. (*misinterpret*) 523.

adj. **unintelligible**, unaccountable, undecipherable, undiscoverable, unknowable, unfathomable; incognizable, inexplicable, inscrutable; inapprehensible, incomprehensible; insolvable, insoluble; impenetrable.

puzzling, as Greek to one, unexplained, paradoxical, enigmatic *or* enigmatical, indecipherable, illegible.

obscure, crabbed, imperspicuous [*rare*], dark, muddy, clear as mud [*colloq.*], seen through a

520. Equivocalness

mist, dim, nebulous, shrouded in mystery; undiscernible etc. (*invisible*) 447; misty etc. (*opaque*) 426; hidden etc. 528; latent etc. 526; mysterious; mystic, mystical, acroamatic *or* acroamatical, metempiric *or* metempirical; transcendental; occult, esoteric, recondite, abstruse.

indefinite etc. (*indistinct*) 447; perplexed etc. (*confused*) 59; undetermined, vague, loose, ambiguous.

inconceivable, inconceptible [*obs.*]; searchless; above-, beyond-, past-comprehension; beyond one's depth; unconceived.

inexpressible, unutterable, ineffable, undefinable, incommunicable.

520. Equivocalness
[having a double sense]

n. **equivocalness** etc. *adj.;* equivocation; double meaning etc. 516; ambiguity, *double entente* [*F.*], double-entendre, pun, paragram [*rare*], *calembour* [*F.*], quibble, equivoque *or* equivoke, anagram; conundrum etc. (*riddle*) 533; word play etc. (*wit*) 842; homonym, homonymy; amphiboly, amphibologism, amphilogism *or* amphilogy [*rare*], anagrammatism, ambilogy, ambiloquy [*obs.*].

Sphinx, Delphic oracle.

equivocation etc. (*duplicity*) 544; white lie, mental reservation etc. (*concealment*) 528; paltering.

v. **equivocate** etc. (*palter*) 544; anagrammatize; be equivocal etc. *adj.;* have two meanings etc. 516.

adj. **equivocal**, ambiguous, amphibolous [*obs.*], doubtful, amphibolic, ambiloquent [*obs.*], ambiloquous, homonymic, homonymous; double-tongued etc. (*lying*) 544; enigmatical, indeterminate.

521. Metaphor

n. **figure of speech**; *façon de parler* [*F.*], way of speaking, colloquialism.

phrase etc. 566; figure, trope, metaphor, tralatition, metonymy, enallage, catachresis, synecdoche, antonomasia; satire, irony, figurativeness etc. *adj.;* image, imagery, metathesis, metalepsis, type, anagoge, simile.

personification, prosopopoeia, allegory, allegorization, apologue, parable, fable.

inference, implication, deduction, allusion, adumbration; euphemism, euphuism, application.

v. **employ metaphor** etc. *n.;* personify, allegorize, fable, adumbrate, shadow forth, apply, allude to.

adj. **metaphorical**, tropical, tralatitious, figurative, catachrestic *or* catachrestical, antonomastic *or* antonomastical, typical, parabolic *or* parabolical, allegoric *or* allegorical, allusive, referential, anagogic *or* anagogical; euphuistic *or* euphuistical, euphemistic *or* euphemistical, ironic, ironical; colloquial.

adv. **as it were**, so to -speak, -say, -express oneself; in a manner of speaking [*colloq.*].

522. Interpretation

n. **interpretation**, definition; explanation, explication; solution, answer; rationale; plain-, simple-, strict- interpretation; meaning etc. 516; *mot d'énigme* [*F.*]; clew etc. (*indication*) 550.

symptomatology, semeiology *or* semiology, diagnosis, prognosis; metoposcopy, physiognomy; paleography etc. (*philology*) 560; oneirology.

translation; rendering, rendition; reddition; literal-, free- translation; key; secret; *clavis* [*L.*], crib, pony, trot [*Eng.*].

comment, commentary; exegesis; expounding, exposition; hermeneutics; inference etc. (*deduction*) 480; illustration, exemplification; gloss, annotation, scholium, note; enucleation, elucidation, dilucidation [*obs.*]; *éclaircissement* [*F.*].

acception [*obs.*], acceptation, acceptance; light, reading, lection, construction, version.

equivalent, -meaning etc. 516; synonym, poecilonym, polyonym [*rare*]; paraphrase, metaphrase; convertible terms, apposition.

dictionary etc. 562; polyglot.

prediction etc. 511; chiromancy *or* cheiromancy, palmistry; astrology.

v. **interpret**, explain, define, construe, translate, render; do into, turn into; transfuse the sense of.

find out etc. (480*a*)- -the meaning of etc. 516; read; spell out, make out; decipher, unravel, disentangle; find the key of, enucleate, resolve, solve; consignify [*rare*]; read between the lines, read into.

elucidate, account for; find-, tell- the cause of etc. 153; throw-, shed- -light, -new light, -fresh light- upon; clear up.

illustrate, exemplify; unfold, expound, comment upon, annotate; popularize etc. (*render intelligible*) 518.

understand by; take-, understand-, receive-, accept- in a particular sense; put a construction on, be given to understand.

adj. **explanatory**, expository; explicative, explicatory; exegetical; construable; hermeneutic *or* hermeneutical, interpretive, interpretative, commentarial, commentatorial, inferential, illustrative, exemplificative, exemplificational, annotative, scholiastic, elucidative; symptomatological; paleographic *or* paleographical.

equivalent etc. 27; paraphrastic, consignificative [*rare*], consignificant, synonymous, poecilonymic, polyonymal [*rare*], polyonymic [*rare*].

metaphrastic, literal etc. 516; polyglot.

adv. **in explanation** etc. *n.;* that is to say, *id est* [*L.*], *videlicet* [*L.*], to wit, namely, in other words.

literally, strictly speaking: in -plain, -plainer--terms, -words, -English; more simply.

523. Misinterpretation

n. **misinterpretation**, misapprehension, misdoubt, misconception, misunderstanding, misacceptation [*obs.*], misconstruction, misapplication; catachresis; eisegesis; cross-reading, cross-purposes; mistake etc. 495.

misrepresentation, perversion, misstatement, exaggeration etc. 549; false -coloring, -construction; abuse of terms; play upon words, *jeu de mots* [*F.*], pun, parody, travesty; double-talk; falsification etc. (*lying*) 544.

v. **misinterpret**, misapprehend, misunderstand, misconceive, misjudge, misdeem, misdoubt, misspell, mistranslate, misconstrue, misapply; mistake etc. 495.

misrepresent, pervert; explain wrongly, misstate; garble etc. (*falsify*) 544; distort, detort [*obs.*]; travesty, play upon words; stretch-, strain-, twist-, wrench-, wring-, wrest- the -sense, -meaning; explain away; put a -bad, -wrong, -erroneous, -false- construction on; give a false coloring; look through dark-, rose-colored- spectacles.

be out; be-, play- at cross-purposes; be off [*slang*], be 'way off [*slang*], be off base [*slang*].

adj. **misinterpreted** etc. *v.;* eisegetical, catachrestic *or* catachrestical; untranslated, untranslatable.

confused, tangled, snarled, mixed, dazed, perplexed, bewildered, rattled [*slang*], benighted.

adv. **at cross-purposes**, at sixes and sevens [*colloq.*]; *à tort et à travers* [*F.*]; all balled up [*colloq.*], in a maze, all fouled up [*slang*].

524. Interpreter

n. **interpreter** (*fem.* interpretress), translator, expositor, expounder, exponent, explainer; demonstrator.

commentator, scholiast, annotator; metaphrast, paraphrast; glossarist, prolocutor.

spokesman, speaker, mouthpiece, foreman of the jury; mediator, delegate, exponent, representative, diplomatic agent, ambassador, plenipotentiary; advocate, judge, Supreme Court.

guide, dragoman, courier, *valet de place* [*F.*], cicerone, showman, barker [*colloq.*], oneirocritic; Oedipus, Joseph; oracle etc. 513.

Section 2. Modes of Communication

525. Manifestation

n. **manifestation**, unfoldment, unfolding; plainness etc. *adj.;* plain speaking; expression; showing etc. *v.;* exposition, demonstration, séance, materialization; exhibition, production; display, show-down [*slang*], show, showing off [*colloq.*]; premonstration [*obs.*].

[thing shown] exhibit, exhibition, exposition, show [*colloq.*], performance.

indication etc. (*calling attention to*) 457; publicity etc. 531; disclosure etc. 529; openness etc. (*honesty*) 543, (*artlessness*) 703; *épanchement* [*F.*]; saliency, prominence.

v. **make** *or* **render manifest** etc. *adj.;* materialize; bring -forth, -forward, -to the front, -into view; give notice; express; represent, set forth, evidence, exhibit; show, -up; expose; produce; hold up-, expose- to view; set-, place-, lay- before -one, -one's eyes; tell to one's face; trot out [*colloq.*], put through one's paces [*colloq.*], show one's paces, show off [*colloq.*]; show forth, unveil, bring to light, display, demonstrate, unroll; lay open; draw out, bring out; bring out in strong relief; call-, bring- into notice; hold up the mirror to; wear one's heart upon his sleeve; show one's -face, -colors; manifest oneself; speak out; make no -mystery, -secret- of; unfurl the flag; proclaim etc. (*publish*) 531.

indicate etc. (*direct attention to*) 457; disclose etc. 529; translate, transcribe, decipher, decode; elicit etc. 480a.

be manifest etc. *adj.;* appear etc. (*be visible*) 446; transpire etc. (*be disclosed*) 529; speak for itself, stand to reason; stare one in the face, loom large, appear on the horizon, rear its head; give -token, -sign, -indication of; tell its own tale etc. (*intelligible*) 518; go without saying, be self-evident.

526. Latency

adj. **manifest**, apparent; salient, striking, demonstrative, prominent, in the foreground, notable, pronounced.

flagrant; notorious etc. (*public*) 531; arrant; stark-staring; unshaded, glaring.

plain, clear, defined, definite, distinct, conspicuous etc. (*visible*) 446; obvious, evident, unmistakable, conclusive, indubitable, not to be mistaken, palpable, self-evident, autoptic *or* autoptical; intelligible etc. 518; clear as -day, -daylight, -noonday; plain as -a pikestaff [*colloq.*], -the sun at noonday, -the nose on one's face [*colloq.*], -way to parish church [*colloq.*].

ostensible; open, -as day; overt, patent, express, explicit; naked, bare, literal, downright, undisguised, exoteric.

unreserved; frank, plain-spoken etc. (*artless*) 703.

barefaced, brazen, bold, shameless, daring, flaunting, risqué [*F.*], loud.

manifested etc. *v.;* disclosed etc. 529; capable of being shown, producible; unconcealable.

adv. **manifestly**, openly etc. *adj.;* before one's eyes, under one's nose [*colloq.*], under one's very eyes, to one's face, face to face, above board, cards on the table, cartes sur table [*F.*], on the stage, in open court, in the open streets, in plain sight, in the open, at the cross-roads, in the market place, in market overt; in the face of -day, -heaven; in- broad-, open- daylight; without reserve; at first blush, prima facie [*L.*], on the face of; in set terms.

526. Latency

n. **latency**, inexpression; hidden-, occult- meaning; obscurity etc. (*unintelligibility*) 519; occultness, mystery, cabala *or* cabbala, cabalism, occultism, mysticism, symbolism, anagoge; silence etc. (*taciturnity*) 585; concealment etc. 528; more than meets the -eye, -ear; Delphic oracle; le dessous des cartes [*F.*], undercurrent; "something rotten in the state of Denmark" [*Hamlet*].

snake in the grass etc. (*pitfall*) 667; secret etc. 533. darkness, invisibility, imperceptibility.

allusion, insinuation, inference, implication; innuendo etc. 527; adumbration.

latent influence, invisible government, power behind the throne, friend at court, wire-puller [*colloq.*], king-maker; "a destiny that shapes our ends" [*Hamlet*].

v. **be latent** etc. *adj.;* lurk, smolder *or* smoulder, underlie, make no sign; escape -observation, -detection, -recognition; lie hid etc. 528.

laugh up one's sleeve; keep back etc. (*conceal*) 528.

involve, imply, implicate, connote, import, understand, allude to, infer, leave an inference; mysticize [*rare*], symbolize; whisper etc. (*conceal*) 528.

adj. **latent**; lurking etc. *v.;* secret, occult, anagogic *or* anagogical, cabalistic *or* cabalistical, symbolic, esoteric, recondite, veiled, symbolic, cryptic *or* cryptical; mystic, mystical; implied etc. *v.;* dormant; abeyant.

unapparent, unknown, unseen etc. 441; in the background; invisible etc. 447; indiscoverable, dark; impenetrable etc. (*unintelligible*) 519; unspied, unsuspected.

undeveloped, unsolved, unexplained, untraced, undiscovered etc. 480a, untracked, unexplored, uninvented.

unexpressed, unmentioned, unpronounced, unsaid, unwritten, unpublished, unbreathed, untalked of, untold etc. 527, unsung, unexposed, unproclaimed, undisclosed etc. 529, not expressed, tacit.

indirect, crooked, inferential; by inference, by implication; implicit; constructive; allusive, covert, muffled; steganographic; understood, underhand, underground; concealed; under cover etc. 528; delitescent.

adv. **secretly** etc. 528; by a side wind; sub silentio [*L.*]; in the background; behind the scenes, behind one's back; on the tip of one's tongue; between the lines; by a mutual understanding; sub rosa [*L.*]; below the surface.

527. Information

n. **information**, advisement [*archaic*], enlightenment, acquaintance, knowledge etc. 490; publicity etc. 531.

mention; acquainting etc. *v.;* instruction etc. (*teaching*) 537; outpouring; intercommunication, communicativeness.

intimation, communication, notice, notification, enunciation, annunciation, announcement, communiqué [*F.*]; representation, round robin, presentment.

report, advice, monition; news etc. 532; return etc. (*record*) 551; account etc. (*description*) 594; statement etc. (*affirmation*) 535; case, estimate, specification.

dispatch *or* despatch, message, wire [*colloq.*], cable, telegram, telex etc. (*news*) 532; telephone, phone [*colloq.*], radiophone, wireless telephone, telegraphone.

informant, authority, teller, annunciator, harbinger, herald, intelligencer [*now rare*], reporter, exponent, mouthpiece; spokesman etc. (*interpreter*) 524; informer, eavesdropper, delator, detective, bull [*slang, U. S.*], sleuth [*colloq.*]; *mouchard* [*F.*], spy, newsmonger; messenger etc. 534; *amicus curiae* [*L.*].

guide, *valet de place* [*F.*], cicerone, pilot, guidebook, handbook; *vade mecum* [*L.*], manual; map, plan, chart, gazetteer; itinerary etc. (*journey*) 266.

hint, suggestion, innuendo, inkling, whisper, passing word, word in the ear, subaudition, subauditur, cue, byplay; gesture etc. (*indication*) 550; gentle-, broad- hint; *verbum sapienti* [*L.*]; word to the wise; insinuation etc. (*latency*) 526.

v. **tell**; inform, -of; acquaint, -with; impart, -to; make acquainted with, apprise, advise, enlighten, awaken.

let fall, mention, express, intimate, represent, communicate, make known; publish etc. 531; notify, signify, specify, convey the knowledge of; retail, render an account; give an account etc. (*describe*) 594; state etc. (*affirm*) 535.

let one know, have one know; give one to understand; give notice; set-, lay-, put- before; point out, put into one's head; put one in possession of; instruct etc. (*teach*) 537; direct the attention to etc. 457.

announce, annunciate; report, -progress; bring-, send-, leave-, write- word; telegraph, wire [*colloq.*], telephone, telex, phone [*colloq.*].

disclose etc. 529; show cause; explain etc. (*interpret*) 522.

hint; give an inkling of; give-, drop-, throw out- a hint; insinuate; allude to, make allusion to; glance at; tip off [*slang*], give one a tip [*colloq.*]; tip the wink [*slang*] etc. (*indicate*) 550; suggest, prompt, give the cue, breathe; whisper, -in the ear.

berate, scold, chide, strafe [*colloq.*], score [*colloq.*], dress down [*colloq.*], reprove, trim [*slang*], rate; give one a -bit, -piece- of one's mind; tell one -plainly, -once for all; speak volumes.

undeceive, unbeguile; set right, correct, open the eyes of, disabuse.

be informed of etc.; know etc. 490; learn etc. 539; get scent of, gather from; sleuth [*colloq.*]; awaken to, open one's eyes to; become -alive, -awake- to; hear, understand; come to one's -ears, -knowledge; reach one's ears; overhear etc. (*hear*) 418; get wise to [*slang*].

adj. **informed** etc. *v.; communiqué* [*F.*]; informational, advisory, intelligential; reported etc. *v.;* published etc. 531.

expressive etc. 516; explicit etc. (*open*) 525, (*clear*) 518; plain-spoken etc. (*artless*) 703.

declaratory, declarative, enunciative, nunciative [*rare*], annunciative [*rare*], enunciatory, insinuant [*rare*]; oral, nuncupative [*said of oral wills*], nuncupative [*said of oral wills*], nuncupatory [*obs.*]; expository; communicative, communicatory.

adv. **from information received**; according to -reports, -suggestion, -rumor; from notice given; by the underground route; as a matter of -general information, -common report; in the air; according to-, from- what one can gather.

528. Concealment

n. **concealment**; hiding etc. *v.;* occultation, mystification.

reticence, reserve, reservation; mental reservation, aside; *arrière pensée* [*F.*], suppression, evasion, white lie, misprision; silence etc. (*taciturnity*) 585; suppression of truth etc. 544; underhand dealing; closeness, secretiveness etc. *adj.;* mystery.

seal of secrecy; freemasonry; screen etc. 530; disguise etc. 530; masquerade; masked battery; hiding place etc. 530.

cryptography, steganography; cipher, code, cable code; sympathetic ink, palimpsest.

stalking, still-hunt, hunt.

stealth, stealthiness; obreption [*obs.*]; slyness etc. (*cunning*) 702.

secrecy, latitancy [*rare*], latitation [*obs.*]; seclusion etc. 893; privacy, secretness, hugger-mugger [*archaic*]; disguise, incognito (*fem.* incognita).

mysticism, occultism, supernaturalism; esotericism, esoterics, esotery.

latency etc. 526; snake in the grass; secret etc. 533; stowaway; blind baggage [*slang*].

masquerader, masker, mask, domino.

v. **conceal**, hide, secrete, put out of sight; lock up, seal up, bottle up.

cover, screen, cloak, veil, shroud; cover up one's tracks; screen from -sight, -observation; draw the veil; draw-, close- the curtain; curtain, shade, eclipse, throw a veil over; becloud, bemask; mask, camouflage, disguise; ensconce, muffle; befog; whisper.

keep- from, -back, -to oneself; keep -snug, -close, -secret, -dark; bury; sink, suppress; keep -from, -out of- -view, -sight; keep in-, throw into- the -shade, -background; stifle, hush up, smother, withhold, reserve; fence with a question; ignore etc. 460.

code, codify; use a -code, -cipher.

529. Disclosure

keep a secret, keep one's own counsel; hold one's tongue etc. (*silence*) 585; make no sign, not let it go further; not breathe a -word, −syllable- about; not let the right hand know what the left is doing; hide one's light under a bushel, bury one's talent in a napkin.

hoodwink; keep−, leave- in -the dark, −ignorance; blind, -the eyes; blindfold, mystify; puzzle etc. (*render uncertain*) 475; bamboozle etc. (*deceive*) 545.

be concealed etc. *v.;* suffer an eclipse; occult, retire from sight, couch; hide oneself; lie -hid, −in ambush, −perdu, −snug, −low [*colloq.*], −close; latitate [*obs.*]; seclude oneself etc. 893; lurk, sneak, skulk, slink, prowl, gumshoe [*slang*]; steal -into, −out of, −by, −along; play at -bopeep, −hide and seek; hide in holes and corners; still-hunt.

adj. **concealed** etc. *v.;* hidden; secret, latitant [*rare*], recondite, mystic, mystical, cabalistic *or* cabalistical, occult, dark; cryptic *or* cyptical, private, privy, *in petto* [*It.*], auricular, clandestine, close, close-mouthed, inviolate; tortuous.

behind a screen etc. 530; under -cover, −an eclipse; in ambush, in hiding, in disguise; in a -cloud, −fog, −mist, −haze, −dark corner; in the -shade, −dark; clouded, wrapt in clouds; invisible etc. 447; buried, underground, perdu; secluded etc. 893.

undisclosed etc. 529, untold etc. 527; covert etc. (*latent*) 526; mysterious etc. (*unintelligible*) 519.

inviolable, irrevealable, confidential; esoteric; not to be spoken of.

furtive, obreptitious, stealthy, feline; skulking etc. *v.;* surreptitious, underhand, hole and corner [*colloq.*]; sly etc. (*cunning*) 702; secretive, clandestine, evasive; reserved, reticent, uncommunicative, buttoned up; close, −as wax; taciturn etc. 585.

adv. **secretly** etc. *adj.;* in secret, in private, in one's sleeve, in holes and corners [*colloq.*]; in the dark etc. *adj.*

januis clausis [*L.*], with closed doors, *à huis clos* [*F.*]; hugger-mugger, in hugger-mugger [*archaic*], *à la dérobée* [*F.*], under the -cloak of, −rose, −table; *sub rosa* [*L.*], *en tapinois* [*F.*], in the background, aside, on the sly [*colloq.*], with bated breath, sotto voce, in a whisper, without beat of drum, *à la sourdine* [*F.*].

behind the veil; beyond -mortal ken, −the grave, −the veil; hid from mortal vision; into the -eternal secret, −realms supersensible, −supreme mystery.

confidentially etc. *adj.;* in−, in strict- confidence; between -ourselves, −you and me; *entre nous* [*F.*], *inter nos* [*L.*], under the seal of secrecy; *à couvert* [*F.*].

underhand, by stealth, like a thief in the night; stealthily etc. *adj.;* behind -the scenes, −the curtain, −one's back, −a screen etc. 530; incognito; *in camera* [*L.*].

529. Disclosure

n. **disclosure**; retection [*obs.*]; unveiling etc. *v.;* deterration [*obs.*], revealment, revelation; divulgement, divulgation [*rare*], divulgence, exposition, exposure, publication, *exposé* [*F.*], whole truth; telltale etc. (*news*) 532.

bursting of a bubble; *dénouement* [*F.*].

acknowledgment, avowance, avowal; confession, confessional; shrift.

narrator etc. 594; talebearer etc. 532.

v. **disclose**, discover, dismask [*obs.*]; draw−, draw aside−, lift−, raise−, lift up−, remove−, tear- the -veil, −curtain; unmask, unveil, unfold, uncover, unseal, unkennel; take off−, break- the seal; lay open, lay bare; expose; open, −up; bare, bring to light; evidence; make -clear, −evident, −manifest; evince.

raise−, drop−, lift−, remove−, throw off- the mask; expose; lay open; undeceive, unbeguile; disabuse, set right, correct, open the eyes of; *désillusionner* [*F.*].

divulge, reveal, break [*obs.*]; let into the secret; reveal the secrets of the prison house; tell etc. (*inform*) 527; rat [*slang*], squeal [*slang*]; breathe, utter, blab, peach [*slang*]; let -out, −fall, −drop, −slip, −the cat out of the bag [*colloq.*], come out with it [*colloq.*], come it [*slang*], betray; tell tales, −out of school; come out with; give vent to, give utterance to; open the lips, blurt out, vent, whisper about; speak out etc. (*make manifest*) 525; break the news; make public etc. 531; unriddle etc. (*find out*) 480a; split.

acknowledge, allow, concede, grant, admit, own, confess, avow, throw off all disguise, turn inside out, make a clean breast; show one's -hand, −cards; unburden−, disburden- one's mind, −conscience, −heart; open−, lay bare−, give one a piece of [*colloq.*]- one's mind; unbosom oneself, "own the soft impeachment" [Sheridan]; say−, speak- the truth; turn informer; turn -King's, −Queen's, −State's- evidence.

be disclosed etc.; transpire, come to light; come in sight etc. (*be visible*) 446; become known, escape the lips; come out, ooze out, creep out, leak out, peep out, crop out, crop forth, crop up; show its -face, –colors; discover etc. itself; break through the clouds, flash on the mind; come to one's ears etc. 527.

adj. **disclosed** etc. v.; revelative, revelatory, revelational, expository, confessional, confessionary, confessory.

int. out with it! 'fess up! [*slang*]; open up! [*colloq*].

530. Ambush
[means of concealment]

n. **ambush**, ambuscade; stalking-horse; lurking-hole, –place; secret path, back stairs; retreat etc. (*refuge*) 666.
hiding place, hidlings [*Scot. & dial. Eng.*]; secret -place, –drawer; recess, hole, cubbyhole, hidie-hole [*Scot.*], holes and corners; closet, crypt, adytum, abditory [*rare*], oubliette [*F.*]; safe, safe-deposit box, safety-deposit box.
screen, cover, shade, blinker; veil, curtain, blind, purdah [*India*], cloak, cloud.
mask, visor *or* vizor, vizard [*archaic*], disguise, masquerade dress, domino.
pitfall etc. (*source of danger*) 667; trap etc. (*snare*) 545.

v. **ambush**, ambuscade; lie in ambush etc. (*hide oneself*) 528; lie in wait for; set a trap for etc. (*deceive*) 545.

adv. aux aguets [*F.*]; januis clausis [*L.*] etc. 528.

531. Publication

n. **publication**; public announcement etc. 527; promulgation, propagation, proclamation, pronouncement, *pronunciamiento* [*Sp.*], pronunciamento, edict, encyclical; circulation, indiction [*rare*], edition, impression, imprint.
publicity, notoriety, currency, flagrancy, cry, hue and cry, *bruit* [*F.*]; bruit, oyez *or* oyes, *vox populi* [*L.*]; report etc. (*news*) 532; telegram, cable [*colloq.*] etc. 532; telegraphy; publisher etc. v.
the press, the Fourth Estate, public press, newspaper, tabloid, journal, gazette, daily, weekly, monthly, quarterly, annual; magazine.
advertisement, ad., placard, bill, flyer [*cant*], leaflet, handbill, *affiche* [*F.*], broadside, broadsheet, poster; circular, –letter; manifesto; notice etc. 527; program *or* programme.

v. **publish**; make -public, –known etc. (*information*) 527; speak of, talk of; broach, utter; put forward; circulate, propagate, promulgate; spread, –abroad; rumor, diffuse, disseminate, evulgate [*obs.*]; put–, give–, send- forth; emit, edit, get out; issue; bring–, lay–, drag- before the public; give -out, –to the world; report, cover [*newspaper cant*]; put–, bandy–, hawk–, buzz–, whisper–, bruit–, blaze- about; drag into the -open day, –limelight [*colloq.*], throw the spotlight on [*colloq.*]; voice, bruit.
proclaim, herald, blazon; blaze–, noise- abroad; sound a trumpet; trumpet–, thunder- forth; give tongue; announce with -beat of drum, –flourish of trumpets; proclaim -from the housetops, –at Charing Cross, –at the crossroads, –at the market cross.
raise a -cry, –hue and cry, -report; set news afloat.
telegraph, cable, wireless [*colloq.*], broadcast, telecast, televise, wire [*colloq.*].
advertise, placard; post, –up; *afficher* [*F.*], publish in the Gazette, send round the crier, cry abroad.
be published etc.; be *or* become public etc. *adj.*; come out; go–, fly–, buzz–, blow- about; get -about, –abroad, –afloat, –wind; find vent; see the light; go forth, take air, acquire currency, pass current; go the rounds, go the round of the newspapers, go through the length and breadth of the land; *virum volitare per ora* [*L.*]; pass from mouth to mouth; spread; run–, spread- like wildfire.

adj. **published** etc. v.; current etc. (*news*) 532; in circulation, public; notorious; flagrant, arrant; open etc. 525; trumpet-tongued; encyclic *or* encyclical, proclamatory, annunciatory, promulgatory; exoteric.
telegraphic, cabled, radiotelegraphic, telegraphed, wireless; radiophonic.

adv. **publicly** etc. *adj.*; in public, in open court, with open doors; in the -limelight, –spotlight [*both colloq.*]; for publication.

int. Oyez! Oyes! notice! flash!

532. News

n. **news**; information etc. 527; piece–, budget- of -news, –information; intelligence, tidings; beat *or* scoop [*newspaper cant*], story, copy [*cant*], print, letterpress.
fresh–, stirring–, old–, stale- news; glad tidings; old–, stale- story; chestnut [*slang*].
message, word, advice, aviso, dispatch *or* despatch; telegram, cable [*colloq.*], wire [*colloq.*], radio [*colloq.*], radiogram, wireless telegram, wireless [*colloq.*], marconigram, pneumatogram, communication, errand, embassy; bulletin; broadcast.
report, rumor, hearsay, on-dit, flying rumor, news stirring, cry, buzz, bruit, fame; talk,

533. Secret

ouï-dire [*F.*], scandal, eavesdropping; town–, table- -talk, –gossip; tittle-tattle; canard, topic of the day, idea afloat.

 narrator etc. (*describe*) 594; newsmonger, scandalmonger; busybody, talebearer, telltale, gossip, tattler, blab, babbler, tattletale, chatterer; informer, squealer [*slang*].

v. **transpire** etc. (*be disclosed*) 529; rumor etc. (*publish*) 531.

adj. **rumored**; publicly–, currently- -rumored, –reported; many-tongued; rife, current, floating, afloat, going about, in circulation, in every one's mouth, all over the town.

 having news value, newsy [*colloq.*], snappy [*slang*].

adv. **as they say**; as the story -goes, –runs; it is said.

 by telegraph, by cable, by radio [*colloq.*], by television, by wireless [*colloq.*].

533. Secret

n. **secret**; dead–, profound- secret; arcanum, mystery; latency etc. 526; Asian mystery; sealed book, secrets of the prison house; *le dessous des cartes* [*F.*].

 enigma, riddle, puzzle, nut to crack, conundrum, charade, rebus, logogriph; monogram, anagram, anagrammatism; Sphinx; *crux criticorum* [*L.*].

 maze, labyrinth, meander [*usually in pl.*], Hyrcynian wood; intricacy.

 problem etc. (*question*) 461; paradox etc. (*difficulty*) 704; unintelligibility etc. 519; *terra incognita* [*L.*] etc. (*ignorance*) 491.

adj. **secret** etc. (*concealed*) 528; involved etc. 248; labyrinthian, labyrinthine, labyrinthic *or* labyrinthical, mazy, meandrous.

 enigmatic *or* enigmatical, anagrammatic *or* anagrammatical, monogrammatic, logogriphic, cryptic *or* cryptical.

534. Messenger

n. **messenger**, angel, envoy, emissary, legate, delegate, nuncio, internuncio, intermediary, go-between; ambassador etc. (*diplomatist*) 758.

 Gabriel, Hermes, Mercury, Iris, Ariel.

 marshal, flag bearer, herald, crier, trumpeter, bellman, pursuivant, *parlementaire* [*F.*], apparitor.

 courier, runner, dak *or* dawk [*India*], estafette *or* estafet, commissionaire; errand boy, chore boy, newsboy.

 mail; post, post office; letter bag, mail bag; postman, mail-man, letter carrier; mail train, mail boat, mailer; aërial mail; carrier pigeon.

 telegraph, cable [*colloq.*], wire [*colloq.*], radiotelegraph, wireless telegraph, wireless [*colloq.*], radio [*colloq.*], television [*colloq.*].

 telephone, phone [*colloq.*], radio-telephone, radiophone, wireless telephone.

 reporter, newspaperman, journalist; gentleman–, representative- of the Press; penny-a-liner; hack writer, special–, war–, own- correspondent; spy, scout; informer etc. 527.

535. Affirmation

n. **affirmation**, affirmance, statement, allegation, assertion, predication, predicate [*logic*], declaration, word, averment; confirmation.

 asseveration, adjuration, swearing, oath, affidavit; deposition etc. (*record*) 551; avouchment, avouch [*rare*], assurance; protest, protestation; profession; acknowledgment etc. (*assent*) 488; legal pledge, pronouncement; solemn -averment, –avowal, –declaration.

 vote, voice; ballot, suffrage; *vox populi* [*L.*].

 remark, observation; position etc. (*proposition*) 514; saying, dictum, sentence, *ipse dixit* [*L.*].

 positiveness, emphasis, peremptoriness; dogmatism etc. (*certainty*) 474; weight.

 dogmatist etc. 887.

v. **assert**; make an assertion etc. *n.;* have one's say; say, affirm, predicate, declare, state; protest, profess; acknowledge etc. (*assent*) 488.

 put forth, put forward; advance, allege, propose, propound; announce etc. 527; enunciate, broach, set forth, hold out, maintain, contend, pronounce, pretend.

 depose, depone, aver, avow, avouch, asseverate, swear, rap [*archaic slang*], affirm; make–, take one's- oath; make–, swear–, put in- an affidavit; take one's Bible oath, kiss the book, vow, *vitam impendere vero* [*L.*]; swear till -one is black in the face, –all's blue [*both colloq.*]; be sworn, call Heaven to witness; vouch, warrant, certify, assure; swear by bell, book, and candle; attest etc. (*evidence*) 467; adjure etc. (*put to one's oath*) 768.

 emphasize; swear by etc. (*believe*) 484; insist upon, take one's stand upon; lay stress on; assert -roundly, –positively; lay down, –the law; raise one's voice, dogmatize, have the last word; rap out; repeat; reassert, reaffirm.

adj. **affirmative**; asserting etc. *v.;* declaratory, predicatory, predicative, predicational, pronunciatory, pronunciative, *soi-disant* [*F.*]; positive; unmistakable, clear; certain etc. 474; express, explicit etc. (*patent*) 525; absolute, emphatic, flat, broad, round, pointed, marked, distinct, decided, assertive, insistent, confident, trenchant, dogmatic, definitive, formal, solemn, categorical, peremptory; unretracted.

predicable, affirmable, attributable.

adv. **affirmatively** etc. *adj.;* in the affirmative.

with emphasis, ex-cathedra, without fear of contradiction.

I must say, indeed, i' faith, let me tell you, why, give me leave to say, marry [*archaic*], you may be sure, I'd have you know; upon my -word, –honor; by my troth, egad [*euphemism*], I assure you; by jingo, by Jove, by George etc. [*all colloq.*]; troth, seriously, sadly [*obs.*]; in –, in sober- -sadness, –truth, –earnest; of a truth, truly, pardie *or* perdy [*archaic*]; in all conscience, upon oath; be assured etc. (*belief*) 484; yes etc. (*assent*) 488; I'll -warrant, –warrant you, –engage, –answer for it, –be bound, –venture to say, –take my oath; in fact, forsooth, joking -aside, –apart; in all -soberness, –seriousness; so help me God; not to mince the matter.

536. Negation

n. **negation**, abnegation; denial; disavowal, disclaimer; abjuration; contradiction, contravention; recusation, protest; recusancy etc. (*dissent*) 489; flat-, emphatic- -contradiction, –denial; *démenti* [*F.*].

qualification etc. 469; repudiation etc. 610; recantation, revocation; retractation etc. 607; rebuttal; confutation etc. 479; refusal etc. 764; prohibition etc. 761.

v. **deny**; contradict, contravene; controvert, give denial to, gainsay, negative, shake the head; take the Fifth [*slang*].

deny -flatly, –peremptorily, –emphatically, –absolutely, –wholly, –entirely; give the lie to, belie.

disclaim, disown, disaffirm, disavow, abjure, forswear, abnegate, renounce; recant etc. 607; revoke etc. (*abrogate*) 756.

dispute, impugn, traverse, rebut, join issue upon; bring *or* call in question etc. (*doubt*) 485; give (one) the lie in his throat.

repudiate etc. 610; set aside, ignore etc. 460; rebut etc. (*confute*) 479; qualify etc. 469; refuse etc. 764.

adj. **denying** etc. *v.;* denied etc. *v.;* revocatory, abjuratory, abnegative [*rare*], contradictory; negative, negatory; recusant etc. (*dissenting*) 489; at issue upon.

adv. **no**, nay, not, nowise, no way [*colloq.*], noways; not a -bit, –whit, –jot; not at all, not in the least, not so; no such thing; nothing of the -kind, –sort; quite the contrary, *tout au contraire* [*F.*], far from it; *tant s'en faut* [*F.*]; on no account, in no respect; by no means, by no manner of means; negatively.

537. Teaching

n. **teaching** etc. *v.;* pedagogics, pedagogy; instruction; edification; education; tuition; tutorship, tutorage, tutelage; direction, guidance; opsimathy [*rare*].

preparation, qualification, training, schooling etc. *v.;* discipline; exercise, exercitation, drill, practice.

persuasion, proselytism, propagandism, propaganda; indoctrination, inculcation, inoculation, initiation.

lesson, lecture, sermon, homily, harangue, disquisition; apologue, parable; discourse, prelection, preachment; explanation etc. (*interpretation*) 522; chalk talk [*colloq.*].

Chautauqua -system, –course; lyceum.

exercise, task; curriculum; course, –of study; grammar, three R's; A. B. C. etc. (*beginning*) 66.

[education] elementary–, primary–, grammar school–, common school–, high school–, secondary–, technical–, college–, collegiate–, military–, university–, liberal–, classical–, academic–, religious–, denominational–, moral–, secular- education; propaedeutics, moral tuition; the humanities, humanism, humane studies.

normal–, kindergarten- -course, –training; vocational -training, –therapeutics; Montessori system.

physical education, physical drill, gymnastics, calisthenics, eurythmics *or* eurhythmics; sloyd.

v. **teach**, instruct, edify, school, tutor; cram [*colloq.*], grind [*colloq.*], prime, coach; enlighten etc. (*inform*) 527.

inculcate, indoctrinate, inoculate, infuse, instill, infix, ingraft *or* engraft, infiltrate; imbue, impregnate, implant; graft, sow the seeds of, disseminate, propagate.

give an idea of; put up to [*slang*]; put in the way of; set right.

sharpen the wits, enlarge the mind; give new ideas, open the eyes, bring forward, "teach the young idea how to shoot" [Thomson]; improve etc. 658.

direct, guide; direct attention to etc. (*attention*) 457; impress upon the -mind, –memory; beat into, –the head; convince etc. (*belief*) 484.

538. Misteaching

expound etc. (*interpret*) 522; lecture; read–, give- a -lesson, –lecture, –sermon, –discourse; incept [*Cambridge Univ., Eng.*]; hold forth, preach; prelect, sermonize, moralize; point a moral.

train, discipline; bring up, –to; educate, form, ground, prepare, qualify, drill, exercise, practice, habituate, familiarize with, nurture, dry-nurse, breed, rear, take in hand; break, –in; tame; preinstruct; initiate, graduate; inure etc. (*habituate*) 613.

put to nurse, send to school.

adj. **educational**; scholastic, academic, doctrinal; disciplinal, disciplinary, instructive, instructional, hortatory, homiletic *or* homiletical, pedagogic *or* pedagogical, didactic; teaching etc. *v.;* taught etc. *v.;* propaedeutic *or* propaedeutical; propagative; cultural, humanistic, humane; pragmatic *or* pragmatical, practical, utilitarian; naturalistic, psychological, scientific, sociological, eclectic, coeducational.

538. Misteaching

n. **misteaching**, misinformation, misintelligence, misguidance, misdirection, mispersuasion [*archaic*], misinstruction, misleading etc. *v.;* perversion; false–, dangerous- teaching; sophistry etc. 477; college of Laputa; the blind leading the blind.

v. **misinform**, misteach, misdescribe, misdirect, misguide, misinstruct, miscorrect; pervert; put on a false–, throw off the- scent; deceive etc. 545; mislead etc. (*error*) 495; misrepresent; lie etc. 544; *spargere voces in vulgum ambiguas* [*Virgil*], preach to the wise, teach one's grandmother to suck eggs [*colloq.*].

render unintelligible etc. 519; bewilder etc. (*uncertainty*) 475; mystify etc. (*conceal*) 528; unteach [*archaic*].

adj. **misteaching** etc. *v.;* unedifying.

539. Learning

n. **learning**; acquisition of -knowledge etc. 490, –skill etc. 698; acquirement, attainment; mental cultivation, edification, scholarship, erudition; acquired knowledge, lore; wide–, general- information; wide reading; self-instruction; study, grind [*colloq.*], reading, perusal; inquiry etc. 461.

docility etc. (*willingness*) 602; aptitude etc. 698.

apprenticeship, prenticeship [*obs. or colloq.*], pupilage, tutelage, novitiate.

examination, matriculation; responsions *or* smalls [*Oxford Univ.*], previous examination *or* little go [*Cambridge Univ., Eng.*], moderations *or* mods. [*Oxford Univ.*], final examination, finals, greats [*Oxford Univ.*], great go, tripos [*both Cambridge Univ., Eng.*].

translation, crib [*student cant*]; pony, trot, horse [*all student slang*].

v. **learn**; acquire–, gain–, receive–, take in–, drink in–, imbibe–, pick up–, gather–, get–, obtain–, collect–, glean- -knowledge, -information, -learning.

acquaint oneself with, master; make oneself -master of, -acquainted with; grind [*college slang*], cram *or* cram up [*colloq.*], get up, coach up [*colloq.*]; learn by -heart, -rote.

read, spell, peruse; con; run–, pore–, thumb- over; wade through, run through, plunge into, dip into; glance–, run the eye- -over, –through; turn over the leaves.

study; be studious etc. *adj.;* consume–, burn- -the midnight oil; mind one's book, bury oneself in.

go to -school, -college, -the university; serve an (*or* one's) apprenticeship, serve one's time; learn one's trade; be informed etc. 527; be taught etc. 537.

adj. **studious**; industrious etc. 682; scholastic, scholarly, well read, widely read, well posted [*colloq.*], erudite, learned; full of -information, –learning, –lore.

teachable; docile etc. (*willing*) 602; apt etc. 698.

adv. at one's books; *in statu pupillari* [*L.*] etc. (*learner*) 541.

540. Teacher

n. **teacher**, trainer, perceptor, instructor, institutor [*obs.*], master, tutor, director, coryphaeus [*Oxford Univ.*], dry nurse [*slang*], coach [*colloq.*], crammer [*colloq.*], grinder [*college slang, Eng.*], don [*Univ. cant*]; governor [*obs.*], bear leader [*humorous*]; governess, duenna; disciplinarian.

professor, lecturer, reader, prelector *or* praelector, prolocutor, preacher; chalk talker, *khoja* [*Turk.*], munshi *or* moonshee [*Moham.*]; pastor etc. (*clergy*) 996; schoolmaster, dominie, usher [*Brit.*], pedagogue, abecedarian; schoolmistress, dame [*rare*], kindergartner, monitor, pupil teacher.

guide; docent, coach, expositor etc. 524; guru [*Hindu*]; mentor etc. (*adviser*) 695; pioneer, apostle, missionary, propagandist; example etc. 22.

professorship etc. (*school*) 542.
tutelage etc. (*teaching*) 537.

adj. **pedagogic** or pedagogical, preceptorial, tutorial, professorial; scholastic etc. 537.

541. Learner

n. **learner**, scholar, student, alumnus (*fem.* alumna, *pl.* alumni), *élève* [*F.*], pupil, schoolboy, schoolgirl; questionist, questioner, inquirer; monitor, prefect; beginner, tyro, abecedarian, alphabetarian.
undergraduate, undergrad. [*colloq.*], freshman, fresh *or* freshie *or* frosh [*slang*], plebe [*West Point cant*], sophomore, soph [*colloq.*], junior, senior; commoner; pensioner, sizar [*both Cambridge Univ., Eng.*]; exhibitioner, scholar [*winner of a scholarship*], fellow commoner [*Eng. Univ.*], demy [*Magdalene Coll., Oxford*]; junior, sophister *or* soph, senior sophister *or* soph, sophister, questionist [*all Eng. Univ.*].
graduate student, post-graduate student, post-doctoral fellow.
class, form, grade, room; promotion, graduation, remove; pupilage etc. (*learning*) 539.
disciple, chela [*India*], follower, apostle, proselyte.
fellow student, *condiscipulus* [*L.*], condisciple, classmate, schoolmate, schoolfellow, fellow pupil.
novice, recruit, tenderfoot [*slang*], neophyte, inceptor, *débutant* [*F.*], catechumen, probationer; apprentice, prentice [*obs. or colloq.*], articled clerk.
adj. in statu pupillari [*L.*], in leading strings, pupillary, monitorial; abecedarian, rudimentary; probationary, probatory, probational; sophomoric *or* sophomoral.

542. School

n. **school**, academy, lyceum, *Gymnasium* [*Ger.*], *lycée* [*F.*], palaestra *or* palestra, seminary, college, educational institution, institute; university, 'varsity [*colloq.*], Alma Mater [*L.*].
[general] day-, boarding-, preparatory *or* prep [*colloq.*], -, elementary-, common-, denominational-, secondary-, endowed-, free-, continuation-, convent-, art-, music-, military-, naval-, technical-, library-, secretarial-, business-, correspondence- school; kindergarten, nursery, day nursery, nursery school, *crèche* [*F.*]; Sunday-, Sabbath-, Bible- school; reform school, reformatory; teachers' training college; university extension -lectures, -course.
[british] primary-, infant-, dame [*hist.*]-, voluntary-, government-, Board-, higher grade-, National-, mission-, missionary-, British and Foreign-, state-aided-, grant-in-aid-, middle-class-, County Council-, training-, normal-, grammar-, collegiate-, high-, upper-, modern-, lower-, County-, County high-, Cathedral-, municipal secondary-, municipal technical-, Friends'-, coeducational *or* dual-, Polytechnic-, King Henry VIII's-, King Edward's-, Queen Elizabeth's-, Queen Mary's-, merchant guild-, Blue-Coat- school; Christ's Hospital; public school (*as* Eton, Harrow, Rugby etc.); school of art, school of arts and crafts, trade school; Royal Naval College, Royal Military Academy (Woolwich), Royal Military College (Sandhurst); training ship for -royal navy, -mercantile marine; College of Preceptors; Royal Academy-, London College-, Trinity College- of Music; Royal College of Organists.
[united states] district-, grade-, parochial-, public-, primary-, grammar-, junior high-, high-, Latin- school; private-, technological-, normal-, kindergarten training- school; summer school; military academy (West Point); naval academy (Annapolis); college, freshwater college [*slang*], jerk water college [*slang*], State university; graduate school, post-graduate school.
class, division, form etc. 541; seminar *or* seminary.
class room, room, school room, recitation room, lecture room, lecture hall, theater *or* theatre, amphitheater *or* amphitheatre.
desk, reading desk, ambo, pulpit, forum, stage, rostrum, platform, hustings, tribune.
schoolbook, textbook, hornbook; grammar, primer, abecedary [*rare*], abecedarium, New England Primer, rudiments, manual, *vade mecum* [*L.*]; encyclopedia *or* encyclopaedia; cyclopedia *or* cyclopaedia; Lindley Murray, Cocker; dictionary, lexicon, thesaurus.
professorship, associate professorship, lectureship, readership, fellowship, preceptorship, tutorship, instructorship; chair.
directorate, board, syndicate; College Board, Board of Regents (N. Y.), School Board, Council of Education; Board of Education; Board-, Prefect- of Studies; Textbook Committee; propaganda.
adj. **scholastic**, academic, collegiate; educational, palaestral *or* palestral, cultural; gymnastic, athletic, physical, eurythmic.
adv. ex-cathedra.

543. Veracity

- *n.* **veracity**; truthfulness, frankness etc. *adj.*; truth, soothfastness [*archaic*], smooth [*archaic*], veridicality, sincerity, candor, honesty, fidelity; plain dealing, *bona fides* [*L.*]; love of truth; probity etc. 939; ingenuousness etc. (*artlessness*) 703.

  the truth the whole truth and nothing but the truth; honest–, unvarnished–, sober- truth etc. (*fact*) 494; unvarnished tale; light of truth.

- *v.* **speak the truth**, tell the truth; speak on oath; speak without -equivocation, –mental reservation; speak by the card; paint in its–, show oneself in one's- true colors; make a clean breast, let it all hang out [*slang*] etc. (*disclose*) 529; speak one's mind etc. (*be blunt*) 703; not lie etc. 544, not deceive etc. 545.

- *adj.* **truthful**, true; veracious, veridical; scrupulous etc. (*honorable*) 939; sincere, candid, frank, open, straightforward, unreserved; open–, frank–, true–, simple- hearted; soothfast [*archaic*], truth-telling, honest, trustworthy; undissembling etc. (dissemble etc. 544); guileless, pure; truth-loving; unperjured; true-blue, as good as one's word; one's word one's bond; unaffected, unfeigned, *bona fide* [*L.*]; outspoken, ingenuous etc. (*artless*) 703; undisguised etc. (*real*) 494.

- *adv.* **truly** etc. (*really*) 494; in plain words etc. 703; in–, with–, of a–, in good- truth; as the dial to the sun, as the needle to the pole; honor bright [*colloq.*]; troth; in good -sooth, –earnest; soothfast [*archaic*], unfeignedly, with no nonsense, in sooth, sooth to say, *bona fide* [*L.*], *in foro conscientiae* [*L.*]; without equivocation; *cartes sur table* [*F.*], from the bottom of one's heart; by my troth etc. (*affirmation*) 535.

544. Falsehood

- *n.* **falsehood**, falseness; falsity, falsification; deception etc. 545; untruthfulness; untruth etc. 546; guile; lying etc. *v.*, misrepresentation; mendacity, perjury, false swearing; forgery, invention, fabrication; subreption; covin [*archaic*].

  perversion–, suppression- of truth; *suppressio veri* [*L.*]; perversion, distortion, false coloring; exaggeration etc. 549; prevarication, equivocation, shuffling, fencing, evasion, fraud; *suggestio falsi* [*L.*] etc. (*lie*) 546; mystification etc. (*concealment*) 528; simulation etc. (*imitation*) 19; dissimulation, dissembling; deceit; *blague* [*F.*].

  sham, pretense, scam [*slang*], pretending, malingering.

duplicity, double dealing, insincerity, tartufism *or* tartuffism, hypocrisy, cant, humbug, fake [*slang*]; casuistry, jesuitism, jesuitry; pharisaism; Machiavelism, "organized hypocrisy"; lip -homage, –service; mouth honor; hollowness; mere -show, –outside; crocodile tears, mealy-mouthedness, quackery; charlatanism, charlatanry; gammon [*Eng. colloq.*], buncombe *or* bunkum *or* bunk, flam: bam [*slang*], flimflam, cajolery, flattery; Judas kiss; perfidy etc. (*bad faith*) 940; *il volto sciolto i pensieri stretti* [*It.*].

unfairness etc. (*dishonesty*) 940; artfulness etc. (*cunning*) 702; misstatement etc. (*error*) 495.

- *v.* **be false** etc. *adj.*, be a liar etc. 548; speak falsely etc. *adv.*; tell a lie etc. 546; lie, fib; lie like a trooper; swear falsely, forswear, perjure oneself, bear false witness.

  falsify, misstate, misquote, miscite, misreport, misrepresent; belie, pervert, distort; put a false construction upon etc. (*misinterpret*) 523.

  prevaricate, equivocate, quibble; palter, –to the understanding; *répondre en Normand* [*F.*]; trim, shuffle, fence, mince the truth, beat about the bush, blow hot and cold [*colloq.*], play fast and loose.

  garble, gloss over, disguise, give a color to; give–, put- a -gloss, –false coloring- upon; color, varnish, cook [*colloq.*], doctor [*colloq.*], dress up, embroider; exaggerate etc. 549; *blague* [*F.*].

  fabricate, invent, trump up, get up; forge, fake [*slang*], hatch, concoct; romance etc. (*imagine*) 515; cry "wolf!"

  dissemble, dissimulate; feign, assume, put on, pretend, make believe; act the old soldier [*colloq.*], play possum; play -false, –a double game; coquet; act–, play- a part; affect etc. 855; simulate, pass off for; counterfeit, sham, make a show of; malinger; say the grapes are sour.

  cant [*dial. Eng.*], play the hypocrite, sham Abram *or* Abraham, *faire pattes de velours* [*F.*], put on the mask, clean the outside of the platter, lie like a thief, lie through one's teeth; hand out–, hold out–, sail under- false colors; "commend the poisoned chalice to the lips" [*Macbeth*]; *spargere voces in vulgum ambiguas* [*Virgil*]; deceive etc. 545.

- *adj.* **false**, deceitful, mendacious, unveracious, fraudulent, dishonest; faithless, truthless, untruthful, trothless [*archaic*]; unfair, uncandid; hollow-hearted; evasive; uningenuous, disingenuous; hollow, insincere, *Parthis mendacior* [*L.*]; forsworn.

545. Deception

collusive, collusory [*obs.*]; artful etc. (*cunning*) 702; perfidious etc. 940; spurious etc. (*deceptive*) 545; untrue etc. 546; falsified etc. *v.*; covinous.

hypocritical, canting, jesuitical, pharisaical; tartufish *or* tartuffish; Machiavellic, Machiavellian *or* Machiavelian; double, –tongued, –handed, –minded, –hearted, –dealing; two-faced, double-faced; Janus-faced; smooth-faced, –spoken, –tongued; plausible; mealy-mouthed; affected etc. 855.

adv. **falsely** etc. *adj.*; *à la Tartufe* [*F.*], with a double tongue; slily etc. (*cunning*) 702.

545. Deception

n. **deception**; falseness etc. 544; untruth etc. 546; imposition, imposture; fraud, deceit, guile; fraudulence, fraudulency; covin [*archaic*]; knavery etc. (*cunning*) 702; misrepresentation etc. (*falsehood*) 544; bluff; straw-bail, straw-bid; spoof [*slang*]; hocus-pocus, *escamoterie* [*F.*], jockeyship; trickery, coggery [*obs.*], pettifoggery, sharp practice, chicanery; *supercherie* [*F.*], cozenage, circumvention, ingannation [*obs.*], collusiveness, collusion; treachery etc. 940; practical joke.

delusion, gullery [*archaic*]; juggling, jugglery; sleight of hand, legerdemain; prestigiation [*obs.*], prestidigitation; magic etc. 992; conjuring, conjuration.

trick, cheat, wile, blind, feint, plant [*slang*], bubble, fetch, catch [*dial.*], chicane, artifice, reach [*obs.*], bite [*obs., colloq.*], juggle, hocus [*archaic*]; thimble-rig, card sharping, artful dodge, swindle; tricks upon travelers; trapan *or* trepan [*archaic*]; stratagem etc. (*artifice*) 702; fake [*colloq. or slang*], hoax; theft etc. 791; ballot-box stuffing, barney [*slang*], bunko *or* bunco, bunko game; confidence -trick, –game; brace–, drop–, gum–, panel–, shell–, skin– game [*all slang*]; gold brick [*colloq.*].

snare, trap, pitfall, Cornish hug, decoy, gin; springe, springle [*obs.*]; noose, hook; bait, decoy duck, stool pigeon, tub to the whale, baited trap, *guet-apens* [*F.*]; cobweb, net, meshes, toils, mouse trap, birdlime; Dionaea, Venus's flytrap; ambush etc. 530; trapdoor, sliding panel, false bottom; spring net, spring gun; mask, masked battery; mine; flytrap; green goods; panel house.

disguise, disguisement; false colors, masquerade, mummery, borrowed plumes; wolf in sheep's clothing etc. (*deceiver*) 548; *pattes de velours* [*F.*].

sham; mockery etc. (*imitation*) 19; copy etc. 21; counterfeit, make-believe, forgery, fraud; lie etc. 546; "a delusion, a mockery, and a snare" [Denman], hollow mockery; whited–, painted-sepulcher; jerry-building, jerryism [*builders' cant*]; man of straw.

tinsel, paste, false jewelry, scagliola, ormolu, mosaic gold, brummagem, German silver, albata, paktong, white metal, Britannia metal, paint.

illusion etc. (*error*) 495; *ignis fatuus* [*L.*] etc. 423; mirage etc. 443.

v. **deceive**, take in, Machiavellize; defraud, cheat, jockey, do [*slang*], *escamoter* [*F.*], cozen, diddle [*dial.*], nab [*slang*], chouse [*colloq.*], bite [*colloq.*], play one false, bilk, cully, jilt [*obs.*], pluck [*rare*], swindle, victimize; abuse; mystify; blind, –one's eyes; blindfold, hoodwink; throw dust into the eyes, "keep the word of promise to the ear and break it to the hope" [*Macbeth*].

impose–, practice–, play–, put–, palm–, foist- upon; snatch a verdict; bluff, –off; bunko *or* bunco, four-flush [*slang*]; gum [*slang*], spoof [*slang*], stuff (a ballot box) [*U. S.*].

circumvent, overreach; outreach, outwit, outmaneuver *or* outmanoeuvre, steal a march upon, give the go-by to [*slang*], leave in the lurch.

insnare, ensnare; set–, lay- a -trap, –snare- for; bait the hook, forelay [*obs.*], spread the toils, lime; decoy, waylay, lure, beguile, delude, inveigle; trapan *or* trepan [*archaic*]; kidnap; let in, hook in; trick; entrap *or* intrap, nick, springe [*rare*], nousel *or* nousle [*obs.*]; blind a trail, enmesh *or* immesh; shanghai, crimp; catch, –in a trap; sniggle, entangle, illaqueate [*rare*], balk, trip up; throw a tub to a whale, hocus.

fool, befool, practice on one's credulity, dupe, gull, hoax, bamboozle [*colloq.*]; hum [*slang or colloq.*], humbug, gammon [*Eng. colloq.*], stuff up [*slang*], stuff [*slang*], sell [*slang*]; play a -trick, –practical joke- upon one; fool to the top of one's bent, send on a fool's errand; make -game, –a fool, –an April fool, –an ass- of; trifle with, cajole, flatter; come over etc. (*influence*) 615; gild the pill, make things pleasant, divert, put a good face upon; dissemble etc. 544.

live by one's wits; cog [*rare*], cog the dice; play at hide and seek; obtain money under false pretenses etc. (*steal*) 791; conjure, juggle, practice chicanery; deacon; jerry-build; pass by trickery, play off, palm off, foist off, fob off [*archaic*].

546. Untruth

mislead etc. (*error*) 495; lie etc. 544; misinform etc. 538; betray etc. 940.
be deceived etc. 547.

adj. **deceptive**, deceptious [*rare*], deceitful, covinous [*law*]; delusive, delusory; illusive, illusory; deceived etc. *v.;* deceiving etc. *v.;* cunning etc. 702; prestigious [*obs.*], prestigiatory [*obs.*]; elusive, insidious, *ad captandum vulgus* [*L.*].

make-believe; untrue etc. 546; mock, sham, counterfeit, snide [*slang*], pseudo, spurious, so-called, pretended, feigned, trumped-up, bogus [*colloq.*], scamped, fraudulent, tricky, factitious, artificial, bastard; surreptitious, illegitimate, contraband, adulterated, sophisticated; unsound, rotten at the core; colorable; disguised; meretricious; jerry-built, jerry [*builders' cant*]; tinsel, pinchbeck, plated; catchpenny; brummagem; simulated etc. 544.

adv. under -false colors, -the garb of, -cover of; over the left [*slang*].

546. Untruth

n. **untruth**, falsehood, lie, story, thing that is not, fib, bounce, crammer [*slang*], tarradiddle *or* taradiddle [*colloq.*], whopper *or* whapper [*colloq.*], *jhuth* [*Hind.*].

fabrication, forgery, invention; misstatement, misrepresentation, perversion, falsification, gloss, *suggestio falsi* [*L.*]; exaggeration etc. 549.

fiction; fable, nursery tale; romance etc. (*imagination*) 515; absurd-, untrue-, false-, trumped up- -story, -statement; thing devised by the enemy; canard; shave [*slang, Eng.*], sell [*colloq.*], hum, [*slang*], whopper [*colloq.*], yarn [*colloq.*], fish story [*colloq.*], tall tale, traveler's tale, Canterbury tale, cock-and-bull story, fairy tale, fake, press-agent's yarn [*colloq.*], hot air [*slang*], claptrap.

myth, moonshine, bosh [*colloq.*], all my eye and Betty Martin [*colloq.*], all my eye [*colloq.*], mare's-nest, farce.

half truth, white lie, pious fraud; mental reservation etc. (*concealment*) 528; irony.

pretense, pretext; false plea etc. 617; subterfuge, evasion, shift, shuffle, make-believe; sham etc. (*deception*) 545; profession, empty words; Judas kiss etc. (*hypocrisy*) 544; disguise etc. (*mask*) 530.

v. **ring untrue**; have a -false meaning, -hidden meaning, -false appearance; be an untruth etc. *n.;* lie etc. 544.

feign, pretend, sham, counterfeit, gammon [*Eng. colloq.*], make-believe.

adj. **untrue**, false, trumped up; void of-, without-foundation; fictive, far from the truth, false as dicer's oaths; unfounded, *ben trovato* [*It.*], invented, fabulous, fabricated, fraudulent, forged; fictitious, factitious, supposititious, surreptitious; illusory, elusory; evasive, satiric *or* satirical, ironical; *soi-disant* [*F.*] etc. (*misnamed*) 565.

547. Dupe

n. **dupe**, gull, gudgeon, *gobemouche* [*F.*], cully, victim, April fool; jay, sucker, pigeon, cull [*all slang*]; laughingstock etc. 857; simple Simon, flat [*colloq.*], greenhorn; fool etc. 501; puppet, cat's-paw.

v. **be deceived** etc. 545, be the dupe of; fall into a trap; swallow-, nibble at- the bait; bite; catch a Tartar.

adj. **credulous** etc. 486.
mistaken etc. (*error*) 495.

548. Deceiver

n. **deceiver** etc. (deceive etc. 545); dissembler, hypocrite; sophist, Pharisee, Jesuit, Mawworm, Pecksniff, Joseph Surface, Tartufe *or* Tartuffe, Janus; serpent, snake in the grass, cockatrice, Judas, wolf in sheep's clothing; jilt; shuffler.

liar etc. (*lie* etc. 544); Tom Pepper, Machiavel, Machiavelist; story-teller, perjurer, false witness, *menteur à triple étage* [*F.*], Scapin; bunko artist, bunko steerer, carpetbagger, capper [*all slang, U. S.*], faker [*slang*], fraud, four-flusher [*slang*], confidence man, grifter, horse coper [*Eng.*], ringer [*slang*], spieler [*colloq.*]; straw bidder; crimp; decoy duck, stool pigeon; rogue, knave, cheat; swindler etc. (*thief*) 792; jobber, gypsy.

impostor, pretender, malingerer, humbug; adventurer, adventuress; Cagliostro, Fernam Mendex Pinto; ass in lion's skin etc. (*bungler*) 701; actor etc. (*stage player*) 599.

quack, charlatan, mountebank, saltimbanco [*obs.*], saltimbanque [*F.*], blagueur [*F.*], empiric, quacksalver [*now rare*], medicaster.

conjuror, juggler, trickster, prestidigitator, necromancer, sorcerer, magician, wizard, mage [*archaic*], medicine man, shaman.

549. Exaggeration

n. **exaggeration**; expansion etc. 194; hyperbole, stretch, strain, coloring; high coloring, caricature, *caricatura* [*It.*]; extravagance etc. (*nonsense*) 497; Baron Munchausen; Munchausenism; men in buckram, big one, yarn [*colloq.*], fringe, embroidery, tall tale, traveler's tale; fish story [*colloq.*], gooseberry [*slang*].

storm-, tempest- in a teacup; much ado about nothing etc. (*overestimation*) 482; puffery etc. (*boasting*) 884; rant etc. (*turgescence*) 577.

false coloring etc. (*falsehood*) 544; aggravation etc. 835.

figure of speech, *façon de parler* [*F.*]; stretch of -fancy, -the imagination; flight of fancy etc. (*imagination*) 515.

v. **exaggerate**, magnify, pile up, aggravate; amplify etc. (*expand*) 194; optimize; overestimate etc. 482; hyperbolize; overcharge, overstate, overdraw, overlay, overshoot the mark, overpraise; make much of, make the most of; strain, -a point; stretch, -a point; go great lengths; spin a long yarn [*colloq.*]; draw-, pull-, use-, shoot with- a (*or* the) longbow [*colloq.*]; deal in the marvelous.

out-Herod Herod, run riot, talk at random.

overcolor, heighten; color -highly, -too highly; *broder* [*F.*], embroider, be flowery; flourish; color etc. (*misrepresent*) 544; puff etc. (*boast*) 884.

underrate, pessimize, underestimate etc. 483.

adj. **exaggerated** etc. *v.;* overwrought; bombastic etc. (*magniloquent*) 577; hyperbolical, on stilts; fabulous, extravagant, preposterous, egregious, *outré* [*F.*], highflying.

Section 3. Means of Communication

550. Indication

n. **indication**; symbolism, symbolization; symptomatology, semeiology *or* semiology, semeiotics *or* semiotics, pathognomy; *Zeitgeist* [*Ger.*], sign of the times.

means of recognition; lineament, feature, trait, trick, earmark, characteristic, diagnostic; divining rod; cloven hoof; footfall.

sign, symbol; index, indice [*obs.*], indicator, point, pointer; exponent, note, token, symptom; dollar mark; type, figure, emblem, cipher, device; representation etc. 554.

motto, epigraph, epitaph, posy [*archaic*].

gesture, gesticulation; pantomime; wink, glance, leer; nod, shrug, beck; touch, cudge; grip, freemasonry; telegraphy, byplay, dumb show; cue; hint etc. 527.

track, spoor, trail, footprint, scent; clew *or* clue, key.

dactylology, dactylography, dactylonomy, dactyliomancy, chirology [*rare*], chiromancy, palmistry; finger print, Bertillon system.

signal, signal post, rocket, blue light, red light; watch fire, watchtower; telegraph, semaphore, flagstaff; fiery cross; calumet, peace pipe; heliograph; guidon; headlight, searchlight, flashlight, spotlight.

mark, line, stroke, score, stripe, streak, scratch, tick, dot, point, notch, nick, blaze; red letter, sublineation, underlining, jotting; print; imprint, impress, impression; note, annotation.

[map drawing] hachure, contour line; isobar, isopiestic line, isobaric line; isotherm, isothermal line; latitude, longitude, meridian, equator.

[typography] dash, hyphen, parentheses, brackets *or* crotchets, apostrophe, question mark, exclamation *or* exclamation point; acute-, grave- accent; long *or* macron, short *or* breve, dieresis, caret, brace, ellipsis, leaders, asterisk, dagger *or* obelisk, double dagger, section, parallels, paragraph, index, asterism, cedilla, guillemets [*rare*], quotation marks *or* quotes [*colloq.*], tilde, circumflex.

[for identification] badge, criterion; countercheck, countermark, countersign, counterfoil, stub, duplicate, tally; label, ticket, billet, letter, counter, check, chip, chop [*Oriental*], dib [*slang*]; broad arrow; government mark; totem; tessera, card, bill; witness, voucher; stamp; *cachet* [*F.*]; trade-, hall- mark; signature; address-, visiting- card; *carte de visite* [*F.*]; credentials etc. (*evidence*) 467; attestation; hand, handwriting, sign manual; cipher; monogram; seal, sigil, signet; autograph, autography; finger print; paraph, brand; superscription; indorsement *or* endorsement; title, heading, docket; tonsure, scalp lock; mortar board [*colloq.*], cap and gown, hood; caste mark; *mot de passe* [*F.*], *mot du guet* [*F.*]; passeparole *or* passparole [*obs.*], shibboleth; watchword, catchword, password; sign, countersign, pass, dueguard, grip; open-sesame; timbrology [*rare*].

insignia; banner, banneret; banderole, bandrol *or* bannerol; flag, colors, streamer, standard, eagle, vexillum, labarum, oriflamme *or* oriflamb; figurehead; ensign; pennant, whip *or* coach-whip, pennon, burgee, blue peter, jack, ancient [*rare*], gonfalon, union jack; "Old Glory" [*colloq.*], quarantine flag; yellow flag, yellow jack; tricolor, *drapeau tricolore* [*F.*], stars and stripes; stars and bars; half-masted flag, union down; red flag; bunting.

551. Record

heraldry, crest; arms, coat of arms; armorial bearings, hatchment; escutcheon *or* scutcheon, achievement, shield, supporters; livery, uniform; cockade, brassard, epaulet, chevron; garland, chaplet, fillet [*antiq.*], love knot, favor.

[of locality] beacon, beacon fire, cresset, cairn, post, staff, flagstaff, hand, pointer, vane, cock, weathercock, weathervane; guide–, hand–, finger–, directing–, sign- post; pillars of Hercules, pharos; balefire, signal fire; *l'Etoile du Nord* [*F.*], North Star, polestar, Polaris; landmark, seamark; lighthouse, balize [*rare*], lodestar *or* loadstar; cynosure, guide; address, direction, name; sign, signboard.

[of the future] warning etc. 668; omen etc. 512; prefigurement etc. 511.

[of the past] trace, record etc. 551.

[of danger] warning etc. 668; fire alarm, burglar alarm; alarm etc. 669.

[of authority] scepter etc. 747.

[of triumph] trophy etc. 733.

[of quantity] gauge etc. 466.

[of distance] milestone, milepost; mileage ticket; milliary [*Rom. antiq.*].

[of disgrace] brand, fool's cap, mark of Cain, stigma, stripes, broad arrow.

[for detection] check, time clock, telltale; test etc. (*experiment*) 463.

notification etc. (*information*) 527; advertisement etc. (*publication*) 531.

call, word of command; bugle call, trumpet call; bell, alarum, cry; battle–, rallying- cry; reveille, taps, last post; sacring bell, Sanctus bell, angelus; pibroch, keen [*Ir.*], coronach [*Scot. & Ir.*], dirge.

v. **indicate**; be the sign of etc. *n.;* denote, betoken; argue, testify etc. (*evidence*) 467; bear the impress of etc. *n.;* connote, connotate, signify.

represent, stand for; typify etc. (*prefigure*) 511; symbolize.

mark; put an indication, put a mark etc. *n.;* note, tick, stamp, nick, earmark; blaze; label, ticket, docket; dot, spot, score, dash, trace, chalk.

print, imprint, impress; engrave, stereotype, electrotype, lithograph; prove, pull, reprint.

make a sign etc. *n.;* signalize; give–, hang out– a signal; beck [*archaic*], beckon; nod; wink, glance, leer, nudge, shrug, tip the wink [*slang*]; gesture, gesticulate; raise–, hold up– the -finger, –hand; saw the air, "suit the action to the word" [*Hamlet*].

wave–, unfurl–, hoist–, hang out– a banner etc. *n.;* wave -the hand, –a kerchief; give the cue etc. (*inform*) 527; show one's colors; give–, sound– an alarm; beat the drum, sound the trumpets, raise a cry.

sign, seal, attest etc. (*evidence*) 467; underscore, underline etc. (*give importance to*) 642; call attention to etc. (*attention*) 457; give notice etc. (*inform*) 527.

adj. **indicative**, indicatory; indicating etc. *v.* connotative, denotative; diacritical, representative, typical, symbolic *or* symbolical, pantomimic, pathognomonic *or* pathognomonical, symptomatic, semeiotic *or* semiotic, sematic, ominous, characteristic, significant, significative, demonstrative, diagnostic, exponential, emblematic, armorial; individual etc. (*special*) 79.

known by, recognizable by; indicated etc. *v.;* pointed, marked.

[capable of being denoted] denotable; indelible.

adv. **symbolically** etc. *adj.;* in token of; in dumb show, in pantomime.

551. Record

n. **trace**, vestige, relic, remains; scar, cicatrix; footstep, footmark, footprint; pug [*India*], track, mark, wake, trail, scent, *piste* [*F.*].

monument, hatchment, achievement; escutcheon *or* scutcheon; slab, tablet, trophy, obelisk, pillar, column, monolith; memorial; memento etc. (*memory*) 505; testimonial, medal, Congressional medal; cross, Victoria cross *or* V. C., iron cross [*Ger.*]; ribbon, garter; commemoration etc. (*celebration*) 883.

record, note, minute; register, registry; roll etc. (*list*) 86; chartulary *or* cartulary, diptych, Domesday book; *catalogue raisonné* [*F.*]; entry, memorandum, indorsement *or* endorsement, inscription, copy, duplicate, docket; notch etc. (*mark*) 550; muniments; deed etc. (*security*) 771; document; deposition, *procés verbal* [*F.*]; affidavit; certificate etc. (*evidence*) 467.

notebook, memorandum book, pocketbook, commonplace book, portfolio; bulletin, bulletin board, score board, score sheet, totalizator [*racing*] tote board [*colloq.*]; card index, file, letter file, pigeonholes; *excerpta* [*L.*], excerpt, extract, adversaria, jottings, dottings.

newspaper, daily, gazette etc. (*publication*) 531; magazine.

calendar, ephemeris, diary, log, log book *or* logbook, journal, daybook, ledger, cashbook, petty cashbook.

archive, scroll, state paper, return, bluebook *or* blue book; almanac *or* almanack, gazetteer, Almanach de Gotha, Statesman's Year-book, Whitaker's Almanack; census report; statistics etc. 86; *compte rendu* [*F.*]; Acts–, Transactions–, Proceedings- of; Hansard's Debates; Congressional Records; minutes, chronicle, annals; legend; history, biography etc. 594.

registration; registry, enrollment *or* enrolment, tabulation; entry, booking; signature etc. (*identification*) 550; recorder etc. 553; journalism.

mechanical record, recording instrument; gramophone, phonograph etc. 418; seismograph, seismometer; speedometer, pedometer, patent log [*naut.*]; ticker, tape; time clock; anemometer etc. (*measurement*) 466; turnstile; cash register; votograph.

v. **record**; put–, place- upon record; chronicle, calendar, excerpt, hand down to posterity; keep up the memory etc. (*remember*) 505; commemorate etc. (*celebrate*) 883; report etc. (*inform*) 527; commit to–, reduce to- writing; put–, set down- -in writing, –in black and white; put–, jot–, take–, write–, note–, set-down; note, minute, put on paper; take–, make- a -note, –minute, –memorandum; summarize, make a return; mark etc. (*indicate*) 550; sign etc. (*attest*) 467.

enter, book; post, post up; insert, make an entry of; mark off, tick off; register, list, docket, enroll, inscroll; file etc. (*store*) 636.

adv. **on record**, on file; in one's -good books, –bad books.

552. Obliteration
[suppression of sign]

n. **obliteration**, erasure, rasure [*rare*]; cancel, cancellation; circumduction [*rare*], deletion, blot; *tabula rasa* [*L.*]; effacement, extinction.

v. **efface**, obliterate, erase, rase [*rare*], expunge, cancel, dele; blot–, take–, rub–, scratch–, strike–, wipe–, wash–, sponge- out; wipe off, rub off; wipe away; deface, render illegible; draw the pen through, rule out, apply the sponge.

be effaced etc.; leave no trace etc. 550; "leave not a rack behind" [*Tempest*].

adj. **obliterated** etc. *v.;* leaving no trace; intestate; unrecorded, unregistered, unwritten; printless, out of print.

int. dele; out with it!

553. Recorder

n. **recorder**, notary, clerk; registrar, registrary [*obs.*], register; prothonotary; amanuensis, secretary, recording secretary, stenographer, scribe, babu [*India*], remembrancer, bookkeeper, *custos rotulorum* [*L.*], Master of the Rolls.

annalist, historian, historiographer, chronicler; biographer etc. (*narrator*) 594; antiquary etc. (*antiquity*) 122; memorialist.

journalist, newspaperman, reporter, interviewer, pressman, publicist, author, editor.

554. Representation

n. **representation**, depiction, depicture; imitation etc. 19; illustration, delineation, depictment; imagery, portraiture, iconography; design, designing; art, fine arts; painting etc. 556; sculpture etc. 557; engraving etc. 558.

photography; radiography, X-ray photography, skiagraphy; spectroheliography, photospectroheliography.

personation, personification; impersonation; drama etc. 599.

drawing, picture, sketch, draft *or* draught; tracing; copy etc. 21.

photograph, photo [*colloq.*], daguerreotype, talbotype, calotype; heliotype, heliograph; print, cabinet, *carte de visite* (*pl. cartes de visite*) [*F.*], ping-pong [*cant*], snapshot.

image, likeness, icon, portrait; striking likeness, speaking likeness; spitting image [*colloq.*]; very image; effigy, facsimile.

figure, figurehead; puppet, doll, figurine, aglet *or* aiglet, manikin, mannequin, lay figure, model, marionette, fantoccini, waxwork, bust; statue, statuette, hieroglyph.

hieroglyphic, anaglyph, diagram, monogram.

map, plan, chart; ground plan, projection, elevation; atlas; outline, scheme; view etc. (*painting*) 556; ichnography, cartography.

radiograph, radiogram, scotograph, skiagraph *or* sciagraph, skiagram *or* sciagram, CAT scan, ultrasound image, X-ray photograph, X-ray [*colloq.*]; spectrogram, spectroheliogram, photospectroheliogram.

delineator, draftsman *or* draughtsman; artist etc. 559; photographer, radiographer, X-ray photographer, skiagrapher, daguerreotypist.

v. **represent**, delineate, depict, depicture, portray, picture, limn, take–, catch- a likeness etc. *n.;* hit off, photograph, daguerreotype; snapshot; figure; shadow -forth, -out; adumbrate; body forth; describe etc. 594; trace, copy, mold *or* mould.

illustrate, symbolize; paint etc. 556; carve etc. 557; engrave etc. 558.

personate, personify, impersonate, dress up [*colloq.*], assume a character, pose as, act; play

555. Misrepresentation

etc. (*drama*) 599; mimic etc. (*imitate*) 19; hold the mirror up to nature.

adj. **representing** etc. *v.*, representative; illustrative; represented etc. *v.*; imitative, figurative; iconic, like etc. 17; graphic etc. (*descriptive*) 594.

Renaissance, trecento, quattrocento, cinquecento, Directoire, Moyen Age.

555. Misrepresentation

n. **misrepresentation**, misstatement, falsification, caricatura [*obs.*], exaggeration; daubing etc. *v.*; bad likeness, daub, scratch; imitation, effigy.

distortion, anamorphosis, anamorphoscope; Claude Lorrain–, concave–, convex- mirror.

burlesque, travesty, parody, takeoff, caricature, extravaganza.

v. **misrepresent**, distort, overdraw, exaggerate, daub; falsify, understate, overstate, stretch.

burlesque, travesty, parody, caricature.

adj. **misrepresented** etc. *v.*; bluesky.

556. Painting and Black and White

n. **painting**; depicting; drawing etc. *v.*; design; perspective; *chiaroscuro* etc. (*light*) 420; composition; treatment; arrangement, values, atmosphere, tone, technique.

historical–, portrait–, miniature–, landscape–, marine–, flower–, poster–, interior–, scene- painting; scenography.

pallet, palette; easel; brush, pencil, stump; black lead, charcoal, crayons, chalk, pastel; paint etc. (*coloring matter*) 428; water–, body–, oil- color; oils, oil paint; varnish etc. 356a; priming; *gouache* [*F.*], tempera, distemper, fresco, water glass; enamel; encaustic painting; mosaic; tapestry, batik; sun painting.

style, school; the grand style, high art, *genre* [*F.*], portraiture; futurist, cubist, vorticist; ornamental art etc. 847; monochrome, polychrome; grisaille.

[schools of painting] Italian–, Bolognese–, Florentine–, Milanese–, Modena–, Parma–, Neapolitan–, Paduan–, Roman–, Umbrian–, Venetian–, British–, Dutch–, Flemish–, French–, German–, Spanish- School; School of Raphael etc.

picture, painting, piece, tableau, canvas; oil painting etc.; fresco, cartoon; easel–, cabinet- picture; drawing, draft *or* draught; pencil etc. drawing, water-color drawing; still life; sketch, outline, study.

portrait etc. (*representation*) 554; whole–, full–, half- length; three-quarters profile; head; miniature; shade, silhouette; profile.

view, landscape, seascape, sea view, seapiece; scene, prospect; interior; panorama, bird's-eye view, diorama.

picture gallery, art gallery, art museum, pinacotheca; studio, *atelier* [*F.*].

photography, skiagraphy, radiography etc. 554; photograph, radiograph etc. 554; scenograph.

v. **paint**, design, limn, draw, sketch, pencil, scratch, shade, stipple, hatch, dash off, chalk out, square up; color, dead color, wash, varnish; draw in pencil etc. *n.*; paint in oils etc. *n.*; stencil; depict etc. (*represent*) 554.

adj. **pictorial**, graphic; painted etc. *v.*; picturesque, genre; historical etc. *n.*; monochrome, polychrome; scenographic; futurist, cubist, vorticist; in the grand style; painty, pastose.

pencil, oil etc. *n.*

adv. in pencil etc. *n.*

557. Sculpture

n. **sculpture**, insculpture [*obs.*]; carving etc. *v.*; statuary, anaglyptics, cermaics.

marble, bronze, terra cotta; ceramic ware, pottery, porcelain, china, earthenware; cloisonné, enamel, faïence, satsuma.

relief, relievo; basso-relievo *or* bassorilievo [*It.*], low relief, bas-relief; alto-relievo *or* alto-rilievo [*It.*], high relief; mezzo-relievo *or* mezzo-rilievo [*It.*]; glyph, intaglio, anaglyph; medal, medallion; cameo.

[schools of sculpture] Aeginetan–, Attic–, Chian–, Pergamene–, Rhodian–, Samian–, Sicyonian- School.

statute etc. (*image*) 554; cast etc. (*copy*) 21; glyptotheca.

[statues] Apollo Belvedere, Venus of Melos *or* Milo, Cnidian Aphrodite, Venus de' Medici, Dying Gaul, Farnese Hercules, Laocoön, Niobe, Silenus and Infant Bacchus, Theseus, Centaur and Eros, Niké *or* Winged Victory of Samothrace, The Wrestlers, Michelangelo's David, Mercury taking Flight, Rodin's The Thinker.

v. **sculpture**, carve, cut, chisel, model, mold; cast.

adj. **sculptured** etc. *v.*; in relief, glyptic, anaglyphic, anaglyptic, ceroplastic. ceramic; Parian; marble etc. *n.*; xanthian.

558. Engraving

n. **engraving**, chalcography, glyptography; line–, mezzotint–, stipple–, chalk- engraving; dry point, bur; etching, aquatint *or* aquatinta; chiseling; plate–, copperplate–, steel–, halftone–, process–, wood- engraving; xylography, lignography, glyptography, cerography, lithography, chromolithography, photolithography, zincography, glyphography, xerography.

graver, burin, etching point, style; plate, stone, wood block, negative; die, punch, stamp.

printing; plate–, copperplate–, anastatic–, color–, lithographic- printing; type printing etc. 591; three-color process.

impression, print, engraving, plate; steel-plate, copperplate; etching; aquatint, mezzotint, lithotint; cut, woodcut; stereotype, graphotype, autotype, heliotype; xylograph, lignograph, glyptograph, cerograph, lithograph, chromolithograph, photolithograph, zincograph, glyphograph; process.

illustration, illumination; half tone; photogravure; rotogravure [*trade name*]; vignette, initial letter, *cul de lampe* [*F.*], tailpiece.

v. **engrave**, grave, insculp [*rare*], stipple, scrape, etch; bite, bite in; lithograph etc. *n.;* print.

adj. **engraved** etc. *v.;* insculptured, glyptographic; "insculp'd upon" [*Merchant of Venice*].

559. Artist

n. **artist**; painter, limner, drawer, sketcher, designer, engraver, chalcographer, glyptographer, graver, line engraver, draftsman *or* draughtsman copyist; enameler *or* enameller, enamelist *or* enamellist; cartoonist, caricaturist.

historical–, landscape–, marine–, flower–, portrait–, genre–, miniature–, scene- painter; carver, chaser, modeler, *figuriste* [*F.*], statuary, sculptor.

Phidias, Praxiteles, Apelles, Raphael, Michelangelo, Titian; Royal Academician.

560. Language

n. **language**; phraseology etc. 569; speech etc. 582; tongue, lingo [*chiefly humorous*], vernacular; mother–, vulgar–, native- tongue; household words; King's *or* Queen's English; dialect, brogue, gobbledegook, patois etc. 563; idiom, idiotism.

confusion of tongues, Babel; *pasigraphie* [*F.*], pasigraphy; universal language, Volapük, Esperanto, Ido; pantomime etc. (*signs*) 550.

linguistics, lexicology, philology, glossology, glottology, comparative philology; Grimm's law, Verner's law; comparative grammar, phonetics; chrestomathy; paleology *or* palaeology, paleography *or* palaeography.

onomatopoeia, betacism, mimmation, myatism, nunnation.

literature, letters, polite literature, *belles lettres* [*F.*], muses, humanities, *litterae humaniores* [*L.*], republic of letters, dead languages, classics; genius–, spirit–, idiom- of a language; scholarship etc. (*knowledge*) 490.

linguist etc. (*scholar*) 492.

v. **express**, say, express by words etc. 566.

adj. **lingual**, linguistic; dialectic; vernacular, current; bilingual; diglot, hexaglot, polyglot; literary; colloquial, slangy.

561. Letter

n. **letter**; character; hieroglyphic etc. (*writing*) 590; type etc. (*printing*) 591; capitals; digraph, trigraph; ideogram, ideograph; majuscule, *majusculoe* [*L.*]; minuscule, *minusculae* [*L.*]; alphabet, ABC, abecedary, christcrossrow *or* crisscross-row [*obs. or dial. Eng.*].

consonant, vowel; diphthong, triphthong; mute, surd, sonant, liquid, labial, palatal, cerebral, dental, guttural; guna, vriddhi [*Skr. gram.*].

syllable; monosyllable, dissyllable, polysyllable; affix, prefix, suffix.

spelling, orthography; phonography, phonetic spelling, phonetics; anagrammatism, metagrammatism.

cipher, monogram, anagram; acrostic, double acrostic, double crostic.

v. spell, orthographize [*rare*]; gunate; transliterate.

cipher, decipher; code, decode; make–, construct- acrostics; design monograms; play anagrams; use–, invent- ciphers.

adj. **literal**; alphabetical, abecedarian; syllabic; majuscular, minuscular; uncial etc. (*writing*) 590.

phonetic, voiced, tonic, sonant; voiceless, surd; mute, labial, palatal, cerebral, dental, guttural, liquid.

562. Word

n. **word**, term, vocable; name etc. 564; phrase etc. 566; root, etymon; derivative; part of speech etc. (*grammar*) 567; ideophone, ideogram, ideograph.

dictionary, lexicon, vocabulary, word book, index, glossary, thesaurus, gradus, delectus, concordance; Rosetta stone.

[science of language] etymology, derivation, glottology *or* glossology, semantics, linguistics; terminology, orismology; translation; pronunciation, orthoëpy; paleology etc. (*philology*) 560; lexicography.

lexicographer, lexicologist, etymologist, linguist, orthoëpist, verbarian; semanticist, glossographer etc. (*scholar*) 492.

verbosity, verbiage, wordiness; loquacity etc. 584.

v. vocalize; etymologize, derive, philologize; index; translate.

adj. **verbal**, literal; titular, nominal.
[similarly derived] conjugate, paronymous; derivative.
verbose, wordy etc. 573; loquacious etc. 584.
adv. **verbally** etc. *adj.;* *verbatim* [*L.*] etc. (*exactly*) 494.

563. Neology

n. **neology**, neologism; newfangled expression; caconym; barbarism, archaism, black letter, monkish Latin; corruption, missaying, antiphrasis; pseudology; idioticon.
play upon words, paronomasia; word play etc. (*wit*) 842; *double-entente* [*F.*] etc. (*ambiguity*) 520; palindrome, paragram, clinch [*now rare*], double entendre pun; abuse of -language, -terms.
dialect, brogue, patois, provincialism, broken English, Anglicism, Briticism, Gallicism, Scotticism, Hibernicism, Americanism; Gypsy lingo, Romany.
lingua franca, pidgin *or* pigeon English; Chinook, Hindustani, kitchen Kaffir, Swahili, Haussa, Volapük, Esperanto, Ido.
jargon, dog Latin, gibberish; confusion of tongues, Babel; babu English, chi-chi [*Anglo-India*].
colloquialism etc. (*figure of speech*) 521; byword; technicality, lingo, slang, cant, argot, *bat* [*Hind.*], macaronics, rhyming slang, St. Giles's Greek, thieves' Latin, peddler's French, flash tongue, Billingsgate, Franglais.
pseudonym etc. (*misnomer*) 565; Mr. So-and-so; "Sergeant What-is-name" [*Kipling*]; what d'ye call 'em, what's his name, thingummy, thingamabob, thingummybob [*all colloq.*]; *je ne sais quoi* [*F.*].
neologist, coiner of words.
v. coin words; Americanize, Anglicize, Gallicize; sling the bat [*slang, Anglo-Ind.*].
adj. neologic, neological; archaic, rare, obsolescent; obsolete etc. (*old*) 124; colloquial, dialectal, dialectic *or* dialectical; slang, cant, flash, barbarous; Anglice [*NL.*].

564. Nomenclature

n. **nomenclature**; naming etc. *v.;* nuncupation [*obs.*], nomination [*obs.*], baptism; orismology; onomatopoeia; antonomasia.
name; appellation, appellative; designation; title; head, heading, caption; denomination; by-name; nickname etc. 565; epithet; what one may -well, -fairly, -properly, -fitly- call.
style, proper name; praenomen, agnomen, cognomen; patronymic, surname; cognomination;

eponym; compellation, description, synonym, antonym; empty -title, -name; title, handle to one's name; namesake.
term, expression, noun; byword; convertible terms etc. 522; technical term; cant etc. 563.
v. **name**, call, term, denominate, designate, style, entitle, clepe [*archaic*], dub [*colloq. or humorous*], christen, baptize, nickname, characterize, specify, define, distinguish by the name of; label etc. (*mark*) 550.
be called etc. *v.;* take-, bear-, go (*or* be known) by-, go (*or* pass) under-, rejoice in- the name of; hight [*archaic*], yclept *or* ycleped [*archaic or humorous*].
adj. **named** etc. *v.;* known as; nuncupatory [*obs.*], nuncupative [*obs.*]; cognominal, titular, nominal, orismological.

565. Misnomer

n. **misnomer**; *lucus a non lucendo* [*L.*]; Mrs. Malaprop; what d'ye call 'em etc. (*neologism*) 563.
nickname, *sobriquet* [*F.*] *or* soubriquet, pet name, little name, by-name; assumed -name, -title; alias; *nom de course* [*F.*], *nom de theâtre* [*F.*], stage name; *nom de guerre* [*F.*], *nom de plume* [*English formation*], pen name, pseudonym; pseudonymity, pseudonymousness.
v. **misname**, miscall, misterm; call out of one's name [*colloq.*], nickname; assume -a name, -an alias; take an -alias, -assumed name.
adj. **misnamed** etc. *v.;* pseudonymous; *soi-disant* [*F.*]; self-called, self-styled, self-christened; so-called, quasi.
nameless, anonymous; without a-, having no- name; innominate, unnamed; unacknowledged; pseudo, bastard.
adv. in no sense; by whatever name, under any name.

566. Phrase

n. **phrase**, expression, locution, set phrase; sentence, paragraph; figure of speech etc. 521; idiom, idiotism; turn of expression; style.
paraphrase etc. (*synonym*) 522; euphemism; euphuism; periphrase etc. (*circumlocution*) 573; motto etc. (*proverb*) 496; phraseology etc. 569.
v. **express**, phrase; word, word it; give -words, -expression -to; voice; arrange in-, clothe in-, put into-, express by- words; couch in terms; find words to express; speak by the card; call, denominate, designate, dub.
adj. expressed etc. *v.;* idiomatic; stylistic.
adv. in -round, -set, -good set- terms; in set phrases; by the card.

567. Grammar

n. **grammar**, accidence, syntax, analysis, praxis, punctuation; parts of speech; jussive; syllabication *or* syllabification, paradigm, syllepsis, synopsis; inflection, case, declension, conjugation; *jus et norma loquendi* [*L.*]; Lindley Murray etc. (*schoolbook*) 542; correct style, philology etc. (*language*) 560.

v. parse, analyze *or* analyse, conjugate, decline, punctuate, syllabicate, syllabize.

adj. grammatical, syntactic *or* syntactical, inflectional; synoptic.

568. Solecism

n. **solecism**; bad–, false–, faulty-grammar; grammatical blunder; *faux pas* [*F.*], error, slip; slip of the pen, *lapsus calami* [*L.*]; slip of the tongue, *lapsus linguae* [*L.*]; slipslop; bull, Hibernianism; barbarism, impropriety.

v. **solecize** *or* solecise, commit a solecism; use -bad, –faulty- grammar; murder the King's (*or* Queen's) English; speak–, write-out of the idiom; break Priscian's head.

adj. **ungrammatical**; incorrect, inaccurate, faulty; improper, incongruous; solecistic *or* solecistical; slipslop.

569. Style

n. **style**, diction, phraseology, wording; manner, strain; composition; mode of expression, idiom, choice of words; mode of speech, literary power, ready pen, pen of a ready writer; grand style, grand manner; command of language etc. (*eloquence*) 582; authorship, artistry; *la morgue littéraire* [*F.*].

v. **word**; express by words etc. 566; write; apply–, employ- the file.

570. Perspicuity

n. **perspicuity** etc. (*intelligibility*) 518; plain speaking etc. (*manifestation*) 525; definiteness, definition; exactness etc. 494; explicitness, lucidness, lucidity, limpidity, clearness.

adj. **lucid** etc. (*intelligible*) 518; limpid, pellucid, clear; explicit etc. (*manifest*) 525; exact etc. 494.

571. Obscurity

n. **obscurity** etc. (*unintelligibility*) 519; involution, crabbedness, confusion; hard words; ambiguity etc. 520; unintelligibility, unintelligibleness; vagueness etc. 475, inexactness etc. 495; what d'ye call 'em etc. (*neologism*) 563; darkness of meaning.

adj. **obscure** etc. *n.;* crabbed; involved, confused.

572. Conciseness

n. **conciseness** etc. *adj.;* brevity, "the soul of wit," laconicism *or* laconism; ellipsis; syncope; abridgment etc. (*shortening*) 201; compression etc. 195; epitome etc. 596; monostich; Spartans; Tacitus.

portmanteau-word [Lewis Carroll]; brunch [breakfast+lunch], squarson [squire+parson]; slithy, *adj.* [slimy+lithe], torrible, *adj.* [torrid +horrible], crowzy, *adj.* [crowded+cozy], motel, *n.* [motor+hotel].

v. **be concise** etc. *adj.;* telescope, laconize; condense etc. 195; abridge etc. 201; abstract etc. 596; come to the point.

adj. **concise**, brief, short, terse, close; to the point, exact; neat, compact; compressed, condensed, pointed; laconic, curt, pithy, trenchant, summary; pregnant; compendious etc. (*compendium*) 596; succinct; elliptical, epigrammatic, crisp; sententious.

adv. **concisely** etc. *adj.;* briefly, summarily; in brief, in short, in a word, in few words; for the sake of brevity, for shortness' sake; to come to the point, to make a long story short, to cut the matter short, to be brief; it comes to this, the long and short of it is, the gist is.

573. Diffuseness

n. **diffuseness** etc. *adj.;* amplification etc. *v.;* dilating etc. *v.;* verbosity, wordiness; verbiage, cloud of words, *copia verborum* [*L.*]; flow of words etc. (*loquacity*) 584; looseness.

tautology, battology, polylogy [*obs.*], perissology [*obs.*]; pleonasm, exuberance, redundance; thrice-told tale; prolixity, longiloquence, longsomeness, circumlocution, ambages [*rare*], periphrase, periphrasis, roundabout phrases; episode; expletive; penny-a-lining; richness etc. 577; padding; drivel, twaddle, drool.

v. **be diffuse** etc. *adj.;* run out on, descant, expatiate, enlarge, dilate, amplify, expand, inflate, pad [*editor's cant*], launch out, branch out; rant.

maunder, prose; harp upon etc. (*repeat*) 104; dwell on, insist upon.

digress, ramble, *battre la campagne* [*F.*], beat about the bush, perorate, spin a long yarn, protract; spin–, swell–, draw- out; battologize *or* battalogize; drivel, twaddle, drool.

adj. **diffuse**, profuse; wordy, verbose, largiloquent [*obs.*], copious, exuberant, pleonastic, lengthy; long, longsome, long-winded, longspun, long drawn out; spun out, protracted, prolix, diffusive, prosing, maundering; circumlocutory, periphrastic, ambagious *or* ambaguious, am-

574. Vigor

bagitory, roundabout; digressive; discursive, excursive; loose; rambling, episodic; flatulent, frothy.

adv. **diffusely** etc. *adj.;* at large, *in extenso* [*L.*]; about it and about.

574. Vigor

n. **vigor**, power, force; boldness, raciness etc. *adj.;* intellectual force; spirit, punch [*slang*], point, piquancy; verve, ardor, enthusiasm, glow, fire, warmth; strong language; gravity, weight, sententiousness.

loftiness, elevation, sublimity, grandeur.

eloquence; command of words, command of language.

adj. **vigorous**, nervous, powerful, forcible, forceful, mordant, biting, trenchant, incisive, graphic, impressive; sensational.

spirited, lively, glowing, sparkling, racy, bold, slashing, crushing; pungent, piquant, full of beans [*slang*], full of pep [*slang*], having punch [*slang*], full of point, pointed, pithy; sententious.

lofty, elevated, sublime, poetic, grand, weighty, ponderous; eloquent.

vehement, petulant, passionate, burning, impassioned.

adv. in -glowing, –good set, –no measured- terms; with his heart on fire; like a ton of bricks [*colloq.*].

575. Feebleness

n. **feebleness** etc. *adj.;* enervation, flaccidity, vapidity, poverty, frigidity.

adj. **feeble**, bald, tame, meager *or* meagre, insipid, watery, nerveless, jejune, vapid, trashy, cold, frigid, poor, dull, dry, languid; colorless, enervated; prosing, prosy, prosaic, unvaried, monotonous, weak, washy, wishy-washy [*colloq.*], sloppy, sketchy, slight; careless, slovenly, loose, disjointed, disconnected, lax; slipshod, slipslop; inexact; puerile, childish; flatulent, rambling etc. (*diffuse*) 573.

576. Plainness

n. **plainness** etc. *adj.;* simplicity, *simplex munditiis* [Hor.], lack of ornamentation, severity; plain talk; plain -terms, –English; Saxon English; household words.

v. **speak plainly**, waste no words, call a spade a spade; plunge *in medias res* [*L.*]; come to the point.

adj. **plain**, simple; unornamented, unadorned, unvarnished; homely, homespun; neat; severe, chaste, pure, Saxon; commonplace, matter-of-fact, natural, prosaic, sober, unimaginative.

dry, unvaried, monotonous etc. 575.

adv. **point-blank**; in plain -terms, words, –English; in common parlance.

577. Ornament

n. **ornament**; floridness etc. *adj.;* turgidity, turgescence *or* turgescency; altiloquence [*obs.*], grandiloquence, magniloquence, declamation, teratology [*obs.*]; well-rounded periods; elegance etc. 578; orotundity.

inversion, antithesis, alliteration, paronomasia; trope; figurativeness etc. (*metaphor*) 521.

flourish; flowers of -speech, –rhetoric; frills, –of style; euphuism, euphemism.

bombast, big-sounding words, high-sounding words; macrology, *sesquipedalia verba* [*L.*], sesquipedalian words, sesquipedality, sesquipedalianism, Alexandrine; inflation, pretension; rant, fustian, highfalutin' [*slang*], buncombe *or* bunkum *or* bunk, balderdash; prose run mad; fine writing; purple patches; Minerva press.

phrasemonger, euphuist, euphemist; word coiner.

v. **ornament**, overlay with ornament, overcharge, overload; euphuize, euphemize; buncomize [*colloq.*]; smell of the lamp.

adj. **ornate**; ornamented etc. *v.;* beautified etc. 847; florid, rich, flowery; euphuistic, euphemistic; sonorous; high- big- sounding; inflated, swelling, tumid; turgid, turgescent; pedantic, pompous, stilted; orotund; high-flown, high-flowing, highfalutin' [*slang*]; sententious, rhetorical, declamatory; grandiose; grandiloquent; magniloquent; altiloquent [*obs.*]; sesquipedal, sesquipedalian; Johnsonian, mouthy; bombastic; fustian; frothy, flashy, flamboyant.

antithetical, alliterative; figurative etc. 521; artificial etc. (*inelegant*) 579.

adv. **ore rotundo** [*L.*], with rounded phrase.

578. Elegance

n. **elegance**, distinction, clarity, purity, grace, felicity, ease; gracefulness, readiness etc. *adj.;* concinnity, concinnation [*rare*], euphony; balance, rhythm, symmetry, proportion, taste, good taste, restraint, nice discrimination, propriety, correctness; Attic salt, Atticism, classicalism, classicism.

well-rounded–, well-turned–, flowing- periods; the right word in the right place; antithesis etc. 577.

purist, classicist, stylist.

v. **flow -smoothly**, –with ease; discriminate nicely, display elegance etc. *n.;* point an antithesis, round a period.

adj. **elegant**, polished, classic *or* classical, classicistic, concinnous [*rare*], correct, Attic, Ciceronian, artistic; chaste, pure, Saxon, academic *or* academical.

graceful, easy, readable, fluent, flowing, tripping; unaffected, natural, unlabored; mellifluous, euphonious; euphemistic; symmetrical, balanced, restrained; rhythmic *or* rhythmical.

felicitous, happy, neat; well–, neatly- -put, –expressed.

579. Inelegance

n. **inelegance**, impurity, vulgarity; want of–, poor–, bad- taste; stiffness etc. *adj.;* "unlettered Muse" [Gray]; cacology, cacography, poor diction, poor choice of words; loose–, slipshod- construction; want of balance, ill-balanced sentences; barbarism; slang etc. 563; solecism etc. 568; mannerism etc. (*affectation*) 855; euphuism, Marinism, Gongorism; fustian etc. 577; cacophony; words that -break the teeth, –dislocate the jaw.

cacographer, barbarian; euphuist, Marinist, Gongorist.

v. **be inelegant** etc. *adj.;* employ inelegance etc. *n.*

adj. **inelegant**, graceless, ungraceful; harsh, abrupt; dry, stiff, cramped, formal, *guindé* [*F.*]; forced, labored; artificial, mannered, ponderous; awkward, uncourtly, unpolished; turgid etc. 577; affected, euphuistic; barbarous, uncouth, grotesque, rude, crude, halting, cacographic *or* cacographical; offensive to ears polite; vulgar, tasteless.

580. Voice

n. **voice**; vocality; organ, lungs, bellows; good–, fine–, powerful etc. (*loud*) 404–, musical etc. 413- voice; intonation; tone etc. (*sound*) 402- of voice.

utterance; vocalization; cry etc. 411; strain, prolation [*archaic*]; exclamation, ejaculation, vociferation, ecphonesis; enunciation, articulation; articulate sound, distinctness; clearness, –of articulation; stage whisper; delivery, attack.

accent, accentuation; emphasis, stress; broad–, strong–, pure–, native–, foreign- accent; pronunciation; orthoëpy; euphony etc. (*melody*) 413; polyphonism, polyphony.

[words similarly pronounced] homonyms.

ventriloquism *or* ventriloquy, ventrilocution, gastriloquism *or* gastriloquy [*rare*]; ventriloquist, gastriloquist [*rare*].

[science of voice], phonology; etc. (*sound*) 402.

v. **speak**, utter, breathe; give utterance, give tongue; cry etc. (*shout*) 411; ejaculate, rap out; vocalize, prolate [*obs.*], articulate, enunciate, pronounce, accentuate, aspirate, deliver, emit; whisper, murmur, whisper in the ear; ventriloquize.

adj. **vocal**, phonetic, oral; ejaculatory, articulate, articulated, distinct, enunciative, accentuated, aspirated; euphonious etc. (*melodious*) 413; whispered.

ventriloquous, ventriloquistic, gastriloquial [*rare*], gastriloquous [*rare*].

581. Aphonia

n. **aphonia** *or* aphony; dumbness etc. *adj.;* obmutescence [*rare*]; absence–, want- of voice; dysphonia *or* dysphony; silence etc. (*taciturnity*) 585; raucity; harsh voice etc. 410, unmusical voice etc. 414; quaver, quavering; falsetto, "childish treble"; deaf-mutism, deaf-muteness, deaf-dumbness, mute, dummy, deaf-mute.

v. **speak low**, speak softly; whisper etc. (*faintness*) 405; keep silence etc. 585.

silence; render -mute, –silent; muzzle, muffle, suppress, smother, gag, strike dumb, dumfound *or* dumbfound dumfounder *or* dumbfounder, mum [*obs.*], drown the voice, put to silence, stop one's mouth, cut one short.

stick in the throat.

adj. **aphonous**, nonvocal, aphonic, dumb, mute, deaf and dumb, deaf-dumb; mum; obmutescent [*rare*], tongue-tied; breathless, tongueless, voiceless, speechless, wordless; mute as a -fish, –stockfish, –mackerel; silent etc. (*taciturn*) 585; muzzled; inarticulate, inaudible.

croaking, raucous, hoarse, husky, dry, hollow, sepulchral, hoarse as a raven; rough.

adv. **with bated breath**, with the finger on the lips; *sotto voce* [*It.*]; in a -low tone, –cracked voice, –broken voice; in broken tones, aside, in an aside.

int. **mum**! hush! sh! silence! whist! whisht! [*dial.*]; chut! etc. (*silence*) 403.

582. Speech

n. **speech**, faculty of speech; locution, talk, parlance, verbal intercourse, prolation [*archaic*], oral communication, word of mouth, parole, palaver, prattle.

oration, recitation, delivery, say [*colloq.*], speech, lecture, prelection *or* praelection, harangue, sermon, tirade, formal speech, peroration; speechifying; soliloquy etc. 589; allocution etc. 586; interlocution etc. 588; salutatory [*U. S.*]; screed; valedictory [*U. S.*].

oratory, elocution, eloquence, rhetoric, declamation; grandiloquence, multiloquence, talkativeness; burst of eloquence; facundity [*obs.*]; flow–, command- of -words, –language; *copia verborum* [*L.*]; power of speech, gift of gab [*colloq.*]; *usus loquendi* [*L.*].

speaker etc. *v.;* spokesman; prolocutor, interlocutor; mouthpiece, Hermes; orator, oratrix, oratress; Demosthenes, Cicero; rhetorician, lecturer, preacher, prelector *or* praelector; elocutionist, reciter, reader; spellbinder; stump–, platform- orator; speechmaker, patterer, monologist, monologuist, improvisator, *improvvisatore* or *improvisatore* [*It.*], *improvvisatrice* or *improvisatrice* [*It.*].

v. **speak**, –of; say, utter, pronounce, deliver, give utterance to; utter–, pour- forth; breathe, let fall, come out with; rap out, blurt out; have on one's lips; have at the -end, –tip-of one's tongue.

soliloquize etc. 589; tell etc. (*inform*) 527; speak to etc. 586; talk together etc. 588.

break silence; open one's -lips, –mouth; lift–, raise- one's voice; give tongue, wag the tongue [*colloq.*]; talk, outspeak; put in a word or two.

declaim, hold forth; make–, deliver- a speech etc. *n.;* speechify [*derisive or humorous*], harangue, stump [*colloq.*], flourish, spout, rant, recite, lecture, prelect *or* praelect, sermonize, discourse, be on one's legs; have–, say- one's say; expatiate etc. (*speak at length*) 573; speak one's mind, go on the–, take the-stump [*U. S.*].

be eloquent etc. *adj.;* have a tongue in one's head, have the gift of gab [*colloq.*] etc. *n.*

pass one's lips, escape one's lips; fall from the -lips, –mouth.

adj. **oral**, lingual, phonetic, not written, nuncupative [*of wills*], unwritten; speaking etc., spoken etc. *v.;* outspoken, facund [*archaic*].

eloquent, oratorical, rhetorical, elocutionary, declamatory; grandiloquent etc. 577; talkative etc. 584; Ciceronian, Tullian.

adv. **orally** etc. *adj.;* by word of mouth, *viva voce* [*L.*], from the lips of; from his own mouth.

583. Stammering
[imperfect speech]

n. **inarticulateness**; stammering etc. *v.;* hesitation etc. *v.;* impediment in one's speech; titubancy [*obs.*], traulism [*obs.*]; whisper etc. (*faint sound*) 405; lisp, drawl, tardiloquence [*rare*]; nasal -tone, –accent; twang; falsetto etc. (*want of voice*) 581; cacology, cacoëpy; broken -voice, –accents, –sentences; brogue etc. 563.

slip of the tongue, *lapsus linguae* [*L.*].

v. **stammer**, stutter, hesitate, falter, hammer [*obs. or dial. Eng.*], balbutiate [*obs.*], balbucinate [*obs.*], haw, hem and haw, be unable to put two words together.

mumble, mutter, maund [*obs.*], maunder; whisper etc. 405; mince, lisp; jabber, gabble, gibber; splutter, sputter; muffle, mump; drawl, mouth; croak; speak thick, speak through the nose; talk incoherently, quaver, snuffle, clip one's words.

murder the language, murder the King's (*or* Queen's) English; mispronounce, missay [*rare*].

adj. **inarticulate**; stammering etc. *v.;* guttural, throaty, nasal; tremulous; affected; stertorous; cacoëpistic.

adv. *sotto voce* etc. (*faintly*) 405.

584. Loquacity

n. **loquacity**, loquaciousness, effusion; talkativeness etc. *adj.;* garrulity; multiloquence, much speaking.

gabble, gab [*colloq.*], jaw [*colloq.*], hot air [*slang*]; jabber, chatter; prate, prattle, cackle, clack; twaddle, twattle, rattle, *caquet* [*F.*], *caqueterie* [*F.*], blabber, *bavardage* [*F.*], bibble-babble, gibble-gabble; small talk etc. (*converse*) 588; Babel.

fluency, flippancy, volubility, flowing tongue; flow, –of words; *flux de -bouche, –mots* [*F.*]; *copia verborum* [*L.*], *cacoëthes loquendi* [*L.*]; *furor loquendi* [*L.*]; verbosity etc. (*diffuseness*) 573; gift of the gab etc. (*eloquence*) 582.

talker; chatterer, chatterbox; babbler etc. *v.;* rattle; "agreeable rattle" [Goldsmith]; ranter; sermonizer, proser, driveler *or* driveller, blatherskite [*colloq.*], blab, jaw-box [*slang*], gas-

bag [*slang*], wind-bag [*slang*], hot-air artist [*slang*]; gossip etc. (*converse*) 588; magpie, jay, parrot, poll *or* polly; *moulin à paroles* [*F.*].
- *v.* **be loquacious** etc. *adj.;* talk glibly, pour forth, patter; prate, palaver, prose, maunder, chatter, blab, gush, prattle, clack, jabber, jaw [*low*], shoot one's mouth off [*slang*]; blather, blatter, blether; rattle, –on; twaddle, twattle; babble, gabble; outtalk; talk oneself -out of breath, –hoarse; talk–, run on- like a mill race; have one's tongue hanging in the middle and wagging at both ends; talk the hind legs off a mule, talk one deaf and dumb, clack like a hen, go on forever; expatiate etc. (*speak at length*) 573; gossip etc. (*converse*) 588; din in the ears etc. (*repeat*) 104; talk at random, talk nonsense etc. 497; be hoarse with talking.
- *adj.* **loquacious**, talkative, garrulous, linguacious [*obs.*], multiloquent *or* multiloquous; chattering etc. *v.;* chatty etc. (*sociable*) 892; declamatory etc. 582; open-mouthed.

  fluent, voluble, glib, flippant; long-tongued, long-winded etc. (*diffuse*) 573.
- *adv.* **glibly** etc. *adj.;* trippingly on the tongue.

585. Taciturnity

- *n.* **silence**, muteness, obmutescence [*rare*], laconism, laconicism, taciturnity, pauciloquy, costiveness [*obs.*], curtness; reserve, reticence etc. (*concealment*) 528.

  man of few words; Spartan, Laconian.
- *v.* **be silent** etc. *adj.;* keep silence; hold one's -tongue, –peace; not speak etc. 582; say nothing; seal-, close-, put a padlock on- the -lips, –mouth; put a bridle on one's tongue; keep one's tongue between one's teeth; make no sign, not let a word escape one; keep a secret etc. 528; have not a word to throw at a dog, not have a word to say; lay-, place- the finger on the lips; render mute etc. 581.

  stick in one's throat.
- *adj.* **silent**, mute, mum; silent as a -post, –stone, –the grave etc. (*still*) 403; dumb etc. 581; unconversable.

  taciturn, laconic, pauciloquent, concise, sententious, sparing of words; close, close-mouthed, close-tongued; costive [*obs.*], inconversable [*obs.*], curt; reserved; reticent etc. (*concealing*) 528.
- *int.* **silence!** tush! mum! hush! chut! [*F.*], hist! tut! not another word! shut up! stop right there! be still! chup! [*Hind.*].

586. Allocution

- *n.* **allocution**, alloquy [*obs.*], address; smoke talk, chalk talk [*both colloq.*]; speech etc. 582; apostrophe, interpellation, appeal, invocation, salutation, salutatory; word in the ear.

  platform etc. 542; plank [*politics*].

  audience etc. (*interview*) 588.

  [feigned dialogue] dialogism.
- *v.* **address**, speak to, accost, make up to [*colloq.*], apostrophize, appeal to, invoke; hail, salute; call to, halloo.

  lecture etc. (*make a speech*) 582; preach, sermonize, harangue, spellbind.

  take aside, take by the button; talk to in private.
- *int.* soho! halloo! hey! hist! hi!

587. Response

etc. see ANSWER 462.

588. Interlocution

- *n.* **interlocution**; collocution, colloquy, converse, conversation, confabulation, confab [*colloq.*], chin-music [*slang*], talk, discourse, verbal intercourse; oral communication, commerce; dialogue, duologue, trialogue.

  "the feast of reason and the flow of soul" [Pope]; *mollia tempora fandi* [*L.*].

  chat, causerie [*F.*], chitchat; small-, table-, tea-table-, town-, village-, idle-talk; tattle, gossip, tittle-tattle; babble, babblement; *tripotage* [*F.*], cackle, prittle-prattle, *on dit* [*F.*]; talk of the -town, –village.

  conference, parley, interview, audience, *pourparler* [*F.*]; *tête-à-tête* [*F.*]; reception, *conversazione* [*It.*]; congress etc. (*council*) 696; powwow.

  hall of audience, durbar [*India*], auditorium, assembly room.

  debate, palaver, logomachy, war of words, controversy, newspaper war.

  talker, gossip, tattler; Paul Pry; tabby [*colloq.*], chatterer etc. (*loquacity*) 584; interlocutor etc. (*spokesman*) 582; conversationist, conversationalist, dialogist.
- *v.* **converse**, talk together, confabulate; dialogue, dialogize; hold-, carry on-, join in-, engage in- a conversation; put in a word; shine in conversation; bandy words; parley; palaver; chat, gossip, tattle; prate etc. (*loquacity*) 584; powwow.

  confer with, discourse with, commune with, commerce with; hold -converse, –conference,

–intercourse; talk it over; be closeted with; talk with one in private, talk with one *tête-à-tête* [*F.*].

adj. **conversing** etc. *v.;* interlocutory; conversational, conversable; discursive *or* discoursive [*obs.*]; chatty etc. (*sociable*) 892; colloquial, confabulatory, *tête-à-tête* [*F.*].

589. Soliloquy

n. **soliloquy,** monology, monologue, apostrophe; monology.

soliloquist, monologist, monologuist, monologian, soliloquizer; speaker etc. 582; Dr. Johnson, Coleridge.

v. **soliloquize,** monologize, monologuize, say–, talk- to oneself; rehearse a speech, address an imaginary audience; address the four walls; say aside, think aloud, apostrophize.

adj. **soliloquizing** etc. *v.;* monologic *or* monological; apostrophic, apostrophal [*rare*].

adv. **aside,** apart.

590. Writing

n. **writing** etc. *v.;* chirography, stelography [*rare*], monography, stylography, cerography, graphology; pencraft, penmanship; quill driving [*humorous*]; typewriting.

stroke–, dash- of the pen; *coup de plume* [*F.*]; line; headline; pen and ink.

manuscript, MS., writing, *litterae scriptae* [*L.*]; these presents [*law*].

character, letter etc. 561; uncial writing, cuneiform character, arrowhead, contraction; Ogham, runes; hieroglyphic, hieratic, demotic, Hebrew, Greek, Cyrillic, Roman; Arabic, Persian, Naskhi *or* Neskhi, Shikasta, Nasta'lik *or* Ta'lik; Brahmi, Devanagari, Nagari; Chinese; script.

shorthand; stenography, brachygraphy, tachygraphy; secret writing, writing in cipher; cryptography, steganography; phonography, pasigraphy, polygraphy [*rare*], logography.

copy; transcript, rescript; rough–, fair- copy; rough draft.

handwriting; signature, sign manual, mark, autograph, monograph, holograph; hand, fist [*colloq.*].

calligraphy; good–, running–, flowing–, cursive–, Italian–, slanting–, perpendicular–, round–, copybook–, fine–, legible–, bold- hand.

cacography, *griffonage* [*F.*], *barbouillage* [*F.*]; bad–, cramped–, crabbed–, illegible- hand; scribble etc. *v.; pattes de mouche* [*F.*], fly tracks; ill-formed letters; pothooks and hangers.

stationery; pen, reed, quill, goose quill; pencil, style, stylograph, stylographic pen, fountain pen; paper, foolscap, parchment, vellum, papyrus, tablet, block, pad, notebook, memorandum book, copybook, commonplace-book; slate, marble, pillar, table; blackboard; ink-bottle, inkhorn, inkpot, inkstand, inkwell; typewriter.

composition, authorship; *cacoëthes scribendi* [*L.*]; graphomania; lucubration, production, work, preparation; screed, article, paper, pamphlet, book etc. 593; essay, theme, thesis; novel, textbook, poem, book of poems, book of verse; compilation, anthology; piece of music, *morceau* [*F.*] etc. (*musical composition*) 415.

transcription etc. (*copy*) 21; inscription etc. (*record*) 551; superscription etc. (*indication*) 550.

writer, scribe, amanuensis, scrivener, secretary, clerk, penman, copyist, transcriber, quill driver [*humorous*]; stenographer, brachygrapher, tachygrapher, phonographer, logographer, cipherer, cryptographer *or* cryptographist, steganographist; typewriter, typist; writer for the press etc. (*author*) 593; chirographer, cerographist; monographist, graphomaniac; calligraphist, calligrapher; cacographer; graphologist.

v. **write,** pen, typewrite, type [*colloq.*]; copy, engross; write out, –fair; transcribe; scribble, scrawl, scrabble, scratch; interline; take down in -shorthand, –longhand; spoil–, stain- paper [*humorous*]; note down; write down etc. (*record*) 551; sign etc. (*attest*) 467; enface.

compose, indite, draw up, draft, formulate; dictate; inscribe, throw on paper, dash off; manifold.

take up the pen, take pen in hand; shed–, spill–, dip one's pen in- ink.

adj. writing etc. *v.;* written etc. *v.;* in writing, in black and white; under one's hand.

uncial, runic, cuneiform, hieroglyphic *or* hieroglyphical, arrowhead etc. *n.*

stenographic, phonographic, brachygraphic, cryptographic, pasigraphic, logographic, tachygraphic; stenographical etc.

adv. *currente calamo* [*L.*]; pen in hand; with the pen of a ready writer; that "the wayfaring men, though fools, shall not err therein" [*Bible*].

591. Printing

n. **printing;** block–, type- printing; linotype, monotype; plate printing etc. (*engraving*) 558; the press etc. (*publication*) 531; composition.

print, letterpress, text, matter; live–, standing–, dead- matter; copy; context, page, column, note, section; catch-word; running head, running title; signature; justification; dummy.

folio etc. (*book*) 593; copy, impression. pull, proof, revise, advance sheets; author's–, galley–, page–, plate–, press- proof; press revise.

typography; stereotype, electrotype; matrix; font *or* fount; pi *or* pie; roman, italics; capitals etc. (*letters*) 561, caps., small caps., upper case, lower case; logotype; type-bar, type-slug; type-body; em, en; type measure, type scale; type casting, type metal, type mold, typograph; type foundry, letter foundry; composing stick, stick; composing -frame. -rule, –stand; foot stick; chase, form, galley, measure, scale, case, boxes; gauge, gauge pin, feed gauge, guide, dabber, gutter, gutter stick; brayer, boss, batter, bank; bearer, guard; bed, blanket, tympan, turtle, platen, bevel, burr, frame, frisket, gripper, quadrat, quad; quoin, slug, slur, ratchet, reglet; guillotine, rounce, cylinder; overlay, underlay, sinkage, macule; platen press, perfecting machine; printing-press, printing-machine; presswork; sheet work; off-cut, off-print, set-off; off-set, smut; turn, turned letter; bookplate, bookstamp, colophon; composing room, press room.

space, 3-em, thick space; 4-em, 5-em, thin space; 6-em, hair space; patent space.

metal type, body, shank, face, shoulder, counter, serif *or* ceriph, stem, beard, groove, feet.

styles of type: Old English, Black Letter, German Text, Gothic, Antique, Clarendon, Boldface *or* Full-face, French Elzevir, Caslon Old Style, Ionic, Script, Typewriter.

point system: 4½ point (diamond), 5 pt. (pearl), 5½ pt. (agate *or* ruby), 6 pt. (nonpareil), 7 pt. (minion), 8 pt. (brevier), 9 pt. (bourgeois), 10 pt. (long primer), 11 pt. (small pica), 12 pt. (pica), 14 pt. (English), 16 pt. (Columbian), 18 pt. (great primer).

printer, compositor, reader, proof reader;- printer's devil; copyholder.

v. **print**; compose; put–, go- to press; pass–, see-through the press; publish etc. 531; bring out; appear in–, rush into- print; set up, stick, make-up, impose, justify, macule *or* mackle, mortise, offset, overrun, rout.

distribute, pi *or* pie, pi a form.

adj. **typographical** etc. *n.;* printed etc. *v.;* in type; solid in galleys; kerned, deckle-edged; bold-faced *or* full-faced; pied.

592. Correspondence

n. **correspondence,** letter, epistle, note, billet, written communication, post card *or* postcard, postal, postal card; missive, circular, favor, *billet-doux* [*F.*]; chit *or* chitty [*India*], letter card [*Brit.*], picture post card; dispatch *or* despatch; bulletin, these presents [*law*]; rescript, rescription [*archaic*]; post etc. (*messenger*) 534.

letter writer, epistolarian, correspondent, writer, communicator; author, contributor.

v. **correspond,** –with; write to, send a letter to; drop a line to [*colloq.*]; start–, begin–, keep up- a correspondence; deluge with -letters, –post cards; communicate by -writing, –letter; let one know by -post, –mail; dispatch *or* despatch, circularize, follow up, bombard; reply, reply by return mail, communicate.

adj. **epistolary,** epistolarian.

593. Book

n. **book,** booklet; writing, work, volume, tome, opuscule *or* opuscle, opusculum; tract, tractate, treatise, *livret* [*F.*], brochure, monograph, pamphlet, codex, libretto; handbook, manual, enchiridion; novel etc. (*composition*) 590; circular, publication; the press etc. 531; chapbook.

part, issue, number, *livraison* [*F.*]; album, portfolio; periodical, serial, magazine, ephemeris, annual, journal.

paper, bill, sheet, broadsheet; leaf, leaflet; fly leaf, page; quire, ream.

pasteboard, cardboard, strawboard, millboard, binder's board; carton.

make-up, bastard title, title, printer's imprint, subtitles, dedication, preface, contents, list of plates *or* illustrations, errata, introduction, text; chapter, section, head, article, paragraph, passage, clause; recto, verso *or* reverso; supplement, appendix, index.

[sizes] folio, quarto (4to *or* 4°); octavo (8vo), cap 8vo, demy 8vo, imperial 8vo, medium 8vo, royal 8vo, post 8vo, pott 8vo, crown 8vo, foolscap 8vo; duodecimo, twelvemo *or* 12mo; sextodecimo, sixteenmo *or* 16mo, octodecimo, eighteenmo *or* 18mo.

bookbinding, bibliopegy; folding, stitching, wire-stitching; tooling; blind–, gold- tooling; binder's title; case, cover; quarter–, half–, three-quarters- bound book; full leather.

[binding materials] paper, paper boards, buckram, cloth, skiver, roan, pigskin, Russia, Turkey morocco, levant morocco, seal, parchment, vellum.

594. Description

work of reference, encyclopedia *or* encyclopaedia, cyclopedia *or* cyclopaedia, dictionary, thesaurus, concordance, anthology; compilation.

writer, author, *littérateur* [*F.*], essayist; pen, scribbler, the scribbling race; free lance; literary hack, Grub-street writer; adjective jerker [*slang*], hack writer, hack, ghost [*cant.*], ghost writer, ink slinger [*slang*]; journalist, publicist, writer for–, gentleman of–, representative of- the press; reporter, correspondent; war–, special- correspondent; knight of the -plume, –pen, –quill [*all humorous*]; penny-a-liner; editor, subeditor, reviser, diaskeuast; scribe etc. 590; playwright etc. 599; poet etc. 597.

the trade, publisher, bookseller; book -salesman, –agent, –canvasser, –solicitor.

bibliopole, bibliopolist, book collector; bookbinder, bibliopegist; bookworm etc. 492; bibliologist, bibliographer, bibliophile, bibliognost, librarian, bibliothec.

bookstore, bookshop, bookseller's shop, *librairie* [*F.*], publishing house.

library, bibliotheca, public library, lending library.

knowledge of books, bibliography, bibliology; book learning etc. (*knowledge*) 490; bookselling, bibliopolism.

594. Description

n. **description**, account, statement, report; *exposé* [*F.*] etc. (*disclosure*) 529; specification, particulars; summary of facts; brief etc. (*abstract*) 596; return etc. (*record*) 551; *catalogue raisonné* [*F.*] etc. (*list*) 86; guidebook etc. (*information*) 527.

delineation etc. (*representation*) 554; sketch, pastel, vignette, monograph; minute-, detailed-, particular-, circumstantial-, graphic- account; narration, recital, rehearsal, relation.

narrative, history; memoir, memorials; annals etc. (*chronicle*) 551; saga; tradition, legend, story, tale, historiette; personal narrative, journal, letters, biography, autobiography, life; obituary, orbit [*cant.*], necrology; adventures, fortunes, experiences, confessions; anecdote, ana.

historiography, chronography; historic Muse, Clio.

work of fiction, novel, romance, short story; detective -story, -yarn; "grue" [Stevenson]; fairy–, nursery- tale; fable, parable, apologue, allegory; dime novel, penny dreadful, shilling shocker [*slang*].

relator etc. *v.; raconteur* [*F.*]; historiographer, chronographer, historian etc. (*recorder*) 553; biographer, fabulist, novelist, story-teller, romancer, spinner of yarns, teller of tales, anecdotist, word-painter; writer etc. 593.

v. **describe**; set forth etc. (*state*) 535; draw a picture, picture; portray etc. (*represent*) 554; characterize, analyze, give words to, narrate, relate, recite, recount, sum up, run over, recapitulate, rehearse, fight one's battles over again; harrow up the soul, hold one breathless, novelize, romance.

unfold etc. (*disclose*) 529- a tale; tell; give–, render- an account of; report, make a report, draw up a statement; throw into -essay form, –book form; stick to the facts, show life as it is; historicize.

detail, particularize, itemize; enter into–, descend to- -particulars, –details.

adj. **descriptive**, graphic, narrative, epic, suggestive, well-drawn; historic *or* historical, historiographical, chronographic *or* chronographical, biographic *or* biographical, autobiographical; traditive [*esp., from ancestors to descendants*], traditional, traditionary; legendary, mythical, fabulous; anecdotic, storied; described etc. *v.;* romantic, idealistic; realistic, true to life; expository.

595. Dissertation

n. **dissertation**, treatise, essay; thesis, theme; tract, tractate, tractation [*obs.*]; discourse, memoir, disquisition, lecture, sermon, homily, pandect, digest; excursus.

investigation etc. (*inquiry*) 461; study etc. (*consideration*) 451; discussion etc. (*reasoning*) 476; exposition etc. (*explanation*) 522.

commentary, commentation, review, critique, criticism, article; leader, leading article; editorial; running commentary.

commentator, critic, essayist, pamphleteer, publicist, reviewer, leader writer, editor, annotator.

v. **comment**, explain, interpret, criticize, illuminate; dissert [*rare*]–, descant–, write–, touch upon a subject; treat of–, take up–, ventilate–, discuss–, deal with–, go into–, canvass–, handle–, do justice to- a subject; show the true inwardness of.

adj. **disquisitional**, disquisitive, disquisitionary [*rare*]; expository, commentarial, commentatorial, critical.

discursive, discoursive, digressive, desultory.

596. Compendium

n. **compendium**, compend, abstract, *précis* [*F.*], epitome, *multum in parvo* [*L.*], analysis, pandect, digest, sum and substance, brief, abridgment, *abrégé* [*F.*], summary, *aperçu* [*F.*], draft, minute, note; excerpt, extract; synopsis, textbook, conspectus, outlines, syllabus, contents, heads, prospectus.
    album; scrap–, note–, memorandum–, commonplace- book.
    fragments, ana, extracts, *excerpta* [*L.*], cuttings; fugitive -pieces, –writings; *spicilegium* [*L.*], flowers, anthology, miscellany, collectanea, analects *or* analecta; compilation.
    recapitulation, *résumé* [*F.*], review.
    abbreviation, abbreviature; contraction; shortening etc. 201; compression etc. 195.
v. **abridge**, abstract, epitomize, summarize; make–, prepare–, draw–, compile- an abstract etc. *n.;* abbreviate etc. (*shorten*) 201; condense etc. (*compress*) 195.
    compile etc. (*collect*) 72; note down, collect, edit.
    recapitulate, review, skim, run over, sum up.
adj. **compendious**, synoptic, analectic; *abrégé* [*F.*], abridged etc. *v.;* abbreviatory; analytic *or* analytical; variorum.
adv. **in short**, in epitome, in substance, in few words.

597. Poetry

n. **poetry**, poetics, poesy, Muse, tuneful Nine, Apollo, Apollo Musagetes, Calliope, Parnassus, Helicon, Pierides, Pierian spring; inspiration, fire of genius, coal from off the altar.
    poem; epic, epic poem; epopee *or* epopoeia, epos, ode, epode, idyl *or* idyll, lyric, eclogue, pastoral, bucolic, georgic, dithyramb *or* dithyrambus, anacreontic, sonnet, roundelay, rondeau, rondel, roundel, rondelet; triolet, sestina, virelay, ballade, cento, ghazal *or* ghazel, madrigal, monody, elegy; amoebaeum, palinode.
    dramatic–, didactic–, narrative–, lyric–, satirical- poetry; satire, opera.
    anthology, posy [*archaic*], garland, miscellany, *disjecta membra poetae* [*L.*].
    song, ballad, lay; love–, drinking–, war–, seasong; lullaby, *aubade* [*F.*]; music etc. 415; nursery rhymes.
    [bad poetry] doggerel, Hudibrastic verse; macaronics, macaronic verse; "not poetry, but prose run mad" [Pope].
    versification, riming *or* rhyming, making verses; prosody; scansion, scanning, orthometry [*rare*].
    canto, stanza, distich, verse, line, couplet, triplet, quatrain; strophe, antistrophe; refrain, chorus, burden; octave, sextet.
    verse, rime *or* rhyme, assonance, crambo [*contemptuous*], meter, measure, foot, numbers, strain, rhythm; ictus, beat, accent; accentuation etc. (*voice*) 580; iambus, iambic, iamb; dactyl, spondee, trochee, anapest etc.; hexameter, pentameter; Alexandrine; anacrusis, antispast, blank verse, Leonine verse, runes, alliteration; *bout-rimé* [*F.*].
    elegiacs etc. *adj.;* elegiac etc. *adj.* -verse, –meter *or* metre, –poetry.
    poet, minor poet; genius, maker [*obs.*], creator; poet laureate; laureate; bard, lyrist, scald *or* skald, scop [*hist.*], idylist *or* idyllist, sonneteer, rhapsodist, epic [*obs.*], epic poet, dithyrambic, satirist, troubadour, trouvère; minstrel; minnesinger, Meistersinger; jongleur, improvisator *or* improvvisatore [*It.*] *or* improvisatore; versifier, rimer *or* rhymer, rimester *or* rhymester; ballad monger, runer; poetaster; *genus irritabile vatum* [*L.*].
v. **poetize**, sing, "lisp in numbers" [Pope], build the stately rime, sing deathless songs, make immortal by verse; satirize; compose epic etc. *adj.* -poetry; string verses together, cap rimes, poeticize, versify, make verses, rime *or* rhyme, scan.
    produce -lame verses, –limping meters, –halting rime.
adj. **poetic** *or* poetical; lyric *or* lyrical; tuneful; epic; dithyrambic etc. *n.;* metrical; acatalectic, catalectic; elegiac, iambic, dactylic, spondaic *or* spondaical, trochaic, anapestic; amoebaeic, Melibean, scaldic *or* skaldic; Ionic, Sapphic, Alcaic, Pindaric, Pierian.

598. Prose

n. **prose**, prosaism, prosaicness, prosaicism [*rare*]; poetic prose; history etc. (*description*) 594.
    prose writer, essayist, monographer, monographist, novelist; *raconteur* [*F.*] etc. 594.
v. **prose**; write -prose, –in prose.
adj. **prosaic**, prosy, prosal [*obs.*]; unpoetical.
    rimeless *or* rhymeless, unrimed *or* unrhymed, in prose, not in verse.

599. The Drama

n. **the drama**, the stage, the theater *or* theatre, the play; theatricals, dramaturgy, histrionic art, mimography, buskin, sock, cothurnus, Melpomene and Thalia, Thespis.

599. The Drama

play, drama, stageplay, piece, five-act play, tragedy, comedy, opera, vaudeville, comedietta, *lever de rideau* [*F.*], curtain raiser, interlude, afterpiece, exode [*Rom. antiq.*], farce, *divertissement* [*F.*], extravaganza, burletta, harlequinade, pantomime, burlesque, *opéra bouffe* [*F.*], ballet, spectacle, masque, *drame* [*F.*], *comédie drame* [*F.*]; melodrama; *comédie larmoyante* [*F.*]; emotional -drama, -play; sensation drama; tragi-comedy; light-, genteel-, low-, farce- comedy, comedy of manners, farcical-comedy; monodrama, monodram *or* monodrame, monologue, duologue, dialogue; trilogy; charade, *proverbe* [*F.*]; mystery, miracle play, morality play.

act, scene, tableau, curtain; introduction, induction [*archaic*], exposition, expository scenes; prologue, epilogue; libretto, book, text, prompter's copy.

performance, representation, show [*colloq.*], *mise en scène* [*F.*], stage setting, stagery [*obs.*], stagecraft, *jeu de théâtre* [*F.*]; acting; gesture etc. 550; impersonation etc. 554; stage business, gag, patter, slap-stick [*slang*], buffoonery.

theater *or* theatre, playhouse, opera house; music hall; amphitheater *or* amphitheatre, circus, hippodrome; moving-picture theater, moving pictures, movies [*colloq.*], films, cinematograph *or* cinema [*colloq., Brit.*]; puppet show, fantoccini; marionettes. Punch and Judy.

auditory, auditorium, front of the house, front [*colloq. and professional*], stalls [*chiefly Eng.*], orchestra seats *or* orchestra, pit [*chiefly Eng.*], parquet, orchestra circle, boxes, balcony, gallery, peanut gallery [*slang*]; dressing rooms, greenroom.

scenery; back scene, flat; drop, drop scene; wing, screen, coulisse, side scene, transformation scene, curtain, act drop; proscenium; fire curtain, asbestos curtain.

stage, movable stage, scene, the boards; trap, mezzanine floor; flies; floats, footlights; limelight, spotlight, colored light, klieg light; orchestra.

theatrical costume, theatrical properties, props [*theat. cant*].

cast, *dramatis personae* [*L.*], persons in the play; role, part, character; repertoire, repertory, *répertoire* [*F.*].

actor, player; stage-, strolling- player; barnstormer, stager [*rare*], old stager; masker, masquer [*rare*], mime, mimer, mimic, mimester [*rare*]; *artiste* [*F.*], performer, star, headliner; comedian, tragedian, *tragédienne* [*F.*], Thespian, Roscius, ham [*slang*], hamfatter [*slang*]; utility, general utility, utility man.

buffoon, pantomimist, clown, *farceur* [*F.*], *buffo* (*pl. buffi*) [*It.*], grimacer, pantaloon, harlequin, columbine; punch, punchinello, *pulcinella* [*It.*].

mummer, guiser [*Eng. & Scot.*], guisard [*Scot.*], gysart [*obs.*], masque [*obs.*], mask.

mountebank, Jack Pudding; tumbler, posture master, acrobat; contortionist; ballet dancer, ballet girl; *coryphée* [*F.*], *danseuse* [*F.*]; chorus girl, chorus singer.

company; first tragedian, prima donna, leading lady; lead; leading man, protagonist; *jeune premier* [*F.*], *débutant* (*fem. débutante*) [*F.*]; light-, genteel-, low- comedian; walking gentleman *or* lady [*obsoles.*], *amoroso* [*It.*], juvenile lead, juvenile; heavy lead, heavy; heavy father, ingenue, *ingénue* [*F.*], *jeune veuve* [*F.*], soubrette, *farceur* (*fem. farceuse*) [*F.*].

mute, figurant, figurante, walking part, supernumerary, super [*theat. cant*], supe [*theat. cant*].

manager; stage-, actor-, acting- manager; *entrepreneur* [*F.*], impresario; angel [*slang*].

[theater staff] property man, prop [*theat. cant*]; costumer, costumier, wig-maker, make-up artist; sceneshifter, grip, stage hand, stage carpenter, machinist, electrician, chief electrician; prompter, call boy; advance agent, publicity agent.

dramatist, playwright, playwriter; dramatic -author, -writer; mimographer, mimist [*obs.*]; dramatic critic.

audience, auditory, house; orchestra etc. *n.*; gallery, the gods [*colloq.*], gallery gods [*collow.*].

v. **act**, play, perform; put on the stage, dramatize, stage, produce, set; personate etc. 554; mimic etc. (*imitate*) 19; enact; play-, act-, go through-, perform-a part; rehearse, spout, gag [*slang*], patter [*slang*], rant; strut and fret one's hour upon the stage; tread the -stage, -boards; make one's début, take a part, come out; star; supe [*slang*].

adj. **dramatic**; theatric *or* theatrical; scenic, histrionic, comic, tragic, buskined, cothurned; farcical, tragi-comic, melodramatic, operatic; stagy *or* stagey; spectacular, stellar, all-star [*cant*]; stagestruck.

adv. **on the stage**, on the boards; in the limelight, in the spotlight; before the floats, before the footlights, before the curtain, before an audience; behind the scenes.

Class 5. Volition

Division 1. Individual Volition

Section 1. Volition in General

600. Will

n. **will**, volition, conation, volitiency, velleity; *liberum arbitrium* [*L.*]; will and pleasure, free will; freedom etc. 748; discretion; choice, inclination, intent, purpose, voluntarism; option etc. (*choice*) 609; voluntariness, spontaneity, spontaneousness; originality.

wish, desire, pleasure, mind, frame of mind etc. (*inclination*) 602; intention etc. 620; predetermination etc. 611; self-control etc. determination etc. (*resolution*) 604; force of will, will power, autocracy, bossiness [*colloq.*].

v. **will**, list [*archaic*]; see fit, think fit; determine etc. (*resolve*) 604; enjoin; settle etc. (*choose*) 609; volunteer.

have a will of one's own; do what one chooses etc. (*freedom*) 748; have it all one's own way; have one's will, have one's own way; use-, exercise- one's discretion; take -upon oneself, –one's own course, –the law into one's own hands; do of one's own accord, do upon one's own authority, do upon one's own responsibility; take responsibility, boss [*colloq.*], take the bit between one's teeth; originate etc. (*cause*) 153.

adj. **voluntary**, volitional, willful *or* wilful; free etc. 748; optional; discretional, discretionary; volitient, volitive; volunteer, voluntaristic; dictatorial, bossy [*colloq.*].

minded etc. (*willing*) 602; prepense etc. (*predetermined*) 611; intended etc. 620; autocratic; unbidden etc. (bid etc. 741); spontaneous; original etc. (*causal*) 153; unconstrained.

adv. **voluntarily** etc. *adj.*; at will, at pleasure; *à volonté* [*F.*], *à discrétion* [*F.*]; *al piacere* [*It.*]; *ad libitum* [*L.*], *ad arbitrium* [*L.*]; as one thinks proper, as it seems good to; *a beneplacito* [*It*].

of one's own -accord, –free will; on one's own responsibility; *proprio-, suo-, ex mero- motu* [*L.*]; out of one's own head; by choice etc. 609; purposely etc. (*intentionally*) 620; deliberately etc. 611.

601. Necessity

n. **involuntariness**; instinct, blind impulse; inborn-, innate- proclivity; native-, natural- tendency; natural impulse, predetermination.

necessity, necessitation, necessitarianism, obligation; compulsion etc. 744; subjection etc. 749; stern-, hard-, dire-, imperious-, inexorable-, iron-, adverse- -necessity, –fate; *anagke* [*Gr.*], what must be.

destiny, destination; fatality, fate, kismet, doom, foredoom, election, predestination; preordination, foreordination; lot, fortune; fatalism; inevitableness etc. *adj.;* spell etc. 993.

fates, Parcae, Sisters three, book of fate; God's will, Heaven, will of Heaven; star, stars; planet, planets; astral influence; wheel of Fortune, Ides of March, Hobson's choice.

last shift, last resort; *dernier ressort* [*F.*]; *pis aller* etc. (*substitute*) 147; necessaries etc. (*requirement*) 630.

necessarian, necessitarian; fatalist; automaton, pawn.

v. **lie under a necessity**; be fated, be doomed, be destined etc., be in for, be under the necessity of; be obliged, be forced, be driven; have no -choice, –alternative; be one's fate to etc. *n.;* be pushed to the wall, be driven into a corner, be unable to help, be swept on, be drawn irresistibly.

destine, doom, foredoom, devote; predestine, preordain; cast a spell etc. 992; necessitate; compel etc. 744.

be decreed, be determined, be destined etc., be written; be written in the -book of fate, –stars.

adj. **necessary**, necessarian, necessitarian; needful etc. (*requisite*) 630.

fated; destined etc. *v.;* fateful, big with fate; set apart, devoted, elect.

compulsory etc. (*compel*) 744; uncontrollable, inevitable, unavoidable, indefeasible, irresistible, irrevocable, inexorable, binding; avoidless, resistless.

involuntary, instinctive, automatic, blind, mechanical; unconscious, unwitting, unthinking; unintentional etc. (*undesigned*) 621; spellbound; impulsive etc. 612.

602. Willingness

adv. **necessarily** etc. *adj.;* of necessity, of course; *ex necessitate rei* [*L.*]; needs must; perforce etc. 744; *nolens volens* [*L.*]; will he nil he, will I nill I, willy-nilly, *bon gré mal gré* [*F.*]; willing or unwilling, *coûte que coûte* [*F.*]; compulsorily, by compulsion, by force.

faute de mieux [*F.*]; by stress of; if need be; *que faire?* [*F.*].

602. Willingness

n. **willingness**, voluntariness etc. *adj.;* willing mind, heart.

disposition, inclination, liking, turn, propensity, propension, propenseness, leaning, animus; frame of mind, humor, mood, vein; bent etc. (*turn of mind*) 820; *penchant* [*F.*] etc. (*desire*) 865; aptitude etc. 698.

docility, docibleness [*rare*], docibility [*rare*], appetency, tractability, tractableness, persuadability, persuadableness, persuasibleness, persuasibility; pliability etc. (*softness*) 324.

geniality, cordiality; goodwill; alacrity, readiness, zeal, enthusiasm, earnestness, forwardness; eagerness etc. (*desire*) 865.

assent etc. 488; compliance etc. 762; pleasure etc. (*will*) 600.

labor of love, self-appointed task, volunteering; gratuitous service; social service, welfare work.

volunteer, unpaid worker, amateur, voluntary [*rare*]; social worker, welfare worker.

v. **be willing** etc. *adj.;* incline, lean to, mind, propend [*rare*], had as lief, would as lief; lend-, give-, turn- a willing ear; have -a, –half a, –a great- mind to; hold to, cling to; desire etc. 865.

acquiesce etc. (*assent*) 488; see think- -good, -fit, -proper; comply with etc. 762.

swallow-, nibble at- the bait; swallow bait, hook, and sinker; swallow bait and all; gorge the hook; have-, make- no scruple of; make no bones of [*colloq.*]; jump at, catch at; go in for, go in at [*both colloq.*]; take up, plunge into, have a go at [*colloq.*]; meet halfway.

volunteer, offer, proffer; offer oneself etc. 763.

adj. **willing**, minded, fain, disposed, inclined, favorable; favorably -minded, -inclined, -disposed; well-disposed, lief [*archaic*], nothing loth; in the -vein, –mood, –humor, –mind.

ready, forward, earnest, eager, zealous, enthusiastic; bent upon etc. (*desirous*) 865; predisposed, desirous, propense.

docile; persuadable, persuasible; suasible, amenable, easily persuaded, facile, easy-going; tractable etc. (*pliant*) 324; genial, gracious, cordial, cheering, hearty; content etc. (*assenting*) 488.

voluntary, gratuitous, spontaneous; unasked etc. (ask etc. 765); unforced etc. (*free*) 748.

adv. **willingly** etc. *adj.;* fain, freely, as lief, heart and soul; with pleasure, with all one's heart, with open arms; with good will, with right good will; *de bonne volonté* [*F.*], *ex animo* [*L.*], *con amore* [*It.*], heart in hand, nothing loath, without reluctance, of one's own accord, graciously, with a good grace; without demur.

à la bonne heure [*F.*]; by all means, by all manner of means; to one's heart's content; yes etc. (*assent*) 488.

int. **surely**! sure! with pleasure! of course! delighted!

603. Unwillingness

n. **unwillingness** etc. *adj.;* indisposition, indisposedness, disinclination, aversation [*rare*], aversion; averseness etc. (*dislike*) 867; nolleity [*rare*], nolition [*rare*]; renitence *or* renitency; reluctance; indifference etc. 866; backwardness etc. *adj.;* slowness etc. 275; want of -alacrity, –readiness; indocility etc. (*obstinacy*) 606.

scrupulousness, scrupulosity; qualms–, twinge- of conscience; delicacy, demur, scruple, qualm, shrinking, recoil; hesitation etc. (*irresolution*) 605; fastidiousness etc. 868.

dissent etc. 489; refusal etc. 764.

forced labor, unwilling service, peonage; compulsion etc. 744; slacker.

v. **be unwilling** etc. *adj.;* nill [*archaic*]; dislike etc. 867; grudge, begrudge; not find it in one's heart to, not have the stomach to.

demur, stick at, scruple, stickle; hang fire, run rusty [*colloq.*], go stale; give up, let down [*slang*]; pull back, be a dead weight, be a passenger in the boat, not pull fair, shirk, slack, shy [*dial. Eng.*], fight shy of, get by [*slang*], duck [*slang*]; recoil, shrink, swerve; hesitate etc. 605; avoid etc. 623.

oppose etc. 708; dissent etc. 489; refuse etc. 764.

adj. **unwilling**; not in the vein, loath *or* loth, shy of, disinclined, indisposed, averse, reluctant, not content; renitent, opposed; adverse etc. (*opposed*) 708; laggard, backward, remiss, slack, slow to; indifferent etc. 866; scrupulous; squeamish etc. (*fastidious*) 868; repugnant etc. (*dislike*) 867; restiff [*obs.*], restive; demurring etc. *v.;* unconsenting etc. (*refusing*) 764; involuntary etc. 601; grudging, forced; irreconcilable.

adv. **unwillingly** etc. *adj.;* grudgingly, with a heavy heart; with -a bad, –an ill- grace; against-, sore against- one's wishes, –one's will, –the grain;

invita Minerva [*L.*]; *à contre coeur* [*F.*]; *malgré soi* [*F.*]; in spite of -one's teeth, -oneself; *nolens volens* [*L.*] etc. (*necessity*) 601; perforce etc. 744; under protest; no etc. 536; if I must I must; not if one can help it; not for the world; far be it from me.

604. Resolution

n. **determination**, will; iron will, unconquerable will; will of one's own, decision, resolution; backbone; clear grit, grit [*U. S. & Can.*]; sand [*slang*]; strength of -mind, –will; resolve etc. (*intent*) 620; intransigence *or* intransigency, *intransigeance* [*F.*]; firmness etc. (*stability*) 150; energy, manliness, vigor; resoluteness etc. (*courage*) 861; zeal etc. 682; desperation; devotion, devotedness.

self-control, *aplomb* [*F.*], mastery over self, self-mastery, self-command, self-possession, self-reliance, self-government, self-restraint, self-conquest, self-denial; moral -courage, –fiber, –strength.

tenacity, perseverance etc. 604*a*; obstinacy etc. 606; game, pluck; fighting cock, game cock; bulldog; British lion.

irreconcilable, intransigent, *intransigeant* [*F.*], bitter-ender [*colloq.*]; fighting minority, militant remnant.

v. **have determination** etc. *n.;* know one's own mind; be resolved etc. *adj.;* make up one's mind; will, resolve, determine; decide etc. (*judgment*) 480; form–, come to- a -determination, –resolution, –resolve; conclude, fix, seal, determine once for all, bring to a crisis, drive matters to an extremity; take a decisive step etc. (*choice*) 609; take upon oneself etc. (*undertake*) 676.

steel oneself, devote oneself to, give oneself up to; throw away the scabbard, kick down the ladder, nail one's colors to the mast, set one's back against the wall, burn one's bridges, grit one's teeth, set one's teeth, set one's jaw, take the bit in one's mouth, put one's foot down, take one's stand, stand firm etc. (*stability*) 150; stand no nonsense, not listen to the voice of the charmer; insist upon, make a point of; set one's heart upon, set one's mind upon.

buckle to; buckle oneself; put–, lay–, set- one's shoulder to the wheel; put one's heart into; run the gauntlet, make a dash at, take the bull by the horns; rush–, plunge- *in medias res* [*L.*]; go in for [*colloq.*].

stick at nothing; make short work of etc. (*activity*) 682; not stick at trifles; go all lengths, go the limit [*slang*], go the whole hog [*slang*], go it blind [*slang*]; go down with one's colors flying; die game; persist etc. (*persevere*) 604 *a;* go through fire and water, "ride in the whirlwind and direct the storm" [Addison].

adj. **resolved** etc. *v.;* determined; strong-willed, strong-minded; resolute etc. (*brave*) 861; self-possessed, earnest, serious; decided, definitive, peremptory, unhesitating, unflinching, unshrinking; firm, iron, game, plucky, tenacious, gritty, indomitable, game to the backbone, game to the last; inexorable, relentless, not to be -shaken, –put down; *tenax propositi* [*L.*]; obstinate etc. 606; steady etc. (*persevering*) 604*a*.

unbending, unyielding; set–, bent–, intent- upon; grim, stern; inflexible etc. (*hard*) 323; cast-iron, irrevocable, irreversible; not to be deflected; firm as Gibraltar.

steeled–, proof- against; *in utrumque paratus* [*L.*].

adv. **resolutely** etc. *adj.;* in earnest, in good earnest; seriously, joking apart, earnestly, heart and soul; on one's mettle; manfully, like a man; with a high -heart, –courage, –hand; with a strong hand etc. (*exertion*) 686.

at all risks, at all hazards, at all events; at any -rate, –risk, –hazard, –price, –cost, –sacrifice; *à bis ou à blanc* [*F.*], cost what it may; *coûte que coûte* [*F.*]; *à tort et à travers* [*F.*]; once for all; neck or nothing; survive or perish, live or die; rain or shine.

604a. Perseverance

n. **perseverance**; continuance etc. (*inaction*) 143; permanence etc. (*absence of change*) 141; firmness etc. (*stability*) 150.

constancy, steadiness; singleness–, tenacity- of purpose; persistence, plodding, patience; sedulity [*rare*] etc. (*industry*) 682; pertinacy [*obs.*], pertinacity, pertinaciousness; iteration etc. 104.

grit, bottom, game, pluck, stamina, backbone, sand [*slang*]; indefatigability, indefatigableness; tenacity, staying power, endurance; bulldog courage.

v. **persevere**, persist; hold -on, –out; die in the last ditch, be in at the death; stick to, cling to, adhere to; stick to one's text; keep on, carry on, hold on; keep to–, maintain- one's -course, –ground; go all lengths, go through fire and water; bear up, keep up, hold up; plod; stick to work etc. (*work*) 686; continue etc. 143; follow up; die in harness, die at one's post.

605. Irresolution

adj. **persevering**, constant; steady, steadfast; undeviating, unwavering, unfaltering, unswerving, unflinching, unsleeping, unflagging, undrooping; steady as time; unintermitting, unremitting; plodding; industrious etc. 682; strenuous etc. 686; pertinacious; persisting, persistent.

solid, sturdy, stanch *or* staunch, true to oneself; unchangeable etc. 150; unconquerable etc. (*strong*) 159; indomitable, game to the last, indefatigable, untiring, unwearied, never tiring.

adv. **without fail**; through evil report and good report, through thick and thin, through fire and water; *per fas et nefas* [*L.*]; sink or swim, at any price, *vogue la galère* [*F.*]; rain or shine, fair or foul, in sickness and in health.

605. Irresolution

n. **irresolution**, infirmity of purpose, indecision, indetermination, undetermination [*rare*], instability; loss of will power, abulia, abulomania; unsettlement; uncertainty etc. 475; demur, suspense; hesitating etc. *v.*, hesitation, hesitancy; wabble *or* wobble; revocability, vacillation; changeableness etc. 149; fluctuation; alternation etc. (*oscillation*) 314; caprice etc. 608; lukewarmness, Laodiceanism.

fickleness, levity, *légèreté* [*F.*]; pliancy etc. (*softness*) 324; weakness; timidity etc. 860; cowardice etc. 862; half measures.

waverer, shilly-shally, ass between two bundles of hay; shuttlecock, butterfly, feather, piece of thistledown; house built on sand; doughface; turncoat, opportunist, Vicar of Bray, Dite Deuchars; Laodicean; timeserver etc. 607.

v. **be irresolute** etc. *adj.*; hang-, keep- in suspense; leave *ad referendum;* think twice about, pause; dawdle etc. (*inactivity*) 683; remain neuter; dilly-dally, hesitate, boggle, hover, dacker *or* daiker [*dial. Eng. & Scot.*], wabble *or* wobble [*colloq.*], shilly-shally, hem and haw, demur, not know one's own mind; debate, balance; dally with, coquet with; will and will not, *chasser-balancer* [*F.*]; go halfway, compromise, make a compromise; be thrown off one's balance, stagger like a drunken man; be afraid etc. 860; let "I dare not" wait upon "I would" [*Macbeth*]; falter, waver.

vacillate etc. 149; change etc. 140; retract etc. 607; fluctuate; pendulate; alternate etc. (*oscillate*) 314; keep off and on, play fast and loose; blow hot and cold etc. (*caprice*) 608; turn one's coat.

shuffle, palter, blink, shirk, trim.

adj. **irresolute**, infirm of purpose, palsied, drifting, double-minded, half-hearted; undecided, unresolved, undetermined; shilly-shally, wabbly *or* wobbly; fidgety, tremulous; hesitating etc. *v.*; off one's balance; abulic; at a loss etc. (*uncertain*) 475.

vacillating etc. *v.*; unsteady etc. (*changeable*) 149; unsteadfast, fickle, unreliable, irresponsible, unstable, unstable as water, without ballast; capricious etc. 608; volatile, frothy; light, lightsome, lightminded; giddy; fast and loose.

weak, feeble-minded, frail; timid etc. 860; cowardly etc. 862; dough-faced; facile; pliant etc. (*soft*) 324; unable to say "no," easy-going.

revocable, reversible.

adv. **irresolutely** etc. *adj.*; irresolvedly; in faltering accents; off and on; on the sands; from pillar to post; seesaw etc. 314.

606. Obstinacy

n. **obstinateness** etc. *adj.*; obstinacy, tenacity; cussedness; perseverance etc. 604a; immovability; old school; inflexibility etc. (*hardness*) 323; obduracy, obduration [*rare*], obdurateness, doggedness, dogged resolution; resolution etc. 604; ruling passion; blind side.

self-will, contumacy, perversity; pervicaciousness [*rare*], pervicacy [*obs.*], pervicacity [*obs.*]; indocility [*obs.*].

bigotry, intolerance, dogmatism; opiniatry [*obs.*], opiniativeness [*rare*]; impersuasibility, impersuadableness, intractableness, incorrigibility; fixed idea etc. (*prejudgment*) 481; fanaticism, zealotry, infatuation, monomania; opinionatedness, opinionativeness.

bigot, opinionist [*obs.*], opinionatist [*obs.*], opiniator [*obs.*], opinator [*obs.*]; stickler, dogmatist, zealot, enthusiast, fanatic, bitter-ender [*colloq.*]; mule.

v. **be obstinate** etc. *adj.*; stickle, take no denial, fly in the face of facts; opinionate [*rare*], be wedded to an opinion, hug a belief; have one's own way etc. (*will*) 600; persist etc. (*persevere*) 604a; have-, insist on having- the last word.

die hard, die fighting, fight to the last ditch, fight against destiny, not yield an inch, stand out.

adj. obstinate, tenacious, stubborn, obdurate, case-hardened; inflexible etc. (*hard*) 323; balky; immovable, not to be moved; inert etc. 172; unchangeable etc. 150; inexorable etc. (*determined*) 604; mulish, obstinate as a mule, pigheaded.

dogged; sullen, sulky; unmoved, uninfluenced, unaffected.

willful or wilful, self-willed, perverse; resty [*dial. Eng.*], restive, pervicacious [*rare*], ungovernable, wayward, refractory, unruly; heady, headstrong; *entêté* [*F.*]; contumacious; cross-grained.

arbitrary, dogmatic, positive, bigoted, opinionated, opinionative, opinionate [*obs.*], opinioned, opiniative [*rare*]; prejudiced etc. 481; creed-bound; prepossessed, infatuated; stiff-backed, stiff-necked, stiff-hearted; hard-mouthed, hidebound; unyielding; impervious, impracticable, impersuasible, impersuadable, unpersuadable; untractable, intractable; incorrigible, deaf to advice, impervious to reason; crotchety etc. 608.

adv. obstinately etc. *adj.;* with set jaw, with sullen mouth; no surrender.

607. Tergiversation

n. **tergiversation**, tergiversating, recantation; palinode, palinody [*rare*]; renunciation; abjuration, abjurement; defection etc. (*relinquishment*) 624; going over etc. *v.;* apostasy; retraction, retractation; withdrawal; disavowal etc. (*negation*) 536; revocation, revokement [*rare*], reversal; repentance etc. 950; *redintegratio amoris* [*L.*].

change of -mind, -intention, -purpose; afterthought.

coquetry, flirtation; vacillation etc. 605.

recidivism, recidivation, backsliding; *volte-face* [*F.*].

turncoat, turn-tippet [*obs.*]; rat [*cant*], apostate, renegade, pervert, deserter, backslider; recidivist; crawfish [*slang*], mugwump, blackleg, scab [*slang*]; proselyte, convert.

timeserver, time-pleaser; timist [*obs.*], Vicar of Bray, trimmer, ambidexter; double dealer; weathercock etc. (*changeable*) 149; Janus; coquet, flirt.

v. **tergiversate**, veer round, wheel round, turn round; change one's- mind, -intention, -purpose, -note; abjure, renounce; withdraw from etc. (*relinquish*) 624; turn a pirouette; go over-, pass-, change-, skip- from one side to another; go to the right-about; box the compass, shift one's ground, go upon another tack.

apostatize, change sides, go over, rat [*cant*], *tourner casaque* [*F.*], recant, retract; revoke; rescind etc. (*abrogate*) 756; recall; forswear, unsay; come -over, -round- to an opinion.

back down, draw in one's horns, eat one's words; eat-, swallow- the leek; swerve, flinch, back out of, retrace one's steps, crawfish, crawl [*both slang*]; think better of it; come back-, return- to one's first love; turn over a new leaf etc. (*repent*) 950.

trim, shuffle, play fast and loose, blow hot and cold, coquet, flirt, be on the fence, straddle, hold with the hare but run with the hounds; *nager entre deux eaux* [*F.*], wait to see how the -cat jumps, -wind blows.

adj. **changeful** etc. 149; irresolute etc. 605; ductile, slippery as an eel, trimming, ambidextrous, timeserving; coquetting etc. *v.*

revocatory, reactionary.

608. Caprice

n. **caprice**, fancy, humor; whim, whimsey or whimsy, whim-wham, crotchet, *capriccio* [*It.*], quirk, freak, maggot, fad, vagary, prank, fit, flimflam, escapade, boutade [*obs.*], wild-goose chase; capriciousness etc. *adj.;* kink.

v. **be capricious** etc. *adj.;* have a maggot in the brain; take it into one's head, take the bit in one's teeth; strain at a gnat and swallow a camel; blow hot and cold; play fast and loose, play fantastic tricks; *tourner casaque* [*F.*].

adj. **capricious**; erratic, eccentric, fitful, hysterical; full of whims etc. *n.;* maggoty; inconsistent, fanciful, fantastic, whimsical, crotchety, kinky, particular, humorsome, freakish, skittish, wanton, wayward; contrary; captious; unreasonable, unrestrained, undisciplined, not amenable to reason, arbitrary; unconformable etc. 83; penny wise and pound foolish; fickle etc. (*irresolute*) 605; frivolous, sleeveless [*obs.*], giddy, volatile.

adv. **by fits**, by fits and starts, without rime or reason, at one's own sweet will; without counting the cost.

609. Choice

n. **choice**, option; discretion etc. (*volition*) 600; preoption; alternative; dilemma, *embarras de choix* [*F.*]; adoption, coöptation; novation [*law*]; decision etc. (*judgment*) 480.

election, poll, ballot, vote, division, voice, suffrage, cumulative vote; plebiscitum, plebiscite, *vox populi* [*L.*], popular decision, referendum; electioneering; voting etc. *v.;* elective franchise; straight ticket, ticket; ballot box.

selection, excerption, gleaning, eclecticism; *excerpta* [*L.*]; gleanings, cuttings, scissors and paste; pick etc. (*best*) 650.

preference, prelation [*rare*]; predilection etc. (*desire*) 865; Apple of Discord; choice of Hercules; Scylla and Charybdis; good and evil.

609a. Absence of Choice

v. **offer for one's choice**, set before; hold out–, present–, offer- the alternative; put to the vote.
choose, elect; coöpt; coöptate [*rare*]; take–, make- one's choice; make choice of, fix upon; use–, exercise–, one's- -discretion, -option; adopt, take up, embrace, espouse.
settle; decide etc. (*adjudge*) 480; list etc. (*will*) 600; make up one's mind etc. (*resolve*) 604.
vote, poll, hold up one's hand, give a (*or* the) voting sign; divide.
select; pick, –and choose; pick–, single- out; excerpt, cull, glean, winnow; sift–, separate–, winnow- the chaff from the wheat; pick up, pitch upon; pick one's way; indulge one's fancy.
set apart, mark out for; mark etc. 550.
prefer; have rather, had (*or* would) as lief; fancy etc. (*desire*) 865; reserve, set one's seal upon; be persuaded etc. 615.
take a decided step, take a decisive step; commit oneself to a course; pass–, cross- the Rubicon; cast in one's lot with; take for better or for worse.

adj. **optional**; coöptative; discretional etc. (*voluntary*) 600; at choice, on approval.
choosing etc. *v.;* eclectic; preferential.
chosen etc. *v.;* choice etc. (*good*) 648; elect, select, popular.

adv. **optionally** etc. *adj.;* at pleasure etc. (*will*) 600; either, –the one or the other; or; at the option of; whether or not; once for all; for one's money.
by choice, by preference; in preference; rather, before.

609a.   Absence of Choice

n. **no choice**, Hobson's choice; first come first served; necessity etc. 601; not a pin to choose etc. (*equality*) 27; any, the first that comes; that or nothing.
neutrality, indifference; indecision etc. (*irresolution*) 605.

v. **be neutral** etc. *adj.;* have no -preference, -choice; waive, not vote; abstain–, refrain–, –from voting; leave undecided; "make a virtue of necessity" [*Two Gentlemen from Verona*].

adj. **neutral**, neuter; indifferent; undecided etc. (*irresolute*) 605.

adv. **either** etc. (*choice*) 609.

610.   Rejection

n. **rejection**, repudiation, exclusion; refusal etc. 764; declination, declinature, withdrawal; averseness.

v. **reject**; set–, lay- aside; give up; decline etc. (*refuse*) 764; exclude, except; pluck up, spurn, cast out.
repudiate, scout, set at naught; fling–, cast–, throw–, toss- -to the winds, –to the dogs, –overboard, –away; send to the right-about; disclaim etc. (*deny*) 536; discard etc. (*eject*) 297, (*have done with*) 678.

adj. **rejected** etc. *v.;* rejectaneous [*obs.*], rejectitious [*obs.*], declinatory; not chosen etc. 609, not to be thought of; out of the question; "declined with thanks."

adv. **neither**, neither the one nor the other; no etc. 536.

611.   Predetermination

n. **predetermination**, predestination, preordination, premeditation, predeliberation; foregone conclusion; *parti pris* [*F.*]; resolve, propendency [*obs.*]; intention etc. 620; project etc. 626; fate, foredoom, necessity.
schedule, list, calendar, docket, slate, register, roster, poll, muster, draft, *cadre* [*F.*], panel.

v. **predetermine**, predestine, preordain, premeditate, preresolve, preconcert; resolve beforehand.
list, schedule, docket, slate, register, poll, empanel, draft.

adj. **premeditated** etc. *v.;* predesigned; prepense, advised, studied, designed, calculated; aforethought; intended etc. 620; foregone.
well-laid, well-devised, well-weighed; maturely considered; cut-and-dried, slated; cunning.

adv. **advisedly** etc. *adj.;* with premeditation, deliberately, all things considered, with eyes open, in cold blood; intentionally etc. 620.

612.   Impulse

n. **impulse**, sudden thought; impromptu, improvisation; inspiration, flash, spurt.
improvisor, extemporizer, *improvvisatore* or *improvisatore* [*It.*]; creature of impulse.

v. flash on the mind.
improvise, extemporize; say what comes uppermost, say what comes first into one's head; act on the spur of the moment, rise to the occasion; spurt.

adj. **extemporaneous**, impulsive, indeliberate [*rare*]; snap; improvised, improvisate, improviso, improvisatory; unpremeditated; unmeditated, improvisatorial, improvisatory, *improvisé* [*F.*]; unprompted, unguided; natural, unguarded; spontaneous etc. (*voluntary*) 600; instinctive etc. 601.

208

613. Habit

n. **habit**, habitude, habituation, assuetude [*obs.*], assuefaction [*obs.*]; wont; run, way; habitual attitude, habitual state of mind, habitual course.

common–, general–, natural–, ordinary- -course, –run, –state- of things; matter of course; beaten -path, –track, –ground.

cacoëthes; bad–, confirmed–, inveterate–, intrinsic etc. (5)- habit; addictedness, addiction, trick.

custom, use, usage, prescription, immemorial usage, practice; prevalence, observance; conventionalism, conventionality; mode, fashion, vogue; etiquette etc. (*gentility*) 852; order of the day, cry; conformity etc. 82; consuetude, dastur *or* dustoor [*India*].

one's old way, old school, *veteris vestigia flammae* [*L.*]; *laudator temporis acti* [*L.*].

rule, standing order, precedent, routine; red tape, red-tapism; pipe clay; rut, groove.

addict, habitué, habitual [*colloq.*], frequenter, case [*slang*], hard case [*slang*], the limit [*slang*].

inurement; training etc. (*education*) 537; seasoning, hardening; radication; second nature, acclimatization; knack etc. (*skill*) 698.

v. **be wont** etc. *adj.*

fall into a custom etc. (*conform to*) 82; tread–, follow- the beaten -track, –path; *stare super antiquas vias* [*L.*]; move in a rut, run on in a groove, go round like a horse in a mill, go on in the old jog-trot way; get wound up in red tape.

habituate, inure, harden, season, caseharden; accustom, familiarize; naturalize, acclimatize; keep one's hand in; train etc. (*educate*) 537.

get into the -way, –knack- of; learn etc. 539; cling to, adhere to; repeat etc. 104; acquire–, contract–, fall into- a -habit, –trick; addict oneself to, take to, accustom oneself to.

be habitual etc. *adj.;* prevail; come into use, become a habit, take root; gain upon one, grow upon one.

adj. **habitual**; accustomary, customary; prescriptive; accustomed etc. *v.;* of -daily, –everyday- occurrence; consuetudinary; wonted, usual, general, ordinary, common, frequent, every day, household, jog-trot; well-trodden, well-known; familiar, vernacular, trite, commonplace, conventional, regular, set, stock, established, stereotyped; prevailing, prevalent; current, received, acknowledged, recognized, accredited; of course, admitted, understood.

conformable etc. 82; according to -use, –custom, –routine; in vogue, in fashion; fashionable etc. (*genteel*) 852.

wont; used to, given to, addicted to, attuned to, habituated to etc. *v.;* in the habit of; habitué [*F.*]; at home in etc. (*skillful*) 698; seasoned; imbued with, soaked in, permeated with, never free from; devoted to, wedded to.

hackneyed, fixed, rooted, deep-rooted, ingrafted *or* engrafted, permanent, inveterate, besetting, naturalized; ingrained etc. (*intrinsic*) 5.

adv. **habitually** etc. *adj.;* always etc. (*uniformly*) 16.

as usual, as is one's wont, as things go, as the world goes, as the sparks fly upwards; as you were [*mil.*]; *more suo* [*L.*], *more solito* [*L.*]; *ex more* [*L.*].

as a rule, for the most part; generally etc. *adj.;* most -often, –frequently.

614. Desuetude

n. **desuetude**, disusage; obsolescence, disuse etc. 678; want of -habit, –use, –practice; inusitation [*rare*]; newness to; new brooms.

nonprevalence; infraction of usage etc. (*unconformity*) 83; "a custom more honored in the breach than the observance" [*Hamlet*].

v. **be unaccustomed** etc. *adj.;* leave off–, cast off–, break off–, cure oneself of–, wean oneself from–, shake off–, violate–, break through–, infringe- a habit, –a custom, –a usage; break one's -chains, –fetters; do old things in a new way, give an original touch, give a new dress to old ideas; disuse etc. 678; wear off.

adj. **unaccustomed**, unused, unwonted, unseasoned, uninured, unhabituated, untrained; new, fresh, original; impulsive etc. *adj.* 612; green etc. (*unskilled*) 699; unhackneyed.

unconventional, unfashionable; dissident, protestant; unusual etc. (*unconformable*) 83; nonobservant; disused etc. 678.

adv. **contrary to -custom**, – usage, –convention; for once, just once; "this time doesn't count."

615. Motive

n. **motive**, springs of action.

reason, ground, call, principle; by-end, by-purpose; mainspring, *primum mobile* [*L.*], keystone; the why and the wherefore; *pro* and *con*, reason why; secret motive, ulterior motive; *arrière pensée* [*F.*]; intention etc. 620.

inducement, consideration; attraction; loadstone; magnet, magnetism, magnetic force; allectation [*obs.*], allective [*obs.*], temptation, enticement, *agacerie* [*F.*], allurement, witchery; bewitchment, bewitchery; charm; spell etc. 993; fascination, blandishment, cajolery; seduction, seducement; honeyed words, voice of the tempter, song of the Sirens; forbidden fruit, golden apple.

persuasibility, persuasibleness, persuadability, persuadableness; attractability; impressibility, susceptibility; softness; persuasiveness, attractiveness; tantalization.

influence, prompting, dictate, instance; impulse, impulsion; incitement, incitation; press, insistence, urge [*rare*], instigation; provocation etc. (*excitation of feeling*) 824; inspiration; persuasion, suasion; encouragement, advocacy; exhortation, hortation; advice etc. 695; solicitation etc. (*request*) 765; lobbyism; pull [*slang*].

incentive, stimulus, spur, fillip, whip, goad, ankus [*India*], rowel, provocative, whet, dram.

bribe, lure; decoy, decoy duck; bait, trail of a red herring; bribery and corruption; sop, sop to Cerberus.

tempter, seducer, seductor, seductress; prompter, suggester, coaxer, wheedler, Siren, Circe, vampire [*colloq.*], vamp [*slang*]; instigator, *agent provocateur* [*F.*]; lobbyist; firebrand, incendiary.

v. **induce**, move; draw, draw on; bring in its train, give an impulse to etc. *n.;* inspire; put up to [*slang*], prompt, call up; attract, beckon.

stimulate etc. (*excite*) 824; spirit, spirit up, inspirit; rouse, arouse, animate, incite, provoke, instigate, set on, actuate; act upon, work upon, operate upon; encourage; pat–, clap- on the -back, -shoulder.

set an example, set the fashion; keep in countenance, back up.

influence, weigh with, bias, sway, incline, dispose, predispose, turn the scale, inoculate; lead, –by the nose; have–, exercise–, influence- -with, –over, –upon; go–, come- round one [*colloq.*]; turn the head, magnetize; lobby [*chiefly U. S.*].

persuade; prevail -with, –upon; overcome, carry; bring round, bring to one's senses; draw–, win–, gain–, talk- over; come over [*colloq.*]; procure, enlist, engage; invite, court.

tempt, seduce, overpersuade, entice, allure, captivate, fascinate, bewitch, carry away, charm, conciliate, wheedle, coax, lure, vamp [*slang*]; inveigle, tantalize, cajole etc. (*deceive*) 545.

bribe, tamper with, suborn, grease the palm, bait with a silver hook, gild the pill, make things pleasant, put a sop into the pan, throw a sop to, bait the hook.

enforce, force; impel etc. (*push*) 276; propel etc. 284; whip, lash, goad, spur, prick, urge; egg on, hound on, hurry on; drag etc. 285; exhort; advise etc. 695; call upon etc., press etc. (*request*) 765; advocate.

be persuaded etc.; yield to temptation, come round [*colloq.*]; concede etc. (*consent*) 762; obey a call; follow -advice, –the bent, –the dictates of; act on principle.

adj. **impulsive**, motive; persuasive, persuasory [*rare*], hortative, hortatory; protreptical [*obs.*]; inviting, tempting, etc. *v.;* suasive, suasory [*obs.*], irresistible, seductive, attractive; fascinating etc. (*pleasing*) 829; provocative etc. (*exciting*) 824.

induced etc. *v.;* disposed; persuadable etc. (*docile*) 602; spellbound; instinct–, taken–, smitten- with; inspired by etc. *v.*

adv. **because**, therefore etc. (*cause*) 155; from this motive, from that motive; for this reason, for that reason; for; by reason of, for the sake of, on the score of, on account of; out of, from, as, forasmuch as.

for all the world; on principle.

615a. Absence of Motive

n. **absence of motive**; caprice etc. 608; chance etc. (*absence of design*) 621.

v. **scruple** etc. (*be unwilling*) 603; have no motive.

adj. **aimless** etc. (*chance*) 621; without rhyme or reason.

adv. **capriciously**, out of mere caprice.

616. Dissuasion

n. **dissuasion**, dehortation [*rare*], expostulation, remonstrance; deprecation etc. 766.

discouragement, dehortative [*rare*], monitory, damper, wet blanket; contraindicant.

curb etc. (*means of restraint*) 752; constraint etc. (*restraint*) 751; check etc. (*hindrance*) 706.

reluctance etc. (*unwillingness*) 603; contraindication.

v. **dissuade**, dehort [*rare*], cry out against, remonstrate, expostulate, warn, contraindicate.

disincline, indispose, shake, stagger; dispirit; discourage, dishearten, disenchant; deter; hold back, keep back etc. (*restrain*) 751; render averse etc. 603; repel; turn aside etc. (*deviation*) 279; wean from; act as a drag etc. (*hinder*) 706; throw cold water on, damp, cool,

chill, blunt, calm, quiet, quench; deprecate etc. 766.
- *adj.* **dissuading** etc. *v.;* dissuasive; dehortatory [*rare*], dehortative [*rare*], expostulatory; monitive [*obs.*], monitory, monitorial.
  dissuaded etc. *v.;* admonitory; uninduced etc. (induce etc. 615); unpersuadable etc. (*obstinate*) 606; averse etc. (*unwilling*) 603; repugnant etc. (*dislike*) 867.

617. Plea

[ostensible motive, ground, or reason]

- *n.* **plea**, pretext; allegation, advocation [*archaic*]; ostensible -motive, –ground, –reason; excuse etc. (*vindication*) 937; color; gloss, guise.
  handle, peg to hang on; room, *locus standi* [*L.*]; stalking-horse, *cheval de bataille* [*F.*], cue.
  loophole, starting-hole [*obs.*]; hole to creep out of, come-off [*colloq.*], way of escape.
  pretense etc. (*untruth*) 546; put-off, subterfuge, dust thrown in the eye; blind; moonshine; mere–, shallow- pretext; lame -excuse, –apology; tub to a whale; false plea, sour grapes; makeshift, shift, white lie; special pleading etc. (*sophistry*) 477; soft sawder [*slang*] etc. (*flattery*) 933.
- *v.* **plead**, allege; shelter oneself under the plea of; creep out of; tell a white lie; excuse etc. (*vindicate*) 937; color, gloss over, lend a color to; furnish a handle etc. *n.;* make a pretext of, make a handle of; use as a plea etc. *n.;* take one's stand upon, make capital out of; pretend etc. (*lie*) 544.
- *adj.* **advocatory** [*rare*], excusing; **ostensible** etc. (*manifest*) 525; alleged, apologetic; pretended etc. 545.
- *adv.* **ostensibly**; under the plea of, under the pretense of.

618. Good

- *n.* **good**, benefit, advantage; improvement etc. 658; greatest–, supreme- good; interest, service, behoof, behalf; weal [*archaic*]; main chance; *summum bonum* [*L.*]; commonwealth [*now rare*], commonweal *or* common weal; "consummation devoutly to be wished" [*Hamlet*]; gain, boot [*archaic*]; profit, harvest.
  boon etc. (*gift*) 784; good turn; blessing, benison; world of good; piece of good -luck, –fortune; nuts [*now Eng. slang*], prize, windfall, godsend, waif, treasure-trove.
  good fortune etc. (*prosperity*) 734; happiness etc. 827.
  [source of good] goodness etc. 648; utility etc. 644; remedy etc. 662; pleasure giving etc. 829.
- *v.* **benefit**, profit, advantage, serve, help, avail, boot [*archaic*], good [*obs.*], do good to.
  gain, prosper, flourish, thrive etc. 734.
- *adj.* **commendable** etc. 931; useful etc. 644; good etc., beneficial etc. 648.
- *adv.* **well**, aright, satisfactorily, favorably, not amiss; all for the best; to one's advantage etc. *n.;* in one's favor, in one's interest etc. *n.*

619. Evil

- *n.* **evil**, ill, harm, hurt, mischief, nuisance; machinations of the devil, Pandora's box, ills that flesh is heir to; mental suffering etc. (*pain*) 828.
  [evil spirit] demon etc. 980.
  [cause of evil] bane etc. 663.
  [production of evil] badness etc. 649; painfulness etc. 830; evildoer etc. 913.
  blow, buffet, stroke, scratch, bruise, wound, gash, mutilation; mortal -blow, –wound; *immedicabile vulnus* [*L.*]; damage, loss etc. (*deterioration*) 659.
  disadvantage, prejudice, drawback.
  disaster, accident, casualty; mishap etc. (*misfortune*) 735; bad job [*colloq.*], devil to pay [*colloq.*]; calamity, bale [*chiefly poetic*], woe, fatal mischief, catastrophe, tragedy; ruin etc. (*destruction*) 162; adversity etc. 735.
  outrage, wrong, injury, foul play; bad turn, ill turn; disservice; spoliation etc. 791; grievance, crying evil.
- *v.* **disserve**, do disservice to, harm, injure, hurt.
  be in trouble etc. (*adversity*) 735.
- *adj.* **disastrous**, bad etc. 649; awry, out of joint; disadvantageous; disserviceable, injurious, harmful.
- *adv.* **amiss**, wrong, ill, to one's cost.

Section 2. Prospective Volition

---

620. Intention

- *n.* **intention**, intent, intentionality; purpose; *quo animo* [*L.*]; project etc. 626; undertaking etc. 676; predetermination etc. 611; design, ambition.
  contemplation, mind, animus, view, purview [*law*], proposal; study; lookout.
  object, aim, end; final cause; *raisòn d'être* [*F.*]; *cui bono* [*L.*]; "the be-all and the end-all" [*Macbeth*]; drift etc. (*meaning*) 516; tendency etc. 176; destination, mark, point, butt, goal, target, bull's-eye, quintain; prey, quarry, game.

621. Chance

    decision, determination, resolve; fixed–, set–, settled- purpose; ultimatum; resolution etc. 604; wish etc. 865; *arrière pensée* [*F.*]; motive etc. 615.

    [study of final causes] teleology.

v. **intend**, purpose, design, mean; have to; propose to oneself; harbor a design; have in -view, –contemplation, –one's eye; have *in petto* [*It.*]; have an eye to.

    bid for, labor for; be after, aspire to *or* after, endeavor after; be at, aim at, drive at, point at, level at; take aim; set before oneself; study to.

    contemplate, meditate; take upon oneself etc. (*undertake*) 676; take into one's head; think of, dream of, talk of; premeditate etc. 611; compass [*legal*], calculate; destine, destinate; propose.

    project etc. (*plan*) 626; have a mind to etc. (*be willing*) 602; desire etc. 865; pursue etc. 622.

adj. **intended** etc. *v.;* intentional, advised, express, determinate; prepense etc. 611; bound for; intending etc. *v.;* disposed, inclined, minded; bent upon etc. (*earnest*) 604; at stake; on the -anvil, –tapis; in view, in prospect, in the breast of; *in petto* [*It.*]; teleological.

adv. **intentionally** etc. *adj.;* advisedly, wittingly, knowingly, designedly, purposely, on purpose, by design, studiously, pointedly; with intent etc. *n.;* deliberately etc. (*with premeditation*) 611; with one's eyes open, in cold blood.

    for; with a view to, with an eye to; in order -to, –that; to the end that, with the intent that; for the purpose of, with the view of, in contemplation of, on account of.

    in pursuance of, pursuant to; *quo animo* [*L.*]; to all intents and purposes.

621. Chance
[absence of purpose]

n. **chance** etc. 156; lot, fate etc. (*necessity*) 601; luck; good luck etc. (*good*) 618; hoodoo, jinx [*slang*], jadoo *or* jadu [*Hind.*]; voodoo, voodooism; swastika *or* swastica, fylfot, gammadion; wheel of chance, Fortune's wheel; mascot.

    speculation, venture, mere–, random- shot; blind bargain, leap in the dark; pig in a poke etc. (*uncertainty*) 475; fluke [*sporting cant*], potluck, flyer [*slang*], flutter [*Eng. slang*]; futures.

    gambling, game of chance; drawing lots; sortilegy, sortition [*obs.*]; *rouge et noir* [*F.*], hazard, ante, chuck-a-luck *or* chuck-luck, crack-loo, craps; faro, faro bank; roulette, pitch and toss, chuck-farthing, cup tossing, heads or tails, cross and pile [*archaic*], dice, dice box, poker-dice; fan-tan [*Chinese*].

    wager; gamble, risk, stake, pyramid, plunge; bet, betting; gambling; the turf.

    gambling house, gaming house, gambling den, pool room, betting-house; bucket shop; joint [*slang*]; parimutuel, totalizator, totalizer tote board; hell; betting ring; Wall Street, Stock Exchange, curb, curb market.

    gambler, gamester, dicer, sport [*cant*], punter, plunger, speculator, hazarder, sucker, bookmaker, bookie [*colloq.*], man of the turf; pool shark [*colloq.*], shark, adventurer.

v. **chance** etc. (*hap*) 156; stand a chance etc. (*be possible*) 470.

    toss up; cast–, draw- lots; leave–, trust- -to chance, –to the chapter of accidents; tempt fortune; chance it, take one's chance; run–, incur–, encounter- the -risk, –chance; stand the hazard of the die.

    speculate, try one's luck, set on a cast, raffle, put into a lottery, buy a pig in a poke, shuffle the cards.

    risk, venture, hazard, stake; ante; lay, –a wager; make a bet, wager, bet, gamble, game, play for; play at chuck-farthing; play the ponies, play the bangtails [*both slang*]; play–, shoot- craps etc.

adj. **fortuitous** etc. 156; unintentional, unintended; accidental; not meant; undesigned, unpurposed; unpremeditated etc. 612; never thought of.

    indiscriminate, promiscuous; undirected, random; aimless, driftless, designless, purposeless, causeless; without purpose.

    possible etc. 470.

adv. **casually** etc. 156; unintentionally etc. *adj.;* unwittingly.

    incidentally, *en passant* [*F.*], by the way.

    at random, at a venture, at haphazard; as luck would have it; in luck; out of luck; by chance, by good fortune; as it may happen.

int. what luck! better luck next time!

622. Pursuit
[purpose in action]

n. **pursuit**; pursuing etc. *v.;* prosecution; pursuance; enterprise etc. (*un*dertaking) 676; business etc. 625; adventure etc. (*essay*) 675; quest etc. (*search*) 461; scramble, hue and cry, game; hobby; still-hunt.

    chase, hunt, *battue* [*F.*], race, steeplechase, hunting, coursing; venation [*obs.*], venery; fox chase, fox hunting; sport, sporting; shooting, angling, fishing, hawking; shikar [*India*].

    pursuer; hunter, huntsman, the field; shikari [*India*], sportman, Nimrod; hound etc. 366.

v. **pursue**, prosecute, follow; run–, make–, be–, hunt–, prowl- after; shadow; carry on etc. (*do*) 680; be absorbed in; engage in etc. (*undertake*) 676; set about etc. (*begin*) 66; endeavor etc. 675; court etc. (*request*) 765; seek etc. (*search*) 461; aim at etc. (*intention*) 620; follow the trail etc. (*trace*) 461; fish for etc. (*experiment*) 463; press on etc. (*haste*) 684; run a race etc. (*velocity*) 274.

tread a path; take–, hold- a course; shape–, direct–, bend- one's -steps, –course; play a game; fight–, elbow- one's way; follow up; take to, take up; go in for; ride one's hobby.

chase, give chase, still-hunt, stalk, shikar [*India*], course, dog, hunt, hound, tread–, follow- on the heels of, etc. (*sequence*) 281; start game.

rush upon; rush headlong etc. (*violence*) 173; ride at, run full tilt at; make a leap at, jump at, snatch at; run down.

adj. **pursuing** etc. *v.;* in quest of etc. (*inquiry*) 461; in pursuit, in full cry, in hot pursuit; on the scent.

adv. **after**; in pursuance of etc. (*intention*) 620.

int. tallyho! yoicks! soho!

623. Avoidance
[absence of pursuit]

n. **avoidance**, evasion, elusion; seclusion etc. 893. avolation [*obs.*], flight; escape etc. 671; retreat etc. 287; recoil etc. 277; departure etc. 293; rejection etc. 610.

abstention, abstinence; forbearance; refraining etc. *v.;* inaction etc. 681; neutrality.

shirker etc. *v.;* slacker, shirk, quitter, eye servant, truant; fugitive, refugee, runaway, runagate, deserter, renegade, backslider; maroon.

v. **abstain**, refrain, spare, not attempt; not do etc. 681; maintain the even tenor of one's way.

eschew, keep from, let alone, have nothing to do with; keep–, stand–, hold- -aloof, –off; take no part in, have no hand in.

avoid, shun; steer–, keep- clear of; fight shy of; keep one's distance, keep at a respectful distance; keep–, get- out of the way; evade, elude, turn away from; set one's face against etc. (*oppose*) 708; deny oneself.

shrink; hang–, hold–, draw- back; recoil etc. 277; retire etc. (*recede*) 287; flinch, blink, blench, shy, shirk, dodge, parry, make way for, give place to.

beat a retreat; turn tail, turn one's back; take to one's heels; run, run away, run for one's life; maroon; cut and run [*colloq.*]; be off, –like a shot; fly, flee, fly–, flee–, run away- from; take flight, take to flight; desert, elope; make off, scamper off, sneak off, shuffle off, sheer off; break–, burst–, tear oneself–, slip–, slink–, steal- -away, –away from; slip cable, part company, turn on one's heel; sneak out of, play truant, give one the go-by [*slang*], give leg bail [*slang*], take French leave, slope [*slang*], decamp, flit, bolt, abscond, levant [*slang, Eng.*], skedaddle [*dial.*], absquatulate, cut one's stick [*slang*], walk one's chalks [*slang*], show the heels, show a clean (*or* light) pair of heels, make oneself scarce [*slang*]; escape etc. 671; go away etc. (*depart*) 293; abandon etc. 624; reject etc. 610.

lead one a dance, lead one a pretty dance; throw off the scent, play at hide and seek.

adj. **avoiding** etc. *v.;* neutral; unsought, unattempted; shy of etc. (*unwilling*) 603; elusive, evasive; fugitive, runaway; shy, wild.

adv. **lest**, in order to avoid.

int. forbear! keep off! hands off! *sauve qui peut!* [*F.*], devil take the hindmost!

624. Relinquishment

n. **relinquishment**, abandonment; desertion, defection, secession, withdrawal; cave of Adullam; *nolle prosequi* [*L.*].

discontinuance etc. (*cessation*) 142; renunciation etc. (*recantation*) 607; abrogation etc. 756; resignation etc. (*retirement*) 757; desuetude etc. 614; cession etc. (*of property*) 782.

v. **relinquish**, give up, abandon, desert, forsake, leave in the lurch; go back on [*colloq.*]; depart–, secede - withdraw- from; back out of [*colloq.*], back down from [*colloq.*]; leave, quit, take leave of, bid a long farewell; vacate etc. (*resign*) 757.

renounce etc. (*abjure*) 607; forego, have done with, drop; nol-pros [*law*]; disuse etc. 678; discard etc. 782; wash one's hands of; drop all idea of.

break off, leave off; desist; stop etc. (*cease*) 142; hold one's hand, stay one's hand; quit one's hold; give over, shut up shop; throw up the -game, –cards.

give up the -point, –argument; pass to the order of the day, move the previous question, table, table the motion.

adj. **unpursued**; relinquished etc. *v.;* relinquishing etc. *v.*

int. avast! etc. (*stop*) 142.

625. Business

n. **business**, occupation, employment, undertaking; pursuit etc. 622; what one is doing, what one is about; affair, concern, matter, case.

626. Plan

task, matter in hand, irons in the fire; thing to do, agendum (*pl.* agenda), work, job, chore, errand, commission, mission, charge, care; duty etc. 926.

exercise; work etc. (*action*) 680; avocation, hobby; press of business etc. (*activity*) 682.

function, part, role, cue; province, lookout [*colloq.*], department, capacity, sphere, orb [*now rare*], field, line; walk, –of life; beat, round, routine; race, career.

office, place, post, chargeship, incumbency, living; situation, berth, billet, appointment, employ [*rare*], service etc. (*servitude*) 749; engagement; undertaking etc. 676.

vocation, calling, profession, cloth, faculty; industry, art; industrial arts; craft, mystery [*obs.*], handicraft; trade etc. (*commerce*) 794.

v. **occupy oneself with**; pass–, employ–, spend- one's time in; employ oneself -in, –upon; concern oneself with; make it one's business etc. *n.;* undertake etc. 676; enter a profession; betake oneself to, turn one's hand to; have to do with etc. (*do*) 680.

be about, be doing, be engaged in, be employed in, be occupied with, be at work on; have one's hands in, have in hand; have on one's -hands, –shoulders; bear the burden; have one's hands full etc. (*activity*) 682.

ply one's task, ply one's trade; drive a trade; carry on–, do–, transact- -business, –a trade etc. *n.;* keep a shop; labor in one's vocation; pursue the even tenor of one's way; attend to business, attend to one's work.

officiate, serve, act; act one's part, play one's part; do duty; serve–, discharge–, perform- the -office, –duties, –functions- of; hold–, fill- -an office, –a place, –a situation; hold a portfolio.

be in the hands of, be on the stocks, be on the anvil; pass through one's hands.

adj. **businesslike**; workaday; professional, vocational; official, functional; humming, busy etc. (*actively employed*) 682.

in hand, on hand; on *or* in one's hands; afoot; on foot, on the anvil; going on; acting.

adv. **in the course of business**, all in the day's work; professionally etc. *adj.*

626. Plan

n. **plan**, scheme, design, project, proposal, proposition, suggestion; resolution, motion; precaution etc. (*provision*) 673; deep-laid etc. (*premeditated*) 611- plan etc.; germ etc. (*cause*) 153.

system etc. (*order*) 58; organization etc. (*arrangement*) 60.

outline, sketch, skeleton, draft *or* draught, ébauche [*F.*], brouillon [*F.*]; rough -cast, –draft *or* draught, –copy; copy; proof, revise.

forecast, program *or* programme, prospectus; carte du pays [*F.*]; card; bill, protocol; order of the day, memoranda, list of agenda; bill of fare etc. (*food*) 298; base of operations; platform, plank, slate, ticket.

role; policy etc. (*line of conduct*) 692.

contrivance, invention, expedient, receipt, nostrum, artifice, device; pipelaying; stratagem etc. (*cunning*) 702; trick etc. (*deception*) 545; alternative, loop-hole; shift etc. (*substitute*) 147; last shift etc. (*necessity*) 601, gadget.

measure, step; stroke, –of policy; masterstroke; trump, trump card, courtcard; cheval de bataille [*F.*], great gun; coup, - d'état [*F.*]; clever–, bold–, good- -move, –hit, –stroke; bright -thought, –idea; great idea.

intrigue, cabal, plot, conspiracy, complot, machination; underplot, counterplot; mine, countermine.

schemer, schemist [*rare*], schematist [*obs.*]; strategist, machinator; Machiavellian, Machiavellist, conspirator; intrigant etc. (*cunning*) 702.

projector, promoter, designer etc. *v.;* organizer, founder (*fem.* foundress), author, artist, builder.

v. **plan**, scheme, design, frame, contrive, project, forecast, sketch; devise, invent etc. (*imagine*) 515; set one's wits to work etc. 515; spring a project; fall upon, hit upon; strike–, chalk–, cut–, lay–, map- out; lay down a plan; shape–, mark-out a course; predetermine etc. 611; concert, preconcert, preëstablish; prepare etc. 673; hatch, –a plot; concoct; take -steps, –measures.

systematize, organize; cast, recast, arrange etc. 60; digest, mature.

plot; counterplot, mine, countermine, dig a mine; lay a train; intrigue etc. (*cunning*) 702.

adj. **planned** etc. *v.;* strategic *or* strategical.

planning etc. *v.;* in course of preparation etc. 673; under consideration, on the tapis, on the carpet, on the table.

627. Method
[path]

n. **method**, way, manner, wise [*rare, exc. in phrases*], gait, form, mode, fashion, tone, guise; modus operandi [*L.*]; procedure etc. (*line of conduct*) 692.

path, road, route, course; line of way, line of road; trajectory, orbit, track, beat, tack.

steps; stair, staircase; flight of -steps, –stairs; ladder, stile; perron.
bridge, footbridge, viaduct, pontoon, stepping-stone, plank, gangway; draw-bridge.
pass, ford, ferry, tunnel; pipe etc. 260.
means of access, adit, entrance, approach, passage, cloister, covered way, lobby, corridor, aisle; alley, lane, vennel [*Scot. & dial. Eng.*], avenue, artery, channel; gateway etc. (*opening*) 260; door, backdoor, backstairs; secret passage; covert way.
roadway, express; thoroughfare; highway, macadam, parkway, boulevard; turnpike–, royal–, state–, coach- road; broad–, King's–, Queen's- highway; beaten -track, –path; horse–, bridle- -road, –track, –path; walk, *trottoir* [*F.*], footpath, pathway, pavement, flags, sidewalk, by-road, crossroad; by–, cross--path, –way; cut; short cut & (*mid-course*) 628; *carrefour* [*F.*]; private–, occupation- road; highways and byways; railroad, railway, trolley track, tramroad, tramway; towpath; causeway; street etc. (*abode*) 189; stairway, gangway; speedway; canal etc. (*conduit*) 350.

adv. **how**; in what way, in what manner; by what mode; so, thus, in this way, after this fashion.
one way or another, anyhow; somehow or other etc. (*instrumentality*) 631; by way of; *via* [*L.*]; *in transitu* [*L.*] etc. 270; on the high road to, on the way to.

628. Mid-course

n. **mid-course**, midway [*rare*], middle way, middle course; moderation; mean etc. 29; middle etc. 68; *juste milieu* [*F.*], *mezzo termine* [*L.*], golden mean, *ariston metron* [*Gr.*], *aurea mediocritas* [*L.*]; fifty-fifty [*colloq.*].
shortcut, crosscut; straight etc. (*direct*) 278 -course, –path; great-circle sailing.
compromise, half measures, half-and-half measures; neutrality.

v. **keep the golden mean**; keep in–, steer–, preserve- -a middle, –an even- course; avoid both Scylla and Charybdis; go straight etc. (*direct*) 278.
compromise, make a compromise, go fifty-fifty [*colloq.*], concede half, go half-way.

adj. **neutral**, average, even, evenly balanced; impartial, moderate; straight etc. (*direct*) 278.

adv. **midway**, in the mean; in moderation.

629. Circuit

n **circuit**, round-about way, digression, detour, circumbendibus [*humorous*], circumambience, circumambiency, circumambulation, ambages, loop; winding etc. (*circuition*) 311; zigzag etc. (*deviation*) 279.

v. **go round about**, circumambulate, perform a circuit, make a circuit, go out of one's way; make a detour; meander etc. (*deviate*) 279.
lead a pretty dance; beat about, –the bush; make two bites of a cherry.

adj. **circuitous**, circumambient, circumambulatory, indirect, roundabout; zigzag etc. (*deviating*) 279; backhanded.

adv. **in a roundabout way**; by a side wind, by an indirect course; from pillar to post.

630. Requirement

n. **requirement**, need, wants, necessities; necessaries, –of life; stress, exigency, pinch, *sine qua non* [*L.*], matter of necessity; case of need, case of life or death.
desideratum etc. (*desire*) 865; want etc. (*deficiency*) 640.
needfulness, essentiality, necessity, indispensability, urgency, prerequisite; the least one can -do, –require.
requisition etc. (*request*) 765 (*exaction*) 741; run; demand for, call for.
charge, claim, command, injunction, mandate, order, precept, ultimatum.

v. **require**, need, want, have occasion for; not be able to do without, not able to dispense with; prerequire.
be necessary etc. *adj.;* stand in need of; lack etc. 640; desiderate; desire etc. 865.
render necessary, necessitate, create a necessity for, call for, put in requisition; make a requisition etc. (*ask for*) 765, (*demand*) 741.

adj. **necessary**; required etc. *v.;* requisite, needful, imperative, essential, indispensable, prerequisite; called for; in demand, in request.
in want of; destitute of etc. 640.
urgent, exigent, pressing, instant, crying, absorbing.

adv. **of necessity**; *ex necessitate rei* [*L.*] etc. (*necessarily*) 601; out of -stern necessity, –bitter need; in a pinch.

631. Instrumentality

n. **instrumentality**; aid etc. 707; subservience *or* subserviency, intermediacy, intermediation, mediation, intervention, medium, intermedium, intermediary, interagent, intermediate, mediating agency, vehicle, hand; agency etc. 170.
minister, handmaid; midwife, *accoucheur* [*F.*], *accoucheuse* [*fem., F.*], obstetrician; servant,

632. Means

slave, maid, valet; friend at court; go-between; cat's-paw; stepping-stone.

key, master–, pass–, latch- key; "open sesame"; passport, *passe-partout* [*F.*], safe-conduct; pull [*slang*], influence.

instrument etc. 633; expedient etc. (*plan*) 626; means etc. 632.

v. **subserve**, minister, mediate, intervene, intermediate, come–, go- between; interpose; pull the -strings, –wires; use one's influence; be instrumental etc. *adj.;* pander to; officiate; tend.

adj. **instrumental**; useful etc. 644; ministerial, subservient, serviceable; mediatorial, intermedial, intermediary, intermediate, intervening; conducive.

adv. **through**, by, *per* [*L.*]; whereby, thereby, hereby; by the agency of etc. 170; by dint of; by *or* in virtue of; through the medium of etc. *n.;* along with; on the shoulders of; by means of etc. 632; by *or* with the aid of etc. (*assistance*) 707.

somehow; *per fas et nefas* [*L.*]; by fair means or foul; somehow or other; by hook or by crook.

632. Means

n. **means**, resources, wherewithal, ways and means; capital etc. (*money*) 800; revenue, income; stock in trade etc. 636; provision etc. 637; reserve, remnant, last resource, a shot in the locker [*colloq.*]; appliances etc. (*machinery*) 633; means and appliances; conveniences; cards to play; expedients etc. (*measures*) 626; two strings to one's bow; wheels within wheels; sheet anchor etc. (*safety*) 666; aid etc. 707; medium etc. 631.

v. **provide the wherewithal**; find–, have–, possess- means etc. *n.;* have something laid by, –for a rainy day; have powerful friends, have friends at court; have something to draw on; beg, borrow, or steal.

adj. **instrumental** etc. 631; **mechanical** etc. 633.

reliable, trustworthy, efficient; honorable etc. (*upright*) 939.

adv. **by means of**, with; by -what, –all, –any, –some- means; wherewith, herewith, therewith; wherewithal.

how etc. (*in what manner*) 627; through etc. (*by the instrumentality of*) 631; with *or* by the aid of etc. (*assistance*) 707; by the agency of etc. 170.

633. Instrument

n. **machinery**, mechanism, engineering.

instrument, organ, tool, implement, utensil, machine, engine, lathe, gin, mill; air–, caloric–, heat–, steam–, internal-combustion- engine; motor.

equipment, gear, tackle, tackling; rigging, apparatus, appliances; plant, *matériel* [*F.*]; harness, trappings, fittings, accouterments *or* accoutrements, impedimenta; equipment, equipage; appointments, furniture, upholstery; chattels; paraphernalia etc. (*belongings*) 780.

mechanical powers; mechanical -advantage, –movements, –contrivances; leverage; fulcrum lever, crow, crowbar, gavelock [*Scot. & dial. Eng.*], jemmy, jimmy, marline spike *or* marlinspike, handspike, arm, limb, wing; oar, paddle etc. (*navigation*) 267.

wheel and axle; wheelwork, clockwork; rolling contact; epicyclic train; revolving lever; wheels within wheels; pinion, crank, winch; cam; capstan etc. (*lift*) 307; wheel etc. (*rotation*) 312; bevel gearing, spur gearing, universal joint; fly wheel, governor, turbine, water wheel; pump, lift-pump, force-pump, hydraulic ram.

pulley, crane, derrick; belt, open belt, crossed belt; cone pulley, stepped speed pulley.

inclined plane; wedge; screw; jack; spring, mainspring; can hook, glut, heald, heddle, loom, shuttle, jenny, parbuckle, sprag.

[tools etc.] hammer etc. (*impulse*) 276; edge tool etc. (*cut*) 253; turnscrew, screw driver *or* screwdriver; borer etc. 262; vise, teeth, etc. (*hold*) 781; nail, rope etc. (*join*) 45; peg etc. (*hang*) 214; support etc. 215; spoon etc. (*vehicle*) 272; arms etc. 727.

handle, hilt, haft *or* heft, shaft, shank, blade, trigger, tiller, rudder, helm, treadle, pedal, key; knocker.

adj. **instrumental** etc. 631.

mechanical, machinal [*rare*]; brachial; propulsive, driving, hoisting, elevating, lifting.

useful, labor-saving, ingenious; simple; complicated; well made, well fitted, sharp, in good order, well equipped.

634. Substitute

n. **substitute** etc. 147; proxy, alternate, stand-in [*colloq.*], understudy; deputy etc. 759; *badli* [*Hind.*].

635. Materials

n. **material**, raw material, stuff, stock, staple; ore. [building material] marble, granite, limestone, freestone, sandstone, brown stone; stone, metal, brick, bricks and mortar; chinking, mortar, lime, chunam [*India*], clay, plaster, daubing, concrete, cement, reinforced concrete; unburnt brick, adobe; composition, compo; slates, tiles; whitewash etc. 223.

wood, timber, clapboard, shingle, shake, puncheon, log, rafter, beam, joist; two-by-four, four-by-four; post, upright, stud, lath; wall board.

materials; supplies, munition, fuel, grist, household stuff; crockery etc. 384; pabulum etc. (*food*) 298; oilcloth, linoleum; ammunition etc. (*arms*) 727; contingents; relay, reënforcement; baggage etc. (*personal property*) 780; means etc. 632.

fabrics, calico, cambric, cashmere, linen, cotton, wool, silk; muslin, lawn, voile, gingham, dimity, broadcloth, homespun, serge, tweed, crêpe de chine, chiffon, satin, velvet.

adj. raw etc. (*unprepared*) 674; finished; wooden etc. *n.;* adobe.

636. Store

n. **stock**, fund, mine, vein, lode, quarry; spring; fount, fountain; well, wellspring [*obs. exc. fig.*]; orchard, garden, farm; milch cow; hen.

stock in trade, supply; heap etc. (*collection*) 72; treasure; reserve, *corps de réserve* [*F.*], reserve fund, nest egg, savings, *bonne bouche* [*F.*].

crop, harvest, vintage, yield, product, gleaning.

store, accumulation, hoard; mow, rick, stack; lumber; relay etc. (*provision*) 637.

storehouse, storeroom, store closet; depository, depot, cache, repository, reservatory [*obs.*], repertory; repertorium [*rare*]; promptuary, warehouse, godown [*Oriental*], entrepôt [*F.*], magazine; buttery, larder, spence [*dial. Eng.*]; garner, granary, grain elevator, silo; cannery, safe-deposit vault, stillroom, bank etc. (*treasury*) 802; armory; arsenal; dock; freight yard, train shed, carbarn, power station; stable, barn, byre, cowhouse, piggery; hen house; fish hatchery; hothouse, conservatory.

quiver, bandolier *or* bandoleer; coffer etc. (*receptable*) 191.

reservoir, cistern, *aljibar* [*Sp. Am.*], tank, pond, mill pond; gasometer.

[collections] library, public library, library of Congress, British Museum, Bodleian, Bibliothek; gallery, art gallery, picture gallery, Louvre, museum, Madame Tussaud's, zoölogical garden, zoo [*colloq.*], aquarium, menagerie.

work of reference, dictionary, lexicon, encyclopedia *or* encyclopaedia, cyclopedia *or* cyclopaedia, thesaurus, atlas, concordance, anthology.

conservation; storing etc. *v.;* storage.

file, letter file, card index, portfolio, budget; photographic -plate, –film; memory.

v. **store**; put by, lay by, set by; stow away; set apart, lay apart; store up, hoard up, treasure up, lay up, heap up, put up, garner up, save up; bank; cache; accumulate, amass, hoard, fund, garner, save.

reserve; keep back, hold back; husband, –one's resources.

deposit; stow, stack, load; harvest; heap, collect etc. 72; lay in store etc. *adj.;* keep, file [papers]; lay in etc. (*provide*) 637; preserve etc. 670.

adj. **stored** etc. *v.;* in store, in reserve, in ordinary; spare, supernumerary.

adv. for a rainy day, for a nest egg, to fall back upon; on deposit.

637. Provision

n. **provision**, supply; grist, –to the mill; subvention etc. (*aid*) 707; resources etc. (*means*) 632; groceries, grocery.

providing etc. *v.;* purveyance; reenforcement; commissariat.

provender etc. (*food*) 298; ensilage; viaticum; ration; emergency–, iron-ration.

caterer, purveyor, provider, commissary, quartermaster, steward, purser, housekeeper, manciple, feeder, batman, victualer *or* victualler, comprador *or* compradore [*China*]; innkeeper, landlord, innholder, mine host, khansamah [*India*], *restaurateur* [*F.*]; grocer, green grocer, huckster, fishmonger, provision merchant; sutler etc. (*merchant*) 797.

provision shop, provision store, meat shop, fish store; market, supermarket, public market; grocery, grocery store.

v. **provide**; make -provision, –due provision for; lay in, –a stock, –a store.

supply, suppeditate [*obs.*]; furnish; find, find one in; arm.

cater, victual, provision, purvey, forage; beat up for; stock, –with; make good, replenish; fill, –up; recruit, feed.

store, have in -store, –reserve; keep, keep by one; have to fall back upon; store etc. 636; provide against a rainy day etc. (*economy*) 817; conserve, keep, preserve, lay by, gather into barns.

638. Waste

n. **consumption**, expenditure, exhaustion; dispersion etc. 73; ebb; leakage etc. (*exudation*) 295; loss etc. 776; wear and tear; waste; prodigality etc. 818; misuse etc. 679; wasting etc. *v.;* rubbish etc. (*useless*) 645.

639. Sufficiency

v. **consume**, spend, expend, use, swallow up; exhaust; impoverish; spill, drain, empty, deplete; disperse etc. 73.

cast–, fool–, muddle–, throw–, fling–, fritter– away; burn the candle at both ends, waste; squander etc. 818.

labor in vain etc. (*useless*) 645; "waste its sweetness on the desert air" [Gray]; cast pearls before swine; employ a steam engine to crack a nut, waste powder and shot, break a butterfly on a wheel; cut blocks with a razor, pour water into a sieve, tilt at windmills.

run to waste; ebb; leak etc. (*run out*) 295; melt away, run dry, dry up; spoil.

adj. **wasted** etc. *v.;* gone to waste, useless, rendered useless, made unavailable; run to seed; dried up; at a low ebb.

wasteful etc. (*prodigal*) 818; penny wise and pound foolish.

639. Sufficiency

n. **sufficiency**, adequacy, enough, wherewithal, *quantum sufficit* [*L.*], satisfaction, competence; no less.

mediocrity etc. (*average*) 29.

fill; fullness etc. (*completeness*) 52; plenitude, plenty; abundance; copiousness etc. *adj.;* amplitude, galore [*rare*], lots [*colloq.*], profusion; full measure; "good measure, pressed down, and shaken together, and running over" [*Bible*].

luxuriance etc. (*fertility*) 168; affluence etc. (*wealth*) 803; fat of the land; "a land flowing with milk and honey" [*Bible*]; cornucopia; horn of -plenty, -Amalthaea; mine etc. (*stock*) 636.

outpouring; flood etc. (*great quantity*) 31; tide etc. (*river*) 348; repletion etc. (*redundance*) 641; satiety etc. 869.

rich man etc. (*wealth*) 803; financier, banker, creditor etc. 805; plutocrat.

v. **be sufficient** etc. *adj.;* suffice; do, just do [*both colloq.*], satisfy, pass muster; have enough etc. *n.;* eat–, drink–, have– one's fill; roll in, swim in; wallow in etc. (*superabundance*) 641; wanton.

abound, exuberate, teem, flow, stream, rain, shower down; pour, pour in; swarm; bristle with; superabound.

render sufficient etc. *adj.;* replenish etc. (*fill*) 52.

adj. **sufficient**, enough, adequate, up to the mark, commensurate, competent, satisfactory, valid, tangible.

moderate etc. (*temperate*) 953; measured.

ample; full etc. (*complete*) 52; plenty, plentiful, plenteous; plenty as blackberries; copious, abundant; abounding etc. *v.;* replete, enough and to spare, flush; chock-full *or* choke-full; well-stocked, well-provided; liberal; unstinted, unstinting, stintless; without stint; unsparing, unmeasured; lavish etc. 641; wholesale.

unexhausted, unwasted; exhaustless, inexhaustible.

rich; luxuriant etc. (*fertile*) 168; affluent etc. (*wealthy*) 803; wantless; big with etc. (*pregnant*) 161.

adv. **sufficiently**, amply etc. *adj.;* full; in abundance etc. *n.;* with no sparing hand; to one's heart's content, *ad libitum* [*L.*], without stint; to the good.

640. Insufficiency

n. **insufficiency**, inadequacy, inadequateness; incompetence etc. (*impotence*) 158; deficiency etc. (*incompleteness*) 53; imperfection etc. 651; shortcoming etc. 304; paucity; stint; scantiness etc. (*smallness*) 32; none to spare; bare subsistence.

scarcity, dearth; want, need, lack, poverty, exigency; inanition, starvation, famine, drought *or* drouth.

dole, mite, pittance; short -allowance, -commons; half rations; banyan day; fast day, Lent.

depletion, emptiness, poorness etc. *adj.;* vacancy, flaccidity; ebb tide; low water; "a beggarly account of empty boxes" [*Romeo and Juliet*]; indigence etc. 804; insolvency etc. (*nonpayment*) 808.

poor man, pauper etc. 804; bankrupt etc. (*nonpayment*) 808.

miser, niggard etc. (*parsimony*) 819.

v. **be insufficient** etc. *adj.;* not suffice etc. 639; kick the beam; come short of etc. 304; run dry.

want, lack, need, require; *caret* [*L.*]; be in want etc. (*poor*) 804; live from hand to mouth.

render insufficient etc. *adj.;* drain of resources; impoverish etc. (*waste*) 638; stint etc. (*begrudge*) 819; put on short -allowance, -commons.

do insufficiently etc. *adv.;* scotch the snake.

adj. **insufficient**, inadequate; too little etc. 32; not enough etc. 639; unequal to; incompetent etc. (*impotent*) 158; perfunctory etc. (*neglect*) 460; deficient etc. (*incomplete*) 53; wanting etc. *v.;* imperfect etc. 651; ill-furnished, ill-provided, ill-stored, ill-off.

short of, out of, destitute of, devoid of, bereft of etc. 789, denuded of; slack, at a low ebb; empty, vacant, bare; dry, drained.

unprovided, unsupplied, unfurnished; unreplenished, unfed; unstored, untreasured; empty-handed.

meager or meagre, poor, thin, scrimp, sparing, stunted, spare, stinted; starved, starveling, emaciated, undernourished, underfed, half-starved, famine-stricken, famished; jejune.

scarce; not to be had, –for love or money, –at any price; scurvy; stingy etc. 819; at the end of one's tether; without resources etc. 632; in want etc. (*poor*) 804; in debt etc. 806; scant etc. (*small*) 32.

adv. insufficiently etc. *adj.;* in default of, for want of; failing.

641. Redundance

n. **redundance**; too much, too many; superabundance, superfluity, superfluence [*obs.*], supersaturation; nimiety [*rare*], transcendency, exuberance, profuseness; profusion etc. (*plenty*) 639; repletion, enough in all conscience, *satis superque* [*L.*], lion's share; more than enough etc. 639; plethora, engorgement, congestion, load, surfeit, sickener; turgescence etc. (*expansion*) 194; overdose, overmeasure, oversupply, overflow; inundation etc. (*water*) 348; avalanche, deluge.

pleonasm etc. (*diffuseness*) 573; too many irons in the fire; *embarras de richesses* [*F.*]; embarrassment of riches; money to burn [*colloq.*].

accumulation etc. (*store*) 636; heap etc. 72; drug, –in the market; glut; crowd; burden.

excess, surplus, overplus; epact; margin; remainder etc. 40; duplicate; surplusage, expletive; work of supererogation; bonus, bonanza.

luxury; extravagance etc. (*prodigality*) 818; exorbitance, lavishment; intemperance etc. 954.

v. **superabound**, overabound; know no bounds, swarm; meet one at every turn; creep with, bristle with; overflow; run–, flow–, well–, brim-over; run riot; overrun, overstock, overlay, overcharge, overdose, overfeed, overburden, overload, overdo, overwhelm, overshoot the mark etc. (*go beyond*) 303; surcharge, supersaturate, gorge, glut, load, drench, whelm, inundate, deluge, flood, drug, –the market; hepatize.

send–, carry- -coals to Newcastle, –owls to Athens; teach one's grandmother to suck eggs [*colloq.*]; *pisces natare docere* [*L.*]; kill the slain, butter one's bread on both sides, put butter upon bacon; employ a steam engine to crack a nut etc. (*waste*) 638.

wallow in; roll in etc. (*plenty*) 639; remain on one's hands, hang heavy on hand, go a-begging *or* go begging; exaggerate etc. 549.

cloy, choke, accloy [*archaic*], suffocate; pile up, lay on thick; lay it on, –with a trowel; impregnate with; lavish etc. (*squander*) 818.

adj. **redundant**; too much, too many; exuberant, inordinate, superabundant, excess, overmuch, replete, profuse, lavish; prodigal etc. 818; exorbitant; overweening; extravagant; overcharged etc. *v.;* supersaturated, drenched, overflowing; running -over, -to waste, -down.

crammed–, filled- to overflowing; gorged, stuffed, smothered, ready to burst; dropsical, turgid, plethoric; full-blooded, haematose *or* hematose; obese etc. 194.

superfluous, unnecessary, needless, supervacaneous [*obs.*], uncalled for, to spare, in excess; over and above etc. (*remainder*) 40; *de trop* [*F.*]; adscititious etc. (*additional*) 37; supernumerary etc. (*reserve*) 636; on one's hands, spare, duplicate, supererogatory, expletory, expletive; *un peu fort* [*F.*].

adv. **over and above**; over much, too much; too far; over, too; without–, beyond–, out of- measure; with . . . to spare; over head and ears; over one's head; up to one's -eyes, –ears; extra; beyond the mark etc. (*overrun*) 303; *acervatim* [*L.*].

642. Importance

n. **importance**, consequence, moment, prominence, consideration, mark, materialness, materiality.

greatness etc. 31; superiority etc. 33; notability etc. (*repute*) 873; weight etc. (*influence*) 175; value etc. (*goodness*) 648; usefulness etc. 644.

import, significance, concern; emphasis, interest.

gravity, seriousness, solemnity; no joke, no laughing matter; pressure, urgency, stress; matter of life and death.

memorabilia, notabilia, great doings; red-letter day.

salient point, outstanding feature; great -thing, –point; main chance, "the be-all and the end-all" [*Macbeth*]; cardinal point; substance, gist etc. (*essence*) 5; sum and substance, gravamen, head and front; important–, principal–, prominent–, essential- part; half the battle; *sine qua non* [*L.*]; breath of one's nostrils etc. (*life*) 359; cream, salt, core, kernel, heart,

643. Unimportance

nucleus; key, keynote; keystone; corner stone; trump card etc. (*device*) 626.

chief, top sawyer, first fiddle, top banana [*cant*], prima donna, triton among the minnows; "it"; the only pebble on the beach; burra (*or* bara) sahib [*India*]; bigwig etc. 875.

v. **be important** etc. *adj.*; be somebody, be something; import, signify, matter, be an object; carry weight etc. (*influence*) 175; make a figure etc. (*repute*) 873; be in the ascendant, come to the front, lead the way, take the lead, play first fiddle, throw all else into the shade; lie at the root of; deserve–, merit–, be worthy of- -notice, –regard, –consideration.

value; attach–, ascribe–, give- importance etc. *n.*- to; care for; set store -upon, –by; mark etc. 550; mark with a white stone, underline; write–, put–, print- in -italics, –capitals, –large letters, –large type, –bold-faced type, -letters of gold; accentuate, emphasize, lay stress on.

make much of; make -a fuss, –a stir, –a piece of work, –much ado- about.

adj. **important**; of importance etc. *n.*; momentous, material; to the point; not to be -overlooked, –despised, –sneezed at [*colloq.*]; egregious; weighty etc. (*influential*) 175; of note etc. (*repute*) 873; notable, prominent, salient, signal; memorable, remarkable; worthy of -remark, –notice; never to be forgotten; stirring, eventful.

in the front rank, first-rate, A1 *or* A number 1 [*colloq.*], first chop [*Anglo-Ind. & colloq.*]; superior etc. 33; considerable etc. (*great*) 31; marked etc. *v.*; rare etc. 137.

grave, serious, earnest, noble, grand, solemn, impressive, commanding, imposing.

urgent, pressing, critical, instant.

paramount, essential, vital, all-absorbing, radical, cardinal, chief, main, prime, primary, principal, leading, capital, foremost, overruling; of vital etc. importance.

significant, telling, trenchant, emphatic, pregnant; *tanti* [*L.*].

adv. **in the main**; materially etc. *adj.*; above all, in the first place, before everything else; *kat' exochen* [*Gr.*], *par excellence* [*F.*], to crown all.

643. Unimportance

n. **unimportance**, insignificance, nothingness, immateriality.

triviality, levity, frivolity, fribble; paltriness etc. *adj.*; poverty; smallness etc. 32; vanity etc. (*uselessness*) 645; matter of indifference etc. 866; no object.

nothing, –to signify, –worth speaking of, –particular, –to boast of, –to speak of; small–, no great–, trifling etc. *adj.*- matter; mere joke, mere nothing; hardly–, scarcely- anything; nonentity, small beer, cipher; no great shakes [*colloq.*], *peu de chose* [*F.*]; child's play.

toy, plaything, popgun, paper pellet, gimcrack, gewgaw, bauble, trinket, bagatelle, kickshaw, knickknack, whimwham, trifle, "trifles light as air" [*Othello*].

trumpery, trash, rubbish, stuff, *fatras* [*F.*], frippery; "leather or prunello" [Pope]; fiddle-faddle [*colloq.*], fingle-fangle; chaff, drug, froth, bubble, smoke, cobweb; weed; refuse etc. (*inutility*) 645; scum etc. (*dirt*) 653.

joke, jest, snap of the fingers, snap of one's thumb; fudge etc. (*unmeaning*) 517; fiddlestick, pack of nonsense, mere farce.

trifle, straw, pin, fig, fico [*archaic*], button, rush; bulrush, feather, half-penny, farthing, brass farthing, doit, peppercorn, iota, tinker's dam (*or* damn), continental, jot, mote, rap, pinch of snuff, old song; cent, mill, picayune; pai, pice [*both India*]; pistareen, red cent.

nine days' wonder, *ridiculus mus* [*L.*]; flash in the pan etc. (*impotence*) 158; much ado about nothing etc. (*overestimation*) 482; tempest–, storm- in a teapot.

minutiae, details, minor details, small fry; dust in the balance, feather in the scale, drop in the ocean, fleabite, pin prick, molehill.

v. **be unimportant** etc. *adj.*; not matter etc. 642; go for–, matter–, signify- -little, –nothing, –little or nothing; not matter a straw etc. *n.*

make light of etc. (*underestimate*) 483; catch at straws etc. (*overestimate*) 482; tumble–, stumble- over one's shadow; make mountains out of molehills, make much ado about nothing.

adj. **unimportant**; of -little, –small, –no- -account, –importance etc. 642; immaterial; nonessential, unessential, irrelevant, not vital, uninteresting; indifferent, amateurish.

subordinate etc. (*inferior*) 34; mediocre etc. (*average*) 29; passable, fair, respectable, tolerable, commonplace; uneventful, mere, common; ordinary etc. (*habitual*) 613; inconsiderable, soso *or* so-so, insignificant, nugatory, inappreciable.

trifling, trivial; slight, slender, light, flimsy, frothy, idle; puerile etc. (*fool*-ish) 499; airy, shallow; weak etc. 160; powerless etc. 158; frivolous, petty, niggling; peddling, piddling, fribbling, fribble, inane, ridiculous, farcical; finical, finicking *or* finicky *or* finikin, mincing, fiddle-faddle [*colloq.*], namby-pamby, wishy-washy [*colloq.*], milk and water, insipid.

paltry, poor, pitiful; contemptible etc. (*contempt*) 930; sorry, mean, meager *or* meagre, shabby, miserable, wretched, vile, scrubby, scrannel [*archaic*], weedy, niggardly, scurvy, beggarly, worthless, twopenny-halfpenny, two-for-a-cent, two-bit, two-by-four, cheap, trashy, catchpenny, gimcrack, trumpery; one-horse.

not worth -the pains, -while, -mentioning, -speaking of, -a thought, -a curse, -a cent, -a rap, -a hair, -a straw etc. *n.;* beneath contempt, below par; not up to -sample, -specification; beneath-, unworthy of- -notice, -regard - consideration; *de lana caprina* [*L.*]; vain etc. (*useless*) 645.

adv. **slightly** etc. *adj.;* rather, somewhat, pretty well, fairly, fairly well, tolerably.

for aught one cares; it matters not, it does not signify; it is of no -consequence, -importance.

int. **no matter**! pish! tush! tut! pshaw! pugh! pooh, -pooh! fudge! bosh! humbug! fiddlestick, -end! fiddledeedee! never mind! *n'importe!* [*F.*]; what signifies! what matter! what boots it! what of that! what's the odds! a fig for! stuff! nonsense! stuff and nonsense!

644. Utility

n. **utility**; usefulness etc. *adj.;* efficacy, efficiency, adequacy; service, use, stead, avail, boot [*archaic*]; help etc. (*aid*) 707; applicability etc. *adj.;* subservience etc. (*instrumentality*) 631; function etc. (*business*) 625; value; worth etc. (*goodness*) 648; money's worth; productiveness etc. 168; *cui bono* etc. (*intention*) 620; utilization etc. (*use*) 677; step in the right direction.

commonweal *or* common weal; commonwealth; public -good, -service, -interest; utilitarianism etc. (*philanthropy*) 910; public servant.

v. **be useful** etc. *adj.;* avail, serve; subserve [*rare*] etc. (*be instrumental to*) 631; conduce etc. (*tend*) 176; answer-, serve- -one's turn, -a purpose.

act a part etc. (*action*) 680; perform-, discharge -a function etc. 625; do-, render- -a service, -good service, -yeoman's service; bestead, stand one in good stead; be the making of; help etc. 707.

benefit etc. (*do good*) 648; bear fruit etc. (*produce*) 161; bring grist to the mill; profit, remunerate.

find one's -account, -advantage- in; reap the benefit of etc. (*be better for*) 658.

render useful etc. (*use*) 677.

adj. **useful**; of use etc. *n.;* serviceable, proficuous [*obs.*], good for; subservient etc. (*instrumental*) 631; conducive etc. (*tending*) 176; subsidiary etc. (*helping*) 707.

advantageous etc. (*beneficial*) 648; profitable, gainful, remunerative, worth one's salt; valuable; invaluable, beyond price, of general utility; prolific etc. (*productive*) 168.

adequate; efficient, efficacious; effective, effectual; expedient etc. 646.

applicable, usable, available, ready, handy, at hand, tangible; commodious, adaptable; of all work.

adv. **usefully** etc. *adj.*

for use, for service; in the public service; for the good of the -people, -public, -service; *pro bono publico* [*L.*].

645. Inutility

n. **inutility**; uselessness etc. *adj.;* inefficacy, futility; ineptitude, inaptitude; inadequacy etc. (*insufficiency*) 640; unfitness; inefficiency etc. (*incompetence*) 158; unskillfulness etc. 699; disservice; unfruitfulness etc. (*unproductiveness*) 169; labor -in vain, -lost, -of Sisyphus; lost -trouble, -labor; work of Penelope; Penelope's web; sleeveless [*obs.*]-, bootless- errand; wild-goose chase, mere farce.

redundance, supererogation etc. 641; tautology etc. (*repetition*) 104.

worthlessness; vanity, *vanitas vanitatum* [*L.*], inanity, nugacity; triviality etc. (*unimportance*) 643.

worthless residue, *caput mortuum* [*L., old chem.*]; waste paper, dead letter; blunt tool.

rubbish, junk, lumber, litter, odds and ends, cast-off clothes; button top; shoddy; rags, orts [*archaic*], leavings, dross, trash, refuse, sweepings, scourings, offscourings, waste, rubble, *débris* [*F.*]; chaff, stubble, broken meat; dregs etc. (*dirt*) 653; weeds, tares; rubbish heap, dust hole; *rudera* [*L.*], deads, slag.

idler; *fruges consumere natus* [Horace] etc. (*drone*) 683.

v. **be useless** etc. *adj.;* go a-begging etc. (*redundant*) 641; fail etc. 732.

labor in vain; seek-, strive- after impossibilities; use vain efforts, roll the stone of Sisyphus, beat the air, lash the waves, *battre l'eau avec un bâton* [*F.*], *donner un coup d'épée dans l'eau* [*F.*], fish in the air, milk the ram, drop a bucket into an empty well, pour water into a sieve, sow the sand; bay the moon; preach-, speak- to the winds; whistle jigs to a milestone; kick against

646. Expedience

the pricks, *se battre contre des moulins* [*F.*]; lock the stable door when the steed is stolen etc. (*too late*) 135; hold a farthing candle to the sun; cast pearls before swine etc. (*waste*) 638; carry coals to Newcastle etc. (*redundance*) 641; wash a blackamoor white etc. (*impossible*) 471.

render useless etc. *adj.;* dismantle, dismast, dismount, disqualify, disable; unrig [*chiefly naut.*]; hamstring, hock *or* hough, cripple, lame etc. (*injure*) 659; spike guns, clip the wings; put out of gear; throw a wrench in the machinery, throw a monkey-wrench into the works.

adj. **useless**, inutile, nugatory, inefficacious, futile, unavailing, bootless; inoperative etc. 158; inadequate etc. (*insufficient*) 640; inservient [*obs.*], inept, inefficient etc. (*impotent*) 158; of no avail etc. (*use*) 644; ineffectual etc. (*failure*) 732; incompetent etc. (*unskillful*) 699; "weary, stale, flat, and unprofitable" [*Hamlet*]; superfluous etc. (*redundant*) 641; dispensable; thrown away etc. (*wasted*) 638; abortive etc. (*immature*) 674.

worthless, valueless, unsalable; not worth a straw etc. (*trifling*) 643; dear at any price.

vain, empty, inane; gainless, profitless, fruitless; unserviceable, unprofitable; ill-spent; effete, barren, sterile, impotent, worn out; unproductive etc. 169; *hors de combat* [*F.*], past work etc. (*impaired*) 659; obsolete etc. (*old*) 124; fit for the dust hole; good for nothing; of no earthly use; not worth -having, —powder and shot; leading to no end, uncalled for; unnecessary, unneeded, superfluous.

adv. **uselessly** etc. *adj.;* to -little, —no, —little or no- purpose.

int. cui bono? [*L.*]; what's the good! what's the use!

646. Expedience
[specific subservience]

n. **expedience** *or* expediency, desirability, desirableness etc. *adj.;* fitness etc. (*agreement*) 23; utility etc. 644; propriety; opportunism; advantage, opportunity; pragmatism, pragmaticism; a working proposition.

high time etc. (*occasion*) 134; suitable time *or* season, tempestivity [*obs.*].

v. **be expedient** etc. *adj.;* suit etc. (*agree*) 23; befit; suit-, befit- the -time, -season, -occasion; produce the goods [*colloq.*].

conform etc. 82.

adj. **expedient**; desirable, advisable, acceptable; convenient; worth while, meet; fit, fitting, due, proper, eligible, seemly, becoming, befitting etc. *v.;* opportune etc. (*in season*) 134; in loco [*L.*]; suitable etc. (*accordant*) 23; applicable etc. (*useful*) 644.

practical, practicable, effective, pragmatic, pragmatical.

adv. **conveniently** etc. *adj.;* in the nick of time; in the right place.

647. Inexpedience

n. **inexpedience** *or* inexpediency, undesirability, undesirableness etc. *adj.;* discommodity, impropriety; unfitness etc. (*disagreement*) 24; inutility etc. 645; disadvantage, disadvantageousness, inconvenience, inadvisability.

v. **be inexpedient** etc. *adj.;* come amiss etc. (*disagree*) 24; embarrass etc. (*hinder*) 706; put to inconvenience.

adj. **inexpedient**, undesirable; unadvisable [*rare*], inadvisable, unsuitable, troublesome, objectionable; inapt, ineligible, inadmissible, inconvenient; incommodious, discommodious; disadvantageous; inappropriate, unfit etc. (*inconsonant*) 24.

ill-contrived, ill-advised; unsatisfactory; unprofitable etc., inept etc. (*useless*) 645; inopportune etc. (*unseasonable*) 135; out of-, in the wrong- place; improper, unseemly.

clumsy, awkward; cumbrous, cumbersome; lumbering, unwieldy, hulky; unmanageable etc. (*impracticable*) 704; impedient etc. (*in the way*) 706.

unnecessary etc. (*redundant*) 641.

648. Goodness
[capability of producing good, good qualities]

n. **goodness** etc. *adj.;* excellence, merit; virtue etc. 944; value, worth, price.

superexcellence, supereminence, quintessence; superiority etc. 33; perfection etc. 650; *coup de maître* [*F.*]; masterpiece, *chef d'oeuvre* [*F.*], prime, flower, cream, *élite* [*F.*], pick, nonesuch [*now rare*], A1 *or* A number 1 [*colloq.*], *nonpareil* [*F.*], *crème de la crème* [*F.*], flower of the flock, cock of the walk, salt of the earth; champion; prodigy, wonder, best ever [*colloq.*].

gem, -of the first water; *bijou* [*F.*], precious stone, jewel, pearl, diamond, ruby, brilliant, treasure; tidbit, good thing; *rara avis* [*L.*], one in a thousand.

beneficence etc. 906.

good man etc. 948.

v. **be beneficial** etc. *adj.;* produce *or* do good etc. 618; profit etc. (*be of use*) 644; benefit; confer a benefit etc. 618.

produce a good effect; be the making of, do a world of good, make a man of; do a good turn, confer an obligation; improve etc. 658.

do no harm, break no bones.

be good etc. *adj.;* be pure gold, be all wool; be the real -thing, −article; look good to [*colloq.*]; excel, transcend etc. (*be superior*) 33; bear away the bell.

stand the -proof, −test; pass muster, pass an examination.

vie, challenge comparison, emulate, rival.

adj. **beneficial,** valuable, of value; serviceable etc. (*useful*) 644; advantageous, profitable, edifying; salutary etc. (*healthful*) 656.

harmless, hurtless; unobnoxious; innocuous, innocent, inoffensive.

favorable; propitious etc. (*hopegiving*) 858; fair.

good, good as gold; excellent; better; superior etc. 33; above par; nice, fine; genuine etc. (*true*) 494.

choice, best, select, picked, elect, *recherché* [*F.*], rare, priceless; unparagoned [*rare*], matchless, peerless, unequaled *or* unequalled, unparalleled etc. (*supreme*) 33; superlatively etc. (33)- good; bully [*slang*], crackerjack [*slang*], gilt-edge *or* gilt-edged [*colloq.*]; superfine, superexcellent; of the first water; first-rate, first-class; highwrought, exquisite, very best, crack [*colloq.*], prime, tip-top [*colloq.*], capital, cardinal; standard etc. (*perfect*) 650; inimitable.

admirable, estimable; praiseworthy etc. (*approve*) 931; pleasing etc. 829; *couleur de rose* [*F.*], precious, of great price; costly etc. (*dear*) 814; worth -its weight in gold, −a king's ransom; priceless, invaluable, inestimable, precious as the apple of the eye.

satisfactory, up to the mark, unexceptionable, unobjectionable; tidy [*colloq.*].

in -good, −fair- condition; unspoiled, fresh; sound etc. (*perfect*) 650.

adv. **beneficially** etc. *adj.;* well etc. 618; for one's benefit.

649. Badness
[capability of producing evil, bad qualities]

n. **hurtfulness** etc. *adj.;* virulence.

bane etc. 663; plague spot etc. (*insalubrity*) 657; evil star, ill wind; hoodoo [*colloq.*], jinx [*slang*], *jadu* [*Hind.*], Jonah; snake in the grass, skeleton in the closet; *amari aliquid* [*L.*]; thorn in the -side, −flesh.

malignity, damnability, damnification, damnifying; malevolence etc. 907; tender mercies [*irony*].

ill-treatment, annoyance, molestation, abuse, oppression, persecution, outrage; misusage etc. 679; *damnum* [*L.*], scathe; injury etc. (*damage*) 659; Mickey, Mickey Finn [*both slang*], knockout drops.

badness etc. *adj.;* peccancy, abomination; painfulness etc. 830; pestilence etc. (*disease*) 655; guilt etc. 947; depravity etc. 945.

bad man etc. 949; evildoer etc. 913.

v. **be hurtful** etc. *adj.;* cause-, produce-, inflict-, work-, do- evil etc. 619; damnify, endamage, hurt, harm, scathe; injure etc. (*damage*) 659; pain etc. 830.

wrong, aggrieve, oppress, persecute; trample-, tread-, bear hard-, put-upon; overburden; weigh -down, −heavy on; victimize; run down, run hard; thwart; molest etc. 830.

maltreat, abuse; ill-use, illtreat; buffet, bruise, scratch, maul; smite etc. (*scourge*) 972; do violence, do a mischief; stab, pierce, outrage.

do mischief, do harm, make mischief, bring-, lead-, get- into trouble; hex, hoodoo [*colloq.*].

destroy etc. 162.

adj. **hurtful,** harmful, scathful [*obs. or dial.*], scatheful, baneful, baleful, injurious, deleterious, detrimental, noxious, pernicious, mischievous, full of mischief, mischief-making, malefic, malignant, nocuous, noisome; prejudicial; disserviceable, disadvantageous; wide-wasting.

unlucky, sinister; obnoxious; untoward, disastrous.

oppressive, burdensome, onerous; malign etc. (*malevolent*) 907.

corrupting etc. (*corrupt* etc. 659); virulent, venomous, envenomed, corrosive; poisonous etc. (*morbific*) 657; deadly etc. (*killing*) 361; destructive etc. (*destroying*) 162; inauspicious etc. 859.

bad, ill, arrant, as bad as bad can be, dreadful; horrid, horrible; dire; rank, peccant, foul, fulsome; rotten, rotten at the core.

unsatisfactory, indifferent; injured etc. deteriorated etc. 659; exceptionable, below par etc. (*imperfect*) 651; ill-contrived, ill-disposed, ill-conditioned.

deplorable, wretched, sad, grievous, lamentable, pitiful, pitiable, woeful etc. (*painful*) 830; mean etc. (*paltry*) 643.

evil, wrong; depraved etc. 945; shocking; reprehensible etc. (*disapproved*) 932.

hateful, −as a toad; abominable, vile, base, villainous, detestable, execrable, cursed, accursed, confounded; damned, damnable,

650. Perfection

damnatory, damnific [*rare*]; infernal; diabolic etc. (*malevolent*) 907.

inadvisable, unadvisable [*rare*] etc. (*inexpedient*) 647; unprofitable etc. (*useless*) 645; incompetent etc. (*unskillful*) 699; irremediable etc. (*hopeless*) 859.

adv. **badly** etc. *adj.;* wrong, ill; to one's cost; where the shoe pinches; with malignity etc. *n.*

650. Perfection

n. **perfection**; perfectness etc. *adj.;* indefectibility; impeccancy, impeccability.

paragon, pink, *beau ideal* [*F.*]; pink–, acme- of perfection; *ne plus ultra* [*L.*]; summit etc. 210. [comparisons] *cygne noir* [*F.*]; Phoenix *or* Phenix; black tulip, *tulipe noir* [*F.*]; philosopher's stone; Koh-i-noor.

model, standard, pattern, mirror, Admirable Crichton; trump, brick, corker, caution, humdinger [*all slang*]; "the observed of all observers" [*Hamlet*], very prince of.

Bayard, *chevalier sans peur et sans reproche* [*F.*]; Roland, Sidney.

masterpiece, masterstroke, prize-winner, prize; superexcellence etc. (*goodness*) 648; transcendence etc. (*superiority*) 33.

v. **be perfect** etc. *adj.;* transcend etc. (*be supreme*) 33.

perfect, bring to perfection, ripen, mature; consummate, crown, put the finishing touch to (*or* upon); complete etc. 729; put in trim etc. (*prepare*) 673; maturate [*rare*].

adj. **perfect**, faultless; indefective [*rare*], indeficient [*rare*], indefectible; immaculate, spotless, impeccable; free from imperfection etc. 651; unblemished, uninjured etc. 659; sound, –as a roach; in perfect condition; scathless [*obs. or dial.*], scatheless, intact, harmless; seaworthy etc. (*safe*) 644; right as a trivet; *in se ipso totus teres atque rotundus* [Hor.]; consummate etc. (*complete*) 52; finished etc. 729; complete in itself; well-rounded.

best etc. (*good*) 648; model, standard; inimitable, unparagoned [*rare*], unparalleled etc. (*supreme*) 33; superhuman, divine; beyond all praise etc. (*approbation*) 931; *sans peur et sans reproche* [*F.*].

adv. **to perfection**; perfectly etc. *adj.; ad unguem* [*L.*]; clean, –as a whistle; with a finish; to the limit.

651. Imperfection

n. **imperfection**; imperfectness etc. *adj.;* deficiency; inadequacy etc. (*insufficiency*) 640; peccability, defection, peccancy etc. (*badness*) 649; immaturity etc. 674.

fault, defect, "little rift within the lute" [Tennyson], weak point; screw loose; flaw etc. (*break*) 70; gap etc. 198; twist etc. 243; taint, attainder; *mésalliance* [*F.*], bar sinister; hole in one's coat; blemish etc. 848; weakness etc. 160; shortcoming etc. 304; drawback; seamy side.

half blood, drop of black blood, touch of the tar-brush [*colloq.*].

mediocrity; no great -shakes, -catch [*both colloq.*]; not much to boast of; one-horse shay; one-horse town; peanut -politics, -policy.

v. **be imperfect** etc. *adj.;* rot before it ripens, bear within it the seeds of decay; have a defect etc. *n.;* lie under a disadvantage; spring a leak. not pass muster, barely pass muster; fall short etc. 304.

adj. **imperfect**; not perfect etc. 650; deficient, defective; faulty, unsound, tainted, specked; mutilated; out of order; out of tune, cracked; leaky; sprung; warped etc. (*distort*) 243; lame; injured etc. (*deteriorated*) 659; peccant etc. (*bad*) 649; frail etc. (*weak*) 160; inadequate etc. (*insufficient*) 640; crude etc. (*unprepared*) 674; incomplete etc. 53; found wanting; below par; short-handed; below-, under- its full -strength, -complement.

indifferent, middling, ordinary, mediocre; average etc. 29; soso *or* so-so; *couci-couci* [*F.*], milk-and-water; tolerable, fair, passable; pretty -well, -good; rather-, moderately- good; good-, well- enough; decent; not bad, not amiss; unobjectionable, admissible, bearable, better than nothing.

secondary, inferior; second-rate, second best; one-horse; two-bit, two-by-four.

adv. **almost** etc.; to a limited extent, rather etc. 32; pretty, moderately; only, considering, all things considered, enough; might be worse.

652. Cleanness

n. **cleanness** etc. *adj.;* purity; cleaning etc. *v.;* purification, defecation etc. *v.;* purgation, lustration; abstersion [*rare*], detersion; aspersion, asperges [*R. C. Ch.*]; epuration [*rare*], mundation [*obs.*], ablution, lavation, colature [*obs.*]; disinfection etc. *v.;* drainage, sewerage.

bath, bathroom, swimming pool, natatorium, swimming bath, public bath, baths, bathhouse, hot bath, sauna etc. 386; lavatory; laundry, washhouse.

cleaner, washerwoman, laundress, dhobi [*India*], laundryman, washerman; scavenger, sweeper; mehtar (*fem.* mehtrani), bhangi [*all India*]; mud lark [*slang*]; sanitation worker, crossing-, street- sweeper, white wings; dustman; sweep.

brush; broom, besom, vacuum cleaner, carpet sweeper; mop, swab, hose; scraper; rake, shovel; sieve, riddle, screen, filter; blotter.

napkin, serviette, cloth, maukin [*obs.*], malkin [*obs.*], handkerchief, towel, sudary, sudarium, face cloth, wash cloth; doily *or* doyley, bib; carving cloth, tablecloth; duster, sponge.

mat, doormat, rug, drugget, cover.

[cleansing agents] wash, lotion, detergent, soap, purifier etc. *v.;* disinfectant; benzene, benzine, benzol, benzolin; bleaching powder, chloride of lime; lye, buck.

dentifrice, tooth paste, tooth powder; mouth wash.

cathartic, purgative, aperient, deobstruent, laxative.

v. **be** *or* **render clean** etc. *adj.*

clean, cleanse; mundify [*obs.*], rinse, wring, flush, full, wipe, mop, sponge, scour, swab, scrub.

wash, lave etc. (*water*) 337; launder, buck; absterge [*rare*], deterge; decrassify; clear, purify; depurate, spurate [*rare*], despumate, defecate; purge, expurgate, elutriate, lixiviate, edulcorate, clarify, refine, rack; percolate, separate, strain, filter, filtrate, drain.

sift, winnow, sieve, bolt, screen, riddle; pick, weed.

comb, rake, scrape, rasp; hackle, heckle, card.

sweep, brush, brush up, whisk, broom, vacuum [*colloq.*].

rout-, clear-, sweep etc.- out; make a clean sweep of, clean house, spruce up [*colloq.*].

disinfect, fumigate, ventilate, deodorize; whitewash.

adj. **clean**, cleanly; pure; immaculate; spotless, stainless, taintless, trig [*dial.*], without a stain, unstained, unspotted, unsoiled, unsullied, untainted, uninfected; sweet, -as a nut.

neat, spruce, tidy, trim, jimp *or* gimp [*Scot. & dial. Eng.*], clean as a new penny, like a cat in pattens; cleaned etc. *v.;* kempt [*archaic*].

abstergent, detergent, depurative, abstersive [*rare*], cathartic, cleansing, purifying.

adv. **neatly** etc. *adj.;* clean as a whistle.

653. Uncleanness

n. **uncleanness** etc. *adj.;* impurity; immundity [*rare*], immundicity [*rare*], mucidness, impurity etc. (of mind) 961.

defilement, contamination etc. *v.;* defoedation [*obs.*]; soilure, soiliness [*obs.*]; abomination; taint, tainture [*obs.*]; fetor etc. 401.

lousiness, pediculosis, pediculation, phthiriasis [*med.*].

decay; putrescence, putrefaction; corruption; mold *or* mould, must, mildew, dry rot, mucor [*rare*], caries [*med.*], rubigo [*obs.*].

slovenry; slovenliness etc. *adj.;* squalor.

dowdy, drab, slut, malkin *or* mawkin [*obs. or dial. Eng.*], slattern, sloven, slammerkin [*obs.*], slammock *or* slummock [*dial.*], drabble-tail, draggle-tail, mud lark [*slang*], dustman, sweep; beast, pig.

dirt, filth, soil, slop; dust, cobweb, flue; smoke, soot, smudge, smut, grime, raff [*dial.*], riffraff; sossle *or* sozzle [*dial.*].

dregs, sordes, grounds, lees; argol; sediment, settlement; heeltap; dross, drossiness; mother [*obs.*], precipitate, *scoriae* [*L.*], ashes, cinders, recrement, slag; scum, froth.

useless refuse, hogwash [*colloq.*], swill, garbage, ditch water, dishwater, bilge-water; rinsings, cheeseparings; sweepings etc. 645; outscourings, offscourings, offscum; *caput mortuum* [*L.*], residuum, sprue, dross, clinker, draff; scurf, scurfiness; exuviae; furfur, dandruff; tartar, fur.

spawn, offal, gurry; carrion; slough, peccant humor, pus, matter, suppuration.

dung, ordure, lienteria; feces *or* faeces, excrement, feculence; excreta etc. 299; sewage, sewerage [*rare in this sense*]; fertilizer, muck; coprolite; guano, manure, compost.

[receptacles] dunghill, colluvies [*med.*]; mixen, midden [*both archaic or dial. Eng.*], bog, laystall [*obs.*]; cesspool; sump [*Scot. & dial. Eng.*], sough [*dial. Eng.*], cloaca, Cloaca Maxima; sink, drain, sewer, common sewer; Cloacina; dust hole; glory hole [*colloq.*].

water-closet, w. c., toilet [*colloq.*], *cabinet d'aisance* [*F.*], latrine, backhouse, necessary, privy, jakes [*rare*], Mrs. Jones; head [*naval slang*].

sty, pigsty, lair, den, Augean stable, sink of corruption; slum, rookery.

mud, mire, quagmire, alluvium, silt, sludge, slime, slush, slosh [*dial.*], sposh.

vermin, louse, flea, nit, bug, chinch; lice etc. 366.

v. **be** *or* **become unclean** etc. *adj.;* rot, putrefy, fester, rankle, reek; stink etc. 401; mold *or* mould, molder *or* moulder; go bad etc. *adj.*

wallow in the mire; slobber, slabber.

render unclean etc. *adj.;* dirt, dirty; soil, smoke, tarnish, slaver, spot, smear; daub, blot, blur, smudge, smutch, smirch; begrease; drabble, dabble, daggle, spatter, slubber [*dial.*]; besmear etc., bemire, beslime, begrime, befoul; splash, stain, distain [*archaic*], maculate, sully, pollute,

654. Health

defile, debase, contaminate, taint, leaven; corrupt etc. (*injure*) 659; cover with dust etc. *n.;* drabble in the mud; roil.

adj. **unclean**, dirty, filthy, grimy; soiled etc. *v.;* not to be handled -without gloves, —with kid gloves; dusty, snuffy, smutty, sooty, smoky; thick, turbid, dreggy; slimy; mussy.

lousy, pedicular, pediculous.

uncleanly, slovenly, slatternly, untidy, sluttish, dowdy, draggle-tailed, drabble-tailed; uncombed, unkempt, unscoured, unswept, unwiped, unwashed, unstrained, unpurified; squalid; lutose, slammocky *or* slummocky [*dial.*], sossly *or* sozzly [*dial.*], sloppy [*colloq.*].

offensive, nasty, coarse, foul, impure, abominable, beastly, reeky, reechy [*dial. Eng.*]; fetid etc. 401.

moldy *or* mouldy, musty, fusty, mildewed, rusty, moth-eaten, mucid, rancid, bad, gone bad, lentiginous *or* lentiginose, touched, reasty [*dial. Eng.*], rotten, corrupt, tainted, high, flyblown, maggoty; putrid, putrefactive, putrescent, putrefied; saprogenic *or* saprogenous; purulent, carious, peccant; fecal, feculent; stercoraceous, excrementitious; scurfy, impetiginous; gory, bloody; rotting etc. *v.;* rotten as -a pear, —cheese.

crapulous etc. (*intemperate*) 954; beastlike; gross etc. (*impure in mind*) 961; fimetarious, fimicolous.

int. pah! faugh! ugh!

654. Health

n. **health**, sanity; soundness etc. *adj.;* vigor; good-, perfect-, excellent-, rude-, robust- health; bloom, *mens sana in corpore sano* [*L.*]; Hygeia; incorruption, incorruptibility; valetude [*obs.*]; good state-, clean bill- of health; eupepsia *or* eupepsy, euphoria *or* euphory; convalescence, upgrade; strength, poise.

v. **be in health** etc. *adj.;* be bursting with -vigor, —pep [*slang*]; never feel better; bloom, flourish. keep body and soul together, keep on one's legs; enjoy -good, —a good state of- health; have a clean bill of health.

return to health; recover etc. 660; get better etc. (*improve*) 658; take a -new, —fresh- lease of life; convalesce, be convalescent; add years to one's life; recruit; restore to health; cure etc. (*restore*) 660.

adj. **healthy**, healthful; in health etc. *n.;* well, sound, whole, strong, blooming, hearty, hale, fresh, green, florid, flush, hardy, stanch *or* staunch, brave, robust, vigorous, weatherproof.

on one's legs; sound as a -roach, —bell; fresh as -a daisy, —a rose, —April; walking on air; hearty as a buck; in -fine, —high- feather; in good case, in full bloom; pretty bobbish [*Eng. dial. or slang*]; bursting with -health, —vigor; in fine fettle; chipper [*colloq.*]; tolerably well, as well as can be expected.

unscathed, uninjured, unmaimed, unmarred, untainted; sound of wind and limb, without a scratch, safe and sound.

sanitary etc. (*health-giving*) 656; sanatory etc. (*remedial*) 662.

655. Disease

n. **disease**; illness, sickness etc. *adj.;* ailing etc. *v.;* "the thousand natural shocks That flesh is heir to" [*Hamlet*]; "all ills that men endure" [Cowley]; morbidity, morbosity [*obs.*]; infirmity, ailment, indisposition; complaint, disorder, malady, distemperature [*archaic*]; valetudinarianism; loss of health, delicacy, delicate health, invalidity, invalidism, invalescence [*rare*]; malnutrition, want of nourishment, cachexia *or* cachexy; prostration, decline, collapse; decay etc. 659.

visitation, attack, seizure, stroke, fit, epilepsy, apoplexy, bloodstroke; palsy, paralysis, motor paralysis, sensory paralysis, hemiplegia, paraplegia *or* paraplegy; *paralysis agitans* [*L.*], shaking palsy, Parkinson's disease; shock; shell-shock [*World War I*].

taint, virus, pollution, infection, contagion; septicaemia *or* septicemia, blood poisoning, pyaemia *or* pyemia, septicity; epidemic; sporadic, endemic; plague, pestilence.

fever, calenture; inflammation; ague; intermittent-, remittent-, congestive-, pernicious- fever; malaria, malarial fever; dengue *or* dandy fever, breakbone fever; yellow fever, yellow jack; typhoid *or* typhoid fever, enteric fever; typhus; eruptive fever; scarlet fever, scarlatina; smallpox, variola; varioloid; vaccinia, cow pox; varicella, chicken pox; rubeola, measles.

eruption, rash, brash, breaking out; canker rash; dartre, exanthema *or* exanthem; scabies, itch, psora; pox; eczema, tetter, psoriasis; lichen, papular rash; lichen tropicus, prickly heat; impetigo; erythema; erysipelas, St. Anthony's fire; urticaria, hives, nettlerash; herpes; herpes zoster, shingles; herpes simplex *and* circinatus, ringworm; miliaria, pemphigus, rupia.

sore, canker, ulcer, fester, boil, gumboil; pimple etc. (*swelling*) 250; carbuncle; gathering; abscess, impostume *or* imposthume [*obsoles.*],

655. Disease

aposteme; Rigg's disease, pyorrhea *or* pyorrhoea; chancre; peccant humor; proud flesh; corruption; enanthem *or* enanthema, gangrene; mortification, sphacelus, sphacelation; slough, caries, necrosis; cancer, carcinoma; tumor, leprosy.

heart disease, carditis, pericarditis, endocarditis, valvular lesion; hypertrophy–, dilatation–, atrophy–, fatty degeneration- of the heart; angina pectoris.

wasting disease, marasmus, emaciation, atrophy; consumption, white plague, tuberculosis, T.B. [*med. cant*], phthisis; pulmonary–, galloping- consumption; pulmonary phthisis, phthisipneumonia, pneumonia; chlorosis, green sickness; anaemia *or* anemia; leucocythaenia *or* leucocythenia.

throat disease, laryngitis, tonsillitis, quinsy, cynanche; bronchitis, diphtheria, whooping cough, pertussis; thrush, canker.

cold, cough; rheum; catarrh, hay fever; influenza, grippe *or* grip; rose cold.

indigestion, dyspepsia, poor digestion, pyrosis, water qualm; cardialgia, heartburn; seasickness, *mal de mer* [*F.*]; nausea; giddiness, vertigo; constipation, autointoxication.

eye disease, trachoma, conjunctivitis, pink eye; cataract, caligo, pin-and-web, *gutta serena* [*L.*].

veneral disease, pox, syphilis; gonorrhea *or* gonorrhoea, blennorrhea *or* blennorrhoea, blennorrhagia.

[various diseases] headache etc. (*physical pain*) 378; goiter *or* goitre, bronchocele, struma, tracheocele; lockjaw, tetanus, trismus; diarrhea *or* diarrhoea, dysentery, bloody flux, flux, issue, hemorrhage; hemorrhoids, piles; cholera, cholera morbus, Asiatic cholera, cholera infantum, summer complaint; colic; jaundice, icterus; apnea; asthma; king's evil, scrofula; rickets, rachitis; appendicitis; gall-stones, biliary calculus, stone; hernia, rupture; varicosis, varicose veins; arteriosclerosis, hardening of the arteries; neuritis; nervous prostration; St. Vitus's dance, chorea; neurasthenia; sciatica; rheumatism, arthritis, lumbago; dropsy, edema; elephantiasis; beriberi; locomotor ataxia; paresis, softening of the brain; bubonic plague; black death; leprosy, elephantiasis; sleeping sickness.

fatal etc. (*hopeless*) 859 -disease etc.; dangerous illness, churchyard cough; general breaking up, break-up of the system.

[disease of mind] idiocy etc. 499; insanity etc. 503.

martyr to disease; cripple; "the halt, the lame, and the blind"; valetudinary, valetudinarian; invalid, patient, case.

sick-room, sick-chamber; hospital etc. 662.

[science of disease] pathology, pathogeny, etiology, nosology, nosography, nosogeny, therapeutics; diagnostics, symptomatology, semeiology, semeiography, prognosis, diagnosis; clinic, polyclinic.

[veterinary] anthrax, splenic fever, woolsorter's disease, charbon, milzbrand, malignant pustule, quarter evil, quarter ill, Texas fever, blackwater, murrain, bighead; blackleg, black quarter; cattle plague, glanders, milk sickness; rinderpest, foot-and-mouth disease, hog cholera; epizoötic; heaves, rot, sheep rot; scabies, mange, distemper.

v. **be** *or* **feel ill** etc. *adj.;* ail, suffer, labor under, be affected with, complain of; droop, flag, languish, halt; sicken, peak, pine, dwindle; gasp; drop down in one's tracks; waste away, fail, lose strength, lose one's grip.

keep one's bed; lay by, lay up; be laid by the heels; lie helpless, –on one's back.

fall a victim to–, be stricken by–, take–, catch- -a disease etc. *n.*, - an infection; break out.

malinger, feign sickness etc. (*falsehood*) 544.

adj. **ailing** etc. *v.;* ill, ill of; taken ill, seized with; indisposed, unwell, sick, squeamish, poorly, seedy [*colloq.*]; affected–, afflicted- with illness; laid up, confined, bedridden, invalided, in hospital, on the sick list; out of health, out of sorts [*colloq.*], under the weather; valetudinary.

unsound, unhealthy; morbose [*obs.*], healthless, infirm, chlorotic, unbraced, cranky [*dial. Eng.*], sickly, weakly, weakened etc. (*weak*) 160; drooping, flagging; lame, halt, crippled, halting; *hors de combat* [*F.*] etc. (*useless*) 645.

touched in the wind, broken-winded, spavined, gasping.

diseased, morbid, tainted, vitiated, peccant, contaminated, poisoned, septic, septical, tabetic, tabid, mangy, leprous, cankered; rotten, –to, –at- the core; withered; palsied, paralytic; dyspeptic; luetic, pneumonic, pulmonic, phthisic *or* phthisical, consumptive, tubercular, tuberculous, rachitic; syntectic *or* syntectical, varicose.

decrepit; decayed etc. (*deteriorated*) 659; incurable etc. (*hopeless*) 859; in declining health; in a bad way, in danger, prostrate; moribund etc. (*death*) 360.

epidemic, epizoötic [*of animals*]; zymotic, contagious; morbific etc. 657.

656. Salubrity

- *n.* **salubrity**, salubriousness, wholesomeness, healthfulness; healthiness etc. *adj.;* Hygeia, Aesculapius.

  fine -air, –climate; eudiometer.

  [preservation of health] hygiene; valetudinarianism; pure air, exercise, nourishment, tonic; immunity; sanitarium, sanatorium; valetudinarian, sanitarian.

- *v.* **be salubrious** etc. *adj.;* make for health, conduce to health; be good for, agree with; assimilate etc. 23.

- *adj.* **salubrious**, salutary, salutiferous [*rare*]; wholesome; healthy, healthful; sanitary, prophylactic; benign, bracing, tonic, invigorating, good for, nutritious; hygeian, hygienic; Hygeian.

  sanative etc. (*remedial*) 662; restorative etc. (*reinstate*) 660; useful etc. 644.

  innoxious, innocuous, innocent; harmless, uninjurious, uninfectious; immune.

657. Insalubrity

- *n.* **insalubrity**, insalubriousness; unhealthiness etc. *adj.;* plague spot; malaria etc. (*poison*) 663; death in the pot, contagion; poisonousness, toxicity.

- *v.* **be insalubrious** etc. *adj.;* disagree with; shorten one's days.

- *adj.* **insalubrious**; unhealthy, unwholesome; noxious, noisome; morbific *or* morbifical, morbiferous; mephitic, septic, azotic, deleterious; pestilent, pestiferous, pestilential; virulent, venomous, envenomed, poisonous, toxic, toxiferous, narcotic; deadly etc. (*killing*) 361.

  innutritious, unnutritious [*rare*], undigestible [*rare*], indigestible, ungenial; uncongenial etc. (*disagreeing*) 24.

  contagious, infectious, catching, taking, communicable, inoculable, epidemic, zymotic, sporadic, endemic, pandemic; epizoötic [*of animals*].

658. Improvement

- *n.* **improvement**, amelioration, melioration, betterment; mend, amendment, emendation; mending etc. *v.;* advancement; advance etc. (*progress*) 282; ascent etc. 305; promotion, preferment; elevation etc. 307; increase etc. 35.

  cultivation, culture, march of intellect, menticulture; race-culture, acculturation, civilization; culture zone; eugenics.

  reform, reformation; revision, radical reform; second thoughts, correction, refinement, elaboration; purification etc. 652; repair etc. (*restoration*) 660; recovery etc. 660.

  revise, revised edition, new edition, new issue.

  reformer, reformist, progressive, radical.

- *v.* **improve**; be–, become–, get- better; mend, amend.

  advance etc. (*progress*) 282; ascend etc. 305; increase etc. 35; fructify, ripen, mature; pick up, come about, rally, take a favorable turn; turn over a new leaf, turn the corner; raise one's head, have sown one's wild oats; recover etc. 660.

  profit by; be better etc. *adj.,* be improved by; turn to -right, –good, –best- account; reap the benefit of; make good use of, make capital out of; place to good account.

  render better, improve, mend, amend, better; ameliorate, meliorate, relieve; correct; repair etc. (*restore*) 660; doctor etc. (*remedy*) 662; purify etc. 652; decrassify.

  improve–, refine- upon; rectify; enrich, mellow, elaborate, fatten.

  refresh, revive; put–, infuse- new blood into; invigorate etc. (*strengthen*) 159; reinvigorate, recruit, renew, make over, revivify, freshen.

  promote, cultivate, advance, forward, enhance; bring forward, bring on; foster etc. 707.

  touch up, rub up, brush up, furbish up, bolster up, vamp up, brighten up, warm up; polish, cook, make the most of, set off to advantage; prune; put in order etc. (*arrange*) 60.

  revise, edit, redact, digest, review, make corrections, make improvements etc. *n.*

  reform, remodel, reorganize; build -afresh, –anew; reclaim, civilize; lift, uplift, inspire; new-model.

  view in a new light, think better of, appeal from Philip drunk to Philip sober.

  palliate, mitigate; lessen etc. (36) an evil.

- *adj.* **better**, –off, –for; all the better for; better advised; improving etc. *v.;* progressive, improved etc. *v.*

  reformatory, emendatory; reparatory etc. (*restorative*) 660; remedial etc. 662.

  corrigible, improvable, curable; accultural.

- *adv.* **on consideration**, on reconsideration, on second thoughts, on better advice; on the mend, on the upgrade; *ad melius inquirendum* [*L.*].

659. Deterioration

- *n.* **deterioration**, debasement; wane, ebb; recession etc. 287; retrogradation etc. 283; decrease etc. 36.

  degeneracy, degeneration, degenerateness; degradation; depravation, depravement [*rare*], depravedness; devolution; depravity etc. 945; demoralization, retrogression; masochism.

660. Restoration

impairment, inquination [*obs.*], injury, damage, loss, detriment, delaceration [*obs.*], outrage, havoc, inroad, ravage, scathe, scath [*dial.*], perversion, prostitution, vitiation, discoloration, pollution, defoedation, poisoning, venenation [*rare*], leaven, contamination, canker, corruption, adulteration, alloy.

decline, declension, declination; decadence *or* decadency; falling off etc. *v.;* caducity [*rare*], senility, decrepitude.

decay, dilapidation, ravages of time, wear and tear; erosion, corrosion, moldiness *or* mouldiness; rottenness; moth and rust, dry rot, blight, marcescence, marasmus, atrophy, collapse; disorganization; *délabrement* [*F.*] etc. (*destruction*) 162; aphid, aphis (*pl.* aphides), plant louse; vine fretter, vine grub; gypsy (*or* gipsy) moth; buffalo carpet beetle etc. (*injurious insects*) 913.

wreck, mere wreck, honeycomb, *magni nominis umbra* [*L.*], jade, rackabones, skate; tacky *or* tackey, plug [*slang*].

v. **deteriorate**; be-, become- -worse, -deteriorated etc. *adj.;* have seen better days, degenerate, fall off; wane etc. (*decrease*) 36; ebb; retrograde etc. 283; decline, droop; go down etc. (*sink*) 306; go downhill, go on from bad to worse, go farther and fare worse; jump out of the frying pan into the fire; avoid Scylla and fall into Charybdis.

run to -seed, -waste; swale [*obs.*], sweal [*obs.*]; lapse, be the worse for; sphacelate; break, break down; spring a leak, crack, start; shrivel etc. (*contract*) 195; fade, go off, wither, molder *or* moulder, rot, rankle, decay, go bad; go to-, fall into- decay; fall "into the sere, the yellow leaf" [*Macbeth*]; rust, crumble, shake; totter, -to its fall; perish etc. 162; die etc. 360.

[render less good] deteriorate; weaken etc. 160; put back; taint, infect, contaminate, poison, empoison, envenom, canker, corrupt, exulcerate [*obs.*], pollute, vitiate, inquinate [*obs.*], debase, embase [*obs.*]; denaturalize, leaven; deflower, debauch, defile, deprave, degrade; ulcerate; stain etc. (*dirt*) 653; discolor, alloy, adulterate, sophisticate, tamper with, prejudice.

pervert, prostitute, demoralize, brutalize; render vicious etc. 945.

embitter, acerbate, exacerbate, aggravate.

injure, impair, labefy [*rare*], damage, harm, hurt, shend, scath [*dial.*], scathe, spoil, mar, despoil, dilapidate, waste; overrun; ravage; pillage etc. 791.

wound, stab, pierce, maim, lame, surbate [*obs.*], cripple, hock *or* hough, hamstring, hit between wind and water, scotch, mangle, mutilate, disfigure, blemish, deface, warp.

blight, rot; corrode, erode; wear away, wear out; gnaw, — at the root of; sap, mine, undermine, shake, sap the foundations of, break up; disorganize, dismantle, dismast; destroy etc. 162.

damnify etc. (*aggrieve*) 649; do one's worst; knock down; deal a blow to; play -havoc, — sad havoc, -the mischief [*colloq.*], -the deuce [*colloq.*], — the very devil [*colloq.*]- -with, — among; decimate.

adj. **deteriorated** etc. *v.;* altered, — for the worse; unimproved etc. (*improve* etc. 658); injured etc. *v.;* sprung; withering, spoiling etc. *v.;* on the -wane, -decline; tabid; degenerate; worse; the —, all the- worse for; out of -repair, — tune; imperfect etc. 651; the worse for wear; battered; weathered, weather-beaten; stale, *passé* [*F.*], shaken, dilapidated, frayed, faded, wilted, shabby, secondhand, threadbare; worn, -to- -a thread, — a shadow, — the stump, — rags; reduced, — to a skeleton; far-gone; tacky.

decayed etc. *v.;* moth-eaten, worm-eaten; mildewed, rusty, moldy *or* mouldy, spotted, seedy, time-worn, moss-grown; discolored; effete, wasted, crumbling, moldering *or* mouldering, rotten, cankered, blighted, marcescent, tainted; depraved etc. (*vicious*) 945; decrepit; broken-down; done, — for, — up [*all colloq.*]; worn-out, used up [*colloq.*]; fit for the -dust hole, — waste-paper basket; past work etc. (*useless*) 645.

at a low ebb, in a bad way, on one's last legs; undermined, deciduous; nodding to its fall etc. (*destruction*) 162; tottering etc. (*dangerous*) 665; past cure etc. (*hopeless*) 859; washed out, run down; fatigued etc. 688; unprogressive, improgressive [*rare*], backward, stagnant, behind the times; retrograde etc. (*retrogressive*) 283; deleterious etc. 649.

adv. **on the down grade**, on the downward track; beyond hope.

660. Restoration

n. **restoration**, restoral [*rare*], restorance [*obs.*]; reinstatement, replacement, rehabilitation, reëstablishment, reconstitution, reconstruction; reproduction etc. 163; renovation, renewal; revival, revivement [*rare*], reviviscence *or* revivescence; refreshment etc. 689; resuscitation, reanimation, revivification, reviction [*obs.*]; reorganization.

reaction; redemption etc. (*deliverance*) 672; restitution etc. 790; relief etc. 834.

recurrence etc. (*repetition*) 104; *réchauffé* [*F.*], *rifacimento* [*It.*].

661. Relapse

renaissance, renascence, rebirth, second youth, rejuvenescence, rejuvenation, new birth; regeneration, regeneracy, regenerateness, regenesis, palingenesis, reconversion; resurgence, resurrection.
redress, retrieval, reclamation, recovery; convalescence; resumption, *résumption* [*F.*]; sanativeness.
cure, recure [*obs.*], sanation [*obs.*]; healing etc. *v.;* redintegration; rectification; instauration; cicatrization; disinfection; delousing, delousement.
repair, repairing, reparation, mending; recruiting etc. *v.;* tinkering.
mender, doctor, physician, surgeon; priest, clergyman, pastor; carpenter, joiner, plumber, tinker, cobbler; reviver, revivor [*rare*], renewer, *vis medicatrix* [*L.*] etc. (*remedy*) 662.
curableness, curability, reparability, restorableness, retrievability, recoverability, recoverableness.

v. **return to the original state**; recover, rally, revive; come to, come round, come to oneself; pull through, weather the storm, be oneself again; get -well, — round, — the better of, — over — up, — about; rise from -one's ashes, — the grave; resurge, resurrect; survive etc. (*outlive*) 110; resume, reappear; come to, — life again; live again, rise again.
heal, heal over, skin over, cicatrize; right itself, heal itself.
restore, put back, place *in statu quo* [*L.*]; reinstate, replace, reseat, rehabilitate, reëstablish, reëstate, reinstall.
reconstruct, rebuild, reorganize, reconstitute; convert, reconvert; recondition, renew, renovate; regenerate; rejuvenate.
redeem, reclaim, recover, retrieve; rescue etc. (*deliver*) 672.
cure, heal, remedy, doctor, physic, medicate; redress, recure; break of; bring round, set on one's legs.
resuscitate, revive, reanimate, revivify, recall to life; reproduce etc. 163; warm up; reinvigorate, refresh etc. 689.
redintegrate, make whole; recoup etc. 790; make good, make all square; rectify; put —, set- -right, — to rights, — straight; set up, correct; put in order etc. (*arrange*) 60; refit, recruit; fill up, — the ranks; reinforce.
repair, mend; put in repair, put in thorough repair; retouch, botch, vamp, tinker, cobble; do up, patch up, plaster up, vamp up; darn, finedraw, heelpiece; stop a gap, stanch *or* staunch, calk *or* caulk, careen, splice, bind up wounds.

adj. **restored** etc. *v.;* redivivus, redivivous [*rare*], reviviscible, convalescent; in a fair way; none the worse; rejuvenated; renascent.
restoring etc. *v.;* restorative, recuperative; sanative, sanatory; reparative, reparatory; curative, remedial.
restorable, recoverable, remediable, retrievable, curable, sanable [*rare*].

adv. *in statu quo* [*L.*]; as you were.

661. Relapse

n. **relapse**, lapse; falling back etc. *v.;* retrogradation etc. (*retrogression*) 283; deterioration etc. 659. [return to, or recurrence of, a bad state] backsliding, recidivation [*obs.*]; recidivism, recidivity; recrudescence.

v. **relapse**, lapse; fall —, slide —, slip —, sinkback; have a relapse, be overcome, be overtaken, yield again to, fall again into; return; retrograde etc. 283; recidivate [*rare*]; fall off etc. 659- again.

adj. **backsliding**, relapsing etc. *v.;* recidivous, recidivistic, recrudescent, retrograde.

662. Remedy

n. **remedy**, help, redress; anthelmintic, vermifuge, helminthagogue; antifebrile, febrifuge; antipoison, antidote, mithridate [*old pharm.*], theriaca *or* theriac, counterpoison; antispasmodic; lithagogue; bracer, pick-me-up [*colloq.*], stimulant, tonic; abirritant, prophylactic, antiseptic, germicide, bactericide, corrective, restorative; alterant, alterative; cathartic etc. 652; specific; emetic, carminative.
materia medica, pharmacy, pharmacology, pharmaceutics, acology, posology, dosology [*rare*]; pathology etc. 655; pharmacopoeia.
narcotic, nepenthe *or* nepenthes, opium, morphine, cocaine, hashish, methadone, bhang, ganja; dope, speed, grass, crystal, angel dust, acid, horse, coke [*all slang*]; sedative etc. 174.
cure; partial —, attempted —, radical —, perfect —, certain- cure; sovereign remedy, panacea, cure-all, catholicon.
physic, medicine, simples, drug, potion, draft *or* draught, dose, pill, bolus, electuary; lincture *or* linctus; medicament; pharmacon.
nostrum, recipe, receipt, prescription; elixir, *elixir vitae* [*L.*], balm, balsam, cordial, tisane, ptisan.
aguweed, boneset; arnica, benzoin, cream of tartar, bitartrate of potash, calomel, mercurous

chloride; catnip, catmint; Epsom salts; feverroot or feverwort, feverweed, friar's balsam, Indian sage; ipecac or ipecacuanha; Peruvian bark, Jesuits' bark, cinchona, quinine or quinin, sassafras, yarrow.

salve, ointment, cerate, oil, lenitive, palliative, lotion, embrocation, liniment.

harquebusade or arquebusade, traumatic, vulnerary, pepastic, maturative, maturant, suppurative; eyewater, collyrium; cosmetic; depilatory.

poultice, cataplasm, vesicatory, plaster, *emplastrum* [*L.*], epithem, sinapism.

compress, pledget; bandage etc. (*support*) 215.

treatment, medical treatment, regimen, diet; dietary, dietetics; *vis medicatrix* [*L.*]; *vis naturae* [*L.*]; *médecine expectante* [*F.*]; bloodletting, bleeding, venesection, phlebotomy, cupping, sanguisuge, leeches; operation, the knife [*colloq.*], surgical operation; major operation; electrolysis, electrolyzation.

healing art, leechcraft [*archaic*], practice of medicine, therapeutics; allopathy, homeopathy, osteopathy, eclecticism, heteropathy; gynecology, gyniatrics, gynecological therapeutics; pediatrics; surgery, chirurgery [*archaic*]; orthopedics, orthopedia or orthopaedia, orthopraxy, orthopraxis, orthopedic surgery; sarcology, organotherapy; hydrotherapy, hydropathy, cold-water cure; faith cure, faith healing, mind cure, psychotherapy, psychotherapeutics; Christian Science, Eddyism; radiotherapy, heliotherapy, serotherapy, serum therapy; aerotherapy, pneumatotherapy; occupational or vocational therapy; dentistry, surgical dentistry; midwifery, obstetrics, tocology.

hospital, infirmary, clinic, *hôpital* [*F.*], general hospital, *hotel-Dieu* [*F.*]; special hospital (cancer, children's, dental, fever, maternity or lying-in, ophthalmic etc); pesthouse, lazarhouse, lazaretto, lazaret; lock hospital [*Eng.*]; *maison de santé* [*F.*]; *Hôtel des Invalides* [*F.*]; sanatarium, sanitarium, sanatorium, springs, baths, spa, pump room, well; hospice; asylum, home; Red Cross; ambulance.

dispensary, dispensatory, drug store, chemist's shop [*Brit.*].

doctor, physician, leech [*archaic*], medical man, disciple of Aesculapius; medical —, general-practitioner; medical attendant, specialist; surgeon, chirurgeon [*archaic*].

consultant, operator; resident, interne; anaesthetist or anesthetist; aurist, oculist, dentist, dental surgeon; osteopath, osteopathist; orthopedist; gynecologist, obstetrician; Christian Science practitioner, faith healer; medical student, medic [*colloq.*]; *accoucheur* (*fem. accoucheuse*) [*F.*], midwife; nurse; registered —, graduate —, trained —, district —, practical —, monthly-, visiting —, nurse; sister, nursing sister; dresser, bonesetter, apothecary, druggist, chemist [*Brit.*], pharmacopolist, pharmaceutist, pharmacist, pharmaceutical chemist, pharmacologist; Aesculapius, Hippocrates, Galen; *masseur* (*fem. masseuse*) [*F.*], massagist, rubber.

[instruments] stethoscope, stethometer, stethograph, respirometer, spirometer, pneumometer, spirograph, pneumatograph, pneumatometer, pulmotor.

v. **apply a remedy** etc. *n.;* doctor [*colloq.*], dose, physic, nurse, minister to, attend, dress the wounds, plaster, poultice; strap, splint, bandage; prevent etc. 706; relieve etc. 834; palliate etc. 658; heal, cure, "kill or cure," work a cure, remedy, stay (disease), snatch from the jaws of death; restore etc. 660; drench with physic; consult, specialize, operate, anaesthetize or anesthetize; straighten, mold or mould; deliver; extract, fill, stop; transfuse, bleed, cup, let blood; electrolyze.

manicure; pedicure; shampoo; massage, rub.

adj. **remedial**; restorative etc. 660; corrective, palliative, healing; sanatory, sanative; prophylactic; salutiferous etc. (*salutary*) 656; medical, medicinal; therapeutic, hypnotic, neurotic, chirurgical [*archaic*], surgical, epulotic [*obs.*], paregoric, tonic, corroborant, roborant; analeptic, balsamic, anodyne, narcotic, sedative, lenitive, demulcent, emollient; detersive, detergent; abstersive, disinfectant; febrifugal, antifebrile; alternative; traumatic, vulnerary.

allopathic, homeopathic, eclectic, hydropathic, heteropathic; aperient, laxative, cathartic, purgative; septic, aseptic, antiseptic; antiluetic, antisyphilitic; anthelmintic, vermifugal; chalybeate, deobstruent; purifying, cleansing, depurative, depuratory; electrolytic or electrolytical.

dietetic, dietary, alimentary; nutritious, nutritive; digestive, digestible, peptic.

remediable, curable; antidotal, alexipharmic, alexiteric.

663. Bane

n. **bane**, curse, hereditary evil, thorn in the flesh; *bête noir* [*F.*], bugbear; evil etc. 619; hurtfulness etc. (*badness*) 649; painfulness etc. (*cause of pain*) 830; scourge etc. (*punishment*) 975; *damnosa hereditas* [*L.*]; white elephant.

664. Safety

rust, worm, helminth, moth, "moth and rust" [*Bible*], fungus, mildew; dry rot; canker, cankerworm; cancer; viper etc. (*evildoer*) 913; demon etc. 980.

sting, fang, thorn, tang [*dial. Eng.*], bramble, brier *or* briar, nettle.

poison, leaven, virus, venom; arsenic, Prussic acid, antimony, tartar emetic, strychnine, tannin *or* tannic acid, nicotine; miasma *or* miasm, effluvium, mephitis, stench; fetor etc. 401; malaria, azote [*rare*], nitrogen, coal gas, illuminating gas, natural gas, gas, poison gas, mustard gas, chlorine, tear gas, lachrymose gas; sewer gas; pest.

Albany hemp, arsenious -oxide, — acid; bichloride of mercury; carbonic acid, — gas; choke damp, black damp, fire damp, afterdamp, marsh gas, methane; cyanide of potassium, carbolic acid, corrosive sublimate; hydrocyanic acid, hydrocyanide; nux vomica, ratsbane.

toxicant, intoxicant, deliriant, delirifacient, hemlock, hellebore, nightshade, deadly nightshade, belladonna, henbane, aconite; banewort, opium, bhang [*India*], ganja [*India*], hemp, cannabin, cannabis, marijuana, hashish; Upas tree.

[science of poisons] toxicology.

adj. **baneful** etc. (*bad*) 649; poisonous etc. (*unwholesome*) 657.

664. Safety

n. **safety**, security, surety, impregnability; invulnerability, invulnerableness etc. *adj.;* danger -past, — over; storm blown over; coast clear; escape etc. 671; means of escape; blow-, safety-, snifting- valve; safeguard, palladium; sheet anchor; rock, tower.

guardianship, wardship, wardenship; tutelage, custody, safe-keeping; preservation etc. 670; guardship [*obs.*], protection, auspices.

protector, guardian; warden, warder; preserver, life saver, custodian, duenna, chaperon, third person.

safe-conduct, escort, convoy; guard, shield etc. (*defense*) 717; guardian angel; tutelary -god, — deity, — saint; *genius loci* [*L.*].

watchdog, bandog; Cerberus.

watchman, patrolman, policeman, police officer, officer, "the finest"; cop, copper, peeler, bobby [*all slang*], blue coat [*colloq.*], constable, roundsman, gendarme [*F.*], military police; detective, tec [*slang*], bull [*slang*], spotter [*slang*]; sheriff, deputy; sentinel, sentry, scout etc. (*warning*) 668.

armed force, garrison, life guard, State guard, militia, regular army, navy; volunteer; marine etc. 726; battleship, man-of-war etc. 726.

[means of safety] refuge etc., anchor etc. 666; precaution etc. (*preparation*) 673; guard, guard rail, hand rail; bulkhead, watertight compartment, safety appliance; bolt, hasp etc. (*pin*) 45; cyclone cellar, dugout, bombproof dug-out; quarantine, *cordon sanitaire* [*F.*].

[sense of security] confidence etc. 858.

judge, justice, judiciary, magistrate, beak [*slang, Eng.*], justice of the peace, J. P.; deemster [*Isle of Man*], hakim [*Oriental*]; chancellor etc. 967.

v. **be safe** etc. *adj.;* keep one's head above water, tide over, save one's bacon [*colloq.*]; ride out —, weather- the storm; light upon one's feet; bear a charmed life; escape etc. 671; possess nine lives.

protect, watch over; make *or* render safe etc. *adj.;* take care of etc. (*care*) 459; preserve etc. 670; cover, screen, shelter, shroud, flank, ward; take charge of; guard etc. (*defend*) 717; garrison; man the -garrison, — lifeboat; secure etc. (*restrain*) 751; intrench *or* entrench, mine, countermine; dig in; fence round etc. (*circumscribe*) 229; house, nestle, ensconce.

escort, support, accompany, convoy.

watch, mount guard, patrol, go on one's beat; do —, perform- sentry go; scout, spy.

take precautions etc. (*prepare for*) 673; "make assurance double sure" [*Macbeth*] etc. (*caution*) 864; take up a loose thread; reef, take in a reef, make all snug, have an anchor to windward, double reef topsails.

seek safety; take —, find- shelter etc. 666; run into port.

adj. **safe**, secure, sure; in safety, in security; in shelter, in harbor, in port; in the shadow of a rock; on *terra firma* [*L.*]; on the safe side; under the -shield of, — shade of, — wing of, — shadow of one's wing; under cover, under lock and key; out of -danger, — the meshes, — harm's way; on sure ground, at anchor, high and dry, above water; unthreatened, unmolested; protected etc. *v.; cavendo tutus* [*L.*]; panoplied etc. (*defended*) 717.

safe and sound etc. (*preserved*) 670; harmless; scatheless etc. (*perfect*) 650; unhazarded; not dangerous etc. 665.

snug, seaworthy, airworthy; watertight, weathertight, weatherproof, waterproof, fireproof; bombproof, shellproof.

defensible, tenable, proof against, invulnerable; unassailable, unattackable; "founded upon a rock" [*Bible*], impregnable, imperdible [*obs.*]; inexpugnable.

protecting etc. *v.*; guardian, tutelary; preservative etc. 670; trustworthy etc. 939.

adv. **ex abundante cautela** [*L.*]; with impunity.

int. **all's well**! all clear! all serene! [*slang*]; safety first! at rest! at ease!

665. Danger

n. **danger**, peril, insecurity, jeopardy, risk, hazard, venture, precariousness, slipperiness; instability etc. 149; defenselessness etc. *adj.*

exposure etc. (*liability*) 177; vulnerability; vulnerable point, heel of Achilles; forlorn hope etc. (*hopelessness*) 859.

[dangerous course] leap in the dark etc. (*rashness*) 863; road to ruin, *facilis descensus Averni* [Vergil], hairbreadth escape.

[approach of danger] cause for alarm; source of danger etc. 667; rock —, breakers- ahead; storm brewing; clouds -in the horizon, — gathering; warning etc. 668; alarm etc. 669.

[sense of danger] apprehension etc. 860.

v. **be in danger** etc. *adj.*; be exposed to —, run into —, incur —, encounter- danger etc. *n.*; run a risk; lay oneself open to etc. (*liability*) 177; lean on —, trust to- a broken reed; feel the ground sliding from under one, have to run for it; have the -chances, — odds- against one.

hang by a thread, totter; tremble on the verge; totter on the brink; sleep —, stand- on a volcano; sit on a barrel of gunpowder, live in a glass house.

endanger; bring —, place —, put- in -danger etc. *n.*; expose to danger, imperil; be proscribed; have one's name on the danger list; be overdue [*naut.*], be despaired of; be under sentence of death; jeopard, jeopardize; put one's head in the lion's mouth; beard the lion in his den; compromise; sail too near the wind etc. (*rash*) 863.

threaten etc. (909) danger; run one hard; lay a trap for etc. (*deceive*) 545.

adventure, risk, hazard, venture, stake, set at hazard; run the gauntlet etc. (*dare*) 861; engage in a forlorn hope.

adj. **in danger** etc. *n.*; endangered etc. *v.*; fraught with danger; dangerous, hazardous, perilous, periculous [*obs.*], parlous [*archaic*], unsafe, unprotected etc. (safe, protect etc. 664); insecure, untrustworthy, unreliable; built upon sand, on a sandy basis; unsound, speculative, wild-cat.

defenseless, guardless, fenceless [*archaic*], harborless, unsheltered, unshielded; vulnerable, expugnable, exposed; open to etc. (*liable*) 177.

aux abois [*F.*], at bay, with one's back to the wall; on the wrong side of the wall, on a lee shore, on the rocks.

precarious, critical, ticklish; slippery, slippy; hanging by a thread etc. *v.*; with a halter round one's neck; between -the hammer and the anvil, — Scylla and Charybdis, — two fires; on the edge, brink, *or* verge of -a precipice, — a volcano, — an abyss, —a pit; in the lion's den, on slippery ground, under fire; not out of the wood; in the condemned cell, under sentence of death; at stake, in question.

unwarned, unadmonished, unadvised; unprepared etc. 674; off one's guard etc. (*inexpectant*) 508.

tottering, unstable, unsteady; shaky, top-heavy, tumble-down, ramshackle, crumbling, waterlogged; helpless, guideless; in a bad way; reduced to —, at- the last extremity; trembling in the balance; nodding to its fall etc. (*destruction*) 162.

threatening etc. 909; ominous, ill-omened; alarming etc. (*fear*) 860; explosive; poisonous; venomous etc. (*insalubrious*) 657; rotten at the core.

adventurous etc. (*rash*) 863, (*bold*) 861.

int. **stop**! look! listen! look out! watch your step! look alive! look slippy! [*colloq.*]; below there! 'ware heads! beware! take care! *prenez garde!* [*F.*].

666. Refuge

[means of safety]

n. **refuge**, sanctuary, retreat, fastness, stronghold, fortress, castle, acropolis; keep, last resort; ward; prison etc. 752; asylum, ark, home, refuge for the destitute; almshouse; hiding place &. (*ambush*) 530; *sanctum sanctorum* [*L.*] etc. (*privacy*) 893.

anchorage, roadstead; breakwater, mole, port, haven; harbor, — of refuge; seaport; pier, jetty, embankment, quay, wharf, landing place; bund, bunder [*both Oriental*]; water wing [*arch.*].

covert, shelter, screen, lee wall, wing, shield, umbrella; dashboard, dasher, splashboard, mud guard *or* mudguard, wheel guard.

wall etc. (*inclosure*) 232; fort etc. (*defense*) 717.

anchor, sheet anchor, sacred anchor [*Gr. & Rom. antiq.*], kedge *or* kedge anchor; Trotman's —, Martin's —, mushroom- anchor; killick; grapnel, grappling iron; mainstay; support etc. 215; check etc. 706; ballast.

667. Pitfall

  means of escape etc. (*escape*) 671; lifeboat, swimming belt, cork jacket, life preserver, buoy, breeches buoy; parachute, plank, stepping-stone.
  safeguard etc. (*protection*) 664.
  jury mast; vent-peg; safety -valve, — lamp; lightning -rod, — conductor.
v. **seek** or **find safety** etc. 664; seek —, take —, find- refuge etc. *n.;* claim sanctuary; head for the hills, take to the high ground; throw oneself into the arms of; break for the tall timber, break for the woods; fly to, reach in time; make port, make the harbor; anchor in the roadstead; crouch in the lee of; reach -shelter, — home, — running water.
  bar the gate, let the portcullis down; lock —, bolt —, make fast- the door; raise the drawbridge.

667. Pitfall
[source of danger]

n. rocks, reefs, coral reef, sunken rocks, snags; sands, quicksands; syrt [*rare*], syrtis [*rare*]; Goodwin sands, sandy foundation; slippery ground; breakers, shoals, shallows, bank, shelf, flat, lee shore, ironbound coast, rockbound coast; rock —, breakers- ahead; derelict.
  abyss, abysm, pit, void, chasm, crevasse.
  whirlpool, eddy, vortex, gurge [*rare*], rapids, undertow; current, tide gate, tide race, maelstrom; eagre, bore, tidal wave.
  pitfall; ambush etc. 530; trapdoor; trap etc. (*snare*) 545; mine, masked battery, spring-gun.
  pest, ugly customer, dangerous person, *le chat qui dort* [*F.*]; crouching tiger; incendiary, firebug [*slang*]; firebrand; hornet's nest.
  sword of Damocles; wolf at the door, snake in the grass, snake in one's bosom, death in the -cup, — pot; latency etc. 526.

668. Warning

n. **warning**, caution, caveat; notice etc. (*information*) 257; premonition, premonishment [*rare*]; prediction etc. 511; symptom, contraindication, lesson, dehortation; admonition, monition; alarm etc. 669.
  handwriting on the wall, *tekel upharsin* [*Heb.*], yellow flag; red flag, red light, fog-signal, foghorn; siren; monitor, warning voice, Cassandra, signs of the times, Mother Cary's chickens, stormy petrel, bird of ill omen, gathering clouds, cloud no bigger than a man's hand, clouds in the horizon, death watch, death lights etc. (*premonitions*) 992a.
  watchtower, beacon, signal post; lighthouse etc. (*indication of locality*) 550.
  sentinel, sentry; watch, watchman; watch and ward; watchdog, bandog, house dog; patrol, vedette, picket, bivouac, scout, spy, spial [*obs.*]; advanced —, rear- guard; lookout, flagman.
  cautiousness etc. 864.
v. **warn**, caution; forewarn, prewarn; admonish, forebode, premonish [*rare*]; give -notice, — warning; menace etc. (*threaten*) 909; put on one's guard; sound the alarm etc. 669; croak.
  beware, ware [*dial.*]; take -warning, — heed at one's peril; look out, keep one's wits about one; keep watch and ward etc. (*care*) 459.
adj. **warning** etc. *v.;* premonitory, monitory, cautionary, admonitory, admonitive [*rare*]; ominous, threatening, lowering, minatory etc. (*threat*) 909; symptomatic, sematic [*biol.*].
  warned etc. *v.;* on one's guard etc. (*careful*) 459, (*cautious*) 864.
adv. with alarm, on guard, after due warning, with one's eyes open; *in terrorem* [*L.*].
int. **beware**! ware! take care! mind —, take care- what you are about! mind! look out! watch your step!

669. Alarm
[indication of danger]

n. **alarm**; alarum, larum [*archaic*], alarm bell, tocsin, *alerte* [*F.*], beat of drum, sound of trumpet, note of alarm, hue and cry, fiery cross; signal of distress; flag at -half-mast, — half-staff; blue lights; war cry, war whoop; warning etc. 668; fog signal, fog bell, fog horn, siren; yellow flag; danger signal; red light, red flag; fire bell, fire alarm, still alarm; burglar alarm; watchman's rattle, police whistle.
  false alarm, cry of wolf; bugbear, bugaboo.
v. **alarm**; give —, raise —, sound —, turn in —, beat- the *or* an -alarm etc. *n.;* warn etc. 668; ring the tocsin; *battre la générale* [*F.*]; cry wolf; half-mast.
adj. **alarmed**; warned; alarming etc. *v.*
int. *sauve qui peut!* [*F.*]; *qui vive?* [*F.*]; who goes there?

670. Preservation

n. **preservation**; safe-keeping; conservation etc. (*storage*) 636; maintenance, support, sustentation [*rare*], conservatism; economy; *vis conervatrix* [*L.*]; salvation etc. (*deliverance*) 672.
  [means of preservation] prophylaxis; preserver, preservative; hygiastics, hygiantics [*both rare*]; hygiene, hygienics; cover, drugget; *cordon sanitaire* [*F.*]; ensilage; dehydration, anhydra-

tion, evaporation; drying, putting up, canning, pickling; tinned goods [*chiefly Brit.*], canned goods; hyanization.

[superstitious remedies] charm etc. 993.

v. **preserve**, maintain, keep, sustain, support; keep -up, — alive; not willingly let die; nurse; cure etc. (*restore*) 660; save, rescue; be —, make- safe etc. 664; take care of etc. (*care*) 459; guard etc. (*defend*) 717; bank, bank up, shore up.

embalm, dry, cure, salt, pickle, season, kyanize, bottle, pot, tin [*chiefly Brit.*], can; dehydrate, anhydrate, evaporate; husband etc. (*store*) 636.

hold one's own; *stare super antiquas vias* [Bacon]; hold —, stand- one's ground etc. (*resist*) 719.

adj. **preserving** etc. *v.;* conservative; prophylactic; preservatory, preservative; hygienic.

preserved etc. *v.;* unimpaired, unbroken, uninjured, unhurt, unsinged, unmarred; safe, — and sound; intact, with a whole skin, without a scratch.

671. Escape

n. **escape**, scape [*obs.*]; avolation [*obs.*], elopement, flight; evasion etc. (*avoidance*) 623; retreat; narrow —, hairbreadth- escape; close call [*colloq.*], close shave, near shave [*colloq.*]; come off, impunity.

[means of escape] loophole etc. (*opening*) 260; path etc. 627; secret -chamber, passage; refuge etc. 666; vent, — peg; safety valve; drawbridge, fire escape.

reprieve etc. (*deliverance*) 672; liberation etc. 750.

refugee etc. (*fugitive*) 623.

v. **escape**, scape [*archaic*]; make —, effect —, make good- one's escape; break jail; get off, get clear off, get well out of; *échapper belle* [*F.*], save one's bacon [*colloq.*], make a get-away [*slang*]; weather the storm etc. (*safe*) 664; escape scot-free.

elude etc., make off etc. (*avoid*) 623; march off etc. (*go away*) 293; give one the slip; slip through the -hands, — fingers; slip the collar, wriggle out of; break loose, break from prison; break — slip —, get- away; find vent, find a hole to creep out of.

adj. escaping, escaped etc. *v.;* stolen away, fled; scot-free.

672. Deliverance

n. **deliverance**, extrication, rescue, ransom; reprieve, reprieval [*rare*], respite; armistice, truce; liberation etc. 750; emancipation; redemption, redeemableness, salvation; exemption; day of grace; riddance; jail (*Brit.* gaol) delivery.

v. **deliver**, extricate, rescue, save, free, liberate, set free, release, emancipate, redeem, ransom; bring -off, — through; *tirer d'affaire* [*F.*], get the wheel out of the rut, snatch from the jaws of death, come to the rescue; rid; retrieve etc. (*restore*) 660; be —, get- rid of.

adj. saved etc. *v.;* extricable, redeemable, rescuable.

int. to the rescue! a rescue! saved!

673. Preparation

n. **preparation**; providing etc. *v.;* provision, providence; anticipation etc. (*foresight*) 510; precaution, preconcertedness, preconcertion, predisposition; forecast etc. (*plan*) 626; rehearsal, note of preparation; dissemination, propaganda.

groundwork, first stone, cradle, stepping-stone; foundation, first rung, scaffold etc. (*support*) 215; scaffolding, *échafaudage* [*F.*].

elaboration; ripening etc. *v.;* maturation, evolution; perfection; concoction, digestion; gestation, hatching, incubation, sitting.

[putting in order] arrangement etc. 60; clearance; adjustment etc. 23; tuning; equipment, outfit, accouterment *or* accoutrement, armament, array.

[preparation of men] training etc. (*education*) 537; inurement etc. (*habit*) 613; novitiate.

[preparation of food] cooking, cookery, culinary art; brewing.

[preparation of the soil] tilling, plowing *or* ploughing, sowing, semination, cultivation.

[state of being prepared] preparedness, readiness, ripeness, mellowness; maturity; *un impromptu fait à loisir* [*F.*].

[preparer] preparer, trainer, coach; teacher etc. 540; pioneer; *avant-courrier* [*F.*], *avant-coureur* [*F.*]; *voortrekker* [*Dutch*]; prophet; forerunner etc. (*precursor*) 64; sappers and miners, pavior, navvy; packer, stevedore, longshoreman; warming pan.

v. **prepare**; get —, make- ready; predispose, address oneself to, get under weigh; make preparations, settle preliminaries, get up, sound the note of preparation.

set *or* put in order etc. (*arrange*) 60; forecast etc. (*plan*) 626; prepare —, plow —, dress- the ground; till —, cultivate- the soil; sow the seed, lay a train, dig a mine; lay —, fix- the -foundations, — basis, — groundwork; dig the foundations, erect the scaffolding; lay the first stone etc. (*begin*) 66.

674. Nonpreparation

roughhew; cut out work; block out, hammer out; lick into shape etc. (*form*) 240.

elaborate, mature, ripen, mellow, season, bring to maturity; nurture etc. (*aid*) 707; hatch, cook, brew; temper, anneal, smelt; barbecue; dry, cure, salt, smoke, infumate [*rare*]; maturate.

equip, arm, man; fit out, fit up; furnish, rig, dress, garnish, betrim, accouter *or* accoutre, array, fettle, fledge; dress up, furbish up, brush up, vamp up; refurbish; sharpen one's tools, trim one's -tackle, — foils; set, prime, attune; whet the -knife, — sword; wind up, screw up; adjust etc. (*fit*) 27; put in -trim, — train, — gear, — working order, — tune, — a groove for, — harness; pack, stow away, stow down, stow, load, store.

prepare for etc.; train etc. (*teach*) 537; inure etc. (*habituate*) 613; breed; rehearse; make provision for; take -steps, — measures, — precautions; provide, provide against; beat up for recruits; open the door to etc. (*facilitate*) 705.

set one's house in order, make all snug; clear decks, clear for action; close one's ranks; shuffle the cards.

prepare oneself; serve an apprenticeship etc. (*learn*) 539; lay oneself out for, get into harness, gird up one's loins, buckle on one's armor, *reculer pour mieux sauter* [*F.*], prime and load, shoulder arms, get up steam; put the horses to, harness, harness up [*colloq.*], hitch up [*colloq.*].

guard against, make sure against; forearm, make sure, prepare for the evil day, have a rod in pickle, have a bone to pick, provide against a rainy day, feather one's nest; lay in provisions etc. 637; make investments; keep on foot, keep going.

be prepared, be ready etc. *adj.;* hold oneself in readiness, watch and pray, keep one's powder dry, lie in wait for etc. (*expect*) 507; anticipate etc. (*foresee*) 510; *principiis obstare* [*L.*]; *venienti occurrere morbo* [*L.*].

adj. **preparing** etc. *v.;* in preparation, in course of preparation, in agitation, in embryo, in hand, in train; afoot, afloat; on foot, on the stocks, on the anvil; under consideration etc. (*plan*) 626; in consultation; brewing, hatching, forthcoming, brooding; in store for, in reserve.

precautionary, provident; preparative, preparatory; provisional, inchoate, under revision; under advisement; preliminary etc. (*precedent*) 62.

prepared etc. *v.;* in readiness; ready, — to one's hand, ready made; cut and dried; made to one's hand, ready cut, made to order, at one's elbow, ready for use, all ready; handy, on the table; in gear; running -smoothly, — sweetly; in working -order, — gear; snug; in practice.

in full feather, in best bib and tucker [*colloq.*]; in —, at- harness; in the saddle, in arms, in battle array, in war paint; up in arms; armed -at all points, — to the teeth, — *cap à pie* [*F.*]; sword in hand; booted and spurred.

in utrumque paratus [Virgil], *semper paratus* [*L.*]; on the alert etc. (*vigilant*) 459; at one's post.

ripe, mature, mellow; pucka *or* pukka *or* pakka [*Hind.*]; practiced etc. (*skilled*) 698; labored, elaborate, high-wrought, smelling of the lamp, worked up.

adv. **in preparation**, in anticipation of; afoot, astir, abroad; abroach; in fine fettle.

674. Nonpreparation

n. **nonpreparation**, unpreparedness; absence of —, want of- preparation; inculture [*obs.*], inconcoction [*obs.*], improvidence.

immaturity, crudity; rawness etc. *adj.;* abortion; disqualification.

[absence of art] nature, state of nature; virgin soil, unweeded garden; rough diamond; neglect etc. 460.

rough copy etc. (*plan*) 626; germ etc. 153; raw material etc. 635.

improvisation etc. (*impulse*) 612.

v. **be unprepared** etc. *adj.;* want —, lack- preparation; lie fallow; *s'embarquer sans biscuits* [*F.*]; live from hand to mouth.

[render unprepared] dismantle etc. (*render useless*) 645; undress etc. 226.

extemporize, improvise; cook up, fix up, vamp.

surprise, drop in on [*colloq.*], pay a surprise visit, drop in [*colloq.*], give a surprise party, take potluck with; take —, catch- unawares; take by surprise, call informally.

adj. **unprepared** etc. (prepare etc. 673); without preparation etc. 673; incomplete etc. 53; rudimental, embryonic, abortive; immature, unripe, *kutcha* or *kachcha* [*Hind.*]; callow, unfledged, unhatched, unnurtured, raw, green, crude; coarse, rough, roughcast, roughhewn; in the rough; rough-edged, unhewn, unformed, unfashioned, unwrought, unlabored, unblown; indigested, undigested; unmellowed, unseasoned, unleavened; uncooked, unboiled, unconcocted; unpolished, uncut, deckle-edged.

untaught, uneducated, untrained, untutored, undrilled, unexercised; unlicked; precocious, premature.

fallow, unsown, untilled, uncultivated.

natural, *in puris naturalibus* [*L.*], in a state of nature; undressed; in dishabille, *en déshabillé* [*F.*], in negligee.
unfitted, disqualified, unqualified, ill-digested; unbegun, unready, unarranged, unorganized, unfurnished, unprovided, unequipped, untrimmed; out of -gear, — kilter *or* kelter [*colloq.*], — order; dismantled etc. *v.*
shiftless, improvident, unthrifty, thriftless, thoughtless, unguarded; happy-go-lucky; slack, remiss; caught napping etc. (*inexpectant*) 508; unpremeditated etc. 612.

adv. **inadvertently**, by surprise, without premeditation; extempore etc. 612.

675. Essay

n. **essay**, trial, endeavor, attempt; aim, struggle, venture, adventure, speculation, *coup d'essai* [*F.*], *début* [*F.*]; probation etc. (*experiment*) 463.

v. **try**, essay; experiment etc. 463; endeavor, strive; tempt, attempt, make an attempt; venture, adventure, speculate, take one's chance, tempt fortune; try one's -fortune, — luck, — hand; use one's endeavor; feel —, grope —, pick- one's way.
try hard, push, make a bold push, use one's best endeavor; do one's best etc. (*exertion*) 686.

adj. **essaying** etc. *v.*; experimental etc. 463; tentative, empirical, problematic *or* problematical, probationary.

adv. **experimentally** etc. *adj.*; on trial, at a venture; by rule of thumb.
if one may be so bold.

676. Undertaking

n. **undertaking**; compact etc. 769; adventure, venture; engagement etc. (*promise*) 768; enterprise, emprise *or* emprize [*archaic*]; pilgrimage; matter in hand etc. (*business*) 625; move; first move etc. (*beginning*) 66.

v. **undertake**; engage —, embark- in; launch —, plunge- into; volunteer; apprentice oneself to; engage etc. (*promise*) 768; contract etc. 769; take upon -oneself, — one's shoulders; devote oneself to etc. (*determination*) 604.
take up, take on, take in hand; tackle [*colloq.*]; set —, go- about; set —, fall- -to, — to work; launch forth; break the ice; set up shop; put in -hand, — execution; set forward; break the neck of a -day's work, — business; be in for [*colloq.*]; put one's hand to; betake oneself to, turn one's hand to, go to do; be in the midst of; begin etc. 66; broach, institute etc. (*originate*) 153; put —, lay- one's -hand to the plow, — shoulder to the wheel.

have in hand etc. (*business*) 625; have many irons in the fire etc. (*activity*) 682.

adj. **undertaking** etc. *v.*; on the anvil etc. 625; available, receptive; full of pep [*colloq.*], peppy [*colloq.*], energetic; adventurous, venturesome.

int. here goes! shoot! [*colloq.*].

677. Use

n. **use**, employ; exercise, exercitation; application, appliance; adhibition, disposal; consumption; agency etc. (*physical*) 170; usufruct; usefulness etc. 644; benefit; recourse, resort, avail; pragmatism, pragmaticism.
[conversion to use] utilization, utility, service, wear.
[way of using] usage, employment, *modus operandi* [*L.*].
user, consumer, purchasing public, buying public; market, public demand, popular demand, demand.

v. **use**, make use of, employ, put to use; apply; put in -action, — operation, — practice; set in motion, set to work.
ply, work, wield, handle, manipulate; play, play off; exert, exercise, practice, avail oneself of, profit by; resort to, lay one's hand to, fall back upon, have recourse to, recur to, take to, take up, betake oneself to; take up with, take advantage of; lay one's hands on, try.
render useful etc. 644; mold *or* mould; turn to -account, — use; convert to use, utilize; administer; work up; call —, bring- into play; put into requisition; call —, draw- forth; press —, enlist- into the service; task, tax, put to task; bring to bear upon, devote, dedicate, consecrate, apply, adhibit, dispose of; make a handle of, make a cat's-paw of.
fall back upon, make a shift with; make the most of, make the best of.
consume, use up, devour, swallow up; absorb, expend; wear, outwear.

adj. **in use**; used etc. *v.*; well-worn, well-trodden.
useful etc. 644; subservient etc. (*instrumental*) 631; utilitarian, pragmatic *or* pragmatical.

678. Disuse

n. **disuse**; forbearance, abstinence; relinquishment etc. 782; desuetude etc. (*want of habit*) 614; disusage.

v. **not use**; do without, dispense with, let alone, not touch, forbear, abstain, spare, waive, neglect; keep back, reserve.
disuse; lay up, lay by, lay on the shelf, lay up in a napkin; shelve; set —, put —, lay- aside;

679. Misuse

leave off, have done with; supersede; discard etc. (*eject*) 297; dismiss, give warning.

throw aside etc. (*relinquish*) 782; make away with etc. (*destroy*) 162; cast —, heave —, throw- overboard; cast to the -dogs, — winds; dismantle etc. (*render useless*) 645.

lie —, remain- unemployed etc. *adj.*

adj. **not used** etc. *v.;* unemployed, unapplied, undisposed of, unspent, unexercised, untouched, untrodden, unessayed, ungathered, unculled; uncalled for, not required.

disused etc. *v.;* done with, run down, worn out, not worth saving.

int. no use!

679. Misuse

n. **misuse**, misusage, misemployment, misapplication, misappropriation.

abuse, profanation, prostitution, desecration; waste etc. 638.

v. **misuse**, misemploy, misapply, misappropriate.

desecrate, abuse, profane, prostitute.

overtask, overtax, overwork, overdrive; squander etc. 818; waste etc. 638.

cut blocks with a razor, employ a steam engine to crack a nut; catch at a straw.

adj. **misused** etc. *v.*

Section 3. Action

680. Action

n. **action**, performance; doing etc. *v.;* perpetration; exercise, exercitation; movement, operation, evolution, work, employment; labor etc. (*exertion*) 686; *praxis* [*L.*], execution; procedure etc. (*conduct*) 692; handicraft; business etc. 625; agency etc. (*power at work*) 170.

deed, act, overt act, stitch, touch, gest *or* geste; transaction, job, doings, dealings, proceeding, measure, step, maneuver *or* manoeuvre, manoeuver *or* manoeuvre, bout, passage, move, stroke, blow; *coup*, — *de main*, — *d'état* [*F.*]; *tour de force* [*F.*] etc. (*display*) 882; feat, exploit; achievement etc. (*completion*) 729; handiwork, craftsmanship, workmanship; manufacture; stroke of policy etc. (*plan*) 626.

actor etc. (*doer*) 690.

v. **do**, perform, execute; achieve etc. (*complete*) 729; transact, enact; commit, perpetrate, inflict; exercise, prosecute, carry on, work, practice, play.

employ oneself, ply one's task; officiate, have in hand etc. (*business*) 625; labor etc. 686; be at work; pursue a course; shape one's course etc. (*conduct*) 692.

act, operate; take action, take steps; strike a blow, mix it up with [*slang*], lift a finger, stretch forth one's hand; take in hand etc. (*undertake*) 676; put oneself in motion; put in practice; carry into execution etc. (*complete*) 729; act upon.

be an actor etc. 690; take —, act —, play —, perform- a part in; participate in; have a -hand in, — finger in the pie; have to do with; be a party to, be a participator in; bear —, lend- a hand; pull an oar, run in a race; mix oneself up with etc. (*meddle*) 682.

be in action; come into operation etc. (*power at work*) 170.

adj. **in action**; doing etc. *v.;* acting; in harness; up to one's ears in work; in the midst of things; on duty; at work; operative; in operation etc. 170.

adv. in the -act, — midst of, — thick of; red-handed, *in flagrante delicto* [*L.*]; while one's hand is in; while one is at it.

681. Inaction

n. **inaction**, passiveness, abstinence from action; watchful waiting; noninterference; Fabian —, *laisser-aller* [*F.*] —, *laisser-faire* [*F.*] —, conservative- policy; neglect etc. 460.

inactivity etc. 683; stagnation, vegetation, loafing, loaf; rest etc. (*repose*) 687; quiescence etc. 265; want of occupation, unemployment, inoccupation; idle hours, idle hands, time hanging on one's hands, *dolce far niente* [*It.*]; shore duty; interregnum; sinecure; soft snap, soft thing, soft touch, cinch [*all four slang*].

v. **not do**, not act, not attempt; be inactive etc. 683; abstain from doing, do nothing, hold, spare; not stir —, not move —, not lift- a -finger, — hand, — foot, — peg; fold one's -arms, — hands; leave —, let- alone; let be, let pass, let things take their course, let it have its way, let well alone, let well enough alone; *quieta non movere* [*L.*]; *stare super antiquas vias* [*L.*]; rest and be thankful, live and let live; lie —, rest- upon one's oars; *laisser aller* [*F.*], *laisser faire* [*F.*]; stand aloof; refrain etc. (*avoid*) 623; keep oneself from doing; remit —, relax- one's efforts; desist etc. (*relinquish*) 624; stop etc. (*cease*) 142; pause etc. (*be quiet*) 265.

wait, lie in wait, bide one's time, take time, tide it over.

cool —, **kick**- one's heels; while away the -time, — tedious hours; pass —, fill up —, beguile- the time; talk against time; waste time etc. (*inactive*) 683.

682. Activity

lie by, lie on the shelf, lie idle, lie to, lie fallow; keep quiet, slug [*obs.*]; have nothing to do, whistle for want of thought; twiddle one's thumbs.

undo, do away with; take down, take to pieces; destroy etc. 162.

adj. **not doing** etc. *v.;* not done etc. *v.;* undone; passive; unoccupied, unemployed; out of -employ, — work, — a job; uncultivated, fallow; *désoeuvré* [*F.*].

adv. **at a stand**, *re infecta* [*L.*], *les bras croisés* [*F.*], with folded arms; with the hands -in the pockets, — behind one's back; *pour passer le temps* [*F.*].

int. **stop**! etc. 142; hands off! so let it be! enough! no more! *bas*! [*Hind.*], *basta*! [*It.*].

682. Activity

n. **activity**; briskness, liveliness etc. *adj.;* animation, life, vivacity, spirit, verve, pep [*slang*], dash, go [*colloq.*], energy; snap, vim.

smartness, nimbleness, agility; quickness etc. *adj.;* velocity etc. 274; alacrity, promptitude; dispatch *or* despatch, expedition; haste etc. 684; punctuality etc. (*early*) 132.

eagerness, zeal, ardor, enthusiasm, *perfervidum ingenium* [*L.*], *empressement* [*F.*], earnestness, intentness; *abandon* [*F.*]; vigor etc. (*physical energy*) 171; devotion etc. (*resolution*) 604; exertion etc. 686.

industry, assiduity; assiduousness etc. *adj.;* sedulity [*rare*], sedulousness; laboriousness; drudgery etc. (*labor*) 686; painstaking, diligence; perseverance etc. 604*a*; indefatigation [*obs.*]; businesslike habits, habits of business.

vigilance etc. 459; wakefulness, sleeplessness, restlessness; insomnia; pervigilium, *insomnium* [*L.*]; racketing.

bustle, hustle [*colloq.*], movement, stir, fuss, ado, bother, fidget, fidgetiness; flurry etc. (*haste*) 684.

officiousness; dabbling, meddling; interference, interposition, intermeddling; butting in [*slang*], horning in [*slang*], intrusiveness, minding others' business, not minding one's own business; tampering with, intrigue.

press of business, no sinecure, plenty to do, a great deal doing [*colloq.*], a lot going on [*colloq.*], many irons in the fire, great doings, busy hum of men, the madding crowd, the thick of things, battle of life, thick of the action.

man of action, busy bee; new broom; sharp fellow, blade; devotee, enthusiast, fanatic, zealot, hummer [*slang*], hustler [*colloq.*], humdinger [*slang*], rustler [*slang*]; live wire, human dynamo [*both colloq.*], live man.

meddler, intermeddler, intriguer, intrigant *or* intriguant, telltale, busybody, pickthank [*archaic*].

v. **be active** etc. *adj.;* busy oneself in; stir, stir about, stir one's stumps [*colloq.*]; bestir —, rouse- oneself; speed, hasten, peg away, lay about one, bustle, fuss; raise —, kick up- a dust; push; make a -fuss, — stir; go ahead, push forward; fight —, elbow- one's way; make progress etc. 282; toil etc. (*labor*) 686; moil, drudge, plod, persist etc. (*persevere*) 604*a;* keep up the ball; keep the pot boiling.

look sharp; have all one's eyes about one etc. (*vigilance*) 459; rise, arouse oneself, hustle [*colloq.*], push [*colloq.*], get up early, be about, keep moving, steal a march, catch a weasel asleep, kill two birds with one stone; seize the opportunity etc. 134; lose no time, not lose a moment, make the most of one's time, not suffer the grass to grow under one's feet, improve the shining hour, make short work of; dash off; make haste etc. 684; do one's best, take pains etc. (*exert oneself*) 686; do —, work- wonders; have a lot of -kick [*colloq.*], — pep [*slang*].

have many irons in the fire, have one's hands full, have much on one's hands; have other -things to do, — fish to fry; be busy; not have a moment -to spare, — that one can call one's own.

have one's fling, run the round of; go all lengths, stick at nothing, run riot.

outdo; overdo, overact, overlay, weigh down, overshoot the mark; make a toil of a pleasure.

have a hand in etc. (*act in*) 680; take an active part, put in one's oar, have a finger in the pie, mix oneself up with, trouble one's head about, intrigue; agitate.

meddle, tamper with, intermeddle, interfere, interpose; obtrude; poke —, thrust- one's nose in; butt in, horn in [*both slang*].

adj. **active**, brisk, — as a lark, — as a bee; lively, animated, vivacious; alive, — and kicking [*colloq.*]; frisky, spirited, stirring.

nimble, — as a squirrel; agile; light-footed, nimble-footed; featly tripping.

quick, prompt, yare [*archaic*], instant, ready, alert, spry, sharp, smart; fast etc. (*swift*) 274; capable, smart as a steel trap, no sooner said than done etc. (*early*) 132; quick as a lamplighter, expeditious; awake, broad awake; go-ahead, live, hustling [*colloq.*]; wide-awake etc. (*intelligent*) 498.

683. Inactivity

forward, eager, ardent, strenuous, zealous, enterprising, in earnest; resolute etc. 604.
industrious, assiduous, diligent, sedulous, notable [*obsoles. in this sense*], painstaking; intent etc. (*attention*) 457; indefatigable etc. (*persevering*) 604a; unwearied, never weary, sleepless, unsleeping, never tired; plodding, hard-working etc. 686; businesslike.
bustling; restless, — as a hyena; fussy, fidgety, pottering; busy as a hen with one chicken.
working, at work, on duty, in harness; up in arms; on one's legs, at call; up and -doing, — stirring; laboring, workday, workaday.
busy, occupied; hard at work, hard at it; up to one's ears in, full of business; busy as a -bee, — housewife.
meddling etc. *v.*; meddlesome, pushing, officious, overofficious, *intrigant* [*F.*].
astir, stirring; agoing, afoot; on foot; in full swing; eventful; on the alert etc. (*vigilant*) 459.
adv. **actively** etc. *adj.*; featly [*archaic*]; with life and spirit, with might and main etc. 686, with haste etc. 684, with wings; full tilt, *in mediis rebus* [*L.*].
int. be —, look- -alive, — sharp! move on! push on! keep moving! go ahead! stir your stumps! [*colloq.*]; *age quod agis!* [*L.*], *jaldi!* [*Hind.*], *jaldi karo!* [*Hind.*], step lively! get a move on!

683. Inactivity

n. **inactivity**; inaction etc. 681; inertness etc. 172; obstinacy etc. 606.
lull etc. (*cessation*) 142; quiescence etc. 265; rust, rustiness.
idleness, remissness etc. *adj.*; sloth, indolence, indiligence [*rare*]; dawdling etc. *v.*; ergophobia, otiosity, hoboism.
dull work; pottering; relaxation etc. (*loosening*) 47; Castle of Indolence.
languor; dullness etc. *adj.*; segnity [*obs.*], segnitude [*obs.*], lentor; sluggishness etc. (*slowness*) 275; procrastination etc. (*delay*) 133; torpor, torpidity, torpescence; stupor etc. (*insensibility*) 823; somnolence; drowsiness etc. *adj.*; nodding etc. *v.*; oscitation, oscitancy; pandiculation, hypnotism, lethargy; statuvolence *or* statuvolism; sand in the eyes, heaviness, heavy eyelids.
sleep, slumber; sound —, heavy —, balmy-sleep; Morpheus; Somnus; coma, trance, catalepsy, hypnosis, ecstasis, dream; hibernation; nap, doze, snooze [*colloq.*], siesta, wink of sleep, forty winks [*colloq.*]; snore; hypnology.
[cause of inactivity] lullaby, *berceuse* [*F.*], *Schlummerlied* [*Ger.*]; anaesthesia *or* anesthesia, anaesthetic *or* anesthetic, opiate, sedative etc. 174.
idler, drone, dawdle [*rare*], dawdler; dead head, stiff, dead one [*all slang*], mopus [*obs.*], do-little, *fainéant* [*F.*], dummy, sleeping partner; afternoon farmer; truant etc. (*runaway*) 623; bummer, bum [*slang*], Weary Willie [*colloq.*], tramp, sundowner [*slang, Austral.*], hobo, fakir *or* fakeer [*Moham.*], sunyasi [*Hind.*]; beggar, cadger [*slang*], lounge lizard [*slang*], lounger, lazzarone, loafer; lubber, lubbard [*rare*]; slow coach etc. (*slow*) 275; opium —, lotus- eater; slug; laggard, sluggard; slumberer, the Dustman, the Sandman; the Fat Boy in Pickwick; dormouse, marmot; waiter on Providence, *fruges consumere natus* [*L.*]; Mr. Micawber.

v. **be inactive** etc. *adj.*; do nothing etc. 681; move slowly etc. 275; let the grass grow under one's feet; take one's time, dawdle, drawl, lag, hang back, slouch; loll, lollop [*colloq., Brit.*], lounge, poke, loaf, loiter; go to sleep over; sleep at one's post, *ne battre que d'une aile* [*F.*].
take it easy, take things as they come; lead an easy life, vegetate, swim with the stream, eat the bread of idleness, goof off [*slang*]; loll in the lap of -luxury, — indolence; waste —, consume —, kill —, lose- time; burn daylight, waste the precious hours.
dally, dilly-dally; idle —, trifle —, fritter —, fool- away time; spend —, take- time in; peddle, piddle; potter, putter, dabble, faddle [*dial. Eng.*], fribble, fiddle-faddle.
sleep, slumber, be asleep; hibernate; oversleep; sleep like a -top, — log, — dormouse; sleep -soundly, — heavily; doze, drowse, snooze [*colloq.*], nap; take a nap etc. *n.*; dream; snore; settle —, go —, go off- to sleep; drop off [*colloq.*]; fall asleep, drop asleep; get some shuteye [*slang*], close —, seal up- -the -eyes, — eyelids; weigh down the eyelids; get sleepy, nod, yawn; go to bed, turn in, hit the hay [*slang*], hit the sack [*slang*], rest in the arms of Morpheus.
languish, expend itself, flag, hang fire; relax.
render idle etc. *adj.*; sluggardize; mitigate etc. 174.

adj. **inactive**; motionless etc. 265; unoccupied etc. (*doing nothing*) 681.
indolent, lazy, slothful, idle, lusk [*obs.*], remiss, slack, inert, torpid, torpescent, sluggish, otiose, languid, supine, heavy, dull, leaden, lumpish; drony, dronish; lazy as Ludlam's dog.
dilatory, laggard; lagging etc. *v.*; slow etc. 275; rusty, flagging; fiddle-faddle; pottering etc. *v.*; shilly-shally etc. (*irresolute*) 605.

686. Exertion

exanimate [*now rare*], soulless; listless; lackadaisical, maudlin.

sleeping etc. *v.;* asleep; fast —, dead —, sound-asleep; in a sound sleep; sound as a top, dormant, comatose; in the -arms, — lap- of Morpheus.

sleepy, sleepful [*rare*], full of sleep, oscitant, dozy, drowsy, somnolent, torpescent; lethargic *or* lethargical, somnifacient; statuvolent, statuvolic; heavy, heavy with sleep; nappy, somnific, somniferous; soporose *or* soporous, soporific, soporiferous; hypnotic; balmy, dreamy; unawakened, unwakened.

sedative etc. 174.

adv. **inactively** etc. *adj.;* at leisure etc. 685; with half-shut eyes, half asleep; in dreams, in dreamland.

684. Haste

n. **haste**, urgency, dispatch *or* despatch, acceleration, spurt *or* spirt, forced march, rush, scurry *or* skurry, scuttle, dash; velocity etc. 274; precipitancy, precipitation, precipitousness etc. *adj.;* impetuosity; *brusquerie* [*F.*]; hurry, drive, scramble, bustle, fuss, fidget, flurry, flutter, splutter.

v. **haste**, hasten; make haste, make a dash etc. *n.;* hurry —, dash —, whip —, push —, press- -on, — forward; hurry, scurry *or* skurry, scuttle along, bundle on, dart to and fro, bustle, flutter, scramble; plunge, — headlong; dash off; rush etc. (*violence*) 173; express, railroad [*colloq.*].

bestir oneself etc. (*be active*) 682; lose -no time, — not a moment, — not an instant; make short work of; make the best of one's -time, — way.

be precipitate etc. *adj.;* jump at, be in haste, be in a hurry etc. *n.;* have -no time —, have not a moment- -to lose, — to spare; work against time, work under pressure.

quicken etc. 274; accelerate, expedite, put on, precipitate, urge, whip, spur, flog, goad.

adj. **hasty**, hurried, brusque; scrambling, cursory, precipitate, headlong, furious, boisterous, impetuous, hot-headed; feverish, fussy; pushing.

in haste, in a hurry etc. *n.;* in hot haste, in all haste; breathless, pressed for time, hard pressed, urgent.

adv. **with haste**, with all haste, with breathless speed; in haste etc. *adj.;* apace etc. (*swiftly*) 274; amain; all at once etc. (*instantaneously*) 113; at short notice etc., immediately etc. (*early*) 132; posthaste; by cable, by telegraph, by wireless [*colloq.*], by airmail, by air, by return mail, by steam [*colloq.*], by forced marches.

hastily, precipitately etc. *adj.;* helter-skelter, hurry-skurry, holus-bolus; slap-dash, slap-bang; full-tilt, full-drive; heels over head, head and shoulders, headlong, *à corps perdu* [*F.*].

by fits and starts, by spurts; hop skip and jump.

int. **rush**! immediate! urgent! look alive! *jaldi karo!* [*Hind.*]; get with it [*colloq.*], get a move on! [*colloq.*], get a wiggle on! [*colloq.*]; quickmarch! [*mil.*], double! [*mil.*]; gallop! charge! [*mil.*].

685. Leisure

n. **leisure**; convenience; spare -time, — hours, –moments; vacant hour; time, — to spare, — to burn [*slang*], — on one's hands; holiday etc. (*rest*) 687; *otium cum dignitate;* ease.

v. **have leisure** etc. *n.;* take one's -time, — leisure, — ease; repose etc. 687; move slowly etc. 275; while away the time etc. (*inaction*) 681; be master of one's time, be an idle man; *desipere in loco* [*L.*].

686. Exertion

n. **exertion**, effort, strain, tug, pull, stress, throw, stretch, struggle, spell, spurt *or* spirt; stroke —, stitch- of work.

"a long pull, a strong pull, and a pull all together"; dead lift; heft [*dial.*]; wear and tear; ado; toil and trouble; uphill —, hard —, warm- work; harvest time.

exercise, exercitation, practice, play, gymnastics, field sports; breather [*colloq.*], racing, running, jumping, riding etc.

labor, work, toil, travail [*rare*], manual labor, sweat of one's brow, swink [*obs.*], operoseness, drudgery, slavery, fag [*colloq., Eng.*], faggery, fagging, hammering; *limae labor* [*L.*]; operosity [*obs.*], operoseness.

trouble, pains, duty; resolution etc. 604; energy etc. (*physical*) 171.

worker, plodder, laborer, drudge, fagger, fag [*Eng. schools*], slave; man of action etc. 682; agent etc. 690; Samson, Hercules.

v. **exert oneself**; exert —, tax- one's energies; use exertion.

labor, work, toil, moil, sweat, fag, swink [*archaic*], toil and moil, drudge, slave, drag a lengthened chain, wade through, strive, strain; make —, stretch- a long arm; pull, tug, ply; ply —, tug at- the oar; do the work; take the laboring oar.

bestir oneself (*be active*) 682; take trouble, trouble oneself.

work hard; rough it; put forth -one's strength, — a strong arm; fall to work, bend the bow; buckle to, set one's shoulder to the wheel etc.

687. Repose

(*resolution*) 604; work like a -horse, — cart horse, — dog, — galley slave, — coal heaver, — Briton; labor —, work- day and night; redouble one's efforts; do double duty; work double -hours, — tides; sit up, burn the candle at both ends, burn the midnight oil; stick to etc. (*persevere*) 604a; work —, fight- one's way; lay about one, hammer at.

do one's best, do one's level best, do one's utmost; take pains; do the best one can, do all one can, do all in one's power, do as much as in one lies, do what lies in one's power; use one's -best, — utmost- endeavor; try one's- -best, — utmost; play one's best card; put one's -best, — right- leg foremost; put one's best foot foremost; have one's whole soul in his work, put all one's strength into, strain every nerve; spare no -efforts, —pains; go all lengths; go through fire and water etc. (*resolution*) 604; move heaven and earth, leave no stone unturned.

adj. laboring etc. *v.*
laborious, hefty [*colloq.*], operose, elaborate; strained; toilsome, troublesome, wearisome, burdensome; uphill; herculean, gymnastic, palaestric *or* palestric, athletic.
hardworking, painstaking, strenuous, energetic, never idle.
hard at work, on the stretch, on the move, on the jump, on the dead jump, on the run.

adv. **laboriously** etc. *adj.;* lustily; *pugnis et calcibus* [*L.*]; with might and main, with all one's might, with a strong hand, with sledge hammer, with much ado; to the best of one's abilities, *totis viribus* [*L.*], *vi et armis* [*L.*], *manibus pedibusque* [*L.*], tooth and nail, *unguibus et rostro* [*L.*], hammer and tongs, heart and soul; through thick and thin etc. (*perseverance*) 604a.
by the sweat of one's brow, *suo Marte* [*L.*].

687. Repose

n. **repose**, rest, silken repose; sleep etc. 683.
relaxation, breathing time; halt, stay, pause etc. (*cessation*) 142; respite.
day of rest, *dies non* [*L.*], Sabbath, Lord's day, Sunday, First Day, holiday, red-letter day; gala day etc. (*amusement*) 840; vacation, recess.

v. **repose**; rest, rest and be thankful; take rest, take one's ease.
lie down; recline, recline on a bed of down, recline on an easychair; go to -rest, — bed, — sleep etc. 683.
relax, unbend, slacken; take breath etc. (*refresh*) 689; rest upon one's oars; pause etc. (*cease*) 142; stay one's hand.

take a holiday, shut up shop; lie fallow etc. (*inaction*) 681.

adj. **reposing** etc. *v.;* unstrained.
holiday, festal, ferial [*rare*]; sabbatic *or* sabbatical.

adv. at rest.

688. Fatigue

n. **fatigue**; weariness etc. 841; yawning, drowsiness etc. 683; lassitude, tiredness, fatigation [*obs.*], sweat.
shortness of breath; anhelation [*rare*], dyspnea, panting, labored breathing.
faintness, fainting, swoon, goneness, exhaustion, collapse, prostration, deliquium, syncope, lipothymy.

v. **be fatigued** etc. *adj.;* yawn etc. (*get sleepy*) 683; droop, sink, flag; lose breath, lose wind; gasp, pant, puff, blow, drop, swoon, faint, succumb.
fatigue, tire, bore, weary, irk [*chiefly impersonal, as*, it irks me], flag, jade, harass, exhaust, knock up, wear out, bleed white, prostrate.
tax, task, strain; overtask, overwork, overburden, overtax, overstrain, fag, fag out.

adj. **fatigued** etc. *v.;* weary etc. 841; drowsy etc. 683; drooping etc. *v.;* haggard; toilworn, wayworn; footsore, surbated [*obs.*], weather-beaten; faint; done, done up, knocked up [*all Brit. colloq.*]; bushed [*slang*], done in; exhausted, used up [*colloq.*], prostrate, spent; overtired, overspent, overfatigued; unrefreshed, unrestored.
ready to drop, all in [*slang*], more dead than alive, dog-weary, dog-tired, walked off one's legs, tired to death, on one's last legs, played out, *hors de combat* [*F.*].
worn, worn out; battered, shattered, pulled down, seedy [*colloq.*], enfeebled, altered.
breathless, windless; short of —, out of -breath, — wind; blown, puffing and blowing; short-breathed; anhelose; broken-winded, short-winded; dyspneal, dyspneic.

689. Refreshment

n. **recuperation**; recovery of strength etc. 159; refreshing, bracing etc. *v.;* restoration, revival etc. 660; repair, refection, refocillation [*obs.*], refreshment, regale, regalement, bait; relief etc. 834.

v. **refresh**; brace etc. (*strengthen*) 159; reinvigorate; air, freshen up, recruit; repair etc. (*restore*) 660; fan, refocillate [*obs.*]; refresh the inner man; get better, raise one's head; recover —, regain —, renew- one's strength etc. 159; perk up.

breathe, respire; drink in the ozone; draw —, take —, gather —, take a long —, regain —, recover- breath.
recuperate; come to oneself etc. (*revive*) 660; feel like a giant refreshed.

adj. **refreshing** etc. *v.;* recuperative etc. 660.
refreshed etc. *v.;* untired, unwearied.

690. Agent

n. **agent**, doer, actor, performer, perpetrator, operator; executor, executrix; practitioner, worker, old stager; mediary, medium, reagent.
minister etc. (*instrument*) 631; representative etc. (*commissioner*) 758, (*deputy*) 759; factor, steward.
servant etc. 746; factotum, general, maid-of-all-work, servant-of-all-work, do-all [*colloq.*].
[comparisons] bee, ant, working bee, termite, white ant; laboring oar; shaft horse.
workman, artisan; craftsman, handicraftsman; mechanic, operative; workingman, laboring man; hewers of wood and drawers of water, laborer, navvy [*Eng.*]; hand, man, day laborer, journeyman, hack; mere tool etc. 633; beast of burden, drudge, fag; lumper, stevedore, roustabout.
maker, artificer, *artifex* [*L.*], artist, wright, manufacturer, architect, contractor, builder, mason, bricklayer, smith, forger, Vulcan; carpenter; platelayer, blacksmith, locksmith, sailmaker, tailor, cordwainer, wheelwright.
machinist, mechanician, engineer, electrician, plumber, gasfitter.
workwoman, charwoman, seamstress *or* sempstress, needlewoman, laundress, washerwoman, "Madonna of the tubs" [Phelps].
coworker, associate, fellow worker, cooperator, colleague, *confrère* [*F.*]; party to, participator in, *particeps criminis* [*L.*], *dramatis personae* [*L.*]; *personnel* [*F.*].

691. Workshop

n. **workshop**, workhouse; laboratory, manufactory, armory, arsenal, mill, factory, *usine* [*F.*], mint, loom; cabinet, bureau, studio, *atelier* [*F.*]; hive, hive of industry; plant; hothouse, hotbed; kitchen; alveary, beehive; bindery, forcing pit, nailery, dock, dockyard, slip, yard, wharf; foundry *or* foundery, forge, furnace; vineyard, orchard, nursery, truck garden, truck farm, farm.
melting pot, crucible, caldron *or* cauldron, mortar, alembic; matrix.

692. Conduct

n. **conduct**, behavior; deportment, comportment; carriage, *maintien* [*F.*], demeanor, guise, bearing, manner, observance.
course —, line- of -conduct, — action, — proceeding; role; process, ways, practice, procedure, *modus operandi* [*L.*]; method etc., path etc. 627.
dealing, transaction etc. (*action*) 680; business etc. 625.
policy, polity; tactics, game, generalship, statesmanship, seamanship; strategy, strategics; plan etc. 626.
management; government etc. (*direction*) 693; stewardship, husbandry, housekeeping, housewifery; *ménage or* menage; *régime or* regime, regimen, economy, economics; political economy.
career, life, course, walk, province, race, record; execution, manipulation, treatment; campaign.

v. **transact**, execute; dispatch *or* despatch, proceed with, discharge; carry -on, — through, — out, — into effect; work out; go through, get through; enact; put into practice; officiate etc. 625.
bear —, behave —, comport —, demean —, carry —, conduct —, acquit- oneself.
run a race, lead a life, play a game; take —, adopt- a course; steer —, shape- one's course; play one's part, play one's cards; shift for oneself; paddle one's own canoe; bail one's own boat.
conduct; manage etc. (*direct*) 693.
deal with, have to do with; treat, handle a case; take -steps, — measures.

adj. **conducting** etc. *v.;* directive, strategic *or* strategical, methodical, business-like, practical, executive; economic.

693. Direction

n. **direction**; management, managery [*obs.*]; government, gubernation [*obs.*], conduct, legislation, regulation, guidance; bossism; legislature; steerage, pilotage; reins, — of government; helm, rudder, needle, compass; guiding star, lodestar *or* loadstar, polestar; cynosure.
ministry, ministration; administration; stewardship, proctorship; chair; agency.
supervision, superintendence; surveillance, oversight; eye of the master; control, charge; auspices; board of control etc. (*council*) 696; command etc. (*authority*) 737.
statesmanship; statecraft, kingcraft, queencraft; premiership, senatorship; director etc. 694; seat, portfolio.

694. Director

v. **direct**, manage, govern, conduct; order, prescribe, cut out work for; head, lead; lead the way, show the way; take the lead, lead on; regulate, guide, steer, pilot; take the helm, be at the helm; have —, handle —, hold —, take- the reins; drive, tool [*cant*], tackle.

superintend, supervise; overlook, oversee, control, keep in order, look after, see to, legislate for; administer, ministrate [*obs.*]; matronize; patronize; have the -care, — charge- of; have —, take- the direction; pull the -strings, — wires; rule etc. (*command*) 737; be the guiding force; have —, hold- -office, — the portfolio; preside, — at the board; take —, occupy —, be in- the chair; pull the stroke oar.

adj. **directing** etc. *v.;* executive, gubernatorial, supervisory; hegemonic *or* hegemonical, predominant; statesmanlike.

adv. **in charge of**, under the guidance of, under the auspices of; in control of, at the helm, at the head of.

694. Director

n. **director**, manager, governor, rector [*rare*], controller, comptroller; superintendent, supervisor; intendant, overseer, overlooker; supercargo, husband [*archaic*], inspector, foreman, ganger [*Eng.*], visitor, ranger, surveyor, aedile *or* edile [*Rom. hist.*], moderator, monitor, taskmaster; master etc. 745; leader, ringleader, agitator, demagogue, corypheus, conductor, fugleman, precentor, bellwether; *caporal* [*F.*], choregus, collector, file leader, flugelman, linkboy.

guiding star etc. (*guidance*) 693; adviser etc. 695; guide etc. (*information*) 527; pilot; helmsman; steersman, steersmate [*obs.*]; wire-puller.

driver, whip, jehu [*humorous*], charioteer; coachman, carman, cabman; postilion, *vetturino* [*It.*], muleteer, *arriero* [*Sp.*], teamster; whipper-in; chauffeur, motorman, engine-driver.

head, headman, chief, principal, president, speaker; chair, chairman; captain etc. (*master*) 745; superior; mayor etc. (*civil authority*) 745; vice-president, prime minister, premier, vizier *or* vizir, grand vizier, eparch.

officer, functionary, minister, official, red-tape, red-tapist, bureaucrat; Jack in office; office bearer, office holder; person in authority etc. 745.

statesman, strategist, legislator, lawgiver, politician, statist [*rare*], statemonger; Minos, Draco; arbiter etc. (*judge*) 967; boss, political dictator, dictator, power behind the throne, kingmaker; secretary, — of state; Reis Effendi; vicar etc. (*deputy*) 759; board etc. (*council*) 696.

steward, factor; agent etc. 758; bailiff, middleman; clerk of works; landreeve; factotum, major-domo, seneschal, housekeeper, shepherd; croupier; proctor, procurator, curator, librarian.

adv. ex officio.

695. Advice

n. **advice**, counsel, adhortation [*obs.*]; word to the wise; suggestion, submonition [*obs.*], recommendation, advocacy; advisement [*archaic*]; consultation.

exhortation etc. (*persuasion*) 615; expostulation etc. (*dissuasion*) 616; admonition etc. (*warning*) 668; guidance etc. (*direction*) 693.

instruction, charge, injunction; Governor's —, President's- message; King's —, Queen's- speech; message, speech from the throne.

adviser, prompter; counsel, counselor; monitor, mentor, Nestor, sage, wise man, wise woman; *magnus Apollo* [*L.*], senator; teacher etc. 540; yogi *or* yogin; physician, leech [*archaic*]; archiater; arbiter etc. (*judge*) 967.

guide, manual, chart etc. (*information*) 527.

consultation, conference, *pourparler* [*F.*], parley, powwow; reference, referment.

v. **advise**, counsel; give -advice, — counsel, — a piece of advice; suggest, prompt, submonish [*obs.*], recommend, prescribe, advocate; exhort etc. (*persuade*) 615.

enjoin, enforce, charge, instruct, call; call upon etc. (*request*) 765; dictate.

expostulate etc. (*dissuade*) 616; admonish etc. (*warn*) 668.

advise with; lay heads —,consult- together; compare notes; hold a council, deliberate, be closeted with.

confer, consult, refer to, call in; follow, follow implicitly; take —, follow- advice; be advised by, have at one's elbow, take one's cue from.

adj. **recommendatory**; hortative etc. (*persuasive*) 615; dehortatory etc. (*dissuasive*) 616; admonitory etc. (*warning*) 668; consultative; dictatory, dictatorial; didactic.

int. go to!

696. Council

n. **council**, committee, subcommittee, comitia [*Rom. hist.*], privy council, court, chamber, cabinet, board, bench, staff.

junta, divan, musnud, sanhedrin *or* sanhedrim [*Jewish antiq.*], amphictyonic council [*Gr.*

hist.]; syndicate; court of appeal etc. (*tribunal*) 966; board of -control, — works; county council, local board, parish council, common council, town meeting; board of overseers; *zemstvo* [*Russ.*].

[ecclesiastical] convocation, synod, congregation, church, chapter, directory, vestry, consistory, conventicle, conclave, convention, classis.

legislature, parliament, congress, national council, states-general, diet.

Duma [*Russia*], Storthing *or* Storting [*Norway*], Rigsdag [*Denmark*], Riksdag [*Sweden*], Knesset [*Israel*], Cortes [*Spain*], Reichsrath *or* Reichsrat [*Austria*], Volksraad [*Dutch*]; Dail Eireann [*Ireland*]; witan, witenagemot *or* witenagemote [*Anglo-Saxon hist.*].

upper house, upper chamber, first chamber, senate, *senatus* [*Rom. hist.*], legislative council, House of Lords, House of Peers; Bundesrath *or* Bundesrat [*Ger.*], federal council, Lagting [*Nor.*], Landsthing [*Den.*].

lower house, lower chamber, second chamber, house of representatives, House of Commons, the house, legislative assembly, chamber of deputies; Odelsting [*Nor.*], Folkething [*Den.*], Reichstag [*Ger.*].

assembly, plenum, caucus, clique; meeting, sitting, séance, *camarilla* [*Sp.*], conference, hearing, session, palaver, *pourparler* [*F.*], durbar [*India*]; quorum; council fire [*N. Am.*], pow-wow.

[representatives] congressman, M. C., senator, representative; member, — of parliament, M. P.; representative of the people; assemblyman, councilor.

adj. curule, congressional, senatorial, parliamentary; synodic *or* synodical.

697. Precept

n. **precept**, direction, instruction, charge; prescript, prescription; recipe, receipt; golden rule; maxim etc. 496.

rule, canon, law, code, *corpus juris* [*L.*], *lex scripta* [*L.*], convention; unwritten law; canon law; act, statute, rubric, stage direction, regulation; model, form, formula, formulary; technicality; nice point, fine point, norm.

order etc. (*command*) 741.

698. Skill

n. **skill**, skillfulness *or* skilfulness, address; dexterity, dexterousness *or* dextrousness, adroitness, expertness etc. *adj.*; proficiency, competence, craft; callidity [*rare*], calliddness, facility, knack, trick, sleight; mastery, mastership; excellence, panurgy [*rare*]; ambidexterity, ambidextrousness; sleight of hand etc. (*deception*) 545.

seamanship, airmanship, marksmanship, horsemanship; rope-dancing; tight-rope —, slack-rope- walking.

accomplishment, acquirement, attainment; art, science; finish, finished execution, technique, technique, practical —, technical- knowledge; technology.

world wisdom, knowledge of the world, *savoir faire* [*F.*]; tact; mother wit etc. (*sagacity*) 498; discretion etc. (*caution*) 864; finesse; craftiness etc. (*cunning*) 702; management etc. (*conduct*) 692; self-help.

cleverness, talent, ability, ingenuity, capacity, parts, talents, faculty, endowment, forte, turn, gift, genius; intelligence etc. 498; sharpness, readiness etc. (*activity*) 682; invention etc. 515; aptness, aptitude; turn for, capacity for, genius for; felicity, capability, *curiosa felicitas* [*L.*], qualification, habilitation.

proficient, expert, adept etc. 700.

masterpiece, masterwork, *coup de maître* [*F.*,] *chef d'oeuvre* [*F.*], *tour de force* [*F.*]; good stroke etc. (*plan*) 626.

v. **be skillful** etc. *adj.*; excel in, be master of; have a turn for etc. *n.*

know what's what, know- a hawk from a handsaw, — what one is about, — on which side one's bread is buttered, — what's o'clock, — what o'clock it is, — what's up, — the time of day, — a thing or two, — the ropes; have cut one's -eyeteeth, — wisdom teeth; see through a millstone; be up to [*all colloq.*]

see one's way, see where the wind lies, see which way the wind blows; have all one's wits about one, have one's hand in; *savoir vivre* [*F.*]; *scire quid valeant humeri quid ferre recusent* [*L*].

look after the main chance; cut one's coat according to one's cloth; live by one's wits; exercise one's discretion, feather the oar, sail near the wind; stoop to conquer etc. (*cunning*) 702; play one's cards well, play one's best card; hit the nail on the head, put the saddle on the right horse.

take advantage of, make the most of; profit by etc. (*use*) 677; make a hit etc. (*succeed*) 731; make a virtue of necessity; make hay while the sun shines etc. (*occasion*) 134.

adj. **skillful** *or* skilful, dexterous *or* dextrous, adroit, expert, apt, handy, quick, deft, ready, slick [*slang*], smart etc. (*active*) 682; proficient, good at, up to, at home in, master of, a good hand at,

699. Unskillfulness

au fait [*F.*], thoroughbred, masterly, crack [*colloq.*], crackerjack [*slang*], accomplished; conversant etc. (*knowing*) 490.

experienced, practiced, skilled; up in, well up in; in practice; competent, efficient, qualified, capable, fitted, fit for, up to the mark, up and coming, trained, initiated, prepared, primed, finished.

clever, cute [*colloq.*], able, ingenious, felicitous, gifted, talented, endowed; inventive etc. 515; shrewd, sharp etc. (*intelligent*) 498; cunning etc. 702; alive to, up to snuff [*slang*], not to be caught with chaff; discreet.

neat-handed, fine-fingered, nimble-fingered, ambidextrous, sure-footed; cut out for [*colloq.*], fitted for.

technical, artistic, scientific, daedalian, shipshapelike, workmanlike, businesslike, statesmanlike.

adv. **skillfully** or skilfully etc. *adj.;* well etc. 618; artistically; with skill, with fine technique, with consummate skill; *secundum artem* [*L.*], *suo Marte* [*L.*]; to the best of one's abilities etc. (*exertion*) 686; like a machine.

699. Unskillfulness

n. **unskillfulness** or unskilfulness etc. *adj.;* want of skill etc. 698; incompetence or incompetency; inability, infelicity, indexterity [*rare*], clumsiness, inaptitude etc. *adj.;* inexperience; disqualification, unproficiency; quackery.

folly, stupidity etc. 499; indiscretion etc. (*rashness*) 863; thoughtlessness etc. (*inattention*) 458, (*neglect*) 460; *sabotage* [*F.*].

mismanagement, misconduct, misfeasance; inexpedience, bad policy, impolicy; maladministration; misrule, misgovernment, misapplication, misdirection.

absence of rule, rule of thumb; bungling etc. *v.;* failure etc. 732; screw loose; too many cooks.

blunder etc. (*mistake*) 495; *étourderie* [*F.*], *gaucherie* [*F.*], act of folly, *balourdise* [*F.*], bungle, botch, botchery; bad job, sad work.

sprat sent out to catch a whale, butterfly broken on a wheel, tempest in a teacup, storm in a teacup, much ado about nothing, wild-goose chase.

bungler etc. 701; fool etc. 501; hen with its head cut off [*colloq.*].

v. **be unskillful** or unskilful, etc. *adj.;* not see an inch beyond one's nose; blunder, bungle, muff [*esp., baseball*], boggle, fumble, botch, mar, spoil, bitch [*obs.*], flounder, stumble, trip; hobble etc. 275; put one's foot in it [*colloq.*]; make a -mess, — hash, — sad work- of [*all colloq.*]; overshoot the mark.

play tricks with, play Puck; mismanage, misconduct, misdirect, misapply, missend.

act foolishly; stultify —, make a fool of —, commit- oneself; play the fool; put oneself out of court; lose one's -head, — senses, — cunning; begin at the wrong end; do things by halves etc. (*not complete*) 730; make two bites of a cherry; play at cross-purposes; strain at a gnat and swallow a camel etc. (*caprice*) 608; put the cart before the horse; lock the stable door when the horse is stolen etc. (*too late*) 135.

not know what one is about, not know one's own interest, not know on which side one's bread is buttered; stand in one's own light, quarrel with one's bread and butter, throw a stone in one's own garden, kill the goose which lays the golden eggs, pay dear for one's whistle, cut one's own throat, burn one's fingers; knock —, run- one's head against a stone wall; bring the house about one's ears; have too many -eggs in one basket (*imprudent*) 863, — irons in the fire.

cut blocks with a razor; hold a farthing candle to the sun etc. (*useless*) 645; fight with —, grasp at- a shadow; catch at straws, lean on a broken reed, reckon without one's host, go on a wild-goose chase; go on a fool's errand, go on a sleeveless errand [*obs.*]; go further and fare worse; fail etc. 732.

mistake etc. 495; take the shadow for the substance etc. (*credulity*) 486; bark up the wrong tree; be in the wrong box, aim at a pigeon and kill a crow; take —, get- -the wrong pig by the tail, — the wrong sow by the ear, — the dirty end of the stick [*all colloq.*]; put the saddle on the wrong horse, put a square thing into a round hole, put new wine into old bottles; lose one's way, miss one's way; fall into a trap, catch a Tartar.

adj. **unskillful** or unskilful etc. 698; unskilled, inexpert; bungling etc. *v.;* awkward, clumsy, unhandy, lubberly, *gauche* [*F.*], maladroit; left-handed, heavy-handed; slovenly, slatternly; gawky.

adrift, at fault.

inapt, unapt; inhabile [*obs.*]; untractable, unteachable; giddy etc. (*inattentive*) 458; inconsiderate etc. (*neglectful*) 460; stupid etc. 499; inactive etc. 683; incompetent; unqualified, disqualified, ill-qualified; unfit; quackish; raw, green, inexperienced, rusty, out of practice.

unaccustomed, unused, untrained etc. 537, uninitiated, unconversant etc. (*ignorant*) 491; unbusinesslike, unpractical, shiftless; unstatesmanlike.

ill-advised, unadvised, misadvised; ill-devised, ill-imagined, ill-judged, ill-contrived, ill-conducted; unguided, misguided; misconducted, foolish, wild; infelicitous; penny wise and pound foolish etc. (*inconsistent*) 608.

700. Proficient

n. **proficient**, expert, adept; dab, dabster [*both colloq. or dial.*], connoisseur etc. (*scholar*) 492; master, — hand; top sawyer, top banana [*cant*], prima donna, première danseuse [*F.*], first fiddle, chef de cuisine [*F.*]; protagonist; past master; mahatma.

nice —, good —, clean- hand; practiced —, experienced- -eye, — hand; marksman; good —, dead —, crack- shot [*colloq.*]; ropedancer, ropewalker, funambulist; contortionist, acrobat; conjuror etc. (*deceiver*) 548; wizard etc. 994.

picked man; medallist, prizeman, honorsman.

veteran; old -stager, — campaigner, — soldier, — file, — hand; man of business, man of the world.

genius; master -mind, — head, — spirit.

pantologist, Admirable Crichton, Jack of all trades; prodigy of learning, quiz kid [*colloq.*], walking encyclopedia, mine of information.

man of cunning; cunning —, sharp- -blade, — fellow; diplomatist, diplomat, Machiavellian; politician, jobber; tactician, strategist.

peculator, forger, coiner; cracksman etc. 792.

701. Bungler

n. **bungler**; blunderer, blunderhead; marplot, fumbler, lubber, clown, lout, duffer [*colloq.*]; stick, poor stick, odd stick [*all colloq.*]; bad —, poor- -hand, — shot; butterfingers [*colloq.*], fumblefist [*colloq.*].

no conjuror; flat, muff, muffer, slow coach [*all colloq.*]; looby, swab [*slang & dial.*], doit, yokel [*Eng.*], clod; awkward squad, novice, greenhorn, blanc-bec [*F.*], galoot [*slang*].

fish out of water, ass in lion's skin, jackdaw in peacock's feathers; quack etc. (*deceiver*) 548; Lord of Misrule, Abbot of Unreason [*both obs. or hist.*].

landlubber, fresh-water sailor, fair-weather sailor, horse marine.

sloven, slattern, traipse *or* trapes [*obs. or dial. Eng.*], slut.

702. Cunning

n. **cunning**, craft; cunningness, craftiness etc. *adj.;* subtlety, subtilty, subtility [*rare*]; the cunning of the -serpent, — Old Boy [*slang*]; artificiality; maneuvering *or* manoeuvring etc. *v.;* temporization; circumvention.

chicane, chicanery; sharp practice, knavery, jugglery; concealment etc. 528; guile [*colloq.*], doubling, duplicity etc. (*falsehood*) 544; foul play.

diplomacy, politics; Machiavellianism *or* Machiavellism; gerrymander, jobbery, back-stairs influence.

artifice, art, device, machination; plot etc. (*plan*) 626; maneuver, stratagem, dodge, artful dodge, wile; trick, trickery etc. (*deception*) 545; ruse, ruse de guerre [*F.*]; finesse, side blow, thin end of the wedge, shift, go-by [*colloq.*], subterfuge, evasion; white lie etc. (*untruth*) 546; juggle, tour de force [*F.*]; tricks -of the trade, — upon travelers; gold brick [*colloq.*], imposture, deception; espièglerie [*F.*]; net, trap etc. 545.

schemer, trickster, keener [*Western U. S.*], Philadelphia lawyer [*colloq.*]; sly boots [*humorous*], fox, reynard; intriguer, intrigant; repeater, floater; man of cunning etc. 700; horse trader; Indian giver [*colloq.*].

Ulysses, Machiavelli *or* Machiavel.

v. **be cunning** etc. *adj.;* have cut one's eyeteeth; contrive etc. (*plan*) 626; live by one's wits; maneuver *or* manoeuvre; intrigue, gerrymander, finesse, double, temporize, stoop to conquer, reculer pour mieux sauter [*F.*], circumvent, steal a march upon; outdo, get the better of, snatch a thing from under one's nose; overreach etc. 545; throw off one's guard; surprise etc. 508; snatch a verdict; waylay, undermine, introduce the thin end of the wedge; be too much for, be too deep for, sell a gold brick to [*colloq.*], give the go-by to [*slang*]; play a deep game, play tricks with; flatter, make things pleasant; have an ax to grind.

adj. **cunning**, crafty, artful; skillful *or* skilful etc. 698; subtle, subtile, feline, vulpine; cunning as a -fox, — serpent; deep, — laid; profound; designing, contriving; intriguing etc. *v.;* strategic, diplomatic, politic, Machiavellian *or* Machiavelian, timeserving; artificial; tricky, tricksy [*rare*], wily, sly, slim [*S. Africa*], insidious, stealthy; underhand etc. (*hidden*) 528; subdolous [*obs.*], double-faced, double-tongued, shifty, deceptive; deceitful etc. 545; crooked; arch, pawky [*Scot. & dial. Eng.*], shrewd, acute; sharp, — as a needle; canny *or* cannie, astute,

703. Artlessness

leery [*slang*], knowing, up to snuff [*slang*], too clever by half, not to be caught with chaff.

adv. **cunningly** etc. *adj.;* slily, on the sly [*colloq.*], by a side wind.

703. Artlessness

n. **artlessness** etc. *adj.;* inartificiality, unsophistication; nature, simplicity; innocence etc. 946; *bonhomie* [*F.*], *naïveté* [*F.*], *abandon* [*F.*], candor, sincerity; singleness of -purpose, –heart; honesty etc. 939; plain speaking; *épanchement* [*F.*].

rough diamond, matter-of-fact man; *le palais de vérité* [*F.*]; *enfant terrible* [*F.*].

v. **be artless** etc. *adj.;* be round with one [Shakespeare]; look one in the face; wear one's heart upon one's sleeve for daws to peck at; think aloud; speak -out, –one's mind; be free with one, call a spade a spade; tell the truth, the whole truth, and nothing but the truth.

adj. **artless**, natural, pure, native, confiding, simple, plain, inartificial, untutored, unsophisticated, *ingénu* [*F.*], unaffected, naïve; sincere, frank; open, –as day; candid, ingenuous, guileless; unsuspicious, honest etc. 939; childlike, innocent etc. 946; Arcadian; undesigning, straightforward, unreserved, above-board; simple-minded, single-minded; frank–, open–, single–, simple- hearted.

matter-of-fact, free-spoken, plainspoken, outspoken; blunt, downright, direct, unpoetical; unflattering, untrimmed, unvarnished.

adv. **in plain -words**, –English; without mincing the matter; not to mince the matter etc. (*affirmation*) 535.

Section 4. Antagonism

704. Difficulty

n. **difficulty**; hardness etc. *adj.;* impracticability etc. (*impossibility*) 471; tough–, hard–, uphill- work; hard–, Herculean–, Augean- task; task of Sisyphus, Sisyphean labor, tough job [*colloq.*], tough proposition [*colloq.*], teaser [*colloq.*], rasper [*slang*], dead weight, dead lift.

dilemma, embarrassment; deadlock; perplexity etc. (*uncertainty*) 475; intricacy; entanglement etc. 59; cross fire; awkwardness, delicacy; delicate ground, thin ice, ticklish card to play, knot, Gordian knot, *dignus vindice nodus* [*L.*], net, meshes, maze; coil etc. (*convolution*) 248; crooked path; involvement; hard road to travel.

vexed question, *vexata quoestio* [*L.*], poser; puzzle etc. (*riddle*) 533; nice–, delicate–, subtle–, knotty- point; paradox; hard–, nut to crack; bone to pick, crux, *pons asinorum* [*L.*], where the shoe pinches.

quandary, nonplus, strait, pass, pinch, rub, pretty pass, stress, brunt; critical situation, crisis; trial, emergency, exigency, scramble.

scrape, hobble, slough, quagmire, hot water [*colloq.*], hornet's nest; sea–, peck- of troubles; pretty kettle of fish [*colloq.*]; pickle, stew, imbroglio, mess, muddle, botch, fuss, bustle, ado; false position; stand; deadlock, dead set; fix, horns of a dilemma, *cul de sac* [*F.*], blind alley; hitch; stumblingblock etc. (*hindrance*) 706.

v. **be difficult** etc. *adj.;* run one hard, go against the grain, try one's patience, put one out; put to one's -shifts; –wit's end; go hard with one, try one; pose, perplex etc. (*uncertain*) 475; pother, bother, nonplus, gravel [*colloq.*], bring to a deadlock; be impossible etc. 471; be in the way of etc. (*hinder*) 706.

be in difficulty etc. *n.;* meet with–, labor under–, get into–, plunge into–, struggle with–, contend with–, grapple with- difficulties; labor under a disadvantage; fish in troubled waters, buffet the waves; swim against the -current, –stream; scud under bare poles; have much ado with, have a hard time of it; come to the -push, –pinch; bear the brunt; grope in the dark, lose one's way, weave a tangled web, walk on eggshells, walk among eggs.

get into a scrape etc. *n.;* bring a hornet's nest about one's ears; be put to one's shifts; flounder, boggle, struggle; not know which way to turn etc. (*uncertain*) 475; *perdre son latin* [*F.*]; stick -at, –in the mud, –fast; come to a -stand, –deadlock; get all -balled up [*slang*], –snarled up, –tangled up, –wound up; hold the wolf by the ears.

render difficult etc. *adj.;* enmesh, encumber, embarrass, ravel, entangle; put a spoke in the wheel etc. (*hinder*) 706; spike one's guns; lead a wild-goose chase, lead a pretty dance.

adj. **difficult**, not easy, hard, tough [*colloq.*]; troublesome, toilsome, irksome; operose, laborious, onerous, arduous, Herculean, formidable; sooner–, more easily- said than done; difficult–, hard- to deal with; ill-conditioned, crabbed; not to be handled with kid gloves, not made with rose water.

awkward, unwieldy, unmanageable; intractable, stubborn etc. (*obstinate*) 606; perverse, refractory, plaguy [*colloq.*], trying, thorny, rugged;

knotted, knotty; invious [*obs.*]; pathless, trackless; labyrinthine etc. (*convoluted*) 248; intricate, complicated etc. (*tangled*) 59; impracticable etc. (*impossible*) 471; not feasible etc. 470; desperate etc. (*hopeless*) 859.

embarrassing, perplexing etc. (*uncertain*) 475; delicate, ticklish, critical, uncertain, thorny, set with thorns; beset with–, full of–, surrounded by–, entangled by–, encompassed with- difficulties.

under a difficulty; in a box; in difficulty, in hot water [*colloq.*], in the suds [*colloq.*], in the soup [*slang*], in a cleft stick, in a fix [*colloq.*], in the wrong box, in a scrape etc. *n.*, in deep water, in a fine pickle [*colloq.*], *in extremis* [*L.*]; between -two stools, –Scylla and Charybdis; on the horns of a dilemma; on the rocks; surrounded by -shoals, –breakers, –quicksands; at cross-purposes; not out of the wood.

reduced to straits; hard–, sorely- pressed; run hard; pinched, put to it, straightened; hard up [*slang*]; hard put to it, hard set [*both colloq.*]; put to one's shifts; puzzled, at a loss, etc. (*uncertain*) 475; at the end of one's tether, at one's wits' end, at a nonplus, at a standstill; graveled, nonplused *or* nonplussed, stranded, aground; stuck–, set- fast; out, put out, out in one's reckoning; up a tree, at bay, *aux abois* [*F.*], driven -into a corner, –from post to pillar, –to extremity, –to one's wit's end, –to the wall; *au bout de son Latin* [*F.*]; out of one's depth; thrown out.

accomplished with difficulty; hard-fought, hard-earned.

adv. **with difficulty**, with much ado; hardly etc. *adj.;* uphill; upstream; against the -stream, –grain; *à rebours* [*F.*]; *invita Minerva* [*L.*]; in the teeth of; at a pinch, upon a pinch; at long odds.

705. Facility

n. **facility**, ease; easiness etc. *adj.;* capability; feasibility etc. (*practicability*) 470; flexibility, pliancy etc. 324; smoothness etc. 255; disencumbrance, disentanglement; deoppilation [*obs.*]; permission etc. 760.

plain–, smooth–, straight- sailing; mere child's play, holiday task; cinch, snap [*both slang*].

all clear, smooth water, fair wind; smooth–, royal- road; clear -coast, –stage, –course; straight course; *tabula rasa* [*L.*]; full play etc. (*freedom*) 748.

v. **be easy** etc. *adj.;* go on–, run- smoothly; have full play etc. *n.;* go–, run- on all fours [*colloq.*]; hit on all -four, –six, –eight, –twelve (cylinders) [*automobile cant*]; obey the helm, work well, work smoothly, work like a machine.

flow–, swim–, drift–, go- with the- -stream, –tide; see one's way; have it all one's own way, have the game in one's own hands; walk over the course, win at a canter, win at a walk, win hands down [*colloq.*]; make little of, make light of, make nothing of; be at home in etc. (*skillful*) 698.

render easy etc. *adj.;* facilitate, smooth, ease, popularize; lighten, –the labor; free, clear; disencumber, disembarrass, disentangle, disengage; deobstruct, unclog, extricate, unravel, unknot, get the kinks out of; untie–, cut- the knot; disburden, unload, exonerate, emancipate, free from, deoppilate [*obs.*]; humor etc. (*aid*) 707; lubricate etc. 332; relieve etc. 834.

leave a hole to creep out of, leave a loophole, leave a way out, leave the matter open; give the reins to, give full play, give full swing; make way for; open the -door to, –way; prepare–, smooth–, clear- the -ground, –way, –path, –road; make all clear for, pave the way, bridge over; permit etc. 760.

adj. **easy**, facile; feasible etc. (*practicable*) 470; easily -managed, –accomplished; within reach, accessible, easy of access, for the million, open to.

manageable, wieldy [*rare*], toward, towardly, tractable; submissive; yielding, ductile; suant *or* suent [*local U. S. & prov. Eng.*]; tractable etc. (*docile*) 602, pliant etc. (*soft*) 324; glib [*obs.*], slippery; smooth etc. 255; on friction wheels, on velvet.

unburdened, disburdened, disencumbered, disembarrassed; exonerated; unloaded, unobstructed, untrammeled; unrestrained etc. (*free*) 748; at ease, light.

at home, quite at home; in one's element, in smooth water.

adv. **easily** etc. *adj.;* readily, smoothly, swimmingly, with no effort, on easy terms, single-handed, with one hand tied behind one's back.

706. Hindrance

n. **prevention**, preclusion, obstruction, stoppage; embolus, clot, embolism; interruption, interception, interclusion [*obs.*], hindrance, impedition [*obs.*]; retardment, retardation; embarrassment, oppilation [*obs.*], striction, constriction, coarctation, stricture, restriction; infarct, infarction; restraint etc. 751; inhibition etc. 761; blockade etc. (*closure*) 261.

707. Aid

interference, interposition; obtrusion; discouragement, discountenance; disapproval, disapprobation, opposition.
impediment, let [*archaic*], obstacle, obstruction, knot, knag; check, hitch, *contretemps* [*F.*], screw loose, grit in the oil; stumbling-block, stumbling-stone; lion in the path; snag; snags and sawyers, sawyer, planter [*local, U. S.*]
bar, stile, barrier; turnstile, turnpike; gate, portcullis; beaver dam; barricade etc. (*defense*) 717; wall, dead wall, breakwater, groin *or* groyne; bulkhead, block, buffer; stopper etc. 263; boom, dam, weir.
check; encumbrance *or* incumbrance; clog, skid, shoe, spoke, brake; drag anchor, drag sail, drag sheet, drift sail, sea anchor, floating anchor; anchor; mushroom–, sheet–, kedge– anchor; kedge, bower; checkrein, bearing rein; bit, snaffle, curb, curb bit; drag, –chain, –weight; load, burden, fardel [*obs.*], onus, millstone round one's neck, impedimenta; dead weight; lumber, pack; nightmare, ephialtes, incubus, old man of the sea; remora [*surg.*]; stay, stop; preventive, prophylactic.
drawback, objection; difficulty etc. 704; insuperable etc. (471) obstacle; trail of a red herring; estoppel [*law*]; ill wind; head wind etc. (*opposition*) 708; trammel, tether etc. (*means of restraint*) 752; holdback, counterpoise.
damper, wet blanket, hinderer, marplot, kill-joy, crape-hanger [*slang*], dog in the manger, Nosy Parker [*colloq.*], buttinsky [*humorous*]; usurper, interloper; opponent etc. 710; filibusterer.

v. **hinder**, impede, filibuster [*U. S.*], impedite [*obs.*], embarrass.
avert, keep off, stave off, ward off; obviate; antevert [*obs.*]; turn aside, draw off, prevent, forfend *or* forefend [*archaic*], nip in the bud; retard, slacken, check, let [*archaic*]; counteract, countercheck; preclude, debar, foreclose, estop [*law*]; inhibit etc. 761; shackle etc. (*restrain*) 751; restrict.
obstruct, stop, stay, bar, bolt, lock; block, –up; choke off; belay, barricade; block–, stop– the way; forlay *or* forelay [*obs.*], dam up etc. (*close*) 261; put on the brake etc. *n.;* scotch–, lock–, put a spoke in– the wheel; put a stop to etc. 142; traverse, contravene; interrupt, intercept; oppose etc. 708; hedge -in, –round; cut off; interclude [*obs.*].
interfere, interpose, intermeddle etc. 682.
encumber *or* incumber; cramp, hamper; clog, –the wheels; cumber; handicap; choke; saddle with, load with; overload, overlay, overwhelm; lumber, trammel, tie one's hands, put to inconvenience; incommode, discommode; discompose; hustle [*colloq.*], corner, drive into a corner.
run foul of, fall foul of; cross the path of, break in upon.
thwart, frustrate, disconcert, balk, foil; faze, feeze *or* feaze; baffle, snub, override, circumvent; defeat etc. 731; spike guns etc. (*render useless*) 645; spoil, mar, clip the wings of; cripple etc. (*injure*) 659; put an extinguisher on; damp; dishearten etc. (*dissuade*) 616; discountenance, throw cold water on, spoil sport; lay–, throw– a wet blanket on; steal one's thunder; cut the ground from under one, take the wind out of one's sails, undermine; be–, stand– in the way of; act as a drag; hang like a millstone round one's neck.

adj. **hindering** etc. *v.;* obstructive, obstruent; intrusive, meddlesome; impeditive, impedient; intercipient [*obs.*]; prophylactic etc. (*remedial*) 662; impedimentary, impedimental.
in the way of, unfavorable; onerous, burdensome; cumbrous, cumbersome; obtrusive.
hindered etc. *v.;* windbound, water-logged, heavy laden; hard pressed.
unassisted etc. (*see* assist etc. 707); single-handed, alone; deserted etc. 624; unseconded.

adv. **in the way**, with everything against one, with one's wheels clogged, through all obstacles; with many difficulties, under many difficulties.

707. Aid

n. **aid**, aidance, assistance, help, opitulation [*obs.*], succor; support, lift, advance, furtherance, promotion; coadjuvancy etc. (*cooperation*) 709.
patronage, auspices, championship, countenance, favor, interest, advocacy.
sustenance, sustentation [*rare*], maintenance, alimentation, nutrition, nourishment; eutrophy; manna in the wilderness; food etc. 298; means etc. 632; subsidy, bounty, subvention.
ministry, ministration; subministration [*obs.*], accommodation.
relief, rescue; help at a dead lift; supernatural aid; *deus ex machina* [*L.*].
supplies, reënforcements, succors, contingents, recruits; support etc. (*physical*) 215; adjunct, ally etc. (*helper*) 711.

v. **aid**, assist, help, succor, lend one's aid; come to the aid of etc. *n.;* contribute, subscribe to; bring–, give–, furnish–, afford–, supply aid etc. *n.;* give–, stretch–, lend–, bear–, hold out- a -hand, –helping hand; give one a -lift,

–cast, –turn; take by the hand, take in tow; help a lame dog over a stile, lend wings to.

relieve, rescue; set up, set agoing, set on one's legs; bear–, pull- through; give new life to, be the making of; reënforce, recruit; set–, put–, push- forward; give -a lift, –a shove, –an impulse- to; promote, further, forward, advance; speed, expedite, quicken, hasten.

support, sustain, uphold, prop, hold up, bolster.

nourish, nurture, nurse, cradle, dry nurse, suckle, foster, cherish, put out to nurse; manure, cultivate, force; foment; feed–, fan- the flame.

serve; do service to, tender to, pander to; administer to, subminister to [*obs.*], minister to; tend, attend, wait on; take care of etc. 459; entertain; smooth the bed of sickness.

oblige, accommodate, consult the wishes of; humor, cheer, encourage.

second, stand by; back, –up; pay the piper, abet; work for, make interest for, stick up for [*colloq.*], stick by, take up the cudgels for; take up–, espouse–, adopt- the cause of; advocate, beat up for recruits, press into the service; squire [*colloq.*], give moral support to, keep in countenance, countenance, patronize, take up; lend one's name to; lend oneself to, lend one's countenance to; smile upon, shine upon; favor, befriend, take in hand, enlist under the banners of; side with etc. (*cooperate*) 709.

be of use to; subserve etc. (*instrument*) 631; benefit etc. 648; render a service etc. (*utility*) 644; conduce etc. (*tend*) 176.

adj. **aiding** etc. *v.*; auxiliary, adjuvant, helpful; coadjuvant etc. 709; subservient, ministrant, ancillary, accessary, accessory, subsidiary.

friendly, amicable, favorable, propitious, well-disposed; neighborly; obliging etc. (*benevolent*) 906; at one's beck.

adv. **with** *or* **by the aid of** etc. *n.;* on–, in- behalf of; in aid of, in the service of, in favor of, in the name of, in furtherance of; on account of; **for** the sake of, on the part of; *non obstante* [*L.*].

int. **help**! save us! to the rescue! this way! *à moi!* [*F.*].

708. Opposition

n. **opposition**, antagonism; oppugnancy, oppugnation [*rare*]; impugnation, impugnment, contrariousness [*rare*], contrariness, contrariety; contravention; counteraction etc. 179; counterplot.

resistance etc. 719; restraint etc. 751; hindrance etc. 706; absence of aid etc. 707.

cross fire, cross current, undercurrent, head wind.

clashing, collision, conflict, discord, want of harmony; filibuster, filibusterism.

competition, two of a trade, rivalry, emulation, race, contest; tug of war.

v. **oppose**, counteract, run counter to; withstand etc. (*resist*) 719; control etc. (*restrain*) 751; hinder etc. 706; antagonize, oppugn, fly in the face of, go dead against, kick against, cross, kick at, fall out with, fall foul of; set–, pit- against; face, confront, cope with; make a -stand, –dead set- against; set -oneself, –one's face- against; protest–, vote–, raise one's voice- against; disfavor, turn one's back upon; set at naught, slap in the face, slam the door in one's face.

thwart, be–, play- at cross-purposes; counterwork, countermine; over-thwart.

encounter, stem, breast; stem–, breast- the -tide, –current, –flood; buffet the waves; beat up against, make head against; grapple with; kick against the pricks etc. (*resist*) 719; contend with *or* against etc. 720; do battle with *or* against etc. (*warfare*) 722.

contradict, contravene; belie; go–, run–, beat–, militate- against; come in conflict with.

compete, emulate etc., 720; rival, spoil one's trade, force out, drive one out of business.

adj. **opposing**, opposed etc. *v.;* adverse, antagonistic, oppugnant, overthwart; contrary etc. 14; at variance etc. 24; at issue, at war with, in controversy with, in opposition; "agin' the government."

in hostile array, front to front, with crossed bayonets, at daggers drawn; up in arms; resistant etc. 719.

unfavorable, unpropitious, unfriendly, hostile, inimical, cross; filibusterous.

competitive, emulous, cut-throat; in rivalry with, in friendly rivalry.

adv. **against**, *versus* [*L.*], counter to, in conflict with, at cross-purposes, cross, contrariwise, unfavorably.

against the -grain, –current, –stream, –wind, –tide; with a head-wind; with the wind -ahead, –in one's teeth.

in spite, in despite, in defiance; in the -way, –teeth, –face- of; across; athwart, overthwart; where the shoe pinches; in one's teeth.

though etc. 30; even; *quand même* [*F.*]; *per contra* [*L.*].

709. Cooperation

n. **cooperation**; coadjuvancy, coadjutorship, coadjument [*rare*], coagency, coefficiency; concert, concurrence, complicity, coadministration, coaction; participation; union etc. 43; coefficacy; combination etc. 48; collusion, collusiveness.

association, alliance, colleagueship, joint stock, copartnership, pool, gentleman's agreement; cartel; confederation etc. (*party*) 712; coalition, federation, fusion; a long pull a strong pull and a pull all together; logrolling, *quid pro quo* [*L.*], freemasonry.

unanimity etc. (*assent*) 488; *esprit de corps* [*F.*], party spirit; clanship, partisanship; concord etc. 714; synergy, synergism.

v. **cooperate**, concur; conduce etc. 178; combine, coadjute, coadjuvate, coact [*rare*], unite one's efforts; keep–, draw–, pull–, club–, hand–, hold–, league–, band–, be banded- together; pool; stand–, put- shoulder to shoulder; act in concert, join forces, fraternize, cling to one another; vote solidly, vote in blocks; conspire, concert, lay one's heads together; confederate, make an agreement with, be in league with; collude, understand one another, play into the hands of, hunt in couples.

side with, take sides with, go along with, go hand in hand with, join hands with, make common cause with, strike in with, unite with, join with, mix oneself up with, take part with, cast in one's lot with; join–, enter into- partnership with; rally round, flock to, follow the lead of; come to, pass over to, come into the views of; be–, row–, sail- in the same boat; sail on the same tack.

participate, be a party to, lend oneself to; chip in [*colloq.*], have a -hand in, –finger in the pie; take–, bear- part in; second etc. (*aid*) 707; take the part of, play the game of; espouse a -cause, –quarrel.

adj. **cooperating** etc. *v.;* in cooperation etc. *n.,* in league etc. (*party*) 712; coadjuvant, coadjutant, coadjutive, coactive, coalitional, hand in glove with; dyed in the wool; synergetic, synergistic.

favorable to etc. 707; unopposed etc. 708.

adv. **unanimously**, as one man etc. 488; shoulder to shoulder, in cooperation with.

710. Opponent

n. **opponent**, antagonist, adversary, oppugnant [*rare*]; adverse party, opposition; enemy etc. 891; assailant.

oppositionist, obstructive; brawler, wrangler, brangler [*rare*], disputant; filibuster, filibusterer, extremist, bitter-ender, irreconcilable, obstructionist, "willful men."

malcontent; demagogue, reactionist; anarchist, anarch; Jacobin, Fenian, Sinn Feiner, Red; Industrial Workers of the World, I. W. W.

rival, competitor, contestant, entrant; the field.

711. Auxiliary

n. **auxiliary**; recruit; assistant; adjuvant, adjutant; *ayudante* [*Sp. Amer.*], co-aid; adjunct; help, helper, helpmate, helping hand; colleague, partner, mate, confrère, cooperator; coadjuvant, coadjutant, coadjutator [*rare*], coadjutor, coadjutrix, collaborator.

ally; friend etc. 890; confidant (*fem.* confidante), *fidus Achates* [*L.*], *alter ego* [*L.*], pal [*slang*], chum [*colloq.*], mate, comate.

aide-de-camp [*F.*], secretary, clerk, associate, marshal; right-hand, right-hand man; candleholder, bottle-holder [*colloq.*]; handmaid; servant etc. 746.

puppet, cat's-paw, creature, jack-straw, tool; jackal; *âme damnée* [*F.*]; satellite, adherent; parasite, dependent, client [*Rom. hist.*].

confederate; complice [*archaic*], accomplice; accessory, –after the fact; *particeps criminis* [*L.*]; *socius criminis* [*L.*].

upholder; votary; sectarian, sectary; seconder, backer, supporter, abettor, advocate, partisan, champion, patron, friend at court, mediator; angel [*slang*].

friend in need, jack at a pinch, special providence, *deus ex machina* [*L.*], guardian angel, fairy godmother, tutelary genius.

712. Party

n. **party**, faction, denomination, class, communion, side, crew, team; band, horde, posse, phalanx; caste, family, gens [*Rom. hist.*], clan etc. 166. Confederates, Conservatives, Democrats, Federalists, Federals, Liberals, Libertarians, Radicals, Republicans, Socialists, Tories, Whigs etc.

community, body, fellowship, solidarity; freemasonry; party spirit etc. (*cooperation*) 709; fraternity, sodality, confraternity, sorority; *familistère* [*F.*], familistery; brotherhood, sisterhood.

fraternal order, Elks, Freemasons, Knights Templars, Odd Fellows, Knights of Pythias; Royal Arcanum etc.

gang, tong [*Chin.*]; Camorra, Kuklux, Kuklux Klan, Molly Maguires, Fenians, Sinn Feiners,

Bolsheviki, Bolshevists, Industrial Workers of the World, I. W. W., Luddites; ring, machine; Tammany, –Hall; junto, cabal, camarilla, brigue [*obs.*].

clique, knot, circle, set, coterie; club, casino.

corporation, corporate body, guild; establishment, company, copartnership, partnership, cahoot [*slang*]; firm, house; joint concern, joint-stock company; cartel, combine [*colloq.*], trust; holding company, consortium, merger.

society, association; institute, institution; union; trades union; league, syndicate, alliance; *Verein, Bund, Zollverein* [*all Ger.*]; combination; *Turnverein* [*Ger.*]; *Liedertafel* etc. (*singing societies*) 416; league–, alliance– offensive and defensive; coalition; federation; confederation, confederacy.

staff; cast, *dramatis personae* [*L.*].

v. **unite**, join; band together; club together etc. (*cooperate*) 709; found a –firm, –house; cement–, form– a party etc. *n.;* associate etc. (*assemble*) 72; federate, federalize, go cahoots [*slang*], go fifty-fifty [*slang*].

adj. **in league**, in partnership, in alliance etc. *n.*
bonded–, banded–, linked etc. (*joined*) 43- together; embattled; confederated, federative, joint, corporate, organized, enleagued, leagued, syndicated; clubbable *or* clubable, fraternal, Masonic, institutional, denominational; cliquish, cliquy *or* cliquey; union-made.

adv. **side by side**, hand in hand, shoulder to shoulder, *en masse* [*F.*], in the same boat.

713. Discord

n. **discord**, disaccord, dissidence, dissonance; disagreement etc. 24; jar, clash, break, shock; jarring, jostling etc. *v.;* screw loose.

variance, difference, dissension, misunderstanding, cross-purposes, odds, *brouillerie* [*F.*]; division, split, rupture, disruption, division in the camp, house divided against itself, "rift within the lute" [*Tennyson*], disunion, breach; schism etc. (*dissent*) 489; feud, faction.

polemics; litigation; strife etc. (*contention*) 720; warfare etc. 722; outbreak, open rupture, breaking off of negotiations, recall of ambassadors, declaration of war.

quarrel, dispute, tiff, bicker, *tracasserie* [*F.*], squabble, altercation, barney [*slang*], *démêlé* [*F.*], snarl, spat [*colloq. or dial.*], towrow [*Scot. & dial Eng.*], words, high words; wrangling etc. *v.;* jangle, brabble [*archaic*], brabblement [*archaic*], cross questions and crooked answers, snip-snap [*rare*]; family jars.

broil, brawl, row [*colloq.*], racket, hubbub, rixation [*obs.*]; embroilment, embranglement, imbroglio, fracas, breach of the peace, piece of work, scrimmage, rumpus [*colloq.*]; breeze [*colloq.*], squall; riot, disturbance etc. (*disorder*) 59; commotion etc. (*agitation*) 315; bear garden, Donnybrook.

subject of dispute, ground of quarrel, battle ground, disputed point; bone -of contention, –to pick; apple of discord, *casus belli* [*L.*]; question at issue etc. (*subject of inquiry*) 461; vexed question, *vexata quaestio* [*L.*], brand of discord.

contentiousness etc. *adj.;* enmity etc. 889; hate etc. 898; troublous times; cat-and-dog life; Kilkenny cats; disputant etc. 710; strange bedfellows.

v. **disagree**; be discordant etc. *adj.;* disaccord, come amiss etc. 24; clash, jar, jostle, pull different ways, conflict, have no measures with, misunderstand one another; live like cat and dog; differ; dissent etc. 489; have a bone to pick with, have a crow to pluck with.

quarrel, fall out, dispute; litigate; controvert etc. (*deny*) 536; squabble, tiff, spat, altercate, row [*colloq.*], brabble, wrangle, jangle, brangle, bicker, nag; spar etc. (*contend*) 720; have words with etc. *n.;* fall foul of.

split; break–, break squares–, part company– with; declare war, try conclusions; join–, put in– issue; pick a quarrel, fasten a quarrel on; sow–, stir up– dissension etc. *n.;* embroil, entangle, disunite, widen the breach; rub one's fur the wrong way; get one all het up [*dial.*]; get one hot under the collar [*colloq.*]; set at odds, set together by the ears; set–, pit– against.

get into hot water, fish in troubled waters, brawl; kick up a -row, –dust [*colloq.*]; turn the house out of window.

adj. **discordant**, dissident; disagreeing etc. *v.;* out of tune, dissonant, harsh, grating, jangling, unmelodious, inharmonious, ajar; on bad terms, dissentient etc. 489; unreconciled, unpacified; inconsistent, contradictory, incongruous, discrepant.

quarrelsome, unpacific; gladiatorial, controversial, polemic, disputatious; factious; litigious, litigant.

at strife, at odds, at loggerheads, at daggers drawn, at variance, at issue, at cross-purposes, at sixes and sevens, at feud, at high words; up in arms, heated, het up [*dial.*], hot under the collar [*colloq.*], together by the ears, in hot water, embroiled; torn, disunited.

714. Concord

n. **concord**, accord, harmony, symphony; homologue, homology, correspondence; agreement etc. 23; sympathy etc. (*love*) 897; response; union, unison, unity; bonds of harmony; peace etc. 721; unanimity etc. (*assent*) 488; league etc. 712; happy family.

rapprochement [*F.*], reunion; amity etc. (*friendship*) 888; alliance, *entente cordiale* [*F.*], good understanding, conciliation, arbitration.

peacemaker, intercessor, interceder, propitiator, mediator.

v. **agree** etc. 23; accord, harmonize with, blend in with; fraternize; be concordant etc. *adj.*; go hand in hand; run parallel etc. (*concur*) 178; understand one another; pull together etc. (*cooperate*) 709; put up one's horses together, sing in chorus.

side with, sympathize with, go with, chime in with, fall in with; come round [*colloq.*]; be pacified etc. 723; assent etc. 488; enter into the -ideas, -feelings- of; reciprocate.

hurler avec les loups [*F.*]; go-, swim- with the stream; get on the band wagon [*slang*].

smooth, pour oil on the troubled waters; keep in good humor, render accordant, put in tune; come to an understanding, meet halfway; keep the peace, remain at peace; mediate, intercede.

adj. **concordant**, congenial; agreeing etc. *v.;* in accord etc. *n.;* harmonious, united, cemented; banded together etc. 712; allied; friendly etc. 888; fraternal; conciliatory; at one with; of one mind etc. (*assent*) 488.

at peace, in still water; tranquil etc. (*pacific*) 721.

adv. **unanimously**, without a dissentient voice; with one voice etc. (*assent*) 488; in concert with, hand in hand; on one's side.

int. make it unanimous! are you with us?

715. Defiance

n. **defiance**; daring etc. *v.;* dare, defial, defi [*slang*]; "dare, dare, and double-dare" [*child's challenge*]; challenge, cartel; threat etc. 909; war cry, war whoop.

v. **defy**, dare, beard; brave etc. (*courage*) 861; bid defiance to; bite the thumb at; set at defiance, set at naught; hurl defiance at; dance the war dance; snap the fingers at, laugh to scorn; disobey etc. 742.

show -fight, -one's teeth, -a bold front; bluster, look big, stand with arms akimbo; double-, shake- the fist; threaten etc. 909.

challenge, call out; throw-, fling- down the -gauntlet, -gage, -glove.

adj. **defiant**; defying etc. *v.;* with arms akimbo; rebellious, bold, insolent, reckless, contemptuous, greatly daring, regardless of consequences.

adv. **in defiance of**, in the teeth of; under one's very nose; in open rebellion.

int. do your worst! come if you dare! come on! just try it! marry come up! [*archaic or dial.*], hoity toity!

716. Attack

n. **attack**; assault, -and battery; onset, onslaught, charge.

base of operations, point of attack; echelon; open order; close formation.

aggression, offense; incursion, inroad, invasion; irruption; outbreak; bucking, estapade [*manège*], *ruade* [*F.*], kicking, kick; punch etc. (*impulse*) 276; *coup de main* [*F.*]; sally, sortie, camisade *or* camisado [*archaic*], raid, foray; run at, run against; dead set at.

storm, storming; boarding, escalade; siege, investment, obsession [*obs.*], bombardment, cannonade, barrage; zero hour.

battue [*F.*], razzia, dragonnade *or* dragoonade; devastation etc. 162; *éboulement* [*F.*].

fire, volley; direct-, ricochet-, plunging-, rolling-, horizontal-, vertical-, platoon-, file-fire; fusilade; fire of demolition, percussion fire; sharpshooting, broadside; raking-, cross-fire; volley of grapeshot, *feu d'enfer* [*F.*].

cut, thrust, lunge, pass, passado [*obs.*], stoccado *or* stoccata [*archaic*], carte (*or* quarte) and tierce, home thrust; *coup de bec* [*F.*].

assailant, aggressor, invader; sharpshooter, dead shot, fusilier, dragoon, Uhlan.

v. **attack**, assault, assail; set upon, fall upon; charge, impugn, break a lance with, enter the lists.

show fight, come on; assume-, take- the offensive; be-, become- the aggressor; strike the first blow, throw the first stone at, fire the first shot; lift a hand-, draw the sword- against; take up the cudgels; advance-, march- against; march upon, invade, harry.

strike at, poke at, thrust at; aim-, deal- a blow at; give-, fetch- one a -blow, -kick; have a -cut, -shot, -fling, -shy- at; be down upon, pounce upon; fall foul of, light into [*colloq.*], pitch into [*colloq.*], launch out against; bait, slap on the face; make a -thrust, -pass, -set, -dead set- at; bear down upon.

close with, come to close quarters, bring to bay, come to blows.

ride full tilt against; let fly at, dash at, run a tilt at, rush at, tilt at, run at, fly at, hawk at, have at, let out at; make a -dash, -rush at; attack tooth and nail; strike home; drive–, press- one hard; be hard upon, run down, strike at the root of.

lay about one, run amuck.

fire upon, fire at, fire a shot at; draw a bead on; shoot at, pop at, level at, let off a gun at; open fire, pepper, bombard, shell, pour a broadside into; fire a volley, fire red-hot shot; spring a mine.

stone, lapidate, pelt; throw - a stone, –stones - at; hurl -at, –against, –at the head of; rock.

beset, besiege, beleaguer; lay siege to, invest, open the trenches, plant a battery, sap, mine; storm, board, scale the walls, go over the top.

cut and thrust, bayonet, give one the bayonet; butt; kick, strike etc. (*impulse*) 276; horsewhip, whip etc. (*punish*) 972.

adj. **attacking** etc. *v.;* aggressive, offensive, incursive, invasive, irruptive, obsidional.

up in arms.

adv. **on the offensive**, on the warpath, amuck, amok. over the top; at bay.

int. "up and at them!"

717. Defense

n. **defense** or defence, protection, guard, ward; shielding etc. *v.;* propugnation [*obs.*]; preservation etc. 670; guardianship.

self-defense, self-preservation; resistance etc. 719.

safeguard etc. (*safety*) 664; screen etc. (*shelter*) 666, (*concealment*) 350; fortification; munition, muniment; bulwark, fosse, trench, mine, countermine, dugout; moat, ditch, intrenchment *or* entrenchment, vallation, rampart, scarp, escarp, counterscarp, vanfoss; dike *or* dyke; parapet, sunk fence, haha, embankment, mound, mole, bank; earthwork, fieldwork; fence, wall, dead wall, contravallation *or* countervallation; paling etc. (*inclosure*) 232; palisade, stockade, stoccado [*obs.*], laager [*S. Africa*], sangar [*India*]; barrier, barricade; boom; portcullis, *chevaux de frise* [*F.*]; abatis *or* abattis, barbed wire entanglements, vallum [*Rom. antiq.*], circumvallation, merlon, battlement, glacis; casemate; buttress, abutment; shore etc. (*support*) 215.

breastwork, banquette, mantelet *or* mantlet, tenaille *or* tenail, ravelin, curtain, demilune, half-moon; bastion, demibastion, redan; vauntmure [*rare*], faussebraie *or* faussebraye, advanced work, hornwork, lunette, outwork; barbican, redoubt, sconce, fortalice; lines.

machicolation, bartizan, loophole, balistraria [*ancient fortification*]; postern gate, sally port.

stronghold, hold, fastness; asylum etc. (*refuge*) 666; keep, donjon, citadel, capitol, castle; tower, –of strength; fortress, propugnaculum, fort, kila [*India*]; barracoon, barrack; pah *or* pa [*N. Z.*]; peel, peel tower, peelhouse; rath [*Ir. antiq.*]; martello tower, blockhouse, wooden walls.

[protective devices] buffer, fender, cowcatcher; apron, mask, gauntlet, thimble; armor *or* armour, shield, buckler, scutum [*Rom. antiq.*], target, targe [*archaic*], aegis, breastplate, cuirass, backplate, habergeon, mail, coat of mail, brigandine, hauberk, lorica, helm [*archaic*], armet, basinet *or* bassinet, sallet *or* salade, greave, jambe, heaume, morion, cabasset, beaver, visor *or* vizor; face guard, helmet, casque, casquetel, siege cap, headpiece; steel helmet, tin -helmet, –hat [*soldiers' cant*]; camail, neckguard; *Pickelhaube* [*Ger.*]; spiked helmet; shako etc. (*dress*) 225; bearskin; vambrace, rerebrace, cubitière, sollerets, pédieux; panoply, caparison, housings; chamfron *or* chamfrain; truncheon etc. (*weapon*) 727; carapace, shell; spines, needles.

defender, protector; Defender of the Faith, *fidei defensor* [*L.*], guardian etc. (*safety*) 664; bodyguard, champion; knight-errant, Paladin; propugnator *or* propugner *or* propugnor [*obs.*]; picket; garrison.

v. **defend**, forfend *or* forefend [*archaic*], fend; shield, screen, shroud; engarrison, garrison, man; fence round etc. (*circumscribe*) 229; fence, intrench *or* entrench; arm, harness [*archaic*], accouter *or* accoutre; guard etc. (*keep safe*) 664; guard against; take care of etc. (*vigilance*) 459; bear harmless; fend–, keep–, ward–, beat- off; hinder etc. 706.

repel, parry, propugn [*obs.*], put to flight; give a warm reception to [*ironical*]; hold - keep- at -bay, –arm's length.

resist invasion, stand siege; be–, stand–, act- on the defensive; show fight; maintain–, stand- one's ground; stand by; hold one's own; bear–, stand- the brunt; fall back upon, hold, stand in the gap.

adj. **defending** etc. *v.;* defensive; mural; armed, –at all points, –cap-a-pie, –to the teeth; panoplied; accoutered *or* accoutred, harnessed [*archaic*], "in complete steel" [*Hamlet*]; iron-plated, ironclad; loopholed, castellated, machicolated, casemated; defended etc. *v.;* proof against, ball-proof, bullet-proof; protective.

adv. **defensively**; on the defensive; in defense; in self-defense; at bay, *pro aris et focis* [*L.*].

718. Retaliation

int. **no surrender**! *"ils ne passeront pas!"* "they shall not pass!" [*the French at Verdun*].

718. Retaliation

n. **retaliation**, reprisal, talion [*rare*], retort; counterstroke, counterblast, counterplot, counterproject; retribution, *lex talionis* [*L.*]; reciprocation etc. (*reciprocity*) 12.
requital, desert; tit for tat, give and take, blow for blow, *quid pro quo* [*L.*], a Roland for an Oliver, measure for measure, diamond cut diamond, an eye for an eye, boomerang, the biter bit, a game at which two can play; reproof valiant, retort courteous.
recrimination etc. (*accusation*) 938; revenge etc. 919; compensation etc. 30; reaction etc. (*recoil*) 277.

v. **retaliate**, retort, turn upon; pay, pay off, pay back; pay in -one's own, -the same- coin; cap, match; reciprocate etc. 148; turn the tables upon, return the compliment; give a *quid pro quo* etc. *n.,* give as much as one takes; give as good as was sent; exchange blows; give and take, exchange fisticuffs; be quits, be even with; pay off old scores.
serve one right, be hoist on one's own petard, throw a stone in one's own garden, catch a Tartar.

adj. **retaliating** etc. *v.;* retaliatory, retaliative, retributive, recriminatory, reciprocal; talionic [*rare*].

adv. **in retaliation**; *en revanche* [*F.*].

719. Resistance

n. **resistance**, stand, front, oppugnation [*rare*], oppugnance, oppugnancy; opposition etc. 708; reniteny, renitence, reluctance [*archaic*], reluctation [*rare*], recalcitrance *or* recalcitrancy, recalcitration; repugnance, repulsion; kicking etc. *v.*
repulse, rebuff, snub.
insurrection etc. (*disobedience*) 742; strike; turn-out [*colloq.*], lockout; barring-out; *levée en masse* [*F.*], *Jacquerie* [*F. hist.*]; rebellion; boycott; riot etc. (*disorder*) 59.

v. **resist**; not submit etc. 725; repugn [*obs.*], reluctate [*rare*], oppugn, withstand; stand up-, strive-, bear up-, be proof-, make head- against; stand, -firm, -fast, -one's ground, -the brunt of, -out; hold -one's ground, -one's own, -out; stick it out [*colloq.*].
face, confront, breast the -wave, -current; stem the -tide, -torrent; grapple with; show a bold front etc. (*courage*) 861; present a front, make a stand, take one's stand.
oppose etc. 708; kick, -against; recalcitrate, kick against the pricks; fly in the face of; lift the hand against etc. (*attack*) 716; withstand -an attack, -a siege, -the onset; rise up in arms etc. (*war*) 722; strike, turn out; draw up a round robin etc. (*remonstrate*) 932; put one's foot down; boycott; revolt etc. (*disobey*) 742; make a riot.
prendre le mors aux dents [*F.*], take the bit between the teeth; sell one's life dearly, die hard, keep at bay; repel, repulse.

adj. **resisting** etc. *v.;* oppugnant, resistive, resistant; refractory etc. (*disobedient*) 742; repugnant; recalcitrant, renitent, repulsive, repellent; up in arms.
proof against; unconquerable etc. (*strong*) 159; stubborn, unconquered; indomitable etc. (*persevering*) 604a; unyielding etc. (*obstinate*) 606.

int. **hands off**! keep off!
never say die! stick it! [*colloq.*]; show what you're made of! give 'em hell! [*colloq.*]; "up, Guards, and at them!" [Wellington—*at Waterloo, as alleged*].

720. Contention

n. **contention**, strife; contest, contestation; struggle; belligerency; opposition etc. 708.
controversy, polemics; debate etc. (*discussion*) 476; war of words, logomachy, litigation; paper war; high words etc. (*quarrel*) 713; sparring etc. *v.*
competition, rivalry; corrivalry, corrivalship; agonism [*obs.*], *concours* [*F.*], match, race, tug of war, horse racing, heat, dash, steeple chase, point-to-point race, handicap; regatta; field day; sham fight, Derby day; turf, sporting, bullfight, tauromachy [*rare*], gymkhana [*orig. Anglo-Indian*]; boat race, torpids [*Oxford Univ.*].
pugilism, boxing, fisticuffs, spar, mill [*cant*], set-to [*colloq.*], round, bout, event; prize fighting; quarterstaff, single stick; gladiatorship, gymnastics; wrestling; catch-as-catch-can-, Greco-Roman (*or* Graeco-Roman)-, Cornish-, Westmorland and Cumberland- style [of wrestling]; jujutsu (*also* jujitsu, jiujutsu, jiujitsu), *samo* [*Jap.*], *kooshti* [*Hind.*]; karate; athletics, athletic sports; games of skill etc. 840.
fracas etc. (*discord*) 713; clash of arms; tussle, scuffle, broil, fray; affray, affrayment [*obs.*]; velitation [*obs.*]; luctation [*rare*], colluctation

[*obs.*], shindy [Brit. *colloq.*], brigue [*obs.*], brabble, scramble, mêlée [*F.*], scrimmage, stramash [*dial. or slang*], free-for-all [*cant*]; free–, stand up–, hand to hand–, running- fight.

conflict, skirmish; encounter, rencounter, rencontre, collision, affair, brush, fight; sharp contest, hard knocks; battle, –royal; combat, action, engagement, just *or* joust, tournament; tilt, tilting; tourney, lists; pitched battle; guerrilla (*or* guerilla)–, irregular- warfare; bush-fighting.

deeds–, feats- of arms; pugnacity; combativeness etc. *adj.;* bone of contention etc. 713.

death struggle, struggle for life or death, Armageddon.

naval engagement, naumachia *or* naumachy, sea fight.

duel, duello [*rare*], single combat, *monomachia* [*L.*] *or* monomachy, satisfaction, *passage d'armes* [*F.*], passage of arms, affair of honor; triangular duel; hostile meeting, digladiation [*archaic*]; appeal to arms etc. (*warfare*) 722.

v. **contend**; contest, strive, struggle, scramble, wrestle; spar, square [*colloq.*]; exchange -blows, –fisticuffs; fib [*slang, Eng.*], jostle *or* justle, tussle, tilt, box, stave [*obs. or dial.*], fence; skirmish; pickeer [*obs.*]; fight etc. (*war*) 722; wrangle etc. (*quarrel*) 713.

contend etc. with; grapple–, engage–, close–, buckle [*obs.*]–, bandy–, try conclusions–, have a brush etc. *n.* –, tilt- with; encounter, fall foul of, pitch into [*colloq.*], clapperclaw [*archaic or dial.*], run a tilt at; oppose etc. 708; reluct.

compete–, cope–, vie–, race- with; outvie, emulate, rival; run a race.

contend etc. for, stipulate for, stickle for; insist upon, make a point of.

join issue, come to blows; be at–, fall to–, go to- loggerheads; set to, come to the scratch, pull a gun [*slang*], exchange shots, measure swords, meet hand to hand; take up the -cudgels, –glove, –gauntlet; tourney, just *or* joust, enter the lists; couch one's lance; give satisfaction; appeal to arms etc. (*warfare*) 722.

lay about one; break the peace.

adj. **contending** etc. *v.;* at loggerheads, at war, at issue.

contentious, combative, bellicose, belligerent, unpeaceful; warlike etc. 722; quarrelsome etc. 901; pugnacious, pugilistic; tauromachian *or* tauromachic [*rare*]; gladiatorial.

athletic, gymnastic, palaestral *or* palestral, palaestric *or* palestric; competitive, rival.

721. Peace

n. **peace**; amity etc. (*friendship*) 888; pacifism; harmony etc. (*concord*) 714; tranquility etc. (*quiescence*) 265; truce etc. (*pacification*) 723; pipe of peace, calumet.

piping time of peace, quiet life; neutrality.

v. **be at peace**; keep the peace etc. (*concord*) 714; make peace etc. 723; pacify; be a pacifist.

adj. **pacific**; peaceable, peaceful; calm, tranquil, untroubled, halcyon; bloodless; neutral, pacifistic, "too proud to fight" [Woodrow Wilson].

722. Warfare

n. **warfare**; fighting etc. *v.;* hostilities; war, arms, the sword; Mars, Bellona, grim-visaged war, *horrida bella* [*L.*]; bloodshed.

appeal to -arms, –the sword; ordeal–, wager- of battle; *ultima ratio regum* [*L.*], arbitrament of the sword, declaration of war.

battle array, campaign, crusade, expedition; mobilization; state of siege; battlefield etc. (*arena*) 728; warpath.

art of war, rules of war, the war game, tactics, strategy, castrametation; generalship, soldiership; military evolutions, ballistics, gunnery; aviation; chivalry; gunpowder, shot, shell, poison gas.

battle, conflict etc. (*contention*) 720; service, campaigning, active service, tented field; kriegsspiel *or* Kriegsspiel [*Ger.*], fiery cross, trumpet, clarion, bugle, pibroch, slogan; war cry, war whoop; battle cry, beat of drum, *rappel* [*F.*], tom-tom; word of command; password, watchword; *passage d'armes* [*F.*].

war to the -death, –knife; *guerre à -mort, –outrance* [*F.*]; open–, trench–, guerrilla (*or* guerilla)–, internecine–, civil- war (*or* warfare).

war medal, military medal, Congressional medal, Victoria Cross, V. C., *croix de guerre* [*F.*], *médaille militaire* [*F.*], iron cross [*Ger.*].

war news, war bulletin, war extra; war correspondent.

v. **arm**; prepare for war; raise–, mobilize- troops; raise up in arms; take up the udgels etc. 720; take up–, fly to–, appeal to- -arms, –the sword; draw–, unsheathe- the sword; dig up the -hatchet, –tomahawk.

war, make war, go to war, declare war, wage war, "let slip the dogs of war" [*Julius Caesar*]; cry havoc; kindle–, light- the torch of war; raise one's banner, send round the fiery cross, hoist the black flag; throw–, fling- away the scabbard; take the field; take the law into one's own hands; do–, give–, join–, engage in–, go to-

723. Pacification

battle; flesh one's sword; set to, fall to, engage, measure swords with, draw the trigger, cross swords; come to -blows, –close quarters; fight; combat; contend etc. 720; battle with, break a lance with.

serve; enroll, enlist; see–, be on– –service, –active service; campaign; wield the sword, shoulder a musket, smell powder, be under fire; spill blood, imbrue the hands in blood; be on the warpath.

carry on -war, –hostilities; keep the field; fight the good fight; take by storm; go over the top [*World War I*]; fight -it out, –like devils, –one's way, –hand to hand; cut one's way -out, –through; sell one's life dearly.

adj. **armed**, –to the teeth, –cap-a-pie; sword in hand; contending, contentious etc. 720; in–, under–, up in– arms; at war with; bristling with arms; in battle array, in open arms, in the field; embattled; battled.

warlike, belligerent, combative, armigerous, bellicose, martial, unpacific, unpeaceful; military, militant; soldier like, soldierly, chivalrous; strategical, civil, internecine; irregular, guerrilla *or* guerilla.

adv. *flagrante bello* [*L.*], in the thick of the fray, in the cannon's mouth; at the sword's point, at the point of the bayonet.

int. **to arms**! *vae victis!* [*L.*] to your tents O Israel! *c'est la guerre!* [*F.*].

723. Pacification

n. **pacification**, conciliation; reconcilement, shaking of hands, calumet, peace pipe; accommodation, arrangement, adjustment; terms, compromise; amnesty, deed of release.

peace offering; olive branch; calumet, –of peace; overture, preliminaries of peace.

truce, armistice; suspension of -arms, –hostilities; truce of God; breathing time; convention; *modus vivendi* [*L.*]; flag of truce, white flag, *parlementaire* [*F.*], cartel.

hollow truce, *pax in bello* [*L.*]; drawn battle.

v. **pacify**, tranquilize, compose; allay etc. (*moderate*) 174; reconcile, propitiate, placate, conciliate, meet halfway, hold out the olive branch, heal the breach, make peace, restore harmony, bring to terms.

make up a quarrel; settle–, arrange–, accommodate- -matters, –differences; set straight; *tantas componere lites* [*L.*]; come to -an understanding, –terms; bridge over; hush up; make it up, make matters up; shake hands; mend one's fences.

raise a siege; put up–, sheathe- the sword; bury the hatchet, lay down one's arms, turn swords into plowshares; smoke the calumet, close the temple of Janus; keep the peace etc. (*concord*) 714; be pacified etc.; come round.

adj. **conciliatory**, pacificatory; composing etc. *v.*; pacified etc. *v.*; accommodative.

724. Mediation

n. **mediation**, mediatorship, mediatization, mediatorialism; intervention, interposition, interference, intermeddling, intercession; parley, negotiation, arbitration; flag of truce etc. 723; good offices, peace offering; diplomatics [*rare*], diplomacy; compromise etc. 774.

mediator, intercessor, peacemaker, make-peace, negotiator, go-between; diplomatist etc. (*consignee*) 758; moderator; propitiator; umpire, arbitrator, referee.

v. **mediate**, mediatize; intercede, interpose, interfere, intervene; step in, negotiate; meet halfway; arbitrate, propitiate; agree to arbitration; submit; *componere lites* [*L.*].

adj. **mediatory**, mediatorial, negotiable; mediating etc. *v.*; propitiatory, diplomatic.

725. Submission

n. **submission**, yielding, acquiescence, compliance, submittal, submissiveness, deference, nonresistance; obedience etc. 743.

surrender, cession, capitulation, resignation, backdown [*colloq.*]; passing under the yoke, laying down one's arms, delivering up the keys (of the city etc.), handing over one's sword.

obeisance, homage, kneeling, genuflexion, curtsy *or* curtsey, kotow *or* kowtow [*Chinese*], salaam *or* salam [*Oriental*], prostration.

v. **submit**, succumb, yield, bend, stoop, accede, relent, resign, defer to.

surrender, –at discretion; cede, capitulate, come to terms, retreat, beat a retreat; lay down–, deliver up- one's arms; lower–, haul down–, strike- one's -flag, –colors; draw in one's horns etc. (*humility*) 879; give -way, –ground, –in, –up; cave in [*colloq.*]; suffer judgment by default; bend, –to one's yoke, –before the storm; reel back; bend–, knuckle- -down, –to, –under; knock under.

humble oneself; eat -dirt, –crow, –the leek, –humble pie; bite–, lick- the dust; be–, fall- at one's feet; crouch before, throw oneself at the feet of; swallow the -leek, –pill; kiss the rod; turn the other cheek; *avaler les couleuvres* [*F.*], gulp down.

pocket the affront; make the best of, make a virtue of necessity; grin and abide, grin and bear it, shrug the shoulders, resign oneself; submit with a good grace etc. (*bear with*) 826.

yield obeisance; obey etc. 743; kneel to, bow to, pay homage to, cringe to, truckle to; bend the -neck, -knee; kneel, fall on one's knees, bow submission, curtsy *or* curtsey, kotow *or* kowtow [*Chinese*].

adj. **submissive**, resigned, crouching, prostrate; downtrodden; surrendering etc. *v.;* down on one's marrowbones [*slang*]; on one's bended knee; nonresisting, unresisting; pliant etc. (*soft*) 324; humble etc. 879; undefended.

untenable, indefensible, insupportable, unsupportable.

726. Combatant

n. **combatant**; disputant, controversialist, polemic, litigant, belligerent; competitor, rival, corrival; fighter, assailant; champion, Paladin; mosstrooper, swashbuckler, fire eater, duelist, swordsman, *sabreur* [*F.*], *beau sabreur* [*F.*]; athlete, wrestler, boxer.

bully, bludgeon man, rough, rowdy, ruffian, tough [*colloq., U. S.*], gunman [*colloq.*], Thug *or* thug; terrorist etc. 887; fighting man, prize fighter, pugilist, bruiser, the fancy [*now rare*], gladiator, fighting-cock, gamecock.

soldier, warrior, brave, man at arms, guardsman, *gendarme* [*F.*]; campaigner, veteran; redcoat, military man, Rajput; armiger, esquire, knight; Amazon.

Janizary *or* Janissary; myrmidon; Mameluke *or* Mamaluke, spahi *or* spahee, bashi-bazouk [*Turk.*], Cossack, Croat, Pandor; irregular, free lance, franc-tireur, tirailleur, guerrilla *or* guerilla, *condottiere* [*It.*], mercenary; bushwhacker, companion; Hessian.

private, -soldier; Tommy Atkins [*Brit.*], doughboy [*slang*], grunt [*slang*], G.I. [*slang*], rank and file, peon, sepoy [*India*], *légionnaire* [*F.*], legionary, food for powder, fodder for cannon, cannon fodder, *Kannonenfutter* [*Ger.*]; spearman, pikeman; archer, bowman; halberdier; musketeer, carabineer, rifleman, sharpshooter, jäger *or* yager, skirmisher; grenadier, fusileer, infantryman, foot soldier, footman [*rare*], light infantryman, chasseur, zouave; artilleryman, gunner, cannoneer, bombardier [*hist.*], matross [*obs.*]; engineer; sapper, -and miner; cavalryman, trooper, sowar [*India*], dragoon; light-, heavy- dragoon; heavy, cuirassier, hussar, lancer; recruit, rookie [*slang*], conscript, drafted man, enlisted man.

officer etc. (*commander*) 745; subaltern, ensign, standard bearer.

horse and foot; cavalry, horse, light horse, mounted rifles; infantry, foot, light infantry, rifles; artillery, horse artillery, field artillery, gunners; military train.

armed force, troops, soldiery, military, forces, Sabaoth, host, the army, standing army, regulars, the line, troops of the line, militia, national guard, state guard, bodyguard, yeomanry, volunteers, trainband, fencibles [*hist.*]; auxiliary, *bersagliere* [*It.*]; garde -nationale, -royale [*F.*]; minuteman [*Am. hist.*]; auxiliary-, reserve- forces; reserves, *posse comitatus* [*L.*], posse; guards, yeomen of the guard, beefeaters [*Eng.*], life guards, household troops, Horse Guards, Foot Guards; Swiss guards.

levy, draft *or* draught; raw levies, awkward squad; Landwehr, Landsturm.

army, *crops d'armée* [*F.*], army corps; host, division, battalia [*rare*], sotnia [*Russ.*], column, wing, detachment, garrison, flying column, brigade, regiment, corps, battalion, squadron, company, battery, subdivision, section, platoon, squad; picket, guard, rank, file; legion, phalanx, cohort, maniple, manipulus [*Rom. hist.*]; cloud of skirmishers.

war horse, charger, destrer *or* destrier [*archaic*].

navy, first line of defense, wooden walls, naval forces, fleet, flotilla, armada, squadron; man-of-war's man etc. (*sailor*) 269; marines.

man-of-war, line-of-battle ship, ship of the line, battleship, warship, ironclad, war vessel, war castle, H.M.S., U.S.S.; superdreadnought, dreadnought, cruiser; armored-, protected- cruiser; torpedo-boat, -destroyer; destroyer, torpedo-catcher, gunboat; submarine, submersible, U-boat; submarine chaser; mine layer, sweeper; turret ship, ram, monitor, floating battery; first-rate, frigate, sloop of war, corvet *or* corvette; bomb vessel; flagship, guard ship, privateer; troopship, transport, tender, storeship, catamaran [*obs.*], fire boat.

aeroplane, airplane, *avion* [*F.*], Fokker, dirigible, blimp; zeppelin etc. (*aeronautics*) 273.

727. Arms

n. **arms**, arm, weapon, deadly weapon; armament, armature; panoply, stand of arms; armor etc. (*defense*) 717; armory etc. (*store*) 636; *apparatus belli* [*L.*]; gunnery; ballistics etc. (*propulsion*) 284.

side arms, *armes blanches* [*F.*], sword; good-, trusty-, naked- sword; cold steel, naked steel,

steel, blade, brand [*archaic*]; broadsword, Toledo, Ferrara, claymore, glaive [*archaic*] *or* glave [*obs.*]; saber *or* sabre, cutlass, hanger, bilbo, falchion, scimitar *or* cimeter [*obs.*], whinyard [*obs.*], rapier, tuck [*hist.*], foil, yataghan (*also* ataghan, attaghan); dagger, poniard, baselard, dirk, stiletto, katar *or* kuttar [*India*], stylet; skean, skean dhu [*Scot.*]; creese *or* kris; dudgeon [*archaic*], bowie knife; bayonet, sword bayonet, sword stick.

ax *or* **axe**, battle ax, Lochaber ax, adaga, poleax *or* poleaxe, halberd *or* halbert, gisarme, tomahawk, bill, black bill, brown bill, partisan.

spear, lance, pike, spontoon, assagai *or* assegai, javelin, jereed *or* jerid, dart, shaft, bolt, reed, arrow; harpoon, gaff, eelspear; weet-weet, womerah, throwing stick, throw stick, boomerang; oxgoad, ankus.

club, war club, waddy [*Austral.*], mace, truncheon, staff, bludgeon, cudgel, shillalah *or* shillelagh, handstaff, quarterstaff; bat, cane, stick, walking-stick, knuckle duster; billy, life-preserver, blackjack, sandbag.

bow, crossbow, arbalest, ballista *or* balista, balister [*obs.*], trebuchet *or* trebucket, catapult, sling; battering-ram etc. (*impulse*) 276.

firearms; gun, piece; artillery, ordnance; siege–, battering- train; park, battery; cannon, gun of position, heavy gun, fieldpiece, field gun, mountain gun, siege gun, seacoast gun; mortar, howitzer, carronade, culverin, basilisk [*obs.*]; falconet, jingal swivel, swivel gun, pedrero *or* pederero, *bouche à feu* [*F.*], smooth bore, rifled cannon; Armstrong–, Lancaster–, Paixhans–, Whitworth–, Parrott–, Krupp–, Vickers–, Benet-Mercié–, Gatling–, Maxim–, machine- gun; pompom, *mitrailleuse* [*F.*]; "seventy-five" [*French rapid-fire 75 mm. field gun*]; Lewis gun; auto-rifle, ten-pounder; bazooka; flame-thrower, *Flammenwerfer* [*Ger.*], *lance-flamme* [*F.*].

small arms; musketry; musket, firelock, fowling piece, rifle, fusil [*obs. or hist.*], escopette *or* escopet, carbine, blunderbuss, musketoon, Brown Bess, matchlock, harquebus *or* arquebus, caliver, hackbut *or* hagbut, shotgun, petronel [*hist.*]; small bore; breechloader, muzzle-loader; gunflint, gunlock, Minié–, Enfield–, Flobert–, Westley Richards–, Snider–, Martini-Henry–, Lee-Metford–, Lee-Enfield–, Mauser–, Mannlicher–, Springfield–, magazine- rifle; needle gun, *chassepot* [*F.*]; wind gun, air gun; automatic -gun, -pistol; automatic; revolver, repeater; shooting iron [*slang*],

shooter [*colloq.*], six-shooter, gun, pistol, pistolet [*obs.*].

missile, bolt, projectile, shot, ball; grape; grape–, canister–, bar–, cannon–, langrage *or* langrel–, round–, chain- shot; slung shot; shrapnel, *mitraille* [*F.*], grenade, hand grenade, rifle grenade; shell, high-explosive shell, *obus explosif* [*F.*], bomb, depth bomb, smoke bomb, gas bomb; bullet; dumdum–, man-stopping–, explosive–, expanding- bullet; petard; infernal machine, torpedo; carcass, rocket; congreve, –rocket; slug, stone, rock, brickbat.

thunderbolt, levin- -bolt, –brand; stroke, stroke of lightning, thunderstone [*obs. or dial. Eng.*].

ammunition; powder, –and shot; explosive; gunpowder, "villanous saltpetre" (*villainous saltpeter*) [*Henry IV.*]; guncotton, pyroxylin *or* pyroxyline, dynamite, melinite, cordite, gelignite, lyddite, nitroglycerin *or* nitrogylcerine, trinitrotoluol, trinitrotoluene, T.N.T.; cartridge; ball cartridge, cartouche, fireball; poison gas, mustard gas, chlorine gas, tear gas etc.

728. Arena

n. **arena**, field, platform; scene of action, theater *or* theatre, walk, course; hustings; stage, boards etc. (*playhouse*) 599; amphitheater *or* amphitheatre, Coliseum, Colosseum; Flavian amphitheater, hippodrome, circus, race course, *corso* [*It.*], turf, cockpit, bear garden, gymnasium, palaestra *or* palestra, ring, lists; tilt-yard, tilting ground; *Campus Martius* [*L.*], *Champ de Mars* [*F.*]; campus, playing field, playground.

battle field, battle ground; field of -battle, –slaughter; No Man's Land [*World War I*]; "over there" [*used in America, esp. of the Western Front in World War I*], "out there" [*corresponding term in Eng.*]; theater–, seat- of war; Aceldama, camp; the enemy's camp.

trysting place etc. (*place of meeting*) 74.

Section 5. Results of Action

729. Completion

n. **completion**; accomplishment, achievement, fulfillment *or* fulfilment; performance, execution; dispatch *or* despatch, consummation, culmination; finish, conclusion; limit, effectuation; close etc. (*end*) 67; terminus etc. (*arrival*) 292; winding up; *finale* [*It.*], *dénouement* [*F.*], catastrophe, issue, upshot, result; final–, last–, crowning–, finishing- -touch, –stroke; last finish, *coup de grâce* [*F.*]; crowning of the edifice; coping stone, copestone, keystone; missing link etc. 53; superstructure, *ne plus ultra* [*L.*], work done, *fait accompli* [*F.*]. elaboration; finality; completeness etc. 52.

v. **complete**, perfect; effect, effectuate; accomplish, achieve, compass, consummate, hammer out; bring to -maturity, –perfection; elaborate.

do, execute, make; go–, get- through; work out, enact; bring -about, –to bear, –to pass, –through, –to a head.

dispatch *or* despatch, knock off [*colloq.*], finish off, polish off; make short work of; dispose of, set at rest; perform, discharge fulfill *or* fulfil, realize; put in -practice, –force; carry -out, –into effect, –into execution; make good; be as good as one's word.

do thoroughly, not do by halves, go the whole hog [*colloq.*]; drive home, be in at the death etc. (*persevere*) 604a; carry through, deliver the goods [*colloq.*], play out, exhaust; fill the bill [*colloq.*].

finish, bring to a close etc. (*end*) 67; wind up, stamp, clinch, seal, set the seal on, put the seal to; give the final touch etc. *n.* to; put the -last, –finishing- touch to; crown, crown all; cap.

ripen, culminate; come to a -head, –crisis; come to its end; die a natural death, die of old age; run its course, run one's race; touch–, reach–, attain- the goal; reach etc. (*arrive*) 292; get in the harvest.

adj. **completing**, final; concluding, conclusive; crowning etc. *v.;* exhaustive, elaborate, complete, mature, perfect, consummate, thorough.

done, completed etc. *v.;* done for [*colloq.*], sped, wrought out; highly wrought etc. (*preparation*) 673; thorough etc. 52; ripe etc. (*ready*) 673.

adv. **completely** etc. (*thoroughly*) 52; to crown all, out of hand; with absolute -perfection, –finish; as a last stroke; as a fitting climax.

730. Noncompletion

n. **noncompletion**, nonfulfillment *or* nonfulfilment, shortcoming etc. 304; incompleteness etc. 53; drawn -battle, –game; work of Penelope; Sisyphean -labor, –toil, –task.

nonperformance, inexecution; neglect of execution; neglect etc. 460.

v. **not complete** etc. 729; leave unfinished etc. *adj.,* leave undone; neglect etc. 460; let alone, let slip; lose sight of.

fall short of etc. 304; do things by halves, scotch the snake not kill it; hang fire; be slow to; collapse etc. 304.

adj. **incomplete** etc. 53; not completed etc. *v.;* uncompleted, unfinished, unaccomplished, unperformed, unexecuted; sketchy; addle, muddled, sterile.

in progress, in hand, on the stocks, in preparation, moving, getting along, going on, proceeding; on one's hands; on the anvil.

adv. *re infecta* [*L.*]; without–, lacking- -the final touches, –the finishing stroke.

731. Success

n. **success**, successfulness; speed; advance etc. (*progress*) 282.

trump card; hit, stroke; lucky–, fortunate–, good- -hit, –stroke; bold stroke, masterstroke; ten-strike [*colloq.*]; *coup de maître* [*F.*], checkmate; half the battle, prize; profit etc. (*acquisition*) 775.

continued success; good fortune etc. (*prosperity*) 734; time well spent.

mastery, advantage over; upper hand, whip hand; ascendancy, expugnation [*obs.*], conquest, victory, walkover [*colloq.*], subdual; subjugation etc. (*subjection*) 749; triumph etc. (*exultation*) 884; proficiency etc. (*skill*) 698; a feather in one's cap [*colloq.*].

victor, victress [*rare*], victrix [*rare*], conqueror, master, champion, winner; master of the -situation, –position.

v. **succeed**; be successful etc. *adj.;* gain one's -end, –ends; crown with success.

gain–, attain–, carry–, secure–, win- -a point, –an object; get there [*colloq.*]; manage to, contrive to; accomplish etc. (*effect, complete*) 729; do–, work- wonders; make a go of it [*colloq.*].

come off -well, –successfully, –with flying colors; make short work of; take–, carry- by storm; bear away the bell; win one's spurs, win the battle; win–, carry–, gain- the -day, –prize, –palm; have the best of it, have it all one's own way, have the game in one's own hands, have the ball at one's feet, have one on the hip; walk over the course; carry all before one, remain in possession of the field; socre a success, strike it rich, hit pay dirt.

make progress etc. (*advance*) 282; win–, make–, work–, find- one's way; speed; strive to some purpose; prosper etc. 734; drive a roaring trade; make profit etc. (*acquire*) 775; reap–, gather- the -fruits, –benefit of, –harvest; strike oil [*slang*], make one's fortune, get in the harvest, turn to good account; turn to account etc. (*use*) 677.

261

triumph, be triumphant; gain–, obtain- -a victory, –an advantage; chain victory to one's car.

surmount–, overcome–, get over- -a difficulty, –an obstacle etc. 706; *se tirer d'affaire* [*F.*]; make head against; stem the -torrent, –tide, –current; weather -the storm, –a point; turn a corner, keep one's head above water, tide over; master; get–, have–, gain- the -better of, –best of, –upper hand, –ascendancy, –whip hand, –start of; distance; surpass etc. (*superiority*) 33.

defeat, conquer, vanquish, discomfit; euchre [*slang*]; overcome, overthrow, overpower, overmaster, overmatch, overset, override, overreach; outwit, outdo, outflank, outmaneuver *or* outmanoeuvre, outgeneral, outvote; take the wind out of one's adversary's sails; beat, beat hollow [*colloq.*], lick [*colloq.*], rout, drub, floor, worst, lick to a frazzle [*colloq.*]; put -down, –to flight, –to the rout, –*hors de combat* [*F.*], –out of court.

settle [*colloq.*], do for [*colloq.*], break the -neck of, –back of; capsize, sink, shipwreck, drown, swamp; subdue; subjugate etc. (*subject*) 749; reduce; make the enemy bite the dust; victimize, roll in the dust, trample under foot, put an extinguisher upon.

checkmate, silence, quell, nonsuit, upset, confound, nonplus, stalemate, trump; baffle etc. (*hinder*) 706; circumvent, elude; trip up, –the heels of; drive -into a corner, –to the wall; run hard, put one's nose out of joint [*colloq.*].

avail; answer, –the purpose; prevail, take effect, do, turn out well, work well, take [*colloq.*], tell, bear fruit; hit it, hit the mark, hit the nail on the head; nick it; turn up trumps, make a hit; find one's account in.

adj. **successful**; prosperous etc. 734; succeeding etc. *v.;* triumphant; flushed–, crowned- with success; victorious; set up [*colloq.*]; in the ascendant; unbeaten etc. (*see* beat etc. *v.*); well-spent; felicitous, effective, in full swing.

adv. **successfully** etc. *adj.;* with flying colors, in triumph, swimmingly; *à merveille* [*F.*], beyond all hope; to some–, to good- purpose; to one's heart's content.

732. Failure

n. **failure**, unsuccess, nonsuccess, nonfulfillment *or* nonfulfilment; dead failure, successlessness; abortion, miscarriage; *brutum fulmen* [*L.*] etc. 158; labor in vain etc. (*inutility*) 645; no go [*colloq.*]; inefficacy; inefficaciousness etc. *adj.;* vain–, ineffectual–, abortive- -attempt, –efforts, flash in the pan, "lame and impotent conclusion" [*Othello*]; frustration; slip 'twixt cup and lip etc. (*disappointment*) 509.

blunder etc. (*mistake*) 495; fault, omission, miss, oversight, slip, trip, stumble, claudication [*obs.*] footfall; false–, wrong- step; *faux pas* [*F.*], titubation, *bévue* [*F.*], *faute* [*F.*], lurch; botchery etc. (*want of skill*) 699; scrape, mess, muddle, botch, fiasco, breakdown; flunk [*colloq.*].

mishap etc. (*misfortune*) 735; split, collapse, smash, blow, explosion.

repulse, rebuff, defeat, rout, overthrow, discomfiture; beating, drubbing; quietus, nonsuit, subjugation; checkmate, stalemate, fool's mate.

losing game, *affaire flambée* [*F.*]

fall, downfall, ruin, perdition; wreck etc. (*destruction*) 162; deathblow; bankruptcy etc. (*nonpayment*) 808.

victim, prey; bankrupt; flunker [*colloq.*], flunky *or* flunkey [*cant*].

v. **fail**; be unsuccessful etc. *adj.;* not succeed etc. 731; make vain efforts etc. *n.;* do–, labor–, toil- in vain; flunk [*colloq.*]; lose one's labor, take nothing by one's motion; bring to naught, make nothing of; wash a black-amoor white etc. (*impossible*) 471; roll the stone of Sisyphus etc. (*useless*) 645; do by halves etc. (*not complete*) 730; lose ground etc. (*recede*) 283; fall short of etc. 304; go to -the wall, –the dogs, –pot [*colloq.*], lick–, bite- the dust; be defeated etc. 731; have the worst of it, lose the day, come off second best, lose; not have a leg to stand on; fall a prey to; succumb etc. (*submit*) 725.

miss, –one's aim, –the mark, –one's footing, –stays [*naut.*]; slip, trip, stumble; make a slip etc., *n.;* make a blunder etc. 495, make a mess of, make a botch of; bitch it [*obs.*], miscarry, abort, go up like a rocket and come down like the stick, reckon without one's host; get the wrong -pig by the tail, –sow by the ear [*colloq.*] etc. (*blunder, mismanage*) 699.

flounder, falter; limp, halt, hobble, titubate; fall, tumble; lose one's balance; fall to the ground, fall between two stools; stick in the mud, run aground, split upon a rock; run–, knock–, dash- one's head against a stone wall; break one's back; break down, sink, drown, founder, have the ground cut from under one; get into -trouble, –a mess, –a scrape; come to grief etc. (*adversity*) 735.

come to nothing, end in smoke; flat out [*colloq.*]; fall -to the ground, –through, –dead, –stillborn, –flat; slip through one's fingers; hang fire, misfire, flash in the pan, collapse;

topple down etc. (*descent*) 305; go to wrack and ruin etc. (*destruction*) 162.

go amiss, go wrong, go cross, go hard with, go on a wrong tack; go on-, come off-, turn out-, work- ill; take a wrong turn, take an ugly turn, be all over with, be all up with; explode; dash one's hopes etc. (*disappoint*) 509; defeat the purpose; sow the wind and reap the whirlwind, jump out of the frying pan into the fire.

adj. **unsuccessful**, successless, stick-it [*Scot.*]; failing, tripping etc. *v.;* at fault; unfortunate etc. 735.

abortive, sterile, impotent, addle, stillborn; fruitless, bootless; ineffectual, ineffective; inefficient etc. (*impotent*) 158; inefficacious; lame, hobbling, *décousu* [*F.*]; insufficient etc. 640; unavailing etc. (*useless*) 645; of no effect.

stranded, aground, grounded, swamped, cast away, wrecked, foundered, capsized, shipwrecked, nonsuited; foiled; defeated etc. 731; struck-, borne-, broken- down; downtrodden; overborne, overwhelmed; all up with [*colloq.*]; plowed *or* ploughed [*Eng. Univ. cant*], plucked [*college cant*].

undone, lost, ruined, broken; bankrupt etc. (*not paying*) 808; played out; done up, done for [*both colloq.*]; deadbeat [*colloq.*], ruined root and branch, *flambé* [*F.*], knocked on the head; destroyed etc. 162.

frustrated, thwarted, crossed, unhinged, disconcerted, dashed; thrown -off one's balance, -on one's back, -on one's beam ends; unhorsed, in a sorry plight; hard hit; stultified, befooled, dished [*colloq.*], hoist on one's own petard; victimized, sacrificed.

wide of the mark etc. (*error*) 495; out of one's reckoning etc. (*inexpectation*) 508; left in the lurch; thrown away etc. (*wasted*) 638; unattained; uncompleted etc. 730.

adv. **unsuccessfully** etc. *adj.;* to little or no purpose, in vain, *re infecta* [*L.*].

733. Trophy

n. **trophy**; medal, prize, palm, laurel, laurels, bays, crown, chaplet, wreath, civic crown; insignia etc. 550; eulogy, citation; fellowship, scholarship; feather in one's cap etc. (*honor*) 873; garland; triumphal arch; Victoria Cross, Congressional medal, *croix de guerre* [*F.*], *médaille militaire* [*F.*], Iron Cross; Pulitzer Prize, Oscar, Emmy; Carnegie medal, Nobel prize; blue ribbon; red ribbon of the Legion of Honor; decoration etc. 877.

triumph etc. (*celebration*) 883; flying colors etc. (*show*) 882.

734. Prosperity

n. **prosperity**, welfare, well-being; affluence etc. (*wealth*) 803; success etc. 731; thrift, roaring trade; good-, smiles of - fortune; blessings; godsend; bed of roses; fat of the land, milk and honey, loaves and fishes, fleshpots of Egypt.

luck; good-, run of- luck; sunshine; fair -weather, -wind; fair wind and no favor; palmy-, bright-, halcyon-days; piping times, tide, flood, high tide.

golden age, golden time, *Saturnia regna* [*L.*], Saturnian age.

man of substance, made man, lucky dog, *enfant gâté* [*F.*], spoiled child of fortune.

upstart, parvenu, *nouveau riche* [*F.*], *narikin* [*Jap.*], skipjack [*dial. Eng.*], mushroom.

v. **prosper**, thrive, flourish; be prosperous etc. *adj.;* drive a roaring trade; go on -well, -smoothly, -swimmingly; sail before the wind, swim with the tide; run -smooth, -smoothly, -on all fours [*colloq.*].

rise-, get on- in the world; work-, make- one's way; look up; lift-, raise-one's head, make one's fortune, feather one's nest, make one's pile [*slang*].

flower, blow, blossom, bloom, fructify, bear fruit, fatten, batten.

keep oneself afloat; keep-, hold-one's head above water; light-, fall-on one's -legs, -feet; drop into a good thing; bear a charmed life; bask in the sunshine; have a good (*or* fine) time of it; have a run, - of luck; have the good fortune etc. *n.* to; take a favorable turn; live -on the fat of the land, -in clover, -on velvet.

adj. **prosperous**; thriving etc. *v.;* in a fair way, buoyant; well off, well to do, well to live [*archaic*], set up [*colloq.*], well to do in the world; at one's ease; rich etc. 803; in good case; in full feather, in high feather; fortunate, lucky, in luck; born with a silver spoon in one's mouth, born under a lucky star; on the sunny side of the hedge.

palmy, halcyon; agreeable etc. 829; *couleur de rose* [*F.*].

auspicious, propitious, providential.

adv. **prosperously** etc. *adj.;* swimmingly; as good luck would have it; beyond all -expectation, -hope; beyond one's deserts; beyond the dreams of avarice.

735. Adversity

n. **adversity**, evil etc. 619; failure etc. 732; bad -ill-, evil-, adverse-, hard- -fortune, -hap, -luck, -lot; frowns of fortune; evil -dispensa-

736. Mediocrity

tion, –star, –genius; ups and downs of life; the sport of fortune; broken fortunes; hard -case, –lines, –life; sea–, peck- of troubles; hell upon earth; slough of despond.

pressure of the times, iron age, evil day, time out of joint; hard–, bad–, sad- times; rainy day, cloud, dark cloud, gathering clouds, ill wind; affliction etc. (*painfulness*) 830; bitter -pill, –draft (*or* draught), –cup; care.

trouble, hardship, curse, blight, blast, load, pressure, humiliation.

misfortune, misventure [*archaic*], mishap, mischance, misadventure, disaster, calamity, catastrophe; accident, casualty, cross, blow, trial, sorrow, visitation, infliction, reverse, check, *contretemps* [*F.*], pinch, rub; backset, comedown, setback.

downfall, fall; losing game; falling etc. *v.*; ruination, ruinousness, undoing; extremity; ruin etc. (*destruction*) 162.

v. **be ill of** etc. *adj.*; go hard with; fall on evil, –days; go on ill; not prosper etc. 734.

come to grief, go downhill, go to rack and ruin etc. (*destruction*) 162, go to the dogs [*colloq.*]; fall, –from one's high estate; decay, sink, decline, go down in the world; have seen better days; bring down one's gray hairs with sorrow to the grave; be all over with, be all up with [*colloq.*]; bring a wasp's (*or* hornet's) nest about one's ears.

adj. **unfortunate**, unblest, unhappy, unlucky, unprosperous, improsperous [*obs.*]; hoodooed [*colloq.*], Jonahed [*slang*], jinxed [*slang*], luckless, hapless; out of luck; in trouble, in a bad way, in an evil plight; under a cloud; clouded; ill off, badly off; in adverse circumstances; poor etc. 804; behindhand, down in the world, decayed, undone; on the road to ruin, on its last legs, on the wane; in one's utmost need; up the creek without a paddle [*colloq.*].

ill-fated, ill-starred, ill-omened; planet-struck, devoted, doomed; inauspicious, unauspicious [*rare*], ominous, sinister, unpropitious; unfavorable; born -under an evil star, –with a wooden ladle in one's mouth.

adverse, untoward; disastrous, calamitous, ruinous, dire, deplorable.

adv. if the worst come to the worst, as ill luck would have it, from bad to worse, out of the frying pan into the fire.

736. Mediocrity

n. **mediocrity**; golden mean etc. (*mid-course*) 628, (*moderation*) 174; moderate–, average- circumstances; respectability.

middle classes, *bourgeoisie* [*F.*].

v. strike the golden mean; preserve a middle course etc. 628.

jog on, get along [*colloq.*], get by [*slang*]; go–, get on- -fairly, –quietly, –peaceably, –tolerably, –respectably.

adj. **middling**, *comme ci comme ça* [*F.*], so-so, fair, fair to middling [*colloq.*], medium, moderate, mediocre, ordinary; second–, third–, fourth- rate.

adv. with nothing to brag about.

Division 2. Intersocial Volition

Section 1. General

737. Authority

n. **authority**; influence, patronage, power, preponderance, credit, prestige, prerogative, jurisdiction; right etc. (*title*) 924.

divine right, dynastic rights, authoritativeness; royalty, regality, imperiality [*rare*]; absoluteness, absolutism, despotism, tyranny; *jus nocendi* [*L.*]; *jus divinum* [*L.*].

command, empire, sway, rule; dominion, domination; sovereignty, supremacy, suzerainty; kinghood, kingship, lordship, headship, chiefdom; patriarchy, patriarchate; leadership, hegemony; seigniory; mastery, mastership, masterdom; government etc. (*direction*) 693; dictation, control.

hold, grasp; grip, gripe; reach; iron sway etc. (*severity*) 739; fangs, clutches, talons; rod of empire etc. (*scepter*) 747.

reign, *régime* [*F.*], dynasty; directorship, dictatorship; protectorate, protectorship; caliphate, pashalic, electorate; presidency, presidentship; administration; consulship, proconsulship; prefecture; seneschalship; magistrature, magistracy.

[governments] empire; monarchy; limited–, constitutional- monarchy; aristarchy, aristocracy; oligarchy, democracy, demagogy; heteronomy;

republic; thearchy; diarchy, duarchy, duumvirate; triarchy, triumvirate; heterarchy [*obs.*]; autocracy, monocracy.

representative government, constitutional government, *vox populi* [*L.*], home rule, dominion rule [*Brit.*], colonial government; self-government, autonomy, self-determination; republicanism, federalism; socialism; collectivism; pantisocracy; *imperium in imperio* [*L.*]; bureaucracy; beadledom, Bumbledom; stratocracy [*rare*], martial law; military -power, –government; feodality, feodatory, feudal system, feudalism.

gynocracy, gynarchy, gynecocracy, matriarchy, matriarchate, metrocracy; petticoat government.

[vicarious authority] commission etc. 755; deputy etc. 759; permission etc. 760.

state, realm, commonwealth, country, power, polity, body politic, *posse comitatus* [*L.*]; toparchy.

ruler; person in authority etc. (*master*) 745; judicature etc. 965; cabinet etc. (*council*) 696; seat of -government, –authority; headquarters.

usurper, tyrant, jack-in-office.

[acquisition of authority] accession; installation etc. 755; usurpation.

v. **authorize** etc. (*permit*) 760; warrant etc. (*right*) 924; dictate etc. (*order*) 741; have–, hold–, possess–, exercise–, exert–, grasp–, seize–, wrest–, wield- authority etc. *n.*

rule, sway, command, control, administer; govern etc. (*direct*) 693; lead, preside over, reign; possess–, be seated on–, occupy–, seize- the throne; sway–, wield- the scepter *or* sceptre; wear the crown.

be at the head of etc. *adj.;* hold–, be in–, fill an-office; hold–, occupy- a post; be master etc. 745.

dominate; have–, get- the -upper, –whip-hand; gain a hold upon, preponderate, dominate, rule the roast; boss [*colloq.*]; override, overrule, overawe; lord it over, hold in hand, keep under, make a puppet of, lead by the nose, turn round one's little finger, bend to one's will, hold one's own, wear the breeches [*colloq.*]; have the ball at one's feet, have it all one's own way, have the game in one's own hand, have on the hip, have under one's thumb; be master of the situation; take the lead, play first fiddle, set the fashion; give the law to; carry with a high hand; lay down the law; "ride in the whirlwind and direct the storm" [*adapted from* Addison]; rule with a rod of iron etc. (*severity*) 739.

assume authority etc. *n.;* ascend–, mount- the throne; take the reins, –into one's hand; assume the reins of government; take–, assume the- command.

be governed by, be in the power of; be under the -rule of, –dominion of.

adj. **ruling** etc. *v.;* regnant, at the head, dominant, paramount, supreme, predominant, preponderant, in the ascendant, influential; gubernatorial; imperious; authoritative, executive, administrative, clothed with authority, official, bureaucratic, departmental, *ex officio* [*L.*], imperative, peremptory, overruling, absolute; hegemonic *or* hegemonical; arbitrary; compulsory etc. 744; stringent.

at one's command; in one's power, in one's grasp; under control; authorized etc. (*due*) 924.

sovereign; regal, royal, royalist, monarchical, kingly; dynastic, imperial, imperialistic; princely; feudal; aristocratic, autocratic; oligarchic etc. *n.;* democratic, republican.

adv. in the name of, by the authority of, at one's command, *de par le Roi* [*F.*], in virtue of; under the auspices of, in the hands of.

at one's pleasure; by a dash (*or* stroke) of the pen; at one's nod; by lifting one's finger; *ex mero motu* [*L.*]; *ex cathedra* [*L.*].

738. Laxity
[absence of authority]

n. **laxity**; laxness, looseness, slackness; toleration etc. (*lenity*) 740; freedom etc. 748.

anarchy, interregnum; relaxation; loosening etc. *v.;* remission; dead letter, *brutum fulmen* [*L.*], misrule; license, licentiousness; insubordination etc. (*disobedience*) 742; mob rule, mob law, mobocracy, ochlocracy; lynch law etc. (*illegality*) 964, nihilism, reign of violence.

[deprivation of power] dethronement, impeachment, deposition, abdication; usurpation.

v. **be lax** etc. *adj.;* *laisser faire* [*F.*], *laisser aller* [*F.*]; hold a loose rein; give the reins to, give rope enough, give a loose to [*obs.*], give a free course to, give free rein to; tolerate; relax; misrule.

go beyond the length of one's tether; have one's -swing, –fling; act without -instructions, –authority; act on one's own responsibility, usurp authority, undermine the authority of.

dethrone, depose; abdicate.

adj. **lax**, loose; slack; remiss etc. (*careless*) 460; weak.

739. Severity

relaxed; licensed; reinless, unbridled; anarchic *or* anarchical, nihilistic; "agin the government"; unauthorized etc. (*unwarranted*) 925; adespotic, undespotic; not imperious etc. (*ruling*) 737.

739. Severity

n. **severity**; strictness, harshness etc. *adj.;* rigor, stringency, austerity; inclemency etc. (*pitilessness*) 914a; arrogance etc. 885; precisianism, formalism.

arbitrary power; absolutism, despotism; dictatorship, autocracy, tyranny, domineering, domination, oppression; assumption, usurpation; inquisition, reign of terror, martial law; iron -heel, –rule, –hand, –sway; tight grasp; brute -force, –strength; coercion etc. 744; strong–, tight- hand.

bureaucracy, red-tapism, pipe-clay, officialism; hard -lines, –measure; tender mercies [*ironical*]; sharp practice.

tyrant, disciplinarian, precisian, martinet, stickler, bashaw, despot, the Grand Panjandrum himself, hard master, Draco, oppressor, inquisitor, extortioner, harpy, vulture; Accipitres, Raptores, raptors [*obs.*], birds of prey.

v. **be severe** etc. *adj.*

arrogate, assume, usurp, take liberties; domineer, bully etc. 885; tyrannize; wrest the law to one's advantage; inflict, wreak, stretch a point, put on the screw; be hard upon; bear–, lay- a heavy hand on; be down upon [*slang*], come down upon [*colloq.*]; illtreat; deal hardly with, deal hard measure to; rule with a rod of iron, chastise with scorpions; dye with blood; oppress, override; trample–, tread- -down, –upon, –under foot; crush under an iron heel, ride roughshod over; rivet the yoke; hold–, keep- a tight hand; force down the throat; coerce etc. 744; give no quarter etc. (*pitiless*) 914a.

adj. **severe**; strict, hard, harsh, dour [*Scot.*], rigid, stiff, stern, rigorous, uncompromising, exacting, exigent, *exigeant* [*F.*], inexorable, inflexible, obdurate, austere, hard-headed, hard-shell [*colloq.*], relentless, Spartan, Draconian, stringent, strict, prudish, precise, puritanical, straitlaced, searching, unsparing, iron-handed, peremptory, absolute, positive, arbitrary, imperative; coercive etc. 744; tyrannical, extortionate, grinding, withering, oppressive, inquisitorial; inclement etc. (*ruthless*) 914a; cruel etc. (*malevolent*) 907; haughty, arrogant etc. 885; precisian, formal, punctilious.

adv. **severely** etc. *adj.;* with a -high, –strong, –tight, –heavy- hand.
at the point of the -sword, –bayonet.

740. Lenity

n. **lenity**, lenitence, lenitency; moderation etc. 174; tolerance, toleration; mildness, gentleness; favor; indulgence, indulgency [*rare*], clemence [*obs.*], clemency, mercy, forbearance, quarter; compassion etc. 914.

v. **be lenient** etc. *adj.;* tolerate, bear with; *parcere subjectis* [*L.*], spare the vanquished, give quarter.

indulge; allow one to -go his own gait, –have his own way, spoil.

adj. **lenient**; mild, –as milk; gentle, soft; tolerant, indulgent, easy, moderate, complaisant, unconcerned, easy-going; clement etc. (*compassionate*) 914; forbearing; long-suffering.

741. Command

n. **command**, order, ordinance, act, fiat, *hukm* [*Hind.*], bidding, dictum, hest, behest, call, beck, nod.

dispatch *or* despatch, message, direction, injunction, charge, instructions; appointment, fixture.

demand, exaction, imposition, requisition, claim, reclamation, revendication [*rare*]; ultimatum etc. (*terms*) 770; request etc. 765; requirement.

decree, dictate, dictation, mandate, caveat, *senatus consultum* [*L.*]; precept; prescript, rescript, writ, ordination, bull, edict, decretal, dispensation, prescription, brevet, placet, *placitum* [*L.*], ukase, firman, hatti-sherif, hatti-humayoun (*or* humayun), warrant, passport, mittimus, mandamus, summons, subpoena, *nisi prius* [*L.*], interpellation, citation; word, –of command; *mot d'ordre* [*F.*]; bugle–, trumpet-call; beat of drum, tattoo; order of the day; enactment etc. (*law*) 963; plebiscite etc. (*choice*) 609.

v. **command**, order, decree, enact, ordain, dictate, direct, give orders.

issue a command; make–, issue–, promulgate- -a requisition, –a decree, –an order etc. *n.;* give the -word of command, –word, –signal; call to order; give–, lay down- the law; assume the command etc. (*authority*) 737; remand.

prescribe, set, appoint, mark out; set–, prescribe–, impose- a task; set to work, put in requisition.

bid, enjoin, charge, call upon, instruct; require, –at the hands of; exact, impose, tax, task; demand; insist on etc. (*compel*) 744.

266

claim, lay claim to, revendicate [*rare*], reclaim.
cite, summon, avoke; call for, send for; subpoena; beckon.
be ordered etc.; receive an order etc. *n.*

adj. **commanding** etc. *v.;* authoritative etc. 737; decretory, decretive, decretal; callable; imperative, jussive; decisive, final, without appeal; interpellative, demanded, commanded etc. *v.*

adv. in a commanding tone; by a -stroke, –dash- of the pen; by order, at beat of drum, on the first summons, to order, at the word of command; by -command, –order, –decree- of; as required, as requested, as ordered, as commanded.

742. Disobedience

n. **disobedience**, insubordination, contumacy; infraction, infringement; violation, noncompliance; nonobservance etc. 773.

revolt, rebellion, mutiny, outbreak, rising, uprising, insurrection, *émeute* [*F.*], riot, tumult etc. (*disorder*) 59; strike etc. (*resistance*) 719; barring out; defiance etc. 715.

mutinousness etc. *adj.;* mutineering; sedition, treason; high–, petty–, misprison of- treason; *praemunire* or premunire; *lèse-majesté* [*F.*]; violation of law etc. 964; defection, secession, Sinn Fein; revolution; overthrow–, overturn- of -government, –authority; *sabotage* [*F.*], sansculottism, bolshevism.

insurgent, mutineer, rebel, revolter, rioter, traitor, *Carbonaro* [*It.*], sansculotte, red republican, *bonnet rouge* [*F.*], communist, Fenian, Sinn Feiner, Red, Bolshevist, *frondeur* [*F.*], seceder, Secessionist [*esp., U. S. hist.*] or Secesh [*colloq. or slang*]; apostate, renegade, runaway, runagate; brawler, anarchist, demagogue; Spartacus, Masaniello, Wat Tyler, Jack Cade; ringleader.

v. **disobey**, violate, infringe; shirk, slide out of, slack; set at defiance etc. (*defy*) 715; set authority at naught, run riot, fly in the face of; take the law into one's own hands; kick over the traces; refuse to support, bolt.

turn–, run- restive; champ the bit; strike etc. (*resist*) 719; rise, –in arms; secede; mutiny, rebel.

adj. **disobedient**; uncomplying, uncompliant; unsubmissive, unruly, ungovernable; breachy, insubordinate, impatient of control; restive, restiff [*obs.*], refractory, contumacious, recusant etc. (*refuse*) 764; recalcitrant; resisting etc. 719; lawless, riotous, mutinous, seditious, insurgent, revolutionary, sansculottic, secessionist.
unobeyed, disobeyed; unbidden.

743. Obedience

n. **obedience**; observance etc. 772; compliance; submission etc. 725; subjection etc. 749; nonresistance; passiveness, passivity, resignation.

allegiance, loyalty, fealty, homage, deference, devotion, constancy, fidelity.

submissiveness, submissness [*obs.*]; ductility etc. (*softness*) 324; obsequiousness etc. (*servility*) 886.

v. **be obedient** etc. *adj.;* obey, bear obedience to; submit etc. 725; comply, answer the helm, come at one's call; do one's bidding, do what one is told, do suit and service; attend to orders; serve -faithfully, –loyally, –devotedly, –without question; give -loyal, –devoted-service; be resigned to, be submissive to.

follow, –the lead of, –to the world's end; serve etc. 746; play second fiddle.

adj. **obedient**, law-abiding, complying, compliant; loyal, faithful, devoted; at one's -call, –command, –orders, –beck and call; under beck and call, under control.

restrainable; resigned, passive; submissive etc. 725; henpecked; pliant etc. (*soft*) 324.
unresisted, unresisting.

adv. **obediently** etc. *adj.;* as you please, if you please; in compliance with, in obedience to; at your -command, –orders, –service.

744. Compulsion

n. **compulsion**, coercion, coaction, constraint; restraint etc. 751; duress, enforcement, press, conscription; eminent domain.

force; brute–, main–, physical- force; the sword, *ultima ratio* [*L.*]; club–, lynch–, mob- law, *argumentum baculinum* [*L.*], *le droit du plus fort* [*F.*]; the force of -might, –right; martial law.

necessity etc. 601; *force majeure* [*F.*], spur of necessity, Hobson's choice.

v. **compel**, force, make, drive, coerce, constrain, enforce, necessitate, oblige.

force upon, press; cram–, thrust–, force- down the throat; say it must be done, make a point of, insist upon, take no denial; put down, dragoon.

extort, wring from; put–, turn- on the screw; drag into; bind, –over; pin–, tie- down; require, tax, put in force; commandeer; restrain etc. 751.

adj. **compelling** etc. *v.;* coercive, coactive; inexorable etc. 739; compulsory, compulsatory; obligatory, stringent, peremptory, binding.

forcible, not to be trifled with; irresistible etc. 601; compelled etc. *v.;* fain to.

adv. **forcibly**; by force etc. *n.*, by force of arms; on compulsion, perforce; *vi et armis* [*L.*], under the lash; at the point of the -sword, -bayonet; by a strong arm.

under protest, in spite of, in one's teeth; against one's will etc. 603; *nolens volens* [*L.*] etc. (*of necessity*) 601; by stress of -circumstances, -weather; under press of; *de rigueur* [*F.*].

745. Master

n. **master**, *padrone* [*It.*], lord, -paramount; commander, commandant, captain, chief, chieftain; paterfamilias [*Rom. law*], patriarch; sahib [*India*], bara (or burra) sahib [*India*], sirdar, sheik; head, senior, governor, ruler, dictator; leader etc. (*director*) 694; boss, baas [*Dutch*]; cockarouse [*obs.*], sachem, sagamore, werowance.

lord of the ascendant; cock of the -walk, -loft, -midden [*archaic*], -roost; gray mare; mistress.

potentate; liege, -lord; suzerain, overlord, overking, sovereign, monarch, autocrat, despot, tyrant, oligarch; boss of bosses [*slang*], godfather [*slang*].

crowned head, emperor, king, anointed king, majesty, imperator, protector, president, stadholder *or* stadtholder, judge.

caesar, kaiser, czar *or* tsar, sultan, soldan [*obs.*], grand Turk, caliph, imam *or* imaum, shah, padishah, sophi, mogul, great mogul, khan, lama, pendragon, tycoon, mikado, inca, cazique; voivode *or* waywode, hospodar, landamman; sayid *or* sayyid, cacique, czarevitch, grand seignior.

prince, duke etc. (*nobility*) 875; archduke, doge, elector; seignior; landgrave, margrave; maharajah, rajah, emir, nizam, nawab etc. (*Indian ruling chiefs*) 875.

empress, queen, sultana, czarina *or* tsarina, princess, infanta, duchess, margravine; czarevna *or* tsarevna, czarina; maharani, rani [*both Hindu*], begum [*Moham.*]; rectoress *or* rectress, rectrix.

regent, viceroy, exarch, palatine, khedive, beglerbeg *or* beylerbey, three-tailed bashaw, pasha *or* bashaw, bey *or* beg, dey, shereef *or* sherif, tetrarch, satrap, mandarin, nabob, burgrave; laird etc. (*proprietor*) 779; commissioner, deputy commissioner, collector, woon *or* wun [*Burmese*].

the authorities, the powers that be, the government, "them above" [Eliot]; staff, *état major* [*F.*], aga, official, man in office, person in authority; sirkar *or* sircar; Sublime Porte.

[military authorities] marshal, field marshal, *maréchal* [*F.*], generalissimo; commander-in-chief, seraskier [*Turk.*], hetman [*Cossack*]; general, brigadier general, brigadier, lieutenant general, major general, colonel, lieutenant colonel, major, captain, ressaldar *or* risaldar [*India*], subahdar *or* subadar [*India*]; centurion, lieutenant, jemadar [*India*], sublieutenant, officer, staff officer, aide-de-camp, brigade major, adjutant, ensign, cornet, cadet, subaltern; non-commissioned officer; sergeant, -major; color sergeant; top-sergeant [*U.S.*], havildar [*India*]; corporal, -major; lance corporal, acting corporal; naik [*India*]; drum major; captain general, knight marshal.

[**civil authorities**] mayor, mayoralty; *maire* [*F.*], prefect, chancellor, archon [*Gr.*], provost, magistrate, syndic; alcalde [*Sp.*], alcaide *or* alcaid; burgomaster, *corregidor* [*Sp.*], seneschal, alderman, warden, constable, portreeve; lord mayor; officer etc. (*executive*) 965; diwan *or* dewan [*India*]; hakim; *fonctionnaire* [*F.*].

[naval authorities] admiral, admiralty; rear-, vice-, port- admiral; commodore, captain, commander, lieutenant; skipper, master, mate, navarch [*Gr. antiq.*].

746. Servant

n. **servant**, retainer, follower, henchman, servitor, domestic, menial, help, lady help [*Brit.*], employee *or* employé; *attaché* [*F.*], official.

subject, liege, liegeman; people, "my people."

retinue, suite, *cortège* [*F.*], staff, court; office force, clerical staff, clerical force, workers, associate workers, employees, the help.

attendant, squire, usher, donzel [*obs.*], apprentice, prentice [*colloq. or dial.*]; page, buttons [*colloq.*], footboy; trainbearer, cupbearer; waiter, tapster, butler, livery servant, lackey, footman, flunky *or* flunkey [*colloq.*]; bearer [*Anglo-Ind.*], boy; hamal [*India*], scout [*Oxford Univ.*], gyp [*Camb. Univ.*], valet, *valet de chambre* [*F.*]; equerry, groom; jockey, hostler *or* ostler, orderly, messenger, gillie *or* gilly, caddie *or* caddy, herdsman, swineherd; barkeeper, bartender, barkeep; boots [*Brit.*]; cad [*Eng. Univ. cant*], bell boy, bellhop [*slang*], tiger, chokra [*India*], boy; counterjumper [*colloq.*]; khansamah *or* khansaman [*India*], khitmutgar [*India*]; yardman, journeyman.

bailiff, castellan *or* castellain, seneschal, chamberlain, major-domo, groom of the chambers.

secretary; under-, assistant- secretary; stenographer, clerk; subsidiary; agent etc. 758; subaltern; underling, understrapper; man.

maid, maidservant; girl, help, handmaid; confidant (*fem.* confidante), *confident* (*fem. confidente*) [*F.*]; lady's maid, abigail, soubrette, amah [*Oriental*], biddy [*colloq.*], *bonne* [*F.*], ayah [*India*]; nurse–, nursery–, house–, parlor–, waiting–, chamber–, kitchen–, scullery-maid; *femme –, fille- de chambre* [*F.*]; *chef de cuisine* [*F.*], *cordon bleu* [*F.*], chef, cook, scullion, Cinderella; pot-walloper; maid–, servant-of all work; slavey [*slang, Eng.*], general servant [*Brit.*], general housework maid, general [*colloq.*]; washerwoman, laundress, bedmaker; charwoman etc. (*worker*) 690.

dependent or dependant, hanger-on, led friend [*obs.*], satellite; parasite etc. (*servility*) 886; led captain; *protégé* [*F.*], ward, hireling, mercenary, puppet, man of straw, creature; serf, vassal, slave, negro, helot; bondsman, bondswoman, bondslave; *âme damnée* [*F.*], odalisque or odalisk, ryot, *adscriptus gleboe* [*L.*], villein or villain [*hist.*], churl or ceorl [*hist.*]; beadsman or bedesman; sizar or sizer [*Camb. & Dublin Univs.*], pensioner, pensionary; client.

badge of slavery; bonds etc. 752.

v. **serve**, minister to, help, coöperate; wait–, attend–, dance attendance–, fasten oneself–, pin oneself- upon; squire, valet, tend, hang on the sleeve of; chore [*dial.*], do the chores [*colloq.*], char [*dial. Eng.*], do for [*colloq.*], fag.

adj. **serviceable**, useful, helpful; cooperative.

serving etc. *v.*; in the train of; in one's -pay, –employ; at one's call etc. (*obedient*) 743; in bonds.

servile, slavish, vernile [*rare*]; subject, thrall, bond; subservient, obsequious, base, fawning, truckling, sycophantic or sycophantical, sycophantish [*rare*], parasitic, cringing.

747. Scepter
[insignia of authority]

n. [**regal**] scepter or sceptre, rod of empire; orb; pall; robes of -state, -royalty; ermine, purple; crown, coronet, diadem, cap of maintenance; triple plume, Prince of Wales's feathers; uraeus, flail [*both Egyptian*]; signet, seal.

[ecclesiastical] tiara, triple crown; ring, keys; miter or mitre, crozier, crook, staff; cardinal's hat; bishop's -apron, –sleeves, –lawn, –gaiters, –shovel hat; fillet.

[military] epaulet or epaulette, star, bar, eagle, crown [*Brit.*], oak leaf, Sam Browne belt; chevron, stripe.

caduceus; Mercury's -staff, –rod, –wand; mace, fasces, ax or axe, truncheon, staff, baton, wand, rod; staff–, rod- -of office, –of authority; insignia–, ensign–, emblem–, badge- of authority; flag etc. (*insignia*) 550; regalia; toga, mantle, decoration; title etc. 877; portfolio.

throne, Peacock throne [*Chinese*], musnud or masnad [*Ar.*]; raj-gaddi, gaddi or guddee [*India*], divan; wool-sack, chair; dais etc. (*seat*) 215.

talisman, amulet, charm, sign.

helm; reins etc. (*means of restraint*) 752.

748. Freedom

n. **freedom**, liberty, independence; license etc. (*permission*) 760; eleutherism [*rare*]; facility etc. 705.

scope, range, latitude, play; free–, full- -play, -scope; free field and no favor; swing, full swing, elbowroom, margin, rope, wide berth; Liberty Hall.

franchise, denization; prerogative etc. (*dueness*) 924.

freeman, freedman, liveryman [*London guilds*], citizen, denizen.

immunity, exemption; emancipation etc. (*liberation*) 750; affranchisement, enfranchisement; right, privilege.

autonomy, self-government, liberalism, free trade; self-determination; noninterference etc. 706; Monroe Doctrine.

free land, freehold; alod or allod, alodium or allodium; frankalmoign or frankalmoigne [*Eng. law*], tenure in (or by) free alms [*Eng. law*]; dead hand, mortmain [*law*].

independent, free lance, freethinker, free trader or freetrader; bushwhacker.

v. **be free** etc. *adj.*; have -scope etc. *n.*, - the run of, –one's own way, –a will of one's own, –one's fling; do what one -likes, –wishes, –pleases, –chooses; go at large, feel at home, paddle one's own canoe; stand on one's rights; stand on one's own legs; shift for oneself.

take a liberty; make free with, make oneself quite at home; use a freedom; take leave, take French leave.

free, liberate, set free etc. 750; give the reins to etc. (*permit*) 760; allow–, give -scope etc. *n.* to; give a horse his head.

make free of; give the -freedom of, –franchise; enfranchise, affranchise.

laisser faire [*F.*], *laisser aller* [*F.*]; live and let live; leave to oneself; leave or let alone, mind one's own business.

adj. **free**, –as air; out of harness, independent, at large, loose, scot-free; left -alone, –to oneself.

unconstrained, unbuttoned, unconfined, unrestrained, unchecked, unprevented, unhindered,

749. Subjection

unobstructed, unbound, uncontrolled, untrammeled, uncaught; in full swing.

unsubject, ungoverned, unenslaved, unenthralled, unchained, unshackled, unfettered, unreined, unbridled, uncurbed, unmuzzled, unvanquished.

unrestricted, unlimited, unconditional; absolute; with unlimited -power, –opportunity; discretionary etc. (*optional*) 600.

unassailed, unforced, uncompelled.

unbiased, unprejudiced, uninfluenced; spontaneous.

free and easy; at–, at one's– ease; *dégagé* [*F.*], quite at home; beyond all bounds; wanton, rampant, irrepressible.

exempt; freed etc. 750; freeborn; autonomous, freehold, alodial *or* allodial; eleutherian [*rare*].

gratuitous, gratis etc. 815; for nothing, for love.

unclaimed, going a-begging.

adv. freely etc. *adj.*; ad libitum [*L.*] etc. (*at will*) 600; with no restraint etc. 751.

749. Subjection

n. **subjection**; dependence, dependency; subordination; thrall, thralldom *or* thraldom, enthrallment *or* enthralment, subjugation, bondage, serfdom; feudalism, feudality; vassalage, villenage *or* villeinage, slavery, enslavement, involuntary servitude; conquest.

service; servitude, servitorship; tendence, employ, tutelage, clientship; liability etc. 177; constraint etc. 751; oppression etc. (*severity*) 739; yoke etc. (*means of restraint*) 752; submission etc. 725; obedience etc. 743.

v. **be subject** etc. *adj.*; be *or* lie at the mercy of; depend–, lean–, hang– upon; fall a prey to, fall under; play second fiddle.

be a -mere machine, –puppet, –doormat, –football; not dare to say one's soul is his own; drag a chain.

serve etc. 746; obey etc. 743; submit etc. 725.

subjugate, subject, tame, break in; master etc. 731; tread -down, –under foot; weigh down; drag at one's chariot wheel; reduce to -subjection, –slavery; enthrall *or* enthral, inthrall *or* inthral, bethrall, enslave, lead captive; take into custody etc. (*restrain*) 751; rule etc. 737; drive into a corner, hold at the sword's point; keep under; hold in -bondage, –leading strings, –swaddling clothes; have at one's -apron strings, –beck and call; have in one's pocket.

adj. **subject**, dependent, subordinate; feudal, feudatory; in subjection to, servitorial [*rare*], under control; in leading strings, in harness; subjected, thrall [*archaic*]; servile, slavish etc. 746; enslaved etc. *v.;* constrained etc. 751; downtrodden; overborne; overwhelmed; under the lash, on the hip, led by the nose, henpecked; the -puppet, –sport, –plaything- of; under one's -orders, –command, –thumb; used as a doormat, treated like dirt under one's feet; a slave to; at the mercy of; in the -power, –hands, –clutches- of; at the feet of; in one's pocket; tied to one's apron strings; uxorious; at one's beck and call etc. (*obedient*) 743; liable etc. 177; parasitical; stipendiary.

adv. **under**; under -orders, –the heel, –command; at one's orders; with no -mind, –will, –soul- of one's own.

750. Liberation

n. **liberation**, disengagement, release, enlargement, emancipation, disenthrallment *or* disenthralment, Emancipation Proclamation; affranchisement, enfranchisement; manumission; discharge, dismissal.

deliverance etc. 672; redemption, extrication, acquittance, absolution; acquittal etc. 970; escape etc. 671.

v. **liberate**, free; set free, set at liberty; render free, emancipate, release; enfranchise, affranchise; manumit; enlarge; demobilize, disband, discharge, disenthrall *or* disenthral, disinthrall *or* disinthral, dismiss; let go, let loose, let out, let slip; cast–, turn– adrift; deliver etc. 672; absolve etc. (*acquit*) 970.

unfetter etc. 751, untie etc. 43; loose etc. (*disjoin*) 44; loosen, relax; unbolt, unbar, unclose, uncork, unclog, unhand, unbind, unchain, unharness; disengage, disentangle; clear, extricate, unloose; reprieve.

become free; gain–, obtain–, acquire- one's -liberty etc. 748; get rid of, get clear of; deliver oneself from; shake off the yoke, slip the collar; break loose, break prison; tear asunder one's bonds, cast off trammels; escape etc. 671.

adj. **liberated** etc. *v.;* out of harness etc. (*free*) 748; foot-loose; breathing free air again; one's own master again.

adv. **at large**, at liberty; adrift.

int. unhand me! let me go! reprieve! go in peace! free!

751. Restraint

n. **restraint**; hindrance etc. 706; coercion etc. (*compulsion*) 744; cohibition [*rare*], constraint, repression; discipline, control.

limitation, restriction, protection, monopoly; prohibition etc. 761; economic pressure.

confinement, restringency [*obs.*], durance, duress; imprisonment; incarceration, coarctation [*obs.*], entombment, mancipation [*obs.*], thrall; thralldom etc. (*subjection*) 749; durance vile, limbo, captivity; blockade; detention camp; quarantine station.

arrest, arrestation [*rare*], arrestment, custody.

keep, care, charge, ward.

curb etc. (*means of restraint*) 752; *lettres de cachet* [*F.*].

repressionist, monopolist, protectionist.

prisoner etc. 754.

v. **restrain**, check; put–, lay- under restraint, put under arrest; enthrall *or* enthral, inthrall *or* inthral, bethrall *or* bethral; restrict; debar etc. (*hinder*) 706; constrain; coerce etc. (*compel*) 744; curb, control; hold–, keep- back, –from, –in, –in check, –within bounds; hold in -leash, –leading strings; withhold.

repress, suppress; keep under; smother; pull in, rein in; hold, –fast; keep a tight hand on; prohibit etc. 761; inhibit, cohibit.

fasten etc. (*join*) 43; enchain, fetter, shackle; entrammel, trammel; bridle, muzzle, hopple, gag, pinion, manacle, handcuff, tie one's hands, hobble, bind, bind hand and foot; swathe, swaddle; pin down, tether, picket; tie, –up, –down; peg -out, –down; keep [*archaic*], secure; forge fetters.

confine; shut -up, –in; clap up, lock up, box up, mew up, bottle up, cork up, seal up, button up; hem in, bolt in, wall in, rail in; impound, pen, coop; inclose etc. (*circumscribe*) 229; cage; incage *or* encage; close the door upon, cloister; imprison, jug [*slang*], immure; incarcerate, entomb; clap–, lay- under hatches; put in -irons, –a strait-waistcoat; throw–, cast- into prison; put into bilboes.

arrest; take -up, –charge of, –into custody; restringe [*rare*], cohibit [*rare*]; take–, make- -prisoner, –captive; captivate [*rare*]; lead -captive, –into captivity; send–, commit-to prison; commit; give in -charge, –custody; subjugate etc. 749.

adj. **restrained**, constrained; imprisoned etc. *v.;* pent up; jammed in, packed in, wedged in; under -restraint, –lock and key, –hatches; in swaddling clothes; on parole; serving–, doing- time [*colloq. or slang*]; in irons, in the guardhouse; in custody etc. (*prisoner*) 754; cohibitive [*rare*]; mancipatory [*Rom. law*]; coactive etc. (*compulsory*) 744.

icebound, windbound, weatherbound; "cabined, cribbed, confined" [*Macbeth*]; in lob's pound, laid by the heels.

stiff, restringent [*obs.*], narrow, prudish, straitlaced, hidebound, barkbound.

adv. **under restraint**, under discipline; in prison, in jail, in durance vile, in confinement; behind bars; in captivity, during captivity; under arrest; under prohibition; within limits, within bounds.

752. Prison
[means of restraint]

n. **prison**, prisonhouse; jail *or* gaol, cage, coop, den, cell; stronghold, fortress, keep, donjon, dungeon, Bastille, oubliette [*F.*], bridewell [*Eng.*], jug [*slang*], house of correction, hulks, tollbooth, panopticon, penitentiary, state prison, guardroom, lockup, roundhouse [*archaic*], watch-house [*obs. or Scot.*], station house, station [*colloq.*], sponging house; house of detention, poky [*slang*], black hole, pen [*also slang for penitentiary*], fold, pinfold *or* penfold, pound; inclosure etc. 232; penal settlement; bilboes, stocks, limbo *or* limbus, quod [*slang*]; hoosegow [*slang*], calaboose [*local*], choky *or* chokey [*Anglo-Ind. or slang, Eng.*]; chauki, thana [*both India*]; workhouse [*U.S.; in England, a workhouse is a poorhouse*], reformatory, reform school; debtor's prison, college [*slang, Eng.*].

Tower, Newgate, Fleet, Marshalsea; King's (*or* Queen's) Bench; Alcatraz, Sing Sing, the Tombs.

[restraining devices] shackle, bond, gyve, fetter, trammel, irons, pinion, manacle, handcuff, strait-waistcoat, hopples; vise *or* vice; bandage, splint, strap.

yoke, collar, halter, harness; muzzle, gag, bit, curb, snaffle, bridle; rein, reins; bearing rein; martingale; leading string; tether, picket, band, guy, chain; cord etc. (*fastening*) 45; cavesson, hackamore [*Western U.S.*], jaquima [*S. W. U. S.*], headstall, lines [*U.S. & dial. Eng.*], ribbons [*colloq.*]; brake.

bar, bolt, lock, padlock; rail, paling, palisade; wall, fence, barrier, barricade.

drag etc. (*hindrance*) 706.

adj. imprisoned etc. (*restrained*) 751.

753. Keeper

n. **keeper**, custodian, *custos* [*L.*], ranger, gamekeeper, warder, jailer *or* gaoler, turnkey, castellan, guard; watch, watchdog, watchman, night watchman, Charley *or* Charlie [*Brit.*]; chokidar

271

754. Prisoner

[Anglo-Ind.], durwan [Anglo-Ind.], hayward; sentry, sentinel, watch and ward; *concierge* [F.], coastguard.
escort, bodyguard; convoy.
guardian, protector, governor, duenna; governess etc. (*teacher*) 540; nurse, *bonne* [F.], amah [*Oriental*], ayah [*India*].

754. Prisoner

n. **prisoner**, convict, captive, *détenu* [F.], collegian [*slang*], close prisoner.
jailbird *or* gaolbird, ticket-of-leave man [*Brit.*], *chevronné* [F.].

v. stand committed, be imprisoned etc. 751.

adj. **imprisoned** etc. 751; in prison, in quod [*slang*], in durance vile, in limbo, in custody, in charge, in chains; behind bars; under lock and key, under hatches.
on parole.

755. Commission
[vicarious authority]

n. **commission**, delegation; consignment, assignment; proxy, power of attorney, procuration; deputation, legation, mission, embassy; agency, agentship; clerkship.
errand, charge, brevet, diploma, exequatur, permit etc. (*permission*) 760.
appointment, nomination, return; charter; ordination; installation, inauguration, investiture; accession, coronation, enthronement.
regency, regentship; vicegerency.
viceroy etc. 745; consignee etc. 758; deputy etc. 759.

v. **commission**, delegate, depute; consign, assign; charge; intrust *or* entrust; commit, –to the hands of; authorize etc. (*permit*) 760.
put in commission, accredit, engage, hire, bespeak, appoint, name, nominate, return, ordain; install, induct, inaugurate, invest, crown; enroll, enlist; give power of attorney to; employ, empower; set–, place- over; send out.
be commissioned, be accredited; represent, stand for; stand in the -stead, –place, –shoes- of.

adj. commissioned etc. *v.*

adv. **instead of**; in one's -stead, –place; as proxy for; *per procurationem* [L.], *in loco parentis* [L.].

756. Abrogation

n. **abrogation**, annulment, nullification; *vacatur* [L.]; *nolle prosequi* [L., *law*]; canceling etc. *v.*; cancel; revocation, revokement; repeal, rescission, defeasance.
dismissal, *congé* [F.], demission [*obs.*]; bounce [*slang*]; deposal, deposition; dethronement; disestablishment, disendowment; secularization, deconsecration; sack [*slang*], walking-papers, walking-ticket [*both colloq.*], yellow cover [*slang*].
abolition, abolishment; dissolution.
counterorder, countermand; repudiation, retractation; recantation etc. (*tergiversation*) 607.
abolitionist, prohibitionist.

v. **abrogate**, annul, cancel; destroy etc. 162; abolish; revoke, repeal, rescind, reverse, retract, recall; overrule, override; set aside; disannul, dissolve, quash, nullify, make void, nol-pros [*law*], declare null and void; disestablish, disendow; deconsecrate.
countermand, counterorder; do away with; sweep–, brush- away; throw overboard, throw to the dogs; scatter to the winds, cast behind.
disclaim etc. (*deny*) 536; ignore, repudiate; recant etc. 607; divest oneself, break off.
dismiss, discard; cast–, turn- off, –out, –adrift, –out of doors, –aside, –away; send off, send away, send about one's business; discharge, get rid of etc. (*eject*) 297; bounce [*slang*]; fire, fire out, sack [*all slang*].
cashier; break; oust; unseat, unsaddle; unthrone, dethrone, disenthrone, depose, uncrown; unfrock, strike off the roll; disbar, disbench.
be abrogated etc.; receive its quietus.

adj. **abrogated** etc. *v.; functus officio* [L.].

int. get along with you! begone! go about your business! away with!

757. Resignation

n. **resignation**, retirement, abdication; renunciation, retractation, retraction, renunciance [*rare*], disclamation, disclaimer, abjuration; abandonment, relinquishment.

v. **resign**; give up, throw up; lay down, throw up the cards, wash one's hands of, abjure, renounce, forego, disclaim, retract; deny etc. 536.
abrogate etc. 756; desert etc. (*relinquish*) 624; get rid of etc. 782.
vacate, –one's seat; abdicate; accept the stewardship of the Chiltern Hundreds [*Eng.*]; retire; tender–, pass in–, hand in- one's resignation.

adj. **abdicant**; resigning etc. *v.;* renunciatory, renunciant [*rare*], abjuratory, disclamatory [*rare*], retractive.

758. Consignee

n. **consignee**, trustee, nominee; committee.
functionary, placeman, curator; treasurer etc. 801; agent, factor, reeve [*Eng. hist.*], steward, gomashta [*India*], bailiff, clerk, secretary, attorney, solicitor, proctor, broker, dalal

[*India*], dubash [*India*]; insurer, underwriter, commission agent, auctioneer, one's man of business; factotum etc. (*director*) 694; caretaker; garnishee; under agent, employé; servant etc. 746.

negotiator, go-between; middleman; shop steward *and* walking delegate [*labor unions*].

delegate; commissary, commissioner; emissary, envoy, commissionaire; messenger etc. 534.

diplomatist, diplomat *or* diplomate, *corps diplomatique* [*F.*], embassy; ambassador *or* embassador, diplomatic agent, representative, resident, consul, legate, nuncio, internuncio, *chargé d'affaires* [*F.*], *attaché* [*F.*]; vicegerent etc. (*deputy*) 759; plenipotentiary.

salesman, traveler, bagman, *commis voyageur* [*F.*], traveling salesman, commercial traveler, drummer [*U. S.*], traveling man; agent for (firm *or* commodity); touter [*colloq.*], barker [*colloq*].

reporter; newspaper–, own–, foreign–, war–, special- correspondent.

759. Deputy

n. **deputy**, substitute, proxy, *locum tenens* [*L.*], *badli* [*Hind.*], delegate, representative, next friend [*law*], pinch hitter [*cant*], *prochein ami* [*F. law*], surrogate, secondary; vice-president, vice-chairman, vice [*colloq.*].

regent, vicegerent, vizier, minister, vicar; premier etc. (*director*) 694; chancellor, prefect, provost, warden, lieutenant, archon [*antiq.*], consul, proconsul [*Rom. antiq.*]; viceroy etc. (*governor*) 745; ambassador; commissioner etc. 758; plenipotentiary, plenipotent; *alter ego* [*L.*].

team, eight, nine, eleven; captain, champion.

v. **be deputy** etc. *n.;* stand–, appear–, hold a brief–, answer- for; represent; stand–, walk- in the shoes of; stand in the stead of.

delegate, depute, empower, commission, substitute, ablegate [*R. C. Ch.*], accredit.

adj. **acting**; vice, viceregal; accredited to; delegated etc. *v.;* representative, plenipotent [*rare*], consular, proconsular.

adv. **in behalf of**, in the place of, as representing, by proxy.

Section 2. Special

760. Permission

n. **permission**, leave; allowance, sufferance; tolerance, toleration; liberty, law, license, concession, grace; indulgence etc. (*lenity*) 740; favor, dispensation, exemption, release; connivance; vouchsafement.

authorization, warranty [*law*], accordance, admission.

permit, warrant, brevet, precept, sanction, authority, firman; *hukm* [*Hind.*]; pass, passport; furlough, license, *carte blanche* [*F.*], ticket of leave; grant, charter, patent.

v. **permit**; give permission etc. *n.,* give power; let, allow, admit; suffer, bear with, tolerate, recognize; concede etc. 762; accord, vouchsafe, favor, humor, gratify, indulge, stretch a point; wink at, connive at; shut one's eyes to.

grant, empower, charter, enfranchise, privilege, confer a privilege, license, authorize, warrant; sanction; intrust etc. (*commission*) 755.

give *carte blanche* [*F.*], give the reins to, give scope to etc. (*freedom*) 748; leave -alone, –it to one, –the door open; open the -door to, –floodgates; give a loose to [*obs.*].

ask–, beg–, crave–, request- -leave, –permission.

let off; absolve etc. (*acquit*) 970; release, exonerate, dispense with.

adj. **permitting** etc. *v.;* permissive, indulgent.

permitted etc. *v.;* patent, chartered, permissible, allowable, lawful, legitimate, legal; legalized etc. (*law*) 963; licit; unforbid [*archaic*], unforbidden; unconditional.

adv. **permissibly**, licitly; by–, with–, on- leave etc. *n.; speciali gratia* [*L.*]; under favor of; *pace* [*L.*]; *ad libitum* [*L.*] etc. (*freely*) 748, (*at will*) 600; by all means etc. (*willingly*) 602; yes etc. (*assent*) 488.

761. Prohibition

n. **prohibition**, inhibition; veto, disallowance; interdict, interdiction; injunction; embargo, ban, taboo *or* tabu, proscription; *index expurgatorius* [*L.*], restriction etc. (*restraint*) 751; hindrance etc. 706; forbidden fruit; Maine law, Volstead Act, 18th amendment.

v. prohibit, inhibit; forbid, put one's veto upon, disallow; bar; debar etc. (*hinder*) 706, forfend *or* forefend [*archaic*].

restrain etc. 751; keep -in, –within bounds; cohibit [*rare*], withhold, limit, circumscribe, clip the wings of, restrict; interdict, taboo *or* tabu; put–, place- under -an interdiction, –the ban; proscribe; exclude, shut out; shut–, bolt–, show- the door; warn off; dash the cup from one's lips; forbid the banns.

adj. **prohibitive**, prohibitory; proscriptive; restrictive, exclusive; forbidding etc. *v.*

prohibited etc. *v.;* not permitted etc. 760; unlicensed, contraband, under the ban of, taboo

762. Consent

or tabu; illegal etc. 964; unauthorized, not to be thought of.

adv. on no account etc. (*no*) 536.

int. forbid it heaven! heaven forbid! etc. (*deprecation*) 766.

hands off! keep off! hold! stop! avast!

762. Consent

n. **consent**; assent etc. 488; acquiescence; approval etc. 931; compliance, agreement, concession; yieldance [*obs.*], yieldingness; accession, acknowledgment, acceptance, agnition [*obs.*].

settlement, adjustment, ratification, confirmation. permit etc. (*permission*) 760; promise etc. 768.

v. **consent**; assent etc. 488; yield assent, admit, allow, concede, grant, yield; come over, come round; give into, acknowledge, agnize [*archaic*], give consent, comply with, acquiesce, agree to, fall in with, accede, accept, embrace an offer, close with, take at one's word, have no objection.

satisfy, meet one's wishes, settle, come to terms etc. 488; not refuse etc. 764; turn a willing ear etc. (*willingness*) 602; jump at; deign, vouchsafe; promise etc. 768.

adj. **consenting** etc. *v.;* complaint, agreeable [*colloq.*], willing, eager; agreed etc. (*assent*) 488; unconditional.

adv. **yes** etc. (*assent*) 488; by all means etc. (*willingly*) 602; if you please, as you please; be it so, so be it, well and good, of course.

763. Offer

n. **offer**, proffer, presentation, tender, bid, overture; proposal, proposition; motion, invitation; candidature, candidacy; offering etc. (*gift*) 784.

v. **offer**, proffer, present, tender; bid; propose, move; make a motion, make advances; start; invite, hold out, place in one's way; put–, place- at one's disposal; put in one's power, make possible, put forward.

hawk about; offer for sale etc. 796; press etc. (*request*) 765; go a-begging; lay at one's feet.

volunteer, come forward, be a candidate; offer–, present- oneself; stand for, bid for; seek; be at one's service.

bribe etc. (*give*) 784; grease the palm [*slang*].

adj. **offering**, offered etc. *v.;* in the market, for sale, to let, disengaged, on hire; at one's disposal.

764. Refusal

n. **refusal**, rejection; noncompliance, incompliance; denial; declining etc. *v.;* declension; declinature; peremptory–, flat–, point blank- refusal; repulse, rebuff; discountenance, disapprobation.

negation, recusancy, abnegation, protest, disclamation, renunciation, disclaimer; dissent etc. 489; revocation etc. 756.

v. **refuse**, reject, deny, decline; nill [*archaic*], turn down [*slang*], abnegate, negate, negative; refuse–, withhold- one's assent; shake the head; close the -hand, –purse; grudge, begrudge, be slow to, hang fire; pass [*at cards*].

stand aloof, be deaf to; turn a deaf ear to, turn one's back upon; set one's face against, discountenance, not hear of, have nothing to do with, wash one's hands of, forswear, set aside, cast behind one; not yield an inch etc. (*obstinacy*) 606.

resist, cross; not grant etc. 762; repel, repulse; shut–, slam- the door in one's face; rebuff; send -back, –to the right about, –away with a flea in the ear [*colloq.*]; deny oneself, not be at home to; discard etc. (*repudiate*) 610; rescind etc. (*revoke*) 756; disclaim, protest; dissent etc. 489.

adj. **refusing** etc. *v.;* restive, restiff [*obs.*]; recusant; uncomplying, noncompliant, incompliant, unconsenting; declinatory, uncomplaisant, disclamatory [*rare*], negatory, protestant; not willing to hear of, deaf to.

refused etc. *v.;* ungranted, out of the question, not to be thought of, impossible.

adv. **no** etc. 536; on no account, not for the world; no thank you; your humble servant [*ironically*], *bien obligé* [*F.*], not on your life!

765. Request

n. **request**, requisition; claim etc. (*demand*) 741; petition, suit, prayer, begging letter, round robin.

motion, overture, application, canvass, address, appeal, apostrophe; imprecation; rogation [*eccl.*]; proposal, proposition.

orison etc. (*worship*) 990; incantation etc. (*spell*) 993.

mendicancy, mendication [*rare*]; asking, begging etc. *v.;* postulation, solicitation, invitation, entreaty, importunity, supplication, instance, impetration, imploration, obsecration, obtestation, invocation, interpellation.

v. **request**, ask, beg, crave, sue, pray, petition, solicit, invite, pop the question [*colloq.*], make bold to ask; beg leave, beg a boon; apply to, call to, put to; call upon, call for; make–, address–, prefer–, put up- a -request, –prayer, –petition; make -application, –a requisition; ask–, trouble- one for; claim etc. (*demand*) 741;

274

offer up prayers etc. (*worship*) 990; whistle for [*colloq.*].

bespeak, canvass, tout [*cant, Eng.*], make interest, court; seek, bid for etc. (*offer*) 763; publish the banns.

entreat, beseech, plead, supplicate, beg hard, implore; conjure, adjure; obsecrate [*rare*], apostrophize, obtest [*rare*]; cry to, kneel to, appeal to; invoke, evoke; impetrate, imprecate, ply, press, urge, beset, importune, dun, tax, clamor for; cry aloud, cry for help; fall on one's knees; throw oneself at the feet of; come down on one's marrowbones [*slang or humorous*].

beg from door to door, send the hat round, go a-begging; mendicate [*rare*], mump, cadge [*dial. or slang, Eng.*], beg one's bread.

dance attendance on, besiege, knock at the door.

adj. **requesting** etc. *v.*, precatory, supplant, supplicant, supplicatory, invocative, invocatory, invitatory, imprecatory, rogatory; postulatory [*rare*], postulant; obsecratory [*rare*], obsecrationary [*rare*]; imploratory [*rare*], mendicant, mendicatory [*obs.*].

importunate, clamorous, urgent, solicitous; cap in hand; on one's -knees, -bended knees, -marrowbones [*slang or humorous*].

adv. **please**, prithee, do, pray; be so good as, be good enough; have the goodness, vouchsafe, will you, I pray thee, if you please.

int. for- God's, –heaven's - goodness', –mercy's- sake! we beseech thee to hear us! help! save me!

766. Deprecation
[negative request]

n. **deprecation**, expostulation; intercession, mediation, protest, remonstrance.

v. **deprecate**, protest, expostulate, enter a protest, intercede for; remonstrate.

adj. **deprecatory**, expostulatory, intercessory, mediatorial.

deprecated, protested.

unsought, unbesought; unasked etc. (*see ask etc.* 765).

Int. **God forbid**! cry you mercy! forbid it Heaven! Heaven forfend (*or* forefend)! Heaven forbid! far be it from! hands off! etc. (*prohibition*) 761.

767. Petitioner

n. **petitioner**, solicitor, applicant, suppliant, supplicant, suitor, candidate, claimant, postulant, aspirant, competitor, bidder; place hunter, pothunter, prizer [*archaic*].

salesman, drummer [*archaic*]; bagman etc. 758; canvasser.

beggar, mendicant, mumper, sturdy beggar, panhandler [*slang*], cadger.

hotel runner [*cant*] touter [*colloq.*], runner [*cant*], steerer, tout [*cant, Eng.*]; barker [*colloq.*].

sycophant, parasite etc. (*servility*) 886.

Section 3. Conditional

---

768. Promise

n. **promise**, undertaking, word, troth, plight, pledge, parole, word of honor, vow; oath etc. (*affirmation*) 535; profession, assurance, warranty, guarantee, insurance, obligation; contract etc. 769; stipulation.

engagement, preengagement; affiance; betrothal, betrothment; marriage -contract, -vow; plighted faith, troth-plight [*Scot. or dial.*], gage d'amour [*F.*].

v. **promise**; give a promise etc. *n.*; undertake, engage; make-, form- an engagement; enter into *or* on an engagement; bind-, tie-, pledge-, commit-, take upon- oneself; vow; swear etc. (*affirm*) 535, give-, pass-, pledge-, plight- one's -word, –honor, –credit, –troth; betroth, plight faith, take the vows, trothplight [*Scot. or dial.*].

assure, warrant, guarantee; covenant etc. 769; avouch, vouch for; attest etc. (*bear witness*) 467.

hold out an expectation; contract an obligation; become bound to, become sponsor for; answer for, be answerable for; secure; give security etc. 771; underwrite.

adjure, administer an oath, put to one's oath, swear a witness.

adj. **promising** etc. *v.*; promissory; votive; under hand and seal, upon oath, upon the Book; upon–, on- affirmation.

promised etc. *v.*; affianced, pledged, bound; committed, compromised; in for it [*colloq.*].

adv. as true as I live; in all soberness; upon my honor; my word for it; my head upon it; I call God to witness; as one's head shall answer for; *ex voto* [*L.*].

768a. Release from engagement

n. **release** etc. (*liberation*) 750.

adj. **absolute**; unconditional etc. (*free*) 748.

769. Compact

n. **compact**, contract, specialty, bundobast [*India*], deal [*colloq.*], agreement, bargain; affidation [*rare*], pact, paction [*chiefly Scot.*], bond, covenant, indenture [*law*].

770. Conditions

stipulation, settlement, convention; compromise, cartel.

negotiation etc. (*bargaining*) 794; diplomacy etc. (*mediation*) 724; negotiator etc. (*agent*) 758.

treaty, protocol, concordat, *Zollverein* [*Ger.*], *Sonderbund* [*Ger.*], charter, Magna Charta *or* Magna Carta, pragmatic sanction.

ratification, completion, signature, seal, sigil, signet, bond.

v. **contract**, covenant, agree for; engage etc. (*promise*) 768; indent.

negotiate, treat, stipulate, make terms; bargain etc. (*barter*) 794.

conclude, close, close with, complete; make-, strike- a bargain; come to -terms, -an understanding; compromise etc. 774; set at rest; settle; confirm, ratify, clinch *or* clench, subscribe, underwrite; indorse, endorse, put the seal to; sign on the dotted line; sign, seal etc. (*attest*) 467; take one at one's word, bargain by inch of candle.

adj. **contractual**, complete; agreed etc. *v.;* conventional; under hand and seal; signed, sealed, and delivered.

adv. **as agreed upon**, as promised, as contracted for; according to the -contract, -bargain, -agreement, on the dotted line [*slang*].

770. Conditions

n. **conditions**, terms; articles, -of agreement; memorandum; clauses, provisions; proviso etc. (*qualification*) 469; covenant, stipulation, obligation, ultimatum, *sine qua non* [*L.*]; *casus foederis* [*L.*].

v. **condition**, make it a condition, stipulate, insist upon, make a point of; bind, tie up; fence in, hedge in, have a string to it [*colloq.*]; make-, come to- -terms etc. (*contract*) 769.

adj. **conditional**, provisional, guarded, fenced, hedged in.

adv. **conditionally** etc. (*with qualification*) 469; provisionally, *pro re nata* [*L.*], on condition; with a string to it [*colloq.*], with strings attached [*colloq.*], with a reservation.

771. Security

n. **security**; guaranty, guarantee; gage, warranty, bond, tie, pledge, *vadium vivum* [*L.*], plight [*rare*], mortgage, *vadium mortuum* [*L.*], debenture, hypothec [*Rom. & civil law*], hypothecation, bill of sale, lien, pawn, pignoration; real security; vadium, collateral, bail; parole etc. (*promise*) 768.

stake, deposit, earnest, handsel *or* hansel, handsale, caution [*Scot. law*].

promissory note; bill, -of exchange; I.O.U.; personal security, covenant.

acceptance, indorsement *or* endorsement, signature, execution, stamp, seal.

sponsor, surety, bail, replevin; mainpernor, mainprise *or* mainprize [*hist. law*]; hostage; godchild, godfather, godmother; sponsion, sponsorship.

recognizance; deed-, covenant- of indemnity.

authentication, verification, warrant, certificate, voucher, docket *or* doquet [*obs.*]; record etc. 551; probate, attested copy.

acquittance, quittance; discharge, release; receipt.

muniments, title deed, instrument; deed, deed poll, indenture; specialty; insurance; charter etc. (*compact*) 769; charter poll; paper, parchment, settlement, will, testament, last will and testament, codicil.

v. **give security**, give bail, give substantial bail; go bail; handsel *or* hansel, pawn, put in pawn, pledge, put up the spout [*slang*], hock [*slang*], impawn *or* empawn [*obs.*], spout [*slang*], impignorate, mortgage, hypothecate.

guarantee, warrant, assure; accept, indorse *or* endorse, underwrite, insure.

execute, stamp; sign, seal etc. (*evidence*) 467.

let, set *or* sett [*Scot. law*]; grant-, take-, hold- a lease; hold in pledge; lend on security etc. 787.

adj. **pledged**, pawned etc. *v.;* secure; impignorate, pignorative [*rare*], in pawn, up the spout [*slang*]; at stake, on deposit, as earnest.

sponsorial, sponsional [*rare*]; as sponsor etc. *n.*

let, leased; held in pledge.

772. Observance

n. **observance**, performance, compliance, acquiescence, concurrence; obedience etc. 743; fulfillment *or* fulfilment, satisfaction, discharge; acquittance, acquittal.

adhesion, acknowledgment; fidelity etc. (*probity*) 939; exact etc. 494- observance; unserving fidelity to.

v. **observe**, comply with, respect, acknowledge, abide by; cling to, adhere to, be faithful to, act up to; meet, fulfill *or* fulfil; carry out, carry into execution; execute, perform, keep, satisfy, discharge; do one's office.

keep faith with; perform-, fulfill-, discharge- acquit oneself of- an obligation; make good; make good-, keep- one's -word, -promise; redeem one's pledge; stand to one's engagement.

adj. **observant**, faithful, true, loyal; honorable etc. 939; true as the dial to the sun, true as the needle to the pole; punctual, punctilious, scrupulous, meticulous; literal etc. (*exact*) 494; as good as one's word.

adv. **faithfully** etc. *adj.;* to the letter.

773. Nonobservance

n. **nonobservance** etc. 772; evasion, inobservance, failure, omission, neglect, laches [*law*], casualness, slackness, laxness, laxity, informality.

lawlessness; disobedience etc. 742; bad faith etc. 940.

infringement, infraction; violation, transgression; piracy.

retractation, repudiation, nullification; protest; forfeiture.

v. **evade**, fail, neglect, omit, elude, give the go-by to [*slang*], cut [*colloq.*], set aside, ignore; shut–, close- one's eyes to.

infringe, transgress, violate, pirate, break, trample under foot, do violence to, drive a coach and four (*or* six) through.

discard, protest, repudiate, fling to the winds, set at naught, nullify, declare null and void; cancel etc. (*wipe off*) 552.

retract, go back from, be off, forfeit, go from one's word, palter; stretch a point, strain a point.

adj. **violating** etc. *v.;* lawless, transgressive; elusive, evasive, slack, lax, casual, slippery; nonobservant.

unfulfilled etc. (*see* fulfill etc. 772).

774. Compromise

n. **compromise**, commutation, composition; middle term, *mezzo termine* [*It.*]; compensation etc. 30; abatement of differences, adjustment, mutual concession.

v. **compromise**, commute, compound; take the mean; split the difference, meet one halfway, give and take; come to terms etc. (*contact*) 769; submit to arbitration, abide by arbitration; patch up, bridge over, arrange; straighten out, adjust, adjust differences; agree; cut a deal [*slang*]; make the best of, make a virtue of necessity; take the will for the deed.

Section 4. Possessive Relations

775. Acquisition

n. **acquisition**; gaining etc. *v.;* obtainment, procuration, procurement; purchase, descent, inheritance; gift etc. 784.

recovery, retrieval, revendication [*rare*], replevin; redemption, salvage, trover; find, *trouvaille* [*F.*], foundling.

gain, thrift; money-making, money-grubbing; lucre, filthy lucre, loaves and fishes, fleshpots of Egypt, the main chance, pelf; emolument etc. (*remuneration*) 973.

profit, earnings, winnings, innings, pickings, perquisite, accruement [*obs.*], net profit; avails; income etc. (*receipt*) 810; proceeds, produce, product; outcome, output; return, fruit, crop, harvest; second crop, aftermath; benefit etc. (*good*) 618.

prize, sweepstakes, trick, pool; kitty, jackpot, pot; wealth etc. 803.

[fraudulent acquisition] subreption; obreption; stealing etc. 791.

v. **acquire**, get, gain, win, earn, obtain, procure, gather; collect etc. (*assemble*) 72; pick, pick up; glean.

find; come–, pitch–, light- upon; come across, come at; scrape -up, –together; get in, reap and carry, net, bag, sack, bring home, secure; derive, draw, get in the harvest.

get hold of, get between one's finger and thumb, get into one's hand, get at; take–, come into–, enter into- possession.

profit; make–, draw- profit; turn to -profit, –account; make capital out of, make money by; obtain a return, reap the fruits of; reap–, gain- an advantage; turn -a penny, –an honest penny; hit the jackpot [*colloq.*], strike it rich; make the pot boil, bring grist to the mill; make–, coin–, raise- money; raise funds, raise the wind [*slang*]; fill one's pocket etc. (*wealth*) 803.

realize, clear; treasure up etc. (*store*) 636; produce etc. 161; take etc. 789.

receive etc. 785; come by, come in for; inherit; step into, –a fortune, –the shoes of; succeed to.

recover, get back, regain, retrieve, revendicate [*rare*], replevin, replevy, redeem, come by one's own.

be profitable etc. *adj.;* pay, answer.

accrue etc. (*be received*) 785.

adj. **acquisitive**, productive, profitable, advantageous, gainful, remunerative, paying, lucrative, acquiring, acquired etc. *v.*

adv. in the way of gain; for money; at interest.

776. Loss

n. **loss**, perdition, deperdition [*archaic*]; forfeiture, lapse.

privation, bereavement; deprivation etc. (*dispossession*) 789; riddance; damage, squandering, waste.

v. **lose**; incur–, experience–, meet with- a loss; miss; mislay, let slip, allow to slip through the

777. Possession

fingers; be deprived of; be without etc. (*exempt*) 777a; forfeit, pay with.
squander; get rid of etc. 782; waste etc. 638.
be lost, lapse.

adj. **losing** etc. *v.;* not having etc. 777a.
deprived of; shorn of, deperdite [*rare*], denuded, bereaved, bereft, minus [*colloq., exc. in math.*], cut off; dispossessed etc. 789; rid of, quit of; out of pocket.
lost etc. *v.;* long lost; irretrievable etc. (*hopeless*) 859; off one's hands.

int. **farewell to**! adieu to! good riddance.

777. Possession

n. **possession**, seizin *or* seisin; ownership etc. 780; occupancy; hold, holding; tenure, tenancy, feodality, feodatory, feud *or* feod, fief, fee, fee tail, fee simple; dependency; villenage *or* villeinage; socage, chivalry, knight service.
bird in hand, *uti possidetis* [*L.*], chose in possession [*rare*].
exclusive possession, impropriation, monopoly, retention etc. 781; prepossession, preoccupancy; nine points of the law; corner, usucapion *or* usucaption [*Rom. law*], prescription.
future possession, heritage, inheritance, heirship, reversion, fee; primogeniture, ultimogeniture.

v. **possess**, have, hold, occupy, enjoy; be possessed of etc. *adj.;* have in hand etc. *adj.;* own etc. 780; command.
inherit; come to, come in for.
monopolize, engross, forestall, regrate, impropriate, appropriate, usucapt [*Rom. law*], have all to oneself; corner; have a firm hold of etc. (*retain*) 781; get into one's hand etc. (*acquire*) 775.
belong to, appertain to, pertain to; be in one's possession etc. *adj.;* vest in.

adj. **possessing** etc. *v.;* worth; possessed of, seized of, master of, usucapient [*Rom. law*]; in possession of; endowed–, blest–, instinct–, fraught–, laden–, charged- with.
possessed etc. *v.;* on hand, by one; in hand, in store, in stock; unsold, unshared; in one's -hands, –grasp, –possession; at one's command, at one's disposal; one's own etc. (*property*) 780.

777a. Exemption

n. **exemption**; absence etc. 187; exception, immunity, privilege, release.

v. **not have** etc. 777; be without etc. *adj.;* excuse.

adj. **devoid of**, exempt from, without, unpossessed of, unblest with; immune from.
not having etc. 777; unpossessed; untenuated etc. (*vacant*) 187; without an owner.
unobtained, unacquired.

778. Participation
[joint possession]

n. **participation**; condominium, cotenancy, joint tenancy; occupancy–, possession–, tenancy- in common; joint–, common- stock; limited partnership, copartnership, partnership; communion; community of -possessions, –goods; communication, communalization; communism, communalism, collectivism, socialism; cooperation etc. 709.
snacks [*obs.*], coportion [*obs.*], picnic, hotchpot *or* hotchpotch, hodgepodge; coheirship, coparcenary *or* coparceny; gavelkind.
participator, sharer, copartner, partner; shareholder; cotenant, joint tenant; tenants in common; coheir, coparcener.
communist, communitarian, communalist, collectivist, socialist.

v. **participate**, partake; share, share in; come in for a share; go shares, go snacks [*obs.*], go cahoots [*slang*], halve; share and share alike.
join in; have a hand in etc. (*coöperate*) 709.
communize, communalize; have–, possess–, be seized- -in common, –as joint tenants etc. *n.*

adj. **partaking** etc. *v.*
communistic, communalistic, socialistic; cooperative, profit-sharing.

adv. **in common**, share and share alike; on shares; in cahoots [*slang*].

779. Possessor

n. **possessor**, holder; occupant, occupier; tenant; person *or* man in possession etc. 777; renter, lodger, lessee, underlessee; zamindar *or* zemindar [*India*]; ryot [*India*]; tenant -on sufferance, –at will, –from year to year, –for years, –for life.
owner; proprietor, proprietress, proprietary; impropriator, master, mistress, lord.
landholder, landowner, landlord, landlady; lord -of the manor, –paramount; heritor [*Scots law*], laird [*Scot.*], vavasor *or* vavasour [*feud. law*]; landed gentry, mesne lord; planter.
beneficiary, *cestui que* (or *qui*) *trust* [*law*], mortgagor.
grantee, feoffee, feoffee in trust, releasee, devisee; legatee, legatary [*rare*].

782. Relinquishment

trustee; holder etc. of the legal estate; mortgagee. right owner, rightful owner.

[future possessor] heir, –apparent, –presumptive; inheritor, reversioner; remainder-man; heiress, inheritress, inheritrix.

780. Property

n. **property**, possession, seizin *or* seisin; tenure etc. (*possession*) 777; *suum cuique* [*L.*], *meum et tuum* [*L.*].

ownership, proprietorship, lordship; seigniory *or* seignory *or* seigneury, seignoralty; empire etc. (*dominion*) 737.

estate, interest, stake, right, title, claim, demand, holding; vested–, contingent–, beneficial–, equitable- interest; use, trust, benefit; legal–, equitable- estate.

absolute interest, paramount estate, freehold; fee, –simple, –tail; estate -in fee, –in tail, –tail; estate in tail -male, –female, –general.

term, limitation, lease, settlement, strict settlement, particular estate; estate -for life, –for years, –*pur autre vie* [*F.*]; remainder, reversion, expectancy, possibility.

dower, dowry, jointure, appanage *or* apanage, inheritance, heritage, patrimony, alimony; legacy etc. (*gift*) 784; Falcidian law, paternal estate, thirds.

assets, belongings, means, resources, circumstances; wealth etc. 803; money etc. 800; what one -is worth, –will cut up for [*colloq.*]; estate and effects.

realty, land, lands; landed–, real- -estate, –property; tenements; hereditaments; corporeal–, incorporeal- hereditaments; acres; ground etc. (*earth*) 342; acquest, mesestead [*archaic*], messuage, toft [*Scot. & dial. Eng.*].

manor, honor [*Eng. feudal law*], domain, demesne; farm, plantation, hacienda [*Sp. Am.*]; alodium *or* allodium etc. (*free*) 748; feoff, fief, feud *or* feod, zamindari *or* zemindari [*India*], arado [*S. W. U. S.*], rancho [*S. W. U. S.*], ranch, spread.

freeholds, copyholds, leaseholds; folkland [*O. Eng. law*].

chattels real; fixtures, plant, heirloom; easement; right of -common, –user.

territory, state, kingdom, principality, realm, empire, protectorate, dependency, sphere of influence, mandate.

personalty; personal -property, –estate, –effects; chattels, goods, effects, movables; stock, –in trade; things, traps [*colloq.*], chattels personal, rattletraps, paraphernalia; equipage etc. 633; parcels [*Eng.*], appurtenances.

impedimenta; luggage, baggage; bag and baggage; pelf; cargo, lading.

income etc. (*receipts*) 810; rent roll; maul and wedges [*U. S.*].

patent, copyright; chose in action; credit etc. 805; debt etc. 806.

v. **possess** etc. 777; be the possessor of etc. 779; own; have for one's -own, –very own; come in for, inherit; enfeoff.

savor of the realty.

belong to; be one's property etc. *n.*; pertain to, appertain to.

adj. **one's own**; landed, praedial *or* predial, manorial, alodial *or* allodial; seigniorial *or* seigneurial; freehold, copyhold, leasehold; feudal *or* feodal; hereditary, entailed, real, personal.

adv. **to one's credit**, to one's account; to the good.

to one and -his heirs for ever, –the heirs of his body, –his heirs and assigns, –his executors, administrators and assigns.

781. Retention

n. **retention**; retaining etc. *v.*; keep [*archaic*], detention, custody; tenacity, firm hold, grasp, gripe, grip, iron grip; bond etc. (*vinculum*) 45.

clutches, tongs, forceps, tenaculum, pincers, nippers, pliers, vise, hook.

fangs, teeth, claws, talons, nail, unguis, tentacle.

paw, hand, finger, wrist, fist, nieve *or* nief [*archaic or dial.*].

captive etc. 754; bird in hand.

v. **retain**, keep; hold, –fast, –tight, –one's own, –one's ground; clinch, clench, clutch, grasp, gripe, hug, have a firm hold of.

secure, withhold, detain; hold–, keep- back; keep close; husband etc. (*store*) 636; reserve; have–, keep- in stock etc. (*possess*) 777; entail, tie up, settle.

adj. **retentive**, tenacious; retaining etc. *v.*

unforfeited, undeprived, undisposed, uncommunicated.

incommunicable, inalienable; in mortmain; in strict settlement.

782. Relinquishment

n. **relinquishment**, abandonment etc. (*of a course*) 624; renunciation, expropriation, dereliction; cession, surrender, dispensation; resignation etc. 757; riddance.

derelict etc. *adj.*; jetsam *or* jettison; abandoned farm; waif, foundling.

783. Transfer

v. **relinquish**, give up, surrender, yield, cede; let go, let slip; spare, drop, resign, forego, renounce, abandon, expropriate, give away, dispose of, part with; lay -aside, -apart, -down, -on the shelf & (*disuse*) 678; set aside, put aside; make away with, cast behind; discard, cast off, dismiss; maroon.

cast-, throw-, pitch-, fling- away, -aside, -overboard, -to the dogs; cast-, throw-, sweep- to the winds; put-, turn-, sweep- away; jettison.

quit one's hold.

supersede, give notice to quit, give warning; be *or* get rid of; be *or* get quit of; eject etc. 297.

rid-, disburden-, divest-, dispossess- oneself of; wash one's hands of.

divorce, unmarry [*rare*]; cut off, desert, disinherit; separate.

adj. **relinquished** etc. *v.;* cast off, derelict; unowned, disowned, disinherited, divorced; unappropriated, unculled; left etc. (*residuary*) 40.

int. away with!

783. Transfer

n. **transfer**, conveyance, assignment, alienation, abalienation; demise, limitation; conveyancing; transmission etc. (*transference*) 270; enfeoffment, bargain and sale, lease and release; exchange etc. (*interchange*) 148; barter etc. 794; substitution etc. 147.

succession, reversion; shifting use, shifting trust; devolution.

v. **transfer**, convey; alien, alienate; assign; enfeoff; grant etc. (*confer*) 784; consign; make over, hand over; pass, hand, transmit, negotiate; hand down; exchange etc. (*interchange*) 148.

change hands, change from one to another; devolve, revert, succeed; come into possession etc. (*acquire*) 775.

disinherit; abalienate [*rare*]; dispossess etc. 789; substitute etc. 147.

adj. **alienable**, negotiable, transferable, reversional, transmissive; inherited.

adv. **by transfer** etc. *n.;* on lease.

784 Giving

n. **giving** etc. *v.;* bestowal, bestowment, donation; presentation, presentment; accordance; concession, cession; delivery, consignment, dispensation, communication, endowment; investment, investiture; award.

charity, almsgiving, liberality, generosity.

[thing given] gift, donation, present, *cadeau* [*F.*]; fairing; free gift, boon, favor, benefaction, grant, offering, oblation, sacrifice, immolation.

grace, act of grace, bonus.

allowance, contribution, subscription, subsidy, tribute, subvention.

bequest, legacy, devise, will, dotation, dot, appanage *or* apanage, dowry, dower; voluntary -settlement, -conveyance etc. 783; amortization.

gratuity, lagniappe *or* lagnappe [*Louisiana*], pilon [*S. W. U. S.*]; alms, largess, bounty, dole, sportule [*obs.*], donative, help, oblation, offertory, honorarium, Peter pence, sportula, Christmas box, Easter offering, vails [*rare*], *douceur* [*F.*], drink money, tip, hand out [*slang*], *pourboire* [*F.*], Trinkgeld [*G*], baksheesh *or* bakshish, cumshaw [*China*], dash *or* dashee [*Africa*]; fee etc. (*recompense*) 973; consideration.

bribe, bait, ground bait; peace offering; handsel *or* hansel; boodle [*slang*], graft [*colloq.*], grease [*slang*].

giver, grantor etc. *v.;* donor, almoner, testator, feoffer, settlor [*law*]; investor, subscriber, contributor; Fairy Godmother [*or l. c.*].

v. **deliver**, hand, pass, put into the hands of; hand-, make-, deliver-, pass-, turn- over; assign dower.

present, give away, dispense, dispose of; give-, deal-, dole-, mete-, squeeze-out; fork over, fork out, shell out [*all slang*].

make a present; allow, contribute, subscribe, furnish its quota.

pay etc. 807; render, impart, communicate.

concede, cede, yield, part with, shed, cast; spend etc. 809; sacrifice, immolate.

give, bestow, donate, confer, grant, accord, award, assign; offer etc. 763.

intrust, consign, vest in.

invest, endow, settle upon; bequeath, leave, devise.

furnish, supply, help; administer to, minister to; afford, spare; accommodate with, indulge with; favor with; shower down upon; lavish, pour on, thrust upon.

bribe, tip; tickle-, grease- the palm [*slang*].

adj. **giving** etc. *v.;* given etc. *v.;* allowed, allowable; concessional; communicable.

charitable, eleemosynary, sportulary [*obs.*], tributary; gratis etc. 815; donative.

adv. **as a free gift** etc. *n.;* in charity; toward the endowment fund.

int. don't mention it! not another word! glad to do it!

785. Receiving

n. **receiving** etc. *v.;* acquisition etc. 775; reception etc. (*introduction*) 296; suscipiency [*rare*], acceptance, admission.
recipient, receiver, suscipient [*rare*], accipient; assignee, devisee; legatee, legatary; grantee, feoffee, donee, relessee, lessee.
beneficiary, sportulary [*obs.*], stipendiary; pensioner, pensionary; almsman.
income etc. (*receipt*) 810.

v. **receive**; take etc. 789; acquire etc. 775; admit.
pocket; take in, catch, touch; put into one's -pocket, –purse; accept; take off one's hands.
be received; come in, come to hand; pass–, fall- into one's hand; go into one's pocket; fall to one's -lot, –share; come–, fall- to one; accrue; have given etc. (784) to one.

adj. **receiving** etc. *v.;* recipient, suscipient [*rare*]; stipendiary, stipendarian, pensionary.
received etc. *v.;* given etc. 784; secondhand.
not given, unbestowed etc. (*see* give, bestow etc. 784).

786. Apportionment

n. **apportionment**, allotment, consignment, assignment, allocation, appointment; appropriation; dispensation, distribution; division, deal; partition, repartition, administration.
portion, dividend, contingent, share, allotment, lot, measure, dose; dole, meed, pittance; *quantum* [*L.*], ration; ratio, proportion, quota, modicum, mess, allowance.

v. **apportion**, divide; distribute, administer, dispense; billet, allot, allocate, detail, cast, share, mete; portion–, parcel–, dole- out; deal, carve.
partition, assign, appropriate, appoint.
participate, come in for one's share etc. 778.

adj. apportioning etc. *v.;* apportioned etc. *v.;* respective.

adv. respectively, each to each; by lot; in equal shares.

787. Lending

n. **lending** etc. *v.;* loan, advance, accommodation, feneration [*obs.*]; mortgage etc. (*security*) 771; investment.
pawnshop, spout [*slang*], *mont de piété* [*F.*], my uncle's [*slang*].
lender, pawnbroker, money lender, usurer, Shylock.

v. **lend**, advance, accommodate with; lend on security; loan; pawn etc. (*security*) 771.
invest; intrust; place–, put- out to interest; place, put; embark, risk, venture, sink, fund.
let, lease, set *or* sett [*Scot. law*], sublet, sublease, underlet; demise.

adj. **lending** etc. *v.;* lent etc. *v.;* come across (*or* down) with the needful [*slang*].

adv. in advance; on loan, on security.

788. Borrowing

n. **borrowing**, pledging, pawning, putting up the spout [*slang*].
borrowed plumes; plagiarism etc. (*thieving*) 791.

v. **borrow**, desume [*obs.*]; pawn, put up the spout [*slang*], patronize my uncle [*slang*].
raise–, take up- money; raise the wind [*slang*]; get the -dough, –needful [*both slang*]; fly a kite, borrow from Peter to pay Paul; run into debt etc. (*debt*) 806.
hire, rent, farm; take a -lease, –demise; take–, hire- by the -hour, –mile, –year etc.
appropriate, adopt, apply, imitate, make use of, take; plagiarize, pirate.
replevy.

adj. borrowed etc. *v.*

789. Taking

n. **taking** etc. *v.;* reception etc. (*taking in*) 296; deglutition etc. (*taking food*) 298; appropriation, prehension [*chiefly zoöl.*], prensation [*obs.*]; capture, caption; apprehension, deprehension [*obs.*]; abreption [*obs.*], seizure; abduction, ablation; subtraction etc. (*subduction*) 38; abstraction, ademption; androlepsia *or* androlepsy.
dispossession; deprivation, deprivement; bereavement; divestment; disinheritance, dishersion; distraint, distress, attachment, execution; sequestration, confiscation; eviction etc. 297.
rapacity, rapaciousness, extortion, predacity; bloodsucking, vampirism; theft etc. 791.
resumption; reprises [*law*], reprisal; recovery etc. 775.
clutch, swoop, wrench; grip etc. (*retention*) 781; haul, take, catch; scramble.
taker, captor, capturer; extortioner *or* extortionist; vampire.

v. **take**, catch, hook, nab [*slang*], bag, sack, pocket, put into one's pocket; receive; accept.
reap, crop, cull, pluck; gather etc. (*get*) 775; draw.

790. Restitution

appropriate, impropriate [*Eng. eccl. law*]; assume, possess oneself of; take possession of; commandeer [*colloq.*]; lay–, clap- one's hands on [*colloq.*]; help oneself to; make free with, dip one's hands into, lay under contribution; intercept; scramble for; deprive of.

seize, abstract; take–, carry–, bear- -away, –off; adeem [*law*]; hurry off–, run away- with; abduct; steal etc. 791; ravish; pounce–, spring- upon; swoop to, swoop down upon; take by -storm, –assault; snatch, reave [*archaic*].

snap up, nip up, whip up, catch up; kidnap, crimp, capture, lay violent hands on.

get–, lay–, take–, catch–, lay fast–, take firm- hold of; lay by the heels, take prisoner; fasten upon, grapple, embrace, grip, gripe, clasp, grab [*colloq.*], make away with, clutch, collar, throttle, take by the throat, claw, clinch, clench, make sure of.

catch at, jump at, make a grab at, snap at, snatch at; reach, make a long arm [*colloq.*], stretch forth one's hand.

disseize *or* disseise; take from, take away from; deduct etc. 38; retrench etc. (*curtail*) 201; dispossess, ease one of, snatch from one's grasp; tear–, tear away–, wrench–, wrest–, wring- from; extort; deprive of, bereave; disinherit, cut off with a shilling; oust etc. (*eject*) 297; divest; levy, distrain, confiscate; sequester, sequestrate; accroach; usurp; despoil, strip, fleece, shear, displume.

absorb etc. (*suck in*) 296; draw off; suck, –like a leach, –the blood of; impoverish, eat out of house and home; drain, –to the dregs; gut, dry, exhaust, swallow up.

retake, resume; recover etc. 775.

adj. **taking** etc. *v.;* privative, prehensile; predacious *or* predaceous, predal [*obs.*], predatory, wolfish, lupine, rapacious, raptorial; ravening, ravenous; parasitic; all-devouring, all-engulfing.

bereft etc. 776.

adv. at one fell swoop.

790. Restitution

n. **restitution**, return; rendition, reddition; restoration, reinstatement, reinvestment, recuperation; rehabilitation etc. (*reconstruction*) 660; reparation, atonement; compensation, indemnification.

recovery etc. (*getting back*) 775; release, replevin, replevy, redemption; reversion; remitter.

v. **restore**, return; give–, carry–, bring- back; render, –up; give up; let go, unclutch; disgorge, regorge; regurgitate; recoup, reimburse, compensate, indemnify, reinvest, reinstate, remit, rehabilitate; repair etc. (*make good*) 660.

recover etc. (*get back*) 775; redeem; take back again; revest, revert.

adj. **restoring** etc. *v.;* recuperative etc. 660; compensatory, indemnificatory; reversionary, redemptive, revertible.

adv. in full restitution; as partial compensation; to atone for.

791. Stealing

n. **stealing** etc. *v.;* theft, thievery, robbery, direption [*rare*]; abstraction, appropriation; plagiary [*rare*], plagiarism, autoplagiarism; rape, depredation; kidnaping *or* kidnapping.

pillage, spoliation, plunder, sack, sackage [*rare*], rapine, brigandage, latrociny [*obs.*], latrocinium [*Rom. law*], highway robbery, holdup [*slang*]; raid, foray, razzia; piracy, privateering, buccaneering; filibustering, filibusterism; burglary, housebreaking; abaction, cattle stealing, cattle lifting [*colloq.*], cattle rustling horse stealing; automobile–, car- stealing.

blackmail, badger game [*cant*], Black Hand [*U. S.*].

peculation, embezzlement; fraud etc. 545; larceny, petty larceny, pilfering, shoplifting.

thievishness, rapacity, predacity, predaciousness; kleptomania.

Alsatia; Whitefriars; den of Cacus, den of thieves.

license to plunder, letters of marque.

v. **steal**, thieve, rob, purloin, pilfer, filch, prig [Brit. *cant*], bag, nim [*obs.*], crib [*colloq.*], cabbage, palm; abstract; appropriate, plagiarize.

disregard the distinction between *meum* and *tuum*.

abduct, convey away, carry off, kidnap, crimp, impress, press [*rare*]; make–, walk–, run- off with; run away with; spirit away, seize etc. (*lay violent hands on*) 789.

plunder, pillage, rifle, sack, loot, ransack, spoil, spoliate, despoil, strip, sweep, gut, forage, levy blackmail, pirate, pickeer [*obs.*], maraud, lift cattle [*colloq.*], poach, rustle, smuggle, run; badger [*cant*], bunko *or* bunco; hold up; bail up, stick up [*both colloq. or slang, Austral.*], filibuster.

swindle, peculate, embezzle; sponge, mulct, rook, bilk, pluck, pigeon [*slang*], thimblerig; diddle [*colloq. or dial.*], fleece; defraud etc. 545; obtain under false pretenses; live by one's wits.

rob–, borrow from- Peter to pay Paul; set a thief to catch a thief.

adj. **thieving** etc. *v.;* thievish, light-fingered, furacious [*rare*]; furtive; piratical; predacious *or* predaceous, predal [*obs.*], predatory; raptorial etc. (*rapacious*) 789.
stolen etc. *v.*

792. Thief

n. **thief**, robber, *homo trium literarum* [*L.*], spoiler, depredator, pillager, marauder; pilferer, rifler, filcher, plagiarist; harpy, shark [*slang*], land rat [*cant*], land pirate, land shark, falcon; smuggler, poacher; abductor, badger [*cant*], kidnaper *or* kidnapper; *chor* [*Hind.*], crook [*slang*], lifter, skin [*slang*], contrabandist, hawk; hold-up, jackleg, rustler [*all three slang*]; spieler [*colloq., Austral.*], sandbagger, sneak thief, strong-arm man.

pirate, corsair, viking, sea king, buccaneer, privateer; Paul Jones.

brigand, bandit, freebooter, thug, dacoit [*India*]; rover, ranger, pickeerer [*obs.*], picaroon, filibuster, rapparee [*Ir.*]; cattle thief, abactor; bushranger, mosstrooper [*hist.*], Bedouin; wrecker; highwayman, footpad, sturdy beggar, knight of the road.

Dick Turpin, Claude Duval, Jonathan Wild, Macheath, Nevison, Jesse James.

pickpocket, dip [*slang*], cutpurse, pickpurse [*rare*], light-fingered gentry; sharper; card sharper, card cheat, Greek; thimblerigger; bunkoman *or* buncoman, rook [*slang*], welsher [*slang*], blackleg [*colloq.*], leg [*slang, Eng.*], diddler [*colloq. or slang*], defaulter; Autolycus, Jeremy Diddler, Robert Macaire, Artful Dodger, trickster; swell mob [*slang*], *chevalier d'industrie* [*F.*]; shoplifter.

swindler, duffer [*Eng.*], peculator; forger, coiner, smasher [*cant, Eng.*], counterfeiter; fence, receiver of stolen goods.

burglar, housebreaker, yeggman *or* yegg [*slang*], cracksman [*slang*], magsman [*slang*], sneak thief; second-story -thief, -man; Bill Sikes, Jack Sheppard.

793. Booty

n. **booty**, spoil, plunder, prize, loot, swag [*cant*]; perquisite, boodle [*polit. cant*], graft [*colloq.*], pork barrel [*polit. cant*], pickings; *spolia opima* [*L.*], prey; blackmail; stolen goods.
adj. **looting**, plundering, spoliative, manubial [*obs.*].

794. Barter

n. **barter**, exchange, scorse [*obs.*], truck system; interchange etc. 148.

a Roland for an Oliver, *quid pro quo* [*L.*], commutation, composition; Indian gift [*colloq.*].

trade, commerce, mercature [*obs.*], buying and selling, bargain and sale; traffic, business, nundination [*obs.*], custom, shopping; commercial enterprise, speculation, jobbing, stockjobbing, agiotage, brokery.

dealing, transaction, negotiation, bargain.
free trade [*opp. to protection*].

v. **barter**, exchange, truck, scorse [*obs.*], swap *or* swop [*colloq. & dial.*]; interchange etc. 148; commutate etc. (*sub titute*) 147; compound for.

trade, traffic, buy and sell, give and take, nundinate [*obs.*]; carry on–, ply–, drive- a trade; be in -business, –the city; keep a shop, deal in, employ one's capital in.

trade–, deal–, have dealings- with; put through a deal with; have truck with; transact–, do- business with; open–, have–, keep- an account with.

bargain; drive–, make- a bargain; negotiate, bid for; haggle, stickle, –for; higgle, dicker, chaffer, huckster, cheapen, beat down; underbid; outbid; ask, charge; strike a bargain etc. (*contract*) 769.

speculate; give–, bait with- a sprat to catch a -herring, –mackerel; buy low and sell high, buy in the cheapest and sell in the dearest market; stag the market [*London Stock Exchange*], rig the market [*Exchange cant*].

adj. **commercial**, mercantile, trading; interchangeable, marketable, staple, in the market, for sale; at a bargain, marked down.
wholesale, retail.

adv. over the counter; in the marts of trade; on the Rialto, on 'change.

795. Purchase

n. **purchase**, emption [*rare*]; buying, purchasing, shopping; preëmption; refusal.
coemption [*Rom. law*]; bribery; slave trade.
buyer, purchaser, emptor [*law*], coemptor, vendee; client, customer, clientele, clientage; patron, employer.

v. **buy**, purchase, invest in, regrate, procure; rent etc. (*hire*) 788; repurchase, buy in.

make–, complete- a purchase; buy over the counter; pay cash for; charge, –to one's account.

shop, market, go a-shopping.
keep in one's pay, bribe, suborn; pay etc. 807; spend etc. 809.

adj. purchased etc. *v.;* emptorial, coemptional, coemptive; cliental.

796. Sale

n. **sale**, vent [*rare*], vend [*Eng.*], disposal; auction, roup [*Scot.*], outcry, vendue, Dutch auction; custom etc. (*traffic*) 794.
salableness, salability, marketability, vendibility, vendibleness.
seller, vender, vendor; consigner; *institor* [*L.*]; rouping wife [*Scot.*]; merchant etc. 797; auctioneer.
salesmanship, selling ability.

v. **sell**, vend, dispose of, make a sale, effect a sale; sell over the counter, sell at auction, sell by [*esp. Brit.*] auction, auction, roup [*Scot.*], outcry; put up to (*or* at) auction; bring to (*or* under) the hammer; offer-, put up- for sale; hawk, bring to market; wholesale; dump, unload, place; offer etc. 763; undersell; dispense, retail; deal in etc. 794; sell -off, -out; turn into money, realize.
let; mortgage etc. (*security*) 771.

adj. **for sale**, under the hammer, in the market.
salable, marketable, vendible, staple, merchantable; in demand, popular.
unsalable etc., unpurchased, unbought; on the shelves, shelved, on one's hands.

797. Merchant

n. **merchant**, trader, dealer, monger, chandler, salesman; money changer, changer [*archaic*]; regrater; shopkeeper, shopman; tradesman, tradespeople, tradesfolk.
retailer; chapman, hawker, huckster, higgler; peddler *or* pedlar, colporteur, cadger, Autolycus; sutler, vivandière, costerman, costermonger; tallyman [*rare*], canvasser, solicitor; cheap Jack, *camelot* [*F.*]; faker [*slang*]; vintner; greengrocer, groceryman, haberdasher.
money-lender, cambist, usurer, moneyer [*obs.*], banker; money-changer, money-broker.
jobber; broker etc. (*agent*) 758; buyer etc. 795; seller etc. 796; bear, bull [*Stock Exchange*].
concern, house, corporation; firm etc. (*partnership*) 712.

798. Merchandise

n. **merchandise**, ware, commodity, effects, goods, article, stock, produce, staple commodity; stock in trade etc. (*store*) 636; cargo etc. (*contents*) 190.

799. Mart

n. **mart**, market, marketplace; fair, bazaar, staple, exchange, stock exchange, Wheat Pit [*Chicago*]; 'change, bourse, curb, hall, guildhall; tollbooth [*Scot. & dial. Eng.*], customhouse; Tattersall's.
shop, stall, booth; wharf; office, chambers, countinghouse, bureau; counter *or* compter [*obs.*].
store etc. 636; department store, finding store [*U. S.*], grindery warehouse, warehouse, wareroom; depot, interposit [*rare*], *entrepôt* [*F.*], emporium, establishment.
market overt, open market.

800. Money

n. **money**, finance; money -matters, -market; accounts etc. 811; funds, treasure, capital, stock; assets etc. (*property*) 780; wealth etc. 803; supplies, ways and means, wherewithal *or* wherewith, sinews of war, almighty dollar, cash.
solvency, responsibility, reliability, solidity, soundness.
sum, amount; balance, balance sheet; sum total; proceeds etc. (*receipts*) 810.
currency, circulating medium, specie, coin, piece, hard cash; dollar, sterling; pounds, shillings, and pence, £ s. d.; guinea; gold mohur [*India*]; eagle, double eagle; pocket, breeches pocket [*colloq.*], wallet, roll, purse; money in hand; *argent comptant* [*F.*], ready [*colloq.*], ready money; Federal-, fractional-, postal- currency; bottom dollar [*colloq.*]; checks, chips.
[slang terms] the needful, rhino, brass, blunt, dust, mopus, tin, salt, chink, dough, jack, moss, rock, dibs, slug [*Calif.* 1849]; buzzard dollar, spondulics, long green; barrel, pile, wad; dough, bread, long green.
precious metals, gold, silver, copper, bullion, ingot, bar, nugget.
petty cash, pocket money, pin money, spending money, change, small coin; long bit, short bit, two bits, quarter [*all U. S.*]; dime, nickel, cent, red cent [*colloq., U.S.*]; doit, stiver, rap, mite, farthing, sou, penny, shilling, tester, groat, rouleau.
wampum, wampumpeag, seawan *or* seawant, roanoke, cowrie.
great wealth, money to burn [*colloq.*]; power-, mint-, barrel-, raft- of money [*all colloq.*]; good-, round-, lump- sum; plum (=£100,-000) [*rare slang*]; million, millions, thousands; crore (= ten million rupees, written Rs. 1,00,00,000) [*India*]; lac *or* lakh, lac of rupees (= 100,000 rupees, written Rs. 1,00,000) [*India*].
[science of coins] numismatics, numismatology, chrysology.

paper money; money-, postal-, post office-order; note, -of hand; bank-, promissory-note; I O U, bond; bill, -of exchange; draft, check [*esp. U.S.*] *or* cheque [*esp. Brit.*], hundi [*India*], order, warrant, coupon, debenture, exchequer bill, assignat, greenback; blueback, shinplaster [*slang*].

remittance etc. (*payment*) 807; credit etc. 805; liability etc. 806.

drawer, drawee; obligor, obligee.

counterfeit-, false-, bad- money; queer [*slang*], base coin, flash note, slip [*obs.*], kite [*slang*]; fancy stocks; Bank of Elegance.

counterfeiter, coiner, moneyer, forger.

v. **total**, amount to, come to, mount up to.

touch the pocket; draw, draw upon; back; indorse etc. (*security*) 771; discount etc. 813.

issue, utter, circulate; fiscalize, monetize, remonetize.

demonetize, deprive of standard value; cease to issue.

coin, counterfeit, forge; circulate bad money, shove the queer [*slang*].

adj. **monetary**, pecuniary, crumenal [*obs.*], fiscal, financial, sumptuary, numismatical; sterling; nummary.

solvent, sound, substantial, good, reliable, responsible, solid, having a good rating; able to pay -20 shillings to the pound, -100 cents on the dollar.

801. Treasurer

n. **treasurer**; bursar, purser, purse bearer; cash keeper, banker; depositary; questor *or* quaestor [*Rom.*], receiver, liquidator, steward, trustee, accountant, expert accountant, Accountant General, almoner *or* almner, paymaster, cashier, teller; cambist; money changer etc. (*merchant*) 797.

financier, Chancellor of the Exchequer, Secretary of the Treasury, minister of finance.

802. Treasury

n. **treasury**, bank, exchequer, almonry, fisc *or* fiscus, hanaper; kutcherry *or* cutcherry *or* kachahri [*India*], bursary; strong box, stronghold, strong room; coffer; chest etc. (*receptacle*) 191; safe; depository etc. 636; cash register, cash box, money-box, till, tiller.

purse, moneybag, portemonnaie, pocketbook, wallet; purse strings; pocket, breeches pocket.

sinking fund; stocks; public-, parliamentary--stocks, -funds, -securities; Consols, *crédit mobilier* [*F.*]; bonds, government bonds, Liberty bonds, savings bonds, three per cents; gilt-edged securities.

803. Wealth

n. **wealth**, riches, fortune, handsome fortune, opulence, affluence; good-, easy- circumstances; independence; competence etc. (*sufficiency*) 639; solvency etc. 800.

capital, money; round sum; great wealth etc. (*treasure*) 800; mint of money, mine of wealth, bonanza, El Dorado, Pactolus, Golconda, Potosi, Philosopher's Stone; the Golden Touch.

long-, full-, well lined-, heavy- purse; purse of Fortunatus; *embarras de richesses* [*F.*].

pelf, Mammon, lucre, filthy lucre; loaves and fishes, fleshpots of Egypt.

means, resources, substance, command of money; property etc. 780; income etc. 810.

provision, maintenance, livelihood; dowry, alimony.

rich man, moneyed man, warm man [*old slang*], man of substance; capitalist, millionaire, tippybob [*slang*], Nabob, Croesus, Midas, Plutus, Dives, Timon of Athens; Danaë.

timocracy, plutocracy.

v. **be rich** etc. *adj.;* roll-, wallow- in -wealth, -riches; have money to burn [*colloq.*].

afford, well afford; command -money, -a sum; make both ends meet, hold one's head above water.

become rich etc. *adj.;* fill one's pocket etc. (*treasury*) 802; feather one's nest, make a fortune; make money etc. (*acquire*) 775.

enrich, imburse [*rare*].

worship Mammon, worship the golden calf.

adj. **wealthy**, rich, affluent, opulent, moneyed, worth a great deal; well-to-do, well off; warm [*old slang*]; well-, provided for.

made of money; rich as - Croesus; rolling in -riches, -wealth; having a power of money etc. (*great wealth*) 800.

flush, -of -cash, -money, -tin [*slang*]; in funds, in cash, in full feather.

solvent etc., 800; pecunious [*rare*], out of debt, all straight.

804. Poverty

n. **poverty**, indigence, penury, pauperism, destitution, want; need, neediness; lack, necessity, privation, distress, difficulties, wolf at the door.

straits; bad-, poor-, needy-, embarrassed-, reduced-, straightened- circumstances; slender-, narrow- means; hand-to-mouth exis-

805. Credit

tence, *res angusta domi* [*L.*], low water [*slang*], impecuniosity.

mendicity, beggary, mendicancy; broken–, loss of– fortune; insolvency etc. (*nonpayment*) 808.

empty -purse, -pocket; light purse; "a beggarly account of empty boxes" [*Romeo and Juliet*].

poor man, pauper, mumper, mendicant, beggar, starveling; *pauvre diable* [*F.*], fakir *or* fakeer [*India*], sunyasi [*India*], schnorrer [*Yiddish*].

v. **be poor** etc. *adj.;* want, lack, starve, live from hand to mouth, have seen better days, go down in the world, come upon the parish; go to -the dogs, –the almshouse, –the poorhouse, –rack and ruin; not have a -penny etc. (*money*) 800, –shot in one's locker; beg one's bread, –from door to door; *tirer le diable par la queue* [*F.*]; run into debt etc. (*debt*) 806.

render poor etc. *adj.;* impoverish; reduce, –to poverty; pauperize, fleece, ruin, bring on the parish.

adj. **poor**, indigent; poverty-stricken; badly–, poorly–, ill- off; poor as -a rat, –a church mouse, –Job, –Job's turkey [*colloq.*]; fortuneless, dowerless, moneyless, penniless; unportioned, unmoneyed; impecunious; out–, short- of -money, –cash; without–, not- worth- a rap etc. (*money*) 800; *qui n'a pas le sou* [*F.*], out of pocket, hard up; out at -elbows, –heels; seedy [*colloq.*], in rags, barefooted; beggarly, beggared, destitute; fleeced, stripped; bereft, bereaved; reduced.

in want etc. *n.;* needy, necessitous, distressed, pinched, straitened; put to one's -shifts, –last shifts; unable to -keep the wolf from the door, –make both ends meet; embarrassed, under hatches; involved etc. (*in debt*) 806; insolvent etc. (*not paying*) 808.

adv. in forma pauperis [*L.*].

805. Credit

n. **credit**, trust, tick [*colloq.*], strap [*slang*], score, tally, account.

paper credit, letter of credit, circular note; duplicate; mortgage, lien, debenture, floating capital; draft, *lettre de créance* [*F.*], securities.

creditor, lender, lessor, mortgagee; dun, dunner; usurer.

v. **credit**, accredit, intrust *or* entrust; keep–, run up- an account with.

place to one's -credit, –account; give–, take- credit; fly a kite [*com. slang*]; have one's credit good for.

adj. **accredited**; of good credit, of unlimited credit; well rated; credited, crediting.

adv. on credit etc. *n.;* to the account of, to the credit of; *à compte* [*F*].

806. Debt

n. **debt**, obligation, liability, indebtment, debit, score.

arrears, deferred payment, deficit, default; insolvency etc. (*nonpayment*) 808; bad debt.

interest; premium; usance [*obs.*], usury; floating -debt, –capital.

debtor, debitor [*obs.*], mortgagor; defaulter etc. 808; borrower.

v. **be in debt** etc. *adj.;* owe; incur–, contract- a debt etc. *n.;* run up -a bill, –a score, –an account; go on tick [*colloq.*]; borrow etc. 788; run–, get- into debt; be over head and ears in debt; be in difficulties; outrun the constable.

answer for, go bail for; back one's note.

adj. **liable**, chargeable, answerable for.

indebted, in debt, in embarrassed circumstances, in difficulties; encumbered *or* incumbered, involved; involved–, plunged–, deep–, over head and ears- in debt; deeply involved; fast tied up; insolvent etc. (*not paying*) 808; minus [*colloq.*], out of pocket.

unpaid; unrequited, unrewarded; owing, due, in arrear, outstanding.

807. Payment

n. **payment**, defrayment; discharge; acquittance, quittance; settlement, clearance, liquidation, satisfaction, reckoning, arrangement.

acknowledgment, release; receipt, –in full, –in full of all demands; voucher.

repayment, reimbursement, retribution; pay etc. (*reward*) 973; money paid etc. (*expenditure*) 809.

ready money etc. (*cash*) 800; stake, remittance, installment *or* instalment.

payer, liquidator etc. 801.

v. **pay**, defray, make payment; pay -down, –on the nail [*slang*], –ready money, –at sight, –in advance; cash, honor a bill, acknowledge; redeem; pay in kind.

pay one's -way, –shot, –footing; pay -the piper, –sauce for all [*both colloq.*], –costs; come down with the needful [*slang*]; shell–, fork- out [*both slang*]; come down with, –the dust [*both slang*]; tickle–, grease- the palm [*both colloq.*]; expend etc. 809; put down, lay down.

discharge, settle, quit [*archaic*], acquit oneself of; foot the bill [*colloq.*]; account with, reckon with, settle with, be even with, be quits with; strike a balance; settle–, balance–, square- accounts with; quit scores [*archaic*]; wipe-, clear- off old scores; satisfy; pay in full; satisfy-, pay in full- all demands; clear, liquidate; pay -up, -old debts.

repay, refund, reimburse, retribute [*obs.*]; make compensation etc. 30; disgorge, make repayment.

adj. **paying** etc. paid etc. *v.;* owing nothing, out of debt, all straight, all clear, clear of encumbrance, clear of debt, above water; unowed, never indebted; solvent etc. 800.

adv. to the tune of [*colloq.*]; on the nail [*slang*], money down, cash down, cash on delivery, C.O.D.

808. Nonpayment

n. **nonpayment**; default, defalcation; protest, repudiation; application of the sponge; whitewashing.

insolvency, bankruptcy, failure; insufficiency etc. 640; run upon a bank; overdrawn account. waste paper bonds; dishonored-, protested- bills; bogus check *or* cheque, rubber check [*colloq.*].

defaulter, bankrupt, insolvent debtor, lame duck [*slang*], man of straw; welsher *or* welcher, stag [*obs.*], levanter, absconder.

v. **not pay** etc. 807; fail, break, stop payment; become -insolvent, -bankrupt; be gazetted; have one's check -dishonored, -protested.

pay under protest; button up one's pockets, draw the purse strings; apply the sponge; pay over the left shoulder [*colloq.*], get whitewashed; swindle etc. 791; run up bills, fly kites [*com. slang*].

protest, dishonor, repudiate, nullify.

adj. **not paying**; in debt etc. 806; behindhand, in arrear; beggared etc., (*poor*) 804; unable to make both ends meet, minus [*colloq.*], worse than nothing.

insolvent, bankrupt, in the gazette, gazetted, ruined.

unpaid etc. (*outstanding*) 806; gratis etc. 815; unremunerated.

809. Expenditure

n. **expenditure**, money going out; outgoings, outlay; expenses, disbursement; prime cost etc. (*price*) 812; circulation; run upon a bank.

[money paid] payment etc. 807; pay etc. (*remuneration*) 973; bribe etc. 973; fee, footing, garnish [*obs.*]; subsidy; tribute; contingent, quota; donation, gift etc. 784.

investment; purchase etc. 795.

deposit, pay in advance, earnest, handsel *or* hansel, installment *or* instalment.

v. **expend**, spend; run-, get- through; pay, disburse; ante, ante up [*both poker*]; pony up [*slang*]; open-, loose-, untie- the purse strings, lay out, shell out [*slang*], fork out [*slang*]; bleed; make up a sum, invest, sink money.

fee etc. (*reward*) 973; pay one's way etc. (*pay*) 807; subscribe etc. (*give*) 784; subsidize; bribe.

adj. **expending**, expended etc. *v.;* sumptuary, lavish, free, free with one's money, liberal; beyond one's income.

expensive, costly, dear, high-priced, precious, high.

810. Receipt

n. **receipt**, value received, money coming in; income, incomings [*rare*], revenue, return, proceeds; gross receipts, net profit; earnings etc. (*gain*) 775; *accepta* [*L.*], avails.

rent, rent roll; rental, rentage [*obs.*], rack-rent.

premium, bonus; sweepstakes, tontine, prize, drawings, hand-out [*slang*].

pension, annuity; jointure etc. (*property*) 780; alimony, pittance, emolument etc. (*remuneration*) 973.

v. **receive** etc. 785; get, have an income of, be in receipt of, have coming in; take money; draw from, derive from; acquire etc. 775; take etc. 789; have in prospect.

yield, bring in, afford, pay, return; accrue etc. (*be received from*) 785.

adj. **receiving**, received etc. *v.;* well-paying, remunerative, interest-bearing; well-, profitably- invested; profitable etc. (*gainful*) 775.

adv. at interest; within one's income.

811. Accounts

n. **accounts**, accompts [*archaic*]; business-, commercial-, monetary- arithmetic; statistics etc. (*numeration*) 85; money matters, finance, budget, bill, score, reckoning, account.

bookkeeping, audit, single entry, double entry; computation, calculation, casting up.

account book, books, ledger; day-, cash-, petty-cash-, pass- book; journal; debtor and creditor-, cash-, running- account; account current; balance, -sheet; *compte rendu* [*F.*], account settled; *acquit* [*F.*], assets, expenditure, liabilities, outstanding accounts; profit and loss -account, -statement; receipts; receipt -in full, -in part, -on account; spread sheet.

accountant, auditor, actuary, bookkeeper; financier etc. 801; accounting party; chartered accountant [*Eng.*], certified public accountant [*U. S.*], C.P.A., bank examiner, bank auditor.

812. Price

- *v.* **keep accounts**, enter, post, post up, book, credit, debit, carry over; take stock; tot up [*colloq.*], add, add up; balance-, make up-, square-, settle-, wind up-, cast up- accounts; make accounts square.
  bring to book, audit, examine the books, tax.
  falsify, surcharge; falsify-, garble- an account; cook-, doctor- an account [*both colloq.*]; cook-, doctor- the books [*both colloq.*].
- *adj.* monetary etc. 800; accountable, accounting; statistical; entered etc. *v.*

812. Price

- *n.* **price**, amount, cost, expense, prime cost, charge, figure, demand, damage [*colloq.*], fare, hire; wages etc. (*remuneration*) 973.
  dues, duty, toll, tax, impost, tariff, cess, sess [*obs.*], tallage *or* tailage [*Old Eng. law*], levy; *abkari* [*India*], capitation, capitation tax, poll tax; doomage, *likin* [*Chinese*], gabel *or* gabelle, salt tax; gavel [*Old Eng. law*], octroi [*F.*], custom, excise, assessment, taxation, benevolence [*hist.*], forced loan; tenths [*hist.*], tithe, exactment, ransom, salvage, towage; brokerage, wharfage, freightage.
  worth, rate, value, par value, valuation, appraisement, money's worth; penny etc. -worth; price current, market price, quotation, current quotation; what it will fetch etc. *v.*
  bill etc. (*account*) 811; shot, scot, scot and lot.
- *v.* **price**; bear-, set-, fix- a price; appraise, assess, doom, charge, demand, ask, require, exact, run up; distrain; run up a bill etc. (*debt*) 806; have one's price; liquidate.
  amount to, come to, mount up to; stand one in [*colloq.*], put one back [*slang*].
  fetch, sell for, cost, bring in, yield, afford.
- *adj.* **priced** etc. *v.*; to the tune of, *ad valorem* [*L.*]; dutiable, taxable, assessable; mercenary, venal.

813. Discount

- *n.* **discount**, abatement, concession, reduction, depreciation, allowance, qualification, set-off, drawback, poundage, agio, percentage; rebate, rebatement, backwardization [*Eng.*], backwardation [*Eng.*], contango [*Eng. Stock Exchange*]; salvage; tare [*com.*], tare and tret.
- *v.* **discount**, bate, rebate, abate, deduct, strike off, mark down, reduce, take off, allow, give, make allowance; depreciate.
- *adj.* **discounting** etc. *v.*; concessional; marked down; depreciative.
- *adv.* **at a discount**, at a bargain, below par, on sale.

814. Dearness

- *n.* **dearness** etc. *adj.*; high-, famine-, fancy- price; overcharge; extravagance; exorbitance, extortion; heavy pull upon the purse.
- *v.* **be dear** etc. *adj.*; cost much, cost a pretty penny [*colloq.*]; rise in price, look up.
  overcharge, bleed [*colloq.*], skin [*slang*], fleece, extort.
  pay too much, pay through the nose [*colloq.*], pay too dear for one's whistle [*colloq.*].
- *adj.* **dear**; high, -priced; of great price, expensive, costly, precious, dear bought; unreasonable, extravagant, exorbitant, extortionate.
  at a premium; not to be had, -for love or money; beyond price, above price; priceless, of priceless value.
- *adv.* **dear**, dearly; at great cost, at heavy cost, at a high price, *à grands frais* [*F.*].

815. Cheapness

- *n.* **cheapness**, low price; depreciation; bargain, *bon marché* [*F.*]; good penny etc. -worth; drug in the market.
  [absence of charge] gratuity; free -quarters, -seats, -admission; free lunch; run of one's teeth [*slang*]; nominal price, peppercorn rent; labor of love.
  deadhead [*colloq.*], dead beat [*slang*], beat [*slang*], sponger.
- *v.* **be cheap** etc. *adj.*; cost little; come down-, fall- in price; be marked down.
  buy for a mere nothing, buy at a bargain, buy dirt-cheap, buy for an old song; have one's money's worth; beat down, cheapen.
- *adj.* **cheap**; low, -priced; moderate, reasonable; inexpensive *or* unexpensive; well-, worth the money; *magnifique et pas cher* [*F.*]; good-, cheap- at the price; dirt-cheap, dog-cheap; cheap as dirt, cheap and nasty [*colloq.*]; peppercorn; catchpenny.
  reduced, half-price, depreciated, shopworn, marked down, unsalable.
  gratuitous, gratis, free, for nothing; costless, expenseless; without charge, not charged, untaxed; scot-free, shot-free, rent-free; free of -cost, -expense; complimentary, honorary, unbought, unpaid for.
- *adv.* **at a bargain**, for a mere song; at cost price, at prime cost, at a reduction; on the cheap [*colloq., Eng.*]; *bon marché* or *à bon marché* [*F.*].

816. Liberality

- *n.* **liberality**, generosity, munificence; bounty, bounteousness, bountifulness; hospitableness, hospitality; charity etc. (*beneficence*) 906; open-, free- hand; open-, large-, free- heart; enough and to spare.

cheerful giver, free giver, patron; benefactor etc. 912.

v. **be liberal** etc. *adj.;* spend–, bleed- freely; shower down upon; open one's purse strings etc. (*disburse*) 809; spare no expense, give *carte blanche* [*F.*]; give with both hands; give the coat off one's back; keep open house, fill one's house with guests.

adj. **liberal**, free, generous; charitable etc. (*beneficent*) 906; hospitable; bountiful, bounteous, ample, handsome; unsparing, ungrudging; unselfish; open–, free–, full- handed; open–, large–, free-hearted; munificent, princely.

adv. **liberally** etc. *adj.;* ungrudgingly; with open hands, with both hands.

817. Economy

n. **economy**, frugality; thrift, thriftiness; care, husbandry, good housewifery, savingness, retrenchment.

savings; prevention of waste, save-all; parsimony etc. 819.

v. **be economical** etc. *adj.;* practice economy, economize, save; retrench, cut down expenses; cut one's coat according to one's cloth, make both ends meet, keep within compass, meet one's expenses, keep one's head above water, pay one's way; husband etc. (*lay by*) 636; save–, invest- money; put out to interest; provide–, save- -for, –against- a rainy day; feather one's nest; look after the main chance [*colloq.*].

adj. **economical**, frugal, careful, thrifty, saving, chary, spare, sparing; parsimonious etc. 819; sufficient; plain.

adv. **sparingly** etc. *adj.; ne quid nimis* [*L.*].

818. Prodigality

n. **prodigality**, prodigence [*obs.*], wastefulness, wastry *or* wastrie [*Scot.*], unthriftiness, waste; profusion, profuseness; extravagance; squandering etc. *v.;* lavishness.

pound-foolishness, pound-folly, penny wisdom.

prodigal, spendthrift, wastethrift, wastrel [*dial. Eng.*], waster, high roller [*slang*], squanderer, spender, spendall, scattergood [*archaic*]; locust; Prodigal Son; Timon of Athens.

v. **be prodigal** etc. *adj.;* squander, lavish, sow broadcast; blow in [*slang*]; pay through the nose etc. (*dear*) 814; spill, waste, dissipate, exhaust, drain, eat out of house and home, overdraw, outrun the constable; run out, run through; misspend; throw good money after bad, throw the helve after the hatchet; burn the candle at both ends; make ducks and drakes of one's money; fool–, potter–, muddle–, fritter–, throw- away one's money; squander one's substance in riotous living; spend money like water; pour water into a sieve, kill the goose that lays the golden eggs; *manger son blé en herbe* [*F.*].

adj. **prodigal**, profuse, thriftless, unthrifty, improvident, wasteful, losel, extravagant, lavish, dissipated, over-liberal; full-handed etc. (*liberal*) 816; overpaid.

penny-wise and pound-foolish.

adv. with an unsparing hand; money burning one's pocket.

int. keep the change! hang the expense!

819. Parsimony

n. **parsimony**, parcity [*obs.*]; parsimoniousness, stinginess etc. *adj.;* stint; illiberality, avarice, tenacity, avidity, rapacity, extortion, malversation, venality, cupidity; lack of prodigality etc. 818; selfishness etc. 943; *auri sacra fames* [*L.*]; cheeseparings and candle ends.

miser, niggard, churl, screw, skin-flint, skin [*slang*], codger [*dial. Eng.*], money-grub [*slang*], muckworm, scrimp [*colloq.*], pinchgut [*obs. or vulgar*], lick-penny, hunks [*colloq.*], curmudgeon, harpy, extortioner, usurer, Hessian [*U.S.*]; pinchfist, pinchpenny [*obs.*].

Harpagon, Euclio, Silas Marner, Daniel Dancer.

v. **be parsimonious** etc. *adj.;* grudge, begrudge, stint, pinch, gripe, screw, dole out, hold back, withhold, starve, famish, live upon nothing, skin a flint [*colloq.*], pinch a sixpence till it squeaks.

drive a bargain, cheapen, beat down; stop one hole in a sieve; have an itching palm, grasp, grab.

adj. **parsimonious**, penurious, stingy, miserly, mean, shabby, peddling, penny wise, near, near as the bark on a tree, niggardly, close; close-handed, close-fisted, fast-handed [*obs.*], hard-fisted, straithanded [*obs.*], tight-fisted; tight [*colloq.*], sparing; chary; grudging, gripping etc. *v.;* illiberal, ungenerous, churlish, hidebound, sordid, mercenary, venal, covetous, usurious, avaricious; greedy, extortionate, rapacious; underpaid.

adv. with a sparing hand.

Class 6. Affections

Section 1. Affections in General

820. Affections

n. **character**, qualities, disposition, affections, nature, spirit, tone; temper, temperament; diathesis, idiosyncrasy; cast-, habit-, frame- of -mind, –soul; predilection, turn; natural–, turn of mind; bent, bias, predisposition, proneness, proclivity, propensity, propenseness, propension, propendency [*obs.*]; vein, humor, mood, grain, mettle, backbone; sympathy etc. (*love*) 897.

soul, heart, breast, bosom, inner man; heart's -core, –strings, –blood; heart of hearts, *penetralia mentis* [*L.*]; secret and inmost recesses of the heart, cockles of one's heart; inmost- heart, –soul.

passion, pervading spirit; ruling–, master- passion; *furore* [*It.*], furor; fullness of the heart, heyday of the blood, flesh and blood, flow of soul.

energy, fervor, fire, verve, force.

v. have *or* possess character etc. *n.;* be of a character etc. *n.;* be affected etc. *adj.;* breathe energy etc. *n.*

adj. **characterized**, affected, formed, molded *or* moulded, cast; attemperate, attempered, tempered; framed.

prone, predisposed, disposed, inclined; having a bias etc. *n.;* tinctured–, imbued–, penetrated–, eaten up- with.

inborn, inbred, ingrained; deep-rooted, ineffaceable, inveterate; congenital, dyed in the wool, implanted by nature, inherent, in the grain.

adv. in one's heart etc. *n.;* at heart; heart and soul etc. 821; in the vein, in the mood.

821. Feeling

n. **feeling**; suffering etc. *v.;* endurance, tolerance, sufferance, experience, response; sympathy etc. (*love*) 897; impression, inspiration, affection, sensation, emotion, pathos, deep sense.

warmth, glow, unction, gusto, vehemence, fervor, fervency; heartiness, cordiality; earnestness, eagerness; *empressement* [*F.*], gush [*colloq.*], ardor, zeal, passion, enthusiasm, verve, *furore* [*It.*], furor, fanaticism; excitation of feeling etc. 824; fullness of the heart etc. (*disposition*) 820; passion etc. (*state of excitability*) 825; ecstasy etc. (*pleasure*) 827.

state of excitement; blush, suffusion, flush; hectic, hectic fever, hectic flush; tingling, thrill, turn, shock; agitation etc. (*irregular motion*) 315; quiver, heaving, flutter, flurry, fluster, twitter, tremor; throb, throbbing; pulsation, palpitation, panting; trepidation, perturbation, ruffle, hurry of spirits, pother, stew [*colloq.*], ferment.

v. **feel**; receive an impression etc. *n.;* be impressed with etc. *adj.;* entertain–, harbor–, cherish- -feeling etc. *n.*

respond; catch the -flame, –infection; enter into the spirit of.

bear, suffer, support, sustain, endure, thole [*obs. or dial.*], aby *or* abye; brook; abide etc. (*be composed*) 826; experience etc. (*meet with*) 151; taste, prove; labor–, smart- under; bear the brunt of, brave, stand.

be agitated, be excited etc., 824; swell, glow, warm, flush, blush, crimson, change color, mantle; darken, whiten, pale; turn -color, –pale, –red, –black in the face; tingle, thrill, heave, pant, throb, palpitate, go pitapat, tremble, quiver, flutter, twitter; shake etc. 315; blench, stagger, reel; look -blue, –black; wince, draw a deep breath.

impress etc. (*excite the feelings*) 824.

adj. **feeling** etc. *v.;* sentient; sensuous, sensorial, sensory; emotive, emotional; of *or* with feeling etc. *n.*

lively, quick, smart, strong, sharp, acute, cutting, piercing, incisive; keen, –as a razor; trenchant, pungent, racy, piquant, poignant, caustic.

impressive, deep, profound, indelible; deep-felt, homefelt, heartfelt; swelling, soul-stirring, heart-expanding, electric, thrilling, rapturous, ecstatic; pervading, penetrating, absorbing.

earnest, wistful, eager, breathless; fervent, fervid, gushing [*colloq.*], warm, passionate, warmhearted, hearty, cordial, sincere, zealous, enthusiastic, glowing, ardent, burning, red-hot, fiery, flaming; boiling, –over.

rabid, raving, feverish, fanatical, hysterical; impetuous etc. (*excitable*) 825; overmastering.

impressed–, moved–, touched–, affected–, penetrated–, seized–, imbued etc. 820- with; devoured by; wrought up etc. (*excited*) 824; struck all of a heap [*colloq.*]; rapt; in a quiver etc. *n.;* enraptured etc. 829.

the heart -big, —full, —swelling, —beating, —pulsating, —throbbing, —thumping, —beating high, —melting, —overflowing, —bursting, —breaking.

adv. **heartily**, heart and soul, from the bottom of one's heart, *ab imo pectore* [*L.*], *de profundis* [*L.*]; at heart, *con amore* [*It.*], devoutly, over head and ears.

821a. Psychology and Psychotherapy

n. **psychology**, psychonomics, abnormal psychology, applied psychology, animal psychology, child psychology, clinical psychology, comparative psychology, differential psychology, dynamic psychology, experimental psychology, existential psychology, faculty psychology, functional psychology, genetic psychology, individual psychology, industrial psychology, parapsychology, rational psychology, self-psychology, structural psychology; physiological psychology, psychobiochemistry, psychobiology, psychophysics; psychoasthenics, psychostatics, psychogenetics; psychotechnics, psychotechnology.

[systems] Freudian psychology; Gestalt psychology *or* configurationism; behavior psychology *or* Watson's psychology; association psychology, mental chemistry.

psychiatry, psychiatrics, neuropsychiatry; prophylactic psychiatry, mental hygiene; psychosomatic medicine; psychosocial medicine.

psychotherapy; group therapy; occupational therapy; recreational therapy; narcotherapy, narcoanalysis, amytal *or* pentothal interview; hypnotherapy, hypnoanalysis; psychosurgery; suggestion therapy; hypnotic suggestion, posthypnotic suggestion; autosuggestion; sleep treatment; shock therapy, electroshock therapy, protein shock therapy, metrazol shock therapy, hypoglycemic shock therapy, insulin shock therapy, insulin coma therapy, convulsive shock therapy; psychoanalysis, depth interview; psychoanalytic therapy, depth psychology; psychognosis; dream analysis, interpretation of dreams, dream symbolism.

psychological test; aptitude test, Oseretsky test, Stanford scientific aptitude test; personality test, Bernreuter personality inventory, Minnesota multiplastic personality inventory; association test, controlled association test, free association test; apperception test, card test; Rorschach test, ink-blot test; intelligence test, I.Q. test; alpha test, beta test, Babcock-Levy test, Binet-Simon test, Goldstein-Sheerer test, Kent mental test, aussage test; Wechsler-Bellevue intelligence scale, Gesell's development schedule, Minnesota preschool scale, Cattell's infant intelligence scale.

psyche, mind; preconscious, foreconscious, coconscious; subconscious, unconscious, submerged mind; libido, libidinal energy, libidinal object; id, ego, superego; ego-ideal, ego-id conflict.

[pathological personality types] neurotic, psychoneurotic, neuropath; maladjusted personality, hostile personality; antisocial personality, sociopath; escapist; psychotic personality; mental defective, ament; hypochondriac; alcoholic.

neurosis, psychoneurosis, functional nervous disorder; pathoneurosis, actual neurosis, anxiety neurosis, blast neurosis, fright neurosis, traumatic neurosis, transference neurosis; compulsion neurosis, obsessional neurosis, obsessive-compulsion neurosis; occupational neurosis, professional neurasthenia; combat *or* war neurosis, battle fatigue, shell-shock; nervous breakdown.

psychosis, psychopathy, psychopathic condition; schizophrenia, functional disintegration, dissociation of personality, split personality, multiple personality; dementia praecox, paranoia, catatonia; hebephrenia, paraphrenia, schizophasia, schizothymia; melancholia, manic-depressive insanity, affective psychosis, cyclothymia; Korsakoff's psychosis, polyneuritic psychosis; amentia, fugue; dementia paralytica; senile dementia, senile psychosis, degenerative psychosis; presenile dementia; psychopathia sexualis, psychosexuality; pharmacopsychosis; arteriosclerotic psychosis, climacteric psychosis, exhaustive psychosis, gestational psychosis, involuntary psychosis, involutional psychosis, metabolic psychosis, organic psychosis, postinfectious psychosis, psychasthenia, psycholepsy, psychokinesia, psychorhythmia, toxic psychosis; moral insanity, psychopathic personality; rabies, hydrophobia.

[neurotic symptoms] anxiety, precordial anxiety, free-floating anxiety; asthenia; hysteria, conversion hysteria, anxiety hysteria; dissociation, emotional instability, flight reaction, immaturity; depression; detachment; passive aggression, passive dependence; phobia, morbid fear, astraphobia (lightning and thunder), acrophobia (heights), agoraphobia (open places), ailurophobia (cats), claustrophobia (confined

822. Sensibility

places), hematophobia (blood), hydrophobia (water), pyrophobia (fire), scotophobia (darkness), toxiphobia (being poisoned), xenophobia (strangers); unresponsiveness, apathy; stupor, catatonic stupor, euphoria, elation.

mania, obsession, compulsion; megalomania, monomania, kleptomania, pyromania, erotomania, dipsomania.

complex, inferiority complex, superiority complex, Oedipus *or* nuclear complex, Electra complex, persecution complex, castration complex; fixation, libido fixation, arrested development; infantile fixation, pregenital fixation; regression.

defense mechanism, psychological *or* sociological adjustive reaction; negativism; escape mechanism; withdrawal; isolation, emotional insulation; autistic thinking; compensation, overcompensation, decompensation; substitution; sublimation; projection; displacement; rationalization; suppression, repression, inhibition, reaction formation.

822. Sensibility

n. **sensibility**, sensibleness, sensitiveness; moral sensibility; impressibility, affectibility; susceptibleness, susceptibility, susceptivity; mobility; vivacity, vivaciousness; tenderness, softness; sentimentality, sentimentalism.

excitability etc. 825; fastidiousness etc. 868; physical sensibility etc. 375; sensitive plant.

sore point, sore place; quick, raw; where the shoe pinches.

v. **be sensible** etc. *adj.;* have a tender, –warm, –sensitive- heart; be all heart.

take to heart, treasure up in the heart; shrink, wince, blench, quiver.

"die of a rose in aromatic pain" [Pope]; touch to the quick; touch–, flick one- on the raw.

adj. **sensible**, sensitive; impressible, impressionable; susceptive, susceptible; alive to, impassionable, gushing [*colloq.*]; warm-hearted, tender-hearted, soft-hearted; tender, soft, maudlin, sentimental, romantic; enthusiastic, impassioned, highflying, spirited, mettlesome, vivacious, lively, expressive, mobile, tremblingly alive; excitable etc. 825; oversensitive, without skin, thin-skinned; fastidious etc. 868.

adv. **sensibly** etc. *adj.;* to the quick, on the raw, to the inmost core.

823. Insensibility

n. **insensibility**, insensibleness; want of sensibility etc. 823; moral insensibility; inertness, inertia, *vis inertiae* [*L.*]; impassibility, impassibleness; inappetency, apathy, phlegm, dullness, hebetude, supineness, insusceptibility, unimpressibility, luke-warmness.

coldness; cold -fit, –blood, –heart; coolness; frigidity, *sang-froid* [*F.*], stoicism, imperturbation etc. (*inexcitability*) 826; nonchalance, unconcern, dry eyes; insouciance etc. (*indifference*) 866; recklessness etc. 863; callousness, callosity, obtundity, brutification; heart of stone, blood and iron, stock and stone, marble, deadness.

neutrality; quietism, vegetation.

torpor, torpidity; obstupefaction [*obs.*], lethargy, coma, trance; sleep etc. 683; inanimation [*rare*], suspended animation; stupor, stupefaction; paralysis, palsy; numbness etc. (*physical insensibility*) 376; analgesia.

stoic, Indian, man of iron, pococurante, pococurantist; the Fat Boy in Pickwick.

trifler, dabbler, dilettante, sciolist etc. 493.

v. **be insensible** etc. *adj.;* have a rhinoceros hide; show insensibility etc. *n.;* not mind, not care, not be affected by; have no desire for etc. 866; have–, feel–, take- no interest in; *nil admirari* [*L.*]; not care a straw etc. (*unimportance*) 643 for; disregard etc. (*neglect*) 460; set at naught etc. (*make light of*) 483; turn a deaf ear to etc. (*inattention*) 458; vegetate.

render insensible, render callous; blunt, obtund, numb, benumb, paralyze, chloroform, deaden, hebetate, stun, stupefy; brutify, brutalize.

insure; harden, harden the heart; steel, case-harden, sear.

adj. **insensible**, unconscious; impassive, impassible; blind to, deaf to, dead to; obtundent, insusceptible *or* unsusceptible, unimpressionable, unimpressible; passionless, spiritless, heartless, soulless, unfeeling; unmoral.

apathetic, unemotional, leucophlegmatic [*obs.*], phlegmatic; dull, frigid; cold cold-blooded, cold-hearted; cold as charity; flat, obtuse, inert, supine, sluggish, torpid, torpedinous [*rare*], torporific; sleepy etc. (*inactive*) 683; languid, half-hearted, tame; numb, numbed; comatose; anaesthetic etc. 376; stupefied, chloroformed, palsy-stricken.

indifferent, lukewarm, Laodicean, careless, mindless, regardless; inattentive etc. 458; neglectful etc. 460; disregarding.

unconcerned, nonchalant, pococurante, insouciant, *sans souci* [*F.*]; unambitious etc. 866.

unaffected, unruffled, unimpressed, uninspired, unexcited, unmoved, unstirred, untouched, unshocked, unstruck; unblushing etc. (*shameless*) 885; unanimated; vegetative.

callous, thick-skinned, pachydermatous, impervious; hard, hardened; inured, casehardened; steeled-, proof- against; imperturbable etc. (*inexcitable*) 826; unfelt.

adv. **insensibly** etc. *adj.*; *aequo animo* [*L.*], without being -moved, -touched, -impressed; in cold blood; with dry eyes, with withers unwrung.

int. never mind! it is of no consequence etc. (*unimportant*) 642; it cannot be helped! it is all the same!

824. Excitation

n. **excitation of feeling**; mental-, mental excitement; suscitation [*obs.*], suscitability [*obs.*], galvanism, high pressure, stimulation, piquancy, provocation, inspiration, calling forth, infection; animation, agitation, perturbation; subjugation, fascination, intoxication, enravishment, ravishment, entrancement; unction, impressiveness etc. *adj.*

trial of temper, *casus belli* [*L.*], irritation etc. (*anger*) 900; passion etc. (*state of excitability*) 825; thrill etc. (*feeling*) 821; repression of feeling etc. 826.

emotional appeal, melodrama; great moment, crisis; sensationalism, yellow journalism.

v. **excite**, affect, touch, move, impress, strike, interest, animate, inspire, impassion, smite, infect; stir-, fire-, warm- the blood; set astir; awake, wake; awaken, waken; call forth; evoke, provoke; raise up, summon up, call up, wake up, blow up, get up, light up; raise; get up the steam, rouse, arouse, stir, fire, kindle, enkindle, illumine, illuminate, apply the torch, set on fire, inflame.

stimulate; exuscitate *or* exsuscitate [*both obs.*], suscitate [*obs.*]; inspirit; spirit up, stir up, work up; infuse life into, give new life to; bring-, introduce- new blood; quicken; sharpen; whet; work upon etc. (*incite*) 615; hurry on, give a fillip, fillip, put on one's mettle.

fan the -fire, -flame; blow the coals, stir the embers; fan, fan into a flame; foster, heat, warm, foment, raise to a fever heat; keep up, keep the pot boiling; revive, rekindle; rake up, rip up.

intoxicate, overwhelm, overpower, *bouleverser* [*F.*], upset, turn one's head; send [*slang*], fascinate; enrapture etc. (*give pleasure*) 829.

penetrate, pierce; stir-, play on-, come home to- the feelings; touch -a string, -a chord, -the soul, -the heart; go to one's heart, go through one, open the wound, turn the knife in the wound; touch to the quick; possess-, pervade-, imbue-, penetrate-, imbrue [*obs.*]-, absorb-, affect-, disturb- the soul; rivet the attention; sink into the -mind, -heart; absorb; prey on the mind.

agitate, perturb, ruffle, fluster, flutter, flurry, shake, disturb, startle, shock, stagger; give one a -shock, -turn; strike all of a heap [*colloq.*], strike dumb, stun, astound, electrify, galvanize, petrify.

irritate, sting; cut; cut to the -heart, -quick; try one's temper; fool to the top of one's bent, pique; infuriate, madden, make one's blood boil; lash into fury etc. (*wrath*) 900.

be excited etc. *adj.*; flash up, flare up; catch the infection; thrill etc. (*feel*) 821; mantle; work oneself up; seethe, boil, simmer, foam, fume, flame, rage, rave; run mad etc. (*passion*) 825; run amuck *or* amok.

adj. **excited** etc. *v.*; wrought up, on the *qui vive*, astir, sparkling; in a -quiver etc. 821, -fever, -ferment, -blaze, -state of excitement; in hysterics; black in the face, overwrought; hot, red-hot, flushed, feverish; all of a -flutter, -twitter; all in a pucker [*colloq.*]; with quivering lips, with trembling lips, with twitching lips, with tears in one's eyes.

raging, flaming; boiling, -over; ebullient, seething; foaming, -at the mouth; fuming; stung to the quick; on one's high ropes; on one's high horse; carried away by passion, wild, raving, frantic, mad, amuck, distracted, beside oneself, out of one's wits, ready to burst, *bouleversé* [*F.*], demoniacal.

lost, *éperdu* [*F.*], tempest-tossed; haggard; ready to sink.

exciting etc. *v.*; impressive, warm, glowing, fervid, swelling, imposing, spirit-stirring, thrilling; high-wrought; soul-stirring, soul-subduing; heart-stirring, heart-swelling, heart-thrilling; agonizing etc. (*painful*) 830; telling, sensational, melodramatic, hysterical; overpowering, overwhelming, more than flesh and blood can bear; yellow.

piquant etc. (*pungent*) 392; spicy, appetizing, stinging, provocative, *provoquant* [*F.*], tantalizing.

adv. at a critical -moment, -period, -point; under a sudden strain; with heart-interest [*cant*]; with plenty of pep [*slang*], with a punch [*slang*]; till one is blue in the face.

825. Excitability
[excess of sensitiveness]

n. **excitability**, impetuosity, vehemence; boisterousness etc. *adj.*; turbulence; impatience, intolerance, non-endurance; irritability etc. (*irascibility*) 901; itching etc. (*desire*) 865; winc-

826. Inexcitability

ing; disquiet, disquietude; restlessness; fidgets, fidgetiness; agitation etc. (*irregular motion*) 315.

trepidation, perturbation, ruffle, hurry, fuss, flurry, fluster, flutter; pother, stew [*colloq.*], ferment; whirl; buck fever [*colloq.*]; stage fright; hurry-scurry *or* hurry-skurry; thrill etc. (*feeling*) 821; state–, fever- of excitement; transport.

passion, excitement, flush, heat; fever, fever-heat; fire, flame, fume, blood boiling; tumult; effervescence, ebullition; boiling, –over; whiff, gust, storm, tempest; scene, breaking out, burst, fit, paroxysm, explosion, outbreak, outburst; agony.

fury; violence etc. 173; fierceness etc. *adj.*; rage, furor, furore [*It.*], desperation, madness, distraction, raving, delirium; frenzy *or* phrensy, hysterics; intoxication; tearing–, raging- passion; towering rage; anger etc. 900.

fixed idea, *l'idée fixe* [*F.*], monomania; fascination, infatuation, fanaticism; Quixotism, Quixotry; *tête montée* [*F.*].

v. **be impatient** etc. *adj.*; not be able to bear etc. 826; bear ill, wince, chafe, champ the bit; be in a stew [*colloq.*] etc. *n.*; be out of all patience, fidget, fuss, not have a wink of sleep; toss, –on one's pillow.

fume, rage, foam; lose one's temper etc. 900; break out, burst out, fly out; go–, fly- -off, –off at a tangent; explode; flare up, flame up, fire up, burst into a flame, take fire, fire, burn; stew [*colloq.*]; boil, –over; rave, rant, tear; go–, run- -wild, –mad; go into hysterics; run riot, run amuck *or* amok; *battre la campagne* [*F.*], *faire le diable à quatre* [*F.*]; play the deuce [*slang*]; raise -Cain, –the mischief, –the devil [*all slang*].

adj. **excitable**, easily excited, in an excitable state; startlish, mettlesome, high-mettled, skittish; high-strung; irritable etc. (*irascible*) 901; impatient, intolerant; moody, maggoty-headed.

feverish, febrile, hysterical; delirious, mad.

unquiet, mercurial, electric, galvanic, hasty, hurried, restless, fidgety, fussy; chafing etc. *v.*

vehement, demonstrative, violent, wild, furious, fierce, fiery, hot-headed, madcap.

overzealous, enthusiastic, impassioned, fanatical; rabid etc. (*eager*) 865.

rampant, clamorous, uproarious, turbulent, tempestuous, tumultuary, boisterous.

impulsive, impetuous, passionate, uncontrolled, uncontrollable, ungovernable, irrepressible, stanchless *or* staunchless, inextinguishable, burning, simmering, volcanic, ready to burst forth.

excited, exciting etc. 824.

adv. in confusion, pell-mell; in trepidation etc. *n.*

int. pish! pshaw! horrors!

826. Inexcitability

n. **inexcitability**, imperturbability, inirritability; even temper, tranquil mind, dispassion; toleration, tolerance, patience.

passiveness etc. (*physical inertness*) 172; hebetude, hebetation; impassibility etc. (*insensibility*) 823; stupefaction.

calmness etc. *adj.*; composure, placidity, indisturbance, imperturbation, *sang-froid* [*F.*], coolness, tranquillity, serenity; quiet, quietude; peace of mind, mental calmness.

equanimity, poise, staidness etc. *adj.*; gravity, sobriety, quietism, Quakerism; philosophy, stoicism, command of temper; self-possession, self-control, self-command, self-restraint; presence of mind.

resignation, submission etc. 725; sufferance, supportance, endurance, longsufferance, forbearance, longanimity, fortitude; patience of Job, "patience on a monument" [*Twelfth Night*], "patience sovereign o'er transmuted ill" [Johnson]; moderation; repression–, subjugation- of feeling; restraint etc. 751; tranquilization etc. (*moderation*) 174.

v. **be composed** etc. *adj.*

laisser faire [*F.*], *laisser aller* [*F.*]; take things -easily, –as they come; take it easy, rub on [*colloq.*], live and let live; take -easily, –coolly, –in good part; *aequam servare mentem* [*L.*].

endure; bear, –well, –the brunt; go through, support, brave, disregard; tolerate, suffer, stand, bide; abide, aby *or* abye; bear with, put up with, take up with, abide with; acquiesce; submit etc. (*yield*) 725; submit with a good grace; resign–, reconcile- oneself to; brook, digest, eat, swallow, pocket, stomach; carry on, carry through; make light of, make the best of, make "a virtue of necessity" [Chaucer]; put a good face on, keep one's countenance; check etc. 751- oneself.

compose, appease etc. (*moderate*) 174; propitiate; repress etc. (*restrain*) 751; render insensible etc. 823; overcome–, allay–, repress- one's excitability etc. 825; master one's feelings; make -one-self, –one's mind- easy; set one's mind at -ease, –rest; calm–, cool- down; gentle, tame, thaw, grow cool.

be borne, be endured, be swallowed; go down.

adj. **inexcitable**, imperturbable; unsusceptible etc. (*insensible*) 823; dispassionate, unpassionate, cold-blooded, unirritable, inirritable; enduring etc. *v.;* stoical, Platonic, philosophic, staid, stayed [*obs.*], sober, –minded; grave; sober–, grave- as a judge; sedate, demure, cool-headed, level-headed.

easy-going, peaceful, placid, calm; quiet, –as a mouse; tranquil, serene; cool, –as -a cucumber, –custard [*both colloq.*]; undemonstrative.

composed, collected; temperate etc. (*moderate*) 174; unexcited, unstirred, unruffled, undisturbed, unperturbed, unimpassioned.

meek, tolerant; patient, –as Job; unoffended; unresisting; submissive etc. 725; tame; content, resigned, chastened, subdued, lamblike; gentle, –as a lamb; *suaviter in modo* [*L.*]; mild, –as mother's milk; soft as peppermint; armed with patience, bearing with, clement, long-suffering, forbearant, longanimous.

adv. "like patience on a monument smiling at grief" [*Twelfth Night*]; *aequo animo* [*L.*], in cold blood etc. 823; more in sorrow than in anger.

int. patience! and shuffle the cards.

Section 2. Personal

827. Pleasure

n. **pleasure**, gratification, enjoyment, fruition, delectation, oblectation [*rare*]; relish, zest; gusto etc. (*physical pleasure*) 377; satisfaction etc. (*content*) 831; complacency.

well-being; good etc. 618; snugness, comfort, ease; cushion etc. 215; *sans souci* [*F.*], mind at ease.

joy, gladness, delight, glee, cheer, sunshine; cheerfulness etc. 836.

treat, refreshment; amusement etc. 840; luxury etc. 377.

happiness, felicity, bliss; beatitude, beatification; enchantment, transport, rapture, ravishment, ecstasy; *summum bonum* [*L.*]; paradise, elysium etc. (*heaven*) 981; third–, seventh- heaven; unalloyed happiness etc.; hedonics, hedonism.

mens sana in corpore sano [Juvenal].

honeymoon; palmy–, halcyon- days; golden -age, –time; Eden, Paradise; Dixie, Dixie land *or* Dixie's land; *Saturnia regna* [*L.*], Arcadia, Cockaigne, happy valley, Agapemone.

v. **be pleased** etc. 829; oblectate [*rare*]; feel–, experience- pleasure etc. *n.;* joy; enjoy–, hug- oneself; be in clover [*colloq.*] etc. 377, be in elysium etc. 981; tread on enchanted ground; fall–, go- into raptures.

feel at home, breathe freely, bask in the sunshine.

enjoy, like, relish; be pleased with etc. 829; receive–, derive- pleasure etc. *n.*- from; take pleasure etc. *n.*- in; delight in, rejoice in, indulge in, luxuriate in; gloat over etc. (*physical pleasure*) 377; love etc. 897; fall for [*slang*]; take to, take a fancy to [*both colloq.*]; have a liking for; enter into the spirit of; take in good part; treat oneself to, solace oneself with.

adj. **pleased** etc. 829; not sorry; glad, gladsome; pleased as Punch; pleased as a child with a new toy.

happy, blest, blessed, blissful, beatified; happy as -a clam at high water [*U. S.*], –a king, –the day is long; thrice happy, *ter quaterque beatus* [*L.*]; enjoying etc. *v.;* joyful etc. (*in spirits*) 836; hedonic.

in a blissful state, in paradise etc. 981, in raptures, in ecstasies, in a transport of delight.

comfortable etc. (*physical pleasure*) 377; at ease; in clover [*colloq.*]; content etc. 831; *sans souci* [*F.*].

overjoyed, entranced, enchanted; raptured, enraptured, enravished, ravished, transported; fascinated, captivated.

with a joyful face, with sparkling eyes.

pleasing etc. 829; ecstatic, beatific *or* beaitifical; painless, unalloyed, without alloy, cloudless.

adv. **happily** etc. *adj.;* with pleasure etc. (*willingly*) 602; with glee etc. *n.*

828. Pain

n. **pain**, mental suffering, dolor, suffering, sufferance [*rare*], ache; smart etc. (*physical pain*) 378; passion.

displeasure, dissatisfaction, discomfort, discomposure, disquiet; *malaise* [*F.*], inquietude, uneasiness, vexation of spirit; taking [*colloq.*]; discontent etc. 832.

dejection etc. 837; weariness etc. 841; anhedonia.

annoyance, irritation, worry, infliction, visitation; plague, bore; bother, botheration [*colloq.*], stew [*colloq.*], vexation, mortification, chagrin, *esclandre* [*F.*]; *mauvais quart d'heure* [*F.*].

care, anxiety, solicitude, trouble, trial, ordeal, fiery ordeal, shock, blow, cark [*archaic*], dole [*archaic*], fret, burden, load.

grief, sorrow, distress, affliction, woe, bitterness, heartache; carking cares [*archaic*]; concern; heavy–, aching–, bleeding–, broken- heart; heavy affliction, gnawing grief.

misery, unhappiness, infelicity, tribulation, wretchedness, desolation; despair etc. 859; extremity, prostration, depth of misery; slough of despond etc. (*adversity*) 735; peck–, sea– of troubles; "the thousand natural shocks that flesh is heir to" [*Hamlet*] etc. (*evil*) 616; miseries of human life; the iron entering the soul; "unkindest cut of all" [*Julius Caesar*].

nightmare, ephialtes, incubus.

anguish, pang, agony, torture, torment; crucifixion, martyrdom, rack; purgatory etc. (*hell*) 982; hell upon earth; iron age, reign of terror.

sufferer, victim, prey, martyr, object of compassion, wretch, shorn lamb.

v. **suffer**, ail; feel–, suffer–, experience–, undergo–, bear–, endure– pain etc. *n.*, smart, ache etc. (*physical pain*) 378; bleed; be the victim of.

labor under afflictions; bear–, stagger under–, take up– the cross; quaff the bitter cup, have a bad time of it; fall on evil days etc. (*adversity*) 735; go hard with, come to grief, fall a sacrifice to, drain the cup of misery to the dregs, "sup full of horrors" [*Macbeth*].

fret, chafe, sit on thorns, be on pins and needles, wince, worry oneself, be in a taking [*colloq.*], fret and fume; take on [*colloq.*], take to heart; cark [*archaic*].

grieve; mourn etc. (*lament*) 839; yearn, repine, pine, droop, languish, sink; give way; despair etc. 859; heart-scald [*dial. Eng.*]; break one's heart; weigh upon the heart etc. (*inflict pain*) 830.

adj. **pained**, afflicted; in–, in a state of–, full of– pain etc. *n.;* suffering etc. *v.;* worried, displeased etc. 830; aching, griped, sore etc. (*physical pain*) 378; on the rack, in limbo; between hawk and buzzard.

uneasy, uncomfortable, ill at ease; in a taking, in a way [*both colloq.*]; disturbed; discontented etc. 832; out of humor etc. 901*a;* weary etc. 841.

unfortunate etc. (*hapless*) 735; to be pitied, doomed, devoted, accursed, undone, lost, stranded; fey [*obs.*]; victimized, a prey to, ill-used.

unhappy, infelicitous, poor, wretched, miserable, woe-begone; cheerless etc. (*dejected*) 837; careworn; heavy laden, stricken, crushed.

concerned, sorry; sorrowing, sorrowful; cut up [*colloq.*], chagrined, horrified, horror-stricken; in–, plunged in–, a prey to– grief etc. *n.;* in tears etc. (*lamenting*) 839; steeped to the lips in misery; heartstricken, heartbroken, heart-scalded [*dial. Eng.*]; broken-hearted; in despair etc. 859.

829. Pleasurableness
[capability of giving pleasure]

n. **pleasurableness**, pleasantness, agreeableness etc. *adj.;* pleasure giving, jucundity [*rare*], jocundity, delectability; amusement etc. 840; goodness etc. 648; manna in the wilderness, land flowing with milk and honey, "the shadow of a great rock in a weary land" [*Bible*]; flowery beds of ease; fair weather.

treat; regale etc. (*physical pleasure*) 377; sweets etc. (*sugar*) 396; dainty, *bonne bouche* [*F.*], titbit *or* tidbit; sweets, sweetmeats, nuts, *sauce piquante* [*F.*], salt, savor; a sight for sore eyes [*colloq.*].

attraction etc. (*motive*) 615; attractiveness, attractability [*rare*], attractableness; invitingness etc. *adj.;* charm, fascination, captivation, enchantment, witchery, seduction, winning ways, amenity, amiability; winsomeness; loveliness etc. (*beauty*) 845; sunny side, bright side.

v. **delight**, charm, becharm, imparadise; gladden etc. (*make cheerful*) 836; win–, gladden–, rejoice–, warm the cockles of– the heart; do one's heart good; bless, beatify; take, captivate, fascinate; enchant, entrance, enrapture, transport, bewitch, ravish, enravish.

cause–, produce–, create–, give–, afford–, procure–, offer–, present–, yield– pleasure etc. 827.

please, satisfy, gratify, –desire etc. 865; slake, satiate, quench; indulge, humor, flatter, tickle; tickle the palate etc. (*savory*) 394; regale, refresh; enliven; treat; amuse etc. 840; take–, tickle–, hit– one's fancy; meet one's wishes.

attract, allure etc. (*move*) 615; stimulate etc. (*excite*) 824; interest.

make things pleasant, make everyone feel happy, popularize, gild the pill, sweeten; smooth–, pour oil upon– the troubled waters.

adj. **pleasurable**, causing pleasure etc. *v.;* laetificant; pleasure-giving; pleasing, pleasant, amiable, agreeable, grateful, gratifying; lief *or* leef [*obs.*], acceptable; dear, beloved; welcome, –as the roses in May; welcomed; favorite; to one's taste, –mind, –liking; satisfactory etc. (*good*) 648.

refreshing; comfortable; cordial; genial; glad, gladsome; sweet, delectable, nice, dainty; delicate, delicious; dulcet; luscious etc. 396; palatable etc. 394.

luxurious, voluptuous; sensual etc. 377.

attractive etc. 615; inviting, prepossessing, engaging; winning, winsome; taking, fascinating, captivating, killing [*colloq.*]; seducing, seductive; heart-robbing; alluring, enticing; appetizing etc. (*exciting*) 824; cheering etc. 836; bewitching; enchanting, entrancing, enravishing.

delightful, charming, felicitous, exquisite; lovely etc. (*beautiful* 845; ravishing, rapturous; heartfelt, thrilling, ecstatic, beatific *or* beatifical, seraphic; empyrean; paradisaic *or* paradisaical; elysian etc. (*heavenly*) 981.

palmy, halcyon, Saturnian.

adv. **to one's delight**, to one's heart's content, in utter satisfaction; at one's ease; in clover; in heaven, in paradise, in elysium; from a full heart.

830. Painfulness
[capability of giving pain]

n. **painfulness** etc. *adj.;* trouble, care etc. (*pain*) 828; trial, affliction, infliction; cross, blow, stroke, burden, load, curse; bitter -pill, –draft *or* draught, –cup; cup–, waters- of bitterness.

annoyance, grievance, nuisance, vexation, mortification, sickener [*rare*], worry, bore, bother, pother, hot water, "sea of troubles" [*Hamlet*], hornet's nest, plague, pest.

source of -irritation, –annoyance; wound, sore subject, skeleton in the closet; thorn in -the flesh, –one's side; where the shoe pinches, gall and wormwood; fly in the ointment; worm at the heart of the rose; crumpled rose-leaf; pea in the shoe.

cancer, ulcer, sting, thorn; canker etc. (*bane*) 663; scorpion etc. (*evildoer*) 913; dagger etc. (*arms*) 727; scourge etc. (*instrument of punishment*) 975; carking care [*archaic*], canker worm of care.

mishap, misfortune etc. (*adversity*) 735; désagrément [*F.*], esclandre [*F.*], rub.

sorry sight, heavy news, provocation; affront etc. 929; "head and front of one's offending" [*Othello*].

infestation, molestation; malignity etc. (*malevolence*) 907.

v. **pain**, hurt, wound; cause–, occasion–, give–, bring–, induce–, produce–, create–, inflict- pain etc. 828.

pinch, prick, gripe etc. (*physical pain*) 378; pierce, lancinate, cut.

hurt–, wound–, grate upon–, jar upon- the feelings; wring–, pierce–, lacerate–, break–, rend- the heart; make the heart bleed; tear–, rend- the heartstrings; draw tears from the eyes; add a nail to one's coffin.

sadden; make unhappy etc. 828; plunge into sorrow, grieve, fash [*Scot.*], afflict, distress; cut up [*colloq.*], cut to the heart.

annoy, incommode, displease, discompose, trouble, disquiet; faze [*U. S.*], feeze *or* feaze [*colloq., U. S. & dial. Eng.*], disturb, cross, thwart, perplex, molest; tease, tire, irk, vex, mortify, wherret [*obs.*], worry, plague, bother, pester, bore, pother, harass, harry, badger, heckle, bait, beset, infest, persecute, importune.

torment, wring, harrow, torture; bullyrag; put to the -rack, –question; break on the wheel, rack, scarify; cruciate [*obs.*], crucify; convulse, agonize; barb the dart; plant a - dagger in the breast, –thorn in one's side.

irritate, provoke, sting, nettle, try the patience, pique, fret, roil rile [*colloq. & dial.*], tweak the nose, chafe, gall; sting–, wound–, cut- to the quick; aggrieve, affront, enchafe [*obs.*], enrage, ruffle, sour the temper; give offense etc. (*resentment*) 900.

maltreat, bite, snap at, assail; smite etc. (*punish*) 972; bite the hand that feeds one.

repel, revolt; sicken, disgust, nauseate; disenchant, offend, shock, stink in the nostrils; go against–, turn- the stomach; make one sick, set the teeth on edge, go against the grain, grate on the ear; stick in one's -throat, –gizzard [*colloq.*]; rankle, gnaw, corrode, horrify, appal, freeze the blood; make the flesh creep, make the hair stand on end; make the blood -curdle, –run cold; make one shudder.

haunt, haunt the memory; weigh–, prey- on the -heart, –mind, –spirits; bring one's gray hairs with sorrow to the grave.

adj. **painful**, causing pain, hurting etc. *v.;* hurtful etc. (*bad*) 649; dolorific *or* dolorifical, dolorous.

unpleasant, unpleasing, displeasing, disagreeable, unpalatable, bitter, distasteful, unpleasing, uninviting, unwelcome, undesirable, undesired; obnoxious; unacceptable, unpopular, thankless.

untoward, unsatisfactory, unlucky, inauspicious, ill-starred, uncomfortable.

distressing; afflicting, afflictive; joyless, cheerless, comfortless, dismal, disheartening; depressing, depressive; dreary, melancholy, grievous, piteous, woeful, rueful, mournful; deplorable, pitiable, lamentable, sad, affecting, touching, pathetic.

irritating, provoking, stinging, annoying, aggravating [*colloq.*], exasperating, mortifying, galling; unaccommodating, invidious, vexatious; troublesome, tiresome, irksome, weari-

831. Content

some; plaguing, plaguesome, plaguy [*colloq.*]; awkward.

importunate; teasing, pestering, bothering, harassing, worrying, tormenting, carking [*archaic*].

insufferable, intolerable, insupportable, unbearable, unendurable; past bearing; not to be -borne, –endured; more than flesh and blood can bear; enough to -drive one mad, –provoke a saint, –make a parson swear [*colloq.*], –try the patience of Job.

shocking, terrific, grim, appalling, crushing; dreadful, fearful, frightful; thrilling, tremendous, dire; heartbreaking, heart-rending, heart-wounding, heart-corroding, heart-sickening; harrowing, rending.

odious, hateful, execrable, repulsive, repellent, abhorrent; horrid, horrible, horrific, horrifying; offensive; nauseous, nauseating; disgusting, sickening, revolting; nasty; loathsome, loathful; fulsome; vile etc. (*bad*) 649; hideous etc. 846.

acute, sharp, sore, severe, grave, hard, harsh, cruel, biting, caustic; cutting, corroding, consuming, racking, excruciating, searching, searing, grinding, grating, agonizing; envenomed; catheretic, pyrotic.

cumbrous, cumbersome, burdensome, onerous, oppressive.

desolating, withering, tragical, disastrous, calamitous, ruinous.

adv. **painfully** etc. *adj.;* with pain etc. 828; deuced *or* deucedly [*slang*]; under torture, in agony, out of the depths.

int. woe's me! alas! that I had ever been born! *hinc illae lacrimae!* [Terence].

831. Content

n. **content**, contentment, contentedness; complacency, satisfaction, entire satisfaction, ease, heart's ease, peace of mind; serenity etc. 826; cheerfulness etc. 836; ray of comfort; comfort etc. (*well-being*) 827.

patience, moderation, endurance; conciliation, reconciliation; resignation etc. (*patience*) 826; quietism.

waiter on Providence; quietist.

v. **be content** etc. *adj.;* rest satisfied, rest and be thankful; take the good the gods provide, let well enough alone, feel oneself at home, hug oneself, lay the flattering unction to one's soul.

take up with, take in good part; assent etc. 488; be reconciled to, make one's peace with; get over it; take heart, take comfort; put up with etc. (*bear*) 826.

render content etc. *adj.;* set at ease, comfort; set one's -heart, –mind- at -ease, –rest; speak peace; conciliate, reconcile, win over, propitiate, disarm, beguile; content, satisfy; gratify etc. 829.

be tolerated etc. 826; go down, go down with [*colloq.*], do.

adj. **content**, contented; satisfied etc. *v.;* at ease, at one's ease, at home; with the mind at ease, *sans souci* [*F.*], *sine curâ* [*L.*], easy-going, not particular; conciliatory; unrepining, of good comfort; resigned etc. (*patient*) 826; cheerful etc. 836.

serene etc. 826; unafflicted, unvexed, unmolested, unplagued; at rest; snug, comfortable; in one's element; not easily perturbed; imperturbable.

satisfactory, adequate, commensurate, sufficient, ample, equal to; satisfying.

adv. to one's heart's content; *à la bonne heure* [*F.*]; all for the best.

int. amen etc. (*assent*) 488; very well! all the better! so much the better! well and good! it will do! that will do! it cannot be helped! done! content! i' faith! [*archaic*]; better and better! good! good for you! put it thar, pard! [*colloq.*].

832. Discontent

n. **discontent**, discontentment; dissatisfaction; "the winter of our discontent" [*Henry VI*]; dissent etc. 489; querulousness etc. (*lamentation*) 839; hypercriticism.

disappointment, mortification; cold comfort; regret etc. 833; repining, taking on [*colloq.*] etc. *v.;* inquietude, vexation of spirit, soreness; heartburning, heart-grief.

malcontent, grumbler, growler, grouch [*slang*], croaker, *laudator temporis acti* [*L.*]; censurer, complainer, faultfinder, murmurer.

The Opposition; Bitter-Enders [*U. S. politics*], Die-Hards; cave of Adullam; indignation meeting.

v. **be discontented** etc. *adj.;* quarrel with one's bread and butter; repine; regret etc. 833; wish one to Jericho, wish one at the bottom of the Red Sea; take on [*colloq.*], take to heart; shrug the shoulders; make a wry face, pull a long face; knit one's brows; look blue, look black, look black as thunder, look blank, look glum.

grumble, take ill, take in bad part; fret, chafe, make a piece of work [*colloq.*], croak; lament etc. 839.

cause discontent etc. *n.;* dissatisfy, disappoint, mortify, put out [*colloq.*], disconcert; cut up; dishearten.

- *adj.* **discontented**; dissatisfied etc. *v.;* unsatisfied, ungratified; dissident; dissentient etc. 489; malcontent, exigent, exacting, hypercritical.
- **repining** etc. *v.;* regretful etc. 833; down in the mouth etc. (*dejected*) 837.
- **glum**, sulky; in high dudgeon, in a fume, in the sulks, in the dumps, in bad humor; sour, sour as a crab; sore as a crab [*colloq.*]; soured, sore; out of humor, out of temper.
- **disappointing** etc. *v.;* unsatisfactory.
- *adv.* **from bad to worse**, out of the frying pan into the fire, in the depths of despair.
- *int.* so much the worse! that's bad! couldn't be worse! worse and worse!

833. Regret

- *n.* **regret**, repining; homesickness, nostalgia; *mal du pays* [*F.*], *maladie du pays* [*F.*]; lamentation etc. 839; penitence etc. 950.
- **bitterness**, heartburning.
- *laudator temporis acti* [*L.*] etc. (*discontent*) 832.
- *v.* **regret**, deplore; bewail etc. (*lament*) 839; repine, cast a longing lingering look behind; rue, rue the day; repent etc. 950; *infandum renovare dolorem* [*L.*].
- prey–, weigh–, have a weight- on the mind; leave an aching void.
- *adj.* **regretting** etc. *v.;* regretful; homesick.
- **regretted** etc. *v.;* much to be regretted, regrettable; lamentable etc. (*bad*) 649.
- *int.* what a pity! hang it *or* hang it all! [*colloq.*].

834. Relief

- *n.* **relief**; deliverance; refreshment etc. 689; easement, softening, alleviation, mitigation, palliation, soothing; lullaby, cradle-song, *berceuse* [*F.*].
- **solace**, consolation, comfort, encouragement; crumb of comfort, balm in Gilead.
- **lenitive**, palliative, restorative etc. (*remedy*) 662; stupe, poultice, fomentation, assuasive; cushion etc. 215.
- *v.* **relieve**, ease, alleviate, mitigate, palliate, soothe; salve; soften, –down; forment, stupe, poultice; assuage, allay, abirritate.
- remedy; cure etc. (*restore*) 660; refresh; pour balm into, pour oil on.
- smooth the ruffled brow of care, temper the wind to the shorn lamb, lay the flattering unction to one's soul.
- **cheer**, comfort, console; enliven; encourage, bear up, pat on the back, give comfort, set at ease; gladden–, cheer- the heart; inspirit, invigorate.
- **disburden** etc. (*free*) 705; take off a load of care.

- **be relieved**; breathe more freely, draw a long breath; take comfort; dry the eyes, dry the tears, wipe the eyes, wipe away the tears; pull oneself together.
- *adj.* **relieving** etc. *v.;* consolatory, soothing; assuaging, assuasive; balmy, balsamic; lenitive, palliative; anodyne etc. (*remedial*) 662; curative etc. 660.

835. Aggravation

- *n.* **aggravation**, heightening; exacerbation; exasperation; overestimation etc. 482; exaggeration etc. 549.
- *v.* **aggravate**, render worse, heighten, embitter, sour; exacerbate, acerbate, exasperate, envenom; enrage, provoke, tease.
- add fuel to the -fire, –flame; fan the flame etc. (*excite*) 824; go from bad to worse etc. (*deteriorate*) 659.
- *adj.* **aggravated** etc. *v.;* worse, unrelieved; aggravable [*obs.*], aggravative, aggravating etc. *v.*
- *adv.* out of the frying pan into the fire, from bad to worse, worse and worse.
- *int.* so much the worse! *tant pis!* [*F.*].

836. Cheerfulness

- *n.* **cheerfulness** etc. *adj.;* geniality, gayety, *L'Allegro* [*It.*], cheer, good humor, spirits; high spirits, animal spirits, flow of spirits; glee, high glee, light heart; sunshine of the -mind, –breast; *gaieté de coeur* [*F.*], *bon naturel* [*F.*].
- **liveliness** etc. *adj.;* life, alacrity, vivacity, animation, *allégresse* [*F.*]; jocundity, joviality, jollity; levity; jocularity etc. (*wit*) 842.
- **mirth**, merriment, hilarity, exhilaration; laughter etc. 838; merrymaking etc. (*amusement*) 840; heyday, rejoicing etc. 838; marriage bell.
- nepenthe *or* nepenthes, lotus; Euphrosyne.
- **optimism** etc. (*hopefulness*) 858; self-complacency; hedonics, hedonism.
- *v.* **be cheerful** etc. *adj.;* have the mind at ease, smile, put a good face upon, keep up one's spirits; view the bright side of the picture, view things *en couleur de rose* [*F.*]; look through rose-colored spectacles; *ridentem dicere verum* [*L.*], cheer up, brighten up, light up, bear up; take heart, cast away care, drive dull care away, perk up; keep a stiff upper lip [*slang*].
- **rejoice** etc.; 838; carol, chirp, chirrup, lilt; frisk, rollic, give a loose to mirth [*obs.*].
- **cheer**, enliven, elate, exhilarate, gladden, inspirit, animate, raise the spirits, inspire; put in good humor; cheer–, rejoice- the heart; delight etc. (*give pleasure*) 829.

837. Dejection

- *adj.* **cheerful**; happy etc. 827; cheery, of good cheer, smiling; blithe; in spirits, in good spirits; breezy, bully [*slang*], chipper [*colloq.*]; in high -spirits, –feather; happy as -the day is long, –a king; gay, gay as a lark; *allegro* [*It.*]; debonair *or* debonaire, light, lightsome, lighthearted; buoyant, bright, free and easy, airy; jaunty *or* janty, rollicky [*colloq.*], canty [*Scot. & dial. Eng.*], "crouse an' canty" [Burns]; hedonic; riant; sprightly, sprightful; spry; spirited, spiritful [*rare*], lively, animated, vivacious; brisk, –as a bee; sparkling; sportive; full of -play, –spirit; all alive.
  sunny, palmy; hopeful etc. 858.
  merry, –as a -cricket, –grig, –marriage bell; joyful, joyous, jocund, jovial; jolly, –as a thrush, –as a sand-boy; blithesome; gleeful, gleesome; hilarious, rattling [*colloq.*].
  winsome, bonny, hearty, buxom.
  playful, playsome; *folâtre* [*F.*], playful as a kitten, tricksy, frisky, frolicsome; gamesome; jocose, jocular, waggish; mirth-loving, laughter-loving, abderian; mirthful, rollicking.
  elate, elated; exulting, jubilant, flushed; rejoicing etc. 838; cock-a-hoop.
  cheering, inspiriting, exhilarating; cardiac *or* cardiacal; pleasing etc. 829; palmy, flourishing, halcyon.
- *adv.* **cheerfully** etc. *adj.;* cheerily, with good cheer; with a cheerful etc. heart; with relish, with zest; on the crest of the wave.
- *int.* **never say die**! come! cheer up! hurrah! etc. 838; "hence loathed melancholy!" begone dull care! away with melancholy!

837. Dejection

- *n.* **dejection**; dejectedness etc. *adj.;* depression, prosternation [*obs.*], mopishness, damp; lowness-, depression- of spirits; weight-, oppression-, damp- on the spirits; low-, bad-, drooping-, depressed- spirits; heart sinking; heaviness-, failure- of heart.
  heaviness etc. *adj.;* infestivity, gloom; weariness etc. 841; *taedium vitae* [*L.*], disgust of life; *mal du pays* [*F.*] etc. (regret) 833; anhedonia.
  melancholy; sadness etc. *adj.;* *Il Penseroso* [*Old It.*], melancholia, dismals, blue devils [*colloq.*], blues [*colloq.*], mopes, lachrymals *or* lacrimals, mumps, dumps [*chiefly humorous*], doldrums, vapors [*archaic*], megrims, spleen [*obsoles.*], horros, hypochondriasis, hypochondria, jawfall [*rare*], pessimism; *la maladie sans maladie* [*F.*], despondency, slough of Despond; disconsolateness etc. *adj.;* hope deferred, blank despondency; voiceless woe.
  prostration, prostration of soul; broken heart; despair etc. 859; cave of despair, cave of Trophonius.
  gravity; demureness etc. *adj.;* solemnity; long face, grave face.
  hypochondriac, seek-sorrow, self-tormentor, *heautontimorumenos* [*Gr.*], *malade imaginaire* [*F.*], *médecin tant pis* [*F.*]; croaker, pessimist; mope, mopus [*dial. Eng. & slang*], damper, wet blanket crape-hanger [*slang*], Job's comforter.
  [cause of dejection] affliction etc. 830; sorry sight; *memento mori* [*L.*]; deathwatch, death's-head, skeleton at the feast.
- *v.* **be dejected** etc. *adj.;* grieve; mourn etc. (lament) 839; take on [*colloq.*], give way, lose heart, despond, droop, sink.
  lower, look downcast, frown, pout; hang down the head; pull-, make- a long face; laugh on the wrong side of the mouth; grin a ghastly smile; look blue, look like a drowned man; lay to heart, take to heart.
  mope, brood over; fret; sulk; pine, pine away; yearn; repine etc. (regret) 833; despair etc. 859.
  refrain from laughter, keep one's countenance; be *or* look grave etc. *adj.;* repress a smile, keep a straight face.
  depress, discourage, dishearten, dispirit; damp, dull, deject, lower, sink, dash, knock down, unman, prostrate, break one's heart; frown upon; cast a gloom on, cast a shade on; sadden; damp-, dash-, wither- one's hopes; weight-, lie heavy-, prey- on the -mind, -spirits; damp-, dampen-, depress- the spirits.
- *adj.* **cheerless**, joyless, spiritless, uncheerful, uncheery, unlively; unhappy etc. 828; melancholy, dismal, somber, dark, gloomy, *triste* [*F.*], clouded, murky, lowering, frowning, lugubrious, funereal, mournful, lamentable, dreadful.
  dreary, flat; dull, –as -a beetle, –ditchwater; depressing etc. *v.;* damp [*archaic*].
  downcast, downhearted, mopy [*colloq.*], "melancholy as a gib cat" [*Henry IV Part I*]; a prey to melancholy; "besieged with sable-coloured melancholy" [*Love's Labour Lost*]; down in the mouth [*colloq.*], down on one's luck [*colloq.*]; heavy-hearted; in the -dumps, –suds [*colloq.*], –sulks, –doldrums; in doleful dumps, in bad humor; sullen; mumpish, dumpish, mopish, moping; moody, glum; sulky etc. (discontented) 832; out of -sorts, –humor, –heart, –spirits; ill at ease, low-spirited, in low spirits, a cup too low; weary etc. 841; discouraged, disheartened, desponding, chapfallen *or* chopfallen, jawfallen [*rare*]; crestfallen.

sad, pensive, *pensieroso* [*It.*], tristful; dolesome, doleful; woe-begone, lachry-mose, in tears, melancholic, hypochondriacal, bilious, jaundiced, atrabilious, saturnine, splenetic; lackadaisical.

serious, sedate, staid, earnest; grave, –as -a judge, –an undertaker, –a mustard pot [*colloq.*]; sober, solemn, demure; grim, grim-faced, grim-visaged; rueful, wan, long-faced.

disconsolate, inconsolable, forlorn, comfortless, desolate, *désolé* [*F.*], sick at heart; soul-sick, heartsick; *au désespoir* [*F.*]; in despair etc. 859; lost.

overcome; broken-down, borne-down, bowed-down; heartstricken etc. (*mental suffering*) 828; cut up [*colloq.*], dashed, sunk; unnerved, unmanned; downfallen, downtrodden; broken-hearted; careworn.

adv. **sadly** etc. *adj.*; with a long face, with tears in one's eyes.

838. Rejoicing
[expression of pleasure]

n. **rejoicing**, exultation, triumph, jubilation, heyday, flush, reveling *or* revelling; merrymaking etc. (*amusement*) 840; jubilee etc. (*celebration*) 883; paean, *Te Deum* [*L.*] etc. (*thanksgiving*) 990; congratulation etc. 896.

smile, simper, smirk, grin; broad grin, sardonic grin.

laughter, giggle, titter, snicker, snigger, crow, cheer, chuckle, shout; Homeric laughter; horse–, hearty- laugh; guffaw; burst–, fit–, shout–, roar–, peal- of laughter; cachinnation; Kentish fire.

risibility; derision etc. 856; "sport that wrinkled Care derides" [Milton].

Momus; Democritus the Abderite; rollicker.

cheer, huzza, hurrah *or* hurra, cheering; shout, yell, college yell; tiger [*colloq.*].

v. **rejoice**; thank–, bless- one's stars; congratulate oneself, hug oneself; rub–, clap- one's hands; smack the lips, fling up one's cap; dance, skip; sing, carol, chirrup, chirp; hurrah *or* hurra; cry for joy, leap with joy, skip for joy; exult etc. (*boast*) 884; triumph; hold jubilee etc. (*celebrate*) 883; sing a *Te Deum*, sing a paean of triumph; make merry etc. (*sport*) 840.

smile, simper, smirk; grin, –like a Cheshire cat [*colloq.*]; mock, laugh in one's sleeve.

laugh, –outright; giggle, titter, snigger, snicker, crow, smicker [*obs.*], chuckle, cackle; burst out; burst into a roar of laughter, burst into a fit of laughter; shout, split [*colloq.*], roar.

shake–, split–, hold both- one's sides; roar–, shake–, nearly die–, die- with laughter.

raise laughter etc. (*amuse*) 840.

adj. **rejoicing** etc. *v.*; jubilant, exultant, triumphant; flushed, elated; laughing etc. *v.*; risible; ready to -burst, –split, –die with laughter [*all colloq.*]; convulsed with laughter; shaking like a jelly with -laughter, –suppressed merriment [*both colloq.*].

laughable etc. (*ludicrous*) 853.

adv. **laughingly**; on a broad grin, in fits of laughter, amid peals of laughter; in triumph; in mockery; with a -roar, –peal, –outburst- of laughter.

int. **hurrah**! huzza! three cheers! right on! hip, hip, hurrah! aha! hail! tolderolloll! Heaven be praised! *tant mieux!* [*F.*], so much the better! good enough! tra-la-la!

839. Lamentation
[expression of pain]

n. **lamentation**, lament, wail, complaint, plaint, murmur, mutter, grumble, groan, moan, whine, whimper, sob, sigh, suspiration, deep sigh; frown, scowl.

cry etc. (*vociferation*) 411; scream, howl, outcry, wail, wail of woe.

weeping etc. *v.*; tear; flood of tears, fit of crying, lachrymation [*rare*], crying; melting mood; "weeping and gnashing of teeth" [Bible].

plaintiveness etc. *adj.*; languishment; condolence etc. 915.

mourning, weeds [*colloq.*], widow's weeds, willow, cypress, crape, deep mourning; sackcloth and ashes; lachrymatory, tear bottle, lachrymals *or* lacrimals; knell etc. 363; dump [*obs.*], death song, dirge, coronach [*Scot. & Ir.*], nenia, requiem, elegy, epicedium; threne [*rare*], menody, threnody; jeremiad *or* jeremiade, ululation, keen [*Ir.*], ullalulla [*Ir.*].

mourner, keener [*Ir.*]; grumbler etc. (*discontent*) 832; Niobe; Heraclitus, Jeremiah, Mrs. Gummidge.

v. **lament**, mourn, deplore, grieve, keen [*Ir.*], weep over; bewail, bemoan; condole with etc. 915; fret etc. (*suffer*) 828; wear–, go into–, put on- mourning; wear -the willow, –sackcloth and ashes; *infandum renovare dolorem* [Virgil] etc. (*regret*) 833; give sorrow words.

sigh; give–, heave–, fetch- a sigh; "waft a sigh from Indus to the pole" [Pope]; sigh "like furnace" [*As You Like It*]; wail.

cry, weep, sob, greet [*archaic or Scot.*], blubber, snivel, bibber, whimper, pule; pipe, pipe one's eye [*both slang, orig. naut.*]; drop–, shed- -tears,

–a tear; melt–, burst– into tears; *fondre en larmes* [*F.*], cry oneself blind, cry one's eyes out; yammer [*dial.*].

scream etc. (*cry out*) 411; mew etc. (*animal sounds*) 412; groan, moan, whine, yelp, howl, yell, ululate; roar; roar–, bellow– like a bull; cry out lustily, rend the air.

show signs of grief; frown, scowl, make a wry face, gnash one's teeth, wring one's hands, tear one's hair, beat one's breast, roll on the ground, burst with grief.

complain, murmur, mutter, grumble, growl, clamor, make a fuss about, croak, grunt, maunder [*obs.*]; deprecate etc. (*disapprove*) 932.

cry out before one is hurt, complain without cause.

adj. **lamenting** etc. *v.;* in mourning, in sackcloth and ashes; ululant, ululative [*obs.*], clamorous; crying–, lamenting– to high heaven, sorrowing, sorrowful etc. (*unhappy*) 828; mournful, tearful; lachrymose, lachrymal *or* lacrimal, lachrymatory, plaintive, plaintful; querulous, querimonious; in the melting mood.

in tears, with tears in one's eyes; with moistened eyes, with watery eyes; bathed–, dissolved– in tears; "like Niobe, all tears" [*Hamlet*].

elegiac, epicedial, threnetic *or* threnetical.

adv. de profundis [*L.*], les larmes aux yeux [*F.*].

int. **alas**! alack! heigh-ho! O dear! ah me! woe is me! lackadaisy! well a day! lack a day! alack a day! wellaway! alas the day! *O tempora, O mores!* [*L.*]; what a pity! *miserabile dictu!* [*L.*]; too true!

840. Amusement

n. **amusement**, entertainment, diversion, divertisement, *divertissement* [*F.*]; reaction, relaxation, solace; pastime, *passe-temps* [*F.*], sport; labor of love; pleasure etc. 827.

fun, frolic, merriment, jollity, joviality, jovialness; heyday; laughter etc. 838; jocosity, jocoseness; drollery, buffoonery, tomfoolery; mummery, mumming, masquing, pageant; pleasantry; wit etc. 842; quip, quirk.

play; game, game of romps; gambol, romp, prank, antic, frisk, rig [*obs. or dial.*], lark [*colloq.*], spree, skylarking, vagary, monkey trick, *fredaine* [*F.*], escapade, *échappée* [*F.*], bout, *espièglerie* [*F.*]; practical joke etc. (*ridicule*) 856.

[dance steps] *gambade* [*F.*], gambado, *pas* [*F.*]; pigeonwing, heel-and-toe, buck-and-wing, shuffle, double shuffle; *chassé* [*F.*], *coupé* [*F.*], grapevine, etc.

[dances] dance, hop [*colloq.*], stag dance, shindig [*slang*]; ball; *bal, bal masqué, bal costumé* [*all F.*], masquerade, masquerade ball, cornwallis [*U. S.*]; mistletoe-bough dance; Dance of Death, *danse macabre* [*F.*]; interpretative dance, step dance, sand dance, *pas seul* [*F.*], skirt dance, folk dance; Morisco *or* morice [*obs.*], morris dance, saraband, fandango, bolero, tarantella, boutade, gavot *or* gavotte, minuet, *allemande* [*F.*], rigadoon, fling, Highland fling, Highland schottische, strathspey, reel, jig, hornpipe, sword dance, breakdown, cakewalk; kantikoy, snake dance; country dance, Scotch reel, Virginia reel, Sir Roger de Coverley, Portland fancy; ballet etc. (*drama*) 599; ragtime [*colloq.*] etc. (*music*) 415; jazz [*slang*]; nautch [*India*].

square dance, quadrille, Lancers, cotillion *or* cotillon [*F.*], German.

round dance, waltz, *valse* [*F.*], polka, mazurka, galop, gallopade *or* galopade, schottische, one-step, two-step, fox-trot, turkey-trot; shimmy.

danse du ventre [*F.*], belly dance, break dance, *chonchina* [*Jap.*], cancan.

dancer, *danseur (fem. danseuse)* [*F.*], *première danseuse* [*F.*], ballet dancer; geisha [*Jap.*]; nautch girl, bayadere [*both India*]; clog–, step–, skirt–, figure-dancer; figurant (*fem.* figurante), Morisco [*obs.*], morris dancer; terpsichorean [*colloq.*]; Terpsichore.

festivity, merrymaking; party etc. (*social gathering*) 892; revels, revelry, reveling *or* revelling, carnival, Saturnalia, jollification [*colloq.*], junket, picnic.

fête champêtre [*F.*], lawn party, garden party, regatta, field day, *fête* [*F.*], festival, gala, gala day; feast, banquet etc. (*food*) 298; regale, symposium, high jinks [*colloq.*], carouse, carousal, brawl; wassail; wake; bust [*slang*], tear [*slang*]; Turnerfest [*Ger.*]; gymkhana [*orig. Anglo-Ind.*]; treat; *ridotto* [*It.*], drum [*obs. or hist.*], kettledrum [*colloq.*], rout [*archaic*]; tea party, tea, tea fight [*slang*]; Kaffee-Klatsch [*Ger.*]; concert etc. (*music*) 415; show [*colloq.*]; play etc. (*drama*) 599; randy [*dial.*]; clambake, fish fry, beefsteak fry, squantum, donation party [*all U. S.*]; bat, bum [*both slang*], jamboree [*slang*].

round of pleasure, dissipation, a short life and a merry one, racketing, holiday making.

rejoicing etc. 838; jubilee etc. (*celebration*) 883.

fireworks, *feu-de-joie* [*F.*], firecrackers, bonfire.

holiday; red-letter day, play day; high days and holidays; high holiday, Bank holiday [*Eng.*]; May day, Derby day [*Eng.*]; Easter Monday, Whitmonday, Twelfth Night, Halloween;

840. Amusement

Christmas etc. 138; Dewali [*Hindu*], Holi *or* Hoolee [*Hindu*]; Bairam, Muharram [*both Moham.*]; wayzgoose [*Printers*], beanfeast [*Eng.*]; Arbor–, Declaration–, Independence–, Labor–, Memorial *or* Decoration–, Thanksgiving- Day; Washington's–, Lincoln's–, King's- birthday; Empire Day [*Brit.*]; Mardi gras, *mi-carême* [*F.*], *feria* [*S. W. U. S.*], *fiesta* [*Sp.*].

place of amusement, theater *or* theatre; concert -hall, –room; ballroom, dance hall, assembly room; moving-picture–, cinema- theater; movies [*colloq.*]; music hall; vaudeville -theater, –show; circus, hippodrome.

park, pleasance *or* plaisance [*archaic*]; arbor; garden etc. (*horticulture*) 371; pleasure–, play–, cricket–, croquet- archery–, polo–, hunting-ground; tennis–, racket–, squash–, badminton-court; bowling- green, –alley; croquet lawn, rink, glaciarium, ice rink, skating rink; golf links, race course, athletic field, stadium; gymnasium, swimming -pool, –bath; billiard room, pool room, casino, shooting gallery; flying horses, roundabout, merry-go-round; swing; *montagne Russe* [*F.*]; aërial railway, scenic railway, roller coaster, chutes, flying boats, etc.

Vauxhall, Ranelagh, Hurlingham; Lord's, Epsom, Newmarket, Doncaster, Sandown Park, Henley, Cowes, Mortlake [*all in Eng.*]; Coney Island; Brooklands, Sheepshead Bay, Belmont Park, Saratoga; New London, Forest Hills, Longwood [*all in U. S.*]; Monte Carlo; Longchamps [*France*]; Flemington [*Melbourne, Australia*].

[sports and games] athletic sports, track events, gymnastics; archery, rifle shooting; tournament, pugilism etc. (*contention*) 720; sporting etc. 622; horse racing, the turf; water polo; aquatics etc. 267.

skating, ice skating, roller skating, sliding; cricket, tennis, lawn tennis, pallone, rackets, squash, fives, trap bat and ball, badminton, battledore and shuttlecock, pall-mall, croquet, golf, curling, hockey, shinny *or* shinney; polo, football, Rugby, rugger [*colloq.*]; association, soccer [*colloq.*]; tent pegging, tilting at the ring, quintain, greasy pole; knur (*or* knurr) and spell [*Eng.*]; quoits, discus; hammer–, horseshoe-throwing; putting the -weight, –shot; hurdling; leapfrog; sack–, potato–, obstacle–, three-legged- race; hop skip and jump; French and English, tug of war; rounders, baseball, basket ball, pushball, captain ball; lacrosse; tobogganing.

blind-man's buff, hunt the slipper, hide and seek, kiss in the ring; snapdragon; cross questions and crooked answers, twenty questions, what's my thought? charades, crambo, dumb crambo, crisscross, proverbs, *bouts rimés* [*F.*]; hop-scotch, jackstones, mumble-the-peg *or* mumblety-peg; ping-pong, tiddledywinks, tipcat.

billiards, pool, pyramids, bagatelle; bowls, skittles, ninepins, American bowls; tenpins, bowling, tivoli.

chess, draughts, checkers *or* chequers, backgammon, dominoes, halma, dice, craps, crap shooting, crap game, "negro golf," "indoor golf" [*both humorous*]; merelles, nine men's morris, gobang, "the royal game of goose" [Goldsmith]; fox and geese; lotto *or* loto etc.

cards; whist, rubber; round game; loo, cribbage, *bésique* [*F.*], euchre, cutthroat euchre, railroad euchre; drole, *écarté*, picquet, all fours, quadrille, omber *or* ombre, reverse, Pope Joan, commit; boston, *vingt et un* [*F.*], quinze, thirty-one, put, speculation, connections, brag, cassino, lottery, commerce, snip-snap-snorem, lift smoke, blind hookey, Polish bank, Earl of Coventry, napoleon *or* nap [*colloq.*]; banker, penny-ante, poker, jack pot; blind–, draw–, straight–, stud–, poker; bluff; bridge, –whist; auction; monte, reversis, squeezers, old maid, fan-tan, fright, beggar-my-neighbor, goat, hearts, patience, solitaire, pairs.

court cards; ace, king, queen, knave, jack, joker; bower; right–, left- bower; dummy; hand; trump; face cards, diamonds, hearts, clubs, spades; pack, deck; flush, full-house, straight, three of a kind, pair, *misère* [*F.*] etc.

toy, plaything, bauble; doll etc. (*puppet*) 554; teetotum; knickknack etc. (*trifle*) 643; magic lantern etc. (*show*) 448; peep–, puppet–, raree–, galanty *or* gallanty–, Punch-and-Judy-show; marionettes; toy-shop; "quips and cranks and wanton wiles, nods and becks and wreathed smiles" [Milton].

sportsman (*fem.* sportswoman), hunter, Nimrod. archer, toxophilite; cricketer, footballer, ball-players etc.

gamester (*fem.* gamestress), sport, gambler; dicer, punter, plunger.

reveler *or* reveller, carouser; master of the -ceremonies, –revels; *arbiter elegantiarum* [*L.*]; *arbiter bibendi* [*L.*].

devotee, enthusiast, follower, fan [*slang*], rooter [*slang*]; turfman.

v. **amuse**, entertain, divert, enliven; tickle, -the fancy; titillate, raise a smile, put in good humor;

841. Weariness

cause–, create–, occasion–, raise–, excite–, produce–, convulse with- laughter; set the table in a roar, be the death of one.

cheer, rejoice; recreate, solace; please etc. 829; interest; treat, regale.

amuse oneself; game; play, –a game, –pranks, –tricks; sport, disport, toy, wanton, revel, junket, feast, carouse, banquet, make merry, drown care; drive dull care away; frolic, gambol, frisk, romp; caper; dance etc. (*leap*) 309; keep up the ball; run a rig, sow one's wild oats, have one's fling, take one's pleasure; paint the town red [*slang*]; see life; *desipere in loco* [Horace], play the fool.

make–, keep- holiday; go a-Maying.

while away–, beguile- the time; kill time, dally.

adj. **amusing**, entertaining, diverting etc. *v.;* recreative, lusory; pleasant etc. (*pleasing*) 829; laughable etc. (*ludicrous*) 853; witty etc. 842; festive, festal; jovial, jolly, jocund, roguish, rompish; playful, –as a kitten; sportive, ludibrious [*obs.*].

amused etc. *v.;* "pleased with a rattle, tickled with a straw" [Pope].

adv. "on the light fantastic toe" [Milton], at play, in sport.

int. *vive la bagatelle!* [*F.*], *vogue la galère!* [*F.*], come on fellows! "hail, hail, the gang's all here!" some party! [*slang*].

841. Weariness

n. **weariness**, defatigation [*obs.*], ennui, boredom; lassitude etc. (*fatigue*) 688; drowsiness etc. 683.

disgust, nausea, loathing, sickness; satiety etc. 869; *taedium vitae* [*L.*] etc. (*dejection*) 837.

tedium, wearisomeness, tediousness etc. *adj.;* heavy hours, dull work, monotony, twice-told tale; "the enemy" [time].

bore, buttonholer, proser, dry-as-dust, fossil [*colloq.*], wet blanket; pill, stiff [*both slang*].

v. **weary**; tire etc. (*fatigue*) 688; bore; bore–, weary–, tire- -to death, –out of one's life, –out of all patience; set–, send- to sleep; buttonhole.

pall, sicken, nauseate, disgust; harp on the same string; drag its -slow, –weary- length along.

never hear the last of; be tired etc. *adj.* of *or* with; yawn; die with *ennui*.

adj. **wearying** etc. *v.;* wearing; wearisome, tiresome, irksome; uninteresting, stupid, bald, devoid of interest, jejune, dry, monotonous, dull, arid, tedious, humdrum, mortal [*colloq.*], flat, prosy, prosing; slow; soporific, somniferous, dormitive, opiate.

disgusting etc. *v.;* unenjoyed.

weary; tired etc. *v.;* drowsy etc. (*sleepy*) 683; uninterested, flagging, used up, worn out, *blasé* [*F.*], life-weary, weary of life; sick of.

adv. **wearily** etc. *adj.;* *usque ad nauseam* [*L.*].

842. Wit

n. **wit**, wittiness; Attic -wit, –salt; Atticism; salt, *esprit* [*F.*], point, fancy, whim, humor *or* humour, drollery, pleasantry.

buffoonery, fooling, farce, tom-foolery; shenanigan [*slang*], harlequinade etc. 599; broad -farce, –humor; fun, *espiéglerie* [*F.*]; *vis comica* [*L.*].

jocularity; jocosity, jocoseness; facetiousness; waggery, waggishness; whimsicality; comicality etc. 853.

smartness, ready wit, banter, persiflage, *badinage* [*F.*], retort, repartee, *quid pro quo* [*L.*]; ridicule etc. 856.

facetiae, quips and cranks; jest, joke, capital joke; *canorae nugae* [*L.*]; standing -jest, –joke; conceit, quip, quirk, crank, quiddity [*rare*], *concetto* [*It.*], *plaisanterie* [*F.*], brilliant idea; merry–, bright–, happy- thought; sally; flash, –of wit, –of merriment; scintillation; *mot*, –*pour rire* [*F.*]; witticism, smart saying, *bon mot* [*F.*], *jeu d'esprit* [*F.*], epigram; jest book; dry joke, *quodlibet* [*L.*], cream of the jest.

word-play, *jeu de mots* [*F.*], play upon words; pun, punning; *double entente* [*F.*] etc. (*ambiguity*) 520; quibble, verbal quibble; conundrum etc. (*riddle*) 533; anagram, acrostic, double acrostic, trifling, idle conceit, turlupinade [*obs.*].

old joke, Joe Miller, chestnut [*slang*]; hoary-headed -joke, –jest; joke–, jest- with whiskers [*humorous*].

v. **joke**, jest, cut jokes; crack a joke, get off a joke; pun; perpetrate a -joke, –pun; make fun of, make merry with; set the table in a roar etc. (*amuse*) 840; tell a good -story, –yarn.

retort, flash back, flash, scintillate; banter etc. (*ridicule*) 856; *ridentem dicere verum* [*L.*]; joke at one's expense.

adj. **witty**, Attic; clever, keen, keen-witted, brilliant, pungent; quick-witted, nimble-witted; smart; jocular, jocose, funny, waggish, facetious, whimsical, humorous; playful etc. 840; merry and wise; pleasant, sprightly, cute [*colloq.*], *spirituel* [*F.*], sparkling, epigrammatic, full of point, *ben trovato* [*It.*]; comic etc. 853.

adv. in joke, in jest, for the jest's sake, in sport, in play.

304

843. Dullness

n. **dullness** or dulness, heaviness, flatness; infestivity etc. 837, stupidity etc. 499; want of originality; dearth of ideas.

prose, matter of fact; heavy book, *conte à dormir debout* [*F.*]; commonplace, platitude.

v. **be dull** etc. *adj.;* hang fire, fall flat; platitudinize, prose, take *au sérieux* [*F.*], be caught napping.

render dull etc. *adj.;* damp, depress, throw cold water on, lay a wet blanket on; fall flat upon the ear.

adj. **dull**, –as ditch water; jejune, dry, unentertaining, uninteresting, unlively, heavy-footed, elephantine; slow of comprehension; insipid, tasteless, slow as molasses [*colloq.*], logy; unimaginative; insulse; dry as dust; prosy, prosing, prosaic; matter-of-fact, commonplace, platitudinous, pointless; "weary, stale, flat, and unprofitable" [*Hamlet*].

stupid, slow, flat, humdrum, monotonous; melancholic etc. 837; stolid etc. 499; plodding.

844. Humorist

n. **humorist**, wag, wit, reparteeist, epigrammatist, punster; *bel esprit* [*F.*], life of the party; joker, jester, Joe Miller, *drôle de corps* [*F.*], galliard or gaillard [*archaic*], spark; *bon diable* [*F.*]; *persifleur* [*F.*], banterer, "Agreeable Rattle" [Goldsmith].

buffoon, *farceur* [*F.*], merry-andrew, mime, tumbler, acrobat, mountebank, charlatan, posture master, harlequin, punch, punchinello, *pulcinella* [*It.*], Scaramouch, clown; wearer of the -cap and bells, –motley; motley fool; pantaloon, gypsy; jack-pudding [*archaic*], Jack-in-the-green; jack-a-dandy; zany; madcap, pickle-herring, witling, caricaturist, grimacer, grimacier.

845. Beauty

n. **beauty**, beautifulness, pulchritude; the beautiful, to kalon [*Gr.*].

beauty unadorned; form, elegance, grace, *belle tournure* [*F.*]; symmetry etc. 242; concinnity, delicacy, refinement, charm, *je ne sais quoi* [*F.*], *nescio quid* [*L.*], style.

comeliness, fairness etc. *adj.;* polish, gloss; good effect, good looks; trigness.

bloom, brilliancy, radiance, splendor or splendour, gorgeousness, magnificence; sublimity, sublimification [*obs.*].

beau ideal, le beau idéal [*F.*]; Venus, Aphrodite, Hebe, the Graces, Peri, Houri, Cupid, Apollo, Hyperion, Adonis, Antinous, Narcissus, Astarte; Helen of Troy, Cleopatra; Venus of Milo, Apollo Belvedere.

[comparisons] butterfly; flower, flow'ret gay; garden, anemone, asphodel, buttercup, crane's-bill, daffodil, lily, lily of the valley, ranunculus, rose, rhododendron, windflower.

the flower of, the pink of; *bijou* [*F.*]; jewel etc. (*ornament*) 847; work of art.

loveliness, pleasurableness etc. 829.

beautifying, beautification [*rare*]; landscape gardening; decoration etc. etc. 847; calisthenics, physical culture.

[science of the perception of beauty] callaesthetics.

v. **be beautiful** etc. *adj.;* shine, beam, bloom; become one etc. (*accord*) 23; set off, become, grace.

render beautiful etc. *adj.;* beautify; polish, burnish; gild etc. (*decorate*) 847; set out.

"snatch a grace beyond the reach of art" [Pope].

adj. **beautiful**, beauteous, handsome; pretty; lovely, graceful, elegant, exquisite, flowerlike, delicate, dainty, refined.

comely, fair, personable, seemly [*obs.*], decent [*archaic*], proper, bonny, good-looking; well-favored, well-made, well-formed, well-proportioned, shapely, zaftig [*colloq.*]; symmetrical etc. (*regular*) 242; harmonious etc. (*color*) 428; sightly, fit to be seen.

bright, bright-eyed; rosy-cheeked, cherry-cheeked; rosy, ruddy; blooming, in full bloom.

goodly, dapper, tight, jimp or gimp [*Scot. & dial. Eng.*], jaunty or janty, trig, natty [*orig. slang*], quaint [*archaic*], trim, tidy, neat, spruce, smart, tricksy [*rare*].

brilliant, shining; beamy, beaming; sparkling, radiant, splendid, resplendent, dazzling, glowing; glossy, sleek; rich, gorgeous, superb, magnificent, grand, fine, sublime.

artistic or artistical, aesthetic; picturesque, pictorial; *fait à peindre* [*F.*], paintable, well-composed, well-grouped, well-varied; curious.

enchanting etc. (*pleasure-giving*) 829; attractive etc. (*inviting*) 615; becoming etc. (*accordant*) 23; ornamental etc. 847; of consummate art.

perfect, unspotted, spotless etc. 650; immaculate; undeformed, undefaced.

passable, presentable, tolerable, not amiss.

846. Ugliness

n. **ugliness** etc. *adj.;* deformity, inelegance; acomia, baldness, alopecia; disfigurement etc. (*blemish*) 848; want of symmetry, inconcinnity

847. Ornament

[rare], "uglification" [Carroll]; distortion etc. 243; squalor etc. (*uncleanness*) 653.

forbidding countenance, vinegar aspect, hanging look, wry face, face that would stop a clock [*colloq.*]; *spretae injuria formae* [Virgil].

eyesore, object, figure, sight [*colloq.*], fright, octopus. specter *or* spectre. scarecrow, hag, harridan, satyr, witch, toad, baboon, monster, Caliban, Aesop; *monstrum horrendum informe ingens cui lumen ademptum* [Virgil].

v. **be ugly** etc. *adj.;* look ill, grin horribly a ghastly smile, grin through a horse collar [*colloq.*], make faces.

render ugly etc. *adj.;* deface; disfigure, defigure [*obs.*], deform, uglify [*rare*], spoil; distort etc. 243; blemish etc. (*injure*) 659; soil etc. (*render unclean*) 653.

adj. **ugly**, –as -sin, –a toad, –a scarecrow, –a dead monkey; plain, coarse; homely etc. (*unadorned*) 849; ordinary, unornamental, inartistic; unsightly, unseemly, uncomely, unshapely, unlovely; sightless [*obs.*], seemless [*obs.*], not fit to be seen; unbeauteous, unbeautiful, beautiless.

bald, bald-headed, acomous, hairless, *chauve* [*F.*], depilous [*rare*], glabrous [*bot.*]; smooth-faced, beardless, whiskerless, clean-shaven.

misshapen, misproportioned; shapeless etc. (*amorphous*) 241; monstrous; gaunt etc. (*thin*) 203; dumpy etc. (*short*) 201; curtailed of its fair proportions; ill-made, ill-shaped, ill-proportioned; crooked etc. (*distorted*) 243.

unprepossessing, hard-featured, hard-visaged; ill-favored, hard-favored, evil-favored; ill-looking; squalid, haggard; grim, grim-faced, grim-visaged; grisly, ghastly; ghostlike, deathlike; cadaverous, gruesome *or* grewsome.

uncouth, ungainly, graceless, inelegant; ungraceful, stiff; rugged, rough, gross, rude, awkward, clumsy, slouching, rickety, gawky, lumping, lumpish, lumbering, hulking *or* hulky, unwieldy.

repellent, forbidding, frightful, hideous, odious, uncanny, repulsive; horrid, horrible; shocking etc. (*painful*) 830.

foul etc. (*dirty*) 653; dingy etc. (*colorless*) 429; gaudy etc. (*color*) 428; tarnished, smeared, besmeared, bedaubed; disfigured etc. *v.;* discolored, spotted, spotty.

showy, specious, pretentious, garish etc. (*ostentatious*) 882.

847. Ornament

n. **ornament**, ornamentation, ornamental art; ornature [*rare*], ornateness, ornation [*rare*], adornment, decoration, embellishment; architecture.

garnish, polish, varnish, French polish, gilding, japanning, lacquer, ormolu, enamel; *champlevé* ware, *cloisonné* ware; cosmetics.

[ornamentation] pattern, diaper, powdering, paneling, graining, inlaid work, pargeting; detail; texture etc. 329; richness; tracery, molding *or* moulding, fillet, listel, strapwork, *coquillage* [*F.*], flourish, *fleur-de-lis* [*F.*], arabesque, fret, anthemion; egg and -tongue, –dart; astragal, zigzag, acanthus, cartouche; pilaster etc. (*projection*) 250; bead, beading; frostwork, tooling; Moresque, Morisco.

embroidery, broidery [*archaic*], needlework, brocade, brocatel *or* brocatelle, bugles, beads, galloon, lace, fringe, border, insertion, *motif* [*F.*], edging, trimming; trappings; drapery, over-drapery, hanging, tapestry, arras; millinery, ermine; *drap d'or* [*F.*].

wreath, festoon, garland, chaplet, flower, nosegay, bouquet, posy; "daisies pied and violets blue" [*Love's Labour Lost*].

tassel, knot; shoulder knot, epaulet *or* epaulette, aglet *or* aiglet, aigulet [*rare*], frog; star, rosette, bow; feather, plume, panache, aigret *or* aigrette; fillet, snood.

jewelry *or* jewellery, *bijouterie* [*F.*] *or* bijoutry; tiara, crown, coronet, diadem; jewel, *bijou* [*F.*], trinket, locket, necklace, bracelet, bangle; armlet, anklet, earring, nose-ring, carcanet [*archaic*], chain, chatelaine, brooch, torque.

gem, precious stone; diamond, brilliant; pearl; sapphire, Oriental topaz, lapis lazuli; ruby, balas *or* balais *or* balas ruby; emerald, beryl, aquamarine, alexandrite; opal, fire opal, girasol *or* girasole; garnet, carbuncle; amethyst, plasma; turquoise *or* turquois; topaz; coral; chalcedony, agate, onyx, sard, sardonyx, chrysoprase, carnelian, cat's-eye, jasper; heliotrope, bloodstone; hyacinth, jacinth, zircon, jargon *or* jargoon; chrysolite, peridot; spinel *or* spinelle, spinel ruby; moonstone, sunstone.

frippery, finery, gewgaw, knickknack, gimcrack, tinsel, spangle, clinquant, pinchbeck, paste; excess of ornament etc. (*vulgarity*) 851; gaud, pride, show, ostentation.

illustration, illumination, vignette; *fleuron* [*F.*]; headpiece, tailpiece, *cul-de-lampe* [*F.*]; purple patches, flowers of rhetoric etc. 577.

virtu, article of virtu, piece of virtu, work of art, bric-a-brac, curio; rarity, a find.

v. **ornament**, embellish, enrich, decorate, adorn, beautify; adonize [*rare*], dandify.

garnish, furbish, polish, gild, varnish, whitewash, enamel, japan, lacquer, paint, grain.

spangle, bespangle, bead, embroider, work; chase, tool, emboss, fret; emblazon, blazon, illuminate; illustrate.

smarten, trim, dizen, bedizen, prink, prank; trick up, trick out, fig out; deck, bedeck, dight [*archaic*], bedight [*archaic*], array; titivate *or* tittivate [*colloq.*], spruce up [*colloq.*]; smarten up, dress, dress up; powder.

become etc. (*accord with*) 23.

adj. **ornamented**, beautified etc. *v.;* ornate, rich, gilt, begilt, tessellated, inlaid, festooned; *champlevé* [*F.*], *cloisonné* [*F.*], topiary [*rare*].

smart, gay, tricksy [*rare*], flowery, glittering; new-gilt, new-spangled; fine; fine as -a Mayday queen, -fivepence, -a carrot fresh scraped, -a fiddle [*all colloq.*]; pranked out, bedight [*archaic*], well-groomed.

in full dress etc. (*fashion*) 852; *en grande -tenue, -toilette* [*F.*]; in one's best bib and tucker, in Sunday best, *endimanché* [*F.*]; dressed to advantage.

showy, flashy; gaudy etc. (*vulgar*) 851; garish *or* gairish, splendiferous [*humorous*], gorgeous.

ornamental, decorative; becoming etc. (*accordant*) 23.

848. Blemish

n. **blemish**, disfigurement, deformity; adactylism; defect etc. (*imperfection*) 651; flaw, maculation; injury etc. (*deterioration*) 659; spots on the sun; eyesore.

stain, blot, spot, spottiness; speck, speckle, blur, freckle, mole, macula, macule, patch, blotch, birthmark; blobber lip, blubber lip, harelip; blain, tarnish, smudge; dirt etc. 653; scar, wem [*obs.*], wen; pustule; whelk; excrescence, pimple etc. (*protuberance*) 250; burn, blister, roughness.

v. **disfigure** etc. (*injure*) 659; uglify [*rare*]; render ugly etc. 846.

adj. **disfigured**; discolored; imperfect etc. 651; blobber-lipped *or* blubber-lipped, harelipped; chapped, specked, speckled, freckled, pitted, bloodshot, bruised; injured etc. (*deteriorated*) 659.

849. Simplicity

n. **simplicity**; plainness, homeliness; undress, nudity, beauty unadorned; chasteness, chastity, restraint, severity, naturalness, unaffectedness.

v. **be simple** etc. *adj.*

render simple etc. *adj.;* simplify, reduce to simplicity, strip of ornament, chasten, restrain.

adj. **simple**, plain, homelike, homish, homely, homespun [*fig.*], ordinary, household.

unaffected, natural, native; inartificial etc. (*artless*) 703; free from -affectation, -ornament; *simplex munditiis* [Horace]; *sans façon* [*F.*], *en déshabillé* [*F.*].

chaste, inornate, severe.

unadorned, unornamented, undecked, ungarnished, unarranged, untrimmed, unvarnished.

bald, flat, blank, dull.

simple-minded, childish, credulous etc. 486.

850. Taste
[good taste]

n. **taste**; good-, refined-, cultivated- taste; delicacy, refinement, fine feeling, gust, gusto, tact, finesse; nicety etc. (*discrimination*) 465; *to prepon* [*Gr.*], polish, elegance, grace.

artistic quality, virtu; dilettanteism, virtuosity, connoisseurship, fine art of living; fine art; culture, cultivation.

"caviare to the general" [*Hamlet*].

[science of taste] aesthetics.

man of taste etc.; connoisseur, judge, critic, conoscente, virtuoso, amateur, dilettante; Aristarchus, Corinthian; Aristotle, Stagirite; Petronius, *arbiter elegantiae* [*L.*], *arbiter elegantiarum* [*L.*].

euphemist, purist, precisian.

v. **display taste** etc. *n.;* appreciate, judge, criticize, discriminate etc. 465.

adj. **in good taste**, tasteful, unaffected, pure, chaste, classical, Attic, cultivated; attractive, charming, dainty; aesthetic, artistic.

refined, tasty [*colloq.*]; prim, precise, formal, prudish; elegant etc. 578; euphemistic.

to one's taste, to one's mind; after one's fancy; *comme il faut* [*F.*]; *tiré à quatre épingles* [*F.*].

adv. **elegantly** etc. *adj.;* with quiet elegance; with elegant simplicity; without ostentation.

851. Vulgarity
[bad taste]

n. **vulgarity**, vulgarism; barbarism, Vandalism, Gothicism; *mauvais goût* [*F.*], bad taste; want of tact; ungentlemanliness, ungentlemanlikeness; ill-breeding etc. (*discourtesy*) 895.

coarseness etc. *adj.;* indecorum, loud behavior [*colloq.*], misbehavior; *gaucherie* [*F.*], awkwardness; boorishness etc. *adj.;* homeliness, rusticity.

lowness, low life, *mauvais ton* [*F.*]; brutality; blackguardism, rowdyism, ruffianism; ribaldry; slang etc. (*neology*) 563.

bad joke, *mauvaise plaisanterie* [*F.*], poor joke, joke in bad taste; practical joke.

852. Fashion

[excess of ornament] gaudiness, tawdriness, gingerbread, false ornament, cheap jewelry; flashy -clothes, -dress; finery, frippery, trickery, tinsel, gewgaw, clinquant.

vulgarian, rough diamond; clown etc. (*commonalty*) 876; Goth, Vandal, Boeotian; snob, cad [*colloq.*], gent [*humorous*]; parvenu etc. 876; frump [*colloq.*], dowdy; slut, slattern etc. 653; tomboy, hoyden, cub, unlicked cub.

v. be vulgar etc. *adj.;* misbehave; talk-, smell of the-shop; show a want of -tact, -consideration; be a vulgarian etc. *n.*

adj. **in bad taste**, vulgar, unrefined, coarse, indecorous, ribald, gross; unseemly, unbeseeming, unpresentable; *contra bonos mores* [*L.*]; ungraceful etc. (*ugly*) 846; dowdy; slovenly etc. (*dirty*) 653; ungenteel, shabby genteel; low etc. (*plebeian*) 876.

extravagant, monstrous, horrid; shocking etc. (*painful*) 830.

ill-mannered, ill-bred, underbred, snobbish, uncourtly; uncivil etc. (*discourteous* 895; ungentlemanly, ungentlemanlike; unladylike, unfeminine; wild, wild as a hawk, wild as an unbacked colt.

uncouth, unkempt, uncombed, untamed, unlicked, unpolished, plebeian; incondite [*rare*]; heavy, rude, awkward; homely, homespun, homebred; provincial, countrified, rustic; boorish, clownish; savage, brutish, blackguard, blackguardly, rowdyish, rowdy.

barbarous, barbaric, Gothic, heathenish, tramontane, outlandish; uncultivated; Bohemian; unclassical, doggerel *or* doggrel.

obsolete etc. (*antiquated*) 124; out of fashion, old-fashioned, out of date, unfashionable.

newfangled etc. (*unfamiliar*) 83; fantastic, fantastical, odd etc. (*ridiculous*) 853; particular; affected etc. 855.

tawdry, gaudy, meretricious, brummagem [*slang*], bedizened, tricked out; obtrusive, flaunting, loud, crass, showy, flashy, garish.

852. Fashion

n. **fashion**, style, *ton* [*F.*], *bon ton* [*F.*], society; good-, polite- society; *monde* [*F.*]; drawing-room, civilized life, civilization, town, *beau monde* [*F.*], high life, court; world; fashionable-, gay- world; height-, pink-, star-, glass- of fashion; "the glass of fashion and the mould of form" [*Hamlet*]; Vanity Fair; Mayfair; show etc. (*ostentation*) 822.

manners, breeding etc. (*politeness*) 894; air, demeanor etc. (*appearance*) 448; *savoir faire* [*F.*]; gentlemanliness, gentility, decorum, propriety, *bienséance* [*F.*]; conventions of society; Mrs. Grundy; dictates of -Society, -Mrs. Grundy; convention, conventionality, the proprieties; punctiliousness, punctilio, form, formality; etiquette, point of etiquette.

mode, vogue, style, the latest thing, *dernier cri* [*F.*], the go [*colloq.*], the rage etc. (*desire*) 865; prevailing taste; dress etc. 225; custom etc. 613.

leader of fashion; *arbiter elegantiarum* [*L.*] etc. (*taste*) 850; man-, woman- of -fashion, -the world; clubman, clubwoman; upper ten thousand etc. (*nobility*) 875; upper ten [*colloq.*]; élite [*F.*] etc. (*distinction*) 873; smart set [*colloq.*]; the four hundred.

v. **be fashionable** etc. *adj.,* be the rage etc. *n.;* have a run, pass current.

follow-, keep up with-, conform to-, fall in with- the fashion etc. *n.;* go with the stream etc. (*conform*) 82; be on (*or* get on) the band wagon [*slang*], be in the swim [*colloq.*]; *savoir -vivre, -faire* [*F.*]; keep up appearances, behave oneself.

set the fashion, bring into fashion; give a tone to society, cut a figure in society [*colloq.*]; brush shoulders with -the nobility, -royalty; appear-, be presented- at court.

keep one's -automobile, -car, -carriage, -yacht, -house in town [*Eng.*], -cottage at Newport; be a member of the best clubs.

adj. **fashionable**; in fashion etc. *n.;* à la mode [*F.*], *comme il faut* [*F.*]; admitted-, admissible- in society etc. *n.;* presentable; punctilious, decorous, conventional etc. (*customary*) 613; genteel; well-bred, well-mannered, well-behaved, well-spoken; gentlemanlike, gentlemanly; ladylike; civil, polite etc. (*courteous*) 894.

dashing, jaunty *or* janty, showy, spirited, fast.

polished, refined, thoroughbred, gently bred, courtly; *distingué* [*F.*], distinguished, aristocratic *or* aristocratical; unselfconscious, self-possessed, poised, easy, frank, unconstrained, unembarrassed, *dégagé* [*F.*].

modish, stylish, swell [*slang*], recherché, récherché [*F.*]; newfangled etc. (*unfamiliar*) 83; all the rage, all the go [*colloq.*].

in -court, -full, -evening- dress; *en grande tenue* [*F.*] etc. (*ornament*) 847.

adv. **fashionably** etc. *adj.;* for fashion's sake; in fear of Mrs. Grundy; in the latest -style, -mode.

int. it isn't done!

853. Ridiculousness

n. **ridiculousness** etc. *adj.;* comicality, oddity etc. *adj.;* drollery; farce, comedy; burlesque etc. (*ridicule*) 856; buffoonery etc. (*fun*) 840; frippery; amphigory *or* amphigouri, doggerel (*or* doggrel) verses; bull, Irish bull, Hibernicism, Hibernianism, Spoonerism; absurdity etc. 497.

fustian, extravagance, bombast etc. (*unmeaning*) 517; anticlimax, bathos; monstrosity etc. (*unconformity*) 83; laughingstock etc. 857; screamer *or* scream [*slang*].

v. **be ridiculous** etc. *adj.;* pass from the sublime to the ridiculous; make one laugh; play the fool, make a fool of oneself, commit an absurdity; ride-, play- the goat [*colloq.*].

make ridiculous, make a goat of [*colloq.*], make a fool of, play a joke on.

adj. **ridiculous**, ludicrous, comic *or* comical, drollish, waggish, quizzical, droll, funny, laughable, risible, farcical, screaming; serio-comic, serio-comical; tragi-comic, tragi-comical; *pour rire* [*F.*].

odd, grotesque; whimsical, —as a dancing bear; fanciful, fantastic, queer, rum [*slang*], quaint, bizarre; eccentric etc. (*unconformable*) 83; strange, outlandish, out-of-the-way, baroque, rococo; awkward etc. (*ugly*) 846.

extravagant, *outré* [*F.*], monstrous, preposterous, absurd, bombastic, inflated, stilted, burlesque, mock heroic.

trivial, doggerel *or* doggrel, gimcrack, contemptible etc. (*unimportant*) 643.

derisive, ironical etc. 856.

854. Fop

n. **fine gentleman**, fop, swell [*colloq.*], dandy, exquisite, coxcomb, beau, macaroni [*hist.*]; blade, blood, buck [*archaic*], man about town, fast man, *roué* [*F.*]; fribble, jemmy [*obs.*], spark, popinjay, puppy [*contemptuous*], prig, *petit maître* [*F.*]; jackanapes, jack-a-dandy, jessamy [*obs.*], man milliner; carpet knight; masher [*slang*], dude [*colloq.*].

fine lady, belle, flirt, coquette, toast.

855. Affectation

n. **affectation**; affectedness etc. *adj.;* acting a part etc. *v.;* pretense etc. (*falsehood*) 544, (*ostentation*) 882; boasting etc. 884; charlatanism, quackery, shallow profundity.

pretension, airs, pedantry, pedantism, purism, precisianism, stiffness, formality, buckram; prunes and prisms; euphuism; teratology etc. (*altiloquence*) 577.

prudery, demureness, mock modesty, *minauderie* [*F.*], sentimentalism; *mauvaise honte* [*F.*], false shame.

mannerism, *simagrée* [*F.*], grimace.

foppery, dandyism, man millinery, coxcombry, coquetry, puppyism, conceit.

affecter *or* affector, performer, actor; pedant, pedagogue, doctrinaire, purist, euphuist, mannerist; grimacier [*rare*]; lump of affectation, *précieuse ridicule* [*F.*], *bas bleu* [*F.*], blue stocking, poetaster; prig; charlatan etc. (*deceiver*) 548; *petit maître* [*F.*] etc. (*fop*) 854; flatterer etc. 935; coquette, prude, puritan, precisian, formalist.

v. **affect**, act a part, put on; give oneself airs etc. (*arrogance*) 885; boast etc. 884; coquet; simper, mince, attitudinize, pose; flirt a fan; languish; euphuize; overact, overdo.

adj. **affected**, full of affectation, pretentious, pedantic, stilted, stagy, theatrical, big-sounding, *ad captandum* [*L.*]; canting, insincere; not natural, unnatural, self-conscious; mannered, *maniéré* [*F.*]; artificial; overwrought, overdone, overacted; euphuistic etc. 577.

stiff, starch, formal, prim, smug, demure, *tiré à quatre épingles* [*F.*], quakerish, puritanical, prudish, pragmatical.

priggish, conceited, coxcomical, foppish, dandified, finical, finicking *or* finicky *or* finikin; mincing, simpering, namby-pamby, sentimental, languishing.

856. Ridicule

n. **ridicule**, derision; sardonic -smile, -grin; irrision [*obs.*], snicker *or* snigger, grin, twit [*rare*]; scoffing etc. (*disrespect*) 929; mockery, quiz, banter, irony, persiflage, raillery, chaff, *badinage* [*F.*]; quizzing etc. *v.;* asteism.

squib, satire, skit, quip, quib [*obs.*].

burlesque, parody, travesty, *travestie* [*F.*]; farce etc. (*drama*) 599; caricature.

buffoonery etc. (*fun*) 840; practical joke, horseplay, roughhouse [*slang*].

v. **ridicule**, deride; laugh at, grin at, smile at; snicker *or* snigger; laugh in one's sleeve; banter, rally, chaff, joke, twit, quiz, poke fun at, roast [*slang*], guy [*colloq.*], jolly [*colloq.*], rag [*slang, Eng.*]; haze; tehee *or* teehee; fleer; play upon, play tricks upon; get the laugh on [*slang*]; fool, –to the top of one's bent; show up.

turn into ridicule; make merry with; make -fun, –game, –a fool, –an April fool- of; rally; scoff etc. (*disrespect*) 929.

burlesque, satirize, parody, caricature, travesty.

857. Laughingstock

be ridiculous etc. 853; raise a laugh etc. (*amuse*) 840; play the fool, make a fool of oneself.

adj. derisive, derisory, mock; sarcastic, ironical, quizzical, burlesque, Hudibrastic, Rabelaisian; scurrilous etc. (*disrespectful*) 929.

adv. in ridicule etc. *n.;* as a joke, to raise a laugh.

int. "What fools these mortals be!" [*Midsummer Night's Dream*].

857. Laughingstock
[object and cause of ridicule]

n. laughingstock, jesting-stock, gazing-stock; butt, game, fair game; April fool etc. (*dupe*) 547, original, oddity; queer–, odd- fish [*colloq.*], figure of fun [*colloq.*]; quiz, square toes; old fogy *or* fogey [*colloq.*].

monkey; buffoon etc. (*jester*) 844; pantomimist etc. (*actor*) 599.

jest etc. (*wit*) 842.

858. Hope

n. hope, hopes; desire etc. 865; fervent hope, sanguine expectation, trust, confidence, reliance; faith etc. (*belief*) 484; affiance, assurance; secureness, security; reassurance.

good -omen, –auspices; promise, well-grounded hopes; good–, bright-prospect; clear sky.

hopefulness, buoyancy, optimism, enthusiasm, heart of grace, aspiration; assumption, presumption; anticipation etc. (*expectation*) 507.

optimist, utopist [*rare*], utopian.

daydream, castles in the air, castles in Spain, *châteaux en Espagne* [*F.*], *le pot au lait* [*F.*], Utopia, millennium; golden dream; dream of Alnaschar; airy hopes, fool's paradise; mirage etc. (*fallacies of vision*) 443; fond hope.

ray of hope; beam–, gleam–, glimmer–, dawn–, flash–, star- of hope; cheer; bit of blue sky, silver lining of the cloud, bottom of Pandora's box, balm in Gilead.

mainstay, anchor, sheet anchor; staff etc. (*support*) 215; heaven etc. 981.

v. hope, trust, confide, rely on, put one's trust in, lean upon; pin one's hope upon, pin one's faith upon etc. (*believe*) 484.

feel–, entertain–, harbor–, indulge–, cherish–, feed–, foster–, nourish–, encourage–, cling to–, live in- hope etc. *n.;* see land; feel–, rest- -assured, –confident etc. *adj.*

hope for etc. (*desire*) 865; anticipate; presume; promise oneself; expect etc. (*look forward to*) 507.

be hopeful etc. *adj.;* look on the bright side of, view on the sunny side, *voir en couleur de rose* [*F.*], make the best of it, hope for the best; hope against hope; put -a good, –a bold, –the best- face upon; keep one's spirits up; take heart, –of grace; be of good -heart, –cheer; flatter oneself, "lay the flattering unction to one's soul" [*Hamlet*].

catch at a straw, hope against hope, count one's chickens before they are hatched.

encourage, hearten, inspirit; give–, inspire–, raise–, hold out- hope etc. *n.;* raise expectations; encourage, cheer, assure, reassure, buoy up, embolden; promise, bid fair, augur well, be in a fair way, look up, flatter, tell a flattering tale.

adj. hopeful, confident; hoping etc. *v.;* in hopes etc. *n.;* secure etc. (*certain*) 484; sanguine, in good heart, buoyed up, buoyant, elated, flushed, exultant, enthusiastic; heartsome [*chiefly Scot.*]; utopian.

fearless; free from–, exempt from- fear, –suspicion, –distrust, –despair; unsuspecting, unsuspicious, undespairing, self-reliant; dauntless etc. (*courageous*) 861.

propitious, promising; probable, on the high road to; within sight of -shore, –land; of–, full of- promise; of good omen; auspicious, *de bon augure* [*F.*]; reassuring; encouraging, cheering, inspiriting, looking up, bright, roseate, *couleur de rose* [*F.*], rose-colored.

adv. hopefully etc. *adj.*

int. God speed! good luck!

859. Hopelessness
[absence, want, or loss of hope]

n. hopelessness etc. *adj.;* despair, desperation; despondency etc. (*dejection*) 837; pessimism.

hope deferred, dashed hopes; vain expectation etc. (*disappointment*) 509.

airy hopes etc. 858; bad -job, –business; gloomy–, clouds on the–, black spots in the- horizon; dark future; slough of Despond, cave of Despair; *immedicabile vulnus* [*L.*].

forlorn hope, *enfant perdu* (*pl. enfants perdus*) [*F.*]; goner [*slang*]; gone -case, –coon [*slang*].

pessimist, Job's comforter; hypochondriac etc. 837; bird of bad omen, bird of ill omen.

v. despair; lose–, give up–, abandon–, relinquish- -all hope, –the hope of; give up, give over; yield to despair; falter; despond etc. (*be dejected*) 837; *jeter le manche après la cognée* [*F.*].

shatter one's hopes; inspire–, drive to- despair etc. *n.;* disconcert; dash–, crush–, destroy-one's hopes; dash the cup from one's lips; undermine one's foundation; take away one's last hope.

- *adj.* **hopeless**, desperate, despairing, gone, in despair, *au désespoir* [*F.*], forlorn; inconsolable etc. (*dejected*) 837; broken-hearted.

  out of the question, not to be thought of; impracticable etc. 471; past -hope, -cure, -mending, -recall; at one's last gasp etc. (*death*) 360; given up, given over.

  undone, ruined; incurable, cureless, immedicable, remediless, beyond remedy; incorrigible; irreparable, irremediable, irrecoverable, irreversible, irretrievable, irreclaimable, irredeemable, irrevocable, immitigable.

  unpropitious, unpromising, inauspicious, ill-omened, threatening, clouded over, lowering, ominous.

860. Fear

- *n.* **fear**, timidity, diffidence, want of confidence; apprehensiveness, fearfulness etc. *adj.*; solicitude, anxiety, care, apprehension, misgiving; feeze [*colloq., U. S.*]; mistrust etc. (*doubt*) 485; suspicion, qualm; hesitation etc. (*irresolution*) 605.

  trepidation, flutter, fear and trembling, perturbation, tremor, quivering, shaking, trembling, throbbing heart, palpitation, ague fit, cold sweat; nervousness, restlessness etc. *adj.*; inquietude, disquietude, heartquake; abject fear etc. (*cowardice*) 862; mortal funk [*colloq.*], heartsinking, despondency; despair etc. 859.

  batophobia, hypsophobia; claustrophobia; agoraphobia.

  fright, affright [*archaic*], affrightment [*archaic*], boof [*slang*], alarm, dread, awe, terror, horror, dismay, consternation, panic, scare, panic fear, panic terror; "terror by night" [*Bible*]; chute [*N. U. S.*], stampede [*of horses*].

  intimidation, terrorism, reign of terror; terrorist.

  [object of fear] bugbear, bugaboo, scarecrow; hobgoblin etc. (*demon*) 980; nightmare, Gorgon, mormo [*obs.*], ogre, Hurlothrumbo, raw head and bloody bones, fee-faw-fum, *bête noire* [*F.*], *enfant terrible* [*F.*].

  alarmist etc. (*coward*) 862.

- *v.* **fear**, stand in awe of; be afraid etc. *adj.*; have qualms etc. *n.*; apprehend, sit upon thorns, eye askance; distrust etc. (*disbelieve*) 485.

  hesitate etc. (*be irresolute*) 605; falter, funk [*colloq.*], cower, crouch; skulk etc. (*cowardice*) 862; take fright, take alarm; start, wince, flinch, shy, shrink, blench; fly etc. (*avoid*) 623.

  grow pale, turn pale, stand aghast; be in a daze; not dare to say one's soul is one's own.

  tremble, shake; shiver, -in one's shoes; shudder, flutter; shake-, tremble- -like an aspen leaf, -all over; quake, quaver, quiver, quail.

  frighten, fright, affright, terrify; inspire-, excite- -fear, -awe; raise apprehensions; bulldoze [*colloq.*], faze [*colloq.*], feeze *or* feaze [*colloq.*]; give-, raise-, sound- an alarm; alarm, startle, scare, cry "wolf," disquiet, dismay, astound; frighten from one's propriety; frighten out of one's -wits, -senses, -seven senses; awe; strike all of a heap [*colloq.*], strike an awe into, strike terror; harrow up the soul, appall *or* appal, unman, petrify, horrify; pile on the agony.

  make one's -flesh creep, -hair stand on end, -blood run cold, -teeth chatter; take away-, stop- one's breath; make one tremble etc.

  daunt, put in fear, intimidate, cow, daunt, overawe, abash, deter, discourage; browbeat, bully; threaten etc. 909; terrorize, put in bodily fear.

  haunt, obsess, beset, besiege; prey-, weigh- on the mind.

- *adj.* **afraid**, fearful, timid, timorous, nervous, diffident, coy, faint-hearted, tremulous, shaky, afraid of one's shadow, apprehensive, restless, fidgety; more frightened than hurt.

  fearing etc. *v.*; frightened etc. *v.*; in fear, in a fright etc. *n.*; haunted with the fear of etc. *n.*; afeard [*dial.*].

  aghast; awe-struck, awe-stricken; horror-struck, horror-stricken; terror-struck, terror-stricken; panic-struck, panic-stricken; frightened to death, white as a sheet; pale, -as -death, -ashes, -a ghost; breathless, in hysterics.

  inspiring fear etc. *v.*; alarming; formidable, redoubtable; perilous etc. (*danger*) 665; portentous; fearful, dread, dreadful, fell, dire, direful, shocking, frightful, terrible, terrific, tremendous; horrid, horrible, horrific, ghastly, awful, awe-inspiring; revolting etc. (*painful*) 830; Gorgonian, Gorgon-like.

- *adv.* *in terrorem* [*L.*].
- *int.* "angels and ministers of grace defend us!" [*Hamlet*].

861. Courage
[absence of fear]

- *n.* **courage**, bravery, valor *or* valour; resoluteness, boldness etc. *adj.*; spirit, daring, gallantry, intrepidity, prowess, heroism, chivalry; contempt-, defiance- of danger; derring-do [*pseudo-archaic*]; audacity; rashness etc. 863; dash; defiance etc. 715; confidence, self-reliance.

862. Cowardice

manhood, manliness, nerve, pluck, mettle, game; heart, –of grace; spunk [*colloq.*], grit, virtue, hardihood, fortitude; firmness etc. (*stability*) 150; heart of oak; bottom, backbone etc. (*perseverance*) 604a; resolution etc. (*determination*) 604; tenacity, bulldog courage.

exploit, feat, deed, act, achievement; heroic, –deed, –act; bold stroke.

brave man, man of courage, man of mettle; a man; hero, demigod, paladin; Hercules, Theseus, Perseus, Achilles, Hector; Bayard, *chevalier sans peur et sans reproche;* Lancelot, Sir Galahad.

brave woman, heroine, Amazon, Joan of Arc.

[comparisons] lion, tiger, panther, bulldog; gamecock, fighting-cock.

dare-devil, fire eater etc. 863.

v. **be courageous** etc. *adj.;* dare, venture, make bold; face–, front–, affront–, confront–, brave–, defy–, despise–, mock- danger; look in the face; look -full, –boldly, –danger- in the face; face; meet, meet in front; brave, beard; defy etc. 715.

bell the cat, take the bull by the horns, beard the lion in his den, march up to the cannon's mouth, go through fire and water, run the gantlet *or* gauntlet.

nerve oneself; take–, muster–, summon up–, pluck up- courage; take heart; take–, pluck up- heart of grace; hold up one's head, screw one's courage to the sticking place; come -to, –up to- the scratch; stand, –to one's guns, –fire, –against; bear up, –against; hold out etc. (*persevere*) 604a.

put a bold face upon; show–, present- a bold front; show fight; face the music.

hearten; give–, infuse–, inspire- courage; reassure, encourage, embolden, inspirit, cheer, nerve, put upon one's mettle, rally, raise a rallying cry; pat on the back, make a man of, keep in countenance.

adj. **courageous**, brave, valiant, valorous, gallant, intrepid, spirited, spiritful; high-spirited, high-mettled, mettlesome, plucky; manly, manful, resolute, stout, stout-hearted; iron-hearted, lion-hearted; heart of oak; Penthesilean.

bold, bold-spirited; daring, audacious; fearless, dauntless, aweless, dreadless [*obs.*]; undaunted, unappalled, undismayed, unawed, unblenched, unabashed, unalarmed, unflinching, unshrinking, unblenching, unapprehensive; confident, self-reliant; bold as -a lion, –brass [*colloq.*].

enterprising, adventurous, venturous, venturesome, dashing, chivalrous; soldierly etc. (*warlike*) 722; heroic.

fierce, savage; pugnacious etc. (*bellicose*) 720.

strong-minded, strong-willed, hardy, doughty [*archaic or humorous*]; firm etc. (*stable*) 150; determined etc. (*resolved*) 604; dogged, indomitable etc. (*persevering*) 604a.

upon one's mettle; up to the scratch; reassured etc. *v.;* unfeared, undreaded.

862. Cowardice
[excess of fear]

n. **cowardice**, pusillanimity; cowardliness etc. *adj.;* timidity, effeminacy.

poltroonery, baseness, dastardness, dastardy, abject fear, funk [*colloq.*]; Dutch courage [*colloq.*]; fear etc. 860; white feather, faint heart; cold feet [*slang*], yellow streak [*slang*].

coward, poltroon, dastard, sneak, recreant; shy–, dunghill- cock; coistrel *or* coistril [*archaic*], milksop, white-liver [*colloq.*], nidget [*obs.*]; slink [*Scot. & dial. Eng.*], cur [*contemptuous*], craven, caitiff; Bob Acres, Jerry Sneak.

alarmist, terrorist, pessimist; sheep in wolf's clothing.

shirker, slacker; runagate etc. (*fugitive*) 623.

v. **quail** etc. (*fear*) 860; be cowardly etc. *adj.*, be a coward etc. *n.;* funk [*colloq.*], cower, skulk, sneak; flinch, shy, fight shy, slink, turn tail; run away etc. (*avoid*) 623; show the white feather.

adj. **cowardly**, coward, fearful, shy, timid, timorous, skittish; poor-spirited, spiritless, soft, effeminate; weak-minded; infirm of purpose etc. 605; weak–, faint–, chicken–, hen–, pigeon-hearted; white–, lily–, milk- livered; smock-faced.

dastard, dastardly, base, craven, sneaking, dunghill, recreant; unwarlike, unsoldierlike; "in face a lion but in heart a deer"; "more like a rabbit than a robber."

unmanned; frightened etc. 860.

adv. with fear and trembling, in fear of one's life, in a blue funk [*colloq.*]; "with groanings that cannot be uttered" [*Bible*].

int. sauve qui peut! [*F.*], devil take the hindmost!

863. Rashness

n. **rashness** etc. *adj.;* temerity, want of caution, imprudence, indiscretion; overconfidence, presumption, audacity; precipitancy, precipitation, impetuosity; levity; foolhardihood, foolhardiness; heedlessness, thoughtlessness etc. (*inattention*) 458; carelessness etc. (*neglect*) 460; desperation; Quixotism, knight-errantry; fire eating.

gaming, gambling; blind bargain, leap in the dark, fool's paradise; too many eggs in one basket.

desperado, rashling [*obs.*], madcap, daredevil, Hotspur, Hector; scapegrace, *enfant perdu* [*F.*]; Don Quixote, knight-errant, Icarus; adventurer; dynamiter *or* dynamitard; fire eater, bully, bravo.

gambler, gamester etc. (*chance*) 621.

v. **be rash** etc. *adj.;* stick at nothing, play a desperate game; run into danger etc. 665; play with -fire, -edge tools; *donner tête baissée* [*F.*]; knock one's head against a wall etc. (*be unskillful*) 699; kick against the pricks; rush on destruction; tempt Providence, go on a forlorn hope.

carry too much sail, sail too near the wind, ride at single anchor, go out of one's depth; go to sea in a sieve.

take a leap in the dark; buy a pig in a poke; bet against a dead certainty.

count one's chickens before they are hatched; reckon without one's host; catch at straws; trust to-, lean on- a broken reed.

adj. **rash**, incautious, indiscreet, injudicious, imprudent, improvident, temerarious; uncalculating, impulsive; heedless; careless etc. (*neglectful*) 460; without ballast, head over heels, heels over head; giddy etc. (*inattentive*) 458.

reckless, wanton, wild, madcap, desperate, devil-may-care, death-defying; hot-blooded, hot-headed, hot-brained; headlong, headstrong; breakneck, foolhardy, harebrained, precipitate.

overconfident, overweening; venturesome, venturous, adventurous, Quixotic; fire-eating.

unexpected; off one's guard etc. (*inexpectant*) 508.

adv. posthaste, *à corps perdu* [*F.*], hand over head [*rare*], *tête baissée* [*F.*], headforemost; happen what may.

864. Caution

n. **caution**; cautiousness etc. *adj.;* discretion, prudence, cautel [*obs.*], heed, circumspection, calculation, deliberation.

foresight etc. 510; vigilance etc. 459; warning etc. 668.

worldly wisdom; "safety first," Fabian policy, "watchful waiting."

coolness etc. *adj.;* self-possession, self-command; presence of mind, *sang-froid* [*F.*], well-regulated mind.

v. **be cautious** etc. *adj.;* take -care, -heed, -good care; have a care; mind, mind what one is about; be on one's guard etc. (*keep watch*) 459; "make assurance double sure" [*Macbeth*].

think twice, look before one leaps, keep one's eye peeled [*slang*], keep one's weather eye open [*colloq.*]; count the cost, look to the main chance; cut one's coat according to one's cloth; feel one's -ground, -way; see how the land lies etc. (*foresight*) 510; pussy-foot; wait to see how the cat jumps; bridle one's tongue; *reculer pour mieux sauter* [*F.*] etc. (*prepare*) 673; let well enough alone, *ne pas reveiller le chat qui dort* [*F.*]; let sleeping dogs lie.

keep out of -harm's way, -troubled waters; keep at a respectful distance, stand aloof; keep-, be- on the safe side.

anticipate; bespeak etc. (*be early*) 132.

lay by; husband one's resources etc. 636.

warn, caution etc. 668.

adj. **cautious**, wary, guarded, guardful [*rare*]; on one's guard etc. (*watchful*) 459; gingerly, precautious [*rare*], suspicious, leery [*slang*]; *cavendo tutus* [*L.*]; *in medio tutissimus* [*L.*]; vigilant; careful, heedful, cautelous [*obs.*], stealthy, chary, shy of, circumspect, prudent, canny [*Scot.*], safe, noncommittal, discreet, politic; sure-footed etc. (*skillful*) 698.

unenterprising, unadventurous, cool, steady, self-possessed; overcautious.

adv. cautiously etc. *adj.*

int. have a care! look out! danger! mind your eye! [*colloq.*]; stop! look! listen! *cave canem!* [*L.*].

865. Desire

n. **desire**, wish, fancy, fantasy; inclination, leaning, bent, mind, animus, partiality, *penchant* [*F.*], predilection; propensity etc. 820; willingness etc. 602; liking, love, fondness, relish.

longing, hankering, yearning, coveting; aspiration, ambition, vaulting ambition; eagerness, zeal, ardor, *empressement* [*F.*], breathless impatience, solicitude, anxiety, overanxiety; impetuosity etc. 825.

need, want, exigency, urgency, necessity.

appetite, appetition, appetence, appetency; sharp appetite, keenness, hunger, stomach, twist; thirst, thirstiness; drought *or* drouth, mouth-watering.

edge of -appetite, -hunger; torment of Tantalus; sweet tooth [*colloq.*], lickerish (*or* liquorish) tooth; longing-, wistful-, sheep's- eyes.

avidity, greed, greediness, covetousness, ravenousness etc. *adj.;* grasping, craving, canine appetite, rapacity; voracity etc. (*gluttony*) 957.

passion, rage, furor, frenzy, mania, manie [*obs.*]; itching palm; inextinguishable desire; itch, itching, prurience, cacoëthes, cupidity,

866. Indifference

lust, concupiscence; kleptomania, dipsomania; monomania, *idée fixe* [*F.*].

[of animals] heat, rut, oestrus.

[person desiring] lover, amateur, votary, devotee, aspirant, solicitant, candidate; cormorant etc. 957; parasite, sycophant.

[object of desire] desideratum, desideration; want etc. (*requirement*) 630; "a consummation devoutly to be wish'd" [*Hamlet*]; attraction, magnet, loadstone, lure, allurement, fancy, temptation, seduction, fascination, prestige, height of one's ambition, idol; whim, whimsey *or* whimsy, whim-wham; maggot; hobby, hobbyhorse [*rare*].

Fortunatus's cap; wishing -cap, –stone, –well; love potion; aphrodisiac.

v. **desire**; wish, wish for; be desirous etc. *adj.;* have a longing etc. *n.;* hope etc. 858.

care for, affect, like, list [*archaic*]; take to, cling to, take a fancy to; fancy; prefer etc. (*choose*) 609; have an eye to, have a mind to; find it in one's heart etc. (*be willing*) 602; have a fancy for, set one's eyes upon; cast sheep's eyes upon, look sweet on [*colloq.*]; take into one's head, have at heart, be bent upon; set one's cap at [*colloq.*], set one's heart upon, set one's mind upon; covet.

hunger–, thirst–, crave–, lust–, itch–, hanker–, run mad- after; raven for, die for; burn to; sigh–, cry–, gape–, gasp–, pine–, pant–, languish–, yearn–, long–, be on thorns–, hope- for; aspire after; catch at, grasp at, jump at.

woo, court, ogle, solicit; fish for, whistle for, put up for [*slang*].

want, miss, need, lack, desiderate, feel the want of; would fain -have, –do; would be glad of.

hunger; be hungry etc. *adj.;* have a good appetite, play a good knife and fork [*colloq.*].

attract, allure; cause–, create–, raise–, excite–, provoke- desire; whet the appetite; appetize, titillate, take one's fancy, tempt; hold out -temptation, –allurement; tantalize, make one's mouth water, *faire venir l'eau à la bouche* [*F.*].

gratify desire etc. (*give pleasure*) 829.

adj. **desirous**; desiring etc. *v.;* orectic, appetitive; inclined etc. (*willing*) 602; partial to [*colloq.*]; fain, wishful, longing, wistful; optative; anxious, curious; at a loss for, sedulous, solicitous.

eager, avid, keen; burning, fervent, ardent; agog; all agog; breathless; impatient etc. (*impetuous*) 825; bent–, intent–, set- on, –upon; mad after, *enragé* [*F.*], rabid, dying for, devoured by desire.

aspiring, ambitious, vaulting, sky-aspiring, high-reaching.

craving, hungry, sharp-set, peckish [*colloq.*], ravening, with an empty stomach, esurient, lickerish, thirsty, athirst, parched with thirst, pinched with hunger, famished, dry, droughty *or* drouthy; hungry as a -hunter, –hawk, –horse, –church mouse.

greedy, –as a hog; overeager, voracious; ravenous, –as a wolf; open-mouthed, covetous, rapacious, grasping, extortionate, exacting, sordid, *alieni appetens* [*L.*]; insatiable, insatiate, unquenchable, quenchless; omnivorous.

unsatisfied, unsated, unslaked.

desirable; desired etc. *v.;* in demand, popular; pleasing etc. (*giving pleasure*) 829; appetizing, appetible; tantalizing.

adv. fain; with eager appetite; wistfully etc. *adj.*

int. would that! would it were! O for! if only! *esto perpetua!* [*L.*].

866. Indifference

n. **indifference**, neutrality; unconcern, insouciance, nonchalance; want of -interest, –earnestness; anorexia *or* anorexy, inappetence *or* inappetency; apathy etc. (*insensibility*) 823; supineness etc. (*inactivity*) 683; disdain etc. 930; recklessness etc. 863; inattention etc. 458; coldness etc. *adj.;* anaphrodisia.

anaphrodisiac *or* antaphrodisiac; lust-quencher, passion-queller.

v. **be indifferent** etc. *adj.;* stand neuter; take no interest in etc. (*insensibility*) 823; have no desire for etc. 865, have no taste for, have no relish for; not care for; care nothing -for, –about; not care a -straw etc. (*unimportance*) 643 -about, –for; not mind.

set at naught etc. (*make light of*) 483; spurn etc. (*disdain*) 930.

adj. **indifferent**, cold, frigid, luke-warm; cool, –as a cucumber; neutral, unconcerned, insouciant, phlegmatic, pocucurantish, pococurante, easy-going, devil-may-care, careless, listless, lackadaisical; half-hearted, unambitious, unaspiring, undesirous, unsolicitous, unattracted, inappetent, all one to.

unattractive, unalluring, undesired, undesirable, uncared for, unwished, unvalued.

insipid etc. 391.

adv. for aught one cares; with utter indifference.

int. **never mind**! who cares! it's all one to me!

867. Dislike

n. **dislike**, distaste, disrelish, disinclination, displacency [*rare*].
reluctance; backwardness etc. (*unwillingness*) 603.
repugnance, disgust, queasiness, nausea, loathing, loathfulness [*rare*], aversion, averseness, aversation [*obs.*], abomination, antipathy, abhorrence, horror; mortal-, rooted- -antipathy, –horror; hatred, detestation; hate etc. 898; animosity etc. 900.
hydrophobia, canine madness; xenophobia, batophobia etc. (*nervousness*) 860; Anglophobia, Germanophobia, Slavophobia etc.
sickener; gall and wormwood etc. (*unsavory*) 395; shuddering, cold sweat.

v. **dislike**, mislike, disrelish; mind, object to; would rather not, not care for; have-, conceive-, entertain-, take- a dislike, -an aversion- to; have no -taste, -stomach- for; shrug the shoulders at, shudder at, turn up the nose at, look askance at; make a -mouth, –wry face, –grimace; make faces.
shun, avoid etc. 623; eschew; withdraw-, shrink-, recoil - from; not be able to -bear, –abide, –endure.
loathe, nauseate, wamble [*obs. or dial. Eng.*], abominate, detest, abhor; hate etc. 898; take amiss etc. 900; have enough of etc. (*be satiated*) 869.
cause dislike, excite dislike; disincline, repel, sicken; make sick, render sick; turn one's stomach, nauseate, disgust, shock, stink in the nostrils; go against the -grain, –stomach; stick in the throat; make one's blood run cold etc. (*give pain*) 830; pall.

adj. **disliking** etc. *v.;* averse to, loath *or* loth, adverse; shy of, sick of, out of conceit with; disinclined; heartsick, dogsick; queasy.
disliked etc. *v.;* uncared for, unpopular, out of favor; repulsive, repugnant, repellent; abhorrent, insufferable, fulsome, nauseous, loathsome, loathful [*rare*], offensive; disgusting etc. *v.;* disagreeable etc. (*painful*) 830.
uneatable, inedible, inesculent [*rare*], unappetizing, unsavory.

adv. **to satiety**, to one's disgust; *usque ad nauseam* [*L.*].

int. faugh! foh! ugh!

868. Fastidiousness

n. **fastidiousness** etc. *adj.;* nicety, meticulosity, hypercriticism, difficulty in being pleased; *friandise* [*F.*], epicurism, *omnia suspendens naso* [*L.*].
discrimination, discernment, perspicacity, perspicaciousness [*rare*], keenness, sharpness, insight.
epicure, gourmet.
[excess of delicacy] prudery, prudishness, primness.

v. **be fastidious** etc. *adj.;* split hairs; hunt for the crumpled rose-leaf.
mince the matter; turn up one's nose at etc. (*disdain*) 930; look a gift horse in the mouth, see spots on the sun; see the mote in one's brother's eye.
discriminate, have nice discrimination; have exquisite taste; be discriminative etc. *adj.*

adj. **fastidious**, nice, delicate, *délicat* [*F.*]; meticulous, finicking *or* finicky *or* finikin, exacting, finical; difficult, dainty, lickerish, squeamish, thin-skinned; queasy; hard-, difficult- to please; querulous, particular, scrupulous; censorious etc. 932; hypercritical; overcritical.
prudish, strait-laced, prim.
discriminative, discriminating, discerning, discriminant [*rare*], judicious, keen, sharp, perspicacious.

869. Satiety

n. **satiety**, satisfaction, saturation, repletion, glut, surfeit; cloyment [*obs.*], satiation; weariness etc. 841.
spoiled child; *enfant gâté* [*F.*]; too much of a good thing, *toujours perdrix* [*F.*]; a diet of cake; *crambe repetita* [*Juvenal*].

v. **sate**, satiate, satisfy, saturate; cloy, quench, slake, pall, glut, gorge, surfeit; bore etc. (*weary*) 841; tire etc. (*fatigue*) 688; spoil.
have enough of, have quite enough of, have one's fill, have too much of; be satiated etc. *adj.*

adj. **satiated** etc. *v.;* overgorged; gorged with plenty, overfed; *blasé* [*F.*], used up [*colloq.*], sick of, heartsick.

int. **enough**! hold! *eheu jam satis!* [*L.*].

870. Wonder

n. **wonder**, marvel; astonishment, amazement, wonderment, bewilderment; amazedness etc. *adj.;* admiration, awe; stupor, stupefaction, stound [*obs.*], fascination; sensation; surprise etc. (*inexpectation*) 508.
note of admiration; thaumaturgy etc. (*sorcery*) 992.

v. **wonder**, marvel, admire; be surprised etc. *adj.;* start; stare; open-, rub-, turn up- one's eyes; gloar [*obs.*]; gape, open one's mouth, hold one's breath; look-, stand- -aghast, –agog;

871. Expectance

look blank etc. (*disappointment*) 509; *tomber des nues* [*F.*]; not believe one's -eyes, -ears, -senses; not be able to account for etc. (*unintelligible*) 519; not know whether one stands on one's head or one's heels.

astonish, surprise, amaze, astound; dumfound *or* dumbfound, dumfounder *or* dumbfounder, startle, dazzle; daze; strike, -with - wonder, -awe; electrify; stun, stupefy, petrify, confound, bewilder, flabbergast [*colloq.*]; stagger, throw on one's beam ends, fascinate, turn the head, take away one's breath, strike dumb; make one's -hair stand on end, -tongue cleave to the roof of one's mouth; make one stare.

take by surprise, take unawares etc. (*be unexpected*) 508.

be wonderful etc. *adj.;* beggar-, baffle- description; stagger belief.

adj. **astonished**, surprised etc. *v.;* aghast, all agog, breathless, agape; open-mouthed; awe-, thunder-, moon-, planet- struck; spellbound; lost in -amazement, -wonder, -astonishment; struck all of a heap [*colloq.*], unable to believe one's senses; like a duck in -a fit, -thunder [*both colloq.*].

wonderful, wondrous; surprising etc. *v.;* unexpected etc. 508; unheard of; mysterious etc. (*inexplicable*) 519; miraculous.

monstrous, prodigious, stupendous, marvelous; inconceivable, incredible, inimaginable [*obs.*], unimaginable; strange etc. (*uncommon*) 83; passing strange.

striking etc. *v.;* overwhelming; wonder-working.

indescribable, inexpressible, ineffable, unutterable, unspeakable.

adv. **wonderfully** etc. *adj.;* fearfully; for a wonder, in the name of wonder; strange to say; *mirabile dictu* [*L.*], *mirabile visu* [*L.*]; to one's great surprise.

with wonder etc. *n.,* with gaping mouth, with open eyes, with upturned eyes; with the eyes starting out of one's head.

int. **lo!** lo and behold! O! heyday! halloo! what! indeed! really! surely! humph! hem! good -lack, -heavens, -gracious! gad so! welladay! dear me! only think! lackadaisy! my stars! my goodness! gracious goodness! goodness gracious! mercy on us! heavens and earth! God bless me! bless us! bless my heart! odzookens! *O gemini!* adzooks! hoity-toity! strong! Heaven save-, bless- the mark! can such things be! zounds! 'sdeath! what on earth! what in the world! who would have thought it! etc. (*inexpectation*) 508; you don't say so! what do you say to that! *nous verrons!* [*F.*], how now! where am I? fancy! do tell! *Ciel!* [*F.*]; what do you know! [*slang*]; what do you know about that! [*slang*], well, I'll be jiggered! [*colloq.*].

871. Expectance
[absence of wonder]

n. **expectance**, expectancy etc. (*expectation*) 507.

imperturbability. imperturbableness, imperturbation, *sang-froid* [*F.*], calmness, unruffled calm, coolness, coldbloodedness, hardheadedness, steadiness, lack of nerves, want of imagination, practicality.

nothing out of the ordinary.

v. **expect** etc. 507; not be surprised, not wonder etc. 870; *nil admirari* [*L.*], make nothing of; take it coolly; be unamazed etc. *adj.;* display imperturbability etc. *n.*

adj. **expecting** etc. *v.;* unamazed, astonished at nothing; *blasé* [*F.*] etc. (*weary*) 841; expected etc. *v.;* foreseen.

imperturbable, nerveless, cool, cool-headed, unruffled, calm, steady, hard-headed, practical, unimaginative.

common, ordinary etc. (*habitual*) 613.

int. no wonder! of course! why not?

872. Prodigy

n. **prodigy**, phenomenon, wonder, wonderment, marvel, miracle; freak, freak of nature, *lusus naturae* [*L.*], monstrosity; monster etc. (*unconformity*) 83; curiosity, infant prodigy, lion, sight, spectacle; *jeu-, coup- de théâtre* [*F.*]; gazingstock; sign; St. Elmo's -fire, -light; portent etc. 512.

what no words can paint; wonders of the world; *annus mirabilis* [*L.*]; *dignus vindice nodus* [*L.*].

detonation; bursting of a -shell, -bomb, -mine; volcanic eruption, peal of thunder; thunderclap, thunderbolt, thunderstone [*obs. or dial. Eng.*].

873. Repute

n. **repute**, reputation; distinction, mark, name, figure; good-, high- repute; note, notability, notoriety, éclat, "the bubble reputation" [*As You Like It*], vogue, celebrity; fame, famousness; renown; popularity, *aura popularis* [*L.*]; approbation etc. 931; credit, *succès d'estime* [*F.*], prestige, talk of the town; name to conjure with.

account, regard, respect; reputability [*rare*], reputableness etc. *adj.;* respectability etc. (*probity*) 939; good -name, -report; fair name.

dignity; stateliness etc. *adj.;* solemnity, grandeur, splendor, nobility, majesty, sublimity; glory, honor; luster etc. (*light*) 420; illustriousness etc. *adj.*

rank, standing, brevet rank, precedence, *pas* [*F.*], station, place, status; position, -in society; order, degree, *locus standi* [*L.*], caste, condition.

graduation, university degree, baccalaureate, doctorate, doctorship; scholarship, fellowship.

eminence; greatness etc. *adj.;* height etc. 206; importance etc. 642; preëminence, supereminence; high mightiness, primacy; top of the -ladder, -tree; elevation; ascent etc. 305; superexaltation, exaltation, dignification [*rare*], aggrandizement; dedication, consecration, enthronement.

celebrity, worthy, hero, man of mark, great card, lion, *rara avis* [*L.*], notability, somebody; "the observed of all observers" [*Hamlet*]; classman; man of rank etc. (*nobleman*) 875; pillar of the -state, -church; "a mother in Israel" [*Bible*].

chief etc. (*master*) 745; first fiddle etc. (*proficient*) 700; scholar, *savant* [*F.*] etc. 492; cynosure, mirror; flower, pink, pearl; paragon etc. (*perfection*) 650; "the choice and master spirits of this age" [*Julius Caesar*]; *élite* [*F.*]; star, sun, constellation, galaxy.

ornament, honor, feather in one's cap, halo, aureole, nimbus; halo-, blaze- of glory; "blushing honors" [*Henry VIII*]; laurels etc. (*trophy*) 733.

posthumous fame, memory, niche in the temple of fame; celebration, canonization, enshrinement, glorification; immortality, immortal name; *magni nominis umbra* [Lucan].

v. **glory in**; be conscious of glory; be proud of etc. (*pride*) 878; exult etc. (*boast*) 884; be vain of etc. (*vanity*) 880.

be distinguished etc. *adj.;* shine etc. (*light*) 420; shine forth, figure; cut a figure, cut a dash [*colloq.*], make a splash [*colloq.*].

surpass, outshine, outrival, outvie, outjump, eclipse; throw-, cast- into the shade; overshadow.

rival, emulate, vie with.

gain *or* **acquire honor** etc. *n.;* live, flourish, glitter; flaunt; play first fiddle etc. (*be of importance*) 642; bear the -palm, -bell; lead the way, take precedence, take the wall of [*obs.*]; gain-, win- -laurels, -spurs, -golden opinions etc. (*approbation*) 931; graduate, take one's degree, pass one's examination; win a -scholarship, -fellowship.

make -a, -some- -noise, -noise in the world; leave one's mark, exalt one's horn, star, have a run, be run after; be lionized, come into vogue, come to the front; raise one's head.

honor; give-, do-, pay-, render- honor to; accredit, pay regard to, dignify, glorify; sing praises to etc. (*approve*) 931; look up to; exalt, aggrandize, elevate, nobilitate [*archaic*]; enthrone, signalize, immortalize, deify, exalt to the skies; hand one's name down to posterity.

consecrate; dedicate to, devote to; enshrine, inscribe, blazon, lionize, blow the trumpet, crown with laurel.

confer *or* reflect honor on etc. *n.;* shed a luster on; redound to one's honor, ennoble.

adj. **distinguished**, *distingué* [*F.*], noted; of note etc. *n.;* honored etc. *v.;* popular; fashionable etc. 852; remarkable etc. (*important*) 642; notable, notorious; celebrated, renowned, in every one's mouth, talked of, famous, famed, far-famed; conspicuous, to the front; foremost; in the -front rank, -ascendant.

in good odor; in favor, in high favor; reputable, respectable, creditable.

imperishable, deathless, immortal, never fading, fadeless, *aere perennius* [*L.*], time-honored.

illustrious, glorious, splendid, brilliant, radiant; bright etc. 420; full-blown; honorific.

eminent, prominent; high etc. 206; in the zenith; at the -head of, -top of the tree; peerless, of the first water; superior etc. 33; supereminent, preëminent.

great, dignified, proud, noble, honorable, worshipful, lordly, grand, stately, august, princely, imposing, solemn, transcendent, majestic, sacred, sublime, heaven-born, heroic, *sans peur et sans reproche* [*F.*]; sacrosanct.

int. **hail**! all hail! *ave!* [*L.*], *viva!* [*It.*], *vive!* [*F.*], long life to! glory-, honor- be to!

874. Disrepute

n. **disrepute**, discredit; ill-, bad- -repute, -name, -odor, -favor; disapprobation etc. 932; ingloriousness, derogation, abasement, debasement; abjectness etc. *adj.;* degradation, dedecoration [*rare*]; "a long farewell to all my greatness" [*Henry VIII*]; odium, obloquy, opprobrium, ignominy.

dishonor, disgrace, shame, crying-, burning-shame; humiliation; scandal, baseness, vileness; turpitude etc. (*improbity*) 940; infamy.

stigma, brand, reproach, imputation, slur, stain, blot, spot, blur; *scandalum magnatum* [*L.*], badge of infamy, blot in one's escutcheon; bend

875. Nobility

sinister, bar sinister, champain, point champain [*her.*]; byword of reproach; object of scorn, hissing [*archaic*]; Ichabod.

tarnish, taint, defilement, pollution.

argumentum ad verecundiam [*L.*]; sense of shame etc. 879.

v. **be inglorious** etc. *adj.;* incur disgrace etc. *n.;* have–, earn- a bad name; put–, wear- a halter round one's neck; disgrace–, expose- oneself.

play second fiddle; lose caste; "pale his uneffectual fire" [*Hamlet*]; recede into the shade; fall from one's high estate; keep in the background etc. (*modesty*) 881; be conscious of disgrace etc. (*humility*) 879; look -blue, –foolish, –like a fool; cut a -poor, –sorry- figure; laugh on the wrong side of the mouth [*colloq.*]; make a sorry face, go away with a flea in one's ear [*colloq.*], slink away.

cause shame etc. *n.;* shame, disgrace, put to shame, dishonor; throw–, cast–, fling–, reflect- dishonor etc. *n.* upon; be a reproach to etc. *n.;* derogate from.

tarnish, stain, blot, sully, taint; discredit; degrade, debase, defile; beggar; expel etc. (*punish*) 972.

stigmatize, vilify, defame, slur, cast a slur upon, impute shame to, brand, post, hold up to shame, send to Coventry; tread–, trample- under foot; show up [*colloq.*], drag through the mud, drag through the mire, heap dirt upon; reprehend etc. 932.

bring low, put down, snub; take down; take down a peg, –lower, –or two [*colloq.*].

obscure, eclipse, outshine, take the shine out of [*colloq.*]; throw–, cast- into the shade; overshadow; leave–, put- in the background; push into a corner, put one's nose out of joint [*colloq.*]; put out, put out of countenance.

disconcert, upset, throw off one's center, discompose; put to the blush etc. (*humble*) 879.

adj. **disgraced** etc. *v.;* blown upon; "shorn of its beams" [*Milton*], shorn of one's glory; overcome, downtrodden; loaded with shame etc. *n.;* in bad repute etc. *n.;* out of -repute, –favor, –fashion, –countenance; at a discount; under -a cloud, –an eclipse; unable to show one's face; in the -shade, –background; out at elbows, down in the world, down on one's uppers [*colloq.*], down and out.

inglorious, nameless, renownless, obscure, unknown to fame, unnoticed, unnoted, unhonored, unglorified.

discreditable, shameful, disgraceful, disreputable, despicable; questionable; unbecoming, unworthy, derogatory; degrading, humiliating, *infra dignitatem* [*L.*], dedecorous [*rare*]; scandalous, infamous, too bad, unmentionable, ribald, opprobrious; arrant, shocking, outrageous, notorious.

ignominious, scrubby, dirty, abject, vile, beggarly, pitiful, low, mean, petty, shabby; base etc. (*dishonorable*) 940.

adv. to one's shame be it spoken.

int. **shame**! fie! for shame! *proh pudor!* [*L.*]; *O tempora! O mores!* [*L.*]; ough! *sic transit gloria mundi!* [*L.*].

875. Nobility

n. **nobility**, rank, condition, distinction, optimacy [*rare*], blood, *pur sang* [*F.*], birth, high descent, order; quality, gentility; blue blood of Castile; "all the blood of all the Howards" [*Pope*]; caste of "Vere de Vere" [*Tennyson*]; *ancien régime* [*F.*].

high life, *haut monde* [*F.*]; upper classes, upper ten [*colloq.*], upper ten thousand; the four hundred; *élite* [*F.*], aristocracy, great folks; fashionable world etc. (*fashion*) 852.

personage–, man- of -distinction, –mark, –rank; notables, notabilities; celebrity, bigwig [*humorous*], magnate, great man, star; big bug, big gun, great gun [*colloq.*]; gilded rooster [*slang*]; *magni nominis umbra* [Lucan]; "every inch a king" [*Lear*].

[the nobility] peerage, baronage; house of -lords, –peers; lords, –temporal and spiritual; noblesse; knightage.

peer, noble, nobleman; lord, lording [*archaic*], lordling; grandee, magnifico, hidalgo; daimio, samurai, *shizoku* [*Jap.*]; don; aristocrat, swell [*colloq.*], three-tailed bashaw; gentleman, squire, squireen [*humorous, Eng.*], patrician; laureate.

gentry, gentlefolk; squirarchy *or* squirearchy, better sort, magnates, primates, optimates; pantisocracy.

king etc. (*master*) 745; atheling [*hist.*]; prince, duke, marquis, earl, viscount, baron, thane [*hist.*], banneret, baronet, knight, chevalier, count, armiger, esquire, laird [*Scot.*]; signior, seignior; *signor* [*It.*], *señor* [*Sp.*], *senhor* [*Pg.*]; boyar *or* boyard [*Russ.*]; effendi, sheik *or* sheikh, emir, shereef *or* sherif, pasha, sahib; palsgrave [*Ger. hist.*], waldgrave, margrave; vavasor [*feudal law*].

empress, queen, princess, duchess, marchioness, viscountess, countess; lady, *doña* [*Sp.*], dona [*Pg.*]; *signora* [*It.*], *señora* [*Sp.*], senhora [*Pg.*]; dame; memsahib.

876. Commonalty

[indian ruling chiefs] raja, rana, rao, rawal, rawat, rai, raikwar, raikbar, raikat; maharaja, maharana, maharao etc.; Gackwar [*lit.* cowherd; *Baroda*]; maharaja bahadur, raja bahadur, rai (*or* rao) bahadur; rai (*or* rao) sahib; jám, thakur [*all Hindu titles*].

nawab, wali, sultan, ameer *or* amir, mir, mirza, mian, khan; Nizam, nawab bahadur, khan bahadur, khan sahib [*all Moham. titles*].

sirdar *or* sardar, diwan *or* dewan [*both Hindu and Moham. titles*].

[honorifics] shahzada ["King's son"], kumar *or* kunwar ["prince"]; mirza [*when appended it signifies* "prince"; *when prefixed,* "Mr."]; arbab ["lord"]; malik ["master"]; khanzada ["son of a khan"]; huzur *or* huzoor ["the presence"].

[female titles] rani, maharani [*Hindu*]; sultana, malikah, begum *or* begam [*Moham.*].

shahzadi, kumari *or* kunwari, raj-kumari, malikzadi, khanam [*all equivalent to* "princess"].

[rank or office] kingship, dukedom, marquisate, earldom; viscountship, viscounty, viscountcy; lordship, baronetcy, knighthood, donship.

v. be noble etc. *adj.*

adj. **noble**, exalted; of rank etc. *n.*; princely, titled, patrician, aristocratic; highborn, well-born; of gentle blood; genteel, *comme il faut* [*F.*], gentlemanlike, courtly etc. (*fashionable*) 852; highly respectable.

adv. in high quarters.

876. Commonalty

n. **commonalty**, democracy; obscurity; low -condition, -life, -society, -company; *bourgeoisie* [*F.*]; mass of -the people, -society; Brown, Jones, and Robinson; Tom, Dick, and Harry; "the four million" [O. Henry]; the peepul [*humorous*]; lower-, humbler- classes, -orders; vulgar-, common- herd; rank and file, *hoc genus omne* [*L.*]; the -many, -general, -crowd, -people, -populace, -multitude, -million, -masses, -mobility [*humorous*], -other half, -peasantry; king Mob; proletariat; *fruges consumere nati* [*L.*], *demos* [*Gr.*], *hoi polloi* [*Gr.*], great unwashed; man in the street.

rabble, -rout; chaff, rout, horde, canaille; scum-, residuum-, dregs- of -the people, -society; mob, swinish multitude, *foex populi* [*L.*]; trash; *profanum-, ignobile- vulgus* [*L.*]; vermin, raff, riffraff, rag-tag and bobtail; small fry.

commoner, one of the people, democrat, plebeian, republican, proletary, proletarian, proletaire, *roturier* [*F.*], John Smith, Mr. Snooks, *bourgeois* [*F.*], *épicier* [*F.*], Philistine, cockney; grisette, demimonde, demimondaine.

peasant, countryman, boor, carl *or* carle [*Scot. or archaic*], churl; villain *or* villein [*obs. or rare*], serf; *terrae filius* [*L.*], kern *or* kerne [*Ir.*], gossoon [*Anglo-Ir.*]; tike *or* tyke [*archaic or dial.*], ryot [*India*], fellah [*Ar. pl.* fellahin *or* fellaheen]; docker, stevedore, longshoreman; swain, clown, hind [*Eng.*], clod, clodhopper, hobnail, yokel, bogtrotter, bumpkin; plowman *or* ploughman, plowboy *or* ploughboy; chuff, hayseed [*slang*], rustic, lunkhead [*colloq.*], loon [*archaic*], rube [*slang*], chaw-bacon [*slang*], tiller of the soil; hewers of wood and drawers of water; sons of Martha; groundling [*obs.*], gaffer, put, cub, Tony Lumpkin [Goldsmith], looby, lout, underling; gamin, street Arab, mudlark.

rough, rowdy, roughneck [*slang*], ruffian, tough [*colloq.*], pot-walloper [*slang*], scullion, slubberdegullion [*obs.*], vulgar-, low- fellow; cad.

upstart, parvenu, skipjack [*dial. Eng.*]; nobody, -one knows; *hesterni quirites* [*L.*], *pessoribus orti* [*L.*]; *bourgeois gentilhomme* [*F.*]; *novus homo* [*L.*], snob, gent [*vulgar or humorous*], mushroom, no one knows who, adventurer; *nouveau riche* (*pl.* nouveaux riches; *fem.* nouvelles riches) [*F.*].

vagabond, beggar, gaberlunzie [*Scot.*], beadsman *or* bedesman [*Scot.*], muckworm, *sans-culotte* [*F.*], tatterdemalion, caitiff, ragamuffin, pariah, outcast of society, tramp, bezonian [Shakespeare], panhandler [*slang*], sundowner [*Austral.*], bum [*slang*], hobo; chiffonier *or* chiffonnier [*rare*], ragman, ragpicker, sweeper, sweep, scrub.

wench, slut, quean, Cinderella.

barbarian, Goth, Vandal, Hottentot, Zulu, savage, Yahoo; unlicked cub, rough diamond.

barbarousness, barbarism, savagery; Boeotia; Philistinism; parvenuism, parvenudom.

v. **be ignoble** etc. *adj.*, be nobody etc. *n.*; be of (*or* belong to) the common herd etc. *n.*

adj. **ignoble**, common, mean, low, base, vile, sorry, scrubby, beggarly; below par; no great shakes etc. (*unimportant*) 643; homely, homespun, vulgar, low-minded; snobbish, parvenu, low bred; menial, underling, servile.

plebeian, proletarian; of -low, -mean- -parentage, -origin, -extraction; lowborn, baseborn, earthborn; mushroom, dunghill, risen from the ranks; unknown to fame, obscure, untitled.

rustic, country, uncivilized; loutish, boorish, clownish, churlish, brutish, raffish; rude, unpolished, unlicked.

barbarous, barbarian, barbaric, barbaresque [De Quincey].
cockney, born within sound of Bow bells.
adv. below the salt.

877. Title

n. **title**, honor; knighthood etc. (*nobility*) 875.
highness, excellency, grace, lordship, worship; reverence; reverend; esquire, sir, master, Mr., *signor* [*It.*], *señor* [*Sp.*], etc. 373; *Mein Herr* [*Ger.*], mynheer; your–, his- honor; serene highness.
madam, *madame* [*F.*] etc. (*mistress*) 374; empress, queen etc. 875.
decoration, laurel, palm, wreath, garland, bays, medal, ribbon, riband, blue ribbon, red ribbon, cordon, cross, crown, coronet, star, garter, fleece; feather, –in one's cap; epaulet *or* epaulette, chevron, *fourragère* [*F.*], colors, cockade; livery; order, arms, coat of arms, shield, escutcheon *or* scutcheon, crest; reward etc. 973; handle to one's name.

878. Pride

n. **pride**; haughtiness etc. *adj.;* high notions, hauteur; vainglory, crest; arrogance etc. (*assumption*) 885; self-importance, pomposity, pompousness; side [*slang*], swank, swagger, toploftiness [*colloq.*].
proud man, highflyer *or* highflier; fine gentleman; fine lady, *grande dame* [*F.*].
dignity, self-respect, *mens sibi conscia recti* [Virgil].

v. **be proud** etc. *adj.;* put a good face on; look one in the face; stalk abroad, perk, perk up, perk oneself up; think no small beer of oneself [*colloq.*]; think no small potatoes of oneself [*colloq.*]; presume, swagger, strut; rear–, lift up– one's head; hold one's head high, look big, take the wall; "bear like the Turk no rival near the throne" [Pope]; carry with a high hand; ride the–, mount on one's- high horse; set one's back up, bridle, toss the head; give oneself airs etc. (*assume*) 885; boast etc. 884.
pride oneself on; glory in, take a pride in; pique–, plume–, hug- oneself; stand upon, be proud of; not hide one's light under a bushel, not put one's talent in a napkin; not think small beer of oneself [*colloq.*] etc. (*vanity*) 880.

adj. **dignified**; stately, proud-crested, lordly, baronial; lofty-minded, high-souled, high-minded, high-mettled, high-plumed, high-flown, high-toned.
proud, haughty, lofty, high, mighty, swollen, puffed up, flushed, blown; vainglorious; purse-proud, fine; proud as -a peacock, –Lucifer; bloated with pride.
supercilious, disdainful, bumptious, magisterial, imperious, high-handed, high and mighty, overweening, consequential; pompous, toplofty [*colloq.*]; arrogant etc. 885; unblushing etc. 880.
stiff, stiff-necked; starched, perked up, stuck up [*colloq.*]; in buckram, strait-laced; prim etc. (*affected*) 855.
on one's dignity; on one's -high horse, –tight ropes, –high ropes; on stilts; *en grand seigneur* [*F.*].

adv. with head erect; *de haut en bas* [*F.*]; with nose in air, with nose turned up; with a sneer, with curling lip.

879. Humility

n. **humility**, humbleness, meekness, lowness, lowliness, lowlihood; abasement, self-abasement; submission etc. 725; resignation.
modesty, timidity etc. 881; verecundity [*obs.*], blush, suffusion, confusion; sense of -shame, –disgrace; humiliation, mortification; letdown, setdown.
condescension; affability etc. (*courtesy*) 894.

v. **be humble** etc. *adj.;* deign, vouchsafe, condescend; humble oneself, demean oneself [*colloq.*]; stoop, -to conquer; carry coals; submit etc. 725; submit with a good grace etc. (*brook*) 826; yield the palm.
lower one's -tone, –note; sing small [*colloq.*], draw in one's horns [*colloq.*], sober down; hide one's -face, –diminished head; not dare to show one's face, take shame to oneself, not have a word to say for oneself; feel–, be conscious of- -shame, –disgrace; be humiliated, be put out of countenance, be shamed, be put to the blush etc. *v.;* receive a snub; eat humble pie, eat crow, eat dirt; drink the cup of humiliation to the dregs.
blush for, blush up to the eyes; redden, change color; color up; hang one's head, look foolish, feel small.
render humble; humble, humiliate; let–, set–, take–, tread–, frown-down; snub, abash, abase, make one sing small [*colloq.*], strike dumb; teach one his distance; take down a peg, –lower; throw–, cast- into the shade etc. 874; stare–, put- out of countenance; put to the blush; confuse, ashame [*rare*], shame, mortify,

disgrace, crush; send away with a flea in one's ear [*colloq.*].

get a setdown.

adj. **humble**, lowly, meek; modest etc. 881; humble-minded, sober-minded; unoffended; submissive etc. 725; servile etc. 886.

condescending; affable etc. (*courteous*) 894.

humbled etc. *v.;* bowed down, resigned; abashed, ashamed, dashed; out of countenance; down in the mouth; down on one's -knees, -marrowbones [*colloq.*], -uppers [*colloq.*]; humbled in the dust, brow-beaten; chapfallen, crestfallen; dumfoundered *or* dumbfoundered, flabbergasted [*colloq.*], struck all of a heap [*colloq.*]; shorn of one's glory etc. (*disrepute*) 874.

adv. **humbly**; with downcast eyes, with bated breath, on bended knee; on all fours; with one's tail between one's legs.

under correction, with due deference.

880. Vanity

n. **vanity**; conceit, conceitedness; self-conceit, self-complacency, self-confidence, self-sufficiency, self-esteem, self-love, self-approbation, self-praise, self-glorification, self-laudation, self-gratulation, self-applause, self-admiration; *amour propre* [*F.*]; selfishness etc. 943.

pretensions, airs, affected manner, mannerism; egoism, egotism, priggism, priggishness; coxcombery, gaudery, vain-glory, elation; pride etc. 878; ostentation etc. 882; assurance etc. 885.

vox et praeterea nihil [*L.*].

egoist, egotist; peacock; coxcomb etc. 854; Sir Oracle etc. 887.

v. **be vain** etc. *adj.;* be vain of; pique oneself etc. (*pride*) 878; lay the flattering unction to one's soul.

have -too high, -an overweening- opinion of -oneself, -one's talents; blind oneself as to one's own merit; not think small beer of oneself [*colloq.*]; strut; put oneself forward; fish for compliments; give oneself airs etc. (*assume*) 885; boast etc. 884.

render vain etc. *adj.;* inspire with vanity etc. *n.;* inflate, puff up, turn one's head.

adj. **vain**, -as a peacock; conceited, overweening, pert, forward; vainglorious, high-flown; ostentatious etc. 882; puffed up, inflated, flushed.

self-satisfied, self-confident, self-sufficient, self-flattering, self-admiring, self-applauding, self-glorious, self-opinionated; *entêté* [*F.*] etc. (*wrong-headed*) 481; wise in one's own conceit, pragmatical [*rare*], overwise, pretentious, priggish; egotistic *or* egotistical; *soidisant* [*F.*] etc. (*boastful*) 884; arrogant etc. 885; assured.

unabashed, unblushing, unconstrained, unceremonious; free and easy.

adv. **vainly** etc. *adj.*

881. Modesty

n. **modesty**; humility etc. 879; diffidence, timidity; retiring disposition; unobtrusiveness; bashfulness etc. *adj.; mauvaise honte* [*F.*]; blush, blushing; verecundity [*obs.*]; self-knowledge.

reserve, constraint; demureness etc. *adj.;* "blushing honors" [*Henry VIII*].

[comparison] violet.

v. **be modest** etc. *adj.;* retire, reserve oneself; give way to; draw in one's horns etc. 879; hide one's face.

keep private, keep in the background, keep one's distance; pursue the noiseless tenor of one's way, "do good by stealth and blush to find it fame" [Pope], hide one's light under a bushel; cast sheep's eyes.

adj. **modest**, diffident; humble etc. 879; timid, timorous, bashful; shy, nervous, skittish, coy, sheepish, shame-faced, blushing, overmodest.

unpretending, unpretentious; unobtrusive, unassuming, unostentatious, unboastful, unaspiring; poor in spirit; deprecative, deprecatory.

reserved, constrained, demure.

abashed, ashamed; out of countenance etc. (*humbled*) 879.

adv. **modestly** etc. *adj.;* quietly, privately; without -ceremony, -beat of drum; *sans façon* [*F.*].

882. Ostentation

n. **ostentation**, display, show, *coup d' oeil* [*F.*], flourish, parade, *étalage* [*F.*], pomp, magnificence, splendor, pageantry, array, state, solemnity; dash [*colloq.*], splash [*colloq.*], splurge [*colloq.*], glitter, strut, pomposity, pompousness; pretense, pretensions, showing off; fuss; grand doings.

demonstration, flying colors; flourish of trumpets etc. (*celebration*) 883; pageant, spectacle, exhibition, exposition, procession, turnout [*colloq.*], set out; grand function; fête, gala, field day, review, march past, promenade, "insubstantial pageant" [*Tempest*].

coup de théâtre [*F.*], stage effect, stage trick; claptrap; *mise en scène* [*F.*], *tour de force* [*F.*], chic [*colloq., F.*].

dress; court-, full-, evening-, ball-, fancy-dress; tailoring, millinery, man millinery, frippery; foppery, equipage.

883. Celebration

ceremony, ceremonial, ritual, form, formality, etiquette, puncto [*obs.*], punctilio, punctiliousness, starchedness, stateliness.

mummery, solemn mockery, mouth honor; tomfoolery; attitudinarianism.

attitudinarian; fop etc. 854; no modest violet.

v. **be ostentatious** etc. *adj.;* come forward, put oneself forward, attract attention, star; make–, cut- a -figure, –dash, –splash, –splurge [*all colloq.*]; strut; blow one's own trumpet; have no false modesty; figure; make a show, –display; glitter.

show off, show one's paces; parade, march past; display, exhibit, put forward, hold up; trot out [*slang*], hand out; sport [*colloq.*], brandish, blazon forth; dangle, –before the eyes; cry up etc. (*praise*) 931; *prôner* [*F.*], flaunt, emblazon, prink, set off, mount, have framed and glazed.

put on the mask; put a -good, –smiling- face upon; clean the outside of the platter etc. (*disguise*) 544.

adj. **ostentatious**, showy, dashing, pretentious, jaunty *or* janty, grand, pompous, high-sounding; turgid etc. (*big-sounding*) 577; garish *or* gairish; gaudy, –as a -peacock, –butterfly, –tulip; flaunting, flashing, flaming, glittering; gay etc. (*ornate*) 847.

splendid, magnificent, sumptuous, palatial.

theatrical, theatric, dramatic, spectacular, scenic, scenical; dramaturgic *or* dramaturgical.

ceremonial, ritual, ritualistic; solemn, stately, majestic, formal, stiff, ceremonious, punctilious, starched, starchy.

en grande tenue [*F.*], in one's best bib and tucker [*colloq.*], in one's Sunday best, *endimanché* [*F.*], chic [*colloq., F.*].

adv. with flourish of trumpet, with beat of drum, with flying colors, with a brass band; at the head of the procession; with no false modesty.

endimanché ad captandum vulgus [*L.*].

883. Celebration

n. **celebration**, solemnization, commemoration, ovation, triumph; lionization.

inauguration, installation, presentation; coronation; *début* [*F.*], coming out [*colloq.*]; Lord Mayor's show [*London, Eng.*]; harvest-home, husking bee, quilting bee; birthday, anniversary, biennial, triennial etc.; centenary, centennial; bicentenary, bicentennial; tercentenary, tercentennial etc.; "the day we celebrate"; red-letter day; trophy etc. 733; jubilation, laudation, paean *or* pean; *Te Deum* etc. (*thanksgiving*) 990; festivity, festival; fête etc.

882; Forefathers' Day [*U. S.*], Independence Day, "the Glorious Fourth"; holiday etc. 840.

triumphal arch, bonfire; salute, salvo, salvo of artillery; *feu de joie* [*F.*], flourish of trumpets, fanfare, colors flying, illuminations.

[wedding anniversaries] *wooden* wedding [5th], *tin* wedding [10th], *crystal* wedding [15th], *china* wedding [20th], *silver* wedding [25th], *golden* wedding [50th], *diamond* wedding [60th].

jubilee, 50th anniversary; diamond jubilee, 60th anniversary.

v. **celebrate**, keep, signalize, do honor to, commemorate, solemnize, hallow; keep high festival, keep holiday; mark with a red letter.

pledge, drink to, toast; hob and nob, hobnob with; present.

inaugurate, install, instate, induct, chair.

rejoice etc. 838; kill the fatted calf, hold jubilee; roast an ox, serve up the Thanksgiving turkey, serve up the Christmas goose; fire a salute, dip the colors, present arms; paint the town red [*colloq.*]; maffick [*colloq., Eng.*].

adj. **celebrating** etc. *v.;* commemorative, celebrated, immortal; solemn, jubilant; kept, kept in remembrance.

adv. **in honor of**, in commemoration of, in celebration of, in memory of; as a toast.

int. **hail**! all hail! "see the conquering hero comes!" "Hail! hail! the gang's all here!"

884. Boasting

n. **boasting** etc. *v.;* boast, vaunt, crake [*obs.*], pretense, pretensions, cock-a-hoopness, braggadocio, braggadocianism, puff [*colloq.*], puffery; flourish, fanfaronade; gasconade, bluff, highfaluting *or* highfalutin, *blague* [*F.*]; side [*slang, Eng.*], swagger, jingoism, spread-eagleism; brag, braggartism *or* braggardism, braggartry, bounce, rant, bluster, bravado, bunk *or* buncombe *or* bunkum; jactation, jactitation, jactancy; venditation [*obs.*], vaporing, rodomontade, bombast, gas [*slang*], hot air [*slang*], fine talking, tall talk, tall story [*both colloq.*], fish story [*humorous*]; magniloquence, teratology [*obs.*], heroics; chauvinism; exaggeration etc. 549; vanity etc. 880; *vox et praeterea nihil* [*L.*]; much cry and little wool, *brutum fulmen* [*L.*].

exultation, gloriation [*obs.*], glorification; flourish of trumpets; triumph etc. 883.

boaster, braggart, braggadocio, fanfaron, pretender, bluffer, blower [*slang*], blower of his own trumpet, windbag [*slang*], hot-air artist [*slang*], Fourth of July orator; Thraso, Gascon; chauvinist, jingo, jingoist; blusterer, swaggerer etc. 887; charlatan, trumpeter; puppy etc. (*fop*) 854.

v. **boast**, make a boast of, brag, vaunt, puff, show off, flourish, crake [*obs.*], crack, trumpet, strut, swagger, *blague* [*F.*], gasconade, vapor; blow [*slang*], four-flush [*slang*], bluff; talk big, draw the long bow, speak for Buncombe; *faire claquer son fouet* [*F.*], blow one's own trumpet; put on side [*slang, Eng.*], swank [*dial. Eng.*]; let the American eagle scream, sing "Rule, Britannia," indulge in jingoism; *se faire valoir* [*F.*], take merit to oneself, make a merit of; holloa before one is out of the wood.

exult; crow, crow over [*both colloq.*], triumph, glory, jubilate, rejoice, maffick [*colloq., Eng.*], throw up one's cap, yell oneself hoarse, cheer.

gloat, gloat over; chuckle; neigh.

adj. **boasting** etc. *v.;* magniloquent, flaming, thrasonic [*rare*], thrasonical, stilted, gasconading, braggart, boastful, pretentious; vainglorious etc. (*conceited*) 880; highfaluting *or* highfalutin; spread-eagle [*colloq. & humorous*].

elate, elated, jubilant, triumphant, exultant; in high feather; flushed, –with victory; cock-a-hoop, cock-a-hoopish; on stilts [*colloq.*].

vaunted etc. *v.*

adv. **vauntingly** etc. *adj.;* in triumph; with a blare of trumpets.

885. Insolence
[undue assumption of superiority]

n. **insolence**, brashness, brazenness, malapertness; haughtiness etc. *adj.;* arrogance, airs; bumptiousness, toploftiness [*colloq.*], assumption, presumption; assumption of infallibility; contumely, disdain, insult; overbearance, domineering etc. *v.;* bluster, swagger, swaggering etc. *v.;* bounce; terrorism; tyranny etc. 739; beggar on horseback; usurpation.

impertinence, cheek [*colloq. or slang*], nerve [*slang*], nerviness [*slang*], sauce [*colloq.*], abuse; sauciness etc. *adj.;* flippancy, dicacity [*obs.*], petulance [*rare in this sense*], procacity [*rare*].

impudence, self-assertion, assurance, audacity, hardihood; front, face, brass, gall [*slang*]; shamelessness etc. *adj.;* effrontery, hardened front, face of brass.

jingoism, chauvinism; *Kultur* [*Ger.*], "might is right," *Macht ist Recht* [*Ger.*].

malapert, saucebox etc. (*blusterer*) 887.

jingo, jingoist, chauvinist; fire eater [*colloq.*]; boaster etc. 884.

v. **be insolent** etc. *adj.;* bluster, vapor, swagger, swell, give oneself airs, snap one's fingers, kick up a dust [*colloq.*]; swear etc. (*affirm*) 535; rap out oaths; roister.

arrogate, assume, presume; make bold, make free; take a liberty, give an inch and take an ell.

outface, outlook, outstare, outbrazen, outbrave; stare out of countenance; brazen out; lay down the law; teach one's grandmother to suck eggs [*colloq.*]; assume a lofty bearing; talk big, look big, put on big looks, act the *grand seigneur;* mount–, ride- the high horse; toss the head, carry with a high hand; tempt Providence; want snuffing [*colloq.*].

domineer, bully, dictate, hector; lord it over; *traiter–, regarder- de haut en bas* [*F.*]; exact; snub, huff, beard, fly in the face of; put to the blush; bear–, beat- down; browbeat, intimidate; trample–, tread- -down, –under foot; dragoon, ride roughshod over; bulldoze [*colloq.*], terrorize.

adj. **insolent**, haughty, arrogant, imperious, magisterial, dictatorial, arbitrary; high-handed, high and mighty; contumelious, supercilious, overbearing, toplofty [*colloq.*], toploftical [*rare*], intolerant, domineering, overweening, high-flown; precocious, assuming, would-be, bumptious.

pert, flippant, fresh [*slang*], brash, cavalier, saucy, forward, impertinent, malapert; impudent, audacious, presumptuous.

brazen, bluff, shameless, aweless, unblushing, unabashed; bold-faced, bare-faced, brazen-faced; dead–, lost- to shame.

blustering, swaggering, hectoring, rollicking, roistering, vaporing, free and easy, devil-may-care, jaunty *or* janty; thrasonic [*rare*], thrasonical, fire-eating [*colloq.*]; "full of sound and fury" [*Macbeth*].

jingo, jingoistic, chauvinistic.

adv. **insolently** etc. *adj.;* with nose in air; with arms akimbo; *de haut en bas* [*F.*]; with a high hand; *ex cathedra* [*L.*].

886. Servility

n. **servility**; slavery etc. (*subjection*) 749; obsequiousness etc. *adj.;* subserviency; abasement, prostration, prosternation [*obs.*]; genuflection etc. (*worship*) 990; toadeating; fawning etc. *v.;* tufthunting, timeserving, flunkyism *or* flunkeyism; sycophancy etc. (*flattery*) 933; humility etc. 879.

sycophant, parasite; toad, toady, toadeater, tufthunter; snob, flunky *or* flunkey, lapdog, span-

887. Blusterer

iel, lick-spit, lick-spittle, smell-feast, *Graeculus esuriens* [*L.*], hanger on, *cavalier (or cavaliere) servente* [*It.*], led captain, carpet knight; timeserver, fortune hunter, Vicar of Bray, Sir Pertinax MacSycophant, pickthank; flatterer etc. 935; doer of dirty work; *âme damnée* [*F.*], tool; reptile; slave etc. (*servant*) 746; *homme de cour* [*F.*], courtier; beat [*slang*], dead beat [*slang*], doughface [*slang*]; heeler, ward heeler [*both polit. cant*]; jackal, sponge, sponger, sucker [*slang*], tagtail, truckler.

v. **cringe**, bow, stoop, kneel, bend the knee; fall on one's knees, prostrate oneself; worship etc. 990.

fawn, crouch, cower, sneak, crawl, sponge, truckle, toady, truckle to, grovel, lick the feet of, lick one's shoes, make a doormat of oneself, kiss the hem of one's garment; be servile etc. *adj.*

pay court to; feed on, fatten on, batten on, dance attendance on, follow at heel, pin oneself upon, hang on the sleeve of, *avaler les couleuvres* [*F.*], keep time to, fetch and carry, do the dirty work of.

go with the stream, follow the crowd, worship the rising sun, hold with the hare and run with the hounds; get on the band wagon; be a timeserver etc. *n.*

adj. **servile**, obsequious; supple, —as a glove; soapy [*slang*], oily, pliant, cringing, abased, dough-faced [*colloq.*], fawning, slavish, groveling, reptilian, sniveling, mealy-mouthed; beggarly, sycophantic, parasitical; abject, prostrate, down on one's marrowbones [*jocular or slang*]; base, mean, sneaking; crouching etc. *v.*; timeserving.

adv. **with servility** etc. *n.*; hat-, cap- in hand; "in a bondman's key" [*Merchant of Venice*]; "with bated breath and whispering humbleness" [*ibid.*].

int. so please you! as my lord wills! don't mind me!

887. Blusterer

n. **blusterer**, swaggerer, vaporer, roisterer, brawler; fanfaron; braggart etc. (*boaster*) 884; bully, terrorist, rough, ruffian, rough-neck [*slang*], tough [*colloq.*], rowdy, bulldozer [*colloq.*], roarer [*slang, obs.*], slang-whanger [*slang*], larrikin [*Austral. & Eng.*]; hoodlum [*colloq.*], hooligan [*slang*], Mohock, Mohawk [*rare*], Drawcansir, swashbuckler, Captain Bobadil, Sir Lucius O'-Trigger, Thraso, Pistol, Parolles, Bombastes Furioso, Hector, Chrononhotonthologos; jingo; desperado, dare-devil, fire eater [*colloq.*]; fury etc. (*violent person*) 173.

puppy etc. (*fop*) 854, jackanapes, bantam-cock; malapert, saucebox [*colloq.*]; minx, hussy.

dogmatist, doctrinaire, Sir Oracle, stump orator etc. 582; prig, Jack-in-office.

Section 3. Sympathetic

888. Friendship

n. **friendship**, amity; friendliness etc. *adj.*; brotherhood, fraternity, sodality, confraternity; sorority, sorosis, sisterhood; harmony etc. (*concord*) 714; peace etc. 721.

firm–, staunch–, intimate–, familiar–, bosom–, cordial–, tried–, devoted–, lasting–, fast–, sincere–, warm–, ardent- friendship.

cordiality, fraternization, association, *entente cordiale* [*F.*], good understanding, *rapprochement* [*F.*], sympathy, fellow-feeling, response, welcomeness; affection etc. (*love*) 897; partiality, favoritism; good will etc. (*benevolence*) 906.

acquaintance, introduction, familiarity, intimacy, intercourse, fellowship, knowledge of.

v. **be friendly** etc. *adj.*, be friends etc. 890, be acquainted with etc. *adj.*; know; have the ear of; keep company with etc. (*sociality*) 892; hold communication with, have dealings with, sympathize with; have a leaning to; bear good will etc. (*benevolent*) 906; love etc. 897; make much of; befriend etc. (*aid*) 707; introduce to.

set one's horses together; have the latchstring out; hold out–, extend- the right hand of -friendship, –fellowship; become friendly etc. *adj.*; make friends etc. (890) with; break the ice, be introduced to; pick up acquaintance; make–, scrape- acquaintance with; get into favor, gain the friendship of.

shake hands with, strike hands with, fraternize, sororize [*rare*], embrace; receive with open arms, throw oneself into the arms of; meet halfway, take in good part.

adj. **friendly**, amicable, amical; well-affected, unhostile, neighborly; brotherly, fraternal, sisterly, sororal [*rare*]; ardent, devoted, sympathetic, harmonious, hearty, cordial, warm-hearted.

friends with, at home with, hand in hand with; on -good, –friendly, –amicable, –cordial, –familiar, –intimate- -terms, –footing; on speaking terms, on visiting terms, on one's visiting list; in one's good -graces, –books.

acquainted, familiar, intimate, thick, hand and glove, hail fellow well met, free and easy; welcome.

892. Sociality

adv. **amicably** etc. *adj.;* with open arms, *à bras ouverts* [*F.*]; *sans cérémonie* [*F.*]; arm in arm.

889. Enmity

n. **enmity**, hostility, antagonism; unfriendliness etc. *adj.;* discord etc. 713; bitterness, rancor; heart-burning; animosity etc. 900; malevolence etc. 907.

alienation, estrangement; dislike etc. 867; aversion, hate etc. 898.

v. **be unfriendly** etc. *adj.;* keep–, hold- at arm's length; be at loggerheads; bear malice etc. 907; fall out; take umbrage etc. 900; harden the heart, alienate, estrange.

adj. **unfriendly**, inimical, hostile; at enmity, at variance, at daggers drawn, at open war with; up in arms against; in bad odor with.

on bad terms, not on speaking terms; cool, cold, cold-hearted; estranged, alienated, disaffected, irreconcilable.

890. Friend

n. **friend**, –of one's bosom; *alter ego* [*L.*], other self; intimate, confidant (*masc.*), confidante (*fem.*), confident; best–, bosom–, fast-friend; *amicus usque ad aras* [*L.*], *fidus Achates* [*L.*]; *persona grata* [*L.*]; well-wisher; neighbor *or* neighbour, acquaintance.

favorer, fautor [*rare*], patron, backer, Maecenas; tutelary saint, good genius, advocate, partisan, sympathizer; ally; friend in need etc. (*auxiliary*) 711.

associate, consociate, compeer, comrade, mate, companion, *camarade* [*F.*], *confrère* [*F.*], colleague, comate, copemate *or* copesmate [*obs.*]; partner; side-partner, copartner, consort; old–, crony; chum [*colloq.*], pal [*slang*], buddy [*slang*]; playfellow, playmate, schoolfellow; bedfellow, bunkie [*colloq.*], bedmate, chamberfellow; classfellow, classman, classmate; roommate, shopmate, shipmate, messmate; fellow–, boon–, pot- companion; fellow-man, stable companion; best man, bridesmaid, maid of honor.

[famous friendships] Pylades and Orestes, Castor and Pollux, Achilles and Patroclus, Diomedes and Sthenalus, Hercules and Iolaus, Theseus and Pirithoüs, Epaminondas and Pelopidas, Nisus and Euryalus, Damon and Pythias, David and Jonathan, Christ and the beloved disciple; Soldiers Three, the Three Musketeers.

par nobile fratrum [*L., often ironical*]; *Arcades ambo* [*L.*].

host, hostess (*fem.*), Amphitryon, Boniface.
guest, visitor, frequenter, habitué, *protégé* [*F.*].
compatriot; fellow–, countryman; fellow townsman, townie [*slang*].

int. "Thank God for a trusty chum!" [Kipling].

891. Enemy

n. **enemy**; antagonist; foe, foeman; open–, bitter- enemy; opponent etc. 710; backfriend [*obs.*], copemate *or* copesmate [*obs.*], "dearest foe"; mortal -aversion, –antipathy; snake in the grass.

public enemy, enemy to society; anarchist, seditionist, traitor, traitress (*fem.*).

892. Sociality

n. **sociality**, sociability, sociableness etc. *adj.;* social intercourse, consociation, intercourse, intercommunion; consortship, companionship, comradeship, fellowship; urbanity etc. (*courtesy*) 894; intimacy, familiarity; clubbability *or* clubability [*colloq.*], clubbism; *esprit de corps* [*F.*]; *morale* [*F.*].

conviviality; good- fellowship, –company; joviality, jollity, *savoir vivre* [*F.*], *joie de vivre* [*F.*], festivity, festive board, walnuts and wine, merrymaking; loving cup; hospitality, heartiness; cheer; "the feast of reason and the flow of soul" [Pope].

welcome, welcomeness, greeting; hearty–, warm–, welcome- reception; hearty welcome; hearty–, warm- greeting; the glad hand [*slang*].

boon companion; good–, jolly-fellow; *bon enfant* [*F.*], bawcock [*archaic*], crony, *bon vivant* [*F.*]; a good mixer [*colloq.*].

social–, family- circle; family hearth; circle of acquaintance, coterie, society, company; club etc. (*association*) 712.

social gathering, social reunion; assembly etc. (*assemblage*) 72; barbecue; bee; corn-husking, corn-shucking; husking, husking-bee; hen party [*colloq.*]; house raising, house-warming, hanging of the crane; infare *or* infair [*Scot. & dial., U. S.*]; smoker, –party [*both colloq.*]; Dutch treat [*colloq.*]; stag, –party [*both colloq.*]; sociable, tamasha [*Hind.*], party, entertainment, reception, levee, at home, *conversazione* [*It.*], soirée [*F.*], matinée; evening–, morning–, afternoon–, garden–, coming-out–, surprise- party; *partie carrée* [*F.*]; kettledrum, drum, drum major, rout [*archaic*], tempest, hurricane; *ridotto* [*It.*]; ball, hunt ball, dance, dinner dance, festival etc. (*amusement*) 840.

[social meals] breakfast, wedding breakfast, hunt breakfast; luncheon, lunch; picnic lunch, basket lunch, picnic; tea, afternoon tea, five o'clock tea, cup of tea, dish of tea [*esp. Brit.*], thé dansant [*F.*], coming-out tea [*colloq.*]; tea party, tea fight [*slang*]; dinner, potluck, bachelor dinner, stag dinner [*colloq.*], hunt dinner; church supper, high tea; banquet etc. 298.

visit, visiting; round of visits; call, morning call; interview etc. (*interlocution*) 588; assignation; tryst, trysting place; appointment.

v. be sociable etc. *adj.;* know; be acquainted etc. *adj.;* associate with, sort with, consort with, keep company with, walk hand in hand with; eat off the same trencher, club together, consort, bear one company, join; consociate [*rare*], intercommunicate, intercommune [*rare*], make acquaintance with etc. (*friendship*) 888; make advances, fraternize, embrace.

visit, pay a visit; interchange -visits, –cards; call at, call upon; leave a card; drop in, look in, look one up, beat up one's quarters [*colloq.*].

receive hospitality; be–, feel–, make oneself- at home with; make free with; crack a bottle with; take potluck with; live at free quarters; find the latchstring out.

entertain; give a party etc. *n.;* be at home, see one's friends, keep open house, do the honors; receive, –with open arms; welcome; give a warm reception etc. *n.* to; kill the fatted calf.

adj. **sociable**, companionable, clubbable *or* clubable [*colloq.*], clubbish; conversable, cozy *or* cosy *or* cosey, chatty, conversational; convivial, festive, festal, jovial, jolly, hospitable.

welcome, –as roses in May; fêted, entertained.

free and easy, hail fellow well met, familiar, intimate, consociate, consociated; associated with etc. *v.;* on visiting terms, acquainted; social, neighborly.

international, cosmopolitan; gregarious.

adv. **sociably** etc. *adj.;* en famille [*F.*], in the family circle; on terms of intimacy; in the social whirl; sans -façon, –cérémonie [*F.*], arm in arm.

893. Seclusion. Exclusion

n. **seclusion**, privacy, retirement, eremitism, anchoretism, anchoritism, reclusion, recess; suspension; snugness etc. *adj.;* concealment, delitescence; rustication, *rus in urbe* [*L.*], ruralism, rurality [*rare*], solitude; solitariness etc. (*singleness*) 87; isolation; "splendid isolation"; loneliness etc. *adj.;* estrangement from the world, voluntary exile; aloofness.

depopulation, desertion, desolation; wilderness etc. (*unproductive*) 169; howling wilderness; rotten borough, Old Sarum [*Eng.*].

retreat, cell, hermitage, cloister; convent etc. 1000; *sanctum sanctorum* [*L.*], study, library, den [*colloq.*].

exclusion, excommunication, banishment, exile, ostracism, proscription; economic pressure; cut, cut direct; dead cut.

unsociability, unsociableness, dissociability, dissociality; inhospitality, inhospitableness etc. *adj.;* domesticity, self-sufficiency, Darby and Joan.

recluse, hermit, eremite, anchoret *or* anchorite, anchorist [*obs.*]; santon; stylite, pillarist, pillar-saint [*all Ch. hist.*]; St. Simeon Stylites; caveman, cave-dweller, troglodyte, Timon of Athens, solitarian [*obs.*], solitaire, ruralist [*obs.*], disciple of Zimmermann, closet cynic, cynic, Diogenes.

outcast, pariah, leper; outsider, rank outsider; castaway, pilgarlic [*low*], wastrel [*dial. Eng.*], losel, foundling; wilding.

v. **be** *or* **live secluded** etc. *adj.;* keep–, stand–, hold oneself- -aloof, –in the background; keep snug; shut oneself up, deny oneself, seclude oneself; creep into a corner, rusticate, dissocialize; retire, –from the world; hermitize; take the veil; abandon etc. 624; sport one's oak [*Univ. slang, Eng.*].

exclude, repel; cut, –dead; refuse to -associate with, –acknowledge; send to Coventry, look cool–, turn one's back–, shut the door- upon; blackball, excommunicate, exile, expatriate; banish, outlaw, maroon, ostracize, proscribe, cut off from, keep at arm's length, draw a cordon round, boycott, embargo, blockade, isolate.

depopulate, dispeople, unpeople; desolate, devastate.

adj. **secluded**, sequestered, retired, delitescent, private, by; in a backwater; out of the world, out of the way; "the world forgetting by the world forgot" [Pope].

unsociable, unsocial, dissocial, inhospitable, cynical, inconversable [*obs.*], unclubbable *or* unclubable [*colloq.*], sauvage [*F.*]; hermitical, eremitic *or* eremitical, anchoretic *or* anchoretical, anchoritic *or* anchoritical, anchoretish, anchoritish, troglodytic.

snug, domestic, stay-at-home.

excluded etc. *v.;* unfrequented, unvisited, unintroduced, uninvited, unwelcome; on the fringe of society; under a cloud, left to shift for oneself; deserted, –in one's utmost need; unfriended, friendless, kithless, homeless, desolate, lorn, forlorn; solitary, lonely, lonesome, isolated, single, estranged; derelict, outcast, outside the gates, "yammering at the bars"; banished etc. *v.;* under an embargo.

uninhabited, unoccupied, untenanted, tenantless, abandoned; uninhabitable.

894. Courtesy

n. **courtesy**; respect etc. 928; good- manners, –behavior, –breeding; manners; politeness etc. *adj.; bienséance* [*F.*], urbanity, comity, gentility, breeding, gentle breeding, cultivation, culture, polish, presence; civility, civilization; amenity, suavity; good temper, good humor, amiability, easy temper, complacency, soft tongue, mansuetude [*archaic*]; condescension etc. (*humility*) 879; affability, complaisance, compliance, *prévenance* [*F.*], amiability, gallantry, chivalry; fine flower of -courtesy, –chivalry.

pink of courtesy, pink of politeness; flower of knighthood, *chevalier sans peur et sans reproche*, Bayard, Sidney, "a verray parfit gentil knight" [Chaucer], Chesterfield; Launcelot, Gawaine, Colonel Newcome; "gentle Shakespeare" [Ben Jonson].

compliment; fair-, soft-, sweet- words; honeyed phrases, ceremonial; salutation, reception, presentation, introduction, *accueil* [*F.*], greeting, recognition; welcome, aboard [*obs.*], respects, *devoir* [*F.*], duty [*archaic*], regards, remembrances; kind -regards, –remembrances; deference, love, best love, empty encomium, flattering remark, hollow commendation; salaams.

[forms of greeting] obeisance etc. (*reverence*) 928; bow, curtsy *or* curtsey, scrape, salaam, kotow *or* kowtow [*China*], bowing and scraping; kneeling; genuflection etc. (*worship*) 990; obsequiousness etc. 886; capping, pulling the forelock, making a leg [*colloq.*], shaking hands, etc. *v.;* grip of the hand; embrace, hug, squeeze, kiss, buss, smack; salute, accolade; loving cup, *vin d'honneur* [*F.*], pledge; love token etc. (*endearment*) 902.

mark of recognition, nod; "nods and becks and wreathed smiles" [Milton]; valediction etc. 293; condolence etc. 915.

v. **be courteous** etc. *adj.;* show courtesy etc. *n.*

mind one's P's and Q's [*colloq.*], behave oneself, be all things to all men, conciliate, speak one fair, take in good part; do the amiable [*colloq.*]; look as if butter would not melt in one's mouth; mend–, mind- one's manners.

do the honors, usher, usher in, receive, greet, hail, bid welcome; welcome, –with open arms; shake hands; hold out–, press–, squeeze- the hand; bid Godspeed; speed the parting guest; cheer, serenade.

visit, wait upon, present oneself, pay one's respects, pay a visit etc. (*sociability*) 892; dance attendance on etc. (*servility*) 886; pay attentions to; do homage to etc. (*respect*) 928; give *or* send one's regards to etc. *n.*

salute; embrace etc. (*endearment*) 902; kiss, –hands; drink to, pledge, hob and nob; move to [*colloq.*], nod to; smile upon.

uncover, cap; touch–, raise–, lift–, take off- the hat; doff the cap; tip the hat to [*slang*]; pull the forelock; present arms; make way for; bow, make one's bow, make a leg scrape, curtsy *or* curtsey, bow and scrape, bob a curtsy, kneel; bow–, bend- the knee; salaam, kotow *or* kowtow [*China*]; prostrate oneself etc. (*worship*) 990.

render polite etc. *adj.;* polish, rub off the -corners, –rough edges; cultivate, civilize, humanize.

adj. **courteous**, polite, civil, mannerly, urbane; well-behaved, well-mannered, well-bred, well-brought up; gently bred; of gentle -manners, –breeding; good-mannered, polished, civilized, cultivated; refined etc. (*taste*) 850; gentleman-like etc. (*fashion*) 852; gallant, chivalrous, chivalric; on one's good (*or* best) behavior.

ingratiating, winning; gentle, mild; good-humored, cordial, gracious, amiable, tactful, affable, familiar; neighborly; obliging, complaisant, complacent, conciliatory.

bland, suave; fine–, fair–, soft- spoken; honey-mouthed, honey-tongued; oily, oily-tongued, unctuous; obsequious etc. 886.

adv. **courteously** etc. *adj.;* with a good grace; with open arms, with outstretched arms, *à bras ouverts* [*F.*]; *suaviter in modo* [*L.*], with perfect courtesy, in good humor.

int. **hail**! welcome! well met! *ave!* [*L.*]; all hail! good -day, –morrow, –morning, –evening, –afternoon, –night! sweet dreams! Godspeed! *pax vobiscum!* [*L.*]; all good go with you! may your shadow never be less!

895. Discourtesy

n. **discourtesy**; ill-breeding; ill–, bad–, ungainly- manners; tactlessness; uncourteousness etc. *adj.;* rusticity, inurbanity, illiberality, incivility, displacency [*obs.*]; lack *or* want of courtesy etc. 894; disrespect etc. 929; procacity [*obs.*], im-

896. Congratulation

pudence, misbehavior, barbarism, barbarity; brutality, brutishness, brutification, blackguardism, conduct unbecoming a gentleman, *grossièreté* [F.], *brusquerie* [F.], vulgarity etc. 851.

bad temper, ill temper; peevishness, surliness; churlishness etc. *adj.;* spinosity, perversity; moroseness etc. (*sullenness*) 901a.

sternness etc. *adj.;* austerity; moodishness, captiousness etc. 901; cynicism; tartness etc. *adj.;* acrimony, acerbity, virulence, asperity.

scowl, black looks, frown; sulks, short answer, rebuff; hard words, contumely; unparliamentary language, personality.

bear, bruin, grizzly, grizzly bear; brute, blackguard, beast; unlicked cub; frump [*colloq.*], crosspatch [*colloq.*]; grouch, old grouch; saucebox etc. 887; crooked stick.

v. **be rude** etc. *adj.;* insult etc. 929; treat with discourtesy; take a name in vain; make bold with, make free with; take a liberty; stare out of countenance, ogle, point at, put to the blush.

cut; turn one's back upon, turn on one's heel; give the cold shoulder; keep at -a distance, -arm's length; look -cool, -coldly, -black- upon; show the door to, send away with a flea in the ear [*colloq.*].

lose one's temper etc. (*resentment*) 900; mump [*dial.*], sulk etc. 901a; frown, scowl, glower, pout; snap, snarl, growl.

render rude etc. *adj.;* brutalize, brutify.

adj. **discourteous**, uncourteous, uncourtly; ill-bred, ill-mannered, ill-behaved, ill-conditioned, unbred; unmannerly, unmannered, impolite, unpolite, uncivil, ungracious, unceremonious, cool; unpolished, uncivilized, ungenteel, ungentlemanlike, ungentlemanly; unladylike; blackguard; vulgar etc. 851; dedecorous [*obs.*]; foul-mouthed, foul-spoken; abusive.

pert, forward, obtrusive, impudent, rude, saucy, procacious [*archaic*], brash; flippant etc. (*insolent*) 885.

repulsive; uncomplaisant, unaccommodating, unneighborly, ungallant; inaffable; ungentle, ungainly, rough, rugged, bluff, blunt, gruff; churlish, boorish, bearish; brutal, brusque, stern, harsh, austere; cavalier.

bad-tempered, ill-tempered, ill-humored; out of -temper, -humor; crusty, tart, sour, crabbed, sharp, short, trenchant, sarcastic, biting, doggish, currish, caustic, virulent, bitter, acrimonious, venomous, contumelious; snarling etc. *v.;* surly, -as a bear; perverse; grim, sullen etc. 901a; peevish etc. (*irascible*) 901; bristling, thorny, spinose, spinous.

adv. **discourteously** etc. *adj.;* with discourtesy etc. *n.*, with a bad grace.

896. Congratulation

n. **congratulation**, gratulation, felicitation; salute etc. 894; condolence etc. 915; compliments of the season; good wishes, best wishes.

v. **congratulate**, gratulate, felicitate; give joy, wish one joy; compliment; tender-, offer- one's congratulations; wish many happy returns of the day, wish a merry Christmas and a happy new year.

congratulate oneself etc. (*rejoice*) 838.

adj. **congratulatory**, gratulatory.

897. Love

n. **love**, affection, sympathy, fellow-feeling; tenderness etc. *adj.;* heart, brotherly love; charity, good will; benevolence etc. 906; attachment; fondness etc. *adj.;* liking; inclination etc. (*desire*) 865; regard, dilection [*obs.*], admiration, fancy.

yearning, *eros* [*Gr.*], tender passion, amour; gyneolatry; gallantry, passion, flame, devotion, fervor, enthusiasm, transport of love, rapture, enchantment, infatuation, adoration, idolatry.

mother love, maternal love, natural affection, *storge* [*Gr.*].

attractiveness, charm; popularity; idol, favorite etc. 899.

god of love, Cupid, Venus, Eros, Kama [*Hindu*]; myrtle; turtle dove, sparrow; cupid amoretto; true lover's knot; love -token, -suit, -affair, -tale, -story; the old story, plighted love; courtship etc. 902; amourette; free-love.

lover, suitor, *fiancé* [*F.*], follower [*colloq.*], admirer, adorer, wooer, amoret [*obs.*], amorist, beau, sweetheart, inamorato, swain, young man [*colloq.*], flame [*colloq.*], love, truelove; leman [*archaic*], Lothario, gallant, paramour, captive; *amoroso, cavaliere servente, cicisbeo, caro sposo* [*all It.*].

ladylove, sweetheart, mistress, inamorata, idol, darling, duck, Dulcinea, angel, goddess, *cara sposa* [*It.*]; betrothed, affianced, *fiancée* [*F.*].

flirt, coquette, amorette.

pair of turtledoves; abode of love; Agapemone [*Ch. hist.*].

v. **love**, like, affect, fancy, care for, take an interest in, be partial to, sympathize with; affection; be in love with etc. *adj.;* have-, entertain-, harbor-, cherish- a love for etc. *n.;* regard, revere; take to, bear love to, be wedded to; set one's affections on; burn; adore, idolize, love to distraction, *aimer éperdument* [*F.*]; dote -on, -upon.

make much of, feast one's eyes on; hold dear, prize; hug, cling to, cherish, caress, fondle, pet.

take a fancy to, look sweet upon [*colloq.*]; become enamored etc. *adj.;* fall in love with, lose one's heart; desire etc. 865.

excite love; win–, gain–, secure–, engage- the -love, –affections, –heart; take the fancy of; have a place in–, wind round- the heart; attract, attach, endear, charm, fascinate, captivate, bewitch, seduce, enamor, enrapture, turn the head.

get into favor; ingratiate–, insinuate–, worm- oneself; propitiate, curry favor with, pay one's court to, *faire l'aimable* [*F.*], set one's cap at [*colloq.*], coquet, flirt.

adj. **loving** etc. *v.;* fond of; taken with [*colloq.*], struck with [*colloq.*], smitten, bitten [*colloq.*]; attached to, wedded to; enamored; charmed etc. *v.;* in love; love-sick; over head and ears in love.

affectionate, tender, sweet upon [*colloq.*], sympathetic, amorous, amatory; fond, erotic, uxorious, ardent, passionate, rapturous, devoted, motherly.

loved etc. *v.;* beloved, well beloved, dearly beloved; dear as the apple of one's eye, nearest to one's heart; dear, precious, darling, pet, little; favorite, popular.

congenial; to–, after- one's -mind, –taste, –fancy, –own heart; in one's good graces etc. (*friendly*) 888.

lovable, adorable, lovely, sweet, attractive, seductive, winning, winsome, charming, engaging, interesting, enchanting, captivating, fascinating, bewitching, amiable; seraphic *or* seraphical, angelic, like an angel.

898. Hate

n. **hate**, hatred, vials of hate; "Hymn of Hate."

disaffection, disfavor; alienation, estrangement, coolness; enmity etc. 889; animosity etc. 900; malice etc. 907; implacability etc. (*revenge*) 919.

umbrage, pique, grudge, dudgeon, spleen, bitterness, bitterness of feeling; ill blood, bad blood; acrimony.

repugnance etc. (*dislike*) 867; odium, unpopularity; detestation, abhorrence, loathing, execration, abomination, aversion, antipathy; demonophobia, gynephobia, negrophobia; Anglophobia etc. 867.

object of hatred, an abomination, an aversion, *bête noire* [*F.*]; enemy etc. 891; bitter pill; source of annoyance etc. 830.

v. **hate**, detest, abominate, abhor, loathe; recoil at, shudder at; shrink from, view with horror, hold in abomination, revolt against, execrate; scowl etc. 895; disrelish etc. (*dislike*) 867.

owe a grudge; bear spleen, bear a grudge, bear malice etc. (*malevolence*) 907; conceive an aversion to.

excite hatred, provoke hatred etc. *n.;* be hateful etc. *adj.;* stink in the nostrils; estrange, alienate, repel, set against, sow dissension, set by the ears, envenom, incense, irritate, rile [*dial. or colloq.*], ruffle, vex, roil; horrify etc. 830.

adj. **hating** etc. *v.;* abhorrent; averse from etc. (*disliking*) 867; set against; bitter etc. (*acrimonious*) 895; implacable etc. (*revengeful*) 919.

unloved, unbeloved, unlamented, undeplored, unmourned, uncared for, unendeared, unvalued; disliked etc. 867.

crossed in love, forsaken, rejected, lovelorn, jilted.

hateful, obnoxious, odious, abominable, repulsive, offensive, shocking; disgusting etc. (*disagreeable*) 830; reprehensible.

invidious, spiteful; malicious etc. 907.

insulting, irritating, provoking.

[mutual hate] at daggers drawn; not on speaking terms etc. (*enmity*) 889; at loggerheads.

899. Favorite

n. **favorite**, pet, fondling, cosset, minion [*rare*], idol, jewel, spoiled child, *enfant gâté* [*F.*]; led captain; crony; apple of one's eye, man after one's own heart; *persona grata* [*L.*].

love, dear, darling, duck, honey, jewel; mopsy *or* mopsey, moppet; sweetheart etc. (*love*) 897.

general–, universal- favorite; idol of the people; matinée idol.

900. Resentment

n. **resentment**, displeasure, animosity, anger, wrath, ire, indignation; exasperation, vexation, bitter resentment, wrathful indignation.

pique, umbrage, huff, miff [*colloq.*], soreness, dudgeon, acerbity, virulence, bitterness, acrimony, asperity, spleen, gall; heartburning, heartswelling; rankling.

ill–, bad- -humor, –temper; irascibility etc. 901; scowl etc. 895; sulks etc. 901*a;* ill blood etc. (*hate*) 898; revenge etc. 919.

irritation; warmth, bile, choler, fume, pucker [*colloq.*], dander [*colloq.*], ferment, excitement, ebullition; angry mood, taking [*colloq.*], pet, tiff, passion, fit, tantrum.

rage, fury; towering -rage, –passion; *acharnement* [*F.*], desperation, burst, explosion, paroxysm, storm; violence etc. 173; fire and fury; vials of wrath; gnashing of teeth, hot blood, high words.

329

901. Irascibility

furies, Erinyes (*sing.* Erinys), Eumenides; Alecto, Megaera, Tisiphone.

[cause of umbrage] affront, provocation, offense; indignity etc. (*insult*) 929; grudge; crow to -pluck, -pick, -pull; red rag, last straw, sore subject, *casus belli* [*L.*]; ill turn, outrage.

buffet, blow, slap in the face, box on the ear, rap on the knuckles.

v. **resent**; take -amiss, -ill, -to heart, -offense, -umbrage, -huff, -exception; not take it as a joke; *ne pas entendre raillerie* [*F.*]; take in bad part, take in ill part.

pout, knit the brow, frown, scowl, lower, snarl, growl, gnarl, gnash, snap; redden, color; look black, look black as thunder, look daggers; bite one's thumb; show-, grind- one's teeth; champ the bit.

be angry; fly-, fall-, get- into a -rage, -passion; fly off the handle, fly off at a tangent; let one's angry passions rise; bridle up, bristle up, froth up, fire up, flare up; foam at the mouth; open-, pour out- the vials of one's wrath.

chafe, mantle, fume, kindle, fly out, take fire; boil, -over; boil with- indignation, -rage; rage, storm, foam; hector, bully, bluster; vent one's -rage, spleen; lose one's temper; have a fling at; kick up a -row, -dust, -shindy [*all slang*]; cut up rough [*slang*], stand on one's hind legs, stamp the foot; stamp-, quiver-, swell-, foam- with rage; burst with anger; raise -Cain, -the devil, -Ned, -the mischief, -the roof [*all slang*]; breathe fire and fury; breathe revenge.

bear malice etc. (*revenge*) 919.

cause anger, raise anger; affront, offend; give -offense, -umbrage; anger; hurt the feelings; insult, discompose, fret, ruffle, roil, heckle, nettle, huff, pique; excite etc. 824; irritate, stir the blood, stir up bile; sting, -to the quick; rile, provoke, chafe, wound, incense, inflame, wrath [*obs.*], make one hot under the collar [*slang*], enrage, aggravate, add fuel to the flame, fan into a flame, widen the breach, envenom, embitter, exasperate, infuriate, kindle wrath; stick in one's craw *or* crop *or* gizzard [*colloq.*]; rankle etc. 919; hit-, rub-, sting-, strike- on the raw.

put out of -countenance, -humor; put (*or* get) one's monkey up [*colloq.*], put (*or* get) one's back up; raise one's -gorge, -dander [*colloq.*], -choler; work up into a passion, make one's blood boil, make the ears tingle, throw into a ferment, madden, drive one mad; lash into -fury, -madness; fool to the top of one's bent; set by the ears; bring a hornet's nest about one's ears.

adj. **angry**, wroth, irate, ireful, wrathful; cross etc. (*irascible*) 901; Achillean; sulky etc. 901*a*; bitter, virulent; acrimonious etc. (*discourteous*) etc. 895; offended etc. *v.;* waxy [*slang, Eng.*], wrought, worked up; indignant, hurt, sore; set against.

warm, burning; boiling, -over; fuming, raging, hot under the collar [*slang*]; *acharné* [*F.*]; foaming, -at the mouth; convulsed with rage; fierce, wild, rageful, furious, mad with rage, fiery, infuriate, rabid, savage; relentless etc. 919; violent etc. 173.

flushed with -anger, -rage; in a- huff, -stew [*colloq.*], -fume, -pucker [*dial. or colloq.*], -wax [*slang*], -passion, -rage, -fury, -taking [*colloq.*]; on one's high ropes [*colloq.*], up in arms; in high dudgeon.

adv. **angrily** etc. *adj.;* in the height of passion; in the heat of -passion, -the moment; in an ecstasy of rage.

int. *tantaene animis caelestibus irae!* [Virgil]; marry come up! zounds! 'sdeath!

901. Irascibility

n. **irascibility**, irascibleness, temper; crossness etc. *adj.;* susceptibility, procacity [*rare*], petulance, irritability, tartness, acerbity, acrimony, asperity, protervity [*rare*]; huff etc. (*resentment*) 900; a word and a blow; pugnacity etc. (*contentiousness*) 720; excitability etc. 825; bad-, fiery-, crooked-, irritable etc. *adj.* - temper; *genus irritable* [*L.*], hot blood.

ill humor etc. (*sullenness*) 901*a;* churlishness etc. (*discourtesy*) 895.

Sir Fretful Plagiary; brabbler, Tartar; shrew, vixen, virago, termagant, dragon, scold, Xanthippe *or* Xantippe, Kate the Shrew; porcupine; spitfire; fire eater etc. (*blusterer*) 887; fury etc. (*violent person*) 173.

v. **be irascible** etc. *adj.;* have a temper etc. *n.,* have a devil in one, be possessed of the devil, have the temper of a fiend; brabble [*archaic or dial.*]; fire up etc. (*be angry*) 900.

adj. **irascible**, bad-tempered, ill-tempered, irritable, susceptible; excitable etc. 825; thin-skinned etc. (*sensitive*) 822; fretful, fidgety; on the fret.

hasty, overhasty, quick, warm, hot, testy, touchy, techy *or* tetchy; like -touch- wood, -tinder, -a barrel of gunpowder; huffy, pettish, petulant, querulous, captious, moody, moodish; fractious, peevish, *acariâtre* [*F.*].

quarrelsome, contentious, disputatious; pugnacious etc. (*bellicose*) 720; cantankerous [*colloq.*], exceptious [*rare*], cross-grained; waspish, snappish, peppery, fiery, passionate, choleric, shrewish, "sudden and quick in quarrel" [*As You Like It*]; restive etc. (*perverse*) 901 *a;* churlish etc. (*discourteous*) 895; cross, –as -crabs, –a bear with a sore head, –a cat, –a dog, –two sticks, –the tongs [*all colloq.*]; sore, sore as a crab [*colloq.*].

in a bad temper; sulky etc. 901*a;* angry etc. 900; resentful, resentive; vindictive etc. 919.

int. pish!

901a. Sullenness

n. **sullenness** etc. *adj.;* morosity, spleen; churlishness etc. (*discourtesy*) 895; irascibility etc. 901; moodiness etc. *adj.;* perversity; obstinacy etc. 606; torvity [*obs.*], thorniness, spinosity; crabbedness etc. *adj.*

ill–, bad- -temper, –humor; sulks, dudgeon, mumps, dumps [*humorous*], doleful dumps [*colloq. or humorous*], vapors [*archaic*], glooming, doldrums, fit of the sulks, bouderie, black looks, scowl; grouch [*slang*]; huff etc. (*resentment*) 900.

v. **be sullen** etc. *adj.;* sulk; frown, scowl, lower, glower, pout, have a hangdog look, glout [*rare or dial.*], grouch, grout.

adj. **sullen**, sulky; ill-tempered, ill-humored, ill-affected, ill-disposed; grouty; in -an ill, –a bad, –a shocking- -temper, –humor; out of - temper, –humor; naggy [*colloq.*], torvous [*obs.*], crusty, crabbed, sour, sore, sore as a crab; surly etc. (*discourteous*) 895.

moody, moodish, spleenish, spleeny, spleenful, splenetic, cankered; cross, cross-grained; perverse, wayward, humorsome; restive, restiff [*rare*], malignant, refractory, ungovernable, cantankerous, intractable, exceptious [*rare*], sinistrous [*obs.*], deaf to reason, unaccommodating, rusty [*dial. Eng.*], froward, cussed [*vulgar*], curst [*archaic or dial.*].

grumpy, glum, grim, grum, morose, frumpish [*obs.*]; in the sulks etc. *n.;* out of sorts; scowling, glowering, growling, grouchy; peevish etc. (*irascible*) 901; dogged etc. (*stubborn*) 606.

902. Endearment
[expression of affection]

n. **endearment**, caress, blandishment, blandiment [*obs.*]; *épanchement* [*F.*], fondling, billing and cooing, dalliance, caressing, embrace, salute, kiss, buss, smack, osculation, deosculation [*obs.*].

courtship, wooing, suit, addresses, the soft impeachment; love-making; calf love [*colloq.*]; amorous glances, ogle, side-glance, sheep's eyes, goo-goo eyes [*slang*]; serenading, caterwauling.

flirting etc. *v.;* flirtation, gallantry; coquetry, spooning [*slang*].

true lover's knot, plighted love, engagement, betrothal; marriage etc. 903; honeymoon; love tale, love token; love letter, *billet-doux* [*F.*]; posy [*archaic*]; valentine.

Strephon and Chloe, 'Arry and 'Arriet.

flirt, coquette; male flirt, philanderer; spoon [*slang*].

v. **caress**, fondle, pet, dandle; pat, –on the -head, –cheek; chuck under the chin, smile upon, coax, wheedle, cosset, coddle, cocker, make much of, cherish, foster, kill with kindness.

clasp, hug, cuddle; fold to the heart, press to the bosom; fold–, strain- in one's arms; take to one's arms; snuggle, nestle, nuzzle; embrace, kiss, buss, smack, blow a kiss; salute etc. (*courtesy*) 894.

make love, bill and coo, spoon [*slang*], toy, dally, flirt, coquet, gallivant *or* galavant; philander; pay one's -court, –addresses, –attentions- to; serenade; court, sweetheart [*colloq. or dial.*], woo; set one's cap at *or* for [*colloq.*]; be *or* look sweet upon [*colloq.*]; ogle, cast sheep's eyes upon, make goo-goo eyes at [*slang*], *faire les yeux doux* [*F.*].

fall in love with, fall over head and ears in love with; win the affections etc. (*love*) 897; die for.

propose; make–, have- an offer; pop the question [*colloq.*]; become engaged, become betrothed; plight one's -troth, –faith.

adj. **caressing** etc. *v.;* "sighing like furnace" [*As You Like It*]; love-sick, spoony *or* spooney [*slang*].
caressed etc. *v.*

903. Marriage

n. **marriage**, matrimony, wedlock, union, intermarriage, miscegenation, marriageability; *vinculum matrimonii* [*L.*], nuptial tie, nuptial knot; match; betrothment etc. (*promise*) 768.

married state, coverture, bed, cohabitation.

wedding, nuptials, Hymen, bridal, espousals, spousals; leading to the altar etc. *v.;* nuptial benediction, epithalamium; sealing.

torch–, temple- of Hymen; saffron -veil, –robe; hymeneal altar; honeymoon.

bridesmaid, maid of honor, matron of honor; usher, best man, bridesman, groomsman; bride, bridegroom.

married man, neogamist [*obs.*], Benedict, partner, spouse, mate, yokemate, husband, man,

consort, baron [*old law & her.*], goodman [*archaic or dial.*], old man.
married woman, wife, wife of one's bosom, wedded wife, rib [*dial. & sportive*], helpmeet, helpmate, better half, ball and chain [*slang*], gray mare, goodwife [*archaic or dial.*], old lady *or* old woman [*vulgar*].
feme, –covert [*law*]; lady [*obs. or uncultivated*]; squaw; matron, matronship, matronage, matronhood.
married couple, man and wife, wedded pair, wedded couple, Darby and Joan, Philemon and Baucis.
affinity, soul-mate; spiritual wife, spiritual husband.
[kinds of marriage] monogamy, monogyny; bigamy, digamy, deuterogamy; trigamy; polygamy, polygyny, polyandry, polyandrism; Mormonism, spiritual wifery (*or* wifeism); levirate.
harem, seraglio; Mormon.
monogamist, monogynist, bigamist etc.; Turk, Bluebeard.
unlawful–, left-handed–, morganatic–, ill-assorted- marriage; *mésalliance* [*F.*], *mariage de convenance* [*F.*].
marriage broker, matchmaker, professional matchmaker, schatchen [*Yiddish*]; matrimonial -agency, –agent, –bureau.

v. **marry**, wive, take to oneself a wife; be married, be spliced [*colloq.*]; go off, go to the world [*obs.*], pair off; wed, espouse, lead to the hymeneal altar, take "for better for worse," give one's hand to, bestow one's hand upon.
marry, join, handfast [*archaic*]; couple etc. (*unite*) 43; be made one; tie the nuptial knot; give away, give in marriage; seal; affy, affiance; betroth etc. (*promise*) 768; publish–, call–, proclaim–, bid- the banns, be asked in church.
remarry, rewed; intermarry, interwed.

adj. **married** etc. *v.;* one, one bone and one flesh.
marriageable, nubile.
engaged, betrothed, affianced.
matrimonial, marital, conjugal, connubial, wedded; nuptial, hymeneal, spousal, bridal; monogamous etc.

904. Celibacy

n. **celibacy**, singleness, single blessedness; bachelorhood, bachelorship; misogamy, misogyny.
virginity, pucelage [*rare*], maidhood [*rare*], maidenhood, maidenhead.
unmarried man, bachelor, Coelebs, agamist, old bachelor; misogamist, misogynist; monk, priest, celibate, religious.
unmarried woman, spinster, maid, maiden; virgin, *feme sole* [*law*], old maid; bachelor-girl, girl-bachelor; nun, sister, vestal, vestal virgin; Diana, St. Agnes.

v. live single, enjoy single blessedness, keep bachelor hall.

adj. **unmarried**, unwedded; wifeless, spouseless; single, celibate, virgin.

905. Divorce. Widowhood

n. **divorce**, divorcement; separation, judicial separation, separate maintenance; *separatio a -mensa et thoro, –vinculo matrimonii* [*L.*].
widowhood, viduity [*rare*], viduage, viduation, weeds; viduate [*eccl.*].
widow, relict, dowager; divorcée; grass widow.
widower; grass widower; cuckold.

v. live separate; separate, divorce, disespouse [*obs.*], put away; cheat on [*slang*]; wear the horns.

906. Benevolence

n. **benevolence**, Christian charity; God's love, God's grace; good will; philanthropy etc. 910; unselfishness etc. 942.
good -nature, –feeling, –wishes; kindness, kindliness etc. *adj.;* loving-kindness, benignity, brotherly love, charity, humanity, kindly feelings, fellow-feeling, sympathy; goodness–, warmth- of heart; warm-heartedness, bonhomie *or* bonhommie, kind-heartedness; amiability, milk of human kindness, tenderness; love etc. 897; friendship etc. 888; toleration, consideration; mercy etc. (*pity*) 914.
charitableness etc. *adj.;* bounty, almsgiving; good works, beneficence, generosity; "the luxury of doing good" [Goldsmith].
acts of kindness, a good turn; good–, kind- -offices, –treatment.
philanthropist, "one who loves his fellow-men" [Hunt], salt of the earth; good Samaritan, sympathizer, well-wisher, *bon enfant* [*F.*]; altruist.

v. **be benevolent** etc. *adj.;* have one's heart in the right place, bear good will; wish well, wish Godspeed; view–, regard - with an eye of favor; take in good part; take–, feel - an interest in; be–, feel- interested- in; have a fellow-feeling for, sympathize with, feel for; fraternize etc. (*be friendly*) 888.
enter into the feelings of others, practice the Golden Rule, do as you would be done by, meet halfway.
treat well; give comfort, smooth the bed of death; do good, do a good turn; benefit etc. (*good-*

ness) 648; render a service, render assistance, give one a hand, be of use; aid etc. 707.

adj. **benevolent**, kind, kindly, well-meaning, amiable, cordial; obliging, accommodating, indulgent, gracious, complacent, good-humored; tender, considerate; warm-hearted, kind-hearted, tender-hearted, large-hearted, broad-hearted, soft-hearted; merciful etc. 914.

good-natured, well-natured, spleenless [*rare*]; sympathizing, sympathetic; complaisant etc. (*courteous*) 894; well-meant, well-intentioned, kindly meant.

full of natural affection, fatherly, motherly, brotherly, sisterly; paternal, maternal, fraternal; sororal [*rare*]; friendly etc. 888.

charitable, beneficent, philanthropical, generous, humane, benignant, bounteous, bountiful.

adv. **with good will**, with a good intention [*rare*], with the best intentions; out of deepest sympathy; in a burst of generosity.

int. **godspeed**! good luck! all good luck go with you! count on me!

907. Malevolence

n. **malevolence**, bad intent, bad intention, unkindness, diskindness [*obs.*]; ill-nature, ill-will, ill-blood, bad blood; enmity etc. 889; hate etc. 898; malice, –prepense, –aforethought; malignance, malignancy, malignity; maliciousness etc. *adj.*; spite, despite, resentment etc. 900.

uncharitableness etc. *adj.*; incompassion [*rare*], incompassionateness [*rare*] etc. 914*a*; gall, venom, rancor, rankling, virulence, mordacity, acerbity; churlishness etc. (*discourtesy*) 895; hardness of heart, heart of stone, obduracy; evil eye, cloven -foot, –hoof.

ill turn, bad turn; affront etc. (*disrespect*) 929; bigotry, intolerance, tender mercies [*ironical*]; "unkindest cut of all" [*Julius Caesar*].

cruelty, cruelness etc. *adj.*; brutality, savagery, ferity, ferocity; outrage, atrocity, ill-usage, persecution; barbarity, inhumanity, immanity [*obs.*], truculence, ruffianism; Inquisition, torture, vivisection.

v. **be malevolent** etc. *adj.*; bear–, harbor- -spleen, –a grudge, –malice; betray–, show- the cloven foot; hurt etc. (*physical pain*) 378; annoy etc. 830; injure, harm, wrong; do harm to, do an ill office to; outrage; disoblige, malign, plant a thorn in the breast; turn and rend one.

molest, worry, harass, haunt, harry, bait, tease; throw stones at; play the devil with; hunt down, dragoon, hound; persecute, oppress, grind, maltreat, ill-treat, ill-use, misuse.

wreak one's malice on, do one's worst, break a butterfly on the wheel; dip–, imbrue- one's hands in blood; show no quarter, have no mercy etc. 914*a*.

adj. **malevolent**, unbenevolent, unbenign; ill-disposed, ill-intentioned, ill-natured, ill-conditioned, ill-contrived; evil-minded, evil-disposed, black-browed; malicious, malign, malignant; rancorous, spiteful, despiteful; treacherous, mordacious, caustic, bitter, envenomed, acrimonious, virulent; unamiable, uncharitable; maleficent, venomous, grinding, galling.

harsh, disobliging, unkind, unfriendly, ungracious, inofficious [*obs.*], invidious; churlish etc. (*uncourteous*) 895; surly, sullen etc. 901*a*.

cold-blooded, cold-hearted; black-hearted, hard-hearted, flint-hearted, marble-hearted, stony-hearted, hard of heart, cold, unnatural; ruthless etc. (*unmerciful*) 914*a*; relentless etc. (*revengeful*) 919.

cruel, brutal, brutish, savage; savage as a -bear, –tiger; ferine, ferocious, feral, inhuman; barbarous, fell, untamed, tameless, truculent, incendiary; blood-thirsty etc. (*murderous*) 361; atrocious; bloody-minded; fiendish, fiendlike; demoniac *or* demoniacal; diabolic *or* diabolical, devilish, infernal, hellish, Tartarean *or* Tartareous, Satanic.

adv. **malevolently** etc. *adj.*; with bad intent etc. *n.*; with the ferocity of a tiger.

908. Malediction

n. **malediction**, malison, curse, imprecation, denunciation, execration; anathema, –maranatha; maranatha [*a misinterpretation*]; ban, proscription, excommunication, commination, thunders of the Vatican, fulmination; aspersion, disparagement, vilification, vituperation.

abuse; foul–, bad–, strong–, unparliamentary- language; billingsgate, sauce [*colloq.*]; blackguardism etc. (*discourtesy*) 895; evil speaking; cursing etc. *v.*; profane swearing, oath; foul invective, ribaldry, rude reproach, scurrility, threat etc. 909; more bark than bite; invective etc. (*disapprobation*) 932.

v. **curse**, accurse, imprecate, damn; curse with bell, book, and candle; invoke–, call down- curses on the head of; call down curses upon one's devoted head; devote to destruction.

execrate, beshrew [*archaic*], scold; anathematize etc. (*censure*) 932; hold up to execration, denounce, proscribe, excommunicate, fulminate,

909. Threat

thunder against; curse up hill and down dale; threaten etc. 909.

swear, curse and swear; swear like a trooper; fall a-cursing, rap out an oath, swear at, damn.

adj. **maledictory**, imprecatory; cursing, cursed etc. *v.*

int. woe to! beshrew! [*archaic*], *ruat coelum!* [*L.*], woe betide! ill betide! confusion seize! damn! confound! blast! curse! devil take! hang! out with! a plague upon! out upon! aroynt! *honi soit!* [*F.*], *parbleu!* [*F.*].

909. Threat

n. **threat**, menace; defiance etc. 715; abuse, minacity [*rare*], minaciousness, intimidation; denunciation; fulmination; commination etc. (*curse*) 908; gathering clouds etc. (*warning*) 668.

v. **threaten**, threat, menace; snarl, growl, gnarl, mutter, bark, bully.

defy etc. 715; intimidate etc. 860; keep–, hold up–, hold out- *in terrorem* [*L.*]; shake–, double–, clinch- the fist at; thunder, talk big, fulminate, use big words, bluster, look daggers.

adj. **threatening**, menacing, mínatory, minacious, comminatory, abusive; *in terrorem* [*L.*]; ominous etc. (*predicting*) 511; defiant etc. 715; under the ban.

int. vae victis! at your peril! do your worst! look out!

910. Philanthropy

n. **philanthropy**, altruism, humanity, humanitarianism, universal benevolence, eudaemonism *or* eudemonism, *deliciae humani generis* [*L.*].

public welfare, commonwealth [*now rare*], commonweal *or* common weal [*now rare*]; socialism, communism; Fourierism, phalansterism *or* phalansterianism, Saint Simonianism; cosmopolitanism, utilitarianism, the greatest happiness of the greatest number, social science, sociology.

public spirit, patriotism, civism, nationality, love of country, *amor patriae* [*L.*].

chivalry, knight errantry; generosity etc. 942.

philanthropist, eudaemonist *or* eudemonist, utilitarian, Benthamite, socialist, communist, cosmopolite, citizen of the world, *amicus humani generis* [*L.*]; altruist etc. 906; "little friend of all the world" [*Kipling*]; knight errant; patriot.

adj. **philanthropic**, altruistic, humanitarian, utilitarian, cosmopolitan; public-spirited, patriotic; humane, large-hearted etc. (*benevolent*) 906; chivalric, chivalrous; generous etc. 942.

adv. pro bono publico [*L.*]; *pro aris et focis* [*Cicero*].

911. Misanthropy

n. **misanthropy**, incivism; egotism etc. (*selfishness*) 943; moroseness etc. 901a; cynicism; want of patriotism etc. 910.

misanthrope, misanthropist, egotist, cynic, man hater, Timon, Diogenes.

woman hater, misogynist.

adj. **misanthropic**, antisocial, unpatriotic; egotistical etc. (*selfish*) 943; morose etc. 901a.

912. Benefactor

n. **benefactor**, savior, protector, good genius, tutelary saint, guardian angel, good Samaritan; friend in need, "a very present help in time of trouble" [*Bible*]; fairy godmother; *pater patriae* [*L.*]; salt of the earth etc. (*good man*) 948; auxiliary etc. 711.

913. Evildoer
[maleficent being]

n. **evildoer**, evil worker, malfeasor; wrongdoer etc. 949; mischiefmaker, marplot; oppressor, tyrant; firebrand, incendiary, fire bug, macher *or* torch [*slang*], pyromaniac, arsonist etc. 384; anarchist, nihilist, destroyer, Vandal, iconoclast, terrorist; Attila, scourge of the human race.

bane etc. 963; torpedo, bomb, U-boat.

savage, brute, ruffian, barbarian, semibarbarian, caitiff, desperado; Apache, gunman, hoodlum [*colloq.*], plug-ugly [*slang*], Redskin, tough [*colloq.*], Mohock, Mohawk [*rare*], bludgeon man, bully, rough, hooligan [*slang*], larrikin [*Austral. & Eng.*], ugly customer, dangerous classes; thief etc. 792; butcher, hangman; cutthroat etc. (*killer*) 361.

wild beast, tiger, leopard, panther, hyena, catamount, catamountain, lynx, cougar, jaguar, puma; bloodhound, hellhound, sleuth-hound; gorilla; vulture.

cockatrice, adder; snake, –in the grass; serpent, cobra, asp, rattlesnake, anaconda; boa; viper etc. (*snake*) 366; *alacrán* [*Sp. Amer.*], alligator, cayman, crocodile, mugger *or* magar [*Hind.*]; Gila monster; octopus.

[*injurious insects*] buffalo carpet beetle, cucumber flea beetle, elm-tree beetle, striped cucumber beetle, Japanese beetle, gypsy (*or* gipsy) moth, brown-tail moth, flat-headed apple-tree borer, peach-tree borer, round-headed apple-tree borer, squash vine borer, bedbug, harlequin cabbage bug, potato bug, buffalo bug, rose bug, squash bug, tent caterpillar; curculio, weevil, snout beetle, billbeetle, billbug, plum curculio; horn fly, white grub, San José scale, onion maggot, clover-seed midge, grain weevil,

bollworm, cankerworm, cutworm, fall webworm, tobacco worm, tomato worm, wireworm; white ant, scorpion, hornet, mosquito, locust, Colorado beetle.
hag, hellhag, beldam, Jezebel.
monster; fiend etc. (*demon*) 980; devil incarnate, demon in human shape; Frankenstein's monster; cannibal, anthropophagus, anthropophagist; bloodsucker, vampire, ogre, ghoul.
harpy, siren, vampire [*colloq.*], vamp [*slang*]; Furies, Eumenides.

914. Pity

n. **pity,** compassion, commiseration; bowels, –of compassion; sympathy, fellow-feeling, tenderness, soft-heartedness, yearning, forbearance, humanity, mercy, clemency; leniency etc. (*lenity*) 740; exorability, exorableness; charity, ruth, long-suffering.
melting mood; *argumentum ad misericordiam* [*L.*]; quarter, grace, *locus poenitentiae* [*L.*].
sympathizer; advocate, friend, partisan, patron, wellwisher, defender, champion.

v. **pity;** have–, show–, take- pity etc. *n.;* commiserate, compassionate; condole etc. 915; sympathize; feel for, be sorry for, yearn over; weep, melt, thaw, enter into the feelings of.
forbear, relent, relax, give quarter, wipe the tears, *parcere subjectis* [*L.*]; give a *coup de grâce* [*F.*], put out of one's misery; be cruel to be kind.
raise *or* **excite pity** etc. *n.;* touch, soften, melt, melt the heart; appeal, –to one's better feelings; propitiate, disarm.
supplicate etc. (*request*) 765; ask for mercy etc. *n.;* cry for quarter, beg one's life, kneel; deprecate.

adj. **pitying** etc. *v.;* pitiful, compassionate, sympathetic, touched.
merciful, clement, ruthful; humane; humanitarian etc. (*philanthropic*) 910; tender, tenderhearted; soft, soft-hearted; unhardened; lenient etc. 740; exorable, forbearing; melting etc. *v.;* weak.

int. for pity's sake! mercy! have–, cry you- mercy! God help you! poor -thing, –dear, –fellow! woe betide! *quis talia fando temperet a lachrymis!* [Virgil].

914a. Pitilessness

n. **pitilessness** etc. *adj.;* inclemency, inexorability, inflexibility, incompassion [*rare*], hardness of heart; want of pity etc. 914; severity etc. 739; malevolence etc. 907.

v. **be pitiless** etc. *adj.;* turn a deaf ear to; claim one's "pound of flesh" [Merchant of Venice]; have no–, shut the gates of- mercy etc. 914; give no quarter.

adj. **pitiless,** merciless, ruthless, bowelless; unpitying, unmerciful, inclement; grim-faced, grim-visaged; uncompassionate, incompassionate [*rare*], uncompassioned; inflexible, relentless, inexorable; unrelenting etc. 919; harsh etc. 739; cruel etc. 907.

915. Condolence

n. **condolence;** lamentation etc. 839; sympathy, consolation.

v. **condole with,** console, sympathize; express–, testify- pity; afford–, supply- consolation; lament with etc. 839; express sympathy for, feel for, send one's condolences; feel -grief, –sorrow- in common with; share one's sorrow.

916. Gratitude

n. **gratitude,** gratefulness, thankfulness; feeling of–, sense of- obligation.
acknowledgment, recognition, thanksgiving, giving thanks; thankful good will.
thanks, praise, benediction; paean; *Te Deum* etc. (*worship*) 990; grace, –before meat, –after meat; thank offering; requital.

v. **be grateful** etc. *adj.;* thank; give–, render–, return–, offer–, tender-thanks etc. *n.;* acknowledge, requite.
feel–, be–, lie- under an obligation; *savoir gré* [*F.*]; not look a gift horse in the mouth; never forget, overflow with gratitude; thank–, bless- one's stars; fall on one's knees.

adj. **grateful,** thankful, obliged, beholden, indebted to, under obligation

int. **thanks!** many thanks! gramercy! much obliged! thank you! thank Heaven! Heaven be praised!

917. Ingratitude

n. **ingratitude,** thanklessness, oblivion of benefits, unthankfulness.
"benefits forgot" [*As You Like It*]; thankless task, thankless office.

v. **be ungrateful** etc. *adj.;* feel no obligation, owe one no thanks, forget benefits; look a gift horse in the mouth.

adj. **ungrateful,** unmindful, unthankful; thankless, ingrate, wanting in gratitude, insensible of benefits.
forgotten; unacknowledged, unthanked, unrequited, unrewarded; ill-requited; ill-rewarded.

int. thank you for nothing! "*et tu Brute!*" [*Julius Caesar*].

918. Forgiveness

n. **forgiveness**, pardon, condonation, grace, remission, absolution, amnesty, oblivion; indulgence; reprieve.

conciliation; reconcilement; reconciliation etc. (*pacification*) 723; propitiation.

longanimity, placability; *amantium irae* [*L.*]; *locus poenitentiae* [*L.*]; forbearance.

exoneration, excuse, quittance, release, indemnity; bill-, act-, covenant-, deed- of indemnity; exculpation etc. (*acquittal*) 970.

v. **forgive**, –and forget; pardon, condone, think no more of, let bygones be bygones, shake hands; forget an injury; bury the hatchet; drown all unkindness; start afresh, make a new start.

let off [*colloq.*], remit, absolve, give absolution; blot out one's -sins, –offenses, –transgressions, –debts; wipe the slate clean; reprieve; acquit etc. 970.

excuse, pass over, overlook; wink at etc. (*neglect*) 460; bear with; allow for, make allowances for; let one down easily, not be too hard upon, pocket the affront.

conciliate, propitiate, placate; beg-, ask-, implore- pardon etc. *n.;* make up a quarrel etc. (*pacify*) 723; let the wound heal.

adj. **forgiving**, placable, conciliatory.

forgiven etc. *v.;* unresented, unavenged, unrevenged.

int. have mercy! cry you mercy! forgive and forget!

919. Revenge

n. **revenge**, revengement [*rare*], vengeance; avengement, avengeance [*obs.*], sweet revenge, vendetta, death feud, blood for blood; eye for an eye, tooth for a tooth, *lex talionis* [*L.*], retaliation etc. 718; day of reckoning.

rancor, vindictiveness, immitigability; implacability; malevolence etc. 907; ruthlessness etc. 914a.

avenger, vindicator [*obs.*], Nemesis, Eumenides.

v. **revenge**, avenge, vindicate [*obs.*]; take revenge, have one's revenge; breathe -revenge, –vengeance; wreak one's - vengeance, –anger; cry quittance; give no quarter, take no prisoners.

have accounts to settle, have a crow to pluck, have a rod in pickle.

keep the wound green; nurse one's revenge, harbor -revenge, –vindictive feeling; bear malice; rankle, rankle in the breast.

have at a disadvantage, have on the hip, have the upper hand, have at one's mercy.

adj. **revengeful**, vengeful, vindictive, rancorous; pitiless etc. 914a; ruthless, rigorous, avenging, retaliative, grudgeful [*rare*].

unforgiving, unrelenting; inexorable, stony-hearted, implacable, relentless, remorseless.

rankling, immitigable; *aeternum servans sub pectore vulnus* [*L.*].

920. Jealousy

n. **jealousy**, jealousness; jaundiced eye; distrust, mistrust, misdoubt, heartburn; envy etc. 921; doubt, envious suspicion, suspicion; "green-eyed monster" [*Othello*]; yellows; Juno.

v. **be jealous** etc. *adj.;* view with jealousy, view with a jealous eye, view with a jaundiced eye; grudge, begrudge.

doubt, distrust, mistrust, suspect, misdoubt, heartburn [*obs.*]; jealouse [*obs. or Scot. & dial. Eng.*].

adj. **jealous**, jealous as a Barbary pigeon; jaundiced, yellow-eyed, envious; beside oneself with -jealousy, –envy.

921. Envy

n. **envy**; enviousness etc. *adj.;* rivalry; *jalousie de métier* [*F.*]; ill-will, spite; jealousy etc. 920.

v. **envy**, covet, grudge, begrudge, burst with envy, break the tenth commandment.

adj. **envious**, individious, covetous, grudging, begrudged; belittling; *alieni appetens* [*L.*].

Section 4. Moral

922. Right

n. **right**; what ought to be, what should be; what is fit etc. *adj.;* fitness etc. *adj.; summum jus* [*L.*].

justice, equity; equitableness etc. *adj.;* propriety; fair play, square deal [*colloq.*], impartiality, measure for measure, give and take, *lex talionis* [*L.*].

scales of justice, evenhanded justice, karma; *suum cuique* [*L.*]; clear stage–, fair field- and no favor; retributive justice, nemesis.

Astraea, Nemesis, Themis, Rhadamanthus.

morals etc. (*duty*) 926; law etc. 963; honor etc. (*probity*) 939; virtue etc. 944.

v. **be right** etc. *adj.;* stand to reason.

see justice done, see one righted, see fair play; do justice to; recompense etc. (*reward*) 973; hold the scales even, give and take; serve one right, put the saddle on the right horse; give every one his due, give the devil his due; *audire alteram partem* [*L.*].

deserve etc. (*be entitled to*) 924.

adj. **right**, good; just, reasonable; fit etc. 924; equal, equable, equitable; evenhanded, fair, square, fair and square.

legitimate, justifiable, rightful; as it should be, as it ought to be; lawful etc. (*permitted*) 760, (*legal*) 963.
    deserved etc. 924.
adv. **rightly** etc. *adj.; à-, au- bon droit* [*F.*], in justice, in equity, in reason.
    without -distinction of, –regard to, –respect to- persons; upon even terms.
int. all right!

923. Wrong

n. **wrong**; what ought not to be, what should not be *malum in se* [*L.*]; unreasonableness grievance; shame.
    injustice; unfairness etc. *adj.;* iniquity, foul play, partiality, leaning, favor, favoritism, nepotism; partisanship, party spirit; undueness etc. 925; unlawfulness etc. 964.
    robbing Peter to pay Paul etc. *v.;* the wolf and the lamb; vice etc. 945.
v. **be wrong** etc. *adj.;* cry to heaven for vengeance.
    do wrong etc. *n.;* be inequitable etc. *adj.;* favor, lean towards; encroach, impose upon; reap where one has not sown; give an inch and take an ell; rob Peter to pay Paul.
adj. **wrong**, wrongful; bad, too bad; unjust, unfair, inequitable, unequitable, unequal, partial, one-sided; injurious.
    unjustifiable, unreasonable, unallowable, unwarrantable, objectionable, improper, unfit; unjustified etc. 925; illegal etc. 964; iniquitous; immoral etc. 945.
    in the wrong, –box; in bad [*slang*], in wrong [*slang*].
adv. **wrongly** etc. *adj.*
int. this is too bad! it will not do!

924. Dueness

n. **dueness**, right, droit [*law*], due, privilege, prerogative, prescription, title, claim, pretension, demand, birthright.
    immunity, license, liberty, franchise; vested -interest, –right.
    sanction, authority, warranty [*law*], charter, licitness, warrant etc. (*permission*) 760; constitution etc. (*law*) 963; tenure; bond etc. (*security*) 771.
    deserts, merits, dues; all that is coming to one [*colloq.*].
    claimant, appellant; plaintiff etc. 938.
v. **be due to** etc. *adj.;* be the due of etc. *n.;* have -right, –title, –claim- to; be entitled to; have a claim upon; belong to etc. (*property*) 780.
    deserve, merit, be worthy of, richly deserve.
    demand, claim; call upon one for, come upon one for, appeal to for; revendicate [*rare*], revindicate, reclaim; exact; insist -on, –upon; challenge; take one's stand, make a point of, require, lay claim to; assert, assume, arrogate.
    make good; substantiate; vindicate a -claim, –right; fit–, qualify- for; make out a case.
    use a right, assert, enforce, put in force, lay under contribution.
    entitle; give *or* confer a right; authorize etc. 760; sanction, sanctify, legalize, ordain, prescribe, allot.
    give every one his due etc. 922; pay one's dues; have one's -due, –rights; stand upon one's rights.
adj. **having a right to** etc. *v.;* entitled to; claiming; deserving, meriting, worthy of.
    privileged, allowed, sanctioned, warranted, authorized; ordained, prescribed, constitutional, chartered, enfranchised.
    prescriptive, presumptive, absolute, indefeasible, unalienable, inalienable, imprescriptible, inviolable, unimpeachable, unchallenged; sacrosanct.
    due to, merited, deserved, condign [*archaic, except of punishment*], richly deserved.
    right, fit, fitting, correct, proper, meet, befitting, becoming, seemly; decorous; creditable, up to the mark, right as a trivet; just–, quite- the thing; *selon les règles* [*F.*]; square, unexceptionable, equitable etc. 922; due, *en règle* [*F.*].
    lawful, licit, legitimate, legal; legalized etc. (*law*) 963; allowable etc. (*permitted*) 760.
adv. **duly**; as is -right, –fitting, –just; unexceptionably; *ex officio* [*L.*], *de jure* [*L.*]; by right, by divine right; *jure divino* [*L.*], *Dei gratia* [*L.*], in the name of.

925. Unueness

[absence of right]

n. **undueness** etc. *adj.; malum prohibitum* [*L.*]; impropriety; illegality etc. 964.
    falseness etc. *adj.;* emptiness–, invalidity- of title; illegitimacy.
    loss of right, disfranchisement, forfeiture.
    assumption, usurpation, tort [*law*], violation, breach, encroachment, presumption, seizure; stretch, exaction, imposition, lion's share.
    usurper, pretender, impostor.
v. **be undue** etc. *adj.;* not be due etc. 924.
    infringe, encroach, trench on, exact; arrogate, –to oneself; give an inch and take an ell; stretch–, strain- a point; usurp, violate, do violence to; get under false pretenses, sail under false colors.

926. Duty

disentitle, disfranchise, disqualify; invalidate.
relax etc. (*be lax*) 738; misbehave etc. (*vice*) 945; misbecome.

adj. **undue**; unlawful etc. (*illegal*) 964; unconstitutional, illicit, unauthorized, unwarranted, unallowed, unsanctioned, unjustified; disentitled, unentitled; disqualified, unqualified; unprivileged, unchartered.
undeserved, unmerited, unearned; unfulfilled. forfeited, disfranchised.
illegitimate, bastard, spurious, false; usurped, tortious [*law*].
improper; unmeet, unfit, unbefitting, unseemly, unbecoming, misbecoming, seemless [*obs.*]; *contra bonos mores* [*L.*]; not the thing, out of the question, not to be thought of; preposterous, pretentious, would-be.

926. Duty

n. **duty**, what ought to be done, moral obligation, accountableness, liability, onus, responsibility; bounden–, imperative- duty; call, –of duty; accountability.
allegiance, fealty, tie; engagement etc. (*promise*) 768; part; function, calling etc. (*business*) 625.
observance, fulfillment, discharge, performance, acquittal, satisfaction, redemption; good behavior.
morality, morals, decalogue; case of conscience; conscientiousness etc. (*probity*) 939; conscience, inward monitor, still small voice within, sense of duty, tender conscience; the hell within [*P.L.*].
propriety, fitness; dueness etc. 924; seemliness, amenableness, amenability, decorum, *to prepon* [*Gr.*]; the thing, the proper thing; the -right, –proper- thing to do.
[science of morals] ethics, ethology [*obs. in this sense*]; deontology, aretology [*obs.*]; moral–, ethical- philosophy; casuistry, polity.

v. **be the duty of**, be incumbent on etc. *adj.;* be responsible etc. *adj.;* behoove, become, befit, beseem; belong to, pertain to; fall to one's lot; devolve on; lie upon, lie on one's head, lie at one's door; rest with, rest on the shoulders of.
take upon oneself etc. (*promise*) 768; be–, become- -bound to, –sponsor for; incur a responsibility etc. *n.;* be–, stand–, lie- under an obligation; stand responsible for; have to answer for; owe it to oneself.
enter upon–, perform–, observe–, fulfill–, discharge–, adhere to–, acquit oneself of–, satisfy- -a duty, –an obligation; act one's part, redeem one's pledge, do justice to, be at one's post; do duty; do one's duty etc. (*be virtuous*) 944.
be on one's good behavior, mind one's P's and Q's; walk the straight path.
impose a duty etc. *n.;* enjoin, require, exact; bind, –over; saddle with, prescribe, assign, call upon, look to, oblige.

adj. **obligatory**, binding; imperative, peremptory; stringent etc. (*severe*) 739; behooving etc. *v.;* incumbent on, chargeable on; under obligation; obliged by, bound by, tied by; saddled with.
due to, beholden to, bound to, indebted to; tied down; compromised etc. (*promised*) 768; in duty bound.
amenable, liable, accountable, responsible, answerable.
right, meet etc. (*due*) 924; moral, ethical, casuistical, conscientious, ethological.

adv. with a safe conscience, as in duty bound on good behavior, on one's own responsibility, at one's own risk, *suo periculo* [*L.*]; *in foro conscientiae* [*L.*]; *quamdiu se bene gesserit* [*L.*]; at one's post.

927. Dereliction of Duty

n. **dereliction of duty**; fault etc. (*guilt*) 947; sin etc. (*vice*) 945; nonobservance, nonperformance, noncoöperation; indolence, neglect, relaxation, infraction, violation, transgression, failure, evasion; eyeservice; dead letter.
slacker, loafer, time-killer; eyeserver, eyeservant; striker; noncoöperator.

v. **violate**; break, break through; infringe; set aside, set at naught; encroach upon, trench upon; trample -on, –under foot; slight, get by [*slang*], neglect, evade, renounce, forswear, repudiate; wash one's hands of; escape. transgress, fail.
call to account etc. (*disapprobation*) 932.

927a. Exemption

n. **exemption**, freedom, irresponsibility, immunity, liberty, license, release, quitclaim [*law*]; exoneration, excuse, dispensation, absolution, franchise [*obs.*], renunciation, discharge; exculpation etc. 970.

v. **exempt**, release, acquit, discharge, quitclaim [*law*], remise, remit; free, set at liberty, let off [*colloq.*], pass over, spare, excuse, dispense with, give dispensation, license; stretch a point; absolve etc. (*forgive*) 918; exonerate etc. (*exculpate*) 970; save the necessity.
be exempt etc. *adj.*

928. Respect

n. **respect**, regard, consideration; courtesy etc. 894; attention, deference, reverence, honor, esteem, estimation, veneration, admiration; approbation etc. 931.
 homage, fealty, obeisance, genuflection, kneeling, prostration; obsequiousness etc. 886; salaam, kotow *or* kowtow [*Chinese*], bow, presenting arms, salute.
 respects, regards, duty, *devoirs* [*F.*], *égards* [*F.*].
 devotion etc. (*piety*) 987.

v. **respect**, regard; revere, reverence; hold in reverence, honor, venerate, hallow; esteem etc. (*approve of*) 931; think much of; entertain-, bear- respect for; look up to, defer to; have-, hold- a high opinion of; pay attention to, pay respect to etc. *n.;* do *or* render honor to; do the honors, hail; show courtesy etc. 894; salute, present arms.
 do *or* pay homage to; pay tribute to, kneel to, bow to, bend the knee to; fall down before, prostrate oneself, kiss the hem of one's garment; worship etc. 990.
 keep one's distance, make room, observe due decorum, stand on ceremony.
 command respect, inspire respect; awe, impose, overawe, dazzle.

adj. **respecting** etc. *v.;* respectful, deferential, decorous, reverential, obsequious, ceremonious, bareheaded, cap in hand, on one's knees; prostrate etc. (*servile*) 886.
 respected etc. *v.;* in high -esteem, -estimation; time-honored, venerable, *emeritus* [*L.*].

adv. **in deference to**; with all respect, with due respect, with the highest respect; with submission.
 excusing the liberty; saving your -grace, -presence; *salva sit reverentia* [*L.*]; *pace tanti nominis* [*L.*].

int. hail! all hail! *hoch!* [*Ger.*]; *esto perpetua!* [*L.*], may your shadow never be less!

929. Disrespect

n. **disrespect**, disesteem, disestimation; disfavor, disrepute, want of esteem, low estimation, disparagement etc. (*dispraise*) 932, (*detraction*) 934; irreverence; slight, neglect; superciliousness etc. (*contempt*) 930.
 indignity, vilipendency [*obs.*], contumely, affront, dishonor, insult, outrage, discourtesy etc. 895; practical joking; scurrility, scoffing; sibilation, hiss, hissing, hoot, irrision [*rare*], derision; mockery; irony etc. (*ridicule*) 856; sarcasm.
 gibe *or* jibe, flout, jeer, scoff, gleek [*obs.*], fleer, taunt, sneer, quip, fling, twit, wipe [*dial. or slang*], slap in the face.

v. **treat with disrespect** etc. *n.;* hold in disrespect etc. (*despise*) 930; misprize, disregard, slight, undervalue, humiliate, depreciate, trifle with, set at naught, pass by, push aside, overlook, turn one's back upon, laugh in one's sleeve; be disrespectful etc. *adj.;* be discourteous etc. 895; set down, browbeat.
 dishonor, desecrate; insult, affront, outrage.
 speak slightingly of; disparage etc. (*dispraise*) 932; vilipend, call names; throw-, fling- dirt; throw mud at; make ride the rail, drag through the mud, point at, indulge in personalities; make mouths [*archaic*], make faces; bite the thumb; take-, pluck- by the beard; toss in a blanket, tar and feather.
 deride, have *or* hold in derision; scoff, barrack [*dial. Eng. & Austral.*], sneer, laugh at, snigger, ridicule, gibe *or* jibe, mock, jeer, taunt, twit, niggle, gleek [*obs.*], gird, flout, fleer; roast [*colloq.*], guy [*colloq.*], rag [*dial. Eng. & college slang*] smoke [*old slang*]; turn into ridicule; burlesque etc. 856; laugh to scorn etc. (*contempt*) 930; lead one a dance, have a fling at, scout, hiss, hoot, mob.
 fool; make game of, make a fool of, make an April fool of; play a practical joke.

adj. **disrespectful**; aweless, irreverent; disparaging etc. 934; insulting etc. *v.;* supercilious etc. (*scornful*) 930; rude, derisive, sarcastic; scurrile, scurrilous, contumelious, contemptuous, insolent, disdainful.
 unrespected, unworshiped, unenvied, unsaluted; unregarded, disregarded.

adv. **disrespectfully** etc. *adj.*

930. Contempt

n. **contempt**, disdain, scorn, sovereign contempt; despisal [*rare*], despiciency [*obs.*], despisement [*rare*]; vilipendency [*obs.*], contumely; slight, sneer, spurn, byword; despect [*rare*].
 contemptuousness etc. *adj.;* scornful eye; smile of contempt; derision etc. (*disrespect*) 929.
 [state of being despised] despisedness.

v. **despise**, contemn, scorn, disdain, feel contempt for, view with a scornful eye; disregard, slight, not mind; pass by etc. (*neglect*) 460; look down

931. Approbation

upon; hold - cheap, –in contempt, –in disrespect; think nothing of, think small beer of [*colloq.*]; make light of; underestimate etc. 483; esteem slightly, esteem of small or no account; take no account of, care nothing for; set no store by; not care a straw etc. (*unimportance*) 643; set at naught, laugh in one's sleeve, snap one's fingers at, shrug one's shoulders, turn up one's nose at, pooh-pooh, "damn with faint praise" [*Pope*].

sneeze at, whistle at, sneer at; curl up one's lip, toss the head, *traiter de haut en bas* [*F.*]; laugh at etc. (*be disrespectful*) 929; point the finger of–, hold up to–, laugh to- scorn; scout, hoot, flout, hiss, scoff at.

spurn, turn one's back upon, turn a cold shoulder upon; tread–, trample- -upon, –under foot; kick; fling to the winds etc. (*repudiate*) 610; send away with a flea in the ear [*colloq.*].

adj. **contemptuous**, disdainful, scornful, withering, contumelious, supercilious, cynical, haughty, cavalier; derisive; with the nose in air, *de haut en bas* [*F.*].

contemptible, despicable; pitiable; pitiful etc. (*unimportant*) 643; despised etc. *v.;* downtrodden; unenvied.

adv. **contemptuously** etc. *adj.*

int. a fig for etc. (*unimportant*) 643; bah! pooh! pshaw! never mind! away with! hang it! fiddledeedee!

931. Approbation

n. **approbation**, approval, approvement [*obs.*], bepraisement, sanction, advocacy; nod of approbation; esteem, estimation, good opinion, golden opinions, admiration; love etc. 897; appreciation, regard, account, popularity, *kudos* [*Gr.*], credit; repute etc. 873.

commendation, praise, laud, laudation; good word; meed–, tribute- of praise; encomium, eulogy, eulogium, *éloge* [*F.*], panegyric, blurb [*slang*]; homage, hero worship; benediction, blessing, benison.

applause, plaudit, clap; clapping, –of hands; acclaim, acclamation; cheer; paean, hosanna; shout–, peal–, chorus–, thunders- of -applause etc.; prytaneum.

winner, prize winner, best seller, corker [*slang*], peach [*slang*], oner [*slang*], the real thing [*colloq.*], the goods [*slang*].

v. **approve**, approbate, think good of, think much of, think well of, think highly of; esteem, value, prize; set great store by.

honor, hold in esteem, look up to, admire; like etc. 897; be in favor of, wish Godspeed; hail, hail with satisfaction, do justice to, appreciate.

stand up for, stick up for [*colloq.*], uphold, hold up, countenance, sanction; clap–, pat- on the back; keep in countenance, indorse *or* endorse; give credit, recommend; mark with a white -mark, –stone.

commend, belaud, praise, laud, compliment, pay a tribute, bepraise; clap, –the hands; applaud, cheer, acclaim, acclamate [*rare*], encore; panegyrize, eulogize, boost [*colloq.*], root for [*slang*], cry up, *prôner* [*F.*], puff; extol, –to the skies; magnify, glorify, exalt, swell, make much of; flatter etc. 933; bless, give a blessing to; have–, say- a good word for; speak - well, –highly, –in high terms- of; sing–, sound–, chant–, resound- the praises of; sing praises to; cheer–, applaud- to the -echo, –very echo.

redound to the -honor, –praise, –credit- of; do credit to; deserve -praise etc. *n.;* recommend itself; pass muster.

be praised etc.; receive honorable mention; be in favor with, be in high favor with; ring with the praises of, win golden opinions, gain credit, find favor with, stand well in the opinion of; *laudari a laudato viro* [*L.*].

adj. **approving** etc. *v.;* in favor of; lost in admiration; commendatory, complimentary, benedictory, laudatory, panegyrical, eulogistic, encomiastic, acclamatory, lavish of praise, uncritical.

approved, praised etc. *v.;* uncensured, unimpeached; popular, in good odor; in high esteem etc. (*respected*) 928; in favor, in high favor.

praiseworthy, commendable, of estimation; deserving–, worthy of- praise etc. *n.;* good etc. 648; meritorious, estimable, creditable, unimpeachable; beyond all praise.

adv. **commendably**, with credit, to admiration; well etc. 618; with three times three.

int. hear hear! good for you! do it again! bully for you! [*slang*], well done! fine! bravo! *bravissimo!* [*It.*], euge! [*Gr. & L.*], *macte virtute!* [*L.*], so far so good! that's right! quite right! one cheer more! may your shadow never be less! *esto perpetua!* [*L.*], long life to! viva! [*It.*], evviva! [*It.*], Godspeed! *valete et plaudite!* [*L.*], encore! [*F.*], bis! [*L. & F.*].

932. Disapprobation

n. **disapprobation**, disapproval, improbation [*obs.*], disesteem, displacency [*rare*]; odium; dislike etc. 867; black list, blackball, ostracism, boycott; index expurgatorius.

disparagement, depreciation, disvaluation, dispraise, discommendation; detraction etc. 934; denunciation; condemnation etc. 971; animad-

932. Disapprobation

version, reflection, stricture, objection, exception, criticism; blame, censure, obloquy; sardonic -grin, –laugh; sarcasm, satire, insinuation, innuendo; bad–, poor–, left-handed- compliment.

sneer etc. (*contempt*) 930; taunt etc. (*disrespect*) 929; cavil, carping, censoriousness; hypercriticism etc. (*fastidiousness*) 868.

reprehension, remonstrance, expostulation, reproof, reprobation, admonition, increpation [*archaic*], reproach; rebuke, reprimand, castigation, jobation [*colloq.*], lecture, curtain lecture, blowup [*colloq.*]; blowing up, trimming, wigging, dressing, dressing down [*all colloq.*]; rating, scolding, correction, set down, rap on the knuckles, *coup de bec* [*F.*], rebuff; slap, slap on the face; home thrust, hit; frown, scowl, black look.

diatribe, jeremiad *or* jeremiade, tirade, philippic.

chiding, upbraiding etc. *v.;* exprobration [*rare*], personal remarks, abuse, vituperation, invective, objurgation, contumely; hard–, cutting–, bitter- words; evil-speaking; bad language etc. 908; personality.

clamor, outcry, hue and cry; hiss, hissing, sibilation, catcall; execration etc. 908.

v. **disapprove**; dislike etc. 867; lament etc. 839; object to, take exception to; be scandalized at, think ill of; view with -disfavor, –dark eyes, –jaundiced eyes; *nil admirari* [*L.*], disvalue, improbate [*obs.*].

frown upon, look grave; bend–, knit- the brows; shake the head at, shrug the shoulders; turn up the nose etc. (*contempt*) 930; look askance, look black upon; look with an evil eye; make a wry face at, make a face at, make a mouth at [*archaic*], set one's face against.

blame; lay–, cast- blame upon; censure, *fronder* [*F.*], reproach, pass censure on, reprobate, impugn, impeach; disbar, unfrock.

accuse etc. 938; impeach, denounce; hold up to -reprobation, –execration; expose, brand, gibbet, stigmatize; show up, pull up [*both colloq.*]; take up; cry "shame" upon; be outspoken; raise a hue and cry against.

reprehend, chide, admonish; berate, betongue; bring–, call- -to account, –over the coals [*colloq.*], –to order; take to task, haul over the coals [*colloq.*], reprove, lecture, bring to book; read a -lesson, –lecture- to; rebuke, correct; reprimand, chastise, castigate, lash, trounce; trim, blow up, give it to, give one fits, give it to one, lay out [*all six colloq.*]; *laver la tête* [*F.*], overhaul.

remonstrate, expostulate, recriminate.

execrate etc. 908; exprobate [*rare*], speak daggers, vituperate; abuse, –like a pickpocket; tongue-lash [*colloq.*], scold, rate, objurgate, upbraid, fall foul of; jaw [*low*]; rail, -at, –in good set terms; bark at, yelp at, anathematize, call names; call by -hard, –ugly- names; avile [*obs.*], revile, vilify, vilipend, bespatter; clapperclaw [*archaic*]; rave–, thunder–, fulminate- against; load with reproaches.

decry, cry down, run down, frown down; exclaim–, protest–, inveigh–, declaim–, cry out–, raise one's voice- against; clamor, hiss, hoot, –catcall, mob; backbite; ostracize, blacklist, boycott, blackball; draw up–, sign- a round robin.

take down, set down; snub, snap one up, give a rap on the knuckles; throw a stone -at, –in one's garden; have a fling at, have a snap at; have words with, pluck a crow with; give one a wipe [*dial. or slang*]; give one a lick with the rough side of the tongue [*colloq.*].

animadvert upon, reflect upon; glance at; cast -reflection, –reproach - a slur- upon; insinuate, "damn with faint praise" [Pope]; "hint a fault and hesitate dislike" [Pope]; not to be able to say much for.

disparage, depreciate, knock [*colloq.*], dispraise, discommend [*rare*], deprecate, speak ill of, not speak well of; condemn etc. (*find guilty*) 971; scoff at, point at; twit, taunt etc. (*disrespect*) 929; sneer at etc. (*despise*) 230; satirize, lampoon; defame etc. (*detract*) 934; depreciate, find fault with, criticize, cut up; pull–, pick- to pieces; take exception; cavil; peck at, nibble at, carp at; be censorious etc. *adj.;* pick -holes, –a hole, –a hole in one's coat; poke holes in; make a fuss about.

incur blame, excite disapprobation, scandalize, shock, revolt; get a bad name, forfeit one's good opinion, be under a cloud, come under the ferule, bring a hornet's nest about one's ears.

take blame, stand corrected; have to answer for.

adj. **disapproving** etc. *v.;* disparaging, condemnatory, damnatory, denunciatory, reproachful, abusive, objurgatory, clamorous, vituperative; defamatory etc. 934.

satirical, sarcastic, sardonic, cynical, dry, sharp, cutting, biting, severe, withering, trenchant, hard upon; censorious, critical, captious, carping, hypercritical; scandalized; fastidious etc. 868; sparing of–, grudging -praise.

disapproved, chid etc. *v.;* in bad odor, blown upon, unapproved; unblest; at a discount, exploded; weighed in the balance and found wanting.

933. Flattery

unlamented, unbewailed, unpitied.
blameworthy, reprehensible etc. (*guilt*) 947; to-, worthy of- blame; answerable, uncommendable, exceptionable, not to be thought of; bad etc. 649; vicious etc. 945.

adv. **reproachfully** etc. *adj.;* with a wry face.

int. it is too bad! it won't do! it will never do! it isn't done! marry come up! [*archaic or dial.*], Oh! come! 'sdeath! [*archaic*].

forbid it Heaven! God forbid! Heaven forbid! out upon it! fie upon it! away with! tut! *O tempora! O mores!* [*L.*]; shame! fie, –for shame! out on you!

tell it not in Gath!

933. Flattery

n. **flattery**, adulation, gloze [*rare*]; blandishment [*rare*], blandiloquence; cajolery; fawning, wheedling etc. *v.;* captation, coquetry, obsequiousness, sycophancy, flunkeyism, toadyism, toadeating, tufthunting, snobbishness.

incense, honeyed words, flummery, buncombe *or* bunkum [*cant or slang*]; blarney, butter, soft soap, soft sawder [*all colloq.*]; rose water.

voice of the charmer, mouth honor; lip homage; euphemism; unctuousness etc. *adj.*

v. **flatter**, praise to the skies, puff; wheedle, cajole, glaver [*obs. or dial.*], coax; fawn, –upon; humor, gloze [*now rare*], soothe, pet, coquet, slaver, butter [*colloq.*], jolly [*colloq.*]; bespatter, beslubber, beplaster, beslaver; lay it on thick, overpraise; cog [*obs.*], collogue [*obs. in this sense*]; truckle to, pander *or* pandar to, pay court to; court; creep into the good graces of, curry favor with, hang on the sleeve of; fool to the top of one's bent; lick the dust.

lay the flattering unction to one's soul, gild the pill, make things pleasant.

overestimate etc. 482; exaggerate etc. 549.

adj. **flattering** etc. *v.;* adulatory; mealy-mouthed, honey-mouthed, honeyed, smooth, smooth-tongued; soapy [*slang*], oily, unctuous, blandiloquent, specious; fine–, fair– spoken; plausible, servile, sycophantic, fulsome; courtierly, courtierlike.

adv. ad captandum.

934. Detraction

n. **detraction**, disparagement, depreciation, vilification, obloquy, scurrility, scandal, defamation, aspersion, traducement [*rare*], slander, calumny, obtrectation [*obs.*], evil-speaking, backbiting, scandalum magnatum [*L.*].

sarcasm, cynicism; criticism (*disapprobation*) 932; invective etc. 932; envenomed tongue; *spretae injuria formae* [*L.*].

personality, libel, lampoon, skit [*Scot. & dial.*], squib, pasquil, pasquinade; *chronique scandaleuse* [*F.*], roorback.

detractor etc. 936.

v. **detract**, derogate, decry, depreciate, disparage; run down, cry down; back-cap; belittle; pessimize [*obs.*]; sneer at etc. (*contemn*) 930; criticize, pull to pieces, pick a hole in one's coat, asperse, cast aspersions, blow upon, bespatter, blacken, vilify, vilipend, avile [*obs.*]; give a dog a bad name, brand, malign; backbite, libel, lampoon, traduce, slander, defame, calumniate, bear false witness against; speak ill of behind one's back.

muckrake; fling dirt etc. (*disrespect*) 929; anathematize etc. 932; dip the pen in gall, view in a bad light.

adj. **detracting** etc. *v.;* defamatory, traducent [*rare*], detractory, derogatory, disparaging, libelous; scurrile, scurrilous, abusive; foul-spoken, foul-tongued, foul-mouthed; slanderous, calumnious, calumniatory; sarcastic, sardonic, satirical, cynical.

935. Flatterer

n. **flatterer**, adulator, eulogist, euphemist; optimist, encomiast, laudator, booster [*colloq.*], whitewasher.

today, toadeater, sycophant, courtier, flattercap [*obs. or dial. Eng.*], pickthank [*archaic or dial.*], Damocles, Sir Pertinax MacSycophant; *flatteur* [*F.*], *prôneur* [*F.*]; puffer, *claqueur* [*F.*], claquer; tout, touter [*both colloq.*], clawback [*obs. or dial. Eng.*], slaverer; doer of dirty work; parasite, hanger-on etc. (*servility*) 886.

adj. flattering etc. 933.

936. Detractor

n. **detractor**, reprover; censor, censurer; cynic, critic, caviler, carper, word-catcher, *frondeur* [*F.*], barracker [*dial. Eng. & Austral.*].

defamer, knocker [*colloq.*], backbiter, slanderer, Sir Benjamin Backbite, lampooner, satirist, traducer, libeler, calumniator, dearest foe, Thersites; Zoilus; good-natured friend [*satirical*]; reviler, vituperator, castigator; shrew etc. 901; muckraker.

disapprover, *laudator temporis acti* [Horace].

adj. black-mouthed, abusive etc. 934.

937. Vindication

n. **vindication**, justification, warrant; exoneration, exculpation, disculpation; acquittal etc. 970; whitewashing.

extenuation, palliation, palliative, softening, mitigation.

plea etc. 617; apology, gloss, varnish; salvo [*rare*], excuse, extenuating circumstances; allowance, –to be made; *locus poenitentiae* [*L.*]; reply, defense *or* defence; recrimination etc. 938.

apologist, vindicator, justifier; defendant etc. 938.

true bill, justifiable charge.

v. **justify**, warrant; be an excuse for etc. *n.;* lend a color, furnish a handle; vindicate, exculpate, disculpate [*rare*]; acquit etc. 970; clear, set right, exonerate, whitewash; clear the skirts of.

extenuate, palliate, excuse, soften, apologize, varnish, slur, gloze; put a -gloss, -good face- upon; mince; gloss over, bolster up, help a lame dog over a stile.

advocate, defend, plead one's cause; stand up for, stick up for [*colloq.*], speak up for; contend for, speak for; bear out, keep in countenance, support; plead etc. 617; say in defense; plead ignorance; confess and avoid, propugn [*obs.*], put in a good word for.

take the will for the deed, make allowance for, do justice to; give one his due, give the Devil his due.

make good; prove the truth of, prove one's case; be justified by the event.

adj. **vindicative**, vindicatory, vindicated, vindicating etc. *v.;* palliative; exculpatory, disculpatory, apologetic.

excusable, defensible, pardonable; venial, veniable [*obs.*]; specious, plausible, justifiable.

938. Accusation

n. **accusation**, charge, imputation, slur, inculpation, exprobration [*rare*], delation; crimination, incrimination, accrimination [*obs.*], recrimination; *tu quoque* argument; invective etc. 932.

denunciation, denouncement [*archaic*]; libel, challenge, citation, arraignment, impeachment, appeachment [*obs.*], indictment, bill of indictment, true bill; lawsuit etc. 969; condemnation etc. 971.

gravamen of a charge, head and front of one's offending, *argumentum ad hominem* [*L.*]; scandal etc. (*detraction*) 934; *scandalum magnatum* [*L.*].

accuser, prosecutor, plaintiff, complainant, libelant, delator, informant, informer.

accused, defendant, prisoner, respondent, corespondent; litigant; panel.

v. **accuse**, charge, tax, impute, twit, taunt with, reproach; brand with reproach; stigmatize, slur; cast a stone at, cast a slur on; criminate, incriminate, inculpate, implicate; call to account etc. (*censure*) 932; take to -blame, -task; put in the black book.

inform against, indict, denounce, arraign; impeach, appeach [*obs.*]; have up, show up [*colloq.*], pull up [*colloq.*]; challenge, cite, lodge a complaint; prosecute, bring an action against etc. 969; blow upon [*colloq.*], squeal [*slang*].

charge with, saddle with; lay to one's -door, -charge; lay the blame on, bring home to; cast-, throw- in one's teeth; cast the first stone at.

have-, keep- a rod in pickle for; have a crow to pluck with.

trump up a charge.

adj. **accusing** etc. *v.;* accusatory, accusative, imputative, denunciatory, recriminatory, criminatory.

accused etc. *v.;* suspected; under -suspicion, -a cloud, -surveillance.

in custody, in detention, in the lockup, in the watch-house, in the jug [*slang*], in stir [*slang*], in the house of detention.

accusable, imputable, indefensible, inexcusable, unpardonable, unjustifiable; vicious etc. 845.

int. look at home! *tu quoque* [*L.*] etc. (*retaliation*) 718.

939. Probity

n. **probity**, integrity, rectitude; uprightness etc. *adj.;* honesty, faith; honor; *bonne foi* [*F.*], good faith, *bona fides* [*L.*]; purity, grace; clean hands.

constancy; faithfulness etc. *adj.;* fidelity, loyalty, incorruption [*archaic*], incorruptibility; trustworthiness etc. *adj.;* truth, candor, singleness of heart; veracity etc. 543; tender conscience etc. (*sense of duty*) 926.

fairness etc. *adj.;* fair play, justice, equity, impartiality, principle.

court of honor, a fair field and no favor; *argumentum ad verecundiam* [*L.*].

punctiliousness, punctilio, delicacy, nicety, scrupulosity, scrupulousness etc. *adj.;* scruple; point, -of honor; punctuality [*rare in this sense*].

dignity etc. (*repute*) 873; respectability, respectableness etc. *adj.*

man of honor, man of his word, gentleman, *gentilhomme* [*F.*], *fidus Achates* [*L.*], preux

940. Improbity

chevalier [*F.*], *galantuomo* [*It.*]; true-penny, trump [*slang*], brick [*slang or colloq.*], true Briton.

v. **be honorable** etc. *adj.;* deal -honorably, —squarely, —impartially, —fairly; speak the truth etc. (*veracity*) 543; draw a straight furrow; tell the truth and shame the Devil, *vitam impendere vero* [*L.*]; show a proper spirit, make a point of; do one's duty etc. (*virtue*) 944; play the game [*colloq.*].

redeem one's pledge etc. 926; keep–, be as good as- one's -promise, —word; keep faith with, not fail.

give and take, *audire alteram partem* [*L.*], give the Devil his due, put the saddle on the right horse.

redound to one's honor.

adj. **upright**; honest, —as daylight; veracious etc. 543; virtuous etc. 944; noble, honorable, reputable, respectable; fair, right, just, equitable, impartial, evenhanded, square; fair–, open- and aboveboard; white [*slang*].

inviolable, inviolate, unviolated, unbroken, unbetrayed; unbought, unbribed.

constant, —as the northern star; faithful, loyal, staunch; true, -blue, -to one's colors, -to the core, —as the needle to the pole; "marble-constant" [*Antony and Cleopatra*]; true-hearted, trusty, trustworthy; as good as one's word, to be depended on, incorruptible, honest as the day.

manly, straightforward etc. (*ingenuous*) 703; frank, candid, open-hearted.

conscientious, tender-conscienced, right-minded, high-principled, high-minded, scrupulous, religious, strict; nice, punctilious, overscrupulous, correct, punctual.

stainless, unstained, untarnished, unsullied, untainted, unperjured, uncorrupt, uncorrupted; innocent etc. 946; pure, undefiled, undepraved, undebauched; *integer vitae scelerisque purus* [Horace]; *justus et tenax propositi* [Horace]; supramundane, unworldly.

chivalrous, jealous of honor, *sans peur et sans reproche* [*F.*]; high-spirited.

adv. **honorably** etc. *adj.; bona fide* [*L.*]; on the square [*colloq.*], in good faith, in all honor, by fair means, *foro conscientiae* [*L.*], with clean hands.

int. on my honor! honor bright! [*colloq.*]; by my faith!

940. Improbity

n. **improbity**, dishonesty, dishonor; deviation from rectitude; disgrace etc. (*disrepute*) 874; fraud etc. (*deception*) 545; lying etc. 544; mouth honor etc. (*flattery*) 933; bad faith, *mala fides* [*L.*], Punic faith, *Punica fides* [*L.*]; infidelity; faithlessness etc. *adj.;* Judas kiss, betrayal; perfidy; perfidiousness etc. *adj.;* treachery, double dealing; unfairness etc. *adj.*

breach of -promise, —trust, —faith; prodition [*obs.*], disloyalty, divided allegiance, hyphenated allegiance [*cant*], treason, high treason; apostasy etc. (*tergiversation*) 607; nonobservance etc. 773.

shabbiness etc. *adj.;* villainy; baseness etc. *adj.;* abjection, debasement, degradation, turpitude, moral turpitude, laxity, trimming, shuffling.

knavery, roguery, rascality, foulplay; jobbing, jobbery, graft [*colloq.*], venality, nepotism; corruption, job, shuffle, fishy transaction; barratry [*law*], sharp practice, heads I win tails you lose.

v. **be dishonest** etc. *adj.;* play false; break one's -word, —faith, —promise; jilt, betray, forswear; shuffle etc. (*lie*) 544; play with marked cards, cheat at cards, live by one's wits, sail near the wind.

disgrace–, dishonor–, lower–, demean–, degrade- oneself; derogate, stoop, grovel, sneak, lose caste; sell oneself, squeal [*slang*], go back on [*colloq.*], go over to the enemy; seal one's infamy.

adj. **dishonest**, dishonorable; unconscientious, unscrupulous; fraudulent etc. 545; knavish; disgraceful etc. (*disreputable*) 974; wicked etc. 945.

false-hearted, disingenuous; unfair, one-sided; double, double-hearted, double-tongued, double-faced; time-serving, crooked, tortuous, insidious, Machiavellian, dark, slippery; fishy [*colloq.*], questionable.

infamous, arrant, foul, base, vile, low, ignominious, blackguard, perfidious, treacherous, perjured; hyphenated [*cant*].

contemptible, abject, mean, shabby, little, paltry, dirty, scurvy, scabby, sneaking, groveling, scrubby, rascally, barratrous [*law*], pettifogging; corrupt, venal; debased, mongrel; beneath one.

low-minded, low-thoughted, base-minded.

derogatory, degrading, undignified, indign [*obs.*], unbecoming, unbeseeming, unbefitting, *infra dignitatem* [*L.*], ungentlemanly, ungentlemanlike; unknightly, unchivalric, unmanly, unhandsome; recreant, inglorious.

faithless, of bad faith, false, unfaithful, disloyal; untrustworthy; trustless, trothless [*archaic*], lost to shame, dead to honor.

adv. **dishonestly** etc. *adj.; mala fide* [*L.*]; like a thief in the night, by crooked paths, by foul means.

int. O tempora! O mores! [Cicero].

941. Knave

n. **knave**, rogue, villain; Scapin, rascal; Lazarillo de Tormes; bad man etc. 949; blackguard etc. 949; barrator *or* barrater [*law*], shyster.

traitor, betrayer, archtraitor, conspirator, Judas, Catiline; reptile, serpent, snake in the grass, wolf in sheep's clothing, sneak, Jerry Sneak, squealer [*slang*], telltale, mischief-maker; trimmer, renegade etc. (*tergiversation*) 607; truant, recreant, slacker; sycophant etc. (*servility*) 886.

942. Disinterestedness

n. **disinterestedness** etc. *adj.;* generosity; liberality, liberalism; altruism; benevolence etc. 906; elevation, loftiness of purpose, exaltation, magnanimity; chivalry, chivalrous spirit, heroism, sublimity.

self-denial, self-abnegation, self-sacrifice, self-devotion, self-immolation, self-control etc. (*resolution*) 604; stoicism, devotion; martyrdom, suttee.

labor of love.

[comparisons] Good Shepherd, Good Samaritan, Bishop Bienvenu [Victor Hugo], Great Heart.

v. **be disinterested** etc. *adj.;* make a sacrifice, lay one's head on the block; put oneself in the place of others, do as one would be done by, do unto others as we would men should do unto us.

adj. **disinterested**, unselfish, self-denying, self-sacrificing, self-devotional.

magnanimous, noble-minded, high-minded; princely, handsome, great, high, elevated, lofty, exalted, spirited, stoical, great-hearted, large-hearted; generous, liberal, chivalrous, heroic, sublime.

unbought, unbribed; uncorrupted etc. (*upright*) 939.

943. Selfishness

n. **selfishness** etc. *adj.;* self-love, self-indulgence, self-worship, self-seeking, self-interest; egotism, egoism; *amour propre* [*F.*] etc. (*vanity*) 880; nepotism; charity that begins at home.

worldliness etc. *adj.;* world wisdom.

illiberality; meanness etc. *adj.*

self-seeker, timeserver, time-pleaser, tufthunter, fortune hunter; jobber, worldling; egotist, egoist, monopolist, nepotist; dog in the manger, *canis in praesepi* [*L.*], "foes to nobleness," temporizer, hyphenate [*cant*], trimmer; hog, road-hog, end-seat hog [*colloq.*].

v. **be selfish** etc. *adj.;* please–, indulge–, pamper–, coddle– oneself; consult one's own –wishes, –pleasure; look after one's own interest; feather one's nest; take care of number one, have an eye to the main chance, know on which side one's bread is buttered; give an inch and take an ell.

adj. **selfish**, self-seeking, self-indulgent, self-interested; wrapt up in self, centered in self; egotistic *or* egotistical, egoistic *or* egoistical.

illiberal, mean, ungenerous, narrowminded; mercenary, venal; covetous etc. 819.

worldly, unspiritual, earthly, earthly -minded, mundane, worldly-minded, worldly-wise; timeserving.

interested; *alieni appetens sui profusus* [Sallust].

adv. **ungenerously** etc. *adj.;* to gain some private ends, from selfish motives, from interested motives.

944. Virtue

n. **virtue**; virtuousness etc. *adj.;* morality; moral rectitude; integrity etc. (*probity*) 939; nobleness etc. 873.

merit, worth, desert, excellence, credit; self-control etc. (*resolution*) 604; self-denial etc. (*temperance*) 953.

well-doing; good actions, good behavior; discharge–, fulfillment–, performance- of duty; well-spent life; innocence etc. 946.

morals; ethics etc. (*duty*) 926; cardinal virtues.

[science of virtue] aretaics (*contrasted with* eudemonism); aretology.

v. **be virtuous** etc. *adj.;* practice virtue etc. *n.;* do–, fulfill–, perform–, discharge- one's duty; redeem one's pledge etc. 926; act well, –one's part; fight the good fight; acquit oneself well; command–, master- one's passions; keep in the right path, keep on the straight and narrow way.

set an example, set a good example; be on one's -good, –best- behavior.

adj. **virtuous**, good; innocent etc. 646; meritorious, deserving, worthy, desertful [*rare*], correct; dutiful, duteous; moral, right, righteous, right-minded; well-intentioned, creditable, laudable, commendable, praiseworthy; above praise, beyond all praise; excellent, admirable; sterling, pure, noble; whole-souled.

exemplary; matchless, peerless, saintly, saintlike; heaven-born, angelic, seraphic, godlike.

adv. **virtuously** etc. *adj.; e merito* [*L.*].

945. Vice

n. **vice**; evildoing, evil courses; wrongdoing; wickedness, viciousness etc. *adj.;* hardness of heart;

946. Innocence

iniquity, peccability, demerit; sin, Adam, old Adam, offending Adam.

immorality, impropriety, indecorum, scandal, laxity, looseness of morals; want of -principle -ballast; knavery, etc. (*improbity*) 940; atrocity, brutality etc. (*malevolence*) 907; obliquity, backsliding, infamy.

depravity, demoralization, pravity, pollution; corruption etc. (*debasement*) 659; profligacy; flagrancy, unnatural desires, unnatural habits, Sadism, Lesbianism, sodomy; lust etc. 961.

lowest dregs of vice, sink of iniquity, Alsatian den; *gusto picaresco* [*L*.].

cannibalism, endocannibalism, endophagy; exocannibalism, exophagy; "long pig" [*humorous*].

weakness etc. *adj.;* infirmity, weakness of the flesh, frailty, imperfection, error; weak side; foible; failing, failure; crying sin, besetting sin; defect, deficiency; cloven foot.

fault, crime; criminality etc. (*guilt*) 947.

reprobate; sinner etc. 949.

[resorts] brothel etc. 961; gambling house etc. 621; joint [*slang*], opium den.

v. **be vicious** etc. *adj.;* sin, commit sin, do amiss, err, transgress; misdemean-, forget-, misconduct- oneself; misdo [*rare*], misbehave; fall, lapse, slip, trip, offend, trespass; deviate from the -line of duty, -path of virtue etc. 944; take a wrong course, go astray; hug a sin, hug a fault; sow one's wild oats.

render vicious etc. *adj.;* demoralize, brutalize; corrupt etc. (*degrade*) 659.

adj. **vicious**; sinful; sinning etc. *v.;* wicked, iniquitous, immoral, unrighteous, wrong, criminal; unprincipled, lawless, disorderly, dissolute, profligate, scampish; worthless, desertless [*rare*], disgraceful, recreant, disreputable; demoralizing, degrading.

miscreated, misbegotten; demoralized, corrupt, depraved; Sadistic, degenerate.

evil-minded, evil-disposed; ill-conditioned; malevolent etc. 907; heartless, graceless, shameless, virtueless, abandoned, lost to virtue; unconscionable; sunk-, lost-, deep-, steeped- in iniquity.

base, sinister, scurvy, foul, gross, vile, black, grave, facinorous [*obs*.], felonious, nefarious, shameful, scandalous, infamous, villainous, of a deep dye, heinous; flagrant, flagitious, atrocious, incarnate, accursed.

diabolic or diabolical, Mephistophelian, satanic, hellish, infernal, stygian, fiendlike, hellborn, demoniacal, devilish, fiendish.

incorrigible, irreclaimable, obdurate, reprobate, past praying for; culpable, reprehensible etc. (*guilty*) 947.

unjustifiable, indefensible, inexcusable, inexpiable, unpardonable, irremissible.

improper, unseemly, indecorous, indiscreet, *contra bonos mores* [*L*.], unworthy, blameworthy, reprehensible, uncommendable, discreditable; naughty, incorrect, unduteous, undutiful.

weak, frail, lax, infirm, imperfect; spineless, invertebrate [*both fig.*]; dotty [*slang*].

adv. wrong; sinfully etc. *adj.;* without excuse.

int. fie upon! it smells to heaven!

946. Innocence

n. **innocence**; guiltlessness etc. *adj.;* incorruption, impeccability, inerrability, inerrableness.

clean hands, clear conscience, *mens sibi conscia recti* [Virgil].

innocent, new-born babe; lamb, dove.

v. **be innocent** etc. *adj.; nil conscire sibi nulla pallescere culpa* [Horace].

acquit etc. 970; exculpate etc. (*vindicate*) 937.

adj. **innocent**, not guilty; unguilty; guiltless, faultless, sinless, stainless, bloodless, spotless; clear, immaculate; *rectus in curia* [*L*.]; unspotted, unblemished, unerring; undefiled etc. 939; unhardened, Saturnian; Arcadian etc. (*artless*) 703; paradisaic or paradisaical, paradisiac or paradisiacal.

inculpable, unculpable [*rare*], unblamed, unblamable, blameless, unfallen, inerrable, above suspicion, irreproachable, irreprovable [*rare*], irreprehensible; unexceptionable, unobjectionable, unimpeachable; salvable; venial etc. 937.

virtuous etc. 944; unreproved, unimpeached, unreproached.

harmless, inoffensive, innoxious [*obs*.], innocuous; dovelike; lamblike; pure, harmless as doves; innocent as -a lamb, -the babe unborn; "more sinned against than sinning" [*Lear*].

adv. **innocently** etc. *adj.;* with clean hands; with a -clear, -safe- conscience.

947. Guilt

n. **guilt**, guiltiness, culpability, criminality, criminousness [*obs*.]; deviation from rectitude etc. (*improbity*) 940; sinfulness etc. (*vice*) 945; peccability.

misconduct, misbehavior, misdoing, misdeed; fault, sin, error, transgression; dereliction, delinquency.

indiscretion, lapse, slip, trip, *faux pas* [*F.*], peccadillo; flaw, blot, omission, failing, failure; blunder, break *or* bad break [*colloq.*].

offense, trespass; misdemeanor, tort [*law*], delict, *delictum* [*L.*]; misfeasance [*law*], misprision, misprision of treason *or* felony [*law*]; malfeasance [*law*], official misconduct, nonfeasance [*law*]; malefaction, malversation, corruption, malpractice; crime, felony, capital crime.

enormity, atrocity, outrage; unpardonable sin, deadly sin, mortal sin; "deed without a name" [*Macbeth*].

corpus delicti [*L.*], body of the crime, substantial facts, fundamental facts, damning evidence.

adj. **guilty**, blamable, culpable, peccable, in fault, censurable, reprehensible, blameworthy.

objectionable, exceptionable, uncommendable, illaudable; weighed in the balance and found wanting.

adv. **in the very act**, *in flagrante delicto* [*L.*], redhanded.

948. Good Man
[good woman]

n. **good man**, worthy.

model, paragon etc. (*perfection*) 650; good example; hero, demigod, seraph, angel; saint etc. (*piety*) 987; benefactor etc. 912; philanthropist etc. 910; Aristides; noble liver, pattern.

salt of the earth; one in ten thousand; a man among men, white man [*slang*]; brick [*slang*], trump [*slang*], rough diamond.

good woman, virgin, innocent; goddess, queen, Madonna, ministering angel, heaven's noblest gift; "a perfect woman, nobly planned" [*Wordsworth*].

949. Bad Man
[bad woman]

n. **bad man**, wrongdoer, worker of iniquity; evildoer etc. 913; sinner, transgressor; the wicked etc. 945; bad example.

rascal, scoundrel, villain, miscreant, budmash [*India*], caitiff, wretch, reptile, viper, serpent, cockatrice, basilisk; tiger, monster; devil etc. (*demon*) 980; devil incarnate; demon in human shape, Nana Sahib; hellhound, rakehell.

roué [*F.*], rake; Sadist, one who has sold himself to the devil, fallen angel, *âme damnée* [*F.*], *vaurien* [*F.*], *mauvais sujet* [*F.*], loose fish [*colloq.*], rounder [*slang*]; lost sheep, black sheep; castaway, recreant, defaulter; prodigal etc. 818.

bad woman, jade, Jezebel, hell-cat, quean, wench, slut; adultress etc. 962.

rough, rowdy, ugly customer, ruffian, bully, tough [*colloq.*], hoodlum etc. 886; Jonathan Wild; hangman; incendiary, fire bug; thief etc. 792; murderer etc. 361.

culprit, delinquent, criminal, malefactor, misdemeanant; felon; convict, jailbird *or* gaolbird, ticket-of-leave man [*Brit.*]; outlaw.

riffraff, scum of the earth; blackguard, *polisson* [*F.*], loafer, sneak, rascalion *or* rascallion; cullion, mean wretch, varlet [*archaic*], kern [*obs.*], *âme-de-boue* [*F.*], *drôle* [*F.*]; cur, dog, hound, whelp, mongrel; losel [*archaic or dial.*], loon *or* lown [*obs. or dial. variant*], ronion *or* ronyon *or* runnion [*obs. or rare*]; outcast, vagabond, runagate; rogue etc. (*knave*) 941.

scamp, scapegrace, rip [*colloq.*], ne'er-do-well, good for nothing, reprobate, scalawag *or* scallawag [*colloq.*], sad dog [*colloq.*], limb [*colloq.*], rapscallion [*all the words in this paragraph are commonly applied jocularly or lightly*].

int. sirrah!

950. Penitence

n. **penitence**, contrition, compunction, repentance, remorse; regret etc. 833.

self-reproach, self-reproof, self-accusation, self-condemnation, self-humiliation; stings-, pangs-, qualms-, prickings-, twinge-, twitch-, touch-, voice- of conscience; "compunctious visitings of nature" [*Macbeth*].

acknowledgment, confession etc. (*disclosure*) 529; apology etc. 952; recantation etc. 607; penance etc. 952; resipiscence [*rare*].

awakened conscience, deathbed repentance, *locus poenitentiae* [*L.*], stool of repentance, cutty stool [*Scot.*], mourners' bench [*local*].

penitent, repentant [*rare*], Magdalen, prodigal son, returned prodigal, "a sadder and a wiser man" [*Coleridge*].

v. **repent**, be sorry for; be penitent etc. *adj.*; rue; regret etc. 833; think better of; recant etc. 607; knock under etc. (*submit*) 725; plead guilty; sing -*miserere*, -*de profundis* [*L.*]; cry *peccavi* [*L.*]; say *culpa mea* [*L.*], own oneself in the wrong; acknowledge, confess etc. (*disclose*) 529; humble oneself; beg pardon etc. (*apologize*) 952; turn over a new leaf, put on the new man, turn from sin; repent in sackcloth and ashes etc. (*do penance*) 952; learn by experience.

reclaim, reform, regenerate, redeem, convert, amend, set straight again, make a new man of, restore self-respect.

951. Impenitence

adj. **penitent**; repenting etc. *v.;* repentant, contrite, softened, melted, touched; conscience-smitten, conscience-stricken; self-accusing, self-convicted.
 penitential, penitentiary; reclaimed; not hardened: unhardened.
adv. mea culpa [*L.*]; de profundis [*L.*].

951. Impenitence

n. **impenitence**, irrepentance, recusancy, recusance; lack of contrition.
 hardness of heart, heart of stone, seared conscience, induration, obduracy; deaf ears.
v. **be impenitent** etc. *adj.;* steel the heart, harden the heart; turn away from the light; die game, die and make no sign.
adj. **impenitent**, uncontrite, obdurate, hard, hardened, seared, recusant, unrepentant; relentless, remorseless, graceless, shriftless.
 lost, incorrigible, irreclaimable.
 unreclaimed, unreformed; unrepented, unatoned.

952. Atonement

n. **atonement**, reparation; compromise, composition; compensation etc. 30; quittance, quits [*rare*], expiation, redemption, reclamation, conciliation, propitiation; indemnification, redress.
 amends, apology, amende honorable [*F.*], satisfaction; peace–, sin–, burnt- offering; scapegoat, sacrifice.
 penance, fasting, maceration, sackcloth and ashes, white sheet, shrift, flagellation, lustration; purgation, purgatory.
v. **atone**, atone for; expiate; propitiate; make amends, make good; reclaim, redeem, repair, ransom, absolve, purge, shrive, do penance, stand in a white sheet, repent in sackcloth and ahses.
 set one's house in order, wipe off old scores, make matters up; pay the forfeit, pay the penalty.
 apologize, express regret, beg pardon, faire l'amende honorable [*F.*], give satisfaction; get–, fall- down on one's knees, –marrowbones [*slang or jocular*].
adj. **propitiatory**, expiatory, sacrifice, sacrificial, sacrificatory [*rare*]; piacular, piaculous [*rare*].

953. Temperance

n. **temperance**, moderation, sobriety, soberness.
 forbearance, abnegation; self-denial, self-restraint, self-control etc. (*resolution*) 604.
 abstinence, abstemiousness, asceticism; Encratism, prohibition; frugality; vegetarianism, teetotalism, total abstinence; system of -Pythagoras, –Cornaro; Pythagorism; Stoicism.
 abstainer, Pythagorean, gymnosophist; nephalist, teetotaler etc. 958; Encratite, vegetarian, fruitarian, hydropot [*rare*]; ascetic etc. 995.
v. **be temperate** etc. *adj.;* abstain, forbear, refrain, deny oneself, spare; know when one has had enough; take the pledge; prohibit; control the -old Adam, –carnal man, –fleshly lusts; refrain from indulgence, look not upon the wine when it is red.
adj. **temperate**, moderate, sober, frugal, sparing, abstemious, abstinent; within compass; measured etc. (*sufficient*) 639.
 Pythagorean; vegetarian, fruitarian; teetotal.

954. Intemperance

n. **intemperance**, sensuality, rakery [*rare*], animalism, carnality; tragalism; pleasure; effiminacy, silkiness; luxury, luxuriousness; lap of -pleasure, –luxury; free-living.
 indulgence; high living, inabstinence, self-indulgence; voluptuousness etc. *adj.;* epicurism, epicureanism, sybaritism.
 dissipation; licentiousness etc. *adj.;* debauchery; crapulence.
 revel, revels, revelry, orgy; drunkenness etc. 959; debauch, carousal, jollification [*colloq.*], high old time [*colloq.*], drinking bout, wassail, saturnalia, excess, too much.
 drug habit; Circean cup; bhang, hashish, opium, hop [*slang*], dope [*slang*], cocaine; drug fiend, dope fiend [*slang*].
v. **be intemperate** etc. *adj.;* indulge, exceed; live -well, –high, –on the fat of the land; eat drink and be merry, look upon the wine when it is red, dine not wisely but too well; give free rein to indulgence etc. *n.;* wallow in voluptuousness etc. *n.;* plunge into dissipation; sensualize, brutify, carnalize.
 revel, rake, live hard, run riot, sow one's wild oats; slake one's -appetite, –thirst; swill; pamper.
adj. **intemperate**, inabstinent, excessive; sensual, self-indulgent; voluptuous, licentious, wild, dissolute, rakish, fast, debauched; orgiastic, Corybantic, Paphian.
 brutish, crapulous, swinish, piggish, hoggish, beastlike, theroid [*med.*].
 luxurious, Epicurean, Sybaritical; bred–, nursed- in the lap of luxury; indulged, pampered; full fed, high fed.
 intoxicated, drunk etc. 959.

954a. Sensualist

n. **sensualist**, Sybarite, voluptuary, Sardanapalus, man of pleasure, carpet knight; epicure, epicurean, *gourmet* [*F.*]; gourmand; glutton etc. 957; pig, hog; votary–, swine- of Epicurus; Heliogabalus; free liver, hard liver; libertine etc. 962; hedonist; tragalist.

955. Asceticism

n. **asceticism**, puritanism, sabbatarianism; cynicism, austerity; total abstinence; nephalism; Yoga.

mortification, maceration, sackcloth and ashes, flagellation; penance etc. 952; fasting etc. 956; martyrdom.

ascetic, anchoret *or* anchorite, *Heautontimorumenos* [*Gr.*]; hermit etc. (*recluse*) 893; puritan, sabbatarian, cynic; bhikshu, sannyasi *or* sanyasi, yogi [*all Hindu*]; dervish, fakir [*both Moham.*]; martyr.

adj. **ascetic**, austere, puritanical; cynical; over-religious; acerb, acerbic.

956. Fasting

n. **fasting**; xerophagy; famishment, starvation.

fast, *jour maigre* [*F.*]; fast day, banyan day; Lent, quadragesima; Ramadan *or* Ramazan [*Moham.*]; spare–, meager- diet; lenten -diet, –entertainment; *soupe maigre* [*F.*], short commons, Barmecide feast; short rations; punishment of Tantalus.

v. **fast**, starve, clem [*obs.*], famish, perish with hunger; dine with Duke Humphrey; make two bites of a cherry; "keep the larder lean."

adj. **fasting** etc.*v.;* lenten, quadragesimal; unfed; starved etc. *v.;* half-starved; hungry etc. 865.

957. Gluttony

n. **gluttony**; greed; greediness etc. *adj.;* voracity.

epicurism, gastronomy; good–, high-living; edacity, gulosity [*rare*], crapulence; guttling, guzzle [*rare*], guzzling; pantophagy.

feast etc. (*food*) 298; good cheer, blow out [*slang*]; *batterie de cuisine* [*F.*].

glutton, gormandizer, gourmand, cormorant, pig, hog etc. (*sensualist*) 954a; guttler, pantophagist; belly-god, Apicius, gastronome.

epicure, *bon vivant* [*F.*], gourmand *gourmet* [*F.*], gourmet.

v. **gormandize**, gorge; overgorge oneself, overeat oneself, glut, satiate, engorge, eat one's fill, cram, stuff, guttle, guzzle, bolt, devour, gobble up; overindulge; gulp etc. (*swallow food*) 298; raven, eat out of house and home; have the stomach of an ostrich; play a good knife and fork etc. (*appetite*) 865; have a capacious -gorge, –maw.

pamper [*obs. as glut*], indulge.

adj. **gluttonous**, greedy; gormandizing etc. *v.;* edacious, omnivorous, pantophagic, pantophagous, voracious, devouring, all-devouring, crapulent, swinish.

pampered [*obs. as* fed to excess]; overfed, overgorged, overindulged.

958. Sobriety

n. **sobriety**; teetotalism, nephalism.

water-drinker; hydropot [*rare*], prohibitionist; teetotaler *or* teetotaller, abstainer, nephalist, Good Templar, band of hope, W. C. T. U. (Women's Christian Temperance Union).

v. take the pledge, swear off.

adj. **sober**, –as a judge; temperate, moderate.

959. Drunkenness

n. **drunkenness** etc. *adj.;* intemperance; drinking etc. *v.;* inebriety, inebriation, ebriety [*rare*], ebriosity [*rare*], insobriety, intoxication; temulence [*rare*], bibacity, wine-bibbing; compotation, potation; deep potations, bacchanals, bacchanalia, bacchanalianism, libations; bender [*slang*].

alcoholism, oinomania, dipsomania; delirium tremens, D. T.'s [*colloq.*]; *mania a potu* [*L.*].

drink, alcoholic drinks, alcohol, blue ruin [*slang*], booze *or* bouse [*colloq.*], "the luscious liquor" [Milton]; grog, port wine, punch; punchbowl, cup, rosy wine, flowing bowl; drop, –too much; dram; beer etc. (*beverage*) 298; *aguardiente* [*Sp.*]; apple-brandy, apple-jack; bourbon; brandy, brandy smesh; chain lightning [*slang*], champagne, cocktail; gin, ginsling; highball, peg [*slang, orig. India*]; burra (*or* bara) peg, chota peg [*both India*]; rum, schnapps, sherry, xeres, sling, usquebaugh, vodka, whisky *or* whiskey, rye; stirrup cup, parting cup, doch-an-dorrach *or* doch-an-dorris [*Scot.*].

illicit distilling; moonshining, moonshine *or* moonshine whisky [*colloq.*], hooch [*slang*], home-brew; white lightning; moonshiner [*colloq.*], bootlegger [*slang*].

drunkard, sot, toper, tippler, bibber, winebibber; hard–, gin–, dram- drinker; soaker [*slang*], sponge [*slang*], tun [*jocose*], love-pot, tosspot, guzzler, guzzle [*rare*], barfly, boozer *or* bouser [*colloq.*], bum [*slang*], tavern haunter, thirsty soul, reveler, carouser, Bacchanal, Bac-

960. Purity

chanalian; Bacchae, bacchante, maenad; devotee to Bacchus.

v. **get** *or* **be drunk** etc. *adj.;* see double; take a -drop, -glass- too much; get smashed [*slang*]; drink, tipple, tope [*colloq.*], booze *or* bouse [*colloq.*], guzzle, swill [*slang*], soak [*slang*], sot [*rare*], bum [*slang*], besot, have a jag on [*slang*], lush [*slang*], bib [*obs. or dial.*], swig [*dial. or colloq.*], carouse; sacrifice at the shrine of Bacchus; take to drinking; drink -hard, -deep, -like a fish; have one's swill [*slang*], drain the cup, splice the main brace [*slang*], take a hair of the dog that bit you.

liquor, liquor up [*both slang*], wet one's -whistle, -clay, -swallow [*colloq. or humorous*]; wet the red lane [*humorous*]; raise the elbow, raise the little finger, hit the booze [*slang*], take a whet; crack a-, pass the- bottle; toss off etc. (*drink up*) 298; go to the -alehouse, -public house, -saloon.

make one drunk etc. *adj.;* inebriate, fuddle [*colloq.*], befuddle, fuzzle [*obs.*], get into one's head.

sell illicitly, bootleg [*slang*].

adj. **drunk**, tipsy, intoxicated, bibacious, inebrious, inebriate, inebriated; in one's cups; in a state of intoxication etc. *n.;* temulent, temulentive [*both rare*]; fuddled [*colloq.*], mellow, cut [*slang*], boozy *or* bousy [*colloq.*], full [*vulgar*], fou [*Scot.*], lit up [*slang*], glorious [*humorous*], fresh [*slang*], merry, elevated; flush, flushed, flustered, disguised [*archaic*], groggy [*colloq.*], beery; top-heavy; pot-valiant, potulent [*obs.*], squiffy [*slang*]; overcome, overtaken [*obs.*], whittled [*obs.*]; screwed, tight, primed, corned, raddled, smashed, stoned, sewed up, lushy [*all slang*], muzzy [*colloq.*], nappy [*rare*], muddled, obfuscated, maudlin; crapulous, blind drunk, dead drunk.

inter pocula [*L.*], in liquor, the worse for liquor; having had a drop too much, half-seas over [*slang*], three sheets in the wind [*sailors' slang*], under the table.

drunk as -a piper, -a fiddler, -a lord, -Chloe, -an owl, -David's sow, -a wheelbarrow [*all colloq.*].

drunken, bibacious, sottish; given-, addicted- to -drink, -the bottle; toping etc. *v.;* primed, -on the hip; heeled [*slang*].

960. Purity

n. **purity**; decency, decorum, delicacy; continence, chastity, honesty, virtue, modesty, shame; pudicity, pucelage [*rare*], virginity.

virgin, vestal, prude; Lucretia, Diana, Athena Parthenos; Joseph, Hippolytus.

adj. **pure**, undefiled, modest, delicate, decent, decorous; *virginibus puerisque* [*L.*]; chaste, continent, virtuous, honest, Platonic.

961. Impurity

n. **impurity**; uncleanness etc. (*filth*) 653; immodesty; grossness etc. *adj.;* indelicacy, indecency, impudicity, obscenity, ribaldry, smut, bawdry, *double entente, équivoque* [*F.*]; pornography.

incontinence, debauchery, libertinism, libertinage, fornication, wenching, venery, dissipation.

concupiscence, lust, carnality, flesh, salacity; pruriency, lechery, lasciviousness, lewdness, lasciviency [*obs.*], lubricity; Sadism, Sapphism, Lesbianism, nymphomania, aphrodisia, satyriasis.

seduction; defloration, defilement, abuse, violation, stupration, rape; incest.

social evil, harlotry, whoredom, concubinage, cuckoldom, adultery, advoutry [*obs.*], crim. con.; free-love.

intrigue, amour, amourette, *liaison* [*F.*], *faux pas* [*F.*], entanglement; gallantry.

[resorts] brothel, bagnio, stew, bawdyhouse, lupanar, house of ill fame, bordel [*obs.*]; Yoshiwara [*Jap.*], red-light district.

harem, seraglio, zenana [*India*].

v. **be impure** etc. *adj.;* debauch, defile, seduce; prostitute; abuse, violate, rape, stuprate [*rare*], deflower; commit adultery etc. *n.;* intrigue.

adj. **impure**; unclean etc. (*dirty*) 653; not to be mentioned to ears polite; immodest, shameless, indecorous, indelicate, indecent, Fescennine; loose, *risqué* [*F.*], coarse, gross, broad, free, equivocal, smutty, fulsome, ribald, obscene, bawdy, pornographic.

concupiscent, prurient, lickerish, rampant, lustful; carnal, carnal-minded; lewd, lascivious, lecherous, libidinous, erotic, ruttish, must *or* musty [*said of elephants*]; salacious, Paphian, voluptuous; goatish, beastly, bestial, incestuous.

unchaste, light, wanton, licentious, adulterous, debauched, dissolute; of loose character, of easy virtue; frail, gay, riggish [*obs.*], incontinent, meretricious, rakish, gallant, dissipated; no better than she should be; on the town, on the streets, on the *pavé* [*F.*], on the loose [*colloq.*].

962. Libertine

n. **libertine**; voluptuary etc. 954*a;* rake, debauchee, loose fish [*colloq.*], rip [*colloq.*], rakehell, fast man; intrigant, gallant, seducer, fornicator, lecher, satyr, goat, whoremonger, *paillard* [*F.*], advocater [*obs.*], adulterer, gay deceiver, Lothario, Don Juan, Bluebeard; chartered libertine.

adultress, advoutress [*obs.*], courtesan, prostitute, strumpet, harlot, whore, hooker [*slang*], punk [*obsoles.*], *fille de joie* [*F.*], woman, woman of the town, streetwalker, Cyprian, miss [*obs.*], piece [*slang*], demirep, wench, trollop, trull, baggage, hussy, drab, bitch [*low*], jade, skit [*obs.*], rig [*obs.*], quean, mopsy [*dial. Eng.*], slut, minx, harridan; unfortunate, –female, –woman; woman -of easy virtue etc. (*unchaste*) 961; wanton, fornicatress; *lorette* [*F.*], *cocotte* [*F.*], *petite dame* [*F.*], grisette; demimondaine; chippy [*slang*]; Sapphist; white slave.

Jezebel, Messalina, Delilah, Thais, Phryne, Aspasia, Lais.

demimonde, erring sisters, fallen women, frail sisterhood.

mistress, concubine, kept woman, doxy, *chère amie* [*F.*]; *bona roba* [*It.*]; spiritual wife.

procurer, pimp, pander *or* pandar, bawd, *conciliatrix* [*L.*], procuress, mackerel [*archaic*], wittol [*obs.*].

963. Legality

n. **legality**, legitimacy, legitimateness; legitimatization, legitimization.

law, code, *corpus juris* [*L.*], constitution, pandect, charter, act, enactment, statute, rule; canon etc. (*precept*) 697; ordinance, institution, regulation; bylaw *or* bye-law; rescript, decree etc. (*order*) 741; ordonnance; standing order; plebiscite etc. (*choice*) 609; legislature.

legal process; form, formula, formality, rite, arm of the law; *habeas corpus* [*L.*]; *fieri facias* [*L.*].

equity, common law; *lex scripta* [*L.*]; *lex non scripta* [*L.*], unwritten law; law of nations, *droit des gens* [*F.*], international law, *jus gentium* [*L.*]; *jus civile* [*L.*]; civil–, canon–, crown–, criminal–, statute–, ecclesiastical- law; *lex mercatoria* [*L.*].

constitutionalism, constitutionality; justice etc. 922.

[science of law] jurisprudence, nomology; legislation, codification, nomography.

v. **legalize**, legitimate, legitimize, legitimatize; enact, ordain; decree etc. (*order*) 741; pass a law, legislate; codify, formulate, formalize, regularize, authorize.

adj. **legal**, legitimate; according to law; vested, constitutional, chartered, legalized; lawful etc. (*permitted*) 760; statutable, statutory; legislatorial, legislative; judicial, juridical; nomistic, nomothetical.

adv. **legally** etc. *adj.;* in the eye of the law; *de jure* [*L.*].

964. Illegality
[absence or violation of law]

n. **lawlessness**; illicitness; breach–, violation- of law; disobedience etc. 742; unconformity etc. 83; arbitrariness etc. *adj.;* antinomy, violence, brute force, despotism, tyranny, outlawry.

mob–, lynch–, club–, Lydford–, martial–, drumhead- law; *coup d'état* [*F.*]; *le droit du plus fort* [*F.*]; *argumentum baculinum* [*L.*].

illegality, informality, unlawfulness, illegitimacy, bar sinister.

trover and conversion; smuggling, bootlegging [*slang*], illicit distilling etc. 959; poaching; simony.

v. **violate the law**, offend against the law, set the law at defiance, ride roughshod over, drive a coach and six through a statute; make the law a dead letter, take the law into one's own hands.

smuggle, run, poach, bootleg [*slang*].

adj. **illegal**; prohibited etc. 761; not allowed, unlawful, illegitimate, illicit, contraband, actionable.

unchartered, unconstitutional; unwarranted, unwarrantable, unauthorized; informal, unofficial, injudicial [*rare*], extra-judicial.

lawless, arbitrary, despotic, despotical; summary, irresponsible; unanswerable, unaccountable.

null and void; a dead letter.

adv. **illegally** etc. *adj.;* with a high hand, in violation of law.

965. Jurisdiction
[executive]

n. **jurisdiction**, judicature, administration of justice; soc, soke [*both A. S. & early Eng. law*]; executive, commission of the peace; magistracy etc. (*authority*) 737; judge etc. 967; tribunal etc. 966.

city government, municipal government, commission government, Oregon plan; municipality, corporation, bailiwick, shrievalty; police, police force; constabulary, Bumbledom.

966. Tribunal

executive officer, officer, commissioner, lord lieutenant [*Brit.*], collector [*India*]; city manager, mayor, alderman, councilor *or* councillor, selectman; bailiff, tipstaff, bumbailiff [*Eng.*], catchpole *or* catchpoll, beadle; sheriff, shrieve [*obs.*], bailie [*Scot.*], constable; policeman, police constable, police sergeant, patrolman etc. 664; *sbirro* [*It.*], alguazil, *gendarme* [*F.*], kavass [*Turk.*], lictor, mace bearer, *huissier* [*F.*], tithingman; excise man, gauger *or* gager, customhouse officer, *douanier* [*F.*]; press gang *or* pressgang.

coroner, aedile *or* edile; reeve, portreeve [*early Eng. hist.*], paritor [*obs.*], *posse comitatus* [*L.*].

bureau, cutcherry [*India*], department, portfolio, secretariat.

v. **judge**, sit in judgment; have jurisdiction over.

adj. **executive**, administrative, judicative, municipal; inquisitorial, causidical; judicatory, judiciary, judicial, juridical.

adv. *coram judice* [*L.*].

966. Tribunal

n. **tribunal**, court, curia, board, bench, judicature, judicatory; court of -justice, –law, –arbitration; inquisition; guild; durbar [*India*], divan [*Oriental*], Areopagus.

justice–, judgment–, mercy-seat; woolsack; bar, bar of justice; dock; forum, hustings, bureau, drumhead; jury-box; witness box, witness stand.

senate-house, town hall, theater *or* theatre; House of Commons, House of Lords; statehouse, townhouse, courthouse.

[British courts], sessions; petty–, quarter–, special–, general- sessions [*Eng. law*]; assizes; eyre, justices in eyre, wardmote, burghmote, barmote, courtleet, court-baron, court of piepoudre [*all old Eng. law*]; superior courts of Westminster; court of -record, –oyer and terminer, –assize, –appeal, –error; High court of -Judicature, –Appeal; Judicial Committee of the Privy Council; Star Chamber; Court of -Chancery, –King's *or* Queen's Bench, –Exchequer, –Common Pleas, –Probate, –Admiralty; Lords Justices'–, Rolls–, Vice Chancellor's–, Stannary–, Divorce–, Palatine–, county–, police- court; Court of Criminal Appeal; Court of Small Causes [*India*]; court of common council; board of green cloth.

[United States courts] United States -Supreme Court, –District Court, –Circuit Court of Appeal; Federal Court of Claims, Court of Private Land Claims; Supreme Court, court of sessions, criminal court, police court, juvenile court, night court [*colloq.*], municipal court.

court-martial (*pl.* courts-martial), drumhead court-martial.

ecclesiastical court, Rota *or* Rota Romana [*R. C. Ch.*]; Court of Arches [*Eng.*].

Papal Court, Curia.

adj. **judicial** etc. 965; appellate; curial.

967. Judge

n. **judge**, justice; justiciar [*Eng. [Scot. hist.*]; justiciary [*Eng. & Scot. hist.*]; chancellor; justice–, judge- of assize; recorder, common serjeant; puisne–, assistant–, county court- judge; conservator–, justice- of the peace; J.P.; "the Great Unpaid" [*Eng.*]; court etc. (*tribunal*) 966; deemster [*Isle of Man & archaic*], moderator, bencher [*archaic*], jurat, magistrate, police magistrate, beak [*slang*]; his worship, his honor, his lordship; the court.

Lord Chancellor, Lord Justice; Master of the Rolls, Vice Chancellor; Lord Chief -Justice, –Baron; Chief Justice; Mr. Justice; Baron, –of the Exchequer.

assessor; arbiter, arbitrator, doomsman *or* domesman [*obs.*], umpire, referee, referendary [*rare*]; revising barrister [*Eng.*], receiver, official receiver; censor etc. (*critic*) 480; barmaster [*Eng.*].

archon, tribune, praetor, ephor, syndic, podesta [*It.*]; mollah, ulema, hakim, mufti, cadi *or* kadi [*all Moham.*]; alcalde [*Sp.*]; Rhadamanthus, Minos, Solomon.

jury, grand jury, petty jury, inquest, panel, country; twelve men in a box.

juror, juryman, talesman; grand-juror, grand-juryman, recognitor; petty-juror, petty-juryman.

litigant etc. (*accusation*) 938.

v. **adjudge** etc. (*determine*) 480; try a case, try a prisoner.

adj. judicial etc. 965.

968. Lawyer

n. **lawyer**, jurist, legist, pundit [*India*], civilian, publicist, jurisconsult, legal adviser, advocate; barrister, barrister-at-law; counsel, counselor *or* counsellor, King's *or* Queen's counsel; K. C.; Q. C.; silk *or* silk gown; junior counsel, stuff *or* stuff gown; leader, serjeant-at-law, bencher, pleader, special pleader; tubman [*Eng. law*], judge etc. 967.

solicitor, attorney, vakil *or* vakeel [*India*], proctor; equity draftsman, conveyancer, notary, –public; scrivener, cursitor [*Eng. law*]; writer, –to the signet; S.S.C.; limb of the law; pettifogger, shyster.

bar, legal profession, gentlemen of the long robe; junior–, outer–, inner– bar; Inns of Court [*Eng.*].

v. **practice law**; practice at (*or* within) the bar, plead; call to (*or* within) the bar, be called to (*or* within) the bar; admitted to the bar, take silk.

disbar, disbench [*Eng. law*], degrade.

adj. learned in the law; at the bar; forensic.

969. Lawsuit

n. **lawsuit**, suit, action, cause; litigation; suit in law; dispute etc. 713.

writ, summons, subpoena, citation, latitat [*Eng. law*]; *nisi prius, venire, venire facias, habeas corpus* [*all L.*].

arraignment, prosecution, impeachment; accusation etc. 938; presentment, true bill, indictment.

arrest, apprehension, committal, commitment; imprisonment etc. (*restraint*) 751.

pleadings; declaration, bill, claim; *procès-verbal* [*F.*], bill of right, information, *corpus delicti* [*L.*]; affidavit, state of facts, libel; answer, replication, plea, demurrer, rebutter, rejoinder; surrebutter, surrejoinder.

suitor, libelant *or* libellant, party to a suit; litigant etc. 938.

hearing, trial; judgment, sentence, finding, verdict etc. 480; appeal, –motion; writ of error; certiorari.

case, decision, precedent; decided case, reports.

v. **go to law**, appeal to the law; bring to -justice, –trial, –the bar; put on trial, pull up; accuse etc. 938; prefer *or* file a claim etc. *n.;* take the law of [*colloq.*], inform against.

cite, summon, summons, serve with a writ, arraign, sue, prosecute, bring an action against, indict, impeach, attach, distrain, commit; apprehend, arrest; give in charge etc. (*restrain*) 751.

empanel a jury, challenge the jurors; implead, join issue; close the pleadings; set down for hearing.

try, hear a cause; sit in judgment; adjudicate etc. 480.

adj. **litigious** etc. (*quarrelsome*) 713; *qui tam, coram judice, sub judice* [*all L.*].

adv. *pendente lite* [*L.*].

970. Acquittal

n. **acquittal**, acquitment [*obs.*]; exculpation, acquittance, clearance, exoneration; discharge etc. (*release*) 750; *quietus* [*L.*], absolution, compurgation, reprieve, respite; pardon etc. (*forgiveness*) 918.

[exemption from punishment] impunity, immunity.

v. **acquit**, exculpate, exonerate, clear; absolve, whitewash, assoil [*archaic*], assoilzie [*Scot.*]; discharge, release; liberate etc. 750.

reprieve, respite; pardon etc. (*forgive*) 918; let off, let off scot-free.

adj. **acquitted** etc. *v.;* uncondemned, unpunished, unchastised; recommended to mercy.

971. Condemnation

n. **condemnation**, conviction, judgment, penalty, sentence; proscription, damnation; death warrant.

attainder, attainture, attaintment.

v. **condemn**, convict, cast [*obs. or dial.*], bring home to, find guilty, damn, doom, sign the death warrant, sentence, pass sentence on, attaint, confiscate, proscribe, sequestrate; nonsuit.

disapprove etc. 932; accuse etc. 938.

stand condemned, be convicted.

adj. **condemnatory**, damnatory; condemned etc. *v.;* nonsuited etc. (*failure*) 732; self-convicted.

972. Punishment

n. **punishment**, punition, chastisement, chastening, correction, castigation; discipline, infliction, trial; judgment; penalty etc. 974; retribution; thunderbolt, Nemesis, Eumenides, the Furies; requital etc. (*reward*) 973; retributive justice; penology.

[forms of punishment] lash, scaffold etc. (*instrument of punishment*) 975; imprisonment etc. (*restraint*) 751; transportation, banishment, expulsion, exile, involuntary exile, ostracism; penal servitude, hard labor; galleys etc. 975; beating etc. *v.;* flagellation, fustigation, cudgeling, gantlet, strappado, estrapade, bastinado, *argumentum baculinum* [*L.*], stick law, rap on the knuckles, box on the ear; blow etc. (*impulse*) 276; stripe, cuff, kick, buffet, pummel; slap, –in the face; wipe [*dial. or slang*], douse *or* dowse [*rare*]; torture, rack; rail-riding, scarpines; picket [*obs.*], picketing; dragonnade.

capital punishment, execution; hanging, shooting etc. *v.;* electrocution, decapitation, decollation, dismemberment; strangling, strangulation,

973. Reward

garrote *or* garrotte; crucifixion, impalement; martyrdom, *auto-da-fé* (*pl. autos-da-fé*) [*Pg.*], *auto-de-fe* [*Sp.*], *noyade* [*F.*], harakiri [*Jap.*], seppuku [*Jap.*], happy dispatch [*jocular*], lethal chamber, hemlock.

v. **punish**, chastise, chasten, castigate, correct, inflict punishment, administer correction, deal retributive justice; tar and feather; masthead, keelhaul.

visit upon, pay; pay out [*colloq.*], serve out [*colloq.*], settle, settle with, do for [*colloq.*], get even with, get one's own back [*slang*], make short work of, give a lesson to, serve one right, make an example of; have a rod in pickle for; give it to, give it one [*both colloq.*].

strike etc. 276; deal a blow to, administer the lash, smite; slap, –the face; smack, cuff, box the ears, spank, thwack, thump, beat, lay on, swinge, buffet; thresh, thrash, pummel, drub, leather [*slang*], trounce, baste, belabor; lace, –one's jacket; dress, dress down, give a dressing, trim [*colloq.*], warm [*dial.*], warm one's jacket [*colloq.*], wipe [*slang*], tund [*obs.*], cob [*dial., Eng.*], bang, strap, comb [*humorous*], lick, larrup [*both colloq.*], wallop [*Scot., dial. Eng. & colloq., U. S.*], cowhide, lambaste [*slang*], lash, whop [*obs.*], flog, scourge, whip, birch, cane, give the stick, switch, flagellate, horsewhip, bastinado, towel [*slang*], rub down with an oaken towel [*slang*], ribroast [*slang*], dust one's jacket [*slang*], fustigate, pitch into [*colloq.*], lay about one, beat black and blue; beat to a -pulp, –mummy, –jelly; give a black eye; hit on the head, crack on the bean [*slang*], sandbag, blackjack, put away [*slang*]; pelt, stone, lapidate.

execute; bring to the -block, –gallows; behead, decapitate, decollate, guillotine; hang, turn off [*slang*]; gibbet, bowstring, dismember, hang draw and quarter; shoot; burn; break on the wheel, crucify; impale *or* empale, flay; lynch; electrocute.

torture, agonize, rack, put on (*or* to) the rack, martyr, martyrize, picket [*obs. or hist.*]; prolong the agony, kill by inches.

banish, exile, transport, deport, expel, ostracize; rusticate; drum out; dismiss, disbar, disbench [*Eng. law*]; strike off the roll, unfrock; post.

suffer, suffer for, suffer punishment; be flogged, be hanged etc.; come to the gallows, dance upon nothing [*ironical*], die in one's shoes; be rightly served.

adj. **punishing** etc. *v.*; penal, punitory, punitive, inflictive, castigatory; punished etc. *v.*

int. à la lanterne! [*F.*].

973. Reward

n. **reward**, recompense, remuneration, prize, meed, guerdon, reguerdon [*obs.*]; price; indemnity, indemnification; quittance, compensation, reparation, redress, retribution, reckoning, acknowledgment, requital, amends, sop; atonement; consideration, return, *quid pro quo* [*L.*]; salvage.

perquisite, perks [*slang*]; vail etc. (*donation*) 784; *douceur* [*F.*], tip; bribe, bait etc. 784; hush-money, smart-money, blackmail; carcelage [*obs.*]; solatium.

allowance, salary, stipend, wages; pay, payment; emolument; tribute; batta [*India*], shot, scot; premium, fee, honorarium; hire; dasturi *or* dustoori [*India*]; mileage.

crown etc. (*decoration of honor*) 877.

v. **reward**, recompense, repay, requite; remunerate, munerate [*obs.*]; compensate; fee, tip, bribe; pay one's footing etc. (*pay*) 807; make amends, indemnify, atone; satisfy, acknowledge.

get for one's pains, reap the fruits of.

adj. remunerative, remuneratory [*rare*], munerary [*obs.*], compensatory, retributive, reparatory [*rare*], reparative.

974. Penalty

n. **penalty**; retribution etc. (*punishment*) 972; pain, pains and penalties; wergild *or* weregild [*hist.*], bloodwite *or* bloodwit [*early Eng. law*]; *peine forte et dure* [*F.*]; penance etc. (*atonement*) 952; the devil to pay.

fine, mulct, amercement, sconce [*Oxford Univ., Eng.*], forfeit, forfeiture, escheat, damages, deodand, sequestration, confiscation, praemunire *or* premunire; domage.

v. **penalize**, fine, mulct, amerce, sconce, confiscate, sequestrate, sequester, escheat, estreat, forfeit.

975. Scourge
[instrument of punishment]

n. **scourge**, whip, lash, strap, thong, cowhide, knout, cat, cat-o'-nine-tails; rope's end; *azote* [*Sp. Am.*], black-snake, bullwhack, kurbash [*Turk.*], chabuk [*Hind.*], quirt, rawhide, sjambok [*S. Africa*].

rod, cane, stick, rattan *or* ratan, birch, birch rod; rod in pickle; switch, ferule, cudgetl, truncheon.

[various instruments] pillory, stocks, whipping post; cucking stool, ducking stool, brank, trebuchet *or* trebucket; triangle, wooden horse, maiden; thumbscrew, boot, rack, wheel, iron heel; treadmill, crank, galleys; bed of Procrustes.

scaffold; block, **ax**, guillotine; stake; cross, gallows, gibbet, tree, drop; noose, rope, halter, bowstring; death chair, electric chair; *mecate* [*Sp.*].

prison, house of correction etc. 752; jailer *or* gaoler.

executioner; electrocutioner; lyncher, garroter *or* garrotter, torturer; headsman, hangman, topsman *or* topping cove [*slang*], Jack Ketch.

malefactor, criminal, culprit, felon, evildoer, misdemeanant; victim, gallows-bird [*slang*], Jack Ketch's pippin [*old slang*].

Section 5. Religious

976. Deity

n. **deity**, Divinity, Godhead, Godship, Omnipotence, Omniscience, Providence.

[quality of being divine] divineness, divinity.

GOD, Lord, Jehovah, The King of Kings, The Lord of Lords, The Almighty, The Supreme Being, The Eternal Being, The Absolute Being, The First Cause; I AM, The All-Father, *Ens Entium* [*L.*], Author of all things, Creator of all things, Author of our being; Cosmoplast, Demiurge; The Infinite, The Eternal; The All-powerful, The Omnipotent, The All-wise, The All-merciful, The All-holy, The All-knowing, The Omniscient.

Deus [*L.*], *Theos* [*Gr.*], *Dieu* [*F.*], *Gott* [*Ger.*], *Dio* [*It.*], *Dios* [*Sp.*], *Deos* [*Pg.*], *Gud* [*Nor., Sw., & Dan.*], *God* [*Du.*], *Bog'* [*Russ.*], Brahmă [*Skr.*], *Deva* [*Skr.*], *Khuda* [*Hind.*], *Allah* [*Ar.*], *Kami* [*Jap.*], *Ten-shu* [*Jap., Christian*], *Jahweh* [*Heb.*].

[attributes and perfections] infinite -power, –wisdom, –goodness, –justice, –truth, –love, –mercy; omnipotence, omniscience, omnipresence; unity, immutability, holiness, glory, light, majesty, sovereignty; infinity, eternity etc. (*perpetuity*) 112.

THE TRINITY, The Holy Trinity, The Trinity in Unity, The Triune God, Triunity, Threefold Unity, "Three in One and One in Three."

I. GOD THE FATHER, The Maker, The Creator, The Preserver.

[functions] creation, preservation, divine government, Theocracy, Thearchy; Providence; ways–, dealings–, dispensations–, visitations– of Providence.

II. GOD THE SON, Jesus Christ; The Messiah, The Anointed, The Saviour, The Redeemer, The Mediator, The Intercessor, The Advocate, The Judge; The Son of God, The Son of Man, The Son of David; The Only-Begotten, The Lamb of God, The Word, Logos; The Man of Sorrows, Jesus of Nazareth, King of the Jews, The Son of Mary, The Risen, Immanuel, Emmanuel, The King of Kings and Lord of Lords, The King of Glory, The Prince of Peace, The Good Shepherd, The Way, The Door, The Truth, The Life, The Bread of Life, The Light of the World, The Vine, The True Vine; The Lord our Righteousness, The Sun of Righteousness.

The Incarnation, The Hypostatic Union, The Word made Flesh.

[functions] salvation, redemption, atonement, propitiation, mediation, intercession, judgment; soteriology.

III. GOD THE HOLY GHOST, The Holy Spirit, Paraclete, The Comforter, The Consoler, The Intercessor, The Spirit of God, The Spirit of Truth, The Dove.

[functions] inspiration, unction, regeneration, sanctification, consolation, grace.

[the deity in other religions] **brahmanism** *or* **hinduism**: Brahm *or* Brahmă (*neuter*), the Supreme Soul *or* Essence of the Universe; Trimurti *or* Hindu trinity *or* Hindu triad: (1) Brahmā (*masc.*), the Creator; (2) Vishnu, the Preserver, (3) Siva *or* Shiva, the Destroyer and Regenerator. For other Hindu deities see 979.

buddhism: the Protestantism of the East; Buddha, the Blessed One, the Teacher, the Lord Buddha.

zoroastrianism: Zerâna-Akerana, the Infinite Being; Ahuramazda *or* Ormazd, the Creator, the Lord of Wisdom, the Wise Lord, the Wise One, the King of Light, the Guardian of Mankind (*opposed by* Ahriman, the King of Darkness).

mohammedanism *or* **islam**: Allah.

judaism: Jehovah.

v. **create**, fashion, make, form, mold *or* mould, manifest.

preserve, uphold, keep, perpetuate, immortalize.

atone, redeem, save, propitiate, expiate; intercede, mediate.

predestinate, predestine, foreordain, preordain; elect, call, ordain.

bless, sanctify, hallow, justify, absolve, glorify.

977. Angel

adj. **almighty**, all-powerful, omnipotent; omnipresent, all-wise, all-seeing, all-knowing, omniscient, supreme.
divine, heavenly, celestial; holy, hallowed, sacred, sacrosanct.
supernatural, superhuman, hyperphysical, superphysical, spiritual, ghostly, supramundane, supersensuous, supersensitive, supersensual, supernormal, unearthly.
theistic; theocratic; deistic; anointed; soterial.

adv. **under God**, by God's will, by God's help, *Deo volente* [*L.*], D. V., God willing; in Jesus' name, in His name, in His fear, to His glory; *jure divino* [*L.*], by divine right.

977. Angel
[beneficient spirits]

n. **angel**, archangel, Messenger of God, guardian angel, ministering spirits, invisible helpers, Choir Invisible, heavenly host, host of heaven, sons of God; morning star; saint.
[celestial hierarchy of pseudo-dionysius] (1) Seraphim (*sing.* seraph, *E. pl.* seraphs), Cherubim (*sing.* cherub, *E. pl.* cherubs; cherubim *or* cherubin *are often treated as sing.*), Thrones; (2) Dominions, Virtues, Powers; (3) Principalities, Archangels, Angels.
Michael, Gabriel, Raphael, Uriel, Chamuel, Jophiel, Zadkiel; Abdiel, Azrael.
madonna, Our Lady, *Notre Dame* [*F.*], Holy Mary, The Virgin, The Blessed Virgin, The Virgin Mary; *Dei Mater* [*L.*], Mother of God; *Regina Coeli* [*L.*], Queen of Heaven; *Regina Angelorum* [*L.*], Queen of Angels; *Stella Maris* [*L.*], Star of the Sea; *Mater Dolorosa* [*L.*]; Zion's Lily; *Alma Mater Redemptoris, Virgo Gloriosa, Virgo Sponsa Dei, Virgo Potens, Virgo Veneranda, Virgo Proedicanda, Virgo Clemens, Virgo Sapientissima, Sancta Virgo Virginum* [*all L.*]; *La Vergine Gloriosa* [*It.*]; *La Grande Vierge* [*F.*].

adj. **angelic**, seraphic, cherubic, archangelic.

978. Satan
[maleficent spirits]

n. **satan**, the Devil, Lucifer, Belial, Beëlzebub, Eblis [*Ar.*], Ahriman [*Zoroastrianism*], Mephistopheles, Mephisto, Shaitan [*Hind.*], Samael, Asmodeus, Satanas [*archaic*], Abaddon [*Heb.*], Apollyon, *le Diable* [*F.*], Deil [*Scot.*], Teufel [*Ger.*], *Diabolus* [*L.*].
his Satanic Majesty, the Prince of the Devils, the Prince of Darkness, the Prince of this world, the Prince of the power of the air; the Tempter, the Adversary, the Evil One, the Evil Spirit, the Archenemy, the Archfiend, the Foul Fiend, the Devil Incarnate, the Father of Lies, the Author of Evil, the Father of Evil, the Old Serpent, the Wicked One, the Common Enemy, the angel of the bottomless pit; the Deuce, the Dickens, the Old Gentleman, Old Nick, Old Scratch, Old Horny, Old Harry, Old Gooseberry [*all slang*].
fallen angels, unclean spirits, devils; the rulers of darkness, the powers of darkness; inhabitants of Pandemonium; demon etc. 980.
moloch, Mammon, Azazel [*Milton*]; Belial [*P. L.*], Beëlzebub [*in P. L., the fallen angel next to Satan*], Loki [*Norse myth.*]
diabolism, devil worship, devil lore, diablerie *or* diablery, diabolology *or* diabology, Satanism, devilism; devilship; devildom; demonry, demonism, demonology, Manichaeism *or* Manicheism; Black Mass, Black Magic, demonolatry, demonomagy; witchcraft etc. (*sorcery*) 992; the cloven hoof; hoofs and horns; demonomy.
diabolist, demonologist, demonologer, demonolater, demonist, demonographer [*rare*], demonomist; Manichaean *or* Manichean.

v. **diabolize** [*rare*], demonize; bewitch, bedevil etc. (*sorcery*) 992; possess, obsess.

adj. **satanic**, diabolic *or* diabolical, devilish, demoniac *or* demoniacal, infernal, hellborn.

979. Mythic and pagan deities

n. **god**, goddess; *deus* [*L.*], *dea* [*L.*]; deva (*fem.* devi) ["the shining ones," *Skr.*]; heathen gods and goddesses; pantheon; theogony.
[Greek and Latin] Zeus, Jupiter *or* Jove (*King*); Apollon, Apollo (*the sun*); Ares, Mars (*war*); Hermes, Mercury (*messenger*); Poseidon, Neptune (*ocean*); Hephaistos, Vulcan (*smith*); Dionysus, Bacchus (*wine*); Pluton *or* Hades [*Gr.*], Pluto *or* Dis [*L.*] (*King of the lower world*); Kronos, Saturn (*time*); Eros, Cupid (*love*); Pan, Faunus (*flocks, herds, forests, and wild life*).
Hera, Juno (*Queen*); Demeter, Ceres (*fruitfulness*); Persephone, Proserpina *or* Proserpine (*Queen of the lower world*); Artemis, Diana (*the moon and hunting*); Athena, Minerva (*wisdom*); Aphrodite, Venus (*love and beauty*); Hestia, Vesta (*the hearth*); Rhea *or* Cybele ("*Mother of the gods,*" *identified with* Ops, *wife of Saturn*); Gaea *or* Ge, Tellus (*earth goddess, mother of the Titans*).
[Norse] Ymir (*primeval giant*), Reimthursen (*frost giants*), Bori (*fashioner of the world*), Bor (*father of Odin*), Odin *or* Woden (*the All-father,*

= *Zeus*); the Aesir *or* Asas; Thor (*the Thunderer*), Balder *or* Baldr (= *Apollo*), Freyr (*fruitfulness*), Tyr *or* Tyrr (*war*), Bragi (*poetry and eloquence*), Höder *or* Hödr (*blind god of the winter*), Heimdall (*warder of Asgard*), Vidar (= *Pan*), Uller *or* Ullr (*the chase*), Forseti (*peacemaker*), Vali (*knowledge and eternal light*), Loki (*evil*).

the Vanir *or* Vans: Njorth *or* Njord (*the winds and the sea*), Frey *or* Freyr (*prosperity and love*), Freya *or* Freyja (*goddess of love and beauty*, = *Venus*).

Frigg *or* Frigga (*wife of Odin*), Hel (*goddess of death*, = *Persephone*), Sif (*wife of Thor*), Nanna (*wife of Balder*), Idun (*goddess of spring, wife of Bragi*), Sigyn (*wife of Loki*).

[Hindu] **vedic gods**: Dyaus (*the Heaven*), Indra (*cloud-compeller*), Varuna (*the sky, also the waters*), Surya (*the sun*, = *Gr.* Helios), Savitar ("*the Inciter," a sun god*), Soma (*the sustainer*), Agni (*fire*), Vavu (*the winds*), the Marutas (*storm gods*), Ushas ("*the Dawn*," *goddess of wisdom*).

brahmanic gods: Brahmâ, Vishnu, Siva *or* Shiva etc. (*Brahmanism*) 976; avatars of Vishnu: (1) Matsya, the fish; (2) Karma, the turtle; (3) Varah, the boar; (4) Narsinh, man-lion; (5) Vaman, the dwarf; (6) Parshuram, a Brahman; (7) Rama; (8) Krishna; (9) Buddha; (10) Kalki; Jagannath *or* Juggernaut (*Krishna*); Ganesha *or* Ganpati (*wisdom*), Hanuman (*monkey god*), Yama (*judge of the dead*).

Sarasvati (*sakti or wife of Brahmâ; goddess of poetry, wisdom, and fine art*), Lakshmi (*wife of Vishnu; goddess of wealth, and prosperity*), Durga *or* Kali (*wife of Siva, conceived as a malignant deity*); Devi ("*the goddess*") *or* Uma ("*light*") *or* Gauri ("*the brilliant*") *or* Parvati ("*the mountaineer," wife of Siva, conceived as a beneficient deity*).

[Egyptian] Ra *or* Amun-Ra (*the sun god*), Neph *or* Nef (*spirit or breath*), Pthah (*demiurge*), Khem (*reproduction*), Mut *or* Maut (= *Gr.* Demeter), Osiris (*judge of the dead*), Isis (*wife of Osiris*), Horus (*the morning sun; son of Osiris and Isis*), Anubis (*jackal-god, brother of Horus, a conductor of the dead*), Nephthys (*sister of Isis*), Set (*evil deity, brother of Osiris*), Thoth (*clerk of the underworld*), Bast *or* Bubastis (*a goddess with head of a cat*), the Sphinx (*wisdom*).

[various] Baal (*Heb. pl.* Baalim) [*Semitic*]; Astarte *or* Ashtoreth (*goddess of fertility and love*) [*Phoenician*]; Bel *Babylonian*]; The Great Spirit [*N. Amer. Indian*]; Mumbo Jumbo [*Sudanese Negroes, an idol or bugaboo*].

nymph, dryad, hamadryad, alseid, wood nymph; naiad, fresh-water nymph; oread, mountain nymph; nereid, sea nymph; limoniad *or* leimoniad, meadow nymph *or* flower nymph; Oceanid, ocean nymph; napaea, glen nymph; potamid, river nymph; Pleiades *or* Atlantides, Hyades, Dodonides.

fairy, fay, sprite *or* spright [*archaic*]; nix (*fem.* nixie), water sprite; the Good Folk, brownie *or* browny, pixy, elf (*pl.* elves), banshee *or* banshie; the Fates *or* Moerae, *Clotho* (Spinner), *Lachesis* (Disposer of Lots), *Atropos* (Inflexible One); gnome, kelpie; faun; peri, nis, kobold, sylph, sylphid; undine, sea maid, sea nymph, mermaid (*masc.* merman); Mab, Oberon, Titania, Ariel; Puck, Robin Goodfellow, Hobgoblin; Leprechaun; denizens of the air; afreet etc. (*bad spirit*) 980.

familiar spirit, familiar, genius, guide, good genius, tutelary genius, daimon, demon *or* daemon, guardian.

mythology, mythical lore, heathen mythology, folklore, fairyism, fairy mythology.

adj. **mythical**, mythic, mythological, fabulous, legendary etc. 515.

fairylike, sylphlike, sylphine, sylphish, sylphidine; elfin, elflike, elfish, nymphlike.

980.   Evil Spirits

n. demon, fiend, devil etc. (*Satan*) 978; evil genius, familiar, familiar spirit; bad–, unclean- spirit; cacodaemon *or* cacodemon, incubus, succubus *and* succuba; daeva *or* deev, bad peri, afreet, lamia, barghest *or* barguest, ogre, ogress, ghoul, vampire, harpy; Fury, the Furies, the Erinyes, the Eumenides; Titan; Friar Rush.

imp, bad fairy, sprite, jinni *or* jinnee (*pl.* jin), genius (*pl.* genii), flibberti-gibbet, ouphe, dwarf, troll, urchin, Cluricaune.

changeling, elf-child, auf, oaf; werewolf, *loup-garou* [*F.*]; satyr.

elemental, sylph, gnome, salamander, nymph [*Rosicrucian*].

siren, nixie, undine, Lorelei.

bugbear, bugaboo, bogy *or* bogey *or* bogie, bug [*obs.*], poker [*rare*], goblin, hobgoblin, boggart *or* boggard.

demonology, demonry etc. (*diabolism*) 978.

adj. demoniac, demoniacal, fiendish, fiendlike, evil, ghoulish; pokerish [*colloq.*], bewitched.

980a.   Specter

n. **specter** *or* spectre, ghost, revenant, apparition, spirit, sprite, shade, shadow, wraith, spook [*now humorous*], phantom, phantasm, fantasm

981. Heaven

[*rare*], idolum; materialization [*Spiritualism*], ectoplasmic manifestation; double, etheric body, etheric self, aura, auric egg, astral body, *mayavi rupa*, ego [*all Theos. and Occultism*]; vision, theophany.

banshee, White Lady, the White Ladies of Normandy, the White Lady of Avenel [Scott]; lemures, larva *or* larvae [*Roman relig.*].

will-o'-the-wisp, Friar's lantern etc. 423.

adj. **spectral**, ghostly, ghostlike, spiritual, wraithlike, weird, uncanny, eerie *or* eery, spooky *or* spookish [*colloq.*], haunted; unearthly, supernatural.

981. Heaven

n. **heaven**; kingdom of -heaven, –God; heavenly kingdom; heaven of heavens, God's throne, throne of God, presence of God; inheritance of the saints in light.

paradise, Eden, Zion, Holy City, New Jerusalem, Heavenly City, City Celestial, abode of the blessed; celestial bliss, eternal bliss, unending bliss, glory, never-ending day.

[mythological heaven or paradise] Olympus; Elysium, Elysian fields, Islands (*or* Isles) of the Blessed, Happy Isles, Fortunate Isles, Arcadia, bowers of bliss, garden of the Hesperides, third heaven, seventh heaven; Valhalla *or* Walhalla [*Scandinavian*]; Nirvana [*Buddhist*]; happy hunting grounds [*N. Amer. Indian*]; *Alfardaws, Assama; Falak al aflak,* ("the highest heaven") [*Mohammedan*].

future state, life after death, eternal home, resurrection, translation; resuscitation etc. 660; apotheosis, deification.

[theosophy] Devachan *or* Devaloka, the land of the Gods.

adj. **heavenly**, celestial, supernal, unearthly, from on high, paradisaic *or* paradisaical, paradisiac *or* paradisiacal, beatific, elysian, Olympian, Arcadian.

982. Hell

n. **hell**, bottomless pit, place of torment; habitation of fallen angels; Pandemonium, Abaddon, Domdaniel; *jahannan* [*Hind.*], Sheol.

hell fire; everlasting -fire, –torment; lake of fire and brimstone; fire that is never quenched, worm that never dies.

purgatory, limbo, gehenna, abyss, Tophet.

[mythological hell] Tartarus, Hades, Avernus, Styx, Stygian creek, pit of Acheron, Cocytus; infernal regions, inferno, shades below, realms of Pluto.

pluto, Rhadamanthus, Erebus, Charon, Cerberus; Persephone, Proserpina *or* Proserpine; Minos, Osiris.

rivers of hell: Styx, Acheron, Cocytus, Phlegethon, Lethe.

adj. **hellish**, infernal, stygian.

983. Theology
[religious knowledge]

n. **theology** (natural and revealed), theosophy, divine wisdom, divinity, hagiology, hagiography, hierography; Caucasian mystery; monotheism, theism, religion; religious -persuasion, –sect, –denomination, –affiliation; creed etc. (*belief*) 484; articles–, declaration–, profession–, confession- of faith.

theologian, theologue [*now rare*], scholastic, divine, schoolman, canonist, theologist [*now rare*], theologus; monotheist, theist; Homoousian (*opp. to* Homoiousian); the Fathers.

adj. **theological**, religious, divine, canonical; denominational; sectarian etc. 984.

983a. Orthodoxy

n. **orthodoxy**; strictness, soundness, religious, truth, true faith; truth etc. 494; soundness of doctrine.

christianity, Christianism; Catholicism, Catholicity; "the faith once delivered to the saints"; hyperorthodoxy etc. 984.

the church, Holy Church, Church Militant, Church Triumphant; Catholic–, Universal–, Apostolic–, Established- Church; the Bride of the Lamb; temple of the Holy Ghost; Church–, body–, members–, disciples–, followers- of Christ; Christians.

true believer; textualist, textuary; canonist etc. (*theologian*) 983; the Orthodox; Christian community; Christendom, collective body of Christians.

canons etc. (*belief*) 484; thirty-nine articles; Apostles'–, Nicene–, Athanasian- Creed; Church Catechism.

adj. **orthodox**, sound, strict, faithful, catholic, schismless, Christian, evangelical, scriptural, literal, divine, monotheistic, theistic; true etc. 494; true blue.

984. Heterodoxy
[sectarianism]

n. **heterodoxy**; error etc. 495; false doctrine, heresy, schism, schismaticism, schismaticalness; recusancy, backsliding, apostasy; materialism, hylotheism; atheism etc. (*irreligion*) 989.

anthropomorphism, anthropopathism, anthropopathy; idolatry etc. 991; superstition etc. (*credulity*) 486.

bigotry etc. (*obstinacy*) 606; fanaticism, iconoclasm; hyperorthodoxy, precisianism; bibliolatry, hagiolatry; sabbatarianism, puritanism.

sectarianism, sectarism [*obs.*], nonconformity; dissent etc. 489; secularism; syncretism; religious sects, the clash of creeds.

protestantism, Arianism, Adventism, Jansenism, Stundism, Erastianism, Calvinism, Quakerism, Methodism, Anabaptism, Puseyism, tractarianism, ritualism, Origenism, Sabellianism, Socinianism, Gnosticism, Mormonism, Second Adventism, materialism, positivism, latitudinarianism, ethicism, deism, higher pantheism, henotheism; monism, philosophical unitarianism etc.; the isms.

anglicanism, Church of England; High-, Low-, Broad-, Free-Church; ultramontanism; monasticism, monkery; Catholicism, Romanism, popery, papism, papistry, papacy, Maryolatry [*usually opprobrious*], Scarlet Woman, Church of Rome; Greek Church. [*Generally speaking, each sect is* orthodox *to itself and* heterodox *to others.*]

judaism; Mohammedanism, Islam, Islamism.

theosophy, New Thought, ethical culture, mental science, mental healing; Christian Science, Eddyism; Spiritualism, Spiritism, occultism; Swedenborgianism.

paganism, heathenism, heathendom; mythology; animism, polytheism, ditheism, tritheism, pantheism; dualism.

gentilism, Babism, Sufiism, Neoplatonism, Brahmanism, Hinduism, Vedantism, Buddhism, Lamaism; Sikhism, Jainism; Confucianism, Taoism; Shintoism, Sabaeanism *or* Sabeanism *or* Sabeism.

pagan, heathen, paynim; *giaour* [*Turk.*], Gheber *or* Ghebre, kafir, non-Mohammedan; gentile; pantheist, polytheist, animist.

misbeliever, heretic, apostate; backslider; antichrist; idolater; skeptic etc. 989.

bigot etc. (*obstinacy*) 606; fanatic, abdal, dervish, iconoclast.

sectarian, sectary, sectarist [*rare*], schismatic; seceder, separatist, recusant, dissenter, nonconformist, nonjuror.

Huguenot, Protestant, Episcopalian; Trinitarian; latitudinarian; limitarian; orthodox dissenter, Puritan, Unitarian, Congregationalist, Independent; Presbyterian, Lutheran, Ubiquitarian, Calvinist, Methodist, Wesleyan; Anabaptist, Baptist; Mormon, Latter-day Saint; Irvingite, Sandemanian, Glassite, Erastian, Sublapsarian, Supralapsarian; Gentoo, Antinomian, Swedenborgian; Adventist, Second Adventist, Bible Christian, Bryanite, Brownian, Dunker, Ebionite, Eusebian; Faith Curer, Faith Christ, Faith Healer, Mental Healer, Christian Scientist; Familist, Jovinianist, Libadist, Restitutionist, Quaker, Shaker, Quietist, Stundist, Tunker etc.

catholic, Roman Catholic, Romanist, Papist, ultramontane; Anglican, Oxford School; tractarian, Puseyite, ritualist; High Churchman.

jew, Hebrew, Rabbinist; Mohammedan, Mussulman, Moslem, Islamite, Osmanli, Motazilite, Shiah, Sunni, Wahabi; Brahman *or* Brahmin; Brahmo; Vedantist, Jain *or* Jaina, Sikh, Parsi *or* Parsee, fire worshiper, Zoroastrian [*erron. called fire worshiper*]; Sufi, Babist, Buddhist; Confucianist, Taoist, Shintoist; Magi, Gymnosophist, Sabian, henotheist, Gnostic, Sadducee, Rosicrucian, Mystic, Occultist, Theosophist, Spiritualist, Spiritist etc.

materialist, hylotheist; positivist, deist, agnostic, atheist etc. 989.

adj. **heterodox**, heretical, unorthodox, unscriptural, uncanonical, unchristian, antiscriptural, apocryphal; antichristian; schismatic, recusant, iconoclastic; sectarian, dissenting, dissident [*now rare*]; Protestant etc. *n.;* secular etc. (*lay*) 997; deistic, agnostic, atheistic; skeptical etc. 989.

bigoted etc. (*prejudiced*) 481, (*obstinate*) 606; superstitious etc. (*credulous*) 486; fanatical; idolatrous etc. 991; visionary etc. (*imaginative*) 515.

judaical; Mohammedan, Islamic *or* Islamitic, Moslem; Brahmanic *or* Brahmanical, Brahminic *or* Brahminical; Buddhist etc. *n.*

popish, papish, papistic *or* papistical, Romish.

pagan, heathen, heathenish, ethnic, ethnical; gentile, paynim; polytheistic, pantheistic, animistic.

985. Revelation
[biblical]

n. **revelation**, inspiration, *afflatus* [*L.*]; theophany, theopneusty.

the bible, the Book, the Book of Books, the Good Book, the Word, the Word of God, Scripture, the Scriptures, Holy Writ, Holy Scriptures, inspired writings, Gospel.

old testament, Septuagint, Vulgate, Pentateuch; Octateuch; the Law, the Jewish Law; the Prophets; major-, minor- Prophets; Hagiographa, Hierographa; Apocrypha.

986. Sacred Writings

new testament; Gospels, Evangelists, Synoptic Gospels, Acts, Epistles, Apocalypse, Revelation; Good Tidings, Glad Tidings.

[hebrew] Talmud, Torah, Mishna, Gemara; Masora *or* Masorah.

inspired writers, inspired penmen; prophet etc. (*seer*) 513; evangelist, apostle, disciple, saint; the Fathers, the Apostolic Fathers; Holy Men of old.

adj. **scriptural**, biblical, sacred, prophetic; evangelical, evangelistic, apostolic, apostolical; inspired, theopneustic, theopneusted [*rare*], apocalyptic, revealed; ecclesiastical, canonical, textuary; Talmudic.

986. Sacred Writings
[non-biblical]

n. The Vedas (Rig-Veda, Yajur-Veda, Sama-Veda, Atharva-Veda), the Upanishads, the Puranas, Sutras, Sastra *or* Shastra, Tantra, Bhagavad Gita [*all Brahmanic*]; Zenda-vesta, A vesta [*Zoroastrian*]; The Koran *or* Alcoran [*Mohammedan*]; Tripitaka, Dhammapada [*Buddhist*]; Granth, Adigranth [*Sikh*]; the Agamas [*Jain*]; the Kings [*Chinese*]; the Eddas [*Scandinavia*].

arcana Coelestia etc. [*Swedenborgian*]; Book of Mormon; "Science and Health with Key to the Scriptures" [*Christian Science*].

[non-biblical prophets and religious founders] Gautama (Buddha); Zoroaster, Confucius, Lao-tse [*Taoism*], Mohammed, Nanak Shah [*Sikhism*], Vaddhamana, "Maha-vira" [*Jainism*], Mirza Ali Mohammed, "Bab-ud-Din" (*Per.* "Gate of the Faith") [*Babism*], Ram Mohun Roy [*Brahmo-Samaj*].

swedenborg, Joseph Smith [*Mormonism*], Mary Baker Eddy [*Christian Science*].

987. Piety

n. **piety**, religion, theism, faith; religiousness, religiosity, holiness etc. *adj.;* saintship; religionism; sanctimony etc. (*assumed piety*) 988; reverence etc. (*respect*) 928; humility, veneration, devotion; prostration etc. (*worship*) 990; grace, unction, edification; sanctity, sanctitude [*rare*]; consecration.

spiritual existence, odor of sanctity, beauty of holiness.

theopathy, beautification, adoption, regeneration, conversion, justification, theodicy, sanctification, salvation, inspiration, bread of life; Body and Blood of Christ.

believer, convert, theist, Christian, devotee, pietist, Saint.

the -good, -righteous, -just, -believing, -elect; the children of -God, -Our Father, -the kingdom, -light.

v. **be pious** etc. *adj.;* have faith etc. *n.;* believe, receive Christ; venerate, adore, worship, perform the acts of devotion; revere etc. 928; be converted etc.; experience the divine illumination [*Mysticism*]; be at one with God, be on God's side, stand up for Jesus, fight the good fight, keep the faith, let one's light shine.

regenerate, convert, edify, sanctify, hallow, keep holy, beatify, inspire, consecrate, enshrine.

adj. **pious**, religious, devout, devoted, reverent, godly, heavenly-minded, humble, pure, pure in heart, holy, spiritual, pietistic, saintly, saintlike; seraphic, sacred, solemn.

believing, faithful, Christian, Catholic.

regenerated; inspired, born-again, consecrated, converted, unearthly, not of the earth, in the world not of it.

elected, adopted, justified, sanctified.

988. Impiety

n. **impiety**; sin etc. 945; irreverence; profaneness etc. *adj.,* profanity, profanation; blasphemy, desecration, sacrilege; scoffing etc. *v.*

[assumed piety] hypocrisy etc. (*falsehood*) 544; pietism, cant, pious fraud; lip-devotion, lip-service, lip-reverence; misdevotion, formalism, austerity; sanctimony, sanctimoniousness etc. *adj.;* pharisaism, precisianism; sabbatism, sabbatarianism; *odium theologicum* [*L.*], sacerdotalism; bigotry etc. (*obstinacy*) 606, (*prejudice*) 481; blue laws.

apostasy, recusancy, hardening, backsliding, declension, perversion, reprobation.

hypocrite etc. (*dissembler*) 548; "Scribes and Pharisees" [*Bible*]; *Rawana-sannyasi* [*Hind.*]; Tartufe, Mawworm, Holy Willie [*Burns*].

bigot, saint [*ironical*]; Pharisee, sabbatarian, formalist, methodist, puritan, pietist, precisian, religionist, devotee, ranter, fanatic; juramentado [*Moro*].

sinner etc. 949; scoffer, blasphemer, sacrilegist [*rare*], sabbath breaker; worldling.

the wicked, the evil, the unjust, the reprobate; sons of -men, -Belial, -the wicked one; children of -the devil, -darkness.

v. **be impious** etc. *adj.;* profane, desecrate, blaspheme, revile, scoff; swear etc. (*malediction*) 908; commit sacrilege.

dissemble, simulate, play the hypocrite, hypocrify [*obs.*], hypocrize [*rare*], snuffle, talk through the nose, talk nasally, hold up the hands in horror, turn up the whites of the eyes; sing psalms for a pretense, make long prayers.

adj. **impious**; irreligious etc. 989; desecrating etc. *v.;* profane, irreverent, sacrilegious, blasphemous.

unhallowed, unsanctified, unregenerate; hardened, perverted, reprobate.

hypocritical etc. (*false*) 544; canting, pietistical, sanctimonious, unctuous, pharisaical, overrighteous, righteous over much.

bigoted, fanatical, hidebound, narrow, illiberal, prejudiced, little; provincial, parochial, insular; priest-ridden.

adv. under the -mask, –cloak, –pretense, –form, –guise- of religion; in blasphemy.

989. Irreligion

n. **irreligion**, indevotion, impiety; ungodliness etc. *adj.;* laxity, apathy, indifference; quietism, passiveness, passivity.

skepticism, doubt; unbelief, disbelief, incredulity, incredulousness etc. *adj.;* want of -faith, –belief; pyrrhonism; doubt etc. 485; agnosticism, freethinking, deism; hylotheism; materialism, rationalism, positivism; nihilism.

infidelity, antichristianity, antichristianism, atheism.

unbeliever, infidel, atheist, antichristian; giaour [*Turk.*], heretic, miscreant [*archaic*], heathen, alien, gentile, Nazarene; *espirit fort* [*F.*], freethinker, skeptic, pyrrhonist, deist, latitudinarian, rationalist; materialist, positivist, nihilist, agnostic, somatist, theophobist.

v. **be irreligious** etc. *adj.;* disbelieve, lack faith; doubt, question etc. 485.

dechristianize, antichristianize [*rare*]; serve Mammon, contend against the light, love darkness rather than light, deny the truth.

adj. **irreligious**; indevout, undevout, devoutless, godless, graceless, ungodly; unholy, unsanctified, unhallowed; atheistic, without God.

skeptical, freethinking, unbelieving, unconverted; incredulous, faithless, lacking faith; deistic, deistical; antichristian, unchristian.

worldly, mundane, earthly, carnal; worldly etc. worldly-minded, unspiritual.

adv. **irreligiously** etc. *adj.*

990. Worship

n. **worship**, adoration, devotion, cult, aspiration, homage, service, humiliation; kneeling, genuflection, prostration; latria, dulia, hyperdulia.

prayer, invocation, supplication, rogation, intercession, orison, holy breathing, petition etc. (*request*) 765; collect, litany, Lord's prayer, paternoster; *Ave Maria* [*L.*]; Hail, Mary; rosary, bead-roll.

revival; anxious–, revival–, camp- meeting.

thanksgiving; giving–, returning- thanks; grace, praise, glorification, paean, benediction, doxology, hosanna, hallelujah *or* halleluiah, alleluia *or* alleluiah; *Te Deum, non nobis Domine, nunc dimittis; O Salutaris* [*all L.*]; *Sanctus, Agnus Dei* [*L.*], *Kyrie Eleison* [*Gr.*], *Gloria* [*L.*], The Annunciation, Tersanctus, Trisagion.

psalm, psalmody; hymn, plain song, chant, chaunt [*archaic*], response, anthem, motet, antiphon, antiphony.

oblation, sacrifice, incense, libation, offering; burnt–, heave–, thank–, votive- offering; offeratory, collection.

discipline, self-discipline, self-examination, self-denial; fasting, penance, confession.

divine service, office, duty; exercises; morning prayer; Mass, matins, nones, complin *or* compline, evensong, vespers, vigils, lauds; undersong, tierce; holyday etc. (*rites*) 998.

prayer book, missal, breviary, Virginal; ritual etc. 998.

worshiper, congregation, communicant, celebrant.

v. **worship**, lift up the heart, aspire; revere etc. 928; adore, do service, pay homage; humble oneself, kneel; bow–, bend- the knee; throw oneself on one's knees, fall down, fall on one's knees; prostrate oneself, bow down and worship; beat the breast.

intone, chant, deacon *or* deacon off [*colloq.*], lead the choir, sing.

pray, invoke, supplicate; put–, offer- up -prayers, –petitions; beseech etc. (*ask*) 765; say one's prayers, tell one's beads, recite the rosary.

give thanks, return thanks, say grace, bless, praise, laud, glorify, magnify, sing praises; give benediction.

propitiate, offer sacrifice, fast, deny oneself; vow, offer vows, give alms.

attend service, attend Mass, go to church, attend divine service; communicate etc. (*rite*) 998; work out one's salvation.

adj. **worshiping** etc. *v.;* devout, devotional, reverent, pure, solemn; fervid etc. (*heartfelt*) 821.

int. **hallelujah** *or* halleluiah! alleluia *or* alleluiah! hosanna! glory be to God! *sursum corda* [*L.*], *Deo gratias* [*L.*].

o Lord! pray God that! God -grant, –bless, –save, –forbid!

991. Idolatry

n. **idolatry**, idolatrousness, idololatry, idolism, idolodoulia, demonism, demonolatry, demonology; idol-, chthonian-, demon-, devil-, fire-worship; zoölatry, fetishism *or* fetichism; ecclesiolatry, heliolatry, bibliolatry, hierolatry [*rare*].

idolization, deification, apotheosis, canonization; hero worship.

sacrifice, idolothyte, hecatomb, holocaust; human sacrifices, immolation, mactation, infanticide, self-immolation, suttee.

idol, golden calf, graven image, fetish *or* fetich, eidolon, *thakur* [*Hind.*], joss [*Chinese*], *lares et penates* [*L.*]; god (*or* goddess) of one's idolatry; Baal, Moloch, Dagon, Juggernaut.

idolater, idolatress, demonolater *or* demonolator, chthonian, fetishist *or* fetichist; idolatrizer, idolizer, idolant [*obs.*], idolaster [*obs.*]; ecclesiolater, heliolater, zoölater, bibliolater.

v. **idolatrize**, idolize; *adorer le veau d'or* [*F.*]; worship -idols, -pictures, -relics; apotheosize, worship, put on a pedestal, prostrate oneself before; make sacrifice to, immolate before; deify, canonize.

adj. **idolatrous**, idololatric [*rare*], idolatric [*rare*], idolistic, chthonian, demonolatrous, fetishic [*rare*], fetishistic *or* fetichistic, idolothyte; worshiping *or* worshipping, prone before, prostrate before, in the dust before, at the feet of; heliolatrous, zoölatrous.

992. Sorcery

n. **sorcery**; occult -art, -sciences; magic, black magic, the black art, necromancy, theurgy, thaumaturgy; demonology, demonomy [*obs.*], demonomancy, demonship; diablerie, bedevilment, witchcraft, witchery; fetishism *or* fetichism; ghost dance, hoodoo, voodoo, voodooism; fire worship, heliolatry; obi *or* obiism, shamanism, vampirism; conjuration, incantation, bewitchment, glamour, enchantment; obsession, possession; exorcism.

divination etc. (*prediction*) 511; sortilege, ordeal, *sortes Vergilianae*; hocuspocus etc. (*deception*) 545.

v. **practice sorcery** etc. *n.;* cast a nativity, cast a horoscope, conjure, exorcise *or* exorcize [*rare in the sense of* conjure], charm, enchant, bewitch, bedevil, overlook, look on with the evil eye, witch, voodoo, hoodoo [*colloq.*]; entrance, fascinate etc. (*influence*) 615; taboo *or* tabu; wave a wand; rub the -ring, -lamp; cast a spell; call up spirits; raise spirits from the dead; raise ghosts, lay ghosts; command jinn *or* genii.

adj. **magic**, magical; witching, weird, cabalistic, talismanic, phylacteric, incantatory; charmed etc. *v.;* Circean; voodoo.

992a. Psychical Research

n. **psychical research**, psychical (*or* psychic) investigation; abnormal psychology; abnormal-, supernormal-, mediumistic-phenomena; mysticism; psychophysics; "psychologist's fallacy" [William James].

the subconscious, the subconscious self, the subliminal self, the higher self; ego etc. 980 *a;* subconsciousness, subliminal consciousness; dual personality, mental duality, secondary consciousness, intuition; multiple personality, mental dissociation, dissociation of personality, functional disintegration; impersonation, obsession, possession.

psychotherapy, psychotherapeutics, psychoanalysis; hysteria, neurasthenia, psychasthenia; over-stimulation; dreams, visions, apparitions, hallucinations, veridical hallucinations; Freud's theory.

mesmerism, animal magnetism; od, odyl *or* odylic force [*obsoles.*], electrobiology; mesmeric trance; hypnotism; hypnosis, hypnoidal state.

[phenomena] **telepathy**, thought transference, thought transmission, telepathic transmission; "malicious animal magnetism" *or* "M. A. P."; telepathic dreams; second sight, clairvoyance, clairaudience, psychometry.

premonitions, previsions, telepathic hallucinations; premonitory apparition, fetch, wraith, double; symbolic hallucinations; death lights, ominous dreams, ominous animals.

automatism, automatic writing, planchette, ouija board, trance writing, spirit writing, psychography; trance speaking, inspirational speaking.

crystal gazing, crystallomancy, crystal vision; hydromancy, lecanomancy, catoptromancy, onychomancy.

spiritualism, spiritism, spirit rapping, "Rochester knockings," table-turning, Poltergeist; spirit manifestations; ghost, specter etc. 980*a;* haunted houses; trance, spirit control, spirit possession; mediumistic communications; séance; materialization.

[theosophy and occultism] astral body etc. 980*a,* *kamarupa* [*Skr.*], desire body; etheric body, *linga sharira* [*Skr.*]; dense body, *sthula sharira* [*Skr.*]; mental body; causal body; bliss body, Buddhic body.

seven principles of man: (1) spirit *or atma* [*Skr.*], (2) spiritual mind, (3) intellect, (4) instinctive mind, (5) prana *or* vital force, (6) astral body, (7) physical body [*Yogi philosophy*].

medium, ecstatica [*rare*], seer, clairvoyant, clairaudient, telepathist; guide, control; mesmerist, hypnotist.

v. **psychologize**; investigate the -abnormal, −suprarational, −supernormal, −the subconscious, −the subliminal; search beyond the threshold, traverse the borderland, know oneself.

mesmerize, magnetize, hypnotize, place under control, subject to suggestion, place in a trance, induce hypnosis.

hold a séance, call up spirits, summon familiar spirits, "call spirits from the vasty deep" [*I Henry IV*]; hold spirit communications; materialize.

adj. **psychical**, psychic, psychal [*rare*], psychological; spiritistic, spiritualistic, spiritual; subconscious, "coconscious" [Morton Prince], subliminal (*opp. to* supraliminal); supernormal, abnormal, suprarational; mystic *or* mystical.

mediumistic, clairvoyant, clairaudient, telepathic; psychometric; hypnoidal, hypnagogic.

993. Spell

n. **spell**, charm, incantation, exorcism, weird [*obs. or Scot.*], cabala *or* cabbala, exsufflation [*obs.*], cantrip *or* contraip *or* contrap [*chiefly Scot.*], runes, abracadabra, open sesame, *or* open-sesame, hocus-pocus, counter-charm, Ephesian letters, bell book and candle, Mumbo Jumbo, evil eye.

talisman, amulet, madstone, periapt, telesm [*archaic*], phylactery, philter *or* philtre, fetish *or* fetich, manito *or* manitou *or* manitu; furcula, furculum, wishbone, merrythought; mascot *or* mascotte, rabbit's foot, hoodoo [*colloq.*], jinx [*slang*], scarabaeus *or* scarab; Om *or* Aum, *Om mani padme hum* [*Buddhist*]; sudarium, veronica, triskelion; swastika, fylfot, gammadion.

wand, caduceus, rod, divining rod, witch hazel, Aaron's rod.

[magic wish-givers] Aladdin's lamp, Aladdin's casket, magic casket, magic ring, magic belt, magic spectacles, wishing cap, Fortunatus's cap; seven-league boots; cap of darkness, Tarnkappe, Tarnhelm.

[fairy lore] fairy ring, fairy circle, fairy round; fernseed, rowan tree, quicken tree [*dial. Eng.*].

994. Sorcerer

n. **sorcerer**, magician, wizard, warlock, necromancer, conjuror, prestidigitator, *prestidigitateur* [*F.*], charmer, exorcist, voodoo, thaumaturge, thaumaturgist, theurgist, image [*poetic*], Magi (*sing.* Magus); diviner, dowser.

sorceress, witch, hag.

medicine man *or* medicine, witch doctor, shaman, shamanist.

vampire, lamia, ghoul; siren, harpy; incubus etc. 980.

astrologer, figure caster [*obs.*], figure flinger [*obs.*]; soothsayer etc. 513.

Katerfelto, Cagliostro, Merlin, Comus; Circe, weird sisters, Graeae *or* Graiae, witch of Endor.

995. Churchdom

n. **churchdom**; church, ministry, apostleship, priesthood, prelacy, hierarchy, church government, pale of the church, christendom.

clericalism, sacerdotalism, episcopalianism, ultramontanism; ecclesiology; theocracy; priestcraft, *odium theologicum* [*L.*]; religious sects etc. 984.

monasticism, monkhood, monachism; celibacy.

[ecclesiastical offices and dignities] cardinalate, cardinalship; primacy, archbishopric, archiepiscopacy; prelacy, bishopric, bishopdom, episcopate, episcopacy, see, diocese; deanery, stall; canonry, canonicate; prebend, prebendaryship, prebendal stall; benefice, incumbency, glebe, advowson, living, cure, charge, cure of souls; rectorship, vicariate, vicarship; pastorate, pastorship, pastoral charge; deaconry, deaconship; curacy; chaplaincy, chaplainship, chaplainry *or* chaplanry [*Scot.*]; abbacy, presbytery.

holy orders, ordination, institution, consecration, induction, reading in [*Eng.*], preferment, translation, presentation.

papacy, pontificate, popedom, See of Rome, the Vatican, the apostolic see.

council etc. 696; conclave, college of cardinals, convocation, conference [*Meth.*], session, synod, consistory, chapter, vestry, presbytery, standing committee; sanhedrin, *congé d'élire* [*F.*].

ecclesiastical courts, consistorial court, court of Arches.

v. **call**, ordain, induct, prefer [*rare*], translate, consecrate, present, elect, bestow

take orders, take the veil, take vows.

adj. **ecclesiastical**, ecclesiological; clerical, sacerdotal, priestly, prelatical, pastoral, ministerial, capitular, theocratic; hierarchical, archiepiscopal; episcopal, episcopalian; canonical; monastic, monachal, monkish; abbatial, abbatical; Anglican; Aaronic, levitical, pontifical, papal, apostolic; ultramontane; priestridden.

996. Clergy

- n. **clergy**, clericals, ministry, priesthood, presbytery, the cloth, the pulpit, the desk.
  clergyman, divine, ecclesiastic, churchman, priest, presbyter, hierophant, pastor, shepherd, minister, clerk in holy orders, parson, sky pilot [*slang*]; father, –in Christ; padre, *abbé* [*F.*], *curé* [*F.*]; reverend; black coat; confessor.
  [dignitaries of the church] ecclesiarch, sacrist, hierarch; patriarch [*Eastern Ch.*]; Abba Salamah, Abuna [*Abyssinian Ch.*]; eminence, reverence, primate, metropolitan, archbishop, bishop, angel [*as in the Cath. Apostolic Ch.*], prelate, diocesan, suffragan, bishop coadjutor, dean, subdean, archdeacon, prebendary, canon, rural dean, rector, vicar, perpetual curate, residentiary, beneficiary, incumbent, chaplain, curate; elder, deacon, deaconess; preacher, reader, Bible reader, lay reader, lecturer; capitular; missionary, propagandist, Jesuit, revivalist, field preacher, colporteur.
  churchwarden, deacon, questman [*hist.*], sidesman; clerk, precentor, choir; almoner, *suisse* [*F.*], verger, beadle, sexton, sacristan; acolyte, thurifer, censor-bearer; choirster, choir boy, member of the choir; soloist, quartet *or* quartette; organist.
  [roman catholic priesthood] Pope, Holy Father, papa [*obs. or rare*], pontiff, high priest, cardinal; archbishop, bishop, bishop coadjutor; canon-regular, canon-secular, confessor, penitentiary, Grand Penitentiary, spiritual director.
  religious, monastic, cenobite, conventual, abbot, prior, monk, friar, lay brother, beadsman *or* bedesman, mendicant, pilgrim, palmer; Jesuit, Franciscan, Friars minor, Minorites; Observant, Capuchin, Dominican, Carmelite; Augustinian; Gilbertine; Austin–, Black–, White–, Gray–, Crossed–, Crutched- Friars; Bonhomme, Carthusian, Benedictine, Cistercian, Trappist, Cluniac, Premonstratensian, Maturine; Templar, Hospitaler; Bernardine, Lorettine, pillarist, stylite; caloyer, hieromonach [*both Eastern Ch.*].
  nun, sister, *religieuse* [*F.*]; priestess, abbess, prioress, canoness; mother superior, superioress, the reverend mother; novice, postulant.
  [jewish] prophet, priest, high priest, Levite; Rabbi, Rabbin, scribe.
  [mohammedan] imam *or* imaum, kahin, kasis, sheik; mullah, murshid, mufti; hadji *or* haji, muezzin [*all Ar.*]; dervish *or* darvesh [*Pers.*], abdal (*pl.* abdali) [*Pers.*], fakir *or* faquir [*Ar.*], beshara [*Hind.*], bashara [*Hind.*], santon [*Turkey*].
  [hindu] Brahman *or* Brahmin, pujari, purohit [*family priest*]; pundit *or* pandit, guru; yogi, sannyasi *or* sanyasi; bhikshu, bhikhari, vairagi *or* bairagi, Ramwat, Ramanandi [*all Hind.*].
  [buddhist] poonghie *or* poonghee [*Burma*], talapoin [*Ceylon & Indo-China*], bonze; lama, Grand Lama *or* Dalai Lama [*Tibet*].
  [various] druid, druidness [*ancient Celts*]; flamen [*Rom. relig. and ancient Britain*]; hierus, hierophant [*Gr. relig.*]; daduchus *or* dadouchos, mystae, epoptae [*Eleusinian Mysteries*].
- v. take orders etc. 995.
- adj. **ordained**, in orders, in holy orders, called to the ministry; the Reverend, the very Reverend, the Right Reverend.

997. Laity

- n. **laity**, flock, fold, congregation, assembly, brethren, people; society; class [*Meth.*], meeting.
  layman, civilian [*obs.*], laic, parishioner, catechumen; secularist.
- v. **laicize**, secularize.
- adj. **secular**, lay, laic *or* laical, congregational, civil, temporal, profane.

998. Rite

- n. **rite**, ceremony, ceremonial, ordinance, observance, function, duty; form, formulary; solemnity, sacrament; incantation etc. (*spell*) 993; service, ministry, ministration; liturgics.
  sermon, preaching, preachment, predication [*obs. or Scot.*], exhortation, religious harangue, homily, lecture, discourse, pastoral.
  [seven sacraments] **baptism**, immersion, christening, chrism; baptismal regeneration; font.
  confirmation, imposition of hands, laying on of hands.
  eucharist, Lord's supper, communion; the sacrament, the holy sacrament; consecrated elements, bread and wine; intinction; celebration, high celebration; *missa cantata* [*L.*]; *asperges* [*L.*]; offertory; introit; consecration; consubstantiation, impanation, subpanation, transubstantiation; real presence; elements; Mass; high–, low–, dry- mass; hunter's (*or* hunting) mass [*obs.*].
  penance etc. (*atonement*) 952; flagellation, maceration, fasting, sackcloth and ashes.
  extreme unction, last rites, viaticum.
  holy orders, ordination etc. (*churchdom*) 995.
  matrimony, marriage, wedlock etc. 903.

worship etc. 990; invocation of saints, canonization, transfiguration, auricular confession, the confessional; absolution; reciting the rosary, telling of beads; processional; thurification, incense, holy water, aspersion.

circumcision; purification; visitation of the sick; burial etc. 363.

[sacred articles] relics, rosary, beads, reliquary, host, cross, rood, crucifix; pyx, pix [*obs.*]; pax, *Agnus Dei* [*L.*], censer, thurible, incensory, patera; urceus, urceole; prayer wheel, prayer machine; Sangraal *or* Sangrael, Holy Grail.

ritual, rubric, canon, ordinal, missal, breviary, Mass book, beadroll; farse; liturgy, prayer book, Book of Common Prayer, *Pietà* [*It.*], euchologion *or* euchology [*Eastern Ch.*], litany, lectionary.

psalter, psalm book, hymn book, hymnal; hymnology, psalmody.

ritualism, ceremonialism; sabbatism, sabbatarianism; ritualist, sabbatarian.

holyday, feast, fast; Sabbath, Passover, Pentecost; Advent, Christmas, Epiphany, Lent; Passion Week, Holy Week; Good Friday, Easter; Ascension Day, Holy Thursday; Whitsuntide, Whitsunday *or* Whit-Sunday [*erroneously,* Whitsun Day]; Trinity Sunday, Corpus Christi; All Saints *or* All Saints' Day, All Souls' Day; love feast, agape; Candlemas *or* Candlemas Day; Lammas, Lammas Day, Lammastide; Michaelmas, Martinmas.

v. **perform service**, do duty, minister, officiate; baptize, dip, sprinkle; confirm, lay hands on; give–, administer–, take–, receive–, attend–, partake of- the -sacrament, –communion, –Holy Eucharist; communicate; celebrate Mass, celebrate; administer–, receive- extreme unction; anele [*obs.*], shrive, absolve; administer–, receive- absolution; confess, make confession; do–, perform–, receive–, inflict- penance; tell one's beads; genuflect; make the sign of the Cross.

excommunicate, ban with bell book and candle.

preach, sermonize, predicate, lecture, address the congregation.

adj. **ritual**, ritualistic, ceremonial; liturgic *or* liturgical; baptismal, eucharistical; paschal.

999. Canonicals

n. **canonicals**, vestments; robe, gown, Geneva gown, frock, pallium, surplice, cotta, cassock; communion cloth, eileton [*Eastern Ch.*], corporal [*Western Ch.*]; scapular *or* scapulary, cope, mozetta *or* mozzetta, amice, scarf, fanon *or* fannel, bands, chasuble, tunicle, dalmatic, alb *or* alba, stole; tonsure, cowl, hood, capuche, calotte; vagas *or* vakas *or* vakass; apron, lawn sleeves, pontificals, pall; miter *or* mitre, tiara, triple crown; shovel–, cardinal's-hat; biretta *or* berretta; crosier *or* crozier, cross staff, pastoral staff; Sanctus bell, sacring bell; seven-branched candlestick; monstrance; censer etc. 998; costume etc. 225.

1000. Temple

n. **temple**, place of worship; house of God, house of prayer; cathedral, minister, church, kirk [*Scot. & dial. Eng.*], chapel, meeting-house, bethel, ebenezer [*Eng.*], conventicle, basilica, fane, holy place, chantry, oratory.

synagogue, tabernacle; mosque, masjid [*Moham.*]; dewal, kan-pati [*both Hindu*], girja [*Hind., Christian*]; pagoda, pagod [*archaic*], kiack [*Buddhist*]; Chinese temple, joss house [*colloq.*]; pantheon.

shrine, dagoba [*India*]; tope, stupa [*Buddhist*], Marabout [*Moham.*].

[interior] altar, sanctuary, Holy of Holies, *sanctum sanctorum* [*L.*], sacristy; sacrarium; communion–, holy–, Lord's- table; table of the Lord; pyx; baptistery, font; piscina; stoup; holy-water stoup, holy-water basin; ambry, aumbry [*archaic*]; sedile; reredos; rood screen, rood beam, chapel screen, jube; rood loft.

chancel, apse, choir, quire [*archaic*], nave, triforium, blindstory, aisle, transept, crypt, porch, cloisters; churchyard, golgotha; calvary, Easter sepulcher; stall, pew, seat, seating; pulpit, ambo, lectern, reading desk; confessional; prothesis, table (*or* altar) of prothesis, chapel of prothesis [*Eastern Ch.*]; credence, baldachin *or* baldaquin; belfry; vestry, chapter house; presbytery; diaconicon *or* diaconicum; mourners' bench, mourners' seat; anxious bench, anxious seat, penitent form.

monastery, priory, abbey, friary, convent, nunnery, cloister.

parsonage, rectory, vicarage, manse, deanery, clergy house; glebe; Vatican; bishop's palace; Lambeth.

adj. **churchly**, claustral, cloistered, monastic, monasterial, monachal, conventual; cruciform.

Index Guide

The numbers refer to the headings under which the words or phrases occur. When the same word or phrase can be used in various senses, the several headings under which it, or its synonyms, will be found are indicated by *italics*. These words in italics are not intended to explain the meaning of the word or phrase to which they are annexed, but only to assist in the required reference.

Italicized references within parentheses are merely suggestive, the parentheses indicating that the term itself is not included in the list referred to.

When the word given in the Index Guide is itself the title or heading of a category, the reference number is printed in bold-face type, thus: **abode 189.**

To keep the Index Guide—necessarily very large—from becoming unwieldy, a considerable number of obsolete, rare, foreign, dialectic, and slang terms have been omitted. Such words, while useful in the text, are not the ones for which synonyms would ordinarily be sought.

Derivatives likewise have been sparingly admitted, since the allied or basic term will serve as a key to the various derived forms; thus, *cold* is given, but not *coldness* or *coldly*. By such means, unnecessary duplication is avoided.

IMPORTANT NOTE

The numbers following all references in this Index Guide refer to the *section numbers* in the text, and *not* to pages. Thus "Aaronic 995" refers to *section* 995, under which the citation will be found. For further ease of reference, the *section* numbers will be found at the *top* of every page.

A

A 1 273, 648
  —at Lloyd's 273
Aaronic 995
A. B. 269
abacist 85
aback 235 take—508
abaction 791
abacus 85
Abaddon 978, 982
abaft 235
abalienate 783
abandon
  depart from 293
  —*a purpose* 624
  —*property* 782
  —*hope* 859
  —*society* 893
abandon *lively* 682
  artless 703
abandoned
  neglected 460
  forsaken 893
  vicious 945
  —*farm* 782
abandonment 757
abase *depress* 308
  degrade 879
abased 886
abasement
  disrepute 874
  servility 886
abash *daunt* 860
  humiliate 879

abashed *modest* 881
abate *lessen* 36
  —*a price* 813
abatement 36
  —*of differences* 774
abatjour 260
abattis 717
abattoir 361
abat-voix 417
abba 166
abbacy 995
abbatial 995
abbatis 717
abbess 996
abbey 1000
abbot 996
abbreviation
  shortening 201
  compendium 596
abbreviatory
  short 201
  compendious 596
abbreviature 596
A B C *beginning* 66
  teaching 537
  letters 561
abdal *fanatic* 984
  clergy 996
abderian 836
abdicant 757
abdicate
  —*a throne* 738
  resign 757
abditory 530
abdomen 221, 250
abdominal 221, 250

abdominoscope 445
abdominous 194
abducent 289
abduct *repel* 289
  take 789
  steal 791
abduction 289
abductor 792
abecedarian
  teacher 540
  learner 541
abecedary *school* 542
  letter 561
aberdevine 366
aberrant
  exceptional 83
  deviating 279
  divergent 291
  erroneous 495
aberration
  (see aberrant)
  variation 20a
  mental—503
abet 707
abettor 711
abeyance *extinction* 2
  suspense 142
  expectation 507
  in—172
abeyant 526
abhor *dislike* 867
  hate 898
abhorrence
  (see abhor)
abhorrent
  painful 830

abide *endure* 1, 106
  remain 110
  continue 141, 143
  dwell 186
  quiet 265
  expect 507
  —*by assent* 488
  observe 772
  —with
  be composed 826
  not—867
abigail 746
abilities
  to the best of one's
  —686
ability *power* 157
  skill 698
abiogenesis 161, 357
abirritate 834
abito 350
abject *vile* 874, 940
  servile 886
  —*fear* 862
abjunction 44
abjuratory 536, 757
abjure *deny* 536
  renounce 607
  resign 757
abkari 812
ablation
  subduction 38
  taking 789
ablaze *heat* 382
  light 420
able *capable* 157
  skillful 698

—*seaman* 269
able-bodied 159
ablegate *displace* 185
  depute 759
ablepsia 442
ablude 15
ablution 652
abnegation
  denial 536
  refusal 764
  forbearance 953
  self—942
abnormal 83
  —*mind* 503
abnormalize 83
aboard *present* 186
  ship 273
  go—293
abode 189 *presage* 511
  take up one's
  —*settle* 150
  locate oneself 184
abodement 511
aboideau 350
abolish (see abolition)
abolition *destroy* 162
  abrogate 756
abolitionist 756
abolitionize 756
abomasum 191
abominable *bad* 649
  foul 653
  hateful 898
abominate
  dislike 867
  hate 898

367

abomination   **accord**

abomination 649
abord 894
aboriginal
  beginning 66
  cause 153
aborigines 188
aborticide 361
abortion
  immaturity 674
  failure 732
abound 639
about *relative to* 9
  nearly 32
  near 197
  around 227
  −*it and about* 573
  −*to* 121
  −*to be* 152
    be−*busy with* 625
    active 682
    beat−629
    come−658
    get−*public* 531
    recover 660
    go−*turn* 311
    going−*news* 532
    put−*turn round* 283
    round−311
    set−676
    turn−*invert* 218
    what it is−454
    what one is−625
above 206−*all*
  superior 33
  important 642
  −*board manifest* 525
    artless 703
    fair 939
  −*comprehension* 519
  −*ground alive* 359
  −*par great* 31
    good 648
  −*praise* 944
  −*price* 814
  −*stairs* 206
  −*suspicion* 946
  −*the mark* 33
  −*water safe* 664
above−mentioned
  preceding 62
  repeated 104
  prior 116
abra 198
abracadabra 993
abrade (*see* abrasion)
Abraham, sham−544
abrasion *paring* 38
  filing 330, 331
abrasive 331
abreast 216, 236
abregé 596
abreption 789
abridge *lessen* 36
  shorten 201
  −*in writing* 572, 596
abridger 201

abridgment
  compendium 596
abroach 673
abroad *extraneous* 57
  distant 196
  uncertain 475
  astir 673
  get−*public* 531
abrogation 756
abrupt *sudden* 113
  violent 173
  steep 217
  unexpected 508
  style 579
abruption 44
abscess 655
abscind 44
abscissa 466
abscission
  retrenchment 38
  division 44
abscond 623
absconder 808
absence
  nonpresence 187
  −*d'esprit* 452
  −*of choice* 609a
  −*of influence* 175a
  −*of intellect* 450a
  −*of mind* 458
  −*of motive* 615a
absent (*see* absence)
absentee 187
absent−minded 458
absinthe 435
absolute
  not relative 1
  great 31
  complete 52
  certain 474
  affirmative 535
  authoritative 737
  severe 739
  free 748
  unalienable 924
  −*establishment* 478
  −*interest property* 980
  make−*confirm* 467
  adjudge 480
Absolute, the 450
absolution 918
absolutism 739
absolve *liberate* 750
  forgive 918
  exempt 927a
  shrive 952, 998
  acquit 970
absonant
  discordant 414
  unreasonable 477
absorb *combine* 48
  take in 296
  consume 677
  −*the mind*
    attention 457
    inattention 458

  −*the soul* 824
absorbed 451
absorbent 296
  (*see* absorb)
absorbing *exigent* 630
  impressive 821
absorption 296
absquatulate 623
abstain *refrain* 623
  disuse 678
  temperance 953
  −*from action* 681
  −*from voting* 609a
abstainer 953, 958
abstemious 953
abstention 623
absterge 652
abstersive 662
abstinence
  (*see* abstain)
  total−953, 955
abstract *separate* 44
  abridge 596
  take 789
  steal 791
  −*idea* 453
  −*oneself*
    inattention 458
  −*thought* 451
    attention 457
  in the−apart 44
  alone 87
abstracted
  inattentive 458
abstraction
  (*see* abstract)
abstruse 519
absurd (*see* absurdity)
  −*statement* 546
absurdity
  impossible 471
  nonsense **497**
  ridiculous 853
abulia 605
Abuna 996
abundance 639
  poor in−832
abundant *great* 31
  enough 639
abuse *deceive* 545
  illtreat 649
  misuse 679
  insolence 885
  malediction 908
  threat 909
  upbraid 932
  violate 961
  −*of language* 563
  −*of terms* 523
abusive
  discourteous 895
  defamatory 934, 936
abut *adjoin* 197
  touch 199
  rest on 215
abutment *defense* 717

abutter 199
aby *remain* 141
  endure 821, 826
abysm 198
abysmal *deep* 208
abyss *space* 180
  interval 198
  depth 208
  pitfall 667
  hell 982
acacia 367
academic *theory* 514
  teaching 537, 542
academical *style* 578
academician 492
  Royal−559
academy 542
acanaceous 253
acanthophorous 253
acanthus 847
acariâtre 901
acarpous 169
acatalectic 597
acatastasia 139
acaudal 38
acaudate 38
accede *assent* 488
  submit 725
  consent 762
accelerate *early* 132
  stimulate 173
  velocity 274
  hasten 684
accelerometer 490a
accension 384
accent *sound* 402
  tone of voice 580
  rhythm 597
accentuate 642
accentuated 581
accentuation 580
accept *assent* 488
  consent 762
  receive 785
  take 789
accepta 810
acceptable
  expedient 646
  agreeable 829
acceptance
  security 771
acceptation
  meaning 516
  interpretation 522
acception 522
access *approach* 286
  easy of−705
  means of−627
accessible
  possible 470
  easy 705
accession *increase* 35
  addition 37
  −*to office* 737, 755
  consent 762
accessory *extrinsic* 6

additive 37
adjunct 39
accompanying 88
aid 707
auxiliary 711
acciaccatura 413
accidence 567
accident *event* 151
  chance 156
  disaster 619
  misfortune 735
  −*of an accident* 156
  fatal−361
accidental *extrinsic* 6
  irrelative 10
  occasional 134
  fortuitous 156
  undesigned 621
accidentalism 156
Accipitres 739
acclamation
  assent 488
  approbation 931
acclamatory 931
acclimatize
  domesticate 370
  inure 613
acclivity 217
accloy 641
accolade 894
accommodate *suit* 23
  adjust 27
  aid 707
  reconcile 723
  give 784
  lend 787
  −*oneself to*
    conform 82
accommodating
  kind 906
accommodation
  (*see* accommodate)
  space 180
  −*train* 272
accompaniment
  adjunct 39
  coexistence **88**
  musical 415
accompanist 416
accompany *add* 37
  coexist 88
  concur 120
  music 416
  escort 664
accomplice 711
accomplish
  execute 161
  complete 729
  succeed 731
accomplishment
  learning 490
  talent 698
accompts 811
accord *uniform* 16
  agree 23
  music 413

368

accordance

assent 488
concord 714
grant 760
give 784
of one's own–600, 602
accordance 23
according–as
  qualification 469
  –to *evidence* 467
  –to *circumstances* 8
  –to Gunter 82
  –to law 963
  –to rule
  conformably 82
accordingly
  logically 476
accordion 417
accordionist 416
accost 586
accouchement 161
accoucheur
  minister 631
  doctor 662
accoucheuse 662
account *list* 86
  adjudge 480
  description 594
  credit 805
  money–811
  fame 873
  approbation 931
  –as *deem* 484
  –for *attribution* 155
  interpret 522
  –with *trade* 794
  pay 807
  call to– *censure* 932
  find one's–in
  useful 644
  success 731
  make no–of
  undervalue 483
  despise 930
  not–for
  unintelligible 519
  on–of *cause* 155
  motive 615
  behalf 707
  on no–536
  send to one's–
  kill 361
  small–643
  take into–
  attend to 457
  qualify 469
  to one's–
  property 780
  turn to–
  improve 658
  use 677
  success 731
  gain 775
accountable
  liable 177
  debit 811

duty 926
accountant
  treasurer 801
  auditor 811
  –general 801
accounting 811
accounts 811
accouple 43
accouter 717
accouterment
  dress 225
  appliance 633
  equipment 673
accoy 174
accredit
  commission 755, 759
  money 805
  honor 873
accredited
  believed 484
  recognized 613
  –to 755, 759
accretion *increase* 35
  coherence 46
accrimination 938
accroach 789
accrue *add* 37
  result 154
  acquire 775
  be received 785, 810
accruement 775
accubation 213
accueil 894
accultural 658
acculturation 658
accumbent 213
accumulate *collect* 72
  store 636
  redundance 641
accumulation
  (see accumulate)
  increase 35
accurate 494
  –knowledge 490
accurse 908
accursed
  disastrous 649
  undone 828
  vicious 945
accusation 938
accuse *disapprove* 932
  charge 938
  lawsuit 969
accustom *habit* 613
accustomary 613
ace *small quantity* 32
  unit 87
  aviator 269a
  cards 840
  within an–197
aceldama *kill* 361
  arena 728
acephalous 59
acequiador 350
acerb 397
acerbate *embitter* 659

aggravate 835
acerbic 955
acerbity
  acrimony 395
  sourness 397
  rudeness 895
  spleen 900, 901
  malevolence 907
acervate 72
acervatim 72, 102, 641
acescence 397
acetaldehyde 490b
acetic 397–acid 397
acetify 397
acetosity 397
acetous 397
acetum 397
achar 393
acharne 900
Achates, fidus–
  friend 890
  faithful 939
ache *cold* 383
  physical 378
  mental 828
Acheron *pit of*–982
achievable 470
achieve *end* 67
  produce 161
  do 680
  accomplish 729
achievement
  hatchment 550
  sign 551
  feat 861
Achillean 900
Achilles–absent 187
  heel of–
  vulnerable 665
aching 383
achromatism 429
achromatization 429
acicular 253
acid 397
acidify 397
aciform 253
acinaciform 253
acknowledge
  answer 462
  assent 488
  disclose 529
  avow 535
  consent 762
  observe 772
  pay 807
  thank 916
  repent 950
  reward 973
  –the corn 529
acknowledged
  custom 613
acme 210
  –of perfection 650
acology 662
acolyte 996

acomia 846
aconite 663
acoumetry 602
acoustic 402, 418
  –organs 418
acoustician 402
acoustics *sound* 402
  hearing 418
acquaint
  –oneself with 539
  –with 527
acquaintance
  knowledge 490
  information 527
  friend 890
  make–with 888
acquest 780
acquiesce *assent* 488
  willing 488
  consent 762
  tolerate 826
acquiescence
  assent 488
  submission 725
  observance 772
acquire *develop* 161
  get 775
  receive 785
  –a habit 613
  –learning 539
acquirement
  knowledge 490
  learning 539
  talent 698
  receipt 810
acquisition
  knowledge 490
  gain **775**
acquisitive 775
acquit *liberate* 750
  accounts 811
  exempt 927a
  vindicate 937
  innocent 946
  absolve 970
acquit oneself
  behave 692
  –of a debt 807
  –of a duty 926
  –of an obligation 772
acquittal 970
acquittance
  receipt 771
acreage 180
acres *space* 180
  land 342
  property 780
Acres, Bob
  coward 862
acrid *pungent* 392
  unsavory 395
acridity *causticity* 171
  pungency 392
  unsavoriness 395
acrimony
  physical 171

discourtesy 895
hatred 898
anger 900
irascibility 901
malevolence 907
acritude 395
acroama 490
acroamatic 490, 519
acrobat *strength* 159
  actor 599
  proficient 700
  mountebank 844
acrobatism 159
acrophobia 821a
acropolis 666
acrospire 167
across *transverse* 219
  opposite 708
acrostic *letter* 561
  wit 842
act *imitate* 19
  physical 170
  –of a play 599
  personate 599
  voluntary 680
  statute 697
  –a part *feign* 544
  –one's part
  business 625
  duty 926
  –upon *physical* 170
  mental 615
  take steps 680
  –up to 772
  –well one's part 944
  –without authority 738
  in the–*doing* 680
  guilt 947
acting *deputy* 759
actinic 420
actinology 420
actinometer 445
action *physical* 170
  voluntary **680**
  battle 720
  law 969
  line of–692
  mix with–170
  put in–677
  suit the–to the
  word 550, 599
  thick of the–682
actionable 964
activate 171
active *physical* 171
  voluntary 682
  –service 722
  –thought 457
activity 682
actor *impostor* 548
  player 599
  agent 690
  affectation 855
Acts *record* 551
  Apostolic 985

369

actual existing 1
  present 118
  real 494
  (*identical* 13)
actuality (*see* actual)
actualize 220
actuary 85, 811
actuate *influence* 175
  incite 615
acuity 253
aculeated 253
acumen 498
acuminated 253
acupuncture 260
acute *energetic* 171
  physically violent 173
  pointed 253
  physically sensible 375
  musical tone 410
  discriminative 465
  perspicacious 498
  cunning 702
  strong feeling 821
  morally painful 830
  –*angle* 244
  –*ear* 418
  –*note* 410
acutely 31
acuteness 465
A. D. 106
adactylism 848
adaga 727
adage 496
adagio *music* 415
  slow 275
Adam *sin* 945
adamant *strong* 159
  hard 323
Adam's ale 337
Adam's needle 253
adapt *agree* 23
  equalize 27
  –*oneself to conform* 82
adaptable
  conformable 82
  useful 644
adaptation
  (*see* adapt)
add *increase* 35
  join 37
  numerically 85
  accounts 811
addendum 39
adder 366, 913
  deafness 419
addict *habit* 613
adding machine 85
additament 39
addition (*see* add)
  adjunction **37**
  thing added 39
  arithmetical 85
addle *barren* 169

incomplete 730
  abortive 732
  –*the wits bewilder* 475
  craze 503
addle–head 501
addle–headed 499
address *compose* 54
  residence 189
  direction 550
  speak to 586
  skill 698
  request 765
addressee 188
addresses
  courtship 902
adduce *bring to* 288
  evidence 467
adduct 288
adeem 789
adelomorphous 83
ademption 789
adenology 329
  intellectual 450
  proficient 698, 700
adept
adequate *power* 157
  sufficient 639
  for a purpose 644
  content 831
adespotic 738
adhere *stick* 46
  –*to persevere* 604a
  habit 613
  –*to a duty* 926
  –*to an obligation* 772
adherent 65, 711
adhesive *sticking* 46
  tenacious 327
  sticky 352
adhibit 677
adhortation 695
adiaphanous 426
adiathermancy 382
adieu *departure* 293
  loss 776
adipocere 356
adipose 355
adit *orifice* 260
  conduit 350
  passage 627
adjacent 197
adjection 37
adjective 39
  –*jerker* 593
adjoin *near* 197
  contact 199
adjourn *postpone* 133
  neglect 460
adjudge 480
adjudicate 480
adjunct *addition* 37
  thing added **39**
  accompaniment 88
  aid 707
  auxiliary 711

adjuration
  affirmation 535
  negation 536
adjure *request* 765
  promise 768
adjust *adapt* 23
  equalize 27
  regulate 58
  prepare 673
  settle 723
  –*differences* 774
adjustment 762, 774
adjutant
  auxiliary 711
  military 745
adjuvant *helping* 707
  auxiliary 711
admeasurement 466
administer
  utilize 677
  conduct 693
  exercise authority 737
  distribute 786
  –*correction* 972
  –*oath* 768
  –*sacrament* 998
  –*to aid* 707
  give 784
administration of justice 965
administrative
  official 737
  judicial 965
admirable
  excellent 648
  virtuous 944
admiral 745
Admiralty, court of – 966
admiration
  wonder 870
  love 897
  respect 928
  approval 931
admirer 897
admissible
  relevant 23
  receivable 296
  tolerable 651
  –*in society* 852
admission (*see* admit)
admit *composition* 54
  include 76
  let in 296
  assent 488
  acknowledge 529
  permit 760
  concede 762
  accept 785
  –*exceptions* 469
  –*of* 470
admitted
  customary 613
  –*maxim etc.* 496
admixture 41

admonish *warn* 668
  advise 695
  reprove 932
admonitory 616
ado *activity* 682
  exertion 686
  difficulty 704
  make much–about important 642
  much–about nothing overestimate 482
  unimportant 643
  unskillful 699
adobe 635
adolescence **131**
Adonis 845
adonize 847
adopt *naturalize* 184
  choose 609
  appropriate 788
  –*a cause aid* 707
  –*a course* 692
  –*an opinion* 484
adoption *religious* 987
adore *love* 897
  worship 990
adorn 847
adown 207
adrift *unrelated* 10
  disjoined 44
  dispersed 73
  uncertain 475
  unapt 699
  liberated 750
  go–deviate 279
  turn–disperse 73
  liberate 750
  dismiss 756
adroit 698
adscititious
  extrinsic 6
  added 37
  redundant 641
adulation 933
adulator 935
Adullam, cave of–
  desertion 624
  discontent 832
adult 131
adulterate *mix* 41
  deteriorate 659
adulterated
  sham 545
adulterer 962
adultery 961
adulthood 131
adultism 131
adumbrate
  darkness 421
  allegorize 521
  represent 554
adumbration
  semblance 21
  darkness 421
  allusion 526

aduncate 245
aduncity 244
adust *arid* 340
  heated 384
  brown 433
adustion 384
advance *increase* 35
  course 109
  progress 282
  assert 535
  improve 658
  aid 707
  succeed 731
  lend 787
  –*against* 716
  –*agent* 599
  –*guard* 234
  –*of learning etc.* 490
  –*upon* 303
  in–precedence 62
  front 234
  precession 280
  in–of superior 33
  in–of one's age 498
advanced 282
  –*in life* 128
  –*work* 717
advancement
  (*see* advance)
  infringement 303
advances, make–
  offer 763
  social 892
advantage
  superiority 33
  increase 35
  influence 175
  benefit 618
  expedience 646
  –*over success* 731
  dressed to–847
  find one's–in 644
  *gain an–*775
  *mechanical–*633
  *set off to–*658
  take–of use 677
  make the most of 698
advantageous
  beneficial 648
  profitable 775
advene 37
Advent 998
advent *futurity* 121
  event 151
  approach 286
  arrival 292
Adventist 984
adventitious
  extrinsic 6
  casual 156
adventive 156
adventure *event* 151
  chance 156
  pursuit 622
  danger 665

adventurer

trial 675
undertaking 676
adventurer
  traveler 268
  experimenter 463
  deceiver 548
  gambler 621
  rash 863
  ignoble 876
adventures
  history 594
adventuress 548
adventurous
  undertaking 676
  bold 861
  rash 863
adversaria 551
adversary 710
Adversary, the–978
adverse *contrary* 14
  opposed 708
  unprosperous 735
  disliking 867
  –*party* 710
adversity 735
advert 457
advertent 457
advertise 531
advice *notice* 527
  news 532
  counsel **695**
  good–695
advisable 646
advise *predict* 511
  inform 527
  counsel 695
  –*with one's pillow* 451
advised
  predetermined 611
  intended 620
  better–658
advisement
  advice 695
  (see advise)
  under–453
adviser *teacher* 540
  counselor 695
advisory 527
advocacy
  approbation 931
advocate
  interpreter 524
  prompt 615
  recommend 695
  aid 707
  auxiliary 711
  friend 890, 914
  vindicate 937
  counselor 968
Advocate, the–
  Savior 976
advocation *plea* 617
advoutress 962
advoutry 961
advowson 995

adynamic 160
adytum *room* 191
  prediction 511
  secret place 530
aedile 965
aegis 717
Aeolian 349
  –*harp* 417
Aeolus 349
aeon 109, 110
aerate 334, 353
aeration 334
aerial *elevated* 206
  navigation 267, 273
  gas 334
  air 338
  –*mail* 534
  –*mail–carrier* 271
  –*navigator* 269
  –*perspective* 428
  –*railway* 840
aerie 189
aeriferous 334
aerification 334
aeriform 334
aerify 334
aeroboat 273
aerobus 273
aerodonetics 267
aerodrome 273
aerodynamics
  navigation 267
  gas 334
  wind 349
aerography 334, 349
aero–hydroplane 273
aerolite 318
aerology *gaseity* 334
  air 338
  wind 349
aeromancy 511
aeromechanic 267, 334
aerometer 338
aerometric 338
aeronat 273
aeronaut 269a
aeronautic 273
  (see aeronautics)
aeronautics
  navigation 267
  air 338
aeroplane 273
  combatant 726
  by–684
aeroplanist 269
aeroscope 338
aeroscopy 334
aerosphere 338
aerostat *balloon* 273
aerostatics 267 334
aerostation 338
aerotherapy 662
aeroyacht 273
aery *gaseous* 334

atmospheric 338
Aesculapius 662
Aesop 846
aesthetic
  sensibility 375
  beauty 845
  taste 850
aestival 125
aestivation 384
aetiology *causes* 155
  life 359
  knowledge 490
  disease 655
afar 196
afeard 860
affable
  condescending 879
  courteous 894
affair *event* 151
  topic 454
  business 625
  battle 720
  –*of honor* 720
affaires, chargé d'– 758
affect *relate to* 9
  tend to 176
  qualify 469
  feign 544
  touch 824
  desire 865
  love 897
affectation 855
affected 583
  –*manner* 880
affected with
  feeling 821
  disease 655
affectibility 822
affecting *pathetic* 830
affection *feeling* 821
  love 897
affectionate 821, 897
affections 820
affettuoso *music* 415
affiance *promise* 768
  trust 858
affianced *love* 897
  marriage 903
affiche 531
affidation 769
affidavit
  affirmation 535
  record 551
  lawsuit 969
affiliation *relation* 9
  kindred 11
  attribution 155
affinal 11
affinitive 9
affinity *relation* 9
  similarity 17
affirmant 488
affirmation
  evidence 467
  assent 488

assert **535**
affirmative 535
affix *add* 37
  sequel 39
  fasten 43
  precedence 62
  letter 561
afflation 349
afflatus *wind* 349
  inspiration 985
afflict 830
  –*with illness* 655
affliction *pain* 828
  infliction 830
  adversity 735
affluence
  sufficiency 639
  prosperity 734
  wealth 803
affluent *river* 348
afflux 286
afford *supply* 784
  wealth 803
  yield 810
  sell for 812
  –*aid etc.* 707
affranchise
  make free of 748
  liberate 750
affray 720
affriction 331
affright 860
affront *molest* 830
  provocation 900
  insult 929
  –*danger* 861
affuse 337
affusion 73
afield 186
afire 382
afloat *extant* 1
  unstable 149
  going on 151
  ship 273
  navigation 267
  ocean 341
  news 532
  preparing 673
  keep oneself–734
  set–*publish* 531
afoot *on hand* 625
  ready 673
  astir 682
afore 116
aforegoing 116
aforehand 116
aforementioned 62, 116
aforesaid
  preceding 62
  repeated 104
  prior 116
aforesighted 116
aforethought 116, 611, 907
aforetime 116

again

a fortiori
  superiority 33
  evidence 467
  reasoning 476
afraid 860–*to say*
  uncertain 4
  be–*irresolute* 605
afreet 980
afresh *repeated* 104
  new 123
African 431
Afric heat 382
Afrikander 57
aft 235
after *in order* 63
  in time 117
  too late 135
  rear 235
  pursuit 622
  –*all for all that* 30
  qualification 469
  on the whole 476
  –*time* 133
  be–*intention* 620
  pursuit 622
  go–*follow* 281
after acceptance 516
after–age 124
afterbirth 63
afterburden 63
afterclap 63, 154, 509
aftercome 65, 154
aftercrop 63, 154, 168
afterdamp 663
afterdinner 117
afterglow
  decrement 40a
  sequence 63
  light 420
aftergrass 63
aftergrowth 65, 154
afterlife 152
aftermath
  sequence 63
  effect 154
  fertile 168
  profit 775
afternoon 126
  –*farmer* 683
afterpain 63
after–part *sequel* 65
  rear 235
afterpiece 63, 599
aftertaste 63, 390
afterthought
  thought 451
  memory 505
  change of mind 607
aftertime 121, 133
afterwards 117
aga 745
again *duplicate* 90
  repeated 104

371

against

—and again 136
come—*periodic* 138
against
 counteraction 179
 anteposition 237
 voluntary opposition 708
 —one's expectation 508
 —one's will 744
 —one's wishes 603
 —the grain
  difficult 704
  painful 830
  dislike 867
 —the stream 704
 —the time when 510
 go— 708
agalloch 400
agamist 904
agape *opening* 260
 curious 455
 expectant 507
 wonder 870
agape *love feast* 998
Agapemone
 pleasure 827
 love 897
agate 847
age *time* 106
 period 108
 course 109
 long time 110
 present time 118
 oldness 124
 advanced life **128**
 from age to— 112
 of— 131
agency *physical* **170**
 instrumentality 631
 means 632
 employment 677
 voluntary action 680
 direction 693
 commission 755
agenda 625
 list of— 626
agent *physical* 153
 worker 686
 voluntary **690**
 consignee 758
 —*provocateur* 615
agentship 755
ages:—ago 122
 for— 110
agglomerate
 cohere 46
 assemble 72
agglutinate 46, 48
aggrandize
 in degree 35
 in bulk 194
 honor 873
aggravate *increase* 35
 vehemence 173
 exaggerate 549

render worse 659
distress 835
exasperate 900
aggravating
 painful 830
aggravation 835
aggregate *whole* 50
 collect 72
 number 84
aggregation 46
aggression 716
aggrieve *injure* 649
 distress 830
aggroup 72
aghast
 disappointed 509
 fear 860
 wonder 870
agile *swift* 274
 active 682
agio 813
agiotage 794
agitate *move* 315
 inquire 461
 activity 682
 excite the feelings 824
 —a *question* 476
agitation (see *agitate*)
 changeableness 149
 energy 171
 motion **315**
 in—*preparing* 673
agitator *leader* 694
aglet 554
aglow *warm* 382
 shine 420
agnate 11
agnition 762
agnomen 564
agnosia 821a
agnostic 487
agnosticism 451, 989
agnus Dei 998
ago 122
agog *expectant* 507
 desire 865
 wonder 870
 (*envious* 455)
agoing 682 set—707
agone 122
agonism 720
agonistic 159
agonize 972
agonizing
 thrilling 824
 painful 830
agony *physical* 378
 mental 828
 —of *death* 360
 —of *excitement* 825
agora 182
agoraphobia 860
agostadero 344
agrarian 371
agree *accord* 23

concur 178
assent 488
concord 714
consent 762
compact 769
compromise 774
—in *opinion* 488
—with *salubrity* 656
agreeable
 consistent 82
 physically 377
 consenting 762
 mentally 829
agreeably to
 conformably 82
agreement 23
 (see *agree*)
 compact 769
agrestic 189, 371
agriculture 342, **371**
agriculturist 342
agronomics 342, 371
agronomist 371
agronomy 342, 371
aground *fixed* 150
 in difficulty 704
 failure 732
agua 337
aguardiente 959
ague 655
ague fit 860
agueweed 662
aguish *cold* 383
aha! *rejoicing* 838
ahead *in front* 234
 procession 280
 go—*progression* 282
Ahriman 978
aid *help* **707**
 charity 906
 —to *memory* 505
 by the—of
 instrument 631
 means 632
aidance 707
aide-de-camp
 auxiliary 711
 officer 745
aider (see *aid*)
aidless 160
aigrette 847
aiguille 253
aigulet 847
ail *sick* 655
 pain 828
aileron 267, 273
ailment 655
aim *direction* 278
 purpose 620
 essay 675
 —a *blow at* 716
 —*high* 305
aimable 278
aimless
 without design 59, 621

without motive 615a
Ainu 372a
air *unsubstantial* 4
 broach 66
 lightness 320
 gas 334
 atmospheric **338**
 wind 349
 tune 415
 appearance 448
 refresh 689
 fashionable 852
 fill the— 404
 fine—salubrity 656
 take— 531
air balloon 273
air bladder 334
air bubble 250
aircraft 273
air cruiser 273
air-drawn 515
air engine 633
air gun 727
air hole 260, 351
airing 266
air line 278
airman 269
airmanship 267, 698
air pipe 349, **351**
airplane 273
air pump 349
airs *affectation* 855
 pride 878
 vanity 880
 arrogance 885
air shaft 351
airship 273
air-tight 261
air tube 351
airward 206
airway 351
airwoman 269a
airworthy 273, 664
airy (see *air*)
 windy 349
 unimportant 643
 gay 836
 —*hopes* 858, 859
 —*tongues* 532
aisle *passage* 260
 way 627
 in *a church* 1000
ait 346
aitchbone 235
ajar *open* 260
 discordant 713
ajee 217
ajutage *opening* 260
 pipe 350
akimbo *angular* 244
 stand— 715
akin *related* 11
 similar 17
alabaster *white* 430
alack! 839
alacran 913

alerte

alacrity *willing* 602
 active 682
 cheerful 836
Aladdin's lamp 993
alameda 189
alar 39
alarm *warning* 668
 notice of danger **669**
 fear 860
 cause for— 665
 give an
 —*indicate* 550
alarmist 862
alarum *loudness* 404
 indication 550
 notice of danger 669
alas! 839
alate 39
alb 999
alba 999
Albany beef 298
Albany hemp 663
albata 430, 545
albatross 366
albeit 30
alberca 343
albescence 430
albication 430
albification 430
albinism 430
albino 443
albinoism 430
Alborah 271
album *book* 593
 compendium 596
albumen
 semiliquid 352
 protein 161, 357
albumin 357
albuminoid 357
Alcaic 597
alcaid 745
alcalde 745, 967
alchemy 144
alcohol 959
alcoholism 959
Alcoran 986
alcove *bower* 191
 hollow 252
Aldebaran 423
alder 367
alderman 745
Alderney 366
ale 298
Alecto 173
alectromancy 511
alehouse 189
 go to the— 959
alembic
 conversion 144
 vessel 191
 furnace 386
 laboratory 691
alert *watchful* 459
 active 682
alerte 669

alertness 457
aleuromancy 511
Alexandrian school 451
Alexandrine
　ornate style 577
　verse 597
　(length 200)
alexandrite 847
alexipharmic 662
alexiteric 662
alfalfa 367
alfilaria 367
alfresco 220
algae 367, 369
algebra 85
algebraist 85
algid 383
algidity 383
algology 369
algorism 85
algorithm 85
alguazil 965
alias 18, 565
alibi 187
alien *irrelevant* 10
　foreign 57
　transfer 783
　gentile 989
alienable 783
alienage 57
alienate *disjoin* 44
　transfer 783
　estrange 889
　set against 898
alienation
　*mental–*503
aliéné 503
alienism 57
alight *stop* 265
　arrive 292
　descend 306
　on fire 382
align *horizontal* 213
　direction 278
aligned 216
alike 17
aliment *food* 298
　(materials 635)
alimentary
　regimen 662
alimentation *aid* 707
alimony *property* 780
　provision 803
　income 810
aliquot *part* 51
　number 84
alive *living* 359
　sentient 375
　intelligent 498
　active 682
　cheerful 836
　–to attention 457
　cognizant 490
　informed 527
　able 698

sensible 822
　–to impressions 375
　–with 102
　keep–continue 143
aljibar 636
alkahest 335
alkali 344
all *whole* 50
　complete 52
　generality 78
　–aboard 293
　–absorbing 642
　–agog 865
　–along 106
　–along of 154
　–at once 113
　–but 32
　–colors 440
　–considered
　　thought 451
　　judgment 480
　–day long 110
　–ears 418
　–eyes and ears 457
　–fours easy 705
　–cards 840
　–hail! welcome 292
　　honor to 873
　　celebration 883
　　courtesy 894
　–hands everybody 78
　–in 688
　–in all 50
　–in good time 152
　–in one's power 686
　–manner of
　　different 15
　　multiform 81
　–one equal 27
　　indifferent 866
　–out completely 52
　　error 495
　–over end 67
　　universal 78
　　destruction 162
　　space 180
　–powerful
　　mighty 159
　　God 976
　　completely 52
　　truly 494
　–right! 922
　–sorts diverse 16a
　　mixed 41
　　multiform 81
　–talk 4
　–the better 831
　–the go 852
　–the rage 852
　–the time 106
　–things to all men 894
　–ways distortion 243
　　deviation 279
　　at–events
　　compensation 30

qualification 469
true 494
resolve 604
at–points 52
at–times 136
in–ages 112
in–directions 278
in–quarters 180
on–hands 488
on–sides 227
Allah 976
allay *moderate* 174
　pacify 723
　relieve 834
　–excitability 826
all–destroying 162
all–devouring 162
allective 615
allege *evidence* 467
　assert 535
　plea 617
allegiance
　obedience 743
　duty 926
allegorization 521
allegory
　similitude 464
　metaphor 521
allegresse 836
allegro *music* 415
　cheerful 836
alleluia 990
all–embracing 56
all–engulfing 162
alleviate
　moderate 174
　relieve 834
alley *court* 189
　passage 260
　way 627
Allhallowmas 138
alliance *relation* 9
　kindred 11
　physical cooperation 178
　voluntary cooperation 709
　party 712
　union 714
allied 48*–to like* 17
alligation 43
alligator 366, 913
　–pear 298
alliteration
　similarity 17
　repetition 104
　style in writing 577
all–knowing 976
allness 52
allocation 60, 786
allocution 586
allodium *free* 748
　property 780
allopathy 662
alloquy 586
allot *arrange* 60

distribute 786
due 924
allow *assent* 488
　admit 529
　permit 760
　consent 762
　give 784
allowable
　permitted 760
　due 924
allowance
　qualification 469
　gift 784
　allotment 786
　discount 813
　salary 973
　make–for forgive 918
　vindicate 937
　*with grains of–*485
alloy *mixture* 41
　combine 48
　solution 335
　debase 659
all–possessed 503
All Saints' Day 138
all–searching 461
all–seeing 976
all–sided 52
All Souls' Day 138
allspice 393
all–star 599
all–sufficient 159
allude *hint* 514
　mean 516
　refer to 521
　latent 526
　inform 527
allure *move* 615
　create desire 865
alluring
　pleasurable 829
allusion 516
allusive 9
alluvial *level* 213
　land 342
　plain 344
alluvion 270, 348
alluvium *deposit* 40
　land 342
　soil 653
all–wise 976
ally *combine* 48
　auxiliary 711
　friend 890
Alma Mater 542
almanac
　chronometry 114
　record 86, 551
　–de Gotha 86
almighty 157
Almighty, the– 976
almond 298
almoner *giver* 784
　treasurer 801
　church officer 996

almonry 801
almost *nearly* 32
　not quite 651
　–all 50
　–immediately 132
alms *gift* 784
　benevolence 906
　worship 990
almshouse 189, 666
almsman 785
Alnaschar's dream
　imagination 515
　hope 858
alod 748
aloes 395
aloes wood 400
aloft 206
alogy 497
alone *single* 87
　unaided 706
　let–not use 678
　not restrain 748
　*never less–*893
along 200*–with*
　added 37
　together 88
　by means of 631
　get–progress 282
　go–depart 293
　go–with concur 178
　assent 488
　cooperate 709
alongside *near* 197
　parallel 216
　laterally 236
aloof *distant* 196
　high 206
　secluded 893
　stand–inaction 681
　refuse 764
　cautious 864
aloofness 893
alopecia 226
aloud 404 *think*
　–soliloquy 589
　naïveté 703
Alp 206
alpenstock 215
Alpha 66
　–and Omega 50
alphabet *beginning* 66
　letters 561
alphabetarian 541
alphabetize 60
alphitomancy 511
alpine *high* 206
Alpine Club
　traveler 268
　ascent 305
already
　antecedently 116
　even now 118
　past time 122
Alsatia *thieving* 791
Alsatian *den* 945
also 37

altar   **analgesia**

altar *marriage* 903
   church 1000
alter 140
   emasculate 158
   –one's *course* 279
   –the *case* 468
alterable 149
alterant 662
alteration
   correlation 12
   difference 15
alterative *remedy* 662
altercation 713
altered *worn* 688
   –for the *worse* 659
alter ego *similar* 17
   auxiliary 711
   deputy 759
   friend 890
alternacy 138
alternate
   reciprocal 12
   vary 20a
   sequence 63
   discontinuous 70
   periodic 138
   substitute 147, 634
   changeable 149
   oscillate 314
alternation 148
alternative
   substitute 147
   choice 609
   plan 626
although
   compensation 30
   counteraction 179
   unless 469
   (*opposition* 708)
altiloquence 577
altimeter 206
altimetry *height* 206
   angle 244
   measurement 466
altitude *height* 206
   –and *azimuth* 466
alto 410, 415 *hill* 206
altogether
   collectively 50
   entirely 52
   the–50, 226
alto-rilievo
   convex 250
   sculpture 557
altruism 910, 942
altruist 906
alum 397
alumina 324
alumnus 541
alveary 370, 691
alveolate 252
alveolus 252
always *uniformly* 16
   generally 78
   during 106
   perpetually 112

habitually 613
a.m. 125
amadou 388
amah 746, 753
amain *violence* 173
   haste 684
amalgam,–ate
   mixture 41
   compound 48
amanuensis
   recorder 553
   secretary 590
amaranthine 112
amaritude 395
amass *whole* 50
   collect 72
   store 636
amassment 72
amateur
   willingness 602
   taste 850
   votary 865
amateurish 643
amatory 897
amaurosis 442
amaze 870
amazement 508
amazingly 31
Amazon *warrior* 726
   courage 861
ambage
   convolution 248
   circumlocution 573
   circuit 629
ambagious
   winding 248
   diffuse 573
ambassador
   interpreter 524
   messenger 534
   representative 758
   deputy 759
amber 356a
   –*color* 436
ambergris 356a
ambidexter
   right and left 238
   fickle 607
   clever 698
ambient 227
ambiguous
   uncertain 475
   unintelligible 519
   equivocal 520
   obscure 571
ambilevous 239
ambilogy 520
ambiloquy 520
ambit 230, 311
ambition
   intention 620
   desire 865
ambitious
   (see *ambition*)
amble *pace* 266
   slowness 275

ambo *school* 542
   pulpit 1000
   alike 17
   friends 890
   bad men 949
ambrosia 298
ambrosial *savory* 394
   fragrant 400
ambulance
   vehicle 272
   hospital 662
ambulation 266
ambuscade 530
ambush *shade* 424
   hiding **530**
   pitfall 667
   lie in–528
ambustion 384
âme damnée
   catspaw 711
   servant 746
   servile 886
   bad man 949
ameer 875
ameliorate 658
amen *assent* 488
   submission 725
   content 831
amenable *liable* 177
   docile 602
   answerable 926
amend *improve* 658
   repent 950
amendatory 30
amendment 658
   18th–761
amends
   compensation 30
   atonement 952
   reward 973
amenity *pleasing* 829
   courtesy 894
amentia 503
amerce 974
American 188
   –*organ* 417
   –*plan* 298
Americanism 563
Americanize 563
amethyst *purple* 437
   jewel 847
amethystine 437
amiable *pleasing* 829
   courteous 894
   loving 897
   kind 906
amianthoid 385
amianthus 385
amicable
   assisting 707
   friendly 888
amice 999
amidships 68
amidst *mixed with* 41
   between 228
amiss 619 come

–*disagree* 24
   mistime 135
   inexpedient 647
   do–945
   go–732
   nothing comes–823
   take–*dislike* 867
   resent 900
amity *concord* 714
   peace 721
   friendship 888
ammeter 157, 272, 490a
ammonia 334, 387
ammonite 248
ammonium chloride 490b
ammunition
   materials 635
   war 727
amnesia 506
amnesty
   pacification 723
   forgiveness 506, 918
amoeba 193, 357
amoebaeic 597
amoebean 63
amoebic 193
amoebiform 81
amoeboid 193
amole 356
among *mixed with* 41
   between 228
amorist 897
amoroso 599
amorous 897
   –*glances* 902
amorphism 241
amorphous
   irregular 83
   formless 241
amortization 784
amotion 270
amount *quantity* 25
   degree 26
   sum of money 800
   price 812
   –to *equal* 27
   number 85
   gross–50
amour *love* 897
   intrigue 961
   –*propre* 880
amourette 897
amphibians 368
amphibious 83
amphibology 520
Amphictyonic council 696
amphigory 497, 853
amphitheater
   prospect 441
   school 542
   theater 599
   arena 728
Amphitryon 890

amphora 191
ample *much* 31
   spacious 180
   large 192
   broad 202
   copious 639
   content 831
amplify *expand* 194
   exaggerate 549
   diffuse style 573
amplitude
   quantity 25
   degree 26
   size 192
   breadth 202
   enough 639
amputate 38
amuck *run–kill* 361
   attack 716
   excite 825
amulet *talisman* 747
   charm 993
amuse *please* 298
   divert 840
amusement 840
   place of–840
amylaceous 352
an *if* 514
ana 594, 596
Anabaptist 984
anachronism
   false time **115**
   inopportune 135
   error 495
anachronize 115
anacoluthon 70
anaconda 913
anacreontic 597
anacrusis 597
anaemia 160
anaemic 429
anaesthesia
   insensibility 376
   numbness 381
   inactivity 683
anaesthetist 662
anaesthetize 376, 662
anaglyph
   representation 554
   sculpture 557
anagoge
   metaphor 521
   latency 526
anagram
   double sense 520
   secret 533
   letter 561
   wit 842
   play–561
anagrammatism 520, 533
anagrammatize 520
analecta 596
analeptic 662
analgesia 823

analogy *relation* 9
  similarity 17
analysis
  decomposition 49
  arrangement 60
  algebra 85
  inquiry 461
  experiment 463
  reasoning 476
  grammar 567
  compendium 596
analyst
  investigator 461
  experimenter 463
analytical
  (see analysis)
analyze *grammar* 567
  describe 594
  (see analysis)
anamorphoscope 555
anamorphosis
  distortion 243
  optical 443
  misrepresentation 555
anapest 597
anaphrodisia 174, 866
anarch 710
anarchist
  opponent 710
  insurgent 742
  enemy 891
  evil doer 913
anarchy *disorder* 59
  social 738
anastatic printing 558
anastomosis
  junction 43
  crossing 219
anastomotic 219
anastrophe 218
anathema 908
anathematize
  curse 908
  censure 932
  detract 934
anatomize *dissect* 44
  investigate 461
anatomy *dissection* 44
  leanness 203
  texture 329
  science 357
  comparative— 368
anatripsis 331
anatriptic 331
ancestor 69, 166
ancestral *bygone* 122
  old 124
  aged 128
ancestry 69, 166
anchor *connection* 45
  stop 265
  safeguard 666
  check 706
  hope 858

at—fixed 150
stationed 184
safe 664
cast—settle 184
arrive 292
sheet—means 632
anchorage
  location 184
  roadstead 189
  refuge 666
anchored *fixed* 150
anchoretic 893
anchorite *recluse* 893
  ascetic 955
ancien régime 875
ancient *old* 124
  flag 550
  —mariner 269
  —times 122
ancientness 122
ancillary 707
ancon 342
and *addition* 37
  accompaniment 88
andante 415
andiron 386
androgynous 83
androlepsia 789
Andromeda 490a
androtomy 372
anecdote 594
anecdotist 594
anele 998
anemograph 349
anemography 349
anemology 349
  anemometer
  wind 349
  measure 466
  record 551
anemometrograph 349
anemometry 349
anemone 845
anemoscope 349
anent 9
aneroid 338, 340
anew *again* 104
  newly 123
anfractuosity 248
angel *messenger* 534
  backer 599, 711
  object of love 897
  good person 948
  supernatural being 977
  bishop 996
  —of death 360
  fallen—bad man 949
  devil 978
  guardian—safety 664
  auxiliary 711
  benefactor 912
angelic 944
angelus 550
anger 900

angina pectoris 655
angiology 329
angle 244
  point of view 448
  try 463
  at an— 217
angle rafter 215
Anglican
  sectarian 984
  ecclesiastical 995
Anglicanism 984
Anglice 563
Anglicism 563
angling 622
Anglophobia 898
angry (see anger)
anguiform 248
anguilliform
  filament 205
  serpentine 248
anguilloid 248
anguillous 248
anguine 366
anguish *physical* 378
  moral 828
angular 244
  —velocity 264
angularity 244
angustation 203
anhedonia 828, 837
anhelation 688
anhydrate 340, 670
anhydration 340
anhydric 340
anhydrous 340
anility *age* 128
  imbecility 499
anima 359—bruta 359
  —divina 359
  —mundi 359
animadvert
  attend to 457
  reprehend 932
animal 366—cries 412
  —economy 359
  —gratification 377
  —life 364
  —magnetism 992a
  —physiology 368
  —spirits 836
  female— 364
animalcular 193
animalcule
  minute 193
  animal 366
animalism
  animality 364
  sensuality 954
animality 364
animalization 364
animastic 450
animate *induce* 615
  excite 824
  enliven 836
animation *life* 359
  animality 364

activity 682
vivacity 836
suspended— 823
animative 359
animism 317, 984
animist 317
animosity *dislike* 867
  enmity 889
  hatred 898
  anger 900
animus
  willingness 602
  intention 620
  desire 865
ankle 244—deep
  deep 208
  shallow 209
anklet 847
ankus 615
ankylosis 150
annalist
  chronologist 115
  recorder 553
annals *chronology* 114
  record 551
  account 594
annatto 434
anneal 673
annex *add* 37, 39
  join 43
annexationist 43
annexe 39
annihilate
  extinguish 2
  destroy 162
anniversary 138, 883
anno 106
annotation
  explanation 522
  note 550
annotator *scholar* 492
  interpreter 524
  commentator 595
annotto 434
announce *herald* 116
  predict 511
  inform 527
  publish 531
  assert 535
announcement
  (see announce)
annoy *molest* 649, 907
  disquiet 830
annoyance 828
  source of— 830
annual *periodic* 138
  plant 367
  book 593
annuity 810
annul *destroy* 162
  abolish 756
annular 247
annularity 249
annulet 247
annunciate
  inform 527

(*publish* 531)
Annunciation, the— 990
annunciative 527
annunciator 527
annunciatory 531
anodyne *lenitive* 174
  remedial 662
  relief 834
anoint *coat* 223
  lubricate 332
  oil 355
Anointed, the 976
anointment
  lubrication 332
  oil 355
anomalous 241
anomaly *disorder* 59
  irregularity 83
anon 132
anonymous 565
anopsia 442
anorexy 866
another *different* 15
  repetition 104
  —time 119
answer
  to an inquiry **462**
  confute 479
  solution 522
  succeed 731
  pecuniary profit 775
  pleadings 969
  —for deputy 759
  promise 768
  go bail 806
  —one's turn 644
  —the helm 743
  —the purpose 731
  —to correspond 9
  require an— 461
answerable
  agreeing 23
  liable 177
  bail 806
  duty 926
  censurable 392
ant 366, 690
Antaeus *strength* 159
  size 192
antagonism
  difference 14
  physical 179
  voluntary 708
  enmity 889
antagonist 710
antagonistic 24
antaphrodisiac 866
antarctic 237, 383
ante 621 *expend* 809
  —up 809
antecedence
  in order 62
  in time 116
antecedent 64
antechamber 191

antedate — appetizing

antedate 115
antediluvian 124
antelope 274, 360
antemundane 124
antenna 379
antepast 510
anteposition 62
anterior *in order* 62
  in time 116
  in place 234
  —*to reason* 477
anteroom 191
antevert 706
anthelion 423
anthelmintic 662
anthem 990
anthemion 847
antherozoid 357
anthology
  writing 590
  book 593
  collection 596
  poem 597
  store 636
anthracite 388
anthrax 655
anthropod 193
anthropogeny 372
anthropoid 372
anthropology
  zoology 368
  mankind 372
anthropomancy 511
anthropomorphism 984
anthropophagus 913
anthroposcopy 511
anthroposophy 372
anthropotomy 372
antic 840
antichristian
  heterodox 984
  irreligious 989
antichronism 115
anticipant 120
anticipate
  anachronism 115
  priority 116
  future 121
  early 132
  expect 507
  foresee 510
  prepare 673
  hope 858
  caution 864
anticipation 120
  (see anticipate)
anticlimax
  decrease 36
  bathos 497, 853
anticlinal 217
anticyclone 265
antidote 662
antigropelos 225
antifebrile 662
antilogarithm 84

antilogy 477
antiluetic 662
antimacassar 223
antimony 663, 490a
Antinomian 984
antinomy 964
Antinous 845
antiorgastic 174
antiparallel 217
antipathy
  contrariety 14
  dislike 867
  hate 898
antiphon *music* 415
  answer 462
  worship 990
antiphonal 462
antiphrasis 563
antipodes
  difference 14
  distance 196
  contraposition 237
antipoison 662
antiquary
  past times 122
  scholar 492
  historian 553
antiquated *aged* 128
  (*out of fashion* 851)
antique 124
antiquity 122
antiscriptural 984
antiseptic 662
antisocial 911
antispasmodic 174, 662
antispast 597
antistrophe 597
antithesis *contrast* 14
  difference 15
  contraposition 237
  style 577
antithesize 14
antitype 22
antler 253
antonomasia
  metaphor 521
  nomenclature 564
antrum 252
anvil *conversion* 144
  support 215
  on the—
  intended 620
  in hand 625, 730
  preparing 673
anxiety *solicitude* 459
  pain 828
  fear 860
  desire 865
anxious (see anxiety)
  —*bench* 1000
  —*expectation* 507
  —*meeting* 1000
  —*seat* 1000
any *some* 25
  part 51

  no choice 609a
  at—rate certain 474
  true 494
  at all hazards 604
anybody 78
anyhow *careless* 460
  in some way 627
aorist 109, 119
aorta 350
apace *early* 132
  swift 274
Apache 913
apache *assassin* 361
aparejo 215
apart *irrelative* 10
  separate 44
  singleness 87
  soliloquy 589
  set— 636
  wide— 196
apartment 191
  —*house* 189
  —*s to let*
  imbecile 450a, 499
apathetic 275
apathy
  incuriosity 456
  insensibility 823
  irreligion 989
ape *monkey* 366
  imitate 19
aperient 652, 662
apéritif 394
aperture 260
apery 19
apex *height* 206
  summit 210
aphelion 196
aphid 366, 659
Aphis 659
aphonic 403, 581
aphonia 581
aphorism 496
aphrodisia 173, 961
aphrodisiac 865
Aphrodite 845
apiarism 370
apiarist 370
apiary 370
apical 210
apiculate 253
apiculture 370
apiece 79
apish 19, 499
apishamore 223
aplomb *stability* 150
  verticality 212
  self—possession 498
  resolution 604
Apocalypse 985
Apocrypha 985
apocryphal
  uncertain 475
  erroneous 495
  heterodox 984
apodeictic 478

apodeixis 478
apodosis 67
apogee 490a
apograph 21
apolaustic 377
Apollo *sun* 318
  music 416
  luminary 423
  beauty 845
  —*Musagetes* 416
  magnus—sage 500
  adviser 695
apologue
  metaphor 521
  teaching 537
  description 594
apology
  substitution 147
  excuse 617
  vindication 937
  penitence 950
  atonement 952
apophysis 250
apoplexy 158
aporia 475
apostasy
  recantation 607
  dishonor 940
  heterodoxy 984
  impiety 988
apostate *convert* 144
  turncoat 607
  seceder 742
  heretic 984
  (*recreant* 941)
apostatize 607
apostle *teacher* 540
  disciple 541
  inspired 985
  —*'s creed* 983a
apostolic 985
  —*church* 983a
  —*see* 995
apostrophe
  typography 550
  address 586
  soliloquy 589
  appeal 765
apostrophize 765
apothecary 662
  —*'s weight* 319
apothegm 496
apotheosis
  resuscitation 163
  heaven 981
  hero worship 991
apozem *liquefy* 335
  fuse 384
apozemial 384
appal *pain* 830
  terrify 860
appanage
  property 780
  gift 784
apparatus 633
apparel 225

apparent *visible* 446
  appearing 448
  probable 472
  manifest 525
  heir— 779
apparition *shade* 362
  fallacy of vision 443
  spirit 980a
  psychical research 992a
  (*appearance* 448)
apparitor
  precursor 64
  messenger 534
appeach 938
appeal *address* 586
  request 765
  —*motion* 969
  —*to*
  call to witness 467
  —*to arms* 722
  —*to for* (*claim*) 924
  court of— 966
appear
  come in sight 446
  show itself 525
  (*come into being* 1)
  —*for* 759
  —*in print* 591
appearance 448
  make one's—
  arrive 292
  to all—to the eye 448
  probable 472
appearances
  keep up— 852
appease 174
appellant
  claimant 924
appellate 966
appellation 564
append *add* 37
  sequence 63
  hang 214
appendage
  addition 37
  adjunct 39
  accompaniment 88
  rear 235
appendicitis 655
appendix 65, 67
apperception 450, 490
appercipient 450
appertain *related to* 9
  component 56
  belong 777
  property 780
appetence 865
appetency 602
appetite 865
  tickle the—
  savory 394
appetitive 865
appetizer 393, 394
appetizing 865

exciting 824
applaud 931
applause 931
apple 298, 369
 —brandy 959
 —butter 396
 —dumpling 298
 —fritters 298
 —jack 959
 —of discord 713
 —of one's eye
  good 648
  love 897
  favorite 899
 —pie 298
 —slump 298
  golden-
  allurement 615
apple green 435
apple-pie order 58
appliance *use* 677
 —s *means* 632
 machinery 633
applicable
 revelant 9, 23
 useful 644
 expedient 646
applicant 767
application *study* 457
 metaphor 521
 use 677
 request 765
apply *appropriate* 788
 —a match 384
 —the mind 457
 —a remedy 662
appoggiato 413
appoggiatura 413
appoint *prescribe* 741
 assign 786
appointment
 business 625
 order 741
 charge 755
 assignment 786
 interview 892
appointments
 gear 633
apportion *arrange* 60
 disperse 73
 allot 786
 (*portion* 51)
apportionment 786
apposition *relation* 9
 relevancy 23
 closeness 199
 paraphrase 522
appraise *estimate* 466
 value 812
appreciate
 realize 450, 451
 measure 466
 judge 480
 know 490
 taste 850
 approve 931

apprehend
 believe 484
 know 490
 fear 860
 seize 969
apprehension
 idea 453
 taking 789
apprehensive 860
apprentice 541
 servant 746
 —oneself 676
apprenticeship
 learning 539
 training 673
apprise 527
appraised of 490
approach *of time* 121
 impend 152
 nearness 197
 move **286**
 path 627
approbation 931
appropinquation 286
appropinquity 197
appropriate *fit* 23
 peculiar 79
 possess 777
 assign 786
 borrow 788
 take 789
 steal 791
 (*expedient* 646)
appropriation
 allotment 786
 taking 789
 stealing 791
approval *assent* 488
 commend 931
approve 488, 931
approximate
 related to 9
 resemble 17
 in mathematics 85
 nearness 197
 approach 286
appulse *meeting* 199
 collision 276
 approach 286
 converge 290
appulsion 199, 276
appurtenance
 adjunct 88
 component 56
 belonging 780
 (*part* 51)
appurtenant
 relating 9
apraxia 821a
apricot *fruit* 298
 color 439
April—fool *dupe* 547
 laughingstock 857
 —showers 149
 make an—fool of
  545

a priori reasoning
 476
apron
 clothing 39, 225
 defense 717
 canonicals 999
apse 1000
à propos *relative* 9
 apt 23
 occasion 134
 (*expedient* 646)
apt *consonant* 23
 tendency 176, 177
 docile 539
 willing 602
 clever 698
 (*intelligent* 498)
 (*expedient* 646)
aqua 337
 —fortis 384
 —regia 384
aquamarine 435, 438
aquarium 370, 636
Aquarius *rain* 348
aquatic 267, 337
aquatics 267
aquatinta 558
aquatist 558
aqueduct 350
aqueous 337
aquiline 244
A. R. 106
Arab *wanderer* 268
 horse 271
araba 272
arabesque 847
Arabian—nights 515
 —perfumes 400
arable 371
arado 780
arbiter *critic* 480
 director 694
 adviser 695
 judge 967
 —bibendi 840
 —elegantiarum
  revels 840
  taste 850
  fashion 852
arbitrament
 judgment 480
 (*choice* 609)
 —of the sword 722
arbitrary
 without relation 10
 irregular 83
 willful 606
 capricious 608
 authoritative 737
 severe 739
 insolent 885
 lawless 964
 —power 739
arbitrate
 adjudicate 480
 mediate 724

arbitration
 concord 714
 compromise 774
 court of—966
 submit to—774
arbitrator 724
arbor *abode* 189
 summerhouse 191
 support 215
 rotation 312
 plaisance 840
Arbor Day 840
arboreal 367
arborescent
 ramifying 242
 rough 256
 trees 367
arboriculture 371
arboriform 242
arc 245
arcade *street* 189
 curve 245
 gateway 260
Arcadia *pleasure* 827
 paradise 981
Arcadian
 pastoral 371
 artless 703
 innocent 946
arcanum 533
arch *great* 31
 support 215
 curve 245
 convex 250
 concave 252
 clever 498
 cunning 702
 triumphal—
 trophy 733
 celebration 883
archaeologist
 antiquary 122
 scholar 492
archaeology 122
archaic *old* 124
archaism
 past times 122
 obsolete phrase 563
archangel 977
archbishop 996
archbishopric 995
archdeacon 996
archduchy 181
archduke 745
archdukedom 180
archebiosis 161
arched roof 245
archenemy, the—978
archer 726, 840
archery 840
Arches, court of—
 tribunal 966
 churchdom 995
archetypal 20
archetype 22, 453
Archeus 359

archfiend 978
archiater 695
archiepiscopal 995
archigenesis 161, 357
archipelago 346
architect
 constructor 164
 agent 690
architectonic 161
architecture
 arrangement 60
 construction 161
 fabric 329
 ornament 847
architrave 210
archive 551
archlute 417
archon *ruler* 745
 deputy 759
 judge 967
archtraitor 941
arclike 245
arctic *northern* 237
 cold 383
arctics 225
arcuation 245
ardent *fiery* 382
 eager 682
 feeling 821
 loving 897
 —expectation 507
 —imagination 515
ardor *vigor* 574
 activity 682
 feeling 821
 desire 865
arduous 704
area 181, 182
arefaction 340
arefy 340
arena *space* 180
 region 181
 field of view 441
 field of battle **728**
arenaceous 330
arenosity 330
areola 247
areolar 219
areometer 321
Areopagus 966
ares 180
arescent 340
aretaics 944
arête 253
aretology 926, 944
Argand lamp 423
argent 430
argentine 430
argil 324
argillaceous 324
argol 653
argosy 273
argot 563
argue *evidence* 467
 reason 476
 indicate 550

377

argufy 476
argument *topic* 454
  discussion 476
  meaning 516
  have the best of an
    –478
Argus–eyed *sight* 441
  vigilant 459
argute 498
aria *composition* 54
  music 415
Arianism 984
arid *unproductive* 169
  dry 340
  uninteresting 841
Ariel *courier* 268
  swift 274
  messenger 534
  spirit 979
arietation 276
arietta 415
aright *well* 618
  (*skillful* 698)
ariolation 511
ariose 413, 415
arise *exist* 1
  begin 66
  happen 151
  mount 305
  appear 446
  –from 154
aristate 253
aristocracy
  power 737
  nobility 875
aristocrat 875
aristocratic 852
Aristotelian 476
Aristotelianism 451
arithmancy 511
arithmetic 85
ark *abode* 189
  asylum 666
  boat 273
arm *part* 51
  power 157
  instrument 633
  provide 637
  prepare 673
  war 722
  weapon 727
  –in arm *together* 88
  friends 888
  sociable 892
  –of the law 963
  –of the sea 343
  make a long–200
armada 726
armadillo 366
Armageddon 361, 720
armament
  preparation 673
  arms 727
armchair 215
armed *defense* 717

–at all points 673
–force 664, 726
armet 717
armful 25
armiger 875
armigerous 722
armillary sphere 466
armipotent 157
armistice
  cessation 142
  deliverance 672
  pacification 723
armless 158
armlet *ring* 247
  gulf 343
armor *defense* 717
  arms 727
  buckle on one's–673
armorial 550
armor–plated 223
armory *assembly* 189
  store 636
  workshop 691
arms 727 (*see* arm)
  heraldry 550
  war 722
  honors 877
  clash of–720
  deeds of–720
  in–*infant* 129
  under–722
  up in–*active* 682
  discord 713
  resistance 719
  resentment 900
  enmity 889
arm's length at–196
  keep at– *repel* 289
  defense 717
  enmity 889
  seclusion 893
  discourtesy 895
Armstrong gun 727
army *collection* 72
  multitude 102
  troops 726
  –list 86
arnica 662
aroint *begone* 297
  malediction 908
aroma 400
aromatize 400
around 227 lie–220
arouse *move* 615
  excite 824
  –oneself 682
arpeggio 413
arpent 180, 200
arquebus 727
arquebusade 662
arraign *accuse* 938
  indict 969
arrange
  set in order 60

organize 357
plan 626
compromise 774
(*prepare* 673)
–in a series 69
–itself 58
–matters *pacify* 723
–music 416
–under 76
arrangement
(*see* arrange)
painting 556
temporary–111
arrant *identical* 31
manifest 525
notorious 531
bad 649
disreputable 874
base 940
arras 847
arrastra 330
array *order* 58
arrangement 60
series 69
assemblage 72
multitude 102
dress 225
prepare 673
adorn 847
ostentation 882
battle–722
arrear, in–
incomplete 53
nonpayment 808
arrears *debt* 806
arrest *stop* 142
restrain 751
in law 969
–the attention **457**
arrière pensée
afterthought 65
mental reservation 528
motive 615
set purpose 620
arriero 694
arrish 168
arrival 292
arrive *happen* 151
reach 292
complete 729
(*stop* 142)
–at a conclusion 480
–at an understanding 488
–at the truth 480a
arroba 319
arrogance
(*see* arrogant)
arrogant *severe* 739
proud 878
insolent 885
arrogate *assume* 885
claim 924
–to oneself
undue 925

arrondissement 181
arrosion 331
arrow *swift* 274
missile 284
arms 727
arrowhead *form* 253
writing 590
arrow–shaped 253
arroyo 350
arsenal *store* 636
workshop 691
(*arms* 727)
arsenic 663
arsenious oxide 663
arson 384
art *representation* 554
business 625
skill 698
cunning 702
(*deception* 545)
–gallery 556
–museum 556
–school 542
fine–850
perfection of–650
work of–
beauty 845
ornament 847
arteriosclerosis 655
artery *conduit* 350
channel 627
artesian well 343
artful *deceitful* 544
cunning 702
–dodge 545, 702
arthritis 655
arthropoda 368
artichoke 298
article *thing* 3
part 51
matter 316
chapter 593
review 595
goods 798
articled clerk 541
articles
–of agreement 770
–of faith *belief* 484
theology 983
thirty–nine–983a
articulates 368
articulation
junction 43
speech 580
articulo, in–
transient 111
dying 360
artifice *plan* 626
cunning 702
(*deception* 545)
artificer 690
artificial *fictitious* 545
cunning 702
affected 855
–language 579
–light 420

artillery
explosion 404
arms 727
–of words 562
artilleryman 726
artisan 690
artist *painter* etc. **559**
contriver 626
agent 690
artiste *music* 416
drama 599
artistic *skillful* 698
beautiful 845
taste 850
–language 578
artistry 569
Artium–Baccalaureus 492–Magister 492
artless 703
artlessness
natural **703**
(*veracious* 543)
arundinaceous 253
aruspex 513
aruspicy 511
as *motive* 615
–broad as long 27
–can be 52
–good as 27
–if similar 17
suppose 514
–it may be
circumstance 8
event 151
chance 156
–it were *similar* 17
metaphor 521
–little as may be 32
–much again 90
–soon as 120
–they say
proverb 496
news 532
–things are 7
–things go *event* 151
habit 613
–to 9
–usual 82
–you were 283
–well as 37
asafetida 395, 401
asbestic 385
asbestos 385
ascend *be great* 31
increase 35
rise 305
improve 658
ascendancy
power 157
influence 175
success 731
ascendant in the–
influence 175
important 642
success 731
authority 737

378

ascension   **athanor**

   repute 873
   lord of the–745
   one's star in the–
      prosperity 734
ascension
   (*see* ascend)
   calefaction 384
Ascension Day 998
ascent (*see* ascend)
   gradient 217
   rise **305**
   glory 873
ascertain *fix* 150
   determine 480
ascertained
   certain 474
   known 490
ascertainment 480a
ascetic 955
asceticism 953, **955**
ascititious *intrinsic* 6
   additional 37
   supplementary 52
ascribe 155
ascription
   (*see* ascribe)
aseptic 662
ash 367, 384
   –*blond* 429
   –*colored* 432
ashamed 879, 881
ash cake 298
ashen 429
ashes *corpse* 362
   dirt 653
   lay in–162
   pale as–
      colorless 429
      fear 860
ashore 342 go
   –*arrive* 292
Ash Wednesday 138
ashy 429
Asian mystery 533
aside *laterally* 236
   whisper 405
   private 528
   –from the purpose 10
   say–589
   set–*displace* 185
   neglect 460
   negative 536
   reject 610
   disuse 678
   abrogate 756
   discard 782
   step–279
asinine *ass* 271
   fool 499
ask *inquire* 461
   request 765
   for sale 794
   price 812
   (*invoke* 990)
   –leave 760

askance 217 eye
   –*fear* 860
   look
   –*vision* 441, 443
   dissent 489
   dislike 867
   disapproval 932
asked in church 903
askew *oblique* 217
   distorted 243
asking (*see* ask)
aslant 217
asleep 683
aslope 217
Asmodeus 978
asomatous 317
asp *animal* 366
   evil doer 913
asparagus 298, 367
Aspasia 962
aspect *feature* 5
   state 7
   situation 183
   appearance 448
aspen leaf
   shake like an–
      motion 315
      fear 860
asperges 998
aspergillum 337
asperity
   roughness 256
   discourtesy 895
   anger 900
   irascibility 901
asperse 934
aspersion
   nonassemblage 73
   cleanness 652
   malediction 908
   rite 998
asphalt *smooth* 255
   resin 356a
asphodel 845
asphyxia 360
asphyxiate 361
aspirant
   candidate 767
   desire 865
aspirate 402, 580
aspirated 681
aspire *rise* 305
   project 620
   hope 858
   desire 865
   worship 990
asportation 270
asquint 217
ass
   beast of burden 271
   fool 501
   –'s bridge
      unintelligible 519
      cheat 548
      bungler 701
   make an–of

delude 545
assafetida 401
assagai 727
assail *attack* 716
   pain 830
assailant
   opponent 710
   attacker 726
assassin,–ate 361
assault 716
   take by–789
assay 463
assayer 463
assemblage **72**
assembly *council* 696
   society 892
   religious 997
assemblyman 696
assembly room 189, 588
assent *belief* 484
   agree **488**
   willing 602
   consent 762
   content 831
assert *affirm* 535
   claim as a right 924
assess *measure* 466
   determine 480
   tax 812
assessor *judge* 967
assets *property* 780
   money 800
   accounts 811
asseverate 535
assiduous 682
assign *commission* 755
   transfer 783
   give 784
   allot 786
   –a duty 926
   –as cause 155
   –dower 784
   –places 60
assignable 270
assignat 800
assignation *tryst* 892
   place of–74
assignee *transfer* 270
   donee 785
assignment 155
assimilate *uniform* 16
   resemble 17
   imitate 19
   agree 23
   transmute 144
assimilation 161
assist 707
assistant 711
assize *measure* 466
   tribunal 966
   justice of–967
associate *mix* 41
   unite 43
   combine 48
   collect 72

accompany 88
   colleague 690
   auxiliary 711
   friend 890
   –professorship 542
   –with *sociality* 892
association
   (*see* associate)
   relation 9
   cooperation 709
   partnership 712
   friendship 888
   –of ideas *intellect* 450
   thought 451
   intuition 477
   hint 514
associational psychology 457
assoil *acquit* 970
   (*liberate* 750)
assoilzie 970
assonance
   agreement 23
   music 413
   poetry 597
assort *arrange* 60
assortment
   collection 72
   class 75
assuage *moderate* 174
   relieve 834
   (–morally 826)
assuasive 174, 834
assuetude 613
assume *believe* 484
   suppose 514
   falsehood 544
   take 789
   insolent 885
   right 924
   –a character 554
   –a form 144
   –authority 737
   –command 741
   –the offensive 716
assumed–name 565
   –position 514
assuming
   insolent 885
assumption
   (*see* assume)
   severity 739
   hope 858
   insolence 885
   seizure 925
assurance
   speculation 156
   certainty 474
   belief 484
   confidence 507
   assertion 535
   promise 768
   security 771
   hope 858
   vanity 880
   insolence 885

make–double sure
   safe 664
   caution 864
assure
   render certain 474
   believe 484
   certify 535
   promise 768
   secure 771
   give hope 858
assured
   self–satisfied 880
assuredly *assent* 488
astatic 320
asteism 856
asterisk 550
astern 235 fall–283
asteroid 318
asthenia 160
astigmatism 443
astir *ready* 673
   active 682
   set–824
astonish 870
astonishing *great* 31
astonishment 508, 870
astound
   be unexpected 508
   excite 824
   fear 860
   surprise 870
astraddle 215
astragal 847
astral 318
   –body 317, 992a
   –influence 601
   –plane 317
astray *at fault* 475
   error 495
   go–*deviate* 279
   sin 945
astriction 43, 195
astride 215
astringent 195, 397
astrolabe 466, 490a
astrology 511, 522
astronomy 490a, 318
astute *wise* 498
   cunning 702
asunder *separate* 44
   distant 196
   as poles–237
asylum *hospital* 662
   retreat 666
   defense 717
asymptote 290
ataghan 727
atajo 72
atavism 145
atelier *studio* 556
   workshop 691
athanasia 112
Athanasian creed 983a
athanor 386

atheism — authorship

atheism 989
atheist 984
atheling 875
athermancy 382
athirst 865
athlete *strong* 159
  combatant 726
athletic *strong* 159
  school 542
  laborious 686
  gymnastic 720
  –sports *contest* 720
  games 840
athletics 720, 840
athwart *oblique* 217
  crossing 219
  opposing 708
Atkins, Tommy–726
Atlantean *great* 31
  strong 159
  supporting 215
Atlantis 515
at large 750
atlas *arrangement* 60
  list 86
  maps 554
  store 636
Atlas *strength* 159
  support 215
atmosphere
  circumambience 227
  air 338
  painting 556
atmospheric blue 438
atole 298
atoll 346
atom
  small in degree 32
  small in size 193
atomism 451
atomize 336
atomizer 336, 400
atoms crush to–162
atomy 193, 203
atonement
  restitution 790
  expiation **952**
  amends 973
  religious 976
atonic 158
atony 158, 160
atrabilious 837
atramentous 431
atrium 191
atrocity
  malevolence 907
  vice 945
  guilt 947
atrophy
  shrinking 195
  disease 655
  decay 659
attach *add* 37
  join 43
  love 897

  legal 969
  –importance to 642
attaché *employé* 746
  diplomatic 758
attachment
  (*see* attach)
  dispossession 789
attack *voice* 580
  disease 655
  assault **716**
attaghan 727
attain *arrive* 292
  succeed 731
  –majority 131
attainable
  possible 470
  (*easy* 705)
attainder *taint* 651
  at law 971
attainment
  knowledge 490
  learning 539
  skill 698
attar 400
attemper *mix* 41
  moderate 174
attempered
  affected 820
attempt 675
  –impossibilities 471
  vain–732
attend *accompany* 88
  be present 186
  follow 117, 281
  apply the mind 457
  medically 662
  aid 707
  serve 746
  –to 418
  –to business 625
  –to one's business 457
  –to orders 743
attendance
  (*see* attend)
  dance–on 866
attendant (*see* attend)
attention 457
  care 459
  respect 928
  attract–882
  call–to 550
  call to–457
  pay–s to 894
  pay one's–s to 902
attentive *mindful* 457
  (*see* attend)
attenuate *decrease* 36
  impotent 158
  reduce 195
  rare 322
attenuated 203
attest
  bear testimony 467
  affirm 535
  adjure 768

attested copy 771
attic *garret* 191
  summit 210
Attic *homespun* 42
  style 578
  wit 842
  taste 850
  –salt 578, 842
Atticism 578
Attila 913
attire 225
attitude
  circumstance 8
  situation 183
  posture 240
attitudinarian 882
attitudinize 855
attollent 307
attorney
  consignee 758
  at law 968
  power of–755
attract
  be powerful 157
  bring towards 288
  induce 615
  allure 865
  excite love 897
  –the attention 457
  visible 446
attraction
  (*see* attract)
  natural power 157
  bring towards 288
attractive
  (*see* attract)
  pleasing 829
  beautiful 845
  taste 850
attractivity 288
attrahent 288
attribute *power* 157
  –s of the Deity 976
  –to 155
attribute
  accompaniment 88
attribution 155
attrite 330, 331
attrition 331
attritus 331
attune *music* 415
  prepare 673
attuned to *habit* 613
aubade 415
auburn 433, 434
auction 796
auctioneer *agent* 758
  seller 796
audacity *courage* 861
  rashness 863
  insolence 885
audible 402
  become–418
  scarcely–405
audience *hearing* 418
  conversation 588

drama 599
  before an–599
audiphone 418
audit *numeration* 85
  examination 461
  accounts 811
auditive 418
auditor *hearer* 418
  accountant 811
auditorium 189, 588
auditory *sound* 402
  hearing 418
  theater 599
  –apparatus 418
  –nerve 418
au fait *knowledge* 490
  skillful 698
Augean–stable 653
  –task 704
auger 262
aught 51
  for–one cares
  unimportant 643
  indifferent 866
  for–one knows
  ignorance 491
  conjecture 514
augment *increase* 35
  thing added 39
  expand 194
augur *soothsayer* 513
  –well 858
augural 511
augurate 511
augury 512
august 31, 873
Augustinian 996
auk 310
Aum 993
aumbry 1000
aunt 11
aura *wind* 349
  sensation 380
  light 420
  astral 980a
aural 418
aureate 436
aurelia 129
aureola 420
aureole 420, 873
aureolin 436
auricle 418
auricomous 436
auricular *hearing* 418
  clandestine 528
  –confession 998
auriculate 418
auriscope 418
auriscopy 418
aurist 418, 662
aurora *dawn* 125
  light 420, 423
  twilight 422
  –australis 423
  –borealis 423
auroral 236

auscultation 418
auspicate 66
auspice *omen* 512
auspices
  influence 175
  prediction 511
  protection 664
  supervision 693
  aid 707
  under the–of 737
auspicious
  opportune 134
  prosperous 734
  hopeful 858
  (*expedient* 646)
austere (*see* austerity)
austerity
  harsh taste 395
  severe 739
  discourteous 895
  ascetic 955
  pietism 988
Austral 237
Australoid 372a
austromancy 511
authentic
  well-founded 1
  evidential 467
  certain 474
  true 484
authentication
  evidence 467
  security 771
author *producer* 164
  designer 554
  writer 593
  projector 626
  –of evil 978
  –of our being 976
  –s proof 591
  dramatic–599
authoritative
  influential 175
  certain 474
  oracular 500
  commanding 741
authority
  influence 175
  testimony 467
  sage 500
  informant 527
  power **737**
  permission 760
  right 924
  do upon one's own–600
  ensign of–747
  person in–745
authorize
  empower 737
  permit 760
  entitle 924
  legalize 963
authorized *due* 924
authorship
  composition 54

autistic thinking

production 161
style 569
writing 590
autistic thinking
  821a
auto 272
autobiography 594
autocar 272
autochthonous 188
autocracy *will* 600
  authority 737
  severity 739
autocrat 745
autocratic *will* 600
  ruling 737
auto–da–fe
  burning 384
  execution 972
autodidactic 490
autograph
  evidence 467
  signature 550
  writing 590
autography 550
autointoxication 655
Autolycus *thief* 792
  peddler 797
automaniac 504
automatic 266, 601
  pistol 727
  –*gun* 727
  –*writing* 992a
automatism 992a
automaton 1
automobile 266, 272
  –*race* 274
automobilist 268
automotive 266
autonomy *rule* 737
  free 748
autoplagiarism 791
autopsy
  post–mortem 363
  vision 441
autoptical *visible* 446
  manifest 525
auto–rifle 727
autotype 558
autumn 126
auxiliary 711
  extra 37
  aid 707
  –*forces* 726
avail *benefit* 618
  useful 644
  succeed 731
  –*oneself of* 677
  of no– 645
available 676
avails 775, 810
avalanche *fall* 306
  redundance 641
avant–courier
  precursor 64
  pioneer 673
avarice 819

avast! *stop* 142, 265
  desist 624
  forbid 761
avatar *change* 140
  Vishnu 979
avaunt! *eject* 297
  disappear 449
ave! *honor* 873
  courtesy 894
Ave Maria 900
avenge 919
avenger 919
avenue *plantation* 371
  way 627
aver 535
average *mean* 29
  neutral 628
  mediocre 651
  –*circumstances* 736
  take an– 466
Avernus 982
averruncate *eject* 297
  extract 301
averse *contrary* 14
  unwilling 603
averseness
  unwillingness 603
  rejection 610
aversion *dislike* 867
  enmity 889
  hate 898
avert 706
  –*the eyes* 442
Avesta 986
aviary 370
aviate 267
aviation 267
aviator 269
avidity *avarice* 819
  desire 865
avile 932, 934
avion 273, 726
aviso 532
avocado 298
avocation 625
avoid 623
avoidance 623
avoidless *certain* 474
  necessary 601
avoirdupois 319
avoke 741
avolation *avoid* 623
  escape 671
avouch 535
avow *assent* 488
  disclose 529
  assert 535
avowal (*see* avow)
avulsion
  separation 44
  extraction 301
await *future* 121
  be kept waiting 133
  impend 152
  expect 507
awake *attentive* 457

careful 459
  intelligent 498
  active 682
  excite 824
awaken *inform* 527
  excite 824
  –*the attention* 457
  –*the memory* 505
award *adjudge* 480
  give 784
aware 490
away *absent* 187
  distant 196
  depart 293
  –*from unrelated* 10
  –*with!* 930, 932
  break–623
  do–with undo 681
  abrogate 756
  fly–293
  get–671
  move–287
awayness 187
awe *fear* 860
  wonder 870
  respect 928
aweless *fearless* 861
  insolent 885
  disrespectful 929
awe–struck 870
awful *great* 31
  fearful 860
  –*silence* 403
awhile 111
awkward *uncouth* 579
  inexpedient 647
  unskillful 699
  difficult 704
  painful 830
  ugly 846
  vulgar 851
  ridiculous 853
  –*squad* 701, 726
awkwardness
  (*see* awkward)
awl 262 –*shaped* 253
awned 253
awning *tent* 223
  shade 424
awry *oblique* 217
  distorted 243
  evil 619
ax *edge tool* 253
  impulse 276
  weapon 727
  –*for beheading* 975
axial 222
axinomancy 511
axiom 496
axiomatic 474
axis *support* 215
  center 222
  rotation 212
axle 312
  wheel and–633
axletree 215

ay 488
ayah *servant* 746
  nurse 753
aye *ever* 112
  yes 488
ayudante 711
azimuth
  horizontal 213
  direction 278
  measurement 466
  –*circle* 212
azoic 358
azote 663 *whip* 975
azotic 657
Azrael 360
azure 438
azurite 490c
azygous *single* 87

B

Baal *divinity* 979
  idol 986
baas *master* 745
babble *rivulet* 348
  faint sound 405
  unmeaning 517
  talk 584, 588
babbler 501 532
babbling *foolish* 499
babe 129
Babel *confusion* 59
  discord 414
  tongues 560
  jargon 563
  loquacity 584
Babism 984
Babist 984
baboon 366, 846
babu 553
  –*English* 563
Bab–ud–Din 986
baby *infant* 129
  posterity 167
  fool 501
  –*blue* 438
  –*grand piano* 417
  –*linen* 225
babyhood 127
babyish 499
baccalaureate 873
baccarat 840
baccate 354
bacchanals 959
Bacchus *drink* 959
bachelor 904
bachelor girl 374,
  904
back *rear* 235
  shoulder 250
  aid 707
  indorse 800
  –*and forth* 148, 314
  –*down recede* 283
  apostatize 607

backer

–*out retire* 283
  change sides 607
  relinquish 624
  –*pedal* 275
  –*to back* 235
  –*up support* 215
  aid 707
  behind one's–
  latent 526
  hidden 528
  come–292
  fall–relapse 661
  give–790
  go–283
  go–from retract 773
  have at one's–215
  hold–avoid 623
  keep–reserve 636
  look–505
  on one's
  –*impotent* 158
  horizontal 213
  failure 732
  pat on the–
  incite 615
  encourage 861
  approve 931
  pay–retaliate 718
  put–deteriorate 659
  restore 660
  send–764
  set one's–against
    the wall 604
  set one's–up
    pride 878
  some time–122
  spring–277
  take–again 790
  trace–505
  turn–283
  turn one's–
  retire 283
  turn one's–upon
  repel 289
  inattention 458
  avoid 623
  oppose 708
  seclusion 893
  discourtesy 895
  disrespect 929
  contempt 930
backbite *traduce* 932
  detract 934
backbiter 936
backbone *intrinsic* 5
  energy 171
  frame 215
  center 222
  grit 604
  persevere 604a
  soul 820
  game to the–604
backcap 934
back door 627
backdown 725
backer 711

381

backfriend ... band

backfriend 891
backgammon 840
background
  distance 196
  rear 235
  in the-latent 526
  ignoble 874
  *keep in the
    -hide* 528
  modest 881
  seclusion 893
  throw into the- 460
backhanded 217, 629
backlash 277
backlog 386, 388
backplate 717
backset
  agriculture 371
  reverse 735
backsettler 188
backside 235
backslider
  turncoat 607
  shirker 623
  apostate 984
backsliding
  regression 283
  tergiversation 607
  relapse 661
  vice 945
  heterodox 984
  impiety 988
backstairs
  ambush 530
  way 627
  -influence 702
backward *tardy* 133
  rear 235
  regression 283
  unwilling 603
  unprogressive 659
backwardation 813
backwards 283
  *-and forwards
    interchange* 148
  oscillation 314
  bend- 325
backwater
  cessation 142
  slowness 275
  regression 283
backwoods 233
backwoodsman
  inhabitant 188
  agriculture 371
bacon 298
  *save one's-
    safety* 644
  escape 671
Baconian method
  461
bacteria 193, 369
bactericide 662
bacteriologist 357
bad 649 *unclean* 653
  wrong 923

-blood hate 898
  malevolence 907
-break 947
-business 859
-case 477
-chance 473
-debt 806
-fairy 980
-faith 940
-grace 895
-habit 613
-hand 701
*-humor
  discontent* 832
  dejection 837
  anger 900
  sullen 901a
-intent 907
-job evil 619
  botch 699
  hopeless 859
-joke 851
-language 908
-luck etc. 735
-man 949
-name 932, 934
-repute 874
-smell 401
-spirit 980
-spirits 837
-taste 851
*-temper
  discourtesy* 895
  resentment 900
  irascibility 901
  sullenness 901a
-time of it 828
-turn evil 619
  malevolence 907
-woman 949
  *from-to worse
    aggravation* 835
  go-decay 853
  deteriorate 659
  *in a-way
    disease* 655
  worse 659
  danger 665
  adversity 735
  in-odor 889
  not a-idea 498
  *on-terms
    discord* 713
  enmity 889
  *put a-construction
    on* 523
  *take in-part
    discontent* 832
  anger 900
  view in a-light 934
badaud 501
badge 550
  -of authority 747
  -of infamy 874
  -of slavery 746
badger 830

stealing 791, 792
-dog 366
-game 791
badinage *wit* 842
  ridicule 856
badli 634, 759
badly off
  adversity 735
  poor 804
badness 649
Baedeker 266
baffle *hinder* 706
  defeat 731
  *-description
    unconformable* 83
  wonder 870
baft 235
bag *put up* 184
  receptacle 191
  protrude 250
  acquire 775
  take 789
  steal 791
  -and baggage 780
bagatelle *trifle* 643
  pastime 840
baggage
  endearment 129
  transference 270
  materials 635
  property 780
  hussy 962
  -car 272
baggala 273
baggy 47
bagman 758, 767
bagnio 961
bagpipes 410, 417
bah! 497, 930
bail *receptacle* 191
  transference 270
  security 771
  -one's own boat 692
  -up 791
  go- 806
  leg- 623
bailiff *director* 694
  servant 746
  factor 758
  officer 965
bailiwick *region* 181
  jurisdiction 965
Bairam 138, 840
bairn 129, 167
bait *fulcrum* 215
  draw 288
  food 298
  trap 545
  lure 615
  refresh 689
  attack 716
  bribe 784
  harass 830
  reward 973
bake 384

baked beans 298
bakehouse 386
baker's dozen 98
baking heat 382
bakshish 784
bal 840
balais 847
balaklava helmet
  225
balance *equal* 27
  mean 29
  compensate 30
  remainder 40
  numberation 85
  weigh 319
  compare 464
  measurement 466
  intelligence 498
  elegance 578
  hesitate 605
  money 800
  accounts 811
  *-accounts with
    pay* 807
  in the- 475
  *off one's-
    irresolute* 605
  fail 732
  the mind losing its-
    503
balanced *stable* 150
  symmetrical 242
  graceful 578
balbucinate 583
balbutiate 583
balcony 250
  theater 599
bald *bare* 226
  style 575
  uninteresting 841
  ugly 846
  plain 849
baldachin 223, 1000
balderdash 497, 517
baldness (see bald)
baldric *belt* 230
  ring 247
bale *bundle* 72
  load 190
  evil 619
  -out 297
baleen 325
balefire 423, 550
baleful 649
balista 727
balister 727
balistraria 717
balize 550
balk *deviate* 279
  disappoint 509
  deceive 545
  hinder 706
balky 283, 606
ball *globe* 249
  missile 284
  shot 727

dance 840
  party 892
  *-at one's feet
    success* 731
  power 737
  *keep up the-
    continue* 143
  active 682
ballad *song* 415
  poem 597
  -monger 597
ballast
  compensation 30
  weight 319
  wisdom 498
  safety 666
  without-rash 863
  vicious 945
ballet *drama* 599
  dance 840
ballet dancer 599
ballista 727
ballistics
  projectiles 284
  war 722
  arms 727
balloon 273, 325
balloonery 267
ballooning 267
balloonist 269
ballot 535, 609
  -box stuffing 545
ball player 840
ballproof 717
ballroom 840
balm *moderate* 174
  lubrication 332
  fragrance 400
  remedy 662
  relief 834
Balmoral *boot* 225
balmy *sleep* 683
balneal 337
balourdise 699
balsam 400, 662
balsamic
  salubrious 834
balustrade
  support 215
  inclosure 232
bam 544
bambino 129
bamboo 367
bamboozle 545
ban *prohibit* 761
  denounce 908
  *-with bell, book, and
    candle* 998
  under the- 906
banana 298, 369
banco regis 968
band *ligature* 45
  assemblage 72
  filament 205
  belt 230
  ring 247

bandage — bask

bandage
  music 415, 416, 417
  party 712
  shackle 752
  –of hope 958
  –s *canonicals* 999
  –together 709
  –with 720
bandage *tie* 43
  ligature 45
  support 215
  cover 223
  remedy 662
  restraint 752
  the eyes–d 442
bandbox 191
banded together
  concurring 178
  party 712
banderole 550
bandit *slayer* 361
  brigand 792
bandmaster 416
bandobast
  (see bundobust)
bandog *animal* 366
  safeguard 664
  warning 668
bandolier 636
bandrol 550
bandurria 417
bandy *exchange* 148
  agitate 315
  –about *publish* 531
  –legged 243
  –words *discuss* 476
  converse 588
bane *evil* 619
  source of evil 663
baneful 649
banewort 663
bang *impel* 276
  sound 406
  beat 972
banish *eject* 297
  seclude 893
  punish 972
  (*exclude* 55)
banister 215
banjo 417
bank *acclivity* 217
  side of lake 342
  store 636
  sand 667
  fence 717
  money 802
  –examiner 811
  –holiday 840
  –of Elegance 800
  –up 670
  sea–342
banker
  man of means 639
  merchant 797
  treasurer 801
  card game 840
bank note 800

bankrupt 640
  –of life 683
bankruptcy
  failure 732
  nonpayment 808
banlieue *near* 197
  circumjacent 227
banner 550
  enlist under the–s
    of 707
  raise one's–722
banneret 875
banns forbid the–761
  publish the–
    ask 765
  marriage 903
banquet *meal* 298
  pleasure 377
  feast 840
banquette 717
banshee 979, 980a
bant 38
bantam cock 887
banter *wit* 842
  ridicule 856
banterer 844
bantling *child* 129
  scion 167
Bantu 372a
banyan *tree* 367
  stint 640
  fast 956
baptize 564, 998
baptism *name* 564
  rite 998
Baptist 984
baptistery 1000
bar *except* 38
  fastening 45
  exclude 55
  hotel 189
  line 200
  support 215
  inclosure 232
  close 261
  music 413
  hindrance 706
  insignia 747
  prison 752
  prohibit 761
  tribunal 966
  legal profession 968
  –room 189
  –sinister *flaw* 651
  disrepute 874
  illegal 964
  –tender 746
baragouin 517
bara hazri 298
bara khana 298
bara sahib 642, 745
barb *spike* 253
  nag 271
  velocity 274
  –the dart *pain* 830
Barbados tar 356

barbarian *alien* 57
  inelegance 579
  uncivilized 876
  evildoer 913
barbaric
  extraneous 57
  vulgar 851
  rude 876
barbarism
  neology 563
  solecism 568
  bad style 579
  vulgarity 851
  discourtesy 895
barbarous
  unformed 241
  neologic 563
  plebeian 876
  maleficent 907
barbate 205, 253
barbecue
  repast 298, 892
  cook 673
barbed 225
  –wire entanglements
    717
barbel 205
barber *wind* 349
barbican 206, 717
barbouillage 590
bard *musician* 416
  poet 597
barded 225
bare *mere* 32
  nude 226
  manifest 525
  disclose 529
  scanty 640
  –possibility 473
  –supposition 514
bareback 226
barebone 203
barefaced 885
barefoot 226
  poor 804
bareheaded *respect* 928
bargain *compact* 769
  barter 794
  cheap 815
  –and sale
    transfer of property
    783
  –for 507
  into the–37
barge 273
bargee 269
barghest 980
barf 383
baritone 408
barium sulphate 430
bark *rind* 223
  flay 226
  ship 273
  yelp 406, 412
  –at *threaten* 909
  censure 932

  –up the wrong tree 699
  –worse than bite 885
  more–than bite 908
barkbound 751
barkeep 746
barkeeper 746
barkentine 273
barker *guide* 524
  tout 758
  petitioner 767
barley 367
barleycorn *little* 193
Barleycorn, Sir John
  298
barm *leaven* 320
  bubbles 353
barmaster 967
Barmecide feast 956
barmote 966
barn 189, 370, 636
barnacles 368, 445
barndoor fowl 366
barney 545, 713
barograph 338, 490a
barometer *air* 338
  measure 466, 490a
  consult the–463
baron *peer* 875
  husband 903
  –of the Exchequer 967
  court–966
baronage 875
baronet 875
baronial 878
baroque 853
baroscope 338
barouche 272
barque 273
barrack
  encampment 184
  abode 189
  shed 223
  jibe 929
  defense 717
barracker 936
barracoon 717
barrage *loudness* 404
  drumming 407
  attack 716
barranco 198
barrator 941
barratrous 940
barratry 940
barred *crossed* 219
  striped 440
barrel *vessel* 191
  cylinder 249
  –organ 417
barrel house 189
barren 169
barricade *fence* 232
  obstacle 706
  defense 717
  prison 752
barrier
  (see barricade)

barring *save* 38
  excluding 55
  except 83
  –out *resist* 719
  disobey 742
barrister 968
  revising–967
barrow *mound* 206
  vehicle 272
  grave 363
barter *reciprocate* 12
  interchange 148
  commerce 794
barway 294
basalt 490c
bas bleu *scholar* 492
  affectation 855
base *low* 207
  lowest part 211
  support 215
  evil 649
  menial 746
  cowardly 862
  shameful 874
  servile 886
  dishonorable 940
  vicious 945
  –coin 800
  –note 408
  –of operations
    plan 626
  attack 716
baseball 840
baseboard 211
baseborn 876
based on
  ground of belief 467
baselard 727
baseless *unreal* 2
  unsubstantial 4
basement *cellar* 191
  lowest part 207, 211
baseness (see base)
  inferiority 34
bashaw *tyrant* 739
  ruler 745
bashful 881
bashfulness 881
bashi-bazouk 726
basilica 1000
basilisk
  unconformity 83
  sight 441
  cannon 737
  serpent 366, 949
basin *dock* 189
  vessel 191, 211
  hollow 252
  plain 344
basis *lowest part* 211
  support 215
  preparation 673
bask
  physical enjoyment
    377
  warmth 382

basket   beat

prosperity 734
  moral enjoyment 827
  —in the sun 384
basket 191—of 190
basket ball 840
bas-relief *convex* 250
  sculpture 557
bass *music* 415
  —*clarinet* 417
  —*note* 408
  —*tuba* 417
  —*viol* 417
basset 446
basset horn 417
bassinet *cradle* 191
  helmet 717
bassoon 417
basso profondo 408
basso-rilievo
  convex 250
  sculpture 557
bastard *spurious* 545
  nameless 565
  illegitimate 925
baste *beat* 276
  punish 972
Bastille 752
bastinado 972
bastion 717
bat *strike* 276
  club 727
  spree 840
batch *quantity* 25
  collection 72
bate *diminish* 36
  subtract 38
  reduce price 813
bateau 273
bated breath with
  —*faint sound* 405
  expecting 507
  hiding 528
  whisper 581
  humble 879
bath 337, 652–s
  remedy 662
  warm—386
Bath chair 272
bathe *immerse* 300
  plunge 310
  water 337
bathhouse 652
batholith 490c
bathometer 208, 341, 466
bathos *anticlimax* 497
  (*ridiculous* 853)
bathroom 191, 652
bathybic 341
bathycolpian 208
bathymeter 208
bathymetry 208
bathypelagic 208
bathysmal 208
batik 556
bating 55

batman 637
baton *support* 215
  scepter 747
batophobia 206, 860, 867
batrachians 368
batta 973
battalia 726
battalion 726
batten 298—on 886
batter *destroy* 162
  beat 276
  pulpiness 354
battered
  worse for wear 659
  tired 688
battering-ram 276
battering train 727
battery *artillery* 726
  guns 727
  floating—726
  plant a—716
battle *killing* 361
  contention 720
  warfare 722
  —*array order* 60
  prepare 673
  war 722
  —*ax* 727
  —*cruiser* 273
  —*cry sign* 550
  war 722
  —*field arena* 728
  —*ground discord* 713
  —*with oppose* 708
  half the—642
  win the—731
battled 722
battledore 325
  —*and shuttlecock interchange* 148
  game 840
battlement
  embrasure 257
  defense 717
battleship 664, 726
battologize 573
battology *repeat* 104
  diffuse style 573
battue *kill* 361
  pursuit 622
  attack 716
bauble *trifle* 643
  toy 840
bauxite 490c
bavardage
  unmeaning 517
  chatter 584
bavin 388
bawarchi-khana 191
bawcock 892
bawd 962
bawdy,-house 961
bawl 411
bawn 189
bay *concave* 252

gulf 343
  cry 412
  brown 433
  at—*danger* 665
  difficulty 604
  defense 717, 719
  —*leaf* 400
  —the moon *useless* 645
  bring to—716
bayadere 840
Bayard 271
bayard *bay* 433
bayberry 400
  —*candle* 423
baygall 345
bayonet *kill* 361
  attack 716
  weapon 727
  at the point of the— *war* 722
  severity 739
  coercion 744
  crossed—s 708
bayou 343
bay rum 400
bays *trophy* 733
  crown 877
baysalt 336
bay window 245, 260
bazaar 799
B.C. 106
be 1—alive with 102
  —all and end all *whole* 50
  intention 620
  importance 642
  —all up with 162
  —off *depart* 293
  eject 297
  retract 773
  —it so 488
  —that as it may 30
beach 342
beach comber 268, 348
beacon *sign* 550
  warning 668
  (*light* 423)
  —*fire* 423, 550
bead 249, 847
beading 847
beadle *janitor* 263
  law officer 965
  church 996
beadledom 737
beadroll *list* 86
  prayers 990
  ritual 998
beads 847
  tell one's—990, 998
beadsman
  servant 746
  clergy 996
beagle 366
beak *face* 234

nose 250
magistrate 967
beaked 245
beaker 191
beam *support* 215
  quarter 236
  weigh 319
  light 420
  measurement 466
  on—ends
  powerless 158
  horizontal 213
  side 236
  fail 732
  wonder 870
beaming
  beautiful 845
beanfeast 840
beans 298
bear *produce* 161
  sustain 215
  carry 270
  animal 366
  admit of 470
  stock exchange 797
  suffer 821
  endure 826
  —a hand 680
  —a sense 516
  —away 789
  —away the bell *best* 648
  success 731
  —company 88
  —date 114
  —down *violent* 173
  insolent 885
  —down upon 716
  —false witness 544
  —fruit *produce* 161
  useful 644
  success 731
  prosper 734
  —hard upon 649
  —harmless 717
  —ill 825
  —off *deviate* 279
  —on 215
  —oneself 692
  —out *evidence* 467
  vindicate 937
  —pain 828
  —the brunt *difficult* 704
  defense 717
  —the burden 625
  —the cross 828
  —the palm *supreme* 33
  —through 707
  —up *approach* 286
  persevere 604a
  relieve 834
  cheerful 836
  —up against *resist* 719
  brave 861
  —upon *relevant* 9, 23

influence 175
  —with *tolerate* 740
  permit 760
  take coolly 826
  forgive 918
  bring to—677
  more than flesh and blood can—824
  unable to—
  excited 825
  dislike 867
bear *savage* 907
  surly 895
  —*garden disorder* 59
  discord 713
  arena 728
  —*leader* 540
  —*pit* 370
  —*skin cap* 225
  helmet 717
bearable 651
beard *hair* 205
  prickles 253
  rough 256
  defy 715
  brave 861
  insolence 885
  pluck by the—
  disrespect 929
bearded *hairy* 256
beardless 127, 226
bearer 271
  funeral 363
  servant 746
bear grass 253
bearing *relation* 9
  support 215
  direction 278
  meaning 516
  demeanor 692
  —*rein* 706, 752
bearings
  circumstances 8
  situation 183
bearish 895
beast *animal* 366
  unclean 653
  discourteous 895
  —of burden
  carrier 271
  laborer 690
beastlike *unclean* 653
beastly *unclean* 653
  impure 961
beat *be superior* 33
  periodic 138
  region 181
  impulse 276
  surpass 303
  oscillate 314
  agitation 315
  crush 330
  sound 407
  verse 597
  line of pursuit 625
  path 627

384

beaten track — being

overcome 731
sponger 886
strike 972
—about *circuit* 629
—about the bush
  try for 463
  evade the point 477
  prevaricate 544
  diffuse style 573
—against 708
—a retreat *retire* 283
  avoid 623
  submit 725
—down *destroy* 162
  cheapen 794, 815, 819
  insolent 885
—hollow 33
—into *teach* 537
—of drum *music* 416
  publish 531
  alarm 669
  war 722
  command 741
  pomp 882
—off 717
—one's breast 839
—the air 645
—the Dutch 508
—time *clock* 114
  music 416
—up *churn* 352
—up against
  oppose 708
—up for *cater* 637
—up for recruits
  prepare 673
  aid 707
—up one's quarters
  seek 461
  visit 892
beaten track
  habit 613
  way 627
  leave the—83
  tread the—82
beatific
  pleasing 827, 829
  heavenly 981
beatification
  piety 987
beating high
  the heart—824
beau
  man 373
  fop 854
  admirer 897
  —catcher 256
  —idéal *perfect* 650
  beauty 845
  —monde *fashion* 852
    (*nobility* 875)
beautiful 845
beautify 845, 847
beautiless 846
beauty 845

—of a lovely woman 374
beaver *covering* 223
  hat 225
  animal 366
  —dam 706
becalm 265
because *cause* 153
  attribution 155
  answer 462
  reasoning 476
  motive 615
bechance 151
becharm 829
bêche de mer 298
beck *rill* 348
  sign 550
  mandate 741
  at one's—*aid* 707
  obey 743
beckon *sign* 550
  motive 615
  call 741
becloud *befog* 353
  dark 421
  dim 422
  hide 528
become *change to* 144
  accord with 23
  behove 926
  —of 151
becoming
  accordant 23
  proper 646
  beautiful 845, 847
  due 924
becripple 158
bed *lodgment* 191
  layer 204
  base 211
  support 215
  for animals 370
  garden 371
  —bugs 366
  —maker 746
  —of down *repose* 687
  —of Procrustes 975
  —of roses
    pleasure 377
    prosperity 734
    brought to—161
    death—360
    go to—*quiet* 265
    sleep 683
    keep one's—*ill* 655
bedarken 421
bedaub *cover* 223
  dirt 653
  (*deface* 846)
bedazzle 420
bedding 215
bedeck 847
bedesman
  (*see* beadsman)
bedevil *derange* 61

diabolize 978
sorcery 992
bedew 339
bedfellow 890
bedgown 225
bedlight 225, 847
bedim 421, 422
bedizen *invest* 225
  ornament 847
  vulgar 851
Bedlam
  —broke loose 59
  candidate for—504
bedog 63
Bedouin 792
bedridden 655
bed rock 211
bedroom 191
bedstead 215
bedtime 126
bedwarf 195
bee 690 *gathering* 892
  —in a bottle 407
  —in one's bonnet 503
  busy—682
  swarm like—s 102
beech *tree* 367
beef 298
beefeater 263, 726
beefheaded 499
beehive *convexity* 250
  for bees 370
  workshop 691
bee line 278
Beelzebub 978
beer 298
beery 959
beeswax 352
beetle *overhang* 206
  project 250
  insect 366
  deafness 419
  —head 501
  blind as a—442
  Colorado—913
beetling 214
beet root 298
beets 298
beet sugar 396
befall 151
befit *agree* 23
  expedient 646
  due 924, 926
befog *becloud* 353
  conceal 528
befool *mad* 503
  deceive 545
befooled
  victimized 732
before *in order* 62
  in time 116
  presence 186
  in space 234
  precession 280
  preference 609
  —Christ 106

—everything 153
—long 132
—mentioned 62, 116
—now 122
—one's eyes
  visible 446
  manifest 525
—one's time 132
—the house 454
  set—one 525
beforehand *prior* 116
  early 132
  foresight 510
  resolve—611
befoul 653
befriend *aid* 707
  friendship 888
befuddle 959
beg Turkish title 745
beg *ask* 765
  —leave 760
  —one's bread 765
  —one's life 914
  —pardon 952
  —the question 477
beget 161
begetter 164, 166
beggar *idler* 683
  petitioner 767
  poor 804
  degrade 874
  low person 876
  —description
    unconformable 83
    nomenclature 564
    wonderful 870
  —my neighbor 840
  —on horseback 885
  —s mounted 885
  sturdy—792
beggared
  bankrupt 808
beggar's-lice 253
beggarly *mean* 643
  vile 874
  vulgar 876
  servile 886
  —account of empty boxes
    insufficient 640
    poor 804
begging—letter 765
  go a—*too much* 641
  useless 645
  offered 763
  free 748
begilt 847
begin 66 —again 104
beginner 541
beginning 66
  still ending and—140
begird 227, 229
beglerbeg 745
begone *depart* 293

ejection 297
abrogate 756
(*disappear* 440)
—dull care 836
begrease 653
begrime 653
begrudge
  unwilling 603
  refuse 764
  stingy 819
  envy 921
beguile *mislead* 495
  deceive 545
  reconcile 831
—the time
  inaction 681
  amusement 840
  —to—many 615
begum 745, 875
behalf *advantage* 618
  aid 707
  in—of 759
behave oneself
  conduct 692
  fashion 852
  courtesy 894
behavior 692
  one's good—
  polite 894
  virtuous 944
behead *kill* 361
  execute 972
behemoth 192
behest 741
behind *in order* 63
  in space 235
  sequence 281
  —bars 754
  —one's back
    missing 187
  —the age *old* 124
    ignorant 491
  —the scenes *cause* 153
    unseen 447
    cognizant 490
    latent 526
    hidden 528
    playhouse 599
  —the veil 528
  —time 115, 133
behindhand *late* 133
  shortcoming 304
  adversity 735
  insolvent 808
behold *see* 441
  look 457
beholden *grateful* 916
  obligatory 926
beholder 444
behoof 618
behoove 926
being *abstract* 1
  concrete 3
  created—366
  human—372
  time—106

385

Bel 979
belabor *buffet* 276
   thump 972
belated *late* 133
   ignorant 491
belaud 931
belay *join* 43
   restrain 706
belch *eject* 297
   emit gas 349
beldam
   grandmother 130
   hag 173, 913
belduque 253
beleaguer, 227, 716
belfry 206, 1000
Belial 978
   sons of– 988
belie *deny* 536
   falsify 544
   contradict 708
belief *credence* **484**
   religious creed 983
   easy of– 472
   hug a– 606
believe (*see belief*)
   suppose 514
   –who may 485
   not–one's senses 870
   reason to– 472
believer *religious* 987
   true– 983a
belike 472
belittle *decrease* 36
   underestimate 483
   detract 934
belittling *envy* 921
bell *time* 106
   sound 417
   sign 550
   alarm– 669
   bear away the–
   goodness 648
   success 731
   repute 873
   –book, and candle
   swear 535
   curse 908
   spell 993
   rite 998
   –boy 746
   –mare 64
   –note 408
   –pepper 393
   –the cat 861
   cracked– 408a
   passing– 363
   peal of–s 407
belladonna 663
belle 374, 854
belles–lettres 560
bellicose
   contentious 720
   warlike 722
bellied 250

belligerent
   contentious 720
   warlike 722
   combatant 726
belling 412
bellman 534
Bellona 722
bellow *loud* 404
   cry 411
   animal cry 412
   wail 839
bellows *wind* 349
   lungs 580
bell–shaped
   globose 249
   concave 252
bellwether *go first* 64
   direct 694
belly *inside* 221
   convex 250
   –*god* 957
bellyful *complete* 52
   enough 639
belomancy 511
belong to *related* 9
   component 56
   included 76
   attribute 157
   property 777, 780
   duty 926
beloved 897
below 207
   –its full strength 651
   –par *inferior* 34
   at a low ebb 207
   contempt 643
   bad 649
   indifferent 651
   discount 813
   ignoble 876
   –stairs 207
   –the mark 32
   –here– 318
belt *inclose* 227
   outline 230
   ring 247
   strait 343
   swimming– 666
belvedere 441
bemask 528
bemingle 41
bemire 653
bemoan 839
bemused 458
bench *support* 215
   council 696
   tribunal 966
Bench, King's– 752
bencher 967, 968
bend *oblique* 217
   angle 244
   curve 245
   incline 278
   deviate 279
   depression 308
   circuit 311

   give 324
   submit 725
   –backward 235
   –one's course 278
   –one's looks upon 441
   –one's steps 622
   –over 250
   –sinister 874
   –the bow 686
   –the brows 932
   –the knee
   bow down 308
   submit 725
   humble 879
   servile 886
   courtesy 894
   respect 928
   worship 990
   –the mind 457
   –to *tend* 176
   –to one's will 737
   –to rules etc. 82
   –towards 278
bender 959
beneath 207
   –contempt 643
   –notice 643
   –one 940
Benedick 903
Benedictine 996
benediction
   gratitude 916
   approval 931
   worship 990
   nuptial– 903
benefaction 784
benefactor 816, **912**
benefice 995
beneficent 906
beneficial *good* 648
   (*useful* 644)
   –interest 780
beneficiary
   possessor 779
   receive 785
   clergy 996
benefit *profit* 618
   use 644, 677
   do good 648
   aid 707
   acquisition 775
   property 780
   benevolence 906
   (*improve* 658)
   –s forgot 917
   reap the–of 731
benevolence *tax* 812
   love 897
   kindness **906**
   universal 910
Bengal heat 382
benighted *dark* 421
   ignorant 491
benightedness 442
benign 656

benignant 906
benison 931
Benjamin's mess
   greater 33
   chief part 50
bent *tendency* 176
   framework 232
   angle 244
   grass 367
   turn of mind 820
   desire 865
   –on *willing* 602
   resolved 604
   intention 620
   desirous 865
   fool to the top of one's– 856
benthal 208
Benthamite 910
benthopelagic 208
benthos 208, 366, 367
ben trovato
   likely 472
   imagination 515
   untruth 546
   wit 842
benumb
   insensible 376
   cold 385
   deaden affections 823
benzine 356, 652
benzoin 662
benzolin 652
beplaster 933
bepraise 931
bequeath 784
bequeathable 270
bequest *gift* 270, 784
   (*acquisition* 775)
berate 527, 932
Berber 372a
berceuse 415
bereavement
   death 360
   loss 776
   take away 789
bereft *poor* 804
   –of life 360
   –of reason 503
berg *iceberg* 383
bergamot 400
Bergsonism 451
beriberi 655
Berkeleyism 451
berlin 272
berloque 407
Bernardine 996
Bernoulli's principle 490d
bersagliere 726
berserk 173
berth *lodging* 189
   bed 215
   office 625
Bertillon system 550
beryl *green* 435

   jewel 847
beseech *request* 765
   pray 900
beseem 926
beset *surround* 227
   follow 281
   attack 716
   entreat 765
   annoy 830
   fear 860
   –with difficulties 704
besetting *general* 78
   habit 613
   –sin 945
beshrew 908
beside *except* 83
   near 197
   alongside 236
   –oneself *mad* 503
   excited 824
   –the mark
   irrelevant 10
   error 495
besides 37
besiege *surround* 227
   attack 716
   solicit 765
   fear 860
bésique 840
beslaver 933
beslime 653
beslubber 933
besmear *cover* 223
   dirt 653
besnow 430
besom 652
besot 959
besotted 481
bespangle 847
bespangled 318
bespatter *dirt* 653
   disapprove 932
   flatter 933
   detract 934
bespeak *early* 132
   evidence 467
   indicate 516
   engage 755
   ask for 765
bespeckle 440
bespot 470
besprinkle *mix* 41
   variegate 440
best *good* 648
   perfect 650
   all for the–
   good 618
   prosper 734
   content 831
   hope 858
   bad is the– 649
   –bib and tucker
   prepared 673
   ornament 847
   ostentation 882
   –ever 646

—intentions 906
—man *marriage* 903
—part *great* 31
 nearly all 50
—room 191
—seller 931
 do one's—*care* 459
 try 675
 activity 682
 exertion 686
 have the—of it **731**
 make the—of it
 overestimate 482
 use 677
 submit 725
 compromise 774
 take easily 826
 hope 858
 make the—of one's
  time 684
 to the—of one's
  belief 484
bestead 644
bestial 961
bestir oneself
 activity 682
 haste 684
 exertion 686
bestow *give* 784
 a benefice 995
 —one's *hand* 903
 —*thought* 451
bestraddle 215
bestrew 73
bestride *mount* 206
 ride 215
bet 621
betacism 560
betake oneself to
 journey 266
 business 625
 use 677
betatron 490d
bête noire *fear* 860
 hate 898
bethel 1000
bethink *think* 451
 remember 505
bethrall
 subjection 749
 restraint 751
betide 151
betimes 132
bêtise 497
betoken *evidence* 467
 predict 511
 indicate 550
betongue 932
betray *disclose* 529
 deceive 545
 dishonor 940
 —itself *visible* 446
betrayer 941
betrim 673
betroth *promise* 768
 marriage 903

betrothal 902
 (*see* betroth)
betrothed 897
better *good* 648
 improve 658
 —half 903
 —sort *beau monde* 875
 for—for worse
 choice 609
 marriage 903
 get—*health* 654
 improve 658
 refreshment 689
 restoration 660
 get the—of 731
 seen—days
  deteriorate 659
  adversity 735
  poor 804
 think—of *correct* 658
 repent 950
betting house 621
betty 374
between 228
 —cup and lip 111
 —ourselves 528
 —the lines 526
 —two fires 665
 far— 198
 lie— 228
betwixt 228
bevel 217
bever 298
beverage 298
bevue 732
bevy *assemblage* 72
 multitude 102
bewail *regret* 833
 lament 839
beware 668
bewilder *put out* 458
 uncertain 475
 astonish 870
bewildered 495, 523
bewitch *fascinate* 615
 please 829
 excite love 897
 diabolize 978
 hoodoo 992
bey 745
beyond *superior* 33
 distance 196
 —compare 31, 33
 —control 471
 —expression 31
 —hope 731, 734
 —measure 641
 —mortal ken 528
 —one's depth
  deep 208
  unintelligible 519
 —one's grasp 471
 —possibility 471
 —praise *perfect* 650
 approbation 931
 virtue 944

—price 814
—question 474
—range 196
—reason 471
—remedy 859
—seas 57
—the grave 528
—the mark
 transcursion 303
 redundance 641
—the veil 528
—the verge 180
go— 303
bezel 217
bezonian 876
bhang 663, 954
bhangi 652
bhikshu 955
bias *influence* 175
 tendency 176
 slope 217
 prepossession 481
 disposition 820
 (*motive* 615)
bib *pinafore* 225
 drink 959
 cleanness 652
bibber *weep* 839
 tope 959
bibble-babble 584
Bible 985
—Christian 984
—oath 535
biblioclams 162
biblioclast 165
bibliognost 593
bibliographer 593
bibliography 593
bibliolatry
 learning 490
 heterodoxy 984
 idolatry 991
bibliologist 593
bibliomancy 511
bibliomania 490
bibliomaniac 492
bibliopegist 593
bibliophile 492, 593
bibliopole 593
bibliotheca 593
bibulous 298
bice 435, 438
bicentenary, 98, 138, 883
bicentennial 98, 138, 883
bicephalous 90
bichhona 215
bichloride of
 mercury 663
bicipital 90
bicker *flutter* 315
 quarrel 713
 (*contend* 720)
bickering 24
bicolor 440

biconjugate 91
bicorn 245
bicuspid 91
bicycle 266, 272
bid *order* 741
 offer 763
 —a long farewell 624
 —defiance 715
 —fair *tend* 176
 probable 472
 promise 511
 hope 858
 —for *intend* 620
 offer 763
 request 765
 bargain 794
 —the banns 903
bidder 767
bidding *command* 741
biddy 746
bide *wait* 133
 remain 141
 take coolly 826
 —one's time 133
 watch 507
 inactive 681
bidental 90
bidet 271
biduous 89
biennial *periodic* 138
 plant 367
 celebration 883
bienséance *polish* 852
 manners 894
bier 363
bifacial 90
bifarious 90
bifid 91
bifold 90
biform *double* 90
 (*two* 89)
bifurcate *bisect* 91
 angle 244
big *in degree* 31
 in size 192
 wide 194
 —bug 875
 —gun 875
 —sounding *loud* 404
 words 577
 affected 855
 —with 161
 —with the fate of 511
 look—*defy* 715
 proud 878
 insolent 885
 talk—885 *threat* 909
bigamist 903
bigamy 903
biggin 191
bighead 655
bight 343
bigot *positive* 474
 prejudice 481
 obstinate 606
 heterodox 984

impious 988
bigwig 875
bijou *goodness* 648
 beauty 845
 ornament 847
bijouterie 847
bike 272
bilabiate 90
bilander 273
bilateral *two* 90
 side 236
bilbao 727
bilboes 752
 put into—751
bile 900
bilge *base* 211
 convex 250
 yawn 260
 —water 653
biliary calculus 655
bilingual 560
bilious 837
bilk *disappoint* 509
 cheat 545
 steal 791
bill *list* 86
 hatchet 253
 placard 531
 ticket 550
 paper 593
 plan 626
 weapon 727
 money order 800
 money account 811
 charge 812
 in law 969
 —and coo 902
 —of exchange
  security 771
 —of fare *food* 298
  plan 626
 —of indictment 938
 —of sale 771
 —s of mortality 360
 true—969
billet *locate* 184
 apportion 786
billet *ticket* 550
 epistle 592
 business 625
 —doux 902
billhook 253
billiard-ball
 round 249
 —room 191
 —table *flat* 213
billiards 840
billingsgate *slang* 563
 curse 908
 (*censure* 932)
billion 98, 102
billow *sea* 348
billows *ocean* 341
billy *kettle* 191
 club 727
billycock 225

387

billy goat   **bleak**

billy goat 373
bimonthly 138
bin 191
bina 417
binary 89
binate 89
bind *connect* 43
   cover 223
   compel 744
   condition 770
   obligation 926
   –hand and foot 751
   –oneself 768
   –over 744
   –up wounds 660
bindery 691
binding
   unavoidable 601
   obligatory 744
bine 367
Binet–Simon test 821a
bing 72
binocular 445
binomial 89
biogenesis 161, 357
biogeny 161
biograph 448
biography 594
biologist 357
biology 357, 359
bion 357
biophore 357
bioplasm 357
biotaxy 357
biotic 357
biparous 89
bipartite 44, 91
biplane 273
biplicity 89
biquadrate 95, 96
birch *tree* 367
   flog 972
   –rod 975
bird 366, 368
   –in hand *have* 777
   keep 781
   –of ill omen
   omen 512
   warning 668
   hopeless 859
   –of paradise 366
   –of passage 268
   –of prey 739
   –'s-eye view
   vision 441
   appearance 448
   painting 556
   –s of a feather 17
   kill two–s with one stone 682
   the–has flown
   absence 187
   escape 671
bird cage 370
birdlime *glue* 45

   trap 545
birdman 269
bird–witted 458
biretta 999
birth *beginning* 66
   production 161
   paternity 166
   nobility 875
   –day suit 226
   –right 924
birthday 138, 883
birthmark 848
birthnight 138
birthplace 153
bis *repeat* 104
   approval 931
biscuit 298
bise 349
bisect 91
bisection *middle* 68
   halve 91
bisexual 83
bishop *punch* 298
   clergy 996
   –coadjutor 996
   –'s palace 1000
   –'s purple 437
bishopric 995
bison 366
bisque *soup* 298
bissextile 138
bistoury 253
bister 433
bisulcate 259
bit *small quantity* 32
   part 51
   time 106
   curb 706, 752
   –between the teeth 719
   –by bit *by degrees* 26
   by installments 51
   in detail 79
   slowly 275
bitartrate of potash 662
bitch *female* 366, 374
   clumsy 699
   fail 732
   impure 962
bite *eat* 298
   physical pain 378
   cold 385
   cheat 545
   dupe 547
   etch 558
   mental pain 830
   –in 259
   –the dust 725
   –the thumb
   anger 900
   disrespect 929
   –the tongue 392
biter bit 718
biting *painful* 378
   cold 383

   pungent 392
   vigorous 574
   painful 830
   discourteous 895
   censorious 932
bito 350
bitten 897
bitter *cold* 383
   taste 392, 395
   painful 830
   acrimonious 895
   hate 898
   angry 900
   malevolent 907
   –pill 735
   –words 932
bitter-ender
   irreconcilable 604
   bigot 606
   opponent 710
bitterly *greatly* 31
bitterness (*see* bitter)
   pain 828
   regret 833
   enmity 889
bitumen 356a
bituminous 388
bivalve 90
bivalves 368
bivouac *encamp* 184
   camp 189
   repose 265
   match 668
biweekly 138
bizarre
   unconformable 83
   ridiculous 853
blab *disclosure* 529
   news 532
   loquacity 584
blabber 584
black *color* 431
   crime 945
   –and blue *beat* 972
   –and white
   chiaroscuro 420
   colorless 429
   record 551
   art 556
   writing 590
   –art 992
   –book 938
   –damp 663
   –death 655
   –eye 972
   –flag 722
   –hole *crowd* 72
   prison 752
   –in the face
   swear 535
   excitement 821
   –lead 556
   –letter *old* 124
   barbarism 563
   print 591
   –looks

   discourteous 895
   sullen 901a
   disapprove 932
   –Magic 978
   –Maria 272
   –quarter 655
   –sheep 949
   –swan 83
   look–*feeling* 821
   discontent 832
   angry 900
   prove that–is white 477
blackamoor 431
   wash a–white 471
blackball *exclude* 55
   banish 893
   disapprove 932
blackberry 298
Black Bess 271
blackbird 366
blackboard 590
black–browed 907
blackcoat 996
blackcock 366
blacken (*see* black)
   defame 934
blackfellow 431
Black friar 996
blackguard
   vulgar 851
   rude 895
   base 940
   vagabond 949
blackguardism 908
Black Hand 791
black–hearted 907
blackjack 361, 727
blackleg *apostate* 607
   disease 655
   thief 792
blacklist 932
blackmail *theft* 791
   booty 793
   bribe 973
black–mouthed 936
blackness 431
blacksmith 690
black snake *whip* 975
blacky 431
bladder 191
blade *edge tool* 253
   man 373
   instrument 633
   sharp fellow 682
   proficient 700
   sword 727
   fop 854
blague 544, 884
blain *lump* 250
   blotch 848
blamable 947
blame *attribute to* 155
   disapprobation 932
   lay–on 938
   take– 932

blameless 946
blameworthy
   disapprove 932
   vice 945
   guilt 947
blanc–bec 701
blanc fixe 430
blanch 429, 430
blancmange 298
bland *mild* 174
   suave 894
blandiloquence 933
blandishment
   inducement 615
   endearment 902
   flattery 933
blank *inexistent* 2
   unsubstantial 4
   absence 187
   closure 261
   –cartridge 158
   –verse 597
   look–
   disappointed 509
   discontent 832
   wonder 870
   point–576
blanket *cover* 223
   warm 384
   toss in a–929
   wet–174
blare 404, 412
blarney 933
blasé *weary* 841
   satiated 869
blasphemy 988
blast *destroy* 162
   explosion 173
   wind 349
   sound 404
   adversity 735
   curse 908
blastoderm 357
blat 412
blatant *loud* 404
   cry 412
   silly 499
blather 584
blatherskite 584
blatter 412, 584
blaze *heat* 382
   light 420
   mark 550
   excitement 824
   –abroad 531
   –d with lights 840
blazer *coat* 225
blazing *luminary* 423
blazon *publish* 531
   repute 873
   ostentation 882
bleach 429, 430
bleachers 444
bleaching powder 652
bleak 383

blear

blear 422
blearedness 443
blear-eyed 443
bleat 412
bleb 250
bleed
  physical pain 378
  remedy 662
  spend money 809
  extort money 814
  moral pain 828
  —freely *liberal* 816
  —white 688
  make the heart—830
bleeding
  hemorrhage 299
  remedy 662
  —heart 828
blemish *deface* 241
  imperfection 651
  injure 659
  ugly 846
  defect 848
blench *avoid* 623
  feeling 821
  fear 860
blend *mix* 41
  combine 48
  melody 413
blennorrhagia 655
blennorrhoea 655
bless *give pleasure* 829
  approve 931
  divine function 976
  worship 990
  —my heart 870
  —one's stars
  rejoice 838
  thanks 916
blessed 827
  abode of the—981
blessedness
  single—904
blessing *good* 618
  approval 931
blessings
  prosperity 734
blest 827—with
  possessed of 777
blether 584
Bletonism 511
blight *deteriorate* 659
  adversity 735
  —hope 509
blighted 659
blimp 726
blind *shade* 424
  cecity 442
  inattentive 458
  ignorant 491
  conceal 528
  screen 530
  deception 545
  instinctive 601
  pretext 617
  insensible 823

—alley 252, 261
—a trail 545
—bargain
  uncertain 475
  purposeless 621
  rash 863
—coal 388
—drunk 959
—hookey 840
—lead the blind 538
—man's buff 840
—man's holiday 422
—of one eye 443
—poker 840
—side *prejudice* 481
  credulity 486
  obstinacy 606
  —the eyes *hide* 528
  deceive 545
—to one's own merit 880
blinders 424, 443
blindfold 528
blindness 442
blindworm 419
blink *wink* 443
  neglect 460
  falter 605
  avoid 623
  (*overlook* 458)
  —at *blind to* 442
blinkard 443
blinker 424, 530
bliss 827 *celestial* 981
blister *convexity* 250
  blemish 848
blithe 836
blizzard 349
bloat *inflate* 194
  boast 884
bloated *expanded* 194
  misshapen 243
  convex 250
  —with pride 878
bloater 298
blob 250
blobber 848—lip 848
block *mass* 192
  support 215
  delineate 230
  dense 321
  hard 323
  fool 501
  writing 590
  hinder 706
  execution 975
  —of buildings 189
  —out *shape* 240
  prepare 673
  —printing 591
  —up *close* 261
  obstruct 706
  bring to the—972
  cut—s with a razor 638
  wood—558

blockade
  surround 227
  close 261
  restrain 751
  seclude 893
blockhead 501
  the bookful—499
blockhouse 717
blockish 499
blonde 429, 430
blood
  consanguinity 11
  fluid 333
  kill 361
  fop 854
  nobility 875
  —boil *excite* 824, 825
  anger 900
  —for blood 919
  —heat 382
  —horse 271
  —poisoning 655
  —red 434
  —relation 11
  —run cold
  painful 830
  fear 860
  —up *excited* 824
  angry 900
  —vessel 350
  dye with—
  severe 739
  hands in—*cruel* 907
  in the—5
  life—359
  new—*improve* 658
  animate 824
  spill—*war* 722
bloodhound 366, 913
bloodless *peace* 721
  virtue 946
bloodlessness 160
bloodletting 297, 662
bloodshed 361, 722
bloodshot 848
bloodstained 361
bloodstone 847
bloodstroke 655
bloodsucker 913
bloodsucking 789
bloodthirsty
  murderous 361
  cruel 907
bloodwite 974
bloody (see blood)
  killing 361
  red 434
  unclean 653
  cruel 907
  —flux 299, 655
  —minded 907
bloom *youth* 127
  blossom 367
  heat 382
  blue 438
  health 654

blues

  prosperity 734
  in full—131
bloomers 225
blooming *red* 434
  healthy 654
  beauty 845
blossom *effect* 154
  flower 161, 367
  prosperity 734
blot *blacken* 431
  error 495
  obliterate 552
  dirty 653
  blemish 848
  disgrace 874
  guilt 947
  —out *destroy* 162
  obliterate 552
blotch *black* 431
  blemish 848
blotchy 431
blotter 652
blouse 225
blow *knock* 276
  wind 349
  blossom 367
  unexpected 508
  disappointment 509
  evil 619
  action 680
  get wind 688
  failure 732
  prosper 734
  adversity 735
  pain 828, 830
  boast 884
  —a kiss 902
  —down 162
  —for blow 718
  —hot and cold *lie* 544
  irresolute 605
  tergiversation 607
  caprice 608
  —in *squander* 818
  —off *disperse* 73
  —one's brains out 361
  —out *food* 298
  tire 406
  darken 421
  gorge 957
  —over *past* 122
  —the coals 824
  —the fire 384
  —the horn 416
  —the trumpet 873
  —up *destroy* 162
  eruption 173
  inflate 194
  wind 349
  excite 824
  objurgate 932, 934
  —upon *accuse* 938
  —valve 664
  come to—s 720, 722
  deal a—at 716
  deal a—to 972

  death—360, 361
blowhole 351
blower 884
blown (see blow)
  fatigued 688
  proud 878
  —upon
  disreputable 874
  censured 932
  —with restless
  violence 173
  storm—over *safe* 664
  peace 721
blowpipe 144, 349
blowth 367
blowzy *swollen* 194
  red 434
blubber *fat* 356
  cry 830
  —lip 848
Blucher boot 225
bludgeon
  weapon 727
  (*strike* 276)
  —man *fighter* 726
  brute 913
blue *sky* 338
  ocean 341
  color 438
  learned 490
  bit of—*hope* 858
  —and red 437
  —and yellow 435
  —blood 875
  —book *list* 86
  record 551
  —devils 837
  —green 435
  —jacket 269
  —laws 988
  —light *signal* 550
  alarm 669
  —moon 110
  —peter *flag* 550
  set sail 293
  points 298
  —ribbon 733, 877
  —ruin 959
  —serene 338
  look—
  disappointed 509
  feeling 821
  discontent 832
  disrepute 874
  out of the—338, 508
  true—*veracity* 543
  probity 939
blueback 800
Bluebeard
  marriage 903
  libertine 962
blueberry 298
  —pie 298
bluefish 298
blueness 438
blues 837

389

bluestocking
  pedant 491
  scholar 492
  affectation 855
bluff *violent* 173
  high 206
  cliff 212
  blunt 254
  deceive 545
  brag 884
  card game 840
  insolent 885
  discourteous 895
  –*off* 545
bluffer *boaster* 884
blunder *error* 495
  absurdity 497
  awkward 699
  failure 732
  indiscretion 947
  –*upon* 156
blunderbuss 727
blunderhead 701
blunderheaded 499
blunt *weaken* 160
  inert 172
  to moderate 174
  obtuse 254
  benumb 376
  to damp 616
  plain–spoken 703
  cash 800
  deaden feelings 823
  discourteous 895
  –*tool* 645
  –*witted* 499
bluntness 254
blur *dim* 443
  dirt 653
  blemish 848
  stigma 874
blurb 931
blurred *invisible* 477
blurt out *disclose* 529
  speak 582
blush *heat* 382
  redden 434
  feel 821
  humbled 879
  modest 881
  at first–see 441
  appear 448
  manifest 525
  put to the–
  humble 879
  browbeat 885
  discourtesy 895
blushing honors
  repute 873
  modesty 881
bluster *violent* 173
  defiant 715
  insolent 885
  resent 900
  threaten 909
blusterer 887

blustering
  (*see* bluster)
  windy 349
Blut und Eisen 159
boa 225
  –*constrictor* 366
boar *animal* 366
  male 373
  wild–366
board *layer* 204
  support 215
  food 298
  hard 323
  directorate 542
  council 696
  attack 716
  tribunal 966
  –*of education* 542
  –*of Regents* 542
  –*of studies* 542
  –*school* 542
  festive–892
  go by the–
  powerless 158
  destruction 162
  go on–293
  on–present 186
  ship 273
  preside at the–693
boarder 188
boards *theater* 599
  arena 728
boardwalk 189
boast 884
  not much to–of 651
boaster 884 *jingo* 885
boastful 884
boasting 884
boat 273–*race* 720
  in the same–
  accompany 88
  party 712
boating 267
boatman 269
boat–shaped 245
boatswain 269
bob *depress* 308
  leap 309
  oscillate 314
  agitate 315
  –*a courtesy* 894
  –*for fish* 463
Bobadil, Captain–887
bobbery 404
bobbin 312
bobbish 654
bobcat 366
bobsled 272
bobtailed 53
bocage 367
bock beer 298
bode 511
bodice 225
bodiless 317
bodily *substantially* 3

  wholly 50
  material 316
  –*enjoyment* 377
  –*fear* 860
  –*pain* 378
bodkin
  go between 228
  perforator 262
body *substance* 3
  whole 50
  assemblage 72
  matter 316
  party 712
  –*and blood of Christ* 987
  –*clothes* 225
  –*color* 556
  –*forth* 554
  –*of doctrine* 490
  –*of knowledge* 490
  –*of water* 348
  –*politic mankind* 372
  authority 737
  in a–together 88
  keep–and soul together 654
bodyguard
  defense 717
  combatant 726
  keeper 753
Boeotian *small* 32
  stupid 499
  fool 501
  vulgar 851
  ignoble 876
bog *swamp* 345
  dunghill 653
  –*trotter* 876
boggart 980a
boggle *hesitate* 605
  awkward 699
  difficulty 704
bogie 980
bogle 980
bogus 545–*check* 808
Bohemian
  unconformity 83
  traveler 268
  ungenteel 851
boil *violence* 173
  effervesce 315
  bubble 353
  heat 382, 384
  ulceration 655
  excitement 824, 825
  anger 900
  –*down* 195
boiled (*see* boil)
  –*beef* 298
  –*eggs* 298
boiler 386
boisterous
  violent 173
  hasty 684
  excitable 825
bold *prominent* 250

  unreserved 525
  vigorous 574
  defiant 715
  brave 861
  –*push essay* 675
  –*relief visible* 446
  –*stroke plan* 626
  success 731
  make–with
  discourtesy 895
  show a–front
  defy 715
  brave 861
bold face *type* 591
boldfaced
  insolent 885
  printing 591
bole 50
bolero 840
boldness (*see* bold)
bolshevism 146, 742
bolshevist 146, 712
bolster *support* 215
  repair 658
  aid 707
  –*up vindicate* 937
bolt *sift* 42, 652
  fasten 43
  fastening 45
  close 261
  move rapidly 274
  propel 284
  run away 370, 623
  safety 664
  escape 671
  hindrance 706
  shaft 727
  shackle 752
  –*food swallow* 298
  gormandize 957
  –*in* 751
  –*out of the blue* 508
  –*the door* 761
  –*upright* 212
bolthead 191
bolus *mouthful* 298
  remedy 662
bomb 404, 406, 727
  –*explosion* 361
  –*vessel* 726
bombard 716
  circularize 592
bombardier 726
bombardon 417
bombast
  overestimation 482
  absurdity 497
  unmeaning 517
  magniloquence 577
  ridiculous 853
  boasting 884
  (*exaggeration* 549)
bombastic
  (*see* bombast)
bomber 269a
bombilation 404, 407

bombinate 407
bombing cruiser 273
bombproof 664
bon:–*diable* 844
  –*enfant social* 892
  kindly 906
  –*mot* 842
  –*ton* 852
  –*vivant* 957
  voyage 267
bona fides
  veracity 543
  probity 939
bonanza *extra* 641
  wealth 803
bonbon 396
bond *tie* 45
  servile 746
  compact 769
  security 771
  money 800
  right 924
  –*of union* 9, 45
bondage 749
bonded together 712
bonds (*see* bond)
  fetters 752
  securities 802
  –*of harmony* 714
  in–service 746
bondsman 746
bone *dense* 321
  hard 323
  strength 159
  –*of contention* 713, 720
  –*to pick*
  difficulty 704
  discord 713
  bred in the–5
  one–and one flesh 903
bonehouse 363
bones (*see* bone)
  corpse 362
  music 417
  break no–648
  make no
  –*willing* 602
bonesetter 662
bonfire 382
  festivity 840
  celebration 883
  make a–of 384
bonhomie *candor* 703
  kindness 906
bonhomme 996
Boniface 890
bonne *servant* 746
  nurse 753
  –*bouche treat* 377
  savory 394
  saving 636
  pleasant 829
bonnet 225
  –*rouge* 742

390

bonny

bonny *cheerful* 836
  pretty 845
bonnyclabber 321
bonus *extra* 641
  gift 784
  money 810
bony 323
bonze 996
booby 501
boodle 784
boof 860
book *part* 51
  register 86
  record 551
  volume **593**
  libretto 599
  enter accounts 811
  at one's–s 539
  –*collector* 593
  –*learning* 490
  –*madness* 490
  –*of fate* 601
  –*of poems* 590
  bring to–
  evidence 467
  account 811
  reprove 932
  mind one's– 539
  school– 542
  without–
  by heart 505
bookbinder 593
bookbinding 593
bookcase 191
booked *dying* 360
bookish 490
bookkeeper 553
bookkeeping 811
bookless
  unlearned 493
bookmaker 156
bookmaking 156
bookseller 593
bookshop 593
bookstore 593
bookworm 492, 593
booly 268
boom *support* 215
  sail 267
  rush 274
  impulse 276
  sound 404
  roll 407
  obstacle 706
  defense 717
boomerang *recoil* 277
  weapon 727
boon 784 *beg a–* 765
  –*companion* 890
boor *clown* 876
boorish *ridiculous* 851
  uncourteous 895
boost *impulse* 276
  praise 931
booster 935
boot *box* 191

dress 225
advantage 618
punishment 975
to–added 37
booted and spurred 673
bootee 225
booth *stall* 189
  shop 799
bootikin 225
bootleg
  drunkenness 959
bootlegging 964
bootless *useless* 645
  failing 732
boots *dress* 225
  servant 746
  what–it 643
booty 35, **793**
booze 959
bo-peep *peep* 441
  hide 528
bordel 961
border *contiguity* 199
  edge 231
  flank 236
  flower bed 371
  ornament 847
  –*upon* 197, 199
borderer 197
bordering 233
  –*upon* 197
bore *diameter* 202
  hole 260
  tide 348
  tidal wave 667
  trouble 828
  plague 830
  weary 841
Boreal *Northern* 237
  cold 383
borean 349
Boreas 349
boredom 841
borer 262
boresome 275
born 359 –*so* 5
  –*to other things* 865
  –*under a lucky star* 734
  –*under an evil star* 735
borne 826 –*down*
  failure 732
  defection 837
borné 499
borough 189
  rotten– 893
borrow *imitate* 19
  receive 788
borrowed plumes
  deception 545
borrower 806
borrowing 788
boscage 367
bosh *absurdity* 497

unmeaning 517
untrue 546
trifling 643
bosk 367
bosky 367
bosom *breast* 221
  mind 450
  affections 820
  –*friend* 890
  –*of one's family* 225
  in the–of 229
boss *knob* 250
  will 600
  politician 694
  rule 737
  master 745
bossiness 600
bossism 693
boston 840
Boston bag 191
botanic 369
  –*garden* 369, 371
botanomancy 511
botany 367, **369**
botch *disorder* 59
  mend 660
  unskillful 699
  difficulty 704
  fail 732
both 89
bother
  uncertainty 475
  bustle 682
  difficulty 704
  trouble 828
  harass 830
botheration 828
bothy 189
bottle *receptacle* 191
  preserve 670
  bee in a– 407
  –*green* 435
  –*holder auxiliary* 177
  mediator 724
  –*up remember* 505
  hide 528
  restrain 751
  crack a– 298
  pass the– 959
  smelling– 400
bottom
  lowest part 211
  support 215
  rear 235
  combe 252
  ship 273
  pluck 604a
  courage 861
  at– 5
  at the–of cause 153
  –*dollar* 67, 800
  –*upwards* 218
  from the–of one's heart veracity 543
  feeling 821
  go to the– 310

probe to the– 461
bottomless 208
  –*pit* 982
bottoms 345
bouderie 901a
boudoir 191 –*cap* 225
bouge 250
bough *part* 51
  curve 245
  tree 367
boughpot 400
bought *flexure* 245
bougie 423
bouilli 298
boulder 249
boulevards 227
bouleversement
  revolution 146
  destruction 162
  excite 824
bounce *eject* 297
  jump 309
  lie 546
  dismiss 756
  boast 884
  insolence 885
  –*upon arrive* 292
  surprise 508
bouncer *ejection* 297
bouncing *large* 192
bound
  circumscribe 229, 233
  swift 274
  leap 309
  certain 474
  –*back recoil* 277
  –*by* 926
  –*for direction* 278
  destination 620
  –*to promise* 768
  responsible 926
  I'll be– 535
boundary 233
bounden duty 926
boundless
  infinite 105
  space 180
bounds 233
  outline 230
  –*of modesty* 881
  –*of possibility* 470
  keep within–
  moderation 174
  shortcoming 304
  restrain 751
  prohibit 761
bountiful *liberal* 816
  benevolent 906
bounty *aid* 707
  gift 784
bouquet *fragrant* 400
  beauty 847
bourdon *staff* 215
  melody 413
  drone 415

box

bourgeois *medium* 29
  type 591
  commoner 876
bourgeon 161, 194
bourn 233, 292
bourse 799
bouse 959
bout *turn* 138
  job 680
  fight 720
  prank 840
  drinking– 954
boutade *absurdity* 497
  caprice 608
boutonnière 400
bovine *ox* 366
  beef-witted 499
bow *fore part* 234
  curve 245
  projection 250
  stoop 308
  fiddlestick 417
  weapon 727
  ornament 847
  servility 886
  reverence 894
  respect 928
  bend the– 686
  –*down worship* 990
  –*out* 297
  –*submission* 725
  –*window* 245, 260
Bow bells 876
bowed down
  lament 837
  humble 879
bowelless 914a
bowels *inside* 221
  conduit 350
  –*full of wrath* 722
  –*of compassion* 914
  –*of the earth* 208
bower *abode* 189
  alcove 191
  cards 840
  –*s of bliss* 981
bowery 424
bowie knife 253, 727
bowl *vessel* 191
  rotate 312
  –*along walk* 266
  swift 274
  flowing– 959
bow-legged 243
bowler *hat* 225
bowling green
  level 213
bowls 840
bowman 726
bowshot 197
bowsprit 234
bowstring
  execution 972, 975
bowwow 412
box *house* 189
  chest 191

    theater 599
    fight 720
    –car 272
    –pleat 258
    –the compass
      direction 278
      rotation 312
      change of mind 607
    –the ear *anger* 900
      strike 972
    –up 751
      horse–272
      in a–704
      musical–417
      wrong–*error* 495
      unskillful 699
      dilemma 704
boxer 726
boy 129 *servant* 746
boyage 127
boyar 875
boycott *eject* 297
    resist 719
    seclude 893
    disapprove 893
boyhood 127
Boyle's Law 490d
boylike 129
brabble *discord* 713
    contest 720
brabbler 901
brace *tie* 43
    fasten 45
    two 89
    strengthen 159
    support 215
    music 413
    typography 550
    refresh 689
    –game 545
bracelet *circle* 247
    ornament 847
bracer 392, 662
brachial 633
brachycephalic
    index 372a
brachygraphy 590
bracing
    salubrious 656
bracken 367
bracket *tie* 43, 45
    couple 89
    support 215
    –s *typography* 550
brackish 392
bract 367
brad 45
bradawl 262
Bradshaw 266
brae 206
brag *cards* 840
    boast 884
braggadocio 482, 884
braggart 482, 884
Brahma 976
Brahman *religion* 984

    priest 996
Brahmanism 976
Brahmi 590
Brahmo 984
braid *tie* 43
    ligature 45
    net 219
    variegate 440
Braille 442
brain *kill* 361
    intellect 450
    skill 498
    rack one's–s 451, 515
    suck one's–s 461
brainless 499
brainpan 450
brainsick 458
brainwork 451
brainy 450, 498
brake *slowness* 275
    copse 367
    check 706
    curb 752
    apply the
      –*slower* 275
    hinder 706
    put the–s on 265
    (see also break)
bramble *thorn* 253
    bane 663
bran 330
brancard 272
branch *member* 51
    posterity 167
    ramify 244
    stream 348
    tree 367
    –off *bifurcate* 91
    diverge 291
    –out *ramify* 91
    diffuse style 573
branchiae 349
branching
    ramous **242**
brand *burn* 384
    fuel 388
    torch 423
    mark 550
    sword 727
    disrepute 874
    censure 932
    stigmatize 934
    –new 123
    –of discord 713
    –with reproach 938
brandish *oscillate* 314
    flourish 315
    display 882
brandy smash 959
brangle 713
brangler 710
brank 975
brash *brittle* 328
    downpour 348
    sickness 655

brashness 885
brasier 386
brass *alloy* 41
    music 416
    insolence 885
    bold as–861
    –band 416, 417
    –colored 439
    –farthing 643
brassard 550
brassière 225
brat 129, 167
brattice 224, 228
bravado 884
brave *healthy* 654
    defy 234, 715
    warrior 726
    bear 821, 826
    courage 861
bravery (see brave)
bravo *assassin* 361
    desperado 863
    applause 931
bravura 415, 416
brawl *cry* 411
    discord 713
    revel 840
brawler *disputant* 710
    rioter 742
    blusterer 887
brawny *strong* 159
    stout 192
bray *grind* 330
    cry 412
Bray, Vicar of–
    tergiversation 607
    servility 886
braze 43
brazen *unreserved* 525
    insolent 885
brazier 191
Brazil tea 298
breach *crack* 44
    gap 198
    quarrel 713
    violation 925
    –of faith 940
    –of law
      unconformity 83
      illegal 964
    –of the peace 713
    custom honored in the–614
breachy 198
    unruly 742
bread 298 beg–765
    selfish 943
    –of idleness 683
    –of life *Christ* 976
    piety 987
    –upon the waters 484
breadbasket 191
breadfruit 298
breadstuffs 298
breadth 202
    chiaroscuro 420

break *fracture* 44
    discontinuity 70
    change 140
    gap 198
    carriage 272
    deviate 279
    crumble 328
    train animals 370
    disclose 529
    discord 713
    cashier 756
    violate 773, 927
    bankrupt 808
    faux pas 947
    –a habit 614
    –a lance *attack* 716
    battle 722
    –a law 83
    –away *depart* 293
    avoid 623
    –bread 298
    –bulk 297
    –camp 293
    –down *destroy* 162
    fall short 304
    decay 659
    fail 732
    –for taller timber 666
    –forth 295
    –ground *begin* 66
    depart 293
    –in *ingress* 294
    domesticate 370
    teach 537
    tame 749
    –in upon *derange* 61
    inopportune 135
    hinder 706
    –jail 671
    –loose *escape* 671
    get free 750
    –no bones 648
    –of 660
    –of day *morning* 125
    twilight 422
    –off *cease* 70, 142
    relinquish 624
    abrogate 756
    –one's neck
      powerless 158
      die 360
    –on the wheel
      physical pain 378
      mental pain 830
      punishment 972
    –open 173
    –out *begin* 66
    violent 173
    disease 655
    excited 825
    –Priscian's head 568
    –prison 750
    –short 328
    –silence 582
    –the heart
      pain 828, 830

    dejection 837
    –the ice 888
    –the neck of *task* 676
    success 731
    –the peace
    violence 173
    contest 720
    –the ranks 61
    –the teeth
      hard words 579
    –the thread 70
    –through a custom 614
    –through the clouds
      visible 446
    disclose 529
    –up *disjoin* 44
    decompose 49
    end 67
    revolution 146
    destroy 162
    –up of the system
      death 360
    disease 655
    –with 713
    –with the past 146
    –word *deceive* 545
    improbity 940
breakable 328
breakbone fever 655
breakdown 840
breaker *of horses* 268
    wave 348
breakers *surf* 348
    shallow 667
    –ahead 665
    surrounded by–704
breakfast 298
breakneck
    precipice 217
    rash 863
breakwater
    refuge 666
    obstruction 706
breast *interior* 221
    confront 234
    convex 250
    meat 298
    mind 450
    oppose 708
    soul 820
    at the–129
    –high 206
    –the current 719
    in the–of 620
breastplate 717
breastwork 717
breath *instant* 113
    breeze 349
    life 359
    animality 364
    faint sound 405
    –of accusation 938
    expect 507
    wonder 870
    in the same–120

breathe … broken

breathe
  not a–of air
  quiet 265
  hot 382
  out of–688
  shortness of–688
  take away one's–
    unexpected 508
  fear 860
  wonder 870
  take–*rest* 265
  refresh 689
  with bated–581
breathe *exist* 1
  blow 349
  live 359
  faint sound 405
  evince 467
  mean 516
  inform 527
  disclose 529
  utter 580
  speak 582
  refresh 689
  –freely *pleasure* 827
  relief 834
  –one's last 360
  –the vital air 359
  not–a word 528
breathing *time* 106
  air 349
  –time *repose* 687
  truce 723
breathing–hole 351
breathless
  voiceless 581
  out of breath 688
  feeling 821
  fear 860
  eager 865
  wonder 870
  –attention 457
  –expectation 507
  –impatience 865
  –speed 684
breech *invest* 225
  rear 235
breeches 225
  –maker 225
  –pocket
  money 800, 802
  wear the–737
breechloader 727
breed *race* 11
  kind 75
  multiply 161
  progeny 167
  animals 370
  rear 537
  (*prepare* 673)
breeding
  production 161
  style 852
  politeness 894
  –place 153
breeze *wind* 349
  discord 713

breezy 836
brethren 997
breve 413
brevet *warrant* 741
  commission 755
  permit 760
  –rank 873
breviary 990, 998
brevier 591
brevipennate 193
brevity *short* 201
  concise 572
brew *mix* 41
  prepare 673
brewing
  impending 152
Briarean 102, 159
Briareus 159, 192
bribe *equivalent* 30
  tempt 615
  offer 763
  gift 784
  buy 795
  reward 809, 973
bribery (see bribe)
bric–a–brac 847
brick *hard* 323
  pottery 384
  material 635
  trump 939, 948
  –color 434
  –over 386
  –red 434
  make–s without
    straw 471
brickbat 727
brickkiln 386
bricklayer 690
bricky 434
bridal 903
bride 903
bridegroom 903
bridesmaid 890, 903
bridesman 903
bridewell 752
bridge
  intermedium 45
  way 627
  card game 840
  –of death 360
  –over *join* 43
  facilitate 705
  make peace 723
  compromise 774
bridle *depart* 293
  restrain 751
  rein 752
  –one's tongue
    silent 585
    cautious 864
  –road 627
  –up 900
brief *time* 111
  space 201
  concise 572
  compendium 596

  –case 191
  hold a–for 759
briefly *anon* 132
brier *sharp* 253
  bane 663
brig 273
brigade *arrange* 60
  military 726
brigadier 745
brigand 792
brigandage 791
brigandine 717
brigantine 273
bright *shine* 420
  color 428
  intelligent 498
  cheery 836
  beauty 845
  glory 873
  –colored 428
  –days 734
  –prospect 858
  –side 829
  –thought *sharp* 498
  good stroke 626
  wit 842
  look at the–side
  cheer 836
  hope 858
brighten up
  furbish 658
bright–eyed 845
brigue *party* 712
  contention 720
brilliant *shining* 420
  music 416
  good 648
  witty 842
  beautiful 845
  gem 847
  glorious 873
  be–*intellectual* 498
  –idea 842
brim 231–over 641
brimful 52
brimstone 388
brindled 440
brine *sea* 341
  salt 392
bring 270–about
  cause 153
  achieve 729
  –back 790
  –back to the memory
    505
  –forth *produce* 161
  extract 301
  –forward
  evidence 467
  manifest 525
  teach 537
  improve 658
  –gray hairs to the
    grave
  adversity 735
  pain 830

  –grist to the mill 644
  –home 775
  –home to 155
  –in *receive* 296
  income 810
  price 812
  –in a verdict 480
  –in its train 88
  –in question 461
  –into being 161
  –into play 677
  –low 874
  –off 672
  –out *discover* 480a
  manifest 525
  publish 591
  –over *persuade* 484
  –round *persuade* 615
  restore 660
  –to *convert* 144
  halt 265
  –to a crisis 604
  –to a point 74
  –to bear 470
  –to bear upon
    relation 9
    action 170
  –together *assemble* 72
  –to life 359
  –to light 480a
  –to maturity
    prepare 673
    complete 729
  –to mind 505
  –to perfection 677
  –to terms 723
  –to trial 969
  –under one's notice
    457
  –up *develop* 161
  vomit 297
  train 370
  educate 537
  –up the rear 235
  –word 527
brink 231
  –of the grave 360
  on the–*almost* 32
  coming 121
  near 197
briny 392–deep 341
brio *music* 415
briquette 388
brisk *prompt* 111
  energetic 171
  active 682
  cheery 836
bristle 253–up
  stick up 250
  angry 900
  –with *plenty* 639
  too much 641
  –with arms 722
bristling *thorny* 253
  discourtesy 895
bristly *rough* 256

Britannia metal 545
Briticism 563
British 188
  –courts 966
  –lion 604
Britisher 188
Briton 188 true–939
brittle 328
brittleness 328
britzka 272
broach *begin* 66
  found 153
  perforate 262
  tap 297
  publish 531
  assert 535
broad *general* 78
  space 202
  lake 343
  emphatic 535
  indelicate 961
  –accent 580
  –arrow 550
  –awake *vigilant* 459
  brisk 682
  –daylight *light* 420
  manifest 525
  –farce 842
  –gauge 466
  –grin 838
  –highway 627
  –hint 527
  –meaning 516
broadcast
  disperse 73, 291
  publish 531
  news 532
  sow–818
broadcloth 219, 635
broaden 78
broadhearted 906
broadhorn 273
broadsheet 531, 593
broad–shouldered
  159
broadside *lateral* 236
  publication 531
  cannonade 716
broadsword 727
Brobdingnagian 159,
  192
brocade 847
brocatelle 847
brochure 593
broder 549
brogan 225
brogue *boot* 225
  dialect 560, 563
broidery 847
broil *heat* 382
  fry 384
  fray 713, 720
broiler *fowl* 298
broken *divided* 51
  discontinuous 70
  weak 160

393

broker   **bully**

   of horses 370
   —*color* 428
   —*down decrepit* 659
   failing 732
   dejected 837
   —English 563
   —*fortune*
     adversity 735
     poverty 804
   —*heart pain* 828
     dejected 837
     hopeless 859
   —*meat* 645
   —*reed* 665
   —*voice* 581, 583
   —*winded disease* 655
     fatigue 688
broker *agent* 758
   merchant 797
brokerage *pay* 812
brokery 794
bromide
   conventionalist 82
bromidium 496
bronchia 351
broncho 271
   —*buster* 370
bronchocele 655
bronze *brown* 433
   sculpture 557
brooch 847
brood *multitude* 102
   family 167
   hatch 370
   —over *think* 451
   mope 837
brooding
   preparing 673
brook *stream* 348
   bear 826
broom
   undergrowth 367
   sweep 652
broomstick 491
broth 298
brothel 945, 961
brother *kin* 11
   similar 17
   equal 27
   —Jonathan 188
brotherhood 712
brotherly
   friendship 888
   love 897
   benevolence 906
brougham 272
brought to bed 161
brouillerie 713
brouillon 626
brow *top* 210
   edge 231
   front 234
browbeat
   intimidate 860
   swagger 885
   disrespect 929

   —en *humbled* 879
brown 433—Bess 727
   —*ocher* 433
   —*stone* 635
   —*stone house* 189, 831
   —*study thought* 451
   inattention 458
   imagination 515
Brownian 984
brownie 979
brownness 433
browse 298
bruin 895
bruise *powder* 330
   hurt 619
   injure 649
bruised *blemished* 848
bruiser 726
bruit 531, 532
brumal 383
brummagem 545
brunch 572
brunette 433
Brünn *man* 372a
Brunswick black 356a
brunt *beginning* 66
   impulse 276
   bear the—
   difficulty 704
   defense 717
   endure 821, 826
   (*resist* 719)
brush *tail* 235
   rough 256
   rapid motion 274
   groom 370
   touch 379
   clean 652
   fight 720
   —*away reject* 297
   abrogate 756
   —up *clean* 652
   furbish 658
   prepare 673
   paint—556
brushwood 367, 388
brusque *violent* 173
   haste 684
   discourtesy 895
Brussels sprouts 298
brustle 407
brutal *vulgar* 851
   rude 895
   savage 907
brutalize (*see* brutal)
   corrupt 659
   deaden 823
   vice 945
brute *animal* 366
   rude 895
   maleficent 913
   —*force strength* 159
   violence 173
   animal 450a

   severe 739
   compulsion 744
   lawless 964
   —*matter matter* 316
   inorganic 358
brutify 954
brutish (*see* brute)
   vulgar 851
   ignoble 876
   intemperate 954
Bryanite 984
bryophites 369
bubble
   unsubstantial 4
   transient 111
   little 193
   light 320
   water 348
   air 353
   error 495
   deceit 545
   trifle 643
   —*burst fall short* 304
   disappoint 509
   fail 732
   —*reputation* 873
   —up *agitation* 315
bubbling 353
bubo 250
bubonic plague 655
buccaneer 791, 792
Bucephalus 271
buck *confront* 234
   leap 309
   stag 366
   male 373
   negro 431
   wash 652
   fop 854
   —*basket* 191
   —*fever* 825
   —*jump* 309
   —*nigger* 431
bucket *receptacle* 191
   load 270
   —*shop* 621
   kick the—360
bucking *attack* 716
buckle *tie* 43
   fastening 45
   distort 243
   curl 248
   —oneself 604
   —on one's armor 673
   —to *resolution* 604
   exertion 686
   —with *grapple* 720
buckler 717
buckram
   affectation 855
   pride 878
   men in—549
buckwheat 367
bucolic
   pastoral 370, 371
   poem 597

bud *beginning* 66
   germ 153
   expand 194
   graft 300
   blossom 367
   —from 154
Buddha 976, 986
Buddhism 976, 984
Buddhist 984
   —priests 996
   —temple 1000
budding *young* 127
   expansion 194
buddy *chum* 890
budge 264
budget *heap* 72
   bag 191
   store 636
   finance 811
   —of *news* 532
budmash 949
buff *skin* 223
   color 436
   native—226
buffalo 366—bug 366
   —*robe* 223
   —*wallow* 343
buffer *hindrance* 706
   defense 717
buffet *strike* 276
   agitate 315
   evil 619
   bad 649
   affront 900
   smite 972
   —the waves
   difficulty 704
   opposition 708
buffet *bar* 189
   cupboard 191
buffle-headed 499
buffo 599
buffoon *actor* 599
   humorist 844
   butt 857
buffoonery
   amusement 840
   humor 842
bug *littleness* 193
   insect 366, 653
bugaboo *alarm* 669
   fear 860
bugbear
   imaginary 515
   alarm 669
   fear 860, 980
buggy 272
bugle *instrument* 417
   war cry 722
   —*call sign* 550
   command 741
bugles *ornament* 847
build *construct* 161
   form 240
   —a campfire 384
   —up *compose* 54

   —upon *belief* 484
   —upon a rock 150
builder 626, 690
building material 635
buildings 189
built on *basis* 211
bulb *knob* 249
   projection 250
bulbul 416
bulge 250
bulk *be great* 31
   whole 50
   size 192
bulkhead
   covering 223
   interjacence 228
   safety 664
   hindrance 706
bulky 31
bull *animal* 366
   male 373
   error 495
   absurdity 497
   solecism 568
   detective 664
   ordinance 741
   stock exchange 797
   —in a china shop 59
   take the—by the horns
   resolution 604
   courage 861
Bull, John— 188
bulla 250
bull calf 501
bulldog
   animal 327, 366
   pluck 604, 604a
   courage 861
bulldoze 860, 885
bulldozer 887
bullet *ball* 249
   arms 727
   (*missile* 284)
   —proof 717
bulletin *list* 86
   news 532
   record 551
   letter 592
   —board 551
bullfight 720
bullhead 501
bullion 800
bull's-eye *center* 222
   lantern 423
   aim 620
bullwhack 975
bullwhacker 370
bully *boat* 273
   first-rate 648
   fighter 726
   jovial 836
   frighten 860
   rashness 863
   bluster 885

bullyrag

bullyrag

    blusterer 887
    resent 900
    threaten 909
    evildoer 913
    bad man 949
    –for you 931
bullyrag 830
bulrush *worthless* 643
bulwark 717
bum *idler* 683
    spree 840
    beggar 876
    drink 959
bumbailiff 965
Bumbledom
    authority 737
    jurisdiction 965
bumboat 273
bummer 683
bump *projection* 250
    thump 276
bumper 52
bumpkin 876
bumptious *proud* 878
    insolent 885
bun 298
bunch *collection* 72
    proluberance 250
bunch-backed 243
buncombe *lie* 544
    bombast 577
    boast 884
    flattery 933
Bund 712
bund *quay* 666
bunder 292, 666
bunderboat 273
bundle *packet* 72
    go 266
    start 284
    –along 274
    –off 234
    –on *hurry* 274
    haste 684
    –out 297
bundobust 60, 769
bung 263, 351
    –up 261
bungalow 189
bunghole 351
bungle 699
bungler 701
bunk *lie* 544
    reside 186
    support 215
bunker 181
bunkie *bedfellow* 890
bunko 545, 791
    –game 545
    –steerer 548
bunkoman 792
bunkum
    (*see* buncombe)
bunt 276
bunting 550
buoy *raise* 307

float 320
refuge 666
hope 858
buoyant *floating* 305
    light 320
    elastic 325
    prosperous 734
    cheerful 836
    hopeful 858
bur *clinging* 46
    rough 256
    in engraving 558
burden *lading* 190
    weight 319
    melody 413
    music 415
    poetry 597
    too much 641
    clog 706
    oppress 828
    care 830
    –of a song
      repetition 104
    –the memory 505
burdensome
    (*see* burden)
    hurtful 649
    laborious 686
    cumbrous 830
bureau *chest* 191
    office 691
    shop 799
    tribunal 966
    department 965
bureaucracy 737
bureaucrat 694
bureaucratic 737
burgee 550
burgeon 161, 194
burgess 188
burgh 189
burgher 188
burghmote 966
burglar 792
    –alarm 550, 669
burglary 791
burgomaster 745
burgrave 745
burial 363
buried *deep* 208
    imbedded 229
    hidden 528
    –in a napkin 460
    –in oblivion 506
burin 558
burke 361
burlesque
    imitation 19
    travesty 21, 555
    absurdity 497
    drama 599
    comic 853
    ridicule 856
burletta 599
burly 192
burn *near* 197

rivulet 348
hot 382
consume 384
neglect 460
near the truth 480a
excited 825
blemish 848
love 897
punish 972
–daylight 683
–in 384
–one's fingers 699
–out 385
–the candle at both
    ends *waste* 638
exertion 686
prodigal 818
–to 865
–up the road 266
burner 423
burning (*see* burn)
    of a corpse 363
    passion 821
    angry 900
    –ghât 363, 384
    –glass 445
    –pain 378
    –shame 874
    –with curiosity 455
burnish *polish* 255
    shine 420
    beautify 845
burnoose 225
burnt (*see* burn)
    red 434
    –offering *atone* 952
    worship 990
    –orange 434
burr 253, 410
burra sahib 642, 745
burro 271
burrow *lodge* 184
    excavate 252
bursar 801
bursary 802
bursat 348
burst *disjoin* 44
    instantaneous 113
    explosion 173
    brittle 328
    sound 406
    paroxysm 825
    bubble–
      disclosure 529
    all over 729
    –away 623
    –forth *begin* 66
    expand 194
    be seen 446
    –in 294
    –into a flame 825
    –into tears 839
    –of anger 900
    –of eloquence 582
    –of envy 921
    –of laughter 838

–out *violence* 173
    egress 295
–upon *arrive* 292
    unexpected 508
–with grief 839
    ready to–
      replete 641
    excited 824
burthen (*see* burden)
bury *inclose* 229
    inter 363
    conceal 528
    –one's talent 528
    –the hatchet 723
busby 225
bush *branch* 51
    lining 224
    jungle 344
    shrub 367
    beat about the–629
    in the–344
bushed 475, 688
bushel *much* 31
    multitude 102
    receptacle 191
    size 192
    hid under a–460
    not hide light under
      a–878
bushfighting 720
bushing 224
Bushman 431
bushranger 792
bushwhacker
    scythe 253
    guerrilla 726
    free lance 748
bushy 256
business *event* 151
    topic 454
    occupation 625
    commerce 794
    full of–682
    man of–
      proficient 700
    consignee 758
    mind one's–
      incurious 456
    attentive 457
    careful 459
    send about one's–
      297
    stage–599
businesslike
    orderly 58
    business 625
    active 682
    practical 692
    skillful 698
buskin *dress* 225
    drama 599
buss *boat* 273
    courtesy 894
    endearment 902
bust 554 *spree* 840
bustee 189

button

bustle *energy* 171
    dress 225
    agitation 315
    activity 682
    haste 684
    difficulty 704
bustling (*see* bustle)
    eventful 151
busy 682
    idly–638, 683
busybody
    curiosity 455
    newsmonger 532
    activity 682
but
    on the other hand
      30
    except 83
    limit 233
    qualifying 469
    –now 118
butcha 129, 167
butcher *kill* 361
    evildoer 913
butchered 53
butler 746
butt *cask* 191
    push 276
    aim 620
    attack 716
    laughingstock 857
    –end 67
    –in 294
butte 206
butter 356
    flattery 933
    –bread on both sides
      641
    –not melt in mouth
      894
buttercup 845
buttered side know
    –skill 698
    selfish 943
    not know–699
butter-fingers 701
butterfly *insect* 366
    variegated 440
    fickle 605
    beauty 845
    gaudy 882
    break–on wheel
      waste 638
    spite 907
butterscotch 396
buttery 636
Buttinsky 294
buttock 235
button *fasten* 43
    fastening 45
    little 193
    hanging 214
    knob 250
    trifle 643
    –up close 261
    restrain 751

buttoned–up   **call**

–up one's pockets 808
   take by the– 586
buttoned–up
   reserved 528
buttonhole *flower* 400
   bore 841
buttonholer 841
buttons *page* 746
button–top
   useless 645
buttress *strength* 159
   support 215
   defense 717
butyraceous 355
buxom 836
buy 795 –and sell 794
   –a pig in a poke 621
buzz *hiss* 409
   insect cry 412
   publish 531
   news 532
   –saw 44
buzzard *bird* 366
   fool 501
   between hawk and–
      agitation 315
   worry 828
   blind as a– 442
   –dollar 800
by *alongside* 236
   instrumental 631
   sequestered 893
   –and by 121, 132
   –itself 87
   –means of 632
   –my troth etc. 535
   –no means 32
   –telegraph 532
   –the by 134
   –the card 82
   –the hour etc.
     hire 788
   –the way *à propos* 9
   beside the purpose 10
   parenthetical 134
   –wireless 532
   go–*pass* 303
   have–one
     provide 637
     possess 777
bye *departure* 293
by–end 615
bygone *past* 122
   forgotten 506
   let–s be bygones 918
bylaw 963
byname 565
by–pass 287
bypast 122
bypath 279
byplay *hint* 527
   gesture 550
by–purpose 615
byre 189, 370, 636

byroad 278, 627
by–room 191
byssus 256
bystander *near* 197
   spectator 444
byway 627
byword *maxim* 496
   cant term 563, 564
   reproach 874
   contempt 930

C

cab 272
cabal *plan* 626
   confederacy 712
cabala *latency* 526
   spell 993
cabalism 526
cabalistic *hidden* 528
   sorcery 992
cabane 273
cabaret 189
cabasset 717
cabbage 298, 791
cabestro 45
cabin *room* 189
   receptacle 191
cabined 751
cabinet *receptacle* 191
   workshop 691
   council 696
   –*picture* 556
cable *link* 45
   dispatch 527
   news 531, 532
   telegraph 534
   by– 684
   –code 528
   slip– 623
   telegraphic– 534
cabled *telegraphic* 531
cabman *traveler* 268
   director 694
caboose 386
cabriolet 272
cacation 299
cachalot 192
cache 636
cachet 550
   lettre de– 751
cachexia
   weakness 160
   disease 655
cachinnation 838
cacique 745
cackle *of geese* 412
   chatter 584
   talk 588
   laugh 838
cacodemon 980
cacoëpy 410, 583
cacoëthes *habit* 613
   itch 865
   –*loquendi* 584

–*scribendi* 590
cacographer 579
cacographic 579
cacography 590
cacology 579, 583
caconym 563
cacophonous
   (*see* cacophony)
cacophony
   stridor 410
   discord 414
   style 579
Cacus, den of– 791
cad *servant* 746
   vulgar 851
   plebeian 876
cadastral survey 466
cadastration 466
cadastre *list* 86
   measurement 466
cadaverous
   corpse 362
   pale 429
   hideous 846
caddy 191
cadeau 784
cadence *pace* 264
   fall 306
   sound 402
   music 415
cadenza 415
cadet *junior* 129
   soldier 726
   officer 745
   –blue 438
cadge 765
cadger *beggar* 767
   huckster 797
cadi 967
cadmium 439
caduceus *insignia* 747
   wand 215, 993
caducity *fugacity* 111
   age 128
   impotence 158
   decay 659
caducous 111
caecal 261
caecum 221, 350
Caesar 745
caesura
   disjunction 44
   discontinuity 70
   cessation 142
   interval 198
café 189
caftan 225
cafuzo 41
cage *receptacle* 191
   restrain 751
   prison 752
Cagliostro
   impostor 548
   sorcerer 994
cahoot 712, 778
cahot 250, 315

cahotage *disorder* 59
   agitation 315
Cain 361
caique 273
cairn *grave* 363
   sign 550
caisson 191, 252
caitiff *churl* 876
   ruffian 913
   villain 949
cajole *flatter* 933
   (*see* cajolery)
cajolery
   imposition 544, 545
   persuasion 615
   flattery 933
cake *stick* 46
   pastry 298, 396
   consolidate 321
   –walk 840
calabash 191
calaboose 752
calambac 400
calambour 400
calamiform 253
calamitous
   adverse 935
   disastrous 830
calamity *killing* 361
   evil 619
   adversity 735
   suffering 830
calash *cap* 225
   vehicle 272
calathiform 252
calcareous 432
calcimine 430
calcinatory 384
calcine 384
calcitrate 276
calcium light 423
calculate *reckon* 85
   investigate 461
   expect 507
   intend 620
   –upon 484
calculated
   tending 176
   premeditated 611
calculating
   prudent 498
   –machine 85
calculation
   (*see* calculate)
   accounts 811
   caution 864
calculous 323
calculus 85, 323
caldron
   (*see* cauldron)
calèche 272
Caledonian 188
calefaction 384
calefy 384
calembour 520
calendar *list* 86

chronicle 114
   record 551
   schedule 611
calender 255
calenture
   delirium 503
   disease 655
calf *young* 129
   animals 366
   fool 501
   –love 902
   golden– 986, 991
Caliban 846
caliber *degree* 26
   size 192
   breadth 202
   opening 260
   intellectual capacity 498
calibrate *degree* 26
   breadth 202
   measure 466
caliche 490a
calico 635
calid 382
calidarium 386
calidity 382
caliginous 421
calipers 466
caliph 745
caliphate 737
calisthenics
   training 537
   beauty 845
caliver 727
calk 660
call *signal* 550
   name 564
   express 566
   motive 615
   visit 892
   sanctify 976
   ordain 995
   at one's– *alert* 682
   obedient 743
   –attention to 457
   –for *require* 630
   order 741
   ask 765
   –forth *resort to* 677
   excite 824
   –in *advice* 695
   –in question 485
   –into being 161
   –into notice 525
   –into play 677
   –names 929, 932
   –of duty 926
   –off the attention 458
   –out *cry* 411
   challenge 715
   –over *number* 85
   –to 586
   –to account 932
   –to mind 505

callable

−to order 741
−to the bar 968
−to the ministry 996
−to witness 467
−up *recollect* 505
  motive 615
  excite 824
−upon *demand* 741
  request 765
  visit 892
  duty 924, 926
−up spirits 992
  within−197
callable 741
callaesthetics 845
callant 129
call boy *theater* 599
callidity 698
calligraphy 590
calling *business* 625
Calliope 597
calliope 404, 417
callithump 173
callosity 323, 823
callous *hard* 323
  obtuse 376
  insensible 823
callow *young* 127
  infant 129
  bare 226
  unprepared 674
calm *physical* 174
  quiet 265
  silent 403
  dissuade 616
  leisure 685
  peace 721
  moral 826
  imperturbable 871
−before a storm 145
−belief etc. 484
  green−below 318
calmant 174
calmative 174
calminant 210
calminate 210
calmness
  expectance 871
  (*see* calm)
calomel 662
caloric 382
  −engine 633
calorie 490d
calorimeter 389
calotte 999
calotype 554
caloyer 996
calumet *token* 550
  −of peace 721, 723
calumniator 936
calumny 934
calvary 1000
Calvinism 984
calyx 191
cam 633
camarade 890

camarilla 712
camber 250
cambist 797, 801
camboose 386
Cambrian 188
cambric 635
camel 271
  −backed 243
  −bird 274
  swallow a−
  caprice 608
  clumsy 699
camelopard 206
camelot 797
cameo *convex* 250
  sculpture 557
camera 445
camera lucida 445
camera obscura 445
camerated 191
camilla 274
camisade 716
camisole 225
camorra 712
camouflage 273, 528
camp *locate* 184
  abode 189
  military 728
  −meeting 990
  −on the trail 281
campagna *space* 180
  plain 344
campaign *tactics* 692
  war 722
  (*plan* 626)
  −hat 225
campaigner 726
campaigning
  travel 266
campaniform
  curved 245
  round 249
  concave 252
campanile 206
campanular 245, 249
campanulous 249
camper 268
campestrian 344
campestrine 344
camphor 356a
camphorated 356a
campus 344, 367, 728
Campus Martius 728
can *power* 157
  mug 191
  preserve 670
  best one−686
  −it be! 870
Canadian 188
canaille 876
canakin 191
canal *opening* 260
  conduit 350
  way 627
  −boat 273
canaliferous 259

canard *rumor* 532
  lie 546
canary 366
cancan *dance* 840
cancel *destroy* 162
  counteract 179
  obliterate 552
  abrogate 756
  repudiate 773
cancellated 219
cancellation 219
cancelli 191
cancellous 219
cancer *disease* 655
  bane 663
  painful 830
candelabrum 423
candelia 349
candent 382, 430
candid *white* 430
  sincere 543
  ingenuous 703
  honorable 939
candidacy 763
candidate
  petitioner 767
  desirous 865
candidature 763
candle 423
  bargain by inch of−769
  burn−at both ends 686
  −ends *remains* 40
  economy 817
candle foot 466
candleholder 711
candlelight 126, 422
Candlemas 138, 998
candle power 466
candlestick 423
  seven−branched−999
candor *veracity* 543
  artlessness 703
  honor 939
candy *dense* 321
  sweet 396
cane *weapon* 727
  punish 972
  scourge 975
  −sugar 396
canescent 430
can hook 633
Canicula 423
canicule 382
canicular 382
caniculated 259
canine 366
  −appetite 865
  −madness 867
canister 191
canker *disease* 655
  deterioration 659
  bane 663
  pain 830

cankered *sullen* 901a
cankerworm 663
  evildoer 913
  care 830
canned goods 670
cannel coal 388
cannery 636
cannibal 913
cannibalism 945
cannikin 191
canning 670
cannon *collision* 276
  loud 404
  arms 727
  −'s mouth *war* 722
  courage 861
cannonade 716
cannonball
  round 249
  swift 274
cannoneer 726
cannot 471
cannular 260
canny *wise* 498
  cunning 702
canoe 273
  paddle one's own−748
canon *regularity* 80
  music 415
  belief 484
  precept 697
  priest 996
  rite 998
  −law 697
canon
  ravine 198, 350
canonical *regular* 82
  inspired 985
  ecclesiastical 995
canonicals 999
canonist 983
canonization
  repute 873
  deification 991
  rite 998
canonize 991
canonry 995
canopus 490a
canopy 223
  −of heaven 318
canorous 413
cant *oblique* 217
  jerk 276
  hypocrisy 544
  neology 563
  impiety 988
cantabile 415
cantankerous 901, 901a
cantata 415
cantatore 416
cantatrice 416
canteen 189, 191
canter *move* 266
  gallop 274

win at a−705
canterbury
  receptacle 191
Canterbury tale 546
cantharides 171
cant hook 276
canticle 415
cantilever 215
canting 855
cantle 51
cantlet *small* 32
  piece 51
canto 597
canton *partition* 44
  area 181
cantonment
  location 184
  abode 189
cantrap 993
canty 836
Canuck 188
canvas *sail* 267
  picture 556
  under press of−274
canvass
  investigate 461
  discuss 476
  dissert 595
  solicit 765
canvasser 767, 797
canzonet *song* 415
caoutchouc 325
cap *be superior* 33
  height 206
  summit 210
  cover 223
  hat 225
  retaliate 718
  complete 729
  salute 894
  −and bells 844
  −and gown 550
  −fits 23
  −in hand *request* 765
  servile 886
  respect 928
  −of maintenance 747
  fling up one's−838
  Fortunatus's−993
  set one's−at 897, 902
capability
  endowment 5
  power 157
  skill 698
  facility 705
capable *quick* 682
  (*see* capability)
capacious *space* 180
  −memory 505
capacitor 490d
capacity *endowment* 5
  power 157
  space 180
  size 192
  intellect 450

cap–a–pie

wisdom 498
office 625
talent 698
meanest–499, 518
cap–a–pie
complete 52
armed–
prepared 673
defense 717
war 722
caparison 225
cape *height* 206
cloak 225
projection 250
(*land* 342)
Cape cart 272
caper *leap* 309
absurdity 497
dance 840
capful *quantity* 25
small 32
–of wind 349
capillament 205
capillary *hairlike* 205
(*thin* 203)
capital *city* 189
top 210
letter 561
important 642
excellent 648
money 800
wealth 803
–*crime* 947
–*punishment* 972
make–out of
pretext 617
acquire 775
capitalist 803
capitals 591
print in–s 642
capitation 85
–*tax* 812
capitol 717
capitular *rule* 80
churchdom 995
clergy 996
capitulate 725
capnomancy 511
capon 298, 373
caponize 38, 158
caporal 694
capote 225
capper 548
capriccio *music* 415
whim 608
caprice 608
out of–615a
capricious
irregular 139
changeable 149
irresolute 605
whimsical 608
capriciously
without motive 615a
(see *capricious*)
capriole 309

capsheaf 210
capsicum 393
capsize *inversion* 218
wreck 731
capsized 732
capstan *lift* 307
machine 633
capstone 210
capsular *concave* 252
capsule *vessel* 191
tunicle 223
captain *mariner* 269
master 745
captation 933
caption 789
heading 66, 564
captious
capricious 608
irascible 901
censorious 932
captivate *induce* 615
restrain 751
please 829
captivated
fascinated 827
captivating
pleasing 829
lovable 897
captivation
attraction 829
captive *prisoner* 754
adorer 897
–balloon 273
lead–749
make–751
captivity 751
captor 789
capture 789
capturer 789
Capuchin 996
caquet 584
car 272
carabineer 726
carack 273
caracole 309
caracoler 266
carafe 191
caramel 396
carapace 717
carat 319
caravan *company* 72
journey 266
vehicle 272
caravansary 189
caravel 273
carbarn 636
carbine 727
carbolic acid 663
carbon 388
carbonaceous 388
Carbonaro 742
carbonate
–of ammonia 392
–of lead 430
carbonic acid 663
carbonization 384

carbonize 384
carboy 191
carbuncle *red* 434
abscess 655
jewel 847
carburetor 272
carcanet 847
carcass *structure* 329
corpse 362
bomb 727
carcelage 973
carcinoma 655
card *unravel* 60
ticket 550
plan 626
comb 652
address–550
by the–82
–*cheat* 792
–*index*
arrangement 60
list 86
record 551
store 636
–s to play 632
great–873
house of–s 328
leave a–892
on the–s *liable* 177
destiny 152
possible 470
playing–s 840
play one's best–686
play one's–692
play one's–s well 698
shuffle the–s
begin again 66
change 140
chance 621
prepare 673
speak by the–
care 459
veracity 543
phrase 566
throw up the–s 757
trump–626
cardboard 593
cardcase 191
cardiac 836
cardialgia 655
Cardigan jacket 225
cardinal *dress* 225
red 434
bird 434
important 642
excellent 648
priest 995, 996
–*bird* 434
–*flower* 434
–*grosbeak* 434
–*points compass* 278
–*virtues* 944
cardinalate 995
cardioid 245
carditis 655

card–sharper 792
card–sharping 545
care *attention* 459
business 625
adversity 735
custody 751
economy 817
pain 828
fear 860
–for *important* 642
desire 865
love 897
–will kill a cat 459
drive–away 840
for aught one–s
unimportant 643
indifferent 866
have the–of 693
take–864
take–of 459
careen *slope* 217
repair 660
career *business* 625
conduct 692
careful *heedful* 459
frugal 817
careless
inattentive 458
neglectful 460
feeble 575
insensible 823
indifferent 866
carelessness
(see *careless*)
caress 902
caret *incomplete* 53
typography 550
want 640
caretaker 758
careworn *pain* 828
dejection 837
cargador 271
cargo
large quantity 31
contents 190
shipment 270
property 780
goods 798
Carib 372a
caribou 366
caricature *likeness* 19
copy 21
exaggerate 549
misrepresent 555
ridicule 856
caricaturist 559, 844
caries 49, 655
cariole 272
carious 653
cark 828
carking 828–*care* 830
carle 876
carlock 352
carman 694
Carmelite 996
carminative 174, 662

carry

carmine 434
carnage 361
carnal *fleshly* 364
intemperate 954
impure 961
irreligious 989
carnalize 954
carnation 434
Carnegie medal 733
carnival 840
carnivore 298
carnivorism 298
carnivorous 298
carol *music* 415, 416
cheerful 836
rejoice 838
carom 276
carouse *feast* 298
festivity 840
intemperance 954
drinking 959
carp at 932
carpenter 690
carper 936
carpet 211–*knight*
fop 854
servile 886
sybarite 954a
–sweeper 652
on the–*topic* 454
project 626
carpetbagger 548
carphology 315
carrefour 627
carriage *gait* 264
transference 270
vehicle 272
aspect 448
conduct 692
keep one's–852
carried (see *carry*)
–away by passion 824
–by acclamation 488
carrier 271
–pigeon 534
carriole 272
carrion *carcass* 362
foul 653
carrom 276
carronade 727
carroty 434
carry *conduce to* 176
support 215
transfer 270
induce 615
–all before one 731
–a point *succeed* 731
–by storm 731
–coals 879
–conviction 484
–in the mind 505
–into execution
complete 729
observe 772
–off *take* 789

cart

 steal 791
 –on
  (see below)
 –oneself 692
 –out *conduct* 692
  complete 729
 –over *transfer* 270
  accounts 811
 –through 692, 729
 –weight *influence* 175
  evidence 467
  importance 642
 –with a high hand
  authority 737
  pride 878
  insolence 885
  reap and– 775
  carry on
   continue 143
   persevere 604a
   pursue 622
   do 680
   conduct 692
  –an argument 476
  –an inquiry 461
  –a trade 794
  –business 625
  –war 722
cart 272–away 185
 –before the horse
  disorder 59
  inversion 218
  bungling 699
 –horse 271
 –load *much* 31
  contents 190
cartage 270
carte *list* 86
 –and tierce 716
 –blanche *power* 157
  permit 760
  liberal 816
 –de visite 550, 554
cartel *defiance* 715
 truce 723
 compact 709, 769
carter 268
Cartesianism 451
Carthusian 996
cartilage *dense* 321
 hard 323
 tough 327
cartilaginous
 hard 323
 tenacious 327
cartographer 466
cartography 466, 554
carton 593
cartoon 21, 556
cartoonist 558
cartouche
 ammunition 727
 ornament 847
cartridge 727
cartulary *list* 86
 record 551

caruncle 250
caruncular 250
carunculation 250
carve *cut* 44
 make 161
 form 240
 furrow 259
 sculpture 557
 apportion 786
 –one's way 282
carvel 273
carver 559
Caryatides 215
casa 189
cascade 348
case *state* 7
 box 191
 sheath 223
 topic 454
 argument 476
 specification 527
 grammar 567
 affair 625
 patient 655
 lawsuit 969
 be the–*exist* 1
 true 494
 –in point *agree* 23
 conform 82
 in–*circumstance* 8
 event 151
 supposition 514
 in good
 –*healthy* 654
 prosperous 734
 make out a–
  evidence 467
  right 924
caseate 321
caseation 321
caseharden
 strengthen 159
 habituate 613
casehardened
 callous 376, 823
 obstinate 606
casein 321
casemate *barrack* 189
 defense 717
casement 260
casern 189
cash *money* 800
 pay 807
 –account 811
 –down 810
 –on delivery 810
 –register 85, 551, 802
 in–803
cashbook 551, 811
cashbox 802
cashier *dismiss* 756
 treasurer 801
cashmere 635
casing 223
casino 712
cask 191

casket *box* 191
 coffin 363
casque *helmet* 717
casquetel 717
Cassandra
 prophet 513
 warning 668
cassino 840
Cassiopeia's Chair 318
cassock 999
cast *mold* 21
 small quantity 32
 add 37
 role 51
 spread 73
 tendency 176
 exuvial 223
 form 240
 throw 284
 tinge 428
 aspect 448
 plan 626
 staff 712
 give 784
 allot 786
 condemn 971
 –about for 463
 –accounts 811
 –adrift *disperse* 73
 eject 297
 liberate 750
 dismiss 756
 –a gloom 837
 –a nativity
  predict 511
  sorcery 992
 –anchor *stop* 265
 arrive 292
 –a shade 421
 –aside 460
 –a slur *discredit* 874
 accuse 938
 –a spell 992
 –aspersions 934
 –away *reject* 610
 waste 638
 lost 732
 –away *care* 836
 –behind one
  forget 506
 refuse 764
 relinquish 782
 –dishonor upon 874
 –down 308
 dejected 837
 –eyes on 441
 –in one's lot with 609
 –in the eye 443
 –in the same mold 17
 –in the teeth 938
 –iron *metal* 323
 resolute 604
 –lots 621

 –luster upon 420
 –of countenance 448
 –of mind 820
 –of the dice 156
 –off *divest* 226
 dismiss 756
 relinquish 782
 –off a habit 614
 –off clothes 645
 –off skin 223
 –off trammels 750
 –one's net 463
 –out 610
 –overboard
  disuse 678
 –reflection upon 932
 –the eyes back 122
 –the eyes over 457
 –the parts 60
 –the skin 226
 –to the dogs 162
 –up *add* 85
 happen 151
 eject 297
 give one a–707
 set on a–621
castaneous 433
castanet 417
castaway *exile* 893
 reprobate 949
 (*impious* 988)
caste *class* 75
 party 712
 rank 873
 –mark 550
 lose–940
castellan *servant* 746
 keeper 753
castellated 717
caster *cruet* 191
 wheel 312
castigate *reprove* 932
 punish 972
castigator 936
casting–vote 480
 –weight 28, 30
castle *at chess* 148
 abode 189
 refuge 666
 defense 717
 –builder 515
 –in the air
  inattention 458
  impossible 471
  imagination 515
  hope 858
castor *hat* 225
Castor and Pollux
 twins 89
 luminary 423
 friends 890
castrametation
 building 189
 war 722
castrate *subduct* 38
 impotent 158

casual *incidental* 6
 chance 156
 uncertain 475
 nonobservant 773
casualty *event* 151
 killed 361
 evil 619
 misfortune 735
casuist 476
casuistic 477
casuistry
 sophistry 477
 falsehood 544
 duty 926
casus belli
 quarrel 713
 irritation 824, 900
cat *boat* 273
 nine lives 359
 animal 366
 keen sight 441
 fall on one's feet 734
 cross 901
 as the–jumps
  event 151
 –and dog life 713
 –in pattens 652
 gib–, tom–*male* 373
 let–out of bag 529
 see how the–jumps
  foresight 510
  fickleness 607
  caution 864
catabasis 36
catacaustic 245
catachresis
 metaphor 521
 misinterpretation 523
cataclasm 44
cataclysm
 convulsion 146
 destruction 162
 deluge 348
 (*redundance* 641)
catacomb 363
catacoustics 402
catafalque 363
catalectic 597
catalepsy 265, 683, 821a
catalo 41
catalogue *arrange* 60
 list 86
 –raisonné 551
catalysis 49
catamaran *vessel* 273
 fighter 726
catamenia 138
catamount 913
cataphonics 402
cataplasm 662
catapult
 propulsion 284
 weapon 727
cataract *waterfall* 348

399

catarrh

blindness 442, 443
catarrh 299
catastrophe
  dénouement 154
  disaster 619
  finish 729
  misfortune 735
  end 67
catastrophic
  revolutionary 146
  (*see* catastrophe)
catboat 273
catcall *whistle* 417
  disapproval 932
catch *imitate* 19
  fastening 45
  song 415
  detect 480a
  gather the meaning 518
  cheat 545
  receive 785
  take 789
  by–es 70
  –a *disease* 655
  –a *glimpse of* 441
  –a *likeness* 554
  –an *idea* 498
  –a *sound* 418
  –at *willing* 602
  desire 865
  –a Tartar *dupe* 547
  retaliate 718
  –at *straws*
  overrate 482
  credulous 486
  unskillful 699
  rash 863
  –by *surprise* 508
  –*drain* 191
  –*fire* 384
  –in a *trap* 545
  –one's *death* 360
  –the *attention* 457
  –the *breath* 349
  –the *ear* 418
  –the *eye* 446
  –the *infection*
  excitation 824
  –*tripping* 480a
  –*up* 789
  no great– 651
catching
  infectious 657
catchpenny
  deceiving 545
  trumpery 643
  cheap 815
catchpoll 965
catchweed 253
catchword
  identification 550
  printing 591
catechesis 461
catechism
  inquiry 461
  creed 484
  church– 983a
catechize 461
catechumen
  convert 144
  learner 541
  laity 997
categorical
  positive 474
  demonstrative 478
  affirmative 535
  –*ly true* 494
categorization 60
category *state* 7
  quantity 25
  class 75
  in the same– 9
catena 69
catenarian 245
catenary 245
catenation 69
cater 637
caterpillar 129
caterwaul
  cat–cry 412
  discord 414
  courting 902
cates 298
catgut 417
  –*scraper* 416
catharsis 821a
cathartic 652, 662
Cathay *cycle of–* 683
cathedral 189, 1000
catheretic 384, 830
Catherine wheel 423
cathexis 821a
cathode 490d
catholic
  universal 78
  religious 987
  –*church* 983a
  Roman– 984
Catholicization 144
catholicon 662
Catiline 941
catnip 662
cat-o'-nine-tails 975
catopsis 441
catoptrics 420
catoptromancy 511
cat's cradle 219
cat's-eye 847
cat's-paw *dupe* 547
  instrumental 631
  use 677
  auxiliary 711
cat's tail 353
cattle
  beasts of burden 271
  animals 366
  –*plague* 655
  –*stealing* 791
  –*thief* 792
  –*truck* 272

Caucasian mystery 983
Caucasoid 372a
caucus *assemblage* 72
  council 696
caudal *end* 67
  rear 235
caudate 214
caudex 215
cauf 370
caught
  –*napping* 458, 491
  –*tripping* 491
cauldron *convert* 144
  vessel 191
  heat 386
  laboratory 691
cauliflower 298
caulk 660
causal 153
causative 153
cause *source* **153**
  lawsuit 969
  –*d by* 154
  final– 620
  take up the–of 707
  tell the–of 522
causeless *casual* 156
  aimless 621
causerie 588
causeway 627
causidical 965
caustic *energetic* 171
  feeling 821
  painful 830
  gruff 895
  malevolent 907
  –*curve* 245
cautel *caution* 864
  (*care* 459)
cauterant 384
cautery 384
caution *warn* 668
  prudence 864
  security 771
  (*care* 459)
  (*advice* 695)
  want of– 863
cavalcade
  procession 69
  journey 266
cavalier
  horseman 268
  insolent 885
  sycophant 886
  discourteous 895
  contemptuous 930
cavaliere servente
  servile 886
  lover 897
cavalry 726
cavalryman 726
cavatina 415
cave *dwelling* 189
  cell 191
  cavity 252

–in *hollow* 252
  submit 725
  –of Adullam
  desertion 624
  discontent 832
  –of Aeolus 349
  –of *despair* 837
caveat *warning* 668
  command 741
cave-dweller 893
cave-in 162
caveman 893
Cavendish 392
cavern (*see* cave)
cavernous 252
cavesson 752
caviar
  hors d'oeuvre 298
  pungent 392
  condiment 393
  (*energy* 171)
  –to the *general* 850
cavil *sophistry* 477
  demur 485
  dissent 489
  censure 932
caviler 936
cavity 252
cavort 315
caw 412
cayenne *pungent* 392
  condiment 393
  (*energy* 171)
cayman 913
cayuse 271
cazique 745
cease 142
  –to *breathe* 360
  –to *exist* 2
ceaseless 112
ceaselessness 69
cecity 442
cedar 367, 400
cede *submit* 725
  relinquish 782
  give 784
cedilla 550
ceil 224
ceiling
  height 206, 210
  cover 223
ceja 367
celebrant 990
celebrate 883
  the Eucharist 998
celebration 883
  repute 873
  rite 998
celebrity 505, 873
  nobility 875
celerity 274
celery 298
Celestial
  Chinaman 188
celestial *physical* 318
  religious 976

cento

heaven 981
  (*delightful* 829)
  –*hierarchy* 977
celibacy 904
celibate 904
cell *abode* 189
  receptacle 191
  cavity 252
  organic 357
  prison 752
  hermitage 893
  –*theory* 357
cellar 191, 207
cellaret 191
cellarway 260
cellular 191, 252
celluloid 19
celsitude 206
cement *attach* 43
  united medium 45
  unite 46, 48
  covering 223
  hard 323
  material 635
  –a *party* 712
cemented
  concord 714
cemetery 363
cenobite 996
cenotaph 363
Cenozoic era 372a, 490c
cense 400
censer 400, 998, 999
censor *critic* 480
  detractor 936
censorious
  judging 480
  disapproving 932
censurable 947
censure 932
censurer 832, 936
census *number* 85
  list 86
  –*report* 551
cent 800
  unimportance 643
centaur 83
Centaurus 490a
centenarian 130
centenary *hundred* 98
  period 138
  celebration 883
centennial
  (*see* centenary)
center *in order* 68
  in space 222
  converge 290
  –*board* 211
  –of *life* 1
  –*round* *assemble* 72
  converge 290
centesimal 99
centimeter 200
centipeds 368
cento 597

400

central   chargé d'affaires

central 68, 222
centrality 222
centralize *combine* 48
centric 222
centricality 222
centrifugal 291
centripetal 290
centrosome 357
centuple 98
centuplicate 98
centuriate 98
centurion 745
century *hundred* 98
  period 108
  long time 110
cephalalgia 378
ceramic 384
  –*ware* 557
ceramics 557
cerate 355, 662
Cerberus *janitor* 263
  custodian 664
  sop for–615
cereal 298, 367
cereals 369
cerebral *phonetic* 561
cerebrate 451
cerebration 451
cerebrum 450
cerecloth 223, 363
cerement
  covering 223
  wax 356
  burial 363
ceremonious 928
ceremony *parade* 882
  courtesy 894
  rite 998
cerise 434
cerograph 558
cerography
  engraving 558
  writing 590
ceromancy 511
ceroplastic 557
certain *special* 79
  indefinite number 100
  sure 474
  belief 484
  true 494
  make–*of* 480*a*
  of a–*age* 128
  to a–*degree* 32
certainly *yes* 488
certainty **474**
certes *surely* 474
  yes 488
certificate
  evidence 467
  record 551
  security 771
certify *evince* 467
  affirm 535
certiorari 969
certitude 474

cerulean 438
cerulescent 438
ceruse 430
cespitose 367
cess *tax* 812
cessation **142**
cession *surrender* 725
  of property 782
  gift 784
cesspool 653
cest 247
cestus *ligtaure* 45
  girdle 247
Cetus 490*a*
chabuk 975
chafe
  physical pain 378
  warm 384
  irritate 825
  mental pain 828, 830
  discontent 832
  incense 900
chaff *trash* 643
  rubbish 645
  ridicule 856
  vulgar 876
  not to be caught with–clever 698
  cunning 702
  winnow–from wheat 609
chaffer 794
chafing dish 386
chagrin 828
chain *fasten* 43
  vinculum 45
  series 69
  measure 200
  interlinking 219
  imprison 752
  ornament 847
  adamantine–*s* 360
  –*lightning* 423
  drink 959
  –*s fireplace* 386
  drag a–749
  drag a lengthened– 686
  in–*s prisoner* 754
chain shot 727
chair *support* 215
  vehicle 272
  professorship 542
  throne 747
  celebration 883
  president 694
  –*car* 272
  in the–693
chairman 694
chaise 272
chalcedony 847
chalcography 558
chalet 189
chalice 191
chalk *earth* 342

  white 430
  mark 550
  drawing 556
  –*out plan* 626
  –*talk* 537, 584
  –*talker* 540
chalky 430
challenge
  question 461
  doubt 485
  claim 924
  defy 715
  accuse 938
  –*comparison* 648
  –*the jurors* 969
chalybeate 662
chamber *room* 191
  council 696
  mart 799
  –*concert* 415
  –*fellow* 890
  –*music* 415
  sick–655
chamberlain 746
chambermaid 746
chameleon *lizard* 366
  changeable 149
  variegated 440
chamfer 259
chamois
  smoothness 255
  leap 306
  animal 366
champ 298–*the bit*
  disobedient 742
  chafe 825
  angry 900
champagne 959
champaign 344
champain 874
champak 400
champion *best* 648
  auxiliary 711
  defense 717
  combatant 726
  victor 731
  representative 759
  pity 914
championship 707
champlevé 847
chance
  absence of cause **156**
  liability 177
  absence of aim **621**
  as–*would have it* 152
  be one's–151
  –*s against one*
  danger 665
  game of–840
  great–472
  small–473
  stand a–*liable* 177
  possible 470
  take one's–675
chanceable 156

chanceful 156
chancel 1000
chancellor
  judge 664, 967
  president 745
  deputy 759
  –*of the exchequer* 801
chancery–*suit*
  delay 133
  court of–966
chandelier 214, 423
chandler 797
change *alteration* **140**
  interchange 148
  mart 799
  small coin 800
  –*about* 149
  –*color* 821
  –*for* 147
  –*hands* 783
  –*of mind* 607
  –*of opinion* 485
  –*of place* 264
  radical–146
  sudden–146
changeable 149
changeableness
  mutable **149**
  irresolute 605
changeful 607
changeling
  substitute 147
  fool 501
changer 797
channel *base* 211
  furrow 259
  opening 260
  conduit 350
  artery 627
chant *song* 415
  sing 416
  worship 990
chanter 416
chanticleer 366
chantress 416
chantry 1000
chaomancy 511
chaos 59
chap *crack* 198
  jaw 231
  fellow 373
chaparajos 225
chaparral 367
chap book 593
chapeau 225
chapel 189, 1000
chaperon
  accompany 88
  guard 459
  safety 664
chapfallen 837, 878
chaplain 996
chaplaincy 995
chaplet *circle* 247
  fragrance 400

  favor 550
  trophy 733
  ornament 847
chapman 797
chaps *chaparajos* 225
chapter *partition* 44
  part 51
  topic 454
  book 593
  council 696
  church 995
  –*and verse*
  evidence 467
  exact 494
  –*of accidents* 156, 621
chapter house 1000
chaqueta 225
char 384
char-à-bancs 272
character *nature* 5
  state 7
  class 75
  oddity 83
  letter 561
  drama 599
  disposition 820
characteristic
  intrinsic 5
  special 79
  mark 550
characterize
  name 564
  describe 594
characterized 820
charade *riddle* 533
  drama 599
charcoal
  fuel 384, 388
  black 431
  drawing 556
charge *fill* 52
  contents 190
  business 625
  mandate 630
  direction 693
  advice 695
  precept 697
  attack 716
  order 741
  custody 751
  commission 755
  bargain for 794
  price 812
  accusation 938
  churchdom 995
  –*d with*
  possessed of 777
  –*on attribute* 155
  in–*prisoner* 754
  justifiable–937
  take–*of safe* 664
  take in–751
chargeable *debt* 806
  –*on duty* 926
chargé d'affaires 758

charger

charger *carrier* 271
   fighter 726
chargeship 625
chariot 272
   drag at one's–
     wheels 749
charioteer *driver* 268
   pilot 694
charitable
   (see charity)
charity *give* 784
   liberal 816
   beneficient 906
   pity 914
   –that begins at home 943
   cold as
     –*insensible* 823
charivari *loud* 404
   clatter 407
   discord 414
charlatan
   ignoramus 493
   impostor 548
   mountebank 844
   boaster 884
charlatanism
   ignorance 491
   falsehood 544
   affectation 855
Charles's wain 318
Charley 753
charm *draw* 288
   motive 615
   talisman 747
   please 829
   beauty 845
   love 897
   attraction 928
   conjure 992
   spell 993
   bear a–d life
     safe 664
     prosperous 734
charmer *sorcerer* 994
   voice of the–
     flattery 933
charming *taste* 850
   (see charm)
charnel house 363
chart *inform* 527
   represent 554
charter
   commission 755
   permit 760
   compact 769
   security 771
   privilege 924
chartered *legal* 963
   –*accountant* 811
   –*libertine* 962
chartulary 86
charwoman
   worker 690
   servant 746
chary *economical* 817

   stingy 819
   cautious 864
Charybdis
   whirlpool 312, 346
   danger 665
chase *emboss* 250
   drive away 289
   killing 361
   forest 367
   pursue 622
   ornament 847
   wild goose–645
chaser 559
chasm *interval* 198
   opening 260
   gully 350
   abyss 667
   (*discontinuity* 70)
chassepot 727
chasser 297
   –*balancer* 605
chasseur 726
chassis 272
chaste *shapely* 242
   language 576, 578
   simple 849
   good taste 850
   pure 960
chasten *moderate* 174
   punish 972
chastened
   subdued spirit 826
chasteness
   (see chaste)
chastise *censure* 932
   punish 972
   –with scorpions 739
chastity 960
chasuble 999
chat 588
château 189
châtelaine 847
chatoyant 440
chattels
   furniture 633
   property 780
chatter 412, 584
chatterbox 584
chattering of teeth
   cold 383
chatti 191
chatty *talkative* 584
   sociable 892
chauffeur 268, 271, 694
chauki 752
chaunt (see chant)
chaussé 225
Chautauqua 537
chauvinism 884, 885
chauvinist 885
chawbacon 876
cheap *worthless* 643
   low price 815
   hold–930
cheapen *haggle* 794

   begrudge 819
cheapness 815
cheat *deceive* 545
   deceiver 548
check *numerical* 85
   cessation 142
   moderate 174
   counteract 179
   slacken 275
   plaid 440
   experiment 463
   measure 466
   evidence 468
   ticket 550
   dissuade 616
   hinder 706
   misfortune 735
   restrain 751
   money order 800
   –in full career 142
   –oneself 829
   –the growth 201
checkered
   diversified 16a
   changeable 149
   variegated 440
checkers 440
   game 840
checkmate
   deadlock 142
   success 731
   failure 732
checkrein 706
checkroll 86
checkstring
   pull the–142
cheek *side* 236
   –by jowl *with* 88
   near 197
cheeks *dual* 89
cheep 412
cheer *repast* 298
   cry 411
   aid 707
   pleasure 827
   relief 834
   mirth 836
   rejoicing 838
   amusement 840
   courage 861
   exult 884
   sociality 892
   welcome 894
   applaud 931
   (*please* 829)
   good–*hope* 858
   high living 957
cheerful 836
   –*giver* 816
cheerfulness 836
cheering 602
cheerless
   unpleasing 830
   dejected 837
cheese 298
cheesecake 298

cheeseparings
   remains 40
   dirt 653
   parsimony 819
cheetah 440
chef de cuisine
   proficient 700
   servant 746
chef–d'oeuvre
   masterpiece 648
   master stroke 698
cheiromancy 522
chela 541
chemical 144
chemical apparatus 490b
chemise 225
chemisette 225
chemistry 490b, 144
   organic–357
cheque 800
chequer 440–*roll* 86
cherish *aid* 707
   love 897
   endearment 902
   –a belief 484
   –an idea etc. 451
   –feelings etc. 821
cheroot 392
cherry 298, 434
   two bites of a–
     overrate 482
   roundabout 629
   clumsy 699
cherry–cheeked 845
cherry–colored 434
chersonese 342
cherub 167, 977
Cherubim 977
Cheshire cat 838
chess 840
chessboard 440
chest *box* 191
   money coffer 802
chestnut
   stale joke 105, 532
   fruit 367
   red 434
chestnut–color 433
cheval–de–bataille
   plea 617
   plan 626
cheval glass 445
chevalier 875
   –d'industrie 792
chevaux de frise
   spikes 253
   defense 717
chevron *obliquity* 217
   rank 550, 747, 877
chevronné 754
chew 298 *tobacco* 392
   –the cud 451
chiaroscuro *light* 420
   gray 432
   painting 556

chimera

chiasm 43, 219
chiasmal 219
chic *show* 882
chicane *sophistry* 477
   deceit 545
   cunning 702
chicanery
   (see chicane)
chi–chi 563
chick 424
chickaree 274
chicken *young* 129
   fowl 298, 366
   reckon–s before
     hatched *hope* 858
   rash 863
   tender as a–*soft* 324
   sensitive 822
   compassionate 914
chicken–hearted 862
chide 527, 932
chief *principal* 642
   master 745
   –part 31
   evidence in–467
chiefdom 737
Chief Justice 967
chieftain 745
chiffon 635
chiffonier 876
chiffonnière 191
chignon 225
chilblains 383
child *infant* 129
   offspring 167
   fool 501
   –of God 987
   –'s play *trifling* 643
   easy 705
childbirth 161
childhood 127
childish *credulous* 486
   foolish 499
   feeble 575
   –*treble* 581
childlike *artless* 703
childly 129
children 167
chiliad 98, 120
chill *cold* 383
   render cold 385
   indispose 616
chilly 383
Chiltern Hundreds 757
chimaera *fish* 368
chime *repetition* 104
   roll 407
   resonance 408
   melody 413
   –in with *agree* 23
   conform 82
   assent 488
   concord 714
chimera *monster* 83
   imaginary 515

chimney — circle

(error 495)
chimney *opening* 260
  airpipe 351
  (*egress* 295)
  —*corner* 189
chin 234
china *ceramic* 384
  art 557
  —*wedding* 883
Chinaman 188
chinch 653
chine 235
Chinese 188
  —*temple* 1000
chink *gap* 198
  sound 408
  money 800
chinking 635
Chinook 349, 563
chip *small* 32
  detach 44
  bit 51
  reduce 195
  counter 550
  —*in* 709
  —*off the old block similar* 17
  copy 21
  offspring 167
chipmunk 274, 366
chipper 654, 836
chippy 962
chirography 590
chirology 550
chiromancy 511, 550
chirp *bird—note* 412
  sing 416
  cheerful 836
  rejoice 838
chirrup (*see* chirp)
chirurgery 662
chisel *fabricate* 161
  form 240
  furrow 259
  tool 262
  sculpture 557
chiseling 558
chit *infant* 129, 167
  small 193
  letter 592
chit-chat 588
chitterlings 221
chivalrous 894
  (*see* chivalry)
chivalry *war* 722
  tenure 777
  courage 861
  philanthropy 910
  honor 939
  generosity 942
chivarras 225
chlamys 225
chloral 376
chloride—*of lime* 652
  —*of sodium* 336
chlorine 435, 663

—*gas* 727
chloroform
  opiate 174
  anaesthetic 376
  mental insensibility 823
chlorosis 655
chlorotic 655
chock-full
  complete 52
  replete 639
chocolate *food* 298
  color 433
choice *will* 600
  election **609**
  excellent 648
  absence of—**609a**
  by—600
  —*of words* 569
  —*spirits* 873
choir *sing* 416
  church music 996
  church 1000
Choir Invisible 977
choirmaster 416
choke *close* 261
  stifle 361
  redundant 641
  hinder 706
  —*off* 706
chokeberry 397
choke damp 663
choke-full
  (*see* chock-full)
chokidar 753
chokra 746
choky 752
choler 900
cholera 655
choleric 901
chondrification 323
choose 609
  do what one—s 748
chop *disjoin* 44
  change 140
  water in motion 348
  indication 550
  —*and change* 140
  —*logic* 476
  —*up* 201
chopfallen 837
chophouse 189
choppiness 348
chopping *large* 192
  —*sea* 348
choppy 348
chops *mouth* 66
  jaws 231
  food 298
chop-suey 298
chor 792
choral 415—*club* 416
  —*society* 416
chord 413
chore 625, 746
  —*boy* 534

chorea 315, 655
choregus 694
chorister *singer* 416
  church singer 996
chorographer 466
chorography 183, 466
chorometer 466
chorus *shout* 411
  song 415
  singers 416
  unanimity 488
  poetry 597
  opera 599
  concord 714
  —*girl* 599
chose—*in action* 780
  —*in possession* 777
chosen 609
chota hazri 298
chouse 545
chowchow 41
chowder 298
chowderhead 501
chow dog 366
chrestomathy 560
chrism 998
Christ 976
  Church of—983a
  receive—987
Christcross 219
Christcross-row 561
christen *name* 564
  rite 998
Christendom 983a, 995
Christian 983a, 987
  —*charity* 906
  —*Science* 984
Christmas *period* 138
  Church festival 998
Christmas box 784
chromatic *color* 428
  —*scale music* 413
chromation 357
chromatism 428
chromatogenous 428
chromatograph 428
chromatography 428
chromatology 428
chromatometer 428
chromato-pseudo-blepsis 443
chromatoscope 428
chromatoscopy 428
chromatrope 428, 445
chrome 436
chromium 490b
chromogen 428
chromolithograph 558
chromometer 428
chromoscope 428
chromosome 357
chromosphere 318

chronic 110, 143
chronicle
  measure time 114
  annals 551
chronicler 553
chronogram 114
chronographer 594
chronography
  measure time 114
  description 594
chronolithograph 558
chronologic 114
chronologize 114
chronology 114
chronometry 114
chrononhoton-thologos 887
chrysalis 129
chrysolite
  greenness 435
  perfection 650
  jewel 847
chrysology 800
chrysoprase 435
chthonian 991
chubby 192
chuck *throw* 284
  beef 298
  animal cry 412
  —*under chin* 902
chucker-out 297
chuck farthing 621
chuckle
  animal cry 412
  laugh 838
  exult 884
chucklehead 501
chuddar 225
chuff 876
chum 711, 890
chummery 189
chunk 51
chunky 201
chupatty 298
Church *building* 189
  infallible 474
  orthodox 983a
  Christendom 995
  temple 1000
  —*of Christ* 983a
  dignitaries of—996
  go to—990
  High—, *Low*—, *etc.* 984
churchdom 995
churchman 996
churchwarden 996
churchyard
  burial 363
  church 1000
  —*cough* 655
churl *boor* 876
churlish *niggard* 819
  rude 895
  sulky 901a

  malevolent 907
churn *agitate* 315
  butter 352
chute 348
chutney 393
chyle 333
chylification 333
chylous 333
cibarious 298
cicada 366
cicatrix 551
cicatrize 660
Cicero 582
cicerone 524, 527
Ciceronian 578, 582
cicisbeo 897
cicuration 370
cider 298
cienaga 345
cigar 392
cilia *hairs* 205
  rough 256
ciliolum 205
cimeter 727
Cimmerian 421
cinch *girth* 45, 370
  facility 705
cinchona 662
cinct 229
cincture 247
cinder *combustion* 384
  dirt 653
  (*remains* 40)
Cinderella
  servant 746
  commonalty 876
cinema 448, 840
cinematograph 448, 559
cinerary 363
cineration 384
cinereous 432
cingle 230
cinnabar 434
cinnamon 393, 433
cinque 98
cinquecento 114, 554
cipher *unsubstantial* 4
  number 84
  compute 85
  zero 101
  concealment 528
  mark 550
  letter 561
  unimportant 643
  writing in—590
Circe *seductor* 615
  sorcerer 994
Circean 992—*cup*
  pleasure 377
  intemperance 954
circination 312
circle *region* 181
  encompass 227
  form 247
  party 712

circling

(assemblage 72)
—of acquaintance 892
—of the sciences 490
   describe a—311
   great—sailing 628
   in—s 312
circling
   convolution 248
circuit region 181
   outline 230
   winding 248
   tour 266
   indirect path 311
   indirect course 629
circuition 311
circuitous
   winding 248
   devious 279
   indirect 311
   —method 629
circular round 247
   publication 531
   letter 592
   pamphlet 593
   —note 805
   —saw 44
circularity 247
circulate circuit 311
   rotate 312
   publish 531
   money 800
circulating medium 800
circulation
   (see circulate)
   —of money 809
   in—news 532
circumambience 629
   (see circumambient)
circumambient 227, 229, 311
circumambulate
   travel 266
   go round 311
circumambulation 629
circumbendibus
   winding 248
   indirect method 629
   (circuition 311)
circumcinct 229
circumcision 44, 998
circumduction 552
circumference 230
circumferential 227, 230
circumflex turn 311
circumflexion 311
circumfluent
   tie round 227
   move round 311
circumforaneous
   traveling 266
   circuition 311
circumfuse 73, 312
circumgyration 312

circumjacence 227
circumlocution
   periphrase 573
   (phrase 566)
   —court 133
   —office 133
circumlocutory 573
circummigration 311
circumnavigate
   navigation 267
   circuition 311
circumnutation 314
circumrotation 312
circumscribe
   surround 229
   limit 233
   circle 311
   limit 761
circumscription 229
circumspection
   attention 457
   care 459
   caution 459
circumstance phase 8
   event 151
   blows of—151
   —of glorious war 722
circumstances
   property 780
   bad—804
   depend on—475
   good—803
   under the—8
circumstantial 8
   —account 594
   —evidence 467
   probability 472
circumstantiality 457, 459
circumstantiate 467
circumvallation
   inclosure 229, 232
   defense 717
   line of—233
circumvent
   environ 227
   move round 311
   cheat 545
   cunning 702
   hinder 706
   checkmate 731
circumvest 225
circumvolant 311
circumvolute 312
circumvolution
   winding 248
   rotation 312
circus buildings 189
   drama 599
   arena 728
cirrocumulus 353
cirrose 353
cirrostratus 353
cirrous 353
cirrus 205, 353

Cistercian 996
cistern receptacle 191
   store 636
cit 188
citadel defense 717
   (refuge 666)
citation summons 467
   trophy 733
cite
   quote as example 82
   as evidence 467
   summon 741
   accuse 938
   arraign 969
cithern 417
citizen inhabitant 188
   freeman 748
   (man 373)
   —of the world 910
citreous 436
citrine 435, 436
city 189 in the—794
civet 400
civic 372 —crown 733
civil warfare 722
   courteous 894
   laity 997
   —authorities 745
   —crown 733
   —law 963
   —service list 86
   —war 722
civilian lawyer 968
   layman 997
civility 894
civilization
   improvement 658
   fashion 852
   courtesy 894
civilize 658
civilized life 852
civism 910
clabber 321
clack clatter 407
   animal cry 412
   talkative 584
clad 225
claim mandate 630
   demand 741
   property 780
   right 924
   lawsuit 969
   —the attention 457
claimant
   petitioner 767
   right 924
clairaudience 450, 992a
clairaudient 450
clair-obscur 420, 421
clairvoyance 450, 513, 992a
clam 298
clamant 411
clambake 840

clamber 305
clammy 352
clamor cry 411
   wail 839
   —against 932
   —for 765
clamorous
   (see clamor)
   loud 404
   excitable 825
clamp fasten 43
   fastening 45
clan race 11
   class 75
   family 166
   party 712
clandestine 528
clang 404
clangor 404, 508
clank 410
clannishness 481
clanship 709
clap shut 261
   explosion 406
   applaud 931
   —on the back 931
   —on the shoulder 615
   —the hands
   rejoice 838
   —together 43
   —up imprison 751
   thunder
   —prodigy 872
clapboard 223, 635
clapperclaw
   contention 720
   censure 932
claptrap
   absurdity 497
   pretense 546
   display 882
claque 72
claquer 935
clarence 272
claret 298 —color 434
clarify 652
clarinet 417
clarion music 417
   war 722
clarity clearness 518
   elegance 578
clash disagree 24
   cross 179
   concussion 276
   sound 406
   oppose 708
   discord 713
   —of arms 720
clashing
   contrariety 14
   wrangle 24
clasp fasten 43
   fastening 45
   stick 46
   come close 197
   belt 230

embrace 902
class arrange 60
   category **75**
   learners 541
   school 542
   party 712
   laity 997
   —fellow 890
classfellow 890
classic old 124
   symmetry 242
   music 415
classical
   elegant writing 578
   taste 850
   —education 537
classicism 578
classicist 578
classics 560
classification 60
classify 60
classis 696
classman 873
   associate 890
classmate 492, 541, 890
class room 542
clatter noise 404
   rattle 407
claudication
   slowness 275
   failure 732
clause part 51
   passage 593
   condition 770
claustral 1000
claustrophobia 860
clavate 250
clavichord 417
clavier 417
claviform 250
clavis opening 260
   interpretation 522
claw tenacity 327
   hook 781
   grasp 789
   —back 935
clawhammer coat **225**
clay soft 324
   earth 342
   corpse 362
   material 635
clay-cold 383
clayey 324
claymore 727
clean entirely 52
   perfect 650
   unstained 652
   —bill of health 654
   —breast disclose 529
   —cut 494
   —forgotten 506
   —hand proficient 700
   —out empty 297
   —sweep

404

cleanly   cloud

revolution 146
destruction 162
with—hands
honesty 939
innocence 946
cleanly 652
cleanness 652
cleanse 652
cleansing 652
clean-up 35
clear *simple* 42
  leap 309
  sound 413
  light 420
  transparent 425
  visible 446
  certain 474
  intelligible 518
  manifest 525
  distinct 535
  perspicuous 570
  easy 705
  liberate 750
  profit 775
  vindicate 937
  innocent 946
  acquit 970
  —articulation 580
  —as day 474
  —conscience 946
  —for action
    prepare 673
  —grit 604
  —of *distant* 196
  —off *pay* 807
  —out *empty* 297
    clean 652
  —sky *hope* 858
  —stage *occasion* 134
    easy 705
    right 922
  —the course 302
  —the ground
    facilitate 705
  —the skirts of 937
  —the throat 297
  —up *light* 420
    intelligible 518
    interpret 522
    coast—664
    get-off 671
    keep—of 623
clearance 970
clear-cut *true* 494
  plain 518
clear-eyed 441
clear-headed 498
clear-sighted
  vision 441
  shrewd 498
clearing 181, 184
clearness (*see* clear)
clear-thinking 498
cleavage *cutting* 44
  structure 329
cleave *sunder* 44

adhere 46
bisect 91
cleaver 253
cledge 342
clef 413
cleft *disjoined* 44
  bisected 91
  chink 198
  in a—stick
    difficulty 704
clem 956
clement *lenient* 740
  long-suffering 826
  compassionate 914
clench *compact* 769
  retain 781
  take 789
clepe 564
clepsydra 114
clerestory 191
clergy 996—list 86
clerical 995, 996
  —error 495
  —staff 746
clericalism 995
clerk *scholar* 492
  recorder 553
  writer 590
  helper 711
  servant 746
  agent 758
  clergy 996
  articled—541
  —of works 694
clerkship
  commission 755
cleromancy 511
clever *intelligent* 498
  skillful 698
  witty 482
  too—by half 702
clew *ball* 249
  inquiry 461
  answer 462
  interpretation 522
  indication 550
  seek a—461
click 406
client *follower* 65
  dependent 711, 746
  customer 795
clientele 795
clientship
  subjection 749
cliff *height* 206
  vertical 212
  steep 217
climacteric 128
climate *region* 181
  weather 338
  fine—656
climatology 338
climatometer 338
climax *supremacy* 33
  summit 210
  turning point 283

climb 305
  fain would I—860
  thou—ing sorrow
    828
clime 181
clinal 217
clinch *fasten* 43
  close 261
  certify 474
  pun 563
  complete 729
  clutch 781
  snatch 789
  —an argument 479
  —the fist at 909
clincher 479
cling *adhere* 46
  —to near 197
  willing 602
  persevere 604a
  habit 613
  observe 772
  desire 865
  love 897
  —to hope 858
  —to one another 709
clinic *disease* 655
  remedy 662
clink *resonance* 408
  stridor 410
clinker *brick* 384
  dirt 653
clinometer
  oblique 217
  angle 244
  (*measurement* 466)
clinquant
  ornament 847
  vulgar 851
Clio 594
clip *shorten* 201
  pace 264
  blow 276
  —one's words 583
  —the wings
    powerless 158
    slow 275
  useless 645
  hinder 706
  prohibit 761
  (*prune* 38)
  (*contract* 195)
clipper 273
clipping
  small piece 51
clique *class* 75
  conclave 696
  party 712
  (*sociality* 892)
cliquish 712
clivers 253
cloaca *conduit* 350
  foul 653
Cloacina 653
cloak *dress* 225
  conceal 528

disguise 530
(*pretense* 546)
clock 114
clockwise 312
clockwork 633 by
  —uniform 16
  order 58
  regular 80
clod *lump* 192
  earth 342
  fool 501
  bungler 701
clodhopper 876
clodpated *stupid* 499
clog *shoe* 225
  hinder 706
cloisonné 557, 847
cloister *arcade* 189
  passage 627
  restraint 751
  seclusion 893
  convent 1000
  (*seclusion* 893)
close *similar* 17
  copy 21
  tight 43
  end 67
  field 181
  court 189
  near 197
  narrow 203
  shut 261
  dense 321
  warm 382
  hidden 528
  concise 572
  taciturn 585
  complete 729
  conclude 769
  stingy 819
  —at hand
  to—morrow 121
  imminent 152
  near 197
  —call 671
  —formation 716
  —in upon
    converge 290
  —inquiry 461
  —one's eyes to
    not attend 458
    set at naught 773
  —one's ranks 673
  —prisoner 754
  —quarters 197
  —approach 286
    attack 716
    battle 722
  —study *thought* 451
    attention 457
  —the door upon
    restrain 751
  —the ears 419
  —the eyes *die* 360
    not see 442
  —the hand *refuse* 764

—with *cohere* 46
  assent 488
  attack 716
  contend 720
  consent 762
  compact 769
  keep—*hide* 528
  retain 781
closely (*see* close)
  —packed 72
closet *receptacle* 191
  ambush 530
closeted with
  conference 588
  advice 695
closure 261
  stopping 142
clot *solidify* 321
  earth 342
  hindrance 706
  (*cohere* 46)
cloth *vocation* 625
  napkin 652
  clergy 996
clothe 225
clothes 225
  —basket 191
  —horse 215
  —press 191
  grave—363
clothier 225
clothing 225
clotpoll 501
clotted 352
  —cream 321, 354
cloture 142
cloud *assemblage* 72
  multitude 102
  wind 349
  mist 353
  darken 421
  dim 422
  shade 424
  semitransparency
    427
  screen 520
  break through the—s
    446
  —capt 206
  —of dust 330
  —of skirmishers 726
  —of smoke 333
  —of words 573
  —over 421, 422
  —s gathering
    dark 421
    danger 665
    warning 668
  —topped 206
  drop from the—s
    508
  in a—*uncertain* 475
    hidden 528
  in the—s *lofty* 206
    inattentive 458
    dreaming 515

405

cloud–built   coherence

under a–
  insane 503
  adversity 735
  disrepute 874
  secluded 893
  censured 932
  accused 938
cloud–built 4
cloudburst 348
clouded
  variegated 440
  dejected 837
  hopeless 859
  –*perception* 499
cloudland 515
cloudless *light* 420
  happy 827
cloudy *dim* 422
  opaque 426
clough 206
clove 198
cloven 91
cloven foot *mark* 550
  malevolence 907
  vice 945
  Satan 978
  see the–480*a*
  show the–907
clover *grass* 367
  luxury 377
  prosperity 734
  comfort 827
  in–377, 827
clown *pantomime* 599
  buffoon 844
  vulgar 851
  rustic 876
cloy *pall* 376
  redundance 641
  satiety 869
cloying 396
cloyment 869
club *combine* 48
  place of meeting 74
  house 189
  association 712
  weapon 727
  sociality 892
  –*law compulsion* 744
  lawless 964
  –*together*
    coöperate 709
clubbability 892
clubbable 712
club–footed 243
clubman 852
club–shaped 250
clubwoman 852
cluck 412
clue (*see* clew)
clump *assemblage* 72
  projecting mass 250
  –*of trees* 367
clumsiness
  (*see* clumsy)
clumsy *unfit* 647

  awkward 699
  ugly 846
Cluniac 996
cluricaune 980
cluster 72
clutch *automobile* 272
  retain 781
  seize 789
clutches 737
  in the–of 749
clutter *be loud* 404
  roll 407
clypeate 245
clypeiform 245
clyster 300
coacervation 72
coach *carriage* 272
  teach 537
  tutor 540, 673
  –*road* 627
  –*up* 539
  drive a–*and six*
    through 964
coach house 191
coachman *travel* 268
  pilot 694
coaction
  concurrence 178
  cooperation 709
  compulsion 744
coactive 709
coadjutant 709, 711
coadjutive 709
coadjutor 711
coadjuvancy 709
coadjuvant 711
coadjuvate 709
coadministration
  709
coadunate 178
coagency *concur* 178
  cooperate 709
coagmentation 72
coagulate *cohere* 46
  densify 321
  thicken 352
  pulpy 354
coagulum 321, 352
co–aid 711
coal 388 *carry–s* 879
  carry–s to
    Newcastle 641
  haul over the–s 932
coal–black 431
coalesce *identity* 13
  combine 48
coalheaver
  work like a–686
coalition
  cooperate 709
  party 712
coaptation 23
coarctate 195, 203
coarctation
  decrease 36
  contraction 195

  narrow 203
  impede 706
  restraint 751
  (*compulsion* 744)
coarse *harsh* 410
  dirty 653
  unpolished 674
  vulgar 851
  impure 961
  –*grain* 329
coast *border* 231
  glide 266
  navigate 267
  land 342
  –*line* 230
coaster 273
coastguard 753
coat *layer* 204
  paint 223
  habit 225
  (*surface* 220)
  –*of arms* 550
  –*of mail* 717
  cut–*according to*
    cloth 698
coatee 225
coating, inner– 224
coax *persuade* 615
  endearment 902
  flatter 933
coaxer 615
cob *horse* 271
  punish 972
cobalt 438
cobble *mend* 660
cobbler
  shoemaker 225
coble 273
cobra 366, 913
cobweb *filament* 205
  light 320
  fiction 545
  flimsy 643
  dirt 653
  –*s of antiquity* 124
  –*s of sophistry* 477
cocaine 376, 662, 954
cochineal 434
cochlea 418
cochleate 248
cock *vane* 338
  bird 366
  male 373
  –*and–bull story* 546
  –*of the walk best* 648
  master 745
  –*the eye* 441
  –*up vertical* 212
  convex 250
  game–861
cockade *badge* 550
  title 877
cock–a–hoop
  gay 836
  exulting 884
cockarouse 745

cockatrice *monster* 83
  serpent 366
  piercing eye 548
  evildoer 913
  miscreant 949
cockboat 273
cockcrow 125
Cocker
  school book 542
  according to–82
cocker *fold* 258
  dog 366
  caress 902
cock–eyed 443
cockle *pucker* 195
  fold 258
  –*s of one's heart* 820
cockleshell 273
cockloft 191
cockney
  Londoner 188
  plebeian 876
cockpit *hold* 191
  arena 728
cockroach 366
cockshut *evening* 126
  dusk 422
cocksure 484
cockswain 269
cocktail 959
cocoa 298
co–conscious 992*a*
coconut–*butter*
  –*oil* 356
cocoon 129
cocotte 962
coction 384
Cocytus 982
C. O. D. *receipt* 810
cod *fish* 298
  shell 223
coddle 902
  –*oneself* 943
code *concealment* 528
  cipher 561
  precept 697
  law 963
  (*compendium* 596)
codex 593
codger 819
codicil *addition* 37
  sequel 65
  testament 771
  (*adjunct* 39)
codification 60
codify *arrange* 60
  conceal 528
  legalize 963
codlin 129
coecum 261
coeducational 537
coefficacy 709
coefficient *factor* 84
  accompany 88
  cooperate 709
Caelebs 904

Coelentera 368
coeliac 221–*flux* 299
coemption 795
coequal 27
coequality 27
coerce *compel* 744
  restrain 751
coetaneous 120
coeternal
  perpetual 112
  synchronous 120
coeternity 110, 112
coeval 120
  –*with birth* 5
coevality 27
coexist *exist* 1
  accompany 88
  synchronism 120
  continuity 199
coexistence
  (*see* coexist)
coextension
  equality 27
  parallelism 216
  symmetry 242
coextensive 216, 242
coffee 298
coffeepot 191
coffeehouse 189
coffer *chest* 191
  store 636
  money chest 802
cofferdam 55
coffin 363
  add a nail to one's–
    830
cog *tooth* 253
  boat 273
  deceive 545
  flatter 933
cogency 157
cogent *powerful* 157
  –*reasoning* 476
coggery 545
cogitate 450, 451
cogitative 451
  –*faculties* 450
cognate *related* 9
  consanguineous 11
  similar 17
cognation 11
cognition 490
cognitive
  –*faculties* 450
cognizance 490
  take–*of intellect* 490
  attention 457
cognomen 564
cognoscence 490
cogwheel 312
cohabitation
  location 184
  marriage 903
coheir 778
cohere 46
coherence *unite* 46

coherent — come

stability 150
dense 321
coherent 23
cohesion 46
cohesive 46, 327
cohibit *restrain* 751
  prohibit 761
  (*counteract*) 179
cohobation 336
cohort 726
cohue 72
coif 225, 370
coiffure 225
coign 244
coil *disorder* 59
  convolution 248
  circuition 311
  radiator 386
  shuffle off this
    mortal– 360
coin *fabricate* 161
  imagine 515
  money 800
  –*money* 775
  –*words* 563
coincide
  (see coincidence)
coincidence
  identity 13
  in time 120
  in place 199
  in opinion 488
coincident 13, 178
coiner *thief* 792
  counterfeiter 800
coinstantaneous 120
coistril 862
coition 43
cojuror 467
coke 388
colander 60, 260
colature 652
cold *frigid* **383**
  color 429, 438
  style 575
  insensible 823
  indifferent 866
  –*comfort* 832
  –*feet cowardice* 862
  –*shoulder*
    discourtesy 895
    contempt 930
  –*steel* 727
  –*storage* 387
  –*sweat fear* 860
  dislike 867
  –*water cure* 662
  in–*blood*
  premediated 611
  purposely 620
  unfeeling 823
  dispassionate 826
  throw–*water on*
    dissuade 616
  hinder 706
  dull 843

coldbloodedness 871
cold–frame 371
cold–hearted
  unfeeling 823
  hostile 889
  malevolent 907
cold–short 328
coleslaw 298
colic 378
Coliseum 728
collaboration 178
collaborator 711
collapse
  prostration 158
  contract 195
  shortcoming 304
  disease 655
  deteriorate 659
  fatigue 688
  failure 732
collar *dress* 225
  circlet 247
  shackle 752
  seize 789
  slip the– 750
collate 54, 464
collateral *relative* 9
  relation 11
  synchronous 120
  parallel 216
  lateral 236
  –*evidence* 467
collation *repast* 298
  comparison 464
colleague
  accompany 88
  associate 690
  cooperation 709
  auxiliary 711
  friend 890
collect *assemble* 72
  opine 480
  understand 518
  compile 596
  acquire 775
  prayer 990
  (*take*) 789
  –*evidence* 467
  –*knowledge* 539
  –*one's thoughts* 451
collectanea
  assemblage 72
  compendium 596
collected *calm* 826
collection
  assemblage 72
  store 636
  offertory 990
collective 78
collectively *whole* 50
  generality 78
  together 88
collectivism 737, 778
collectivist 778
collector
  director 694, 745

colleen 129
college 542
  –*board* 542
  –*education* 537
  –*yell* 838
  go to– 539
collide 276
collie 366
collier 273
colliery 252
colligate 72
collimate 216
collimation 216, 278
colliquation 335
collision *clash* 179
  percussion 276
  opposition 708
  encounter 720
collocate *arrange* 60
  assemble 72
  place 184
collocution 588
collogue *wheedle* 933
colloid 490b
collop 51
colloquial
  figure of speech 521
  language 560
  neology 563
  conversation 588
  –*meaning* 516
colluctation 720
collusion *deceit* 545
  conspiring 709
collusive 544
colluvies 653
collyrium 662
cologne 400
colon *punctuation* 142
  intestine 350
colonel 745
colonial 188
colonist 188, 294, 295
colonization 184
colonize 184
colonnade *series* 69
  houses 189
colony
  region 181, 184
  settlement 188
colophon 65
colophony 356a
color *hue* **428**
  tone 431
  redden 434
  appearance 448
  probability 472
  disguise 544
  paint 556
  plead 615
  plea 617
  be angry 900
  all–*s* 440
  change–
    shame 879
  –*too highly* 549

–*up redden* 434
  blush 879
  give a–*to*
  change 140
  qualify 469
  probable 472
  falsehood 544
  lend a–*to plea* 617
  vindicate 937
  man of– 431
  show in true–*s* 543
colorable
  ostensible 472
  deceptive 545
Colorado beetle 913
coloration 428
coloratura 415, 416
color–blindness 443
colored (see color)
  –*man* 431
  –*spectacles* 424
colorimeter 428
coloring (see color)
  meaning 516
  –*matter* 428
  false– 523
colorless *weak* 160
  pale 429
  feeble 575
color–printing 558
colors *ensign* 550
  decoration 877
  false– 544, 545
  flying–*display* 882
  celebration 883
  lower one's– 735
  nail one's–*to the*
    mast 604
  show one's–
    manifest 525
  disclose 529
  true to one's– 939
color–sergeant 745
colossal 192
Colosseum 728
colossus *strength* 159
  size 192
  height 206
colporteur 797, 996
colt *young* 129
  horse 271
  fool 501
colter 253
colubrine 366
columbarium 189
columbine 599
columella 215
columelliform 215
column *series* 69
  height 206
  support 215
  cylinder 249
  caravan 266
  monument 551
  printing 591
  troop 726

colures 318
coma
  inactive 683
  insensible 376, 823
comate 711, 890
comb *teeth* 253
  clean 652
  punish 972
combat 720, 722
  –*plane* 273
combatant 726
combative 720, 722
combe 252
comber *wave* 348
combination 48
  arithmetical 84
  party 712
  –*of fortuitous*
    circumstances 621
combine *unite* 48
  component 56
  concur 178
  partnership 712
  cooperate 709
combustible 388
combustion 384
come *happen* 151
  approach 286
  arrive 292
  cheer up! 836
  out upon! 932
  –*about* 658
  –*across discover* 480a
  –*after sequence* 63
    posterior 117
  –*amiss*
    disagreeable 24
    ill–timed 135
  –*and go* 314
  –*at one's call* 743
  –*back* 283
  –*before* 116
  –*by* 775
  –*down with* 807
  –*first superior* 33
    precede 62
  –*forth egress* 295
    appear 446
  –*forward* 763
  –*from follow* 154
    hail from 292
  –*in ingress* 294
    receipt 785
  –*in for*
    property 778, 780
  –*into existence be* 1
    begin 66
  –*into operation* 170
  –*into the views of*
    cooperate 709
  –*into the world* 359
  –*into use* 613
  –*into view* 446
  –*near* 286
  –*of* 154
  –*of age* 131

comedown — companionship

-off *loose* 44
event 151
escape 671
-off *well* 731
-on *future* 121
destiny 152
I defy you 715
attack 716
-out *disclosure* 529
publication 531
on the stage 599
-out of *effect* 154
egress 295
-out with
disclose 529
speak 582
-over *influence* 615
consent 762
-round *period* 138
conversion 144
belief 484
assent 488
change of mind 607
influence 615
restoration 660
be pacified 723
consent 762
-short of *inferior* 34
fall short 304
-to *equal* 27
whole 50
arithmetic 85
future 121
become 144
destiny 152
effect 154
inherit 777
money 800
price 812
-to a determination 604
-to a head *climax* 33
complete 52
-to a stand 142
-together *assemble* 72
converge 290
-to hand 785
-to life 359
-to nothing
unproductive 169
fail 732
-to oneself 660
-to one's knowledge 527
-to one's senses 502
-to pass *state* 7
event 151
-to pieces 44
-to terms *assent* 488
contract 769
-to the point
specialty 79
attention 457
concise 572
-to the front 303
-to the rescue 672

-to the same thing 27
-under 76
-upon *unexpected* 508
acquire 775
claim 924
-what may 474
cut and-again 639
it-s to this concisely 572
comedown 306, 735
comedy *drama* 599
comic 853
comely 240, 845
come-off
loophole 617
comestible 298
comet *wanderer* 268
star 318
omen 512
cometary 111
comfit 396
comfort *pleasure* 377
delight 827
content 831
relief 834
a man of- 834
give- 906
comfortable
pleasing 829
Comforter 976
comforter
wrap 223, 384
comfortless
painful 830
dejected 837
comic *wit* 842
ridiculous 853
coming (see come)
impending 152
-events
prediction 511
-out *celebration* 883
-time 121
comitia 696
comity 894
comma 142
command *high* 206
requirement 630
authority 737
order **741**
possess 777
*at one's-
obedient* 743
-a view of 441
-belief 484
-of language
writing 574
speaking 582
-of money 803
-one's passions 944
-one's temper 826
-respect 928
commandant 745
commandeer 744, 789

commander
mariner 269
chief 745
commander-in-chief 745
commanding
(see command)
important 642
comme il faut
taste 850
fashion 852
genteel 875
commemorate 883
commence 66
commend 931
-the poisoned chalice 544
commendable 944
commendably 931
commensurate
accordant 23
numeral 85
adequate 639
content 831
comment *reason* 476
judgment 480
interpretation 522
explain 595
commentary 595
commentator 492, 524
commerce
conversation 588
barter 794
cards 840
commercial
-*arithmetic* 811
-*traveler* 758
commination 908, 909
commingle 41
comminute 330
commiserate 914
commissariat 637
commissary
consignee 758
commission *task* 625
delegate **755**, 759
-of the peace 965
commissioner 745, 758
commissionnaire
messenger 534
consignee 758
commissure 43
commis-voyageur 758
commit *do* 680
delegate 755
cards 840
arrest 969
-an *absurdity* 853
-oneself *clumsy* 699
promise 768
-oneself to a course 609

-to *memory* 505
-to *prison* 751
-to *sin* 945
-to the *flames* 384
-to *writing* 551
commitment 969
committee
council 696
consignee 758
(*director*) 694
commix 41
commode 191
commodious 644
commodity 798
commodore 745
common *general* 78
ordinary 82
plain 344
grass 367
agriculture 371
habitual 613
trifling 643
base 876
-*consent* 488
-*council* 966
-*course* 613
-*herd* 876
-*law old* 124
law 963
-*measure* 84
-*origin* 153
-*parlance* 576
-*run* 78, 613
-*saying* 496
-*school* 537
-*sense* 498, 502
-*sewer* 653
-*stock* 778
-*weal mankind* 372
good 618
utility 644
philanthropy 910
in-related 9
participate 778
make-cause 709
right of- 780
tenant in- 778
commonalty 876
commoner 541, **876**
commonplace
usual 82
known 490
maxim 496
plain 576
habit 613
unimportant 643
dull 843
-*book record* 551
compendium 596
Common Pleas, Court of- 966
commons 298
commonweal
mankind 372
good 618
utility 644

philanthropy 910
commonwealth
region 181
mankind 372
utility 644
state 737
commorant 188
commotion 315
communalism 778
commune
township 181
commune with 588
-oneself 451
communicable 784
communicant 990
communicate *join* 43
tell 527
give 784
sacrament 998
communication
news 532
oral- 582, 588
communicative 527
communion
society 712
participation 778
sacrament 998
-*table* 1000
hold-with 888
communiqué 527
communist *rebel* 742
participation 778
philanthropy 910
communitarian 778
community
party 712
-*at large* 372
-*of goods* 778
-*singing* 415
commutation
difference 15
compensation 30
substitution 147
interchange 148
compromise 774
barter 794
commuter 268
commutual 12
compact *joined* 43
united 87
compressed 195
compendious 201
dense 321
bargain **769**
compactness
(see compact)
compages *whole* 50
structure 329
compagination 43
companion *match* 17
accompaniment 88
stairway 305
friend 890
companionable 892
companionless 87
companionship 892

408

companionway 305
company *assembly* 72
  actors 599
  party, partnership 712
  troop 726
  sociality 892
  (*merchants* 791)
  bear–88
  in–with 88
comparable 9
comparative
  degree 26
  compare 464
  –*anatomy* 368
  –*estimate* 464
comparatively 32
compare 464
  –*notes* 695
comparison 464
compartition 44
compartment
  part 51
  region 181
  place 182
  cell 191
  carriage 272
compass
  degree 26
  space 180
  surround 227
  circumscribe 233
  circuition 311
  measure 466
  intent 620
  guidance 693
  achieve 729
  box the
  –*azimuth* 278
  rotation 312
  –about 229
  –of thought 498
  in a small–193
  keep within–
  moderation 174
  fall short 304
  economy 817
  points of the–236
compassion 914
  object of–828
compassionate 914
compatible
  consentaneous 23
  possible 470
compatriot
  inhabitant 188
  friend 890
compeer *equal* 27
  friend 890
compel 744
compellation 564
compelled 744
compendious
  inclusive 56
  short 201
compendium 596

compensate
  make up for 30
  restore 790
  requite 973
compensation 30
compensatory 30, 790
compete 708, 720
competence
  power 157
  sufficiency 639
  skill 698
  wealth 803
competition
  opposition 708
  contention 720
competitor
  opponent 710
  combatant 726
  candidate 767
compilation
  composition 54
  collect 72
  writing 590
  book 593
  compendium 596
compile 54, 72
complacent
  pleased 827
  content 831
  courteous 894
  kind 906
complain 839
  –without cause 839
complainant 938
complainer 832
complaint *illness* 655
  murmur 839
  lodge a–938
complaisant
  lenient 740
  courteous 894
  kind 906
complanate 251
complement
  counterpart 14
  adjunct 39
  remainder 40
  part 52
  arithmetic 84
complemental 12
complete *entire* 52
  accomplish 729
  conclude 769
  –answer 479
  –circle 311
  in a–degree 31
completeness 52
  unity 87
completion 729
complex 59
complexion *state* 7
  color 428
  appearance 448
complexity 59
complexus 50, 59

compliance
  conformity 82
  submission 725
  obedience 743
  consent 762
  observance 772
  courtesy 894
compliant
  (*see* compliance)
complicate
  derange 61
complicated
  disorder 59
  convolution 248
  mechanical 633
complice 711
complicity 709
compliment
  courtesy 894
  congratulate 896
  praise 931
  –s of season 896
  poor–932
complimentary 815
complot 626
comply
  (*see* compliance)
compo *coating* 223
  material 635
component 56
comport–oneself 692
  –with 23
compos 502
compose
  make up 54, 56
  arrange 60
  produce 161
  moderate 174
  music 416
  write 590
  printing 591
  pacify 723
  assuage 826
composed
  self–possessed 826
composer *music* 413
composing
  –frame 591
  –room 591
  –rule 591
composite 41
composition 54
  (*see* compose)
  combination 48
  piece of music 415
  picture 556
  style 569
  writing 590
  building material 635
  compromise 774
  barter 794
  atonement 952
compositor 591
compost 653
composure 826

compotation 298, 959
compote 298
compound *mix* 41
  combination 48
  yard 232
  compromise 774
  –arithmetic 466
  –for *substitute* 147
  barter 794
  (*stipulate* 769)
comprador 637
comprehend
  compose 54
  include 76
  know 490
  understand 518
comprehensibility 518
comprehension
  (*see* comprehend)
  intelligence 498
comprehensive
  wholesale 50
  inclusive 56, 76
  general 78
  wide 192
  –argument 476
compress
  contract 195
  curtail 201
  condense 321
  remedy 662
compressed 572
compressible 322
comprise 76
comprised be–in 1
comprobation
  evidence 467
  demonstration 478
compromise
  dally with 605
  mid–course 628
  danger 665
  pacify 723
  compact 769
  compound 774
  atone 952
compromised
  promised 768
compter 799
compte rendu
  record 551
  accounts 811
  (*abstract* 596)
comptroller
  director 694
  (*master* 745)
compulsion 744
  forced labor 603
compulsion neurosis 821a
compulsory 601, 744
compunction 950
compurgation
  evidence 467

  acquittal 970
compurgator 467
computable 85
compute 37, 85
computation
  addition 37
  accounts 811
comrade 890
comradeship 892
con *think* 451
  get by heart 505
  learn 539
conation *agency* 170
  tendency 176
  will 600
conative 170, 176
conatus 176
concamerate 245
concatenation
  junction 43
  continuity 69
  –of circumstances 621
concave 252
  –mirror 555
concavity 252
conceal *invisible* 447
  hide 528
  cunning 702
concealment 528
concede *assent* 488
  admit 529
  permit 760
  consent 762
  give 784
conceit *idea* 453
  overestimation 482
  folly 499
  supposition 514
  imagination 515
  wit 842
  affectation 855
  vanity 880
conceited
  dogmatic 481
conceivable 470
conceive *begin* 66
  teem 168
  note 450
  believe 484
  understand 490
  imagine 515
  concent 413
concentrate
  assemble 72
  centrality 222
  converge 290
concentric 216, 222
concentricity 216
conception
  (*see* conceive)
  intellect 450
  idea 453
  guiding–453
concern *relation* 9
  event 151

concerning   confuse

care 459
business 625
importance 642
firm 797
grief 828
—oneself with 625
concerning
  relative to 9
  (*topic* 454)
concert *agreement* 23
  synchronous 120
  music 415
  act in—709
  —*hall* 189
  —*master* 416
  —*measures* 626
  —*piece* 415
  in—*musical* 413
  concord 714
concertina 417
concerto 415
concert room 840
concession
  permission 760
  consent 762
  giving 784
  discount 813
concetto 842
conch 204, 215
concha 418
conchate 245
conchiform 245
conchoid 245
conchology 223
concierge 263, 753
conciliate
  talk over 615
  pacify 723
  satisfy 831
  courtesy 894
  atonement 952
conciliatory
  (*see* conciliate)
  concord 714
  courteous 894
  forgiving 918
conciliatrix 962
concinnity
  agreement 23
  style 578
  beauty 845
concise 572
  taciturn 585
conciseness 572
concision 201
conclave *assembly* 72
  council 696
  church 995
conclude *end* 67
  infer 480
  resolve 604
  complete 729
  compact 769
conclusion
  (*see* conclude)
  sequel 65

eventuality 151
effect 154
judgment 480
foregone—611
hasty—481
try—*s* 476
conclusive
  (*see* conclude)
  final 67
  answer 462
  evidential 467
  certain 474
  proof 478
  manifest 525
  —*reasoning* 476
concoct *lie* 544
  plan 626
  prepare 673
concomitant
  accompany 88
  same time 120
  concurrence 178
concord *agree* 23
  music **413**
  assent 488
  harmony **714**
  (*amity* 888)
concordance
  dictionary 562, 593, 636
concordant 178
concordat 769
concours 720
concourse
  assemblage 72
  convergence 290
  —*of atoms* 621
concremation 384
concrete *mass* 46
  density 321
  hardness 323
  materials 635
concretion 46
concubinage 961
concubine 926
concupiscence
  desire 865
  impurity 961
concur *coexist* 120
  causation 178
  converge 290
  assent 488
  concert 709
concurrence *crisis* 43
  coagency **178**
  observance 772
concurrent 178, 216
concussion 276
condemn 971
condemnation
  censure 932
  conviction **971**
condemnatory 971
condesation
  brevity 201
  (*see* condense)

condense
  compress 195
  dense 321
condensed 572
condescend 879
condescension 879
condign 924
condiment 393
condisciple 541
condition *state* 7
  modification 469
  supposition 514
  term 770
  repute 873
  rank 875
  in—*plump* 192
  in good—648
  in perfect—650
  on—770
  physical—316
conditional 8
conditions 770
condolence 914, **915**
condone 918
condottiere
  traveler 268
  fighter 726
conduce
  contribute 153
  tend 176
  concur 178
  avail 644
conducent 176
conducive 631
conduct *transfer* 270
  procedure **692**
  lead 693
  —*an inquiry* 461
  —*to* 278
  safe—*passport* 631
  safety 664
conduction 264
conductivity 157
conductor *guard* 268
  conveyer 271
  music 416
  director 694
  lightning—666
conduit 350
conduplicate 89
condyle 250
cone *round* 249
  pointed 253
cone-shaped 253
conestoga wagon 272
confab 588
confabulation 588, 821a
confection 396
  confectionery 396
confederacy
  cooperation 709
  party 712
confederate
  combine 48
  auxiliary 711

Confederates 712
confer *advise* 695
  give 784
  —*benefit* 648
  —*power* 157
  —*privilege* 760
  —*right* 924
  —*with* 588
conference
  (*see* confer)
  council 696
  churchdom 995
conferva 367
confess *assent* 488
  avow 529
  penitence 950
  —*and avoid* 937
confession
  (*see* confess)
  worship 990
  auricular—998
  —*of faith* 983
confessional
  disclosure 529
  rite 998
  temple 1000
confessions
  biography 594
confessor 996
confidant
  auxiliary 711
  maid 746
  friend 890
confidante
  servant 746
  friend 890
confidence *trust* 484
  expectation 507
  deception 545
  hope 858
  courage 861
  —*man* 548
  —*trick* 545
  in—528
confident
  (*see* confidence)
  affirm 535
confidential 528
confiding 703
configuration 240
confine *place* 182
  circumscribe 229
  border 231
  limit 233
  imprison 751
confined
  narrow judgment 481
  ill 655
confinement
  childbed 161
confines of
  on the—197
confirm
  corroborate 467
  assent 488

consent 762
compact 769
rite 998
confirmation 535
confirmatory 480
confirmed 150
  —*habit* 613
confirmist 488
confiscate *take* 789
  condemn 971
  penalty 974
confiture 298, 396
conflagration 384
conflation 54
conflexure 245
conflict
  disagreement 24
  opposition 708
  discord 713
  contention 720
  warfare 722
conflicting
  contrary 14
  counteracting 179
  —*evidence* 468
confluence
  junction 43
  convergence 290
  river 348
confluent 290
conflux *assemblage* 72
  convergence 290
conform *assent* 488
conformable
  agreeing 23
  concurrent 178
conformation 240
conformity 82
  concurrence 178
  —*to rule* 494
confound *disorder* 61
  destroy 162
  not discriminate 465a
  perplex 475
  confute 479
  defeat 731
  astonish 870
  curse 908
confounded *great* 31
  bad 649
confraternity
  party 712
  friendship 888
confrère *colleague* 711
  friend 890
confrication 331
confront *face* 234
  compare 464
  oppose 708
  resist 719
  —*danger* 861
  —*witnesses* 467
Confucius 986
confuse *derange* 61
  perplex 458

obscure 519
not discriminate 465a
abash 879
confused *disorder* 59
  invisible 447
  uncertain 475
  perplexed 523
  style 571
  harmoniously–81
confusion
  (*see confuse*)
  obscurity 571
  –of tongues 560, 563
  –of vision 443
  –seize 908
  –worse confounded 59
  in–*excited* 825
confutation 479
confute 479
congé *departure* 293
  abrogation 756
  –d'elire 995
congeal *dense* 321
  cold 385
congener *similar* 17
  included 76
congeneric *similar* 17
congenerous 9, 17
congenial *agreeing* 23
  concord 714
  love 897
  (*expedient* 646)
congenital 5
  inborn 820
congenite 5
Congeries 72
congestion 641
conglaciation 385
conglobation 72
conglomerate
  cohere 46
  assemblage 72
  dense 321
conglutinate 46
congratulate 896
  –oneself 838
congratulation 896
congregation
  assemblage 72
  worshipers 990
  laity 997
congregational 995
Congregationalist 984
congress *assembly* 72
  convergence 290
  conference 588
  council 696
congressional 696
  –medal 551, 722
congressman 696
congreve *fuel* 388
  –rocket 727
congruence 23

congruous
  agreeing 23
  (*expedient* 646)
conical *round* 249
  pointed 25
conifer 369
conjectural 514
conjecture 514
conjoin 43
conjoint 48
conjointly 37
conjugal 903
conjugate
  combined 48
  words 562
  grammar 567
  –in all its tenses etc. 104
conjugation
  junction 43
  pair 89
  phase 144
  contiguity 199
  grammar 567
conjunction
  junction 43
  contiguity 199
  in–with 37
conjunctive 48
conjuncture
  contingency 8
  occasion 134
conjure *deceive* 545
  entreat 765
  sorcery 992
  –up 506
  –up a vision 515
  name to–with 873
conjurer *deceiver* 548
  sorcerer 994
connate *intrinsic* 5
  related 9
  kindred 11
  cause 153
connation 11
connatural *related* 9
  uniform 16
  similar 17
connaturality 13
connature 13, 16
connect *relate* 9
  link 43
connection *kin* 11
  coherence 46
connective 45
conned , well–490
connivance 760
connive *overlook* 460
  cooperate 709
  allow 760
connivent 286
connoisseur
  critic 480
  scholar 492
  taste 850
connoisseurship 850

connotate 550
connotation 516
connote *mean* 516
  indicate 550
connubial 903
conoscente 850
conquer 731
conquered
  (*failure* 732)
conqueror 731
conquest 749
consanguinity 11
conscience
  knowledge 490
  moral sense 926
  awakened–950
  clear–946
  in all–*great* 31
  affirmation 535
  qualms of–603
  stricken–950
  tender–926
  honor 939
conscientious 926
  faithful 21
  scrupulous 939
  (*veracious* 543)
  (*virtuous* 944)
conscious
  intuitive 450
  knowledge 490
  –of disgrace 874
  –of glory 873
consciousness 450
  subliminal–992a
conscript 726
conscription 744
consecrate *use* 677
  dedicate 873
  sanctify 987
  holy orders 995
consecration *rite* 998
consectary 478
  –reasoning 476
consecution 63
consecutive
  following 63
  continuous 69
  posterior 117
  –fifths 414
consecutively
  slowly 275
consension 23
consensus 23, 488
consent *assent* 488
  compliance 762
  with one–178
consentaneity 23
consentaneous
  agreeing 23
  concurrent 178
  (*expedient* 646)
consequence
  event 151
  effect 154
  importance 642

in–478
of no–643
take the–s 154
consequent 63
consequential
  deducible 478
  arrogant 878
consequently
  reasoning 476
  effect 154
conservation
  permanence 141
  storage 636
  preservation 670
conservatism 141, 670
conservative 141
  –policy 681
Conservatives 712
conservator of the peace 967
conservatory
  receptacle 191
  floriculture 371
  furnace 386
  store 636
conserve *sweet* 396
  store 637
consider *think* 451
  attend to 457
  examine 461
  adjudge 480
  believe 484
considerable
  in degree 31
  in size 192
  important 642
considerate
  careful 459
  judicious 498
consideration
  purchase money 147
  thought 451
  idea 453
  attention 457
  qualification 469
  inducement 615
  importance 642
  gift 784
  benevolence 906
  respect 928
  requital 973
  deserve–642
  in–of
  compensation 30
  reasoning 476
  on–658
  take into–
  thought 451
  attention 457
  under–*topic* 454
  inquiry 461
  plan 626
considered
  (*see* consider)
  all things–

judgment 480
premeditation 611
imperfection 651
consign *transfer* 270
  commission 755
  property 783
  give 784
  –to oblivion 506
  –to the flames 384
  –to the tomb 363
consignee 270, 758
consigner 796
consignificative 522
consignment
  commission 755
  gift 784
  apportionment 786
consilience 178
consimilarity 17
consist–in 1
  –of 54
consistence
  density 321
consistency
  uniformity 16
  agreement 23
consistent 82
  –ly with 82
consistory
  council 696
  church 995
consociate 890, 892
consolation *relief* 834
  condole 915
  religious 976
console *table* 215
consolidate
  unite 46, 48
  condense 321
Consols 802
consommé 298
consonance 16
consonant
  agreeing 23
  musical 413
  letter 561
  (*expedient* 646)
consort *accompany* 88
  associate 892
  spouse 903
  –with 23
consortium 23
consortship 892
conspection 441
conspectus 596
conspicuous
  visible 446
  famous 873
  –by his absence 187
conspiracy 626
  –of silence 460
conspirator 626
  traitor 941
conspire *concur* 178
  cooperate 709
constable *safety* 664

411

governor 745
officer 965
constancy 743
constant *uniform* 16
 continuous 69
 regular 80
 frequent 136
 periodic 138
 immutable 150
 exact 494
 persevering 604a
 faithful 939
 –flow 69
constellation
 stars 318
 luminary 423
 glory 873
consternation 860
constipate 321
constipation
 closure 261
 density 321
constituency 609
constituent 56, 609
constitute
 compose 54, 56
 produce 161
constituted by 1
constitution *nature* 5
 state 7
 composition 54
 structure 329
 charter 924
 law 963
 higher law than– 926
constitutional
 walk 266
 –*government* 737
constitutive 153
constrain *compel* 744
 restrain 751
 abash 881
constraint
 contraction 195
 [*see* constrain]
constrict 195
constriction 706
constringe 195
constringency 195
construct *compose* 54
 produce 161
 organize 357
construction
 production 161
 form 240
 structure 329
 meaning 522
 put a false–upon 523
constructive
 creative 161
 latent 526
 –*evidence* 467
constructor 164
construe 522

consubstantiation 998
consuetude 613
consul 758, 759
consular 759
consulship 737
consult *remedy* 662
 advise 695
 –*one's own wishes* 943
 –*one's pillow* 133
 –*the wishes of* 707
consultant 662
consultation 695
consume *decay* 49
 destroy 162
 waste 638
 use 677
 time time 106
 inactivity 683
consumer *user* 677
consuming 830
consummate *great* 31
 complete 52
 be perfect 650
 completed 729
 –*skill* 698
consummation
 end 67
 completion 729
 –*devoutly to be wished good* 618
 desire 865
consumption
 [*see* consume]
 decrease 36
 shrinking 195
 disease 655
consumptive 655
contact *contiguity* 199
 touch 379
 come in–
 arrive 292
contagion
 transfer 270
 unhealthy 657
contagious 655, 657
contain
 be composed of 54
 include 76
 contained in 1
container
 receptacle 191
contaminate *soil* 653
 spoil 659
contaminated
 diseased 655
contamination 653, 659
contango 813
contemn 930
contemper 48, 174
contemplate
 view 441
 intellect 450
 think 451

expect 507
purpose 620
contemplation
 [*see* contemplate]
contemporaneous 120
contemporary 120
contemporation 174
contempt 930
 –*of danger* 861
contemptible
 unimportant 643
 dishonorable 940
contemptuous
 defiant 715
 disrespectful 929
 disdainful 930
contend *reason* 476
 assert 535
 fight 720
 –*for vindicate* 937
 –*with difficulties* 704
content *assenting* 488
 willing 602
 calm 826
 satisfied 831
 to one's heart's– sufficient 639
 success 731
contention 720
contentious 901
contents
 ingredients 56
 list 86
 components 190
 book 593
 synopsis 596
conterminate *end* 67
 limit 233
conterminous 199
contesseration 72
contest 708, 720
contestant 710
context 591
contexture 329
 (*state* 7)
contiguity 199
contiguous 197
continence 960
continent 342
continental *trifle* 643
continentals 225
contingency
 junction 43
 event 151
 uncertainty 475
 expectation 507
contingent *extrinsic* 6
 conditional 8
 casual 156
 liable 177
 possible 470
 uncertain 475
 supply 635
 aid 707
 allotted 786

donation 809
–*duration* 108a
–*interest* 780
continual
 perpetual 112
 frequent 136
continuance 117, 143
continuation *affix* 37
 adjunct 39
 sequence 63
 sequel 65
 –*school* 542
continuations
 trousers 225
continue *exist* 1
 endure 106, 110
 persist 143
continued 69
 –*existence* 112
 –*success* 731
continuing 143
continuity 16, 69
continuous 69
contortion
 distortion 243
 convolution 248
 (*ugliness* 846)
contortionist 599
contortuosity 243
contour *outline* 230
 appearance 448
 –*line* 550
contra 14 *per*–708
contraband
 deceitful 545
 prohibited 761
 illicit 964
contrabandist 792
contrabasso 417
contraclockwise 283
contract *shrink* 195
 narrow 203
 promise 768
 bargain 769
 (*decrease* 36)
 (*curtail* 201)
 –*a debt* 806
 –*a habit* 613
 –*an obligation* 768
contractible 195
contractility 195
 (*elasticity* 325)
contraction 195
 shorthand 590
 compendium 596
contractive 36, 464
contractor 690
contractual 769
contradict
 contrary 14
 dissent 489
 deny 536
 oppose 708
contradiction
 difference 15
 answer 462

contradictoriness 15
contradictory
 evidence 468
 discordant 713
contradistinction 15
contrafagotto 417
contraindicant 616
contraindicate
 dissuade 616
 warning 668
contralto 408
contraposition
 inversion 218
 reversion 237
contrapuntal 415
contrapuntist 413
contrariety 14, 15, 708
contrariness 708
contrariwise 148, 708
contrary *opposite* 14
 antagonistic 179
 captious 608
 opposing 708
 –*to expectation*
 improbable 473
 unexpected 508
 –*to reason* 471
 quite the–536
contrast
 contrariety 14
 difference 15
 comparison 464
contrastive 15
contrate wheel 247
contravallation 717
contravene
 contrary 14
 counteract 179
 counterevidence 468
 deny 536
 hinder 706
 oppose 708
contre–coup 277
contrectation 379
contretemps
 ill timed 135
 hindrance 706
 misfortune 735
contribute *cause* 153
 tend 176
 concur 178
 aid 707
 give 784
contribution 784
 lay under– take 789
 due 924
contributor
 correspondent 592
 giver 784
contributory *extra* 37
contrition
 abrasion 331
 penitence 950
contrivance 626

412

contrive *produce* 161
  plan 626
  –to *succeed in* 731
contriving
  cunning 702
control *power* 157
  influence 175
  aviation 273
  regulate 693
  authority 737
  restrain 751
  board of– 696
  get–of 175
  under–
    obedience 743
  subjection 749
controller 694
controversial
  discussion 476
  discordant 713
controversialist 476, 726
controversy
  discussion 476
  interlocution 588
  contention 720
controvert *deny* 536
controvertible
  uncertain 475
  debatable 476
  untrue 495
contumacy
  obstinacy 606
  disobedience 742
contumely
  arrogance 885
  rudeness 895
  disrespect 929
  scorn 930
  reproach 932
contund 330
contuse 330
conundrum *pun* 520
  riddle 533
  wit 842
  (*problem* 461)
convalesce 654
convalescence 654, 660
convection 270, 490a
convene 72
convenience 685
conveniences 632
convenient 646
convent 1000
  –*school* 542
conventicle
  assembly 72
  council 696
  chapel 1000
convention
  assembly 72
  canon 80
  council 696
  law 697
  treaty of peace 723

compact 769
  –*of society* 852
conventional
  customary 613
conventionalism 613
conventionalist 82
conventionality 613
conventionalize 82
conventual *monk* 996
  convent 1000
converge 290
convergence 290, 372a
convergent 286, 290
conversable *talk* 588
  sociable 892
conversant *know* 490
  skillful 698
conversation 588
conversational 588
  sociable 892
conversationist 588
conversazione
  interlocution 588
  social gathering 892
converse
  reverse 14, 237
  talk 588
  hold high– 539
conversely 148, 168
conversible 144
conversion 144
  trover and– 964
convert *change* 140
  change to 144
  opinion 484
  tergiversation 607
  penitent 950
  religion 987
  –*to use* 677
convertible
  identical 13
  equal 27
  –*terms* 522
convex 250
  –*lens* 445, 490a
  –*mirror* 555
convexity 250
convey *transfer* 270
  mean 516
  assign 783
  –*away* 791
  –*the knowledge of* 527
conveyable 270
conveyance
  (*see* convey)
  vehicle 272
conveyancer 968
conveyancing 783
convict *convince* 484
  prisoner 754
  condemned 949
  condemn 971
conviction
  confutation 479

belief 484
  prove guilty 971
convince *confute* 479
  belief 484
  teach 537
  easily–d 486
convincing
  conclusive 478
convivial 892
convocate 72
convocation
  assemblage 72
  council 696
  church 995
convoke 72
convolution *coil* **248**
  rotation 312
convoy *transfer* 270
  accompany 88
  guard 664
  escort 753
convluse *derange* 61
  violent 173
  agitate 315
  bodily pain 378
  mental pain 830
convulsed with
  –*laughter* 838
  –*rage* 900
convulsion
  (*see* convulse)
  disorder 59
  revolution 146
  in–s 315
convulsive shock therapy 821a
coo 412
cook *heat* 384
  falsify 544
  improve 658
  prepare 673
  servant 746
  –*accounts* 811
  too many–s 699
cooker *range* 386
cookery 673
cook house 191
cookie 298
cookshop 189
cookstove 386
cool *moderate* 174
  cold 383
  refrigerate 385
  gray 432
  dissuade 616
  inexcitable 826
  cautious 864
  indifferent 866
  imperturbable 871
  unfriendly 889
  discourteous 895
  –*down*
    become sane 502
    be composed 826
  –*one's heels*
    kept waiting 133

inaction 681
  look–upon
  unsocial 893
  take–ly 826
cooler 387
cool–headed
  judicious 498
  unexcitable 826
coolie *bearer* 271
cooling 385
coolness (*see* cool)
  insensibility 823
  estrangement 898
coomb 252
coon's age 110
coop *abode* 189
  restrain 751
  prison 752
cooperate 709
cooperation
  physical 178
  voluntary **709**
  participation 778
cooperative
  concurring 178
  cooperating 709
  helpful 746
cooperator 690, 711
cooptative 609
cooptation 609
coordinate *equal* 27
  arrange 60
  measure 466
cop 664
copal 356a
coparcener 778
copartner
  accompanying 88
  participator 778
  associate 890
copartnership
  cooperation 709
  party 712
  participation 778
cope *equal* 27
  oppose 708
  contend 720
  canonicals 999
copemate *enemy* 891
coping 204, 210
  –*stone top* 210
  completion 729
copious
  productive 168
  diffuse style 573
  abundant 639
coportion 778
copper *money* 800
copper–colored 433
copperhead 366
copperish 433
copperplate
  engraving 558
coppery 433
coppice 367
coprolite 653

coprophilia 821a
copse 367
copula 45
copulation 43
copy *imitate* 19
  facsimile 21
  prototype 22
  duplicate 90
  record 561
  represent 554
  write 590
  for the press 591
  plan 626
copyhold 780
copyholder 591
copyist *imitator* 19
  artist 559
  writer 590
copyright 780
coquelicot 434
coquet *lie* 544
  change the mind 607
  affected 855
  love 897
  endearment 902
  flattery 938
  –*with irresolute* 605
coquette
  affected 854, 855
  flirt 897, 902
coquillage 847
coracle 273
coral *animal* 368
  red 434
  ornament 847
  –*reef* 667
coralline 434
cor Anglais 417
corbeille 191
corbel 215
cord *tie* 45
  size 192
  filament 205
cordage 45, 192
cordate 245
cordial *pleasure* 377
  dram 392
  willing 602
  remedy 662
  feeling 821
  grateful 829
  friendly 888
  courteous 894
  benevolent 906
cordiality
  goodwill 602
  fervor 821
  friendship 888
cordiform 245
cordite 727
cordon *inclosure* 232
  circularity 247
  decoration 877
  –*bleu* 746
  –*sanitaire safety* 664
  preservation 670

corduroy   **count**

corduroy 259
  –road 259
cordwain 223
cordwainer
  shoemaker 225
  artificer 690
core *center* 222
  gist 5, 642
  true to the–939
corespondent 938
coriaceous 327
Corinthian 850
corium 223
corival (*see* corrival)
cork *plug* 263
  lightness 320
  –jacket 666
  –up *close* 261
  restrain 751
corking pin 45
corkscrew *spiral* 248
  perforator 262
  circuition 311
corky *shriveled* 195
  dry 340
cormorant *desire* 865
  gluttony 957
corn *projection* 250
  food 298
  –fed 192
  –husk 223
  –husking 892
  –shuck 223
Cornaro 953
corncake 298
corndabs 298
corndodgers 298
cornea 441
corned 959
corneous 323
corner *plight* 7
  place 182
  receptacle 191
  angle 244
  discommode 706
  monopoly **777**
  creep into a–893
  drive into a–706
  in a dark–528
  push into a–874
  rub off–s 82
  turn a–311
  turn the–658
cornerstone
  support 215
  importance 642
cornet *music* 417
  officer 745
cornetist 416
cornice 210
corniculate 253
cornification 323
Cornish hug 545
corno 417
cornopean 417
cornstarch 298

cornucopia 639
cornute
  projecting 250
  sharp 253
cornwallis 840
corollary *adjunct* 39
  deduction 480
corona *summit* 210
  circularity 247
coronach 415, 550, 839
coronation
  enthronement 755
  celebration 883
coroner 965
coronet *hoop* 247
  insignia 747
  jewel 847
  title 877
corporal
  corporeal 316
  officer 745
corporate *joined* 43
  combine 48
  party 712
  –body 712
corporation *bulk* 192
  convex 250
  association 712
  merchants 797
  jurisdiction 965
corporeal 3, 316
  –hereditaments 780
  –nature 364
corporeity 3, 316
corposant 423
corps *assemblage* 72
  troops 726
  –de reserve 636
corpse 362
  –candle 423
corpulence 192
corpulent 192, 194
corpus 316–delicti
  guilt 947
  lawsuit 969
  –juris *precept* 697
  law 963
corpuscle *small* 32
  little 193
corradiation *focus* 74
  convergence 290
corral
  circumscribe 229
  inclosure 232
  round up 370
correct *orderly* 58
  true 494
  inform 527
  disclose 529
  improve 658
  repair 660
  due 924
  censure 932
  honorable 939
  virtuous 944

  punish 972
  –ear 416, 418
  –memory 505
  –reasoning 476
  –style
    grammatical 567
    elegant 578
correction
  (*see* correct)
  house of–752
  under–879
corrective 662
correctness
  (*see* correct)
  elegance 578
corregidor 745
correlation *relation* 9
  reciprocity **12**
correlative 9, 17
correspond *agree* 23
  write 592
correspondence
  correlation 12
  similarity 17
  agreement 23
  writing **592**
  concord 714
correspondent
  reciprocal 12
  messenger 534
  letter writer 592
  journalist 593
  consignee 758
corresponsive 178
corridor *place* 191
  passage 627
  –s of time 109
  –train 272
corrigendum 495
corrigible 658
corrival 726
corrivalry 720
corrivation 348
corroborant 662
corroboration
  evidence 467
  assent 488
corrode *burn* 384
  erode 659
  afflict 830
corrosion
  (*see* corrode)
corrosive
  (*see* corrode)
  acrid 171
  destructive 649
  –sublimate 663
corrugate *derange* 61
  constrict 195
  roughen 256
  rumple 258
  furrow 259
corrupt
  (*see* corruption)
corrupting
  noxious 649

corruption
  decomposition 49
  neology 563
  foulness 653
  disease 655
  deterioration 659
  improbity 940
  vice 945
  guilt 947
corsage 225
corsair *boat* 273
  pirate 792
corse 362
corselet 225
corset 225
corso 728
cortège *adjunct* 39
  continuity 69
  accompaniment 88
  journey 266
  suite 646
cortes 696
cortex *cortical* 223
coruscate 420, 498
corvet *ship* 273
  man–of–war 726
corvette (*see* corvet)
Corvus 490a
Corybantic 503, 954
coryphée 599
Corypheus
  teacher 540
  director 694
coscinomancy 511
cosey 892
cosine 217
cos lettuce 298
cosmetic *remedy* 662
  ornament 847
cosmical 318
cosmogony 318
cosmography 318
cosmology 318
cosmoplast 976
cosmopolitan
  abode 189
  mankind 372
  sociality 892
  philanthropic 910
cosmorama 448
cosmos 60, 318
Cossack 726
cosset *darling* 899
  caress 902
cost 812–price 815
  –what it may 604
  pay–s 807
  to one's–evil 619
costate 259
costermonger 797
costive *compact* 321
  taciturn 855
costless 815
costly 809, 814
costume 225

  theatrical–599
costumé 225 bal–840
costumer 225, 599
costumier 225
  theatrical 599
cosy *snug* 377
  sociable 892
cot *abode* 189
  bed 215
  –betty 374
cotangent 217
cote 189
cotenancy 778
coterie *class* 75
  junto 712
  society 892
coterminous 120
cothurnus 599
cotidal 341
cotillion 840
cotquean 374, 501
cottage 189
cottager 188
cotter 188
cotton 205, 635
cottonseed oil 356
Cottrell process 490b
cotyledon 367
couch *lie* 213
  bed 215
  stoop 308
  lurk 528
  –in terms 566
  –one's lance 720
  lone–of everlasting sleep 360, 363
couchant 213
couci–couci 651
cougar 913
cough 349
  churchyard–655
coulee 211, 350
couleur de rose
  good 648
  prosperity 734
  view en–836
coulisse 599
Coulomb's Law 490d
council *senate* 696
  church 995
  cease thy–695
  –fire 696
  –of education 542
  hold a–695
councilor 696
counsel *advice* 695
  lawyer 698
  keep one's own–528
  take–*think* 451
  inquire 461
  be advised 695
count *clause* 51
  item 79
  compute 85

414

countable

estimate 480
lord 875
—*the cost* 864
—*upon believe* 484
expect 507
countable 85
countenance *face* 234
appearance 448
favor 707
approve 931
—*falling
disappointment* 509
dejection 837
keep in—*conform* 82
induce 615
encourage 861
vindicate 937
*keep one's
—brook* 826
not laugh 837
out of—*abashed* 879
put out of—874
stare out of—885
counter *contrary* 14
number 84
table 215
rear 235
reverse 237
token 550
shopboard 799
—*to* 708
lie nailed to the— 934
over the—*barter* 794
buy 795
sell 796
run—179
counteract
compensate 30
physically 179
hinder 706
voluntarily 708
counteraction 179
counterbalance 30
counterblast
counteract 179
answer 462
retaliate 718
counterchange
correlation 12
interchange 148
countercharge 462
countercharm 993
countercheck
mark 550
hindrance 706
counterclaim 30
counterclockwise 283
countercurrent 312
counterevidence 468
counterfeit
imitate 19
copy 21
simulate 544
sham 545

untrue 546
—*presentment* 21
counterfeiter 800
counterfoil 550
counterjumper 746
countermand 756
countermarch
journey 266
regression 283
regression 283
countermark 550
countermine
excavate 252
intrigue 626
oppose 708
defense 717
countermotion 283
counterorder 756
counterpane 223
counterpart
identity 13
complement 14
match 17
copy 21
duplicate 90
reverse 237
counterplot *plan* 626
oppose 708
retaliate 718
counterpoint 14, 413
counterpoise
compensate 30
weight 319
hinder 706
(*counteract* 179)
counterpoison 662
counterpole 14
counterproject 718
counterprotest 468
counter-revolution 146
counterscarp 717
counterscript 21
countersign
evidence 467
assent 488
mark 550
counterstatement 462
counterstroke 718
countertransference 821a
countervail
outweigh 28
compensate 30
evidence 468
counterweigh 319
counterwork 708
countess 875
countinghouse 799
countless 105
countrified *rustic* 189
vulgar 851
country *region* 181
abode 189
rural 371

state 737
jury 967
—*seat* 189
—*town* 189
love of—910
country-dance 840
countryman
commonalty 876
friend 890
countryside 182
county 181
—*council* 696
—*council school* 542
—*court* 966
coup
instantaneous 113
action 680
—*de grâce end* 67
deathblow 361
completion 729
pity 914
punishment 972
—*de main
violence* 173
action 680
attack 716
—*de maître
excellent* 648
skillful 698
success 731
—*d'état revolution* 146
plan 626
action 680
lawless 964
coupé 272
coupelet 272
couple *unite* 43
fastening 45
combine 48
two 89
—*d with added* 37
accompanied 88
coupler 45
couplet 89, 597
coupon 800
courage 861
—*oozing out* 862
moral—604
courageous 861
courier *traveler* 268
interpreter 524
messenger 534
course *order* 58
continuity 69
time 106, **109**
layer 204
motion 264
locomotion 266, 267
direction 278
dinner 298
river 348
habit 613
pursuit 622
way 627
conduct 692
arena 728

bend one's—266
—*of action* 692
—*of business* 625
—*of events* 151
—*of inquiry* 461
—*of preparation* 673
—*of study* 537
—*of things* 151
—*of time* 121
—*runs smooth* 734
follow as of—478
hold a—278
in due—109, 134
in the—*of
during* 106
*keep one's
—progress* 282
persevere 604a
*let things take their
— continue* 143
inaction 681
mark out a—626
of—*conformity* 82
effect 154
certain 474
assent 488
necessity 601
custom 613
consent 762
expect 871
run its—*end* 67
complete 729
take a—622
take its—151
courser *horse* 271
swift 274
courses 138
coursing *kill* 361
pursue 622
court *close* 181
house 189
hall 191
invite 615
pursue 622
council 696
retinue 746
solicit 765
gentility 852
wish 865
woo 902
flatter 933
tribunal 966
bring into—467
—*card* 626
—*of honor* 939
friend at—711
pay—*to servile* 886
love 897, 902
flatter 933
put out of—731
courteous 894
courtesan 962
courtesy
politeness **894**
show—*respect* 928
courthouse 189

courtier *servile* 886
flatterer 935
—*like* 933
courtly 852
courtship 902
courtyard 182
cousin 11
cove *cell* 191
hollow 252
bay 343
covenant *compact* 769
condition 770
security 771
covenantor 488
Coventry Earl of
—*cards* 840
send to—*eject* 297
disrepute 874
seclusion 893
cover *compensate* 30
include 76
superpose, lid 223
dress 225
stopper 263
course 298
hat h 370
conceal 528
retreat 530
report 531
keep clean 652
keep safe 664
preserve 670
—*up one's tracks* 528
—*with dust* 653
under—*hidden* 528
pretense 545
safe 664
covercle 223
covering 223
coverlet 223
Coverley, Sir Roger
de—840
covert *abode* 189
shade 424
invisible 447
latent 526
refuge 666
—*way* 627
feme-e 903
coverture 903
covet *desire* 865
envy 921
covetous *miserly* 819
covey *assemblage* 72
multitude 102
covin 544, 545
cow *animal* 366
female 374
intimidate 860
—*pony* 271
coward 862
cowardice 862
cowardly 862
cowboy 370
cowcatcher 717
cower *stoop* 308

fear 860
cowardice 862
servile 886
cowherd 370
cowhide *lash* 972
whip 975
cowhouse 189
cowkeeper 370
cowl *sacerdotal* 999
(dress 225)
cowled 223
cowlstaff 215
coworker 690
coworking 178
cow-puncher 370
coxcomb 854
coxcombry
affectation 855
vanity 880
coxswain 269
coy *timid* 860
modest 881
coyote 366
cozen 545
crab
crustacean 298, 368
sourness 397
–like motion
deviation 279
regression 283
crab apple 397
crabbed *sour* 397
unintelligible 519
obscure style 571
difficult 704
uncivil 895
sulky 901a
crabmeat 298
crack *split* 44
discontinuity 70
instantaneous 113
fissure 198
furrow 259
brittle 328
sound 406
excellent 648
injure 659
skillful 698
boast 884
–a bottle *food* 298
social 892
drunken 959
–a joke 842
–of doom *end* 67
future 121
destruction 162
–one's invention 515
–shot 700
crack-brained
insane 503
(foolish 499)
cracked
unmusical 410
mad 503
faulty 651
–*bell* 408a

–*voice* 581
cracker *biscuit* 298
firework 406
crackerjack 33, 648, 698
crackle 406
crack-loo 621
cracksman 792
cradle *beginning* 66
infancy 127
origin 153
placing 184
bed 215
crossing 219
training 673
aid 707
–hole 259
–song 415, 834
in the– 129
craft *shipping* 273
business 625
skill 698
cunning 702
craftsman 690
craftsmanship 680
crag *cliff* 212
pointed 253
hard 323
land 342
craggy *rough* 256
craichy 160
craig *height* 206
crake 884
cram *crowd* 72
stuff 194
choke 261
teach 537
learn 539
gorge 957
–down the throat
compel 744
crambo 597
crammed 52
–to overflowing 641
crammer *teacher* 540
lie 546
cramp *fastening* 45
paralyze 158
weaken 160
little 193
compress 195
spasm 315, 378
hinder 706
cramped *style* 579
cramp iron 45
cran 191
cranberry 298
cranch (see **craunch**)
crane *angle* 244
elevate 307
bird 366, 386
–neck 245
crane's-bill 845
cranial index 372a
craniology etc. 450
cranium 450

crank *fanatic* 504
instrument 633
wit 842
treadmill 975
–shaft 272
crankle *fold* 258
crankling *rough* 256
cranky *weak* 160
ill health 655
cranny 198
crape *crinkle* 248
mourning 839
craps 621
crapulence
intemperance 954
gluttony 957
drunken 959
crash *destruction* 162
collision 276
brittle 328
sound 406
crasis *nature* 5
coherence 48
composition 54
crass *great* 31
dense 321
semifluid 352
unintelligent 493
bad taste 851
–ignorance 491
crassamentum 321, 352
crassitude
breadth 202
density 321
thickness 352
crate *receptacle* 191
crater *deep* 208
hollow 252
craunch *shatter* 44
chew 298
pulverize 330
cravat 225
crave *ask* 765
desire 865
craven *cowardly* 862
craw 191
crawfish 298
recede 283
apostatize 607
crawl *elapse* 109
creep 275
withdraw 283
apostatize 607
servile 886
crawly 380
crayon 556
crazy *weak* 160
mad 503
creak 410
creaking 410
cream *emulsion* 352
oil 356
yellow 436
important part 642
best 648

–*color white* 430
yellow 436
–of tartar 662
–of the jest 842
creamy 352
crease 258
create *cause* 153
produce 161
imagine 515
created *being* 366
creation (see **create**)
effect 154
world 318
creative 20, 153
creativeness 18, 20
Creator 976
creator *producer* 164
poet 597
creature *thing* 3
effect 154
animal 271, 366
man 372
slave 746
–comforts *food* 298
pleasure 377
the–*food* 298
crèche 542
credence *belief* 484
church 1000
credenda 484
credential 467
credible *possible* 470
probable 472
belief 484
credit *belief* 484
influence 737
pecuniary 805
account 811
repute 873
approbation 931
desert 944
to one's–
property 780
creditable *right* 924
credit mobilier 802
creditor 639, 805
credulity 486
(heterodoxy 984)
credulous 486, 849
–person *dupe* 547
creed *belief* 484
theology 983
Apostles'– 983a
–bound 606
creek *interval* 198
water 343
creel 191
creep *crawl* 275
tingle 380
(inactivity 683)
–in 294
–into a corner 893
–into the good graces of 933
–out 529
–upon one 508

–with *multitude* 102
redundance 641
creeper 367
creeping
sensation 380
–thing 366
creepy 380
creese 727
cremation
of corpses 363
burning 384
crematorium 363
crematory 384
crème
–de la crème 648
–de menthe 435
–glacée 298
Cremona 417
crenate 257
crenelate 257
crenelle 257
crenulate 257
creole 57
crêpe de Chine 635
crepitant 406
crepitation 406
crepuscle *dawn* 125
dusk 422
crepuscular 125
crescendo *increase* 35
musical 415
crescent *increasing* 35
street 189
curve 245
–shaped 253
crescive 35
cress 298
cresset *signal* 550
(*luminary* 423)
crest *climax* 33
summit 210
pointed 253
tuft 256
sign 550
armorial 877
pride 878
crestate 253
crestfallen
dejected 837
humble 879
cretaceous 430
crevasse 198, 667
crevice 198
crew *assemblage* 72
inhabitants 188
mariners 269
party 712
crib *bed* 215
translation 522, 539
steal 791
cribbage 840
cribbed *confined* 751
cribble 260
cribriform 260
Crichton, Admirable
– scholar 492

perfect 650
proficient 700
crick *pain* 378
cricket *insect* 366
 game 840
 —*ground level* 213
cricketer 840
crier 534
 send round the—531
crim. con. 961
crime *guilt* 947
criminal *vicious* 945
 culprit 949
 malefactor 975
 (—*conversation* 961)
 —*law* 963
criminality 947
criminate 938
crimp *crinkle* 248
 notch 257
 brittle 328
 deception 545
 deceiver 548
 take 789
 steal 791
crimple 258
crimson *color* 434
 feeling 821
cringe *submit* 725
 servility 886
cringing *servile* 746
crinite 256
crinkle *angle* 244
 convolution 248
 ruffle 256
 fold 258
crinoid 368
crinoline 225
cripple *disable* 158
 weaken 160
 injure 659
crippled *disease* 655
crisis *conjuncture* 8
 contingency 43
 present time 118
 opportunity 134
 event 151
 strait 704
 bring to a—604
 come to a—729
crisp *rumpled* 248
 rough 256
 brittle 328
 style 572
Crispin 225
crisscross 219, 840
criterion *test* 463
 evidence 467
 indication 550
crithomancy 511
critic *judge* 480
 taste 850
 detractor 936
 and stand a—480
critical *contingent* 8
 opportune 134

discriminating 465
judicious 480
important 642
dangerous 665
difficult 704
censorious 932
nothing if not—480
criticism
 judgment 480
 dissertation 595
 disapprobation 932
 detraction 934
criticize
 discriminate 465
 judge 480
 disapprove 932
 detract 934
critique
 (*see* criticism)
 discrimination 465
critter 271
croak *cry* 412
 hoarseness 581
 stammer 583
 warning 668
 discontent 832
 lament 839
croaker 832, 837
Croat 726
crochet *obstinacy* 608
crock 191
crockery 384
crocodile 366, 913
crocodile tears 54
crocus *yellow* 436
Croesus 803
croft 189, 232
cromlech 363
crone *veteran* 130
 fool 501
crony *friend* 890
 sociality 892
 favorite 899
crook *support* 215
 curve 245
 deviation 279
 thief 792
crooked *sloping* 217
 distorted 243
 angular 244
 deviating 279
 latent 526
 crafty 702
 ugly 846
 dishonorable 940
 —*path* 704
 —*stick discourtesy* 895
 —*temper* 901
 —*ways* 279
croon 405
crop *stomach* 191
 harvest 154
 shorten 201
 eat 298
 store 636
 gather 775

take 789
—*out reproduce* 163
visible 446
disclose 529
—*up begin* 66
take place 151
reproduction 163
second —*fertile* 168
profit 775
cropped
 fragmentary 51
cropper *fall* 306
croquet *game* 840
 —*ground level* 213
croquette 298
crore 98
crosier 215, 999
cross *mix* 41
 support 215
 across 219
 pass 302
 interment 363
 oppose 708
 failure 732
 disaster 735
 refuse 764
 vex 830
 decoration 877
 fretful 901
 punishment 975
 rites 998
 —*and pile* 621
 —*debt* 30
 —*fire interchange* 148
 difficulty 704
 opposition 708
 attack 716
 —*purposes*
 contrary 14
 disorder 59
 error 495
 misinterpret 523
 unskillful 699
 difficulty 704
 opposition 708
 discord 713
 —*questions*
 inquiry 461
 discord 713
 game 840
 —*sea* 348
 —*swords* 722
 —*the mind* 451
 —*the path of* 706
 —*the Rubicon* 609
 —*fire* 722
 red—662
crossbar 219
crossbarred 219
crossbow 727
crossbreed 41, 83
crosscut 628
crossed 219
 —*bayonet* 708
 —*in love* 898
cross—examine 461

cross—eye 443
cross—grained
 rough 256
 obstinate 606
 irascible 901
 sulky 901a
crosshatch 259
crossing 219—*the bar death* 360
crosspatch 895
crossroad 627
crossruff 314
cross—shaped 219
crosswise 219
crotch 91, 244
crotchet *music* 413
 misjudgment 481
 caprice 608
crouch *lower* 207
 stoop 308
 fear 860
 servile 886
 —*before* 725
croup 235
croupier 694
crow *bird* 366
 cry 412
 black 431
 rejoice 838
 boast 884
 as the—*flies* 278
 —*to pluck discord* 713
 anger 900
 accuse 938
 pluck a—*with* 932
crowbar 633
crowd *assemblage* 72
 multitude 102
 close 197
 redundance 641
 the masses 876
 —*is not company* 892
 —*in the*—*mixed* 41
 the madding—893
crowded 72, 102, 197
 (*see* crowd)
crown *top* 210
 circle 247
 be perfect 650
 complete 729
 trophy 733
 scepter 747
 install 755
 jewel 847
 decoration 877
 reward 973
 —*ed head* 745
 —*law* 963
 —*of sorrow* 828
 —*wheel* 247
 —*with laurel* 873
 —*with success* 731
 to—*all* 33, 642
crowning (*see* crown)
 superior 33
 end 67

—*point* 210
crown—post 215
crow's—foot *age* 128
crow's nest
 nautical 210
crozier 747
crucial *crossing* 219
 proof 478
 —*test* 463
cruciate
 cruciform 219
 physical pain 378
 mental pain 830
crucible *dish* 191
 conversion 144
 furnace 386
 experiment 463
 laboratory 691
 put into the—163
cruciferous 219
crucifix 219, 998
crucifixion
 anguish 828
 (*see* crucify)
cruciform 219, 1000
crucify
 physical torture 378
 mental agony 830
 execution 972
crude *color* 428
 inelegant 579
 unprepared 674
cruel *painful* 830
 inhuman 907
 —*as death* 907
 —*only to be kind* 830
cruelly *much* 31
cruelty (*see* cruel)
cruet 191
cruise *navigation* 267
cruiser 726
cruller 298
crumb *small* 32
 bit 51
 powder 330
 (*part* 51)
 (*little* 193)
 —*of comfort* 834
crumble *decrease* 36
 weak 160
 destruction 162
 brittle 328
 pulverize 330
 spoil 659
 —*into dust*
 decompose 49
 —*under one's feet* 735
crumbling
 (*see* crumble)
 dangerous 665
crumbly 330
crumenal 800
crump *distorted* 243
 curved 245
crumple *ruffle* 256
 fold 258

crunch | current

up *destroy* 162
crush 195
crunch *shatter* **44**
  chew 298
  pulverize 330
crupper 235
crusade 361, 722
cruse 191
crush *crowd* 72
  destroy 162
  compress 195
  shatter 328
  pulverize 330
  humble 879
  (*injure* 649)
  –one's hopes
    disappoint 509
    hopeless 859
  –under an iron heel
    739
crushed *unhappy* 828
crush hat 225
crushing *vigorous* 574
  painful 830
crust 223
crustacean 366, 368
crusty
  discourteous 895
  sullen 901a
crutch *support* 215
  angle 244
crux *cross* 219
  difficulty 704
Crux 490a
cry *stridor* 410
  human **411**
  animal 412
  publish 531, 532
  call 550
  voice 580
  vogue 613
  weep 839
  –aloud *implore* 765
  –and little wool
    overrate 482
    boast 884
    disappoint 509
  –before hurt 839
  –down 932, 934
  –for 865
  –for joy 838
  –for vengeance 923
  –out against
    dissuade 616
    censure 932
  –shame 932
  –to beseech 765
  –up 931
  –wolf *false* 544
    alarm 669
  –you mercy
    depreciate 766
    pity 914
    forgive 918
    far–to 196
    full–*loud* 404

raise a–550
crying (*see* cry)
  urgent 630
  –evil 619
  –shame 874
  –sin 945
crypt *cell* 191
  grave 363
  ambush 530
  altar 1000
cryptic *uncertain* 475
  concealed 528
  secret 533
cryptography
  unintelligibility 519
  hidden 528
  writing 590
crystal *hard* 323
  water 337
  transparent 425
  –gazing 992a
  –oil 356
  snow–383
crystalline *dense* 321
  transparent 425
crystallinity 321
crystallization 321, 323
crystallize 321
crystallomancy 511
crystallose 396
cub *young* 129
  offspring 167
  vulgar 851
  clown 876
  unlicked–241
cubby-hole 191, 530
cube
  three dimensions 92, 93
  form 244
cubeb 393
cubicle 191
cubist 556
cubit 200
cucking stool 975
cuckold 905
cuckoldom 961
cuckoo *imitation* 19
  repetition 104
  bird 366
  sound 407
  cry 412
  songbird 416
cucullate 223
cucumber 298
  –green 435
cuddle 902
cuddy 271
cudgel *beat* 276
  weapon 727
  punish 975
  –one's brains
    think 451
    imagine 515
  take up the–s

aid 707
attack 716
contention 720
cudgeling
  punishment 972
cue *humor* 5
  role 51, 625
  hint 527
  watchword 550
  plea 617
  take one's–from 695
cue rest 215
cuff *sleeve* 225
  blow 276
  punishment 972
cuirass 717
cuirassier 726
cuisine 298
culbute *inversion* 218
  fall 306
cul-de-lampe
  engraving 558
  ornament 847
cul-de-sac
  concave 252
  closed 261
  difficulty 704
culet 211
culinary 298–art 673
cull *dupe* 547
  choose 609
  take 789
cullender 260
cullibility 486
cullion 949
cully *deceive* 545
  dupe 547
culm 388
culminate
  maximum 33
  height 206
  top 210
  complete 729
culpability *vice* 945
  guilt 947
culprit 949, 975
cult 990
cultivate *till* 365, 371
  sharpen 375
  improve 658
  prepare 673
  aid 707
  courtesy 894
cultivated
  courteous 894
  –taste 850
cultivation
  (*see* cultivate)
  knowledge 490
cultivator 371
cultural 537, 542
cultural anthropology 372a
culture *knowledge* 490
  improvement 658

taste 850
courtesy 894
culverin 727
culvert 350
cumber *load* 319
  obstruct 706
cumbersome
  incommodious 647
  disagreeable 830
cumbrous 830
cummerbund 225
cumshaw 784
cumulative
  assembled 72
  evidential 467
  –evidence 467
  –vote 609
cumulous 353
cumulus 353
cunctation *delay* 133
  (*inactivity* 683)
cuneate 244
cuneiform 244, 372a
  –character 590
cunning *prepense* 611
  sagacious 698
  artful 702
  –fellow 700
cup *vessel* 191
  hollow 252
  beverage 298
  remedy 662
  tipple 959
  between–and lip 111
  bitter–828
  –of humiliation 879
  –that cheers etc. 298
  –too low 837
  –tossing 621
  dash the–from one's lips 509
  in one's–s 959
cupbearer 746
cupboard 191
cupel 384
cupellation 336, 384
Cupid *beauty* 845
  love 897
cupidity *avarice* 819
  desire 865
cupola *height* 206
  dome 223, 250
cupping 662
cup-shaped 252
cur *dog* 366
  sneak 949
curable 658, 660, 662
curacy 995
curate 996
curative 660
curator 694, 758
curb *moderate* 174
  slacken 275
  dissuade 616
  chance 621

check 706
restrain 751
shackle 752
mart 799
–bit 706
–roof 244
curcuma paper 463
curd *density* 321
  pulp 354
  (*cohere* 46)
curdle *condense* 321
  make the blood– 830
curdled 352
cure *reinstate* 660
  remedy 662
  preserve 670
  benefice 995
curé 996
cure-all 662
cureless 859
curfew 126
curia 966
curio 847
curiosity
  unconformity 83
  inquiring 455
  phenomenon 872
curious *exceptional* 83
  inquisitive 455
  true 494
  beautiful 845
  desirous 865
curiously *very* 31
curl *bend* 245
  convolution 248
  hair 256
  cockle up 258
  –cloud 353
  –paper 256
  –up one's lip 930
curling *game* 840
curling tongs 386
curly 248
curmudgeon
  miser 819
currants 298
currency
  publicity 531
  money 800
current *existing* 1
  general 78
  present 118
  happening 151
  –of water 348
  –of air 349
  rife 531, 532
  language 560
  habit 613
  danger 667
  –account 811
  against the–708
  –belief 488
  –of events 151
  –of ideas 451
  –of time 109

curricle

go with the—82
pass—believed 484
fashion 852
stem the—708
curricle 272
curricular 272
curriculum 537
currish 895
curry rub 331
condiment 393
—favor with love 897
flatter 933
currycomb 370
curse bane 663
adversity 735
painful 830
malediction 908
(evil 619)
cursed bad 649
cursitor 968
cursive 573
cursory transient 111
inattentive 458
hasty 684
take a—view of 457
neglect 460
curst sullen 901a
curt short 201
concise 572
taciturn 585
curtail retrench 38
shorten 201
(decrease 36)
(deprive 789)
—ed of its fair proportions
distorted 243
ugly 846
curtailment
decrease 36
(see curtail)
curtain shade 424
hide 528, 530
theater 599
fortification 717
behind the—
invisible 447
inquiry 461
knowledge 490
close the—528
—lecture 932
—raiser
drama 66, 599
raise the—529
rising of the—448
curtal 201
curtate 201
curtsy stoop 308, 314
submit 725
polite 894
curule 474, 696
curvate 245
curvature 245
curve 245
curved 245
curvet leap 309

turn 311
oscillate 314
agitate 315
curvilinear 245
—motion 311
cushat 366
cushion pillow 215
soft 324
relief 834
cusp angle 244
sharp 253
cuspidor 191
cussed 901a
cussedness 606
custard pie 298
custodian 753
custody safe 664
captive 751
retention 781
in—prisoner 754
accused 938
take into—751
custom old 124
habit 613
barter 794
sale 796
tax 812
fashion 852
—honored in breach 614
customary
(see custom)
regular 80
customer 795
customhouse 799
—officer 965
custos 753
—rotulorum 553
cut geld 38
divide 44
bit 51
discontinuity 70
absent 187
interval 198
curtail 201
layer 204
form 240
notch 257
blow 276
depart 293
eject 297
reap 371
physical pain 378
cold 385
neglect 460
carve 557
engraving 558
road 627
attack 716
affect 824
mental pain 830
ignore 893
discourtesy 895
tipsy 959
—according to cloth
economy 817

caution 864
—across 302
—adrift 44
—a figure
appearance 448
fashion 852
repute 873
display 882
—along 274
—and come again
repeat 104
enough 639
—and dried
arranged 60
prepared 673
—and run 274, 293, 623
—and thrust 716
—a poor figure 874
—away 274
—blocks with a razor
sophistry 477
waste 638
misuse 679
—both ways 468
—capers 309
—dead 893
—direct 893
—down destroy 162
shorten 201
level 213
fell 308
kill 361
—down expenses 817
—in two 91
—it out 142
—jokes 842
—off subduct 38
disjoin 44
depart 293
kill 361
impede 706
bereft 776
divorce 782
secluded 893
—off with a shilling 789
—of one's jib 448
—one's own throat 699
—one's stick
depart 293
avoid 623
—one's way through 302
—open 260
—out surpass 33
substitute 147
plan 626
—out for 698
—out work
prepare 673
direct 693
—short stop 142
destroy 162
shorten 201

silence 581
—the first turf 66
—the ground from under one
confute 479
hinder 706
—the knot 705
—to pieces 162
kill 361
—to the heart 824, 308
—to the quick 830
—up root and branch 162
—up divide 44
destroy 162
pained 828
give pain 830
discontented 832
dejected 837
censure 932
—up rough 900
have a—at 716
short—628
unkindest—of all
pain 828
malevolence 907
what one will—up for 780
cutaneous 223
cutcherry 802, 965
cute 698
cuteness 498
cuticle 223
cutis 223
cutlass 727
cutlery 253
cutpurse 792
cutter 273 sleigh 272
cutthroat killer 361
opposition 708
evil doer 913
cutting sharp 253
cold 383
affecting 821
painful 830
reproachful 932
cuttings excerpta 596
selections 609
cuttlefish 368
cutty stool 950
cwt. hundred 98
weight 319
cyanic 438
cyanogen 438
cycle time 106
period 138
circle 247
journey 266
vehicle 272
—of indiction 108
cyclic 138
cyclist 268
cycloid 247
cyclone rotation 312
wind 349

dabbled

cyclonic 349
Cyclopean strong 159
huge 31, 192
cyclopedia
knowledge 490
book 542, 593
store 636
Cyclops monster 83
mighty 159
huge 192
cygnet 366
Cygnus 490a
cylinder
rotundity 249
automobile 272
cylindric 249
cymbal 417
cymbiform 245
cymophane 440
cymophanous 440
cynanche 655
cynic recluse 893
misanthrope 911
detractor 936
ascetic 955
closet—
unsociable 893
cynical
contemptuous 930
censorious 932
detracting 934
cynicism
discourtesy 895
Cynic philosophy 451
Cynosure 423
cynosure sign 550
direction 693
repute 873
Cynthia 318
—of the minute 149
cypher (see cipher)
cypress interment 363
mourning 839
Cyprian 962
Cyrenaic school 451
cyst 191
cytology 357
cytoplasm 357
czar 745
czarevna 745
czarina 745
czarevitch 745

D

dab paint 223
morsel 32
slap 276
clever 700
dabble water 337
dirty 653
meddle 682
fribble 683
dabbled wet 339

419

dabbler 493, 823
dabster 700
dachshund 366
dacker 605
dacoit 792
dactyl 597
dactyliomancy 511
dactylography 550
dactylology 419, 550
dactylonomy
  numeration 85
  symbol 550
dad 166
dado 211
daedal *various* 15
  diversified 16a
  variegated 440
Daedalian
  convoluted 248
  artistic 698
daeva 980
daft 503
daffodil 845
dagger
  typography 550
  weapon 727
  air drawn– 515
  at–s drawn
  opposed 708
  discord 713
  enmity 889
  hate 898
  –*of the mind* 860
  looks–s anger 900
  threat 909
  plant–in breast
  give pain 830
  speak–s 932
daggle *hang* 214
  dirty 653
dagoba 1000
Dagon 991
daguerreotype
  represent 554
dahabeah 273
Dail Eireann 696
daily *frequent* 136
  periodic 138
  newspaper 531
  –*occurrence*
  normal 82
  habitual 613
daimio 875
dainty *food* 298
  savoring 394
  pleasing 829
  delicate 845
  tasty 850
  fastidious 868
dairy 191
dais *support* 215
  throne 747
daisy–*pied* 847
  fresh as a– 654
dak 534
  –*bungalow* 189

dalal 758
dale *valley* 252
dally *delay* 133
  irresolute 605
  inactive 683
  amuse 640
  fondle 902
dalmatic 999
Daltonism 443
dam *parent* 166
  close 261
  pond 343
  obstruct 706
damage *evil* 619
  injure, spoil 659
  loss 776
  price 812
damages 974
damascene 440
damask 434
dame *woman* 374
  teacher 540
  lady 875
damn *malediction* 908
  condemn 971
  –*with faint praise*
  932, 934
damnability 649
damnable 649
damnatory *evil* 649
  disapprove 932
  condemn 971
damnify *damage* 649
  spoil 659
Damocles
  –*sword of–* 667
damoiseau 129
damoiselle 129
Damon and Pythias
  890
damp *moderate* 174
  moist 339
  cold 385
  dissuade 616
  hinder 706
  depress 837
  dull 843
  –*the sound* 408a
dampen 339
damper *cake* 298
  furnace 386
  faintness 405
damsel *youth* 129
  female 374
damson 437
Danaë 803
dance *jump* 309
  oscillate 314
  agitate 315
  rejoice 838
  sport 840
  –*attendance*
  waiting 133
  follow 281
  servant 746
  petition 765

  servility 886
  –*music* 415
  –*steps* 840
  –*the back step* 283
  –*the war dance* 715
  –*upon nothing* 972
  lead one a–
  run away 623
  circuit 629
  difficult 704
  practical joke 929
  lead the– 175
dancer 840
dander 900
dandi 272
Dandie Dinmont
  366
dandify 847
dandiprat 193
dandle 902
dandruff 653
dandy *litter* 266, 272
  ship 273
  fop 854
dandyism 855
danger 665–*past* 664
  –*signal* 669
  in–liable 177
  –*source of–* 667
dangerous
  (*see danger*)
  –*classes* 913
  –*illness* 655
  –*person* 667
dangle *hang* 214
  swing 314
  display 882
dangler 281
Daniel *sage* 500
  judge 967
  –*come to judgment*
  480
dank 339
danseuse 599
Dan to Beersheba
  complete 52
  extent 180
dapper *little* 193
  elegant 845
dapple–gray 432
dappled 432, 440
Darby and Joan
  secluded 893
  married 903
dare *confront* 234
  defy 715
  face danger 861
  –*not* 860
  –*say probable* 472
  believe 484
  suppose 514
dare–devil
  courage 861
  rash 863
  bluster 887
daring *unreserved* 525

  courageous 861
  –*imagination* 515
dark *obscure* 421
  dim 422
  color 428
  black 431
  blind 442
  invisible 447
  unintelligible 519
  latent 526
  joyless 837
  insidious 940
  –*ages* 491
  –*amid the blaze of*
  noon 442
  –*cloud* 735
  –*lantern* 423
  in the–ignorant 491
  keep–hide 528
  leap in the–
  experiment 463
  chance 621
  rash 863
  view with–eyes 932
darken *obscure* 422
  look black 821
  –*over* 421
darkened 421
darkle 422
darkling 421
darkly
  see through a glass–
  443
darkness
  (*see dark*) 421
  children of– 988
  –*of meaning* 571
  powers of– 978
darksomeness 421
darky 431
darling *beloved* 897
  favorite 599
darn 660
dart *swift* 274
  propel 284
  missile 727
  –*to and fro* 684
dartre 655
Darwinian 357
Darwinism 357
dash
  small quantity 32
  mix 41
  start 146
  swift 276
  fling 284
  mark 550
  courage 861
  cut a–repute 873
  display 882
  –*at resolution* 604
  attack 716
  –*cup from lips* 761
  –*down* 308
  –*hopes*
  disappoint 509

  fail 732
  dejected 837
  despair 859
  –*off compose* 54
  paint 556
  write 590
  active 682
  haste 684
  –*of the pen* 590
  –*on* 274
dashboard 666
dashed (*see* dash)
  humbled 879
dasher 666
dashing
  fashionable 852
  brave 861
  ostentatious 882
dastard 862
dasturi 973
data *evidence* 467
  reasoning 476
  supposition 514
datal 114
date *time* 106
  chronology 114
  to this– 118
  up to– 123
dateless 124
datum (*see* data)
daub *cover* 223
  bad painting 555
  dirt 653
daubing 635
daughter 167
daunt 860
dauntless 858, 861
davenport 191, 215
dawdle *tardy* 133
  slow 275
  inactive 683
dawn *precursor* 64
  begin 66
  priority 116
  morning 125
  light 420
  dim 422
  glimpse 490
day *period* 108
  present time 118
  light 420
  all– 110
  all in–'s work 625
  clear as–
  certain 474
  intelligible 518
  manifest 525
  close of– 126
  –*after day*
  diuturnal 110
  frequent 136
  –*after the fair* 135
  –*after to–morrow*
  121
  –*and night*
  frequent 136

420

day–bed   deciduous

—before yesterday 122
—by day
  repeatedly 104
  time 106
  periodic 138
—of judgment 121
—of rest 686
—one's own 731
—s gone by 122
—s numbered
  transient 111
  death 360
—s of week 138
  decline of— 126
  denizens of the— 366
  happy as the—is long 827, 836
  have had its— 124
  open as— 703
  order of the— 613
  red letter— 642
  see the light of— 446
day-bed 215
day-blindness 443
daybook record 551
  accounts 811
daybreak
  morning 125
  dim 422
daydream fancy 515
  hope 858
daydreamer 515
daydreaming 458
day-laborer 690
daylight morning 125
  light 420
  see—intelligible 518
daypeep 125
dayspring 125
day-star 318, 423
daze 420, 870
  in a— 860
dazed inattentive 458
  uncertain 475
  confused 523
dazzle light 420
  blind 422, 443
  put out 458
  astonish 870
  awe 928
dazzling (see dazzle)
  beautiful 845
deacon 996 juggle 545
  intone 990
deaconry 995
dead complete 52
  obsolete 124
  inert 172
  colorless 429
  lifeless 360
  insensible 376
  —against contrary 14
  oppose 708
  —asleep 683
  —beat powerless 158

sponger 886
—certainty 474
—color 556
—cut 893
—drunk 959
—failure 732
—flat 213
—heat 27
—languages 560
—letter impotent 158
  unmeaning 517
  useless 645
  laxity 738
  exempt 927
  illegal 964
—lift exertion 686
  difficulty 707
—march 275, 363, 415
—of night
  midnight 126
  dark 421
—one 460
—reckoning
  numeration 85
  measurement 466
—secret 533
—set against 708
—set at attack 716
—shot 284, 700, 716
—silence 403
—slow 275
—sound 408a
—stop 142
—to 823
—wall hindrance 706
  defense 717
—water 142, 343
—weight 706
  more–than alive 688
deaden
  weaken 158
  moderate 174
  insensible 376
  muffle 405, 408a
  benumb 823
deadened 381
deadhead 815
deadhouse 363
deadlock cease 142
  stoppage 265
  difficulty 704
deadly killing 361
  pernicious 649
  unhealthy 657
  —sin 947
  —weapon 361, 727
deads 645
deaf 419
  inattentive 458
  —and dumb 581
  —ears 419
  —to insensible 823
  —to advice 606
  —to reason 901a
  turn–ear to

neglect 460
unbelief 487
refuse 764
deafen loud 404
deaf–mute 419, 581
deaf–mutism 581
deafness 419
deal much 31
  arrange 60
  compact 769
  allot 786
—a blow injure 659
  attack 716
  punish 972
—board 323
—in 794
—out scatter 73
—with treat of 595
  handle 692
  barter 794
dealbation 430
dealer 797
dealings action 680
  have–with
  trade 794
  friendly 888
dean age 128
  clergyman 996
deanery office 995
  house 1000
dear expending 809
  high priced 814
  loved 897
  favorite 899
—at any price 646
—me wonder 870
  O—! lament 839
dearborn 272
dearness 814
dearth 640
—of ideas 843
death 360
  be the–of one
  amuse 840
—defying 863
—in the pot
  unhealthy 657
  hidden danger 667
  do to–361
  house of–363
  in at the–arrive 292
  persevere 604a
  pale as–colorless 429
  fear 860
  put to–361
  still as–265
  violent–361
deathbed 360
—repentance 950
death bell 363
deathblow end 67
  killing 361
  failure 732
death chair 975
death fire 423

deathless
  perpetual 112
  fame 873
deathlike silent 403
  hideous 846
death's–head 837
death–song 839
death–struggle 720
death–warrant 971
deathwatch 668, 837
debacle
  revolution 146
  destruction 162
  violence 173
  downfall 306
  torrent 348
debar hinder 706
  restrain 751
  prohibit 761
debark 292, 342
debarment 55
debase depress 308
  foul 653
  deteriorate 659
  degrade 874
debased lowered 207
  dishonored 940
debatable 475
—point 454
debate reason 476
  talk 588
  hesitate 605
  dispute 720
debauch spoil 659
  intemperance 954
  impurity 961
debauchee 962
debenture
  security 771
  money 800
  credit 805
debility 160
debit debt 806
  accounts 811
debitor 806
debonair 836
debouch 293, 295
debouchment 293
debris fragments 51
  crumbled 330
  useless 645
debt 800
—of nature 360
  get out of–807
  out of–803
debtor 806
—and creditor 811
début beginning 66
  essay 675
débutant learner 541
  drama 599
decade ten 98
  period 108
  celebration 883
decadence 659
decagon 98, 244

decagonal 98
decahedral 98
decalescence 382
decalogue 926
decamp go away 293
  run away 623
decant 270
decanter 191
decapitate kill 361
  punish 972
decarbonized iron 313
decare 98
decarnate 317
decastyle 98
decasyllable 98
decay decrease 36
  decomposition 49
  shrivel 195
  unclean 653
  disease 655
  spoil 659
  adversity 735
—of memory 506
  natural–360
decayed (see decay)
  old 124
  rotten 160
decease 360
deceit falsehood 544
  deception 545
  cunning 702
deceitful (see deceit)
deceive 545
deceived in error 495
  duped 547
deceiver 548 gay–962
decemvir 98
decennial 138
decennium 108
decent mediocre 651
  pure 960
decentralize 49
deception 545, 702
deceptive
  sophistical 477
  deceiving 545
  cunning 702
—reasoning 477
decession 293
dechristianize 989
decibel 490d
decide
  turn the scale 153
  judge 480
  choose 609
decided great 31
  ended 67
  certain 474
  resolved 604
  take a–step 609
deciduous
  transitory 111
  falling 306
  vegetation 367
  spoiled 659

421

decimal

decimal
  numeration 84
  tenth 98, 99
decimalize 99
decimate *subtract* 38
  tenth 99
  few 103
  weaken 160
  kill 361
  play havoc 659
decipher 522, 525, 561
decision
  judgment 480
  resolution 604
  intention 620
  law case 969
decisive *certain* 474
  proof 478
  commanding 741
  take a—step 609
deck *floor* 211
  cards 840
  beautify 847
deckle-edged 674
declaim 582
  —against 932
declamatory
  style 577
  speech 582
declaration
  evidence 467
  affirmation 535
  law pleadings 969
  —of faith *belief* 484
  theology 983
  —of war 713, 722
declarative 527
declaratory
  meaning 516
  inform 527
declare 535
declension
  (see decline)
  grammar 567
  backsliding 988
declensions 5
declination
  (see decline)
  deviation 279
  divergence 291
  measurement 466
  rejection 610
declinatory 764
declinature 764
decline *decrease* 36
  old 124
  weaken 160
  descent 306
  grammar 567
  be unwilling 603
  reject 610
  disease 655
  become worse 659
  adversity 735
  refuse 764

—of day 126
—of life 128
declivitous 217, 306
declivity *slope* 217
  descent 306
declivous 306
decoction 335, 384
decode 525, 561
decollate 972
décolletée 225
decolor 429
decoloration 429
decolorize 429
decompose 49
decomposition 49
decompound 49
deconsecrate 756
decoration
  trophy 733
  insignia 747
  ornament 847
  title 877
Decoration Day 840
decorous
  (see decorum)
  proper 924
  respectful 928
decorticate 226
decorum *fashion* 852
  duty 926
  purity 960
decoy *draw* 288
  deceive 545
  deceiver 548
  entice 615
decrassify 652, 658
decrease *in degree* 36
  in size 195
decree *judgment* 480
  order 741
  law 963, 969
decrement
  decrease 36
  thing deducted 40a
  contraction 195
decrepit *old* 128
  impotent 158
  weak 160
  disease 655
  decayed 659
decrepitate 406
decrepitation 490b
decrepitude
  (see decrepit)
decrescence 36
decrescendo 36
decretal 741
decretive 741
decry *underrate* 483
  censure 932
  detract 934
decumbent 213, 214
decuple 98
decursive 306
decurtation 201
decussate 219

decussation 219
dedecorous
  disreputable 874
  discourteous 895
dedicate *use* 677
  inscribe 873
dedication *book* 593
  (see dedicate)
deduce *deduct* 38
  infer 480
deducible
  evidence 467
  proof 478
deduct *retrench* 38
  deprive 789
deduction
  (see deduce)
  decrement 40a
  reasoning 476
  inference 521
deductive 476
deed *transference* 270
  evidence 467
  record 551
  act 680
  security 771
  —s of arms 720
  —without a name 947
deem 484
deemster 664, 967
deep *great* 31
  profound 208
  sea 341
  sonorous 404
  cunning 702
  —color 428
  —game 702
  —in debt 806
  —knowledge 490
  —mourning 839
  —note 408
  —potations 959
  —reflection 451
  —sea 208
  —sense 821
  —sigh 839
  —study 457
  —toned 413
  in—water 704
  plough the—267
deep-dyed
  intense 171
  black 431
  vicious 945
deepen *increase* 35
deep-felt 821
deep-laid *plan* 626
deeply (see deep)
deep-mouthed
  resonant 408
  bark 412
deep musing 458
deep-read 490
deep-rooted
  stable 150
  strong 159

belief 484
  habit 613
  affections 820
deep-seated 208
  interior 221
deer 366
  in heart a—862
deev 980
deface
  destroy form 241
  obliterate 552
  injure 659
  render ugly 846
defalcation
  incomplete 53
  contraction 195
  shortcoming 304
  nonpayment 808
defamation
  (see defame)
defamatory 932, 934
defame *shame* 874
  censure 932
  detract 934
defamer 936
defatigation 841
default *incomplete* 53
  shortcoming 304
  neglect 460
  insufficiency 640
  debt 806
  nonpayment 808
  in—of 187
  judgment by—725
defaulter *thief* 792
  nonpayer 808
  rogue 949
defeasance 756
defeat *confute* 479
  succeed 731
  failure 732
  —one's hope 509
defecate 652
defecation 299
defect *decrement* 40a
  incomplete 53
  imperfect 651
  failing 945
defection
  relinquishment 624
  imperfection 651
  disobedience 742
defective
  incomplete 53
  insufficient 640
  imperfect 651
defend (see defense)
defendant 938
  defender 914
defense *answer* 462
  resist 717
  vindication 937
defenseless
  impotent 158
  weak 160
  exposed 665

deflower

defense mechanism 821a
defensible *safe* 664
  excusable 937
defensive alliance 712
defer *put off* 133
  neglect 460
  —to *assent* 488
  submit 725
  respect 928
deference
  submission 725
  obedience 743
  humility 879
  courtesy 894
  respect 928
deferment 460
defial 715
defiance 715
  threat 909
  —of danger 861
  in—*opposition* 708
  set at—*disobey* 742
defiant 715
deficiency
  (see deficient)
  vice 945
  —of blood 160
deficient *inferior* 34
  incomplete 53
  shortcoming 304
  insufficient 640
  imperfect 651
deficit
  incompleteness 53
  debt 806
defigure 846
defile *interval* 198
  march 266
  dirt 653
  spoil 659
  shame 874
  impure 961
define *limit* 233
  explain 522
  name 564
definite *special* 79
  limited 233
  visible 446
  certain 474
  exact 494
  intelligible 518
  manifest 525
  perspicuous 570
definition
  interpretation 521
definitive *final* 67
  affirmative 535
  decided 604
deflagration 384
deflate 195
deflect *curve* 245
  deviate 279
deflower *spoil* 659
  violate 961

422

defluent 348
defluxion *egress* 295
   flowing 348
defoedation 653, 659
deform 241, 846
deformed 243
deforming 241
deformity
   distortion 243
   ugliness 846
   blemish 848
defraud *cheat* 545
   swindle 791
defray 807
defrayment 807
deft *suitable* 23
   clever 698
defunct 360, 362
defy *confront* 234
   set at defiance 715
   disobey 742
   threaten 909
   –*danger* 861
dégagé *free* 748
   fashion 852
degeneracy 659
degenerate
   deteriorate 659
   vice 945
deglutition 298
degradation
   deterioration 659
   shame 874
   dishonor 940
degrade *disbar* 968
   (see degradation)
degree 26 *term* 71
   honor 873
   by–*s* 26
   by slow–*s* 275
   in no–107
   no–4
degustation 390
dehisce 260
dehiscence 260
dehort *dissuade* 616
   advise 695
dehydrate 340, 670
dehydration 340, 670
deification 981
deify *honor* 873
   idolatry 991
deign *condescend* 762
   consent 879
deism *heterodoxy* 984
   irreligion 989
deistic 976, 989
Deity 976
   tutelary–664
dejection
   excretion 299
   melancholy 837
déjeuner 298
dejudication 480
dekko 457
delaceration 659

delaminate 204
delation 133, 938
delator 527, 938
delay 133, 460
dele 162, 552
delectable *savory* 394
   agreeable 829
delectation 827
delectus 562
delegate *transfer* 270
   interpreter 524
   messenger 534
   commission 755
   consignee 758
   deputy 759
delegated *acting* 759
delegation 755
delete 162
deleterious
   pernicious 649
   unwholesome 657
deletion 552
deletory
   destructive 162
deliberate *slow* 275
   think 451
   attentive 457
   leisure 685
   advise 695
   cautious 864
deliberately
   (see deliberate)
   late 133
   with premeditation 611
deliberation
   (see deliberate)
delicacy *weak* 160
   slender 203
   dainty 298
   texture 329
   savory 394
   delicate ear 418
   exact 494
   scruple 603
   ill health 655
   difficult 704
   pleasing 829
   beauty 845
   taste 850
   fastidious 868
   honor 939
   pure 960
delicate (see delicacy)
   color 428
   brittle 328
delicatessen 394
délice 377
delicious *taste* 394
   pleasing 829
delict 947
delictum 947
delight
   pleasure 377, 827
   pleasing 829
Delilah 962

delimit 233
delineate *outline* 230
   represent 554
   describe 594
delineavit 556
delinquency 304, 947
delinquent 949
deliquation 335
deliquesce 36, 335
deliquescent 335, 348
deliquium
   paralysis 158
   fatigue 688
deliriant 663
delirifacient 663
delirious 503, 825
delirium *raving* 503
   passion 825
   –*tremens* 959
delitescence
   invisible 447
   latency 526
   seclusion 893
deliver *transfer* 270
   utter 580, 582
   remedy 662
   rescue 672
   liberate 750
   give 784
   relieve 834
   –*as one's act and deed* 467
   –*a speech* 582
   –*judgment* 480
   –*the goods* 729
deliverance 672
delivery (see deliver)
   bring forth 161
dell 252
Delphic oracle
   prophetic 513
   equivocal 520
   latent 526
Delphinus 490a
delta *triad* 92
   land 342
delude *error* 495
   deceive 545
deluge *crowd* 72
   water 337
   flood 348
   redundance 641
delusion (see delude
   insane 503
   self–*credulous* 486
delve *dig* 252
   till 371
   –*into inquire* 461
demagogue
   director 694
   malcontent 710
   rebel 742
demagogy 737
demand *inquire* 461
   user 677
   order 741

   ask 765
   price 812
   claim 924
   in–*require* 630
   salable 795
   desire 865
   public–677
demarcate 233
demarcation 233
dematerialize 317
demean oneself
   conduct 692
   humble 879
   dishonor 940
demeanor *aid* 448
   conduct 692
   fashion 852
demency 503
dement 61
dementate 503
démenti 536
dementia 503
demerit 945
demesne *abode* 189
   property 780
demi– 91
demigod *hero* 861
   angel 948
   –*Authority* 737
demigration 266
demijohn 191
demi-jour 422
demimondaine 876
demimonde
   plebeian 876
   licentious 962
demirep 962
demise *death* 360
   transfer 783
   lease 787
demisemiquaver 413
demission 756
demitint 421
Demiurge 976
demiurgic 153
demivolt 309
demobilize 750
democracy *rule* 737
   commonalty 876
democratic 737
Democrats 712
Democritus 838
demoiselle 129
demolish 479
demolishment 162
demon *violent* 173
   bane 663
   familiar spirit 979
   devil 980
   –*in human shape* 913, 949
   –*worship* 991
demonetize 800
   wicked 945
demoniacal
   malevolent 907

   furious 824
demonist 978
demonize 978
demonology
   demons 980
   sorcery 992
demonophobia 898
demonry 980
demonstration
   number 85
   proof 478
   manifest 525
   ostentation 882
   ocular–441, 446
demonstrative
   manifest 525
   indicative 550
   vehement 825
demonstrator 524
demoralize
   unnerve 158
   spoil 659
   vicious 945
Demosthenes 582
demulcent *mild* 174
   soothing 662
demur *disbelieve* 485
   dissent 489
   unwilling 603
   hesitate 605
demure *grave* 826
   sad 837
   affected 855
   modest 881
demurrage 133
demurrer 969
den *abode* 189
   study 191
   sty 653
   prison 752
   seclusion 893
   –*of thieves* 791
denary 98
denaturalize
   corrupt 659
denaturalized
   abnormal 83
dendriform 242, 367
dendroid 242
dendrology 369
Deneb 490a
dengue fever 655
denial *negation* 536
   refusal 764
   self–953
denigrate 431
denization 748
denizen
   inhabitant 188
   freeman 748
   –*s of the air* 979
   –*s of the day* 366
denominate 566
denomination
   class 75
   name 564

denominational — design

sect 712
religious—983
denominational
dissent 489
party 712
theological 983
—*education* 537
denominator 84
denotative 550
denote *specify* 79
mean 516
indicate 550
dénouement *end* 67
result 154
disclosure 529
completion 729
denounce *curse* 908
disapprove 932
accuse 938
dense *crowded* 72
close 321
vegetation 365
ignorant 493
density 321
dent *hollow* 252
notch 257
dental 561
dentate 257
denticulated
sharp 253
notched 257
denticulation 257
dentifrice 652
dentiphone 418
dentist 662
dentistry 662
denude 226
denuded *loss* 776
—*of insufficient* 640
denunciation 909
(*see* denounce)
deny *dissent* 489
negative 536
refuse 764
—*oneself avoid* 623
seclude 893
temperate 953
ascetic 990
deobstruct 705
deobstruent 652, 662
deodand 974
deodorant 399
deodorize 399
clean 652
deodorizer 399
deontology 926
deoppilation 705
deorganization 61
deosculation 902
deoxidation 140
deoxidization 140
depart 293—from
differ 15
deviate 279
relinquish 624
—*this life* 360

departed
nonexistent 2
department *class* 75
region 181
business 625
bureau 965
—*store* 799
departmental 737
departure 293
new—66
point of—293
depend *hang* 214
contingent 475
—*on circumstances* 475
—*upon*
be the effect of 154
evidence 467
trust 484
to be—*ed on*
certain 474
reliable 484
honorable 939
dependence 46
dependency
relation 9
property 777, 780
dependent *effect* 154
liable 177
hanging 214
puppet 711
servant 746
subject 749
deperdition 776
dephlegmation 340
dephlegmatory 340
depict 554, 556
describe 594
depiction (*see* depict)
depilation 226
depilatory 662
depilous 226
deplete 638
depletion 640
deplorable *bad* 649
disastrous 735
painful 830
deplore *regret* 833
complain 839
remorse 950
deploy 194
depone 535
deponent 467
depopulate *eject* 297
desert 893
deport 972
deportation
removal 270
emigration 297
deportment 692
depose *evidence* 467
declare 535
dethrone 738, 756
deposit *place* 184
transference 270
precipitate 321

store 636
security 771
payment 809
depositary 801
deposition
see depose, deposit
record 551
depository 636
depot *station* 266
store 636
shop 799
depotentiate 158
deprave *spoil* 659
depraved *bad* 649
vicious 945
depravity 945
depreciation 766
pity 914
disapprove 932
deprecative 881
deprecatory 766, 881
depreciate
disrespect 929
(*see* depreciation)
depreciation
decrease 36
underestimate 483
discount 813
cheap 815
censure 932
detraction 934
accusation 938
depreciator 483
depredation 791
depredator 792
deprehension 789
depress
(*see* depression)
depressing
painful 830
depression
lowness 207
depth 208
concavity 252
dent 257
furrow 259
lowering 308
dejection 837
dullness 843
deprivation 789
deprive *subduct* 38
take 789
—*of life* 361
—*of power* 158
—*of property* 789
—*of strength* 160
deprived of 776
de profundis
lamentation 839
penitence 950
depth *physical* 208
mental 498
—*beyond depth* 104
—*bomb* 208, 727
—*of misery* 828
—*of thought* 451

—*of winter* 383
out of one's—304, 310
depthless 209
depurate *clean* 652
improve 658
depurative 652
depuratory 662
deputation 755
depute 755, 759
deputies, chamber of—696
deputy 759 *police* 664
—*commissioner* 745
dequantitate 36
deracinate 2
derail 142
derange *insane* 503
deranged 503
derangement 61
mental—503
derby *hat* 225
Derby—*day* 720
derelict *ship* 273
land 342
source of danger 667
relinquished 782
outcast 893
dereliction
relinquishment 624, 782
guilt 947
—*of duty* 927
deride *ridicule* 856
disrespect 929
contempt 930
derisive 582, 853
(*see* deride)
derivate 155
derivation
origin 153, 154, 155
verbal 562
derivative 562
derive *attribute* 155
deduce 480
word 562
acquire 775
income 810
derm 223
dermal 223
dermatogen 223
dermatography 223
dermatoid 223
dermatology 223
dermatopathy 223
dermatophyte 223
dermatoplasty 223
dermic 223
dermis 223
dermoid 223
dernier cri 123
derogate
underrate 483
disparage 934
dishonor 940
—*from* 874

derogatory
shame 874
dishonor 940
derrick 307, 633
derring-do 861
dervish 955, 984, 996
descant *precursor* 64
music 415
diffuseness 573
loquacity 584
dissert 595
descend *slope* 217
go down 306
—*to particulars*
special 79
describe 594
descendant 120, 167
descent 69
lineage 166
fall **306**
inheritance 775
describe 594
description *kind* 75
name 564
narration 594
descriptive 594
descry 441
desecrate *misuse* 679
disrespect 929
profane 988
desert
unproductive 169
space 180
empty 187
plain 344
run away 623
relinquish 624
retaliation 718
divorce 782
merit 924, 944
deserted *outcast* 893
deserter 607, 623
desertion (*see* desert)
desertless 945
deserve
be entitled to 924
merit 944
—*belief* 484
—*notice* 642
deserving 924
déshabille
(*see* dishabille)
desiccate 340
desiccator 340
desiderate *need* 630
desire 865
desideratum
inquiry 461
requirement 630
desire 865
design *prototype* 22
composition 54
delineation 554
painting 556
intention 620
plan 626

424

designate *specify* 79
  call 564
  express 566
designation *kind* 75
designed
  aforethought 611
designer 559, 626
designing
  cunning 702
designless 621
desinence *end* 67
  discontinuance 142
desirability 646
desirable 646
desire 865 *will* 600
  have no–*for* 866
desirous *ready* 602
  desiring 865
desist *discontinue* 142
  relinquish 624
  inaction 681
desk *box* 91
  support 215
  school 542
  pulpit 1000
  the–996
désobligeant
  carriage 272
desolate *alone* 87
  ravage 162
  afflicted 828
  dejected 837
  secluded 893
desolating
  painful 830
desolation
  (*see* desolate)
despair *grief* 828
  hopeless 859
despatch
  (*see* dispatch)
despect 930
desperado *rash* 863
  blusterer 887
  evil doer 913
desperate *great* **31**
  violent 173
  impossible 471
  resolved 604
  difficult 704
  excitable 825
  hopeless 859
  rash 863
  anger 900
despicable
  trifling 643
  shameful 874
  contemptible 930
despise 930
  –*danger* 861
despite 30, 907
  in–708
despoil *injure* 659
  take 789
  rob 791
despond *dejected* 837

fear 860
despot 745
despotism
  authority 737
  severity 739
  arbitrary 964
despumate 652
desquamate 226
desquamation 223, 226
dess 204
dessert 298
destination *end* 67
  arrival 292
  intention 620
destine 620
destiny *chance* 152
  fate 601
  fight against–606
destitute
  insufficient 640
  poor 804
  refuge for–666
desto 415
destrier 726
destroy *demolish* 162
  injure 659
  –*hopes* 859
  –*life* 361
destroyed
  (*see* destroy)
  inexistent 2
  failure 732
destroyer 165
  naval 726
  evil doer 913
destruction
  (*see* destroy)
destructive *bad* 649
  mutually–361
destructor 165
desuetude 614
  disuse 678
desultory
  disordered 59
  fitful 70
  multiform 81
  irregular in time 139
  changeable 149
  deviating 279
  agitated 315
  discursive 595
desume 788
detach 44
detached
  irrelated 10
  loose 47
detachment *part* 51
  army 726
detail *item* 79
  describe 594
  allot 786
  ornament 847
  attention to–457, 459
  in–51

detailed
  circumstantial 8
details *minutiae* 32
  unimportant 643
detain 781
detect 480a
detective 527, 664
detent 45
detention 781
  –*camp* 751
  house of–752
  in house of–938
deter *dissuade* 616
  alarm 860
deterge *clean* 652
detergent 652, 662
deteriorate 659
deterioration 659
determinable 278
determinate
  special 79
  exact 474
  conclusive 480
  intended 620
determinative 67
determine *end* 67
  define 79
  cause 153
  direction 278
  satisfy 462
  make sure 474
  judge 480
  discover 480a
  resolve 604
determined
  resolute 604
deterration 529
detersion 652
detersive 662
detest *dislike* 876
  hate 898
detestable 649
dethronement
  anarchy 738
  abrogation 756
detonate *explode* 173
  sound 406
detonation 404, 406, 872
detortion *form* 243
  meaning 523
detour *curve* 245
  circuit 629
detract *subduct* 38
  underrate 483
  defame 934
  slander 938
detraction 934
detractor 936
detrain 292
detriment *evil* 619
  deterioration 659
detrimental 649
detrital 330
detrition 330
detritus *fragments* 51

transference 270
powder 330
detrude *cast out* 297
  cut down 308
detruncate 38
detrusion
  (*see* detrude)
detrusive 308
deuce *two* 89
  devil 978
  –*is in him* 608
  play the–825
deuced *great* 31
  painful 830
deux ex machina
  aid 707
  auxiliary 711
deuterogamy 903
deva 979
Devanagari 590
devastate *destroy* 162
  havoc 659
  depopulate 893
devastation 162
develop *increase* 35
  produce 161
  expand 194
  evolve 313
development 194
devexity *bending* 217
  curvature 245
deviate *vary* 20a
  change 140
  turn 279
  diverge 291
  circuit 629
  –*from* 15
  –*from rectitude* 940
  –*from virtue* 945
deviation 279
deviatory 311
device *motto* 550
  expedient 626
  artifice 702
devil
  seasoned food 392
  evil doer 913
  bad man 949
  Satan 978
  demon 980
  –*in one*
  headstrong 863
  temper 901
  –*may care rash* 863
  indifferent 866
  insolent 885
  –*'s tattoo* 407
  –*take* 908
  –*take the hindmost
  run away* 623
  haste 684
  cowardice 862
  –*to pay disorder* 59
  violence 173
  evil 619
  failure 732

penalty 974
  –*worship* 978
  fight like –s 722
  give the–*his due
  right* 922
  vindicate 937
  fair 939
  have a–503
  machinations of the
  –619
  play the–*with
  injure* 659
  malevolent 907
  printer's–591
devil–dog 269
devilish *great* 31
  bad 649
  malevolent 907
  vicious 945
devious *curved* 245
  deviating 279
  circuitous 311
devisable 270
devise *imagine* 515
  plan 626
  bequeath 784
  –*d by the enemy* 546
devisee
  transference 270
  possess 779
  receive 785
deviser 164
devitalize 158
devoid *absent* 187
  empty 640
  not having 777a
devoir *courtesy* 894
  respect 928
devolution 659, 783
devolve 783–*on* 926
Devonian Period
  490c
Devonshire cream
  321
devote *destine* 601
  employ 677
  consecrate 873
  –*oneself to* 604
  –*the mind to* 457
  –*to destruction* 908
devoted *habit* 613
  ill–fated 735
  obedient 743
  undone 828
  love 897
devotee *zealot* 682
  sports 840
  aspirant 865
  pious 987
  fanatic 988
devotion
  (*see* devotee, devoted) *love* 897
  piety 987
  worship 990
  self–942

devour

devour *destroy* 162
  eat 298
  gluttony 957
devoured by
  feeling 821
devouring element
  382
devout 987, 990
devoutless 989
devoutly 821
dew 339
Dewali 138
dewan 745
dewy 339 –eve 126
dexter 238
dexterous 238, 698
dextrality 238
dextrorsal 238
dey 745
dhobi 652
dhoti 225
dhow 273
dhu 431
diablerie 992
diabolic *bad* 649
  malevolent 907
  wicked 945
  satanic 978
diabolist 978
diabolology 978
diacaustic 245
diaconicum 1000
diacoustics 402
diacritical 15, 550
diadem 747, 847
diaeresis 49, 550
diagnosis 465, 522, 655
diagnostic
  distinguishable 15
  special 79
  experiment 463
  discriminative 465
  indication 550
  (*intrinsic* 5)
diagnostics 655
diagonal 217
diagram 554
dial 114 *measure* 466
  as the–to the sun
  veracious 543
  faithful 772
dialect 563
dialectic
  argument 476
  language 56
dialogism 586
dialogue 588, 599
diameter 202
diametrical 237
  –ly opposite
  contrariety 14
  contraposition 237
diamond *lozenge* 244
  goodness 648
  ornament 847

 –cut diamond
  cunning 702
  retaliation 718
  –wedding 883
  rough –703
Diana *moon* 318
  chaste 960
diapason 413
diaper 847
diaphanous 425
diaphonics 402
diaphoresis 299
diaphragm *middle* 68
  partition 228
diaporesis 475
diarrhea 290
diary *journal* 114
  record 551
diaskenast 593
diastase 320
diastatic 320
diaster 161
diastole 194
diatessaron 413
diathermancy 384
diathermic 384
diathesis *nature* 5
  state 7
  temperament 820
diatom 193
diatomic 193
diatonic 413
diatribe 932
dib 550
dibasic acid 490a
dibble *perforator* 262
  till 371
dibs 800
dicacity 885
dice *chance* 156, 621
  on the–470
dicer 621, 840
dichotomy *bisect* 91
  angle 244
dichroic 443
dichroism 440
dickens 978
dicker *ten* 98
  haggle 794
dictagraph 418
dictate *write* 590
  enjoin 615
  advise 695
  authority 737
  command 741
dictator 745
dictatorial
  certain 474
  narrow 481
  willful 600
  insolent 885
dictatorship 737, 739
diction 569
dictionary *list* 542
  words 562
  book 593

 store 636
dictophone 418
dictum *maxim* 496
  affirmation 535
  command 741
didactic 537
didder 383
diddle 545
dido 309
diduction 44
die *mould* 22
  expire 360
  burn out 385
  engraving 558
  –and make no sign 951
  –a violent death 361
  –away *dissolve* 4
  decrease 36
  cease 142
  –for *desire* 865
  endearment 902
  –for one's country 360
  –from the memory 536
  –game 951
  –hard *obstinate* 606
  resist 719
  –in harness
  continue 143
  persevere 604a
  –in one's shoes 972
  –in the last ditch 604a
  –of a rose in
  aromatic pain 822
  –out *pass away* 2
  vanish 4
  –with ennui 841
  –with laughter 838
  hazard of the–621
  never say–604a
  not willingly let–670
  the–is cast 601
dieresis 49, 550
dies –faustus 731
  –infaustus 732
  –irae 919, 982
  –non never 107
  rest 687
diet *food* 298
  remedy 662
  council 696
  spare –956
dietetics 662
differ 15 *discord* 713
  –in opinion 489
  –toto coelo
  contrary 14
  dissimilar 18
difference 15
  (see *differ*)
  numerical 84
  –engine 85

 perception of –465
 split the –774
different 15
  multiform 81
  –time 119
differentia 15
differential
  differing 15
  number 84
  gear 272
  –calculus 85
  –thermometer 389
differentiate 79
differentiation
  calculation 85
  discrimination 465
differentiative 15
difficult 704
  –to please 868
difficulties
  poverty 804
  in–806
difficulty 704
  question 461
diffide 485
diffident *fearful* 860
  modest 881
diffluent 348
diffuse *mix* 41
  disperse 73
  publish 531
  style 573
  (*permeate* 186)
diffuseness 104, **573**
diffusion 73, 372a, 490a
diffusive *dispersed* 73
  verbose 573
dig *deepen* 208
  excavate 252
  till 371
  –in intrench 664
  –the foundations 673
  –up 480a
  –up the tomahawk 722
digamy 903
digenesis 161
digest *arrange* 60
  boil 384
  think 451
  dissertation 595
  compendium 596
  plan 626
  improve 658
  prepare 673
  brook 826
digestible 662
digestion 673
digestive 662
diggings 189
dight *dress* 225
  ornament 847
digit 84 *morsel* 32
digitated 253
digladiation 720

 diglot 560
dignified 31
dignify 873
dignitary *clergy* 996
dignity *greatness* 31
  glory 873
  pride 878
  honor 939
digraph 561
digress *deviate* 279
  style 573
digression *circuit* 629
digressive 595
dijudication 480
dike *gap* 198
  fence 232
  furrow 259
  gulf 343
  conduit 350
  defense 717
dilaceration 44
dilapidation 659
dilation (see *dilate*)
dilate *increase* 35
  swell 194
  widen 202
  rarefy 322
  expatiate 573
dilation 194
dilatory *slow* 275
  inactive 683
dilection 897
dilemma *state* 7
  uncertain 475
  logic 476
  choice 609
  difficulty 704
dilettante
  connoisseur 492
  dabbler 823
  taste 850
dilettantism
  knowledge 490
  taste 850
diligence *coach* 272
diligent *active* 682
  –thought 457
dilly–dally
  irresolution 605
  inactivity **683**
dilogy 104
dilucidation 522
diluent 335
dilute *weaken* 160
  water 337
diluvian 124
dim *dark* 421
  faint 422
  invisible 447
  unintelligible 519
  –eyed 443
dime 800 –novel 594
dimension 192
dimidiate 91
diminish *lessen* 36
  reduce 103

diminish

diminuendo   **disconnected**

    contract 195
    —the number 103
diminuendo
    music 415
diminution 36, 195
diminutive *degree* 32
    size 193
dimity 635
dimness 422
dimple *concavity* 252
    notch 257
dim-sightedness 443
    unwise 499
din 404—*in the ear*
    repeat 104
    drum 407
    loquacity 584
    —of arms 716
dine 298
    —with Duke
      Humphrey 956
dingdong 407
dinghy 273
dingle 252 *door* 232
dingy *dark* 421, 422
    colorless 429
    black 431
    gray 432
dining room 191
dinner 298
    —jacket 225
dint *power* 157
    concavity 252
    blow 276
    by—of
      instrumentality 631
diocesan 996
diocese 181, 995
Diogenes
    recluse 893
    cynic 911
    lantern of—
      inquiry 461
Dionaea 545
dioptrics 420
diorama *view* 448
    painting 556
diorism 465
dip *slope* 217
    concavity 252
    load 270
    direction 278
    insert 300
    descent 306
    depression 308
    plunge 310
    water 337
    baptize 998
    —into *glance at* 457
    inquire 461
    learn 539
    —one's hands into
      take 789
diphthong 561
diphyletic 89, 167
diploma *evidence* 467

    commission 755
diplomacy
    artfulness 702
    mediation 724
    negotiation 769
diplomatic
    (see diplomacy)
    —agent 758
diplomatist
    messenger 534
    consignee 758
dipper 191
Dipper 318
dipsomania
    insanity 503
    desire 865
    drunkenness 959
dipsomaniac 504
diptych *list* 86
    record 551
dire *hateful* 649
    disastrous 735
    grievous 830
    fearful 860
direct *straight* 246
    teach 537
    artless 703
    command 741
    —attention to 457
    —one's course
      motion 278
      pursuit 622
    —the eyes to 441
directable 278
direction (see direct)
    tendency 278
    indication 550
    management 693
    precept 697
directive 692
directly *soon* 132
director *teacher* 540
    college 542
    manager **694**
    master 745
directorship 737
directory *list* 86
    council 696
diremption 44
direption 791
dirge *funeral* 363
    song 415
    lament 839
dirigible
    balloon 273, 726
    direction 278
dirk 727
dirt 653—*cheap* 815
    throw—*defame* 874
    disrespect 929
dirtiness (see dirty)
dirty *dim* 222
    opaque 426
    unclean 653
    disreputable 874
    dishonorable 940

    —end of stick 699
    —sky 353
    —weather 349
    do—work *servile* 886
    flatterer 935
diruption 162
disability
    impotence 158
disable 158
    weaken 160
disabled 158
disabuse *inform* 527
    disclose 529
disaccord 713
    —with 15
disadvantage
    evil 619
    inexperience 647
    at a—34
    lie under a—651
disadvantageous
    disastrous 619
    inexpedient 647
    bad 649
disaffection
    dissent 489
    enmity 889
    hate 898
disaffirm 536
disagree
    (see disagreement)
disagreeable
    unpleasing 830
    dislike 867
disagreement
    difference 15
    incongruity 24
    dissent 489
    discord 713
disallow 761
disannul 756
disappear 449
disappearance 449
disappointment
    balk **509**
    fail 732
    discontent 832
disapprobation
    hindrance 706
    refusal 764
    disapproval 932
disapprove 932
disapprover 936
disarm *disable* 158
    weaken 160
    reconcile 831
    propitiate 914
disarrange 61
disarray *disorder* 59
    undress 226
disaster *killing* 361
    evil 619
    failure 732
    adversity 735
    calamity 830
disastrous *bad* 649

disavow 536
disband *separate* 44
    disperse 73
    liberate 750
disbar *abrogate* 756
    disapprove 932
    punish 968, 972
disbelief 485
    religious 989
disbelieve 485, 989
disbench
    abrogate 756
    disbar 968
    punish 972
disbowel 297
disbranch 44
disburden
    facilitate 705
    —oneself of 782
    —one's mind 529
disburse 809
disc *surface* 220
    front 234
discard *eject* 297
    relinquish 624
    disuse 678
    abrogate 756
    refuse 764
    repudiate 773
    surrender 782
    —from one's thoughts 458
discarded 495
discarnate 317
disceptation 476
discern *see* 441
    know 490
discernible 446
discerning 498
discernment 498, 868
discerptible 51
discerption 44
discharge
    violence 173
    propel 284
    emit 297
    excrete 299
    sound 406
    acquit oneself 692
    complete 729
    liberate 750
    abrogate 756
    pay 807
    exempt 927a
    acquit 970
    —a duty 926, 944
    —a function
      business 625
      utility 644
    —an obligation 772
    —from the memory 506
    —from the mind 458
    —itself *egress* 295
    river 348

discind 44
disciple *pupil* 541
    Christian 985
disciplinarian
    master 540
    martinet 739
discipline *order* 58
    follower 65
    teaching 537
    training 673
    restraint 751
    punishment 972
    religious 990
disclaim *deny* 536
    repudiate 756
    objure 757
    refuse 764
disclaimer 536
disclamation
    (see disclaim)
disclose 529
disclosure 529
    discovery 480a
discoid *broad* 202
    layer 204
    frontal 220
    flat 251
discoloration 429
discolored
    shabby 659
    ugly 846
    blemish 848
discomfit 731
discomfiture 732
discomfort
    physical 378
    mental 828
discommend 932
discommode
    hinder 706
discommodious
    useless 645
    inexpedient 647
discompose
    derange 61
    put out 458
    hinder 706
    pain 830
    disconcert 874
    anger 900
discomposure 828
disconcert *derange* 61
    distract 458
    disappoint 509
    hinder 706
    discontent 832
    confuse 874
disconcerted
    hopeless 859
    (*failure* 732)
disconformity 83
discongruity 15, 24
disconnect 44, 70
disconnected
    divided 51
    feeble 575

427

disconnection
  irrelation 19
  disjunction 44
  discontinuity 70
disconsolate 837
discontent 832
discontinuance
  cessation 142
  relinquishment 624
discontinuity 70
discontinuous 70
discord
  disagreement 24
  of sound 414
  of color 428
  dissension 713
discordance
  (see discord)
discount *decrease* 36
  decrement 40a
  money 813
  at a–disrepute 874
  disapproved 932
discountenance
  disfavor 706
  refuse 764
discourage
  dissuade 616
  sadden 837
  frighten 860
  (*disfavor* 706)
discourse *teach* 537
  speech 582
  talk 588
  dissert 595
  sermon 998
discourtesy 895
discouse 202
discover *perceive* 441
  solve 462
  find 480a
  disclose 529
  –*itself be seen* 446
discovery 480a
discredit *disbelief* 485
  dishonor 874
discreditable
  vicious 945
discreet *careful* 459
  cautious 864
  (*clever* 698)
discrepancy 20a, 471
discrepant
  differing 15
  disagreeing 24
  discordant 713
discrepate 15
discrete *separate* 44
  disjunctive 70
  single 87
discretion *will* 600
  choice 609
  skill 698
  caution 864
  surrender at– 725
  years of– 131

discriminate
  (see discrimination)
discrimination
  difference 15
  nice perception 465
  wisdom 498
  taste 850
  fastidiousness 868
disculpate 937
discumbency 213
discursion 266
discursive
  moving 264
  migratory 266
  wandering 279
  –*faculties* 450
  argumentative 476
  diffuse style 573
  conversable 588
  disserting 595
discus 840
discuss *eat* 298
  reflect 451
  inquire 461
  reason 476
  dissert 595
discussion
  (see discuss)
  open to– 475
  under– 461
discutient 73
disdain
  indifference 866
  fastidious 868
  pride 878
  insolence 885
  contempt 930
disdainful
  (see disdain)
  disrespectful 929
disease 655
diseased 655
  –*mind* 503
disembark 292, 342
disembarrass 705
disembodied 317
disembody
  decompose 49
  disperse 73
  spiritualize 317
disembogue *emit* 295
  eject 297
  flow out 348
disembowel 297, 301, 361
disembroil 60
disenable 158
disenchant
  discover 480a
  dissuade 616
  displease 830
disencumber 705
disendow 756
disengage *detach* 44
  facilitate 705
  liberate 750

disengaged *to let* 763
disentangle
  separate 44
  arrange 60
  unroll 313
  decipher 522
  facilitate 705
  liberate 750
disenthrall 750
disenthrone 756
disentitle 925
disespouse 905
disestablish
  displace 185
  abrogate 756
disesteem
  disrespect 929
  censure 932
disfavor *oppose* 708
  hate 898
  disrespect 929
  view with– 932
disfigure *deface* 241
  injure 659
  deform 846
  blemish 848
disfranchise 925
disfurnish 226
disgorge *emit* 297
  flow out 348
  restore 790
  pay 807
disgrace *shame* 874
  dishonor 940
  sense of– 879
disgraceful *vice* 945
disgruntle 509
disgruntled 509
disguise *conceal* 528
  mask 530
  falsify 544
  untruth 546
disguised
  (see disguise)
  –*in drink* 959
disgust *taste* 395
  offensive 830
  weary 841
  dislike 867
  hatred 898
  –*of life* 837
disgusting
  (see disgust)
dish *destroy* 162
  plate 191
  scoop out 252
  food 298
  –*of tea* 892
dishabille
  undress 225
  unprepared 674
dishearten
  dissuade 616
  pain 830
  discontent 832
  deject 837

dished 732
disherison 789
dishevel *loose* 47
  disorder 61
  disperse 73
  intermix 219
dishevelment 59
  (see *dishevel*)
dishing 252
dishonest *false* 544
  base 940
dishonor
  disrepute 874
  disrespect 929
  baseness 940
  –*bills* 808
dishwater 653
disillusion 509
disinclination 867
disincline
  dissuade 616
  dislike 867
disinclined 603
disinfect *purify* 652
  restore 660
disinfectant 388, 662
disingenuous
  false 544
  dishonorable 940
disinherit 782, 783, 789
disinheritance 789
disintegrate
  separate 44
  decompose 49
  pulverize 330
disintegration 49
disinter *exhume* 363
  discover 480a
disinterested 942
disinvigorate 158
disjoin 44
disjointed *disorder* 59
  powerless 158
  feeble 575
disjointure 44
disjunction 44
disjunctive 70
disk (see *disc*)
diskindness 907
dislike 867
  reluctance 603
  hate 898
dislimb 44
dislocate *separate* 44
  put out of joint 61
dislocated *disorder* 59
  dislodge
  displace 185
  eject 297
disloyal 940
dismal *depressing* 830
  dejected 837
  –*universal hiss* 930
dismantle *destroy* 162
  divest 226

dismask 529
dismast
  render useless 645
  injure 659
  disuse 678
dismay 860
dismember
  separate 44
  disperse 73
  execute 972
dismemberment 972
dismiss *discard* 678
  liberate 750
  abrogate 756
  relinquish 782
  punish 972
  –*from the mind* 452, 458
dismount *arrive* 292
  descend 306
  render useless 645
disniche 185
disobedience 742
  nonobservance 773
disoblige 907
disomatous 90
disorder *confusion* 59
  derange 61
  turbulent 173
  disease 655
  –*ed intellect* 503
disorderly
  unprincipled 945
disorganize
  derange 61
  destroy 162
  spoil 659
disorganized 59
disorientation 279
disown 536
disowned 782
dispansion 194
disparage
  underrate 483
  disrespect 929
  dispraise 932
  detract 934
disparagement 908
disparate 15
disparity *different* 15
  dissimilar 18
  disagreeing 24
  unequal 28
  isolated 44
dispart 44
dispassionate 826
  –*opinion* 484
dispatch *eject* 297
  eat 298
  kill 361
  message 527
  news 532
  epistle 592

428

dispel

expedition 682
haste 684
conduct 692
complete 729
command 741
—food 298
happy—972
dispel *scatter* 73
destroy 162
displace 185
repel 289
dispensable
useless 645
dispensary 662
dispensation
(see dispense)
command 741
license 760
relinquishment 782
exemption 927a
—s of Providence 976
dispense *disperse* 73
give 784
apportion 786
retail 796
—with *disuse* 678
permit 760
exempt 927a
dispeople *eject* 297
expatriate 893
dispermy 89
disperse *separate* 44
scatter 73
diverge 291
waste 638
dispersion 73
chromatic—428
—of light 420
dispersive 73
dispirit
discourage 616
sadden 837
displace *derange* 61
remove 185
displacement
derange 61
remove 185
transfer 270
displacency
dislike 867
incivility 895
disapprobation 932
displant 185
display *appear* 448
show 525
parade 882
displease 830
displeasure 828
anger 900
displosion 173
displume 789
disport 840
disposal (see dispose)
at one's—777
dispose *arrange* 60
tend 176

induce 615
—of *use* 677
complete 729
relinquish 782
give 784
sell 796
disposed *minded* 620
—to doubt 487
disposition
temperament 5
order 58
arrangement 60
inclination 602
mind 820
dispossess
transfer 783
take away 789
—oneself of 782
dispraise 932
dispread 73
disprize 483
disproof
counter evidence 468
confutation 479
disproportion
irrelation 10
disagreement 24
disprove 479
disputable
uncertain 475
doubt 485
disputant
(see dispute)
opponent 710
combatant 726
disputatious
(see dispute)
irritable 901
dispute *disagree* 24
discuss 476
doubt 485
deny 536
discord 713
in—461
disqualification
incapacitate 158
useless 645
unprepared 674
unskillful 699
disentitle 925
disqualify
(see disqualification)
disquiet
changeable 149
agitation 315
excitement 825
uneasiness 828
give pain 830
disquietude
apprehension 860
disquiparant 10, 28
disquisit on 537, 595
disregard
overlook 458
neglect 460
make light of 483

insensible to 823, 826
disrespect 929
contempt 930
—of time 115
disrelated 10
disrelish *dislike* 867
hate 889
disreputable 874
vicious 945
disrepute 874, 929
disrespect 929
despise 930
disrespectful 929
disrobe 226
disruption
disjunction 44
destruction 162
discord 713
dissatisfaction
sorrow 828
discontent 832
dissatisfied 832
make—509
dissect
anatomize 44, 49
investigate 461
disseize 789
dissemblance 18
dissemble 544, 988
dissembler 548
disseminate
scatter 73
pervade 186
publish 531
teach 537
dissemination
(see disseminate)
preparation 673
dissension 713
sow—898
dissent *disagree* 489
refuse 764
heterodoxy 984
dissenter 489
dissentient 24, 489
dissenting 487, 489
dissentious 24
dissepiment 228
dissertation 595
disserve 619
disservice
disadvantage 619
useless 645
disserviceable
bad 649
disastrous 619
dissever 44
discontinue 70
dissidence
disagreement 24
dissent 489
discord 713
discontent 832
heterodoxy 984
dissilience 173

dissimilarity 16a, **18**
dissimilitude, 15, 16 a 24
dissimulate 544
dissipate *scatter* 73
destroy 162
pleasure 377
prodigality 818
amusement 840
intemperance 954
dissolute 961
dissipated 961
dissipative 73
dissociability 893
dissocial 893
dissociate 44
dissociation
irrelation 10
separation 44
dissogeny 161
dissoluble 51, 335
dissolute
profligate 945
intemperate 954
dissolute 961
dissolution
(see dissolve)
decomposition 49
end 67
destruction 162
death 360
dissolvable 51, 335
dissolve *vanish* 2, 4
liquefy 335
disappear 449
abrogate 756
dissolvent 335
dissolving views 448, 449
dissonance
disagreement 24
unmusical 414
discord 713
dissonant 15, 713
dissuade 616
dissuasion 616
dissuitable 24
dissyllable 561
distain *dirty* 653
ugly 846
distal 196
distance 196
overtake 282
go beyond 303
defeat 731
angular—244
—of time
long time 110
past 122
keep at a—
discourtesy 895
keep one's—
avoid 623
modest 881
respect 928
teach one his—879

distraction

distant 196
distaste 867
distasteful 830
distemper *color* 428
painting 556
disease 655
distend 194
distended 192
distich 89, 597
distichous 91
distill *come out* 295
extract 301
evaporate 336
drop 348
distillate 490d
distillation 336
distinct *disjoined* 44
audible 402
visible 446
intelligible 518
manifest 525
express 535
articulate 580
distinction
difference 15
greatness 31
discrimination 465
elegance 578
fame 873
rank 875
—without a difference 27
lacking —465a
distinctive
different 15
savory 394
—feature 79
distingué *fashion* 852
repute 873
distinguisn
perceive 441
discriminate 465
—by the name of 564
distinguishable 15
distinguished
superior 33
repute 873
distinguishing 15
distort (see distortion)
distortion
obliquity 217
twist **243**
of vision 443
misinterpret 523
falsehood 544
misrepresent 555
ugly 846
(misjudge 481)
distract 458
distracted
confused 475
insane 503
excited 824
distraction
passion 825
love to—897

429

distrain *take* 789
  appraise 812
  attach 969
distrait 458
distraught 475, 503
distress *distraint* 789
  poverty 804
  affliction 828
  cause pain 830
  signal of–669
distribute *arrange* 60
  disperse 73
  type 591
  allot 786
distribution
  (see distribute)
distributor
  electrical 272
district
  to partition 44
  area 181
  –*court* 966
distrust *disbelief* 485
  fear 860
distrustful 487
disturb *derange* 61
  change 140
  displace 185
  agitate 315
  excite 824
  distress 828, 830
disturbance
  disorder 59
disunion
  disagreement 24
  separation 44
  disorder 59
  discord 713
disunite *separate* 44
  break with 713
disunity 24
disuse *desuetude* 614
  relinquish 624
  unemploy **678**
disused 124, 678
disvaluation 932
disvalue 932
ditch *inclosure* 232
  hollow 252
  trench 259
  water 343
  conduit 350
  defense 717
ditch water 653
ditheism 984
dithyramb *poetry* 597
dithyrambic
  wild 503
ditto *identity* 13
  repetition 104
  say–*to* 488
ditty 415–*bag* 191
diurnal 138
diuturnal 110
diuturnity 110
divagate 279

divan *sofa* 215
  council 696
  throne 747
  tribunal 966
divaricate *differ* 15
  bifurcate 91
  fork 244
  diverge 291
divarication 16a
dive *resort* 189
  swim 267
  plunge 310
  –*into inquire* 461
divellicate 44
diverge
  (see divergence)
divergence
  nonuniformity 16a
  difference 15
  dissimilarity 18
  variation 20a
  disagreement 24
  deviation 279
  separation 291
divers *different* 15
  multiform 81
  many 102
  –*colored* 440
diverse 15
diversiform 81
diversify
  (see diversity)
  vary 20a
  change 140
diversion *change* 140
  deviation 279
  pleasure 377
  amusement 840
diversity *difference* 15
  irregular 16a
  dissimilar 18
  multiform 81
  –*of opinion* 489
divert *turn* 279
  deceive 545
  amuse 840
  –*the mind* 452, 458
divertissement
  drama 599
  amusement 840
Dives 803
divest *denude* 226
  take 789
  –*oneself of*
    abrogate 756
    relinquish 782
divestment 226
divide *separate* 44
  part 51
  arrange 60
  arithmetic 85
  bisect 91
  measure 466
  vote 609
  apportion 786
dividend *part* 51

  number 84
  portion 786
dividers 466
divination
  prediction 511
  sorcery 992
divine *predict* 511
  guess 514
  perfect 650
  of God 976, 983, 983a
  clergyman 996
  –*right authority* 737
  due 924
  –*service* 990
diviner 994
diving 267–*bird* 310
divining rod *sign* 550
  magic 993
Divinity *God* 976
  theology 983
divisible (see divide)
  number 84
division (see divide)
  part 51
  class 75
  arithmetic 85
  school 542
  election 609
  discord 713
  military 726
divisor 84
divorce *separation* 44
  relinquish 782
  matrimonial **905**
Divorce Court 966
divorcée 905
divulge 529
divulsion 44
diwan 745
dixi 535
Dixie's land 827
dizen 225, 847
dizzard 501
dizziness (see dizzy)
dizzy *dim–sighted* 443
  confused 458
  vertigo 503
  –*height* 206
  –*round* 312
do *fare* 7
  suit 23
  produce 161
  cheat 545
  act 680
  complete 729
  succeed 731
  I beg 765
  all one can–686
  –*as done by* 906, 942
  –*a service useful* 644
  aid 707
  –*as one pleases* 748
  –*as others do* 82
  –*away with*
    destroy 162

    eject 297
    abrogate 756
  –*battle* 722
  –*business* 625
  –*for destroy* 162
    kill 261
    conquer 731
    punish 972
  –*good* 906
  –*harm* 907
  –*honor* 873
  –*into translate* 522
  –*justice to* 595
  –*like* 19
  –*little* 683
  –*no harm* 648
  –*nothing* 681
  –*nothing but* 136
  –*one's bidding* 743
  –*one's office* 772
  –*over* 223
  –*tell* 508
  –*the work* 686
  –*up* 660
  –*without* 678
  –*wrong* 923
  have to–*with* 680, 692
  plenty to–682
  thing to–625
doch–an–dorrach 959
docile *of horses* 370
  learning 539
  willing 602
docimastic 463
docimasy 463
dock *diminish* 36
  cut off 38
  port 189
  shorten 201
  store 636
  tribunal 966
  –*walloper* 269
docked
  incomplete 53
docket *list* 69, 86
  evidence 467
  note 550
  record 551
  schedule 611
  security 771
  on the–454
dockyard 691
doctor
  learned man 492
  prevaricate 544
  improve 658
  restore 660
  remedy 662
  after death the–135
  –*accounts* 811
  when–*s disagree* 475
doctorate 873
doctorship 873

doctrinaire
  positive 474
  pedant 492
  theorist 514
  affectation 855
  blusterer 887
doctrinal 537
doctrine *tenet* 484
  knowledge 490
document 551
documentary 467
  –*evidence* 467
dodder 160
dodecahedron 244
dodge *follow* 63
  change 140
  shift 264
  deviate 279
  oscillate 314
  pursue 461
  avoid 623
  stratagem 702
  (*deceive* 545)
doe *swift* 274
  deer 366
  female 374
doer *originator* 164
  agent 690
doff 226–*the cap* 894
dog *follow* 63, 281
  animal 366
  male 373
  pursue 622
  wretch 949
  cast to the–*s*
    destroy 162
    reject 610
    disuse 678
    abrogate 756
    relinquish 782
  –*in manager* 943
  –*in office* 737
  –*s of war* 722
  go to the–*s*
    destruction 162
    fail 732
    adversity 735
    poverty 804
  hair of–*that bit you* 959
dogcart 272
dog–cheap 815
dog days 382
doge 745
dogged *obstinate* 606
  valor 861
  sullen 901a
doggedness 606
  (see dogged)
dogger 273
doggerel *verse* 597
  ridiculous 851, 853
doggish 895
doghole 189
dog Latin 563
dogma *tenet* 484

dogmatic   **down**

    theology 983
dogmatic *certain* 474
    positive 481
    assertion 535
    obstinate 606
dogmatism
    (*see* dogmatic)
dogmatist 887
dogmatization 474
dog's age 110
dog's-ear 258
dogsick 867
dog star 423
dogtrot 275
dog-weary 688
doily 852
doing up and—682
    what one is—625
doings *events* 151
    actions 680
    conduct 692
doit *trifle* 643
    coin 800
dokhma 363
dolce far niente 681
doldrums
    dejection 837
    sulks 901a
dole *mite* 32
    scant 640
    give 784
    allot 786
    parsimony 819
    grief 828
doleful 837
doll *small* 193
    image 554
dollar 800—mark 550
dollish 129
dolor *physical* 378
    moral 828
dolorous 830
dolphin 341
dolt 501
doltish 499
domain *class* 75
    region 181
    property 780
dome *high* 206
    covering 223
    convex 250
Domesday book
    list 86
    record 551
domesman 967
domestic
    inhabitant 188
    home 189
    interior 221
    servant 746
    secluded 893
    —animals 366
domesticate
    locate 184
    acclimatize 613
    —animals 370

domesticize 370
domicile 189
domiciled
    inhabitating 186
domiciliary 188
    —visit 461
dominant
    influence 175
    note in music 413
dominate
    influence 175
    rule 737
domination 175, 737, 939
domineer
    tyrannize 739
    insolence 885
Dominican 996
Dominie 540
dominion 181, 737
    —rule 737
domino *dress* 225
    mask 530
    concealment 528
    game 840
don *put on* 225
    man 373
    scholar 492
    tutor 540
    noble 875
Do-na 875
donate 784
donation
    compensation 30
    gift 784
    —party 840
donative 784
done *finished* 729
    —for *impotent* 158
    spoilt 659
    failure 732
    —up *impotent* 158
    tired 688
    have—with *cease* 142
    relinquish 624
    disuse 678
    work—729
donee 270, 785
donga 252
donjon *defense* 717
    prison 752
donkey *ass* 271
    fool 501
Donna 374
Donnybrook
    disorder 59
    discord 713
donor 784
donship 875, 877
donzel 746
doodle 501 *music* 416
doodlesack 410, 417
dooly 272
doom *end* 67
    fate 152
    destruction 162

death 360
    judgment 480
    necessity 601
    assess 812
    sentence 971
    —sealed *death* 360
    adversity 735
doomage 812, 974
doomed 735, 828
doomsday *end* 67
    future 121
    till—112
door *entrance* 66
    cover 223
    brink 231
    barrier 232
    opening 260
    passage 627
    at one's—197
    beg from door to—765
    close the—upon 751
    death's—360
    keep within—s 265
    lie at one's—926
    open a—to
    liable 177
    open the—to
    receive 296
    facilitate 705
    permit 760
    show the—to
    eject 297
    discourtesy 895
    (*prohibit* 761)
doorkeeper 263
doormat 652
doorway 260
dope 465, 662
Doppler effect 490d
Dorado, El 803
dormancy 172
dormant *inert* 172
    latent 526
    asleep 683
dormer 260
dormeuse 272
dormitive 841
dormitory 191
dormouse 683
dorp 189
dorsal 235
dorser 191
dorsigerous 215
dorsum *back* 235
    hump 250
dory 273
dose *quantity* 25
    part 51
    medicine 662
    apportion 786
dosser 191
dossil *cover* 223
    stopper 263
dot *small* 32
    point 180a

place 182
    little 193
    variegate 440
    mark 550
dot *dowry* 784
dotage *age* 128
    imbecility 499
dotard *old* 130
    foolish 501
dotation 784
dote *drivel* 499, 503
    —upon 897
dotted 440
douanier 965
double *similar* 17
    increase 35
    duplex 90
    substitute 147
    fold 258
    turn 283
    finesse 702
    specter 980a
    wraith 992a
    —acrostic *letters* 561
    wit 842
    —a point 311
    —eagle 800
    —entry 811
    —meaning 520
    —quartet 415
    —reef topsails 664
    —sure 474
    —the fist 909
    —up
    render powerless 158
    in quick time 274
    march at the—274
    see—dim sight 443
    drunk 959
    work—tides 686
double bass 417
double-dealer 607
double-dealing
    lie 544
    cunning 940
double-distilled 171
double-dyed 428
double-edged 171
double entente
    ambiguity 520
    impure 961
double-faced
    lie 544
    cunning 702
    dishonorable 940
double-handed 544
double-headed 90
double-hearted 940
double-minded 605
double-ripper 272
double-runner 272
double-shot 171
double-shotted 171
doublet 225
double-talk 523
doublets 89

double-tongued
    lie 544
    cunning 702, 940
doubling 702
doubt *uncertain* 475
    disbelieve **485**
    skeptic 989
doubtful
    uncertain 475
    equivocal 520
    —meaning
    unintelligible 519
    (*equivocal* 520)
    more than—473
doubtless *certain* 474
    belief 484
    assent 488
douceur *gift* 784
    reward 973
douche 337
dough *inelastic* 324
    pulp 354
    money 800
doughboy 726
doughface 605, 886
doughnut 298
doughty 159, 861
dour 739
douse *blow* 276, 972
    immerse 310
    splash 337
Dove
    Holy Ghost 976
dove *bird* 366
    innocent 946
    roar like sucking—174
dove-color 432
dovecote 189
dovetail *agree* 23
    join 43
    intersect 219
    intervene 228
    angle 244
    insert 300
dowager *lady* 374
    widow 905
dowdy *dirty* 653
    vulgar 851
dower *property* 780
    bequest 784
    wealth 803
dowerless 804
down *upland* 180
    below 207
    sleep 306
    cast down 308
    light 320
    bear—upon 716
    bed of—*pleasure* 377
    repose 687
    be—upon *attack* 716
    severe 739
    come—306
    —in price 815
    —in the mouth 837

431

downcast

—on one's
  marrowbones 886
—on one's uppers 879
  get—306
  go—sink 306
  calm 826
  go—like a stone 310
  money—807
  take—lower 308
  rebuff 874
  humble 879
downcast
  descendent 306
  dejected 837
—eyes 879
downcome 306
down-easter 188
downfall
  destruction 162
  fall 306
  earth 342
  failure 732
  misfortune 735
down-grade 306
down-hearted 837
downhill *sloping* 217
  descent 306
  go—*adversity* 735
downpour 348
down-reaching 208
downright *absolute* 31
  manifest 525
  sincere 703
downs *uplands* 180
  heights 206
  wolds 344
down-trodden
  submission 725
  vanquished 732
  subject 749
  dejected 837
  disrepute 874
  contempt 930
downwards 306
downy *smooth* 255
  plumose 256
  soft 324
dowry *property* 780
  bequest 784
  provision 803
dowse 276
dowser 994
doxology 990
doxy 962
doyen 128, 130
doyley 652
doze 683
dozen 98
drab *color* 432
  slut 59, 653
  hussy 962
drabble 653
drachm 319
Draco *ruler* 694
  severe 739
draff 653

draft
  (see also draught)
  decrement 40a
  traction 285
  drawing 554, 556
  write 590
  abstract 596
  list 611
  plan 626
  physic 662
  combatant 726
  check 800, 805
—off *displace* 185
  transfer 270
drafted man 726
draft-horse 271
drag *elapse* 109
  carriage 272
  crawl 275
  traction 285
  impediment 706
—a chain *tedious* 110
  exertion 686
  subjection 749
—along 106
—anchor 706
—into *implicate* 54
  compel 744
—into open day 531
—on *endure* 106, 110
  continue 143
—sail *check* 706
—sheet 706
—slow length
  long 200
  weary 841
—through mire
  disrepute 874
  disrespect 929
—towards *attract* 288
  put on the—275
draggle 285, 653
draggle-tail 59
drag-net *all sorts* 78
dragoman 524
dragon
  monster 83, 366
  violent 173
  irascible 901
dragon fly 366
dragonnade
  attack 716
  punish 972
dragoon *attack* 716
  soldier 726
  compel 744
  insolent 885
  worry 907
drain *dike* 232
  flow out 295
  empty 297
  dry 340
  conduit 350
  waste 638
  clean 652
  unclean 653

  exhaust 789
  dissipate 818
—into 348
—of resources 640
—the cup *drink* 298
  drunken 959
—the cup of misery 828
drainage (see drain)
drake *male* 373
  fire—423
dram *drink* 298
  weight 319
  pungent 392
  stimulus 615
—drinking 959
drama 599
dramatic
  musician 416
  drama 599
  ostentation 882
—author 599
—poetry 597
dramatis personae
  mankind 372
  play 599
  agents 690
  party 712
dramatist 599
dramatize 599
dramaturgic 882
dramaturgy 599
drap d'or 847
drape 225
draper 225
drapery 225
drastic 171
draught
  (see also draft)
  depth 208
  traction 285
  drink 298
  stream of air 349
  delineation 554, 556
  plan 626
  physic 662
  troops 726
—off 73
draughts *game* 840
draughtsman
  artist 559
Dravidian 372a
draw *compose* 54
  pull 285
  delineate 554, 556
  money 800
—a bead on 716
—a curtain 424
—and quarter 972
—an inference 480
—a parallel 9
—a picture 594
—aside 279
—a straight furrow 939
—back *regret* 283

  avoid 623
—breath *refresh* 689
  feeling 821
  relief 834
—down 153
—forth *extract* 301
  use 677
—from 810
—in 195
—in one's horns
  tergiversation 607
  humility 879
—lots 621
—near *time* 121
  approach 286
—off *eject* 297
  hinder 706
  take 789
—off the attention 458
—on *time* 121
  event 151
  induce 615
—on futurity 132
—out *protract* 110
  late 133
  prlong 200
  extract 301
  discover 480a
  exhibit 525
  diffuse style 573
—over *induce* 615
—poker 840
—profit 775
—the line 465
—the pen through 552
—the sword
  attack 716
  war 722
—the teeth of 158
—the veil 528
—together *assemble* 72
  cooperate 709
—towards 288
—up *order* 58
  stop 265
  write 590
—up a statement 594
—upon *money* 800
drawback
  decrement 40a
  evil 619
  imperfection 651
  hindrance 706
  discount 813
drawbridge *way* 627
  escape 671
drawcansir 887
drawee 800
drawer *receptacle* 191
  artist 559
—of water 690
drawers *garment* 225
drawing
  delineation 554, 556

drawing knife 253
drawing-room
  assembly 72
  room 191
  fashion 852
—car 272
drawl *prolong* 200
  creep 275
  in speech 583
  sluggish 683
drawn *equated* 27
—battle
  pacification 723
  incomplete 730
dray 272
dray horse 271
drayman 268
dread 860
dreadful *great* 31
  bad 649
  dire 830
  depressing 837
  fearful 860
dreadless 861
dreadnought
  coat 225
  battleship 726
dream *unsubstantial* 4
  error 495
  fancy 515
  sleep 683
  psychotherapy 992a
—of *think* 451
  intend 620
—on other things 458
  golden—858
dreamer
  madman 504
  imaginative 515
dreamlike 4
dreamy
  unsubstantial 4
  inattentive 458
  imaginative 515
  sleepy 683
drear 16
drearisome 16
dreary *uniform* 16
  solitary 87
  melancholy 830, 837
dredge *collect* 72
  extract 301
  raise 307
dredging machine 307
dregs *remainder* 40
  density 321
  refuse 645
  dirt 653
—of the people 876
—of vice 945
drench *drink* 298
  water 337
  physic 370
  redundance 641
—with physic 662

drencher 348
drenching 337
　−rain 348
dress *uniformity* 16
　agree 23
　equalize 27
　clothes 225
　prepare 673
　ornament 847
　ostentation 882
　−down *berate* 527
　−the ground 371
　−to advantage 847
　−up *falsehood* 544
　represent 554
　−wounds 662
　full−852
dress clothes 225
dress coat 225
dress suit 225
dresser *sideboard* 215
　surgeon 662
dressing
　reprimand 932
　punish 972
dressing gown 225
dressmaker 225
dribble *flow out* 295
　drop 348
dribbling 32
driblet 25, 32
dried 340
drier 340
drift *accumulate* 72
　distance 196
　tunnel 260
　motion 264
　float 267
　transfer 270
　direction 278
　deviation 279
　approach 286
　air 338
　wind 349
　meaning 516
　intention 620
　−sail 706
　snow−383
drifter *neglecter* 460
drifting *irresolute* 605
driftless 621
drill *crossing* 219
　bore 260
　auger 262
　teach 537
　prepare 673
drink *swallow* 296
　liquor 298
　tipple 959
　−in *imbibe* 296, 298
　−in learning 539
　−in the ozone 689
　−one's fill *enough* 639
　−to *celebrate* 883
　courtesy 894
drinkable 298

drinker 959
drinking bout 954
drinking song 597
drink money 784
drip *ooze* 295
　flow 348
dripping *wet* 339
　fat 356
drive *assemblage* 72
　airing 266
　impel 276
　propel 284
　urge 615
　haste 684
　direct 693
　compel 744
　−a bargain *barter* 794
　parsimony 819
　−a coach and six
　　through 83
　−ahead *progress* 282
　−at *mean* 516
　intend 620
　−care away 836
　−from *repel* 289
　−home 729
　−in 300
　−into a corner
　　difficult 704
　　hinder 706
　defeat 731
　subjection 749
　−matters to an
　　extremity 604
　−on *progress* 282
　−one hard 716
　−out 297
　−to despair 859
　−to the last 133
　−trade *business* 625
　barter 794
drive gate 260
drivel *slobber* 297
　imbecile 409
　mad 503
　diffuseness 573
driveler *fool* 501
　loquacious 584
driver *coachman* 268
　director 694
driveway 260
driving rain 348
drizzle 348
drizzly 348
drogher 273
drole *cards* 840
drollery
　amusement 840
　wit 842
　ridiculous 853
dromedary 271
drone *slow* 275
　sound 407, 412, 413
　music 415
　inactive 683
drool *drivel* 297

diffuseness 573
droop *weak* 160
　pendency 214
　sink 306
　disease 655
　decline 659
　flag 688
　sorrow 828
　dejection 837
drop
　small quantity 32
　discontinue 142
　powerless 158
　bring forth 161
　fell 213
　pendent 214
　spherule 249
　emerge 295
　fall 306
　trickle 348
　relinquish 624
　discard 782
　gallows 975
　−a hint 527
　−all idea of 624
　−asleep 683
　−astern 283
　−by drop
　　by degrees 26
　in parts 51
　−dead 360
　−from the clouds 508
　−game 545
　−in *arrive* 292
　immerse 300
　sociality 892
　−in one's tracks 361
　−in the ocean
　　trifling 643
　−into a good thing
　　734
　−into the grave 360
　−off *decrease* 36
　die 360
　sleep 683
　−serene 442
　−the mask 529
　−the subject 458
　−too much 959
　let−308
　ready to
　−*fatigue* 688
dropping fire 70
drop scene 599
dropsical *swollen* 194
　redundant 641
droshki 272
dross *remainder* 40
　trash 643
　rubbish 645
　dirt 653
drought *dryness* 340
　insufficiency 640
　thirst 865
droughty 340
drouk 337

droukit 339
drove *assemblage* 72
　multitude 102
drover 370
drown *affusion* 337
　kill 361
　ruin 731, 732
　−care 840
　−the voice 581
drowsy *slow* 275
　sleepy 683
　weary 841
drub *defeat* 731, 732
　punish 972
drudge *plod* 682
　labor 686
　worker 690
drudgery 686
drug *superfluity* 641
　trash 643
　remedy 662
　−habit 954
　−in the market 815
　−store 662
drugget *cover* 223
　clean 652
　preserve 670
druggist 662
druid 996
drum *repeat* 104
　cylinder 249
　sound 407
　musician 416
　music 417
　party 892
　beat of−*signal* 550
　alarm 669
　war 722
　command 741
　parade 882
　−fire 407
　−out 972
　ear−418
　muffled−*funeral* 363
　nonresonance 408a
drumhead
　lawless 964
　tribunal 966
drum major 416, 745
drummer 416
　traveler 758, 767
drunk 959
　−with choler 900
drunkard 959
drunken 959
　reel like a−man 315
drunkenness 959
dry *arid* 340
　style 575, 576, 579
　hoarse 581
　scanty 640
　preserve 670
　exhaust 789
　tedious 841
　thirsty 865
　cynical 932

−as dust *dull* 843
−goods 329
−joke 842
−land 342
−the tears 834
−up 340 *waste* 638
　on−land 342
　run−640
　with−eyes 823
dryad *tree* 367
　nymph 979
Dryasdust
　antiquarian 122
dry land 342
dryness 340
dry nurse *teach* 537
　teacher 540
　aid 707
dry point 558
dry rot *dirt* 653
　decay 659
　bane 663
duad 89
dual 89, 90
　−personality 992a
dualism 984
duality 89
duarchy 737
dub 564, 566
dubash 758
Dubhe 490a
dubiosity 475
dubious 475
dubitation
　uncertainty 475
　(*unbelief* 485)
duchess *mistress* 745
　nobility 875
duchy 181
duck *zero* 101
　stoop 308
　plunge 310
　bird 298, 366
　water 337
　darling 897, 899
　−in thunder 870
　play−s and drakes
　recoil 277
　prodigality 818
ducking stool 975
duckling 129
duck pond 370
duct 350
ductibility 324
ductile *tractile* 285
　flexible 324
　trimming 607
　easy 705
　docile 743
ductility 490a
　(see ductile)
dud 304
dude 854
dudgeon *dagger* 727
　discontent 832
　churlishness 895

433

duds

hate 898
anger 900
sullenness 901a
duds 225
due *expedient* 646
　owing 806
　proper 924, 926
　–*respect* 928
　–*sense of* 498
　–*time soon* 132
　–*to*
　　cause and effect 154, 155
　　give–weight 465
　　give his–to
　　right 922
　　vindication 937
　　fair 939
　　in–course 109
　　occasion 134
dueguard 550
duel 720
duelist 726
duello 720
dueness 924
duenna *teacher* 540
　guardian 664
　keeper 753
dues 812
duet 415
duffer *ignoramus* 493
　bungler 701
　smuggler 792
dug 250
dugout *dwelling* 189
　tench 232
　boat 273
　safety 664
　defense 717
duke *ruler* 745
　noble 875
dukedom 877
dulcet *sweet* 396
　sound 405
　melodious 413
　agreeable 829
dulcify 174, 324, 396
dulcimer 417
dulcin 396
Dulcinea 897
dulcorate 396
dulia 990
dull *weak* 160
　unintelligent 32, 493
　inert 172
　moderate 174
　blunt 254
　slow 275
　insensible 376
　sound 405
　dim 422
　color 428
　colorless 429
　stolid 499
　style 575
　inactive 683

unapt 699
callous 823
dejected 837
weary 841
prosing 843
simple 849
–*of hearing* 419
–*sight* 443
dullard 501
dullish *blunt* 254
dullness 843
duly 924
dulse 367
duma 696
dumb *ignorant* 493
　voiceless 581
　–*animal* 366
　–*friend* 366
　–*show* 550
　strike–*astonish* 870
　humble 879
dumb-waiter 307
dumdum bullet 727
dumfound
　disappoint 509
　silence 581
　astonish 870
　humble 879
dummy *substitute* 147
　impotent 158
　speechless 581
　printing 591
　inactive 683
　cards 840
dump *unload* 297
　music 415
　sale 796
　lament 839
　–*cart* 272
dumps *discontent* 832
　dejection 837
　sulk 901a
dumpy *little* 193
　short 201
　thick 202
dun *din* 422
　colorless 429
　gray 432
　importune 765
　creditor 805
dunce *ignoramus* 493
　fool 501
dunderhead 501
dune 206
dung 653
dungeon 752
dunghill *dirt* 653
　cowardly 862
　baseborn 876
　–*cock* 366
Dunker 984
duo 415
duodecimal 99
duodecimo *little* 193
　book 593
duodenal 221

duodenary 98
duodenum 221, 350
duologue
　interlocution 588
　drama 599
dupe *credulous* 486
　deceive 545
　deceived **547**
duplex 90 –*house* 189
duplicate *copy* 21
　double 90
　repetition 104
　tally 550
　record 551
　redundant 641
　pawn 805
duplication
　imitation 19
　doubling **90**
　repetition 104
duplicature *fold* 258
duplicity *duality* 89
　falsehood 544
durability 141
durable *long time* 110
　permanent 141
　stable 150
durance 751 *in*–754
duration 106
　contingent–108a
durbar *conference* 588
　council 696
　tribunal 966
dure 106
duress *compulsion* 744
　restraint 751
Durga 979
Durham boat 273
during 106
　–*pleasure etc.* 108a
durity 323
durwan 263, 753
dusk *evening* 126
　half-light 422
dusky *dark* 421
　dim 422
　black 431
dust *levity* 320
　powder 330
　corpse 362
　trash 643
　dirt 653
　money 800
　come to–*die* 360
　–*in the balance* 643
　–*one's jacket* 972
　humbled in the–879
　kick up a–885
　level with the–162
　lick the–*submit* 725
　fail 732
　make to bite the – 731
　throw–*in the eyes blind* 442
　deceive 545

plead 617
turn to–
　deorganized 358
　die 360
duster 652
dust hole 519
　fit for the–
　useless 645
　dirty 653
　spoilt 659
dustman *cleaner* 652
dustoor 613
dustoori 973
dust storm 330
dusty *powder* 330
　dirt 653
Dutch–*auction* 796
　–*cap* 225
　–*courage* 862
　–*oven* 386
　–*treat* 892
　high–519
　it beats the–508
Dutchman 57
　flying–515
dutiable 812
dutiful 944
duty *business* 625
　work 686
　tax 812
　courtesy 894
　obligation **926**
　respect 928
　worship 990
　rite 998
　do one's–*virtue* 944
　on–680, 682
duumvirate 737
Duval, Claude–792
D.V. 470
dwarf *lessen* 36
　small 193
　elf 980
dwell *reside* 186
　abide 265
　–*upon descant* 573
dweller 188
dwelling *location* 184
　abode **189**
dwindle *lessen* 36
　shrink 195
　droop 655
dyad 193
dyadic 89
dye 428
　–*d in the wool* 709, 820
dying 360
dyke (*see* dike)
dynamic 157
　–*energy* 157
dynamics 276
dynamitard 863
dynamite 727
dynamize 171
dynamo 157

ear

dynamograph 276
dynamometer 276, 466
dynasty 737
dyne 490d
dysentery 299
dysmerogenesis 161
dysmeromorph 357
dyspepsia 655
dyspeptic 655
dysphonia 581
dysphoria 149
dyspnea 688

E

each 79
　–*in his turn* 148
　–*other* 12
　–*to each* 786
eager *willing* 602
　active 682
　consenting 762
　ardent 821
　desirous 865
　–*expectation* 507
eagle *bird* 366
　standard 550
　insignia 747
　coin 800
　–*eye sight* 441
　intelligence 498
　–*winged swift* 274
eagre 348, 667
ean 161
ear *of corn* 154
　hearing 418
　all–418
　come to one's–s 527
　sin in the–*loud* 404
　drum 407
　–*for music* 416, 418
　have the–*of belief* 484
　friendship 888
　in at one–*out at the other*
　inattention 458
　forget 506
　lend an–*hear* 418
　attend 457
　make the–*s tingle anger* 900
　meet the–418
　nice–418
　no–419
　not for–*s polite* 961
　offend the–410
　prick up the–*s attention* 457
　expectation 507
　pull about one's–*s* 308
　quick–418

earache   educational

    reach one's–s 527
    ring in the–408
    set by the–s
        discord 713
        hate 898
        resentment 900
    split the–s 404
    together by the–s
        discord 713
    up to one's–s
        redundance 641
        active 682
        willing–602
    word in the–586
earache 378
eardrop 214
eardrum 418
eared 419
earl 875
earldom 877
earless 419
earliness 132
early 132 get up–682
earmark 550
ear muffs 384
earn 775
earnest *willing* 602
    determined 604
    emphatic 642
    pledge 771
    pay in advance 809
    eager 821
    serious 837
    in–*affirmation* 535
    veracious 543
    strenuous 682
earnings 775
ear–piercing 410
earring 847
earshot 197
    out of–405
ear–splitting 402, 404
earth *ground* 211
    world 318
    land 342
    corpse 362
    –flax 385
    what on
    –*inquiry* 461
    wonder 870
earthenware
    baked 384
    sculpture 557
earthling 372
earthly 318
earthly–minded
    selfish 943
    irreligious 989
earthquake
    revolution 146
    violence 173
earthwork 717
ear–witness 467
ease *abate* 36
    bodily 377

    style 578
    leisure 685
    facility 705
    mental 827
    content 831
    at one's–
        prosperous 734
    –off *deviate* 297
    –one of *take* 789
    mind at–
        cheerful 836
    set at–*relief* 834
    take one's–687
easel *support* 215
    painting 556
    –picture 556
easement
    property 780
    relief 834
easily (see easy)
    –accomplished 705
    –affected 375
    –deceived 486
    –persuaded 602
    let one down–918
east *side* 236
    direction 278
Easter *period* 138
    rite 998
    –Monday
        holiday 840
    –offering *gift* 784
    –sepulcher 1000
eastern 236
Easterner 57
easting 196
eastward 236
easy *gentle* 275
    style 578
    facile 705
    –ascent 217
    –chair *support* 215
    repose 687
    –circumstances 803
    –of belief 472
    –sail *moderate* 174
    slow 275
    –temper 894
    –terms 705
    –to understand 518
    –virtue 961
    make one self–
        about 484
    take it–*inactive* 683
    inexcitable 826
easy–going
    willing 602
    irresolute 605
    lenient 740
    inexcitable 826
    contented 831
    indifferent 866
eat *food* 298
    tolerate 826
    –dirt 725
    –heartily 298

    –off the same
        trencher 892
    –one's fill *enough* 639
    gorge 957
    –one's words 607
    –out of house and
        home *take* 789
    prodigal 818
    gluttony 957
eatable 298
eatables 298
eaten up with 820
eating 298
eating house 189
eau de Cologne 400
eau sucrée 396
eaves 250
eavesdropper
    curiosity 455
    informer 527
eavesdropping
    hearing 418
    news 532
ebb *decrease* 36
    contract 195
    regress 283
    recession 287
    tide 348
    waste 638
    spoil 659
    –and flow 314
    –of life 360
    low–36 *low* 207
    depression 308
    insufficient 640
ebb tide *decrease* 36
    low 207
    dry 340
ebenezer 1000
Ebionite 984
Eblis 978
ebon 431
ebony 431
éboulement 162, 716
ebriety 959
ebullience
    (see ebullient)
    calefaction 384
ebullient *violent* 173
    hot 382
    excited 824
ebulliometer 384
ebullioscope 384
ebullition *energy* 171
    violence 173
    agitation 315
    heating 384
    excitation 825
    anger 900
eburin 430
écarté 840
ecbatic 155
eccentric *irregular* 83
    exterior 220
    foolish 499
    crazed 503

    capricious 608
ecchymosis 299
ecclesiarch 996
ecclesiastic
    church 995
    clergy 996
ecclesiastical
    canonical 985
    temple 1000
    –law 963
ecclesiolatry 991
ecco 457
eccrinology 299
ecdemic 220
ecderon 223
échafaudage 673
echelon *arrange* 60
    oblique motion 279
    attack 716
echinate 253
echinodermata 368
echo *similarity* 17
    imitate 19
    copy 21
    repeat 104
    recoil 277
    resonance 408
    answer 462
    assent 488
    applaud to the–931
echoes awaken–404
echolalia 821a
echoless 403
éclat 873
eclectic *teaching* 537
    choice 609
eclecticism 451, 662
eclipse *surpass* 33
    disappearance 449
    hide 528
    outshine 873, 874
    partial–*dim* 422
    total–*dark* 421
    under an
    –*invisible* 447
    out of repute 874
ecliptic 318
eclogue 597
ecology 357
economic 692
    –pressure 751
economical 817
economics 692
economize 817
economy *order* 58
    preservation 670
    conduct 692
    frugality **817**
    (*plan* 626)
    animal–359
ecphonesis 580
ecrhythmic 139
ecrhythmus 139
écru 426, 433
ecstasis 683
ecstasy *frenzy* 515

    transport 821
    rapture 827
ecstatic 829
ecstatica 992a
ecteron 223
ectoderm 223
ectogenous 161
ectomorphy 372a
ectropic 218
ectype 21
ecumenical 78
edacity 957
Edda 986
eddish 168
Eddy, Mary Baker– 986
eddy *whirlpool* 348
    current 312, 490a
    danger 667
Eden *heaven* 827
    (*pleasure* 827)
edentate 254
edge *energy* 171
    height 206
    brink **231**
    deviate 279
    cutting–253
    –in 228
    –of hunger 865
    –one's way 282
    set on–256
    take the–off 174
edge tools 253
    play with–863
edgewise 217
edging *obliquity* 217
    border 231
    ornament 847
edible 298
edict 531, 741
edification
    building 161
    teaching 537
    learning 539
    piety 987
edifice 161
edifying *good* 648
edile 965
edit *publication* 531
    compile 596
    revise 658
    (*printing* 591)
edition 531 new–658
editor *recorder* 553
    book 593
    commentator 595
editorial 595
educate *teach* 537
    (*prepare* 673)
educated 490
education
    teaching 537
    knowledge 490
    man of–492
educational 537
    school 542

435

educe

educe *extract* 301
  discover 480a
educt 40
education 40a
edulcorate
  sweeten 396
  clean 652
eel *convolutions* 248
  fish 298
  –*spear* 727
  wriggle like an–315
efface *destroy* 162
  disappear 449
  obliterate 552
  –*from the memory* 506
effect *consequence* 154
  complete 729
  carry into–692
  in–5
  take–731
  to that–516
  with crushing–162
effective *substantial* 3
  capable 157
  influential 175
  useful 644
  practical 646
effects *property* 780
  goods 798
effectual
  influential 175
  success 731
effectually 52
effectuate 729
effeminacy
  (*see* effeminate)
effeminate *weak* 160
  womanlike 374
  timorous 862
  sensual 954
effeminize 158
effendi 875
effervesce *energy* 171
  violence 173
  agitate 315
  bubble 353
  excited 825
effervescent
  (*see* effervesce)
  aerated 338
effete *old* 128
  weak 160
  useless 645
  spoiled 659
efficacious
  (*see* efficient)
efficient *power* 157
  agency 170
  reliable 632
  utility 644
  skill 698
effigy *copy* 21
  representation 554
efflation 349
efflorescence 330

effluence *egress* 295
  flow 348
effluent 295
effluvious 398
effluvium *vapor* 334
  odor 398
efflux *egress* 295
  (*flow* 348)
efformation 240
effort 686
effrontery 885
effulgence 420
effuse
  pour out 295, 297
  excrete 299
  speech 582
effusion [*see* effuse]
  loquacity 584
  –*of blood* 361
effusive 295
eft 366
eftsoon 113, 117, 132
egad 535
egest 297
egesta 299
egestion 297
egestive 297
egg *beginning* 66
  cause 153
  food 298
  –*and dart ornament* 847
  –*on* 615
  too many–*s in one basket*
  unskillful 699
  (*imprudent* 863)
  walk among–*s* 704
eggplant 298
egg-shaped 247, 249
eggshell 223
ego *intrinsic* 5
  immaterial 317
  astral body 980a
  non–6
egohood 5
ego-id conflict 821a
egoism 880
egoist 880
egotism
  overestimation 482
  vanity 880
  cynicism 911
  selfishness 943
egotist 482
egotistical
  (*see* egotism)
  narrow 481
egregious
  exceptional 83
  absurd 497
  exaggerated 549
  important 642
egregiously
  greatly 31
  supremely 33

egress 295
egurgitate 295
Egyptian
  –*darkness* 421
  –*deities* 979
eiderdown 223, 324
eidoloclast 165
eidolon 453, 991
eidouranion 318
eight *number* 98
  boat 273
  representative 759
eighty 98
eileton 999
Einstein theory 451, 490a
eisegesis 523
eisteddfod 72
either *choice* 609
  happy with–605
ejaculate *propel* 284
  utter 580
eject 297
ejecta 299
ejection *displace* 185
  emit 297
  excretion 299
ejective 297, 299
ejector 349
eke *also* 37
  –*out complete* 52
  spin out 110
ekka 272
elaborate
  improve 658
  prepare 673
  laborious 686
  work out 729
elaboration
  (*see* elaborate)
elaine 356
élan 276
elapse *flow* 109
  pass 122
elastic (*see* elasticity)
  –*fluid* 334
elasticity *power* 157
  strength 159
  energy 171
  spring **325**
elate *cheer* 836
  rejoice 838
  hope 858
  vain 880
  boast 884
elbow *angle* 244
  projection 250
  push 276
  at one's–*near* 197
  advice 695
  –*one's way*
  progress 282
  pursuit 622
  active 682
  out at–*s*
  undress 226

  poor 804
  disrepute 874
elbowchair 215
elbow grease 331
elbowroom *space* 180
  freedom 748
eld 122, 124, 128
elder *older* 124
  aged 128
  veteran 130
  clergy 996
eldern 124, 128
El Dorado 803
Eleatic school 451
elect *choose* 609
  good 648
  predestinate 976
  pious 987
  churchdom 995
election *numerical* 84
  necessity 601
electioneering 609
elective franchise 609
elector 609, 745
electorate 737
  constituency 609
Electra complex 821a
electric *carrier* 271
  vehicle 272
  trolley 273
  swift 274
  sensation 821
  excitable 825
  –*bath* 386
  –*blue* 438
  –*car* 273
  –*chair* 975
  –*fan* 349
  –*light* 423
  –*stove* 386
  –*torch* 423
electrician 690
electricity 157, 388
electrification 157
electrify
  locomotion 266
  unexpected 508
  excite 824
  astonish 870
electrobiology 992
electrocute 361, 972
electrocution 361, 972
electrocutioner 975
electrodynamics 157
electrodynamometer 157
electrokinetics 157
electrolier 423
electrolysis 49, 662
electrolyze 49, 662
electromagnetism 157
electrometer 157

eleventh hour

electrometric 157
electromotion 157
electromotive force 157
electron 32
electrophorus 157, 490a
electroscope 157
electrostatics 157, 490a
electrotype 21, 550, 591
electuary 662
eleemosynary 784
Elegance, Bank of– 800
elegance *in style* 578
  beauty 845
  taste 850
elegy *interment* 363
  poetry 597
  lament 839
element
  substantiality 3
  component 56
  beginning 66
  cause 153
  matter 316
  devouring–382
  in one's–*facility* 705
  content 831
  out of its–185
elemental *simple* 42
  Rosicrucian 980
elementary *simple* 42
  –*education* 537
elements
  Eucharist 998
elench 477
elephant *large* 192
  carrier 271
  animal 366
  white–*bane* 663
elephantiasis 655
elephantine *huge* 192
  dull 843
eleutherian 748
elevated *tipsy* 959
elevation *height* 206
  vertical 212
  raising **307**
  plan 554
  loftiness 574
  repute 873
  angular–244
  –*of mind* 942
  –*of style* 574
  improvement 658
  glory 873
elevator *ascent* 305
  descent 306
  elevation 307
eleven 98
  representative 759
eleventh hour
  evening 126

436

late 133
opportune 134
elf *infant* 129
  little 193
  fairy 979
elicit *cause* 153
  draw out 301
  discover 480a
  manifest 525
eligible 646
eliminant 299
eliminate *subduct* 38
  simplify 42
  exclude 55
  weed 103
  extract 301
eliminative 299, 350
elision *separation* 44
  shortening 201
elite *best* 648
  distinguished 873
  aristocrat 875
elixation 384
elixir 5, 662
  find the—of life 471
elk 366
ell 200 *take an*
  —take 789
  insolence 885
  wrong 923
  undue 925
  selfish 943
ellipse 247
ellipsis *shorten* 201
  typography 550
  style 572
ellipsoid 247, 249
elliptic 247
elm *tree* 367
elocation
  displace 185
  transfer 270
elocution 582
elocutionist 582
elongate 200
elongation
  distance 196
  lengthening 200
elopement *avoid* 623
  escape 671
eloquence *style* 569
  speech 582
  action is— 582
  to try thy— 582
else 37
elsewhere 187
elsewise 18
elucidate 82, 522
elucidative 522
elude *sophistry* 477
  avoid 623
  escape 671
  succeed 731
  palter 773
elusive (see elude)
  deceptive 545

elusory *untrue* 546
elutriate 652
elysian *delightful* 829
  heavenly 981
Elysium *bliss* 827
  paradise 981
elytron 223
emanciated *lean* 203
  starved 640
emanciation
  shrinking 195
  thinness 203
  disease 655
emanant 295
emanate *follow* 117
  go out of 295
  excrete 299
  —from 544
emanation *egress* 295
  vapor 353
  odor 398
emancipate
  deliver 672
  facilitate 705
  free 748, 750
emasculate
  castrate 38
  impotent 158
  (*weaken* 160)
embalm
  interment 363
  perfume 400
  preserve 670
  —*in the memory* 505
embankment
  esplanade 189
  refuge 666
  fence 717
  (*inclosure* 232)
embargo *stoppage* 265
  prohibition 761
  seclusion 893
embark *transfer* 270
  depart 293
  invest 787
  —*in begin* 66
  engage in 676
embarras
  —*de choix* 609
  —*de richesses*
    redundance 641
    wealth 803
embarrass
  render difficult 704
  hinder 706
embarrassed
  poor 804
  in debt 806
embarrassing
  uncertain 475
embarrassment
  (see embarrass)
embase 659
embassy *errand* 532
  commission 755
  consignee 758

embattled
  arranged 60
  leagued 712
  war array 722
embay 229
embed *locate* 184
  base 215
embellish 847
embers 384
embezzle 791
embitter
  deteriorate 659
  aggravate 835
  acerbate 900
emblazon *color* 428
  ornament 847
  display 882
emblem 550
  —*of authority* 747
embodied 316
embody *join* 43
  combine 48
  form a whole 50
  compose 54
  include 76
  materialize 316
embogue 297
embolden *hope* 858
  encourage 861
embolic 261
embolism
  interjacence 228
  closure 261
  insertion 300
  hindrance 706
embolus 261, 706
embonpoint 192
embosomed
  lodged 184
  interjacent 228
  circumscribed 229
emboss *convex* 250
  ornament 847
embouchure 260
embow 245
embowel 297
embrace *compose* 54
  include 76
  inclose 227
  choose 609
  take 789
  friendship 888
  sociality 892
  courtesy 894
  endearment 902
  —*an offer* 762
embrangle
  derange 61
embranglement
  discord 713
embrasure *notch* 257
  opening 260
embrocate 370
embrocation 662
embroider
  variegate 440

lie 544
exaggerate 549
ornament 847
embroidery
  adjunct 39
  exaggeration 549
embroil *derange* 61
  discord 713
embroilment
  disorder 59
embrown 433
embryo *beginning* 66
  cause 153
  in—destined 152
  preparing 673
embryologist 357
embryology 357, 359, 368
embryonic *little* 193
  immature 674
emendation 658
emerald *green* 435
  jewel 847
emerge 295
emergency
  circumstance 8
  junction 43
  occasion 134
  event 151
  difficulty 704
emergent 295
emeritus *sage* 500
  respected 928
emersion 295
emery *sharpener* 253
  —*paper smooth* 255
emesis 297
emetic 297, 662
émeute 742
emication 420
emigrant *stranger* 57
  traveler 268
emigrate
  remove 266
  egress 295
emigration
  (see emigrate)
eminence *height* 206
  fame 873
  church dignitary 996
eminently 33
emir *master* 745
  noble 875
emissary
  messenger 534
  consignee 758
emission 297
emissive 297
emit *eject* 297
  publish 531
  voice 580
  —*vapor* 336
Emmanuel 976
emmeleia 413
emmet 193
emollient 662

emolument
  acquisition 775
  receipt 810
  remuneration 973
emotion 821
emotional 821
  —*appeal* 824
empale *transfix* 260
  execute 972
empanel *list* 86, 611
  jury 969
empennage 273
emperor 745
  positiveness 535
emphasis *accent* 580
emphasize 535
emphatic
  positive assertion 535
  important 642
emphatically
  much 31
empierce 260
empire *region* 181
  dominion 737
  domain 780
empirema 476
empiric 548
empirical
  experiment 463
  essay 675
empiricism 451, 463
emplastrum 662
employ *business* 625
  use 677
  servitude 749
  commission 755
  —*one's capital in* 794
  —*oneself* 680
  —*one's time in* 625
  in one's— 746
employee *servant* 746
  agent 758
employer 795
employment
  (see employ)
  action 680
empoison 659
emporium 799
empower *power* 157
  commission 755
  delegate 759
  permit 760
empress 745, 877
emprise 676
emptiness
  (see empty)
emption 795
emptor 795
  caveat— 769
emptorial 795
empty *clear* 185
  vacant 187
  deflate 195
  drain 297
  ignorant 491

empty–handed   engulf

waste 638
deficient 640
useless 645
beggarly account of
  –boxes
poverty 804
–*encomium* 894
–one's *glass* 298
–*purse* 804
–*sound* 517
–*stomach* 865
–*title name* 564
undue 925
–*words* 546
empty-handed 640
empty-headed 491
empurple 434, 437
empyrean *sky* 318
  blissful 829
empyreuma 401
empyrosis 384
emu 366
emulate *imitate* 19
  goodness 648
  rival 708
  compete 720
  glory 873
emulsify 352
emulsion 352
emunctory 295, 350
en–*bloc* 50–*masse* 50
  –*passant*
    parenthetical 10
    transient 111
    à propos 134
  –*rapport* 9
  –*règle order* 58
    conformity 82
  –*route journey* 266
    progress 282
enable 157
enact *drama* 599
  action 680
  conduct 692
  complete 729
  order 741
  law 963
enallage
  metaphor 521
  (*substitute* 147)
enamel *coating* 223
  painting 556
  porcelain 557
  ornament 847
enameler 559
enamor 897
enanthema 655
encage 751
encamp *locate* 184
  abode 189
encase 223
encaustic painting 556
enceinte
  with child 161
  region 181

inclosure 232
enchafe 830
enchain *restrain* 751
  (*join* 43)
enchant *please* 829
enchanged
  pleased 827
enchanting
  beautiful 845
  love 897
enchantment
  sorcery 992
enchase 43, 223, 259
enchymatous 194
enchyridion 593
encincture 227, 229
encircle *include* 76
  surround 227
  go round 311
  revolve 312
Encke 490a
enclave *close* 181
  boundary 233
enclose (see *inclose*)
enclosure
  (see *inclosure*)
enclothe 225
encomiast 935
encomium 931
encompass 227
  –*with gloom* 422
encore *again* 104
  approbation 931
encounter
  undergo 151
  clash 276
  meet 292
  withstand 708
  contest 720
  –*danger* 665
  –*risk* 621
encourage
  animate 615
  aid 707
  comfort 834
  hope 858
  embolden 861
Encratism 953
Encratite 953
encroach
  transcursion 303
  do wrong 923
  infringe 925
  –*upon* 927
encrust 223
encuirassed 223
encumber
  difficulty 704
  hindrance 706
encumbrance
  (see *encumber*)
encyclical 531
encyclopedia
  knowledge 490
  book 542, 593
  store 636

encyclopedical 78
encysted 229
end *termination* 67
  effect 154
  object 620
  at an–142
  come to its–729
  –in smoke 732
  –of life 360
  –of one's tether
  sophistry 477
  ignorant 491
  insufficient 640
  difficult 704
  –one's *days* 360
  –s of the earth 196
  –to end *space* 180
  touching 199
  length 200
  on–212
  one's journey's–292
  put an–to
  destroy 162
  kill 361
end-all 67
endamage 649
endanger 665
endear 897
endearment 902
endeavor *pursue* 622
  attempt 675
  –after 620
  use one's best–686
endemic *special* 79
  interior 221
  disease 655
endenizen 184
endermic 223
enderon 223
endimanche
  adorned 847
  display 882
endive 298
endless
  multitudinous 102
  infinite 105
  lasting 110
  perpetual 112
endlong 200
endogamy 372a
endogenous 567
endome 223
endomorphic 221
endophagy 945
endorse (see *indorse*)
endorsement
  (see *indorsement*)
endosmose 302
endow
  confer power 157
endowed with
  possessed of 777
endowment
  intrinsic 5
  power 157
  talent 698

gift 784
endue 157
endurable 110
endurance
  (see *endure*)
  perseverance 604a
  patience 831
endure *exist* 1
  time 106
  last 110
  continue 141, 143
  undergo 151
  feel 821
  submit to 826
  –for ever 112
  –*pain* 828
  unable to–867
enduring
  remembered 506
endways 200
endwise 200, 212
enema 300, 337
enemy *time* 841
  foe 891
  –to society 891
  the common–978
  thing devised by the
    –546
energetic (see *energy*)
  undertaking 676
energize 157
energumen 504
energy *power* 157
  strength 159
  physical **171**
  resolution 604
  activity 682
  passion 820
enervate *paralyze* 158
  weaken 160
enervated 575
enervation 160, 575
enface 590
enfant–*gâté*
  prosperity 734
  satiety 869
  favorite 899
  –*perdu hopeless* 859
  reckless 863
  –*terrible artless* 703
  object of fear 860
enfeeble 160
enfeebled
  worn out 688
enfeoffment 783
Enfield rifle 727
enfilade
  lengthwise 200
  pierce 260
  pass through 302
enfold 229
enforce *urge* 615
  advise 695
  compel 744
  require 924
enfranchise *free* 748

liberate 750
permit 760
enfranchised
  privileged 924
engage *bespeak* 132
  induce 615
  undertake 676
  do battle 722
  commission 755
  promise 768
  compact 769
  –the attention 457
  –with 720
  I'll–*affirmation* 535
engaged *marriage* 903
  be–*mistime* 135
  –in *attention* 457
engagement
  business 625
  battle 720
  endearment 902
engaging *pleasing* 829
  amiable 897
engarrison 717
engender 161
engild 439
engine 633
engine driver 268
engineer
  engine driver 268
  mechanician 690
  military 726
engineering 633
engird 227
English *native* 188
  broken–563
  –*horn* 417
  –*philosophy* 451
  king's–560
  murder the king's–
    568
  plain
  –*intelligible* 518
  interpreted 522
  style 576
Englishman 188
engobe 223
engorge *swallow* 296
  gluttony 957
engorgement
  swallowing 296
  too much 641
engrail 256
engrave *furrow* 259
  mark 550
  –in the memory 505
engraver 559
engraving 558
engross *write* 590
  possess 777
  –the thoughts
  thought 451
  attention 457
engulf *destroy* 162
  swallow up 296
  plunge 310

enhance / epicene

enhance *increase* 35
  improve 658
enhancement 35
enharmonic 413
enigma *question* 461
  unintelligibility 519
  secret 533
enigmatic
  uncertain 475
  obscure 519
  (*hidden* 528)
enigmatical 520
enjoin 600 *advise* 695
  command 741
  prescribe 926
enjoy *physically* 377
  possess 777
  morally 827
  –a state 7
  –health 654
enjoyment (*see* enjoy)
enkindle *heat* 384
  excite 824
  (*induce* 615)
enlarge *increase* 35
  swell 194
  in writing 573
  liberate 750
  –the mind 537
enlarged views 498
enlighten
  illumine 420
  inform 527
  teach 537
enlightened
  knowledge 490
enlist *engage* 615
  war 722
  commission 755
  –into the service 677
  –under the banners of 707
enlisted man 726
enliven *delight* 829
  inspirit 834
  cheer 836
  amuse 840
enmesh 545, 704
enmity 889
ennead 98
enneahedral 98
enneastyle 98
ennoble 873
ennui 841
enormity *crime* 947
enormous *great* 31
  bid 192
  –number 102
enough *much* 31
  no more! 142
  sufficient 639
  moderately 651
  satiety 869
  –and to spare 639
  –in all conscience 641

–to drive one mad 830
  know when one has had–953
enrage *provoke* 830
  aggravate 835
  incense 900
enragé 865
enrapture *excite* 824
  beautify 829
  love 897
enraptured 827
enravish *beatify* 829
enravished 827
enravishment 824
enrich *improve* 658
  wealth 803
  ornament 847
enrobe 225
enroll *list* 86
  record 551
  enlist 722
  commission 755
  –troops 722
ens *essence* 1
ensample 22
ensanguined 361
ensate 253
ensconce *conceal* 528
  safety 664
ensconced
  located 184
ensemble 50
Ens Entium 976
enshrine
  circumscribe 229
  repute 873
  sanctify 987
  –in the memory 505
ensiform 253
ensign *standard* 550
  officer 726
  master 745
  –of authority 747
ensilage 637, 670
enslave 749
ensnare 545
ensphere 227
ens rationis 1, 451
ensue *follow* 63, 117
  happen 151
ensure 474
entablature 210
entail *cause* 153
  tie up property 781
entangle *interlink* 43
  derange 61
  ravel 219
  entrap 545
  embroil 713
entangled *disorder* 59
  –by difficulties 704
entanglement
  (*see* entangle)
  impurity 961
entelechy 161

entente cordiale
  agreement 23
  alliance 714
  friendship 888
enter *list* 86
  go in 294
  note 551
  account 811
  –a profession 625
  –in *converge* 290
  –into an engagement 768
  –into details *special* 79
  describe 594
  –into the composition of 56
  –into the feelings of 914
  –into the ideas of *understand* 518
  concord 714
  –into the spirit of *feel* 821
  delight 827
  –into one's views 488
  –the lists *attack* 716
  contention 720
  –the mind 451
  –upon 66
enteritis 221
enterology 221
enteropothy 221
enterotomy 221
enterprise
  pursuit 622
  undertaking 676
  commercial–794
enterprising
  energetic 171
  active 682
  courageous 861
entertain
  bear in mind 457
  support 707
  amuse 840
  sociality 892
  –an idea 451
  –an opinion 484
  –doubts 485
  –feeling 821
entertainment
  (*see* entertain)
  repast 298
  pleasure 377
enthrall
  subjection 749
  restraint 751
enthrone 873
enthronement 755
enthusiasm *vigor* 574
  willingness 602
  eagerness 682
  feeling 821
  hope 858
  love 897

enthusiast
  madman 504
  obstinate 606
  active 682
  sports 840
enthusiastic
  imaginative 515
  willing 602
  sensitive 822
  excitable 825
  sanguine 858
enthymeme 476
entice 615
enticement 615
enticing 829
entire *whole* 50
  complete 52
  continuous 69
  –horse 373
entirely *much* 31
entirety (*see* entire)
entitle *name* 564
  give a right 924
entity 1
entomb *inter* 363
  imprison 751
entombment 363
entomology 368
entourage
  situation 183
  surroundings 227
entozoön 193
entrails 221
entrain 293
entrammel 751
entrance
  beginning 66
  ingress 294
  means of access 627
  enrapture 827, 829
  magic 992
  give–to 296
entranced 515
entrancement 824
entrant 710
entrap *deceive* 545
  (*imperil* 665)
entreat 765
entrée *reception* 296
  dish 298
  give the–296
  have the–294
entremet 298
entrepôt *store* 636
  mart 799
entrepreneur 599
entre-sol 191
entrust
  commission 755
  give 784
  credit 805
entry *beginning* 66
  ingress 294
  record 551
entwine *join* 43
  intersect 219

convolve 248
enucleate 522
enumerate 85
  –among 76
enunciate *inform* 527
  affirm 535
  voice 580
envelop 225
envelope *covering* 223
  inclosure 232
envenom *deprave* 659
  exasperate 835
  hate 898
  anger 900
envenomed *bad* 649
  insalubrious 657
  painful 830
  malevolent 907
  –tongue 934
envious 920
  –suspicion 920
environ 227
environment 183, 227
environs 197
  in such and such 183
envisage 220
envoy *messenger* 534
  consignee 758
envy 921
enwrap 225
enzyme 320
Eolian harp 417
Eolus 349
eon 106, 110
epacme 62
epact 641
epagoge 476
eparch 694
epact 108
epaulet *badge* 550
  insignia 747
  ornament 847
  decoration 877
epergne 191
ephemera 193
ephemeral 111
ephemerality 111
ephemerid 193
ephemeris
  calendar 114
  record 551
  book 593
ephemeron 111
Ephesian letters 993
ephialtes
  physical pain 378
  hindrance 706
  mental pain 828
ephor 967
epic *descriptive* 594
  poetry 597
epicarp 223
epicedium 839
epicene *multiform* 81

439

epicure

exceptional 83
epicure *fastidious* 868
  sybarite 954a
  glutton 957
epicurean 954
Epicureanism 451
Epicurus, system of 954
epicycle 247
epicycloid 247
epidemic *general* 78
  disease 655
  insalubrity 657
epidermal 223
epidermis 223
epigastrium 250
epigenesis 161
epigram *wit* 842
epigrammatic
  concise 572
epigrammatist 844
epigraph 550
epilepsy 315
epilogue *sequel* 65
  end 67
  drama 599
Epiphany 998
episcopacy 995
episcopal 995
Episcopalian 984
episcopate 995
episode *adjunct* 39
  discontinuity 70
  interjacence 228
episodic *irrelative* 10
  style 573
epistle 592
Epistles 985
epistyle 210
epitaph 363, 550
epithalamium 903
epithelium 223
epithem 662
epithet 564
epitome
  miniature 193
  short 201
  concise 572
  compendium 596
epitomist 201
epitomization 201
epitomizer 201
epizoötic 655, 657
epoch *time* 106
  period 108
  instant 113
  date 114
  present time 118
epochal 108
epode 597
eponym 564
epopoea 597
Epsom salts 662
epulation 298
epulotic 662
epuration 652

equable *uniform* 16
  equitable 922
equal *even* 27
  be parallel 216
  equitable 922
  –*chance* 156
  –*times* 120
  –*to power* 157
equality 27
  identity 13
equalize 213
equanimity 826
equate 27
  compensate 30
equation 37, 85
equator *middle* 68
  world 318, 550
equatorial 68
equerry 746
equestrian 268
equestrienne 268
equibalanced 27
equidistant 68, 216
equilibration 27
equilibrium 27
equine *carrier* 271
  horse 366
equinox *spring* 125
  autumn 126
equip *dress* 225
  prepare 673
equipage *vehicle* 272
  instruments 633
  display 882
equiparable 9
equiparant 9, 27
equiparate 27
equipment *gear* 633
  (see equip)
equipoise 27
equipollence 27
equiponderant 27
equitable *wise* 498
  just 922
  due 924
  honorable 939
  –*interest* 780
equitation 266
equity *right* 922
  honor 939
  law 963
  –*draftsman* 968
  in–922
equivalent
  correlated 12
  identical 13
  equal 27
  compensation 30
  substitute 147
  translation 522
equivocalness
  dubious 475
  double meaning **520**
  impure 961
equivocate
  sophistry 477

  palter 520
  lie 544
equivocation
  (see equivocate)
  quirk 481
  without–543
équivoque
  double meaning 520
  impure 961
era *time* 106
  period 108
  date 114
  –*of indiction* 108
eradicate *destroy* 162
  eject 297
  extract 301
eradication 103
erase *destroy* 162
  rub out 331
  obliterate 552
Erastian 984
erasure (see erase)
Erato 416
Eratosthenes 490a
ere 116–*long* 132
  –*now* 116 *past* 122
  –*then* 116
Erebus *dark* 421
  hell 982
erect *build* 161
  vertical 212
  straight 246
  raise 307
  –*the scaffolding* 673
  with head–878
erection *building* 161
  elevation 307
eremite 893
erewhile 116, 122, 132
ergo 476
ergophobia 683
ergotism 480, 489
ergotize 485
Erinyes 173
eriometer 445
eristic 476
ermine *covering* 223
  badge of authority 747
  ornament 847
erode 36, 659
erosion (see erode)
erotic *amorous* 897
  impure 961
erotomania 821a
err–*in opinion* 495
  –*morally* 945
  to-is human 495
errand *message* 532
  business 625
  commission 755
errand boy 534
errant 279
erratic *irregular* 139
  changeable 149

  wandering 279
  capricious 608
erratum 495
errhine 349
erroneous 495
error *fallacy* **495**
  vice 945
  guilt 947
  court of–966
  writ of–969
erst 66, 122
erstwhile 122
erubescence 434
eructate 297
eructation 297, 349
erudite 490, 500, 539
erudition
  knowledge 490
  learning 539
erumpent 295
eruption
  revolution 146
  violence 173
  egress 295
  ejection 297
  explosion 406
  disease 655
  volcanic–872
eruptive
  (see eruption)
eruptivity 297
erysipelas 655
erythroblast 357
escalade
  mounting 305
  attack 716
escalator 305, 307
escalop 248
escamoter 545
escapade
  absurdity 497
  freak 608
  prank 840
escape *flight* **671**
  liberate 750
  evade 927
  –*notice etc.*
  invisible 447
  inattention 458
  latent 526
  –*the lips a*
  disclosure 529
  speech 582
  –*the memory* 506
  means of–664, 666
escarp
  fortification 717
escarpment
  stratum 204
  height 206
  oblique 217
eschar 204
escharotic
  caustic 171
  pungent 392
eschatology 67

establish

escheat 145, 974
eschew *avoid*
  dislike 867
esclandre 828, 830
escopet 727
escort *accompany* 88
  safeguard 664
  keeper 753
escritoire 191
esculent 298
escutcheon 550, 551
esophagus 350
esoteric *private* 79
  unintelligible 519
  concealed 528
esotericism 528
espalier 232
especial 79
especially *more* 33
Esperanto 560, 563
espial 441
espionage *looking* 441
  inquiry 461
esplanade *houses* 189
  flat 213 (*plain* 344)
espousals 903
espouse *choose* 609
  marriage 903
  –*a cause aid* 707
  cooperate 709
esprit *shrewdness* 498
  wit 842
  bel–844
  –*de corps bias* 481
  cooperation 709
  sociality 892
  (*party* 712)
  –*fort thinker* 500
  irreligious 989
espy 441
esquire *rank* 875
  title 877
essay *experiment* 463
  writing 590
  dissertation 595
  endeavor **675**
essayist
  author 593, 595
esse 1
essence *being* 1
  nature 5
  scent 398
  meaning 516
  (*important part* 642)
essential *real* 1
  intrinsic 5
  great 31
  required 630
  important 642
  –*nature* 3
essentially
  substantially 3
establish *settle* 150
  create 161
  place 184
  evidence 467

440

established — evil speaking

demonstrate 478
—*equilibrium* 27
established
 permanent 141
 habit 613
 —*church* 983a
establishment
 party 712
 shop 799
estafette 268, 534
estaminet 189
estate *condition* 7
 kind 75
 property 780
 come to man's—131
esteem *believe* 484
 approve 931
 in high—928
estimable 648
estimate *number* 85
 measure 466
 adjudge 480
 information 527
 —*too highly* 482
estimation
 (see esteem,
  estimate)
estival 382
estop 706
estrade 213
estrange *disjoin* 44
 alienate 889
 hate 898
estranged
 secluded 893
estrapade *attack* 716
 punishment 972
estreat 974
estuary 343
estuation 384
esurient 865
et cetera *add* 37
 include 76
 plural 100
état major 745
etch *furrow* 259
 engraving 558
etching 54, 558
Eternal, The—976
eternal 112
 —*home* 981
 —*rest* 360
 into the—*secret* 528
eternalize 112
eterne 112
eternity 112 *an*—110
 launch into—360,
  361
 palace of—543
ether *space* 180
 lightness 320
 rarity 322
 vapor 334
 anesthetic 376
ethereal 4
etheric body 980a

etheric double 317
ethical 926
 —*culture* 984
ethicism 984
ethics 926
Ethiop *black* 431
Ethiopian 431
 —*'s skin*
  unchangeable 150
ethnic 984
ethnography 372a
ethnology 372
ethology 926
etiolate *bleach* 429
 whiten 430
etiology
 (see aetiology)
etiquette *custom* 613
 fashion 852
 ceremony 882
etymologist 492, 562
etymologize 562
etymology 562
etymon *origin* 153
 verbal 562
Eucharist 998
euchology 998
euchre 840 *defeat* 731
eucrasy 41
eudaemonism 910,
 944
eudaemonist 910
eudiometer *air* 338
 salubrity 656
eudiometry 338
eugenics 658
eulogist 935
eulogize 482
eulogy 733, 931
Eumenides
 violence 173
 fury 900
 evildoers 913
 revenge 919
eumerogenesis 161
eunuch 158
eunuchize 158
eupepsia 654
euphemism
 metaphor 521
 affirmation 535
 phrase 566
 style 577, 578
 flattery 933
euphemist
 man of taste 850
 flatterer 935
euphonium 417
euphony *melody* 413
 elegant style 578
euphoria 654
Euphrosyne 836
euphuism
 metaphor 521
 elegant style 577
 affected style 579

affectation 855
euphuize 855
Eurasian 41
eureka! *answer* 462
 discovery 480a
Euripus 343
European plan 298
eurythmic 542
eurythmics 242, 537
eurythmy 242
Eusebian 984
Eustachian tube 418
Euterpe 416
euthanasia 360
eutrophy 707
evacuate *quit* 293
 excrete 295
 emit 297
evacuation 299
evade *sophistry* 477
 avoid 623
 not observe 773
 exempt 927
evagation 279
evanescent *small* 32
 transient 111
 little 193
 disappearing 449
evangelical 983a,
 985
Evangelists 985
evanid 160
evaporable 334
evaporate
 unsubstantial 4
 transient 111
 vaporize 336
 dry up 340
evaporation
 vaporization 336
 dryness 340
 cloud 353
 preserving 670
evaporator 336
evasion *sophistry* 477
 quirk 481
 concealment 528
 falsehood 544
 untruth 546
 avoidance 623
 escape 671
 cunning 702
 nonobservance 773
 dereliction 927
evasive (see evasion)
eve 126 *on the*—*of*
 transient 111
 prior 116
 future 121
evection 61
even *uniform* 16
 equal 27
 still more 33
 level 213
 parallel 216
 straight 246

flat 251
 smooth 255
 although 469
 neutral 628
 in spite of 708
 be—*with*
 retaliate 718
 pay 807
 —*course* 628
 —*now* 118
 —*off* 27
 —*so for all that* 30
 yes 488
 —*temper* 826
 —*tenor uniform* 16
 order 58
 regularity 80
 —*terms* 922
 pursue the—*tenor*
 continue 143
 avoid 623
 business 625
even—**handed**
 just 922
 honorable 939
evening 126
 —*dress* 225
 —*star* 423
 shades of—422
evenness (see even)
 symmetry 242
evensong 126, 990
event 151 *bout* 720
 in the—*of*
  circumstance 8
 eventuality 151
 destiny 152
 supposition 514
 justified by the—937
eventful 151
 remarkable 642
 stirring 682
eventide 126
eventual *future* 121
eventuality 151
eventually *effect* 154
eventuate 151
ever *invariable* 16
 perpetually 112
 —*and anon* 136
 —*changing* 149
 —*recurring* 104
 —*so little* 32
 —*so long* 110
 —*so many* 102
everduring 112
evergreen
 continuous 69
 lasting 110
 always 112
 fresh 123
 plant 367, 369
everlasting
 perpetual 112
 destined 152
 —*fire* 982

—*life* 152
evermore 112
eversible 140
eversion 140, 218
evert 140, 218
every *general* 78
 periodic 138
 at—*turn* 186
 —*day conformity* 82
 frequent 136
 habit 613
 —*description* 81
 —*hand against one*
  891
 —*inch* 50
 —*other* 138
 —*whit* 52
 in—*mouth*
  assent 488
  news 532
  repute 873
 in—*quarter* 180
 in—*respect* 194
 on—*side* 22
everybody 78
every one 78
 —*his due* 922
 —*in his turn* 148
everywhere *space* 180
 presence 186
evict 297
evidence 467
 manifestation 525
 disclosure 529
 ocular—446
evident *visible* 446
 certain 474
 manifest 525
evidential 467
evil *harm* 619
 badness 649
 demoniac 980
 impious 988
 —*day adversity* 735
 —*eye vision* 441
 malevolence 907
 disapprobation 932
 spell 993
 —*favored* 846
 —*fortune* 735
 —*genius* 980
 —*hour* 135
 —*one* 978
 —*plight* 735
 —*spirits* 980
 —*star* 649
 prepare for—673
 through—*report etc.*
  604a
evildoer 913, 975
evildoing 945
evil—**minded**
 malevolent 907
 vicious 945
evil speaking
 malediction 908

441

censure 932
detraction 934
evince *show* 467
prove 478
disclose 529
evirate 158
eviscerate *eject* 297
extract 301
eviscerated 4
eviternal 112
evoke *cause* 153
call upon 765
excite 824
evolution
numerical 85
production 161
motion 264
circuition 311
turning out **313**
organization 357
training 673
action 680
military –s 722
evolutionary 264, 313
evolve *discover* 480a
evolved from 154
(*and see* evolution)
evolvement 313
evulgate 531
evulsion 301
evviva! 931
ewe *sheep* 366
female 374
ewer 191
ex–animo 602
–dono 784
–more 613
–officio *officer* 694
authority 737
duty 924
–parte 467
–post facto 122, 133
–tempore *instant* 113
occasion 134
–voto 768
exacerbate
increase 35
exasperate 173
pervert 659
aggravate 835
exact *similar* 17
copy 21
true 494
literal 516
style 572
require 741
tax 812
insolence 885
claim 924, 926
–meaning 516
–memory 505
–observance 772
–truth 494
exacting *severe* 739
discontented 832

grasping 865
exaction (*see* exact)
undue 925
exactly *literally* 19
just so 488
exactness (*see* exact)
exaggeration
increase 35
expand 194
overestimate 482
magnify **549**
misrepresent 555
exalt *increase* 35
elevate 307
extol 931
(*boast* 884)
–one's horn 873
exalted *high* 206
repute 873
noble 875
magnanimous 942
examination
(*see* examine)
evidence 467
on–463
undergo–461
examine
attend to 457
inquire 461
–the books
accounts 811
example *pattern* 22
instance 82
bad–949
good–948
make an–*of* 974
set a good–944
exanimate *dead* 360
supine 683
exanthema 655
exarch 745
exasperate
exacerbate 173
aggravate 835
enrage 900
excavate 252
excavation 252
excecation 442
exceed *surpass* 33
remain 40
transgress 303
intemperance 954
exceedingly
(*greatly* 31)
excel *surpass* 33
–in *skillful* 698
excellence
goodness 648
virtue 944
excellency *title* 877
excelsior 305
except *subduct* 38
exclude 55
reject 610
exception
unconformity 83

qualification 469
exemption 777a
disapproval 932
take–*qualify* 469
resent 900
exceptionable
bad 649
guilty 947
exceptional
unimitated 20
extraneous 57
uncomfortable 83
in an–*degree* 31
exceptions 901, 901a
excern 297
excerpt 551, 609
excerpta *parts* 51
compendium 596
selections 609
excerption 609
excess *remainder* 40
redundance 641
intemperance 954
excessive *great* 31
exchange
reciprocity 12
interchange 148
saloon 189
transfer 783
barter 794
mart 799
bill of–771
–*blows etc.*
retaliation 718
battle 720
Exchequer 802
Baron of–967
Court of–966
–*bill* 800
excise 812
exciseman 965
excision 38
excitability
excitement **825**
irascibility 901
excitant 171
excitation 824
excitative 171
excite *energy* 171
violence 173
impassion 824
–*an impression* 375
–*attention* 457
–*desire* 865
–*hope* 811
–*love* 897
excited 173
–*fancy* 515
excitement 824, 825
anger 900
exclaim 411
–*against* 932
exclamation
typography 550
utterance 580
exclude *sift* 42

leave out 55
reject 610
prohibit 761
banish 893
exclusion 55, 57
exclusive *simple* 42
omitting 55
special 79
irregular 83
forbidding 761
–*of* 38
–*possession* 777
–*thought* 457
excogitate
ruminate 450
thought 451
imagination 515
excommunicate
banish 893
curse 908
rite 998
(*exclude* 55)
excoriate 226
excrement
excretion 299
dirt 653
excrescence
projection 250
blemish 848
excreta *excretion* 299
dirt 653
excretion 297, **299**
excretory 295, 299, 350
excruciating
physical pain 378
mental pain 830
exculpate *forgive* 918
vindicate 937
acquit 970
excursion 266, 311
excursionist 268
excursive
deviating 279
–*style* 573
excursus 595
excuse *plea* 617
exempt 777a
forgive 918
exempt 927a
vindicate 937
execrable *bad* 649
offensive 830
execrate *hate* 898
curse 908
execute *kill* 361
(*see* execution)
execution *music* 416
action 680
conduct 692
signing 771
observance 772
punishment 972
carry into–
complete 729
put in–

undertaking 676
executioner 975
executive *conduct* 692
directing 693
authority 737
judicature 965
executor 690
to one and his–*s*
etc. property 780
exegesis 522
exegetical 522
exemplar 22
exemplary 944
exemplify *quote* 82
illustrate 522
exempt *free* 748
dispensation 927a
–*from absent* 187
unpossessed 777a
exemption
exception 83
qualification 469
deliverance 672
permission 760
nonpossession **777a**
nonliability **927a**
exenterate 297
exequatur 755
exequies 363
exercise
operation 170
teach 537
task 625
use 677
act 680
exert 686
(*prepare* 673)
–*authority* 737
–*discretion* 600
–*power* 157
–*the intellect* 451
exercises 990
exercitation
(*see* exercise)
exergue 231
exert *use* 677
–*authority* 737
–*oneself* 686
exertion *physical* 171
effort **686**
exertive 170
exfoliate 226
exhalation
ejection 297
excretion 299
vapor 336
breathing 349, 353
odor 398
exhale 349
exhaust *paralyze* 158
deflate 195
of an automobile 272
waste 638
fatigue 688
complete 729
drain 789

exhausted

squander 818
exhausted
  inexistent 2
exhaustion
  (see exhaust)
exhaustive
  complete 52
  –*inquiry* 461
exhaustless
  infinite 105
  enough 639
exhibit *evidence* 467
  show 525
  display 882
exhibition
  (see exhibit)
  scholarship 541
exhilarate 836
exhilarating gas 376
exhort *persuade* 615
  advise 695
exhortation
  sermon 998
  (see exhort)
exhume
  past times 122
  disinter 363
exigeant 739
exigency *crisis* 8
  requirement 630
  dearth 640
  difficulty 704
  need 865
exigent *exacting* 739
  discontented 832
exiguity 193
exiguous 193
exile *transport* 185
  banish 893
  punish 972
  (*eject* 297)
  voluntary–893
exility 203
existence *being* **1**
  thing 3
  –*in time* 118
  destiny 152
  –*in space* 186
  come into–151
exit *departure* 293
  egress 295
  disappear 449
  give–to 297
exode 599
exodus 293
exogamy 372a
exogenous 367
exomorphic 220
exonerate
  disburden 705
  release 760
  forgive 918
  exempt 927a
  vindicate 937
  acquit 970
exophagy 945

exorable 914
exorbitant
  enormous 31
  redundant 641
  dear 814
exorcism 992, 993
exorcist 994
exordium 64, 66
exosmose 302
exosmosis 302
exostosis 250
exoteric *open* 525
  public 531
exothermic reaction 490d
exotic *alien* 10
  exceptional 83
  plant 367
expand *increase* 35
  swell 194
  –*in breadth* 202
  rarefy 322
  –*in writing* 573
expanse *space* 180
  size 192
  plain 344
expansion 194
expansive 194
expatiate *range* 266
  –*in writing* etc. **573**
  –*in discourse* 584
expatriate *deport* 295
  banish 893
expect
  look forward to 507
  hope 858
  not wonder 871
  (*future* 121)
  reason to–472
expectance 871
expectancy 780, 871
expectant 121, 507
expectation 507
  beyond–508
  hold out an–768
expected 507
  as well as can be–654
expectorate 297
expedience 646
expedient *plan* 626
  means 632
  useful 646
expedite *early* 132
  quickening 274
  hasten 684
  aid 707
expedition
  (see expedite)
  march 266
  activity 682
  war 722
expel *push* 284
  eject 297
  punish 972
  (*displace* 185)

expend *waste* 638
  use 677
  pay 809
  –*itself* 683
expenditure 809
  accounts 811
expense *price* 812
  joke at one's–842
  spare no–816
expenseless 815
expenses 809
expensive 809, 814
experience
  meet with 151
  knowledge 490
  undergo 821
  learn by–950
experienced 698
  –*eye* etc. 700
experiences
  narrative 594
experiment *trail* **463**
  endeavor 675
experimental 463
  –*philosophy* 316
expert *skillful* 698
  proficient 700
  –*accountant* 801
expiate 952, 976
expiration
  (see expire)
expire *end* 67
  run its course 109
  breathe 349
  die 360
expired *past* 122
explain *exemplify* 82
  answer 462
  interpret 522
  comment 595
  (*inform* 527)
  (*teach* 537)
  –*away* 523
  –*wrongly* 523
explainer 524
explanation
  (see explain)
expletive *diffuse* 573
  redundant 641
expletory 641
explication 522
explicit *meaning* 516
  clear 518
  potent 525
explicitness 570
explode *burst* 173
  sound 406
  confute 479
  failure 732
  passion 825
exploded *past* 122
  antiquated 124
  error 495
  blown upon 932
  (see explosion)
exploit *action* 680

courage 861
exploitation 461
exploration 461
explore
  investigate 461
  experiment 463
explorer 268
explosion
  (see explode)
  revolution 146
  violence 173
  loudness 404
  sound 406
  anger 900
explosive 727
  dangerous 665
exponent
  numerical 84
  interpreter 524
  informant 527
  index 550
export 295
expose *denude* 226
  confute 479
  disclose 529
  censure 932
  –*oneself*
  disreputable 874
  –*to danger* 665
  –*to view* *visible* 446
  manifest 525
exposé
  confutation 479
  disclosure 529
  description 594
exposed *bare* 226
  –*to liable* 177
exposition
  (see expose)
  explanation 522
  indication 550
  drama 599
  exhibition 882
expositor
  interpreter 524
  teacher 540
expository
  explaining 522
  informing 527
  disclosed 529
  disserting 595
expostulate
  dissuade 616
  advise 695
  deprecate 766
  reprehend 932
exposure (see expose)
  appearance 448
  –*to weather* 338
expound *interpret* 522
  teach 537
expounder 524
express
  carrier 268, 271
  rapid 274
  squeeze out 301

extend

mean 516
declare 525
inform 527
language 560
intentional 620
transit 627
haste 684
–*by words* 566
–*car* 272
–*regret* 952
–*sympathy for* 915
–*train* 272
expressed 566
well–578
expression
  (see express)
  musical–416
  aspect 448
  nomenclature 564
  phrase 566
  mode of–569
  new fangled–563
expressive
  meaning 516
  sensibility 822
expressman 271
exprobation
  censure 932
  accusation 938
expropriation 782
expugnable 665
expugnation
  success 731
  (*taking* 789)
expuition 297
expulsion (see expel)
  exclusion 55
expunge *destroy* 162
  efface 552
expurgate 652
exquisite *savory* 394
  excellent 648
  pleasurable 829
  beautiful 845
  fop 854
exquisitely *very* 31
exradio 420
exsiccate 340
exspuition 297
exsudation 299
exsufflation 993
extant 1
extasy (see ecstasy)
extemporaneous
  (see extempore)
  transient 111
extempore
  instant 113
  early 132
  occasion 134
  offhand 612
  unprepared 674
extemporize 612
extemporizer 612
extend *expand* 194
  prolong 200

extended

(*increase* 35)
—to 196
extended *spacious* 180
  long 200
  broad 202
extendibility 324
extensibility 324, 325
extensile 324
extension
  (*see* extend)
  increase 35
  continuance 143
  space 180
  —of time 110
extensive *great* 31
  wide 180
  —knowledge 490
extent *degree* 26
  space 180
  length 200
extenuate *decrease* 36
  weaken 160
  excuse 937
extenuated 203
extenuating 937
  —circumstances
    qualification 469
    excuse 937
extenuatory 469
exterior 57, 220
exteriority 220
exterminate 162
extermination 301
exterminator 165
extern 220
external 220
  —evidence 467
  —senses 375
externalize 220
exterritorial 220
extinct *inexistent* 2
  past 122
  old 124
  destroyed 162
  darkness 421
extincteur 385
extinction
  obliteration 552
  —of life 360
extinguish
  destroy 162
  blow out 385
  darken 421
extinguisher 165
  put an—upon
  hinder 706
  defeat 731
extinguishment 2
extirpate 2, 301
extispicious 511
extispicy 511
extol *overestimate* 482
  praise 931
extort *extract* 301
  compel 744
  despoil 789

extorted *dissent* 489
extortion
  dearness 814
  rapacity 819
extortionate
  severe 739
  dear 814
  rapacious 819
  grasping 865
extortioner 789, 819
extra *additional* 37
  supernumerary 641
  ab—220
extract *take out* 301
  record 551
  quotation 596
  remedy 662
extraction 301
  paternity 166
  —of roots 85
extractor 301
extradition
  deportation 270
  expulsion 297
extrados 220
extrajudicial 964
extralimitary 220
extramundane 220, 317
extramural 220
extraneous
  extrinsic 6
  not related 10
  foreign 57
  exterior 220
extraneousness 57
extraordinary
  great 31
  exceptional 83
extraregarding 220
extraterrene 220
extraterrestrial 220
extraterritorial 220
extravagance
  (*see* extravagant)
extravagant
  inordinate 31
  violent 173
  absurd 497
  foolish 499
  fanciful 515
  exaggerated 549
  excessive 641
  high-priced 814
  prodigal 818
  vulgar 851
  ridiculous 853
extravaganza
  fanciful 515
  misrepresentation 555
  drama 599
extravagation 303
extravasate
  egress 295
  ejection 297

extreme
  inordinate 31
  end 67
  —unction 998
extremist 710
extremity *end* 67
  adversity 735
  tribulation 828
  at the last—665
  drive matters to an —604
extricate *take out* 301
  deliver 672
  facilitate 705
  liberate 750
extrinsicality 6
extrinsic evidence 467
extrusion *eject* 297
  excrete 299
extrusive 297
exuberant—*style* 573
  redundant 639
exudation *egress* 295
  excretion 299
exudative 295
exude 295
exulcerate 659
exult *rejoice* 838
  boast 884
exultant *hopeful* 858
exulting *cheerful* 836
exunge 356
exuviae 223, 653
  (*remains* 40)
exuvial 226
exuviate 226
eye *circle* 247
  opening 260
  organ of sight 441
  appear to one's—446
  before one's—
  front 234
  visible 446
  manifest 525
  cast the—s on
  see 441
  cast the—s over
  attend to 457
  catch the—457
  close the—s
  blind 442
  death 360
  sleep 683
  dry—s 823
  —askance 860
  —disease 655
  —glistening 824
  —like Mars 441
  —of a needle 260
  —of the master 693
  —s draw straws 683
  —s of a lynx 459
  —s open *attention* 457
  care 459
  intention 620

  —s opened
  disclosure 529
  —s out 442
  fix the—s on 457
  have an—to
  attention 457
  intention 620
  desire 865
  have one's—s about one 459
  in one's—*visible* 446
  expectant 507
  in the—of the law 963
  in the—s of *appearance* 448
  belief 484
  keep an—upon 459
  look with one's own —s 459
  mind's—515
  open the—s to 480*a*
  set one's—upon 865
  shut one's—s to *inattention* 458
  permit 760
  to the—s 448
  under the—s of 186
  up to one's—s 641
  with moistened—s 839
  with open—s 870
eyeglass 445
eyelashes 256
eyeless 442
eyelet 260
eye opener 508
eyesight 441
eyesore *ugly* 846
  blemish 848
eyeteeth
  have cut one's— *adolescence* 131
  skill 698
  cunning 702
eyewater 662
eyewitness
  spectator 444
  evidence 467
eyot 346
eyre 966
eyrie 189

F

Fabian policy
  delay 133
  inaction 681
  caution 864
fable *error* 495
  metaphor 521
  fiction 546
  description 594
fabric *state* 7

  effect 154
  texture 329
  —s 635
fabricate *compose* 54
  form 56
  make 161
  invent 515
  falsify 544
fabrication *lie* 546
fabulist 594
fabulous *enormous* 31
  imaginary 515
  untrue 546
  exaggerated 549
  descriptive 594
  mythical 979
faburden 413
façade 234
face *exterior* 220
  covering 223
  line 224
  front 234
  aspect 448
  oppose 708
  resist 719
  impudence 885
  change the—of 146
  —about 279
  —of the country 344
  —of the thing *appearance* 448
  —the music 861
  —to face *front* 234
  contraposition 237
  manifest 525
  fly in the—of *disobey* 742
  in the—of *presence* 186
  opposite 708
  look in the—*see* 441
  proud 878
  make—s *distort* 243
  ugly 846
  disrespect 929
  not show—
  disreputable 874
  bashful 879
  on the—of
  manifest 525
  on the—of the earth
  space 180
  world 318
  put a good—on
  sham 545
  calm 826
  cheerful 836
  hope 858
  pride 878
  display 882
  vindicate 937
  set one's—against 708
  show—against 708
  show—*present* 186
  visible 446

face cloth   **fall**

to one's—525
wry—378
face cloth
  cleanness 652
face guard 717
facet 220
facetiae 842
facetious 842
facia 234
facile *willing* 602
  irresolute 605
  easy 705
facile princeps 33
facilitate 705
facility *skill* 698
  easy 705
facing *covering* 223
  lining 224
facinorous 945
façon de parler
  figure of speech 521
  exaggeration 549
facsimile *copy* 21
  duplication 90
  representation 554
fact *existence* 1
  event 151
  certainty 474
  truth 494
  in—535
faction *company* 72
  party 712
  feud 713
factious 24, 713
factitious 545, 546
factor *numerical* 84
  agent 690
  director 694
  consignee 758
  (*merchant* 797)
factory 691
factotum *agent* 690
  manager 694
  employé 758
facts *evidence* 467
  summary of—594
factual 1
facula 420
faculties 450
  in possession of
    one's—502
faculty *power* 157
  profession 625
  skill 698
facundity 582
fad *bias* 481
  caprice 608
faddle 683
fade *vanish* 4
  transient 111
  become old 124
  droop 160
  grow dim 422
  lose color 429
  disappear 449
  spoil 659

—away *cease* 142
  disappear 449
—from the memory
  506
—out 129
fadeless 873
fadge 23
faeces [*see* feces]
fag *labor* 686
  fatigue 688
  drudge 690
  —end *remainder* 40
  end 67
fagot *bundle* 72
  fuel 388
  —voter 4
Fahrenheit scale
  490d
faïence 557
fail *droop* 160, 655
  shortcoming 304
  be confuted 479
  not succeed 732
  not observe 773
  not pay 808
  dereliction 927
failing (*see* fail)
  incomplete 53
  insufficient 640
  vice 945
  guilt 947
  —heart 837
  —luck 735
  —memory 506
  —sight 443
  —strength 160
failure 732
fain *willing* 602
  compulsive 744
  wish 865
fainéant 683
faint
  small in degree 32
  impotent 158
  weak 160
  sound 405
  dim 422
  color 429
  swoon 688
  damn with—*praise*
    930, 932, 934
  —heart *fear* 860
  cowardice 862
  wooing 902
faintness *sound* **405**
  (*see* faint)
fair *in degree* 31
  pale 429
  white 430
  wise 498
  important 643
  good 648
  moderate 651
  mart 799
  beautiful 845
  just 922

honorable 939
  by—means or foul
    631
—chance 472
—copy *copy* 21
  writing 590
—field *occasion* 134
  freedom 748
—game 857
—name 873
—play 922, 923
—question 461
—sex 374
—weather 734
  pleasurableness 829
—weather sailor 701
—wind 705
—words 894
  in a—way
  tending 176
  probable 472
  convalescent 658
  hopeful 858
fairing 784
fairly *intrinsically* 5
  slightly 643
  get on—736
fair-spoken
  courtesy 894
  flattery 933
fairway 267
fairy *fanciful* 515
  fay 979
  imp 980
  —lore 993
  —tale 594
  fabrication 546
fairyism 979
fairyland 515
fait accompli
  certain 474
  complete 729
faith *belief* 484
  hope 858
  honor 939
  piety 987
  declaration of—983
—cure 662
—curer 984
—healing 662
  i'—535
  keep—with
  observe 772
  plight—*promise* 768
  love 902
  true—*orthodox* 983a
  want of—
  incredulity 487
  irreligious 989
faithful (*see* faith)
  like 17
  copy 21
  exact 494
  obedient 743
—memory 505

—to 772
faithless *false* 544
  dishonorable 940
  skeptical 989
fake *imitation* 19
  concoct 544
  swindle 545
  untruth 546
faker 548, 683, 797
fakir 804, 955, 996
falcade 309
falcate *pointed* 244
  carved 245
falchion 727
Falcidian law 780
falciform (*see* falcate)
falcon 792
falconet 727
faldstool 215
fall *autumn* 126
  happen 151
  perish 162
  slope 217
  regression 283
  descend 306
  die 360
  fail 732
  adversity 735
  vice 945
—a cursing 908
—a prey to
  defeated 732
  subject 749
—asleep 683
—astern *rear* 235
  regress 283
—at one's feet 725
—away 195
—back *return* 283
  recede 287
  relapse 661
—back upon *use* 677
  defense 717
—dead *die* 360
—down *collapse* 304
  worship 990
—down before 928
—flat on the ear 843
—foul of *blow* 276
  hinder 706
  oppose 708
  discord 713
  attack 716
  contention 720
  censure 932
—from one's high
    estate
  adversity 735
  disrepute 874
—from the lips 582
—in *order* 58
  continuity 69
  event 151
—in love with 897
—in price 815
—in the way of 186

—in with *agree* 23
  conform 82
  converge 290
  discover 480a
  concord 714
  consent 762
—into *conversion* 144
  river 348
—into a custom
  conform to 82
—into a habit 613
—into a passion 900
—into a trap 547
—into decay 659
—into oblivion 506
—into raptures 827
—of day 125
—off *decrease* 36
  deteriorate 659
—off again 661
—of snow 383
—of the curtain 67
—of the leaf 126
—of the mercury 338
—on one's knees
  submit 725
  servile 886
  gratitude 916
  worship 990
—out *happen* 151
  quarrel 713
  enmity 889
—short *inferior* 34
  contract 195
  shortcoming 304
—through *fail* 732
—to *eat* 298
  take in hand 676
  do battle 722
—to dust 328
—to one's lot
  event 151
  chance 156
  receive 785
  duty 926
—to pieces
  disjunction 44
  destruction 162
  brittle 328
—to the ground
  be confuted 479
  fail 732
—to work 686
—under *inclusion* 76
  subjection 749
—under one's notice
    457
—upon *discover* 480a
  unexpected 508
  devise 626
  attack 716
—upon the ear 418
  have to—back upon
  provision 637
  let—*lower* 308
  inform 527

fallacy / fast

water—348
fallacy *sophistry* 477
  error 495
  show the—of 497
fallen angel
  bad man 949
  Satan 978
fallible *uncertain* 475
  sophistical 477
falling—*action* 154
  —star *world* 318
  luminary 423
  —weather 348
fallow
  unproductive 169
  yellow 436
  unready 674
  inactive 681
false *sophistry* 477
  error 495
  untrue 544, 546
  spurious 925
  dishonorable 940
  —alarm 669
  —coloring
    misinterpretation 523
  falsehood 544
  —construction 523, 544
  —doctrine 984
  —expectation 509
  —hearted 940
  —impression 495
  —light *vision* 443
  —money 800
  —ornament 851
  —plea *untruth* 546
  plea 617
  —position 704
  —pretenses *steal* 791
  —prophet
    disappoint 509
    (*pseudo*—*revelation*) 986
  —reasoning 477
  —scent *error* 495
  mislead 538
  —shame 855
  —statement 546
  —step 732
  —teaching 538
  —witness *deceiver* 548
  detraction 934
falsehood 544, 546
falsetto *squeak* 410
  music 415
  want of voice 581
falsification 555
falsify *error* 495
  falsehood 544, 546
  misrepresent 555
  —accounts 811
  —one's hope 509
falsity (*see* false)
falter *slow* 275

stammer 583
hesitate 605
slip 732
hopeless 859
fear 860
fame *greatness* 31
  memory 505
  renown 873
familiar *known* 490
  habitual 613
  sociable 892
  affable 894
  spirit 979, 980
  on—terms 888
familiarity
  (*see* familiar)
familiarize *teach* 537
  habit 613
Familist 984
familistery 712
family *kin* 11
  pedigree 69
  class 75
  ancestors 166
  posterity 167
  domestic 221
  party 712
  —circle 892
  —jars 713
  —likeness 17
  —tie 11
  —tree 166
  happy—714
  in the bosom of one's—221
  in the—way 161
famine 640
  —price 814
famine-stricken 640
famish *stingy* 819
  fasting 956
famished
  insufficient 640
  hungry 865
famous 873
famously *much* 31
fan *strike* 276
  blow 349
  cool 385
  refresh 689
  stimulate 824
  enthusiast 840
  —into a flame
    anger 900
  —the embers 505
  —the flame
    violence 173
  heat 384
  aid 707
  excite 824
  flirt a—855
fanatic *dogmatist* 474
  madman 504
  imaginative 515
  zealot 682
  religious—988

fanatical
  dogmatic 474
  misjudging 481
  insane 503
  emotional 821
  excitable 825
  heterodox 984
  overrighteous 988
fanaticism
  dogmatism 474
  obstinacy 606
  (*see* fanatical)
fanciful
  imaginative 515
  capricious 608
  ridiculous 853
  —projector 515
fancy *think* 451
  idea 453
  believe 484
  suppose 514
  imagine 515
  caprice 608
  choice 609
  pugilism 726
  wit 842
  desire 865
  love 897
  after one's—850
  —dog 366
  —price 814
  —stocks 800
  indulge one's—609
  take a—to
    delight in 827
  desire 865
  take one's
    —please 829
fandango 840
fane 1000
fanfare *loudness* 404
  celebration 883
fanfaron 887
fanfaronade 884
fangs *venom* 663
  rule 737
  retention 781
fanlight 260
fanlike 202
fannel 999
fanon 999
fan-shaped 194
fantasia 415
fantastic *odd* 83
  absurd 497
  imaginative 515
  capricious 608
  bad taste 851
  ridiculous 853
fantasy
  imagination 515
  desire 865
fantoccini
  representation 554
  drama 599
faquir (*see* fakir)

far—and near 180
  —and wide 31, 180, 196
  —as the eye can see 180
  —away 196
  —be it from
    unwilling 603
  deprecation 766
  —between
    disjunction 44
  few 103
  interval 198
  —from it *unlike* 18
  shortcoming 304
  no 536
  —from the truth 546
  —off 196
farad 490d
farce *absurdity* 497
  untruth 546
  drama 599
  wit 842
  ridiculous 853
  mere—
    unimportant 643
  useless 645
farceur *actor* 599
  humorist 844
farcical *absurd* 497
  ridiculous 853
fardel *bundle* 72
  hindrance 706
fare *state* 7
  food 298
  price 812
  bill of—*list* 86
farewell
  departure 293
  relinquishment 624
  loss 776
  —to greatness 874
far-famed 31, 873
far-fetched 10
far-flung 180
far-gone *much* 31
  insane 503
  spoiled 654
farina 330
farinaceous 330
farm *till* 371
  productiveness 636
  property 780
  rent 788
farmer 371
  afternoon—683
farmhouse 189
faro 621—bank 621
farrago 59
farrier 370
farrow *produce* 161
  litter 369
  multitude 102
farse 998
far-sighted
  vision 441

foresight 510
farther 196
  (*see* further)
farthing *quarter* 97
  worthless 643
  coin 800
  —candle 422
farthingale 225
fasces 747
fascia *band* 205
  circle 247
fasciate 247
fascicle 51, 72
fasciculated 72
fascinate
  influence 615
  excite 824
  please 829
  astonish 870
  love 897
  conjure 992
fascinated
  pleased 827
fascination
  (*see* fascinate)
  infatuation 825
  desire 870
  (*spell* 993)
fascinator *wrap* 384
fascine 72
fash 830
fashion *state* 7
  form 240
  custom 613
  method 627
  ton **852**
  create 976
  after a—*middling* 32
  after this—627
  be in the—488
  follow the—82
  for—'s sake 852
  man of—852
  set the
    —*influence* 175
  authority 737
fast *joined* 43
  steadfast 150
  rapid 274
  fashionable 852
  intemperate 954
  not eat 956
  worship 990
  rite 998
  —and loose
    sophistry 477
  falsehood 544
  irresolute 605
  tergiversation 607
  caprice 608
  —asleep 683
  —by 197
  —day 640, 956
  —friend 890
  —man *fop* 854
  libertine 962

446

fasten

stick–704
fasten *join* 43
  hang 214
  restrain 751
  –a quarrel upon 713
  –on the mind 451
  –upon 789
fastening 45
fast–handed 819
fastidious 868
  censorious 932
fastidiousness 868
fastigium 210
fasting *worship* 990
  penance 952
  abstinence **956**
fastness *asylum* 666
  defense 717
fat *corpulent* 192
  expansion 194
  unctuous 355
  oleaginous 356
  in the fire
    disorder 59
    violence 173
  –of the land
    pleasure 377
    enough 639
    prosperity 734
    intemperance 95
  kill the–ted calf
    celebration 883
    sociality 892
fata Morgana
  ignis fatuus 423
fatal 361–*disease* 655
  –gift of beauty 845
fatalism 601
fatality 601
fate *end* 67
  necessity 601
  predetermination 611
  chance 621
  be one's–156
  sure as–474
fateful 601
Fates 601
fat–headed 499
father *eldest* 128
  paternity 166
  priest 996
  Apostolical–s 985
  –upon 155
  gathered to one's–s 360
  heavy–599
Father, God the–976
fatherhood 166
fatherland 181, 189, 342
fatherless 158
fatherly 906
fathership 166
Fathers, the–983
fathom *length* 200
investigate 461
solve 462
measure 466
discover 480a
knowledge 490
fathomless 208
fatidical 511
fatigation 688
fatigue 688
  (*weariness* 841)
fatihah 66
fatiloquent 511
fatling 298
fatness (see fat)
fatras 643
fatten *expand* 194
  improve 658
  prosperous 734
  –on *parasite* 886
  –upon *feed* 298
fatuity 499
fat–witted 499
faubourg 227
fauces 231
faucet 263
faugh! 867
fault *break* 70
  rift 198
  error 495
  imperfection 651
  failure 732
  vice 945
  guilt 947
  at–*uncertain* 475
  ignorant 491
  unskillful 699
  find–with 932
fault–finder 832
faultless *perfect* 650
  innocent 946
faulty *imperfect* 651
faun 978
fauna 366
fault: comme il–
  taste 850
  fashion 852
fauteuil 215
fautor 890
faux pas *failure* 732
  misconduct 947
  intrigue 961
favaginous 252
faveolate 252
favilious 432
favonian 349
favor *resemble* 17
  badge 550
  letter 592
  aid 707
  indulgence 740
  permit 760
  gift 784
  partiality 923
  appearances in–of 472
  –with 784
get into–
  friendship 888
  love 897
  in–*repute* 873
  approbation 931
  in–of *approve* 931
  under–of 760
  view with–906
favorable
  occasion 134
  willing 602
  good 648
  aid 707
  –*prospect* 472
  –to 709
  take a–turn
    improve 658
    prosperity 734
favorably *well* 618
favorer 890
favorite *pleasing* 829
  beloved 897, **899**
favoritism
  friendship 888
  wrong 923
favose 252
fawn *animal* 366
  brown 433
  cringe 886
  flatter 933
fawn–colored 433
fawning *servile* 746
fay 979
faze *disconcert* 706
  bother 830
  daunt 860
fealty *obedience* 743
  duty 926
  respect 928
fear 860
fearful *incredible* 31
  painful 830
  timid 862
fearfully *much* 31
  wonderfully 870
fearless *hope* 858
  courage 861
feasible *possible* 470
  easy 705
feast *period* 138
  repast 298
  pleasure 377
  revel 840
  rite 998
  –one's eyes 897
feast of reason
  conversation 588
  –and flow of soul
    sociality 892
feat *action* 680
  courage **861**
  –of arms 720
  –of strength 159
feather *class* 75
  tuft 256
  light 320
irresolution 605
trifle 643
ornament 847
decoration 877
–in one's cap
  honor 873
  decoration 877
–in the scale 643
–in one's nest
  prepare 673
  prosperity 734
  wealth 803
  economy 817
  selfish 943
–the oar 698
  hear a–drop 403
  in full–*prepared* 673
  prosperous 734
  rich 803
  in high–*health* 654
  cheerful 884
  pleased with a–840
feather bed 324
feathered tribes 366
feathery 149, 256
featly 682
feature *character* 5
  component 56
  form 240
  appearance 448
  lineament 234, 550
feaze 60
  (see also faze)
febricity 382
febrifacient 383
febrific 382
febrifuge 662
febrile 382, 825
fecal 299, 653
feces *excretion* 299
  foulness 653
feculence 653
fecund 168
fecundate 161
federal 48
  –currency 800
federalism 737
federalists 712
federate 48, 712
federation 712
fee *possession* 777
  property 780
  pay 809
  reward 973
feeble *weak* 160
  illogical 477
  (*scanty* 32)
feeble–minded
  imbecile 499
  irresolute 605
feebleness *style* 575
feed *eat* 298
  fodder 370
  fuel 388
  supply 637
  –the flame 707

fellow

fee–faw–fum
  bugbear 860
feel *sense* 375
  touch 379
  emotion 821
  –for *try* 463
  benevolence 906
  pity 914
  –grief 915
  –one's way *essay* 675
  caution 864
  –the pulse 461
  –the want of 865
feeler 379
  inquiry 461
  experiment 463
feeling 821
  –of sense 916
feet *low* 207
  walkers 266
  at one's–*near* 197
  subjection 749
  humility 879
  fall at one's–
    submit 725
  fall on one's–
    prosper 734
  lick the–of
    servile 886
  light upon one's–
    safe 664
  spring to one's–307
  throw oneself at the–
    of *entreat* 765
feign 544, 546
feigned 545
feint 545
felicitate 896
felicitious *agreeing* 23
  –*style* 23
  skillful 698
  successful 731
  pleasant 829
felicity *elegance* 578
  happiness 827
feline *cat* 366
  stealthy 528
  cunning 702
fell *destroy* 162
  mountain 206
  lay flat 213
  skin 223
  knock flat 251
  lay low 308
  plain 344
  dire 860
  malevolent 907
fellah 876
fellow *similar* 17
  equal 27
  companion 88
  dual 89
  man 373
  scholar 492
  –commoner 541

447

fellow–companion
890
fellow–countryman
890
fellow–creature 372
fellow–feeling
  friendship 888
  love 897
  benevolence 906
  pity 914
fellowless 28
fellow–man 890
fellowship
  academic 542
  partnership 712
  rank 873
  friendship 888
  good– 892
fellow–student 541
felo–de–se 361
felon 949, 975
felonious 945
felony 947
felt *texture* 219
  heart– 821
felucca 273
female 374
feme covert 903
feme sole 904
feminality
  weakness 160
  woman 374
feminine 374
feminity 374
femme de chambre
746
fen 345
fence *enclose* 232
  evade 544
  defense 717
  fight 720
  prison 752
  thief 792
  (*safety* 664)
  (*refuge* 666)
  –round 229
  –with a question 528
  on the– 607
  word– 477
fenced 770
fenceless 665
fencibles 726
feneration 787
fend 717
fender 717
Fenian
  malcontent 710
  party 712
  rebel 742
fenny 345
feodal 780
feodality
  government 737
  possession 777
feoff *property* 780
feoffee *possessor* 779

receiver 785
feoffer 784
ferae naturae 366
feria 840
ferine 907
ferment *disorder* 59
  energy 171
  violence 173
  agitation 315
  lightness 320
  effervesce 353
  sour 397
  emotion 821
  excitement 824, 825
  anger 900
fermentation
  (see *ferment*)
  acetous– 397
fern 367–*plants* 369
fern–shaped 242
ferocity *violence* 173
  brutality 907
Ferrara *sword* 727
ferret 366–out
  be curious 455
  inquire 461
  discover 480a
ferruginous 433
ferry *transfer* 270
  way 627
ferryboat 273
ferryman 269
fertile *productive* 168
  (*abundant* 639)
  –*imagination* 515
fertilization 161, 168
fertilize 168
fertilizer 653
ferule 975
  come under the–
  932
fervent *hot* 382
  desirous 865
  –*hope* 858
fervid *hot* 382
  heartfelt 821
  excited 824
fervor *heat* 382
  passion 820
  animation 821
  love 897
Fescennine 961
festal *eating* 298
  holiday 687
  social 892
fester *corrupt* 653
  disease 655
festival *regularity* 138
  celebration 883
  –*chorus* 416
festivity
  amusement 840
  celebration 883
  sociality 892
festoon *curve* 245
  ornament 847

fetch *bring* 270
  arrive 292
  evasion 545
  sell for 812
  –and carry
  servile 886
  –a sigh 839
  –one a blow
  strike 276
  attack 716
  –water in a sieve 471
fetch *wraith* 992a
fete *amusement* 840
  gala 882
fetich (see *fetish*)
feticide 361
fetid 401
fetish 991, 993
fetishism 992
fetor 663
fetter *restrain* 751
  shackle 752
fettle 7, 673
fetus 129, 153
feu de joie
  amusement 840
  celebration 883
feud *discord* 713
  possession 777
  property 780
  death– 919
feudal
  government 737
  tenure 780
feudatory 749
fever *heat* 382
  disease 655
  excitement 825
feverish *hot* 382
  hurry 684
  animated 821
  excited 824
feverwort 662
few 103 a–100
  –and far between 70
  –words *concise* 572
  taciturn 585
  compendium 596
fewness 103
fey 828
fez 225
fiancée 897
fiasco 732
flat 741
flat lux 161
fib *falsehood* 544, 546
  thump 276
fiber *link* 45
  filament 205
  resolution 604
fibrilliferous 205
Fichteanism 451
fickle *changeable* 149
  irresolute 605
fictile 240
fiction *untruth* 546

(*fancy* 515)
  work of– 594
fictitious 515, 546
fictive 546
fid 392
fiddle *play* 416
  violin 417
fiddledeedee
  absurd 497
  unimportant 643
  contempt 930
fiddle–faddle
  absurdity 497
  unmeaning 517
  trifle 643
  dawdle 683
fiddler 416
fiddlestick 417
  –end 643
fidei defensor 717
fidelity *truth* 494
  veracity 543
  obedience 743
  observance 772
  honor 939
fidget *changes* 149
  activity 682
  hurry 684
  excitability 825
fidgety *irresolute* 605
  fearful 860
  irascible 901
fiducial 150
fiduciary 484
fidus Achates
  auxiliary 711
  friend 890
fie *disreputable* 874
  –upon it *censure* 932
field *scope* 180
  region 181
  plain 344
  agriculture 367, 371
  business 625
  arena 728
  property 780
  beasts of the– 366
  –of blood 361
  –of inquiry *topic* 454
  inquiry 461
  –of view *vista* 441
  idea 453
  the–*competitors* 710
  take the– 722
field day
  contention 720
  amusement 840
  display 882
field glass 445
field marshal 745
field piece 727
field preacher 996
field work 717
fiend *ruffian* 913
  demon 980
fiendish 945

fiendlike
  malevolent 907
  wicked 945
  fiend 980
fierce *violent* 173
  passion 825
  daring 861
  angry 900
fieri facias 963
fiery *violent* 173
  hot 382
  strong feeling 821
  excitable 825
  angry 900
  irascible 901
  –cross *indication* 550
  alarm 669
  warfare 722
  –furnace 386
  –*imagination* 515
  –ordeal 828
fiesta 840
fife 410, 417
fifer 416
fifth 98, 99
fifty 98 go–fifty 628
fig *food* 298
  unimportance 643
  –out 857
  –tree 367
fight *contention* 720
  warfare 722
  –against destiny 606
  –it out 722
  –one's battles again
  594
  –one's way
  –shy *avoid* 623
  coward 862
  pursue 622
  active 682
  exertion 686
  –the good fight 944
  show–defense 717
  courage 861
fighter 726
fighting cock
  tenacity 604
  combatant 726
  courage 861
fighting man 726
figment 515
figurante 599
figurate number 84
figuration 240
figurative
  metaphorical 521
  representing 554
  –*style* 577
figure *number* 84
  form 240
  appearance 448
  metaphor 521
  indicate 550
  represent 554
  price 812

figure flinger

ugly 846
cut a–*repute* 873
display 882
–to oneself 515
–of speech 521
exaggeration 549
poor–874
figure flinger 994
figurehead *sign* 550
representation 554
figurine 554
figuriste 559
filaceous 205
filament 205
filamentiferous 205
filamentous 256
filch 791
filcher 762
file *subduct* 38
arrange 60
row 69
assemblage 72
list 86
reduce 195
smooth 255
pulverize 330
record 551
store 636
soldiers 726
–a claim 969
–exceptions 469
–leader 694
–off *march* 266
diverge 291
on–551
file-fire 716
filgurate 420
filial 167
filiality 155
filiate 155
filiation
consanguinity 11
attribution 155
posterity 167
filibeg 225
filibuster *delay* 133
impede 706
obstructionist 710
plunder 791
thief 792
filibusterer 707, 710
filibustering 791
filibusterous 708
filiciform 242
filicoid 242
filiform 205
filigree 219
filings 330
filius nullius 925
filius terrae 876
fill *complete* 52
occupy 186
contents 190
stuff 224
provision 637
remedy 662

eat one's–957
–an office
business 625
government 737
–ed to overflowing 641
–one's pocket 803
–out *expand* 194
–the bill 729
–time 106
–up *compensate* 30
compose 54
close 261
restore 660
–up the time
inaction 681
have one's–
enough 639
satiety 869
fille-de chambre 746
–de joie 962
filled
–to overflowing 641
fillet *band* 45
filament 205
circle 247
indication 550
ornament 847
filling *stuffing* 224
fillip *impulse* 276
propulsion 284
stimulus 615
excite 824
filly 271
film *layer* 204
opaque 426
semitransparent 427
–over the eyes
dim sight 443
ignorant 491
filmy *texture* 329
filter *percolate* 295
clean 652
filth 653
filthy 653
filtrate 652
filtration 490d
fimbria 256
fimbriated 256
fimetarious 653
fimicolous 653
fin 267
final *ending* 67
completing 729
commanding 741
court of–appeal 474
–cause 620
–stroke 729
–touch 729
have the–word 153
finale *end* 67
completion 729
finality 67, 729
finally *for good* 141
eventually 151
on the whole 476

finance *money* 800
account 811
minister of–801
financier 639, 801
finch 366
find *eventuality* 151
adjudge 480
discover 480a
acquire 775
–a clue to 480a
–credence 484
–in *provide* 637
–it in one's heart 602
–means 632
–one's account in 644
–oneself *be* 1
present 186
–one's way 731
–one's way into 294
–out 480a
–the cause of 522
–the key of 522
–the meaning 522
–to one's cost 509
–vent 671
fin-de-siècle 123
finding *judgment* 480
lawsuit 959
–store 799
fine *small* 32
large 192
thin 203
rare 322
not raining 340
exact 494
good 648
beautiful 845
adorned 847
proud 878
mulct 974
–air 656
–arts 554
–by degrees 30
–feather *strong* 159
healthy 654
–feeling 850
–frenzy 515
–gentleman *fop* 854
proud 878
–grain 329
–lady 854, 878
–powder 330
–talking *overrate* 482
boast 884
–time of it 734
–voice 580
–writing 482, 577
in–*end* 67
after all 476
one–morning 106
some–morning 119
finedraw 660
fine-fingered 698
fineness (*see* fine)
finery *ornament* 847

vulgarity 851
fine-spoken
courtesy 894
flattery 933
finespun *thin* 203
sophistry 477
finesse *tact* 698
artifice 702
taste 850
(*deception* 545)
finest the–*police* 664
finestill 336
fine-toned 413
finger *touch* 379
hold 781
at one's–s' end
near 197
know 490
remember 505
–in the pie *cause* 153
interfere 228
act 680
active 682
cooperate 709
–on the lips
aphony 581
taciturnity 585
–'s breadth 203
lay the–on
point out 457
discover 480a
life a–680
not lift a–681
point the–at 457
turn round one's little–737
fingerling 193
finger post 550
finger print
evidence 467
dactylology 550
finger stall 223
fingle-fangle 643
finical *trifling* 643
affected 855
fastidious 868
finicality 457
finicking *trifling* 643
affected 855
fastidious 868
finis 67
finish *end* 67
symmetry 242
skill 698
complete 729
finished *absolute* 31
perfect 650
skilled 698
finishing–stroke 361
–touch 729
finite 32
finnan haddie 298
Finno-Ugric 372a
fiord 343, 490a
fir *tree* 367
–balsam 400

fire extinguisher

fire *energy* 171
eject 297
heat 382
make hot 384
fuel 388
shoot 406
dismiss 756
excite 834, 825
between two–s 665
catch–384
passion 820
–and fury 900
–and sword 162
–at 716
–a volley 716
–off 284
–of genius 498
–the blood 824
–up *excite* 825
anger 900
go through–and water
resolution 604
perseverance 604a
courage 861
hell–982
on–382
open–*begin* 66
play with–863
take–*excitable* 825
angry 900
under–*danger* 665
war 722
fire alarm 550, 669
fire annihilator 385
firearms 727
fireball *fuel* 388
arms 727
fire balloon 273
fire barrel 388
fire bell 669
firebox 386
firebrand *fuel* 388
instigator 615
dangerous man 667
incendiary 913
fire brigade 385
fire bug 384, 913, 949
firecracker 406, 840
fire curtain
theater 599
firedamp 663
fire department 385
firedog 386
firedrake 423
fire-eater
courage 861
fighter 726
jingo 885
blusterer 887
fire-eating
rashness 863
insolence 885
fire engine 385
fire escape 671
fire extinguisher 385

449

firefly   **flashy**

firefly 423
fireless cooker 386
fire light 422
firelock 727
fireman *stoker* 268
   extinguisher 385
fire-new 123
fireplace 386
fireproof 385 *safe* 664
fireside 189
firewood 388
firework *fire* 382
   luminary 423
   amusement 840
fire worship 382, 991
fire worshipper 984
firing *fuel* 388
   explosion 406
firkin 191
firm *junction* 43
   stable 150
   hard 323
   resolute 604
   partnership 712
   merchant 797
   brave 861
   –*belief* 484
   –*hold* 781
   stand– 719
firman *decree* 741
   permit 760
firmness (see firm)
first 66 at–sight 448
   come back to–love
      607
  –and foremost 66
  –and last 87
  –blow 716
  –blush *morning* 125
   vision 441
   appearance 448
   manifest 525
  –cause 976
  –come first served
      609a
  –fiddle
   importance 642
   proficient 700
   authority 737
  –impression 66
  –line 234
  –move 66
  –opportunity 132
  –stage 66
  –stone
   preparation 673
   attack 716
  –that comes 609a
   great–Cause 976
   in the–place 153
   of the–water
   best 648
   repute 873
   on the–summons
      741
firstborn 124, 128

first-class *best* 648
first fruits 154
firstling *eldest* 128
   effect 154
first-rate
   important 642
   excellent 648
   man-of-war 726
firth 343
fisc 802
fiscal 800
fiscalize 800
fish *food* 298
   sport 361, 622
   animal 366
   zoology 368
  –for *seek* 461
   experiment 463
   desire 865
  –for compliments
      880
  –fry 840
  –glue 352
  –hatchery 370, 636
  –in the air 645
  –in troubled waters
   difficult 704
   discord 713
  –out *inquire* 461
   discover 480a
  –out of water
   disagree 24
   unconformable 83
   displaced 185
   bungler 701
  –story 546, 549
  –up *raise* 307
   find 480a
   food for–es 362
   other–to fry
   ill–timed 135
   busy 682
   queer– 857
fisherman 361
fishery 370
fishing *kill* 361
   pursue 622
fishing boat 273
fishmonger 637
fish pond *pool* 343
   pisciculture 370
fish-tail 267
fishy transaction 940
fisk *run* 266
   speed 274
fissile 328
fission 44
fissure *break* 44
   chink 198
fist *handwriting* 590
   grip 781
   shake the–*defy* 715
   threat 909
fisticuffs 720
fistula 260
fit *state* 7

agreeing 23
equal 27
paroxysm 173
agitation 315
caprice 608
expedient 646
disease 655
excitement 825
anger 900
right 922
due 924
duty 926
by–s and starts
irregular 59
discontinuous 70
agitated 315
capricious 608
haste 684
–for 698, 924
–of abstraction 458
–of crying 839
–out *dress* 225
prepare 673
–to be seen 845
in–s 315
think– 600
fitchet 401
fitchew 401
fitful *irregular* 139
changeable 149
capricious 608
fittings 633
five 98 division by– 99
–act play 599
–and twenty 98
fives *game* 840
fix *dilemma* 7
join 43
arrange 60
establish 150
place 184
immovable 265
solidify 321
resolve 604
difficulty 704
–the eyes upon 441
–the foundations 673
–the memory 505
–the thoughts 457
–the time 114
–upon *discover* 480a
choose 609
fixed *intrinsic* 5
durable 110
permanent 141
stable 150
quiescent 265
habitual 613
–*idea* 481, 825
–opinion 484
–periods 138
–purpose 620
fixity 141, 265
fixture
appointment 741
property 780

fizgig 423
fizz 409
fizzle 304, 353
  –out 304
fizzy 353
flabbergast
  astonish 870
flabbergasted
  humbled 879
flabby 324
flabelliform 194
flabellum 349
flaccid *weak* 160
  soft 324
  empty 640
flaccidity (see flaccid)
  feeble style 575
flag *weak* 160
  flat stone 204
  floor 211
  smoothness 255
  slow 275
  plant 367
  sign 550
  path 627
  infirm 655
  inactive 683
  tired 688
  insignia 747
  weary 841
  –of truce 723
  –ship 726
  lower one's– 725
  red–*alarm* 669
  yellow–
    warning 668
    alarm 669
flag bearer 534
flagellation
  penance 952
  asceticism 955
  flogging 972
  rite 998
flagelliform 205
flageolet 417
flagitious 945
flagman 668
flagon 191
flagrant *great* 31
  manifest 525
  notorious 531
  atrocious 945
flagration 384
flagstaff *tall* 206
  signal 550
flagstone 204
flail 276
flake 204 snow– 383
flam 544
flambé 732
flambeau 423
flamboyant 577
flame *fire* 382
  light 420
  luminary 423
  passion 824, 825

love 897
add fuel to the– 173
catch the–
  emotion 821
consign to the–s
    384
–colored *red* 434
orange 439
–thrower 727
–up 825
in–s 382
flamen 996
flaming *violent* 173
  feeling 821
  excited 824
  ostentatious 882
  boasting 884
flamingo 366
flannel 384
flange *support* 215
  rim 231
  projection 250
flank *side* 236
  protect 664
flannel 384
flap *adjunct* 39
  hanging 214
  move to and fro 315
  –the memory 505
flapdoodle 517
flapjack 298
flapper *girl* 129
flapping *loose* 47
flare *violent* 173
  glare 420
  –up *excited* 824, 825
  angry 900
flaring *color* 428
flash *instant* 113
  violent 173
  fire 382
  light 420
  wit 842
  eyes–fire 900
  –across the memory
    505
  –back 842
  –in the pan
    unsubstantial 4
    impotent 158
    unproductive 169
    failure 732
  –note 800
  –of wit 842
  –on the mind
    thought 451
    disclose 529
    impulse 612
  –tongue 563
  –up *excited* 824
  –upon *unexpected* 508
flashing
  ostentatious 882
flashlight 423, 550
flashy *gaudy color* 428
  –*style* 577
  ornament 847

flask — flourish

tawdry 851
flask 191
flat *inert* 172
  story 191
  low 207
  horizontal 213
  paint 223
  vapid 391
  low tone 408
  musical note 413
  positive 535
  dupe 547
  back-scene 599
  shoal 667
  bungler 701
  insensible 823
  dejected 837
  weary 841
  dull 843
  simple 849
  fall–732
  –*contradiction* 536
  –*house* 189
  –*out* 304, 732
  –*refusal* 764
flatboat 273
flatiron 255, 386
flatness 251
flatsided 203
flatten 251
flatter *deceive* 545
  cunning 702
  please 829
  encourage 858
  approbation 931
  adulation 933
  –*oneself probable* 472
  hope 858
  –*the palate* 394
flatterer 935
flattering
  –*remark* 894
  –*tale hope* 858
  –*unction to one's soul content* 831
  vain 880
  flattery 933
flattery *falsehood* 544
  adulation **933**
flattish 251
flatulent *gaseous* 334
  air 338
  wind 349
  –*style* 573, 575
flatus *gas* 334
  wind 349
flaunt *flourish* 873
  display 882
flaunting *gaudy* 428
  unreserved 525
  ridiculous 853
flautist 416
flavor 390
flavoring 393
flavous 436
flaw *break* 70

crack 198
error 495
imperfection 651
blemish 848
fault 947
–*in an argument* 477
flax comb 253
flaxen 436
flay *divest* 226
  punish 972
flea *jumper* 309
  insect 366
  dirt 653
  –*in one's ear*
  repel 289
  eject 297
  refuse 764
  disrepute 874
  abashed 879
  discourteous 895
  contempt 930
flea-bite 643
flea-bitten 440
fleck 440
flecked 440
flection 279
fled *escaped* 671
fledge 673
flee *avoid* 623
fleece *tegument* 223
  strip 789
  rob 791
  impoverish 804
  surcharge 814
fleer *ridicule* 856
  insult 929
fleet *unsubstantial* 4
  transient 111
  ships 273
  swift 274
  navy 726
Fleet *prison* 752
fleeting 111
flesh *bulk* 192
  animal 364
  mankind 372
  carnal 961
  –*and blood substance* 3
  materiality 316
  animality 364
  affections 820
  gain–194
  ills that–*is heir to evil* 619
  disease 655
  in the–359
  make the–*creep pain* 830
  fear 860
  one–903
  way of all–360
  weakness of the–945
flesh color 434
fleshly 316

fleshpots 298
fleshy *of fruit* 354
fleur-de-lis 847
fleuron 847
flexible *pliant* 324
  easy 705
flexion *curvature* 245
  fold 258
  deviation 279
flexuosity 248
flexuous 248, 348
flexure *curve* 245
  fold 258
flibbertigibber 980
flicker *changing* 149
  waver 314
  flutter 315
  light 420
  dim 422
flickering
  irregular 139
flies *insects* 366
  theater 599
flight *flock* 102
  volitation 267
  swiftness 274
  departure 293
  avoidance 623
  escape 671
  –*of fancy* 515
  –*of stairs ascent* 305
  way 627
  –*of time* 109
  put to–*propel* 284
  repel 717
  vanquish 731
flighty *inattentive* 458
  mad 503
  fanciful 515
flimflam *lie* 544
  caprice 608
flimsy *copy* 21
  weak 160
  rarity 322
  soft 324
  sophistical 477
  trifling 643
flinch *swerve* 607
  avoid 623
  fear 860
  cowardice 862
fling *propel* 284
  jig 840
  jeer 929
  –*aside* 782
  –*away reject* 610
  waste 638
  relinquish **782**
  –*down* 308
  –*to the winds destroy* 162
  not observe 773
  have a–*at attack* 716
  resent 900
  disrespect 929

censure 932
have one's–
  active 682
  laxity 738
  freedom 748
  amusement 840
flint *hard* 323
flint-hearted 907
flip *beverage* 298
flippant *fluent* 584
  pert 885
  discourteous 895
flipper *paddle* 267
flirt *propel* 284
  changer 607
  coquette 854, 902
  love 897
  endearment 902
  –*a fan affectation* 855
flirtation 902
flit *elapse* 109
  changeable 149
  move 264
  travel 266
  swift 274
  depart 293
  run away 623
flitter *small part* 32
  changeable 149
  flutter 315
flitting *evanescent* 111
flivver 272
float *establish* 150
  navigate 267
  boat 273
  buoy up 305
  lightness 320
  before the–s
  on the stage 599
  –*before the eyes* 446
  –*in the mind thought* 451
  imagination 515
  –*on the air* 405
floater *schemer* 702
floating (see float)
  rumored 532
  –*anchor* 706
  –*battery* 726
  –*capital* 805
  –*debt* 806
  –*hotel* 273
floccillation 315
flocculence 324
flocculent *woolly* 256
  soft 324
  pulverulent 330
flock *assemblage* 72
  multitude 102
  laity 997
  –s *and herds* 366
  –*together* **72**
floe *ice* 383
flog 684, 972
flood *much* 31
  crowd 72

water 337
river 348
abundance 639
redundance 641
prosperity 734
–*of light* 420
–*of tears* 839
stem the–708
floodgate *limit* 233
  egress 295
  conduit 350
  open the–s
  eject 297
  permit 760
flood mark 466
flood tide *increase* 35
  complete 52
  height 206
  advance 282
  water 337
floor *level* 204
  base 211
  horizontal 213
  support 215
  overthrow 731
  ground–191
flop 315
flora 369
floral 367
floret 367
floriculture 371
florid *music* 416
  color 428
  red 434
  –*style* 577
  health 654
florist 371
floss 256
flotation (see float)
flotilla *ships* 273
  navy 726
flotsam and jetsam 73
flounce *trimming* 231
  jump 309
  agitation 315
  (*move quickly* 274)
flounder *change* 149
  toss 315
  uncertain 475
  bungle 699
  difficulty 704
  fail 732
  (*blunder* 495)
flour 330
flourish
  brandish 314, 315
  vegetate 365, 367
  exaggerate 549
  language 577
  speech 582
  gain 618
  healthy 654
  prosperous 734
  ornament 847
  repute 873

flourishing / fool

display 882
boast 884
(*succeed* 731)
—of trumpets
loud 404
publish 531
ostentation 882
celebrate 883
boast 884
flourishing
(*see* flourish)
cheerful 836
flout *disrespect* 929
contempt 930
(*ridicule* 856)
flow *course* 109
hang 214
motion 264
stream 348
murmur 405
abundance 639
—from *result* 154
—in 294
—into *river* 348
—of ideas 451
—of soul
conversation 588
affections 820
cheerful 836
social 892
—of time 109
—of words 582, 584
—out 295
—over 641
—with the tide 705
flower *essence* 5
produce 161
plant 367
prosper 734
beauty 845
ornament 847
repute 873
—of age 131
—of flock 648
—of life 127
—painting 556, 559
full many a—447
floweret 367
flowering plant 367
flowerlike *beauty* 845
flowers *anthology* 596
—of rhetoric 577
flowery
ornamental 847
be—*exaggerate* 549
flowing (*see* flow)
—*periods* 578
fluctuate *change* 149
oscillate 314
irresolute 605
flue *opening* 260
air–pipe 351
down 320
dust 653
fluent *differential* 84
fluid 333

stream 348
—language 578
speech 584
fluff 256, 320
fluffy 256
flugelman 694
fluid 333
—in motion **347**
fluidity 333
fluke *chance* 156, 621
hook 244
flume 350
flummery
unmeaning 517
flattery 933
flump 406
flunk 732
flunker 732
flunky *servant* 746
servile 886
flunkyism 933
fluorescence 425, 490d
flurry *disconcert* 458
hurry 684
agitation 821, 824
excitability 825
flush *flat* 251
flood 348
heat 382
light 420
color 428
red 434
abundant 639
wash 652
health 654
feeling 821
passion 825
rejoicing 838
cards 840
in liquor 959
—of cash 803
flushed (*see* flush)
red 434
excited 824
cheerful 836
hopeful 858
proud 878
vain 880
—with rage 900
—with success 731
—with victory 884
fluster *distract* 458
move 821
excite 824, 825
flustered *tipsy* 959
flute *furrow* 259
music 417
flutist 416
flutter *variable* 149
agitation 315, 824
hurry 684
emotion 821
excite 825
fear 860
fluvial 348

fluviograph 348
fluvio–marine 344
fluviometer 348
fluvioterrestrial 318
flux *conversion* 144
motion 264
liquefaction 335
flow 348
—and reflux 314
—of time 109
fluxion 84
fluxions 85
fly *vanish* 4
flap 39
time 109
transient 111
burst 173
minute 193
wings 267
vehicle 272
swift 274
depart 293
break 328
insect 366
lose color 429
shun 623
—aloft 305
—at 716
—back 277
—from 623
—in the face of
oppose 708
resist 719
disobey 742
insolence 885
—in the face of facts
misjudge 481
obstinate 606
—kites *borrow* 788
credit 805
not pay 808
—off 291
—open 260
—out *violent* 173
excitable 825
angry 900
—to arms 722
—tracks *writing* 590
flyblown 653
flyboat 273
flyer *aviator* 269a
advertisement 531
flying (*see* fly)
—boat 273
—colors *success* 731
display 882
celebrate 883
—column 726
—fish 83
—rumor 532
Flying Dutchman 269
fly leaf
interjacent 228
book 593
flytrap 545

fly wheel 312, 633
foal *young* 129
horse 271
foam *violent* 173
boil 315
spray 353
excitement 824, 825
—with rage 900
foamy 320
fob 191—off 545
focal 222
focus **74** *nucleus* 153
center 222
bring into a—
collect 72
convergence 290
in—*visible* 446
out of—*dim* 447
fodder *food* 298
for animals 370
(*provision* 637)
—for cannon 726
foe 891
—s to nobleness 943
foehn 349
foeticide 361
foetor 401
foetus (*see* fetus)
fog *mist* 353
uncertainty 475
in a—*hidden* 528
London—*yellow* 436
fog bell 669
foggy *opaque* 426
fog horn 669
fog signal 668, 669
fogy *fool* 501
laughingstock 857
foible 945
foil *contrast* 14
lamina 204
baffle 706
weapon 727
defeat 731
foiled 732
foin 276
foist *ship* 273
—in 228
—upon 545
Fokker *combatant* 726
folâtre 836
fold *bisect* 91
inclosure 232
plait **258**
prison 752
congregation 997
—in one's arms 902
—one's arms 681
—to the heart 902
—up 225
foliaceous 204
foliage 367
foliate *page* 85
foliated 204
foliation 204
folio 593

foliole 367
folk 372
folkland 780
folklore 124, 979
folkway 372a
follicle *cyst* 191
hollow 252
follicular 260
follow *be similar* 17
—in order 63
conform to 82
—in time 117
—in motion 281
understand 518
pursue 622
obey 743
—advice 695
—from *result from* 154
be proved by 478
—implicitly 486
—the dictates of 615
—the example of 19
—the lead of
cooperate 709
—suit *imitate* 19
—the trail 461
—up *continue* 143
circularize 592
persevere 604a
follower (*see* follow)
sequel 65
learn 541
servant 746
lover 897
escort 988
folly *building* 189
irrationality **499**
act of—
mismanagement 699
foment *stimulate* 173
warm 384
promote 707
excite 824
relieve 834
fonctionnaire 745
fond 897—*hope* 858
fondle 902
fondling *favorite* 899
endearment 902
fondness *desire* 865
font *origin* 153
type 591
rite 998
altar 1000
fontanel 260
food *eatables* **298**
(*materials* 635)
(*provision* 637)
—for powder 726
—for the mind 454
preparation of—673
fool 501 *deceive* 545
ridicule 856
disrespect 929
a—s bolt 499
—away 638

452

foolhardy

—away money 818
—away time 683
—'s errand
   deceived 545
   unskillful 699
—'s mate 732
—'s paradise
   unsubstantial 4
   misjudgment 481
   disappoint 509
   hope 858
   rash 863
—s rush in 499
—to the top of one's
   bent *excite* 824
   anger 900
   flatter 933
   make a—of oneself
   bungle 699
   ridiculous 853
   motley—844
   play the—*folly* 499
   amusement 840
foolhardy 863
fooling *humor* 842
foolish 499
   act—ly 699
   look—*disrepute* 874
   shame 879
foolscap *sign* 550
   paper 590
foot *length* 200
   stand 211
   meter 579
   at—'s pace 275
   at the—of 207
   —by foot 51
   —it *journey* 266
   dance 309
   —the bill 807
   keep on
   —*continue* 143
   support 215
   prepare 673
   not stir a—681
   on—*existing* 1
   during 106
   event 151
   action 170
   journey 266
   topic 454
   business 625
   preparing 673
   active 682
   one—in the grave
   age 128
   death 360
   put one's—down
   resolved 604
   put one's—in
   bungle 699
   set—on land 342
   trample under—930
football
   subjection 749
   game 840

footballer 840
footboy 746
footbridge 627
foot candle 466
footfall *motion* 264
   indication 550
   stumble 732
foot guards 726
footing
   circumstances 8
   addition 37
   rank 71
   influence 175
   situation 183
   foundation 211
   support 215
   payment 809
   be on a—*state* 7
   friendly—888
   get a—*location* 184
   pay one's—807
footlights *stage* 599
foot—loose
   liberated 750
footman 746
footmark 551
footpad 792
foot passenger 268
footpath 627
foot pound 466
footprint 550, 551
foot soldier 726
foot—sore 688
footstep *trace* 551
footstool 215
foot—stove 386
foot ton 466
foot—warmer 386
fop 854
foppery *display* 882
foppish *affected* 855
for *cause* 155
   tendency 176
   reason 476
   motive 615
   intention 620
   —all that
   notwithstanding 30
   qualification 469
   —a season 106
   —a time 111
   —aught one knows
      156
   —better for worse 78
   —ever 16, 112
   —example 82
   —form's sake 82
   —good *complete* 52
   diuturnity 110
   permanence 141
   —nothing 815
   —the most part
   great 31
   general 78
   special 79
   —the nonce 118

—the time being 106
have—*price* 812
forage *food* 298
   provision 637
   steal 791
forage cap 225
foramen 260
foraminous 260
forasmuch as
   relating to 9
   cause 155
   reason 476
   motive 615
foray *attack* 716
   robbery 791
forbear *avoid* 623
   spare 678
   lenity 740
   sufferance 826
   pity 914
   abstain 953
forbearance 918
forbid 761 God
   —*dissent* 489
   deprecation 766
   censure 932
   prayer 990
forbidden fruit
   seduction 615
   prohibition 761
forbidding
   prohibitive 761
   ugly 846
force *assemblage* 72
   power 157
   strength 159
   agency 170
   energy 171
   violence 173
   cascade 348
   agriculture 371
   significance 516
   —of *style* 574
   urge 615
   cultivate 707
   compulsion 744
   passion 820
   armed—726
   brute—964
   —down the throat
   severe 739
   compel 744
   —majeure 744
   —of argument 476
   —of arms 744
   —of will 600
   —one's way
   progression 282
   passage 302
   —open 173
   put in—924
forced *irrelative* 10
   —*style* 579
   unwilling 603
   —labor 603
   —loan 812

—march 744
forceful 171, 574
forceless 175a
forcemeat 298
forceps *extraction* 301
   grip 781
forces 726
forcible (*see* force)
   —*separation* 301
forcing house 371
forcing pit 691
ford *passage* 302
   way 627
fore 116, 234
fore–and–aft
   complete 52
   lengthwise 200
   —schooner 273
fore–and–after 273
forearm 673
forebears 166
forebode 511, 668
forecast *foresight* 510
   prediction 507, 511
   plan 626
   (*prepare* 673)
foreclose 706
foreday 125
foredoom 152, 601, 611
forefathers
   ancestors 166
   (*veteran* 130)
Forefathers' Day 883
forefend *prohibit* 761
   (*hinder* 706)
   (*guard* 717)
forefinger 379
forefront 66, 234
forego *relinquish* 624
   renounce 757
   surrender 782
foregoing
   preceding 62
   prior 116
foregone *past* 122
   —conclusion
   prejudged 481
   predetermined 611
foreground 234
   in the—*manifest* 525
forehead 234
foreign *alien* 10
   extraneous 57
   —accent 580
   —parts 196
foreigner 57
forejudge
   prejudge 481
   foresight 510
foreknow 510
foreknowledge 510
foreland *height* 206
   projection 250
forelay 706

forge

forelock
   take time by the—
   early 132
   occasion 134
forelooper 64
foreman 694
foremost *superior* 33
   beginning 66
   front 234
   in advance 280
   important 642
   reputed 873
forenoon 125
forensic 968
foreordain
   destine 152
   predestinate 976
foreordination
   necessity 601
fore part 234
forerun *precede* 62
   prior 116
   go before 280
forerunner
   precursor 64
   preparer 673
   (*omen* 512)
foresee *expect* 507
   foreknow 510
foreseen 871
foreshadow 511
foreshorten 201
foreshow 511
foresight 510
   caution 864
forest 367
   —primeval 367
forestall *prior* 116
   early 132
   possession **777**
   (*expect* 507)
   (*prepare* 673)
forester 371
forestry 371
foretaste 510
foretell 511
forethought 510
   vigilance 459
foretoken 511
forever 16, 112
forewarn *predict* 511
   warn 668
foreword 64
forfeit *fail* 773
   lose 776
   penalty 974
   —one's good opinion 932
forfeiture
   disfranchisement 925
forfend *hinder* 706
   defend 717
forgather 72
forge *imitate* 19
   produce 161
   furnace 368

453

forged — fragrant

trump up 544
foundry 691
—*ahead* 282
—*fetters* 751
forged *false* 546
forger *maker* 690
  thief 792
  counterfeiter 800
forgery *deception* 545
forget 506
  —*benefits* 917
  —*injury* 918
  —*oneself* 945
  hand—cunning 699
forgetful 506
forgive 918
forgiveness 918
forgo (*see* forego)
forgotten *past* 122
  ingratitude 917
  —*by the world* 893
fork *bifid* 91
  pointed 244
  —*lightning* 423
  —*out give* 784
  pay 807
  expenditure 809
forking 291
forlay 706
forlorn *dejected* 837
  hopeless 859
  deserted 893
  —*hope danger* 665
  hopelessness 859
  rashness 863
form *state* 7
  likeness 21
  make up 54
  order 58
  arrange 60
  convert 144
  produce 161
  bench 215
  shape **240**
  organization 357
  educate 537
  pupils 541
  school 542
  manner 627
  beauty 845
  fashion 852
  etiquette 882
  law 963
  create 976
  rite 998
—*a party* 712
—*a resolution* 604
—*part of* 56
formal (*see* form)
  regular 82
  definitive 535
  style 579
  severe 739
  taste 850
  affected 855
  stately 882

—*speech* 582
formaldehyde 490b
formalism 739, 988
formalist 82, 988
formality (*see* formal)
  ceremony 852
  affectation 855
  law 963
formalize 963
formation
  composition 54
  production 161
  shape 240
formative *causal* 153
  form 240
  —*notion* 453
formed (*see* form)
  attempered 820
former *in order* 62
  prior in time 116
  past 122
formerly 66, 119
formic acid 490b
formication 380
formidable
  difficult 704
  terrible 860
formless 241
formula *rule* 80
  arithmetic 84
  maxim 496
  precept 697
  law 963
formulary 998
formulate 590
fornication 961
fornicator 962
forsake 624
forsaken 898
forsooth 535
forswear *deny* 536
  lie 544
  tergiversation 607
  refuse 764
  transgress 927
  improbity 940
fort *refuge* 666
  defense 717
fortalice 717
forte 698
forth 282 *come*
  —*egress* 295
  visible 446
  go—depart 293
forthcoming
  destiny 152
  preparing 673
forthright 113, 132
forthwith 132, 507
fortification
  defense 717
fortify *strengthen* 159
fortitude
  endurance 826
  courage 861
fortnightly 138

fortress *refuge* 666
  defense 717
  prison 752
fortuitous
  adventitious 6
  chance 156
  undesigned 621
  —*combination of circumstances* 621
  —*concourse of atoms* 59
fortuity 156
fortunate
  opportune 134
  successful 731
  prosperous 734
Fortunatus's—*cap*
  wish 865
  spell 993
  —*purse* 803
fortune *chance* 156
  fate 601
  wealth 803
  be one's—151
  evil—735
—*s narrative* 594
  good—734
  make one's—
  succeed 731
  wealth 803
  tempt—*hazard* 621
  essay 675
  trick of—509
  try one's—675
  wheel of—601
fortune hunter
  servile 886
  selfish 943
fortuneless 804
fortune teller 513
fortune telling 51
forty 98—*winks* 683
Forty-Niner 463
forum *place* 182
  school 542
  tribunal 966
forward *early* 132
  front 234
  transmit 270
  advance 282
  interjection 286
  willing 602
  improve 658
  active 682
  help 707
  vain 880
  insolent 885
  uncourteous 895
  bend—234
  come—*in sight* 446
  offer 763
  display 882
  —*in knowledge* 490
  move—282
  press—*haste* 684
  put—*aid* 707

  offer 763
  put oneself—88
  set—676
foss 348
fosse *inclosure* 232
  ditch 259
  defense 717
  (*interval* 198)
fossil *remains* 40
  ancient 124
  hard 323
  organic 357
  dry bones 362
fossilization 357
fossilize 357
foster *aid* 707
  excite 824
  caress 902
  —*a belief* 484
fou 959
foul *collide* 276
  bad 649
  dirty 653
  ugly 846
  base 940
  vicious 945
  fall—*of oppose* 708
  quarrel 713
  attack 716
  fight 720
  censure 932
  —*fiend* 978
  —*invective* 908
  —*language*
    malediction 908
  —*odor* 401
  —*play evil* 619
    cunning 702
    wrong 923
    improbity 940
  run—*of impede* 706
foul-mouthed
  uncourteous 895
foulness (*see* foul)
foul-spoken
  detraction 934
foumart 401
found *cause* 153
  support 215
foundation
  stability 150
  base 211
  support 215
  lay the—*s* 673
  sandy—667
  shake to its—*s* 315
founded—*on base* 211
  evidence 467
  well—472
founder
  originator 164
  sink 310
  projector 626
  fail 732
  religious—*s* 986
foundling *trover* 775

  derelict 782
  outcast 893
foundry 691
fount *type* 591
fountain *source* 153
  river 348
  store 636
  —*pen* 590
fountainhead 210
four 95—*in hand* 272
  —*score etc.* 98
  —*times* 96
  from the—*winds* 278
  on all—*s identity* 13
  agreement 23
  horizontal 213
  easy 705
  prosperous 734
  humble 879
four-flush 545, 884
fourfold 96
Four Hundred 852, 875
Fourierism 910
four-oar 273
four-poster 215
fourragère 877
foursquare 244
fourth 96, 97
  musical 413
Fourth Estate 531
four-wheeler 272
fowl 298, 366
fowling piece 727
fox *animal* 366
  cunning 702
  —*chase* 622
  —*hunting* 622
foxhound 366
foxy *brown* 433
fox terrier 366
fox trot *dance* 840
fracas *disorder* 59
  noise 404
  discord 713
  contention 720
fraction *part* 51
  numerical 84
  less than one **100a**
Foxy Quiller 804
fractional 100*a*
  —*currency* 800
fractious 901
fracture
  disjunction 44
  discontinuity 70
  fissure 198
fragile *weak* 160
  brittle 328
fragment *small* 32
  part 51
  little 193
  extract 596
fragmentary 100*a*
fragrance **400**
fragrant 400

454

frail — front

—weed 392
frail *weak* 160
  brittle 328
  irresolute 605
  imperfect 651
  failing 945
  impure 961
  —sisterhood 962
frailty (see frail)
frame *intrinsicality* 5
  condition 7
  make 161
  support 215
  border 231
  form 240
  substance 316
  structure 329
  contrive 626
  —of mind
  inclination 602
  disposition 820
  have—d and glazed 822
frame house 189
framework
  support 215
  structure 329
franchise *freedom* 748
  right 924
  exemption 927a
Franciscan 996
franc-tireur 726
frangible 328
frank *open* 525
  sincere 543
  artless 703
  honorable 939
  —as rain 703
frankalmoigne 748
Frankenstein 913
Frankfurter 298
frankincense 400
frantic *violent* 173
  delirious 503
  excited 824
fraternal *brother* 11
  leagued 712
  concord 714
  friendly 888
  (*benevolent* 906)
  —order 711
fraternity *brothers* 11
  party 712
  friends 888
fraternize *combine* 48
  cooperate 709
  agree 714
  sympathize 888
  associate 892
fratricide 361
Frau 374
fraud *falsehood* 544
  deception 545
  impostor 548
  dishonor 940
  pious—988

fraudulent
  (see fraud)
  untruth 546
fraught *full* 52
  pregnant 161
  possessing 777
  (*sufficient* 639)
  —with danger 665
fray *rub* 331
  battle 720
  in the thick of the— 722
frayed *worn* 659
freak 608
  —of nature 83
freckle 848
freckled 440, 848
fredaine 840
free *detached* 44, 47
  unconditional 52
  deliver 672
  unobstructed 705
  liberate 748, 750
  expending 809
  gratis 815
  liberal 816
  insolent 885
  exempt 927a
  impure 961
  —and easy
  cheerful 836
  vain 880
  insolent 885
  friendly 888
  sociable 892
  —companion 726
  —fight 720
  —from *simple* 42
  —from imperfection 650
  —gift 784
  —giver 816
  —lance 523, 726, 748
  —land 748
  —liver 954a
  —living 954
  —love 897, 961
  —lunch 815
  —play 170, 748
  —quarters *cheap* 815
  hospitality 892
  —space 180
  —stage 789
  —trade *commerce* 794
  —translation 522
  —will 600
  make—of 748
  make—with
  frank 703
  take 789
  sociable 892
  uncourteous 895
freebooter 792
freeborn 748
free-burning 388
freedman 748

freedom 748
free-handed 816
freehold 780
freely *willingly* 602
freeman 748
Freemason 711
freemasonry
  unintelligible 519
  secret 528
  sign 550
  cooperation 709
  party 712
free-spoken 703
freestone 635
freethinker 487, 748, 989
free thought 487
free trader 748
freeze 376, 385
  —the blood 830
freezing 383
  —machine 387
  —mixture 387
freight *lade* 184
  cargo 190
  transfer 270
  —train 272
  —yard 636
freightage 270, 812
freighter *carrier* 271
  vessel 273
French 188
  —beans 298
  —gray 432
  —horn 417
  —leave *avoid* 623
  freedom 748
  —philosophy 451
  —polish 847
  peddler's— 563
Frenchman 188
frenetic 503
frenzy *madness* 503
  imagination 515
  excitement 825
frequency 136
frequent
  in number 104
  in time 136
  in space 186
  habitual 613
frequenter 613
fresco *cold* 383
  painting 556
  al—*out of doors* 220
  in the air 338
fresh *extra* 37
  new 123
  flood 348
  cold 383
  color 428
  remembered 505
  novice 541
  unaccustomed 614
  good 648
  healthy 654

  pert 885
  tipsy 959
  —breeze 349
  —color 434
  —news 532
freshen 689
freshet 348
freshman 492, 541
freshness (see fresh)
fresh-water
  —college 542
  —sailor 701
fret *suffer* 378
  grieve 828
  gall 830
  discontent 832
  sad 837
  ornament 847
  irritate 900
  —and fume 828
fretful 901
fretwork 219
Freud's theory 992a
friable *brittle* 328
  pulverulent 330
friandice 868
friar 996 Black—s 996
  —Rush 980
  —'s balsam 662
  —'s lantern 423
friary 1000
fribble *slur over* 460
  trifle 643
  dawdle 683
  fop 854
fricassee 298
frication 331
friction *force* 157
  obstacle 179
  rubbing 331
  on-wheels 705
fried—brains 298
  —eggs 298
  —sole 298
friend *auxiliary* 711
  wellwisher 890
  sympathizer 914
  be—s 888
  —at court 631
  next—759
  see one's—s 892
friendless 893
friendliness 888
friendly *amicable* 714
friendship 888
frieze 210, 329
frigate
  man-of-war 726
  (*ship* 273)
fright *cards* 840
  alarm 860
frighten 860
frightful *dreadful* 830
  ugly 846
frightfully *much* 31
frigid *cold* 383

  —style 575
  callous 823
  indifferent 866
frigidarium 387
frigorific 385
frill *border* 231
  convolution 248
frills 577
  —of style 577
fringe *border* 231
  lace 256
  exaggeration 549
  ornament 847
frippery *trifle* 643
  ornament 847
  finery 851
  ridiculous 853
  ostentation 882
  (*dress* 225)
friseur 225
frisk *prance* 266
  leap 309
  absurdity 497
  gay 836
  amusement 840
frisky *brisk* 682
  in spirits 836
frith *chasm* 198
  strait 343
  forest 367
fritiniancy 412
fritter *small* 32
  —away *lessen* 36
  waste 638
  (*misuse* 679)
  —away time 683
frivolity
  (see frivolous)
frivolous
  unreasonable 477
  foolish 499
  capricious 608
  trivial 643
friz *curl* 245, 248
  fold 258
frock *dress* 225
  canonicals 999
  —coat 225
frog *leaper* 309
  ornament 847
frolic 840
frolicsome 836
from *motive* 615
  —day to day 106, 138
  —end to end 52
  —that time 117
  —this cause 155
  —time immemorial 122
  —time to time 136
frond 367
fronder *censure* 932
frondeur *disobey* 742
  detract 936
front *first* 66
  wig 225

455

frontage

fore part **234**
resist 719
insolence 885
bring to the–
manifest 525
come to the–
surpass 303
important 642
repute 873
–*danger* 861
–*of the house* 599
–*rank* 234
–*to front* 708
in–280
in the–*rank*
important 642
repute 873
present a–719
frontage 234
frontal 220
frontier *vicinity* 199
limit 233
fronting *opposite* 237
frontispiece 64
frost *cold* 383
semitransparent 427
whiten 430
–*over* 427
frost-bite 383
frosted 427, 430
–*glass* 427
frost smoke 353
frostwork 847
froth *bubble* 353
trifle 643
dirt 653
–*up angry* 900
frothy 353
–*style* 573, 577
irresolute 605
frounce 258
frow 374
froward 901a
frown *lower* 837
scowl 839
discourteous 895
angry 900
sulky 901a
disapprove 932
–*down abash* 879
–*s of fortune* 735
frowzy 401
frozen 383, 385
fructiferous 168
fructify *produce* 161
be productive 168
improve 658
prosper 734
fructuous 168
frugal *economical* 817
temperate 953
fruit *result* 154
produce 161
profit 775
forbidden–615
–*tree* 367

reap the–s
succeed 731
reward 973
fruitarian 953
fruit-bearing 168
fruitful 168
fruition 161, 827
fruitless
unproductive 169
useless 645
failure 732
frumenty 298
frump *vulgar* 851
unmannerly 895
frumpish *sulky* 901a
frustrate
counteract 179
prevent 706
(*defeat* 731)
frustrated 732
frustum 51
fry *shoal* 102
child 129
heat 384
small–
unimportant 643
commonalty 876
frying pan 386
out of–*into fire*
worse 659
clumsy 699
failure 732
misfortune 735
aggravation 835
fuchsine 434
fucoid 367
fuddled 959
fudge *unmeaning* 517
trivial 643
(*nonsense* 497)
fuel *combustible* **388**
materials 635
add–*to the flame*
increase 35
heat 384
aggravate 835
anger 900
fugacious 111
fugitive *transient* 111
emigrant 268
avoiding 623
(*escape* 671)
–*writings* 596
fugleman *pattern* 22
director 694
fugue 415
fulciment 215
fulcrum *support* 215
mechanical power 633
(*leverage* 175)
fulfill *complete* 729
–*a duty* 926
–*an obligation* 772
fulgent 420
fulgurant 420

fulgurite 260
fuliginosity 426
fuliginous *dim* 422
opaque 426
black 431
full *circumstantial* 8
much 31
complete 52
large 192
loud 404
abundant 639
cleanse 652
–*age* 131
–*bloom health* 654
beauty 845
–*colored* 428
–*cry aloud* 404
bark 412
pursuit 622
–*dress dress* 225
ornament 847
fashion 852
show 882
–*drive* 274
–*feather prepared* 673
–*force* 159
–*gallop* 274
–*heart* 820
–*house cards* 840
–*many* 102
–*measure* 639
–*of business* 682
–*of incident* 151
–*of meaning* 516
–*of people* 186
–*of point* 842
–*of whims* 608
–*play facility* 705
freedom 748
–*scope* 748
–*score* 415
–*size* 192
–*speed* 274
–*steam ahead* **282**
–*stop cease* 142
rest 265
–*swing strong* 159
active 682
successful 731
free 748
–*tide* 348
–*tilt active* 682
haste 684
–*view* 446
hands–*active* 682
receipt in–807
full-blown
expanded 194
glorious 873
full-blooded 641
full-fed 954
full-flavored 392
full-grown
adolescent 131
large 192
(*expanded* 194)

full-handed
liberal 816
prodigal 818
full-length 556
full-mouthed 411, 412
full *circumstantial* 8
fullness (*see* **full**)
in the–*of time* 109
full-toned 413
fully 31
fulminate *violent* 173
propel 284
loud 404
malediction 908
threat 909
–*against accuse* 932
fulsome
nauseous 395
fetid 401
bad 649
abhorrent 867
adulatory 933
impure 961
fulvescent 436
fulvid 436
fulvous 436
fumarole 490c
fumble *derange* 61
handle 379
grope 463
awkward 699
fumbler 701
fume *violent* 173
exhalation 334, 336
air pipe 351
heat 382
odor 398
excitement 824
be impatient 825
anger 900
–*s of fancy* 515
in a
–*discontented* 832
fumid 426
fumigate
vaporize 336
cleanse 652
fumigator 388
fun *amusement* 840
humor 842
make–*of* 856
funambulist 700
function *algebra* 84
office 170
business 625
utility 644
pomp 882
duty 926
functionary
director 694
consignee 758
fund *store* 636
invest 787
(*abundance* 639)
sinking–802
fundament 235

fundamental
intrinsic 5
base 211
support 215
–*bass* 413
–*note* 413
fundamentally
very 31
funds 800 *in*–803
public–802
funebrial 363
funeral *procession* 69
interment 363
–*director* 363
–*pace* 275
–*pyre* 423
–*ring* 363
funerary 363
funereal
interment 363
dismal 837
fungate 365
fungi 369
fungiform 249
fungoid 369
fungologist 369
fungology 369
fungosity
projection 250
fungous 367, 369
fungus *projection* 250
vegetable 367
fetor 401
bane 663
funicle 205
funk *fear* 860
cowardice 862
funnel *opening* 260
conduit 350
air pipe 351
funnel-shaped 252
funny *odd* 83
boat 273
humorous 842
comic 853
fur *covering* 223
hair 256
warm 384
dirt 653
furacious 791
furbelow 231
furbish *improve* 658
prepare 673
adorn 847
furcate 244
furcation 91
furcula 993
furcular 91, 244
furculum 91, 244
furfur 653
furfuraceous 330
Furies *anger* 900
evildoers 913
furiosity 173
furious *violent* 173
haste 684

furiously

passion 825
anger 900
furiously *much* 31
furl 312
furlong 200
furlough 760
furnace 386
 workshop 691
 like a—hot 382
 *sighing like—
  lament* 839
 in love 902
furnish *provide* 637
 prepare 673
 give 784
 —*a handle* 617
 —*aid* 707
 —*its quota* 784
furniture 633
 (*property* 780)
furor *insanity* 503
 emotion 820, 821
 passion 825
 desire 865
 —*scribendi* 592, 594
furore (*see* furor)
furrow 259
Fürst 745
further *extra* 37
 distant 196
 aid 707
 *go—and fare worse
  worse* 659
 bungle 699
 *not let it go—*528
furthermore 37
furtive
 clandestine 528
 stealing 791
 (*false* 544)
furuncle 250
fury *violence* 173
 excitation 825
 anger 900
 demon 980
 *filled with—*825
furze 367
fuscous 433
fuse *join* 43
 combine 48
 heat 382, 384
 torch 388
 (*melt* 335)
fuselage 273
fusel oil 356
fusiform *pointed* 253
fusil 727
fusileer 716, 726
fusillade *killing* 361
 attack 716
fusion *union* 48
 heat 384, 490a
 cooperation 709
fuss *agitation* 315
 activity 682
 haste 684

difficulty 704
excitement 825
ostentation 882
*make a—about
 importance* 642
lament 839
disapprove 932
fussy *circumstantial* 8
 crochety 481
 bustling 682
 excitable 825
fustee 41
fustian *texture* 329
 absurd 497
 unmeaning 517
 —*style* 577, 579
 ridiculous 853
fustic 436
fustigate 972
fusty *old* 124
 fetid 401
 dirty 653
futile 645
futility 499, 645
future 121
 expected 507
 *eye to the—*510
 —*possession* 777
 —*state destiny* 152
 heaven 981
 *in the—*152
futurist 556
futurity **121**
fuzzle 959
fuzzy 447
fylfot 993

G

gab 584
 *gift of the—*582
gabardine 225
gabble 583, 584
gabelle 812
gaberlunzie 876
gable *side* 236,
 —*end* 67
gad 266
gadabout 268
gadget 626
gaff 727
gaffer *old* 130
 man 373
 clown 876
gag *silence* 403
 render mute 581
 dramatic 599
 muzzle 751
 imprison 752
 (*taciturnity* 585)
gage *measure* 466
 security 771
 throw down the—
 715
gage d'amour 768

gaggle 412
gaieté de coeur 836
gaiety (*see* gay) 836
gaillard 844
gain *increase* 35
 advantage 618
 acquisition 775
 —*a point* 731
 —*a victory* 731
 —*credit* 931
 —*ground progress* 282
 improve 658
 —*head* 175
 —*laurels* 873
 —*learning* 539
 —*one's ends* 731
 —*over* 615
 —*private ends* 943
 —*strength* 35
 —*the confidence of*
  484
 —*the start
  priority* 116
 early 132
 —*time protract* 110
 early 132
 late 133
 —*upon approach* 286
 pass 303
 become a habit 613
gainful *useful* 644
gainless 646
gainsay 536
gairish (*see* garish)
gait *walk* 264
 manner 627
gaiter 225
gala *festival* 840
 display 882
 —*day* 687
galactic circle 318
galantuomo 939
galavant 902
galaxy *assemblage* 72
 multitude 102
 stars 318
 luminary 423
 glory 873
gale 349
galeiform 245
Galen 662
galimatias 497
galiongee 269
galiot 273
gall *hurt* 378
 bitter 395
 annoy 830
 insolence 885
 anger 900
 malevolence 907
 *dip the pen in—*934
gallant *brave* 861
 courteous 894
 love 897
 licentious 961, 962
gallantry (*see* gallant)

dalliance 902
**gallanty-show
 spectacle** 448
 amusement 840
galleon 273
gallery *room* 191
 passage 260
 spectators 444
 auditory 599
 museum 636
 *picture—*556
galley *ship* 273
 furnace 386
 printing 591
 punishment 972, 975
 —*proof* 591
 work like a—slave
  686
galliass 273
Gallic 188
Gallicism 563
Gallicize 562
galligaskin 225
gallimaufry 41
gallinaceous 366
gallipot 191
gallium 490d
gallivant 902
galloon 847
gallop *pass away* 111
 ride 266, 370
 scamper 274
galloping *fast* 274
 —*consumption* 655
galloway 271
gallows *kill* 361
 punishment 975
 *come to the—*972
gallstone 655
galoot 701
galopade 840
galore 102, 639
galvanic *power* 157
 excitable 825
galvanism *force* 157
galvanize 157, 824
galvanometer 157,
 466
galvanoscope 157
gamache 225
gambade *leap* 309
 prank 840
gambado *gaiter* 225
 leap 309
gambit 66
gamble
 chance 156, 621
gambler 463, 840
gambling
 chance (156) 621
 sport 840
 rashness 863
gambling house 621,
 945
gamboge 436
gambol 309, 840

gap

gambrel roof 244
game *food* 298
 animal 366
 savory 394
 resolute 604
 persevering 604a
 aim 620
 gamble 621
 pursuit 622
 tactics 692
 amusement 840
 laughingstock 857
 brave 861
 —*at which two can
  play* 718
 —*in one's hands
  easy* 705
 succeed 731
 command 737
 —*to the last* 604a
 —*up* 732
 *make—of
  deceive* 545
 ridicule 856
 disrespect 929
 *play the—of
  cooperate* 709
gamecock *fighter* 726
 tenacity 604
 pluck 861
gamekeeper 370, 753
gamesome 836
gamester *chance* 621
 play 840
 rash 863
gametal 163
gametangium 357
gamete 357
gamic 161
gamin 876
gaming (*see* game)
gaming house 621
gammadion 621, 993
gammer *old* 130
 woman 374
gammon
 false 544, 545
 untruth 546
gamey 392
gamut 413
gander 373
gang *assemblage* 72
 go 264
 party 712
ganger 694
gangrene 655
gangway *opening* 260
 way 627
ganja 663
gantlet 972 *run the—
 resolution* 604
 dare 861
gaol 752 —*delivery* 672
gaoler *keeper* 753
 punishment 975
gap *discontinuity* 70

gape — gent

chasm 198
  stand in the–717
gape *open* 260
  curiosity 455
  wonder 870
  –for *desire* 865
gaping (see gape)
  expectant 507
gar 161
garage 191, 272
garb 225
  under the–of 545
garbage 653
garble *take from* 38
  exclude 55
  misinterpret 523
  falsify 544
  –accounts 811
garbled *incomplete* 53
garde–nationale 726
  –royale 726
garden *grounds* 189
  horticulture 371
  source of supply 636
  beautiful 845
  botanic–371
  zoological–370
gardener 371
gardens *street* 189
gare 266
gargle 337
gargoyle 350
garish *light* 420
  color 428
  ornament 847
  gay 845
  tawdry 851
  display 882
gari–wala 268
garland *circle* 247
  fragrance 400
  sign 550
  poetry 597
  trophy 733
  ornament 847
  decoration 877
garlic *condiment* 393
  fetid 401
garment 225
garner *store* 636
  (*collect* 72)
garnet 434, 847
garnish *addition* 39
  prepare 673
  fee 809
  ornament 847
garnishee 758
garniture *dress* 225
garran 271
garret *room* 191
  top 210
garrison
  occupant 188
  safety 664
  defense 717
  soldiers 726

garron 271
garrote
  render powerless 158
  kill 361
  punishment 972
garrulity 584
garter *fastening* 45
  decoration 877
  –blue 438
garth 181
gas *gaseity* 334
  fuel 388
  light 420
  bombast 884
  –bomb 727
  –meter 334
  –stove 386
gasconade 884
gaseity 334
gaseous
  unsubstantial 4
  of gas 324
  vaporous 336
gash *cut* 44
  interval 198
  wound 619
gasification 334, 336
gasiform 334
gasify 334
gaskins 225
gaslight 423
gasoline 272, 356
gasometer 636
gasp *blow* 349
  droop 655
  poison 663
  fatigue 688
  at the last–360
  –for *desire* 865
gassy 349
gastric 191, 298
gastriloquism 580
gastromancy 511
gastronomy 298, 957
gastroscope 445
gate *beginning* 66
  inclosure 232
  mouth 260
  barrier 706
  –way *way* 627
  water–350
gâteau 298
gatekeeper 263
Gath, tell it not in–
  conceal 528
  disapprove 932
gather *collect* 72
  expand 194
  fold 258
  conclude 480
  acquire 775
  take 789
  –breath 689
  –flesh 194
  –from one
    information 527

–fruits 731
–grapes from thorns 471
gathered
  –to one's fathers 360
gathering
  assemblage 72
  abscess 655
  –clouds *dark* 421
  shade 424
  omen 512
  danger 665
  warning 668
  adversity 735
gathering place 74
Gatling gun 727
gauche *clumsy* 699
gaucherie 699
  vulgarity 851
gaud *ornament* 847
gaudery *vanity* 880
gaudy *color* 428
  vulgar 851
  showy 882
gauge 466 *rain*–348
  wind–349
gauger 965
gaunt *bulky* 192
  lean 203
  ugly 846
gauntlet *glove* 225
  armor 717
  fling down the–715
  take up the–720
Gautama 986
gauze *shade* 424
  semitransparent 427
gavel *worth* 812
  sheaf 72
gavelkind 778
gavelock 633
gavot 840
gawk 501
gawky *awkward* 699
  ugly 846
  (*ridiculous* 853)
gay *color* 428
  cheerful 836
  adorned 847
  showy 882
  dissipated 961
  –deceiver 962
  –world 852
gayety (see gay) 836
Gay–Lussac's law 490d
gaze 441
gazebo 441
gazelle *swift* 274
  animal 366
gazer *spectator* 444
gazette
  publication 531
  record 551
  in the–
  bankrupt 808

gazetteer *list* 86
  information 527
  record 551
gazingstock
  ridiculous 857
  wondrous 872
geanticline 245
gear *clothes* 225
  automobile 272
  cogwheel 312
  harness 633
  in–673
  out of–*disjoin* 44
  derange 61
  useless 645
  unprepared 674
gearwheel 312
gehenna 982
Geist 982
gelatin 352
gelatinize 352
gelatinous 352
geld *subduct* 38
  impotence 158
gelding *horse* 271
  male 373
gelid 383
gelidity 383
gelignite 727
geloscopy 511
gem *excellence* 648
  ornament 847
  (*perfect* 650)
geminate 90
gemination 161
Gemini *twins* 89
  O–! 870
gemma 153
gemmation 194
gemmule 153
gemot 72
gendarme *safety* 664
  soldier 726
  police 965
gender 75
genealogy *line* 69
  paternity 166
general *whole* 50
  generic 78
  habitual 613
  servant 690, 746
  officer 745
  –breaking up 655
  –conception 25
  –favorite 899
  –information 490
  –meaning 516
  –public 372
  –run 613
  the
  –*commonalty* 876
  things in–151
generalissimo 745
generality *mean* 29
  universal **78**
generalize 476

generally 16
  –speaking 613
generalship
  tactics 692
  warfare 722
generate *produce* 161
  productive 168
generation
  consanguinity 11
  period 108
  production 161
  mankind 372
  rising–167
  spontaneous–161
  wise in one's–498
generative 153, 161
generator
  producer 164
  of automobile 272
generic 78
generosity
  greatness 31
  giving 784
  liberality 816
  benevolence 906
  disinterestedness 942
generous
  (see generosity)
genesis *beginning* 66
  production 161
genet 271
Genethliacs 511
genetic 5, 161
genetous 5
Geneva gown 999
genial *productive* 161
  sensuous 377
  warm 382
  willing 602
  delightful 829
  (*renascent* 163)
geniality (see genial)
  cheerfulness 836
geniculated 244
genital 161
genitor 166
geniture 161
genius *intellect* 450
  talent 498
  poet 597
  skill 698
  proficient 700
  familiar spirit 979
  evil–980
  –borrows nobly 19
  –for 698
  –loci 664
  –of a language 560
  good–*friend* 898
  benefactor 912
  spirit 979
  man of–492
  tulelary–711
genre *painting* 556
gens 712
gent *vulgar* 851

458

genteel

commonalty 876
genteel *fashion* 852
  rank 875
  (*polite* 894)
 —*comedy* 599
gentile *heterodox* 984
 without religion 989
gentilhomme 939
gentility *fashion* 852
  rank 875
  politeness 894
gentium, jus–963
gentle *moderate* 174
  slow 275
  train 370
  faint sound 405
  lenient 740
  meek 826
  cool down 826
  courteous 894
 —*blood* 875
 —*breeding* 894
 —*hint* 527
 —*slope* 217
gentlefolk 875
gentleman *male* 373
  squire 875
  man of honor 939
 —'s *agreement* 23, 709
  the old–978
  walking–599
gentlemanly
  fashionable 852
gentleness
  (see *gentle*)
Gentoo 984
gentry 875
  landed–779
genuflexion
  bowing 308
  submission 725
  servility 886
  courtesy 894
  respect 928
  worship 990
genuine *true* 494
  good 648
genus 75
geochemistry 490c
geodesic 318, 342
geodesist 85, 318, 342
geodesy 342, 466, 490a
geognost 342
geognosy 342
geogony 342
geographer 318, 342
geography 183, 342
geoid 249
geologist 342
geology 490c, 342, 358
geomancer 513
geomancy 511

geometrician 85
geometry 466
geophilous 342
geoponics 342, 371
georama 448
georgics 342, 371
geosyncline 245
germ *cause* 153
  littleness 193
  plan 626
 —*cell* 357
 —*plasm* 357
German *dance* 840
 —*band* 416
 —*philosophy* 451
 —*silver* 430, 545
 —*tinder* 388
germane
  relevant 23
  (*related* 9)
germicide 662
germinal 153
 —*matter* 357
germinate 194, 365
 —*from* 154
germination 161
gerocomy 128
gerontic 128
gerrymander 702
gest 680
Gestalt psychology 821a
geste 515
gestation
  propagation 161
  carriage 270
  maturation 673
gesticulate 550
gesture *hint* 527
  indication 550
get *become* 144
  beget 161
  acquire 775
 —*ahead* 35
 —*ahead of* 33
 —*along* 282
 —*along with you*
   ejection 297
   dismissal 756
 —*a sight of* see 441
   comprehend 490
 —*at* 480a
 —*away* 287
 —*back* *retire* 283
   regain 775
 —*better* 658
 —*by heart* 505
 —*down* *swallow* 298
   descend 306
 —*for one's pains* 973
 —*home* 292
 —*in* *collect* 72
   gather 775
 —*into harness* 673
 —*into the way of* 613
 —*into trouble* 732

 —*loose* 44
 —*near* 286
 —*off* *depart* 293
   escape 671
 —*on* *advance* 282
   prosper 734
 —*out* *eject* 297
   extract 301
   publish 531
 —*over*
   recover from 660
   succeed 731
   be content 831
 —*over the ground* 274
 —*ready* 673
 —*rid of* 42, 672
 —*the best of* 731
 —*the gist of* 457
 —*there* 731
 —*the wrong pig by the tail* 699, 732
 —*through* *end* 67
   transact 692
   complete 729
   expend 809
 —*to extend to* 196
   arrive 292
 —*together* 72
 —*up* *ascend* 305
   raise 307
   learn 539
   fabricate 544
   prepare 673
   rise early 682
   foment 824
 —*you gone* 297
gettings 35
get-up *form* 240
gewgaw *rifle* 643
  ornament 847
  vulgar 851
geyser 382, 384
gharri 272
 —*wallah* 268
ghastly *pale* 429
  hideous 846
  frightful 860
ghaut 203
ghazal 597
ghee 356
ghetto 189
ghost *shade* 362
  fallacy of vision 443
  soul 450
  writer 593
  apparition 980a
 —*dance* 992
 —*of a chance* 473
  give up the–360
  pale as a–
   colorless 429
   fear 860
Ghost, Holy–976
ghostlike *ugly* 846
ghostly
  intellectual 450

  supernatural 976, 980a
ghoul *evildoer* 913
  demon 980
ghurry 108, 114
ghyll 348
giant *large* 192
  tall 206
 —*refreshed* *strong* 159
  refreshed 689
 —'s *strides*
   distance 196
   swift 274
giaour *heterodox* 984
  irreligion 989
gibber *stammer* 583
gibberish
  absurdity 497
  nonsense 517
  neology 563
gibbet *stigmatize* 932
  execute 972
  gallows 975
gibble-gabble 584
gibbous *globose* 249
  convex 250
gib-cat *male* 373
gibe *disrespect* 929
  (*ridicule* 856)
giddy *inattentive* 458
  vertiginous 503
  irresolute 605
  capricious 608
  bungling 699
giddy-head 501
giddy-headed 458
giddy-paced 315
gift *compensation* 30
  power 157
  transference 270
  talent 698
  given 784
  expenditure 809
 —*of the gab* 582
  look a–*horse in the mouth*
   fastidious 868
   ungrateful 917
gifted 698
gig 273
gigantic *strong* 159
  large 192
  tall 206
giggle 838
Gilbertine 996
gild *coat* 223
  yellow 436
  color 439
  ornament 847
 —*ed rooster* 875
 —*refined gold* 641
 —*the pill* *deceive* 545
  tempt 615
  please 829
  flatter 933
gilding (*see gild*)

girlish

Gilead, balm in–
  relief 834
  hope 858
gill *ravine* 252
  brook 348
 —s *respiration* 349
gillie 746
gilt 436, 847
gilt-edged
  excellent 648
 —*securities* 802
gimbals 312
gimcrack *weak* 160
  brittle 328
  trifling 643
  ornament 847
  ridiculous 853
  (*useless* 645)
gimlet 262
gimp *clean* 652
  pretty 845
gin *trap* 545
  instrument 633
  intoxicating 959
ginger 171
gingerbread
  weak 160
  vulgar 851
  (*ornament* 847)
gingerly
  moderately 174
  carefully 459
  cautiously 864
  (*slowly* 275)
gingham 635
gingle 408
gin palace 189
gipsy *wanderer* 268
  cheat 548
  wag 844
 —*lingo* 563
giraffe 206, 366
girandole 423
girasol 847
gird *bind* 43
  strengthen 159
  surround 227
  jeer 929
 —*up one's loins*
   brace 159
   prepare 673
girder *bond* 45
  beam 215
girdle *bond* 45
  circumference 230
  circle 247
  put a–*round about the earth* 274, 311
girl *young* 129
  female 374
  servant 746
girl bachelor 904
girleen 129
girlhood 127
girlish 374

459

girllike

girllike 129
girt 229
girth *bond* 45
　circumference 230
gisarme 727
gist *essence* 5
　meaning 516
　important 642
gite 265
gittern 417
give *yield* 324
　melt 382
　bestow 784
　discount 813
　–a horse his head 748
　–and take
　　compensation 30
　　interchange 148
　　retaliation 718
　　compromise 774
　　barter 794
　　equity 922
　　honor 939
　–attention 418
　–a turn to 140
　–away 782, 784
　　in marriage 903
　–back 790
　–birth to 161
　–chase 622
　–consent 762
　–cry 411
　–ear 418
　–expression to 566
　–forth 531
　–in *submit* 725
　–in charge
　　restrain 751
　–in custody 751
　–in to *consent* 762
　–it one *censure* 932
　　punish 972
　–light 420
　–notice *inform* 527
　　warn 668
　–one credit for 484
　–one the slip 671
　–one to understand 527
　–out *emit* 297
　　publish 531
　　bestow 784
　–over *cease* 142
　　relinquish 624
　　lose hope 859
　–place to
　　substitute 147
　　avoid 623
　–play to the
　　imagination 515
　–points to 27
　–quarter 740
　–rise to 153
　–security 771
　–the go-by 623

–the lie 536
–the mind to 457
–the once-over 461
–tongue 531
–up
　not understand 519
　reject 610
　relinquish 624
　submit 725
　resign 757
　surrender 782
　restore 790
　hopeless 859
–up the ghost 360
–way *weak* 160
　brittle 328
　submit 725
　pine 828
　despond 837
　modest 881
given (see give)
　circumstances 8
　supposition 514
　received 785
　–over *dying* 360
　–time 143
　–to 613
　–up 360
giver 784
giving 784
gizzard 191
　stick in one's– 900
glabrate 226
glabrous 226, 255
glacial 383
glaciarum 840
glaciate 385
glaciation 383
glacier 383
glacis 217, 717
glad *pleased* 827
　pleasing 829
　–rags 225
　–tidings 532
　would be–of 865
gladden 834, 836
glade *hollow* 252
　opening 260
　shade 424
gladiate 253
gladiator 726
gladiatorial 713, 720
　–combat 361
gladsome 827, 829
glair 352
glaive 727
glamour 992
glance *touch* 379
　look 441
　sign 550
　–at *take notice of* 457
　allude to 527
　censure 932
　–off *deviate* 279
　diverge 291
　–coal 388

see at a–498
gland 221–cell 221
glanders 655
glandule 221
glare *light* 420
　stare 441
　imperfect vision 443
　visible 446
glaring (see glare)
　great 31
　color 428
　visible 446
　manifest 525
glass *vessel* 191
　smooth 255
　brittle 328
　transparent 425
　lens 445
　–of fashion 852
　–too much 959
　live in a–house
　brittle 328
　visible 446
　danger 665
　musical, musicales 47
　see through a–
　　darkly 491
glass-coach 272
Glassite 984
glassy (see glass)
　shining 420
　colorless 429
glaucous 435
glave 727
glaver 933
glaze 255 *ice* 383
gleam *small* 32
　light 420
　visibility 446
glean *choose* 609
　acquire 775
glebe *land* 342
　ecclesiastical 995
　church 1000
glee *music* 415
　satisfaction 827
　merriment 836
gleek 929
glen 252
glib *voluble* 584
　facile 705
glide *lapse* 109
　move 264
　travel 266
　aviation 267
　(*slow* 275)
　–into *conversion* 144
glimmer *light* 420
　dim 422
　visible 446
　slight knowledge 490, 491
glimpse *sight* 441
　knowledge 490
glint 420, 441

glissade 306
glisten 420
glitter *shine* 420
　be visible 446
　illustrious 882
glittering
　ornament 847
　display 882
gloaming 126, 422
gloar *look* 441
　wonder 870
gloat-on *look* 441
　–over *pleasure* 377
　look 441
　delight 827
globated 249
globe *sphere* 249
　world 318
　on the face of the– 318
globe-trotter 268
globe-trotting 441
globoid 249
globularity 249
globule *small* 32
　spherule 249
glochidiate 253
glomeration 72
gloom *darkness* 421
　dimness 422
　sadness 837
gloomy *dark* 421
　sad 837
　–horizon 859
gloriation 884
glorification
　(see glorify)
glorify *honor* 873
　approve 931
　worship 990
glorious
　illustrious 873
　tipsy 959
glory *light* 420
　honor 873
　heaven 981
　–be to God 990
　–dies not 873
　–in 878
　King of– 976
gloss *smooth* 255
　sheen 420
　interpretation 522
　falsehood 546
　plea 617
　beauty 845
　–of novelty 123
　–over *neglect* 460
　sophistry 477
　falsehood 544
　plead 615
　vindicate 937
glossarist 524
glossary *list* 86
　dictionary 562
　(*interpretation* 522)

gnat

glossographer 492
glossologist 492
glossology 560, 562
glossy (see gloss)
glottology 560, 562
glout 901a
glove 225
　take up the– 720
　throw down the– 715
glover 225
glow *warm* 382
　shine 420
　color 428
　visibility 446
　style 574
　passion 821
glower *glare* 443
　discourteous 895
　sullen 901a
glowing (see glow)
　red 434
　orange 439
　excited 824
　beautiful 845
　–terms 574
glowworm 423
gloze *flatter* 933
　vindicate 937
glucose 396
glue *cement* 45
　cementing 46
　semiliquid 352
glum *discontented* 832
　dejected 837
　sulky 901a
glume 223
glut *wedge* 633
　redundance 641
　satiety 869
glutinous 327, 352
glutinousness 327
glutton 954a, 957
gluttony 957
　(*desire* 865)
glycerine
　lubrication 332
　oil 356
glyph 557
glyphography 558
glyptography 558
glyptotheca 557
glyster 300
gnarl *kink* 59
　distort 243
　convexity 250
　anger 900
　threat 909
gnarled *twisted* 59
　rough 256
　dense 321
gnarly 256
gnash one's teeth
　lament 839
　angry 900
gnat *little* 193

460

gnaw   **good**

strain at a–etc.
  caprice 608
gnaw *eat* 298
  rub 331
  injure 659
gnawing
 –grief 828, 830
 –pain 378
gnome 496, 980
gnomic 496
gnomon 114
Gnostic 984
Gnosticism 451
gnu 366
go *cease to exist* 2
  energy 171, 682
  move 264
  recede 287
  depart 293
  jade 429
  disappear 449
  fashion 852
  as things–613
  come and–314
  give the–by to
    neglect 460
  deceive 545
  avoid 623
  not observe 773
 –about
  turn round 311
  published 531
  undertake 676
 –about your business
  ejection 297
  dismissal 756
 –across 302
 –after *in time* 117
  in motion 281
 –against 708
 –ahead *precede* 280
  advance 282
  active 682
 –all lengths 604*a*
  complete 52
  resolve 604
  exertion 686
 –aloft 305
 –astray 495
 –away 293
 –back 283
 –back on 624
 –bad 659
 –bail 771
 –before 280
 –beyond 303
 –by *conform to* 82
  elapse 109
  past 122
  outrun 303
  subterfuge 702
 –by the board 158
 –by the name of 564
 –cahoots 712
 –deep into 461
 –down *sink* 306

  decline 659
 –down with
  believed 484
  tolerated 826
  content 831
 –farther and fare
    worse 659
 –for nothing
  sophistry 477
  unimportant 643
 –forth *depart* 293
  publish 531
 –from one's word
    773
 –halves 91
 –hand in hand
  accompany 88
  same time 120
 –hard 704
 –in 294
 –in for *resolution* 604
  pursuit 622
 –into *ingress* 294
  inquire 461
  dissert 595
 –mad 503
 –near 286
 –no further
  keep secret 528
 –off *explode* 173
  depart 293
  die 360
  wither 659
  marry 903
 –on *time* 106
  continue 143
  advance 282
 –on for ever 112
 –on ill 735
 –on the stump 582
 –out *cease* 142
  egress 295
  extinct 385
 –out of one's head
    506
 –over *passage* 302
  explore 461
  apostate 607
  faithless 940
 –round 311
 –shares 778
 –the limit 52, 604
 –through
  meet with 151
  pass 302
  explore 461
  perform 599
  conduct 692
  complete 729
  endure 826
 –through fire and
    water 604*a*
 –to extend 196
  travel 266
  direction 278
  remonstrance 695

 –to glory 162, 360
 –to pieces 162
 –to sleep 683
 –to war 722
 –under 162
 –up 305
 –West *die* 360
 –with *assent* 488
  concord 714
 –with the stream
  conform 82
  servile 886
goad *for oxen* 370
  motive 615
  quicken 684
go-ahead 171, 682
goal *end* 67
  reach 292 *object* 620
  reach the–
  complete 729
goat *jumper* 309
  lecher 962
  he–*male* 373
goatee 256
goatish 961
gob *sailor* 269
  jaws 298
gobang 840
gobbet *small piece* 32
  food 298
gobble *cry* 412
  gormandize 957
  eat 298
gobemouche *fool* 501
  dupe 547
go-between
  interjacent 226
  instrumental 631
  mediate 724
  agent 758
goblet 191
goblin 980
  (*bugbear* 860)
gocart 722
GOD 976
  for–'s sake 765
 –bless me! 870
 –bless you
  farewell 293
 –forbid 766
 –forsaken 196
 –grant 990
 –knows 491
 –'s acre 363
 –'s grace 906
 –'s love 906
 –'s own country 189
 –'s will 601
 –willing 470
  house of–1000
  kingdom of–981
  sons of–977
  to–be true 772
god 979
  household–s 189
  the–s

  gallery 444, 599
  tutelary–664
godchild 771
goddess *love* 897
  good woman 948
  heathen 979
  she moves a–374
godfather 771
Godhead 976
godlike 987
godly 944
godmother 771
godown 636
godsend *good* 618
  prosperity 734
Godspeed
  farewell 293
  hope 858
  courtesy 894
  benevolence 906
  approbation 931
goer *horse* 271
goes (see **go**)
  as one–270
  here–676
goggle 441
goggle-eyed 443
goggles 445
going (see **go**)
  general 78
  rumor 532
 –on
  incomplete 53, 730
  current 151
  transacting 625
 –to happen 152
goiter 655
Golconda 803
gold *yellow* 436
  orange 439
  money 800
  all is not–486
 –brick 545, 702
 –mohur 800
  worth its weight in–
    648
  write in letters of–
    642
golden (see **gold**)
 –age *prosperity* 734
  pleasure 827
 –apple 615
 –calf *wealth* 803
  idolatry 991
 –dream
  imagination 515
  hope 858
 –mean
  moderation 174
  mid-course 628
 –opinions 931
 –opportunity 134
 –rule *precept* 697
 –season of life 127
 –wedding 883
  music's–tongue 415

golf 840
Golgotha *burial* 363
  churchyard 1000
Goliath *strength* 159
  size 192
gomashta 758
gondola 273
gondolier 269
gone (see **go**) *past* 122
  absent 187
  dead 360
  hopeless 859
 –bad 653
 –by *antiquated* 124
 –case 859
 –coon 859
 –out of one's
    recollection 506
 –where the woodbine
    twineth 771
goneness 688
goner 859
gonfalon 550
gong 417
goniometer *angle* 244
  measure 466
gonorrhea 655
good *complete* 52
  palatable 394
  assent 488
  benefit **618**
  beneficial 648
  right 922
  virtuous 944
  pious 987
  as–as 197
  be–enough 765
  be so–as 765
  do– 906
  for–*diuturnal* 110
  permanent 141
 –actions 944
 –as one's word
  veracity 543
  observance 772
  probity 939
 –at 698
 –at the price 815
 –auspices 858
 –behavior
  contingent 108*a*
  duty 926
  virtue 944
 –bye 293
 –chance 472
 –cheer *food* 298
  cheerful 826
 –circumstances 803
 –condition 192
 –day *arrival* 292
  departure 293
  courtesy 894
 –effect *goodness* 648
  beauty 845
 –enough
  not perfect 651

good–for–nothing   grand

–fellow 892
–fight *war* 722
  virtue 944
–for *useful* 644
  salubrious 656
–fortune 734
–Friday 138, 998
–genius *friend* 890
  benefactor 912
  god 979
–hand 700
–humor *concord* 714
  cheerfulness 836
  amuse 840
  courtesy 894
  kindly 906
–intention 906
–judgment 498
–lack! 870
–living *food* 298
  gluttony 957
–look out 459
–looks 845
–luck 734
–man *man* 373
  husband 903
  worthy **948**
–manners 894
–morrow 292
–name 873
–nature 906
–offices
  mediation 724
  kind 906
–old time 122
–omen 858
–opinion 931
–pennyworth 815
–repute 873
–sense 498
–society 852
–taste 850
–tasting 394
–temper 894
–thing 648
–time *early* 132
  opportune 134
  prosperous 734
–turn *kindness* 906
–understanding 714
–wife *woman* 374
  spouse 903
–will *willingness* 602
  benevolence 906
–woman 948
–word *approval* 931
  vindication 927
–works 906
  in–case 192
  in–odor *repute* 873
  approbation 931
  in one's–books 888
  in one's–graces 888
  make–*evidence* 467
  provide 637
  restore 660

complete 729
substantiate 924
vindicate 937
atone for 952
put a–face upon
cheerful 836
proud 878
so far so–931
take in–part
pleased 827
courteous 894
kind 906
think–931
to–purpose 731
to the–780
turn to–account 731
what's the–645
good–for–nothing
  impotence 158
  useless 645
good–looking 845
goodly *great* 31
  large 192
  handsome 845
good–natured 906
goodness
  (*see* good) **648**
  virtue 944
–gracious! 870
–of heart 906
have the
  –*request* 765
goods *effects* 780
  merchandise 798
Goodwin sands 667
goody 374
goose *bird* 298, 366
  hiss 409
  game of–840
  giddy as a–458
  –egg *zero* 101
  –flesh 383
  –grass 253
  kill the–with golden
    eggs *bungler* 699
    prodigal 818
gooseberry *fruit* 298
  yarn 549
–eyes 441, 443
old–978
goosecap 501
goosequill 590
goose–skin 383
Gordian knot
  tangled 59
  difficulty 704
  (*problem* 461)
gore *gusset* 43
  stab 260
  blood 361
gorge *ravine* 198, 350
  fill 641
  satiety 869
  gluttony 957
  (*eat* 298)

–the hook 602
raise one's–900
gorge–de–pigeon 432, 440
gorgeous *color* 428
  beauty 845
  ornament 847
Gorgon 860
gorilla 366, 913
gormandize *eat* 298
  gluttony 957
gorse 367
gory *murderous* 361
  red 434
  unclean 653
gospel *certainty* 474
  doctrine 484
  truth 494
  take for–484
Gospels 985
gossamer
  filament 205
  light 320
  texture 329
gossamery
  unsubstantial 4
  weak 160
  light 320
gossip *news* 532
  babbler 584
  conversation 588
gossoon 876
Goth *vulgar* 851
  barbarian 876
gothamite 501
Gotham, wise men of 501
gothic *amorphous* 241
Gothicism 851
gouache 556
gouge *concave* 252
  perforator 262
goulash 298
gourmand
  sensualist 954a
  glutton 957
gourmet
  fastidious 868
  sybarite 954a
gout 378
goût 390
govern *direct* 693
  authority 737
governess 540
government
  (*see* govern)
  ruling power 745
  divine–976
  –bonds 802
  –mark 550
  –s *authority* 737
  –school 542
  petticoat–699
governor *father* 166
  tutor 540
  director 694

ruler 745
keeper 753
–'s message 695
gowk 501
gown *dress* 225
  canonicals 999
gownsman 492
grab *take* 789
  miser 819
grabble 379
grace *style* 578
  permission 760
  concession 784
  elegance 845
  polish 850
  title 877
  pity 914
  forgiveness 918
  honor 939
  piety 987
  worship 990
  act of–784
  God's–906
–before meat 916
  heart of–861
  in one's good–s 888
  say–990
  submit with a good
    –826
  with a bad–603
  with a good–
    willing 602
    courteous 894
graceful *elegant* 578
  beautiful 845
  tasteful 850
graceless
  inelegant 579
  ugly 846
  vicious 945
  impenitent 951
  irreligious 989
Graces 845
gracile 203
gracious *willing* 602
  courteous 894
  kind 906
  good–870
gradatim *in order* 58
  continuous 69
  slow 275
gradation *degree* 26
  order 58
  continuity 69
gradatory 26
grade *degree* 26
  classify 60
  term 71
  obliquity 217
  ascent 305
  class 541, (75)
  at–219
  –crossing 219
gradient 217, 305
gradual *degree* 26
  continuous 69

slow 275
graduate *adjust* 23
  degree 26
  divide 44
  arrange 60
  series 69
  measure 466
  scholar 492
  teaching 537
  rank 873
  –school 542
graduated scale 466
graduation *class* 541
  rank 873
gradus 86, 562
Graecist 492
graft *join* 43
  locate 184
  insert 300
–a *plant* 371
  teach 537
  bribe 784
  improbity 940
grain *essence* 5
  small 32
  tendency 176
  little 193
  rough 256
  weight 319
  texture 329
  powder 330
  paint 428
  temper 820
  ornament 847
  against the–
    rough 256
    unwilling 603
    opposing 708
–elevator 636
–oil 356
–s of allowance
  qualification 469
  doubt 485
  in the–820
  like–s of sand
    incoherent 47
grallatory 267
gramercy 916
gram–fed 192
graminivorous 298
grammar
  beginning 66
  teaching 537
  school 542
  language **567**
  bad–568
  comparative–560
  –school 537
grammarian 492
grammatical 567
  –blunder 568
grammatism 561
gramophone 417, 418, 551
granary 636
grand *august* 31

462

grandam · grim

grandam
- *vigor* 574
- *important* 642
- *handsome* 845
- *glorious* 873
- *ostentatious* 882
- —climacteric 128
- —doings 882
- —juror 967
- —manner *solecism* 568
- —piano 417
- —seignior 745
- —style 556, 568
- —tour 266
- —Turk 745
- —vizier 694

grandam 130
grandchildren 167
grandee 875
grandeur *greatness* 31
- *vigor* 574
- *repute* 873

grandfather
- *veteran* 130
- *paternity* 166

grandiloquent 577
grandiose 482, 577
grandmother
- *maternal* 166
- *simple* 501
- *teach*—538

grandness (see grand)
grandsire *veteran* 130
- *paternity* 166

grandstand 444
grange 189
granger 371
granite 323, 635
granivorous 298
- *qualification* 469
- *unbelief* 485

granny 130
granolithic
- *pavement* 255

grant *admit* 529
- *permit* 760
- *consent* 762
- *confer* 784
- *God*—990
- —a lease 771
- —in—aid school 542

granted 488 take for
- —believe 484
- *suppose* 514

grantee
- *transference* 270
- *possessor* 779
- *receiver* 785

grantor 784
granular 330
granulate 330
granulated 330
- —sugar 386

granule 32
grapefruit 298
grapes 298 *sour*—
- *unattainable* 471

grandam
- *falsehood* 544
- *excuse* 617

grapeshot *attack* 716
- *arms* 727

graphic
- *intelligible* 518
- *painting* 556
- *vigorous* 574
- *descriptive* 594

graphology 590
graphomania 590
graphomaniac 590
graphometer 244
graphophone 417
graphotype 558
grapnel 666
grapple *fasten* 43
- *clutch* 789
- —with—a question 461
- —difficulties 704
- *oppose* 708
- *resist* 719
- *contention* 720

grappling iron
- *fastening* 45
- *safety* 666

grasp *comprehend* 518
- *power* 737
- *retain* 781
- *seize* 789
- —at 865
- —of intellect 498
- in one's—737
- *possess* 777
- tight—*severe* 739

grasping *miserly* 819
- *covetous* 856

grass *fell* 213
- *vegetation* 367
- —widow 905
- let the—grow under
  one's feet
- *neglect* 460
- *inactive* 683
- not let the—etc.
  active 682

grasshopper 309, 366
grassland 367
grassplot 371
grassy 367
grate *arrangement* 60
- *rub* 330
- *physical pain* 378
- *stove* 386
- —on the ear
  harsh sound 410
- —on the feelings 830

grated *barred* 219
grateful
- *physically pleasant*
  377
- *agreeable* 829
- *thankful* 916

grater 330
gratification
- *animal*—377

moral—827
gratify *permit* 760
- *please* 829

gratifying 377, 829
grating (see grate)
- *lattice* 219
- *stridor* 410

gratis 815
gratitude 916
gratuitous
- *inconsequent* 477
- *supposititious* 514
- *voluntary* 602
- *free* 748
- *payless* 815
- —service 602

gratuity *gift* 784
- *gratis* 815

gratulate 896
gravamen 642
- —of a charge 938

grave *great* 31
- *furrow* 259
- *tomb* 363
- *somber* 428
- *engrave* 558
- *important* 642
- *composed* 826
- *distressing* 830
- *sad* 837
- *heinous* 945
- —in the memory 505
- —note 408
- look—*disapprove* 932
- on this side of the—
  359
- rise from the—660
- silent as the—403
- sink into the—360
- without a—363

gravel *earth* 342
- *puzzle* 704

graven image 991
graveolent 401
graver 558
gravestone 363
gravitate *descend* 306
- *weigh* 319
- —towards 176

gravity *force* 157
- *weight* 319
- *vigor* 574
- *importance* 642
- *sedateness* 826
- *seriousness* 827
- center of—222
- specific—*weight* 319
- *density* 321

gravy 298, 333
gray *color* 428, **432**
- bring—hairs to the
  grave
- *adversity* 735
- *harass* 830
- —friar 996
- —hairs 128

—mare *ruler* 737
- *master* 745
- *wife* 903

graybeard 130
graze *touch* 199
- *browze* 298
- *rub* 331
- *touch* 379

grazier 370
grease *lubricate* 332
- *oil* 355, 356
- *graft* 784
- —the palm *tempt* 615
- *give* 784
- *pay* 807

greasy 355
great *much* 31
- *big* 192
- *glorious* 873
- *magnanimous* 942
- (*important* 642)
- —bear 318
- —circle sailing 628
- —coat 225
- —doings
  importance 642
- *bustle* 682
- —First Cause 153
- —folks 875
- —gun 626, 875
- —hearted 942
- —is the glory 873
- —Mogul 745
- —moment 824
- —number 102
- —quantity 31
- —Spirit 979
  the—adventure
  death 360

greater 33
- —number 102
- —part 31
- *nearly all* 50

greatest 33 —good 618
greatness 31
greave 225
grebe 310
Greco—Roman
- —philosophy 450

greed *desire* 865
- *gluttony* 957

greedy *avaricious* 819
Greek *Grecian* 188
- *unintelligible* 519
- *sharper* 792
- —Church 984
- —deities 979
- —Kalends 107
- —philosophy 451
  St. Giles's—563

green *new* 123
- *young* 127
- *lawn* 344
- *grass* 367, 371
- *sour* 397
- *color* 435

credulous 486
- *novice* 491
- *unused* 614
- *healthy* 654
- *immature* 674
- *unskilled* 699
- board of—cloth 966
- —goods 545
- —old age 128
- —peas 298
- —sickness 655

greenback 800
green—eyed monster
  920
greengrocer 797
greenhorn *novice* 493
- *dupe* 547
- *bungler* 701

greenhouse
- *receptacle* 191
- *horticulture* 371

greenish 435
greenness **435**
greenroom 599
greens 298, 367
greensward 344, 367
greenwood 367
greet *weep* 839
- *hail* 894

greeting *sociality* 892
gregarious 892
grenade 727
grenadier *tall* 206
- *soldier* 726

grey (see gray)
greyhound *swift* 274
- *animal* 366

griddlecake 298
gridelin 437
gridiron *crossing* 219
- *stove* 386

grief 828
- come to—735

grievance *evil* 619
- *painful* 830
- *wrong* 923

grieve *mourn* 828
- *pain* 830
- *dejected* 837
- *complain* 839

grievous *bad* 649
- *painful* 830

grievously *very* 31
griffe 41
griffin *newcomer* 57
- *monster* 83

griffonage 590
grig *merry* 836
grill 382, 384
- *question* 461

grille 219
grill room 189
grim *resolute* 604
- *painful* 830
- *doleful* 837
- *ugly* 846

463

grimace

discourteous 895
sullen 901a
—faced 914a
—visaged war 722
grimace
distortion 243
affectation 855
grimacer actor 599
humorist 844
affected 855
Grimaldi 490a
Grimaldi man 372a
grimalkin 366
grimy 652
grin laugh 838
ridicule 856
—a ghastly smile
dejected 837
ugly 846
—and abide 725
grind reduce 195
sharpen 253
pulverizer 330
pain 378
teaching 537
learn 539
oppress 907
—one's teeth 900
—the organ 416
grinder teacher 330
grindery warehouse 799
grinding severe 739
distressing 830
grindstone
sharpener 253
pulverizer 330
grip bag 191
paroxysm 315
indication 550
sceneshifter 599
power 737
retention 781
clutch 789
—of the hand 894
gripe (see grip)
pain 378
parsimony 819
gripes 378
grippe 655
gripsack 191
grisaille gray 432
painting 556
grisard 130
grisette woman 374
commonalty 876
libertine 962
grisly 846
grist quantity 25
materials 635
provision 637
—to the mill
useful 644
acquire 775
gristle dense 321
tough 327

gristmill 330
grit strength 159
powder 330
resolution 604
stamina 604a
—in the oil
hindrance 706
gritty hard 323
grizzled gray 432
variegated 440
grizzly 895
groan cry 411
lament 839
groat 800
grocer 637
groceries 637
groceryman 797
grog drink 298
intoxicating 959
groin 244
groom
tend a horse 370
servant 746
groomed, well—847
groomsman 903
groove furrow 259
habit 613
move in a—82
put in a—for 673
grope feel 379
experiment 463
try 675
(inquire 461)
—in the dark
blind 442
difficult 704
gross great 31
whole 50
number 98
ugly 846
vulgar 851
vicious 945
impure 961
—credulity 486
—receipts 810
grossièreté 895
grossness (see gross)
grot (see grotto)
grotesque odd 83
distorted 243
—style 579
ridiculous 853
grotto alcove 191
hollow 252
grouch sullen 901a
ground cause 153
region 181
situation 183
base 211
fell 213
support 215
coating 223
land 342
plain 344
evidence 467
teach 537

motive 615
plea 617
above—359
down to the—52
dress the—371
fall to the—732
get over the—274
go over the—302
—bait 784
—cut from under one 732
—floor chamber 191
low 207
base 211
—hog day 138
—of quarrel 713
—on attribute 155
—plan 554
—sliding from under one danger 665
—swell agitation 315
waves 348
level with the—162
maintain one's—
persevere 604a
play—840
prepare the—673
stand one's—
defend 717
resist 719
grounded
stranded 732
—on basis 211
evidence 467
well—490
groundless
unsubstantial 4
illogical 477
erroneous 495
groundling 876
grounds dregs 653
groundwork
substantiality 3
precursor 64
cause 153
basis 211
support 215
preparation 673
group marshal 60
cluster 72
grouse 298, 366
grout vinculum 45
sullen 901a
grouty 901a
grove group 72
street 189
glade 252
wood 367
grovel below 207
move slowly 275
cringe 886
base 940
grow increase 35
become 144
expand 194
vegetation 365, 367

—from effect 154
—into 144
—less 195
—like a weed 365
—old gracefully 128
—rank 365
—taller 206
—together 46
—up 194
—upon one 613
grower 164
growl blow 349
cry 412
complain 839
discourtesy 895
anger 900
threat 909
growler cab 272
discontented 832
sulky 901a
grown up 131
growth (see grow)
development 161
—in size 194
tumor 250
vegetation 367
groyne 706
grub
small animal 193
food 298
—up eradicate 301
discover 480a
grudge unwilling 603
refuse 764
stingy 819
hate 898
anger 900
envy 921
bear a—907
owe a—898
grudging
unwilling 603
envious 921
—praise 932
gruel 298, 352
gruesome 846
gruff harsh sound 410
discourteous 895
(morose 901a)
grum harsh sound 410
morose 901a
grumble cry 411
complain 832, 839
grume 321, 354
grumose 321
grumous dense 321
pulpy 354
grumpy 901a
Grundy, Mrs. 852
grunt
animal sound 412
complain 839
G string loincloth 225
guano 653
guarantee
promise 768

guided by

security 771
guaranty 771
guard stopper 263
traveling 268
safety rail 664
defense 717
soldier 726
sentry 753
advanced—668
—against prepare 673
defense 717
—ship protection 664
man-of-war 726
mount—care 459
safety 664
off one's
—inexpectant 508
on one's
—careful 459
cautious 864
rear—668
throw off one's—
cunning 702
guarded
conditions 770
guardian safety 664
defense 717
keeper 753
—angel helper 711
benefactor 912
spirit 977
guardianship 664, 717
guardless 665
guardroom 752
guardsman 726
gubernation 693
gubernatorial 693, 737
gudgeon 547
guerdon 973
guerrilla 722, 726
guess 514
guesswork 514
guest 890
the parting—892
guffaw 838
guggle gush 348
bubble 353
resound 408
cry 412
guidable 278
guidance (see guide)
guide model 22
—a horse 370
teach 537
teacher 540
indicate 550
direct 693
director 694
advise 695
familiar spirit 979
—philosopher and friend 695
guidebook 527
guided by, be—

464

guideless

conform 82
guideless 665
guidepost 550
guiding star 693
guidon 550
guild *society* 712
  tribunal 966
guildhall 799
guile *deceit* 544, 545
  cunning 702
guileless
  veracious 543
  artless 703
guillemets 550
guillotine
  decapitate 361, 972
  ax 975
guilt 947 (*vice* 945)
guiltless 946
guilty 947 find–971
  plead–950
guimpe 225
guinea 800
guisard 599
guise *state* 7
  dress 225
  appearance 448
  plea 617
  mode 627
  conduct, 692
guiser 599
guitar 417
gulch 198, 350
gules 434
gulf *interval* 198
  deep 208
  lake **343**
gulfy 312
gull *bird* 366
  deceive 545
  dupe 547
gullet *throat* 260, 350
gullible 486
gully *gorge* 198
  hollow 252
  evening 260
  conduit 350
gulosity 957
gulp *swallow* 296
  take food 298
  –*down credulity* 486
  submit 725
gum *fastening* 45
  fasten 46
  resin 356a
  cheat 545
  –*elastic* 325
  –*game* 545
gumbo 298
gumminess 327
gummosity 352
gummous 352, 356a
gummy *tenacious* 327
  semiliquid 352
  resinous 356a

gumption 498
gumshoe
  be concealed 528
gun *report* 406
  weapon 284, 727
  blow great–*s* 349
  –*s loudness* 404
  sure as a–474
guna 561
gunate 561
gunboat 726
guncotton 727
gunflint 727
gunman 361, 726, 913
gunner 284, 726
gunnery 284, 722, 727
gunpowder
  warfare 722
  ammunition 727
  not invent–665
  sit on barrel of–501
gunshot 197
gurge *eddy* 312
  torrent 348
gurgle *flow* 348
  bubble 353
  faint sound 405
  resonance 408
gurgoyle 350
guru *scholar* 492
  teacher 540
  holy man 996
gurry 653
gush *flow out* 295
  flood 348
  overestimation 482
  loquacity 584
  ardor 821
gushing *egress* 295
  emotional 821
  impressible 822
gusset 43
gust *wind* 349
  physical taste 390
  passion 825
  moral taste 850
gustable 298
gustation 390
gustative 390
gustful 390, 394
gustless 391
gusto (*see* gust)
  physical pleasure 377
  emotion 821
gusty 349
gut *destroy* 162
  opening 260
  strait 343
  eviscerate 297
  sack 789
  steal 791
guts *inside* 221
gutta 442–*serena* 442
gutter *groove* 259

conduit 350
guttle 957
guttural *letter* 561
  inarticulate 583
guy *vinculum* 45
  tether 752
  grotesque 853
guzzle *gluttony* 957
  drunkenness 959
guzzler 959
gybe 279
gymkhana 720
gymnasium *hall* 189
  school 542
  arena 728
gymnast *strong* 159
gymnastic *strong* 159
  school 542
  athletic 720
gymnastics
  training 537
  exercise 686
  contention 720
  sport 840
gymnosophist
  abstainer 953
  sectarian 984
gynaeceum 374
gynaecic 374
gynandrous 83
gynarchy 737
gynecocracy 737
gynecology 662
gyneolatry 897
gynephobia 898
gyniatrics 662
gynics 374
gyp 746
gypsy 268
gyral 312
gyrate 312
gyrocar 312
gyromancy 511
gyroplane 312
gyroscope 312
gyrostat 312
gyrostatics 312
gysart 599
gyve 311, 752

H

habeas corpus 963
haberdasher 225, 797
habergeon 717
habiliment 225
habilitation 698
habit *essence* 5
  coat 225
  custom **613**
  –*of mind* 820
  –*s of business* 682
  want of–614
habitant 188, 371

habitat 189
habitation 189
habit maker 225
habitual *orderly* 58
  normal 80
  ordinary 82
  customary 613
habituate *train* 537
  accustom 613
habituation 82, 613
habitude *state* 7
  habit 613
habitué 613
hachure 550
hacienda *abode* 189
  property 780
hack *cut* 44
  shorten 201
  horse 271
  vehicle 272
  writer 593
  worker 690
  –*writer* 534
  literary–593
hackamore 752
hackbut 727
hackee 274
hackery 272
hackle 44
  comb 253, 652
hackman 268
hackney coach 272
hackneyed
  known 490
  trite 496
  habitual 613
haddock 298
Hades 982
hadji *traveler* 268
  priest 996
haematobious 5, 161
haematose 641
haemorrhage
  (*see* hemorrhage)
haft 633
hag *ugly* 846
  wretch 913
  witch 994
haggard *insane* 503
  tired 688
  wild 824
  ugly 846
haggis 298
haggle *cut* 44
  chaffer 794
hagiographa 985
hagiology 983
hagioscope 260
ha-ha *ditch* 198
  defense 717
haik 225
hail *welcome* 292
  ice 383
  call 586
  rejoicing 838
  honor to 873

half

  celebration 883
  courtesy 894
  salute 928
  approve 931
  –*fellow well met friendship* 888
  sociality 892
  –*from* 293
hailstone 383
hair *small* 32
  filament 205
  roughness 256
  –*breadth escape danger* 665
  escape 671
  –'s *breadth near* 197
  narrow 203
  –*s on the head multitude* 102
  make one's–stand on end
  distressing 830
  fear 860
  wonder 870
  to a–494
hairdresser 225
hairif 253
hairless 226
hair-splitting 480
hairy *rough* 256
hajj 266
hakim *safety* 664
  master 745
  judge 967
halberd 727
halberdier 726
halcyon *calm* 174
  peace 721
  prosperous 734
  joyful 827, 829
  cheerful 836
  –*birds omen* 512
hale 654
half 91–*a dozen*
  six 98
  several 102
  –*a gale* 349
  –*a hundred* 98
  –*and half equal* 27
  mixed 41
  incomplete 53
  –*distance* 68
  –*light* 422
  –*mast* 669
  –*masted flag* 550
  –*measures incomplete* 53
  vacillating 605
  mid–course 628
  –*moon* 245
  –*price* 815
  –*rations* 640
  –*scholar* 493
  –*seas over* 959
  –*sight* 443
  –*speed moderate* 174

465

half–baked

   slow 275
  –the battle
    important 642
   success 731
  –tint 421
  –truth 546
  see with–an eye
   intelligent 498
  intelligible 518
  manifest 525
half–baked
  ignorant 491
  imbecile 499
half–blind 443
half blood *mixture* 41
  unconformity 83
  imperfect 651
half–breed 41
half–frozen 352
half–hearted
  irresolute 605
  insensible 823
  indifferent 866
half–learned 491
half–learning 491
half–melted 352
halfpenny *trifle* 643
half–starved
  insufficient 640
  fasting 956
half–tone 421, 558
half–way *small* 32
  middle 68
  between 228
  go–*irresolute* 605
  mid–*course* 628
  meet–*willing* 602
  compromise 774
half–witted 499, 501
hall *chamber* 189
  receptacle 191
  mart 799
  –mark 550
  –of audience 588
  –s of time 109
  music–599
hallelujah 990
Halley 490a
halloo *cry* 411
  look here! 457
  call 586
  wonder 870
hallow *celebrate* 883
  respect 928
hallowed 976
Halloween 138
Hallowmas 138
hallucination
  error 495
  insanity 503
  psychical research 992a
halo *light* 420
  glory 873
halomancy 511
halser 45

halt *cease* 142
  weak 160
  rest 265
  go slowly 275
  lame 655
  fail 732
  at the–265
halter *rope* 45
  restraint 752
  punishment 975
  wear a–874
  with a–round one's neck 665
halting *style* 579
  –place 292
halve (*see* half)
halves do by–
  neglect 460
  not complete 730
  go–778
  not do by–729
ham *house* 189
  meat 298
hamadryad 979
hamal 746
hamfatter 599
hamiform 245
Hamitic 372a
hamlet 189
hammer *repeat* 104
  knock 276
  stammer 583
  between the–and the anvil 665
  –at *think* 451
  work 686
  –out *form* 240
  thought 451
  prepare 673
  complete 729
  under the–
   auction 796
hammock 215
hamous 245
hamper *basket* 191
  obstruct 706
hamstring
  incapacitate 158
  render useless 645
  injure 659
hamulate 245
hanaper 802
hand
  measure of length 200
  side 236
  mariner 269
  transfer 270
  man 372
  organ of touch 379
  indicator 550
  writing 590
  medium 631
  agent 690
  grasp 781
  cards 840

  transfer 783
  at–*present* 118
  future 121
  destined 152
  near 197
  useful 644
  bad–590
  bird in–781
  come to–*arrive* 292
  received 785
  fold one's–s 681
  give one's–to *marry* 903
  good–*writing* 590
  skill 698
  proficiency 700
  –and glove 888
  –back 683
  –down *record* 551
  transfer 783
  –in hand *joined* 43
  accompanying 88
  same time 120
  concur 178
  coöperate 709
  party 712
  concord 714
  friend 888
  social 892
  –in one's chips 360
  –of death 360
  –organ 417
  –over *transfer* 783
  give 784
  –over head
   inattention 458
   neglect 460
   reckless 863
  –s off! *avoid* 623
  leave alone 681
  prohibition 761
  –to hand
   touching 199
   transfer 270
   fight 720, 722
  have a–in *cause* 153
  act 680
  cooperate 709
  have one's–in
   skill 698
  have one's–s full 682
  helping–707, 711
  hold in–*rule* 737
  hold out the
   –*courtesy* 894
  hold up the
   –*vote* 609
  in–*incomplete* 53
  business 625
  preparing 673
  not finished 730
  possessed 777
  money 800
  in the–s of *authority* 737

  subjection 749
  keep one's–in 613
  lay–s on
   discover 480a
   use 677
   take 789
   rite 998
  live from–to mouth
   insufficient 640
   unprepared 674
   poor 804
  much on one's–s 682
  no–in 623
  on one's–s
   business 625
   redundant 641
   not finished 730
   for sale 796
  on the other–468
  poor–701
  put into one's–s 784
  put one's–to 676
  ready to one's–673
  shake–s 918
  stretch forth one's– 680
  take by the–707
  take in– *teach* 537
  undertake 676
  time hanging on one's–
   inaction 681
   leisure 685
   weary 841
  try one's–675
  turn one's–to 625
  under one's–
   in writing 590
   promise 768
   compact 769
  with the –s in the pockets 681
hand–bag 191
hand–barrow 272
handbill 531
handbook *travel* 266
  information 527
  book 593
handbreadth 200
hand camera 445
hand car 272
handfast 903
handful *quantity* 25
  small 32
  few 103
hand gallop 274
hand grenade 727
handicap *equalize* 27
  incumber 706
  race 720
handicraft
  business 625
  working 680
handicraftsman 690

hang

handiwork *effect* 154
  doing 680
handkerchief
  clothes 225
  cleaner 652
handle *feel, touch* 379
  dissert 595
  plea 617
  instrument 633
  use 677
  manage 693
  furnish a–937
  –a case 692
  –to one's name
   name 564
   honor 877
  make a–of 677
handmaid
  instrumentality 631
  auxiliary 711
  servant 746
hand mirror 445
hand post 550
handsel *begin* 66
  security 771
  gift 784
  pay 809
handsome *liberal* 816
  beautiful 845
  disinterested 942
  –fortune 803
  –is that handsome does 816
handspike 633
handstaff 727
handwriting
  evidence 467
  signature 550
  autograph 590
  –on the wall
   warning 668
handy *near* 197
  useful 644
  ready 673
  dexterous 698
hang *lateness* 133
  pendency 214
  kill 361
  curse 908
  execute 972
  –about 133, 197
  –back 133, 623
  –by a thread 665
  –down the head 837
  –fire *late* 133
  cease 142
  unproductive 169
  inert 172
  slow 275
  reluctance 603
  inactive 683
  not finish 730
  fail 732
  refuse 764
  –in doubt 485
  –in suspense 605

466

hangar   **harsh**

—in the balance 133
—it! *regret* 833
   contempt 930
—on *accompany* 88
—on hand 641
—on the sleeve of
   servant 746
   servility 886
   flattery 933
—out *display* 882
—out a light 420
—out a signal 550
—out one's shingle
   184
—over *destiny* 152
   height 206
   project 250
   (*futurity* 121)
—over the head 152
—together *joined* 43
   cohere 46
   concur 178
   cooperate 709
—up *delay* 133
—up the fiddle 67
—upon *effect* 154
   dependency 749
—upon the lips of 418
hangar 191, 273
hang-dog look 901*a*
hanger *weapon* 727
hanger-on
   accompaniment 88
   servant 746
   servile 886
   pothooks and -s 590
hanging (*see* hang)
   oblique 217
   elevated 307
   ornament 847
   —look 846
hangman
   evildoer 913
   bad man 949
   executioner 975
hangnail 214
hank *tie* 45
hanker 865
Hansard 551
hansom 272
hap 156
haphazard
   chance 156, 621
hapless
   unfortunate 735
   (*miserable* 828)
   (*hopeless* 859)
haplography 495
haply *possibly* 470
   (*by chance* 156)
happen 151
  —as it may
   chance 621
  —what may
   certain 474
   reckless 863

happening 151
happiness
   (*see* happy)
   the greatest–of the
     greatest number
     910
happy *fit* 23
   opportune 134
   style 578
   glad 827
   cheerful 836
  —as a clam 827
  —dispatch 972
  —go lucky 674
  —hunting grounds
    981
  —release 360
  —returns of the day
    896
  —thought 842
  —valley 515, 827
    imagination 515
    delight 827
harakiri 361, 972
harangue
   teaching 537
   speech 582
   allocution 586
harass *fatigue* 688
   vex 830
   worry 907
harbinger
   precursor 64
   omen 512
   informant 527
harbor *abode* 189
   haven 292
   refuge 666
   cherish 821
  —a design 620
  —an idea 451
  —revenge 919
  —*natural*–343
harborless 185, 665
hard *strong* 159
   dense 323
   physically insensible
    376
   sour 397
   difficult 704
   severe 739
   morally insensible
    823
   grievous 830
   impenitent 951
   blow–349
   go- difficult 704
   failure 732
   adversity 735
   pain 828
  —a-lee 273
  —and fast rule 80
  —a-port 273
  —at it 682
  —at work 682
  —bargain 819

—by 197
—case 735
—cash 800
—earned 704
—fought 704
—frost 383
—heart
   malevolent 907
   vicious 945
   impenitent 951
—hit 732
—knocks 720
—life 735
—lines *adversity* 735
   severity 739
—liver 954*a*
—lot 735
—master 739
—measure 739
—names 932
—necessity 601
—nut to crack 704
—of belief 487
—of hearing 419
—pressed *haste* 684
   difficulty 704
   hindrance 706
—put to it 704
—set 704
—tack 298
—task 703
—time 704
—to believe 485
—to please 868
—up *difficulty* 704
   poor 804
—upon *nearness* 197
   attack 715
   severe 739
   censure 932
—winter 383
—words *obscure* 571
   rude 895
   censure 932
—work 686
—hit–276
—look–at 441
—not be too–upon
   918
—strike– *energy* 171
   impulse 276
—try–675
—work–686
harden (*see* hard)
   strengthen 159
   accustom 613
  —the heart
    insensible 823
    enmity 889
    impenitence 951
hardened
   impious 988
  —front *insolent* 885
hardening *habit* 613
hard-favored 846
hard-featured 846

hard-fisted 819
hard-handed 739
hard-headed 498,
  871
hard-hitting 518
hardihood
   coverage 861
   insolence 885
hardiness (*see* hardy)
hardly *scarcely* 32
   deal-with 739
  —any *few* 103
  —anything *small* 32
   unimportant 643
  —ever 137
hard-mouthed 606
hardness 323
hardpan 211
hard-shell 739
hardship 735
hard-visaged 846
hardware 323
hardy *strong* 159
   healthy 654
   brave 861
hare 274, 298
  hold with the–and
    run with the
    hounds *fickle* 607
   servile 886
harebrained
   giddy 458
   rash 863
   (*foolish* 499)
   (*mad* 503)
harelip 243, 848
harem *household* 189
   woman 374
   marriage 903
   imputrity 961
haricot 298
hariff 253
hariolation 511
hark *hear* 418
   attention 457
  —back 283
harl 205
harlequin
   changeable 149
   nimble 274
   motley 440
   pantomimic 599
   humorist 844
harlequinade 599
harlot 962
harlotry 961
harm *evil* 619
   badness 649
   malevolence 907
harmattan 349
harmful 619
harmless
   impotent 158
   good 648
   perfect 650
   salubrious 656

   safe 664
   innocent 946
   bear–717
harmonica 417
harmonics 413
harmoniphon 417
harmonist 413
harmonious
   (*see* harmony)
   concurring 178
harmonium 417
harmonization 413
harmonize
   arrange 60
   conform 82
   concur 178
   music 416
harmony
   agreement 23
   order 58
   music 413
   color 428
   concord 714
   peace 721
   friendship 888
   want of–414
harness *fasten* 43
   fastening 45
   accouterment 225
  —a horse 370
   instrument 633
   prepare 673
   restraint 752
  —up 293
   in– *prepared* 673
   in action 680
   active 682
   subjection 749
harp *repeat* 104
   musical instrument
    417
   weary 841
Harpagon 819
harper 416
harpoon 727
harpsichord 417
harpy *relentless* 739
   thief 792
   miser 819
   evildoer 913
   demon 980
harquebus 727
harridan *hag* 846
   trollop 962
harrier 366
harrow
   agriculture 371
  —up the soul 860
   under the–378
harrowing 830
harry *pain* 830
   attack 716
   persecute 907
Harry, old–978
harsh *acrid* 171
   sound 410

467

harshness

style 579
discordant 713
severe 739
disagreeable 830
morose 895
malevolent 907
–voice 581
harshness (see harsh)
hart deer 366
male 373
hartshorn 392
harum-scarum
disorder 59
inattentive 458
haruspice 513
haruspicy 511
harvest evening 126
effect 154
profit 618
store 636
acquisition 775
get in the–
complete 729
succeed 731
–home
celebration 883
–time exertion 686
has been 122
harsh mix 41
cut 44
confusion 59
food 298
make–699
hashed 53
hashish 663, 954
hasp fasten 43
fastening 45
safety 664
hassock 215
hastate 253
haste velocity 274
activity 682
hurry **684**
hasten promote 707
hasty transient 113
hurried 684
impatient 825
irritable 901
hasty pudding 298
hat 225
cardinal's–999
–in hand 886
send round the–765
shovel–999
hatch produce 161
gate 232
opening 260
incubate 370
fabricate 544
shading 556
plan 626
prepare 673
–a plot 626
hatchel 253
hatches, under–
restraint 751

prisoner 754
poor 804
hatchet cutting 253
dig up the–722
throw the helve
after the–818
hatchet-faced 203
hatchet man 361
hatchment
funeral 363
arms 550
record 551
hatchway 260
hate dislike 867
hatred 898
hateful noxious 649
painful 830
hatrack 215
hatred (see hate)
object of–898
hatter 225
hatti-sherif 741
hattock 72
hauberk 717
haugh 344
haughty proud 878
insolent 885
contemptuous 930
haul drag 285
catch of fish etc. 789
–down one's flag 725
haunch 236
haunt focus 74
presence 186
abode 189
alarm 860
persecute 907
–the memory
remember 505
trouble 830
haunted 980a
hautboy 417
hauteur 878
haut monde 875
Havana cigar 392
have confute 479
ken 490
possess 777
–a high opinion of
928
–a jag on 959
–an ax to grind 702
–at 716
–done! 142
–for one's own 780
–in store destiny 152
provision 637
–it discover 480a
believe 484
–it your own way
submission 725
–no choice 609a
–no end 112
–nothing to do with
10
–one's rights 924

–one know 527
–other fish to fry 135
–rather 609
–some knowledge of
490
–the advantage
unequal 28
superior 33
–the start 116
–to 620
–to do with 9
–up 638
haven arrival 292
refuge 666
haversack 191
havildar 745
havoc destruction 162
cry– war 722
play– spoil 659
haw 583
hawk spit 297
bird 366
stammer 583
swindler 792
between–and
buzzard
agitation 315
worry 828
eye of a–498
–about publish 531
offer 763
sell 796
–at 716
know a–from a
hand saw
discriminate 465
skill 698
hawker 797
hawk-eyed 441
hawking chase 622
hawser 45
haycock 72
hay fever 655
hay-seed 876
hayward 753
hazard
chance 156, 621
danger 665
all is on the–349
at all–s 604
–a conjecture 514
–a proposition 477
haze mist 353
uncertainty 475
joke 856
in a– hidden 528
hazel 433
hazy 427
he 373
head precedence 62
beginning 66
class 75
summit 210
coiffure 225
lead 280
froth 353

person 372
intellect 450
topic 454
wisdom 498
picture 556
nomenclature 564
chapter 593
direct 693
director 694
master 745
as one's–shall
answer for 768
at the–of
direction 693
authority 737
repute 873
bow the–308
bring to a–729
can't get out of
one's–595
come into one's–
451
come to a–729
from–to foot 200
gain–175
get into one's–
thought 451
belief 484
intoxicate 959
give a horse his–
748
hang one's–879
have in one's–490
have no–506
–above water
safe 664
prosperous 734
wealth 803
–and front
important 642
–and front of one's
offending
provocation 830
charge 938
–and shoulders
irrelevant 10
complete 52
haste 684
–clothes 225
–over heels
inversion 218
rotation 312
–tone 410
–voice 410
hold one's–up 307
knock one's–against
impulse 276
unskillful 699
fail 732
knock on the–361
lie on one's–926
lift up one's–878
make–against
oppose 708
resistance 719
success 731

make neither–nor
tail of 519
never entered into
one's–458
not know whether
one stands on–or
heels
uncertain 475
wonder 870
off one's–503
on one's–218
over–and ears
deep 641
debt 806
love 897
put into one's–
supposition 514
information 527
put out of one's–
458
run in the–505
take into one's–
thought 451
caprice 608
intention 620
trouble one's–about
457
turn the–824
with–erect 878
headache 378
headdress 225
header 310
headfirst 173
headforemost
violent 173
rash 863
headgear 225
heading prefix 64
beginning 66
indication 550
title 564
headland height 206
projection 250
(land 342)
headlight 423, 550
headline 590
headlong hurry 684
rush 863
rush– violence 173
headman 694
headmost front 234
precession 280
headpiece
summit 210
intellect 450
helmet 717
ornament 847
headquarters
focus 74
abode 189
authority 737
headrace 350
heads
compendium 596
–I win tails you lose
unfair 940

headship　　　　　　　　　　　　　　　　　　　　　　　　　　　　　　　　hedgehog

　　–or tails 156, 621
　　lay–together
　　　　advice 695
　　　　cooperate 709
headship 737
headsman 975
headspring 153
headstall 752
headstone 215, 363
headstrong
　　　violent 173
　　　obstinate 606
　　　rash 863
headway *space* 180
　　　navigation 267
　　　progression 282
　　　departure 293
head wind 708
headwork 451
heady *sparkling* 353
　　　obstinate 606
heal *restore* 660
　　　cure 662
　　–the breach
　　　pacify 723
　　let the wound–
　　　forgive 918
heald 633
　　　healing art 662
health 654
　　–resort 189
healthful 654, 656
healthiness 656
healthy 654, 656
heap *quantity* 31
　　　collection 72
　　　multitude 102
　　　store 636
　　　too many 641
　　–indiscriminately
　　　465a
　　　rubbish–645
hear *audition* 418
　　　be informed 527
　　–a cause *adjudge* 480
　　　lawsuit 969
　　–and obey 743
　　–hear! 931
　　–out 457
　　not–of *refuse* 764
hearer 418
hearing 418
　　(see hear)
　　　gain a–175
　　　give a–418
　　　hard of–419
　　　out of–196
　　　within–197
hearken 457
hearsay 467, 532
　　–evidence 467
hearse 363
heart *intrinsicality* 5
　　　cause 153
　　　interior 221
　　　center 222

　　　mind 450
　　　willingness 602
　　　essential 642
　　　affections 820
　　　courage 861
　　　love 897
　　　a–untainted 939
　　　at–820, 821
　　　beating–821, 824
　　　break the–830
　　　by– *memory* 505
　　　do one's–good 829
　　　from bottom of–
　　　　543
　　　go to one's–824
　　　have a place in the
　　　　–897
　　–and soul
　　　completely 52
　　　willing 602
　　　resolute 604
　　　exertion 686
　　　feeling 821
　　–bleeding for 914
　　–disease 655
　　–expanding 821
　　–failing one
　　　dejection 837
　　　fear 860
　　–far from fraud 939
　　–in hand 602
　　–in right place 906
　　–leaping into one's
　　　　mouth 824
　　–leaping with joy
　　　pleasure 827
　　　rejoicing 838
　　–of grace 858
　　–of oak *strong* 159
　　　hard 323
　　–of stone
　　　insensible 823
　　　malevolent 907
　　–'s core *mind* 450
　　　affections 820
　　–sinking *fear* 860
　　–to conceive 698
　　　in good–858
　　　know by–490
　　　lay to–837
　　　learn by–539
　　　lift up the–990
　　　lose–837
　　　lose one's–897
　　　man after one's own
　　　　–899
　　　nearest to one's–
　　　　897
　　　not find it in one's–
　　　　603
　　　put one's–into 604
　　　set one's–upon 604
　　　take– *content* 831
　　　hope 858
　　　courage 861
　　　take to–

　　　sensibility 822
　　　discontent 832
　　　dejection 837
　　　anger 900
　　　to one's–'s content
　　　willing 602
　　　enough 639
　　　success 731
　　　content 831
　　　warm–822
　　　wind round the–
　　　　897
　　　with a heavy–603
　　　with all one's–602
heartache 828
heartbreaking
　　　affecting 821
　　　painful 830
heartbroken 828
heartburn 655
heartburning
　　　discontent 832
　　　regret 833
　　　enmity 889
　　　anger 900
heart–corroding 830
hearten *hope* 858
　　　courage 861
heartfelt *emotion* 821
　　　pleasure 829
hearth *home* 189
　　　fireplace 386
heartily (see hearty)
heartless
　　　insensible 823
　　　vicious 945
heartquake 860
heartrending 830
heart–robbing 829
heart's–ease 831
heartshaped 245
heartsick
　　　dejection 837
　　　dislike 867
　　　satiety 869
heart–sickening 830
heart–sinking 860
heartsome 858
heart–stirring 824
heartstricken 828
**heartstrings, tear
the–** 830
heartswelling
　　　excitation 824
　　　resentment 900
hearty *willing* 602
　　　healthy 654
　　　feeling 821
　　　cheerful 836
　　　friendly 888
　　　social 892
　　–laugh 838
　　–meal 298
　　–reception 892
heat *warmth* 382
　　　make hot 384

　　　contest 720
　　　excitement 824, 825
　　　desire 865
　　　dead–27
　　–of passion 900
heated *hot* 382
　　　quarrelsome 713
　　–imagination 515
heat engine 633
heater 386
heath *moor* 344
　　　plant 367
heathen *pagan* 984
　　　irreligious 989
　　–mythology 979
heathendom 984
heathenish
　　　vulgar 851
heather *moor* 344
　　　plant 367
heaume 717
**heautonti-
moreumenos**
　　　croaker 837
　　　ascetic 955
heave *raise* 307
　　　emotion 821
　　–a sigh 839
　　–in sight 446
　　–the lead *depth* 208
　　　measure 466
　　–to 265
heaven *bliss* 827
　　　paradise 981
　　　call–to witness 535
　　　for–'s sake 765
　　–be praised
　　　rejoicing 838
　　　gratitude 916
　　–forfend! 766
　　–knows
　　　uncertain 475
　　　ignorant 491
　　　in the face of–525
　　　light of–420
　　　the–s 180, 318
　　　move–and earth
　　　　686
　　　will of–601
heaven–born
　　　wise 498
　　　repute 873
　　　virtue 944
heaven–directed 498
heaven–kissing 206
heavenly *celestial* 318
　　　rapturous 829
　　　divine 976
　　　of heaven 981
　　–bodies 318
　　–host 977
　　–kingdom 981
heavenly–minded
　　　987
heavenward 305
heave offering 990

heaves 655
heavy *great* 31
　　　inert 172
　　　weighty 319
　　　stupid 499
　　　actor 599
　　　sleepy 683
　　　dull 843
　　　brutish 851
　　–affliction 828
　　–cost 814
　　–dragoon 726
　　–father 599
　　–gun 727
　　–hand *clumsy* 699
　　　severe 739
　　–heart *loth* 603
　　　pain 828
　　　dejection 837
　　–hours 841
　　–news 830
　　–on hand 641
　　–on the mind 837
　　–sea *agitation* 315
　　　waves 348
　　–sleep 683
　　–wet 298
heavy–footed
　　　dull 843
heavy–laden
　　　hindrance 706
　　　unhappy 828
hebdomadal 138
Hebe 845
hebetate 823, 826
hebetic 127
hebetude *imbecile* 499
　　　insensible 823
　　　inexcitable 826
hebetudinous 499
Hebraist 492
Hebrew
　　　unintelligible 519
　　　Jew 984
hecatomb *number* 98
　　　sacrifice 991
heckle *comb* 253, 652
　　　harry 830
hectic *hot* 382
　　　red 434
　　　flush 821
　　–fever 821
　　–flush 821
Hector *brave* 861
　　　rash 863
　　　bully 887
hector *domineer* 885
　　　resent 900
heddle 633
hedge *compensate* 30
　　　circumjacence 227
　　　inclosure 232
　　–in *circumscribe* 229
　　　hinder 706
　　　conditions 770
hedgehog 253

469

hedgerow 232
hedonic 827, 836
hedonism 377, 451, 827
hedonist 954a
hedonistic 377
heed *attend* 457
  care 459
  beware 668
  caution 864
heedful 457
heedless
  inattentive 458
  neglectful 460
  forgetful 506
  rash 863
heel *follow* 63
  support 215
  lean 217
  tag 235
  deviate 279
  go round 311
  −*of Achilles* 665
  iron−975
  turn on one's−
  go back 283
  go round 311
  avoid 623
heeler 886
heelpiece *sequel* 65
  back 235
  repair 660
heeltap *remainder* 40
  dress 653
heels *lowness* 207
  at the−*of near* 197
  behind 235
  cool one's−681
  follow on the−*of* 281
  −*over head*
  inverted 218
  hasty 684
  rash 863
  laid by the−751
  lay by the−789
  show a light pair of −623
  take to one's−623
  tread on the−*of near* 197
  follow 281
  approach 286
heft *weight* 319
  handle 633
  exertion 686
hefty *laborious* 686
Hegelianism 451
hegemonic 33
hegemony
  influence 175
  direction 693
  authority 737
hegira 293
Heidelberg man 372a

heifer 366
heigho! 839
height *degree* 26
  altitude **206**
  summit 210
  at its−*great* 31
  supreme 33
  draw oneself up to his full−307
heighten *increase* 35
  elevate 307
  exaggerate 549
  aggravate 835
heinous 945
heir *futurity* 121
  posterity 167
  inheritor 779
heirloom 780
heirship 777
heliacal 318
helical 248
Helicon 597
Heliogabalus 954a
heliograph *signal* 550
  picture 554
heliography *light* 420
  painting 556
heliolater 382
heliolatry 382, 991
heliology 420
heliometer 420
heliometry 420
Heliophagous 420
Helios 318, 423
helioscope 445
heliotherapy 420, 662
heliotrope *purple* 437
  ornament 847
heliotype 437, 554, 558
helium 490b
helix 248
hell *abyss* 208
  gaming house 621
  gehenna **982**
  −*broke loose* 59
  −*upon earth*
  misfortune 735
  pain 828
  −*within* 926
hellborn *vicious* 945
  satanic 978
hellebore 663
hell−**cat** 949
Hellenist 492
hellhag 913
hellhound
  evildoer 913
  bad man 949
hellish
  malevolent 907
  vicious 945
  hell 982
  (*bad* 649)
helm *handle* 633

scepter 747
(*authority* 737)
answer the−743
at the−693
obey the−705
take the−693
helmet *hat* 225
  armor 717
helminth 663
helminthagogue 662
helminthology 368
helmsman 269, 694
helot 746
help *benefit* 618
  utility 644
  remedy 662
  aid 707
  servant **746**
  give 784
  −*oneself to* 789
  it can't be−*ed*
  submission 725
  never mind 823
  content 831
  God−*you* 914
  so−*me God* 535
helper 711
helpful 746
helpless
  incapable 158
  exposed 665
helpmate
  auxiliary **711**
  wife 903
helpmeet 903
helter−**skelter**
  disorder 59
  haste 684
hem *edge* 231
  fold 258
  indeed! 870
  −*in inclose* 229
  restrain 751
  kiss the−*of one's garment* 886
hematite 490c
hemeralopia 443
hemi− 91
hemiplegia 376
hemisphere 181
hemispheric 250
hemlock *herb* 367
  unsavoriness 395
  bane 663
  punishment 972
hemorrhage 299
hemorrhoids 655
hemp *filament* 205
  poison 663
hen *bird* 366
  female 374
  source of supply 636
  −*party* 892
  −*with one chicken busy* 682
henbane 663

hence
  arising from 155
  departure 293
  deduction 476
henceforth 121
henchman 746
hencoop 370
hen−**headed** 458
hen−**hearted** 862
henhussy 374, 501
henna 433, 439
henotheism 984
henpecked
  obedient 743
  subject 749
hepatize 641
heptad 98, 193
heptagon 98, 244
heptahedral 98
heptamerous 98
heptangular 98
herald *precursor* 64
  precede 116
  precession 280
  predict 511
  informant 527
  proclaim 531
  messenger 534
heraldry 550
herb 367
herbaceous 367
herbage 367
herbal 369
Herbartianism 451
herbivore 298
herbivorous 298
herborize 369
herculean *great* 31
  strong 159
  exertion 686
  difficult 704
Hercules
  strength 159
  size 192
  support 215
  pillars of− *limit* 233
  mark 550
herd *assemblage* 72
  multitude 102
herder 370
herdsman 746
here *situation* 183
  presence 186
  arrival 292
  come−! 286
  −*and there dispersed* 73
  few 103
  place 182, 183
  −*below* 318
  −*goes* 676
  −*there and everywhere diversity* 16a
  space 180
  omnipresence 186

−*to*−*day and gone tomorrow* 111
hereabouts *site* 183
  near 197
hereafter 121
  destiny 152
hereby 631
hereditament 780
hereditary *intrinsic* 5
  derivative 154, 167
  property 780
heredity 154, 167
herein 221
heresy *error* 495
  religious 984
heretic 489, 984
heretical 495, 984
heretofore 122
hereupon 106
herewith
  accompanying 88
  means 632
heritage *futurity* 121
  possession 777
  property 780
heritor 779
hermaphrodite 83
  −*brig* 273
hermeneutics 522
Hermes 582
hermetically 261
hermit *recluse* 893
  ascetic 955
hermitage *house* 189
  cell 191
  seclusion 893
hermitize 893
hernia 655
hero *brave* 861
  glory 873
  good man 948
  −*worship approbation* 931
  idolatry 991
Herod, out−**Herod**− 549
heroic (*see hero*)
  magnanimous 942
  mock−853
heroics 884
heroism 861
heron 366
herpes 655
herpetology 368
herring *fish* 298
  pungent 392
  −*pond* 341
  trail of a red−615, 706
herring−**gutted** 203
hesitate
  uncertain 475
  skeptical 485
  stammer 583
  reluctant 603
  irresolute 605

Hesperian   **hiss**

   fearful 860
Hesperian 236
Hesperides
   garden of the–981
Hesperus 423
Hessian 726, 819
Hessian boot 225
hest 741
heterarchy 737
heteroclite 83, 139
heterodox 487, 489
heterodoxy 984
heterogamy 161, 357
heterogeneity 15, 16a
heterogeneous
   unrelated 10
   different 15
   mixed 41
   multiform 81
   exceptional 83
heterogenesis 161
heteromorphism 16a
heteronomy 737
heteropathy 662
heterotopy 185
hetman 745
hew *cut* 44
   shorten 201
   fashion 240
   –down 213, 308
hewers of wood
   workers 690
   commonalty 876
hexad 98, 193
hexaglot 560
hexagon 98, 244
hexahedral 98
hexahedron 98, 244
hexameter 98, 597
hexangular 98
hexastyle 98
heyday
   exultation 836, 838
   festivity 840
   wonder 870
   –of the blood 820
   –of youth 127
hiation 260
hiatus *interval* 198
   (*discontinuity* 70)
hibernal 383
hibernate 683
Hibernian 188
Hibernicism
   absurdity 497
   neology 563
hiccup 349
hickory shirt 225
hid
   –under a bushel 460
hidalgo 875
hidden 528
   –meaning 526
hide *skin* 223

   conceal 528
   –and seek
   deception 545
   avoid 623
   game 840
   –diminished head
   inferior 34
   decrease 36
   humility 879
   –one's face
   modesty 881
hidebound
   strait-laced 751
   stingy 819
   bigoted 988
hideous 846
hiding place
   abode 189
   ambush 530
   refuge 666
hie *go* 264
   speed 274
   –to 266
hiemal 383
hierarch 996
hierarchy 995
hieratic 372a
hieroglyphic
   representation 554
   letter 561
   writing 590
hierographa 985
hierography 983
hierolatry 991
hieromancy 511
hierophant 996
hieroscopy 511
higgle 794
higgledy-piggledy 59
higgler 797
high *much* 31
   lofty 206
   of game 298
   fetid 401
   treble 410
   foul 653
   noted 873
   proud 878
   from on–981
   –and dry *stable* 150
   safe 664
   –and mighty
   pride 878
   insolence 885
   –art 556
   –as heaven 67
   –celebration 998
   –color *color* 428
   red 434
   exaggerate 549
   –days and holidays 840
   –descent 875
   –glee 836
   –hand *violent* 173

   resolved 604
   authority 737
   severe 739
   pride 878
   insolence 885
   lawless 964
   –in tone *white* 430
   –life *fashion* 852
   rank 875
   –living
   intemperance 954
   gluttony 957
   –mass 998
   –mightiness 873
   –note 410
   –notions 878
   –places 210
   –pressure *power* 157
   energy 171
   excitation of feeling 824
   –price 814
   –priest 996
   –principled 939
   –repute 873
   –school 542
   –seas 341
   –tide *wave* 348
   prosperity 734
   –time *late* 133
   occasion 134
   –treason
   disobedience 742
   dishonor 940
   –words *quarrel* 713
   anger 900
   in a–degree 31
   in–automobile 274
   in–esteem 928
   in–feather
   strong 159
   health 654
   cheerful 836
   boasting 884
   in–quarters 875
   in–spirits 836
   on–206
   on one's–ropes
   excitation 824
   pride 878
   anger 900
   on the–road to
   way 627
   hope 858
   ride the–horse 878
   think–ly of 931
highball 959
highbinder 361
highborn 875
high-brow
   pedantry 491
higher 33, 206
   –education 490
   –pantheism 984
highest 210
   –heaven 981

highfaluting 577, 884
high-fed 954
high-flavored 392
highflier
   madman 504
   proud 878
high-flown
   absurd 497
   imaginative 515
   style 577
   proud 878
   vain 880
   insolent 885
highflyer
   madman 504
highflying
   exaggerated 549
   ostentatious 822
highlands 206
high-low 225
high-mettled
   excitable 825
   brave 861
high-minded
   honorable 939
   magnanimous 942
highness *title* 877
high-pitched 410
high-plumed 878
high-priced 809
high-reaching 206, 865
high-roller 818
high-seasoned 392
high-souled 878
high-sounding
   loud 404
   words 577
   display 882
high-spirited
   brave 861
   honorable 939
high-strung 825
hight 564
high-toned 410, 878
highwater
   completeness 52
   height 206
   crater 337
   –mark *measure* 466
highway 627
   –s and byways 627
highwayman 792
high-wrought
   good 648
   prepared 673
   excited 824
hike 260
hiker 268
hilarity 836
hill *height* 206
   convexity 250
   ascent 305
   –station 189
hill-dwelling 206
hillock 206

hilly 206
hilt 633
hind *back* 235
   deer 366
   clown 876
   on one's–legs
   elevation 307
   anger 900
hinder *impede* 706
   (*counteract* 179)
   (*prohibit* 761)
hindermost *end* 67
   back 235
hind quarters 235
Hindu *deities* 979
   priests 996
   temples 1000
Hinduism 976, 984
Hindustani 563
hindrance 706
hindward 235
hinge *fasten* 43
   fastening 45
   cause 153
   depend upon 154
   rotate 312
hinny 271
hint *reminder* 505
   suppose 514
   inform 527
   –a fault etc. 932
   take a–498
hinterland 235
hip 236 have on the–
   confute 479
   success 731
   authority 737
   subjection 749
hip bath 386
hipped *deranged* 503
hippish 503
hippocentaur 80
Hippocrates 219, 662
hippocratic 360
hippodrome
   drama 599
   arena 728
hippogriff 83
Hippolytus 960
hippophagy 298
hippopotamus 192, 366
hip rafter, 215
hip roof 223
hire *commission* 755
   borrowing 788
   price 812
   reward 973
   (*purchase* 795)
   on–763
hireling 746
hirsute 256
hispid 256
hiss *sound* 409
   animal cry 412
   disrespect 929

471

hist

    contempt 930
    disapprobation 932
hist hush! 585, 586
histogenesis 161
histology 329, 368
historian 553
historic 594
historical 594
    –painter 559
    –painting 556
historicize 594
historiette 594
historiographer 553, 594
historiography 594
history pedigree 69
    the past 122
    record 551
    narrative 594
    prose 598
    natural–357
histrionic 599
hit chance 156
    strike 276
    reach 292
    succeed 731
    censure 932
    (punish 972)
    good–626
    –off 554
    –one's fancy 829
    –on the raw 900
    –the mark 731
    –upon chance 156
    discover 480a
    plan 626
    make a–731
    palpable–276
hitch fasten 43
    cessation 142
    concurrence 178
    hang 214
    jerk 315
    –a horse 370
    difficulty 704
    hindrance 706
hither direction 278
    arrival 292
    come–286
hitherto 122
Hittite 372a
hive multitude 102
    location 184
    abode 189
    apiary 370
    workshop 691
H. M. S. 726
hoar aged 128
    white 430
    –frost 383
hoard 636
    –s after–s 819
hoarse husky 405
    harsh 410
    voiceless 581
    talk oneself–584

hoary (see hoar)
    old 124
hoax 545
hob support 215
    stove 386
    –and nob
    celebration 883
    courtesy 894
hobble limp 275
    awkward 699
    difficulty 704
    fail 732
    shackle 751
hobbledehoy 129
hobby crotchet 481
    pursuit 622
    avocation 625
    desire 865
hobbyhorse 272
hobgoblin fearful 860
    demon 980
hobnail 876
hobo tramp 268
    neglect 460
    idler 683
    vagabond 876
hoboism 266, 683
Hobson's choice
    necessity 601
    no choice 609a
    compulsion 744
hock maim 645
hockey 840
hocus 545
hocus–pocus
    interchange 148
    unmeaning 517
    cheat 545
    conjuration 992
    spell 993
hod receptacle 191
    vehicle 272
hoddy–doddy 501
hodgepodge 41, 59
hoe vehicle 272
    agriculture 371
hoecake 298
hog animal 366
    selfishness 943
    sensualist 954a
    glutton 957
    go the whole–604
    greedy as a–865
hog's back 206
hog wallow 343
hog wash 653
hoist 307–a flag 550
    –on one's own petard
    retaliation 718
    failure 732
    –the black flag 722
hoity–toity
    defiance 715
    wonder 870
hold cohere 46
    contain 54

    remain 141
    cease 142
    go on 143
    happen 151
    receptacle 191
    cellar 207
    base 211
    support 215
    halt 265
    believe 484
    be passive 681
    defend 717
    power 737
    restrain 751
    prohibit 761
    possess 777
    retain 781
    enough! 869
    gain a–upon 737
    get–of 789
    have a firm–781
    have a–upon 175
    –a council 695
    –a high opinion of 928
    –a lease 771
    –aloof absence 187
    distrust 487
    avoid 623
    –a meeting 72
    –an argument 476
    –a situation 625
    –authority 737
    –back avoid 623
    store 636
    restrain 751
    retain 781
    miserly 819
    –both one's sides 838
    –converse 588
    –fast restrain 751
    retain 781
    –forth teach 537
    speak 582
    –good
    demonstration 478
    truth 494
    –hard 265
    –in hand 737
    –in remembrance 505
    –in solution 335
    –off 623
    –office 693
    –on
    continue 141, 143
    persevere 604a
    –one's breath
    wonder 870
    –oneself in readiness 673
    –oneself up 307
    –one's ground 141
    –one's hand
    cease 142
    relinquish 624
    –one's own

home

    preserve 670
    defend 717
    resist 719
    –one's tongue 585
    –out
    (see below)
    –the scales 466
    –to 602
    –together junction 43
    cooperate 709
    –up
    (see below)
    –up one's head 861
    quit one's–782
    take–175
holdback 706
holder 779
holdfast 45
holding tenancy 777
    property 780
    –company 712
hold out continue 106
    affirm 535
    persevere 604a
    resist 719
    offer 763
    brave 861
    –expectation
    predict 511
    promise 768
    –temptation 865
hold up continue 143
    support 215
    not rain 340
    aid 707
    display 882
    extol 931
    –one's hand sign 550
    threat 600
    –the mirror 525
    –to execration
    curse 908
    censure 932
    –to scorn 930
    –to shame 874
    –to view 525
hold–up 791, 792
hole state 7
    place 182
    hovel 189
    receptacle 191
    cave 251
    opening 260
    ambush 530
    –and corner
    place 182
    peer into–461
    hiding 528, 530
    –in one's coat 651
    –to creep out of
    plea 617
    escape 671
    facility 705
Holi 138
holiday leisure 685
    repose 687

    amusement 840
    celebration 883
    –task easy 706
holiness God 976
    piety 987
holloa 411
    –before one is out of the wood 884
hollow unsubstantial 4
    completely 52
    incomplete 53
    depth 208
    concavity 252
    –sound 408 gruff 410
    specious 477
    voiceless 581
    beat–731
    –commendation 894
    –truce 723
hollow–hearted 544
hollowness
    (see hollow)
holm 345, 346
holocaust kill 361
    sacrifice 991
    (destruction 162)
holograph 590
holt 367
holus–bolus 684
Holy of God 976
    pious 987
    –breathing 990
    –day 998
    –Ghost 976
    –Grail 998
    –men of old 985
    –orders 995
    –place 1000
    –Scriptures 985
    –Spirit 976
    –Thursday 998
    –water 998
    –week 998
    keep–987
    temple of the– Ghost 983a
homage
    submission 725
    fealty 743
    reverence 928
    approbation 931
    worship 990
homaloid 251
home focus 74
    habitation 189
    near 197
    interior 221
    arrival 292
    country 342
    hospital 662
    refuge 666
    at–party 72
    present 186
    within 221
    at ease 705
    social gathering 892

home–bred   horseplay

    at–in *knowledge* 490
    skill 698
    at–with
        friendship 888
    be at–*to visitors* 892
    bring–to
        evidence 467
        belief 484
        accuse 938
        condemn 971
    come–292
    drive–729
    eternal–98
    feel at–*freedom* 748
        pleasure 827
        content 831
    from–187
    get–292
    go from–293
    go–283
    –rule 737
    –stroke 170
    –thrust *attack* 716
        censure 932
    look at–
        accusation 938
    make oneself at–
        free 748
        sociable 892
    not be at–764
    stay at–265
    strike–*energy* 171
    attack 716
home–bred 851
home–felt 821, 824
home–grown 367
homeless
    unhoused 185
    banished 893
homelike 849
homeliness 851
    (see homely)
homely *language* 576
    unadorned 849
    common 851, 876
homeopathic
    small 32
    little 193
homeopathy 662
homesick 833
homespun *simple* 42
    texture 219, 329, 635
homestall 189
homestead 189
homeward bound 292
homicide 361
homiletical 537
homily *teaching* 537
    advice 595
    sermon 998
hominy 298
homish 849
homme de cour 886
homocentric 68

homogeneity
    relation 9
    identity 13
    uniformity 16
    simplicity 42
homogenesis 161
homoiousia 17
homoiousian 983
homologate 23
homologue 714
homology *relation* 9
    uniformity 16
    equality 27
    concord 714
homonym
    equivocal 520
    vocal sound 580
homonymy 520
homoousia 13
homoousian 983
homophonic 402
homophony 402, 413
homunculus 193
hone 253
honest *veracious* 543
    honorable 939
    pure 960
    –meaning 516
    –truth 494
    turn an–penny 775
honey *sweet* 396
    favorite 899
    –sweet 396
    milk and–734
honeybee 366
honeycomb
    concave 252
    opening 260
    deterioration 659
honeyed–phrases 894
    –words
        allurement 615
        flattery 933
honeymoon
    pleasure 827
    endearment 902
    marriage 903
honey–mouthed
    courteous 894
    flatter 933
honor *demesne* 780
    glory 873
    title 877
    respect 928
    approbation 931
    probity 939
    affair of–720
    do–to 883
    do the–s
        sociality 892
        courtesy 894
        respect 928
    his–*judge* 967
    –a bill 807
    –be to 873
    –bright *veracity* 543

    probity 939
    in–of 883
    man of–939
    upon my–535
    word of–768
honorable (see honor)
    reliable 632
honorarium *gift* 784
    reward 973
honorary 815
honored 500
    (see honor)
hooch 298
hood *cap* 225
    automobile 272
    distinction 550
    cowl 999
hooded 223
hoodlum 887, 913
hoodoo *chance* 621
    bane 649
    sorcery 992
hoodooed 735
hoodwink *ignore* 491
    blind 442
    hide 528
    deceive 545
hoof 211
hook *fasten* 43
    fastening 45
    hang 214
    curve 245
    deceive 545
    retain 781
    take 789
    by–or by crook 631
hooked 244, 245
hooker *ship* 273
Hooke's law 490d
hookey, blind–840
hooklike 245
hook–shaped 245
hooligan 887, 913
hoop *circle* 247
    cry 411
hoot *cry* 411, 412
    deride 929
    contempt 930
    censure 932
hop *leap* 309
    dance 840
    –skip and jump
        leap 309
        agitation 315
        haste 684
        game 840
    –the twig 360
hope 858
    band of–958
    beyond all–734
    dash one's–s 837
    excite–511
    foster–858
    –against hope 858
    –deferred
        dejection 837

    lamentation 859
    –for *expect* 507
    desire 865
    –for the best 858
    well grounded–472
hopeful *infant* 129
    probable 472
    hope 858
hopelessness 471, 859
hop garden 371
hop–o'–my–thumb 193
hopper 191
hopple 751
hopples 752
hopscotch 840
horary 108
horde *assemblage* 72
    party 712
    commonalty 876
horehound 400
horizon *distance* 196
    view 441
    expectation 507
    (*future* 121)
    gloomy–859
horizontality 213
horizontally 213, 251
horn *receptacle* 191
    pommel 215, 249
    sharp 253
    music 417
    draw in one's–s
        recant 607
        submit 725
        humility 879
    exalt one's–873
    –in 294
    –of plenty 639
    –s of a dilemma
        reasoning 476
        difficulty 704
    wear the–s 905
hornbook 542
horned 245
hornet *evildoer* 913
    –'s nest *pitfall* 667
        difficulty 704
        adversity 735
        painful 830
        resentment 900
        censure 932
hornpipe 840
horn–shaped 253
hornwork 717
horny 323
Horny, old–978
horologer 114
horology 114
horoscope 511
horrible *great* 31
    noxious 649
    dire 830
    ugly 846
    fearful 860

horrid (see horrible)
    vulgar 851
horrific (see horrible)
horrified *pain* 828
    fear 860
horrify *pain* 830
    terrify 860
horripilation 383
horrisonous 410
horror *fear* 860
    dislike 867
    view with–898
horrors *dejection* 837
    cup full of–828
horror–stricken 828
hors de combat
    impotent 158
    useless 645
    tired out 688
    put–731
hors d'oeuvre 298, 394
horse *hang on* 214
    stand 215
    carrier 271
    animal 366
    male 373
    translation 539
    cavalry 726
    –and foot 726
    –artillery 726
    –box 272
    –car 272
    –cloth 225
    –coper 548
    –doctor 370
    –guards 726
    –laugh 838
    –leech 370
    –litter 272
    –marine 268, 701
    –racing–*pastime* 840
    contention 720
    –sense 498
    –soldier 726
    –stealing 791
    –track 627
    –trainer 370
    like a–in a mill 613
    put thes to 673
    put up one's–s at 184
    put up one's–s together
        concord 714
        friendship 888
    ride the high–885
    take–266
    war–726
    work like a–686
horseback 266
horseman 268
horsemanship
    riding 266
    skill 698
horseplay 856

473

horse power

horse power 466
horse-radish 298, 393
horseshoe 245
  –crab 368
horseshoer 370
horsewhip 972
horsewoman 268
hortation
  persuasion 615
  advice 695
hortatory 537, 615
horticulture 371
horticulturist 369
hosanna *praise* 931
  worship 990
hose *stockings* 225
  pipe 350
  cleanness 652
hosier 225
hospice *house* 189
  hospital 662
hospitable *liberal* 816
  social 892
hospital 662 in–655
hospitality
  (see hospitable)
Hospitaller 996
hospodar 745
host *collection* 72
  multitude 102
  army 726
  friend 890
  rite 998
  –in himself 175
  –of heaven 977
  reckon without
    one's– *error* 495
  unskillful 699
  rash 863
hostage 771
hostel 189
hostelry 189
hostile *disagreeing* 24
  opposed 708
  enmity 889
  –meeting 720
  in–array 708
hostilities 722
hostility 889
hostler 746
hot *violent* 173
  warm 382
  pungent 392
  red 434
  orange 439
  excited 824
  irascible 901
  blow–and cold
  inconsistent 477
  falsehood 544
  tergiversation 607
  caprice 608
  –air bombast 884
  –bath 382, 386
  –blood *rash* 863

angry 900
irascible 901
–dog *sausage* 298
–springs 382, 384
–water *difficulty* 704
quarrel 713
painful 830
–wave 382
in–haste 684
in–pursuit 622
make–384
hotbed *cause* 153
center 222
workshop 691
hot-brained 863
hotchpot *mixture* 41
confusion 59
participation 778
hotel 189–keeper 188
–runner 767
Hotel des Invalides 662
hot-headed
hasty 684
excitable 825
hothouse
conservatory 371
furnace 386
store 636
workshop 691
hotpress 255
Hotspur 863
Hottentot 431, 876
hough 659
hound *fellow* 63
animal 366
hunt 622
persecute 907
wretch 949
hold with the hare
  but run with the–s 607
–on 615
hour *period* 108
point of time 113
present time 118
–after hour 110
improve the shining
  –682
one's–is come
occasion 134
death 360
the long–s 106
hourglass
chronometer 114
contraction 195
narrow 203
Houri 845
hourly *time* 106
frequent 136
periodical 138
house *lineage* 69
assembly 72
family 166
locate 184
abode 189

theater 599
make safe 664
council 696
firm 712
merchant 797
bring the–about
  one's ears 699
eat out of–and
  home
prodigal 818
gluttony 957
–built on sand 160
–divided against
  itself 713
–of cards 160
–of Commons 966
–of correction
  prison 752
  punishment 975
–of death 363
–of detention 752
–of God 1000
–of Lords 875, 966
–of peers 875
–of prayer 1000
–of Representatives 696
keep–184
set one's–in order 952
turn–out of window 713
turn out of–and
  home 297
housebreaker 792
housebreaking 791
house dog 366
household
inhabitants 188
abode 189
–gods 189
–stuff 635
–troops 726
–words *known* 490
language 560
plain 576, 849
householder 188
housekeeper 637, 694
housekeeping 692
houseless 185
housemaid 746
house raising 892
houseroom 180
housetop *summit* 210
proclaim from–531
housewarming 892
housewife 682
bag 191
housewifery
conduct 692
economy 817
housing *lodging* 189
covering 223
horse-cloth 225
hovel 189
hover *impend* 152

high 206
rove 266
soar 267
ascend 305
air 338
irresolute 605
–about *move* 264
–over *near* 197
how *way* 627
means 632
–comes it?
attribution 155
inquiry 461
–now 870
howbeit 30
however *degree* 26
notwithstanding 30
except 83
howitzer 727
howker 273
howl *blow* 349
protracted sound 407
human cry 411
animal cry 412
lamentation 839
howling 412
–wilderness
unproductive 169
secluded 893
hoy 273
hoyden *girl* 129
rude 851
hub *centrality* 222
circularity 247
convexity 250
hubbub *stir* 315
noise 404
outcry 411
discord 713
hubby 250
huckleberry 298
huckster
provision 637
barter 794
merchant 797
huddle *disorder* 59
derange 61
collect 72
hug 197
–on 225
Hudibrastic 856
–verse 597
hue 428–and cry
cry 411
proclaim 531
pursuit 622
alarm 669
–of dungeons 982
raise a–and cry 932
hueless 429
huff *insolence* 885
anger 900
huffy 901
hug *cohere* 46
border on 197
retain 781

humble

courtesy 894
love 897
endearment 902
–a belief 606
–a sin 945
–oneself *pleasure* 827
content 831
rejoicing 338
pride 878
–the shore
navigation 267
approach 286
huge *in degree* 31
in size 192
hugger-mugger 59, 528
Huguenot 984
huissier 965
huke 225
hukm 741, 760
hulk *body* 50
ship 273
hulking 193
hulks 752
hulky *big* 192
unwieldly 647
ugly 846
hull 50
hullabaloo *noise* 404
shout 411
hum *faint sound* 405
continued sound 407
animal sound 412
sing 416
deceive 545, 546
busy–of men 682
human 372
–face divine 234
–race 372
–sacrifices 991
–system 364
humane
benevolent 906
philanthropic 910
merciful 914
–studies 537
–teaching 537
humanism 451, 537
humanistic 537
humanitarian 910
humanitarianism 372
humanities
letters 560
humanize 894
humation 363
humble *inferior* 34
meek 879
modest 881
pious 987
eat–pie 725
–oneself *meek* 879
penitent 950
worship 990
–r classes 876
your–servant

humble–minded   hysteron proteron

dissent 489
refusal 764
humble–minded 879
humbug *falsehood* 544
  deception 545
  deceiver 548
  trifle 643
humdinger 682
humdrum *weary* 841
  dull 843
  (*prose* 598)
humectate *water* 337
  moisture 339
humid 339
humiliate *humble* 879
  disrespect 929
humiliation
  adversity 735
  disrepute 874
  sense of shame 879
  worship 990
  self–950
humility
  meekness 879
  piety 987
hummer 682
humming top 417
hummock *hill* 206
  hump 250
humor *essence* 5
  tendency 176
  liquid 333
  disposition 602
  caprice 608
  aid 707
  indulge 760
  affections 820
  please 829
  wit 842
  flatter 933
  (*fun* 840)
  in the–602
  out of–901a
  peccant
  –*unclean* 653
  disease 655
humorist 844
humorous 842
humorsome
  capricious 608
  sulky 901a
hump 250
humpbacked 243
Hun *destroyer* 165
hunch 250
hunchbacked 243
hundi 800
hundred *number* 98
  many 102
  region 181
hundredth 99
hundredweight 319
hunger 865
hungry 865
hunks 819
hunt *follow* 63

inquiry 461
pursuit 622
–*after* 622
–*down* 907
–*in couples* 17, 709
–*out inquiry* 461
  discover 480a
–*the slipper* 840
hunter *horse* 271
  killer 361
  pursuer 622
  sportsman 840
  place–767
hunting *killing* 361
  sporting 622
hunting ground 840
huntsman 268, 361
hurdle 272
hurdy–gurdy 417
hurl 284–*against* 716
  –*defiance* 715
hurly–burly 315
hurrah 411, 836, 838
hurricane
  tempest 349
  (*violence* 173)
  –*deck* 210
hurry *haste* 684
  excite 825
  –*forward* 684
  –*off with* 789
  –*of spirits* 821
  –*on* 615
  –*skurry* 825
hurst 367
hurt
  physical pain 378
  evil 619
  maltreat 649
  injure 659
  –*the feelings*
    pain 830
    anger 900
  more frightened
    than–860
hurtful 649
hurtle 276
hurtless 648
husband *store* 636
  director 694
  spouse 903
husbandman 371
husbandry
  agriculture 371
  conduct 692
  economy 817
hush *moderate* 174
  stop 265
  silence 403
  taciturn 585
  –*up conceal* 528
  pacify 723
hush money
  compensation 30
  reward 973
husk *covering* 223

strip 226
husking bee 892
husky *strong* 159
  dry 340
  dog 366
  faint sound 405
  hoarse 581
hussar 726
hussif 191
hussy *girl* 129
  blusterer 887
  libertine 962
hustings *school* 542
  arena 728
  tribunal 966
hustle *perturb* 61
  push 276
  agitate 315
  activity 682
  hinder 706
hustler 682
hustling 682
hut 189
hutch 189
huzur 373
huzza 411, 838
hyacinth *jewel* 847
hyacinthine 437
Hyades 318
hyaline
  ocean 318, 341
  transparency 425
hyalite 425
hyaloid 425
hybernation 683
hybrid *mixture* 41
  exception 83
hydra
  monster 83, 366
  productive 168
hydra–headed 163
hydrant 348
hydrargyrum 274
hydrate of amyl 356
hydraulics 348
hydrocephalus 194
hydrocyanic acid 663
hydrocyanide 663
hydrocycle 272
hydrodynamics
  fluid 333
  stream 348
hydrodynamometer 348
hydrography 341
hydrokinetics 333, 348
hydrology 333
hydrolysis 49
hydromancy 511, 992
hydromechanics 348
hydromel 396
hydrometer 321, 333, 348

hydrometrograph 348
hydrometry 333
hydropathy 662
hydrophobia 867
hydrophone 333
hydrophthalmus 194
hydroplane 273
hydroplaning 267
hydropot 953, 958
hydroscope 114
hydrostat 333
hydrostatics 333, 348
hydrotherapy 662
hydrotic 337
hydrous 337
Hydrus 490a
hyemal 383
hyena 913
hyetograph 348
hyetology 348
hyetometer 348, 466
hyetometrograph 348
hygeian 656
hygiantics 670
hygiene 656, 670
hygienic 656, 670
hygienics 670
hygre 348
hygrometer 349
hygrometry 339
hyle 316
hylic 316
hylism 316
hylocist 316
hylotheism
  materiality 316
  heterodoxy 984
  irreligion 989
hylotheist 316
Hymen 903
hymeneal 903
hymn
  song 415
  worship 990
  –*of Hate* 898
hymn book 998
hymnody 54
hymnology 415
hypallage 218
hypaxis *existence* 1
hyperbaton 218
hyperbola 245
hyperbole 549
hyperborean
  far 196
  opposite 237
  cold 383
hypercriticism
  misjudgment 481
  discontent 832
  fastidiousness 868
  censure 932
hyperdulia 990
Hyperion 423, 845

–*to a satyr* 14
hyperorthodoxy 984
hyperphysical 450, 976
hypertrophy 194
hyphen 45, 550
hyphenate 943
hyphenated 940
  –*allegiance* 940
hypnagogic 992a
hypnology 683
hypnosis
  insensibility 376
  inactivity 683
  psychical research 992a
hypnotic
  remedy 662
  sleep 683
hypnotism 683, 992a
hypocaust 386
hypochondriac
  insanity 503
  madman 504
  low spirits 837
  hopelessness 859
hypochondriasis 837
hypocrisy
  falsehood 544
  religious–988
hypocrite 548
  play the–544
hypocritical 544
hypodermic 223
hypostasis 3
hypostatic union 976
hypothecate 771
hypothenuse 217
hypothesis 514
hypothesize 514
hypothetical
  uncertain 475
  supposed 514
  imaginative 515
hypped *insane* 503
  dejected 837
hypsography 206, 466
hypsometer 206
hypsometry 206, 466
hypsophobia 206, 860
hysteria
  insanity 503
  psychotherapy 992a
hysteric *violent* 173
hysterical
  spasmodic 608
  emotional 821
  excitable 825
hysterics 173 in
  –*excited* 824
  frightened 860
hysterology 218
hysteron proteron 218

I   imaginable

I

I 79
iambic 597
iambus 597
Icarus *navigator* 269
   descent 306
   rash 863
   fate of– 306
ice *cold* 383
   refrigerate 385
   refrigeratory 387
iceberg 383
ice boat 273
icebound 383
   restraint 751
ice box 385, 387
ice-built 383
ice canoe 273
ice chest 385
ice cream 298
ice field 383
ice float 383
ice floe 383
ice house 387
ice machine 387
ice pack 383
icequake 383
ice water 298
ice yacht 273
Ichabod 874
ichnography 554
ichor 333
ichthyocol 352
ichthyology 368
ichthyomancy 511
ichthyotomy 368
ichthyophagous 298
icon 554
iconoclasm 984
iconoclast
   destroyer 165
   evildoer 913
iconography 554
icosahedron 244
icterine 436
icterus 436
ictus 597
icy 383
idea
   small quantity 32
   notion 453
   (*belief* 454)
   (*inkling* 490)
   give an–of 537
ideal *unreal* 2
   completeness 52
   erroneous 495
   imaginary 515
idealism 451
idealistic 594
ideality
   intellect 450
   imagination 515
idealize 515

idée fixe 481
identical 13
identification
   identity 13
   comparison 464
   discovery 480a
identity 13
ideogram 561
ideograph 561
ideology 450
ideophone 402, 562
ideophonous 402
Ides of March 601
idiocrasy *essence* 5
   tendency 176
idiocy 499, 503
idiom 560, 566
idiomatic *special* 79
idioplasm 357
idiosyncrasy
   essence 5
   speciality 79
   unconformity 83
   tendency 176
   temperament 820
idiot 501
   tale told by an– 517
idiotic *foolish* 499
idioticon 563
idiotism *folly* 499
   language 560
   phrase 566
idle *foolish* 499
   trivial 643
   slothful 683
   be an-man
   leisure 685
   –conceit 842
   –hours 681
   –talk 588
   –time away 683
   lie–inaction 681
idler 645, 683
Ido 560, 563
idol *desire* 865
   favorite 899
   fetich 991
   –of the people 899
idolater 984, 991
idolatrize 991
idolatry *love* 897
   image-worship 991
idolize *love* 897
   idolatrize 991
idoloclast 165
idolum 980a
idoneous 23
idyl 597
idylist 597
if *circumstance* 8
   qualification 469
   supposition 514
   –possible 470
   –you please 765
igloo 189
igneous 382

ignis fatuus
   luminary 423
   phantom 443
ignite 384
ignition
   calefaction 384
   automobile 272
ignoble 876
ignominy *shame* 874
   dishonor 940
ignoramus 493
ignorance 491
   keep in– 528
   plead– 937
ignorant 491
ignore *neglect* 460
   incredulity 487
   not known 491
   repudiate 756, 773
iguana 366
ileum 221, 350
ilk 13
ill *evil* 619
   badness 649
   sick 655
   as–luck would have it 135
   bird of–omen 668
   do an–office to 907
   go on–fail 732
   adversity 735
   house of–fame 961
   –at ease pain 828
   dejection 837
   –betide 908
   –blood hate 898
   malevolence 907
   –humor anger 900
   sullenness 901a
   –luck 735
   –name 874
   –off insufficient 640
   adversity 735
   poor 804
   –repute 874
   –s that flesh is heir to evil 619
   disease 655
   –temper evil 619
   –turn evil 619
   affront 900
   spiteful 907
   –usage 907
   –will 907, 921
   –wind bad 649
   hindrance 706
   adversity 735
   look– 846
   take–discontent 832
   anger 900
ill-adapted 24
ill-advised
   foolish 499
   inexpedient 647
   unskillful 699
ill-affected 901a

illapse *conversion* 144
   ingress 294
illaqueate 545
ill-assorted 24
illation 480
illaudible 947
ill-behaved 895
ill-boding 512
ill-bred *vulgar* 851
   rude 895
ill-conditioned
   bad 649
   difficult 704
   discourteous 895
   malevolent 907
   vicious 945
ill-conducted
   unskillful 699
ill-contrived
   inexpedient 647
   bad 649
   unskillful 699
   malevolent 907
ill-defined 447
ill-devised
   foolish 499
   unskillful 699
ill-digested 674
ill-disposed *bad* 649
   sullen 901a
   spiteful 907
illegality 964
illegible 519
   render– 552
   –hand 590
illegitimate
   deceitful 545
   undue 925
   illegal 964
ill-fated 135, 735
ill-favored 395
ill-furnished 640
illiberal
   narrow-minded 481
   stingy 819
   uncourteous 895
   selfish 943
   bigoted 988
illicit *undue* 925
   illegal 964
ill-imagined
   foolish 499
   unskillful 699
illimited 105
ill-intentioned 907
illiteracy 491
illiterate 491, 493
ill-judged *foolish* 499
   unskillful 699
ill-judging 481
ill-made
   distorted 243
   ugly 846
ill-mannered
   vulgar 851
   rude 895

ill-marked
   invisible 447
ill-natured 907
illogical
   sophistical 477
   erroneous 495
ill-omened
   untoward 135
   danger 605
   adverse 735
   hopeless 859
ill-proportioned 243
ill-provided 640
ill-qualified 699
ill-requited 917
ill-rewarded 917
ill-shaped *ugly* 846
ill-spent 646
ill-starred 135, 735
ill-tempered 901
ill-timed 135
illtreat *bad* 649
   severe 739
   malevolent 907
illuminant 388, 420
illuminate
   enlighten 420
   color 428
   comment 595
   ornament 847
illuminati 492
illumination
   (*see illuminate*)
   book illustration 558
   celebration 883
illumine *lighten* 420
   excite 824
ill-use 907
ill-used 828
illusion
   fallacy of vision 443
   error 495
illusive
   unsubstantial 4
   sophistical 477
   erroneous 495
   deceitful 545, 546
illusory (*see illusive*)
illustrate
   exemplify 82
   interpret 522
   represent 554
   engravings 558
   ornament 847
illustrious 873
image *likeness* 17
   appearance 448
   idea 453
   metaphor 521
   representation 554
   graven–idol 991
   –in the mind 453
imagery *fancy* 515
   metaphor 521
   representation 554
imaginable 470

imaginary
non-existing 2
fancied 515
-quantity 84
imagination 515
imaginative 515
imaum prince 745
priest 996
imbecile
incapable 158
ignorant 493
foolish 499
fool 501
imbecility
impotence 158
folly 499
unmeaningness 517
imbed locate 184
base 215
insert 300
imbedded 229
imbibe 296
-learning 539
imbibitory 296
imbrangle 61
imbricate 223
imbrication 223
imbroglio disorder 59
difficulty 704
discord 713
imbrue
impregnate 300
moisten 339
-one's hands in
blood killing 361
war 722
-the soul 824
imbue mix 41
impregnante 300
moisten 339
tinge 428
teach 537
imbued
combination 48
affections 820
-with belief 484
habit 613
feeling 821
imburse 803
imitate copy 19
appropriate 788
imitation copying 19
copy 21
representation 554
misrepresentation 555
imitative
imitating 19
music 415
imitator 19
immaculate
perfect 650, 847
clean 652
innocent 946
(excellent 648)
immanence 5

immanent 5, 132
Immanity 907
immanuel 976
immaterial
unsubstantial 4
immaterialist 317
immaterality
spiritual 317
trifling 643
immaterialize 317
immature new 123
unprepared 674
immeasurable
great 31
infinite 105
immediate
continuous 69
immediately
instantly 113
early 132
immedicable 859
immelodious 414
immemorial 124
from time-122
-usage 613
immense great 31
infinite 105
-size 192
immensity
infinity 105
size 192
immerge
introduce 300
dip 337
immerse insert 300
submerge 310
dip 337
immersed in 229
immersion
(see immerse)
baptism 998
immesh 545
immethodical 59, 139
immigrant alien 57
traveler 268
entering 294
immigration
migration 266
entrance 294
imminent
destined 152
approaching 286
immiscible 47
immission 296
immitigable
violence 173
hopeless 859
revenge 919
immix 41
immixture 41
immobility
immutability 150
quiescence 265
(resolution 604)
immoderately 31

immodest 961
immolation
killing 361
giving 784
sacrifice 991
immoral wrong 923
vicious 945
immortal
diuturnal 110
perpetual 112
glorious 873
celebrated 883
her-part 112
immortalize
perpetuate 112
preserve 976
immotile 265
immovable stable 150
quiescent 265
obstinate 606
(resolved 604)
immundicity 653
immune
innocuous 656
(see immunity)
immunity
freedom 748
exemption 777a
right 924
exemption 927a
acquittal 970
immure imprison 751
(inclose 229)
immutable stable 150
deity 976
imo pectore, ab- 821
imp child 167
demon 980
(evildoer 913)
(bad man 949)
impact contact 43
impulse 276
insertion 300
touch 379
impair 659
impairment 659
impale transfix 260
execute 972
impalpable small 193
powder 330
intangible 381
impanation 998
imparadise 829
imparity 28
impart inform 527
give 784
impartial
judicious 498
neutral 628
just 922
honorable 939
-opinion 484
impassable
closed 261
impossible 471

(difficult 704)
impasse 7
impassible 823
impassion 824
impassionable 822
impassioned
-language 574
sentimental 822
excited 825
impassive 823
impatient 825
-of control 742
impawn 771
impeach censure 932
accuse 938
go to law 969
impeachment 738
(see impeach)
soft-902
impeccability
faultless 650
innocent 946
impecunious 804
impede 179, 706
impediment 706
-in speech 583
impedimenta
instrument 633
luggage 780
impel push 276
induce 615
impend future 121
destiny 152
overhang 206
impending 132
(see impend)
impenetrable
closed 261
solid 321
unintelligible 519
latent 526
(hidden 528)
impenitence 951
imperative
require 630
command 737
severe 739
commanding 741
duty 926
imperator 745
imperceptible
small 32
minute 193
slow 275
invisible 447
latent 526
impercipient 376
imperdible 664
imperfect
incomplete 53
failing 651
vicious 945
-vision 143
imperfection 651
inferiority 34
vice 945

imperfectly 32
imperforate 261
imperial
trunk 191
beard 256
authority 737
imperil 665
imperious
command 737
proud 878
arrogant 885
-necessity 601
imperishable
eternal 112
stable 150
glorious 873
impermanent
transient 111
(changeable 149)
impermeable
closed 261
dense 321
impersonal
general 78
neuter 316
impersonate 554
imperspicuity 519
impersuasible 606
impertinent
irrelevant 10
insolent 885
(disagreeing 24)
(inexpedient 647)
imperturbable
inexcitable 826
contented 831
unamazed 871
impervious
closed 261
impossible 471
insensible 823
-to light 426
-to reason 606
impetiginous 653
impetrate 765
impetuosity
(see impetuous)
impetuous
boisterous 173
hasty 684
excitable 825
rash 863
eager 865
impetus 276
impiety 988, 989
impignorate 787
impinge 276
impious 988
impish 980
implacable
hatred 898
unforgiving 919
(wrath 900)
implant
insert 296, 300
teach 537

implanted
  ingrained 5
  adventitious 6
  —by nature 820
implausible 473
implead 969
implement 633
impletion 52
implex 41
implicate
  involve 54, 526
  accuse 938
implicated
  related 9
  component 56
implication
  disorder 59
  meaning 516
  metaphor 521
  latency 526
implicit 526
  —belief 484
implied (*see* imply)
implore 765
imply *evidence* 467
  mean 516
  involve 526
  (*metaphor* 521)
impolicy 699
impolite 895
imponderable 4, 320
imporous *closed* 261
  dense 321
import
  put between 228
  ingress 294
  take in 296
  insert 300
  mean 516
  involve 526
  be of consequence 642
importance
  greatness 31
  consequence **642**
  attach—to 642
  attach too much—to 482
  of no—643
important 642
importune *ask* 765
  pester 830
impose *print* 591
  order 741
  awe 928
  —upon *credulity* 486
  deceive 545
  be unjust 923
imposing
  important 642
  exciting 824
  glorious 873
imposition
  (*see* impose)
  undue 925
  —of hands 998

impossibilities
  seek after—645
impossibility 471
impossible 471
  deception 702
  refusal 764
  (*difficulty* 704)
  —*quantity algebra* 84
impost 812
impostor 548, 925
impostume 655
imposture 545
impotence 158
impotent 732
  —*conclusion* 732
  —to rise 158
impound
  imprison 751
  (*inclose* 229)
impoverish
  weaken 160
  waste 638
  despoil 789
  render poor 804
impracticable
  impossible 471
  misjudging 481
  obstinate 606
  difficulty 704
impracticality 471
imprecation
  prayer 765
  curse 908
imprecatory 765, 908
impregnable
  strong 159
  safe 664
impregnate *mix* 41
  combine 48
  fecundate 161, 168
  insert 300
  teach 537
  —with *cloy* 641
impresario 599
imprescriptible 924
impress *effect* 154
  cause sensation 375
  mark 550
  excite feeling 824
  —upon the mind
  memory 505
  teach 537
impressed with
  belief 484
  feeling 821
impressibility 375
impressible
  motive 615
  sensibility 822
impression *effect* 154
  sensation 375
  idea 453
  belief 484
  publication 531
  mark 550
  engraving 558

  print 591
  emotion 821
  make an *act* 171
  thought 451
impressionable 375, 822
impressive
  language 574
  important 642
  feeling 821, 824
imprimit 558
imprimus 66
imprint *publisher* 531
  indication 550
  —in the memory 505
imprison
  circumscribe 229
  restrain 751
  punish 972
improbability 473
improbate 932
improbity 940
impromptu 612
improper
  incongruous 24
  foolish 499
  solecistic 568
  inexpedient 647
  wrong 923
  unmeet 925
  vicious 945
  —time 135
impropriate
  possess 777
  take 789
impropriator 779
impropriety
  (*see* improper)
improve 658
  —the occasion 134
  —the shining hour 682
  —upon 658
improvement 658
improvident
  careless 460
  not preparing 674
  prodigal 818
  rash 863
improvisator 416, 582
improvisatore
  speech 582
  poetry 597
  impulse 612
improvise
  imagination 515
  extemporize 612
  unprepared 674
improviser 612
imprudent
  neglectful 460
  rash 863
  (*unwise* 699)
impudence
  insolence 885

  discourtesy 895
impudent
  insolent 885
  discourteous 895
impudicity 961
impugn *deny* 536
  attack 716
  blame 932
impugnation 708
impugnment 708
impuisance 158
impulse *push* 276
  sudden thought **612**
  motive 615
  blind—601
  creature of—612
  give an—to
  propel 284
  aid 707
impulsive
  (*see* impulse)
  intuitive 477
  unaccustomed 604
  excitable 825
  rash 863
impunctual 133
impunity
  escape 671
  acquittal 970
  with—*safely* 664
impurity
  inelegance 579
  foul 653
  licentious **961**
imputation
  ascribe 155
  slur 874
  accuse 938
in 221 go—294
  —a jiffy 113
  —and out 314
  —a rut 16
  —as much as
    relation 9
    degree 26
  —for *undertake* 676
    promise 768
  —s and outs 182
in—camera 528
  —*extenso whole* 50
  diffuse 573
  —*loco* 23
  —*medias res* 68
  —*propria persona* 79, 186
  —*re* 9
  —*statu quo* 141
  —*statu quo ante bellum* 140
  —*toto* 52
  —*transitu*
    transient 111
    transfer 270
inability
  want of power 158
  want of skill 699

  —to discriminate 465a
inabstinent 954
inaccessible
  distant 196
  impossible 471
inaccordant 24
inaccurate *error* 495
  solecism 568
inacquiescent 24
inaction *inertness* 172
  not doing 681
inactivity 683
  inertness 172
inadequacy
  (*see* inadequate)
inadequate
  unequal 28
  powerless 158
  insufficient 640
  useless 645
  imperfect 651
  (*weak* 160)
inadmissible
  incongruous 24
  excluded 55
  extraneous 57
  inexpedient 647
inadvertence 458
inadvisable 647, 649
inaffable 895
inalienable
  retention 781
  right 924
inamorata 897
inane *void* 4
  incogitancy 452
  unmeaning 517
  insufficient 640
  trivial 643
  useless 645
inanimate 360
  —matter 358
inanition 158
inanity (*see* inane)
inappetency
  insensibility 823
  indifference 866
inapplicable
  irrelation 10
  disagreement 24
inapposite
  irrelation 10
  disagreement 24
inappreciable
  in degree 32
  in size 193
  unimportant 643
inapprehensible
  stolid 499
  unintelligible 519
inappropriate
  unconsonant 24
  inexpedient 647
inapt *incongruous* 24
  impotent 158

inarticulate

 useless 645
 inexpedient 647
 unskillful 699
inarticulate 581, 583
inartificial 703
inartistic 846
inasmuch *whereas* 9
 however 26
 because 476
inattention 458
inattentive 419, 458
inaudible *silence* 403
 faint sound 405
 deaf 419
 voiceless 581
inaugural
 precursor 64
inaugurate *begin* 66
 install 755
 celebrate 883
inauguratory 66
inauspicious
 untimely 135
 untoward 649
 adverse 735
 hopeless 859
inbeing 5
inborn *intrinsic* 5
 affections 820
 (*habit* 613)
 —*proclivity* 601
inbound 294
inbred (see inborn)
inca 745
incage 751
incalculable *much* 31
 infinite 105
incalescence 382
incandescence 382
incantation
 invocation 765
 spell 993
incantatory 992
incapable
 impotent 158
 (*weak* 160)
incapacious 203
incapacitate 158
incapacity
 impotence 158
 ignorance 491
 stupidity 499
 (*weakness* 160)
incarcerate
 imprison 751
 (*surround* 229)
incarnadine 434
incarnate *intrinsic* 5
 materiality 316
 to incorporate 364
 vicious 945
 devil—bad man 949
 Satan 978
incarnation 316, 976
incase *cover* 223
 surround 229

incautious *rash* 863
 (*neglect* 460)
incendiary
 destroy 162
 burn 384
 influence 615
 pitfall 667
 malevolent 907
 evildoer 913
 bad man 949
incensation 400
incense *fuel* 388
 fragrant 400
 hate 898
 anger 900
 flatter 933
 worship 990
 rite 998
 —*breathing* 400
 —*burner* 400
incension
 burning 384
incensorium 400
incentive 615
incept 66, 537
inception 66
inceptive
 beginning 66
 causal 153
 generative 168
inceptor 541
incertitude 475
incessant
 repeated 104
 ceaseless 112
 frequent 136
incest 961
inch *small* 32
 length 200
 move slowly 275
 measure 466
 by—es 275
 give an—and take
  an ell 789
 —*by inch*
 by degrees 26
 in parts 51
 slowly 275
 not see an—beyond
  one's nose 699
 *not yield an—*606
 *to an—*494
inchoation
 beginning 66
 preparation 673
incide 44
incidence 278
incident 151
 *full of—*151
incidental *extrinsic* 6
 circumstance 8
 irrelative 10
 occurring 151
 casual 156
 liable 177
 chance 621

—*music* 415
incinerate 384
incinerator 384
incipience 66
incircumspect 460
incise *cut* 44
 furrow 259
incision *cut* 44
 furrow 259
incisive *energy* 171
 vigor 574
 feeling 821
incite *exasperate* 173
 urge 615
incitement
 (see incite)
incivility 895
incivism 911
inclasp 229
inclement
 violent 173
 cold 383
 severe 739
 pitiless 914a
inclination
 (see incline)
 descent 306
 will 600
 affection 820
 desire 865
 love 897
incline *tendency* 179
 slope 217
 direction 278
 willing 602
 induce 615
 —*an ear to* 457
inclined *oblique* 217
 intended 620
 —*plane* 633
inclose
 place within 221
 surround 227
 hem in 229
inclosure *region* 181
 envelope **232**
 fence 752
include
 composition 54
 —*in a class* 76
inclusion 76
inclusive *additive* 37
 component 56
 class 76
inclusory 56
incogitance 452
incoction 674
incognito 528
incognizable 519
incoherence
 physical **47**
 mental 503
incombustible 385
income *means* 632
 profit 775
 property 780
 wealth 803

 receipt 810
incomer
 immigrant 294
incoming *ingress* 294
 receipt 810
incommensurable
 irrelation 10
 (*disagreeing* 24)
 —*quantity* 84, 85
incommode
 hinder 706
 (*trouble* 830)
 (*incommodious* 647)
incommodious 647
incommunicable
 unmeaning 517
 unintelligible 519
 retention 781
incommutable 150
incomparable
 superior 33
 (*good* 648)
incompassionate 914a
incompatibility 15
incompatible 24
incompetence
 inability 158
 incapacity 499
 unskillful 699
incomplete
 fractional 51
 not complete 53, 730
incompleteness 53
 noncompletion 730
incomplex 42
incompliance 764
incomprehensible
 infinite 105
 unintelligible 519
incomprehension 491
incompressible 321
inconceivable
 unthought of 452
 impossible 471
 improbable 473
 incredible 485
 unintelligible 519
 wonder 870
inconceptible 519
inconcinnity
 disagreement 24
 ugliness 846
inconclusive 477
inconcoction 674
incondite 851
inconformity 15
incongruous
 differing 15
 disagreeing 24
 faulty 568
 discordant 713
inconnection
 irrelation 10
 disjunction 44

incorrigible

inconsequence
 irrelation 10
inconsequential
 illogical 477
inconsiderable
 small 32
 fractional 100a
 unimportant 643
inconsiderate
 thoughtless 452
 inattentive 458
 neglectful 460
 foolish 699
inconsistent
 contrary 14
 disagreeing 24
 illogical 477
 absurd 497
 foolish 499
 discordant 713
 capricious 608
inconsolable 837
inconsonant
 disagreeing 24
 fitful 149
inconspicuous 447
inconstant 149
incontestable
 strong 159
 certain 474
incontiguous 196
incontinent 961
incontinently 132
incontrollable 173
incontrovertible
 certain 474
 (*stable* 150)
inconvenience 647
 *put to—*706
inconvenient 135, 647
inconversable
 taciturn 585
 unsociable 893
inconvertible
 continuing 143
 (*stable* 150)
inconvincible 487
incorporality 317
incorporate
 combine 48
 include 76
 materialize 316
 immaterial 317
 animality 364
incorporation
 (see incorporate)
incorporeal 317
 —*hereditaments* 780
incorrect *illogical* 477
 erroneous 495
 solecism 568
 vicious 945
incorrigible
 obstinate 606
 hopeless 859

479

incorruptible

vicious 945
impenitent 951
incorruptible
honorable 939
incorruption
probity 939
innocence 946
(health 654)
incrassate
increase 194
density 321
—fluids 352
(thick 202)
increase—*in degree* **35**
—in number 102
—in size 194
incredible *great* 31
impossible 471
improbable 473
doubtful 485
wonderful 870
incredulity
unbelief **487**
religious—989
increment
increase 35
addition 37
adjunct 39
expansion 194
increpation 932
incriminate 938
incrust *coat* 223
line 224
incubate 370
incubation 673
incubus
hindrance 706
pain 828
demon 980
inculcate 537
inculcated 6
inculpable 946
inculpate 938
inculture 674
incumbency
business 625
churchdom 995
incumbent
inhabitant 188
high 206
weight 319
duty 926
clergyman 996
incumber 706
incumbered 806
incumbrance 706
incunabula 66, 127
incur 177—*a debt* 806
—a loss 776
—blame 932
—danger 665
—disgrace 874
—the risk 621
incurable
ingrained 5
disease 655

hopeless 859
incuriosity 456
incursion *ingress* 294
attack 716
incurvation 245
incus 418
indagation 461
indebted *owing* 806
gratitude 916
duty 926
indecent 961
indeciduous 150
indecipherable 519
indecision 605
indecisive 475
indeclinable 150
indecorous
vulgar 851
vicious 945
impure 961
indeed *existing* 1
very 31
assent 488
truly 494
assertion 535
wonder 870
indefatigable
persevering 604a
active 682
indefeasible
stable 150
certainty 474
necessity 601
due 924
indefectible 650
indefensible
powerless 158
submission 725
accusable 938
wrong 945
indeficient 650
indefinite *great* 31
every 78
infinite 105
aoristic 119
misty 447
uncertain 475
inexact 495
vague 519
indeliberate 612
indelible *stable* 150
memory 505
mark 550
feeling 821
indelicate 961
indemnification 790, 952
indemnificatory 30
indemnity
compensation 30
forgiveness 918
reward 973
deed of—771
indent *list* 86
scallop 248
indentation 252, 257

indenture
compact 769
security 771
(evidence 467)
(record 551)
independence
irrelation 10
freedom 748
wealth 803
Independence Day 138, 840
Independent 984
independent
(see independence)
indescribable
great 31
wonderful 870
indesinent 112
indestructible 150
indeterminate
chance 156
uncertain 475
equivocal 520
irresolute 605
indevotion 989
index *arrangement* 60
exponent 84
list 86
sign 550
words 562
index expurgatorius 761
indexterity 699
Indian—file 69
—*gift* 794
—*giver* 702
—*rubber* 325
—*ruling chiefs* 875
—*sage* 662
—*summer* 126
—*weed* 392
indicate *specify* 79
direct attention to 457
mean 516
mark 550
indication 75, **550**
indicative
evidence 467
indicating 550
indicatory 550
indicolite 438
indict *accuse* 938
arraign 969
indiction 108, 531
indifference
incuriosity 456
unwillingness 603
no choice 609a
insensibility 823
unconcern **866**
irreligion 989
matter of—643
indifferent
(see indifference)
unimportant 643

bad 649
indigence
insufficiency 640
poverty 804
indigene 188
indigenous
intrinsic 5
inhabitant 188
indigested 674
indigestible 657
indigestion 655, 657
indigitate 457
indign 940
indignation 900
—*meeting* 832
iron—722
indignity *affront* 900
insult 929
indigo 438
indiligence 683
indirect *oblique* 217
devious 279
latent 526
circuitous 629
indiscernible 447
indiscerptible
whole 50
unity 87
dense 321
indiscoverable 526
indiscreet *rash* 863
blamable 945
(neglectful 460)
(unskillful 699)
indiscrete 48
indiscretion *guilt* 947
(see indiscreet)
indiscriminate
mixed 41
unarranged 59
multiform 81
casual 621
indiscrimination 465a
indispensable 630
indispose
dissuade 616
indisposed
unwilling 603
sick 655
—*to believe* 487
indisputable 474
indissoluble
joined 43
whole 50
stable 150
dense 321
indissolvable
(see indissoluble)
indistinct *dim* 447
(vague 519)
indistinction 465a
indistinguishable
identical 13
invisible 447
indiscriminate 465a

indulge

indisturbance
quiescence 265
inexcitation 826
indite 54, 590
individual *whole* 50
special 79
unity 87
person 372
individuality
speciality 79
unity 87
individualize 79
indivisible *whole* 50
dense 321
indocility
incapacity 158
obstinacy 606
indoctrinate 537
Indo-European 372a
indolence 683, 927
indomitable
strong 159
determined 604
persevering 604a
resisting 719
courage 861
indoor 221
indoors 221
indorse *evidence* 467
assent 488
ratify 769
security 771
—*a bill* 800
approve 931
indorsee 270
indorsement
mark 550
record 551
indorser 488
indraft *gulf* 343
current 348
wind 349
indubitable 474, 525
induce *cause* 153
power 157
produce 161
motive 615
induct *receive* 296
inaugurate 883
inductance 490d
induction *inquiry* 461
reasoning 476
drama 599
appointment 755
—*of a priest* 995
inductive 476
indue 157
indulge *lenity* 740
allow 760
please 829
intemperance 954
—*in* 827
—*in reverie*
inattention 458
fancy 515
—*oneself* 943

indulgence / infuse

   –one's fancy 609
   –with *give* 784
indulgence
   (*see* indulge)
   absolution 918
indulgent *kind* 906
induration
   hardening 323
   impenitence 951
industrious
   studious 539
   (*see* industry)
industry *business* 625
   activity 682
   hive of–691
indweller 188
indwelling 5
inebriety 959
inedible 867
ineffable *great* 31
   unmeaning 517
   wonderful 870
ineffaceable 820
ineffectual
   incapable 158
   useless 645
   failing 732
   –attempt 732
   pale its–fire 422
inefficacious
   incapable 158
   useless 645
   failing 732
inefficient 158
inelastic *soft* 324
   –fluid 333
inelasticity 326
inelegance
   in language **579**
   ugly 846
ineluctable 474
inept *incapable* 158
   useless 645
   (*inexpedient* 647)
inequality 24, **28**
inequation 28
inequitable 923
ineradicable
   intrinsic 5
   stable 150
inerrable 946
inert (*see* inertness)
inertia 172
inertness
   physical **172**
   inactive 683
   moral 823
inessential 10
inestimable 648
inevitable *certain* 474
   destiny 601
inexact *erroneous* 495
   feeble 575
inexcitability 826
inexcusable
   accusable 938

   vicious 945
inexecution 730
inexhaustibility 105
inexhaustible 104,
   639
inexistence 2
inexorable
   unavoidable 601
   resolved 604
   stern 739
   compelling 744
   pitiless 914a
   revengeful 919
   (*wrathful* 900)
   (*malevolent* 907)
inexpectation 508
inexpedience 647,
   699
inexpensive 815
inexperience
   ignorant 491
   unskillful 699
inexpert 699
inexpiable 945
inexplicable 519
inexpressible
   great 31
   unmeaning 517
   unintelligible 519
   wonderful 870
inexpressibles 225
inexpression
   latency 526
inexpressive 517
inexpugnable 664
inextension 180a
   littleness 193
   immateriality 317
inextinguishable
   stable 150
   strong 159
   excitable 825
   –desire 865
inextricable
   coherent 46
   disorder 59
   impossible 471
   (*difficult* 704)
infallibility 474
   assumption of–885
infallible 474
infamy *shame* 874
   dishonor 940
   vice 945
infancy
   beginning 66
   youth 127
infant 129 *fool* 501
Infanta 745
infanticide
   killing 361
   sacrifice 991
infantine 129
   foolish 499
infantry 726
infarct 261, 706

infarction 261, 706
infare 892
infatuation
   misjudgment 481
   credulity 486
   folly 499
   insanity 503
   obstinacy 606
   passion 825
   love 897
infeasible 471
infect *mix with* 41
   contaminate 659
   excite 824
infection
   transference 270
   disease 655
infectious 270, 657
infecund 169
infelicitous 24, 828
infelicity
   inexpertness 699
   misery 828
infer *presume* 472
   deduce 480
   imply 526
inference
   reasoning 476
   judgment 480
   implication 521
   latency 526
   by–467
inferential
   demonstrative 478
   construable 522
   latent 526
inferior
   (*see* inferiority)
   low 207
inferiority
   in degree **34**
   in size 195
   imperfection 651
   personal–34
infernal *bad* 649
   malevolent 907
   wicked 945
   satanic 978
   –machine 727
   –regions 982
infertility 169
infest 830
infestivity *sad* 837
   dull 843
infibulation 43
infidel 487, 989
infidelity
   dishonor 940
   irreligion 989
infiltrate *mix* 41
   intervene 228
   interpenetrate 294
   ooze 295
   receive 296
   moisten 337, 339
   teach 537

infiltration
   passage 302
   (*see* infiltrate)
infinite 105
   –goodness 976
Infinite, the– 976
infinitely *great* 31
infinitesimal
   small 32
   little 193
   –calculus 85
infinity 105
infirm *weak* 160
   disease 655
   vicious 945
   –of purpose 605
infirmary 662
infirmity (*see* infirm)
infix 537
infixion 300
inflame
   render violent 173
   burn 384
   excite 824
   anger 900
   (*incite* 615)
inflamed *red* 434
   (*see* inflame)
inflammable
   burn 384
   fuel 388
inflammation
   heating 384
   disease 655
inflammatory
   heated 384
   (*see* inflame)
inflate *increase* 35
   expand 194
   blow 349
inflated *style* 573, 577
   ridiculous 853
   vain 880
inflation (*see* inflate)
   rarefaction 322
inflect 245
inflection *change* 140
   curvature 245
   grammar 567
inflectional 567
inflexible *hard* 323
   resolved 604
   obstinate 606
   stern 739
   a will–906
   –in faith 159
inflexion
   (*see* inflection)
inflict *act upon* 680
   severity 739
   –evil 649
   –pain *bodily pain* 378
     mental pain 830
   –punishment 972
infliction
   adversity 735

   mental pain 828,
     830
   punishment 972
inflorescence 161
influence *cause* 153
   change 140
   physical –**175**
   tendency 176
   inducement 615
   instrumentality 631
   authority 737
   (*importance* 642)
   absence of–**175a**
   make one's–felt 175
   sphere of–780
influenza 655
influx 294
inform 527–against
   accuse 938
   go to *law* 969
informal *irregular* 83
   lawless 964
informality
   nonobservance 773
informant 527, 938
information
   knowledge 490
   communication **527**
   lawsuit 969
   pick up–539
   wide–539
informed 527
informity 241
infraction
   infringement 303
   disobedience 742
   nonobservance 773
   exemption 927
   –of usage
     unconformity 83
     desuetude 614
infrangible
   combined 46
   dense 321
infrequency 137
infrequent 137
infrigidation 385
infringe
   transgress 303
   disobey 742
   not observe 773
   undueness 925
   dereliction 927
   –a law 83
infructuose 169
infumate 340, 673
infundibular
   concave 252
   hole 260
infuriate *violent* 173
   excite 824
   anger 900
infuscate 431
infuse *mix* 41
   insert 300
   teach 537

infused — insist

—courage 861
—life into 824
—new blood 658
infused 6
infusible 321
infusion (see infuse)
  liquefaction 335
infusoria 193
ingannation 545
ingate 350
ingathering 72
ingemination 90
ingenerate 5
ingenious
  original 515
  instrumental 633
  skillful 698
ingenit 5
ingénu *artless* 703
ingénue *actress* 599
ingenuity 698
ingenuous *artless* 703
  (*sincere* 543)
  (*honorable* 939)
ingesta 298
ingestion 296
ingestive 296
ingle 388
ingle side 189
inglorious
  disreputable 874
  dishonorable 940
ingluvies 191
ingot 800
ingraft *add* 37
  join 43
  insert 300
  teach 537
ingrafted *extrinsic* 6
  habit 613
ingrain *insinuate* 228
  texture 329
  color 428
ingrained *intrinsic* 5
  combined 48
  habit 613
  character 820
ingrate 917
ingratiate 897
ingratiating 894
ingratitude 917
ingredient 56
ingress 294
  forcible—300
ingressive 294
ingurgitate 296
ingustible 391
inhabile 699
inhabit 186
inhabitant 188
inhalation
  (see inhale)
inhale *receive* 296
  breathe 349
  smoke 389
  smell 398

inharmonious 15,
  713—*color* 428
  —*sound* 414
inhere in 56
inherence 5
inherent 56, 820
inherit *acquire* 775
  possess 777
inheritance
  property 780
  —*of the saints* 981
inherited *intrinsic* 5
  transfer 783
inheritor 779
inhesion 5
inhibit *hinder* 706
  restrain 751
  prohibit 761
  (*restrain* 615)
inhospitable 893
inhuman 907
inhume 363
inimaginable
  impossible 471
  improbable 473
  wonderful 870
inimical *contrary* 14
  opposition 708
  enmity 889
inimitable
  nonimitation 20
  unequal 28
  supreme 33
  very good 648
  perfect 650
iniquity *wrong* 923
  vice 945
  worker of—949
inirritability 826
initial 66—*letter* 558
initiate *begin* 66
  receive 296
  teach 537
initiated *skillful* 698
initiatory 296
inject 300 *fluid* 337
injudicial 964
injudicious 499, 863
injunction
  command 630
  advice 695
  command 741
  prohibition 761
injure *evil* 619
  damage 659
  spite 907
injurious 619, 923
  —*insects* 913
injury *evil* 619
  badness 649
  damage 659
injustice 923
ink 431
  before the—is dry
    132
  pen and—590

ink-blot test 821a
inkhorn 590
inkle 45
inkling *knowledge* 490
  supposition 514
  information 527
inkslinger 593
inkwell 590
inlaid 847—*work* 847
inland 221
inlay 300, 440
inlet *beginning* 66
  interval 198
  opening 260
  ingress 294
  —*of the sea* 343
inly 221
inmate 188, 221
inmost 221—*nature* 1
  —*soul* 820
  —*thoughts* 451
  to the-core 822
inn 189
innate 5 (*habit* 613)
  —*proclivity* 601
innavigable 471
inner 221
  —*coating* 224
  —*man intellect* 450
  affections 820
  —*reality* 1
innermost 221
  —*recesses* 221
innings *land* 342
  acquisition 775
innkeeper 188, 637
innocence 946
innocent *child* 167
  fool 501
  good 648
  healthy 656
  artless 703
  guiltless 946
  good woman 948
innocuous *good* 648
  healthy 656
  innocent 946
innominables 225
innominate 565
innovation
  variation 20a
  new 123
  change 140
innoxious
  salubrious 656
  innocent 946
innuendo *hint* 527
  censure 932
innumerable 105
innutritious 657
inobservance 773
  (*disobedience* 742)
inoccupation 681
inoculate *insert* 300
  teach 537
  influence 615

inoculated 48
inoculation
  (see inoculate)
inodorous 399
inoffensive *good* 648
  innocent 946
inofficious 907
inoperative
  powerless 158
  unproductive 169
  useless 645
inopportune
  untimely 135
  inexpedient 647
inordinate *great* 31
  excessive 641
inorganic 358
inorganic chemistry
  490b
inorganization 358
inornate 849
inosculate *join* 43
  combined 48
  intersect 219
  convoluted 248
inquest 461, 967
inquietude
  changeable 149
  uneasy 828
  discontent 832
  apprehension 860
  (*motion* 264)
inquinate 659
inquire 461—*into* 595
inquirer 461, 541
inquiring 461
  —*mind* 455
inquiry 461
inquisition
  inquiry 461
  severity 739
  tribunal 966
inquisitive 455
inquisitorial
  prying 455
  inquiry 461
  severe 739
  jurisdiction 965
inroad *ingress* 294
  trespass 303
  devastation 659
  invasion 716
insalubrity 657
insanity 61, **503**
insatiable 865
inscribe *write* 590
  blazon 873
inscription
  (see inscribe)
  interment 363
  record 551
inscroll 551
inscrutable 519
insculpture 557
insculptured 558
insecable *junction* 43

unity 87
insect 366, 368
  minute 193
  injurious—s 913
  —*cry* 412
insecure *danger* 665
  (*uncertain* 475)
insensate *foolish* 499
  insane 503
insensibility *slow* 275
  physical **376**
  moral **823**
  —*of benefits* 917
  —*to the past* 506
insensible *numb* 381
  (see insensibility)
inseparable
  junction 43
  coherence 46
insert *locate* 184
  interpose 228
  enter 294
  put in 300
  record 551
  —*itself* 300
insertion 300
  ornament 847
inservient 645
insessorial 206
inseverable
  junction 43
  unity 87
inside 221—*out* 218
  —*part music* 415
  turn—*out* 529
insidious
  deceitful 545
  cunning 702
  dishonorable 940
insight 490, 868
insignia 550
  —*of authority* 747
insignificant
  unmeaning 517
  unimportant 643
insincere 544, 855
insinuate
  intervene 228
  ingress 294
  insert 300
  latency 526
  hint 527
  ingratiate 897
  blame 932
  (*suppose* 514)
  (*mean* 516)
insipid *tasteless* 391
  style 575
  trifling 643
insipidity
  tasteless **391**
  indifferent 866
insist *argue* 476
  command 741
  —*upon affirm* 535
  dwell on 573

insistence

be determined 604
contend 720
compel 744
conditions 770
due 924
insistence (*see* insist)
influence 615
insnare 545
insobriety 959
insolation 340, 382, 384
insolence 885
insolent *defiant* 715
arrogant 885
disrespectful 929
insoluble *dense* 321
unintelligible 519
insolvable 519
insolvent *poverty* 804
debt 806
nonpayment 808
insomnium 682
insouciance
thoughtlessness 458
supineness 823
indifference 866
inspan 293
inspect *look* 441
attend to 457
inspector
inquisitor 461
judge 480
director 694
inspiration
breathing 349
wisdom 498
imagination 515
impulse 612
motive 615
feeling 821
Deity 976
revelation 985
religious–987
inspirator 349
inspire *breathe* 349
prompt 615
improvement 658
animate 824
cheer 836
–*courage* 861
–*hope* 858
–*respect* 928
inspired 615
–*writers* 985
inspirit *incite* 615
animate 824
cheer 834
hope 858
encourage 861
inspiriting
hopeful 858
inspissate *dense* 321
semiliquid 352
instability 149, 605
install *locate* 184
commission 755

celebrate 883
installment
portion 51
payment 807, 809
instance *example* 82
motive 615
solicitation 765
instant *moment* 113
present 118
destiny 152
required 630
importance 642
active 682
lose not an–684
on the–132
instantaneity 113
instanter 113, 132
instate 883
instauration 660
instead 147
instigate 615
instigator 615
instill *imbue* 41
introduce 296
insert 300
teach 537
instinct *intellect* 450
intuition 477
impulse 601
brute–450a
–*with motive* 615
possession 777
instinctive *inborn* 5
institute *begin* 66
cause 153
produce 161
academy 542
society 712
–*an inquiry* 461
institution
academy 542
society 712
political–963
church 995
institutional 712
institutor 540
instruct *teach* 537
advise 695
precept 697
order 741
instructed 490
instruction
(*see* instruct)
instructional 537
instructive 537
instructor 540
instructorship 542
instrument
implement 633
security 771
musical–417
optical–445
instrumental 631
–*music* 415
instrumentalist 416
instrumentality 631

instrumentation 54, 60
insubordinate 742
insubstantial
inexistent 2
unsubstantial 4
immaterial 317
–*pageant* 882
insubstantiality
disappearance 449
(*see* insubstantial)
insufferable
painful 830
dislike 867
insufficiency 640
insufflation 349
insular *unrelated* 10
detached 44
single 87
region 181
island 346
narrow 481
bigoted 988
insulate 44, 346
insulin shock therapy 821a
insulse *stupid* 499
dull 843
insult *insolence* 885
rudeness 895
offense 900
disrespect 929
insulting 898
insuperable 471
–*obstacle* 706
insupportable 725, 830
insuppressible 173
insurance 768, 771
insure *make sure* 474
obtain security 771
insurer
underwriter 758
insurgent 146, 742
insurmountable 471
insurrection
resistance 719
disobedience 742
insurrectionary 146
insusceptible 823
–*of change* 150
intact *permanent* 141
perfect 650
preserved 670
intactness
completeness 52
(*see* intact)
intaglio *mold* 22
concave 252
sculpture 557
intake *automobile* 272
intangible *little* 193
numb 381
integer *whole* 50
number 84
unity 87

integral 50
–*calculus* 85
–*part* 56
integrant 56
integrate
consolidate 50
(*complete* 52)
integrity *whole* 50
completeness 52
probity 939
virtue 944
integument 223
intellect 450
absence of–450a
exercise of the–451
intellection 450, 451
intellectual 450
–*force* 574
–*powers* 450
intelligence
mind 450
capacity 498
news 532
intelligencer 527
intelligent 498
intelligential 527
intelligibility 518
(*perspicuity* 570)
intelligible 518
intemperance 954
drunkenness 959
intempestive 115, 135
intempestivity 135
intend 620
intendant 694
intended *will* 600
predetermined 611
intense *great* 31
energetic 171
–*color* 428
–*thought* 457
intensify *increase* 35
stimulate 171
intensity *degree* 26
greatness 31
energy 171
intensive 35
intent *attention* 457
well 600
design 620
active 682
–*upon desire* 865
resolved 604
to all–*s and purposes* 27, 52
intention 620
bad–607
good–906
inter 363
interact 12
interaction
working 170
(*intermedium* 228)
interactive 148
interagent 228, 631

interest

intercalate 228
intercalation 228, 300
intercede
be concordant 714
mediate 724, 976
deprecate 766
interceder 714
intercept *hinder* 706
take 789
intercession
(*see* intercede)
worship 990
Intercessor 976
intercessor 714
interchange 148
barter 794
–*visits etc.* 892
interchangeable 12
intercipient 706
interclude 706
intercollegiate 148
intercolumnar 228
intercommunication 527
intercommunion 892
interconnection 9, 12
intercostal 228
intercourse
friendship 888
sociality 892
verbal–582, 588
intercross 219
intercurrence
interchange 148
interjacence 228
passage 302
interdenominational 148
interdependence 12
interdict 761
interdigitate
intersect 219
intervene 228
interest *concern* 9
influence 175
curiosity 455
advantage 618
importance 642
property 780
debt 806
excite 824
please 829
amuse 840
devoid of–841
feel an–*in* 906
–*bearing* 810
make–*for* 707
not know one's own–699
place out at–
lend 787
economy 817
take an–*in*
curiosity 455

483

interested / introduce

love 897
take no-in
insensibility 823
indifference 866
want of-866
interested *selfish* 943
interesting
lovable 897
interfacial 228
interfere *disagree* 24
counteract 179
intervene 228
activity 682
thwart 706
mediate 724
interferometer 193
interfuse 48
interfusion 41
intergrowth 228
interim *time* 106
short time 111
interior 221
painting 556
interiority 221
interjacence
middle 68
coming between **228**
interject *interpose* 228
insert 300
interlace *join* 43
combine 48
twine 219
interlacement 41
interlard *mix* 41
combine 48
interpolate 228
interleave 228
interline
interpolate 288
write 590
interlineal 228
interlineation 37, 300
interlink *join* 43
twine 219
interlobular 228
interlocation 228
interlocular 228
interlocution 588
interlocutor 582
interloper
extraneous 57
intervene 228
obstruct 706
interlude *time* 106
dramatic 599
intermarriage 903
intermarry 903
intermaxillary 228
intermeddle
interfere 682
hinder 706
intermeddling 724
intermedial 228, 631
intermediary 534, 631

intermediate
mean 29
middle 68
intervening 228
ministerial 631
-time 106
intermediation
agency 170
intermedium
mean 29
link 45
intervention 228
instrument 631
(*means* 632)
interment **363**
insertion 300
intermigration 266
interminable
infinite 105
eternal 112
long 200
intermingle 41
intermission
time 106
discontinuance 142
intermit *interrupt* 70
recur 138
discontinue 142
intermittence
time 106
periodicity 138
intermittent 138
intermix 41, 48
intermolecular 228
intermundane 228
intermutation 148
intern 221
internal *intrinsic* 5
interior 221
-evidence 467
internasal 228
international
reciprocal 12
interchange 148
sociality 892
-law 963
interne 662
internecine 361
-war 722
interneural 228
internodal 228
internuncio
messenger 534
diplomatist 758
interoceanic 228
interosseal 228
interpel 142
interpellation
inquiry 461
address 586
summons 471
command 741
appeal 765
interpenetration
interjacence 228
ingress 294

passage 302
interplanetary 228
interpolar 228
interpolation
analytical 85
interpose 228
insertion 300
interpose
intervene 228
act 682
hinder 706
mediate 724
interposit 799
interposition
(see interpose)
interpret 522, 595
interpretation 516, **522** (*answer* 462)
interpreter **524**
interradial 228
interregnum
intermission 106
transient 111
discontinuance 142
interval 198
inaction 681
laxity 738
(*discontinuity* 70)
interrelation 9, 12
interrenal 228
interrogate 461
interrogation 461
typography 550
interrupt
discontinuity 70
cessation 142
hinder 706
interruption
derangement 61
interval 198
interscapular 228
interscholastic 148
intersect 219
intersection 198, 219
interseptal 228
interspace
interval 198
interior 221
intersperse *diffuse* 73
interpose 228
(*music* 41)
interstate 148
interstellar 228
interstice 198
interstitial
internal 221
interjacent 228
intertanglement 41
intertexture
mixture 41
intersection 219
tissue 329
intertribal 148
intertwine *unite* 43
cross 219
intertwist 43, 219

interurban 148
interval *degree* 26
-of time 106
-of space **198**
-in music 413
at-s
discontinuously 70
at regular-s 138
intervalvular 228
intervascular 228
intervene
-in order 70
-in time 106
-in space 228
be instrumental 631
mediate 724
(*agent* 758)
intervener 228
interventricular 228
intervert *change* 140
deviate 279
intervertebral 228
interview
conference 588
society 892
interviewer 553, 554
intervolved 43
interweave *join* 43
cross 219
interjacence 228
interwork 148
interworking 170
intestate 552
intestine 221, 350
inthrall
subjection 749
restraint 751
intimacy 888
intimate *special* 79
close 197
tell 527
friendly 888
friend 890
intimately *joined* 43
intimation 527
intimidate
frighten 860
insolence 885
threat 909
intinction 998
into *go*-294
put-300
run-300
intolerable 830
intolerance
prejudice 481
obstinacy 606
impatience 825
insolence 885
malevolence 907
intolerant 489
intomb 363
intonation *sound* 402
musical 413
voice 580
intone *sing* 416

worship 990
intort 248
intoxicant *bane* 663
intoxicated 959
intoxication
excitement 824, 825
inebriation 959
intracanal 221
intracellular 221
intractable
obstinate 606
difficult 704
sullen 901a
intrados 221
intralobular 221
intramarginal 221
intramolecular 221
intramundane 221
intramural 221
intransient 110
intransigence 604
intransigent 604
intransitive 110
intransmutable
diuturnal 110
stable 150
intraocular 221
intrap 545
intraregarding 221
intraseptal 221
intratelluric 221
intrauterine 221
intravascular 221
intravenous 221
intraventricular 221
intrench *safety* 664
defend 717
-on 303
intrepid 861
intricacy 533
intricate *confused* 59
convoluted 248
difficult 704
intrigant
meddlesome 682
cunning 702
libertine 962
intrigue *plot* 626
activity 682
cunning 702
licentiousness 961
intriguer *activity* 682
cunning 702
intrinsic 5 *forming* 56
-evidence 467
-habit 613
-truth 494
intrinsicality **5**
introception 296
introduce *lead* 62
interpose 228
precede 280
insert 300
-new blood 140
-new conditions 469
-to 888

484

introducer 164
introduction
  (see introduce)
  preface 64
  reception 296
  drama 599
  friendship 888
  courtesy 894
introductory
  precursor 64
  beginning 66
  priority 116
  receptive 296
introgression 294
introit 296, 998
intromissive 296
intromit *receive* 296
intromittent 296
introspection
  look into 441
  attend to 457
introspective 451
introvert 218
intrude *interfere* 24
  inopportune 135
  intervene 228
  enter 294
  trespass 303
intruder 57
intrusion
  (see intrude)
intrusive 706
intrusiveness 682
intrust *commit* 755
  lend 787
intuition *mind* 450
  unreasoning **477**
  knowledge 490
  subconsciousness 992a
intumescence
  swell 194
  convex 250
intussuscept 14, 218
intwine *join* 43
  twist 248
inunction 223
inundate *effusion* 337
  flow 348
  redundance 641
inurbanity 895
inure *habituate* 613
  train 673
inured *insensible* 823
inurn 363
inusitate 20
inusitation 614
inutility 645
invade *ingress* 294
  trespass 303
  attack 713
invaginate 14, 218
invagination 218, 357
invalid *powerless* 158
  illogical 477

  diseased 655
  undue 925
invalidate *disable* 158
  weaken 160
  confute 479
invalidity *disease* 655
invaluable 644, 648
invariable *intrinsic* 5
  uniform 16
  conformable 82
  stable 150
invasion *ingress* 294
  attack 716
invective 932
inveigh 932
inveigle *deceive* 545
  seduce 615
invent *imagine* 515
  lie 544
  devise 626
invented *untrue* 546
invention (see invent)
  composition 54
inventive *skillful* 698
inventor 164
inventory 86
inverse *contrary* 14
  upside down 218
inversion
  derangement 61
  change 140
  of position **218**
  contraposition 237
  reversion 145
  language 577
invertebracy 158
invertebrate
  impotent 158
  frail 945
invest *impower* 157
  clothe 225
  surround 227
  besiege 716
  commission 755
  give 784
  lend 787
  expend 809
  –in *locate* 184
  purchase 795
  –money 817
  –with *ascribe* 155
investigate 461
investiture
  appointment 755
investment
  clothing 225
  (see invest)
  make–s 673
investor 784
inveterate *old* 124
  established 150
  inborn 820
  –belief 484
  –habit 613
invidious *painful* 830
  hatred 898

  spite 907
  envy 921
invigilation 459
invigorate
  strengthen 159
  improve 658
  inspirit 834
invigorating
  healthy 656
invincible 159
inviolable *secret* 528
  right 924
  honor 939
inviolate
  permanent 141
  secret 528
  honorable 939
invious *closed* 261
  pathless 704
invisibility **447**
invisible *small* 193
  not to be seen 447
  concealed 526
  –government 526
  –helpers 977
invitation (see invite)
invitatory 765
invite *induce* 615
  offer 763
  ask 765
  –the attention 457
inviting (see invite)
  pleasing 829
invocation
  (see invoke)
invocative 765
invoice 86
invoke *address* 586
  implore 765
  pray 990
  –curses 908
  –saints 998
involucrum 223
involuntary
  necessary 601
  unwilling 603
  –servitude 749
involution
  (see involve)
  algebra 85
involutional psychosis 821a
involve *include* 54
  derange 61
  wrap 225
  evince 467
  mean 516
  latency 526
involved *disorder* 59
  convoluted 248
  secret 533
  obscure style 571
  in debt 806
involvement 61, 704
invulnerable 664
inward *intrinsic* 5

  inside 221
  incoming 294
  –monitor 926
inweave 219, 300
inwrap 225
inwrought 5
ion 490d
Ionian school 451
Ionic 597
iota *small* 32
  trifle 643
  (*minute* 193)
I O U *security* 771
  money 800
ipecacuanha 662
ipse dixit
  certainty 474
  affirmation 535
ipso facto 1
irascibility **901**
irate 900
iridescent 440
iridosmine 323
Iris *traveler* 268
  messenger 534
iris *rainbow* 440
  eye 441
irisated 440
irisation 440
Irish 188–green 435
Irishism 497
Irishman 188
irk 688, 830
irksome *tiresome* 688
  difficult 704
  painful 830
  weary 841
iron *strength* 159
  smooth 255
  hard 323
  resolution 604
  –*age adversity* 735
  pain 828
  –cross 551, 733
  –entering into the soul 828, 830
  –gray 432
  –grip 159
  –gripe 781
  –heel 739
  –necessity 601
  –rule 739
  –sway 739
  –will 604
  rule with a rod of– 739
iron–bound coast
  land 342
  danger 667
ironclad *covering* 223
  defense 717
  man of war 726
iron–handed 739
iron–hearted 861
ironic (see irony)
iron mold 434

  irons 752 fire–386
  –in the fire
  business 625
  redundance 641
  active 682
  unskillful 699
  put in–751
irony
  figure of speech 521
  untruth 546
  ridicule 856
irradiate 420
irrational *number* 84
  illogical 477
  silly 499
irreclaimable
  hopeless 859
  vicious 945
  impenitent 951
irreconcilable
  unrelated 10
  discordant 24
  unwilling 603
  intransigent 604
  opponent 710
  enmity 889
irrecoverable
  past 122
  hopeless 859
  (*lost* 776)
irredeemable
  hopeless 859
  (*lost* 776)
irreducible
  discordant 24
  out of order 59
  unchangeable 150
irrefragable 478
irrefutable
  certain 474
  proved 478
irregular *diverse* 16a
  out of order 59
  multiform 81
  against rule 83
  –*in recurrence* 139
  distorted 243
  guerrilla 722
  combatant 726
irregularity **139**
irrelation 10
irrelevant
  unrelated 10
  unaccordant 24
  sophistical 477
  unimportant 643
irreligion **989**
irremediable
  bad 649
  hopeless 859
  (*spoiled* 659)
  (*lost* 776)
irremissible 945
irremovable 141, 150
irreparable
  hopeless 859

irrepentance   jerky

(bad 649)
(spoiled 659)
(lost 776)
irrepentance 951
irreprehensible 946
irrepressible
   violent 173
   free 748
   excitable 825
irreproachable 946
irreprovable 946
irresilient 326
irresistible
   strong 159
   demonstration 478
   necessary 601
   impulsive 615
irresoluble 150
irresolution 605
irresolvable 87
irresolvedly 605
irrespective 10
irresponsible
   vacillating 605
   exempt 927a
   arbitrary 964
irretrievable
   stable 150
   lost 776
   hopeless 859
irrevealable 528
irreverence
   disrespect 929
   impiety 988
irreversible
   stable 150
   resolute 604
   hopeless 859
   (*past*) 122)
irrevocable
   stable 150
   necessary 601
   resolute 604
   hopeless 859
irrigate 337
irriguous 339
irrision *ridicule* 856
   disrespect 929
irritable *excitable* 825
   irascible 901
irritate *violent* 173
   excite 824
   pain 830
   provoke 898
   incense 900
irritating
   (*see* irritate)
   stringent 171
irritation
   (*see* irritate)
   pain 828
   source of–830
irruption *ingress* 294
   invasion 716
Irvingite 984
is–to be 152 that–118

ischiagra 378
ischialgia 378
Ishmael 83
isinglass 352
Isis 979
Islam 976
Islamism 984
island 44, **346**
islander 188
isle 346
isobar 338, 550
isobath 27
isocheimal 383
isochronal 27, 114
isochronize 120
isochronous 114, 120
isogamy 17, 161, 357
isolate *detach* 44
   seclude 893
isolated *unrelated* 10
   single 87
isomorph 240
isomorphism 240
isonomy 27
isoperimetric 27
isopiestic line 338, 550
isopolity 27
isotherm 550
isothermal 382
isotonic 413
isotope 490d
isotropy 27
issue *distribute* 73
   focus 74
   event 151
   effect 154
   posterity 167
   depart 293
   egress 295
   stream 348, 349
   inquiry 461
   publication 531
   book 593
   ulcer 655
   dénouement 729
   money 800
   at–*discussion* 476
   dissent 489
   negation 536
   opposition 708
   discord 713
   contention 720
   in–461
   –a command 741
   join–*lawsuit* 969
issueless 169
isthmus
   connection 45
   narrow 203
   land 342
it *importance* 642
italics *mark* 550
   printing 591
   put in–
   importance 642

itch *titillation* 380
   disease 655
   desire 865
itching 380
   –palm 819
item *addition* 37, 39
   part 51
   speciality 79
   integer 87
itemize , 79, 594
iterance 104
iteration 104
itinerant *moving* 266
   traveler 268
itinerary *journey* 266
   guidebook 527
ivory 430
ivy *cling like*–46
Ixion 312

J

jab 276
jabber *unmeaning* 517
   stammer 583
   chatter 584
jacal 189
jacent 213
jacet, hic–363
jacinth 847
jack *rotation* 312
   ensign 550
   cards 840
Jack *sailor* 269
   –at a pinch 711
   –Cade 742
   –in office *director* 694
   bully 887
   –Ketch 975
   –of all trades 700
   –o' lantern 423
   –Pudding *actor* 599
   humorist 844
   –tar 269
jack-a-dandy
   buffoon 844
   fop 854
jackal *auxiliary* 711
   sycophant 886
jackanapes *fop* 854
   blusterer 887
jackass 271
jack boot 225
jackeroo 57
jacket 225 cork–666
jackleg 792
jackpot 775, 840
jackstones 840
Jacobin 710
Jacob's ladder 305
Jacquerie *tumult* 719
jactation 315
jactitation *tossing* 315
   boasting 884
jaculation 284

jade *horse* 271
   worn–*out* 659
   fatigue 688
   low woman 876
   scamp 949
   drab 962
jadu 621, 649
jag 257 *burden* 190
   dent 257
jäger 726
jagged 244, 256
jaguar 440, 913
jail 752
jailbird *prisoner* 754
   bad man 949
jailer *keeper* 753
   punisher 975
jakes 653
jalousie 351, 424
jam *squeeze* 43
   pulp 354
   sweet 298, 396
   –in *interpose* 228
Jamaica
   –bayberry 400
   –pepper 393
jamb 215
jamboree 840
jammed in
   restraint 751
jampan 272
jane *woman* 374
jangle
   harsh sound 410
   quarrel 713
janissary 726
janitor 263
Jansenist 984
janty (*see* jaunty)
January 138
Janus *deceiver* 607
   tergiversation 607
   close the temple of
   –723
Janus-faced 544
japan *coat* 223
   resin 356a
   ornament 847
jaquima 752
jar *clash* 24
   vessel 191
   agitation 315
   stridor 410
   discord 713
   –upon the feelings 830
jardinière 191
jargon *absurdity* 497
   no meaning 517
   unintelligible 519
   neology 563
jarring 24, 414
jasper 435, 847
jaundice 436
jaundiced *yellow* 436
   prejudiced 481

dejected 837
jealous 920
view with–eyes
disapprove 932
jaunt 266
jaunting car 272
jaunty *gay* 836
   pretty 845
   stylish 852
   showy 882
   insolent 885
Javanese 372a
javelin 727
jaw *chatter* 584
   scold 932
jaw-fallen 837
jaws *mouth* 231
   eating 298
   –of death 360
jay 584 *dupe* 547
jazz *music* 415
   dance 840
   –band 416
jealous 920
   –of honor 939
jealousy 920
   suspicion 485
jeer *flout* 929
   (*joke* 842)
   (*banter* 856)
Jehovah 976
Jehu *traveler* 268
   director 694
jejune *incomplete* 53
   unproductive 169
   insipid 391
   style 575
   scanty 640
   wearying 841
   dull 843
jejunum 221, 350
jell 352
jellify 352
jelly 352
   beat to a–972
jellyfish 368
jemadar 745
jemmy *lever* 633
   dandy 854
jennet 271
jenny 633
jeopardy 665
jerboa 309
jereed 727
jeremiad *lament* 839
   invective 932
   (*accusation* 938)
Jericho, send to–297
jerk *start* 146
   throw 284
   pull 285
   agitate 315
jerkin 225
jerks, by–70
   the–315
jerky 315

jerry

jerry *deceived* 545
jerry-build 545
jerry-building 545
jerry-built 160, 545
Jerry Sneak
　coward 862
　knave 941
Jersey *cow* 366
jersey *clothing* 225
jessamy
　affectation 855
jest *trifle* 643
　wit 842
jest book 842
jester 844
jesting stock 857
Jesuit *deceiver* 548
　priest 996
jesuitical
　sophistical 477
　deceitful 544
Jesus 976
jet *stream* 348
　–black 431
jetsam 782
jettison 782
jetty *projection* 250
　harbor 666
jeu–de mots 842
　–d'esprit 842
　–de theatre 599
jewel *gem* 648
　ornament 847
　favorite 899
　–s five words long 648
jewelry 847 false–545
jew's-harp 417
Jezebel *wicked* 913
　wretch 949
　courtesan 962
jhil 345
jhilmil 351
jib *reverse* 140
　front 234
　recoil 276
　regression 283
　cut of one's–
　form 240
　appearance 448
jibe *concur* 178
jiffy 113
jig *dance* 840
　(*music* 415)
jigger 215, 272
jilt *disappoint* 509
　deceive 545
　deceiver 548
　dishonor 940
jilted 898
jimp 845
jingal 727
jingle 408
jingo *boaster* 884
　insolence 885
　blusterer 887

jingoism 884, 885
jinks, high–840
jinn 980
jinrikisha 266, 272
jitney 272
jiujitsu 720
jiva 157
job *business* 625
　action 680
　unfair 940
　tough–704
Job–'s comforter
　dejection 837
　hopeless 859
　patience of–826
　poor as–804
jobation 932
jobber *deceiver* 548
　tactician 700
　merchant 797
　trickster 943
jobbernowl 501
jobbery *cunning* 702
　improbity 940
jobbing *barter* 794
jockey *rider* 268
　deceive 545
　servant 746
jocose *gay* 836
　witty 842
jocoseness *fun* 840
jocular *gay* 636
　droll 842
jocund *gay* 836
　sportive 840
Joe Miller *wit* 842
　humorist 844
jog *push* 276
　shake 315
　–on *continue* 143
　trudge 266
　slow 275
　advance 282
　mediocrity 736
　–the memory 505
jogger
　memory aid 505
joggle 315
jog-trot
　uniformity 16
　trudge 266
　slow 275
　habit 613
John Doe and Richard Roe 4
Johnsonian 577
join *connect* 43
　assemble 72
　contiguous 199
　arrive 272
　party 712
　sociality 892
　marry 903
　–battle 722
　–forces 708
　–hands 708

–in 778
–in the chorus 488
–issue *discuss* 476
　deny 536
　quarrel 713
　contend 720
　lawsuit 969
–the choir invisible 360
–the majority 360
–with 709
joining *meeting* 292
joint *junction* 43
　part 51
　accompanying 88
　concurrent 178
　meat 298
　low resort 621, 945
　–concern 712
joint stock
　cooperation 709
　participation 778
joint tenancy 778
jointure 780
joist 215
joke *absurdity* 497
　trifle 643
　wit 842
　ridicule 856
　in–842
　mere–643
　no–*existing* 1
　important 642
　practical–
　deception 545
　ridicule 856
　disrespect 929
　take a–498
joker 844 *cards* 840
joking apart
　affirmation 535
　resolution 604
jole 236
jollification
　amusement 840
　intemperance 954
jollity *amusement* 840
　sociality 892
jolly *plump* 192
　marine 269
　gay 836
　flattery 933
　–boat 273
　–fellow 892
jolt *impulse* 276
　agitation 315
jolthead 501
Jonah 621, 649
Jones
　Davy–'s locker 360
　Paul–792
jongleur 597
jonquil 436
Jordan 360
jornada 200
jorum 191

Joseph 960
　–'s coat 440
joss 991
joss-house 1000
joss-stick 388
jostle *rush* 276
　jog 315
　clash 713
　contend 720
　(*disagree* 24)
jot *small* 32
　unimportant 643
jotting *indication* 550
　record 551
joule 490d
jounce 315
journal *annals* 114
　newspaper 531
　record 551
　magazine 593
　narrative 594
　accounts 811
journalism 551
journalist
　recorder 553
　representation 554
　author 593
journey 266
　–'s end 292
journeyman
　artisan 690
　servant 746
joust 720
Jove 979 sub
　–out of doors 220
　air 338
jovial *gay* 836
　amusement 840
　social 892
Jovinianist 984
jowl 236
joy 827 give one–896
　–rider 274
joyful 836
joyless *painful* 830
　sad 837
J. P. 967
Juan, Don–962
jubbah 225
jube 1000
jubilant *gay* 836
　rejoicing 838
　celebrating 883
　boastful 884
jubilate 884
jubilee
　anniversary 138
　celebration 883
jucundity 829
Judaism 984
Judas *deceiver* 548
　knave 941
　–kiss *hypocrisy* 544
　base 940
judge *intellect* 450
　decide 480

jumper

interpreter 524
justice 664
master 745
taste 850
magistrate **967**
–in a lump 465a
Judge *deity* 976
Judgment, Day of–67
judgment
　intellect 450
　discrimination 465
　decision **480**
　wisdom 498
　condemnation 971
　sentence 972
judgment seat 966
judication 480
judicatory 965, 966
judicature 965, 966
judicial 965
　–astrology 511
　–murder 361
　–separation 905
judiciary 664
judicious 498
jug 191
juggernaut *kill* 361
　god 979
　idolatry 991
juggle *deceive* 545
　cunning 702
juggler 548
jugglery 545
jugulate 361
juice **333**
juiceless 340
juicy 339
jujube 396
julep 396
julienne *soup* 298
jumble *mixture* 41
　confusion 59
　derange 61
　indiscrimination 465a
Jumbo 192
jument 271
jump
　sudden change 146
　leap 309
　neglect 460
　at one–113
　–about 315
　–at *willing* 602
　pursue 622
　hasten 684
　consent 762
　seize 789
　desire 865
　–over 460
　–to a conclusion
　misjudge 481
　credulous 486
　–up 307, 309
jumper *clothing* 225

487

junction   keystone

   vehicle 272
junction 43
juncture
   circumstance 8
   junction 43
   period 134
jungle *disorder* 59
   vegetation 367
jungly 365
junior *secondary* 34
   youth 127
   student 492
juniority 34
juniper 367
junk 273 *lumber* 645
junket *dish* 298
   merrymaking 840
Juno 920
junta 696
junto 712
jupe 225
jupiter 979
juramentado 988
Jurassic Period 490c
jurat 967
juridical 965
jurisconsult 968
jurisdiction 965
   authority 737
jurisprudence 963
jurist 968
juror 967
jury 967
   impanel a–969
   –box 966
   –mast *substitute* 147
   refuge 666
juryman 967
jussive 567, 741
just *accurate* 494
   right 922
   equitable 939
   pious 987
   –as *similar* 17
   same time 120
   –do 639
   –in time 134
   –now 118
   –out 123
   –reasoning 476
   –so 488
   –then 113
   –the thing
      agreement 23
      exact 494
just *tilt* 720
juste milieu
   middle 68
   moderation 174
   mid-course 628
justice *judge* 664
   right 922
   honor 939
   magistrate 967
   administration of
     965

   bring to–969
   court of–966
   do–to eat 298
   duty 926
   praise 931
   vindicate 937
   –seat 966
   not do-to 483
   retributive–972
justiciary 967
justifiable *right* 922
   vindication 937
justification
   printing 591
   vindication 937
   religious 987
justle *push* 276
   contend 720
jut 214
jute 205
jut out 250
jutting over 214
jutty 250
juvenescent 127
juvenile *youth* 127
   actor 599
juxtaposition 199

K

Kaa 366
Kabyle 372a
kachcha 674
kadi 967
kaffiyeh 225
kahin 996
kail 840
kaiser 745
kal 121
kala jagah 189
kala pani 341
kaleidophon 445
kaleidoscope 149,
   428, 445
Kali 979
kalpa 106, 109
kangaroo 309, 366
Kantianism 451
kantikoy 840
karma 922
karoo 169
karyaster 357
karyoplasmic 357
karyosome 357
kassis 996
Katerfelto 994
kavass 965
kayak 273
K. C. 968
keck 297
keddah 261
kedge *navigate* 267
   anchor 666
keel 211
   –upwards 218

keel boat 273
keelhaul 972
keen *energetic* 171
   sharp 253
   sensible 375
   cold 383
   intelligent 498
   poignant 821
   lament 550, 839
   eager 865
   –blast 349
keener
   mourner 363, 839
   schemer 702
keen-eyed 441
keenness (*see* keen)
   fastidiousness 868
keen-sighted 498
keen-witted 842, 498
keep *do often* 136
   persist 141
   continue 143
   food 298
   store 636
   provision 637
   refuge 666
   preserve 670
   citadel 717
   custody 751
   prison 752
   observe 772
   retain 781
   celebrate 883
   preserve 976
   –accounts 811
   –a good look out for
     507
   –alive *life* 359
   preserve 670
   –aloof *absence* 187
   distance 196
   avoidance 623
   –an account with 805
   –an eye upon 459
   –apart 44
   –a secret 528
   –a shop 625
   –a stiff upper lip 836
   –away 187
   –back *late* 133
   conceal 528
   dissuade 616
   not use 678
   restrain 751
   retain 781
   –body and soul
     together *life* 359
   health 654
   –close 781
   –company 88
   –firm 150
   –from *conceal* 528
   refrain 623
   not do 681
   restrain 751
   –going *continue* 143

   move 264
   –hold 150
   –holy 987
   –house 184
   –in *restrain* 751
   prohibit 761
   –in ignorance 528
   –in mind 505
   –in order 693
   –in sight 459
   –in suspense
     uncertainty 475
   irresolution 605
   –in the thoughts 505
   –in view
     attend to 457
   remember 505
   expect 507
   –moving 682
   –off *avoid* 623
   avert 706
   defend 717
   resist 719
   prohibition 761
   –on *do often* 136
   continue 143
   persevere 604a
   –one in countenance
     conformity 82
   induce 615
   aid 707
   encourage 861
   –one's bed 655
   –one's countenance
     unexcitable 826
   sad 837
   –one's course 282
   –one's ground 141
   –one's hand in 613
   –one's head above
     water 731
   –one's promise 772
   –one's word 939
   –on foot
     continuance 143
   support 215
   –on one's legs 654
   –out of the way 187
   –out of harm's way
     864
   –pace with *equal* 27
   same time 120
   –quiet 265
   –silence 585
   –the ball rolling 143
   –the field 143, 722
   –the peace 714
   –time *punctual* 132
   –to 604a
   –together 709
   –to oneself 528
   –under *authority* 737
   subjection 749
   restraint 751
   –up (*see below*)
   –waiting 133

   –watch 459
   –within bounds 304
keeper 370, **753**
keeping *congruity* 23
   in–82
   safe–safety 664
   preservation 670
keeping room 191
keepsake 505
keep up *continue* 143
   preserve 670
   stimulate 824
   –a correspondence
     592
   –appearances 852
   –one's spirits 836
   –the ball *active* 682
   amusement 840
   –the memory of 505
   –with 274
keg 191
kelpie 271, 979
Kelvin scale 490d
kempt 652
ken *sight* 441
   knowledge 490
kennel *hovel* 189
   hole 251
   conduit 350
Kentish fire 838
képi 225
Kepler 490a
kerbstone 233
kerchief 225
   wave a–550
kern *harden* 321
   low fellow 876
   varlet 949
kernel *heart* 5
   central 222
   important 642
kerosene 356
ketch *ship* 273
Ketch, Jack–975
ketones 490b
kettle *vessel* 191
   caldron 386
   –of fish *disorder* 59
   difficulty 704
kettledrum
   music 417
   tea-party 892
key *cause* 153
   opener 260
   music 413
   color 428
   interpretation 522
   indication 550
   instrument 631, 633
   emblem of authority
     747
keyhole 260
keynote *model* **22**
   rule 80 *music* 413
keystone *support* 215
   motive 615

kahka / known

importance 642
   completion 729
kahka 225, 433
khamsin 349
khan *inn* 189
   governor 745
khansamah 637, 746
khedive 745
khitmutgar 746
khoja 540
khudd 217
kiack 1000
kibitka 272
kick *impulse* 276
   recoil 277
   pungency 392
   assault 716
   spurn 930
   punish 972
   –against *oppose* 708
   resist 719
   –against the pricks
     useless 645
     rash 863
   –one's heels
     kept waiting 133
     nothing to do 681
   –over the traces 742
   –the beam
     unequal 28
     come short of 34
     insufficiency 640
   –up a dust *active* 682
     discord 713
     insolent 885
   –up a row
     violent 173
     discord 713
kickshaw *food* 298
   trifle 643
kid *child* 129, 167
kiddish 129
kid gloves
   not to be handled
     with–*dirty* 653
   difficult 704
kidnap *deceive* 545
   take 789
   steal 791
kidnaper 792
kidney *class* 75
   organ 221
   –beans 298
kila 717
kilderkin 191
Kilkenny cats 713
kill 361
   –the fatted calf 883
   –the goose with
     golden eggs 699
   –the slain 641
   –time *inactivity* 683
     amusement 840
   –two birds with one
     stone 682
   –with kindness 902

killick 666
killing 361
   delightful 829
killing time 126
kill–joy 706
kiln 386
kilometer 200
kilowatt 466
kilt 225
kilter *state* 7
   out of–674
kimbo 244
kimono 225
kin 75
kind *class* 75
   benevolent 906
   –regards 894
   –words 906
   pay in–807
kindergarten 537, 542
kindergartner 540
kindle *cause* 153
   produce 161
   quicken 171
   inflame 173
   set fire to 384
   excite 824
   incense 900
kindling 384
   –wood 388
kindly 906
kindness 906
kindred 11
kine 366
kinematics 264, 276, 490a
kinetics 276
king 745 *cards* 840
   every inch a–
     authority 737
   rank 875
King–'s Bench
   prison 752
   court 966
   –Death 360
   –of Kings 976
   –'s counsel 968
   –'s English 560
   –'s evidence 529
   –'s evil 655
   –'s highway 627
   –'s speech 695
   –'s yellow 436
kingcraft 693
kingdom *region* 181
   property 780
   –of heaven 981
kingly 737
king–maker 526, 694
king–post 215
kingship 877
kink *knot* 59
   convolution 248
   crick 378
   whim 608

kinsfolk 11
kinsman 11
kiosk *house* 189
kip 215
kipper 298
kirk 1000
kirtle 225
kismet 601
kiss *touch* 379
   courtesy 894
   endearment 902
   –in the ring 840
   –the book 535
   –the hem of one's
     garment 928
   –the rod 725
kit *class* 75
   knapsack, bottle 191
   fiddle 417
kitchen *room* 191
   workshop 691
   –kaffir 563
   –maid 746
kitchener 386
kite *fly* 273
   bill 800
   fly a–*credit* 805
   insolvency 808
kith 11
kithless 87
kitten *young* 129
   bring forth 161
   playful as a–836, 840
kittereen 272
kitty *profit* 775
kleptomania
   insanity 502
   stealing 791
   desire 865
kleptomaniac 504
knack 698
   get into the–613
knag 706
knap 306
knapsack 191
knarl 59
knave *deceiver* 548
   cards 840
   rogue 941
knavery *deception* 545
   cunning 702
   improbity 940
   vice 945
knead *mix* 41
   mold 240
   soften 324
   touch 379
knee *angle* 244
   bend the–*stoop* 308
   submission 725
   down on one's–
     humble 879
   fall on one's–s
     beg 765
     atone 952

   on one's–s *beg* 765
   respect 928
   on the–s of the
     gods 152
knee–deep 208, 209
kneel *stoop* 308
   submit 725
   beg 765
   servility 886
   courtesy 894
   ask mercy 914
   respect 928
   worship 990
knell 363
   strike the death–361
knickerbockers 225
knickers 225
knickknack 643, 847
knife 253–pleat 248
   play a good–and
     fork *eat* 298
   appetite 865
knight 875–errant
   defender 717
   rash 863
   philanthropist 910
   –marshal 745
   –of the road 460
   –service 777
   –'s move 279
   –Templar 712
knighthood 877
knit 43–the brow
   discontent 832
   anger 900
   disapprobation 932
   well–159
knob *pendency* 214
   ball 249
   protuberance 250
knobby 206, 250
knock *blow* 276
   sound 406
   dispraise 932
   (*punish* 972)
   hard–s 720
   –at the door
     death 360
     request 765
   –down *destroy* 162
     lay flat 213
     lower 308
     injure 659
     dishearten 837
   –off *complete* 729
   –one's head against 699
   –on the head *kill* 361
   –out 162
   –out blow 162
   –over 162
   –under 725
   –up 688
knock–down
   argument 479

knocked–on the head
   failure 732
   –to atoms 162
knocker
   instrument 633
   detractor 936
knock–kneed 243, 244
knock–out 67
   –drops 649
knoll 206
knot *ligature* 45
   entanglement 59
   group 72
   length 200
   intersection 219
   distortion 243
   round 249
   convexity 250
   dense 321
   difficulty 704
   hindrance 706
   junto 712
   ornament 847
   tie the nuptial–903
   true lover's
     –*love* 897
   endearment 902
knotted *rough* 256
knout 975
know *believe* 484
   knowledge 490
   friendly 888
   associate 892
   I'd have you–
     attend 457
     assertion 535
   I–better 536
   –by heart 505
   –for certain 484
   –no bounds *great* 31
   infinite 105
   redundance 641
   –nothing of 491
   –one's own mind 604
   –what one is about 698
   –what's what 698
   –which is which 465
   not that one–s 491
knowing 702
knowingly 620
knowledge 490
   (see know)
   acquire–539
   come to one's–527
   –of the world 698
   practical–698
known 490
   become–529
   –as 564
   –by 550
   make–*inform* 527
   publish 531
   well–490
   habitual 613

knuckle 244
   —down 725
knuckle-duster 727
knur 250
knurl 250, 256
knurly 256
knurr and spell 840
kobold 979
kodak 445
koh-i-noor 650
koniology 330
kooshti 720
Koran 986
Korsakoff's
   psychosis 821a
kos 200
kowtow *bow* 308
   submission 725
   courtesy 894
   respect 928
kraal 189
kraken 83
kriegspiel 722
kris 727
Krishna 979
krupp 727
kucha 160, 321
kudos 931
Kuklux 712
Kultur 885
kurbash 975
kutcherry 802, 965
kyanization 670
kyanize 670
kyle 343

L

laager 717
labarum 550
labefy 659
label 550
labent 306
labial *lip* 231
   phonetic 561
labor *parturition* 161
   work 680
   exertion 686
   hard—
   punishment 972
   —for 620
   —in one's vocation 625
   —in vain
      fall short 304
      useless 645
   —of love *willing* 602
      amusement 840
      disinterested 942
   —under *state* 7
      disease 655
      difficulty 704
      feeling 821
      affliction 828
      mountain in— 638

laboratory 691
Labor Day 138, 840
labored *style* 579
   prepared 673
   —study 457
laborer 686, 690
laboring 686
   —man 690
   —oar 686
laborious *active* 682
   exertion 686
   difficult 704
labor-saving 633
labyrinth *disorder* 59
   convolution 248
   internal ear 418
   secret 533
   (*difficulty* 704)
labyrinthine 533
lac *number* 98
   resin 356a
   —of rupees 800
laccolith 490c
lace *stitch* 43
   netting 219
   ornament 847
   —one's jacket 972
lacerable 328
lacerate 44, 378
   —the heart 830
laches *neglect* 460
   nonobservance 773
lachrymation 837
   —gas 663
laciniate 256
lack *incompleteness* 53
   require 630
   insufficient 640
   destitute 804
   want 865
   —faith 989
   —of contrition 951
   —preparation 674
   —wit 501
lackadaisical
   inactive 683
   melancholy 837
   indifferent 866
lackadaisy!
   lament 839
   wonder 870
lackaday 839
lackbrain 499, 501
lacker (*see* lacquer)
lackey 746
lackluster 422, 429
laconic 572, 585
laconicism 572
laconize 572
lacquer *covering* 223
   resin 356a
   adorn 847
lacrosse 840
lacteal 352
lactescence 352, 430
lacuna *gap* 198

pit 252
lacustrine 343
   —dwelling 189
lad 129
ladder *ascent* 305
   way 627
   kick down the— 604
laddie 129
lade *load* 184
   transfer 185, 270
   contents 190
   —out 297
laden 52 *heavy—* 828
   —with 777
lading *contents* 190
   property 780
   bill of— list 86
ladino 41, 271
ladle *receptacle* 191
   transfer 270
   vehicle 272
lady *woman* 374
   rank 875
   wife 903
   —help 746
Lady day 138
ladylike *womanly* 374
   fashionable 852
   (*courteous* 894)
ladylove 897
lady's maid 746
laetificant 829
lag *linger* 275
   follow 281
   dawdle 683
lager beer 298
laggard *unwilling* 603
   inactive 683
lagoon 343
lagniappe 784
laical 997
laicize 997
laid-back 174
   —by the heels 751
   —low 160
   —on one's back 158
   —up 655
lair *den* 189
   sty 653
laird *master* 745
   proprietor 779
   nobility 875
Lais 962
laisser—aller,—faire
   permanence 141
   neglect 460
   inaction 681
   laxity 738
   freedom 748
   inexcitable 826
laity 997
lake *water* **343**
   pink 434
   —dwelling 189
   —of fire and
      brimstone 982

lakh 98
laky *red* 434
Lama *ruler* 745
   prince 996
Lamarckism 357
lamb *infant* 129
   food 298
   animal 366
   gentle 826
   innocent 946
   go out like a— 174
   *lion lies down with
      —* 721
lamba-chauki 215
lambaste 972
lambency 379
lambent *touching* 379
   —flame heat 382
   light 420
Lambeth 1000
lambkin 167, 223
Lamb of God 976
lame *incomplete* 53
   impotent 158
   weak 160
   imperfect 651
   disease 655
   injury 659
   failing 732
   (*bad* 649)
   (*lax* 738)
   *help a—dog over a
      stile aid* 707
   vindicate 937
   —conclusion
      illogical 477
   failure 732
   —duck 808
   —excuse 617
lamellar 204
lamentable *bad* 649
   painful 830
   sad 837
lamentably *very* 31
lamentation 839
   (*regret* 833)
lamenter 363
lamia *demon* 980
   sorcerer 994
lamina *part* 51
   layer 204
laminate 204
Lammas 998
lamp 423 *—shells* 368
   rub the— 992
   safety— 666
   *smell of the
      —style* 577
   prepared 673
lamplight 423
lamplighter
   quick 682
lampoon *censure* 932
   detraction 934
lampooner 936
lampreys 368

lanate 255, 256
lance *pierce* 260
   throw 284
   spear 727
   *break a—with
      attack* 716
   warfare 722
   couch one's— 720
   —corporal 745
lanceolate 253
lancer 726
lancet *sharp* 253
   piercer 262
lanciform 253
lancinate
   bodily pain 378
   mental pain 830
land *arrive* 267, 292
   ground 342
   estate 780
   *how the—lies
      circumstances* 8
   experiment 463
   foresight 510
   hug the— 286
   in the—of the living 359
   *—flowing with milk
      and honey* 168
   make the— 286
   on— 342
   see— 858
landamman 745
landau 272
landed *property* 780
   —gentry 779
   —estate 780
landgrave 745
landholder 779
landing place
   stage 215
   arrive 292
   refuge 666
landlady 779
landlocked 229
landloper 268
landlord
   innkeeper 637
   possessor 779
landlubber 268, 342, 701
landmark *limit* 233
   measurement 466
   indication 550
landowner 779
landreeve 694
landscape
   prospect 448
   —gardening
   agriculture 371
   beauty 845
   —painter 559
   —painting 556
landshark 792
landslide 306
landslip 306

490

landsman

landsman 268, 342
Landsturm 726
landsurveying 466
Landwehr 726
lane *street* 189
  opening 260
  way 627
langrage shot 727
langrel 727
Langrenus 490a
langsyne 122
language 560
  command of—582
  strong— *vigor* 574
  malediction 908
languid *weak* 160
  inert 172
  slow 275
  —*style* 575
  inactive 683
  torpid 823
languish *decrease* 36
  ill 655
  inactive 683
  repine 828
  affect 855
  —for 865
languishing 160
languishment
  lament 839
languor (*see* languid)
laniate 162
lank *long* 200
lanky *thin* 203
  tall 200, 206
lantern *window* 260
  lamp 423
  —jaws 203
  —of Diogenes 461
  magic—448
lanthanide series 490b
lanuginous 256
Laocoön 557
Laodicean 823
lap *flap* 39
  abode 189
  eager 204
  support 215
  interior 221
  wrap 225
  encompass 227, 229
  drink 298
  circuition 311
  —of waves 405
  —of luxury
    pleasure 377
    inactivity 683
    voluptuousness 954
lapdog *animal* 366
  servile 886
lapel 39, 258
lapidate *kill* 361
  attack 716
  punish 972
lapideous 323

lapidescence 323
lapidify 323, 357
lapis lazuli *blue* 438
  jewel 847
lappet 39
lapse *course* 109
  past 122
  conversion 144
  fall 306
  degeneracy 659
  relapse 661
  loss 776
  vice 945
  guilt 947
  —of memory 506
  —of time 109
lapsus linguae
  mistake 495
  solecism 568
  stammering 583
larboard 239
larceny 791
larch 367
lard 355, 356
lardaceous 355
larder 636
  contents of the—298
lares et penates
  home 189
  idols 991
large *quantity* 31
  size 192
  at—*diffuse* 573
  free 748
  liberated 750
  become—194
  —number 102
  —type 642
large-hearted
  liberal 816
  benevolent 906
  disinterested 942
larger 194
largess 785
largest 784
largest portion 192
larghetto *slow* 275
  music 415
largiloquent
  verbose 573
largo *slow* 275
  music 415
lariat 45
larigo 45
lark *ascent* 305
  bird 366
  musician 416
  spree 840
  with the—
    morning 125
larmier 210
larrigan 225
larrikin 887, 913
larrup 972
larum *loud* 404
  alarm 669

larva 129, 193
larynx 351
lascar 269
lascivious 961
lash *tie together* 43
  violence 173
  whip 370
  incite 615
  censure 932
  punish 972
  scourge 975
  —into fury 900
  —the waves 645
  under the
    —compelled 744
    subject 749
lashes *hair* 256
lass *girl* 129
  (*woman* 374)
lassitude *fatigue* 688
  weariness 841
lasso *tie* 45
  loop 247
last *abide* 1
  model 22
  —*in order* 67*
  endure 106
  durable 110
  —in time 122
  continue 141
  at—133
  at the—extremity 665
  breathe one's—360
  die in the—ditch 604a
  game to the—604a
  go to one's—home 360
  —but one etc. 67
  —finish 729
  —for ever 112
  —gasp 360
  —home 363
  —post 550
  —resort 666
  —shift 601
  —sleep 360
  —stage 67
  —straw 153
  —stroke 729
  —touch 729
  —word
    affirmation 535
    obstinacy 606
  —year etc. 122
  never hear the—of 104
  on-legs *weak* 160
  dying 360
  spoiled 659
  adversity 735
lastingness 141
latch *fasten* 43
  fastening 45
latchet 45

latchkey 631
latchstring
  find the—out 892
  have the—out 888
late *past* 122
  new 123
  tardy 133
  dead 360
  too—135
lately *formerly* 122
  recently 123
latency 526
lateness 133
latent *inert* 172
  concealed 526
  influence 526
later 117
laterality 236
lateritious 434
latest 118
lateward 132, 133
lath 205, 635
  thin as a—203
lathe *region* 181
  conversion 144
  machine 633
lather *lubrication* 332
  bubble 353
lathi 215
lathy 203
latifoliate 202
Latin—deities 979
  thieves'—563
latitancy 528
latitat 969
latitude *extent* 180
  region 181
  breadth 202
  measurement 466
  map drawing 550
  freedom 748
  —and longitude
    situation 183
latitudinarian
  heterodox 984
  irreligious 989
latration 412
latria 990
latrine 653
latrocinium 791
latrociny 791
latter *sequent* 63
  past 122
Latter-day Saint 984
latterly 123
lattice *crossing* 219
  opening 160
  opening 260
laud *praise* 931
  worship 990
laudable 944
laudanum 174
laudation 883
laudator 935
laudatory 931

law

laugh 838—at
  ridicule 856
  sneer 929
  (*undervalue* 483)
  —in one's sleeve
    latent 526
    ridicule 856
    disrespect 929
    contempt 930
  —on the wrong side
    of one's mouth
    disappointed 509
    dejected 837
    in disrepute 874
  —to scorn *defy* 715
    despise 930
  make one—853
  raise a—840
laughable 853
laughing-gas 376
  no—matter 642
laughingstock 857
laughter (*see* laugh)
  —holding both his
    sides 838
laughter-loving 836
launch *begin* 66
  boat 273
  propel 284
  —forth 676
  —into 676
  —into eternity 360, 361
  —out 573
  —out against 716
laundress
  washerwoman 652
  agent 690
  servant 746
laundry *room* 191
  heat 386
  clean 652
laundryman 652
laureate 875
  poet—597
laurel *trophy* 733
  glory 873
  decoration 877
  (*reward* 973)
  repose on one's—s 265
lava *excretion* 299
  semiliquid 352
lavage 300
lavatory 386, 652
lave *water* 337
  clean 652
lavement 300
lavender *color* 437
laver la tête 932
lavish *profuse* 641
  give 784
  expend 809
  squander 818
  —of praise 931
law *regularity* 80

law–abiding   leather

statute 697
permission 760
legality 963
court of–966
give the–737
go to–969
Jewish–985
–of the Medes and Persians 80
lay down the–
certainty 474
affirm 535
command 741
learned in the–
practice–968 968
set the–at defiance 964
so many–s 947
take the–into one's own hands
war 722
disobedience 742
lawless 964
take the–of 969
law-abiding 743
lawful *permitted* 760
due 924
legal 963
lawgiver
director 694
(*master* 745)
lawless *irregular* 83
mutinous 742
nonobservant 773
vicious 945
arbitrary 964
lawn *plain* 344
sward 367
agriculture 371
fabric 635
–sleeves 999
–tennis 840
lawsuit 969
lawyer 968
lax *incoherent* 47
soft 324
error 495
–*style* 575
remiss 738
nonobservant 773
dishonorable 940
licentious 945
irreligious 989
laxative 652
remedial 662
laxity 738
laxness 738, 773
lay *arrangement* 60
moderate 174
place 184
ley 344
music 415
poetry 597
bet 621
secular 997
–about one

active 682
exertion 686
attack 716
content 720
punish 972
–apart *exclude* 55
relinquish 782
–aside *neglect* 460
reject 610
disuse 678
give up 782
–at one's feet 763
–at the door of 155
–bare 529
–before 527
–brother 996
–by *store* 636
provide 637
sickness 655
disuse 678
–by the heels 162
–claim to 924
–down
(see below)
–eggs 161
–figure
thing of naught 4
model 22
representation 554
–hands on *use* 677
take 789
rite 998
–heads together
advise 695
cooperate 709
–in *eat* 298
store 636
provide 637
–in ruins 162
–in the dust 162
–it on thick
cover 223
too much 641
flatter 933
–on 972
–one's account for 484
–oneself open to 177
–oneself out for 673
–one's finger upon 480a
–one's head on the block 942
–on the table 133
–open *divest* 226
opening 260
show 525
disclose 529
–out *destroy* 162
horizontal 213
–corpse 363
plan 626
expend 809
–over 133
–siege to 716
–stress on 642

–the ax at the root of tree 162
–the first stone 66
–the flattering unction to one's soul *content* 831
relief 834
–the foundations
originate 153
prepare 673
–to attribute 155
rest 265
–together 43
–to one's charge 938
–train 626
–under hatches 751
–under restraint 751
–up *store* 636
sickness 655
disuse 678
–waste 162
lay down *locate* 184
horizontal 213
assert 535
renounce 757
relinquish 782
pay 807
–a plan 626
–one's arms
passification 723
submission 725
–one's life 360
–the law *certain* 474
assert 535
command 741
insolence 885
layer 204
layette 225
layman 997
laystall 653
lazar house 662
lazy *inactive* 683
(*slow* 275)
lazzarone 683
lb. 319
lea *land* 342
plain 344
leach 295, 335
leachy 335
lead *supremacy* 33
in order 62
influence 175
tend 176
soundings 208
–in motion 280
heavy 319
induce 615
direct 693
authority 737
heave the–466
–a dance
run away 623
circuit 629
difficulty 704
disrespect 929
–a life 692

–astray 495
–by the nose 737
–captive *subject* 749
restraint 751
–on 693
–one to expect 511
–the choir 990
–the dance 280
–the way
precedence 62
begin 66
precession 280
importance 642
direction 693
repute 873
–to no end 645
–to the altar 903
red–434
take the–
influence 175
importance 642
authority 737
leadable 298
leaden *dim* 422
colorless 429
gray 432
inactive 683
leader *precursor* 64
dissertation 595
director 694
counsel 968
–writer 595
leaders
typography 550
leadership 737
leading *beginning* 66
important 642
–article 595
–lady *actress* 599
–note *music* 413
–part 175
–question 461
–strings
childhood 127
child 129
pupil 541
subject 749
restraint 751, 752
leads 223
leaf *part* 51
layer 204
plant 367
–of a book 593
–green 435
turn over a new–658
leafage 367
leafless 226
leaflet 531
leafy 256
league *combine* 48
length 200
cooperation 709
party 712
leak *crack* 198
dribble 295

waste 638
–out *disclosure* 529
spring a–
injury 659
leakage (see leak)
leaky *oozing* 295
imperfect 651
lean *thin* 203
oblique 217
–on 215
–to *shed* 191
willing 602
–towards *favor* 923
–upon *belief* 484
subjection 749
hope 858
leaning *tendency* 176
willingness 602
desire 865
friendship 888
favoritism 923
lean-witted 499
leap
sudden change 146
ascent 305
jump 309
by–s and bounds 274
–in the dark
experiment 463
uncertain 475
chance 621
rash 863
–with joy 838
make a–at 622
leapfrog 840
leaping 309
leap year 138
learn 539
–by experience 950
–by heart 505
learned 490, 539
–man 492
learner 492, **541**
learning
knowledge 490
acquisition of–**539**
lease
property 270, 780
lending 787
grant a–771
–and release 783
take a new–of life 654
leasehold 780
leash *tie* 43
three 92
hold in–751
least–*in quantity* 34
–*in size* 193
at the–32
leather *skin* 223
touch 327
beat 972
–or prunello 643
nothing like–481

492

leave *remainder* 40
  part company 44
  relinquish 624
  permission 760
  bequeath 784
  French—623
  give me—*to say* 535
  —*alone inaction* 681
  freedom 748
  permit 760
  —*a loophole* 705
  —*an inference* 526
  —*a place* 293
  —*in the lurch
    pass* 303
  decisive 545
  —*it to one* 760
  —*no trace
    disappear* 449
  obliterate 552
  —*off cease* 142
  desuetude 614
  relinquish 624
  disuse 678
  —*out* 55
  —*out of one's
    calculation* 460
  —*the beaten track* 83
  —*to chance* 621
  —*to oneself* 748
  —*undecided* 609a
  —*undone* 730
  —*void regret* 833
  —*word* 527
    take—*depart* 293
    freedom 748
leaven *component* 56
  cause 153
  lighten 320
  qualify 469
  deterioration 659
  bane 663
leavings *remainder* 40
  useless 645
lecher 962
lechery 961
lectern 1000
lection *special* 79
  interpretation 522
lectionary 998
lecture *teach* 537
  speak 582
  dissertation 595
  censure 932
  sermon 998
  —*room* 542
lecturer *teacher* 540
  speaker 582
  preacher 996
lectureship 542
led—*captain
  follower* 746
  servile 886
  favorite 899
  —*by the nose* 749
ledge *height* 206

horizontal 213
  shelf 215
  projection 250
ledger *list* 86
  record 551
  accounts 811
lee *front* 234
  side 236
leech *remedy* 662
  physician 695
Lee Enfield rifle 727
leef 829
leek 401 *eat the
  —recant* 607
  submit 725
Lee–Metford rifle 727
leer *stare* 441
  dumb show 550
leery 702
lees 321, 653
**lee shore
  danger** 665, 667
leet, court—966
lee wall 666
leeward 236
leeway *tardy* 133
  space 180
  navigation 267
  progression 282
  shortcoming 304
left *residuary* 40
  sinistral 239
  —*alone* 748
  —*bower* 840
  —*in the lurch* 732
  —*to shift for oneself* 893
  over the—545
  pay over the—
    shoulder 808
left—**handed**
  clumsy 699
  —*compliment* 932
  —*marriage* 903
leg *support* 215
  walker 266
  food 298
  thief 792
  best—*foremost* 686
  fast as—*s will carry* 274
  keep on one's—*s* 654
  last—*s spoiled* 659
  fatigue 688
  —*bail* 623
  light on one's—*s* 734
  make a—894
  not a—*to stand on
  illogical* 477
  confuted 479
  failure 732
  off one's—*s
  propulsion* 284
  on one's—*s*

upright 212
  elevation 307
  speaking 582
  in health 654
  active 682
  free 748
  set on one's—*s* 660
**legacy
  transference** 270
  property 780
  gift 784
legadero 45
legal *permitted* 760
  legitimate 924
  relating to law 963
  —*adviser* 968
  —*estate* 780
  —*pledge* 535
legality 963
legalize 963
legate 534
legatee *transferee* 270
  possessor 779
  receiver 785
legation 755
legato 415
legend *record* 551
  description 594
legendary
  imaginary 515
  mythical 979
legerdemain
  change 146
  trick 545
  (*cunning* 702)
leggings 225
leghorn 225
legible 518—*hand* 590
legion *multitude* 102
  army 726
legionary 726
legislation
  government 693
  legality 963
legislative
  —*assembly* 696
legislator 694
legislature 72, 696
legist 968
legitimate *true* 494
  permitted 760
  right 922
  due 924
  legal 963
legume 298, 367
legumin 321
leguminous 365, 367
Leibnitzianism 451
leiodermatous 255
leisure *spare time* 685
  (*opportunity* 134)
  at one's—*late* 133
leisurely *slowly* 275
leman 897
lemma 476
lemon *fruit* 298

sour 397
  color 436
  —*pie* 298
lemures 980
lend 787—*a hand* 680
  —*aid* 707
  —*countenance* 707
  —*oneself to
    assent* 488
  cooperate 709
  —*on security* 789
  —*wings to* 707
lender *creditor* 805
lending 787
  —*library* 593
length 200 *at
  —in time* 133
  full—*portrait* 556
  go all—*s
    resolution* 604
  activity 682
  exertion 686
  go great—*s* 549
  —*and breadth of* 50
  —*and breadth of the
    land space* 180
  publication 531
  —*of time* 110
lengthen *increase* 35
  make long 200
  —*out diuturnity* 110
  late 133
lengthwise 200, 251
lengthy *long* 200
  diffuse 573
lenient *moderate* 174
  mild 740
  compassionate 914
lenify 174
lenitive
  moderating 174
  lubricant 332
  qualification 469
  remedy 662
  relieving 834
lenity 740
lens 445
lens—**shaped** 245
Lent *fasting* 956
  rite 998
lenten 956
lenticular *curved* 245
  convex 250
lentiginous 330, 653
lentor *slowness* 275
  spissitude 352
  inactivity 683
  (*inertness* 172)
lentous 352
Lenz's law 490d
leonine verses 597
leopard
  variegated 440
  —'s *spots
    unchanging* 150
leper *outcast* 892

lepidote 330
Leprechaun 979
leprosy 655
lerret 273
Lesbianism 945, 961
lèse–majesté 742
less *inferior* 34
  subduction 38
  —*than no time* 113
lessee *possessor* 779
  receiver 785
lessen
  —*in quantity or degree* 36
  —*in size* 195
  —*an evil* 658
lesson *teaching* 537
  warning 668
  give a—*to
    punish* 972
  read a—*to
    censure* 932
  say one's—
    memory 505
lessor 805
lest 623
let *hindrance* 706
  permit 760
  least 771
  lend 787
  sell 796
  apartments to—
    fool 499
  —*alone besides* 37
  permanence 141
  quiescence 265
  avoid 623
  disuse 678
  inaction 681
  not complete 730
  free 748
  —*be permanence* 141
  continuance 143
  inaction 681
  —*blood* 297
  —*down depress* 308
  humble 879
  —*down easily
    forgive* 918
  —*fall drop* 308
  inform 527
  speak 582
  —*fly violence* 173
  propel 284
  —*fly at* 716
  —*go neglect* 460
  liberate 750
  relinquish 782
  restitution 790
  —"*I dare not*" *wait
    upon "I would"* 605
  —*in interpose* 228
  admit 296
  trick 545
  —*into inform* 490
  disclose 529

lethal

-off *violent* 173
propel 284
permit 760
forgive 918
exempt 927a
acquit 970
-one *know* 527
-out *disperse* 73
lengthen 200
eject 297
disclose 529
liberate 750
-out at 716
-pass 460
-slip
miss an opportunity 135
neglect 460
not complete 730
lose 776
relinquish 782
-the matter stand over 133
-things take their course 143
-up *cease* 142
-well alone
content 831
caution 864
to- 763
lethal *deadly* 361
(*pernicious* 649)
-chamber 972
lethargy
inactivity 683
insensibility 823
Lethe, waters of 506
lethiferous
deadly 361
(*pernicious* 649)
letter *mark* 550
character **561**
epistle 592
-card 592
-of credit 805
-writer 592
to the- 494
letter bag 534
letter carrier 271, 534
lettered 490
letterpress 532, 591
letters *knowledge* 490
language 560
description 594
in large- 642
-of marque 791
man of- 492
lettre de créance 805
lettres de cachet 751
lettuce 298
leucoderma 430
leucopathy 430
leucophlegmatic 823
leucorrhea 299

Levant *east* 236
levant *plain* 349
abscond 623
levanter *wind* 349
defaulter 808
levée *assemblage* 72
sociality 892
-en masse 719
level *uniform* 16
equal 27
destroy 162
horizontal 213
flat 251
smooth 255
lower 308
-at *direct* 278
intend 620
attack 716
-best 686
-crossing 219
-with the ground 207
level-headed 826
lever *cause* 153
instrument 633
de rideau 599
leverage 175
leviathan 192
levigate *simpleness* 42
smoothness 255
rub down 330
levin 420, 423
-bolt 727
levirate 903
Levite 996
levitical 995
levity *lightness* 320
irresolution 605
trifle 643
jocularity 836
rashness 863
levy *muster* 72
military 726
distrain 789
demand 812
lewd 961
Lewis gun 727
lex-mercatoria 963
-scripta 697
-scripta et nonscripta 963
-talionis
retaliation 718
right 922
lexicographer 562
lexicography 562
lexicologist 492, 562
lexicology 560
lexicon *list* 86
dictionary 542, 562, 594
ley 344
liabilities 811
liability 177 *debt* 806
duty 926
liaison 961
liar 548

libadist 984
libation *potation* 298
drunkenness 959
worship 990
libel *detraction* 934
accusation 938
libelant 938, 969
libeler 936
liberal *inclusive* 76
ample 639
expending 809
generous 816
disinterested 942
-education
knowledge 490
teaching 537
over- 818
liberalism
freedom 748
liberality *giving* 784
generosity **816**
Liberals 712
liberate *deliver* 672
free 748, 750
liberation 750
(*disjunction* 44)
libertinage 961
libertine 962
libertinism 961
liberty *occasion* 134
freedom 748
permission 760
right 924
exemption 927a
at-*liberated* 750
gain one's- 750
-bonds 802
set at-*free* 750
exempt 927a
take a-*arrogate* 739
make free 748
insolence 885
discourtesy 895
libidinous 961
Libra 490a
librarian 593, 694
library *room* 191
books 593
repository 636
seclusion 893
librate 314
libration 314
-in latitude 314
-of the moon 314
libretto *book* 593
opera 599
lice 366
license *laxity* 738
permission 760
right 924
exemption 927a
-to plunder 791
licentiate 492
licentious *lax* 738
dissolute 954
debauched 961

libadist 984...
lichen 367
lich gate 363
licit *permitted* 760
due 924
lick *lap* 298
touch 379
conquer 731
punish 972
-into shape 240
-one's chops 298
-the dust 933
lickerish *savory* 394
desirous 865
fastidious 868
licentious 961
lickpenny 819
lick-spittle
servile 886
(*flatterer* 935)
licorice 396
lictor 965
lid 223
lie *situation* 183
presence 186
recline 213
falsehood 544
untruth 546
awkward at a- 544
give the-to 536
-at one's door 926
-at the root of 153
-by 681
-down *flat* 213
rest 687
-fallow 674
-hid 528
-in *be* 1
give birth 161
-in ambush 528
-in a nutshell 32
-in one's power 157
-in wait for
expect 507
inaction 681
-on 215
-over *defer* 133
destiny 152
-still 265
-to *quiescence* 265
inaction 681
-under 177
-under a necessity 601
white- 617
Liederkranz 416
Liedertafel 416
lief *pleasant* 829
as-*willing* 602
choice 609
liege 745, 746
liegeman 746
lien *security* 771
credit 805
lienteria 653
lieu 182 in-of 147
lieutenant *officer* 745

deputy 759
lord- 965
life *essence* 5
events 151
vitality **359**
biography 594
activity 682
conduct 692
cheerful 836
animal- 364
battle of- 682
come to- 660
infuse-into
excite 824
-and spirit 682
-beyond the grave 152
-or death *need* 630
important 642
contention 720
-to come 152
put-into 359
recall to- 660
see- 840
support- 359
take away- 361
tenant for- 779
Life, the 976
lifeblood *intrinsic* 5
vital 359
lifeboat *boat* 273
safety 666
life-giving 168
life guard 664, 726
lifeless *inert* 172
dead 360
lifelike 17
lifelong 110
life preserver 666, 727
life saver 664
life-size 192
lifetime 108
life-weary 841
lift *raise* 307
improvement 658
aid 707
-a finger 680
-cattle 791
-hand against 716
-one's head 734
-the mask 529
-the voice *shout* 411
speak 582
-up the eyes 441
-up the heart 990
lifting power 273
lift smoke 840
ligament 45
ligation 43
ligature 45
light *state* 7
small 32
window 260
velocity 274
arrive 292

494

lighten

descend 306
levity 320
kindle 384
match, illuminant 388
luminosity **420**
luminary 423
—*in color* 429
white 430
aspect 448
knowledge 490
interpretation 522
unimportant 643
easy 705
gay 836
loose 961
blue—*signal* 550
bring to—
discover 480a
manifest 525
disclose 529
children of—987
come to—529
false—443
foot—s 599
half—422
in one's own—699
—*and shade* 420
—*comedy* 599
—*fantastic toe* 309
—*heart* 836
—*horse* 726
—*infantry* 726
—*of heel* 274
—*of truth* 543
—*purse* 804
—*under a bushel*
hide 528
not hide 878
modesty 881
—*up illumine* 420
excite 824
cheer 836
—*upon one's feet* 664
—*upon chance* 156
arrive at 292
discover 480a
acquire 775
make—*of*
underrate 483
easy 705
inexcitable 826
despise 930
obstruct the—426
see the—*life* 359
publication 531
throw—*upon* 522
transmit—425
lighten
make light 320
illume 420
facilitate 705
lighter *boat* 273
lighterman 269
light-fingered 791, 792

light-footed *fleet* 274
active 682
light-headed 149, 503
lighthouse 550
lightless 421
light-minded 605
lightning *velocity* 274
flash 420
spark 423
omen 512
brief as the—421
—*express* 272
—*speed* 274
Light of the World 976
lightsome
luminous 420
irresolute 605
cheerful 836
lign-aloes 400
ligneous 367
lignite 388
lignography 558
ligulate 205, 245
like *similar* 17
relish 394
enjoy 827
wish 865
love 897
do what one—s 748
—*a shot* 274
—*master like man* 19
look—448
likely 470, 472
think—507
—*to* 176
likeness *copy* 21
portrait 554
bad—555
likewise 37
likin 812
liking *willingness* 602
desire 865
love 897
have a—*for* 827
to one's—829
lilac *color* 437
Liliputian 193
lilt *cheery* 836
sing 416
lily *botany* 369
white 430
beauty 845
paint the—641
lily-livered 862
lima beans 298
limae labor
improve 658
toil 686
limature
pulverulence 330
friction 331
limb *member* 51
instrument 633
scamp 949

—*of the law* 968
limber *fleet* 272
pliable 324
limbo *prison* 751, 752
pain 828
purgatory 982
lime *fruit* 298, 367
sour 397
entrap 545
limekiln 386
limelight
luminary 423
publicity 531
theater 599
limerick 497
limestone 635
limine, in—66
limit *complete* 52
end 67
circumscribe 229
boundary 233
qualify 469
completion 729
restrain 751
prohibit 761
limitarian 984
limitation (*see* limit)
estate 780, 783
limitative 8
limited
—*in quantity* 32
—*in size* 193
—*train* 272
to a—*extent*
imperfect 651
limitless 105
limn 554, 556
limner 559
limousine 272
limp *weak* 160
slow 275
supple 324
fail 732
limpid 425, 570
limy 432
lin *lake* 343
river 348
linaloa *fragrance* 400
lincture 662
linden 367
line *fastening* 45
lineage 69
continuous 69
ancestors 166
descendants 167
length 200
no breadth 203
string 205
lining 224
outline 230
straight 246
direction 278
music 26, 413
appearance 448
measure 466
mark 550

writing 590
verse 597
vocation 625
army and navy 726
between the—s 526
boundary—233
draw the—465
in a— *continuous* 69
straight 246
in a—*with* 278
—*engraving* 558
—*of action* 692
—*of battle* 69
—*of battle ship* 726
—*of march* 278
—*of road* 627
—*of steamers* 273
—*s cue* 51
read between the—s 522
sounding—208
straight—246
troops of the—726
lineage *kindred* 11
series 69
ancestry 166
posterity 167
lineament
outline 230
feature 240
appearance 448
mark 550
linear *continuity* 69
pedigree 166
length 200
linen 225, 635
linen draper 225
liner 273
lines *fortification* 717
reins 752
hard—*adversity* 735
severity 739
linger *protract* 110
delay 133
loiter 275, 291
—*on time* 106
lingo *language* 560
neology 563
linguacious 584
lingua franca 563
lingual *language* 560
speech 582
linguiform 245
linguist 492, 562
linguistic families 372a
linguistics 560, 562
lingulate 245
liniment
ointment 356
remedy 662
lining 224
link *relation* 9
connect 43
connecting—45
part 51

liqueur

term 71
crossing 219
torch 423
missing—*wanting* 53
completing 729
linkboy 694
linked together
party 712
linn 343, 348
linoleum 223, 635
linotype 591
linseed oil 356
linsey-woolsey 41, 329
linstock 388
lint 223
lintel 215
lion *animal* 366
courage 861
prodigy 872
repute 873
come in like a—173
heard—s *roar* 861
in the—s *den* 665
—*in the path* 706
—*lies down with the lamb* 721
—'s *share more* 33
chief part 50
too much 641
undue 925
lioness 374
lion-hearted 861
lionize *curiosity* 455
repute 873
lip *beginning* 66
edge 231
side 236
prominence 250
between cup and— 111
finger on the —s
silent 581
speechless 585
hang on the—s *of* 418
—*homage flattery* 933
—*service*
falsehood 544
hypocrisy 988
—*wisdom* 499
open one's—s
speak 582
seal the—s 585
smack the—*taste* 390
savory 394
lipothymy 688
lipotype 187
lippitude 443
liquation 382
liquefaction 333, **335**
—*by heat* 384
liquefy 382, 335
liquescence 335
liqueur
drink 298, 392

495

liquid   log

    sweet 396
liquid *fluid* 333
    sound 405
    letter 561
    –*diet* 298
liquidate *pay* 807
    access 812
liquidator 801
liquidity 333
liquor *potable* 298
    fluid 333
    in–959
    –*up* 959
liquorish
    (*see* lickerish)
lisp 583
lissom 324
list *arrange* 69
    catalogue 86
    strip 205
    leaning 217
    fringe 231
    hear 418
    record 551
    will 600
    choose 609
    schedule 611
    arena 728
    desire 865
    enter the–*s*
    attack 716
    contend 720
listed 440
listel 847
listen 418
    be–*ed to* 175
    –*to* 457
    –*to reason* 498
listless
    inattentive 458
    inactive 683
    indifferent 866
litany *worship* 990
    rite 998
literal *imitated* 19
    exact 494
    –*meaning* 516
    manifest 525
    letter 561
    word 562
    –*meaning* 516
    –*translation* 522
literary 560
    –*hack* 593
    –*man* 492
    –*power* 569
literati 492
literatim (*see* literal)
literature
    learning 490
    language 560
lithagogue 662
lithe 324
lithic 323
lithify 323
lithium 490b

lithograph 550, 558
lithoidal 358
lithology 358
lithomancy 511
lithotint 558
litigant *litigious* 713
    combatant 726
    accusation 938
litigation *quarrel* 713
    contention 730
    lawsuit 969
litigious 713
litotes 483
litter *disorder* 59
    derange 61
    multitude 102
    brood 167
    support 215
    vehicle 266, 272
    bedding for cattle 370
    useless 645
littérateur
    scholar 492
    author 593
Little–Bear 318
    –Mary 191
little–*in degree* 32
    –*in size* 193
    darling 897
    mean 940
    bigoted 988
    cost–815
    do–683
    –*by little degree* 26
    slowly 275
    –*did one think* 508
    –*name* 565
    –*one* 129
    make–*of* 483
    signify–643
    think–*of* 458
    to–*purpose*
    useless 645
    failure 732
littleness 193
littoral 342
liturgics 998
liturgy 998
lituus 215
live *exist* 1
    continue 141
    dwell 186
    life 359
    glowing 382
    activity 682
    repute 873
    –*again* 660
    –*and let live*
    inaction 681
    freedom 748
    inexcitability 826
    –*by one's wits* 545
    –*circuit* 157
    –*from hand to mouth* 674

    –*hard* 954
    –*in hope* 858
    –*in the memory* 505
    –*man* 682
    –*matter* 591
    –*on* 298
    –*rail* 157
    –*to explain* 485
    –*to fight again* 110
    –*upon nothing* 819
    –*wire hustler* 682
    we–*in deeds* 680
livelihood 803
liveliness (*see* lively)
livelong 110
lively *leap* 309
    keen 375
    –*style* 574
    active 682
    acute 821
    sensitive 822
    sprightly 836
    –*imagination* 515
    –*pace* 274
liver *organ* 221
    hard–954a
    white–862
liver-colored 433
livery *suit* 225
    color 428
    badge 550
    decoration 877
    –*servant* 746
liveryman 748
livid *dark* 431
    gray 432
    purple 437
living *life* 359
    business 625
    benefice 995
    good–957
    –*beings* 357
    –*room* 191
    –*soul* 372
    –*thing* 366
livraison 51, 593
livret 593
lixiviate 295, 335, 652
lixivium 335
lizard 366
    lounge–683
llama 271
llano 180, 344, 367
Lloyd's register 86
lo! *attention* 457
    wonder 870
load *quantity* 31
    fill 52
    lade 184
    cargo 190
    weight 319
    store 636
    redundance 641
    hindrance 706
    adversity 735

    anxiety 828
    oppress 830
    –*the memory* 505
    –*with* 607
    –*with reproaches* 932
    prime and–673
    take off a–*of care* 834
load line 466
loadstar (*see* lodestar)
loadstone
    attraction 288
    motive 615
    desire 865
loaf *mass* 192
    dawdle 683
    –*sugar* 396
loafer *stroller* 268
    inactive 683
    bad man 949
loafing *inaction* 681
loam 342
loan 787
loath *unwilling* 603
    dislike 867
loathe *dislike* 867
    hate 898
loathing (*see* loathe)
    weariness 841
loathsome
    unsavory 395
    painful 830
    dislike 867
loaves and fishes
    prosperity 734
    acquisition 775
    wealth 803
lobby *chamber* 191
    way 627
lobbyism 615
lobe *part* 51
    pendency 214
    –*of ear* 418
lobelia 434
lobiform 245
lob's pound, in–751
lobster 298, 368
lobule 418
local 183–*board* 696
    –*habitation*
    location 184
    abode 189
locale 183
locality 182, 183
localize 184
locate 184 *be*–*d* 183
location 182, **184**
loch 343
Lochaber ax 727
lock *fasten* 43
    fastening 45
    tuft 256
    canal 350
    hindrance 706
    prison 752
    dead–265

    in the–*up* 938
    –*hospital* 662
    –*stock and barrel* 50
    –*the stable door too late* 135
    useless 645
    unskillful 699
    –*up hide* 528
    imprison 751
    –*weir* 350
    under–*and key*
    safe 664
    restraint 751
    prisoner 754
locker 191
locket 847
lockjaw 655
lockout *exclusion* 55
    insurrection 719
locksmith 690
lockup *prison* 752
locofoco 388
locomobile 266, 272
locomotion 264
    –*by air* 267
    –*by land* 266
    –*by water* 267
locomotive *travel* 266
    carriage 271
locos y niños 450
locular 191
locum tenens
    substitute 147
    inhabitant 188
    deputy 759
locust *insect* 366
    prodigal 818
    evildoer 913
    swarm like–*s* 102
locution 566, 582
lode 636
lodestar
    attraction 288
    indication 550
    direction 693
lodestone
    (*see* loadstone)
lodge *place* 184
    presence 186
    dwelling 189
    –*a complaint* 938
lodgement 184
lodger *inhabitant* 188
    possessor 779
lodging 189
loess 490c
loft *garret* 191
    top 210
lofty *high* 206
    –*style* 574
    proud 878
    insolent 885
    magnanimous 942
log *length* 200
    velocity 274
    fuel 388

measurement 466
record 551
—*book* 551
—*canoe* 273
—*house* 189
—*line* 466
 heave the—466
 sleep like a—683
logan 314
loganberry 298
logarithm 84
logger 371
loggerhead 501 at—s
 discord 713
 contention 720
 hate 898
logic 476
—*of facts* 467
logician 476
logistics 85
logography 590
logogriph 533
logomachy
 discussion 476
 words 588
 dispute 720
logometer 85
logometric 84
Logos 976
logotype 591
logrolling 709
logy 843
loin *back* 235
 side 236
 gird up one's—s
 strong 159
 prepare 673
loin cloth 225
loiter *tardy* 133
 slow 275
 lag 281
 inactive 683
 (*temporize* 110)
Loki 978
loll *sprawl* 213
 recline 215
 inactive 683
lollipop 396
lollop 683
lolly 383
loma 206
London man 372a
lone 87
lonely 893
lonesome 893
long—*in time* 110
—*in space* 200
 typography 550
 diffuse 573
 draw the—*bow* 549
 go to one's—*account* 360
—*ago* 122
—*and the short whole* 50
 concise 572

—*but* 800
—*clothes* 129
—*drawn out* 573
—*duration* 110
—*expected* 507
—*face discontent* 832
 dejection 837
—*for* 865
—*home interment* 363
—*life to glory* 873
 approval 931
—*odds chance* 156
 improbability 473
 difficulty 704
—*pending* 110
—*pull and strong pull* 285
—*range* 196
—*robe* 968
—*run average* 29
 whole 50
 destiny 152
—*sea* 348
—*since* 122
—*time* 110
 make a—*arm exertion* 686
 seize 789
 take a—*breath refreshment* 689
 relief 834
longanimity
 inexcitable 826
 forgiving 918
longboat 273
long chair 215
longevity
 diuturnal 110
 age 128
longevous 110
longhead
 wise man 500
long-headed
 wise 498
longiloquence 573
longing 865
longinquity 196
longish 200
longitude
 situation 183
 length 200
 measurement 466
 map drawing 550
longitudinal 200
long-limbed 200
long-lived 110
longness 200
longshoreman
 waterman 269
 preparer 673
 plebeian 876
long-sighted
 dim-sighted 443
 wise 498
 foresight 518
longsomeness 573

longspun 573
long-standing
 diuturnal 110
 old 124
long-suffering
 lenity 740
 inexcitable 826
 pity 914
longways 217
long-winded 573
loo 840
looby *fool* 501
 bungler 701
 clown 876
look *small degree* 32
 see 441
 appearance 448
 attend to 457
—*about take care* 459
 seek 461
—*after care* 459
 direction 693
—*ahead* 510
—*another way* 442
—*back* 122
—*before one leaps* 864
—*behind the scenes* 461
—*beyond* 510
—*black or blue feeling* 821
 discontent 832
 dejection 837
—*down upon* 930
—*foolish* 874
—*for seek* 461
 expect 507
—*forwards future* 121
 foresight 510
—*here* 457
—*in the face sincerity* 703
 courage 861
 pride 878
—*into attend to* 457
 inquire 461
—*like similarity* 17
 appearance 448
—*on* 186
—*out care* 459
 seek 461
 expect 507
 warning 668
—*over examine* 461
—*round seek* 461
—*sharp* 682
—*through seek* 461
—*to care* 459
 duty 926
—*up prosper* 734
 high price 814
 hope 858
 visit 892
—*upon as adjudge* 480
 believe 484

—*up to repute* 873
 respect 928
 approbation 931
looker-on 444
looking
—*before and after* 441, 673
—*forward to* 507
looking-glass 445
lookout *view* 448
 intention 620
 business 625
 sentinel 668
loom *magnify* 31
 destiny 152
 dim 422
 dim sight 443
 come in sight 446
 instrument 633
 weave 691
—*large* 525
—*of the land* 342
loon *diving bird* 310
 fool 501
 clown 876
 rascal 949
loony 501
loop *curve* 245
 circle 247
 circuit 629
 looping the—267
loophole *opening* 260
 vista 441
 plea 617
 device 626
 escape 671
 fortification 717
loose *detach* 44
 incoherent 47
 pendent 214
 desultory 279
 illogical 477
 vague 519
—*style* 575
 lax 738
 free 748
 liberate 750
 debauched 961
 at a—*end* 685
 give a—*to*
—*imagination* 515
 laxity 738
 permit 760
 indulgence 954
 let—750
—*character* 961
—*fish bad man* 949
 libertine 962
—*morals* 945
—*rein* 738
—*suggestion* 514
—*thread* 495
 leave a—460
 take up a—664
 on the—961
 screw—713

loosen *make loose* 47
 let loose 750
looseness 573
loot *steal* 791
 booty 793
lop 201—*and top* 371
looped *incomplete* 53
looper 321
lop-sided 28
loquacious 562, 584
loquacity 562, **584**
lorcha 273
Lord, lord *ruler* 745
 nobleman 875
 God 976
—*Chancellor* 967
—*it over authority* 737
 insolence 885
—*Justices* 966, 967
—*lieutenant* 965
—*of Lords* 976
—*of creation* 372
—*of the manor* 779
—*of thy presence* 745
—'s *day* 687
—'s *prayer* 990
—'s *supper* 998
—'s *table* 1000
 O—*worship* 990
 the—*knows* 491
lordling 875
lordly *repute* 873
 pride 878
Lord Mayor 745
—'s *show* 883
lordship
 authority 737
 property 780
 title 877
 judge 967
lore 490, 539
lorette 962
Lorettine 996
lorgnette 445
loricated *clothed* 223
lorica 717
lorn 893
lorry 272
lose *forget* 506
 unintelligible 519
 fail 732
 loss 776
—*an opportunity* 135
—*breath* 688
—*caste disrepute* 874
 dishonor 940
—*color* 429
—*flesh* 195
—*ground slow* 275
 regression 283
 shortcoming 304
—*heart* 837
—*hope* 859
—*labor* 732
—*no time active* 682

497

losel

haste 684
—one's balance 732
—one's cunning 699
—one's head
  bewildered 475
—one's heart 897
—one's life 360
—oneself
  uncertain 475
—one's— 151
—one's reason 503
—one's temper 900
—one's way
—sight of *blind* 442
  disappear 449
  neglect 460
  oblivion 506
  not complete 730
—the clew
  uncertain 475
  unintelligible 519
—the day 732
—time 683
  wander 279
  unskillful 699
  difficulty 704
  no time to— 684
losel 893, 949
losing game
  failure 732
  misfortune 735
loss *decrement* 40a
  death 360
  evil 619
  deterioration 659
  privation **776**
  at a—uncertain 475
  at a—for
  desiring 865
—of fortune 804
—of health 655
—of life 360
—of right 925
—of strength 160
lost *nonexisting* 2
  absent 187
  invisible 449
  abstracted 458
  uncertain 475
  failure 732
  loss 776
  over-excited 824
  pain 828
  dejection 837
  impenitent 951
—in admiration 931
—in astonishment 870
—in iniquity 945
—in thought 458
—labor 645
—to shame
  insolent 885
  improbity 940
  bad man 949
—to sight 449
—to view 449
—to virtue 945

lot *state* 7
  quantity 25
  group 72
  multitude 102
  necessity 601
  chance 621
  sufficient 639
  allotment 786
  be one's— 151
  cast in one's—with
  choose 609
  cooperate 709
  cast-s 621
  fall to one's— 156
  in—s 51
  where one's—is cast 189
lota 191
loth (see loath)
Lothario *lover* 897
  libertine 962
lotion *liquid* 337
  clean 652
  remedy 662
loto 840
lotto 156, 840
lottery *chance* 156
  cards 840
  put into a— 621
lotus-eater 683
loud *noisy* 404
  unreserved 525
  bad taste 851
loudness 404
lough 343
lounge *chamber* 191
  inactive 683
  (*quiet* 275)
—lizard 683
loup garou 980
louse 653
lousiness 653
lousy 653
lout *fool* 501
  clown 876
louver 349, 351
lovable 897
love *desire* 865
  courtesy 894
  affection **897**
  favorite 899
  abode of— 897
  God's—906
  labor of—
  willing 602
  inexpensive 815
  amusement 840
  disinterested 942
—affair 897
—all trust a few 864
—of country 910
  make— 902
  no—lost 713
  not for—or money
  scarce 640
  dear 814

love knot *token* 550
loveliness (see lovely)
lovelock 256
lovelorn 898
lovely *beautiful* 845
  lovable 897
love making 902
love pot 959
lover (see love)
love-sick 897, 902
love story 897, 902
love token 897, 902
loving cup *social* 892
  courteous 894
loving-kindness 906
low *small* 32
  not high 207
—sound 405
  moo 412
  vulgar 851
  disreputable 874
  common 876
  ata-ebb small 32
  inferior 34
  depressed 308
  waste 638
  deteriorated 659
  bring- 308
  in—automobile 275
—comedy 599
—condition 876
—estimation 929
—fellow 876
—green tent 363
—life 851
—note 408
—origin 876
—price 815
—spirits 837
—tide 207
—tone *black* 431
  mutter 581
—water *low* 207
  dry 340
  insufficient 640
  poor 804
lowborn 876
low-brow
  ignorance 491
lower *inferior* 34
  decrease 36
  hang 214
  depress 207, 308
  dark 421
  dim 422
  predict 511
  sad 837
  irate 900
  sulky 901a
—case 591
—one's flag 725
—one's note 879
—orders 876
—quality 34
lowering *hanging* 214
  ominous 668

hopeless 859
lowermost 207
lowlands 207
lowliness 879
lowly 879
low-minded
  vulgar 876
  base 940
lown *fool* 501
  knave 949
lowness (see low) **207**
  humility 879
loxic 217
loxodromic 217
loy 272
loyal *obedient* 743
  observant 772
  honorable 939
lozenge 244
lubbard (see lubber)
lubber *slow* 683
  bungler 701
lubberly *huge* 192
  awkward 699
lubricant 332
lubricate *oil* 332, 355
  smooth 255
lubrication
  smooth 255
  oil **332**
lubricity *slippery* 255
  lubrication 332
  unctuous 355
  impure 961
lubricous 332
lucent 420
lucid *luminous* 420
  transparent 425
  intelligible 518
  rational 502
—style 570
—interval 502
lucidity (see lucid)
lucifer 388
Lucifer 306, 423, 978
lucimeter 445
luck *chance* 156, 621
  prosperity 734
  as—may have it 470
luckless 735
lucky *occasion* 134
  successful 731
lucrative 775
lucre *gain* 775
  wealth 803
Lucretia 960
luctation 720
lucubration 451, 590
luculent 420
lucus a non lucendo
  dissimilar 18
  misnomer 565
Luddites 712
ludibrous 840
ludicrous 853
luetic 655

lumpish

luff 267
lug *flap* 39
  pull 285
—ear 418
luggage 270, 780
—van 272
lugger 273
lugubrious 837
lukewarm
  temperate 382, 383
  torpid 823
  indifferent 866
lukewarmness
  irresolution 605
  (see lukewarm)
lull *cessation* 142
  mitigate 174
  silence 403
—by soft zephyrs 349
—to sleep 265
lullaby *moderate* 174
  song 415
  verses 597
  inactivity 683
  relief 834
lumbago 378
lumbar 235
lumber *disorder* 59
  slow 275
  store 636
  useless 645
  hindrance 706
lumbering *unfit* 647
  ugly 846
lumber house
—of books 539
lumberjack 371
lumberman 371
lumber room 191
lumbriciform 249
lumen 490d
luminary *star* 318
  light **423**
  sage 500
luminosity 420
luminous *light* 420
  intelligible 518
lummox 501
lump *whole* 50
  chief part 51
  amass 72
  mass 192
  projection 250
  weight 319
  density 321
  in the— 50
—of affection 855
—sugar 396
—sum 800
—together *join* 43
  combine 48
  assemble 72
lumper 690
lumpish (see lump)
  ignorant 493
  inactive 683

Luna — mail

ugly 846
Luna 318
lunacy 503
lunar 318
 —*caustic* 384
lunate 245
lunatic 503, 504
lunation 108
lunch 298
luncheon 298
lunge *impulse* 276
 attack 716
lungi 225
lungs *wind* 349
 loudness 404
 shout 411
 voice 580
luniform, etc. 245
lunkhead 501, 876
lupanar 961
lupine 789
Lupus 490a
lurch *incline* 217
 sink 306
 oscillation 314
 failure 732
 leave in the—
 outstrip 303
 deceive 545
 relinquish 624
 left in the—
 defeated 732
lurcher *dog* 366
lure *draw* 288
 deceive 545
 entice 615
lurid *dark* 421
 dim 422
 reddish brown 433
lurk *unseen* 447
 latent 526
 hidden 528
lurking place 530
luscious *savory* 394
 grateful 829
lush *vegetation* 365
 drunkenness 959
lushy 959
lusk 683
lusory 840
lust *desire* 865
 concupiscence 961
 —*quencher* 866
luster *brightness* 420
 chandelier 423
 glory 873
lustily *loud* 404
 exertion 686
 *cry out—*839
lustless 158
lustration
 purification 652
 atonement 952
lustrous *shining* 420
lustrum 108
lusty *strong* 159

big 192
lute *cement* 45, 46
 guitar 417
luteolous 436
luteous 436
lutescent 436
Lutheran 984
lutose 653
luxation 44
luxuriant *fertile* 168
 rank 365
 sufficient 639
luxuriate 365—*in*
 pleasure 377
 delight 827
luxurious
 pleasant 377
 delightful 829
 intemperate 954
luxury *physical*—377
 redundance 641
 enjoyment 827
 sensuality 954
 —*of doing good* 648
lycanthropy 503
lyceum 537, 542
lyddite 727
Lydford law 964
Lydian measure 415
lye 652
lying *decumbent* 213
 deceptive 544
 faithless 986
lymph *fluid* 333
 water 337
 transparent 425
lymphatic *slow* 275
 fluid 333, 337
 conduit 350
lynch 972
 —*law* 744, 964
lyncher 975
lynx 366
lynx-eyed *sight* 441
 careful 459
 intelligence 498
Lyra 490a
lyre 417
lyric *music* 415, 416
 —*poetry* 597
lyrist 597
lyssa 867

M

Mab 979
mabap 166
macadamize 255
macaroni 854
macaronic
 absurdity 497
 neology 563
 verses 597
macaroon 298
mace *weapon* 727

scepter 747
mace bearer 965
macerate 337, 354
maceration
 saturation 337
 atonement 952
 asceticism 955
 rite 998
Macheath 792
Machiavel 702
Machiavellism
 falsehood 544
 cunning 702
 dishonesty 940
machicolation
 notch 257
 fortification 717
machination
 plan 626
 cunning 702
 —*s of the devil* 619
machinator 626
machine
 automobile 272
 instrument 633
 party 712
 *be a mere—*749
machine gun 727
machinery 633
machinist
 *theatrical—*599
 workman 690
macilent 203
mackerel 298
 mottled 440
 procuress 962
 —*headed*
 —*sky* 349, 353
mackinaw 225
mackintosh 225
mackle 591
macrobiotic 110
macrocolous 200
macrocosm 318
macrogamete 357
macrology 577
mactation 991
macula 848
maculate
 unclean 653
maculation
 variegation 440
 blemish 848
mad *insane* 503
 excited 824
 (*violent* 173)
 *drive one—*900
 *go—*825
 —*after* 865
 —*with rage* 900
madam 374, 877
madbrained 503
madcap *violent* 173
 lunatic 504
 excitable 825
 buffoon 844
 rash 863

madder *color* 434
made—*man* 734
 —*to one's hand* 673
madefaction 339
madid 339
madman 504
madness (see *mad*)
Madonna *good* 948
 angel 977
 pious 987
madrigal *music* 415
 verses 597
madstone 993
Maecenas *friend* 890
Maelstrom *whirl* 312
 water 348
 pitfall 667
maestro 415
maffick *exult* 884
magazine *record* 551
 book 593
 store 636
 —*rifle* 727
Magdalen 950
mage 994
Magellanic Clouds
 490a
magenta 434, 437
maggot *little* 193
 fancy 515
 caprice 608
 desire 865
maggoty *fanciful* 515
 capricious 608
 unclean 653
 —*headed*
 excitable 825
Magi *sage* 500
 sect 984
magic *influence* 175
 prediction 511
 sorcery 992
 —*lantern*
 instrument 445
 show 448
magician 548, 994
magilp 356a
magisterial
 proud 878
 insolent 885
magistery 330
magistracy
 authority 737
 jurisdiction 965
magistrate *safety* 664
 ruler 745
 justiciary 967
magistrature 737
magma 41, 490a
Magna Charta 769
magnanimity 942
magnate 875
magnet *attract* 288
 desire 865
magnetic
 powerful 157

magnetism
 power 157
 influence 175
 attraction 288
 motive 615
 *animal—*992
magnetite 288
magnetize *power* 157
 influence 175
 attraction 288
 motive 615
 conjure 992
magneto
 automobile 272
magneto-electricity
 157
magnetometer 157
magnetomotive 157
magnetoscope 157
magnificent
 large 192
 fine 845
 grand 882
 (*magnanimous* 942)
magnifico 875
magnifier 445
magnify *increase* 35
 enlarge 194
 overrate 549
 approve 931
 praise 990
magniloquent
 language 577
 boast 884
magnitude
 quantity 25
 greatness 31
 size 192
magnolia 367
magnum bonum 618
Magnus Apollo 500
magpie 584
magsman 792
maharajah 745, 875
maharani 745, 875
mahat 450
mahatma 450, 700
mahlstick 215
mahogany *color* 433
maid *girl* 129
 servant 631, 746
 spinster 904
 —*of honor* 890, 903
maidan 344, 371
maiden *first* 66
 girl 129
 punishment 975
 —*meditation* 451
 —*speech* 66
maidenhood 904
maidenly 374
maiger *fasting* 956
mail *post* 270, 534
 armor 717
 —*bag* 534
 —*boat* 534

mailable

-car 272
-coach 272
-steamer 273
-train 534
mailable 270
mailer 534
maim *cripple* 158
  injure 659
main *tunnel* 260
  ocean 341
  land 342
  conduit 350
  principal 642
  in the-
  intrinsically 5
  greatly 31
  on the whole 50
  principally 642
  -chance *chance* 156
  good 618
  important 642
  profit 775
  look to the-*chance*
  foresight 510
  skill 698
  economy 817
  caution 864
  selfish 943
  -force *strength* 159
  violence 173
  compulsion 744
  -part 31, 50
  plow the-267
  with might and-686
Maine law 761
mainland 342
mainmast 206
mainpernor 771
mainprise 771
mainspring
  cause 153
  instrument 633
  (*motive* 615)
mainstay *support* 215
  refuge 666
  hope 858
maintain
  permanence 141
  continue 143
  sustain 170
  support 215
  assert 535
  preserve 670
  -one's course
  presevere 604a
  -one's ground 717
  -the even tenor of
    one's way 623
maintenance
  (*see* maintain)
  wealth 803
maintien 692
maison de santé 662
maize 367
majestic *grand* 31
  glorious 873

stately 882
majesty *king* 745
  rank 873
  deity 976
major *greater* 33
  officer 745
  -domo *director* 694
  retainer 746
  -general 745
  -key 413
  -part *great* 31
  all 50
majority
  superiority 33
  plurality 100
  multitude 102
  age 131
  join the-360
majuscalae 561
make *constitute* 54, 56
  render 144
  produce 161
  form 240
  arrive at 292
  complete 729
  compel 744
  create 976
  -acquainted with
  inform 527
  learn 539
  -after 622
  -a fuss
  importance 642
  activity 682
  -a go of it 731
  -a piece of work 832
  -a present 784
  -a push 682
  -a requisition
  demand 741
  ask for 765
  -a speech 582
  -a splurge 882
  -away with
  destroy 162
  kill 361
  -a wry face 867
  -believe 544, 545,
    546
  -choice of 609
  -fast 43
  -for 278
  -fun of *wit* 842
  ridicule 856
  -good
  compensation 30
  complete 52, 729
  establish 150
  evidence 467
  demonstrate 478
  provide 637
  restore 660
  -haste 684
  -hay while the sun
    shines 134
  -interest 765

-its appearance 446
-known 527
-light of
  underestimate 483
  easy 705
-love 902
-money 775
-much of
  exaggerate 549
  importance 642
-no doubt 484
-no secret of 525
-no sign *latent* 526
  hidden 528
-nothing of
  unintelligible 519
  not wonder 871
-off *run away* 623
  escape 671
-off with 791
-oneself master of
  539
-one's escape 671
-one's fortune 734
-one's mouth water
  298
-one's way *go on* 302
  prosper 734
-one's word 772
-out *see* 441
  evidence 467
  demonstrate 478
  discover 480a
  know 490
  intelligible 518
  interpret 522
  due 924
-over *transfer* 783
  give 784
-peace 723, 724
-public 531
-ready 673
-sure *stable* 150
  prepare 673
-terms 769
-the best of 725
-the land 292
-things pleasant 702
-time 110
-towards 278
-up
  (*see below*)
-use of 677, 788
-way *progress* 282
  (*improve* 658)
-way for
  substitution 147
  avoid 623
maker *artificer* 690
  (*producer* 164)
Maker, the-976
makeshift
  substitute 147
  excuse 617
make up *complete* 52
  compose 54

printing 591
-accounts 811
-a quarrel 723
-a sum 809
-for 30
-matters 952
-one's mind
  judgment 480
  belief 484
  resolve 604
-to approach 286
  address 586
make-up
  composition 54
  printing 591
  book 593
makeweight
  inequality 28
  compensation 30
  completeness 52
making be the-of
  utility 644
  goodness 648
  aid 707
malachite 435
malacology 368
maladministration
  699
maladroit 699
malady 655
mala fides 940
malaise
  bodily pain 378
  mental pain 828
malapert 885, 887
malappropriate 24
Malaprop, Mrs.-565
Malapropism 495
mal à propos
  discordant 24
  inopportune 135
malaria
  unhealthy 657
  poison 663
malarial fever 655
Malay 372a
malconformation
  243
malcontent
  opposition 710
  discontent 832
male *strong* 159
  man 373
  -animal 373
  -flirt 902
malediction 908
malefaction 947
malefactor 949, 975
malefic 649
maleficent 907
  -being 913
malevolence 907
malfeasance 647
malfeasor 913
malformation
  distortion 243

man

(*ugliness* 846)
malformed 241
malgre 179
malice *hate* 898
  spite 907
  bear-*revenge* 919
  -prepense 907
malign *bad* 649
  malevolent 907
  detract 934
malignant 649, 901a,
  907
malignity 173, 907
malinger 544, 548,
  655
malison 908
malkin *mop* 652
  slattern 653
mall *walk* 189
  opening 260
  club 276
malleable *soft* 324
  (*facile* 705)
mallet 276
malleus 418
malnutrition 655
malodor 401
malpractice 974
malt liquor 298
maltreat
  injure 649
  aggrieve 830
  molest 907
malversation
  rapacious 819
  guilt 947
mamelon 250
Mameluke 726
mamma 166
mammal 366, 368
mammalogy 368
mammiform 250
mammilla 250
Mammon 803
mammoth 192
man *adult* 131
  mankind 372
  male **373**
  prepare 673
  workman 690
  defend 717
  servant 746
  courage 861
  husband 903
  make a-of *good* 648
  brave 861
  -among men 948
  -and a brother 372
  -and wife 903
  -at-arms 726
  -in office 745
  -in the street 876
  -of action 682, 686
  -of letters 271
  -of straw 545, 746
  -'s estate 131

manacle — marker

one's–of business 758
 Son of–976
 to a–488
manacle *restraint* 751
 fetter 752
manage *influence* 175
 direct 693
 –to *succeed* 731
manageable *easy* 705
management
 conduct 692
 skill 698
manager *stage*–599
 director 694
managery 693
man bird 269
mancipation 751
manciple 637
mandamus 741
mandarin 745
mandate
 requirement 630
 command 741
mandible 298
mandola 417
mandolin 417
mandragora 174
mandrel 312
manducation 298
mane 256
man-eater 361
manège *riding* 266
 equestration 370
manes 362
maneuver
 operation 680
 stratagem 702
 (*scheme* 626)
manful *strong* 159
 resolute 604
 brave 861
mange 380, 655
manger 191
mangle *separate* 44
 smooth 255
 injure 659
mangled 53
 (see mangle)
mango 298
mangosteen 298
mangy 380, 655
man hater 911
manhood 131, 861
mania *insanity* 503
 desire 865
 –a *potu* 959
maniac 504
Manichaeism 451, 978
manichord 417
manicure 662
manie 865
manifest *list* 86
 visible 446
 obvious 525

disclosure 529
 (*appear* 448)
 (*intelligible* 518)
manifestation 525
manifesto 531
manifold
 multiform 81
 multitude 102
 automobile 272
 writing 590
 –*linguist* 492
manikin *dwarf* 193
 image 554
manipulate
 handle 379
 use 677
 conduct 692
manito 993
mankind 372
manlike 131
manly *adolescent* 131
 strong 159
 male 373
 brave 861
 upright 939
manna *food* 396
 –in the wilderness
 aid 707
 pleasing 829
mannequin 554
manner *kind* 75
 style 569
 way 627
 conduct 692
 by all–of means 536
 by no–of means 602
 in a–32
 to the–born 5
mannered 579
mannerism
 special 79
 unconformity 83
 affectation 855
 vanity 880
mannerly 894
manners *breeding* 852
 politeness 894
man-of-war
 ship 273, 664
 combatant 726
man-of-war's man 269
manometer 490d
manor 780
 lord of the–779
 –house 189
manorial 780
mansard 223
 –roof 244
manse 1000
mansion 189
manslaughter 361
mansuetude 894
mantelpiece 215

mantilla 225
mantle *spread* 194
 dress 225
 foam 353
 shade 424
 redden 434
 robes 747
 flush 821, 824
 anger 900
mantlet *cloak* 225
 defense 717
mantology 511
manual *guide* 527
 schoolbook 542
 book 593
 advice 695
 –*labor* 686
manubial 793
manufactory 691
manufacture 161, 680
manufacturer 690
manu forti 604, 686, 739
manumission 750
manumotor 272
manure
 agriculture 371
 dirt 653
 aid 707
manuscript 21, 590
many 102
 frequency 136
 for–a day 110
 –irons in the fire 682
 –men many minds 489
 –times *repeated* 104
 frequent 136
 the–876
many-colored 428, 440
manyplies 191
many-sided
 multiform 81
 sides 236
many-tongued 532
map *information* 527
 representation 554
 –of days outworn 236
 –out 626
maple 367–sugar 396
 –syrup 396
mar *deface* 241
 spoil 659
 botch 699
 obstruct 706
marabou 41
Marabout 1000
marah 395
maranatha 908
marasmus
 shrinking 195
 atrophy 655
 deterioration 659

Marathon race 274
maraud 791
marauder 792
marble *ball* 249
 hard 323
 sculpture 557
 tablet 590
 materials 635
 insensible 823
marble–constant 939
marbled 440
marble-hearted 907
marcescence 659
march *region* 181
 journey 266
 progression 282
 music 415
 dead–363
 forced–684
 –against 716
 –of events 151
 –off 293
 –of intellect
 knowledge 490
 improvement 658
 –of time 109
 –on a point 278
 –past 882
 –with 199
 on the–264
 steal a–*advance* 280
 go beyond 303
 deceive 545
 cunning 702
March, Ides of–601
marches 233
marchioness 875
marchpane 298
marcid 203
marconigram 532
marcor 203
Mardi gras 840
mare *horse* 271
 female 374
marechal 745
mare's–nest 497, 546
mare's–tail *wind* 349
 cloud 353
margin *space* 180
 edge 231
 redundance 641
 latitude 748
marginate 231
margrave *master* 745
 nobility 875
Maria 490a
mariage de convenance 903
marigraph 348
marinate 337
marine *fleet* 273
 sailor 269
 oceanic 341
 safety 664

soldier 726
 –*painter* 559
 –*painting* 556
 tell it to the–s 497
mariner 269
Marinism 579
Mariolatry 991
marionette
 representation 554
 drama 599
marish 345
marital 903
maritime
 navigation 267
 ship 273
 oceanic 341
mark *degree* 26
 term 71
 take cognizance 450
 attend to 457
 measurement 466
 indication 550
 record 551
 writing 590
 object 620
 importance 642
 repute 873
 beyond the–303
 leave one's–873
 man of–*repute* 873
 rank 875
 –of Cain 550
 –off 551
 –of recognition 894
 –out *choose* 609
 plan 626
 command 741
 –time
 chronometry 114
 halt 265
 expectation 507
 –with a red letter 883
 –with a white stone 931
 near the–197
 overshoot the–699
 put a–upon 457
 save the–870
 up to the–
 enough 639
 good 648
 skill 698
 due 924
 wide of the–
 distant 196
 error 495
 within the–304
marked (see mark)
 great 31
 special 79
 affirmed 535
 in a–degree 31
 –down *cheap* 815
 well–446
marker *interment* 363

market   **matter**

market *provision* 637
  consumer 677
  buy 795
  mart 799
  bring to–796
  buy in the cheapest etc.–794
  in the–*offered* 763
  barter 794
  sale 796
  –*garden* 371
  –*overt manifest* 525
  –*place street* 189
  mart 799
  –*price* 812
  public–637
  rig the–794
marketable 794, 796
marksman 700
marksmanship 698
marl 342
marmalade 396
marmoreal 430
marmot 683
maroon *brown* 433
  red 434
  fugitive 623
  abandon 782
  outlaw 893
marplot *bungler* 701
  obstacle 706
  malicious 913
marque, letters of– 791
marquee 223
marquetry
  variegated 440
marquis 875
marquisate 877
marriable 131
marriage 903
  ill–*assorted*–904
  –*bell* 836
  –*broker* 903
marriageable
  adolescent 131
  nubile 903
married 903
  –*man* 903
  –*woman* 903
marrow *essence* 5
  interior 221
  central 222
  (*meaning* 516)
  (*importance* 642)
  chill to the–385
marrowbones, one's
  – *submit* 725
  beg 765
  humble 879
  servile 886
  atonement 952
marrowless 158
Marrubium 400
marry *combine* 48
  assertion 535

wed 903
–*come up*
defiance 715
anger 900
censure 932
Mars 722–*orange* 439
marsh 345–*gas* 663
marshal *arrange* 60
  messenger 534
  auxiliary 711
  officer 745
Marshalsea 752
marshy 345
marsupial 191, 368
mart 799
martello tower 206, 717
martial 722
  court–966
  –*law severe* 739
  compulsory 744
  illegal 964
  –*music* 415
martinet 739
martingale 752
Martinmas 998
martyr
  bodily pain 378
  mental pain 828
  ascetic 955
  punishment 972
  –*to disease* 655
martyrdom
  killing 361
  agony 378, 828
  unselfish 942
  punishment 972
marvel *wonder* 870
  prodigy 872
  –*whether* 514
marvelous *great* 31
  wonderful 870
  deal in the–549
Masaniello 742
mascot 621, 993
masculine *strong* 159
  male 373
mash *mix* 41
  disorder 59
  soft 324
  semiliquid 352
  pulpiness 354
masher 854
masjid 1000
mask *dress* 225
  shade 424
  concealment 528
  ambush 530
  deceit 545
  shield 717
  put on the–544
masked *concealed* 528
  –*battery* 667
masker 599
masochism 659
mason 690

Masonic 712
Masorah 985
masque 599
masquerade
  dress 225
  concealment 528
  deception 545
  frolic 840
  –*dress* 530
masquerader 528
Mass *worship* 990
  Eucharist 998
  –*book* 998
mass *quantity* 25
  much 31
  whole 50
  heap 72
  size 192
  gravity 319
  density 321
  in the–50
  –*of society* 876
massacre 361
massage 324, 331, 379, 662
masses, the–876
masseur 331, 662
massicot 436
massive *huge* 192
  heavy 319
  dense 321
mast 206
mastaba 363
master, Master
  boy 129
  influence 175
  man 373
  know 490
  understand 518
  learn 539
  teacher 540
  director 694
  proficient 698, 700
  succeed, conquer 731
  ruler 745
  possession 777
  possessor 779
  title 877
  eye of the–693
  hard–739
  –*hand* 700
  –*key open* 260
  instrument 631
  –*mariner* 269
  –*mind sage* 500
  proficient 700
  –*of Arts* 492
  –*of one's time* 685
  –*of self* 604
  –*of the position* 731
  –*of the revels* 840
  –*of the Rolls recorder* 553
  judge 967
  –*of the situation success* 731

authority 737
–*one's feelings* 826
–*one's passions* 944
–*passion* 820
–*spirit of the age sage* 500
repute 873
past–700
masterdom 737
masterpiece *good* 648
  perfect 650
  skill 698
masterstroke
  plan 626
  masterpiece 650
  success 731
masterwork 698
mastery *success* 731
  authority 737
  get the–*of* 175
masthead *punish* 972
mastic *viscid* 352
  resin 356a
masticate 298, 354
mastiff 366
mastology 368
mat *support* 215
  woven 219
  roughness 256
  doormat 652
matador 361
match *similar* 17
  copy 19
  equal 27
  fuel 388
  retaliate 718
  contest 720
  marriage 903
matchless *unequal* 28
  supreme 33
  virtuous 944
  best 648
  (*perfect* 650)
matchlock 727
matchmaker
  marriage 903
mate *similar* 17
  equal 27
  duality 89
  auxiliary 711
  master 745
  friend 890
  wife 903
  check–732
maté 298
mater, *alma*–542
  –*familias* 166
material
  substance 316
  stuff 635
  important 642
  –*existence* 316
  –*for thought* 454
  –*point* 32
materialism
  matter 316

heterodoxy 984
irreligion 989
materiality
  substantiality 3
  matter 316
  importance 642
materialization
  materiality 316
  manifestation 525
  spiritualism 992a
materialize 316, 446
materials 635
materia medica 662
matériel 316, 633
maternal
  parental 166
  benevolent 906
  –*love* 897
maternity 166
mathematical
  precise 494
  –*point* 193
mathematician 85
mathematics 25
mathesis 25
matin 125
matinée 892
  –*idol* 899
matins 125, 990
matrass 191
matriarch 166
matriarchy 737
matriculate 539
matrimonial 903
  –*agency* 903
matrimony
  mixture 41
  wedlock 903
matrix *mold* 22
  printing 591
  workshop 691
matron *woman* 374
  married 903
  –*of honor marriage* 903
matronize 459, 693
matronly *age* 128
  adolescent 131
matross 726
matter *substance* 3
  copy 21
  material world 316
  topic 454
  meaning 516
  printing 591
  business 625
  importance 642
  pus 653
  in the–*of* 9
  –*in dispute* 461
  –*in hand topic* 454
  business 625
  –*nothing* 643
  –*of course conformity* 82
  certain 474

matter-of-fact   Meistersinger

habitual 613
—of fact *event* 151
  certainty 474
  truth 494
—of indifference 866
—of no consequence 4
—s *affairs* 151
  no— 460
  the wreck of— 59
  what— 643
  what's the—
  curiosity 455
  inquiry 461
matter-of-fact
  prosaic 576
  artless 703
  dull 843
mattock 253
mattress 215
maturate 650, 673
maturative 662
mature *old* 124
  adolescent 131
  conversion 144
  scheme 626
  perfect 650
  improve 658
  prepare 673
  completing 729
  —*thought* 451
Maturine 996
maturity (see mature)
  bring to— 729
matutinal
  morning 125
  (*early* 132)
matzo 298
maudlin *inactive* 683
  sentimental 822
  drunk 959
mauger 30, 179
maukin 652
maul *hammer* 276
  hurt 649
  —and wedges 780
maund *basket* 191
  mumble 583
maunder
  diffuse style 573
  mumble 583
  loquacity 584
  lament 839
Maundy Tuesday 138
Maurolycus 490a
Mauser rifle 727
mausoleum 363
mauvais—*goût* 851
  —quart d'heure 828
  —sujet 949
  —ton 851
mauve 437
mavis 366, 416
maw 191
mawkish 391

mawworm
  deceiver 548
  sham piety 988
maxim 80, **496**
maximal 33
Maxim gun 727
maximum
  supreme 33
  summit 210
may be 470 *as it—* 156
May Day 840
May fly 111
mayhap 470
mayor 745
maypole 206
May queen 847
mazard 298
maze *convolution* 248
  enigma 533
  difficulty 704
  (*ignorance* 491)
  in a—*uncertain* 475
mazed 503
mazurka 840
mazy 533
me 317
mead *plain* 344
  field 367
  sweet 396
meadow *plain* 344
  —*land* 371
meager *small* 32
  incomplete 53
  thin 203
  —*style* 575
  scanty 640
  poor 643
  —*diet* 956
meal *repast* 298
  powder 330
mealy-mouthed
  falsehood 544
  servile 886
  flattering 933
mean *average* **29**
  small 32
  middle 68
  interjacent 228
  signify 516
  intend 620
  contemptible 643
  stingy 819
  shabby 874
  ignoble 876
  sneaking 886
  base 940
  selfish 943
  golden— 174
  —*nothing* 517
  —*parentage* 876
  —*wretch* 949
  take the— 774
meander
  convolution 248
  deviate 279
  circuition 311

  river 348
  maze 533
meandering
  diffuse 573
meaning 516
meaningless 517
meanness
  inferiority 34
  (see mean)
means *appliances* **632**
  property 780
  wealth 803
  by all— 602
  by any— 632
  by no— 536
  —of access 627
  —of recognition 550
mean-spirited 481
meantime 106
meanwhile 106
measles 655
measurable 466
  within—*distance* 470
measure *extent* 25
  degree 26
  moderation 174
  music 413
  compute 466
  verse 597
  proceeding 626
  action 680
  apportion 786
  angular— 244
  full— 639
  —of inclination 217
  out of— 641
  without— 641
measured
  moderate 174
  sufficient 639
  temperate 953
measureless 105
  in—*content* 831
measurement 25, 466
measures
  have no—with 713
  —of length 200
  take—*plan* 626
  prepare 673
  conduct 692
meat 298 *broken—* 645
mecate 975
mechanic 690
mechanical
  automatic 601
  machinery 633
  —*powers* 633
  —*record* 551
mechanician 268, 690
mechanics 276, 490a
mechanism 633
medaglia 235
medal *record* 551
  sculpture 557

  palm 733
  decoration 877
medalist 700
medallion 557
meddle 682
meddlesome 706
Medes and Persians, law of the—
  rule 80
  permanent 141
medial 29, 68, 228
mediant 413
mediary *agent* 690
mediastinum 228
mediate *concord* 714
  (see mediation)
mediation *agency* 170
  instrumentality 631
  intercession 724
  deprecation 766
  Christ 976
Mediator
  Saviour 976
mediator 524, 711, 714
medical 662
  —*attendant* 662
  —*student* 662
medicament 662
medicaster 548
medicate
  compound 41
  heal 660
medicine 662
  —*man* 548, 994
mediety *middle* 68
  (*central* 222)
medieval 124
medievalism 122
mediocrity
  average 29
  smallness 32
  imperfect 651
  —of fortune **736**
meditate
  think 450, 451
  contemplate 620
meditation 451
mediterranean
  middle 68
  interjacent 228
medium *mean* 29
  middle 68
  atmosphere 227
  interjacent 228
  color 428
  spiritualism 450
  oracle 513
  instrument 631
  agent 690
  mediocre 736
  seer 992a
  transparent— 425
mediumship 450
medley
  mixture 41, 42

  disorder 59
  music 415
  chance— 156
medullary 324
meed *apportion* 786
  reward 973
  —of praise 931
meek *gentle* 826
  humble 879
meet *agreement* 23
  assemble 72
  touch 199
  converge 290
  arrive 292
  expedient 646
  fulfill 772
  proper 924
  make both ends—
  wealth 803
  economy 817
  —half way *willing* 602
  concord 714
  pacification 723
  mediation 724
  compromise 774
  friendship 888
  benevolence 906
  —hand to hand 720
  —in front 861
  —one at every turn
  present 186
  redundant 641
  —one's death 360
  —one's expenses 817
  —one's wishes
  consent 762
  pleasurable 829
  —the ear 418
  —the eye 446
  —with *event* 151
  find 480a
  —with attention 457
  unable to make both ends—
  poverty 804
  not pay 808
meeting (see meet)
  junction 43
  hostile— 720
  —of minds 23
  place of— 74
meetinghouse
  hall 189
  chapel 1000
megacosm 318
Megaera 173
megalomania 482
megaphone 404, 418
megascope 445
megatherium 124
megilp 356a
megrims *fits* 315
  pain 378
  melancholy 837
mehtar 652
Meistersinger 597

melancholia
  insanity 503, 821a
  dejection 837
melancholy
  distressing 830
  dejection 837
  away with–836
Melanesian 431
mélange 41
melée *disorder* 59
  contention 720
Melibean 597
melic 413
melinite 727
meliorate 658
melliferous
  sweet 396
mellifluous
  music 413
  –language 478
mellow *old* 128
  grow into 144
  soft 324
  sound 413
  color 428
  improve 658
  prepare 673
  tipsy 959
melodeon 417
melodic 415
melodious 413
melodist 416
melodrama 599, 824
melody 413
Melpomene 599
melt *vanish* 111
  convert 144
  liquefy 335
  heat 382
  fuse 384
  pity 914
  –away cease to exist 2
  unsubstantial 4
  decrease 36
  disappear 449
  waste 638
  –in the air 405
  –into one 48
  –into tears 839
  –the heart 914
melting pot 691
member *part* 51
  component 56
  mankind 372
  councilor 696
  –of the cast 372
membranaceous 204
membrane 204
membranous 204
memento 505
memoir 594, 595
memorabilia
  affairs 151
  reminiscences 505
  important 642
memorable 151, 642

memorandum
  memory 505
  record 551
  system 626
  conditions 770
  –book 551, 590
  compendium 596
memorial record 551
Memorial Day 138, 840
memorialist 553
memorialize 505
memorials 594
memoriam, in–
  tomb 363
  memory 505
memoria technica 505
memory 505
  store 636
  fame 873
  *alive in–*506
  *failing–*506
  in the–of man 122
  –runneth not to the contrary 124
  *short–*506
memsahib 374, 875
men–*may come* 348
menace 909
ménage 692
menagerie
  collection 72
  animals 370
  store 636
mend *improve* 658
  repair 660
  –one's fences 723
  –one's manners 894
mendacity 544
mendicancy
  begging 765
  poverty 804
mendicant
  beggar 765, 767
  poor 804
  monk 996
mendicity 804
menhir 372a
menial *servant* 746
  rustic 876
meniscal 245
meniscus 245, 445
menses 138, 299
menstrual 138
menstruum 335
mensuration 466
mental 450
  –acquisitiveness 455
  –calm 826
  –cultivation 539
  –excitement 824
  –healing 984
  –pabulum 454
  –philosophy 450

  –poise 498
  –reservation 528, 543
  –suffering 828
mentality 450
mentalize 451
mentation 451
menticulture 490, 658
mention 527
  above–ed 104
  not worth–ing 543
mentor *sage* 500
  teacher 540
  adviser 695
mentum 234
menu *list* 86
  food 298
Mephistopheles 978
Mephistophelian 945
mephitic *fetid* 401
  deleterious 654
mephitis 663
meracious 392
mercantile 794
mercatoria, lex–963
mercature 794
mercenary
  soldier 726
  servant 746
  price 812
  parsimonious 819
  selfish 943
mercer 225
merchandise **798**
merchant **797**
merchantable 795
merchantman 273
merciful 914
merciless 914a
mercurial
  changeable 149
  mobile 264
  quick 274
  excitable 825
mercurous chloride 662
Mercury *traveler* 268
  quick 274
  messenger 534
  –'s rod 747
mercy *lenity* 740
  pity 914
  at the–of liable 177
  subject 749
  *cry you–*766
  for–'s sake 765
  *have no–*914a
  –on us! 870
  –seat 966
mere *simple* 32
  lake 343
  trifling 643
  buy for a–nothing 815
  –nothing small 32
  trifle 643

  –pretext 617
  –words 477
  –wreck 659
merelles 840
meretricious
  false 495
  vulgar 851
  licentious 961
merge *combine* 48
  include 76
  insert 300
  plunge 337
  –in 56
  –into become 144
merged 228
merger 712
meridian *region* 181
  room 125
  summit 210
  light 420
  map drawing 550
  –of life 131
meridional 125, 237
meringue 298
merit *goodness* 648
  due 924
  virtue 944
  make a–of 884
  –notice 642
merito, e–944
meritorious 931
mermaid *monster* 83
  ocean 341
  mythology 979
merman 341
meroblast 357
merogenesis 161
merriment
  cheerful 836
  amusement 840
merry *cheerful* 836
  drunk 959
  make–sport 840
  make–with wit 842
  ridicule 856
  –and wise 842
  –as the day is long 836
  –heart 836
  wish a–Christmas etc. 896
merry-andrew 844
merry-go-round 840
merrymaking
  revel 840
  sociality 892
merrythought 842, 993
mersion 337
mesa 344
mésalliance
  ill–assorted 24
  marriage 903
meseems 484
mesh *interstices* 198

  crossing 219
meshes *trap* 545
  difficulty 704
  –of sophistry 477
mesial *middle* 68
  (central 222)
mesilla 344
mesmerism 992
mesmerist 992a
mesne 228–*lord* 779
mesoblast 357
mesocephalic index 372a
mesons 490d
Mesozoic Era 490c
mess *mixture* 41
  disorder 59
  derangement 61
  meal 298
  difficulty 704
  portion 786
  make a–
  –unskillful 699
  fail 732
message *dispatch* 527
  intelligence 532
  command 741
Messalina 962
messenger
  traveler 268
  cloud 353
  envoy **534**
  servant 746
  –balloon 463
Messiah 976
messmate 890
messuage 189, 780
mestee 41
mestizo 41
metabatic 264
metabola 140
metabolism 140, 357
metabolize 140
metacenter 222
metachronism 115
metage 466
metagenesis 140
metagrammatism 561
metal 635
  *Britannia–*545
metalepsis 521
metallic *harsh* 410
metallurgy 358
metamorphosis 140
metamorphotic 81
metaphor
  comparison 464
  figure **521**
  (analogy 17)
metaphrase 522
metaphrast 524
metaphrastic 516
metaphysics 450
metaplasm 357
metasomatism 140

metastasis
  change 140
  inversion 218
  displacement 270
metathesis
  change 140
  inversion 218
  displacement 270
  metaphor 521
mete *measure* 466
  distribute 786
  —out *give* 784
metempirical 519
metempsychosis 140
meteor
  heavenly body 318, 353
  luminary 423
meteoric
  transient 111
  violent 173
  light 420
meteorite 318
meteorology 338, 353
meteoromancy 466
meter *length* 200
  measure 333, 466
  versification 597
methane 663
metheglin 396
methinks 484
method *order* 58
  way **627**
  want of— 59
methodical
  arranged 60
  regular 80, 138
  businesslike 692
Methodist 984
methodist
  formalist 988
methodize 58, 60
Methuselah 130
  old as— 128
  since the days of— 124
metic 57
meticulosity 457, 459, 868
meticulous *exact* 494
  observant 772
  fastidious 868
métis 83
metogenesis 161
metonymy 521
metopic 234
metoposcopist 234, 448
metoposcopy
  front 234
  appearance 448
  interpret 522
metrical
  measured 466
  verse 597
metrocracy 737

metrology 466
metropolis 189, 222
metropolitan
  archbishop 996
mettle *energy* 171
  spirit 820
  courage 861
  man of— 861
  on one's—
    resolved 604
  put on one's—
    excite 824
    encourage 861
mettlesome
  energetic 171
  sensitive 822
  excitable 825
  brave 861
meum et tuum 777, 780
  disregard distinction between— 791
mew *molt* 226
  cry 412
  —up 751
mewed up 229
mewl 412
mews 189
mezzanine floor
  house 191
  theater 599
Mezzofanti 492
mezzo rilievo
  convex 250
  sculpture 557
mezzotint 259, 421, 558
miasm 663
miasma 663
mica 527
micaceous 204
mi-careme 840
Micawber 460
Michaelmas 998
mickle 31
Micomicon 519
microbe 193
microbic 193
microcosm 193
microgamete 357
micrography 193
micrometer 193
micromorph 193
micron 193
microörganism 193
microphone 418
microphyte 193
microscope *little* 193
  vision 441
  optics 445
microscopic 32, 193
microspore 357
microzoa 193
microzyme 193
mid 68
Midas 803

mid-course 29, **628**
midday 125
midden 653
middle—*in degree* 29
  —*in order* **68**
  —*in space* 222
  interjacent 228
  —age 131
  —classes 736
  —constriction 203
  —course 628
  —man *director* 694
    agent 758
  —state 29
  —term 68
  compromise 774
middle-aged 131
middleman 328
middlemost 222
middling *small* 32
  imperfect 651
  mediocre 736
middy 269
  —blouse 225
Midgard 318
midge 193
midland 342
midmost 68
midnight
  night 126
  dark 421
  —blue 438
  —oil 539
midriff *middle* 68
  interjacence 228
midshipman 269
midships 68
midst—*in order* 68
  central 222
  interjacent 228
  in the—of
    mixed with 41
    doing 680
midsummer 125
  —day 138
midway 68, 628
midwife
  instrument 631
  remedy 662
midwifery
  production 161
  surgery 662
mien 448
miff 900
might *power* 157
  violence 173
  energy 686
mightless 158
mighty *much* 31
  strong 159
  large 192
  haughty 878
mignonette 435
migraine 378
migrate 266
mikado 745

milch cow
  productive 168
  animal 366
  store 636
mild *moderate* 174
  warm 382
  insipid 391
  lenient 740
  calm 826
  courteous 894
milden 324
mildew *dirt* 653
  bane 663
mildewed *spoiled* 659
mile 200
mileage 200, 973
  —ticket 550
milestone 50
  whistle jigs to a— 645
militant 722
military 722 *warfare*
  soldiers 726
  —authorities 745
  —band 416, 417
  —education 537
  —power 737
  —school 542
  —time 132
  —train 726
militate against 708
militia 664, 726
milk *moderate* 174
  semiliquid 352
  —cows 370
  white 430
  mild 740
  flow with—and honey *plenty* 639
  prosperity 734
  pleasant 829
  —a he-goat into a sieve 471
  —and water *weak* 160
  insipid 391
  unimportant 643
  imperfect 651
  —of human kindness 906
  —sickness 655
  —the ram 645
  —white 430
milk-livered 862
milksop *impotent* 158
  fool 501
  coward 862
milky (see **milk**)
  semitransparent 427
  white 430
  become— 427
Milky Way 318, 423
mill *indent* 257
  pulverize 330
  machine 633
  unimportance 643
  workshop 691

  fight 720
  like a horse in a— 312
millboard 593
millenary 98, 120
millennium
  number 98
  period 108
  futurity 121
  utopia 515
  hope 858
millesimal 99
millet seed 193
milliard 98
milliary 550
milliner 225
  man— 854
millinery *dress* 225
  ornament 847
  display 882
  man— 855
million 98
  multitude 102
  people 372
  populace 876
  for the—
  intelligible 518
  easy 705
millionaire 803
mill pond *level* 213
  pond 343
  store 636
mill race 343, 348
millstone 330
mime *player* 599
  buffoon 844
mimeography 19
mimic *imitate* 19
  actor 599
mimmation 560
mimography 599
minacity 909
minaret 206
minatory 668
minauderie 855
mince *cut up* 44
  slow 275
  food 298
  stammer 583
  affected 855
  extenuate 937
  —the matter 868
  —the truth 544
  not—the matter *affirm* 525
  artless 703
mincemeat 298
  make—of 162
mince pie 298
mincing 855
  —steps 275
mind *intellect* 450
  attend to 457
  take care 459
  believe 484
  remember 505

minded

will 600
willing 602
purpose 620
warning 668
desire 865
dislike 867
bear in–*thought* 451
attention 457
bit of one's–527
food for the–454
give one a piece of
 one's–529
give the–to 457
have a–to
willing 602
desire 865
in the–*thought* 451
topic 454
willing 602
make one's–easy
 826
make up one's–
 opinion 484
resolve 604
–at ease 827
–cure 662
–one's book 539
–one's business
 incurious 456
 attentive 457
–'s eye 515
–what one is about
 864
never–*neglect* 460
unimportant 643
not know one's own
 –605
not–866
out of–506
set one's–upon 604
speak one's
 –*say* 582
 blunt 703
 to one's–*taste* 850
 love 897
 the public–488
 willing–602
minded *willing* 602
 intending 620
mindful *attentive* 457
 memory 505
mindless
 inattentive 458
 imbecile 499
 forgetful 506
 insensible 823
mine *sap* 162
 hollow 252
 open 260
 snare 545
 intrigue 626
 store 636
 abundance 639
 damage 659
 intrench 664
 pitfall 667

attack 716
defense 717
dig a–*plan* 626
prepare 673
–layer 726
–of wealth 803
spring a–
 unexpected 508
attack 716
miner 252
 sapper and–726
mineral 358–oil 356
mineralize 358
mineralogy 358
Minerva invita
 unwilling 603
 difficult 704
Minerva press
 fustian 577
mingle 41
miniature
 small 32, 193
 portrait 556
 –*painter* 559
Minié rifle 727
minikin 32, 193
minim *small* 32
 music 413
minimifidian 487
minimize 36, 483
minimum *small* 32
 inferior 34
minion 899
minister
 instrumentality 631
 remedy 662
 agent 690
 director 694
 aid 707
 deputy 759
 give 784
 clergy 996
 rites 998
 –to *help* 746
ministerial
 clerical 995
ministering–angel
 948–*spirit* 977
ministration
 direction 693
 aid 707
 rite 998
ministry
 direction 693
 aid 707
 church 995
 clergy 996
 rite 998
 minimum 434
 miniver 223
 minnesinger 597
 minnow 193
 minor *inferior* 34
 infant 129
 –*key* 413
 –*poet* 597

Minorites 996
minority *few* 103
 youth 127
Minos 694
minotaur 83
minster 1000
minstrel
 musician 416
 poet 597
minstrelsy 415
mint *mold* 22
 fragrance 400
 workshop 691
 wealth 803
 –*julep* 298
minuend 38
minuet *music* 415
 dance 840
minus *inexistent* 2
 less 34
 subtracted 38
 absent 187
 deficient 304
 loss 776
 in debt 806
 nonpayment 808
minusculae 561
minute
 circumstantial 8
 –in degree 32
 special 79
 –of time 108
 instant 113
 –in size 193
 record 551
 compendium 596
 (*unimportant* 643)
 –account 594
 –attention 457
 to the–132
minutemen 726
minuteness *care* 459
minutiae *small* 32
 details 79
 unimportant 643
minx *girl* 129
 malapert 887
 wanton 962
miosis 483
mir 188
Mira 490a
miracle
 exceptional 83
 prodigy 872
 –*play* 599
miraculous
 wonderful 870
mirage 443
mire 653
mirror *imitate* 19
 reflector 445
 perfection 650
 glory 873
 hold the–up to
  nature 554
 hold up the–525

magic–443
mirth 836
misacceptation 523
misadventure
 contretemps 135
 adversity 735
 (*evil* 619)
 (*failure* 732)
misadvised 699
misanthropy 911
misapply
 misinterpret 523
 misuse 679
 mismanage 699
misapprehend
 mistake 495
 misinterpret 523
misappropriate 679
misarrange 61
misbecome 925
misbegotten
 crooked 243
 vicious 945
misbehave
 vulgar 851
 vice 945
misbehavior
 discourtesy 895
 guilt 947
misbelief 485
misbeliever 487, 984
miscalculate
 misjudge 481
 err 495
 disappoint 509
miscall 565
miscarry 732
miscegenation 41,
 903
miscellany
 mixture 41
 collection 72
 generality 78
 compendium 596
 poetry 597
mischance *evil* 619
 misfortune 735
 (*failure* 732)
mischief 619 do–649
 make–649
mischief–maker
 evildoer 913
 knave 941
mischievous 649
miscible 41
miscite 544
miscompute
 misjudge 481
 mistake 495
misconceive
 mistake 495
 misinterpret 523
misconception 495,
 523
misconduct
 bungling 699

Mishna

guilt 947
–*oneself* 945
misconjecture 481
misconstrue 523
miscorrect 538
miscount 495
miscreance 485
miscreant 487, 949
miscreated 945
misdate 115
misdeed 947
misdemean 945
misdemeanant 949,
 975
misdemeanor 947
misdescribe 538
misdevotion 988
misdirect
 misteach 538
 unskillful 699
misdo 945
misdoing 947
misdoubt 485, 523
mise en scène
 appearance 448
 drama 599
 display 882
misemploy 679
miser 640, 819
miserable *small* 32
 contemptible 943
 unhappy 828
miserably *very* 31
misère 840
miserere *sing*–950
misericordia
 Domini 470
miserly 819
misery 828
 put out of one's–
 914
misesteem 481
misestimate
 misjudge 481
 (*mistake* 495)
misfeasance
 bungling 699
 guilt 947
misfire 732
misfortune
 adversity 735
 unhappiness 830
 (*evil* 619)
 (*failure* 732)
misgiving *doubt* 485
 fear 860
misgovern 699
misguide *error* 495
 misteaching 538
misguided 699
mishap *evil* 619
 failure 732
 misfortune 735
 painful 830
mishmash 59
Mishna 985

misinform 538
misinformed 491
misinstruct 538
misintelligence 538
misinterpretation 523
misjoined 24
misjudgment
  sophistry 477
  misjudge **481**
  (*error* 495)
mislay *derange* 61
  lose 776
mislead *error* 495
  misteach 538
  deceive 545
mislike 867
mismanage 699
mismatch
  difference 15
  disagreement 24
misname 565
misnomer 565
misogamist
  celibacy 904
  misanthropy 911
misogyny 904
mispersuasion 538
misplace *derange* 61
  displace 185
misplaced
  intrusive 24
  unconformable 83
  displaced 185
  (*disorder* 59)
misprint 495
misprision
  concealment 528
  guilt 947
  −of treason 742
misprize
  underrate 483
  disrespect 929
mispronounce 583
misproportion 241
misproportioned
  distortion 243
  ugly 846
misquote 544
misreckon
  misjudge 481
  mistake 495
misrelation 10
misrelish 867
misreport *err* 495
  falsify 544
misrepresent
  misinterpret 523
  misteach 538
  lie 544
misrepresentation
  555 *untruth* 546
misrule
  misconduct 699
  laxity 738
  Lord of−701

miss *girl* 129
  neglect 460
  error 495
  unintelligible 519
  fail 732
  lose 776
  want 865
  courtesan 962
  −one's aim 732
  −one's way
    uncertain 475
    unskillful 699
  −stays 304
missa cantata 998
missal 990, 998
missay *neology* 563
  stammering 583
missend 699
misshapen
  shapeless 241
  distorted 243
  ugly 846
missile 727
missing *nonexistent* 2
  absent 187
  disappear 449
  −link *wanting* 53
  completing 729
mission *business* 625
  commission 755
missionary
  teacher 540
  clergyman 996
  −school 542
missive 592
misspell 523
misspend 818
misstate *mistake* 495
  misrepresent 523
  falsify 544
misstatement
  error 495
  untruth 546
  misrepresentation 555
mist *cloud* 353
  dark 424
  semitransparency 427
  (*dim* 422)
  in a−528
  −before the eyes 443
  −s of error 495
  seen through a−519
mistake *error* 495
  misconstrue 523
  mismanage 699
  failure 732
  lie under a−495
misteaching 538
mister 373
misterm 565
misthink 481
mistime 135
mistral 349
mistranslate 523

mistress *lady* 374
  master 745
  possessor 779
  love 897
  concubine 962
mistrust 485
misty (*see* mist)
  become−427
misunderstand
  misinterpret 523
misunderstanding
  disagreement 24
  error 495
  discord 713
misuse 679
misventure 135
mite *bit* 32
  infant 129
  small 193
  arachnid 368
  dole 640
  money 800
miter *junction* 43
  angle 244
  crown 747, 999
mithai 396
mithridate 662
mitigate *abate* 174
  improve 658
  relieve 834
  (*calm* 826)
mitigation
  (*see* mitigate)
  qualification 469
  extenuation 937
mitosis
  production 161
mitraille 727
mitrailleuse 727
mitten 225, 384
mittimus 741
mix 41 *disorder* 59
  −oneself up with
    meddle 682
    cooperate 709
mixed *confused* 523
  (*see* mix)
mixen 653
mixture 41 *mere*
  −*disorder* 59
Mizar 490a
mizzen 235−mast 235
mizzle 293, 348
mnemonics 505
mnemotecnhics 505
Mnemosyne 505
moan *faint sound* 405
  cry 411
  lament 839
moat *inclosure* 232
  ditch 259
  canal 350
  defense 717
mob *crowd* 72
  vulgar 876
  hustle 929

  scold 932
  king−876
  −cap 225
  −law *authority* 738
  compulsion 744
  illegality 964
mobcap 225
mobile *inconstant* 149
  movable 264
  sensitive 822
  mobility the−876
mobilization 72, 264, 722
mobilize 264
  −troops 722
mobocracy 738
moccasin 225
mock *imitate* 17, 19
  repeat 104
  erroneous 495
  deceptive 545
  chuckle 838
  ridicule 856
  desrespect 929
  −danger 861
  −modesty 855
  −sun 423
  −turtle soup 298
mockery (*see* mock)
  unsubstantial 4
  −delusion and snare
  sophistry 477
  deception 545
  solemn−882
mocking bird 19
modal 6, 7, 8
mode *state* 7
  music 413
  habit 613
  method 627
  fashion 852
  −of expression 569
model *copy* 21
  prototype 22
  rule 80
  form 240
  representation 554
  sculpture 557
  perfection 650
  good man 948
  −after 19
  −condition 80
  new−658
modeler 559
moderate *small* 32
  allay **174**
  slow 275
  neutral 628
  sufficient 639
  lenient 740
  cheap 815
  temperate 953
  −circumstances
    mediocrity 736
moderately
  imperfect 651

moderation 174
  inexcitability 826
  patience 831
  (*see* moderate)
moderato *music* 415
moderator
  moderation 174
  lamp 423
  director 694
  mediator 724
  judge 967
modern 123
  −philosophy 451
modernist 123
modernity 123
modernization 123
modest *small* 32
modesty *humility* **881**
  purity 960
  mock−855
modicum *little* 32
  allotment 786
modification
  difference 15
  variation 20a
  change 140
  qualification 469
modillion 215
modiolus 215
modish 852
modiste 225
modulate 469
modulation
  change 140
  music 413
module 22
modulus 84
modus operandi 627, 692
modus vivendi 723
mofussil 181
mogul 745
Mohammed 986
Mohammedan 984
  −priests 996
  −temples 1000
Mohammedanism 976
Mohawk
  swaggerer 887
  evildoer 913
moider
  inattention 458
  uncertain 475
moiety 51, 91
moil *plod* 682
  exertion 686
moisture *wet* 337
  humid **339**
moke 219
molar 250
molasses 352, 396
mold *condition* 7
  matrix 22
  convert 144
  form 240

molded

structure 329
earth 342
vegetation 367
model 554
carve 557
decay 653
remedy 662
turn to account 677
create 976
molded 820–on 19
molder *decay* 653
deteriorate 659
molding 847
moldy *fetid* 401
unclean 653
deteriorated 659
mole *wound* 206
prominence 250
refuge 666
defense 717
spot 848
molecular 32
molecule 193
mole-eyed 443
molehill *little* 193
low 207
trifling 643
molest *trouble* 830
molestation
damage 649
malevolence 907
mollah *judge* 967
mollescence 324
mollify *allay* 174
soften 324
(*mental calm* 826)
mollusca 368
mollusk 366, 368
mollycoddle 158, 372
Moloch *slaughter* 361
demon 978
heathen deity 991
molt 226
molten *liquefied* 384
(*heated* 335)
molybdenum 490b
molybdomancy 511
moment–*of time* 113
importance 642
for the–111
lose not a–684
not have a–682
on the spur of the–612
momentous 151
momentum 276
Momus 838
monachal 1000
monachism 995
monad 87, 193
monarch 745
monarchical 737
monarchy 737
monastery 1000
monastic 995
monasticism 995

monde 852
monetary 800
–*arithmetic* 811
monetize 800
money 800
wealth 803
bad–800
command of–803
for one's–609
made of–803
make–775
–*burning one's pocket* 818
–*coming in* 810
–*down* 807
–*going out* 809
–*market* 800
–*matters* 811
–*paid* 809
–*'s worth useful* 644
price 812
cheap 815
raise–788
save–817
throw away one's–818
money bag 802
money box 802
money broker 797
money changer
merchant 797
treasurer 801
moneyed 803
money-grubbing 775
moneyless 804
monger 797
Mongoloid 372a
mongoose 366
mongrel *mixture* 41
anomalous 83
dog 366
base 949
moniliform 249
monism 984
monition
information 527
warning 668
(*advice* 695)
monitor *oracle* 513
pupil teacher 540, 541
director 694
adviser 695
war ship 726
inward–926
–*building* 189
monitory
prediction 511
dissuasion 616
warning 668
monk 904, 996
monkery 984
monkey *imitative* 19
support 215
catapult 276

animal 366
ridiculous 857
–*trick absurdity* 497
sport 840
–*up* 900
play the–499
monkeyshine 497
monkhood 995
monkish Latin 553
monochord 417
monochrome
no color 429
painting 556
monoclinous 83
monocracy 737
monoculous 443
monocycle 272
monodic 402
monodrame 599
monody *poem* 597
lament 839
monogamist 903
monogamy 903
monogram
cipher 533
indication 550
diagram 554
letter 561
monograph
writing 590
description 594
monographer 598
monolith 551
monolithic 983a
monologist 582, 589
monologue
soliloquy 589
drama 599
monomachy 720
monomania
insanity 503
obstinacy 606
excitability 825
monomaniac 504
monophonic 402
monoplane 273
monoplanist 269a
monopolist 751, 943
monopoly
restraint 751
possession 777
monospermous 87
monostich 572
monosyllable 561
monotheism 983
monotone 104
monotonous
uniform 16
equal 27
repetition 104
permanent 141
–*style* 575
weary 841
dull 843
monotony
(*see* monotonous)

monotype 591
Monroe Doctrine 748
monsoon 348, 349
monster *exception* 83
large 192
ugly 846
prodigy 872
evildoer 913
ruffian 949
monstrance 191, 999
monstrosity
(*see* monster)
distortion 243
monstrous
excessive 31
exceptional 83
huge 192
ugly 846
vulgar 851
ridiculous 853
wonderful 870
montagne Russe
slope 217
sport 840
mont de piété 787
monte 840
Montgolfier 273
month 108
monthly 138
–*nurse* 662
monticle 206
monticoline 206
monument *tall* 206
tomb 363
record 551
monumentalize 112
moo 412
mood *nature* 5
state 7
change 140
tendency 176
willingness 602
temper 820
moodish *rude* 895
irascible 901
sullen 901a
moods and tenses
difference 15
variation 20a
moody *furious* 825
sad 837
sullen 901a
moolvi 492
moon *period* 108
changes 149
world 318
bay the–645
jump over the–309
man in the–515
–*blindness* 443
–*glade* 422
–*of green cheese credulity* 486
–*shaped* 245
moonbeam *light* 420

dim 422
mooncalf 501
moon-eyed 443
moonlight 422
moonraking 458
moonshine
unsubstantial 4
dim 422
absurdity 497
unmeaning 517
untrue 546
excuse 617
–*revelers* 979
moonstone 847
moonstruck
insane 503
wonder 870
Moon's type 442
moor *fasten* 43
open space 180
locate 184
highland 206
plain 344
moored firm 150
moorings
connection 45
location 184
moorish *marshy* 345
moorland 180, 206
moose 366
moot *inquire* 461
argue 476
–*point topic* 454
question 461
mooted *supposed* 514
mop *roughness* 256
cleanness 652
mopboard 211
mope 837
mope-eyed 443
moppet 167, 899
mopsy 962
mopus *dreamer* 515
drone 683
money 800
sad 837
moraine 270
moral *judgment* 480
maxim 496
right 922
duty 926
virtuous 944
–*certainty* 474
–*courage* 604
–*education* 537
–*obligation* 926
–*philosophy mind* 450
duty 926
–*support* 707
–*tuition* 537
–*turpitude* 940
point a–537
moralism 451
moralize 476
morals *duty* 926

508

morass   move

virtue 944
morass 345
moration 133
moratorium 133
moratory 133
morbid 655
morbific 657
morceau 32, 415
mordacity 907
mordant *keen* 171
  pungent 392
  color 428
  vigorous 574
more *superior* 33
  extra 37
  –last words 65
  –or less *quantity* 25
  small 32
  inexact 495
  –than a match for *superior* 33
  strong 159
  –than enough 641
  –than flesh and blood can bear 830
  –than meets the eye 526
  –than one 100
moreover 37
mores, O–932
Moresque 847
morganatic marriage 903
morgue 363
  –*littéraire* 569
moribund *dying* 360
  sick 655
morient 360
morion 717
morisco 840
mormo 860
Mormon 984
Mormonism
  polygamy 903
  heterodoxy 984
morning 125
  –dress 225
  –noon and night *diuturnal* 110
  frequent 136
  –star 423, 977
moron 501
morose *rude* 895
  sulky 901a
morosis 499, 503
Morpheus 683
morphine 662
morphological index 372a
morphology 357
  form 240
  zoölogy 368
morphon 357
morris
  nine men's–840

morris-chair 215
morris dance 840
morrow 121
morsel *small* 32
  portion 51
  food 298
mortal *transient* 111
  fatal 361
  man 372
  wearisome 841
  –antipathy 867
  –blow 619
  –coil 362
  –funk 860
  –remains 362
  –sin 947
mortality
  evanescence 111
  death 360
  mankind 372
  bills of–360
mortar *cement* 45
  conversion 144
  pulverizer 330
  crucible 691
  cannon 727
  –board 550
mortgage *security* 771
  lend 787
  sale 796
  credit 805
mortgagee
  possessor 779
  creditor 805
mortgagor
  possessor 779
  creditor 805
mortgagor
  possessor 779
  debtor 806
mortician 363
mortiferous *fatal* 361
  (*unhealthy* 657)
mortification
  death 360
  disease 655
  pain 828
  vexation 830
  discontent 832
  humilation 879
  asceticism 955
mortise *unite* 43
  intersect 219
  interjacence 228
  printing 591
mortmain 748
  in–781
Morton's fork 475
mortuary *death* 360
  interment 363
mosaic *mixture* 41
  multiform 81
  variegation 440
  painting 556
  –gold *deception* 545
Moslem 984

mosque 1000
mosquito 366, 913
moss *tuft* 256
  elasticity 325
  marsh 345
  vegetation 367, 369
  money 800
moss-grown 659
mosstrooper
  fighter 726
  thief 792
most 31 at–32
  for the–part *generally* 78
  habit 613
  make the–of *overestimate* 482
  exaggerate 549
  improve 658
  use 677
  skill 698
  make the–of one's time 682
  –often 136
  the–33
mot 496
Motazilite 984
mote *small* 32
  light 320
  –in the eye *dim-sighted* 443
  misjudging 481
motet 990
moth 366, 663
moth-eaten *old* 124
  unclean 653
  deteriorated 659
mother *parent* 166
  mold 653
  –superior 996
  –tongue 560
  –wit 498
motherhood 166
motherland 166, 181, 189
motherly *love* 897
  kind 906
mother-of-pearl 427, 440
motif 454
motiferous 264
motile 264
motion
  change of place **264**
  topic 454
  plan 626
  proposal 763
  request 765
  make a–763
  –downwards 306
  –from *recession* 287
  repulsion 289
  –into *ingress* 294
  reception 296
  –out of 295
  –through 302

  –towards *approach* 286
  attraction 288
  –upwards 305
  put in–284
  put oneself in–680
  set in–677
motionless 265
motive **615**
  absence of–**615a**
  –power 264
motivity 264
motley *multiform* 81
  variegated 440
  wearer of the–844
motor *motion* 264
  journey 266
  carrier 271
  vehicle 272
  instrument 633
  –paralysis 376
motor bus 272
motor car 272
motorcycle 266, 272
motorial 264
motorist 268
motorium 264
motorize 266
motorman 268, 694
motory 264
motte 367
mottled 440
motto *maxim* 496
  device 550
  phrase 566
mouchard 527
mould (see mold)
mound *large* 192
  hill 206
  defense 717
mount *greatness* 31
  increase 35
  hill 206
  ascend 305
  raise 307
  display 882
  –guard *care* 459
  safety 664
  –up to *money* 800
  price 812
mountain *large* 192
  hill 206
  weight 319
  make–s of molehills 482
  –brought forth mouse *disappoint* 509
  –flax 385
mountaineer 268
mountainous 206
mountebank
  quack 548
  drama 599
  buffoon 844
mounted rifles 726

mourn *grieve* 828
  lament 839
mourner 839
mourners' bench 1000
mournful
  afflicting 830
  sad 837
  lamentable 839
mourning *dress* 225
  in–*black* 431
  lament 839
mouse *little* 193
  animal 366
  search 461
  mountain brought forth–509
  –over 451, 461
  not a-stirring 265
mouse-colored 432
mousehole 260
mouser 366
mouse trap 545
mousseux 353
Mousterian group 372a
mouth *entrance* 66
  receptacle 191
  brink 231
  opening 260
  eat 298
  estuary 343
  drawl 583
  down in the–879
  make–s 929
  –honor *falsehood* 544
  show 882
  flattery 933, 940
  –wash 652
  –watering 865
  open one's–582
  pass from–to mouth 531
  stop one's–581
  word of–582
mouthful *quantity* 25
  small 32
  food 298
mouthpiece
  speaker 534
  information 527
  speech 582
mouthy *style* 577
moutonné 250
movable *motion* 26
  transference 270
movables 780
move *begin* 66
  motion 264
  propose 514
  induce 615
  undertake 676
  act 680
  offer 763
  excite 824
  good–626

509

moved with

—back 287
—forward 282
—from 287
—heaven and earth 686
—in a groove 82
—off 293
—on progress 282
  activity 682
—out of 295
—quickly 274
—slowly 275
—to 894
on the—293
moved with 821
moveless 265
movement
  motion 264
  music 415
  action 680
  activity 682
mover 164
movies
  theater 448, 599, 840
moving 185
  keep—682
  —pictures 448, 599
  —picture machine 445
mow shorten 201
  smooth 255
  agriculture 371
  store 636
  —down destroy 162
  level 213
moxa 384
mozetta 999
M. P. 696
Mr. man 373
  gentleman 877
Mrs. 374
M. S. 590
much 31 make-of
  important 642
  friends 888
  love 897
  endearment 902
  approval 931
  —ado exertion 686
  difficulty 704
  —ado about nothing
  overestimate 482
  exaggerate 549
  unimportant 643
  unskillful 699
  —cry and little wool 884
  —speaking 584
  —the same identity 13
  similarity 17
  equality 27
  not say—for 932
  think—of respect 928
  approbation 931
muchness 31
mucid semiliquid 352

unclean 653
mucilage 352
muck 653
muckle 31
muckrake 934
muckraker 936
muckworm miser 819
  lowborn 876
mucor 653
mucosity 352
mucous 352
mucronate 253
mucronulate 253
muculent 352
mucus 352
mud marsh 345
  semiliquid 352
  dirt 653
  clear as—519
  stick in the—704
muddle disorder 59
  derange 61
  inattention 458
  render uncertain 475
  absurd 497
  difficulty 704
  blunder 732
  —away 638
  —one's brains 475
muddled 730, 959
muddle-headed 499
muddy moist 339
  dim 422
  opaque 426
  color 429
mudguard 666
mud lark dirty 653
  commonalty 876
muezzin 996
muff incapable 158
  dress 225
  effeminacy 374
  warmth 384
  bungle 699
  bungler 701
muffer bungler 701
muffle wrap 225
  silent 403
  faint 405
  nonresonant 408a
  conceal 528
  voiceless 581
  stammer 583
muffled faint 405
  latent 526
  —drums funeral 363
  nonresonance 408a
muffler dress 225
  wrap 384
  silencer 405, 408a
mufti undress 225
  judge 967
  priest 996
mug cup 191
  face 234
  pottery 384

mugger 913
muggy moist 339
mughouse 189
mugient 412
mugwump 607
Muharram 138
mulada 72
mulatto mixture 41
  exception 83
mulct steal 791
  fine 974
mule mongrel 83
  beast of burden 271
  obstinate 606
muleteer 694
muliebrity 374
mulish 606
mull
  prominence 250
  sweeten 396
  —over 451
mullah 492, 996
mulligatawny 298
mullion 215
multangular 244
multifarious
  irrelevant 10
  diverse 16a
  multiform 81
multifid divided 51
multifold 81, 102
multiformity 81
multigenerous 81
multilateral
  sides 236
  angles 244
multilocular 191
multiloquence
  speech 582
  loquacity 584
multinominal 102
multiparity 168
multiparous 168
multipartite 44
multiphase 81
multiple product 84
  numerous 102
multiplex 81
multiplicand 84
multiplication
  arithmetic 85
  multitude 102
  reproduction 163
  productiveness 168
multiplicator 84
multiplicity 102
multiplier 84
multiply
  (see multiplication)
multipotent 157
multisonous 404
multitude
  number **102**
  (assemblage 72)
  many-headed—102
  the—876

mugger 913
multum in parvo 596
multure 330
mum mute 581
  taciturn 585
mumble chew 298
  mutter 583
mumble peg 840
mumblety 840
Mumbo Jumbo
  god 979
  spell 993
mummer 599
mummery
  absurdity 497
  imposture 545
  masquerade 840
  parade 882
  (ridicule 856)
mummify 357, 363
mumming 840
mummy dry 340
  corpse 362
  brown 433
  beat to a—972
mump mutter 583
  beg 765
mumper beggar 767
  pauper 804
mumpish sad 837
mumps dejection 837
  sullenness 901a
mumpsimus 495
munch 298
Munchausen 549
munchil 272
mundane world 318
  selfish 943
  irreligious 989
mundation 652
mundivagant 266
munerary 973
munerate 973
municipal 965
munificent 816
muniment
  evidence 467
  record 551
  defense 717
  security 771
munition
  materials 635
  defense 717
munshi
  learned man 493
  teacher 540
muon 32
mural 717
murder 361
  —the King's English
  solecism 568
  stammering 583
  the—is out 529
murderer 361
muricated 253
murky dark 421

opaque 426
  black 431
  gloomy 837
murmur purl 348
  sound 405
  voice 580
  complain 839
murmurer 832
murrain 655
Murray travel 266
  Lindley—542
murrey 434
muscadine 400
muscle 159
muscular 159
muse 451
  (see musing)
Muse poetry 597
  historic—594
  —of fire 597
  unlettered—579
museology 72
Muses, the—416
musette 417
museum collection 72
  store 636
mush food 298
mushroom
  unsubstantial 4
  new 123
  fungus 367
  upstart 734
  lowborn 876
  —anchor 706
  —s food 298
  fungi 369
  spring up like—s 163
music 415—box 417
  —of the spheres
  order 58
  universe 318
  set to—416
musical 413, 415, 416
  —ear musician 416
  hearing 418
  —instruments **417**
  —note 413
  —voice 580
musicale 415
music hall
  playhouse 599
  amusement 840
musician 416
musing
  thought 451
  —on other things 458
  thick-eyed—837
musk 400
musket 727
  shoulder a—722
musketeer 726
musketry 727
musk ox 366
muskrat 400
musk root 400

muslin
  semitransparent 427
  fabric 635
musnud *support* 215
  council 696
  scepter 747
muss 59, 61
mussuk 191, 348
Mussulman 984
mussy 61, 653
must *necessity* 601
  mucor 653
  compulsion 744
mustache 256
mustang 271
mustard *pungent* 392
  condiment 393
  after meat–135
mustard gas 663, 737
mustard seed 193
musteline 433
muster *collect* 72
  numeration 85
  schedule 611
  –*courage* 861
  not pass–651
  pass–639
muster roll *list* 86
  (*record* 551)
musty 961
  smelling 401
  foul 653
mutable
  changeable 149
  (*irresolute* 605)
mutation 140
mutatis mutandis
  correlation 12
  change 140
  interchange 148
mute *funeral* 363
  silent 403
  sordine 405, 408a, 417
  letter 561
  speechless 581
  taciturn 585
  drama 599
  deaf–419
  render–581
mutescence 408a
mutilate *retrench* 38
  deform 241
  injure 659
mutilated
  incomplete 53
  imperfect 651
mutilation *evil* 619
mutineer 742
mutiny *revolution* 146
  disobedience 742
  (*resistance* 719)
mutter
  faint sound 405
  imperfect speech 583

grumble 839
  threaten 909
mutton 298
  –*chop* 298
muttonhead 501
mutton-headed 499
mutual *correlative* 12
  interchange 148
  –*concession* 774
  –*understanding* 23
muzzle *powerless* 158
  edge 231
  opening 260
  silence 403
  render speechless 581
  restrain 751
  gag 752
muzzle-loader 727
muzzy *confused* 458
  in liquor 959
myatism 560
mycologist 369
mycology 369
mynheer 877
myology 329
myomancy 511
myopia 443
myriad
  ten thousand 98
  multitude 102
myrmidon 726
myrrh 400
myrtle *tree* 367
  love 897
myself *I* 79
  immateriality 317
mysterious
  invisible 447
  uncertain 475
  obscure 519
  concealed 528
mystery
  (*see mysterious*)
  latency 526
  secret 533
  play 599
  craft 625
  into the supreme– 528
mystic *obscure* 519
  concealed 528
  psychic 992a
mysticism
  thought 451
  latency 526
  concealment 528
mystify *falsify* 477
  unintelligible 519
  hide 528
  misteach 538
  deceive 545
myth *fancy* 515
  untruth 546
mythic *deities* 979
mythical
  descriptive 594

mythogenesis 515
mythology *gods* 979
  heathen 984

N

nab *deceive* 545
  seize 789
Nabob *master* 745
  wealthy 803
Naccarati's Index 372a
nacreous 440
nadir 211
naevose 440
nag *horse* 271
  quarrel 713
Nagari 590
naggy 901a
Naiad *ocean* 341
  mythology 979
naik 745
nail *fasten* 43
  fastening 45
  measure of length 200
  peg 214
  hard 323
  relain 781
  hit the right–*on the head*
  discover 480a
  skill 698
  on the–*present* 118
  pay 807
nailery 691
naïveté 703
naked *denuded* 226
  manifest 525
  –*eye* 441
  –*fact* 151
  –*sword* 727
  –*truth* 494
namby-pamby
  trifling 643
  affected 855
name *indication* 550
  appellation 564
  appoint 755
  celebrity 873
  assume a–565
  call–*s disrespect* 929
  disapprobation 932
  fair–873
  good–873
  in the–*of aid* 707
  authority 737
  due 924
  –*to conjure with* 873
nameless
  anonymous 565
  obscure 874
namely *special* 79
  interpretation 522
namesake 564

nanny goat 374
nap *down* 256
  texture 329
  sleep 683
nape *back* 235
napha water 400
naphtha 356
naphthalene 490b
napiform 245
napkin 652
  buried in a–460
  lay up in a–678
napless 226
napoleon *cards* 840
napping
  inattentive 458
  inexpectant 508
  dull 843
  catch–508
nappy *frothy* 353
  tipsy 959
Narcissus 845
narcosis 376, 381
narcotherapy 821a
narcotic
  unhealthy 657
  remedy 662
  (*bad* 649)
narcotization 381
narikin 123
Narragansett 271
narration 594
narrator 529
narrow *contract* 195
  thin 203
  qualify 469
  constrained 751
  bigoted 988
  –*end of the wedge* 66
  –*escape* 671
  –*gauge* 466
  –*house* 363
  –*means* 804
  –*search* 461
narrow-minded
  bigoted 481
  selfish 943
narrowness 203
narrows 343
narrow-souled 481
nasal 349–*accent* 583
nascent 66
nasty *unsavory* 395
  foul 653
  offensive 830
  cheap and–815
natal *birth* 66
  indigenous 188
  –*day* 138
natation 267
natatorium 652
nathless 30
nation 372
  law of–*s* 963
national 372

–*guard* 726
nationality
  nation 372
  patriotism 910
nationwide 78
native *inhabitant* 188
  indigenous 367
  artless 703
  –*accent* 580
  –*land* 189
  –*soil* 189
  –*tendency* 601
  –*tongue* 560
nativity *birth* 66
  cast a–*predict* 511
  sorcery 992
natty 845
natural *intrinsic* 5
  musical note 413
  true 494
  fool 501
  plain 576
  –*style* 578
  spontaneous 621
  not prepared 674
  artless 703
  simplicity 849
  –*affection* 897
  –*course of things* 613
  –*death death* 360
  completion 729
  –*gas* 388
  –*history* 357
  –*impulse* 601
  –*meaning* 516
  –*order of things* 82
  –*philosophy* 316
  –*state* 80
  –*theology* 983
  –*turn* 820
naturalist 357
naturalistic 537
naturalization
  conformity 82
  conversion 144
  location 184
naturalize *habit* 613
naturalized
  inhabitant 188
naturally 154
nature *essence* 5
  rule 80
  tendency 176
  world 318
  reality 494
  artlessness 703
  affections 820
  animated–357
  in–'*s garb* 226
  organized–357
  second–613
  state of–*naked* 226
  raw 674
naught *nothing* 4
  zero 101
  bring to–732

511

naughty

set at—
make light of 483
opposition 708
disobey 742
not observe 773
disrespect 929
contempt 930
naughty 945
naumachia 720
nausea *weariness* 841
disgust 867
nauseate
unsavory 395
give pain 830
nauseous
unsavory 395
unpleasant 830
disgusting 867
nautch 840
nautch girl 840
nautical 267, 273
—*almanac* 86
nautilus 368
naval 267, 273
—*authorities* 745
—*engagement* 720
—*forces* 627
—*school* 542
navarch 745
nave *middle* 68
center 222
circularity 247
church 1000
navel *middle* 68
center 222
navicular 245
naviform 245
navigation 267
navigator 269
navvy *pioneer* 673
laborer 690
navy *ships* 273
fighters 664, 726
—*blue* 438
—*list* 86
nawab 745, 875
nay 536—*rather* 14
Nazarene 989
naze 250
ne plus ultra
supreme 33
complete 52
distance 196
summit 210
limit 210
perfection 650
completion 729
neap
going down 195
low 207
—*tide* 36
near *like* 17, 19
—*in space* 197
—*in time* 121
soon 132
impending 152

approach 286
stingy 819
bring—17
come—286
draw—197
—*at hand* 132
—*one's end* 360
—*run* 32
—*side* 239
—*sight* 443
—*the mark* 32
—*the truth* 480a
—*upon* 32
sail—*the wind*
skillful 698
rash 863
nearly 32—*all* 50
nearness 9, **197**
nearsighted 443
neat *simple* 42
order 58
form 240
in writing 572, 576, 578
clean 652
spruce 845
—'s *foot oil* 356
neat-handed 698
neatherd 370
neb 250
nebula *stars* 318
mist 353
nebular *dim* 422
nebulous *misty* 353
obscure 519
necessarian 601
necessaries 630
necessarily
cause and effect 154
necessary
(see *necessity*)
necessitarianism 601
necessitate 630
necessity *fate* **601**
predetermination 611
requirement 630
compulsion 744
indigence 804
need 865
make a virtue of—698
neck *contraction* 195
narrow 203
break one's—360
—*and crop*
completely 52
turn out—297
—*and neck* 27
—*of land* 342
—*or nothing*
resolute 604
rash 863
neckcloth 225
necklace *circle* 247
ornament 847

necrology
obituary 360
biography 594
necromancer 548, 994
necromancy 511, 992
necrophilia 821a
necropolis 363
necropsy 363
necroscopic 363
necrosis 655
nectar *savory* 394
sweet 396
nectareous 394, 396
need *necessity* 601
requirement 630
insufficiency 640
indigence 804
desire 865
friend in—711
in one's utmost—735
needful *necessary* 601
requisite 630
money 800
do the—*pay* 807
needle *sharp* 253
perforator 262
compass 693
foliage 367
as the—*to the pole*
veracity 543
observance 772
honor 939
—*in a bottle of hay* 475
needle gun 727
needle-shaped 253
needless 641
needle-witted 498
needlewoman 690
needlework 847
ne'er 107
ne'er-do-well 949
nefarious 945
negation 536, 764
negatory 764
negative
inexisting 2
contrary 14
prototype 22
quantity 84
confute 479
deny 536
photograph 558
refuse 764
prove a—468
neglect 460
disuse 678
leave undone 730
omit 773
evade 927
disrespect 929
—*of time* 115
négligé 225
negligence 460
negligent 460

negotiable
transferable 270
mediatory 724
negotiate *leap* 309
mediate 724
bargain 769
transfer 783
traffic 794
negotiator
go-between 724
agent 758
negress 431
Negrillo 193, 431
Negrito 193, 431
negro *black* 431
slave 746
negrophobia 898
negus 298
neif 781
neigh *cry* 412
boast 884
neighbor
near 197, 199
friend 890
neighborhood 197, 227
neighborly *aid* 707
friendly 888
social 892
courteous 894
neither 610
—*here nor there*
irrelevant 10
absent 187
—*more nor less*
equal 27
true 494
—*one thing nor another* 83
nekton 366
nem. con. 488
Nemesis
vengeance 919
justice 922
punishment 972
ncnia 839
neo-criticism 451
neogamist 903
Neo-Hegelianism 451
Neo-Lamarckism 357
neologism 123
neologist 123
neology 563
neophyte 144, 541
Neoplatonism 451, 984
neoteric 123
neo-voluntarism 451
nepenthe *remedy* 662
cheer 836
nephalism 953, 955
nephelognosy 353
nephelometer 353

neuter

nephew 11
nephograph 353
nephology 353
nephoscope 353
nepotism *nephew* 11
wrong 923
dishonest 940
selfish 943
Neptune 341, 490a
Nereid *ocean* 341
mythology 979
nerve *strength* 159
courage 861
with exposed—*s* 378
nerveless
impotent 158
—*style* 575
imperturbable 871
nervous *weak* 160
style 574
timid 860
modest 881
nescience 491
ness 250
nest *cradle* 153
lodging 189
—*of boxes* 204
nest egg 636
nestle *lodge* 186
safety 664
endearment 902
nestling 129, 167
Nestor *veteran* 130
sage 500
advice 695
net *remainder* 40
receptacle 191
intersection 219
inclosure 232
snare 545
difficulty 704
gain 775
—*profit gain* 775
receipt 810
nether 207
nethermost 207, 211
netlike 219
netting 219
nettle *bane* 663
sting 830
incense 900
network *disorder* 59
crossing 219
neural 235
neuralgia 378
neurasthenia 158, 655, 992a
neurology 329
neuropsychiatry 821a
neurosis 821a
neurotic 662
neuter *matter* 316
no choice 609a
remain
—*irresolute* 605

512

neutral

stand
   –indifferent 866
neutral *mean* 29
   no choice 609a
   avoidance 623
   mid–course 628
   pacific 721
   indifferent 866
   –tint *colorless* 429
   gray 432
neutrality
   mid–course 628
   peace 721
   insensibility 823
   indifference 866
neutralize
   compensate 30
   counteract 179
nevée 383
never 107 it will–do
   inexpedient 647
   prohibit 761
   discontent 832
   disapprobation 932
   –a one 4
   –dying 112
   –ending 112
   –fading *perpetual* 112
   glory 873
   –forget 916
   –hear the last of 841
   –indebted 807
   –mind *neglect* 460
   unimportant 643
   insensible 823
   indifferent 866
   contempt 930
   –more 107
   –otherwise 16
   –say die
   persevere 604a
   cheerful 836
   hope 858
   –so 31
   –tell me 489
   –thought of 621
   –tired *active* 682
   –tiring
   persevering 604a
   –to be forgotten 642
   –to return 122
   –was seen the like 83
neverness 107
nevertheless 30
ne vile fano 987, 1000
new *different* 18
   extra 37
   novel 123
   unaccustomed 614
   give–life to *aid* 707
   stimulate 824
   –birth 660
   –blood *change* 140
   improve 658
   excite 824

–brooms
   desuetude 614
   active 682
–chum 57
–conditions 469
–departure 66
–edition
   repetition 104
   reproduction 163
   improvement 658
–ethical movement 451
–ideas 537
–woman 374
   put on the–man 950
   turn over a–leaf
   change 140
   repent 950
   view in a–light 658
newborn *new* 123
   infant 129
Newcastle, carry coals to–641
newcomer 57, 294
New England Primer 542
newfangled
   unfamiliar 83
   new 123
   change 140
   neology 563
newfashioned 123
new–fledged 129
Newfoundland dog 366
Newgate 572
new–gilt 847
new–model
   convert 144
   revolutionize 146
   improve 658
newness 123
news 532
newsboy 534
newsmonger
   curious 455
   informant 527
   news 532
newsmongery 455
newspaper
   publish 531
   record 551
   –correspondent 758
   –war 588
newspaperman 554
newsy 532
newt 366
New Thought 984
Newton 490d
New Year's Day 138
next *following* 63
   later 117
   future 121
   near 197
   –friend 759

–of kin 11
–to nothing 32
–world 152
Niagara 348
niasis 501
niaiserie 517
nib *cut* 44
   end 67
   summit 210
   point 253
nibble *eat* 298
   –at *censure* 932
   –at the bait *dupe* 547
   willing 602
nice *savory* 394
   discriminative 465
   exact 494
   good 648
   pleasing 829
   fastidious 868
   honorable 939
   (*taste* 850)
   –ear 418
   –hand 700
   –perception 465
   –point 697, 704
nicely *completely* 52
Nicene Creed 983a
niceness (see **nice**)
nicety 494
niche *recess* 182
   receptacle 191
   angle 244
   –in the temple of fame 873
nick *notch* 257
   deceive 545
   mark 550
   –it 731
   –of time 134
nickel 800
Nick, Old–978
nicknack 643
nickname 564, 565
nicotine *pungent* 392
   poison 663
nictate 443
nictitate 443
nidget 862
nidification 189
nidor 398
nidorous 401
nidus *cradle* 153
   nest 189
niece 11
niggard
   insufficiency 640
   miser 819
   (*trifling* 643)
niggle *mock* 929
niggling *trifling* 643
nigh 197
nighness 197
night 421
   labor day and–686
   –and day 136

–watchman 753
   orb of–318
nightcap 225
nightfall 126, 422
nightgown 225
nightingale 366, 416
nightmare
   bodily pain 378
   dream 515
   incubus 706
   mental pain 828
   alarm 860
nightshade 663
nightshirt 225
nighttide 126
nightwalker 268
nightwalking 266
nigrescence 431
nigricant 431
nigrification 431
nihilism 738, 989
nihilist 165, 913
nihilistic 738
nihility *inexistence* 2
   unsubstantiality 4
nil *inexistence* 2
   unsubstantiality 4
nill *unwilling* 603
   refuse 764
nilometer 348
Nilote 372a
nim 791
nimble *swift* 274
   active 682
   (*skillful* 698)
nimble–fingered 698
nimble–footed 274
nimble–witted
   intelligence 498
   wit 842
nimbus *cloud* 353
   halo 420
   glory 873
nimiety 641
Nimrod *slayer* 361
   hunter 622
nincompoop 501
nine 98 *team* 759
   –day's wonder
   transient 111
   unimportant 643
   –lives 359
   –men's morris 840
   –points of the law 777
   tuneful–*music* 416
   poetry 597
ninefold 98
ninepins 840
ninety 98
ninny 501
Niobe *all tears* 839
   –of nations 828
nip *cut* 44
   destroy 162
   shorten 201

no

   dram 298
   freeze 385
   pungent 392
   –in the bud *kill* 361
   hinder 706
   –up 789
nipperkin 191
nippers 327, 781
nipple 250
Nirvana 2, 981
nis 979
nisi prius
   summons 741
   lawsuit 969
nisus 176
nitency 420
niter 392
nitric acid 384
nitrogen 663
nitroglycerin 727
nitrous oxide 376
niveous *white* 430
nix *nothing* 101
   absence 187
   fairy 979
nixie *fairy* 979
nizam 745
nizy 501
no *zero* 101
   dissent 489
   negation 536
   refusal 764
   and–mistake 474
   at–great distance 197
   at–hand 32
   at–time 107
   have–business there 83
   have–end
   perpetual 112
   in–degree 32
   –chicken *aged* 128
   grown up 131
   –choice *necessary* 601
   neutral 609a
   –conjuror *fool* 501
   bungler 701
   –consequence 643
   –doubt *certain* 474
   assent 488
   –end of great 31
   multitude 102
   length 200
   –go *shortcoming* 304
   failure 732
   –less 639
   –longer 122
   –man's land
   arena 728
   –matter *neglect* 460
   unimportant 643
   –more *inexistent* 2
   past 122
   dead 360
   –more than 32

Noah's ark — not

−object 643
−one 4
−one knows who 876
−other *same* 13
one 87
−scholar 493
−sooner said than done
instantaneous 113
early 132
−stranger to 490
−such thing
nonexistent 2
unsubstantial 4
contrary 14
dissimilar 18
−thank you 764
−wonder 871
on−account 761
unable to say−605
with−interval 199
Noah's ark
mixture 41
assemblage 72
nob 210
Nobel prize 733
nobilitate 873
nobility 875
noble *great* 31
important 642
rank 873
peer 875
upright 939
disinterested 942
virtuous 944
−liver 948
−scorn 919
noblesse 875
noblesse oblige 875
nobody
unsubstantial 4
zero 101
absence 187
lowborn 876
−home
want of intellect 450a
−knows
ignorance 491
−knows where
distance 196
−present 187
−would think 508
noctambulation 266
noctambulist 268
noctivagant
travel 266
dark 421
noctograph 442
nocturnal *night* 126
dark 421
black 431
nocturne 415
nocuous 649
nod *wag* 314
assent 488

signal 550
sleep 683
command 741
bow 894
(*hint* 527)
−of approbation 931
−of assent 488
nodding to its fall
destruction 162
descent 306
noddle *summit* 210
head 450
noddy 501
node 250
nodose 256
nodosity *convex* 250
rough 256
nodule 87, 250
noggin 191
noise *sound* 402
loud 404
make a−in the world 873
−abroad 531
noiseless 403
noisome *fetid* 401
bad 649
unhealthy 657
noisy 404
nolition 603
nolleity 603
nolle prosequi 624
nomad 268
nomadic 266
nomadization 266
Nomancy 511
nom de guerre 565
nom de plume 565
nomenclature 564
nominal
unsubstantial 4
word 562
name 564
−price 815
nomination
naming 564
appointment 755
nominee 758
nomistic 965
nomography 963
nomology 963
nomothetical 965
non−ens 2−*esse* 2
−sequitur 477
nonaddition 38
nonadmission 55
nonage 127
nonagenarian 130
nonappearance 447
nonary 98
nonassemblage 73
nonattendance 187
nonbeing 2
non−Biblical
−prophets 986
−writings **986**

nonce 118 for the−
present 118
occasion 134
nonchalance
neglect 460
insensibility 823
indifference 866
noncohesive 47
noncoincidence 14
noncommissioned officer 745
noncommittal 864
noncompletion 730
noncompliance
disobedience 742
refusal 764
nonconductive 175a
nonconformity
exception 83
dissent 489
sectarianism 984
nonconsent 489
noncooperation 927
nondescript 83
none 101−else 87
−in the world 4
−the worse 660
−to spare 640
nonendurance 825
nonentity
inexistence 2
unsubstantial 4
unimportant 643
nonessential
extrinsic 6
unimportant 643
nonesuch
unconformity 83
goodness 648
nonexistence 2
nonexpectance 508
nonextension 180a
nonfeasance 947
nonfulfillment 730, 732
−of one's hopes 509
nonidentical 18
nonillion 102
nonimitation 20
noninclusion 55
noninterference
inaction 681
freedom 748
nonius 466
nonjuror
dissent 489
heterodox 984
nonny 501
nonobjective 317
nonobservance
inattention 458
desuetude 614
infraction **773**
dereliction 927
nonpareil 28, 648
nonpayment 808

nonperformance
noncompletion 730
dereliction 927
nonpertinence 10
nonplus
uncertain 475
difficulty 704
conquer 731
nonpreparation 674
nonprevalence 614
nonresidence 187
nonresistance
submission 725
obedience 743
nonresonance 408a
nonsense
absurdity 497
unmeaning 517
trash 643
talk−folly 499
to varnish−499
nonsubjective 316
nonsubsistence 2
nonsuccess 732
nonsuit *defeat* 731
fail 732
condemn 971
nonunderstanding 452
nonuniformity 16a
nonvocal 581
noodle 501
nook *place* 182
receptacle 191
corner 244
noölogy 450
noon *midday* 125
noonday *midday* 125
light 420
clear as−
intelligible 518
manifest 525
nooning 125
noontide 420
nooscopic 450
noose *ligature* 45
loop 247
snare 545
gallows 975
N or M 78
norm 697
normal *intrinsic* 5
average 29
orderly 58
regular 80, 82
perpendicular 212
sane 502
−condition *rule* 80
normalcy 80, 502
normality
(see *normal*)
normalize 58
Norse mythology 979
North 278
−and South 237

−Pole 383
−Star 550
northeaster 349
norther 349
northerly 237
northern 237
−lights 423
−star *constant* 939
northward 237
Northwest passage 311
nose *prominence* 250
curiosity 455, 461
smell 398
lead by the−
induce 615
govern 737
led by the−749
−out 461
not see beyond one's−
misjudge 481
folly 499
unskillful 699
put one's−out of joint *defeat* 731
disrepute 874
(*supplant* 147)
speak through the− 583
thrust one's−in
interjacence 228
busy 682
under one's−
present 186
near 197
manifest 525
defy 715
nose dive
aeronautics 267
nosegay *fragrance* 406
ornament 847
nosey *curious* 455
nosology 655
nostalgia 833
nostology 128
nostril 351
breath of one's−s 359
stink in the−s 401
nostrum
contrivance 626
remedy 662
not *negation* 536
(*dissent* 489)
it will−do 923
−à bit 536
−a few 102
−a leg to stand on 158
−a little 31
−allowed 964
−amiss *good* 618
mediocre 651
pretty 845
−any 101

514

nota bene   **nuptial**

  –a particle 4
  –a pin to choose 27
  –a soul 101
  –at all 32
  –bad 651
  –bargain for 508
  –come up to 34
  –expect 508
  –fail 939
  –far from 197
  –fit to be seen 846
  –following 477
  –for the world
     unwilling 603
     refusal 764
  –grant 764
  –guilty 946
  –hardened 950
  –having *absent* 187
     exempt 777a
  –hear of 764
  –included 55
  –know what to make
     of 519
  –matter
     unimportant 643
  –mind *insensible* 823
     contempt 930
  –often 137
  –of the earth 987
  –one 101
  –on speaking terms
     889
  –on your life 764
  –particular 831
  –pay 808
  –quite 32
  –reach 304
  –right 503
  –seldom 136
  –sorry 827
  –the thing 925
  –to be borne 830
  –to be despised 642
  –to be had
     impossible 471
     insufficient 640
  –to mention
     together with 37
  –to be put down 604
  –to be thought of
     incogitancy 452
     impossible 471
     refusal 764
     hopeless 859
     undue 925
     disapprobation 932
  –trouble oneself
     about 460
  –understand 519
  –vital
     unimportant 643
  –vote 609a
  –within previous
     experience 137
  –wonder 871

  –worth *trifling* 643
     useless 645
     what is– 546
     what ought– 923
nota bene 457
notabilia 642
notabilities 875
notable *great* 31
  manifest 525
  important 642
  active 682
  distinguished 873
notables 875
notably 31
notary *recorder* 553
  lawyer 968
notation 85
notch *gully* 198
  nick 257
  mark 550
note *music* 413
  take cognizance 450
  remark 457
  explanation 522
  sign 550
  record 551
  printing 591
  epistle 592
  minute 596
  money 800
  fame 873
  change one's– 607
  make a–of 551
  –of admiration 870
  –of alarm 669
  –of preparation 673
     of– 873
  take–of 457
notebook *record* 551
  compendium 569
  writing 590
noted *known* 490
  famous 873
noteworthy *great* 31
  exceptional 83
  important 642
nothing *nihility* 4
  zero 101
  trifle 643
  come to–
     fall short 304
     fail 732
  do– 681
  for– 815
  go for– 643
  good for– 646
  make–of
     underestimate 483
     fail 732
  –comes amiss 831
  –in it 4
  –loth 602
  –more to be said 478
  –of the kind
     unlike 18
     negation 536

  –on 226
  –to do 681
  –to do with 764
  –to go upon 471
  –to signify 643
     take–by 732
     think of– 930
     worse than– 808
nothingness 2
notice *intellect* 450
  observe 457
  review 480
  information 527
  warning 668
  bring into– 525
  deserve– 642
  give–*manifest* 525
  inform 527
  indicate 550
  –is hereby given
     publication 531
  –to quit 782
     short– 111
     take–of 450
     this is to give– 457
     worthy of– 642
noticeable 31
notification
  information 527
  (*publication* 531)
notion *idea* 453
  (*belief* 484)
  (*knowledge* 490)
  have no–of 489
notional *fanciful* 515
notionalist 514
notoriety
  publication 531
  fame 873
notorious *known* 490
  public 531
  famous 873
  infamous 874
Notre Dame 977
notturno 415
notwithstanding 30,
  179
nought
  unsubstantiality 4
  (see *naught*)
noun 564
nourish 707
nourishment
  food 298
  aid 707
nous 498
nousle 545
nouveau riche 123
novaculite 253
novation 140, 609
Nova Zembla 383
novel *dissimilar* 18
  new 123
  unknown 491
  tale 594
  (*romance* 515)

  (*fiction* 546)
novelist 594, 598
novelize 594
novena 98, 108
novenary 98
novice *ignoramus* 493
  learner 541
  bungler 701
  religious 996
novitiate
  learning 539
  training 673
novocain 376
novus homo
  stranger 57
  upstart 876
now 118
  –and then 136
  –or never 134
noways 32, 536
nowhere 187
nowise *small* 32
  negation 536
noxious *bad* 649
  unhealthy 657
noyade *kill* 361
  punish 972
nozzle *projection* 250
  opening 260
  for water 337
  air pipe 351
nuance *difference* 15
  discrimination 465
nubiferous 353, 426
nubilation 426
nubile *adolescent* 131
  marriage 903
nubilous 426
nuclear 222
nuclear energy 490d
nucleolus 357
nucleus *middle* 68
  cause 153
  center 222
  kernel 642
nudation 226
nude 226
nudge 550
nudity 226, 849
nugacity
  absurdity 497
  folly 499
  inutility 645
nugatory
  powerless 158
  useless 645
nuggar 273
nugget *mass* 192
  money 800
nuisance *evil* 619
  annoyance 830
null *inexistent* 2
  unsubstantial 4
  absent 187
  declare–and void
     abrogation 756

  nonobservance 773
  –and void
     powerless 158
     unproductive 169
     illegal 964
  (*inexistence* 2)
nullah 198, 252
nullibiety 187
nullicity 187
nullifidian 487
nullify *inexistence* 2
  compensate 30
  destroy 162
  abrogate 756
  not observe 773
  not pay 808
nullity *inexistence* 2
  unsubstantiality 4
numb
  physically insensible
     376, 381
  morally insensible
     823
number *part* 51
  abstract – 84
  count 85
  plural 100
  –of a magazine etc.
     593
  –among 76
  –of times 104
  take care of–one
     943
numbered, days–
  kill 361
  necessity 601
  hopeless 859
  –with the dead 360
numberless 105
numbers *many* 102
  verse 597
numbness 381
numdah 223
numerable 85
numeral 84, 85
numeration 85
numerator 84
numerical 85
numerous 102
numismatics 800
nummary 800
numps 501
numskull 493, 501
nun 904, 996
nunc dimittis 990
nuncio *messenger* 534
  diplomatist 758
nuncupation
  naming 564
nuncupative 527, 582
nuncupatory
  informing 527
nundination 794
nunnation 560
nunnery 1000
nuptial 903–**knot** 903

515

nuptials 903
nurse *remedy* 662
  preserve 670
  help 707
  servant 746
  custodian 753
  put to–537
nursery *infancy* 127
  nest 153
  room 191
  garden 371
  school 542
  plants 691
  –*rhymes* 597
  –*tale fiction* 546
  narrative 594
nursling 129
nurture *feed* 298
  educate 537
  prepare 673
  aid 707
  –*a belief* 484
  –*an idea* 451
nut 298 *madman* 504
  –*to crack riddle* 533
  difficulty 704
  –*oil* 365
nutation 314
nut-brown 433
nutmeg 393
  –*grater* 330
nuts *good* 618
  pleasing 829
nutshell *small* 32
  lie in a– *little* 193
  compendium 596
nutriment 298
nutrition 707
nutritious *food* 298
  healthy 656
  remedy 662
nux vomica 663
nuzzle 902
nyctalopia 443
nymph *child* 129
  woman 374
  mythology 979
  elemental 980
  sea–341
nympha 129
nymphomania 821a
nystagmus 443

O

O! *wonder* 870
  discontent 932
  –*for desire* 865
oaf *fool* 501
oak *strong* 159
  tree 367, 369
  heart of–*hard* 323
  brave 861
oakleaf *insignia* 747
oakum 205

oar *paddle* 267
  oarsman 269
  instrument 633
  laboring–686
  lie upon one's–s 681
  ply the–
  navigate 267
  exert 686
  pull an–680
  put in an–
  interpose 228
  busy 682
  rest on one's–
  cease 142
  quiescence 265
  repose 687
  stroke–693
oar-shaped 245
oarsman 269
oasis *separate* 44
  land 342
oath *assertion* 535
  bad language 908
  –*helper* 467
  rap out–s 885
  upon–768
oatmeal 298
oats 367
obbligato
  accompaniment 88
  music 415
obconic 245
obduction 223
obdurate
  obstinate 606
  severe 739
  malevolent 907
  graceless 945
  impenitent 951
obedience 743
obeisance *bow* 308
  submission 725
  courtesy 894
  reverence 928
obelisk *tall* 206
  monument 551
Oberon 979
obese 194
obesity 192
obey 743
  be subject to 749
  –*a call* 615
  –*rules* 82
  –*the helm* 705
obfuscate *dark* 421
  opaque 426
obfuscated *drunk* 959
obi 992
obiism 992
obit *death* 360
  interment 363
  post–360, 363
obiter dictum
  irrelevant 10
  occasion 134

interjacent 228
obituary *death* 360
  biography 594
object *thing* 3
  matter 316
  intention 620
  ugly 846
  disapprove 932
  be an–
  important 642
  –*lesson* 537
  –*to dislike* 867
objectify 220
objection
  hindrance 706
  disapproval 932
  no–762
objectionable
  inexpedient 647
  wrong 923
  guilty 947
objective *extrinsic* 6
  material 316
objectize 220
objurgate 932
oblate 201
  –*spheroid* 249
oblation *gift* 784
  religious–990
  (*offer* 763)
oblectation 827
obligation
  necessity 601
  promise 768
  conditions 770
  debt 806
  confer an–
  good 648
  feeling of–916
  under an–
  gratitude 916
  duty 926
oblige *benefit* 707
  compel 744
  duty 926
obliged *grateful* 916
  duty 926
  be–601
obligee 800
obliging *helping* 707
  courteous 894
  kind 906
obliquation 279
obliquity *slope* 217
  vice 945
  –*of judgment* 481
  –*of vision* 443
obliterate 2, 162
obliteration 552
  –*of the past* 506
oblivion 506
  inexistence 2
  forgiveness 918
  –*of benefits* 917
  –*of time* 115
  redeem from–505

oblivious 506
oblong 200
  –*spheroid* 249
obloquy *disrepute* 874
  disapprobation 932
  detraction 934
obmutescence
  voiceless 581
  taciturn 585
obnoxious
  pernicious 649
  unpleasing 830
  hateful 898
  –*to liable* 177
obnubilated 422
oboe 417
obovate 247
obreption 528, 775
obscene *dirty* 653
  indecent 961
obscure *dark* 421
  dim 422
  unseen 447
  uncertain 475
  unintelligible 519
  eclipse 874
  ignoble 876
obscurity
  (*see obscure*)
  unsubstantiality 4
  latency 526
  style **571**
obsecration 765
obsecratory 765
obsequies 363
obsequious
  servile 746, 886
  courteous 894
  respectful 928
obsequiousness 933
observance *rule* 82
  attention 457
  habit 613
  practice 692
  fulfillment **772**
  duty 926
  rite 998
Observant *friar* 996
observation
  intellect 450
  idea 453
  attention 457
  assertion 535
observatory 318
observe
  (*see observance, observation*)
  –*a duty* 926
  –*rules* 82
observer
  aviator 269a
  spectator 444
obsess *haunt* 860
  bedevil 978
  sorcery 992
obsession (*see obsess*)

siege 716
obsidional 716
obsolescence 614
obsolescent 563
obsolete *old* 124
  words 563
  effete 645
obstacle *moral*–706
  (*physical*–179)
obstetrician 631
obstetrics
  production 161
  surgery 662
obstinacy 606
  prejudice 481
obstipation 261
obstreperous
  violent 173
  loud 404
obstruct *close* 261
  hinder 706
  –*the passage of light* 426
obstructionist 710
obstructive
  opponent 710
obstruent 706
obstupefaction 823
obtain *exist* 1
  get 775
  –*under false pretense* 791
obtainable 470
obtenebration 421
obtestation
  entreaty 765
obtrectation 934
obtrude *interfere* 228
  insert 300
  meddle 682
  (*obstruct* 706)
obtruncate 201
obtrusion
  interference 228
  obstruction 706
obtrusive
  interfering 228
  vulgar 851
  rude 895
obtund *mitigate* 174
  blunt 254
  deaden 376
  paralyze 823
obtundent 823
obtundity 823
obtuse *blunt* 253
  insensible 376
  imbecile 499
  dull 823
  –*angle* 244
obumbrate 421
obverse 234
obviate 706
obvious *visible* 446
  clear 518
  manifest 525

516

ocarina

ocarina 417
occasion *juncture* 8
  opportunity 134
  cause 153
  befit the— 646
  have—for 630
  on the present— 118
  on the spur of— 612
occasional 134, 475
occasionally 136
Occident 236
occiput 235
occision 361
occlusion 261
occult
  unintelligible 519
  latent 526
  hidden 528
  —art 992
occultation
  disappearance 449
  concealment 528
occultism *latency* 526
  concealment 528
  heterodoxy 984
  psychic 992a
occupancy
  presence 186
  possession 777
  (*property* 780)
  —in common 778
occupant
  inhabitant 188
  proprietor 779
occupation
  business 625
  in the—of 188
  —road 627
occupied 682—*by* 188
  —with attention 457
  business 625
occupier *dweller* 188
  possessor 779
occupy *presence* 186
  possess 777
  —a post 737
  —oneself with
    attend 457
    business 625
  —the chair 693
  —the mind
    thought 451
    attention 457
  —time 106
occur *exist* 1
  follow 117
  happen 151
  —in a place 186
  —to the mind 451
occurrence 151
  circumstance 8
  of daily— 613
occursion 276
ocean 341—*basin* 341
  —greyhound 273
  —lane 341

—of dreams 4
  plow the— 267
ocean-going 273
oceanography 341
Oceanus 341
ocelot 440
ocher *brown* 433
  orange 439
  yellow— 436
ocherous 436, 439
ochlocracy 738
o'clock 114
  know what's— 698
octad 193
octagon 98, 244
octahedron 244
octangular 98
octastyle 98
Octateuch 985
octave *eight* 98
  period 108
  music 413
  poetry 597
octavo 98, 593
octennial 138
octodecimo 593
octogenarian 130
octonary 98
octopus
  mollusk 366, 368
  monster 846, 913
octoroon 41
octroi 812
octuple 98
ocular 441
  —demonstration
    see 441
    visible 446
  —inspection 441
oculist 662
odalisque 746
odd *remaining* 40
  exception 83
  single 87
  insane 503
  vulgar 851
  ridiculous 853
  —fish 857
Odd Fellows 712
oddity
  laughingstock 857
oddments 51
odds *inequality* 28
  chance 156
  discord 713
  at—disagreement 24
  discord 713
  long— 704
  —against one 665
  —and ends
    remainder 40
    mixture 41
    part 51
    useless 645
  the—are 472
  what's the— 643

ode 597
od force 992
Odin 979
odious
  disagreeable 830
  ugly 846
  hateful 898
odium *disgrace* 874
  hatred 898
  blame 932
odium theologicum
  pedantry 481
  pietism 988
  church 995
odograph 200
odometer 200
odontalgia 378
odontoid
  prominent 250
  sharp 253
odor 398 *in bad—* 932
  —of sanctity 987
O. D. shirt 225
odylic force 992
oedematous
  swollen 194
  soft 324
Oedipus *answer* 462
  expounder 524
Oedipus complex 821a
oenomancy 511
o'er (*see* over)
oestrus 865
oeuvres 161
of—*all things* 33
  —a piece uniform 16
    similar 17
    agreeing 23
  —course
    conformity 82
    effect 154
  —late 123
  —no effect 169
  —old 122
  —one mind 23
off 196 *be—* 623
  keep— 623
  make—with 791
  move— 287
  —and on
    periodical 138
    changeable 149
    irresolute 605
  —one's balance 605
  —one's guard
    neglect 260
    inexpectant 508
  —one's hands 776
  —one's head 503
  —one's legs
    carry one— 284
    dance one— 309
  —one's mind 452
  —side 238
  —the track 475

  —with you 297
  sheer— 287
  stand— 287
  start— 293
  take—one's hands 785
  throw—one's center 874
  throw—the scent
    uncertain 475
    avoid 623
offal 653
offend *pain* 830
  vice 945
  —against the law 964
offender
  —never pardons 918
offense *attack* 716
  anger 900
  guilt 947
offensive
  unsavory 395
  fetid 401
  foul 653
  aggressive 716
  displeasing 830
  distasteful 867
  obnoxious 898
  —and defensive
    alliance 712
  —to ears polite 579
offer *volunteer* 602
  proposal 763
  give 784
  —a choice 609
  —for sale 796
  —of marriage 902
  —oneself 763
  —sacrifice 990
  —the alternative 609
  —up prayers 990
offering *gift* 784
  burnt— 990
  sin— 952
offertory *gift* 784
  worship 990
  rite 998
offhand *soon* 132
  inattentive 458
  careless 460
  spontaneous 612
  (*unprepared* 674)
office *doing* 170
  room 191
  business 625
  mart 799
  worship 990
  do an ill— 907
  do one's— 772
  good—s mediate 724
  kind 906
  hold— 693
  kind—s 906
  man in— 694
  —force 746
  —holder 694

oily

officer *director* 694
  soldier 726
  commander 745
  constable 965
offices
  kitchen etc. 191
official *certain* 474
  true 494
  business 625
  man in office 694
  authoritative 737
  master 745
  servant 746
  —receiver 967
officialism 739
officiate *business* 625
  instrumentality 631
  act 680
  conduct 692
  religious 998
officious 682
offing *distance* 196
  ocean 341
offprint 21
offsaddle 292
offscourings
  useless 645
  dirt 653
offscum 653
offset *compensation* 30
  offspring 167
  counteract 179
  printing 591
offshoot *adjunct* 39
  part 51
  effect 154
  offspring 167
offspring
  posterity 167
offtake 40a
offuscate *dark* 421
  opaque 426
often *repeated* 104
  frequent 136
  most— 613
Ogham 590
ogle *look* 441
  desire 865
  rude 895
  endearment 902
ogre *bugbear* 860
  evildoer 913
  demon 980
Ohm's law 490d
oil *lubricate* 332
  grease 355, **356**
  fuel 388
  —on the troubled waters 174
  —stove 386
  pour—on relieve 834
oilcloth 223, 635
oil painting 556
oilskins 225
oily *smooth* 255
  greasy 355

517

servile 886
courteous 894
flattery 933
oinomania 959
ointment
  lubrication 332
  grease 356
  remedy 662
old 124
  die of–age 729
  of–122
  –age 128
  –bachelor 904
  –clothes 225
  –fogy *fool* 501
    laughingstock 857
  –glory 550
  –gold 439
  –joke 842
  –maid *cards* 840
    spinster 374, 904
  –man *veteran* 130
    husband 903
  –man of the sea 706
  –Nick 978
  –school
    antiquated 124
    obstinate 606
    habit 613
  –soldier 392
  –song *repetition* 104
    trifle 643
    cheap 815
  –stager *veteran* 130
    proficient 700
  –story *repetition* 104
    stale news 532
    love 897
  –stuff *repetition* 104
  –times 122
  –woman *fool* 501
    effeminacy 374
    wife 903
  –womanish 499
  –world 124
    one's–way 613
    pay off–scores 718
older 128
old-fangled 124
old-fashioned 124
oldness 124
oldster 130
oldwife 130
oleagine 356
oleaginous 355
olein 356
olfactible 398
olfactory 398
  –organ 250
olibanum 400
olid 401
oligarch 745
oligarchy 737
olio 41
olivaceous 435
olive 367

olive branch
  infant 129
  offspring 167
  pacification 723
olive drab 225
olive green 435
olivine 435
olla podrida 41
Olympus 981
Om 993
omasum 191
omber 840
ombrometer 348
omega *end* 67
omelet 298
omen 512
ominate 511
ominous
  predicting 511
  danger 665
  warning 668
  adverse 735
  hopeless 859
omission
  incomplete 53
  exclusion 55
  neglect 460
  failure 732
  nonobservance 773
  guilt 947
omit (*see* omission)
omitted *inexistent* 2
  absent 187
omnibus 272
omnifarious 81
omnific 168
omniform 81
omnigenous 81
omnipotence
  power 157
  God 976
omnipresence
  presence 186
  God 976
omniscience
  knowledge 490
  God 976
omnium-gatherum
  mixture 41
  confusion 59
  assemblage 72
omnivorous
  eating 298
  desire 865
  gluttony 957
omophagic 298
omphalos 68
on *forwards* 282
  –account of 155
  –a large scale 31
  –all accounts 52
  –all fours *identity* 13
    agreement 23
  –an average 29
  –a par 27
  –foot *duration* 106

event 151
doing 170
–no account 32
–no occasion 107
–one's head 218
–one's travels 57
–that account 155
–the brink of 32
–the cards 152
–the dot 113, 132
–the increase 35
–the movement 113
–the move 264
–the nail 118
–the other hand 30
–the part of 9
–the point of 111
–the present occasion 118
–the whole 50
–time 132
onager 271
once
  different time 119
  past 122
  seldom 137
  at–
  instantaneously 113
  soon 132
  –for all *final* 67
  infrequency 137
  tell one–527
  determine–604
  choose 609
  –in a blue moon 137
  –in a way 137
  –more *twice* 90
  –again 104
  –upon a time
    time 106
    different time 119
    formerly 122
on dit *news* 532
  talk 588
one *identical* 13
  whole 50
  unity 87
  somebody 372
  married 903
  all–to 823
  as–man
  unanimous 488
  cooperation 709
  at–with *agree* 23
  concur 178
  concord 714
  both the–and the other 80
  from–to another
  transfer 783
  make–of 186
  neither–nor the other 610
  of–accord 488
  on–side *oblique* 217
  lateral 236

–and a half 87
–and all *whole* 50
general 78
unanimous 488
–and the same 13
–at a time 87
–bone and one flesh 903
–by one *separately* 44
  respectively 79
  unity 87
–consent *concur* 178
  assent 488
–fell swoop
  instantaneous 113
  violent 173
–fine morning 106
–idea
  narrow mind 481
  –in a way 83
  –in ten thousand
    good 648
    good man 948
  –jump 113
  –leg in the grave 160
  –mind *concur* 178
    assent 488
  –of these days 121
  –or two 100
  –thing with another 476
  –way or another 627
  the–or the other 609
  with–voice 488
one-eyed 443
one-horse 643, 651
oneirocritic 524
oneirology 522
oneiromancy 511
oneness 87
onerous *bad* 649
  difficult 704
  burdensome 706
  troublesome 830
oneself 13
  be–again 660
  have all to–777
  kill–361
  take merit to–884
  take upon–*will* 600
  undertake 676
  talk to–589
  true to–604a
one-sided
  misjudging 481
  wrong 923
  dishonorable 940
one-step *dance* 840
ongoing 282
onion 298, 393, 401
onlooker 444
only *small* 32
  simple 42
  single 87
  imperfect 651

–think 870
–yesterday 123
onomancy 511
onomatopoeia
  language 560
  nomenclature 564
onset *beginning* 66
  attack 716
onslaught 716
ontogenesis 161
ontogeny 161
ontologism 451
ontology 1
onus *burden* 706
  duty 926
onward 282
onychomancy 511
onyx 847
oöcyte 357
oodles 102
oögamy 18, 357
oögenesis 161
oögonium 357
oöphyte 357
oösperm 357
oösphere 357
oöspore 357
ooze *emerge* 295
  flow 348
  semiliquid 352
  –out *disclosure* 529
opacity 426
opal 847–*glass* 427
opalescent
  semitransparent 427
  variegated 440
opaline 427
opaque 426
open *begin* 66
  expand 194
  unclose 260
  manifest 525
  reveal 529
  frank 543
  artless 703
  (*intelligible* 518)
  break–173
  in–court
  manifest 525
  publish 531
  in the–338
  lay–226
  lay oneself–to 177
  leave the matter– 705
  –a case 476
  –a discussion 476
  –air *outside* 220
  atmosphere 338
  –air concert 415
  –and above board 939
  –arms *willing* 602
  warfare 722
  friendship 888
  social 892

opening

   courtesy 894
- country 344
- enemy 891
- eyes *see* 441
   attention 457
   discovery 480a
   expectation 507
   inform 527
   undeceive 529
   teach 537
   predetermination 611
   wonder 870
- fire 716
- house 892
- into *conversion* 144
   river 348
- market 799
- one's mind 529
- one's purse strings 809
- order 194, 716
- question,
   question 461
   uncertain 475
- rupture 713
- sesame *opening* 260
   key 631
   spell 993
- space 180
- the ball
   precedence 62
   beginning 66
- the door to
   cause 153
   facilitate 705
   permit 760
- the lips 529
- the lock 480a
- the sluices 297
- the trenches 716
- to *liable* 177
   facile 705
- to discussion 475
- to suspicion 485
- to the view 446
- up *begin* 66
   disclose 529
- war *war* 722
   enmity 889
   throw 296
- with - doors 531

opening *beginning* 66
   opportunity 134
   space 180
   gap 198
   aperture 260

open-handed 816
open-hearted
   veracious 543
   artless 703
   liberal 816
   honorable 939

open-mouthed
   cry 411
   expectation 507

   speak 582
   loquacious 584
   desire 865
   wonder 870

opera *music* 415
   poetry 597
   drama 599
   (*see* opus)
- glass 445
- house 599

opéra bouffe 599
opera-hat 225
operant 170
operate *cause* 153
   produce 161
   act 170
   remedy 662
   work 680
- upon *motive* 615

operation
   (*see* operate)
   arithmetical - 85
   in - 680
   put in - 677
   surgical - 662

operative *acting* 170
   doing 680
   workman 690

operator *surgeon* 662
   doer 690

operculated 261
operculum 223, 261
operetta 415
operose *toilsome* 686
   difficult 704
ophicleide 417
ophidian 366
ophiology 368
ophiomancy 511
ophite 440
ophthalmia 443
ophthalmic 441
opiate 174, 841
opine 484
opiniative 484
opiniator 606
opiniatre 481
opinion 484
   give an - 480
   have too high an - of oneself 880
   popular - 488
   system of - s 484
   wedded to an - 606

opinionate
   narrow-minded 481
   obstinate 606

opinionated 474, 606
   self - 880

opinionative 474
opinioned
   narrow 481

opinionist
   positive 474
   obstinate 606

opitulation 707

opium

opium *soothe* 174
   deaden sense 376
   narcotic 662
   intemperance 954
- den 945

opium eater 683
oppossum 366
oppidan 188, 189
oppilation 706
opponent
   antagonist 710
   enemy 891

opportune
   well timed 134
   expedient 646

opportunism 646
opportunist 605
opportunity 134, 646
   lose an - 135

oppose *contrary* 14
   counteract 179
   front 234
   evidence 468
   clash 708

opposed (*see* oppose)
   unwilling 603

opposite *contrary* 14
- scale 30
- side 237

opposition 706, **708**
   (*see* oppose)
   the - 710

oppositionist 710
oppress *molest* 649
   severe 739
   malevolence 907

oppressive *hot* 382
   painful 830

oppressor *tyrant* 739
   evildoer 913

opprobrium 874
oppugnance 719
oppugnant 708, 710, 719

oppugnation
   opposition 708
   resistance 719

opsimathy 537
optative 865
optic 420
optical 441
- devices 441
- instruments **445**

optician 445
optics *light* 420
   sight 441
   optical instruments 445

optimacy 875
optimates 875
optimism
   overestimation 482
   hopeful 858

optimist 482, 935
optimize 482, 549
option 609

optional 600
optometer 445
optometry 445
opulence 803
opus *composition* 54
   production 161
   music 413

opuscule 593
or *yellow* 436
   alternative 609

oracle *sage* 500
   prediction 511
   prophet **513**

Oracle, Sir -
   positive 474
   vanity 880
   blusterer 887

oracular *answer* 462
   ambiguous 475
   wise 498, 500
   prediction 511

oral *evidence* 467
   declaratory 527
   voice 580
   speech 582
- communication 588
- evidence 467

orange *fruit* 298
   round 249
   color **439**

orangery 371
oration 582
   funeral - 363

orator 582
oratorical 582
oratorio 415
oratory *speaking* 582
   place of prayer 1000

orb *region* 181
   circle 247
   luminary 423
   eye 441
   sphere of action 625
- of day *sun* 318
   luminary 423
- of night 318

orbicular 247
orbiculation 249
orbit *circle* 247
   heavens 318
   path 627

orbital index 372a
orchard 371, 636, 691

orchestra *music* 415
   musicians 416
   instruments 417
   theater 599

orchestral 415
- score 415

orchestrate 413, 416
orchestration 60, 413
orchestrion 417
orchid 369
orchotomy 158
ordain *command* 741

ordinary

   commission 755
   due 924
   legal 963
   God 976
   church 995

ordained *due* 924
   clergy 996

ordeal *experiment* 463
   trouble 828
   sorcery 992
- of battle 722

order *regularity* 58
   class 75
   requirement 630
   direct 693
   command 741
   money 800
   rank 873
   quality 875
   decoration 877
   law 963
   at one's - 743
   call to - 932
   in - 620
   in working - 673
   keep in - 693
   money - 800
- of the day
   conformity 82
   events 151
   habit 613
   plan 636
   command 741
- of your going 684
   out of - 651
   pass to the - of the day 624
   put in - 60
   recur in regular - 138
   set in - 60
   set one's house in - 673
   standing - 613
   under - s 749

orderless 59
orderly *regular* 58, 80
   arrange 60
   conformable 82
   servant 746
- of succession 63
- of things 80

orders, holy - 995
   in - 996

ordinal 998
ordinance
   command 741
   law 963
   rite 998

ordinary *usual* 82
   meal 298
   habitual 613
   imperfect 651
   mediocre 736
   ugly 846
   simple 849

ordinate | outline

ordinate
  in-*store* 636
  -condition *rule* 80
  -course of things 613
ordinate 466
ordination
  arrangement 60
  measurement 466
  command 741
  commission 755
  church 995
  rite 998
ordnance 727
ordonnance 963
ordure 653
ore 635
oread 979
orectic 865
organ *music* 417
  voice 580
  instrument 633
  -of the soul 580
  -point 408, 413
organic *state* 7
  structural 331
  protoplastic 357
  -change 146
  -chemistry 357, 490a
  -remains 357
  dead 362
organism 329, 366
organist 416, 996
organization
  arrangement 60
  production 161
  structure 329
  animated nature 357
organize *arrange* 60
  produce 161
  animated nature 357
  plan 626
  (*prepare* 673)
organized
  (*see* organize)
  -hypocrisy 544
  -massacre 361
  -murder 361
organizer 626
organography 329
organology 329
organotherapy 662
orgasm 173
orgiastic 954
orgies 954
oriel *recess* 191
  corner 244
  window 260
  chapel 1000
Orient *East* 236
  sunrise 420
Oriental 236
  -philosophy 451
orientate 236
orifice *beginning* 66
  opening 260
oriflamme 550
Origenism 984

origin *beginning* 66
  cause 153
  derive its-154
original *dissimilar* 18
  not imitated 20
  model 22
  individual 79
  exceptional 83
  cause 153
  invented 515
  unaccustomed 614
  laughingstock 857
  return to-state 660
originality *will* 600
  want of-843
originate *begin* 66
  cause 153
  invent 515
  -in 154
originative 153, 168
originator 164
Orion 490a
Orion's belt 318
orismology *word* 562
  name 564
orison *request* 765
  worship 990
ormolu *sham* 545
  ornament 847
Ormazd 976
ornament
  in writing 577
  adornment **847**
  glory 873
  excess of-851
ornamental art 847
  painting 556
ornamentation 847
ornate-*writing* 577
  ornamental 847
orniscopy 511
ornithology 368
ornithomancy 511
orotund 577
orotundity 249, 577
Orpheus 416
orpiment 436
orrery 318
orthodox
  comfortable 82
  -*religion* 983a
  -dissenter 984
orthodoxy 983a
orthoepist 562
orthoepy 562, 580
orthogonal 212
orthography 561
orthology 494
orthometry
  measurement 466
  prosody 597
orthopedist 662
orthopraxy 662
orts *remnants* 40
  useless 645
  (*trifles* 643)

oryctology
  minerals 358
  organic remains 368
O Salutaris 990
oscillation
  change 149
  motion **314**
  center of-222
oscitancy *opening* 260
  sleepy 683
osculation
  contact 199
  touch 379
  endearment 902
osculature 43
Osiris 979
Osmanli 984
osmiridium 323
osmosis 302
Ossa on Pelion
  heap 72
  weight 319
osseous 323
ossify 323
ossuary 363
ostensible
  appearance 448
  probable 472
  manifest 525
  plea 617
ostentation 847, **882**
ostentatious 845, 882
osteology 329
osteopathy 662
ostiary *mouth* 260
  doorkeeper 263
  estuary 343
ostium 260
ostler 746
ostracism
  (*see* ostracize)
ostracize *exclude* 55
  eject 297
  banish 893
  censure 932
  punish 972
ostrich 274, 366
  stomach of an-957
otalgia 378
other *different* 15
  extra 37
  do unto-s as we
    would men
    should do unto
    us 942
  enter into the
    feelings of-s 906
  every-138
  in-words 522
  just the-way 14
  -extreme 14
  -self *friend* 890
  -side of the shield
    468
  -than 18
  -things to do 683

  -time 119
  the-day 123
otherwise 18
otic 418
otiose 169, 683
otiosity 683
otography 418
otologist 418
otology 418
otopathy 418
otoplasty 418
otorrhea 418
otoscope 418
otoscopy 418
ottar, otto (*see* attar)
otter hound 366
ottoman 215
oubliette *ambush* 530
  prison 752
ough! 874
ought-to be 922
  -to be done 926
ouija board 992a
ounce *weight* 319
ouphe 980
Our Lady 977
ourselves 372
oust *eject* 297
  dismiss 756
  deprive 789
out *exterior* 220
  in error 495
  come-446
  go-*egress* 295
  cool 385
  -and out 52
  -at elbows 874
  -at heels 804
  -in one's reckoning
    495
  -of
    (*see below*)
  -upon it
    malediction 908
    censure 932
  -with it *disclose* 529
    obliterate 552
    play-729
    send-297
    time-of joint 735
    waters-337
outbalance
  compensate 30
  superiority 33
outbid 794
outbound 295
outbrave 885
out-brazen 234, 885
outbreak
  beginning 66
  violence 173
  egress 295
  discord 713
  attack 716
  revolt 742
  passion 825

outburst *violence* 173
  egress 295
  revolt 825
outcast
  unconformable 83
  Pariah 876
  secluded 893
  bad man 949
outcome *effect* 154
  egress 295
  produce 775
outcry *noise* 404, 411
  auction 796
  complaint 839
  censure 932
outdo *superior* 33
  transcursion 303
  activity 682
  conquer 731
outdoor 220
outdoors 338
outer 220
outermost 220
outface 885
outfit *clothes* 225
  equipment 673
outflank *flank* 236
  defeat 731
outflow 295
outgate 295
outgeneral 731
outgo 303
outgoing 295
outgoings 809
outgrow 194
outgrowth 65, 154
out-Herod
  superior 33
  bluster 174
  (*exaggerate* 549)
outhouse 191
outing 266
outjump
  transcursion 303
  repute 873
outlandish *foreign* 10
  extraneous 57
  irregular 83
  barbarous 851
  ridiculous 853
outlast 110
outlaw *irregular* 83
  secluded 893
  reprobate 949
outlawry 964
outlay 809
outleap 303
outlet *opening* 260
  egress 295
outlie 196
outline *contour* **230**
  form 240
  features 448
  sketch 554
  painting 556
  plan 626

520

outlines rudiments 66
  principles 596
outlive survive 110
  continue 141
outlook view 448
  outstare 885
outlying
  remaining 40
  exterior 220
outmaneuver
  trick 545
  defeat 731
outmarch 274
outnumber 102
out of motive 615
  insufficient 640
  get—the way 623
  get well—671
  go—one's way 629
  —all proportion 31
  —breath 688
  —cash 804
  —character 24
  —conceit with 867
  —countenance
    disrepute 874
    humbled 879
  —danger 664
  —date
    anachronism 115
    old 124
    ill—timed 135
  —doors 220, 338
  —earshot 419
  —employ 681
  —favor 867
  —focus 447
  —gear disorder 59
    powerless 158
    unprepared 674
  —hand soon 132
    completed 729
  —harness 748
  —health 655
  —hearing distant 196
    not hear 419
  —humor
    discontent 832
    anger 900
  —joint disorder 59
    impotent 158
    evil 619
  —kilter 59
  —luck 735
  —one's depth
    deep 208
    shortcoming 304
    difficult 704
    rash 863
  —one's mind 503
  —one's power 471
  —one's reckoning
    uncertain 475
    error 495
    inexpectation 508
    disappointment 509

—one's teens 131
—one's wits 824
—order disorder 59
  unconformity 83
  imperfect 651
—patience 825
—place disorder 59
  unconformable 83
  displaced 185
  inexpedient 647
—pocket loss 776
  poverty 804
  debt 806
—print 552
—range 196
—reach distant 196
  impossible 471
—repair 659
—repute 874
—season 135
—shape 243
—sight completeness 52
—sorts disorder 59
  dejection 837
—spirits 837
—the common 83
—the perpendicular 217
—the question
  impossible 471
  dissent 489
  rejection 610
  hopeless 859
  refusal 764
  undue 925
—the sphere of 196
—the way
  irrelevant 10
  unimitated 20
  exceptional 83
  absent 187
  distant 196
  ridiculous 853
  secluded 893
—the world dead 360
  secluded 893
—time unmusical 414
  imperfect 651
  spoiled 659
  discord 713
—work 681
  put—sight
  invisible 447
  neglect 460
  conceal 528
  turn—doors 297
outogeny 357
outpost distant 196
  circumjacent 227
  front 234
outpouring egress 295
  information 527
  abundance 639
output egress 295
  produce 775
outrage violence 173

evil 619
badness 649
injury to 659
resentment 900
malevolence 907
disrespect 929
guilt 947
outrageous
  excessive 31
  violent 173
  scandalous 874
outrank 33, 62
outré exceptional 83
  exaggerate 549
  ridiculous 853
outreach distance 196
  deception 545
outreckon 482
outre mer 196
outride 303
outrider 64
outrigger support 215
  boat 273
outright 52
outrival superior 33
  surpass 303
  fame 873
outrun 303
  —the constable
    debt 806
    prodigal 818
outscourings 653
outset beginning 66
  departure 293
outshine glory 873
  eclipse 874
outside extraneous 57
  exterior 220
  appearance 448
  clean the—of the platter
    ostentation 882
    mere—544
  —car 272
outsider 57, 893
outskirts distant 196
  environs 227
outspan 292
outspeak 582
outspoken say 582
  artless 703
  be—censure 932
outspread 202
outstanding
  remaining 40
  outside 220
  —accounts 811
  —debt 806
outstare 885
outstart 66
outstep 303
outstretched 202
  with—arms 894
outstrip 303
outtalk 584
outvie contend 720

shine 873
outvote 731
outward 220
  —bound 293, 295
outwear 677
outweigh exceed 33
  predominate 175
  (unequal 28)
outwit deceive 545
  defeat 731
outwork defense 717
outworn 124
oval 247, 249
ovarian 353
ovary 357
ovate 247, 249
ovation procession 69
  triumph 883
  (trophy 733)
oven 386 like an
  —hot 382
over more 33
  remainder 40
  end 67
  past 122
  high 206
  too much 641
  all—completed 729
  all—with
    destroyed 162
    dead 360
    failure 732
    adversity 735
    danger—664
    fight one's battles—again 594
    get—660
    hand—783
    make—784
  —again repeatedly 104
  —against 237
  —all 200
  —and above
    superior 33
    added 37
    remainder 40
    redundance 641
  —head and ears
    complete 52
    height 206
    feeling 821
  —the border 196
  —the hills and far away 196
  —the mark 33
  —the way 237
  set—755
  turn—218
overabound 641
overact bustle 682
  affect 855
overall 225
overanxiety 865
overarch 223
overawe sway 737
  intimidate 860

respect 928
overbalance
  unequal 28
  compensation 30
  superior 33
overbear
  influence 175
overbearing 885
overboard throw—
  eject 297
  reject 610
  disuse 678
  abrogate 756
  relinquish 782
overborne failure 732
  subjection 749
overburden
  redundant 641
  bad 649
  fatigue 688
overcast cloudy 353
  dark 421
  dim 422
overcautious 864
overcharge
  exaggerate 549
  style 577
  redundance 641
  dearness 814
overcloud 353
overcoat 225
overcolor 549
overcome
  counteract 179
  induce 615
  conquer 731
  sad 837
  disgraced 874
  tipsy 959
  —an obstacle 731
overconfident
  credulous 486
  rash 863
overcredulous 486
overcurious 455
overdate 115
overdistention 194
overdo
  redundance 641
  bustle 682
  affectation 855
overdone—meat 298
overdose 641
overdraw
  exaggerate 549
  misrepresent 555
  prodigal 818
overdrawn account 808
overdrive misuse 679
overdue 115, 133
overeager 865
overeat oneself 957
overestimation 482
overfatigued 688
overfed 869, 957

overfeed 641
overflow *stream* 348
  redundance 641
  –with gratitude 916
overgo 303
overgorged
  satiety 869
  gluttony 957
overgrown *much* 31
  large 192
  expanded 194
overhang *high* 206
  pendency 214
overhanging
  destiny 152
  pendency 214
overhasty 901
overhaul *count* 85
  attend to 457
  inquire 461
  censure 932
overhead 206
overhear *hear* 418
  be informed 527
overjoyed 827
overjump 303
overlap *inwrap* 225
  go beyond 303
overlay *layer* 204
  cover 223
  exaggerate 549
  excess 641
  overdo 682
  hinder 706
  –with ornament
    writing 577
overleap 303
overliberal 818
overlie 223
overload
  ornament 577
  redundance 641
  hinder 706
overlook *slight* 458
  neglect 460
  superintend 693
  forgive 918
  disparage 929
  bewitch 992
overlooked 642
  not to be– 642
overlooker 694
overlord 745
overlying 206
overman 33
overmaster 731
overmastering 821
overmatch
  unequal 28
  superior 33
  strength 159
  conquer 731
overmeasure 641
overmodest 881
overmost 210
overmuch 641

overnight 122
overofficious 682
overpaid 816
overpass *exceed* 33
  transgress 303
overpersuade 615
overplus
  remainder 40
  excess 641
overpoise 179
overpower
  counteract 179
  subdue 731
  emotion 824
overpowering
  strong 159
overpraise
  overrate 482
  exaggerate 549
  flatter 933
overprize 482
overrate 482
overreach *pass* 303
  deceive 545
  baffle 545
overreckon 482
overrefinement 477
over-religious 955
override *superior* 33
  influence 175
  pass 303
  hinder 706
  defeat 731
  authority 737
  severity 739
  abrogate 756
overrighteous 988
overrule *control* 737
  cancel 756
overruling
  important 642
overrun *presence* 186
  spread 194
  motion beyond **303**
  printing 591
  redundance 641
  despoil 659
overscrupulous 939
oversea 57, 341
overseas cap 225
oversee 693
overseer 694
oversensitive 822
overset
  invert 218
  level 308
  subvert 731
overshadow
  darken 353, 421
  repute 873
  disrepute 874
overshoot the mark
  go beyond 303
  exaggerate 549
  overdo 682
  clumsy 699

oversight
  inattention 458
  error 495
  superintendence 693
  failure 732
overskip 303
oversleep 683
overspent 688
overspread
  disperse 73
  be present 186
  cover 233
overstate 549, 555
overstep 303
overstock 641
overstrain *extol* 482
  fatigue 688
oversupply 641
overt 525–*act* 680
overtake 292
overtaken *tipsy* 959
overtask *misuse* 679
  fatigue 688
overtax 679, 688
overthrow
  revolution 146
  destroy 162
  level 308
  confute 479
  vanquish 751
overthrown
  vanquished 732
overthwart 708
overtired 688
overtone 413
overtop *surpass* 33
  height 206
  (*perfection* 650)
overtrustful 486
overture
  precursor 62, 64
  music 415
  offer 763
  request 765
overturn
  revolution 146
  destroy 162
  invert 218
  level 308
  confute 479
overvalue 482
overweening
  excess 641
  rash 863
  pride 878
  conceit 880
  insolence 885
overweigh *exceed* 33
  influence 175
  overrate 482
overwhelm *ruin* 162
  redundant 641
  thwart 706
  affect 824
overwhelmed
  defeated 732

  subjection 749
overwhelming
  strong 159
  wonderful 870
overwise 880
overwork *misuse* 679
  fatigue 688
overwrought
  exaggerated 549
  emotion 824
  affectation 855
overzealous 825
ovicell 357
oviform 249
ovo, in– 153
ovoid 247, 249
ovule 247
ovum 357
owe 806
  –it to oneself 926
owelty 27
owing *debt* 806
  attribution 155
owl *bird* 366
  fool 501
  –'s light 422
  –s to Athens 641
  screech– 412
own *assent* 488
  divulge 529
  possess 777
  property 780
  act on one's–
    responsibility 738
  after one's–heart 897
  at one's–risk 926
  come by one's– 775
  condemned out of
    one's–mouth 479
  hold one's– 737
  look after one's–
    interest 943
  look with one's–
    eyes 459
  out of one's–head 600
  –flesh and blood
    consanguinity 11
owner
  possessor 779
  without an– 777a
ownership
  property 780
ox *animal* 366
  male 373
  hot enough to roast
    an– 382
Oxford school 984
Oxford shoe 225
oxgoad 727
oxidation 357
oxreim 45
ox–tail soup 298
oxygen 359
oxygon 244

oyer and terminer,
  court of– 966
oyes 531
oyez! *hear* 418
  publication 531
oyster 298–*plant* 298
  –*stew* 298

P

P mind one's–'s and Q's
  care 459
  polite 894
  duty 926
pabulum *food* 298
  material 316
  mental– 454
pace *walk* 264
  journey 266
  measure 466
  keep–with
  concur 178
  velocity 274
  –up and down 266
  put through one's–s 525
  show one's–s
    ostentation 882
pace *permission* 760
  –tanti nominis 928
pachydermatous
  physically– 376
  morally– 823
pacific 721
pacification 723
pacifism 721
pacify *allay* 174
  (*compose* 823)
  (*forgive* 918)
pack *arrange* 60
  assemblage 72
  locate 184
  squeeze 195
  prepare 673
  burden 706
  –off *depart* 293
  eject 297
  –of nonsense 643
  –up 229
  send–ing 297
package
  assemblage 72
packer 673
packet
  assemblage 72
  ship 273
pack horse 271
pack saddle 215
pack thread 205
pact 769
Pactolus 803
pad *thicken* 194
  line 224
  horse 271
  diffuseness 573

padding   **Pantheon**

    writing 590
padding *lining* 224
    stopper 263
    soft 324
    diffuseness 573
paddle *walk* 266
    row 267
    oar 633
    —one's own canoe
      conduct 692
      free 748
    —steamer 273
paddock 232
Paddy *Irishman* 188
paddy *rice* 330
padishah 745
padlock *fastening* 45
    fetter 752
    put a—on one's lips
      585
padre 996
padrone 745
paean *rejoicing* 838
    celebration 883
    gratitude 916
    approbation 931
    worship 990
pagan 984
    —deities 979
paganism 984
page *numeration* 85
    printing 591
    book 593
    attendant 746
pageant *spectacle* 448
    amusement 840
    show 882
pagination 85
pagoda 206, 1000
pagri 225
pah 717
pai 643
pail 191
paillard 962
paillasse 215
pain *physical*—**378**
    moral—**828**
    penalty 974
painfulness 830
painfully *very* 31
painless 827
pains 686
    get for one's—973
    —and penalties 974
    take—686
painstaking
    active 682
    laborious 686
paint *coat* 223
    color 428
    deceive 545
    delineate 556
    ornament 847
    —the lily 641
    —the town red 840
painter *rope* 45

    artist 559
painting 54, **556**
painty 556
pair *similar* 17
    combine 48
    couple 89
    —horses 272
    —off *average* 29
    marry 903
pair-oar 273
pairs *cards* 840
pajamas 225
pakka (*see* pucka)
paktong 545
pal *ally* 711
    chum 890
palace 189
    bishop's—1000
    —car 272
Paladin *defense* 717
    combatant 726
palaeocrystic 124
palaeology
    (*see* paleology etc.)
palaestra *school* 542
    arena 728
palaestral
    strength 159
    school 542
    contention 720
palaestric
    exertion 686
    (*see* palaestral)
palang 215
palanquin 266, 272
palatable *savory* 394
    pleasant 829
palatal *phonetic* 561
palate 390
    tickle the—394
palatial *palace* 189
    ostentatious 882
palatinate 181
palatine 745
Palatine Court 966
palaver
    unmeaning 517
    speech 582
    loquacity 584
    colloquy 588
    council 696
pale *region* 181
    inclosure 232
    limit 233
    dim 422
    colorless 429
    frightened 860
    —its ineffectual fire
      dim 422
    out of repute 874
    —of the church 995
    turn—*lose color* 429
    emotion 821
    fear 860
pale-faced 429
paleoanthropic 124

paleography *past* 122
    philology 560
Paleolithic Age 372a
paleology *past* 122
    language 160
paleontology 357, 368
paleozoic 124, 372a
paleozoology 357
palestra
    (*see* palaestra etc.)
paletot 225
palette 556
palfrey 271
palimpsest 147, 528
palindrome
    inversion 218
    neology 563
paling *fence* 232
    prison 752
palingenesis 163, 660
palinody 607
palisade *defense* 717
    prison 752
    —s *cliff* 212
palki 272
pall *mantle* 225
    funeral 363
    disgust 395
    insignia 747
    weary 841
    dislike 867
    satiety 869
    canonicals 999
    —bearer 363
palladium *safety* 664
    (*defense* 717)
pallet *support* 215
    painter's—556
palliament 225
palliate *moderate* 174
    mind 658
    relieve 834
    extenuate 937
    moderation 174
palliative 174
    qualification 469
    remedy 662
pallid 429
pallium 999
pall-mall 840
pallone 840
pallor 429
palm
    measure of length 200
    tree 367, 369
    touch 379
    trophy 733
    steal 791
    laurel 877
    bear the—873
    grease the
    —*induce* 615
    give 784
    itching—865

    —off 545
    —upon 545
    win the—731
palmated 257
palmer *traveler* 268
    clergy 996
palmiped 219
palmist 513
palmistry 500, 511, 522
palm oil 356
palmy *prosperous* 734
    pleasant 829
    joyous 836
    —days *prosperity* 734
    pleasure 827
palpable *material* 316
    tactile 379
    obvious 446
    manifest 525
    (*intelligible* 518)
    —obscure 421
palpate 379
palpation 379
palpitate *tremble* 315
    emotion 821
    fear 860
palpus 379
palsgrave 875
palsied (*see* palsy)
    irresolute 605
palsy *impotence* 158
    physical insensibility 376
    disease 655
    mental insensibility 823
    (*weakness* 160)
palter *falsehood* 544
    shift 605
    elude 773
paltering 520
paltry *small* 32
    unimportant 643
    mean 940
paludal 345
pampas 344, 367
pamper *indulge* 954
    gorge 957
pamphlet 590, 593
pamphleteer 595
pan 191
panacea 662
panache *plume* 256
    ornament 847
panama *hat* 225
Pan-American 78
Pan-Anglican 78
pancake 298
pancratiast 159
pandar (*see* pander)
Pandean pipes 417
pandect
    knowledge 490
    dissertation 595
    compendium 596

    code 963
pandemic 657
Pandemonium 982
    inhabitants of—978
pandemonium 59, 404, 414
pander *pimp* 962
    —to *instrument* 631
    help 707
    flatter 933
pandiculation
    expansion 194
    opening 260
    sleepy 683
Pandoor 726
Pandora's box 619
    bottom of—858
pan-dowdy 298
paned 440
panegyric 931
panegyrize 482
panel *list* 86
    partition 228
    accused 938
    jury 967
    —game 545
    sliding—545
paneling 847
pang *physical*—378
    moral 828
Pan-Germanic 78
Pangloss 492
panhandler 876
panharmonic 78
Pan-Hellenic 78
pani 337
panic 860—*fear* 860
panier 225
pannel 213
pannier 191
panoply 490
    defense 717
    arms 727
panopticon 752
panorama *view* 448
    painting 556
panoramic 78, 446
    —view 441
pan-
phenomenalism 451
Panpipes 417
Panslavic 78
pansophism 490
pant *heat* 382
    fatigue 688
    emotion 821
    —for 865
pantaloon
    old man 130
    pantomimist 599
    buffoon 844
pantaloons 225
pantheism 451, 984
Pantheon *gods* 979
    temple 1000

panther
  variegation 440
  courage 861
pantile *roof* 223
  conduit 350
pantisocracy 737, 875
pantologist
  scholar 492
  proficient 700
pantology 490
pantometer 244
pantomime *signs* 550
  drama 599
pantophagous 298
pantophagy 298, 957
pantry 191
pants 225
panurgy 698
pap *mamma* 250
  pulp 354
papa *father* 166
Papa *pope* 996
papacy 984
papal 995
paper *cover* 223
  white 430
  writing 590
  book 593
  security 771
  (*record* 551)
  –credit 805
  –money 800
  –pellet 643
  –war *discussion* 476
  contention 720
papery *weak* 160
Paphian
  intemperate 954
  impure 961
papilionaceous 242
papilla 250
papillote 256
papistry 984
papoose 129, 167
pappous 256
Papuan 431
papula 250
papule 250
papulose 250
papyrus 590
par 27 above–648
  below–*low* 207
  imperfect 651
  –excellence 33
  –value 812
parable *metaphor* 521
  teaching 537
  description 594
parabola *curve* 245
parabolic
  metaphorical 521
paracentesis 297
parachronism 115
parachute
  balloon 273

  means of safety 666
Paraclete 976
paracme 63
parade *procession* 69
  walk 189
  journey 266
  ostentation 882
paradigm 22, 567
paradisaic 829, 946
Paradise *bliss* 827
  heaven 981
  in–827
paradox
  absurdity 497
  obscurity 519
  difficulty 704
  (*mystery* 528)
paradoxical
  uncertain 475
  absurd 497
  unintelligible 519
paraffin 356
paragon *perfect* 650
  glory 873
  good man 948
paragram
  ambiguous 520
  neology 563
paragraph *part* 51
  indication 550
  phrase 566
  article 593
paraleipsis 460
parallax 196
parallel *similarity* 17
  imitate 19
  –*position* 216
  symmetry 242
  draw a–464
  –s *indication* 550
  run–178
parallelism 216
  agreement 23
  equality 27
  comparison 464
parallelize 464
parallelogram 244
paralogism 477
paralysis
  impotence 158
  physical insensibility 376
  disease 655
  moral insensibility 823
paralyze 158, 376, 823
paramount
  supreme 33
  important 642
  authority 737
  lord–*master* 745
  possessor 779
  –estate 780
paramour 897
paranoia 503

paranoiac 504
parapet 717
paraph 550
paraphernalia
  machinery 633
  belonging 780
paraphrase
  imitation 19
  copy 21
  meaning 516
  synonym 522
  phrase 566
paraphrast 524
paraphrastic
  imitative 19
  interpretation 522
paraphrenia 821a
parapsychology 821a
parasite *follower* 65
  puppet 711
  petitioner 767
  desire 865
  servile 886
  flatterer 935
parasitic
  servile 746, 886
  subjection 749
  grasping 789
parasol *covering* 223
  shade 424
parboil 384
parbuckle 633
Parcae 601
parcel *divide* 44
  part 51
  group 72
  –out *arrange* 60
  allot 786
  part and–66
parcels *property* 780
parch *dry* 340
  heat 382
  bake 384
parched 340
  –with thirst 865
parchment
  writing 590
  security 771
parcity 819
pardon 918 beg–952
  general–506
  –me 489
pardonable 937
pare *cut* 38
  reduce 195
  peel 204
  divest 226
  (*scrape* 331)
  –down *shorten* 201
paregoric 662
parenchyma
  materiality 316
  structure 329
parent 166
parentage
  consanguinity 11

  paternity 166
parenthesis
  discontinuity 70
  inversion 218
  interjacence 228
  indication 550
  by way of
  –*occasion* 134
parenthetical
  irrelative 10
paresthesia 821a
parget 223
pargeting 847
parhelion 423
pariah
  commonalty 876
  outcast 83, 893
parian *sculpture* 557
paries 236
parietal 236
parietes 224
paring (see pare)
  small 32
  (*part* 51)
paring-knife 253
parish 181
  bring to the–804
  come upon the–804
parishioner 997
paritor 965
parity 17, 27
park *house* 189
  vale 252
  plain 344
  trees 367
  artillery 727
  pleasure ground 840
  –paling 232
parlance 582
  in common–576
parlementaire
  messenger 534
  flag of truce 723
parley *talk* 588
  mediation 724
parliament 696
parliamentary 696
  –securities 802
parlor 191
parlor car 272
parlor maid 746
parlous 665
Parnassus 597
parochial
  regional 181
  narrow 481
  bigoted 988
parody *imitation* 19
  copy 21
  absurdity 497
  misinterpret 523
  misrepresentation 555
  travesty 856
parole *speech* 582
  on–*restraint* 751

  prisoner 754
  promise 768
Parolles 887
paronomasia
  neology 563
  ornament 577
paronymous 9, 562
parotid 221
paroxysm
  violence 173
  agitation 315
  emotion 825
  anger 900
parquet 440, 599
parquetry 440
parricide 361
parrot *imitation* 19
  bird 366
  loquacity 584
  repeat like a–505
parrotism 19
parry *confute* 479
  avert 623
  defend 717
parse *analysis* 461
  grammar 567
Parsi 382, 984
parsimony 819
parsnip 298
parson 996
parsonage 1000
part *divide* 44
  portion 51
  diverge 291
  music 413
  book 593
  role 599
  function 625
  duty 926
  act a–*action* 680
  bear–in 709
  component–56
  for my–79
  fractional–100a
  in–*a little* 32
  on the–of 707
  –and parcel 56
  –by part 51
  –company
    disjunction 44
    avoid 623
    quarrel 713
  –of speech 567
  –song 415
  –with *relinquish* 782
  give 784
  play a–in
  influence 175
  principal–642
  take an active–682
  take a–in 680
  take no–in 623
  take–with
  cooperate 709
  take the–of 709
partake 778

parterre

   –of the sacrament 998
parterre *level* 213
   cultivation 371
   (*vegetation* 367)
parthenogenesis 161
partial *unequal* 28
   part 51
   special 79
   fractional 100a
   misjudging 481
   unjust 923
   –shadow 422
partiality
   preponderance 33
   desire 865
   friendship 888
   love 897
partially *a little* 32
   partly 51
partibility 44
particeps criminis
   doer 690
   auxiliary 711
participate
   cooperate 709
   share 778
   –in *be a doer* 680
participation 778
participator
   agent 690
particle *small* 32
   grain 333
particular *item* 51
   event 151
   attentive 457
   careful 459
   exact 494
   capricious 608
   odd 851
   fastidious 868
   in–79
   –account 594
   –estate 780
particularization 75
particularize
   special 79
   describe 594
particularly *very* 31
   more 33
particulars
   speciality 79
   description 594
parting 44–cup 959
Partington, Mrs. 471
parti pris 611
partisan *follower* 65
   auxiliary 711
   weapon 727
   friend 890
   sympathizer 914
partisanship
   warped judgment 481
   cooperation 709
   wrong 923

partition *divide* 44
   wall 228
   allot 786
partlet 366
partly 51
partner *companion* 88
   auxiliary 711
   sharer 778
   friend 890
   spouse 903
   sleeping–683
partnership
   party 712
   join–with 709
partridge 298
parts *intellect* 450
   skill 698
   wisdom 498
parturient 161
parturition 161
party *assemblage* 72
   special 79
   person 372
   association 712
   sociality 892
   –spirit
   warped judgment 481
   cooperation 709
   wrong 923
   –to *action* 680
   agent 690
   cooperate 709
   –to a *suit* 969
   –wall 228
party-colored 428, 440
parvenu *new* 123
   successful 734
   vulgar 851
   lowborn 876
parvenuism 876
parvitude 193
pas *precedence* 62
   term 71
   precession 280
   rank 873
Pascal's law 490d
paschal 998
pasha 745, 875
pashalic 737
pasigraphy 560, 590
pasquil 934
pasquinade 934
pass *predicament* 7
   conjuncture 8
   be superior 33
   course 109
   lapse 122
   happen 151
   interval 198
   defile 203
   move 264
   transfer 270
   move through 302
   exceed 303

   vanish 449
   indication 550
   way 627
   difficulty 704
   thrust 716
   passport 760
   at cards 764
   –as *property* 783, 784
   barely–651
   barely–muster 651
   let it–460
   make a–at 716
   –a *law* 963
   –and repass 302
   oscillate 314
   –an examination
   goodness 648
   repute 873
   –an opinion 480
   –away *cease to exist* 2
   end 67
   transient 111
   past 122
   cease 142
   die 360
   –by *course* 109
   inattention 458
   neglect 460
   deception 545
   disrespectful 929
   –comprehension 519
   –current 484
   –in one's checks 360
   –in review
   attention 457
   inquiry 461
   –in the mind 451
   –into 144
   –into one's hand 785
   –judgment 480
   –muster
   conform to 82
   sufficient 639
   good 648
   approbation 931
   –off *be past* 122
   egress 295
   –off for 544
   –on 282
   –one's time in 625
   –one's word 768
   –out of 295
   –out of sight 449
   –over *exclude* 55
   cross 302
   die 360
   give 784
   forgive 918
   exemption 927a
   –over to 709
   –sentence on 971
   –the eyes over 457
   –the fingers over 379
   –the Rubicon 609
   –through *event* 151
   motion 302

   –through one's hands 625
   –time *exist* 1
   time 106
   do nothing 681
   –to 144
   –to the order of the day 624
   –under the name of 564
   pretty–704
passability 174
passable *small* 32
   unimportant 643
   imperfect 651
   pretty 845
passado 716
passage (*see* pass)
   part 51
   conversion 144
   street 189
   corridor 191
   opening 260
   navigation 267
   deviation 279
   moving through 302
   music 413
   –in a book 593
   means of access 627
   action 680
   cut a–260
   force a–302
   –of arms 720
passage d'armes 722
passamezzo 415
pass book 811
passé *antiquated* 124
   aged 128
   spoiled 659
passed away 122
passenger 268
   –train 272
passeparole 550
passe partout
   key 260
   instrument 631
passer-by 444
passetemps 840
passim *dispersed* 73
   place 182
   situation 183
passing *very* 31
   transient 111
   –away *death* 360
   –bell 363
   –strange 870
   –word 527
passion
   emotion 820, 821
   excitability 825
   pain 828
   desire 865
   love 897
   anger 900
   –queller 866
   ruling–606

passionate *style* 575
   warm 825
   irascible 901
passionless 823
Passion week 998
passive *inert* 172
   inaction 681
   obedient 743
   inexcitable 826
passiveness
   irreligion 989
pass-key 631
Passover 998
passport
   instrumentality 631
   order 741
   permission 760
password *answer* 461
   sign 550
   military 722
past 122, 124
   danger–664
   insensibility to the–506
   obliteration of the–506
   –bearing 830
   –comprehension 519
   –cure 859
   –dispute 474
   –one's prime 128
   –perfect 122
   –performances 465
   –praying for 945
   –recollection 506
   –work *useless* 645
   impaired 659
   thing of the–124
paste *cement* 45
   to cement 46
   pulp 352, 354
   sham 545
   tinsel 847
   scissors and–609
pasteboard 593
pastel 556, 594
pasticcio
   imitation 21
   mixture 41
pastil 400
pastime 840
pastiness (*see* pasty)
pastor 996
pastoral
   bucolic 370, 371
   music 415
   poem 597
   religious 995
   sermon 998
pastorale 415
pastose 556
pastry *food* 298
   sweets 396
pasturage
   meadow 344
   herbage 367

pasture
   meadow 232, 344, 367
   food 298
pasty *tart* 298
   like paste 352
pat *pertinent* 23
   strike 276
   (*expedient* 646)
   –on the back
     induce 615
     comfort 834
     encourage 861
     approve 931
   –on the cheek 902
   –on the head
     endearment 902
Patagonian 206
patch *small* 32
   change 140
   region 181
   blemish 848
   –up *restore* 660
     compromise 774
patchwork
   mixture 41
   discontinuous 70
   variegation 440
pate *summit* 210
   brain 450
pâté 298
patefaction 260
patella 191
patent *open* 260
   manifest 525
   license 760
   property 780
   –log 274, 466, 551
pater *father* 166
patera *cup* 191
   sacramental 998
paterfamilias 166
paternal *father* 166
   benevolent 906
   –domicile 189
   –estate 780
paternity 166
paternoster 990
pater patriae 912
path *direction* 278
   way 627
   cross the–706
   secret–530
pathetic 830
pathless *spacious* 180
   closed 261
   difficult 704
pathognomonic 550
pathognomy 550
pathology 655, 662
pathos 821
patience
   perseverance 604a
   endurance 826
   moderation 831
   cards 840

patient *sick* 655
patois 560, 563
patriarch *veteran* 130
   ancestors 166
   master 745
   priest 996
patriarchal
   ancient 124
   ancestral 166
patriarchy 737
patrician 875
patrimony 780
patriot 910
Patristic philosophy 451
patrol *walk* 266
   safeguard 664
   (*warning* 668)
   –wagon 272
patrolman 664, 965
patron *auxiliary* 711
   customer 795
   liberality 816
   friend 890
   sympathizer 914
patronage
   influence 175
   aid 707
   authority 737
patronize
   supervise 693
   aid 707
patronymic 564
patten 225
patter *strike* 276
   sound 407
   unmeaningness 517
   talk 584
   theater 599
patterer 582
pattern *model* 22
   indication 550
   perfection 650
   ornament 847
   good man 948
patulous 194, 260
pauciloquy 585
paucity *small* 32
   few 103
   scanty 640
Paul Jones 792
Paul Pry *curious* 455
   prattle 588
paunch 191, 250
pauper 640, 804
pause *discontinue* 70
   cease 142
   quiescence 265
   doubt 485
   irresolution 605
   repose 687
   –for a reply 142
pave *cover* 223
   (*prepare* 673)
   –the way 705
pavé, on the–961

pavement *base* 211
   covering 223
   path 627
pavilion 189
paving 211
pavior 673
pavonine 440
paw *touch* 379
   retention 781
pawky 702
pawl 45
pawn 601, 771, 788
pawnbroker 787
pawnshop 787
pax *hush!* 403
   pyx 998
   –vobiscum 894
pay *compensation* 30
   profitable 775
   defray 807
   expend 809
   income 810
   punish 972
   remunerate 973
   in one's
   –servant 746
   hired 795
   –attention to 457
   –a visit 892, 894
   –back 718
   –down 807
   –dues 924
   –homage
     submission 725
     worship 990
   –in advance 809
   –in full 807
   –in one's own coin 718
   –no attention etc. to 458, 460
   –off 718
   –old debts 807
   –one's respects 894
   –one's way
     defray 807
     economy 817
   –out 972
   –regard to 484
   –the debt of nature 360
   –the penalty 952
   –the piper 707
   –through the nose 814
   –too much 814
paying guest 188
paymaster 801
payment 30, 807
   remuneration 973
paynim 984
pea 249, 369
peace *silence* 403
   concord 714
   amity 721
   at–714

   commission of the– 965
   justice of the–967
   keep the–
     moderation 174
     concord 714
   make–723
   make–with 831
   Prince of–976
   speak–831
peaceable
   moderate 174
peaceful
   inexcitable 826
peacemaker 714
   mediator 724
   contented 831
peace offering
   pacification 723
   mediation 724
   gift 784
   atonement 952
peace pipe 550
peach 298, 529
peach-colored 434
pea-coat 225
peacock
   variegation 440
   proud 878
   vain 880
   gaudy 882
   jackdaw in–'s feathers 701
pea-green 435
pea-jacket 225
peak *height* 206
   summit 210
   sharp 253
   sicken 655
peaked 203, 253
peal *loud* 404
   roll 407
   –of bells 407
   –of laughter 838
pear 298
pearl *goodness* 648
   ornament 847
   glory 873
   cast–s before swine 638
   mother-of–440
   –white 430
pearly
   semitransparent 427
   color 428
   white 430
   gray 432
   variegated 440
pear-shape 249
peasant 876
peat 388–bog 345
pebble *little* 193
   hard 323
peccability
   imperfection 651
   vice 945

   guilt 947
peccable 947
peccadillo 947
peccant *bad* 649
   unclean 653
   diseased 655
   –humor 653, 655
peccary 401
peccavi 950
peck *much* 31
   multitude 102
   eat 298
   –at *censure* 932
   –of troubles
     difficulty 704
     adversity 735
     pain 828
peckish 865
Pecksniff 548
pectinated 253
peculate 791
peculator 792
peculiar *special* 79
   exceptional 83
peculiarly *greatly* 31
   more 33
pecuniary 800
pecunious 803
pedagogic 537, 540
pedagogue
   scholar 492
   teacher 450
   pedantic 855
pedal 633
   –point 408, 413
pedant *scholar* 492
pedantic
   half-learned 491
   –style 577
   affected 855
pedantry
   narrow mind 481
peddle *meddle* 683
peddler 797
   –'s French 563
peddling *trifling* 643
   miserly 819
pederero 727
pedestal 215
   place on a–307
pedestrian 268
pediatrics 662
pedicel 215
pedicle 214, 215
pediculation 653
pediculosis 653
pediculous 653
pedicure 662
pedigree
   continuity 69
   ancestry 166
pediment *capital* 210
   base 215
pedlar (*see* peddler)
pedometer 200, 466, 551

peduncle 215
pedunculate 215
peek 441
peel *layer* 204
  skin 223
  uncover 226
  −off *separate* 44
peeler 664
peelhouse 717
peep *chirp* 412
  look 441
  −behind the curtain 461
  −into the future 510
  −of day 125
  −out *visible* 446
  disclosure 529
peephole 260
Peeping Tom 455
peep show *view* 448
  amusement 840
peer *equal* 27
  pry 441
  inquire 461
  lord 875
  −out 446
peerage 875
peerless *unequaled* 28
  supreme 33
  best 648
  glorious 873
  virtuous 944
  (*perfect* 650)
peevish *cross* 895
  irascible 901
peg *grade* 71
  hang 214
  project 250
  drink 959
  come down a−306
  let down a−308
  not stir a−*quiet* 265
  inaction 681
  −away *activity* 682
  −on *journey* 266
  −to hang on *plea* 617
Pegasus 271, 490a
pegology 348
pegomancy 511
pegs *legs* 266
Peking man 372a
pelagic 341
pelerine 225
pelf *gain* 775
  property 780
  money 803
pelican 366
pelisse 225
pellet 249 *paper*−643
pellicle *film* 204
  skin 223
pellmell 59, 825
pellucid 425, 570
peloric 242
pelt *skin* 223
  dress 225

  throw 276
  attack 716
  punish 972
peltate 245
peltry 223
pen *inclosure* 232
  write 590
  writer 593
  restrain 751
  imprison 752
  draw the−*through* 552
  −and ink 590
  −in hand 590
  ready−569
  slip of the −*error* 495
  solecism 568
  stroke of the−*write* 590
  authority 737
  command 741
pena 206
penal 972
  −*servitude* 972
  −*settlement* 752
penalize 974
penalty 971, 974
penance
  atonement 952
  penalty 974
  worship 990
penchant *willing* 602
  desire 865
  love 897
pencil *bundle* 72
  −of light 420
  write 590
pencil drawing 556
pencraft 590
pendant *match* 17
  pendency 214
  −world 318
pendency *time* 106
  hanging 214
pendragon 745
pendulate 605
pendulous
  hanging 214
  oscillating 314
pendulum *hang* 214
  motion of a−314
Penelope, work of−
  useless 645
  incomplete 730
peneplain 344
penetralia 221
penetrate *ingress* 294
  passage 302
  sagacity 498
  −the soul 824
penetrated with
  belief 484
  feeling 821
penetrating
  sagacious 498

  feeling 821
  −glance 441
penetration 465
penguin 310, 366
peninsula 342
penitence 950
penitentiary 752
  confessor 996
penknife 253
penman 590
  inspired−985
penmanship 590
pen name 565
pennant 550
penniless 804
  a−lass 804
pennon 550
penny 800
  cost a pretty−814
  in for a−in for a pound 768
  no−no paternoster 812
  not have a−804
  −ante 840
  −dreadful 594
  −trumpet 410
  −whistle 410, 417
  turn a−775
penny−a−liner
  envoy 534
  writer 593
penny−a−lining
  diffuse style 573
pennyweight 319
penny wise 819
  −and pound foolish
  caprice 608
  waste 638
  prodigal 818
pennyworth 812
penology 972
pensée, arrière−528
penseroso 837
pensile 214
pension *income* 810
pensioner *learner* 541
  servant 746
  receiver 785
pensive
  thoughtful 451
  sad 837
penstock 350
pentad 193
pentagon 98, 244
pentahedron 244
pentameter 98, 597
pentangular 98
pentastyle 98
Pentateuch 985
Pentecost 998
Penthesilean 861
penthouse 191
pent up 751
  −in one's memory 505

penultimate 67
penumbra 421
penurious 819
penury *poverty* 804
  (*scantiness* 640)
peon 726
peonage 603
people
  consanguinity 11
  multitude 102
  location 184
  inhabit 186
  mankind 372
  subjects 746
  commonalty 876
  laity 997
pep 171, 682
  full of−574
pepastic 662
pepper *pungent* 392
  condiment 393
  attack 716
  (*energy* 171)
pepper−and−salt
  gray 432
  variegated 440
peppercorn 643
  cheap 815
  −rent 815
peppery *irascible* 901
pepsin 320
peptic 662
per 631−*contra*
  contrariety 14
  counterevidence 468
  opposition 708
  −saltum
  discontinuous 70
  instantaneous 113
  −se 87
peradventure 470
peragrate 266
perambulate 266
perambulator
  measure of length 200
  vehicle 272
perambulatory 266
perceivable 446
perceive
  be sensible of 375
  see 441
  know 490
percentage
  number 84
  discount 813
perceptible 446
perception *idea* 453
  knowledge 490
perceptive 375, 465
perch *location* 184
  abide 186
  habitation 189
  height 206
  support 215
  −up 307

perchance
  by *chance* 156
  possibly 470
perching 206
percipience 450
percolate
  ooze out 295
  liquefaction 335
  water 337
  stream 348
  clean 652
percolator 191
percursory 458
percussion 276
  center of−222
percussive 277
perdition
  destruction 162
  ruin 732
  loss 776
perdu 528 *enfant*
  −hopeless 859
  rash 863
perdure 106
perdy 535
peregrination 266
peregrinator 268
peremptory
  assertion 535
  firm 604
  authoritative 737
  rigorous 739
  compulsory 744
  duty 926
  −denial 536
  −refusal 764
perennate 106
perennial
  continuous 69
  diuturnal 110
  −plants 367
perennity 112
pererration 266
perfect *great* 31
  entire 52
  excellent 650
  complete 729
perfection 650
  bring to−729
  let us go on unto− 650
perfidy 940
perfiate 349
perforate 260
perforator 262
perforce *necessity* 601
  compulsion 744
perform *produce* 161
  do 170
  −*music* 416
  action 680
  achieve 729
  fulfill 772
  −a circuit 629
  −a duty 926
  −a function 644

527

performable

- —a funeral 363
- —an obligation 772
- —a part *drama* 599
  action 680
- —a service 998
- —the duties of 625

performable 470

performance
 (*see* perform)
 effect 154

performer
 musician 416
 actor 599
 agent 690
 affectation 855

perfume 400
perfumery 400
perfunctory
 incomplete 53
 neglect 460

perhaps *possibly* 470
 supposition 514
 (*chance* 156)

peri *beauty* 845
 mythology 979

periapt 993
pericarp 191
pericranium 450
periculous 665
peridot 847
perigee 490a
perihelion 197, 490a
peril 665 at your—909
 take heed at one's—668

perimeter 230
period *end* 67
 point 71
 —*of time* 106, **108**
 recurrence 138
 at fixed—s 138
 well rounded—s 577, 578

periodical
 recurring 138
 book 593

periodicity 138
peripatetic
 journey 266
 traveler 268

Peripatetic school 451
periphery 230
periphrase
 phrase 566
 diffuse 573

periplus 267
periscope 441
periscopic 446
 —*lens* 445

perish *cease to exist* 2
 be destroyed 162
 die 360
 decay 659
 —with cold 383
 —with hunger 956

perishable 111
perissology
 diffuseness 573
 (*loquacity* 584)

peristalsis 221
peristaltic 248
peristyle 189
periwig 225
periwinkles 298
perjured 940
perjurer 548
perjury 544
perk *dress* 225
 —up *elevate* 307
 revive 689
 cheer 836

perked up *proud* 878
perlustration 441
permanence
 uniformity 16
 durability 110
 unchanging **141**
 unchangeable 150

permanent
 habitual 613

permeable 260
permeate
 insinuate 228
 pervade 186
 pass through 302

permissible
 permitted 760
 (*lawful* 924)

permission **760**
permissive 760
permit 760
permitting 760
 weather etc.—469, 470

permutation
 numerical—84
 change 140
 interchange 148

pernicious 649
pernicity 274
perorate *end* 67
 diffuse style 573

peroration *sequel* 65
 end 67
 speech 582

perpend *partition* 228
 think 451

perpendicular 212, 246

perpension
 attention 457

perpetrate 680
 —a pun etc. 842

perpetrator 690
perpetual 112
 frequent 136
 —*curate* 996

perpetually 16, 112
perpetuate 112
 continue 143
 establish 150

preserve 976
perpetuity 112
perplex *derange* 61
 distract 458
 uncertainty 475
 bother 830

perplexed
 confused 59, 523
 convoluted 248

perplexity *disorder* 59
 uncertainty 475
 unintelligibility 519
 difficulty 704
 (*ignorance* 491)

perquisite 775, 973
perquisition 461
perron 627
perscrutation 461
persecute *oppress* 649
 annoy 830
 malevolence 907

persecution complex 821a

Perseids 490a
perseverance
 continuance 143
 persistence **604a**

persevere 143, 604a
persiflage 842, 856
persifleur 844
persist *duration* 106
 permanence 141
 continue 143
 persevere 604a

persistence 110
persistent 110, 143
person
 substantiality 3
 man 372
 without distinction of—s 922

personable 845
personage 372
persona grata
 friend 890
 favorite 899

personal (*see* person)
 special 79
 subjective 317
 —*narrative* 594
 —*property* 780
 —*security* 771

personality
 (*see* personal)
 discourtesy 895
 disrespect 929
 censure 932
 detraction 934

personalty 780
personate *imitate* 19
 represent 554

personify
 allegory 521
 represent 554

personnel
 constituent 56

doer 690
perspective *view* 448
 expectation 507
 painting 556
 aerial—428
 in—200

perspicacity
 sight 441
 intelligence 498
 fastidiousness 868

perspicuity
 intelligibility 518
 style **570**

perspiration
 exudation 295
 excretion 299
 in a—382

perstringe 457
persuadability 602, 615
persuadable 602
persuade *belief* 484
 induce 615
 (*advise* 695)

persuasibility
 willingness 602

persuasion
 opinion 484
 teaching 537
 inducement 615
 religious—983

persuasive 615
 —*reasoning* 476

pert *vain* 880
 insolent 885
 discourteous 895

pertain to *relate to* 9
 included under 76
 power 157
 belong 777
 property 780
 duty 926

pertinacity 604a
pertinent *relative* 9
 congruous 23
 (*applicable* 644)

pertingent 199
perturbation
 derange 61
 ferment 171
 agitation 315
 emotion 821
 excitation 824, 825
 fear 860

pertusion 260
pertussis 655
peruke 225
peruse 539
Peruvian bark 662
pervade *influence* 175
 extend 186
 affect 821
 —the soul 824

pervading spirit 820
perverse
 obstinate 606

petrify

difficult 704
churlish 895
sulky 901a

perversion
 sophistry 477
 misinterpretation 523
 misteaching 538
 falsehood 544
 untruth 546
 injury 659
 impiety 988

perversity
 (*see* perverse)

pervert
 (*see* perversion)
 convert 144
 recant 607

perverted
 in error 495

pervestigation 461
pervicacious 606
pervigilium 682
pervious 260, 295
pessimism
 overrate 482
 underrate 483
 dejection 837
 hopeless 859

pessimist 482, 862, 859
pessimize 549, 934
pessomancy 511
pest *bane* 663
 painfulness 830

pester 830
pesthouse 662
pestiferous 657
pestilence 655
pestle 330
pet *love* 897
 favorite 899
 fondle 902
 flatter 933

petal 367
petard 727
 hoist on one's own—
 retaliation 718
 failure 732

Peter pence 784
petiole 367
petition *ask* 765
 pray 990

petitioner 767
petitio principii 477
petit maitre 854
petname 565
petrel *warning* 668
petrify *dense* 321
 hard 323
 organization 357
 freeze 385
 thrill 824
 affright 860
 astonish 870

528

petrol   **pidgin English**

petrol 356
petroleum 356
pétroleur 384
petrology 358
petronel 727
petticoat *dress* 225
   woman 374
   –*government* 737
pettifogger 968
pettifogging
   sophistry 477
   dishonorable 940
pettish 901
petty *shallow* 32
   little 193
   unimportant 643
   –*cash* 800, 811
   –*cashbook* 551
   –*larceny* 791
   –*sessions* 966
   –*treason* 742
petulance
   insolence 885
   irascibility 901
petulant
   –*language* 574
pew *cell* 191
   church 1000
pewter 41
phaeton 272
Phaëthon 306, 423
phalansterism 910
phalanx *party* 712
   army 726
   (*assemblage* 72)
phantasm
   illusion 443
   appearance 448
   imagination 515
phantasmagoria 448
phantasy *idea* 453
   imagination 515
phantom *unreal* 4
   corpse 362
   fallacy of vision 443
   imaginary 515
   specter 980a
pharisaical
   falsehood 544
   false piety 988
Pharisee *deceiver* 548
   pietist 988
pharmaceutist 662
pharmacology 662
pharmacopoeia 662
pharmacopolist 662
pharmacy 662
pharos 550
phase *aspect* 8
   transition 144
   form 240
   appearance 448
   assume a new–144
   have many–*s* 149
   view in all its–*s* 461
phasis 448

phasma 443
pheasant 298
phenix (*see* phoenix)
phenomenon
   event 151
   appearance 448
   prodigy 872
phial 191 (*see* vial)
Phidias 559
philander 902
philanderer 902
philanthropical 906, 910
philanthropy 910
philippic 932
Philistine
   conformity 82
   unintellectual 491
   bourgeois 876
philologist 492
philologize 562
philology 560
philomath 492
philomel 416
philosopher
   intellect 450
   scholar 492
   sage 500
   –'*s stone* 650
philosophical
   thoughtful 451
   calm 826
   –*unitarianism* 984
philosophy
   intellect 450
   thought 451
   knowledge 490
   calmness 826
   moral–450
   –*of the mind* 450
philter 993
phiz *face* 234
   look 448
phlebotomy
   ejection 297
   remedy 662
phlegm *viscid* 352
   insensibility 823
phlegmatic *dull* 32
   slow 275
   indifferent 866
phlogiston 382
Phoebe 318
Phoebus *sun* 318
   luminary 423
phoenix *exception* 83
   reproduction 163
   paragon 650
   restoration 660
phone *telephone* 534
phonetic *sound* 402
   tonic 561
   voice 580
   speech 582
   –*spelling* 561
phonetics 560, 561

phonic 402, 418
phonics 402
phonocamptic 402
phonograph 417, 418, 551
phonography
   sound 402
   letter 561
   writing 590
phonorganon 418
phosphorescence
   light 420
   luminary 423
phosphorus 423
photics 420
photodrama 448
photogenic 420
photograph *like* 17
   picture 556
photographer 445
photography
   light 420
   optical instruments 445
   representation 554
   painting 556
photogravure 558
photolithograph 558
photolithography 420
photology 420
photometer *light* 420
   optical instrument 445, 466
photometry 420
photomicrography 420
photon 32, 490d
photophony 402
photoplay 448
photospectro-heliography 554
photosphere 318
phototelegraphy 420
phototherapy 420
phragma 228
phrase *music* 413
   language **566**
phrasemonger 577
phraseology 569
phrenetic
   deranged 503
   madman 504
phrenitis 503
phrenologist 448
phrenology 448, 450
Phryne 962
phthiriasis 653
phthisis 655
phthisozoics 361
phylacteric
   sorcery 992
phylactery
   maxim 496
   spell 993
phyletic 166

phylogeny 161, 357
phylum 75
physic *cure* 660
   remedy 662
   throw–to the dogs 662
physical 316, 542
   –*culture* 845
   –*drill* 537
   –*education*
     material 316
     teaching 537
   –*force strength* 159
     compulsion 744
   –*pain* **378**
   –*pleasure* **377**
   –*science* 316
physician 662, 695
physicism 316
physics 316, **490d**
physiogeny 161
physiognomy
   face 234
   appearance 448
   interpret 522
physiology
   organization 357
   life 359
   vegetable–369
physique *strength* 159
   animality 364
phytivorous 298
phytobiology 369
phytology 369
phyton 369
phytopathologist 369
phytotomy 369
phytozoaria 193
pi 591
piacular 952
pianino 417
pianissimo 415
pianist 416
piano *gentle* 174
   slow 275
   music 415
   –*player* 417
   –*score* 415
pianoforte 417
piazza 182, 189, 191
pibroch *music* 415
   indication 550
   war 722
pica 591
picacho 206
picaroon 792
picayune 643
pick *ax* 253
   eat 298
   select 609
   best 648
   clean 652
   gain 775
   –*a quarrel* 713
   –*holes*

   censure 932, 934
   –*one's steps* 459
   –*one's way* 675
   –*out extract* 301
   select 609
   –*the brains of* 461
   –*the lock* 480a
   –*to pieces*
     separate 44
     destroy 162
     find fault 932
   –*up learn* 539
     get better 658
     gain 775
pickaninny 129
pickax 253
picked 648–*men* 700
pickeer 720
pickeerer 792
pickelhaube 717
picket *join* 43
   locate 184
   fence 229
   guard 668
   defense 717
   soldiers 726
   restrain 751
   imprison 752
   torture 972
pickings *gain* 775
   booty 793
pickle *condition* 7
   macerate 337
   pungent 392
   condiment 393
   preserve 670
   difficulty 704
   have a rod in–673
pickle-herring 844
pick-me-up 392, 662
pickpocket 792
   abuse like a–932
pickthank *busy* 682
   servile 886
picnic *food* 298
   participation 778
   amusement 840
picot *edge* 257
picquet 840
pictorial *painting* 556
   beauty 845
picture
   appearance 448
   representation 554
   painting 556
   description 594
   –*post card* 592
   –*to oneself* 515
picture gallery 556
picturesque
   painting 556
   beauty 845
piddle *dawdle* 683
piddling 643
pidgin English 563

pie

pie *food* 298
  sweet 396
  printing 591
piebald 440
piece *adjunct* 39
  bit 51
  change 140
  painting 556
  drama 599
  cannon 727
  coin 800
  courtesan 962
  fall to–s 162
  give a–of advice 695
  in–s 330
  make a–of work about 642
  of a–42
  –*of a good fortune* 618
  –*of music* 415
  –*of news* 532
  –*of work discord* 713
  –*out* 52
  –*together* 43
  pull to–s 162
pièce
  –*de résistance* 298
  –*justificative* 467
piecemeal 51
pied 440
pier 666
pierce *perforate* 260
  insert 300
  bodily pain 378
  chill 385
  hurt 649
  wound 659
  affect 824
  mental pain 830
  –*the head* 410
  –*the heart* 830
piercer 262
piercing *cold* 383
  loud 404
  shrill 410
  intelligent 498
  feeling 821
  –*eye* 441
  –*pain* 378
pier glass 445
Pierian spring 597
Pierides 416
pietas 998
pietism 988
pietist 987, 988
piety 987
pig *animal* 366
  sensual 954a
  –*in a poke uncertain* 475
  chance 621
  rash 863
  –*together* 72
pigeon *bird* 298, 366

  dupe 547
  steal 791
  gorge de–440
pigeon-hearted 862
pigeonhole
  receptacle 191
  hole 260
  shelve 460
piggery 636
piggin 191
piggish 954
pig-headed
  foolish 499
  obstinate 606
pigment 428
pigmy (*see* pygmy)
pignoration 771
pig-sticking 361
pigsty 653
pigtail 214
Pigwiggen 193
pike *hill* 206
  sharp 253
  fish 366
  weapon 727
pikeman 726
pikestaff *tall* 206
  plain 525
pilaster *support* 215
  projection 250
  ornament 847
pile *heap* 72
  multitude 102
  edifice 161
  velvet 256
  store 636
  money 800
  (*house* 189)
  funeral–363
  –*on the agony* 860
  –*up exaggeration* 549
  redundance 641
pile-driver 276
pile-dwelling 189
pileous 256
piles 655
pilfer *steal* 791
pilferer 792
pilgarlic *outcast* 893
pilgrim *traveler* 268
  palmer 996
pilgrimage
  journey 266
  undertaking 676
pill *sphere* 249
  medicine 662
  bore 841
  bitter–735
pillage *injury* 659
  theft 791
pillager 792
pillar *stable* 150
  lofty 206
  support 215
  monument 551
  tablet 590

  from–*to post transfer* 270
  agitation 315
  irresolute 505
  circuit 629
  –*of the state etc.* 873
  –s *of Hercules* 550
pillarist 996
pillion 215
pillory 975
pillow *support* 215
  soft 324
  consult one's–*temporize* 133
  reflect 451
pillowcase 223
pilon 784
pilose 256
pilot *mariner* 269
  inform 527
  guide 693
  director 694
pilot balloon
  experiment 463
pilot boat 273
pilot bread 298
pilot jacket 225
Pilsener beer 298
pimento 393
pimp 962
pimple *tumor* 250
  blemish 848
pin *fasten* 43
  fastening 45
  locate 184
  sharp 253
  axis 312
  trifle 643
  might hear a–*drop* 403
  not a–*to choose equal* 27
  no choice 609a
  –*down compulsion* 744
  restraint 751
  –*oneself upon serve* 746
  servile 886
  –*one's faith upon* 484
  point of a–193
pinacotheca 556
pinafore 225
pince-nez 445
pincers 781
pinch *emergency* 8
  contract 195
  pain 378
  chill 385
  need 630
  difficulty 704
  grudge 819
  hurt morally 830
  (*insufficiency* 640)
  in a–704

  jack at a–711
  –*of snuff* 643
  where the shoe–es 830
pinchbeck *sham* 545
  jewelry 847
pinched (*see* pinch)
  thin 203
  poor 804
  –*with hunger* 865
pinchfist 819
pinchgut 819
pinching *cold* 383
  miserly 819
Pindaric 597
pine *tree* 367
  disease 655
  dejection 837
  suffer in mind 828
  –*away* 837
  –*for* 865
pineapple 298, 369
pinery 371
pingpong
  photograph 554
  game 840
pin grass 367
pinguid 355
pinguify 355
pinhole 260
pinion *fasten* 43
  wing 267
  instrument 633
  restrain 751
  fetter 752
pink *indent* 257
  pierce 260
  thrust 276
  color 434
  perfection 650
  glory 873
pink of *beauty* 845
  –*courtesy* 894
  –*fashion* 852
  –*perfection* 650
  –*politeness* 894
pin money 800
pinna 418
pinnace 273
pinnacle 210
pinprick 180a, 643
pins *legs* 266
  –*and needles bodily pain* 378
  numb 381
  mental pain 828
pioneer *precursor* 64
  leader 234
  agriculture 371
  teacher 540
  prepare 673
pious 987–*fraud untruth* 546
  false piety 988
pipe *tube* 260
  conduit 350

pit

  vent 351
  sound 410
  cry 411
  music 416, 417
  weep 839
  no–*no dance* 812
  –*of peace* 721
  –*one's eye* 839
  –s *stridor* 410
pipe clay *habit* 613
  strictness 739
piped 260
pipe dream 458, 515
pipelaying 626
piper 416 *pay the*
  –*aid* 707
  payment 807
piping–*hot* 382–*time peace* 721
  prosperity 734
pipkin 191
piquant *pungent* 392
  –*style* 574
  impressive 821
pique *excite* 824
  pain 830
  hate 898
  anger 900
  –*oneself pride* 878
piracy 773
piragua 273
pirate *plagiarize* 788
  steal 791
  thief 792
pirogue 273
pirouette
  inversion 218
  evolution 312
  turn a–607
Pisa, tower of–217
pis-aller
  substitute 147
piscatorial 366
pisciculture 370
piscina *drain* 350
  altar 1000
piscine 350
pish! *absurd* 497
  trifling 643
  excitable 825
  irascible 901
pistareen 643
piste 551
pistol 727
Pistol 887
pistol shot 197
piston 263
pit *deep* 208
  hole 252
  opening 260
  grave 363
  theater 599
  abyss 667
  bottomless–982
  –*against opposition* 708

pitapat

discord 713
—against one another 464
—of Acheron 982
pitapat *agitation* 315
  rattle 407
  feeling 821
  excitation 824
pitapatation 315
pitch *degree* 26
  term 71
  location 184
  height 206
  summit 210
  verticality 212
  obliquity 217
  throw 284
  descent 306
  depression 308
  reel 314
  resin 356a
  musical—413
  black 431
  have absolute—416
  —and toss 621
  —dark 421
  —into *attack* 716
  contend 720
  punish 972
  —of one's breath 411
  —one's tent 292
  —overboard 782
  —upon *reach* 292
  discover 480a
  choose 609
  get 775
  touch—653
pitched battle 720
pitcher 191
pitchfork *vehicle* 273
  throw 284
  rain—s 348
pitch pipe 417
piteous *painful* 830
piteously *much* 31
pitfall *snare* 545
  danger **667**
pith *gist* 5
  strength 159
  interior 221
  center 222
  meaning 516
  important part 642
pithless 158
pithy *meaning* 516
  concise 572
  vigorous 574
pitiable *bad* 649
  painful 830
  contemptible 930
pitied, to be—828
pitiful
  unimportant 643
  bad 649
  disrepute 874
  pity 914

pitiless 914a
  revengeful 919
  (*malevolent* 907)
pittance *quantity* 25
  dole 640
  allotment 786
  income 810
pitted *blemish* 848
pituitous 352
pity 914 *express*—915
  for—'s sake 914
  what a—*regret* 833
  lament 839
pivot *junction* 43
  cause 153
  support 215
  axis 312
pivotal 222
pix *box* 191
  assay 563
  rites 998
pixy 979
pizzicato 415
placable 918
placard 531
placate *pacify* 723
  forgive 918
place *circumstances* 8
  order 58
  arrange 60
  term 71
  occasion 134
  situation **182**, 183
  locate 184
  abode 189
  office 625
  invest 787
  sell 796
  rank 873
  give-to 623
  have—1
  in—183
  in—of 147
  make a—for 184
  out of—185
  —in order 60
  —itself 58
  —to one's credit 805
  —upon record 551
  —under *include* 76
  take—151
place hunter 767
placeman 758
placenta 63
placentals 368
placet 741
placid 826
placket 260
plafond 223
plagiarism
  imitation 19
  borrowing 788
  theft 791
plagiarist 792
plagiarize
  (*see* plagiarism)

plagihedral 217
plague *disease* 655
  pain 828
  worry 830
  —of sighing and grief 837
plague spot 657
plaguy *difficult* 704
  troublesome 830
plaice 298, 367
plaid *shawl* 225
  variegation 440
plaidoyer 476
plain *horizontal* 213
  country **344**
  obvious 446
  meaning 518
  manifest 525
  style 576
  artless 703
  economical 817
  ugly 846
  simple 849
  —dealing 543
  —English 576
  —interpretation 522
  —question 461
  —sailing 705
  —sense 498
  —speaking
    manifest 525
    frank 703
  —terms *intelligble* 518
  interpreted 522
  language 576
  —truth 494
  —words 703
plainly 525
  tell one—527
plainness 576
plains, lunar 490a
plain song 990
plain-spoken
  manifest 525
  frank 703
plaint *cry* 411
  lament 839
plaintiff 938
plaintive 839
plaisance
  (*see* pleasance)
plaisanterie 842
plaister 223
plait *weave* 219
  fold 258
plan *itinerary* 266
  information 527
  representation 554
  scheme **626**
planchette 992a
planchment 223
plane *horizontal* 213
  flat 251
  smooth 255
  soar 305
  inclined—633

planet *world* 318
  fate 601
planetarium 318, 490a
planet-struck
  adversity 735
  wonder 870
planimetry 466
planing 267
plank *board* 204
  platform 586, 626
  path 627
  safety 666
plankton 366, 367
plant *place* 184
  insert 300
  vegetable 367
  agriculture 371
  trick 545
  tools 633
  property 780
  —a battery 716
  —a dagger in the breast 830
  —a thorn in the side 830
  —oneself 184
plantain *banana* 298
plantation
  location 184
  agriculture 371
  estate 780
planter 188, 779
  snag 706
plant house 659
plash *lake* 343
  stream 348
  faintness 405
  sound 408
plashy 345
plasm 22
plasma 357, 847
plasmatic 240
plasmature 240
plasmic 240
plaster *cement* 45
  covering 223
  remedy 662
  —up *repair* 660
plasterwork 223
plastic *alterable* 149
  form 240
  soft 324
  (*facile* 705)
plat *weave* 219
  ground 344
plate *dish* 191
  layer 204
  covering **223**
  flat 251
  food 298
  engraving 558
  —printing 558, 591
plateau *level* 213
  plain 344
plated 545

play

plate layer 690
platform
  horizontal 213
  support 215
  stage 542
  scheme 626
  arena 728
  —*orator* 582
platitude
  unmeaning 517
  dull 843
  (*absurdity* 497)
Plato 490a
Platonic
  contemplative 451
  inexcitable 826
  chaste 960
  —bodies 244
  —Idea 317
  —Ideal 317
Platonism 317, 451
Platonist 317
platoon *army* 726
  (*assemblage* 72)
  —fire 716
platter *receptacle* 191
  layer 204
  flat 251
  clean the outside of the—544
plaudit 931
plausible
  probable 472
  sophistical 477
  false 544
  flattery 933
  vindication 937
play *operation* 170
  influence 175
  scope 180
  oscillation 314
  music 416
  drama 599
  use 677
  action 680
  exertion 686
  freedom 748
  amusement 840
  at—840
  bring into—677
  full of—836
  full—175
  give—to the imagination 515
  in—842
  —a deep game 702
  —a game *pursue* 622
  conduct 692
  pastime 840
  —a part *false* 544
  drama 599
  action 680
  —at cross purposes
    confusion 59
    misinterpret 523
  —fast and loose

531

playa — ply

falsehood 544
irresolute 605
tergiversation 607
caprice 608
—first fiddle
 importance 642
 repute 873
—for chance 621
—gooseberry 459
—havoc 659
—hide and seek
 hide 528
 avoid 623
—into the hands of 709
—of colors 440
—off 545
—of light 420
—one a trick
 disappoint 509
 deceive 545
—one false
 disappoint 509
 falsehood 544
 deception 545
—one's best card
 exertion 686
 skill 698
—one's part
 business 625
 conduct 692
—on the feelings 824
—possum 544
—second fiddle
 inferior 34
 subject 749
—'s the thing 599
—the deuce
 excitement 825
—the devil with
 malevolence 907
—the fool *folly* 499
 clumsy 699
 amusement 840
 ridiculous 853
 ridicule 856
—the monkey 499
—tricks with
 unskillful 699
 cunning 702
—truant 623
—upon *deceive* 545
 ridicule 856
—upon words
 misinterpret 523
 neology 563
 wit 842
—with 460
playa 342, 344
playday 840
played out *end* 67
 fatigue 688
 completion 729
 failure 732
player *musician* 416
 instrument 417

actor 599
—piano 417
playfellow 890
playful 836
—imagination 515
playground
 arena 728
 games 840
playhouse 599
playing field 728
playmate 890
playsome 836
plaything *trifle* 643
 toy 840
 make a—of 749
playwright 599
plaza 189
plea *answer* 462
 argument 476
 excuse **617**
 vindication 937
 lawsuit 969
plead *answer* 462
 argue 467
 plea 617
 beg 765
—guilty 950
—one's cause 937
pleader *lawyer* 968
pleading, special— 477
pleadings 969
pleasance
 demesne 189
 pleasure ground 840
pleasant
 agreeable 829
 amusing 840
 witty 842
 make things—
 deceive 545
 induce 615
 please 829
 flatter 933
pleasantry 840, 842
please 829 as you—
 obedience 743
 do what one—s 748
 if you
—obedience 743
 consent 762
 request 765
—oneself 943
pleasing 394, 829
pleasurableness 829
pleasure
 physical—**377**
 will 600
 moral—**827**
 dissipation 954
 at—600
 at one's—737
 during—108a
 give—829
 make toil of—682
 man of—954a

take one's—840
will and—600
with—*willingly* 602
pleasure-giving 829
pleasure ground
 demesne 189
 amusement 840
pleat 219, 258
plebe 493, 541
plebeian 851, 876
plebiscite
 judgment 480
 choice 609
pledge *promise* 768
 security 771
 borrow 788
 drink to 883, 894
 hold in—771
—oneself 768
—one's word 768
 take the—
 temperance 771
 sobriety 958
pledget *lining* 224
 stopper 263
 remedy 662
Pleiades *cluster* 72
 stars 318
plenary *full* 31
 complete 52
plenipotent
 power 157
plenipotentiary
 interpreter 524
 consignee 758
 deputy 759
plenitude 639
 in the—of power 159
plenteous 168, 639
plenty *multitude* 102
 sufficient 639
—to do 682
plenum *substance* 3
 space 180
 matter 316
pleonasm
 repetition 104
 diffuseness 573
 redundance 641
plerophory 484
plethora 641
plexiform 219
plexure 219
plexus 219
pliable 324
pliant *soft* 324
 irresolute 605
 facile 705
 servile 886
plicature 258
pliers *extractor* 301
 holder 781
plight *state* 7
 circumstance 8
 promise 768

security 771
 evil—735
—one's faith 902
—one's troth 768, 902
plighted love
 love 897
 endearment 902
Plimsoll mark 466
plinth *base* 211
 rest 215
plod *journey* 266
 slow 275
 persevere 604a
 work 682
plodder *worker* 686
plodding 604a, 682
 dull 843
plot—*of ground* 181
 plain 344
 measure 466
 plan 626
 the—thickens
 assemblage 72
 events 682
plough (see plow)
plover 366
plow *furrow* 259
 agriculture 371
—in 228
—one's way 266
—the ground
 prepare 673
—the waves 267
plowable 371
plowboy 876
plowed *failure* 732
plowman 371
plowshare 253
pluck *music* 416
 cheat 545
 resolution 604
 persevere 604a
 take 789
 steal 791
 courage 861
—a crow with 932
—out 301
—up reject 610
—up courage 861
plucked 732
plucky 604
plug *close* 261
 stopper 263
 blow 276
 deterioration 659
plugugly 913
plum *number* 98
 money 800
—pudding 298
plumage 256
plumb *vertical* 212
 straight 246
 close 261
 measure 466
plumber 690
plumb line 212

plum-colored 437
plume *feather* 256
 ornament 847
 borrowed—s 788
—oneself 878
plumigerous 256
plummet *depth* 208
 verticality 212
plumose 256
plump
 instantaneous 113
 fat 192
 tumble 306
 plunge 310
 unexpected 508
—down 306
—upon 292
plumper
 expansion 194
 vote 609
plumpness
 (see plump)
plumule 167
plunder *gain* 35
 steal 791
 booty 793
 (ravage 659)
plunge *revolution* 146
 insert 300
 dive **310**
 immerse 337
 chance 621
 hurry 684
—headlong 684
—in medias res
 plain language 576
 resolute 604
—into *adventure* 676
—into difficulties 704
—into dissipation 954
—into sorrow 830
plunged—in debt 806
—in grief 828
plunger
 gambler 463, 621, 840
pluperfect 122
plurality 33, **100**
plus 37
plush 256
Pluto 982
 realms of—982
plutocracy 803
plutocrat 639
plutonic 382
Plutus 803
pluvial 348
pluviograph 348
pluviometer 348
pluviometry 348
ply *layer* 204
 fold 258
 use 677
 exert 686
 request 765
—a trade 794

532

plytophagous   **polygon**

–one's task 680
–one's trade 625
plytophagous 298
p. m. 126
pneuma 450
pneumatics 334, 338
pneumatogram 532
pneumatograph 662
pneumatology 334, 450
pneumatolytic 334
pneumatometer 334, 662
pneumatonomy 334
pneumatoscope 334
pneumatoscopic 317
pneumatotherapy 662
pneumometer 662
pneumonia 655
poach *steal* 791
  illegality 964
poached eggs 298
poacher 792
poachy 345
pock 250
pocket *place* 184
  pouch 191
  diminutive 193
  receive 785
  take 789
  money 800
  treasury 802
  brook 826
  button up one's– 808
  out of–*loss* 776
  debt 806
  –the affront
    submit 725
    forgive 918
  touch the–800
pocketbook 551
  purse 802
pocket handkerchief 225
pocket money 800
pocket pistol
  bottle 191
pococurante
  insensible 823
  indifferent 866
pod *receptacle* 191
  covering 223
podagra 378
podesta 967
poem 597
poesy 597
poet 597
poetaster *poet* 597
  affectation 855
poetic *style* 574
  –*vigor* 574
  –*prose* 598
poetize 597
poeticize 597

poetry 597
pogrom 361
poignancy
  physical energy 171
  pungency 392
  feeling 821
poignant 378
  (see poignancy)
poignard
  (see poniard)
point *condition* 8
  degree 26
  small 32
  end 67
  term 71
  integer 87
  time 106
  poignancy 171
  no magnitude 180a
  place 182
  speck 193
  sharp 253
  topic 454
  mark 550
  vigor 574
  intention 620
  wit 842
  punctilio 939
  at the–of 197
  at the–of the bayonet 173
  at the–of the sword
  violence 173
  severity 739
  compulsion 744
  come to the–
  special 79
  attention 457
  reasoning 476
  plain language 576
  culminating–210
  disputed–713
  from all–s 180
  full of–574
  give–s to 27
  go straight to the–278
  in–*relative* 9
  agreeing 23
  conformable 82
  in–of fact 1
  knotty–704
  make a–of
  resolution 604
  contention 720
  compulsion 744
  conditions 770
  due 924
  honor 939
  on the–of
  transient 111
  future 121
  –a moral 537
  –an antithesis 578
  –at *direction* 278
  direct attention 457

  intend 620
  discourtesy 895
  disrespect 929
  censure 932
  –at issue 454
  –in dispute 461
  –of attack 716
  –of convergence 74
  –of death 360
  –of etiquette 852
  –of honor 939
  –of land 250
  –of the compass 278
  –of view *view* 441
  aspect 448
  –out *indicate* 79
  –the reason 155
    draw attention 457
    inform 527
  –system 591
  –the finger of scorn 930
  –to *attribute* 155
  direction 278
  probable 472
  predict 511
  mean 516
  to the–*concise* 572
  material 642
point-blank
  direct 278
  plain language 576
  refusal 764
point champain 874
point d'appui 215
pointed *great* 31
  sharp 253
  affirmation 535
  marked 550
  concise 572
  language 574
pointedly
  intention 620
pointer *dog* 366
  discrimination 465
  indicator 550
pointless 254, 843
point-to-point race 720
poise *balance* 27
  weight 319
  measurement 466
  health 654
  inexcitability 826
poison *injure* 659
  bane 663
  –gas 663, 722, 727
poisoned 655
  commend the–chalice 544
poisonous 657, 665
poke *pocket* 191
  loiterer 275
  dawdle 683
  pig in a–
  uncertain 475

  chance 621
  rash 863
  –at *thrust* 276
  attack 716
  –fun at 856
  –one's nose in 455, 682
  –out *project* 250
  –the fire 384
poker 386 *cards* 840
poker dice 621
pokerish 980
polacca 273
polacre 273
polar 210
  –coordinates 466
  –lights 423
Polaris 423, 490a
polariscope 445
polarity *duality* 89
  counteraction 179
  contraposition 237
polarization 490d
pole
  measure of length 200
  tall 206
  summit 210
  axis 222
  oar 267
  rotation 312
  from–to pole 180
  greasy–840
  opposite–s 237
  –vault 309
poleax 727
polecat 401
polemic
  discussion 476
  discord 713
  contention 720
  combatant 726
polemoscope 445
polestar
  attraction 288
  luminary 423
  indication 550
  direction 693
  (*guide* 695)
police *regulate* 58
  guardian 965
  –court 966
  –dog 366
  –officer 664
  –magistrate 967
  –van 272
  –whistle 669
policeman
  safeguard 664
  jurisdiction 965
policy *plan* 626
  conduct 692
polish *smooth* 255
  rub 331
  furbish 658
  beauty 845

  ornament 847
  taste 850
  politeness 894
  –off *finish* 729
Polish bank 840
polished
  –*language* 578
  fashionable 852
  polite 894
polisson 949
polite 894
  offensive to ears–579
  –*literature* 560
  –*society* 852
politeness 894
politic *wise* 498
  cunning 702
  cautious 864
  (*skillful* 698)
  body–*mankind* 372
  government 737
political economy 692
politician
  director 694
  proficient 700
politics 702
polity *conduct* 692
  state 737
  duty 926
polka 415, 840
poll *count* 85
  list 86
  vote 609
  schedule 611
pollard *little* 193
  short 201
  tree 367
polloi, hoi 876
poll tax 812
pollute *soil* 653
  corrupt 659
  disgrace 874
  (*dishonor* 940)
pollution *disease* 655
  vice 945
Pollux 490a
polo 840
Poltergeist 992a
poltroon 862
polyandry 903
polychord 417
polychromatic
  colored 428
  variegated 440
polychrome 440
  painting 556
polyclinic 655
polycoustics 402
polygamy 903
polygastric 191
polyglot
  translation 522
  language 560
polygon *buildings* 189

533

polygraphy

figure 244
polygraphy 590
polylogy 573
polymorphic 81
polymorphism 357
Polynesian 372a
Polyphemus 159, 192
polyphonism 580
polyphony 402
polypus 250
polyscope 445
polysyllable 561
polytheism 984
pomade 356
pomatum 356
Pomeranian 366
pommel *support* 215
 round 249
 beat 972
pomologist 369
pomology 369
Pomona 369
pomp 882
pompom 727
pomposity 878, 882
pompous *inflated* 482
 language 577
 pride 878
poncho 225
pond *lake* 343
 store 636
 fish–370
ponder 451
ponderable
 matter 316
 weight 319
ponderation
 weighing 319
 judgment 480
ponderous *heavy* 319
 –*style* 574, 579
poniard 727
pons asinorum
 unintelligible 519
 difficulty 704
pontiff 996
pontifical 995
pontificals 999
pontificate 995
pontoon *vehicle* 272
 boat 273
 way 627
pony 271
 translation 522, 539
 –up *expend* 809
poodle 366
pooh, pooh!
 absurd 497
 unimportance 643
 contempt 930
pool *lake* 343
 coöperate 709
 prize 775
 billiards 840
 –*room* 621
 –*shark* 621

poonghie 996
poop 235
poor *incomplete* 53
 weak 160
 emaciated 203
 –*reasoning* 477
 –*style* 575
 insufficient 640
 trifling 643
 indigent 804
 unhappy 828
 cut a–figure 874
 –hand 701
 –head 499
 –in spirit 881
 –man 640, 804
 –thing 914
poorhouse 189
poorly 655–off 804
poorness (*see* poor)
 inferiority 34
poor-spirited 862
pop *bubble* 353
 noise 406
 concert 415
 unexpected 508
 –a question 461
 –at 716
 –in *ingress* 294
 insertion 300
 –off *die* 360
 –the question
 request 765
 endearment 902
 –upon *arrive* 292
 discover 480a
pope *infallibility* 474
 priest 996
popedom 995
Pope Joan 840
popery 984
popgun *trifle* 643
popinjay 854
poplar *tall* 206
 tree 367
poppy *sedative* 174
poppy-cock 517
populace 876
popular *choosing* 609
 salable 795
 desirable 865
 celebrated 873
 favorite 897
 approved 931
 –concert 415
 –demand 677
 –opinion 488
popularize
 render intelligible
 518
 facilitate 705
 make pleasant 829
population
 inhabitants 188
 mankind 372
populous *crowded* 72

multitude 102
presence 186
porcelain *baked* 384
 sculpture 557
porch *entrance* 66
 lobby 191
 mouth 231
 opening 260
 (*way* 627)
porcupine
 prickly 253
 touchy 901
pore *opening* 260
 egress 295
 conduit 350
 –over *look* 441
 apply the mind 457
 learn 539
porism *inquiry* 461
 judgment 480
pork 298
pornographic 961
porous *open* 260
 outgoing 295
 spongy 322
 liquescent 335
porpoise 192, 366
porraceous 435
porridge 298, 352
porringer 191
port *abode* 189
 sinistral 239
 gait 264
 arrival 292
 carriage 448
 harbor 666
 –admiral 745
 –fire 388
 –wine 959
portable *small* 193
 transferable 270
 light 320
portage 270
portal *entrance* 66
 mouth 231
 opening 260
 (*way* 627)
portamento 270
portative *small* 193
 transferable 270
 (*light* 320)
portcullis
 hindrance 706
 defense 717
portemonnaie 802
portend 511
portent 512
portentous
 prophetic 511
 fearful 860
porter *janitor* 263
 carrier 271
porterage 270
porterhouse steak
 298
portfolio *case* 191

book 593
file 636
direction 693
authority 747
jurisdiction 965
porthole 260
portico *entrance* 66
 room 191
portière 424
portion *part* 51
 allotment 786
 –out 786
portional 100a
portly 192
portmanteau 191
 –word 572
portrait 554
 –painter 559
 –painting 556
portraiture 554, 556
portray 554
portreeve *master* 745
 functionary 965
portress 263
posada 189
pose *situation* 183
 form 240
 inquiry 461
 puzzle 475
 difficulty 704
 affectation 855
 –as 554
poser 461
Poseidon 341
posited 184
position
 circumstances 8
 term 71
 situation 183
 proposition 514
 assertion 535
 –in society 873
positive *real* 1
 great 31
 strict 82
 certain 474
 narrow–minded 481
 belief 484
 unequivocal 518
 assertion 535
 obstinate 606
 absolute 739
 (*precise* 494)
 Philosophie–316
 –color 428
 –degree 31
 –fact 474
 –quantity 84
Positivism 451
positivism
 heterodoxy 984
 irreligion 989
posnet 191
posology 662
posse *collection* 72
 party 712

posterior

in–470
–comitatus
collection 72
army 726
authority 737
jurisdiction 965
possess 777
 bedevil 978
 –a state 7
 –knowledge 490
 –oneself of 789
 –the mind 484
 –the soul 824
possessed 777
 –with a devil 503
possession 777, 780
 sorcery 992
 come into–775, 783
 in one's–777
 person in–779
 put one in–of 527
 remain in–of the
 field 731
possessor 779
possibility
 chance 156
 liability 177
 may be 470
 property 780
 –upon a possibility
 475
possible
 (*see* possibility)
post *fastening* 45
 list 86
 situation 183
 location 184
 support 215
 send 270
 swift 274
 publish 531
 mail 534
 beacon 550
 record 551
 employment 625
 accounts 811
 stigmatize 874
 punish 972
 at one's
 –persist 604a
 prepared 673
 on duty 926
 drive from–to pillar
 704
 stand like a–265
postal 592
 –currency 800
postboy 268
post card 592
post chaise 272
postdate 115
postdiluvial 117
poster 531
posterior *in order* 63
 in time 117
 in space 235

534

posteriority 117
posteriority *futurity* 121
  descendants 167
  hand down to—
    record 551
  fame 873
postern *portal* 66
  back 235
  opening 260
postexist 1
postexistence 152
postfix 37
postgraduate 492
  —school 542
posthaste *swift* 274
  haste 684
  rash 863
post-horse 271
posthumous
  subsequent 117
  late 133
  —fame 873
posthypnotic
  suggestion 821a
postilion *rider* 268
  guide 694
postliminary
  subsequent 117
  late 133
postlude 65
postman 271, 534
postmeridian 126
post-mortem
  death 360
  interment 363
postnate 117
post-obit 360, 363
post office 534
  —order 800
postpone 133, 460
postprandial 117
postscript 37, 65
postulant *asking* 765
  petitioner 767
  nun 996
postulate
  reasoning 476
  axiom 496
  supposition 514
postulation
  supposition 514
  request 765
postulatory 765
posture
  circumstances 8
  situation 183
  form 240
posture master
  player 599
  buffoon 844
posy *bouquet* 400
  motto 550
  poem 597
  flowers 847
pot *much* 31
  mug 191

heat 384
  saucepan 386
  preserve 670
  stakes 775
  death in the— 657
  go to—
    destruction 162
    failure 732
  keep the—boiling
    continue 143
    active 682
  le—au lait
  imagination 515
  hope 858
  make the—boil 775
potable 298
potage 298
potager 191
Potomac
  all quiet on— 721
potation *beverage* 298
  tippling 959
potato 298
pot-bellied 194
pot companion 890
potency 157, 175, 470
potent 157, 159, 175
potentate 745
potential *inexistent* 2
  powerful 157
potentiality
  power 157
  possibility 470
potentialize 171
pother *disorder* 59
  difficult 704
  feeling 821
  excitement 825
  annoyance 830
pot herbs 393
pothooks 386, 517, 590
pothouse 189
pot hunter 767
potion *beverage* 298
  pungency 392
  medicine 662
potluck *eating* 298
  chance 621
  sociality 892
Potosi 803
potpourri *mixture* 41
  fragrance 400
  music 415
pottage 298
pottering
  faddling 683
potter's field 361, 363
potter's wheel 144
pottery *baked* 384
  art 557
pottle 191
potulent *drink* 298
  drunken 959
pot-valiant 959

pot-walloper
  voter 609
  servant 746
  commoner 876
pouch 191
poultice *pulp* 354
  remedy 662
  relief 834
poultry 366
pounce upon
  unexpected 508
  attack 716
  seize 789
pound—inclose 232
  weight 319
  bruise 330
  —the piano 416
  imprison 752
poundage 813
pounds shillings and pence 800
pour *emerge* 295
  rain 348
  sufficient 639
  it never rains but it —s 641
  —a broadside into 716
  —forth eject 297
  speak 582
  loquacity 584
  —in converge 290
  ingress 294
  sufficiency 639
  —on lavish 784
  —out 295, 297
  —out blood like water 361
  —water into a sieve
    waste 638
    prodigality 818
  —with rain 348
pourboire 784
pourparler
  interlocution 588
  advice 695
  council 696
pousse-café 392
pout *project* 250
  sad 837
  discourteous 895
  irate 900
  sulky 901a
poverty *style* 575
  insufficiency 640
  unimportance 643
  indigence **804**
  —of blood 160
  —of intellect 452, 499
powder 330
  food for— 726
  gun— 727
  keep one's—dry 673
  not worth— 645
  —and shot 727
  smell— 722

waste— 638
powdered
  variegated 440
powdering
  ornament 847
powdery 330
power *much* 31
  numerical 84
  multitude 102
  efficacy 157
  influence 175
  loud 404
  —of style 574
  authority 737
  do all in one's— 686
  give— 760
  in the—of
    authority 737
    subjection 749
  literary— 569
  —of attorney 755
  —of money 800
  —station 636
powerful *strong* 159
  —voice 580
powerless
  impotent 158
  weak 160
powerlessness 175a
powers that be 745
powwow 696
  palaver 588
pox 655
praam 273
practicable
  possible 470
  practical 646
  (easy 705*)*
practical *substantial* 3
  acting 170
  teaching 537
  practicable 646
  executive 692
  imperturbable 871
  —joke absurdity 497
  deception 545
  ridicule 856
  disrespect 929
  —knowledge 698
practicality
  (see practical*)*
practically
  intrinsically 5
practice *arithmetic* 85
  training 537
  habit 613
  exertion 686
  conduct 692
  in—prepared 673
  skilled 698
  out of— 699
  —law 968
  put in—use 677
  action 680
  conduct 692
  complete 729

practice *train* 537
  use 677
  act 680
  —at the bar 968
  —on one's credulity 545
  —upon
    experiment 463
    deceive 545
practiced *skilled* 698
  —eye 700
  —hand 700
practitioner
  medical— 662
  doer 690
praecognita 467
praedial 342, 371
praemunire 742, 974
praenomen 564
praetor 967
pragmatic
  narrow 481
  teaching 537
  practical 646
  —sanction 769
pragmatical
  pedantic 855
  vain 880
pragmatism
  philosophy 451
  expedience 646
  use 677
prahu 273
prairie *space* 180
  plain 344
  vegetation 367
  —dog 366
  —schooner 272
praise *thanks* 916
  commendation 931
  worship 990
praiseworthy
  commendable 931
  virtue 944
prance *move* 266
  leap 309
  dance 315
prank *caprice* 608
  amusement 840
  adorn 847
prate 584
prattle *talk* 582
  chatter 584
pravity 945
prawns 298
praxis *grammar* 567
  action 680
Praxiteles 559
pray *beg* 765
  worship 990
prayer *request* 765
  worship 990
  house of— 1000
  —of Ajax 421
prayer book 990, 998
prayer wheel 998

preach

preach *teach* 537
   allocution 586
   predication 998
   –to the winds 645
   –to the wise 538
preacher *teacher* 540
   speaker 582
   priest 996
preachment 998
preadamite
   antique 124
   veteran 130
preamble 62, 64
preapprehension 481
prebend 995
prebendary 996
precarious
   transient 111
   uncertain 475
   dangerous 665
precatory 765
precaution *care* 459
   expedient 626
   safety 664
   preparation 673
precede *superior* 33
   –in order 62
   –in time 116
   –in motion 280
precedence 62
   rank 873
   (see precede)
precedent
   (see precede)
   prototype 22
   precursor 64
   priority 116
   habit 613
   legal decision 969
   follow–s 82
precentor
   musician 416
   leader 694
   priest 996
precept
   requirement 630
   maxim 697
   order 641
   permit 760
preceptor 540
precession
   –in order 62
   –in motion 280
précieuse ridicule 855
precinct *region* 181
   place 182
   environs 227
   boundary 233
precious *great* 31
   excellent 648
   expending 809
   valuable 814
   beloved 897
   –metals 800
   –stone *goodness* 648

   ornament 847
precipice *vertical* 212
   slope 217
   dangerous 667
   on the verge of a– 665
precipitancy
   haste 684
   rashness 863
precipitate *early* 132
   sink 308
   consolidate 321
   refuse 653
   haste 684
   rash 863
   –oneself 306
precipitous 217
précis 596
precise *exact* 494
   severe 739
   taste 850
precisely *imitation* 19
   assent 488
precisian 739, 850
precisianism
   affectation 855
   heterodoxy 984
   overreligious 988
preclude 706
preclusion 55
preclusive 55
precocious *early* 132
   immature 674
   pert 885
precognition
   forethought 490
   knowledge 510
precompose 56
preconception 481
preconcert
   predetermination 611
   plan 626
precursal 511
precurse 511
precursor
   –in order 62, **64**
   –in time 116
   (*predict* 511)
   (*presage* 512)
predacious 789, 791
predacity 789
predatory *taking* 789
   thieving 791
predecessor 64
predeliberation
   foresight 510
   predetermination 611
predella 215
predesigned 611
predestination
   fate 152
   necessity 601
   predetermination 611

   Deity 976
predetermination 601, **611**
predial *land* 342
   agriculture 371
   manorial 780
predicament *state* 7
   circumstances 8
   junction 43
   character 75
predicate *forecast* 507
   affirm 535
   preach 998
predict 511
prediction 511
predilection *bias* 481
   affection 820
   desire 865
   (*love* 897)
predispose
   motive 615
   prepare 673
predisposed
   willing 602
predisposition
   tendency 176
   affection 820
predominance 157
   (see predominant)
predominant
   influence 175
   directing 693
   authority 737
predominate
   superior 33
preeminent
   superior 33
   celebrated 873
preemption 795
preengage *early* 132
preengagement 768
preestablish 626
preexamine 461
preexist *existence* 1
   priority 116
   (*past* 122)
preface *precedence* 62
   precursor 64
   book 593
prefect *learner* 541
   ruler 745
   deputy 759
   –of studies 542
prefecture 737
prefer *choose* 609
   –a claim 969
   –a petition 765
preference 62
preferment
   improvement 658
   ecclesiastical–995
prefigure
   prediction 511
   (*indication* 550)
prefix 62, 64
preglacial 124

pregnable 158
pregnant
   producing 161
   productive 168
   predicting 511
   –style 572
   important 642
   –with meaning 516
prehensile 789
prehension 789
prehistoric 124
preinstruct 537
prejudge 481
prejudicate 481
prejudice
   misjudge 481
   evil 619
   detriment 659
prejudicial 649
prelacy 995
prelate 996
prelation 609
prelect *expound* 531
   teach 537
   speech 582
prelection 537, 582
prelector 540, 582
prelibation 510
preliminaries
   –of peace 723
   settle–673
preliminary
   preceding 62
   precursor 64
   reception 296
   (*prior* 116)
prelude *prefix* 62
   precursor 64
   beginning 66
   music 415
   (*priority* 116)
premature *early* 132
   unripe 674
premeditate
   predetermine 611
   intend 620
premices 154
premier *director* 694
   vicegerent 759
   –pas 66
premiership 693
premise *prefix* 62
   announce 511
premises
   precursor 64
   prior 116
   ground 182
   evidence 467
   logic 476
premium *debt* 806
   receipt 810
   reward 973
   at a–814
premonish 668
premonition 668, 992a

prepotency

premonitory
   prediction 511
   warning 668
Premonstratensian 996
premonstration
   appearance 448
   prediction 511
   manifestation 525
premunire
   (see praemunire)
prenotion
   misjudgment 481
   foresight 510
prensation 789
prentice 541
prenticeship 539
preoccupancy
   possession 777
preoccupation
   inattention 458
preoption 609
preordain 611
   destiny 152
   necessity 601
   Deity 976
preparation 673
   music 413
   instruction 537
   writing 590
   in course of
   –plan 626
preparatory
   preceding 62
prepare 673
   –the way 705
prepared *predict* 507
   deft 698
preparedness 673
preparing
   destined 152
prepense
   spontaneous 600
   predetermined 611
   intended 620
   malice–907
prepollence 157
preponderance
   superiority 33
   influence 175
   dominance 737
   (*importance* 642)
prepossessed
   obstinate 606
prepossessing 829
prepossession
   prejudice 481
   possession 777
preposterous
   great 31
   absurd 497
   imaginative 515
   exaggerated 549
   ridiculous 853
   undue 925
prepotency 157

536

Pre-Raphaelite

Pre-Raphaelite 122, 124
prerequire 630
prerequisite 630
preresolve 611
prerogative
  authority 737
  right 924
presage *predict* 511
  omen 512
presbyopia 443
presbyter 996
Presbyterian 984
presbytery 995, 996, 1000
prescience 510
prescient 510, 511
prescious 511
prescribe *direct* 693
  advice 695
  order 741
  entitle 924
  enjoin 926
prescript *precept* 697
  decree 741
prescription
  remedy 662
prescriptive *old* 124
  unchanged 141
  habitual 613
  due 924
presence *in space* **186**
  appearance 448
  breeding 824
  in the –of *near* 197
  –chamber 191
  –of God 981
  –of mind *calm* 826
  cautious 864
  real–998
  saving one's–928
present–*in time* 118
  –*in space* 186
  offer 763
  give 784
  church preferment 995
  at–118
  –a bold front 861
  –a front 719
  –arms *courtesy* 894
  respect 928
  –in spirit 187
  –itself *event* 151
  visible 446
  thought 451
  –oneself *presence* 186
  offer 763
  courtesy 894
  –*time* **118**
  instant 113
  –to the mind
  attention 457
  memory 505
  –to the view 448
  these –s *writing* 590

epistle 592
presentable 845, 852
presentation
  (*see* present)
  celebration 883
  courtesy 894
presentiment
  instinct 477
  prejudgment 481
  foresight 510
presently 132
presentment
  information 527
  law proceeding 969
preservation
  continuance 141
  conservation **670**
  Divine attributes 976
preserve *sweets* 396
  provision 637
  (*see* preservation)
  –a middle course 628
preserver
  safeguard 664
preshow 511
preside–at the board
  direction 693
  –over *authority* 737
presidency 737
president *director* 694
  master 745
  –'s message 695
press *crowd* 72
  closet 191
  weight 319
  public–531
  printing 591
  book 593
  move 615
  compel 744
  offer 763
  solicit 765
  go to–591
  –agent's yarn 546
  –in 300
  –into the service
  use 677
  aid 707
  –of business 682
  –on *course* 109
  progression 282
  haste 684
  –one hard 716
  –out 301
  –proof 591
  –to the bosom 902
  under–of 744
  writer for the–593
pressed, hard–704
  –for time 684
pressgang 965
pressing *need* 630
  urgent 642
pressman 554
press room 591

pressure *power* 157
  influence 175
  weight 319
  urgency 642
  adversity 735
  center of–222
  high–824
presswork 591
Prester John 515
prestidigitation 545
prestidigitator 548
prestige *bias* 481
  authority 737
  fascination 865
  fame 873
prestigiation 545
prestissimo 415
presto *instantly* 113
  music 415
prestriction 442
presumable 472
presume
  probability 472
  misjudge 481
  believe 484
  suppose 514
  hope 858
  pride 878
presumption
  (*see* presume)
  probability 472
  expectation 607
  rashness 863
  arrogance 885
  unlawfulness 925
presumptive
  probable 472
  supposed 514
  due 924
  heir–779
  –evidence
  evidence 467
  probability 472
presumptuous 885
presuppose
  misjudge 481
  suppose 514
presurmise
  foresee 510
  suppose 514
pretend *assert* 535
  simulate 544
  untruth 546
pretended 545
pretender
  deceiver 548
  braggart 884
  unentitled 925
pretending 544
pretense
  imitation 19
  falsehood 544
  untruth 546
  excuse 617
  ostentation 882
  boast 884

prim

pretension
  ornament 577
  affectation 855
  due 924
pretentious
  inflated 482
  specious 846
  affected 855
  vain 880
  ostentatious 882
  boasting 884
  undue 925
preterience 111
preterit 122
preterition 122
preterlapsed 122
pretermit 460
preternatural 83
pretext *untruth* 546
  plea 617
pretty *much* 31
  imperfectly 651
  beautiful 845
  –fellow 501
  –good 651
  –kettle of fish, pass, etc. *disorder* 59
  difficulty 704
  –quarrel 720
  –well *much* 31
  little 32
  trifling 643
preux chevalier 939
prevail *exist* 1
  superior 33
  general 78
  influence 175
  habit 613
  succeed 731
  –upon 615
prevailing 78
  –taste 852
prevalence
  (*see* prevail)
prevaricate
  falsehood 544
  (*equivocate* 520)
prévenance 894
prevene 116
prevenient
  precedent 62
  early 132
prevent 706
prevention
  prejudice 481
  hindrance 706
  –of waste 817
preventive 55
previous–in time 116
  (–in order 62)
  move the–question 624
  not within–experience 137
prevision 510
prewarn 668

prey *food* 298
  quarry 620
  booty 793
  victim 828
  fall a–to
  be defeated 732
  subjection 749
  –on the mind
  excite 824
  regret 833
  fear 860
  –on the spirits 837
  –to grief 828
  –to melancholy 837
price
  consideration 147
  value 648
  money **812**
  at any–604a
  beyond–814
  cheap at the–815
  have one's–812
  of great–*good* 648
  dear 814
  reward 973
price current 812
priceless *valuable* 648
  dear 814
prick *sharp* 253
  hole 260
  sting 378
  sensation of touch 380
  incite 615
  mental suffering 830
  kick against the–s
  useless 645
  resistance 719
  –up one's ears
  hear 418
  curiosity 455
  attention 457
  expect 507
prickle *sharp* 253
  sensation of touch 380
prickly 253
pride *ornament* 847
  loftiness **878**
  take a–in 878
prie-dieu 215
priest 904, 996
priestcraft 995
priestess 996
priesthood 995, 996
priest-ridden
  false piety 988
  churchdom 995
prig *steal* 791
  puppy 854
  affected 855
  blusterer 887
priggish *affected* 855
  vain 880
prim *taste* 850
  affected 855

prima donna

proud 878
prima donna
  actress 599
  important 642
  proficient 700
primacy
  superiority 33
  celebrity 873
  church 995
prima facie *sight* 441
  appearance 448
  probable 472
  —*meaning* 516
  manifest 525
primal 66
primary *initial* 66
  cause 153
  important 642
  —*color* 428
  —*education* 537
primate 996
primates 875
prime *initial* 66
  primeval 124
  early 132
  teach 537
  important 642
  excellent 648
  prepare 673
  in one's—131
  —*and load* 673
  —*cost price* 812
  cheap 815
  —*minister* 694
  —*mover* 153, 164
  —*number* 84
  —*of life youth* 127
  adolescence 131
  —*of the morning* 125
primed *skilled* 698
  tipsy 959
primer
  automobile 272
  schoolbook 542
primeval 124
primices 154
primigenous 124
priming 556
primitive *old* 124
  cause 153
primogenial
  beginning 66
primogeniture
  old 124
  age 128
  posterity 167
  heritage 777
primordial
  original 20
  old 124
  cause 153
primordiate 124
primordium 153
primrose—*colored* 436
prince *perfection* 650

master 745
nobility 875
—*of darkness* 978
Prince Albert coat 225
princely
  authoritative 737
  liberal 816
  famous 873
  noble 875
  generous 942
princess 745, 875
principal
  important 642
  director 694
  —*part great* 31
  whole 50
principality
  region 181
  property 780
principally 33
principia 66, 496
principle *intrinsic* 5
  rule 80
  cause 153
  element 316
  reasoning 476
  tenet 484
  maxim 496
  motive 615
  probity 939
  on—615
  want of—945
prink *adorn* 847
  show off 882
print *news* 532
  mark 550
  engraving 558
  letterpress 591
  out of—552
printer 591
printing 591
  —*press* 591
prior—*in order* 62
  —*in time* 116
  clergy 996
priority 116, 234
priory 1000
prism *angularity* 244
  optical instrument 445
  see through a—443
prismatic *color* 428
  variegated 440
prison 752
  cast into—751
  in—751, 754
prisoner *restraint* 751
  captive **754**
  accused 938
  take—*restrain* 751
  seize 789
pristine 122
prithee 765
prittle-prattle 588
privacy *conceal* 528

seclude 893
private *special* 79
  hidden 528
  secluded 893
  in—528
  keep—881
  —*road* 627
  —*soldier* 726
  talk to in—586, 588
  to gain some—*ends* 943
privateer
  combatant 726
  robber 792
privateering 791
privately 881
privation *loss* 776
  poverty 804
privative 789
privilege *freedom* 748
  permission 760
  exemption 777a
  due 924
privity *relation* 9
  knowledge 490
privy *hidden* 528
  latrines 653
  —*to* 490
Privy Council
  tribunal 966
prize *good* 618
  masterpiece 650
  palm 733
  gain 775
  booty 793
  love 897
  approve 931
  —*open* 173
  win the—731
prizer 767
prize fighter 726
prize fighting 720
prizeman 700
prizewinner 650, 931
pro—*and con*
  reasoning 476
  motive 615
  —*bono publico*
  utility 644
  philanthropy 910
  —*formâ* 82
  —*re natâ*
  circumstances 8
  relation 9
  special 79
  occasion 134
  conditions 770
  —*tanto degree* 26
  small 32
  —*tempore* 111
proa 273
probability
  chance 156
  likelihood **472**
probable *hopeful* 858
probate *security* 771

production

(*evidence* 467)
Probate, Court of—966
probation *trial* 463
  demonstration 478
probationary 463
  learner 541
  essay 675
probationer 541
probative 478
probator 461
probe *depth* 208
  perforator 262
  investigate 461
  measure 466
probity 939
problem *topic* 454
  question 461
  enigma 533
problematic 675
problematical
  uncertain 475
  (*hidden* 528)
proboscis 250
procacity
  insolence 885
  rudeness 895
  irascibility 901
procedure
  method 627
  action 680
  conduct 692
proceed *time* 109
  advance 282
  —*from* 154
  —*with* 692
proceeding
  incomplete 53
  event 151
  action 680
  not finished 730
  course of—692
  —*s records* 551
proceeds *gain* 775
  money 800
  receipts 810
procerity 206
process *projection* 250
  engraving 558
  conduct 692
  (*action* 680)
  in—*of time*
  posterior 117
  legal—963
  —*of time course* 109
procession
  continuity 69
  march 266
  ceremony 882
processional *rite* 998
procès verbal
  record 551
  law proceeding 969
prochronism 115
proclaim 531
proclamatory 531

proclivity
  tendency 176
  proneness 820
  (*disposition* 602)
proclivous 217
Proclus 490a
proconsul 759
proconsulship 737
procrastination
  delay 133
  neglect 460
  inactivity 683
procreant 161, 168
procreate
  produce 161
  productive 168
procreative 153, 168
procreator 166
procrustean 82
  —*law* 80
Procrustes
  stretch on the bed of—27
proctor *officer* 694
  consignee 758
  lawyer 968
proctorship 693
procumbent 213
procuration 170, 755
procurator 694
procure *cause* 153
  induce 615
  get 775
  buy 795
procurement 170
procuress 962
prod 276
prodigal *lavish* 641
  extravagant 818
prodigality 818
prodigious *much* 31
  wonderful 870
prodigy *exception* 83
  genius 492
  élite 648
  wonderful 872
  —*of learning* 700
prodition 940
prodromal 116
prodrome 64
produce *increase* 35
  cause 153
  effect 154
  create 161
  prolong 200
  show 525
  stage 599
  fruit 775
  merchandise 798
  —*itself* 446
producer 164
product *multiple* 84
  effect 154
  gain 775
production 161
  composition 54

productive

    writing 590
    (*see* produce)
productive *cause* 153
    power 157
    imagination 515
    acquiring 775
productiveness 168
proem 64, 66
proemial
    preceding in order 62
    beginning 66
profane *desecrate* 679
    impious 988
    laical 997
    —*swearing* 908
profess
    (*see* profession)
profession
    assertion 535
    pretense 546
    business 625
    promise 768
    enter a—625
    —*of faith belief* 484
    theology 983
professional
    business 625
    —*matchmaker* 903
professor
    learned man 492
    teacher 540
professorship 542
proffer 602, 763
proficient
    knowledge 490
    skill 698
    adept **700**
proficuous 644
profile *outline* 230
    side 236
    appearance 448
    portraiture 556
profit *increase* 35
    advantage 618
    utility 644
    acquisition 775
    —*and loss account* 811
    —*by use* 677
profitable *useful* 644
    good 648
    gainful 775
    (*receipts* 810)
profitless 646
profligacy 945
profluent
    progressive 282
    stream 348
profound *great* 31
    deep 208
    learned 490
    wise 498
    sagacious 702
    feeling 821
    —*attention* 457

    —*knowledge* 490
    —*secret* 533
profundity
    (*see* profound)
profuse
    diffuse style 573
    redundant 641
    prodigal 818
profusion
    multitude 102
    plenty 639
prog 298
progenerate 161
progenitive 163
progenitor 166
progeny 167
prognathism 372a
prognosis
    foresight 510
    prediction 511
    interpretation 522
    disease 655
prognostic 507, 511, 512
prognosticate 511
program *catalogue* 86
    music 415
    publication 531
    plan 626
progress *growth* 144
    motion 264
    advance 282
    (*improvement* 658)
    in
    —*incomplete* 53, 730
    in mid—270
    make—282
    —*of science* 490
    —*of time* 109
progression
    gradation 58
    series 69
    numerical—84
    motion **282**
progressive
    continuous 69
    course 109
    advancing 282
    improving 658
prohibition 761
    exclusion 55
    temperance 953
prohibitionist 756, 958
prohibitive 55, 761
project *bulge* 250
    impel 284
    intend 620
    plan 626
projectile 727
projecting 214
projection *map* 554
projector
    promoter 626
prolation *voice* 580
    speech 582

prolegomena 64
prolepsis *precursor* 64
    anachronism 115
proletarian 876
proliferous 163, 168
prolific 168
proligerous 163
prolix 573
prolixity 573
prolocutor
    interpreter 524
    teacher 540
    speaker 582
prologue *precursor* 64
    drama 599
    what's past is—122
prolong *protract* 110
    late 133
    continue 143
    lengthen 200
prolongation
    sequence 63
    protraction 110
    posterity 117
    continuance 143
prolusion 64
promenade *walk* 266
    display 882
Promethean 359
    —*spark* 359
prominence
    (*see* prominent)
prominent
    convex 250
    manifest 525
    important 642
    eminent 873
prominently
    much 31
    more 33
promiscuous
    mixed 41
    irregular 59
    indiscriminate 465a
    casual 621
promise *predict* 511
    engage **768**
    hope 858
    keep one's—939
    keep—*to ear and break to hope* 545
    —*of celestial worth* 511
    —*oneself expect* 507
    hope 858
promissory 768—note
    security 771
    money 800
promontory
    height 206
    projection 250
    land 342
promorphology 357
promote *improve* 658
    aid 707

promoter
    planner 626
promotion *class* 541
    improvement 658
prompt *early* 132
    remind 505
    tell 527
    induce 615
    active 682
    advise 695
    (*quick* 274)
    —*book* 505
    —*memory* 505
prompter *theater* 599
    tempter 615
    adviser 695
promptuary 636
promulgate 531
    —*a decree* 741
pronation and supination 218
prone *horizontal* 213
proneness
    tendency 176
    disposition 820
prôner
    ostentation 882
    praise 931
prôneur 935
prong 91
pronounce
    judge 480
    assert 535
    voice 580
    speak 582
pronounced 31, 525
pronouncement 531, 535
pronunciation 562, 580
pronunciative 535
proof *hard* 323
    insensible 376
    test 463
    demonstration 478
    indication 550
    printing 591
    draft 626
    ocular—446
    —*against strong* 159
    resolute 604
    safe 664
    defense 717
    resistance 719
    insensible 823
proof reader 591
prop *support* 215
    help 707
propaedeutic 537
propaedeutics 537
propagable 168
propaganda
    teaching 537
    school 542
    preparation 673
propagandism 537

propitiate

propagandist
    teacher 540
    priest 996
propagate
    droduce 161
    be productive 168
    publish 531
    teach 537
propel 284
propeller 284, 312
propend 602
propendency
    predetermination 611
    inclination 820
propense 602
propension 820
propensity
    tendency 176
    willingness 602
    inclination 820
proper *special* 79
    expedient 646
    handsome 845
    due 924
    (*right* 922)
    in its—*place* 58
    —*name* 564
    —*time* 134
    show a—*spirit* 939
    the—*thing duty* 926
properties, theatrical—
    costume 225
    drama 599
property *power* 157
    possessions **780**
    wealth 803
property-man 599
prophasis 510
prophecy 511
prophet *oracle* 511
    seer 513
    preparer 673
    priest 996
    non-Biblical—*s* 986
prophetess 513
prophetic *predict* 511
    revelation 985
Prophets, the—985
prophylactic
    healthful 656
    remedy 662
    preservative 670
    hindrance 706
prophylaxis 670
propinquity 197
propitiate *pacify* 723
    mediate 724
    calm 826
    content 831
    love 897
    pity 914
    forgive 918
    atone 952
    worship 990

propitiator — prudent

propitiator 714, 724
propitious *timely* 134
  beneficial 648
  helping 707
  prosperous 734
  auspicious 858
proplasm 22
proportion *relation* 9
  mathematical 84
  sum 85
  symmetry 242
  elegance 578
  allotment 786
proportionate
  agreeing 23
proportions
  space 180
  size 192
proposal 765
  plan 626
propose *suggest* 514
  broach 535
  intend 620
  offer 763
  offer marriage 902
  –a *question* 461
proposition
  supposition 454
  reasoning 476
  project 626
  suggestion 514
  offer 763
  request 765
propound *suggest* 514
  broach 535
  –a *question* 461
proprietary 779
proprietor 779
proprietorship 780
propriety
  agreement 23
  elegance 578
  expedience 646
  fashion 852
  right 922
  duty 926
propugn *resist* 717
  vindicate 937
propugnaculum 717
propulsion 284
propulsive 276, 284, 633
propylon 66
prore 234
prorogue 133
proruption 295
prosaic *usual* 82
  slow 275
  –*style* 575
  dry 576
  dull 843
prosaism *prose* 598
prosal 598
proscenium
  front 234
  theater 599

proscribe
  interdict 761
  banish 893
  curse 908
  condemn 971
  (*exclude* 77)
prose *diffuse style* 573
  prate 584
  not verse **598**
  –run mad *ornate* 577
  poetical 597
  –*writer* 598
prosecute *pursue* 622
  act 680
  accuse 938
  arraign 969
  –an *inquiry* 461
prosecutor 938
proselyte
  conversion 144
  learner 541
  convert 607
proselytism 537
proser 841
prosody 597
prosopopoeia 521
prospect *futurity* 121
  view 448
  probability 472
  expectation 507
  landscape painting 556
  good–858
  in–*intended* 620
prospector 463
prospective 121, 507
prospectively 121, 50
prospectus *list* 86
  foresight 510
  compendium 596
  scheme 626
prosper 618, 734
prosperity **734**
prospicience 510
prostate 221
prosternation
  dejection 837
  servility 886
prostitute
  corrupt 659
  misuse 679
  impure 961
  courtesan 962
prostrate
  powerless 158
  destroyed 162
  low 207
  horizontal 213
  depress 308
  laid up 655
  exhausted 688
  submissive 725
  dejected 837
  servile 886
  fall–306
  –oneself *servile* 886

  obeisance 928
  worship 990
prostration
  (see *prostrate*)
  sickness 655
  submission 725
  pain 828
prosy *feeble style* 575
  weary 841
  dull 843
prosyllogism 476
protagonist *actor* 599
  proficient 700
protasis *precursor* 64
  beginning 66
  maxim 496
protean 81, 149
protect *safe* 664
protected cruiser 726
protection
  influence 175
  defense 717
  restrain 751
protectionist 751
protective 717
  –*devices* 717
protector 664, 717
  master 745
  keeper 753
protectorate 737
  realm 780
protégé *servant* 746
  friend 890
proteid 357
proteiform 149
protein
  semiliquid 352
  organic 357
proteolysis 49
protervity 901
protest *dissent* 489
  assert 535
  deny 536
  refuse 764
  deprecate 766
  not observe 773
  not pay 808
  counter–468
  enter a–766
  –against *oppose* 708
  disapprove 932
  under
  –*unwilling* 603
  compulsion 744
Protestant 984
protestant
  dissenting 489
  unaccustomed 614
  refusing 764
Protestantization 144
protested bills 808
Proteus 149
prothesis 1000
prothonotary 553

protocol *scheme* 626
  compact 769
  (*record* 551)
  (*warrant* 771)
protogenal 153
protohistoric 124
protoplasm
  prototype 22
  organization 357
protoplasmic 240, 357
protoplast 22, 357
prototypal
  original 20
prototype 22
  prediction 511
protoxide of nitrogen 376
protozoa 357, 368
protract *time* 110
  late 133
  lengthen 200
  diffuse style 573
protreptical 615
protrude 250
protrusile 250
protrusive 250
protuberance 250
protypify 511
proud *dignified* 873
  lofty 878
  –*flesh* 250
prove *arithmetic* 85
  turn out 151
  try 463
  demonstrate 478
  indicate 550
  affect 821
  –one's *case*
  vindication 937
  –*true* 494
provender *food* 298
  provision 637
proverb *maxim* 496
  (*phrase* 566)
proverbial 490
provide *furnish* 637
  –against *prepare* 673
  –against a rainy day 817
provided
  conditionally 8
  qualification 469
  supposition 514
  (*conditions* 770)
  –for 803
  well–639
providence
  foresight 510
  preparation 673
  divine government 976
Providence 976
  waiter on–*idle* 683
  contented 831
provident *careful* 459

  wise 498
  prepared 673
providential
  opportune 134
  fortunate 734
provider 637
province
  department 75
  region 181
  office 625
  career 692
  (*duty* 926)
provincial
  (see *province*)
  narrow 481
  vulgar 851
  impiety 988
provincialism
  neology 563
provision *food* 298
  supply **637**
  preparation 673
  wealth 803
  (*materials* 635)
  –*shop* 637
provisional 475
  circumstances 8
  temporary 111
  uncertain 475
  expectation 507
  preparing 673
provisions
  conditions 770
proviso
  qualification 469
  condition 770
provisory 111
provoke *cause* 153
  incite 615
  excite 824
  vex 830
  aggravate 835
  anger 900
  –*desire* 865
  –*hatred* 898
provoquant 824
provost *master* 745
  deputy 759
prow 234
prowess 861
prowl *walk* 266
  lurk 528
  –after 622
proximate *next* 63
  near 197
  –*cause* 153
proximity *near* 197
  adjacent 199
proximo 121
proxy 634, 755
  by–147, 759
prude *affected* 855
  chaste 960
prudent *careful* 459
  wise 498
  cautious 864

540

prudery

(*skillful* 698)
prudery
  affectation 855
  fastidiousness 868
prudish *severe* 739
  stiff 751
  taste 850
  (*see* prudery)
pruina 383
prune *take away* 38
  lop 201, 371
  repair 658
  –s and prisms 855
prunello
  leather or–643
prurience *desire* 865
  lust 961
prurient 380, 961
Prussian blue 438
Prussic acid 663
pry *look* 441
  curiosity 455
  inquire 461
  –into the future 510
  –open 173
prytaneum 931
psalm *music* 415
  worship 990
psalm book 998
psalmody 415
psalter 998
psaltery 417
psammous 330
psephomancy 511
pseudo *simulated* 17
  imitative 19
  sham 545
  misnomer 565
pseudoblepsis 443
pseudology 563
pseudonym 565
pseudonymity 565
pseudoscope 445
pshaw *trifling* 643
  excitement 825
psora 380, 655
psychasthenia 992*a*
psyche 450, 821*a*
psychic 450
psychical 450
  –*research* 450, **992a**
psychoanalysis 450
psychogenesis 450
psychological 450, 537
psychologico-spiritualistic school 451
psychologize 992*a*
psychology 821*a*, 450
psychomancy 511
psychometry 450
psychoneurosis 821*a*
psychopath 450
psychophysicist 450
psychophysics 450

psychosis 821*a*
psychotherapy 821*a*, 662, 992*a*
psychrometer 349
pteridophytes 369
ptisan 662
ptyalism 299
ptyalize 297
puberty 127
pubescent 131
public, *general*–372
  make–531
  –demand 677
  –enemy 891
  –good 644
  –library 593
  –mind 593
  –opinion 488
  –press 531
  –school 542
  –servant 644
  –spirit 910
  –welfare 910
  purchasing–677
publication
  production 161
  disclosure 529
  promulgation **531**
  book 593
public house 189
  go to the–959
publicist 554, 593, 968
publicity 531
publish 531
  –the banns 765
publisher 593
puce 433, 437
pucelage *youth* 127
  celibacy 904
  purity 960
Puck 274, 979
  play–699
pucka *permanent* 141
  solid 321
  valid 494
  ripe 673
pucker *contracted* 195
  fold 258
  anger 900
  in a–*excited* 824
pudder *disorder* 59
pudding *food* 298
  soft 324
  pulpy 354
  sweets 396
  in–*time* 132
puddle 343
pudgy 201
pudicity 960
puerile *boyish* 129
  foolish 499
  feeble 575
  trifling 643
puerperal 161
puff *inflate* 194

  wind 349
  tartlet 396
  pant 688
  boast 884
  praise 931
  flatter 933
  –of smoke 330
  –up *vanity* 880
puffed up
  inflated 482
  pride 878
puffer 935
puffery 884
puffy 194
pug *short* 201
  dog 366
  footprint 551
puggaree 225
pugilism 720
pugilist 726
pugilistic 720
pugnacity
  contentiousness 720
  irascibility 901
puisne *young* 127
puissant *powerful* 157
  strong 159
puke 297
pulchritude 845
pulcinella *actor* 599
  buffoon 844
pule *cry* 411, 412
  weep 839
pull *superiority* 33
  power 157
  influence 175, 615, 631
  row 267
  draw 285
  attraction 288
  indicate 550
  printing 591
  a long and a strong – *cooperate* 709
  –about one's ears 308
  –an oar 680
  –by the sleeve 505
  –different ways 713
  –down *destroy* 162
  lay low 308
  –in 751
  –out 301
  –the check string 142
  –the wires 693
  –through *restoration* 660
  aid 707
  –together 709
  –to pieces *separate* 44
  destroy 162
  censure 932
  detract 934
  –towards *attract* 288
  –up *stop* 142
  rest 265

  root out 301
  reprimand 932
  accuse 969
  –upon the purse 814
  strong–*exertion* 686
pulled down
  weak 160
  fatigued 688
pullet 129
pulley 633
Pullman car 272
pullulate
  produce 161, 168
  multiply 168
  grow 194
pulmonary 349
pulmonate 349
pulmonic 655
pulmotor 349, 662
pulp 354
pulpiness 354
pulpit *rostrum* 542
  clergy 996
  church 1000
pulsate *periodic* 138
  oscillate 314
  agitate 315
pulsation *feeling* 821
pulse (*see* pulsate)
  vegetable 367
  feel the–*inquire* 461
  test 463
pulsion 276
pultaceous 354
pulverable 330
pulverize 330, 358
pulverulence 330
pulvil 400
puma 913
pummel (*see* pommel)
pump *shoe* 225
  water supply 348
  inflate 349
  inquire 461
  instrument 633
pumpkin 298
pump room
  house 189
  remedy 662
pun *similarity* 17
  absurdity 497
  ambiguity 520
  misinterpretation 523
  neology 563
  wit 842
punce 276
Punch *buffoon* 844
  –and Judy 599
punch *mold* 22
  perforate 260
  perforator 262
  nag 271
  strike 276, 716
  beverage 298
  engrave 558

puppet

  vigor 574
punchbowl *vessel* 191
  hollow 252
  tippling 959
puncheon 635
  vessel 191
  perforator 262
puncher 262
punchinello 599, 844
punctated 440
punctilio *fashion* 852
punctilious *exact* 494
  severe 739
  observant 772
  ostentation 882
  scrupulous 939
puncto 882
punctual *early* 132
  periodical 138
  exact 494
  observance 772
  scrupulous 939
punctuation 567
puncture 260
pundit
  learned man 492
  sage 500
  lawyer 968
pung 272
pungency 392
  physical energy 171
  taste 392
pungent *pain* 378
  taste 392
  odor 398
  vigor 574
  feeling 821
punish 972
punishment 972
punition 972
punitive 972
punk 962 *fuel* 388
punkah 349
punster 844
punt *row* 267
  boat 273
punter 840
puny 193
pup *infant* 129
  give birth 161
  dog 366
pupa 129
pupil–*of the eye* 441
  student 492
  learner 541
pupilage
  youth 127
  learning 539
pupillary 541
puppet *little* 193
  dupe 547
  effigy 554
  auxiliary 711
  tool 746
  be the–of 749
  make a–of 737

puppet show
  drama 599
  amusement 840
puppy *infant* 129
  dog 366
  fop 854
  braggart 884
  blusterer 887
puppyism 855
Purana 986
purblind
  dim sight 443
  weak judgment 481
purchase *support* 215
  acquisition 775
  buy **795**
purchase money 147
purchaser 147
purdah
  screen for women 374
  shade 424
  ambush 530
pure *simple* 42
  true 494
  truthful 543
  —*style* 576, 578
  clean 652
  artless 703
  —*taste* 850
  honorable 939
  virtuous 944
  innocent 946
  chaste 960
  devout 987, 990
  —*accent* 580
  —*color* 428
  —*eyed faith* 987
purée 298, 352
purely *much* 31
  little 32
purgation
  cleansing 652
  atonement 952
purgative 652
purgatory
  suffering 828
  atonement 952
  hell 982
purge *cast out* 297
  clean 652
  atone 952
  (*improve* 658)
purify *clean* 652
  improve 658
purist *style* 578
  taste 850
  affected 855
  Pharisee 988
puritan *Pharisee* 988
Puritan 984
puritanical
  severe 739
  affected 855
  ascetic 955
purity 960 (*see* pure)
purl *stream* 348

  faint sound 405
  music 416
purlieus *near* 197
  surrounding 227
purloin 791
purple *violet* **437**
  insignia 747
  —*and fine linen* 377
purport *meaning* 516
  (*intent* 620)
purpose 600, 620
  for the—*of* 176
  infirm of—605
  on—620
  serve a—644
  tenacity of—604a
  to no—
    shortcoming 304
    useless 645
    failure 732
  to some—731
purposeless 621
purpure 437
purr 405, 412
purse *contract* 195
  money 800
  treasury 802
  long—803
  —*up* 195
  put into one's—785
purse bearer 801
purse-proud 878
purser 637, 801
purse strings
  draw the—
    not pay 808
  open the—
    disburse 809
pursuance 63, 143
pursuant to 620
pursue *continue* 143
  follow 281
  aim 622
  —*a course* 680
  —*an inquiry* 461
  —*the tenor of one's*
    way
    incuriosity 456
    business 625
    modesty 881
pursuer 65, 281, 622
pursuit 622
pursuivant 534
pursy 194
purulent 653
purvey 637
purview 620
pus 352, 415, 653
Puseyite 984
push *exigency* 8
  impel 276
  progress 282
  propel 284
  essay 675
  activity 682
  come to the—704

—*aside neglect* 460
  disrespect 929
—*forward active* 682
  aid 707
—*from* 289
—*on haste* 684
—*out eject* 297
—*to the last* 133
pushball 840
pushing 282, 284
pusillanimity 862
puss 366
  play—*in the corner*
    interchange 148
pussy-foot
  cautious 864
pustule *pimple* 250
  blemish 848
put *place* 184
  fool 501
  invest 787
  cards 840
  clown 876
  neatly—576
—*about turn back* 283
  go round 311
  publish 531
—*a case cite* 82
  suppose 514
—*a construction on*
    522
—*a mark upon* 457
—*an end to end* 67
  stop 142
  destroy 162
—*oneself* 361
—*a question* 461
—*aside exclude* 55
  inattention 458
  neglect 460
  disuse 678
—*away*—*thought* 452
  relinquish 782
  divorce 905
—*back turn back* 283
  deteriorate 659
  restore 660
—*before inform* 527
—*by* 636
—*down destroy* 162
  record 551
  conquer 731
  compel 744
  pay 807
  humiliate 874
—*forth expand* 194
  suggest 514
  publish 531
  assert 535
—*a question* 461
—*strength* 686
—*forward suggest* 514
  publish 531
  ostentation 882
—*in,* —*into*
  (*see below*)

—*in commission* 755
—*in force*
  complete 729
  compel 744
—*off late* 133
  divest 226
  depart 293
  plea 617
—*on clothe* 225
  deceive 544
  hasten 684
  affect 855
—*oneself out of*
    court
    sophistry 477
    bungling 699
—*one's hand to* 676
—*one's nose out of*
    joint 33
—*one's trust in* 484
—*on paper* 551
—*out*
  (*see below*)
—*right* 660
—*the horses to* 673
—*the saddle on the*
    right horse 155
—*the seal to*
  complete 729
  compact 769
—*to*
  (*see below*)
—*together join* 43
  combine 48
  assemble 161
—*to inconvenience*
    647
—*up*
  (*see below*)
—*upon deceive* 545
  oppress 649
putative
  attributed 155
  believed 484
  supposed 514
put in *arrive* 292
  insert 300
—*an affidavit* 535
—*a word speak* 582
  converse 588
—*hand* 676
—*mind* 505
—*motion* 264
—*one's head* 514
—*one's pocket* 785
—*order* 60
—*practice* 692
—*remembrance* 505
—*shape* 60
—*the place of* 147
—*the way of* 470
—*trim arrange* 60
  prepare 673
put out *destroy* 162
  outside 220
  extinguish 385

  darken 421
  distract the attention
    458
  uncertain 475
  difficult 704
  discontent 832
—*of countenance* 874,
    900
—*of gear* 158
—*of joint* 61
—*of one's head* 458
—*of one's misery* 914
—*to nurse* 707
—*to order* 59
putrefaction 49, 653
putrefy 49, 653
putrescence 49, 653
putrid 653
puttee 225
putter *dally* 683
putting up
  canning 670
put to *attribute* 155
  request 765
—*death* 361
—*it* 704
—*one's oath* 768
—*press* 591
—*rights* 60
—*sea* 203
—*shame* 874
—*silence* 581
—*task* 677
—*the blush* 879
—*the door* 26
—*the proof* 463
—*the question* 830
—*the rack* 830
—*the sword* 361
—*the vote* 609
—*use* 677
putty 45
put up *assemble* 72
  locate 184
  store 636
—*a petition*
—*a prayer request* 765
  worship 990
—*a shutter* 424
—*for* 865
—*for sale* 796
—*the sword* 723
—*to* 615
—*to auction* 796
—*with substitute* 147
  bear 826
puzzle *uncertain* 475
  conceal 528
  enigma 533
puzzled 475, 533
  (*ignorant* 491)
puzzle-headed 499
puzzling
  unintelligible 519
pyaemia 655
Pygmy 431

pygmy

pygmy 193
pyknic type 372a
Pylades and Orestes 890
pylon 260
pyramid *heap* 72
  height 206
  point 253
  chance 621
pyramids
  billiards 840
pyre 363, 423
pyretic 383
pyrexia 382
pyriform 245, 249
pyrolator 382
pyrolatry 382
pyrology 282
pyromancy 511
pyromaniac 384, 913
pyrometer 389
pyrosis 655
pyrotechnics 382, 423
pyrotechnic sponge 388
pyrotechny 382
pyrotic 830
pyroxylin 727
pyrrhonism
  incredulity 487
  irreligion 989
Pythagorean 953
  —*school* 451
Pythia *oracle* 513
Python 366, 513
python *snake* 366
Pythoness *oracle* 513
pyx *vessel* 191
  experiment 463
  rites 998
  temple 1000

Q

Q. C. 968
Q. E. D. 478
quack *cry* 412
  impostor 548
quackery
  falsehood 544
  want of skill 699
  affectation 855
quacksalver 548
quad 189
quadrable 96
Quadragesima 956
quadrangle
  quaternity 95
  house 189
  angular 244
quadrant *angle* 244
  circle 247
  measurement 466
quadrate with 23

quadratic 95
quadrature *four* 95
  angle 244
quadrennial 138
quadric 95
quadricycle 272
quadrified 97
quadrifoil 95
quadrifoliate 97
quadriform 95
quadrigeminal 97
quadrilateral
  quaternity 95
  sides 236
  angles 244
quadrille 840
quadrillion 102
quadripartition 97
quadriplanar 97
quadrireme 273
quadrisect 97
quadrisection 97
quadriserial 97
quadroon 41
quadrumanous 97
quadruped 366
quadruplet 95
quadruplication 96
quaff 298
  —*the bitter cup* 828
quaggy 345
quagmire *marsh* 345
  dirty 653
  difficult 704
quail *bird* 298
  fear 860
  cowardice 862
quaint *odd* 83
  pretty 845
  ridiculous 853
quake *oscillate* 314
  shake 315
  cold 383
  fear 860
Quaker 984 —*gray* 432
  —*gun* 158
quakerish *prim* 855
  calm 826
Quakerism 984
qualification
  (*see* qualify)
  power 157
  modification 469
  skill 698
  discount 813
qualify *change* 140
  modify 469
  deny 536
  teach 537
  (*prepare* 673)
  —*for* 924
qualities
  character 820
quality *nature* 5
  power 157
  tendency 176

good taste 850
nobility 875
qualm *disbelieve* 485
  unwilling 603
  fear 860
—s *of conscience* 950
quandary *state* 7
  uncertainty 475
  difficulty 704
quantify 25
quantity 25 *much* 31
  multitude 102
quantum *amount* 25
  allotment 786
quarantine 664
  —*flag* 550
  —*station* 751
quark 32
quarrel 24, 713
  —*with one's bread and butter*
  bungling 699
  discontent 832
quarrelsome 901
quarry *object* 620
  mine 636
quart 97
quarter *cut up* 44
  fourth 95
  quadrisection 97
  period 108
  region 181
  locate 184
  abode 189
  side 236
  direction 278
  forbearance 740
  coin 800
  mercy 914
  give—914
  give no—*kill* 361
  severe 739
  pitiless 914a
  —*of a hundred* 98
  —*upon* 184
quarter-deck 210
quarter evil 655
quartermaster 637
quartern 95
quarteron 41
quarters *abode* 189
  take up one's—184
quarter sessions 966
quarterstaff
  contention 720
  weapon 727
quartet *four* 95
  music 415
  church 996
quarto 95, 593
quartz 323
quash *destroy* 162
  annul 756
quasi *similar* 17
  supposed 514
quassation 315

quassia 395
quaternity 95
quatrain 597
quatrefoil 95
quattrocento 114, 554
quaver *oscillate* 314
  shake 315
  sound 407
  music 413, 416
  aphony 581
  imperfect speech 583
  fear 860
quay *houses* 189
  harbor 666
quean 876, 962
queasiness *dislike* 867
queasy *fastidious* 868
Quechuan 372a
queen 745 *cards* 840
  title 877
  good woman 948
queencraft 693
Queen's-Bench
  prison 732
  court 966
  —*counsel* 968
  —*English* 560
  —*evidence* 529
  —*highway* 627
  —*speech* 695
queer *singular* 83
  ridiculous 853
  —*fish* 857
quell *destroy* 162
  moderate 174
  quiescence 265
  subdue 731
quench *destroy* 162
  cool 385
  dissuade 616
  gratify 829
  satiate 869
quenchless 865
querimonious 839
querist 461
quern 330
quernstone 330
querulous
  complaining 839
  fastidious 868
  irritable 901
query 461
quest 461
question *inquiry* 461
  doubt 485
  deny 536
  in-event 151
  topic 454
  inquiry 461
  danger 665
  pop the—902
  put to the—830
  —*at issue* 461
questionable
  uncertain 475

doubtful 485
disreputable 874
improbity 940
questioner 455
questionist 541
questionless
  certain 541
questor 801
queue 65, 214
quib 856
quibble *sophistry* 477
  quirk 481
  unmeaning 517
  equivocation 520
  falsehood 544
  wit 842
  verbal
  —*absurdity* 497
quick *transient* 111
  rapid 274
  alive 359
  intelligent 498
  active 682
  skillful 698
  feeling 821
  sensibility 822
  irascible 901
  cut to the—824
  probe to the—461
  —*as thought* 113
  —*ear* 418
  —*eye* 441
  —*in response* 375
  —*succession* 136
  —*time* 274
  sting to the—
  pain 830
  anger 900
  to the
  —*physically* 375
  mentally 822
  touch to the—822, 824
quicken *work* 170
  violence 173
  come to life 359
  promote 707
  excite 824
quickening power 170
quickly *soon* 132
quicksand *danger* 667
  difficulty 704
  —*of deceit* 545
quick-scented 398
quickset hedge 232
quicksilver
  changeable 149
  energy 171
  motion 264
  velocity 274
quick-witted 842
quid *essence* 1
  pungency 392
quid pro quo
  compensation 30

543

   substitution 147
   interchange 148
   retaliation 718
   barter 794
   wit 842
   reward 973
quidam 372
quiddity *essence* 5
   quibble 477
   wit 842
quidnunc 455
quiescence 265
quiet *calm* 174
   rest 265
   silence 403
   dissuade 616
   leisure 685
   inexcitability 826
   all–on Potomac 721
   keep–681
 –life 721
quietism
   quiescence 265
   insensibility 823
   inexcitability 826
   content 831
   irreligion 989
quietly *modest* 881
   get on–736
quietude 826
quietus *death* 360
   failure 732
   acquittal 970
   give a–361
   receive its–756
quill 590
   my gray goose–590
quill–driver 590
quillet 477
quilt *covering* 223
   variegated 440
quinary 98
quincunx 98
quinine 662
quinquefid 99
quinqueliteral 99
quinquennial 138
quinquennium 108
quinquepartite 99
quinquesect 99
quinquesection 99
quinsy 655
quint 98
quintain *aim* 620
   game 840
quintal 319
quintessence 5
quintet 98, 415
qintroon 41
quintuple 98
quintuplicate 98
quinze 840
quip *amusement* 840
   wit 842
   ridicule 856
   disrespect 929

quire *singers* 416
   paper 593
   church 1000
quirk *sophistry* 477
   misjudgment 481
   caprice 608
   amusement 840
   wit 842
quirt 975
quit *depart* 293
   relinquish 624
   pay 807
 –claim 927a
 –of *loss* 776
   relinquish 782
 –one's hold 782
 –scores 807
qui–tam 969
quitclaim 270, 927a
quite 52
 –another thing
   irrelevant 10
   unlike 18
 –the reverse 14
 –the thing 23
quits *equal* 27
   atonement 952
   be–with
   retaliation 718
   pay 807
quittance *security* 771
   payment 807
   forgiveness 918
   atonement 952
   reward 973
quitter *avoidance* 623
quiver *receptacle* 191
   oscillation 314
   agitation 315
   shiver 383
   store 636
   feeling 821
   sensibility 822
   fear 860
   in a–921, 824
 –with rage 900
qui–vive 669
   on the–459
Quixote, Don–
   mad 504
   rash 863
quixotic *fanciful* 515
   rash 863
quixotism 825
quiz *ridicule* 856
   laughingstock 857
quizzical
   ridiculous 853
quod *prison* 752
   in–754
quodlibet *inquiry* 461
   sophism 477
   wit 842
quoits 840
quondam 122
quorum 696

quota *quantity* 25
   number 84
   contingent 786
   expenditure 809
   furnish its–784
quotation
   imitation 19
   conformity 82
   evidence 467
   price 812
 –marks 550
quote 82 *evidence* 467
quoth *affirmative* 535
   speech 582
quotidian 138
quotient 84
quotiety 25, 136
quotum 25

R

Ra 423
rabat 225
rabbet 43
Rabbi 996
Rabbinist 984
rabbit 298
   productive 168
rabble *assemblage* 72
   mob 876
rabid *insane* 502
   emotion 821, 652
   eager 865
   angry 900
rabies 503, 821a
raccoon 366
raccroc 156
race *relation* 111
   sequence 69
   kind 75
   lineage 166
   run 274
   stream 343, 348
   conduit 350
   pungency 392
   course 622
   business 625
   culture 658
   career 692
   opposition 708
   contention 720
   one's–is run 360
   run a–720
   run in a–680
   run one's–729
race course 728
race horse *horse* 271
   swift 274
racer *vehicle* 272
rachidian 222
rachis 235
rachitis 655
racial 166
raciness 574
rack *receptacle* 191

   frame 215
   cloud 253
   physical pain 378
   purify 652
   anguish 828
   torture 830
   punish 972
   instrument of torture 975
   go to–and ruin 735
   on the–507
 –one's brains
   thought 451
   imagination 515
 –rent 810
rackabones 659
racket *agitation* 315
   loud 404
   roll 407
   discord 414, 713
racket court 840
racketing *active* 682
   amusements 840
rackets 840
rackety *loud* 404
raconteur 594
racy *strong* 171
   pungent 392
 –style 574
   feeling 821
raddle *weave* 219
raddled *tipsy* 959
radial 291
radiance *light* 420
   beauty 845
radiant *diverging* 291
   beauty 845
   glorious 873
radiate 73, 291
radiated 242
radiation 242, 291, 490a
radiator 386
radical *essential* 5
   complete 52
   algebraic root 84
   cause 153
   important 642
   reformer 658
 –change 146
 –cure 662
 –reform 658
radically *greatly* 31
radication 153, 613
radicle 153
radiculose 367
radio 534
radioactive
   energy 171
   calefaction 384
   light 420
radioactivity 490d
radiogram 532, 554
radiograph 421, 554, 556
radiography 556

radiology 420
radiometer *light* 420
   optical instrument 445
   measurement 466
radiometry 420
radiomicrometer 389
radiophone 527, 531, 534
radiophony 402
radioscopy 420
radiotelegraph 434
radiotelegraphic 431
radiotelegraphy 420
radiotelephone 534
radiotherapy 420, 662
radish 298
radium 384
 –emanation 420
radius *length* 200
   width 202
radix 84, 153
radoter 499
radoteur 501
raff *refuse* 653
   rabble 876
   (*miscreant* 949)
raffle 621
raft 273
rafter 215
rag *small* 32
   (*part* 51)
ragamuffin 876
rage *violence* 173
   influence 175
   excitement 824, 825
   fashion 852
   desire 865
   wrath 900
   the battle–s 722
ragged 226
ragout 298
rags *clothes* 225
   useless 645
   do to–384
   tear to–162
   worn to–659
ragtag
 –and bobtail 876
ragtime *music* 415
   dance 840
raid *attack* 716
   pillage 791
rail *inclosure* 232
   prison 752
 –at 932
 –in *circumscribe* 229
   restrain 751
railing 232
raillery 856
rail–riding 972
railroad *travel* 266
   method 627
   expedite 684

railway   **rate**

railway 627
  –speed 274
  –station 266
raiment 225
rain *stream* 348
  sufficient 639
  –of blood *omen* 512
  –or shine *certain* 474
  at all hazards 604
rainbow 440
  omen 512
rain chart 348
rain gauge 348
rainless 340
rains *monsoon* 348
rainy 348
  provide against a–
    day *prepare* 673
  economy 817
  –day *adversity* 735
  –season 348
raise *increase* 35
  produce 161
  elevate 212, 307
  leaven 320
  excite 824
  –a cry 531
  –a dust 682
  –a hue and cry
    against 932
  –alarm 860
  –a laugh 840
  –anger 900
  –a question
    inquire 461
    doubt 485
  –a report 531
  –a siege 723
  –a storm 173
  –Cain 900
  –expectations 858
  –funds 775
  –hope 511
  –money 788
  –one's banner 722
  –one's head
    improve 658
    refresh 689
    prosperity 734
    repute 873
  –one's voice
    affirm 535
  –one's voice against
    932
  –spirits from the
    dead 992
  –the finger 550
  –the mask 529
  –the spirits 836
  –the voice *shout* 441
  –the wind *gain* 775
    borrow 788
  –troops 722
  –up *vertical* 212
    excite 824
raised *convex* 250

raiser *producer* 164
raisins 298
raison d' être 620
rajah 745, 875
rajput 726
rake *drag* 285
  gardening 371
  clean 652
  profligate 949
  intemperance 954
  libertine 962
  –out 301
  –up *collect* 72
    extract 301
    recall 505
    excite 824
  –up evidence 467
rakehell 949, 962
raking fire 716
rakish
  intemperate 954
  licentious 961
rallentando 415
rally *arrange* 60
  improve 658
  restore 660
  ridicule 856
  encourage 861
  –round *order* 58
  coöperate 709
rallying cry
  indication 550
  encouragement 861
rallying point 74
ram *impulse* 276
  sheep 366
  male 373
  man-of-war 726
  milk the–645
  –down *close* 261
    dense 321
  –in 300
Ramadan 138, 956
ramage 367
ramble *stroll* 266
  wander 279
  folly 499
  delirium 503
  digress 573
rambler 269
rambling
  irregularity 139
ramification *part* 51
  bisection 91
  posterity 167
  filament 205
  symmetry 242
  divergence 291
ramify *angularity* 244
  (*see* ramification)
rammer *plug* 263
  impeller 276
ramose 242
  (*rough* 256)
ramp *obliquity* 217
  climb 305

  leap 309
rampage 173
rampant *violent* 173
  prevalent 175
  vertical 212
  raised 307
  free 748
  vehement 825
  licentious 961
rampart 717
ramrod 263, 276
ramshackle 665
ranch 780
rancho 189
rancid *fetid* 401
  unclean 653
rancor *enmity* 889
  malevolence 907
  revenge 919
randan 273
randem *vehicle* 272
random *casual* 156
  uncertain 475
  aimless 621
  talk at
    –sophistry 477
    exaggerate 549
    loquacity 584
    –experiment 463
    chance 621
randy 840
range *extent* 26
  collocate 60
  series 69
  term 71
  class 75
  space 180
  distance 196
  nearness 197
  roam 266
  direction 278
  stove 386
  freedom 748
  long–196
  –itself 58
  –under,–with 76
  within–177
ranger *director* 694
  keeper 753
  thief 792
rangy *long* 200
rani 745, 875
rank *prevalent* 1
  degree 26
  thorough 31
  collocate 60
  precede 62
  row 69
  term 71
  vegetation 365
  fetid 401
  estimate 480
  bad 649
  soldiers 726
  glory 873
  nobility 875

  fill up the–s 660
  man of–875
  –and file
    continuity 69
    soldiers 726
    commonalty 876
  –outsider *outcast* 893
  risen from the–s
    876
rankle *unclean* 653
  corrupt 659
  painful 830
  animosity 900
  malevolence 907
  revenge 919
ransack *seek* 461
  deliver 672
  plunder 791
  price 812
  atonement 952
  –one's brains
    thought 451
    imagination 515
ransom 672, 952
rant *unmeaning* 517
  exaggeration 549
  diffuse style 573
  turgescence 577
  speech 582
  acting 599
  excitement 825
  boasting 884
ranter *talker* 584
  false piety 988
rantipole 458
ranunculus 845
rap *blow* 276
  sound 406
  trifle 643
  money 800
  not worth a–804
  –on the knuckles
    angry 900
    censure 932
    punish 972
  –out *affirm* 535
    voice 580
    speak 582
  –out oaths
    insolence 885
    malediction 908
rapacity *taking* 789
  stealing 791
  avarice 819
  greed 865
rape *seizure* 791
  violation 961
rape oil 356
rapid 274–*slope* 217
  –strides *progress* 282
  velocity 274
  –succession 136
rapids 348, 667
rapier 727
rapine 791
rapparee 792

rappee 392
rappel 722
rapport 9, 23
rapprochement
  concord 714
  friendship 888
rapscallion 949
rapt *thought* 451
  attention 457
  inattention 458
  emotion 821
raptorial *taking* 789
  stealing 791
raptors 739
rapture *bliss* 827
  love 897
rapturous 221, 827
rara avis
  exceptional 83
  good 648
  famous 873
rare *unique* 20
  exceptional 83
  few 103
  infrequent 137
  underdone 298
  tenuous 322
  neologic 563
  choice 648
raree show
  appearance 448
  amusement 840
rarefaction
  expand 194
  render light 322
rari nantes 103
rarity 322, 847
rascal *knave* 941
  bad man 949
rascality 940
rase *obliterate* 552
rash *skin disease* 655
  reckless 863
  (*careless* 460)
rasher 204
rashness 863
rasorial 366
rasp *powder* 330
  rub 331
  clean 652
raspberry 298
rasper *difficult* 704
rasure 552
rat *animal* 366
  recant 607
  –s in the upper story
    503
  smell a–
    discover 480a
    doubt 485
rataplan 407
ratatat 407
ratchet 253
rate *quantity* 25
  degree 26
  motion 264

545

rath … rebound

measure 466
estimation 480
berate 527
price, tax 812
abuse 932
at a great–274
rath *early* 132
fort 717
rather *a little* 32
trifling 643
have–609
have–not 867
–good 651
ratification
confirm 467
affirm 488
consent 762
compact 769
ratio *relation* 9
degree 26
proportion 84
apportionment 786
ratiocination 476
ration *food* 298
provision 637
allotment 786
rational–*quantity* 84
intellectual 450
reasoning 476
judicious 498
sane 502
rationale *cause* 153
attribution 155
answer 462
interpretation 522
rationalism
philosophy 451
reasoning 476
irreligion 989
rationalization 821a
ratlings 215
ratsbane 663
rattan 975
ratten 158
rattle *noise* 406, 407
music 417
confuse 458
prattle 584
death–360
–on 584
rattle-brained 499
rattled
inattentive 458
confused 523
rattle-headed 499
rattlesnake 366, 913
rattletraps 780
rattling 836
–*pace* 274
raucity 410
raucous *strident* 410
hoarse 581
ravage *destroy* 162
despoil 659
–s of time 659
rave *madness* 503

excitement 824, 825
–against 932
ravel *untwist* 60
derange 61
entangle 219
solve 480a
difficulty 704
raveled 59
ravelin 717
raven *bird* 366
black 431
hoarse 581
gorge 957
–for 865
ravening *violent* 173
desire 865
ravenous
grasping 789
desirous 865
raver 504
ravine *interval* 198
narrow 203
dike 259, 350
raving *mad* 503
feeling 821
excitement 824, 825
ravish *seize* 789
please 829
ravished *pleased* 827
ravishment 824
raw *immature* 123
sensitive 378
cold 383
color 428
unprepared 674
unskilled 699
sensibility 822
on the–375
–head and bloody
bones 860
–levies 726
–material 635
rawboned 203
rawhide 975
ray *fish* 368
light 420
–of comfort 831
thou living–450
rayah 745
Rayleigh wave 490c
rayless 421
raze *destroy* 162
level 213
friction 331
–to the ground
lower 308
razor 253
cut blocks with a–
waste 638
misuse 679
unskillful 699
keen as a–821
razzia *destruction* 162
attack 716
plunder 791
reabsorb 296

reach *degree* 26
equal 27
distance 196
fetch 270
arrive at 292
plain 344
river 348
deceive 545
grasp 737
take 789
–of thought 498
–the ear *hearing* 418
information 527
–to *distance* 196
length 200
within–*near* 197
possible 470
reaction
compensation 30
counteraction 179
recoil 277
restoration 660
reactionary
reversion 145
tergiversation 607
reactionist
opponent 710
read *interpret* 522
learn 539
–a lecture 537
well–490
readable 578
reader *teacher* 540
speaker 582
printer 591
clergyman 996
readership 542
readily 705
reading *specialty* 79
knowledge 490
interpretation 522
learning 539
–at sight *music* 415
–in 995
reading desk 1000
readjust *agree* 23
equalize 27
readmit 296
ready *expecting* 507
willing 602
useful 644
prepare 673
active 682
skillful 698
cash 800
get–673
make–673
–made 673
–memory 505
–money 800
–pen 569
–to burst forth 825
–to sink 824
–wit 842
reaffirm 535
reagent 463, 690

real *existing* 1
–*number* 84
true 494
liberal 516
property 780
–estate 780
–property 780
–security 771
realgar 434
realism 494
realistic 494, 594
realize *speciality* 79
intellect 450
think 451
discover 480a
believe 484
conceive 490
imagine 515
accomplish 729
acquire 775
sell 796
really *wonder* 870
(*very* 31)
realm *region* 181
people 372
government 737
property 780
realty 342, 780
ream 593
reamer 262
reanimate
reproduce 163
life 359
resuscitate 660
reap *shorten* 201
agriculture 371
take 789
–and carry 775
–the benefit of
be better for 658
–the fruits
succeed 731
acquire 775
reward 973
–the whirlwind
product 154
failure 732
–where one has not
sown 154, 923
reaper 371
reappear
repetition 104
reproduce 163
visible 446
restore 660
(*frequent* 136)
rear *sequel* 65
end 67
bring up 161
erect 212
back 235
elevate 307
teach 537
in the–281
–its head
manifest 525

–one's head
pride 878
rear admiral 745
reason *cause* 153
intellect 450
thought 451
argue 476
wisdom 498
motive 615
by–of 615
feast of–588
for this–462
in–*moderate* 174
sanity 502
right 922
listen to–498
–in a circle 477
–why *cause* 153
motive 615
stand to
–*certain* 474
proof 478
manifest 525
what's the–? 461
without rime or–
615a
reasonable
moderate 174
probable 472
judicious 498
sane 502
cheap 815
right 922
–*prospect* 472
reasoner 476
reasoning 476
–faculties 450
reasonless 499
reasons 476
reassemble 72
reassert 535
reassure *hope* 858
courage 861
reasty *fetid* 401
unclean 653
reave 789
rebate *deduction* 38
discount 40a
moderate 174
discount 813
rebatement 36, 813
rebec 417
rebel *revolution* 146
disobedience 742
(*resistance* 719)
rebellion
revolution 146
insurrection 719
revolt 742
rebellious *defiant* 715
(see rebellion)
rebellow 412
rebirth 660
reboation 412
rebound *recoil* 277
regression 283

546

rebuff

rebuff
   (*counteraction* 179)
   on the– 145
rebuff *recoil* 277
   resist 719
   repulse 732
   refuse 764
   discourtesy 895
   censure 932
rebuild 660
rebuke 932
rebus 533
rebut *answer* 462
   counter evidence 468
   confute 479
   deny 536
rebuttal (*see* rebut)
rebutter *ansswer* 462
   law pleadings 969
recalcitrance 719
recalcitrant 742
recalcitrate
   recoil 277
   resist 719
recalesce 382
recall *recollect* 505
   recant 607
   cancel 756
   –to life 660
recant *deny* 536
   retract 607
   resign 756
recapitulate
   enumerate 85
   repeat 104
   describe 594
   summarize 596
recast *revolution* 146
   scheme 626
recede *move back* 283
   move from 287
   –into the shade 874
receipt *scheme* 626
   prescription 662
   precept 697
   security 771
   payment 807
   –of *money* 810
   –in full 807
   –s *accounts* 811
receive *include* 76
   admit 296
   belief 484
   assent 488
   acquire 775
   take in 785
   take 789
   –*money* 810
   welcome 892, 894
   –Christ 987
received *known* 490
   habitual 613
   (*conformable* 82)
   –*maxim* 496
receiver *vessel* 191
   assignee 785, 967
   treasurer 801

–of stolen goods 792
receiving 785
recension 85
recent *lately* 122
   new 123
receptacle 191
   (*storehouse* 636)
reception
   comprehension 54
   inclusion 76
   arrival 292
   ingestion 296
   interview 588
   receiving 785
   welcome 892, 894
   warm– 892
reception room 191
receptive
   undertaking 676
   (*see* reception)
recess *receptacle* 191
   corner 244
   regression 283
   ambush 530
   vacation 687
   retirement 893
recesses *interior* 221
   secret–of one's
   heart 820
recession
   motion from 287
recessive 287
réchauffé *copy* 21
   repetition 104
   food 298
   made hot 384
   restored 660
recherché
   unimitated 20
   good 648
   fashionable 852
recidivation
   regression 283
   relapse 661
recidivism 607
recidivist 607
recipe *remedy* 662
   precept 697
recipient
   receptacle 191
   receiving 785
reciprocal *mutual* 12
   –*quantity* 84
   retaliation 718
reciprocate
   correlation 12
   interchange 148
   assent 488
   concord 714
   retaliate 718
reciprocitist 12
reciprocity 12, 148
recision 38
recital *music* 415
recitation (*see* recite)
recitativo 415

recite *enumerate* 85
   speak 582
   narrate 594
reciter 582
reck 459
reckless *careless* 460
   defiant 715
   rash 863
reckon *count* 85
   –*among* 76
   –upon *believe* 484
   –*expect* 507
   –with 807
   –without one's host
   unskillful 699
   fail 732
   rash 863
reckoning
   numeration 85
   measure 466
   expectation 507
   payment 807
   accounts 811
   reward 973
   day of– 919
reclaim *improve* 658
   restore 660
   command 741
   due 924
   atonement 952
reclaimed
   penitent 950
reclamation *land* 342
   (*see* reclaim)
recline *lie flat* 213
   depress 308
   response 687
   –on 215
reclivate 248
recluse 893
recognition
   (*see* recognize)
   courtesy 894
   thanks 916
   means of– 550
recognitor 967
recognizable
   visible 446
   intelligible 518
   –by 550
recognizance 771
recognize *see* 441
   attention 457
   discover 480a
   assent 488
   know 490
   remember 505
   permit 760
   (*affirm* 535)
recognized
   influential 175
   customary 613
   (*conformable* 82)
   –*maxim* 496
recoil *reaction* 179
   repercussion 277

Red

reluctance 603
   shun 623
   from which
      reason–s 471
   –at *hate* 898
   –from *dislike* 867
recollect 505
recommence 66
recommend
   advise 695
   approve 931
   (*induce* 15)
   –itself
   approbation 931
recompense
   reward 973
   (*pay* 809)
recompose
   combine 56
reconcile *agree* 23
   pacify 723
   content 831
   forgive 918
   –oneself to 826
recondite *obscure* 519
   hidden 528
recondition 660
reconnoissance 441
reconnoiter *see* 441
   inquire 461
reconsideration 451
   on– 658
reconstitute 660
reconstruct 660
reconvert 660
record 551
   discrimination 465
   career 692
   break the– 33
   Congressional–s
      551
   court of– 966
recorder 553
   judge 967
recording
   –*instrument* 551
   –*secretary* 554
recount 594
recoup 30, 790
recourse 677
recovery
   improvement 658
   reinstatement 660
   getting back 775
   restitution 790
   –of strength 689
recreant
   coward 862
   base 940
   knave 941
   vicious 945
   bad man 949
recreation 840
recrement 653
recriminate 932
recrimination 938

recriminatory 718, 938
recrudescence 661
recruit *alien* 57
   strength 159
   learner 541
   provision 637
   health 654
   repair 658
   reinstate 660
   refresh 689
   aid 707
   auxiliary 711
   soldier 726
   beat up for–s
   prepare 673
   aid 707
rectal 221
rectangle 244
rectangular
   perpendicular 212
   angle 244
rectify *degree* 26
   straighten 246
   improve 658
   reëstablish 660
rectilinear 246
rectitude *probity* 939
   virtue 944
rector *director* 694
   clergyman 996
rectorship 995
rectory 1000
rectrix 745
rectum 221, 350
recubant 213, 217
recueil 54
recumbent
   horizontal 213
   oblique 217
recuperation 689, 790
recuperative 660
recur *repeat* 104
   frequent 136
   periodic 138
   –to 677
   –to the mind 505
recure 660
recurrence
   (*see* recur)
recursion 292
recurvity 245
recusancy
   impiety 988
   (*see* recusant)
recusant
   dissenting 489
   denying 536
   disobedient 742
   refusing 764
   impenitent 951
   heterodox 984
   (*unwilling* 603)
Red
   anarchist 146, 710

red 434
- and yellow 439
- book *list* 86
- cap *porter* 271
- cent 643, 800
- cross 662
- flag 550, 668
- hot *great* 31
  - *violent* 173
  - *hot* 382
  - *emotion* 821
  - *excited* 824
- lead 434
- letter *mark* 550
  - *celebrate* 883
- letter day
  - *important* 642
  - *rest* 687
  - *amusement* 840
  - *celebration* 883
- light 550, 668
- light district 961
- ocher 434
- pepper 393
- republican 742
- tape 613, 694
- with mirth 892
  turn—*feeling* 821
redact 54, 658
redan 717
redargue 479
redcoat 726
red-complexioned 434
redden *color* 434
  humble 879
  angry 900
reddish-brown 433, 434
reddition
  interpretation 522
  restitution 790
redeem
  compensate 30
  substitute 147
  reinstate 660
  deliver 672
  regain 775
  restore 790
  pay 807
  penitent 950
  atone 952
- from oblivion 505
- one's pledge
  observe 772
  duty 926
Redeemer 976
redemption
  (see redeem)
  liberation 750
  duty 926
  salvation 976
  (*preservation* 676)
redemptioner 295
red-faced 434
red giant 490a

red-handed
  murder 361
  in the act 680
  guilty 947
redict 905
redintegrate 660
redivivus 660
redness 382, 434
redolence *odor* 398
  fragrance 400
redouble *increase* 356
  duplication 90
  repeat 104
- one's efforts 686
redoubt 717
redoubtable 860
redound to
  conduce 176
- one's honor
  glory 873
  approbation 931
  honor 939
redress *restore* 660
  remedy 662
  atonement 952
  reward 973
Redskin 913
red-tapist 694
redtop *grass* 367
reduce *lessen* 36
  pare 38
- in number 103
  weaken 160
  contract 195
  shorten 201
  lower 308
  subdue 731
  discount 813
- in strength 160
- the speed 275
- to *convert* 144
- to a mean 29
- to ashes 384
- to demonstration 478
- to order 60
- to poverty 804
- to powder 330
- to subjection 749
- to writing 551
reduced (see reduce)
  impoverished 804
- to a skeleton 659
- to straits 704
- to the last extremity 665
reductio ad absurdum
  reasoning 476
  confutation 479
reduction
  (see reduce)
  arithmetical 85
  conversion 144
  at a—815
- of temperature 385

reductive 36
redundance
  superiority 33
  diffuseness 573
  too much 641
  inutility 645
  (*remainder* 40)
redundancy 104
reduplication
  imitation 19
  doubling 90
  repetition 104
reecho *imitate* 19
  repeat 104
  resonance 408
reechy 653
reed *weak* 160
  writing 590
  arrow 727
- instrument 417
  trust to a broken— 699
reed-shaped 253
reedy 253
reef *slacken* 275
  shoal 346
  make safe 664
  danger 667
  double-topsails 664
reek *gas* 334
  vaporize 336
  liquid 337
  hot 382
  fester 653
reeking *moist* 339
  unclean 653
reel *rock* 314
  spool 312
  agitate 315
  music 415
  dance 840
- back *yield* 725
reembody *junction* 43
  combination 48
reenforce *add* 37
  strengthen 159
  restore 660
  aid 707
reinforcement
  increase 35
  addition 37
  adjunct 39
  materials 635
  provision 637
  aid 707
reenter 245
reentering angle 244
reentry 292
reestablish 660
refashion 163
refect *strengthen* 159
refection *meal* 298
  refreshment 689
  (*restoration* 660)
refectory 191
refer to *relate* 98

  include 76
  attribute 155
  cite 467
  take advice 695
referable *relative* 9
  attributable 155
referee *judgment* 480
  judge 967
  mediation 724
reference (see refer)
referendary 967
referendum 609
referential 521
refine *sensibility* 375
  clean 652
- upon 658
refined *taste* 850
  fashionable 852
refinement
  discrimination 465
  wisdom 498
  improvement 658
  elegance 845
  taste 850
  over—477
refit 660
reflect *imitate* 19
  think 450, 451
- dishonor 874
- light 420
- upon *censure* 932
reflecting
  thoughtful 498
reflection (see reflect)
  light 420
  idea 453
  cool—came 498
reflector *mirror* 445
reflex *copy* 21
  recoil 277
  regressive 283
reflexion 21, 277
  resonance 408
  light 420
refluence *recoil* 277
  regress 283
  reflux 348
reflux *decrease* 36
  recoil 277
  regress 283
  current 348
refocillate
  strengthen 159
  refresh 689
reform *convert* 144
  improve 658
- school 542, 752
reformation 658
reformatory
  school 542
  prison 752
reformer 658
reformist 658
refound 144
refraction
  deviation 279

  light 420
  fallacy of vision 443
refractivity 420
refractometer 420
refractory
  obstinate 606
  difficult 704
  mutinous 742
  sullen 901a
refrain *repetition* 104
  poetry 597
  avoid 623
  do nothing 681
  temperate 953
  (*unwilling* 603)
  (*reject* 610)
- from laughter 837
- from voting 609a
refresh *strengthen* 159
  cool 385
  refit 658
  restore 660
  recruit 689
  relieve 834
- the inner man 689
- the memory 505
refreshing
  bodily pleasure 377
  mental delight 829
refreshment *food* 298
  recruiting 689
  delight 827
refrigerant 387
refrigeration
  anaesthetic 376
  making cold 385
refrigerator 385
refrigeratory 387
reft 44
refuge 666
refugee *emigrant* 268
  fugitive 623
refulgence 420
refund *pay* 807
  (*restore* 790)
refurbish 673
refusal 764
  preemption 795
refuse *remains* 40
  useless 645
  not consent 764
- assent 489
- to associate with 893
- to believe 487
- to hear 460
refute 479
refuted 495
regain 775
- breath 689
regal 737
regale *feast* 298
  physical pleasure 377
  refresh 689
  pleasing 829
  amusement 840

regalia — remainder

regalia 747
regality 737
regard *relation* 9
  view 441
  attention 457
  judge 480
  credit 873
  love 897
  respect 928
  approbation 931
  have–to 457
  merit–642
  pay–to *believe* 484
  honor 873
  –as 484
regardful
  attentive 457
  careful 459
regardless
  inattentive 458
  insensible 823
regards *courtesy* 894
  respect 928
regatta
  contention 720
  amusement 840
regelate 385
regency 755
regenerate
  reproduce 163
  restore 660
  penitence 950
  piety 987
regeneration
  conversion 144
  divine function 976
  baptismal–998
regent *governor* 745
  deputy 759
regicide 361
régime
  circumstances 8
  conduct 692
  authority 737
  ancien–875
regimen *diet* 298
  remedy 662
regiment
  assemblage 72
  army 726
regimentals 225
region 181, 342
regional 181, 189
register *arrange* 60
  list 86
  chronicle 114
  furnace 386
  record 551
  recorder 553
  schedule 611
registrar 553
registration 551
registry 114
  record 551
reglet 591
regnant *influence* 175

authority 737
regorge 790
regrade 283
regrate 777, 795
regrater 797
regress 287
regression 283, 287
regret *sorrow* 833
  penitence 950
regretted, to be–833
regrowth 163
reguerdon 973
regular *uniform* 16
  complete 52
  order 58
  arrangement 60
  rule 80
  conformity 82
  periodic 138
  symmetric 242
  habitual 613
  by–intervals 58
  –return 138
regularity
  (see *regular*)
regularize *legal* 963
regulars 726
regulate *adjust* 23
  order 58
  arrange 60
  direct 693
regulated by
  conformity 82
regulation
  precept 697
  law 963
  (*command* 741)
regulative principle 453
Regulus 490a
regurgitate
  return 283
  flow 348
  restore 790
rehabilitate
  reconstruct 660
  restore 790
rehearse *repeat* 104
  try 463
  describe 594
  drama 599
  prepare 673
Reichsrath 696
reign *influence* 175
  government 737
  –of terror
  severity 739
  fear 860
  –of violence 738
reimburse *restore* 790
  pay 807
rein
  means of restraint 752
  (*moderate* 174)
  (*counteract* 179)

–in *retard* 275
  restrain 751
reindeer 271, 366
reinforce
  (see *reënforce*)
reinforcement
  (see *reenforcement*)
reinless 738
reins (see *rein*)
  direction 693
  give–to the *imagination* 515
  give the–to *facilitate* 705
  lax 738
  permit 760
  hold the–693
  take the– *authority* 737
reinstall 660
reinstate 660, 790
reinvest 790
reinvigorate 689
reiterate 104
reject *exclude* 55
  eject 297
  refuse 764
rejected *hateful* 898
rejection 610
rejoice *exult* 838
  amuse 840
  –in 827
  –in the name of 564
  –the heart *gratify* 829
  cheer 836
rejoicing 838
rejoin *assemble* 72
  arrive 292
rejoinder *answer* 462
  law pleadings 969
rejoining *meeting* 292
rejuvenescence 660
rekindle *ignite* 384
  excite 824
  (*incite* 615)
relapse *turn back* 145
  regression 283
  fall back **661**
relate *narrate* 594
  –to *refer* 9
related *kin* 11
relation 9 *kin* 11
  narrative 594
relationship 9
relative
  comparative 464
  –*position* 9
relativism 451
relax *loose* 47
  weaken 160
  moderate 174
  slacken speed 275
  soften 324
  inactive 683
  repose 687

misrule 738
  liberate 750
  relent 914
  –one's efforts 681
  –the mind 452
relaxation (see *relax*)
  amusement 840
  dereliction 927
relaxed *weak* 160
relay *materials* 635
  provision 637
release *death* 360
  deliver 672
  liberate 750
  exempt 760
  from engagement 768a
  security 771
  exemption 777a
  restore 790
  repay 807
  forgive 918
  exempt 927a
  discharge 970
  deed of–723
relegate *banish* 55
  transfer 270
  remove 297
relent *moderate* 274
  soften 324
  submit 725
  pity 914
relentless *resolute* 604
  severe 739
  wrathful 900
  malevolent 907
  revenge 919
  impenitent 951
relessee *possessor* 779
  receiver 785
relevancy
  pertinence 9
  congruity 23
relevé 298
reliability
  (see *reliable*)
  solvency 800
reliable *certain* 474
  trustworthy 632
reliance
  confidence 484
  expectation 507
  hope 858
relic *remainder* 40
  reminiscence 505
  token 551
relics *corpse* 362
  sacred 998
relict 905
relief *composition* 54
  silhouette 230
  prominence 250
  aid 707
  comfort **834**
  bas–*convex* 250
  sculpture 557

in *strong*
  –*visible* 446
  manifest 525
relieve *improve* 658
  aid 707
  comfort 834
relievo *convex* 250
  sculpture 557
religieuse 996
religion *theology* 983
  piety 987
  under the mask of 988
religionist 988
religious *celibacy* 904
  honorable 939
  theological 983
  pious 987
  over–955
  –*education* 537
  –*persuasion* 983
  –*sects* 984
relinquish 624, 782
  –a purpose 624
  recant 607
  –hope 859
  –life 360
  –property 782
relinquishment 624, 782 *resignation* 757
reliquary *box* 191
  sacred 998
reliquiae 362
relish *pleasure* 377
  taste 390
  condiment 393
  savory 394
  delight 827
  desire 865
relucent *light* 420
reluct 720
reluctance
  dissuasion 616
  unwilling 603
  dislike 867
reluctation 719
relume *ignite* 384
  light 420
rely *believe* 484
  hope 858
  (*expect* 507)
remain *abide* 1
  be left 40
  endure 106
  long time 110
  continue 141
  be present 186
  stand 265
  –firm 150
  –in one's mind 505
  –in possession of the field 731
  –neuter 605
  –on one's hands 641
remainder 40
  estate 780

549

remainder–man — reprieve

in–*posterior* 117
remainder–man 779
remains *remainder* 40
  corpse 362
  vestige 551
  organic–357
remand *defer* 133
  order 741
remanet 40
remark *observe* 457
  affirmation 535
  worthy of–642
remarkable *great* 31
  exceptional 83
  important 642
remarry 993
remediable
  restore 660
  remedy 662
remedial 660, 662
remediless 859
remedy *restore* 660
  cure **662**
remember 505
remembered 505, 506
remembrance 505
remembrances 894
rememoration 505
remiform 245
remigration
  regression 283
  arrival 292
  egress 295
remind
  remember 505
  recollect 506
  that–s me 134
reminder 505
reminiscence 505
remise 927a
remiss *neglectful* 460
  reluctant 603
  shiftless 674
  idle 683
  lax 738
remission
  cessation 142
  moderation 174
  laxity 738
  forgiveness 918
  exemption 927a
remit (*see* remission)
  –*one's efforts* 681
remittance
  payment 807
remittent 138
remitter 790
remnant
  remainder 40
  reserve 632
remodel *convert* 144
  revolutionize 146
  improve 658
remollient 324
remonetize 800

remonstrance
  dissuasion 616
  deprecation 766
  censure 932
remora *cohere* 46
  hindrance 706
remorse 950
remorseless 919
remote *not related* 10
  distant 196
  –*age* 122
  –*cause* 153
  –*future* 121
  –*region* 196
remotion 270
removal (*see* remove)
remove *subduct* 38
  term 71
  displace 185
  transfer 270
  recede 287
  depart 293
  dinner 298
  extract 301
  school 541
  –*the mask* 529
removedness
  distance 196
remuda 72
remugient 412
remunerate
  reward 973
remunerative
  useful 644
  gain 775
  receipt 810
Renaissance 554
renaissance 660
renascent 163
rencounter
  contact 199
  meeting 292
  fight 720
rend 44–*the air*
  loud 404
  cry 411
  lament 839
  –*the heartstrings* 830
render *convert* 144
  interpret 522
  give 784
  restore 790
  –*an account*
  inform 527
  describe 594
  –*a service* 644
rendezvous
  assemble 72
  focus 74
rendition
  interpretation 522
  restore 790
renegade *convert* 144
  traveler 268
  turncoat 607
  shirker 623

disobey 742
  apostate 941
renew *twice* 90
  repeat 104
  reproduce 163
  recollect 505
  restore 660
  –*one's strength* 689
reniform 245
renitence
  counteraction 179
  hardness 323
  elasticity 325
  unwillingness 603
  resistance 719
renounce
  disavow 536
  recant 607
  relinquish 624
  resign 757
  –*property* 782
  repudiate 927
  (*deny* 536)
renovate
  reproduce 163
  restore 660
renovated *new* 123
renovation
  (*see* renovate)
renown 505, 873
renowned 31
renownless 874
rent *tear* 44
  fissure 198
  hire 788
  purchase 795
rentage 810
rental 810
renter 779
rent–free 815
rent roll *property* 780
  receipts 810
rents *houses* 189
renunciation
  (*see* renounce)
  refusal 764
  exemption 927a
reorganize
  convert 144
  improve 658
  restore 660
repair *mend* 658
  make good 660
  refresh 689
  out of–659
  –*to* 266
reparation
  (*see* repair)
  restitution 790
  atonement 952
  reward 973
reparative 30
repartee *answer* 462
  wit 842
reparteeist 844
repartition 786

repass 314
repast 298
repay *pay* 807
  reward 973
repeal 756
repeat *imitate* 19
  duplication 90
  iterate 104
  reproduce 163
  affirm 535
  –*by rote* 505
repeated *frequent* 136
  iteration 104
repeater *watch* 114
  cunning 702
  firearm 727
repel *repulse* 289
  deter 616
  defend 717
  resist 719
  refuse 764
  give pain 830
  disincline 867
  banish 893
  excite hate 898
repellent (*see* repel)
repent 950
repentant
  my–tears 951
repercuss 277, 289
repercussion
  recoil 277
  (*counteraction* 179)
répertoire 599
repertory 599, 636
repetend
  arithmetical 84
  iteration 104
repetition
  imitation 19
  iteration **104**
  (*copy* 21)
  (*twice* 90)
repine *pain* 828
  discontent 832
  regret 833
  sad 837
  (*repent* 950)
replace *substitute* 147
  locate 184
  restore 660
replenish *complete* 52
  fill 637
repletion *filling* 639
  redundance 641
  satiety 869
replevin *security* 771
  recovery 775
  restore 790
replica 21, 90
replication
  answer 462
  law pleadings 969
reply *answer* 462
  vindicate 937
report *noise* 406

  judgment 480
  inform 527
  publish 531
  rumor 532
  record 551
  statement 594
  good–873
  –*progress* 527
  through evil report and good–604a
reporter
  informant 527
  messenger 534
  journalist 554, 593
  consignee 758
reports *law* 969
repose *quiescence* 265
  leisure 685
  rest **687**
  –*confidence in* 484
  –*on support* 215
  evidence 467
  –*on one's laurels* 142
reposit 184
repository 636
repoussé 250
reprehend 932
reprehensible
  obnoxious 898
  vicious 945
  guilty 947
represent *similar* 17
  imitate 19
  exhibit 525
  intimate 527
  denote 550
  delineate 554
  commission 755
  deputy 759
  (*describe* 594)
  –*to oneself* 515
representation
  (*see* represent)
  copy 21
  portrait **554**
  drama 599
representative
  typical 79
  agent 690
  legislator 696
  commissioner 758
  deputy 759
  –*government* 737
  –*of the people* 696
  –*of the press messenger* 534
  writer 593
repress *restrain* 751
  (*moderate* 174)
  (*counteract* 179)
  –*a smile* 837
  –*one's feelings* 826
repressionist 751
reprieve *lateness* 133
  deliverance 672
  deliberate 750

550

reprimand — rest

pardon 918
respite 970
reprimand 932
reprint *copy* 21
  reproduce 163
  indicate 550
reprisal
  retaliation 718
  resumption 789
reprise *decrement* 40a
reproach *disgrace* 874
  blame 932
  accusation 938
reprobate
  disapproved 932
  vicious 945
  bad man 949
  sinner 988
reprobation
  censure 932
  sin 988
reproduce *match* 17
  imitate 19
  repeat 104
  renovate 163
reproduction 163
  copy 21
  (*see* reproduce)
reproductive 163
reproof 932
  –*valiant* 718
reprove *berate* 527
  disapprove 932
reprover 936
reptatorial 275
reptile
  animal 366, 368
  servile 886
  knave 941
  miscreant 949
republic *people* 372
  government 737
  –*of letters* 560
republican
  government 737
  commonalty 876
republicanism 737
Republicans 712
repudiate *exclude* 55
  deny 489
  reject 610
  abrogate 756
  violate 773
  not pay 808
  evade 927
repugn 719
repugnance
  contrariety 14
  incongruity 24
  resistance 719
  dislike 867
  hate 898
  (*unwillingness* 603)
repulse *recoil* 277
  repel 289
  resist 719

failure 732
refusal 764
repulsion 289, 719
repulsive
  (*see* repulse)
  unsavory 395
  painful 830
  ugly 846
  disliked 867
  discourteous 895
  hateful 898
repurchase 795
reputable
  honored 873
  honorable 939
reputation 505, 873
repute 873
request 765 in–630
  –*permission* 760
requiem *lament* 839
  (*funeral* 363)
  (*music* 415)
require *need* 630
  insufficient 640
  exact 741
  compel 744
  price 812
  due 924
  duty 926
  –*explanation* 519
requirement 630
requisite 630
requisition
  exaction 741
  request 765
  put in–*use* 677
  order 741
requital
  retaliation 718
  gratitude 916
  punishment 972
  reward 973
requite 148
reredos 1000
rescind *cut off* 44
  abrogate 756
  refuse 764
rescission 44, 756
rescript *answer* 462
  transcript 590
  letter 592
  order 741
rescriptive
  prohibition 761
rescue
  preserve 670
  deliver 672
  aid 707
research 461
reseat 660
resection 44
reseda 435
resemblance 17, 21
resent 900
resentful 901
resentment 900

reservation
  concealment 528
  mental–528
  equivocation 520
  untruth 546
  with a–38
reservatory
  receptacle 191
  store 636
reserve
  concealment 528
  silence 585
  choice 609
  means 632
  store 636
  disuse 678
  retain 781
  shyness 881
  in–*destined* 152
  prepared 673
  –*forces* 726
  –*oneself* 881
reservoir 153, 636
resiance 189
resiant 186
reside 186
residence 189
  have one's legal–*at* 184
resident
  consignee 758
  present 186
  inhabitant 188
residential 186
residentiary 186, 188
  clergy 996
residue 40
residuum
  remainder 40
  dregs 653
  commonalty 876
resign *give up* 757
  relinquish 782
  –*one's being* 360
  –*one's breath* 360
  –*oneself submit* 725
  not mind 826
resignation
  (*see* resign)
  submission 725
  obedience 743
  abdication **757**
  renunciation 782
  endurance 826
  humility 879
resilience
  regression 283
  elasticity 325
resin 356a
resipiscence 950
resist *oppose* 179
  withstand 719
  disobey 742
  refuse 764
  –*invasion* 717
resistance 708, 719

(*see* resist)
résistance, pièce de–298
resisting
  tenacious 327
resistivity 490d
resistless *strong* 159
  necessity 601
resolute
  determined 604
  brave 861
resolution
  (*see* resolve)
  decomposition 49
  conversion 144
  music 413
  topic 454
  investigation 461
  mental energy **604**
  intention 620
  scheme 626
  courage 861
resolvable into
  equal 27
  convertible 144
resolve *change* 140
  liquefy 335
  investigate 461
  discover 480a
  interpret 522
  determine 604
  predetermine 611
  intend 620
  –*into convert* 144
  –*into elements* 49
resolvent
  decomposition 49
  dispersion 73
  liquefaction 335
resonance *sound* 402
  ringing **408**
resorb 296
resorbent 296
resort *assemble* 72
  focus 74
  dwelling 189
  converge 290
  last–601
  –*to be present* 186
  travel 266
  employ 677
resound *loud* 404
  ring 408
  –*praises* 931
resources *means* 632
  property 780
  wealth 803
respect *relation* 9
  observe 772
  fame 873
  salutation 894
  deference **928**
  in no–536
  with–*to* 9
respectability
  mediocrity 736

repute 873
probity 939
respectable
  unimportant 643
  distinguished 873
  upright 939
  highly–875
respectful 928
  –*distance avoid* 623
  cautious 864
respective *special* 79
  apportioned 786
respectless 458
respects *courtesy* 894
  deference 928
resperse 73
respiration 349
respirator 349
respire *breathe* 349
  live 359
  refresh 689
respirometer 662
respite
  intermission 106
  defer 133
  pause 142
  deliver 672
  repose 687
  reprieve 970
  (*escape* 671)
resplendent
  luminous 420
  splendid 845
respond *accord* 23
  answer 462
  feel 821
respondent 462
  accused 938
response
  answer 462, **587**
  concord 714
  feeling 821
  friendship 888
  worship 990
responsibility
  solvency 800
  duty 926
responsible 177, 926
responsions 539
responsive 375
rest *remainder* 40
  pause 141
  cessation 142
  support 215
  quiescence 265
  death 360
  music 403, 413
  inaction 681
  repose 687
  at–*interment* 363
  repose 687
  content 831
  –*and be thankful inaction* 681
  repose 687
  –*assured belief* 484

restaurant

hope 858
— on *support* 215
— on one's oars 142, 687
— satisfied 831
— upon *evidence* 467
  confide 484
— with *duty* 926
  set at—*answer* 462
  ascertain 474
  complete 729
  compact 769
  set one's mind at
  —*calm* 826
  set the question at
  —*prove* 478
  adjudge 480
restaurant 189, 298
restaurateur
  provider 637
restful 265
restiff (*see* restive)
resting place
  support 215
  quiet 265
  arrival 292
restitution 790
  restoration 660
Restitutionist 984
restive *averse* 603
  obstinate 606
  disobedient 742
  refusal 764
  perverse 901a
restless
  changeable 149
  moving 264
  agitated 315
  active 682
  excited 825
  fearful 860
restoration 660
restorative
  salubrious 656
  remedial 662
  relieving 834
restore *reinstate* 660
  refresh 689
  return 790
  —*equilibrium* 27
  —*harmony* 723
  —to health 654
restrain *dissuade* 616
  curb 751
  (*moderate* 174)
restrainable
  obedient 743
restrained 578, 751
restraining devices 752
restraint *elegance* 578
  compulsion 744
  restraining 751
  simplicity 849
  self—*stoicism* 826
  temperance 953

restrict *hinder* 706
  restrain 751
  prohibit 761
  (*circumscribe* 229)
restriction 469
restringency 751
resty 606
result *remainder* 40
  posteriority 117
  eventuality 151
  effect 154
  conclusion 480
  completion 729
resultance 154
resultant
  combination 48
  effect 154
resume *begin* 66
  repeat 104
  change 140
  restore 660
  take 789
résumé 596
resumption
  restoration 660
  taking 789
resupination 213
resurge 163
resurgent 163
resurrection
  reproduction 163
  heaven 981
resuscitate
  reproduce 163
  reinstate 660
retable 215
retail *distribute* 73
  inform 527
  barter 794
  sell 796
retailer 797
retain *stand* 150
  keep 781
  —one's reason 502
  —the memory of 505
retainer 746
retake 789
retaliation *retort* 718
  revenge 919
retard *later* 133
  slower 275
  hinder 706
retch 297
retection 529
retention 781
retentive *keeping* 781
  —*memory* 505
retentivity 505
reticence
  concealment 528
reticle 219
reticulation
  crossing 219
  convolution 248
reticule 191
retiform 219

retina 441
retinue *followers* 65
  series 69
  servants 746
retire *absence* 187
  move back 283
  recede 287
  resign 757
  modest 881
  seclusion 893
  —from sight
  disappear 449
  hide 528
  —into the shade
  inferior 34
  decrease 36
retiring *concave* 252
  —*color* 438
  —*disposition* 881
retold 104
retort *crucible* 144
  receptacle 191
  vaporizer 336
  boiler 386
  answer 462
  confutation 479
  retaliation 718
  wit 842
  —*courteous* 718
retouch *restore* 660
  (*improve* 658)
retrace 63, 505
  —one's steps 607
retract *recant* 607
  annul 756
  abjure 757
  violate 773
  (*deny* 536)
retraction
  (*see* retract)
retreat *resort* 74
  absence 187
  abode 189
  regression 283
  recede 287
  ambush 530
  refuge 666
  escape 671
  give way 725
  seclusion 893
  beat a—623
retreating
  concave 252
retrench *subduct* 38
  shorten 201
  lose 789
  economize 817
retribution
  retaliation 718
  payment 807
  punishment 972
  reward 973
retributive 973
  —*justice* 922
retrieve *restore* 660
  acquire 775

retriever *dog* 366
retroaction
  counteraction 179
  recoil 277
  regression 283
retroactive *past* 122
retrocession
  reversion 145
  regression 283
  recession 287
retroflexion 218
retrograde
  contrary 14
  moving back 283
  recession 287
  deteriorated 659
  relapsing 661
retrogression
  regression 283
  deterioration 659
  relapse 661
retrorse 145
retrospection
  past 122
  reversion 145
  thought 451
  memory 505
retroussé 201, 307
retroversion 218
retrude 289
return *list* 86
  repeat 104
  periodic 138
  reverse 145
  recoil 277
  regression 283
  arrival 292
  answer 462
  report 551
  relapse 661
  appoint 755
  profit 775
  restore 790
  proceeds 810
  reward 973
  in—*compensation* 30
  —thanks
  gratitude 916
  worship 990
  —the compliment
  interchange 148
  retaliate 718
  —to the original state 660
reunion *junction* 43
réunion *assemblage* 72
  concord 714
  point de—74
  social—892
reveal 529—itself 446
reveille 550
revel *amuse* 840
  dissipation 954
  —in *enjoy* 377
revelation
  discovery 480a

disclosure 529
  theological 985
Revelation 985
reveler 840
  drunkard 959
reveling *disorder* 59
  rejoicing 838
revelry 954
revenant 361, 980a
revendicate
  claim 741
  acquisition 775
  due 924
revenge 919 breathe
  —*anger* 900
revenue 810
  means 632
  —*cutter* 273
reverberate
  recoil 277
  sound 408
reverbatory 386
revere *love* 897
  respect 928
  piety 987
revered *sage* 500
reverence *title* 877
  respect 928
  piety 987
  clergy 996
reverenced 500
reverend *title* 877
  clergy 996
  —*sir* 130
reverent *pious* 987
  worship 990
reverential
  respectful 928
reverie
  train of thought 451
  inattention 458
  imagination 515
reversal
  inversion 218
  revolution 607
  irresolute 605
reverse *contrary* 14
  return 145
  inversion 218
  —of a medal 235
  anteposition 237
  adversity 735
  abrogate 756
  cards 840
  —of the shield 468
reverseless 150
reversible
reversion
  (*see* reverse)
  posteriority 117
  return 145
  possession 777
  property 780
  succession 783
  remitter 790
reversioner 779

552

reversis 840
revert *repeat* 104
   return 145
   turn back 283
   revest 790
   –*to* 457
revest 790
reviction 660
review *consider* 457
   inquiry 461
   judge 480
   recall 505
   dissertation 595
   compendium 596
   revise 658
   parade 882
reviewer 480, 595
revile *abuse* 932
   blaspheme 988
reviler 936
revise *copy* 21
   consider 457
   printing 591
   plan 626
   edit 658
revising barrister 967
revision 658
   under– 673
revisit 186
revival
   reproduction 163
   life 359
   restoration 660
   worship 990
revivalist 996
revive *reproduce* 163
   refresh 658
   resuscitate 660
   excite 824
revivify *reproduce* 163
   life 359
   resuscitate 660
revocable 605
revocation 536
revoke *recant* 607
   cancel 756
   (*deny* 536)
   (*refuse* 764)
revolt *contrariety* 14
   revolution 146
   resist 719
   disobey 742
   shock 830
   disapproval 932
   –*against hate* 898
   –*at the idea*
     dissent 489
revolting
   painful 830
revolution
   periodicity 138
   change 146
   rotation 312
revolutionary 146, 742

revolutionize 140, 146
revolve
   (*see* revolution)
   –*in the mind* 451
revolver 727
revulsion
   reversion 145
   revolution 146
   inversion 218
   recoil 277
revulsive 276
revulsively 145
reward 30, **973**
reword 104
rewriting 21
Reynard *animal* 366
   cunning 702
rez de chaussée
   room 191
   low 207
rhabdology 85
rhabdomancy 511
rhadamanthus
   judge 967
   hell 982
rhamphoid 245
rhapsodical
   irregular 139
rhapsodist
   fanatic 504
   poet 597
rhapsodize 497
rhapsody
   discontinuity 70
   nonsense 497
   fancy 515
rheometer 157
rheostat 490d
rhetoric *speech* 582
   flowers of– 577
rheum *excretion* 299
   fluidity 333
rheumatism 378
rhino 800
rhinoceros 366–*hide*
   physically insensible 376
   morally insensible 823
rhipidate 194
rhizanthous 367
rhododendron 845
rhomb 244
rhomboid 244
rhubarb 298
rhumb 278
rhyme (*see* rime etc.)
rhythm
   periodicity 138
   melody 413
   elegance 578
   verse 597
rhythmic 413, 578
rhythmical–*style* 578
riant 836

rib *support* 215
   ridge 250
   wife 903
ribald *vulgar* 851
   disreputable 874
   impure 961
ribaldry 908
ribband (*see* ribbon)
ribbed *furrowed* 259
ribbon *tie* 45
   filament 205
   record 551
   decoration 877
ribbons *reins* 752
riboast 972
rice 330, 367
ricebird 298
rich *savory* 394
   color 428
   language 577
   abundant 639
   wealthy 803
   beautiful 845
   ornament 847
   –*gifts wax poor* 907
   –*man* 639, 803
riches 803
richly *much* 31
   –*deserve* 924
rick *accumulation* 72
   store 636
rickety *weak* 160
   ugly 846
   imperfect 651
rickrack 257
ricksha 272
ricochet 277
rid *deliver* 672
   get–of eject 297
   liberation 750
   loose 776
   relinquish 782
riddance 672, 776, 782
riddle *arrange* 60
   crossing 219
   sieve 260
   secret 533
   sift 652
   (*question* 461)
ride *get above* 206
   move 266
   –*a horse* 370
   –*and tie*
     periodicity 138
   journey 266
   –*at anchor* 265
   –*full tilt at*
     pursue 622
     attack 716
   –*hard* 274
   –*in the whirlwind*
     will 604
     rule 737
   –*one's hobby* 622
   –*out the storm* 664

–*roughshod*
   violence 173
   severity 739
   insolence 885
   illegality 964
   –*the waves* 267
rider *affix* 37
   appendix 39
   equestrian 268
ridge *narrow* 203
   height 206
   prominence 250
ridicule 856
   disrespect 929
ridiculous *absurd* 497
   foolish 499
   trifling 643
   grotesque 853
ridiculousness 853
riding *district* 181
   journey 266
ridotto *gala* 840
   rout 892
rifacimento
   repetition 104
   resuscitation 660
rife *general* 78
   influence 175
riffle 348
riffraff *dirt* 653
   commonalty 876
   bad folk 949
rifle *musket* 406, 727
   plunder 791
   –*grenade* 727
rifled cannon 727
rifleman 726
rifler 792
rifles 726
rifle shooting 840
rift *separation* 44
   fissure 198
rig *dress* 225
   vehicle 272
   prepare 673
   frolic 840
   strumpet 962
   –*the market* 794
   run the–upon 929
rigadoon 840
rigging *ropes* 45
   gear 225
   instrument 633
riggish 961
right *dextral* 238
   straight 246*true* 494
   freedom 748
   property 780
   just **922**
   privilege 924
   duty 926
   honor 939
   virtuous 944
   bill of– 969
   by– 924
   have a–to 924

   hit the–nail on the head
   discover 480a
   skill 698
   in one's–mind
     wise 498
     sane 502
   in the–place 646
   keep the–path 944
   –*about*
     (*see below*)
   –*ahead* 234
   –*and left space* 180
   circumjacence 227
   lateral 236
   –*angle* 212
   –*as a trevet* 650
   –*ascension* 466
   –*away* 113, 143
   –*bower* 840
   divine–of kings 737
   –*establishment* 478
   –*hand*
     (*see below*)
   –*itself* 660
   –*line* 246
   –*man in the right place* 23
   –*owner* 779
   –*passage* 279
   –*thing to do* 926
   –*word in the right place* 578
   set–inform 527
   disclose 529
   step in the–direction 644
   that's– 931
right–about
   go to the–
   circuit 311
   tergiversation 607
   send to the–
   eject 297
   reject 610
   refuse 764
   to the– 283
   turn to the–
   inversion 218
   deviation 279
righteous
   virtuous 944
   –*overmuch* 988
   the– 987
Righteousness
   Lord our– 976
   Sun of– 976
rightful 922
   –*owner* 779
right hand *power* 157
   dextrality 238
   help 711
   not let the–know what the left is doing 528
   –*of friendship* 888

right–handed ... roll

right–handed 238
right–minded
  sanity 502
  probity 939
  virtue 944
rights, put to–
  restore 660
  set to–*arrange* 60
  stand on one's–748
rigid *regular* 82
  hard 328
  exact 494
  severe 739
  (*stubborn* 606)
rigmarole
  unmeaning 517
  (*absurd* 497)
rigor 383, 494, 739
  (*compulsion* 744)
  –*mortis* 360
rigorous *exact* 494
  severe 739
  revengeful 919
  –*establishment* 478
Rigsdag 696
riksdag 969
rile *annoy* 830
  hate 898
  anger 900
rilievo *convex* 250
  sculpture 557
rill 348
rim 231, 272
rime *chink* 198
  frost 383
rime or **rhyme**
  similarity 17
  melody 413
  poetry 597
  without–or reason
    absurd 497
  caprice 608
  motiveless 615a
rimeless *prose* 598
rimester 597
rimer 262
rimiform 259
rimose 198
rimple 258
rimulose 198
rind *covering* 223
  flay 226
rinderpest 655
ring *fastening* 45
  pendency 214
  circle 247
  loud 404
  resonance 408
  clique 712
  arena 728
  have the true–494
  in a–fence
    circumscription 229
    inclosure 232
  –dove 366
  –in the ear 408

  –the changes
    repeat 104
    change 140
    changeable 149
  –the tocsin 669
  –*untrue* 546
  –with the praises of 931
  rub the–902
ring–dove 416
ringent 260
ringer *impostor* 548
ringleader
  director 694
  mutineer 742
ringlet *circling* 247
  hair 256
ringworm 655
rink 840
rinse 652
rinsings 653
riot *confusion* 59
  derangement 61
  violence 173
  discord 713
  resist 719
  mutiny 742
  –in *pleasure* 742
  run–*activity* 682
  excitement 825
  intemperance 954
rioter 742
riotous 173
rip *open* 260
  bad man 949
  libertine 962
  –*open* 260
  –up *tear* 44
  excite 824
riparian 342
ripe *of cheese* 298
  prepared 673
  –*age old* 128
  grown up 131
ripen *perfect* 650
  improve 658
  prepare 673
  complete 729
  –into 144
ripicolous 342
riposte 462
ripple *ruffle* 256
  shake 315
  water 348
  murmur 405
riprap 215
rire, pour–853
rise *grow* 35
  begin 66
  revolt 146, 742
  slope 217
  progress 282
  ascend 305
  stir 682
  –above 31, 206
  –again 660

  –from 154
  –in arms 722
  –in price 814
  –in the world 734
  –up *elevation* 307
risible *laughable* 838
  ridiculous 853
  (*wit* 842)
rising (see rise)
  –generation
    youth 127
    posterity 167
  –ground *height* 206
  slope 217
  –of the curtain
    beginning 66
    appearance 448
  worship the–sun 886
risk *chance* 621
  danger 665
  invest 787
  at all–s 604
  at any–604
risqué 961
rite *law* 963
  religious **998**
  funeral–363
ritornel 62, 64
ritornello 104
ritual *ostentation* 882
  worship 990
  rite 998
ritualism
  religious sect 984
rival *emulate* 648
  oppose 708
  opponent 710
  compete 720
  combatant 726
  outshine 873
rivalry *envy* 921
rive 44
rivel 258
river 348
  –of death 360
  –s of hell 982
rivet *fasten* 43
  fastening 45
  –in the memory 505
  –the attention
    attend 457
    excite 824
  –the eyes upon 441
  –the yoke 739
riveted *firm* 150
rivulation 219, 248
rivulet 348
rivulose 248
rixation 713
riziform 249
road *street* 189
  direction 278
  way 627
  on the–
    transference 270

  progression 282
  approach 286
  on the high–to 278
  –to ruin
    destruction 162
  danger 665
  adversity 735
road book 266
road hog *traveler* 268
  selfishness 943
roads *lake* 343
roadstead
  location 184
  abode 189
  refuge 666
roadster 271, 272
roadway 627
roam 266
roan *horse* 271
  color 433
roanoke 800
roar *violence* 173
  blow violently 349
  sound 404, 407
  bellow 411, 412
  laugh 838
  weep 839
roarer 887
roaring *great* 31
  –*trade* 731, 734
roast *heat* 384
  inquire 461
  ridicule 856
  rib–972
  –and boiled 298
  –an ox 883
  –beef etc. 298
  rule the–737
roasting *heat* 382
rob *juice* 352
  pulp 354
  plunder 791
  –Peter to pay Paul
    compensation 30
  steal 791
  wrong 923
robber 792
robbery 791
robe *covering* 223
  dress 225
  canonicals 999
  –s of state 747
robin 366
Robin Goodfellow 979
roborant 662
robust *strong* 159
  healthy 654
roc 83
Rochester knockings 992a
Rocinante 271
rock *firm* 150
  oscillate 314
  hard 323
  land 342

  safety 664
  danger 667
  attack 716
  money 800
  build on a–150
  –ahead 665
  –bound coast 342
  –oil 356
  split upon a–732
rockaway 272
rocket *rapid* 274
  rise 305
  light 423
  signal 550
  arms 727
  go up like a–and come down like the stick 732
rocking–stone 314
rocking–chair 215
rocky 323
rococo 847
rod *support* 215
  measure 466
  scourge 975
  divining 993
  kiss the–725
  –in the pickle
    prepared 673
  accusation 938
  punishment 972
  scourge 975
  –of empire 747
  sounding–208
rodomontade
  overestimation 482
  unmeaning 517
  boast 884
  (*absurdity* 497)
roe *deer* 366
  female 374
rogation *request* 765
  worship 990
rogue *cheat* 548
  knave 941
  scamp 949
  –'s march 297
roguery 940
roguish *playful* 840
roil 653, 898
roister 885
roisterer 887
Roland for an Oliver
  retaliation 718
  barter 794
role *drama* 599
  business 625
  plan 626
  conduct 692
roll *list* 86
  fillet 205
  convolution 248
  rotundity 249
  make smooth 255
  move 264

roll call   round

   wind 311
   rotate 312
   rock 314
   flow 348
   sound 407
   record 551
   money 800
   –along 312
   –in *plenty* 639
     redundance 641
   –in riches 803
   –in the dust 731
   –into one 43
   –in wealth 803
   –of honor 86
   –on 109
   –on the ground 839
   –up 312
   –up in 225
   strike off the–
     abrogate 756
     punish 872
     (*degrade* 874)
roll call 85
roller *fillet* 45
   round 249
   clothing 255
   rotate 312
   –coaster 840
   –skates 266, 272
rollers *billows* 348
rollic 836
rollicker 838
rollicking
   frolicsome 836
   blustering 885
rolling 348–pin 249
   –stock 272
   –stones 149, 312
Rolls, Master of the
   recorder 553
   judge 967
   Court 966
romaine 298
roman 591
Roman Catholic
   423, 984
romance
   absurdity 497
   imagination 515
   untruth 546
   fable 594
romancer
   story–teller 594
Romantism 984
romantic
   imaginative 515
   descriptive 594
   sensitive 822
   romanticism 515
Romany 563
Rome, Church of–
   984
   do at–as the
     Romans do 82
romp *child* 129

   violent 173
   game 840
rondeau *music* 415
Röntgen ray 420
rood *length* 200
   cross 219, 998
rood loft 100
roof *house* 189
   summit 210
   cover 223
   (*height* 206)
   (*summit* 210)
rookie 726
roofless 226
rook *steal* 791
   thief 792
rookery *nests* 189
   dirt 653
room *occasion* 134
   space 180
   presence 186
   chamber 191
   class 541
   classroom 542
   plea 617
   assembly–840
   in the–of 147
   make–for
   opening 260
   respect 928
roomer 188
roommate 890
roomy 180
roorback 934
roost *abode* 189
   bed 215
rooster 366
root *algebraic*–84
   cause 153
   place 184
   abide 186
   base 211
   etymon 562
   cut up–and branch
     162
   lie at the–of 642
   pluck up by the–s
     301
   –and branch 52
   –for *applaud* 931
   –out *eject* 297
   extract 301
   discover 480a
   strike at the–of 716
   take–*influence* 175
   locate 184
   habit 613
rooted *old* 124
   firm 150
   located 184
   habit 613
   (*permanent* 141)
   deep–820
   –antipathy 867
   –belief 484
rooter *sports* 840

rope *fastening* 45
   cord 205
   freedom 748
   scourge 975
   give–enough 738
   –of sand
     incoherence 47
     weakness 160
     impossible 471
   –'s end 975
ropedancer 700
ropedancing 698
ropy 352
roquelaure 225
roric 339
rorid 339
Rorschach test 821a
rosa, sub–528
rosary 990, 998
roscid 339
Roscius 599
rose *pipe* 350
   fragrant 400
   red 434
   beauty 845
   bed of–s
     pleasure 377
     prosperity 734
   couleur de–*red* 434
   good 648
   prosperity 734
   hope 858
   under the–528
   welcome as the–s
     in June
   pleasing 829
   sociality 892
roseate *red* 434
   hopeful 858
rose-colored
   hope 858
rosehead 350
rosette 847
rose water
   moderation 174
   flattery 933
   not made with–704
Rosicrucian 984
rosin *rub* 331
   resin 356a
Rosinante 271
roster 69, 86
rostrate 245
rostriferous 245
rostrum
   beak 234
   pulpit 542
rosy 434–wine 959
rosy-cheeked 845
rot *decay* 49
   putrefy 653
   disease 655
   decay 659
rota *list* 86
   period 138
   court 966

rotation
   periodicity 138
   motion round **312**
rote, by–505
   know–490
   learn–539
roti 298
rotogravure 558
rotten *weak* 160
   bad 649
   foul 653
   decayed 659
   (*fetid* 401)
   –at the core
     deceptive 545
     diseased 655
   –borough 893
   –in state of Denmark
     702
rotund 249
rotunda 189
rotundity 249
roturier 876
roué 949
rouge 434
rouge et noir 621
rough *violent* 173
   shapeless 241
   uneven 256
   pungent 392
   unsavory 395
   sour 397
   sound 410
   raucous 581
   unprepared 674
   fighter 726
   ugly 846
   low fellow 876
   bully 887
   churlish 895
   evildoer 913
   bad man 949
   in the–241
   –and tumble 59
   –breathing 402
   –copy *writing* 590
   –unprepared 674
   –diamond
     amorphism 241
     artless 703
     vulgar 851
     commonalty 876
     good man 948
   –draft 590, 626
   –guess 514
   –it 686
   –sea 348
   –side of the tongue
     censure 932
   –weather *violent* 173
     wind 349
roughcast
   covering 223
   shape 240
   roughness 256
   scheme 626

   unpolished 674
roughhew *form* 240
   prepare 673
rough-house 173
roughly *nearly* 197
roughness 256
   blemish 848
   (see rough)
roughrider 268
roulade 415
rouleau *assemblage* 72
   cylinder 249
   money 800
roulette 621
round *series* 69
   revolution 138
   –of a ladder 215
   curve 245
   circle 247
   rotund 249
   music 415
   fight 720
   all
   –circumjacent 227
   bring–*restore* 660
   come–*periodic* 138
   recant 607
   persuade 615
   dizzy–312
   get–660
   go–311
   go one's–s 266
   go the–
     publication 531
   go the same–104
   in–numbers
     mean 29
   nearly 197
   make the–of 311
   –a corner 311
   –and round
     periodic 138
     rotation 312
   –assertion 535
   –game 840
   –like a horse in a
     mill 613
   –number *number* 84
   multitude 102
   –of life 151
   –of pleasures
     pleasure 377
     amusement 840
   –of the ladder 71
   –of visits 892
   –pace 274
   –robin
     information 527
     petition 765
     censure 932
   –sum 800
   –terms 566
   –trot 274
   –up *cattle* 370
   run the–of
     active 682

roundabout   run

turn–*invert* 218
retreat 283
revolve 311
roundabout
  circumjacent 227
  deviation 279
  circuit 311
  amusement 840
  –phrases 573
  –way 629
rounded 247
  –periods 577, 578
roundelay 597
rounder 949
rounders 840
roundhouse 752
roundlet 247
round-shouldered 243
round-up 72
roup 796
rouse *stimulate* 615
  excite 824
  –oneself 682
rouser 83
rousing 171
roustabout 460, 690
rout *agitation* 315
  printing 591
  overcome 731
  discomfit 732
  rabble 876
  assembly 892
  put to the–731
  –out 652
route 627 en–270
  en–for 282
routine *uniform* 16
  order 58
  rule 80
  periodic 138
  custom 613
  business 625
rove *travel* 266
  deviate 279
rover *traveler* 268
  pirate 792
roving commission 475
row *disorder* 59
  series 69
  violence 173
  street 189
  navigate 267
  discord 713
  –in the same boat 88
rowdy *rough* 726
  vulgar 851
  blusterer 887
  bad man 949
rowel *sharp* 253
  stimulus 615
rowen 168
rower 269
rowlock 215
royal 737–road

way 627
easy 705
Royal Academician 559
royalist 737
royalty 737
royne 298
ruade *impulse* 276
  attack 716
rub *friction* 331
  touch 379
  massage 662
  difficulty 704
  adversity 735
  painful 830
  –down *lessen* 195
  powder 330
  –a horse 370
  –down with an oaken towel 972
  –off 552
  –off corners 82
  –on *slow* 275
  progress 282
  inexcitable 826
  –one's eyes 870
  –one's hands 838
  –on the raw 900
  –out 552
  –up 658
  –up the memory 505
rubadub 407
rubber *eraser* 331
  masseur 662
  whist 840
rubberneck 444, 455
rubbers 225
rubbing 379
rubbish
  unmeaning 517
  trifling 643
  useless 645
rubble 645
rube 501, 876
rubefaction 434
rubeola 655
rubescence 434
Rubicon *limit* 233
  pass the–*begin* 66
  cross 303
  choose 609
rubicose 434
rubicund 434
rubicundity 382, 434
rubiform 434
rubify 434
rubiginous 433
rubigo 653
rubious 434
rubric *precept* 697
  liturgy 998
rubricate *redden* 434
ruby *red* 434
  gem 648
  ornament 847
ruck 258

ruction 297
rudder 273, 633, 693
rudderless 158
ruddle 434
ruddy *red* 434
  beautiful 845
rude *violent* 173
  shapeless 241
  strident 410
  ignorant 491
  inelegant 579
  ugly 846
  vulgar 851
  uncivilized 876
  uncivil 895
  disrespect 929
  –health 654
  –reproach 908
rudera 645
rudiment
  beginning 66
  cause 153
rudimental *small* 193
  immature 674
rudimentary
  small 193
  learner 541
rudiments
  knowledge 490
  school 542
rue *bitter* 395
  regret 833
  repent 950
rueful *painful* 830
  sad 837
ruff 225
ruffian *combatant* 726
  maleficent 913
  scoundrel 949
ruffianism 851, 907
ruffle *disorder* 59
  derange 61
  roughen 256
  fold 258
  feeling 821
  excite 824, 825
  pain 830
  irritate 898
  anger 900
rufous 433, 434
rufulous 434
rug *support* 215
  covering 223
rugged *shapeless* 241
  rough 256
  difficult 704
  ugly 846
  churlish 895
rugose 256
rugulose 256
ruin *destruction* 162
  evil 619
  failure 732
  adversity 735
  poverty 804
  (*decay* 659)

ruined
  nonpayment 808
  hopeless 859
ruinous *painful* 830
ruins *remains* 40
rule *normal* 29
  regularity **80**
  influence 175
  length 200
  measure 466
  decide 480
  custom 613
  precept 697
  government 737
  law 963
  absence of–699
  as a–613
  by–82
  golden–697
  obey–s 82
  –of three 85
  –of thumb
    experiment 463
    unreasoning 477
    essay 675
    unskilled 699
ruler 737, 745
ruling passion
  obstinacy 606
  character 820
rum *queer* 853
  drink 959
rumal 225
rumble 407
rumen 191
ruminate *chew* 298
  think 450, 451
rummage 461
rummer 191
rumor *publicity* 531
  report 532
rumored 531
  publicly–532
rump *remainder* 40
  rear 235
  beef 298
rumple *disorder* 59
  derange 61
  roughen 256
  fold 258
rumpus *confusion* 59
  violence 173
  discord 713
  (*contention* 720)
run *rule* 29
  generality 78
  repetition 104
  time 106
  course 109
  continuance 143
  eventuality 151
  motion 264
  speed 274
  trend 278
  cards 281
  liquefy 335

flow 348
habit 613
demand 630
smuggle 791
contraband 964
have a–*fashion* 852
repute 873
have–of 748
he that–s may read 525
near–197
race is–729
–abreast 27
–a chance
  probable 472
  chance 621
–after *pursue* 622
in *repute* 873
–against *impact* 276
oppose 708
attack 716
–amuck *violent* 173
kill 361
attack 716
–a race *speed* 274
conduct 692
contend 720
–a rig 840
–a risk 665
–at 716
–a tilt at *attack* 716
contend 720
–away *avoid* 623
(*escape* 671)
–away with *take* 789
steal 791
–away with a notion
misjudge 481
credulous 486
–back 283
–counter 468
–counter to 708
–down *pursue* 622
bad 649
attack 716
depreciate 932
detract 934
–dry *waste* 638
insufficient 640
–foul of 276
–hard *danger* 665
difficult 704
success 731
–high *great* 31
violent 173
–in *introduce* 228
–in a race *act* 680
–in couples 17
–in the head *think* 451
remember 505
–into *conversion* 144
insert 300
–into danger 665
–into debt 806
–its course

runabout

course 109
complete 729
past 122
—*like mad* 274
—*low* 36
—*mad insane* 503
passion 825
—*mad after* 865
—*of luck fortune* 156
prosperity 734
—*of one's teeth* 815
—*of things* 151
—*on* 143, 460
—*on in a groove* 613
—*out end* 67
course 109
past 122
antiquated 124
egress 295
prodigal 818
—*out on* 573
—*over count* 85
—*in the mind* 451
examine 457
describe 594
synopsis 596
overflow 641
—*parallel* 178
—*riot violent* 173
exaggerate 549
redundance 641
active 682
disobey 742
intemperance 954
—*rusty* 603
—*smooth easy* 705
prosperous 734
—*the eye over see* 441
learn 539
—*the fingers over* 379
—*the gauntlet* 861
—*through uniform* 16
influence 175
be present 186
kill 361
expend 809
prodigal 818
—*to seed age* 128
deterioration 659
—*to waste* 638
—*up increase* 25
build 161
—*up an account credit* 805
debt 806
charge 812
—*up bills not pay* 808
—*upon a bank bankrupt* 808
expenditure 809
—*wide open* 274
—*wild* 173
time-s 106
runabout 268
vehicle 272
runagate *traveler* 268

fugitive 623
disobey 742
bad man 949
runaway *traveler* 268
avoidance 623
renegade 742
rundle *circle* 247
convolution 248
rotundity 249
rundlet 191
runer 597
runes *writing* 590
poetry 597
spell 993
rung 215
runlet 348
runnel 348
runner *branch* 51
courier 268
conduit 350
messenger 534
petitioner 767
running
continuous 69
—*account* 811
—*commentary* 595
—*fight* 720
—*hand* 590
—*over* 641
—*water* 348
the mind—upon 451
the mind—upon other things 458
runnion 949
runt 193
rupture
disjunction 44
disease 655
quarrel 713
rural *village* 189
agricultural 371
—*dean* 893
ruralist 893
ruse *cunning* 702
(deception 545)
rush *crowd* 72
vigor 171
violence 173
velocity 274
water 348
plant 367
trifle 643
haste 684
make a—at 716
—*in medias res* 604
—*into print* 591
—*on destruction* 863
—*to a conclusion misjudge* 481
credulous 486
—*upon* 622
rus in urbe
abode 189
secluded 893
rushlight *dim* 422
candle 423

rusk 298
russet 433
Russian bath 386
rust *fungus* 369
brown 433
red 434
decay 659
canker 663
inaction 683
moth and— 659
—*colored* 433, 434
—*of antiquity* 122
rustic *village* 189
agricultural 371
vulgar 851
clown 876
rusticate *punish* 972
seclude 893
rusticity
vulgarity 851
impolite 895
rustle *faint sound* 405
protracted sound 407
sibilation 409
rusty *dirty* 653
decayed 659
sluggish 683
unskillful 699
sulky 901a
(old 128)
(unserviceable 645)
run—averse 603
rut *regularity* 80
furrow 259
habit 613
desire 865
ruth 914
ruthless *savage* 907
pitiless 914a
revengeful 919
rutilant 420
ruttish 961
rye 367, 959
ryot *servant* 746
possessor 779
commonalty 876

S

Sabaeanism 382, 984
sabaoth 726
sabbatarian
ascetic 955
sectarian 984
false piety 988
ritualistic 998
Sabbath *rest* 687
rite 998
—*breaker* 988
sabbatic 687
sabbatism 988
sabe 498
Sabellianism 984
saber *kill* 361
weapon 727

sable 223, 431
sabotage
destruction 162
unkillfulness 699
disobedience 742
sabreur *slayer* 361
soldier 726
sabulosity 330
sabulous 330
sac 191 —*de nuit* 225
sacatra 41
saccharify 396
saccharin 396
saccharinity 396
saccharize 396
saccular 191
saccule 191
sacerdotal 995
sacerdotalism 372a, 988
sachem 745
sachet 400
sack *bag* 191
dismissal 756
gain 775
take 789
plunder 791
give the—to 297
sackbut 297
sackcloth and ashes
lament 839
atonement 952
ascetic 955
rite 998
sack-coat 225
sacrament 998
sacrarium 1000
sacred *dignified* 873
holy 976
revelation 985
piety 987
—*anchor* 666
—*nine* 416
—*writings* **986**
sacrifice *destroy* 162
gift 784
atonement 952
worship 990
idolatry 991
at any— 604
fall a— 828
make a— 942
make the supreme 360
—*to Moloch* 361
self— 942
sacrificed 732
sacrilege 988
sacring bell 550
sacristan 996
sacristy 1000
sacrosanct
honorable 873
inviolable 924
holy 976
sad *great* 31

sagacious

color 428
gray 432
bad 649
painful 830
dejected 837
—*disappointment* 509
—*dog* 949
—*times* 735
—*work* 699
sadden 830, 837
saddle *attribute* 155
support 215
meat 298
in the— 673
—*blanket* 223
—*on add* 37
join 43
—*on the right horse discovery* 480a
skill 698
right 922
fair 939
—*on the wrong horse mistake* 495
bungle 699
—*with add* 37
quarter on 184
clog 706
impose a duty 926
accuse 938
saddlebags 191
saddle-shaped 250
Sadducee 984
sadiron 253, 386
sadism 945, 961
sadist 949
sadness 837 *in—without joking* 535
safe *cupboard* 191
ambush 530
secure 664
treasury 802
caution 864
on the—side cautious 864
—*and sound health* 654
—*bind, safe find* 864
—*conscience duty* 926
innocent 946
safe-conduct 631
safe-keeping 670
safety 664
—*bicycle* 272
—*first* 864
—*in valor* 861
—*match* 388
—*valve* 666
saffron *color* 436
sag *oblique* 217
curve 245
saga 594
sagacious
intelligent 498
foresight 510
(skillful 698)

557

sagamore 745
sage *wise* 498
   wise man **500**
   adviser 695
   –*maxim* 496
Sagitta 490*a*
sagittary 83
sagittate 253
sagum 225
Sahara 169
sahib 373, 745, 875
saic 273
said *preceding* 62
   repeated 104
   prior 116
   it is–532
   more easily–than
     done 704
   thou hast–488
sail *navigate* 267
   ship 273
   set out 293
   easy–174
   full–274
   press
   press of–274
   –before the wind 734
   –near the wind 698
   –too near the wind
     863
   shorten–275
   take in–174
   take the wind out
     of one's–s 706
   too much–863
   under–267
sailing, *plain*–705
   –*vessel* 273
sailor 269
   fair weather–701
saint *angel* 977
   revelation 985
   piety 987
   false piety 988
   –*abroad* 548
   tutelary–664
Saint
   –Anthony's fire 655
   –Bernard *dog* 366
   –Elmo's fire 423, 872
   –Martin's summer
     126
   –Swithin, reign of–
     348
   –Swithin's day 138
   –Tib's eve 107
   –Vitus's dance 315,
     655
saintly *virtuous* 944
   pious 987
Saint's day 138
Saint Simonianism
   910
sake
   for goodness'–765
   for the–of

motive 615
aid 707
salaam *obeisance* 725
   courtesy 894
   respect 928
salable 796
salacity 961
salad 41–*oil* 356
salade 717
salamander
   elemental 83, 980
   furnace 386
   salamandrine 384
sal ammoniac 392
salary 973
sale 796 bill of–771
   for– *offer* 763
   barter 794
salebrosity 256
salesman 758, 767,
   797
salesmanship 796
salicylic acid 490*b*
salient *projecting* 250
   sharp 253
   manifest 525
   important 642
   –*angle* 244
   –*point* 642
saline 392
saliva *excretion* 299
   lubrication 332
salivant 297
salivate 297, 332
salle-à-manger
   191
sallow *colorless* 429
   yellow 436
sally *issue* 298
   attack 716
   wit 842
sally port *egress* 295
   fortification 717
salmagundi 41
salmis 298
salmon *fish* 298
   red 434
salmon-colored 434
salon 191
saloon 191 *bar* 189
salsify 298
salt *sailor* 269
   pungent 392
   condiment 393
   importance 642
   preserve 670
   money 800
   wit 842
   below the–876
   –of the earth
     goodness 648
     goodman 948
   –tax 812
   –water 341
   worth one's–644
saltant 315

saltation 309
saltatory 315
saltimbanco 548
saltpeter *pungent* 392
   gunpowder 727
salubrity 656
salutary *healthful* 656
   (*remedial* 662)
salutation (see salute)
salutatory 582, 587
salute *allocution* 586
   celebration 883
   courtesy 894
   kiss 902
   respect 928
salutiferous
   (see salutary)
salvable 946
salvage
   acquisition 775
   tax 812
   discount 813
   reward 973
salvation
   preservation 670
   deliverance 672
   religious 976
   piety 987
   work out one's–990
salve
   lubrication 332, 355
   remedy 662
   relieve 834
salver 191
salvo *exception* 83
   explosion 406
   qualification 469
   excuse 937
   (*condition* 770)
   –of artillery
     celebration 883
sal-volatile 392
Samaol 978
Samaritan, good
   benevolent 906
   benefactor 912
sambar 366
Sam Browne belt
   747
same 13
   all the–to 823
   at the–time
     compensatory 30
     synchronous 120
   go over the–ground
     104
   in the–boat 709
   in the–breath
     instantaneous 113
     synchronous 120
   of the–mind 488
   on the–tack 709
sameness 16
samiel 349
samisen 417
samo 720

samovar 191
samp 298
sampan 273
sample 82
Samson 159
samurai 875
sanation
   restoration 660
sanative *remedial* 662
sanatorium 189, 662
sanctification 976
sanctify
   authorize 926
   piety 987
sanctimony 988
sanction
   permission 760
   dueness 924
   approbation 931
   to–vice 945
sanctitude 987
sanctity 987
sanctuary *refuge* 666
   altar 1000
   claim– 666
sanctum *chamber* 191
   –sanctorum
     abode 189
     privacy 893
     temple 1000
sanctus 900
   –bell 550, 999
sand *powder* 330
   resolution 604
   built upon–665
   sow the–645
sandal 225
sandalwood 400
sandbag 727, 972
sandbagger 792
sand-blind 442
Sandemanian 984
sandpaper 255
sands *danger* 667
   –*danger* 667
   –on the seashore
     multitude 102
sand storm 330
sandstone 635
sandwich-wise 228
sandy *yellow* 436
   red 434
sane 502
sangar 717
sang-froid
   insensibility 823
   inexcitability 826
   presence of mind 864
sangraal 998
sanguinary 361
sanguine *red* 434
   hopeful 858
   –expectation
     expect 507
     hope 858
   –imagination 515

sanguineous 434
sanguisage 662
sanhedrin
   council 696
   churchdom 995
sanies 333
sanious 333
sanitarian 656
sanitarium 189, 656,
   662
sanitary 656
sanity *mental* **502**
   bodily–654
sannyasi 804, 955,
   996
sans 187–cérémonie
   friendly 888
   social 892
   –façon *simple* 849
     modest 881
     social 892
   –pareil 33
   –peur et sans
     reproche
     perfect 650
     heroic 873
     honorable 939
   –souci *insensible* 823
     pleasure 827
     content 831
sans-culotte
   revel 742
   commonalty 876
sans-culottic 146
sans-culottism 146
sans Dieu rien 976
Sanskrit 124
Sanskritist 492
santon *hermit* 893
   priest 996
sap *essence* 5
   destroy 162
   excavate 252
   juice 333
   damage 659
   attack 716
   –the foundations
     162, 659
sap-headed 499
sapid 390
sapient 498
sapless *weak* 160
   dry 340
sapling 129, 367
saponaceous 355
saporific 390
sapper *excavator* 252
   soldier 726
sappers and miners
   preparers 673
Sapphic 597
sapphire *blue* 438
   gem 847
sapphism 961
sapphist 962
sappy *young* 127

saprogenic

juicy 333
  foolish 499
saprogenic 653
saraband 840
sarcasm
  disrespect 929
  censure 932
  detraction 934
sarcastic *ridicule* 856
  discourteous 895
sarcology 662
sarcoma 250
sarcophagus 363
sarculation 103
sard 847
Sardanapalus 954a
sardines 298
sardonic *censure* 932
  detraction 934
  –*grin laughter* 838
  ridicule 856
  discontent 932
sardonyx 847
sargasso 367
Sargasso Sea 367
sark 225
sarmentum 51
sartorial 225
sash 247
sassafras 662
Sastra 986
Satan 978
satanic
  malevolent 907
  vicious 945
  diabolic 978
satchel 191
sate 869
satellite
  companion 88
  follower 281
  heavenly body 318
  auxiliary 711
  servant 746
satiate 52, 376
satiety *sufficient* 639
  pleasant 829
  cloy 869
  (*redundance* 641)
satin 219, 329, 635
  smoothness 255
satire *metaphor* 521
  poetry 597
  ridicule 856
  censure 932
satiric *untruth* 546
satirical 932
  detraction 934
satirist *poet* 597
  detractor 936
satirize 597
satisfaction
  (*see* satisfy)
  duel 720
  pleasure 827
  atonement 952

hail with –931
satisfactorily 618
satisfactory
  (*see* satisfy)
  good 648
satisfy *answer* 462
  convince 484
  sufficient 639
  consent 762
  observance 772
  pay 807
  gratify 829
  content 831
  satiate 869
  reward 973
  –*an obligation* 926
  –*oneself* 484
satisfying 831
satrap *governor* 745
  (*deputy* 759)
satsuma 557
saturate *fill* 52
  moisten 339
  satiate 869
Saturn 490a
saturnalia *disorder* 59
  games 840
  intemperance 954
  –*of blood* 361
Saturnian
  pleasing 829
  innocent 946
  –*age* 734
Saturnia regna
  prosperity 734
  pleasure 827
saturnine 837
satyr *ugly* 846
  libertine 962
  demon 980
satyriasis 821a
sauce *adjunct* 39
  mixture 41
  condiment 393
  abuse 908
  pay–for all 807
  *what is–for the
    goose* 27
saucebox
  blusterer 887
saucepan 191
sauce piquante
  condiment 393
  pleasing 829
saucer 191 –*eyes* 441
saucy *insolent* 885
  flippant 895
sauerkraut 298
sauna 382
saunter
famble 266
  dawdle 275
sausage 298
sauvage 893
sauve qui peut
  run away 623

alarm 669
  haste 684
  cowardice 862
savage *violent* 173
  vulgar 851
  brave 861
  boorish 876
  angry 900
  malevolent 907
  evildoer 913
savagery (*see* savage)
savanna 344, 367
savant *knowledge* 490
  learned man 492
  sage 500
save *subduct* 38
  exclude 55
  except 83
  store 636
  preserve 670
  deliver 672
  economize 817
  God–990
  –*and except* 83
  –*money* 817
  –*one's bacon* 671
  –*the necessity* 927a
  –*us* 707
save-all 817
saving 817
  –*clause* 469
  –*one's presence* 928
savings *store* 636
  economy 817
savior *benefactor* 912
Savior 976
savoir faire *skill* 698
  fashion 852
savoir vivre
  skill 698
  fashion 852
  sociality 892
savor 390 –*of
  resemble* 17
  –*of the reality* 780
savoriness 394
savorless 391
savory 390, 394
savvy 490, 498
saw *cut* 44
  jagged 257
  maxim 496
  –*the air gesture* 550
sawder, *soft–
  flattery* 933
sawdust 330
sawney 501
saxhorn 417
Saxon
  style of language
    576, 578
say *nearly* 32
  turn 138
  assert 535
  express 560
  speak 582

have one's–535,
    582
  not–I did it 938
  –*by heart* 505
  –*no* 489
  –*nothing* 585
  –*one's prayers* 990
  –*to oneself* 589
  –*what comes
    uppermost* 612
  that is to–522
  *what do you–to
    that* 870
  you don't–so 870
sayid 745
saying *maxim* 496
  assertion 535
sbirro 965
scab *apostate* 607
scabbard 191
  *throw away the–
    resolution* 604
  war 722
scabby 940
scabies 380, 655
scabrous 256
scaffold *support* 215
  preparation 673
  execution 975
  (*way* 627)
  (*means* 632)
scagliola 223, 545
scaithless
  (*see* scathless)
scalawag 949
scald *burn* 382, 384
  poet 597
scale *portion* 51
  series 69
  term 71
  slice 204
  skin 223
  mount 305
  weigh 319
  gamut 413
  measure 466
  printing 591
  hold the–s 480
  hold the–s even
    922
  –*s falling from the
    eyes see* 441
  disclose 529
  –*s of justice* 922
  –*the heights* 305
  –*the walls* 716
  *turn the–
    reversion* 145
  influence 175
  counter evidence 468
  motive 615
scalene 243
scaling ladder 305
scallion 298
scallop
  convolution 248

notch 257
scalp 226
scalpel 253
scalp lock 256, 550
scaly 223
scamble 44
scamp *neglect* 460
  rascal 949
scamped *sham* 545
scamper *speed* 274
  –*off* 623
scampish 945
scan *see* 441
  attend to 457
  inquire 461
  know 490
  prosody 597
scandal *news* 532
  obloquy 934
scandalize 932
scandalmonger 532
scandalous
  disreputable 874
  vicious 945
scandent 305
scansion 597
scant *small* 32
  few 103
  little 193
  narrow 203
  insufficient 640
scantling *model* 22
  scrap 32
  dimensions 192
  (*part* 51)
scanty (*see* scant)
scape 671
scapegoat
  substitute 147
  atonement 952
scapegrace
  reckless 863
  rascal 949
scaphoid 245
scapin *cheat* 548
  knave 941
scapulary 999
scar *shore* 342
  record 551
  blemish 848
  he jests at–s 830
scarab 993
Scaramouch 844
scarce *incomplete* 53
  few 103
  infrequent 137
  insufficient 640
  *make oneself–
    absent* 187
  run away 623
scarcely 32 –*any* 103
  –*anything* 643
  –*ever* 137
scarcity (*see* scarce)
scare 860
scarecrow *ugly* 846

559

scarf

frighten 860
scarf *dress* 225
  canonicals 999
scarfskin 223
scarify *notch* 257
  torment 830
scarlatina 655
scarlet 434
  –Woman 984
scarp *oblique* 217
  defense 717
scarpines 972
scathe *badness* 649
  injury 659
  (*evil* 619)
  (*bane* 663)
scatheless *perfect* 650
  (*secure* 664)
  (*saved* 672)
scatter *derange* 61
  disperse 73
  diverge 291
  –to the winds
  destroy 162
  confute 479
scatter–brained
  inattentive 458
  insane 503
scatterling 268
scavenger 652
scene *appearance* 448
  painting 556
  drama 599
  excitement 825
  –of action 728
scene painter 559
scene painting 556
scenery 448, 599
sceneshifter 599
scenic 599, 882
scenography 54, 556
scent *smell* 398
  discovery 480a
  disbelieve 485
  knowledge 490
  sign 550
  trail 551
  get-of 527
  on the–622
  on the right–462
  put on a new–279
  –from afar 510
  throw off the–623
scent bag 400
scent bottle 400
scent container 400
scented 400
scentless 399
scepter 33, **747**
  sway the–737
schatchen 903
schedule 86, 611
Schelling's
  philosophy 451
schematism 60
schematist 626

scheme *draft* 554
  plan 626
schemer 626, 702
schenk beer 298
scherzo 415
schesis 7
schism *dissent* 489
  discord 713
  heterodoxy 984
schismless 983a
schist 490c
schistose 204
schnapps 959
schnorrer 804
scholar *erudite* **492**
  learner 541
  rank 873
scholarly 539
scholarship
  knowledge 490
  learning 539
  trophy 733, 873
scholastic
  knowledge 490
  teaching 537, 540
  learning 539
  school 542
  theology 983
Scholasticism 451
scholiast 492, 524
scholium *maxim* 496
  interpretation 522
school *herd* 72
  system of opinions
    484
  knowledge 490
  teaching 537
  academy **542**
  painting 556
  go to–539
  –bag 191
  –days 127
  send to–537
  –of art 542
  –s of painting 556
  –s of sculpture 557
schoolbook 542
schoolboy *lad* 129
  learner 541
  (*tyro* 193)
  a–s tale 111
  familiar to every–
    490
schoolfellow 541
schoolgirl 129, 541
schoolman
  scholar 492
  theologian 983
schoolmaster 540
  –abroad
    knowledge 490
    learning 537
schoolmistress 540
schoolroom 191, 542
schooner 273
  receptacle 191

Schopenhauer's
  philosophy 451
schrod 298
sciamachy 497
sciatica 378
science *knowledge* 490
  skill 698
  –of language 562
  –of virtue 944
scientific *exact* 494
  teaching 537
scopophilia 821a
scrabble
  unmeaning 517
  scribble 590
scrag 203
scraggy *lean* 193
  amorphous 241
  rough 256
  (*ugly* 846)
scramble
  confusion 59
  climb 305
  pursue 622
  haste 684
  difficulty 704
  contend 720
  seize 789
scrambled eggs 298
scranch 330
scrannel 643
scrap *small* 32
  piece 51
  child 129
  (*minute* 193)
scrapbook 596
scrape *subduct* 38
  reduce 195
  pulverize 330
  abrade 331
  –the fiddle 416
  mezzotint 558
  clean 652
  difficulty 704
  mischance 732
  bow 894
  –together *assemble* 72
  acquire 775
scraper 652
scratch *groove* 259
  abrade 331
  unmeaning 517
  mark 550
  daub 555
  draw 556
  write 590
  hurt 619
  wound 649
  come to the–
    contention 720
    courage 861
  mere–209
  old–978
  –out 552
  –the head 461
  up to the–861

without a–670
scrawl
  unmeaning 517
  write 590
scrawny 203
screak 411
scream *blow* 349
  cry 411
  wail 839
screaming 853
screech 411, 412
screed 86, 590
screen
  sift 60
  crossing 219
  sieve 260
  shade 424
  hide 528
  hider 530
  side scene 599
  sift 652
  safety 664
  shelter 666
  defense 717
  –from sight 442
screw *fasten* 43
  fastening 45
  distortion 243
  oar 267
  propeller 284
  rotation 312
  instrument 633
  miser 819
  put on the–
    severity 739
    compel 744
  –loose *insane* 503
  imperfect 651
  unskillful 699
  hindrance 706
  attack 713
  –one's courage to the
    sticking place 861
  –up *fasten* 43
  strengthen 159
  prepare 673
  –up the eyes 443
screw–driver 633
screwed *drunk* 959
screw–shaped 248
screw steamer 273
scribble *compose* 54
  unmeaning 517
  write 590
scribbler 593
scribe *recorder* 553
  writer 590, 593
  priest 996
scrimmage
  discord 713
  contention 720
scrimp *short* 201
  insufficient 640
  stingy 819
scrip 191
script 590

sconce

scriptural
  orthodox 983a
Scripture *certain* 474
  revelation 985
scrivener *writer* 590
  lawyer 968
scrofula 655
scroll *list* 86
  record 551
scrub *short* 201
  rub 331
  bush 367
  clean 652
  dirty person 653
  commonalty 876
scrubby *small* 193
  trifling 643
  disreputable 874
  vulgar 876
  shabby 940
scruple
  small quantity 32
  weight 319
  doubt 485
  reluctance 603
scientist *reasoner* 476
  learned man 492
scimitar 727
  –shaped 253
scintilla
  small 32, 193
  spark 420, 423
scintillate
  (see scintillation)
  intelligence 498
scintillation *heat* 382
  light 420
  wit 842
sciolism 491
sciolist 493
sciomancy 511
scion *part* 51
  child 129
  posterity 167
scission 44
scissors 253
  –and paste 609
scissure 198
sclerotics 195
scobs 330
scoff *ridicule* 856
  deride 929
  impiety 988
  –at *despise* 930
  censure 932
scold *berate* 527
  shrew 901
  malediction 908
  censure 932
  (*detractor* 936)
scolecoid 248
scollop
  convolution 248
  notch 257
sconce *top* 210
  candlestick 423

560

scone　　**secondhand**

brain 450
defense 717
mulct 974
scone 298
scoop *depression* 252
　perforator 262
scop 597
scope *degree* 26
　occasion 134
　extent 180
　meaning 516
　freedom 748
　(*intention* 620)
scorch 382, 384
scorcher 268, 274
scorching *violent* 173
score *compose* 54
　arrangement 60
　count 85
　list 86
　twenty 98
　indent 257
　furrow 259
　music 415
　berate 527
　mark 550
　credit 805
　debt 806
　accounts 811
　on the—of relation 9
　motive 615
　–*a success* 731
　–*board* 551
　–*sheet* 551
scores *many* 102
scoriaceous 384
scoriae *ash* 384
　dirt 653
　(*useless* 645)
scorify 384
scorn 930
scorpion *insect* 368
　painful 830
　evildoer 913
　(*bane* 663)
　chastise with—s 739
scorse 794
scot *reward* 973
scotch *notch* 257
　injure 659
　–*the snake maim* 158
　insufficient 640
　noncompletion 730
　–*the wheel* 706
scot-free *escape* 671
　free 748
　cheap 815
　exempt 927a
　escape— escape 671
　let off–970
scotograph 554
scotomy 443
Scotsman 188
Scotticism 563
scoundrel 949
scour *run* 274

rub 331
clean 652
–*the country* 266
–*the plain* 274
scourge *bane* 663
　painful 830
　punish 972
　instrument of
　　punishment **975**
　–*of the human race*
　　913
scourings 645
scout *vanguard* 234
　aviator 269a
　spectator 444
　feeler 463
　messenger 534
　reject 610
　patrol 664
　warning 668
　servant 746
　disrespect 929
　disdain 930
　(*looker* 444)
　(*underrate* 483)
　(*ridicule* 856)
scow 273
scowl *complain* 839
　frown 895
　anger 900
　sullen 901a
　disapprobation 932
　–*of night* 982
　probity 939
　make no—of 602
scrupulous
　careful 459
　incredulous 487
　exact 494
　reluctant 603
　observant 772
　fastidious 868
　punctilious 939
scrutator 461
scritinizer 461
scrutiny *attention* 457
　inquiry 461
scrutoire 191
scud *sail* 267
　speed 274
　shower 348
　cloud 353
　–*under bare poles*
　　704
scuffle 720
scull *row* 267
scullery 191
scullion 746
sculptor 559
sculpture *form* 240
　carving **557**
scum *foam* 353
　dirt 653
　–*of the earth* 949
　–*of society* 876
scupper 350

scurf 653
scurrility 908
scurrilous
　ridicule 856
　disrespect 929
　detraction 934
scurry *haste* 274, 684
　excitability 825
scurvy *insufficient* 640
　unimportant 643
　base 940
　wicked 945
scut 235
scutate 245
scutcheon
　standard 550
　honor 877
scutiform 245, 251
scuttle *destroy* 162
　receptacle 191
　speed 274, 684
　–*along*
　haste 684
scutum 717
Scylla and
Charybdis
　between–
　danger 665
　difficulty 704
scyphiform 252
scythe 253
　–*of Time* 106
scytho *pointed* 244
　sharp 253
sea *multitude* 102
　ocean 341
　at–341
　uncertain 475
　go to–293
　heavy–315
　–*of doubt* 475
　–*of troubles*
　difficulty 704
　adversity 735
sea anchor 706
seaboard 342
seacoast 342
　–*gun* 727
sea dog 269
sea duck 310
seafarer 269
seafaring 267, 273
sea fight 720
seagirt 346
seagoing 267, 341
sea green 435
sea king 791
seal *matrix* 22
　close 261
　animal 366
　evidence 467
　mark 550
　resolve 604
　complete 729
　authority 747
　compact 769

security 771
marriage 903
break the–529
–*brown* 433
–*of secrecy* 528
–*one's infamy* 940
–*the doom of* 162
–*the lips* 585
–*up restrain* 751
under–769
sealed 261
　hermetically–261
　one's fate is–601
　–*book ignorance* 491
　unintelligible 519
　secret 533
sealing 903
sealing wax 747
seals *insignia* 747
seam 43
sea-maid 979
seaman 269
seamanship
　conduct 692
　skill 698
seamark 550
seamless 50
sea mosses 368
seamstress 225, 690
seamy side 651
séance *assemblage* 72
　manifestation 525
　council 696
　spiritualism 992a
seapiece 556
seaport 666
sear *dry* 340
　burn 384
　deaden 823
　–*and yellow leaf*
　　age 128
　–*ed conscience* 951
search 455, 461
searching *severe* 739
　painful 830
searchless 519
searchlight 423, 550
sea serpent 83
seashore 342
seasickness 655
seaside 342
sea slug 298
seas, lunar 490a
season *mix* 41
　time 106
　pungent 392
　accustom 613
　preserve 670
　prepare 673
seasonable *fit* 23
　early 132
　opportune 134
sea song 597
seasoning
　condiment 393

seat *place* 183
　locate 184
　abode 189
　support 215
　rump 235
　direction 693
　judgment–966
　–*of government* 737
　–*of war* 728
seated 184
　firmly–150
sea urchins 368
sea view 556
seawant 800
seaway 180
seaweed 367
seaworthy 273, 341,
　664
sebaceous 355
secant 44, 219
secede *dissent* 489
　relinquish 624
　disobey 742
seceder *heterodox* 984
secern 299
Secessionist 742
seclude 893
seclusion 893
second *duplication* 90
　–*of time* 108
　instant 113
　–*in music* 413, 415
　abet 707
　one's–*self* 17
　play or sing a–416
　play–fiddle
　obey 743
　subject 749
　disrepute 874
　–*best imperfect* 651
　failure 732
　–*childhood age* 128
　imbecility 499
　–*crop fertile* 168
　profit 775
　–*edition* 104
　–*nature* 613
　–*sight foresight* 510
　clairvoyance 992a
　–*thoughts sequel* 65
　thought 451
　improvement 658
　–*to none* 33
　–*youth* 660
secondary *inferior* 34
　following 63
　imperfect 651
　deputy 759
　–*education* 537
　–*evidence* 467
seconder 711
secondhand
　imitation 19
　old 124
　deteriorated 659
　received 785

561

secondly 90
second–rate 651
secrecy (*see* secret)
secret *key* 522
  latent 526
  hidden 528
  riddle **533**
  in the– 490
  keep a–*silent* 585
  –motive 615
  –passage 627
  –place 530
  –writing 590
secretariat 965
secretary *desk* 191
  recorder 553
  writer 590
  director 694
  auxiliary 711
  servant 746
  consignee 758
secrete 299
  conceal 528
secretion 299
secretive 528
secretory 299
sect 75
  religious– 983, 984
sectarian *dissent* 489
  ally 711
  heterodox 984
sectary 65
section *division* 44
  part 51
  class 75
  indication 550
  printing 591
  chapter 593
  troops 726
sector *part* 51
  circle 247
secular *centenary* 98
  periodic 138
  laity 997
  –education 537
secularism 984
secularization 756
secundines 63
secundum artem
  conformable 82
  skillful 698
secure *fasten* 43
  bespeak 132
  belief 484
  safe 664
  restrain 751
  engage 768
  gain 775
  confident 858
  –an object
    success 731
securities 805
security *safety* 664
  pledge **771**
  hope 858
  lend on– 787

sedan 272
sedan chair 272
sedate *thoughtful* 451
  calm 826
  grave 837
sedative *calming* 174
  remedy 662
sedentary 265
sedge 367
sedile 1000
sediment 321, 653
sedimentary
  remainder 40
sedition 742
seditionist 891
seduce *entice* 615
  love 897
  debauch 961
seducer 962
seduction
  pleasing 829
  desire 865
seductress 615
sedulous *active* 682
  desirous 865
see *view* 441
  look 457
  believe 484
  know 490
  bishopric 995
  –after 459
  –at a glance 498
  –daylight 480a
  –double 959
  –fit 600, 602
  –justice done 922
  –life *amusement* 840
  –one's way
    foresight 510
    intelligible 518
    skill 698
    easy 705
  –service 722
  –sights 455
  –the light *born* 359
    published 531
  –through
    discover 480a
    intelligence 498
  –to *attention* 457
    care 459
    direction 693
  we shall– 507
seed *small* 32
  cause 153
  posterity 167
  grain 330
  agriculture 371
  run to–*age* 128
  lose health 659
  –plants 369
  sow the– 673
seedling 129, 367
seed plot
  productive 168
  agriculture 371

seedtime of life 127
seedy *weak* 160
  disease 655
  deteriorated 659
  exhausted 688
  needy 804
seeing 441–that
  circumstance 8
  reasoning 476
seek *inquire* 461
  pursue 622
  offer 763
  request 765
  –safety 664
seek–sorrow 837
seel 217
seem 448
  as it–s good to 600
seeming 488
seemingly 472
seemless *ugly* 846
  undue 925
seemliness *duty* 926
seemly *expedient* 646
  handsome 845
  due 924
seep 295, 337
seepage 337
seer *veteran* 130
  madman 504
  oracle 511, 513
  sorcerer 994
seesaw 12, 314
seethe *moisture* 339
  hot 382
  make hot 384
  excitement 824
seething caldron 386
segar 392
segment 44, 51
segnitude 683
segregate
  not related 10
  separate 44
  exclude 55
segregated
  incoherent 47
seignior *master* 745
  nobility 875
seigniory
  authority 737
  property 780
seine *net* 232
seisin (*see* seizin)
seismic 314
seismograph 314, 551
seismology 314, 490c
seismometer 276, 490c
seismoscope 314
seize *take* 789
  rob 791
  –an opportunity 134
  –the present hour 134

seized with
  disease 655
  feeling 821
seizin *possession* 777
  property 780
seizure 315, 925
sejunction 44
seldom 137
select *specify* 79
  choose 609
  good 648
selection 75
selectman 965
Selene 318
self *identity* 13
  specialty 79
  –abasement 879
  –accusing 950
  –admiration 880
  –annulling 497
  –applause 880
  –assertion 885
  –called 565
  –command
    resolution 604
    caution 864
    (*temperance* 953)
  –communing 451
  –complacency
    cheerful 836
    vanity 880
  –confidence 880
  –conquest
    resolution 604
    (*temperance* 953)
  –conscious 855
  –consultation 451
  –contradictory 471, 497
  –control 604
  –convicted 950
  –conviction *belief* 484
    penitent 950
    condemned 971
  –council 451
  –deceit *error* 495
  –deception
    credulity 486
  –defense 717
  –delusion 486, 347
  –denial
    disinterested 942
    temperance 953
    penance 990
  –depreciation 483
  –determination 737, 748
  –detraction 483
  –discipline 990
  –educated 490
  –esteem 880
  –evident *certain* 474
    manifest 525
  –examination 990
  –existing 1
  –government

authority 737
  freedom 748
  (*virtue* 944)
  –help 698
  –immolation 991
  –importance 878
  –indulgence
    selfishness 943
    intemperance 954
  –instruction 539
  –interest 943
  –knowledge 881
  –love 943
  –luminous 423
  –made 490
  –opinionated 481
  –opinioned
    narrow–minded 481
    (*foolish* 499)
    (*obstinate* 606)
  –possessed 852
  –possession
    sanity 502
    resolution 604
    inexcitability 826
    caution 864
  –praise 880
  –preservation 717
  –reliance
    resolution 604
    hope 858
    courage 861
  –reproach 950
  –respect *pride* 878
  –restraint 826, 953
  –sacrifice 942
  –satisfied 880
  –seeker 943
  –seeking 943
  –starter
    automobile 272
  –styled 565
  –sufficiency 893
  –sufficient 880
  –taught 490
  –tormentor 837
  –will 606
selfish 943
selfishness **943**
selfsame 13
sell *absurdity* 497
  deception 545
  untruth 546
  sale 796
  –for 812
  –off 796
  –oneself 940
  –one's life dearly
    resist 719
    fight 722
  –out 796
seller 796
selliform 250
selling ability 796
selvage 231
semaphore 550

sematic

sematic 668
semblance
  similarity 17
  imitation 19
  copy 21
  probability 471
  wear the–of
    appearance 448
semeiology 522, 655
semeiotics 550
semen 153
semester 108
semi–91
semibarbarian 913
semibreve 413
semicircle 247
semicircular 245
semicolon 142
semidiaphanous 427
semifluid 352
semiliquidity 352
semilunar 245
seminal *causing* 153
seminar 542
seminary 542
semination
  preparation 673
semiopaque 427
semipellucid 427
semiquaver 413
Semitic 372a
semitone 413
semitransparency 427
sempervirid 110, 123
sempiternal 112
sempiternity 110, 112
senary 98
senate 72, 696
senate house 966
senator *counsel* 695
  councillor 696
senatorship 693
send *transfer* 270
  propel 284
  –about one's business 289
  –adrift 597
  –a letter to 592
  –away *repel* 289
  eject 297
  refuse 764
  –for 741
  –forth *propel* 284
  publish 531
  –off 284
  –out *eject* 297
  commission 755
  –word 527
seneca–oil 356
senectitude 128
senescence 128
seneschal
  director 694
  master 745

servant 746
seneschalship 737
senile 128, 158, 499
  –dementia 499, 821a
senior *age* 128
  student 492
  master 745
seniority *oldness* 124
  age 128
señor 877
sensation
  physical sensibility 375
  emotion 821
  wonder 870
sensational
  language 574
  exciting 824
sensation drama 599
sensations of touch 380
sense *wisdom* 498
  meaning 516
  accept in a
    particular–522
  deep–821
  in no–565
  –of duty 926
senseless
  insensible 376
  absurd 497
  foolish 499
  unmeaning 517
senses *external*–375
  intellect 450
  sanity 502
sensibility
  physical–**375**
  moral **822**
sensible *material* 316
  wise 498
sensitive 375, 822
  –plant 822
sensorial 821
sensorium 450
sensual *pleasure* 377
  intemperate 954
sensualist 954a
sensualize 954
sensuous
  sensibility 375
  pleasure 377
  feeling 821
sentence *decision* 480
  maxim 496
  affirmation 535
  phrase 566
  lawsuit 969
  condemnation 971
  my–is for war 722
sententious
  concise 572
  –*language* 574, 577
  taciturn 585
sentiment
  –*physically* 375

–*morally* 821
sentiment *idea* 453
  (*opinion* 484)
  (*maxim* 496)
sentimental
  sensitive 822
  affected 855
sentinel *guard* 263
  guardian 664
  watch 668
  keeper 753
sentry 664, 668, 753
sepal 367
separable 44
separate *disjoin* 44
  exclude 55
  bisect 91
  diverge 291
  clean 652
  divorce 782, 905
  –into elements 49
  –maintenance 905
  –the chaff from the wheat
  discriminate 465
  select 609
separation
  (see *separate*)
separatist 489, 984
  disjunction 44
separative 49
seposition
  disjunction 44
  exclusion 55
sepoy 726
seppuku 972
sept *kin* 11
  class 75
  clan 166
septal 228
septenary 98
septennial 138
Septentrional 237
septet 415
septic 655, 657, 662
septicemia 655
septicity 655
septimal 98
septuagenary 98
septuagesimal 98
Septuagint 985
septulum 228
septum 228
septuple 98
sepulcher 363
  whited–545
sepulchral
  interment 363
  resonance 408
  stridor 410
  hoarse 581
sepulture 363
sequacious 63, 117
sequacity *soft* 324
  tenacity 327

sequel *following* **65**
  –*in time* 117
  sequence 281
  (*addition* 39)
sequela 63, 65
sequence–*in order* **63**
  –*in time* 117
  motion **281**
  logical–476
sequent 63, 117
sequester *take* 789
  confiscate 974
  (*hide* 528)
sequestered
  secluded 893
sequestrate *seize* 789
  condemn 971
  confiscate 974
sérac 383
seraglio *abode* 189
  woman 374
  marriage 903
  impurity 961
seraph *saint* 948
  angel 977
seraphic *blissful* 829
  virtuous 944
  pious 987
Seraphim 977
seraphina 417
seraskier 745
sere (see *sear*)
  –and yellow leaf 128
serein *dew* 339
  rain 348
serenade *music* 415
  compliment 894
  endearment 902
serene *pellucid* 425
  calm 826
  content 831
  –highness 877
serf *slave* 746
  clown 876
serfdom 749
serge 635
sergeant 745
serial *continuous* 69
  periodic 138
  book 593
seriatim *in order* 58
  continuously 69
  each to each 79
  slowly 275
series *continuity* 69
  number 84
serif 591
serio–comic 853
serious *great* 31
  resolved 604
  important 642
  dejected 837
seriously 535
serjeant
  common–967
  –*at–law* 968

serviceable

sermon *lesson* 537
  speech 582
  dissertation 595
  pastoral 998
  funeral–363
sermonize 586
sermonizer 584
serosity *fluid* 333
serotherapy 662
serotine 133
serpent *tortuous* 248
  snake 366
  hiss 409
  wind instrument 417
  wise 498
  deceiver 548
  cunning 702
  evildoer 913
  knave 941
  demon 949
  great sea–515
  the old–978
serpentine 248
serrated *angular* 244
  notched 257
serried *crowded* 72
  dense 321
serum *lymph* 333
  water 337
servant *minister* 631
  agent 690
  help 711
  retainer **746**
  –of all work 690
serve *benefit* 618
  business 625
  utility 644
  aid 707
  warfare 722
  obey 743
  servant 746
  (*work* 680)
  –an apprenticeship 539
  –as a substitute 147
  –faithfully 743
  –one right
    retaliation 718
    right 922
    punish 972
  –one's turn 644
  –out 972
  –with a writ 969
service *good* 618
  utility 644
  use 677
  warfare 722
  servitude 749
  worship 990
  rite 998
  at one's–763
  press into the–677
  render a–*utility* 644
  benevolence 906
serviceable
  instrumental 631

servile

useful 644
good 648
servant 746
servile *servant* 746
  subject 749
  ignoble 876
  obsequious 886
servility
  obsequious **886**
  (*flattery* 933)
  (*see* servile)
servitor 746
servitorship 749
servitude 749
  penal–972
sesame, open–
  opening 260
  watchword 550
  spell 993
sesqui–87
sesquipedalian
  long 200
sess 812
sessile 46
session *council* 696
  churchdom 995
sessions *law* 966
sestet 415
set *condition* 7
  join 43
  coherence 46
  compose 54
  group 72
  class 75
  firm 150
  tendency 176
  situation 183
  place 184
  form 240
  sharpen 253
  direction 278
  go down 306
  dense 321
  stage 599
  habit 613
  prepare 673
  gang 712
  impose 741
  make a dead–at 716
  –about *begin* 66
  undertake 676
  –abroach 73
  –afloat *originate* 153
  publish 531
  oppose 708
  quarrel 713
  hate 898
  angry 900
  (*counteract* 179)
  –against one another 464
  –agoing *impulse* 276
  propulsion 284
  aid 707
  –an example
  model 22

motive 615
–apart *separate* 44
exclude 55
select 609
–a price 812
–aside *displace* 185
disregard 458
neglect 460
negative 536
reject 610
disuse 678
annul 756
refuse 764
not observe 773
relinquish 782
dereliction 927
–at ease 831
–at hazard 665
–at naught
make light of 483
reject 610
oppose 708
defy 715
disobey 742
not observe 773
dereliction 927
–at trap for 545
–at rest *end* 67
answer 462
adjudge 480
complete 729
compact 769
–before *inform* 527
choice 609
–before oneself 620
–by 636
–by the ears 898
–down
(*see below*)
–foot on 294
–forth *show* 525
assert 535
describe 594
–forward 293
–free 750
–going (*see* –agoing)
–in *begin* 66
rain 348
–in motion *move* 264
use 677
–in order 60
–in towards 286
–no store by
make light of 483
despise 930
–off *compensation* 30
depart 293
improve 658
discount 813
adorn 845
display 882
–on 615
–on a cast 621
–one's affections on 897
–one's back up 878

–one's cap at
love 897
endearment 902
–one's face against
oppose 708
refuse 764
disapprove 932
–one's hand to 467
–one's heart upon
resolve 604
desire 865
–one's seal to 467
–one's teeth 604
–one's wits to work
think 451
imagine 515
plan 626
–on fire *ignite* 384
excite 824
–on foot 66
–on its legs
establish 150
–on one's legs
strengthen 159
restore 669
–out *arrange* 60
begin 66
depart 293
decorate 845
display 882
–over 755
–phrase 566
–purpose 620
–right *inform* 527
disclose 529
teach 537
reinstate 660
vindicate 937
–sail 293
–store by 642
–straight
straighten 246
pacify 723
–terms *manifest* 525
phrase 566
style 574
–the eyes on 441
–the fashion
influence 175
authority 737
fashion 852
–the seal on 729
–the table in a roar 840
–to *contend* 720
war 722
–to music 416
–too high a value upon 482
–to rights 60
–to work
undertake 676
impose 741
–up *originate* 153
strengthen 159
produce 161

upright 212
raise 307
successful 731
prosperous 734
–upon *resolved* 604
attack 716
desirous 865
(*intending* 620)
–up shop 676
–watch 459
setaceous 256
setarious 253
setback 306, 735
set down *record* 551
humiliate 879
slight 929
censure 932
give one a–
confute 479
–a cause for hearing 969
–as 484
–for 484
–in writing 551
–to 155
setiferous 256
set-off *printing* 591
setose 256
sett *lease* 771, 787
settee 215
setter 366
settle *regulate* 60
establish 150
be located 184
bench 215
come to rest 265
subside 306
kill 361
decide 480
choose 609
vanquish 731
consent 762
compact 769
pay 807
–accounts *pay* 807
accounts 811
–down
adolescence 131
stability 150
moderate 174
locate onseelf 184
–into 144
–matters 723
–preliminaries 673
–property 781
–the question 478
–to sleep 683
–upon *give* 784
–with *pay* 807
settled (*see* settle)
ended 67
account–811
–opinion 484
–principle 496
–purpose 620
settlement (*see* settle)

sexual congress

location 184
colony 188
dregs 653
compact 769
deed 771
property 780
strict–781
settler 188
settlings 321
settlor 784
seven 98
in–league boots 274
wake the–sleepers 404
Seven Seas 341
seventy 98
seventy–five *gun* 727
sever 44
severable 44
several *special* 79
plural 100
many 102
–times 104
severalize 465
severally *divided* 44
respectively 79
severalty 44
severe *energetic* 171
symmetry 242
exact 494
–*style* 576
harsh 739
painful 830
simple 849
critical 932
severely *very* 31
severity 739
(*see* severe)
sew 43
sewage *excretion* 299
filth 653
sewed up
drunk 959
sewer *drain* 350
cloaca 653
sewerage
drainage 652
filth 653
sewer gas 663
sewing silk 205
sex *kind* 75
women 374
fair–374
sexagenarian 130
sexagenary 98, 99
sexagesimal 98
sextan 98
sextant *angle* 244
circle 247
sextennial 138
sextet 98 *verse* 597
sextodecimo 593
sexton *interment* 363
clergy 996
sextuple 98
sexual congress 43

shabbiness

shabbiness
  (see shabby)
  inferiority 34
shabby *trifling* 643
  deteriorated 659
  stingy 819
  mean 874
  disgraceful 940
  (*bad* 649)
shabby genteel 851
shack 189
shackle *fastening* 45
  hinder 706
  restrain 751
  fetter 752
shad 298
shade *degree* 26
  small quantity 32
  manes 362
  darkness 421
  dimness 422
  shadow **424**
  color 428
  conceal 528
  screen 530
  paint 556
  ghost 980a
  distribution of–421
  in the–*hidden* 528
  out of repute 874
  shadow of a
    –*small* 32
    dim 422
  throw all else into
    the–642
  throw into the–
    surpass 303
    conceal 528
    glory 873
  thrown into the–
    inferior 34
    disrepute 874
  under the–*of* 664
  without a–*of doubt* 474
shades–*below* 982
  –*of death* 360
  –*of difference* 15
  –*of evening* 422
  welcome ye–424
shading 421–*off* 26
shadow
  unsubstantial 4
  copy 21
  small 32
  remains 40
  hands
  follow 63
  accompaniment 88
  thin 203
  pursue 235, 622
  sequence 281
  cloud 353, 422
  dark 421
  shade 424
  inquire 461
  dream 515

  ghost 980a
  disdains the–878
  fight with a–699
  follow as a–281
  may your–*never be less courtesy* 894
  respect 928
  approbation 931
  partial–422
  –*forth dim* 422
  predict 511
  metaphor 521
  represent 554
  –*of coming events* 511
  –*of the tomb* 363
  take the–for the substance
    credulous 486
    mistake 495
    unskillful 699
  under the–*of one's wing* 664
  without a–*of turning* 141
  worn to a–*thin* 203
  worse for wear 659
shadowy *inexistent* 2
  unsubstantial 4
  shady 424
  invisible 447
shaft *deep* 208
  frame 215
  pit 252, 260
  air pipe 351
  handle 633
  weapon 727
  (*missile* 284)
shaggy 256
shagreen 223
shah 745
shaitan 978
shake *totter* 149
  weak 160
  vibrate 314
  agitation 315
  shiver 383
  trill 407
  music 416
  dissuade 616
  shingle 635
  injure 659
  impress 821
  excited 824
  fear 860
  –hands
    pacification 723
    friendship 888
    courtesy 894
    forgive 918
  –off 297
  –off the yoke 750
  –one's faith 485
  –one's sides 838
  –the head *dissent* 489
  deny 536

  refuse 764
  disapprove 932
  –to pieces 162
  –up 315
shakedown *bed* 215
shaker 984
shakes, no great– *trifling* 643
  imperfect 651
shaking prairie 344
shako *hat* 225
  helmet 717
shaky *weak* 160
  in danger 665
  fearful 860
shallop 273
shallow
  unintelligent 32
  not deep 209
  ignorant 491
  ignoramus 493
  foolish 499
  trifling 643
  –*pretext* 617
  –*profundity* 855
shallow-brain *fool* 501
shallowness 209
  (see shallow)
shallow-pated 499
shallows *danger* 667
sham *falsehood* 544
  deception 545
  untruth 546
  –*fight* 720
shaman 548, 994
shamanism 992
shamble *dawdle* 275
  stagger 315
shambles 361
shame *disrepute* 874
  wrong 923
  censure 932
  chastity 960
  cry–upon 932
  false–855
  for–874
  sense of–879
  –the devil 939
  to one's–be it spoken 874
shamefaced 881
shameful
  disgraceful 874
  profligate 945
shameless
  unreserved 525
  impudent 885
  profligate 945
  indecent 961
shamianah 223
shampoo 662
shamrock 92
shandrydan 272
shanghai 545
shank *support* 215

  printing 591
  instrument 633
shanks 266
  –'s mare 266
shanty 189
shape *state* 7
  harmonize 82
  form 240
  aspect 448
  (*state* 7)
  (*convert* 144)
  –one's course
    direction 278
    pursuit 622
    conduct 692
  –out a course *plan* 626
shapeless
  amorphous 241
  ugly 846
shapely *form* 240
  symmetrical 242
  comely 845
share *part* 51
  participate 778
  allotted portion 786
  –and share alike 778
  –one's sorrow 915
shareholder 778
shark *fish* 366, 368
  thief 792
  (*cheat* 548)
sharp *energetic* 171
  violent 173
  acute 253
  sensible 375
  pungent 392
  –*sound* 410
  musical tone 413
  intelligent 498
  active 682
  clever 698
  cunning 702
  feeling 821
  painful 830
  rude 895
  censorious 932
  look–*take care* 459
  be active 682
  –appetite 865
  –contest 720
  –ear 418
  –eye 441
  –fellow *active* 682
  proficient 700
  –frost 383
  –lookout
    vigilance 459
    expectation 507
  –pain 378
  –practice
    deception 545
    cunning 702
  severity 739
  improbity 940
sharpen (see sharp)

sheer

  excite 824
  –one's tools 673
  –one's wits 537
sharpener 253
sharper *thief* 792
  (*cheat* 548)
sharpness 253
  fastidiousness 868
sharp-set 865
sharpshooter 716, 726
sharpshooting 716
Shastra 986
shatter *disjoin* 44
  render powerless 158
  destroy 162
shatterbrained 503
shattered *weak* 160
  fatigued 688
shave *reduce* 195
  shorten 201
  layer 204
  smooth 255
  grate 330
  lie 546
shaving *small* 32
  layer 204
  filament 205
  (*part* 51)
shawl 225, 384
shay 272
she 374
sheaf 72
shear *reduce* 195
  shorten 201
  –sheep 370
  take 789
shears 253
sheath *receptacle* 191
  envelope 223
sheathe *moderate* 174
  line 224
  clothe 225
  –the sword 723
sheathing 223, 224
shebeen 189
shed *scatter* 73
  building 189
  emit 297
  give 784
  –a luster on 873
  –blood 361
  –light upon 420
  –tears 839
sheen 420
sheep 366
sheep dog 366
sheepfold 232
sheepish 881
sheep's eyes
  desire 865
  modest 881
  endearment 902
sheer *mere* 32
  simple 42
  complete 52

565

sheet

deviation 279
–off *avoid* 623
  (*depart* 293)
sheet *layer* 204
  covering 223
  paper 593
  –of fire 382
  –of water 343
  white–*penance* 952
  winding–363
sheet anchor
  safety 664, 666, 706
  hope 858
sheet lightning 423
sheet work 591
sheik *ruler* 745
  priest 996
shelf *support* 215
  rock 667
  on the
  –*powerless* 158
  disused 678
  inaction 681
shell *cover* 223
  coffin 363
  bomb 404, 727
  bombard 716
  warfare 722
  –*game* 545
  –out 807, 809
shellac 356a
shellback 269
shellfish 366
shellproof 664
shell–shaped 245
shell–shock 655
shelter *safety* 664
  refuge 666
  –oneself under plea
    of 617
sheltie 271
shelve *lateness* 133
  locate 184
  slope 217
  neglect 460
  disuse 678
shelved *unsalable* 796
shelving beach 217
shenanigan 842
shend 659
sheol 982
shepherd
  tender of sheep 370
  director 694
  pastor 996
Shepherd, the Good
  –976
shepherd's dog 366
Sheppard, Jack–792
sherbet 298
shereef *governor* 745
  noble 875
sheriff 664, 965
sherry 959
Shetland 271
Shiah 984

shibboleth 550
shield *heraldry* 550
  safety 664
  buckler 666
  defend 717
  scutcheon 877
  look only at one
    side of the–481
  reverse of the
  –*rear* 235
  counter evidence 468
  under the–of 664
shield–shaped 245
shift *change* 140
  convert 144
  substitute 147
  changeable 149
  displace 185
  chemise 225
  more 264
  transfer 270
  deviate 279
  prevaricate 546
  plea 617
  cunning 702
  (*expedient* 626)
  last–601
  left to–for oneself
    893
  make a–with
  substitute 147
  use 677
  put to one's–s
  difficulty 704
  poverty 804
  –for oneself
  conduct 692
  freedom 748
  –off *defer* 133
  –one's ground 607
  –one's quarters 264
  –the scene 140
  –to and fro 149
shifting (*see* shift)
  transient 111
  –sands 149
  –trust or use 783
shiftless
  unprepared 674
  inhabile 699
shifty 702
shikar 622
shillalah 727
shilling 800
  cut off with a–789
  –shocker 594
shilly–shally 605
shimmer 420
shimmy *dance* 840
shin *climb* 305
shindig 840
shindy 720
shine *light* 420
  beauty 845
  glory 873
  –forth 873

–in conversation 588
–upon *illumine* 420
  aid 707
  take the–out of 874
shingle
  covering 223, 635
  powder 330
  –house 189
shining (*see* shine)
  –light *sage* 500
shinny 840
shinplaster 800
shintiyan 225
shiny 420
ship *lade* 190
  transfer 270
  vessel **273**
  one's–coming in
    803
  –of the line 726
  take–sail 267
  depart 293
ship biscuit 298
shipboard, on–273
shipentine 273
shipload *much* 31
  cargo 190
  (*abundance* 639)
shipman 269
shipmate 890
shipment
  contents 190
  transfer 270
shippen 189
shipping 273
shipshape *order* 58
  conformity 82
  skill 698
shipwreck
  destruction 162, 361
  vanquish 731
  failure 732
shire 181
shirk *shuffle* 605
  avoid 623
  disobey 742
shirred eggs 298
shirt 225
shirt waist 225
Shiva 976
shivaree 414
shive *small piece* 32
  layer 204
shiver *small piece* 32
  divide 44
  destroy 162
  filament 205
  shake 315
  brittle 328
  cold 383
  fear 860
  go to–s 162
  –in one's shoes 860
shivery *brittle* 328
  powdery 330
shizoku 875

shoal *assemblage* 72
  multitude 102
  shallow 209
shoals *danger* 667
  surrounded by
  –*difficulty* 704
shock *sheaf* 72
  violence 173
  concussion 276
  agitation 315
  unexpected 508
  discord 713
  affect 821
  move 824
  pain 828
  give pain 830
  dislike 867
  scandalize 932
  (*contest* 720)
shocking *bad* 649
  painful 830
  ugly 846
  vulgar 851
  fearful 860
  disreputable 874
  hateful 898
  in a–temper 901a
shockingly *much* 31
shod 225
shoddy 645
shoe *support* 215
  dress 225
  hindrance 706
  stand in the–s of
    commission 755
  deputy 759
  where the–pinches
    badness 649
  difficulty 704
  opposition 708
  sensibility 822
  painful 830
shoemaker 225
shog 173
shoot *offspring* 167
  expand 194
  dart 274
  propel 284
  kill 361
  vegetable 367
  pain 378
  execute 972
  –ahead 282
  –ahead of 303
  –at 716
  –out beams 420
  –up *increase* 35
  prominent 250
  grow 365
  (*ascend* 305)
  teach the young
    idea to–537
shooter *pistol* 727
shooting (*see* shoot)
  chase 622
  –pain 378

–star *world* 318
  luminary 423
  omen 512
shooting coat 225
shooting iron 727
shop *buy* 795
  mart 799
  keep a–*business* 625
  trade 794
  shup up–*end* 67
  cease 142
  relinquish 624
  rest 687
  smell of the–851
shopkeeper 797
shoplifter 792
shoplifting 791
shopman 797
shopmate 890
shopping 794, 795
shop–worn
  cheap 815
shore *support* 215
  border 231
  land 342
  buttress 717
  hug the–286
  on–342
  –up 215, 669, 670
shoreless 180
shorn *cut short* 21
  divided 51
  deprived 776
  –lamb 828
  –of its beams
  dim 422
  inglorious 874
short *not long* 201
  brittle 328
  typography 550
  concise 572
  uncivil 895
  at–notice
  transient 111
  early 132
  come–of, fall–of
  inferior 34
  shortcoming 304
  insufficient 640
  in–*concisely* 572
  compendium 596
  make–work of
  destroy 162
  active 682
  haste 684
  complete 729
  conquer 731
  punish 972
  –allowance 640
  –answer 895
  –bit *money* 800
  –breath 688
  –by 201
  –commons
  insufficiency 640
  fasting 956

shortage

—cut *straight* 246
  mid—*course* 628
—distance 197
—life and merry 840
—measure 53
—of *small* 32
  inferior 34
  subtraction 38
  incomplete 53
  shortcoming 304
  insufficient 640
—of cash 804
—rations 956
—sea 348
shortage 53
shortbread 298
shortcoming
  inequality 28
  inferiority 34
  motion short of **304**
  noncompletion 730
shorten 201—sail 275
shorthand 590
short—handed 651
shorthorn 366
short—lived 111
shortly *soon* 132, 507
shortness 201
  for—sake 572
shorts 225
shortsighted
  myopic 443
  misjudging 481
  foolish 499
short—winded
  weak 160
  fatigue 688
short—witted 499
shot *missile* 284
  variegated 440
  guess 514
  war material 722, 727
  price 812
  reward 973
  bad—701
  exchange—s 720
  good—700
  have a—at 716
  like a—113
  not have a—in one's locker 804
  off like a—623
  random
  —experiment 463
  chance 621
  round—727
  —in the locker 632
shot—free 815
shotgun 727
should be
  no better than she—961
  what—922
shoulder *support* 215
  projection 250

shove 276
  printing 591
  broad—ed 159
  cold—289
  have on one's—s 625
  on the—s of
  high 206
  elevated 307
  instrumentality 631
  rest on the—s of 926
—a musket 722
—arms 673
—to shoulder
  cooperate 709
  party 712
—to the wheel
  resolution 604
  undertaking 676
  shrug the—s
  (see shrug)
  take upon one's—s 676
shoulder knot 847
shout *loud* 404
  cry 406, 411
  rejoice 838
  (*voice* 580)
shove 276 give a—to
  aid 707
shovel *receptacle* 191
  transfer 270
  vehicle 272
  fire iron 386
  cleanness 652
  —away 297
shovel hat 999
show *occasion* 134
  visible 446
  appear 448
  draw attention 457
  evidence 467
  demonstrate 478
  manifest 525
  drama 599, 840
  ornament 847
  parade 882
  dumb—550
  make a—544
  mere—544
  peep—840
—a light pair of heels 623
—cause 527
—fight *defy* 715
  attack 716
  defend 717
  brave 861
—forth 525
—in front 303
—itself 446
—of *similarity* 17
  probability 472
—off *display* 882
  boast 884

—one's cards 529
—one's colors 550
—one's face
  presence 186
  manifest 525
  disclose 529
—one's hand 529
—one's teeth 715
—up *visible* 446
  manifest 525
  ridicule 856
  degrade 874
  censure 932
  accuse 938
show—down 525
shower *assemblage* 72
  shower bath 337
  rain 348
—bath 337, 386
—down
  abundance 639
—down upon *give* 784
  liberal 816
showman 524
showy *color* 428
  ugliness 846
  ornament 847
  tawdry 851
  fashionable 852
  ostentatious 882
shrapnel 727
shred *small* 32
  filament 205
  (*part* 51)
shrew 901
shrewd *knowing* 490
  wise 498
  cunning 702
  (*clever* 698)
shriek 410, 411
shrievalty 965
shrieve 965
shrift *confession* 529
  absolution 952
shriftless 951
shrill *loud* 404, 410
  cry 411
shrimp 193, 298
shrine *receptacle* 191
  tomb 363
  temple 998, 1000
shrink *decrease* 36
  shrivel 195
  go back 283, 287
  unwilling 603
  avoid 623
  sensitive 822
—from *fear* 860
  dislike 867
  hate 898
shrive 952
shrivel *contract* 195
  fold 258
  (*decrease* 36)
shriveled *thin* 203
  (*small* 193)

shroud *covering* 223
  invest 225
  funeral 363
  hide 528
  safety 664
  defend 717
—ed in mystery 519
shrub *plant* 367
  plantation 371
shrug *sign* 550
  (*hint* 527)
—the shoulders
  dissent 489
  submit 725
  discontent 832
  dislike 867
  contempt 930
  disapprobation 932
shrunk *little* 193
  shrink 195
shudder *cold* 383
  fear 860
  make one
—*painful* 830
—at *aversion* 867
  hate 898
shuffle *mix* 41
  derange 61
  change 140
  interchange 148
  changeable 149
  move slowly 275
  agitate 315
  falsehood 544
  untruth 546
  irresolute 605
  recant 607
  improbity 940
  patience and—the cards 826
—off *run away* 623
—off this mortal coil 360
—on 266
—the cards
  begin again 66
  change 140
  chance 621
  prepare 673
shuffler 548
shun *avoid* 623
  dislike 867
shunt *transfer* 270
  deviate 279
  remove 287
shunted *shelved* 460
shut 261—in 751
—one's ears *deaf* 419
  not believe 487
—oneself up 893
—one's eyes to
  not attend to 458
  neglect 460
  not believe 487
  permit 760
  not observe 773

sick

—out *exclude* 55
  prohibit 761
—the eyes 442
—the door 761
—the door in one's face 764
—the door upon 893
—the gates of mercy 914a
—up *close* 261
  confute 479
  imprison 751
  (*inclose* 229)
  taciturnity 585
—up shop *end* 67
  cease 142
  relinquish 624
  repose 687
shutter 424
shuttle
  correlation 12
  oscillate 314
  instrument 633
shuttlecock 605
shuttlewise 314
shy *deviate* 279
  draw back 283
  propel 284
  avoid 623
  fearful 860
  cowardly 862
  modest 881
  fight—of 623
  have a—at 716
—cock 862
—of *doubtful* 485
  unwilling 603
  cautious 864
  dislike 867
—of belief 487
Shylock 787
shyster 941, 968
Siamese 372a
Siamese twins 89
sib 11
Siberia 383
sibilation *hiss* **409**
  disrespect 929
  disapprobation 932
sibling 372a
sibyl *oracle* 513
  ugly 846
sibylline 511
—leaves 513
sic *imitation* 19
  exact 494
siccation 340
siccity 340
sick *ill* 655
  make one—
  painful 830
  aversion 867
—at heart 837
—of *weary* 841
  dislike 867
  satiated 869

sick chamber

visitation of the– 998
sick chamber 655
sicken *nauseate* 395
　disease 655
　pain 830
　weary 841
　disgust 867
sickener
　too much 641
sickle *pointed* 244
　sharp 253
sickle-shaped 245
sickly *weak* 160
sickness 655
sick room 655
side *consanguinity* 11
　edge 231
　laterality 236
　party 712
　at one's–197
　from–to side 314
　look only at one–of the shield 481
　on every–227
　on one–243
　on one's–714
　pass from one–to another 607
　–*by side*
　　accompaniment 88
　　near 197
　　laterality 236
　　party 712
　–*issue* 39
　–*with aid* 707
　　cooperate 709
　　concord 714
　take up a–476
　wrong–up 218
side arms 727
side blow 702
sideboard 191
side dish 298
side drum 417
sideling 237, 279
sidelong 236, 237, 279
side partner 891
sideration 318
sidereal 318
siderite 288
sideromancy 511
sidesaddle 215
side scene 599
sidesman 996
sidetrack 279, 287
sidewalk 627
sideways *oblique* 217
　lateral 236
side wind *oblique* 217
　circuit 629
　cunning 702
sidewinder 276
sidewipe 276
sidewise 237

sidle *oblique* 217
　lateral 236
　deviate 279
siege 716 *lay-to* 716
　state of–722
siege cap 717
siege gun 727
siege train 727
siesta 683
sieve *sort* 60
　crossing 219
　perforate 260
　sift 652
　pour water into a–waste 638
　lavish 818
　stop one hole in a– 819
sift *simplify* 42
　sort 60
　inquire 461
　discriminate 465
　clean 652
　–*the chaff from the wheat* 609
sifter 219
sigh 839 –*for* 865
sighing 839
　–*like furnace* 902
sight *much* 31
　multitude 102
　vision 441
　appearance 448
　ugly 846
　prodigy 872
　at–soon 132
　seeing 441
　dim–443
　in–446
　in–of near 197
　seen 441
　keep in–457
　within–of shore 858
sightless *blind* 442
　invisible 447
　ugly 846
sightly 845
sight-reading
　music 415
sights, see–455
sight-seeing 441
sight-seer
　spectator 444
　curiosity 455
sight-singing 415
sigil *seal* 550
　evidence 769
sigmoid 245, 248
sign *attest* 467
　omen 512
　indication 550
　record 551
　write 590
　talisman 747
　compact 769
　prodigy 872

　give–of 525
　make no–585
　–*s of the times*
　omen 512
　warning 668
　–*s of the zodiac* 318
signal *great* 31
　eventful 151
　sign 550
　important 642
　give the–741
　–*of distress* 669
signalize *indicate* 550
　glory 873
　celebrate 883
signally 31
signal light 423
signal post 550, 668
signature
　mark, identification 550
　writing 590
　printing 591
　compact 769
　security 771
signboard 550
signet
　mark, identification 550
　sign of authority 747
　compact 769
　(*evidence*) 467
　writer to the–968
significant
　(*see signify*)
　evidence 467
　importance 642
　(*clear* 518)
signifies, what–643
signify *forebode* 511
　mean 516
　inform 527
　indication 550
signior 875
sign manual 550, 590
signor 877
sign painting 555
signpost 550
sike 348
Sikes, Bill–792
silence *disable* 158
　no sound **403**
　confute 479
　latency 526
　concealment 528
　aphony 581
　taciturn 585
　check 731
silencer 405, 408a
silent (*see silence*)
silhouette
　outline 230
　appearance 448
　portrait 556
siliquose 191

silk
　texture 219, 329, 635
　smooth 255
　soft 324
　make a–purse out of a sow's ear 471
　–*gown barrister* 968
silken 255
　–*repose* 687
silkiness
　voluptuousness 954
sill 215
silly *credulous* 486
　imbecile 499
　insane 503
silo 636
silt *dirt* 653
　(*remainder* 40)
silvan 367
silver *bright* 420
　white 430
　gray 432
　money 800
　bait with a–hook 615
　German–545
　–*footed queen* 318
　–*lining of the cloud* 858
　–*wedding* 883
silver-toned 413
silviculture 371
simagrée 855
simian 499
similarity 17
　–*of form* 240
simile *similarity* 17
　comparison 464
　metaphor 521
similitude *likeness* 17
　copy 21
simious 499
simmer *agitation* 315
　boil 382, 384
　excitement 824
simmering 825
Simon, Simple–547
Simon Pure
　the real–494
Simeon Stylites 893
simony 964
simoon 349, 382
simous 243
simper *smile* 838
　affectation 855
simple *mere* 32
　unmixed 42
　credulous 486
　ignorant 493
　silly 499
　–*language* 576
　instrumental 633
　hero 662
　artless 703

single

　unadorned 849
　–*duty* 926
　–*meaning* 516
simple-hearted 543
simple-minded 849
simpleness 42
Simple Simon 501, 547
simpleton 501
simplicity 849
　ignorance 491
　(*see* simple)
simplify (*see* simple)
　elucidate 518
simply *little* 32
　singly 87
　more
　–*interpreted* 522
simulate *resemble* 17
　imitate 19
　cheat 544
　impiety 988
simultaneous 120
sin *vice* 945
　guilt 947
Sinaean 188
sinapism 662
since
　under the circumstances 8
　after 117
　cause 155
　reason 476
sincere *veracious* 543
　ingenuous 703
　feeling 821
sine 217
sine die *never* 107
　defer 133
sine qua non
　required 630
　important 642
　condition 770
sinecure 681 *no*–682
sinew 159
sinewless 158
sinews of war
　money 800
sinewy 159
sinful 945
sing *blow* 349
　bird cry 412
　music 416
　poetry 597
　rejoice 838
　–*in the shrouds* 349
　–*out* 411
　–*praises approve* 931
　worship 990
　–*small* 879
singe 382, 384
singer *musician* 416
　poet 597
singing club 416
single *unmixed* 42
　unit 87

single—foot   **slabber**

   secluded 893
   unmarried 904
   ride at—anchor 863
   —*combat* 720
   —*entry* 811
   —*file* 69
   —*out* 609
single—foot 275
single—handed
   one 87
   easy 705
   unassisted 706
single—minded 703
singleness (*see* single)
   —*of heart artless* 703
   probity 939
   —*of purpose*
      perseverance 604a
      artless 703
single—seater 273
singlestick 720
singsong 16, 414
singular *special* 79
   exceptional 83
   one 87
singularly *very* 31
   nonconformity 83
sinister *left* 239
   bad 649
   adverse 735
   vicious 945
   bar—imperfect 651
   disrepute 874
sinistrality 239
sinistrorsal 239
sinistrous *sullen* 901a
Sinitic 372a
sink *disappear* 4, 111
   destroy 162
   descend 306
   lower 308
   submerge 310
   neglect 460
   conceal 528
   cloaca 653
   fatigue 688
   vanquish 731
   fail 732
   adversity 735
   invest 787
   pain 828
   depressed 837
   (*decay* 659)
   —*back* 661
   —*in the mind*
      thought 451
      memory 505
      excite 824
   —*into oblivion* 506
   —*into the grave* 360
   —*money* 809
   —*of corruption* 653
   —*of iniquity* 945
   —*or swim*
      certainty 474
      perseverance 604a

sinking *heart*—837
   —*fund* 802
sinless 946
sinned against
   more—than sinning 946
sinner 949
Sinn Feiner 710, 712, 742
sin offering 952
sinologist 492
sinuous 217, 248
sinus 252
sip *small* 32
   drink 298
siphon 348, 350
sippet 298
sir *man* 373
   title 877
   —*Oracle* 887
sircar 745
sirdar 745
sire 166
siren *sea nymph* 341
   musician 416
   musical instrument 417
   seducing 615
   warning 668
   alarm 669
   evildoer 913
   evil spirit 980
   sorcerer 994
   —*strains* 415
   song of the—*s* 615
sirene
   musical instrument 417
siriasis 503
sirius 423
sirkar 745
sirloin 298
sirocco *wind* 349
   heat 382
sirrah! 949
siskin 366
sissy *milksop* 158
sister *kin* 11
   likeness 17
   nurse 662
   celibacy 904
sisterhood *party* 712
   friendship 888
   frail—962
sisterly 906
sisters,—*three* 601
   weird—994
Sisyphus *task of*—
   useless 645
   difficult 704
   (*not complete* 730)
sit 308 *hatch* 370
   —*down settle* 184
   lie 213
   stoop 308
   —*in judgment*

adjudge 480
   jurisdiction 965
   lawsuit 969
   —*on* 215
   —*on thorns*
      annoyance 828
      fear 860
   —*up for* 133
site 182, 183
sith *circumstance* 8
   reason 476
sitting (*see* sit)
   incubation 673
   convocation 696
   —*up late* 133
   work 686
sitting room 191
situation
   circumstances 8
   place **183**
   location 184
   business 625
   out of a—185
situs 183
sitz bath 386
Siva 976
six 98
   —*of one and half a dozen of the other* 27
sixes and sevens *at*
   —*disorder* 59
   discord 713
six—shooter 727
sixty 98
sizar 746
size *magnitude* 31
   glue 45
   arrange 60
   dimensions **192**
   viscid 352
   —*up* 480
sizz 409
sizzle 409
sjambok 975
skald 597
skate *locomotion* 266
   vehicle 272
   deterioration 659
skating 840
skating rink 840
skean 727
skean dhu 727
skedaddle 274, 623
skeel 191
skeesicks 949
skein 219 *tangled*—59
skeletal 203
skeleton *remains* 40
   essential part 50
   thin 203
   support 215
   corpse 362
   plan 626
   reduced to a—659
   —*in the closet*

bad 649
   painful 830
skeptic
   agnostic 485, 984
skepticism
   thought 451
   doubt 485
   incredulity 487
   irreligion 989
sketch *delineate* 230
   form 240
   represent 554
   paint 556
   describe 594
   outline 626
sketcher 559
sketchy *incomplete* 53
   feeble 575
   unfinished 730
skew 217
skewbald 440
skewer 45
ski 225, 266, 272
skiagram 421, 554
skiagraph 421
skiagraphy
   shadow 421
   representation 554, 556
skid *support* 215
   hindrance 706
skies (*see* sky)
   exalt to the—873
   praise to the—933
skiff 273
skill **698**
   acquisition of—539
   game of—840
skillet 191, 386
skillful 698
skim *move* 266
   navigate 267
   rapid 274
   neglect 460
   summarize 596
skimp 460
skin *outside* 220
   tegument 223
   peel 226
   thief 792
   mere—*and bone* 203
   —*a flint*
      impossible 471
      parsimony 819
   —*game* 545
   —*over* 660
   wet to the—339
   with a whole—670
   without—822
skin—deep
   shallow 32, 209
   external 220
skinlike 223
skinned thick—376
   thin—375
skinny *thin* 203

all skin 223
skip *depart* 293
   jump 309
   neglect 460
   rejoice 838
   (*amusement* 840)
skipjack
   prosperous 734
   lowborn 876
skipper
   sea captain 269
   captain 745
skippet 191
skippingly 70
skirmish 720
skirmisher 726
skirt *appendix* 39
   pendent 214
   dress 225
   surrounding 227
   edge 231
   side 236
   woman 374
   hang upon the—*s of* 281
   on the—*s of*
   near 197
skirt—dance 840
skirting 231
skit *ridicule* 856
   detraction 934
   prostitute 962
skittish
   capricious 608
   excitable 825
   timid 862
   bashful 881
skittles 840
skive 204
skulk *hide* 528
   cowardly 862
skull 450
skullcap 225
skunk 366, 401
skunk cabbage 401
skurry 684
sky *summit* 210
   world 318
   air 338
sky—aspiring 865
sky—blue 438
skylark 305
skylarking 840
skylight 260
sky line 196
skyrocket 305
skyscraper 210
skyward 210, 305
slab *layer* 204
   support 215
   flat 251
   puddle 343
   viscous 352
   record 551
slabber *slaver* 297
   unclean 653

slabsided   **sluggish**

slabsided 200, 203
slack *loose* 47
   weak 160
   inert 172
   slow 275
   cool 385
   coal 388
   unwilling 603
   insufficient 640
   unprepared 674
   inactive 683
   lax 738
   nonobservant 773
slacken *loosen* 47
   moderate 174
   neglect 460
   repose 687
   hinder 706
   one's pace 275
slacker 623, 927
slade 252
slag *embers* 384
   rubbish 645
   dirt 653
   (*remains* 40)
slake *quench* 174
   gratify 829
   satiate 869
   (*content* 831)
   —*one's appetite*
   intemperance 954
slam *shut* 261
   slap 276
   snap 406
   —the door in one's
    face *oppose* 708
   refuse 764
slammerkin 653
slammock 653
slander 934
slanderer 936
slang 563
slang-whanger 887
slangy 560
slant 217
slap *instantly* 113
   strike 276
   censure 932
   punish 972
   —in the face
    opposition 708
    attack 716
    anger 900
    disrespect 929
    disapprobation 932
   —the forehead 461
slap-bang 406
slap-dash 684
slap-stick 599
slash 44
slashing *style* 574
slate *list* 86
   writing tablet 590
   schedule 611
   plan 626
   —*loose mad* 503

slate-colored 432
slates *roof* 223
slattern *disorder* 59
   dirty 653
   bungler 701
   vulgar 851
   (*negligent* 460)
slatternly
   (*see* slattern)
   unskillful 699
slaughter 361
slaughterhouse 361
slave *servant* 631, 746
   worker 686
   a—to 749
   —to no sect 984
   —*trade* 795
slaver *ship* 273
   slobber 297
   dirt 653
   flatter 933
slavery *toil* 686
   subjection 749
slavish
   servile 746, 886
   subject 749
slay 361
slave 59
sleazy 160
sled 272
sledge 272
sledge hammer 276
   with a—*destroy* 162
   exertion 686
sleek *smooth* 255
   pretty 845
sleep *inactivity* 683
   balmy—683
   last—360
   not have a wink of—
    825
   put to—376
   rock to—*smooth* 174
   send to—841
   —at one's post 683
   —upon *defer* 133
    consider 451
   —with one eye open
    459
sleeper *support* 215
   wake the seven—s
    404
sleeping car 272
sleeping partner 683
sleepless *active* 682
sleepwalker 268
sleepwalking 266
sleepy 683
sleet 383
sleeve *skein* 219
   dress 225
   hang on the—of 746
   in one's—*hidden* 528
   laugh in one's—
    latency 526
   rejoice 838

   hope 856
   wear one's heart
    upon one's
   —*manifest* 525
   artless 703
sleeveless *foolish* 499
   unreasonable 608
   —*errand useless* 645
   unskillful 699
sleigh 272
sleight *skill* 698
   —of hand
   deception 545
   (*interchange* 146)
slender *small* 32
   thin 203
   trifling 643
   —*means* 804
sleuth 527
   —*hound* 913
slice *cut* 44
   piece 51
   layer 204
slick *smooth* 255
   smart 698
slicker 225
slide *elapse* 109
   smooth 255
   pass 264
   locomotion 266
   descend 306
   —back 661
   —in 228
   —into 144
slide valve 263
sliding
   amusement 840
sliding panel 545
sliding rule 85
slight *small* 32
   shallow 209
   rare 322
   neglect 460
   disparage 483
   feeble 575
   trifle 643
   dereliction 927
   disrespect 929
   contempt 930
slight-made 203
slily
   surreptitiously 544
   craftily 702
slim 203 *cunning* 702
slime *viscous* 352
   dirt 653
sling *hang* 214
   project 284
   weapon 727
   drink 959
slink *hide* 528
   cowardice 862
   —*away avoid* 623
   disrepute 874
   (*escape* 671)
slinky 203

slip *small* 32
   elapse 109
   child 129
   strip 205
   descend 306
   error 495
   workshop 691
   fail 732
   false coin 800
   vice 945
   guilt 947
   give one the—671
   let—*liberate* 750
   lose 776
   relinquish 782
   let—the dogs of war
    722
   —away 187, 623
   —*cable* 623
   —in (*or* —into) 294
   —of the pen 495, 568
   —of the tongue
    solecism 568
    stammering 583
   —on 225
   —over *neglect* 460
   —the collar
    escape 671
    free oneself 750
   —the memory 506
   —through the fingers
    miss an opportunity
    135
    escape 671
    fail 732
   —'twixt cup and lip
    509
slipper 225
   hunt the—840
slippery *transient* 111
   smooth 255
   greasy 355
   uncertain 475
   vacillating 607
   dangerous 665
   facile 705
   nonobservant 773
   faithless 940
   —*ground* 667
slipshod 575
slipslop *absurdity* 497
   solecism 568
   weak language 575
slit *divide* 44
   chink 198
   furrow 259
sliver 51
slobber *drivel* 297
   slop 337
   dirt 653
sloe *black* 431
slogan 722
sloop 273
   —of-war 726
slop *spill* 297
   water 337

   dirt 653
slope *oblique* 217
   run away 623
sloping 306
sloppy *moist* 339
   marsh 345
   style 575
slops *clothes* 225
slosh 337, 653
slot 260
sloth 683
slouch *low* 207
   oblique 217
   move slowly 275
   inactive 683
slouching *ugly* 846
slough *covering* 223
   divest 226
   quagmire 345
   dirt 653
   difficulty 704
   adversity 735
   (*remains* 40)
   —of Despond 859
sloughy 226
sloven *untidy* 59
   bungler 701
   vehicle 272
slovenly *untidy* 59
   careless 460
   style 575
   dirty 653
   awkward 699
   vulgar 851
slow *tardy* 133
   inert 172
   moderate 174
   motion 275
   inactive 683
   wearisome 841
   dull 843
   be-to *unwilling* 603
   not finish 730
   refuse 764
   by—degrees 26
   march in—time 275
   —down 174
   —movement
    music 415
slow-burning 388
slow coach 701
slowness 275
slowworm 419
sloyd 537
slubber *unclean* 653
   (*inactive* 683)
slubberdegullion 876
sludge 653
slug *slow* 275
   printing 591
   inaction 681
   inactivity 683
   bullet 727
   money 800
sluggard 275, 683
sluggish *inert* 172

570

sluice

callous 823
sluice *limit* 233
  egress 295
  river 348
  conduit 350
  open the–s 297
slum 653
slumber 683
slummock 653
slump 304, 306
slung shot 727
slur *stigma* 874
  gloss over 937
  reproach 938
  –over *neglect* 460
  slight 483
  (*exclude* 55)
  (*inattention* 458)
  (*conceal* 528)
slush *marsh* 345
  semiliquid 352
  dirt 653
slut *untidy* 59
  dog 366
  dirty 653
  wench 876
  unchaste 962
  (*neglect* 460)
sly *shrewd* 498
  stealthy 528
  cunning 702
  (*false* 544)
slyboots 702
smack
  small quantity 32
  mixture 41
  boat 273
  impulse 276
  taste 390
  courtesy 894
  kiss 902
  strike 972
  –of *resemble* 17
  –the lips *pleasure* 277
  taste 390
  savory 394
  rejoice 838
small– *in degree* 32
  –*in size* 193
  become–195
  esteem of–account 930
  feel–879
  not think–beer of oneself 880
  of–account 643
  on a–scale 32, 193
  –arms 727
  –beer 643
  –bore 727
  –chance 473
  –coin 800
  –fry *littleness* 193
  unimportant 643
  commonalty 876
  –hours 125

–matter 643
–number 103
–part 51
–talk 588
think no–beer of oneself 878
think–beer of 930
smallclothes 225
smaller *in degree* 34
  in size 195
smallness 32
smalls 225
smalt 438
smart *pain* 378
  active 682
  clever 698
  feel 821
  grief 828
  witty 842
  pretty 845
  ornamental 847
  –pace 274
  –saying 842
  –set 852
  –under 821
smarten 847
smart money 973
smash *destruction* 162
  failure 732
smasher 792
smatch 390
smatterer 493
smattering 491
smear *cover* 223
  grease 355
  soil 653
smeared 426
smell 398, 401
  bad–401
  –a rat 485
  –of the lamp
    ornate style 577
  prepared 673
  –powder 722
smell-feast 886
smelling bottle 400
smelt *heat* 384
  prepare 673
smicker 838
smile *cheerful* 836
  rejoice 838
  raise a–840
  –at 856
  –of contempt 930
  –of fortune 734
  –upon *aid* 707
  courtesy 894
  endearment 902
smirch *blacken* 431
  dirty 653
smirk 838
smite *maltreat* 649
  excite 824
  afflict 830
  punish 972
  (*strike* 276)

smith 690
smitten *love* 897
  –with *moved* 615
smock *clothing* 225
  wrinkle 258
smock-faced 862
smock frock 225
smoke *dust* 330
  vapor 336
  heat 382
  tobacco 392
  discover 480a
  suspect 485
  unimportant 643
  dirt 653
  end in–
    shortcoming 304
    failure 732
  –the calumet of peace 723
smoke bomb 727
smoked glasses 424
smokejack 312
smoke screen 424
smokeshaft 351
smoker *concert* 892
smokestack 260, 351
smoke talk 584
smoking hot 382
smoking jacket 225
smoking room 191
smoky *opaque* 426
  dirty 653
smolder *inert* 172
  burn 382
  latent 526
smooth *uniform* 16
  calm 174
  make level 213
  flat 251
  not rough 255
  easy 705
  –as glass 255
  –down 174
  –over 174
  –sailing 705
  –the bed of sickness *aid* 707
  benevolence 906
  the ruffled brow of care 834
  –the way *facilitate* 705
  –water *easy* 705
smooth bore 727
smoothly
  (*see* smooth)
  go on
  –*prosperous* 734
smoothness 255
smooth-tongued
  lie 544
  flatter 933
smother *repress* 174
  kill 361
  suppress 528

stifle sound 581
restrain 751
(*abide* 826)
smudge *fuel* 388
  blackness 431
  dirt 653
  blemish 848
smug *affected* 855
smuggle
  introduce 228
  steal 791
  illegal 964
  (*ingress* 294)
smuggler 792
smut *black* 431
  dirt 653
  impurity 961
  (*blemish* 848)
smutch 431
smutty *black* 431
  impure 961
snack
  small quantity 32
  food 298
snacks, go–778
snaffle 706, 752
snag *projection* 250
  sharp 253
  danger 667
  hindrance 706
snail *slow* 275
  mollusk 368
snake *coil* 248
  draw 285
  serpent 366
  hissing 409
  miscreant 913
  scotch the–640
  –in the grass
    hidden 528
    deceiver 548
    bad 649
    source of danger 667
    evildoer 913
    knave 941
snakelike 248, 366
snakestone 248
snap *break* 44
  time 106
  shut 261
  eat 298
  brittle 328
  noise **406**
  impulse 612
  activity 682
  cheapness 815
  rude 895
  –at *seize* 789
  bite 830
  censure 932
  –of the fingers
    trifle 643
  –one's fingers at
    defy 715
    insolence 885
    despise 930

snipe

–one up *censure* 932
–the thread 70
–up *seize* 789
snapdragon 840
snappish 901
snappy *news* 532
snap shot 554
snare *deception* 545
  (*source of danger* 667)
snare drum 417
snarl *growl* 412
  discord 713
  rude 895
  angry 900
  threaten 909
snarled *confused* 523
snatch
  small quantity 32, 51
  seize 789
  by–es 70
  –at *pursue* 622
  seize 789
  –a verdict
    deceive 545
    cunning 702
  –from one's grasp 789
  –from the jaws of death 672
sneak *hide* 528
  coward 862
  servile 886
  base 940
  knave 941
  bad man 949
  –off, –out of 623
  –thief 792
sneakers *shoes* 225
sneer *disparage* 929
  contempt 930
  blame 932
sneeze *blow* 349
  snuffle 409
  not to be–d at 642
  –at *despise* 930
snick
  small quantity 32
  part 51
snicker *rejoicing* 838
  ridicule 856
snide 545
sniff *blow* 349
  odor 398
  discovery 480a
sniffle 349
snifting valve 664
snigger *laugh* 838
  ridicule 856
  disrespect 929
sniggle 545
snip *small quantity* 32
  cut 44
  tailor 225
snipe 298, 366

snippet   **solve**

snippet 32
snip-snap 713
snivel *weep* 839
sniveling *servile* 886
snob *vulgar* 851
   plebeian 876
   servile 886
snobbishness
   flattery 933
snood *headdress* 225
   circle 247
snooze 683
snore *noise* 441
   sleep 683
snort 411, 412
snorter 83
snout 250
snow *ship* 273
   ice 383
   white 430
snow avalanche 383
snow ball 72, 383
snow blindness 443
snow-bound 383
snowdrift 72
snowshoes 225, 266, 272
snowslide 306, 383
snowslip 306, 383
snowstorm 383
snub *short* 201
   hinder 706
   cast a slur 874
   humiliate 879
   bluster 885
   censure 932
snub-nosed
   distortion 243
   (*ugly* 846)
snuff *blow* 349
   pungent 392
   odor 398
   go out like the—of a candle 360
   —out *destroy* 162
   dark 421
   —up *inhale* 296
   smell 398
   up to—*skillful* 698
   cunning 702
snuff-color 433
snuffle *blow* 349
   hiss 409
   stammer 583
   hypocrisy 988
snuffy 653
snug *closed* 261
   comfortable 377
   safe 664
   prepared 673
   content 831
   secluded 893
   keep—*conceal* 528
   seclude 893
   make all
   —*prepare* 673

snuggery 189
snuggle 902
snugness 827
so *similar* 17
   very 31
   therefore 476
   method 627
   —be it *assent* 488
   consent 762
   —far so good 618
   —let it be 681
   —much the better
   content 831
   rejoicing 838
   —much the worse
   discontent 832
   aggravation 835
   —to speak *similar* 17
   metaphor 521
soak *immerse* 300
   water 337
   moist 339
   drunkenness 959
   —up 340
soap *lubricate* 332
   oil 356
soapy *unctuous* 355
   service 886
   flattery 933
soar *great* 31
   height 206
   fly 267
   rise 305
   air 338
sob 839
sober *substantial* 3
   moderate 174
   wise 498
   sane 502
   plain 576
   grave 837
   temperate 953
   abstinent 958
   in—*sadness*
   affirmation 535
   —down 174, 502
   humility 879
   —*senses* 502
   —*truth fact* 494
sober-minded 502
   calm 826
   humble 879
soberness 953
sobriety 958
sobriquet 565
soc *jurisdiction* 965
socage 777
so-called
   deception 545
   misnomer 565
sociable *carriage* 272
   sociality 892
social *mankind* 372
   sociable 892
   —*circle* 892
   —*evil* 961

—gathering 892
—*science* 910
—*service* 602
—*smile* 906
—*worker* 602
socialism
   government 737
   participation 778
   philanthropy 910
Socialists 712
sociality 892
society *mankind* 372
   party 712
   fashion 852
   sociality 892
   laity 997
   position in—873
sociological 537
   —school 451
sociology 910
sociopath 821a
socius criminis 711
sock *hosiery* 225
   drama 599
sockdolager 67, 479
socket *receptacle* 191
   concave 252
socle 215
Socratic method 461
Socratic school 451
sod 344
   beneath the—363
sodality *party* 712
   friendship 888
   (*sociality* 892)
sodden *moist* 339
   boiled 384
sofa 215
soft *stop!* 142
   weak 160
   moderate 174
   smooth 255
   not hard 324
   moist 339
   marsh 345
   silence! 403
   —*sound* 405
   dulcet 413
   credulous 486
   silly 499
   lenient 740
   tender 822
   timid 862
   (*docile* 602)
   (*irresolute* 605)
   own the—
   impeachment 529
   —buzzing *slander* 934
   —*music* 415
   —*pedal* 405
   —sawder *plea* 617
   flattery 933
   —snap 681
   —soap *oil* 356
   flattery 933
   —thing 681

—tongue,—words 894
soften (*see soft*)
   moderate 174
   relieve 834
   pity 914
   palliate 937
   penitent 950
   —down 834
softening 324
   —of the brain 158
softer sex 374
soft-hearted 914
softling 160
softness 324
   persuasibility 615
soft-spoken 894
soggy 339
soho *attention* 457
   parley 586
   hunting 622
soi-distant
   asserting 535
   misnomer 565
   vain 880
soil *region* 181
   land 342
   dirt 653
   deface 846
   (*spoil* 659)
   (*blemish* 848)
   till the—
   agriculture 371
   prepare 673
soilure 653
soirée 892
sojourn *dwell* 186
   abode 189
   (*rest* 265)
sojourner 188
soke 181
solace *relief* 834
   recreation 840
   —oneself with
   pleasure 827
solar 318 —system 318
solatium 973
sola topi 225
soldan 745
solder *join* 43
   cement 45
   cohere 46
soldier 726
soldierlike *war* 722
   brave 861
sole *alone* 87
   base 211
   support 215
   fish 298
   *feme—*904
solecism
   ungrammatical 568
   (*sophistry* 477)
solemn
   affirmation 535
   important 642
   grave 837

glorious 873
ostentatious 882
commemoration 883
religious 987
worship 990
—*avowal* 535
—*declaration* 535
—*mockery* 882
—*silence* 403
solemnity *rite* 998
solemnization 883
sol-fa 416
solfeggio 415
solferino 434, 437
solicit *induce* 615
   request 765
   desire 865
   —the attention 457
solicitor *agent* 758
   petitioner 767
   merchant 797
   lawyer 968
solicitous 765, 865
solicitude *care* 459
   pain 828
   anxiety 860
   desire 865
solid *complete* 52
   dense 321
   certain 474
   learned 490
   exact 494
   wise 498
   persevering 604a
   —in galleys 591
solidarity *party* 712
solidify 48, 321
solidity (*see* solid)
   solvency 800
solidungulate 366
soliloquist 589
soliloquy 589
soliped 366
solitaire *game* 840
   hermit 893
solitary *alone* 87
   secluded 893
solitude 87, 893
solmization 415
solo 415
soloist 996
Solomon 498, 500
Solon 498, 500
solstice *dance* 372a
soluble *fluid* 333
   liquefy 335
solus 87
solution *fluid* 333
   liquefaction 335
   music 413
   answer 462
   explanation 522
   —of continuity 70
solve *liquefy* 335
   discover 480a
   unriddle 522

solvency

solvency (see solvent)
solvent
  decomposition 49
  liquefier 335
  diluent 337
  sound 800
  moneyed 803
  payment 807
Somali 372a
somatics 316
somatist 316, 989
somatologist 316
somatology 316
somber *dark* 421
  color 428
  black 431
  gray 432
  sad 837
sombrero 225
some
  indefinite quantity 25
  small quantity 32
  more than one 100
  at—other time 119
  in—degree degree 26
  small 32
  in—place 182
  —ten or a dozen 102
  —time ago 122
  —time or other 119
somebody *person* 372
  important 642
  distinguished 873
somehow 155
  —or other *cause* 155
  instrument 831
somersault 218
something *thing* 3
  small degree 32
  matter 316
  —else 15
  —like 17
  —or other 475
sometimes 136
somewhat *a little* 32
  a trifle 643
somewhere 182
  —about 32
somnambulism
  walking 266
  trance 515
somnambulist
  walker 268
  dreamer 515
somnifacient 683
somniferous
  sleepy 683
  weary 841
somnolence 683
Somnus 683
son 167
  (see sons *below*)
Son, God the—976
sonant 402, 561
sonata 415

Sonderbund 769
song *music* 415
  poem 597
  death—death 360
  lament 839
  for a mere—815
  love—597
  no—no supper 812
  old—643
song bird 416
song leader 416
songster 416
soniferous 402
sonification 402
sonnet 597
sonneteer 597
sonorescence 402
sonorous *sound* 402
  loud 404
  language 577
sons—of Belial 988
  —of God 977
  —of Martha 876
sontag 225
soon *transient* 111
  future 121
  early 132
  expected 507
  too—for 135
sooner—or later
  another time 119
  future 121
  —said than done 704
soot *black* 431
  dirt 653
sooth *prediction* 511
  in good—543
soothe *allay* 174
  relieve 834
  flatter 933
  (*calm* 826)
soothing
  faint sound 405
  —syrup 174
soothsay 511
soothsayer *oracle* 513
  magician 994
soothsaying 511
sootiness 421
sop *small quantity* 32
  food 298
  sodden 339
  fool 501
  inducement 615
  reward 973
  —in the pan 615
  —to Cerberus 458
soph *scholar* 492
  student 541
Sophism 451
sophism
  bad logic 477
  absurdity 497
sophist *scholar* 492
  dissembler 548
sophister 492

student 541
sophistical 477
sophisticate *mix* 41
  debase 659
sophisticated
  spurious 545
sophistry 477
sophomore 492, 541
soporific *sleepy* 683
  weary 841
soporose 683
soprano 410
sorcerer 548, **994**
sorcery 511, **992**
sordes 653
sordet 417
sordid *stingy* 819
  covetous 865
sordine 405, 408a, 417
sore *bodily pain* 378
  disease 655
  mental suffering 828, 830
  discontent 832
  anger 900
  —place 822
  —subject 830, 900
sorely *very* 31
sorghum 396
sorites 476
sororal 906
sorority 712, 888
sorosis 888
sorrel 433
sorrow 828
  give—words 839
  more in—than anger 900
  patient 826
  forgiveness 918
sorry *trifling* 643
  grieved 828
  mean 876
  (*small* 32)
  (*bad* 649)
  be—for *pity* 914
  repent 750
  cut a—figure 874
  in a—plight
  failure 732
  make a—face 874
  —sight *painful* 830
  sad 837
sort *degree* 26
  arrange 60
  kind 75
  —with *sociality* 892
sortable 23
sortes
  chance 156, 621
  —Virgilianae
  sorcery 992
sortie 716
sortilege
  prediction 511
  sorcery 992

sortilegy 621
sortition 621
sorts, out of—
  ill health 655
  sulky 901a
so—so *small* 32
  trifling 643
  imperfect 651
sossle 653
sot *fool* 501
  drunkard 959
soterial 976
soteriology 976
sotnia 726
sotto voce
  faint sound 405
  conceal 528
  voiceless 581
sou *money* 800
soubrette 599, 746
soufflé 298
sough *conduit* 350
  faint sound 405
  cloaca 653
soul *essence* 5
  person 372
  intellect 450
  genius 498
  affections 820
  (*whole* 50)
  (*important* 642)
  flow of—588
  have one's whole—
    in his work 686
  not a—187
  not dare to say
    one's—is his own
  subjection 749
  fear 860
  —of wit 572
soulless *inactive* 683
  insensible 823
soul—mate 903
soul—sick 837
soul—stirring
  emotion 821
  excitement 824
sound *great* 31
  conformable 82
  stable 150
  strong 159
  fathom 208
  —of a fish 334
  bay 343
  noise **402**
  resonance 408
  investigate 461
  measure 466
  true 494
  wise 498
  sane 502
  good 648
  perfect 650
  healthy 654
  solvent 800
  orthodox 983a

southpaw

catch a—418
full of—and fury
  unmeaning 517
  insolent 885
safe and—*health* 654
  preserved 670
—a retreat 283
—asleep 683
—a trumpet
  publish 531
  alarm 669
—mind 502
—of limb 654
—of wind 654
—reasoning 476
—sleep 683
—the alarm
  indication 550
  warning 668
  alarm 669
  fear 860
—the horn 416
—the note of
  preparation 673
—the praises of 931
soundable 310
sounding 402
  big—577
  —brass 517
sounding—board 417
soundings 208
soundless
  unfathomable 208
  silent 403
soundness
  —of doctrine 983a
soup *food* 298
  semiliquid 352
soupçon *small* 32
  mixture 41
sour *acid* 397
  discontented 832
  embitter 835
  uncivil 895
  sulky 901
  —grapes
  impossible 471
  excuse 617
  —the temper 830
source *beginning* 66
  cause 153
sourdet 417
sourdine 417 à la
  —*noiseless* 405
  concealed 528
soured 832
  discontented 832
sourness 397
souse *plunge* 306, 310
  water 337
south *direction* 278
  north and—
  opposite 237
Southern 237
—Cross 318
southpaw 239

573

South Pole

South Pole 383
southward 237
souvenir 505
sovereign *superior* 33
  all-powerful 159
  authoritative 737
  ruler 745
  —*contempt* 930
  —*remedy* 662
sovereignty 737
  (*see* sovereign)
sow *scatter* 73
  pig 366
  agriculture 371
  female 374
  get the wrong—by
    the ear
  misjudgment 481
  error 495
  mismanage 699
  fail 732
  —*broadcast* 818
  —*dissension*
    discord 713
    hate 898
  —one's wild oats
    improve 658
    amusement 840
    vice 945
    intemperance 954
  —the sand 645
  —the seed
    prepare 673
  —the seeds of
    cause 153
    teach 537
sowar 726
sower 371
sozzle 653
spa *town* 189
  sanatorium 662
space *music* 26, 413
  arrange 60
  time 106
  occasion 134
  extension 180
  printing 591
  celestial—s 318
spaddle 272
spade 272
  call a—a spade
    plain language 576
    straightforward 703
spade husbandry
  371
spahi 726
span *similarity* 17
  join 43
  link 45
  duality 89
  time 106
  transient 111
  small 193
  distance 196
  near 196
  length 200

short 201
—*of horses* 272
  measure 466
spangle *spark* 420
  ornament 847
spaniel *dog* 366
  servile 886
  (*flatterer* 935)
Spanish fly 171
spank *swift* 274
  flog 792
spanking *large* 192
  —*pace* 274
span-new 123
spar *beam* 214
  quarrel 713
  contend 720
spare *small* 193
  meager 203
  refrain 623
  store 636
  scanty 640
  redundant 641
  disuse 678
  inaction 681
  relinquish 782
  give 784
  economy 817
  exempt 927a
  temperate 953
  enough and to—639
  not a moment to—
    682
  —*diet* 956
  —no expense 816
  —no pains 686
  —room 180
  —time 685
  to—641
spared, be— *live* 359
  it cannot be—630
sparge 337
spargefaction
  scatter 73
  wet 337
sparger 337
sparing (*see* spare)
  small 32
  economy 817
  parsimony 819
  temperate 953
  —of praise 932
  —of words 585
  with a—hand 819
  with no—hand 639
spark *small* 32
  heat 382
  light 420
  luminary 423
  wag 844
  fop 854
  as the—s fly
    upwards
  habit 613
sparkle *bubble* 353
  glisten 420

sparkling
  vigorous 574
  excitement 824
  cheerful 836
  wit 842
  beauty 845
  with—eyes 827
spark plug 272
sparrow *bird* 366
  love 897
sparse 73, 103
sparseness 73, 103, 137
Spartacus 742
Spartan 739
spasm
  sudden change 146
  violence 173
  agitation 315
  pain 378
spasmodic
  discontinuous 70
  irregular 139
  changeable 149
  violent 173
  —*cholera* 655
spat
  production 161, 167
  quarrel 713
spathic 204
spats 225
spatter *dirt* 653
  (*damage* 659)
  (*defame* 634)
spatterdash 225
spatula *receptacle* 191
  vehicle 272
spavined 655
spawn
  offspring 161, 167
  productiveness 168
  dirt 653
spay 38, 158
speak *voice* 580
  speech 582
  —for 937
  —for itself
    intelligible 518
    manifest 525
  —ill of *censure* 932
    detract 934
  —low 581
  —of *meaning* 516
    publish 531
    speak 582
    (*describe* 594)
  —one fair 894
  —out *make*
    manifest 525
    artless 703
    artless 703
  —softly 581
  —to 586
  —up 411
  —up for 937
  —volumes 467

—well of 931
speaker
  interpreter 524
  soliloquy 589
  chairman 694
speaking 582
  much—584
  on—terms 888
  —*likeness* 554
  —of 134
  way of—521
speaking trumpet 418
spear *pierce* 260
  weapon 727
spearman 726
spear-shaped 253
special *particular* 79
  (*intrinsic* 5)
speciality 79
specialize 79, 662
special pleader 968
special pleading
  sophistry 477
specialty *compact* 769
  security 771
specie 800
species *kind* 75
  appearance 448
  human—372
specific *special* 79
  remedy 662
  —*gravity* 321
specification *class* 75
  description 594
specify
  particularize 79
  tell 527
  name 564
specimen 82
specious *probable* 472
  sophistical 477
  showy 846
  flattering 933
  pardonable 937
speck
  small quantity 32
  inextension 180a
  (*dot* 193)
  (*blemish* 848)
specked *imperfect* 651
speckle *variegate* 440
  blemish 848
spectacle
  appearance 448
  prodigy 872
  show 882
  drama 599
spectacles 441, 445
spectacular 599, 882
spectator 197, **444**
specter
  fallacy of vision 443
  ugly 846
  ghost 361, 980a, 992a

spell

spectral *inexistence* 2
  unsubstantial 4
  uncanny 980a
spectrogram 554
spectroheliogram 554
spectroheliography 554
spectrometer 445
spectroscope
  light 420
  color 428
  optical instrument 445
spectrum *color* 428
  variegation 440
  optical illusion 443
speculate *view* 441
  think 451
  suppose 514
  chance 621
  essay 675
  traffic 794
speculation
  experiment 463
  cards 840
speculative
  thought 451
  experiment 463
  supposition 514
  unsound 665
speculator
  experiment 463
  theorist 514
  chance 621
sped *completed* 729
speech 582
  figure of—521
  parts of—567
  —from the throne 695
  —of angels *music* 415
speechify 582
speechless 403, 581
speechmaker 582
speed *journey* 266
  velocity 274
  activity 682
  help 707
  succeed 731
  —mania 274
  —maniac 268
  —the parting guest 293
  with breathless—684
speedily *soon* 132
speedometer 200, 274, 551
  automobile 272
speedway 626
spell *period* 106
  influence 175
  read 539
  letter 561
  necessity 601
  motive 615
  exertion 686

spellbind — spontaneous

charm **993**
cast a– 992
wonder 870
–out *interpret* 522
spellbind 586
spellbound 601, 615
spelling 561
spence 636
spencer 225
spend *effuse* 297
  waste 638
  give 784
  purchase 795
  expend 809
  –*freely* 816
  –*one's time in* 625
  –*time* 106
  –*time in* 683
spendthrift 818
spent *weak* 160
  tired 688
sperm 153
spermaceti 356
spermary 357
spermatic 168
spermatize 168
spermatophytes 369
spermatozoön 357
sperm gland 357
spew 297
sphacelate 659
sphacelation 655
spacelus 655
sphere *rank* 26
  space 180
  region 181
  ball 249
  world 318
  business 625
  –*of influence* 786
spheroid 249
spherule 249
sphery 318
sphinx *monster* 83
  oracle 513
  ambiguous 520
  riddle 533
spial 668
spice
  small quantity 32
  mixture 41
  pungent 392
  condiment 393
spiced *taste* 390
spicilegium
  assemblage 72
  allocution 596
spick and span 123
spiculate 253
spicules 490d
spiculum 253
spicy *fragrant* 400
  exciting 824
spider *animal* 368
  receptacle 191
  pan 386

spieler 548, 792
spigot 263
spike *sharp* 253
  pierce 260
  plug 263
  (*pass through* 302)
  –*guns powerless* 158
  useless 645
spikebit 262
spike team 92, 272
spile 263 –*hole* 351
spill *filament* 205
  stopper 263
  shed 297
  splash 348
  match 388
  waste 638
  lavish 818
  (*misuse* 679)
  –*and pelt* 59
  –*blood* 722
spin *journey* 266
  aviation 267
  rotate 312
  –*a long yarn exaggerate* 549
  –*out protract* 110
  late 133
  prolong 200
  diffuse style 573
spinach 298
spinal 222, 235
spindle 312
spindle-shanks 203
spindle-shaped 253
spindrift 353
spine 253
spinel 847
spineless *weak* 945
spinet *copse* 367
  harpsichord 417
spinney 367
spinosity
  unintelligible 519
  discourtesy 895
  sullenness 901a
spinous *prickly* 253
Spinozism 451
spinster 374, 904
spinuliferous 253
spiny 253
spiracle 260, 351
spiral 248, 311
spire *height* 206
  peak 253
  soar 305
spiriferous 248
spirit *essence* 5
  immateriality 317
  intellect 450
  meaning 516
  vigorous language 574
  stimulate 615
  activity 682
  affections 820

courage 861
ghost 361, 980
evil–**980**a
keep one's–*up hope* 858
–*away* 791
–*control* 992a
–*of my dream* 515
–*of myrcia* 400
–*up induce* 615
excite 824
unclean– 978
with life and– 682
Spirit, the Holy– 976
spirited *language* 574
  active 682
  sensitive 822
  cheerful 836
  dashing 852
  brave 861
  generous 942
spiritism 317, 992a
spiritist 317, 450
spiritistic 317
spiritless
  insensible 823
  sad 837
  cowardly 862
spiritoso *music* 415
spirit rapping 992a
spirits *drink* 298
  cheer 836
spirit-stirring 824
spiritual
  immaterial 317
  psychical 450
  divine 976
  pious 987
  –*director* 996
  –*existence* 987
  –*wife* 903, 962
spiritualism
  immateriality 317
  intellect 450
  heterodoxy 984
  psychical research 992a
spiritualist 317
spiritualize 317
spirituel 842
spiroid 248
spirograph 662
spirometer 662
spirt *eject* 297
  stream 348
  haste 684
  exertion 686
spirtle *disperse* 73
  splash 348
spissitude *dense* 321
  viscid 352
spit *pointed* 253
  perforate 260
  eject 297, 299
  rain 348
  –*fire irascible* 901

spite 907 *envy* 921
  in–*of*
  disagreement 24
  counteraction 179
  opposition 708
  in–*of one's teeth unwilling* 603
spiteful
  malevolent 907
  hating 898
spittle 299
spittoon 191
splanchnic 221, 329
splanchnology 221, 329
splash *affuse* 337
  stream 348
  spatter 653
  parade 882
  make a–*fame* 873
  display 882
splashboard 666
splayfooted 243
spleen
  melancholy 837
  hatred 898
  anger 900
  sullen 901a
  harbor– 907
spleenless 906
splendiferous 851
splendor *bright* 420
  beautiful 845
  glorious 873
  display 882
splenetic *sad* 837
  morose 901a
splice *join* 43
  cross 219
  interjacent 228
  repair 660
  –*the main brace tipsy* 959
spliced, be–
  marriage 903
splint 215, 662, 752
splinter
  small piece 32
  divide 44
  filament 205
  brittle 328
  (*part* 51)
split *divide* 44
  bisect 91
  brittle 328
  divulge 529
  quarrel 713
  fail 732
  laugh 838
  –*hairs discriminate* 465
  sophistry 477
  –*one's sides* 838
  –*the difference mean* 29
  compromise 774

–*the ears loud* 404
  stridor 410
  deafness 419
  –*the lungs* 411
  –*upon a rock* 732
splurge 882
splutter *energy* 171
  spit 297
  stammer 583
  haste 684
spoil *waste* 638
  vitiate 659
  botch 699
  hinder 706
  lenity 740
  plunder 791
  booty 793
  satiate 869
  (*bad* 649)
  –*s of time* 106
  –*sport* 706
  –*trade* 708
spoiled child
  satiated 869
  favorite 899
  –*of fortune* 734
spoiler 792
spoke *radius* 200
  tooth 253
  obstruct 706
  put a–*in one's wheel render powerless* 158
  hinder 706
spokesman
  interpreter 524
  speaker 582
spoliate 791
spoliative 793
spondee 597
sponge *stopper* 263
  moisten 339
  dry 340
  pulpiness 354
  marine animal 368
  clean 652
  despoil 791
  drunkard 959
  apply the–
  obliterate 552
  nonpayment 808
  –*out* 552
sponger 886
sponging-house 752
spongy *porous* 252
  soft 324
  squashy 345
sponsion 771
sponsor *witness* 467
  security 771
  be–*for promise* 768
  obligation 926
sponsorship 771
spontaneous
  voluntary 600
  willing 602

575

spontoon — squeamish

impulsive 612
—generation 357
spontoon 727
spoof 545
spook 361, 980a
  fish 368
spool 312
spoon *receptacle* 191
  ladle 272
  bill and coo 902
  born with a silver— in one's mouth 734
spoondrift 353
Spoonerism 495
spoonful *some* 25
  small quantity 32
spoon-meat 298
spoony *foolish* 499
  lovesick 902
spoor 550
sporaceous 330
sporadic
  unassembled 73
  infrequent 137
  disease 655, 657
spore 330
sporogenous 161
sporophyte 357
sporous 330
sport *killing* 361
  chase 622
  amusement 840
  show off 882
  (*enjoyment* 827)
  in—pastime 840
  humor 842
  —*of fortune* 735
  —*one's oak* 893
  the—of 749
sporting *killing* 361
  contention 720
  amusement 840
  —*dog* 366
sportive *gay* 836
  frolicsome 840
sportsman 361, 622, 840
sportswoman 840
sportulary 784, 785
sportule 784
sporule 330
sposh 653
spot *inextension* 180a
  place 182
  discover 480a
  mark 550
  dirt 653
  blemish 848
  blot 874
  (*decoloration* 429)
  (*sully* 846)
  (*disgrace* 940)
  on the—
  —*instantly* 113
  present time 118

soon 132
in one's presence 186
spotless *perfect* 650
  clean 652
  innocent 946
  (*beautiful* 845)
spotlight 423, 550, 599
spotted
  variegated 440
  damaged 659
  ugly 846
spotter *aviator* 269a
spousal 903
spouse *companion* 88
  married 903
spouseless 904
spout *egress* 295
  flow out 348
  conduit 350
  speak 582
  act 599
  pawn 771
  (*lend* 787)
sprag 633
sprain *powerless* 158
  weak 160
sprat
  —*to catch a herring barter* 794
  —*to catch a whale bungling* 699
sprawl *length* 200
  horizontal 213
  descend 306
spray *sprig* 51
  atomizer 336
  foam 353
  foliage 367
  flowers 400
spread *enlarge* 35
  disperse 73
  universalize 78
  expanse 180
  expand 194
  diverge 291
  meal 298
  publish 531
  —*abroad* 531
  —*a shade* 421
  —*canvas* 267
  —*out* 194
  —*sail* 267
  —*the toils* 545
  —*to* 196
spread-eagle 884
spree 840
sprig *branch* 51
  infant 129
sprightly *cheerful* 836
  witty 842
spring *early* 125
  source 153
  strength 159
  velocity 274
  recoil 277

fly 293
leap 309
elasticity 325
rivulet 348
instrument 633
store 636
remedy 662
—*a leak imperfect* 651
  damage 659
—*a mine destroy* 162
  unexpected 508
  attack 716
—*a project* 626
—*back* 277
—*from* 154
—*of life* 131
—*s of action* 615
—*tide flood* 31, 35, 52
  high 206
  water 337
  wave 348
  (*abundance* 639)
—*to one's feet* 307
—*up begin* 66
  event 151
  grow 194
  ascend 305
  visible 446
—*upon* 508, 789
spring balance 319
springe 545
Springfield rifle 727
spring gun 545, 667
springle 545
spring-net 545
springtide *youth* 127
springy 325
sprinkle *add* 37
  mix 41
  scatter 73
  wet 337, 348
  variegate 440
  baptize 998
sprinkler 337
sprinkling
  small quantity 32
sprint 274
sprit *sprout* 167
  support 215
sprite *good spirit* 979
  demon 980
sprout *grow* 35, 365
  offspring 167
  expand 194
  —*from result* 154
spruce *tree* 367
  neat 652
  beautiful 845
  —*up* 652, 847
sprue 653
sprung *imperfect* 651
  damaged 659
spry *active* 682
  cheerful 836
  (*skillful* 698)
spud 272

spume 353
spunk 861
spun out
  long time 110
  diffuse style 573
spur *pointed* 250
  sharp 253
  —*a horse* 370
  incite 615
  quicken 684
  on the—of the moment
  instantly 113
  now 118
  soon 132
  opportune 134
  impulse 612
  win—s succeed 731
  glory 873
spurious
  erroneous 495
  false 544
  deceptive 545
  illegitimate 925
spurn *reject* 610
  disdain 930
spurred 253
spurt *transient* 111
  swift 274
  gush 348
  impulse 612
  haste 684
  exertion 686
spurtle 73
sputum 299
sputter *emit* 297
  splash 348
  stammer 583
spy *see* 441
  spectator 444
  inquire 461
  informer 527
  emissary 534
  scout 664
  warning 668
spyglass 445
squab *large* 192
  short 201
  broad 202
  bench 215
  nestling 298
squabble 713
squad *assemblage* 72
  soldiers 726
squadron *fighters* 726
  (*crowd* 72)
  (*ships* 273)
squalid *dirty* 653
  unsightly 846
squall *violent* 173
  wind 349
  cry 411
  quarrel 713
squalor 653
squamate 223
squamiferous 223

squamous *layer* 204
  skin 223
squander *waste* 638
  misuse 679
  lose 776
  prodigal 818
squandering 776
squantum 840
square *congruous* 23
  compensate 30
  four 95
  place 182
  houses 189
  perpendicular 212
  form 244
  measure 466
  sparring 720
  justice 924
  honorable 939
  make all— 660
  on the— 939
  —*accounts pay* 807
  account 811
  put a—thing into a round hole 699
  —*deal* 922
  —*inches* 180
  —*piano* 417
  —*the circle* 471
  —*up* 556
  —*with* 23
  —*yards* 180
square-toes 857
squash *destroy* 162
  flatten 251
  blow 276
  fruit 298
  soft 324
  marsh 345
  semiliquid 352
  pulpiness 354
  hiss 409
  —*pie* 298
squashy 345, 352
squat
  locate oneself 184
  little 193
  short 201
  thick 202
  low 207
  sit 308
  (*ugly* 846)
squatter 188
squaw *woman* 374
  wife 903
squeak
  human cry 411
  animal cry 412
  disclosure 529
  (*weep* 839)
squeal (*see* squeak)
squealer 532, 941
squeamish
  unwilling 603
  sick 655
  fastidious 868

(*censorious* 932)
squeeze *contract* 195
   condense 321
   embrace 894
   (*narrow* 203)
squeeze out
   extract 301
   give 784
squeezers 840
squelch 162, 251
squib *sound* 406
   lampoon 856
   detraction 934
squid 368
squidgy 201
squiffy 959
squint *look* 441
   defective sight 443
squirarchy 875
squire *aid* 707
   attendant 746
   gentry 875
squireen 875
squirm 315
squirrel *swift* 274
   animal 366
   nimble 682
squirt *eject* 297
   sport 348
stab *pierce* 260
   kill 361
   pain 378, 649
   injure 659
stability 16, **150**
   (*quiescence* 265)
   (*perseverance* 604a)
stabilize 150
stable *firm* 150
   house 189, 370
   store 636
   lock the–door when the steed is stolen
   too late 135
   useless 645
   bungling 699
  –*companion* 890
  –*equilibrium* 150
staccato 415
stack *assemblage* 72
   store 636
staddle 215
   infant 129
stadtholder 745
staff *support* 215
   music 413, 415
   signal 550
   council 696
   party 712
   weapon 727
   chief 745
   retinue 746
   (*directors* 694)
   (*hope* 858)
   pastoral–999
  –*officer* 745
  –of honor 128

  –of life 298
  –of office 747
stag *deer* 366
   male 373
   defaulter 808
   sociality 892
  –*dance* 840
  –*party* 892
  –the market 794
stage *degree* 26
   term 71
   time 106
   position 183
   layer 204
   platform 215
   forum 542
   drama 599
   arena 728
   come upon the–446
   go off the
  –*depart* 293
   on the–*manifest* 525
   theatrical 599
  –*business* 599
  –*direction* 697
  –*effect display* 882
  –*manager* 599
  –*name* 565
  –*play* 599
  –*player* 599
  –*whisper* 580
stagecoach 272
stagecraft 599
stager *player* 599
   doer 690
   old–130
stage–struck 599
stagger *slow* 275
   totter 314
   agitate 315
   unexpected 508
   dissuade 616
   feeling 821
   affect 824
   astonish 870
  –*belief doubt* 485
  –like a drunken man *irresolute* 605
staggers 315
Stagirite 850
stagnant *inert* 172
   quiescent 265
   unprogressive 659
stagnate 265
   (*persist* 141)
stagnation
   inertness 172
   quiescence 265
   inaction 681
stagy *drama* 599
   affected 855
staid *wise* 498
   calm 826
   grave 837
stain *coating* 223
   color 428

   dirt 653
   spoil 659
   blemish 848
   disgrace 874
   (*deface* 846)
   (*dishonor* 940)
  –*paper writing* 590
stained, travel–266
stainless *clean* 652
   honorable 939
   innocent 946
stair 305, 627
staircase 305
stairway 305, 306
stake *fastening* 45
   wager 621
   danger 665
   security 771
   property 780
   lay down 807
   execution 975
   at–*intended* 620
   in danger 665
stalactite 224
stalagmite 224
stale *old* 124
   insipid 391
   deteriorated 659
   (*undesired* 866)
  –flat and unprofitable 645
  –*news* 532
stalemate 731, 732
stalk *support* 215
   walk 266
   chase 622
  –*abroad generality* 78
   proud 878
stalking 528
stalking–horse
   ambush 530
   plea 617
stall *lateness* 133
   cessation 142
   abode 189
   receptacle 191
   support 215
   theater 599
   mart 799
   churchdom 995
   cathedral 1000
   finger–223
stallion *horse* 271
   male 373
stalwart *strong* 159
   large 192
   (*tall* 206)
stamina *strength* 159
   perseverance 604a
stammel 434
stammering 583
stamp *character* 7
   prototype 22
   kind 75
   form 240
   mark 550

   engraving 558
   complete 729
   security 771
   (*record* 551)
  –in the memory 505
  –out *destroy* 162
   extinguish 385
  –the foot *anger* 900
stampede 860
stanch– *a flow* 348
   persevering 604a
   health 654
   reinstate 660
   honest 939
  –*belief* 484
stanchion 215
stanchless 825
stand *exist* 1
   rank 71
   time 106
   long time 110
   permanent 141
   support 215
   quiescence 265
   difficulty 704
   resistance 719
   brook 821
   patience 826
   brave 861
   at a–681
   come to a–704
   make a–*oppose* 708
   resist 719
  –a chance
   possible 470
   probable 472
  –*aghast* 870
  –*aloof avoidance* 623
   inaction 681
   refuse 764
  –at attention 507
  –at ease 458
  –by *near* 197
   aid 707
   defend 717
  –committed 754
  –fair for 472
  –fast 143, 265
  –fire 861
  –firm *stability* 10
   remain 265
   resist 719
  –first 66
  –for *indicate* 550
   deputy 759
   candidate 763
  –forth *visible* 446
  –in need of 630
  –in one's own light 699
  –in the shoes of 147
  –in the way of 706
  –no nonsense 604
  –of arms 727
  –off *recede* 287
   avoid 623

  –on 215
  –one in 812
  –one in good stead 644
  –one's ground
   preserved 670
   resist 719
  –on one's rights 748
  –out *project* 250
   visible 446
   obstinate 606
  –over 133
  –siege 717
  –still *remain* 141
   stop 265
   difficulty 704
  –the brunt 717
  –the hazard of the die 621
  –the proof 648
  –the test *true* 494
   good 648
  –to one's engagement 772
  –to reason *proof* 478
   manifest 525
   right 922
  –up
   (*see below*)
  –upon *pride* 878
  –well in the opinion of 931
   take one's
  –*resolve* 604
   resist 719
   due 924
   take one's–upon
   reasoning 476
   affirm 535
   plea 617
standard *model* 22
   degree 26
   average 29
   rule 80
   measure 466
   flag 550
   good 648
   perfect 650
standard bearer 726
standardize 58, 466
standing *footing* 8
   degree 26
   long time 110
   permanence 141
   situation 183
   note 873
  –*army* 726
  –dish *rule* 80
   permanent 141
  –jest *wit* 842
  –order *custom* 613
   legality 963
  –water 343
standpatter 150
standpipe 348
standpoint 183, 441

577

standstill *pause* 265
  (see stand still
    above)
stand up *vertical* 212
  elevate 307
  —against *resist* 719
  —fight 720
  —for *applaud* 931
  vindicate 937
stannary court 966
stanza 597
stapes 418
staple *fastening* 45
  whole 50
  peg 214
  texture 329
  material 635
  trade 794
  salable 795
  mart 799
  —commodity 798
star *luminary* 423
  actor 599
  act as a star 599
  destiny 601
  direction 693
  insignia 747
  ornament 847
  glory 873
  noble 875
  decoration 877
  display 882
  —in the ascendant
  success 731
  prosperity 734
  —of fashion 852
starboard 238
starch *stiff* 323
  viscid 352
  affected 855
star-chamber 966
starched *proud* 878
  ostentatious 882
starchy *formal* 882
stare *look* 441
  curiosity 455
  wonder 870
  make one—870
  —one in the face
  destiny 152
  manifest 525
  —out of countenance
  humiliate 879
  insolent 885
  discourteous 895
starfish 368
stargazing 318
staring 446
stark *very* 31
  sheer 32
  complete 52
  hard 323
  —blind 442
  —mad 503
stark-naked 226
stark staring 31

manifest 525
  —mad 503
starlight 422
starlike *pointed* 253
starling 366
starry 318
  —cope of heaven 318
stars (see star)
  worlds 318
  bless one's—916
  —and stripes 550
  —in the firmament
  multitude 102
  under the—338
star-shaped 253
start *begin* 66
  sudden change 146
  arise 151
  impulse 276
  move 284
  depart 293
  leap 309
  unexpected 508
  suggest 514
  crack 659
  offer 763
  fear 860
  wonder 870
  by fits and—s 608
  get the—*precede* 280
  success 731
  give a—to *impel* 276
  have the—*prior* 116
  early 132
  get before 280
  —a doubt 485
  —afresh 66
  —a question 461
  —game 622
  —off 293
  —up *project* 250
  arise 305
  appear 446
starting— hole
  plea 617
  —point *departure* 293
  reasoning 476
startle *doubt* 485
  unexpected 508
  excite 824
  fear 860
  wonder 870
startling 508
starlish 825
starvation
  (see starve)
  insufficiency 640
  fasting 956
starve *cold* 383, 385
  poverty 804
  parsimony 819
  fast 956
starveling *thin* 203
  insufficient 640
  poor 804
state *condition* 7

term 71
speciality 79
nation 372
inform 527
affirm 535
government 737
realm 780
ostentation 882
robes of—747
secretary of—694
—aided school 542
—of affairs 151
—of excitement 821
—of facts *lawsuit* 969
—of siege 722
—paper 551
—room 191
statecraft 693
stated *settled* 150
  at—periods 138
state guard 664, 726
statehouse 966
stately *grand* 873
  proud 878
  pompous 882
statement
  affirmation 535
  description 594
statemonger 694
stateroom 191
states-general 696
statesmanlike 698
statesmanship 692, 693
statewide 78
static 157, 319
statics *strength* 159
  gravity 319
station *degree* 26
  term 71
  place 182
  situation 183
  locate 184
  journey 266
  prison 752
  rank 873
stationary
  permanent 141
  quiescent 265
stationery 590
station house 752
statist 694
statistical 85, 811
statistician 85
statistics
  numeration 85
  lists 86
statuary *sculpture* 557
  sculptor 559
statue 554
  still as a—265
statuette 554
stature 206
status *position* 8
  terms 71
  situation 183

repute 873
status quo *past* 122
  unchanged 145
  restoration 660
statute *act* 697
  law 963
statutory 963
statuvolence 683
staunch (see stanch)
stave *music* 413, 415
  contention 720
  —in *concave* 252
  hole 260
  —off *defer* 133
  hinder 706
stay *time* 106
  wait 133
  continue 141
  stop 142
  dwell 186
  support 215
  not move 265
  not move 265
  neglect 460
  repose 687
  prevent 706
  (dissuade 616)
  (refuge 666)
  —at home 893
  —away 187
  —one's hand
  cease 142
  relinquish 624
  rest 687
stayed (see staid)
staying power 604a
stays *corset* 225
stead 644 in the—of
  substitution 147
  commission 755
  deputy 759
  stand one in good—
    644
steadfast *stable* 150
  persevering 604a
  (quiescent 265)
  —belief 484
  —thought 457
steadfastly 136
steady *regular* 80
  periodic 138
  stable 150
  persevering 604a
  cautious 864
  imperturbable 871
steal 791 —along
  creep 275
  hide 528
  —a march *prior* 116
  early 132
  precede 280
  deceive 545
  active 682
  cunning 702
  —away *avoid* 623
  (escape 671)

—on the ear 405
—upon one
  unexpected 508
stealing 791
stealth
  concealment 528
stealthy 528
  cunning 702
  caution 864
steam *navigate* 267
  gas 334
  vaporize 336
  bubbles 353
  heat 382
  get up—673
  —up 171
  under sail and—274
  under—267
steamboat 273
steam engine 633
  —to crack a nut
  waste 638
  redundance 641
  misuse 679
steamer
  automobile 272
  ship 273
  —track 341
stearine 356
steatopygia 372a
steed 271
steel *strong* 159
  sharp 253
  hard 323
  sword 727
  harden the sensibility
    823
  —blue 438
  —gray 432
  —oneself 604
  —square 466
  —the heart 951
steeled against
  resolved 604
  insensible 823
steel engraving 558
steelyard *weigh* 319
  measurement 466
steep *height* 206
  cliff 212
  slope 217
  sloping 306
  soak 337
steeped 337
  —in iniquity 945
  —in misery 828
steeple *high* 206
  spire 253
steeplechase
  swift 274
  pursuit 622
  contest 720
steer *beast* 366
  male 373
  direct 693
  —clear *turn aside* 279

578

steerable — stir

steerable
  avoid 623
  —for *direction* 278
  —one's course
    conduct 692
steerable 278
steerage 279, 693
steerer *tout* 767
steersman
  mariner 269
  director 694
steganographic 526
steganography
  unintelligible 519
  hidden 528
  writing 590
stellar *starry* 318
  dramatic 599
stellated 253
stelography 590
stem *origin* 153
  ancestor 166
  front 234
  stalk 367
  oppose 708
  —the tide *stop* 142
  resist 719
  —the torrent
    succeed 731
  —to stern 200
stench 401, 663
stencil 556
stenographer 554, 746
stenographic 590
  —*report* 551
stenography 590
stent 233
stentor *cry* 411
stentorian *loud* 404
step *degree* 26
  term 71
  support 215
  motion 264, 366
  measure 466
  expedient 626
  act 680
  (*means* 632)
  but a—197
  dance the back—283
  not stir a—265
  —by step *degree* 26
  order 58
  seriatim 69
  slowly 275
  —forward 282
  —in *mediate* 724
  —in the right
    direction 644
  —into *acquire* 775
  —into the shoes of
    sequence 63
    posteriority 117
    substitution 147
  —lively 682
  —of time 109
  —on

  be supported by 215
  —out 360
  —short 275
  take a decisive—609
steppe 180, 344, 367
stepping-stone
  link 45
  way 627
  instrument 631
  resource 666
  preparation 673
steps *way* 627
  bend one's
  —*travel* 266
  direction 278
  flight of—305
  retrace one's—283
  take—*plan* 626
  prepare 673
  conduct 692
  tread in the—of 281
stercoraceous 653
stercoral 653
stereognosis 379
stereography 591
stereometry 466
stereoscope 445
stereoscopic 446
stereotype *mark* 550
  engraving 558
  printing 591
stereotyped
  stable 150
  habit 613
sterile
  unproductive 169
  uncompleted 730
  abortive 732
sterling *true* 494
  virtuous 944
  (*good* 648)
  —*coin* 800
stern *rear* 235
  resolute 604
  severe 739
  discourteous 895
  —*necessity* 601
  —*truth* 494
sternmost 235
sternutation
  sneeze 349
  sound 409
sternway 267
stern-wheeler 273
stertorous *sound* 402
  voice 583
stet 150
stethograph 466, 662
stethometer 662
stethoscope 418, 466, 662
stevedore *load* 52
  location 184
  carrier 271
  preparation 673
  commonalty 876

stew *food* 298
  heat 382
  cook 384
  difficulty 704
  emotion 821
  excitement 825
  annoyance 828
  bagnio 961
  (*confusion* 59)
  in a—*angry* 900
steward *caterer* 637
  agent 690
  director 694
  consignee 758
  treasurer 801
stewardship
  conduct 692
  direction 693
stewpan 386
stichomancy 511
stick *adhere* 46
  time 106
  cease 142
  continue 143
  staff 215
  stab 260
  remain quiet 265
  fool 501
  bungler 701
  weapon 727
  scourge 975
  dirty end of the—699
  give the—to 972
  —at *doubt* 485
  —*averse* 603
  —at nothing
    resolve 604
    active 682
    rash 863
  —fast *firm* 150
  difficulty 704
  —in 300
  —in one's gizzard
    pain 830
    anger 900
  —in the mud
    come short 304
    fail 732
  —in the throat
    hoarse 581
    not say 585
    dislike 867
  —*law* 972
  —out 250
  —to continue 143
  persevere 604a
  —up *vertical* 212
    elevate 307
    rob 791
  —up for *aid* 707
    applaud 931
    vindicate 937
stickit 732
stickle *reluctant* 603
  obstinate 606

  —for *contend* 720
  barter 794
stickler 606
  severity 739
sticky *cohering* 46
  viscid 352
stiff *rigid* 323
  neglect 460
  style 579
  severe 739
  bore 841
  ugly 846
  affected 855
  haughty 878
  pompous 882
  —*breeze* 349
stiffen 323
stiffneck *pain* 378
stiff-necked 606
stiffness (see *stiff*)
  stability 150
stifle *kill* 361
  silence 403
  conceal 528
  (*destroy* 162)
stifled *faint sound* 405
stifling *hot* 382
stigma *indication* 550
  disgrace 874
stigmatize 874
  censure 932
  accuse 938
stile *way* 627
  hindrance 706
  help a lame dog
    over a—707
stiletto *piercer* 262
  dagger 727
still
  on the other hand 30
  moderate 174
  not moving 265
  vaporization 336
  furnace 386
  silent 403
  (*notwithstanding* 179)
  (allay *excitement* 826)
  in—water 714
  —be doing 686
  —less 467
  —life *matter* 316
  painting 556
  —more *superior* 33
  evidence 467
  —small voice 405
stillatitious 348
stillborn *dead* 360
  failure 732
still-hunt 528, 622
stillicidium 348
stillroom 636
stilted *elevated* 307
  —*style* 577

  ridiculous 853
  affected 855
  boasting 884
stilts *support* 215
  on—*high* 206
  elevated 307
  hyperbolical 549
  proud 878
  boasting 884
stimulant 171, 662
stimulate *energy* 171
  violence 173
  incite 615
  excite 824
stimulating
  (see *stimulate*)
  suggestive 514
stimulus 615
sting *pain* 378
  tingle 380
  poison 663
  excite 824
  mental *suffering* 830
  anger 900
  —on the raw 900
stinging *pungent* 392
stingo 298
stingy 819
stink 401
  —in the nostrils
    unpleasant 830
    dislike 867
    hate 898
stinkball 401
stinkpot 401
stint *degree* 26
  limit 233
  scanty 640
  begrudge 819
stintless 639
stipend *salary* 973
stipendiary
  subject 749
  receiving 785
stipple *variegate* 440
  painting 556
  engraving 558
stipulate *bargain* 769
  conditions 770
  —for 720
stipulation 60, 768
stir *energy* 171
  move 264
  agitation 315
  sensibility 375
  activity 682
  emotion 824
  make a
  —*important* 642
  active 682
  —about 682
  —a question
    inquiry 461
    discuss 476
  —one's stumps
    walk 266

579

stirps

    active 682
   —the blood *excite* 824
   anger 900
   —the embers
    rekindle 163
   excite 824
   —the feelings 824
   —the fire 384
   —up *mix* 41
   violent 173
   excite 824
   (*incite* 615)
   —up dissension 713
stirps *kin* 11
   source 153
   paternity 166
stirring *events* 151
   important 642
   active 682
   —*news* 532
stirrup *support* 215
   with a foot in the—
    293
stirrup cup 293, 959
stitch *junction* 43
   pain 378
   work 680
   —in *time* 132
   —of *work* 686
stiver 800
stoat 360, 401
stoccado 717
stock *kinship* 11
   quantity 25
   origin 153
   paternity 166
   collar 225
   food 298
   fool 501
   habitual 613
   materials 635
   store 636
   property 780
   merchandise 798
   money 800
   (*offspring* 166)
   in—777
   laughing—857
   lay in a—637
   —in trade *means* 632
   store 636
   property 780
   merchandise 798
   —with 637
   take—*inspect* 457
   accounts 811
stockade 717
stocked, well—639
stock exchange 621, 799
stocking 225
stockjobbing 794
stocks *prison* 752
   funds 802
   punishment 975
   on the—*business* 625

   preparation 673
   —and stones
    matter 316
   insensible 823
stock-still 265
stocky 201
stoep 191
stogy 392
stoic (see stoicism)
Stoicism 451
stoicism
   insensibility 823
   inexcitability 826
   disinterested 942
   temperance 953
stoke 388
stoker 268
stole 999
stolen 793—away 671
   —*goods* 793
stolid *unintelligent* 32
   stupid 499
   dull 843
stomach *pouch* 191
   taste 390
   brook 826
   desire 865
   not have the—to
    603
   —of an ostrich 957
   turn the—830
stomacher 225
stomachic 191
stone *heavy* 319
   dense 321
   hard 323
   kill 361
   lithography 558
   material 635
   attack 716
   weapon 727
   punish 972
   cast the first—at 938
   corner—642
   go down like a—310
   heart of
   —*insensible* 823
   cruel 907
   key—642
   mark with a white—
    642
   musical—s 417
   no—unturned
   inquiry 461
   exertion 686
   philosopher's—662
   precious—648
   stepping—627
   —dead 360
   —of Sisyphus 645
   throw a—at
   attack 716
   censure 932
   accuse 938
   throw a—in one's
    own garden

   clumsy 699
   retaliation 718
   throw—s at
    malevolent 907
stone-blind 442
stone-colored 432
stone-deaf 419
Stonehenge 372a
stone's throw 197
stoneware 384
stony 323
stony-hearted
   malevolent 907
   revengeful 919
stook 72
stool 215
   between two—s 704
   —of repentance 950
stool pigeon 545, 548
stoop *receptacle* 191
   slope 217
   lower 308
   submit 725
   humble 879
   servile 886
   dishonorable 940
   —to conquer
    cunning 702
stop *end* 67
   lateness 133
   cease 142
   close 261
   rest 265
   station 266
   silent 403
   remedy 662
   inaction 681
   hinder 706
   prohibit 761
   put a—to 142
   —a flow 348
   —a gap repair 660
   —payment 808
   —short
   discontinue 142
   cease to move 265
   —short of 304
   —the breath 361
   —the ears 419
   —the mouth
   confute 479
   gag 581
   —the sound 408a
   —the way 706
   —to consider 485
   —up 261
stopcock 263
stop-gap
   substitute 147
   stopper 263
stoppage *end* 67
   cessation 142
   hindrance 706
stopper 263
store *location* 184
   stock 636

   shop 799
   (*collection* 72)
   (*abundance* 639)
   in—*destiny* 152
   preparing 673
   lay in a—637
   set no—483
   set-by
   important 642
   commend 931
   —away 184
   —in the memory 505
   —of knowledge 490
storehouse 636
storeroom 636
storeship *ship* 273
   ship of war 726
storge *love* 897
storied *descriptive* 594
stork 366
storm *crowd* 72
   convulsion 146
   violence 173
   agitation 315
   wind 349
   attack 716
   passion 825
   anger 900
   ride the—267
   —brewing 665
   —in a teacup
   overrate 482
   exaggerate 549
   unimportance 643
   blunder 699
   —is up 349
   take by
   —*conquer* 731
   seize 789
storthing 696
story *rooms* 191
   layer 204
   lie 546
   history 594
   as the—goes 532
   the old—897
story-teller 548, 594
stot 366
stound 870
stoup *cup* 191
   altar 1000
stour 59 *large* 192
stout *strong* 159
stout-hearted 861
stove *fireplace* 386
   —in 252
stow *locate* 184
   pack close 195
   store 636
stowage *space* 180
   location 184
stowaway 528
strabism 443
straddle 266
   tergiversation 607
Stradivarius 417

strait

strafe 527
straggle *stroll* 266
   deviate 279
straggler 268
straggling
   disjunction 44
   disorder 59
straight *vertical* 212
   rectilinear 246
   direction 278
   cards 840
   all—*rich* 803
   solvent 807
   —course 628
   —descent 167
   —lined 246
   —poker 840
   —sailing 705
   —shot 278
   —ticket 609
   —up *vertical* 212
straighten
   make straight 246
   remedy 662
   —out 774
straightforward 278
   truthful 543
   artless 703
   honorable 939
straightness 246
straightway 132
strain *race* 11
   continuity 69
   weaken 160
   operation 170
   violence 173
   percolate 295
   transgress 303
   sound 402
   melody 415
   overrate 482
   exaggerate 549
   style 569
   voice 580
   poetry 597
   clean 652
   effort 686
   fatigue 688
   —a point
   go beyond 303
   exaggerate 549
   not observe 773
   undue 925
   —at a gnat and
    swallow a camel
    608
   —every nerve 686
   —in the arms 902
   —one's ears 418
   —one's eyes 441
   —one's invention 515
   —the meaning 523
   —the throat 411
strainer *sieve* 260
strait *interval* 198
   water 343

580

straitened ... stringent

difficulty 704
—s *poverty* 804
straitened *poor* 804
strait-handed 819
strait-laced
  severe 739
  restraint 751
  fastidious 868
  haughty 878
strait-waistcoat
  restrain 751
  means of restraint 752
stramash 720
strand *thread* 205
  land 342
stranded
  stuck fast 150
  in difficulty 704
  failure 732
  pain 828
strange *unrelated* 10
  exceptional 83
  ridiculous 853
  wonderful 870
  —*bedfellows* 713
  —*to say* 870
strangely *much* 31
stranger
  extraneous 57
  a—to ignorant 491
strangle
  render powerless 158
  contract 195
  kill 361
strangulation
  (see **strangle**)
  punishment 972
strap *fasten* 43
  fastening 45, 752
  remedy 662
  punish 972
  instrument of punishment 975
strappado 972
strapping *strong* 159
  big 192
  —*pace* 274
strapwork 847
stratagem
  deception 545
  plan 626
  artifice 702
strategic *plan* 626
  artifice 702
strategist
  planner 626
  director 694
  proficient 700
strategy *conduct* 692
  warfare 722
  (*skill* 698)
strath 252
strathspey 840
stratification
  layers 204

structure 329
stratocracy 737
stratum 204
stratus 353
straw *scatter* 73
  light 320
  unimportant 643
  *catch at—*s
  overrate 482
  credulous 486
  misuse 679
  unskillful 699
  hope 858
  rash 863
  care not a—
  indifference 866
  despise 930
  in the—161
  man of—
  unsubstantial 4
  cheat 548
  insolvent 808
  low person 876
  not worth a—
  trifling 643
  useless 645
  —*bail* 545
  —*bid* 545
  —*bidder* 548
  —to show the wind 463
  the eyes drawing—s 683
strawberry 298
strawboard 593
straw-colored 436
stray *dispersion* 73
  exceptional 83
  traveler 268
  deviate 279
  (*stroll* 266)
streak *long* 200
  narrow 203
  furrow 259
  light 420
  stripe 440
  mark 550
streaked *crossed* 219
  variegated 440
stream *assemble* 72
  move 264
  —*of fluid* **347**
  —*of water* 348
  —*of air* 349
  —*of light* 420
  abundance 639
  against the—708
  —of events 151
  —of time 109
  with the—
  conformity 82
  progression 282
  assent 488
  facility 705
  concord 714
  fashion 852

servility 886
streamer *flag* 550
streamful 348
streaming *loose* 47
  dispread 73
streamlet 348
street *houses* 189
  way 627
  man in the—876
  —*musician* 416
  —*piano* 417
streets
  in the open—525
  on the—961
streetwalker 962
strength *quantity* 25
  degree 26
  greatness 31
  vigor 159
  energy 171
  tenacity 327
  animality 364
  health 654
  put all one's—into 686
  —of mind 604
  tower of—717
strengthen
  increase 35
  reinforce 37
strengthless 160
strenuous
  energetic 171
  persevering 604a
  active 682
  exertion 686
Strephon and Chloe 902
stress *emphasis* 580
  requirement 630
  importance 642
  strain 686
  difficulty 704
  by—*of necessity* 601
  lay—on
  reasoning 476
  —of circumstances
  compulsion 744
  —of weather 349
stretch *expanse* 180
  expand 194
  extend 200
  plain 344
  exaggerate 549
  misrepresent 555
  exertion 686
  encroach 925
  at a—69
  mind on the
  —*thought* 451
  on the—*exertion* 686
  —a point
  —*exceptional* 83
  go beyond 303
  exaggerate 549
  severity 739

permit 760
  not observe 773
  undue 925
  exempt 927a
  —away to
  —*distance* 196
  —forth one's hand
  —*act* 680
  take 789
  —of the imagination 515, 549
  —the meaning 523
  —to *distance* 196
  length 200
  upon the—
  attention 457
stretcher *support* 215
  vehicle 272
strew 73
striae *furrows* 259
  variegation 440
striated 259, 440
stricken *pain* 828
  terror—860
  —in years 128
strict *faithful* 21
  in conformity 82
  exact 494
  severe 739
  conscientious 939
  orthodox 983a
  —*inquiry* 461
  —*interpretation* 522
  —*search* 461
  —*settlement* 780
strictly speaking
  exact 494
  interpreted 522
stricture
  constriction 203
  hindrance 706
  censure 932
stride *distance* 196
  motion 264
  walk 266
strident 410
strides make—282
  rapid—274
stridor 410
strife *discord* 713
  contention 720
strigate 440
strike *operate* 170
  hit 276
  resist 719
  disobey 742
  impress 824
  beat 972
  (*astonish* 870)
  —a balance
  equalize 27
  mean 29
  pay 807
  —a bargain
  contract 769
  barter 794

—a blow *act* 680
—a light *set fire to* 384
  light 420
—all of a heap
  excite 824
  frighten 860
—at 716
—at the root of 162
—dumb *dumb* 581
  wonder 870
  humble 879
—hard 171
—home 171
—in with *imitate* 19
  assent 488
  cooperate 709
—off *exclude* 55
—off the roll
  abrogate 756
  punish 972
  —oil 731
—one 451
—one's flag 725
—on the raw 900
—out *exclude* 55
  destroy 162
  invent 515
  obliterate 552
  scheme 626
—out something new
  sudden change 146
  invention 515
—root 150
—sail 275
—tents 293
—terror 860
—the eye 457
—the first blow 716
—the iron while it is hot 134
—the lyre 416
—the mind 457
—up 416
—with wonder 870
striking 525
—*likeness* 554
strikingly *greatly* 31
string *tie* 43
  ligature 45
  continuity 69
  filament 205
  musical note 413
—together *arrange* 60
  continuity 69
—*alphabet* 442
—beans 298
—orchestra 416
—quartet 415, 416
  with a—to it 770
stringed
  instruments 417
stringent
  energetic 171
  authoritative 737
  strict 739
  compulsory 744

581

strings
  music 416, 417
  leading–541
  pull the
  –*influence* 175
  direct 693
  two–*to one's bow* 632
stringy
  filamentous 205
  tough 327
striolate 440
strip *narrow* 203
  filament 205
  divest 226
  take 789
  rob 791
stripe *length* 200
  variegation 440
  mark 550
  insignia 747
  blow 972
stripling 129
stripped *poor* 804
strive *endeavor* 675
  exert 686
  contend 720
  –*against* 720
stroke *impulse* 276
  touch 379
  mark 550
  evil 619
  expedient 626
  disease 655
  action 680
  success 731
  painful 830
  at a–113
  good–626
  –*of death* 360
  –*of policy* 626
  –*of the pen*
    writing 590
    command 741
  –*of time* 113
  –*of word* 686
  –*the wrong way* 256
stroll 266
strolling player 599
strong *great* 31
  powerful 159
  energetic 171
  tough 327
  taste 390
  pungent 392
  fetid 401
  resolved 604
  healthy 654
  feeling 821
  wonderful! 870
  by a–*arm* 744
  smell–*of* 398
  –*accent* 580
  –*argument* 476
  –*arm man* 792
  –*box* 802
  –*language* 574
  –*point* 476
  –*pull* 686
    with a–*hand*
    resolution 604
    exertion 686
    severity 739
  strong-headed 498
  stronghold *refuge* 666
    defense 717
    prison 752
  strong-minded
    wisdom 498
    courage 861
  strong-room 802
  strong-scented 398
  strong-willed 604, 861
strop 253
strophe 597
strow 73
struck
  (see stricken, strike)
  awe–860
  –*all of a heap*
    emotion 821
    wonder 870
  –*down defeated* 732
  –*with love* 897
structural 7, 240
structure
  production 161
  form 240
  texture 329
  organization 357
  (*house* 189)
struggle *essay* 675
  exert 686
  difficulty 704
  contend 720
strum 416
struma 655
strumpet 962
strut *walk* 266
  pride 878
  parade 882
  boast 884
  –*and fret one's hour upon the stage*
    life 359
    drama 599
strychnine 663
stub 550
stubbed 201
stubble *remains* 40
  useless 645
stubborn *strong* 159
  hard 323
  obstinate 606
  resistance 719
stubby 201
stucco *cement* 45
  covering 223
stuck (see stick)
  –*fast firm* 150
  difficulty 704
stuck-up 878
stud *hanging peg* 214
  knob 250
  horses 271
  –*poker* 840
studded *many* 102
  spiked 253
  variegated 440
student 492, 541
studied
  predetermined 611
  (*willful* 600)
studio *room* 191
  painting 556
  workshop 691
studious
  thoughtful 451
  docile 539
  intending 620
study *copy* 21
  room 191
  thought 451
  attention 457
  research 461
  learning 539
  painting 556
  intention 620
  seclusion 893
  –*in anatomy* 203
stuff *substance* 3
  contents 190
  expand 194
  line 224
  matter 316
  texture 329
  absurdity 497
  unmeaning 517
  deceive 545
  material 635
  trifle 643
  overeat 957
  –*and nonsense*
    unsubstantial 4
    unmeaning 517
  –*in* 300
  –*the memory with* 505
  –*up close* 261
    hoax 545
  such–*as dreams are made of* 515
stuffed *crammed* 641
  –*eggs* 298
stuffing *contents* 190
  lining 224
  stopper 263
stuffy *dense* 321
  sultry 382
stultified *failure* 732
stultify 497
  –*oneself* 699
stultiloquy 497
stumble *fall* 306
  flounder 315
  error 495
  unskillful 699
  failure 732
  –*on chance* 556
  discover 480a
stumblingblock
  difficulty 704
  hindrance 706
stump *remainder* 40
  trunk 51
  walk 266
  drawing 556
  speak 582
  stir your–*s*
  active 682
  –*along slow* 275
  worn to the–659
stump orator 582
stumpy *short* 201
stun
  physically insensible 376
  loud 404
  deafen 419
  unexpected 508
  morally insensible 823
  affect 824
  astonish 870
Stundist 984
stung (see sting)
  –*to the quick* 824
stunt *shorten* 201
stunted *small* 193
  contracted 195
  meager 640
stupa 363
stupe 834
stupefaction 826
stupefy
  –*physically* 376
  –*morally* 823
  astonish 870
stupendous *great* 31
  large 192
  wonderful 870
stupid *misjudging* 481
  credulous 486
  unintelligent 499
  tiresome 841
  dull 843
stupor
  insensibility 376, 823
  wonder 870
stupration 961
sturdy *strong* 159
  persevering 604a
  –*beggar beggar* 767
  thief 792
sturgeon 298
stutter 583
sty *inclosure* 189, 232
  dirt 653
Stygian *dark* 421
  diabolic 945
  infernal 982
  cross the–*ferry*
  die 360
  –*shore death* 360
style *state* 7
  time 114
  painting 556
  graver 558
  name 564
  phrase 566
  diction 569
  writing 590
  beauty 845
  fashion 852
stylet *awl* 262
  dagger 727
stylish 852
stylist 578
stylite 996
Stylites, Simeon– 893
stylography 590
styptic 397
Styx 982
suanpan 85
suant 705
suasible 602
suasion 615
suave 894
suavity 894
sub 34
subacid 397
subacidity 397
subaction 330
subahdar 745
subalpine 206
subaltern *inferior* 34
  soldier 726
  officer 745
  servant 746
subaqueous 208
subarborescent 242
subastral 318
subaudition 527
subclavate 250
subcommittee 696
subconscious 450, 992a –*self* 317, 450
subcontrary 237
subcutaneous 221, 223
subdean 996
subdichotomy 91
subditious 147
subdivide 44
subdivision *part* 51
  military 726
subdolous 702
subdominant 413
subdual 731
subduction
  subtraction 38
  (*taking* 789)
subdue *calm* 174
  faint sound 405
  succeed 731
subdued *morally* 826
subeditor 593

suberose 320
subitaneous 113
subito 113
subjacency 34, 207
subjacent 207
subject *influence* 175
  liable 177
  topic 454
  meaning 516
  servant 746
  enthrall 749
  be–ed to 177
  —*matter* 516
  —*of dispute* 713
  —*to examination* 461
  —*of inquiry* 461
  —*of thought* 454
  —*to qualification* 469
  uncertain 475
subjection 749
subjective *intrinsic* 5
  immaterial 317
  intellectual 450
subjoin 37, 63
subjoinder 462
subjugate
  conquer 731
  subject 749
subjugation
  defeat 732
  moral impression 824
subjunction 43
subjunctive 37
Sublapsarian 984
sublation 38
sublet 787
sublease 787
sublevation 307
sublieutenant 745
sublimate *elevate* 307
  lighten 320
  vaporize 336
sublime *greatness* 31
  high 206
  language 574
  beauty 845
  glory 873
  magnanimous 942
  from the—to the ridiculous 853
Sublime Porte 745
subliminal 450
  —*consciousness* 450, 992a
  —*self* 317
sublimity
  (*see* sublime)
sublineation 550
sublunary 318
submarine 208
  boat 726
  —*chaser* 726
submediant 413
submerge *destroy* 162
  immerse 300

plunge 310
steep 337
submergible 310
submersible 310, 726
submersion
  depth 208
  plunge 310
subministration 707
submission 725
  obedience 643
  with– 928
submissive
  tractable 705
  enduring 826
  humble 879
  (*penitent* 950)
submit *propound* 514
  mediate 724
  yield 725
  —*to arbitration* 774
submittal 725
submonish 695
submultiple 84
subordinacy 34
subordinate
  inferior 34
  unimportant 643
  subject 749
subordination
  order 58
  (*obedience* 743)
suborn *induce* 615
  purchase 795
  bride 784)
subpanation 998
subpoena
  command 741
  lawsuit 969
subreption
  falsehood 544
  acquisition 775
subrogate 147
subscribe *assent* 488
  aid 707
  agree to 769
  give 784
subscriber
  (*see* subscribe)
subscript 37, 65
subscription *gift* 784
subsequent
  —*in order* 63
  —*in time* 117
  —*time* 121
subserviency
  servility 886
subservient
  instrumental 631
  aid 707
  servile 746
subside *decrease* 36
  sink 306
subsidiary *extrinsic* 6
  aid 707
  servant 746
  (*tending* 176)

subsidy *aid* 707
  gift 784
  pay 809
subsist *exist* 1
  continue 141, 106
  live 359
subsistence *food* 298
subsoil *interior* 221
  earth 342
substance *thing* 3
  intrinsicality 5
  quantity 25
  inside 221
  matter 316
  texture 329
  meaning 516
  important part 642
  wealth 803
  in– 596
  man of– 803
substantial *existing* 1
  hypostatic 3
  material 316
  dense 321
  true 494
  —*meaning* 516
substantialism 316
substantialist 316
substantiality 3
substantialize 316
substantially
  intrinsically 5
  —*true* 494
substantiate
  materialize 316
  evidence 467
  make good 924
substantive *existing* 1
  substantial 3
substitute *change* 147
  means **634**
  deputy 759
substitution **147**
substratum
  substance 3
  layer 204
  base 211
  support 215
  interior 221
  materiality 316
substructure 211
subsultory 315
subsultus 315
subsume 76
subtend 237
subterfuge
  sophistry 477
  quirk 481
  lie 546
  pretense 617
  cunning 702
subterrane 252
subterranean 208
subtile *light* 320
  rare 322
  —*texture* 329

subtility 498
subtilize *rarefy* 322
  sophistry 477
subtilty 322
subtle *slight* 32
  light 320
  rarity 322
  texture 329
  color 428
  cunning 702
  —*point* 704
  —*reasoning* 476
subtlety *sophistry* 477
  wisdom 498
subtraction
  subduction 38
  arithmetic 85
  taking 789
subtrahend
  subtract 38
  number 84
subulate 253
suburb *town* 189
  near 197
  environs 227
subvention
  support 215
  aid 707
  gift 784
subversion
  revolution 146
subvert *destroy* 162
  invert 218
  depress 308
succedaneum 147
succeed *follow* 63
  posterior 117
  success 731
  transfer 783
  —*to acquire* 775
success 731
succession
  sequence 63
  continuity 69
  repetition 104
  posteriority 117
  transfer 783
  in quick– 136
  in regular– 138
  —*of ideas* 451
  —*of time* 109
successless 732
successor *sequel* 65
  posterior 117
succinct 572
succor 707
succotash 298
succubus 980
succulent
  nutritive 298
  juicy 333
  semiliquid 352
  pulpy 354
succumb *fatigue* 688
  yield 725
  fail 732

(*obey* 743)
succussion 315
such– *a one* 372
  —*as* 17
  —*being the case* 8
  —*like* 17
suchwise 8
suck *draw off* 297
  drink 298
  take 789
  —*in* 296
  —*the blood of* 789
sucker 260 *dupe* 547
  servility 886
sucking pig 298
suckle 707
suckling *infant* 129
sucrose 386
suction *force* 157
  reception 296
Sudanic 372a
sudarium 652, 993
sudary 652
sudation 299
sudatorium 386
sudatory 386
sudden *transient* 111
  instantaneous 113
  soon 132
  unexpected 508
  —*and quick in quarrel* 901
  —*burst* 508
  —*death* 360
  —*thought* 612
sudorific 382
suds *froth* 353
  in the–difficulty 704
  dejected 837
sue *demand* 765
  go to law 969
suet 356
suffer
  physical pain 378
  disease 655
  allow 760
  feel 821
  endure 826
  moral pain 828
  —*for* 972
  —*punishment* 972
sufferance 826
  tenant on– 779
suffice 639
sufficiency **639**
sufficient *enough* 639
  economical 817
  satisfactory 831
suffix *adjunct* 39
  sequence 63
  sequel 65
  letter 561
sufflation 349
suffocate *kill* 361
  excess 641
suffocating *hot* 382

583

suffocation

fetid 401
suffocation
  death 361
suffragan 996
suffrage 609 *vote* 535
suffragette 374
suffragist 609
suffusion *mixture* 41
  feeling 821
  blush 879
Sufi *religious sect* 984
Sufism 984
sugar 396
sugar loaf
  pointed 253
sugary 396
suggest *suppose* 514
  inform 527
  advise 695
  –*itself thought* 451
  fancy 515
  –*a question* 461
suggester *tempter* 615
suggestion *plan* 626
  advice 695
suggestive
  reminder 505
  significant 516
  descriptive 594
suicidal
  destructive 162
suicide *killing* 361
sui generis 20, 83
suigenetic 163
suisse *beadle* 996
Suisse
  point d'argent point
  de–812
suit *accord* 23
  series 69
  class 75
  clothes 225
  expedient 646
  petition 765
  courtship 902
  do–*and service* 743
  follow–19
  law–969
  love–897
  –in law 969
  –the action to the word 550
  –the occasion 646
suitable 23, 646
  –*season* 134
suit case 191
suite *sequel* 65
  series 69
  retinue 746
  –of rooms 191
suitor *petitioner* 767
  lover 897
  lawsuit 969
sulcated 259
sulcus 259
sulkiness (*see* sulky)

discourtesy 895
sulky *carriage* 272
  obstinate 606
  discontented 832
  dejected 837
  sullen 901a
sulks 895
sullen *obstinate* 606
  gloomy 837
  discourteous 895
  sulky 901a
sullenness 901a
sully *dirty* 653
  dishonor 874
  (*deface* 846)
sulphite 83
sulphur 388
sulphur-colored 436
sultan 745
sultry 382
sum *add* 37
  number 84
  money 800
  –and substance
  meaning 516
  synopsis 596
  important part 642
  –*total* 800
  –*up reckon* 85
  discriminate 465
  description 594
  compendium 596
sumless 105
summarize 551, 596
summation 37, 85
summary
  transient 111
  early 132
  short 201
  concise 572
  compendious 596
  illegal 964
  –of facts 594
summer *season* 125
  support 215
  heat 382
  –*lightning* 423
  –*school* 542
summerhouse 191
summerset 218
summit *top* **210**
  (*superiority* 33)
summon
  command 741
  lawsuit 969
  (*accuse* 938)
  –up *memory* 505
  excite 824
  –up *courage* 861
summons
  evidence 467
  command 741
  lawsuit 969
sump *base* 211
  inlet 343
  slough 345

cess 653
sumpter-horse 271
sumptuary
  money 800
  expenditure 809
sumptuous 882
sum total 50
sun *heavenly body* 318
  luminary 423
  glory 873
  as the–at noonday
  bright 420
  certain 474
  plain 525
  bask in the–377
  farthing candle to the–645
  going down of the–126
  –oneself 384
  under the
  –*space* 180
  world 318
Sun of Righteousness 976
sunbeam 420
  –s from cucumbers 471
sunburn 384
sunburnt 433
Sunday 138, 687
  –best *ornament* 847
  show 882
  –school 542
sunder 44
sundial 114
sun dog 423
sundown 126
sundowner 460, 876
sundry 102
sunflower 369
sunk (*see* sink)
  deep 208
  –fence 717
  –in iniquity 945
  –in oblivion 508
sunken rocks 667
sunless 421
sunlight 420
Sunni 984
sunny *warm* 382
  luminous 420
  cheerful 836
sunny side 829
  –of hedge 734
  view the–858
sun painting 556
sunrise 125, 236
sunset 126, 236
  at–133
  –glow 420
sunshade *cover* 223
  shade 424
sunshine *light* 420
  prosperity 734
  happy 827

cheerful 836
sunshiny 382
sunstone 847
sunstroke
  heat 384
  madness 503
sun-up 125
sun worship 382
sunyasi (*see* sannyasi)
  retaliation 718
  punishment 972
sup *small quantity* 32
  feed 298
  –full of horrors 828
supawn 298
super *theatrical* 599
superable *possible* 470
  (*easy* 705)
superabound 641
  sufficiency 639
superadd 37
superannuated 128, 158
superb 845
supercargo 694
supercherie 545
supercilious
  proud 878
  insolent 885
  disrespectful 929
  scornful 930
superdreadnought 726
supereminence
  goodness 648
  repute 873
supererogation
  redundant 641
  useless 645
  (*activity* 682)
superexaltation 873
superexcellence 648
superfetation
  added 37
  productive 168
superficial
  shallow 209
  outside 220
  misjudging 481
  ignorant 491
  –extent 180
superficies 220
superfine 648
superfluitant 305
superfluity
  remainder 40
  redundance 641
superfluous
  remaining 40
  redundant 641
  useless 645
superhuman
  perfect 650
  godlike 976
superimpose 233
superimposed 206

supervacaneous

superincumbent
  above 206
  heavy 319
superinduce
  change 140
  cause 153
  produce 161
superintend 693
superintendent 694
superior
  greater 33
  –in size 194
  high 206
  important 642
  good 648
  director 694
superiority **33**
superjunction 37
superlative 33
superman 33
supernal *height* 206
  summit 210
  heavenly 981
supernatant *high* 206
  ascent 305
supernatural
  deity 976
  spectral 980a
  –aid 707
supernaturalism 528
supernormal 20, 976
supernumerary
  adjunct 39
  theatrical 599
  reserve 636
  redundant 641
  (*remainder* 40)
superphysical 450, 976
superplus 40
superpose *add* 37
  cover 223
supersaturate 641
superscription
  mark 550
  writing 590
  (*evidence* 467)
supersede
  substitute 147
  disuse 678
  relinquish 782
supersensible
  –regions 317, 318
supersensitive 976
supersensual 976
supersensuous 976
superstition 486
  religious–984
superstitious 486, 984–remedies 670
superstratum 220
superstructure 729
supertonic 413
supervacaneous
  redundant 641
  (*useless* 645)

supervene
  be added 37
  succeed 117
  happen 151
supervise 693
supervisor 694
supervisory 693
supination 213
supine *horizontal* 213
  inverted 218
  sluggish 683
  mentally torpid 823
suppeditate 637
supper 298
  full of–954a
supplant 147
supple *soft* 324
  servile 886
supplement
  addition 37
  adjunct 39
  completion 52
suppletory 37
suppliant *begging* 765
  beggar 767
supplicate *beg* 765
  pity 914
  worship 990
supplies
  materials 635
  aid 707
  money 800
supply *store* 636
  provide 637
  give 784
  –*aid* 707
  –*deficiencies* 52
  –*the place of* 147
support *perform* 170
  sustain 215
  evidence 467
  escort 664
  preserve 670
  aid 707
  feel 821
  endure 826
  vindicate 937
  –*life* 359
supporter
  auxiliary 711
supporters
  heraldic 550
suppose 472, 514
supposing
  provided 469
supposition 514
supposititious
  unattested 468
  untrue 546
suppress *destroy* 162
  conceal 528
  silent 581
  restrain 751
suppression
  (*see* suppress)
  –*of truth* 544

suppuration 653
suppurative 663
suppute 85
supralapsarian 984
supramundane 939
supremacy
  superior 33
  authority 737
supreme 33
  summit 210
  authority 737
  almighty 976
  in a–degree 31
  –*good* 618
  –*principle* 450
Supreme Being 976
surbate 659
surbated 688
surcease 142
surcharge
  redundance 641
  (*dear* 814)
  falsify 811
surcingle 45
surcost 225
surd *number* 84
  silent 403
  deaf 419
  phonetic 561
sure *certain* 474
  belief 484
  assent 488
  safe 664
  make–against 673
  make–of
  inquire 461
  take 789
  on–ground 664
  security 771
  to be–assent 488
  you may be–
  affirmation 535
sure–footed
  careful 459
  skillful 698
  cautious 864
surely 870
sureness (*see* sure)
surety *certainty* 474
  safety 664
surf *tide* 348
  foam 353
surface *outside* 220
  texture 329
  lie on the–
  intelligible 518
  manifest 525
  skim the–
  slur over 460
  –*car* 272
surfeit
  redundance 641
  satiety 869
surge *swarm* 72
  swell 305
  rotation 312

wave 348
surgeon 662
surgery 662
surly *gruff* 895
  sullen 901a
  unkind 907
surmise 510, 514
surmount *tower* 206
  summit 210
  transcursion 303
  ascent 305
  –*a difficulty* 731
surmountable 470
surname 564
surpass *be superior* 33
  grow 194
  go beyond 303
  outshine 873
surplice 999
surplus *remainder* 40
  redundance 641
surplusage 641
surprise
  nonexpectation 508
  take unawares 674
  wonder 870
  –*party* 892
surprisingly 31
surrebut 462
surrebutter
  answer 462
  pleadings 969
surrejoin 462
surrejoinder 462
surrender *submit* 725
  relinquish 782
  (*obey* 743)
  no–obstinate 606
  defense 717
  –*one's life* 360
surreptitious
  furtive 528
  deceptive 545
  untrue 546
surrogate 147, 759
surround
  circumjacent 227
  circumscribe 229
surroundings 227
surtout *coat* 225
surveillance *care* 459
  direction 693
  *under–*938
survene 151
survey *view* 441
  measure 466
surveyor 466, 694
survive *remain* 40
  long time 110
  permanent 141
susceptibility
  power 157
  tendency 176
  liability 177
  sensibility 375
  motive 615

impressibility 822
irascibility 901
susceptive 177
suscipient 785
suscitate *cause* 153
  produce 161
  stir up 173
  excite 824
suspect *doubt* 485
  suppose 514
suspected *accused* 938
suspectless 484
suspend *defer* 133
  discontinue 142
  hang 214
  neglect 460
suspended
  animation 823
suspenders 45
suspense
  cessation 142
  uncertainty 475
  expectation 507
  irresolution 605
  in–inert 172
suspension
  lateness 133
  cessation 142
  hanging 214
  music 413
  seclusion 893
  –*of arms* 723
suspicion *doubt* 485
  incredulity 487
  knowledge 490
  supposition 514
  fear 860
  cautious 864
  jealousy 920
  *under–*938
suspiration 839
suspire 359
sustain *continue* 143
  strength 159
  perform 170
  support 215
  preserve 670
  aid 707
  endure 821
sustained note 413
sustaining power
  170
sustenance 298, 707
sustentation
  (*see* sustain)
  food 298
sustentative 215
sustention 215
susurration 405
sutler *purveyor* 637
  merchant 797
suttee *killing* 361
  burning 384
  unselfishness 942
  idolatry 991
sutteeism 361

suture 43
suzerain 745
suzerainty 737
swab *dry* 340
  clean 652
  lubber 701
swaddle *clothe* 225
  restrain 751
swaddling clothes in
  –*infant* 129
  subjection 749
swag *hang* 214
  lean 217
  curve 245
  drop 306
  oscillate 314
  booty 793
swage 174
swagger *pride* 878
  boast 884
  bluster 885
swaggerer 482, 884,
  887
swagsman 268
swain *man* 373
  rustic 876
  lover 897
swale 659
swallow *swift* 274
  gulp 296
  eat 298
  bird 366
  believe 484
  credulous 486
  brook 826
  –*flight* 274
  –*the bait dupe* 547
  willing 602
  –*the leek recant* 607
  submit 725
  –*up destroy* 162
  store 636
  use 677
  take 789
  –*whole* 465a
swallow–tailed coat
  225
swamp *destroy* 162
  marsh 345
  defeat 731
swamped *failure* 732
swampy *moist* 339
swan 366–*bath* 341
  –*road* 341
  –*song* 360
swap *exchange* 148
  blow 276
  barter 794
sward 344, 367
swarm *crowd* 72
  multitude 102
  climb 305
  bees 370
  sufficiency 639
  redundance 641
swarthy 431

swartness 431
swash *affuse* 337
  spurt 348
swashbuckler
  fighter 726
  blusterer 887
swashy 339
swastika 621, 993
swath 72
swathe *fasten* 43
  clothe 225
  restrain 751
sway *power* 157
  influence 175
  lean 217
  oscillate 314
  agitation 315
  induce 615
  authority 737
  –to and fro 149
sweal 659
swear *affirm* 535
  promise 768
  curse 908
  just enough to–by 32
  –at 908
  –a witness 768
  –by *believe* 484
  –false 544
sweat *exude* 295
  excretion 299
  heat 382
  exertion 686
  fatigue 688
  cold–860
  in a–382
  –of one's brow 686
  –over 451
sweater 225
Swedenborg 986
Swedenborgian
  religious sect 984
sweep *space* 180
  curve 245
  navigation 267
  rapid 274
  bend 279
  clean 652
  dirty fellow 653
  steal 791
  make a clean–of 297
  –along 264
  –away *destroy* 162
  eject 297
  abrogate 756
  relinquish 782
  –off 297
  –of time 109
  –out *eject* 297
  clean 652
  –the chords 416
sweeper
  cleaner 652, 876
  war vessel 726

sweeping *whole* 50
  complete 52
  inclusive 76
  general 78
  –change 146
sweepings *useless* 645
  dirt 653
  (*trifle* 643)
sweepstakes *gain* 775
  receipt 810
sweet *saccharine* 396
  melodious 413
  color 428
  clean 652
  agreeable 829
  lovely 897
  love 897
  endearment 902
  –potatoes 298
  –smell 400
  –tooth *desire* 865
  –wine 396
  –words 894
sweeten 396, 829
sweetheart 897, 902
sweetmeat 396, 829
sweetness 396
  –and light 829
sweets *pastry* 298
  sugar 396
  treat 829
sweet-scented 400
swell *increase* 35
  expand 194
  convexity 250
  wave 348
  sound 404
  emotion 821
  fop 854
  nobility 875
  swagger 885
  extol 931
  (*increase* 35)
  ground
  –*agitation* 315
  –out *diffuse style* 573
  –over 250
  –the ranks of 37
  –with rage 900
swelling
  expansion 194
  prominence 250
  –*style* 577
  excitement 824
swell mob 792
swelter 382
sweltry 382
swerve *variation* 20a
  change 140
  deviate 279
  demur 603
  tergiversation 607
  –from 287
swift 274
swig *drink* 298
  drunkenness 959

swill *drink* 298
  uncleanness 653
  intemperance 954
  drunkenness 959
swim *navigate* 267
  float 305
  light 320
  dim-sightedness 443
  –against the stream 704
  –in *pleasure* 377
  abundance 639
  –with the stream *conformity* 82
  inactivity 683
  –with the tide *prosperity* 734
swimming–*eyes* 443
  –head 503
  –bath 652
  –belt 666
  –bladder 334
  –pool 652
swimmingly
  easily 705
  success 731
  prosperity 734
swindle *cheat* 545
  peculate 791
swindler *cheat* 545
  peculate 791
swindler *cheat* 548
  thief 792
swine 366
  cast pearls before 638
  –of Epicurus 954a
swineherd 746
swing *operation* 170
  space 180
  hang 214
  oscillate 314
  freedom 748
  amusement 840
  full–*active* 682
  success 731
  give full– *facilitate* 705
  have one's–738
swinge 972
swinging *great* 31
swinish
  intemperance 954
  gluttony 957
  –multitude 876
swink 686
swirl 312, 348
swish 409
switch *deviate* 279
  recede 287
  flog 972
  rod 975
swivel *hinge* 312
  cannon 727
swivel-eye 443
swollen *expanded* 194

  proud 878
swoon *powerless* 158
  fatigue 688
swoop
  descend 274, 306
  seize 789
  at one fell–173
swop 794
sword *weapon* 727
  at the point of the– 722 *severity* 739
  compulsion 744
  subjection 749
  draw the–*war* 722
  flesh one's–*war* 722
  measure–s 720, 722
  put to the–361
  –of Damocles 667
  –in hand *prepare* 673
  war 722
  turn–s into plowshares 723
sword-shaped 253
swordsman 726
Sybarite 954a
sybaritism 954
syce 268
sycophancy
  flattery 933
sycophant *follower* 65
  petitioner 767
  desirer 865
  servile 886
  flatterer 935
sycophantic 746
syenite *blue* 438
syllabicate 567
syllable 561
  breathe not a–528
syllabus *list* 86
  compendium 596
syllepsis 567
syllogism 476
syllogistic 476
sylph 979, 980
sylvan 367
symbol
  mathematical–84
  sign 550
symbolic *latent* 526
  indicative 550
symbolize
  latency 526
  indicate 550
  represent 554
symmetrical
  regular 80
  form 240
  elegant 578
  (*see* symmetry)
symmetry *equality* 27
  order 58
  conformity 82
  centrality 222
  regular form **242**
  elegance 578

  beauty 845
  want of–846
sympathetic
  (*see* sympathy)
  –ink 528
  –tear 906
sympathize
  (*see* sympathy)
sympathizer
  partisan 890
sympathy
  concord 714
  friendship 888
  love 897
  kindness 906
  pity 914
  condolence 915
symphonic 415
  –poem 415
symphonious 413
symphony
  overture 64
  music 415
  concord 714
symphysis 43
symposium *meal* 298
  festival 840
  (*drunken* 959)
symptom 550, 668
symptomatic 668
symptomatology 522, 550, 655
synaeresis 48, 54
synagogue 1000
synchronic 120
synchronism **120**
synchysis 218
synclinal 217
syncopate 195
syncopation 195, 415
syncope
  impotence 158
  contraction 195
  musical 413
  rhetoric 572
  fatigue 688
syncretic
  derangement 61
syncretism
  disagreement 24
  heterodoxy 984
syncretize 48
syndic *ruler* 745
  judge 967
syndicate
  directorate 542
  council 696
  league 712
synecdoche 521
synergism 709
synergy 178, 709
syngenic 5
synizesis 48, 54
synod *council* 696
  church 995
  (*assemblage* 72)

synonym
  meaning 516
  interpretation 522
  nomenclature 564
synonymize 516
synopsis
  arrangement 60
  list 86
  grammar 567
  compendium 596
synovia
  lubrication 332
  oil 356
synovial 332
syntactic 567
syntagma 60
syntax 567
syntectic 655
synthesis
  combination 48
  composition 54
  reasoning 476
synthetic 476
syringe *water* 337
  stream 348
syrinx 410
syrt 667
syrup 352, 396
system *order* 58
  rule 80
  plan 626
  —of knowledge 490
  —of opinions 484
systematic *regular* 80
systematize *order* 58
  arrange 60
  organize 357
  plan 626
systole 195
  —and diastole 138, 314
syzygy 199

T

T to a—494
tab 39
tabard 225
tabasco 393
tabby *mottled* 440
  gossip 588
tabefaction 195
tabernacle *house* 189
  temple 1000
tabes 195
tabescent 195
tabetic 195, 203, 655
tabic 203
tabid *shrunk* 195
  thin 203
  disease 655
  deteriorated 659
table *arrangement* 60
  list 86
  defer 133

  layer 204
  support 215
  flat 251
  repast 298
  neglect 460
  writing 590
  on the
  —preparing 673
  —of the Lord 1000
  turn the—s 218
  under the
  —hidden 528
  drunk 959
tableau *list* 86
  appearance 448
  painting 556
  theatrical 599
tablecloth 652
table d'hôte 298
table-land
  horizontal 213
  plain 344
tablespoon 191
tablet *layer* 204
  flat 251
  record 551
  writing 590
  —s of the memory 505
table talk *news* 532
  conversation 588
table-turning 992
tableware 191
tablier 225
tablinum 191
taboo *prohibited* 761
  magic 992
tabor 417
tabouret 215
tabret 417
tabular 60
tabula rasa
  inexistence 2
  absence 187
  ignorance 491
  obliterated 552
  facility 705
tabulate *arrange* 60
  series 69
  list 86
tabulation *record* 551
tace 403
tachygraphy 590
tacit *implied* 516
  latent 526
taciturnity 585
Tacitus
  concise style 572
tack *join* 43
  nails 45
  change course 140
  direction 278
  turn 279
  way 627
  —to add 37
  wrong—732

tackle *fastening* 45
  gear 633
  undertake 676
  manage 693
tacky 352 *dowdy* 659
tact *touch* 379
  discrimination 465
  wisdom 498
  skill 698
  taste 850
  want of—851
tactful (*see* tact)
  affable 894
tactician 700
tactics *conduct* 692
  warfare 722
  (*plan* 626)
  (*skill* 698)
tactile 379
taction 379
tactlessness 895
tactual 379
tadpole 129
taenia 205
taeniate 205
taffeta 255
taffy 396
tag *small* 32
  addition 37
  fastening 45
  follow 63, 235
  sequel 65
  end 67
  point 253
  animal 366
  game 840
  (*adjunct* 39)
tagtail 886
tail *sequel* 65
  end 67
  pendent 214
  rear 235
  aeronautics 273
  estate—780
  —off *decrease* 36
  turn—623
tail coat 225
tailless 38
tailor *clothier* 225
  workman 690
tailoress 225
tailoring *clothes* 225
  finery 882
tailpiece
  sequel 65, 235
  engraving 558
  ornament 847
tailrace 350
taint *imperfection* 651
  dirt 653
  decay 659
  disgrace 874
tainted *fetid* 401
  diseased 655
taintless 652
taj 225

tajo 259
take *eat* 298
  believe 484
  know 490
  understand 518
  succeed 731
  receive 785
  appropriate 788, 789
  captivate 829
  give and—718
  —aback
    unexpected 508
    astonish 870
  —a back seat 34
  —a course 692
  —action 680
  —a disease 655
  —advice 695
  —after 17
  —a hint 498
  —a leaf out of
    another's book 19
  —a lease 788
  —a liberty 748
  —a likeness 554
  —an account of
    enumerate 85
  —an ell 885
  —an infection 655
  —a peep 441
  —aside 586
  —a turn 140
  —away *annihilate* 2
    subtract 38
    remove 185
    seize 789
  —away life 361
  —back again 790
  —by
    (*see below*)
  —care *warning* 668
    cautious 864
  —care of 459
  —comfort
    constant 831
    relief 834
  —coolly 826
  —down *swallow* 298
    depress 308
    record 551
    dismantle 681
    humiliate 874
    censure 932
  —easily 826
  —effect *event* 151
    act 170
  —exception 932
  —fire 384
  —flight 623
  —for
    (*see below*)
  —from *subtract* 38
    seize 789
  —heart *contented* 831
    cheerful 836
  —heed 864

  —hold of *cohere* 46
    seize 789
  —hold of the mind 484
  —ill 832
  —in
    (*see below*)
  —it believe 484
    suppose 514
    —its course
    continue 143
    event 151
  —its rise *begin* 66
    result 154
  —leave of 624
  —measures 626
  —money 810
  —no care of 460
  —no denial
    obstinate 606
    compel 744
  —no interest in 823
  —no note of 460
  —no note of time 115
  —notice 457
  —off
    (*see below*)
  —on
    (*see below*)
  —one at one's word 769
  —one's chance
    chance 621
    essay 675
  —one's choice 609
  —oneself off 293
  —one's fancy
    pleasing 829
    desire 865
  —one's oath 535
  —one with another 29
  —on trust 484
  —out *extract* 301
    obliterate 552
  —part with 709
  —pattern by 19
  —pen in hand 590
  —place 151
  —possession of 789
  —precedence
    superior 33
    precede 62
  —root *firm* 150
    located 184
  —ship 267
  —steps *prepare* 673
    act 680
  —stock 85
  —the air line 278
  —the back track 283
  —the cake 33
  —the consequences 154
  —the field 722
  —the good the gods provide 831

587

take by

- the lead 62
- the place of 147
- the shine out of 33
- the stump 582
- things as they come
  inactivity 683
  inexcitable 826
  relief 834
- time *duration* 106
  late 133
  leisure 685
- time by the forelock 132
- to *habit* 613
  pursuit 622
  use 677
  like 827
  desire 865
  love 897
- to heart *pain* 828
  discontent 832
- to pieces *disjoin* 44
  dismantle 681
- up
  (*see below*)
- upon oneself
  undertake 676
  promise 768
- warning 668
- wing 293

take by-surprise 508
- the button 586
- the hand *aid* 707

take for 484
- better for worse 609
- gospel 486
- granted 472, 484

take in *include* 54
  shorten 201
  admit 296
  understand 518
  deceive 545
  receive money 785
- an idea 498
- good part
  be calm 826
  be pleased 827
  content 831
- hand *teach* 537
  undertake 676
  aid 707
- sail 275

take into-account
  include 76
  discriminate 465
  qualify 469
- consideration 451
- custody 751
- one's head
  suppose 514
  caprice 608

taken be-*die* 360
- ill 655
- with 897

take off *mimic* 19
  destroy 162

remove 185
  divest 226
  burlesque 555
  discount 813
- one's hands 785
- the hat 894

take on
  discontent 832
  melancholy 837
- credit 484
- trust 484

taker 789

take up *elevate* 307
  inquire 461
  dissent 595
  choose 609
  undertake 676
  arrest 751
  borrow 788
  censure 932
- a case 476
- an inquiry 461
- arms 722
- money 788
- one's abode 184
- one's pen 590
- the cudgels
  attack 716
  contend 720
- with *attention* 457
  use 677
  content 831

taking 789
  infectious 657
  in a-*pained* 828
  angry 900
- off *death* 360

talapoin 996

talbotype 554

tale *counting* 85
  narrative 594
  thereby hangs a- 526
  twice-told-
  diffuse style 573
  weary 841

talebearer 529, 532

talent 264, 698
  bury one's-in a napkin 528
  not put one's-in a napkin 878

talesman 967

talionic 718

taliped 243

talisman *insignia* 747
  charm 993

talismanic 992

talk *unsubstantial* 4
  rumor 532
  speak 582
  conversation 588
  small-588
- against time
  time 106
  protract 110

inaction 681
- at random
  illogical 477
  loquacity 584
- big *boast* 884
  insolent 885
  threat 909
- glibly 584
- nonsense 497
- of *signify* 516
  publish 531
  intend 620
- of the town
  gossip 588
  dame 873
- oneself out of breath 584
- over *confer* 588
  persuade 615
- together 588
- to in private 586
- to oneself 589

talkative 584

talkativeness 582, 584

talked of 873

talker 584, 588

talking , fine-
  overestimation 482

tall *great* 31
  high 206
- talk 884

tallage 812

tallies 85

tallow 356
- candle 423

tallow-faced 429

tally *agree* 23
  numeration 85
  list 86
  sign 550
  credit 805
- with *conform* 82

tallyho 622

tallyman 797

talma 225

Talmud 985

talon 327

talons *authority* 737
  claws 781

talus 217

tamasha 892

tambourine 417

tame *inert* 172
  moderate 174, 826
  domesticate 370
  teach 537
  feeble 575
  subjugate 749
  insensible 823
  calm 826

tameless *violent* 173
  malevolent 907

Tammany 712

tam-o'-shanter 225

tamper *mallet* 276

- with *alter* 140
  seduce 615
  injure 659
  meddle 682

tampion 263

tam-tam 417

tan *color* 433

tandem *at length* 200
  vehicle 272

tang *taste* 390
  pungency 392
  bane 663

tangent 199, 379
  fly off at a-
  deviate 279
  diverge 291
  excitable 825

tangible *material* 316
  touch 379
  exact 494
  sufficient 639
  useful 644

tangle *derange* 61
  matted 219

tangled *disordered* 59
  confused 523
  weave a-web
  difficulty 704

tank *reservoir* 636
  (*receptacle* 191)

tankard 191

tannin 663

tantalize *balk* 509
  induce 615
  desire 865

tantalizing
  exciting 824

Tantalus torment of-
  expectation 507
  desire 865

tantamount *equal* 27
  synonymous 516

tantara 407

tanti 642

tantivy *speed* 274

tantra 986

tantrum 900

tap *open* 260
  plug 263
  hit 276
  let out 295, 297
  sound 406
  turn on the-297

tape *string* 205
  (*fastening* 45)

taper *contract* 195
  narrow 203
  candle 423
- to a point 253

tapestry *painting* 556
  ornament 847

tapir 366

tapis on the-
  event 151
  topic 454
  intention 620

task

  plan 626

taproot 153

tapster 746

tar *cover* 223
  sailor 269
  pitch 356a
- and feather
  disrespect 929
  punish 972

tarantella 315

tarantism 315

tarboosh 225

tardigrade 275

tardiloquence 583

tardy *dilatory* 133
  slow 275

tare *discount* 40a
- and tret 813

tares 645

target 620, 717

tariff 812

tarn 343

tarnish
  discoloration 429
  soil 653
  deface 848
  disgrace 874
  (*damage* 659)

tarpaulin 223

tarpon 298

tarradiddle 546

tarred 356a

tarriance 133

tarry *remain* 110
  later 133
  continue 141
  stay 265
- for *expect* 507

tart *pastry* 298, 396
  acid 397
  rude 895
  irascible 901

tartan 440

tartane 273

Tartar *choleric* 901
  catch a-*dupe* 547
  unskillful 699
  retaliation 718
  (*failure* 732)

tartar *sourness* 397
  dirt 653
- emetic 663

Tartarean 907

tartarize 397

Tartarus 982

Tartuffe
  hypocrisy 544
  deceiver 548
  impiety 988

task *lesson* 537
  business 625
  put to use 677
  fatigue 688
  command 741
  hard-704
  set a-741

taskmaster

take to–932
–the memory 505
taskmaster 694
tassel 214, 847
tastable 390
taste *sapidity* **390**
  elegance 578
  experience 821
  good taste **850**
  man of–850
  –good 394
  –of quality 5
  to one's–*savory* 394
  pleasant 829
  love 897
tasteful 850
tasteless *insipid* 391
  inelegant 579
tasty 390, 394, 850
tatter
  small quantity 32
tatterdemalion 876
tatters *garments* 225
  tear to–162
Tattersall's 799
tattle 588
tattler
  newsmonger 532
  gossip 588
tattletale 532
tattoo *drumming* 407
  mottled 440
  summons 741
tau 219
taught (see teach)
  fastened 43
taunt *disrespect* 929
  reproach 938
  (*ridicule* 856)
tauromachy 720
Taurus 490a
taut 43
tautologize 104
tautology
  repetition 104
  diffuse style 573
tautophony 104
tavern 189
  –haunter 959
tawdry 851
tawed leather 327
tawny *brown* 433
  yellow 436
tax *inquire* 461
  employ 677
  fatigue 688
  command 741
  compel 744
  request 765
  accounts 811
  impost 812
  accuse 938
  –one's energies 686
  –the memory 505
taxable 812
taxation 812

taxi 272
taxicab 272
taxidermy 368
taxis 60
taxonomy 60
tazza 191
tea 298
teach 537
  –one's grandmother
    redundant 641
    impertinent 885
teachable 539
teacher **540**, 673
teaching **537**
  false–538
teacup, storm in a–
  overrate 482
  exaggerate 549
tea gown 225
teak 367
teal 298
team *continuity* 69
  assemblage 72
  conveyance 272
  crew 712
  representative 759
teamster 694
tea party 892
teapot 191
teapoy 215
tear *weeping* 839
  draw–s 830
  shed–s 839
  –s in one's eyes
    excited 824
    sad 837
tear *separate* 44
  violence 173
  move rapidly 274
  excite 825
  spree 840
  –asunder one's bonds 750
  –away from 789
  –oneself away 623
  –one's hair 839
  –out 301
  –to pieces
    separate 44
    destroy 162
  –up *destroy* 162
tearful 839
tear gas 663, 727
tease *annoy* 830
  aggravate 835
  spite 907
teaser *difficult* 704
teasing 830
teat 250
tea-table talk 588
technical
  conformable 82
  workmanlike 698
  –education 537
  –knowledge 698
  –school 542

–term 564
technicality
  special 79
  cant term 563
  formulary 697
technique
  painting 556
  skill 698
technology 698
techy 901
tectiform 223
tectology 357
ted 73
tedge 350
Te Deum 990
tedious 841
  while away the– hours 681
tedium 841
tee 66
teem *produce* 161
  productive 168
  abound 639
  –with *multitude* 102
teemful 168
teeming *crowd* 72
teemless 169
teens 98
  in one's–127, 129
teeter 314
teeth *grinders* 330
  holders 781
  armed to the–
    prepared 673
    defense 717
    warfare 722
  between the–405
  cast in one's–938
  chattering of–
    cold 383
  grind one's–900
  have cut one's eye– 698
  in one's–
    opposition 708
    compulsion 744
  in the–of
    difficulty 704
    opposition 708
  make one's–chatter
    cold 385
    fear 860
  run of one's–815
  set one's–604
  set the–on edge
    scrape 331
    saw 397
    stridor 410
    pain the feelings 830
  show one's–900
teetotalism
  temperance 953
  sobriety 958
teetotum *rotation* 312
  toy 840
teg 366

tegumen 223
tegument 223
tehee 856
teichopsia 442
teinoscope 445
telamon 215
telegony 154
telegram 527, 531, 532
telegraph
  velocity 274
  inform 527
  messenger 534
  signal 550
  by–*haste* 684
telegraphic 531
telegraphone 527
telegraphy
  publication 531
telekinesis 264
telemeter 200
teleology 620
telepathic 450
telepathy 450, 992a
telephone 418
  inform 527
  messenger 534
telephony 402
telescope 441, 445, 572 *collide* 276
telescopic 196
telesm 993
telethermometer 389
tell *count* 85
  influence 175
  evidence 467
  inform 527
  speak 582
  describe 594
  succeed 731
  let me–you 535
  –a lie 544
  –fortunes 511
  –fortunes 511
  –how 155
  –its own tale 518
  –of 467
  –off 85
  –one plainly 527
  –one's beads 990, 998
  –tales *disclose* 529
  –the cause of 522
  –the truth 543
  who can–475
teller *treasurer* 801
telling *influential* 175
  graphic 518
  important 642
  exciting 824
  with–effect
    energy 171
    influence 175
telltale *news* 532
  indicator 550
  knave 941

tempt

telluric 318
temerity 863
temper *nature* 5
  state 7
  moderate 174
  elasticity 323
  pliability 324
  qualify 469
  prepare 673
  affections 820
  irascibility 901
  command of–826
  lose one's–900
  out of–901a
  –the wind to the shorn lamb 834
  trial of–824
tempera 556
temperament
  nature 5
  tendency 176
  musical 413
  affections 820
temperance 174, **953**
temperate
  moderate 174
  mild 826
  abstemious 953
temperature 382
  increase of–384
  reduction of–385
tempest *violence* 173
  agitation 315
  wind 349
  exaggeration 549
  excitement 825
tempestivity 134
tempest-tossed
  excited 824
Templar 996
  good–958
temple *house* 189
  side 236
  church **1000**
  –of the Holy Ghost 983a
temporal
  transient 111
  chronological 114
  laical 997
  lords–and spiritual 875
temporary 111
  –expedient 147
temporize
  protract 110
  defer 133
  cunning 702
  (*occasion* 134)
temporizer 943
tempt *entice* 615
  attempt 675
  desire 865
  –fortune *hazard* 621
  essay 675
  –Providence *rash* 863

temptation — thank

temptation
  arrogate 885
  —the appetite 394
temptation
  —hath a music 615
tempter 615
  Satan 978
  voice of the—615
temulence 959
ten 98—thousand 98
  —to one 472
tenable 664
tenacity *coherence* 46
  toughness **327**
  memory 505
  resolution 604
  perservance 604a
  obstinacy 606
  retention 781
  avarice 819
  —of life 357
  —of purpose 604a
tenaculum 781
tenancy 777
tenant *present* 186
  occupier 188
  possessor 779
tenantless
  absence 187
  seclusion 893
tenax propositi
  determined 204
  honorable 939
tend *conduce* 176
  —animals 370
  minister 631
  aid 707
  serve 746
  —stock 370
  —towards
    direction 278
tendence 176, 749
tendency 176
tender *slight* 32
  ship 273
  soft 324
  color 428
  war vessel 726
  offer 763
  susceptible 822
  affectionate 897
  benevolent 906
  compassionate 914
  —age 127
  —conscience *duty* 926
    (*honor* 939)
  —heart *susceptible* 822
    kind 906
    compassionate 914
  —mercies
    (ironical)
    badness 649
    severity 739
    cruelty 907
  —one's resignation
    757
  —passion 897

—to 707
tenderfoot 57, 541
tenderling 158
tendon 45
tendril *fastening* 45
  runner 51, 367
  infant 129
  filament 205
  convoluted 248
tenebrous 421
tenement *house* 189
  apartment 191
  property 780
  —of clay 362
tenet *belief* 484
  (*theology* 983)
tenez 142
tenfold 98
tennis 840
tenor *course* 7
  degree 26
  directions 278
  high note 410
  violin 417
  meaning 516
  (*musician* 416)
  pursue the noiseless
    —of one's way
    881
  —horn 417
tenpins 840
ten pounder 727
tense *hard* 323
tensibility 325
tensile 325
tension *strength* 159
  length 200
ten-strike 731
tensure 200
tent *abode* 189
  covering 223
  pitch one's—
    locate 184
    arrive 292
tentacle 781
tentative *inquiry* 461
  experimental 463
  essaying 675
tented field 722
tenter-hook 214
  on—s 507
tenth 99
tenths *lithe* 812
tent pegging 840
tenuity *smallness* 32
  thinness 203
  rarity 322
tenuous (*see* tenuity)
  unsubstantial 4
tenure *possession* 777
  property 780
  due 924
tepee 189, 223
tepefaction 384
tepefy 384
tephramancy 511

tepid *warm* 382
  half cold 383
tepidarium 386
teratism 83
teratogenic 83
teratology
  unconformity 83
  distortion 243
  altiloquence 577
  boasting 884
tercentenary 98, 883
terceron 41
terebration
  opening 260
  (*passage through*
    302)
tergal 235
tergiversate 140, 607
tergiversation
  regress 283
  change of mind **607**
tergum 235
term *end* 67
  place in series **71**
  period of time 106
  limit 233
  word 562
  name 564
  lease 780
termagant 901
terminable 233
terminal *end* 67
  limit 233
terminate *end* 67
  limit 233, 292
  journey 266
termination 67, 151
terminology 562
terminus *end* 67
  limit 233
  journey 266
  arrival 292
termite 366, 690
termless 105
terms (*see* term)
  circumstances 8
  reasoning 476
  pacification 723
  conditions 770
  bring to—723
  come to—*assent* 488
  pacify 723
  submit 725
  consent 762
  compact 769
  couch in—566
  in no measured—
    574
  on friendly—888
ternal 94
ternary 93, 490a
ternion 92
Terpsichore
  music 416
  dancing 840
terra cotta *baked* 384

  brown 433
  sculpture 557
terra firma
  support 215
  land 342
terra incognita 491
terrace *houses* 189
  level 213
terrain 181
terraqueous 318
terrene *world* 318
  land 342
terrestrial 318
terret 45
terre verte 435
terrible *vast* 31
  fearful 860
terribly *greatly* 31
terrier *list* 86
  auger 262
  dog 366
terrific *painful* 830
  fearful 860
terrify 860
terrine 191
territorial *land* 342
territory *region* 181
  property 780
terror 860
  King of—s 360
  reign of
  —severity 739
  pain 828
terrorism 860
  insolence 885
terrorist
  combatant 726
  intimidator 860
  coward 862
  blusterer 887
  evildoer 913
terrorize 860, 885
Tersanctus 900
terse 572
tertian *periodic* 138
tertiary 92, 93
tertium quid
  dissimilar 18
  mixture 41
  combination 48
  unconformable 83
terza 93
terzetto 415
tessellated
  variegated 440
  ornament 847
tessellation 440
tesserae *mosaic* 440
  counters 550
test 463
testa 223
testaceology 223
testaceous 223
testament
  security 771
  (*record* 551)

Testament 985
testamur 467
testator 784
tester *bedspread* 215
  sixpence 800
testicle 357
testify *evidence* 467
  sign 550
testimonial 551
testimony 467
testy 901
tetanus 655
tetchy 901
tête-à-tête *two* 89
  near 197
  confer 588
tether *fasten* 43
  locate 184
  restrain 751
  means of restraint
    752
  go beyond the
    length of one's—
    738
tethered *firm* 150
tetrachord 413
tetract 95
tetrad 95, 193
tetragon 95
tetragram 95
tetrahedral 253
tetrahedron 95, 244
tetrarch 745
tetter 655
Texas fever 655
text *prototype* 22
  topic 454
  meaning 516
  printing 591
  book 593
  libretto 599
textbook *school* 542
  synopsis 596
  (*teaching* 537)
  —committee 542
textile *woven* 219
  texture 329
textuary
  orthodox 983a
  revelation 985
texture *mixture* 41
  roughness 256
  fabric **329**
  (*condition* 7)
Thais 962
Thalia 599
thallogens 369
Thames
  never set the—on
    fire *fool* 501
  bungler 701
thana 752
thane *nobility* 875
  (*master* 745)
thank 916
  no—you 764

thankful

   —one's stars
    rejoice 838
  —you for nothing 917
thankful 916
  rest and be–
    quiescence 265
    content 831
thankless *painful* 830
  ungrateful 917
thank offering 916
thanks 916
Thanksgiving 138, 840
thanksgiving
  gratitude 916
  worship 990
thanks to
  caused by 155
that 79 at–time 119
  —being so 8
  —is 118
  —is to say 79
  —or nothing 609a
thatch *roof* 223
  roughness 256
  furrow 259
  (*top* 210)
thaumatrope 445
thaumaturgist 994
thaumaturgy 992
thaw *melt* 335
  heat 382
  calm the mind 826
  pity 914
Thearchy
  authority 737
  Diety 976
theater *spectacle* 441
  classroom 542
  drama 599
  arena 728
  amusement 840
  tribunal 966
  –staff 599
theatrical 599
  affected 855
  ostentatious 882
theca 223
thé dansant 892
theft 791
theism
  monotheism 983
  piety 987
theist 983
theistic *of God* 976
theme *topic* 454
  writing 590
  dissertation 595
Themis 922
then *time* 106
  priority 116
  therefore 476
thence *caused by* 155
  departure 293
  therefore 476
thenceforward 121

theocracy *Diety* 976
  church 995
theodicy 987
theodolite 244, 466
theogony 161, 979
theologian 983
theology 983
theomancy 511
theopathy 987
theophany 980a, 985
theophobist 989
theopneustic 985
theorbo 417
theorem *topic* 454
  maxim 496
  supposition 514
theoretical 514, 515
theorist 514
theorize 155, 514
theory *attribution* 155
  knowledge 490
  supposition 514
theosophist 981, 984, 992a
theosophy 983
therapeutics 537, 655, 662
there *situation* 183
  presence 186
thereabouts
  almost 32
  place 183
  near 197
thereafter 117
thereby 631
  —hangs a tale 154
therefore
  attribution 155
  reasoning 476
  judgment 480
  motive 615
therein 221
thereof 9
theretofore 116
thereupon *time* 106
  after 117
therewith
  accompanying 88
  means 632
theriac 662
thermae 382, 386
thermal 382
thermantidote 349
thermogenesis 382
thermology 382
thermolysis 49
thermometer
  heat **389**
  measure 466
thermometrograph 389
thermopile 389
thermoscope 389
thermostat 389
Thersites 936
thesaurus *list* 86

school 542
words 562
book 593
store 636
thesis *theme* 454
  proposition 514
  writing 590
  dissertation 595
  (*affirmation* 535)
Thespian 599
Thetis 341
theurgist 994
theurgy 992
thews and sinews 159
thick *middle* 68
  crowded 72
  numerous 102
  broad 202
  dense 321
  semiliquid 352
  turbid 426
  dirty 653
  friends 888
  come–102
  in the–of
  imbedded 228
  action 680
  lay it on–*cover* 223
  redundance 641
  flattery 933
  —of the action 682
  —of the fray 722
  through–and thin
  violent 173
  persevere 604a
thick–coming
  many 102
  repeated 104
  frequent 136
  —fancies 515
thicken 35
  the plot–s 682
thicket 72, 367
thick–headed 499
thickness 202
thick–ribbed 159
  —ice 383
thickset *short* 201
  broad 202
  dense 321
thick–skinned
  physically 376
  morally 823
thick–skull
  imbecile 499
  fool 501
thief 792
  like a–in the night
  unexpected 508
  concealment 528
  dishonorable 940
  set a–to catch a thief 791
thievery 791
thieves' Latin 563

thievish 791
thill 215
thimble 717
  (*concave* 252)
thimbleful 32
thimblerig 545
thimblerigger 792
thin *subduct* 38
  few 103
  small 193
  narrow 203
  rare 322
  scanty 640
  —end of the wedge 66
  —out 371
thing *substance* 3
  matter 316
  just the–924
  the–926
  —of naught 4
  —to do 625
things *events* 151
  clothes 225
  chattels 780
  as–go 613
thingumbob 563
think
  cogitate 450, 451
  believe 484
  as one–s proper 600
  only–873
  reason to–472
  —aloud *soliloquy* 589
  artless 703
  —better of *recant* 607
  improve 658
  —fit *will* 600
  willing 602
  —highly 931
  —ill 932
  —likely 472
  —no more of
  inattention 458
  forgive 918
  —of *intend* 620
  —out 457
  —twice *irresolute* 605
  cautious 864
  —upon *remember* 505
thinker 500
thinking 451
  —principle 450
thinness 203
thin–skinned
  physically sensible 375
  morally sensitive 822
  fastidious 868
  irascible 901
third 93 *trisection* 94
  music 413
  —degree 461
  —heaven 981
  —part 94

thought

  —person 664
  —power 92
thirdly 93
thirds 780
thirst 865
  —for glory 716
  —for knowledge 455
thirsty 865–*soul* 959
thirteen 98
thirty–nine articles 983a
thirty–one *cards* 840
this 79
  at–time of day 118
  —that or the other 15
thistle *prickly* 253
thistledown *light* 320
thither 278
thole 821
thole pin 215
thong *fastening* 45
  scourge 975
Thor 979
thorn *sharp* 253
  bane 663
  painful 830
  plant a–830
  spiteful 907
  —in the flesh 830
  —in the side
  badness 649
  annoyance 830
  on–s for
  longing 865
  sit on–s
  physical pain 378
  moral pain 828
  fear 860
thorniness
  (see *thorny*)
  sullenness 901a
thorny *prickly* 253
  difficult 704
  discourteous 895
thorough 52, 729
thoroughbass 413
thoroughbred
  intrinsic 5
  horse 271
  skill 698
  fashionable 852
thoroughfare
  opening 260
  way 627
  (*passage* 302)
thoroughgoing 52
thoroughly do–729
thoroughpaced 31
thorp 189
though
  compensation 30
  qualification 469
  opposition 708
  (*counteraction* 179)
thought *little* 32
  reflection **451**

thoughtful

idea 453
(*maxim* 496)
give a–to 457
not to be–of
reject 610
prohibit 761
organ of–450
quick as–274
seat of–450
subject of–454
the power of–451
–of 454
–reading 450
–transference 450, 992a
want of–458
who could have 508
thoughtful
reflecting 451
wise 498
thoughtless
incogitant 452
inattentive 458
careless 460
improvident 674
thousand *number* 98
many 102
one in a–*good* 648
good man 948
thrall 746, 751
thralldom 749
thrash *punish* 972
Thraso 887
Thrasonic 884, 885
thrawn 217
thread *arrange* 60
series 69
weak 160
filament 205
pass through 302
hang by a–665
life hangs by a–360
not have a dry–339
–one's way
journey 266
passage 302
worn to a–659
threadbare *bare* 226
deteriorated 659
threadlike 205
thread paper 203
threat 909
threaten *future* 121
destiny 152
danger 665
(*alarm* 669)
threatening
warning 668
unhopeful 859
three 93 sisters–601
–color process 558
–per cent 802
–R's 537
–sheets in the wind 959
–times three

number 98
approbation 931
three–decker
house 189
threefold 93
three–score 98
–years and ten 128
three–tailed bashaw
master 745
nobility 875
threne 839
threnetic 838
threnody 839
thresh 972–out 461
threshold
beginning 66
edge 231
at the–*near* 197
–of an inquiry 461
thrice 93–happy 827
–is he armed 922
–told tale 573
thrid 302
thrift *prosperity* 734
gain 775
economy 817
thriftless 674, 818
thrill *touch* 380
feeling 821
excitation 824
thrilling *pleasing* 829
painful 830
thrive *prosper* 73
gain 618
(*succeed* 732)
throat *opening* 260
air pipe 350, 351
cut the–361
force down the–739
stick in one's–
voiceless 581
speechless 585
take by the–789
–disease 655
throaty 583
throb *oscillate* 314
agitate 315
emotion 821
throbbing–heart 860
–pain 378
throe *revolution* 146
violence 173
agitation 315
physical pain 378
(*moral pain* 828)
birth–161
throne *abode* 189
seat 215
emblem of authority 747
ascend the–737
occupy the–737
–of God 981
throng 72
throttle
render powerless 158

close 261
kill 361
seize 789
–down 275
through *owing to* 154
viâ 278
by means of 631
(*passage* 302)
get–729
go–one 824
–thick and thin
complete 52
violence 173
perseverance 604a
throughout
totality 50
completeness 52
–the world 180
throw *impel* 276
propel 284
exertion 686
–a tub to catch a whale 545
–a veil over 528
–away *eject* 297
reject 610
waste 638
relinquish 782
–away the scabbard 722
–cold water on 616
–doubt upon 485
–down *destroy* 162
lower 308
–good money after bad 818
–in 228
–into the shade
superior 33
lessen 36
surpass 303
important 642
(*repute* 873)
–off (*see below*)
–of the dice 156
–oneself at the feet of 725
–oneself into the arms of
safety 664
–on paper 590
–open *open* 260
admit 296
–out
(*see below*)
–over *destroy* 162
–overboard
exclude 55
destroy 162
eject 297
abrogate 756
–up
(*see below*)
throwback 145
throw off 297
–all disguise 529

–one's guard
inexpectation 508
cunning 702
–the mask 529
–the scent
misdirect 538
avoid 623
throw out *propel* 284
eject 297
–a feeler 379
–a hint 527
–a suggestion 514
–of gear *disjoin* 44
derange 61
thrown out 704
throw up *eject* 297
resign 757
–one's cap 884
–the game 624
thrum 416
thrush 366, 416
thrust *push* 276
attack 716
–down one's throat 744
–in *insert* 300
(*interpose* 228)
–one's nose in 682
–upon 784
thud 406, 408a
thug
murderer 361, 726
bandit 792
thuggee 361
thuggery 361
thumb *touch* 379
bite the–929
one's fingers all–s 699
rule of–
experiment 463
unreasoning 477
essay 675
–over 539
–s down! 361
under one's–
authority 737
subjection 749
thumb print
evidence 467
thumbscrew 975
thump *beat* 276
noise 406
nonresonance 408a
–the piano 416
punish 972
thumping *great* 31
big 192
thunder *violence* 173
noise 404
omen 512
prodigy 872
threaten 909
look black as–
discontented 832
angry 900

–against
malediction 908
censure 932
–at the top of one's voice 411
–by 274
–forth 531
–of applause 931
–s of the Vatican 908
thunderbolt
weapon 727
prodigy 872
thunderburst 406
thunderclap
noise 406
unexpected 508
prodigy 872
thunderhead 353
thundering
immense 31
big 192
thunderstorm 173
thunderstruck 870
thundertube 260
thurible 400, 998
thurifer 400
thuriferous 400
thurification
fragrance 400
rite 998
thus *circumstance* 8
therefore 476
–far *little* 32
limit 233
thwack *beat* 276
punish 972
thwart *across* 219
wrong 649
obstruct 706
oppose 708
annoy 830
thwarted 732
thyroid 221
thyrsus 215
tiara *insignia* 747
jewelry 847
canonicals 999
tic douloureux 378
tick *oscillation* 314
insect 368
sound 407
mark 550
credit 805
go on–806
–off *record* 551
ticket 550 *plan* 626
ticket of leave 760
–man *prisoner* 754
bad man 949
tickle *touch* 380
please 829
amuse 840
(*physical pleasure* 377)
–the fancy 829, 840
–the palate 394

592

tickler

    –the palm *give* 784
      pay 807
tickler *pungency* 392
tickling 380
ticklish *touch* 380
    uncertain 475
    dangerous 665
    difficult 704
tidal wave 348, 667
tidbit *food* 298
    gem 646
    good 648
    pleasing 829
tide *time* 106
    ocean 341
    wave 348
    abundance 639
    prosperity 734
    against the–708
    drift with the–
      facile 705
    go with the–
      conformity 82
    high etc.–348
    stem the–708
    swim with the–
      prosperity 734
    –of eloquence 582
    –of events 151
    –of time 109
    –over *time* 106
    defer 133
    safe 664
    inaction 681
    succeed 731
    –race 348, 667
    turn of the–210
tidings 532
tidy *orderly* 58
    arrange 60
    covering 223
    good 648
    clean 652
    pretty 845
tie *relation* 9
    equality 27
    fasten 43
    fastening 45
    neckcloth 225
    security 771
    obligation 926
    nuptial–903
    ride and–266
    –down *hinder* 706
    compel 744
    restrain 751
    –oneself *promise* 768
    –the hands
      render powerless 158
      restrain 751
    –s of blood 11
    –up *restrain* 751
    condition 770
    entail 771
tiebeam 45
tied up *in debt* 806

tier *continuity* 69
    layer 204
tierce *triality* 92
    worship 990
    carte and–716
tiff *quarrel* 713
    anger 900
tiffin 298
tigella 367
tiger *violent* 173
    servant 746
    cheer 838
    courage 861
    savage 907
    evildoer 913
    bad man 949
tight *fast* 43
    closed 261
    smart 845
    drunk 959
    keep a–hand on 751
    on one's–ropes 878
    –grasp 739
    –hand 739
tighten 43
    contract 195
tight-fisted 819
tights 225
tigress 374
tike 876
tilbury 272
tilde 550
tile *roof* 223
    hat 225
    –loose *insane* 503
tiler *sentinel* 263
till *up to the time* 106
    coffer 191
    cultivate 371
    treasury 802
    –doomsday 112
    –now 122
    –the soil *prepare* 673
tillable 371
tiller *instrument* 633
    money-box 802
    –of the soil
      agriculture 342, 371
    clown 876
tilmus 315
tilpah 223
tilt *slope* 217
    cover 223
    propel 284
    fall 306
    contention 720
    full-direct 278
    active 682
    haste 684
    ride full–at
    pursue 622
    attack 716
    run a–at 716
    –over 218
    –up 307

    –with 720
tilth 371
tilting 720
    –at the ring 840
tilt-yard 728
timbal 417
timber *trees* 367
    materials 635
timbre 413
timbrel 417
timbrology 550
time 106
    adjust 58
    instant 113
    leisure 685
    against–*haste* 684
    at–s 136
    course of–109
    employ one's–in 625
    glass of–106
    in–*course* 109
    early 132
    destiny 152
    measure–114
    no–*instantly* 113
    soon 132
    no–to lose *need* 630
    haste 684
    no–to spare 684
    ravages of–659
    slow–275
    take–*slow* 275
    inaction 681
    inactive 683
    there being–s when 136
    –after time 104
    –and again 104
    –being 118
    –clock 550, 551
    –drawing on 121
    –enough 132
    –gone by 135
    –hanging on one's hands
      inaction 681
      leisure 685
      weariness 841
    –has been 122
    –immemorial 122
    –is out of joint 106
    –of day 113
    –of life *duration* 106
    now 118
    age 128
    –out of mind 122
    –to come 121
    –to spare 685
    –up *transient* 111
    occasion 134
    –was 122
    –wasted 106
    true–113
    waste–683
timeful 134

time-honored
    old 124
    repute 873
    respected 928
timekeeper 114
timeless 135
timely *early* 132
    opportune 134
timeous 134
timepiece 114
timepleaser 607, 943
times *present* 118
    events 151
    hard–735
    many–136
timeserver 607, 943
timeserving
    tergiversation 607
    cunning 702
    servility 886
    improbity 940
    selfishness 943
time-worn *old* 124
    age 128
    deteriorated 659
timid *fearful* 860
    cowardly 862
    humble 881
timidity (see timid)
    humility 879
timist 607
timocracy 803
Timon of Athens
    wealth 803
    seclusion 893
    misanthrope 911
timorous (see timid)
timothy 367
timpano 417
tin *preserve* 670
    money 800
    –oven 386
    –wedding 883
tinct 428
tinction 428
tinctorial 428
tincture
    small quantity 32
    mixture 41
    color 428
tinctured
    disposition 820
tinder *fuel* 388
    irascible 901
tine 253
tinge
    small quantity 32
    mix 41
    color 428
tingent 428
tingible 428
tingle *pain* 378
    touch 380
    emotion 821
    make the ears–900
tink 408

tithing

tinker *repair* 660
    (*improve* 658)
tinkle *faint sound* 405
    resonance 408
tinkling cymbal 517
tinned goods 670
tinnient 408
tinsel *glitter* 420
    sham 545
    ornament 847
    frippery 851
tint 428
tintamarre 404
tintinnabulary 408
tintinnabulation 408
tiny 193
tip *end* 67
    summit 210
    cover 223
    discrimination 465
    give 784
    (*pay* 807)
    on–toe *high* 206
    expect 507
    –off 465
    –the wink 550
tipcat 840
tippet 214, 225
tipple *drink* 298
    tope 959
tippler 959
tippybob 803
tipstaff 965
tipsy 959
tiptop *summit* 210
    good 648
tirade *speech* 582
    censure 932
tirailleur 726
tire *invest* 225
    automobile 272
    fatigue 688
    worry 830
    weary 841
tiresome (see tire)
tisane 662
Tisiphone 173
tissue *whole* 50
    assemblage 72
    matted 219
    texture 329
tit *small* 193
    pony 271
Titan *strength* 159
    size 192
    sun god 423
    demon 980
Titaness 192
Titanic 159
titanic 31, 192
titbit *savory* 394
    pleasing 829
tit for tat 718
tithe *tenth* 99
    tax 812
tithing 181

tithingman 965
Titian red 434
titillate *amuse* 840
  provoke desire 865
titillation
  pleasure 377
  touch 380
titivate 847
title *indication* 550
  name 564
  book 593
  authority 747
  right to property 780
  distinction **877**
  right 924
titled 875
title deed 771
title-page 66
titration 490b
titter 838
tittle
  small quantity 32
  inextension 180a
  to a– 494
tittle-tattle *news* 532
  small talk 588
titubancy 583
titubate *fall* 306
  fail 732
titular *word* 562
  nomenclature 564
tivoli 840
tmesis 218
T.N.T. 727
to *direction* 278
  lie–681
  –a certain degree 32
  –a great extent 31
  –all intents and
    purposes
    equally 27
    whole 52
  –a man 78
  –and fro 12, 148, 314
  –a small extent 32
  –be sure 488
  –come *future* 121
    destiny 152
  –crown all 33, 642
  –do 59
  –some extent 26
  –the credit of 805
  –the end of the
    chapter 52
  –the end of time 112
  –the full 52
  –the letter 19
  –the point 23
  –the purpose 23
  –this day 118
  –wit 79
toad *hateful* 649
  ugly 846
  –under a harrow 378
toadeater *servile* 886
  sycophant 935

toadeating
  flattery 933
toadstool 367
toadying 886
toadyism 933
toast *roast* 384
  celebrate 883
  –brown 433
toaster 386
tobacco 392
toboggan 272
tobogganing 840
toby 191
toccata 415
tocogony 161
tocology 161, 662
tocsin 669
tod 319
today 118
toddle *walk* 266
  limp 275
toddy 298
toe 211
  on the light
    fantastic–
  jump 309
  dance 840
toes turn up the–
  die 360
toft 189, 780
toga *coat* 225
  robes 747
  assume the–virilis
    131
together
  accompanying 88
  same time 120
  come–290
  get–72
  hang–709
  lay heads–695
  –with *added to* 37
    accompanied by 88
toggery 225
toil *activity* 682
  exertion 686
  –of a pleasure 682
  –s *trap* 545
    (*danger* 667)
    (*wile* 702)
toilet 225–water 400
toilette 225
  en grande–847
toilsome 686
  difficult 704
toilworn 688
token 550 give
  –*manifest* 525
  –of remembrance 505
tolderrolloll 838
Toledo 727
tolerable *a little* 32
  trifling 643
  not perfect 651
  passable 845
toleration *laxity* 738

lenity 740
permission 760
feeling 821
calmness 826
benevolence 906
toll *sound* 407
  tax 812
  –the knell 363
tollbooth *prison* 752
  market 799
toluene 490b
tom *male* 373
tomahawk 727
tomato 298
tomb 363
  lay in the–363
  –of the Capulets 506
tombola 156
tomboy 129, 851
tombstone 363
tomcat 373
tome 593
tomentose 256
tomfool 501
tomfoolery
  absurdity 497
  amusement 840
  wit 842
  ostentation 882
Tommy Atkins 726
tomnoddy 501
Tom o' Bedlam 504
to-morrow 121
  –and to-morrow
    repetition 104
    course of time 109
tompion 263
tomtit 193
Tom Thumb 193
tom-tom *music* 417
  military 722
ton *weight* 319
  fashion 852
tonality *music* 413
  light and shade 420
tone *state* 7
  strength 159
  tendency 176
  sound 402
  music 413
  color 428
  painting 556
  method 627
  disposition 820
  give a–to 852
  –down *moderate* 174
  darken 421
  discolor 429
  –of voice 580
  –poem 415
tong 712
tonga 272
tongs *fire irons* 386
  retention 781
tongue *projection* 250
  food 298

touch 379
taste 390
language 560
bite the–392
bridle one's–585
give–404, 580
have a–in one's
  head 582
hold one's–403
keep one's–between
  one's teeth 585
on the tip of one's–
  near 197
forget 506
latent 526
speech 582
slip of the–
  error 495
  solecism 568
  stammering 583
–cleave to the roof
  of one's mouth
  870
–of land 342
–running loose 584
wag the–582
tongue-lash
  berate 932
tongueless 581
tongue-shaped 245
tongue-tied 581
tonic
  musical note 413
  phonetic 561
  healthy 656
  medicine 662
tonicity *strength* 159
tonic sol-fa 415
tonjon 272
tonnage 192
tonneau 272
tonsillitis 655
tonsils 351
tonsure 550, 999
tonsured 226
tontine 810
tony 501
Tony Lumpkin 876
too *also* 37
  excess 641
  in a–great degree
    31
  –bad *disreputable* 874
    wrong 923
    censure 932
  –far 641
  –hot to hold one 830
  –late 133
  –late for 135
  –little 640
  –many 641
  –much (see below)
  –soon 132
  –soon for 135
  true *regret* 833
    lamentation 839

too much
  redundance 641
  intemperance 954
  have–of 869
  make–of 482
  –for 471
  –of a good thing 869
tool *instrument* 633
  steer 693
  cat's-paw 711
  servile 886
  edge– 253
  mere– 690
tooling 847
toot 406, 416
tooth *fastening* 45
  projection 250
  sharp 253
  roughness 256
  notch 257
  texture 329
  taste 390
  sweet–desire 865
  fastidious 868
  –and nail
    violence 173
    exertion 686
    attack 716
  –of time 106, 551
  –paste 652
  –powder 652
toothache 378
toothed 253
toothful 392
toothless 254
tooth-shaped 253
toothsome 394
tootle 407, 416
top *supreme* 33
  summit 210
  roof 223
  automobile 272
  spin 312
  at the–of one's
    speed 274
  at the–of one's
    voice *loud* 404
    shout 411
  at the–of the tree
    873
  fool to the–of one's
    bent 545
  from–to toe 200
  sleep like a–683
  –of the ladder 873
  –to bottom
    completely 52
toparchy 737
topaz *yellow* 436
  jewel 847
top banana 642
top-boot 225
tope *tomb* 363
  trees 367
  drink 959
  temple 1000

topek 189
toper 959
topfull 52
top-gallant mast
  height 206
  summit 210
top-heavy
  unbalanced 28
  inverted 218
  dangerous 665
  tipsy 959
Tophet 982
topiary 847
topic 454
  –of the day 532
topical 183
toploftiness 878, 885
topmast 206
topmost 210
topographer 466
topography 183, 466, 550
topple *unbalanced* 28
  perish 162
  decay 659
  –down *fall* 306
  –over 28, 306
topsail schooner 273
top sawyer 700
top-sergeant 745
topsy-turvy 59, 218
tor 206
torch *fuel* 388
  luminary 423
  apply the–824
  light the–of war 722
  –of Hymen 903
Tories 712
torment *physical* 378
  moral 828, 830
  place of–982
tormina 378
torminous 378
torn (*see* tear)
  discord 713
tornado *whirl* 312
  wind 349
  (*violence* 173)
torose 250
torpedinous 823
torpedo *vehicle* 272
  detonator 406
  weapon 727
  evildoer 913
torpedo boat 726
torpescent 683
torpid *inert* 172
  inactive 683
  insensible 823
torpor (*see* torpid)
torpids 720
torporific 823
torque 847
torrefy 340, 384
torrent *violence* 173

rapid 274
flow 348
rain in–s 348
torrid 382
torsion 248
torso 50
tort 925, 947
torticollis 378
tortile 248
tortious 925
tortive 248
tortoise 275
tortoise-shell 440
tortuous *twisted* 248
  concealed 528
  dishonorable 940
torture *physical* 378
  moral 828, 830
  cruelty 907
  punishment 972
  –a question 476
torturer 975
torturous 378
torvity 901a
toss *derange* 61
  throw 284
  oscillate 314
  agitate 315
  –in a blanket 929
  –off *drink* 298
  –on one's pillow 825
  –overboard 610
  –the head *pride* 878
  insolence 885
  contempt 930
  –up 156, 621
tosspot 959
tot *child* 129, 167
  –up 811
total *add* 37
  whole 50
  number 84, 85
  –abstinence
  temperate 953
  ascetic 955
  –eclipse 421
  sum–800
totality 52
totalizator 551, 621
totally 52
tote 270
totem 550
totemism 372a
totient 84
totitive 84
totter *changeable* 149
  weak 160
  limp 275
  oscillate 314
  agitate 315
  decay 659
  danger 665
  –to its fall 162
touch *relate to* 9
  small quantity 32
  mixture 41

contact 199
sensation **379, 380**
music 416
test 463
indication 550
act 680
receive 785
excite 824
pity 914
in–with 9
some–of nature's glow 318
–and go *instant* 113
–soon 132
–changeable 149
–easy 705
–on 516
–on the raw 822
–the guitar 416
–the hat 894
–the heart 824
–to the quick 822
–up 658
–upon *treat on* 595
touched *crazy* 503
  tainted 653
  compassion 914
  penitent 950
  –in the wind 655
  –with *feeling* 821
touchhole 351
touching 830
touchstone 463
touchwood *fuel* 388
  irascible 901
touchy 901
tough *coherent* 46
  violence 173
  tenacious 327
  difficult 704
  ruffian 726, 876
  larrikin 887
  bully 913
toupee 256
tour 266
tour de force
  skill 698
  stratagem 702
  display 882
touring car 272
tourist 268
tournament 720
tourney 720
tourniquet 263
tournure *outline* 230
  form 240
  appearance 448
tousle 61
tout *solicit* 765
  petitioner 767
  flatterer 935
tout ensemble 226
touter *agent* 758
  solicitor 767
  eulogist 935
tow 285 take in

–aid 707
towardly 705
towards 278
  draw–288
  move–286
towel *clean* 652
  flog 972
tower *stability* 150
  edifice 161
  abode 189
  height 206
  soar 305
  safety 664
  check 706
  defense 717
  prison 752
  –above 31
  –of silence 363
  –of strength
  strong 159
  influential 175
towering *great* 31
  violent 173
  large 192
  high 206
  –passion 900
  –rage 825
tow-headed 429
town *city* 189
  fashion 852
  all over the–532
  man about–854
  on the–961
  talk of the–873
townhall 966
townhouse 189, 966
township 181
townsman 188
town talk *news* 532
  gossip 588
towpath 627
towrow 713
toxic 657
toxicant 663
toxicology 663
toxiferous 657
toxophilite 840
toy *trifle* 643
  amusement 840
  fondle 902
toy dog 366
toyshop 840
tracasserie 713
trace *follow* 63
  inquire 461
  discover 480a
  mark 550
  record 551
  delineate 554
  –back 122
  –out 480a
  –to 155
  –up 461
tracery *lattice* 219
  curve 245
  ornament 847

traces *harness* 45
trachea 351
tracheocele 655
trachoma 655
tracing 21
track *travel* 266
  trace 461
  spoor 550
  record 551
  way 627
  in one's–s 113
  –events 840
trackless *space* 180
  difficult 704
  –trolley 273
tract *region* 181
  book 593
  dissertation 595
  –of time 109
tractable
  malleable 324
  willing 602
  easy 705
tractarian 984
tractate 595
tractile *traction* **285**
  soft 324
traction 285
tractive 285
tractor 272
trade *business* 625
  traffic 794
  drive a–625
  learn one's–539
  the–*booksellers* 593
  –with 794
  tricks of the–702
  two of a–708
trader 797
trademark 550
tradesman 797
trade union 712
trade wind 349
tradition *old* 124
  description 594
traditionalism 451
traditive 594
traduce 934
traducer 936
traffic 794
tragalism 954
tragalist 954a
tragedian 599
tragedy *drama* 599
  evil 619
tragic *drama* 599
tragical 830
tragi-comedy 599
tragi-comic 853
trail *sequel* 65
  pendent 214
  slow 275
  traction 285
  odor 398
  inquiry 461
  track 550

trailer

record 551
follow in the—of 281
—of a red herring 615, 706
—of the serpent 945
trailer *vehicle* 272
train *sequence* 63, 281
  sequel 65
  series 69
  pendent 214
  vehicle 272
  traction 285
  —*animals* 370
  teach 537
  accustom 613
  prepare 673
  bring in its—615
  in—673
  in the—*of following* 281
  servant 746
  lay —*scheme* 626
  prepare 673
  put in—673
  siege—727
  —*of reasoning* 476
  —*of thought* 451
trainband 726
train bearer 746
trained 698
trainer—*of horses* 268
  —*of animals* 370
  teacher 540
training
  education 537
train oil 356
traipse 275
trait *speciality* 79
  appearance 448
  mark 550
traitor
  disobedient 742
  enemy 891
  knave 941
traitress 891
trajection 297
trajectory 627
tralatitious 521
tralineate 279
tralucent 425
tram 272
trammel *hinder* 706
  restrain 751
  fetter 752
  cast—*s off* 750
tramontane
  foreign 57
  distant 196
  wind 349
  outlandish 851
tramp *stroll* 266
  stroller 268
  vagabond 460, 876
  on the—264
tramper 268

trample—*in the dust*
  destroy 162
  prostrate 308
  —*out* 162
  —*under foot vanquish* 731
  not observe 773
  disrepute 874
  insolence 885
  dereliction 927
  contempt 930
  —*upon badness* 649
  severity 739
tramway 627
trance *dream* 515
  sleep 683
  lethargy 823
tranquil *calm* 174
  quiet 265
  peaceful 721
  —*mind* 826
tranquilize
  moderate 174
  pacify 723
  soothe 826
transact *act* 680
  conduct 692
  —*business* 625
  —*business with* 794
transaction *event* 151
  action 680
  —*s of record* 551
transalpine 196
transanimation 140
transatlantic 196
transcalency 384
transcend *great* 31
  superior 33
  go beyond 303
transcendency 641
transcendent
  unequal 28
  superior 33
  glorious 873
  (*perfect* 650)
transcendental
  intellectual 450
  unintelligible 519
transcendentalism 450, 451
transcolate *exude* 295
  (*stream* 348)
transcribe *copy* 19
  manifest 525
  write 590
transcript *copy* 21
  writing 590
transcursion 303
transept *church* 1000
transeunt 111
transfer *copy* 21
  displace 185
  —*of things* 270
  —*of property* **783**
transferable 270, 783
transferee 270

transference 270
transfiguration
  change 140
  divine—908
transfix 260
transfixed *firm* 150
transforation 260
transform 140
transformation
  scene 599
transfuse *mix* 41
  transfer 270
  remedy 662
  —*the sense of* 522
transgress
  go beyond 303
  infringe 773
  violate 927
  sin 945
transgression
  guilt 947
transgressor 949
transience 111
transient
  time 109, 111
  changeable 149
  traveler 268
transilience
  revolution 146
  transcursion 303
transit *conversion* 144
  angularity 244
  motion 264
  transference 270
  measurement 466
transition 144, 270
transitional
  change 140
transitory 111
translate
  interpret 522
  manifest 525
  word 562
  promote 995
translation
  transference 270
  crib 539
  word 562
  resurrection 981
translator 524
transliterate 561
translocate 185
translocation 270
translucence 425
translumination 425
transmarine 196
transmigration
  change 140
  conversion 144
transmission
  moving 270
  automobile 272
  passage 302
  —*of property* 783
transmit 270, 302
  transfer 783

—*light* 425
transmogrify 140
transmorphism 140
transmutation
  change 140
  conversion 144
transom 215, 349
transparency **425**
transparent
  transmitting light 425
  obvious 518
transpierce 260
transpire
  evaporate 336
  appear 525
  be disclosed 529
transplace 270
transplant 270, 371
transplendent 420
transpontine 196
transport
  transfer 270
  ship 273
  war vessel 726
  excitement 825
  delight 827
  please 829
  punish 972
  (*emotion* 821, 824)
  —*of love* 897
transportation 144
transported
  overjoyed 827
transposal 148, 218
transpose
  invert 14, 218
  exchange 148
  displace 185
  transfer 270
  —*music* 413
transshape 140
transshipment 185
transubstantiation
  change 140
  sacrament 998
transudatory 295
transude *ooze* 295
  pass 302
  (*stream* 348)
transume *change* 140
transumption
  transfer 270
transverse
  change 140
  oblique 217
  crossing 219
tranter 271
trap *closure* 261
  gig 272
  snare 545
  stage—599
  pitfall 667
  fall into a—*dupe* 547
  clumsy 699
  lay a—*for* 545

tread

trapan 545
trapdoor *opening* 260
  snare 545
  pitfall 667
trapes 701
trappings *adjunct* 39
  clothes 225
  equipment 633
  ornament 847
Trappist 996
traps *clothes* 225
  baggage 780
trash *unmeaning* 517
  trifling 643
  useless 645
  riffraff 876
trashy— *style* 575
traulism 583
traumatic 662
travail *childbirth* 161
  labor 686
trave 215
travel 266
  —*out of the record* 10, 477
traveler 268
  bagman 758
  tricks upon—s
  deception 545
  cunning 702
  —'s *tale untruth* 546
  exaggeration 549
traveling 266
  —*bag* 191
  —*salesman* 758
traverse
  contravene 179
  move 266
  pass 302
  negative 536
  obstruct 706
travestie *copy* 21
  ridicule 856
travesty *imitate* 19
  misinterpret 523
  burlesque 555
  ridicule 856
travis 215
trawl 285, 463
trawler 273
tray 191
treacherous 907, 940
  —*memory* 506
treachery
  deception 545
  dishonesty 940
treacle *thick* 352
  sweet 396
tread *motion* 264
  walk 266
  —*a path journey* 266
  pursuit 622
  —*down harsh* 739
  humble 879
  —*in the steps of* 19
  —*on the heels of* 281

treadle

  −the beaten track
    conformity 82
    habit 613
  −the boards 599
  −the stage 599
  −under foot
    destroy 162
    subjection 749
    disrepute 874
    insolence 885
    contempt 930
  −upon *persecute* 649
treadle 633
treadmill 312, 975
treason *revolt* 742
  treachery 940
treasure *store* 636
  goodness 648
  money 800
  −trove 618
  −up in the memory 505
treasurer 801
treasury 802
treat
  physical pleasure 377
  manage 692
  bargain 769
  delight 827, 829
  amusement 840
  −of 595
  −oneself to 827
  −well 906
treatise 593, 595
treatment
  painting 556
  conduct 692
  ill−649
  medical−662
treaty 769
treble *three* 93
  shrill 410
  (*music* 413)
  childish−581
trebucket 727, 975
trecento 114, 554
tree *pedigree* 69, 166
  plant 367
  gallows 975
  as the−falls 151
  top of the−210
  −of knowledge 493
  up a−704
treelike 367
treenail 45
trefoil 92
trek 266
trekker 268
trellis 219
tremble *fluctuate* 149
  weakness 160
  shake 315
  cold 383
  emotion 821
  fear 860
  make one−860

trembling
  −in the balance
  uncertain 475
  danger 665
  −prairie 344
  −to its fall
  destruction 160
tremellose 352
tremendous
  painful 830
  fearful 860
tremendously 31
tremor *agitation* 315
  emotion 821
  fearful 860
tremulous
  agitated 315
  −*voice* 583
  irresolute 605
  fear 860
trench *dike* 232
  furrow 259
  defense 717
  open the−es 716
  −on *near* 197
  trespass 303
  moral trespass 925
  −upon 927
trenchant
  energetic 171
  assertive 535
  concise style 572
  vigorous language 574
  important 642
  emotion 821
  discourteous 895
  censure 932
trencher *plate* 191
  layer 204
trend *tendency* 176
  bend 278
  deviate 279
trennel 45
trepan *opening* 260
  borer 262
  snare 545
trepang 298
trephine 260, 262
trepidation
  agitation 315
  emotion 821
  excitement 825
  fear 860
trespass
  go beyond 303
  vice 945
  guilt 947
tress 256
trestle 215
trews 225
trey 92
triacid base 490b
triad 92, 193
triadelphous 94
triagonal 244

trial *inquiry* 461
  experiment 463
  essay 675
  difficulty 704
  adversity 735
  suffering 828, 830
  lawsuit 969
  punishment 972
  on−463
  −of temper 824
triality 92
trialogue 588
triangle
  triality 92, 244
  music 417
  punishment 975
triangular 94
  −duel 720
triarch 92
triarchy 737
tribe *race* 11
  assemblage 72
  class 75
  clan 166
tribulation 828
tribunal 966
tribune *rostrum* 542
  judge 967
tributary *river* 348
  giving 784
tribute *donation* 784
  money paid 809
  reward 973
  pay−to *respect* 928
  approbation 931
tricapsular 94
trice 113−up 43
tricennial 138
Trichinopoli cheroot 392
trichogenous 256
trichoid 256
trichosis 226
trichotomy 94
trichroism 440
trick *deception* 545
  indication 550
  habit 613
  contrivance 626
  skill 698
  artifice 702
  −at cards 775
  play−s *bungle* 699
  cunning 702
  amusement 840
  ridicule 856
  −of fortune 509
  −out *adorn* 847
  vulgar 851
  −s of the trade 702
trickery *deceit* 545
  finery 851
trickiness (see tricky)
trickle *ooze* 295
  stream 348
trickster *deceiver* 548

  schemer 702
  rogue 792
trickster myth 372a
tricksy *crafty* 702
  cheery 836
  pretty 845
  ornamented 847
tricky *deceiving* 545
  cunning 702
tricolor
  variegated 440
  flag 550
tricuspid 94
tricycle 272
trident 92, 94, 341
tridental 94
tried *tested* 463
triennial
  periodical 138
  plant 367
  celebration 883
triennium 92
trifid 94
trifle *small* 32
  neglect 460
  folly 499
  unimportant 643
  not stick at−s 604
  not to be−d with 744
  −time away 683
  −with *neglect* 460
  deceive 545
  disrespect 929
trifler 460 *fool* 501
trifling 499, 643
  wit 842
trifoliate 94
triforium 1000
triform 92
trifurcate 94
trig 652, 845
trigamy 903
trigger 633
  draw the−722
trigon 92, 244
trigonal 94
trigonometry 244
trigrammatic 94
trigraph 561
trilateral
  triplication 93
  sides 236
  angles 244
trilogistic *triple* 93
trilogy *drama* 599
trill *stream* 348
  sound 407
  music 413, 415, 416
  thousand−s 402
trillion 98
trilobite 368
trim *slate* 7
  adjust 27
  dress 225
  form 240

  garden 367
  lie 544
  waver 605
  change sides 607
  clean 652
  beautify 845
  adorn 847
  scold 932
  flog 972
  (*prepare* 673)
  in−*order* 58
trimmer *fickle* 607
  apostate 941
  timeserver 943
trimming *border* 231
  ornament 847
  dishonesty 940
Trimurti 92, 976
trinal 92
trine 93
trinitrotoluene 727
trinitrotoluol 727
trinity 92
Trinity, Holy−976
trinket *trifle* 643
  ornament 847
trinkgeld 784
trinomial 92
trio *three* 92
  music 415
trionym 92
trip *jaunt* 266
  run 274
  fall 306
  leap 309
  mistake 495
  bungle 699
  fail 732
  vice 945
  guilt 947
  −up *deceive* 545
  overthrow 731
tripartition 94
tripedal 93
tripetalous 94
triphthong 561
triplane 273
triplasic 93
triple *increase* 35
  triplication 93
  −crown 999
triplet *three* 92
  verse 597
triplication 93
triplicity 92
triplopia 92
tripod *triality* 92
  support 215
  furnace 386
tripodal 94
tripotage 588
tripping (see trip)
  style 578
  nimble 682
  caught−491
trippingly 584

597

tripsis 330
Triptolemus 371
triquetral 94
trireme 92, 273
Trisagion 900
triseme 92
trisection 94
triskelion 92, 993
trismus 655
triste 837
tristful 837
trisula 92
trisulcate *trisected* 94
  furrow 259
trite *known* 490
  conventional 613
  –*saying* 496
tritheism 984
Triton *sea* 341
  –*among the minnows*
    superior 33
  huge 192
  important 642
trituration 330
triumph *procession* 69
  success 731
  trophy 733
  exult 838
  celebrate 883
  boast 884
triumvirate 92, 737
triune 93
Triune God 976
triunity 92
trivet *support* 215
  stove 386
  right as a–
    perfect 650
  due 924
trivial *unmeaning* 517
  trifling 643
  useless 645
  ridiculous 853
  (*small* 32)
troat 412
trocar 262
trochaic 597
trochee 597
trochilic 312
trodden *down–*749
  well–habitual 613
  used 677
troglodyte 893
troll *roll* 312
  fairy 980
trolley 266, 271, 273
  –*car* 272
trollibus 273
trollop 59, 962
trombone 417
troop *assemblage* 72
  soldiers 726
  raise–s 722
trooper 726
  *lie like a–*544
  *swear like a–*908

troopship 726
trope 521
Trophonius, cave of
  –837
trophoplasm 357
trophy *record* 551
  palm **733**
tropical 382
  metaphorical 521
trot *run* 266, 370
  velocity 274
  translation 539
  –*out manifest* 525
  display 882
troth *belief* 484
  veracity 543
  promise 768
  *by my–*535
  *plight one's–*902
trothless *false* 544
  dishonorable 940
trotters 266, 298
trottoir 627
troubadour 597
trouble *disorder* 59
  derange 61
  exertion 686
  difficulty 704
  adversity 735
  pain 828
  painful 830
  *bring into–*649
  *get into–*732
  in–evil 619
  adversity 735
  *take–*686
  –*one for* 765
  –*oneself* 686
  –*one's head about*
    682
troubled (*see* trouble)
  fish in–waters 704
troublesome
  inexpedient 647
  exertion 686
  difficult 704
  painful 830
troublous 59
  violent 173
  –*times* 713
trough *hollow* 252
  trench 259
  conduit 350
trounce *censure* 932
  punish 972
troupe 72
trousers 225
  *put on long–*131
trousseau 225
trout 298
trouvaille 775
trouvère 597
trover *acquisition* 775
  unlawful 964
trow *think* 451
  believe 484

know 490
trowel 191
troy weight 319
truant *absent* 187
  runaway 623
  idle 682
  apostate 941
truce *lateness* 133
  cessation 142
  deliverance 672
  peace 721
  pacification 723
  *flag of–*724
  –*of God* 142
trucidation 361
truck *summit* 210
  vehicle 272
  barter 794
  –*driver* 268, 271
  –*farm* 691
  –*garden* 371, 691
truckle–bed 215
truckler 886
truckle to *submit* 725
  servile 886
  flatter 933
truckling *servile* 746
truckman 268
truculent 907
trudge *walk* 266
  move slowly 275
true *real* 1
  straight 246
  assent 488
  accurate 494
  veracious 543
  faithful 772
  honorable 939
  orthodox 983a
  see in its–colors
    480a
  –*bill vindicate* 937
  accuse 938
  lawsuit 969
  –*faith* 983a
  –*meaning* 516
  –*to nature* 17
  –*to oneself* 604a
  –*saying* 496
true–blue 494
true–hearted 543,
  939
truelove 897
truelover's knot
  love 897
  endearment 902
trueness (*see* true)
true–penny 939
truffles 298
truism *axiom* 496
  unmeaning 517
trull 962
truly *very* 31
  assent 488
  really 494
  indeed 535

trump *perfect* 650
  cards 840
  honorable 939
  good man 948
  –*card device* 626
  success 731
  –*up falsehood* 544
  accuse 938
  turn up–s 731
trumped up
  counterevidence 468
  deception 545
  untruth 546
trumpery
  unmeaning 517
  trifling 643
trumpet *music* 417
  war cry 722
  boast 884
  *ear–*418
  flourish of–s
  ostentation 882
  celebration 883
  boasting 884
  penny–skill 410
  sound of
  –*alarm* 669
  *speaking–*418
  –*blast* 404
  –*call signal* 550
  command 741
  –*forth* 531
trumpeter
  musician 416
  messenger 534
  boaster 884
trumpet–toned
  shrill 410
trumpet–tongued
  loud 404
  public 531
truncate *shorten* 201
  formless 241
truncated
  incomplete 53
truncheon
  weapon 727
  staff of office 747
  instrument of
    punishment 975
trundle *propel* 284
  roll 312
  –*bed* 215
trunk *whole* 50
  origin 153
  paternity 166
  box 191
trunk hose 225
trunnion *support* 215
  projection 250
truss *tie* 43
  pack, packet 72
  support 215
trust *belief* 484
  property 780
  credit 805

hope 858
  –*to a broken reed*
    699
  –*to the chapter of*
    accidents 621
trusted 484
trustee *consignee* 758
  possessor 779
  treasurer 801
trustful 484
trustless 940
trustworthy
  certain 474
  belief 484
  –*memory* 505
  veracious 543
  reliable 632
  honorable 939
truth *exactness* **494**
  veracity 543
  probity 939
  *arrive at the–*480a
  in–certainly 474
  *love of–*543
  of a
  –*affirmation* 535
  veraciously 543
  prove the–of 937
  *religious–*983a
  speak the
  –*disclose* 529
  veracity 543
Truth, Spirit of–976
truthless 544
truth–loving 543
truth–telling 543
trutination 319
try *experiment* 463
  adjudge 480
  endeavor 675
  use 677
  lawsuit 969
  –*a case* 967
  –*a cause* 480
  –*a prisoner* 967
  –*conclusions*
    discuss 476
  quarrel 713
  contend 720
  –*one difficulty* 704
  –*one's hand* 675
  –*one's luck* 621
  –*one's temper* 824
  –*one's utmost* 686
  –*the patience* 830
trying *fatigue* 688
  difficulty 704
tryst 74, 892
trysting place 74
tsar 745
tub 191, 386
  –*to a whale*
    deception 545
  excuse 617
tuba 417
tubate 260

tubby 201
tube 260
tubercle 250
tubercular 655
tuberculosis 655
tuberosity 250
tubman 968
tubular 260
tubulated 260
tubule 260
tuck *adjunct* 39
   fold 258
   dagger 727
   –in *locate* 184
   eat 298
   insert 300
tucker 225
tuft *collection* 72
   rough 256
tufted 256
tufthunter *servile* 886
   selfish 943
tufthunting
   servility 886
   flattery 933
tug *ship* 273
   pull 285
   effort 686
   –of war 720
   athletic sport 840
tuition 537
tulip *variegated* 440
   gaudy 882
Tullian 582
tumble *derange* 61
   destruction 162
   fall 306
   agitate 315
   fail 732
   rough and–59
tumble–down
   weak 160
   tottering 665
tumbler *glass* 191
   actor 599
   buffoon 844
tumbrel 272
tumefaction 194
tumid *expanded* 194
   –*style* 577
   (*big* 192)
tumor *expansion* 194
   prominence 250
tump 206
tumult *disorder* 59
   agitation 315
   revolt 742
   emotion 825
tumultuous
   (*see* tumult)
   violent 173
tumulus 363
tun *receptacle* 191
   large 192
   drunkard 959
tuna 298

tunable 413
tund 972
tundra 344
tune *music* 415, 416
   in–413
   out of–
   unmusical 414
   imperfect 651
   deteriorated 659
   put in–*prepare* 673
   concord 714
   to the–of
   quantity 25
   payment 807
   price 812
   –up 416
tuneful *music* 413
   poetry 597
   –nine *musician* 416
   poet 597
tuneless 414
tunic 225
tunicle 999
tuning fork 417
tunker 984
tunnage 192
tunnel *concave* 252
   opening 260
   passage 627
tup *sheep* 366
   male 373
tu quoque–argument
   counterevidence 468
   confutation 479
   accuse 938
turban 225
turbary 367
turbid *opaque* 426
   foul 653
turbinal 248
turbinated
   convoluted 248
   rotation 312
turbine 267, 284,
   312, 633
   –steamer 273
turbiniform 245, 248
turbinoid 248
turbulence
   violence 173
   agitation 315
   excitation 825
   (*disorder* 59)
turbulent
   (*see* turbulence)
   disorderly 59
Turcism 984
tureen 191
turf *elasticity* 325
   lawn 344
   grass 367, 371
   fuel 388
   gambling 621
   races 720
   race course 728
   amusement 840

turfman 840
turgid *expanded* 194
   –*style* 577
   redundant 641
   ostentatious 882
   (*exaggerated* 549)
Turk *polygamist* 903
   grand–745
turkey 298–trot 840
Turkish bath 386
turlupinade 842
turmeric paper 463
turmoil *confusion* 59
   violence 173
   agitation 315
turn *state* 7
   crisis 134
   period of time 138
   change 140
   tendency 176
   form 240
   curve 245
   blunt 254
   stroll 266
   deviate 279
   recession 287
   circuition 311
   rotate 312
   music 413
   willingness 602
   aptitude 698
   affections 820
   emotion 821
   trepidation 860
   by–s *periodic* 138
   interchange 148
   come in its–138
   do a good–*good* 648
   benevolent 906
   each in its–148
   give one a–*aid* 707
   excite 824
   ill–907
   in–*order* 58
   periodic 138
   in his–148
   meet one at every–641
   one's luck–s 735
   serve one's–644
   take a favorable–658
   take a wrong–732
   to a–494
   –about
   interchange 148
   –a corner
   go round 311
   succeed 731
   –a deaf ear to
   deaf 419
   refuse 764
   –adrift *disperse* 73
   eject 297
   –and turn about
   interchange 148

   changeable 149
   –and twist 248
   –a penny 775
   –aside *change* 140
   deviate 279
   hinder 706
   –away *eject* 297
   not look 442
   avoid 623
   dismiss 756
   relinquish 782
   –back *reversion* 145
   regression 283
   –color 821
   –down 258
   –end for end 14
   –for 698
   –from *repent* 950
   –in go to bed 683
   –in an alarm 669
   –inside out 529
   –into *conversion* 144
   translate 522
   –money 796
   –ridicule 856
   –of expression 566
   –off 972
   –of mind 820
   –of the cards 156
   –of the table 156
   –of the tide
   reverse 145
   invert 218
   –one's attention from 458
   –one's back upon
   oppose 708
   refuse 764
   disrespect 929
   contempt 930
   –one's hand to 625
   –on one's heel
   avoid 623
   discourtesy 895
   –on the tap 297
   –out *become* 144
   happen 151
   exterior 220
   clothes 225
   eject 297
   insurrection 719
   –well 731
   –ill 732
   dismiss 756
   display 882
   –over
   (*see below*)
   –round *inversion* 218
   revolve 311
   rotate 312
   recant 607
   –one's little finger 737
   –tail *go back* 283
   run away 623
   cowardice 862
   –the brain 503

   –the corner
   change 140
   improve 658
   –the eyes upon 441
   –the head *induce* 615
   excite 824
   astonish 870
   vanity 880
   hate 898
   –the house out of window 713
   –the mind to 457
   –the other cheek 725
   –the scale *unequal* 28
   superior 33
   change 140
   reverse 145
   cause 153
   counterevidence 468
   induce 615
   –the stomach
   unsavory 395
   aversion 867
   –the tables
   contrary 14
   countervail 468
   retaliate 718
   –the tide 145
   –to account *use* 677
   profit 775
   –to good account 658
   –topsy–turvy
   invert 14
   derange 61
   invest 218
   –turtle 218
   –under 258
   –up
   (*see below*)
   –upon
   depend upon 154
   retaliate 718
   –upside down 14
turnable 384
turncoat
   conversion 144
   changeableness 149
   irresolution 605
   tergiversation 607
turned up *short* 201
Turnerfest 840
turning point *crisis* 8
   end 67
   occasion 134
   reversion 145
   cause 153
   summit 210
   limit 233
turnip 298
turnip-shaped 245
turnkey 753
turnout *carriage* 272
   laborers' strike 719
   procession 882
turn over *give* 784
   invert **218**

599

—a new leaf
  change 140
  improve 658
  repent 950
 —in the mind 451
 —the leaves
  peruse 457
  learn 539
 —to 270
turnover *pastry* 298
turnpike 706
 —road 627
turnscrew 633
turnspit 312, 366, 386
turnstile 551, 706
turntippet 607
turn up *happen* 151
  visible 446
  unexpected 508
 —one's eyes
  wonder 870
  hypocrisy 988
 —one's nose at
  aversion 867
  fastidious 868
  contempt 930
Turnverein 712
turpentine and beeswax 255
Turpin, Dick–792
turpitude
  disgrace 874
  dishonor 940
turquoise *blue* 438
  jewel 847
turret 206
turret ship 726
turtle *savory* 394
 —soup 298
turtledoves 897
tush *silence* 403
  taciturn 585
  trifling 643
tusk 253
tussle 720
tut (*see* tush)
  censure 932
tutelage *teaching* 537
  learning 539
  safety 664
  subjection 749
tutelary *safety* 664
 —genius *auxiliary* 711
  god 979
 —god 664
 —saint *friend* 890
  benefactor 912
tutor *cultivate* 375
  teach 537
  teacher 540
tutorial 540
tutorship 537, 542
tuxedo coat 225
tuyère 386
twaddle *absurd* 497

unmeaning 517
diffuseness 573
talk 584
twain 89 in–44
twang *taste* 390
  pungency 392
  sound 402
  stridor 410
  music 416
  voice 583
twattle (*see* twaddle)
tweak 378
 —the nose 830
tweed 219, 635
tweedle *touch* 379
twelfth 99
twelve 98
twentieth 118
twenty etc. 98
twice 90
twice-told tale
  repeat 104
  weary 841
twiddle 379
twig 51 hop the–360
twilight *morning* 125
  evening 126
  dusk 422
 —sleep 376
twill *crossing* 219
  convolution 248
  fold 258
twin *similar* 17
  accompanying 88
  two 89
  duplicate 90
 —screws 284
 —six 272
twine *string* 205
  intersect 219
  convolution 248
 —round *join* 43
  circumjacence 227
twinge *pain* 378
  (*mental suffering* 828, 830)
 —of conscience 603
twinkle
  instantaneous 113
  light 420
  dimness 422
twinkling of an eye
  in the–113
twinning 490c
twins 11
twire 315
twirl *convolute* 248
  revolve 311
  rotate 312
twist *join* 43
  thread 205
  oblique 217
  crossing 219
  distort 243
  convolution 248
  deviate 279

bend 311
prejudice 481
insanity 503
fault 651
appetite 865
twit *deride* 856
  disrespect 929
  censure 932
  accuse 938
twitch *pull* 285
  pain 378
  mental–828
twitching 315
twitter *agitation* 315
  cry 412
  music 416
  emotion 821
  excitement 824
'twixt 228
two 89
  fall between–stools 732
  game at which–can play 718
  in–places at once 471
  kill–birds with one stone 682
  make–bites of a cherry
  circuitous 629
  not eat 956
 —dozen 98
 —meanings 520
 —of a trade 708
 —or three 100
 —score 98
 —souls 87
 —strings to one's bow 632
  unable to put–words together 583
two-by-four 643
two-edged 253
two-faced
  deceitful 544
twofold 90
two-seater 273
two-sided 90
two-step *dance* 840
Tycho 490a
tycoon 745
tyg 191
tyke 876
tymbal 417
tympani 417
tympanitis 418
tympanum *top* 210
  ear 418
tympany 194
type *essential* 5
  similarity 17
  pattern 22
  class 75
  form 240

prediction 511
metaphor 521
indication 550
letter 561
printing 591
 —for the blind 442
typescript 21
typesetting 54
typewrite 590
typewriting 590
typhonic 349
typhoon *wind* 349
  (*violent* 173)
typical *special* 79
  conformable 82
  metaphorical 521
  significant 550
typify 511
typist 590
typography 591
tyranny *authority* 737
  severity 739
  illegality 964
tyrant *authority* 737
  severe 739
  ruler 745
  evildoer 913
tyre 230
tyro *ignoramus* 493
  learner 541

U

uberty *luxuriance* 168
  (*sufficiency* 639)
ubiety 186
ubiquitarian 984
ubiquity 186
U-boat 208, 726
udder 191
udometer 348
ugh! 867
uglification 846
ugliness 846
ugly 846
  call by–names 932
  take an–turn 732
 —customer
  source of danger 667
  evildoer 913
  bad man 949
uhlan 716, 726
ukase 741
ukulele 417
ulcer *disease* 655
  care 830
ulcerate 659
ulema *judge* 967
uliginous 352
ullalulla 839
ulster 225
ulterior *extra* 37
  extraneous 57
 —in time 121
 —in space 196

ultima ratio 744
 —regum 722
ultimate 67
 —cause 153
ultimately
  difference 15
  future 121
  latest 133
ultima Thule 196
ultimatum
  definite 474
  intention 620
  requirement 630
  terms 770
ultimeter 244
ultimo 122
ultimogeniture 777
ultra *great* 31
  superior 33
ultramarine 438
ultramicroscope 445
ultramontane
  foreign 57
  distant 196
  heterodox 984
  church 995
ultramundane 196
ultrasonic frequency 490d
ultra-violet rays 420
ululate 412, 839
ululation 407, **412**
Ulysses 702
umbilicus 222
umbra 421
umbrage *shade* 424
  hatred 898
  take–*anger* 900
umbrageous 421
umbrella
  covering 223
  shade 424
  protection 666
umpire *judgment* 480
  mediator 724
  judge 967
unabashed *bold* 861
  vain 885
  insolent 885
unabated 31
unable 158
 —to say "No" 605
unacceptable 830
unaccommodating
  disagreeing 24
  disagreeable 830
  discourteous 895
  sulky 901a
unaccompanied 87
unaccomplished 730
unaccountable
  exceptional 83
  unintelligible 519
  irresponsible 927a
  arbitrary 964

600

unaccustomed   uncircumspect

   (*wonderful* 870)
unaccustomed
   unusual 83
   unused 614
   unskillful 699
unachievable 471
unacknowledged
   ignored 489
   nameless 565
   unrequited 917
unacquainted 491
unacquired 777a
unactuated (616)
unadmonished 665
unadorned *style* 576
   simple 849
   beauty–845
unadulterated
   simple 42
   genuine 494
   (*good* 648)
unadventurous 864
unadvisable 647
unadvised
   dangerous 665
   unskillful 699
unaffected
   genuine 494
   sincere 543
   –*style* 578
   obstinate 606
   artless 703
   insensible 823
   simple 849
   taste 850
   (*physically callous* 376)
unafflicted 831
unaided
   weak 160
   (*unsupported* 706)
unalarmed 861
unalienable 924
unallayed 159
unallied 10
unallowable 923
unallowed 925
unalloyed 42
   –*happiness* 827
   –*truth* 494
unalluring 866
unalterable 150
unaltered
   identical 13
   stable 150
   (*unchanged* 141)
unamazed 871
unambiguous 518
unambitious 866
unamiable 907
unanimated 823
unanimity
   agreement 23
   assent 488
   accord 714
unannexed 44

unanswerable
   demonstrative 478
   irresponsible 927a
   arbitrary 964
   (*certain* 474)
unanswered 478
unanticipated 508
unappalled 861
unappareled 226
unapparent
   latent 526
   (*invisible* 447)
unappeasable 173
unappetizing 867
unapplied 678
unappreciated 483
unapprehended 491
unapprehensive 861
unapprised 491
unapproachable
   great 31
   infinite 105
   distant 196
unapproached
   unequal 28
   superior 33
unappropriated 782
unapproved 932
unapt *incongruous* 24
   impotent 158
   unskillful 699
   (*inexpedient* 647)
unarmed 158
unarranged
   disorder 59
   unprepared 674
unarrayed 226, 849
unartificial 849
unascertained
   uncertain 475
   ignorant 491
unasked
   voluntary 602
   not asked 766
unaspiring
   indifferent 866
   modest 881
unassailable 664
unassailed 748
unassembled 73
unassisted *weak* 160
   unaided 706
   –*eye* 441
unassociated 44
unassuming 881
unatoned 951
unattached 44
unattackable 664
unattainable 471
unattained 732
unattempted 623
unattended 87
   –*to* 460
unattested
   not evidence 468
   (*unrecorded* 552)

unattracted
   indifferent 866 (616)
unattractive 866
unauthenticated
   improved 468
   uncertain 475
   inexact 495
unauthoritative
   uncertain 475
unauthorized
   prohibited 761
   undue 925
   lawless 964
unavailing *useless* 645
   failure 732
unavenged 918
unavoidable
   certain 474
   necessary 601
unavowed 489
unawakened 683
unaware *ignorant* 491
   unexpecting 508
unawed 861
unbalanced 28
unbar 750
unbearable 830
unbeaten 123
unbeauteous 846
unbecoming
   incongruous 24
   disreputable 874
   undue 925
   dishonorable 940
   –*a gentleman* 895
unbefitting *inapt* 24
   undue 925
   improbity 940
   (see unbecoming)
unbegotten 2
unbeguile *inform* 527
   disclose 529
unbegun
   unprepared 674
unbeheld (447)
unbelief 485
   irreligion 989
   (*incredulity* 487)
unbelievable 485
unbeliever *infidel* 989
unbelieving 485
unbeloved 898
unbend *straighten* 246
   repose 687
   –*the mind* 452
unbending *hard* 323
   resolute 604
unbenevolent 907
unbenign 907
unbent 246
unbeseeming
   vulgar 851
   dishonorable 940
unbesought
   not ask 766
   (*spontaneous* 602)

unbestowed (785)
unbetrayed 939
unbewailed 932
unbiased *wise* 498
   free 748
   (*spontaneous* 602a)
unbidden *willful* 600
   disobedient 742
unbigoted 498
unbind *detach* 44
   release 750
unblamable 946
unblamed 946
unblemished
   perfect 650
   innocent 946
unblenching 861
unblended 42
unblest
   unfortunate 735
   not approved 932
   –*with* 777a
unblown 674
unblushing
   proud 878
   vain 880
   imprudent 885
unboastful 881
unbodied 317
unboiled 674
unbolt *liberate* 750
   (*unfasten* 44)
unbookish 491
unborn *not existing* 2
   destined 152
   (*future* 121)
unbosom oneself 529
unbought
   not bought 796
   honorary 815
   honorable 939
   unselfish 942
unbound *free* 748
   exempt 927a
unbounded
   infinite 105
   (*great* 31)
   (*large* 192)
   (*space* 180)
unbrace *weaken* 160
   relax 655
unbreathed 526
unbred 895
unbribed
   honorable 939
   disinterested 942
unbridled *violent* 173
   lax 738
   free 748
unbroken *entire* 50
   continuous 69
   preserved 670
   unviolated 939
   –*extent* 69
unbruised 50
unbuckle 44

unburden
   –*one's mind* 529
unburdened 705
unburied 362
unbuttoned 748
uncalculating 863
uncalled for
   redundant 641
   useless 645
   not used 678
uncandid
   insincere 544
   morose 907
uncanny *ugly* 846
   spectral 980a
uncanonical 984
uncared for
   neglected 460
   indifferent 866
   disliked 867
   hated 898
uncase (226)
uncate 245
uncaught *free* 748
uncaused 156
unceasing 112, 143
uncensured 931
unceremonious
   vain 880
   discourteous 895
uncertain
   irregular 139
   not certain 475
   doubtful 485
   embarrassing 704
   in an–*degree* 32
uncertainty 475
unchain *unfasten* 44
   liberate 750
unchained *free* 748
unchallenged
   assent 488
   due 924
unchangeable
   stable 150
   persevering 604a
unchanged 16, 141
unchangingly 136
uncharitable 907
unchartered
   undue 925
   illegal 964
unchaste 961
unchastised 970
unchecked 748
uncheckered 141
uncheerful 837
unchivalric 940
unchristian
   heterodox 984
   irreligious 989
uncial 590
unciform 245
uncinated 244
uncircumscribed 180
uncircumspect 460

uncivil *vulgar* 851
  rude 895
uncivilized *low* 876
  uncourteous 895
unclad 226
unclaimed 748
unclassed (59)
unclassical 851
unclassified (59)
uncle *kin* 11
  my–'s
  pawnshop 787
unclean 653
  –spirit 978, 980
uncleanness 653
Uncle Sam 188
unclipped 50
unclog *facilitate* 705
  liberate 750
unclose *open* 260
  liberate 750
unclothed 226
unclouded *light* 420
  visible 446
  (*joyful* 827)
unclubbable 893
unclutch 790
uncoif 226
uncoil *evolve* 313
  (*straighten* 246)
uncollected (73)
uncolored
  achromatic 429
  true 494
  (*veracious* 543)
uncombed
  dirty 653
  vulgar 851
uncombined
  simple 42
  incoherent 47
uncomeatable 471
uncomely 846
uncomfortable
  annoyed 828
  annoying 830
uncommendable
  blamable 932
  bad 945
  guilt 947
uncommensurable 24
uncommon
  unimitated 20
  exceptional 83
  infrequent 137
uncommonly 31
uncommonness 137
uncommunicated 781
uncommunicative 528
uncompact 322
uncompassionate 914a
uncompelled 748

uncomplaisant 764 (895)
uncompleted
  incomplete 53
  unfinished 730
  failure 732
uncomplying
  disobedient 742
  refusing 764
uncompounded 42
uncompressed
  light 320
  rare 322
uncompromising
  conformable 82
  severe 739
unconcealable 525
unconceived
  uncreated 12
  unintelligible 519
unconcern
  insensible 823
  indifferent 866
unconcerned
  tolerant 740
  (see unconcern)
unconcocted 674
uncondemned 970
unconditional
  complete 52
  free 748
  permission 760
  consent 762
  release 768a
unconducive 175a
unconfined 748
unconfirmed 475
unconformity
  disagreement 24
  irregularity 83
unconfused
  methodical 58
  clear 518
unconfuted
  demonstrated 478
  true 494
uncongealed 333
uncongenial
  disagreeing 24
  insalubrious 657
unconnected
  irrelative 10
  disjointed 44
  discontinuous 70
  illogical 477
unconquerable
  strong 159
  persevering 604a
  –will 604
unconquered 719
unconscientious 940
unconscionable
  excessive 31
  unprincipled 945
unconscious
  ignorant 491

insensible 823
unconsenting
  unwilling 603
  refusing 764
unconsidered 452
unconsolidated 47
unconsonant 24
unconspicuous
  invisible 447
  (*latent* 526)
unconstitutional
  undue 925
  illegal 964
unconstrained
  free 748
  fashion 852
  unabashed 880
  will 600
unconsumed
  remaining 40
uncontested 474
uncontradicted 488
uncontrite 951
uncontrollable
  violent 173
  necessity 601
  emotion 825
uncontrolled *free* 748
  excitability 825
uncontroverted 488
unconventional 83, 614
unconversable 585
unconversant
  ignorant 491
  unskilled 699
unconverted
  dissenting 489
  irreligious 989
unconvinced 489
uncooked 674
uncopied 20
uncork 750
uncorrupted
  upright 939
  (*innocent* 946)
uncounted 475
uncouple (44)
uncourteous 895
uncourtly
  inelegant 579
  vulgar 851
  rude 895
uncouth–*style* 579
  ugly 846
  vulgar 851
  (*ridiculous* 853)
uncouthness
  (see uncouth)
  amorphism 241
uncover *denude* 226
  open 260
  disclose 529
  bow 894
uncreated 2
uncritical 931

uncropped 50
uncrown 756
unction
  lubrication 332
  emotion 821, 824
  divine functions 976
  piety 987
  extreme–998
  lay the flattering–to one's soul
  relief 834
  hope 858
unctuous *oily* 355
  bland 894
  flattering 933
  hypocritical 988
unctuousness 355
unculled *unused* 678
  relinquished 782
unculpable 946
uncultivated
  ignorant 491
  fallow 674
  vulgarity 851
uncurbed 748
uncurl 246
uncustomary
  exceptional 83
  (*desuetude* 614)
uncut 50, 674
undamaged (648)
undamped 340
undated
  without date 115
  waving 248
undaunted 861
undazzled 498
undebauched
  honorable 939
  (*innocent* 946)
undecayed (648)
undeceive *inform* 527
  disclose 529
undeceived
  knowing 490
undecennary 98
undecided
  inquiring 461
  uncertain 475
  irresolute 605
  leave–609a
undecipherable 519
undecked 849
undecomposed 42
undefaced 845, 847
undefended 725
undefiled *honest* 939
  innocent 946
  chaste 960
undefinable
  uncertain 475
  unmeaning 517
  unintelligible 519
undefined
  invisible 447
  uncertain 475

(*unintelligible* 519)
undeformed 845, 847
undemolished 50
undemonstrable 485
undemonstrated 475
undemonstrative 826
undeniable 474, 478
undeplored 898
undepraved 939
undeprived 781
under *less* 34
  below 207
  subject to 749
  range–76
  –age 127
  –agent 758
  –breath 405
  –cover *covered* 223
  hidden 528
  safe 664
  –foot
  (*see below*)
  –full strength 651
  –lock and key 664
  –one's control 743
  –one's eyes 446
  –press of 744
  –protest *dissent* 489
  compulsion 744
  –restraint 751
  –seal 467
  –subjection 749
  –the circumstances 8
  –the head of 9
  –the mark 34
  –the sun 1
  –way 282
underbid 794
underbreath 405
underbred 851
underclothing 225
undercurrent
  cause 153
  stream 348, 349
  latent 526
  opposing 709
underdone 298
underestimation 483
underfed 640
underfoot 207
  tread–739
undergo 151
  –a change 144
  –pain 828
undergraduate 541
underground *low* 207
  deep 208
  latent 526
  hidden 528
undergrowth 367
underhand *latent* 526
  hidden 528
  –dealing 528
underhung 250
underlay 591

underlessee 779
underlet 787
underlie *low* 207
  latent 526
underline *mark* 550
  emphatic 642
underling
  servant 746
  clown 876
undermine
  impotence 158
  burrow 252
  damage 659
  stratagem 702
  hinder 706
undermost 211
underneath 207
undernourished 640
undern–song 900
underpaid 819
underpin 215
underplot 626
underprop 215
underrate 483, 549
underreckon 483
underscore 550
undersecretary 746
undersell 796
underset 215
undershirt 225
undershot 250
undersign *testify* 467
  (*write* 590)
undersized 193
undersong 104
understand *note* 450
  know 490
  intelligible 518
  latent 526
  be informed 527
  give one to – 572
  – *by meaning* 516
  interpret 522
  – *one another*
  coöperate 709
  concord 714
understanding
  intellect 450
  intelligence 498
  come to an–
  assent 488
  intelligible 518
  agree 714
  pacification 723
  compact 769
  good–concord 714
  friendship 888
  with the– 469
understate 555
understood
  meaning 516
  implied 526
  customary 613
  (*metaphorical* 521)
understrapper 746
understudy 634

undertake
  endeavor 676
  promise 768
undertaker 363
undertaking
  business 625
  enterprise **676**
undertone 405
undertow 348, 667
undervalue 483, 929
undervest 225
underwood 367
underwrite
  promise 768
  compact 769
  insurance 771
underwriter 758
undescribed 83
undeserved 925
undesigned
  chance 621
undesigning
  artless 703
undesirable
  inexpedient 647
  painful 830
undesired 830
  indifferent 866
undesirous 866
undespairing 858
undestroyed
  existing 1
  whole 50
  persisting 141
undetermined
  chance 156
  inquiry 461
  uncertain 475
  unintelligible 519
  irresolute 605
undeveloped
  latent 526
undeviating
  uniform 16
  unchanged 150
  straight 246
  direct 278
  persevering 604a
undevout 989
undigested *crude* 674
  (*unarranged* 59)
undignified 940
undiminished
  great 31
  not diminished 35
  whole 50
undirected
  erratic 279
  casual 621
undiscernible
  visible 447
  unintelligible 519
undiscerning
  blind 442
  inattentive 458
undisciplined 608

(*unskillful* 699)
undisclosed
  latent 526
  hidden 528
undiscoverable 519
undiscovered 526
undiscriminating 465a
undisguised *true* 494
  manifest 525
  sincere 543
  (*meaning* 516)
undismayed 861
undisposed of
  not used 678
  kept 781
undisputed 474
undissembling 543
undissolved *entire* 50
  dense 321
undistinguishable 465a
undistinguished 465a
undistorted
  straight 246
  true 494
undistracted 457
undisturbed
  quiescent 265
  repose 685
  unexcited 826
  (*in order* 58)
undiversified 16
undivided *whole* 50
  complete 52
undivulged (528)
undo *untie* 44
  reverse 145
  destroy 162
  neutralize 179
  not do 681
undoing *ruin* 735
undone *failure* 732
  adversity 735
  pained 828
  hopeless 859
undoubted 474
undraped 226
undreaded 861
undreamt of 452
undress *clothes* 225
  nude 226
  simple 849
undressed
  unprepared 674
  (*unadorned* 849)
undried 339
undrilled 674
undriven (602)
undrooping
  persevering 604a
  (*active* 682)
undueness 925
undulate *wave* 248
  oscillate 314

undutiful 945
undyed (429)
undying
  perpetual 112
  immutable 150
unearned 925
unearth *eject* 297
  disinter 363
  inquire 461
  discover 480a
unearthly
  immaterial 317
  Deity 976
  spectral 980a
  heavenly 981
  pious 987
uneasy 149, 828
uneatable 867
unedifying 538
uneducated
  ignorant 491
  unprepared 674
unembarrassed
  facility 705
  dégagé 852
unembodied 317
unemotional 823
unemployed
  not used 678
  inactive 681
unemployment 681
unencumbered
  easy 705
  exempt 927a
unendeared 898
unending 112
unendowed 158
  – *with reason* 450a
unendurable 830
unenjoyed *weary* 841
unenlightened
  ignorant 491
  foolish 499
  (*dark* 421)
unenslaved 748
unenterprising 864
unentertaining 275, 843
unenthralled 748
unentitled 925
unenvied
  not respected 929
  despised 930
unequal *inequality* 28
  irregular 139
  inequitable 923
  – *to insufficient* 640
  (*impotent* 158)
unequaled
  inequality 28
  superior 33
  good 648
unequipped 674
unequitable 923
unequivocal *great* 31
  sure 474

clear 518
unerring *certain* 474
  tone 494
  innocent 946
unessayed 678
unessential
  extrinsic 6
  irrelative 10
  unimportant 643
unestablished 185
uneven *diverse* 16a
  unequal 28
  irregular 139
  rough 256
uneventful 643
unexact 495
unexaggerated 494
unexamined 460
unexampled
  unimitated 20
  unequaled 28
  unconformity 83
unexceptionable
  good 648
  legitimate 924
  innocent 946
unexcitable 826
unexcited 823, 826
unexciting 174
unexecuted 730
unexempt 177
unexercised
  unprepared 674
  unused 678
  (*unskilled* 699)
unexerted 172
unexhausted
  vigorous 159
  abundant 639
unexpanded
  not expanded 195
  narrow 203
unexpected
  exceptional 83
  inexpectation 508
  rash 863
  (*wonderful* 870)
unexpensive 815
unexplained
  not known 491
  unintelligible 519
  latent 526
unexplored
  neglected 460
  ignorant 491
  unseen 536
unexposed 526
unexpressed 536
unexpressive 517
unextended 317
unextinguished
  raging 173
  burning 382
unfaded *color* 428
  (*perfect* 650)
unfading 112, 141

603

unfailing · uninfluenced

unfailing 141
unfair *false* 544
  unjust 923
  dishonorable 940
unfaithful 940
unfallen 946
unfaltering 604a
unfamiliar 83
unfashionable
  unconformable 83
  unaccustomed 614
  vulgar 851
unfashioned
  formless 241
  unwrought 674
unfasten 44
unfathomable
  infinite 105
  deep 208
  mysterious 519
unfavorable
  out of season 135
  hindrance 706
  obstructive 708
  adverse 735
  –chance 473
unfeared 861
unfeasible 471
unfed *deficient* 640
  fasting 956
unfeeling
  physically– 376
  numb 381
  morally– 823
unfeigned 543
unfelt 823
unfeminine
  manly 373
  vulgar 851
unfertile 169
unfetter *release* 750
  (*unfasten* 44)
unfettered *free* 748
  (*spontaneous* 600)
unfinished
  incomplete 53
  not completed 730
unfit *inappropriate* 24
  impotence 158
  inexpedient 647
  unskillful 699
  wrong 923
  undue 925
unfitness
  inutility 645
  (see unfit)
unfitted
  not prepared 674
unfix 44
unfixed *mutable* 149
  (*irresolute* 605)
unflagging
  persevering 604a
  (*active* 682)
unflammable 385
unflattering *true* 494

  artless 703
  (*sincere* 543)
  unflavored 391)
unfledged
  young 127, 129
  callow 674
unfleshly 317
unflinching *firm* 604
  persevering 604a
  brave 861
unfoiled (731)
unfold *straighten* 246
  evolve 313
  interpret 522
  disclose 529
  –a tale 594
unfoldment
  (see unfold)
  manifestation 525
unforbidden 760
unforced *willing* 602
  free 748
unforeseen
  unexpected 508
  (*wonderful* 870)
unforfeited 781
unforgettable 506
unforgiving 919
unforgotten 505
unformed
  shapeless 241
  unshaped 674
unfortified *pure* 42
  powerless 158
unfortunate
  ill–timed 135
  failure 732
  adversity 735
  unhappy 828
  –woman 962
unfounded
  untruth 546
  (*falsehood* 544)
unfrequent 137
unfrequented 893
unfriended
  powerless 158
  secluded 893
unfriendly
  opposed 708
  hostile 889
  malevolent 907
unfrock *dismiss* 756
  disapprobation 932
  punish 972
unfrozen *warm* 382
  (*liquefied* 335)
unfruitful 169
unfulfilled
  nonobservance 773
  undue 925
unfurl *unfold* 313
  –a flag manifest 525
  signal 550
unfurnished
  insufficient 640

  unprepared 674
ungainly *ugly* 846
  rude 895
ungallant 895
ungarmented 226
ungarnished 849
ungathered 678
ungenerous
  stingy 819
  selfish 943
ungenial 657
ungenteel *vulgar* 851
  rude 895
ungentle *violent* 173
  rude 895
ungentlemanly
  vulgar 851
  rude 895
  dishonorable 940
ungifted 32, 499
unglorified 874
unglue
  incoherence 47
  (*disjoin* 44)
ungodly 989
ungovernable
  violent 173
  disobedient 742
  passionate 825
ungoverned 748
ungraceful
  –language 579
  ugly 846
  vulgar 851
ungracious
  uncivil 895
  unfriendly 907
ungrammatical 568
ungranted 764
ungrateful 917
ungratified
  discontent 832
  (*pain* 828)
ungrounded
  unsubstantial 4
  erroneous 495
ungrudging 816
unguarded
  neglected 460
  spontaneous 612
  unprepared 674
  (*dangerous* 665)
  in an–moment
  unexpectedly 508
unguent 332, 356
unguiculate 245
unguided
  ignorant 491
  impulsive 612
  unskilled 699
unguilty 946
unguinous 355
unguis 781
unhabitable 187
unhabituated 614
unhackneyed 614

unhallowed
  impious 988
  irreligious 989
unhand 750
unhandled 123
unhandseled 123
unhandsome 940
unhandy 699
unhappy
  adversity 735
  pain 828
  dejected 837
  make– 830
unharbored 185
unhardened
  tender 914
  innocent 946
  penitent 950
unharmonious
  incongruous 24
  unmusical 414
unharness
  liberate 750
  (*disjoin* 44)
unhatched *callow* 674
unhazarded 664
unhealthy *ill* 655
  unwholesome 657
unheard of
  exceptional 83
  new 123
  improbable 473
  ignorant 491
  wonderful 870
unheated 383
unheed 460
unheeded 460
unheeding 458
unhelped (708)
unhesitating
  belief 484
  resolved 604
unhewn *formless* 241
  unprepared 674
unhindered 748
unhinge *derange* 61
  make powerless 158
unhinged
  impotent 158
  insane 503
  failure 732
unholy 989
unhonored 874
unhook (44)
unhoped 508
unhorsed 732
unhostile 888
unhouse 297
unhoused 185
unhurt 670
unicorn
  monster 83
  carriage 272
  (*prodigy* 872)
unideal *existing* 1
  no thought 452

  true 494
unidentical 18
unification
  combination 48
  one 87
uniflorous 87
unifoliolate 87
uniform
  homogeneous 16
  simple 42
  orderly 58
  regular 80
  dress 225
  symmetry 242
  livery 550
uniformity 16
unigenital 87
uniglobular 87
unijugate 89
uniliteral 87
unilluminated 421
unilobed 87
unilocular 87
unimaginable
  impossible 471
  improbable 473
  wonderful 870
unimaginative
  plain 576
  dull 843
  expectant 871
unimagined
  existing 1
  true 494
unimitated 20
unimodular 87
unimpaired
  preserved 670
  (*good* 648)
unimpassioned 826
unimpeachable
  certain 474
  true 494
  due 924
  approved 931
  innocent 946
unimpeached 931, 946
unimpelled (616)
unimportance 643
unimpressed 838
unimpressible 823
unimproved 659
unincited (616)
unincreased 36
unincumbered
  easy 705
  exempt 927a
uninduced 616
uninfected 652
uninfectious 656
uninflammable 385
uninfluenced
  obstinate 606
  unactuated 616
  unrestricted 748

604

uninfluential
  inert 172
  no influence 175a
uninformed 491
ingenuous 544
uninhabit
  absence 187
  secluded 893
uninhabitable 187, 893
uninhabited 187, 893
uninitiated
  ignorant 491
  unskillful 699
uninjured *perfect* 650
  healthy 654
  preserved 670
uninjurious 656
uninquisitive 456
uninspired
  unexcited 823
  (*unactuated* 616)
uninstructed 491
unintellectual
  incogitant 452
  imbecile 499
unintellectuality 450a
unintelligent 32, 499
unintelligibility 519, 571
unintelligible 519
  –style 571
  render– 538
unintended 621
unintentional
  necessary 601
  undesigned 621
uninterested
  incurious 456
  weary 841
  dull 843
uninteresting 643
unintermitting
  unbroken 69
  durable 110
  continuing 143
  persevering 604a
uninterrupted
  continuous 69
  perpetual 112
  unremitting 893
  –existence 112
unintroduced 893
uninured
  unaccustomed 614
  (*unprepared* 674)
uninvented 526
uninvestigated 491
uninvited 893
uninviting 830
union *agreement* 23
  junction 43
  combination 48
  concurrence 178
  party 712

  concord 714
  marriage 903
  –down flag 550
union jack 550
union pipes 417
unique *dissimilar* 18
  original 20
  unequal 28
  exceptional 83
  alone 87
unirritable 826
unirritating 174
unison *agreement* 23
  melody 413
  concord 714
  (*uniform* 16)
  in–melody 413
unisulcate 259
unit 87
Unitarian 984
unitary 87
unite *join* 43
  combine 48
  component 56
  assemble 72
  concur 178
  converge 290
  party 712
  (*agree* 23)
  –in pairs 89
  –one's efforts 709
  –with coöperate 709
united *coherent* 46
  concord 714
United States courts 966
unity *identity* 13
  uniformity 16
  whole 50
  complete 52
  single 87
  concord 714
  –of time 120
Unity, Trinity in– 976
universal 78
  –Church 983a
  –concept 450
  –favorite 899
  –joint 272, 633
  –language 560
  –ly present 186
  –predicament 25
universality 52
universalize 78
universe 318
university 542
  go to the– 539
  –degree 873
  –education 537
unjust *wrong* 923
  impious 988
unjustifiable
  wrong 923
  inexcusable 938
  wicked 945

unjustified 923
  undue 925
unkempt *rough* 256
  unclean 653
  vulgar 851
unkennel *eject* 297
  disclose 529
unkind 907
  –est cut of all 828
unkindness *hard–* 907
unknightly 940
unknit (44)
unknot 705
unknowable 519
unknowing 491
unknown
  ignorant 491
  latent 526
  –quantities 491
  –to fame
    inglorious 874
    lowborn 876
unlabored–*style* 578
  unprepared 674
unlace (44)
unlade 297
unladylike
  vulgar 851
  rude 895
unlamented
  hated 898
  disapproved 932
unlatch 44
unlawful *undue* 925
  illegal 964
unlearn 506
unlearned 491
unleavened 674
unless *circumstances* 8
  except 83
  qualification 469
  (*condition* 770)
unlettered 491
  –Muse 579
unlicensed 761
unlicked
  unprepared 674
  vulgar 851
  clownish 876
  –cub shapeless 241
  unmannerly 895
unlike 18
unlikely 471, 473
unlimber 323
unlimited *great* 31
  infinite 105
  free 748
  –space 180
unlink (44)
unliquefied 321
unlively *grave* 837
  dull 843
unload *displace* 185
  eject 297
  disencumber 705
  sell 796

unlock *unfasten* 44
  discover 480a
  (*explain* 462)
unlooked for 508
unloose *unfasten* 44
  liberate 750
unloved 898
unlovely 846
unlucky
  inopportune 135
  bad 649
  unfortunate 735
  in pain 830
unmade 2
unmaimed 654
unmake 145
unman *castrate* 38
  render powerless 158
  madden 837
  frighten 860
unmanageable
  unwieldy 647
  perverse 704
unmanly
  effeminate 374
  dishonorable 940
unmanned
  dejected 837
  cowardly 862
unmannered 895
unmannerly 895
unmarked 460
unmarred *sound* 654
  preserved 670
unmarried 904
unmask
  disclose 529
  (*show* 525)
unmatched
  different 15
  dissimilar 18
  unparalleled 20
  unequal 28
unmeaningness 517
unmeant 517
unmeasured
  infinite 105
  undistinguished 465a
  abundant 639
unmeditated
  impulsive 612
  (*undesigned* 621)
unmeet 925
unmellowed 674
unmelodious 414, 713
unmelted 321
unmentionable 874
unmentionables 225
unmentioned 526
unmerciful
  pitiless 914a
  (*malevolent* 907)
unmerited 925
unmethodical 59

unmindful
  inattentive 458
  neglectful 460
  ungrateful 917
unmingled 42
unmissed 460
unmistakable
  certain 474
  intelligible 518
  manifest 525
  affirmation 535
  (*visible* 446)
unmitigable 173
unmitigated *great* 31
  complete 52
  violent 173
unmixed 42
unmodified (141)
unmolested *safe* 664
  content 831
unmoneyed 804
unmoral 823
unmourned 898
unmoved
  quiescent 265
  obstinate 606
  insensible 823
  (*resolute* 604)
  (*uninduced* 616)
unmusical 414
  –voice 581
unmuzzle 748
unnamed 565
unnatural
  exceptional 83
  affected 855
  spiteful 907
unnecessary
  redundant 641
  useless 645
  inexpedient 647
unneeded 645
unneighborly 895
unnerved
  powerless 158
  weak 160
  dejected 837
unnoted *neglected* 460
  ignoble 874
unnoticed 460, 874
unnumbered 105
unnurtured 674
unobeyed 742
unobjectionable
  good 648
  pretty good 651
  innocent 946
unobnoxious 648
unobscured 420
unobservant 458
unobserved 460
unobstructed
  clear 705
  free 749
  (*unopposed* 709)
unobtainable 471

605

unobtained

unobtained 777a
unobtrusive 881
unoccupied
  vacant 187
  unthinking 452
  doing nothing 681
  inactive 683
  leisured 685
  secluded 893
unoffended
  enduring 826
  humble 879
unofficial 964
unoften 137
unopened 261
unopposed 709
unordinary 20, 83
unorganized 358
  unprepared 674
  —*matter* 358
unornamental 846
unornamented
  —*style* 576
  simple 849
unorthodox 984
unostentatious 881
unowed 807
unowned 782
unpacific
  discordant 713
  warfare 722
unpacified 713
unpack *unfasten* 44
  take out 297
unpaid *debt* 806
  honorary 815
  —*worker*
  volunteer 602
unpalatable
  unsavory 395
  disagreeable 830
  (*dislike* 867)
unparagoned
  supreme 33
  best 648
  perfect 650
unparalleled
  unlimited 20
  unequaled 28
  supreme 33
  exceptional 83
  best 648
unpardonable
  inexcusable 938
  wicked 945
unparliamentary
  language
  discourteous 895
  cursing 908
unpassable 261
unpassionate 826
unpatriotic 911
unpatterned 28
unpeaceful
  contention 720
  war 722

unpeered 28
unpeople
  emigration 297
  banishment 893
  (*displace* 185)
unperceived
  neglected 460
  unknown 491
  (*latent* 526)
unperformed 730
unperjured
  truthful 543
  honorable 939
unperplexed 498
unpersuadable
  obstinate 606
unpersuaded 616
unperturbed 826
unphilosophical 499
unpierced 261
unpin (44)
unpitied 932
unpitying
  pitiless 914a
  (*angry* 900)
  (*malevolent* 907)
unplaced 185
unplagued 831
unpleasant 830
unpleasing 830
unplumbed 104
unpoetical *prose* 598
  matter of fact 703
unpointed *blunt* 254
unpolished *rough* 256
  inelegant 579
  unprepared 674
  vulgar 851
  rude 895
unpolite 895
unpolluted *good* 648
  perfect 650
unpopular
  disagreeable 830
  dislike 867
unpopularity
  hatred 898
unportioned 804
unpossessed 777a
unpracticed (699)
unprecedented
  exceptional 83
  rare 137
unprejudiced 498, 748
unpremeditated
  impulsive 612
  undesigned 621
  unprepared 674
unprepared 674
unprepossessed 498
unprepossessing 846
unpresentable 851
unpretending 881
unpretentious 881
unprevented 748

unprincipled 945
unprivileged 925
unprized 483
unproclaimed 526
unproduced
  inexistent 2
unproductive
  useless 645
unproductiveness 169
unproficiency 699
unprofitable
  unproductive 169
  useless 645
  inexpedient 647
  bad 649
unprogressive 659
unprolific 169
unpromising 859
unprompted 612
unpronounced
  latent 526
unpropitious
  ill-timed 135
  opposed 708
  adverse 735
  hopeless 859
unproportioned
  (*disagreeing* 24)
unprosperous 735
unprotected 665
unproved 477
unprovided
  scanty 640
  unprepared 674
unprovoked (616)
unpublished 526
unpunctual
  tardy 133
  untimely 135
  irregular 139
unpunished 970
unpurchased 796
unpurified 653
unpurposed 621
unpursued 624
unqualified
  incomplete 52
  impotent 158
  certain 474
  unprepared 674
  inexpert 699
  unentitled 925
  —*truth* 494
unquelled 173
unquenchable
  strong 159
  desire 865
unquenched
  violence 173
  heat 382
unquestionable
  certain 474
unquestionably
  assent 488
unquestioned 474

agreed upon 488
unquiet *motion* 264
  agitation 315
  excitable 825
unravel *untie* 44
  arrange 60
  straighten 246
  evolve 313
  discover 480a
  interpret 522
  disembarrass 705
  (*solve* 462)
unreached 304
unread *ignorant* 491
unready 674
unreal *not existing* 2
  unsubstantial 4
  erroneous 495
  imaginary 515
unreasonable
  impossible 471
  illogical 477
  misjudging 481
  foolish 499
  capricious 608
  exorbitant 814
  unjust 923
  unreasoning 452
unreclaimed 951
unrecognizable 146
unreconciled 713
unrecorded 552
unrecounted 55
unrecumbent 212
unreduced 31
unrefined 851
unreflecting 458
unreformed 951
unrefreshed 688
unrefuted *proved* 478
  true 494
unregarded
  neglected 460
  unrespected 929
unregenerate 988
unregistered 552
unreined 748
unrelated 10
unrelenting
  pitiless 914a
  revengeful 919
  (*malevolent* 907)
unreliable
  uncertain 475
  vacillating 605
  insecure 665
unrelieved 835
unremarked 460
unremembered 506
unremitting
  continuous 69, 143
  continuing 110
  persevering 604a
  (*industrious* 682)
unremoved 184
unremunerated 808

unroll

unrenewed 141
unrepaid (806)
unrepealed 141
unrepeated *single* 87
  few 103
unrepentant 951
unrepining 831
unreplenished 640
unreported (526)
unrepressed 173
unreproached 946
unreproved 946
unrequited
  owing 806
  ingratitude 917
unresented
  forgiven 918
unresenting
  enduring 826
unreserved
  manifest 525
  veracious 543
  artless 703
unresisted 743
unresisting 725
unresolved 605
unrespected 929
unrespited 971
unrest *changeable* 149
  moving 264
unrestored
  fatigue 688
unrestrained
  capricious 608
  unencumbered 705
  free 748
unrestricted
  undiminished 31
  free 748
unretracted 535
unrevealed (528)
unrevenged 918
unreversed 143
unrevoked 143
unrewarded
  unpaid 806
  ingratitude 917
unrhymed 598
unriddle
  find out 480a
  disclose 529
  (*interpret* 522)
unrig 645
unrighteous 945
unrip 260
unripe *youth* 127
  sour 397
  unprepared 674
  —*fruit* 397
unrivaled
  unequaled 28
  supreme 33
  (*good* 648)
unrivet (44)
unrobe (226)
unroll *evolve* 313

606

unromantic

display 525
(*unravel* 47)
(*straighten* 246)
unromantic 494
unroof (226)
unroot *extract* 301
(*destroy* 162)
unruffled *calm* 174
quiet 265
unaffected 823
placid 826
imperturbable 871
(*in order* 58)
unruly *violent* 173
obstinate 606
disobedient 742
unsaddle 756
unsafe 665
unsaid 526
unsalable *useless* 645
selling 796
cheap 815
unsaluted 929
unsanctified 475
impiety 988
irreligion 989
unsanctioned 925
unsated 865
unsatisfactory
inexpedient 647
bad 649
displeasing 830
discontent 832
unsatisfied
discontented 832
desirous 865
unsavoriness 395
unsavory *insipid* 391
not savory 395
inedible 867
unsay *recant* 607
(*negation* 536)
unscanned 460
unscathed 654
unscattered (72)
unscholarly 491
unschooled
ignorant 491
(*unskillful* 699)
unscientific
illogical 477
(*erroneous* 495)
unscoured 653
unscreened (665)
unscrew (44)
unscriptural 984
unscrupulous 940
unseal 529
unsearched 460
unseasonable
inappropriate 24
ill-timed 135
(*inexpedient* 647)
unseasoned
unaccustomed 614
unprepared 674

unseat *displace* 185
abrogate 756
unseconded
unassisted 706
unseemly
inexpedient 647
ugly 846
vulgar 851
undue 925
vicious 945
unseen *invisible* 447
neglected 460
latent 526
unsegmentic 357
unseldom 136
unselfconscious 852
unselfish 816, 942
unseparated 46
unserviceable 645
unservient 645
unsettle *derange* 61
unsettled *mutable* 149
displaced 185
uncertain 475
–in one's mind 503
unsevered 50
unsex 146
unshackle (*untie* 44)
(*liberate* 750)
unshackled (*free* 748)
unshaded
manifest 525
unshaken *strong* 159
(*resolute* 604)
–belief 484
unshapely 241, 846
unshapen
amorphous 241
(*ugly* 846)
unshared 777
unsheathe
(*uncover* 226)
–the sword *war* 722
unsheltered 665
unshielded 665
unshifting 143
unship 297
unshipment 185
unshocked 823
unshorn 50
unshortened 200
unshrinking
determined 604
courageous 861
unsifted 460
unsightly 846
unsinged 670
unskilled 699
unskillfulness 699
unslaked 865
unsleeping
persevering 604a
active 682
unsmooth 256
unsociable 893
unsocial 893

unsoiled 652
unsold 777
unsolder (*disjoin* 44)
(*incoherence* 47)
unsoldierlike 862
unsolicitous 866
unsolved 526
unsophisticated
simple 42
genuine 494
artless 703
(*good* 648)
unsorted 59
unsought *avoided* 623
unrequested 766
unsound *weak* 160
illogical 477
erroneous 495
deceptive 545
imperfect 651
speculative 665
(*unhealthy* 655)
–mind 503
unsown 674
unsparing
abundant 639
severe 739
liberal 816
with an–hand 818
unspeakable *great* 31
wonderful 870
unspecified 78
unspent 678
unspied 526
unspiritual 316
unspoiled *good* 648
unspoken (581)
unspotted *clean* 652
beautiful 845
innocent 946
unstable
changeable 149
inverted 218
vacillating 605
precarious 665
–equilibrium 149
unstaid 149
unstained *clean* 652
honorable 939
unstatesmanlike 699
unsteadfast 605
unsteady *mutable* 149
irresolute 605
in danger 665
(*fickle* 607)
unstinted 639
unstirred 823, 826
unstopped
continuing 143
open 260
unstored 640
unstrained
turbid 653
relaxed 687
–meaning 516
unstrengthened 160

unstruck 823
unstrung 160
unstudied 460
unsubject 748
unsubmissive 742
unsubstantial 4
weak 160
immaterial 317
rare 322
erroneous 495
imaginary 515
unsubstantiality 4
unsuccess 732
unsuccessful 732
unsuccessive 70
unsuitable
incongruous 24
inexpedient 647
–time 135
unsullied *clean* 652
honorable 939
(*guiltless* 946)
unsung 526
unsupplied 640
unsupported
weak 160
(*unassisted* 706)
–by evidence 468
unsuppressed 141
unsurmountable 471
unsurpassed 33
unsusceptible 823
unsuspected
belief 484
latent 526
unsuspecting
hopeful 858
unsuspicious
belief 484
artless 703
hope 858
unsustainable
erroneous 495
unsustained
error 495
(*weak* 160)
(*unassisted* 706)
unswayed (616)
unsweet 395, 414
unswept 653
unswerving
straight 246
direct 278
persevering 604a
unsymmetric
uncomfortable 83
unsymmetrical
irregular 59
shapeless 241
distorted 243
unsympathetic 24
unsystematic 59, 139
untack (44)
untainted *pure* 652
healthy 654
honorable 939

untoward

untalked of 526
untamed *rude* 851
ferocious 907
untangled (58)
untarnished
honorable 939
(*innocent* 946)
untasted 391
untaught
ignorant 491
untrained 674
untaxed 815
unteach 538
unteachable
foolish 499
unskillful 699
untempted (616)
untenable
powerless 158
illogical 477
undefended 725
secluded 893
untenanted 187
unthanked 917
unthankful 917
unthankfulness 915
unthawed *solid* 321
cold 383
unthinkable 471
unthinking
unconsidered 452
involuntary 601
unthought of
unconsidered 452
neglected 460
unthreatened 664
unthrifty
unprepared 674
prodigal 818
unthrone 756
untidy *in disorder* 59
slovenly 653
untie *liberate* 750
(*loose* 44)
–the knot 705
until 106 (108)
–now 118
untilled 674
untimely 135
–end 360
untinged *simple* 42
(*uncolored* 429)
untired 689
untiring 604a
untitled 876
untold *countless* 105
uncertain 475
latent 526
secret 528
untouched
disused 678
insensible 823
untoward
ill-timed 135
bad 649
unprosperous 735

607

unpleasant 830
untraced 526
untracked 526
untractable
  obstinate 606
  unskillful 699
untrained
  unaccustomed 614
  unprepared 674
  unskilled 699
untrammeled
  easy 705
  free 748
untranslatable 523
untranslated 20, 523
untraveled 265
untreasured 640
untried *new* 123
  not decided 461
untrimmed
  unprepared 674
  matter-of-fact 703
  simple 849
untrodden *new* 123
  impervious 261
  not used 678
untroubled *calm* 174
  peaceful 721
untrue *erroneous* 495
  unveracious 546
untrustworthy
  uncertain 475
  erroneous 495
  danger 665
  dishonorable 940
untruth 546
untruthfulness 544
untunable 414
unturned 246
untutored
  ignorant 491
  unprepared 674
  artless 703
untwine 313
untwist *evolve* 313
  (*separate* 44, 47)
  (*straighten* 246)
unused
  unaccustomed 614
  unskillful 699
unusual 83
unusually *very* 31
unutterable *great* 31
  unmeaning 517
  wonderful 870
unvalued
  underrated 483
  undesired 866
  disliked 898
unvanquished 748
unvaried *uniform* 16
  monotonous 104
  continuing 143
  -style 575, 576
unvarnished
  true 494, 543

  -style 576
  matter-of-fact 703
  simple 849
  -tale true 494
  veracious 543
unvarying 143
unveil *manifest* 525
  disclose 529
  (*manifest* 525)
unventilated 261
unveracious 544
unversed
  ignorant 491
  (*unskilled* 699)
unvexed 831
unviolated 939
unvisited 893
unvitiated (648)
unwakened 683
unwarlike 862
unwarmed 383
unwarned
  unexpected 508
  danger 665
unwarped judgment
  498
unwarrantable
  wrong 923
unwarranted 923
  illogical 477
  undue 925
  illegal 964
unwary *neglectful* 460
  (*rash* 863)
unwashed 653
  great- 876
unwaste (639)
unwatchful 460
unwavering 604a
unweakened 159
unwearied
  persevering 604a
  indefatigable 682
  refreshed 689
unweave 60
unwedded 904
unweeded garden
  674
unweeting 491
unweighed 460
unwelcome
  disagreeable 830
  unsocial 893
unwell 655
unwept 831
unwholesome 657
unwieldy *large* 192
  heavy 319
  cumbersome 647
  difficult 704
  ugly 846
unwilling *dissent* 489
  -service 603
unwillingness 603
unwind *evolve* 313
  (*straighten* 246)

unwiped 653
unwisdom 499
unwise 499
unwished 866
unwithered 159
unwitnessed (526)
unwitting
  ignorant 491
  involuntary 601
unwittingly
  undesignedly 621
unwomanly 373
unwonted
  unimitated 20
  unusual 83
  unaccustomed 614
unworldly 939
unworn 159
unworshiped 929
unworthy
  shameful 874
  vicious 945
  -of belief 485
  -of notice 643
unwrap 246
unwrinkled 255
unwritten *old* 124
  latent 526
  obliterated 552
  spoken 582
  -law 697, 963
unwrought 674
unyielding *stable* 150
  tough 323
  unbending 604
  obstinate 606
  resisting 719
unyoke (44)
up *aloft* 206
  vertical 212
  ascent 305
  effervescing 353
  excited 824
  all-with
  destruction 162
  failure 732
  adversity 735
  prices looking- 814
  the game is- 735
  time- 111
  -and at them 716
  -and coming 698
  -and doing 682
  -and down 314
  -for discussion 454
  -in 698
  -in arms
  prepared 673
  active 682
  opposition 708
  attack 716
  resistance 719
  warfare 722
  -on end 212
  -to
  (*see below*)

Upanishads 986
upas tree 663
upbear *support* 215
  raise 307
upbraid 932
upcast 305, 307
upgrade 305, 654
upgrow 206
upgrowth
  expansion 194
  ascent 305
upheaval 146, 307
upheave 307
uphill *acclivity* 217
  ascent 305
  laborious 686
  difficult 704
uphoist 307
uphold *continue* 143
  support 215
  evidence 467
  aid 707
  praise 931
  preserve 976
upholder 488, 711
upholstery 633
upland 180
uplands 206, 344
uplift *elevation* 307
  improvement 658
upon—*my honor* 535
  -oath 535
  -which after 117
  future 121
upper 206—*case*
  printing 591
  -classes 875
  -hand influence 175
  success 731
  sway 737
  -story summit 210
  intellect 450
  wisdom 498
  -ten thousand 875
uppermost
  summit 210
  say what comes-
    612
  -in one's thoughts
    memory 505
  -in the mind
    thought 451
  topic 454
  attention 457
upraise 307
uprear 307
upright
  vertical 212
  straight 246
  honest 939
  -piano 417
uprise 305
uprising 146, 742
uproar *disorder* 59
  violence 173
  noise 404

uproarious
  excitable 825
uproariousness 404,
  825
uproot *extract* 301
  (*destroy* 162)
ups and downs of
  life *events* 151
  adversity 735
upset *destroy* 162
  invert 218
  throw down 308
  defeat 731
  excite 824
  disconcert 874
upshot *result* 154
  judgment 480
  completion 729
  (*end* 67)
upside down 218
upstairs 206
upstart *newness* 123
  prosperous 734
  plebeian 876
upstream
  with difficulty 704
up to *time* 106
  power 157
  knowing 490
  skillful 698
  -one's ears 641
  -one's eyes 641
  -snuff 702
  -the brim 52
  -the mark equal 27
  sufficient 639
  good 648
  due 924
  -the scratch 861
  -this time time 106
  past 122
upturn 210
upturned 305, 307
upward 305
  -flight 305
upwards 206—*of*
  more 33
  plurality 100
uranic 318
uranography 318
uranolite 318
uranology 318
uranometry 318
urban 189
urbane 894
urceole 998
urceus 191, 998
urchin *child* 129, 167
  small 193
  wretch 949
urge *violence* 173
  impel 276
  incite 615
  hasten 684
  beg 765
urgency *need* 865

urgent

(see urgent)
urgent required 630
  important 642
  haste 684
  request 765
urn vase 191
  funeral 363
  heater 386
  cinerary – 363
Ursa Major 318, 490a
Ursa Minor 318, 490a
usable 644
usage custom 613
  use 677
  (rule 80)
usance 806
use habit 613
  waste 638
  utility 644
  employ **677**
  property 780
  be of–to aid 707
  benevolence 906
  in– 677
  make good – of 658
  – a right 924
  – loosely 465a
  – one's discretion 600
  – one's endeavor 675
  – up 677
used to 613
used up
  deteriorated 659
  fatigue 688
  weary 841
  satiated 869
useful
  instrumental 633
  utility 644
  serviceable 746
  render – 677
useless
  unproductive 169
  wasted 638
  inutility 645
user 677 right of – **780**
Ushas 979
usher attendant 263
  receive 296
  teacher 540
  servant 746
  courtesy 894
  marriage 903
  – in precedence 62
  begin 66
  herald 116
  precession 280
  announce 511
  – into the world 161
usine 691
usquebaugh 959
ustulate 384
ustulation 384
usual ordinary 82

  customary 613
usucapion 777
usufruct 677
usurer lender 787
  merchant 797
  credit 805
  miser 819
usurious 819
usurp assume 739
  seize 789
  illegal 925
  – authority 738
usurpation
  (see usurp)
  authority 737
  insolence 885
usurper 706, 737
usury 806
utensil recipient 191
  instrument 633
utilitarian
  teaching 537
  useful 677
  philanthropy 910
utilitarianism 451
utility 644 general
  – actor 599
utilize 677
utmost 33
  do one's – 686
  – height 210
Utopia visionary 515
  hopeful 858
utricle 191
utter extreme 31
  distribute 73
  disclose 529
  publish 531
  speak 580, 582
  money 800
utterance (see utter)
utterly completely 52
uttermost 31
  to the – parts of the earth space 180
  distance 196
uxoricide 361
uxorious 750, 897

V

vacancy (see vacant)
  – of mind 452
vacant void 4
  absent 187
  thoughtless 452
  unmeaning 517
  scanty 640
  – hour 685
  – mind folly 499
vacate displace 185
  absent 187
  depart 293
  resign 757
vacation repose 687

  (leisure 685)
vacatur 756
vaccine 366
vache 191
vacillate
  changeable 149
  undulate 314
  waver 605
vacuity 187, 452
vacuolar 357
vacuolation 161
vacuolization 161
vacuometer 338, 446
vacuous
  unsubstantial 4
  absent 187
  (inexistent 2)
vacuum absence 187
  – cleaner 652
vade mecum
  information 527
  schoolbook 542
vadium 771
vagabond
  wanderer 268
  low person 876
  rogue 949
vagabondage 266
vagary absurdity 497
  imagination 515
  whim 608
  antic 840
vagas 999
vaginate 223
vagitus 129
vagrant
  changeable 149
  roving 266
  traveler 268
  deviating 279
vague unsubstantial 4
  uncertain 475
  unreasoning 477
  unmeaning 517
  obscure 519
  – language 571
  – suggestion 514
vails donation 784
  reward 973
  (expenditure 809)
vain unreal 2
  unprofitable 645
  conceited 880
  in – failure 732
  labor in –
  come short 304
  useless 645
  fail 732
  take a name in – 895
  use – efforts 645
  – attempt 732
  – expectation 509
vainglorious
  haughty 878
  vain 880
  boasting 884

vakas 999
vakil 968
valance 231
vale 252 – of years 128
valediction adieu 293
  courtesy 894
valedictorian 293
valedictory 582
valentine 902
valet 631, 746
  – de chambre 746
  – de place
  interpreter 524
  guide 527
valetudinarian
  invalid 655
  salubrity 656
valetudinarianism 655
Valhalla 981
valiant 861
valid confirmed 150
  powerful 157
  strong 159
  true 494
  sufficient 639
  (influential 179)
  – reasoning 476
valise 191
vallation 717
valley 252
  – of the shadow of death 360
vallum 717
valor 861 for – 733
valorization 480
valuable useful 644
  good 648
value color 428
  measure 466
  estimate 480
  importance 642
  utility 644
  goodness 648
  price 812
  approbation 931
  of priceless – 814
  set a – upon 482
  – received 810
  – s painting 556
valueless 646
valve stop 263
  conduit 350
  safety – safety 664
  refuge 666
  escape 671
vambrace 717
vamose 293
vamp change 140
  seduce 615
  improvise 674
  – up change 140
  improve 658
  restore 660
  prepare 673
vampire tempter 615

variable

  taking 789
  evildoer 913
  demon 980
vampirism
  extortion 789
  sorcery 992
van beginning 66
  front 234
  wagon 272
  in the – 234
  precession 280
vancourier 64
Vandal destroyer 165
  vulgar 851
  commonalty 876
  evildoer 913
Vandalic 241
vandalism 851
vandyke 257
vandyke brown 433
vane
  changeableness 149
  wind 338, 349
  indication 550
vanfoss 717
vanguard 234
vanilla 298
vanish unsubstantial 4
  transient 111
  disappear 449
  (cease to exist 2)
vanishing small 32
  little 193
  disappearing 449
vanity useless 645
  conceit **880**
Vanity Fair 852
vanquish 731
vantage ground
  superiority 33
  power 157
  influence 175
  height 206
vapid insipid 391
  – style 575
  (unattractive 866)
vaporarium 386
vaporization 336
vapor gas 334
  bubbles 353
  fancy 515
  boast 884
  insolence 885
  – bath 386
vaporer 887
vaporific 336
vaporous
  unsubstantial 4
  vaporization 336
  imaginative 515
  (opaque 426)
vapors dejection 837
vaquero 370
vargueno 191
variable irregular 139
  changeable 149

irresolute 605
variance *difference* 15
  disagreement 24
  discord 713
  at–*enmity* 889
  at–*with* 489
  at–*with the fact* 471
variation
  difference 15
  dissimilarity 18
  diverseness **20a**
  number 84
  chance 140
  music 415
varicella 655
varicose 655
varied 15
  –*assortment* 81
variegated 428, 440
variegation 440
variety *difference* 15
  class 75
  multiformity 81
  exception 83
  –*the spice of life* 81
variform 81
variola 655
variometer 157, 466
variorum 596
various *different* 15
  many 102
  –*places* 182
  –*times* 119
varlet 949
varnish
  overlay 223
  resin 352, 356a
  sophistry 477
  falsehood 544
  painting 556
  decorate 847
  excuse 937
Varuna 318, 979
vary *differ* 15
  dissimilar 18
  variation 20a
  change 140
  fluctuate 149
vascular *cells* 191
  holes 260
  pipes 350
vasculum 191
vase 191
vassal 746
vassalage 749
vast *great* 31
  spacious 180
  large 192
  –*learning* 490
vasty 180, 192
  –*deep* 341
vat 191
Vatican
  churchdom 995
  temple 1000

thunders of the– 908
vaticide 361
vatication 511
vaudeville 599
vault *cellar* 191
  curve 245
  convexity 250
  leap 309
  tomb 363
  –*of heaven* 318
vaulted *curved* 245
  concave 252
vaulting *superior* 33
  aspiring 865
vaunt 884
vauntmure 717
vaurien 949
vavasour
  possessor 779
  nobleman 875
veal 298
vection 270
Vedanta 451
Vedantism 984
Vedas 986
vedette 668
Vedic 124
veer *change* 140
  deviate 279
  go back 283
  change intention 607
vega 344
vegetability 365
vegetable 298, **367**
  –*kingdom* 367
  –*life* 365
  –*oil* 356
  –*physiology* 369
vegetality 365
vegetarian 298, 367, 953
vegetarianism 298
vegetate *exist* 1
  grow 194, 365, 367
  inactive 683
  insensible 823
vegetation 365
  inaction 681
vegetative 365, 367
vegetism 365
vehemence
  violence 173
  feeling 821
  emotion 825
vehement
  –*language* 574
vehicle *carriage* **272**
  instrument 631
vehicular 272
veil *covering* 225
  shade 424
  conceal 528
  ambush 530
  draw aside the– 529
  take the

–*seclude* 893
  church 995
veiled 475
  (*invisible* 447)
vein *intrinsicality* 5
  tendency 176
  thin 203
  thread 205
  conduit 350
  humor 602
  mine 636
  affections 820
  in the– 602
  not in the– 603
veined 440
veinlet 205
veldt 344
veldtschoen 225
velitation 720
velleity 600
vellicate 315
vellicating 392
vellicative 315, 392
vellum 590
velo 466
veloce *music* 415
velocimeter 274
velocipede 272
velocity
  rate of motion 264
  swiftness **274**
  angular– 244
velumen 255
velutinous 255
velvet *smooth* 255
  pile 256
  pleasure 377
  fabric 635
  on–easy 705
velveteen 255
vena 350
venal *price* 812
  stingy 819
  dishonest 940
  selfish 943
venation 622
vend 796
vendaval 349
vendee 795
vender 796
vendetta 919
vendible 796
venditation 884
vendor 796
vendue 796
veneer *layer* 204
  covering 223
venenation 659
venerable
  old 124
  aged 128
  sage 500
  respected 928
venerated 500
veneration
  respect 928

piety 987
veneral disease 655
venery *killing* 361
  hunting 622
  impurity 961
venesection
  ejection 297
  remedy 662
Venetian blinds 351, 424
vengeance 919
  cry to heaven for– 923
  with a–greatly 31
  violent 173
vengeful 919
venial 937
venire 969–*facias* 969
venison 298, 394
vennel 627
venom *bane* 663
  malignity 907
venomous *bad* 649
  poisonous 657
  dangerous 666
  rude 895
  maleficent 907
venose 205
vent *opening* 260
  egress 295
  air pipe 351
  disclose 529
  escape 671
  sale 796
  find–egress 295
  passage 302
  publish 531
  escape 671
  give–to emit 297
  disclose 529
  –*one's rage* 900
  –*one's spleen* 900
ventage 351
venter 191
venthole 260, 351
ventiduct 351
ventilabrum 349
ventilate *begin* 66
  air 338
  wind 349
  discuss 595
  –*a question*
  inquiry 461
  reasoning 476
ventilative 349
ventilator *wind* 349
  air pipe 351
ventose 349
ventosity 349
vent peg *stopper* 263
  safety 666
  escape 671
ventricle 191
ventricose 250
ventriloquism 580
ventriloquist 580

venture
  experiment 463
  presume 472
  chance 621
  danger 665
  try 675
  undertaking 676
  invest 787
  courage 861
  I'll–to say 535
venturesome
  undertaking 676
  brave 861
  rash 863
venue 74, 183
venula 205
Venus
  luminary 318, 423
  –'s *flytrap* 545
  beauty 845
  love 897
veracity 543
veranda 191
verbal 562
  –*intercourse*
  speech 582
  interlocution 588
  –*quibble*
  absurdity 497
  wit 842
verbarian 562
verbatim
  imitation 19
  exact 494
  literal 516
  words 562
  –*report* 551
verbiage
  unmeaning 517
  words 562
  diffuse 573
  (*absurdity* 497)
verbigeration 821a
verbosity *words* 562
  diffuse 573
  loquacity 584
verdant
  vegetation 367
  green 435
verd antique 435
verdict *opinion* 480
  lawsuit 969
  snatch a–cheat 545
  cunning 702
verdigris 435
verdine 435
verditer 435
verdure
  vegetation 307
  green 435
verecundity
  humility 879
  modesty 881
Verein 712
verge *tendency* 176
  near 197

610

vergent · vinculum

edge 231
limit 233
direction 278
vergent 67
verger 996
veridical 467, 543
　—*hallucination* 992a
veriest 31
verification *test* 463
　warrant 771
verificative 467
verify 463
　evidence 467
　demonstrate 478
　find out 480a
verily *truly* 494
　(*positively* 32)
verisimilitude 472
veritable 1, 494
verity 494
verjuice 397
vermeology 368
vermes 368
vermicelli 298
vermicular
　convoluted 248
　worm 366
vermiculation 221
vermiform 248, 249
vermifuge 662
vermilion 434
vermin *animal* 366
　unclean 653
　base 876
vernacular
　native 188
　internal 221
　language 560
　habitual 613
vernal *early* 123
　spring 125
vernier
　minuteness 193
　—*scale* 466
Vernunft 450
veronica 993
verruca 250
versatile
　changeable 149
　(*irresolute* 605)
　(*fickle* 607)
verse *division* 51
　poetry 597
versed in
　knowledge 490
　(*skill* 698)
versicolor 440
versify 597
version *special* 79
　change 140
　interpretation 522
Verstand 450
versus *towards* 278
　against 708
vert 435
vertebra 215, 222

vertebral 222, 235
　—*column* 222
vertebrate 368
vertebration 357
vertex 210
vertical 212, 246
　—*rays* 382
verticality 212
verticity 312
vertigo *rotation* 312
　delirium 503
verve *imagination* 515
　vigorous language 574
　activity 682
　feeling 821
very 31—*best* 648
　—*image* 554
　—*many* 102
　—*minute* 113
　—*much* 31
　—*picture* 17
　—*small* 32
　—*thing identity* 13
　agreement 23
　exact 494
　—*true assent* 488
　—*well content* 831
vesicatory 662
vesicle *cell* 191
　covering 223
　globe 249
vesicular *cells* 191
　holes 260
vesper 126
vespers 126, 990
vespertine
　evening 126
vessel *receptacle* 191
　tube 260
　ship 273
vest *place* 184
　dress 225
　—*in belong to* 777
　give 784
vesta *match* 388
vestal 960—*virgin* 904
vested *fixed* 150
　legal 963
　—*in located* 184
　—*interest given* 780
　due 924
vestibule *entrance* 66
　room 191
　hearing 418
vestige 551
vestigial 193
vestment *dress* 225
　canonicals 999
vestry *council* 696
　churchdom 995
　church 1000
vesture 225
vesuvian *match* 388
vet *veterinarian* 370
veteran *old* 130

adept 700
warrior 726
veterinarian 370
veterinary art 370
veto 761
vettura 272
vetturino 694
vetust 124
vex 830, 898
vexation
　pain 828, 830
　—*of spirit* 828
　discontent 832
vexatious 830
vexed question
　difficulty 704
　discord 713
vexillum 550
via *direction* 278
　way 627
viable 359
viaduct 627
viagraph 466
vial 191
　—*s of hate* 898
　—*s of wrath* 900
via lactea 318
viameter 200
viands 298
viaticum
　provision 637
　rite 998
viatometer 200
vibrate 314
　—*between two extremes* 149
vibratile 314
vibration 314, 408
vibratiuncle 314
vibrative 314
vibratory
　changeable 149
vibrograph 314
vibroscope 314
vicar *deputy* 759
　clergyman 996
　—*of Bray changeableness* 149
　tergiversation 607
　servility 886
vicarage 1000
vicarial 147
vicariate 995
vicarious
　substitute 147
vicarship 995
vice *pinion* 752
　deputy 759
　wickedness 945
vice-admiral 745
vice-chairman 759
Vice-Chancellor 967
　—'s *Court* 966
vicegerency 755
vicegerent 758, 759
vicenary 98

vice-president 694, 759
vice-regal 759
viceroy *governor* 745
　deputy 759
vicesimal 98
vice versâ
　reciprocal 12
　contrary 14
　interchange 148
vicinage 197, 227
vicinal 197
vicinism 145
vicinity 197, 227
vicious 173, 945
　render—659
　—*reasoning* 477
vicissitude
　changeable 149
　(*change* 140)
victim *dupe* 547
　defeated 732
　sufferer 828
　culprit 975
victimize *kill* 361
　deceive 545
　injure 649
　baffle 731
victimized 828
victor 731
victoria *carriage* 272
Victoria Cross 551, 722, 733
victory 731
victrola 417, 418
victual *provide* 637
victuals 298
videlicet
　specification 79
　namely 522
　(*example* 82)
viduation 905
viduity 905
vie *good* 648
　—*with contend* 720
　(*oppose* 708)
vielle 417
view *sight* 441
　appearance 448
　attend to 457
　opinion 484
　landscape painting 556
　intention 520
　bring into—525
　come into—446
　commanding—441
　in—*visible* 446
　intended 420
　expected 507
　keep in—457
　on—448
　present to the—448
　—*as* 484
　—*halloo* 411
　—*in a new light* 658

—*s tenet* 484
　with a—*to* 620
viewer 444
viewless 447
viewpoint 441, 453
vigesimal 98
vigil *care* 459
vigilance *care* 459
　wisdom 498
　activity 682
vigilant 864
vigils *worship* 990
vigneron 371
vignette
　engraving 558
　sketch 594
　embellishment 847
vigor *strength* 159
　energy 171
　style 574
　resolution 604
　health 654
　activity 682
viking 792
vile *valueless* 643
　hateful 649
　painful 830
　disgraceful 874
　plebeian 876
　dishonorable 940
　vicious 945
vilification 908
vilify *shame* 874
　censure 932
　detract 934
　(*disrespect* 929)
　(*contempt* 930)
vilipend
　disrespect 929
　censure 932
　detract 934
vilipendency 930
villa 189
village 189—*talk* 588
villager 188
villain *servant* 746
　serf 876
　rascal 949
villainous *evil* 649
　wicked 945
　—*saltpeter* 727
villainy 940
vellein (*see* villein)
villenage
　subjection 749
　tenure 777
villi 256
villous 256
vim 171, 682
vina 417
vinaceous 434
vinaigrette 400
vincible *impotent* 158
　(*weak* 160)
vincture 43
vinculum 45

vindicate
  evidence 467
  avenge 919
  justify 937
  –a *right* 924
vindication 937
vindicator
  revenge 919
vindictive
  irascible 901
  revengeful 919
vine 367
vinegar 397
  –*aspect* 846
vine-grower 371
vinegrub 659
vineyard *tillage* 371
  workshop 691
vingt et un 840
viniculturist 371
vintage
  agriculture 371
  store 636
vintner 797
viol 417
violaceous 437
violate *disobey* 742
  nonobservance 773
  undue 925
  dereliction 927
  ravish 961
  –a *law* 83
  –a *usage* 614
  –the *law* 964
violence 173
  arbitrary 964
  do-to bad 649
  nonobservance 773
  undue 925
violent 173
  excitable 825
  in a–*degree* 31
  lay-hands on 789
  –*death death* 360
  kill 361
violet 437
  modesty 881
violin 417
violinist 416
violoncello 417
violone 417
viper *snake* 366
  bane 663
  evildoer 913
  bad man 949
viperine 366
virago 901
virent 435
virescence 435
virgate 246
virgin *new* 123
  girl 129
  spinster 904
  good woman 948
  pure 960
  –*soil ignorance* 491

  untilled 674
virginal 900
virginals 417
Virginia
  crooked as–fence 243
  –*reel* 840
viridian 435
viridity 435
virile *adolescent* 131
  strong 159
  manly 373
virtu 847, 850
virtual *inexistent* 2
  unsubstantial 5
  –*image* 443
virtually 5
  (*truly* 494)
virtue *power* 157
  courage 861
  goodness 944
  purity 960
  by–of power 157
  instrumentality 631
  in–of authority 737
  make a–of necessity no choice 609a
  skill 698
  submit 725
  compromise 774
  bear 826
virtueless 945
virtuosity *taste* 850
virtuoso 415, 416, 850
virtuous *virtue* 944
  purity 960
virulence *energy* 171
  noxiousness 649
  insalubrity 657
  discourtesy 895
  anger 900
  malevolence 907
virus *disease* 655
  poison 663
vis inertiae
  power 157
  inertness 172
  insensibility 823
visa 488
visage *front* 234
  appearance 448
vis-à-vis
  contrariety 14
  front 234
  opposite 237
  carriage 272
viscera 221
visceral 221, 329
viscid 327, 352
viscidity 327
viscount 875
viscountship 877
viscous 352
viscum 45
vise 327, 752, 781

Vishnu 979
visibility 446
visible 446
  (*intelligible* 518)
  become–448
  be–448
  darkness–421
vision *sight* 441
  phantasm 443
  dream 515
  specter 980a
  psychical research 992a
  organ of–441
visionary *inexistent* 2
  unsubstantial 4
  impossible 471
  imaginary 515
  heterodox 984
  (*untrue* 495)
visionless 442
visit *arrival* 292
  social 892
  courtesy 894
  –*behind the scenes* 461
  –*upon* 972
visitation *disease* 655
  adversity 735
  suffering 828
  (*evil* 619)
  –*of the sick* 998
  –s *of Providence* 976
visiting 892
  on–terms
  friendship 888
  sociality 892
  –*card* 550
visitor *immigrant* 294
  director 694
  friend 890
visor 530
vista *convergence* 260
  sight 441
  appearance 448
  expectation 507
  –*of time* 109
visual 441 –*organ* 441
visualize 220
vitability 359
vital *life* 359
  important 642
  –*air* 359
  –*force* 359
  –*part* 3
  –*principle* 1
vitalic 359
vitality *stability* 150
  strength 159
  life 359
vitalize 359
vitals 221
vitiate *deteriorate* 659
vitiated *diseased* 655
viticulture 371
vitreform 425

vitreous *hard* 323
  transparent 425
vitrescent 323
vitrics 191
vitrify 323
vitrine 191
vituperate 932
vituperation 908
vituperator 936
viva! *glory* 873
  praise 931
vivace *music* 415
vivacious *active* 682
  sensitive 822
  cheerful 836
vivandière 797
vivarium 370
viva voce 582
vive *glory be to* 873
  on the qui–824
vivid *energetic* 171
  sensibility 375
  light 420
  color 428
  graphic 518
  (*powerful* 157)
  still–
  remembering 506
vivify *strength* 159
  life 359
vivisection *pain* 378
  cruelty 907
vixen *fox* 366
  female 374
  shrew 901
viz. (see *videlicet*)
vizier *director* 694
  deputy 759
vizor *mask* 530
  shield 717
vlei 345
vocable 562
vocabulary 562
vocal *music* 415
  voice 580
  –*score* 415
vocalist 416
vocalize 562, 580
vocation *business* 625
  (*duty* 926)
vocational 625
  –*therapy* 662
  –*training* 537
vociferation *loud* 404
  cry 411
  voice 580
vogue *custom* 613
  fashion 852
  fame 873
voice *sound* 402
  cry 411
  judgment 480
  promulgate 531
  affirmation 535
  express 566
  human–580

  choice 609
  (*belief* 484)
  give one's–for 488
  make one's–heard 175
  raise one's
  –*shout* 411
  speak 582
  still small–
  faint sound 405
  conscience 926
  want of–581
  warning–668
  –*against dissent* 489
  oppose 708
  –*of the charmer* 933
  –*of the tempter* 615
voiceless 561, 581
  –*woe* 837
void *unsubstantial* 4
  absence 187
  emit 297
  abyss 667
  (*inexistence* 2)
  null and–964
  –*of foundation* 546
  –*of reason* 450a
  –*of suspicion* 484
voidance 297
voile 635
voiturier 268
voivode 745
volant 267
Volapük 560, 563
volatile *transient* 111
  light 320
  gaseous 334
  vaporizable 336
  assent 488
  irresolute 605
  capricious 608
  –*alkali* 334
vol-au-vent 298
volcanic *violent* 173
  heat 382
  burnt 388
  excitable 825
volcanism 490c
volcano *violence* 173
  furnace 386
  pitfall 667
  on a–danger 665
volitation 267
volitient 600
volksraad 696
volley *collection* 72
  violence 173
  report 406
  attack 716
  (*impulse* 276)
volplane 267
volplaning 267
Volstead Act 761
volt 490d
voltaic 157
  –*electricity* 157

voltameter 157
volt ampere 466
volte-face 283, 607
voltigeur 726
voluble 584
volume *great* 31
  bulk 192
  book 593
  speak–s
  evidence 467
  intelligible 518
  inform 527
  –of smoke 330
voluminous *great* 31
  bulky 192
voluntarism 600
voluntary
  prelude 62, 64
  music 415
  willing 602
  donation 784
  –opposition 179
  –school 542
volunteer *will* 600
  willing 602
  safety 664
  endeavor 676
  combatant 726
  offer 763
voluptuary
  sensualist 954a
  libertine 962
voluptuous
  pleasure 377
  delightful 829
  intemperate 954
  impure 961
volutation 311
volute 248
vomit 297
vomitive 297
vomitory *opening* 260
  exit 295
  ejection 297
voodoo 621, 992, 994
voorlooper 64
voortrekker 64, 673
voracious *desire* 865
  glutton 957
Vorspiel 415
Vorstellung 515
vortex *rotation* 312
  agitation 315
  river 348
vorticist 556
vorticular 312
votary *auxiliary* 711
  devotee 865
vote *affirmation* 535
  choice 609
  have the deciding–
    153
  –for 488
voter 609
votive 768
  –offering 990

votograph 551
vouch *assert* 535
  –for 467
voucher *evidence* 467
  indication 550
  security 771
  payment 807
  (*record* 551)
vouchsafe *permit* 760
  consent 762
  ask 765
  condescend 879
vow *affirmation* 535
  promise 768
  worship 990
  take–s 995
vowel 561
vox populi *assent* 488
  publication 531
  choice 609
  authority 737
voyage 267
voyager 268
voyeurism 821a
vraisemblance 472
vug 252
vuggy 252
Vulcan 690
vulgar *inelegant* 579
  lowborn 876
  –tongue 560
vulgarian
  bad taste 851
vulgarity
  inelegance 579
  want of refinement
    851
Vulgate 985
vulnerable 665
vulnerary 662
vulpine 702
vulture *bird* 366
  harpy 739
  evildoer 913

W

wabble *slow* 275
  oscillate 314
  irresolution 605
wad *line* 224
  money 800
wadding *lining* 224
  stopper 263
  soft 324
waddle 275
waddy 727
wade 267
  –in blood 361
  –through *learn* 539
  exertion 686
wadi 490c
wafer *cement* 45
  thin 203
  lamina 204

waffle 298–irons 386
waft *transfer* 270
  blow 349
wafted, be–267
wag *oscillate* 314
  agitate 315
  joker 844
  –on *journey* 266
  progression 282
wager 621
  –of battle 722
  –of law 467
wages 973
wage war 722
waggery *wit* 842
waggish *cheery* 836
  ridiculous 853
waggle *oscillate* 314
  agitate 315
Wagnerian 415
wagon 272
wagoner 268
wagonette 272
wagonload *much* 31
Wahabi 984
waif *godsend* 618
  derelict 782
waifs and estrays
  dispersed 73
  wanderers 268
wail 412, 839
wain 272
wainscot *base* 211
  lining 224
waist 203
waistcoat 224, 225
  put in a strait–751
wait *tarry* 133
  inaction 681
  lie in–for 530
  –for 507
  –impatiently 133
  –on *accompany* 88
  aid 707
  –to see how the wind
    blows 607
  –upon *serve* 746
  call on 894
waiter *servant* 746
  –on Providence
  neglect 460
  inactive 683
  content 831
waiting 507
  be kept–133
waiting maid 746
waits 416
waive *defer* 133
  not choose 609a
  not use 678
wake *sequel* 65
  rear 235
  funeral 363
  trace 551
  excite 824
  amusement 840

  enough to–the dead
    404
  follow in the–of
    281
  –the thoughts 457
  –up *imagination* 515
  excitation 824
wakeful *careful* 459
  active 682
waldgrave 875
wale 250
waler 271
Walhalla 981
walk *region* 181
  move 266
  slowness 275
  business 625
  way 627
  conduct 692
  arena 728
  –ed off one's legs
    688
  –in the shoes of 19
  –off with 791
  –of life 625
  –one's chalks
  depart 293
  run away 623
  –over the course
  easy 705
  succeed 731
  –the earth 359
walker 268
walking delegate 758
walking gentleman
  599
walking papers 756
walking-stick 727
walk-over
  success 731
wall *vertical* 212
  parietes 224
  inclosure 232
  refuge 666
  obstacle 706
  defense 717
  prison 752
  driven to the–
  difficulty 704
  go to the–
  destruction 162
  fail 732
  pushed to the–
  necessity 601
  take the–*repute* 873
  pride 878
  –eyed 442
  –in *circumscribe* 229
  restrain 751
  wooden–s 726
wallaby 309
wallet 191, 800
wallop 315, 972
wallow *low* 207
  plunge 310
  rotate 312

  pool 343
  –in *pleasure* 377
  superabundance 641
  –in *riches* 803
  –in the mire 653
  –in *voluptuousness*
    954
wallsend 388
Wall Street 621
walnut 298, 367
  across the –s 299
walrus 366
waltz *music* 415
  dance 840
wamble *vacillate* 149
  slowness 275
  oscillate 314
  dislike 867
  (*irresolute* 605)
wampum 800
wan *pale* 429
  sad 837
wand *scepter* 747
  magic 993
  wave a–992
wander *move* 264
  journey 266
  deviate 279
  delirium 503
  the attention–s 458
wanderer 268
wandering
  exceptional 83
  –Jew 268
Wanderjahr 266
wanderlust 266
wane *decrease* 36
  age 128
  contract 195
  decay 659
  one's star on the–
    735
  wax and–140
wanigan 273
want
  inferiority 34
  incompleteness 53
  shortcoming 304
  requirement 630
  insufficiency 640
  poverty 804
  desire 865
  their–s but few 831
  –of consideration 458
  –of discernment
    465a
  –of distinction 465a
  –of esteem 929
wanting
  incomplete 53
  absent 187
  imbecile 499
  found–*imperfect* 651
  disapproval 932
  guilt 947
wantless 639

wanton
  uncomfortable 83
  capricious 608
  sufficiency 639
  unrestrained 748
  amusement 840
  rash 863
  impure 961
  harlot 962
  (*inconsiderate* 460)
wapentake 181
war 361, 722 at
  –*disagreement* 24
  contention 720
  at–with opposed 708
  fighting 722
  declare–713
  man of–727
  seat of–728
  –*correspondent* 722
  –*news* 722
  –*of words talk* 588
  contention 720
warble 416
war castle 726
war cry *alarm* 669
  defiance 715
  war 722
ward *part* 51
  parish 181
  safety 664
  asylum 666
  dependent 746
  restraint 751
  –*heeler* 886
  –*off hindrance* 706
  defense 717
  watch and–*care* 459
  keeper 753
war dance
  defiance 715
warden *guardian* 664
  master 745
  deputy 759
warder *porter* 263
  guardian 664
  keeper 753
  –*of the brain* 505
wardmote 966
wardrobe 225
wardship 664
ware *warning* 668
  merchandise 798
warehouse *store* 636
  mart 799
warfare 361, 722
  discord 713
war horse 726
warlike 722
warlock 994
warm *violent* 173
  near 197
  hot 382
  make hot 384
  red 434
  orange 439

wealthy 803
  ardent 821
  excited 824
  angry 900
  irascible 901
  flog 972
  –*bath* 386
  –*imagination* 515
  –*man* 803
  –*reception repel* 717
  welcome 892
  –*the blood* 824
  –*the cockles of the heart* 829
  –*up improve* 658
  resuscitate 660
  –*work* 686
warmed up
  repeated 104
war medal 722
warm–hearted
  feeling 821
  sensibility 822
  friendship 888
  benevolence 906
warming 384
warming pan
  locum tenens 147
  heater 386
  preparation 673
warmth
  vigorous language 574
warn *dissuade* 616
  caution 668
  (*forebode* 511)
  –*off* 761
warning *omen* 512
  caution 668
  (*advice* 695)
  give–*dismiss* 678
  relinquish 782
  –*voice alarm* 666
warp *change* 140
  tendency 176
  contract 195
  distort 243
  navigate 267
  deviate 279
  prejudice 481
  deteriorate 659
  –*and weft* 329
war paint
  preparation 673
warpath 722
warped
  narrow–minded 481
  imperfect 651
warrant *evidence* 467
  protest 535
  order 741
  permit 760
  promise 768
  security 771
  money order 800
  justify 937

death–*die* 360
  kill 361
  condemn 971
  I'll–you 535
warranted 924
warranty
  permission 760
  promise 768
  security 771
  sanction 924
warren 168
warrior 726
warship 726
wart 250
war whoop 715, 722
wary *cautious* 864
  (*careful, vigilant* 459)
wash *cover* 223
  water 337
  marsh 345
  color 428
  paint 556
  cleanse 652
  –*down* 298
  –*one's hands of relinquish* 624
  depute 757
  refuse 764
  part with 782
  dereliction 927
  –*out discolor* 429
  obliterate 552
wash cloth 652
washerman 652
washerwoman 652, 690
washhouse
  furnace 386
  cleansing 652
washout 162, 348
washy *weak* 160
  unmeaning 517
  feeble style 575
wasp *insect* 366
  narrow 203
  bring a–'*s nest about one's ears* 735
waspish *violent* 173
  irascible 901
  (*discourteous* 895)
wassail *beverage* 298
  feast 840
  drunkenness 954
waste *decrease* 36
  decrement 40a
  destroy 162
  unproductive 169
  space 180
  contract 195
  plain 344
  consumption **638**
  useless 645
  spoiled 659
  misuse 679

loss 776
  prodigality 818
  run to–
  superfluity 641
  deteriorate 659
  –*away* 655
  –*of years* 151
  –*time inactive* 683
  watery–341
wasted *weak* 160
  deteriorated 659
wasteful 818
waste paper
  of no force 158
  –*bonds* 808
waste pipe 350
waster *neglect* 460
  prodigal 818
wastethrift 818
wasting 638
  wide–649
wastrel *vagrant* 268
  neglect 460
  outcast 893
watch *company* 72
  clock 114
  observe 441
  attend to 457
  take care of 459
  expect 507
  guardian 664
  warning 668
  keeper 573
  death–*death* 360
  warning 668
  on the–*vigilant* 459
  expectant 507
  –*and ward care* 459
  keeper 573
  –*for* 507
watchdog
  guardian 664
  warning 668
  keeper 753
watcher 459
watchet 438
watch fire 550
watchful 459–*waiting*
  inaction 681
  caution 864
watchhouse 752
  in the–938
watchman
  guardian 664
  sentinel 668
  keeper 753
watchman's rattle 417
watchtower *view* 441
  signal 550
  warning 668
watchword *sign* 550
  military 722
water 337
  –*animals* 370
  transparent 425

back–283
  cast one's bread upon the–*s* 638
  depth of–208
  great–*s* 341
  hold–*proof* 478
  truth 494
  [*keep one's head above*]–664
  land covered with– 343
  of the first–648
  pour–*into a sieve* 638
  running–348
  spend money like– 818
  throw cold–*on* 174
  walk the–*s* 267
water carrier 348
water color 556
water course 350
watercress 298
water cure 662
water dog 269, 361
water drinker 958
watered
  variegated 440
waterfall 348
water gap 350
water glass 556
water gruel 160
watering–*cart* 348
  –*place* 189
  –*pot* 348
waterless 340
water–logged
  powerless 158
  danger 665
  hindrance 706
waterman 269
watermelon 298
water nymph 979
water pipe 350
water polo 840
waterproof *dress* 225
  dry 340
  protection 664
water qualm 655
waters
  on the face of the– 180
  –*of bitterness* 830
  –*of oblivion* 506
watershed 210
water spaniel 366
waterspout 348
water–tight
  closed 261
  dry 340
  protection 664
water wheel 633
waterworks 350
watery *wet* 337
  moist 339
  feeble style 575

watt

-eyes 839
-grave 360
watt 490d
wattle 219
wattmeter 157
Wat Tyler 742
wave *sinuous* 248
  oscillate 314
  -of water 348
  (see *waive*)
  -a banner 550
  -a wand 992
waver *changeable* 149
  doubt 485
  irresolute 605
waverer 605
waves 341
  buffet the-
  navigate 267
  difficult 704
  oppose 708
  lash the- 645
  plow the- 267
waveson 73
wavy 248
wax *increase* 35
  become 144
  expand 194
  soft 324
  lubrication 332
  viscid 352
  substance 356
  close as- 528
  -and wane 140
wax candle 423
waxed 356a
waxwork 554
waxy *unctuous* 355
  irate 900
way *degree* 26
  space 180
  habit 613
  road 627
  by the-
  in transitu 270
  accidental 621
  by-of direction 278
  method 627
  fall in the-of 186
  fight one's-
  pursue 622
  warfare 722
  find its- 302
  gather- 267
  get into the-of 613
  go one's- 293
  go your- 297
  have one's own-
  will 600
  easy 705
  succeed 731
  authority 737
  freedom 748
  have-on 267
  in a bad- 655
  in a-pained 828

in the-near 197
in the-of
  hinder 706
  oppose 708
  it must have its- 601
  let it have its- 681
long-off 196
make one's-
  journey 266
  progression 282
  passage 302
  prosperity 734
make- 302
make-for
  substitution 147
opening 260
turn aside 279
avoid 623
facilitate 705
courtesy 894
not know which-to turn 475
on the- 282
place in one's-
  offer 763
put in the-of
  enable 470
teach 537
see one's- 490
show the- 693
under-move 264
sail 267
progression 282
depart 293
-in 294
-of escape 617
-of speaking 521
-of thinking 484
-out 295
wing one's- 267
Way, the- 976
wayfarer 268
wayfaring 266
waylay *deception* 545
  cunning 702
wayless 261
ways 692
  inall manner of- 278
  -and means
  means 632
  money 800
wayward
  changeable 149
  obstinate 606
  capricious 608
  sullen 901a
wayworn *journey* 266
  fatigue 688
wayzgoose 840
weak *feeble* 160
  water 337
  insipid 391
  illogical 477
  foolish 499

-style 575
irresolute 605
trifling 643
lax 738
compassionate 914
vicious 945
(*small* 32)
expose one's-point
confute 479
-point illogical 477
imperfection 651
-side folly 499
vice 945
weaken *decrease* 36
  diminish 38
  enfeeble 160
  refute 468
weakened
  unhealthy 655
weaker vessel 374
weak-headed 499
weak-hearted 862
weakly *unhealthy* 655
weak-minded 499
weakness 160
  -of the flesh 945
weal 618
  common- 644
weald 367
wealth *property* 780
  riches **803**
wean
  change opinion 484
  change habit 614
  -from dissuade 616
  -one's thoughts from 506
weanling 129
weapon *arms* 727
  (*instrument* 633)
weaponless 158
wear *decrease* 36
  clothes 225
  deflect 279
  use 677
  better to-out 686
  -and tear waste 638
  injury 659
  exertion 686
  -away cease 142
  deteriorate 659
  -off cease 142
  desuetude 614
  -on 109
  -out deteriorate 659
  tire 688
  -the breeches 737
weariness *ennui* **841**
wearing
  wearisome 841
  -apparel 225
wearisome *slow* 275
  laborious 686
  fatiguing 688
  painful 830
weary *fatigue* 688

painful 828
sad 837
ennuyant 841
-flat, stale, and unprofitable 843
-waste 344
weasand *throat* 260
  pipe 351
weasel 366, 441
  catch a-asleep
  impossible 471
  active 682
  -words 517
weather 338
  rough etc.
  -violent 173
  wind 349
  -the storm
  stability 150
  recover 660
  safe 664
  succeed 731
  under the- 655
  -bureau 513
  -permitting 469, 470
  -prophet 513
  -vane 149
weather-beaten
  weak 160
  damaged 659
  fatigue 688
weather-bound 751
weathercock
  changeable 149
  wind 349
  indication 550
  fickle 607
weathered 659
weather gauge 338
weatherglass 338
weatherproof
  healthy 654
  safe 664
weathertight 664
weather vane
  (see *vane*)
weatherwise 338
  foresight 510
  indication 550
  (*prediction* 511)
weave *compose* 54
  produce 161
  interlace 219
  -a tangled web 704
weazen 193, 195
web *intersection* 219
  texture 329
web-footed 219
webwork 59
Wechsler–Bellevue intelligence scale 821a
wed 903
wedded 903–*pair* 903
  -to belief 484
  habit 613

weighed

loving 897
-to an opinion
  misjudgment 481
  obstinacy 606
wedding 903
  -anniversaries 883
wedge *join* 43
  angular 244
  sharp 253
  instrument 633
  thin edge of the-
  begin 66
  insinuate 228
  cunning 702
  -in 228
wedged in
  imprisoned 751
wedlock 903
wee 193
  -sma' hours 125
weed *exclude* 55
  few 103
  plant 367
  agriculture 371
  cigar 392
  trifle 643
  clean 652
  -out eject 297
  extract 301
weeds *dress* 225
  useless 645
  mourning 839
  widowhood 905
weedy *thin* 203
  trifling 643
week 108
weekly 138
ween *judge* 480
  believe 484
  know 490
weep *lament* 839
  pity 914
weet *judgment* 480
  knowledge 490
weetless 491
weet-weet 727
weft 329
weigh *influence* 175
  lift 307
  heavy 319
  ponder 451
  under-(see *way*]
  -anchor 267, 293
  -carefully
  discriminate 465
  -down aggrieve 649
  -on the heart 830
  -heavy on 649
  -on the mind
  regret 833
  dejection 837
  fear 860
  -with 615
weighbridge 319
weighed (see *weigh*)

615

weighing machine   whet

   —and found wanting
     inferior 34
     disapproved 932
weighing machine
  466
weight *influence* 175
   contents 190
   gravity 319
   affirmation 535
   vigor 574
   importance 642
   attach–to 484
   carry–175
   drag–706
   have–*evidence* 467
   throw one's–into
     the scale 175
weightless 320
weights and
  measures 466
weighty (*see* weight)
   evidence 467
weir *inclosure* 232
   conduit 350
   hindrance 706
weird *spectral* 980a
   mystic 992
   spell 993
   –sisters 994
Weismannism 357
welcome *arrival* 292
   grateful 829
   friendly 888
   sociality 892
   reception 894
weld *join* 43
   cohere 46
welfare 734
   –work 602
   –worker 602
welkin *worlds* 318
   air 338
   make the–ring **411**
well *much* 31
   origin 153
   deep 208
   exude 295
   pool 343
   flow 348
   assent 488
   good 618
   store 636
   healthy 654
   spa 662
   act–944
   all's–664
   drop a bucket into
     an empty–645
   get–660
   go on–734
   let–alone
     quiescence 265
     inaction 681
   think–of 931
   treat–906
   turn out–731

   –and good *assent* 488
     consent 762
     content 831
   –done! 931
   –enough *not much* 32
     imperfect 651
   –out 295
   –over 641
   –up in 698
   –with 888
     work–731
welladay *lament* 839
   wonder 870
well–advised 498
well–affected 888
well–behaved
   genteel 852
   courteous 894
well–being
   prosperous 734
   happy 827
well–beloved 897
well–born 875
well–bred *genteel* 852
   (*courteous* 894)
well–composed 845
well–defined
   visible 446
   exact 494
   predetermined 611
   (*plan* 626)
well–devised 611
well–disposed 602,
  707
well–doing 944
well–done *cooked* 298
well–favored 845
well–formed 240,
  845
well–fed 192
well–founded
   existent 1
   probable 472
   certain 474
   –*belief* 484
   true 494
well–grounded
   existent 1
   informed 490
   –*hope* 858
well–grouped 845
wellhead 153
well–informed 490
Wellington boots
  225
well–intentioned
   benevolent 906
   virtuous 944
well–knit *strong* 159
well–known
   knowledge 490
   habitual 613
well–laid 611
well–made *form* 240
   beauty 845
well–mannered 894

well–marked 446
well–meaning 906
well–meant 906
well–met 894
well–natured 906
well–nigh *almost* 32
   near 197
well–off
   prosperous 734
   rich 803
well–proportioned
  240, 845
well–provided 639
well–regulated
   order 58
   conformity 82
   circumspect 864
well–set 242
well–spent
   successful 731
   virtuous 944
wellspring 153, 636
well–timed 134
well–to–do
   prosperous 734
   rich 803
well–turned periods
  578
well–weighed 611
wellwisher 890, 906,
  914
Welsh 188–rabbit 298
welsher *swindler* 792
   nonpayment 808
welt 321
welter *plunge* 310
   roll 311
   –in one's blood 361
wem 848
wen 250, 848
wench *girl* 129
   woman 374
   peasant 876
   impure 962
wenching 961
wend 266
were, as you–660
wergild 974
werewolf 980
werowance 745
Wesleyan 984
west *lateral* 236
   direction 278
westing 196
Westminster
   superior courts of–
     966
westward 236
wet *water* 337, 348
   moist 339
   just enough to–
     one's feet 209
   –blanket *dissuade* 616
     hindrance 706
   sadden 837
   weary 841

   dull 843
   –one's whistle
     drink 298
     tipple 959
wether 366
whack 276
whacking
   large 31, 192
whale *large* 192
   mammal 366
   sprat to catch a–
     699
   tub to a–
     deception 545
     excuse 617
whalebone 325
whaler 273
whap 276
wharf *houses* 189
   refuge 666
   workshop 691
   mart 799
wharfage 812
wharf boat 273
what *inquiry* 461
   wonder 870
   and–not 81
   know–'s what
     discriminate 465
     intelligent 498
     skill 698
   –d'ye call 'em 563
   –in the world
     singular 83
     wonderful 870
   –is the reason? 461
   –next 455
   –on earth *singular* 83
   –'s his name 563
   –signifies 643
whatever 78
   –may happen 474
wheal 250
wheat 367
   winnow the chaff
     from the–609
Wheat Pit *mart* 799
wheedle *coax* 615
   endearment 902
   flatter 933
wheedler 615
wheel *circle* 247
   convexity 250
   bicycle 272
   deviate 279
   turn back 283
   circuition 311
   rotation 312
   rack 975
   break on the–
     pain 478
     punish 972
   get the–out of the
     rut 672
   scotch the–706
   –about 279

   –and axle 633
   –guard 666
   –of Fortune
     changeable 149
     chance 156
     rotation 312
     necessity 601
   –round *inversion* 218
     tergiversation 607
   –s within wheels
     entangled 59
     machinery 633
wheelbarrow 272
wheel chair 272
wheelman 268, 269
wheelwork 633
wheelwright 690
wheeze *blow* 349
   hiss 409
wheezy 409
whelk 250, 848
whelm 641
whelp *infant* 129
   production 161
   dog 366
   rogue 949
when *inquiry* 461
   (*different time* 119)
   in the time–106
whence
   attribution 155
   departure 293
   inquiry 461
   reasoning 476
where *presence* 186
   inquiry 461
   –am I? 870
whereabouts
   place 182
   situation 183
   near 197
whereas *relating to* 9
   because 476
whereby 631
wherefore
   attribution 155
   inquiry 461
   reasoning 476
   judgment 480
   motive 615
wherein 221
whereness 186
whereupon *time* 106
   different time 119
   after 121
wherever 180, 182
wherewith *means* 632
   money 800
wherewithal 639
wherret 830
wherry 273
whet *sharpen* 253
   meal 298
   incite 615
   excite 824
   take a–*tipple* 959

whether

−the appetite 865
−the knife 673
whether 514
  −or not 609
whetstone 253
which at−time 119
  know−is which 465
whiff *wind* 349
  excitement 825
whiffle 349
Whig 274, 712
while *time* 106
  (*same time* 120)
  in a−132
  −away time *time* 106
  inaction 681
  pastime 840
  worth−646
whilom 122
whilst 106
whim *fancy* 515
  caprice 608
  wet 842
  desire 865
whimper 839
whimsical (*see* whim)
  ridiculous 853
whimsey *fancy* 515
  caprice 608
  desire 865
whimwham
  imagination 515
  caprice 608
  unimportance 643
whin 367, 407
whine *cry* 411
  complain 839
whinyard 727
whip *coachman* 268
  strike 276
  stir up 315
  −a horse 370
  indication 550
  urge 615
  hasten 684
  director 694
  flog 972
  scourge 975
  −and spur *swift* 274
  −away *depart* 293
  −hand *success* 731
  authority 737
  −in 300 *collect* 72
  −on 684
  −off 293
  −up 789
whipcord 205
whipped cream 298
whipper−in 694
whippersnapper 129
whipping post 975
whipster 129
whir *rotate* 312
  sound 407
whirl *rotate* 312
  flurry 825

whirligig 312
whirlpool *rotate* 312
  agitation 315
  water 348
  danger 667
whirlwind *disorder* 59
  agitation 315
  wind 349
  reap the
  −*product* 154
  fail 732
  ride the−
  resolution 604
  authority 737
whisk *rapid* 274
  circuition 311
  agitation 315
  sweep 652
  −off 297
whisker 256
whisket 191
whisky 272, 298, 959
whisper
  faint sound 405
  tell 527
  conceal 528
  voice 580
  stammer 583
  stage−580
  −about *disclose* 529
  publish 531
  −in the ear *voice* 580
whist *hush* 403
  cards 840
whistle *wind* 349
  hiss 409
  stridor 410
  play music 416
  musical instrument 417
  clean as a−
  thorough 52
  perfect 650
  neatly 652
  pay too dear for one's−
  inexpedient 647
  unskillful 699
  dear 814
  wet one's
  −*drink* 298
  tipple 959
  −at 930
  −for *request* 765
  desire 865
  −for want of thought
  inaction 681
  −jigs to a milestone 645
whit *small* 32
  (*part* 51)
white 430
  probity 939
  mark with a−stone
  important 642
  approve 931

  stand in a−sheet 952
  −ant 690
  −as a sheet 860
  −feather 862
  −flag 723
  −friar 996
  −frost 383
  −heat 382
  −horses 348
  −lead 430
  −lie *equivocal* 520
  concealment 528
  untruth 546
  plea 617
  −liver 862
  −metal 430, 545
  −of the eye 441
  −plague 655
  −slave 962
  −wings *cleaner* 652
whitechapel
  vehicle 272
white dwarf 490a
whiten 429, 430
whiteness 430
whitening 430
whites 299
whitewash *cover* 223
  whiten 430
  materials 635
  cleanse 652
  ornament 847
  justify 937
  acquit 970
whitewashed
  get−808
whitewasher 935
whitey brown 433
whither *tendency* 176
  direction 278
  inquiry 461
whiting *fish* 298
  pigment 430
whitish 430
whitleather
  tough 327
Whitmonday 840
Whitsuntide 998
whittle *cut* 44
  knife 253
whittled *drunk* 959
whiz 409
who 461
  −would have thought?
  inexpectation 508
  wonder 870
whole *entire* 50
  healthy 654
  go the−hog 729
  make−660
  on the
  −*reasoning* 476
  judgment 480
  the−time 106

  −truth *truth* 494
  disclosure 529
  veracity 543
wholesale
  large scale 31
  whole 50
  abundant 639
  trade 794
  sell 796
wholesome 502, 656
whole−souled 944
wholly *entirely* 50
  completely 52
whoop 411
  −ing cough 655
  war−*defiance* 715
  warfare 722
whop *flog* 972
whopper *size* 192
  lie 546
whopping *huge* 192
whore 962
whoredom 961
whoremonger 962
whorl 248
whortleberry 298
who's who 86
why *cause* 153
  attribution 155
  inquiry 461
  indeed 535
  motive 615
wibble−wabble 314
wick *fuel* 388
  luminary 423
wicked 945 the
  −*bad men* 949
  impious 988
  the−one 978
wickedness 945
wicker 219
wicket *entrance* 66
  gateway 260
wide *general* 78
  space 180
  broad 202
  in the−world 180
  −apart *different* 15
  −awake *hat* 225
  intelligent 298
  −away 196
  −berth 748
  −of distant 196
  −of the mark
  distance 196
  deviation 279
  error 495
  −of the truth 495
  −open *expanded* 194
  opening 260
  −reading 539
  −world 180, 318
widen 194
  −the breach
  quarrel 713
  anger 900

wildfire

widespread *great* 31
  dispersed 73
  space 180
  expanded 194
widow 905
widowhood 905
width 202
wield *brandish* 315
  handle 379
  use 677
  −*authority* 737
  −the sword 722
wieldy 705
wife 903
wifeless 904
wig 225
wigging 932
wight 373
wigmaker 599
wigwam 189, 223
wild *unproductive* 169
  violent 173
  space 180
  plain 344
  vegetation 365
  inattentive 458
  mad 503
  shy 623
  unskilled 699
  excited 824, 825
  untamed 851
  rash 863
  angry 900
  licentious 954
  run−825
  sow one's−oats
  grow up 131
  improve 658
  amusement 840
  vice 945
  intemperance 954
  −animals 366
  −beast *fierce* 173
  −cinnamon 400
  −clove 400
  −duck 298
  −goose chase
  caprice 608
  useless 645
  unskillful 699
  −*imagination* 515
Wild, Jonathan
  thief 792
  bad man 949
wildcat 366, 665
wilderness
  disorder 59
  unproductive 169
  space 180
  solitude 893
  −of sweets 827
wildfire 382
  spread like−
  violence 173
  influence 175

wilding

expand 194
publication 531
wilding 893
wildness (see wild)
wile *deception* 545
  cunning 702
will *volition* 600
  resolution 604
  testament 771
  gift 784
  *at–*600
  have one's own–
    600 *freedom* 748
  make one's–
    death 360
  *tenant at–*779
  –and will not 605
  –be 152
  –for the deed
    compromise 774
    vindication 937
  –he nil he 601
  –of Heaven 601
  –power 600
  –you 765
willful *voluntary* 600
  obstinate 606
willingness 602
willing 762
  –or unwilling 601
will-o'-the-wisp
  luminary 423
  imp 980
willow 367, 839
  –whistle 410, 417
willy-nilly
  necessity 601
  compulsion (744)
willy-willy *gale* 349
wilted 659
wily 702
wimble 262
wimple 225
win *succeed* 731
  get 775
  –the affections
    love 897
  –golden opinions 931
  –the heart
    pleasing 829
  –laurels 873
  –over belief 484
  induce 615
  content 831
wince *bodily pain* 378
  emotion 821
  excitement 825
  mental pain 828
  flinch 860
winch *lift* 307
  instrument 633
wind, *n.*
  velocity 274
  blast **349**
  life 359
  against the–

direction 278
opposition 708
before the–
direct 278
prosperous 734
cast to the–s
repudiate 610
disuse 678
not observe 773
relinquish 782
*close to the–*278
fair–
*get–*531
hit between–and
  water 659
*in the–*151, 152
in the–'s eye 278
*lose–*688
*outstrip the–*274
preach to the–s 645
*raise the–*775
sail near the–
direction 278
skill 698
sharp practice 940
scatter to the–s 756
see how the–blows
direction 278
experiment 463
foresight 510
fickle 607
see where the–lie
  698
short–ed 688
sound of–and limb
  654
sport of–s and
  waves 315
take the–out of
  one's sails
render powerless 158
hinder 706
defeat 731
to the four–s
space 180
*touched in the–*655
what's in the–? 461
–ahead 708
–and weather
  permitting
  qualification 469
  possibility 470
wind, *v.*
  twirl 248
  deviate 279
  meander 311
  –round one's finger
    175
  –round the heart 897
  –the horn 416
  –up strengthen 159
  prepare 673
  complete 729
  –accounts 811
  –upward ascent 305
windbound 706

windfall 618
windflower 845
wind gauge 349
wind gun 727
winding 248, 311
winding sheet 363
windings and
  turnings 248
wind instruments
  417
windjammer 273
windlass 307
windless 688
windmill 312
window 260
  make the–s shake
    loud noise 404
windpipe 351
wind-up *end* 67
windward, to–
  lateral 236
  direction 278
windy 349
wine 298
  put new–into old
    bottles 699
winebibbing 959
wine-colored 434
wine cooler 387
wine-red 434
wing *adjunct* 39
  part 51
  side 236
  fly 267
  food 298
  side scene 599
  instrument 633
  refuge 666
  army 726
  clip the–s 275
  lend–s to 707
  on the–motion 264
  flying 267
  transference 270
  departure 293
  on the–s of the
    wind 274
  take–journey 266
  fly 267
  depart 293
  under the–of
    safe 664
  –one's flight 293
  –one's way 267
  with–s active 682
wing-chair 215
winged *swift* 274
wink *nictitate* 443
  indicate 550
  tip the–indicate 550
  inform 527
  –at be blind to 442
  neglect 460
  permit 760
  forgive 918
  –of sleep 683

winner 731, 931
winning (see win)
  pleasing 829
  courteous 894
  lovable 897
winnings 775
winnow *sift* 42
  exclude 55
  inquire 461
  pick 609
  clean 652
  –the chaff from the
    wheat
    discriminate 465
winsome *pleasing* 829
  cheerful 836
  love 897
winter *season* 126
  cold 383
  –of our discontent
    832
wintry 383
wipe *dry* 340
  clean 652
  disrespect 929
  flog 972
  give one a–
    rebuke 932
  –away obliterate 552
  –off old scores
    pay 807
  atone 952
  –the eyes relieve 834
  –the tears pity 914
wire *ligature* 45
  filament 205
  inform 527
  news 532
  messenger 534
  telegraph 534
  pull the–s 693
wire-drawn *long* 200
wireless 274, 531,
  534 *by–*684
  –telegram 532
  –telegraph 534
  –telephone 527
wire-puller 526, 694
wireworm 913
wiry *strong* 159
wis 514
wisdom 498
  have cut one's–
    teeth 698
  *worldly–*864
wise
  intelligent 498
  sage 500
  manner 627
  *in such–*8
  –after event 135
  –in one's own
    conceit 880
  –man 500
  –maxim 496
  *word to the–*695

with

wiseacre
  ignoramus 493
  sage 500
  fool 501
wish *will* 600
  intention 620
  desire 865
  do what one–es 748
  *not what we–*865
  –at the bottom of the
    Red Sea 832
  –is father to the
    thought
    misjudge 481
  credulous 486
  hope 858
  desire 865
  –joy 896
  –well 906
wishbone 993
wishing cap 865, 993
wishing stone 865
wishing-well 865
wish-wash
  unmeaning 517
wishy-washy
  weak 160
  insipid 391
  unmeaning 517
  feeble style 575
  unimportant 643
wisket 191
wisp 72
wistful *thought* 451
  feeling 821
  desirous 865
wit *intellect* 450
  wisdom 498
  humor **842**
  humorist 844
  a–with dunces 492
  at one's–'s end
  uncertain 475
  difficulty 704
  *mother–*498
  *soul of–*572
  *to–*522
witan 696
witch *oracle* 513
  ugly 846
  sorceress 994
  (proficient 700)
witchcraft 978, 992
witchery
  attraction 615
  pleasing 829
  sorcery 992
witching time
  midnight 126
  dark 421
wit-cracker 844
witenagemote 696
with *added* 37
  mixed 41
  ligature 45
  accompanying 88

618

withal

    means 632
    (*joined*) 43)
    go—178
    —all its parts 52
    —a sting to it 770
    —a vengeance
      great 31
      complete 52
    —a witness 31
    —regard to 9
withal *in addition* 37
    accompanying 88
withdraw *subduct* 38
    absent 187
    turn back 283
    recede 287
    depart 293
    —from *recant* 607
    relinquish 624
    dislike 867
withdrawal
    (*see* withdraw)
    rejection 610
withe 45
wither *shrink* 195
    decay 659
    —one's hopes 837
withered *weak* 160
    disease 655
withering *harsh* 739
    painful 830
    contempt 930
    censure 932
withers 250—unwrung
    strong 159
    insensible 323
withhold *hide* 528
    restrain 751
    prohibit 761
    retain 781
    stint 819
    —one's assent 764
within 221
    derived from—5
    keep—221
    place—221
    —an ace 32
    —bounds *small* 32
    shortcoming 304
    restraint 751
    —call 197
    —compass
      shortcoming 304
      temperate 953
    —one's memory 505
    —reach *near* 197
    easy 705
    —the mark 304
without *unless* 8
    subduction 38
    exception 83
    absence 187
    exterior 220
    circumjacent 227
    exemption 777a
    derived from—6

    not be able to do—
      630
    —a dissentient voice
      488
    —a leg to stand on
      158
    —alloy 827
    —a rap 804
    —a shadow of turning
      141
    —ballast *irresolute* 605
    unprincipled 945
    —ceasing 136
    —ceremony 881
    —charge 815
    —end *infinite* 105
    perpetual 112
    —exception 16
    —excuse 945
    —fail *certain* 474
    persevering 604a
    —fear of
      contradiction 535
    —God 989
    —limit 105
    —measure 105
    —notice 508
    —number 105
    —parallel 33
    —reason 499
    —regard to 10
    —reluctance 602
    —reserve 525
    —rhyme or reason
      615a
    —stint 639
    —warning 508
withstand *oppose* 708
    resist 719
    (*counteract*) 179)
withy 45
witless 491
witling *fool* 501
    wag 844
witness *see* 441
    spectator 444
    evidence 467
    voucher 550
    call to—467
witness box 966
wits 450
    all one's—about one
    care 459
    intelligence 498
    skin 698
    live by one's—
      deceive 545
      skill 698
      cunning 702
      steal 791
      dishonorable 940
    one's—gone a wool-
      gathering 458
    set one's—to work
      think 451
      invent 515

    plan 626
witsnapper 844
witticism 842
wittingly 620
wittol 962
witty 842, 844
    be—498
wive 903
wivern 83
wizard *sage* 500
    deceiver 548
    proficient 700
    sorcerer 994
    —of the air 269
wizen *wither* 195
    throat 260
woe *pain* 828
    evil 619
    —betide
      malediction 908
      pity 914
    —is me 839
    —to 908
woebegone 828
    sad 837
woeful *bad* 649
    painful 830
woefully *very* 31
wold 344
wolf *ravenous* 865
    cry—*false* 544
    alarm 669
    fear 860
    hold the—by the
      ears 704
    keep the—from the
      door 359
    unable to keep the—
      from the door
      804
    —and the lamb 923
    —at the door
      source of danger 667
      poverty 804
    —in sheep's clothing
      deceiver 548
      knave 941
wolfish 789
woman *adult* 131
    human 374
    —of the town 962
    —perfected 374
    —the lesser man 374
woman hater 911
womanhood 131, 374
womanish 374
womankind 374
womanly
    adolescent 131
    feminine 374
womb *cause* 153
    interior 221
    —of time *future* 121
    destiny 152
womerah 727
wonder *exception* 83

words

    superexcellence 646
    astonishment **870**
    prodigy 872
    do—s *activity* 682
    succeed 731
    for a—870
    nine days'—643
    not—507
    —s of the world 872
    —whether
      uncertain 475
      ignorant 491
      suppose 514
wonderfully
    greatly 31
wonderworking 870
wondrous 870
wont *habitual* 613
    (*conformity* 82)
won't do, it—
    disapproval 932
woo *desire* 865
    courtship 902
wooer 897
wood *trees* 367
    material 635
    not out of the—
      danger 665
      difficulty 704
    —lot 232
woodbine
    gone where the—
      twineth 771
woodchuck day 138
woodcut 558
woodcutter 371
wooded, well—256
wooden 635
    —horse 975
    —spoon 493
    —walls *defense* 717
    men—of—war 726
wood engraving 558
woodlands 367
wood—note 412
wood nymph 979
wood pavement 255
wood pigeon 366
woodwind 416
woody 367
woof 329
wool *flocculent* 256
    warm 382
    wrap 384
    fabric 635
    much cry and little
      —482
woolgathering 458
woolly 255, 256
woolpack *cloud* 353
woolsack *pillow* 215
    authority 747
    tribunal 966
woon 745
word *maxim* 496
    intelligence 532

    assertion 535
    volable **562**
    phrase 566
    command 741
    promise 768
    give the—741
    good as one's—
      veracious 543
      complete 729
      probity 939
    in a—572
    keep one's—939
    man of his—939
    not a—to say
      silent 585
      humble 879
    pass—550
    put in a—582
    take at one's—
      believe 484
      consent 762
    upon my—535
    watch—*military* 722
    —and a blow
      hasty 684
      contentious 720
      irascible 901
    —for word
      imitation 19
      truth 494
    —it 566
    —of command
      indication 550
      military 722
      command 741
    —in the ear
      information 527
      allocution 586
    —of honor 768
    —of mouth 582
    —to the wise
      intelligible 518
      advice 695
Word *Deity* 573
    —of God 985
wordbook 86
word-catcher 936
wordiness 562, 573
wording 569
wordless 581
word painter 594
word painting 515
word play
    equivocal 520
    neology 563
    wit 842
words *quarrel* 713
    bandy—588
    bitter—932
    choice of—569
    command of—574
    express by—566
    flow of
    —eloquence 582
    loquacity 584
    mere—*sophistry* 477

wordy

unmeaning 517
no—can paint 872
play of— 842
put into— 566
war of
—*interlocution* 588
contest 720
—*that burn* 574
—*with censure* 932
wordy 562, 573
work *product* 154
operation 170
pass and repass 302
ferment 320
writing 590
book 593
business 625
use 677
action 680
exertion 686
ornament 847
at—*in operation* 170
business 625
doing 680
active 682
earth—717
field—717
hard—*exertion* 686
difficulty 704
piece of—
importance 642
discord 713
stick to—604a
stitch of—686
stroke of—686
—*a change* 140
—*against time* 684
—*for* 707
—*hard exertion* 686
difficult 704
—*ill* 732
—*in* 228
—*of art*
beauty 845, 847
(*painting* 556)
(*sculpture* 557)
(*engraving* 558)
—*of fiction* 594
—*of reference* 636
—*one's way*
progress 282
ascent 305
exertion 686
succeed 731
—*towards tend* 176
—*up*
(*see below*)
—*upon influence* 175
incite 615
excite 824
—*out conduct* 692
complete 729
—*out one's salvation* 990
—*well easy* 705
successful 731

—*wonders active* 682
succeed 731
workability 490
workable 490
workableness 470
workaday
business 625
active 682
worker 686, 690, 746
workhouse 691
prison 752
working *acting* 170
active 682
—*bee* 690
—*man* 690
—*order* 673
—*towards* 176
workman 690
workmanlike 698
workmanship
production 161
action 680
works (see work)
board of—696
good—906
—*of the mind* 451
workshop 691
work up
prepare 673
use 677
excite 824
—*into form* 240
—*into a passion* 900
workwoman 690
world *great* 31
events 151
space 180
universe **318**
mankind 372
fashion 852
(*events* 151)
all the—*over* 180
as the—*goes* 613
a—*of* 102
citizen of the—910
come into the—359
follow to the's *end* 743
for all the—615
give to the—531
knowledge of the— 698
man of the—
proficient 700
fashion 852
not for the—
dissent 489
refusal 764
organized—357
pendent—173
Prince of this—978
rise in the—734
throughout the—180
—*and his wife* 102
—*beyond the grave* 152

—*forgetting, by the world forgot* 893
—*of good good* 618
do good 648
—*principle* 359
—*soul* 359
—*spirit* 359
—*to come* 152
—*wisdom skill* 698
caution 864
selfishness 943
—*without end* 112
worldling *selfish* 943
impious 988
worldly *selfish* 943
irreligious 989
—*wisdom* 864
worldwide *great* 31
universal 78
space 180
worm *small* 193
spiral 248
animal 366, 368
bane 663
food for—s 362
—*in* 228
—*oneself ingress* 294
love 897
—*one's way slow* 275
passage 302
—*out* 480a
—*that never dies* 982
worm-eaten 659
wormwood
gall and—395
worn *weak* 160
damage 659
fatigue 688
well—*used* 677
worn-out 659
weary 841
worry *vexation* 828
tease 830
harass 907
worse *deteriorated* 659
aggravated 835
—*for wear* 160
worship *title* 877
servility 886
venerate 987
religious **990**
idolize 991
demon—991
idol—991
fire—991
his—967
place of—1000
—*Mammon* 803
—*the rising sun* 886
worshiper 990
worshipful 873
worst *defeat* 731
do one's—*injure* 659
spite 907
do your
—*defiance* 715

threat 909
have the—*of it* 732
make the—*of* 482
worst come to the—
certain 474
bad 649
hopeless 859
worth *value* 644
goodness 648
possession 777
price 812
virtue 944
penny—812
what one is—780
—*a great deal* 803
—*one's salt* 644
—*the money* 815
—*while* 646
worthless *trifling* 643
useless 645
profligate 945
—*residue* 645
worthy *famous* 873
virtuous 944
good 948
—*of* 924
—*of belief* 484
—*of blame* 932
—*of noble wife* 905
—*of notice* 642
—*of remark* 642
wot 490
would—*fain* 865
—*that!* 865
would-be *pert* 885
usurping 925
wound *evil* 619
injure 659
pain 830
anger 900
(*badness* 649)
deep—s 830
keep the—*green* 919
—*the feelings* 830
woven fabrics 219
wrack *destruction* 162
(*evil* 619)
go to—*and ruin*
perish 162
fail 732
bankrupt 804
wraith 980a, 992a
wrangle
disagreement 24
reason 476
unbelief 485
dissent 489
quarrel 713
contend 720
wrangler
reasoner 476
scholar 492
opponent 710
wrangling
(see *wrangle*)
wrap *cover* 223

wristers

clothe 225
warmth 384
wrapped in
attention 457
—*clouds* 528
—*self* 943
—*thought* 458
wrapper 223, 225
inclosure 232
wraprascal 225
wrath 900
wreak *violent* 173
harsh 739
—*one's anger* 919
—*one's malice on* 907
wreath *woven* 219
circle 247
fragrance 400
trophy 733
ornament 847
honor 877
wreathe *weave* 219
wreathy 248
wreck *remainder* 40
destruction 162
damage 659
defeat 732
wrecker 792
wrench *disjoin* 44
draw 285
extract 301
twist 311
seize 789
wrest *distort* 243
—*from* 789
—*the sense* 523
wrestle 720
wrestler 726
wretch *sufferer* 828
sinner 949
wretched
unimportant 643
bad 649
unhappy 828
wretchedly *small* 32
wriggle *oscillate* 314
agitate 315
—*into* 294
—*out of* 671
wright 690
wring *twist* 248
pain 378
clean 652
torment 830
—*from extract* 301
compel 744
take 789
—*one's hands* 839
—*the heart* 830
wringing wet 339
wrinkle 258
wrinkled *aged* 128
wrist *retention* 781
(*instrument* 633)
wristband 225
wristers 384

620

writ evidence 467
  order 741
  lawsuit 969
Writ, Holy–985
write compose 54
  style 569
  writing 590
  lived to–593
  –down record 551
  –out 590
  –to 592
  –upon 595
  –word 527
writer write 590
  correspondent 592
  author 593
  story–teller 594
  dramatic–599
  pen of a ready–569
  –to the Signet 968
writhe distort 243
  agitate 315
  pain 378
writing
  composition 54
  penmanship 590
  book 593
  put in–551
  –in cipher 590
written 590 it is
  –necessity 601
wrong evil 619
  injury 649
  spite 907
  improper **923**
  vice 945
  begin at the–end 699
  go–732
  in the–error 495
  wrong 923
  in the–place 647
  own oneself in the 950
  –box unskillful 699
  difficulty 704
  wrong 923
  –course 945
  –in one's head 503
  –side of the wall 665
  –side out 218
  –side up 218
  –sow by the ear
    blunder 699
    failure 732
  –step 732
wrongdoer 949
wrongdoing 945
wrongful 923
wrongheaded 481
wrought highly
  –prepared 673
  complete 729
  –iron 323
  –out 729
  –up excited 824

angry 900
wry oblique 217
  distorted 243
  –face pain 378
  discontent 832
  lamentation 839
  ugly 846
  disapproval 932
wuther 349
wynd 189
wyvern 83

X

xanthein 436
xanthian 557
xanthic 436
xanthin 436
Xanthippe scold 901
xanthite 436
xanthocarpous 436
xanthocroia 436
xanthochroid 436
xanthocyanopia 436, 443
xanthophyll 436
xebec 273
xenodochium 189
xenogenesis 161
xenophobia 867
xeres 959
xerophagy
  fasting 956
xiphoid 253
xiphopagus
  unconformity 83
X–ray photograph 554
X–ray photography 554
X–rays 420, 490d
xylograph 558
xylography 558
xylophagous 298
xylophone 417
x, y, z, 491

Y

yach 508
yacht 273
yachting 267
yaffle 25
yager 726
Yahoo 702
yak 366
yam 298
Yama 979
yammer 839
yank 285
Yankee 188
yap 406, 411, 412
yard abode 189
  length 200

inclosure 232
  workshop 691
yardarm to yardarm 197
yardman 746
yare 682
yarn filament 205
  untruth 546
  exaggeration 549
  mingled–41
  spin a long–549
  diffuse style 573
yarr 412
yarrow 662
yataghan 727
yaup 411, 412
yaw 279
yawl ship 273
  cry 412
yawn open 260
  sleepy 683
  tired 688
  weary 841
yawning gulf 198
  deep 208
y–cleped 564
yea more 33
  assent 488
yean 161
year time 106
  period 108
  all the–round 110
  since the–one 124
  tenant from–to year 779
  –after year 104
year–book 138
yearling 129, 366
yearly 138
yearn pain 828
  sad 837
  –for desire 865
  pity 914
yearning love 897
years 128
  come to–of discretion 131
  in–128
  tenant for–779
  –ago 122
  –old 128
yeast leaven 320
  bubbles 353
yell cry 406, 410, 411
  cheer 838
  complain 839
yellow 436
  sensational 824
  –and red 439
  –complexioned 436
  –cover 756
  –fever 655
  –flag 550, 668
  –journalism 824
  –streak 862
yellow–eyed 920

yellowish 436
yellowness 436
yellows 920
yelp cry 406, 412
  whine 839
  –at execrate 932
yeoman farmer 371
  man 373
  –of the guard 263, 726
  –'s service 644
yeomanry 726
yerk strike 276
  (attack 716)
yes assent 488
  consent 762
yesterday past 122
  of–new 123
yet
  in compensation 30
  exception 83
  time 106
  prior 116
  past 122
  qualification 469
yew 367
yield soft 324
  submit 725
  consent 762
  resign 782
  furnish 784
  gain 810
  price 812
  –assent assent 488
  consent 762
  –obeisance 725
  –one's breath 360
  –the palm inferior 34
  humility 879
  –to despair 859
  –to temptation 615
  –up the ghost 360
yielding soft 324
  facile 705
  submissive 725
yodel 416
yoga 955
yogi intellect 450
  adviser 695
  ascetic 955
  priest 996
  –philosophy 992a
yo–ho 411, 457
yoho 457
yoick 411
yoicks 411, 622
yoke join 43
  vinculum 45
  couple 89
  –a horse 370
  subject 749
  means of restraint 752
  rivet the–739
yokel tyro 701
  rustic 876

yokemate 903
yolk 436
yonder that 79
  distant 196
yore 122
Yoshiwara 961
you–don't say so 870
  –'re another 718
young 127–man
  lover 897
youngling 129
youngster 129
younker 129
youth age **127**
  lad 129
youthful 127
yucca 253
yule 138–candle 512
  –log 388, 512
yuletide 138

Z

Zadkiel 513
zaffer 438
zambo 41
zambomba 417
zany 501
zarp 664
zeal willingness 602
  activity 682
  feeling 821
  desire 865
zealot dogmatist 474
  obstinate 606
  active 682
  (resolute 604)
zealotry 606
zealous (see zeal)
zebra 366, 440
zebrule 41
zebu 366
Zeeman effect 490a
Zeitgeist 550
zemindar 779
zemindary 780
zemstvo 696
zenana abode 189
  woman 374
  impurity 961
Zendavesta 986
zendik 487
zenith climax 31
  height 206
  summit 210
  in the–repute 873
zephyr 349
Zeppelin 273, 726
zero nothing 4
  nought **101**
  –hour 716
zest relish 394
  enjoyment 827
zetetic 461
Zeus 979

621

zigzag *oblique* 217
  angle 244
  deviating 279
  oscillating 314
  cicuit 629
  ornament 847
Zimmermann
  disciple of– 893
zincograph 558
zincography 558
zingaro 268
Zion 981
zip 409
zircon 847
zither 417
zocle 215
zodiac *zone* 230
  worlds 318
zodiacal light 423
zoëtic 359
Zoilus 936
Zollverein
  compact 769
  association 712
zone *region* 181
  layer 204
  belt 230
  circle 247
zoo 370
zoogloea 357
zoographer 368
zoographist 368
zoography 368
zoohygiantics 370
zooid 357
zoolatry 991
zoological 366
  –*garden* 370, 636
zoologist 357
zoology 368
zoonomy 368
zoophorous 210
zoophyte 366
zoospore 357
zootomy 368
zoril 401
Zoroaster 986
Zoroastrian 382, 984
Zoroastrianism 382, 976
zouave 726
zounds *wonder* 870
  anger 900
Zulu 876
zygote 357
zyme 320
zymogenic 320
zymologic 320
zymotic *disease* 655
  unhealthy 657

HOW TO USE
ROGET'S UNIVERSITY THESAURUS

The most common use for a thesaurus is to find a word that precisely fits a thought you wish to express.

Let us assume that you have written this sentence:

The ship sailed at dawn.

You may be dissatisfied with the word *ship* because it does not specify precisely the type of ship you have in mind. You think for a moment but cannot bring to mind the word you should use. Rather than spend any more time trying to recall the word, you turn to your *Roget University Thesaurus*.

First you look up *ship* in the index to the thesaurus. On page 566, column 3, you find the following:

---

sheet   **short**

deviation 279
—off *avoid* 623
(*depart* 293)
sheet *layer* 204
  covering 223
  paper 593
  —of fire 382
  —of water 343
  white—*penance* 952
  winding—363
sheet anchor
  safety 664, 666, 706
  hope 858
sheet lightning 423
sheet work 591
sheik *ruler* 745
  priest 996
shelf *support* 215
  rock 667
  on the
  —*powerless* 158
  disused 678
  inaction 681
shell *cover* 223
  coffin 363
  bomb 404, 727
  bombard 716

shibboleth 550
shield *heraldry* 550
  safety 664
  buckler 666
  defend 717
  scutcheon 877
  look only at one
    side of the—481
  reverse of the
  —*rear* 235
  counter evidence 468
  under the—of 664
shield-shaped 245
shift *change* 140
  convert 144
  substitute 147
  changeable 149
  displace 185
  chemise 225
  more 264
  transfer 270
  deviate 279
  prevaricate 546
  plea 617
  cunning 702
  (*expedient* 626)
  last—601

—in conversation 588
—upon *illumine* 420
  aid 707
  take the—out of 874
shingle
  covering 223, 635
  powder 330
  —house 189
shining (see shine)
  —light *sage* 500
shinny 840
shinplaster 800
shintiyan 225
shiny 420
ship *lade* 190
  transfer 270
  vessel **273**
  one's—coming in
    803
  —of the line 726
  take—*sail* 267
  depart 293
ship biscuit 298
shipboard, on—273
shipentine 273
shipload *much* 31
  cargo 190

shoal *assemblage* 72
  multitude 102
  shallow 209
shoals *danger* 667
  surrounded by
  —*difficulty* 704
shock *sheaf* 72
  violence 173
  concussion 276
  agitation 315
  unexpected 508
  discord 713
  affect 821
  move 824
  pain 828
  give *pain* 830
  dislike 867
  scandalize 932
  (*contest* 720)
shocking *bad* 649
  painful 830
  ugly 846
  vulgar 851
  fearful 860
  disreputable 874
  hateful 898
  in a—*temper* 901a

—star *world* 318
  luminary 423
  omen 512
shooting coat 225
shooting iron 727
shop *buy* 795
  mart 799
  keep a—*business* 625
  trade 794
  shup up—*end* 67
  cease 142
  relinquish 624
  rest 687
  smell of the—851
shopkeeper 797
shoplifter 792
shoplifting 791
shopman 797
shopmate 890
shopping 794, 795
shop-worn
  cheap 815
shore *support* 215
  border 231
  land 342
  buttress 717
  hug the—286

The words listed under **ship** are keys to larger listings of words that are related to it in various ways. For instance, the subentry *transfer* would lead you to a list of words that are close in meaning to the sense of *ship* that means to transfer (transport, convey, carry, etc.).

Obviously, transfer is not the meaning of *ship* that you have in mind. You are looking for a type of vessel, and you find that *vessel* is also a subentry of **ship**, so you know your thesaurus will help you. The number that follows *vessel*, 273, is the number of the category of words that will include the word you are looking for.